Encyclopedia of World Literature in the 20th Century

Encyclopedia of
in the

IN FIVE VOLUMES

World Literature 20th Century

STEVEN R. SERAFIN, General Editor

WALTER D. GLANZE, Associate Editor

VOLUME 5: Supplement and Index

A Frederick Ungar Book
CONTINUUM · NEW YORK

1993
The Continuum Publishing Company
370 Lexington Avenue
New York, NY 10017

Distributed to Libraries by Gale Research, Inc.
835 Penobscot Bldg., Detroit, Michigan 48226

Copyright © 1993 by The Continuum Publishing Company

Printed in the United States of America

Library of Congress Cataloging-in-Data
(Revised for volume 5)

Encyclopedia of world literature in the 20th century.

Includes bibliographies and index.
1. Literature, Modern—20th century—Bio-bibliography.
2. Literature, Modern—20th century—Encyclopedias.
I. Klein, Leonard S.
PN771.E5   1981   803   81-3357
ISBN 0-8044-3135-3 (v. 1)
ISBN 0-8044-3136-1 (v. 2)
ISBN 0-8044-3137-x (v. 3)
ISBN 0-8044-3138-8 (v. 4)
ISBN 0-8264-0571-1 (v. 5: Supplement and Index)

Board of Advisers

v

Contributors to Volume 5

Hédi Abdel-Jaouad
Mas'adī
Memmi
al-Shābbī

Cecil A. Abrahams
Head

Robert Acker
Blatter
Böni
Brinkmann
German Literature
Gomringer
Jandl
Mayröcker
Meyer
Mon
Muschg
Regler
Rosei
Walter

Ali Jimale Ahmed
Deressa
Kenyan Literature

Roger Allen
Egyptian Literature
Faraj
Munīf
Tāmir
Wannūs

Paul Anderer
Kobayashi

Verena Andermatt-Conley
Cixous

Melvin S. Arrington, Jr.
Gallegos Lara
Gorostiza
Salazar Bondy

John M. Asfour
al-Māghūt

Aida A. Bamia
Algerian Literature
Ghallāb
Ibn Hadūqa
Wattār

Lowell A. Bangerter
Braun
Heym
Kant
Kirsch

Harold Barratt
Anthony
Selvon

Paul Barrette
Aquin
Canadian Literature
Ferron
Godbout
Theriault
Tremblay

Carl D. Bennett
Richardson

Mary G. Berg
  Hernández, L. J.
  Naranjo
  Odio
  Oreamuno
  Valenzuela

Jason Berner
  Keneally
  Sexton
  Thurber
  Triana

Robert L. Berner
  Jacobson

Neil K. Besner
  Gallant

Delys M. Bird
  Jolley

Issa J. Boullata
  Jabrā

Laurence A. Breiner
  Brathwaite

Deming Brown
  Bakhtin

Charlotte H. Bruner
  Emecheta

Leonard Casper
  Santos
  Ty-Casper

Peter J. Chelkowski
  Al-e Ahmad
  Hoveyda
  Iranian Literature
  Sa'edi

Chia-ning Chang
  Yosano

Chung Ling
  Yü

Alice R. Clemente
  Jorge

Catherine Cobham
  al-Kharrāt

Carli Coetzee
  Breytenbach
  Brink
  South African Literature: In Afrikaans

Arthur B. Coffin
  Bierce

Karen Colligan-Taylor
  Ōba

Miriam Cooke
  Haqqī
  al-Shaykh

Carlo Coppola
  Ali
  Ezekiel
  Ghose
  Indian Literature

Marcel Cornis-Pope
  Blandiana
  Sorescu

Maja E. Cybulska
  Iwaniuk

Sandra Messinger Cypess
  Gambaro

Bogdan Czaykowski
  Polish Literature

Margaret H. Decker
  Kao

Wijnie E. de Groot
  Nooteboom

Ed C. M. de Moor
  'Aql
  al-Hājj
  al-Khāl

Terri DeYoung
  Sāyigh

Dinh-Hoa Nguyen
  Khái-Hưng

Nguyễn Tuân
Vietnamese Literature
Vũ Hoàng Chương

Paul B. Dixon
Piñon

Inés Dölz-Blackburn
Buenaventura
Marín Cañas

Dorothy Driver
South African Literature: In English

Helga Druxes
Hofmann
Kipphardt
Leutenegger
Meckel

Evelio Echevarría
Caballero Calderón
Carrasquilla
Jaimes Freyre

Helen Regueiro Elam
Bloom

Sarah English
Irving
McMurtry

John D. Erickson
French Literature

Joseph Ferdinand
Phelps

Rosario Ferreri
Levi
Sereni

Donald M. Fiene
Dovlatov
Osorgin

Zbigniew Folejewski
Polish Literature

Jean-François Fourny
Foucault

Karen Wilkes Gainey
Pym

Eric J. Gangloff
Kinoshita

John F. Garganigo
Belli
Dragún

Dick Gerdes
Bryce Echenique

Van C. Gessel
Endō

Sabah Ghandour
'Awwād
Mīna

James Gibbs
Rotimi

John R. Givens
Shukshin

Frances Devlin Glass
Australian Literature

Janet N. Gold
Alegría, C.
Cardenal
Central American Literature

Howard Goldblatt
Chinese Literature

Luis F. González-Cruz
Piñera

Luis T. González-del-Valle
Arniches
Echegaray
Palacio Valdés

Helena Goscilo
Petrushevskaya
Tolstaya

Theodora Rapp Graham
Brookner

Robert Greenup
Betjeman
le Carré

Gabriele Griffin
  Weldon

Clara Gyorgyey
  Csoóri

Igor Hájek
  Czechoslovak Literature
  Holub
  Klíma

Kenneth E. Hall
  Alvarez Gardeazabal
  Cepeda Samudio
  Goldemberg
  Rovinski
  Szichman

Talat Sait Halman
  Ağaoğlu
  Cansever
  Cumalı
  Dilmen
  İlhan
  Necatigil
  Turkish Literature

Walid Hamarneh
  Farmān
  al-Ghītānī
  Ismā'īl

Geraldine Harcourt
  Tsushima

John J. Hassett
  Dorfman

Evelyn J. Hawthorne
  Mais

Adnan Haydar
  Abū Mādī

Ben A. Heller
  Girri
  Mutis
  Padilla

Theo Hermans
  Berge

David K. Herzberger
  Benet
  Torrente Ballester

Julia Cuervo Hewitt
  Cabrera
  Ferré
  Garro
  Novás Calvo
  Zapata Olivella

Mildred A. Hill-Lubin
  Aidoo

Hosea Hirata
  Japanese Literature
  Murakami
  Nishiwaki

Keith Hitchins
  Goran

Poul Houe
  Hultberg
  Larsen

Niels Ingwersen
  Reich
  Tafdrup

Salma Khadra Jayyusi
  'Abd al-Sabūr
  al-Malā'ika

D. Barton Johnson
  Sokolov
  Yerofeev

W. P. Kenney
  Burke
  Cain
  Chandler
  Du Bois
  Gaines
  Hammett
  Hayden
  Killens
  Marshall
  Wilson, A.

Ludmila M. Kerman
  Brouwers

Robert F. Kiernan
American Literature
Auchincloss
Strand
Wright

Bettina L. Knapp
Chedid

Jack Kolbert
Modiano
Wiesel

Jürgen Koppensteiner
Austrian Literature
Bauer
Szyszkowitz

Renée Larrier
Condé
Schwarz-Bart

Wendy Larson
Wang

Alma H. Law
Radzinsky
Vysotsky

Alexis Levitin
Andrade

Morton P. Levitt
Coover
Johnson
Renault

David A. Lowe
Russian Literature

Elizabeth Lowe
Fonseca
Scliar
Telles

William Luis
Arenas

Thomas E. Lyon
Viñas

Margareta Martin
Tuuri

Danielle Marx-Scouras
Boudjedra
Chraïbi
Kristeva

Russell McDougall
Herbert

George R. McMurray
Argentine Literature
Argueta
Azuela
Chilean Literature
Edwards
Ibargüengoitia
Mexican Literature
Poniatowska
Ramírez
Skármeta
Solares
Spota

Jaroslav Med
Holan

Samia Mehrez
Dunqul

Ronald Meyer
Iskander
Lipkin
Lisnyanskaya

Vasa D. Mihailovich
Kiš
Nastasijević
Pavić

Stephen Miller
Conde
Espriu
Grau
Otero
Pardo Bazán
Rodoreda

Margo Milleret
Boal

William E. Mishler
  Jacobsen
  Sandel
  Uppdal

Charles Molesworth
  Ashbery
  DeLillo
  Postmodernism
  Snyder

Naomi Hoki Moniz
  Callado

Michela Montante
  Eco

Mildred Mortimer
  Djebar

Charles A. Moser
  Dalchev
  Dimitrova

Warren Motte
  Perec

Brian Murray
  Bates
  English Literature
  Lodge
  Scott
  Wolfe

Eunice D. Myers
  Chacel

Nadeem Naimy
  Gibran

Virgil Nemoianu
  Romanian Literature

Cornelis Nijland
  Nu'ayma

Harley D. Oberhelman
  Allende

Fergal O'Doherty
  Durcan
  Irish Literature

Wole Ogundele
  Nigerian Literature

William Over
  Gray
  Hurston
  Inge
  Kennedy
  Momaday
  Wilson, L.

Oyekan Owomoyela
  Osofisan

Dennis Paoli
  Friel
  Kinsella

Kathleen Parthé
  Abramov
  Rasputin

Lon Pearson
  Alegría, F.
  Guzmán
  Lafourcade
  Teillier

Mattityahu Peled
  Taymūr

Janet Perez
  Spanish Literature

Charles A. Perrone
  Melo Neto

Michael A. Peterman
  Davies

Sanford Pinsker
  Ozick

Beth Pollack
  Costantini

Laurence M. Porter
  Wittig

Richard N. Porter
  Nagibin

John Povey
Coetzee
Rive

Janet M. Powers
Desai
Mukherjee
Rushdie

M. Byron Raizis
Plaskovitis
Taktsis
Tsirkas

Lillian S. Robinson
Angelou
Feminist Criticism
Kumin
Olsen
Rich
Rukeyser
Tyler
Williams

Jorge Rodríguez-Florido
Laguerre
Novo

Sven Hakon Rossel
Christensen
Danish Literature
Madsen
Nordbrandt
Stangerup

Leonid Rudnytzky
Kostenko
Kotsyubynsky
Rudenko
Shevchuk
Stus
Ukrainian Literature

Ivan Sanders
Hungarian Literature
Konrád
Nádas

George D. Schade
Lihn
Pareja Diezcanseco

Gregory A. Schirmer
Trevor

George C. Schoolfield
Bargum
Donner
Kihlman
Tikkanen

C. S. Schreiner
Poststructuralism

Robert Scott
Aguilera Malta
Bombal
Wolff

Clinton B. Seely
Das

Helen Segall
Voynovich

Eric Sellin
Ben Jelloun
Khatibi
Tchicaya U Tam'si

Virginia Shen
Carranza
Gaitán Durán
Lynch
Mejía Vallejo

Muhammad Siddiq
Darwīsh
Habībī
Kanafānī
Palestinian Literature

William L. Siemens
Moreno-Duran

Rimvydas Šilbajoris
Lithuanian Literature

Juris Silenieks
Glissant

Nicasio Silverio
Ballagas
Veloz Maggiolo

Malcolm Silverman
Buarque
Ribeiro, D.

Jan I. Sjåvik
Fløgstad
Hauge
Solstad

Sam L. Slick
Carballido
Pacheco
Pellicer
Sabines

David A. Smyth
Siburapha

Jill Stephen
Historicism

Irwin Stern
Brazilian Literature
Faria
Gonçalves
Saramago

Donna George Storey
Furui

William L. Stull
Carver

Margaret D. Sullivan
Beattie
Berger
Ignatow
Paley
Walker
White

Mihály Szegedy-Maszák
Esterházy
Mészöly

Mildred Tahara
Ariyoshi

William Tay
Pai

Robert Thacker
Munro

Chezia Thompson-Cager
Lovelace

Robert Donald Thornton
Scottish Literature

Michael Thorpe
Amadi

Anne Tomiche
Lyotard

Shawkat M. Toorawa
Hijāzī

Egil Törnqvist
Norén

Geneviève Troussereau
Lacan

Martin Tucker
Literature and Exile

William J. Tyler
Ishikawa

Luiz Fernando Valente
Ribeiro, J. U.

Eamonn Wall
Mahon
Montague

Lars G. Warme
Ekman
Lindgren
Swedish Literature
Trotzig

Michael V. Williams
Bichsel

Raymond Leslie Williams
Colombian Literature

David Wills
Deconstruction
Derrida

Tadeusz Witkowski
Barańczak
Krynicki
Zagajewski

CONTRIBUTORS TO VOLUME 5

Hal Wylie
Bemba
Depestre

Horacio Xaubet
Hernández, F.
Peri Rossi
Sánchez

Donald A. Yates
Denevi
Guido

Ying-hsiung Chou
Mo

Lorraine M. York
Ondaatje

B. M. Young
Inoue

M. J. L. Young
al-'Ujaylī

Leon I. Yudkin
Appelfeld
Grossman
Israeli Literature
Kahana-Carmon
Kenaz
Megged
Schutz
Shabtai
Tammuz
Yehoshua

Humayun Zafar Zaidi
Hyder

Ilinca Zarifopol-Johnston
Cioran

Harry Zohn
Lasker-Schüler
Lind
Soyfer

Virpi Zuck
Kilpi

Abbreviations for Periodicals, Volume 5

A&E	Anglistik & Englischunterricht	*ArielE*	Ariel: A Review of International English Literature
AAS	Asian and African Studies		
ABnG	Amsterdamer Beiträge zur Neueren Germanistik	*ArielK*	Ariel
		ArQ	Arizona Quarterly
ACLALSB	ACLALS Bulletin	*Atenea: Revista de Ciencia, Arte y Literatura de la Universidad de Concepción*	
Actualidades:	*Consejo Nacional de la Cultura, Centro de Estudios Latinoamericanos "Romulo Gallegos"/Caracas, Venezuela*		
		AUC	Anales de la Universidad de Chile
		AUMLA	AUMLA: Journal of the Australasian Universities Language and Literature Association: A Journal of Literary Criticism and Linguistics
AfrSR	The African Studies Review		
AGald	Anales Galdosianos		
AHR	Afro-Hispanic Review	*BAC*	Boletín de la Academia Colombiana
AIQ	American Indian Quarterly		
AJFS	Australian Journal of French Studies	*BALF*	Black American Literature Forum
		BF	Books from Finland
AL	American Literature	*BHS*	Bulletin of Hispanic Studies
ALEC	Anales de la Literatura Española Contemporánea	*BlackI*	Black Images: A Critical Quarterly on Black Arts and Culture
ALHis	Anales de Literatura Hispanoamericana	*Boundary*	Boundary 2: A Journal of Postmodern Literature and Culture
ALR	American Literary Realism, 1870–1910	*BR/RB*	The Bilingual Review/La Revista Bilingüe
ALS	Australian Literary Studies	*BSIS*	Bulletin of the Society for Italian Studies
ALT	African Literature Today		
AmerP	American Poetry	*BSUF*	Ball State University Forum
AN	Acta Neophilologica	*CA*	Cuadernos Americanos
AnUS	Annual of Urdu Studies	*Callaloo: A Black South Journal of Arts and Letters*	
APR	The American Poetry Review		
AR	The Antioch Review	*CanL*	Canadian Literature
Arabica: Revue d'Études Arabes		*CarQ*	Caribbean Quarterly
		CasaA	Casa de las Américas

CASS	Canadian-American Slavic Studies
CBAA	Current Bibliography on African Affairs
CCur	Cross Currents: A Yearbook of Central European Culture
CE	College English
CE&S	Commonwealth Essays and Studies
CelfanR	Revue Celfan/Celfan Review
CentR	The Centennial Review (E. Lansing, MI)
CFM	Canadian Fiction Magazine
CFrC	Contemporary French Civilization
CH	Crítica Hispánica
CHA	Cuadernos Hispanoamericanos

Chasqui: Revista de Literatura Latinoamericana

CJIS	Canadian Journal of Irish Studies
CL	Comparative Literature
CLAJ	College Language Association Journal
CLAQ	Children's Literature Association Quarterly
CLEAR	Chinese Literature: Essays, Articles, Reviews
CNIE	Commonwealth Novel in English
Colóquio	Colóquio/Letras

Confluencia: Revista Hispánica de Cultura y Literatura

ConL	Contemporary Literature
CP	Concerning Poetry
CQ	The Cambridge Quarterly
CREL	Cahiers Roumains d'Études Littéraires: Revue Trimestrielle de Critique, d'Esthétique et d'Histoire Littéraires
Crit	Critique: Studies in Modern Fiction

Critique: Revue Générale des Publications Françaises et Étrangères

CritQ	Critical Quarterly
CSP	Canadian Slavonic Papers
CTR	Canadian Theatre Review
Dada	Dada/Surrealism
DeltaES	Delta: Revue du Centre d'Études et de Recherche sur les Écrivains du Sud aux États-Unis

Diacritics: A Review of Contemporary Criticism

Dimension: Contemporary German Arts and Letters

DLB	Dictionary of Literary Biography
DLit	Discurso Literario: Revista de Temas Hispánicos
DQR	Dutch Quarterly Review of Anglo-American Letters
DU	Der Deutschunterricht: Beiträge zu seiner Praxis und Wissenschaftlichen Grundlegung
DUJ	Durham University Journal

Eco: Revista de la Cultura de Occidente

ECr	L'Esprit Créateur
ECW	Essays on Canadian Writing

Edebiyat: A Journal of Middle Eastern Literatures

EF	Études Françaises
EI	Études Irlandaises
EinA	English in Africa
Éire	Éire-Ireland: A Journal of Irish Studies (St. Paul, MN)
ELWIU	Essays in Literature (Macomb, IL)
Ensayistas	Los Ensayistas: Georgia Series on Hispanic Thought
ESC	English Studies in Canada

Escritura: Revista de Teoría y Crítica Literarias

ExTL	Explicación de Textos Literarios
FMLS	Forum for Modern Language Studies

Folio: Essays on Foreign Languages and Literatures

FR	The French Review
FrF	French Forum

Frontiers: A Journal of Women Studies

FSt	Feminist Studies
GaR	The Georgia Review
GL&L	German Life and Letters
GQ	The German Quarterly
GR	Germanic Review
GSlav	Germano-Slavica: A Canadian Journal of Germanic and Slavic Comparative Studies
HAHR	Hispanic American Historical Review
HAR	Hebrew Annual Review

HC	The Hollins Critic
HisJ	Hispanic Journal
Hispam	Hispamérica: Revista de Literatura
Hispania: A Journal Devoted to the Interests of the Teaching of Spanish and Portuguese	
Hispano	Hispanófila
Horizontes: Revista de la Universidad Católica de Puerto Rico	
HR	Hispanic Review
HudR	The Hudson Review
I&L	Ideologies and Literature
Ibero	Iberoromania
IBLA: Revue de l'Institut des Belles Lettres Arabes	
IFR	International Fiction Review
IFRev	International Folklore Review
IJMES	International Journal of Middle East Studies
IJSLP	International Journal of Slavic Linguistics and Poetics
Imagine: International Chicano Poetry Journal	
IndL	Indian Literature
Inti: Revista de Literatura Hispánica	
IonC	Index on Censorship
IowaR	The Iowa Review
IranS	Iranian Studies: Journal of the Society for Iranian Studies
IS	Italian Studies
IUR	Irish University Review: A Journal of Irish Studies
JapQ	Japan Quarterly
JArabL	Journal of Arabic Literature
JASt	Journal of Asian Studies
JATJ	Journal of the Association of Teachers of Japanese
JBalS	Journal of Baltic Studies
JBlS	Journal of Black Studies
JCF	Journal of Canadian Fiction
JCL	The Journal of Commonwealth Literature
JCSR	Journal of Canadian Studies/Revue d'Études Canadiennes
JIWE	The Journal of Indian Writing in English
JNT	Journal of Narrative Technique
JPC	Journal of Popular Culture
JPrag	Journal of Pragmatics
JRS	Journal of Russian Studies
JSoAL	Journal of South Asian Literature
JSSB	Journal of the Siam Society
KanQ	Kansas Quarterly
KFQ	Keystone Folklore
KR	The Kenyon Review
KRQ	Romance Quarterly (formerly Kentucky Romance Quarterly)
LALR	Latin American Literary Review
L&P	Literature and Psychology
LangQ	The USF Language Quarterly
LATR	Latin American Theatre Review
LBR	Luso-Brazilian Review
LE&W	Literature East and West
LHY	Literary Half-Yearly
LitR	Literary Review
Lituanus: Baltic States Quarterly of Arts & Sciences	
LM	London Magazine
LOS	Literary Onomastics Studies
LPer	Literature in Performance: A Journal of Literary and Performing Art
MAL	Modern Austrian Literature
MAWAR	MAWA Review
MCL	Modern Chinese Literature
MD	Modern Drama
Merkur: Deutsche Zeitschrift für europäisches Denken	
MFS	Modern Fiction Studies
MHL	Modern Hebrew Literature
MichA	Michigan Academician: Papers of the Michigan Academy of Science, Arts, and Letters
ML	Modern Languages
MLN	Modern Language Notes
MLR	The Modern Language Review
MLS	Modern Language Studies
MN	Monumenta Nipponica
Monatshefte: Für Deutschen Unterricht, Deutsche Sprache und Literatur	

Mosaic: A Journal for the Interdisciplinary Study of Literature

MP   Modern Philology: A Journal Devoted to Research in Medieval and Modern Literature

MQ   Midwest Quarterly: A Journal of Contemporary Thought

MQR   Michigan Quarterly Review

MR   Massachusetts Review: A Quarterly of Literature, the Arts and Public Affairs

MRRM   Monographic Review/Revista Monográfica

Neohelicon: Acta Comparationis Litterarum Universarum

NER   New England Review and Bread Loaf Quarterly

NewC   The New Criterion

NewL   New Letters: A Magazine of Fine Writing

NewR   New Republic

NGC   New German Critique: An Interdisciplinary Journal of German Studies

NGS   New German Studies

NHQ   The New Hungarian Quarterly

NLH   New Literary History: A Journal of Theory and Interpretation

Novel: A Forum on Fiction

NRF   Nouvelle Revue Française

NWR   Northwest Review

NYRB   New York Review of Books

NYT   New York Times

NYTBR   New York Times Book Review

NYTMag   New York Times Magazine

NZSJ   New Zealand Slavonic Journal

Obsidian II: Black Literature in Review

OLR   The Oxford Literary Review

OnsE   Ons Erfdeel: Algemeen-Nederlands Tweemaandelijks Cultureel Tijdschrift

OSP   Oxford Slavonic Papers

PA   Présence Africaine

P&R   Philosophy and Rhetoric

Paragraph: The Journal of the Modern Critical Theory Group

Parnassus: Poetry in Review

PCL   Perspectives on Contemporary Literature

PCP   Pacific Coast Philology

PFr   Présence Francophone: Revue internationale de langue et de littérature

Plaza: Revista de Literatura

Plural: Revista Cultural de Excelsior

PMLA: Publications of the Modern Language Association of America

PoetryR   Poetry Review (London, England)

PolR   The Polish Review

POMPA   Publications of the Mississippi Philological Association

PoT   Poetics Today

PPNCFL   Proceedings of the Pacific Northwest Conference on Foreign Languages

PQ   Philological Quarterly

PR   Partisan Review

Prismal/Cabral: Revista de Literatura Hispánica/ Caderno Afro-Brasileiro Asiático Lusitano

PStud   Portuguese Studies

QQ   Queen's Quarterly

Quimera: Revista de Literatura

RaJAH   The Rackham Journal of the Arts and Humanities

RAL   Research in African Literatures

RCEH   Revista Canadiense de Estudios Hispánicos

RCF   The Review of Contemporary Fiction

RChL   Revista Chilena de Literatura

RCLL   Revista de Crítica Literaria Latinoamericana

REH   Revista de Estudios Hispánicos

Renascence: Essays on Value in Literature

Renditions: A Chinese-English Translation Magazine

RevI   Revista/Review Interamericana

Review: Latin American Literature and Arts

RHLQCF   Revue d'histoire littéraire du Québec et du Canada Français

RHM   Revista Hispánica Moderna

RI   Revista Iberoamericana

RIB	Revista Interamericana de Bibliografía/Inter-American Review of Bibliography
RLJ	Russian Language Journal
RLMC	Rivista di Letterature Moderne e Comparate
RLT	Russian Literature Triquarterly
RNL	Review of National Literatures
RR	Romanic Review
RusR	Russian Review
SAF	Studies in American Fiction
SAJL	Studies in American Jewish Literature
SatR	Saturday Review
SBR	Swedish Book Review
ScanR	Scandinavian Review
SCL	Studies in Canadian Literature
SCR	South Carolina Review
SDR	South Dakota Review
SEEA	Slavic and East European Arts
SEEJ	Slavic and East European Journal
SEER	The Slavonic and East European Review
SFR	Stanford French Review
SHR	Southern Humanities Review
Siglo	Siglo XX/20th Century
Signs: Journal of Women in Culture and Society	
SlavR	Slavic Review: American Quarterly of Soviet and East European Studies
SLitI	Studies in the Literary Imagination
Slovo: Časopis Staroslavenskog Zavoda u Zagrebu	
SoR	The Southern Review
Southerly: A Review of Australian Literature	
SovL	Soviet Literature
SR	Sewanee Review
SS	Scandinavian Studies
SSF	Studies in Short Fiction
SSR	Scottish Slavonic Review
StTCL	Studies in Twentieth Century Literature
Studies: An Irish Quarterly Review	
SubStance: A Review of Theory and Literary Criticism	

SWR	Southwest Review
Symposium: A Quarterly Journal in Modern Foreign Literatures	
T&K	Text & Kontext
TCL	Twentieth Century Literature
TCrit	Texto Crítico
TDR	The Drama Review
Theoria: A Journal of Studies in the Arts, Humanities and Social Sciences	
TJ	Theatre Journal
TLS	[London] Times Literary Supplement
TRev	Translation Review
TuK	Text + Kritik: Zeitschrift für Literatur
UDR	University of Dayton Review
UkrR	The Ukrainian Review: A Quarterly Magazine Devoted to the Study of the Ukraine
UQ	Ukrainian Quarterly: Journal of East European and Asian Affairs
UTQ	University of Toronto Quarterly: A Canadian Journal of the Humanities
UWR	University of Windsor Review (Windsor, Ontario)
VQR	Virginia Quarterly Review
WAL	Western American Literature
WB	Weimarer Beiträge
Westerly: A Quarterly Review	
WHR	Western Humanities Review
WLT	World Literature Today
WLWE	World Literature Written in English
WR	Western Review
WS	Women's Studies: An Interdisciplinary Journal
WSlA	Wiener Slawistischer Almanach
WVUPP	West Virginia University Philological Papers
YES	Yearbook of English Studies
YFS	Yale French Studies
YR	The Yale Review
ZAA	Zeitschrift für Anglistik und Amerikanistik
ZS	Zeitschrift für Slawistik
ZSP	Zeitschrift für Slavische Philologie

Illustrations

Acknowledgments

For permission to reproduce the illustrations in this volume,
the editors and publisher are indebted to the following:

ISABEL ALLENDE	Photo by Thomas Victor, courtesy of Alfred A. Knopf, Inc., N.Y.
ELECHI AMADI	Heinemann, Oxford
MAYA ANGELOU	Photo by Tim Richmond, courtesy of Random House, N.Y.
MICHAEL ANTHONY	Heinemann, Oxford
REINALDO ARENAS	Photo by Dolores Koch, courtesy of Grove Press, Inc., N.Y.
ANDRÉE CHEDID	Serpent's Tail, London
E. M. CIORAN	Photo by Jacques Sassier, courtesy of Arcade Publishing, N.Y.
HÉLÈNE CIXOUS	des femmes, Paris
ROBERTSON DAVIES	Photo by Jerry Bauer, courtesy of Viking, N.Y.
ARIEL DORFMAN	Photo by Thomas Victor, courtesy of Viking, N.Y.
SERGEY DOVLATOV	Photo by Jerry Bauer, courtesy of Weidenfeld & Nicolson, N.Y.
UMBERTO ECO	Photo by Kent Phillips, courtesy of Indiana University Press, Bloomington
KJARTAN FLØGSTAD	Photo by Anne Britt Kiluik, courtesy of Louisiana State University Press, Baton Rouge
MAVIS GALLANT	Photo by Frank Grant, courtesy of Random House, N.Y.
STEFAN HEYM	German Information Center, N.Y.
MIROSLAV HOLUB	Photo by Mark Lumley, courtesy of Bloodaxe Books Ltd, Newcastle upon Tyne
THOMAS KENEALLY	Photo by Jerry Bauer, courtesy of Simon & Schuster, N.Y.
GEORGE KONRÁD	Photo by Layle Silbert, courtesy of Harcourt Brace Jovanovich, Inc., N.Y.
PRIMO LEVI	Photo by Jerry Bauer, courtesy of Simon & Schuster, N.Y.
EARL LOVELACE	Heinemann, Oxford
LARRY MCMURTRY	Photo by Lee Marmon, courtesy of Simon & Schuster, N.Y.
BHARATI MUKHERJEE	Photo by Tom Victor, courtesy of Grove Press, Inc., N.Y.
ʿABD AL-RAHMĀN MUNĪF	Pantheon Books, N.Y.
MURAKAMI HURUKI	Photo by Eizo Matsumura
ADOLF MUSCHG	German Information center, N.Y.
CEES NOOTEBOOM	Louisiana State University Press, Baton Rouge
MILORAD PAVIĆ	Photo by Ivo Eterović, courtesy of Alfred A. Knopf, Inc., N.Y.
NÉLIDA PIÑON	Photo by Ulf Andersen, courtesy of Alfred A. Knopf, Inc., N.Y.
SALMAN RUSHDIE	Photo by Jerry Bauer, courtesy of Viking, N.Y.
JOSÉ SARAMAGO	Photo by S. Fischer, courtesy of Harcourt Brace Jovanovich, Inc., N.Y.
SIMONE SCHWARZ-BART	Photo by Anaïk Frantz, courtesy of Seuil, Paris
HANĀN AL-SHAYKH	Interlink Publishing Group, Inc., N.Y.
HENRIK STANGERUP	Lindhart and Ringhof, Copenhagen
MÄRTA TIKKANEN	Finnish Literature Information Centre
TATYANA TOLSTAYA	Photo by Jerry Bauer, courtesy of Alfred A. Knopf, Inc., N.Y.
WILLIAM TREVOR	Photo by Jerry Bauer, courtesy of Viking, N.Y.
LUISA VALENZUELA	Photo by Brendan Hennessy, courtesy of Simon & Schuster, N.Y.
ALICE WALKER	Photo by Jean Weisinger, courtesy of Harcourt Brace Jovanovich, Inc., N.Y.
WANG MENG	Photo by Perry Link, courtesy of University of Washington Press, Seattle
FAY WELDON	Photo by Mark Gerson, courtesy of Viking, N.Y.
A. B. YEHOSHUA	Photo by Horst Tappe, courtesy of Doubleday, N.Y.
ADAM ZAGAJEWSKI	Photo by Virginia Schendler, courtesy of Farrar, Straus & Giroux, Inc., N.Y.

Preface to the Supplement

This Supplement to the *Encyclopedia of World Literature in the 20th Century* is designed to complement the four-volume Revised Edition by providing an enlarged treatment of significant literary activity during the century and throughout the world. The breadth and complexity of this literature demands progressive study, analysis, and evaluation, and the Supplement serves as a comprehensive and authoritative guide for this purpose. Responsive to the needs of scholarly and general readers alike, the Supplement provides new, expanded, and revised information necessary to the assessment and appreciation of the growth and development of modern world literature. The decade preceding the publication of this Supplement has been one of the most extraordinary in modern history, dominated by the impact of unprecedented social and political upheaval and historic redefinition of national boundaries. We have witnessed events that have altered the shape of the world and the terms by which we discuss literature. The sociopolitical as well as literary ramifications of these alterations have yet to fully realize themselves and be understood. However, we have made every attempt to incorporate these recent developments within the context of the Supplement.

The Supplement contains survey articles on some thirty-five national literatures. Designed as a continuation of volumes 1 to 4 of the *Encyclopedia*, the survey articles in the Supplement focus primarily on the literary activity during the last decade and since the publication of the Revised Edition. The survey articles discuss the work of mature writers who continue to make a significant literary contribution as well as new and emerging writers who have produced work of popular interest and critical importance.

The core of the Supplement, like that of the Revised Edition, is the separate articles on major and representative writers. The Supplement contains articles for more than four hundred authors of national or international significance. Selected by the general editor in conjunction with the board of advisers, the authors receiving separate articles in the volume reflect three basic criteria governing inclusion. They are: (1) established authors of early or mid-century whose oeuvre and literary reputation continue to exert a significant influence in the present; (2) authors of late-century who have made a substantial literary contribution; (3) authors of outstanding achievement from less familiar literatures. In order to fulfill its purpose as a reference work, the Supplement attempts to be comprehensive rather than faddish in the selection of authors. It is also important to maintain the international scope of the *Encyclopedia*. Thus, many authors—American, British, European—who are well known to English-speaking readers do not receive separate entries but are instead treated within the survey articles of national literatures. Many of the authors from the less familiar literatures have limited exposure to English-speaking readers, and a significant number to date have not been translated into English or have not generated criticism in English of scholarly merit. For these authors, the Supplement serves as the primary source of reference to English-speaking readers.

Similar to volumes 1 to 4 of the Revised Edition, topical articles are included in the Supplement to reflect literary trends, movements, or bodies of critical thought that have influenced modern world literature. The Supplement includes articles on deconstruction, feminist criticism, historicism, literature and exile, postmodernism, and poststructuralism.

STEVEN R. SERAFIN

The general editor wishes to express his appreciation, first, to the hundreds of individuals whose contributions have helped to make this Supplement a reference work of distinction. He is most indebted to those scholars listed in the board of advisers, whose generosity of time and expertise provided proportion, balance, and consistency in the preparation of the volume. The editor wishes to acknowledge the exceptional contribution of the following individuals: Roger Allen for Arabic literatures, George R. McMurray for Spanish American literature, Howard Goldblatt for Chinese literature, Hosea Hirata for Japanese literature, John D. Erickson for French literature, and the late John Povey for African literatures.

The editors are especially grateful for the guidance of Werner Mark Linz, publisher of Continuum, and Evander Lomke, managing editor.

Finally, the general editor offers his gratitude to Dennis Paoli for his advice and support during the project and to Jason Berner and Geneviève Trousserean for their invaluable editorial assistance, all of whom are affiliated with Hunter College of the City University of New York.

Encyclopedia of World Literature
in the 20th Century

'ABD AL-SABŪR, Salāh

Egyptian poet, dramatist, and critic; b. 3 May 1931; d. Aug. 1981, Cairo

S. is the most prominent Egyptian poet since the mid-1950s. He obtained a degree from Cairo University in 1951 and worked mainly in cultural avenues all his life, first as teacher and journalist, then in several administrative positions, the last of which was as director of the General Organization of Egyptian Books. His premature death put an end to a most flourishing literary career.

He is the earliest Egyptian poet to achieve a modernist approach in the form and content of his poetry. As early as his first collection, *Al-nās fī bilādī* (1957; people in my country), he demonstrated a radical departure from the language, structure, and attitudinal characteristics of the inherited poetry. His sentence constructions were relaxed, and his vocabulary, intonations, and rhythms were greatly deelevated from the original eloquence and loud rhythms of Arabic verse, and his attitude and vision were markedly different. This is perhaps his greatest achievement, arrived at, in good measure, unwittingly. For although his experiment with language was as conscious as it was instinctive, his actual awareness, at that early period, of the other modernist dimensions of his work was perhaps not equal to the depth of the experiment itself. From the outset, S. was able to achieve modernity both in form and content. Early in his work, just as in the works of almost all Arab poets of the 1950s, the contemporary Arab predicament is fully recognized, yet he depicts it not in the loud, direct tones of protest and dissent typical of his contemporaries, but in the quiet tones and demure stance of the modernist poet. The problem of modernity in contemporary Arabic poetry has not mainly been a problem of language and form; these two elements had been more radically revolutionized than other equally important elements. The main problem has been one of tone and attitude, two elements that proved highly resistant to change, which stipulates first, a de-elevated, declassed status for the poet who has traditionally viewed himself as prophet, leader, and liberator, and secondly, a vision that recognizes the helpless situation of the individual in an Arab world constantly subject to internal coercion and external aggression. S. instinctively realized all this, as well as the necessity to deelevate diction and approximate it to the living language of the people around him, without ever vulgarizing it. He is not an heir to self-assertiveness or demonstrative heroics, and his psychological and intellectual make-up—modest, gentle, urbane, and sophisticated—enabled him to achieve the necessary shift from the heroic stance and the aristocratic, old-world grandeur to the urban (sometimes even plebeian) contemporary expression. S.'s occasional employment of irony, as in his long poem "Hikāyat al-mughannī 'l-hazīn" (story of the sad minstrel), published in *Ta'ammulāt fī zaman jarīh* (1971; reflections on a wounded era), is subtle and highly effective and could have been achieved only because the poet's concept of himself and his role had changed dramatically. S. could see himself and everyone else as victims, not heroes, of the times. His protagonist uncovers a world of fraud, complicity, and false situations, but in his strife against this world he discovers that he is an integral part of it and that his life is controlled by its pernicious forces. His rebellion against his predicament is not a direct attempt to influence this world, but an expression of suffering reflecting the receptive stance of a victim who is acted upon by events. This suffering invariably helps transform the world of the reader through a recognition of his or her own similar situation. S.'s revolution in form, language, and syntax is supported by a genuine transformation of vision and depression of tone, all elements combining to reflect a precocious modernist spirit anticipating the works of such modernists as Sa'dī Yūsuf (b. 1943) and the younger poets of the 1980s.

S. has also rendered a major contribution to the verse drama in Arabic, writing highly experimental plays. In his first play, *Ma'sāt al-Hallāj* (1964; tragedy of al-Hallāj), a tragedy, he incorporated the Greek principle of the fall of the manifestly doomed hero. Al-Hallāj, a famous mystic and staunch defender of the poor, was crucified for heresy in Baghdad in 922. Despite his precarious position as a spokesman for social justice, which made him undesirable to the authorities of his time, he was tempted, out of the joy and fulness of his heart, to divulge that he had achieved direct union with God, and the judges rose immediately to indict him, convincing the very people whom he had defended of his heresy. In other plays, S. diversified both his form and themes. *Musāfir layl* (1969; night traveler) is a symbolic black comedy, and *Al-Amīra tantazir* (1970; the princess waits) is a fairy tale-like story that celebrates the advent of hope and the rise to action after a long period of inertia and despair. Technically, S. manipulated dramatic poetry to convey the language and themes of daily life without loss to its poetic quality.

S.'s whole oeuvre is furthermore informed by cogent ideas and a definite stance toward both Arab life and the general universal condition, colored, where relevant, by deep empathy. His is one of the few poetic experiments to merge thought and art in a subtle mélange that sacrifices neither.

His many prose writings, though not of the same order as his poetic and dramatic works, still reflect an original mind; and such works as his book on classical Arabic poetry, *Qirā'a jadīda li shi'rinā 'l-qadīm* (1968; a new reading in our old poetry), are a departure from the usual way this poetry has been treated previously. Perhaps his most interesting prose work is his book on his own career as poet, *Hayātī fi 'l-shi'r* (1969; my life in poetry).

To sum up, S. is a notable experimenter and innovator, a poet with a sense of the tragic who reflects a vision of a broken world full of victims and failed endeavors. Yet he is sparse of emotion, devoted to questions, free of absolutes, completely stripped of heroics, and marvelously free of sentimentality. Addressing great universals and major national and human issues, he probes deeply into the meaning of life, combining the opposing poles of the tragic and the ironic, a truly tormented soul that finds no rest. As a true modernist, he has never accepted the conventional or catered to the expectations of the audience. Instead, his work is marked by an inversion of tradition and focuses on aspects of experience never before broached in poetry. His theme spans diverse aspects of experience ranging from a wide spectrum of communal preoccupations, to the cycle of life and death, to the joy of love and the desolation of its absence and to the diverse disappointments of life.

FURTHER WORKS: *Afkār qawmiyya* (1960); *Aswāt al-'asr* (1960); *Aqūlu lakum* (1961); *Ahlām al-fāris al-qadīm* (1964); *Hattā naqhar al-mawt* (1966); *Wa tabqā 'l-kalima* (1970); *Shajar al-layl* (1970); *Rihla 'alā 'l-waraq* (1971); *Madīnat al-'ishq wa 'l-hikma* (1972); *Al-nisā' hīna yatahattamna* (1976); *Al-ibhār fi 'l-dhākira* (1979); *Kitāba 'alā wajh al-rīh* (1980); *Mashārif al-khamsīn* (1981)

BIBLIOGRAPHY: Badawi, M. M., *A Critical Introduction to Modern Arabic Poetry* (1975), 209, 216–18, 260; Jayyusi, S. K., *Trends and Movements in Modern Arabic Poetry* (1977) Vol. 2, passim; Ayyad, S. M., and N. Witherspoon, *Reflections and Deflections: A Study of the Contemporary Arab Mind through its Literary Creations* (1986), 200–11; Badawi, M. M., *Modern Arabic Drama in Egypt* (1987), 220–28; Jayyusi, S. K., "Modernist Poetry in Arabic," in *Cambridge History of Arabic Literature,* Vol. 4, forthcoming

SALMA KHADRA JAYYUSI

ABRAMOV, Fyodor

Russian novelist, short-story writer, and critic, b. 29 Feb. 1920, Verkola; d. 14 May 1983, Leningrad

A. is one of the most famous of the many Russian peasant writers who played an important role in post-Stalinist literature. Born in the Arkhangel region of northern Russia, A. studied at Leningrad University before volunteering for the front in World War II, where he is rumored to have worked for the Soviet counterintelligence unit SMERSH. After recovering from his war wounds, he joined the Communist Party in 1945, continued his studies, and received his graduate degree in 1951. In the early 1950s, he was a professor of Soviet literature in Leningrad and an influential critic; after the success of his first novel at the end of the 1950s, he devoted himself entirely to his writing.

A. began publishing literary criticism in 1949. His controverisal essay "Lyudi kolkhoznoy derevni v poslevoennoy proze" (1954; kolkhoz peasants in postwar prose) was one of several important attacks in the early Thaw years on Socialist Realist collective-farm novels. While undermining this type of hackneyed Soviet prose, A. praised the works of a number of writers, including Valentin Ovechkin (1904–1968) and Vladimir Tendryakov (q.v.). In many ways A.'s essay served as a blueprint for the evolution of collective-farm literature into "village prose," the largest and most coherent body of aesthetically and ideologically significant literature to be published in the U.S.S.R. in the decades between Stalin's death in 1953 and the advent of glasnost in the mid-1980s.

Unlike his fellow village-prose writers, who worked mostly in smaller forms or loosely constructed memoirs, A. began with the novel. He is best known for his four-volume series, set in the northern Russian village of Pekashino. *Bratya i syostry* (1958; brothers and sisters) began the chronicle of the Pryaslin family in the early years of World War II. While other Soviet writers focused on the battlefield itself or on the "hero cities" of the Soviet Union, A. was interested in how the war was experienced on the ''second front'' in the Russian village. *Dve zimi i tri leta* (1968; *Two Winters and Three Summers*, 1984) is the second and best-known part of this tetralogy, and covers the immediate postwar years when the task of rebuilding turns out to be as exhausting as the war effort. In his novels A. unites the reformist, nostalgic, and lyrical tendencies of village prose with elements of the epic and chronicle. He successfully captures the texture of Soviet life by reflecting the impact of major events on one small but ultimately representative area of the country. The third volume, *Puti-pereputya* (1973; at the crossroads), concentrates on the corrupt, unjust, and ineffective administration of collectivized agriculture, which so often undermined the hard work of the northern peasants. The final volume, *Dom* (1978; the house), takes the villagers into the early 1970s. While there is a tragic death in the Pryaslin family at the end of *Dom,* there is also a melancholy-luminous atmosphere that reassures the reader that not all traditional Russian peasant values have been lost. These novels were well received in the Soviet Union, and A. was awarded the State Prize for Literature in 1975.

While A. is primarily known for his Pekashino series, he wrote successfully in a number of other genres. The book-length essay *Vokrug da okolo* (1963; *The New Life,* 1963) contained his most frank and controversial appraisal of the kolkhoz system. He says here bluntly what had been introduced with greater subtlety in his fiction. This essay was seen in the West as an important example of Thaw literature, more critical but less artistic than Aleksandr Solzhenitsyn's (q.v.) *Odin den v zhizni Ivana Denisovicha* (1962; *One Day in the Life of Ivan Denisovich,* 1963). A. was severely criticized at home for being too negative about the kolkhoz system, and he was able to publish very little between 1963 and 1968.

In his numerous short stories, A. chronicles the gradual fading of traditional rural ways in northern Russia. Sometimes he listens to the narratives of older villagers who recall the years before the Revolution and before collectivization; in other stories he focuses on the younger people who escape the countryside as soon as they can, and only return to boast about their wider knowledge of the modern world. A. also favored very short lyrical essays, which include such material as his own reminiscences about rural life, transcripts of conversations with villagers, and northern folklore. Some of these selections were published during his lifetime as *Trava-murava* (1982; the thick green grass), while further selections from his extensive notebooks were published posthumously as ''Dom v Verkole'' (1986; the house in Verkola). Among the many ''delayed'' works that

appeared in the glasnost years, one of the most noteworthy is A.'s ''Poezdka v proshloe'' (1989; a journey into the past). This story, which A. worked on between 1963 and 1974, reveals some hard truths about the government's treatment of the kulaks during the process of collectivization in terms of one man's dramatic act of repentance.

A. was among the most talented and productive writers of Russian village prose, which makes him one of the most important literary figures of the post-Stalinist period. He championed the use of folk and regional speech in literature to reflect accurately the psychology of peasant characters and to preserve this rich linguistic heritage against the influence of an impoverished urban language. A.'s prose style stands in sharp contrast to the mostly homogeneous language of Socialist Realist novels. A. was in no way a dissident writer, but he always sought to write as honestly as possible about the contemporary peasant and life in the Russian countryside, and in this way to undo the damage that had been done to the rural theme in literature since 1917.

FURTHER WORKS: *Bezottsovshchina* (1962); *Derevyannye koni* (1972); *Poslednyaya okhota* (1973); *Izbrannoe* (1975); *Sobranie sochinenii* (1980); *Babiley* (1981); *Povesti i rasskazy* (1985); *Chem zhiven—kormimsya* (1986); *Pashnya zhivaya i mertyaya* (1987, with Antonin Chistyakov). FURTHER VOLUME IN ENGLISH: *The Swans Flew By and Other Stories* (1986)

BIBLIOGRAPHY: Brown, D., *Soviet Russian Literature since Stalin* (1978), 233–37; Hosking, G., *Beyond Socialist Realism* (1980), 56–57; Brown, E. J., *Russian Literature since the Revolution* (rev. ed., 1982), 299–301; Marsh, R. J., *Soviet Fiction since Stalin* (1986), 173–76; Lowe, D. A., *Russian Writing since 1953* (1987), 85–86; Shneidman, N. N., *Soviet Literature in the 1980s* (1989), 97–101; Gillespie, D., ''Ironies and Legacies: Village Prose and Glasnost,'' *FMLS*, 27, 1 (Jan. 1991), 70–84

KATHLEEN PARTHÉ

ABŪ MĀDĪ, Īliyyā

Lebanese poet (writing in Arabic), b. 1889, Muhayditha; d. 1957, Brooklyn, N.Y., U.S.A.

A. M. is hailed by Arab critics as the foremost poet among *al-Mahjariyyūn,* a group of mainly Lebanese writers who emigrated to the U.S. and South America in the early 1900s and who are credited with innovations in the idiom, form, and content of Arabic poetry and prose. In 1900 A. M. left Lebanon for Egypt and lived there until

1911, the date of the publication of his first poetry collection, *Dīwān Tadhkār al-mādī* (remembering the past), which launched his career as a gifted young poet employing monometers and mono-rhymes in the classical traditional manner. That same year, he emigrated to the U.S., where he soon distinguished himself as poet and journalist and came into close contact with the members of the Society of the Pen, which he helped found in 1916. Three other collections, *Dīwān Īliyyā Abū Mādī* (1919; the divan of I. A. M.), *al-Jadāwil* (1927; streams), and *al-Khamā'il* (1940; gardens), appeared in New York. *Tibr wa Turāb* (1960; gold dust and earth) was published posthumously in Beirut, Lebanon, by his brother.

A. M. is a controversial poet. While *Dīwān Tadhkār al-mādī* brought him immediate recognition, critics of his poetry pointed to linguistic and stylistic weaknesses, which some blamed on his youth and lack of literary education. Others saw in those early stages little more than occasional poems in the overwhelming poetic tradition of the time. In the second collection, A. M. emerges as a strong imitator of his predecessors and contemporaries in the Arab world, but imitation, strong as it was in many of his poems, left him no room for poetic creation, and his personality remained submerged in a time and space not his own, in a poetic idiom foreign to his social reality. The reception of this collection by the members of the Society of the Pen was, to say the least, lukewarm, this in spite of the fact that the leader of *al-Mahjariyyūn,* Kahlil Gibran (q.v.), wrote the short foreword to the volume.

A new stage in A. M.'s development as a poet coincides with his participation in the pioneering literary activities of his compatriots and the theoretical discussions they had on the nature of poetry, most prominently in A. M.'s literary journal *al-Sāmir* (1929–1957). Through their influence, especially in their own experimentation in the language of poetry, A. M. came to realize that only the inauguration of a new language can contribute to modern Arabic poetry.

The poems of *al-Jadāwil,* which earned him his distinction as a strong modern poet, were written between 1919 and 1927, the most important formative years of A. M.'s career. This was a new kind of poetry, contemplative, romantic, lyrical, and dramatic, a true revolution in both the content and the form of Arabic poetry. Some of the poems of this collection have become household items in the Arab world and have contributed to the romantic trend that ensued. The artificial abstract form of A. M.'s earlier collections gave way to a vital organic unity, a poetic distance that allowed the movements in the poems to grow without the poet's interference. Experimentation in meter and

rhythmic variations characterize this collection, and the naive rationality of the poetry that preceded reverted here to a romanticism of dreams and visions, a poetry of color and music, unknown to the classical poetic tradition.

However, despite the enthusiastic praise of his friends and readers in the Americas and the Arab world, A. M. soon returned to his old imitative stage. His enthusiasm for the modern poetic manifesto of the Society of the Pen waned, perhaps because he was intensely aware of his larger public in the Arab world at that time, which often viewed the innovations of *al-Mahjariyyūn* with suspicion. Thus in *al-Khamā'il* and later on in *Tibr wa Turāb* A. M. exhibits an anxiety of influence that pulled him back and forth between his Arab heritage and his new Western sensibility.

In the development of modern Arabic poetry, A. M. remains one of the most important voices in the early decades of the 20th c. However, his innovations, strong as they were, lacked the philosophical conviction and the depth of Gibran, the most prominent member of the Society of the Pen.

BIBLIOGRAPHY: Badawi, M. M., *A Critical Introduction to Modern Arabic Poetry* (1975), 188–91; Jayyusi, S. K., *Trends and Movements in Modern Arabic Poetry* (1977), Vol. 1, 123–35, 326–28; Ostle, R. C., "I. A. M. and Arabic Poetry in the Inter-War Period," in Ostle, R. C., ed., *Studies in Modern Arabic Literature* (1975), 34–45

ADNAN HAYDAR

AĞAOĞLU, Adalet

Turkish novelist and dramatist, b. 1929, Nallıhan

A leading writer of fiction and drama, A. enjoys prestige as Turkey's premier woman novelist in the last quarter of the 20th c. In 1950 she graduated from the University of Ankara with a degree in French language and literature. She had taken up writing in 1946 when she contributed reviews and essays on the theater to the Ankara daily *Ulus*. In 1948–1949 she published poetry in the literary journal *Kaynak*. In 1951 she joined the staff of Radio Ankara, where she worked successively as a librarian, dramaturge, and chief of literary programs and radio plays. From the mid-1960s to 1970 she served as consultant to the Turkish radio and television administration. In recent years she was a columnist for the Istanbul dailies *Milliyet* and *Cumhuriyet*.

A. first attracted attention as a dramatist: Her 1964 play *Evcilik Oyunu* (1964; the marriage game) earned considerable praise from the critics. It is a well-made play that deals in ingenious ways with matrimonial crisis. *Çatıdaki Çatlak* (perf. 1965, pub. 1969; crack in the roof), *Tombala* (1969; lottery), and *Kendini yazan şarkı* (1976; the song that wrote itself) are remarkable for their explorations into the psychological motivations of the principal characters and for a Pinteresque flavor, especially in their dialogue. Her *Üç oyun* (1973; three plays), containing *Bir kahramanın ölümü* (death of a hero), *Çıkış* (exit), and *Kozalar* (cocoons), somewhat reminiscent of Samuel Beckett (q.v.), won the Drama Prize of the Turkish Language Society in 1974.

A.'s entry into the world of fiction in 1973 with *Ölmeye yatmak* (lying down to die) earned her a great deal of accolades and stimulated much debate about the innovations she introduced. This first novel, which interfuses incisive psychological portrayals, news items, and stream-of-consciousness (q.v.) techniques, is a masterwork dealing with political oppression, personal crisis, women's subjugation, and violations of human rights in modern Turkey. Although complete in itself, *Ölmeye yatmak* stands as the first part of a trilogy, together with *Bir düğün gecesi* (1979; a wedding night) and *Hayır* (1987; no). *Bir düğün gecesi,* perhaps the most lyrical of A.'s novels, was awarded Turkey's three major literary prizes. Her first collection of short stories, *Yüksek gerilim* (1974; high tension), which contains mostly conventional realistic stories, won the Sait Faik Prize in 1975.

Fikrimin ince gülü (1976; my mind's tender rose), a widely acclaimed novel of social injustice and private anguish, was banned by the military government of the early 1980s. Dealing mainly with the alienation of the Turkish guest workers in Germany, this book is A.'s most effective exposé of class differences, economic exploitation, and materialistic fetishism. Her second collection of short stories, *Sessizliğin ilk sesi* (1978; first sound of silence), broke new ground in introspective and surrealistic fiction: Some of the stories here can be seen as the quintessence of her best novels. *Yazsonu* (1980; summer's end), which the author herself identified as "a novelization of the creative act," represents a further foray into the realm of imaginative mysterium as do many of the masterful pieces in her third collection of short stories, *Hadi gidelim* (1982; come on, let's go).

In 1984 A. published *Üç beş kişi* (a few people), a novel of the social and personal dilemmas arising from the exodus from the countryside into the urban areas. In quick succession came *Göç temizliği* (1985; clean-up for moving), an avowedly autobiographical novel.

A. collected some of her essays and articles on literature in a volume entitled *Geçerken* (1986; in passing). A number of her radio and television plays produced in Turkey, France, and Germany remain unpublished, as do some of her stage works. In 1991 A. saw publication of her avant-garde play *Çok uzak fazla yakın* (very far—too close).

Her novella *Ruh üşümesi* (1991; soul shivering), which is subtitled "a chamber novel," combines a powerful eroticism with flights of the imagination, making it one of the most compelling works of sexual enactments in the history of Turkish fiction.

A.'s experiments with form and substance of fiction, her explorations into the minds of her protagonists, her deft ways of evoking moods and atmosphere, and her singular style have secured a permanent place for her in the literature of Turkey in the 20th c.

BIBLIOGRAPHY: Ervin, E. W., "Narrative Technique in the Fiction of A. A.," *Edebiyat,* 1, 1 (1987), 128–46

TALAT SAIT HALMAN

AGUILERA MALTA, Demetrio

Ecuadorean novelist, dramatist, and short-story writer, b. 24 May 1909, Guayaquil; d. 29 Dec. 1981, Mexico City, Mexico

A. M. started out as a teacher and later served his country as minister of culture. As his reputation as a writer grew, he took up residency in Mexico and in his later years was invited by universities in the U.S. as a writer in residence. In 1981 his native country honored him with the Eugenio Espejo Prize, the most distinguished literary prize awarded in Ecuador.

A. M. began his career with short stories in *Los que se van* (1930; those who leave), a volume that also included stories by Joaquín Gallegos Lara (q.v.) and Enrique Gil Gilbert (1912–1973). The book portrayed the violent, broken lives of the *cholos* or half-castes of Guayaquil and was both condemned and praised for the crude naturalism of its language and characterizations. In *Don Goyo* (1933; *Don Goyo,* 1980), A. M.'s first novel, the *cholo* is still his subject, but the regionalism of the mangrove swamps near Guayaquil is tinged with a magical quality, especially in the portrayal of the patriarchal tribal chief, Don Goyo Quimi, whom the *cholos* perceive as an almost mythical being at one with the surrounding natural world. *La isla virgen* (1942; the virgin island) similarly mixes reality and myth. The white man Nestor is the opposite of Don Goyo as he exploits the natural environment of San Pancracio. Nature, personified as woman, eventually takes its revenge on the one who would violate her. These two novels represent A. M.'s epic regionalist stage. In retrospect, they can be seen as precursors of the Latin American magic realism (q.v.) of the 1950s and 1960s.

A. M. spent the next decade writing mainly drama, although he composed journalistic fiction as well. For his farces, satires, and atmospheric theatrical pieces he is considered one of the outstanding dramatists of Latin America. In the mid-1960s A. M. returned to the novel with the publication of *La caballaresa del sol* (1964; *Manuela,* 1967), *El Quijote de El Dorado* (1965; the Quixote of El Dorado), and *Un nuevo mar para el rey* (1965; a new ocean for the king), three historico-biographical novels about Simón Bolívar, Francisco de Oreana, and Vasco Núñez de Balboa respectively. Well written but rather conventional and straightforward in form and style, they hardly anticipate his last and most imaginative period of magic-realist satire.

This last period saw the publication of *Siete lunas y siete serpientes* (1970; *Seven Serpents and Seven Moons,* 1976) and *El secuestro del general* (1973; *Babelandia,* 1984). The former is an expressionistic tour de force, a hallucinatory comedy set in the mythical island town of Santorontón and the surrounding coastal area of Ecuador. The regionalism of the earlier novels, however, is here subordinated to allegory as A. M. invents a self-contained microcosm for the unfolding of the archetypal story of the human fall from paradise in Latin America. On the one hand are the evil, satanical characters (representing the politician, the military, the exploitative upper class, and the institutional church), driven by lust and desire for power, who wreak their different kinds of destruction on Santorontón. Combating them are the forces for Good, the effigy of the burned Christ, the good Father Cándido, Doctor Balda, and the Earth Mother Clotilde, who represent authentic Christianity, scientific enlightenment, and nostalgia for a lost paradise respectively. Myth (Christian, Indian, African), legend, dream, and sheer fantasy permeate the novel; evil characters are transformed into crocodiles, serpents, and toads as they rape, murder, and pillage; the burned Christ carries on a dialogue with the good priest Cándido; and redemption occurs through the erotic rituals of the African shaman Bulu-Bulu. An often-incantatory prose style intensifies this radically defamiliarized reality. *El secuestro del general* is equally phantasmagorical but more grotesque in its use of Black Humor (q.v.).

A. M. is a committed writer with a passion for social justice who has assimilated the vision and techniques of magic realism over the years. Rather than deepen our understanding of reality, however, the techniques are used to bring into focus a sociopolitical message. Because of this, it is unlikely that A. M. will ever have the wide international readership of a Gabriel García Márquez (q. v.).

FURTHER WORKS: *Canal Zone* (1935); *¡Madrid!* (1936); *España leal* (1938); *Lázaro* (1941); *No bastan los átomos* (1955); *Dientes blancos* (1955); *El tigre* (1956); *Honorarios* (1957); *Trilogía Ecuatoriana* (1957); *Una cruz en la sierra maestra* (1960); *Infierno negro* (1967); *Fantoche* (1970); *Muerte, S.A.* (1970); *Teatro completo* (1970); *Jaguar* (1977)

BIBLIOGRAPHY: Davis, J., "The 'Episodios Americanos' of A. M.," *Foreign Language Quarterly,* 9 (1970), 43–47; Luzuriaga, G., "La evolución estilística del teatro de A. M.," *LATR,* 3, 2 (Spring 1970), 39–44; Davis, J., "The 'Episodios Americanos', cont.," *Foreign Language Quarterly,* 9 (1971), 49–53; Monsanto, C., "*Infierno negro:* drama de protesta social," *Duquesne Hispanic Review,* 10 (1971), 11–22; Carter, B., "La novelística de A. M.: Enfoques y pareceres," *Chasqui,* 3 (1973), 66–70; Koldewyn, P., "Protesta guerrillera y mitológica: Novela nueva de A. M.," *Nueva Narrativa Hispanoamericana,* 5 (1975), 199–205; Rabassa, C. C., *D. A. M. and Social Justice* (1980)

ROBERT SCOTT

AIDOO, Ama Ata

(formerly Christina Ama Ata Aidoo) Ghanaian dramatist, poet, short-story writer, and novelist (writing in English), b. 23 Mar. 1942, Abeadzi Kyiakor

Educated at Wesley Girls School, Cape Coast, and the University of Ghana (in Legon), where she earned a B.A. with honors in 1964 and became a research fellow in African studies after graduation, A. participated in an international seminar at Harvard University in 1966 and studied creative writing at Stanford University. She has traveled extensively in Africa, the U.S., and Europe as a writer, teacher, and consultant. Beginning in 1970 she was based as a lecturer in English at the University of Cape Coast; but in January 1982, she accepted the appointment of secretary for education for Ghana and served until June 1983. Since September 1983, A. has lived in Harare, Zimbabwe.

While yet a student, A. won prizes for her short stories and witnessed the production of her first play, *The Dilemma of a Ghost* (perf. 1964, pub. 1965). Classified most often as a dramatist, A. has written in the major genres. All of her works, however, reflect the influence of the oral tradition, especially storytelling, which she states has power and pertinence for the contemporary writer and audience. While her creations are set primarily in Africa, particularly Ghana, and address the problems and situations of that continent, they are designed to engage her worldwide audience toward the recognition that the issues affect us all and, furthermore, that her readers too have a responsibility to help resolve these ills.

The Dilemma of a Ghost, her first play, adopts structural and thematic elements from the traditional dilemma tale as it dramatizes the conflicts that result when an African male who has been studying in the U.S. returns to Ghana with his African-American wife. *Anowa* (1969), the second dramatic piece, based on a legend which A. says her mother told her, emphasizes the interlocking systems of gender, race, and class, especially as these structures impact on the lives of women. The beautiful, strong-minded, nonconforming Anowa, whose name provides the title, is the model for the other independent female figures who dominate the later works and who, along with their rebellious ideas, have earned for their creator the title of "feminist."

The short stories, many published in journals before being collected in *No Sweetness Here* (1970), illustrate, even more keenly, her ability to employ the techniques and performance skills of the oral artist and concurrently to serve as a voice for the African woman. These eleven tales explore themes of motherhood, womanhood, childhood, the family, marriage, and other issues confronting postindependent Africa.

A.'s poetry also first appeared in anthologies and journals. In addition, her plays, short stories, and longer pieces display her dynamic flair for combining narrative and poetry. *Someone Talking to Sometime* (1985), a volume of poems, takes one on a journey to experience the pain, hurt, and foolishness that African people have suffered on the continent, in the U.S., and throughout the world. Another subject, which emerged in the short stories, but receives prominence here and in *Our Sister Killjoy; or, the Reflections of a Black-Eyed Squint* (1977), is neocolonialism, the system of oppression and abuse by African leaders and the educated elites against their own struggling people. The collection appeals for an end to the suffering and strife.

Our Sister Killjoy; or, the Reflections of a Black-Eyed Squint and *Changes: A Love Story* (1991) represent A.'s contribution to the novel. Both works are similar in that they present the independent, educated, professional female protagonist in a book-length, poetic-prose form that defies conventional categories. *Changes,* subtitled "A Love Story," which is a surprise, since A. had vowed never to write on such a "frivolous" topic, moves closer in shape toward its Western counterpart.

Nevertheless, this most recently published piece of fiction provides the provocative treatment and twist that characterize the writings of this author.

"Experimental," "innovative," "inimitable," "stimulating," "engaging," and "committed" describe this multitalented African female writer and her writings. Sometimes angry, sometimes witty, incisive yet sensitive, possessing remarkable insight into the human condition, A. blends the legacy of her African oral inheritance with the Western borrowings to produce eloquent and dazzling creations. For too long, neglected and underrepresented in critical circles, possibly because of publishing problems, availability of the books, and the originality in her performances, A. now appears to be gaining the recognition her powerful literature deserves.

FURTHER WORKS: *The Eagle and the Chickens and Other Stories for Children* (1986); *Birds and Other Poems for Children* (1987)

BIBLIOGRAPHY: Brown, L. W., "A. A. A.: The Art of the Short Story and Sexual Roles in Africa," *WLWE,* 13 (1974), 172–83; Adelugba, D., "Language and Drama: A. A. A.," in Jones, E. D., ed., *ALT,* 8 (1976), 72–84; Brown, L. W., "A. A. A.," *Women Writers in Black Africa* (1981), 84–121; Hill-Lubin, M., "The Relationship of African-Americans and Africans: A Recurring Theme in the Works of A. A. A.," *PA,* 124 (1982), 190–201; Elder, A., "A. A. A. and the Oral Tradition: A Paradox of Form and Substance," in Jones, E. D., et al., eds., *Women in African Literature Today* (1987), 109–18; Owusu, K., "Canons under Siege: Blackness, Femaleness, and A. A. A.'s *Our Sister Killjoy,*" *Callaloo,* 13, 2 (Spring 1990), 341–63

MILDRED A. HILL-LUBIN

AL-E AHMAD, Jalal

Iranian novelist, short-story writer, essayist, critic, editor, and translator, b. 1923, Tehran; d. 1969, Khalif Abad Assalam

The major Persian writer of fiction and nonfiction of the 20th c., A. is regarded by some as the best prose writer in Persian since the middle of the 13th c. He was born to a religious Muslim family; his father and four other members of the family were Shi'ite clerics, and when he was twenty, A. was sent to the holy city of Najaf in Iraq to be trained as a cleric. At the age of twenty-one, A. broke off from his family and joined the Tudeh Communist Party. In 1946 A. became an editor of the Tudeh monthly magazines *Mardom* and *Rahbar,* as well as many other party publications.

In the autumn of 1947, A. left the main core of the Tudeh party and was active in a splinter group that was not aligned with Moscow, and finally broke off with the communists. During the early 1950s, at the time of nationalization of oil by Mosaddeq, A. gravitated to the National Front Movement and was very active in the Third Force Party. From the mid-1950s until his death, A. was the main social critic and spokesman for the nonestablishment Iranian intelligentsia. In the last decade of his life, as he started to battle Western influences in Iran, he moved along the curve toward the point of his departure, to the Shi'ite Muslim environment. What he once criticized and even ridiculed, now he defended and considered the Twelver Shi'ism as the basic fabric of the Iranian civilization. During his lifetime he traveled almost a complete circle. As he propagated these views through his writing, he could be considered a precursor of the Islamic revolution that took place ten years after his death.

He received a high-school education by attending classes in the evening, working during the day in the Tehran bazaar as an electrician, watchmaker, and leather merchant. A. graduated from Tehran Teachers' College in 1946. He worked as a teacher almost the rest of his life. In 1950 A. married Simin Daneshvar (b. 1921), a writer, translator, and art-history professor. On the literary scene he appeared in the spring of 1945 with a short story, "Ziarat" ("The Pilgrimage," 1949), published in the literary magazine *Sokhan*. This was followed by four collections of stories, *Did va bazdid* (1946; the exchange of visits), *Az ranji ke mibarim* (1947; our suffering), *Se tar* (1948; the sitar), and *Zan-e ziadi* (1952; the superfluous wife). A fifth collection appeared posthumously as *Panj dastan* (1974; five stories). The love and the compassion for the ordinary people of Iran led A. to become a self-taught ethnographer who traveled around the country doing field work. This is reflected in his fiction writing, especially in his short stories, which are slices of everyday life. They are like blown-up frames of a movie reel, complete with sound track on which the colloquial speech patterns and characteristics of various social classes are recorded. The devotion of A. to the Iranian people is best underscored in the title of a collection of his stories translated into English and published in the U.S. as *Iranian Society: An Anthology of Writings by J. A. A.* (1982). In his long fictional narratives, A. is even more forceful in his social criticism. The first book, called *Sargozasht-e kanduha* (1955; the tale of the beehives), is an allegory of the exploitation of Iranian natural resources by foreign powers. Using the time-honored symbolism of the animal world, A. was able to deflect the pen of the censor. The most-ac-

claimed and most-read work of A. is *Modir-e madraseh* (1958; *The School Principal,* 1974). This masterpiece of narration and social criticism was reprinted many times, and a great number of copies, by Iranian standards, were sold. It is a first-person narrative of an elementary-school teacher who manages to become the principal of a school on the outskirts of Tehran. It is an indictment of the educational system of Iran and of Iranian society as a whole. Like many of his short stories, *Modir-e madraseh* is in great measure based on A.'s autobiographical material. The simple and direct prose makes the book very readable and credible. Another example of the first-person narrative is A.'s last novel, *Nafrin-e zamin* (1968; the cursing of the land). Again the main protagonist is a school teacher, but this time in a rural setting. In this book A. deals not only with education but with land reform, mechanized farms, and military conscription. The book also shows that the author, toward the end of his life, was more interested in cultural anthropology than in literature.

Nun wa'l qalam (1961; *By the Pen,* 1988) is regarded by the literary critics as his most mature work, and written in accordance with the modern standard of novel writing. It seems that the action of the book takes place in the capital of Safavid Esfahan, at the time of the growth of Shi'ism in Iran. The book, however, is not a historical novel since the city and the empire are in the realm of the imaginary. The title of the novel stems from chapter sixty-eight of the Koran, which is called "The Pen." That chapter starts with the letter "N," the meaning of which has not been determined by the scholars of the scriptures—it is therefore called a mystical letter.

Outside of Iran, A.'s most famous work belongs to nonfiction. It is a passionate attack on the Westernization of Iran under the Pahlavi monarchy, bearing the title of *Gharbzadegi* (1962; *Plagued by the West,* 1982). This work was also translated into English as *Gharbzadegi-Westruckness* (1982) and *Occidentosis: A Plague from the West* (1984). The plague is the Western encroachment in the East, infectious and sapping the vital strength of old countries like Iran. *Gharbzadegi* had a great impact on Iranian literary circles, on other intellectuals, and indirectly on the masses, as A. argued in it that the traditional Shi'ite Muslim values are the foundation of the Iranian masses.

To the nonfiction genre belong many works, especially his ethnographic studies. A. wrote travel accounts of his journeys to the Soviet Union, western Europe, and Iranian provinces. One of the most telling travelogues is his *Khasi dar miqat* (1964; *Lost in the Crowd,* 1985). In April of 1964, A. undertook a hajj, the pilgrimage to the most holy Muslim shrine in Mecca. *Khasi dar miqat* is an excellent description of the hajj and its rituals. Though A. at that time was moving toward the position of his origin in a strong religious framework, in the book he still comes through as a religious skeptic. Skeptic he was not, however, when he thought about the political application of the hajj as the great opportunity to mobilize Muslims against Western domination.

In Iran the role of the admired writer, especially an *engagé* one, can be compared only to that of eastern Europe: writers that are seen as mirrors of the conscience of the nation and its guiding beacons. There is no doubt that A. was such a writer.

BIBLIOGRAPHY: Kamshad, H., *Modern Persian Prose Literature* (1966), 125–27; Yarshater, E., "The Modern Literary Idiom," *Iran Faces the Seventies* (1971), 284–320; Hillmann, M. C., "The Mobilization of Iran," *LE&W*, 20, 1–4 (Jan.–Dec. 1976), 61–64; Chelkowski, P., "The Literary Genres in Modern Iran," in Lenczowski, G., ed., *Iran under the Pahlavis* (1978), 333–64; Yarshater, E., Foreword to *Plagued by the West* (1982), ix–x; Yarshater, E., ed., *Persian Literature* (1988), 301–2; Hillmann, M. C., *Iranian Culture: A Persianist View* (1990), 119–44; Clinton, J. W., "A. A. J.," in Yarshater, E., ed., *Encyclopaedia Iranica* (1982), Vol. 1, 745–47

PETER J. CHELKOWSKI

ALEGRÍA, Claribel

Salvadoran-Nicaraguan poet and novelist, b. 12 May 1924, Esteli, Nicaragua

A. is a prize-winning poet and novelist of renown who has also contributed to the growing body of testimonial literature from Central America. She was born in Nicaragua and moved with her family to El Salvador as a young child when her father, an anti-interventionist during the U.S. occupation of Nicaragua, was forced into exile. A. has subsequently lived in the U.S., Europe, and Mexico and other Latin American countries. She received her B.A. from George Washington University and is married to U.S.-born journalist Darwin J. Flakoll, with whom she has collaborated on a number of projects including a novel as well as books of testimony and Central American history. In 1979, with the victory of the FSLN (Sandinista Front for National Liberation), A. returned to live in Nicaragua. She continues to travel extensively and to speak and write about the social and political situation in Central America, particularly in El Salvador and Nicaragua, the two countries she considers her homeland.

A.'s poetic expression has evolved thematically from the self-reflective meditations of the young poet in her first book, *Anillo de silencio* (1948; ring of silence), which evokes life and death, past and present, in her search for her identity, to the still self-reflective but more socially and politically committed voice of her later work. A constant self-questioning and looking inward, captured in metaphors of mirrors, islands, prisons, walls, caves, and grottoes, evolves toward a looking outward and an identification of the lyric voice with the voices of those who have struggled, resisted, disappeared, or otherwise suffered in the name of justice. A. finds the fullness of her lyric voice and personal identity within a tradition of socially committed poetry which she evokes in one of the central poems of *Sobrevivo* (1978; I survive), "Sorrow" (title in English), a powerful dream poem of searching for, mourning, and becoming one with Pablo Neruda (q.v.), Roque Dalton (1935–1975), and other poets whose lives and deaths were indictments of repression. Although her themes as well as the sophistication of her use of metaphor have evolved, her language has remained characteristically straightforward, at times colloquial and conversational.

The impulse to reclaim her Central American heritage and to participate actively in exposing the lies and injustices of history is first apparent in the novel *Cenizas de Izalco* (1966; *Ashes of Izalco*, 1988), written collaboratively by A. and Flakoll. Employing the technique of the found manuscript, in this case the diary of the narrator's mother's lover, the novel uncovers/unmasks, with the protagonist's reading of the diary, an infamous chapter of Salvadoran history: the massacre by government troops of over thirty thousand peasants in 1932. A. herself as a child in Santa Ana, El Salvador, witnessed this massacre, thus *Cenizas de Izalco* is a combination of personal testimony and fictional narrative, as well as a way for A. to bear witness to history while attempting to reinscribe herself in the life of the country where she locates her roots.

Carmen, the protagonist of *Cenizas de Izalco*, is a Salvadoran woman married to a middle-class North American and living in the U.S. In *Album familiar* (1984; *Family Album*, 1989) A. explores once again the dilemma of the middle-class Central American woman who lives elsewhere, in this case in Paris, and who struggles with distance, separation, and commitment, eventually finding her salvation and the key to her identity by deciding to work for the FSLN in Paris. A. takes the challenge of commitment a step further for the protagonist of *Despierta, mi bien despierta* (1986; wake up, my love, wake up), a Salvadoran woman married to a member of the country's ruling oligarchy. Through her relationship with a young revolutionary she becomes aware of the repressive situation in her country and her husband's complicity in a mass murder. She leaves her husband, thereby solving an identity crisis as well as her problems of boredom and political ignorance.

In 1983 A. and Flakoll published *No me agarran viva* (*They Won't Take Me Alive,* 1987), an account of the life and death of a young Salvadoran woman who is a member of the FMLN (Farabundo Marti Front for National Liberation). Based on interviews with friends and relatives of the protagonist, Eugenia, the text weaves together letters, personal testimonies, discussions of Salvadoran history, and dramatizations of scenes and conversations in which issues such as machismo within revolutionary organizations, the fate of the children of revolutionaries, and the evolving role of women in social struggles in Central America are illuminated. *No me agarran viva* represents what A. herself calls her *letras de emergencia* (emergency or crisis writing), texts that emerge from the writer's awareness and commitment and that respond to the brutal realities of contemporary Central American life. Death, whether the result of poverty or political repression, is a grim fact of life in Central America, and A. confronts this reality from a variety of perspectives, but always from a deeply personal and impassioned stance.

Whether in the form of poetry, prose, testimony, or a hybrid of these genres, such as *Luisa en el país de la realidad* (1987; *Luisa in Reality-land,* 1987), A.'s texts are characterized by a female narrator's search for or declaration of her identity. Memory, the dead, imagination and imaginary interlocutors, love, and commitment aid the protagonists in their discovery of and subsequent battles against hypocrisy, machismo, and bourgeois complacency. Their hope or salvation is often found in their willingness to reidentify with their roots and with the disenfranchised in their political struggle.

A. is one of a small but growing number of women who are recognized by their male literary counterparts in Central America and whose production, quantitatively as well as qualitatively, is professional. To her credit, A. has managed to fuse the personal with the political to create texts important in their scope and powerful in their emotional content. Her attention to the concerns of women has contributed to the elevation of the female character in Central American literature to a higher level of autonomy and agency.

FURTHER WORKS: *Suite de amor, angustia y soledad* (1951); *Vigilias* (1953); *Acuario* (1955); *Tres cuentos* (1958); *Huésped de mi tiempo* (1961); *Vía única* (1965); *Aprendizaje* (1970); *Pagaré a cob-*

rar y otros poemas (1973); *El detén* (1977); *La encrucijada salvadoreña* (1980, with Darwin J. Flakoll); *Homenaje a El Salvador* (1981); *Suma y sigue* (1981); *Flores del volcán* (1982; *Flowers from the Volcano,* 1982); *Poesía viva* (1983); *Nicaragua: La revolución sandinista* (1983, with Darwin J. Flakoll); *Para romper el silencio: Resistencia y lucha en las cárceles salvadoreñas* (1984, with Darwin J. Flakoll); *Pueblo de Dios y Mandinga* (1985); *Y este poema río* (1988). FURTHER VOLUME IN ENGLISH: *Woman of the River* (1988)

BIBLIOGRAPHY: Papastamatiu, B., "La sobrevida poética de C. A.," *CasaA,* 110 (Sept.–Oct. 1978), 148–50; Peri Rossi, C., "Cuatro poetas latinoamericanas," *Hora de poesía* (Barcelona), 8 (Mar.–Apr. 1980); Arenal, E., "Two Poets of the Sandinista Struggle," *FSt,* 7, 1 (Spring 1981), 19–27; Benedetti, M., Introduction to *Suma y sigue. Antología* (1981), 9–16; Forché, C., "Interview with C. A.," *IonC,* 13, 2 (Apr. 1984), 11–13; Yúdice, G., "Letras de Emergencia: C. A.," *RI,* 51, 132–33 (July–Dec. 1985), 953–64; Saporta Sternbach, N., "C. A.," in Marting, D. E., ed., *Spanish American Women Writers* (1990), 9–19

JANET N. GOLD

ALEGRÍA, Fernando

Chilean critic, novelist, and poet, b. 26 Sept. 1918, Santiago

Currently the dean of Latin American critics, A. is a prolific writer of nearly fifty books and more than one hundred articles and is the Sadie Dernham Pater Professor in the Humanities at Stanford University. A graduate of the University of Chile (1939), he earned a Ph.D. in Romance linguistics at the University of California, Berkeley, in 1947, and won a Guggenheim fellowship. For the next twenty years, he held full-time positions at both Berkeley and the University of Chile, spending roughly half the year in each post. Since 1967 he has taught at Stanford, where he also served recently as department chair. During his illustrious career A. has lectured at more than 100 universities.

In 1970 President Salvador Allende named him cultural attaché in Washington, D.C. But after the September 1973 coup that placed General Augusto Pinochet in power, A. was refused entrance to Chile and could not return for more than ten years. Because he personally identified with the exiles and their political plight, A. became one of the most vociferous of the Chilean exiles, founding and editing the *Revista de Literatura Chilena en el Exilio* (1974), now entitled *Literatura Chilena: Creación y Crítica.* He also edited an anthology,

Chilean Writers in Exile (1982), which includes his *War Chorale,* an English translation of his *Coral de guerra* (1979).

A. initiated his novelistic pursuits at age twenty with the publication of *Recabarren* (1938; Recabarren), a fictionalized biography of Luis Emilio Recabarren. A printer turned journalist, Recabarren founded Chile's Socialist Party in 1912, which in 1921 changed its name to the Communist Party when it joined the Third International.

But at age seventeen A. had also published his first critical article, "El paisaje y sus problemas" (1935; the landscape and its problems), in the leading Chilean journal *Atenea.* Thus for more than fifty years A. has been able to maintain an amazing equilibrium in both areas: fiction and criticism.

Following *Recabarren,* A. published *Lautaro, ljoven libertador del arauco* (1943; *Lautaro,* 1944), another fictionalized history, which won the Farrar & Rinehart Prize in New York (1943). A. feels that for a nation to be worthy of its heroes it must cause them to transcend history, recalling them to the public mind in terms of the present as well as projecting them into the future. As a young Araucanian Indian, Lautaro helped the fierce tribes of the Arauco region of Chile gain freedom from the imperialist Spanish. Thus A.'s Lautaro becomes a model for Chileans of the early 1940s to thrust off the yoke of foreign imperialism, Nazi influences, or threatening dictators. In a more recent work, *Allende, mi vecino el presidente* (1989; *Allende, My Neighbor the President,* 1990), A. turns again to a fictionalized biography or history.

In much of his later fiction A. varies his fictionalizing of history to create in his books two distinct views of humanity. The Hispanic immigrant in the U.S. is the subject of one group of novels, including *Caballo de copas* (1957; *My Horse Gonzalez,* 1964) and *Amerika, Amerikka, Amerikkka, manifiestos de Vietnam* (1970; Amerika, Amerikka, Amerikkka, exposés about Vietnam, pub. in English as *The Funhouse,* 1986). A. pictures the plight of displaced Chileans and other migrant Hispanics in these works, and it is his exceptional view of the interfacing of the two cultures in his writings (the U.S. and the Hispanic) that will cause A. to be remembered and makes this fiction of the two cultures of major importance.

Testimonial literature, which replaced Socialist Realism (the proletarian novel) in leftist writing, is the second type of novel to which A. has recently turned. A. reproduces in his testimonial fiction paragraphs of magazine articles, swatches of voices in the wind, radio reports, oral anecdotes, letters, and a diary juxtaposed with a fictional account of a photographer's torture at the hands of the junta and his eventual death. A.'s

attack on the despotic mentality of the Pinochet military régime and the cruelty predominant in Chile after the 1973 coup appear in *El paso de los gansos* (1975; goose-step march, pub. in English as *The Chilean Spring,* 1980). *Coral de guerra* is another testimonial novel, in the pattern of William Faulkner's (q.v.) soliloquy novel, *As I Lay Dying* (1930).

A. returned again to a "fictionalized reality" in his autobiography, *Una especie de memoria* (1983; a kind of memoir), which, like *Mañana los guerreros* (1964; tomorrow the warriors), centers on the focal year 1938. It was a key year for his generation, known as the Generation of 1938, which was a group of novelists who through their literature helped established Marxist governments in Chile in 1938 and 1970. A. is one of the few of that large group who are still active in their writing. Their prose style is metaphorical and poetic.

As a poet, A. is not widely known in his own country because of his years of exile; yet, ironically, his poems are often recited by the masses or sung by international stars like Joan Baez, without the public realizing that A. is the author.

The winner of numerous national and international prizes for his writing, including the Medalla de Oro y Placa (1981), A.'s books have been widely disseminated through numerous editions and translated into eight languages. In his creative writing he inserts eroticism and humor, often championing the poor and making national heroes believably human in order to motivate the reader to participate in cultural change.

FURTHER WORKS: *Ideas estéticas de la poesía moderna* (1939); *Leyenda de la ciudad perdida* (1942); *Ensayo sobre cinco temas de Thomas Mann* (1949); *Camaleón* (1950); *Walt Whitman en Hispanoamérica* (1954); *La poesía chilena; orígenes y desarrollo del siglo XVI al XIX* (1954); *El poeta que se volvió gusano y otras historias verídicas* (1956); *Breve historia de la novela hispanoamericana* (1959); *El cataclismo* (1960); *Las noches del cazador* (1961); *Las fronteras del realismo; literatura chilena del siglo XX* (1962); *Viva Chile M . . . !* (1965); *Genio y figura de Gabriela Mistral* (1966); *La novela hispanoamericana del siglo XX* (1967); *Los días contados* (1968); *Como un árbol rojo* (1968; bilingual ed.); *La maratón del Palomo* (1968); *Los mejores cuentos de F. A.* (1968); *La venganza del general* (1969); *La literatura chilena contemporanea* (1969); *Literatura y revolución* (1970); *La ciudad de arena* (1974); *Retratos contemporáneos* (1979); *Los trapecios* (1985); *Nueva historia de la novela hispanoamericana* (1986); *La rebelión de los placeres* (1990). FURTHER VOLUMES IN ENGLISH: *Ten Pastoral*

Psalms (1968; bilingual ed.); *Instructions for Undressing the Human Race* (1969); *Changing Times/ Cambio de Siglo* (1972; bilingual ed.); *Changing Centuries: Poems* (1984; bilingual ed.)

BIBLIOGRAPHY: Giacomán, H. F., ed., *Homenaje a F. A.: Variaciones interpretativas en torno a su obra* (1972); Correas de Zapata, C., "Talking with A.," *Américas,* 24, 8 (1972), 9–12; Ruiz, R., *F. A.: vida y obra* (1979); Reeves, R. E., "Bibliografía de F. A.," *TCrit,* 7, 22–23 (1981), 31–58; Semprún de Donahue, M. de, *Figuras y contrafiguras en la poesía de F. A.* (1981); Valenzuela, V., *F. A.: el escritor y su época* (1985); Epple, J. A., ed., *Para una fundación imaginaria de Chile: La obra literaria de F. A.* (1987); Columbus, C. K., " 'Affective' Strategies for Social Change: A.'s *The Chilean Spring,*" *Mosaic,* 22, 1 (Winter 1989), 101–11

LON PEARSON

ALGERIAN LITERATURE

See Volume 1, page 45.

Born in the turmoil of the fight for the recovery of independence, Algerian literature was endowed with a vigor that did not abandon it in the post-independence period. A particularly profuse literary production characterized the 1980s, bringing new life and vitality onto the Algerian cultural scene. Among the various revolutions that shaped postindependence life in Algeria, the cultural revolution received special attention for more than one reason. There was the need to assert the national identity through the reinforcement of the national language, Arabic, as well as a great desire to open the gates of education to all the people, a process referred to as the democratization of education. It gave all children access to schools, particularly those who were once barred from the educational system. The concern with the rapid installation of the educational machine was almost feverish on the part of the responsible authorities. Many saw it as the means to join the world's advanced nations. A long period of search for the best educational system that would be uniquely Algerian was underway. An unexpressed desire for uniqueness and individuality seemed to guide these efforts. Regardless of the motivations and the outcome, however, the focus of attention was on the reinstitution of Arabic as the national language and the Arabization of the country. A natural overflow of Arabic writings was expected to follow, gradually displacing the literature written in French. But contrary to all expectations, literary production in French showed an unabated growth.

The debate on the use of French continued to funnel heated discussions and passionate arguments much similar to the ones heard twenty years earlier. Individual efforts at solving the dilemma were made by some writers. Kateb Yacine (q.v.) turned his attention to the theater, producing plays using spoken Algerian in the dialogue. Rachid Boudjedra (q.v.) chose to publish his novels in Arabic first, followed by a French translation. All the predictions of the death of French literature proved wrong.

While the theme of the war of independence did not abandon the scene, it acquired a new character and served a different purpose. The anticolonial feeling found expression in a new reading of history as the writers traveled back to the precolonial period for a source of inspiration. Their national identity was achieved as they claimed their Arab-Islamic or Berber-Islamic heritage, leaning on the historical significance of the events of this far-away past to interpret and assess the present. It is a tendency that manifests itself equally in the literatures written in Arabic and in French. The writers using these two languages shared also the same concern for the failure of the revolution to fulfill its promises, particularly after the disintegration of the agrarian reform. Both groups devised ingenious ways to convey their message of disapproval, depending heavily on either a true or imagined return of a *maquisard* to cast a critical look on their society or using symbols from Algerian folklore.

The war of independence as a theme did not disappear, only its function changed as it became a tool to denounce hypocrites and parasites. Long after the war ended, the fighters and the martyrs continued to haunt Algerian literature. If Al-Tāhir Wattār (q.v.) imagined only the return of the martyrs of the revolution, Rachid Mimouni (b. 1945) portrayed the life of a fighter who returns to his village after he was presumed dead. Ironically, at a time and place where festivities were being held to celebrate the memory of the fighters and bury their remains in earmarked cemeteries, the hero of the novel spends his time and energy trying to prove that he is alive. His adventures are a real odyssey related in *Le fleuve detourné* (1982; the deviated river). The official position vis-à-vis the martyrs of the revolution is the subject of another novel by Taher Djaout (b. 1954) entitled *Les chercheurs d'os* (1984; the bones seekers). The book portrays the painful awakening of a young man in search of his brother's bones. During his search he questions the real motives of the living in this hunt for the bones of the dead, which he sees in its essence as a means to confirm their death. Wasini Al-A'raj (b. 1954), on the other hand, depends purely on imagination in *Hal al-*

Dunya (1987; the condition of the world) when he pushes a martyr out of the frame of a picture in a courtroom and gives him the opportunity to criticize the judge who was preaching morality while his past activities in the years of the war spoke to the contrary.

An added novelty in the literature written in French is the growing number of women novelists and essayists. While some maintained a continuity in their literary production, others changed vocation such as Aisha Lemsine (b. 1942), who after publishing two novels shifted to journalistic investigation with *L'ordalie des voix* (1983; the trial of the voices), a platform for Arab women's opinions. Some women writers simply fell into silence after a promising start, such as Yamina Mechakra (b. 1953), who earned praise for her novel *La grotte éclatée* (1979; the shattered cave). Another feature of the last decade is the appearance of an unprecedented phenomenon among the young members of the new generation of Algerians born in France. For various reasons mainly related to the great difficulties in the acculturation process and the periodical resurgence of racism, many expressed a long suppressed rage over their conditions. Their voice is, in a special way, the silent cry of their parents who, handicapped by their illiteracy, failed to raise the vital issues that confronted them in the early years of emigration. The writings of the Maghribi youth, predominantly Algerian, is known as "Beur" literature.

As far as the various literary genres are concerned, all seem to be flourishing both in Arabic and in French. Drama, however, made little progress, and the rare published texts do not find their way to the stage. The opposite situation occurred when some plays were performed but their manuscripts were never published; an example is Yacine's *Mohammad prend ta valise* (1971; Mohammad, grab your suitcase).

The Arabic literary movement witnessed a certain change in its trend since the first quarter of the 20th c. with the gradual ascendency of the novel and the continued abundant production of short stories and, to a lesser extent, poetry. While the established novelists continued to write at a somewhat slower pace, a number of younger writers, armed with a solid Arabic education, appeared on the literary scene. The literature of the 1980s is also characterized by the absence of inhibition in dealing with previously taboo subjects such as sexual relations and love. The reserve manifested by writers such as Mouloud Feraoun or Mohammad Dib (qq.v.) vanished almost totally with the writers of the new generation.

The growing political power of the Berber movement benefited its folk literature as it became the center of attention leading to the collection,

translation, and interpretation of Berber poetry, as well as the appearance of periodicals in Amazigh language.

In Arabic

The Novel

The scene of the novel continues to be dominated by the names of the two pioneers Al-Tāhir Wattār and ʿAbd al-Hamīd ibn Hadūqa (q.v.). The former walked the bridge of the war of independence between his first novel, *Al-Laz* (1974; Laz), and one of his latest works, *Al-ʿIshq wa-al-Mawt fi al-zaman ul-Harāshī* (1978; passion and death in the Harrachi time). His hero, Al-Laz, who loses his mind in the first novel, recovers his sanity in the latter book. His latest novel, *Tajriba fi al-ʿIshq* (1990; an experience in passion), marks a turning point in his career stylistically and thematically, although he does not abandon his political revendication, which extends here beyond the borders of Algeria and tackles various Arab causes. Hadūqa continued the tendency manifested in his earlier novels to mix politics and love. In *Bana al-Subh* (1980; the morning appeared) he draws a picture of the complex and corrupt life in the city, whereas in *Al-Jāziya wa-al Darāwish* (1983; the Jaziya and the dervishes) Hadūqa returns to the country, which seems to exercise a special fascination on the author. He did not falter, however, on his feminist position portraying assertive women in his novels, in the rural and the urban environments. Although these two veteran novelists gradually moved away from the war themes, the younger writers revived the subject, as if the evocation of this major event in the history of their country was a national duty and a sign of patriotism. One such novelist, Mirzāq Biqtash (b. 1945) centers the action of his two books, *Tuyūr fi al-Zāhira* (1981; birds at noon) and *Al-Buzah* (1983; uniform wearers), on the war through the eyes of children. Wasini al-Aʿraj showed less involvement with the war of independence without ignoring it totally. With a tendency toward philosophical reflection he cast a critical eye on the postindependence period and its shortcomings, describing the disenchantment of the people and their efforts at maintaining a source of hope in an increasingly deteriorating situation. The hero of his novel *Waqāʾiʿ rajul Ghamara Sawb al-Bahr* (1983; the adventures of a man who ventured toward the sea) goes in search of the missing elements in society. Al-Aʿraj brings to the Arabic novel in Algeria a poetic prose that added a great limpidity and fluidity to the language. He also broke the hard skin of certain social taboos by talking freely about love and sexual relations. In spite of his openness in dealing with this topic he succeeds in sublimating it. Although greatly concerned with the social realities and their handicapping effect on his people, Al-A'raj probes deeply in his inner self for a variety of emotions and soul-searching that is unprecedented in the Arabic Algerian novel.

The Short Story

While the novel tried to infuse a sense of hope in the midst of a problematic reality, the short story was generally less optimistic in its approach. It revealed a world of fear, anxiety, failure, and shattered dreams. Emigration increased but failed to bring happiness in spite of the material prosperity it generally provided. Wives in particular resented their husbands' departures, fearful and apprehensive of their marriage to foreign women or their indulgence in the sins of the West. The health and security of the emigrant men was a constant worry. Many collections carry at least one story on the subject. In his collection *Al-Aswāt* (1985; the voices) Ammar Belhassan (b. 1953) entitles one of his short stories "Rahīl warā'a Khayt al-Damm" (setting out on the trace of blood drops). Al-A'raj devoted his collection *Alam al-Kitāba 'An Ahzān al-Manfā* (1980; the painful process of writing about the sorrows of exile) in its entirety to an evocation of his love for his country and returned to the theme in his collection *Asmāk al-Barr al-Mutawahhish* (1986; the fish of the savage shore). A greater maturity is apparent in the thinking of the characters of these writers as the decision to return to their homeland is dictated primarily by the desire to serve it.

Armed with little experience and much difficulty, the Algerians had to face a tough reality after the euphoria of freedom. As if overwhelmed by the magnitude of the responsibility and the accumulation of problems through the years, they found themselves in a "wasteland." Algeria suffered from the usual postindependence problems of the Third World countries such as exploitation, a growing number of parasites, a distorted sense of patriotism, a race for positions, and quick wealth. Added to these major problems were the daily vexations of life in the form of crowded and slow-running buses, traffic jams, housing crisis, the high cost of living, exacting social duties, and shortages of vital consumer goods. Seemingly insignificant, these material problems impacted profoundly on the psychology of the individuals. In "Humūm Saghīra," (1986; little worries) Ahmad Mannur's (b. 1945) hero echoes the other writers' concerns, lamenting the shortage of spare parts for his car, which forced him to use the overcrowded public transportation. This solution caused him unhappiness at work and at home and made him ponder on the policy of his government. The housing crisis, for example, which led to jamming more than one family in tiny apartments, caused not only continuous frictions between the inhabitants but also a loss of privacy impacting on marital relations, job performance, and productivity as a whole. A poignantly realistic account of such a painful experience is given in Mustaphā Natur's (b. 1950) " 'Usr al-Wilāda" (difficult delivery) from his collection *Ahlām al-Jiyād al-mafjū'a* (1985; dreams of the frightened horses).

Voicing their frustration and anger on paper was for many writers the only escape from a reality that entrapped them. Frustrations exploded also in the popular and old form of singing known as *Al-Rai'*. Revived in the 1980s the *Rai* songs are profane and pernicious in their content and express an antiestablishment stand. They acted as a cry of freedom against the multiple restrictive laws of the government and were used by the "Beur" in France as an identity symbol.

Poetry

Algerian poetry took a few strides on the way to modernity in the 1970s and continued on this path in the 1980s. Yet the poetic production is weaker quantitatively as if more writers opted for prose. Some of the poets who achieved renown in the past, such as Ahlām Mostaghānmī (b. 1953), faded from the literary scene, while new names appeared. The themes in the more recent production revolve generally around the homeland and the memory of the martyrs of the revolution; there is also an interest in the Arab nation and the obstacles facing Arab unity. Sarcasm on the erosion of Arab wealth by the rulers is expressed in a manner reminiscent of the Syrian Nizār Qabbānī (b. 1923). Sarcasm is also present in Zeinab al-A'waj's (b. 1956) *Arfudu An Udajjan al-Atfāl* (1983; I refuse to see the children exploited), where a deep revendicative tone dominates the collection. The memory of the martyrs is usually evoked to stress their betrayal by the ruling power. But a note of hope pierces through her poems as well as those of the poets of her generation who believe in the rising sun. There is also a concern for the well-being of society and for justice as conceived from a socialist point of view, a predominant position among the poets of the 1980s. The Palestinian problem remained central to a number of poems, as it did in the short stories. In *Atfāl Port-Said Yuhājirūn Ilā Awwal May* (1983; the children of Port-Said emigrate to the first of May), 'Abd al-'Alī Razzāqī (b. 1949) expressed consternation at the state of Jerusalem and the war in Lebanon while the Arab rulers were indulging in their pleasures. A feeling of brotherhood for the Arabs motivated the poet to fight for the Arab cause, now that his country was free. Although full of anger, the language of the poems is subdued by the beauty of the imagery and a more flowing poetic style. Reading Razzāqī or Al-A'waj's poetry, one can't help but notice the impact of known Arab poets on their writings, in particular the Palestinian Mahmūd Darwīsh (q.v.). It is quite obvious that the true literary revival in the language of poetry took place in the 1980s with the growing number of Algerians studying in the *Mashriq*. Their interests and literary experience encompassed vaster spheres than those of their predecessors. These recent collections are written in free verse and reveal a tendency to experiment in form.

In French

It is possible to say without exaggeration that literature using the French language bloomed in Algeria in the last decade and a half contrary to all expectations. Works written in French were published both in France and Algeria, even by national publishing houses such as L'Édition Nationale du Livre, previously known as Société Nationale d'Édition et de Diffusion (SNED). Some of the peculiarities of this literature are the versatility of its authors and their disregard for the adoption of a strict literary genre in a single book. Many mixed poetry and prose in the same work, while others contributed in separate works to poetry, the novel, the short story, and even drama. Acting as ethnologists, some writers collected folk literature. Mouloud Mammeri's (q.v.) efforts centered on Mohand Si-Mohand (1840?–1906), a renowned Berber poet, while Rabah Belamri (b. 1946) published popular tales.

The Novel

There is nevertheless a major difference between this literature and that of the colonial period and the early postindependence era. The new approach is that of a recovered entity and rediscovered roots. The young writers such as Taher Djaout and Habib Tangour (b. 1947) seem comfortably anchored in their history and at ease in their identity, neither embarrassed by the use of French nor apologetic. Acting as truly independent thinkers, they do not seem concerned by the danger of being claimed by another culture. *They own the language that once owned them.* Their appearance on the cultural scene is the anticlimax of the clash of civilizations that marked many of the works and lives of their predecessors. Taher Djaout jour-

neyed back in history in *L'invention du désert* (1987; the invention of the desert) to trace the steps of the ancestors, the Almoravids. His contemporary Habib Tangour roamed history from the Jahiliyya to the Abbasid periods, contrasting past and present to assess and condemn conditions in Algeria. His novel *Le vieux de la montagne* (1983; the old man and the mountain) reveals the disillusionment of the people with their country's government. This return to precolonial history is neither an escape from reality nor an emotional consolation in past glories. It is rather a measuring rod for the present. A shift in outlook characterizes the works of established novelists such as Rachid Boudjedra and Assia Djebar (q.v.). Boudjedra introduced a triumvirate of action in his most recent novels, moving from the past to the present to autobiographical information. This triple direction forms usually the woven text of his books. He embarked also on a triple-narrative and multiple-time sequences where the action moves freely, allowing him to give his own interpretation of the present by superimposing it on the past. Most events lead usually to incidents that marked deeply his personal life, such as his mother's death related in *La prise de Gibraltar* (1987; the conquest of Gibraltar). It is evoked parallel to the incident that led to the death of a large number of women killed by the French forces as they demonstrated in 1955 in Constantine. A more restricted narration of his autobiography appeared in *La macération* (1985; the maceration) through the rewriting of the *A Thousand and One Nights* for a film scenario. The novel is a new look at the more recent history of Algeria and the life of the novelist's father already evoked in *La répudiation* (1969; the repudiation) under a less flattering image.

Rachid Boudjedra's case raises a question of classification if we are to consider his novels written in French as simple translations of those he writes first in Arabic, a process he began with *Le démantèlement* (1982; the fragmentation), entitled *Al-tafakkuk* in Arabic (1982). Two reasons dictate Boudjedra's inclusion in the section of the literature written in French. His readers are predominantly those of the French version of his novels, and his insistence on publishing the French and Arabic versions of his novels almost simultaneously reinforces the feeling among many critics that his Arabic novels are, contrary to his assertions, mere translations of the novels he writes first in French. A style heavily marked by French images and sentence constructions alien to Arabic strengthens this theory.

In this new phase of their production the novelists narrate their life through the windows of history with the comfort of a traditional storyteller like a purgation. There is clearly in Boudjedra's writings and in that of Assia Djebar's an abandonment of the self and the absence of the studentlike attitude desiring to impress the teacher-master characteristic of their early works. Djebar continued in her two most recent novels, *L'amour la fantasia* (1985; *Fantasia; an Algerian Cavalcade,* 1989) and *Ombre Sultane* (1987; *A Sister to Scheherazade,* 1987), to champion women's causes, but without the romantic spirit of her first few novels. Both in these new works and in the documentary films she produced, *La Zerda et les chants de l'oublie* (1982; the Zerda and the songs of forgetfulness) and *La Nouba des femmes du Mont Chenoua* (1978; the Nouba of the women of Mount Chenoua), she gave a historical perspective of women's importance in society, stressing their role in the history of their country. While relying heavily on autobiographical information in the *L'amour la fantasia,* she enters the evocative and symbolic world of Shahrazad (Sherazade, Scheherazade) in *Ombre Sultane.* There she juxtaposes two lives, the traditional and the modern, considering the future with some apprehension at the possibility of seeing women failing to play a role in a world they helped create.

The reader should not be misled in thinking, however, that the novelists abandoned the task of political criticism. A veteran of the novel, Mouloud Mammeri, described the disillusionment of the intellectuals in their country's régime in *La traversée* (1982; the crossing). Equally critical of the political realities of his country is the young and promising novelist Rachid Mimouni. In *Le fleuve détourné* he denounced the government policy and its exploitation of socialism and the spirit of the revolution in order to dominate the people. In another novel, *Tombeza* (1984; Tombeza), he raised the question of traitors who benefited from the times of war and peace, a theme dear to Hadūqa. Another literary figure, Mohammad Dib, a veteran novelist, poet, and short-story writer, drew gradually away from his early concern with the sociopolitical problems of his country to pursue an old favorite topic, that of words and their fleeting meaning. Emanating from his short story "La dalle écrite" (1966; the inscribed stone), the pursuit of an ever-escaping significance of words continued to haunt him in his later work. Through Habel in the novel bearing the same name and Eid in *Les terrasses d'orsol* (1985; the roofs of Orsol) Dib chased death and love, playing what seemed like a hide-and-seek game with these major emotions in a person's life. Much of his reflection revolved around the thin line where reality and imagination are intertwined, where illusion often predominates over truth. One theme to which Dib remained faithful throughout his work is his high regard for women, who often play the role of the rescuer.

The character of Shahrazad was revived in more than one novel, possibly as part of this return trip to the roots. A new writer, Leïla Sebbar (b. 1941), gives the heroine of the *A Thousand and One Nights* a place of honor in her works. Three of her books carry her name as part of the title, the first one is *Sherazade, 17 ans, brune, frisée, les yeux verts* (1982; Sherazade, age 17, brunette, curly hair and green eyes), then *Les carnets de Sherazade* (1985; Sherazade's notes), and the most recent book, *Le fou de Sherazade* (1991; crazy about Sherazade). Although belonging to two worlds, those of her French mother and her Algerian father, and living in France, Sebbar is attached to Algeria, where she found her identity. She followed in her predecessors' footsteps, particularly Kateb Yacine, for whom she has a special admiration, as she gives Jaffar in *J. H. cherche âme sœur* (1987; J. H. looking for a soul sister) the novel *Nedjma* (1956; Nedjma) to read while in prison. Like Yacine, she moves her characters from one novel to the other. Thus Jaffar, Sherazade, and Julien appear in *Les carnets de Sherazade,* and *J. H. cherche âme sœur.* The three reappear in *Le fou de Sherazade,* as Jaffar meets Sherazade in Beirut in the midst of a cross fire by invisible snipers. When they depart, Sherazade conveys Nedjma's protection on him. The significance of Sherazade's role is explained in the last novel through a commentary made by one of the characters, Pierrot; he interprets her endless talk as a means to protect herself against rape.

Sebbar centered her attention on the identity problems of the generation of emigrant children and their relation to their country of origin. After her own personal odyssey, she seemed to have reached a situation of comfort. At ease with her identity, she moved beyond the borders of France and Algeria, taking her characters to Beirut and Jerusalem with an effort to stress the brotherhood of the two peoples, Palestinians and Israelis. Sebbar stands at the demarcation line between the writers who live in self-imposed exile in France and the second generation of Algerians commonly known as the "Beur."

The "Beur," the new generation of Algerians born in France and citizens of their parents' country of exile, drew attention to themselves through a number of highly autobiographical novels published in the 1980s. Their works are cries of anger and calls for help. Projected into the midst of a Western society due to circumstances beyond their control, they found themselves oscillating between two cultures and at ease in neither. Children of a failed acculturation, they found in writing an outlet for their confusion and loss. Although most are so far the authors of a single book, some managed to achieve fame, such as Mehdi Charef (b. 1952), who wrote *Le thé au harem d'Archi Ahmed* (1983;

Tea in the Harem, 1989). Another ''Beur,'' Farida Belghoul (b. 1958?), wrote the best novel in this genre, *Georgette* (1986; Georgette). Each writer deals with a certain aspect of the life of the ''Beur.'' While Charef described the despair and poverty of the emigrants' lives, transforming them into professional thieves at an early age, Belghoul concentrated on a life between two cultures and the lack of understanding between parents and children. This budding literature is still in the making; only the future will reveal whether it was an impetuous, one-time event or the first step on a serious literary movement.

This new literature of the 1980s, whether ''Beur'' or that of the self-exiled writers such as Ali Boumadhi (b. 1934) or Rabah Belamri (b. 1946) adopts a more descriptive style, faithful to reality and reminiscent of that of the early works of the 1950s—as if this new generation of Algerian writers is motivated by the desire to testify like its predecessors.

The Short Story

This literary genre continued to be widely used and published. It fulfilled the same role played by the Arabic short story and acted as a platform of dissatisfaction and frustration. The short story deals with seemingly unimportant incidents such as queuing for various kinds of purchases, or the race for stocking on merchandise, clearly a major preoccupation of the people always fearful of food or other shortages. Hamid Skif (b. 1951), however, dramatizes this banality in either a tragicomical art describing the rise and fall of a refrigerator or a pathetic glorification of tomato paste in *Les nouvelles de la maison du silence* (1986; news from the house of silence). For Assia Djebar, more versed in the novel, the few short stories she published, and also her collection carrying the title of Delacroix's painting, *Femmes d'Alger dans leur appartement* (1980; women of Algiers in their apartment), there is not much new. The author continued her description of the women's world, their gestures and their dreams of the outside world as imagined from behind their closed doors. If there is an impressive number of published collections of short stories, there are more works that appeared separately in the national press. The message, however, remains the same.

Poetry

It seems difficult to talk about Algerian poetry without mentioning one of its champions, Mohammad Dib. Here more even than in the novel, Dib reveals his almost obsessive concern with the language, with words and their magical effects. Thematically, however, his poetry remains within the boundaries of his novels. *Omneros* (1975; Omnero) raised the usual reflection on love and death, whereas *O vive* (1987; Oh! long life) is a testimony of the author's deep affection and respect for women. Contrary to the younger generation of poets, Dib, Bashir Hadj-Ali (b. 1920), Malek Alloula (b. 1939), and Jamal-Eddine Bencheikh (b. 1930) deal with poetry as artists, whereas the others used it as a channel for their anger. Few among the poets of the 1980s produced significant numbers of poems to trace a certain continuity in their progression or to speak at all of any kind of evolution.

Some veteran poets, though, deserve more attention. Both Djamal Amrani (b. 1935) and Noureddine Aba (b. 1921) made a comeback in the last decade. The latter is endowed with a humanitarian outlook on the world's problems and manifested a particular concern for the Palestinian cause in collections such as *L'aube à Jerusalem* (1979; dawn in Jerusalem) and *Tel Zaatar s'est tu à la tombée de la nuit* (1981; Tel Zaatar was quiet at sunset). Amrani deals with national problems and is known as the chronicler of the war of independence. His latest collections, such as *Jours couleur de soleil* (1979; days with the color of the sun) and *Entre la dent et la mémoire* (1981; between tooth and memory), reveal an interest in the present while maintaining a link with the past.

This genre remains much alive and fed continuously by new contributions and experimentations, many written by unknown poets. For most members of this young generation poetry is perceived as an expression of freedom.

BIBLIOGRAPHY: Mortimer, M., *The Algerian Novel in French, 1954–1965* (1972); Dejeux, J., *Situation de la littérature maghrébine de langue française* (1982); Bouzar, W., *Lectures maghrebines: Essai* (1984); Djaout, T., *Les mots migrateurs* (1985); Bonn, C., *Le roman algérien de langue française* (1985); Mostaghanmi, A., *Algérie: Femmes et écritures* (1985); Yahiaoui, F., *Roman et société coloniale dans l'Algérie de l'entre-deux-guerres* (1985); Lacheraf, M., *Écrits didactiques sur la culture, l'histoire et la société en Algérie* (1988); Bonn, C., *Anthologie de la littérature algérienne* (1990); Achour, C., *Anthologie de la littérature algérienne de langue française* (1990); Mortimer, M., *Journeys through the French African Novel* (1990)

AIDA A. BAMIA

ALI, Ahmed

Pakistani novelist, short-story writer, poet, essayist, and translator (writing in Urdu and English), b. 1 July 1910, Delhi, India

A., Pakistan's best-known living author, writes in both English (novels, poetry, essays) and Urdu (short stories). His numerous translations into English include poetry from Indonesian, Urdu, and Chinese, and the Koran from Arabic.

Educated in English-medium schools, A. received his B.A. and M.A. in English literature from Lucknow University. In addition to writing, he has had several other careers: a teacher of English in India, China, Pakistan, and the U.S.; a diplomat serving in the Pakistan foreign service in both China and Morocco; a public-relations advisor to several large Pakistani corporations; and a small businessman. He was awarded the Star of Distinction by the Government of Pakistan in 1980.

In 1932 A. and three friends published an anthology of ten short stories and a one-act play entitled *Angare* (burning coals). Attacking middle-class Muslim mores and attitudes, these works satirized religious hypocrisy, male chauvinism, and society's indifference to the poor. The book caused a major uproar, due primarily to the authors' cavalier treatment of Islam and the Koran. During this controversy the book was publicly burned, the authors denounced in the press and from the pulpit, and their lives threatened. Contests were even held to find the best way to punish them for their blasphemy. The volume was quickly proscribed, a ban that remains in force to this day.

Later, in 1936, A. played a key role in organizing the first meeting of the All-India Progressive Writers' Association, which, with encouragement from various European leftist writers, spread Marxist ideology and Socialist Realism (q.v.) to authors in India's dozen major languages. This organization remained a major force on the Indian literary scene for nearly two decades. As it grew increasingly doctrinaire in the late 1930s, A. broke with the group and assumed a literary stance more concerned with aesthetics and less encumbered by politics. At this time he also started writing in English.

A.'s first volume of short stories, *Shole* (1936; flames), contains about half of his corpus in this genre. These works show an acute social consciousness in which A. derides conservative Muslim social, political, and religious thinking. Several are highly symbolic and deftly use interior monologue and stream of consciousness (q.v.). A second volume of short stories, *Hamari gali* (our lane), appeared in 1942, the title story from which is considered A.'s best. It was published in A.'s own English translation in *New Writing* (1937). Highly autobiographical and richly textured, it is set in A.'s Kucha Pundit neighborhood of Old Delhi and depicts a variety of colorful, minutely etched characters who live out their hapless lives in superstition and fear.

A. traveled to England in 1939, where, assisted by E. M. Forster (q.v.), he was able to place his first English language novel, *Twilight in Delhi,* with the prestigious Hogarth Press, which published it to considerable critical acclaim in the following year, one of only two works by Asian writers this press ever printed. A.'s masterpiece, this novel vividly and poignantly details the downward slide in the fortunes of several generations of a well-to-do Muslim family in Delhi at the start of this century. It is considered one of the most distinctive novels in Commonwealth literature.

A.'s poetry is deeply influenced by his stays in China, first in 1947–1948 as a British Council visiting professor of English in Nanking, when he started his study of Chinese, and later as a diplomat in 1951–1952. The themes of this poetry are similar to those found in the novels: the fading of youth and the evanescence of life, the loss of friends either through death or abandonment, the sadness of potential unrealized, and the emptiness of success achieved. Often modeled on classical Chinese lyrics, many of A.'s poems are collected in *Purple Gold Mountain* (1960).

As an essayist A. has published seven volumes of literary criticism, including *Mr. Eliot's Penny World of Dreams* (1942) and *Ghalib: Two Essays* (1969). An indefatigable translator, A. has published *The Flaming Earth: Poems from Indonesia* (1949), one of the earliest English-language collections of poetry from Southeast Asia, and four anthologies of classical Urdu poetry, the most important of which is *The Golden Tradition* (1973). In 1980 he completed his highly acclaimed translation of the Koran from Arabic, which he considers his magnum opus, currently in its ninth printing. He has translated and published in journals the works of a number of prerevolutionary Chinese poets, and has edited several English-language literary journals and books of creative writing from Asia and Africa.

A.'s prose style is a striking combination of opulent lyricism and stark realism, suffused with ellipses and purposely antiquated language that gives his fiction an epic, almost biblical, quality. Much of the diction of his early poetry is similarly textured, but later poems reflecting Chinese influences are remarkable in their simplicity of language. A man who moves with equal ease between West and East, A. has served as an important, though often unrecognized, intellectual and artistic link between these two polarities. Through his creative writings, scholarly publications, and translations, he has brought Asia and some of its choicest literary works to the often indifferent attention of the West.

ISABEL ALLENDE

ELECHI AMADI

MAYA ANGELOU

MICHAEL ANTHONY

FURTHER WORKS: *Break the Chains* (1932); *Poetry: A Problem* (1934); *The Land of Twilight* (1937); *Teaching of Poetry* (1940); *Qaid khana* (1944); *Maut se pahle* (1945); *Muslim China* (1949); *The Falcon and the Hunted Bird* (1950); *The Bulbul and the Rose* (1960); *Ocean of Night* (1964); *The Failure of an Intellect* (1968); *Ghalib: Selected Poems* (1969); *The Problem of Style and Technique in Ghalib* (1969); *The Shadow and the Substance: Principles of Reality, Art and Literature* (1977); *Of Rats and Diplomats* (1985)

BIBLIOGRAPHY: Brander, L., "Two Novels of A. A.," *JCL*, 3 (1967), 76–86; Anderson, D., "A. A. and *Twilight in Delhi*," *Mahfil, A Quarterly of South Asian Literature*, 7, 1–2 (1971), 81–86; Anderson, D., "A. A. and the Growth of the Pakistani Literary Tradition in English," *WLWE*, 16, 2 (1975), 436–49; Kumar, A., "*Twilight in Delhi*: A Study in Lyricism," *IndL*, 19, 2 (1976), 25–38; Coppola, C., "The Short Stories of A. A.," *Studies in the Urdu Gazal and Prose Fiction* (1979), 214–42; Coppola, C., "The Poetry of A. A.," *JIWE*, 8, 1–2 (Jan.–July 1980), 63–76; Nevin, A., "Historical Imagination and the Novels of A. A.," *JIWE*, 8, 1–2 (Jan.–July 1980), 3–13; Coppola, C., "The *Angare* Group: The *Enfants Terribles* of Urdu Literature," *AnUS*, 1 (1981), 57–69; King, B., "From *Twilight to Midnight*: Muslim Novels of India and Pakistan," *The Worlds of Muslim Imagination* (1986), 243–59; Coppola, C., "The All-India Progressive Writers' Association: The European Phase," *Marxist Influences and South Asian Literature* (1988), 1–41

CARLO COPPOLA

ALLENDE, Isabel

Chilean novelist and short-story writer, b. 2 Aug. 1942, Lima, Peru

A. was born to diplomat parents residing in Peru, but at the age of three her father abandoned the family, and she and her mother returned to Chile. The focus of her early childhood was on her mother, and there was little contact with her father's side of the family except for a close relationship with an uncle, Salvador Allende Gossens, elected president of Chile in 1970. When A. was ten, her mother married another diplomat, Ramón Huidobro, who became a strong paternal figure in her childhood. A. traces her interest in storytelling to the tales she heard from her maternal grandparents and from the servants in the kitchen of the family estate. The fact that her mother gave her a notebook in which she could write her early impressions was another stimulus that ultimately led to a career in writing. Her early work in journalism and television was cut short by the 1973 coup d'état that resulted in the death of President Allende and the beginning of a sixteen-year military dictatorship under General Augusto Pinochet. Forced to leave Chile in 1975 as a result of the harsh treatment meted out to leftist supporters of the Allende government, her career as a writer of fiction began in Venezuela, where she and her family lived for over a decade as expatriates. Her first two novels show a growing nostalgia for Chile and for family members still there, but her third novel is set in her adopted country, Venezuela. A. now lives in the U.S.

A.'s first novel, *La casa de los espíritus* (1982; *The House of the Spirits*, 1985), was written as a long letter to her centenarian grandfather who was near death in Chile. Unable to publish the novel in Venezuela, A. sent the manuscript to the well-known literary agent Carmen Balcells, who facilitated its publication by Plaza & Janés in Spain. It is a panoramic view of Chile during the first seventy-five years of the 20th c. and of the vicissitudes of the Trueba family: the wrathful founder, Esteban Trueba; his hypersensitive wife; and the legitimate and illegitimate children sired by the founder. Its scope and purpose have often been compared to Gabriel García Márquez's (q.v.) *Cien años de soledad* (1967; *One Hundred Years of Solitude*, 1970). Dominant in the novel are the themes of Latin American politics, feminism, and the importance of writing. The novel contains many autobiographical details and integrates the plot with Chilean history.

In her second novel, *De amor y de sombra* (1984; *Of Love and Shadows*, 1987), A. explores the themes of repression and dictatorship as a photographer and his journalist girlfriend investigate a common crime that leads them to an unbelievable massacre ordered by the dictatorship. The two find love while they uncover a violent world of poverty, ignorance, misery, sickness, and torture. Whereas the action has a fictional setting, readers familiar with the Pinochet dictatorship would recognize the events as accurate and plausible. Although Chile is never mentioned in the novel, A. asserts that it is based on an event that took place there in 1978.

Eva Luna (1987; *Eva Luna*, 1988), although set in Venezuela, continues many of the themes seen in the first two novels. It recounts the life of the protagonist, born in the lower classes but blessed with a remarkable skill: storytelling. She uses this skill to get food, shelter, sex, and ultimately love, while she turns mundane events into extraordinary works of fiction and television scenarios. There are many autobiographical episodes that explore the themes of feminism, politics, journalism, and censorship against the backdrop of 20th-c. Venezuela. This novel contains a rich admixture of intertextuality in which A. probes the relationship between writing and reality, between herself the author and Eva Luna her creation, and between political reality and the television scripts Eva writes. A.'s most recent publication is a collection of twenty-three short stories, purportedly the ones Eva Luna wrote during the course of the third novel. *Cuentos de Eva Luna* (1990; *The Stories of Eva Luna,* 1991) is a collection of tales that have the common thread of love as their focus.

In less than a decade A.'s reputation in the field of contemporary fiction has risen meteorically. She continues to explore in particular the themes of feminism, politics, and the art of writing as seen in her three novels, all of which have been translated into twenty-one languages.

FURTHER WORKS: *Civilice a su troglodita* (1974); *La gorda de porcelana* (1983); *El plan infinito* (1991)

BIBLIOGRAPHY: Agosín, M., "Entrevista a I. A./ Interview with I. A.," *Imagine,* 1, 2 (1984), 42–56; Coddou, M., ed., *Los libros tienen sus propios espíritus* (1986); Moody, M., "I. A. and the Testimonial Novel," *Confluencia,* 2, 1 (Fall 1986), 39–43; Moody, M., "Entrevista con A.," *DLit,* 4, 1 (Autumn 1986), 41–53; Gordon, A., "A. on Love and Shadow," *ConL,* 28, 4 (Winter 1987), 530–42; Earle, P. G., "Literature as Survival: A.'s *The House of the Spirits,*" *ConL,* 28 (1987), 543–54; Coddou, M., *Para leer a I. A.* (1988); Foster, D., "I. A. Unveiled," *Mother Jones,* 13, 10 (Dec. 1988), 42–46; Antoni, R., "Parody or Piracy: The Relationship of *The House of the Spirits* to *One Hundred Years of Solitude,*" *LALR,* 16, 32 (July–Dec. 1988), 16–28; Mitgang, H., "A. Explores Her Novels and Herself," *NYT,* 4 Feb. 1988, 16; Meyer, D., "Exile and the Female Condition in I. A.'s *De amor y de sombra,*" *IFR,* 15, 2 (Summer 1988), 151–57; Hart, P., *Narrative Magic in the Fiction of I. A.* (1989); Talmor, S., "The House of the Truebas," *DUJ,* 81, 2 (June 1989), 309–12; Levine, L. G., "I. A.," in Marting, D. E., ed., *Spanish American Women Writers* (1990), 20–30

HARLEY D. OBERHELMAN

"Living on" was a persistent tradition in I. A.'s family on her mother's side, and her late grandmother—the main model for Clara del Valle, "Clara la clarividente," in *The House of the Spirits*—had been practicing since premature death what Grandfather had always preached in life, with her periodic messages and visitations. The letter to Grandfather got longer, and longer. A year later (1982) it had grown to five-hundred pages. It was a diary in retrospect, a family chronicle, an au-

tobiography, a political testimony, a group portrait and contemporary history, a series of experiments with magic. In other words, a novel. A. was a journalist in search of a complementary medium. Aesthetically, she would now participate in the basic ritual of Latin American literature: a celebration of reality. Ethically, she wanted to bear witness to social injustice, political violence, and repression—having been motivated by the betrayal and murder by right-wing conspirators of an uncle on her father's side, President Salvador Allende . . . .

In what circumstances was the novel under consideration written? In [a] 1986 lecture . . . A. stressed the importance of the "moment of history the writer is born into," especially in Latin America, a world of great "struggles and defeats, brutality and magic." Increasingly aware of the New World's five-hundred-year tradition of violence, she matured intellectually with her uncle's socialist movement and became a novelist at her reactionary grandfather's death. Thus, her book is the celebration of a momentous social struggle in which those two figures were principals. Only fictitious names are used in the story, for places as well as for people, but the implications are obvious: this was to be a composite testimony of many voices . . . written with a recent exile's sense of urgency, and a family member's intimacy.

Peter G. Earle, "Literature as Survival: A.'s *The House of the Spirits,*" *ConL,* 28, 4 (Winter 1987), 543–45

While the first few sentences of *The House of the Spirits* seem to belong to [Gabriel] García Márquez and *One Hundred Years of Solitude,* the last few—which, ironically enough, are much the same—belong to I. A. "Rarely has a new novel from Latin America consciously or unconsciously owed more to its predecessors; equally rare is the original utterance coming out of what is now a collective literary tradition." That this is A.'s first novel does not excuse the presence of García Márquez (as the critics suggest), though it might explain it, perhaps in terms of a problem facing all post-Boom Latin American novelists, new and other-wise, who wish to follow in the tradition of magical realism: How does one get beyond *One Hundred Years of Solitude,* since all writing in the genre would seem, in the end, a rewriting of this novel? A. begins with this premise—consciously or unconsciously—and in the rewriting she discovers her own novel, one very different from *One Hundred Years of Solitude.* . . . *The House of the Spirits* . . . reads, initially, like a parody of García Márquez's novel, though not a *conscious* sort of parody. . . . But A. does not use García Márquez's language as an exposé to destroy it, speaking *through* it in her own language; rather, A. uses his language as a means to discover her own language, which she *substitutes* for García Márquez's. In other words, we would have trouble isolating a representing discourse which is simultaneously present, and at odds with the represented discourse: there is no obvious wink at the reader. We can, however, contrast an "initial" discourse with a "final" discourse, which *are* at odds with each other. A. begins speaking in a represented language—a language not her own, but García Márquez's, though perhaps she is not aware of it—and through this language she discovers her own representing language. It is as though A. "unconsciously" parodies García Márquez early in the novel, then stumbles happily onto her own language—her own story—in the end. But is there unconscious parody . . . or are we simply speaking here of inattentive writing? Are we simply comparing an established master with a first novelist?

Robert Antoni, "Parody or Piracy: The Relationship of *The House of the Spirits* to *One Hundred Years of Solitude*," *LALR*, 16, 32 (July–Dec. 1988), 16

Chilean author I. A.'s second novel, published in Spain in 1984, confirms the impression made by *La casa de los espíritus* . . . of her skill as a storyteller. This time, however, instead of an epic portrayal of four generations of women, she has chosen a more limited historical perspective focusing on a transforming experience in the life of one young woman. Still, A. remains true to the moral imperative behind all her writing, which is to bear witness through literature to a time and place in Latin-American history: "All those of us who write and are fortunate enough to be published ought to assume the responsibility for serving the cause of freedom and justice. We have a mission to accomplish in the front lines. In the face of the obscurantism that oppresses various countries on our continent, we must offer words, reason and hope. Literature must be placed at the service of mankind. Ideas are the worst enemy of barbarism." Like *La casa de los espíritus, De amor y de sombra* . . . is a novel set in an unnamed country, which is unmistakably the author's homeland, under the dictatorship of an unnamed general, obviously Augusto Pinochet, in approximately 1978. As much as it is a tale of female self-discovery, it is equally, from beginning to end, a repudiation of military regimes and the mentality that sustains them.

Doris Meyer, "Exile and the Female Condition in I. A.'s *De amor y de sombra*," *IFR*, 15, 2 (Summer 1988), 151

Despite the incredibly painful and difficult material that A. writes about, neither she nor her novels are filled with a sense of pessimism or despair. A. has often said in her public lectures that such emotions are paralyzing. She believes profoundly in the ability of the human spirit to endure. It is perhaps for this reason that her novels are ultimately so uplifting as well as entertaining. A born storyteller, A. renders tribute to this gift in her most recent work, *Eva Luna* . . . , a modern picaresque novel about a 20th-c. Scheherazade who spins tales to survive in a politically unstable Latin American society.

It is difficult for one who has met I. A. not to immediately find pieces of her in all her female characters. They share her sharp intelligence, playful sense of humor, force of decision, love of words, romantic temperament, desire to live life as if it were a novel, and healthy sense of female identity. A. is a dynamic and exuberant public speaker who attracts packed audiences

wherever she speaks. Her lectures are much like her novels themselves: a thoughtful blend of the personal and the political, a call for bearing witness, and a strong statement on the power of women and their ability to create a new morality in times of violence. A. has recently posed for herself in public forums the difficult questions: "For whom do I write? Why do I write?" If her answers are as complex as the questions themselves, they nonetheless can be synthesized in the following words: "I feel that writing is an act of hope, a sort of communion with our fellow men, a tiny bit of light. I certainly write for myself, but mainly for others. For those who have no voice and for those who are kept in silence. I write for you. I write so that people will love each other more."

Linda Gould Levine, "I. A.," in Diane E. Marting, ed., *Spanish American Women Writers* (1990), 22

There are many elements in *Eva Luna* that will sound familiar to the reader of *La casa de los espíritus*. At the heart of the story is an independent female deeply attached to her mother's spirit, a child who drags around a stuffed animal, and who later evokes her mother's spirit while she is unjustly in jail. There is also a house filled with mummies and occasional spirits, a charming eccentric who believes in tarot cards and astrology, a mention here and there of auras, the occasional attempt at clairvoyance, and a prophetic dream or two. But for all of this, *Eva Luna* is a new and fresh novel, and if some of her characters are similar, they are in new situations and settings. After all, Faulkner's Compsons resurfaced again and again, and no one ever seemed too surprised to see the themes of incest, degeneracy, or suicide recur in Yoknapatawpha County. Besides, as was the case in *De amor y de sombra*, in *Eva Luna* the strictly "magical" occurrences in this new novel are few. The beautiful transsexual Mimí nurses a host of superstitions, and Eva seems to find this endearing, but she does not take them particularly seriously. Eva also "speaks" to her dead mother from time to time, and occasionally "sees" her, but on the literal narrative plane there is nothing more magical about this than the persistence of memory. Once again, there is a deliberate attempt to undercut the superstitions through which some of the characters (and readers?) view the world.

Patricia Hart, *Narrative Magic in the Fiction of I. A.* (1989), 170–71

ALVAREZ GARDEAZABAL, Gustavo
Colombian novelist, b. 31 Oct. 1945, Tuluá

A. G. is one of the most prominent Colombian novelists to emerge from the shadow of the Nobel Prize-winning novelist Gabriel García Márquez (q.v.). Born in the small town of Tuluá, A. G. briefly studied engineering at Medellín, then attended the Universidad del Valle in Cali, from which he received his Licenciatura de Letras in 1970, writing a thesis titled "La novelística de la violencia en Colombia'' (1970; the novel of violence in Colombia); he began writing fiction soon thereafter. He was a faculty member at the same university during much of the 1970s and in the early 1980s, when he also wrote a newspaper column. Although A. G. has generally lived in Colombia, finding in his home region a source of inspiration, he lived for a brief period in the U.S. in 1985. His novel *El divino* (1986; the divine) was written with a Guggenheim fellowship. A. G. has been involved in politics; he joined (and later left) the Movimiento Cívico in Colombia. He was their representative to the National Assembly. After his Guggenheim fellowship in the U.S. in 1985, he returned to Colombia and later became Alcalde (mayor) of Tuluá (1988–1990). A. G. has frequently been controversial, both as a professor and as an outspoken writer uninhibited about denouncing political chicanery by those in power.

A. G. began his novelistic career, after a self-admitted false start with *Piedra pintada* (1965; painted rock), with a trilogy concerning the epoch known unhappily to Colombians as ''La Violencia,'' a period stretching from about 1948 to about 1960, during which political violence was endemic. This trilogy, consisting of *La tara del papa* (1971; the tare of the Papa), *Cóndores no entierran todos los días* (1972; condors don't bury every day), and *Dabeiba* (1973; Dabeiba), creates a complex portrait of the self-destructive and apocalyptic environment of violence and stresses the corrupting effects of the political struggle between liberals and conservatives. The hallmarks of the style of A. G. appear in these works. For instance, *Cóndores,* the story of León María Lozano, the cheese seller who becomes the leader of a powerful gang of killers for the conservatives, is told by means of innovative use of temporal reference, foreshadowings, and linguistic tags (such as the frequent use of *dizque,* ''they say'') that emphasize the oral quality of the narrative and establish the implied reader as having prior knowledge of the town and at least some of the events.

Much of the work of A. G. has been centered in the town of Tuluá, which acquires mythical and exaggerated qualities through his treatment of its inhabitants and social history. The mythifying tendency, which is nevertheless satirical and corrosive, is strongly present in *El bazar de los idiotas* (1974; *Bazaar of the Idiots,* 1991), which presents the story of two miracle-working idiots, using complex techniques of narrative organization and repetition to present a humorous and grotesque chronicle that attacks both religious superstition and faith in the efficacy of science.

El titiritero (1977; the puppet master) concerns violence arising from student demonstrations at the Universidad del Valle in Cali. The title refers to the manipulation of characters carried out by the novelist as well as to political manipulation and the distortion of truth by historians. The novel is an advance over the previous work of A. G., pointing toward his later novels, such as the complex *Los míos* (1981; my people) and *Pepe Botellas* (1984; Pepe Botellas) in its self-reflexive nature and collage of materials. His two subsequent novels, *El divino* and *El último gamonal* (1987; the last boss), while somewhat less ''major,'' continue his critique of political and religious hypocrisy.

As Raymond L. Williams and others have noted, A. G. shares certain features with García Márquez, such as a cultivation of an ''exotic'' regional locale, a participation in innovative narrative strategies, an emphasis on orality, and a preoccupation with Colombian history. But A. G. has attained a strong and unmistakable style that is the mark of the truly individual artist. His work has gradually grown in complexity and richness, with its particular hallmarks being a complicated play on the nature of historical versus fictional ''truth,'' typically carried out by means of a deceptively chatty narrative voice that draws the reader into a fascinating world of uncertainties and speculations about chronicled events, which nevertheless are meticulously and richly detailed. As have other Colombian novelists such as Eduardo Caballero Calderón, Alvaro Cepeda Samudio (qq.v.), and García Márquez, A. G. has frequently concentrated on the period of ''La Violencia.'' Recipient of numerous prizes for his work, he is one of the major writers now producing in Latin America.

FURTHER WORKS: *Cuentos del Parque Boyacá* (1978); *Manual de crítica literaria* (1980); *Cali* (1990); *Los sordos ya no hablan* (1991)

BIBLIOGRAPHY: Williams, R. L., ed., *Aproximaciones a G. A. G.* (1977); Gyurko, L. A., ''The Phantasmagoric World of G.,'' *HisJ,* 2, 1 (Fall 1980), 27–40; Williams, R. L., ''Structure and Transformation of Reality in A. G.: *El bazar de los idiotas,*'' *KRQ,* 27, 2 (1980), 244–61; Bell, S. M., ''Hacia el apocalipsis: la violencia en los cuentos de A. G.,'' *CH,* 3, 1 (1981), 3–16; Luchting, W. A., '' 'Yo no fui': la poética de la no responsabilidad. *El titiritero,* de G. A. G.,'' *CA,* 236, 3 (1981), 208–21; Souza, R. D., ''*Los míos* and the Burden of History,'' *Chasqui,* 11, 2–3 (Feb.–May 1982), 38–41; Williams, R. L., ''El tiempo en la novela: observaciones en torno al tiempo en la novela colombiana contemporánea,'' *ExTL,* 11, 2 (1982–1983), 11–28; Souza, R. D., ''Caos y orden en dos novelas de A. G.,'' *El café literario* (Bogotá), 6, 36 (1983), 9–12; Thompson, J., ''The Creation of Myth with the

Idiot as Hero in *El bazar de los idiotas,*" *ArielK,* 1, 1 (Fall 1983), 2–8; Sklodowska, E., "*Pepe Botellas* de A. G.: ironías de un discurso histórico," *Revista de estudios colombianos,* 1 (1986), 17–22; Souza, R. D., *La historia en la novela hispanoamericana moderna* (1988), 129–48; Tittler, J., "*El último gamonal:* entrega final de la telenovela biográfica de A. G.," *Revista de estudios colombianos,* 9 (1990), 32–37; Williams, R. L., *The Colombian Novel, 1844–1987* (1991), 172–82

KENNETH E. HALL

AMADI, Elechi

Nigerian novelist and dramatist (writing in English), b. 12 May 1934, Aluu (near Port Harcourt)

A. belongs to a minority eastern riverine nation (tribe), the Ikwere. He studied at the Government College in Umuahia, and graduated in science from the University of Ibadan. He has been land surveyor, army officer, and teacher, serving as the only leading eastern Nigerian writer in the federal army during the Biafran War (1966–1970). Subsequently he joined the Rivers State government, heading the ministry of information and later its education ministry.

A.'s early novels, like Chinua Achebe's (q.v.), are set in his traditional African world, but unlike Achebe's, which are shadowed by the colonial intrusion, treat exclusively that world's life of "tradition, propriety, and decorum." There is no alien disruption, no contrasting authorial perspective reflecting rational scepticism or modern change. Ihuoma, the "pure" heroine of A.'s first novel, *The Concubine* (1966), may be seen either in classical tragic terms, doomed by her link with the divine to be denied human life and love, or as a pathetic figure overshadowed by unlucky circumstances.

The Great Ponds (1969) more fully portrays than in Achebe a warrior society in action, showing in harsh measure the cost of intervillage and interclass violence. What again, as in *The Concubine,* has engaged us, is not how these events may be explained, but A.'s compassionate and thoughtful rendering of the tragedy's effects, in motive and behavior, upon those involved. This again distinguishes *The Slave* (1978), whose protagonist, Olumati, is denied an impossible happiness and takes refuge in slavery to a shrine, as in another society such a man might have become reclusive or suicidal.

A. describes *Sunset in Biafra: A Civil War Diary* (1973) as "an intimate personal story" of his experiences during the Nigerian Civil War. His narrative is dispassionate, understated, stoical; his

experience of human folly and corruption, of human weakness and division, convinced him of the deep-rooted menace of tribalism, "the herd instinct." This account of the psychological effects of captivity is relatively measured and matter-of-fact next to Wole Soyinka's (q.v.) *The Man Died* (1972), but more balanced overall, more credible even in its recognition that the tragedy and guilt alike were shared. A similarly sober viewpoint pervades the novel *Estrangement* (1986). Set in the war's aftermath, it portrays the struggle to regain normalcy, individual and communal.

A. has been overshadowed by Achebe, chiefly perhaps because he ignores the colonial encounter; furthermore, his English style is comparatively stilted, less idiomatic. He can, however, match Achebe in representing and interpreting the life and values of traditional village society, even surpassing him in his patient development of close relationships and familial attachments.

FURTHER WORKS: *Isiburu* (1973); *Pepper Soup* [and] *Ibadan* (1977); *Ethics in Nigerian Culture* (1982)

BIBLIOGRAPHY: Niven, A., "The Achievement of E. A.," in Rutherford, A., ed., *Commonwealth* (1971), 92–100; Palmer, E., *An Introduction to the African Novel* (1972), 117–28; Obiechina, E. N., *Culture, Tradition and Society in the West African Novel* (1975); Taiwo, O., *Culture and the Nigerian Novel* (1976), 197–209; Burness, D., ed., *Wanasema: Conversations with African Writers* (1985), 4–10

MICHAEL THORPE

AMERICAN LITERATURE

See Volume 1, page 57.

The 1980s saw a general retreat in American literature from the surrealistic and confessional modes of expression that dominated new writing during the late 1960s and early 1970s. The retreat was due in part to a natural flux of taste, for periods of extreme style tend to engender a reactionary taste for tradition. Probably the retreat was due also to a habitual conservatism of Americans that reasserted itself as the disenchantments of the Vietnam period faded from consciousness. The 1970s esteem for arcane gamesmanship in fiction, for confrontation in the theater, and for extraordinary doses of candor in poetry came gradually to seem excessive, even manic. In their place came revivals of narrative realism, naturalistic dramaturgy, and—to a lesser extent—poetic formalism. Postmodernism (q.v.) did not disappear from the literary scene, assuredly, but its more obvious vaunts suffered diminished prestige.

Fiction

Among the most important writers of the 1980s were four novelists of long-standing reputation and established achievement who continued to publish major work as a matter of course: Saul Bellow, John Updike, Gore Vidal, and Philip Roth (qq.v.). Bellow's *The Dean's December* (1982) received mixed reception, but the story collection *Him with His Foot in His Mouth* (1984), the novel *More Die of Heartbreak* (1987), and two novellas, *The Bellarosa Connection* (1989) and *A Theft* (1989), are works of daunting intelligence that reaffirm Bellow's eminence as a Nobel laureate. Updike's foray into theology in *Roger's Version* (1986) struck many readers as tendentious, but a delightful comedy entitled *The Witches of Eastwick* (1984) and comedies of manners called *S.* (1988), *Rabbit Is Rich* (1981), and *Rabbit at Rest* (1990)—announced as the last of the Harry "Rabbit" Angstrom series—are as topical and lucidly written as the best in Updike's oeuvre. Gore Vidal has such divergent impulses as a novelist that the occasional blunder seems inevitable, but a satiric misfire like *Duluth* (1983) is redeemed by the magisterial *Lincoln* (1984), *Empire* (1987), and *Hollywood* (1990), all of which contain the absorbing period detail and dexterous wit that have come to distinguish Vidal's ongoing chronicle of American history. Finally, Philip Roth proved himself once again an anatomist of generational Jewish conflict in an omnibus compilation of *The Ghost Writer* (1979), *Zuckerman Unbound* (1981), and *The Anatomy Lesson* (1983), published as *Zuckerman Bound* (1985). Even more impressive is *The Counterlife* (1986), in which the author's comically aggrieved Jewishness finds expression in a deconstructionist tour de force.

This cluster of established novelists writing at the top of their form was augmented by a number of other writers whose achievements in the period brought to a kind of fulfillment the promise of earlier work, among them Reynolds Price (b. 1933), Peter Taylor (b. 1917), Don DeLillo, Anne Tyler, Larry McMurtry, and Toni Morrison (qq.v.). Price climaxed a long and distinguished career of writing about the North Carolina up-country with the comically compelling *Kate Vaiden* (1986). Taylor's achievement was similar when he crowned forty years' worth of short stories with *A Summons to Memphis* (1986), a first novel so adroit that it could serve as a textbook of novelistic method. DeLillo cemented a gathering reputation for hard-edged, rather chilling fictions with *White Noise* (1985) and *Libra* (1988). With equal force, Anne

Tyler nailed down her reputation as a master of the crisply written comedy of manners in a series of fine novels, among them *Dinner in the Homesick Restaurant* (1982), *The Accidental Tourist* (1985), and *Breathing Lessons* (1988). None of these writers, however, fulfilled his or her early promise so astonishingly as Larry McMurtry and Toni Morrison. In a series of fictions about the American West, McMurtry is engaged in a revisionist mythologizing of that region akin to what Faulkner did for Mississippi, and in *Lonesome Dove* (1985), an epic tale of a Texas cattle drive, he has written what is assuredly a masterpiece. In *Beloved* (1987), Morrison has written a commensurate work: an awesomely imagined and brutally powerful chronicle of slavery and its aftermath in rural Ohio several years after the Civil War.

Other reputations declined somewhat in the decade. Norman Mailer's (q.v.) attempts at genre fiction in *Ancient Evenings* (1983), *Tough Guys Don't Dance* (1984), and *Harlot's Ghost* (1991) did nothing to buttress his once-substantial reputation, and Ishmael Reed's (q.v.) *Reckless Eyeballing* (1986) and *The Terrible Threes* (1989) contributed only to a consensus that the 1970s overrated his screwball humor. Indeed, any number of literary reputations declined because novelists like Reed continued to write in an aggressively postmodern mode that seemed in the 1980s a dated, one-note mannerism of the 1970s. The critical reception of both *Letters* (1979) and *Sabbatical* (1982) suggested that the postmodern cleverness of John Barth (q.v.) had reached the point of unreadability, and the outsize *The Tidewater Tales* (1987) inspired at least one critic to a post-postmodern reversal of the Mies van der Rohe theorem: that more is less. *The Last Voyage of Somebody the Sailor* (1991) offered readers no relief from Barth's ponderous jocosity. Neither did Kurt Vonnegut, Jr. (q.v.), appear to develop in any significant way in the 1980s. *Galápagos* (1985), *Bluebeard* (1987), and *Hocus Pocus* (1990) are as inventive and funny as anything Vonnegut published between 1967 and 1975 but are ideationally and stylistically too much of that period. It is increasingly said of Vonnegut that he is a genre novelist—limited to the genre of the Vonnegut novel. Something similar might be said of William Gaddis (q.v.), whose *Carpenter's Gothic* seemed in 1985 too much of the 1970s in its obsession with authenticity and phoniness, with situational ethics, and with the way we speak now. Other writers who seemed locked into the 1960s and 1970s mode of extravagance and saw their reputations decline somewhat in the 1980s include Joseph Heller (q.v.), whose *God Knows* (1984) and *Picture This* (1988) failed the comic standard of his earlier *Catch-22* (1961), and John Irving (q.v.), whose *The Hotel New Hampshire* (1981), *The Cider House Rules* (1985), and *A Prayer for Owen Meany* (1989) lacked the carefully edged insouciance of *The World According to Garp* (1978).

Several novelists of the middle rank with distinctive but not distinctively postmodern signatures enjoyed more stable reputations than postmodernists like Barth and Vonnegut: notably Louis Auchincloss, Joyce Carol Oates, E. L. Doctorow, and Joan Didion (qq.v.). Among these novelists of the middle rank in America, no one gives that rank more distinction than Auchincloss. A prolific writer, he has published over a long career a work of fiction almost every year, and in recent novels like *Diary of a Yuppie* (1986) and *The Lady of Situations* (1990) he has continued to take the ethical pulse of America with elegant, underappreciated art. The even more prolific Oates is less reliable than Auchincloss in her craft. In *You Must Remember This* (1987) she broke with the gothicism that had preoccupied her in such novels as *Bellefleur* (1980) and *A Bloodsmoor Romance* (1982), only to return to gothicism in *Because It Is Bitter and Because It Is My Heart* (1990); but even when her taste for overwrought gothicism is under control, Oates's fictions continue to bear the impress of hasty writing. Doctorow has been marginally more successful than Oates in laying claim to seriousness of intent, but his distinctive compound of historical and fictional characters in *World's Fair* (1985) and *Billy Bathgate* (1989) is essentially the same as that in *Ragtime* (1975), and it has come to seem a gimmick that limits him to midrank achievement. The journalistic writings of Joan Didion have helped to steady her reputation in a period when it might have faltered on the basis of her fiction. Certainly the terse and elliptic style that gave such distinction to *A Book of Common Prayer* (1977) failed to enliven *Democracy* (1984).

A galaxy of relatively new writers has especially invigorated American fiction since 1980, nudging it decisively toward realism and away from the nonlinear, surrealistic novels that dominated the late 1960s and 1970s. No writers are more notable in this regard than those associated with what is voguishly termed "hick chic": Louise Erdrich (b. 1954), whose novels *Love Medicine* (1984), *The Beet Queen* (1986), and *Tracks* (1988) have given life to the people of North Dakota; her husband and collaborator Michael Dorris (b. 1945), under whose name has been published *A Yellow Raft in Blue Water* (1987); Carolyn Chute (b. 1947), whose extraordinary novels *The Beans of Egypt, Maine* (1985) and *Letourneau's Used Auto Parts* (1988) deal with poverty, squalor, and sometimes hilarious violence in rural slums of the Northeast; Jayne Anne Phillips (b. 1952), whose novel *Machine*

Dreams (1984) and collection of stories *Fast Lanes* (1987) give voice to assorted down-and-outers; Bobbie Ann Mason (b. 1940), whose *In Country* (1985) and *Spence & Lila* (1988) are pitch-perfect novels of rural Kentucky; Ivan Doig (b. 1939), whose *Dancing at the Rascal Fair* (1987) is set in turn-of-the-century Montana; and John Casey (b. 1939), whose toweringly beautiful *Spartina* (1989) plumbs unromantically the life of a Rhode Island fisherman.

Another group of writers not identified specifically with "hick chic" but interested in kindred subjects like ethnicity, the rural sensibility, and the suburban experience is part of this drift toward representative realism. No one built a major reputation more suddenly in that regard than William Kennedy (q.v.), the success of whose *Ironweed* (1983) was followed by the successful reprinting in 1983 of *Legs* (1975) and *Billy Phelan's Greatest Game* (1978), the three novels making up his so-called "Albany" trilogy. In *Quinn's Book* (1988), a picaresque novel, Kennedy employs his native Albany, New York, once again. Women writers were an especially impressive presence in this area of fiction, both statistically and qualitatively. Mary Gordon (b. 1949) wrote compellingly of Irish-Catholic women too dominated by men in *Final Payments* (1978) and *The Company of Women* (1980). She has enlarged that focus in the even more accomplished *Men and Angels* (1985) and *The Other Side* (1989). Gloria Naylor (b. 1950) wrote no less compellingly of the plight of black women in *The Women of Brewster Place* (1982), *Linden Hills* (1985), and *Mama Day* (1988); Alice Walker (q.v.), of two black sisters facing terrible burdens of awareness in an epistolary novel entitled *The Color Purple* (1982); and Alice McDermott (b. 1953), of growing up in 1960s suburbia in a hauntingly beautiful novel entitled *That Night* (1987).

Fiction identifiable with the ongoing Southern Renaissance seems also a part of this drift toward representative realism—novels like Madison Smartt Bell's (b. 1957) *A Soldier's Joy* (1989), James Wilcox's (b. 1949) *Sort of Rich* (1989), John Ed Bradley's (b. 1959) *Tupelo Nights* (1988), and Padgett Powell's (b. 1952) *Edisto* (1984). But of particular distinction among such new-South, realistic novels are once again a number of works by women: Josephine Humphreys's (b. 1945) *Dreams of Sleep* (1984) and *Rich in Love* (1987); Gail Godwin's (b. 1937) *A Southern Family* (1987); Mary Lee Settle's (b. 1918) quintet about the West Virginia coal country, brought to completion with *The Killing Ground* (1982), and also her *Charley Bland* (1989); Lee Smith's (b. 1944) *Oral History* (1983) and *Fair and Tender Ladies* (1988); Ellen Gilchrist's (b. 1935) *The Anna Papers* (1988); and

Jill McCorkle's (b. 1958) *Tending to Virginia* (1987).

Postmodern metafictionists remain a significant part of the literary scene, but they ceased in the 1980s to enjoy the critical deference they received in the late 1960s and 1970s. John Hawkes's *Adventures in the Alaskan Skin Trade* (1985) and *Whistlejacket* (1988), Robert Coover's (qq.v.) *Gerald's Party* (1986) and *Pinocchio in Venice* (1991), Joseph McElroy's (b. 1930) *Women and Men* (1987), Gilbert Sorrentino's (b. 1929) *Rose Theatre* (1987), Ronald Sukenick's (b. 1932) *Blown Away* (1986), and Constance Urdang's (b. 1922) *American Earthquakes* (1988) found only limited audiences, not just because they are inherently difficult books, but because their self-reflexive conceits and multidimensional, nonlinear combinations of fantasy, joke, and horror seem to many readers a throwback to the intellectual temper of the early 1970s. Indeed, since the mid-1980s, a group of mostly young writers greatly celebrated by the media and known irreverently as the "Brat Pack" has commandeered the reputation for insouciant up-to-datedness that the metafictionists once enjoyed. Membership in the group is ongoing and undefined, but it is generally thought to include Madison Smartt Bell, Jay McInerney (b. 1955), David Leavitt (b. 1961), Mary Gaitskill (b. 1954), Gordon Lish (b. 1934), Tama Janowitz (b. 1957), Bret Easton Ellis (b. 1964), Jill Eisenstadt (b. 1963), Richard Ford (b. 1944), T. Coraghessan Boyle (b. 1948), and Ron Hansen (b. 1947). The group's most estimable publications to date are Leavitt's *Family Dancing* (1984) and *The Lost Language of Cranes* (1986), Boyle's *World's End* (1987) and *East Is East* (1990), and Eisenstadt's *From Rockaway* (1987).

A surprising development in American fiction since 1980 has been the sudden proliferation of collections of short stories, a proliferation due in great part to a new interest in their publication by university and small presses. Story collections from the commercial presses tend still to favor the enigmatic minimalism endorsed by the influential *New Yorker* magazine, as in Mark Strand's (q.v.) *Mr. and Mrs. Baby* (1985) and Frederick Barthelme's (b. 1943) *Natural Selection* (1990), but diversity and plurality are everywhere else the hallmarks of a short-story renaissance. Among the many well-remarked collections of the period are T. Coraghessan Boyle's *If the River Was Whiskey* (1989); Harold Brodkey's (b. 1930) *Stories in an Almost Classical Mode* (1988); Raymond Carver's (q.v.) *What We Talk About When We Talk About Love* (1981), *Cathedral* (1983), and *Where I'm Calling From* (1988); Richard Ford's *Rock Springs* (1987); Ellen Gilchrist's *Victory Over Japan* (1984); Amy Hempel's (b. 1951) *Reasons to Live* (1985);

Peter Matthiessen's (b. 1927) *Midnight Turning Gray* (1984); Mary Morris's (b. 1947) *The Bus of Dreams* (1985); Mary Robinson's (b. 1949) *An Amateur's Guide to the Night* (1983); and Tobias Wolff's (b. 1945) *In the Garden of the North American Martyrs* (1981).

Poetry

There has been much talk since 1980 of a poetry renaissance in America, the talk inspired by an increase in the publication of poetry by small and university presses. Volumes of selected and collected poems by established writers have been especially numerous. The late Anne Sexton (q.v.) was memorialized in a *Complete Poems* in 1981; Robert Creeley (q.v.) amassed thirty years of verses for a *Collected Poems* in 1982; and the years since then have seen volumes of selected or collected poems from such important figures as John Ashbery, Robert Bly, David Ignatow, Adrienne Rich (qq.v.), A. R. Ammons (b. 1926), Marvin Bell (b. 1937), Hayden Carruth (b. 1921), Carolyn Kizer (b. 1925), Stanley Kunitz (b. 1905), Gregory Orr (b. 1947), Charles Simic (b. 1938), W. D. Snodgrass (b. 1926), and Richard Wilbur (b. 1921). Few of these collections proffer definitive overviews, however. Allen Ginsberg (q.v.) was enshrouded in 1984 in a massive *Collected Poems,* but that apparent summation of his oeuvre did not preclude a *New and Selected Poems* the very next year. In many ways, the publication of selected or collected poems has become a *pro tempore* event; except in a few cases, it no longer signals the summation of a career.

Indeed, unexpected shifts of direction and startling achievements of poetic maturity have in many instances followed upon the publication of such collections. In *Sweet Will* (1985), Philip Levine (b. 1928) moves beyond the scathing social pronouncements that typify his *Selected Poems* (1984) to a poetry of resignation and pity; in *Axe Handles* (1983), Gary Snyder (q.v.) avoids the angry abstractions of his earlier poems and seems, abruptly, a man who has discovered peace; and in the feminist poems of *Yin* (1984) and *The Nearness of You* (1986), Carolyn Kizer softens the rhetoric of her collected poems in *Mermaids in the Basement: Poems for Women* (1984). In a wholly unforeseen development, John Ashbery has moved away from the clotted, overpacked lines that were a Whitmanesque feature of his work to publish in collections like *A Wave* (1984) and *April Galleons* (1987) relatively straightforward poems touched pleasantly with nostalgia. In a contrary drift, A. R. Ammons has brought to startling maturity a style that evokes not only Whitman's aesthetic of inclusion but Dickinson's sudden turns of abstraction and elliptical grammar. Ammons's *Sumerian Vistas* (1987) is especially distinguished in this regard—a collection as evocatively American as it is aesthetically bewitching.

Other established poets have written importantly without notably changing direction or effecting a shift in their reputation. In the fine poems of *Mirrors* (1983) and *Memory Gardens* (1986), Robert Creeley continues to eschew symbolism, as he has for his whole career; in *A Few Days* (1985), James Schuyler (1923–1991) manifests the taut, sharp-eyed inventiveness that one has come to expect from him; and in *The One Day* (1988), Donald Hall (b. 1928) evokes landscapes with his distinctive particularity, grace, and melancholy. In the lovely *In Time and Place* (1986), John Hollander (b. 1929) continues to be wholly high cultural—a resolute champion of the canonical modes of poetry; in *An Oregon Message* (1987), William Stafford (b. 1914) creates once again his unlikely combinations of precise form and ineffable content; and in *The Continuous Life* (1990), Mark Strand pursues the elusive concord between words and wordlessness that has long preoccupied him.

The recent poems of James Merrill and W. S. Merwin (qq.v.) have confounded all foresight—as, perhaps, genius should. Under the title *The Changing Light at Sandover*, Merrill assembled in 1982 the previously scattered parts of a 560-page poem that records his half-playful, half-serious experiments in communication with the spirit world through the medium of the Ouija board. The poem raises and attempts to resolve such important questions about visionary experience that it might be placed squarely in the tradition of Dante, Wordsworth, and Blake. It is certainly the most important long poem of recent decades. *Late Settings* (1985) and *The Inner Room* (1988) are not as experimental as *Sandover* but as collections they are distinctive and unforeseen in their return to a verbal filigree abandoned in *Sandover*. Merwin is even more than Merrill a poet of inexplicable drift. Of the many poets who turned inward in the 1960s, he was the most successful in rendering images that floated freely in psychological space, but since the 1970s he has been moving fluidly from the visionary to the phenomenal and partway back again. Indeed, the poems in collections like *Opening the Hand* (1983) and *The Rain in the Trees* (1988) seem to be located in fissures of consciousness, dream, and memory. Few American poets active today are writing as clearly as Merrill and Merwin at the top of their form.

The central preoccupation of American poetry for several decades has been the creation of the so-called "authentic" voice, a voice that successfully conveys intimacy, sincerity, and a commitment to explorations of the self. More than any other poet, Robert Bly formulated that voice in his 1962 collection *Silence in the Snowy Fields*, and a legion of American poets continues to emulate the task Bly set himself. In their view, the inflated, rhetorical language of the Moderns was an evasion of the self; thus, they favor content rather than form, honest subjectivity rather than fictive personae, and simplicity of syntax rather than elegant interdynamics of texture and sound. Among the newly substantial and important voices in American poetry that bring distinction to this voice are C. K. Williams (b. 1936), Ellen Bryant Voigt (b. 1943), Tess Gallagher (b. 1943), Mary Oliver (b. 1935), and Mary Jo Salter (b. 1954). For several books now, and especially in *Flesh and Blood* (1987), Williams has been writing in long, capacious lines that suit his capaciousness of spirit; Voigt has manifested in *The Forces of Plenty* (1983) and in *The Lotus Flowers* (1987) a style that is successfully intimate and flexible; and Gallagher, in her *Amplitude: New and Selected Poems* (1987), has demonstrated a fine ability with anecdotal poems that are decorous only on their surface. Mary Oliver, who won a Pulitzer Prize in 1983 for *American Primitive*, is one of the purest lyricists writing today. And Mary Jo Salter is Oliver's equal. In two collections to date, *Henry Purcell in Japan* (1985) and *Unfinished Painting* (1989), she has proven herself an extraordinarily graceful and even exquisite lyricist.

But currents of discontent with the "authentic" voice are discernible in the period since 1980. It is indicative of that discontent that one of the most talked-about texts in recent years is Vikram Seth's (b. 1952) *The Golden Gate* (1986), a novel-poem in intricate rhyme and meter that chronicles the lives and crises of a group of San Francisco Yuppies. Seth's poem is a striking instance of the so-called New Narrative, which seeks relief from free-verse spontaneity in traditional meters and rhymes, and relief from the prevailing lyricism of contemporary American poetry in narrative and dramatic verse. The New Narrative has much in common with the so-called New Formalism, of which Amy Clampitt (b. 1920) has become the most representative figure through a series of collections that she has gowned in academic learning and traditional poetic craftsmanship, among them *What the Light Was Like* (1985) and *Archaic Figure* (1987). Gjertrud Schnackenberg (b. 1953) is also interesting as a New Formalist, although her poems in *The Lamplit Answer* (1985) are so carefully studied and insistently referential that they might have been excised from T. S. Eliot's (q.v.) *The Waste Land* (1922). A more interesting New Formalist than either Clampitt or Schnackenberg is Marilyn Hacker (b. 1942), who seems to work exclusively in such traditional forms as sestinas, sonnets, and ballads, but with a lightness and irony that seem contemporaneously necessary and of which Clampitt and Schnackenberg seem incapable.

If the New Narrative and the New Formalism currents of discontent agitate the poetic scene, they fail as yet to disrupt a flow of influence from the established American poets to their temporal successors. To that extent, the period since 1980 has lacked the discontinuities in tradition that are the hallmark of an authentic renaissance. Talented poets like Dana Gioia (b. 1950) and Susan Ludvigson (b. 1942) seem to filter Robert Bly's influence through the immediate influence of Mark Strand; W. S. Merwin might claim a disciple in David St. John (b. 1949); James Merrill, in Pamela Alexander (b. 1948) and Alfred Corn (b. 1943). The influence of Wallace Stevens (q.v.) is everywhere evident, notably so in the work of J. D. McClatchy (b. 1945), Pattiann Rogers (b. 1940), and George Bradley (b. 1953). Indeed, in a volume entitled *Terms To Be Met* (1986), Bradley makes clear that he has learned a great deal not only from Stevens but from those whom Stevens taught. Thus, he mimics without apology John Ashbery's plangent tone, John Hollander's intellectual allusiveness, and Richard Howard's (b. 1929) apostrophes. For better or worse, such respectful continuities define the present situations of American poetry.

Drama

The runaway economics of Broadway in recent years has engendered a notable caution regarding the production of untested work—to the extent that fully two-thirds of the plays that reached Broadway during the 1980s were revivals or were pretested successes that had their origin either off-Broadway, in London's West End, or in the American regional theaters. Although less subject than Broadway to the economic risks of original presentation, theaters located elsewhere than Broadway tended to share Broadway's conservatism and consequently to favor the presentation of realistic plays already established as stageworthy. There was also a clear preference for works sweet-tempered and nonthreatening. The confrontational dynamics and expressionistic staging of the preceding decades survived in scattered productions and in the work of militantly experimental houses like Ellen Stewart's (b. 1928) La Mama Experimental Theatre Club and Richard Foreman's (b. 1937) Ontological-Hysteric Theatre, but the general conservatism of the American stage was conspicuous. No manifestos or movements dynamized the scene as they did in the 1960s and 1970s.

In such a commercial climate, even *éminences grises* failed to command Broadway audiences for works inferior to their masterpieces, notably Arthur Miller with *The American Clock* (1982), Tennessee Williams with *Clothes for a Summer Night* (1983), and Edward Albee (qq.v.) with *Lolita* (perf. 1981) and *The Man Who Had Three Arms* (perf. 1982). Younger playwrights like Lanford Wilson and David Mamet (qq.v.) tended to dominate the stage in their stead. Wilson is widely thought to have emerged as Broadway's most satisfying dramatist of the period, especially in a series of linked plays that includes *5th of July* (1979), *Talley's Folly* (1980), and *Talley & Son* (1986). Mamet's masterpiece remains *American Buffalo* (1977), probably the most important American play of the 1970s, but more recent plays like *Glengarry Glen Ross* (1984) and *Speed-the-Plow* (1988) are comparably energized, the former by rhythms of scatologic dialogue that Mamet raises almost to the level of poetry. On the basis of his wisecracking comedies, Neil Simon (b. 1927) has not generally been considered a serious playwright, but in an autobiographical trilogy composed of *Brighton Beach Memoirs* (1984), *Biloxi Blues* (1986), and *Broadway Bound* (1987), and in the darker, somewhat more tonally ambitious *Lost in Yonkers* (1992), he created a stageworthy mix of nostalgia and cynicism that has gained him a new respect. David Rabe's (b. 1940) and Terrence McNally's (b. 1939) status on Broadway was greatly complicated by the casting of their plays. Rabe's *Hurlyburly* (1985) is a minor work more esteemed than it would otherwise have been for having been cast with movie stars, and McNally's *The Rink* (1985) was a sturdy drama whose reception was probably less than it should have been because of excessively glamorous casting. McNally was more successful off-Broadway with *The Lisbon Traviata* (1986) and *Frankie and Johnny in the Clair de Lune* (1987).

Important newcomers, one or more of whose plays have received a Broadway imprimatur, include A. R. Gurney, Jr. (b. 1930), Tina Howe (b. 1937), David Henry Hwang (b. 1957), Wendy Wasserstein (b. 1950), and Beth Henley (b. 1952). Gurney is the author of an engaging stream of plays many of which evoke affectionately the world of WASP America in the 1930s and 1940s, among them *The Middle Ages* (1985), *The Dining Room* (1982), and *The Cocktail Hour* (1989). Howe came to attention with a delicately imaginative play entitled *Painting Churches* (1984) and the equally impressive *Coastal Disturbances* (1987), after which an oddly thin play, *Approaching Zanzibar* (1989), was a disappointment. Hwang is best known for the sturdy and elegantly implicational *M. Butterfly* (1988), which bears out the promise of his earlier, more evanescent dramas. After a considerable success off-Broadway with *Uncommon Women and Others* (1978) and a modest success with *Isn't It Romantic?* (1985), Wasserstein came to Broadway with *The Heidi Chronicles* (1990) and deservedly won almost every theatrical prize of the year. Henley had a comparable success on Broadway with *Crimes of the Heart* (1982), a very funny play about three sisters living in Mississippi in 1974. She crowned that success with *The Miss Firecracker Contest* (1985), a delightful comedy about Southern oddballs, and in *The Lucky Spot* (perf. 1987) she assembled an assortment of waifs, strays, and misfits for an uproarious celebration of Christmas 1934 in the first taxi-dance hall in Pigeon, Louisiana. A certain vogue for Southern plays like Henley's was discernible, although not always with characters of Henley's madcap sort. A more genial ambience was achieved by Robert Harling (b. 1951) in *Steel Magnolias* (1988) and by Alfred Uhry (b. 1936) in a charming, two-character play entitled *Driving Miss Daisy* (1987).

But the major American playwright since 1980 and probably for a decade before that is Sam Shepard (q.v.), who resists offering his work to Broadway theaters in his stated preference for the less-commercial theaters of off-Broadway. Shepard's early plays were characterized by expressionistic staging and folkloric themes, but with *Curse of the Starving Class* (1976) and *Buried Child* (1979) he began to explore through a more naturalistic dramaturgy the subject of family relationships, especially among the unsophisticated and itinerant. *True West* (1981), *Fool for Love* (1983), and *A Lie of the Mind* (1987) are fine, chiseled installments in that apparently autobiographical exploration, and they are works that clearly establish Shepard as the most prestigious and theatrically exciting American playwright of his generation.

Like Shepard, a number of dramatists who built their reputations in the confrontational theater of the 1960s and 1970s have continued to write for the off- and off-off-Broadway theater while participating in the general drift of that theater back to the linear plots, coherent personae, and explicable themes that it once spurned as Broadway pabulum. Israel Horovitz (b. 1939) charmed audiences greatly with a trilogy of such plays based on Morley Ferlog's memoirs of a Jewish-Canadian youth—*Today I Am a Fountain Pen* (perf. 1986) being the best of them—and John Guare (b. 1938) charmed other audiences with *Six Degrees of Separation* (1990) and with the unabashed melodrama of two installments in a projected tetralogy: *Lydie Breeze* (1982) and *Gardenia* (1982). A penchant

for autobiographical plays seems a part of this off-Broadway accommodation of realism at the same time that it seems a residue of 1960s confessionalism, as in Albert Innaurato's (b. 1948) *Coming of Age in SoHo* (1985) and *Gus & Al* (1989). Realism redivivus was especially influential in the work of August Wilson (q.v.), who brought such integrity to the writing of plays like *Fences* (1986) and *The Piano Lesson* (1990) that they are thought emblematic of all that is best in the recent off-Broadway theater.

Significant new dramatists on the off- and off-off-Broadway scene include John Patrick Shanley (b. 1951), the author of what he calls an "emotionally connected" tetralogy that began with *Danny and the Deep Blue Sea* (1984) and concluded with *Italian American Reconciliation* (1989); Marsha Norman (b. 1947), the author of a nicely mordant play entitled *'night Mother* (1983); Harvey Fierstein (b. 1954), the author of the vital and funny *Torch Song Trilogy* (1981); Richard Greenberg (b. 1958), whose *Eastern Standard* (1989) is as notable for its romantic sophistication as for its subversive punch; and Jane Wagner (b. 1935), the author of a witty, one-woman play called *The Search for Signs of Intelligent Life in the Universe* (1986).

It is arguable, however, that the most vital wellsprings of American drama since 1980 are no longer to be found off- and off-off-Broadway but in the regional theaters. Companies in Louisville, San Francisco, Washington, Dallas, Chicago, Minneapolis, and Los Angeles began to develop national prominence in the 1960s, and they have continued to flourish despite potentially ruinous cutbacks in funding. The number of such nonprofit, professional companies now exceeds four hundred nationwide, and only ten percent of them are based in New York City. Concomitant with such growth, regional theaters have become a significant supplier of the Broadway and off-Broadway theaters—a supplier, even, of intact productions. It was the American National Theater in Washington, for instance, that gave Broadway one of its most distinguished productions of the 1980s, a 1985 revival of *The Iceman Cometh* that united the actor Jason Robards and the director José Quintero in a reprise of their legendary 1956 collaboration. Major Broadway successes of the period that originated in regional theaters include Mark Medoff's (b. 1940) *Children of a Lesser God* (1980), which had its genesis at the Mark Taper Forum in Los Angeles; John Pielmeier's (b. 1949) *Agnes of God* (1982), which traveled to New York from the Actor's Theatre of Louisville; and August Wilson's *Ma Rainey's Black Bottom* (1985), which was first staged by Yale Repertory.

BIBLIOGRAPHY: Perloff, M., "The Word As Such: Language Poetry in the Eighties," *APR*, 13, 3 (May–June 1984), 15–22; Klinkowitz, J., *Literary Subversions: New American Fiction and the Practice of Criticism* (1985); Mernit, S., "The State of the Short Story," *VQR*, 62, 2 (Spring 1986), 302–11; Andrews, B., et al., "Is There, Currently, an American Poetry? A Symposium," *AmerP*, 4, 2 (1987), 2–40; Delbanco, N., ed., special issue of "Contemporary American Fiction, I," *MQR*, 26, 4 (Fall 1987); McCaffery, L., and S. Gregory, eds., *Alive and Writing: Interviews with American Authors of the 1980s* (1987); McCaffery, L., "The Fictions of the Present," in Elliott, E., et al., eds., *Columbia Literary History of the United States* (1988), 1161–77; Austin, A., "The Present State of Black Theatre," *TDR*, 32, 3 (1988), 85–100; Delbanco, N., ed., special issue of "Contemporary American Fiction, II," *MQR*, 27, 1 (Winter 1988); Johnson, C. R., *Being and Race: Black Writing since 1970* (1988); Klinkowitz, J., "The New American Novel of Manners," *NWR*, 26, 3 (1988), 90–95; Feirstein, F., ed., *Expansive Poetry* (1989); McClatchy, J. D., *White Paper: On Contemporary American Poetry* (1989); Bly, R., *American Poetry: Wildness and Domesticity* (1990); Clarke, G., ed., *The New American Writing: Essays on American Literature since 1970* (1990); Hendin, J., "Fictions of Acquisition," in Mills, N., ed., *Culture in an Age of Money* (1990), 216–33; Hendin, J., "A Material Difference: Notes on the Newness of 1980s Fiction," *Dissent*, 37, 1 (1990), 49–57; Pinsker, S., *Bearing the Bad News: Contemporary American Literature and Culture* (1990); Saltzman, A. M., *Designs of Darkness in Contemporary American Fiction* (1990)

ROBERT F. KIERNAN

ANDRADE, Eugénio de

(pseud. of José Fontinhas) Portuguese poet, b. 19 Jan. 1923, Povoa da Atalaia

A. is Portugal's best-known living poet. Born in a village not far from the Spanish border, he was raised by a much beloved mother, whose death in 1956 deeply affected him. His feelings for his father may be deduced from the total absence of that figure in his work. After studies in Castelo Branco, Lisbon, and Coimbra, A. entered the civil service and worked in the department of public health and welfare until his retirement in 1983. From 1950 to the present, he has lived alone in the northern city of Porto.

Although he began to publish in his teens, A. has rejected his early work and prefers to consider *As Mãos e os Frutos* (1948; hands and fruit) the book that began his career. That work has been

followed to date by nineteen more volumes of poetry, two prose works, two children's books, numerous anthologies, and translations into Portuguese of poets such as Federico García Lorca and Yannis Ritsos (qq.v.). A.'s poetry has been translated into at least twenty languages, his complete works are currently being published in French, and four volumes have appeared in English translation. He has won Portugal's three most prestigious literary awards: the Critics' Award in 1986 and the Grande Premio for Poetry and the D. Dinis Award in 1989.

A.'s poetry has always exhibited a carefully evoked simplicity. Through naked word and image, he strives to convey what he calls "the rough or sweet skin of things." Distrustful of abstractions, he focuses on the world of matter, proclaiming a love for "words smooth as pebbles, rough as rye bread. Words that smell of clover and dust, loam and lemon, resin and sun." His limpid and highly musical style engraves sharp images of the things of this earth, while evoking powerful fluctuations of desire, joy, loss, and regret. The four classical elements of earth, water, fire, and air are never absent from his work. Nor is the human body, which the poet sees as "a metaphor for the universe." The critic Luis Miguel Nava (dates n.a.) draws together the three strands of A.'s poetic vision when he observes that "nature, the body, and the word meet on the same plane and in some way intermingle or merge."

A.'s pagan attachment to the body, its senses, and the world of things that surround it is accompanied, in his later works, by a deepening sense of impending death. Collections such as *Branco no branco* (1984; *White on White,* 1987) reveal an unresolved tension between nostalgia and resignation, with memory playing an important role as mixed blessing. "Shadow's weight," the cold sea, the threat of snow add poignancy and intensity to the characteristic life-affirmative lyricism of A.'s expression.

Marguerite Yourcenar (q.v.) has referred to "the well-tempered clavier" of A.'s poems, Ángel Flores (b. 1900) speaks of his "enduring language that becomes richer at every reading," and the Spanish writer Angel Crespo (b. 1926) proclaims that "his voice was born to baptize the world." Subtle musicality, deceptively simple imagery, and a richness of metaphor and symbolic suggestiveness combine to make A. the most popular contemporary poet in Portugal and, with the exception of Fernando Pessoa (q.v.), the most widely translated Portuguese poet of the 20th c.

FURTHER WORKS: *Adolescente* (1942); *Pureza* (1945); *Os amantes sem dinheiro* (1950); *As palavras interditas* (1951); *Até amanhã* (1956); *Cor-*

ação do dia (1958); *Mar de setembro* (1961); *Ostinato rigore* (1964); *Obscuro domínio* (1971); *Véspera da água* (1973); *Escrita da terra e outros epitáfios* (1974); *Limiar dos pássaros* (1976); *Memória doutro rio* (1978; *Memory of Another River,* 1988); *Matéria solar* (1980); *O peso da sombra* (1982); *Aquela nuvem e outras* (1986); *Contra a obscuridade* (1987); *Vertentes do olhar* (1987); *O outro nome da terra* (1988); *Rente ao dizer* (1992). FURTHER VOLUME IN ENGLISH: *Inhabited Heart: The Selected Poems of E. de A.* (1985)

BIBLIOGRAPHY: Sayers, R. S., "E. de A.," in Bede, J.-A., and W. B. Edgerton, eds., *Columbia Dictionary of Modern European Literature,* rev. 2nd ed. (1980), 21–22; Sayers, R. S., "Portuguese Poetry of Today and E. dc A.," *CP,* 17, 2 (Fall 1984), 137–54; Bedate, P. G., Introduction to *Inhabited Heart* (1985), vii–x; Levitin, A., Afterword to *White on White* (1987), 57–60; Levitin, A., Introduction to *Memory of Another River* (1988), 1–6

ALEXIS LEVITIN

ANGELOU, Maya

American autobiographer and poet, b. 4 Apr. 1928, St. Louis, Mo.

A. has written poetry, plays for stage, screen, and television, and songs. A performer, she has appeared on three continents as a dancer, singer, and actress; her frequent American television appearances in these roles, as well as filling the functions of interviewer and panelist in discussions of race-related current issues, have made her one of the most widely known figures in African-American cultural life. But it is as the author of a multivolume memoir, still in progress, that she has made the deepest impression. Her life—as experience and as artifact—is the creation of hers that the reading public knows best.

A. spent part of her childhood in her birthplace with her mother, part with her grandmother in Stamps, Arkansas, in what she understood to be exile, and her adolescence in San Francisco. In California she spent much of her adult years, during which, as the successive installments of her autobiography outline, she has also lived and worked in New York, Africa, and Europe.

Although A.'s memoirs are her own story filtered through a number of narrative and even fictional conventions, many of the issues they raise consciously evoke generalizations about the content and meaning of black female life in the middle third of the 20th c. Thus her treatment of the sexual abuse that she suffered as a child is at once personal and archetypal. And the highly individual

personalities of her mother and grandmother also point to broad conclusions about both the limitations and the power of black women in a racist society.

In her various autobiographical volumes, beginning with *I Know Why the Caged Bird Sings* (1970), A. discusses her experiences as a single mother, as San Francisco's first black female streetcar conductor, as a prostitute, as an artist, as a civil-rights worker, and as a black American expatriate living in Africa in the first heady years after independence. She worked with Martin Luther King, Jr., in New York, met with Malcolm X when he visited Ghana, was briefly married to a prominent African, and toured Europe in *Porgy and Bess,* and her memoirs connect all these experiences to her inner growth, what the title of one of the volumes calls *The Heart of a Woman* (1981).

Another theme that runs through the autobiography from the first volume on is what might be called the heart of a *writer*. More precisely, the autobiography is about the making of a writer under the particular social and cultural conditions of Southern black female life. In this by no means linear development, A. as narrator goes from the sexually molested child traumatized into aphonia, a literal not speaking, to a conscious subject who felt that Shakespeare, as she read him at age nine, spoke to and for her, to someone who could make use, for her own writing, of the canonical materials of white male Western culture and the languages of African-American folk life. In her collections of poetry, the influence of black American culture, especially musical and religious culture—spirituals and sorrow songs, gospel music, and popular sayings—is even more evident than in the autobiography, as A. translates her cultural heritage into the raw materials of a deliberate and sometimes overly self-conscious art.

FURTHER WORKS: *Just Give Me a Cool Drink of Water 'fore I Diiie* (1971); *Gather Together in My Name* (1974); *Oh Pray My Wings Are Gonna Fit Me Well* (1975); *Singin' and Swingin' and Gettin' Merry Like Christmas* (1976); *And Still I Rise* (1978); *Poems* (1981); *Shaker, Why Don't You Sing?* (1983); *All God's Children Need Traveling Shoes* (1986); *Now Sheba Sings the Song* (1987); *I Shall Not Be Moved* (1990)

BIBLIOGRAPHY: Smith, S. A., "The Song of a Caged Bird: M. A.'s Quest after Self-Acceptance," *SHR,* 7 (Fall 1973), 365–75; Butterfield, S., *Black Autobiography in America* (1974), 203–9; Kent, G. E., "M. A.'s *I Know Why the Caged Bird Sings* and Black Autobiographical Tradition," *KanQ,* 7 (1975), 272–78; Neubauer, C.

E., "Displacement and Autobiographical Style in M. A.'s *The Heart of a Woman*," *BALF*, 17, 3 (Fall 1983), 123–29; Evans, M., ed., *Black Women Writers (1950–1980): A Critical Evaluation* (1984), 6–24, 25–36; Ramsey, P. R., "Transcendence: The Poetry of M. A.," *CBAA*, 17, 2 (1984–1985), 139–53; Froula, C., "The Daughter's Seduction: Sexual Violence and Literary History," *Signs*, 11, 4 (Summer 1986), 621–44; Gilbert, S., "M. A.'s *I Know Why the Caged Bird Sings:* Paths to Escape," *Mount Olive Review*, 1, 1 (Spring 1987), 39–50; Cudjoe, S. R., "M. A.: The Autobiographical Statement Updated," in Gates, H. L., Jr., ed., *Reading Black, Reading Feminist* (1990), 272–306

LILLIAN S. ROBINSON

Her genius as a writer is her ability to recapture the texture of the way of life in the texture of its idioms, its idiosyncratic vocabulary and especially in its process of image-making. The imagery holds the reality, giving it immediacy. That she chooses to recreate the past in its own sounds suggests to the reader that she accepts the past and recognizes its beauty and its ugliness, its assets and its liabilities, its strength and its weakness. Here we witness a return to and final acceptance of the past in the return to and full acceptance of its language, the language a symbolic construct of a way of life. Ultimately M. A.'s style testifies to her reaffirmation of self-acceptance, the self-acceptance she achieves within the pattern of the autobiography.

Sidonie Ann Smith, "The Song of a Caged Bird: M. A.'s Quest after Self-Acceptance," *Southern Humanities Review*, 7 (Fall 1973), 375

In many ways, *I Know Why the Caged Bird Sings* resembles Richard Wright's *Black Boy*. The setting is a small segregated town in the rural South; the parents have sent the children to live with relatives, one of whom owns a general store; Maya and her brother are forced to attend church, where they amuse themselves by making fun of the more zealous members of the congregation; the preacher comes to dinner and eats all the chicken; there is constant friction between the blacks and the poor whites; the fact of her oppression gradually intrudes on the writer's consciousness when she observes what happens around her—the hypocritical speeches of the white superintendent in their segregated school, the refusal of a white dentist to fix her teeth after her grandmother has salvaged his business; her brother helps fish a decomposed Negro body out of the pond while whites stand around and tell malicious jokes; the local sheriff gives them casual warnings whenever the Klan is about to go on a rampage; and finally, she migrates to a Northern city. M. A.'s complex sense of humor and compassion for other people's defects, however, endow her work with a different quality of radiance; she does not have Wright's mortal seriousness, or his estrangement, and does not take his risks. . . .

The distance in M. A.'s work is achieved by her sense of humor. She has the power of joking at herself, of re-creating the past in a comic spirit without belittling the other people involved and of capturing the pathetic and tragic overtones of the laughter without being overwhelmed by them. Frightened of a ghost story about the dead Mrs. Taylor, a woman who had always screamed her orders in the store because she was half deaf, A. remarks, "the thought of that voice coming out of the grave and all the way down the hill from the cemetery and hanging over my head was enough to straighten my hair." As in Langston Hughes, the humor is often a way of shattering racist images by using them. She knows that the "superstitious" dread Negroes are supposed to have for graveyards is the butt of racist jokes and has felt the perpetual torture of trying to make her hair conform to white standards of beauty; both experiences are subdued, and controlled, by the comic purpose. It is the fear, and the author's ability to laugh at her insecurities, that we remember most—the caged bird's mastery of her song.

Stephen Butterfield, *Black Autobiography in America* (1974), 203–9

In *Heart of a Woman*, A. deliberately strives to capture the individual conversational styles of her relatives and friends. In a sense, her friends and acquaintances become "characters" in the story of her life, and like any good writer of fiction, she attempts to make their conversations realistic and convincing. With some of the people who figure in her autobiography, there is no objective measure for credibility other than the reader's critical appreciation for life itself. If the conversant in question is not well-known beyond the scope of the autobiography, A. need only ensure that the dialogue attributed to the individual be consistent with his character as delineated in the text itself. Yet many of her friends and associates were either highly successful celebrities or popular political figures, and the conversations recorded in her life story have points of reference beyond the autobiographical text. In other words, readers can test the degree of verisimilitude in the recorded dialogues with either firsthand knowledge or second-hand sources of information about the celebrities' lives.

It is highly probable, for example, that many of A.'s readers are already familiar with the rhetorical styles of Martin Luther King, Jr., and Malcolm X, and the popular lyrics of Billie Holiday. In fact the lives of these three people in such accounts as *Why We Can't Wait*, *The Autobiography of Malcolm X*, and *Lady Sings the Blues* have in many ways become part of our contemporary folk history. A. adds a personalized quality to her recollections of conversations with these individuals and many others. The record of their conversations in *Heart of a Woman* brings them to life again, because the autobiographer is sensitive to and even somewhat self-conscious about the accurate reconstruction of their individual styles.

Since memory is not infallible, fictionalization comes into play whenever the autobiographer reconstructs or, perhaps more correctly, recreates conversation. While the autobiographer relies on invention, he or she creates the illusion of an infallible memory that records exactly the feel of a place and the words spoken there.

Carol E. Neubauer, "Displacement and Autobiographical Style in M. A.'s *The Heart of a Woman*," *BALF*, 17, 3 (Fall 1983), 124–25

Unlike her poetry, which is a continuation of traditional oral expression in Afro-American literature, A.'s prose follows classic technique in nonpoetic Western forms. The material in each book while chronologically marking her life is nonetheless arranged in loosely structured plot sequences which are skillfully controlled. In *Caged Bird* the tenuous psyche of a gangly, sensitive, withdrawn child is traumatically jarred by rape, a treacherous act from which neither the reader nor the protagonist has recovered by the book's end. All else is cathartic: her uncles' justified revenge upon the rapist, her years of readjustment in a closed world of speechlessness despite the warm nurturing of her grandmother, her granduncle, her beloved brother Bailey, and the Stamps community; a second reunion with her vivacious mother; even her absurdly unlucky pregnancy at the end does not assuage the reader's anticipatory wonder: isn't the act of rape by a trusted adult so assaultive upon an eight-year-old's life that it leaves a wound which can never be healed? Such reader interest in a character's future is the craft from which quality fiction is made. Few autobiographers however have the verve to seize the drama of such a moment, using one specific incident to control the book but with an underlining implication that the incident will not control a life.

The denouement in *Gather Together in My Name* is again sexual: the older, crafty, experienced man lasciviously preying upon the young, vulnerable, and, for all her exposure by that time, naïve woman. While foreshadowing apprehension guided the reader to the central action in the first work, Maya presses the evolvement in *Gather Together* through a limited first-person narrator who seems to know less of the villain's intention than is obvious to the reader. Thrice removed from the action, the reader sees that L. D. Tolbrook is nothing but a slick pimp, that his seductive sexual refusals can only lead to a calamitous end; that his please-turn-these-few-tricks-for-me-baby-so-I-can-get-out-of-an-urgent-jam line is an ancient inducement for susceptible females, but Maya the actor in the tragedy cannot. She is too much in love. Maya, the author, through whose eyes we see a younger, foolish "self," so painstakingly details the girl's descent into the brothel that Black women, all women, have enough vicarious example to avoid the trap. Again, through using the "self" as role model, not only is Maya able to instruct and inspire the reader but the sacrifice of personal disclosure authenticates the autobiography's integral depth.

Just as the title of *Gather Together* is taken from a New Testament injunction for the travailing soul to pray and commune while waiting patiently for deliverance and the *Caged Bird* title is taken from a poem by the beloved Paul Laurence Dunbar, who gave call to A.'s nascent creativity, the title of the third work, *Singin' and Swingin' and Gettin' Merry Like Christmas,* is a folkloric title symbolic of the author's long-deserved

ascent to success and fulfillment. This volume's plot and tone are lifted above adroit reenactments of that native humor so effective in relieving constant struggle in Black life which is holistically balanced in the first two books. The buoyancy is constant because Maya (who had theretofore been called Marguerite or Ritie all her life) the singer, Maya the dancer, Maya the actress, had shed the fearful image of "typical" unwed Black mother with a dead-end destiny. She knew she was more than that. But the racist and sexist society—which had relegated her to dishwasher, short-order cook, barmaid, chauffeur, and counter clerk; which had denied her entrance into secure employment and higher education in the armed services; and which programmed her into a familiar void when the crush of changing modernity even eradicated the avenues which partially liberated her foremothers—seemed invincible. The culmination of her show business climb is a dual invitation: either to replace Eartha Kitt in the Broadway production of *New Faces* or to join the star-studded cast of *Porgy and Bess,* which began a world tour in 1954. From that climax the settings shift to such faraway places as Rome, Venice, Paris, Yugoslavia, Alexandria, Cairo, Athens, and Milan; and the narrator, character, and reader view life from glorious vistas auspiciously removed from the world of that dejected girl in Stamps, Arkansas.

Sondra O'Neale, "Reconstruction of the Composite Self," in Mari Evans, ed., *Black Women Writers (1950–1980): A Critical Evaluation* (1984), 32–33

The public achievements have been many and yet the private motivation out of which her writing generates extends beyond the mere search for words as metaphors for purely private experience. Her poetry becomes both political and confessional. Significantly, one sees in her autobiographies a role-modeling process—one paradigmatic for other women—while not allowing the didactic to become paramount in either the poetry or the autobiographies.

Her autobiographies and poetry reveal a vital need to transform the elements of a stultifying and destructive personal, social, political and historical milieu into a sensual and physical refuge. Loneliness and human distantiation pervade both her love and political poetry, but are counterposed by a glorification of life and sensuality which produces a transcendence over all which could otherwise destroy and create her despair. This world of sensuality becomes a fortress against potentially alienating forces, i.e., men, war, oppression of any kind, in the real world.

Priscilla R. Ramsey, "Transcendence: The Poetry of M. A.," *CBAA*, 17, 2 (1984–1985), 140

It was the culmination of a number of factors at the end of the sixties that led to the outpouring of writings by Afro-American women. First, the inherent shortcomings of the nationalism of the Black Power movement; second, the increased social and economic pressures that led to the rapid deterioration of the urban centers of America; third, the rise of the feminist movement that made Afro-American women more conscious of their particularity; and, fourth, the increasing tensions in black male-female relations. . . . All of these factors led to a special kind of problematic to which the Afro-American woman had to address herself, adding a new and dynamic dimension to American literature. [Mel] Watkins's contention that the white media exploited the rift between black men and women that this literature examined, leading subsequently to the popularity of black women writers, possesses some degree of truth.

It is out of these conditions and in response to these specific concerns that M. A. offered her autobiographical statements: *I Know Why the Caged Bird Sings* (1970), *Gather Together in My Name* (1974), *Singin' and Swingin' and Gettin' Merry Like Christmas* (1976), *The Heart of a Woman* (1981), and *All God's Children Need Traveling Shoes* (1986). Although her last two works examine the manner in which the events of the sixties impacted upon her life, they were produced in a time when some of the social and political fervor of the 1970s had abated and thus allowed for a more sober assessment. Needless to say, the political currents of the time are more prominent in the last two segments of her statement. As a statement, A. presents a powerful, authentic, and profound signification of Afro-American life and the changing concerns of the Afro-American woman in her quest for personal autonomy, understanding, and love. Such a statement, because of the simple, forthright, and honest manner in which it is presented, is depicted against the larger struggle of Afro-American and African peoples for their liberation and triumphs. It is a celebration of the struggle, survival, and existence of Afro-American people.

Selwyn R. Cudjoe, "M. A.: The Autobiographical Statement Updated," in Henry Louis Gates, Jr., ed., *Reading Black, Reading Feminist* (1990), 284–85

ANTHONY, Michael

Trinidadian novelist, short-story writer, and historian, b. 10 Feb. 1932, Mayaro

After his education in Mayaro and San Fernando, A. worked as a molder in an iron foundry; but he quit this job in 1954 and went to London, where he hoped to establish a writing career. He was, however, at odds with the social and racial climate in England, and he returned to Trinidad in 1970 after a two-year sojourn in Brazil, where he served in Trinidad's diplomatic corps. He has lived in Trinidad since then, and has had a long and rewarding career with the island's National Cultural Council.

Although he began his literary career as a poet, A. abandoned this after receiving discouraging comments from the editors of the BBC's "Caribbean Voices," a particularly important forum for aspiring West Indian writers in the 1950s, and turned his talents to fiction where he found his voice. Of his six novels, collected short stories, and various concise histories of Trinidad and To-

bago, *The Games Were Coming* (1963), *The Year in San Fernando* (1965), *Green Days by the River* (1967), and *Cricket in the Road, and Other Stories* (1973) are outstanding achievements. Mayaro, a seaside community on Trinidad's southeastern coast, has exercised a tenacious hold on A.'s imagination, and its mystique pervades his fiction. *Green Days by the River,* one of his finest explorations of a youngster's developing consciousness, is set in Mayaro; and so too are several of his short stories. But Mayaro is more than merely a lush setting for the action; its rustic charm and arcadian resonances suggest a timelessness and immutability that are congenial to A.'s artistic temperament. In *All That Glitters* (1981), A.'s most recently published novel, some of these symbolic resonances are set alongside the community's workers, individuals such as Clunis, a mere coconut picker, who, for all his rough exterior and disconcerting brashness, is as genuine and reliable as the Mayaro tides.

A.'s emphasis on the strong, dour character, especially the husbandless wife and mother, is one of his important contributions to West Indian fiction. Many of A.'s women are stoic persons who withstand the vicissitudes of life with admirable fortitude. For instance, the drunkard's wife in the short story "Drunkard of the River" (1960) perseveres despite her husband's frequent brutalities. The world is a place of much hardship for other characters such as the dogged protagonist of "The Girl and the River" (1955), A.'s first short story, and certainly one of his best efforts. For Leon Seal, the obsessed cyclist of *The Games Were Coming,* an austere regimen (which eventually alienates his otherwise pliable girlfriend) is the price he pays for winning the prestigious fifteen-mile race, which is a test of his physical and moral fiber.

A.'s characters, the growing youngster notably, are uncommonly sensitive and largely vulnerable. Many of them, consequently, come to grief. Several of these youngsters can be found in A.'s short stories, and some are early, but well-rounded, preparations for the more complex adolescents of the novels. In *The Year in San Fernando* and *Green Days by the River* A. uses the first-person narrator's shifting perceptions to explore with compelling sensitivity and effectiveness the maturing responses of two young heroes who must come to terms with the sober and sometimes sordid realities of the adult world. At the end of his sometimes harrowing sojourn in San Fernando, Francis, whose status in the Chandles's household is little more than a house slave, changes profoundly: he has acquired a deeper understanding of the driven Chandles family, and he has become less psychologically dependent upon others; and

Shellie, the boy hero of *Green Days by the River*, after his symbolic baptism of fire and cleansing in the Edenic Cedar Grove, eventually understands that maturity is accepting the consequences of one's actions and decisions.

A.'s prose is another excellent feature of his best work. Although it can be emotionally charged, it is a prose of compelling sparseness—even of the tightness of poetry—and is often characterized by an effective blending of tone, rhythm, and figurative language. The clarity and simplicity of his prose remind one of Ernest Hemingway's (q.v.), and indeed A. has said that *A Farewell to Arms* (1929) was a fictional catalyst for him.

A.'s fiction is palpably West Indian, and it is tenaciously rooted in the physical reality of the West Indies. He examines the lives of men and women who are severely circumscribed by poverty and deprivation with candor and sympathy. His best work, moreover, shows a sensitive understanding of the West Indian personality, and this, together with his explorations of the physical and metaphysical contours of his society and his probing of the child psyche, assures him a permanent place in the history of West Indian literature.

FURTHER WORKS: *Sandra Street, and Other Stories* (1973); *Glimpses of Trinidad and Tobago* (1974); *King of the Masquerade* (1974); *Profile Trinidad: A Historical Survey from the Discovery to 1900* (1975); *Folk Tales and Fantasies* (1976); *Streets of Conflict* (1976); *The Making of Port of Spain* (1978); *Bright Road to El Dorado* (1982); *Port of Spain in a World at War 1939–1945* (1983); *First in Trinidad* (1985); *Heroes of the People of Trinidad and Tobago* (1986); *A Better and Brighter Day* (1987); *Towns and Villages of Trinidad and Tobago* (1988)

BIBLIOGRAPHY: Edwards, P., and K. Ramchand, "The Art of Memory: M. A.'s *The Year in San Fernando*," *JCL*, 7 (July 1969), 59–72; Sander, R., "The Homesickness of M. A.," *LHY*, 16, 1 (1975), 95–125; Luengo, A., "Growing Up in San Fernando: Change and Growth in M. A.'s *The Year in San Fernando*," *ArielE*, 6, 2 (1975), 81–95; Niven, A., "My Sympathies Enlarged: The Novels of M. A.," *CE&S*, 2 (1976), 45–62; Ramchand, K., *An Introduction to the Study of West Indian Literature* (1976), 143–54; Noel, D., "The Muses Inhabit Mayaro: M. A.'s *Cricket in the Road*," *IFR*, 5 (1978), 61–62; Barratt, H., "M. A. and Earl Lovelace: The Search for Selfhood," *ACLALSB*, 5, 3 (1980), 62–73; Smyer, R. I., "Enchantment and Violence in the Fiction of M. A.," *WLWE*, 21, 1 (Spring 1982), 148–59; Barratt, H., "M. A.: A Critical Assessment," *Bim*, 66–67 (1983), 157–64; Carter, S., "M. A.'s

All That Glitters: A Golden West Indian Experimental Mystery," *Journal of West Indian Literature,* 2 (1987), 41–54

HAROLD BARRATT

APPELFELD, Aharon

Israeli novelist and short-story writer, b. 16 Feb. 1932, Tschernovitz, Bukovina

A. reached Palestine in the wake of World War II in 1947, after surviving the period of the Holocaust by wandering the forests. Deprived of any primary or secondary education, he sidestepped these first stages, and studied Hebrew and Yiddish literature at the Hebrew University, Jerusalem. Hebrew has always been his sole literary language.

Although A.'s first literary foray was into poetry, he began publishing stories, of which his first collection, *Ashan* (smoke), appeared in 1962. This set the tone for his later work, as his stories are oblique reflections of the Jewish disaster in Europe. A.'s heroes and heroines have so absorbed the past that their current lives are often merely reflexes to what has gone before. They continue to exist in the shadow of a past experience that penetrated so deeply they could never shake it off or live a renewed, Israeli life.

A.'s sentences are short, the language deployed spare and only minimally rooted in Hebrew sources, although remote from the common Israeli argot. This helps to locate the text at some remove from contemporary Israel and toward the world of the deracinated Jew of central Europe. The action is usually situated in the prewar period, where the trapped individual is held in an enclosed space, speeding toward a future known by the reader, as in *Badenheim* (1980; *Badenheim 1939,* 1981). Or, it is placed in a postwar setting, as in *1946* (1980; 1946), with the intervening phase passed over. In the latter case, as in *Haor venakutonet* (1971; the skin and the coat), the protagonists are entirely locked into their past, scarcely alluding to the contemporary scene, stunted in a state of developmental paralysis. It is in such novels as *Badenheim* and *Tor haplaot* (1978; *The Age of Wonders,* 1981), where the action is dense and the narrative content forces the pace, that the author's strength is most manifest. In such stories, there is less tendency to luxuriate in repetition and poetic representation of paralysis. The old world is seen at its most confident, in its cultural and human value, and in its weakness, its self-deception and denial. As in the representation of the Holocaust in the media, the train serves as a powerful and culminating image of removal and dislocation, and both of these novellas conclude with its use. But then, too, other primary images are frozen in time and space in the record of the narrator.

Captured in A.'s prose is not the white heat of violence, the coals themselves, but rather the residue of the embers. The parallel concern is with the mental disposition among mid-European Jews that prevailed in the pre-Holocaust period. When Jews were separated from their Christian environment and compatriots, they could not understand why. Denial is uncomfortable, but where could anger and frustration be directed?

A.'s prose is oblique and the endings are open. However, an ironic dialogue is established with the reader, who, inevitably, in the light of history, knows more of the outcome than does the narrator. For all the narrative vagueness, the fiction is more or less located in time and place. When the factors are concretized as in *Badenheim* and *Tor haplaot,* the story is most effective. In such works, individual circumstance exemplifies national fate.

FURTHER WORKS: *Bagay haporeh* (1963); *Kfor al haaretz* (1965); *Beqomat haqarqa* (1968); *Adney hanahar* (1971); *Haor vehakutonet* (1971); *Keishon haayin* (1973); *Kemeah edim* (1975); *Masot beguf shlishiy* (1979); *Mikhvat haor* (1980); *Hakutonet vehapasim* (1985); *Ritspat esh* (1988); *Katerina* (1989). FURTHER VOLUMES IN ENGLISH: *Tzili: The Story of a Life* (1983); *The Retreat* (1985); *To the Land of the Cattails* (1987); *The Immortal Bartfuss* (1988); *For Every Sin* (1989)

BIBLIOGRAPHY: Yudkin, L. I., *Escape into Siege: A Survey of Israeli Literature Today* (1974), 118–23; Coffin, E. A., "A.'s Exceptional Universe; Harmony out of Chaos," *Hebrew Studies* (1983), Vol. 24, 85–98; Yudkin, L. I., *1948 and After: Aspects of Israeli Fiction* (1984), 31–32, 162–64; Nesvisky, M., "A. A.: A Profile," *Present Tense,* 12, 2 (Winter 1985), 58–60

LEON I. YUDKIN

'AQL, Sa'īd

Lebanese poet, b. 4 July 1912, Zahla

A. is known as the most successful Arab interpreter of French 19th-c. symbolist theory. Born in the Christian town of Zahla, he studied, like the famous Khalīl Mutrān (1870–1949), at its well-known Oriental School, where he became acquainted with the classics of Ahabic poetry and with 20th-c. neoclassic poets like Ahmad Shawqī (1868–1932) and Bishāra al-Khūrī (1885–1968). He was inspired by his readings of the Koran, the Bible, and Phoenician legends in his first works, but got his symbolist ideas from the works of

French symbolists like Abbé Henri Brémond (1865–1933), Paul Valéry (q.v.), and Stéphane Mallarmé (1842–1898). He wrote his most famous work, *al-Majdaliyya* (1937; the Magdalen), at the age of twenty-five. This long narrative poem is considered to be the best example in Arabic of symbolist poetry. A.'s symbolist experiment gave later poets a basis to build on. He also wrote a number of plays, and for many years he was the literary editor of the Beirut newspaper *Lisān al-Hāl.* He founded the weekly *Lubnān* and a publishing house, and has been considered as the architect of "Lebanonism."

A. started his literary career with a Bible-inspired poetic drama, *Bint Yaftāh* (1935; Jephtah's daughter). In this tragedy, with a theme chosen from the Book of Judges, he presented a mixture of romantic and classical poetry, but with a strong element of lyricism. It was followed by *al Majdaliyya,* characterized by Salmā Khadrā Jayyūsī as "one of the most charming poems in modern Arabic" and in it "A. proves himself a master of magic effects of sound and rhythm, manipulating the sounds of vowels and consonants with skill, and exploiting their latent musical power." The poem is a celebration of beauty but shows a lack of realism, and it overlooks the sexual implications of Mary Magdalene's story. This idealistic view of human love seems to be characteristic of A.'s love poetry in general. It is only a small step to the exaggerations that have been noted in A.'s work and which led some critics to call him more a romantic than a symbolist poet.

In 1944 A. published the verse drama *Qadmūs* (Qadmūs), which embodied his ideas on Lebanese nationalism. Here we find the influence of Phoenician mythology. Qadmūs, prince of Sidon, is in search of his sister Europe, who is in the power of Zeus. He has to fight a dragon before he can get his sister back. A. used the theme to defend his nationalistic ideas of Phoenicianism and to oppose Arab nationalism that prevailed at the time. *Qadmūs* is considered to be the first poetic drama in modern Arabic literature.

The poems he wrote between 1932 and 1949 were published in the volume *Rindalā* (1950; Rindalā). They are mostly love poems with little evidence of the poet's own experience with women. The beloved woman in this poetry assumes mythical dimensions, and the poet insists on a distance between him and his beloved. Not fulfillment but glorification seems to be the main objective of the poet. Here one finds again the romantic touch that is reminiscent also of old Udhrite poetry.

In 1960 there followed a collection of short poems in the same vein, written from 1932 onward, entitled *Ajmalu minki? Lā!* (more beautiful than you? no!). A. also introduced the use of

REINALDO ARENAS

ANDRÉE CHEDID

E. M. CIORAN

HÉLÈNE CIXOUS

dialect elements in his poetry and caused a shock with his volume of experimental poetry in Lebanese dialect, *Yārā* (1961; Yara), written in Latin characters.

At that time, A. had already lost his leading position in the circle of Lebanese poets, after having fought "a losing battle with the avant-garde poets of the fifties," such as Yūsuf al-Khāl and Adūnis (qq.v.). But they all owed to him to a greater or lesser extent their awareness of symbolist language. His poetry was the beginning of one of the most fertile symbolist trends as represented in the avant-garde poetry of the 1950s.

FURTHER WORKS: *Lubnān in hakā* (1960); *Ka's likhimr* (1961); *Ajrās al-yāsmīn* (1971); *Kitāb al-ward* (1972); *Qasā'id mīn daftarihā* (1973); *Kummā 'l-a'mida* (1974); *Khummāsiyyāt* (1978)

BIBLIOGRAPHY: Durtal, J., *S. 'A.: un grand poète libanais* (1970); Jayyusi, S. K., *Trends and Movements in Modern Arabic Poetry* (1977), Vol. 2, 475–509; Nasr, N. S., *S. A. Faylasufan* (1980); Jayyusi, S. K., ed., *Modern Arabic Poetry: An Anthology* (1987), 57–60

ED C. M. DE MOOR

AQUIN, Hubert

Canadian novelist and journalist (writing in French), b. 24 Oct. 1929, Montreal; d. 15 Mar. 1977, Montreal

A. received the traditional "classical" education at the Jean-Jacques-Olier, Sainte-Croix, and Sainte-Marie schools, following which he attended the University of Montreal where he received his M.A. in philosophy (1951). He completed his studies with a three-year stint at the Institute for Political Studies in Paris. Upon his return to Canada, he obtained employment at government institutions, first at Radio Canada as a writer, from 1954 to 1960, and then, until 1963, at the National Office for Film (Office national du film), where he was involved in the production of various films. From 1961 to 1971 he was director of the magazine *Liberté*.

Politically involved in the revolutionary changes taking place in the Province of Quebec, in the RIN (Rassemblement pour l'Indépendance Nationale), he was imprisoned for terrorist activity, and specifically for carrying weapons. It was during this incarceration that he wrote his first novel, *Prochain épisode* (1965; *Prochain épisode*, 1967). This was followed by others: *Trou de mémoire* (1968; *Blackout*, 1974), *L'antiphonaire* (1969; *The Antiphonary*, 1973), and *Neige noire* (1974; *Ham-*

let's Twin, 1974). During these same years, he taught at the University of Quebec at Montreal, SUNY Buffalo, and Carleton University.

The noninitiated reader finds A.'s books difficult to access: The Quebec political scene and A.'s passionate involvement in it are important dimensions in his works; his exposure to and the influence by contemporary writers such as the French New Novelists have a direct bearing on his writing style, with its nontraditional approach to chronology and its unwillingness to adhere to stock techniques of characterization.

Prochain épisode exploded onto the literary scene in 1965, thoroughly disliked by a number of readers because of its mystifying style, but also greatly admired by many others who had the patience, training, and commitment necessary for understanding a work that does not make comprehension easy for the reader. On the one hand, it is the story of the author-narrator, imprisoned for political activity, telling his tale, who he is, what he has done; on the other hand, it is a detective story unfolding in Switzerland with flashbacks to Quebec in which the hero, madly in love with K.—a mystery woman with ties to his past in Quebec, and involved in his endeavor—pursues an enemy of his political group. But this enemy, who becomes one or two more characters, and who is all-knowing, and has wealth and impeccable tastes, eludes the author. Intermingled are thus a passionate love story, taking place mainly in the past, in a Quebec lovingly evoked along with political commitments and attachments to it; a quest in Switzerland by the author for the enemy, who turns out to be his double; and the subsequent betrayal, capture, and imprisonment, which provide the author-narrator the time and place to recreate who he is, what he has done, and what will take place in the next episode.

Trou de mémoire continues the disrupted-disruptive process characteristic of the first novel by presenting a "story" told by different narrators who are free to add to the basic tale, change it, and explain or elaborate events that were presented only superficially. Here, too, in addition to A.'s reflections and preoccupations with the act of writing, we find involvement with politics and the revolution, love and violence (with rape evoking the British domination of Quebec), and intoxication and clear-headedness. The reader is kept in suspense, waiting for the pieces to fall into place.

These preoccupations are explored further in *L'antiphonaire*, a fragmented, disconnected story, part of it taking place in the 16th c., the other in the 20th, each replying to the other, as would the texts in an antiphonary, presenting oppositions and unions of the sexes, with accompanying violence and retribution in the form of rapes and murders and suicide (the latter also found in *Trou de mémoire*).

Neige noire transposes these interests to the film, evoking the pure lands of the north (northern Norway), where the filmmaker Nicolas plans to immolate his wife Sylvia, who will be segmented cinematographically, intermingling the female figure regenerated into other female figures who become a couple. The themes of death and rebirth, which form the basis of the work, present a new type of society and world order.

It is not so much for his stories that A. is interesting, but rather for his narrative techniques and his philosophical preoccupations, and for his grappling with the issues of politics, writing, activism, and life versus death. His political position led him to quarrel with many, among them René Lévesque. He refused to accept the Governor-General's Award in 1969. He received an award from the Province of Quebec (1970), as well as the David Prize (1972), the Press Prize (1974), and the Great Literary Prize of the city of Montreal (1975). His suicide in 1977 was a tragic event for the literature of Quebec and North America.

FURTHER WORKS: *Point de fuite (essai)* (1971); *Blocs erratiques* (1977)

BIBLIOGRAPHY: Smart, P., *H. A., Agent double* (1973); Martel, J., "Bibliographie analytique d'H. A. 1947–1982," *RHLQCF,* 7 (Winter–Spring 1984), 79–229; Martel, J., "Mise à jour (1983–1984) de la bibliographie analytique d'H. A.," *RHLQCF,* 10 (Summer–Autumn 1985), 75–112; Mocquais, P.-Y., *H. A. ou La quête interrompue* (1985); Sheppard, G., and A. Yanacopoulo, *Signé H. A.: Enquête sur le suicide d'un écrivain* (1985); Lemire, M., et al., *Dictionnaire des œuvres littéraires du Québec* (1982), Vol. 3, passim; (1984), Vol. 4, passim; (1987), Vol. 5, passim; New, W. H., *A History of Canadian Literature* (1989), 284–86

PAUL BARRETTE

ARENAS, Reinaldo

Cuban novelist and short-story writer, b. 16 July 1943, Perronales; d. 7 Dec. 1990, New York, N.Y., U.S.A.

Before his premature death, A. was one of the most talented Cuban and Latin American writers in recent memory. Although he is known mainly as a novelist and a short-story writer, he also wrote plays, poetry, and essays. Born and raised in Perronales, a town near Holguín in the former province of Oriente (now Holguín), A. was an only child raised by his mother, aunts, and grandparents. As a teenager A. participated in the rebel uprising against Batista. After the triumph of the Cuban revolution of 1959, he studied agricultural accounting and worked on a poultry farm. In 1962 A. traveled to Havana where he abandoned his line of work; he became a researcher at the José Martí National Library, from 1963 to 1968, and wrote fiction. A. belongs to the second generation of writers of the Cuban revolution. Initially, he identified with the new government, but later, because of his writings and life-style, A. fell from grace and was arrested in 1973 and 1974, and sent to a rehabilitation camp until 1976. During the Mariel boatlift of 1980, A. fled the island and lived in New York; he contracted AIDS and subsequently committed suicide in his Manhattan apartment in 1990.

A.'s literature can be characterized by its attempt to free itself from the confines of any restriction, be it literary, historical, political, social, or sexual. His *Celestino antes del alba* (1967; Celestino before the dawn), a novel that invents its own reality, won a mention in the 1965 National Contest sponsored by the UNEAC (National Union of Cuban Writers and Artists). This was A.'s first and only novel published in Cuba. The others were either smuggled out of the country or written in exile.

With A.'s second novel, *El mundo alucinante* (1969; *Hallucinations, 1971*), he received international acclaim; although the novel had been awarded an honorable mention by the UNEAC in 1966, it was not published in Cuba. Instead, it was published in France in 1968 where it obtained *Le Monde*'s First Prize for the best foreign novel of the year. *El mundo alucinante* is based on the life of friar Servando Teresa de Mier (1765–1827) and highlights his travels and persecutions for expressing his own ideas. The novel follows in theme and structure the friar's memoirs and recalls A.'s own life. It is written in the first, second, and third persons and suggests a continuous rewriting of events from different perspectives, but also a complete view of the events narrated.

In 1972 an unauthorized collection of stories, *Con los ojos cerrados* (with closed eyes), appeared in Uruguay. It was written after A. completed his first two novels; like them, it received an honorable mention by the UNEAC. *Con los ojos cerrados* contains two stories worth noting. "Comienza el desfile" (the parade begins) opens the volume and narrates the enthusiastic reception given to Castro's rebels as they entered the protagonist's home town; and "La vieja Rosa" (repub. 1980; *Old Rosa*, 1989) is a powerful novelette about an unyielding landowner in the revolution. After his exile, A. rewrote *Celestino antes del alba* and *Con los ojos cerrados;* the first was retitled *Cantando en el pozo* (1982; *Singing from the Well,* 1987) and the other *Termina el desfile* (1981; end of the parade). The story that gives title to the collection symbolically is placed at the end. It was written in exile and is a dramatic account of the takeover of the Peruvian Embassy, which preceded the Mariel boatlift. This story closes a chapter in the writer's life.

El palacio de las blanquísimas mofetas (1980; *Palace of the White Skunks,* 1990) was written in 1972 and was smuggled out of Cuba in 1973, appearing first in French in 1975. It narrates the economic, political, cultural, and psychological traumas of a family in the Cuban countryside. In 1976 A. began to rewrite *Otra vez el mar* (1982; *Farewell to the Sea,* 1986), which he wrote in 1969 and completed in New York. The original manuscript entrusted to a friend disappeared; the second version was confiscated by the authorities. The third version, smuggled out of Cuba, takes place after a six-day vacation and provides two viewpoints, that of Hector and of his wife, but in reality they are part of the protagonist's imagination. Both of these novels are a continuation of *Celestino antes del alba.*

After arriving in the U.S., A. founded Mariel in 1983, a periodical and publishing house, to give publicity to intellectuals who opposed the Castro government. In addition, he published four more novels. The first is *Arturo, la estrella más brillante* (1984; Arturo, the brightest star) which documents the life of a homosexual in a government rehabilitation camp in the late 1960s. In the end, his lover/executioner is transformed into his mother. The second one is *La loma del Angel* (1987; *Graveyard of the Angels,* 1987) and follows the pattern of the 19th-c. Cuban antislavery narrative as it rewrites Cirilo Villaverde's (1812–1894) *Cecilia Valdés* (1882; Cecilia Valdés), Cuba's national novel. A. describes the past from a contemporary perspective to suggest the continuity between slavery in the 19th c. and its manifestation under the present government. The two other works of fiction are *El portero* (1989; *The Doorman,* 1991), which takes place in New York and describes the protagonist's life in the city, and *Viaje a La Habana* (1990; journey to Havana), which gathers three novelettes about a Cuban exile who returns to the island.

A. was a versatile writer. His works include *El central* (1981; *El Central,* 1984), a long poem conceived while he was forced to work on a sugarcane plantation, *Persecución* (1985; persecution), an experimental play, and *Necesidad de libertad* (1986; need for liberty), a collection of essays. All of these works denounce the political, moral, social, and sexual oppressions of Cuban society by the Castro government. At the time of his death, A. left five unpublished manuscripts: the novels "El asalto" (the attack) and "El color del verano" (the color of summer), a collection of short stories, "Adios a mamá" (goodbye, mother), an autobiography, "Antes que a nochezza" (before the knight falls), and a collection of documents, "Un plebiscito de Fidel Castro" (plebiscite for Fidel Castro).

A. was a gifted writer with an extraordinary imagination. He was one of the few internationally renowned writers whose work is hardly known in his own country. But given the nature of his work and his stature in the world community, A.'s reputation will outlast the present administration and he will receive his overdue recognition in Cuba.

FURTHER WORKS: *Voluntad de vivir manifestándose* (1989); *Leprosorio* (1990); *Meditaciones de Saint-Nazaire* (1990)

BIBLIOGRAPHY: Borinsky, A., "Re-escribir y escribir: A., Menard, Borges, Cervantes, Fray Servando," *RI,* 41, 92–93 (July–Dec. 1975), 605–16; Rodríguez Monegal, E., "The Labyrinthine World of R. A.," *LALR,* 8, 16 (1980), 126–31; Santí, E. M., "Entrevista con R. A.," *Vuelta,* 4, 47 (1980), 18–25; Méndez Rodena, A., *"El palacio de las blanquísimas mofestas:* Narración historiográfica o narración imaginaria?," *Revista de la Universidad de México,* 27 (1983), 14–21; Barreda, P., "Vestirse al desnudo, borrando escribirse: *El central* de R. A.," *Boletín de la Academia Puertorriqueña de la Lengua Española,* 12 (1984), 25–37; Olivares, J., "Carnival and the Novel: R. A.'s *El palacio de las blanquísimas mofetas,*" *HR,* 53, 4 (Autumn 1985), 467–76; Volek, E., "La carnavalización y la alegoría en *El mundo alucinante* de R. A.," *RI,* 51, 130–31 (Jan.–June 1985), 125–48; Rozencvaig, P., *R. A.: narrativa de la trangresión* (1986); Bejar, E. C., *La textualidad de R. A.* (1987); Bush, A., "The Riddled Text: Borges and A.," *MLN,* 103, 2 (Mar. 1988), 374–97; Luis, W., "Present and Future Antislavery Narratives and R. A.'s *Graveyard of the Angels,*" *Literary Bondage: Slavery in Cuban Narrative* (1990), 238–47; Soto, F., *"Celestino antes del alba:* escritura subversiva/sexualidad," *RI,* 57, 154 (Jan.–Mar. 1991), 345–54; Valero, R., *Otra vez el mar* de R. A.," *RI,* 57, 154 (Jan.–Mar. 1991), 355–63; Solotorevsky, M., "El relato literario como configurador de un

referente histórico: *Termina el desfile* de R. A.,''
RI, 57, 154 (Jan.–Mar. 1991), 365–69

WILLIAM LUIS

ARGENTINE LITERATURE

See Volume 1, page 110.

Fiction

Since the 1960s, Argentina has been governed mostly by military régimes, the principal exception being the period since 1983 when democracy was restored. Thus, much of the nation's recent literature reflects the conditions of life under heavy-handed dictators. During the past decade, however, the deteriorating economic situation has begun to occupy center stage, and, with the granting of freedom of the press, subjects previously considered taboo have been treated with increasing audacity.

Although they published their major works before 1980, the three most influential writers of fiction during the above-mentioned period are Jorge Luis Borges, Ernesto Sábato, and Julio Cortázar (qq.v.). Borges, who died in 1986, is famous for his impeccably stylized, metaphysical short stories based on philosophical themes; the novels of Sábato, who holds a Ph.D. in physics, reflect his turn to the humanities for solutions to present-day problems and his search for the elusive Argentine identity. Cortázar's death in 1984 ended his career as the author of novels and fantastic tales that still fascinate a wide reading public.

José Bianco (1908–1986) and Adolfo Bioy Casares (q.v.) are two of the leading representatives of the older generation. Both belong to an elite group of intellectuals that wrote for *Sur,* the prestigious literary journal that downplayed realism and advocated more sophisticated forms of writing. Bianco and Bioy Casares eschew politics, preferring to engage their readers in flights of fantasy, psychological speculations, and aesthetic reflections. Examples of their works are Bianco's *La pérdida del reino* (1972; the loss of the kingdom) and Bioy Casares's *La aventura de un fotógrafo en La Plata* (1985; the adventure of a photographer in La Plata), in which a photographer's grappling with his art parallels the author's creative process.

Of the novelists born during the 1920s and 1930s, Manuel Puig (q.v.) is considered the most original. Puig writes in colloquial Argentine Spanish to depict the stultifying aspects of small-town life as well as the oppression and sexism in the national culture. He also reveals a fascination with the movies, which he views as an escape for the average citizen trapped in a meaningless day-to-day existence. He is an innovator in his use of postmodernist techniques. His novels of the 1980s include *Sangre de amor correspondido* (1982; *Blood of Requited Love,* 1984), a sordid evocation of adolescent love with brutal insights into the human psyche, and *Cae la noche tropical* (1989; *Tropical Night Falling,* 1991), which depicts lonely Argentines living in exile.

Other important authors of Puig's generation are Humberto Costantini, David Viñas (qq.v.), Tomás Eloy Martínez (b. 1934), Abel Posse (b. 1934), and Enrique Medina (b. 1937). Costantini's most successful novel is *De dioses, hombrecitos y policías* (1979; *The Gods, the Little Guys, and the Police,* 1984), a bitter allegory of the torture and disappearance of liberals under a ruthless military régime. An implacable Marxist critic of Argentine society, Viñas is best known for his attack on the military establishment in *Los hombres de a caballo* (1967; men on horseback). Eloy Martínez is the author of Argentina's finest nonfiction novel, *La novela de Perón* (1985; *The Perón Novel,* 1988), an engrossing account of the famed president's life, climaxing with his return from Spain in 1973. *Los perros del paraíso* (1983; *The Dogs of Paradise,* 1989), by Posse, recounts the Spanish conquest of the New World with leaps into the present and comic resonances of Gabriel García Márquez's (q.v.) *Cien años de soledad* (1967; *One Hundred Years of Solitude,* 1970). One of Argentina's best-selling novelists, Medina has been criticized for his lurid, brutal sensationalism, but he is a gifted narrator whose frankness has softened attitudes toward many forbidden topics. His *Perros de la noche* (1977; night dogs), about the depraved behavior of an abandoned brother and sister, typifies his condemnatory portraits of his homeland.

Argentina has produced more exceptionally talented women novelists than any other Spanish American country. A few of the long list of names are Sylvina Bullrich (b. 1915), Beatriz Guido, Marta Lynch, Luisa Valenzuela (qq.v.), and Marta Traba (1930–1983). An outspoken feminist, Bullrich writes in a realistic mode about political corruption, the suffering of the impoverished, and, in her satirical novel *La bicicleta* (1986; the bicycle), about the decline of Argentina's standing among nations. Guido also indicts Argentine society in her realistic novels such as *El incendio de las vísperas* (1964; the fire of vespers), a tale of the oligarchy's moral decay under Perón. A militant leftist and feminist, Lynch has left a legacy of intricately designed novels and stories, a fine example of which is *Los años de fuego* (1980; the years of fire). Critics also see Valenzuela as a feminist, but her nonrealistic approach to literature evokes Borges and Cortázar. Her *Cambio de armas* (1982; *Other Weapons,* 1985) is a grouping of sophisticated tales delineating male-female relationships. A prolific political and social critic, Marta Traba is best known for her *Conversación al sur* (1981; *Mothers and Shadows,* 1986), about the complex relationship between two leftist women brutalized by a tyrannical regime.

The younger generation of talented fiction writers (those born after 1940) includes, among others, Mario Szichman (q.v.), Ricardo Piglia (b. 1941), Osvaldo Soriano (b. 1943), Cecilia Absatz (b. 1943), Jorge Asís (b. 1946), Mempo Giardinelli (b. 1947), and Reina Roffé (b. 1951).

Poetry

Borges inevitably first comes to mind when the subject of 20th-c. Argentine poetry is broached. Although he is considered an intellectual interested in literature and philosophy, Borges also poeticizes Buenos Aires and Argentina's colorful past. But his fascination with philosophical systems and aesthetics does indeed find expression in much of his poetry. Having become completely blind in the mid-1950s, he began to show a preference for classical meters because they were easier for him to memorize than blank verse. One detects in his subsequent poems a more intimate tone, underscoring his philosophical meditations on time, death, and solitude. In *La cifra* (1982; the figure), one of his last collections, he still longs for the ultimate poetic revelation.

Three other widely known poets are Alberto Girri (q.v.), Olga Orozco (b. 1920), and Alejandra Pizarnik (1936–1972). Girri's work resembles Borges's in its philosophical content, but he is more obscure than his renowned colleague. He is also more pessimistic, viewing the world as a labyrinth of fear and hatred, and Western culture as degenerate and evil. His poems in *El ojo* (1964; the eye) and *Envíos* (1966; dispatches) underscore his sombre world vision.

Orozco first became known as a member of the 1940 Generation, but during the 1960s she elicited greater interest. Difficult to comprehend, her work remains outside the range of many readers. She has obviously been influenced by symbolism and surrealism (qq.v.) and seems obsessed with a desire to return to a vaguely described unity—perhaps her childhood—that existed before the Fall. She also obsessively searches for God, attempting to transcend the limitations imposed by him on humanity. *La oscuridad es otro sol* (1967; darkness is another sun) unfolds permutations of a single persona, that of the poet, and *Cantos de Berenice* (1977; songs to Berenice), tells of an enchantress reaching out to her alter ego in the realm of the dead.

Often compared to Sylvia Plath (q.v.), Pizarnik apparently committed suicide. The three major themes of her work are death, love, and poetry—death representing infinite peace, love inevitably turning into disenchantment, and poetry becoming an escape from loneliness. Pizarnik uses avantgarde techniques such as disjointed expression, illogical connections, and hermetic allusions, imbuing her poems with an oneiric quality. Her last collection, *El infierno musical* (1971; the musical hell), represents a desperate quest for self-identity and poetic perfection.

Argentine poetry of the 1960s is characterized by realistic, everyday language and an optimistic but revolutionary tone. Typical in this decade of worldwide turmoil are the works of Juan Gelman (b. 1930) and Noé Jitrik (b. 1928). Gelman denounces dictatorship and the bourgeois establishment in *Cólera buey* (1963; oxlike anger) and *Poemas* (1968; poems); Jitrik vents his fury against injustice in *Addio a la mama* (1965; farewell to mama).

Since the 1970s, because of adverse political and economic conditions, poets have fluctuated between frustration and resignation, but at the same time many have withdrawn to the subjective realm as a means of escape from reality. Thus surrealism is still alive, as indicated by the lasting influence of older poets such as Orozco, Juan L. Ortiz (1896–1978), Enrique Molina (b. 1910), César Fernández Moreno (b. 1919), Roberto Juarroz (b. 1925), and Raúl Gustavo Aguirre (b. 1927), the latter perhaps the nation's leading surrealist.

The Essay

Argentina has produced many fine essayists, two of whom, Ezequiel Martínez Estrada (1895–1964) and Eduardo Mallea (1903–1982), have brilliantly analyzed the Argentine character. Although Peter G. Earle laments the decline of the essay, there are signs that the genre is being revived.

The novelist Sábato not only condemns authoritarianism and the excessive mechanization in today's world but also, like Martínez Estrada and Mallea, analyzes the Argentine character, focusing on its national and European traits. Many of his essays have been collected in *La robotización del hombre y otras páginas de ficción y reflexión* (1981; the robotization of humans and other pages of fiction and reflection). Early in his career Borges wrote elegantly stylized essays on literary and philosophical topics and occasionally fused essay and fiction into his unique mode of expression. In a somewhat similar manner, Cortázar combined the essay and personal whims as, for example, in *Territorios* (1978; territories), a series of amusing pieces on painting. In *Último round* (1969; last round) Cortázar predicts the eventual utopian fulfillment of the goals of Marxist economics and aesthetics.

In *Indios, ejércitos y fronteras* (1983; Indians, armies, and frontiers) Viñas condemns the slaughter of Indians during the 19th c. and also criticizes Domingo Faustino Sarmiento (1811–1888), the well-known politician who encouraged European immigration at the expense of the "uncivilized tribes" of the pampa. The injustice of the military regime of the 1970s is exposed in graphic detail in *Preso sin nombre, celda sin número* (1981; *Prisoner without a Name, Cell without a Number,* 1981), by Jacobo Timerman (b. 1923), a Jewish journalist imprisoned for thirty months.

Two prominent women essayists are Victoria Ocampo (1890–1979) and Marta Traba, the above-mentioned novelist. Founder of *Sur,* which she directed from 1931 until its demise in the early 1970s, Ocampo published ten volumes of essays entitled *Testimonios* (1935–1977; testimonies), dealing principally with Argentine and foreign literatures. Traba wrote extensively on painting, literature, and politics; the breadth of her knowledge is demonstrated in her *Siglo XX en las artes plásticas latinoamericanas: Un guía* (1982–1983; 20th c. in Latin American plastic arts: a guide).

Argentina's finest literary critics include Enrique Anderson Imbert (b. 1910) and the poet Jitrik. A fiction writer and longtime professor in the U.S., Anderson Imbert is the author of *Crítica interna* (1961; internal criticism) and many other texts. Jitrik has published several volumes on critical theory including *La vibración del presente: Trabajos críticos sobre textos y escritores latinoamericanos* (1987; the vibration of the present: critical studies of Latin American texts and writers).

Under the repressive military régime from 1976 until 1983, a program known as *El Proceso* (Process of National Restoration) was implemented to effect a return to the nation's traditional roots, with its commitment to the Catholic church and the patriarchal family. This program also suppressed liberal elements such as Peronists, Zionists, organized labor, and middle-class intellectuals. In *La cultura nacional: Examen crítico* (1987; the national culture: critical examination) essayist Eduardo S. Calamaro (b. 1940) rejects *El Proceso* and proclaims the need to reestablish pluralism to encourage the nation's dynamic cultural growth. Calamaro's study is an example of the diversity of ideas being fostered by the newly created democracy.

Drama

Under the military dictatorship, dramatists were threatened with censorship or worse if they were too bold in their criticism of the authorities. In 1981, faced with a decline in the number of plays produced and the diminishing audiences, an association of dramatists, directors, and actors formed the *Teatro Abierto* (Open Theater), an experiment by which the three groups collaborated in the writing and producing of plays, their purposes being to revitalize the theater and achieve greater freedom of expression. Critics agree that the experiment has been at least moderately successful.

Argentine theater of the past two decades fluctuates between traditional realism and vanguardism. The principal practitioners of realism are Carlos Gorostiza (b. 1920), Roberto Cossa (b. 1934), and Ricardo Talesnik (b. 1935). Gorostiza develops the themes of human responsibility and the choices people are forced to make under stress; in *Los prójimos* (1967; *Neighbors,* 1970) witnesses to a woman's murder refuse to become involved in the judicial process. Cossa and Talesnik collaborated in *El avión* (1970; the airplane), an excellent example of political drama. An acerbic satire as well, it sketches the reactions on different social levels to the imminent arrival of an airplane carrying the long-awaited general (Juan Perón), who did indeed return from exile three years later. The play's dramatic tension derives from the clash between the fanatical Peronists' ebullient mood of anticipation and the mounting apprehension on the part of the upper-middle-class citizens, who detest the populist leader.

The most important representatives of Argentina's vanguardist theater are Griselda Gambaro, Osvaldo Dragún (qq.v.), Eduardo Pavlovsky (b. 1933), and Ricardo Monti (b. 1945). Gambaro is linked to the existentialist Theater of the Absurd (q.v.), but she is also a practitioner of the theater of cruelty. Her most successful plays include *El campo* (1965; *The Camp,* 1971), in which a Nazi concentration camp becomes a metaphor for Argentina, and *Las paredes* (1964; the walls), dramatizing the interrogation of a youth by government henchmen. The most important single influence on Dragún is Bertolt Brecht (q.v.), whose techniques serve to denounce social injustice and assail hypocrisy. Although it was written early in his career, the most celebrated of his works is still a trilogy of one-act tragicomedies entitled *Historias para ser contadas* (1957; stories to be told). Pavlovsky, educated as a psychiatrist, is Argentina's leading creator of psychodrama. He, like Gambaro, has been influenced by the Theater of the Absurd, but he is best known for his theater of cruelty. His most widely presented work is *El señor Galíndez* (1976; Mr. Galíndez), a shocking exposé of torture and mutilation systematically practiced by the Argentine authorities. Monti has been lauded as one of Argentina's most innovative and serious voices in the contemporary theater. His works display a mélange of surrealism and the grotesque, which he utilizes to explore both national and universal concerns. His most overtly political work is *Historia tendenciosa de la clase media argentina* (1971; tendentious history of the Argentine middle class), whose central character is the Old Whore, a symbol of the nation.

Despite its numerous political and economic crises over the past half century, Argentina, a country of only thirty-two million citizens, has created an impressive volume of literary works. Mario Vargas Llosa (q.v.) believes that if writers were satisfied with the status quo, there would be no need for literature. Argentine writers have had many reasons to express their dissatisfaction, which they have done with artistry and increasing openness. With the recent reestablishment of democracy, one can expect the large quantity and high quality of Argentine letters to continue unabated.

BIBLIOGRAPHY: Foster, D. W., *Currents in the Contemporary Argentine Novel* (1975); Zubatsky, D. S., "Annotated Bibliography of Latin American Author Bibliographies: Argentina & Uruguay," *Chasqui*, 8, 2 (Feb. 1979), 47–95; Foster, D. W., "The Demythification of Buenos Aires in Selected Argentine Novels of the Seventies," *Chasqui*, 10, 1 (Nov. 1980), 3–25; Borello, R. A., et al., *El ensayo argentino, 1930–1970* (1981); Zayas de Lima, P., *Diccionario de autores teatrales argentinos, 1950–1980* (1981); Himelblau, J., "The Argentine Avant-Garde Theater," *Symposium*, 39, 2 (Summer 1985), 104–12; Foster, D. W., "Narrativa testimonial argentina durante los años del 'Proceso,' " in Jara, R., and H. Vidal, eds., *Testimonio y literatura* (1986), 138–54; Running, T., "El lenguaje como tema en la poesía argentina actual," *Letras*, 15–16 (Apr.–Aug. 1986), 150–66; Balderston, D., et al., eds., *Ficción y política: La narrativa argentina durante el proceso militar* (1987); McMurray, G. R., *Spanish American Writing since 1941: A Critical Survey* (1987), 14–18, 23–27, 39–42, 52–58, 132–39, 191–95, 224–31, 310–18; Rizk, B. J., *El nuevo teatro latinoamericano: Una lectura histórica* (1987); Robino, A., "La poesía argentina de hoy," *Río de la Plata: Culturas*, 7 (1988), 121–32; Sosnowski, S., ed., *Represión y reconstrucción de una cultura: El caso argentino* (1988); Kohut, K., and A. Pagni, eds., *Literatura argentina hoy: De la dictadura a la democracia* (1989); Lértora Mendoza, C. A., "Panorama del pensamiento argentino actual," *Ensayistas*, 26–27

(1989), 117–60; Rojo, G., *Crítica del exilio: Ensayos sobre literatura latinoamericana actual* (1989); Guerra Cunningham, L., ed., *Splintering Darkness: Latin American Women Writers in Search of Themselves* (1990).

GEORGE R. MCMURRAY

ARGUETA, Manlio

Salvadoran novelist and poet, b. 24 Nov. 1935, San Miguel

A. is considered El Salvador's most important living novelist and one of Central America's most prominent men of letters. In 1956, while studying at the National University in San Salvador, he joined a circle of young writers, the so-called Generation of 1956, who opposed the military dictatorship ruling the country at that time. A. began his career as a poet, but he is much better known for his four novels, three of which have won literary prizes. Forced into exile in 1972, he lives in Costa Rica, where he founded and still directs the Salvadoran-Costa Rican Institute of Culture.

The settings of A.'s first novel, *El valle de las hamacas* (1970; the valley of the hammocks), are El Salvador and Nicaragua during the régime of the Salvadoran dictator José María Lemus (1956–1960). The political and social conflicts in both nations are dramatized through the lives of two lovers, Rosaura and Raúl, who become separated when Raúl leaves El Salvador for Nicaragua to command a group of Sandinistas. To explain the historical background of the strife, A. inserts into the text a lengthy chronicle of Pedro de Alvarado's conquest of Central America more than four centuries ago. A. also utilizes innovative techniques such as interior monologues, temporal and spatial dislocations, and shifting points of view to intensify individual sentiments and broaden the narrative focus.

Caperucita en la zona roja (1977; Red Riding-hood in the red zone) resembles A.'s first novel in several respects. The protagonists are, once again, two lovers (in this case Alfonso and Hormiga) who suffer long separations for political reasons; both novels juxtapose episodes set in different time frames and narrated from different points of view; and both depict clashes between government troops and protesters. The temporal dimensions of *Caperucita en la zona roja*, however, are restricted to the mid-1970s, and the relationship between the two lovers receives closer scrutiny, especially when Hormiga becomes involved in the "red zone" of forbidden political activities.

Un día en la vida (1980; *One Day of Life,* 1983), A.'s most highly acclaimed novel to date, is written in a more direct, coherent style, its principal narrator being a middle-aged peasant woman, Lupe Fuentes, whose growing awareness of social injustice provides the major theme as well as the unifying plot thread. The foreground action lasts only twelve hours, but in this short time frame Lupe's monologues evoke her childhood, her marriage to José at the age of fifteen, and, most important, the recent changes in their lives. Although the year of the foreground action is never revealed, it is probably in the late 1970s. The novel was published in 1980, the year El Salvador's civil war began and also the year of the assassination of Archbishop Salvador Oscar Arnulfo Romero, who is depicted as a harsh critic of the government. Furthermore, the chain of events underscores the tense environment that must have existed just prior to the wholesale violence.

Perhaps the strongest feature of the novel is its capacity to rivet the reader's attention on the tragic lives of its characters. Although illiterate, Lupe is obviously an intelligent woman whose devotion to her family and dedication to her religion reinforce her resolve to survive the violence swirling around her. The evolving role of the Catholic church also generates much of the action, reflecting the liberation theology that had spread throughout Latin America. And still another voice is that of an unidentified soldier whose fanatical hatred of "communists" results from his training by "gringo" army officers. Sprinkled with biblical symbols (Lupe's husband José ultimately emerges as a Christ figure), *Un día en la vida* is a fine example of the artistically conceived social-protest novel.

A.'s most recent work of fiction, *Cuzcatlán donde bate la Mar del Sur* (1986; *Cuzcatlán Where the Southern Sea Beats,* 1987), portrays several generations of a peasant family who, like the previous protagonists, suffer the atrocities of right-wing régimes determined to suppress all traces of opposition. But this novel is more complex, consisting of narrative fragments that compel the reader to realign events and uncover cause-and-effect relationships. Other passages allude to precolonial Cuzcatlán (the pre-Columbian name for El Salvador) and elements of Mayan mythology, which serve to elucidate the present-day situation.

In its entirety A.'s oeuvre offers a moving tribute to his compatriots' struggle for justice. His artistic treatment of the tragic political and social realities of El Salvador has attracted readers from many parts of the world.

FURTHER WORKS: *De aquí en adelante* (1967); *Poemas* (1967); *En el costado de la luz* (1968); *Las bellas armas reales* (1979)

BIBLIOGRAPHY: McMurray, G. R., "The Novels of El Salvador's M. A.," *Proceedings of the Rocky Mountain Council on Latin American Studies* (1984), 192–97; Martínez, Z. N., "M. A.," *Hispam*, 14, 42 (Dec. 1985), 41–54; Rodríguez Hernández, R., "La nueva novela histórica hispanoamericana: *La insurrección* y *Un día en la vida*," *TCrit*, 13, 36–37 (1987), 153–63; Santos, R., ed., *And We Sold the Rain: Contemporary Fiction from Central America* (1988), 201–2; Martin, G., *Journeys through the Labyrinth: Latin American Fiction in the Twentieth Century* (1989), 331; Beverley, J., and M. Zimmerman, *Literature and Politics in the Central American Revolutions* (1990), 192–94

GEORGE R. MCMURRAY

ARIYOSHI Sawako

Japanese dramatist, short-story writer, novelist, and essayist; b. 21 Jan. 1931, Wakayama City; d. 30 Aug. 1984, Tokyo

When A. was born, in Wakayama City, her father was employed by the New York branch of the Yokohama Species Bank. Her mother came from the distinguished Kimoto family in Wakayama. Besides A., the couple had two sons. When A. was four years old, her family moved to Java (Jakarta, Indonesia); they lived a privileged life for the next few years, with natives serving as maids and houseboys. A precocious child, A. read avidly the works of Natsume Sōseki (q.v.) and Arishima Takeo (1878–1923).

Because of the tense international situation, the family soon returned to Tokyo. In fact, A. moved many times in the course of her childhood. Because she was extremely sensitive, her exposure to life abroad gave her an opportunity to see with new eyes Japan's rich cultural tradition, as well as Japanese society closed to outsiders. Her novel *Kinokawa* (1959; *The River Ki,* 1980) vividly describes details from the lives of her maternal grandmother, her mother, and the author herself as a child and a young adult.

During the bleak postwar years, her father, sensing her utter disenchantment with Japan, introduced A. to the Kabuki theater. This was the beginning of A.'s lifelong interest in the Japanese theater tradition. As the years went by, she became thoroughly familiar with Nō, Kabuki, and Bunraku plays. In later years she studied the modern theater of the West and grew to appreciate greatly the classical ballet and Western opera. Yet, she also appreciated the painting and decorative arts of Japan, enhanced by formal lessons in the Yabunouchi school of tea ceremony, and she amassed a fine collection of art and tea utensils.

Soon after graduating from Tokyo Women's College in 1952, A. joined the editorial staff of a publishing company. It was during this phase in her career that she contributed to a literary coterie magazine, *Hakuchigun*. Between 1954 and 1956, she was employed by the Azuma Kabuki Association, performing secretarial duties and assisting in stage productions. A. began to be published in the 1950s. Active as both a dramatist and a writer of short stories, novels, and essays, A. would be classed together with such writers as Sono Ayako (b. 1931), Kurahashi Yumiko (b. 1935), Ōba Minako (q.v.), and Kōno Taeko (b. 1926) for her intellect and literary talent.

A dance drama that A. wrote, based on a Nō play, was performed at the Shimbashi Embujō Theater in 1956. At this early stage in her career, it was already clear that A.'s two loves were literature and the theater. In subsequent years A., besides writing original plays or adaptations of other works, saw her novels and short stories adapted for the stage, the cinema, and television. Even after her death, her works continued to inspire stage productions and television films. Her novel *Hishoku* (1964; not because of color) is scheduled to be made into an American film; the screenplay is being written by Veline Hasu Houston (dates n.a.), an Amerasian poet and dramatist.

In November 1959 A. received a Rockefeller grant to study at Sarah Lawrence College in New York during the winter and spring terms. During her stay there, she studied the playwright Christopher Fry. In August 1960 she made her way to Europe and returned to Japan via the Middle East after spending nearly a year abroad. Her novels *Hishoku* and *Pueruto riko nikki* (1964; Puerto Rico diary) were written as a result of having lived on the American East Coast for a time.

In June 1961 A. was invited to Mainland China along with other Japanese writers. This was the first of her many trips to this country. Years later, in the summer of 1978, she was given an opportunity to view firsthand what life was like in a commune. At the same time she lectured on environmental pollution, a social problem in which she was deeply interested. A book about her impressions of China, *Ariyoshi Sawako no Chūgoku repōto* (the China report of A. S.), was published in 1979.

In March 1962 A. married Jin Akira, the director of the Art Friend Association. A daughter, Tamao, was born to the couple in 1963, but the next year A. and Jin Akira were divorced. Throughout this crisis in her private life, A. continued to write.

She traveled widely from 1956 to 1970, going as far as New Guinea, where she stayed for about a month, working in the jungles with a Japanese woman anthropologist. In November 1970 she accepted an invitation to be a writer-in-residence at the University of Hawaii at Manoa and taught a graduate seminar on the Kabuki plays of Tsuruya Namboku IV. She returned to Japan via mainland U.S. and Europe, at the time deeply interested in the problem of caring for the elderly. *Kōkotsu no hito* (1972; *The Twilight Years,* 1984), recounts the moving story of Shigezō, a senile old man, and his caregivers.

A. received the Mainichi Cultural Prize for her historical novel *Kazunomiyasama otome* (1978; her highness princess Kazu). In retrospect it appears that the author had mentally exhausted herself in conducting research for the novel and imagined herself as one or the other of the characters in the novel who undergo great hardships in the 1860s when Japan was on the threshold of the modern period. Nevertheless A. continued to write and travel. During the last year of her life, she traveled to England and Wales.

One characteristic of A.'s writing is that, unlike other Japanese women writers, she is not known for her love stories. As a professional writer she believed that there were too many issues more important than love. Indeed, she wrote about a great many subjects: racial and other social prejudices, environmental pollution, caring for the elderly, the role of women in society, among other topics. Although her early short stories about artists and artisans dedicated to their craft are of interest, she will probably be best remembered for her social-problem novels. "Kiyu no shi" (1962; the death of Kiyu) describes a prostitute who commits suicide rather than becoming the mistress of an American merchant; A. attempts to trace the beginning of Japanese prejudice against Caucasians in this short story. In *Hishoku* A. has as her main character a Japanese war bride married to a black American. While living in Harlem, the heroine observes for herself the racial prejudice toward blacks and Hispanics in the U.S.

A. lived through a remarkable period in the modern history of Japan, and she thought deeply about the social problems that many industrial nations are facing. Her approach, however, was unique in that she focused on the victims of a social problem, be it radiation disease, caring for the elderly, or environmental pollution. She was deeply sympathetic to the less fortunate in the strictly stratified Japanese society—the pariahs and underprivileged, those who are not blessed with an impressive pedigree and fine upbringing, and she saw clearly the bigotry and prejudice of the Japanese toward these and other outsiders. Whether they are victims of the U.S. atomic-bomb blasts of August 1945 or victims of environmental pollution, they will be affected for generations.

As a divorced woman with a daughter to raise and educate, A. thought deeply about the position of women in Japanese society. She wrote about prostitutes and princesses, housewives and old women. Because, as a rule, women have had to struggle harder than men, they emerge as final victors in many of her stories. In A.'s works, none of them typical "love stories" or unrelentingly gloomy autobiographical works so characteristic of other Japanese woman writers, A. makes her characters come alive.

A. died of heart failure in her home in Tokyo in the summer of 1984. In January 1986 the media announced that an Ariyoshi Memorial museum would be established at the site of the Kimoto estate in Wakayama City. The plans include an adjacent branch of the Wakayama Municipal Library, and the museum will display A.'s personal possessions and original manuscripts. That she will be honored in the home of her maternal grandmother, the setting of *Kinokawa,* is most fitting, since a number of her works were set in Wakayama Prefecture.

A.'s works have a wide appeal to readers of all age groups. She often spent years planning and doing research for a particular work, whether it was a historical novel or a work treating a modern social problem. Her works have been translated into Chinese, English, and a number of European languages. A. will doubtless be remembered as a unique writer who admirably contributed to the great tradition of outstanding Japanese women writers in our time.

FURTHER WORKS: *Shojorento* (1957); *Dangen* (1957); *Masshiroke no ke* (1957); *Zuihitsu* (1958); *U-Tsui anjusan* (1958); *Hana no inochi* (1958); *Eguchi no sato* (1958); *Geisha warutsu Itariano* (1959); *Watashi wa wasurenai* (1960); *Shin onna daigaku* (1960); *Kitō* (1960); *Sanbaba* (1961); *Onna deshi* (1961); *Ariyoshi Sawako shū* (1961); *Hina no nikki* (1962); *Kōge* (1962); *Kyakko* (1962); *Sarashina fujin* (1962); *Heiten jikan* (1962); *Sukezaemon yondai ki* (1962); *Arita gawa* (1963); *Wakakusa no uta* (1963); *Renbu* (1963); *Karinui* (1963); *Kinokawa* (1964; *The River Ki,* 1980); *Onnayakata* (1965); *Ichi no ito* (1965); *Hidaka gawa* (1966); *Aka jishi: A gidayū* (1967); *Ranbu* (1967); *Hanaoka Seishū no tsuma* (1967; *The Doctor's Wife,* 1978); *Fushin no toki* (1968); *Midaremai* (1968); *Umikura* (1968); *Onna futari no Nyūginia* (1969); *Watakushi wa wasurenai* (1969); *Izumo no Okuni* (1969); *Furu Amerika ni sode* (1970); *Shibazakura* (1970); *Kaminaga hime* (1970); *Yūhigaoka Sangōkan* (1971); *Shimmyo* (1971); *Keitonsbiru jiken no kunin* (1972); *Boke no hana*

(1973); *Mō kyojo kō* (1973); *Sarasa fujin* (1973); *Nidai no ikeri* (1973); *Masagoya Omine* (1974); *Boshi Hen'yo* (1974); *Fukugō osen* (1975); *Kinugawa* (1975); *Yu-chi Tso-ho-tzu hsiao shuo hsuan* (1977); *Aoi tsubo* (1977); *Fukugō osen sono go* (1977); *Shojo rentō* (1978); *Akujo ni tsuite* (1978); *Kazunomiyasama otome* (1978) *Nihon no Shimajima, mukashi to ima* (1981)

BIBLIOGRAPHY: Heinrich, A. V., " 'Startling Resonances': Some Comparative Feminist Issues," in Balakian, A., et al., eds., *Proceedings of the Xth Congress of the International Comparative Literature Association* (1985), Vol. 2, 608–13; Allen, L., "A Critique of A. S.: *Hanaoka Seishu no tsuma,*" in Chapman, J., and D. Steeds, eds., *Proceedings of the British Association for Japanese Studies, 1984* (1985), 42–53

MILDRED TAHARA

ARNICHES, Carlos

Spanish dramatist, b. 11 Oct. 1866, Alicante; d. 16 Apr. 1943, Madrid

A. spent his early years in the provincial city of Alicante, where he staged short plays as a child while in school. During these years he had as a classmate Joaquín Dicenta (1863–1917), an important dramatist, novelist, and journalist years later. In 1880 A. and his family moved to Barcelona soon after his father was relieved of his post as paymaster at a factory as a result of local political intrigues. From this experience, A. developed a hatred for politics, an attitude that is reflected in his play *Los caciques* (1920; the bosses). In Barcelona, where he worked for its most important newspaper, *La Vanguardia,* he remained until 1885. Subsequently, he went to Madrid where, after serious financial difficulties, which led to his many contacts with the slum districts, he began to stage his plays and to publish them. He remained in Madrid for over fifty years. There he became a leading intellectual figure as reflected by his appointment as president of the Círculo de Bellas Artes in 1916, a cultural institution that has remained very important. In 1936, at the beginning of the Spanish Civil War, A. became an exile in Argentina, thus bringing his theater to the New World. Upon his return to Madrid in 1940, he resumed his activities as a dramatist.

A prolific author, A. was a master of the *sainete* (one-act farces) and the *zarzuela* (musical comedies), theatrical representations considered in Spain part of the *género chico* (petit genre), works that involve short, popular dramatic or dramatic-musical playlets, skits, or operettas, generally one act in length. These plays often depicted the plight of the lower classes in Madrid by capturing aspects of their language and customs. Over half of A.'s plays were written in collaboration with numerous other dramatists: among them, José Lopéz Silva (1861–1925), Joaquín Abati (1865–1936), and Enrique García Alvarez (1873–1931). It was specifically from García Alvarez that A. derived a keen understanding of the development of plots and the use of dialogue.

Without a doubt, A.'s fundamental contribution to drama stemmed from his ability to define the significance of the Madrilenian *sainete*. This paradigm became apparent with *El santo de la Isidra* (1898; Isidra's saint). Often the most important characters of the *sainete* were a rascal/pimp courageous in appearance but in fact a coward, and an honest blue-collar worker who was in love with a good and sophisticated girl who, in turn, was being seduced by the boastful rascal. Overall, the *sainete* confronts its readers/spectators with a clear conflict between good and evil, between a worker's respect for the prevailing social values as supported by the middle class and a rascal who attempts to intimidate those surrounding him as he violates the prevailing social codes. All this is portrayed by means of language that attempts, in an artificial and clever way, to capture a popular flavor appealing to the masses and conforming to the stereotypical views held by the middle class on the usual behavior of the masses. The language in much of A.'s works depends heavily on comical effects that hide many of the technical deficiencies of his works. Among A.'s best *sainetes* are *Las estrellas* (1904; the stars) and *La flor del barrio* (1919; the flower of the district).

A. evolved from a *sainetero* to the writing of protest plays such as *Los caciques* and *La heroica villa* (1921; the heroic town) in which he criticized, respectively, political tyranny and provincial hypocrisy. From there he went to write "grotesque tragedies" in which, by means of caricature and exaggeration, he aimed to produce a tragicomic effect. Among A.'s grotesque plays are *Es mi hombre* (1921; that is my man), *La locura de Don Juan* (1923; Don Juan's madness), and *La diosa rie* (1931; the goddess smiles).

Overall, the theater of A. provides the current reader and spectator with an understanding of the Spanish stage during the early years of the 20th c. in both artistic and social terms. Furthermore, it constitutes the beginning of a break with a referential conception of dramatic art as it favors a more stylized view of the cosmos as evidenced by the use of carefully selected stereotypical situations and language.

FURTHER WORKS: *Casa editorial* (1888); *La verdad desnuda* (1888); *Sociedad secreta* (1889); *El reclamo* (1893); *Los bandidos* (1896); *La guardia amarilla* (1897); *El último chulo* (1899); *La cara de Dios* (1899); *La divisa* (1902); *Los guapos* (1905); *El Premio Nobel* (1911); *La casa de Quirós* (1915); *El mirar de sus ojos* (1922); *La dichosa honradez* (1923); *El señor Badanas* (1930); *El hombrecillo* (1941)

BIBLIOGRAPHY: Pérez de Ayala, R., *Las máscaras: ensayos de crítica teatral* (1919), Vol. 1, 117–98; Berenguer Carísomo, A., *El teatro de C. A.* (1937); Deleito y Piñuela, J., *Estampas del Madrid teatral de fin de siglo* (1946), 211–21, 363–69; Ramos, V., *Vida y teatro de C. A.* (1966); Monleón, J., ed., *C. A.: teatro* (1967); Seco, M., *A. y el habla de Madrid* (1970); McKay, D. R., *C. A.* (1972); Ruiz Ramón, F., *Historia del teatro Español: Siglo XX* (1986), 38–48

LUIS T. GONZÁLEZ-DEL-VALLE

ASHBERY, John

American poet and art critic, b. 28 July 1927, Rochester, N.Y.

A. was raised in upper New York State, and attended Harvard, where he wrote a long study of Wallace Stevens (q.v.) for the famous critic F. O. Mathiessen (1902–1950). In 1955 he moved to Paris, where he was art editor for the international edition of the *Herald Tribune*. After returning to America in 1965, he resided in New York City, where he served on the editorial board of *Art News*. Often associated with Frank O'Hara (q.v.), Kenneth Koch (b. 1925), and James Schuyler (1923–1991), A. became known as one of the "New York School" of poets. In the late 1960s, his reputation began to grow, and in 1975 he won the Pulitzer Prize, the National Book Award, and the National Book Critics Circle Award. From this point on he was increasingly recognized as the leading American poet, and his influence was felt in the work of dozens of young poets. He has won virtually every literary award including the Bollingen Prize (1984) and a MacArthur Prize fellowship (1985).

A.'s first full-length book, *Some Trees* (1956), was chosen by W. H. Auden (q.v.) for the Yale Series of Younger Poets. The introduction by Auden linked A. to a Rimbaudian, protosurrealist tradition, but A. disliked the distant tone of the elder poet, and when the book was later reprinted he had the introduction dropped. However, the question of A.'s use of French models and tradition continues to be an important part of the criticism and controversy his extremely challenging poetry has instigated. A. read, among others, the French surrealist Raymond Roussel (q.v.), and learned from him the use of "specious simile," in which the reader is told rather less than would be conveyed by simple description. This playful, alogical device combines with others—such as frequently shifting pronominal reference and sentence subordination, and paragraph-length associative structures—to create a virtual polymorphous perversity of syntax. With *The Tennis Court Oath* (1962) this alogicality reached even greater heights, and some of those who defended A., like Harold Bloom (q.v.), found this volume impenetrable.

However, with the next two volumes, *Rivers and Mountains* (1966) and *The Double Dream of Spring* (1970), A. was well on his way to achieving one of the most distinctive styles in American poetry. Though he has spoken of his reluctance to discuss his work, A. has said that he writes "mainly for escapist purposes" and that "we need all the escapism we can get and even that isn't going to be enough." But because he often escapes into the dream landscapes of his own emotional life, and because he can never escape from his own vast and deeply cultured learning, A. writes a poetry that is often obsessive in its anxiety. States of great lyrical pleasure vie with moments of terror and anticipated loss. Conversely, moments of great loss and pain are won through until an air of wisdom, extremely rare in contemporary poetry, begins to seem easy of achievement. A campy sense of humor is seldom absent for long, but there is also a philosophical meditativeness, and the combination of these two attitudes is distinctive. This distinctiveness accounts for the willingness of many critics, despite the density of texture at both the level of the line and the overall metaphoric structure of the lyric argument, to venture readings of an often subjective sort.

In 1975 A. published the prize-winning book that more than any other defined him: *Self-Portrait in a Convex Mirror*. The title poem, based on a painting by Parmigianino that A. says had haunted him for a long time, explores the instability of the self with a thoroughness that surpasses most of the modernist works, which use the same subject matter. Indeed, the poem is one of the central texts of postmodernism (q.v.), and at the same time fully reveals how A. continues to rework many of the problems of romanticism (q.v.). The key struggle in the book is perhaps the question of how to integrate transcendent or sublime insights and feelings into ordinary waking reality, and to achieve this integration while facing the self that is at once an empty container and an inescapable given. By pursuing his own reflective

energies beyond any boundary of wit or irony or aesthetic decorum, A. was able to write his most emotionally resonant poem.

With *Three Poems* (1977) A. challenged even his most inventive critics, for this was a book-length meditation in prose. The sentences resembled his earlier verse, combining sinuous syntax and mundane vocabulary, flights of association and cold marches through his own emotional detritus. The "poem" eventually yields to a patient reader, and not surprisingly its themes and claims and concerns are those of the first five books. But especially notable is A.'s willingness, even his calculated commitment, to using clichéd constructions, phrases, and expressions, as if his first charge were to redeem the fallenness of existence in its most mundane language.

With *Houseboat Days* (1977) and *April Galleons* (1987) A. further perfected his lyric invention, being perhaps slightly less elliptical in his presentation. But *As We Know* (1979) and *Shadow Train* (1981) were felt by some to be of lesser intensity. *As We Know* contained the long "Litany," published in two columns, and *Shadow Train* was comprised exclusively of poems written in four quatrains. *A Wave* (1985) returned to the mix of long and medium-length lyrics that dominated most of the previous volumes. With *Flow Chart* (1991) A. again experimented with a book-length format, and produced a single work as long as *Three Poems*. This poem contains a double sestina, along with a welter of beautifully made sentences, moments of fine lyric control, and long passages of nearly indecipherable complexity. It shows how attached A. is to narrative, as moments and scenes rush by, clipped and elliptical, always suggesting some weighty revelation is at hand, yet always avoiding any firm sense of closure.

A.'s stature now seems nearly indisputable, and he has come to dominate the last third of the American century as Robert Lowell dominated the middle and T. S. Eliot (qq.v.) the first third. Many of his critics have dampened, at least somewhat, the often polemic discussion that surrounded his work in the early 1970s, and have settled into the more difficult task of making discriminations inside what has grown into a large body of work. Most of the reviews of *Flow Chart* began with the assumption that it was high-quality poetry from an acknowledged master, and proceeded to praise it accordingly. However, almost no one offered a reading of the poem or even indicated how utterly baffling much of the book is. In "Litany" A. asked for critics who would be more responsive and yet probing. But having become a major poet, A. may have to settle for praise and respect.

AUCHINCLOSS

FURTHER WORKS: *Turandot and Other Poems* (1953); *A Nest of Ninnies* (1969, with James Schuyler); *Three Plays* (1978); *Selected Poems* (1985); *Reported Sightings: Art Chronicles, 1957–1987* (1988); *Hotel Lautréamont* (1991)

BIBLIOGRAPHY: Bloom, H., ''J. A.: The Charity of the Hard Moments,'' *Salmagundi*, 22–23 (1973), 103–23; Packard, W., comp., *The Craft of Poetry* (1974), 111–32; Kalstone, D., *Five Temperaments* (1977), 170–99; Molesworth, C., *The Fierce Embrace* (1979), 163–83; Shapiro, D., *J. A.* (1979); Lehman, D., ed., *Beyond Amazement; New Essays on J. A.* (1980); Breslin, P., ''Warpless and Woofless Subtleties,'' *Poetry*, 137 (1980), 42–50; Vendler, H., ''Understanding A.,'' *New Yorker*, 16 Mar. 1981, 119–35; Altieri, C., *Self and Sensibility in Contemporary American Poetry* (1984), 132–64; Ross, A., *The Failure of Modernism* (1986), 159–208

CHARLES MOLESWORTH

AUCHINCLOSS, Louis

American novelist, b. 27 Sept. 1917, Lawrence, Long Island, N.Y.

A.'s birth into a relatively old and prominent family in New York society has afforded him an insider's understanding of the dramas of wealth, arrogance, and infidelity that are his frequent themes as a novelist of manners. Indeed, he records in a memoir entitled *A Writer's Capital* (1974) that he began at an early age to see in terms of story both his family and the society in which he moved. But A.'s family chose to immerse him in a tribal world of grandparents and cousins as much as in the haut monde, and from that immersion may have come a detachment from society that balances his insider's understanding. From his long career as a lawyer specializing in estates and trusts, A. seems to have derived an especially useful perspective as a novelist of manners: a sense that American society is a microcosm of the country's politics and power.

A.'s most impressive novel is generally thought to be *The Rector of Justin* (1964), which takes the form of a journal kept by a young teacher in an exclusive preparatory school modeled on the Groton School in Massachusetts, where A. was once a student. In a series of five memoirs incorporated into the teacher's journal, the founding headmaster of the school is seen from widely different viewpoints that keep open the question of his character and influence, whether good or bad. Some readers were unhappy to see in the headmaster a portrait of Endicott Peabody, who was Rector of Groton

from 1884 to 1940, but *The Rector of Justin* is less a roman à clef than a novel of character enriched with a sense of the society that produced such a headmaster and finally brought his era to an end.

The grounding of characters like the Rector of Justin in social history, often in a dynastic overview, is a staple of A.'s fiction. *The House of Five Talents* (1960) and *Portrait in Brownstone* (1962) trace the lives of single families through several generations and illumine brightly the style of patrician life in New York and Newport from the last decades of the 19th c. to the mid-20th c. *The Winthrop Covenant* (1976) is a sequence of nine stories that trace between 1630 and 1975 the rise and fall of the Puritan ethic through the lives of still another New England–New York dynasty. *Watchfires* (1982) is a Civil War novel that covers three generations in the life of a family. Based in several respects upon the life of the journalist Walter Lippmann, *The House of the Prophet* (1980) invites comparison with *The Rector of Justin* inasmuch as its central narrative subsumes a number of other narratives spread over sixty years of American political history.

Indeed, almost all of A.'s fictions are historical in some mode. In dealing with European and British material, he relies less upon the illuminations of a dynastic or temporal sweep and more upon the recreation of contexts and personages. *The Cat and the King* (1981) is based on the memoirs of the second Duc de St. Simon and set at the court of Versailles. *Exit Lady Masham* (1983) is a fictive memoir of life at the court of Queen Anne that includes among its historical characters Sarah Churchill, the Duchess of Marlborough, Robert Harley, the Earl of Oxford, and Jonathan Swift, the pamphleteer and poet. In novels not overtly historical, A. tends to be historically allusive or literarily historical. *The Dark Lady* (1977), for instance, reprises the dark lady of Shakespeare's sonnets in a Hippolytus-Phaedra story about a failed actress who finds a career in politics after World War II. In *The Country Cousin* (1978) the title character tries energetically to understand her life in the 1930s in terms of a Victorian novel. In *The Lady of Situations* (1990) another title character fancies herself a Brontë sister invested with wit and ambition but divested of moors and genius.

It bears emphasis that A. is in none of his works simply a historian of manners. Indeed, because he is invariably concerned with issues of morality and psychology that transcend particular strata of society and time, A.'s fictions are part of a historical drift of the novel of manners into the realms of the psychological novel and the novel of character.

If many of his protagonists feel trapped between an outmoded, rapidly vanishing past and a present that they can inhabit only with misgivings, other protagonists are troubled by atemporal feelings of inadequacy that set them on self-destructive courses, both personally and professionally.

Such protagonists are particularly evident in A.'s novels that deal with the world of law and finance: *The Great World and Timothy Colt* (1956), *Venus in Sparta* (1958), *Pursuit of the Prodigal* (1959), *The Embezzler* (1966), *A World of Profit* (1968), and *I Come As a Thief* (1972). With his usual care, A. details the social backgrounds of the attorneys, stockbrokers, and trust officers in these novels, and he details with equal precision the hierarchies and behavioral codes of the firms in which they work. But his focus is the beleaguered psyches of his characters, who play out in venal criminality their long-established insecurities and maladjustments. That Wall Street glides inexorably into rottenness while they do so does not explain adequately their malfeasances, any more than does the society into which they were born, or does time, with its changing conventions. Yet A.'s novels are typically at their best when such factors impinge upon the characters, shadowing their already dark psychological development with changing social prescriptions.

A. is justly famous for his novels of manners and particularly for his New York novels about bankers and lawyers, but the same straightforward style, psychological acuity, and command of period detail that characterize those works give distinction to his collections of short stories and his nonfiction. Each of his story collections is unified by a theme or a set of recurring characters that invites a reading almost like that of a novel—as, indeed, novels like *The Book Class* (1984) and *Fellow Passengers* (1989) seem reciprocally to invite the reading proper to a story sequence. Among the best of A.'s numerous story collections are *The Injustice Collectors* (1950), *Powers of Attorney* (1963), *Second Chance: Tales of Two Generations* (1970), *The Partners* (1974), and *Skinny Island* (1987). A.'s substantial body of nonfiction includes two collections of literary and historical essays, *Reflections of a Jacobite* (1961) and *Life, Law and Letters* (1979); a collection of essays on American women writers, *Pioneers and Caretakers* (1965); a book of Shakespearean criticism, *Motiveless Malignity* (1969); an edition of an 1890s diary, *Maverick in Mauve* (1983); a short study of Henry James (q.v.) and longer studies of the court of Queen Victoria and of women in the age of Louis XIV; and popular biographies of Edith Wharton (q.v.) and Cardinal Richelieu.

Critics have tended to label A. a novelist of manners writing in the tradition of John P. Mar-

quand and John O'Hara (qq.v.), despite the fact that A.'s interests as a storyteller extend beyond the problems of social class that preoccupied the two older writers. A. himself consistently claims as his literary mentors Henry James and Edith Wharton, even referring to himself on occasion as a Jacobite. The difference between the two sets of antecedents measures the range of A.'s talent, for he is at once a popular novelist and a writer who is allusive, insightful, and literary in the best sense.

FURTHER WORKS: *The Indifferent Children* (1947); *Sybil* (1952); *A Law for the Lion* (1953); *The Romantic Egoists* (1954); *Edith Wharton* (1961); *Ellen Glasgow* (1964); *Tales of Manhattan* (1967); *On Sister Carrie* (1968); *Henry Adams* (1971); *Edith Wharton: A Woman in Her Time* (1971); *Richelieu* (1972); *Reading Henry James* (1975); *Persons of Consequence: Queen Victoria and Her Circle* (1979); *Unseen Versailles* (1981); *Three "Perfect" Novels and What They Have in Common* (1981); *Narcissa and Other Fables* (1983); *False Dawn: Women in the Age of the Sun King* (1984); *Honorable Men* (1985); *Diary of a Yuppie* (1986); *The Golden Calves* (1988); *The Vanderbilt Era: Profiles of a Gilded Age* (1989); *Love without Wings: Some Friendships in Literature and Politics* (1991)

BIBLIOGRAPHY: Kane, P., "Lawyers at the Top: The Fiction of L. A.," *Crit*, 7, 2 (1964–1965), 36–46; Macaulay, R., "Let Me Tell You about the Rich . . .," *KR*, 27 (1965), 645–71; Tuttleton, J., "L. A.: The Image of Lost Elegance and Virtue," *AL*, 43 (1972), 616–32; Long, R., "The Image of Gatsby in the Fiction of L. A. and C. D. B. Bryan," *Fitzgerald/Hemingway Annual*, 4 (1972), 325–28; Tuttleton, J. W., *The Novel of Manners in America* (1972), 236–61; Westbrook, W., "L. A.'s Vision of Wall Street," *Crit*, 15, 2 (1973), 57–66; Tuttleton, J. W., "Capital Investment," *SR*, 82 (1974), 48–52; Bryer, J. R., *L. A. and His Critics: A Bibliographical Record* (1977); Milne, G., *The Sense of Society: A History of the American Novel of Manners* (1977), 236–53; Vidal, G., *Matters of Fact and of Fiction* (1977), 27–38; Dahl, C., *L. A.* (1986); Parsell, D. B., *L. A.* (1988)

ROBERT F. KIERNAN

AUSTRALIAN LITERATURE

See Volume 1, page 145.

The two decades from 1970 to 1990 have marked a growing sophistication and maturity in Australian literature: state patronage (on a small scale) of promising and established writers through the Arts Council of Australia; increasing confidence on the part of publishers that a national and international market exists for Australian literature; an increasing commitment to teaching it in schools and universities; a proliferation of literary prizes and festivals; the establishing of many journals and magazines that analyze the culture and its artifacts; the successful translation of many novels to the screen; and the development in 1978 of the Association for the Study of Australian Literature. In addition, many literary biographies and autobiographies have been written; for example, Dorothy Green's (1915–1991) monumental study of Henry Handel Richardson, *Ulysses Bound* (1973), Brian Matthew's (b. 1936) postmodern *Louisa* (1987), and Dorothy Hewett's (b. 1923) left-wing *Wild Card: An Autobiography 1923–1958* (1990). All of these factors have resulted in an unprecedented production of literary works and an energetic discussion of them.

Accelerated immigration after World War II from countries other than the United Kingdom and Ireland (the traditional sources of migrants) has necessitated further redefinitions of Australian identity. The bush-based, male-dominated nationalism of the 1890s, fashionable again in the 1940s and 1950s, was seen as not true to the largely urbanized character of the Australian experience. The first postwar migrants from Italy, Greece, and central and eastern Europe experienced some pressure to assimilate. In the 1980s, with the government officially committed to a policy of multiculturalism and ethnic diversity, there has been a tendency for a literature by writers from a migrant background that celebrates ethnicity from within the ethnic culture. This represents a challenge in a substantially monolingual society to an historically monolithic nationalist ideology. The earlier generation of migrant writers, which included such writers as Judah Waten (1911–1985) and David Martin (b. 1915), has been augmented by the very considerable literary gifts of Lebanese-born David Malouf (b. 1934), poet, novelist, essayist, librettist, and literary critic, who lives partly in Australia and partly in Tuscany. He is perhaps most famous as a writer of poetic novels of great diversity; his *An Imaginary Life* (1978) chronicles the last years of Ovid in exile and charts subtly how language mediates experience. The newer groups of Asian migrants have yet to find powerful literary voices.

Aboriginal writing in English is a relatively new phenomenon in Australian literature, and it has been given considerable momentum, and practical financial assistance, by the Aboriginal Arts Board and the Aboriginal Publications Foundation. David Unaipon (1873–1967) produced the first book to be published by an Aboriginal writer in 1929, *Native Legends*. Chief among the next generation of writers are Kath Walker (b. 1920), who adopted her tribal name, Oodgeroo Noonuccal, in the late 1980s, and Kevin Gilbert (b. 1933), who have both been deeply influenced by the Black Power movement in the U.S. Oodgeroo Noonuccal's poetry, activist speeches, and stories for children constitute a defiant and proud assertion of her Aboriginal identity. Mudrooroo Narogin (formerly Colin Johnson, b. 1939), reared in a white orphanage, is the most substantial Aboriginal novelist to date. In *Wildcat Falling* (1965), the first Aboriginal novel in Australia, he writes of the plight of the dispossessed urban Aboriginal; in his best novel to date, *Doctor Wooreddy's Prescription for Enduring the Ending of the World* (1983), he deals with the genocidal history of the Tasmanian Aborigines, and tells it, significantly in an empoweringly ironic voice, from the point of view of the black man. The development of a national touring theater group has brought to white and black audiences a variety of Aboriginal plays, including the impressive trilogy of plays by Jack Davis (b. 1917), *The First Born* (published as *Kullark* and *The Dreamers,* 1982, and *No Sugar,* 1986). Since 1988, the bicentenary of white settlement in Australia, Aboriginal literature has been given a decided impetus, and white Australia is enjoying increased access to the works of this culture, both in its traditional and more modern manifestations.

In the late 1970s and 1980s, Patrick White (q.v.) maintained his place as a major symbolic novelist concerned with exploring sprirituality and the problematics of gender in prose that was always confrontationist, poetic, and experimental. The output and reputation of Christina Stead continued to grow until her death in 1983, and Xavier Herbert (qq.v.) secured his place in Australian literary history with the publication of his epic *Poor Fellow My Country* (1975). Thomas Keneally (q.v.), self-confessedly aiming at the serious but middlebrow and cosmopolitan reader, has won international acclaim for novels that delve into the ethics of particular historical events, notably *Confederates* (1979) and *Schindler's Ark* (1982; pub. in the U.S. as *Schindler's List,* 1982).

In the fertile literary environment of the late 1970s and 1980s, a new generation of writers has emerged. Most celebrated is Peter Carey (b. 1943), whose blending of the surreal and the real in his 1988 Booker Prize–winning *Oscar and Lucinda* (1988) owes something to Gabriel García Márquez's (q.v.) magic realism (q.v.) and his postcolonial stance, but it is indigenous and original in its satiric and self-consciously literary explorations of human failure. Several writers of the younger generation, notably Rodney Hall (b. 1935), Gerald Murnane (b. 1939), and Tim Winton (b. 1960), concern themselves with the mythology of their family, culture, or racial group, often doing so in visionary ways. A few, primarily Frank Moorhouse (b. 1938), David Ireland (b. 1927), and David Foster (b. 1944), are more boldly transgressive of their culture.

Many female novelists have emerged in these two decades, and with them new definitions of fiction and of national identity: Elizabeth Jolley (q.v.), Jessica Anderson (b. 1916), and Olga Masters (1919–1986) are women who began to be published in their maturity; alongside these are a group of younger women whose consciousnesses have to some extent been constructed by feminism, notably Helen Garner (b. 1942), Beverly Farmer (b. 1941), Kate Grenville (b. 1950), and Barbara Hanrahan (b. 1939). Their fiction often demonstrates the gynocritical preference for realism, but sometimes they exploit and remake older genres like gothic and romance, or invent new ones in an attempt to explore *différence*. Two expatriate writers, Janet Turner Hospital (b. 1942) and Shirley Hazzard (b. 1931), write with a poignant consciousness of having been girls in Australia, and explore in very different ways what it means to be both Australian and cosmopolitan.

Although in the late 1970s and 1980s poetry has been to some extent eclipsed as a form, a substantial new talent has emerged in Les Murray (b. 1938). His laconic voice and his focus on the ordinary rural man are reminiscent of bush balladry, but he is profoundly religious in proclaiming the sacredness of the land and of the need to live in intimacy with it. Similarly, Judith Wright (q.v.) continues her passionate attack on historical and contemporary abuses of the land and its original inhabitants in both poetry, biography, and political speeches. Much celebrated, A. D. Hope (b. 1907) continues to write measured, witty, formal, intertextual poetry that reflects his sense of respect for the poetry of the past, and poetry that at the same time incorporates his fascination with science and new ideas. Unlike the expatriate Peter Porter's (b. 1929) trenchant urbanity and sophistication, Bruce Dawe (b. 1930) satirizes, often ruefully, suburban Australia and its political institutions. Wit, irony, and precise observation, often of the predicament of women, mark the poetry of Gwen Harwood (b. 1920), Rosemary Dobson (b. 1920), and Fay Zwicky (b. 1933).

Since 1970 small independent theaters (La Mama, La Boîte, The Hole in the Wall, Jane Street, The Ensemble) and a wide range of community and alternative theaters have continued to play a seminal role in the development of new experimental theater works. Although some (like The Pram Factory and Nimrod) are defunct, many new theaters have taken over their functions. The National Playwrights' Conference is another venue in which new plays are workshopped before being produced commercially. Significantly, most of the prestigious, serious, professional theaters in the capital cities demonstrate substantial commitment to new Australian plays, and restage older ones, thus creating the sense of an Australian theatrical tradition, which did not exist twenty years ago. A new feature of Australian theater is its parochial nature, and while state companies regularly share production and actors, audiences tend to be less appreciative of imported productions. At the level of writing, such regionalism is coming to be seen as a strength rather than as a liability, as monolithic notions of national identity come under scrutiny.

While social-realist theater and comedy of manners dominate the commercial venues and David Williamson (b. 1942) is the acknowledged master of these genres, there has been in the 1970s and 1980s a greater diversity in form and content, notably by Stephen Sewell (b. 1953), and nonnaturalistic exploratory forms are often successful, as is evident in the work of Dorothy Hewett, Louis Nowra (b. 1950), and Ron Elisha (b. 1951). While these writers' works are still concerned with issues of national identity, as are the novelists and the poets, the definitions are less narrow and less prescriptive than they were in the 1950s and 1960s and more self-consciously cosmopolitan, and there is a deepening and darkening of vision in terms of the issues debated.

BIBLIOGRAPHY: Fitzpatrick, P. H., *After "The Doll"*: *Australian Drama since 1955* (1979); Docker, J., *In a Critical Condition: Reading Australian Literature* (1984); Green, H. M., *A History of Australian Literature: Pure and Applied*, rev. ed. (2 vols., 1984–1985); Wilde, W. H., J. Hooton, and B. Andrews, *The Oxford Companion to Australian Literature* (1985); Holloway, P., ed., *Contemporary Australian Drama*, rev. 2nd. ed. (1987); Daniel, H., *Liars: Australian New Novelists* (1988); Hergenhan, L., ed., *The Penguin New Literary History of Australia* (1988); Gelder, K., and P. Salzman, *The New Diversity: Australian Fiction, 1970–1988* (1989); McLaren, J. D., *Australian Literature: An Historical Introduction* (1989); Whitlock, G., ed., *Eight Voices of the Eighties* (1989); Davis, J., S. Muecke, M. Narogin, and M. Shoemaker, eds., *Paperbark: A Col-*

lection of Black Australian Writings (1990); Radic, L., *The State of the Play: The Revolution in the Australian Theatre since the 1960s* (1991)

FRANCES DEVLIN GLASS

AUSTRIAN LITERATURE

See Volume 1, page 149.

In the 1970s and 1980s the discussion about whether there was a distinct Austrian literature once again flared up at international scholarly conferences. By that time, Austria had established her national identity. With most of today's Austrians demonstrating an unsentimental and pragmatic attitude toward their country, they no longer need a "spiritual"—and often artificial—concept of what constitutes Austria or is "Austrian." Unlike the post-World War II generation, today's Austrians do not find it necessary to use the literature that is being written in their country as a tool to help establish their individuality and set them apart from the Germans. They accept the fact that, with some exceptions, most new literary work to come out of their country after World War II has been published in Germany (until recently, in the Federal Republic of Germany). They also realize that, without readers in Germany, all talk about Austrian literature would be academic, and they are pleased to know that many of the most prominent "German" writers are actually from Austria. Peter Handke, Thomas Bernhard, Ernst Jandl, Friederike Mayröcker (qq.v.), Elfriede Jelinek (b. 1946), Peter Turrini (b. 1944), Christoph Ransmayr (b. 1954), and Barbara Frischmuth (b. 1941) are just a few examples.

While it is true that many literary works that originated in Austria are connected with the country's history, there is no consensus as to history's actual role in literature. According to Claudio Magris's (b. 1939) study *Der habsburgische Mythos in der österreichischen Literatur* (1966; the Habsburg myth in Austrian literature), escapism and attempts to portray the Habsburg era as a "harmonious blend of races and cultures" (Wolfschütz) and to glorify the myth of the supranational Austro-Hungarian Empire are predominant in Austrian literature, even after the collapse of the monarchy. Magris sees evidence of this in authors as diverse as Franz Grillparzer (1791–1872), Adalbert Stifter (1805–1868), Arthur Schnitzler (1862–1931), and Joseph Roth (q.v.).

Following Magris, the German critic Ulrich Greiner (b. 1945) also emphasizes the retrospective aspect of Austrian literature. The title of his book, *Der Tod des Nachsommers* (1979; the death of the Indian Summer), is indicative of his view.

It contains an allusion to Stifter's novel *Der Nachsommer* (1857; *Indian Summer*, 1985) with its atmosphere of passivity and "political calm." Having adopted Stifter as the "grandfather of Austrian literature," Greiner sees the majority of contemporary Austrian writers displaying apolitical, ahistoric, artificial, and narcissistic attitudes. They have, in his opinion, renounced politics out of a sense of frustration and a lack of vision for their country's future. Instead, they have subscribed to an ideology of "conflict avoidance," retreating into a world of radical subjectivism, into an ivory tower of aestheticism.

Greiner's perspectives have some validity, yet they do not show the complete picture. There are indeed a number of writers in the 1970s who have rejected reality out of their conviction that it is uncertain what reality is. Examples are Peter Handke, who in his novel *Die Stunde der wahren Empfindung* (1975; *A Moment of True Feeling*, 1977) raises the question whether there is objectivity beyond human sensations. Likewise, Gerhard Roth (b. 1942), in his novels *Der große Horizont* (1974; the great horizon) and *Ein neuer Morgen* (1976; a new morning), introduces characters who frequently experience multilayered, dreamlike realities and are incapable of living their lives firsthand. Gert Jonke (b. 1946) also, particularly in his satirical novel about the art world, *Schule der Geläufigkeit* (1977; school of dexterity), manipulates his characters between dream and reality.

While these and other writers do not deny their emphasis on subjectivism and nonideology, many of them reject the notion that they are apolitical and lack social consciousness. On the contrary, they see themselves carrying out a revolt—albeit in the aesthetic sphere. They insist on their individuality and do not want to be part of any group or school. In H. C. Artmann's (b. 1921) terms they are "unarmed individual anarchists with an Austrian character." Artmann, to this day one of Austria's most popular writers of poetry, stresses the freedom of the "poetic act." All art is to be value-free, spontaneous, and free of public criticism.

Writing in the vein of Magris and Greiner, the Viennese critic and novelist Robert Menasse (b. 1954), in his essay "Die sozialpartnerschaftliche Ästhetik" (1990; the aesthetics of social partnership), blames the Austrian system of cooperation between government, labor, and industry in virtually all fields of economic policy, affectionately known as "social partnership," for that subgenre of literature that can indeed be seen as apolitical and antirealistic. Social partnership has, as Menasse points out correctly, been a cornerstone of

Austrian politics, it has had a deep effect on public consciousness. Not surprisingly, writers are not exempt from its appeal. Social partnership has a tendency to smooth over conflict and promotes compromise and consensus among the country's main group interests. While most Austrians cherish the system for having brought about political stability and economic success, Menasse—and others—reject it as antidemocratic, and they repudiate it for fostering a "naive ideology of harmony." Unlike their colleagues in the Federal Republic of Germany where authors such as Heinrich Böll and Günter Grass (qq.v.) actively participated, as artists and citizens, in the political life of their country, Austrian writers, Menasse laments, have succumbed to the "aesthetics of social partnership," resulting in a retrogressive attitude, in a renunciation of social and political involvement.

It is difficult to refute Magris, Greiner, and Menasse altogether. However, the idea that contemporary literature in Austria, much of which has been known under labels such as "new subjectivity" or "new sensitivity," is either obsessed with the past or totally apolitical and artificial has indeed become an "undesirable cliché." For example, it does not do justice to one important movement of Austrian prose writers known as *Anti-Heimatliteratur* (antiregional literature). A diverse group of writers, some of them using dialect, they introduced a brand of literary regionalism that was not only experienced as a novelty but also created a shock effect upon its readers. While traditional regional literature as exemplified by the popular Karl Heinrich Waggerl (1897–1973) extols the virtues of rural life and stresses harmony, tranquillity, and decency, antiregional writers destroy all romantic myths of sweet landscapes and strong peasants. On the contrary, they give the theme of rural life a savage and ironic twist that has no precedent.

On the basis of his first novel, *Schöne Tage* (1974; *Beautiful Days,* 1976), Franz Innerhofer (b. 1944) became the most prominent exponent of *Anti-Heimatliteratur,* but he is not the only one. Elfriede Jelinek's *Die Liebhaberinnen* (1975; *The Brassiere Factory,* 1987), Michael Scharang's (b. 1941) *Der Sohn des Landarbeiters* (1976; the son of a farm worker), and Gernot Wolfgruber's (b. 1944) *Herrenjahre* (1976; living like a lord) also stress the negative personal and social aspects of the region and take an aggressive attitude. Hans Lebert (b. 1919), Gerhard Fritsch (1924–1969), and George Saiko (1892–1962) are forerunners of this movement. Other writers who have portrayed their country in a critical fashion are Helmut Zenker (b. 1949), Josef Haslinger (b. 1955), and Brigitte Schwaiger (b. 1949), whose novel *Wie kommt das*

Salz ins Meer (1977; *Why Is There Salt in the Sea?,* 1988) became an international best-seller.

In the 1980s no clear trends can be observed in Austrian literature. Many writers who, over the years, have become household words, are still productive: Jandl, Handke, Roth, Jelinek, Frischmuth, to name just a few. A number of new talents have emerged though. With his novel *Die letzte Welt* (1988; *The Last World,* 1990), which is based on Ovid's *Metamorphoses* and has been acclaimed as a modern masterpiece throughout Europe and the U.S., Christoph Ransmayr (b. 1954) created a huge best-seller. Alois Brandstetter (b. 1938), Peter Rosei (q.v.), Josef Winkler (b. 1953), Klaus Hoffer (b. 1942), and Julian Schutting (b. 1937) have gained increased prominence in the literary scene of their country.

In the world of theater, Thomas Bernhard together with Peter Turrini, Felix Mitterer (b. 1948), and Wolfgang Bauer (q.v.) are the dominant figures. Turrini and Mitterer are social critics who have outraged their audiences many times but whose plays have become important features on the contemporary stage and on television. Bauer, whose celebrity results from his early unconventional plays *Magic Afternoon* (1968; title in English) and *Change* (1969; title in English), has to this day remained faithful to his message: Desiring directness, immediacy, and naturalness, we all suffer from alienation in a characterless society. Bernhard's stormy relationship with his native country culminated in controversy over his will. Banning the sale of his books and prohibiting all performances of his plays in Austria, he sent a final signal of his animosity toward his native country, with which all of his writing was closely involved. With his final play, *Heldenplatz* (1988; heroes' square), which deals with the *Anschluß,* Hitler's annexation of Austria in 1938, and its repercussions on the life of an Austrian Jewish family, Bernhard created an unprecedented outcry. Focusing on Austrian complicity in the events of 1938 and dispelling the myth of Austrian innocence, the play touched the nation's sore spot.

Coming to terms with the past, something largely ignored in Austria, became a hot topic during the 1980s. Peter Henisch (b. 1943), Elisabeth Reichart (b. 1953), Gerald Szyszkowitz (q.v.), and Erich Hackl (b. 1954) are in the forefront of those writers who successfully attempted to address issues that had been suppressed until the time of the 1986 presidential elections that brought Kurt Waldheim to power. *Die kleine Figur meines Vaters* (1987; *Negatives of My Father,* 1990) by Henisch, *Puntigam oder Die Kunst des Vergessens* (1988; *Puntigam or The Art of Forgetting,* 1990) by Szyszkowitz, and *Abschied von Sidonie* (1989; *Farewell Sidonia,* 1991) by Hackl, candid accounts of the years in Austria between 1938 and 1945, have appeared in American editions.

Contemporary Austrian poetry, largely ignored by the reading public, is characterized by many lines of development. Traditional, experimental, and postexperimental writings have coexisted for many decades. In addition to Jandl, Mayröcker, and Artmann, some of those who have maintained their reputation as the leading poets are Ilse Aichinger (b. 1921), Christine Busta (1915–1987), Erich Fried (1921–1988), Kurt Klinger (b. 1928), Alfred Kolleritsch (b. 1931), also the editor of Austria's leading literary journal, *manuskripte,* Doris Mühringer (b. 1920), and Gerhard Rühm (b. 1930).

Even though many of Austria's contemporary writers feel alienated from their native country, most of them want to be *Austrian* writers. Literature has traditionally taken a backseat in Austria compared to music and the performing arts. Nevertheless, the country's literary scene remains vibrant and vital. Having received much international acclaim, Austrian literature has also found increasing recognition as a unique entity.

BIBLIOGRAPHY: Greiner, U., *Der Tod des Nachsommers: Aufsätze, Porträts, Kritiken zur österreichischen Gegenwartsliteratur* (1979); Best, A., and H. Wolfschütz, eds., *Modern Austrian Writing: Literature and Society after 1945* (1980); Weber, N., *Das gesellschaftlich Vermittelte der Romane österreichischer Schriftsteller seit 1970* (1980); Polheim, K. K., ed., *Literatur aus Österreich. Österreichische Literatur: Ein Bonner Symposion* (1981); Adel, K., *Aufbruch und Tradition: Einführung in die österreichische Literatur seit 1945* (1982); Bartsch, K., et al., eds., *Für und wider eine österreichische Literatur* (1982); Zeman, H., ed., *Studien zur österreichischen Erzählliteratur der Gegenwart* (1982); Aspetsberger, F., and H. Lengauer, eds., *Zeit ohne Manifeste? Zur Literatur der siebziger Jahre in Österreich* (1987); Bormann, A. von, ed., *Sehnsuchtsangst: Zur österreichischen Literatur der Gegenwart* (1987); Daviau, D. G., ed., *Major Figures of Contemporary Austrian Literature* (1987); McVeigh, J., *Kontinuität und Vergangenheitsbewältigung in der österreichischen Literatur nach 1945* (1988); Hardin, J., and D. G. Daviau, eds., *DLB: Austrian Fiction Writers after 1914* (1989); Zeman, H., ed., *Die österreichische Literatur: Ihr Profil von der Jahrhundertwende bis zur Gegenwart (1880–1980)* (2 vols., 1989); Menasse, R., *Die sozialpartnerschaftliche Ästhetik: Essays zum österreichischen Geist* (1990); "Special Issue: The Current Literary Scene in Austria," *MAL,* 23, 3–4 (1990)

JÜRGEN KOPPENSTEINER

'AWWĀD, Tawfīq Yūsuf

Lebanese novelist, poet, dramatist, and essayist, b. 28 Nov. 1911, Bhirsaf; d. 1988, Lebanon

A. was a well-known Lebanese literary figure and a diplomat. He got his primary education in Bhirsaf, a village in Mount Lebanon. In 1923 he moved to Beirut to study at St. Joseph's University, where his literary talents became apparent. A Catholic publishing house solicited him to translate two novels from French into Arabic. He accepted on a condition that he would sign only his initials on the translation, because he wanted the first published work signed with his full name to be of his own creation. A. worked as a journalist and contributed a great deal to the literary scene until 1946 when he was appointed as the consul of Lebanon to Argentina. He then worked in several diplomatic positions in Lebanon and abroad until he retired in 1975. A. died in 1988, a victim of the Lebanese civil war.

A.'s literary corpus, though meagre in number, is varied and rich in genre and subject matter. His first collection of short stories, *Al-sabī al-a'raj* (1936; the lame boy), was well received in the literary circles at that time. A.'s writing was immediately acclaimed as that of a social reformer, and his literary techniques as innovative in the methods of storytelling. A.'s subject matter is derived from his immediate surroundings depicting an exploitative upper class, the tyranny of a patriarchal society and corrupt clergy, the effects of modernization on traditional values, urban versus rural beliefs, and the oppressed condition of women. Although A.'s style suffers sometimes from authorial intrusion, he nevertheless experimented with new literary techniques, by using first-person narrative voice as opposed to the traditionally omniscient narrator; and by employing a story within a story, a technique that goes back to *A Thousand and One Nights;* also by manipulating time and flashbacks.

A.'s novel *Al-raghīf* (1939; a loaf of bread) shows his sensitivity and his internalization of the historical period he had witnessed as a child, mainly the Ottoman occupation and the famine that struck Lebanon during World War I. A. focuses in this novel on three major issues, the bread that every individual is entitled to have, the liberation from Ottoman rule, and an Arab identity for Lebanon. The novel is divided into five chapters, each of which represents a stage in Arab revolt against the Ottomans. These stages follow the development of a spike of grain: the soil, the seed, the rain, the spike of grain, and the harvest. A.'s artistic success in this novel lies in his ability to transform a purely Lebanese setting into an Arab revolt.

Tawāhīn Bayrūt (1972; *Death in Beirut,* 1976) is a prophetic novel, for it lays bare most of the issues contributing to the outbreak of the Lebanese civil war in 1975. It takes place in Beirut after the defeat of 1967, and its main characters are university students demonstrating and demanding a better-equipped national institution, a firmer stand against Israel especially after its attack on the Lebanese international airport in 1968, and the elimination of sectarianism as a major element in Lebanon's political system. Tamima, the heroine of the novel, acts as a sounding board for the revolutionary ideas tested in the novel. Being a woman of a lower class and a Shi'ite from the south, Tamima's aspirations and actions for self-realization and freedom are doomed to failure. A.'s well-orchestrated novel with his clear vision for a better future for Lebanon, and his perception of the contradictory tendencies of human nature, heralded him to be a master in the novel's art form.

While working as a diplomat, A. stopped publishing but never stopped writing. After eighteen years of being away from the literary scene, A. published *Al-sā'ih wa-al-turjumān* (1962; the tourist and the interpreter), which won him the Lebanese prize of the Society's Book's Friends for best play. The philosophical dialogue in this play takes place in the Ba'alabak ruins in Lebanon between the tourist representing the search for knowledge and the interpreter representing the documentation of history. In 1973 A. published a collection of poems, *Qawāfil al-zamān* (caravans of time), two-line poems in which he followed the traditional prosaic Arabic rhyme and meter. A. also experimented with the prose poem in *Mansiyyāt* (1985; forgotten pieces).

A.'s contribution to the Lebanese intellectual atmosphere in particular and to Arabic literature in general is undeniable. While the Egyptian "New School" in the 1920s and 1930s was advocating new approaches to literature, A. was already experimenting with fresh narrative techniques in Lebanon. His critical articles on different genres and literary figures attest to his wide range of interest in the literary sphere. It was no surprise when UNESCO in 1974 chose him as one of the world's literary figures representing the spirit of his age. The organization also recommended that his entire oeuvre be translated into different languages.

FURTHER WORKS: *Qamīs al-sūf* (1937); *Al-'adhāra* (1944); *Fursān al-kalām* (1963); *Ghubār al-ayyām* (1963); *Matar al-saqī'* (1982); *Hisād al-'umr* (1983)

BIBLIOGRAPHY: Allen, R., *The Arabic Novel* (1982), 52–55; Allen, R., ed., *Modern Arabic Literature* (1987), 61–65; Cooke, M., *War's Other Voices: Women Writers on the Lebanese Civil War* (1987), 89; Accad, E., *Sexuality and War: Literary Masks of the Middle East* (1990), 99–110

SABAH GHANDOUR

AZUELA, Arturo
Mexican novelist, b. 30 June 1938, Mexico City

The grandson of Mariano Azuela (q.v.), the most famous novelist of the Mexican Revolution, A. received his Ph.D. in mathematics from Mexico's National University, where he has served as both professor and administrator. He has lectured in universities throughout Latin America and the U.S. in the fields of mathematics, literature, and the history of science. A. has also served as president of the Confederation of Latin American Writers.

El tamaño del infierno (1973; the dimensions of hell), A.'s first novel, portrays four generations of a family, beginning in the late 19th c. and ending soon after the massacre of Tlatelolco in 1968. One of the principal characters is Uncle Jesús, who fled to Cuba after killing his fiancée's brother. Some seventy years later, having become a legendary figure among members of his family, he returns unexpectedly to die in his homeland. Two major aspects of *El tamaño del infierno* are its episodes depicting salient historical events in 20th-c. Mexico and its well-drawn characters, several of whom are taken from A.'s family. One of these is Mariano Azuela, whose real life is clearly reflected in the chain of events, especially during the Mexican Revolution and his subsequent years in Mexico City, where he practiced medicine and became the venerated family patriarch. Another interesting aspect of this work is its narrative techniques, including its multiple narrators and its frequent use of interior monologues.

Even more complex is *Un tal José Salomé* (1975; a certain José Salomé), the theme of which is the destruction of a town (Rosedal) when it is absorbed by an expanding metropolis, more than likely Mexico City. The life of the eponymous protagonist is the principal unifying thread of the novel, whose structure is characterized by a montage of episodes widely separated in both time and space. Thus voices of the past express the nostalgia of a world that has been all but severed from its roots. As the final lines suggest, however, the mythical soul of Rosedal endures in the memory of the town's oldest citizen and in the telluric image of an ancient elm that has survived the encroachment of voracious developers.

A.'s most successful novel to date, *Manifestación de los silencios* (1979; *Shadows of Silence,* 1985), portrays a group of intellectuals who become alienated from Mexican society because of the intolerable corruption and injustice around them. The foreground action begins in the mid-1960s when José Augusto Banderas, the leading character, kills a man and flees to Europe. During the subsequent decade (the novel ends in 1976, at the close of President Luis Echeverría's term of office) Banderas's friends evoke in desultory fashion details of his life, his broken love affair with Laura, his murder of her lover, his escape, and, at the end of the novel, his arrest in Edinburgh and return to Mexico where he is sentenced to twelve years in prison. The most important of the various narrators is Gabriel, a journalist and friend of José Augusto's who is imprisoned briefly after the massacre of Tlatelolco and who, in the final pages, leaves Mexico with a manuscript that turns out to be the novel itself. *Manifestación de los silencios* is replete with violence reflecting the turbulent years of its plot, both in and outside of Mexico. It is especially significant because of its adroit manipulation of narrative technique and its implicit condemnation of the flaws in Mexican society.

A.'s next novel, *La casa de las mil vírgenes* (1984; the house of the thousand virgins), records the history of the eponymous house of prostitution, which is located in Santa María de la Ribera, a section of Mexico City. Founded in 1892 and demolished during the 1960s, the brothel is remembered by numerous narrators, the most important of whom is Aliba, an employee of the brothel for many years. Aliba's recollections, along with those of other narrators, gradually transform "the house of the thousand virgins" into a mythical place from where many of the major events of recent Mexican history are scrutinized. Thus the Mexican Revolution, the Cristero rebellion of the 1920s, President Lázaro Cárdenas's expropriation of the oil industry in 1938, and the student demonstrations of the 1960s are interwoven with tales of violence and murder in the brothel, leading ultimately to its destruction. Although this novel is fraught with ironic ambiguity, due in part to the opinionated Aliba's unreliability, its blend of history and myth sheds light on Mexico's past.

The protagonist of *El don de la palabra* (1984; the gift of speech) is a successful middle-aged actress named Ana María who, while returning to her homeland (Spain), recalls her many years of residence in Mexico, her divorce from her womanizing husband Antonio, her rebellious daughter Adriana, and her wide circle of friends who have supported her in her career. Thus the novel dramatizes two journeys into the past, one evoked by Ana María and the other experienced by her in 1983, the year she returns to her former home in Spain. The least challenging of A.'s works, *El don de la palabra* demonstrates the author's skill not only in developing believable characters, but also in shifting smoothly between present and past tenses, thus creating a fluid, dynamic plot structure. The temporal transitions achieve greater credibility, moreover, because, through the frequent use of free indirect discourse, the omniscient narrator focuses on the character's field of vision to shorten the distance between the character and reader and, at the same time, to convey vital plot information.

A.'s most recent novel, *El matemático* (1988; the mathematician) is one of his most interesting from both a literary and a philosophical standpoint. The plot involves an English mathematician, Philip Cunningham, who, in the final hours of 1999, looks back on his life, along with the major events of the 20th c. His personal recollections include the death of his wife, the upbringing of his two children, one studying in Scotland and the other in Italy, and his fractured relations with his mistress, with whom he becomes reunited at the end of the novel. But the principal thrust of this work is Cunningham's professional career and his efforts as a mathematician to understand the world around him. Thus, although he has at times been optimistic about the capability of science to solve human problems, he has also experienced existential uncertainties caused by the gap between the sciences and the humanities. As both a humanist and a scientist, A. is quite possibly depicting his own personal efforts to come to grips with this dilemma. Like most of his other novels, *El matemático* expands literary and psychological dimensions through frequent shifts in the point of view and temporal fluctuations triggered by free association.

In their entirety A.'s writings dramatize numerous aspects of 20th-c. Mexican reality and, at the same time, convey their author's existential concerns for the fate of contemporary society. His narrative skill and sensitivity to the vagaries of human behavior have made him one of Mexico's leading men of letters.

BIBLIOGRAPHY: Tatum, C. M., on *Un tal José Salomé, WLT,* 50, 2 (Spring 1976), 379; Anadón, J., "Entrevista con A. A.," *Hispam,* 11, 33 (1983), 61–78; Quinteros, I., "El mundo que parecía ser nuestro en *Un tal José Salomé," CA,* 259, 2 (1985), 205–18; Foxley, C., "*La casa de las mil vírgenes:* Convocación y parodia," *RChL,* 29 (Apr. 1987), 39–56; Rodríguez Padrón, J., "La original narrativa de A. A.," *RI,* 55 (July–Dec. 1989), 148–49, 1033–46; McMurray, G. R., on *El matemático, Chasqui,* 18, 2 (Nov. 1989), 107–9

GEORGE R. MCMURRAY

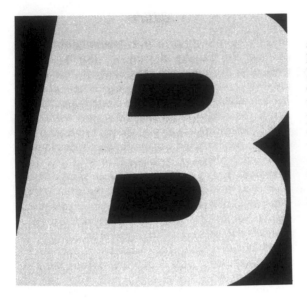

BAKHTIN, Mikhail Mikhailovich

Russian aesthetician, literary theorist, and philosopher, b. 16 Nov. 1895, Orel; d. 7 Mar. 1975, Moscow

B. spent much of his life in provincial cities and towns, in poorly paid intellectual and literary activities. Educated at Odessa and St. Petersburg universities, he lived mainly in Nevel, Vitebsk, Leningrad, and Saransk between 1918 and 1969. In Saransk he taught literature at the Mordovian State University. In Leningrad he was arrested for political reasons and sent into a six-year exile on a collective farm in Kazakhstan. He spent the years of World War II in Moscow, where he also lived from 1969 until his death in 1975. Wherever he lived, B. became the center of intellectual circles involving diverse humanistic interests and innovative thinking.

B.'s fields of interest included philosophy, psychology, folkloristics, linguistics, anthropology, and aesthetics. He is best known for his writings on literary theory and criticism, with special emphasis on the functions of language and on the novel as an art form. His most prominent and influential books are *Problemy tvorchestva Dostoevskogo* (1929, rev. ed., 1963; *Problems of Dostoevsky's Poetics,* 1973) and *Tvorchestvo Fransua Rable i narodnaja kul'tura srednevekov'ja* (1965; *Rabelais and his World,* 1968), and posthumously published collections of articles show him to have been a thinker of remarkable breadth and depth.

The basis of B.'s approach to aesthetics was his conception of language, which he perceived in terms of dialogue. The individual word, phrase, or sentence should not be considered as autonomous or self-contained, but rather as an utterance conditioned by the fact that it is exchanged between an individual speaker, with all his social and personal peculiarites, and a listener who also has his own peculiarities. Each speaker is more or less aware of the linguistic environment and values of his listener, and the speaker subsumes the listener's point of view. The listener is thus an active participant in the utterances of the speaker. Any dialogue, moreover, is governed by the particular time and place—the social, cultural, and historical situation in which it occurs. Properly apprehended, therefore, language is not a fixed phenomenon with a stable set of values and meanings, but a fluid, dynamic medium that expresses constantly changing psychological and social circumstances.

For B. the concept of dialogue involved not only speaking, but thought processes as well. When we think, we are aware of the voices and values of other people, which we in fact share and which live within us. Thought itself is therefore a form of unspoken dialogue between ourselves and others. Since society is made up of a multiplicity of voices, an accurate depiction of reality must involve a dialogic representation of these diverse and conflicting points of view. The literary form best suited for such a representation is the novel.

B. viewed the novel not as a fixed literary canon but as a tendency subverting established literary norms, a force observable even in classical Greece. The novel is an elastic and comprehensive literary entity, a developing, exploratory response to the popular and democratic urge for various kinds of individual and social expression. It embraces all levels, varieties, and possibilities of language. As exemplified in the works of Fyodor Dostoevsky (1821–1881), the novel achieves psychological and social profundity through "polyphony," a portrayal of the complex relationships between the individual voices of characters and the perspectives they represent. In Dostoevsky, the most striking example of polyphony is the use by one character, in interior monologue, of the speech of another character, to form a kind of subjective, unspoken dialogue.

B.'s book on Rabelais as well as his commentary on Dostoevsky and Nikolay Gogol (1809–1852) often emphasize the concept of medieval carnival, a folk celebration that mocks and defies established authority. Through laughter and parody, the spirit of carnival attacks the dogma and pomposity of official social ranks. By dwelling on the drollery of the world, carnival achieves a temporary liberation from the prevailing order. It is the element of carnival, according to B., that provides the novel with much of its social, psychological, and moral interest and depth.

Specialists in numerous fields—including linguistics, philosophy, sociology, and cultural history—find B.'s writings relevant to their interests, and partisans of particular tendencies, such as semiotics and structuralism (q.v.), claim at least part of B. for their own.

FURTHER WORKS: *Voprosy literatury i estetiki* (1975); *Estetika slovesnogo tvorcestva* (1979). [It is assumed that B. is also the author of works published under the name of others: Voloshinov, V. N., *Marksizm i filosofiya yazyka* (1930; *Marxism and the Philosophy of Language,* 1973); Voloshinov, V. N., *Freidizm: Kriticheskii Ocherk* (1927; *Freudianism: A Marxist Critique,* 1976); Medvedev, P. N., *Formal'nyi metod v literaturovedenii* (1928; *The Formal Method in Literary Scholarship,* 1978).] FURTHER VOLUMES IN ENGLISH: *Speech Genres and Other Late Essays* (1979); *The Dialogic Imagination* (1981); *Art and Answerability: Early Philosophical Essays* (1990)

BIBLIOGRAPHY: Ivanov, V. V., "The Significance of M. M. B.'s Ideas on Sign, Utterance and Dialogue for Modern Semiotics," in Baran, H., ed., *Semiotics and Structuralism* (1976), 310–67; Tamarchenko, A., "M. M. B.," *Freidizm: Kriticheskii Ocherk* (1983), 225–80; Clark, K., and M. Holquist, *M. B.* (1984); Morson, G. S., and C. Emerson, eds., *Rethinking B.: Extensions and Challenges* (1989); Morson, G. S., and C. Emerson, *M. B.: Creation of a Prosaics* (1990)

DEMING BROWN

BALLAGAS, Emilio
Cuban poet and translator, b. 7 Nov. 1908, Camaguey; d. 11 Sept. 1954, Havana

B. earned a Ph.D. in education in 1933 and a second Ph.D. in philosophy in 1945, both from the University of Havana, and was professor of literature at various institutions from 1933 until the year of his death. Besides his poetry B. was also an important translator from English and French into Spanish.

B. is considered one of Cuba's most original poetic voices. Although his work includes an important vein of poetry of the Négritude (q.v.), as in *Cuaderno de Poesía Negra* (1934; black poetry notebook), B. is today better known for the innocent, pure poetry of his first book, *Júbilo y Fuga* (1931; rejoicing and flight) and for the tortured intimism of his later books *Elegía sin nombre* (1936; nameless elegy), *Nocturno y elegía* (1938; nocturne and elegy), and *Sabor eterno* (1939; taste of the eternal). In these books B. expressed the existential anguish of the poet alienated from society with no recourse even to religious succor, which B. felt had been denied him because of the self-perceived sinfulness of his life. It is this counterpoint of the poet's guilt and the transparent

innocence of much of his poetry that distinguishes B.'s production from that of other poets of his generation. B. traveled from the pure, virginal, jubilant production of his first book to the elegiac, self-absorbed, melancholy of *Nocturno y elegía* and *Sabor eterno*.

Even though B. was at first better known for his poems of the black experience, the critical consensus now leans toward an enhanced appreciation of his later books, and a lessening of the interest in his Négritude poems, considering the latter largely as the picturesque product of an outsider. The initial interest in this poetry may have been rooted on B.'s publication of two groundbreaking anthologies of black poetry as well as on the central theme of his Ph.D. dissertation.

FURTHER WORKS: *Antología de poesía negra hispanoamericana* (1935); *Nuestra Señora del Mar* (1943); *Mapa de la poesía negra americana* (1946); *Décimas por el júbilo martiano en el Centenario del Apóstol José Martí* (1953)

BIBLIOGRAPHY: Vitier, C., *Obra poética de E. B.* (1955); Augier, A., *E. B.: Orbita de E. B.* (1965); Rice, A. P., *E. B.: Poeta o poesía* (1966); Pallas, R., *La poesía de E. B.* (1973)

NICASIO SILVERIO

BARAŃCZAK, Stanisław
Polish poet, literary critic, scholar, and translator, b. 13 Nov. 1946, Poznań

B., the most prolific representative of the New Wave in Polish literature and its main theoretician, graduated from Adam Mickiewicz University in Poznań (1969). During his student years, toward the end of the 1960s, he established with Ryszard Krynicki (q.v.) the poetic group "Attempts." Like Krynicki, he was considered an advocate of the so-called "linguistic poetry," and like other poets of the New Wave he expressed the social experience of the entire "Generation of '68" in his writing.

B.'s generational experience, the so-called March events of 1968, strongly influenced his first collection of programmatic articles, *Nieufni i zadufani. Romantyzm i klasycyzm w młodej poezji lat sześćdziesiątych* (1971; the distrustful and the overconfident: romanticism and classicism in the young poetry of the 1960s). Referring to the binary divisions into opposite and consecutive literary currents, the author distinguished two models of poetry, which in fact meant two different attitudes toward the world. The object of B.'s attack—classical tendencies of the 1960s—was characterized by poets' escaping from everyday life into the world of myth, avoiding the conversational idiom, and, as well, their inability of depicting social reality. In accepting the variant of a romanticism termed "dialectical," B. sought to unmask the antinomies of the social order. Consequently, his program turned into a vote of no-confidence in the political situation prevailing under real existing socialism.

B.'s early volumes of poetry, *Korekta twarzy* (1968; proofreading of a face), *Jednym tchem* (1970; in one breath), and *Dziennik poranny* (1971; morning diary), focused on a critique of the official language of the time. Irony and other devices adopted by B. usually liberated a series of associations that concealed derision of official press releases and slogans blazed onto banners and posters. They were meant to "teach how to think" and alert the reader to the danger of accepting in good faith everything that the indoctrinators served up.

The main characteristic of B.'s literary persona in the early and mid-1970s is vagueness. This persona is deprived of a sense of personal identity. He carries a feretory in Catholic processions as well as a standard or banner in communist parades. He attends meetings condemning "rabblerousers" or "Zionists," and relies on the authority of others. He does not speak his own language; he uses a communist newspeak instead. All those features contributed to the image of the literary hero of the time and were most fully reflected in the volumes *Sztuczne oddychanie* (1974; artificial respiration) and *Ja wiem, że to niesłuszne* (1977; I know it's not correct). Neither of these books was officially published in Poland.

In 1975 B. became openly involved in protests against the restrictions of constitutional rights, and one year later he served as a cofounder of the Workers' Defense Committee (KOR). As a result of his political activity, he was fired from the post of assistant professor at the Adam Mickiewicz University, and his works were banned from official literary circulation by the censor. At the same time B., along with Krynicki, Adam Zagajewski (q.v.), and several others, started publishing the underground quarterly *Zapis*. In B.'s volume *Tryptyk z betonu, zmęczenia i śniegu* (1980; triptych of concrete, weariness, and snow), containing poems written in the late 1970s, a political reality constitutes the context within which the existential situation of an individual is described. New, metaphysical tones then appeared in the poet's works.

After "Solidarity" had come into existence, B. was allowed to leave Poland and to take up the duties as the Jurzykowski Professor of Polish Language and Literature at Harvard University. The imposition of martial law in Poland in December 1981 found him abroad. A series of B.'s poems, "Przywracanie porządku" ("The Restoration of Order," 1989), included in the volume *Atlantyda* (1986; Atlantis), remains a testimony to the poet's commitment to social questions, but political and moral problems are not isolated from the author's private life. Cross sections of these two commitments are also present in poems included in B.'s émigré volume *Widokówka z tego świata* (1988; postcard from this world). The scene and the very nature of the problems change, but the relationship between the world and the specific poetic ego remains as discordant and distrustful as it ever was. B.'s attitude toward language in general and the language of propaganda in particular is another characteristic of the author's faithfulness to his principle of distrust. B.'s playing with the conversational idiom and with the style of "bureaucratese" writing still produces splendid poetic effects. Yet the primary function of these games is not to expose the duplicity of this language, rather its mechanical and unreflective nature.

B.'s dualistic and internally split vision of the world has always been experienced in a dramatic way. The methods that reflect its semantic instability include paronomasia, ironically used homonyms, enjambment designed to play with the reader's expectations, and more and more frequently assonant rhyme. Rhyme in B.'s poetry is ostentatiously and purposefully casual, as if the author were suggesting that his world does not lend itself to rhymes.

B.'s literary criticism is strictly connected with his poetry through his system of the accepted literary values and through the author's passionate attitude toward the world. B. is interested in those writers whose works stimulate cognitive and moral questions as well as the techniques of persuasion themselves. He is also one of the most brilliant translators of English and Russian literatures.

During his literary career B. has been awarded several prestigious prizes, which include the Kościelskis Prize (1972), the Jurzykowski Prize (1980), and the Terrence Des Prés Prize (1989).

FURTHER WORKS: *Ironia i harmonia* (1973); *Język poetycki Mirona Białoszewskiego* (1974); *Etyka i poetyka: Szkice 1970–78* (1979); *Knebel i słowo* (1980); *Książki najgorsze* (1981); *"Bo tylko ten świat bólu"* (1981); *Wiersze prawie zebrane* (1981); *Czytelnik ubezwłasnowolniony. Perswazja w masowej kulturze literackiej PRL* (1983); *Uciekinier z Utopii. O poezji Zbigniewa Herberta* (1984; *The Fugitive from Utopia: The Poetry of Zbigniew Herbert*, 1987); *Przed i po. Szkice o poezji krajowej przełomu lat siedemdziesiątych i osiemdziesiątych* (1988); *Tablica z Macondo albo osiemnaście prób wytłumaczenia po co i dlaczego się*

pisze (1990); *159 wierszy* (1990). FURTHER VOL-
UMES IN ENGLISH: *Where Did I Wake Up?* (1978);
Under My Own Roof (1980); *Selected Poems: The
Weight of the Body* (1989); *Breathing under Water
and Other East European Essays* (1990)

BIBLIOGRAPHY: Witkowski, T., "The Poets of the
New Wave in Exile," *SEEJ*, 33, 2 (Summer
1989), 204–16; Aaron, J., "Selected Poems: The
Weight of the Body, S. B.," *Erato/Harvard Book
Review*, 15–16 (Spring–Summer 1990), 10–11;
Pettingell, P., "Exiled Poets," *The New Leader*,
53, 3 (1990), 19–20; Bernstein, R., "Breathing
under Water in Poland," *NYT*, 30 Aug. 1990,
C18; Cviić, C., "Communicating in Gurgles No
More: Dissident's Insight," *Washington Times*,
24 Sept. 1990, F3; Crawford, R., "History As
Curse," *PoetryR*, 18, 3 (1991), 35–36

TADEUSZ WITKOWSKI

BARGUM, Johan

Finnish novelist, short-story writer, and dramatist
(writing in Swedish), b. 13 May 1943, Helsinki

B.'s maternal grandmother, with whom he spent
much of his childhood, was the prolific novelist
Margaret von Willebrand-Hollmerus (1894–1982);
his mother, Viveca Hollmerus (b. 1920), made a
brief but critically acclaimed sally into novella
writing during the 1950s. His own career has been
that of the disciplined professional author, without
any ancillary calling and without advocating any
particular economic or political cause—in contrast
to some of his contemporaries in Finland's Swedish literature. Even in his early, radical years, he
was never a polemicist; before all else, he has
been interested in the psychological interplay of
his characters. However, his works for various
forms of theater—including cabaret, radio, and
television—show a clear concern with society's
ills, as do many of his narratives, with their har-
ried, uprooted, and often vaguely seedy protagonists.

B. made his debut with the six novellas collected in *Svartvitt* (1965; black-white), of which
"Kravbudet" ("The Demand Bid," 1974), about
a young man estranged from, yet attached to, a
religious father, has been translated into English.
The entire collection bears what became one of
B.'s hallmarks, his interjection of sudden violence
into normal and even humdrum circumstances.
Femte advent (1967; fifth advent) is ostensibly a
novel but might better be called a collection of
portraits, from the Christmas season, of lonely or
unhappy people, among them a father snubbed by
his son, a suicidal nymphomaniac, and a drunken
Santa Claus. *Tre två ett* (1969; three two one)

continues the exploration of violence, as it intrudes
upon and is occasionally perpetrated by a television soundman, the prodigal son of a well-to-do
Finland-Swedish family, who comes up against
fascist perverts and admirable working men. The
book is B.'s closest approach to the aggressive
social criticism so often practiced by other writers
from the minority during the revolutionary 1960s,
notably Jörn Donner, Christer Kihlmann (qq.v.),
and the poet Claes Andersson (b. 1937), with
whom B. would collaborate on a number of short
plays.

The urge to depict cruelty, debasement, and
callousness was put under stricter artistic control
during the next decade. *Finsk rulett* (1971; Finnish
roulette) demonstrates how the weak are inevitably
abused by the relatively stronger—a waitress, sexually harassed by the owner of the bar where she
works, knocks him unconscious, steals a small
sum from the till, and flees to a villa in the Finnish
skerries, accompanied by her exploitative and unbalanced boyfriend, another of B.'s upper-class
youths, who is eventually killed by the police.
However, before the young woman is apprehended
and sent to prison, she meets three decent men of
a simpler stamp—refugees from a prosperous society that has no further use for them. Two are
pensioners, the one shunted aside by an ambitious
son, the other accompanied by his devoted but
ineffectual offspring. The novel marked not so
much a shift of themes as a refinement of B.'s
favorite techniques: a cinematographic presentation of action scenes, and a careful construction
of atmosphere—here some unusually warm September days, when summer homes (one of them
taken over by the fugitives) are already closed.

In *Mörkrum* (1977; darkroom), B. began to
cultivate a form that would be especially his own,
the quasi-detective novel in which a puzzle is
ostensibly solved while leaving the investigator
still baffled. A free-lance photographer (somewhat
come down in the world, but deeply devoted to
his grandmother and his young daughter) interests
himself in the cause of death of a retired farmer,
relocated to Helsinki and neglected by his children. The fascination with familial relationships
continues in *Den privata detektiven* (1980; the
private detective), in which a former police inspector, a single parent, tries to discover what his
daughter's guilty secret may be. In running down
the sordid answer, the investigator frequents the
streets and courtyards of the Helsinki section called
Katajanokka, with its grand but often shabby
apartment houses from the turn of the century.
The strained web of the family returns in *Pappas
flicka* (1982; daddy's girl). A woman in early
middle age, with faint artistic ambitions, is able
to cope neither with her beloved father's death nor

with her practical-minded husband and daughter, nor with the young man who serves as her model: the last-named is revealed to be her illegitimate half-brother. *Sommarpojken* (1984; the summer boy) is comprised to an even greater extent of a main character's dipping into the past; at his mother's funeral, the narrator decides to locate his father, an effort that makes him relive the summers he spent as the poor-boy companion of rich children at a seaside cottage. Found at last, the father—a pop singer of the 1940s—turns out to be quite senile.

While in *Sommarpojken* the seeker is led down the paths of memory by his late mother's old dog, the short-story collection *Husdjur* (1986; pets) has the animal attachments of human beings at its very center: The seven stories are three pet stories in actual (and wry) fact, including "Bonnie" ("Bonnie," 1989), and four tales in which animals function as mirrors or role models or symbols. The quartet reveals a new aspect of B.'s talent, an ability to slide over into the credibly fantastic. The gift is developed further in "Arkitekten" (the architect), the first of the three novellas of *Resor* (1988; journeys); a daughter suspects that her father, in retirement at his summer place, has first been visited and then crushed by the giant elk of death. A masterpiece, it is accompanied by "Förläggaren" (the publisher), a painfully comic account of a lazy poet, a phrase maker who cuckolds his long-suffering protector, and by "Regissören" (the director), a flashback to a nasty childhood that has led to a severe disorder of personality. Most recently, in *Den svarta portföljen* (1991; the black briefcase), B. has taken up the mystery novel again (this time amidst the savageries of the international drug trade): A tired reporter—with a meddlesome mother and her dog—tries to unlock a dangerous riddle, racing through the Helsinki locales in which B. is so much at home.

All B.'s narratives are compact; in his deliberate craftsmanship and his deft suggestion of emotional nuances he may seem a descendant of the Finland-Swedish author Runar Schildt (1888–1925), whose novellas "Hemkomsten" (1919; the homecoming) and "Häxskogen" (1920; witchwood) B. rewrote for the stage in 1980 and 1984 respectively. His own dramas are less intricately wrought than his narratives, perhaps because they are often topical; extremely effective, they range from the impudent reviews of the 1960s and the plays of the early 1970s, about the trials of small businessmen, collected in *Tre skådespel* (1974; three plays), to *Finns det tigrar i Congo?* (1990; are there tigers in the Congo?), done in collaboration with the director Bengt Ahlfors (b. 1937), dealing with AIDS.

BIBLIOGRAPHY: Widén, G., "J. B.s Analyses," *BF*, 16 (1982), 66–76

GEORGE C. SCHOOLFIELD

BATES, H(erbert) E(rnest)

English novelist and short-story writer, b. 16 May 1905, Rushden, Northamptonshire; d. 29 Jan. 1974, Canterbury, Kent

B., one of the most accomplished short-story writers of his generation, was born into an aspiring working-class family living in a small town in the English Midlands. By his own account, B. spent much of his childhood in happy exploration of the surrounding countryside; and, indeed, rural characters and locations appear frequently in his fiction.

Although B. was a good student, he chose not to pursue a university education. Instead, he began his working career as a reporter for the *Northampton Chronicle* and wrote fiction on the side. B.'s early work greatly impressed Edward Garnett (1868–1937), one of Britain's most influential literary editors. With Garnett's help, B.'s first novel, *The Two Sisters*, was published in 1926.

B., still in his early twenties, now also began publishing short fiction at a prodigious pace; much of this—collected in such volumes as *Day's End and Other Stories* (1928) and *Seven Tales and Alexander* (1929)—shows the influence, in structure and tone, of Anton Chekhov (q.v.), whose stories the young B. particularly admired. By the mid-1930s, B. was frequently described as one of Britain's most industrious and promising younger writers, employing a lean but often richly descriptive and highly atmospheric style that would continue to characterize his finest fiction. *The Woman Who Had Imagination and Other Stories* (1934) shows B. reaching his artistic maturity; many critics, including Graham Greene (q.v.), praised the volume's deft depictions of country life and its often humorous treatment of highly memorable characters. Of these, the old but still spirited Uncle Silas—who appears in both "The Wedding" and "The Lily"—proved so popular that B. continued to feature him in a series of stories later published as *My Uncle Silas* (1939) and *Sugar for the Horse* (1957).

Another collection of stories, *Cut and Come Again* (1935), also brought B. wide acclaim. This volume contains several of his best-known stories, including "The Mill," a vivid but harsh portrayal of rural life that reveals something of the Thomas Hardy-like naturalism that occasionally surfaces in B.'s fiction and counterbalances the more gently romantic strain that undoubtedly played a large part in his wide appeal. Indeed, B. is a writer of considerable emotional range, capable of convincingly conveying the sadness and cruelty of life as well as its delights and pleasures.

During the 1930s, B. published several of his finest novels, including *The Fallow Land* (1932) and *The Poacher* (1935), both of which show the hard side of rural life while celebrating, in varying ways, the strength and ingenuity that survival in the country often requires.

In 1941 B. joined the air ministry, and spent World War II writing a series of stories designed to help build morale during the conflict's duration. These pieces, appearing under the pseudonym of "Flying Officer X," were collected in *The Greatest People in the World and Other Stories* (1942) and *How Sleep the Brave and Other Stories* (1943). They proved highly popular, and B.'s authorship of them soon became widely known.

In *Fair Stood the Wind for France* (1944), B. centers on a wounded English pilot trapped in occupied territory. With its precise prose and avoidance of both melodrama and propaganda, this is the best of the "Officer X" books, and remains one of the more enduring English novels about the war published during the 1940s. The lesser-known *Dear Life* (1950) also focuses on the war and its aftermath, but more darkly; it is now rightly considered to be one of B.'s most compelling novels.

After the war, B. continued to earn his living with his pen. Much of the work he came to produce—including such novels as *The Sleepless Moon* (1956) and *A Crown of Wild Myrtle* (1962)—cannot be ranked much higher than the general run of popular fiction published during the 1950s and 1960s. In such novels as *The Darling Buds of May* (1958) and *A Breath of French Air* (1959) B. portrays the comical and lusty Larkins, a family of junk dealers from Kent; doing so, he brings rather bluntly to the fore the same keen interest in sexuality that had more subtly informed much of his earlier fiction. B.'s Larkin novels were among the most profitable of his career. However, they are generally dismissed by critics who see them as proof that, regrettably, B. came to abandon his artistic ambitions in favor of brisk and steady sales.

Undoubtedly, much of B.'s later fiction shows evidence of distraction and haste. But during his final phase he also produced *Love for Lydia* (1952), his most autobiographical novel, which features some of his strongest characterizations and an especially vivid depiction of life in the English Midlands during the 1920s. *The Triple Echo* (1970) is a superbly constructed novella that deals intriguingly with, among other things, questions of sexual identity. Such works demonstrate once more

that B. is an unusually gifted writer whose achievement in both the novel and the short story is significant and deserves increasing recognition.

FURTHER WORKS: *Catherine Foster* (1929); *The Hessian Prisoner* (1930); *Charlotte's Row* (1931); *The Black Boxer* (1932); *Sally Go Round the Moon* (1932); *The Story without an End and The Country Doctor* (1932); *Thirty Tales* (1934); *The Duet* (1935); *Flowers and Faces* (1935); *A House of Women* (1936); *Down the River* (1937); *Something Short and Sweet* (1937); *Spella Ho* (1938); *The Flying Goat* (1939); *Country Tales* (1940); *The Beauty of the Dead and Other Stories* (1940); *The Seasons and the Gardener* (1940); *In the Heart of the Country* (1942); *The Bride Comes to Evensford* (1943); *Country Life* (1943); *There's Freedom in the Air: The Official Story of the Allied Air Forces from the Occupied Countries* (1944); *The Cruise of the Breadwinner* (1946); *The Tinkers of Elstow* (1946); *The Purple Plain* (1947); *Edward Garnett: A Memoir* (1950); *The Scarlet Sword* (1950); *Colonel Julian and Other Stories* (1951); *The Country of White Clover* (1952); *The Face of England* (1952); *The Feast of July* (1954); *The Daffodil Sky* (1955); *The Watercress Girl and Other Stories* (1959); *An Aspidistra in Babylon: Four Novellas* (1960); *The Day of the Tortoise* (1961); *Now Sleeps the Crimson Petal and Other Stories* (1961); *The Golden Oriole: Five Novellas* (1962); *Achilles and Diana* (1963); *Oh! To Be in England* (1963); *The Fabulous Mrs. V.* (1964); *A Moment in Time* (1964); *The Wedding Party* (1965); *The Distant Horns of Summer* (1967); *The Four Beauties: Four Novellas* (1968); *The White Admiral* (1968); *The Wild Cherry Tree* (1968); *A Little of What You Fancy* (1970); *The Blossoming World* (1971); *The World in Ripeness* (1972); *A Fountain of Flowers* (1974); *The Vanished World: An Autobiography* (1979)

BIBLIOGRAPHY: Cavaliero, G., "The Enduring Land: H. E. B.," *The Rural Tradition in the English Novel, 1900–1939* (1977), 196–200; Vannatta, D. P., *H. E. B.* (1983); Baldwin, D. R., "Atmosphere in the Stories of H. E. B.," *SSF*, 21, 3 (Summer 1984), 215–22; Gindin, J., "A. E. Coppard and H. E. B.," in Flora, J. M., ed., *The English Short Story, 1880–1945* (1985), 113–41; Baldwin, D. R., *H. E. B.: A Literary Life* (1987)

BRIAN MURRAY

BAUER, Wolfgang

Austrian dramatist, poet, and novelist, b. 18 Mar. 1941, Graz

B. has been in the spotlight as one of Austria's most talked-about writers for over thirty years. Born in Graz and still residing in that city, he began to write while still young. Initially he attended law school; then, finding that too unimaginative, he took up French and geography. However, he decided against a teaching career and moved to Vienna to study drama. After a few semesters he returned to Graz to establish himself as a writer. With the exception of one novel, *Der Fieberkopf: Ein Roman in Briefen* (1967; the fever head: an epistolary novel), two volumes of poetry, *Das stille Schilf* (1969; the quiet reed) and *Das Herz* (1981; the heart), occasional short prose, and some journalism, B. has limited himself to drama.

B.'s early works are in the tradition of existentialist philosophy and the Theater of the Absurd (q.v.). *Party for Six* (1967; title in English) forms a bridge between his absurd plays and the later realistic ones. Despite the play's ultrarealistic form and setting, the author's intentions to undermine conventional concepts of reality are obvious. By not presenting the party but only what is incidental to it, B. wants to demonstrate that everything that "really" happens either may or may not be presented on stage.

B.'s best-known play is *Magic Afternoon* (1968; title in English). In the 1969–1970 theater season it was among the six plays most frequently performed in German-speaking countries. Translated into many languages, it has been widely produced throughout the world. *Magic Afternoon* is the story of the boredom, the frustrations, and the violence of four young people. While the play's success has largely been attributed to B.'s having captured in it the spirit of the youth culture of the 1960s, it transcends time and place and can be seen as a study of cultural alienation and as a parable for human isolation and loneliness. Although *Magic Afternoon* has become a classic of sorts, it also established B.'s reputation as an author of chaos and perversion.

Change (1969; title in English), a provocative play about manipulation and countermanipulation, is in many ways similar to *Magic Afternoon*. Although frequently interpreted as a "mirror of the times," it too reflects B.'s existential anguish and illustrates his view that humans are no more than puppets—manipulated.

The artificial world of the culture industry, of film, pop music, and the theater, is the topic of *Film und Frau* (1971; *Shakespeare the Sadist*, 1972) and *Silvester oder Das Massaker im Hotel Sacher* (1971; New Year's Eve or the massacre in the Sacher Hotel). The characters in these plays all suffer from alienation and boredom and are without recognizable individuality.

Gespenster (1974; *Ghosts*, 1978), because of its earthy language and some obscenities, caused an uproar when shown on television and led to accusations of pornography and degenerate art. With a scanty and outright nonsensical plot, the play portrays individuals who, while aware of the emptiness and senselessness of their situation, mistakenly believe that they can live with substitute identities.

Magnetküsse (1976; magnetic kisses), a surrealistic crime thriller about a writer of detective stories, presents an almost identical message. Its hero's appeal for human freedom goes unheard, his quest for authenticity leads to insanity. Parallels between B.'s play and the portrayals of American culture by Jerzy Kosinski (q.v.) in literature and Roman Polanski in film are striking.

In *Memory Hotel* (1980; *Memory Hotel*, 1981), on the other hand, B., for the first time, expresses hope that the struggle for human liberation may not be futile after all. While the play, again, is a chaotic sequence of happenings, there are indications that a meaningful life and happiness are possible.

Despite the refusal of the public to go along with his philosophical plays, B. single-mindedly continued to write in this vein. With borderlines between dream and reality blurred and their logic limited only by the boundaries of imagination, his plays *"Woher kommen wir? Was sind wir? Wohin gehen wir?"* (1982; *Singapore Sling*, 1983), *Ein fröhlicher Morgen beim Friseur* (1983; a happy morning in the barber shop), and *Das kurze Leben der Schneeflocken* (1983; the short life of the snowflakes) read like a drama cycle with a common theme. While *Ein fröhlicher Morgen* is a fun-filled parable for the senselessness of the world, *Woher kommen wir?* reflects the author's conviction that the process of acculturation has destroyed the harmony that existed in prehistoric times. *Herr Faust spielt Roulette* (1987; Mr. Faust plays roulette), a play about a person's loss of identity, has philosophical implications too. B.'s Faust version has been praised as a bold interpretation of the world as a place of an infernal game of chance, but, with the stage once again becoming the scene of dreams, it has also strained viewers and critics alike to the point of total frustration. Nevertheless, his latest play to date, *"Ach, armer Orpheus"* (1991; "oh, poor Orpheus"), is an indication that B. has remained faithful to himself. In this play, a takeoff on the Orpheus myth, the hero, a writer reminiscent of those in previous plays, constantly moves between dream and reality. All rules of logic are suspended; only the logic of dreams carries weight.

B.'s seriousness as a dramatist, which has often been questioned, cannot be denied. Humor, situation comedy, witty dialogues, use of dialect and jargon, spontaneity and turbulence, combined with elements of American pop culture are some key ingredients of his plays. Whether the author presents his message realistically or in a surrealistic fashion, it is obvious that his plays contain a clearly recognizable continuity of ideas. They are all concerned with basic questions of human existence and a search for a meaningful life. The prestigious literary prizes B. has been awarded in Austria are an indication that he has finally been accepted in his native country as a major exponent of the contemporary theater with a growing international reputation.

FURTHER WORKS: *Mikrodramen* (1964); *Romeo und Julia: Mikrodrama* (1969); *Katharina Doppelkopf und andere Eisenbahnstücke* (1973); *Die Sumpftänzer: Dramen, Prosa, Lyrik aus zwei Jahrzehnten* (1978); *Pfnacht: Komödie in 3 Akten* (1980); *Batyscaphe 17–26 oder Die Hölle ist oben* (1980); *Woher kommen wir? Wohin gehen wir? Dramen und Prosa mit bisher unveröffentlichten und neuen Stücken* (1982); *In Zeiten wie diesen: Ein Drehbuch* (1984); *Werke in sieben Bänden:* Vol. 1. *Einakter und frühe Dramen* (1987), Vol. 2. *Schauspiele 1967–1973* (1986), Vol. 3. *Schauspiele 1975–1986* (1986), Vol. 4. *Der Fieberkopf: Ein Roman in Briefen* (1986), Vol. 6. *Kurzprosa, Essays und Kritiken* (1989); *Das Lächeln des Brian de Palma: Stück* (1988); *"Ach, armer Orpheus!"* in *manuskripte,* 106 (1989), 121–40. FURTHER VOLUME IN ENGLISH: *Change and Other Plays* (1973)

BIBLIOGRAPHY: Haberland, P. H., "Duality, the Artist, and W. B.," *MAL,* 11, 2 (1978), 73–86; special B. issue, *TuK,* 59 (1978); Rorrison, H., "The 'Grazer Gruppe,' Peter Handke and W. B.," in Best, A., and H. Wolfschütz, eds., *Modern Austrian Writing: Literature and Society after 1945* (1980), 252–66; Carpenter, C. A., "The Plays of Bernhard, B., and Handke: A Checklist of Major Critical Studies," *MD,* 23, 4 (Jan. 1981), 484–91; Melzer, G., *W. B.: Eine Einführung in das Gesamtwerk* (1981); Stefanek, P., "Aus einem Gespräch mit W. B. (Graz) über Kritik, Stückeschreiben, Theater, Regie und Publikum," *MAL,* 18, 2 (1985), 79–89; Koppensteiner, J., "W. B.," in Daviau, D. G., ed., *Major Figures of Contemporary Austrian Literature* (1987), 67–88; "W. B. im Gespräch," in Friedl, H., ed., *Die Tiefe der Tinte* (1990), 10–26

JÜRGEN KOPPENSTEINER

BEATTIE, Ann

American short-story writer and novelist, b. 8 Sept. 1947, Washington, D.C.

B. received her B.A. from American University in 1969 and her M.A. from the University of Connecticut in 1970. She has been visiting writer and lecturer at the University of Virginia at Charlottesville (1975–1977), Briggs-Copeland Lecturer in English at Harvard University (1977–1978), and was awarded a Guggenheim fellowship in 1978. B. received a Distinguished Alumnae Award from American University and an award of excellence from the American Academy and Institute of Arts and Letters.

B. began publishing short fiction in the *New Yorker* in 1974, and many of the stories that are later collected in book form were first published in that magazine. In 1976 her first such collection, *Distortions,* was published along with her first novel *Chilly Scenes of Winter.* The characters in her early works are aging hippies, alienated, helpless, and often hopeless. They drift lethargically through the apathy of the 1970s that followed the activism and idealism that was so much a part of the lives of many young Americans a decade earlier. Some are literally drifters, moving from place to place almost randomly. Others are shallow, shiftless dropouts, wandering in and out of relationships, self-absorbed but lacking in self-knowledge. Most characters tend to be marking time, unwilling or unable to act, waiting, often in dread, to be acted upon.

In these early works B. focuses more on details of discrete moments rather than on the unfolding of events that constitutes traditional narrative. Her themes are underscored by the accumulation of mundane details and by the lack of action, structure, or resolution. The prose itself is direct, almost flat. Short, simple sentences work to establish mood rather than to build a carefully constructed plot. Most critics agree that her early style is most effective in her shorter works. The novels tend to suffer for the lack of plot and structure. However, *Chilly Scenes of Winter* was extremely popular, and B. was quickly acclaimed as chronicler of the lost souls of the 1960s. She herself strongly objects to such a label as being a reductive assessment of her work.

Secrets and Surprises (1978), *Jacklighting* (1981), and *The Burning House* (1982), all collections of short stories, show indications that B.'s style is beginning to evolve. Although many of the stories are still plotless and peopled by directionless, powerless, passionless men and women, there is evidence in others that B. is working more on character development. And in her second novel, *Falling in Place* (1980), it seems clear that she sets out to address some of the negative criticism *Chilly Scenes of Winter* received. The pace has picked up, the cast of characters has expanded, there are several centers of action, and there is even a climax.

In *Love Always* (1985) and *Picturing Will: A Novel* (1989), B.'s adult characters live somewhat denser lives, and the children are far more fully realized. The structure of these longer works is also somewhat stronger, yet it is still in the short-story form that B. continues to excel. Many of the pieces collected in *Where You'll Find Me* (1986) and most clearly those in *What Was Mine* (1991) show B.'s maturing vision and her marked tendency to move away from the cool, ironic stance in favor of a more sensitive and sympathetic view of the men, women, and children in these stories. In contrast to the earlier characters, most of whom were in their thirties, we now also meet people who are older and who must face tragedies more profound than loss of innocence and compromised idealism. There is a sadder, slightly more tender, note to their confusion and suffering. Many of the stories touch on issues concerning old age, illness, and death; others explore family relations, changing circumstances, and shifting affections. In the best of these stories, there is a recognition of the effects of time, a stronger and deeper focus, and a more profound sense of moral understanding that confirms B.'s continuing evolution as a major American writer.

FURTHER WORKS: *Spectacles* (1985); *Alex Katz* (1987)

BIBLIOGRAPHY: Gelfant, B. H., "A. B.'s Magic Slate or The End of the Sixties," *NER*, 1 (1979), 374–84; Bell, P. K., "Marge Piercy and A. B.," *Commentary,* 70 (July 1980), 59–61; Gerlach J., "Through 'The Octascope': A View of A. B.," *SSF*, 17, 4 (Fall 1980), 489–94; Murphy, C., *A. B.* (1986); Centola, S. R., "An Interview with A. B.," *ConL,* 31, 4 (Winter 1990), 405–22

MARGARET D. SULLIVAN

BELLI, Carlos Germán

Peruvian poet, b. 15 Sept. 1927, Lima

B. is one of the most expressive poetic voices of contemporary Peruvian and Latin American poetry. A descendant of Italian immigrants, B. began writing poetry at age thirty. His poems have gained recognition in all of Latin America, and a number of them have been translated into English and Italian.

In a country that enjoys a rich poetic tradition, B. has managed to establish a unique voice. His poetry manifests a deep preoccupation with a language based on the intricate verbal processes of Spanish Golden Age poetry displaced from its original context, coupled with a formalism that is both stringent and experimental. His language, confessional and symbolic, with its vocabulary of neologisms, is based on a variety of traditions and influences. On more than one occasion B. has discussed his affinity with surrealism (q.v.), especially in the early stages of his career. After a brief encounter with "letrismo," or poetry that relies on the iconic power of the word for its impact, and on automatic writing, B. discovered the poetry of the modernists. Undertaking a systematic study of Rubén Darío (q.v.), the leading poet of the movement, B. became intrigued by the formal beauty of modernist poetry and the refined eroticism he found in Darío's poems.

Although he relished the linguistic freedom provided by automatic writing, he soon turned toward the classical tradition with its closed, rigid forms. Influenced by Luis de Góngora y Argote (1562–1627), Fernando de Herrera (1534–1597), Francisco Medrano (1570?–1607), Francisco de Quevedo y Villegas (1580–1645), and other masters of Spanish Golden Age poetry, B. became obsessed by the formal aspects of this poetry as he copied the external forms, the meters and the rhymes, in the same manner that Renaissance painters imitated the masters. These intricate verbal processes, typical of Baroque poetry, with its disjointed syntax, stylistic formulae, and daring images, evoke a pastoral world of classical mythology, and form the basis of B.'s poetry. This is poetry that presents extreme difficulties for the reader. It is an intricate process elaborated with attention to detail and dominated by the tension produced by multiple points of focus, shocking contrasts, and subtle interplay of spatial and temporal forms. If it is easy to lose oneself in this labyrinth, there is also a reward for the attentive reader who is able to see a coherent architecture in B.'s work. This is poetry that is always expressed in a language that is charged with deep human feelings and a sense of humility.

In his first books of poems, *Poemas* (1958; poems) and *Dentro y fuera* (1960; inside and out), B. established the basic lines of his entire poetic production. Chief among them is the preoccupation with the theme of alienation that is caused by socioeconomic conditions. The poet feels excluded from a world dominated by those who have power. Another constant in his poetry is the theme of suffering, which is expressed in poems dedicated to his brother, Alfonso, who has been confined to a wheelchair since early childhood. His brother's suffering is equated to the suffering of humankind in general, and it symbolizes a sense of exclusion from the joys of life. The poet and his brother are viewed as imperfect beings destined to suffer the harshest physical and metaphysical privations.

The poet's fragmented voice, in a world that is beyond his control, seeks a sense of integration and liberation through the evocation of a utopic world based on the pastoral tradition. The poet, however, is frustrated in this attempt. His poetry captures the tension produced by two diametrically opposing forces, one that attempts to pull the poet apart, the other that seeks integration.

In *Oh hada cibernética* (1962; oh cybernetic fairy) B. expresses his faith in the power of science to deliver humans from the burden of labor. Technology will allow the poet to find the necessary free time to dedicate himself to his own poetic production. With the passing of time, this desire also becomes frustrated. In the same volume he expresses the desire to achieve a physical and metaphysical union with Filis, the ideal woman of the pastoral tradition. However, the poet soon discovers that this union is only possible through the poetic word itself. Each poem then becomes a small step in the long voyage of self-definition.

The poems of *El pie sobre el cuello* (1964; the foot on the neck) intensify the theme of the poet's suffering as a direct result of his metaphysical as well as his socioeconomic condition. This collection is followed by *Por el monte abajo* (1966; rushing down the mountain), with its predominant tone of exasperation, which is only assuaged by the appearance of a woman, an ideal even more generalized than Filis, as a positive force capable of alleviating the suffering of the poet. It is this idealized woman who restores the poet's humanity and faith in himself. B. experiments with larger poems in *Sextinas y otros poemas* (1970; sestinas and other poems), where the metric form of the Petrarchan canzone predominates. In this collection B.'s poetry becomes more sensual; it assumes an erotic posture that will become even more evident in subsequent works.

He achieves his highest level of complexity and intellectualization in the poems of *En alabanza del bolo alimenticio* (1979; in praise of undigested food), where the physical and natural processes are coupled with a complex process of regeneration. In *Canciones y otros poemas* (1982; songs and other poems) B. achieves a perfect sense of synthesis of his entire poetic production. The last poem of the collection, "Cuando el espíritu no habla por la boca" (when the spirit does not speak through the mouth) is the perfect symbiosis of the poetic word and the sexual act as a means toward transcendence. This same existential posture is also implicit in his latest books of poems: *Más que señora humana* (1986; more than a human lady), *El buen mudar* (1987; the big move), and

En el restante tiempo terrenal (1988; what is left of this terrestrial time).

B.'s poetry may best be summed up in the words of his compatriot, the renowned writer Mario Vargas Llosa (q.v.), who says: "B.'s is a poetry for difficult times, like our own times, for societies in which the life of the spirit and culture seem to languish, without grandeur, in the midst of general indifference."

FURTHER WORK: *Antología personal* (1988)

BIBLIOGRAPHY: Hill, W. N., "The Poetry of C. G. B.," *BHS*, 47 (1970), 327–39; Lasarte, F., "Pastoral and Counter-Pastoral: The Dynamics of B.'s Poetic Despair," *MLN*, 94, 4 (1979), 301–20; Garganigo, J. F., *C. G. B.: antología crítica* (1988)

JOHN F. GARGANIGO

BEMBA, Sylvain

Congolese novelist, dramatist, and journalist (writing in French), b. 17 Feb. 1934, Sibiti

Columnist, broadcaster, and administrator, B. turned to fiction at least partly for political reasons. His country, Congo, is known both for its intense literary development and its active political life. The so-called "Les Trois Glorieuses" days of the 1963 revolution accelerated progressive activities and led to B. receiving a commission from the Movement of the Revolution to write one of his first plays, *Une eau dormante* (1973; dormant water). B.'s keen interest in political reform led to his arrest for his participation in the 1973 coup attempt, for which he received a three-year suspended sentence.

After first studying public administration, B. went to Strasbourg, France, to work on a degree in journalism before entering governmental service as an administrator. At about the same time, he began to write the articles and short stories for which he is known. In the 1950s he was one of the major contributors to the review *Liaison*, which played a major role in the flowering of Congolese and all of francophone African letters. From 1958 to 1961 he wrote a regular column for *Le Petit Journal de Brazzaville*. In 1963 his story "La chambre noire" (the dark room) won the Grand Prix de la Nouvelle Africaine. By the late 1960s B. had risen to director of the Agence Congolaise d'Information, from which he moved on to administer the radio and television stations of Brazzaville. In 1970 he became the director of information and in 1972 the director of cultural affairs of the Congo. In 1973 he had served one month as minister of information before his arrest.

Considered one of his country's most talented and hardworking writers, B. has divided his time and energy between the theater and prose fiction. After publishing a number of plays in the 1970s and making a trip to the U.S. (a tour with other African writers sponsored by Crossroads Africa), which included participation in the 1979 African Literature Association meeting at Indiana University, he turned to the novel and produced four significant additions to African literature in the early 1980s, before turning back to the theater.

It was B.'s journalism and political interests that had propelled him into literature. Toward the end of his years as a newspaper columnist he strung together several columns into a dramatic narrative that led to experimentation with short didactic plays and the commission for *Une eau dormante*. These early short dramas, such as *L'enfer c'est Orféo* (1970; hell is Orpheus), *L'homme qui tua le crocodile* (1972; the man who killed the crocodile), and *Un foutu monde pour un blanchisseur trop honnête* (1977; a screwed-up world for a too-honest laundryman), were soon seen as "classics" of the new nation. B.'s early theater culminated in his most important drama to date, *Tarantelle noire et diable blanc* (1976; black tarantella and white devil), which analyzes Congolese history from 1890 to 1930 in three episodes and eleven scenes. *Tarantelle* is a Brechtian "morality play" that uses dramatic irony, distancing techniques, modern rhetorical figures, myth, the fantastic, and characters like the Sacred Tree/Men and Zombis to interpret the Congo's colonial heritage.

The central concern of *Rêves portatifs* (1979; portable dreams) is the relation of film to freedom. B. hangs all the diverse happenings on the story of a projectionist at the moment of independence, fictionalizing and interpreting the play of historical forces and figures in the first phases of national development. The projectionist, an African Everyman intoxicated with his power to project history and myth, is unable to comprehend the nefarious nature of Western mass culture imported into the Third World; he dreams his own film, or "cynical cynema," a "page from African history" (as seen through Hollywoodian lenses), a saga of cash, sex, and blood in the jungle. The forces of enlightenment sink under the weight of alienation, as native leaders equal the deserted colonizers in corruption. *Le soleil est parti à M'Pemba* (1982; the sun has left for M'Pemba), more unified and less baroque, uses a fantastic "phono-videograph" to tell the story of an extended family in a rapid rerun of recent African history, showing the transmutations from colonialism to independence in the transformations of psyches, identities, and family institutions.

Léopolis (1984; Leopolis), a short playful comic novel, B.'s most integrally structured, recounts the quest of a young black woman from Baltimore for the legendary African hero Febrice M'PFum. The detective romance, a fictionalized biography of Patrice Lumumba, seems to be an attempt to decode the inscrutable mask of the meteoric prime minister, using the means of the New Novel (q.v.), scrambling realities and myths, reworking legends (Tarzan) and conventional interpretations to see Africa in a new light, or a new caricature, to take African culture out of the museum and into the political arena. Lumumba is humanized in the genial Fabrice, champion *joueur de dames,* who wins the African Trianon from the rich planter, only to see it dynamited in the ensuing revolution. But Fabrice/Lumumba emerges from the psychological hall of mirrors a new hero for our (African) times.

FURTHER WORKS: *Bio-bibliographie des écrivains congolais* (1979, with Leopold Mamonsono); *Les cargonautes* (1984); *Cinquante ans de musique du Congo-Zaire* (1984); *Profession avouée: sorcier de la famille* (1986); *Théâtre* (1989)

BIBLIOGRAPHY: Chemain, R., "Le théâtre militant: entretien avec S. B.," *Notre Librairie,* 38 (Sept. 1977), 87–93; Chemain, R., *Panorama critique de la littérature congolaise contemporaine* (1979); Ndzanga-Konga, A., "S. B.: Je suis un élève perpétuel . . .," *Bingo,* 379 (1984), 25–27; Malanda, A., "L'œuvre de S. B.," *PA,* 130, 2 (1984), 93–117; Malanda, A., "Entretien avec S. B.," *Nouvelles du Sud,* 1 (1985), 127–35; Condé, M., "S. B.: Je suis un aventurier cérébral," *Africa,* 168 (1985), 59; Makhele, C., "S. B. ou le syndrôme du miroir brisé," *Notre Librairie,* 92–93 (March 1988), 97–99; Wylie, H., "The Dancing Masks of S. B.," *WLT,* 64, 1 (Winter 1990), 20–24

HAL WYLIE

BENET, Juan

Spanish novelist, short-story writer, and essayist, b. 7 Oct. 1927, Madrid

B. studied at the School of Engineering in Madrid and was a successful civil engineer long before he won recognition as a writer. However, his work building roads and dams is crucial to the formation of his fiction, since his long stays in isolated portions of northern Spain provided him with material for the physical and psychological backdrop of Región, the mythical area in which much of his fiction takes place. Apart from his focus on engineering, B. was also deeply immersed as a youth in the literary milieu of Madrid. He attended the literary *tertulia* of novelist Pío Baroja (q.v.) in the 1940s and in 1953 participated in the important literary magazine *Revista Española*. Also during this period, B. read the complete works of William Faulkner (q.v.), the writer who would exert the most direct influence on his style, technique, and thematic concerns of time, war, and decay.

Volverás a Región (1967; *Return to Región*, 1975), the first of B.'s "Región" cycle of novels, is an important work in the development of postwar Spanish fiction. It represents a radical break with the norms of social realism (q.v.) that characterize the major Spanish narrative of the 1950s and 1960s, and it has a marked influence on the young generation of novelists beginning to write near the end of the Franco regime. The novel explores the decay of the fictional Región (similar to Faulkner's Yoknapatawpha County) during the 20th c. and is structured by the memories of its two principal characters, Dr. Sebastian and Marré Gamallo. Most importantly, *Volverás a Región* offers a compendium of traits that form the cornerstone of much of B.'s fiction: the themes of ruin and decay, a concern for history and the way in which it is narrated, the destructive flow of time, and a sense of the world as profoundly enigmatic and inexplicable. B.'s style and technique in the novel likewise reveal the principal characteristics of his future narrative. His sentences are frequently the length of full pages, and are replete with complex obtrusions, parentheses, ambiguous interpolations, and shifts in narrative perspective.

B.'s next two Región novels, *Una meditación* (1970; *A Meditation*, 1982) and *Un viaje de invierno* (1972; a winter's journey), won the author wide acclaim as one of Spain's most distinguished and complex novelists. Written in the first person, *Una meditación* is indeed a meditation by the narrator on the past. Using a Proustian memory and Faulknerian style, the narrator scrutinizes the period from 1920 to 1970 in an attempt to recover and understand the nature of his family, his friends, and the meaning of his life in the vicinity of Región. *Viaje* is more abstract than B.'s previous fiction (its characters are mere apparitions moving through a fatalistic winter's journey toward death), but the same labyrinthine style, accompanied by digressions placed in the margins of the text, make the novel one of B.'s most difficult to read.

B.'s fiction since *Un viaje de invierno* has both continued the author's exploration of Región and expanded into other areas. His best-selling *El aire de un crimen* (1980; the air of a crime), though set in Región, is a detective novel that appropriates and subverts traditional norms associated with the genre. In *En la penumbra* (1989; in the penumbra) B. moves outside Región to represent the meditations of two women on their lives as they await their mysterious destiny.

It remains in Región, however, where B.'s most important writing lies. *Saúl ante Samuel* (1980; Saul in the presence of Samuel) continues the author's saga of the civil war in Región. B. pursues fully in this novel the tragic consequences of the war. He urges that we understand the irredemptive destruction of the conflict and affirms that humankind's fall into despair cannot be prevented.

In his most recent trilogy of Región and the civil war, *Herrumbrosas lanzas* (1983–1986; rusty lances), B. probes the origin of the conflict in the 19th c. and lays out battle strategies in highly detailed fashion. Although the style and technique of the novels appear to shed much of their surface complexity, they assert a structural and ideological foundation similar to the most abstruse of B.'s earlier fiction: enigma as narrative determinant, the aporias of time as the core of ambiguity, and the essential contingency of all narration as the mediator of reality and truth.

As an essayist and literary theorist B. has written on a wide range of topics from a variety of perspectives. He is most frequently concerned with language and the epistemological questions raised by narrative discourse: how words mean; the grasping together of language to constitute narration; the uniqueness of a literary work outside of social and historical determinants. In *La inspiración y el estilo* (1965; inspiration and style) B. probes the way in which the use of language determines not only how writers write, but also what they write, and he explores as well the theoretical question of how language lends permanence to a literary work. In *El ángel del Señor abandona a Tobías* (1976; the angel of the Lord abandons Tobit) B. compares the narrative techniques of prose and painting and explores how they frame the reader's understanding of a text. In a lengthy segment in *Tobías* he attacks linguistic study and the obsession for developing a science of language in the face of the essential indeterminacy and ambiguity of how words mean.

B. has clearly emerged in the past two decades as one of Spain's most important novelists. His commingling of a complex prose style with a vision of despair and decay in modern Spain makes his fiction both sophisticated as literature and incisive as sociohistoric commentary. His novels have at times been criticized as too difficult and as resisting all modes of interpretive closure. In B.'s view, however, full coherence, the absence of enigma, and resolution of the problematic would make the world, as well as literature, a much impoverished place to explore.

FURTHER WORKS: *Nunca llegarás a nada* (1961); *Puerta de tierra* (1970); *Teatro* (1970); *Una tumba* (1971); *5 narraciones y 2 fábulas* (1972); *La otra casa de Mazón* (1973); *Sub rosa* (1973); *En ciernes* (1976); *¿Qué fue la guerra civil?* (1976); *Cuentos completos* (2 vols., 1977); *En el estado* (1977); *Del pozo y del Numa* (1978); *Trece fábulas y media* (1981); *Una tumba y otros relatos* (1981); *La moviola de Eurípides* (1982); *Otoño en Madrid hacia 1950* (1987); *Londres* (1989)

BIBLIOGRAPHY: Herzberger, D. K., *The Novelistic World of J. B.* (1976); Summerhill, S. J., "Prohibition and Transgression in Two Novels of J. B.," *The American Hispanist*, 4, 36 (May 1979), 20–24; Cabrera, V., *J. B.* (1983); Compitello, M. A., *Ordering the Evidence: "Volverás a Región" and Civil War Fiction* (1983); Manteiga, R., et al., eds., *Critical Approaches to the Writings of J. B.* (1984); Herzberger, D. K., "Numa and the Nature of the Fantastic in the Fiction of J. B.," *StTCL*, 8, 2 (Spring 1984), 185–96; Vernon, K., ed., *J. B.* (1986); Margenot, J. B., "Cartography in the Fiction of J. B.," *Letras Peninsulares*, 1, 3 (Winter 1988), 331–43

DAVID K. HERZBERGER

BEN JELLOUN, Tahar

Moroccan novelist, poet, and essayist (writing in French), b. 1 Dec. 1944, Fez

B. J., born in Fez, moved with his family to Tangier when he was eighteen. There he attended the French *lycée*. He went on to study philosophy at the university in Rabat, where he collaborated with the avant-garde group associated with the journal *Souffles* and published his first poems, *Hommes sous linceul de silence* (1971; men under a shroud of silence), and his first novel, *Harrouda* (1973; Harrouda). B. J. then went to France, where he earned a doctorate in psychiatric social work while counseling North African immigrant workers. His second novel, *La réclusion solitaire* (1976; Solitaire, 1988), fictionalized some of his case histories of sexual dysfunction among male immigrants, files that also formed the basis for his doctoral dissertation, subsequently published in a popular edition as *La plus haute des solitudes* (1977; the deepest solitude). Many of his works, such as *Moha le fou, Moha le sage* (1978; Moha the madman, Moha the wise man), *La prière de l'absent* (1981; prayer for the absent), *L'enfant de sable* (1985; The Sand Child, 1987), and *La nuit*

sacrée (1987; *The Sacred Night*, 1989), invoke psychological data, psychosomatic effects, Freudian symbolism, androgyny and male-female ambivalence, and imagery pertinent to B. J.'s work with impotent immigrants.

B. J.'s early works attracted a small, devoted following but also elicited criticism from some who felt that he had distanced himself from his native Moroccan culture and should rather be considered a "European" stylist. This change appears to have been based on his urbane narrative techniques and his sometimes journalistic approach to his subjects, but it seems quite unfair since B. J.'s works contain many passages whose full appreciation requires recognition on the reader's part of the significant impact Arabic language, Koranic imagery, and other Maghrebian cultural givens have had on B. J.'s French discourse.

B. J.'s celebrity became international after the publication of *L'enfant de sable* and its sequel, *La nuit sacrée,* the latter having been awarded France's most prestigious literary prize, the Prix Goncourt, in 1987. This award seemed only to fan the debate concerning B. J.'s relative Frenchness. And yet B. J., like Abdelkebir Khatibi (q.v.), has repeatedly contended that he is able to use the French language without forfeiting his Moroccan soul. After the Goncourt, B. J. was reported in a syndicated press dispatch to have said that "Arabic is my wife, French is my mistress, and I have been unfaithful to both." The very debate and a need to clarify his position may have contributed in part to the thrust of B. J.'s *Les yeux baissés* (1991; with lowered eyes), a story of the itinerary that leads a young woman from rural Morocco to France, her acquisition of the French language, and a desire to write in French. The protagonist is an allegory of the francophone experience, and the novel functions on two levels, as straight narrative and as a layer of symbolic references to biculturalism and bilingualism.

Most of B. J.'s novels combine social and/or political questions with the disquieting psychological hurts, shortcomings, and yearnings of individuals. His finest novels are *Harrouda*, a haunting "psychospatial" tale of the quite different urban experiences of the two cities, Fez and Tangier, in which B. J. grew up, a tale reminiscent of Khatibi's *La mémoire tatouée* (1971; the tatooed memory), which inspired B. J.; *Moha le fou, Moha le sage*, whose story is told in the poetic, discontinuous ramblings of the confused and tortured mind of Moha, who nevertheless speaks eloquently on behalf of the downtrodden and disenfranchised; *La prière de l'absent*, a novel that recounts a somewhat obscure quest to the south of Morocco by a little band of strange bedfellows—two mentally troubled men, Boby and Sindibad, an old woman, and an infant of destiny who has come under their care—during which we are afforded glimpses of the resistance to colonization by Krim in the north and Ma-al-Aynayn in the south as well as numerous allusions to, among other things, the Koran, as well as surrealism and the Theater of the Absurd (qq.v.), Moroccan policy on the Spanish Sahara (including the government-sponsored *Marche verte,* or Green March), classic Arabic-language poets, and a prime intertextual source in Maghrebian literature, *A Thousand and One Nights; L'écrivain public* (1983; the public scribe), a less well-known novel that brilliantly intertwines narratives in letters, diaries, reminiscences, and dreams; and the diptych of *L'enfant de sable* and *La nuit sacrée,* which tells of the psychological malformation of a girl raised as a boy by her father and her subsequent retrieval of her female identity in a journey of inward questioning, self-realization through erotic manipulation, and, ultimately, violence.

Two works published since B. J. won the Prix Goncourt warrant special mention: *Jour de silence à Tanger* (1990; *Silent Day in Tangier,* 1991), which is the interior monologue of an old man whose waning days are articulated primarily in the listless introspection of reliving ancient, often erotic, memories; and the previously mentioned *Les yeux baissés,* in which B. J. once again has taken as his protagonist a woman, but in this instance one who incarnates many of the problems and preoccupations of the modern Maghrebian francophone writer. The message of *Les yeux baissés* is theorizing yet often playful, as when the young woman, who aspires to be a writer, seeks advice and encouragement from a "famous writer" who tells her the plot of one of his novels, which we recognize as that of B. J.'s own *La prière de l'absent.* Thus, even as we tend to identify the young woman's creative and cultural journey with that of B. J., the author lightly intervenes from without his alter ego.

B. J.'s poetry has been conceived in several styles, ranging from brief enigmatic texts to surrealistic prose poems, of which the best possess rich imagery and a compelling lyricism. Representative poems may be found in the 1983 edition of *Les amandiers sont morts de leurs blessures, suivi de À l'insu du souvenir* (the almond trees have died from their wounds, followed by beyond the ken of memory), which includes such earlier collections as *Cicatrices du soleil* (1972; sun scars) and *Le discours du chameau* (1974; the camel's speech).

FURTHER WORKS: *Grains de peau, Asilah* (1974); *La mémoire future* (1976); *La fiancée de l'eau, suivi de Entretiens avec M. Saïd Hammadi, ouv-* *rier algérien* (1984); *Hospitalité française: Racisme et immigration maghrébine* (1984)

BIBLIOGRAPHY: Gontard, M., *La Violence du texte* (1981), 64–79; Pallister, J. L., "T. B. J. and the Poetry of Refusal," *CelfanR,* 2, 3 (May 1983), 34–36; Tenkoul, A., *Littérature marocaine d'écriture française* (1985), 100–25; Déjeux, J., "T. B. J., romancier, poète et essayiste marocain," *Lettres & Cultures de Langue Française,* 12 (1987), 1–5; Mouzouni, L., *Le roman marocain de langue française* (1987), 108–29; Déjeux, J., "Réception critique de *La nuit sacrée* de T. B. J. dans la presse européenne," *Sindbad* (Rabat), 67 (1988), 22–29; Silva, E. R. da, "T. B. J.: Identité arabe/ expression française," *PFr,* 34 (1989), 63–71; Taleb-Khyar, M. B., "T. B. J. and *The Water's Bride:* Introductory Notes," *Callaloo,* 13, 3 (Summer 1990), 396–425; Abdel-Jaouad, H., "Sacrilegious Discourse," *Middle East Report,* 163 (Mar.–Apr. 1990), 34–36; Rosen, M., "Interview—A Conversation with T. B. J.: Toward a World Literature?," *Middle East Report,* 163 (Mar.–Apr. 1990), 30–33; Cazenave, O., "Gender, Age, and Narrative Transformations in *L'enfant de sable* by T. B. J.," *FR,* 64, 3 (Feb. 1991), 437–50; Erickson, J. D., "Writing Double: Politics and the African Narrative of French Expression," *StTCL,* 15, 1 (Winter 1991), 101–22; Revillon, N., "*L'enfant endormi:* Une lecture de *La prière de l'absent* de T. B. J.," *Itinéraires et Contacts de Culture,* 14 (1991), 90–98; Sellin, E., "Signes migrateurs: Approche transculturelle d'une lecture de la littérature maghrébine d'écriture française," *Itinéraires et Contacts de Culture,* 14 (1991), 42–50

ERIC SELLIN

BERGE, H(ans) C(ornelius) TEN

Dutch poet, prose writer, and translator, b. 24 Dec. 1938, Alkmar

In the 1960s and 1970s T. B. lived in Amsterdam, where he studied Spanish; in 1979 he moved to Zutphen where he still lives as a lecturer at the Visual Arts Academy in nearby Arnhem. He has traveled extensively in central Europe and in North and Central America. These journeys have stimulated his strong ethnological interests, which he developed largely through self-study.

T. B. made his debut as a poet in 1964. His first three collections, reprinted together in *Gedichten* (1969; poems), employ a bare, halting diction, a language full of discontinuities and pared down to essentials, so as to evoke powerful emotions while avoiding the risk of sentimentality. The poems, usually grouped into cycles, range widely in scope and theme and incorporate numerous literary and historical references, from Antarctic expeditions to medieval fairs and the Spanish invasion of Mexico seen through the eyes of the vanquished. Many of T. B.'s early poems use montage techniques to build multilayered narrative sequences in which different viewpoints and voices are juxtaposed; the technique derived from Ezra Pound (q.v.), some of whose *Cantos* T. B. also translated into Dutch (1970).

Since the 1970s T. B.'s poetic diction has become more fluent and melodious, and more intent on combining innovative and traditional elements. *Va-banque* (1977; all or nothing) explores the notion of writing as a game of chance, involving play, risk, and high stakes. The volume *Nieuwe gedichten* (1981; new poems) counterpoints overtly political poems and autobiographical pieces in which the boundaries between fact and fiction are skillfully obscured. Impressive in their epic sombreness are the *Texaanse elegieën* (1983; Texan elegies), a symbolic descent into the underworld of the 20th c. The *Liederen van angst en vertwijfeling* (1988; songs of anguish and despair) revolve around meditations on art and on death, the latter mostly in a Mexican setting. *Overgangsriten* (1992; rites of passage), however, strikes a much more positive chord.

The openness to the outside world which much of T. B.'s poetry has consistently displayed in its method and thematic range is confirmed in a long series of literary and ethnological translations. Several among these have visible traces in T. B.'s original poetry and prose. They include renderings of contemporary poets—Kenneth White (b. 1936), Christopher Middleton (b. 1926), Mark Strand, and Gunnar Ekelöf (qq.v)—but also versions of texts outside the Western tradition, such as Japanese Nō plays and Aztec sacral and secular hymns. His work in the ethnological field culminated in a three-volume annotated collection of myths and fables of North American Indians, Eskimo, and Siberian peoples.

T. B.'s early stories show the hand of the poet in their meticulous wording, visual imagery, and imaginative power. His protagonists are typically émigrés, travelers with an uncertain destination, rootless wanderers in some undefined border region who have at best a tenuous grip on reality and on themselves.

The novel *Een geval van verbeelding* (1970; a case of delusion), which was subsequently reissued in revised form as the two interlinked novellas *Zelfportret met witte muts* (1985; self-portrait with a white woolen hat) and *Matglas* (1982; frosted glass), is set among Polish émigrés in western Europe and contrasts the cautious, guarded life-style of Stefan K., a doctor, with the high-risk existence of the girl Hannele. The book's elusive style, however, prevents a factual reconstruction of the denouement. T. B.'s most ambitious novel to date, *Het geheim van een opgewekt humeur* (1986; the secret of a cheerful mood), interweaves the modern story of a three-cornered relationship with a semihistorical account of a case of incest in 16th-c. Mexico and myths derived from Ovid's *Metamorphoses*. The various narrative strands, all embedded one into the other, contain subtle parallels and inversions, focusing on the notion of incest and hence on the opposition between nature and culture.

T. B.'s literary oeuvre has been described in terms of assemblage, the product of a sophisticated *bricoleur,* a "do-it-yourselfer," who combines lyrical with intellectual and critical impulses, a consciously international outlook, and an anthropological interest with an exceptionally fine sense of language. But the imaginative worlds that T. B. builds, whether in prose or in verse, consistently deal with discontinuities, ruptures, and uncertainties. In their radical questioning of our cultural and ideological assumptions they are profoundly unsettling.

FURTHER WORKS: *Poolsneeuw* (1964); *Swartkrans* (1966); *Personages* (1967); *Canaletto en andere verhalen* (1969); *De witte sjamaan* (1973); *Een schrijver als grenskozak* (1977); *Het meisje met de korte vlechten* (1977); *De beren van Churchill* (1978); *Levenstekens en doodssinjalen* (1980); *De mannenschrik* (1984); *Mythen en fabels van noordelijke volken* (3 vols., 1987); *De verdediging van de poëzie* (1988); *Een Italiaan in Zutphen* (1990). FURTHER VOLUME IN ENGLISH: *The White Shaman, Selected Poems* (1991)

BIBLIOGRAPHY: De Moor, W., "Anonymous Restless Forms: The Dutch Writer, T. B.," *BA,* 47, 2 (Spring 1973), 266–72; *T. B. Informatie* (1987); special T. B. issue, *Yang* (1988); Hermans, T., "T. B. Transmontanus: wat doen de feiten ertoe als er fiktie bestaat?," *OnsE,* 32, 4 (Sept.–Oct. 1989), 545–53; Hermans, T., "Translation and the Indirect Route: An Approximation to H. C. T. B.'s Disparate Worlds," in Westerweel, B., and T. D'haen, eds., *Something Understood: Studies in Anglo-Dutch Literary Translation* (1990), 305–17

THEO HERMANS

BERGER, Thomas

American novelist, short-story writer, and dramatist, b. 20 July 1924, Cincinnati, Ohio

B. served in the U.S. Army for three years (1943–1946), after which he completed his B.A. with honors at the University of Cincinnati in 1948. He worked as a librarian at the Rand School of Social Science (1948–1951) and pursued graduate study at Columbia University from 1950 to 1951. B. was a staff member of the *New York Times* (1951–1952), served as associate editor of *Popular Science Monthly* (1952–1953), and wrote film criticism for *Esquire* (1972–1973). He has been distinguished visiting professor at Southampton College (now the Southampton Campus of Long Island University), New York (1975–1976), lecturer at Yale University (1981–1982), and Regents' lecturer at the University of California, Davis (1982). His awards and honors include a Dial fellowship (1962); the Western Heritage Award (1965) and the Richard and Hinda Rosenthal Award, National Institute of Arts and Letters (1965), both for *Little Big Man* (1964); the Ohioana Book Award (1982) for *Reinhart's Women* (1981); and a Pulitzer Prize nomination (1984) for *The Feud* (1983).

B. has published seventeen novels, two plays, and numerous short stories. The novels *Crazy in Berlin* (1958), *Reinhart in Love* (1962), *Vital Parts* (1970), and *Reinhart's Women* follow the main character, Carlo Reinhart, from his days as a young G.I. during World War II through middle age in the 1970s. Two of B.'s novels, *Little Big Man,* set among the Cheyennes in the American Old West, and *Neighbors* (1981), a dark, Beckett-like tale, have been made into films, released in 1970 and 1981 respectively.

B.'s work is always carefully researched, but his methods, he claims, are not systematic in a scholarly sort of way—he reads extensively in the areas that interest him, taking very few notes, and then allows his imagination to take hold, transmuting "facts" into the truths of his fiction. B. is a master of satire and myth bashing, but that is perhaps the limit of generalizing possible in discussing his work. His range is enormous and each work must be judged on its own terms. Risky, too, is any attempt to categorize B.'s novels too strictly by genre, although B. has commented that his "conscious intention is always to write as conventional an example" of the genre within which he is working, "to celebrate it, to identify and applaud its glories." Thus *Regiment of Women* (1973) seems an experiment in science fiction, while *Who Is Teddy Villanova?* (1977) might be called a detective novel. And with his retelling of the legend of the Knights of the Round Table, B. enters the realm of fantasy/mythology in *Arthur Rex* (1978).

Many critics have described B.'s work as scathing social commentary, but B. says he is not so much interested in parodying social ills as he is in

exploring the creative possibilities of language. Nor does B. think of himself as a writer of comedy, and he asserts that he is rarely if ever consciously trying to be funny. Instead he feels that "my way of looking at things, which is not humorless, no doubt tends to mislead the careless." And while B. does not suggest that he is "in the same league as the author of *Ein Hungerkünstler,*" much of his work is comic in the sense that Franz Kafka's (q.v.) work can be said to be comic. The nightmare is real, and there is nothing to do but laugh. And, indeed, it is Kafka's lesson—that the seemingly mundane can suddenly turn sinister—that much of B.'s prose reexamines and reshapes. Language can blur, can obscure reality, but it also presents and represents reality. B.'s rhetoric *is* the reality, and when the action, person, or concept being scrutinized is viewed from another angle, reality shifts just as quickly as perception does.

The breadth, depth, and variety of B.'s visions along with his exciting manipulation of the English language through which he presents them make him one of the most challenging writers working in the U.S.

FURTHER WORKS: *Killing Time* (1967); *Other People* (1970); *Sneaky People* (1975); *Granted Wishes* (1984); *Nowhere* (1985); *Being Invisible* (1987); *The Houseguest* (1988); *The Burglars* (1988); *Changing the Past* (1989); *Meeting Evil* (1992)

BIBLIOGRAPHY: Schickel, R., "Bitter Comedy," *Commentary,* 50, 1 (July 1970), 76–80; Romano, J., "Camelot and All That," *NYTBR,* 12 Nov. 1978, 3, 62; Schickel, R., "Interviewing T. B.," *NYTBR,* 6 Apr. 1980, 1, 21–22; Landon, B., *T. B.* (1989); Landon, B., "The Measure of *Little Big Man,*" *SAF,* 17, 2 (Autumn 1989), 131–42

MARGARET D. SULLIVAN

BETJEMAN, Sir John

British poet, b. 28 Aug. 1906, London; d. 19 May 1984, Trebetherick, Cornwall

B., perhaps the most popular of all 20th-c. British poets, is celebrated for his light, almost comic, and often satiric depictions of England's recent past. B.'s father was a prosperous London businessman, and the young B. grew up in an affluent London suburb. He was sent to a private preparatory school where T. S. Eliot (q.v.) was one of his teachers. B. attended Magdalen College, Oxford, in 1925, where he was mentored by C. M. Bowram (1898–1971) and tutored by C. S. Lewis (q.v.). While at Magdalen, B. met Evelyn Waugh (q.v.) who became his lifelong friend. Even with such a solid scholastic foundation, B. was not a serious student, and he left Oxford in 1928 with no degree after failing his divinity examination. While at the university, B. had developed his interest in English architecture into a considerable knowledge on the subject, and after a year of teaching he took a position as assistant editor of the *Architecture Review* in 1931.

Soon after taking this position, B. published his first collection of poetry, *Mount Zion* (1931). The volume met with moderate sales, and four more collections were published over the next seventeen years. But B.'s first major success was the publication of his *Collected Poems* (1958). This collection was a best-seller and drew enthusiastic response from readers and critics alike. The poems were performed on the radio in a regular BBC series of readings, serialized in the *London Daily Mail,* and enthusiastically endorsed by the royal family, Princess Margret in particular. In 1960 the poetic autobiography *Summoned by Bells* was published, followed by four more collections, *High and Low* (1966), *A Nip in the Air* (1974), *Church Poems* (1981), and *Uncollected Poems* (1982). All of these volumes met with considerable success, and B.'s fame as a poet continued to grow. In 1969 he was knighted, and in 1972 he succeeded Cecil Day Lewis (q.v.) as poet laureate of England.

Paralleling his career as a poet is B.'s career as an architectural historian of some note. He is both highly regarded and prolifically published in this field. B. was the editor of several of the *Collins Guides* of England, and the author of numerous articles and several volumes of architectural history. His nonfiction publications include *Ghastly Good Taste* (1933), *First and Last Loves* (1952), and *English Churches* (1964, with Basil Clarke).

B.'s poetry is marked by his extremely vivid, solid depiction of the very real landscape of modern England. B.'s subjects are drawn from the everyday experience of British life. He writes in conventional forms and meters, and his language is very open and accessible. His tone is most often light though often nostalgic. His poetry examines the conjunction of the comic and the tragic that is symptomatic of the conservative individual in rapidly changing modern society. B. invokes images of churches, houses, and markets as they exist only in memory, and likewise depicts the structures of social class and Anglicanism as they once were or as they once seemed in childhood. It is through this template of the past that B. views the modern world, his active nostalgia creating a ritual of reassurance. That he has struck a familiar cord is evidenced by his poetry's tremendous popular success. This unprecedented popularity has remained B.'s singular accomplishment.

FURTHER WORKS: *Continual Dew* (1937); *An Oxford University Chest* (1938); *Antiquarian Prejudice* (1939); *Old Lights for New Chancels* (1940); *John Piper* (1944); *New Bats in Old Belfries* (1945); *Slick but Not Streamlined* (1947); *A Few Late Chrysanthemums* (1954); *Poems In the Porch* (1954); *A Ring of Bells* (1962); *The Best of B.* (1978); *Collected Poems* (4th ed., 1979); *Uncollected Poems* (1982)

BIBLIOGRAPHY: Stanford, D., *J. B.: A Study* (1961); Press, J., *B.* (1974); Stapleton, M., *B.: A Bibliography of Writings by and about Him* (1974); Taylor-Martin, P., *J. B.: His Life and Work* (1983); Hillier, B., *Young B.* (1988)

ROBERT GREENUP

BICHSEL, Peter

Swiss short-story writer, novelist, essayist, and journalist (writing in German), b. 24 Mar. 1935, Luzern

B. is one of the best-known contemporary Swiss fiction writers and essayists. Born in Luzern, B. was raised in Olten, where he passed a quiet and introspective childhood. Following pedagogical studies in Solothurn, B. taught at an elementary school in Zuchwil (1957–1968). Increasingly involved in literary activity, B. participated in the Literary Colloquium in West Berlin (1963), and in 1965 soared to prominence after the publication of his *Frau Blum* collection of stories. Apart from his work as a writer of fiction, B. is an influential columnist whose numerous articles on literary and cultural topics have appeared in a variety of newspapers. B. has also taught and lectured extensively abroad. He is married and resides in Bellach.

B.'s rise to eminence was occasioned by the appearance of his first major work, *Eigentlich möchte Frau Blum den Milchmann kennenlernen* (1964; *And Really Frau Blum Would Very Much Like to Meet the Milkman,* 1968), a group of twenty-one miniatures focusing on the commonplace activities of the ordinary middle-class characters. Unable to establish genuine human contact with others, and vaguely aware of a missing dimension in their lives, B.'s essentially passive figures seem ossified in the loneliness and isolation of daily routine.

Evident in a subsequent volume of stories, *Kindergeschichten* (1969; *Stories for Children,* 1971), is B.'s fascination with the individual's place in a world of "dead" knowledge that has lost its power to compel human belief and acceptance. Probably the best known of these stories is "Ein Tisch ist ein Tisch" ("A Table Is a Table"), in which an old man, hoping to create for himself a fresh world of sensory experience, gives new names to familiar objects only to end in the utter frustration of linguistic isolation.

B.'s stories reveal a narrative starkness approaching that of the fairy tale. Far from being traditional heroes, his sparsely drawn characters often resemble marionettes in their apparent simplicity. Notably absent in his work is an emphasis on the social, sexual, and philosophical problems frequently explored by other writers. B.'s approach to the story is essentially that of the unspoken. In contrast to earlier practitioners of short fiction, B. is reluctant to move into the clear light of day the problems affecting the average *petit bourgeois*. His is the art of the intimation, and of the narrative gap. Focusing on the concrete, his sentences are unfailingly simple in structure and diction, and without rhetorical flourish.

Apart from his contributions to the Swiss short story, B. is also known as a novelist, essayist, newspaper columnist, and sometime radio commentator. In the novel *Die Jahreszeiten* (1967; the seasons) B. reveals another of his auctorial preoccupations: the writer's relationship to the process of writing, and the unavoidable contrasts and contradictions implicit in that relationship. An account of a man's frustrating attempt at writing a novel, *Die Jahreszeiten* resembles an antinovel in its questioning of the traditional values and assumptions of fiction. B.'s essays embrace a broad range of literary, political, and cultural topics, and are marked by pithiness, economy, and a straightforward clarity of style. *Des Schweizers Schweiz* (1969; the Switzer's Switzerland), his earliest volume of essays, evoked widespread discussion and controversy with its unambiguous critique of contemporary Swiss culture. B. has also made a number of radio commentaries and addresses, and several of his works have been adapted for presentation on radio and television.

B.'s current reputation rests above all on his standing as a short-story writer of considerable talent. Early in his career the winner of the prestigious Prize of Group 47 (1965), B. is the holder of many additional literary awards and distinctions. Widely read both at home and abroad, B.'s best-known stories have been translated into numerous foreign languages. Although B.'s approach to fiction has often sparked critical controversy, there remains a strong consensus for his position as a leading writer of his generation.

FURTHER WORKS: *Versuche über Gino* (1960); *Das Gästehaus* (1965, with Walter Höllerer, et al.); *Geschichten zur falschen Zeit* (1979); *Der Leser, das Erzählen* (1982); *Schulmeistereien* (1985); *Der*

Busant; von Trinkern, Polizisten und der schönen Magelone (1985); *Irgendwo anderswo; Kolumnen, 1980–1985* (1986); *Im Gegenteil; Kolumnen, 1986– 1990* (1990)

BIBLIOGRAPHY: Bucher, W., and G. Ammann, *Schweizer Schriftsteller im Gespräch* (1970), Vol. 1, 13–47; Peukert, K., *Die Genese des Wissens in P. B.'s "Kindergeschichten"* (1973); Sherry, C., "Translating P. B.: Some Remarks," *Dimension,* 10 (1977), 66–73; Sell, R., "Stagnation und Aufbruch in B.s *Milchmann- und Kindergeschichten," ABnG,* 9 (1979), 255–73; Bänziger, H., *P. B.: Weg und Werk* (1984); Hoven, H., ed., *P. B.: Auskunft für Leser* (1984); Bohm, A., "Narratives for a Post-Heroic Age: P. B.'s Short Prose," *UDR,* 19, 2 (Summer 1988), 55–68; Ward, D., "A Swiss Author and His Languages: An Interview with P. B.," *Monatshefte,* 80, 1 (Spring 1988), 9–21

MICHAEL V. WILLIAMS

BIERCE, Ambrose

American short-story writer, journalist, and poet, b. 24 June 1842, Horse Cave, Ohio; d. 11 Jan. 1914, Ojinaga, Mexico

The tenth of thirteen children, B. had a varied life and a controversial career as a writer. While a teenager, B. lived on a farm in northern Indiana and worked as a printer's assistant on *The Northern Indianan,* an antislavery paper. Beyond high school, his only formal education was a year (1859) at the Kentucky Military Institute. With the outbreak of the Civil War, B. enlisted in the Ninth Indiana Infantry. Subsequently commissioned, he served as topographical officer on General William B. Hazen's staff and fought in several battles including the one that later provided the setting for "Chickamauga" (1889), one of his best stories.

After the Civil War, General Hazen recruited B. as engineering attaché on an inspection tour of military posts in the Montana Territory, which eventually concluded in San Francisco, where B. found employment at the U.S. Sub-Treasury and continued to educate himself. In 1867 B. was first published in the *Californian* and in the following year in *The Golden Era* and the *News Letter.* When he became editor of the *News Letter* in 1868, he began to write "The Town Crier" column, which was soon recognized in New York and London for its acerbic wit and keen satire. In 1871 *The Overland Monthly* published "The Haunted Valley," his first story to appear in print. B. and his new wife moved to England in 1872, where he wrote and contributed to *Fun* and *Figaro*. Returning after three years to San Francisco, B. began, by 1887, to write for William Randolph Hearst's *San Francisco Examiner*. Although often resigning from Hearst's employ, B. worked more or less regularly for the publisher until 1909, when he resigned from *Cosmopolitan*. From 1900 to 1913, B. lived and worked mainly in Washington; late in 1913, at the age of seventy-one, B. departed Washington for a long-planned trip through Mexico to South America. Although the date and place of his death are uncertain, all available evidence indicates that he was killed on 11 January 1914, during the battle of Ojinaga in Mexico.

B. has always been a controversial figure, in person and in his works. During the 1890s, he was best known for his searing newspaper columns; many public figures and venerable institutions came under his severe scrutiny. It is difficult to locate B. in a period or movement, however, because he consistently put himself at odds with the views and values of his time. During the 20th c. he has been best known for his short stories, which have continued to hold a popular audience.

Even though he included the subconscious as a primary factor in many of his best stories, B. thought of himself as a "true realist": "The test of truth is Reason," he wrote, "not Faith." Presumably differentiating his own practice from that of others, he wrote elsewhere that "realism" is "the art of depicting nature as it is seen by toads." He frequently took exception to the work of William Dean Howells (1837–1920), whom he referred to as "Miss Nancy" Howells. In London B. acquired the sobriquet "Bitter Bierce"; while others wrote about utopias, he described dystopias. His satires are in the tradition of Rabelais, La Rochefoucauld, Swift, and Voltaire, all authors he studied. In addition to his challenging experiences in the Civil War, Stoicism was a major influence on his philosophical outlook, as one might expect of the son of Marcus Aurelius Bierce and of the nephew of Lucius Verus Bierce, who published a book on Stoicism in 1855. B. himself especially praised Epictetus.

The 1890s saw the publication of most of B.'s major volumes. His books published before this date bore various pseudonyms. A collection of stories, *Tales of Soldiers and Civilians* (pub. in England as *In the Midst of Life*, the title by which it is now known), appeared in 1892. In collaboration with Dr. Gustav A. Danziger, a dentist and sometime translator, B. published an adaptation of Richard Voss's *Der Mönch von Berchtesgaden* under the title *The Monk and the Hangman's Daughter*, which appeared first serially in the *Examiner* (1891), and in book form the next year. Also in 1892, B. published *Black Beetles in Am-*

ber, a gathering of his satirical verse. Another collection of short stories, published in 1893, bore the title *Can Such Things Be?* In 1881 B. began including items in a weekly newspaper column that he gathered in *The Cynic's Word Book* (1906), which title was forced upon him, he claimed, by the times and his publisher. When he edited his twelve-volume *Collected Works* (1909–1912), however, he changed the title of this work to *The Devil's Dictionary* (1911).

Although popularly known as "bitter" (as noted), "wicked," and "devilish," B. was, in fact, humane, generous, and compassionate. Clearly, B.'s work influenced Kate Chopin (1851–1904) and Stephen Crane (1871–1900). B. was profoundly interested in the ways faulty perception and communication troubled the lives of humans. Repeatedly his stories ask: Is a human being a rational creature? "Chickamauga" and "An Occurrence at Owl Creek Bridge" (1890), probably his best-known stories, turn on startling ironies about the ability of human beings to sort out reality, both physical and psychological. Because of these qualities in his fiction, B. has been "discovered" again, this time by reader-response theorists and semiologists. He has also attracted international interest among creative artists. Like Poe, he has been popular in France. Robert Enrico's *Au cœur de la vie* (1962) is a three-part film based on "Chickamauga," "An Occurrence at Owl Creek Bridge," and "The Mocking-Bird" (1891). In South America, toward which he was traveling when he disappeared at Ojinaga, B. has influenced Carlos Fuentes, Jorge Luis Borges, and Julio Cortázar (qq.v.). Japanese author Ryñosuke Akutagawa (q.v.) has also expressed indebtedness to B.

Until we have a comprehensive scholarly assessment of B.'s voluminous work (he included only about a third of his journalism in his *Collected Works),* it will be difficult to determine his rank and role in literature. In the interim, however, his fiction—in some ways surrealistic and anticipating modern science fiction—will continue to engage the common reader.

FURTHER WORKS: *The Fiend's Delight* (1873, pseud. Dod Grile); *Nuggets and Dust* (1873, pseud. Dod Grile); *Cobwebs from an Empty Skull* (1874, pseud. Dod Grile); *The Dance of Death* (1877, pseud. William Herman); *The Dance of Life: An Answer to The Dance of Death* (1877, pseud. Mrs. J. Milton Bowers); *Fantastic Fables* (1899); *Shapes of Clay* (1903); *A Son of the Gods and a Horseman in the Sky* (1907); *The Shadow on the Dial and Other Essays* (1909); *The Letters of A. B.* (1922)

BIBLIOGRAPHY: McWilliams, C., *A. B.: A Biography* (1929); Fatout, P., *A. B.: The Devil's Lex-*

icographer (1951); Fatout, P., *A. B. and the Black Hills* (1956); Woodruff, S. C., *The Short Stories of A. B.: A Study in Polarity* (1964); Grenander, M. E., *A. B.* (1971); Davidson, C. N., ed., *Critical Essays on A. B.* (1982); Davidson, C. N., *The Experimental Fictions of A. B.* (1984); Saunders, R., *A. B.: The Making of a Misanthrope* (1984)

ARTHUR B. COFFIN

BLANDIANA, Ana

(pseud. of Otilia-Valeria Coman) Romanian poet, translator, and essayist, b. 25 Mar. 1942, Timişoara

Born in Timişoara, southwestern Romania, B. attended high school in Oradea and studied for a degree in philology at the University of Cluj. After graduation (1967), she served as poetry editor for *Viaţa Românească* and *Amfiteatru.* In 1975 she moved to a position as librarian at the Institute of Fine Arts in Bucharest, a job which she later gave up to work as a free-lance writer, publishing poetry and two regular columns in *Contemporanul* and *România literară.* In the mid-1980s B. was banned from all Romanian publications because of her dissident poems. An active participant in the December 1989 uprising against Ceauşescu's dictatorial régime, B. was elected to the newly constituted Council of the National Salvation Front, but resigned from it as soon as its neocommunist leanings became apparent. B. is now a major rallying figure in the prodemocratic opposition.

Though her poems appeared in *Tribuna* from Cluj as early as 1959, B. could not publish her first volume until 1964, after the process of de-Stalinization had started. *Persoana întîia plural* (first person plural) surprised critics with its fresh, uninhibited treatment of subjective emotion and exuberant imagery. Her second volume, *Călcîiul vulnerabil* (1967; the vulnerable heel), toned down the youthful rhetoric, introducing a more reflexive, self-questioning style that was to become B.'s distinctive feature. By the end of the decade, B. was the acknowledged leader of a group of women poets who had made essential contributions to the "poetic revival of the 1960s." While B. has never allowed herself to be categorized as a "woman poet" ("poetry, like truth, like freedom, cannot be categorized into great and small, good and bad, male and female"), her poetry balanced from the start existential and sociocultural concerns, an imaginative exploration of individual experience with an emphasis on broader sociophilosophical issues such as women's lot and experience.

B.'s subsequent volumes of verse, *A treia taină* (1970; the third enigma), *Cincizeci de poeme* (1970;

fifty poems), *Octombrie, noiembrie, decembrie* (1972; October, November, December), and *Poezii* (1974; poems), deepened and darkened this twofold concern. Very little of B.'s earlier expansive rhetoric survived in these poems: The reflection is internalized or impersonal—the motifs of sleep, silence, inner reflection predominate—the line is terse and nervous, devoid of "ornaments." Sentimentality is here refused in favor of an austere, detached mapping of essentials; poetry is no longer a transcription of emotional states, but an intense scrutiny of life, an act of skeptical cognition. Feminine themes are present—maternity, feminine sexuality, woman's spiritual needs—but they are broached from a transpersonal perspective that allows important moral and philosophical questions to be asked. The main emphasis is on cosmic "spending," on existential and poetic dissipation. And yet B.'s vision remains hopefully dialectic, highlighting alternatives, redefining the boundaries between nature and spirit, love and death, individual desire and norm. The competing terms are often described by striking oxymorons: Death is "clear," despair is "happy" and "gentle," light is "ferocious," darkness is "clean" and "tender," "loneliness is a happy town." B.'s deliberately ambivalent, antipoetic style calls into question traditional literary discourse, its problematic claims to truth. Words become the poet's necessary "adversaries" in a lucid dialogue about the limitations of art.

B.'s recent poems continue to reevaluate critically the relation of literature to existential and social truth. *Somnul din somn* (1977; the sleep in sleep), *Ora de nisip* (1983; *The Hour of Sand,* 1990), and *Stea de pradă* (1985; predatory star) are underwritten by a sterner moral and metaphysical perspective, but also by a clearer understanding of a time of great personal and national crisis. B.'s sparse, thinly veiled imagery denounces collective compromises as in the famous lines that got an entire editorial board fired after their publication: "I believe we are vegetal people / How otherwise to account for this compliant / Shedding of our leaves. . . ." By and large, B.'s poetic evolution parallels the broader course of contemporary Romanian poetry: expansive and lyrical in the early 1960s; philosophically skeptical and self-ironic in the 1970s; politically engaged and questioning in the 1980s.

B.'s prose reflections published over the years in two short columns have been collected in *Calitatea de martor* (1970; rev. 2nd ed., 1972; the mark of a witness) and *Eu scriu, tu scrii, el, ea scrie* (1976; I write, you write, he, she writes). These pages of an ongoing "antidiary" gloss with aphoristic crispness Romania's recent cultural history, exposing its social and moral faults. B.'s gift for sharp observation and controversy is also reflected in *Convorbiri subiective* (1971; subjective dialogues) and *O discuţie la masa tăcerii şi alte convorbiri subiective* (1976; a discussion around the silent table and other subjective colloquies)—two collections of spirited interviews coauthored with her husband, Romulus Rusan (b. 1935).

FURTHER WORKS: *Cele patru anotimpuri* (1977); *Cea mai frumoasă dintre lumile posibile* (1978); *Intîmplări din grădina mea* (1980); *Proiecte de trecut; Proze* (1982). FURTHER VOLUMES IN ENGLISH: *Poeme/Poems* (1982); *Don't Be Afraid of Me: Collected Poems* (1985); *Silent Voices* (1986)

BIBLIOGRAPHY: Micu, D., Preface to *Poeme/Poems* (1982), 9–18; Buduca, I., "La qualité de poète: A. B.," *CREL*, 4 (1983), 87–91; Adcock, F., Introduction to *Silent Voices* (1986), 10–14; Jay, P., and A. Cristofovici, Preface to *The Hour of Sand* (1990), 6–9; Chamberlain, L., "Mysteries and Visions," *TLS*, 19–25 Jan. 1990, 59

MARCEL CORNIS-POPE

BLATTER, Silvio
Swiss novelist and short-story writer (writing in German), b. 25 Jan. 1946, Bremgarten

B. studied to be an elementary-school teacher and taught for six years in Aarau. He then worked at various jobs in industry and studied at the University of Zurich. For a short time he directed radio plays for Swiss Radio. Since 1976 he has devoted himself entirely to his writing. He has won numerous literary awards, including the Conrad Ferdinand Meyer Prize (1974), and in 1984 was elected president of the German-Swiss P.E.N. Club. He lives in Zurich.

B.'s work portrays the everyday life of the Swiss in microscopic detail and examines the role that nature, alienation, and homeland play in the Swiss mentality. His works are often socially committed, and he frequently experiments with narrative techniques.

B.'s first major work, *Schaltfehler* (1971; switching error), examines the dehumanizing effect that piecework has on fourteen workers in a large factory. He also explores the world of work in his long story *Genormte tage, verschüttete zeit* (1976; conformist days, spilled time). Here he shows how demeaning, monotonous work has destroyed even the private life of the protagonist, Stöhr. In both cases B. uses nonconventional techniques to force his readers to disengage themselves from the story and reflect on its contents.

B. continues this duality of experimental narrative coupled with contemporary social problems

in other works as well. *Mary Long* (1973; title in English) is a lengthy discourse on the possibilities of prose fiction combined with an exploration of Swiss identity; *Love Me Tender* (1980; title in English) examines the world of sports through a variety of perspectives; and *Die schneefalle* (1981; the snow trap) investigates the debilitating influence of the police apparatus and the mass media in contemporary society and is constructed in a mazelike fashion so that the reader must participate in deciphering the fragments.

B.'s magnum opus to date is a trilogy set in the Freiamt, a Catholic region in the predominantly Protestant canton of Aarau, which is located near Zurich: *Zunehmendes heimweh* (1978; increasing homesickness), *Kein schöner land* (1983; no more beautiful country), and *Das sanfte gesetz* (1988; the gentle law). These novels describe and examine the lives of a number of individuals in and around the fictive Villinger family, who live in B.'s hometown of Bremgarten. All of the characters' hopes, dreams, thoughts, and actions are interwoven with each other in montage fashion to form a gigantic pastiche of Swiss society. The present is often related to the past, and the characters seem to be constantly searching for their own identity within their regional and national frameworks. B. thus critically investigates the whole concept of what it means to be Swiss, incorporating a number of factors, including the influence of religion, nature, and tradition.

Most contemporary Swiss authors investigate in one way or another the phenomenon of Switzerland in their works, and B. is at the foreground of this movement. His piercing observations and his committed stance together with his intriguing stylistic innovations make him one of the leading young authors in the German-speaking world.

FURTHER WORKS: *Brände kommen unerwartet* (1968); *Eine wohnung im erdgeschoß* (1970); *Nur der könig trägt bart* (1973); *Flucht und tod des Daniel Zoff* (1974); *Wassermann* (1986); *Das blaue haus* (1990)

BIBLIOGRAPHY: Böll, H., "Aussichten eines Zwanzigjährigen," *Der Spiegel*, 25 Sept. 1978, 220–21; Bernasconi, C., "Auf dem Weg zum Meistererzähler," *Börsenblatt*, 43, 7 (1987), 236–41; Ester, H., "Heimat und Identität im Werk S. Bs," in Acker, R., and M. Burkhard, eds., *Blick auf die Schweiz* (1987), 61–79

ROBERT ACKER

BLOOM, Harold
American literary critic, b. 11 July 1930, Bronx, N.Y.

B. is one of the most influential critics of this century. Born in The Bronx, New York, to a working-class family, he attended Cornell University and received his Ph.D. from Yale University in 1955. He is the author of eighteen books ranging from studies of romantic poetry to an important redefinition of influence, and from American poetry to Sigmund Freud (q.v.), cabala and the Bible. As general editor for Chelsea House's Modern Critical Views and other series, he has written over five-hundred introductions that together constitute sharp and precise illuminations of a vast range of writers in the Western tradition. Among his many distinctions and awards are NEH and Guggenheim fellowships and a MacArthur grant. In 1987 he was the Charles Eliot Norton Professor of Poetry at Harvard. He is Sterling Professor of the Humanities at Yale and Berg Professor of English at New York University.

A prolific critic best known for his theoretical works on influence, B. began his career with an attack on New Critical methods of reading whose effect was to neglect romantic poetry. New Criticism's (q.v.) emphasis on form, irony, resolution, closure, and a poem frozen in space was inadequate to the specific energies of the romantic poem, which insisted on the breaking of form, on the poem as a fragment of a greater original vision, and on time as a disruption of space. Bloom's first three books—*Shelley's Mythmaking* (1959), *The Visionary Company* (1961), and *Blake's Apocalypse* (1963)—reopened the study of romantic poems as texts aware of their fragmentary status and of an imaginative vision that exceeded their rhetoric.

B.'s importance as a critic is due in large part to his tetralogy on influence: *The Anxiety of Influence* (1973), *A Map of Misreading* (1975), *Kabbalah and Criticism* (1975), and *Poetry and Repression* (1976). In these four books B. reverses the traditional notion of influence as a straightforward "handing over" and articulates a theory of tradition as a battleground in which each poet must confront and overcome the precursor poet in order to make a space for himself in the tradition. The poet's condition can be defined as "belated," and each successive poet, coming ever later upon the scene of poetry, must struggle to turn his belatedness into earliness. Earliness for B. constitutes originality, which stands in a peculiar alignment with difficulty. Each poet, in the process of overcoming the precursor, increases the difficulty of poetic tradition, so that there is an uneasy relationship between difficulty and strength.

The distinction between strong and weak poets is crucial to B.'s theory. Strong poets shape the tradition and in turn are the field of battle for those who come later; weak poets are forgettable, despite whatever political or cultural considerations

might be brought to bear on their work. B. is uncompromising on the question of poetic strength, and rewrites the history of tradition as a history of influence-relations, of overturning and overcoming.

Because tradition is overcrowded and space difficult to achieve, influence in its traditional sense stands in opposition to originality. To be original is to break with the past in a moment of freedom. B. is careful to point out, however, that a poem is "an achieved anxiety." Freedom lies in the process of writing the poem, while the finished text is always a failure of that original vision. In this respect, his theory of influence recovers the high romantic notion of the fragment. The fragment is a fact of poetic life, and anxiety its most telling symptom and driving force.

Through this tetralogy and the seven books that follow, B. articulates and refines the "revisionary ratios" by which influence relations can be mapped. The peculiar effect of a poem whose power and originality turn belatedness into earliness is that it produces the illusion that the later poet has influenced the earlier one. The Greek name B. assigns to this phenomenon in *The Anxiety of Influence* is *apophrades,* the return of the dead, but under conditions in which the latecomer leaves the house open to the ghosts, without fear of silence or suppression. In *Wallace Stevens: The Poems of Our Climate* (1976) B. extends these ratios to construct a theory of "poetic crossings" by which the poet becomes and knows himself to be a poet. In a turn from British romantic poetry to American poetry, B. continues his studies of the high romantic tradition, canonizing Stevens (q.v.) as the heir of a tradition haunted by its very strength.

A critic's canonization of a poet falls well within the purview of influence-relations that B. studies. Because the meaning of a poem wanders between poems, or as B. says, "the meaning of a poem is that there is, or rather was, another poem," criticism plays an important role in articulating that wandering. What B. calls for as essential to criticism is a "diachronic rhetoric," which he himself provides: a way of reading poems that will take into account the powerful effect of time and loss.

B.'s wide-ranging work on influence and on the Western canon draws writers into uncommon and original relations. Two such examples are Freud and cabala. Freud provides B. with the notion of a text as a living psyche, driven by desire toward an end it cannot possibly achieve and propelled into sublime moments by repression. Cabala provides him with the idea of creation as fall—the "catastrophe theory of creation." If in the beginning there is already a flaw, then the poet can offer us that "lost first chance," placing himself (and us) at an origin where freedom and self-creation are possible.

B.'s compelling intervention in literary criticism has had the effect of deidealizing literary relations. Contrary to traditional literary history, which traces influence-relations in chronological fashion, B. insists on the phenomenon of influence as a radical reversal that makes poetic freedom and poetic self-identification possible. His favored trope is *metalepsis,* a "trope-reversing trope" that turns late into early, and which signals the momentary and agonistic triumph of the belated poem. Equally compelling is B.'s argument against deconstruction's (q.v.) insistence on language as a final limit. *Metalepsis* allows a reversal that is also transcendence, a triumph over time and over the limits of language. B.'s theory of poetic influence, which he terms "antithetical criticism," has transformed criticism's view of literary tradition and of the poet's response to its extraordinary wealth.

Equally important is B.'s articulation of the role of the critic. Contrary to established practice, which demands a critic's objectivity in relation to the text, B. insists on the critic's uncompromising subjectivity—"There are no texts; there are only ourselves"—on a response to the text that is itself "a spark and an act," and inseparable from literature.

Though the closest term to define his work is literary criticism, in his most recent work B. has widened the meaning of the term by breaking down normative distinctions between sacred and secular literature. *Ruin the Sacred Truths: Poetry and Belief from the Bible to the Present* (1989), winner of the Christian Gauss Award for the best book of literary criticism, moves from Homer and the Bible to Samuel Beckett (q.v.) as it studies the powerful discontinuities of the Western tradition. *The Book of J* (1990), a best-seller, argues that this text, which has given rise to so much biblical commentary, is the work of one writer, a woman, and that the God it depicts bears little resemblance to the God of normative religion. His latest book is *The American Religion* (1992). And he is at work on a book to be titled *The Western Canon.* An eminent critic who has stirred controversy again and again by his wholly original readings, B. has forged new paths for literary criticism and, in the tradition of Emerson and Longinus, brought it once again into kinship with great literature.

FURTHER WORKS: *Yeats* (1970); *The Ringers in the Tower: Studies in Romantic Tradition* (1971); *Figures of Capable Imagination* (1976); *The Flight to Lucifer* (1979); *Agon: Towards a Theory of Revisionism* (1982); *The Breaking of the Vessels* (1982); *Poetics of Influence* (1988)

BIBLIOGRAPHY: Burke, K., "Father and Son," *NewR,* 12 Apr. 1975, 23–24; Said, E. W., "The Poet As Oedipus: A Map of Misreading," *NYTBR,* 13 Apr. 1975, 23–25; Hollander, J., "Poetic Misprision," *Poetry,* 127 (1976), 222–34; Hartman, G. H., *Criticism in the Wilderness* (1980), 42–62; Riddel, J., "Juda Becomes New Haven," *Diacritics,* 10 (1980), 17–34; Smith, J. H., ed., *The Literary Freud* (1980), ix–xix; Wordsworth, A., "An Art That Will Not Abandon the Self to Language," in Young, R., ed., *Untying the Text* (1981), 207–22; Handelman, S. A., *The Slayers of Moses* (1982), 179–223; de Man, P., *Blindness and Insight,* rev. ed. (1983), 267–76; Axelrod, S. G., "H. B.'s Enterprise," *MP,* 81, 3 (Feb. 1984), 290–97; Fite, D., *H. B., The Rhetoric of Romantic Vision* (1985); Mileur, J.-P., *Literary Revisionism and the Burden of Modernity* (1985); Moynihan, R., *A Recent Imagining* (1986), 3–47; Salusinszky, I., *Criticism in Society* (1987), 45–73; Weis, A., *Paris Review* (Spring 1991), 178–232; Elam, H. R., "H. B.," in Jay, G. S., ed., *DLB: Modern American Critics since 1955* (1988), 32–48; Renza, L., "Influence," in Lentricchia, F., and T. McLaughlin, eds., *Critical Terms for Literary Study* (1990), 186–202

HELEN REGUEIRO ELAM

BOAL, Augusto
Brazilian dramatist, director, and theoretician, b. 1931, Rio de Janeiro

B. is known as a major dramatist and director of Brazil's experimental group Arena Theater of São Paulo, and is recognized as Latin America's most significant theoretician of popular theater. Although his university training was in chemistry, B. became interested in the theater in 1950. After two years of study at Columbia University with John Gassner, he returned to Brazil schooled in playwriting and method acting. From 1956 to 1971 he was associated with Arena Theater, first as codirector and then as director. As a director, B. was instrumental in renovating Brazilian theater. His desire to define a dramatic format that was truly Brazilian led him to help develop new forms of dramatic interpretation for actors, encourage new methods of playwriting for dramatists, and eventually produce new theories of theater. He was jailed, tortured, and exiled by the military dictatorship in 1971. In 1979 he established a theater center in Paris. Since 1986 B. has based his activities in Rio de Janeiro, although he continues to direct plays and conduct workshops in Europe, North and South America, and Africa.

As a dramatist, B.'s interest in renovating the theater process led him to combine a consciousness-raising aesthetic focused on the problems of Brazil's working class with experiments in Bertolt Brecht's (q.v.) distancing techniques. *Revolução na América do Sul* (1960; revolution in South America) is a lesson in the corruption, deception, and violence of politics as perceived through the experiences of one needy individual. The play's circuslike atmosphere, the short scenes, and the use of music as a thematic component became essential ingredients for B.'s later drama. Together with Gianfrancesco Guarnieri (b. 1934) B. authored two more plays while associated with Arena Theater, *Arena conta Zumbi* (1965; Arena tells the story of Zumbi) and *Arena conta Tiradentes* (1967; Arena tells the story of Tiradentes). Both plays rework historic fights for liberty as a means of commenting on the failed leftist reforms of the early 1960s and the ensuing imposition of a repressive military régime. Each play experiments with techniques that encourage the audience to emulate the past by becoming actors in their own history.

While at Arena Theater B. began developing his theories of popular theater, that is, theater that turns over part of the acting to the audience so that drama becomes a means of enacting change. After B.'s exile, he published several books explaining the theory and practice of popular theater. He gained international recognition for *Teatro do oprimido* (1975; *Theater of the Oppressed*, 1979), a treatise on how theater from Aristotle to Eugène Ionesco (q.v.) has usurped the transformative power of the audience. The final portion of the book outlines the Joker system, a method for simultaneously presenting and analyzing a performance. The key figure in the system is the Joker, a facilitator who participates in and questions the actions of the drama as it progresses. Newspaper Theater, an improvisation based on articles taken from the daily newspaper, and Invisible Theater, a prearranged kind of drama that takes place in public areas such as bus stations, parks, or grocery stores, encourage performers to engage the audience in making drama a vehicle for analysis and understanding of community problems. In *Stop: c'est magique!* (1980; stop: this is magic), B. shows how his European audiences, whose concerns are more psychological than social, were trained to stop the action on stage, take the place of a performer, and change the action in progress.

B. was an instrumental figure in revitalizing Brazilian theater during a critical time of its development. As Arena's director he contributed both organizational and creative foundations that have been widely adopted in Brazil. His plays brought new topics, treatments, and techniques to the stage and to Brazil's growing theater audience. As a theoretician B. is both original and revolu-

tionary in his presentation of the political relationship between the action on stage and the potential for action among those in the audience.

FURTHER WORKS: *Marido magro, mulher chata* (1957); *José, do parto a sepultura* (1962); *Tio Patinhas* (1968); *Torquemada* (1971); *200 exercícios e jogos para o ator* (1977); *Técnicas Latinoamericanas de teatro popular* (1977); *Crônicas de nuestra América* (1977); *A deliciosa e sangrenta aventura latina de Jane Spitfire* (1977); *Murro em ponta de faca* (1978); *A tempestade e As mulheres de Atenas* (1979); *Milagre no Brasil* (1979); *O corsário do Rei* (1985)

BIBLIOGRAPHY: Bisset, J. I., "Victims and Violators: The Structure of Violence in *Torquemada*," *LATR*, 15, 2 (Spring 1982), 27–34; Capo, K. E., "Performance of Literature As Social Dialectic," *LPer*, 4, 1 (Nov. 1983), 31–36; Carlson, M. A., *Theories of the Theatre* (1984), 475–76; Schechter, J., "The Jokers of A. B.," *Durov's Pig: Clowns, Politics, and Theater* (1985), 158–63; Albuquerque, S. J., "Conflicting Signs of Violence in A. B.'s *Torquemada*," *MD*, 29, 3 (Sept. 1986), 452–59; Enright, R., "To Dynamize the Audience: Interview with A. B.," *CTR*, 47 (1986), 41–49; Milleret, M., "Acting into Action: Teatro Arena's *Zumbi*," *LATR*, 21, 1 (Fall 1987), 19–27; special B. section, *TDR*, 34, 3 (1990), 24–87

MARGO MILLERET

BOMBAL, Maria Luisa

Chilean novelist and short-story writer, b. 8 July 1910, Viña del Mar; d. 6 May 1980, Santiago

After her father's death in 1922, B. was taken by her mother to Paris, where she lived until finishing her university degree in philosophy and literature at the Sorbonne. In 1931 she returned to Chile, living for two years on the family country estate in the south. In 1933 she accompanied her friend Pablo Neruda to Buenos Aires where she developed friendships with numerous writers, among them Federico García Lorca and Jorge Luis Borges (qq.v.). In this very creative environment, she wrote and published her two brief novels, *La última niebla* (1935; *The House of Mist*, 1947), which included the two stories "El árbol" (the tree) and "Las islas nuevas" (the new islands), and *La amortajada* (1938; *The Shrouded Woman*, 1948). After a thirty-year stay in Washington, D.C., where she lived with her second husband, B. once again returned to her native Chile, living out the remainder of her years in Santiago.

Despite B.'s limited production, two short novels and a handful of short stories, she is highly

regarded today as an innovator. Her narratives are
a radical departure from the picturesque regionalism and social protest of her Chilean contemporaries. Plot as action worked out in a process of
cause and effect to a resolution or conclusion is
not central to her work. Instead, in an evocative,
poetic prose, reminiscent of French symbolism
(q.v.) and influenced by the later vanguardist
movement, she elaborates in an almost musical
fashion the inner emotional states of her alienated
female protagonists. Secondary characters are
viewed subjectively through the prism of an emotionally colored consciousness; atmospheric settings function as metaphorical projections of inner
feelings; and the tone is pervasively one of melancholy.

La última niebla is a retrospective first-person
narrative of no more than fifty pages in which an
unnamed woman records over a period of some
years, in a highly evocative and lyrical prose, her
reflections on the reality or unreality of what most
probably was an erotic dream. Denied her passionate desire for sensual love in her arid marriage,
the woman weaves an elaborate fantasy around an
imagined night of sexual union with a wraithlike
male figure who has all the trappings of Carl
Gustav Jung's (q.v.) *animus*. Gradually she becomes aware of the illusory nature of the experience, ultimately resigning herself to the sterility
of her marriage and the utter conventionality of
her mundane existence. In the first half of the
novel, images of mist, water, and leaves—and in
general of the erotic qualities of nature—create a
dreamlike atmosphere in which reality and fantasy
are ambiguously blended. By the end of the novel,
images of death, old age, and suicide prevail.

La amortajada, a somewhat longer work, is
also strongly retrospective in its narrative structure. Here, however, the protagonist, whose name
is Ana María, lies dead in her casket at her wake,
reflecting mentally on her past relationships with
those who approach her one by one to pay their
last respects—her young cousin (the passion of
her life), her sister, her children, her father, her
male confidant, her husband, and her priest. The
narrative is for the most part third-person *style
indirect libre* but slips from time to time into first
person and occasionally into the perspective of
one of the other characters. Despite these surface
shifts, all voices are subsumed under the single
voice or high-level stream-of-consciousness (q.v.)
of Ana María. Again, the themes are failed relationships and erotic passion denied. In general,
the novel illustrates the profound disparity between
Ana María's naive Edenic expectations and the
realities encountered in her relationships, between
her wish-fulfillment concept of God as dispenser

of sensual happiness and the God of her disillusionment who gave her anguish and suffering instead. In the end, she welcomes not only her "first
death" but also her "second death" as she slips
gradually into sweet oblivion.

The third work on which B.'s reputation rests
is the short story "El árbol." Here Brigida, the
child-woman protagonist, is carried by music
through three distinct stages in her failed marriage
to an older and indifferent man. Unlike the novels,
however, the story contains a hint of optimism. In
the epiphany of self-illumination, she seems to
have matured, able perhaps to make an independent life for herself apart from her husband and
beyond the protection of the "maternal" rubber
tree outside the house where she had lived.

Although B.'s themes are limited, and although
she never really received due recognition in her
native Chile, she is universally considered a consummate stylist. In her lyricism, in her psychological orientation, and in her ambiguous fusion of
reality and fantasy, she is a precursor of what has
been called the "new narrative" in Latin America.

FURTHER WORKS: "Mar, cielo y tierra" (1940);
"Trenzas" (1940); "Washington, ciudad de las
ardillas" (1943); "La historia de María Griselda"
(1946); "La maja y el ruiseñor" (1976)

BIBLIOGRAPHY: Campbell, M., "The Vaporous
World of M. L. B.," *Hispania,* 44, 3 (Sept.
1961), 415–19; Debicki, A., "Structure, Imagery,
and Experience in M. L. B.'s 'El árbol,' " *SSF,*
8 (Winter 1971), 123–29; Levine, L., "M. L. B.
from a Feminist Perspective." *RevI,* 4 (1974),
148–61; Adams, M. I., "M. L. B.: Alienation
and the Poetic Image," *Three Authors of Alienation* (1975), 15–35; Nelson, E., "The Space of
Longing: *La última niebla," The American Hispanist,* 3 (1977), 7–11; Orlandi, C., "Mist, Light
and Libido: *La última niebla," KRQ,* 26, 2 (1979),
231–42; Rodríguez-Peralta, P., "M. L. B.'s Poetic Novels of Female Estrangement," *REH,* 14
(1980), 139–55

ROBERT SCOTT

BÖNI, Franz

Swiss novelist and short-story writer (writing in
German), b. 17 June 1952, Wintherthur

B. studied business and worked as a tradesman
and itinerant salesman from 1973 to 1979. He then
decided to give up this occupation and become a
full-time writer. He has won several prizes in
Switzerland and Germany, including the Conrad

Ferdinand Meyer Prize (1980). He now resides in Zurich.

All of B.'s stories are set in the valleys and forests of the Lower Alps in Switzerland, but the country he portrays is one of disease, squalor, and extremely difficult work. His characters are obsessed with the struggle to survive and are haunted by poverty. They are devoid of love and compassion, and see little meaning in their bizarre and cruel existence, which they long to escape through death. B. has created here the epitome of an antihomeland literature, which itself is a metaphor for the alienation and despair rampant in contemporary capitalist societies.

Almost all of B.'s protagonists are on a journey in search of something they never find in a direct parallel to the meaningless quests of Franz Kafka's (q.v.) characters. In *Die wanderarbeiter* (1981; the itinerant workers) the character A. leaves home for the hard physical labor of a factory, which allows him no time for other pursuits. Franz Zuber in *Schlatt* (1979; Schlatt) also leaves home to find work and returns six years later with a lung disease. In *Hospiz* (1980; hostel) an itinerant peddler endures daily hardships until a storm forces him to stay in a hostel, perhaps for the rest of his life. In *Ein wanderer in alpenregen* (1981; a wanderer in the alpine rain) young people travel into the Alps where they cannot enjoy the beauties of nature but instead encounter ignorant peasants, hard work, and death.

B.'s stories appear to have for the most part autobiographical traits, and this is particularly true of his three-part chronicle about the life of the laborer Nowak: *Wie die zeit vergeht* (1988; how time passes) covers the time 1955–1970, *Die alpen* (1983; the Alps) the period 1970–1980, and *Alle züge fahren nach Salem* (1984; all trains travel to Salem) the period 1980–1984. Nowak grows up in a small Swiss town and tries to escape his dreary existence by delving into popular culture and by traveling to Italy, but he only finds himself surrounded by death and depression. He then decides to leave home for good to work in a small industrial town, but his series of demanding jobs make him more depressed than before. Suicides and death abound everywhere. The city is just as dehumanizing and cruel as the Alpine landscape.

Die residenz (1988; the city of residence) also portrays the negative elements of the city. Franz Kramer grows up in a farm milieu that he refuses to accept. He longs to flee to the capital city to work as a secretary in the castle there. His letters of application are in vain. Finally he travels to the city, Despina, and after many attempts manages to find a position. However, at the height of his career he decides to leave the city, because it has almost destroyed him. He meets Maya, his former love from the village, but their future together is uncertain. Kramer realizes that all his searching for fulfillment has been for naught.

B. is one of the most significant contemporary Swiss-German writers and his antihomeland, antiutopian philosophy shares many features with several other Swiss, Austrian, and German authors. Through distortion and hyperbole he wishes to underscore the bizarre and cruel components of contemporary existence and debunk the myths about Swiss society. Yet B. is prone to description instead of analysis, which produces a pessimistic worldview devoid of the possibility of change and progress.

FURTHER WORKS: *Der knochensammler* (1980); *Sagen aus dem schächental* (1982); *Alvier* (1982); *Der johanniterlauf* (1984); *Die fronfastenkinder: Aufsätze 1966–1985* (1985); *Das zentrum der welt* (1987); *Am ende aller tage* (1989)

BIBLIOGRAPHY: Moser, S., ''Sprachzwerg und Sprachriese,'' *Schweizer Monatshefte,* 12 (1979), 1009–13; Nef, E., ''Ausweglose Topologie,'' *Schweizer Monatshefte,* 3 (1983), 253–57; Hultberg, H., ''Der Wanderer: über F. B.,'' *T&K,* 11, 2 (1983), 370–81; Michaelis, R., ''Nachrichten von Archipel Gletscher oder Bild und Begriff der Heimat bei F. B.,'' *Manuskripte,* 28 (1988), 111–16

ROBERT ACKER

BOUDJEDRA, Rachid

Algerian novelist, screenwriter, and poet (writing in French and Arabic) b. 5 Sept. 1941, Aïn Beida

B. was one of the few Algerian writers of his generation to receive a bilingual education. Although he grew up near Constantine, Algeria, B. studied in Tunis, where Arabic continued to be a language of instruction. At the age of sixteen, he became a freedom fighter for the National Liberation Front during the Algerian revolution. After independence, B. studied philosophy in Paris and completed a thesis on the work of Louis-Ferdinand Céline (q.v.), an author who has greatly influenced his own work. From 1966 to 1972, he taught philosophy in Algeria, France, and Morocco. He has since resided in Algeria, where he has been an adviser to the minister of information and culture, and taught at the Institute of Political Science in Algiers. B. is a militant atheist and Marxist.

One of the few truly bilingual writers of the Maghreb, B. is the leading novelist of postindependence Algeria. The author of eleven novels and several volumes of poetry, B. has also written numerous screenplays for Algerian films, as well as sociological texts on Algerian cinema and society. The recipient of many literary prizes, B.'s work has been translated into a dozen languages. B. is perhaps best known for his first novel, *La répudiation* (1969; the repudiation), and for the screenplays to Mohamed Lakhdar-Hamina's *Chronique des années de braise* (chronicle of the years of embers), golden medal award winner of the 1975 Cannes Film Festival, and Ahmed Rachedi's *Ali au pays des mirages* (Ali in the country of mirages), winner of the Carthage and Moscow film festivals of 1980 and 1981. Although B.'s first six novels were written in French, he decided, in 1981, to write exclusively in Arabic. He subsequently assists Antoine Moussali (dates n.a.) in translating his works into French.

B. published his first work, *Pour ne plus rêver* (1965; to no longer dream), in Algeria. Although dreams can liberate us, writes B., reality must be transformed. Marked by a revolutionary mystique and violence, these poems are clearly the work of a twenty-year-old who fought for the independence of his country. Nevertheless, for B., the liberation of a country does not necessarily imply the liberation of its people. Algerian women remain victims of traditional society. In "La mariée" (the bride) B. boldly depicts the wedding night of an Algerian bride as a sanctioned ritual of rape. This poem set the tone for B.'s successive works, all of which denounce the condition of traditional Algerian women.

Published in Paris, *La répudiation* established B. as the writer of a new literary generation. The first novel of postrevolutionary Algeria, *La répudiation* denounces a corrupt and lascivious society where sociopolitical and cultural abuses are legitimatized by religious practices and cultural traditions. Although B. focuses his attack on the feudal structure of the traditional family, he also faults the Algerian patriarchs for acquiescing to 130 years of colonialism and for aborting the revolution. Written in a brutal, visceral, and syncopated style, where the boundaries between the real, the delirious, and the oneiric are erased by a narrative voice seeking to exorcize the hold of the past through the subversion of sexual taboos, *La répudiation* is one of the most original texts of Maghrebian literature.

The historic past of Algeria, which is already present in *La répudiation,* becomes even more important in *L'insolation* (1972; insolation), where B. continues to examine the violence that underlies contemporary Algerian society. In *Topographie idéale pour une agression caractérisée* (1975; the ideal topography for a downright attack), the Paris metro becomes the ultimate site of racist aggression, whereas in *Le vainqueur de coupe* (1981; the winner of the cup) a French soccer stadium turns into the political arena of the Algerian War. Based on actual historical events, these novels examine acts of violence that are the direct result of the French-Algerian past.

In *Les 1001 années de la nostalgie* (1979; the 1001 years of nostalgia) and *Ma'rakat al-zuqāq* (1986; *La prise de Gibraltar,* 1987; the conquest of Gibraltar) B. juxtaposes episodes of the legendary Arab past with those of contemporary Algerian history. In rewriting history as a fictional narrative, B. seeks to release the hold of the past on the collective identity of a people. Writing becomes a form of liberation from both historical traumas and myths. In *Al-tafakkuk* (1981; *Le démantèlement,* 1982; the bringing down) a young woman born at the eve of the Algerian revolution deconstructs history as she engages in dialogue with a martyr of the revolution. (Beginning with *Le démantèlement,* B. published first in Arabic, then in French.)

The exorcism of the past is of a more personal vein in such novels as *Al marth* (1984; *La macération,* 1985; the maceration) and *Layliyyāt imra'a arik*—(1985; *La pluie,* 1987; the rain). In *La pluie* B. adopts the voice of an Algerian woman to write about the taboos of contemporary society. *Fawdā al-ashyā'* (1990; *Le désordre des choses,* 1991; the disorder of things) centers on three main characters who represent different facets of Algerian society and history: a communist *pied noir* (French Algerian) guillotined during the Algerian War, an Algerian youth brutally tortured during the October 1988 uprisings, and the narrator's mother, falsely accused of adultery. As in *La répudiation,* the personal and the political converge in the mother figure, whose confinement and suffocation becomes the traumatic center of the novel.

B. brings a rich and original perspective to Maghrebian literature. He has always affirmed that writing must be rooted in the local and the particular, and that a writer can only address the problems of his society from within. Nevertheless, as an atheist and a Marxist, he maintains a dissident attitude with respect to the cultural traditions and political structures that paralyze his country. Perfectly bilingual, B. moves comfortably back and forth between the "Orient" and the West, between Islam and psychoanalysis, between eroticism and mysticism, between literary modernity and the golden age of Arab literature.

FURTHER WORKS: *Naissance du cinéma algérien* (1971); *La vie quotidienne en Algérie* (1971); *Journal palestinien* (1972); *L'escargot entêté* (1977); *Likah* (1983; *Greffe,* 1984)

BIBLIOGRAPHY: Bouraoui, H., "Politique et poétique dans l'univers de. B.," *PFr,* 14 (1977), 11–

29; Déjeux, J., *Littérature maghrébine de langue française*, rev. ed. (1980), 381–404; Harrow, K., "Metaphors for Revolution: Blood and Schizophrenia in B.'s Early Novels," *PFr*, 20 (1980), 5–19; Bensmaïn, A., *Crise du sujet, crise de l'identité. Une lecture psychanalytique de R. B.* (1984); Bonn, C., *Le roman algérien de langue française* (1985), 237–79; Gafaïti, H., *B. ou la passion de la modernité* (1987); Gafaïti, H., "R. B.: The Bard of Modernity," *RAL,* 23, 2 (1992), 89–102

DANIELLE MARX-SCOURAS

BRATHWAITE, Edward Kamau

(born Lawson Edward Brathwaite) Barbadian poet and critic, b. 11 May 1930, Bridgetown

Educated at Harrison College in Barbados, B. went on to study history at Cambridge, graduating with honors in 1953. In 1950 B. began publishing poems and a few stories in Barbados and in England. After Cambridge, he worked for the ministry of education in what is now Ghana until 1962. While in Africa, B. published the first of his many essays on West Indian literature. When he returned to the Caribbean, he took a position teaching history at the University of the West Indies in Jamaica. Apart from studies at Sussex leading to his doctorate (1968) and numerous fellowships abroad, B. has remained in Jamaica, where in 1983 he was appointed professor of social and cultural history.

During the late 1960s, B. achieved international recognition with three books of poems, published in rapid succession and subsequently reissued in one volume as *The Arrivants* (1973). In *Rights of Passage* (1967) various black voices, from their different situations, all ask a version of the same question: What constitutes "home" for the descendants of Africans living in the diaspora? *Masks* (1968), in the course of a visionary pilgrimage to Ghana that reverts from the present to the golden age of the Ashanti empire, first offers and then rejects the predictable answer: "Africa." But this experience of Africa, by cleansing the poet's perceptions, makes it possible for B. in *Islands* (1969) to recognize a wealth of African survivals in the Caribbean and to bring to light the region's repressed culture, its gods and rituals, whether African or indigenous in origin. As a whole the trilogy celebrates the resourcefulness with which, even in adverse circumstances of slavery and colonialism, Caribbean peoples have taken possession of their world. In so doing, *The Arrivants* transcends its origins in the Black Power politics of the 1960s. Apart from the import of its themes and B.'s conclusions about them, it is also signif-

icant for its demonstration of the poetry inherent in the rhythms and resources of Caribbean English, and for the complex architecture of lyric forms that it achieves across the span of three volumes.

Like *The Arrivants*, B.'s earliest literary criticism is concerned with exile and diaspora. In response to the migration of so many Caribbean writers away from the region, B. insists on the social function of the contemporary writer, and emphasizes the nourishment that derives from the crucial relationship between writers and their local audience. Not surprisingly, B. was the first West Indian author of unquestionably "literary" verse to present himself widely as a performer of his work, going so far as to produce a commercial recording of his reading of *The Arrivants*.

The mid-1970s was a transitional period for B.; his title pages after 1976 identify the poet as Edward Kamau, and the change symbolizes his continuing attention as both poet and professional historian to the role played by African cultures in shaping contemporary Caribbean society. "The African Presence in Caribbean Literature" (1974) is the best known of several essays in which B. documents what he calls "Africa-in-the-Caribbean." At the same time he has offered provocative analyses of the dynamics by which different cultures interact; he has pursued the study of "inter-culturation" most extensively in *The Development of Creole Society in Jamaica 1770–1820* (1971) and *Contradictory Omens: Cultural Diversity and Integration in the Caribbean* (1974). During this period, B. also completed important bibliographies of Caribbean culture and literary history.

Other Exiles (1975), a retrospective collection of thirty poems from the years 1950–1975, presents personal poetry, in contrast to the public poetry of *The Arrivants*: there are several unusually intimate poems, as well as portraits sketched from his travels as a student in Europe. A complementary volume, *Black+Blues* (1976), offers a more unified set of twenty-three poems preoccupied with imagery of relics, totems, fetishes, ruins, shards. There is a strong sense that these "fragments" are *survivals,* the past alive in the present, though damaged or broken, and that attention to them can bring them to life. While there are desperate, even incendiary voices in these poems, the characteristic movement of the book is a kind of metaphysical optimism familiar from *The Arrivants*.

B.'s second trilogy, which has no collective title, appeared over the course of a decade. *Mother Poem* (1977) depicts the experience of Caribbean women, ranging from the poet's own mother to the personified island of Barbados itself. *Sun Poem* (1982) focuses on fathers and male ancestors, while the central figures of *X/Self* (1987) are the various "children" of those parents, a gallery of personalities formed or deformed by the experience of colonialism throughout the world. This trilogy is at once autobiographically intimate and mythologically vast in its conception of the cycles of history and the dynamics of culture; its ambitious scale, and its radical experiments with language (based ultimately on Caribbean speech) make it less immediately accessible than *The Arrivants*. *X/Self* is B.'s most innovative work to date—though it is, paradoxically, also his most comic.

As a historian B. has situated African survivals within the dynamics of cultural contact. As a critic he may strive to define narrowly a "West Indian aesthetic," yet his *History of the Voice* (1984) is an essential study of the interactions between oral and scribal poetry. As a poet, B. acknowledges the early influence of T. S. Eliot, but his career has really been shaped in amiable contention with two West Indians; B.'s accomplishment is best measured in relation to the work of Derek Walcott, a confessional poet of consummate technique, and that of George Lamming (qq.v.), who first gave voice to the life and landscape of Barbados. Of the three, it is B. who has most affected the art of a younger generation, both in the West Indies and in Britain.

FURTHER WORKS: *Four Plays for Primary Schools* (1964); *Odale's Choice* (1967); *Folk Culture of the Slaves in Jamaica* (1970); *Caribbean Man in Space and Time* (1974); *Days & Nights* (1975); *Our Ancestral Heritage: A Bibliography of the English-Speaking Caribbean* (1977); *Wars of Respect: Nanny, Sam Sharpe and the Struggle for People's Liberation* (1977); *Barbados Poetry: A Checklist/Slavery to the Present* (1979); *Jamaica Poetry: A Checklist/Slavery to the Present* (1979); *Third World Poems* (1983); *Colonial Encounter: Language* (1984); *Roots: Literary Criticism* (1986); *Jah Music* (1986); *Sappho Sakyi's Meditations: Savacou* 16 (1989)

BIBLIOGRAPHY: Ramchand, K., *An Introduction to the Study of West Indian Literature* (1976), 127–42; Lewis, M. W., *Notes to Masks* (1977); Dash, M., "E. B.," in King, B., ed., *West Indian Literature* (1979), 210–27; Rohlehr, G., *Pathfinder: Black Awakening in The Arrivants of E. K. B.* (1981); Baugh, E., "E. B. As Critic: Some Preliminary Observations," *CarQ*, 28, 1–2 (May–June 1982), 66–75; Rohlehr, G., "Megalleons of Light," *Jamaica Journal*, 16, 2 (1983), 81–87; Brown, L. W., *West Indian Poetry* (1984), 146–68; Brathwaite, D. M., *EKB: His Published Prose & Poetry 1948–1986* (1986)

LAURENCE A. BREINER

BRAUN, Volker

German poet, dramatist, and novelist, b. 7 May 1939, Dresden

Early employment experience in a printing shop, as a construction worker, and as a machinist provided important background for B.'s first literary creations. From 1960 to 1964 he studied philosophy at the Karl Marx University in Leipzig (now Leipzig University). Then he worked as a drama producer for the Berlin Ensemble. Between 1967 and 1971 he devoted himself exclusively to his writing, but since 1971 he has again produced plays in theaters in Leipzig and Berlin. Among the literary awards that he has received are the Heinrich Heine Prize (1971), the Heinrich Mann Prize (1980), and the Bremen Literature Prize (1986).

B.'s creative works reflect his perceptions of the constant tension that has existed between professed and actual reality in the society where he lives. His writings are noted for their intensive treatment of political and social problems, their focus on the harsh nature of the worker's world, and their visible highlighting of the establishment's failure to respond to individual needs. During the course of his early artistic development, B. repeatedly came into conflict with the official cultural policies of the German Democratic Republic. These confrontations ultimately led to his expulsion from the directorate of the East German Writers' Union in 1976, when he openly opposed the government's action in revoking the citizenship of the controversial poet Wolf Biermann (q.v.).

The essential character of B.'s early lyric poetry is suggested in the title of his first book of verse, *Provokation für mich* (1965; provocation for me). Dissatisfaction is the formative principle for lines containing original images derived from the workplace and its conditions, city and rural landscapes, and human relationships of friendship and love. His poems express an inner longing for change and demand introspection and self-examination from the reader.

In later collections, including *Wir und nicht sie* (1970; we and not they), *Gegen die symmetrische Welt* (1974; against the symmetrical world), and *Training des aufrechten Gangs* (1979; training to walk upright), B. softened his tone somewhat. Rebelliousness and impatience are replaced by reflection and analysis, polemic by the dialectic of present and future, and tension by a more relaxed, even cheerful mood that accompanies concrete suggestions of strategies for overcoming problems. *Langsamer knirschender Morgen* (1987; slow crackling morning), however, contains satirical poems and epigrams that focus on uncomfortable questions concerning ethics and responsibility. They present a new demonstration of B.'s penchant for sharply pointed social criticism.

From the official cultural perspective of the German Democratic Republic, B.'s dramatic works, with their frank and inexorable exposure of social contradictions and conflicts, were even less comfortable than his poetry. In early plays, such as *Kipper Paul Bauch* (1966; tipper Paul Bauch), *Freunde* (1971; friends), and *Hinze und Kunze* (1973; Hinze and Kunze), by stressing the disparity between the ideal of socialist production and the real mechanical tedium of physical labor, and between the adulation of male productivity and the repression of female contributions to production, B. underscored the danger inherent in sacrificing fulfillment of personal needs on the altar of community demands. His dramas attempt to represent the life of the workers as part of a historical process, but they specifically illustrate his belief that the individual can and should constructively affect the flow of history and the development of society. Subsequent works, including *Guevara; oder, Der Sonnenstaat* (1975; Guevara; or, the sun state), *Der große Frieden* (1979; the great peace), *Simplex Deutsch* (1981; German simplex), and *Transit Europa* (1987; Europe in transit), show greater maturity in their dramatic tone and their portrayal of realistic characters. They are also particularly notable for their demonstration of B.'s special mastery of sexual metaphor.

The central concerns and themes of B.'s poems and dramas also inform his prose fiction and essays. Social criticism takes on an especially personal note in the analytically autobiographical segments of *Das ungezwungene Leben Kasts* (1972; rev. ed., 1979; Kast's unconstrained life), where honest rejection of dictated conceptions of life under socialism is couched in language and descriptions that are filled with earthy vitality. In the controversial *Hinze-Kunze-Roman* (1985; Hinze-Kunze novel), however, with its open treatment of sexual themes, the artistic impact of B.'s attack on political hypocrisy and repression is reduced by tastelessness of presentation that is only partially offset by the uniqueness of the work.

The strength of B.'s commitment to personal involvement in the processes of political and social change is perhaps most readily visible in some of his essays and occasional pieces. The collections *Es genügt nicht die einfache Wahrheit* (1975; the simple truth is not enough) and *Verheerende Folgen mangelnden Anscheins innerbetrieblicher Demokratie* (1988; devastating consequences of the insufficient likelihood of internal democracy), besides being essays of high quality dealing with specific writers, works, and theoretical problems of art and literature, represent pointed treatments of environmental, social, and other issues, in which

B. defends his right to assume a critical, revolutionary stance with respect to reality.

The nonconformity that made B. a controversial literary figure in the German Democratic Republic, his open, frank, and critical examination of contemporary problems, his gift for creating effective satire, and his open advocacy of cultural reform combine to make him one of the most significant and interesting writers to emerge in East Germany after 1960.

FURTHER WORKS: *Vorläufiges* (1966); *Kriegserklärung. Fotogramme* (1967); *Die Kipper* (1972); *Gedichte* (1972); *Stücke 1* (1976); *Unvollendete Geschichte* (1977); *Poesie Album 115* (1977); *Der Stoff zum Leben* (1977); *Tinka* (1977); *Im Querschnitt V. B.* (1978); *Gedichte* (1979); *Stücke 2* (1981); *Berichte von Hinze und Kunze* (1983); *Stücke* (1983); *Archaische Landschaft mit Lösungen* (1983); *Rimbaud, ein Psalm der Aktualität* (1985; *Rimbaud, a Topical Psalm*, 1989); *Stücke 3* (1987); *Bodenloser Satz* (1990); *Texte in zeitlicher Folge* (1990)

BIBLIOGRAPHY: Arnold, H., ed., *V. B.* (1972); Subiotto, A., "The Lyric Poetry of V. B.," *GDR Monitor,* 4 (1980–1981), 1–13; Wallace, I., *The GDR under Honecker 1971–1981* (1981), 43–62; Rosellini, J., *V. B.* (1983); Wallace, I., "V. B.'s Lyric Poetry: Problems of Reception," in Gerber, M., ed., *Studies in GDR Culture and Society,* Vol. 3 (1983), 179–93; Cosentino, C., "V. B.'s *Geschichten von Hinze und Kunze:* A New Look at an Old Problem," in Gerber, M., ed., *Studies in GDR Culture and Society* (1984), Vol. 4, 95–106; Profitlich, U., *V. B.* (1985); Hilton, J., "Back to the Future—V. B. and the German Theatrical Tradition," in Sebald, W. G., ed., *A Radical Stage: Theater in Germany in the 1970s and 1980s* (1988), 124–44; Dart, J., "The Death of a Provocateuse: Some Thoughts on V. B.'s *Tinka,*" *GDR Monitor,* 20 (1988–1989), 65–79

LOWELL A. BANGERTER

BRAZILIAN LITERATURE

See Volume 1, page 320.

The military dictatorship that ruled Brazil from 1964 to 1985 and the struggling democracy following in its aftermath have so thoroughly conditioned the orientation of Brazilian literature over the last quarter century that they merit attention.

The military coup d'état in March 1964 was a result of the social upheaval under a democratically elected government. The sudden resignation of President Jânio Quadros, the assumption of power by his vice president (the supposedly left-leaning João "Jango" Goulart), continuing work-ers' protests in the cities, and the massive literary campaigns in the impoverished northeast fueled hostility toward democracy among the military and its supporters in the traditional Brazilian elite.

While the initial military period (1964–1968) was seen as a brief detour in Brazil's democratic path, the regime confronted an internal guerrilla insurgency and continuing demands for improving conditions of the majority of Brazil's then seventy million inhabitants living in dire circumstances. Five "Institutional Acts" were decreed, which gradually curtailed citizens' rights. "Institutional Act 5" of December 1968 established prior cen-sorship and had disastrous effects on culture. It also signaled the beginning of a despotic campaign of suppression, torture, and murder against "sus-pect" elements in the society.

By 1977 the international outcry against these human-rights abuses led the regime to foresee a gradual return to democracy: A general amnesty was decreed, opposition political parties formed, and some elections were allowed. The 1984 pop-ular campaign for a direct vote for a civilian president failed. The military choice for president, Tancredo Neves, died on the night before assum-ing office in 1985. Vice-president-to-be José Sar-ney, a collaborationist politician associated with the traditional Brazilian brand of clientelist politics (and a literary figure), became the first nonmilitary president of Brazil since 1964.

The exit of the military led to a euphoria that soon turned to national depression. The military's much-heralded "economic miracle," financed by loans from international banks and governments, began to fade when the nation was unable to service these debts. The Sarney administration proved to be a debacle. In 1989 Fernando Collor de Melo, a young, minor political figure was elected president. His promises to control wild inflation, bring a better life to all Brazilians, and protect the atmosphere—generally to remedy the conditions that had led the society of 155 million people into a total economic and social tailspin—have faltered.

During the initial period of dictatorship, the neorealist or social novelists of the 1930s and 1940s—Rachel de Queiroz, Érico Veríssimo and Jorge Amado (qq.v.)—remained active, but pow-erful works of fiction by a newer group of writers (who are now established masters) appeared. An-tônio Callado's (q.v.) *Quarup* (1967; *Quarup*, 1970), as well as some of his later novels, raised the issue of Brazil's Indians to a philosophical level about the nation's future existence. Carlos Heitor Cony (b. 1926) published a semiautobio-graphical novel, *Pessach, a travessia* (1967; "Passover, the Crossing," selection in *Jewish*

Spectator [Winter 1984]), which narrates a middle-class Brazilian's political "awakening" and his participation in a guerrilla movement. Osman Lins's (1924–1978) collection of stories, *Nove, novena* (1966; nine, novena) reflected the world of social injustice surrounding him. More significantly, in these stories he engages in a debate about the artist's role in society. This last concern is preem-inent in his novel *Avalovara* (1973; *Avalovara*, 1980), in which the author requires his reader's active participation in the writing process. Stylistic originality is also a concern of Autran Dourado's (b. 1926) work, notably *O risco do bordado* (1970; *Pattern for a Tapestry*, 1974).

Regionalism, a major tradition of Brazilian lit-erature, had assumed an important reorientation under the influence of João Guimarães Rosa (q.v.). It continued to thrive in different reformulations in the works of Josué Montello (b. 1917) from Maranhão state, Herberto Sales (b. 1917) from Bahia state, and J. J. Veiga (b. 1915) from Goiás state, among many others.

Poets of the stature of Drummond de Andrade (1902–1987), Mário Quintana (b. 1906), and João Cabral de Melo Neto (q.v.) were extremely active. The unity of the "concretists" poets, who had appeared in 1956 led by Haroldo de Campos (b. 1929), Augusto de Campos (b. 1931), and Décio Pignatari (b. 1927), began to dissipate in the early 1960s with a flood of tangential move-ments concerned with the use and image of the poetic word. Among the most important move-ments were Mário Chamie's (b. 1933) "praxis poetry"; "semiotic poetry," which offered code poems or collages lacking words; and the "process poem," whose poets declared the autonomy of the poem itself over its being written or read. Tradi-tional approaches to poetry—lyric, religious, philosophical—continued from a new angle. Lin-dolf Bell's (b. 1938) "poetic catechism move-ment" was preoccupied with social justice rather than religious issues. Moacyr Félix's (b. 1926) "street guitar movement" was aimed at mass participation in and comprehension of poetry as a path toward knowledge. Among the younger re-gionalist poets of note are Marcus Accioly (b. 1943) from Pernambuco state, Ruy Espinheira Filho (b. 1942), and the members of the "pocket lyre group" in Bahia state.

Brazilian theater was active in social causes throughout these years. The Popular Culture Cen-ters were hotbeds of thematically leftist plays aimed at mobilization of the poor. The Opinião Theater Group under the direction of dramatist Oduvaldo Viana Filho (1936–1974) put on the *Show Opinião* in late 1964, which eloquently interwove song and individual testimony into a highly charged protest against the newly installed military regime. Viana

Filho's greatest success—and perhaps the most important Brazilian drama of the last thirty years—was *Rasga coração* (1974; render heart). Using techniques of the Brechtian realist theater and the musical revue, Viana Filho debated the role of political existence in Brazil since the 1920s. The Arena Theater of São Paulo, under the direction of Augusto Boal (q.v.) and Gianfrancesco Guarnieri (b. 1934), and the Oficina group, led by José Celso Martínez (dates n.a.), brought the debate over the national identity and direction to the forefront of discussion in highly successful allegorical musicals inspired by Brazil's past.

Literary criticism turned from superficial impressionism toward professionalism in the 1960s. Antônio Cândido (b. 1918) published *Literatura e sociedade* (1965; literature and society), which led to a new emphasis on textual analysis; his disciples are among the leading literary critics of contemporary Brazil. Two other major figures of criticism of the last quarter century are Afrânio Coutinho (b. 1911) and Wilson Martins (b. 1921).

The "Institutional Act 5" of 1968 led to direct confrontations with the military censors, who attempted to prevent the publication or representation of any work even slightly critical of the political status quo. Writers began to be persecuted: Callado and poet Ferreira Gullar (b. 1930) were jailed; Boal was tortured; and drama came to an almost total halt owing to censorship or lack of resources.

Several works of fiction were banned outright. For example, Ignácio de Loyola Brandão's (b. 1936) novel *Zero* (1975; *Zero*, 1984) appeared first in Italian, but was prohibited in Brazil just after publication. *Zero* is a cinematic portrait of squalor of urban life in a fictitious country resembling Brazil; the protagonist's only possible salvation is turning to revolution to attain his "freedom." Brandão has subsequently published major works at the heartbeat of Brazilian life: *Não verás país nenhum* (1981; *And Still the Earth*, 1985), about the total atmospheric devastation of a future Brazil, and *O beijo não vem na boca* (1985; the kiss is not on the mouth). Rubem Fonseca (q.v.), arguably Brazil's most popular novelist today, published a collection of stories, *Feliz ano novo* (1975; happy new year), that was banned by the regime for gross violence and pornography. Fonseca believes that the stories did no more than reflect the violence instilled in the society by military repression.

Writers sought new avenues for their expression of rage and resistance toward the regime through subtle or direct allegory, parody, testimonial literature, nonfiction fiction and (auto)biography. Oswaldo Franca Júnior's (1936–1989) allegory *Um dia no Rio* (1969; a day in rio) has two parallel plots: the beginning of the students' protest against the regime and a small-time businessmen's schemes for rapid wealth during the "economic miracle"—both are doomed to failure. Ivan Ângelo (b. 1936) published *A festa* (1976; *The Celebration*, 1982), an allegory in which a historical event of the turn of the century represents the sociohistorical present of injustice in Brazil. It is notable for its unique puzzlelike structure and innovative use of language. Ângelo also published a collection of stories, *Casa de vidro* (1979; *Tower of Glass*, 1986), which further dramatized the nation's continuing dilemma.

Testimonial literature presented the marginalized elements of Brazilian society—those who live without the benefit of law and justice—particularly in urban centers. For example, João Antônio's (b. 1937) short fiction, such as *Leão de chácara* (1975; the bouncer), is set in the slums of São Paulo and Rio. Very unsubtle and nonfiction fiction appeared based on the real events: these novels were not only a form of protest, but also served as a means of documentation of events whose publication had been censored. Among these novels, Carlos Heitor Cony's *O caso Lou* (1975; the Lou file) and works by José Louzeiro (b. 1932) are of particular interest. Darcy Ribeiro's (q.v.) *Maíra* (1976; *Maíra*, 1984) was yet another neo-Indianist appeal for justice for the indigenous Brazilians. In this novel, Indian civilization is portrayed as equal to that of other Brazilian races.

Outstanding women writers began to be noticed by the mid-1970s. Clarice Lispector's (q.v.) reputation as Latin America's preeminent woman writer grew to international proportions by the early 1990s. Maria Alice Barroso (b. 1926), Lygia Fagundes Telles, and Nélida Piñon (qq.v.) were outspoken about military repression and produced significant works of literature on the Brazilian woman's situation during the regime and afterward.

Contemporaneously with this protest fiction, a "poetry of suffocation" by younger poets expressed the mood of helplessness and alienation pervading the society. Unable to obtain mainstream publishing contracts, they turned to mimeographing their own poetry and handing it out for free. Many of the poets of the "mimeograph generation" became important figures of the 1980s: Ana Cristina César (1952–1983), Cacaso (pseud. of Antônio Carlos de Brito, 1944–1987), and Chico Alvim (dates n.a.). Chico Buarque (q.v.), the master of protest song since the 1960s, was gradually recognized as a major poet and dramatist.

Overall, Brazilian theater was devastated by censorship. The social dramas of Leilah Assunção (b. 1943) and Consuelo de Castro (b. 1946) gained national attention and, consequently, were often censored. Many of the professional theatrical organizations went into bankruptcy and closed. Smaller alternative theater groups became common in the 1970s. José Vicente's (b. 1945) Ipanema Theater became the center of *tropicalismo,* the nationalistic, all-arts-inclusive movement, which had begun in 1967 and lasted through the early 1970s. *Tropicalismo* sought the reevaluation of Brazilian culture within the context of the modern technologies of cultural representation. Perhaps the culmination of this movement in the theater came in 1978 when director José Alves Antunes Filho's (b. 1929) adaptation of Mário de Andrade's (q.v.) 1928 nativist classic *Macunaíma* was staged and became an international hit.

The beginning of amnesty and the easing of censorship led to a flood of memoirs and testimonies about the 1960s and 1970s by the political and inner exiles, such as Fernando Gabeira (b. 1943), who had participated in the kidnaping of the American ambassador in 1969, and Pedro Nava (1903–1984). These memoirs sought to reclaim the recent past for all Brazilians.

New national literary concerns appeared in the early 1980s: the growth to dominance of urban Brazil; feminist concerns; the predominance of a young (under-thirty) population; ecological questions; the black Brazilian experience; and the role of the immigrant within the culture.

Some of the most successful works of recent fiction reflect the contradictions of a society hell-bent on industrialization and urbanization. In João Ubaldo Ribeiro's (q.v.) *Vila Real* (1979; Vila Real) backlanders struggle for survival against an encroaching company. Márcio Souza (b. 1946) dealt mockingly with serious issues of internal and external neocolonialism in Brazil's Amazon in novels such as *O imperador do Acre* (1976; *The Emperor of the Amazon,* 1980) and *Mad Maria* (1980; *Mad Maria,* 1985). Rubem Fonseca's novels revitalized the 1930s detective-novel genre from a purely Brazilian angle.

Several subcategories of fiction are of note in recent years. The gay life-style is dealt with in the works of writers such as João Silvério Trevisan (b. 1944), as in his *Em nome do desejo* (1983; in the name of desire), who also published a sociocultural history of homosexuality in Brazil: *Devassos no paraíso* (1986; *Perverts in Paradise,* 1986); and Herbert Daniel (b. 1944), who, in addition, has been an AIDS activist. Cassandra Rios (dates n.a.) has written numerous works of fiction about lesbian and bisexual activities; she is a best-selling author within her category. Afro-Brazilian writers have appeared in several urban centers. In São Paulo, the literary journal *Cuadernos Negros* publishes both fiction and poetry of these writers; the younger generation includes

Adão Ventura (b. 1946), José Carlos Limeira (b. 1951), Eli Semog (b. 1952), and Eustáquio Rodrigues (dates n.a.). Moacyr Scliar (q.v.) has distinguished himself as the most successful narrator of the Jewish-Brazilian immigrant experience.

The short story or ministory continues to be the most popularly read literary form. The newest generation of short-fiction writers focuses on the dilemmas of the young Brazilians who came to maturity during the regime. The widening generation conflict, the use of drugs, the flaunting of sex, the television and technological ages are repeated themes of stories by Luís Fernando Emediato (b. 1951), Domingos Pellegrini, Jr. (b. 1949), João Gilberto Noll (b. 1947), and Caio Fernando Abreu (b. 1948).

Satire about the oftentimes surprising reality of Brazilian existence has become an important subcategory of short fiction and the Brazilian *crônica.* Luís Fernando Veríssimo's (b. 1936) *O analista de Bagé* (1983; the analyst from Bagé), a satirical view of Brazilian life, has become the all-time best-seller of Brazilian literature. Carlos Eduardo Novaes's (b. 1940) satires are of a similar nature, although his targets are the fleeting politicians of the moment.

Short fiction about the contemporary Brazilian woman's situation merits special note. Sônia Coutinho (b. 1939) has published both short fiction, such as *Uma certa felicidade* (1976; a certain happiness), and an important novel, *Atire em Sofia* (1989; shoot Sofia), in which women see themselves as outcasts in a macho society. Hilda Hilst's (b. 1930) and Márcia Dénser's (b. 1949) fiction uses blatant profanity to describe the life-style of newly liberated Brazilian women.

"Concert poetry" performed in restaurants, bars, on the beach, and during soccer games became popular in Rio of the mid-1980s among younger poets who express no particular attitude or approach of note. Some of the principal figures are Glória Horta (b. 1954), Suzana Vargas, Alex Polari, Régis Bonvicino, and Daisy Damas (dates n.a.), who openly cultivate the "poema pornô," the pornographic poem.

Theater literally struggles for survival. Nonetheless, innovative works have been written and produced by Naum Alves de Souza, Maria Adelaide Amaral (dates n.a.), and Mauro Rasi (b. 1954). Gerald Thomas (b. 1955) has launched punk versions of classical dramas.

Solid literary criticism reflecting both nationalist and internationalist orientations flourishes with several preeminent figures, including Fábio Lucas (b. 1931), Silviano Santiago (b. 1936), Affonso Romano de Sant'Anna (b. 1937), Luís Costa Lima (b. 1937), Roberto Schwarz (b. 1938), João Alexandre Barbosa (b. 1937), Davi Arrigucci, Jr.

(dates n.a.), José Guilherme Merquior (1941–1991), Walnice Galvão (dates n.a.), and Flora Sussekind (b. 1955), among many others.

Over this quarter century, the traditional social preoccupation of Brazilian literature has been reinforced and is now the predominant concern of literary activity. Without doubt, Brazilian writers view this approach as a form of participatory democracy, which the society as a whole has yet to fully enjoy.

BIBLIOGRAPHY: Lowe, E., *The City in Brazilian Literature* (1982); Haberly, D. T., *Three Sad Races: Racial Identity and National Consciousness in Brazilian Literature* (1983); Patai, D., *Myth and Ideology in Contemporary Brazilian Fiction* (1983); Brookshaw, D., *Race and Color in Brazilian Literature* (1986); Lobo, L., ''Women Writers in Brazil Today,'' *WLT*, 61, 1 (Winter 1987), 49–54; Brookshaw, D., *Paradise Betrayed: Brazilian Literature of the Indian* (1988); Stern, I., ed., *Dictionary of Brazilian Literature* (1988); DiAntonio, R. E., *Brazilian Fiction: Aspects and Evolution of the Contemporary Narrative* (1989); Reis, R., ed., *Toward Socio-Criticism* (1991)

IRWIN STERN

BREYTENBACH, Breyten
South African poet, novelist, and short-story writer (writing in Afrikaans and English), b. 16 Sept. 1939, Bonnievale

B. is the most important Afrikaans poet of his generation, and has also attained some fame as a painter. It is, however, through his political views and imprisonment by the South African government that he has become most prominent. In 1958 and 1959 he studied art and Afrikaans literature at the University of Cape Town. He left South Africa for Europe in 1960, settling in Paris where, in 1962, he married his Vietnamese wife, Hoang Lien. He became increasingly involved in anti-apartheid activities and in 1975 was arrested in South Africa on charges of terrorism and imprisoned until 1982. Subsequent to his release he has lived in Paris and continues to be an important critic of the South African situation.

B.'s first published works are *Katastrofes* (1964; catastrophes), a collection of short stories, and *Die ysterkoei moet sweet* (1964; the iron cow must sweat), a volume of poetry. In the poem ''Bedreiging van die siekes'' (threat of the sick ones), B. introduces himself to his readers as a harmless poet whose task it is to acknowledge the imminence and inevitability of death; and in ''Oop-

maak'' (opening up) from *Katastrofes* he presents himself as a spy setting out each day to build his case against life.

In these two early works, the twenty-five-year-old B.'s obsessional concern with degeneration and decay is countered, as in his later works, by the enduring possibilities of acts of creativity, and also by his love for his often-apostrophized wife. In *Die ysterkoei moet sweet* a number of poems relating to Zen Buddhism are included—an influence that critics have been much concerned with, often ascribing B.'s associative technique to this philosophy.

The most political of B.'s works, verging on invective, is *Skryt: om 'n sinkende skip blou te verf* (1972; shrite [a composite of shit, write, chalk, shrine, stride]: to paint a sinking ship blue), banned in South Africa until 1982. His visit to South Africa in 1973 is recounted in *'n Seisoen in die Paradys* (1976; *A Season in Paradise*, 1980), published under the name B. B. Lasarus. The title invokes Arthur Rimbaud's (1854–1891) *Une saison en enfer* (1873), with the implication that the return to his country of birth offered B. some respite; the nom de plume similarly invokes a resurrection.

After B.'s release from imprisonment, he published a number of works, collectively titled *Die ongedanste dans* (the undanced dance): *Eklips* (1983; eclipse), *'Yk'* (1983; gauge), *Buffalo Bill* (1984; Buffalo Bill), and *Lewendood* (1985; living death). This cycle consists of long, somewhat formless poems, reminiscent of Ezra Pound (q.v.). Some of these poems have been rendered into English by the poet in *Judas Eye and Self-Portrait/Deathwatch* (1988). *The True Confessions of an Albino Terrorist* (1984) is an autobiographical text on his imprisonment (originally published in English and untranslated into Afrikaans); he recounts his interrogation and trial, and explores the condition of imprisonment.

B. has increasingly published in English, distancing himself publicly from the Afrikaans language and Afrikaner culture. *End Papers* (1986) contains reflections on South African society and culture written between 1967 and 1985. The novel *Memory of Snow and Dust* (1989) is, as is the case with much of B.'s work, a complex blend of autobiography and symbolism. It offers a reflection on exile by means of three characters living in Paris, one of them a white author who comes to South Africa and is arrested and sentenced to death for a murder he did not commit. In *All One Horse* (1989) twenty-seven short prose pieces and twenty-seven watercolors by the author are collected.

Breytenbach has been awarded the most prestigious Afrikaans language prize, the Hertzog Prize, which he declined for ideological reasons; he has also received the CNA award five times.

FURTHER WORKS: *Huis van die dowe* (1967); *Kouevuur* (1969); *Lotus* (1970); *Om te vlieg: 'n opstel in vyf ledemate en 'n ode* (1971); *Met ander woorde: vrugte van die droom van stilte* (1973); *De boom achter de maan* (1974); *Voetskrif* (1976); *Blomskryf* (1977); *Die miernes swel op* (1980); *Mouroir (bespieëlende notas van 'n roman)* (1983); *Mouroir: Mirrornotes of a Novel,* 1984); *Notes of Bird* (1984); *Boek (deel een): dryfpunt* (1987); *Soos die so* (1990). FURTHER VOLUMES IN ENGLISH: *And Death White As Words: An Anthology of the Poetry of B. B.* (1978); *In Africa Even the Flies Are Happy: Selected Poems, 1964–1977* (1978)

BIBLIOGRAPHY: Van der Merwe, P. P., "B. B. and the Poet Revolutionary," *Theoria,* 56 (May 1981), 51–72; Cope, J., *The Adversary Within: Dissident Writers in Afrikaans* (1982), 165–82; Dis, A. van, "I am not an Afrikaner any more," *IonC,* 12, 3 (June 1983), 3–6; Des Prés, T., "Rimbaud's Nephew," *Parnassus,* 11, 2 (1983–1984), 83–102; David, C., "B. B.: Le point de non-retour est atteint," *Nouvel Observateur,* 2–8 Aug. 1985, 32; Moore, G., "The Martian Descends: The Poetry of B. B.," *ArielE,* 16, 2 (Apr. 1985), 3–12; Coetzee, J. M., "A Poet in Prison," *Social Dynamics,* 11, 2 (1985), 72–75; Roberts, S., "B. B.'s Prison Literature," *CentR,* 30, 2 (Spring 1986), 304–13; Jacobs, J. U., "B. B. and the South African Prison Book," *Theoria,* 68 (1986), 95–105; Egan, S., "B.'s *Mouroir:* The Novel As Autobiography," *JNT,* 18, 2 (Spring 1988), 89–104; Coetzee, J. M., "B. and the Censor," *Raritan,* 10, 4 (Spring 1991), 58–84

CARLI COETZEE

BRINK, André P(hilippus)

South African novelist, dramatist, and literary critic (writing in Afrikaans and English), b. 29 May 1935, Vrede, Free State

B. is one of the most popular South African novelists and an important critic of Afrikaans literature. He studied at Potchefstroom University, where he obtained an M.A. in English literature in 1958 and in Afrikaans literature in 1959. From 1959 to 1961 he studied at the Sorbonne in Paris. B. was a lecturer in the Afrikaans department at Rhodes University from 1961, and took up a position in the English department at the University of Cape Town in 1991. It is as spokesman for the Writers of the Sixties that he first gained prominence.

In a significant article, to some extent the manifesto of the group, "Oor religie en seks" (1964; on religion and sex), B. argued for a literature that was not limited by Calvinist morality. His own early works are formally experimental and attempt a treatment of sexuality, especially feminine sexuality. The first of these works is *Lobola vir die lewe* (1962; bride price for life), but his *Die ambassadeur* (1963; *The Ambassador,* 1964) marks his highest literary achievement. The novel, which has often been likened to Lawrence Durrell's (q.v.) *The Alexandria Quartet* (4 vols., 1957–1960), is narrated from five different perspectives. The work is the account of a relationship between a South African ambassador and a woman he meets in Paris; she is one of the childlike sylphs B. is criticized for limiting female characters to. A later work, *Orgie* (1965; orgy), again dealing with a sexual ménage à trois involving such a woman, is formally the most experimental of B.'s works.

B.'s five novels of the 1970s are a return to a more conventional form, but were significantly new thematically in Afrikaans. The first of these, *Kennis van die aand* (1973; *Looking on Darkness,* 1974), was the first book by an Afrikaans writer to be banned under the 1963 censorship legislation; it was unbanned in 1982. What distinguishes these novels is a concern with the South African actuality, characterized by state violence and injustice. The novels include *'n Oomblik in die wind* (1975; *An Instant in the Wind,* 1977); *Gerugte van reën* (1978; *Rumours of Rain,* 1978); *'n Droë wit seisoen* (1979; *A Dry White Season,* 1980); and *Houd-den-bek* (1982; *A Chain of Voices,* 1982). The last of these was written simultaneously in Afrikaans and English.

B.'s *States of Emergency* (1988) was published in English only. Explicitly utilizing postmodernist literary techniques, the novel explores the relationship between romantic love and the state of emergency declared in South Africa in 1986; B. has said in an interview that he regards the political situation as a starting point for attempts at exploring the loneliness of the human condition. In his most recent novel, *An Act of Terror* (1991), a history of South Africa is presented, reconstructed by the main character, Thomas Landman, through the chronicle of thirteen generations of his family in the country, culminating in his own political resistance.

B. has made a significant contribution to Afrikaans literature by his numerous translations of European literary works, as well as his literary criticism. He is a prolific author, and not all of his works are of equal quality. As one of the proponents of the "Sestigers," his formal experimentation and exploration of new themes, especially sexuality and South African politics, have been significant.

FURTHER WORKS: *Die meul teen die hang* (1958); *Die gebondenes* (1958); *Die band om ons harte* (1959); *Eindelose weë* (1960); *Bakkies en sy maats—die bende* (1961); *Caesar* (1962); *Orde en chaos* (1962); *Platsak* (1962); *Pot-pourri* (1962); *Sempre diritto* (1963); *Olé* (1965); *Bagasie* (1965); *Elders mooiweer en warm* (1965); *Miskien nooit: 'n somerspel* (1967); *Aspekte van die nuwe prosa* (1967); *Midi* (1969); *Parys-Parys: retoer* (1969); *Fado* (1970); *Die verhoor* (1970); *Die rebelle* (1970); *Die poësie van Breyten Breytenbach* (1971); *Kinkels innie kabel* (1971); *Die bobaas van die boendoe* (1973); *Afrikaners is plesierig* (1973); *Die geskiedenis van Oom Kootjie Emmer van Witgatworteldraai* (1973); *Portret van die vrou as 'n meisie* (1973; *Portrait of the Woman as a Young Girl,* 1973); *Brandewyn in Suid-Afrika* (1973; *Brandy in South Africa,* 1973); *Dessertwyn in Suid-Afrika* (1974; *Dessert Wine in South Africa,* 1974); *Die klap van die meul* (1974); *Die wyn van bowe* (1974); *Pavane* (1974); *Aspekte van die nuwe drama* (1974); *Voorlopige rapport* (1976); *Die hamer van die hekse* (1976); *Jan Rabie se 21* (1977); *Toiings op die langpad* (1979); *Tweede voorlopige rapport* (1980); *'n Emmertjie wyn* (1981); *Heildronk* (1981); *Die fees van die malles* (1982); *Die muur van die pes* (1984; *The Wall of the Plague,* 1985); *Literatuur in die strydperk* (1985); *Waarom literatuur?* (1985); *Vertelkunde: 'n inleiding tot die lees van verhalende tekste* (1988); *Die eerste lewe van Adamastor* (1988); *Die kreef raak gewoond daaraan* (1991). FURTHER VOLUMES IN ENGLISH: *Why Literature?* (1981); *Mapmakers: Writing in a State of Siege* (1983)

BIBLIOGRAPHY: Woods, D., "Brave Truths of a Rebel Author," *Observer,* 23 Sept. 1979, 11; Cope, J., *The Adversary Within: Dissident Writers in Afrikaans* (1982), 124–41; Herbert, H., "Courage in a Land of Darkness," *Guardian,* 6 May 1982, 10; Nkosi, L., "Escaping from the Laager," *TLS,* 16 Sept. 1983, 996; Viola, A., "A. B. and the Writer in State and Siege," *CE&S,* 7, 2 (Spring 1985), 64–71; MacDermott, D., "A Narrow Beam of Light: A Reading of Two Novels by A. B.," *WLWE,* 28, 2 (Autumn 1988), 178–88

CARLI COETZEE

BRINKMANN, Rolf Dieter

German poet, novelist, and short-story writer, b. 16 Apr. 1940, Vechta; d. 23 Apr. 1975, London, England

After high school B. held a variety of temporary jobs. In 1962 he moved to Cologne, where he studied at the Teachers College from 1963 to 1965. He gave this up to become a full-time writer. He was never financially successful but managed to keep his head above water with several small publications, with editorial tasks, and with scholarships, such as at the Villa Massimo in Rome (1972–1973) and at the University of Texas at Austin (1974). He was killed in an automobile accident while visiting London. He had almost ceased publishing after 1970, and many of his works appeared posthumously.

B. began publishing collections of his poems in 1962, but they received little critical attention, primarily because they appeared in limited editions of a few hundred copies or less. Only with the collections *Was fraglich ist wofür* (1967; what is questionable why) and *Die piloten* (1968; the pilots), and with the anthology *Standphotos: gedichte 1962–1970* (1980; still photos: poems 1962–1970) did he reach a wider public. B. began in a rather solipsistic, introverted vein but quickly emerged as the leading German-language pop poet. His poems have a snapshot quality by which he tries, through a series of very short lines, to capture a transitory occurrence of everyday reality, which is full of banality, brutality, and sex. The poems constitute a radical break thematically and stylistically with the German poetic tradition. B.'s last collection of poems, *Westwärts 1 & 2* (1975; westward 1 & 2), published shortly after his death and containing the poems written between 1970 and 1974, became a best-seller. It marks a return to a somewhat more standard verse form, although B. is still interested in experimentation. His thematics are also more traditional: criticism of society, praise of the simple life, and admiration for other authors.

B. was heavily influenced by the American pop movement and was largely responsible for introducing it to German readers. He edited three important and seminal works on this topic: *ACID: neue amerikanische szene* (1969; acid, new American scene, with Ralf-Rainer Rygulla), *Frank O'Hara: lunch poems und andere gedichte* (1969; Frank O'Hara: lunch poems and other poems), and *Silver screen: neue amerikanische lyrik* (1969; silver screen; new American poetry). B. believed that pop culture would help free German society from its inhibiting constraints.

B. also wrote a limited number of prose works, and most of them have an autobiographical flavor. The stories in his first collection, *Die umarmung* (1965; the embrace), are intensely personal, sexually graphic, and painfully exact in their descriptions. In his next collection, *Raupenbahn* (1966; caterpillar ride), he writes about youth and youth culture. In his novel *Keiner weiβ mehr* (1968; no one knows more) he describes a familial situation where consumerism inhibits any truly intimate relationships. In all these stories there is a sense of depression and suffering and an urge to rebel against all societal constraints. Most of the prose works written between 1965 and his death, together with other material, were published as *Der film in worten* (1982; the film in words).

B.'s stay at the Villa Massimo in Rome resulted in three diarylike posthumous publications: *Rom, blicke* (1979; Rome, views), *Erkundungen für die präzisierung des gefühls für einen aufstand* (1987; inquiries about making the feelings for a revolution more precise), and *Schnitte* (1988; cuts). They are large collages of photographs, found material, quotations, postcards, prose, and other material. They show an extremely lonely and tortured individual trying to find meaning in life and lashing out against everything and anything that infringes on his freedom.

Although partially ignored and then almost forgotten during his lifetime, B. has achieved in death what eluded him before, namely recognition as one of the most daring and innovative writers in postwar Germany.

FURTHER WORKS: *Ihr nennt es sprache* (1962); *Le chant du monde* (1964); *Ohne neger* (1966); *& gedichte* (1966); *Godzilla* (1968); *Gras* (1970); *Wold's end* (1973); *Burgruine hochburg* (1984); *Erzählungen* (1985); *Eiswasser an der guadelupe str.* (1985); *Der brand auf der festung hochburg 1684* (1985)

BIBLIOGRAPHY: special B. issue, *TuK,* 71 (July 1981); Lampe, G. W., *Ohne Subjektivität: Interpretationen zur Lyrik R. D. B.s vor dem Hintergrund der Studentenbewegung* (1983); Richter, H., *Ästhetik der Ambivalenz: Studien zur Struktur ''postmoderner'' Lyrik, exemplarisch dargestellt an R. D. Bs Poetik und der Gedichtband ''Westwärts 1 & 2''* (1983); Schulz, G., ''Bandblasen der Seele: zur frühen Prosa und späten Lyrik R. D. Bs,'' *Merkur,* 39, 11 (Nov. 1985), 1015–20; Schenk, H., *Das Kunstverständnis in den späteren Texten R. D. Bs* (1986); Späth, S., ''Rettungsversuche aus dem Todesterritorium'': zur Aktualität der Lyrik R. D. Bs* (1986)

ROBERT ACKER

BROOKNER, Anita

British novelist and art historian, b. 16 July 1928, London

A Londoner by birth and residence, B. is the daughter of Polish Jews, her father born in Poland, her mother in England. Educated at James Allen's Girls' School, she read history at King's College, University of London, and received a Ph.D. in art history from the Courtauld Institute. During the next twenty years B. established a distinguished academic career and published widely recognized studies of 18th- and 19th-c. art. From 1959 to 1964 she was a visiting lecturer in the history of art at the University of Reading. In 1964 she was appointed lecturer at the Courtauld Institute and has continued there as a reader in the history of art since 1977. A Fellow of New Hall, Cambridge University, B. was the first woman to be named Slade Professor of Art at Cambridge (1967–1968). Her brief early studies of Ingres, David, and Watteau led to major critical works: *The Genius of the Future: Studies in French Art Criticism* (1971), *Greuze: The Rise and Fall of an Eighteenth-Century Phenomenon* (1972), and *Jacques-Louis David: A Personal Interpretation* (1980).

In 1980 B. began writing fiction and by 1985 had declared she would not return to art criticism. Since the appearance of *A Start in Life* (pub. in U.S. as *The Debut*) in 1981, she has published eleven novels to date, one each year through 1991.

From her early work to *Hotel du Lac* (1984), awarded the Booker Prize, and subsequently in fiction of enlarged scope and increasing complexity, B.'s writing has won critical acclaim for its nuance, subtlety, and wit. In some measure a satirist of contemporary relations between women and men, B. explores the inducements and rewards marriage held for earlier generations of women and captures the confusion and self-doubt of younger, independent women with careers but without love or the satisfactions of marriage. Discursive in the manner of Henry James and Edith Wharton (qq.v.), B.'s fiction reveals the pleasures and agonies, hopes and disillusions of her major characters through a stream of narrative commentary, frequently with little dialogue.

B.'s first four novels center on intelligent, educated career women—two are academics, one a librarian-turned-writer, another a novelist—plagued by loneliness and the prospect of the single life. In *A Start in Life* Ruth Weiss, like several B. characters the only child of disappointed, inept parents, finds her identity as a young woman through reading and eventually earns a Ph.D. as a Balzac specialist. While Ruth accepts a short-lived compromise marriage and continues her teaching career, the central characters in the next two novels must negotiate the expectations of egocentric men or rapacious couples parading as friends only to find themselves alone at the end. Kitty Maule of *Providence* (1982) and Frances Hinton of *Look at Me* (1983) both meet with rejection by men unworthy of them.

Like these novels, *Hotel du Lac* is a cautionary tale. Edith Hope, at thirty-nine a more urbane, self-accepting woman than earlier B. figures, manages to be objective about the hare and tortoise race of competitive females her novels depict and about her secret affair with a married man. On the brink of marriage to a conventional type who would have her relinquish her writing, she bolts and winds up—at her friends' urging—at a Swiss resort hotel in the midst of some of B.'s most colorful and amusing characters. Offered a marriage of convenience by a charming, intelligent but altogether unscrupulous man who promises her plenty of material for her fiction, Edith is tempted but decides the single state she has created for herself in London is preferable to this cynical arrangement.

B.'s work following *Hotel du Lac* has moved in new and unpredictable directions. Earlier criticism pointed out parallels in her portrayals of single women to Barbara Pym's (q.v.) "excellent women" who find no men to match them. However, the more recent novels demonstrate B.'s ability to work with a richer social fabric and to create characters with complex histories struggling to maintain a delicate balance in worlds foreign to them.

In *Family and Friends* (1985) and *Latecomers* (1988) B. introduces a number of European exiles who have established outwardly successful lives in England after World War II. The former, structured brilliantly around four photographs of wedding parties, suggests a play by Anton Chekhov (q.v.). *Latecomers* is a study in contrasts: of business partners who had escaped to London from war-torn Germany as boys; of their close friendships and marriages; of their two unlikely children. In both works B. reveals—with impressive insight—the psychological dimensions of vastly different characters. With a light but devastating wit she anatomizes a society in transition..

In those writers she has identified as the touchstones of 19th-c. writing—Dickens, James, Trollope, Stendhal, Flaubert, and Zola—B. locates the close scrutiny, moral scruple, and indignation she values in fiction. The contemporary women novelists she admires, among them Rosamund Lehmann (b. 1901), Elizabeth Taylor (1912–1975), Edith Templeton (b. 1916), Mavis Gallant, and Fay Weldon (qq.v.), exemplify the restrained yet passionate storytelling and incisive social analysis of which she herself is master.

B.'s stylistic skill is evident in the painterly qualities of her descriptions and in the deft weaving of references to literary works, paintings, sculptures, and myth into details about her characters' careers and personalities. Sensuous renderings of objects, clothing, rooms, and landscapes

create a rich atmosphere that offsets the more serious moral concerns of her writing.

FURTHER WORKS: *An Iconography of Cecil Rhodes* (1956); *J. A. Dominique Ingres* (1965); *Jacques-Louis David* (1967); *Watteau* (1968); *A Misalliance* (1986); *A Friend from England* (1987); *Lewis Percy* (1989); *Brief Lives* (1990); *A Closed Eye* (1991)

BIBLIOGRAPHY: Jebb, J., "Unblinking," on *Hotel du Lac*, *Spectator*, 22 Sept. 1984, 26–27; Tyler, A., "A Solitary Life Is Still Worth Living," on *Hotel du Lac*, *NYTBR*, 3 Feb. 1985, 1, 31; Wilson, A. N., "Significant Silences," on *Family and Friends*, *TLS*, 6 Sept. 1985, 973; Haffenden, J., *Novelists in Interview* (1985), 57–85; Kakutani, M., on *The Misalliance*, *NYT*, 25 Mar. 1987, C23; Guppy, S., "Interview: The Art of Fiction XCVII: A. B.," *Paris Review*, 109 (1987), 146–69; Hosmer, R. E., "A. B." in Brook, J. M., ed., *DLB: Yearbook 1987* (1988), 293–308; Bawer, B., "Doubles and More Doubles," on *Latecomers*, *NewC*, 7, 8 (Apr. 1989), 67–74; Sadler, L. V., *A. B.* (1990); Lopate, P., on *Lewis Percy*, *NYTBR*, 11 Mar. 1990, 10

THEODORA RAPP GRAHAM

BROUWERS, Jeroen

Dutch novelist and short-story writer, b. 30 Apr. 1940, Batavia, Indonesia

When B. was born in Indonesia, it was a Dutch colony. From 1943 until the end of World War II, B. was imprisoned in Indonesia by the Japanese occupying forces with his mother, grandmother, and sister. In 1948 the family returned to the Netherlands. B. spent six years (1950–1956) at Catholic boarding schools. After working as a journalist for a year and a half, he moved to Belgium in 1964, where he started to work for a publishing company as an executive secretary and editor. He made his literary debut in 1964. After his Belgian period, which ended on a depressive note, B. moved back to the Netherlands in 1976, where he started to write novels, polemic essays, and literary contributions for newspapers and periodicals. In 1982 he was awarded the Flemish-Geuzen Prize for his complete oeuvre.

In B.'s work no book stands on its own; themes and constants are carried from one book to another, motifs repeat themselves, a new publication can cover an earlier one by improving it or by perfecting it. Writing like this is a necessity for B. In his work one meets him as a person who is in conflict with society and himself: He is pursued by an everlasting feeling of insignificance. His writing is centered around an "I" whose biographical data fit the life of B. His point of departure, especially after his Belgian period, is one of having lost the right track. This situation can be explained from earlier experiences, such as his childhood years before the Japanese concentration camp, his experiences in that camp, his years at boarding schools, a failed marriage, and a feeling of doom about his own future.

One can divide B.'s work into two phases. In Amsterdam and Brussels he started writing and slowly became a novelist. His debut, *Het mes op de keel* (1964; the knife at the throat), shows a preference for apocalyptic situations and mythological imagination. In the novel *Joris Ockeloen en het wachten* (1967; Joris Ockeloen and the waiting), for which he received the Vijverberg Prize (1967), B. uses magical realistic processes to attain his mirror effects. His stories reflect in one another; questions asked in one work are answered in another. B. considers this early work an exercise for his later work, which develops at the end of the Belgian period and brings us to his second phase.

In *Zonder trommels en trompetten* (1973; without drums and trumpets) B. deals with a number of themes: literature, death, the past, (impossible) love, materialized in events and thoughts that preoccupy him at that moment and which at the same moment make him the person he is. Each theme has its own voice. This process suggests that all events and the themes they represent illustrate one another and that they sometimes become one. This technique reaches its height in *Zonsopgangen boven zee* (1977; sunrises above the sea).

Bezonken rood (1981; *Sunken Red*, 1990) is perhaps his most important work. Important is the memory of bygone years, of the things that made him what he is. In this work B. describes his life in a Japanese concentration camp. At that time he still had a warm relationship with his mother, which lasted until the end of their stay there, when his mother was humiliated and abused by the Japanese. As of that moment he was lost: "My mother was the most beautiful mother, at that moment I stopped loving her." This experience has determined B.'s relations with other people, especially loved ones.

De zondvloed (1990; the deluge) completes the impressive and baroque "Indian trilogy"—the first part being *Het verzonkene* (1979; the submerged), and the second part, *Bezonken rood*. In addition, it synthesizes at the same time the complete works of B. It is considered a masterpiece, a phenomenon that one does not find easily in Dutch literature. In *De zondvloed* B. pursues his futile search for his lost love, the continuation of his search in "Orpheus," the first story of his debut, *Het mes op de keel.*

Until 1979 B. did not have a large audience. But his polemic activities and his work *Bezonken rood* caused quite a stir in the Netherlands, and his writings were discussed in public debates. B.'s works now attract a large public, which became apparent when his book *De laatste deur* (1983; the last door) was reprinted three times within one year. B. continues to cover all dramatic periods of his life. His work *Zomervlucht* (1990; summer escape) deals with a man's mid-life crisis. The work consists of a chain of associations that all fall into place. *Zomervlucht* is of course part of his biography: "I am the stories that I tell."

FURTHER WORKS: *De toteltuin* (1968); *Groetjes uit Brussel* (1969); *Zachtjes knetteren de letteren* (1975); *Klein leed* (1977); *Mijn Vlaamse jaren* (1978); *De nieuwe revisor* (1979); *Kladboek* (1979); *De Bierkaai* (1980); *Zonder onderschriften* (1980); *Et in Arcadia ego* (1981); *De spoken van Godfried Bomans* (1982); *Alleen voor Vlamingen* (1982); *Es ergo sum* (1982); *Zonder onderschriften* (1983); *Verhalen en levensberichten* (1983); *Winterlicht* (1984); *De levende stilte van Stig Dagerman* (1985); *De sprong* (1985); *Hij is reeds aan de overzijde* (1985); *Helene Swart* (1985); *De achterhoek* (1987); *De oude Faust* (1987); *Sire, er zijn geen Belgen* (1988); *De versierde dood* (1989); *Groetjes uit Brussel* (1989)

LUDMILA M. KERMAN

BRYCE ECHENIQUE, Alfredo (Marcelo)

Peruvian novelist, short-story writer, and journalist, b. 19 Feb. 1939, Lima

B. E. was born into a distinguished aristocratic family and seemed destined to become a writer: His mother, who admired French culture, had baptized him with the second name Marcelo in honor of Marcel Proust (q.v.). In 1964 B. E. graduated from law school, but he also received a degree in literature, writing a thesis on the function of dialogue in the works of Ernest Hemingway (q.v.). That same year he boarded a steamer for Europe to study and write there.

B. E. began his writing career after finishing law school and while continuing his doctoral studies at the Sorbonne. Beginning in 1968, he taught for twelve years at the Sorbonne and the Universities of Nanterre and Vincennes. Between 1980 and 1984, he taught Latin American literature and culture at the Paul Valéry University in Montpelier, France. More recently he has lectured at other European, Latin American, and North American universities. B. E. currently resides in Madrid, Spain.

B. E. is an accomplished fiction writer and journalist. To date, he has written two volumes of short stories and five novels. His works have been translated into fifteen languages (although English is not one of them). B. E. is an exciting feature-story writer for popular journals and newspapers throughout the Hispanic world. He has written extensively about his travels in Europe and Latin America. In November 1988 he was commissioned by Spain's most important newspaper, *El Pais,* to visit Prague, Czechoslovakia, and write a series of articles analyzing the political scene in that country. Currently he writes a daily column for the opinion page of another newspaper, *Diario 16.* He has also been appointed to be a judge for the Premio Cervantes, the Hispanic world's most prestigious literary prize.

His short stories in *Huerto cerrado* (1968; closed orchard), which received a special mention at the Casa de las Américas literary competition in La Habana in 1967, and his first novel, *Un mundo para Julius* (1970; a world for Julius), gave him instant literary fame, not only in Peru, but also in literary circles from Mexico City, Caracas, and Buenos Aires to Europe. While B. E. has written four additional novels—his most recent was published in 1989—readers find themselves returning to his first novel. Like his other works, *Un mundo para Julius* is a novel based heavily on personal experience. Much of the novel is autobiographical, for references to Julius's childhood and schooling are similar to the author's experiences at his grandfather's mansion or at the grade school run by North American nuns and priests in Lima. A charming, well-written piece of literature, it is about a youngster's first years of life until he reaches eleven. However, adult and child perspectives intermingle to create poignant irony, great humor, and penetrating social commentary about the relatively uncomplicated, rich, upper-class strata of Peruvian society in Lima in the 1950s. In Peru this novel has become an integral part of the nation's literary canon, and in other countries it has achieved prominence as well. The writing of the novel in 1969 and its publication in 1970 coincided with the 1969 coup d'état that took credit for expropriating vast land holdings belonging to Peru's oligarchy; not surprisingly, here literature and history fuse to symbolize the destruction of Peru's long-established ruling classes. Despite this first, political reading of the novel, making it very much a novel of its time, it won the Peruvian Premio Nacional de Literatura in 1972 and continues to generate lasting interest for contemporary readers. The novel is not only an engagingly corrosive portrayal of the pretentious, morally blind Peruvian oligarchy and its transition to the dominant nouveau riche class subsidized by an influx of North American capitalism in the

1950s; it is also an early postmodern urban novel in which the bildungsroman motif and its curious, questioning, sentimental protagonist Julius bring together elements of the drama of lost innocence, black comedy of manners, playful parody, and social satire. Translated into many foreign languages, it won first prize for the best foreign novel in translation in France in 1974. As we begin to review the importance of the so-called "boom" period of the 1960s—the fictional works of Carlos Fuentes, Mario Vargas Llosa, Julio Cortázar, Gabriel García Márquez (qq.v.), and others—this novel ranks among the first works to emphasize the art of storytelling in which the notably oral tone of the novel handily juxtaposes invention and representation, hyperbole and reality, multiple points of view and the free indirect style, in addition to interior monologue. The incorporation of these elements into the novel does not place it among those in which the allusion to societal fragmentation is the goal, as in the narrative worlds of Vargas Llosa's and Fuentes's early novels; it creates instead an obvious hierarchy of class and ethnic differences in Peru.

FURTHER WORKS: *Muerte de Sevilla en Madrid* (1972); *La felicidad ja ja* (1974); *A vuelo de buen cubero; y otras crónicas* (1977); *Tantas veces Pedro* (1977); *Todos los cuentos* (1979); *La vida exagerada de Martín Romaña* (1981); *Magdalena y otros cuentos* (1986); *Crónicas personales* (1988); *La última mudanza de Felipe Carrillo* (1988); *El hombre que hablaba de Octavia de Cádiz* (1989); *Dos señoras conversan* (1990)

BIBLIOGRAPHY: Bensoussan, A., "A. B. E., le principe d'innocence," *Co-textes,* 9 (May 1985), 45–53; Eyzaguirre, L., "A. B. E. o la reconquista del tiempo," *RCLL,* 11, 21–22 (1985), 215–21; Gutierrez Mouat, R., "Lector y narratario en dos relatos de B. E.," *Inti: Revista de Literatura Hispánica,* 24–25 (Fall–Spring 1986–1987), 107–26; Ruiz Fajardo, G., "Entrevista epistolar a A. B. E.," *Plaza: Revista de Literatura,* 12 (Spring 1987), 7–12; Eyzaguirre, L., "La última mudanza de B. E.," *Hispam,* 18, 53–54 (Aug.–Dec. 1989), 195–202; Rodriguez-Peralta, P., "The Subjective Narration of B. E.'s *La vida exagerada de Martín Romaña*," *HisJ,* 10, 2 (Spring 1989), 139–51; Padura Fuentes, L., "Retrato y voz de A. B. E.," *Plural: Revista Cultural de Excelsior,* 224 (May 1990), 35–40

DICK GERDES

BUARQUE, Chico

(abbrev. of Francisco Buarque de Hollanda) Brazilian composer, poet, and dramatist, b. 19 June 1944, Rio de Janeiro

B., son of a renowned historian, grew up in São Paulo, in an environment enriched by his family's contacts with Brazil's artistic and intellectual elites. By the mid-1960s, he had already gained fame in his own right, fast becoming the country's leading contemporary bard, recording artist, and dramatist. B. soon came to embody the entire youth culture, especially in its persistent opposition to the excesses of the recently installed military dictatorship. Censorship, corruption, physical abuse, uncontrolled capitalism, foreign economic influence, and American cultural domination became recurrent themes as well as an increasingly cruel reality for B., as it was for many others of his generation; and, in fact, it even motivated him, at the end of the decade, to seek, for a time, voluntary exile abroad.

His early songs already demonstrated pronounced social overtones, a tendency later to incur repeated bouts with government censors. Such was the case, for example, of his "Pedro Pedreiro" (1965; Peter the stonemason), a troubling narrative whose musical poetics focus on the unenviable life-style of Rio's exploited working class. In the same year, B. also undertook his first theatrical project, creating the musical setting for *Morte e vida Severina* (1955; death and life of Severina), by famed poet João Cabral de Melo Neto (q.v.). The trend was soon to be expanded upon considerably. Indeed, in the realm of theater, alive with intensified protest of a sociohistorical nature, his controversial *Roda viva* (spinning wheel) came out in 1968; and three other pieces—all modern-day classics—followed, either authored or coauthored by B.: *Calabar—O elogio da traição* (1973; Calabar—the praise of treachery), *Gota d'água* (1975; a drop of water) and *Opera do malandro* (1978; hustler's opera). In addition, the 1970s also witnessed his hugely successful entry into cinematic song writing as well as the appearance of *Fazenda modelo* (1974; model farm), a novelette. Loosely inspired by George Orwell's (q.v.) *Animal Farm* (1945), the allegorical narrative, too, became a best-seller by satirizing the regime through unmistakable hyperbole.

Roda viva, B.'s two-act *comédia musical,* is actually tragic, exhibiting musical instances, complete with versification and chorus, in no way detrimental to a prevalent dramatic venue. It is a structural mix that he adheres to, as well, in his remaining works. The play centers on the progressive makeover, by cynical promoters, of a humble singer, first into a pop-music idol in the Beatles mold, and then, when tastes change, into a Brazilianized, engagé version of country and western crooner. It is B.'s metaphor for the nation's perennial debate around the multiple binom of exploiter-exploited, rich-poor, foreign-autoch-

thonous, city-countryside, even good-bad. The protagonist, overwhelmed by, as it were, the capitalist exigencies of show business—synthesized symbolically in the title—commits suicide, at which point his widow is already being groomed to succeed him. *Roda viva* proved to be a high point of 1960s theater, in terms of expression and innovative choreography, as well as of forceful protest in a Brazil fast knuckling under to military repression. Not surprisingly, the play was eventually banned.

Calabar—O elogio da traição, coauthored with filmmaker Ruy Guerra, was struck down early on by government censorship. In fact, it was not even allowed to be staged until 1980; and its immediate popularity was assured only through unobstructed publication in book form. The play deals, in a revisionist and, again, farcical light, with the real-life title figure and his role during Holland's protracted, 17th-c. occupation of northeastern Brazil. He is Calabar, who, in being hanged as a traitor to the Portuguese cause, has, much like Benedict Arnold, long since been turned into the embodiment of unpatriotic betrayal. However, doubts are raised as to his true motives, no longer detached from the convoluted, parallel web of intrigue and deception that so dominates both story line and character development. Indeed, Calabar's central role, achieved without his ever appearing in person, is extrapolated in light of the remaining and, for the most part, equally historical figures, all of whom also perform some or other rite of betrayal. This predominant motif, parodically alluded to in the subtitle, proves overwhelming, as well as a demythologizing reflection on all Brazilian institutions, past and, most significantly, present. Structurally, too, *Calabar* breaks with traditionalism through cinemalike shifts that reinforce the anarchic independence of each scene.

B.'s next play, coauthored with Paulo Pontes (1941?–1976), is decisively more tragic than comic. *Gota d'água,* a musical recreation of Euripides's *Medea,* is adapted to the sociolinguistic realities of the contemporary urban masses, and set, rather prototypically, in the working-class outskirts of Rio. The preface to the printed version, in fact, makes unambiguous reference to the ideological questions and collateral thematic baggage that the drama attempts to address: the dehumanizing consequences of a jungle capitalism where the elite co-opts promising have-nots; the need to stress popular culture over imported values; and the primacy of the spoken word vis-à-vis the dramatic art form.

The story line, like the Greek tragedy by which it is inspired, is fleshed out in verse, complete with a choral presence—made up, appropriately, of raucous washwomen. Fortunately, neither compromises the pulsating spontaneity of the present day. Action centers on Jasão, who, after overnight fame with his title samba, abandons longtime companion Joana for another who is more socially advantageous. In desperation, Joana completes the trajectory of this "*carioca* tragedy," killing their children and then committing suicide. Myth and harsh reality join to provide for familiar themes around *Milagre* excesses, like corruption, real-estate speculation, and the manipulation of the masses. More than ever, it is B.'s songs that engender the desired feeling of popular perspective, especially his title composition, alive with rhythm and metaphor.

Ópera do malandro is considered B.'s most ambitious stage production and, as implied in the title, the one where musical discourse is most significant. The composer-dramatist, working alone, based it on John Gay's *Beggar's Opera* (1798) as well as *The Three-Penny Opera* (1955) of Bertolt Brecht (q.v.) and Kurt Weill (1900–1950). From the former comes a milieu imbibed with prostitutes and criminal elements designed to reflect vice on all levels of society; from the latter comes the basic cast of characters and melodramatic scheme, as well as many structural details. B.'s parodied hybrid proves itself as much a musical comedy as a sweeping satire, set not in contemporary Brazil but during the pre-1945 *Estado Novo* of dictator Getúlio Vargas. Once again, chronological dislocation serves as metaphor for more recent and familiar abuses, namely multinational penetration, import substitution, and runaway consumerism. Meanwhile, an especially caricatured cast personifies varied segments of the venal power structure. However, it is the demise of the popular, implicitly endearing title institution, in favor of the detached, upper-echelon chicanery so much a part of post-1964 Brazil, which overrides *Ópera do malandro*. The spectator's unavoidable nostalgia for a fascistoid state, in turn, derides, by its very appeal, the bitter realities of 1970s Brazil—a perception little diminished by the censorship to which the theatrical production was subjected.

The author's sole piece of prose fiction, *Fazenda modelo,* also enjoyed wide success, although admittedly more for what it said (and when) than for any particular aesthetic qualities. In occupying the outer limits of zoomorphology, the satire allegorizes, with precision, Brazil's most frightening post-1964 period. The author subtitles this grotesque vision a "Novelette of Cattle-Raising," prefacing it with a mock-serious paean to his good intentions and concluding it with a technical bibliography. Such realist trappings, together with visual references like maps, diary entries, statistical data, and a newspaper article, serve well to "document" the surrealism of unfolding events.

Over twenty short chapters, through various first-person narrator-witnesses, and in strict linear progression, *Fazenda modelo* traces the brief and tragic history of the modern, cost-effective bovine enterprise. April 1, the parodied date of the March 31 coup that in 1964 brought the military to power, is the explicit divider. Before, the microcosm was just a farm, somewhat chaotic, commercially stagnant, and refreshingly relaxed. Remembered throughout by a nostalgic populace, this Paradise Lost, fleetingly recounted in the first chapter, stands in sharp contrast to the remaining hundred odd pages of progressive, galloping misery.

Such is the touching humanoid nature, particularly of the half-dozen focused head of cattle, that its essentially caricatured presentation proves no impediment to evoking reader empathy. Indeed, the emotional vulnerability, palpable sexuality, and miserable fate of all the bovine characters, less the megalomaniacal Juvenal and his robotized, technocratic, and often sadistic subordinates, include, as well, the generic ingredients for Greek tragedy, modern totalitarianism, and 20th-c. genocide. (Repression, for instance, is delegated to a cadre whose names all begin with the non-Brazilian letter *K,* and, in their totality, sound unabashedly Germanic.) In such an atmosphere, the fact that docile cattle are bred for a profit, slaughtered, and consumed (at one in-house barbecue for ranch administrators, in particular) assumes anthropophagous proportions. None dares to oppose an end to weaning, to dehorning, or to emasculation, while sperm harvesting and artificial insemination make comforting companionship and carnal knowledge near impossible.

This model farm utilizes tools for all too familiar, state-of-the-art repression and jungle capitalism: it manipulates the medium of television; it co-opts the most promising (or potentially rebellious) bulls; it erects electrified fences; and it encourages trigger-happy police. It also freezes minimum wage, outlaws strike action, exports its best production, becomes dependent on foreign capital, and is influenced by so-called "invisible interests." The need for the sacrifice of the majority, in the name of an economic "miracle" of benefit to few, is routinely harped upon by elitist Juvenal in his official pronouncements, and proves the antithesis of the folksy and resigned informality of the novel's narrator-witnesses. Furthermore, neighboring areas, hitherto untouched, are cleared for cattle raising, in the process eliminating the native, nondomesticated population. The reign of terror only ends when the bovine citizenry is "phased out" and, in its place, soy bean is anticlimactically planted. There is no justice, no happy ending, no hope, only an experiment gone wrong. The experiment in question, as is plain to see in the author's thinly veiled invective, is not the paradidatic, nonliterary style of his novella but rather the régime itself.

B. is, first and foremost, a poet and song writer—with well over two hundred musical pieces—whose active commitment to social justice has, unlike with less talented figures, enriched rather than prejudiced his creativity. His varying artistic endeavors—lyrical, musical, theatrical, and fictional—continue to distinguish him in terms of versatility, just as his sense of originality and willingness to experiment with combined art forms promises to keep him in the vanguard of the nation's 1968 Generation.

BIBLIOGRAPHY: Lowe, E., on *Gota d'água, BA,* 50, 4 (Fall 1976), 859; Woodyard, G., "The Dynamics of Tragedy in *Gota d'água,*" *LBR,* 15 (Summer 1978), 151–60; Schoenbach, P. J., "Themes and Directions of the Brazilian Theatre: 1973–1978," *LATR,* 13, 2 (Summer 1980), 43–50; Rego, E. d. S., and C. A. Perrone, *MPB: Contemporary Brazilian Pop Music* (1985), 6–7; Perrone, C. A., "C. B.," in Stern, I., ed., *Dictionary of Brazilian Literature* (1988), 67–68; Perrone, C. A., *Masters of Contemporary Brazilian Song: MPB, 1965–1985* (1989), 1–44; Perrone, C. A., "Dissonance and Dissent: The Musical Dramatics of C. B.," *LATR,* 22, 2 (Spring 1989), 81–94

MALCOLM SILVERMAN

BUENAVENTURA, Enrique

Colombian dramatist, theater director, and critic, b. 1925, Cali

B. studied in the Saint Librada of Cali School where after learning notions of architecture, painting, and sculpture, he developed his lifelong love for art. As a journalist for the newspaper *El Pacífico,* he met an Argentinian theater director and traveled with him as his assistant through South America. When the group dissolved, B. began a wandering life in which he made a living performing the most various trades: journalist in Caracas and Trinidad, theater director in Argentina, sailor in the Caribbean, cook in Buenos Aires, actor and teacher of voodoo and Latin America's religious influence in Brazil and Bolivia, all experiences that he would later incorporate in his endeavors as a dramatist or theater director. In 1962 B. founded a theater company, Experimental Theater of Cali (TEC), with which he has produced about one-hundred plays; some of them have been presented in Europe and the U.S., including Puerto Rico. All TEC plays are a collective creation, although

B. is the principal author and always the director. Some plays have had many variants throughout the years.

B.'s most important concern in his theater is to achieve a universalization of culture in Colombia, rejecting cultural colonialism and commercialization of the arts. In this pursuit, national traditions and folkloric roots are important. At the same time, he wishes to eradicate persistent social problems and to transform the social structure. Therefore, B.'s theater is didactic and ideological and has reached a political and philosophical tone. Based both in the past and in contemporary history, the reality he conveys is, however, stylized, poetic, and visionary since B. perceives his theater as an instrument of change. The public participates in all performances, making each event unique and changeable, popular, and collective. Therefore, B. believes that there is a dramatic literature but that theater is not a literary genre since it only exists when it confronts a public.

As a theatrical theoretician, B. has written many articles. His research has led him into acting methods and stage techniques that have influenced many groups in Latin America.

One of the most famous of B.'s plays is *En la diestra de Dios padre* (1958; on the right-hand side of our father) with five versions based on a tale of the Colombian writer Tomás Carrasquilla (q.v.). The play shows medieval roots, presenting the influence of miracle plays and morality plays. B.'s sympathies in this play are with the poor, in spite of their being presented in a degrading and deformed way and with satiric humor.

Los papeles del infierno (1968; papers of hell) is a strong and poetic presentation of corruption, exploitation, suffering, injustice, and alienation. Farce and pantomine are some of the resources that make the characters seem grotesque. Enclosed in their suffocating spiritual reality, these characters are puppets of their passions, and the only liberating mechanism is violence.

In *La historia de una bala de plata* (1979; story of a silver bullet) the attack is on colonialism on a Caribbean island. Mythical-magic elements and the voodoo tradition add a cultural dimension to the theme and enrich it aesthetically. The 1980 Casa de las Américas Prize was bestowed on B. for this play.

B., considered by many the father of Colombian theater, has created an original oeuvre based on the Colombian reality and adapting contributions of the world theater and the great dramatists of the 20th c. With an irreverent and desacralized approach, he tries to restore dignity to the common person, advocating human rights. The New Theater in Latin America is greatly indebted to B. and looks toward him for guidance.

FURTHER WORKS: *El misterio de los Reyes Magos* (1957); *El monumento* (1959); *Los inocentes* (1966); *La trampa* (1967); *Tirano Banderas* (1968); *El convertible rojo* (1969); *Un requien por el padre Las Casas* (1971); *La denuncia* (1973); *Se hizo justicia* (1977); *Seis horas en la vida de Frank Kulak* (1979); *Ópera bufa* (1982); *El encierro* (1987); *La estación* (1990)

BIBLIOGRAPHY: McIntyre, C., et al., "Charlando con E. B.," *Prismal/Cabral,* 9–10 (Spring 1983), 82–89; González-Cajiao, F., *Historia del teatro en Colombia* (1986), 307, 335, 380–81; Velasco, M., *El nuevo teatro colombiano y la colonizacion cultural* (1987), 89–143; Perales, E., *Teatro hispanoamericano contemporáneo 1967–87* (1989), 132–33, 141; "B.," *El tiempo,* 6 April 1990, 2A
INÉS DÖLZ-BLACKBURN

BURKE, Kenneth

American critic, poet, novelist, and short-story writer, b. 5 May 1897, Pittsburgh, Pa.

A college dropout (he attended both Ohio State and Columbia), B. has lectured at a number of American colleges and universities; his longest affiliation, lasting from 1943 through 1962, was with Bennington College. B. has been the recipient of a number of honors, including a Guggenheim fellowship and a grant from the Rockefeller Foundation; in 1981 he was awarded the National Medal for Literature. His memberships include the National Institute of Arts and Letters and the American Academy of Arts and Sciences. And he has been for much of this century one of the most formidable and provocative mavericks on the American cultural scene.

B.'s fiction and poetry are of more than passing interest, but, most would agree, it is in a series of remarkable books of literary, social, and cultural criticism beginning with *Counter-Statement* (1931) that B. has produced his most impressive work. In this first book, some of whose contents were actually written as early as the mid-1920s, B.'s interests are more specifically, or narrowly, literary than they would be later. His discussions of literary form have achieved the status of classics within the tradition of literary formalism (q.v.). Even here, however, B.'s is a formalism with a difference. Rather than focusing on the work of literature as an autonomous object and defining form as essentially the system of relationships internal to that object, in the manner of the New Criticism (q.v.) that would by mid-century have established itself as the dominant version of American literary formalism, B. saw form in more open, dynamic, and human terms; in B.'s famous for-

mulation, "the creation of an appetite in the mind of the auditor and the adequate satisfying of that appetite." Once one concedes that form is consummated in the mind of the auditor, the concept of the literary work as closed autonomous form gives way to the idea of the literary work in vital relation to its readers and their world.

The introduction of the "auditor" into the equation suggests an opening to the sociology of literature, and indeed to still broader sociocultural considerations, that would characterize B.'s later work, although that work would never abandon the interest in the literary work as one of the most significant forms of human action. The difference is that the literary work becomes for B. most importantly one form of human action, specifically of what he comes to call "symbolic action"; B. moves beyond the formalist tendency to valorize what distinguishes literature from the rest of human behavior to an insistence that literature be seen as part of human behavior. The implication for critical method is that the barring from criticism of such "extrinsic" interests as the biographical, the historical, the ethical, the political—a negative strategy associated with critical formalism and especially, in the U.S., with the New Criticism—constitutes in B.'s view an unacceptable narrowing of the critical act, which, for B., has as its "main ideal . . . to use all that is there to use."

The exploration of symbolic action in all its implications that is a principal motif of B.'s work in the 1930s broadens in the 1940s and 1950s toward the development of a full-fledged system, the "dramatism" whose exposition is the burden of two of B.'s most impressive and important books, *A Grammar of Motives* (1945) and *A Rhetoric of Motives* (1950). These were originally intended to form the first and second volumes of a trilogy, but the third, B.'s "Symbolic of Motives," never appeared, even though B. apparently completed, and published in the form of articles, virtually all of the materials that would have made it up. Critics differ on the issue of whether dramatism, which aspires to nothing less than the study of the full range of human relations through the analogy of drama, is the fully achieved and coherent synthesis that B. was apparently aiming for, but at the very least the effort generated more insights, more revelations, and more intellectual provocations than most critics produce in a lifetime. In *A Grammar of Motives* the concept of the Pentad (Scene, Act, Agent, Agency, Purpose) as an instrument for the analysis of motives provides a point of departure for an intellectual display that is at once dazzling, playful, and deeply serious, as B. manages to bring the entire history of philosophy under the umbrella of his five terms. In

A Rhetoric of Motives, the daring subsumption of poetry under the heading of rhetoric (in the context of the 1950s, a case of flagrant critical heresy), and the radical exploration of rhetoric and its workings that such an act entails, exhilarates as it disorients and, finally, illuminates by providing one of the "perspectives by incongruity" characteristic of B.'s contributions to modern social thought, contributions whose declared overriding aim is the "purification of war."

All the while that he was engaged in system building and in applying his system to interests that ranged far beyond the "literary" in the narrow sense, B. remained a perceptive and illuminating reader of texts. He differed from the New Critics, who were during the same period establishing an orthodox notion of "close reading," in that B.'s readings of individual texts were exercises in an evolving critical method and were offered in part as examples of that method in action. A consequence is that B. in his practical criticism is never concerned exclusively with the uniqueness of the work before him, although he certainly would not deny that uniqueness; a passion to classify is always involved as well.

Dramatism is deeply concerned with language and with the function of linguistic forms, including literary forms, within society at large. In the 1960s, B.'s work, while never abandoning any of its earlier attitudes, begins to place a greater emphasis on language as such, with a corresponding reduction of the interest in the tensions between verbal acts and the nonverbal scenes of those acts that mark the great works of dramatism. He begins to place increased stress on the ways in which "nonverbal" reality may be regarded as in fact determined by the verbal. B. gives this new emphasis the name of "logology," and in *The Rhetoric of Religion: Studies in Logology* (1961) B., whose work has more than once been described in terms of a secularized Christianity, explores the relations of logology and theology, considering such matters as the likeness between words about words (one way of defining "logology") and words about The Word (one way of defining "theology").

At his best, B. throughout his career, both by precept and by example, has suggested ways beyond the destructive dichotomies of criticism. He has shown us that a sensitivity to literary form can coexist with, indeed is essential to, an understanding of the social functions of literature. And he has shown us that an adequate understanding of society requires that we "read" society with the sensitivity a fine critic brings to a literary text. We are also beginning to appreciate the degree to which he anticipated the interests and insights of structuralism and deconstruction (qq.v.) years be-

fore either of those terms had become current; indeed dramatism and logology may be regarded as rivals of those two intellectual movements. Much of B.'s placing of literature within its sociocultural context, including the relation of literature to the dynamics of power, seems to foreshadow the concerns of the new historicism (q.v.) as well. And recent commentators have noted further that the B. who so eloquently and ingeniously developed the definition of form in terms of the appetites of the auditor quoted above, was a reader-response critic before we knew the name for it; it is not clear that we have had a better one. Given the scope of B.'s interests, and the intensity of thought and imagination he has brought to those interests, we classify B. as a critic simply for want of a better word.

FURTHER WORKS: *The White Oxen and Other Stories* (1924); *Towards a Better Life: Being a Series of Epistles or Declamations* (1932); *Permanence and Change: An Anatomy of Purpose* (1935); *Attitudes toward History* (1937); *The Philosophy of Literary Form: Studies in Symbolic Action* (1941); *Book of Moments: Poems 1915–1954* (1955); *Perspectives by Incongruity* (1964); *Terms for Order* (1964); *Language As Symbolic Action: Essays on Life, Literature, and Method* (1966); *Collected Poems 1915–1967* (1968); *The Complete White Oxen: Collected Short Fiction of K. B.* (1968); *Dramatism and Development* (1972); *Selected Correspondence of K. B. and Malcolm Cowley* (1988)

BIBLIOGRAPHY: Parkes, H. B., *The Pragmatic Test: Essays on the History of Ideas* (1941), 202–20; Duffey, B., "Reality as Language: K. B.'s Theory of Poetry," *WR,* 12 (1948), 132–45; Hyman, S. E., *The Armed Vision: A Study in the Methods of Modern Literary Criticism* (1948), 347–94; Knox, G. A., *Critical Moments: K. B.'s Categories and Critiques* (1957); Frank, A. P., *K. B.* (1969); Rueckert, W. H., ed., *Critical Responses to K. B.* (1969); Booth, W. C., *Critical Understanding: The Powers and Limits of Pluralism* (1979), 99–137; Hartman, G. H., *Criticism in the Wilderness: The Study of Literature Today* (1980), 86–114; Kimberling, C. R., *K. B.'s Dramatism and Popular Arts* (1982); Rueckert, W. H., *K. B. and the Drama of Human Relations,* 2nd ed. (1982); White, H., and M. Brose, eds., *Representing K. B.* (1982); Lentricchia, F., *Criticism and Social Change* (1983); Heath, R. L., *Realism and Relativism: A Perspective on K. B.* (1986); Henderson, G. E., *K. B.: Literature and Language As Symbolic Action* (1988); Simons, H., and T. Melia, eds., *The Legacy of K. B.* (1989)

W. P. KENNEY

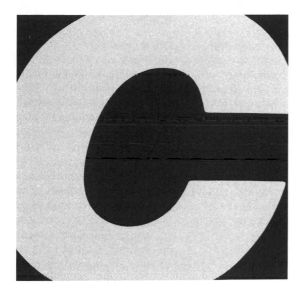

CABALLERO CALDERÓN, Eduardo

Colombian novelist, essayist, and journalist, b. 6 Mar. 1910, Bogotá

A single novel published in 1952 made C. C. internationally known, but by then he had already acquired within his native country a reputation as a journalist, above all, and as an author of essays and a diplomat. *El Cristo de espaldas* (1952; Christ betrayed) was the work that placed him in the forefront of Spanish American fiction.

Born to an elitist family of highland landowners, C. C. began his career as a journalist for a prestigious conservative paper, Bogotá's *El Tiempo*. This activity gave him the necessary experience to enter the field of letters. He was also elected to the house of representatives, and then to the senate. From politics he transferred to diplomacy, representing his country in Latin American cities as well as in Paris. In 1967 he returned to Bogotá and dedicated himself fully to writing.

C. C. began with shorter novels, of which the first one of importance was *El arte de vivir sin soñar* (1943; the art of living without dreaming), an ingenious tale starring two wise scholars from an Asian Salem of the past, where people knew how to dream; after much wandering the two men find themselves in Salem, Oregon, a typical city of the drab Western civilization, whose citizens no longer dream. It is a pessimistic view of modern Western life. C. C. abandoned then the novel for some ten years and built a reputation as an essayist. Main works in this genre were *Latino América: un mundo por hacer* (1944; Latin America: a world to make come true), a sociological reflection of his travels, and *El nuevo príncipe: ensayo sobre las malas pasiones* (1945; the new prince: an essay on bad passions), an almost apocalyptic preview of a society ruled by the despots of modern times—governments, supported by barbaric crowds. This latter book already indicated the path the author

had begun to take and has kept to present: his treatment of the good and bad sides in the human being or, simply, Good versus Evil.

Beginning in 1948, Colombia was immersed into a state of civil war. Nationally known as *La Violencia,* this event lasted almost ten years. Famous Colombian authors, including Gabriel García Márquez (q.v.) and C. C. himself, based their most respected fiction on that genocide. In 1952, as noted, C. C. published *El Cristo de espaldas.* It is the story of a young priest whose high ideals and valiant efforts to bring peace and justice to a highland community beset by violence fail altogether, defeated by a feudalistic system and by human propensity to evil. The priest, himself a new Christ, submits to false accusations and to defeat with no other reward than that of his self-sacrifice. In the somber, but beautifully recounted story, C. C., like most Colombian writers, displayed the pure Castillian Spanish that astonishes Spanish academicians themselves.

Rural themes dominate a good part of C. C.'s fiction. *Siervo sin tierra* (1954; serf without land) is the typical novel of social protest save for the lack of a dogma or revolutionary appeal. It depicts the world of the destitute Colombian highlander who is simply born with his life and even his family already mortgaged to the feudal overlord. In *Manuel Pacho* (1962; Manuel Pacho) the novelist descends from the frigid moors into the torrid plains of eastern Colombia, to portray the unassimilable plainsman that for centuries has been bypassed by modern civilization. In *Caín* (1969; Cain) C. C. repeats a myth that recurs in his novels. Cain, the man unwanted by the gods, in this novel redeems himself through the love of a woman, his own unfaithful wife in this case.

Convinced that he should participate in the contest for the Premio Nadal, C. C. won in 1965 the prestigious prize with the manuscript of a novel that was published in Barcelona a year later. *El buen salvaje* (1966; the noble savage) takes place in Paris. It is the biography of an abulic, uprooted Latin American alienated by a semifossilized European society. In part this work voices the author's opinion that existentialism (q.v.) is more positive in Latin America than it can be in Europe, owing to the more optimistic outlook of life that exists on this side of the Atlantic.

Consistency has so far been the common denominator in the literature of C. C. In his fiction and in his essays he maintains a humanistic creed; he points to the redeeming sides of the individual, if not of the masses, while at the same time condemning that demoniac side of human nature that bases its values on greed and on privilege.

FURTHER WORKS: *Caminos subterráneos* (1936); *Tipacoque: estampas de provincia* (1941); *Sur-*

américa, tierra del hombre (1944); *Breviario del Quijote* (1947); *Cervantes en Colombia* (1948); *Cartas colombianas* (1949); *Ancha es Castilla* (1950); *Diario de Tipacoque* (1950); *Cuentos infantiles* (1953); *La penúltima hora* (1955); *Americanos y europeos* (1957); *Obras* (3 vols., 1963–1964); *Yo, el alcalde: soñar un pueblo para después gobernarlo* (1971); *Azote de sapo* (1976)

BIBLIOGRAPHY: Kirsner, R., "Four Colombian Novels of 'La Violencia,' " *Hispania*, 49, 1 (1966), 70–74; Menton, S., *La novela colombiana: planetas y satélites* (1978), 189–216; Arango, M. A., *Gabriel García Márquez y la novela de la violencia en Colombia* (1985), 91–110; Williams, R. L., "Colombia," in Foster, D. W., comp., *Handbook of Latin American Literature* (1987), 153–90

EVELIO ECHEVARRÍA

CABRERA, Lydia

Cuban short-story writer, folklorist, and ethnological essayist, b. 20 May 1900, Havana

C. is a leading authority on Afro-Cuban (q.v.) cultures and folklore. Her contributions to Cuban literature include short stories based on African oral traditions taken to Cuba by slaves, as well as detailed investigations on the presence of those African traditions in Cuban society. Her work is a careful blend of childhood memories, research, and imagination: a mixture of documentation and poetry, the fantastic and the surreal, universal aspects of the human condition and regional characteristics of the Cuban Creole. C., the youngest daughter of a prominent Cuban family, was tutored at home among Afro-Cuban servants where she was free to explore her own imagination from an early age. In her youth, she accompanied her father to literary cafés, where only men gathered, and by age fourteen she published her first writings in *Cuba y América,* a prestigious political and literary magazine her father directed. In 1922, C. went to Paris to study at the École du Louvre and Beaux Arts. There she met Teresa de la Parra (1895–1936), Lucien Lévy-Bruhl (1857–1939), and Paul Valéry (q.v.) and became familiar with Leo Frobenius (1873–1938) and with vanguard movements in art, especially the techniques in cubism and surrealism (qq.v.), with which she later experimented in her short stories. During this time, C. also became interested in oriental civilizations whose religion and myths reminded her of the stories she had heard in her childhood from black Cuban servants. While vacationing in Havana, C. came in contact with Afro-Cuban believers, and in 1930, during another visit to the island,

she established permanent contact with a poor community predominantly black, which would later become one of the main sources of information for her research.

In 1932 Teresa de la Parra contracted tuberculosis, and C. accompanied her to a sanatorium in Leysin. There, with the initial objective of entertaining the Chilean poet, C. wrote a series of short stories that recaptured humorously anecdotes she had heard from servants in her childhood. These were later collected, translated, and published in France (1936), where there was an increasing interest in African art, and four years later in Cuba as *Cuentos negros de Cuba* (1940; Cuban black stories). In 1935, C. went with Teresa de la Parra to Madrid, where she established a friendship with the Chilean poet Gabriela Mistral (q.v.), who, at this time and in later years, encouraged C. to continue writing. In 1936, when Teresa de La Parra died and the Spanish Civil War broke out, C. returned first to Paris and then, in 1939, permanently to Cuba. In 1942 she began a serious study of Afro-Cuban religion and folklore throughout the island. She also translated Aimé Césaire's (q.v.) *Cahier d'un retour au pays natal* (1939; *Memorandum on My Martinque,* 1947) which was published with illustrations by the Cuban painter Wilfredo Lam. It was C. who exerted a deep influence on Lam's shift to an Afro-Cuban imagery. In 1948 C. published her second collection of short stories, *¿Por qué? Cuentos negros de Cuba* (1948; why? Cuban black stories). Though a continuation in theme and style of her first book, these twenty-eight anecdotes show a more refined lyricism and philosophical humor than her earlier stories. However, it was C.'s monumental book *El monte: notas sobre las religiones, la magia, las supersticiones y el folklore de los negros criollos y del pueblo de Cuba* (1954: the forest [bush/mount]: notes on the religion, magic, superstitions, and folklore of black Creoles and the Cuban people) that finally established C. as a major intellectual figure, as the author of a unique testimonial account of Afro-Cuban beliefs and lore. In 1957 C. published *Anagó: Vocabulario lucumí* (Anagó: Lucumí vocabulary), a dictionary of Spanish and Lucumí (the Yoruba-derived language spoken in Cuba). A year later, C. published another monumental work, *La sociedad secreta Abakuá* (1958; the Abakuá secret society), the first detailed and objective account of the rites, ceremonies, and beliefs of a secret society commonly known in Cuba as *ñáñigos,* related in their traditions to Carabalí nations in Africa.

In 1960 C.'s work came to a temporary halt. With the triumph of the Cuban revolution, C. resettled in Miami, Florida, and twelve years of silence went by before she initiated, if not the most important period of her work, definitely the most prolific, all of it from research material she had gathered in Cuba. Among the books of C.'s second period we find a third collection of short stories, *Ayapá: Cuento de jicotea* (1971; ayapá: tortoise stories), a group of nineteen anecdotes in which *hicotea*, a Caribbean land turtle, appears as the main character. Although cubanized as *jicotea*, C.'s stories of the Afro-Cuban turtle closely resemble the African fables of tortoise, a folkloric and mythological symbol of the Yorubas. C.'s carefully elaborated stories of *jicotea* play with the same philosophical humor and irony that characterize all of C.'s work, while, and at the same time, recapturing through imagination an ancestral African tradition present in Cuba. Three years later, returning again to the narrative form she used in *El monte,* C. published *Yemayá y Ochún* (1974; Yemonja and Oshun), a collection of various myths and legends about the Lucumí (Yoruba) deities Yemayá, the feminine force of the ocean waters, and Ochún, the feminine force of the fresh waters, love, and fertility. C. also published two other important dictionaries: *Vocabulario congo* (1984; Congo [Bakongo] vocabulary), a dictionary of the Bantu languages spoken in Cuba, and *La lengua sagrada de los ñáñigos* (1988; the sacred language of the ñáñigos), a dictionary of the Carabalí languages utilized in the ceremonies of the Abakuá society.

Most of C.'s research took place in the western provinces of the island, where Afro-Cuban lore was best preserved, but her findings and publications are applicable to the traditions of nearly all African descendants in Cuba. Next to the work of Fernando Ortiz (1881–1969), C.'s writing is considered to be the most vast, prolific, and detailed work done on Afro-Cuban cultures. While the importance of C.'s monumental research has at times caused critics to give scant attention to the aesthetic value of her work of fiction, C. is a master storyteller, and should rank among the best and most innovative short-story writers in Spanish America.

FURTHER WORKS: *Refranes de negros viejos* (1955); *Otán iyebiyé: las piedras preciosas* (1970); *La laguna sagrada de San Joaquín* (1973); *Anaforuana: ritual y símbolos de la iniciación en la sociedad secreta Abakuá* (1975); *Francisco y Francisca: chascarrillos de negros viejos* (1976); *La regla kimbisa del Santo Cristo del Buen Viaje* (1977); *Itinerarios del insomnio: Trinidad de Cuba* (1977); *Reglas de congo, palomonte mayombe* (1979); *Koeko iyawó, aprende novicia: pequeño tratado de regla lucumí* (1980); *Cuentos para adultos, niños y retrasados mentales* (1983); *La medicina popular de Cuba: médicos de antaño,* *curanderos, santeros y paleros de hogaño* (1984); *Los animales en el folklore y la magia de Cuba* (1988)

BIBLIOGRAPHY: Ortiz, F., "L. C. (Una cubana afroamericana)," *Crónica,* 3 (Mar. 1949), 7–8; Zambrano, M., "L. C., poeta de la metamorfosis," *Orígenes,* 7, 25 (1950), 11–15; Acosta Saignes, M., "*El monte* de L. C.," *Revista Bimestre Cubana,* 71 (1956), 153–87; Gonzalez, M. P., "Cuentos y recuentos de L. C.," *Revista Cubana,* 1, 2 (1959), 153–61; Novás Calvo, L., "El monte," *Papeles de Son Armadans,* 150 (Sept. 1968), 298–304; Perera, H., *Idapo: El sincretismo de los cuentos negros de L. C.* (1971); Valdes-Cruz, R., *Lo ancestral africano en la narrativa de L. C.* (1974); Sánchez, R., ed., *Homenaje a L. C.* (1978); Hiriart, R., *L. C., vida hecha arte* (1978); Hiriart, R., *Más cerca de Teresa de la Parra: diálogos con L. C.* (1980); Simo, A. M., *L. C.: An Intimate Portrait* (1984); Castellanos, I., and J. Inclan, eds., *En torno a L. C.: cincuentenarios de Cuentos negros de Cuba 1936–1986* (1987); Soto, S., *Magia e historia en los "Cuentos negros," "¿Por qué?" y "Ayapá" de L. C.* (1988)

JULIA CUERVO HEWITT

CAIN, James M.

American novelist, journalist, short-story writer, and screenwriter, b. 1 July 1892, Annapolis, Md.; d. 7 Oct. 1977, Hyattsville, Md.

C., whose father was a college administrator and professor of English, graduated in 1910 from Washington College, of which his father was president at the time. After giving some thought to a career as an opera singer, an interest perhaps reflecting the musical training his mother had completed before her marriage, C. decided while in his early twenties that he would be some kind of writer. He first realized that ambition in journalism, working under Walter Lippmann (1889–1974) at the *New York World* from 1924 until the paper's demise in 1931, and writing articles for H. L. Mencken's (q.v.) *American Mercury* during the same period. Lippmann and Mencken were, of course, among the giants of the American cultural scene at this time, and C. enjoyed a cordial personal relationship with both men. Following the end of the *World,* C. worked at the *New Yorker,* but he found the environment uncongenial, and after nine months moved to Hollywood to embark on what would prove to be an undistinguished career as a screenwriter.

As a writer of fiction, C. was a late starter. He was already in his forties when he produced the "native American masterpieces back to back," to borrow the language of Ross Macdonald (1915–1983), that continue to stand as the foundation of his critical reputation: *The Postman Always Rings Twice* (1934) and "Double Indemnity" (1936), serialized in *Liberty* magazine. These and two other novels of the prewar period—*Serenade* (1937) and *Mildred Pierce* (1941)—along with *The Butterfly* (1947) represent for many critics C. at his best. Complicating the picture, of course, is that all five of these novels have been adapted as films, at least one of which (*Double Indemnity*, 1944) is arguably superior to its source, while another (*Mildred Pierce*, 1945) won an Academy Award for Joan Crawford, who created one of the screen's great roles. It is difficult to know just at present how much of C.'s stature is derived from the cinematic afterlife of his fiction.

But to turn to that fiction today is to be convinced once again of its power, if not of its depth or complexity. C. is frequently classified as one of the American hard-boiled writers (although he denied the relevance of this term to his work) on the basis, at least in part, of the combination in his fiction of a vernacular style (C. generally prefers a first-person narrator), a frequently violent subject matter, and an absence of moralizing. In a typical C. novel, characters who are in themselves neither impressive nor heroic engage our fascinated attention, sympathy, and—at times at least—a kind of guilty identification as they are compelled to destructive and often self-destructive acts by drives that they are pretty much incapable of understanding. They may stand for our frightened recognition of the presence within ourselves of similarly powerful and mysterious drives. The first-person narration encourages such an identification, but it performs other functions as well. Because the story is told in the past tense—that is, the narration itself represents the narrator's confrontation of the consequences of his actions—the first-person narration has a kind of distancing effect; we are reminded, even as C.'s art works on our empathic imagination, where these compulsions and the actions based on them "must" lead. We can thus entertain these dark imaginings without surrendering to them; a kind of immunization occurs.

The first-person narration serves yet another function. If the characters don't understand the forces that compel them, the narrative as a whole is not necessarily any more illuminating on the question. One does not go to C. for psychological insight. Rather, we accept the psychological limitations of the novel as representing the narrator's limitations.

In only one of the five key texts, *Mildred Pierce*, does C. attempt third-person narration. This may contribute to the lack of concentration in the novel, a quality some critics have seen as shapelessness. And it may be that at this point in his career C. simply was not ready to take on the challenges involved in creating a woman narrator. Even here, though, the sense of the third-person narrator as a kind of "masculine" voice and presence creates an artful tension within a generally sympathetic portrait of a woman, while at least partly "motivating" the blind spots that may exist in that portrait.

Mildred herself, in her combination of drive and domesticity, is an interesting variation on the C. woman. Even the most homicidally driven of these women yearn for the stability of the domestic life; and even the most domestic, Mildred, is driven. A feminist critic might find sexism implicit in this image, and perhaps the only appropriate reply is that there is as little sociological as psychological insight in C.'s fiction, but that the unresolved paradoxes of his characters, including the "masculine" drive of his women and the "feminine" vulnerability of his men, are yet another source of their narrative power.

A sympathetic critic has argued that C.'s style and technique function best when theme, character relationships, and milieu are kept simple. This suggests something of C.'s limitations and perhaps indicates why his successes come relatively early and constitute in all a rather small portion of his oeuvre. The narrative in his best work is as driven as the characters, and the characters, combinations of powerful psychological simplification and actions to which they are driven, but for which they ultimately accept responsibility (and perhaps that is the morality of the hard-boiled), assume the dimensions of archetype. One suspects, one hopes, that there will always be readers for whom C. is a discovery.

FURTHER WORKS: *Our Government* (1930); *Love's Lovely Counterfeit* (1942); *Three of a Kind* (1943); *Past All Dishonor* (1946); *Sinful Woman* (1947); *The Moth* (1948); *Jealous Woman* (1950); *The Root of His Evil* (1951); *Galatea* (1953); *Mignon* (1962); *The Magician's Wife* (1965); *Rainbow's End* (1975); *The Institute* (1976); *The Baby in the Icebox and Other Short Fiction* (1981); *Cloud Nine* (1984); *The Enchanted Isle* (1985); *60 Years of Journalism* (1985); *Career in C Major and Other Fiction* (1986)

BIBLIOGRAPHY: Farrell, J. T., *Literature and Morality* (1947), 79–87; Van Nostrand, A. D., *The Denatured Novel* (1960), 126–32; Wilson, E., "The Boys in the Back Room: J. M. C. and John O'Hara," *NewR*, 11 Nov. 1962, 665–66; Oates, J. C., "Man under Sentence of Death: The Novels of J. M. C.," in Madden, D., ed., *Tough Guy Writers of the Thirties* (1968), 110–28; Madden, D., *J. M. C.* (1970); Hoopes, R., *C.* (1982); Root, R., "Hard-Boiled Tragedy: J. M. C.'s Classical Design," *Clues: A Journal of Detection*, 5, 2 (Fall–Winter 1984), 48–57; Madden, D., *C.'s Craft* (1985); Skenazy, P., *J. M. C.* (1989); Hilfer, T., *The Crime Novel: A Deviant Genre* (1990), 55–62

W. P. KENNEY

CALLADO, Antônio

Brazilian novelist, essayist, journalist, and dramatist, b. 26 Jan. 1917, Niterói

C. had a typical middle-class upbringing and spent most of his childhood in Niterói, Petrópolis, and Teresópolis. After his father's death, his family moved to Rio de Janeiro, where he studied law and worked as a journalist. In 1941 C. went to work at the BBC in England and from 1944 to 1947 at the French Radio in France. Although his "years of exile" in Europe were happy, C. felt a profound longing for Brazil and a deep desire to return and rediscover his own country. Back in Brazil, he worked for *Jornal do Brasil* and became known for the coverage of the most critical political, social, and economic issues in the 1950s and 1960s: the status of the Indians, the vast unexplored Amazons region, the burgeoning organization of the peasant leagues in the northeast, and the plight of the *favelados*.

However, it is in his literary works that all these issues are presented with a coherent vision of what the critic Ligia Chiappini Moraes Leite calls a "national and populist project of Brazilian culture." Although C. acknowledges that technically and stylistically he is influenced by his readings of James Joyce, Marcel Proust, and Alain Robbe-Grillet (qq.v.), C. as many other Brazilian intellectuals at the time was reevaluating the concept of Brazilian identity and was fully committed to creating a literature that is meant to be accessible to the masses.

His project—via landmark works such as *Os sertões* (1902; *Rebellion in the Backlands*, 1944) by Euclides da Cunha (1866–1909) and *Macunaíma* (1928; *Macunaíma*, 1984) by Mário de Andrade (q.v.)—is a continuation of the 19th-c. romanticism movement to build a national identity. Thus his novels are a kaleidoscopic voyage across Brazil, in an effort to portray what he found to be its multiple and genuine realities: the Indians in the Amazon forest, the peasants in Pernambuco and the backlands of Bahia, the colonial towns of Minas Gerais, the swamps of the Pantanal in the Midwest, and, back to the city, Rio de Janeiro.

His works can be roughly divided in two groups, religious and political, with his novel *Quarup* (1967; *Quarup*, 1970) serving as the divider. In the first phase there are two novels: *Assunção de Salviano* (1954; the assumption of Salviano) and *Madona de cedro* (1957; cedar Madonna). Although these novels present situations that are critical of the traditional church and the Communist Party in Brazil, their focus is the more universal theme of the struggle for grace and redemption. Frequently compared to the works of Graham Greene (q.v.), C.'s oeuvre is permeated by religious concerns, Catholicism being an important element in the daily lives of the people of his generation. This religious feeling, together with the messianic and martyrdom message, is present in his later books, shifting the focus from the individual religious, sexual sin to the social sin perceived in society.

Quarup, a title taken from an Indian ritual of death and resurrection, is seen as one of the most influential books during the 1960s and 1970s in Brazil. The novel—considered realist by many critics—is a sweeping epic portrait of Brazil, of its people and institutions. C. presents a mosaic of the conflicting ideologies and problems that afflict the country through each one of his characters, such as the Europocentric point of view versus the indigenists; the urban (therefore peripheral: cities along the coast) versus the countryside (the Amazon, the mythical matriarchal center); the land-owning versus the dispossessed; the nationalist Left versus capitalist colonialism. All these themes are kept together by the story of Nando, a priest who wants to convert Indians to Christianity and eventually abandons the robe to become a revolutionary guerrilla hero. This is an optimistic novel, messianic and redemptive with both Christian and Marxist messages.

Bar D. Juan (1971; *Bar D. Juan*, 1972) and *Reflexos do baile* (1978; reflections of the ball) are political urban novels that are more pessimistic. The first is about the disillusionment and paralysis surrounding the revolutionary cause, the second a fragmented testimonial of the chaotic period of terrorist acts and violent military persecution and repression.

Sempreviva (1981; *Sempreviva*, 1988), awarded the Goethe Institute Prize for fiction in 1982, is the story of an exile, a prodigal son, who returns to Brazil before the political amnesty to seek revenge for the death of his beloved woman. But Brazil, the Edenic mother country, is an illusion, and its nature, beneath its benevolent tropical lusciousness, has a dark, sinister, and rotten side. This novel, dense in literary and religious symbols, is a cathartic literary and mystical effort to capture the meaning of recent events in Brazilian history, in this case the underworld of torturers of the military régime and their victims, the tortured.

C.'s *Expedição Montaigne* (1982; Montaigne expedition) and *Concerto Carioca* (1985; carioca concert), like all his novels, unfold and expand themes central to the question of Brazilian identity, in particular the survival of the Indians. Furthermore, it exposes and satirizes the dilemma of the New World intellectual and his attempt to define what is unique about Brazilian identity without escaping his colonial attachment to European tradition.

FURTHER WORKS: *Cidade assassinada* (1954); *Retrato de Portinari* (1956); *Frankel* (1957); *O colar de coral* (1957); *Pedro Mico* (1957); *Os industriais da Seca e os Galileus* (1959); *Uma rede para Iemanjá* (1961); *Maria Chica* (1964); *Forró do Engenho Cananéia* (1964); *Tempo de Arraes* (1964); *Vietnã do norte* (1977); *A revoluta da Cachaça* (1983)

BIBLIOGRAPHY: Galagher, D., on *Quarup, NYTBR* (14 June 1970), 4; Aiex, N. C., "The Reality of Myth: A. C.'s *Assunção de Salviano*," *PCL* (1979), 131–37; Aiex, N. C., "From Rhetoric to Revolution: A. C.'s *Bar D. Juan*," *Seleta* (1980), 131–37; Moraes Leite, L. C., "Quando a Pátria Viaja: Uma leitura dos romances de A. C.," in Zilio, C., J. L. Lafetá, and L. C. Moraes Leite, eds., *O Nacional e o Popular* (1982), 120–234

NAOMI HOKI MONIZ

CANADIAN LITERATURE

See Volume 1, page 395.

In English

The diversity and abundance of English Canadian literature of a high quality continued undiminished through the 1980s and early 1990s, with contributions by authors with established reputations as well as by new, younger members of the world of letters. The identity crisis, always close to the surface in many realms of Canadian matters—the constant challenge to maintain a distinctness in the face of a powerful neighbor sharing the same language and many spiritual values—continues to be a general concern, but is a special concern in French Canadian literature, manifesting itself recently (1988–1989) in uneasiness with or opposition to a Free Trade agreement with the U.S. Fears of being unable to maintain a viable existence on the one hand, especially with the menace of a separated Quebec, with its threat of creating a divided anglophone country, and, on the other hand, the continued immigration, with Asiatics

establishing residence in British Columbia and elsewhere, with Indians and other commonwealth members and others settling in other anglophone provinces, have created tensions that are reflected in literature. The important continued activity of gifted women writers, both in English and in French, has added to the various dimensions explored in Canadian letters.

Literary quality is partly maintained through the support of the Canada Council, established in 1957, which has continued to give financial assistance to allow artists to pursue their art. This has resulted occasionally in creating the type of literature that is appealing to an elite, with a high level of literary sophistication; indeed, many Canadian authors have advanced degrees, including doctorates, from leading institutions of higher learning in Canada and the U.S.—such as Hugh MacLennan (q.v.), Hugh Hood (b. 1928), Louis Dudek (b. 1918), Eli Mandel (b. 1922), James Reany (b. 1926), Robert Kroetsch (b. 1927), Elizabeth Brewster (b. 1922), and John Thompson (1938–1976)—and many others have played important roles in the world of higher education. This involvement with the academic world—many of the leading writers are teachers of English or creative writing—obviously leaves its mark on their works, with many authors being very conscious of the most recent literary theories and very aware of current aesthetic concerns.

Some of English Canada's most important literary figures died within the last decade: F. R. Scott (1899–1985), Milton Acorn (1923–1986), Al Purdy (1918–1986), Margaret Laurence (q.v.) in 1987, George Ryga (1932–1987), and, in 1990, Morley Callaghan, Hugh MacLennan, and Northrop Frye (qq.v.). Since most of these writers continued to be productive, their absence will be noticed. Significant among their latest works were Scott's *Collected Poems* (1981), Acorn's *Dig Up My Heart* (1983), Purdy's *The Stone Bird* (1981), *Piling Blood* (1984), and *The Collected Poems of Al Purdy* (1986), Laurence's *Dance on the Earth: A Memoir* (1989), Callaghan's *A Time for Judas* (1983), *Lost and Found Stories* (1985), *A Wise Old Man on the Road* (1988), and Frye's *The Great Code* (1982), *Divisions on a Ground* (1982), *Myth and Metaphor: Selected Essays 1974–1988* (1990), and *Words with Power: Being a Second Study of the Bible and Literature* (1990).

Although Marshall McLuhan (1911–1980) published his most important work during the 1950s and 1960s—*The Mechanical Bride* (1951), *The Gutenberg Galaxy* (1962), *Understanding Media* (1964), and, with Jerome Agel (b. 1930) of the U.S., *The Medium Is the Massage* (1967) and *War and Peace in the Global Village* [sic: *Massage*]—his contributions to the Canadian intellectual climate have not been forgotten. Indeed, recent works—*Letters of Marshall McLuhan* (1987) and *Marshall McLuhan: The Medium and the Messenger* (1989)—are reminders of his importance. He is among the most original thinkers Canada has produced.

Canadians who have recently made significant contributions to the world of literature include Robertson Davies (q.v.), who completed his Simon Darcourt trilogy: *The Rebel Angels* (1981), *What's Bred in the Bone* (1985), and *The Lyre of Orpheus* (1988); Alice Munro (q.v.) with *The Moons of Jupiter* (1982), *The Progress of Love* (1986), and *Friend of My Youth* (1990); Timothy Findley (b. 1930) with *Famous Last Words* (1981), *Not Wanted on the Voyage* (1984), and *The Telling of Lies* (1986); Margaret Atwood (q.v.), who continues to be one of Canada's most widely read authors, with *Bodily Harm* (1981), *Bluebeard's Egg* (1983), *The Handmaid's Tale* (1985), and *The Cat's Eye* (1988); Mavis Gallant (q.v.), particularly significant in the world of the short story, with *Home Truths* (1981), *What Is To Be Done?* (1983), *Overhead in a Balloon* (1985), *Paris Notebooks: Essays and Reviews* (1986), and *In Transit* (1988); and Mordecai Richler (q.v.) with *Home Sweet Home* (1984) and *Solomon Gursky Was Here* (1989). Among other writers who have been on the literary scene and continue to have an audience are the poets Irving Layton (q.v.) with *A Wild Peculiar Joy* (1982), *The Gucci Bag* (1983), and *Dance with Desire* (1986); Robert Kroetsch, with *Field Notes* (1981), *Alibi* (1983), *Advice to My Friends* (1985), and *The Lovely Treachery of Words: Essays Selected and New* (1989); Dorothy Livesy (b. 1909) with *The Phases of Love* (1983), *Feeling the Worlds* (1984), and *The Self-Completing Tree: Selected Poems* (1986); and Ralph Gufstafson (b. 1909) with *Directives of Autumn* (1984), *Plummets and Other Partialities* (1987), and *Winter Prophecies* (1987).

Michael Ondaatje (q.v.) has continued to be active in the world of verse as well as in prose: *Running in the Family* (1982), *Secular Love* (1984), *In the Skin of a Lion* (1987), and *The Cinnamon Peeler* (1991). John Metcalf (b. 1938) has produced novels, short stories, and works of criticism: *General Ladd* (1980), *Kicking against the Pricks* (1982), *The Bumper Book* (1986), and *Adult Entertainment: Short Fiction* (1986).

In the world of the theater, Timothy Findley and David French (b. 1939) have made important contributions, the latter with *Leaving Home* (1972), *Of the Fields, Lately* (1973), *Jitters* (1980), and *Salt Water Moon* (1984), works that have made him one of Canada's most important dramatists. Other successful writers for the stage are Sharon Pollock (b. 1936), with *Blood Relations* (1980), *Whiskey Six* (1983), and *Doc* (1984), and Ken

Mitchell (b. 1940), with *Gone the Burning Sun* (1984) and *The Plainsman* (1985).

Particularly sensitive to the ethnic diversity of Canada are Rudy Wiebe (b. 1934), with *Peace Shall Destroy Many* (1964), *The Temptation of Big Bear* (1973), and *Where Is the Voice Coming From?* (1974); and many writers who focus on the Jewish experience, among them Norman Levine (b. 1923), C. J. Newman (b. 1935), and Mordecai Richler; as well as a writer who deals with the Japanese-Canadian experience, Joy Kogawa (b. 1935), with *Obason* (1981). Similar sensitivity is displayed by Bharati Mukherjee (q.v.), with *Darkness* (1985), *The Middleman and Other Stories* (1988), and *Jasmine* (1989), and her husband, Clark Blaise (b. 1940), with *Lunar Attractions* (1979), *Lusts* (1983), and *Resident Alien* (1986).

In a tradition so rich in important women writers who do not avoid what could be called women's concerns, some occupy a special niche because of their specific focus, such as Jane Rule (b. 1931), with *The Desert of the Heart* (1964), *Lesbian Images* (1975), *Contract with the World* (1980), and *Inland Passage and Other Stories* (1985), and Mary Meigs (b. 1917), with *The Medusa Head* (1983).

In French

The ebullient literary scene in French continued unabated, fermented by the changing dramatic political environment, with votes on separatism, the instituting of language laws, and the state of suspense created by the Lake Meech Accords. Among the most eminent recent writers are Hubert Aquin, Jacques Ferron, Jacques Godbout, Yves Theriault, and Michel Tremblay (qq.v.).

Other important and successful writers continued to publish in the 1980s: Gabrielle Roy (q.v.) revealed more of her personal life in her final works: *Ces enfants de ma vie* (1977; *Children of My Heart*, 1979), *De quoi t'ennuies-tu, Eveline?* (1982; What's bothering you, Eveline?), her autobiography, *La détresse et l'enchantement* (1984; distress and enchantment), and some of her correspondence, *Ma chère petite soeur: Lettres à Bernadette 1943–1970* (1988; my dear little sister: letters to Bernadette 1943–1970). Anne Hébert (q.v.), following on the success of her 1970 novel *Kamouraska* (*Kamouraska*, 1973), continued in this genre: *Héloïse* (1980; *Heloise*, 1982), *Les fous de Bassan* (1982; *In the Shadow of the Wind*, 1983), and *Le premier jardin* (1988; the first garden). Hébert is above all a poet, and one always striking feature of her novels is the poetic dimension present in the imagery, style, and structure. Marie-Claire Blais (q.v.) has continued to produce novels characterized by a rich prose style and a rather pessimistic vision of the world, often with alienated individuals, among them homosexuals and lesbians: *Le loup. Roman* (1972; *The Wolf,* 1974), *Une liaison parisienne* (1975; *A Literary Affair,* 1979), *Les nuits de l'underground* (1978; *Nights in the Underground: An Exploration of Love,* 1979), *Le sourd dans la ville* (1979; *Deaf to the City,* 1981), *Visions d'Anna ou Le vertige* (1982; visions of Anna or vertigo), and *Pierre* (1984; Pierre).

Gérard Bessette (b. 1920) has been an outstanding figure in Quebec letters for his critical contributions—*Une littérature en ébullition* (1968; a literature in ebullition), *Histoire de la littérature canadienne-française par les textes* (1968; history of French-Canadian literature through texts)—in addition to his purely literary career. Some of his most important novels are *Le Libraire* (1960; *Not for Every Eye,* 1962), *L'incubation* (1965; *Incubation,* 1967), and *Le semestre* (1979; the semester). From one novel to another the style varies, going from realistic to imitative of the *nouveau roman.*

Claire Martin (b. 1914) in the space of approximately ten years created a body of novelistic works that brought her much acclaim. The theme of love and the traditional aspects of Quebec life are among those she develops in *Avec ou sans amour* (1958; with or without love), *Doux-Amer* (1960; *Best-Man,* 1983), and *Dans un gant de fer* (1965; *In an Iron Glove,* 1968).

Antonine Maillet (b. 1929) received the Goncourt Prize, the prestigious French literary award, for her novel *Pélagie-la-charrette* (1979; *Pélagie,* 1982), a story about Acadians, which brought her international acclaim. In recent years she has written plays as well as novels.

Louise Maheux-Forcier (b. 1929), musician and novelist, won a certain fame for her first novel, *Amadou* (1963; tinder, or punk), which features a lesbian relationship amidst torn heterosexual rapports.

Claude Jasmin's (b. 1930) works have often been marked by the political climate, such as *Ethel et le terroriste* (1964; *Ethel and the Terrorist,* 1965), which evokes the confrontations of the early 1960s.

Louky Bersianik (b. 1930) is particularly concerned in her literary works with women and their role in civilization. *L'Euguélionne* (1976; *The Euguelionne,* 1981) and *Pique-nique sur l'Acropole* (1979; picnic on the Acropolis) established her as one of the leading feminist voices in Canada.

Roch Carrier (b. 1937), whose prose works have been well received throughout Canada, explores the Quebec mentality confronted with an all-enveloping English world in such works as *Les enfants du bonhomme dans la lune* (1979; *The*

Hockey Sweater and Other Stories, 1979) and *Il n'y a pas de pays sans grand-père* (1977; *No Country without Grandfathers,* 1981). Recent works have taken him to other lands: *L'ours et le kangourou* (1986; the bear and the kangaroo) and *Un chameau en Jordanie* (1988; a camel in Jordan).

Jacques Poulin (b. 1937) is a novelist whose works are reflective of the political scene in Quebec. However, his *Volkswagen Blues* (1984; title in English) finds his protagonists roaming through the U.S.

Susanne Paradis (b. 1936) has been one of Quebec's most productive writers, with books of poetry—*Un goût de sel* (1983; a taste of salt) and *Effets de l'œil* (1986; effects of the eye)—and novels: *Miss Charlie* (1979; title in English) and *La ligne bleue* (1985; the blue line)—as well as works of literary criticism.

André Major (b. 1942), with *Le cabochon* (1964; the headstrong kid) and *L'épouvantail* (1974; *The Scarecrows of Saint Emmanuel,* 1977), Yves Beauchemin (b. 1941), with *Le matou* (1981; *The Alley Cat,* 1986), and Louis Caron (b. 1942), with *L'emmitouflé* (1977; *The Draft Dodger,* 1980), all reflect involvement with contemporary issues in their novels.

Victor-Lévy Beaulieu (b. 1945) has displayed an uncommon energy in many areas—as an essayist, in *Pour saluer Victor Hugo* (1971; to salute Victor Hugo), *Jack Kérouac: Essai-poulet* (1972; *Jack Kerouac: A Chicken Essay,* 1975); as a dramatist, in *En attendant Trudot* (1974; waiting for Trudot); as a novelist, in *Les grands-pères* (1975; *The Grandfathers,* 1975) and *L'héritage* (1987; the inheritance); and finally as a publisher: as the founder and director of the series ''Bibliothèque Québécoise.''

In poetry, Gerald Godin (b. 1938), whose works have been based on *joual,* the language of the common people, is one of the most popular of Quebec poets; he has published many collections, among them *Ils ne demandaient qu'à brûler, poèmes 1960–1986* (1987; they asked only to burn, poems 1960–1986). Paul Chamberland (b. 1939) followed up on his *Terre Québec* (1964; Quebecland) with *L'enfant doré* (1980; the golden child), *Aléatoire instantané & Midsummer 82* (1983; instantaneous aleatoriness & midsummer 82), *Compagnons chercheurs* (1984; seeker companions), and *Phoenix intégral and Après Auschwitz, Poèmes 1975–1987* (1988; integral phoenix and after Auschwitz, poems 1975–1987), in which the stress is on humankind, sexuality, and the simple life. Nicole Brossard (b. 1943) has emerged as one of the important literary figures in contemporary Quebec, known both for her prose and poetic works, and appreciated especially by those who feel tyrannized by the masculine codes in the language;

among her works are *Le centre blanc (poèmes 1965–1975)* (1978; the white center, poems 1965–1975), *Amantes* (1980; *Lovhers*, 1986), *Picture Theory* (1982; title in English), *double impression (poèmes et textes 1967–1984)* (1984; double impression, poems and texts 1967–1984), and *Domaines d'écriture* (1985; domains of writing); her efforts lead her to redirect communication by the abandonment of such imposed "patriarchal" features of the language as chronology and linearity. Madeleine Gagnon (b. 1938) accompanies her in this effort, in works such as *Les fleurs du Catalpa* (1986; the catalpa flowers).

Other poets, some from earlier generations, such as Rina Lasnier (b. 1915), Roland Giguère (b. 1929), and Jacques Brault (b. 1933), continue to have their admirers. Lasnier's poems have been collected in *Poèmes* (1972; poems) and *L'ombre jetée I et II* (2 vols., 1988–1989; the shadow cast). Giguère, painter as well as poet, has produced *L'âge de la parole, poèmes 1949–1960* (1965; the age of speech, poems 1949–1960), *Forêt vierge folle* (1978; mad virgin forest), and *La main au feu* (1987; the hand in the fire). Brault's recent works include *Moments fragiles* (1984; fragile moments) and *Poèmes I, Mémoire, La Poésie ce matin. L'en dessous l'admirable* (1986; Poems I, memory, poetry this morning, the admirable underneath).

The world of the stage has flourished in the last decades, with many theaters enjoying success, with the production of many new plays, with great numbers of active theatergoers, and, most important, with the contributions of gifted creative artists. In addition to Michel Tremblay, others have played important roles in this success, among them Jean-Claude Germain (b. 1939), Réjean Ducharme (b. 1941), and Marie Laberge (b. 1940).

BIBLIOGRAPHY: Wilson, E., *O Canada, An American's Notes on Canadian Culture* (1965); Reid, M., *The Shouting Signpainters. A Literary and Political Account of Quebec Revolutionary Nationalism* (1972); Lemire, M., et al., *Dictionnaire des œuvres littéraires du Québec* (5 vols., 1980–1987); Weiss, J. M., "The Contemporary Theater and Its Public in Quebec," *Québec Studies,* 1 (1983), 166–77; Powe, B. W., *A Climate Charged* (1984); Keith, W. J., *Canadian Literature in English* (1985); Schwartzwald, R., "Literature and Intellectual Realignments in Quebec," *Québec Studies,* 3 (1985), 32–56; Cagnon, M., *The French Novel of Quebec* (1986); Weiss, J. M., *French-Canadian Theater* (1986); Mailhot, L., and P. Nepveu, *La poésie québécoise des origines à nos jours* (1986); Andersen, M., "Subversive Texts: Québec Women Writers," *SCL,* 13, 2 (1988) 127–41; Hamel, R., et al., *Dictionnaire des auteurs de langue française en Amérique du nord* (1989); New, W. H., *A History of Canadian Literature* (1989); Royer, J., *Introduction à la poésie québécoise: les poètes et les œuvres des origines à nos jours* (1989); Benson, E., and L. W. Conolly, *The Oxford Companion to Canadian Theatre* (1989); Kandiuk, M., *French-Canadian Authors: A Bibliography of Their Works and of English-Language Criticism* (1990)

PAUL BARRETTE

CANSEVER, Edip

Turkish poet, b. 8 Aug. 1928, Istanbul; d. 27 May 1986, Istanbul

One of Turkey's leading modernist poets, C. had a relatively uneventful life. Having left his graduate studies at Istanbul's School of Business Administration, he worked as an antique dealer at the Covered Bazaar for nearly four decades. His earliest poems were published in literary magazines when he was only sixteen years old. In 1951 he published a small magazine called *Nokta,* which lasted through eight issues.

C.'s first two collections of poetry, *İkindi üstü* (1947; in the afternoon) and *Dirlik-düzenlik* (1954; living in harmony), exhibit the influence of his immediate predecessors, especially the group known as *Garip* (Strange), which had sought to liberate new poetry from strict stanzaic forms and jaded conventions and to make its style direct, idiomatic, humorous, and populist. At this stage, C. was writing as a young bourgeois-bohemian, but his promise as a powerful new voice was already apparent. It was with *Yerçekimli karanfil* (1957; the gravitational carnation) that he burst on the literary scene as a major innovator to contend with. Few collections have been as controversial, and even fewer have had as enduring an impact. In a sharp departure from all the earlier norms of the Turkish poetic tradition and renouncing the *Garip* movement, C. and some of his contemporaries, including Cemal Süreyya (q.v.), Turgut Uyar (1927–1985), and Ece Ayhan (b. 1931), launched a brave new poetry, which at first came to be known as "meaningless" or "absurd" and later took the more neutral name "The Second New." C. and his friends made a curious but scintillating mélange of surrealism and existentialism (qq.v.), casting it into unabashedly obscurantist but engagingly lyrical forms of verse. Their wild thrusts of imagination elicited such criticism as "gibberish," "word salad," and "distortion of language." "The Second New," however, succeeded in overcoming the vehement attacks and endured as a profoundly influential aesthetic ideology.

C.'s *Umutsuzlar parkı* (1958; the park of the hopeless) and *Petrol* (1959; petroleum) continued to bring him harsh criticism for egregious innovation and much praise for opening new horizons. It would be realized in the next decade that C. and the movement had once and for all asserted the poet's creative autonomy by freeing him from political commitment, ready-made forms, jaded tradition, pat idiom, and the like. The result was essentially a dazzling narcissism.

In *Nerde Antigone* (1961; where is Antigone) C. moved into a restless alienation, exploring the predicaments of the modern human being in the realm of ancient mythology and new myths. This search led him in *Tragedyalar* (1964; tragedies) and *Çağrılmayan Yakup* (1969; Jacob uninvited) to a strong dramatic narrative style that conveys both dark despair and glimmers of hope. As the titles suggest, these books evoke the spirit of ancient tragedy and biblical lore. In these two books, C. achieved a grandeur of vision and a grand design.

From 1970 until his death, C.'s poetic art evolved as a new, more serene quest for happiness in the midst of a cruel, turbulent world. *Kirli ağustos* (1970; dirty August) and *Sonrası kalır* (1974; the rest shall remain) are stimulating yet tranquil statements about an immutably troubled life in which perhaps the only salvation may be found in simple pleasures and the rich realm of the imagination. *Ben Ruhi Bey Nasılım* (1976; I Ruhi Bey, how am I) and *Sevda ile sevgi* (1977; love and affection) contain many of C.'s most heartwarming poems about ordinary people and the joys and the tender sorrows of love. These are all, however, poems of intriguing subtlety, with a uniquely ingenious style. *Şairin seyir defteri* (1980; poet's log book) is perhaps C.'s most openly personal, if not autobiographical, collection of poems.

In 1981 C.'s complete poems were published in a volume entitled *Yeniden* (anew), stimulating new critical assessments of his poetic career. Critics were unanimous in recognizing that C. had brought important dimensions to modern Turkish poetry. C. published two more collections, *Bezik oynayan kadınlar* (1982; women playing bezique) and *İlkyaz şikayetçileri* (1984; complainers of spring), which contain some of his most impressive and consummate poems. Winner of the 1958 Yeditepe Poetry Prize for *Yerçekimli karanfil* and the Poetry Prize of the Turkish Language Society in 1977 for *Ben Ruhi Bey Nasılım*, C. was given the Literary Award of the Sedat Simavi Foundation in 1981 for his complete poems, *Yeniden*. C. will continue to enjoy high prestige as one of the towering figures of Turkish poetry in the second half of the 20th c.

TALAT SAIT HALMAN

CARBALLIDO, Emilio
Mexican dramatist, b. 25 May 1925, Córdoba, Veracruz

Although C. grew up and has spent most of his life in Mexico City, he has maintained specific ties to Veracruz for both professional and familial reasons. C. graduated from the National University of Mexico with an M.A. in drama and English literature. The author has traveled, lectured, and taught throughout the world; his knowledge of world theater is quite extensive. In addition to having written some one hundred dramatic works for stage, opera, and film, and having received numerous awards for his work, he has also been active as a director, drama professor, and editor of *Tramoya,* a drama journal.

Since the late 1940s, C., in association with a variety of collaborators, has worked tirelessly to change and upgrade the dramatic arts and drama in Mexico, both in terms of style and substance. In the 1970s, C. turned his attention to fostering young playwrights, ultimately collecting and publishing their works in anthologies, notably *Teatro joven de México* (1973; young theater of Mexico), *Más teatro joven* (1979: more young theater), and *9 obras jovenes* (1985; 9 young works).

By 1949 C. had already written and produced or published several short dramatic pieces, and at the age of twenty-five he saw the debut of his first full-length play, *Rosalba y los Llaveros* (1950; Rosalba and the Llaveros). The work was directed by C.'s close friend Salvador Novo (q.v.), and it was an immediate critical success. Set in Veracruz, like many of C.'s works, it treats the clash of values and outlooks between a cosmopolite from Mexico City and her provincial relatives of Otalitlán, Veracruz.

C. followed *Rosalba y los Llaveros* with several other substantial works during the 1950s, including the comedy *La danza que sueña la tortuga* (1955; the dance of which the turtle dreams), a portrait of two middle-aged, single sisters seeking identity and liberation from an overprotective brother in the provincial setting of Veracruz. The following year, C. produced *La hebra de oro* (1956; the golden thread), in which, for the first time, he intertwines his already established theatrical realism with elements of fantasy. The result was a stunning and innovative production that relied on a wide array of experimental and pyrotechnical gimmicks. Various critics consider *La hebra de oro* C.'s most important dramatic work because of its great impact on the development of Mexican theater. Yet another highly successful play followed: *Felicidad* (1957; felicity). It was a semicomedic presentation of marital infidelity, egotism, and spousal oppression. C.'s stature was further elevated when *Felicidad* won the Ruíz de Alarcón Prize for Drama (1957).

During the 1960s C. produced numerous significant dramatic works, including *El relojero de Córdoba* (1960; the clockmaker from Córdoba), another of the author's clever mixes of reality and fantasy. Another success appeared with *El día que se soltaron los leones* (1963; the day they let the lions loose). In this work C. undertook, as a primary focus, social and political criticism of Mexico's repressive society and government. *El día que se soltaron los leones* won the Casa de las Américas Drama Prize in 1963. C. continued to explore new boundaries in his theater, being particularly drawn to the fantastic and magic, laced with realism. He wrote works based on Greek mythology, of which *Medusa* (1966; Medusa) is a fine example. At the same time, however, C. continued to produce traditional theater. Two better-known pieces are the comedies *¡Silencio, pollos pelones, ya les van a echar su maíz!* (1963; shut up, you damn chickens, you'll get your corn) and *Te juro, Juana, que tengo ganas* (1965; I swear to you, Juana, that I want you).

During the 1970s C. produced two works that deserve particular mention: *Un vals sin fin sobre el planeta* (1970; an endless waltz around the world) and *Las cartas de Mozart* (1975; the Mozart letters). In the latter, set in 19th-c. Mexico City, a mysterious young beggar-violinist, while interacting with a middle-class family, slowly metamorphosizes into a young Mozart.

The 1980s have seen yet more of C.'s dramatic works produced and published. *Orinoco* (1982; Orinoco), one of C.'s greatest theatrical successes, treats the plight of two erstwhile and broken-down show girls (prostitutes) who discover themselves floating down the Orinoco River in Venezuela on a boat abandoned by its crew. The pathetic, but comedic, interaction-argumentation between the two imperiled travelers informs the actions and plot. C. continues to enjoy great success in Mexican theater, producing a variety of dramatic works at regular intervals. His *Ceremonia en el templo del tigre* (1986; ceremony in the temple of the tiger) is dedicated to the dark side of Mexican agrarian reform and the intransigent feudalism in the countryside. Violence and despair, with a backdrop of oppression, pervade the book.

Aside from his drama, C. is also an accomplished narrative writer. His novellas *La veleta oxidada* (1956; the oxidized weathervane) and *El norte* (1958; *The Norther*, 1968) were well received, particularly the latter. *El norte* possessed, for its time, a clever alternating of temporal places (past and present) portraying both the birth and death of the sexual relationship between a young man and an older woman. C.'s fine collection of short stories, *La caja vacía* (1962; the empty box), also deserves mention.

Generally considered to be one of Latin America's most prolific dramatists, C. is unquestionably the principal personage in Mexico's rich world of theater. He has distinguished himself by producing an extremely varied body of dramatic work that is notable for both its quantity and quality. C.'s literary and dramatic legacy will be long-lasting and of immense significance.

FURTHER WORKS: *La zona intermedia* (1948); *La triple porfía* (1949); *Medalla al mérito* (1949); *El lugar y la hora* (1957); *D. F.* (1957, rev. ed., 1984); *Las estatuas de marfil* (1960); *Teatro* (1960); *Teseo* (1962); *14 obras en un acto* (1962); *Las vistaciones del diablo* (1965); *Las noticias del día* (1968); *El sol* (1970); *Yo también hablo de la rosa* (1970); *Almanaque de Juárez* (1972); *El arca de Noé* (1974); *Acapulco, los lunes* (1978); *Un pequeño día de ira* (1978); *Fotografía en la playa* (1979); *Tres comedias* (1981); *Tiempo de ladrones; La historia de Chucho el Roto* (1983); *A la epopeya, un gajo* (1983); *Los zapatos de fierro* (1983); *El tren que corría* (1984); *Jardín con animales* (1985); *Teatro para adolescentes* (1985); *Teatro para obreros* (1985); *Avanzada: más teatro joven* (1985); *La rosa de dos aromas* (1986); *El pizarrón encantado* (1988); *Teatro 2* (1988); *19 veces el D. F.* (1989). FURTHER VOLUME IN ENGLISH: *The Golden Thread and Other Plays* (1970)

BIBLIOGRAPHY: Holzapfel, T., "A Mexican Medusa," *MD*, 12 (1970), 231–37; Oliver, W. I., *Voices in the Spanish American Theater* (1971), passim; Bravo-Elizondo, P., *El teatro hispanoamericano de crítica social* (1975), 62–72; Dauster, F., *Ensayos sobre teatro hispanoamericano* (1975), 143–88; Lyday, L. F., and G. W. Woodyard, eds., *Dramatists in Revolt* (1976), 19–36; Peden, M. S., "E. C.: Curriculum operum," *TCrit*, 2, 3 (1976), 94–112; Peterson, K., "Existential Irony in Three C. Plays," *LATR*, 10, 2 (Spring 1977), 29–35; Peden, M. S., *E. C.* (1979); Bixler, J. E., "A Theater of Contradictions: The Recent Works of E. C.," *LATR*, 18, 2 (Spring 1985), 57–65; Cortés, E., "Las novelas cortas de E. C.: Temática y técnica," in Paolini, G., ed., *La Chispa '87: Selected Proceedings* (1987), 81–87; Taylor, D., "Mad World, Mad Hope: C.'s *El día que se soltaron los leones*," *LATR*, 20, 2 (Spring 1987), 67–76; Troiano, J. J., "Illusory Worlds in Three Stories by E. C.," *HisJ*, 10, 2 (Spring 1989), 63–79; Bixler, J. E., "E. C.," in Sole, C. A., ed., *Latin American Writers* (1989), Vol. 3, 1289–94; Taylor, D., *Theatre of Crisis: Drama and Politics in Latin America* (1991), 148–80

SAM L. SLICK

Perhaps we can discover the existential moral of *Medusa* by comparing the proud and distant pose of Sartre's Orestes at the end of *The Flies* with Perseus' final rigidity. Orestes, who in the course of the play changes from a mild and compromising youth into a man of resolute action, ultimately resists the gods' authority in the name of personal and responsible freedom. When Jupiter reminds Orestes that he will have to pay with suffering for the discovery that he is a free man, the Sartrean hero tells him proudly: "Men are free and human life begins on the other side of despair." From this viewpoint, Perseus' hardness of character, his incapacity for affection is the price he pays for his independence from the gods. For his recognition that men are not the toys of the gods or any other power, he must accept as a condition of his existence a state of anguish and estrangement.

In conclusion, *Medusa* is a play about man's quest for moral autonomy in life and politics. It offers a powerful message for the Latin American countries where the masses are oppressed by religion and unjust governments which, from the liberal point of view, are little more than puppet regimes of U. S. imperialism. A daring director could shape *Medusa* into an explosive drama of social revolution.

Tamara Holzapfel, "A Mexican Medusa," *MD*, 12 (1970), 237

E. C. is one of Mexico's leading authors, having written a large number of plays, novels, and short stories, as well as scenarios for various films. His playwrighting underwent a very real sea-change when he traveled abroad in the Mexican foreign service. His present work reflects an encounter with the techniques of modern European theater, such as the Berliner Ensemble. In 1966 C. enjoyed a great success with *I Too Speak of the Rose*. It is an epic drama with expressionist controls that explores human possibilities from political, psychological, moral, and metaphysical points of view. All of this seems ponderous, but quite the opposite is the case. More recently his play *Medusa,* a contemporary interpretation of the Perseus myth, was chosen as the main theatrical offering in Mexico City during the period of the Olympics.

William I. Oliver, *Voices of Change in the Spanish American Theater* (1971), ix

E. C. has written many different kinds of plays: one-act vignettes, plays with historical settings, political commentary, and fantasies. The fantasy plays explore the psychological and archetypal delineations of human freedom. *Medusa, Teseo,* and *Las estatuas de marfil,* a trilogy, deal more singlemindedly with the characteristically existential notion of freedom as action, seeking to explore "how far a free agent can escape from his particular situation in his choices." But these three plays include as many styles. *Medusa* is fantastic and heavily symbolic, and *Teseo,* the least complex of the three, is a one-act fantasy. *Las estatuas de marfil* is entirely realistic, but it is the most subtle and difficult. Together, the plays are three variations on a single theme, and C., through symbol and elegantly metaphorical plot, has incorporated the existential irony that is characteristic of Sartre's drama.

Karen Peterson, "Existential Irony in Three C. Plays," *LALR,* 10, 2 (Spring 1977), 29

C. has changed the course of Mexican theater. In spite of his reservations about the term, C. contributed a number of works to the body of Mexican neo-realistic/costumbristic plays; more importantly, he has raised Mexican theater above the customarily limited level of that genre. C. introduced music, humor, poetry, formal innovation, and his own unique blend of realism and fantasy into the post-World War II Mexican theater. His activities as a teacher and administrator of several schools of theater (Instituto Politécnico Nacional, Bellas Artes, and the cultural program of the University of Veracruz) have influenced the course of the careers of Mexico's current generation of young dramatists.

C. has a true sense of theater. He has created a concept of theater that is universal and enduring. His prose fiction is significant, but C. is at his best when he is his most theatrical, employing all the devices that enhance the direct communication that is theater's particular province. "Teseo" and *Medusa, El relojero de Córdoba,* the trilogy *El lugar y la hora,* utilize the magic of myth. "El espejo," "Medalla al mérito," *La hebra de oro,* and "Yo también hablo de la rosa" delve inventively into levels of individual consciousness. The basically theatrical values of music, dance, and ritual are used innovatively in "Silencio, pollos pelones," *Las cartas de Mozart,* and *El día que se soltaron los leones.* The cathartic power of humor permeates his plays. Serious Mexican theater was rocked out of its conventions by the affectionate warmth, the broad burlesque, the puckish fun of C.'s humor. . . .

C.'s place in Latin American theater is well-established. He is among the half-dozen most important Latin dramatists of this century. His reputation as a prose writer is less secure, but he has made important contributions to fiction. C. loves to travel, and he has taught and lectured in many countries, spreading the warmth of his personality. His work has been performed throughout Latin America, on the Continent, and in many colleges and universities in the United States, exposing this major talent to ever wider audiences. C.'s mark on literature is assured.

Margaret Sayers Peden, *E. C.* (1979), 175–76

C. is undoubtedly the most prolific and versatile of contemporary Latin American dramatists. Since 1948, he has written over one hundred dramatic works, including operas, film scripts, librettos, adaptations, and children's theater. His works traverse the gamut of dramatic styles, from macabre fantasy to strict provincial realism, from allegorical farce to plays of explicit social protest. Despite the structural, technical, and topical diversity of his theater, there are certain C. trademarks: the compassionate portrayal of characters, particularly women, from either the capital or the Veracruz provinces; the gentle humor present in even his most socially committed pieces; the distinctly Mexican setting and language; and the fusion of diverse dramatic styles and levels of reality within individual works. . . .

Today, after forty years in the limelight of Mexican theater, C. shows no sign of slowing down. With a boundless energy, he continues to write one or two plays a year, travel widely, and foment the national theater in every way possible. By sharing his broad knowledge of the theater with the current generation of young playwrights, he is ensuring that the renaissance of Mexican theater will continue well into the future. His varied and limitless creative talents are apparent in the many works that he himself has contributed to this vital, cultural movement. With each new play, he discovers a different way of transforming Mexican reality into art and thus of providing a meaningful yet artistic representation of modern man. While fully aware of the social and economic inequities present in his society, C. never allows his protest to dominate his art, but rather subtly voices his concerns through such vehicles as farcical exaggeration, historical perspectives, and parallels between fiction and reality. By successfully adapting form to content and incorporating imaginative elements into his portrayal of daily life and human relationships, C. has achieved a lasting theater of universal transcendence, meaning, and appeal.

Jacqueline Eyring Bixler, "E. C.," in Charles A. Sole ed., *Latin American Writers* (1989), 1290–92

Readers of Latin American theater may be surprised to find a chapter on E. C. . . . in a study of theater of crisis. C.'s plays, especially the two emphasized here— *El día que se soltaron los leones* . . . and *Yo también hablo de la rosa*. . . —are playful and expansive, calling for elaborate and complicated sets, large casts, bright colors, and music. These plays do not seem to belong to a violent, grotesque world of oppression and crisis. No one overtly torments or tortures anyone else; death comes only to those who deserve it. Compared with much Latin American drama in general and with all the other plays included here in particular, C.'s theater seems joyful, almost optimistic. This is no "poor" theater; there is no call to action associated with "revolutionary" theater. Nor are C.'s plays "committed," "popular," or didactic in any straightforward sense. But commentators will be deceived by C.'s playfulness if they do not recognize that these plays speak to revolution; they are profoundly "popular" . . . they offer a liberating vision of Mexican culture which evades the tugs of the West and yet resists the temptation to fall back onto some native traditionalism.

Diana Taylor, *Theatre of Crisis: Drama and Politics in Latin America* (1991), 148

CARDENAL, Ernesto

Nicaraguan poet, b. 20 Jan. 1925, Granada

Poet, Marxist revolutionary, and Catholic priest, C. is one of Latin America's most important lit-

erary figures. After studying in Mexico and in New York at Columbia University, C. returned to Nicaragua where he participated in the unsuccessful "April Conspiracy" (1954) to overthrow the dictator Somoza. In 1957 he entered the Trappist monastery in Gethsemani, Kentucky, where he was profoundly influenced by Thomas Merton's philosophy of nonviolence. Upon being ordained a Catholic priest in 1965, C. founded the religious community of Solentiname on an island in Lake Nicaragua. Increased government brutality in the 1970s, coupled with his study of Marxism and "liberation theology," inspired C. to become a member of the FSLN (Sandinista Front for National Liberation) and to espouse the doctrine of armed struggle.

One of the hallmarks of C.'s work, when viewed in its entirety, is a constant growth and renewal. His major themes—love (of women in his early poems, later of the Nicaraguan people, God, and the entire universe), history, Nicaragua, revolution—are expressed with great commitment and clarity and indicate the passionate evolution of a writer who has done much to popularize poetry and to stretch the limits of poetic expression.

C. began writing in the early 1940s, but it was not until he became familiar with the poetry of Ezra Pound (q.v.), whose influence he openly acknowledges, that he began to adopt some of the technical devices that would become characteristic of his own poetic style, which he called *exteriorismo,* a term coined by C. and one of his early mentors, José Coronel Urtecho (b. 1906). This is a direct, unadorned poetry, composed of what C. calls the elements of real life. Through the use of a collage technique which often creates the effect of a cinematographic montage of images, C. retells history, narrates political events, gives lessons in economy and indigenous cultures, ponders the injustices of capitalism, and expresses his love of the people and his hatred of dictatorships. C. insists that nothing lies outside the realm of the poetic and freely incorporates proper names, statistical data, fragments of letters, information from newspapers, and passages quoted directly from historical chronicles. In accordance with his stated intention of clarity and intelligibility, his language is unpretentious, conversational, and often colloquial. Realizing that the history of the New World has been written largely by invaders and conquerors, C. has taken on the task of inserting history into poetry and in effect has rewritten significant portions of Latin American history. In poems such as "Raleigh" (1949; Raleigh) and "Con Walker en Nicaragua" (1950; "With Walker in Nicaragua," 1962), C. recreates the vision of the New World as seen through the eyes of foreigners. *La Hora O* (1966; *Zero Hour*, 1968), which has become a revolutionary classic in Latin America, begins with a portrayal of the Central American dictatorships of the 1930s. It examines the United Fruit Company's presence in the "Banana Republics" and tells of Nicaraguan patriot Augusto César Sandino's resistance to U.S. intervention in his country. It concludes with the "April Conspiracy" of 1954 against Somoza, thereby linking past and present in Nicaragua's continuing fight for self-determination. Like many of his poems, *La Hora O* is epic in scale and prophetic in tone. History is manifest through quotidian detail yet perceived with teleological vision. Explicit in C.'s vision is the kingdom of heaven on earth. Rather than an otherworldly or unattainable dream, he sees a classless society living in peace as a goal to be achieved in the present. His study of pre-Colombian Amerindian cultures convinced him that a model of a classless society was to be found in the indigenous communities of America. The poems in *Homenaje a los indios americanos* (1969; *Homage to the American Indians,* 1973) were inspired by this utopian vision of the past. "Economía de Tahuantinsuyu" ("Economy of Tahuantinsuyu"), for example, by juxtaposing images from a peaceful barter economy where there is no hunger or unemployment, with tourists snapping photos of indigent peasants and announcements of stock-market prices, condemns capitalism and posits an indigenous socialism as a lost but recoverable possibility.

When C. visited Cuba for several months in 1970, he was impressed with the accomplishments of the revolution and Cuba's progress toward building a just society created by the "New Man." He began to question his strict adherence to the philosophy of nonviolence and came to accept the necessity of armed resistance in the struggle to create a society based on true Christian principles. He became increasingly supportive of the FSLN in the 1970s, working to encourage revolutionary activism in Nicaragua, as demonstrated by poems such as "Canto nacional" (1972; national song) and "Oráculo sobre Managua" (1973; *Oracle over Managua,* 1973). By 1977 the Solentiname commune, C.'s experiment in creating a small-scale ideal Christian society, had become a Sandinista cell and was subsequently destroyed by Somoza's National Guard. C. declared himself an active member of the FSLN and in 1979 assumed the position of minister of culture in the newly formed Sandinista government.

C.'s poetry during the approximately ten years after the Sandinista victory reflects his full-time involvement in the reconstruction of Nicaragua. Collected in the bilingual edition *Flights of Victory/Vuelos de victoria* (1985), poems such as "Ocupados" ("Busy") and "Reflexiones de un ministro" ("Reflections of a Minister") speak of the visionary prophet and the practical man of action who have fused in the service of building a cultural democracy on a national level. In his enthusiasm for the revolution, his vision, as evidenced in "Waslala" ("Waslala"), is so insistently optimistic and supportive as to appear almost ingenuous. In the context of the difficulties facing the Sandinistas during the reconstruction, these poems may also be read as affirmations of a poet immersed in the historical moment, who sees his country's need for new myths and heroes and answers the call.

As minister of culture, C. was instrumental in establishing workshops where writing poetry based on the principles and techniques of *exteriorismo* was taught to farmers, workers, and soldiers, many of whom had only recently achieved literacy. C.'s themes and style have exercised profound influence among younger writers in Nicaragua and throughout Latin America. The poet-priest-revolutionary with the gray hair and beard, the unassuming style of dress, and the characteristic black beret, whose ability to write history into poetry and whose profound love for the individual, the collective, and the planet is manifest in his poetry along with his disdain of greed, consumerism, and injustice, is an example of the Latin American ideal of the socially committed writer.

FURTHER WORKS: *Gethsemani, KY* (1960); *Epigramas: poemas* (1961); *Oración por Marilyn Monroe y otros poemas* (1965); *El estrecho dudoso* (1966); *Salmos* (1967; *Psalms,* 1981); *Vida en el amor* (1970; *To Live Is To Love,* 1974); *Canto nacional* (1972); *En Cuba* (1972; *In Cuba,* 1974); *El evangelio en Solentiname* (1975; *The Gospel in Solentiname,* 1982); *La santidad de la revolución* (1976); *Tocar el cielo* (1981); *Quetzalcoatl* (1986); *Cántico cósmico* (1989). FURTHER VOLUMES IN ENGLISH: *The Psalms of Liberation and Struggle* (1971); *Marilyn Monroe, and Other Poems* (1975); *"Apocalypse," and Other Poems* (1977); *Zero Hour, and Other Documentary Poems* (1980); *With Walker in Nicaragua, and Other Early Poems, 1949–1954* (1984); *From Nicaragua with Love* (1986)

BIBLIOGRAPHY: Oviedo, J., "E. C.: un místico comprometido," *CasaA,* 11, 53 (Nov.–Dec. 1969), 29–48; Benedetti, M., "E. C.: evangelio y revolución," *CasaA,* 63 (1970), 175–83; Arellano, J., "E. C.: de Granada a Gethsemani (1926–1957)," *CHA,* 289–90 (1974), 163–83; Brotherston, G., *Latin American Poetry: Origins and Presence* (1975), 173–77; García Cambeiro, F., *E. C., poeta de la liberación latinoamericana* (1975); Fraire, I., "Pound and C.," *Review,* 18 (1976),

36–42; Zimmerman, M., "E. C. after the Revolution," *Flights of Victory* (1985), 9–32: Beverley, J., and M. Zimmerman, *Literature and Politics in the Central American Revolutions* (1990), 66–72

JANET N. GOLD

CARRANZA, Eduardo

Colombian poet, literary critic, essayist, polemicist, journalist, and translator, b. 23 July 1913, Apiay; d. 13 Feb. 1985, Bogotá

C. was educated in Bogotá by the Brothers of the Christian Schools and as a young man studied to become a teacher. He taught Spanish and Colombian literature at universities and cultural centers in both countries. Since 1934 he has gained increasing national recognition for the publication of his poetic works, for his collaboration in the cultural journal *Revista de Las Indias,* for editing literary pages in the newspaper *El Tiempo* of Bogotá, for his directorship of the National Library, and for his activities as a diplomat. C. was a member of the Colombian Spanish Academy. In 1939 C. founded the most important poetic group of Colombia, *Piedra y Cielo* (Stone and Sky), a name taken from a poetic notebook of the Spanish poet Juan Ramón Jiménez (q.v.). C., along with Jorge Rojas (b. 1911), Arturo Camacho Ramírez (1910–1982), Carlos Martín (b. 1914), Tomás Vargas Osorio (1908–1941), and Gerardo Valencia (b. 1911), worked intensively during the 1930s and 1940s to show, first, an ascensional impulse to transcend the traditionalism of Colombian poetry, followed by a countervailing terrestrial impulse to touch the stone of Latin America and her hard reality. This heterogeneous group worked to achieve a cohesion of style, vocabulary and syntax, meters and stanzas, metaphors and themes. Although each writer possessed in his work his own personality and characteristics, all departed from the same aesthetic position, which emphasized an eagerness for novelty and formal discipline, a predilection for illogical images, a disdain for the narrative, a respect for forms, an appreciation of classic and modern Hispanic writers, and a use of sentimentalism to create a world of fantasy and sensibility. In essence, the poets of *Piedra y Cielo* were more outspoken than genuinely revolutionary in their cultivation of a poetry of restraint, more artistic than vital as they tried to make the word more intense while firing the atmosphere of Colombian poetry with an enriched poetic sensibility.

Although C.'s favorite themes are universal—nature, woman, childhood, memories, dreams, intimacy, sorrow, melancholy, death, and religious topics—his transcendental attitude and sensitive spirit, as well as the temporal and spacial perspectives of his poetry, with its picturesque vision and lyric strength, distinguish him from other poets of his time. His beautiful poems "La niña de los jardines" (1936; the girl of the gardens) and "Soneto insistente y soneto con una salvedad" (1944; insistent sonnet and sonnet with a salvation) are the best examples of his poetic sensibility and spirit.

Beyond his successful translations of Paul Verlaine (1844–1896), Paul Eluard, and Guillaume Apollinaire (qq.v.), C. has enjoyed a literary career brilliant in its own right; the critical success of his books has seldom been matched by that of other Colombian authors. C.'s work is characterized by graceful sensuality, refinement, and a vague melancholy. Critics have reproached C.'s works for their lack of human depth and concern for the most vital social problems of contemporary existence. Nevertheless, his treatments of love, nature, melancholy, and nostalgia have ensured his position among contemporary Hispanic writers. Although the Colombian poetic generation of today has criticized C.'s traditionalism and his rejection of the significant European and American literary currents, it is precisely his focus on uniquely Hispanic forms and themes that lends strength to his poetry.

FURTHER WORKS: *Canciones para iniciar una fiesta* (1936); *Seis elegías y un himno* (1939); *Ellas, los días y las nubes* (1941); *Sombra de las muchachas* (1941); *Azul de ti* (1944); *Los grandes poetas americanos* (1944); *Canto en voz alta* (1945); *Las santas del paraíso* (1945); *Éste era un rey* (1945); *Los días que ahora son sueños* (1946); *Diciembre azul* (1947); *Amor* (1948); *El olvidado y Alhambra* (1957); *El corazón escrito* (1967); *Los pasos contados* (1970); *El insomne* (1974); *Hablar soñando y otras alucinaciones* (1974); *Epístola mortal y otras soledades* (1975); *Leyendas del corazón y otras páginas abandonadas* (1976); *Lección de poesía para los jóvenes de Cundinamarca* (1980); *20 pemas* (1982); *Carranza* (1985)

BIBLIOGRAPHY: Núñez Segura, J. A., *Literatura colombiana* (1967), 448–54; De Francisco, G. S., *Gran reportaje a E. C.* (1978); García Maffla, J., "El movimiento poético de 'Piedra y Cielo,' " *RI,* 50, 128–29 (July–Dec. 1984), 683–88; Charry Lara, F., *Poesía y poetas colombianos* (1985), 87–92, 105–15; Rozo de Moorhouse, T., "La palabra en la poesía de E. C.," *Thesaurus,* 40, 2 (1985), 415–22; Álvarez Restrepo, A., "E. C. y la poesía colombiana," *BAC,* 36, 153 (July–Sept.

1986), 163–81; Williams, R. L., *The Colombian Novel, 1844–1987* (1991), 43

VIRGINIA SHEN

CARRASQUILLA, Tomás

Colombian novelist, short-story writer, and essayist, b. 17 Jan. 1858, Santo Domingo; d. 19 Dec. 1940, Medellín

Early this century C. shone alone in the fiction of his native country. He might have risen to greater heights had not Colombia produced after the 1920s a brilliant corps of novelists. Today C. is read only within Colombia and especially within his native region of Antioquia.

C. led a rather uneventful life. Sustaining himself with clerical and bureaucratic posts, he devoted himself wholeheartedly to literature. Unmarried, stricken by blindness in old age, he was confined to a wheelchair for the last fifteen years of his life.

C. did not issue his first book until he was almost forty. He began with *Frutos de mi tierra* (1896; fruits of my native land), in which he began to set the pace he was to pursue throughout his literary life. It was the typical realist novel, describing bourgeois people with personal problems in ordinary circumstances. The title of this first novel also indicated the strong regionalistic bent he was to impress on his works. Other similar novels were *Grandeza* (1910; greatness), a biting satire of characters drawn from the Colombian upper and middle classes, their economic and social climbing; and *El padre Casafús* (1914; Father Casafús), written to expose the evils of religious intransigence. But the short novel was C.'s forte. In the mid-1920s he reached his peak. *El zarco* (1925; the blue-eyed boy) is a moving saga of human charity on behalf of a defenseless child. It was followed by *Ligia Cruz* (1926; Ligia Cruz), this being the name of a heroine terminally ill with tuberculosis, once again a powerful story of charity and of transformation through self-sacrifice. Then came *La marquesa de Yolombó* (1928; the marquise of Yolombó), considered C.'s foremost work. Basically a historical novel, it portrays an ambitious Creole woman whose loyalty to Mother Spain and her King is severely tested by the Independence upheaval. More important than the plot itself is the masterful recreation of the times and of peasants, miners, slaves, and Spanish noblemen, all adorned with a magnificent lore.

Several short stories by C. are found in anthologies. "En la diestra de Dios Padre" (1897; in the right hand of Our Lord) is a diverting tale of wit, wholly drawn from local lore. "A la plata!" (1901; money! money!), his best-known short story,

definitely naturalistic, ridicules false parental honor that crumbles down when greed appears. But instead of the scientific structure of the literature of theses, C. reduced his naturalism to a simple description of bad passions and of sordid situations. In nearly all his fiction, both long and short, he put to use his autobiographical material, drawing a good many characters from the people he used to meet in his native Antioquia, as well as in Bogotá, the Colombian capital. Other recourses he employed were regionalism, psychology, and folklore. He did not use regionalism for static pictures but rather to give characters and situations a peculiarity all their own. His psychology was seldom deep; his characters lack internal development, but they are convincingly portrayed, like any live person found in the streets of Medellín or Bogotá. Folklore shows mainly in the speech of the farmers and hillmen that populate his fiction.

C. is not easy to classify. Having been active a good part of the 20th c., he is a modern realist. The lore and the local types he constantly employed placed him as a forerunner of the Spanish American nativistic school of the 1930s. However, he always refrained from entering into the realm of the literature of social protest, which was also a part of the nativistic movement of those years. Although a liberal who advocated freedom and tolerance, he did not allow any ideology to have a voice in his fiction.

With the several novels incorporated into the trilogy of *Memorias de Eloy Gamboa: hace tiempos* (1935–1936; memories of Eloy Gamboa: time ago) the creative power of C. came to an end. Blind, he had to dictate every line to a family member. This trilogy, the most psychological of his works, depicts the mental and spiritual evolution of a child guided by outside influences, both adequate and inadequate. Other works by this venerated Colombian were his essays called *Homilías* (1906; homilies), in which he set down his own literary principles: be sincere and free of affectation; endeavor to write "a national work with modern information"; maintain faithfulness to your native land and to "the hymn of life." And while stating that he had neither school nor favorite authors, his modern realism can be described as parallel to that of Spaniard Vicente Blasco Ibáñez (q.v.).

Because of a defective technique, none of C.'s works can be called a masterpiece, but critics have always judged him as the uniformly good writer that prepared the ground for the vigorous Colombian and Spanish American novel of the midcentury. Labeled "a realist and an idealist," he exhibits the exemplary honesty of the artist that lived for literature alone.

FURTHER WORKS: *Salve, Regina* (1903); *Entrañas de niño* (1914); *Dominicales* (1934); *De tejas arriba* (1936); *Obras completas* (2 vols., 1958)

BIBLIOGRAPHY: Sanín Cano, B., *Letras colombianas* (1944), 199–201; Wade, G. E., "An Introduction to the Colombian novel," *Hispania,* 30, 4 (1947), 467–83; Curcio Altamar, A., *Evolución de la novela en Colombia* (1957),139–48; Sylvester, N., *The "Homilías" and "Dominicales" of T. C.* (1970); Menton, S., *La novela colombiana: planetas y satélites* (1978), 109–44; Levy, K. L., *T. C.* (1980); Williams, R. L., "Colombia," in Foster, D. W., comp., *Handbook of Latin American Literature* (1987), 153–90; Levy, K. L., "T. C.," in Solé, C. A., ed., *Latin American Writers* (1989), Vol. 1, 343–50

EVELIO ECHEVARRÍA

CARVER, Raymond

American short-story writer and poet, b. 25 May 1938, Clatskanie, Oreg.; d. 2 Aug. 1988, Port Angeles, Wash.

Like his literary hero Anton Chekhov (q.v.), C. was a child of the working poor, born in a mill town on the Columbia River dividing Oregon from Washington State. Married at nineteen and father of two before he turned twenty-one, C. experienced during his "first life" many of the vicissitudes he depicts in his writings: spirit-breaking ennui and underemployment, domestic "dis-ease" culminating in divorce, and life-threatening alcoholism. A comparatively tranquil and productive "second life" commenced in 1977, when C. stopped drinking, began his decade-long association with the writer Tess Gallagher (b. 1943), and steadily gained recognition as the foremost short-story writer of his generation. In 1983 the American Academy awarded C. one of its first Strauss "Livings," a fellowship bringing him five years of substantial income. C. and Gallagher married shortly before his death from lung cancer at age fifty.

The bulk of C.'s early fiction is contained in his first short-story collection, *Will You Please Be Quiet, Please?* (1976). In these twenty-two stories written over fifteen difficult years, C. fuses Chekhov's lyrical realism with the cryptic expressionism of Franz Kafka (q.v.). This deceptively simple mode of fabulation charges ordinary experience with uncanny significance, typically with an undertone of menace. For the most part, C.'s early characters are inarticulate working people whose sensibilities exceed their powers of expression. As the title story indicates, the mood of the book is anxious and interrogative. Stories such as "The

Father," "Neighbors," and "Fat" end with antiheroes on the brink of crisis, their unvoiced conflicts unresolved. Critical recognition followed when *Will You Please Be Quiet, Please?* was nominated for a National Book Award.

A transitional middle period in C.'s fiction begins with the commencement of his postalcoholic "second life" in 1977. Over the course of five interlocking books, C. reinvents his art as his stories pass through a purgatorial dialectic of expansion, compression, and reexpansion in new forms. The opening phase of this process begins with *Furious Seasons, and Other Stories* (1977), an interim collection of eight stories, seven of which C. would revise for subsequent books. Next, following the "theory of omission" proposed by Ernest Hemingway (q.v.), C. cut his stories "to the marrow, not just to the bone" for his so-called "minimalist" masterpiece, *What We Talk About When We Talk about Love* (1981). As the lengthy title intimates, these seventeen tightly elliptical stories expose a painful gap between expression and feeling, talk and love, in the lives of men and women whose relationships have been fouled by alcoholism, infidelity, and the failure of youthful hopes. The arresting fusion of style and subject matter won C. acclaim as "a full-grown master," but it also left him at an artistic crisis point. As the stories in *What We Talk About When We Talk about Love* amply demonstrate, the outcome of failed communication is silence—for character and author alike. To avoid this impasse, C. executed a stylistic turnabout over the next two years, restoring and expanding previously pared-down stories and writing new ones in a richer, fuller, and more hopeful key. The first fruits of this widening phase are gathered in *Fires: Essays, Poems, Stories* (1983). The harvest follows in *Cathedral* (1983), a book of twelve new and expanded stories that won C. nominations for the Pulitzer Prize and National Book Critics Circle Award. In the title story and others such as "Feathers," "Fever," and "A Small, Good Thing" (the last story a revision/expansion of "The Bath" in *What We Talk About*), characters find their lives subtly transfigured as silence and isolation give way to compassion and community. A chapbook, *If It Please You* (1984), provides a concluding illustration of C.'s "more generous" mode of realism.

Although C. won fame as a fiction writer, his first calling had been poetry. Writing in the vernacular lyric-narrative mode of William Carlos Williams (q.v.) and Charles Bukowski (b. 1920), C. published three small-press books of poems before his first short-story collection appeared: *Near Klamath* (1968), *Winter Insomnia* (1970), and *At Night the Salmon Move* (1976). Moreover, even as C. devoted himself to fiction in the late

1970s and early 1980s, he remained an occasional poet. In 1984, after years away from the Pacific Northwest, C. returned to his homeland and his early calling. The result was two poetry collections, *Where Water Comes Together with Other Water* (1985) and *Ultramarine* (1986), books that chart the changing course of C.'s life and art, including his deepening preoccupation with mortality. For these poems, C. shared the 1985 Levinson Prize.

C. returned to fiction in 1986–1987 with seven new stories eventually collected in *Where I'm Calling From* (1988), a burst of creativity that heralded further work to come. In retrospect, however, C.'s untimely death marks this efflorescence as his final phase. Stories of this period—among them "Boxes," "Blackbird Pie," and "Elephant"—are typically longer, looser, and more openly reflective than C.'s previous fiction. Their texture is novelistic and their tone autumnal, with C. freely exploring the interplay of character and incident. The capstone of the group is "Errand," C.'s last-written work of fiction. There, taking for his subject the final days of Chekhov, C. validates the life-transforming power of fiction over fact. Even as his own death approached, C. continued writing, completing a last book of poems, *A New Path to the Waterfall* (1989), in the closing weeks of his life.

Despite C.'s foreshortened career, his contributions to late-20th-c. literature are substantial. C. reinvented realism for postmoderns, set in motion the short-story renaissance of the 1980s, and gave voice to a formerly submerged population. By precept and example he served as mentor to an emerging generation of "post-postmodern" realists whose fiction is, like his, at once representational and self-interrogating. Following Chekhov, C. set himself a modest but enduring goal: "a bringing of the news from one world to another." At a deeper level, as one of his contemporaries observed, "The process of Mr. C.'s fiction is to transform our perception."

FURTHER WORKS: *Dostoevsky: A Screenplay* (1985, with Tess Gallagher); *Conversations with R. C.* (1990); *C. Country: The World of R. C.* (1990, with Bob Adelman); *No Heroics, Please: Uncollected Writings* (1991)

BIBLIOGRAPHY: Boxer, D., and C. Phillips, *"Will You Please Be Quiet, Please?:* Voyeurism, Dissociation, and the Art of R. C.," *IowaR,* 10 (Summer 1979), 75–90; Chénetier, M., "Living On/Off the 'Reserve': Performance, Interrogation, and Negativity in the Works of R. C.," in Chénetier, M., ed., *Critical Angles* (1986), 164–90; special "Minimalist Fiction" section, *Mississippi Review,* 40–41 (1985), 7–94; Stull, W. L., "Beyond Hopelessville: Another Side of R. C.," *PQ,* 64, 1 (Winter 1985), 1–15; Saltzman, A. M., *Understanding R. C.* (1988); Meyer, A., "Now You See Him, Now You Don't, Now You Do Again: The Evolution of R. C.'s Minimalism," *Crit,* 30, 4 (Summer 1989), 239–51; Stull, W. L., "R. C.," in Brook, J. M., ed., *DLB Yearbook: 1988* (1989), 199–213; Halpert, S., ed., *. . . When We Talk About R. C.* (1991); Nesset, K., " 'This Word Love': Sexual Politics and Silence in Early R. C.," *AL,* 63, 2 (June 1991), 292–313; Campbell, E., *R. C.: A Study of the Short Fiction* (1992)

WILLIAM L. STULL

CENTRAL AMERICAN LITERATURE

See Volume 1, page 434.

Although confederation has been a recurring aspiration of the isthmus, nationalism, complicated by the powerful presence of foreign economic and military interests, has kept the six Spanish-speaking republics politically separate yet culturally similar. Sectarian politics, repressive governments, national and regional rivalries, and a social organization based on a ruling oligarchy that controls an impoverished rural agricultural sector form the context that has produced six national literatures with a distinct Central American flavor. Geographic and cultural isolation have encouraged the development of the dual phenomena of active literary groups dedicated to the cultivation and celebration of local figures, as well as the desire to transcend the local and produce a universal literary expression. Numerous literary journals of varying life spans have been vital to these efforts and continue to publish the works of new as well as established writers, although the recent appearance of publishing companies such as Guaymuras (Honduras), Editorial Nueva Nicaragua (Nicaragua), and EDUCA (Costa Rica) has created the opportunity for Central American authors to become known internationally. Whereas dictatorships, whether the strong-man régimes of the first half of the 20th c. or the military governments of the latter decades, typically have repressed any literature construed as oppositional, this censorship has in effect encouraged international communication and solidarity among writers, many of whom have lived in exile for significant periods of time. Central American literature has been influenced by and large by the same major currents as its Mexican and South American neighbors, although not all trends and genres have been developed with equal skill or enthusiasm in each of the six countries. Belize, the seventh Central

American country, gained independence from Britain in 1981 and ·is beginning to produce a national literature, as evidenced by Zee Edgell's (b. 1950) novel *Beka Lamb* (1982), about daily life in the preindependence colony formerly known as British Honduras.

Guatemala. The seat of government for the entire isthmus during the colonial period, Guatemala was also the cultural center and continued to be for a number of years after independence. The University of San Carlos in Guatemala City was the region's first and most reputable institution of higher learning and was attended by students from all the Central American countries. This long and venerable cultural history and the rich traditions of the indigenous peoples of Guatemala are two important factors that have contributed to one of Central America's most developed literatures. The modernist trend that dominated much of Latin American literature, particularly poetry, at the turn of the century had its followers in Guatemala as well, but the best writers of this tendency are known primarily for their prose. Enrique Gómez Carrillo (1873–1927), immensely popular during his lifetime, wrote chronicles from Paris and Buenos Aires that were published in newspapers and periodicals throughout Latin America for over thirty years. His trilogy *Tres novelas inmorales* (1899; three immoral novels) is set in the aristocratic salons and bohemian cafés of turn-of-the-century Paris. They are refined, sensual, and antibourgeois, in the modernist style. Rafael Arévalo Martínez (1884–1975)—whose short story "El hombre que parecía un caballo" (1914; the man who looked like a horse) has frequently been anthologized for its unique approach to human psychology—was also an important novelist.

The Estrada Cabrera and Ubico dictatorships inspired the anti-imperialist and *indigenista* works of writers of the 1920s and 1930s, notably Miguel Angel Asturias (q.v.), winner of the Nobel Prize in 1967, and Luis Cardoza y Aragón (b. 1904), whose prose work *Guatemala las líneas de su mano* (1955; Guatemala the lines of your hand) is a highly personalized and all-encompassing study of Guatemala. The period of social and political reform known as the October Revolution ran from 1944 to 1954. This decade saw a proliferation of cultural events and a significant growth in the number of books and journals published. A number of literary groups were formed, among them Saker-ti (Quiché for "dawn"), a coalition of artists, writers, and intellectuals of various leftist ideologies whose stated goal was to create a democratic, nationalist, and realist art. This renaissance of literary activity ended in 1954 when Arbenz was deposed in a military coup. Many

writers were radicalized by the repression and censorship of the military régime and became known collectively as the "Committed Generation." Some were forced into exile, some joined the newly formed guerrilla groups and combined writing with active involvement in the political struggle; many were killed or disappeared. Otto René Castillo (1936–1967) epitomized the romantic ideal of combining literary work with militancy. He founded the journal *Lanzas y letras* that published the work of the Committed Generation. His volume of poetry *Vámonos patria a caminar* (1965; *Let's Go!*, 1971) is a heroic call to action in direct, simple language. Its best-known poem, "Intelectuales apolíticos" ("Apolitical Intellectuals"), a condemnation of apathetic intellectuals and aesthetic snobs, exemplifies the moralistic quality of his poetry. He was tortured and killed in 1967, thus solidifying his legendary status in Central American literary history.

Military governments and social and political problems continue to dominate the cultural consciousness of Guatemala, but since the late 1960s literature has expressed more complex and diverse responses to this national reality. The novel, whose practitioners have become increasingly engaged in formal experimentation, continues to hold a place of prominence in Guatemalan letters. Drawing on indigenous myth, irony, and wordplay, Arturo Arias (b. 1950) treats the theme of the erasure of historical memory and an individual's attempts to reconstruct his own and his country's past in *Después de las bombas* (1979; *After the Bombs*, 1990). Women writers are now more visible. Margarita Carrera (b. 1929), the first woman graduate in literature from the University of San Carlos, has an impressive output in poetry, essay, journalism, and literary criticism. Ana María Rodas (b. 1937) is representative of an increasingly popular feminist poetry, as evidenced in her *Poemas de la izquierda erótica* (1973; poems of the erotic Left), while Rigoberta Menchú (b. 1959), a Quiché Indian woman, exemplifies the recent appearance of indigenous voices. Her autobiography, *Me llamo Rigoberta Menchú* (1983; *I, Rigoberta Menchú*, 1985), as told to Venezuelan anthropologist Elisabeth Burgos-Debray, combines lyrical descriptions of the beliefs and customs of her community with eyewitness accounts of social injustice against the indigenous population of Guatemala. This kind of testimonial narrative has become one of the most vital literary forms in Guatemala today. Mario Payeras (dates n.a.), one of the founders of Guatemala's Guerrilla Army of the Poor, wrote *Días de la selva* (1980; *Days of the Jungle*, 1983) to describe the experiences of this group in the highlands, while Víctor Montejo (b. 1952), a school teacher working in a remote village, narrates the destruction of the village by the army in 1982 in *Testimony: Death of a Guatemalan Village* (1987), which to date has not been published in a Spanish edition.

El Salvador. In a region characterized by a pronounced division of classes and sectarian politics, El Salvador may well be the nation that has struggled the most with the dichotomies rural/urban, traditional/reformist, reformist/revolutionary. It is the smallest of the Central American countries as well as the most densely populated. A persistent interest in defining that which is truly Salvadoran has generated literary responses that range from highly romanticized and sentimental portraits of the national landscape and the humble country dweller, to harshly realistic depictions of social injustice, tyrannical dictators, and a violent military. With few exceptions, Salvadoran narrative shuns the magic realism (q.v.) so prevalent in other parts of Latin America. The massacre in 1932 by government troops of over 30,000 native Salvadorans and subsequent attempts by Indians to hide their identity by abandoning traditional dress and customs significantly erased the indigenous population, already greatly reduced since colonial times. Modern El Salvador is largely a mestizo nation, unlike neighboring Guatemala, where the indigenous influence persists in the national psyche.

Alberto Masferrer (1868–1932) is often considered the first genuinely national writer. He was a friend of Rubén Darío (q.v.), but did not adopt the modernist aesthetic, using instead a clear, expository prose to develop essays that promoted his democratic humanism. Alfred Espino (1902–1928) continues to be one of El Salvador's most widely read poets. He cultivated a sentimental *costumbrism* of rural themes and idealized landscapes that extolled the virtues of family and tradition. His only book, *Jícaras tristes* (1936; sad water gourds), was published posthumously. Arturo Ambrogi (1876–1936) represented a departure from Espino's romantic vision. His chronicles and short stories project a vision more akin to naturalism (q.v.). Salarrué (pseud. of Salvador Salazar Arrué, 1899–1975) was influential in popularizing the regionalist short story in Central America. In *Cuentos de barro* (1927; stories of clay) he portrays rural peasant and working-class life, recreating with great skill the rich Salvadoran vernacular.

Alice Lardé (b. 1896) introduced a sensual feminine eroticism to Salvadoran poetry with *Alma viril* (1925; virile soul), but it was Claudia Lars (pseud. of Carmen Brannon, 1899–1974) who first achieved a high level of professionalism among women writers. Both Lars and Salarrué correspond chronologically to the avant-garde generation, but neither participated in the formal experimentation of this school. Lars's poetry is lucid, distilled, and sincere. She skillfully blends the personal and the universal in poems of children, friends, and nature and in intimate philosophical meditations.

In the early 1950s a group of university-based writers was formed that, like their Guatemalan counterpart, came to be known as the Committed Generation. Members included Roque Dalton (1935–1975), Roberto Armijo (b. 1937), Mercedes Durand (b. 1933), Eugenio Martínez Orantes (b. 1932), and Manlio Argueta (q.v.). Not part of the group, but of kindred spirit, is Claribel Alegría (q.v.). Primarily poets, they were young, idealistic, highly socially and politically aware, iconoclastic, and antibourgeois. Dalton, who had been influenced by Guatemalan poet Otto René Castillo also became a legendary figure because of the circumstances of his death. His self-proclaimed poetry of "ugly words" is didactic, ironic, and self-mocking. His ambitious and original *Las historias prohibidas del pulgarcito* (1974; the forbidden stories of Tom Thumb) is a collage-poem of Salvadoran history. Many of the writers of this group live in exile. Argueta's novels are banned by the Salvadoran government, but have been widely translated. *Un día en la vida* (1980; *One Day of Life,* 1983) portrays Salvadoran peasants in their struggle against military repression. The writers of the Committed Generation who chose to stay in El Salvador, such as Martínez Orantes, have had to negotiate the perils of censorship. The most prolific and respected of the current generation of writers living in the El Salvador is David Escobar Galindo (b. 1943). He has served as director of the National Library, director of the ministry of culture's journal, *Cultura,* and has published over forty-two books of poetry, prose, and theatre.

Honduras. It is the most sparsely populated of the Central American republics, as well as the poorest. The capital city, Tegucigalpa, located in the central highlands, was, until the second half of the 20th c., extremely isolated from other centers of population. The presence of the Standard and United Fruit Companies has largely determined the economy of much of the country. Although it has had its share of dictatorships and military governments, Hondurans often claim that the acute class distinctions that characterize other Central American countries exist in a more modified form in Honduras, since the oligarchy never amassed extreme wealth as did the ruling families of El Salvador and Guatemala, for example.

Isolation notwithstanding, Honduran writers at the turn of the century kept informed of international literary trends largely through the efforts of Froylán Turcios (1875–1943), who founded and/or directed numerous newspapers and literary journals, notably *Esfinge* and *Ariel,* which published the work of Honduran writers as well as excerpts of classics of world literature, and *Boletín de la defensa nacional,* an important political paper that denounced the occupation of Tegucigalpa by U.S. Marines in 1924. Turcios chronicled his most interesting life in *Memorias* (memories), published posthumously in 1980.

Romanticism, which swept the literary youth of Tegucigalpa at the end of the 19th c., remained popular well into the 20th. Lucila Gamero de Medina's (1873–1964) novel *Blanca Olmedo* (1903; Blanca Olmedo) employs the language and characterizations of romanticism in a scathing attack on the clergy. José Antonio Domínguez (1869–1903) is considered by critics to represent the transition from romanticism to modernism. His themes are often patriotic, but his concern for musicality in verse heralded this fundamental preoccupation of modernism (q.v.). His most important work, ''Himno a la materia'' (hymn to matter), is an ambitious long poem that addresses the philosophical question of humanity's spiritual and material nature and finds answers in a romantic scientism. A poet of modernist sensibilities who achieved international acclaim was Juan Ramón Molina (1875–1908). His lyric persona oscillates between the poles of an innocent lyricism and a worldly despair. His work was collected in *Tierras, mares y cielos* (1911; lands, seas, and skies).

One of the most creative and noteworthy periods of Honduran literature was that of the ''Generation of '35.'' Their penchant for gathering in local cafés and the bohemian self-concept they shared contributed to their group identity, although they published no literary manifesto, as was common among avant-garde groups of the time. Of particular interest is the poetry of Claudio Barrera (pseud. of Vicente Alemán, 1912–1971), Jacobo Cárcamo (1916–1959), and Daniel Laínez (1914–1959). Influenced by the Spanish Civil War and personally affected by the dictatorship of Carías Andino, several writers of this generation turned to social and political themes after an initial period of experimentation with avant-garde techniques. Laínez is known for his skillful use of rural manners of speech. All experimented with the themes and rhythms of the then popular *negrista* poetry.

Clementina Suárez (b. 1902), the grande dame of Honduran poetry, began her career with the romantic and formally traditional *Corazón sangrante* (1930; bleeding heart), but soon abandoned the sonnet in favor of the free verse with which she expressed her feminine sexuality and celebrated love, motherhood, freedom, and social commitment. Her work has been collected in *El poeta y sus señales* (1969; the poet and her signs).

The exploitation of national territory by foreign interests has been a major concern of Honduran prose writers. Coupled with a search to define and describe the national identity, these two elements inform the novels of Marcos Carías Reyes (1905–1949), Paca Navas (1900–1969), and Ramón Amaya Amador (1916–1966). Prolific novelist Argentina Díaz Lozano (b. 1912) won international acclaim for her autobiographical work *Peregrinaje* (1944; *Pilgrimage,* 1945). Contemporary fiction writers tend to be more experimental in technique and wide-ranging in theme, although the Honduran milieu prevails. Marcos Carías Zapata's (b. 1938) *Una función con mobiles y tentetiesos* (1980; function with mobiles and roly-poly toys) is a linguistic and structural tour de force. Julio Escoto (b. 1944) has achieved an international reputation for his short stories and novels. Roberto Castillo's (b. 1950) short fiction is a rich blend of magic realism, irony, and humor. Recent Honduran poetry is inspired largely by social concerns and a desire to create an awareness of the national reality. Roberto Sosa's (b. 1930) finely crafted and deeply sensitive poetry has been widely translated; of note are *Los pobres* (1968; *The Poor,* 1983) and *Los días difíciles* (1971; *The Difficult Days,* 1983). The best of the young poets include José Luis Quesada (b. 1948), Rigoberto Paredes (b. 1948), and María Eugenia Ramos (b. 1959).

Nicaragua. Poetry is without a doubt the favored genre in what has been called a country of poets. It was the homeland of Rubén Darío, undisputed master of modernism. Regarded as a national hero, Darío exercised significant influence over Central American poetry in the first two decades of the 20th c. The group Vanguardia emerged in 1928 as a reaction to the aesthetic of Darío's modernism. Their mentor was José Coronel Urtecho (b. 1906). His famous ''Oda a Rubén Darío'' (1927; ode to Rubén Darío) signaled his generation's iconoclastic break with the past and its ambitious project to recreate Nicaraguan literature employing history, folklore, myth, and popular language. Pablo Antonio Cuadra (b. 1912) epitomized this effort in *Poemas nicaragüenses* (1933; Nicaraguan poems).

Cuadra has edited some of the most important literary journals of Nicaragua, including *El pez y la serpiente,* which introduced many poets of the ''Generation of '40'' whose members include Ernesto Cardenal (q.v.), Ernesto Mejía Sánchez (b. 1923), and Carlos Martínez Rivas (b. 1924). Unlike the Vanguardists, this group was united in its opposition to the Somoza dictatorship and formed a bridge between the more individualistic, disorganized iconoclasm of the preceding generation and the Sandinista poets of the 1960s and later. Cardenal is without doubt the major figure in contemporary Nicaraguan cultural life. He has profoundly influenced poetic production in Nicaragua through the poetry workshops he founded in 1979 as minister of culture.

Living up to its reputation as a country of poets, Nicaragua claimed the distinction, during the Sandinista government (1979–1989), of having several political leaders who are also writers, including President Daniel Ortega (b. 1945) and Vice President Sergio Ramírez (q.v.).

Several women have emerged since the 1960s whose poetry ensures the representation of a previously marginalized sector of society. The major figures, known as "The Six," are Gioconda Belli (b. 1948), Vidaluz Meneses (b. 1944), Rosario Murillo (b. 1951), Michele Najlis (b. 1946), Yolanda Blanco (b. 1954), and Daisy Zamora (b. 1950). Collectively, their poetry attempts to define and celebrate femininity in the revolutionary context. Belli has also written a novel, *La mujer habitada* (1985; the inhabited woman), that explores gender relationships among revolutionaries.

The narrative, while less developed than poetry, has existed in various forms, from a picturesque depiction of rural customs and speech in the work of Mariano Fiallos Gil (1907–1964), to the political novels of Hernán Robleto (1898–1969), such as his *Sangre en el trópico* (1930; blood in the tropics), or *Trágame tierra* (1969; let the earth swallow me) by Lisandro Chávez Alfaro (b. 1929). More recently, Omar Cabezas (dates n.a.) has contributed to the testimonial narrative with *La montaña es algo más que una inmensa estepa verde* (1982; *Fire from the Mountain,* 1985), an autobiographical account of his participation in the Sandinista struggle against Somoza. Sergio Ramírez is widely considered the most accomplished short-story writer of Nicaragua today.

Costa Rica. Like the other republics of the isthmus, Costa Rican literature begins to acquire its unique national contours at the turn of the century. Among those writers who comprised the Generation of 1900, *costumbrism*—narrative sketches of manners and social customs, with an emphasis on the use of colloquial language—was the preferred mode. An early practitioner of *costumbrism* laced with naturalism was Joaquín García Monge (1881–1958), also the founder and director of *Repertorio Americano* (1919–1958) an influential and unusually long-lived journal of international circulation. In contrast to García Monge's critical attitude in displaying the ignorance and foibles of society, Manuel González Zeledón's (1864–1936) stories and essays portray a simpler

and more idyllic national reality. Aquileo J. Echeverría's (1866–1909) highly popular *Concherías* (1905; peasant ways) humorously employs colorful rural speech. Carmen Lyra (pseud. of María Isabel Carvajal, 1888–1949) legitimized children's literature, which continues to be a respected genre in Costa Rican letters, with *Los cuentos de mi tía Panchita* (1920; my Aunt Panchita's stories), still read and loved by Costa Rican school children. Other writers of children's literature include Lilia Ramos (1903–1988), Carlos Luis Saenz (1899–1984), and Lara Ríos (pseud. of Marilín Echeverría, dates n.a.).

A wave of narrative fiction that denounced social injustice appeared in the 1940s, including *Mamita Yunai* (1941; Mommy United Fruit) by Carlos Luis Fallas (1909–1966), *El sitio de las abras* (1950; where the clearings are) by Fabián Dobles (b. 1918), and *Puerto Limón* (1950; Puerto Limón) by Joaquín Gutiérrez (b. 1918). While narratives of regionalism and social denunciation continue to be popular, cultivated by Julieta Pinto (b. 1922), Quince Duncan (b. 1940), and others, a number of Costa Rican writers have produced fiction more akin to the technical and thematic experiments of the modern period. A pioneer who openly rejected regionalism in favor of the urban psychological novel was Yolanda Oreamuno (q.v.), author of *La ruta de su evasión* (1948; the route of their escape). Other women have enriched the novel with their innovative contributions. Carmen Naranjo (q.v.) has written *Los perros no ladraron* (1966; the dogs did not bark), an existential novel, and *Diario de una multitud* (1974; diary of a crowd), a collage of urban voices. Anacristina Rossi's (b. 1952) *María la noche* (1985; Maria the night) won a national novel award in 1985. Its exploration of feminine sensuality and its lyrical approach to reality is unusual in Costa Rican women's fiction, although recent women's poetry is often openly celebratory of female sexuality and questioning of gender roles. A precursor was Eunice Odio (q.v.); whose *Los elementos terrestres* (1948; terrestial elements) is a collection of eight long poems that project a mystical-erotic vision of gender relations. A noteworthy recent example is *La estación de fiebre* (1982; the season of fever) by Ana Istarú (b. 1960).

A number of poets and novelists, including Istarú and Samuel Rovinski (q.v.) have also written for the stage. Daniel Gallegos (b. 1930) is one of Costa Rica's outstanding dramatists.

Panama. This country, which separated from Colombia in 1903 to become an independent republic, has since then been identified primarily as the site of the Panama Canal, with the rights to the Canal ceded to the U.S. Panama's relations with the U.S. have greatly influenced its history, politics, economy, and self-image; so it is not surprising that the Canal should play a prominent role in Panamanian letters.

Modernism was in fashion when Panama became a nation. Darío Herrera (1870–1914), whose works remain uncollected, mastered the mellifluous prose and verse of this school. Ricardo Miró (1883–1940) founded the literary journal *Nuevos ritos* (1907–1917), which published the works of Panamanian modernists. María Olimpia de Obaldía (b. 1891), considered Panama's national poet, wrote domestic and patriotic verse. Demetrio Korsi (1899–1957), author of *Cumbia* (1936; Cumbia), is Panama's best-known writer of the *negrista* poetry popular in the 1930s.

Rogelio Sinán (b. 1904) experimented with surrealist techniques in poetry as well as narrative. The most important Panamanian writer of this century, Sinán has influenced other avant-garde poets such as Ricardo J. Bermúdez (b. 1914). Novels that depict Canal themes have been popular throughout the century, particularly in the 1950s and 1960s. Sinán's *Plenilunio* (1947; full moon), which describes the destructive effects of the Canal on the city using innovative narrative techniques, is the best known of this genre. Another significant contribution is Joaquín Beleño's (b. 1922) trilogy *Luna verde* (1951; green moon), *Curundú* (1963; Curundo), and *Gamboa Road Gang* (1963; title in English).

Denunciation of imperialism and social injustice is prevalent in recent Panamanian literature. Esther María Osses (1914–1991), whose poetry is gentle and intimate, writes forceful essays and literary criticism celebrating popular liberation struggles. Bertalicia Peralta (b. 1939) and Pedro Rivera (b. 1939) are important voices of protest in poetry and short fiction, while novelists Carlos Francisco Changmarín (b. 1922) and Eustorgio Chong Ruiz (b. 1934) exemplify this tendency in the novel. A number of contemporary writers are experimenting with narrative techniques, such as the uninterrupted interior monologue of *El último juego* (1977; the last game) by Gloria Guardia de Alfaro (b. 1940).

BIBLIOGRAPHY: Ramírez, S., *La narrativa centroamericana* (1969); García, I., *Historia de la literatura panameña* (1977); Sandoval de Fonseca, V., *Resúmen de literatura costarricense* (1978); Gallegos Valdés, L., *Panorama de la literatura salvadoreña* (1981); Acevedo, R. L., *La novela centroamericana* (1982); Albizúrez Palma, F., and C. Barrios, *Historia de la literatura guatemalteca* (1982); Arellano, J. E., *Panorama de la literatura nicaragüense,* 4th ed. (1982); Armijo, R., Introduction to *Poesía contemporanea de Centro-*

américa (1983); Menton, S., *Historia crítica de la novela guatemalteca,* 2nd ed. (1985); Paredes, R., and M. Salinas Paguada, *Literatura hondureña* (1987); Engelbert, J., Introduction to *And We Sold the Rain: Contemporary Fiction from Central America* (1988); Beverley, J., and M. Zimmerman, *Literature and Politics in the Central American Revolutions* (1990)

JANET N. GOLD

CEPEDA SAMUDIO, Alvaro

Colombian novelist, journalist, and short-story writer, b. 30 Mar. 1926, Ciénaga (or Barranquilla); d. 12 Oct. 1972, New York, N.Y., U.S.A.

C. S. was a member of the Group of Barranquilla, a set of Colombian "coastal" writers that included Alfonso Fuenmayor (b. 1917), Germán Vargas (b. 1919), and Gabriel García Márquez (q.v.). He worked prolifically as a journalist from his days as a college student in the 1940s until the time of his death from cancer. From 1949 until 1951, he lived in the U.S., pursuing journalistic and literary studies at Columbia University. His short stories appeared sporadically in the early 1950s and were first collected in the volume *Todos estábamos a la espera* (1954; we were all waiting), whose title story is one of his most accomplished and shows strong influence by Ernest Hemingway (q.v.). As have many Colombian and Latin American writers of his generation, C. S. owed great debt to the work of North American authors such as Hemingway, William Faulkner, and William Saroyan (qq.v.), as well as to Hollywood film noir. He wrote prolifically about film and founded the Cine Club of Barranquilla in 1957. He also directed several short subjects, including *La langosta azul* (1954; the blue lobster).

As critical literature has noted, C. S. fits well within the *costeño* (coastal) tradition of Colombian literature, which Raymond L. Williams characterizes as ethnically mixed, with cosmopolitan and popular underpinnings. C. S.'s *La casa grande* (1962; *La Casa Grande,* 1991) employs Faulknerian strategies such as interior monologue as well as cinematic technique reminiscent of John Dos Passos (q.v.) to present a collective and symbolic yet highly intimate "history" of the 1928 massacre of banana workers during a strike in the Colombian town of Ciénaga. The perspectivism of the novel, seen in its accomplished presentation of similar events from different points of view and parts of a time sequence, evinces the long-standing interest of C. S. not only in cinema but also in painting. Williams stresses its combination of written and oral qualities, noting its importance as a precursor of García Márquez's *Cien años de so-*

ledad (1967; *One Hundred Years of Solitude,* 1970). The concern of *La casa grande* with oral culture and the function of memory in recording and sifting historical events foreshadows not only the famous novel of García Márquez but also the work of Colombian novelist Gustavo Alvarez Gardeazábal (q.v.).

The cosmopolitanism of the coastal tradition, that is, its relative openness because of its nature as a port, may in part explain the appeal for C. S. of foreign, especially North American, literary models as well as the varied nature of his career in journalism. C. S. dealt in his columns not only with subjects of local Colombian interest (soccer, local and national politics, and familiar locales) but also with problems of nuclear armament, with questions concerning the recently formed United Nations, with the influence of the U.S. on Latin America in general, and even with the opposition of French communists to the influence of Mickey Mouse on French culture, a position that he attacked. In general, as his editor and commentator Jacques Gilard notes, C. S. adopted a democratic socialist stance. His posture might be appropriately compared to that of George Orwell (q.v.), who though in sympathy with socialist ideals did not shrink in his journalism as in his fiction from opposing chicanery and hypocrisy from left or right.

C. S. also commented at length on cinema, generally favoring Italian neorealism, British postwar cinema, and newer trends in European film over the productions of Hollywood. As Gilard points out when noting this tendency to glorify productions (such as some of the British ones) that have paled with the years in contrast with such phenomena as film noir from Hollywood, C. S. was perhaps sated with Hollywood movies, since these dominated the market during World War II, and thus considered the other films a relief of sorts. In any case, despite his frequent attacks on the Hollywood system, his fiction, especially *Todos estábamos a la espera,* shows probable influence not only from writers such as Hemingway but also from film noir.

C. S. is often cited as an important innovator in Colombian fiction shortly preceding the publication of *Cien años de soledad.* His untimely death left unanswered the question of his further development as a creative artist. He has at the very least contributed one masterpiece, *La casa grande,* and one important collection of stories, *Todos estábamos a la espera.* And he has served as an inspiration to other Latin American writers, including not only García Márquez but also, for example, Argentine Mario Szichman (q.v.), who was his journalistic colleague and who modeled his first novel, *Crónica falsa* (1969; false chroni-

cle) after *La casa grande.* The recent translation into English of *La casa grande* will make available to a wider reading public the work of an interesting and energetically creative writer.

FURTHER WORKS: *Los cuentos de Juana* (1972); *Antología* (1977)

BIBLIOGRAPHY: Mena, L. I., "*La casa grande*: el fracaso de un orden social," *Hispam,* 1, 2 (Dec. 1972), 3–17; Gilard, J., Introduction to *Todos estábamos a la espera* (1980), 9–44; Gilard, J., "A. C. S., el experimentador tropical," *Quimera,* 26 (1982), 63–65; Ruffinelli, J., *Crítica en marcha: ensayos sobre literatura latinoamericana* (2nd ed., 1982), 146–47; Gilard, J., Introduction to *En el margen de la ruta (periodismo juvenil—1944–1955)* (1985), v–xc; special C. S. section in Williams, R. L., and A. Pineda Botero, comps., *De ficciones y realidades: perspectivas sobre literatura e historia colombianas. Memorias del Quinto Congreso de Colombianistas* (1989), 41–120; Menton, S., "La novelística de la costa colombiana: especulaciones históricas," in Neumeister, S., ed., *Actas del IX Congreso de la Asociación Internacional de Hispanistas* (2 vols., 1989), 629–34

KENNETH E. HALL

CHACEL, Rosa

Spanish novelist, short-story writer, essayist, and poet, b. 3 June 1898, Valladolid

C. studied painting and sculpture before becoming a writer. At age eight she began art classes in Valladolid. After moving to Madrid, she studied at the School of Arts and Professions and then at the Saint Ferdinand High School of Fine Arts. When bad health curtailed these studies, she joined the Atheneum of Madrid, thus beginning her formal association with the world of letters. There she met Ramón Gómez de la Serna and later the critic and philosopher José Ortega y Gasset (qq.v.), who invited her collaboration in the leading intellectual journals of the period. She became Ortega's artistic follower and, thus, a member of the Generation of 1927. This group considered artistic expression and content equally important; therefore, psychological perceptions and interior monologue prevail over traditional novelistic plot in their works. C. manages to balance polished writing, intellectual exploration of personality, and genuine emotion.

At the Spanish Academy in Rome (1922–1929), C. wrote *Estación. Ida y vuelta* (1930; station, round trip), a *Künstlerroman* influenced by James Joyce's (q.v.) *A Portrait of the Artist As a Young*

Man (1916) and by Ortega and Marcel Proust (q.v.). The novel is an antecedent of the French New Novel (q.v.). The word *estación* means both train station and season; thus, the title refers to the protagonist's round trip by train as well as to the cyclic nature of the work, a return of a season.

During this period C. published a book of vanguard sonnets, *A la orilla de un pozo* (1936; beside a well). She was preparing a biographical novel about Teresa Mancha—commissioned by Ortega for the series "Extraordinary Lives of the 19th Century"—when the Spanish Civil War began, delaying its publication indefinitely. During and after the war C. lived and traveled in Europe, finally emigrating with her family to Rio de Janeiro in 1940. She divided her time between Brazil and Buenos Aires. In the latter, she collaborated with the leading critics of her day, among them Victoria Ocampo (1891–1979), the editor of *Sur*.

Teresa (1941; Teresa) was finally published in Buenos Aires, when the Spanish political situation prevented its publication in Spain. The novel explores the themes of political exile and the ostracism and alienation experienced by a woman who defies 19th-c. mores. This fictional biography of the mistress of Spain's revolutionary romantic poet José Espronceda (1808–1842) portrays a bittersweet passion worthy of the romantic movement. The novel was C.'s second published in Spain, finally appearing in 1963, thirty-three years after *Estación*.

Her third novel, *Memorias de Leticia Valle* (1945; memories of Leticia Valle), was planned in Italy before 1930. This novel in diary form presents the themes of jealousy, artistic education, and possible child molestation, from the perspective of a precocious adolescent female. One of C.'s best novels, *La sinrazón* (1960; beyond reason), is another confessional diary. The protagonist examines the existence and will of God as well as his own reason for being. His quest leads him beyond reason *(razón)* to *la sinrazón*, a term which literally means "without reason," while also connoting injury and injustice. The work, published in Spain in 1970, won the prestigious Critics' Prize in 1977.

C.'s *Barrio de Maravillas* (1976; *The Maravillas District,* 1992) had won the same prize the year before. This is the first volume in a trilogy that C. describes as a history of her literary generation. *Barrio de Maravillas* covers the period from the turn of the century until World War I. *Acrópolis* (1984; the Acropolis) follows the same female artists from 1914 to 1931. The trilogy concludes with *Ciencias naturales* (1988; natural science), tracing one protagonist's many years of exile in Buenos Aires until her return to Spain after Francisco Franco's death. C.'s prose reaches

its zenith in this series, a female bildungsroman, combining interior monologue, omniscient narrative, Platonic dialogue, brilliant descriptions, and the narrator's philosophical-aesthetic discussion.

During her long exile C. also published short stories about life in Spain, Brazil, and Argentina, collecting them in *Icada, nevda, diada* (1971; nothingness). Its topics include double suicide, the exercise of one's will to overcome difficulties, self-created realities, a child's view of the world, and the artist's worldview. C. visited Europe in 1961, researching *La confesión* (1971; confession), a comparative analysis of the confessional essays of Kierkegaard, Rousseau, and St. Augustine. With a Guggenheim fellowship, C. spent two years in New York City, writing a book-length essay, *Saturnal* (1972; saturnalia). In 1974 C. returned to Spain to live.

In Madrid C. continues to write in several genres. These include an autobiography of her early years, *Desde el amanecer* (1972; since dawn), and a two-volume diary under the general title *Alcancía* (1982; potpourri). Of special interest is a published collection of unfinished works, *Novelas antes de tiempo* (1981; novels before their time), in which she discusses the ideas and techniques used in each embryonic work presented, finally explaining how she will finish each, time permitting. Time is a primary concern for this nonagenarian who fears that she will not complete her many projects.

This author's basic style has not changed during her more than sixty years of writing, though it has matured and become increasingly concentrated. If the tragedy of the Spanish Civil War had been avoided, and C. had continued her craft uninterrupted in Spain, she probably would have been one of the most respected Spanish novelists of her day; had the financial exigencies of exile been avoided, she doubtless would have been more prolific. Spain's best critics have recently bestowed many honors on C., including the National Spanish Literature Prize (1988) and that of Castile and León (1991). They recognize that C. is one of the last surviving novelists of the Generation of 1927 and is indisputably one of its best.

FURTHER WORKS: *Sobre el piélago* (1952); *Ofrenda a una virgen loca* (1961); *Versos prohibidos* (1978); *Timoteo Pérez Rubio y sus retratos del jardín* (1980); *Los títulos* (1981); *Rebañaduras* (1986); *La lectura es secreto* (1989); *Balaam y otros cuentos* (1989)

BIBLIOGRAPHY: Aguirre, F., "R. C., como en su playa propia," *CHA,* 296 (1975), 298–315; Myers, E. D., "Narcissism and the Quest for Identity in R. C.'s *La sinrazón,*" *PCL,* 8 (1982), 85–90; Myers, E. D., "*Estación. Ida y vuelta*: R. C.'s

Apprenticeship Novel," *HisJ*, 4, 2 (Spring 1983), 77–84; Porlán, A., *La sinrazón de R. C.* (1984); Johnson, R., "*Estación. Ida y vuelta,* de R. C.: Un nuevo tiempo para la novela," in Burgos, F., ed., *Prosa hispánica de vanguardia* (1986), 201–8; Myers, E. D., "*Teresa*: R. C.'s Novel of Exile and Alienation," *MRRM*, 2 (1986), 151–58; Mangini, S., "Women and Spanish Modernism: The Case of R. C.," *ALEC*, 12, 1–2 (1987), 17–28; Newberry, W., "R. C.'s *Barrio de Maravillas*: The Role of the Arts and the Problem of Spain," *HisJ*, 9, 2 (Spring 1988), 37–44; special C. issue, *Anthropos*, 85 (1988); Mangini, S., ed., "Introducción:" *Estación: Ida y vuelta* (1989), 11–69; special C. homage, *Letras peninsulares* 3, 1 (Spring 1990), 11–82; *R. C.: Premio nacional de las letras españolas, 1987* (1990)

EUNICE D. MYERS

CHANDLER, Raymond

American novelist, short-story writer, and screenwriter, b. 23 July 1888, Chicago, Ill.; d. 26 Mar. 1959, La Jolla, Cal.

C. came late to a literary career. After the divorce of his parents, C. was taken at the age of eight by his mother to England, where he received a classical education at Dulwich College Preparatory School in London. Returning to the U.S. in 1912, he served in World War I as a soldier in the Canadian army, in which he enlisted while visiting British Columbia in 1917. After the war he entered the oil business in California, rising from the position of accountant to executive status before he was fired in 1932 for drinking and absenteeism. It was this turn in his life, occurring as it did in the middle of the Depression, that led C., who as a young man between 1908 and 1911 had published some poetry and translations, to consider whether he might be able to make a living as a writer.

By the time C. published his first short story in 1933, hard-boiled detective fiction had been an established literary subgenre, a mainstay of the "pulp" magazines of the period, for a full decade. "Knights of the Open Palm," by Carroll John Daly (1889–1958), widely regarded as the first hard-boiled detective story, had appeared in *Black Mask* in June 1923, and Dashiell Hammett's (q.v.) "Arson Plus," the debut of Hammett's "Continental Op," was published in October of the same year; by 1933, Hammett had published four novels as well. C., then, is hardly one of the founding fathers of the literary subgenre with which his name is so strongly associated, even though he was in fact older than both Daly and Hammett.

The pulps, printed on cheap paper, aimed at a largely male mass audience, paying writers by the word, held out to the unemployed C. the hope of earning money as a writer, however remote the world of pulp fiction was from C.'s earlier literary efforts. C. prepared himself for his first submission by carefully studying representative samples of pulp fiction, especially fiction published in the most respected of the pulps, *Black Mask*. He gave almost obsessively close attention to the work of Erle Stanley Gardner (1889–1970), who would later become one of the most prolific and prosperous of American writers of detective fiction. In all, C. spent five months writing his first story, "Blackmailers Don't Shoot," which appeared in *Black Mask* in December 1933, when C. was forty-five years old.

There is something comic, perhaps something pathetic, about C.'s painstaking approach to publication in the pulps. But the seriousness of C.'s apprenticeship is revealing and characteristic; no writer would be more devoted to the cause of establishing the artistic seriousness of the hard-boiled crime and detective fiction, which, for him, represented the pulps' most significant contribution to American literary culture. And, for C., this contribution must not be assigned to a critical ghetto called "popular fiction."

C.'s most famous affirmation of the authentic literary value of the right sort of detective fiction (the sort, of course, he was himself engaged in writing) is the essay "The Simple Art of Murder," first published in the *Atlantic Monthly* in December 1944. In this frequently reprinted essay, C. dismisses as unworthy of serious critical attention the formal detective story, associated with writers like Agatha Christie (1891–1976) and Dorothy L. Sayers (1893–1957), that had flourished, especially in England, in the period between the two world wars, the so-called "Golden Age" of detective fiction. He championed instead the work of the "realist[s] in crime," his name for the writers of hard-boiled detective fiction, and especially the work of Hammett, whose best fiction, in C.'s view, had established the artistic value of detective fiction. And yet, C. goes on to say, what Hammett has achieved is not quite enough. Hammett's style lacks echoes, and his heroes (the Continental Op, Sam Spade in *The Maltese Falcon*) are not completely satisfying. In C.'s much quoted formulation, "Down these mean streets a man must go who is not himself mean. . . . He is the hero, he is everything." And this hero, it seems, is essential in providing the "quality of redemption" present in "everything that can be called art."

For C., "everything that can be called art" most emphatically includes his own fiction; and if Anglo-American critics are unable to see that, it is because in their fixation on subject matter and theme, they fail to appreciate writing as writing, by which C. seems to mean all that a writer adds to his subject matter. And it is C.'s goal to provide in his detective fiction those qualities missing, at least in C.'s judgment, even from Hammett at his best.

Above all in Philip Marlowe, the detective protagonist of his novels, C. provides his version of the hero, his "knight" as some critics would have it. Marlowe is beyond question C.'s most important creation and his most important contribution to hard-boiled detective fiction. At once cynical wisecracker and romantic idealist, he is a more complex figure than the code heroes of Hammett's fiction. Where Hammett emphasized surfaces, rarely offering more than a glimpse of the inner life of his protagonists, C. insists upon the psychological and, above all, the ethical richness of the inner life of Marlowe. In his role as narrator, Marlowe constantly comments on, judges, and tries against overwhelming odds to find hints of redemption in the mean streets that constitute his environment. The meaness is as much spiritual as socioeconomic. C. exploits the freedom of the detective hero, unlimited by a clearly defined class position, to move freely within the existing class structure. Marlowe in his investigations becomes the instrument by which C. brings us into confrontation with a fictional world of considerable range and complexity that is also a stylized but incisive portrait of Southern California as it sprawls toward midcentury. The tension between the romantic sensibility of the hero and the demands of survival in the threatening world C. depicts generates the celebrated C. style, an amalgam of tough talk, baroque simile, and that American vernacular which the American-born, but British-educated, C. always heard as a quasi-foreign tongue. It also generates the moral tension between the detective's need to know the world as it is and the idealist's desire to see the world as it might be that is yet another source of the power of C.'s best fiction.

C.'s most successful novels are his first two, *The Big Sleep* (1939) and *Farewell, My Lovely* (1940). The tensions that characterize and organize C.'s work are here most fully in play. The sixth novel in the series, *The Long Goodbye* (1953), is admired by many critics, but others find that the tensions of the best work have collapsed as Marlowe slides into a cynicism and self-pity from which the author does not succeed in distancing himself.

Like many American writers of his generation, C. worked as a screenwriter. Although his experience working on Alfred Hitchcock's *Strangers on a Train* (1951) was not a happy one, his work

as a collaborator on the script of Billy Wilder's *Double Indemnity* (1943), based on the novella by James M. Cain (q.v.), and his script for *The Blue Dahlia* (1945) have earned him an honored place among Hollywood scriptwriters.

C. ranks with Hammett as one of the two most influential writers of hard-boiled detective fiction. In fact, much of the fiction of this sort written since the 1950s is rather more in the spirit of C. than of Hammett. Although critics remain divided on the question of the relative merits of the two writers, there is little dissent from the proposition that they are the two finest writers of hard-boiled detective fiction.

FURTHER WORKS: *The High Window* (1942); *The Lady in the Lake* (1943); *Five Murderers* (1944); *Five Sinister Characters* (1945); *Finger Man and Other Stories* (1946); *The Little Sister* (1949); *The Simple Art of Murder* (1950); *Pickup on Noon Street* (1952); *Playback* (1958); *R. C. Speaking* (1962); *Killer in the Rain* (1964); *C. before Marlowe: R. C.'s Early Prose and Poetry* (1973); *The Notebooks of R. C.* (1976); *Selected Letters of R. C.* (1981)

BIBLIOGRAPHY: Elliott, G., "Country Full of Blondes," *The Nation,* 23 Apr. 1960, 354–60; Durham, P., *Down These Mean Streets a Man Must Go: R. C.'s Knight* (1963); Ruhm, H., "R. C.: From Bloomsbury to the Jungle—And Beyond." in Madden, D., ed., *Tough Guy Writers of the Thirties* (1968), 171–85; Lid, R., "Philip Marlowe Speaking," *KR,* 31 (1969), 153–78; Jameson, F., "On R. C.," *SoR,* 6 (Summer 1970), 624–50; MacShane, F., *The Life of R. C.* (1976); Gross, M., ed., *The World of R. C.* (1977); Knight, S. T., *Form and Ideology in Crime Fiction* (1980), 135–67; Speir, J., *R. C.* (1981); Arden, L., "A Knock at the Backdoor of Art: The Entrance of R. C.," in Benstock, B., ed., *Art in Crime Writing* (1983), 73–96; Newlin, K., *Hardboiled Burlesque: R. C.'s Comic Style* (1984); Wolfe, P., *Something More Than Night: The Case of R. C.* (1985); Marling, W., *R. C.* (1986); Lehman, D., *The Perfect Murder* (1989), 135–67

W. P. KENNEY

CHEDID, Andrée

Egypto-Lebanese-French novelist, poet, dramatist, and short-story writer (writing in French), b. 20 Mar. 1920, Cairo, Egypt

C. is one of the best-known and respected French writers, her works fusing ancient and modern ways, European and Middle-Eastern concepts embedded in a verbal and luminous canvas studded with images, symbols, premonitions, and mystery. Since C.'s parents were separated when she was very young, she was sent to boarding schools in Cairo and in Paris. She had little family life but always maintained a warm and loving relationship with both her father and mother. C. received a B.A. degree in journalism from the American University in her native city. In June 1988 she was awarded an honorary doctor's degree from the same university. Married at the age of twenty-one, she lived from 1942 to 1945 in Lebanon and moved to Paris in 1946.

C. has repeatedly said that she is the product of two civilizations, two ways of life, two psyches. Her childhood days and her early memories, particularly those associated with Egypt, played an important role in her formation as a writer, as evidenced in her novels; *Le sommeil délivré* (1952; *From Sleep Unbound*, 1983), *Jonathan* (1955; Jonathan), *Le sixième jour* (1960; *The Sixth Day*, 1988), *Le survivant* (1963; the survivor), *L'autre* (1969; the other), *La cité fertile* (1972; the fertile city), *Nefertiti et le rêve d'Akhnaton* (1974; Nefertiti and Akhnaton's dream), *Les marches de sable* (1981; steps into the sand). Her writings are a complex of endlessly shifting emotional climates, of disclosing and secreting shapes and hues—energy patterns—that are then transmuted into human beings or into landscapes.

Because C.'s writings for the most part are situated in Egypt, they all bear the veneer of the Middle East as well as the modernism (q.v.) of her adopted land, France. C.'s characters are endowed with a sense of proximity and distance, rootedness and rootlessness. They are paradigms of a personal quest and a collective search: the need to communicate not only with one's own multileveled self but also with those organic and inorganic forces that surround each being. Her works, then, are stamped with universal feelings as well as with personal yearnings, each set apart or opposed to the other.

C.'s themes vary with her novels. The female protagonist of *Le sommeil délivré* is the product of a certain type of contemporary Middle Eastern upbringing with its harsh and brutal customs, particularly in regard to women, whose earthly existence is wholly devoted to serving certain specific purposes: to service the male and to procreate. *Jonathan*, a rite of passage, deals with the choice that many young Christians make in the Middle East between religion and revolution. The classically constructed *Le sixième jour*, focusing on the cholera epidemic raging in Egypt in 1948, may be seen as a death-and-resurrection myth. *L'autre* is a canticle, a hymn, to life. It is also an exploration into the complex problem of human relationships in general. The archetypal mother figure, a prac-

titioner of the ancient art of dance, reigns in *La cité fertile* as she sweeps into the story, arrests the reader's attention, then vanishes only to return moments later, energizing feeling, act, and word. A combination of history and fiction, *Nefertiti et le rêve d'Akhnaton* plunges the reader back into a remote period, 1388–1344 B.C. in Egypt, when the pharaoh Akhnaton rebelled against polytheism in favor of monotheism, favoring the concept of one God as manifested in the visible Sun. In *Les marches de sable* three women—people of all seasons—undertake the desert experience, withdrawing from the world, from life itself, in an attempt to discover an answer to their unfulfilled lives.

Poetry is humanity's common language. For C. poems are to a great extent plainchants in honor of life; hymns to the earth and the heavens, to the vastness of the cosmic experiences. C., the poet, belongs to no group, no school. Her poetry is her own, a unique distillation of what she has experienced and felt most deeply. Whether in *Textes pour une figure* (1949; texts for a face), *Textes pour un poème* (1950; texts for a poem), or *Textes pour le vivant* (1953; texts for the living), C.'s stanzas contain all sorts of aromatic flavors, collages of sensual arabesques, and disquieting abstractions. Hers is a poetry divested of all sentimentality and any taint of romanticism. Solidly structured, each word, line, verse is hewn from her inner being, anchored to her psyche, while its meanings, rhythms, and sensations impact through pleromatic spheres.

The philosophical and thematic import of C.'s theater, as dramatized in *Les nombres* (1968; numbers), *Bérénice d'Égypte* (1968; Bérénice of Egypt), *Le montreur* (1969; the puppeteer), and *Échec à la reine* (1984; queen's checkmate), is relevant to today's problems: issues such as large-scale war, pollution, questions of identity, and fulfillment are broached. Her protagonists are flesh-and-blood beings, but they also are atemporal, archetypal, arising from the deepest layers of the unconscious. They do not develop psychologically as in conventional theater. When they move about on stage weaving intricate patterns in space, each becomes an energy center, diffusing its own aura which either attracts or repels the others.

C.'s writings speak to audiences today. They are direct, unvitiated, divested of all preciosity and rococo elaboration. Unsparing in the authenticity of the feelings or sensations she seeks to convey, she innoculates her readers with pain and torment, if these are deemed necessary, to disclose the acute nature of the protagonist's struggle. Language for C. is *being*: a catalyst that acts and reacts on the reader visually, spiritually, and aesthetically.

FURTHER WORKS: *Textes pour la terre aiméee* (1955); *Terre et poésie* (1956); *Terre regardée* (1960); *Double pays* (1965); *Contre-chant* (1969); *Visage premier* (1972); *Fêtes et lubies* (1973); *Prendre corps* (1973); *Fraternité de la parole* (1975); *Cérémonial de la violence* (1976); *Grandes oreilles, toutes oreilles* (1976); *Lubies* (1976); *Le cœur et le temps* (1977); *Cavernes et soleils* (1979); *Les corps et le temps suivi de l'Étroite Peau* (1979); *Le cœur suspendu* (1981); *L'étrange Mariée* (1983); *Épreuves du vivant* (1983); *Grammaire en fête* (1984); *La maison sans racines* (1985; *The Return to Beirut,* 1989); *Mondes Miroirs Magies* (1988); *L'enfant multiple* (1989); *Poèmes pour un texte (1970–1991)* (1991)

BIBLIOGRAPHY: Knapp, B. L., *French Novelists Speak Out* (1976), 57–64; Izoard, J., *A. C.* (1977); "Huit questions posées à l'auteur," in *À la rencontre d'A. C.* (1981); Knapp, B. L., *A. C.* (1984); Linkhorn, R., ed., *The Prose and Poetry of A.C.* (1990); special C. issue *Sud,* 94–95 (1991)

BETTINA L. KNAPP

CHILEAN LITERATURE

See Volume 1, page 456.

Fiction

Chilean literature of the past two decades reflects the conditions under the socialist regime of President Salvador Allende (1970–1973) and the military dictatorship headed by General Augusto Pinochet (1973–1989). Since the death of Pablo Neruda (q.v.) in 1973, fiction writer José Donoso (q.v.) has been Chile's most widely acclaimed living man of letters, and although politics has seldom been a major theme in his works, his novels published since 1973 do indeed dramatize some of the salient issues treated by other Chilean writers of this period. After *El obsceno pájaro de la noche* (1970; *The Obscene Bird of Night,* 1973), usually considered the last major accomplishment of the "boom," Donoso published *Casa de campo* (1978; *A House in the Country,* 1983), a self-conscious, fantasy-laced tale about a greedy bourgeois family (the Venturas) who browbeat their servants and ruthlessly subjugate the native population living in the vicinity of their sprawling estate (Marulanda). This sophisticated, entertaining novel can be read as a political allegory of Allende's rise and fall. Although Donoso had moved to Spain of his own free will long before the military coup in his homeland, he treats the problems of the exile in *El jardín de al lado* (1981; the garden next door), a technically complex novel with two narrators (a husband and his wife) and

feminist overtones. *La desesperanza* (1986; *Curfew,* 1988), Donoso's most overtly political work to date, focuses on the funeral of Matilde Urrutia, Neruda's widow, and the return to Chile of a popular singer who witnesses the harsh repression of the Pinochet government. Donoso's other recent fiction includes *La misteriosa desaparición de la marquesita de Loria* (1980; the mysterious disappearance of the Marquise de Loria), a psychological story of a young Nicaraguan widow consumed by animal instinct, and *Taratuta. Naturaleza muerta con cachimba* (1990; Taratuta. still life with a pipe), two novelettes, the first of which describes the process of inventing a story about a Russian terrorist, and the second, the account of a bourgeois couple's liberation from a dull existence when they discover the world of art.

Chile's other major contemporary novelists include María Luisa Bombal, Jorge Edwards, Antonio Skármeta, Isabel Allende, Enrique Lafourcade, Ariel Dorfman, and Fernando Alegría (qq.v.). Although all of these authors except Bombal have based at least some of their works on the Chilean political experience of the past two decades, those who fled into exile (Skármeta, Allende, and Dorfman) quite naturally seem more preoccupied with the subject.

Among Chile's many other writers of fiction are Hernán Valdés (b. 1934), Poli Délano (b. 1936), Diamela Eltit (b. 1949), and Antonio Ostornol (b. 1954). Délano is best known for his novel *En este lugar sagrado* (1977; in this sacred place). The introspective protagonist finds himself in the men's restroom of a movie theater when the 1973 military coup occurs, and terrified of being arrested, he remains there for three days, evoking episodes of his past that provide insight into his, and Chile's, present situation. Valdés's *Tejas Verdes* (1974; *Diary of a Chilean Concentration Camp,* 1985) can be read as a novel, but in reality it is a compelling memoir the author wrote after he was released from Tejas Verdes, a concentration camp for enemies of the military government. Valdés composed his text in the form of a diary, using stylistic and structural devices to involve his readers in the horrors he experienced during the most hellish period of his life.

Representatives of a younger generation, Eltit and Ostornol have been classified as postmodernist writers whose experimental techniques require considerable concentration on the part of the reader. Eltit is also a strongly committed feminist, as demonstrated by her novel *Lumpérica* (1983; Lumpérica). In it she not only rebels against male domination and parodies such luminaries as Neruda, Gabriel García Márquez, and Julio Cortázar (qq.v.), but denounces the repression of the military dictatorship as well. Also resonant with political overtones, Ostornol's *El obsesivo mundo de Benjamín* (1982; Benjamin's obsessive world) presents a forty-two-year-old paralytic confined to a wheelchair, who vents his frustrations with his family by murdering his domineering mother with a sword that formerly belonged to his English grandfather.

Poetry

Despite the censorship imposed by the Pinochet régime, Chilean poets refused to be stifled. Major currents in the genre include poetry of protest, existential poetry, and poetry influenced by surrealism (q.v.). Since the death of Neruda, Nicanor Parra (q.v.) has been the nation's most widely read poet. Although he was strongly influenced by surrealism, Parra is known primarily for his antipoetry, which rejects traditional forms of verse and reexamines the purpose and nature of the genre. Thus his language tends to be unadorned, concrete, and often grotesquely humorous and bitterly satirical. An inveterate nonconformist, he rejects the bourgeois establishment, criticizes Allende's socialist government, and abhors Pinochet's military regime. Two of Parra's more recent collections of poems are *Prédicas y sermones del Cristo de Elqui* (1977) and *Nuevos sermones y prédicas del Cristo de Elqui* (1979), published together in translation as *Sermons and Homilies of the Christ of Elqui* (1985). In these hilarious verses, Parra dons the mask of a preacher taken from Chilean folklore in order to parody, with his solemn tone and absurd assertions, the Pinochet régime. In 1986, at the age of seventy-two, Parra became vitally concerned with environmental pollution and the danger of a nuclear holocaust. Thus, as Skármeta has observed, his career has come full circle: In 1954 he had written a poem entitled "Defensa del árbol" ("Defense of the Tree," 1960), and today he is publishing poems in defense of the environment.

Besides Parra, major contemporary Chilean poets include Enrique Lihn, Jorge Teillier (qq.v.), Oscar Hahn (b. 1938), and Raúl Zurita (b. 1951). A longtime resident of the U. S., Hahn writes in a range of styles that have been described as medieval, baroque, expressionist, surrealist, modernist, and vanguardist. He is known above all for his verses of erotic love, for his obsession with death, and for his apocalyptic visions of a nuclear holocaust. The title of his first collection, *Esta rosa negra* (1961; this black rose), becomes a metaphor for the dreaded nuclear cloud, which in turn is identified with copulation and death. Erotic love, with lovers imagined as both victims and killers, is a subject treated in *Arte de morir* (1979; art of dying) and *Mal de amor* (1981; illness of love),

the latter having been banned for several years by Chilean government censors. *Imágenes nucleares* (1983; nuclear images), which contains Hahn's famous poem "Visión de Hiroshima" (vision of Hiroshima), intensifies the author's apocalyptic visions, whereas *Flor de enamorados* (1987; flower of lovers) consists of a group of medieval love poems transformed by modern stylistic techniques.

Zurita is considered by some critics as Chile's most original poetic voice since Neruda. His style is characterized by a colloquial, everyday idiom, but, unlike Parra, Zurita sees language as sacred, a vehicle through which he neither mocks nor destroys but rather seeks an epiphany of the "poetic absolute" or of the "promised land" he would like Chile to become. As a result of his incarceration and torture after the military coup, Zurita created a Dantesque metaphor of his homeland in two of his most widely read collections: *Purgatorio* (1979; purgatory) and *Anteparaíso* (1982; on the border of paradise). More recently, in *El amor de Chile* (1987; the love of Chile), he has turned his gaze to the spectacular Chilean landscape for inspiration.

Essay

Some of Chile's best-known men of letters have followed the Latin American tradition of making personal involvement in affairs of state a basis for their aesthetic expression of ideas. Three fiction writers mentioned above fit into this category: Alegría, Edwards, and Dorfman. Fernando Alegría is an excellent literary critic who has shown a vital interest in politics as well. His *Literatura y revolución* (1971; literature and revolution) contains essays on subjects ranging from Alejo Carpentier, Miguel Angel Asturias (qq.v.), and Cortázar to Latin American society as reflected in the contemporary novel and the political implications of antiliterature. Alegría's *Nueva historia de la novela hispanoamericana* (1986; new history of the Spanish American novel) is one of the most perceptive and complete treatments of the subject. And his *Una especie de memoria* (1983; a kind of memory) is a fascinating recollection of his youth in Chile and of the ideological currents of that time.

Jorge Edwards is well known throughout the Hispanic world for his journalistic articles and essays, many of which combine politics and literature. Some of his finest pieces have been collected in *Desde la cola del dragón* (1977; from the tail of the dragon), which treats, among other subjects, the political polarization of Chile during Allende's term of office, the shadow of Arthur Rimbaud (1854–1891) in French politics during the 1970s, and, in the final essay, the policies of

Felipe González of Spain for his moderate left-wing views (as opposed to those of Fidel Castro and his hard-line supporters). Edwards's *Adios poeta* (1990; good-bye, poet) is an engrossing memoir recalling his friendship and professional relationships with Neruda and other literary figures over a period of many years.

A brilliant analyst of both popular and high culture, Ariel Dorfman has collected in *Some Write to the Future* (1991) a group of articles he published in professional journals and had translated into English for American readers. The essays on García Márquez, Jorge Luis Borges (q.v.), and other renowned writers point out the coexistence in Spanish American fiction of metaphor, abstraction, the mundane, and the fantastic, all of which, Dorfman hopes, will eventually coalesce and bring about a better understanding of the vast region's richly textured reality—thus the title of the volume. Another long, provocative essay deals with recent examples of the testimonial genre in Chilean letters, that is, books that have been published by Pinochet's ex-prisoners. Here Dorfman demonstrates how the desire to remember, to accuse, and to inspire has enabled the authors of these texts to win the battle they once thought they had lost as human beings.

Drama

Before 1973 the majority of contemporary Chilean plays were produced in the universities. After the military coup, many dramatists fled into exile as censorship and adverse economic conditions became major obstacles to the presentation of their works. By the mid-1980s, however, some of the exiled dramatists had returned, and the theater was gradually regaining its creative impulses. As censorship eased, the political themes of injustice, fear, and torture became increasingly prevalent, along with the use of nightmares, black humor, and elements of the absurd.

Leading dramatists of the older generation include Isadora Aguirre (b. 1919), Fernando Debesa (b. 1921), Jorge Díaz (b. 1930), Sergio Vodanovic (b. 1926), Luis Alberto Heiremans (1928–1964), Alejandro Sieveking (b. 1934), and Egon Wolff (q.v.). Aguirre, known for her social criticism, her satire of the middle class, and her adroit manipulation of Brechtian techniques, demonstrates her sympathy for the exploited classes, whose lives are depicted in her highly acclaimed *Los papeleros* (1963; the trash collectors). Her *Lautaro* (1982; Lautaro), which draws some political parallels with modern Chile, dramatizes the epic struggle of the Mapuche Indians against the Spaniards during the 16th c. Another of her historical dramas, *Diálogo de fin de siglo* (1989; end-of-century dialogue), is based on the suicide of Chilean President José Manuel Balmaceda in 1891. Aguirre uses an impressive array of avant-garde techniques in *El retablo de Yumbel* (1987; the altarpiece of Yumbel) to dramatize the disappearance of nineteen Allende officials soon after the military coup.

Debesa, who has also been influenced by Bertolt Brecht (q.v.), delves into history in what is still considered his best work, *Bernardo O'Higgins* (1961; Bernardo O'Higgins). This drama recreates the last days of Chile's national hero, who evokes a montage of episodes from his past, revealing his human reactions to crucial moments of history. Debesa's *Ca-ta-ion* (1979; ca-ta-ion), the title of which imitates the babble of a retarded child, is a psychological drama of solitude stemming from the lack of communication between a poverty-stricken divorcée and her son.

As Spanish America's leading dramatist of the absurdist tradition, Jorge Díaz utilizes irony, black humor, and physical violence to convey a grotesque, nonrealistic world vision reminiscent of Eugène Ionesco, Samuel Beckett, and Harold Pinter (qq.v.). Although his dramas develop the themes of alienation and lack of purpose in human existence, they tend to concentrate more heavily on political and social issues than does the French Theater of the Absurd (q.v.). One of Díaz's early plays, *El cepillo de dientes* (1961; the toothbrush), remains his most widely performed and perhaps his best to date. The overriding theme of lack of communication evolves through a series of ritualistic games enacted by a couple, He and She, who invent preposterous situations usually leading to a violent climax. *El lugar donde mueren los mamíferos* (1963; *The Place Where the Mammals Die,* 1971) continues the absurd tone of Díaz's work. Here a charitable organization is in danger of disappearing for lack of welfare recipients. The disaster is prevented by the discovery of Rusty, a starving slum dweller who arrives at the organization headquarters in a crate and who eventually hangs himself because everything is offered him except the food he needs to stay alive. This play is obviously a satire on false charity, but it can also be read as a political allegory about the exploitation of the Third World by developed nations.

Sergio Vodanovic is best known for his satirical portraits of contemporary middle-class Chilean society. In 1959 he achieved wide recognition for his prize-winning *Deja que los perros ladren* (let the dogs bark), an attack on political corruption. His masterwork, however, is *Viña: Tres comedias en traje de baño* (1964; *Viña: Three Beach Plays,* 1971), a trilogy of one-act plays limning Chile's rigid social stratification and the masks, role playing, and alienation characteristic of such a divided society. *El delantal blanco (The White Uniform)*, the most memorable of the three, presents a snobbish upper-class woman with her maid on the beach at Viña del Mar, Chile's most fashionable summer resort. When the two exchange clothing so that the woman can see the world through the eyes of her maid, the ensuing episodes are replete with both social and psychological implications. The political events of the 1970s provide the background for two of Vodanovic's more recent works: *Igual que antes* (1973; same as ever), telling of the breakup of a wealthy industrialist's family under Salvador Allende's régime; and *¿Cuántos años tiene un día?* (1970; how many years does a day have?), about four television journalists who, despite the repression on the heels of the 1973 military coup, remain in Chile, determined to assist in the nation's struggle for cultural survival.

Despite his short life, Luis Alberto Heiremans ranks as one of Chile's finest modern dramatists. *Moscas sobre el mármol* (1951; flies on the marble) represents a despairing view of life, its protagonist being a man named Julián who devises a plan to kill his friend Ernesto because he and Julián's wife are in love. When the plan backfires, causing Julián's death, his mother rejoices because she no longer has to share him with his wife. Heiremans weaves everyday reality, biblical myth, and the modern theme of solitude into the fabric of his most celebrated drama, *El Abanderado* (1962; the standard-bearer). The setting is a rural community where a religious festival is being prepared. El Abanderado, a bandit of local renown, is handed over to the police by a former friend, El Tordo, when he (El Abanderado) returns home to see his mother after many years of absence. Representations of a Christ figure and Judas Iscariot, El Abanderado and El Tordo are two of several biblical figures evoked in this play.

Well known for his penetrating psychological portraits and ingenious fusion of fantasy and reality, Alejandro Sieveking left Chile after the 1973 military coup but returned to his homeland in 1984. His *Animas de día claro* (1962; souls in the light of day) is based on the Chilean superstition that the spirits of those who die without having accomplished their lifetime goals remain on earth until their desires are satisfied. The setting is a dilapidated farmhouse where five deceased sisters, all spinsters, continue to dwell, each seeking some form of self-fulfillment. Though eighty years of age, Berta (the youngest of the sisters) is suddenly rejuvenated by the arrival of Eulolio, a handsome young man who, despite rumors that the house is haunted, wants to buy the property. The miracle of Berta's and Eulolio's relationship is celebrated by the sudden flowering of trees that have been

barren for many years. *Pequeños animales abatidos* (1974; small abject animals) was inspired by the military coup of the previous year, its political subject being presented by the artful juxtaposition of living and dead characters swept up in rapidly changing time sequences. Also published in 1974, *La mantis religiosa (The Praying Mantis, 1983)*, is a murder mystery freighted with powerful psychological, sexual, and mythical overtones.

Three other fine dramatists are Juan Radrigán (b. 1937), Jaime Miranda (b. 1956), and Carlos Cerda (b. 1956). Known for his strong political commitment, Radrigán portrays members of the proletariat, especially those living in the slums of Santiago, where his works are often performed. His sympathetic but realistic portrayal of the miserable lives of the dispossessed is underscored by the authenticity of their speech and by his incitement to resist the oppression to which they are subjected. Typical of his creations is *Hechos consumados* (1981; consummated deeds), a riveting dialogue between a penniless, ill-fated couple. More complex and elaborately staged, *El toro por las astas* (1982; the bull by the horns) takes place in a brothel (a metaphor of Chile under Pinochet), outside of which a war (the repression) rages. Miranda lived in exile in Venezuela, where he wrote his *Testimonio sobre la muerte de Sabrina* (1979; testimony about the death of Sabrina), a denunciation of the military régime, and upon his return to Chile he presented his highly praised, autobiographical *Regreso sin causa* (1984; return without cause). Cerda achieved prominence with his *Lo que está en el aire* (1986; what is in the air), a moving treatment of *los desaparecidos* (Chileans arrested and eliminated after the coup).

For a country with a population of just under thirteen million people, Chile has produced an astonishingly rich literature. Despite the censorship of the 1970s and 1980s, Chilean writers never ceased to depict and denounce the tragic reality they were witnessing. Thus shortly before his death, Enrique Lihn asserted before the Society of Chilean Writers that Chilean literature owed a great deal to General Pinochet. It is still too soon to assess the nation's creative production since the return to democracy, but it seems logical to assume that along with complete freedom of the press the floodgates have already been opened to an even greater surge of literary activity.

BIBLIOGRAPHY: Dorfman, A., "Literatura chilena y clandestinidad," *Escritura*, 4 (1977), 307–14; Promis Ojeda, J., *La novela chilena actual* (1977); Villegas, J., *Interpretación de textos poéticos chilenos* (1977); Foster, D. W., *Chilean Literature: A Working Bibliography of Secondary Sources* (1978); Foster, D. W., "Latin American Documentary Narrative,'' *Alternate Voices in the Contemporary Latin American Narrative* (1985), 1–44; Jara, R., *Los límites de la representación: La novela chilena del golpe* (1985); Rojo, G., *Muerte y resurrección del teatro chileno: 1973–1983* (1985); Alegría, F., *Nueva historia de la novela hispanoamericana* (1986), 329–436; Jofre, M. A., *Literatura chilena en el exilio* (1986); Guerra Cunningham, L., ''Polivalencias de la confesión en la novela chilena del exilio,'' *Texto e ideología en la narrativa chilena* (1987), 227–49; McMurray, G. R., *Spanish American Writing since 1941: A Critical Survey* (1987), 58–63, 132–39, 195–97, 310–18; Pinedo, J., ''La ensayística y el problema de la identidad, 1960–1988,'' *Ensayistas,* 22–25 (1987–1988), 231–64; Carrasco Muñoz, I., ''Poesía chilena de la última década (1977–1987),'' *RChL,* 33 (Apr. 1989), 31–46; Rojo, G., *Crítica del exilio: Ensayos sobre literatura latinoamericana actual* (1989); Dorfman, A., ''Political Code and Literary Code: The Testimonial Genre in Chile Today,'' *Some Write to the Future* (1991), 133–95

GEORGE R. MCMURRAY

CHINESE LITERATURE

See Volume 1, page 456.

Literature from Mainland China

China had seventeen years from the founding of the People's Republic in 1949 to get its plans and institutions in place and working. They were not good years—some, in fact, were quite awful—but there was always activity, always a sense of movement; it wasn't long enough, however, and literature barely had a chance. For with the advent of the Cultural Revolution (1966–1976) the sterility of literary activities matched the general tenor of life, as Chinese society began to unravel. The death of Mao in 1976 and the fall of the Gang of Four began the emancipation process, but writers, usually the first to raise their voices on behalf of society and the individual, were understandably cautious about resuming this notoriously risky endeavor.

Toward the end of 1977, a literary phenomenon known as ''scar literature'' appeared, with courageous editors publishing thinly veiled fictional accounts of institutionalized cruelty and oppression during the chaotic decade. In a milieu characterized more by bewilderment than understanding of what had happened—and why—these writings, typified by the story ''Pan chu-jen'' (1977; the head teacher) by Liu Hsin-wu (Liu Xinwu, b. 1942), served to unite the people in their common suffering. They also, more by design than

coincidence, fixed the blame for China's contemporary ills on Lin Piao (Lin Biao) and the Gang of Four.

The years 1978 and 1979 have been grandiosely termed a golden era of modern Chinese history. Popular demands for reform, highlighted by the establishment of ''Democracy Wall,'' for the righting of political wrongs, and for literary and artistic freedom spawned a liberalization movement that was manifested in a corpus of exposé literature often classified as neorealism (q.v.). The richest harvest was reaped in fiction, as writers turned a critical eye not to the Cultural Revolution, but to the crippled society left in its wake. Ranging from melodrama (though not nearly as maudlin as the somewhat sophomoric ''scar'' stories) to biting satire, these works revealed aspects of society and personal views that would have been heretical in the socialist-realist literature of the preceding period. One of the most successful writers was Kao Hsiao-sheng (Gao Xiaosheng, q.v.), who wrote about the southern Chinese countryside with caustic humor, compassion, and outrage against bureaucratic excesses and mistakes. ''Li Shun-ta tsao-wu'' (1979; ''Li Shunda Builds a House,'' 1983) relates the tale of a peasant whose goal of building a modest home is frustrated by three decades of political campaigns, only to be realized once he resigns himself to the ways of New China: ''back-doorism,'' bribery, and other tricks. The sense of betrayal is palpable in this and other stories by Kao and his contemporaries.

Poetry also played a significant role in exposing social ills and official malfeasance. The long, prosaic poem ''Chiang-chün pu-neng che-yang tso'' (1979; ''General, You Must Not Do This,'' 1983) by Yeh Wen-fu (Ye Wenfu, b. 1944) is a frontal attack on special privileges, easily the most galling of the many forms of social misconduct to the average Chinese citizen.

The screenplay *Chia-ju wo shih chen-te* (1979; *If I Were for Real,* 1983) by Sha Yeh-hsin (Sha Yexin, b. 1939) is yet another attack on the deeply entrenched practice of granting special privileges to people in power and those in their often extensive circles. Concerned with a young man who is mistaken for the son of a member of the Central Committee and thus treated as royalty, the screenplay was deemed so blatantly critical that it had to be filmed not in China but in Taiwan.

Ultimately it was a journalist, a former ''rightist,'' who most powerfully captured the spirit of the writing community during that period of nearly unprecedented liberalization. ''Jen-yao chih-chien'' (1979; ''People or Monsters?,'' 1983) by Liu Pin-yen (Liu Binyan, b. 1925) is a long piece of reportage that exposes a web of corruption created by a powerful official in China's northeast, thereby setting the tone for a genre of writing that captured the fancy of Chinese readers for a number of years.

In November 1979 the Fourth Congress of Chinese Literary and Artistic Workers was convened in Beijing, with more than 3,200 delegates in attendance: The mood was upbeat and hopeful, as a call went out for support of the Four Modernizations, increased intellectual freedom, and a renewed commitment to socialist ideals. Unhappily, instead of prolonging the "literary spring," the congress proved to be the beginning of the end, for a scant two months later, Teng Hsiao-p'ing (Deng Xiaoping) demanded an end to a tolerance of dissent, the closing down of "democracy walls" once and for all, and the suspension of all unofficial journals. He also reaffirmed the wisdom of the purges of the 1950s, which had led inexorably to the horrors of the 1960s and 1970s. People like Liu Pin-yen, Yeh Wen-fu, and Sha Yeh-hsin were subjected to the very criticisms they had warned against with such eloquence and passion. Yet in the midst of this oppressive climate, a remarkable memoir of life during the Cultural Revolution was quietly published: *Kan-hsiao liu-chi* (1981; *Six Chapters from My Life "Downunder,"* 1983) by Yang Chiang (Yang Jiang, b. 1911) is at once a story of deep marital affection and institutional brutality set in the labor camps to which intellectuals were sent, some for nearly a decade, and is considered by some to be a parable on the effects of Maoism on contemporary Chinese society.

By 1981, as leftism made a rebound and neorealism lost its official patronage, a minicampaign was launched against a filmscript entitled *K'u-lien* (1981; unrequited love) by Pai Hua (Bai Hua, b. 1930); it is the story of an overseas artist who returns to China in the wave of patriotism after 1949, only to suffer disillusionment and, ultimately, ignominious death. When his daughter asks him on his deathbed, "Father, you love this country, but does this country love you?" the reader is struck by the degree of cynicism created by three decades of political oppression. The criticism that followed pitted two generations of artists against one another, the older generation generally serving as mouthpieces for powerful bureaucrats. The campaign spread to include a new literary phenomenon pejoratively termed *meng-lung* ("obscure" or "misty") poetry. Actually a form of verse akin to Anglo-American imagism (q.v.), "misty" poetry was created by poets like Pei Tao (Bei Dao, b. 1950), Shu T'ing (Shu Ting, b. 1952), and Ku Ch'eng (Gu Cheng, b. 1957), who gained an enthusiastic, if occasionally befuddled, audience for their difficult, innovative, fresh, and passionate verse. Pei Tao's line "I do not believe!" typifies the mood of alienation that gripped these young victims of the Cultural Revolution.

By 1983 those in charge of literary production were sufficiently concerned over attempts by writers to stretch the boundaries of acceptable literary forms and contents to launch yet another campaign, the short-lived, ill-conceived, and troubling attack against "spiritual pollution" (by which was meant humanism, modernism, and a view that alienation is historically compatible with Marxism). "Misty" poetry was still under the gun, as was the "modernist" fiction of the man slated to become minister of culture, Wang Meng (q.v.), author of the novel *Pu-li* (1979; *Bolshevik Salute,* 1989), and of creators of new expressions of individuality, such as the "humanist" first novel *Ren a! ren* (1980; *Stones of the Wall,* 1985) by Tai Hou-ying (Dai Houying, b. 1938). The architects of the campaign also kept a wary eye on the influx of literature from Taiwan, a phenomenon that had its beginnings at the turn of the decade; for while the earliest representatives of Taiwanese fiction and poetry were critical of Taiwan society, later offerings painted a more appealing picture of the island province. Particularly popular were the artistic stories of Pai Hsien-yung (q.v.) and the highly politicized nativist fiction of Huang Ch'un-ming (b. 1939) and Ch'en Ying-chen (b. 1936). Within a few years Taiwanese popular fiction would be the rage in China, particularly among the young.

By the middle of the decade an uneasy truce existed between literary bureaucrats and writers who lacked official patronage. In the novel *Nan-jen te i-pan shih nü-jen* (1985; *Half of Man Is Woman,* 1986) Chang Hsien-liang (Zhang Xianliang, b. 1936) uses sexual impotence both as a metaphor for political incompetence and as an observable consequence of political oppression; in this and subsequent works he describes how the baleful legacy of the Cultural Revolution is firmly entrenched in contemporary society, embraced by hordes of bureaucrats whose "rice bowls" would be threatened by implementation of institutionalized political, economic, and cultural reforms. While it would be an overstatement to say that Chang's novels broke down literary barriers erected against descriptions of sexuality, they and similar works by female writers such as Wang An-i (Wang Anyi, b. 1954), Chang Hsin-hsin (Zhang Xinxin, b. 1954), and Chang K'ang-k'ang (Zhang Kang-kang, b. 1950), as well as the feminist fiction of Chang Chieh (Zhang Jie, b. 1937), helped make Chinese fiction of the mid-1980s a bit less prudish and moralistic.

In 20th-c. Chinese poetry, generations sometimes span but a few years. It did not take long for "misty" poetry to spawn "postmisty" and other ephemeral schools of avant-garde poets interested in linguistic experimentation, the exultation of ancient cultural and literary traditions, and, in some cases, little more than sensationalism. The one-time "misty" poet Yang Lien (Yang Lian, b. 1955) used for his later inspiration China's ancient myths and legends, a move that linked him with a group of fiction writers known collectively as the *hsün-ken* (root-seeking) school, who captured a broad readership in China and the West by evoking cultural and historical roots in stories that blend heightened linguistic experimentation with a rural-based, nonideological approach to writing. China's past—ancient and recent—is at the core of the writing of novelists like Mo Yen (Mo Yan, q.v.), Han Shao-kung (Han Shaogong, b. 1953), the Tibetan Zhaxi Dawa (b. 1959), the Moslem Chang Ch'eng-chih (Zhang Chengzhi, b. 1948), and more. A series of "king" novellas by Ah Ch'eng (A Cheng, b. 1949), including the renowned "Ch'i-wang" (1984; "The Chess King," 1990), were held up as models of Chinese writing that succeeds by using a non-Westernized idiom while merging past and present.

The most resilient theme in 1980s literature was reform, including prescriptive, upbeat fiction like the factory stories of Chiang Tzu-lung (Jiang Zilong, b. 1941), as well as the more critical, even cynical, stories and novels that followed in the latter half of the decade. One does not emerge optimistic from a reading of *T'ien-t'ang suan-t'ai chih ko* (1988; a song of garlic in paradise county) by Mo Yen, *Fu-tsao* (1987; *Turbulence,* 1991) by Chia P'ing-wa (Jia Pingwa, b. 1954), or *Chen-nü* (1985; virgin widows) by Ku Hua (Gu Hua, b. 1942). Besides revealing the resistance to social reform in certain sectors, these works offer little hope for improvement, at least over the short haul. As though to underscore the pessimism, the government launched yet another political campaign in early 1987, this one targeted at "bourgeois liberalization" (once again an oblique swipe at such Western bugaboos as modernism); it culminated in the expulsion from the party of Liu Pinyen and others. An autumnal chill settled over the writing community during the next couple of years, when the best Chinese literature was published not on the mainland, but in Taiwan. World attention to Chinese culture was captured not by translations of novels, but by their cinematic adaptations, many of which won international prizes.

The decade of the 1980s in China closed with a general clampdown after the June Fourth violence at T'ien-an-men (Tiananmen), which has nearly driven literature underground or into hibernation. Magazines were shut down, editors fired, and censorship reinstituted. Except for writers with official patronage, literary activities have been limited to the stories and poems of a handful of youthful innovators and the occasional offering of an established author; more often than not, even this is published first outside of China, sometimes in translation. The work of Wang Shuo (b. 1958), Yü Hua (b. 1960), and Su T'ung (Su Tong, b. 1963), among others, bears watching, owing to its tone of alienation and cynicism as well as its linguistic and technical innovations. Meanwhile, a burgeoning corpus of expatriate literature is emerging from the pens of writers whose residence in the West is taking on the appearance of permanent domicile; stories by Ai Pei (Ai Bei, b. 1956) and the poetry of Pei Tao and others continue to appear both in Chinese and in translation.

Literature from Taiwan

The past two decades in Taiwan, the other major venue of Chinese literature, have witnessed several significant swings in literary activities and output, not surprising, given the startling changes in Taiwanese politics and society during that period. The most notable achievements of the 1960s, a decade of experimentation and growth, involved Westernized fiction and verse. By the mid-1970s, however, as the Cultural Revolution wound down across the Taiwan Strait, Taiwan was the scene of a protracted debate over nativist writing, which can be viewed in part as a national affirmation movement while Taiwan was suffering a series of political reverses. Literary modernism, a hallmark of the previous decade, was attacked as a symptom of Western cultural imperialism, and replaced by a more politicized corpus that was extremely well received by the populace. Stories of rural Taiwan by Huang Ch'un-ming, Ch'en Ying-chen, and Wang Chen-he (1940–1990), using a mixture of standard Mandarin and local dialect, portrayed Taiwan in the grip of a wrenching social transition and increasing international isolation. Frequently prescriptive in its conception and generally mimetic in nature, this engagé literature reached a broad readership that was denied novelists like Wang Wen-hsing (b. 1939), whose experimental novels *Chia-pien* (1978; family crisis) and *Pei-hai te jen* (1981; backed against the sea) confounded all but the most dedicated readers.

The 1980s saw the return of a more urban-based literature, as a younger group of novelists and poets, many of them women, drew closer to the mass media in their work and gained wide popularity. Novelists like Hsiao Sa (b. 1953), whose work has been characterized as journalistic realism, and Li Ang (b. 1952), the most daring novelist of her day, illuminated the lives, quotidian and spectacular, of contemporary women; occasionally they caused sensations in their own right, as did Li Ang's feminist novel *Sha Fu* (1983; *The Butcher's Wife,* 1986), with its graphic descriptions of sex and violence. Pai Hsien-yung created yet another controversy with the publication of *Nieh-tzu* (1983; *Crystal Boys,* 1990), the first modern novel on a gay theme. Both were reprinted on the mainland.

Taiwan's economic miracle of the late 1980s, coupled with profound political changes that would not have seemed possible only a few years earlier, had broad and immediate effects on literature. Many of the older generation of writers, such as the poet and essayist Yü Kuang-chung (q.v.), were more involved with literary patronage than creative writing, while a few innovative writers like Chang Hsi-kuo (b. 1944) and Chang Ta-ch'un (b. 1957) continued to expand the boundaries of literature, experimenting in detective fiction, science fiction, magic realism (q.v.), and more. However, it was a "brat pack" of aggressively promoted young novelists who captured the lion's share of the market with a more "popular" brand of fiction, including romances, thrillers, and sexually explicit novels.

A trend toward more "consumer-oriented" literature is occurring wherever Chinese literature is written (including Hong Kong and overseas Chinese communities). While the issue of whether or not the 1990s or the 21st c. will witness Chinese political unification is open to debate, an astonishing measure of literary unification—owing to creative cross-fertilization and a Chinese readership that transcends political borders—is already a fait accompli.

BIBLIOGRAPHY: Goldblatt, H., ed., *Chinese Literature for the 1980s* (1982); Lau, J. S. M., ed., *The Unbroken Chain: An Anthology of Taiwan Fiction since 1926* (1983); Lee, Y., ed., *The New Realism: Writings from China after the Cultural Revolution* (1983); Siu, H., and Z. Stern, eds., *Mao's Harvest: Voices from China's New Generation* (1983); Link, P., ed., *Roses and Thorns: The Second Blooming of the Hundred Flowers in Chinese Fiction, 1979–1980* (1984); McDougall, B. S., ed., *Popular Chinese Literature and Performing Arts in the People's Republic of China, 1949–1979* (1984); Duke, M. S., *Blooming and Contending: Chinese Literature in the Post-Mao Era* (1985); Kinkley, J. C., *After Mao: Chinese Literature and Society, 1978–1981* (1985); Duke, M. S., ed., *Modern Chinese Women Writers: Critical Appraisals* (1989); Tai, J., comp., *Spring Bamboo: A Collection of Contemporary Chinese Short Stories* (1989); Carver, A. C., and S. Y. Chang, eds., *Bamboo Shoots after the Rain: Contemporary Stories by Women Writers of Taiwan* (1990); Goldblatt, H., ed., *World's Apart: Recent Chinese Writing and Its Audiences* (1990); Siu, H. F., ed., *Furrows, Peasants, Intellectuals, and the State* (1990); Duke, M. S., ed., *Worlds of Modern Chinese Fiction* (1991); special Chinese literature issue, *WLT,* 65, 3 (Summer 1991)

HOWARD GOLDBLATT

CHRAÏBI, Driss

French-Moroccan novelist (writing in French), b. 15 July 1926, El Jadida (fomerly Mazagan, French Morocco)

C. is the leading Moroccan writer of the so-called "Generation of '52." He is the author of twelve novels, which were published in Paris. The recipient of many literary prizes, C.'s works have been translated into English, Arabic, Italian, German, and Russian. C. was one of a token few native Moroccans to pursue secondary studies in a French *lycée.* At the age of nineteen, he left for Paris to study chemical engineering and neuropsychiatry. After becoming disillusioned with science, he abandoned his formal studies and traveled throughout Europe and to Israel. He has been a writer and producer for the National Radio and Television Broadcasting System in France, where he has resided for the past forty years.

C.'s first novel, *Le passé simple* (1954; *The Simple Past,* 1990) was published at the height of the French-Moroccan conflict. Still the object of critical controversy, this invective text was aimed as much at Moroccan patriarchal society as at French colonial rule. Attacked by his compatriots for having betrayed his country at a time when it was seeking independence from France, C. also became the pawn of French journalists who used *Le passé simple* to legitimate the need for French rule in Morocco. C. was so disturbed by the controversy surrounding his novel that he publicly disowned it in 1957, only to reget his action later. *Le passé simple* was banned in Morocco until 1977.

Unlike other Maghrebian writers of his generation, C. did not hesitate to denounce the autochthonous forces that precipitated and intensified colonialism. He was the first Maghrebian writer to portray the social injustice, corruption, hypocrisy, and opposition to change in his society. He was also the first Moroccan to write about the oppression of women and children in an Islamic, patriarchal society. *Le passé simple* remains the precursor text for the novels of decolonization that burst onto the literary scene in the 1960s and 1970s.

Hailed by critics as a classic tale of revolt against the father, *Le passé simple* is perhaps more a novel about love for a cloistered mother who also symbolizes the sequestered homeland. Although a number of Maghrebian francophone writers employ the mother figure as a symbol of loss and victimization, C. considers her as the basis for sociopolitical change in the Maghreb. She becomes a symbol of Third World liberation in *La civilisation, ma mère!* . . . (1972; *Mother Comes of Age,* 1984). For C., the future of the Maghreb depends on the social evolution of its women, the last colonized of the earth.

C. has never denied that he became a writer thanks to the aberrant historical context of colonialism. As a youth growing up in French Morocco, he was caught in the clash between two irreconcilable societies and cultures. His difficult youth might have conditioned him for a life of solitude and exile, but it has also made him an advocate for understanding among peoples in a world torn apart by national, ethnic, sexual, and religious differences.

C. has written on both the Arab world and the West. *Les boucs* (1955; *The Butts,* 1983) was the first novel to depict the abject conditions of North African immigrant workers in France. In *L'âne* (1956; the ass) C. took a hard look at Third World independence. In *Un ami viendra vous voir* (1967; a friend will come to see you) he depicted the alienation of women in postindustrial consumer society. In C.'s work, displaced peoples from the four corners of the globe come together in the common quest for freedom and happiness, peace with oneself and others.

In 1967 C. confessed that not only had it taken him ten years to exorcize his past and write *Le passé simple,* but it had also taken him eleven more years as well as five more novels to bridge the gap that separated him from his past. In writing about both the Arab world and the West, C. felt that Maghrebian francophone literature could play a fundamental role in bridging two very different worlds. Although he never denied the tremendous impact of French culture on his writing, he never renounced his Moroccan origins.

Succession ouverte (1962; *Heirs to the Past,* 1969) depicts the return to the native land. C.'s most recent novels, *Une enquête au pays* (1981; *Flutes of Death,* 1985), *La mère du printemps (l'Oum-er-Bia)* (1982; *Mother Spring,* 1989), and *Naissance à l'aube* (1986; *Birth at Dawn,* 1990) are dedicated to his people, the Moroccan Berbers. The last two novels explore the Arab-Islamic conquest of Morocco and Andalusia. In writing about the historic past of his people, C. adopts a sensuous and mystical style. An ancient people's survival over time takes the form of a hymn to life.

C. has always insisted that we view him as nothing more than a writer of French expression. He believes that literature transcends national boundaries. Neither French nor Moroccan, C.'s cross-cultural writing shows how national, ethnic, and cultural differences can come together at the crossroads of tolerance for diversity.

FURTHER WORKS: *De tous les horizons* (1958); *La foule* (1961); *Mort au Canada* (1975); *L'inspecteur Ali* (1991)

BIBLIOGRAPHY: Yetiv, I., *Le thème de l'aliénation dans le roman maghrébin d'expression française* (1972), 88–113; Déjeux, J., *Littérature maghrébine de langue française,* rev. ed. (1980), 276–300; Monego, J. P., *Maghrebian Literature in French* (1984), 108–25; Kadra-Hadjadji, H., *Contestation et révolte dans l'œuvre de D. C.* (1986); special C. issue, *CelfanR,* 5, 2 (Feb. 1986); Marx-Scouras, D., "A Literature of Departure: The Cross-Cultural Writing of D. C.," *RAL,* 23, 2 (1992), 131–44

DANIELLE MARX-SCOURAS

CHRISTENSEN, Inger
Danish poet and novelist, b. 16 Jan. 1935, Vejle

C. received her teacher's certificate in 1958 from Århus Teachers' College. Her first poems were published in the journal *Hvedekorn* between 1955 and 1959, a period in which she acquainted herself thoroughly with classic and modern poetry under expert guidance of the poet and critic Poul Borum (b. 1934), who was her husband at that time. A further source of inspiration was Noam Chomsky's (b. 1928) linguistic philosophy, which corresponded to her own thoughts on the power and purpose of language. C. has received numerous prizes and has been a member of the Danish Academy since 1978.

C.'s poetry and prose treat from various viewpoints the same principal theme: fearing the unknown, the individual escapes into established roles, which can be self-chosen but also imposed by society. These roles are seen as restrictive in our relationship to ourselves as well as to the external world and therefore not giving the desired security but, on the contrary, an increased sense of alienation. The language of poetry becomes the tool of imagination and liberation, which is able to penetrate and revive dead reality, creating new experiences reflected in language itself.

In a romantic fashion the *writing* self is placed in the center of all epistemological activity. In her first two poetry collections, *Lys* (1962; light) and *Græs* (1963; grass), C. focuses on the disquieting world of writing: on the gaining of self-knowledge but also on the fear of losing the self during the creative act. The brief, condensed prose poems are based on these themes: nearness versus distance and the tension between ordinary everyday life and the creative moments of inspiration seen in the context of nature, love, and death.

The two volumes anticipate C.'s principal work, and the greatest poetic achievement of Danish literature of the 1960s, the epic *Det* (1969; it). Structured strictly symmetrically, like a musical composition or a chemical experiment, the work stages its own creation, reaching back to the beginning of time, a modern cosmogony, and simultaneously it absorbs the political and social questions of the period. Shaped in a flowing verbal creativity with rhymed stanzas, prose, and song lyrics, *Det* concludes with a stirring exploration of the human being's existential conditions. Only the creative self is able to overcome the dominant split between language and experience and thus make possible a movement from initial chaos to an increasingly more refined differentiation within human life, a movement that is mirrored in the text itself. On the external, social level C. shows an obvious sympathy with the outsider, the rebel; on the textual level she defends openness and the determination to break up and venture into the unknown. Both levels meet in an overpowering tribute to the individual's integration into the fellowship of all human beings as well as into the cycle of nature, which is perhaps only Utopia: "I have attempted to tell about a world that does not exist in order to make it exist."

Linguistic experimentation as well as the analysis of creation and creativity was anticipated in C.'s two novels *Evighedsmaskinen* (1964; the eternity machine) and *Azorno* (1967; Azorno), but here it is seen in relation to the experience of love. The first is a Christ allegory about the incarnation of love in human beings and in society; the second is an epistolary and diary novel, in which various women try to explain their relationship with the man who has given the novel its title—a poet and Kierkegaardian seducer. Filled with jealousy, they all manipulate what they write down, whereby reality is turned into fiction. In her novel *Det malede værelse* (1976; the painted room), about the Italian Renaissance painter Mantegna, related to the fantastical story in the tradition of Isak Dinesen (q.v.), C. attempts to maintain a synthesis of art and reality, image and life. Through three different narrators C. seeks to reach an understanding of the world as a creative process, of which art is a highly integrated part, but without ever reaching a final answer to the question of reality as being a form of art and art being a form of reality.

Det malede værelse concludes by letting one of the narrators, the ten-year-old son of the painter, walk into his father's painting as a symbol of the child's ability to transgress the borders by which the adult is confined. This unspoiled ability to

experience life both in its mythic and basic form is illustrated in the poetry volume *Brev i april* (1979; letter in April). Externally C. describes a journey to southern Europe with a child, whose precise observations of the surrounding world open up new and unexpected perspectives for the first-person narrator, the writing self, which in its turn provokes creative wonder and change. A related awareness of death is found in the collection *Alfabet* (1981; alphabet), now directly connected with linguistic awareness. Formally C.'s use of the alphabet and sequences of numbers as the elements in the creative process links the volume to *Det*. New, however, is an ecological aspect, as C. attempts to reveal the demolishing forces of modern civilization, which is also evident in a disintegration of language. Her poems point to destruction and doom in a setting in which not even love is seen as a redeeming possibility.

C.'s entire oeuvre, which also includes a series of radio plays, published in *En vinteraften i Ufa* (1987; a winter's evening in Ufa), must be read as one single comprehensive linguistic and philosophical experiment to capture an elusive reality. C. is unquestionably the most prolific and distinguished Danish representative of the so-called "systemic" poetry, the theory that proposes that poetry is a linguistic construction guiding the author as a means of cognition by searching for reality in the words—between and outside the words—but always captured with the help of words. For a writer of less stature than C. such attempts could have approached a mathematical problem. However, C. is eminently successful in reaching far beyond such mechanical constructions through her visionary insights into the human mind and spirit, her enthralling mythic associations as well as an overwhelmingly fertile metaphoric imagination.

FURTHER WORKS: *Intriganterne* (1972); *Del af labyrinten* (1982); *Den store ukendte rejse* (1982)

BIBLIOGRAPHY: Nied, S., "Letting Things Be: I. C.'s 'Alphabet,' " *ScanR*, 70, 4 (Dec. 1982), 24–26; Wamberg, B., ed., *Out of Denmark* (1985), 135–48

SVEN HAKON ROSSEL

CIORAN, E(mil) M.

Romanian philosopher and essayist (writing in Romanian and French), b. 8 Apr. 1911, Răşinari

Born in Romania, C. has lived in Paris since 1937 and is recognized as France's most original living existentialist philosopher. The son of a Greek Orthodox priest, he studied philosophy at the University of Bucharest, where he wrote a thesis on Henri Bergson (q.v.). Along with Eugène Ionesco, the absurdist dramatist, and Mircea Eliade (qq.v.), the philosopher of religions, he participated in Romania's cultural renaissance during the 1930s, the politically troubled interwar period. Though younger than either Ionesco or Eliade, C. was no less interesting. His first published book, *Pe culmile disperării* (1934; *On the Heights of Despair*, 1992), was awarded the King Carol II Foundation for Art and Literature Prize (1934). It expresses the nihilistic-apocalyptic sensibilities of the young generation of Romanian intellectuals and foreshadows the main themes of his later philosophical essays. It is thus highly significant as the original source spring of this modern philosopher's thought. By the time he left Romania for Paris on a fellowship from the French Institute in Bucharest, C. was the published author of four books. Since then, he has been living modestly in Paris, doing part-time free-lance work as translator and manuscript reader and writing his books. His first book written in French, *Précis de décomposition* (1949; summary of decay), was accepted by Gallimard in 1947, but C. retrieved it and rewrote it entirely four times. Writing in French was, according to him, "the most difficult task of my life," something akin to putting on a "straitjacket."

C.'s work consists mainly of collections of essays: *Syllogismes de l'amertume* (1952; syllogisms of bitterness), *La tentation d'exister* (1956; *The Temptation To Exist*, 1968), *La chute dans le temps* (1964; *The Fall into Time*, 1970), *De l'inconvénient d'être né* (1973; of the inconvenience of being born). The themes of his work are the themes of postmodern Western civilization: despair and decay, absurdity and alienation, futility and the irrationality of existence, the need for total self-awareness, and consciousness as agony. C.'s style is a unique combination of linguistic elegance and profound thought. Aphorism is his trademark; in turns lyrical and ironical, poetical and paradoxical, he rejects the technique of dry philosophical argument in favor of suggestive, graceful, and vivid formulations that reveal the intellectual and spiritual agony of the philosopher's mind in playful yet gripping ways. The Romanian C. of the 1930s is wilder and more passionate yet not totally unrelated to the French—and much better known— C. of the later decades. The French C. is a Nietzsche distilled through Chamfort, an elegant and ironic stylist who has curbed the fiery lyricism of his youth with moral aphorisms, because he knows, as he puts it in *Le mauvais demiurge* (1969; the evil creator), that "a moralist's first duty is to depoetize his prose."

Writing and philosophizing are for C. organically related to suffering. A running theme throughout his oeuvre is that sickness and suffering have "lyrical virtues" that alone lead to "metaphysical revelations." "To suffer is to generate knowledge," he writes, and he views his life and his work as the metamorphosis of tears turned into thoughts. The impulse to write in order to free himself of his obsessions motivates his entire work. As he put it in a recent interview with the Spanish philosopher Fernando Savater (b. 1938), "writing is for me a form of therapy."

C.'s work is characterized by a dramatic tension between the suffering, problematic man—the organic and lyrical thinker—and his archenemy, the philosopher or the sage, the abstract man, a distinction reminiscent of Nietzsche's Dionysian and Socratic types. A connoisseur of despair, that state of heightened lucidity that is the "negative equivalent of ecstasy," the lyrical thinker rejects the intellectual optimism of the abstract human and those philosophical systems that only manage to reduce the profound to the expressible. For C. "a cry of despair is more revealing than the most subtle thought."

Savater calls C's philosophical discourse "antipedagogical." It tackles major philosophical themes but deliberately resists taking shape as an informative and constructive discourse. It does not aspire to produce anything "new" on the subject, thus renouncing false pretensions to originality. His destructive discourse, going against the grain of traditional philosophical practice, unremittingly seeks to expose the contradictions inherent in any philosophical system, and cultivates with relish all contraries, conferring upon them equally little significance.

C. may be a specialized taste, too sharp and bitter for many palates and, paradoxically, too lyrical and melodramatic for some others. Yet Jean-Paul Sartre (q.v.) has always had a large following in English, and C. is a better pure writer than Sartre or any of the postwar French existentialists. His stylistic incisiveness has led some French critics to put him in the same class as Paul Valéry (q.v.), an ultimate accolade of linguistic purity. But the shocking, bracing verve of his existential despair—and good humor—admits his philosophical prose to the great tradition of Nietzsche and Kierkegaard.

FURTHER WORKS: *Cartea amăgirilor* (1936); *Schimbarea la față a României* (1937); *Lacrimi și sfinți* (1937); *Histoire et utopie* (1960); *Valéry face à ses idoles* (1970); *Joseph de Maistre: Essai sur la pensée réactionnaire* (1977); *Écartèlement* (1979); *Exercices d'admiration* (1986); *Aveux et anathèmes* (1987). FURTHER VOLUME IN ENGLISH: *Anathemas and Admirations* (1991)

BIBLIOGRAPHY: Mauriac, C., *L'alittérature contemporaine* (1958), 159–68; Sontag, S., Introduction to *The Temptation To Exist* (1968), 7–29; Said, E., "Amateur of the Insoluble," *HudR*, 21, 4 (1968–1969), 769–73; Savater, F., *Nihilismo y acción* (1970); Auden, W. H., "The Anomalous Creature," *NYTBR*, 28 Jan. 1971, 16, 20; Caws, P., "The Temptation To Exist," *NYTBR*, 14 Mar. 1971, 5; Savater, F., *Ensayo sobre C.* (1974)

ILINCA ZARIFOPOL-JOHNSTON

CIXOUS, Hélène

French fiction writer, essayist, and dramatist, b. 5 June 1937, Oran, Algeria

C., a major contemporary French writer, is known for her fictional texts, her poetic essays, and her plays. Born in Oran, Algeria, she became aware of social injustices—colonialism, anti-Semitism, antifeminism—at an early age and, in her words, learned to fight. She moved to Paris during her adolescence. C. studied English literature and became a professor of English. In Paris C. moved quickly to the forefront of the intellectual scene. She published her 800-page thesis *L'exile de Joyce ou l'art du remplacement* (1968; *The Exile of James Joyce,* 1972). She will always remain indebted to James Joyce (q.v.) for his work on language and on the relation between living and writing. Marked by the intellectual climate of 1968, C. defines herself against existentialism and Socialist Realism (qq.v.) with their insistence on artistic realism. She writes experimental texts that claim to be more to the Left and subversive because they question the self and break the circuit between reader and writer. *Dedans* (1969; *Inside,* 1986), focusing on C.'s childhood and her coming to writing as a result of her father's death, was awarded the Médicis Prize in 1969. *Le troisième corps* (1970; the third body), *Les commencements* (1970; the beginnings), and *Neutre* (1972; neuter) are written at the intersection of biography and her readings of Freud, Joyce, Kleist, Shakespeare, and others. C. considers writing as an ongoing self-analysis and a path toward a freeing of the self.

At the same time, she militates for a transformation of the academy. In 1970 C. was appointed by the government to found the experimental University, Paris VIII–Vincennes, where she started the Center for Research in Feminine Studies in 1974. In 1970, with Tzvetan Todorov (b. 1939) and Gérard Genette (b. 1930), she founded the review *Poétique,* which proposed to study texts for their poetic merit rather than through chronological ordering.

Since for C. writing *is* life, her ongoing meditations lead to an abundant production. One of her major preoccupations is the undoing of what she calls the phallocentric, masculine, unified self. This critique makes her a champion of the woman's cause. Two polemical texts, "Le rire de la Méduse," (1975; "The Laugh of the Medusa," 1976) and "Sorties" in *La jeune née* (1975; *The Newly Born Woman,* 1986), written in collaboration with Catherine Clément (b. 1939), urge women to break their silence and come to writing. As in all her other texts, C. affirms life against death. These "manifestos" were followed by numerous texts—militant texts to, from, and with woman—that appeared in a woman's publishing house, "des femmes," C. wrote a new feminine genesis, *Souffles* (1975; breathings), and a transformation of the feminine imaginary, *LA* (1976; she/there). She invented a new feminine myth of writing that would displace the masculine orphic myth based on the death of woman in *Illa* (1980; Illa).

C.'s encounters with Heidegger's writings about poetry or coming to language and with the writings of the Brazilian novelist Clarice Lispector (q.v.) are decisive. Under the influence of Heidegger and Lispector, C. began to write texts that emphasize the *approach* of people, things or nature. She wrote about the paradox of riches through poverty and of the infinitely small. However, "L'approche de Clarice Lispector" (1979; the approach of Clarice Lispector) marks a new departure.

A renewed interest in history directed C. toward theater and the stage, to which her encounter with theater director Ariane Mnouchkine gave her access. Issues in cultural pluralism prompted her to write an essay on Nelson Mandela, "La séparation du gâteau" (1982; the separation of the wedding cake), for the collective volume *Pour Nelson Mandela,* and her historical plays about Southeast Asia, *L'histoire terrible mais inachevée de Norodom Sihanouk, roi du Cambodge* (1985; the terrible and unfinished story of Norodom Sihanouk, king of Cambodia) and *L'Indiade ou l'Inde de leurs rêves* (1988; the Indiad or the India of their dreams). Though historically accurate, C.'s epic theater wants to capture the essence of the human. Highly philosophical, it meditates on human destiny. It distinguishes between power struggles in contemporary politics and the love for humans exemplified by Norodom Sihanouk and especially by Gandhi.

A critique of totalitarianism in eastern Europe led C. to a reading of Russian poets. She read and wrote about how these poets responded positively or negatively to their historical situation in an unpublished play, *Anna Akhmatova,* and a piece of lyrical, theatrical fiction with multiple voices, *Manne* (1988; manna) that links Mandela with

Anna Akhmatova and Osip Mandelstam (qq.v). Her studies of Marina Tsvetaeva (q.v.), carried out in her seminars, have been published in *Readings* (1991).

C. characterizes the shifts in her writing as going from the scene of the unconscious to that of history. Yet she never relinquishes the unconscious. She continues to publish fictional texts that resemble more and more meditations on writing and on the state of the author. Who is an author? With whom do I write? Who in me writes when *"I"* is always more than one? are some of the questions that make up texts like *Le livre de Promethea* (1983; *The Book of Promethea,* 1991), written in the quick of life and burning with positive passion; *Jours de l'an* (1989; days of the year), a collection of meditations on writing and on beginnings; *L'ange secret* (1991; the secret angel/the secret stake), on the secret of writing and on the problem of saying *"I"* in the writing scene. These texts hint at what truly motivates C., that is, writing itself as a self-reflective activity. If some of these recent texts tend to be ethereal, her new epic theater has been quite successful.

By the very nature of her enterprise, that is, of writing as living, C. keeps on producing texts. The underlying constants have been an undoing of the unified or narcissistic subject that wants to control the world or the other. C. affirms life against death, insists on undoing repression, be it personal or collective. Her lesson may be that political moves should never lead to simple power reversals but to the affirmation that *"I"* is always more than one.

FURTHER WORKS: *Le prénom de Dieu* (1967); *Un vrai jardin* (1971); *Tombe* (1973); *Prénoms de personne* (1974); *Portrait du soleil* (1974); *Révolutions pour plus d'un Faust* (1975); *Un K. incompréhensible: Pierre Goldman* (1975); *Partie* (1976); *Portrait de Dora* (1976; *Portrait of Dora,* 1977); *Angst* (1977); *La venue à l'écriture* (1977, with Annie Leclerc and Madeleine Gagnon); *Préparatifs de noces au-delà de l'abîme* (1978); *Vivre l'orange/To Live the Orange* (1979; bilingual ed.); *Anankè* (1979); *Ou l'art de l'innocence* (1981); *Limonade tout était si infini* (1982); *La prise de l'école de Madhubaï* (1984); *Entre l'écriture* (1986); *La bataille d'Arcachon* (1987); *L'heure de Clarice Lispector* (1989). FURTHER VOLUMES IN ENGLISH: *Reading with Clarice Lispector* (1990); *"Coming To Writing" and Other Essays* (1991)

BIBLIOGRAPHY: Andermatt-Conley, V., *H. C.: Writing the Feminine* (1984; rev. ed., 1991); Moi, T., "H. C.: an imaginary utopia," *Sexual/Textual Politics* (1985), 102–26; Willis, S., "Mistranslation: *Vivre l'orange,*" *SubStance,* 16 (1987), 76– 83; Guégan-Fisher, C., *La cosmogonie d'H. C.* (1988); Rossum-Guyon, F. van, and M. Diaz-Diocaretz, *H.C., chemins d'une écriture* (1990); Wilcox, H., et al., *The Body and the Text: H. C., Reading and Teaching* (1990); Motard-Noar, M., *Les fictions d'H. C.* (1991); Shiach, M., *H. C.* (1991)

VERENA ANDERMATT-CONLEY

COETZEE, J(ohn) M.

South African novelist and translator (writing in English), b. 9 Feb. 1940, Cape Town

Born in South Africa, C. worked as an applications programer (1962–1963) and a systems programer (1964–1965) in England. He received his M. A. from the University of Cape Town in 1963. From 1968 to 1971 C. was an assistant professor of English at the State University of New York at Buffalo, and he received his Ph.D. from the University of Texas in 1969. In 1972 he became a lecturer in English at the University of Cape Town, where he is currently professor of literature.

From South Africa one anticipates realistic reportage disguised as fiction that spills forth political anger. Such expectation scarcely prepares the reader for C., with his bizarre imagination depicting psychotic cruelties, for his surrealistic world where violence is elevated into apocalypse. The first response is likely to be horrified revulsion, the motivations being so inhumane, the acts so irrational as to have gone beyond the remedy of pity. C. deliberately explores the inner neurosis that engenders brutality. His work is conceived as pure nightmare, yet there is an underlying alternative perception that the intolerable events are closely linked to the pathology of his country.

His first publication, *Dusklands* (1974), consists of two unrelated stories. The first, "The Vietnam Project," written while C. was in the U.S., is a kind of science fiction. A pentagon psychologist attempts to give justification to the murderous incidents during the Vietnam War. His lunatic rationalizations infect his own morality, bringing him to a madness that can only be assuaged by an act of irrational violence. The theme, linking violence to a passionate but distorted commitment, presages C.'s later work, as does the structure. The explications are advanced, not by authorial intervention, but by monologue, the self-convicting commentary of the central character.

The second story of *Dusklands* is "The Narrative of Jacobus Coetzee," which is said to be a direct translation of a 1760 diary recording a disastrous exploration into the interior and a calamitous conflict with the natives who inflict harsh cruelties and then in turn are subjected to an even more vicious revenge. The highly detailed descriptions of the bodily sufferings and the passion with which they are inflicted become characteristic of C.'s later fiction.

In the Heart of the Country (1976; pub. in the U.S. as *From the Heart of the Country,* 1982) is set on a remote South African farm and displays C.'s reconstruction of the Boer world leavened by his extreme imagination. A daughter, reconciled to a spinster's role as the servant of her brutal father, is so incensed when he remarries that she murders him twice. One slaughter is a Freudian dream, but each is described in such exact detail that we are unsure which is intended as the reality. The contrivance of the structure makes all events questionable. Each paragraph of first-person narrative is numbered—a tiresome device presumably intended to increase the sense of disjointed experience. There is a question as to whether she is seduced by a servant or raped. The tensions between mistress and servant take on a fierce escalation toward murderous violence. So typical in C.'s work, there is an exactly depicted reality that exists alongside the fanciful neurotic degeneration. In 1976 *In the Heart of the Country* was awarded the CNA Prize, South Africa's highest literary award.

Waiting for the Barbarians (1980) takes C. into a deeper level of perception where violence and eroticism meet. The events take place on the barely defined border between "The Empire" and "The Barbarians." Under the command of an amiable magistrate, the fort survives comfortably until an inspection commanded by a sadist, Colonel Joll, demands an end to such tolerance. The harmless Barbarians are captured and treated with savage barbarity. Moralities are transposed. The magistrate's tentative protests are partly political, but also intimate and instinctive. He finds a strange salvation as he washes the tortured feet of a Barbarian girl. Before long the magistrate is in jail, along with the Barbarian captives. In turn, such are the twists of this metaphor, he becomes a Barbarian, starved and ill-treated until he seems only an animal. But within that experience he learns a deeper truth about survival and the necessities that human dignity requires in the face of "barbarity." C.'s terrible vision, when taken from that metaphoric frontier, is replicated in the present, where the barbarous battle between the confident torturers and the anxious humanitarians continues. *Waiting for the Barbarians* was awarded the Geoffrey Faber Memorial Prize (1980) and the James Tait Black Memorial Prize (1980).

Life and Times of Michael K. (1983) takes further the quest for human dignity in an atrocious society. Michael suffers from an ugly harelip birth deformity that condemns him to public scorn, yet he exposes a defiant resilience. After a violently destructive riot in Cape Town, he takes his dying mother back to the farm of her childhood memories, but she dies on the way. By now conditions have deteriorated and riots have become a full civil war. There are army posts, prison camps, work camps, and the constant oppression of authority. He falls into each trap, and yet in every case he escapes. His very innocence helps him to survive. All he seeks is the permission to cultivate a plot of land, which, in wartime, amounts to treason. After a series of torture and suffering, he ends up in a hospital camp where his determined passive resistance enrages the doctor, whose long, intimate monologue openly expresses C.'s theme. The doctor recognizes in Michael's unyielding stoicism the means of moral survival—the method of challenging a régime that has turned his noble role as healer into that of prison warder. *Life and Times of Michael K.* won the Booker Prize in 1983.

C.'s powerful work has attracted considerable attention. Many Western literary intellectuals adulate his unremitting search for the truths buried deeply in the human psyche. The more radical find his work elitist, in that its subtlety conceals the open denunciations they prefer.

FURTHER WORKS: *Foe* (1987); *A Land Apart: A Contemporary South African Reader* (1987, with André Brink); *White Writing* (1988); *Age of Iron* (1990)

BIBLIOGRAPHY: Penner, A. R., *Countries of the Mind: The Fiction of J. M. C.* (1989); Wright, D. N. T., "Fiction As Foe: The Novels of J. M. C.," *IFR,* 16, 2 (Summer 1989), 113–18; Attwell, D., "The Problem of History in the Fiction of J. M. C.," *PoT,* 11, 3 (Fall 1990), 579–615; Goddard, K., and J. Read, *J. M. C.: A Bibliography* (1990); Attwell, D., "On the Question of Autobiography: Interview with J. M. C.," *Current Writing: Text and Reception in Southern Africa,* 3, 1 (1991), 117–22; Gallagher, S. V., *A Story of South Africa: J. M. C.'s Fiction in Context* (1991); Stephenson, G., "Escaping the Camps: The Idea of Freedom in J. M. C.'s *Life and Times of Michael K.,*" *CNIE,* 4, 1 (Spring 1991), 77–87; Attwell, D., ed., *Doubling the Point: J. M. C., Essays and Interviews* (1992)

JOHN POVEY

COLOMBIAN LITERATURE

See Volume 1, page 483.

The literature in Colombia of the 20th c. has been dominated by two writers: José Eustacio Rivera and Gabriel García Márquez (qq.v.). Few other writers have established truly national and international reputations, although Colombia has a proud tradition in poetry, and a group of outstanding modern novelists that includes Héctor Rojas Herazo (b. 1922), Fanny Buitrago (b. 1945), Albalucía Angel (b. 1939), Rafael Humberto Moreno-Durán, Manuel Mejía Vallejo, Manuel Zapata Olivella, Gustavo Alvarez Gardeazábal, and Alvaro Cepeda Samudio (qq.v.).

The century was opened amidst a cultural identity crisis, as intellectuals debated whether Colombian literature should be "European" or "national" in its vision and sources. A group of writers identified as *modernistas,* located mostly in Santa Fe de Bogotá, argued in favor of a cosmopolitan aesthetic program that some intellectuals considered too European in conception to be considered authentically Colombian. The major *modernista* poets were José Asunción Silva (1865–1896), who wrote at the end of the 19th c., and Guillermo Valencia (1873–1943), who wrote at the beginning of the 20th c. The strongest opposition to this fin de siècle *modernismo* came from the region of Antioquia, from writers such as Tomás Carrasquilla (q.v.), Francisco de Paula Rendón (1855–1917), and Alfonso Castro (1878–1943). Carrasquilla set forth an aesthetic program that included both a sense of modernity and regional focus. According to Carrasquilla, such a literary program would constitute a literary independence for Colombia. In contrast with the cosmopolitan tastes of the *modernistas,* Carrasquilla defended a realist-naturalist type of fiction that carefully located characters in their regional environment. His major novels were *Frutos de mi tierra* (1896; fruits of my native land), *Grandeza* (1910; greatness), and *La marquesa de Yolombó* (1926; the marquise of Yolombó). These works, as well as other novels and short fiction, were satirical critiques of contemporary Colombian society and nostalgic evocations of an idyllic, rural 19th-c. Colombia.

In addition to Carrasquilla, the most recognized turn-of-the-century novelists were Eustaquio Palacios (1830–1898), Soledad Acosta de Samper (1833–1913), José Manuel Marroquín (1827–1928), and José María Vargas Vila (1860–1933). Palacios, Acosta de Samper, and Marroquín were committed to the political ideas of a conservative political regime identified in Colombia as the Regeneration. Palacios and Marroquín wrote novels of local color and local customs; Acosta de Samper was more concerned with essays and bibliographies, although she did publish several historical novels that contained lengthy political and philosophical statements in the works. Vargas Vila was one of Colombia's most prolific novelists and,

although he was one of Colombia's most fecund and widely read novelists ever, he never wrote a work considered "major." His novels contain scandalous plots, typically embellished with sexual practices considered taboo during the period, thus making them prohibited reading for generations of Colombian students. They were also viewed as literarily unacceptable for Regeneration Intellectuals and their Conservative heirs.

The major novelist of the 1920s was unquestionably José Eustasio Rivera. His writing responded to the nationalistic attitudes predominant in the 1920s and the attempts to establish a "national culture." This nationalistic project found its expression in the work of the pioneers of Colombian theater: Antonio Alvarez Lleras (1892–1956) and Luis Enrique Osorio (1896–1966). Rivera's now classic novel *La vorágine* (1924; *The Vortex,* 1935) was a timely response to this nationalistic period, and remained the model for several generations of Colombian novelists. It relates the story of the narrator-protagonist's flight to the jungle with his lover and his discovery of social injustice among the indigenous workers exploited there. Other novelists of the period, all traditionalists in theme and technique, were Arturo Suárez (1887–1977), Luis López de Mesa (1884–1967), Daniel Samper Ortega (1895–1943), and Gregorio Sánchez Gómez (1895–1942).

The 1930s and 1940s were dominated by the poets. The predominant literary activity of the 1930s was the founding of the *Piedra y Cielo* (Stone and Sky) group of poets in 1939 by the poet Jorge Rojas (b. 1911). The poets Rojas, Eduardo Carranza (q.v.), Arturo Camacho Ramírez (b. 1910), Carlos Martín (b. 1914), Tomás Vargas Osorio (1908–1941), and Gerardo Valencia (b. 1911) are commonly placed in this generation of writers, who espoused inspiration from the poetry of the Spaniards Juan Ramón Jiménez, Rafael Alberti (qq.v.), and Gerardo Diego (1896–1987). Active novelists during the 1930s were César Uribe Piedrahita (1897–1951), Eduardo Zalamea Borda (1907–1963), and Bernardo Arias Trujillo (1903–1938). These three writers sustained patterns established by Rivera. All three addressed issues of national identity and social conflict in a rural setting. Unlike Rivera, however, Uribe Piedrahita, Zalamea Borda, and Arias Trujillo exhibit a sharp awareness of oral culture and interest in assimilating it into their national novel projects. In 1944 the *Cántico* group (in obvious homage to the Spanish poet Jorge Guillén) was established by Jaime Ibáñez (b. 1919). The major novelists of the 1940s were Rafael Gómez Picón (b. 1900), Ernesto Camargo Martínez (b. 1910), Jaime Ardila Casamitjana (b. 1919), and Jaime Ibáñez. They addressed middle-class concerns to a middle-class readership, communicating a sense of the emotional and psychological experience of Colombia's middle class in this period. They were the pioneers of the modern novel in Colombia.

The first truly recognized modern novelistic production to have impact in Colombia, however, was constituted by three novels: *La hojarasca* (1955; *Leafstorm,* 1972) by García Márquez, *La casa grande* (1962; *La Casa Grande,* 1991) by Alvaro Cepeda Samudio, and *Respirando el verano* (1962; breathing the summer) by Héctor Rojas Herazo. All three of these novelists, who rightfully consider themselves patently Faulknerian, brought the standard narrative strategies commonly associated with the modern novel to Colombia. Each of the three relates stories of Colombia's decadent aristocracy, adopting a plethora of Faulknerian narrative strategems. *La hojarasca* and *La casa grande* are related to the presence of the American Fruit Company on the Caribbean coast. The first deals with the effects of this foreign presence in a formerly traditional town; the latter dramatizes the massacre of striking banana workers by government soldiers, a historical event of 1928.

Significant contributions to the modern novel in Colombia during the 1960s were Manuel Mejía Vallejo's *El día señalado* (1964; the appointed day), García Márquez's *Cien años de soledad* (1967; *One Hundred Years of Solitude,* 1970), and Rojas Herazo's *En noviembre llega el arzobispo* (1967; the archbishop arrives in November). Each of these novels is considered the major work by its respective author. Less known modern works that were highly experimental in narrative technique were *Después de la noche* (1964; after the night) by Eutiquio Leal (b. 1928), *El terremoto* (1966; the earthquake) by Germán Pinzón (b. 1934), and *Los días más felices del año* (1966; the happiest days of the year) by Humberto Navarro (b. 1932).

By the mid-1960s, modern and postmodern Colombian novelists were fully immersed in the writing of international fiction, rather than the traditional, regional, and oral cultures. Numerous factors had transformed Colombia and its novel. The irreverent *Nadaístas,* primarily poets, successfully scandalized the still predominantly conservative and conventional cultural establishment. Whether or not the poetry and proclamations of Gonzalo Arango (dates n.a.) and his *Nadaísta* cohorts will be judged of permanent value remains to be seen. Nevertheless, their rebellious textual and extratextual postures had a profound impact on literary tastes and paved the way for ongoing modern and postmodern literary activity in Colombia. The *Nadaísta* novel prize provided an outlet for the publication and distribution of the most experimental fiction of the time, even though the national con-

cern for understanding and evaluating the civil war of the 1950s (La Violencia) was deemed much more important than novels of technical experimentation.

The novel of major impact during this period was García Márquez's *Cien años de soledad,* and the most resonant literary event of the 1960s was the international heralding of this novel. A second round of the García Márquez phenomenon took place in 1982, when he received the Nobel Prize. During the late 1960s and early 1970s, aspiring writers in Colombia often spoke of the "shadow" that García Márquez cast upon them. The general crisis of literary modernism (q.v.) experienced in the West had a double edge in Colombia: On the one hand, García Márquez produced in 1967 one of the most celebrated texts of the supposedly exhausted modern tradition of the West; on the other hand, this modern product enjoyed such an enormous success that it made fiction writing afterward a formidable task in Colombia. By the mid-1970s the shadow of García Márquez's Macondo proved less burdensome as several writers, such as Moreno-Durán, Albalucía Angel, Gustavo Alvarez Gardeazábal, and Marco Tulio Aguilera Garramuño (b. 1949) found new, non-Macondian directions for the Colombian novel. Previously marginal and repressed discourses surfaced in the 1970s and 1980s as part of a new, postmodern attitude. They were discourses not necessarily related to the novel of La Violencia or Macondo.

García Márquez's may well be the most significant enterprise of modern fiction by a single author. Since the publication of *Cien años de soledad,* a pinnacle of the modern novel in Colombia and Latin America, García Márquez has written four novels: *El otoño del patriarca* (1975; *The Autumn of the Patriarch,* 1976), *Crónica de una muerte anunciada* (1981; *Chronicle of a Death Foretold,* 1981), *El amor en los tiempos del cólera* (1985; *Love in the Time of Cholera,* 1988), and *El general en su laberinto* (1990; *The General in His Labyrinth,* 1990). In his total fiction, García Márquez appropriated some of the narrative techniques of modernism (such as fragmentation, collage, and multiple points of view) and used these techniques in what is an identifiable modernist project—the seeking of order and the expression of the ineffable in a world lacking order and waiting to be named. In many ways, all of García Márquez's novels published since 1975 represent a rupture from the fiction of Macondo. His recent novels are far less complex in structure than *El otoño del patriarca,* but nevertheless represent a continuation of his modern project.

Several writers have assimilated the strategems of modern fiction, among them Fanny Buitrago, Manuel Zapata Olivella, and Héctor Rojas Herazo.

In addition to her short fiction, Buitrago has published the novels *El hostigante verano de los dioses* (1963; the harrassing summer of the gods), *Cola de zorro* (1970; fox tail), *Los pañamanes* (1979; the *pañamanes*), and *Los amores de Afrodita* (1983; Afrodite's loves). Much of her fiction emanates from the culture of the Caribbean coast. Several voices narrate *El hostigante verano de los dioses*, the totality of which communicates the state of boredom endured by a spiritually exhausted generation of young people. *Cola de zorro* is Buitrago's most complex work and shares some of the generational attitudes found in her first novel: The characters lack clear direction and their existence tends to be boring. It deals with human relations within the context of a large, extended family. *Los pañamanes*, set on a Caribbean island, portrays the conflicts between, on the one hand, the legends and traditions in a disappearing oral culture on the island and, on the other hand, modernization and its ''beautiful people'' that are taking over. In *Los amores de Afrodita* Buitrago recurs to popular culture in a manner reminiscent of Manuel Puig (q.v.).

Zapata Olivella has published six novels, including two works during the 1980s, *Changó, el gran putas* (1983; Changó, the big s.o.b.) and *El fusilamiento del diablo* (1986; the shooting of the devil). His most ambitious novel, the massive *Changó, el gran putas*, is broad in scope, spanning three continents and six centuries of African and African-American history. Zapata Olivella synthesizes a variety of voices and oral cultures in this saga of a people's striving for liberation. *El fusilamiento del diablo* is a historical novel about the death of an African-Colombian political leader.

Rojas Herazo has published a trilogy of novels consisting of the aforementioned *Respirando el verano* and *El noviembre llega el arzobispo*, and *Celia se pudre* (1986; Celia rots). These novels evoke the premodern, oral world of Celia, the central character of this trilogy, and her family. *Celia se pudre* is the summa of the world of Cedrón, the small town on the Caribbean coast where the three novels take place.

A group of younger writers has experimented with new directions for the Colombian novel in the 1970s and 1980s. Besides Moreno-Durán, Angel, and Aguilera Garramuño, Darío Jaramillo Agudelo (b. 1947), Rodrigo Parra Sandoval (b. 1937), and Alberto Duque López (b. 1943) have pursued an innovative and postmodern project during this period. Cosmopolitan in interests, most of them have preferred to write abroad. Moreno-Durán has published four novels and a volume of short stories; the roots of this work are not found in the empirical reality of Colombia but rather in modernist literature; they are all playful novels whose linguistic excesses make language their main subject. Angel's work has changed dramatically since the publication of her first work, *Los girasoles en invierno* (1970; sunflowers in the winter); her recent fiction, *Misiá Señora* (1982; the missus) and *Las andariegas* (1984; the travelers), is part of a feminist project that emanates directly from feminist theory and fiction. Aguilera Garramuño began his writing career with a self-conscious reaction against the work of García Márquez in his parodic *Breve historia de todas las cosas* (1975; brief history of everything); in *Paraísos hostiles* (1985; hostile paradises), a dialogue on fiction and philosophy, he moves away from the context of Colombia and García Márquez, but he continues in the metafictional mode. Jaramillo Agudelo's only novel, *La muerte de Alec* (1983; the death of Alec), is also a metafiction—in this case, a self-conscious metafiction on the function of literature. *Mateo el flautista* (1968; Mateo the flutist) is an experimental novel that offers two versions of the life of Mateo, the protagonist.

Contemporary Colombian theater and poetry have also undergone a renovation. In theater, Enrique Buenaventura (q.v.) and Santiago García (b. 1943) have been the main innovators. Buenaventura's *En la diestra de Dios Padre* (1958; on the right-hand side of our father) and García's *Guadalupe, años sin cuenta* (1975; Guadalupe, uncounted years) are both elaborate reworkings of previous texts. The new poets who have renovated poetic language in Colombia include Juan Gustavo Cobo Borda (b. 1948), María Mercedes Carranza (b. 1945), Giovanni Quessep (b. 1939), and Darío Jaramillo Agudelo (dates n.a.).

BIBLIOGRAPHY: Franco, J., *The Modern Culture of Latin America: Society and the Artist* (1967); Brushwood, J. S., *The Spanish American Novel: A Twentieth-Century Survey* (1975); Pope, R. D., ''*La vorágine:* la autobiografía de un intelectual,'' in Pope, R. D., ed., *The Analysis of Literary Texts: Current Trends in Methodology* (1980), 256–67; González Echevarría, R., ''*Cien años de soledad:* Novel As Myth and Archive,'' *MLN*, 99, 2 (Mar. 1984), 358–80; Ortega, J., *Poetics of Change: The New Spanish-American Narrative* (1984); Magnarelli, S., *The Lost Rib: Female Characters in the Spanish-American Novel* (1985); Lewis, M. A., *Treading the Ebony Path: Ideology and Violence in Contemporary Afro-Colombian Prose Fiction* (1987); Gass, W. H., ''The First Seven Pages of the Boom,'' *LALR*, 15, 29 (Jan.–June 1987), 33–56; McMurray, G. R., *Spanish American Writing since 1941: A Critical Survey* (1987); Alonso, C. J., *The Spanish American Regional Novel: Modernity and Autochthony* (1990)

RAYMOND LESLIE WILLIAMS

CONDE (ABELLÁN), Carmen

(pseud.: Florentina del Mar) Spanish poet, essayist, novelist, anthologist, writer of children's books, b. 15 Aug. 1907, Cartagena

In 1978 C. was the first woman ever elected as a member of the Spanish Royal Academy of the Language. Coming from a lower-middle-class family that had to spend six years in Melilla, the north African Spanish presidio, for economic reasons, the young C. began as an office worker at age fifteen. But her love of literature led first to a modest scholarship and finally in 1930 to a degree from normal school. In the meantime she began to be paid for her contributions to the literary sections of truly prestigious newspapers in Madrid such as *El Imparcial, El Sol, Informaciones,* and *El Heraldo de Madrid.* During this period, she met local poets and married one, Antonio Oliver Belmás (1903–1968), who had just published his first volume of poetry and was at the time earning his living as a telegrapher. She also continued to write, especially under the influence of Juan Ramón Jiménez and with the friendship of Miguel Hernández (qq.v.).

The advent of the Spanish Republic in conjunction with her and Oliver's history of work led them to become staunch supporters of the Republic's egalitarian programs. Most typical of this commitment is their work founding, directing, and teaching in the Popular University of Cartagena, their hometown. During the war years of 1936–1938, C. did work for her university degree in the Republican stronghold of Valencia, but it was not accepted in postwar Spain. Following some political difficulties during this time, she and Oliver settled in Madrid and came to attain and participate in the increasingly comfortable cultural life the capital offered to professor-writers such as themselves.

Although C. cultivates many fields of writing, it seems that her poetry is the most important. And in the wake of a problematic pregnancy in 1933 that left her both childless and incapable of further conception, and of the Civil War and World War II, her best poetry demonstrates an extraordinary love for life and awareness of the horror of anything that destroys it. In collections of her verse, such as *Mujer sin Edén* (1947; *Woman without Eden,* 1986), *Sea la luz* (1947; let there be light), *Mientras los hombres mueren* (1953; while the men die), and *Derribado arcangel* (1960; overthrown archangel), C. as human being and woman registers powerfully the conditions and limits of human possibilities and the yearning for a more perfect world. Nonetheless, and perhaps as a consequence of the difficult socioeconomic conditions that both she and her husband had to

overcome, C.'s poetry, notably *Empezando la vida* (1955; beginning life), and personal philosophy take life on its own terms. Struggle is concomitant with our condition and must be accepted. In C. this attitude extends so far as to thanking her father for her childhood and early youth of privations and work because they prepared her for the wars and their aftermath that were in store for Spain and the whole world.

As a much-published author with a long career behind her, C. is well known but still not the object of much academic study. In the Spain of the last hundred years much has been made of literary generations or groupings by age and shared socioaesthetic interests. By age C. would belong to either the Generation of 1927 or the Generation of 1936, but her production has been too varied and personal for easy insertion into one of the generations. As a result she presents a singular figure in contemporary Spanish poetry; since her name appears infrequently in discussions of poets belonging to given pre- or postwar generations, it normally appears by itself, or has until the pronounced flowering of interest in women writers during the 1980s by readers and critics with a feminist sensibility. In any case, C.'s poetry will always remain an eloquent and powerful expression of the mid-century crisis when humankind had to reassess its past and future in a way made new and urgent by the extent of wartime destruction and the numbers of people touched by it. Moreover, her *Mujer sin Edén* calls into question basic structures of human society when half of it is considered inferior from the moment of birth.

FURTHER WORKS: *Brocal* (1929); *Júbilos* (1934); *Don Juan de Austria* (1943); *Los enredos de Chismecita* (1943); *La amistad en la literatura española* (1944); *Dios en la poesía española* (1944); *La poesía de la eternidad* (1944); *Vidas contra su espejo* (1944); *Soplo que va y no vuelve* (1944); *Don Alvaro de Luna* (1945); *Aladino* (1945); *Ansia de la gracia* (1945); *Mi fin en el viento* (1947); *Cartas a Katherine Mansfield* (1948); *Mi libro de El Escorial* (1949); *En manos del silencio* (1950); *Iluminada tierra* (1951); *Cobre* (1953); *Las oscuras raices* (1953); *Vivientes de los siglos* (1954); *Poesía femenina viviente* (1955); *Los monólogos de la hija* (1959); *En un mundo de fugitivos* (1960); *Poemas del mar menor* (1962); *Jaguar puro inmarchito* (1963); *Viejo venís y florido* (1963); *Acompañando a Francisca Sánchez* (1964); *Once grandes poetisas américohispanas* (1967); *Obra poética (1929–66)* (1967); *Un pueblo que lucha y canta* (1967); *Menéndez Pidal* (1969); *Poesía amorosa contemporánea* (1969); *Gabriela Mistral* (1970); *A este lado de la eternidad* (1970); *Poesía femenina española* (2 vols., 1967, 1971); *Canci-*

onero de la enamorada (1971); *El caballito y la luna* (1974); *Corrosión* (1975); *Cita con la vida* (1976); *Días por tierra* (1977); *El tiempo es un río lentísimo de fuego* (1978); *Al encuentro de Santa Teresa* (1979); *Poesía ante el tiempo y la inmortalidad* (1979); *La noche oscura del cuerpo* (1980); *Escritoras místicas españolas* (1981); *Desde nunca* (1982); *Cuentos para niños de buena fe* (1982); *Derramen su sangre las sombras* (1983); *Antología poética* (1985); *Juan Ramón Jiménez* (n.d.)

BIBLIOGRAPHY: Alonso, D., *Poetas españoles contemporáneos*, 3rd ed. (1965), 339–44; Fernández-Barros, E., "Doña C. C., en la Academia," *REH*, 14 (1980), 41–49; Galerstein, C. L., ed., *Women Writers of Spain: An Annotated Bio-Bibliographical Guide* (1986), 77–81; Newton, C., "El discurso heroico de C. C.," *MRRM*, 6 (1990), 61–70; Richards, J. C., "The Word without End: Mythic and Linguistic Revision in C. C. A.'s *Mujer sin Edén*," *MRRM*, 6 (1990), 71–80

STEPHEN MILLER

CONDÉ, Maryse

Guadeloupean novelist, short-story writer, dramatist, and critic, b. 11 Feb. 1937, Pointe-à-Pitre

C. is Guadeloupe's best-known writer. She was born into a middle-class family, and her early schooling took place on the island, but she earned a college degree and doctorate in comparative literature at the Sorbonne. During the 1960s she taught in Guinea, Ghana, and Senegal, and during the 1970s at various universities in Paris. She currently resides in Guadeloupe, where she continues her writing, but also teaches part of each year at the University of California, Berkeley, where she is a tenured professor of French. Her husband, Richard Philcox, translates many of her works.

Although C.'s first works were plays, she made her mark on the literary scene by writing novels. The first two—*Hérémakhonon* (1976; *Heremakhonon*, 1982) and *Une saison à Rihata* (1981; *A Season in Rihata*, 1988)—feature Guadeloupean women protagonists in search of their identity. They leave the island, spend time in France, and eventually settle in postcolonial West Africa, an Africa that has been devalorized by the French and romanticized by African writers. There they attempt to reconcile these two opposing images, but are unsuccessful. As a result of C.'s protagonists' failure and her depiction of newly independent countries dominated by dictators, C. has been accused by some critics of perpetuating negative views of Africa.

The two-volume historical novel *Ségou: les murailles de terre* (1984; *Segu*, 1987) and *Ségou: la terre en miettes* (1985; *The Children of Segu*, 1989) seems designed to answer her critics. While the first two novels are partly set in present-day imaginary African countries, the actual Bambara empire of 18th- and 19th-c. Mali with its rich cultural heritage provides the background of *Ségou*. The disruptions brought on by colonialism, slavery, and the influx of Islam and Christianity are seen affecting several generations of the Traouré family. So thoroughly researched and detailed, the work also includes historical and ethnographical notes, genealogies, and maps. In 1986 C.'s interest in history is again demonstrated with the publication of *Moi, Tituba sorcière . . . Noire de Salem* (1986; *I, Tituba, Black Witch of Salem*, 1992), which won the Grand Prize for Women's Literature. C. adds to what little is already known about Tituba, a woman from Barbados brought to Salem, where she was implicated and arrested in the witch trials. Marginalized in contemporary texts, C. allows her to narrate her own story. C.'s latest novels—*La vie scélérate* (1987; *Tree of Life*, 1992), which received the bronze medal from the French Academy, *Traversée de la mangrove* (1989; mangrove crossing), and *Les derniers rois mages* (1992; the last Magi kings)—take place in Guadeloupe and thus represent a third phase in her novel production, which also is characterized by the integration of Creole into a French text.

C., innovative thematically and technically, is one of the French Caribbean's most prolific writers, having also published short stories, children's stories, plays, anthologies, and critical essays. When her characters cross national boundaries, she not only explores the relationships among people of the African diaspora, but she constructs bridges between the Caribbean, Africa, Europe, and the U. S. as well.

FURTHER WORKS: *Le morne de Massabielle* (1970); *Dieu nous l'a donné* (1972); *La mort d'Oluwemi Ajumako* (1973); *La civilisation du bossale* (1978); *Cahier d'un retour au pays natal: Césaire: analyse critique* (1978); *La parole des femmes* (1979); *Pays mêlé suivi de Nanna-ya* (1985); *Haïti chérie* (1987); *Pension les Alizés* (1988); *En attendant le bonheur* (1988); *Victor et les barricades* (1989); *An tan revolisyon* (1989); *Hugo le terrible* (1990)

BIBLIOGRAPHY: Ngate, J., "M. C. and Africa: The Making of a Recalcitrant Daughter," *CBAA*, 19, 1 (1986–1987), 5–20; Satineau, M., "Références politiques dans un roman antillais: *Une saison à Rihata* de M. C.," *Cahiers du CEDAF*, 4, 1–3 (1987), 362–76; Lionnet, F., "Happiness Deferred: M. C.'s *Hérémakhonon* and the Failure of

Enunciation," *Autobiographical Voices: Race, Gender, Self-Portraiture* (1989), 167–90; Snutgen, J., "History, Identity, and the Constitution of the Female Subject: M. C.'s *Tituba*," *Matatu*, 6, 3 (1989), 55–73; Chamoiseau, P., "Considérations sur *Traversée de la mangrove*: une analyse du dernier roman de M. C.," *Antilla*, 364 (1990), 34–39; Clark, V. A., "Developing Diaspora Literacy: Allusion in M. C.'s *Hérémakhonon*," in Davies, C. B., and E. S. Fido, eds., *Out of the Kumbla: Caribbean Women and Literature* (1990), 303–19; Smith, A., "The Semiotics of Exile: M. C.'s Fictional Works," *Callaloo*, 14, 2 (Spring 1991), 381–88

RENÉE LARRIER

COOVER, Robert

American novelist, b. 4 Feb. 1932, Charles City, Ia.

C. received his B.A. at Indiana University (1953) and his M.A. from the University of Chicago (1965). He served as fiction editor of the *Iowa Review* from 1974 to 1977. C. has taught at various colleges and universities and is currently at Brown University. He has received increasing critical acclaim and popular interest, as well as various awards, including the Faulkner Award (1966), a Rockefeller fellowship (1969), and Guggenheim fellowships in 1971 and 1974.

Although there is much that seems radically new in C.'s short stories and novels, they are demonstrably in the long line of American fiction whose origin is in Mark Twain's (1835–1910) *Adventures of Huckleberry Finn* (1884). We find in his work the same passion for the rhythms of an American spoken language, the same often critical concern with aspects of contemporary American culture, and the same immersion in American realities. In the wake of the great modernists and in response to an explosive new world, C., along with Thomas Pynchon, John Barth, Donald Barthelme, E. L. Doctorow, and John Hawkes (qq.v.), has helped to forge a developing new American fiction that is very much in tune with the old. What they have added to Twain's example—this is especially true of C., Pynchon, Doctorow, and Barth—is an explicit involvement with American history and an endeavor to create from it a new mythopoesis. In the new process, a new reality emerges; C., like Hawkes, has at times been called a surrealist. Yet it is clear that, however unlimited his characters' actions may appear to be (by reason or convention), they consistently reflect a reality that is recognizably American.

The early stories collected in *Pricksongs and Descants* (1969) set the tone for all the longer

fictions to follow: at their most effective, they display a wonderful inventiveness, a rare facility for language, and the ability to look at old models from new perspectives. At their weakest, they are self-indulgent and strain for effect. But, even then, they never fail to provoke. Illustrative is "The Brother," which views the Flood from the perspective of Noah's younger brother, a much better man than his sibling yet another of those who fail to survive. In C.'s revisionist version of the biblical myth, the moral imperative is reversed, and our modern heritage becomes both more questionable and more understandable: Our universal ancestor is a man so self-absorbed that survival becomes his sole goal; he is easy enough for us to recognize in our own world.

There is a similar ambiguity in *The Origin of the Brunists* (1966), C.'s first novel, whose frame purports to be historical but which also borrows from myth; but history and myth alike are now C.'s creations. A mine disaster in a dying small town: ninety-seven miners die, and one survives. Around him, Giovanni Bruno, a cult forms, aided by a cynical local newspaperman. The town is divided; the cultists are driven from the town, and their icon is institutionalized; his sister dies a martyr; the mines close; the town stagnates further; the new religion, driven elsewhere, prospers. Echoes of mythopoesis, inverted, are everywhere: comic, irreverent, and also serious.

In *The Universal Baseball Association* (1968), a middle-aged accountant invents a game of baseball played with dice and accompanied by an elaborate set of statistics. But the child's game turns serious, and, gradually, it takes over the life of its creator; its characters supplant those from the world outside in his life. In the final chapter, only they appear; he too is absent in his own account of what is ostensibly his life. Again, the life-giving potential of myth is replaced with irony.

C.'s most ambitious novel is *The Public Burning* (1977), a powerful if sometimes excessive account of the Rosenberg spy case and trial of the early 1950s, a work based on close knowledge of the public record and an extraordinary imagination. Among the principal characters are Richard Nixon, ambitious and amoral vice president, and Uncle Sam, personification of the individualistic American tradition. C.'s Nixon is hateful, comic, and strangely sympathetic. Desperate for affection, he very nearly makes love with Ethel Rosenberg on the electric chair in Sing Sing prison. The scene is tasteless, in a sense, yet it is also very funny. And C. makes us believe that it is potentially true to the characters. It is exceeded only by the novel's conclusion, in which the national spirit is passed from Uncle Sam to Nixon by a graphically detailed act of sodomy, followed by the public execution of the Rosenbergs in Times Square, presided over by Betty Crocker for a national television audience. For an ahistorical people, C. suggests, only an exaggerated mythopoesis may serve; but it serves badly. In the midst of a nation marked everywhere by fertility archetypes, there is only sterility. (It is worth noting that the printed text of this novel is not quite what C. originally wrote but that the publishers evidently insisted on some changes because of a feared, but never actually threatened, libel suit by former President Nixon.)

Much of C.'s subsequent work seems almost consciously lesser: shorter works in a minor key, which investigate individual aspects of American culture but never coalesce completely as fictions. *A Political Fable* (1980) is a reprinting in book form, in an election year, of the early election-year novella "The Cat in the Hat for President" (1968). It is a comic-book vision turned brutally serious. Its somewhat surreal protagonist (he is able to lead out of a television set all the characters that it contains) satirizes and at the same time represents the failings of the American electoral system and sensibility. Published as a limited edition between hard covers, the short story *Charlie in the House of Rue* (1980) follows and subverts the ineffable Charlie Chaplin, who proves here limited, human, effable indeed. He starts through this house with all his familiar gestures and moves, troubled perhaps but surely in control. But then matters change and turn ominous and offensive. It is a very dark comedy that C. finds at the heart of the king of comedy. The roots of *Spanking the Maid* (1982) are in the domination fantasies of the Marquis de Sade (1740–1814), with all their pseudo-philosophical claptrap, in Victorian flagellation tales and in the fictions of Alain Robbe-Grillet (q.v.). But it turns these sources on their tail; the master continues to discipline her because the manuals say that he must, and she accepts because she is learning so much from him about life. But in the end, their play is more wordplay than sexual or psychological, as if James Joyce and not Sigmund Freud (qq.v.) or de Sade were his true master.

In *Whatever Happened to Gloomy Gus of the Chicago Bears?* C. returns, indirectly, to the Richard Nixon character of *The Public Burning*. But Gus (whose real name is Dick and who went to Whittier College) seems the fulfillment of the other Dick's wishes (as athlete and lover) but becomes, ironically, a political radical; he is killed by strike-breakers and police in a march on a steel plant. His tragicomic failure and futile death, allied to the references to both Nixon and Jay Gatsby, make clear that this is another of C.'s readings of the American Dream, our central myth gone awry.

Pinocchio in Venice (1991) is C.'s first major work in more than a decade. It is, like so much of his work, ingenious, wildly comic, marvelously inventive, and it builds on his long-term interests in language, myth, and national character (although here that character may be more Italian than American). But it, too, is ultimately not fully satisfying. From Collodi comes the idea of a puppet given life but remaining a puppet—not only Pinocchio but all his old puppet friends speak and act (as do various animals)—but C. adds to this idea a new, metaphoric dimension. Human potential, human foibles are thus revealed. But we cannot empathize with C.'s hero. The brilliance of the conception and of the writing is not transformed into emotion, may even detract from it at times. We note the ties to C.'s earlier work and his sustained mythic vision. But we remain less moved by Pinocchio's fate than by those of Noah's brother, or the Rosenbergs, or even Richard Nixon. C. remains one of our most vital and challenging novelists. Yet we may feel that he has never quite fulfilled all aspects of his potential.

FURTHER WORKS: *The Water Pourer* (1972); *A Theological Position* (1972); *Hair o' the Chine* (1979); *After Lazarus: A Filmscript* (1980); *The Convention* (1982); *In Bed One Night and Other Brief Encounters* (1983); *Gerald's Party* (1986)

BIBLIOGRAPHY: Bacchilega, C., "Folktales, Fictions and Meta-Fictions: Their Interaction in R. C.'s *Pricksongs and Descants*," *New York Folklore*, 6, 3–4 (1980), 171–84; McCafferey, L., "R. C. on His Own and Other Fictions: An Interview," *Genre*, 14, 1 (1981), 45–63; LeClair, T., "The Garden in the Machine: Three Postmodern Pastorals," *MichA*, 13, 4 (1981), 405–20; Mazurek, R. A., "Metafiction, the Historical Novel, and C.'s *The Public Burning*," *Crit*, 23, 3 (Spring 1982), 29–42; Andersen, R., "The Artist in C.'s Uncollected Stories," *SHR*, 17, 4 (1983), 315–24; Gordon, L. G., *R. C.: The Universal Fiction-making Process* (1983); Lee, L. L., "R. C.'s Moral Vision: *Pricksongs and Descants*," *SSF*, 23, 1 (Winter 1986), 63–69; Caldwell, R. C., Jr., "Of Hobby-Horses, Baseball, and Narrative: C.'s *Universal Baseball Association*," *MFS*, 33, 1 (Spring 1987), 161–71; Mackey, L., "R. C.'s Dirty Stories: Allegories of Reading in 'Seven Exemplary Fictions,'" *IowaR*, 17, 2 (Spring–Summer 1987), 100–21; special C. issue, *DeltaES*, 28 (June 1989); Orlov, P. A., "A Fiction of Fantastic 'Facts': R. C.'s *The Public Burning*," in Sorkin, A. J., ed., *Politics and the Muse: Studies in the Politics of Recent American Literature* (1989)

MORTON P. LEVITT

COSTANTINI, Humberto

Argentine novelist, short-story writer, and dramatist, b. 1924, Buenos Aires; d. 7 June 1987 (or 31 May), Buenos Aires

C. contributed to Argentine narrative, novel and short story, and poetry. He garnered the Municipal Prize (Premio Municipal) for literature from the City of Buenos Aires for *Una vieja historia de caminantes* (1967; an old story about travelers) and for *Háblenme de Funes* (1970; talk to me about Funes). From 1977 until 1983, C. lived in Mexico in self-imposed exile after the disappearance of a friend during the time of the military dictatorship in Argentina. In 1979 he won the distinguished Casa de las Américas Prize for narrative with *De dioses, hombrecitos y policías* (1979; *The Gods, the Little Guys and the Police*, 1984).

Thematically C. follows the lines of a social realist, portraying the social and political realities of his native land and continent. He fuses this palpable reality with a knowledge of classic myths and legends. This fusion allows C. to recreate and to incorporate both elements into a contemporary daily setting using the urban environment of Buenos Aires to frame his works. Originally recognized for his efforts as a short-story writer, he was also an accomplished writer of novels, poetry, and theater. His collection of short stories *De por aquí nomás* (1958; just through here) is a first work. The individual stories are of unequal quality and originality. It is in this collection that C.'s style begins to shape itself. He continued to write short stories and to publish them in literary journals such as *Plural* in Mexico. Some of his short stories may clearly be classified as belonging to fantastic literature and are not in the same realistic vein as his novels.

C. imbues his novels with humor, satire, and commiseration for his fellow countryfolk, for it is often the common citizenry who unwittingly suffer the injustices of the system they do not understand and in which they find themselves trapped.

During his exile in Mexico, C. wrote *De dioses, hombrecitos y policías*. Banned in Argentina by the military, it was released there in 1984 after the free election of Alfonsín as president. The novel examines the Argentine national reality from which the author himself fled in the 1970s. In it C. denounces the random killing of innocent people at the hands of a paramilitary group. People are tortured and killed or "disappeared," which is the euphemism used to refer to this form of execution. There are no popular leaders or revolutionary figures as the target or focus of his novels. Their strength lies in the fact that they illustrate that the victims of repression are often unaware of the evil and untimely death that awaits them. The police, depicted as a paramilitary group, are not immune from their fate. They, too, are trapped by their providence to carry out orders they do not understand and fear to question.

Only two of C.'s novels have been translated into English, *De dioses, hombrecitos y policías* and *La larga noche de Francisco Sanctis* (1984; *The Long Night of Francisco Sanctis*, 1985). The latter characterizes the dilemma of helping one's associates by forewarning them of impending disaster and safeguarding oneself from personal harm. It is from these two novels, particularly the former, that C. is known to English-speaking readers.

Both novels thematically deal with the effect that the political turbulence in Argentina has on the average citizen. But Argentina may stand for numerous other countries where the exact same forms of repression thrive. Therefore, C.'s work takes on a universal tone embodying all unjust governments and the devastation wrought by them.

FURTHER WORKS: *Un señor alto, rubio, de bigotes* (1963); *Tres monólogos* (1964); *Cuestiones con la vida* (1966); *Libro de Trelew* (1973); *Más cuestiones con la vida* (ca. 1974); *Bandeo* (1975); *En la noche* (1985)

BIBLIOGRAPHY: Mastrángelo, C., *El cuento argentino,* 2nd ed. (1975), 96; Cortés Gaviño, A., "Hombrecitos cotidianos," *Plural: revista cultural de Excelsior,* 9, 108 (Sept. 1980), 74–76; Hunt, L., *NYTBR,* 29 Apr. 1984, 34

BETH POLLACK

CSOÓRI, Sándor

Hungarian poet and essayist, b. 3 Feb. 1930, Zámoly

The finest populist poet of his generation, C. was born in a small village in western Hungary to a poor Protestant peasant family. He attended local schools and reached early maturity during the war years. C. published his first volume of poems, *Felröppen a madár* (1954; the bird takes wing), while still in his twenties. The book was an instant success; it won him the József Attila Prize (1954) and a seat on the editorial board of the Budapest literary magazine *Szabad Ifjúság*. In the early 1950s C. represented the Communist Party-inspired poet of the people: the country boy singing in simple rhymes about the rural poor and the joy of building socialism. However, the 1956 revolt profoundly altered both C.'s political views and his direct poetic diction. Showing the influence of such poets as Federico García Lorca and Paul

Éluard (qq.v.), his verse gradually abandoned naive imagism in favor of a more thorough treatment of a few basic themes: love, solitude, nature, and his native roots. This change became apparent in his next collection of poems, *Menekülés a magányból* (1962; escape from solitude).

In the 1960s, frustrated by the economic and psychological privations of his country, C. branched into prose. His essays in *Tudósítás a toronyból* (1963; report from the tower) are a blend of autobiography, sociography, folklore, and poetic social criticism in the manner of the poet Gyula Illyés (q.v.), his long-time mentor. In 1964, after a trip to Cuba, he wrote an exuberant travelogue, *Kubai napló* (1965; Cuban diary), praising Fidel Castro and Che Guevera. From the early 1970s C. has collaborated regularly on film scripts with directors Ferenc Kósa and Sándor Sára. Their first movie, *Tízezer nap* (1963; ten thousand days), won the Grand Prix at Cannes (1964). He also continued to publish poetry and prose. In a major volume of essays *Nomád napló* (1979; nomadic diary), C. advocated reliance on nonpolitical ethical values and an adherence to the folklore tradition, broadening his personal concerns into a yearning for universal social justice. He reached new heights in his new books of poetry *Tizedik este* (1980; the tenth evening), *Tenger és diólevél* (1982; sea and chestnut leaf), and *Kezemben a zöld ág* (1985; green twig in my hand). These volumes read like a romantic portrait of the artist himself, yet in them C. actually assumes varying poetic personae who speak movingly of the experience of death and past loves.

The heritage of romanticism blends in C.'s work with surrealist effects, which he claims to have learned from folk poetry. In each poem the hero is C. himself, an intellectual who has never ceased to be a peasant. In a world leveled by thoughtless modernization, he searches for ways to preserve uniqueness in the world. The poems illuminate his spiritual torment, unravel his deep feelings of isolation, while offering a taste, however slight, of that zestful natural condition from which he and his people were wrenched in the haphazardly transformed postwar world. In another prose volume, *Készülődés a számadásra* (1987; preparing for the reckoning), C. blamed himself and his generation for not speaking the whole truth about Hungary's ills: high suicide rates and low birth rates, diminished national consciousness, and general apathy. In a terse, poetic style he tried to instill a new moral awareness in his contemporaries.

More recently C. found himself at the center of a new political movement, being regarded a kind of spiritual leader of the people. As editor of *Hitel,* a cultural journal identified with the Hungarian Democratic Forum, the leading political party, he has become an ardent spokesman for the new patriotism and a defender of the nation's populist tradition. He has also become internationally known in the past few years. Several of his works have been translated into English and German, and in 1981 he won Austria's prestigious Herder Prize.

C.'s style is a mixture of the traditional and the modern. His imagery is sensuous and natural, but his themes are those of a dislocated visionary. Behind his serene and delicate poetic lines there is always the wistful attempt to capture the unfathomable richness of fast-fading worlds as well as the sadness of universal transience. Nevertheless, C. is a highly respected national poet in Hungary today because his finest works transcend politics and also deal with survival, including national, cultural survival.

FURTHER WORKS: *Ördögpille* (1957); *A költő és a majompofa* (1966); *Második születésem* (1967); *Faltól falig* (1969); *Párbeszéd a sötétben* (1973); *Utazás félálomban* (1974); *Sose harmadnapon* (1976); *A látogató emlékei* (1977); *Jóslás a te idődről* (1979); *Iszapeső* (1980); *A félig bevallott élet* (1982); *Elmaradt lázálom* (1982); *Várakozás a tavaszban* (1983); *Csoóri breviárium* (1988); *A világ emlékművei* (1989). FURTHER VOLUMES IN ENGLISH: *Wings of Knives and Nails* (1981); *Memory of Snow* (1983); *Barbarian Prayer: Selected Poems* (1989)

BIBLIOGRAPHY: Vajda, M., ed., *Modern Hungarian Poetry* (1977), 233–38; Tezla A., ed., *Ocean at the Window* (1980), 277–300; Czigány, L., *The Oxford History of Hungarian Literature* (1984), 460–62; Gömöri, G., on *Készülődés a számadásra*, WLT, 62, 3 (Summer 1988), 486; Gömöri, G., on *Barbarian Prayer: Selected Poems*, WLT, 64, 3 (Summer 1990), 500; Mottram, E., "Before the Revolution: Poetry by S. C.," NHQ, 118 (1990), 112–16

CLARA GYORGYEY

CUMALI, Necati

Turkish poet, dramatist, fiction writer, and essayist, b. 1921, Florina (now Greece)

One of Turkey's most versatile and prolific authors, C. graduated from the faculty of law at Ankara University at the age of twenty. He worked for brief periods for the ministry of public education, the office of the Turkish press attaché in Paris, and Radio Istanbul. From 1950 to 1957 he practiced law in Urla and Izmir, where he had spent much of his early life. In the 1960s he lived some time in Tel Aviv and Paris, where his wife was an attaché. During the second half of his adult life he has been an independent writer.

In the 1940s, C. attracted attention with his simple, straightforward poems which, like the work of his contemporaries Orhan Veli Kanık (1914–1950) and Melih Cevdet Anday (q.v.) among others, dealt with the life of an average person. C.'s poems often celebrated the beauty of nature and sometimes lamented the harsh realities of rural life. His youthful sentiments ranged from tenderness to open protest. His earliest collections, *Kızılçullu yolu* (1943; road to Kızılçullu), *Harbe gidenin şarkıları* (1945; songs of those gone to war), *Mayıs ayı notları* (1947; notes of May), and *Güzel aydınlık* (1951; lovely light), contain effortlessly accomplished poems of romantic involvements, life's simple pleasures, and the poignancy of poverty and war.

C.'s 1955 collection entitled *İmbatla gelen* (borne on the southern wind) features poems in the same vein, but also the striking narrative cycle "Karakolda" (in the precinct) about a blood feud in a rural village, composed like a folk elegy, which is perhaps his most powerful long poem. His *Güneş çizgisi* (1957; line of the sun), *Yağmurlu deniz* (1968; rainy sea), which combined the two previous books with a selection of new poems, *Başaklar gebe* (1970; pregnant are the grains), and *Ceylan ağıdı* (1974; antelope's elegy) chart the course of his transition to a compelling concern about social and political upheaval in Turkey and abroad. In this period, C. visited and resided in several foreign cities, including Paris, New York, Sofia, and Leningrad, which inspired many fine poems. *Yağmurlu deniz* won the coveted poetry prize of the Turkish Language Society in 1969.

Bozkırda bir atlı (1981; a rider in the steppes) and *Yarasın beyler* (1982; to your health, gentlemen) are kaleidoscopic collections containing his lyric, satiric, political, and elegiac poems. In 1980 C. published his collected poems under the title *Aç güneş* (hungry sun) and in 1983 brought out an enlarged collection, *Tufandan önce* (before the deluge).

C.'s novels deal mainly with the dramas of rural life with which he became familiar during his formative years and later as a country lawyer. They are filled with action and memorable characters. The narrative style is remarkably lucid and crisp. His first novel, *Tütün zamanı* (1959; tobacco time), later reissued as *Zeliş* (1971; Zeliş) after the principal character, is a touching story of the life and love of an immigrant girl. *Yağmurlar ve topraklar* (1973; rains and the soil) is a stirring narrative of political turmoil, idealism gone awry, struggle against exploiters, and intellectual restlessness in Turkey in the early 1950s. *Acı tütün* (1974; bitter tobacco) and *Aşk da gezer* (1975;

love too drifts) consolidated C.'s fame as a major novelist.

In the short-story genre C. has secured himself a place of high distinction. His collections *Yalnız kadın* (1955; lonely woman), *Değişik gözle* (1956; with a fresh eye), *Ay büyürken uyuyamam* (1969; I cannot sleep while the moon grows larger), *Kente inen kaplanlar* (1976; tigers swooping on the city), *Dilâ Hanım* (1978; Lady Dilâ), *Revizyonist* (1979; revisionist), *Yakubun koyunları* (1979; Jacob's sheep), and others contain a number of the most consummate short stories written in the Turkish language. *Değişik gözle* won the Sait Faik Prize in 1957. C. was awarded the prize once again in 1977 for his collection *Makedonya 1900* (1976; Macedonia 1900), stories based on the experiences and recollections of his parents.

C.'s novella *Susuz yaz* (1962; dry summer), which he had also written as a play by the same name, was made into a film and enjoyed success in Turkey and abroad, winning the Berlin International Film Festival Award in 1963. (The English translation of the play is included in T. S. Halman's *Modern Turkish Drama*, 1976.)

As a translator, C. has done two volumes of selected poems by Langston Hughes and Guillaume Apollinaire (qq.v.), in 1961 and 1965 respectively. His collections of essays *Niçin aşk* (1971; why love), *Senin için ey demokrasi* (1976; for you, o democracy), and *Etiler mektupları* (1982; letters from Etiler) contain some of his best critical pieces on literature and politics. His *Yeşil bir at sırtında* (1990; riding a green horse) is a collection of reminiscences and reflections.

C.'s plays have enjoyed successful runs at Turkish theaters and have been collected in many volumes. *Boş beşik* (1949; empty cradle), made into a film in 1955, won first prize at the Erlangen International Theater Festival (Germany) in 1955. *Nalınlar* (1962; *The Clogs,* 1982) was a huge success at Istanbul's Kent Players Theater. Most recently, *Derya gülü* (1963) was published in English as *Sea Rose* (1991). These three plays dramatize touching and sometimes humorous episodes of villagers and fishing people of Anatolia. C.'s other plays often deal with urban situations and universal themes. *Bir sabah gülerek uyan* (1990; wake up laughing one morning) is a bittersweet play, a wry comedy of errors, depicting the disquietude of some Turkish intellectuals. *Dün neredeydiniz* (1981; where were you yesterday) was awarded the Ministry of Culture Prize (1981). The range of imagination, the clever plots with surprising denouements, crisp dialogue, and fascinating characters have made C.'s plays highly interesting to watch and to read.

Few Turkish writers have achieved as impressive a success in so many genres—poetry, novel, short story, drama, essays, translations—as has C. His fame will probably endure as one of the most energetic creative forces in the literature of the Turkish republic.

TALAT SAIT HALMAN

CZECHOSLOVAK LITERATURE

See Volume 1, page 520.

Czech Literature

The division of Czech literature into three streams—"official," exile, and *samizdat*—caused by the repression of independent intellectual activities in the wake of the Soviet invasion in 1968, lasted much longer than was deemed possible. On the domestic scene, few imaginative developments of any significance were tolerated for twenty years by a neo-Stalinist régime whose main concern was the preservation of the status quo. Very few of the writers who fell into disfavor after 1968 could hope for a relaxation in the official attitude to themselves and their work. Even a revocation of their previously expressed views, which was a humiliating condition of return into public life, seldom achieved more than limited results.

Among those who after considerable harassment did issue a statement vaguely in support of the authorities was Bohumil Hrabal (q.v.), but that part of his work that he was subsequently allowed to publish in Czechoslovakia was not the best and appeared only in emasculated versions. However, the unexpurgated originals as well as some unpublished manuscripts were either circulated in *samizdat* editions or printed abroad. Most noteworthy of them were *Příliš hlučná samota* (1976; *Too Loud a Solitude,* 1986), which presented a grotesque view of the world from the perspective of a wastepaper warehouse, and *Obsluhoval jsem anglického krále* (1982; *I Served the King of England,* 1989), a bizarre story of a physically stunted and morally deficient careerist. Both were written in the early 1970s when there was little chance of ever seeing them in print. Some of the dilemmas and problems of conscience the author himself faced in the 1970s and 1980s while living in fear of the secret police were later hinted at in his autobiographical trilogy *Svatby v domě* (1987; weddings in the house), *Vita nuova* (1987; new life), and *Proluky* (1986; vacant lots), published in Canada.

The work of Vladimír Páral and Ladislav Fuks (qq.v.), who never were expelled from the ranks of "official" writers, was also affected by political pressures. As he tried to adjust to new circumstances, Páral lost much of the creative drive and critical bite that he had shown in the 1960s, and his once innovative technique was getting worn out by overuse and repetition. This became especially apparent when he embraced the popular fashion of science fiction, which swept through Czechoslovakia in the 1980s. One novel that stood above several that Páral produced during that decade was *Válka s mnohozvířetem* (1986; war with the multibeast), an ecological variation on Karel Čapek's (q.v.) classic *Válka s mloky* (1936; *War with the Newts,* 1937). Fuks's writing suffered a sharp decline from which it had barely started to recover by the end of the 1980s.

Official literature produced little of genuine interest. The promising authors of the 1970s such as Jiří Navrátil (b. 1939), Václav Dušek (b. 1944), or Jiří Švejda (b. 1949) soon found themselves restricted by an invisible barrier of political taboos. Attempts to break the self-imposed bonds of private and intimate themes and to venture into a wider world inevitably led to failure. Although many writers treated in photographic detail the manifestations of moral decay rampant throughout the land, they could not, even if they had dared to, state the obvious, namely, that corruption was an attribute of a stagnant system. Social criticism, which had to bypass the pivotal role of the omnipotent Communist Party, lacked credibility. The picture it painted did not correspond with the reality familiar to readers from their everyday experience.

A number of young authors were granted the opportunity to enter literature during this period, although not the chance properly to deploy their talent. In a stifling environment where mediocrity and convention ruled, there was little scope for nonconformity or experiment. Compromise with the ruling ideology could rarely be avoided. One of the more noticeable of his generation, Zdeněk Zapletal (b. 1951), progressed from early autobiographical books, which followed the fortunes of a small group of young friends, to a broadly conceived novel, *Půlnoční běžci* (1986; midnight runners), in which he endeavored to present a cross section of Czech life in the mid-1980s. The general impression given by this ambitious undertaking, obviously influenced by contemporary American fiction, was that of all-pervading frustration and futility. Nonetheless, conspicuous lacunae in the setting demonstrated yet again that certain subjects remained unmentionable.

Writing of this kind was regarded as occupying a "gray zone" between officialdom and dissent. In the latter part of the 1980s, some gifted new authors, such as Alexandra Berková (b. 1949) and the dramatist Karel Steigerwald (b. 1945), managed to find a refuge in it and were able to publish as long as they could keep up the precarious balancing act.

Hardly any of the censored and self-censored books issued officially during the 1970s and 1980s had a hope of arousing interest in the West. One of the voices that continued to be listened to was that of the poet Miroslav Holub (q.v.). Despite having publicly recanted in 1973, he did not publish in Czechoslovakia until 1982. Throughout that period, however, Holub's already substantial reputation abroad, particularly in the English-speaking countries, grew steadily as his new verse appeared there in translation. It overshadowed the rest of the rather excessive output of poetry in all three streams of Czech literature. Only the work of a handful, notably Karel Šiktanc (b. 1928) or Ivan Diviš (b. 1924), may prove to be lasting.

The books that were most frequently translated in the West were those written either by the banned authors living in Czechoslovakia or by those who had left the country after 1968. The road to recognition was paved for them by the remarkably vigorous Czech cultural and literary community in exile. Most efficient in this respect were two publishing houses, Sixty-Eight Publishers, Toronto, run by the writer Zdena Salivarová (b. 1933) and her husband Josef Škvorecký (q.v.), and Index, Cologne. Books of writers silenced at home could thus be printed in Czech abroad alongside those of writers living in exile. As they were subsequently smuggled back into the country, they helped to counteract to some extent the effects of the politically imposed divisions of Czech literature.

Of those who had settled in the West, Milan Kundera (q.v.) was soon after his emigration in 1975 acknowledged to be the most influential. His new, intricately structured novels, *Kniha smíchu a zapomnění* (1981; first pub. in English as *The Book of Laughter and Forgetting*, 1980), *Nesnesitelná lehkost bytí* (1985; first pub. in English as *The Unbearable Lightness of Being*, 1984), and *Nesmrtelnost* (1992; first pub. in English as *Immortality*, 1991), achieved spectacular success throughout the noncommunist world, but some of their aspects evoked mixed reactions in Czechoslovakia. It was felt that Kundera was taking too many liberties with the representation of his native country. No such criticism was leveled against Josef Škvorecký, who became a much honored Czech-Canadian author while enjoying undiminished popularity at home. Škvorecký located even some of his new work written in exile in the Czechoslovakia of his youth. That applies, for instance, to the account of his alter ego, Danny Smiřický's salad days, *Prima sezóna* (1975; *The Swell Season*, 1982). Danny appeared also in *Příběh inženýra lidských duší* (1977; *The Engineer of Human Souls*, 1984), a broadly conceived fresco of nearly half a century of life beset by tumultuous events in both eastern Europe and the West. Elsewhere, Škvorecký turned to an unconventional rendering of events from the past. In *Scherzo*

capriccioso (1984; *Dvořák in Love,* 1986) he dealt with the Czech composer's stay in the U.S.; in *Nevěsta z Texasu* (1992; a bride from Texas) he investigated the participation of Czech volunteers in the American Civil War.

Among the exiled Czech writers who gained recognition from Western readers and audiences during the two decades were Jiří Gruša (b. 1938), Pavel Kohout (b. 1928), and Arnošt Lustig (q.v.). The works of dozens of others, including Jaroslav Vejvoda (b. 1940) and Vlastimil Třešňák (b. 1950), who did not really embark on their careers as authors until they had left Czechoslovakia, were translated less often.

The awarding of the Nobel Prize in 1984 to the poet Jaroslav Seifert (q.v.) was a great encouragement to the "dissident" or "alternative" culture maintained in Czechoslovakia by the community of banned artists and intellectuals of which he was a distinguished member. Unfortunately, it proved nearly impossible to adequately transpose into different environments the emotional intensity of Seifert's work so much cherished at home. This was not a problem encountered by the radio plays, short stories, and novels of Ivan Klíma (q.v.); they were increasingly finding a positive response in the West, as were many other writers that appeared either on their own or in anthologies. Particularly well received were a collection of Ludvík Vaculík's (q.v.) *feuilletons, A Cup of Coffee with My Interrogator* (1987), and his fictional, although not entirely fictitious, diary, *Český snář* (1983; Czech book of dreams.)

A large proportion of the outstanding books published over the past twenty years were written by women authors, both those living in Czechoslovakia and abroad. The subtle, contemplative short stories of Eda Kriseová (b. 1940) are an example of the former, Zdena Salivarová's novel *Honzlová* (1972; *Summer in Prague,* 1975), written in Canada, but taking place in Czechoslovakia, of the latter.

New plays by Václav Havel (q.v.), unperformed in Czechoslovakia, were being staged all over the world. After the three one-act plays *Audience* (1975; *Audience,* 1978), *Vernisáž* (1976; *Private View,* 1978), and *Protest* (1978; *Protest,* 1978), based on the personal experience of a dissident, the greatest success was achieved by Havel's contemporary adaptation of the Faustian legend, *Pokoušení* (1986; *Temptation,* 1986), particularly in the production of the Royal Shakespeare Company.

Since the late 1960s, Czech literature had become better known throughout the world than ever before in its history. It was a remarkable achievement, considering that most of the universally acclaimed authors were living in exile or were being persecuted while struggling against adverse political conditions at home.

In view of the role that a relatively few of these writers and intellectuals played in preserving essential human values under an oppressive régime and in a climate of social morass and moral decline, it could be regarded as a symbolic act of historical justice that after the "velvet revolution" of November 1989, which brought forty years of communist rule in Czechoslovakia to an end, Václav Havel was elected president of the Republic. As the country regained its freedom, the conditions were created for the separate streams of Czech literature to merge together. The transformation of a totalitarian system into democracy, however, proved to be more difficult than had been foreseen, and it soon became apparent that full integration could not be achieved overnight. It did not help that with the arrival of political pluralism and new economic circumstances Czech culture found itself occupying, perhaps temporarily, a less prominent place in public life than had been its tradition.

As old restrictions were lifted, hundreds of new private publishers mushroomed and a profusion of previously banned and half-forgotten books flooded the market. In addition, an uncontrolled outburst of hitherto unknown commercialism caused the near collapse of the well established publishing houses with a forty-year reputation and of the distribution trade. The generation that had achieved prominence in the 1960s and in most cases suffered subsequent banning or exile enjoyed a comeback, with their books being sold in hundreds of thousands of copies. It was obvious, nonetheless, that the change had come too late for many of them and that the public, though acknowledging them as a worthy reminder of the past, had in the meantime become attuned to a slightly different taste. At the same time, dozens of new names were emerging of young authors who had never been involved either with the communist régime or in the dissident movement and were resolved to go their own way. Only the future would be able to tell whether their contribution to Czech literature was as significant as that of their predecessors.

BIBLIOGRAPHY: Hájek, I., "The rule of the average," *IJSLP*, 33 (1978), 702–19; French, A., *Czech Writers and Politics 1946–1969* (1982); Hájek, I., "Precarious Survival," *Formations*, 1, 1 (Spring 1984), 114–21; Pynsent, R. B., "Social Criticism in Czech Literature of 1970s and 1980s Czechoslovakia," *Bohemia*, 27 (1986), 1–36; Hájek, I., "Changing Attitudes in Recent Czech Fiction," in McMillin, A., ed., *Aspects of Modern Russian and Czech Literature* (1989), 214–23

IGOR HÁJEK

DALCHEV, Atanas

Bulgarian poet, translator, and essayist, b. 12 June 1904, Thessaloniki, Greece; d. 17 Jan. 1978, Sofia

A native of Greece, D. arrived in Bulgaria as a child and received most of his education there. Between 1927 and 1929 he lived in Italy and France, visiting London; in 1936–1937 he was in France again. In Bulgaria he worked at various times as a teacher, school inspector, and school principal, as well as a translator. After the communist seizure of power in 1944 he was with the ministry of information, and also edited a journal.

D. occupies a special place in the history of Bulgarian literature. Initially, in the 1920s, he had links with the symbolist poets, but soon moved away from them. The titles of his principal pre-1944 collections reflect the stages of his creative life at that period: *Prozorets* (1926; window), *Parizh* (1930; Paris), and *Angelut na Shartur* (1943; angel of Chartres). During the worst Stalinist years in Bulgaria, D. was among the very few who retreated into stubborn silence rather than acquiesce to political demands upon literature. He subsequently became a model for the younger generation of poets of the 1960s, a culturally more liberal time when D. himself returned to the scene with a thin but valuable volume of "Notes on Poetry, Literature, and Criticism" entitled *Fragmenti* (1967; fragments).

One of these "fragments" might serve as an epigraph to D.'s entire lifework: "Temperance is a virtue in literature as well." D.'s poems rarely run to more than a few stanzas, and his whole lifetime's original poetic output can easily be contained in one small volume. His vocabulary is deceptively simple, and at first glance seemingly easy to translate. D. was an intensely private man, who exposed no more of himself to his reader's view than necessary. Several of his earlier poems employ the image of the window, a delimited opening that enables him to watch others' lives from afar while he himself remains unobserved.

D. always kept his distance from the world. The theme of loneliness is a prominent one in 20th-c. Bulgarian literature, and D. contributed much to its elaboration. Thus in "Nosht" (1929; night) he surveys the night through his own reflection in the window, and concludes: "three times blacker, heavier becomes the gloom / and my own loneliness." In "Vecher" (1930; evening) the persona thinks of great cities he has known, such as Naples and Paris, and wishes he could somehow participate more fully in the life of society instead of consistently retreating from it.

The philosophical note sounded in "Vecher" attains even more concrete expression in a poem like "Kukuvitsa" (1964; cuckoo), where the poet recalls his Greek childhood and the popular belief that the cuckoo's call numbers the years of life remaining to the hearer. The poet stops his ears, refusing to listen, not because he is afraid, but because he is convinced it is wrong to seek to know the future. Whoever seeks knowledge of the future will discover not life, but death, although D. realizes full well that we cannot forever avoid Death, "the eternal bandit."

D. adopts a classical approach to life and literature. His writing is usually extraordinarily clear, and he finds universal meaning, not in historic individuals or events, but in the everyday objects of our century that lie close at hand, in ordinary people like a man bearing an advertising board whom most of us scarcely notice. In his writing D. reflected in miniature both the enduring traits of the Bulgarian character—thrown into relief through the experiences of a "Bulgarian abroad"— and the passing literary fashions in his native land, but he did so through the prism of his powerful individuality, which was simultaneously earthy and philosophical. His place among the small number of great Bulgarian lyric poets of this century is secure.

FURTHER WORKS: *Stikhotvoreniya* (1928); *Stikhotvoreniya* (1965); *Balkon* (1972); *Stikhotvoreniya. Fragmenti* (1974); *Stikhotvoreniya. Fragmenti. Misli i vpechatleniya* (1978); *Suchineniya* (2 vols., 1984)

BIBLIOGRAPHY: Statkov, D., "A. D.'s poetische Welt," *ZSP*, 34, 2 (1969), 254–76; Mozejko, E., "The Poetry of A. D.," *Proceedings of the Second Bulgaro-Scandinavian Symposium*, Uppsala Slavic Papers, 13, 1 (1982), 85–95

CHARLES A. MOSER

DANISH LITERATURE

See Volume 1, page 536.

Most of the trends shaping Danish literature in the 1960s and 1970s continue in the following two decades. The neorealist novel retains its dominance. It was introduced by Anders Bodelsen and Christian Kampmann (qq.v.) in the mid-1960s, analyzing the psychological impact of the modern welfare state. With his novel *Rolig flugt* (1974; quiet escape), the story of a middle-aged bureaucrat who tries to break with his previous life, the somewhat older Bent William Rasmussen (b. 1924) emerges as a gifted prose writer who develops the neorealist novel into a scathing account of a society in the process of rapid moral and political dissolution.

Already in the 1960s Thorkild Hansen (q.v.) turned the neorealist novel into documentaries. Whereas Hansen employed historical material to elucidate contemporary existential problems, Ebbe Reich (q.v.), since the 1970s, has continued his development of the documentary genre into a critique of contemporary politics. In the 1980s, a renewed interest in historical material focusing on personalities rather than periods becomes noticeable, with a series of biographical narratives, several of which have been translated into the major European languages. Particularly noteworthy is the three-volume series (1981–1991) by Henrik Stangerup (q.v.), structured on the philosophy of Søren Kierkegaard. Stangerup's sister, Helle Stangerup (b. 1939), a writer of detective novels, has been particularly successful with her portrayals from Danish national history, *Christine* (1985; *In the Courts of Power,* 1988), and *Spardame* (1989; queen of spades), whereas Dorrit Willumsen (b. 1940) chose an internationally known woman, Madame Tussaud, as the protagonist of her fascinating fictional account *Marie* (1983; *Marie,* 1986). The novel, like Willumsen's other works since her debut in 1965, is based on an experience of absurdity and loneliness, which makes us change roles to discover our own identity. Willumsen's interest in role problems received a masterful expression in a preceding novel, *Manden som påskud* (1980; the man as pretext) which, incidentally, makes no distinction between the predicaments of modern man and woman, putting a distance between Willumsen and contemporary feminist writers, and, at the same time, indicates the change in direction in Danish women's literature since the 1960s and 1970s.

A particular subgenre within the documentary literature of the 1970s is the so-called confessional literature and the roman à clef. It was inspired by the focusing within the feminist movement on the more private aspects of human relations, and it was anticipated by the hidden autobiographical features in earlier works by Henrik Stangerup and Christian Kampmann. Indeed, a few years later they both contributed significantly to the confessional genre, as did the poet Tove Ditlevsen (1918–1976) with her novels *Gift* (1971; married/poison) and *Vilhelms værelse* (1975; Vilhelm's room), both merciless revelations of the destructive tendencies within marriage. Ditlevsen's novels were followed and partly imitated by a large number of less talented women writers, contributing—sometimes with a degree of sensationalism—to the breaking of taboos regarding alcoholism and sexuality.

Similar or related problems, but seen in a broader social context—often incorporating the motif of alienation in modern capitalist society—result in a partial return in the 1970s to the tradition of social realism of the 1930s and, like then, often accompanied by criticism of the establishment with distinct socialist undertones, focusing on the outsiders of the social mainstream. Whereas Ulrik Gräs (b. 1940) with his novel *Fatimas hånd* (1971; Fatima's hand) uses the milieu of the provinces as a backdrop for his attacks on the middle class, Kirsten Thorup (b. 1942) presented with epic breadth a much wider scope in her four-volume cross section of Danish society from the 1950s until today, which began with the novel *Lille Jonna* (little Jonna) in 1977. Thorup made her debut during the 1960s and was inspired by French absurdism and the psychiatry of R. D. Laing, which is reflected in her novel *Love from Trieste* (1969; *Love from Trieste,* 1980). Her first step toward describing a lower-class milieu was taken with the novel *Baby* (1973; *Baby,* 1980), but it is the books about Jonna that have made Thorup one of the most popular writers in today's Denmark. Like her great predecessor and model Martin Andersen Nexø (1869–1954), Thorup manages—through an admirable myth-creating imagination—to raise her narrative above pure description, turning her characters and their dramatic fate into symbolic expressions of humankind's continuous striving toward a better and different life.

The realistic novel continues to find successful exponents during the 1980s. Jørgen Christian Hansen (1956–1989), in his trilogy *Guldsmeden* (1981; the goldsmith), *Hermelinen* (1982; the stoat), and *Knæleren* (1983; the praying mantis), offers fascinating insights into the world of childhood experience; Klaus Lynggaard (b. 1956), in his *Martin og Victoria* (1985; Martin and Victoria) and *Victorias år* (1986; Victoria's years), provides, in all likelihood, the most comprehensive portrayal of the 1970s. Whereas Lynggaard focuses on the experiences of youth, Arthur Krasilnikoff (b. 1941) uses the recollections of a woman suffering from cancer to render a picture of Denmark from the viewpoint of an older generation.

Due to relative political stability in the realm of foreign policy, Danish writers in the post-Vietnam War era are much less politically active—in connection with Denmark's entering the European Economic Community in 1972 political writing experienced a revival—but otherwise all political engagement takes the form of ecological debate. This development was furthered by the trend among a number of the Marxist-oriented writers of the 1960s, which Hans-Jørgen Nielsen (1941–1991) has labeled "attitudinal relativism." This forms the basis of his own works from the manifesto *"Nielsen" og den hvide verden* (1968; "Nielsen" and the white world) to the novel *Fodboldenglen* (1979; the soccer angel). This relativistic approach rejects the existence of set political norms in the same way as it denies the possibility of comprehending reality as something absolute.

The same turning-away from militant positions can be noticed in women's literature, which after 1968 launched provocative attacks—fictive and nonfictive—on a male dominated and oppressive society. Initially, a series of documentary reports were issued, such as *Kvinder på fabrik* (1971; women in factories) or *Kvindernes bog* (1972; women's book), which were succeeded by more personal, subjective accounts, such as Suzanne Brøgger's (b. 1944) *Fri os fra kærligheden* (1974; *Deliver Us from Love*, 1976). Brøgger provides an excellent example of the development of Danish feminist literature, maturing into discussions of gender roles and moving from semidocumentary or autobiographical accounts, such as the kaleidoscopic *Crème fraîche* (1978; sour cream), toward pure fiction, such as the highly acclaimed epic poem *Tone* (1981; Tone). Brøgger's continued, unorthodox attempt at orienting herself in the contemporary world is also, mixed with religious elements, reflected in her latest work, *Den pebrede susen* (1986; the peppery soughing).

Whereas Brøgger's works are primarily public displays of her private life, other women writers choose a more general social—sometimes political—context. Charlotte Strandgaard (b. 1943) in her novel *Lille menneske* (1982; little human being) subscribed to a psychological approach; Inge Eriksen (b. 1935) displayed a more political orientation; Dea Trier Mørch (b. 1941) wrote a bestselling collective novel about a group of women in a Copenhagen maternity ward, *Vinterbørn* (1976; *Winter's Child*, 1986), abandoning her previous leftist orientation in a stirring account of solidarity and compassion.

Also within poetry there is a development away from programmatic feminism. The early 1970s were dominated by poetry collections that in many cases can only claim to be poetry by being printed in the form of shorter lines, which earned them the derogatory label of "broken prose." Granted, the poetry of Marianne Larsen (q.v.) also deals with gender roles and sex discrimination. But it is removed from the intimate sphere of the majority of the works of "broken prose" in her advocacy of the liberation of the abandoned individual within the framework of political liberation, of a dream of community as expressed in the title of *Der er et håb i mit hoved* (1981; there is a hope in my head). Larsen's latest collections, *Hvor du er* (1987; where you are) and *I timerne og udenfor* (1987; in hours and outside), do mark a stronger orientation toward the personal realm in line with the general trend of the 1980s.

The linguistic experiments of the so-called systemic or concrete poets, like Inger Christensen (q.v.) and Per Højholt (b. 1928), and of a prose writer such as Svend Åge Madsen (q.v.), who established structures or "systems" of language material as sound, syntax, or image as both means and origin of cognition, developed in the 1980s, under the influence of the linguistic theories of Ludwig Wittgenstein (1889–1951), into an even more scripturally oriented approach in the works of Jens Smærup Sørensen (b. 1946), Peter Laugesen (b. 1942), Henning Mortensen (b. 1939), and the younger Dan Turèll (b. 1946). To them *language* is identical with petrifaction and conformity, whereas *script* expresses rebellion, something that is alive and liberating. Klaus Høeck (b. 1938) recast language as a mirror of the problems of reality's unending mass of material by working with mathematical paradigms to structure his five-volume work *Rejse* (1971–1973; journey). His poetry collection of 608 pages, *Hjem* (1985; home), a grandiose attempt to encircle God, is a major work of the 1980s and can be seen as one avenue of "escaping" the linguistic system.

Generally, with all of the systemic writers an orientation toward the outer world took place. Both Inger Christensen and Svend Åge Madsen comment increasingly on contemporary events, Smærup Sørensen moved via exact realism toward the fantastic in his novel *Mit danske kød* (1980; my Danish flesh), and Højholt abandons his experiments in *Turbo* (1968; turbo), in which language has become depersonalized to a degree that the poet lets a swirl of words spread more or less accidentally all over the pages, in favor of the realistic and humorous, and quite popular, *Gittes monologer* (1981–1983; Gitte's monologues). With his novel *Vangebilleder* (1975; pictures from Vangede) Turèll has replaced his previous systemic, computer-generated poetry with topographic realism, in his succeeding works incorporating beat and rock music as well as the detective genre in a flow of books of greatly fluctuating quality but always provocative and characterized by a skillful command of the smallest nuances of the language.

A central feature of women's literature since the 1960s has been the placement of alternative values against the norms of a rationalist and technological society. This feature is not only a question of focusing more strongly on feelings and emotional experiences, but is also expressed in grassroot movements to fight pollution and the destruction of the environment. Chief works in this ecologically oriented literature are the older Thorkild Bjørnvig's (q.v.) poetry collections *Abeguder* (1981; monkey gods) and *Epimeteus* (1990; Epimeteus). Bjørnvig's ecological poems express an organic interdependence with animals, plants, and the earth's resources, an orientation that, during the 1970s, in the prose works of Ib Michael (b. 1943) and Vagn Lundbye (b. 1933) encompasses a sincere fascination with nature peoples who treat the natural world with greater sensitivity than our Western industrial society: Lapps, Eskimos, and Native Americans. A pronounced interest in their myths and religious beliefs is reflected in Lundbye's *Alvidende fortællinger* (1986; omniscient tales), whereas Michael's latest book, the best-selling *Kilroy Kilroy* (1989; Kilroy Kilroy) is a supenseful novel of identity.

The overall development of Danish literature within the last twenty years from an exclusive, modernistic, and experimenting attitude to a linguistic and stylistic openness and thematic accessibility stressing the aesthetic values of literature peaks in the 1980s, in particular among the poets of the decade. A work that both corresponds to this characteristic and, at the same time, also with supreme forcefulness eludes any categorization is the 537 prose-lyrical monologues entitled *Requiem* (1985; requiem) by Peer Hultberg (q.v.). In this monumental work Hultberg has laid open the complex concerns and questions of contemporary civilization, analyzing its emptiness and richness, its fragmentation and coherence.

In general, the poets of the 1980s are individualists not concerned with sociological or ideological analyses but rather with their own sensitive selves as they are exposed to impressions from the world of the media, pop culture, and breathtaking technology. Michael Strunge (1958–1986) came to be the almost cultist figurehead of this new generation, voicing disorientation and despair in a series of nine explosive and high-strung, often surrealist poetry collections. F. P. Jac (b. 1955), a brilliant linguistic equilibrist, protects himself in a poetic universe created around his self as the omniscient center, disrespectfully raiding Danish poetic tradition as well as contemporary slang.

Poetic tradition, in particular the sources of symbolism and early modernism, are rediscovered:

Baudelaire, Mallarmé, and Rimbaud, as well as T. S. Eliot and Ezra Pound (qq.v.), blending with texts often inspired by rock and punk musicians, such as Bob Dylan and David Bowie. This eclectic—or rather postmodernist—approach finds its most talented expression in Bo Green Jensen's (b. 1955) seven-volume cycle of poems, *Rosens veje* (the roads of the rose), completed in 1986. More subdued and reflective are the poems of Søren Ulrik Thomsen (b. 1956), notably in collections from *City Slang* (1982; title in English) to *Nye digte* (1987; new poems), analyzing the creative process and the role of the poem as the point of departure for experiencing present life. The poetry of Pia Tafdrup (q.v.) is characterized by the same lucidity and speculative sophistication. Since her debut in 1981 and reaching a highpoint with *Hvid feber* (1986; white fever), she has continuously attempted to merge her experiences of the erotic and of nature and her awareness of the necessity both to dream and to live this life, into images of rhythmic and sensual beauty.

Contemporary Danish literature is both dynamic and innovative. The topics seem endless: physical and spiritual love, euphoric experiences and Apocalypse, the stony wilderness of the metropolis, provincial idylls and distant exotic places and mythical utopias.

BIBLIOGRAPHY: Rossel, S. H., *A History of Scandinavian Literature, 1870–1980* (1982); Wamberg, B., ed., *Out of Denmark* (1985); Zuck, V., ed., *Dictionary of Scandinavian Literature* (1990); Rossel, S. H., *A History of Danish Literature* (1992)

SVEN HAKON ROSSEL

DARWĪSH, Mahmūd

Palestinian poet, b. 13 Mar. 1941, Birwa, Palestine (now Israel)

D. is by far the best-known Palestinian poet alive. He was born in Birwa, a small village near Acre. During the war of 1948, his family, like so many others, fled the advancing Israeli army to Lebanon, where they lived as refugees for one year. When they "infiltrated" back into Israel, Birwa was no longer in existence. It had been razed by the Israeli army, and a new Jewish settlement stood on its ruins. The family relocated to another Arab village where D. grew up as an "internal" refugee. These traumatic childhood experiences of uprootedness and dislocation left an indelible mark on the poet's nascent consciousness.

By way of formal education, D. attended only elementary and secondary Arab schools in Galilee. After graduating from secondary school, he moved to Haifa to work in journalism. In 1961 he joined the Israeli Communist Party and remained active in its ranks until his permanent departure from Israel in 1971. Since then he has led a somewhat nomadic life, moving from one to another of the following capitals: Cairo, Beirut, London, Paris, and Tunis. He has been active in Palestinian national politics and has occupied several important positions in the cultural apparatus of the Palestine Liberation Organization. Currently, he is a member of the PLO's Executive Committee and chief editor of the Palestinian literary and cultural periodical *al-Karmel,* which is published in Nicosia. In 1969 D. was awarded the Lotus Prize by the Union of Afro-Asian Writers.

D. began writing poetry at an early age. His first collection, *'Asāfīr bilā ajniha* (1960; wingless birds), appeared when he was only nineteen. Mostly traditional in form and style, the love lyrics of this collection have a modest artistic value. For this reason the poet disregarded this collection when compiling his collected works, which began to appear in 1973. It was his second collection, *Awrāq al-zaytūn* (1964; olive leaves), that established his reputation and gained him the epithet "poet of the Palestinian resistance," by which he is still widely known in much of the Arab world.

In general, it is possible to distinguish three distinct phases in D.'s poetry. The first phase spans the period before his departure from Israel in 1971, the second from 1971 to 1982, and the third from 1982 to the present. Thematically, D.'s poetry deals with little else besides the loss of Palestine. In fact, it is so steeped in Palestinian affairs that some knowledge of Palestinian history may be necessary for the proper appreciation of the poetry. But, while D.'s preoccupation with Palestinian concerns has remained constant, his treatment of these concerns has varied and evolved considerably through the years.

Like all the poems of the first phase, the poems of *Awrāq al-zaytūn* deal with two general topics: love and politics. The political poems stand out for their powerful polemics and fiercely defiant tone. Against Zionist claims on Palestine, they affirm the indissoluble historical bond between Palestinians and their land. A primary objective of these poems is precisely this: to strengthen the resolve of the Palestinian peasants in resisting Israeli attempts to dislodge them from their ancestral land. All artistic and aesthetic considerations are strictly subordinated here to this political imperative. Hence the simple form and direct style of these poems. D.'s poetic credo of this phase, contained in his poem "'An al-shi'r" (1964; "On Poetry," 1980), celebrates clarity as the highest virtue of poetry.

This combination of political and rhetorical qualities found a responsive chord in the Arab reading public. Some of D.'s best-known patriotic poems, such as "Bitāqat huwiyyah" (1964; "Identity Card," 1970) date from this early phase and are included in this collection. And although D. himself has long since outgrown the direct declamatory style of these poems and refuses to read them in public, most Arab readers know him for little else.

The image of an open wound is the dominant metaphor for Palestine in D.'s poetry. The pained awareness of loss and injury that pervades these poems, however, is largely alleviated by two positive factors that give D.'s poetry during this phase an optimistic outlook. The first factor is the moral rightness of the Palestinian cause. The second is the assumed solidarity of national liberation movements with the Palestinian people. Being a Marxist, D. assumed the inevitable success of the struggle for national liberation throughout the world, including Palestine. Incidentally, Palestine, in the poems of this phase, is exclusively identified with the peasantry and the working class.

The love poems of *Awrāq al-zaytūn* foreshadow the eventual transformation of the beloved female into the beloved homeland that is characteristic of D.'s subsequent poetry. The transformation appears complete in D.'s next collection, *'Āshiq min filastīn* (1966; *A Lover from Palestine,* 1970). This intimate love relationship between poet and land grows steadily more intense until it reaches the fervor of mystical union in D.'s later poems.

D.'s encounter with the reality of the Arab world proved disillusioning and occasioned a withdrawal from certainty and an inward turn in his poetry. The common things of daily life in the homeland, such as the faces of family and friends and the topography of the landscape, become the object of poetic meditation in exile. A gripping note of nostalgia to Galilee, Haifa, Mount Carmel, and the coast of Palestine reverberates through the poems of the second phase. D.'s first collection in exile, *Uhibbuki aw lā uhibbuki* (1972; I love you, I love you not), suggests the direction and scope of the change in his poetry. Away from the homeland, it becomes a constant struggle to retain intact the details of its identifying characteristics. The words picture, memory, and dream join those of wound and death as key terms in D.'s poetic diction. In the working of dream and memory the body of the beloved female blends imperceptibly with that of the homeland until they become virtually indistinguishable.

While the introspective turn imparts to D.'s poetry a more personal, almost confessional quality, his progressively more frequent appeal to the prophetic tradition of the three great monotheistic religions imparts to it a universal dimension. The cross, crucifixion, and especially wounds and sac-

ROBERTSON DAVIES

ARIEL DORFMAN

SERGEY DOVLATOV

UMBERTO ECO

rificial death are permanent motifs (tropes) in D.'s poetry. D. also makes extensive use of the Old Testament prophets, notably Isaiah and Jeremiah on whom he frequently calls to condemn Israel's acts of injustice against the Palestinians. *Uhibbuki aw lā uhibbuki* begins with seventeen psalms to Palestine. In tone and style D.'s moving lamentations echo those of the Old Testament which D., being bilingual in Arabic and Hebrew, is able to read in the original.

D.'s poetic output has continued unabated during the third phase. Two important poems he wrote after the 1982 Israeli invasion of Lebanon, however, have already left a strong mark on this phase. Both *Qasīdat Bayrūt* (1982; ode to Beirut) and *Madīh al-zill al-'ālī* (1983; a eulogy for the tall shadow) are narrative poems of substantial length. The subject of both is the heroic Palestinian resistance to the Israeli siege of Beirut during the summer of 1982. Following the tradition of the classical Arab poets, D. abandons the subjective voice of the lyricist and sings the collective heroics of his people in the plural voice. Stanzaic in form, both poems mark a return to a simpler, more direct, and clearer style than the poems of the second phase. Of the two poems, the second is considerably longer and more accomplished artistically. It introduces into modern Arabic poetry the city (Beirut) and the sea (Mediterranean) as objects of sustained poetic interest. But it also continues D.'s cultivation of the prophetic voice. Here, D. assumes the voice of the Prophet of Islam, Muhammad, to chastise the Arab régimes for abandoning the Palestinians and the Lebanese to the Israeli onslaught. D.'s harshest invectives are reserved for the oil-rich Arab monarchies. No other modern Arab poet has used the language, style, and motifs of the Koran and the prophetic tradition as effectively as does D. in this poem.

FURTHER WORKS: *Ākhir al-layl* (1967); *Yawmiyyāt jurh filastīnī* (1969); *al-'Asāfīr tamūt fī al-jalīl* (1970); *Muhāwalah raqm 7* (1974); *Tilka sūratuhā wa-hādhā intihār al-'āshiq* (1975); *Ahmad al-za'tar* (1976); *A'rās* (1977); *Hiya ughniyah* (1986); *Dhākirah li-al-nisyān* (1986); *Fī wasf hālatinā* (1987). FURTHER VOLUMES IN ENGLISH: *Selected Poems* (1973); *The Music of Human Flesh* (1980); *Victims of a Map* (1984, with Samīh al-Qāsim and Adonis); *Sand and Other Poems* (1986)

BIBLIOGRAPHY: Al-Messiri, A. W., and K. Boullata, Introduction to *A Lover from Palestine* (1970), 5–11; Johnson-Davies, D., Introduction to *The Music of Human Flesh* (1980), 7–19; Bennani, B., "Translating Arabic Poetry: An Interpretive, Intertextual Approach," in Rose, M. G., ed., *Translation Spectrum: Essays in Theory and Prac-*tice (1981), 135–39; Backmann, P., "Pushkin's Eagle and M. D.'s Nest," in al-Qadi, W., ed., *Studia Arabica et Islamica* (1981), 27–37; "Three Poems," *IonC,* 13, 4 (Aug. 1984), 30–32; McBeath, N., "On the Translation of Poetry: Further Comments," *The Linguist,* 25, 2 (1986), 74–76

MUHAMMAD SIDDIQ

DAS, Jibanananda

Indian poet (writing in Bengali), b. 18 Feb. 1899, Barisal, British India (now Bangladesh); d. 22 Oct. 1954, Calcutta

D. grew up in Barisal, a small town on the northeastern edge of the Sundarban jungle, some fifty miles inland from the Bay of Bengal. He received his education first at home from his parents, later in a local school and college, and then in Calcutta, earning his M.A. in English at Calcutta University. D. taught English literature at various colleges in Calcutta, Delhi, and Barisal. A shy person, he avoided politics and social interactions generally, acquiring early on the epithet of the "most alone of poets." In 1946, anticipating the independence of the subcontinent from Britain the following year with the concomitant partition of Bengal into East Pakistan and the province of West Bengal in India, D. left his beloved ancestral home for good and moved with his family to what was for him the inimical environment of big-city Calcutta.

D.'s initial book was of little consequence. His second volume, *Dūsara pāndulipi* (1936; gray manuscripts), contains the exotic West-Asian imagery typical of D.'s earlier writings, as well as two features that can be said to be his poetic signature: deep involvement in his natural surroundings and interaction with a fantasized, idealized woman who is at times solace incarnate and at other times the cause of his great psychological distress. "Kyāmpe" (1932; "In Camp," 1962) from this collection speaks with revulsion of a deer hunt using for decoy a doe in heat, which as a metaphor becomes "that woman" who allures her victim to emotional death.

Between the publication of his first and second books, D. composed—but never published—a series of sonnets posthumously titled *Rūpasī Bāmlā* (1957; *The Beauteous Bengal: Rupasi Bangla,* 1987) in which he luxuriated in the flora and fauna of his subtropical birthplace. Though a song by Rabindranath Tagore (q.v.) became Bangladesh's national anthem, D.'s sonnets epitomized for the Bangladeshi freedom fighters during the independence struggle in 1971 the very essence of their homeland. D.'s third volume, *Banalatā Sena* (1942;

Banalata Sena)—republished twice in his lifetime in expanded editions—was named for his most famous poem, "Banalatā Sena" (1935; "Banalata Sen," 1962) whose eponymous heroine succors the poet-narrator both in this lonely and exhausting life and for the thousands of years his spirit has wandered throughout the Indian subcontinent.

The advent of World War II and the pressure from politically committed fellow writers may have, during the late 1930s and 1940s, nudged D. into looking away from his personalized universe and toward the greater world. His fourth book, *Mahāprthibī* (1944; world at large), included all the poems from the *Banalatā Sena* volume plus a number of lyrics that reflect consternation and sometimes utter confusion about the plight at present, and the future, of humanity—including the powerful "Āta bachara āgera ekadina" (1938; "A Day Eight Years Ago," 1962) in which he tries to fathom the suicide of an acquaintance. D.'s fifth and last volume to contain all new poetry, *Sātati tārāra timira* (1948; darkness of seven stars), reveals a continuation of the befuddlement engendered in him by the war years. The "darkness" mentioned in the title pervades this collection. An expanded *Banalatā Sena,* replete with more poetry from the earlier prewar period, appeared in 1952 to considerable public acclaim. The anthology *Jībanānanda Dāśera śrestha kabitā* (1954; best poems of J. D.) garnered India's first-ever Sahitya Akademi Prize (1955) for Bengali, a national literary award.

Though known primarily as a poet, D. wrote novels and short stories, none of them published during his lifetime, however. The three seemingly complete novels date from the latter half of the 1940s, around the time or just after D. moved permanently to Calcutta, and have noticeable autobiographical elements.

As more and more of D.'s unpublished poetry and prose becomes available, there may be some reevaluation of what are his finest contributions to Bengali literature, but his ranking as a poet is quite likely secure. The majority of critics consider him the second most important Bengali poet of the century, second only to Tagore. D.'s language could not be imitated by subsequent poets, for as Buddhadeva Bose (1908–1974)—D.'s first, initially most supportive, and, to date, most enduring critic—stated, D. created a language all his own, a mix of high style and colloquial, of indigenous and foreign words. D.'s example, while inimitable, emboldened others. His sensuous depiction of the Bengal countryside may never be surpassed. His poetry from the 1940s and 1950s, more obtuse than his earlier work, has yet to be comprehended thoroughly and appreciated. It is D.'s poetry of

the late 1920s and the 1930s upon which his reputation was made and still stands.

FURTHER WORKS: *Jharā pālaka* (1927); *Kabitāra kathā* (1956); *Belā abelā kālabelā* (1961); *Jībanānanda Dāśera śrestha kabitā* (1970, Dhaka edition); *Jībanānanda Dāśera kābyagrantha* (2 vols., 1970–1971); *Jībanānanda Dāśera galpa* (1972); *Mālyabāna* (1973); *Sudarśanā* (1973); *Sutīrtha* (1977); *Manabihangama* (1979); *Āloprthibī* (1982); *Jībanānanda Dāśera kābya sambhāra* (1982); *Samālocanā samagra* (1983); *Jībanānanda samagra* (1985); *Jalāpaihāti* (1985); *Jībanānanda Dāśera premera kabitā* (n.d.). FURTHER VOLUME IN ENGLISH: *Banalata Sen: Poems* (1962)

BIBLIOGRAPHY: Bose, B., *An Acre of Green Grass* (1948), 45–47, 56–57; Lago, M. M., and T. Gupta, "Pattern in the Imagery of J. D.," *JASt,* 24, 4 (1965), 637–44; Chakravarty, J., "The Spectrum of Modern Bengali Poetry," *Bengali Literature* (May 1967), 9–19; Cevet, D., "A Note on Bengali Poetry," *Bengali Literature* (Winter 1969), 34–45; Bose, A., "J. D.," in Ghose, N., ed., *Studies in Modern Bengali Poetry* (1968), 21–41; Dasgupta, C., *J. D.* (1972); Mukherjee, D., "J.—A World of New Sensibility," *IndL,* 20, 5 (1977), 97–100; Dimock, E. C., Jr., "Reflections on Two Poems by J. D.," *The Sound of Silent Guns and Other Essays* (1989), 33–51; Seely, C. B., *A Poet Apart: A Literary Biography of the Bengali Poet J. D. (1899–1954)* (1990)

CLINTON B. SEELY

DAVIES, Robertson

Canadian dramatist, novelist, and critic. b. 28 Aug. 1913, Thamesville, Ontario

D. is one of Canada's most prominent novelists, having enjoyed an international reputation since the late 1940s. His work weds an acute sense of Ontario as a point of origin with a striving to reach levels of culture and artistic recognition not possible within the narrow provincial and national confines that characterized the country well into the 1950s. Born in southwestern Ontario, he also lived in Renfrew and Kingston before attending Upper Canada College in Toronto. His movements followed the growing success of his father, Rupert Davies (later Sir Rupert), in the newspaper (also radio and television) business. D.'s education continued at Queen's University, then at Oxford, where he completed his doctorate in 1938. Returning to Canada after working briefly with Tyrone Guthrie's Old Vic Company, D. has lived mostly in Toronto and Peterborough. In the latter city he edited his father's paper, the *Peterborough Examiner,* for nearly twenty years before being appointed the founding Master of Massey College at the University of Toronto in 1961. He retired in 1987.

D.'s first published work was his Oxford dissertation *Shakespeare's Boy Actors* (1939). It reflects his deep interest in theater, nurtured by his parents and sought out at every opportunity during his youth. That interest has continued in collections celebrating Canada's Stratford Festival (1953–1955), his involvement in the *Revels History of Drama in English* (Vol. 6), and his *The Well-Tempered Critic* (1981). His great ambition was to be a dramatist, in particular by perpetuating the kind of rich theatrical experience he associated with Henry Irving and the English touring companies he saw in Canada. Those ambitions were further nurtured at Oxford and under Guthrie.

Married and back in Canada during the war, he threw himself into playwriting. The most ambitious of these works he sent back to England, without result. He also wrote one-act plays for amateur companies participating in the Dominion Drama Festival. While he wrote several three-act plays exploring the effects of Canada upon the tastes and aspirations of people of large vision, *At My Heart's Core* (1950) and *Fortune, My Foe* (1949), his most fertile relation was with the Crest Theatre (Toronto), which produced two full-length plays, *A Jig for the Gypsy* (1954) and *Hunting Stuart* (1972) in 1954 and 1955. Another, *Love and Libel,* made it briefly to Broadway in 1960. Despite ongoing frustrations with the theater, D. has continued to write plays, mostly on request. His most notable later effort, *Question Time* (1975), uses the occasion of the arctic plane crash of a prime minister to construct a Jungian reading of the problems of the Canadian psyche.

The kind of writer D. became owed much to his early circumstances. First there was the problem of coming to grips with the powerful personalities of his parents and the alien rough-and-ready world of rural Ontario. Secondly he had to find room in the workaday world of journalism to develop his creative skills even as he had to struggle to find an audience for his plays in a country only marginally interested in theater. Not surprisingly, two other voices emerged in the 1940s: one the urbane and knowledgeable voice of D. as professional book reviewer and cultural commentator; the other the discursive gadfly voice of his comical alter ego Samuel Marchbanks, whose curmudgeonly observations on daily life became a staple of Saturday's *Examiner* and a syndicated column. The quality of D.'s reviews led Alfred Knopf to ask him to compile a collection, *A Voice from the Attic* (1960), while D. later collected and arranged the Marchbanks "diaries" into three volumes (1947–1967).

In the early 1950s D. began to explore the possibilities of fiction. His first novel, *Tempest-Tost* (1951), dealt with the problems besetting an amateur company that mounts an outdoor Shakespearean production. Brimful of D.'s knowledge of theater and dramaturgy, the book is simultaneously a satiric look at the pretensions and mixed motives of the townsfolk involved. It was followed by *Leaven of Malice* (1954) and *A Mixture of Frailties* (1958), the three together comprising "the Salterton trilogy," after the small university city in which they are mostly set.

The first phase of D.'s career as a novelist owes much to the realist tradition, particularly satirists like Evelyn Waugh and Sinclair Lewis, and his early fascination with Sigmund Freud (qq.v.) and oedipal relationships. Near the center of interest is Solly Bridgetower, a young Canadian with an Oxford degree and theatrical aspirations who lives under the pall of his socially prominent, formidable, and manipulative mother. In presenting the misadventures that follow from a false engagement announcement linking Solly to the daughter of his deceased father's academic enemy, *Leaven of Malice* studies the problems of a small-city newspaper and satirizes Salterton's social order and manners.

With *A Mixture of Frailties,* D. sought to investigate character more deeply. While the plot has a heavily satiric Salterton frame, its concern is the education of a young artist. Monica Gall, a singer of unpromising social background, receives a grant from the Bridgetower trust to study in Europe under the tutelage of a leading conductor, Sir Benedict Domdaniel. Education for Monica amounts to both professional and character training at the hands of several experts. In dramatizing the education of an artist as world-class singer, Davies plays with numerous distinctions between romance and reality, emphasizing the importance of tough-minded teachers and the difficult moral problems that follow from committing oneself above all to art. While flawed in several ways, this is D.'s first novel to focus upon the imperialism of art and to probe the relation of the artist to her roots.

The second of D.'s trilogies deservedly earned him a much larger audience. After a relatively fallow decade, he wrote *Fifth Business* (1970), *The Manticore* (1972), and *World of Wonders* (1975), a.k.a. "the Deptford trilogy," after the southwestern Ontario town where the action begins. *Fifth Business,* which is regarded by many as D.'s finest novel, is the private memoir of Dunstan Ramsay, a bachelor and retired school teacher whose deeper life has involved a career of writing about mythology, saints, and "psychological truth," and a lifelong friendship with one of Canada's most prominent public figures, Boy Staunton. The narrative traces Ramsay's life and interaction with Staunton, his "lifelong friend and enemy" over the six decades leading to Staunton's extraordinary death. At the heart of the book is the aging Ramsay's sense of his own worth, which the world and even those close to him easily overlook. Underpinned by D.'s increasing fascination with Jung, the novel is Ramsay's apologia for his life as "fifth business" in the lives of others and as hero of his own compelling adventure.

Constructed around the question of who killed Boy Staunton, the trilogy becomes explicitly Jungian in *The Manticore*. Seeking to recover from his father's death, David Staunton, a Toronto lawyer, seeks analysis in Switzerland. His treatment is abetted by a tougher form of self-recognition administered by a grotesque Swiss, Liesl Vitzliputzli, who has become Ramsay's close friend. *World of Wonders* recalls the life of a third Deptfordian, Paul Dempster (born prematurely as a result of an "accident" involving Staunton and Ramsay), who has gone on to world fame as the magician Magnus Eisengrim. Very much a celebration of theater, deception, and the links between psychology, religion, and art, the novel brings the relations among the three Deptfordians full circle and explicates Boy's death. At the same time it celebrates the individuated life of the wolfish artist and the hard-nosed wisdom of those who, having been truly tested by life, know themselves and what most matters in human experience.

D.'s third—or "Cornish"—trilogy uses Renfrew (Blairlogie) and Massey College (Plowright College) as its bases. It comprises a still more exhaustive look at the mixed motives of those Canadians driven by higher aspirations, be they scholars, artists, ministers, or students. By means of two narrative voices, *The Rebel Angels* (1981) investigates the world of academia both for its human interest and its serious scholarly purposes. *What's Bred in the Bone* (1985) uses narrating angels to reconstruct the life and death of Blairlogie-born Francis Cornish, an overlooked painter whose facility in creating works that seem to belong to the past raises significant questions about the nature of the creative act. *The Lyre of Orpheus* (1988) returns to the university setting dramatizing an attempt, sponsored by the Cornish Trust, to create and perform an opera begun by Hoffman but left only in note form. D.'s tenth novel, *Murther and Walking Spirits,* appeared in 1991.

As D. has become more confident with the novel, he has become increasingly flamboyant in his use of technique, plot, and character. Always

a storyteller and a keen dispenser of interesting information, he has, however, sought mystery rather than disruption in his techniques. Politically his outlook is conservative, sympathetic to the world of the wealthy and the unabashedly cosmopolitan. Still, his work celebrates distinction of character and record of achievement, whatever its roots. Consistently he has remained a commentator on Canadian life and the uneasy attitude of Canadians to the arts, vigorously defending a life in art or in the pursuit of deeper kinds of understanding as the most worthwhile way to live. He has won many awards and honors in Canada and was the first Canadian to be elected an honorary member (1980) of the American Academy and Institute of Arts and Letters.

FURTHER WORKS: *The Diary of Samuel Marchbanks* (1947); *Overlaid: A Comedy* (1948); *Eros at Breakfast and Other Plays* (1949); *The Table Talk of Samuel Marchbanks* (1949); *Fortune, My Foe* (1949); *At My Heart's Core* (1950); *A Jig for the Gypsy* (1954); *Marchbanks' Almanack* (1967); *Four Favourite Plays* (1968); *Stephen Leacock* (1970); *Hunting Stuart and Other Plays* (1972); *One Half of R. D.: Provocative Pronouncements on a Wide Range of Topics* (1977); *The Enthusiasms of R. D.* (1979); *Brothers in the Black Art* (1981); *High Spirits* (1982); *The Mirror of Nature* (1983); *The Papers of Samuel Marchbanks* (1985)

BIBLIOGRAPHY: McPherson, H., "The Mask of Satire: Character and Symbolic Pattern in R. D.'s Fiction," *CanL,* 4 (Spring 1960), 18–30; Roper, G., "R. D., *Fifth Business* and 'That Old Fantastical Duke of Dark Corners, C. G. Jung,' " *JCF,* 1 (Winter 1972), 33–39; special D. issue, *JCSR,* 12 (Feb. 1977); Grant, J. S., *R. D.* (1978); Lawrence, R. G., and S. L. Macey, eds., *Studies in R. D.'s Deptford Trilogy* (1980); special D. issue, *Canadian Drama,* 7, 2 (1981); Monk, P., *The Smaller Infinity: The Jungian Self in the Novels of R. D.* (1982); Stone-Blackburn, S., *R. D., Playwright: A Search for the Self on the Canadian Stage* (1985); Peterman, M. A., *R. D.* (1986); Cameron, E., ed., *R. D.: An Appreciation* (1991)

MICHAEL A. PETERMAN

The ore of his manufacture is mined from the rocky ground of his homeland; he merely works it his own way. He is pedestrian, meticulous, balanced—very much the Canadian, very much the teacher. He takes the raw materials of his existence, the quaint elements of Southern Ontario, and welds them into a mosaic that glows alive with digression, qualification and illumination. In this regard, the fictional Dunstan Ramsay and the factual R. D. are one. It goes beyond coincidence that they share the same initials, howbeit in reversed order; for reversed order is what *Fifth Business* is about. According to D., Canadians get themselves backwards because they cannot reconcile their reality with their image.

Wilfred Cude, "Miracle and Art in *Fifth Business* or Who the Devil is Liselotee Vitziputzli?" in Elspeth Cameron, ed., *R. D.: An Appreciation* (1981), 117

At the centre of each novel in the Deptford trilogy, then, is a character who strives for the integration of public and private selves that is D.'s ideal. D. takes David Staunton only part way along the journey towards self-knowledge, but Dunstan Ramsay and Magnus Eisengrim are presented as characters who have had considerable success in their pursuit of maturity. Neither character, though, is entirely convincing in that D. is unable to integrate all the complex elements at work in their personalities. Thus, rich ambiguity is replaced by a degree of confusion. This is not to deny, though, that the Deptford trilogy provides considerable insight into some central issues of human personality. D.'s analysis of the ways in which the Persona can overwhelm the rest of the personality is masterly, and through his sometimes certain and sometimes faltering analysis of the development of Dunstan Ramsay, David Staunton and Magnus Eisengrim he increases the reader's awareness of the proper relationship that should exist between public and private selves.

David M. Monaghan, "People in Prominent Positions: A Study of the Public Figure in the Deptford Trilogy," *Studies in R. D.'s Deptford Trilogy* (1980), 55

The very language of his fiction is shaped by his aesthetic of ambivalence, of paradox. Decorum, though, weighs more heavily on language than on imagery, limiting the extent of formal dislocation in D.'s work. Under the highlighting eye of the dialogic imagination, which brings together within the same text the intersecting planes of the French Renaissance, of Marxist Russia and of Calvinist Ontario, a carnivalesque element of D.'s writing emerges. The shifting horizon offered by such a multiplicity of perspectives illuminates the heterogeneity that is a characteristic of R. D.'s fictional world.

Barbara Godard, "Writing Paradox, the Paradox of Writing: R. D.," in Elspeth Cameron, ed., *R. D.: An Appreciation* (1981), 253

The two views—one maintaining D. is a monologist with fixed hierarchical values and the other maintaining D. is a dialogist pitting one authority against others without reaching fixed conclusions—are radically opposed. And our understanding of D.'s ideology depends entirely on which of the two we endorse. If he is a monologist, it follows that his world view is elitist. But, if he is a sophisticated deconstructionist, deliberately using post-modern techniques in a Bakhtinian way, he displays an ideology that recognizes the relativity, and possibly the irrationality, of life.

Elspeth Cameron, Introduction to *R. D.: An Appreciation* (1981), 6

What Carl Jung called the process of "individuation" provides a kind of general goal for many of D.'s characters, but it is individuation of a highly particularized stamp. D.'s later novels are increasingly preoccupied with the distinction between egotism and egoism, between selfishness and enlightened self-interest in men of special prominence, be they intellectuals, artists, or priests. The egoism of the hero figure—and D.'s novels and plays are seldom without heroes who are egoists— dominates his work. It is an egoism that he shows to be hard and harrowingly won. His characters typically have much to battle against. Domineering parents, threatening rivals, culturally imposed attitudes, and debilitating circumstances conspire to constrain native gusto and inhibit healthy selfhood in his sensitive protagonists. Battles rage around them on the social and psychological levels. Browbeating, advantage taking, jockeying for position, and playing upon the weaknesses of others come to seem the normal course of behavior. Inequity of power in a hostile world is everywhere apparent. The vulnerable ego must learn how to survive and to assert its own specialness in its own terms.

Michael Peterman, *R. D.* (1986), Preface

D.'s critical output spans an astonishing range. He "was there" and responding to almost every Canadian literary work of significance in the forties, and he continued to tackle an amazing number (considering his other activities) in succeeding decades. Fiction drew the bulk of his attention, but he also reviewed poetry, criticism, biography, reference works, and humour. Usually he felt it a waste of time to discuss a book he did not like, so his response to those he did review was typically generous. He responded to felicitous style, to effective story-telling, to bright imagination, to strong characterization, and could admire any one of these even in the absence of the others. Although he was positive, however, he did not fail to make distinctions. His reviews are witty and enjoyable in themselves, but they also picked the winners. A list of the books he regarded as significant when they first appeared reads now like the syllabus for a course in Canadian literature.

Judith Skelton Grant, ed., *The Well-Tempered Critic: One Man's View of the Arts and Letters in Canada* (1981), 14

DECONSTRUCTION

Deconstruction, or *la déconstruction,* is, in the first place, a word French philosopher Jacques Derrida (q.v.) has used to translate the German words *Destruktion* and *Abbau* in the writings of Martin Heidegger (1889–1976). His choice of the word demonstrates, among other things, the difficulty of translation in general, not because he holds that there is some untouchable original sense to be preserved, but rather because all meaning occurs as a result of a break in the origin—impulse, idea, word—that is supposed to give rise to it.

"Deconstruction" now has the general sense, in journalistic parlance especially, of "critiquing by dismantling," but in relation to Derrida's work it covers the set of ideas and strategies by means of which he seeks to analyze and displace what he finds to be the metaphysical underpinnings, or "logocentrism," of Western thought. In the terms of Derrida's analysis, Western philosophy, at least since Socrates and Plato, has reasoned and advanced its truth thanks to a series of oppositions—truth/error, man/woman, speech/writing, nature/culture, and so on—where the second term is perceived as a falling away from the first, which therefore assumes priority—anteriority and authority—over it. The now "classic" deconstruction is that of the opposition that, philosophers and common sense have consistently maintained, obtains between speech and writing. Derrida shows, by taking the theoreticians of language at their word, that speech in fact has all the negative characteristics attributed to writing, such as distance or absence, error or ambiguity. He finds the two to be structurally indistinguishable, for although writing functions in the absence of its producer, speech similarly involves a "spacing" that prevents it from operating within any intact contextual confines.

Deconstruction thus aims to modify the model of reasoning that relies on such hierarchical thinking, according to whose logic thought can and should reduce to a single, simple unity—God, truth, the idea, the origin—for that has led to the repression of much in Western culture that has been deemed secondary, derivative, or peripheral. Derrida seeks to challenge the hierarchy by giving prominence to the second, repressed term, but he does so through what he calls "a double writing," developing forms of analysis and types of discourse that will avoid reestablishing the old hierarchy by simply reversing its terms. For in challenging that way of thinking, deconstruction wants to avoid imposing itself as a new single, simple truth. Indeed, for Derrida, tradition condemns us, generally speaking, to the logocentric framework, and in spite of the revolutionary impact of his ideas, he sees any process of change as being, from our perspective, interminable. His own effort of deconstruction involves rereading the texts through which logocentrism expresses itself, from the writings of Plato, *La dissémination* (1972; *Dissemination,* 1982), to those of Sigmund Freud and Jacques Lacan (qq.v.), *La carte postale* (1980; *The Post Card,* 1987), from Nietzsche's views on women, *Éperons* (1978; *Spurs,* 1979), to Speech Act Theory, *Limited Inc.* (1990; first pub. in En-

glish as *Limited Inc.,* 1988), from Kant's discourse on the status of the work of art, *La vérité en peinture* (1978; *The Truth in Painting,* 1987), to discussion of the nuclear deterrent, "No Apocalypse, Not Now" (1984) and the use of the word "apartheid," "Racism's Last Word" (1985). His contention is that Western thinking's will-to-singularity is of necessity impossible to sustain in practice, and he thus develops his analyses starting from the lapses, contradictions, and ambiguities that inevitably arise in a piece of writing. From this point of view deconstruction can be considered not so much a word or a set of strategies even, as a state of affairs; something that occurs, or is, and which thereby shows the paradoxes and difficulties of such central tenets of philosophy (and much else), as existence, the event, and being.

From the late 1960s and early 1970s, Derrida's work gained much exposure in the U.S., and it was taken up in particular by academics in literature departments at various institutions such as Yale, Johns Hopkins, and Cornell. Derrida's presence as a regular visiting faculty member, especially at Yale, led to the establishment of what became known as the Yale School, whose members included the scholars Paul de Man (1919–1983) and J. Hillis Miller (b. 1928). In spite of the often brilliant analyses of literary and philosophical texts that such authors, inspired by Derrida's ideas, produced, it was felt that his ideas had lost their edge in translation and, in their application as a form of literary analysis, amounted to little more than a search for the contradictions or impasses in a text or piece of reasoning.

Although it is true that for some time Derrida was wary of the way in which the term "deconstruction" had taken on the specific sense it gained in literary criticism, and downplayed his own uses of the word, he seemed loath to prescribe what the correct form of deconstruction should be. He was therefore accused more and more of being apolitical and of retreating from the real world into the idealism of the text. That accusation came especially from humanists and social scientists who had been schooled in Marxism, and saw the possibility of its extension in the structuralist movement that Derrida's work had to some extent grown out of. Central to their judgment was the appearance of *Glas* (1974; *Glas,* 1986), a book that was variously described as "vulgar," "diabolical," "corrupting," and "obscurantist," for its playing off of Jean Genet (q.v.) against Hegel and its radicalization of the practice of double writing. Later, a number of published pieces explicitly demonstrated Derrida's concern with political issues. By that time, however, attacks on deconstruction, especially in the U.S., were coming more from the right, which saw it as a dangerous form of skepticism and as an important item on the radical agenda that the children of the 1960s, now tenured professors, were forcing down the throats of the American student population. When it was revealed in the late 1980s that Derrida's most obvious precursor, Heidegger, was more active in Nazi politicking than had previously been thought, and that de Man had published anti-Semitic newspaper articles in Belgium in his youth, deconstruction's detractors of whatever ilk cited such facts as more evidence of the moral and political bankruptcy of its ideas. At this writing books and press articles that mention or discuss deconstruction from those points of view continue to appear, whereas Derrida's work is discovered crossing over into more and more diverse fields.

One way of summing up the philosophical tradition that Derrida deconstructs would be in terms of the opposition between inside and outside. Where does the inside end and the outside begin? What is the status of the threshold or frame? These are questions that philosophy has never stopped asking, mostly by trying to avoid asking them, or by presuming to be able to easily separate itself from the objects—art, literature, science—that it addresses. Literature often functions as the outside of philosophy, something the latter seeks not to be in claiming to represent truth and not fiction, but something that philosophical writing, from references to myth made by Socrates to Jean-Jacques Rousseau's *Confessions* (1782; *The Confessions of Jean-Jacques Rousseau*, 1904), seems both tempted and threatened by. This has led a philosopher like Richard Rorty (b. 1931) to collapse the difference between philosophy and other writing, but for Derrida the relation is more complicated, and many of his texts concentrate on it.

On the other hand, deconstruction is interested in borders and margins in general, contending that the points at which, and the means by which, a domain or discipline attempts to close itself off from what it is not in order to define itself, offer the most productive areas for analysis. Paradoxically, definition is made possible by the same means through which it proves its own impossibility, for the inside depends on the outside for its definition and is thus "infected" by it structurally rather than accidentally.

Relations between inside and outside form the basis of Derrida's work on the visual arts, and have led to the proliferation of deconstruction(s) in the fields of painting, film, architecture, and the law. For such fields, whose practice—works of art, buildings, cases—is held to be clearly distinguishable from its theory, the introduction of deconstruction's ideas has raised some fundamental questions concerning that separation, and, as

is to be expected, deconstruction itself has undergone interesting developments and modifications.

Articles by Derrida on Kant's theory of aesthetic judgment and Heidegger's analysis of Van Gogh were published in book form in 1978 (*La vérité en peinture*) along with analyses of works by two contemporary artists, Valerio Adami (b. 1935) and Gérard Titus-Carmel (b. 1941), who have been inspired by his writings. Those essays provide incisive questioning about the status of the work of art and its relation to what *supports* it, in all senses of that word, as well as idiosyncratic readings that seriously challenge the norms of art criticism. Scholars have tried, in retrospect, to assign the label "deconstructionist" to any number of modern artists, but there is no identifiable school of painters or sculptors who call themselves that. Nor are there such filmmakers, although traditional cross-fertilization between literary studies and film studies in the academy meant that deconstruction, drawing on Derrida's notion of writing and his work on painting, made a relatively early appearance in that field.

It is in architecture and law that deconstruction has made some of its most important inroads. Interest shown in Derrida's work by architects such as Bernard Tschumi (b. 1944) and Peter Eisenman (b. 1932) gave rise to articles by him on their work, and later a collaborative project by Derrida and Eisenman was commissioned by Tschumi. There has been intense debate by architects and others over the foundations of the discipline and the presuppositions, concerning form and function for instance, upon which it is based. For a number of architects, the questioning inherent in Derrida's work has been used in conjunction with a revived interest in the Russian Constructivist movement, such that the word "deconstruction" has been modified to "deconstructivism." In recent years, deconstructivist architecture, or deconstruction in architecture, was the subject of an important exhibition at the Museum of Modern Art in New York and a forum at the Tate Gallery in London. Derrida has said that architecture may be regarded as a testing ground for deconstruction, examining the extent to which the foundations of thinking are tied up with thinking about foundations, that is to say about construction or building in general.

The importance of deconstruction for legal studies arises quite simply from the emphasis Derrida's ideas give to questions of interpretation. Deconstruction is but one form of a general revival of theoretical thinking that draws on a number of those known as poststructuralists (Derrida himself rejects the appellation), and that involves critique of the impartiality and freedom from political, social, or economic bias that is supposed to found the law in a democracy. But the matter comes into sharpest relief in the case of constitutional law, where proponents of the doctrine of "original intent" are challenged by those who advocate an activist judiciary. Since, for deconstruction, meaning only comes about as a result of a break in original intent, there would be no sense in attempting to retrieve an original meaning, such as that intended by the Founding Fathers, that is no longer accessible and cannot be second-guessed. Interpretation of the law, or of any text, necessarily becomes an active process, a form of writing that involves the production of new meanings.

The debate deconstruction has initiated over the operations of meaning, which touch on matters of communication and coding in general, carries over into fields seemingly as far apart as information and computing systems, and immunology and biotechnology. In fact, one way Derrida has suggested deconstruction be approached is in terms of a theory of the virus, a system with a life of its own yet imbedded within our own, difficult to prevent or track yet perhaps providing the basis for a rethinking of the origins of life. The effect of deconstruction is similarly to open language and sense-making processes in general to a whole range of possibilities, exciting yet often threatening, that do not submit to the control systems traditionally in force in Western thought.

BIBLIOGRAPHY: De Man, P., *Blindness and Insight: Essays in the Rhetoric of Contemporary Criticism* (1971); Miller, J. H., "Steven's Rock and Criticism as Cure," *GaR,* 30 (1976), 5–33, 330–48; Rorty, R., "Philosophy As a Kind of Writing: An Essay on Derrida," *NLH,* 10 (1978), 141–60; Bloom, H., et al., *Deconstruction and Criticism* (1979); Ropars-Wuilleumier, M. -C., *Le texte divisé* (1981); Culler, J., *On Deconstruction: Theory and Criticism after Structuralism* (1982); Norris, C., *Deconstruction: Theory and Practice* (1982); Ryan, M., *Marxism and Deconstruction* (1982); Arac, J., et al., eds., *The Yale Critics: Deconstruction in America* (1983); Krupnick, M., ed., *Displacement: Derrida and After* (1983); Harvey, I. E., *Derrida and the Economy of Difference* (1986); Llewelyn, J., *Derrida on the Threshold of Sense* (1986); Melville, S., *Philosophy beside Itself: On Deconstruction and Modernism* (1986); Sallis, J., ed., *Deconstruction and Philosophy: The Texts of Jacques Derrida* (1987); Weber, S., *Institution and Interpretation* (1987); Brunette, P., and D. Wills, *Screen/Play: Derrida and Film Theory* (1989); Papadakis, A., C. Cooke, and A. Benjamin, eds., *Deconstruction: Omnibus Volume* (1989); Rapaport, H., *Heidegger and Derrida: Reflections on Time and Language* (1989); special Deconstruction issue, *Cardozo Law Review,* 11, 5–6 (1990)

DAVID WILLS

DELILLO, Don

American novelist, b. 20 Nov. 1937, New York, N.Y.

D. is a novelist of considerable satiric power, but one who pictures personal identities and relationships within an encompassing vision of social power that is by turns paranoid, up-to-date, manic, rootless, and obsessive. Raised as a Roman Catholic, D. attended Fordham University in New York City, and now resides in Westchester County, N.Y. His critical reception has been slow to gather force, though he won the American Book Award in 1985, and his novel on the John F. Kennedy assassination, *Libra* (1988), was a main selection of the Book-of-the-Month Club, and was for a few weeks on the best-seller lists. He is a novelist who bears some resemblance to Saul Bellow and Norman Mailer (qq.v.) in that he works in modes and genres that can appeal to both popular and academic audiences, and yet he generally spurns the spotlight of the media that often shines on (and shadows) successful novelists in America.

D. began as a novelist with a book called *Americana* (1971), but it was in his second novel, *End Zone* (1972), that his ability to conjoin popular subject matter with formal inventiveness was clearly displayed. Football becomes not only a game described with a phenomenological complexity, it is depicted as both national ritual and neurosis, even to the point that death and other cosmic questions seem natural extensions of the reflections that surround its power. The tour de force of the book is a description of a key game from the point of view of one of the players; here D. overturns the normal expectations of chronology and narrative pattern in a language that owes more to James Joyce (q.v.) than to sports journalism.

D. continued his immersion in popular culture with *Great Jones Street* (1973), about a rock-music star who has withdrawn from the pressures of publicity and contemporary mores. Turning to the genre of science fiction, D. created in *Ratner's Star* (1976) a truly paranoid vision of the social forms that have been variously labeled as the information society, the postindustrial age, and the totally administered society. Again the novel's main figure is both seer and victim, perceptive analyst and passive witness to the energies of an organized scheme that defies placement or full discovery.

Players (1977) and *Running Dog* (1978) are novels imbued with sinister plot elements, shadowy characters, and a thoroughly paranoid atmosphere. *The Names* (1982) centers on a cult and a serial murder plot, both of which are modeled on current events; D. clearly uses the newspaper and other information media for material even as he explores their corrosive effects on our sense of social stability and "normal" personality types. These three novels further established D. as a very flexible stylist. *Players,* for example, contained superb dialogue written with the surest of ears for how people really converse.

White Noise (1985) is perhaps D.'s most uninhibitedly satiric work, dealing as it does with an "airborne toxic event" (the widespread emission of a dangerous gas) and something called a program in Hitler studies. Few American novels have so thoroughly captured the hilarity and the terror of our cultural detritus. But with *Libra* D.'s fiction finally attracted the sort of widespread attention that is often the obsession and the bane of his characters. Many conservative reviewers and columnists, such as George Will, saw the novel as suggesting that America is a country dominated by, or at least represented by, conspiratorial psychopathic killers. Will said, for example, that D. has created "yet another exercise [that] blam[es] America for Oswald's act of derangement." With *Mao* (1991), D. continued to explore the values and conundrums of a mass society that is both fascinated and befuddled by the images and violence that it produces.

One of the central questions that bedevils readers of D.'s fiction is whether it critically questions the paranoia that dominated American society in the postwar era or whether it embodies (and even exults in) that paranoia. As a result of his skill at reworking popular genres, and his fascination with the apparently superficial aspects of modern life—and its semantic systems from brand names and media images to bureaucratic doublespeak—D. is a novelist of potentially wide appeal. But because of his acute intelligence and his awareness of complex thought, from systems theory to postmodern philosophy and cultural criticism, he can also be read as an art novelist in the tradition of high skepticism. In this case his predecessors are not only Joyce and Mailer, but also Flaubert and Franz Kafka (q.v.).

BIBLIOGRAPHY: Bryson, N., "City of Dis: The Fiction of D. D.," *Granta,* 2 (1980), 145–57; Nadeau, R., *Readings from the New Book on Nature: Physics and Metaphysics in the Modern Novel* (1981), 161–81; LeClair, T., *In the Loop: D. D. and the Systems Novel* (1987); DeCurtis, A., "Matters of Fact and Fiction," *Rolling Stone,* 17 Nov. 1988; Lentricchia, F., ed., *Introducing D. D.* (1991)

CHARLES MOLESWORTH

DENEVI, Marco

Argentine novelist, short-story writer, and dramatist, b. 12 May 1922, Sáenz Peña

D. was born in the Buenos Aires suburb of Sáenz Peña and there spent most of his adult years. Reflective by nature, he became an omnivorous reader and enjoyed the benefits of a tranquil, sheltered childhood and adolescence. He earned a degree in law but chose not to go into legal practice, accepting instead a position as legal consultant with the Argentine National Postal Savings Bank in Buenos Aires. This was the only job he ever held. It was in 1968, with his literary reputation then firmly established, that he decided to resign his post and undertake writing full time—a most uncommon determination for a Latin American writer. Indeed, in both commitment and dedication D.'s has been an exemplary literary career.

His maiden effort, a novel entitled *Rosaura a las diez* (1955; *Rosa at Ten O'Clock,* 1964), won the prestigious Kraft Prize for a new work by an Argentine author. The award probably surprised the contest judges as much as D., since until then he had never written a single word for publication. An extraordinarily suspenseful and engaging narrative, the novel relates from multiple perspectives the circumstances leading up to the murder of a young woman in a dingy Buenos Aires hotel room. It became an immediate best-seller and has proven to be one of the most popular works of Argentine fiction of this century.

Following the performance and publication of a play, *Los expedientes* (1957; the dossiers), dealing with the dehumanizing effects of a sprawling bureaucracy, D. entered another fiction competition. Chosen from over 3,000 manuscripts submitted from all over Spanish America, D.'s novelette, *Ceremonia secreta* (1960; *Secret Ceremony,* 1961) won first prize in the contest sponsored by the Spanish-language edition of *Life* magazine. Less colloquial, more poetic and intense in style than *Rosaura a las diez,* it nonetheless recounted once more a parable of haunting loneliness.

In the decade following the publication of *Rosaura a las diez,* D. wrote a number of short stories and began to accumulate scores of brief, humorous, and ironic sketches that dealt in a satirical way with the commonplaces of literature and history. These sketches were collected under the apt title *Falsificaciones* (1966; falsifications)

171

and revealed a reserved, sophistic, and playful side to D.'s character that stood in contrast, for example, to the mood of his novelette of the same year, *Un pequeño café* (1966; a small café). The latter, linked in theme and treatment to D.'s earlier spellbinding narratives, tells the story of a lonely, resentful government employee, smothered by the massive bureaucracy in which he toils, who is swept up into a heady adventure involving love, deception, and power. The longer stories of this period were collected in *El emperador de la China y otros cuentos* (1970; the emperor of China and other tales) and *Parque de diversiones* (1970; amusement park). Generally more realistic than the "falsificaciones," these stories demonstrate D.'s ability to observe and dramatize aspects of contemporary life in Buenos Aires and to communicate them in an elegant, entrancing prose style that still remains persuasively colloquial.

During the 1970s, D. produced a novel, *Los asesinos de los días de fiesta* (1972; the holiday murderers), and a total of six collections of short stories and sketches. For the last of these, *Parque de diversiones II* (1979; amusement park II), another abundant miscellany, he prepared this seemingly apologetic statement: "Incapable of articulating my critical ideas (concerning the world we live in) as an essayist might do, I fall back on the only resources at my disposal: the literary (or supposedly dramatic) confection, the minitale, the aphorism." *Los asesinos de los días de fiesta* came to represent for him a failure to deal effectively with his subject—a family of amoral brothers and sisters who invade and occupy a murky mansion in a suburb of Buenos Aires—and eighteen years later he would extensively revise and rewrite it under the title *Música de amor perdido* (1990; music of lost love).

In the 1980s D. changed his tone and his focus. In *Amarinta, o el poder* (1982; Amarinta, or the power) he offered his frankest and most personal work, a book that he dedicated to the memory of his mother and in which he included several sensitive autobiographical pieces. There is little impersonal artifice here, and an uncharacteristic sense of nostalgia invades each page.

Beginning in 1981, D. wrote a long series of moralistic and didactic essays for the Buenos Aires newspaper *La Nación* in which he took the Argentine people to task for the deplorable state in which the country found itself. For a writer who had always avoided the limelight, belonged to no writers organizations, and who zealously protected his personal life, these heatedly controversial columns constituted a huge step. The years of Perón's return to Argentina, his death, the presidency of his wife, Isabel, the "dirty war," the military coups, and the Faulkland Islands disaster encom-

passed a period when many prominent voices in Argentina remained silent. D. was not to be counted among them.

D.'s three novels of the 1980s, *Manuel de historia* (1985; Manuel of history), *Enciclopedia secreta de una familia argentina* (1987; secret encyclopedia of an Argentine family), and *La república de Trapalanda* (1989; the republic of Trapalanda), all deal directly with contemporary Argentine experience and can be seen as unmistakably admonitory in intent.

D. has come a long way from his family's peaceful garden in Sáenz Peña. Art and morality have eventually found in him an exemplary and eloquent spokesman. His contributions to both the literature and the civic perception of his country are unique and incalculable.

FURTHER WORKS: *Ceremonia secreta y otros cuentos* (1965); *Falsificaciones* (2nd ed., 1969); *Hierba del cielo* (1973); *Antología precoz* (1973); *Salón de lectura* (1974); *Los locos y los cuerdos* (1975); *Reunión de desaparecidos* (1977); *Robotobor* (1980); *Obras completas* (6 vols., 1980–1989); *Páginas de M. D., seleccionadas por el autor* (1983)

BIBLIOGRAPHY: Yates, D. A., "M. D.: An Argentine Anomaly," *Kentucky Foreign Language Quarterly*, 9, 3 (1962), 162–67; Yates, D. A., Introduction to *Ceremonia secreta y otros cuentos* (1965), 1–4; Gyurko, L., "Romantic Illusion in D.'s *Rosaura a las diez*," *IBERO*, 3 (1971), 357–73; Yates, D. A., "Un acercamiento a M. D.," in Pupo-Walker, E., ed., *El cuento hispanoamericano ante la crítica* (1973), 223–34; Revel Grove, I., *La realidad calidoscópica de la obra de M. D.* (1974); Feeny, T., "The Influence of Wilkie Collins's *The Moonstone* on M. D.'s *Rosaura a las diez*," *RLMC*, 31 (1978), 225–29; Yates, D. A., "M. D.," in Solé, C. A., ed., *Latin American Writers* (1989), Vol. 3, 1265–69

DONALD A. YATES

DEPESTRE, René

Haitian poet and novelist (writing in French), b. 29 Aug. 1926, Jacmel

Known for using literature as a tool of liberation, D. is considered a leader of the radical or Marxist critique of Négritude (q.v.). Coming of age during World War II, D. was influenced by Jacques Roumain (q.v.) and the surrealist literary movement. As a student in Port-au-Prince, he published his first book, *Étincelles* (1945; sparks), which gave him national fame and the financial means to start a literary-political journal, *La Ruche*. Its subsequent banning set off a youth revolt that helped overthrow the dictatorial regime. D.'s militancy led to a short prison term, followed by a wandering life of exile, first in Paris and later in various Third World countries. During this time, he published a second collection of poems, *Gerbe de sang* (1946; spurt of blood). He was deported in 1950, but he continued his political writing, publishing *Végétations de clarté* (1951; vegetations of light) and *Traduit du grand large* (1952; translated from the high seas), which he subtitled "Poem of My Enchanted Land." He returned to Haiti in 1957, where his refusal to collaborate with the Duvalier régime forced him to leave for Cuba in 1959. D.'s reputation earned him an invitation from Che Guevara to play an important role in the development of the Cuban publishing house *Casa de las Américas*. While in Cuba, D. also participated in Creole radio programs broadcast to Haiti.

D.'s most important poetic works were written in Cuba, and they reflect the optimism of the early days of the revolution: *Journal d'un animal marin* (1964; journal of a marine animal), *Un arc-en-ciel pour l'occident chrétien* (1967; *A Rainbow for the Christian West*, 1972), and *Cantata de octubre a la vida y a muerte del Comandante Ernesto che Guevara* (1968; October cantata on the life and death of comandante Ernesto Che Guevara). His theoretical work, *Por la revolución por la poesía* (1968; for revolution for poetry), consolidated a theory of Third World *littérature engagée*. In the 1970s he began to be more active in prose than poetry, publishing a volume of short stories, *Alléluia pour une femme-jardin* (1973; hallelujah for a woman-garden). His first novel, *El palo ensebado* (*Festival of the Greasy Pole*, 1990), was published in 1975. The poems of *Poète à Cuba* (1976; poet in Cuba) mark an explosive culmination of his revolutionary poetry and record his alienation from communist Cuba, which he left in 1978 for Paris and a job with UNESCO. Two works published in 1980 signify the end of D.'s militancy: *Bonjour et adieu à la négritude* (hello and good-bye to Négritude) and *En état de poésie* (in the state of poetry). In 1986 D. retired to a small town in the south of France. His *Hadriana dans tous mes rêves* (1988; Hadriana in all my dreams) won the Renaudot Prize (1988). In 1990 he reused the title *Journal d'un animal marin* for a volume of selected poems.

Un arc-en-ciel pour l'occident chrétien marshals the voodoo gods of Haiti and black heroes from around the world in a humorous literary assault on imperialist America. D. dramatizes the plight of the "Wretched of the Earth" in this mythic epic made up of a number of shorter poems, each devoted to a *loa* (god) or hero. D. admits that the agrarian gods are powerless against the nuclear "monsters" of the U.S., but uses the heroism of Patrice Lumumba, Malcolm X, and Charlemagne Peralte, the martyred Haitian leader, to rally resistance among the oppressed. *Por la revolución por la poesía* defines the responsibilities of the Third World writer in two essays, then explores particular case studies.

Poète à Cuba contrasts the healthy optimism of poets from the new countries of the world with the decadence of European writers, sketching a vision of innocence and wholeness rooted in community and harmony derived from the early days of the Cuban revolution. He sees Eros as an important factor in revolution and dramatizes autobiographical scenes, playing them against historical revolutionary panoramas. *Hadriana dans tous mes rêves* is a tongue-in-cheek use of realism to study the causes of the current stagnation in Haiti. D. presents the planned marriage of Hadriana as an allegory of a Utopian Haiti. This marriage would be the synthesis of Haitian national dichotomies: black versus mulatto, Creole versus French, Catholic versus voodoo, peasant versus urban. But the reconciliation is dashed by the zombification of the bride, just as Duvalier's domination destroyed the unity achieved during the American occupation.

FURTHER WORKS: *Minerai noir* (1956); *Trente ans de pouvoir noir en Haiti* (1976); *Le mât de Cocagne* (French version of *El palo ensebado* with major changes, 1979); *Eros dans un train chinois* (1990)

BIBLIOGRAPHY: Warner, K., "R. D.: The Not So Terrible 'Enfant Terrible,'" *BlackI*, 3 (1974), 46–54; Dayan, J., Introduction to *A Rainbow for the Christian West* (1977); Wylie, H., "R. D. Speaks of Négritude, Cuba & Communist Eros," *The GAR*, 33 (Feb. 1979), 14–21; Cailler, B., "L'efficacité poétique du vaudou dans *Un arc-en-ciel pour l'occident chrétien* de R. D.," *FR*, 53 (Oct. 1979), 47–59; Jones, B., "Comrade Eros: Erotic Vein in the Writing of R. D.," *CarQ*, 27, 4 (Dec. 1981), 21–30; Wylie, H., "Creative Exile: Dennis Brutus and R. D.," in Parker, C. A., et al., eds., *When the Drumbeat Changes* (1981), 279–93; Wylie, H., "Négritude and Beyond," in Anyidoho, K., et al., eds., *Interdisciplinary Dimensions of African Literature* (1985), 43–51; Dayan, J., "Hallelujah for a Garden-Woman: The Caribbean Adam and His Pretext," *FR*, 59 (Mar. 1986), 581–95; Couffon, C., *R. D.* (1986)

HAL WYLIE

DERESSA, Solomon

Ethiopian poet, journalist, and translator (writing in Amharic, English, and French), b. 14 July 1937, western Wollega

Born in the heart of Oromo country in the rugged mountains of Wollega during the five-year Italian occupation of Ethiopia, D. attended school and university in Addis Ababa. At the university he studied English literature and philosophy. Heavily influenced by his grandfather, an oral historian, D., as a young boy, fell in love with Ethiopian folk poetry and the Azmari (minstrel) tradition. During a five-year sojourn in Europe he pursued a law degree and participated in the cultural life of the African diaspora in Paris. In 1965–1966 he worked as a translator and reporter for the United Nations Radio Service in New York.

Ethiopian poetry in Amharic is heavily dominated by the Qene (classical poetry). The literati of the Coptic Church who take pride in their pedigree by quoting from Ge'ez (an old Ethiopic language) are the saint guardians of classical poetry. D.'s early interest in the folk poetry made him realize the potential inherent in Ethiopian poetic tradition. Yet he could not agree with the prosodic rigidity of classical poetry. *Li'jnett* (1970; youth) is a challenge to classical poets. The subtitle is *Forty and a Half,* an allusion to the forty-four Tabots (covenant of infinite holiness). The poet seems to suggest that forty and a half could equally be as sacred, since the number is only a socially agreed-upon convention. Naturally, the Church was up in arms. It saw the poems as impudent, destructive, and iconoclastic. D. *was* certainly an iconoclast. In one of the poems, he exhorts a poet friend to stop being reverent of fathers so that "you yourself" will become a father.

The clergy was not the only institution that was offended. Traditional poets were also not pleased with the poems, not so much for their profanity as for their stylistic transgressions. In one poem, D. gives a new rendition to a popular song by truck drivers traveling the treacherous road between Mossawa and Addis Ababa. The traditionalists were offended by the poeticization of what they deemed doggerel. Across the border in Somalia, a new love poetry called Balwo gave the clergy and the classical poets a temporary respite from their war of words, so that they could jointly fight the new genre. To the priest, the new form smacked of profanity; to the classical poet, it was a degenerate form. Yet D. and his counterparts in Somalia continued to write poetry that defied the constraints of the traditional form.

D.'s Amharic poems, aside from their symbolic innocence, accomplish three purposes. First, by experimenting with language, the poet challenges the tradition by throwing the gauntlet. Secondly, he provides an alternative to the tradition by using free verse. Finally, he taunts the traditionalist to situate him and his poetry.

D. also writes poetry in English and French. These poems are scattered in many journals and anthologies, which span across time and continents. A short poem, "Prayers," harkens on a theme that is also found in the Amharic poems—the retrogressive dimension of tradition. The Ethiopian novelist Daniachew Worku (b. 1936) uses this poem as an epigram for his 1973 novel *The Thirteenth Sun.* Another collection of D.'s poetry is *Tone of Silence, A Mid-Century African Portrait,* for which the manuscript is, unfortunately, lost. D. is also featured in many anthologies including *Poems of Black Africa* (1975), edited by Wole Soyinka (q.v.).

D.'s Ethiopian poems tend to be bawdy, playful, and belligerent. His concern is that of cultural criticism. The impish defiance of the poetic voice and its unabashed "Do I care?" stance sometimes foster an attitude in which the play on words becomes an end in itself. In contrast, his poems in English and French are lyrical and self-reflexive and generally tend to be less critical. We can detect a tinge of surrealistic influence in the French poems. The same sensibilities, however, run through all his poems. One can legitimately state that D. is the precursor of modern Ethiopian poetry. His daring experimentations with Amharic have been inspirational for many young poets in Ethiopia.

ALI JIMALE AHMED

DERRIDA, Jacques

French philosopher and literary theorist, b. 15 July 1930, El-Biar, Algeria

Born into a Jewish family in French Algeria, where he spent his childhood and adolescence, D. moved to Paris in 1949 to prepare for his university studies. He was associated with the literary group *Tel Quel* in the 1960s and began a major writing career in 1962 with his translation of Edmund Husserl's (1859–1938) *L'origine de la géométrie.* Since then he has continued to publish prolifically, diversifying his writing to cover fields from philosophy to literature, painting, architecture, law, and political issues. D. has lectured in many countries and since 1966 has been a regular visitor to the U.S. Previously at the École Normale Supérieure in Paris, in 1983 he was appointed professor of philosophy at the École des Hautes Études en Sciences Sociales. He lives outside of Paris.

From the time of his first publications, D.'s work has stirred controversy over the extent of its challenge to traditional ways of thinking and writing. Although calling himself a philosopher, D. questions the foundations of philosophy and the means by which it attempts to define and circumscribe other disciplines or domains. He has pursued this line of questioning through highly idiosyncratic analyses of both classical and modern philosophical works, testing the strategies by which those works seek, and fail, to control their own meaning. D. contends that it is logically impossible to suppose, as Western thinking traditionally does, that meaning emerges from an identifiable source or point of origin, such as a thought, or word, or author, and that that origin contains the first and final sense of whatever it produces. His ideas were most notably developed in terms of the treatment of the relation between speech and writing in the works of thinkers as far apart historically as Plato, Rousseau, and Ferdinand de Saussure (q.v.). In *De la grammatologie* (1967; *Of Grammatology,* 1972) D. analyzes the work of such writers to uncover their systematic denigration of writing as exterior, secondary, and derivative, a marker of absence and error, as opposed to the supposed interior and living presence represented by speech.

It is often in literature and in philosophy's reluctant but common recourse to literary effects, such as rhetoric in general, and metaphor and analogy in particular, that D. uncovers exemplars of the competing forces that threaten, of necessity, to derail logical discourse. The most striking example of this confrontation between the literary and the philosophical is *Glas* (1974; *Glas,* 1986), a 365-page book, beginning and ending in midsentence, composed of two main columns that oppose the meditations on absolute knowledge of Hegel, and the celebrations of homosexuality and criminality of Jean Genet (q.v.). There are no explicit connections between the two columns but an unlimited play of cross-fertilization occurs across the blank space separating them, suggesting the role of chance and excess, and the type of leap into the abyss of the unknown that underscores any discursive event and is necessary, according to D., for any meaning to emerge.

D.'s essays on the visual arts and architecture have grown out of an interest shown in his work by a variety of scholars and artists, but they also attest to the extent to which his writings challenge traditional disciplinary boundaries. In *La vérité en peinture* (1978; *The Truth in Painting,* 1987) he gives his earlier ideas "graphic" illustration by examining how our ideas about meaning in the plastic arts assume a clear delimitation of the work, by means of its frame, allowing the spectator or critic to go straight to the supposed center and seat of meaning. D. argues that no work can clearly delineate its inside from its outside, and that the frame, unsure of its status in this respect, demonstrates that quandary.

D. has pursued his interest in the plastic and spatial arts with essays on architecture that continue to pose the question of relations between inside and outside and the sense of a "dwelling" both in physical terms and in terms of philosophy as a dwelling place for thinking. Most recently he was involved in a collaboration to create a garden at the Parc de la Villette in Paris and curated an exhibition of drawings at the Louvre: *Mémoires d'aveugle: L'autoportrait et autres ruines* (1990; memoirs of the blind: the self-portrait and other ruins).

In spite of charges of apoliticism, D. has been active in various political causes: resisting French government moves to reduce the teaching of philosophy in school while at the same time promoting a radical reworking of that discipline, speaking out against racism in his own country, working with dissident groups in communist eastern Europe, writing on behalf of a free and democratic South Africa and the rights of the Palestinians. Recently in the U.S., D. and his work, which now commonly goes by the name of deconstruction (q.v.), have been the target of conservative groups that associate his ideas with challenges to the integrity of the literary canon, and to an established and unchanging understanding of the values of Western civilization. Deconstruction is cited as a coercive orthodoxy in the humanities and has thus become embroiled in the debate over "political correctness." At the same time his ideas on reading and the definition of textuality have found one of their most direct applications in law, where questions of interpretation and the possibility of linguistically demonstrable truth are fundamental to the operation of a legitimate modern society.

D. continues to publish work as diverse as essays on the concept of the university—*Du droit à la philosophie* (1990; of the right to philosophy)—a book that relates questions of culture and human rights to the emergence of the new Europe—*L'autre cap* (1991; the other cape)—and an autobiographical "confession" somewhat modeled after St. Augustine, recounting his mother's illness and his own circumcision—"Circonfession," published in *J. D.* (1991, with Geoff Bennington). After initial enthusiasm from his compatriots, then a great degree of disaffection following the appearance of *Glas* and his "exportation" to the U.S., D.'s reputation in France seems to have been restored at the same time as he has achieved worldwide renown as one of the century's major thinkers.

FURTHER WORKS: *La voix et le phénomène* (1967; *Speech and Phenomena*, 1973); *L'écriture et la différence* (1967; *Writing and Difference*, 1978); *La dissémination* (1972; *Dissemination*, 1982); *Marges de la philosophie* (1972; *Margins of Philosophy*, 1982); *Positions* (1972; *Positions*, 1981); *L'archéologie du frivole: Lire Condillac* (1976; *The Archeology of the Frivolous: Reading Condillac*, 1981); *Éperons: Les styles de Nietzsche* (1978; *Spurs: Nietzsche's Styles*, 1979); *La carte postale: De Socrate à Freud et au-delà* (1980; *The Post Card: From Socrates to Freud and Beyond*, 1987); *L'oreille de l'autre* (1982; *The Ear of the Other*, 1985); *D'un ton apocalyptique adopté naguère en philosophie* (1983; "Of an Apocalyptic Tone Recently Adopted in Philosophy," *OLR*, 6, 2 [1984], 3–37); *Signéponge/Signsponge* (1983); *Lecture de droit de regards* (1985; "Right of Inspection," *Art & Text*, 38 [1989]); *Parages* (1986); *Schibboleth—pour Paul Celan* (1986); *De l'esprit: Heidegger et la question* (1987; *Of Spirit: Heidegger and the Question*, 1989); *Feu la cendre* (1987; *Cinders*, 1992); *Psyché: Inventions de l'autre* (1987); *Ulysse gramophone: Deux mots pour Joyce* (1987); *Mémoires—pour Paul de Man* (1988; first pub. in English as *Mémoires—for Paul de Man*, 1986); *Limited Inc.* (1990; first pub. in English as *Limited Inc.*, 1988); *Le problème de la génèse dans la philosophie de Husserl* (1990)

BIBLIOGRAPHY: Said, E. W., "The Problem of Textuality: Two Exemplary Positions," *CritI*, 4, 4 (Summer 1978), 673–714; Rorty, R., "Philosophy As a Kind of Writing: An Essay on D.," *NLH*, 10, 1 (Autumn 1978), 141–60; Johnson, B., "The Frame of Reference: Poe, Lacan, D.," *The Critical Difference: Essays in the Contemporary Rhetoric of Reading* (1980), 110–46; Lacoue-Labarthe, P., and J.- L. Nancy, eds., *Les fins de l'homme: À partir du travail de J. D.* (1981); Hartman, G. H., *Saving the Text: Literature/D./ Philosophy* (1981); Culler, J., *On Deconstruction: Theory and Criticism after Structuralism* (1982); Kofman, S., *Lectures de D.* (1984); Wood, D., and R. Bernasconi, eds., *D. and Différance* (1985); Ulmer, G. L., *Applied Grammatology: Post(e)-Pedagogy from J. D. to Joseph Beuys* (1985); Gasché, R., *The Tain of the Mirror: D. and the Philosophy of Reflection* (1986); Norris, C., *D.* (1987); Kamuf, P., ed., *A D. Reader: Between the Blinds* (1991); Bennington, G., "Derridabase," in Bennington, G., and J. Derrida, *J. D.* (1991).

DAVID WILLS

Every one of D.'s extraordinarily brilliant readings since and including *De la grammatologie* . . . builds from and around that point in a text around which its own heterodox textuality, distinct from its message or meanings, is organized, the point also *toward* which the text's textuality moves in the shattering dissemination of its unorganizable energy. These points are words that are anticoncepts, bits of the text in which D. believes, and where he shows, the text's irreducible textuality to lie. These anticoncepts, antinames, counterideas escape definite or decidable classification. That is why they are only textual and why also they are heterodox. D.'s method of deconstruction functions then to release them, just as the climactic moment in each of *his* texts is a *performance* by these anticoncepts, these *mere* words. Thus what D. points toward is "une scène d'écriture dans une scène d'écriture et ainsi sans fin, par necessité structurelle marquée dans le texte." Only words that are *syncatégorèmes*—words having, like the copula, a syntactic function but capable of serving semantic ones too—can reveal textuality in its element. These words are of an infinite, hence disseminative, pliability: they mean one thing *and* another (rather like Freud's antithetical primal words), but D.'s interest in them is that it is they, and not the big ideas, that *make* a text the uniquely written phenomenon that it is, a form of *supplementarity* to (or something necessarily in excess of) formulable meaning. And this supplementarity is that property of the text capable of repeating itself *(a)* without exhausting itself and *(b)* without keeping anything (for instance, a secret hoard of meaning) in reserve.

Edward W. Said, "The Problem of Textuality: Two Exemplary Positions," *CritI*, 4, 4 (Summer 1978), 694

Books tell the truth about things. Texts comment on other texts, and we should stop trying to test texts for accuracy of representation: "reading . . . cannot legitimately transgress the text toward something other than it, toward the referent (a reality that is metaphysical, historical, psychobiographical, etc.) or toward a signifier outside the text whose content could take place, could have taken place outside of language, that is to say, in the sense that we give here to that word, outside of writing in general. . . . There is nothing outside of the text." D. regards the need to overcome "the book"—the notion of a piece of writing as aimed at accurate treatment of a subject, conveying a message which (in more fortunate circumstances) might have been conveyed by ostensive definition or by injecting knowledge straight into the brain—as justifying his use of any text to interpret any other text. The most shocking thing about his work—even more shocking than, though not so funny as, his sexual interpretations of the history of philosophy—is his use of multilingual puns, joke etymologies, allusions from anywhere to anywhere, and phonic and typographical gimmicks. It is as if he really thought that the fact that, for example, the French pronunciation of "Hegel" sounds like the French word for "eagle" was supposed to be relevant for comprehending Hegel. But D. does not want to comprehend Hegel's books; he wants to play with Hegel. He doesn't want to write a book about the nature of language; he wants to play with the texts which other people have thought they were writing about language.

Richard Rorty, "Philosophy As a Kind of Writing: An Essay on D.," *NLH*, 10, 1 (Autumn 1978), 146–47

Surely the fact that words are powerful is as important as that *written* words are powerful in a way that may be more basic still. There is a problem here, because *representation* (the realm of what is signified) and *rhetoric* (the signifying act that values oral performance) are seen as coconspirators. The rhetoric that interests D. derives solely from the specific power of the *written:* from texts in which language discloses its groundlessness and injures the notion of substance too well for a "cure of the ground." Traditional rhetoric, however, as the art of persuasion, relies on a smooth consensual calculus of means and ends. Specific verbal devices are isolated as if they effectively corresponded to specific mental or affectional states. . . . As a highly sophisticated and teachable art this rhetoric has the same aim, if not the same lightness, as Nietzsche's *aesthetic,* which is said to keep us from a Dionysian stupor, from foundering absolutely *(zu Grunde gehen).*

For D., the rhetoric of representation, especially when insisted on as a science, is a sham; it is not a science but a pragmatic and consensual exercise; one that can distract from the true cogency of speech by interposing a mechanistic model of communication. Like Heidegger, he wants to liberate language from a doctrinal effectiveness that is honorific rather than authentic, accommodating rather than awe-inspiring. . . .

Since D. himself has stressed that the written sign is indefeasibly poison and cure, and that intertextuality also is radically ambivalent in that its mirror-play at once builds up the reality-effect and deconstructs it, this final chapter becomes, among other things, a counterstatement to D. It is not a refutation but rather a different turn in how to state the matter. A restored theory of representation should acknowledge the deconstructionist challenge as necessary and timely, if somewhat self-involved—that is, only occasionally reflective of analogies to its own project in religious writing and especially in literary writing. A child acts, Wordsworth wrote, "As if his sole vocation / Were endless imitation"; and in D. there is the same strong "antitheatrical prejudice," an attempt in the name of maturity (and no longer of religion) to put away childish things, to overcome imitation. Yet the bonding involved in imitation may indeed be "endless" and therefore self-subverting.

Geoffrey H. Hartman, *Saving the Text: Literature/D./ Philosophy* (1981), 120–21

Those who champion a "historical approach" or chide deconstruction for refusing to appreciate the historical determination of meaning offer a dubious alternative. A "historical approach" appeals to historical narratives—stories of changes in thinking and of the thoughts or beliefs appropriate to distinguishable historical periods—in order to control the meaning of rich and complex works by ruling out possible meanings as historically inappropriate. These historical narratives are produced by interpreting the supposedly less complex and ambiguous texts of a period, and their authority to authorize or control meanings of the most complex texts is certainly questionable. The history invoked as ultimate reality and source of truth manifests itself in narrative constructs, stories designed to yield meaning through narrative ordering. In *Positions* D. emphasizes his distrust of the concept of history, with its entire logocentric system of implications, but notes that he frequently uses the term *history* in a critical way, in order to reinscribe its force. . . . D. uses history against philosophy: when confronted with essentialist, idealizing theories and claims to ahistorical or transhistorical understanding, he asserts the historicity of these discourses and theoretical assumptions. But he also uses philosophy against history and the claims of historical narratives. Deconstruction couples a philosophical critique of history and historical understanding with the specification that discourse is historical and meaning historically determined, both in principle and in practice.

Jonathan Culler, *On Deconstruction: Theory and Criticism after Structuralism* (1982), 129

My contention is that D.'s marked interest in literature, an interest that began with his questioning the particular ideality of literature, has in his thinking never led to anything remotely resembling literary criticism or to a valorization of what literary critics agree to call literature. Paradoxically, D.'s initial inquiry into the ideality of the literary object had the effect of situating his work at the margins not only of philosophy but of literature as well.

Such an observation does not mean, however, that D.'s philosophy is without any relevance to literary criticism. Rather it implies that the importance of D.'s thinking for the discipline of literary criticism is not immediately evident, and that any statement of its relevance to that discipline requires certain mediating steps beforehand. So-called deconstructive criticism, which, however important, is but an offspring of New Criticism, has not, to my knowledge, undertaken these preparatory steps and has done little more than apply what it takes to be a method for reading literary texts to the unproblematized horizon of its discipline. As a result, the genuine impact that D.'s philosophy could have on literary criticism has not been, or at best has hardly been, noticed. The following remarks are not intended to offer a "true" version of deconstructive criticism but only to clarify some of the preliminaries which any deconstructive criticism would have to observe.

If it were possible to draw one major proposition from D.'s statements on literature, it would certainly not be that everything is literature, but on the contrary that "there is no—or hardly any, ever so little—literature". . . . How are we to understand this seemingly provocative claim? What this statement first of all suggests is that Aristotle's production of *the concept* of literature in the *Poetics* (in the aftermath of Plato's determination of poetry as *mimesis*) inaugurates the history of literature as a history in which the certification of literature's birth, the declaration of its name, coincides with its disappearance. Literature, says D., was born of that history, which lasted until the 19th c., and died of that history. . . .

The interpretation of mimesis as subject to truth, as a mimetologism that proclaims the priority and precedence of the imitated over imitation, subjects literature to a status of metaphoric secondariness. Accordingly, literature possesses no specificity of its own and is reducible to its signified, its message, the truth it expresses. Yielding from the outset to the constraints of its philosophical conceptualization, literature, like philosophy, includes "the project of effacing itself in the face of the signified content which it transports and in general teaches." The specificity of philosophy and literature alike rests on this systematic curtailment of the signifier. Consequently, reading is in essence always a transcendental reading in search of the signified. D. writes of "the entire history of texts, and within it the history of literary forms in the West," that it "has almost always and almost everywhere, according to some fashions and across very diverse ages, lent itself to this *transcendental* reading, in that search for the signified."

Rodolphe Gasché, *The Tain of the Mirror: D. and the Philosophy of Reflection* (1986), 255–56

DESAI, Anita

(formerly Anita Mazumdar) Indian novelist, short-story writer, and author of children's books (writing in English), b. 24 June 1937, Mussorie

Born of a Bengali father and a German mother, D. was educated in Delhi at Queen Mary's Higher Secondary School and Miranda House, Delhi University, where she received a B.A. in English literature in 1957. Married in 1958, D. became the mother of four children. Her first three novels, published in the 1960s and early 1970s, are not particularly successful in terms of plot or character. Her most recent writing, however, displays a sensitivity to subtle emotions and family reverberations that some critics have referred to as Chekhovian, although this sort of intuitive awareness emanates from a distinctly feminine sensibility.

Voices of the City (1965) offers us a unique perception of Calcutta seen through the minds of three siblings who come from an aristocratic family in the northern reaches of India close to the Himalayas. The younger sister, Amla, is a young woman artist who comes to Calcutta to work and is immediately struck by the way in which that city has transformed her brother and sister. Amla sees Calcutta as a monster born of the marsh, an ambivalent goddess preying upon people who live there. Thus, Nirode drifts from a job as editor of a literary magazine to writing a play, his physical body diminished by the coffeehouse life-style to which he is addicted. Monisha's diary shows her confined to an orthodox Hindu role as daughter-

in-law in the household of a wealthy old Calcutta family; she cannot bear her stifling existence and commits suicide to protest the theft of her being.

Fire on the Mountain (1977), D.'s fourth novel, is also an exploration of place and its effect on the consciousness of three women, oppressed and crippled at various stages of their lives. The novel is set in Kasauli, a hill station with rocks, pines, and a sweeping view in every direction. Nanda Kaul, an older woman now widowed, comes to this place of light and air, freed finally from domestic responsibilities as hostess, wife, and mother. Her calm is disturbed by a visit from a great-grandchild, Paka, whose psychotic preoccupation with fire brings ruin to the hill community at a moment when the social fabric is being ripped apart by winds of change. Against this relationship, a third woman, Ila Das, struggles to earn a living as a social worker in a vain attempt to offset the genteel upbringing that has rendered her economically helpless.

Clear Light of Day (1980) is also the study of a city, Delhi, where urban history is interwoven with that of a middle-class Hindu family. Bim is a competent woman professor who still lives in the family home in Old Delhi, caring for Baba, the retarded younger brother, and assuming a role as keeper of the family. The relationship of Bim's house to the history of her family is that of Delhi to the history of India. The deepest selves of the family are rooted there, yet the past is multiple, not single, for conflicting memories of that place and the relationships it sheltered are held by all who lived there. Bim, as caretaker of both house and memories, resents the expense of spirit involved, yet realizes, paradoxically, that time the destroyer is also time the preserver. Bim's lifestyle as an independent thinking spirit raises questions, for her superhuman strength in giving without taking leads ultimately to a sterile existence.

The same sort of woman has turned up in several of D.'s recent novels: a newly heroic and thoroughly modern model of the saintly Indian woman. Those qualities that enabled the traditional woman to survive in an arranged marriage are those of D.'s independent woman, who is autonomous, yet bound up with caring for others. She has her own well of emotional strength with no need to draw on nourishment from others. No longer bound by traditional expectations, she is able to assert her need for independence, pursue a career, or decide not to marry or care for children. Although D. offers negative examples of women unable to realize their own needs because of oppression by traditional customs, she also presents the difficulties faced by newly liberated women in giving their lives purpose. The feminist message, that women are senselessly harmed by denial of opportunities for self-realization, comes through loud and clear; but so does the question of what an independent woman's identity might be.

In D.'s *In Custody* (1984) she explores the character of Nur, an Urdu poet fallen on hard times, appreciated only by Deven, a professor of Hindi who would rather be teaching Urdu. Both Deven and Nur verge on the comic, as D. gently mocks a fading literary tradition that persists despite absence of a cultural environment to nourish it. Though able to admire Urdu poetry to the extent of rendering Deven's love for it convincing, D. also comes at the tradition with a feminist perspective, which leads to satire. A venerated poet drinks literally the wine of which the *ghazals* speak (in Persian or Urdu literature, poems consisting of discrete couplets on love or philosophical themes), only to become an alcoholic. Devotee of women, Nur in old age is subject to the whims of two females who give him no peace. In Deven, D. creates a poetry-loving hero, so caught up in illusions that others take advantage of him. Yet Deven breaks free of his illusions by twice crossing over into the feminine: through the acceptance of a caretaker role, and by glimpsing the anguish of Nur's wife, who forces him to consider the viewpoint of woman, the other, the role to which Urdu tradition confines her.

Baumgardner's Bombay (1988) examines the life of a retired German businessman who had come to India in his youth to escape the Holocaust and stayed on in his old age. His needs are few, his companions a German woman expatriate and a menagerie of stray cats. Only when he reaches out in a rare moment of risk-taking to a drug-crazed German hippie is he punished for deviating from his reclusive existence. Nazi hatred surfaces in violence like that which had claimed his mother years before. In this novel, D. explores her own heritage, loading the text with untranslated passages in German (her first language), a source of frustration for the non-German speaking reader. *Baumgardner's Bombay* resembles Kamala Markandaya's (q.v.) novel, *The Nowhere Man* (1972): both deal with elderly gentlemen living out their years in someone else's culture. Yet D. presents the European out of his element, victim not of Indian communalism but of German anti-Semitism, which has resurfaced and hunted him down in his place of exile.

Read chronologically, D.'s novels demonstrate her constant experimentation and progressive maturation as a writer. In recent work, she has grappled with powerful themes: emotional poverty confronted by the liberated woman, the demise of a rich cultural tradition, and evil inherent in the German legacy of anti-Semitism. Her characters, although firmly rooted in reality, have become increasingly symbolic of particular philosophical stances in a multicultural universe. Her plots are steeped in irony while at the same time faithfully portraying life as lived in contemporary India. By scrutinizing small corners of India's diverse society, D. has created an astonishing mosaic of peoples and places within the subcontinent.

Place is always at the heart of her fiction, acting upon her characters, and casting the sort of spell that only a unique landscape can. One comes to understand that India is a country of many unique places, each caught in the struggle of a postcolonial identity crisis. In D.'s writing, place becomes a metaphor for individuals coming to grips with personal journeys into a world they never intended on. She accurately renders tumultuous changes in Indian society from the standpoint of an educated, Westernized sensibility. Although the underclass is not dealt with sympathetically in her writing, D. meets the Western reader on his or her own ground, causing one to ponder a future in which social harmony becomes increasingly elusive.

FURTHER WORKS: *Cry, The Peacock* (1963); *Bye-Bye, Blackbird* (1971); *The Peacock Garden* (1974); *Where Shall We Go This Summer?* (1975); *Cat on a Houseboat* (1976); *Games at Twilight and Other Stories* (1978); *Village by the Sea: An Indian Family Story* (1982)

BIBLIOGRAPHY: Belliappa, M., *A. D.: A Study of Her Fiction* (1971); Ramachandra Rao, B., *The Novels of Mrs. A. D.* (1977); Prasad, M., *A. D. the Novelist* (1981); Sharma, R. S., *A. D.* (1981); Srivastava, R. K., *Perspectives on A. D.* (1984); Jain, J., *Stairs to the Attic: The Novels of A. D.* (1987); Bande, U., *The Novels of A. D.: A Study in Character and Conflict* (1988); Kanwar, A., *Virginia Woolf and A. D.: A Comparative Study* (1989); Jena, S., *Voice and Vision of A. D.* (1989)

JANET M. POWERS

DİLMEN, Güngör

(also known as Güngör Dilmen Kalyoncu), Turkish dramatist and translator (writing in Turkish and English), b. 1930, Tekirdağ

One of Turkey's prominent dramatists, D. was educated at Istanbul's British High School and did his graduate work at the Department of Classical Philology at the University of Istanbul, and he studied theater arts at Yale University and the University of Washington, Seattle (1961–1964). He served as a play editor for the Istanbul City Theaters (1964–1966) and at the theater department of Turkish Radio (1966–1968). He lectured at Durham University, England, from 1970 to

1972. Since the late 1980s he has been teaching at the Istanbul State Conservatory and Bosphorus University as well as working for the Istanbul Municipal Theaters.

Most of D.'s major plays deal with mythological themes and Anatolian, Ottoman, and modern Turkish history. His first play, *Midas' ın kulakları* (perf. 1959, pub. 1965; the ears of Midas), which earned him immediate fame, is the first part of "The Trilogy of Midas," of which the second part is *Midas' ın altınları* (1970; the gold of Midas), and the third part, *Midas' ın kördüğümü* (1975; Midas's Gordian knot). This trilogy, written in a poetic style, dramatizes the three best-known legends relating to the Phrygian king.

D.'s second play is *Canlı maymun lokantası* (1965; live monkey restaurant). Originally written in English, it is a strong indictment of modern colonialism in Hong Kong. His *Ak tanrılar* (1975; white gods) unfurls the conquest of the Aztec Empire, pitting Cortez against Montezuma. *Kurban* (1967; sacrifice/victim) portrays, in a loose adaptation of the Medea theme, the victimization of an Anatolian peasant woman.

Akad' ın yayı (perf. 1967, pub. 1983; the bow of Akkad) is one of the most effective Turkish dramatizations of an ancient myth: Akkad's bow in the Canaanite land. The same book contains *Deli Dumrul* (1979; Dumrul the mad), drawn from the millennium-old Turkish national epic (*The Book of Dede Korkut*, twice translated into English). The play shows how the Angel of Death confronts the protagonist Deli Dumrul with arduous tests. Among D.'s plays based on early Turkish history are *Bağdat Hatun* (perf. 1972, pub. 1982; Lady Bağdat), about the Ilhanid princess demonically driven to become a queen who stopped at nothing (not even the death of her father and brothers and the loss of her unborn child), and *Hasan Sabbah* (1983; Hasan Sabbah), about the political visionary who created a terrorist organization of assassins hell-bent to destroy the Seljuk state in the 11th c.

D. has also written plays dealing with late Ottoman history. These include *İttihat ve Terakki* (1969; the party of union and progress), a docudrama about the misguided idealism and the corrupt regime of "The Young Turks"; *İnsan ve devlet* (perf. 1984, pub. 1990; man and the state), the tragic story of an eminent statesman who pits himself against the empire's powers that be; and *Aşkımız Aksaray' ın en büyük yangını* (1991; our love is the greatest fire of Aksaray), the heartrending tale of the unrequited love of an ex-odalisque for an Armenian musician, leading to her setting one of Istanbul's most destructive fires. D.'s 1992 play *Hakimiyet-i milliye aşevi* (national sovereignty diner) deals with the behind-the-scenes politics of the Turkish struggle for independence in the early 1920s.

Also a leading translator, D. has provided Turkish versions of *Antigone* and *King Oedipus* of Sophocles, *The Persians* and *The Oresteia* of Aeschylus, and August Strindberg's (q.v.) *The Ghost Sonata*.

Ben, Anadolu (1985; *I, Anatolia,* 1991) is perhaps D.'s most celebrated work. It portrays, in separate vignettes, women from Anatolian mythology and history in Act I and numerous Ottoman Turkish women in Act II. It is a one-actress play depicting poignant, sometimes funny or bittersweet, dramatic moments in the lives of Anatolian women. Turkey's most famous actress Yıldız Kenter presented *Ben, Anadolu* scores of times in Turkey and special English-language performances at London's Queen Elizabeth Hall, New York's Lincoln Center, Moscow's Art Theater, Washington's Kennedy Center, and also in Germany, Denmark, Canada, the Netherlands, and other places.

No Turkish dramatist has claimed an expanse of history larger than D.'s terra firma. Few have been as successful in creating vivid action and lyrical dialogue. Most of his plays have beautifully crafted poetic passages. His work, at its best, transposes myths, legends, and history into engrossing dramatic experiences and creates powerful tragic characters. He has received wide critical acclaim for having brought new dimensions to the modern Turkish theater. His dramas are remarkable for the universality of their themes, characters, and human concerns.

D. has won virtually all of the major drama prizes of Turkey, including the İbrahim Şinasi Efendi Award (1964), the İlhan İskender Prize (1966–1967), the Turkish Language Society Award (1977), the Muhsin Ertuğrul Prize (1979), and the Ankara Sanat Kurumu Prize (1991)

BIBLIOGRAPHY: Halman, T. S., ed., *Modern Turkish Drama* (1976), 237–84

TALAT SAIT HALMAN

DIMITROVA, Blaga

Bulgarian poet, prose writer, and translator, b. 2 Jan. 1922, Byala Slatina

Brought up in the ancient capital of Turnovo, D. graduated in Slavic philology from Sofia University in 1945, shortly after the communist seizure of power in 1944. In 1946 she left to do graduate work in the Soviet Union, completing a dissertation on Vladimir Mayakovsky (q.v.) in 1950. All during her career she has written consistently and prolifically, producing lyric poems, narrative poems, lyrical novels, plays, travel impressions, essays, journalism, and translations. By the mid-1980s D. had become a leading advocate of democratic reforms, and after the fall of the communist dictatorship she ran for parliament in the elections of 1990. In January 1992 she was elected vice president of Bulgaria.

D. began publishing shortly before World War II, and her early poems demonstrate both her lyric gift and her orientation toward the everyday; they are also traditional in form. Her attitude toward the terrible times of 1943 already demonstrated that she had a deep understanding of historical catastrophe but nevertheless affirmed that life was good.

Although never a party member, D. sympathized with certain communist objectives at the beginning. In 1950, after the death of the communist prime minister Georgi Dimitrov (no relation), D. brought out a small volume, *Stikhove za vozhda* (verses on the leader), a cluster of chronologically arranged biographical lyrics on Dimitrov, clearly influenced by Mayakovsky in their fabricated enthusiasm for the new political order. In recent years, however, D. has avoided mentioning this collection.

In 1952–1954 D. spent two years as a construction worker in the Rhodope mountains, an experience that found romanticized expression in the moderately modernist novel *Putuvane kum sebe si* (1965; journey to oneself), a story of a woman who wishes to do a man's work in this world without ceasing to be a woman.

Putuvane kum sebe si was the first of several novels, generally relatively short and as modernist in their approach as they could be under Bulgarian circumstances. They include *Otklonenie* (1967; deviation), *Lavina* (1971; avalanche), and *Litse* (1981; face), a book literally "imprisoned" by the authorities until the end of the decade. D. also traveled to Vietnam on at least five occasions during the course of the Vietnam War, describing her experiences in *Podzemno nebe: Vietnamski dnevnik* (1972; subterranean heaven: a Vietnam diary) and using them as material for lyric poems describing the admirable behavior of ordinary people confronting the adversities of war.

For years D. wrote in the shadow of Bulgaria's best-known 20th-c. woman poet, Elisaveta Bagryana (q.v.). When the latter effectively withdrew from the literary scene, D. not only succeeded her as the country's leading woman poet and literary intellectual, but also became one of her chief interpreters through such volumes as *Mladostta na Bagryana* (1975; Bagryana's youth), written in

collaboration with her critic-husband Yordan Vasilev; it contains reminiscences, portraits, and detailed poetic analyses of which perhaps only another poet is capable.

Still, it is as a lyric poet that D. has made her mark in Bulgarian literature. For most of her career she has been a consistent modernist, though not an extreme one. She is very much aware of language as a medium, but also of language as an artifact created by an entire culture over many centuries. She has visited western Europe on several occasions, and values its cultural achievements, but her strongest commitment is to her own people's roots, both distant and more to hand. She pays explicit tribute to the older generation of Bulgarian poets—including Bagryana and Atanas Dalchev (q.v.)—who helped create the more immediate culture in which she moved. And she honors her father and mother, whose declining days she has recorded in moving lyrics. She is sustained, not constricted, by her links with past generations. She incorporates the legacy of the past into her own personality, which she will transmit to others in its entirety only when she dies.

In recent years, as Bulgarian cultural constraints have loosened, D.'s writing has become progressively more complex and difficult, as it deals with some of the deepest issues of human existence. In 1968 she wrote: "The guilty feeling of a transit passenger—/this never deserts me." In 1990 she published a long poem, *Tranzit* (transit), an allegory of her country's contemporary difficulties cast in the form of reflections of an airline passenger delayed by bad weather. "But we shall certainly take off!" are her final words.

D. is now something of an elder "statesman" of Bulgarian culture. In the past she was not a hero, but neither did she commit any actions of which she need be deeply ashamed. She has publicly admitted her earlier shortcomings and, more important, paid eloquent tribute to those few who, unlike her, at critical points raised protesting voices. A bout with cancer in addition to recent political developments has made her resolve to write each of her poems "as if it were her last," and not to distort the truth as she perceives it. This moral determination, coupled with her linguistic mastery, has made her perhaps the foremost literary figure of contemporary Bulgaria.

FURTHER WORKS: *Pesni za Rodopite* (1954); *Na otkrito* (1956); *Do utre* (1959); *Liliana* (1959); *Svetut v shepa* (1962); *Ekspeditsiya kum idniya den* (1964); *Obratno vreme* (1966); *Osudeni na lyubov* (1967); *Migove* (1968); *Ime* (1971); *Impulsi* (1972); *Kak* (1974); *Zabraneno more* (1976); *Gong*

(1976); *Prostranstva* (1980); *Glas* (1985); *Labirint* (1987); *Mezhdu* (1991). FURTHER VOLUME IN ENGLISH: *Because the Sea Is Black* (1989)

BIBLIOGRAPHY: Phillipov, V., "Experimentation in Present-Day Bulgarian Drama (B. D.'s *Dr. Faustina*)," in Birnbaum, H., and T. Eekman, eds., *Fiction and Drama in Eastern and Southeastern Europe* (1980), 305–25; Zdanys, J., "Voices from the Other Europe," *YR*, 79, 3 (1990), 470–73

CHARLES A. MOSER

DJEBAR, Assia

(pseud. of Fatima-Zohra Imalayen) Algerian novelist (writing in French), b. 4 Aug. 1936, Cherchell

D. is Algeria's most prominent woman writer. Known primarily as a novelist, she has also written poetry, plays, and short stories, and has produced two films. Born in Cherchell, a small coastal town near Algiers, D. completed secondary school studies in Algiers, did a preparatory year at the Lycée Fénelon in Paris in 1954, and the following year became the first Algerian woman admitted to the prestigious École Normale Supérieure de Sèvres in France. Joining in the Algerian student strike of 1956, in the early years of the Algerian independence struggle, she skipped final exams and wrote her first novel, *La soif* (1957; *The Mischief*, 1958).

D.'s earliest protagonist is a cultural hybrid. Half-French, half-Algerian, Nadia faces none of the constraints imposed upon traditional Arab women in colonial Algeria. She moves freely in public space and, when not sunbathing on the beach, drives around town in a flashy sports car. Below the surface of this portrait of a hedonist existence, the reader encounters a serious study of psychological development.

Dalila, the protagonist of *Les impatients* (1958; the impatient ones), typifies young women of the Algerian bourgeoisie just before the independence struggle. She expresses the impatience of a generation trying to free itself from an atrophied and hypocritical patriarchal society. D.'s first two novels complement each other: *La soif* depicts the breakup of a marriage viewed through the heroine's eyes; *Les impatients* centers upon the disintegration of a prospective marriage between the heroine and her fiancé. In D.'s early fiction, marriage and freedom seem incompatible.

At the end of the Algerian War (1954–1962), D. turned to the subject of women and war. With *Les enfants du nouveau monde* (1962; children of the new world) she focused on the collective experience of Algerian women awakening to new demands and using the war experience as a catalyst for personal growth. This novel also reworks a theme elaborated in *Les impatients,* the relationship between private and public space, the former reserved for women traditionally barred from public or male domain.

In historical terms, *Les alouettes naïves* (1967; the skylarks) is a sequel to *Les enfants du nouveau monde,* for it is set at the close of the war that had just begun in the previous novel. Introducing the multiplicity of scenes and characters, the emphasis upon daily life, and the lyrical prose of the earlier work, it is a text in which the combat provides a backdrop to the experiences of a young couple. D. now experiments with chronology and introduces an Arab woman assuming her sexuality within the couple. For the novelist, this work ends her first cycle in which female protagonists rebel against patriarchy, participate in the revolution, and expect a new order within which they may claim a public role in public space.

Beginning in the 1980s, D.'s quest for individual and collective identity led her to examine the legacy of the French conquest of 1830 via French Orientalist paintings and historical documents in French archives. *Femmes d'Alger dans leur appartement* (1980; women of Algiers in their apartment), a collection of short stories that takes its title from Delacroix's painting, reveals D.'s new emphasis upon women bonding to struggle against an Algerian patriarchy that replaced the French colonial order. Women warriors discovered that with independence they had been excluded from the new order and were still denied access to public space and power.

L'amour, la fantasia (1985; *An Algerian Cavalcade,* 1989) alternates between an autobiographical journey and historical accounts of the French conquest of 1830 and the Algerian War. In search of women's contribution to Algerian history, D. uses documents and correspondence of the period as well as oral history of the Algerian revolution. She privileges the written and the spoken word as forms of liberation.

In *Ombre sultane* (1987; *A Sister to Scheherazade,* 1987) D. establishes bonds between traditional and emancipated women who share a common experience: patriarchy. The novel charts the process of liberation by which a cloistered and veiled woman discovers the language and meaning of revolt. Finally, D.'s most recent work, *Loin de Medine* (1991; far from Medina), resuscitates the memory of seventeen historical women of the early years of Islam.

D.'s work has evolved in style from a linear first-person narrative wedded to realism to polyphonic postmodern texts. In the past three decades of her literary career, she has never departed from the commitment to explore the North African Muslim woman's world in all its contradictions and complexities.

FURTHER WORKS: *Poèmes pour l'Algérie heureuse* (1969); *Rouge l'aube* (1969); *La nouba des femmes du Mont Chenoua* (1979); *La Zerda ou les chants d'oubli* (1982)

BIBLIOGRAPHY: Zimra, C., "In Her Own Write: The Circular Structures of Linguistic Alienation in A. D.'s Early Novels," *RAL*, 1, 2 (1980), 206–23; Mortimer, M., "The Evolution of A. D.'s Feminist Conscience," in Wylie, H., et al., eds., *Contemporary African Literature* (1983), 7–14; Déjeux, J., *A. D.* (1984); Le Clézio, M., "A. D.: Écrire dans la langue adverse," *Contemporary French Civilization*, 9, 2 (1985), 230–44; Mortimer, M., "Language and Space in the Fiction of A. D. and Leila Sebbar," *RAL*, 19, 3 (1988), 301–11; Mortimer, M., *Journeys through the French African Novel* (1990), 147–64

MILDRED MORTIMER

DONNER, Jörn

Finnish novelist and journalist (writing in Swedish), b. 5 Feb. 1933, Helsinki

D. was born into an affluent family but, as a very young man, turned violently against his patrician background, coediting the radical journal *Arena* (1951–1954) with Christer Kihlman (q.v.) and writing several clumsy semiautobiographical novels, culminating with *Jag, Erik Anders* (1957; I, Erik Anders). Further, in an effort to present his Marxist accusations to a variety of audiences, he frequently contributed to the Finnish-language communist-dominated *Vapaa Sana*, the tabloid *Nya Pressen,* and the liberal *Hufvudstadsbladet,* the last association continuing through the 1960s. In 1980, politically transformed and now famous, D. returned as a columnist to *Hufvudstadsbladet,* the country's largest Swedish paper; he also appears regularly in the Finnish *Aamulehti,* the second-largest member of Finland's Finnish-language press. His journalistic skills were also brought to bear in his pictures of postwar Europe, *Rapport från Berlin* (1958; *Report from Berlin,* 1968), *Rapport från Donau* (1962; report from the Danube), and *Världsboken* (1968, the world book). His skill in the globetrotting genre was applied to a more tractable topic in *Sverigeboken* (1973; the Sweden book), an unflattering picture of the social paradise to which he had transferred his activities during the 1960s, when he became the leading film critic of the major Stockholm daily *Dagens Nyheter.*

Simultaneously, under the aegis of Ingmar Bergman, to whom he devoted a book, *Djävulens ansikte* (1962; *The Films of Ingmar Bergman,* 1972), he became a director of some distinction, first in Sweden and then in Finland. Back on home ground, he began to observe his native land more objectively than before, in the large *Nya boken om vårt land* (1967; the new book about our country)—a title alluding to a school classic from the 19th c.—where D. presented his plans for an unabashedly capitalistic Finnish society. His own talents as an administrator and businessman were of great value to him as head of the Swedish Film Institute and then as chairman of the Finnish Film Foundation. In public life he also served as a Helsinki city commissioner from 1968 to 1972 and again from 1985 to the present, and, since 1987, as a representative of the Swedish People's Party in Finland's parliament.

It is hard to believe that D., in the midst of so much activity (frequently punctuated by trips around the world), could have time for literary creation; his manifold daily or weekly reflections on Finland's and Europe's public life—collected in *Sagt och gjort* (1976; seen and done), *Hemåt i höstregn* (1985; homeward in autumn rain), and *Motströms* (1988; against the current)—might well have absorbed all his authorial energy. However, during the last two decades, he has produced two series of books that guarantee him a place in Finland's literary history. A figure of national fame and notoriety, altogether willing to inform his fellow citizens of their opportunities and their shortcomings, his works have been widely translated into Finnish. The one set is concerned with D. himself, an ongoing record of his attitudes and shifts of opinion, illustrated by telling anecdotes and meaningful facts. The journal he kept of his alternate service as a pacifist in *På ett sjukhus* (1961; at a hospital) had been a preparatory step in this direction; in *Sommar av kärlek och sorg* (1971; summer of love and grief) D. discussed, among much else, his rejection of his leftist phase; another such account, ostensibly more personal, was *Jag, J. J. D.* (1980; I, J. J. D.). Yet, even here, D. was less concerned with self-analysis than with giving his opinions on what he saw and, very often, questioned. In general, he is a keen detector of large political or social patterns but not a sensitive observer of individuals.

D.'s other major concern has been a suite of novels about the fate of a Finland-Swedish industrial dynasty from 1939 to the 1960s. The grand undertaking began with *Nu måste du* (1974; now you must, repub. as *Den sista sommaren,* 1989, the last summer), dealing with the great firm United Metals, and the persons surrounding it. The central figure at the start was Gabriel Berggren, a man of humble origins who married into the family twice, but as the cycle progressed, the spotlight was often moved to a woman, Angela, and her wartime affair with a German officer in *Angelas krig* (1976; Angela's war) and *Angela och kärleken* (1981; Angela and love), where it emerged that the German was homosexual. Other novels in this cycle include *Jakob och friheten* (1978; Jakob and freedom), *Gabriels dag* (1982; Gabriel's day), *Far och son* (1985; father and son), and *Frihetens fångar* (1988; prisoners of freedom). D. has a sovereign command of his settings, at home and abroad, and his narrative, particularly in the later volumes, is leavened by scenes of burlesque humor. But D.'s characterizations are often superficial, and his situations often reminiscent of John Galsworthy's (q.v.) Forsyte novels or the once-popular Jalna series of the Canadian Mazo De la Roche (1885–1961), or television's family epics.

In many respects, D. would remind Americans of William F. Buckley (b. 1925)—in his self-assurance, in his vast knowledge, and in his conservative nonconformism. His enormous industry, his attention to financial detail, and the range of his views have led a Finnish critic to compare him to Balzac. Certainly, he is a major figure in Finland's contemporary letters and public life; it is doubtful, though, that he is an author with a compelling vision or deep human insights.

FURTHER WORKS: *Välsignade liv!* (1951); *Slå dig inte till ro* (1952); *Våra filmproblem—filmipulamme* (1953, with Martti Savo); *Brev* (1954); *Bordet* (1957); *Helsingfors—Finlands ansikte* (1961, with K. G. Roos); *Tapaus Naisenkuvia* (1970); *Marina Maria* (1972); *Ihmisen ääni* (1980); *Dagbok från filminstitutet 1978–1982* (1982); *Presidenten* (1986)

BIBLIOGRAPHY: Schoolfield, G. C., "The Postwar Novel of Swedish Finland," *SS,* 34 (1962), 85–110; Lehtola, E., "J. D.—Action Man," *BF,* 20 (1986), 10–13

GEORGE C. SCHOOLFIELD

DORFMAN, Ariel

Chilean novelist, short-story writer, essayist, poet, and dramatist, b. 6 May 1942, Buenos Aires, Argentina

D. began his writing career as an essayist with a widely read book on the theme of violence in contemporary Spanish American fiction, *Imaginación y violencia en América* (1970; imagination and violence in America), and a second book that became an instant best-seller in Latin America entitled *Para leer al Pato Donald* (1971; How To

Read Donald Duck, 1975), which casts a sardonic look at pop culture in the U.S. But in recent years it has been in the area of fiction that D. has attracted the greatest attention. Although born in Argentina, his family lived in the U.S. for ten years before settling in Chile in 1954. Between 1971 and 1973 he served on the board of directors of Quimantú, the government publishing house, and taught courses at the National University in Santiago on children's literature and mass media. As an ardent supporter of Salvador Allende's Popular Unity government he was forced into exile (France, Holland, and the U.S.) following the military coup of 11 September 1973, and it was only in 1983 that he was permitted to return to Chile by the Pinochet regime. Today he divides his time between Santiago and the U.S., where he is professor of literature and Latin American studies at Duke University. The years of exile, however, have left their mark on his literature. His are texts deeply imbued with a sense of loss and nostalgia for a world violently erased by political currents, and they reflect a spirit of relentless resistance to the forces of oblivion.

D.'s first novel, *Moros en la costa* (1973; *Hard Rain,* 1990), was written in 1972, and by the time it was published, the author had taken refuge in the Argentine embassy in Santiago in the hope of escaping the wave of violence unleashed by the Pinochet regime against its political enemies. The novel is a socioliterary chronicle whose twenty-seven narrative sequences contain book reviews, editorials, newspaper articles, letters, movie scripts, and interviews. D.'s first work of fiction written in exile is *Cría ojos* (1979: opening eyes), a highly political collection of short stories whose principal image is a society suffocated by dictatorship. The title of the collection is an inversion of a popular Spanish refrain that underscores the negative consequences of one's behavior. D.'s inversion, on the other hand, suggests a far more positive experience. To "open eyes" for the author implies a growing awareness of one's reality and a call to action against the forces of oppression.

In writing his next novel D. drastically changed his style in the hope that he could sufficiently disguise his authorship and elude the rejection of the official censor in Chile. *Viudas* (1981; *Widows,* 1983) is the story of a village beset by political terror. Absent are all direct and indirect references to Chile and the Pinochet government. Events take place at the end of World War II in a country whose identity is never stated explicitly. Characters' surnames and geographic details prompt the reader to identify it initially as Greece during the Nazi occupation, but Longa, the name of the fictional village, is really a metaphor for all communities throughout the world whose loved ones have disappeared at the hands of dictators. While *Viudas* is laconic and lean in its prose, *La última canción de Manuel Sendero* (1982; *The Last Song of Manuel Sendero,* 1987) is a complex novel whose labyrinthine structure and multiplicity of narrative voices taxes the abilities of even the most sophisticated readers. The text is composed of three apparently distinct narrative threads whose fusion produces a moving and often comic portrayal of the struggle against abusive power.

In *Máscaras* (1988; *Mascara,* 1988) D. moves beyond the question of exile and leads his reader into a chilling Orwellian world that explores the elusive identity of power and the infinite number of masks that it utilizes in presenting its face to the world. This elusiveness is reflected in the structure of the novel itself as the reader confronts a narrative world that continually slips from his grasp. Linguistic signs are unstable. Narrators become narratees, victimizers the victims, voyeurs the spied-upon, and the powerful the powerless, in an unrelenting process of transformation and disguise. More than anything else he has written, this is D.'s most compelling statement on power and the price paid by a society that makes it its principal goal.

D.'s fiction tends to be structurally open, pointing toward an alternative political reality that transcends an apparently frozen present. While his texts offer few specific details about what that future political culture might look like, it is obviously one based on notions of collective responsibility, the defense of human rights, and a just distribution of power. Each of his narrative texts closes with an implicit "to be continued," with a sense that the final chapter in this long and arduous campaign has not yet been written. As his fiction evolves, D. tends to move farther away from any semblance of realism as a narrative strategy to one that is increasingly allegorical in nature.

FURTHER WORKS: *Superman y sus amigos del alma* (1974); *Ensayos quemados en Chile* (1974); *Culture et résistance au Chili* (1978); *La última aventura del llanero solitario* (1979); *Reader's nuestro que estás en la tierra: ensayos sobre el imperialismo cultural* (1980); *Pruebas al canto* (1980); *Hacia la liberación del lector latinoamericano* (1984); *Patos, elefantes y héroes: la infancia como subdesarrollo* (1985); *Dorando la píldora* (1985); *Los sueños nucleares de Ronald Reagan* (1986); *Cuentos para militares* (1986); *Sin ir más lejos* (1986). FURTHER VOLUMES IN ENGLISH: *The Empire's Old Clothes* (1983); *Death and the Maiden* (1990); *Some Write to the Future* (1991)

BIBLIOGRAPHY: Claro-Mayo, J., "D., cuentista comprometido," *RI,* 47, 114–15 (Jan.–June 1981),

339–45; Flora, C. B., "Roasting Donald Duck: Alternative Comics and Photonovels in Latin America," *JPC,* 18, 1 (Summer 1984), 163–83; Wisenberg, S. L., "A. D.: A Conversation," *Another Chicago Magazine,* 18 (1988), 196–210; Bennetts, L., "A. D., Agonized Exile, Writes To Fight," *NYT,* 14 Apr. 1988, C33; Atwan, R., on "Mascara," *NYTBR,* 6 Nov. 1988, 14; Boyers, P., and J. C. Lértora, "Ideology, Exile, Language: An Interview with A. D.," *Salgamundi,* 82–83 (Spring–Summer 1989), 142–63; Incledon, J., "Liberating the Reader: A Conversation with A. D.," *Chasqui,* 2, 1 (May 1991), 95–107

JOHN J. HASSETT

DOVLATOV, Sergey (Donatovich)

Russian novelist, journalist, and short-story writer, b. 3 Sept. 1941, Ufa; d. 24 Aug. 1990, New York, N.Y., U.S.A.

Born of a Jewish father and an Armenian mother and bearing the Russian name of his stepfather, D. was a true representative of Soviet culture, though he wrote only in Russian. His birthplace was the Ural city of Ufa, where his family had been evacuated at the onset of the war, but D. grew up in Leningrad. He studied Finnish philology at Leningrad University, but tired of it and was dismissed from the institution. Drafted into the army, D. was assigned to a military unit in the far north guarding strict-regime labor camps for habitual criminals. Discharged from the army in 1965, D. became a reporter and as well began to submit stories to magazines; few were published. Active in a circle of young writers, D. knew Iosif Brossky (b. 1940), and worked for a time as secretary to Vera Panova (q.v.), who took him under her protection. From 1972 through 1975 D. worked for a leading daily newspaper in Tallinn, chiefly writing human-interest stories. He was much in demand for his humor, but finally lost his position because of doubtful political company he kept. In addition, a book of stories scheduled for publication was canceled. On returning to Leningrad, D. began to circulate some of his writings in samizdat and to send others to the émigré press abroad. When the latter works appeared in print, D. was harassed by the authorities, jailed for nine days, but finally allowed to emigrate in 1978 to the U.S. He settled with his family in Queens, N.Y., where he found permanent work as a scriptwriter and announcer for Radio Liberty. D. found the time to write fourteen slender volumes during his American period, six of them translated into English. By the end of the 1980s, D. was not only well known in the U.S.—but he was beginning to be published in the U.S.S.R.

But then D. died tragically of a massive heart attack at forty-nine.

Perhaps because of his journalistic background, D. was partial to short fiction. His novels, however, were brief, really novellas. In fact, none of his books was longer than 150 pages. Ten of his stories were published in the *New Yorker* between 1980 and 1989, unprecedented for a Russian émigré and a remarkable testimony to D.'s implicit critical acceptance in the U.S.

Of D.'s four novels, the first is the weakest, but also the cause of some excitement owing to its having been published illegally abroad—appearing first in *Vremia i my*, the Israeli periodical, and then in book form as *Nevidimaia kniga* (1978; *The Invisible Book*, 1979). This work is somewhat fragmented, consisting chiefly of humorous and ironical quotations, anecdotes, observations, political jokes, gossip, and lamentations—all directed, though loosely, to the author's predicament as a samizdat writer who has reached the end of his rope. Because most of the names in it are changed, this text approximately qualifies as a novel.

Zona: Zapiski nadziratelia (1981; *The Zone: A Prison Camp Guard's Story*, 1986) is based in nearly every detail on biographical fact. It takes an existentialist view of guards and prisoners, perceiving them as in essence the same. D. implicitly challenges the rigid anticommunism of Aleksandr Solzhenitsyn's (q.v.) *Gulag* fiction. Also, despite a number of horrible Dostoyevskian events, *Zona* offers considerable humor. For instance, a sergeant earns the nickname "Fidel," after he is asked in a political exam to name any Politburo member and replies, "Castro."

Though not as harrowing as *Zona*, *Inostranka* (1986; *A Foreign Woman*, 1991) is also remarkable for its setting: Queens, N.Y., in the 1980s. It is rare that an émigré writer like D., who hardly learned a word of English, would attempt to treat in a fictional work the myriad details of a foreign culture. The foreign girl of the title, Marusia, is the purely Russian daughter of well-to-do Communist Party members; she lives in the center of the Jewish-Russian émigré community in Forest Hills; and she falls in love with and marries a fifty-year-old Latin-American "ne'er-do-well" named Rafael Gonzáles. By providing a detailed biography of the heroine, D. is able to satirize upper-class Soviet life as well as middle-class émigré life and lower-class American life. It is a tour de force of Gogolian humor. In 1990 *Inostranka* was reprinted in the Soviet journal *Oktiabr'*.

D.'s final novel, *Filial* (1990; branch office), concerns the operation of a radio station similar to Radio Liberty (called "Radio Third Wave"), a Slavic conference in Los Angeles, and the sudden appearance at the latter of the author-narrator's first wife, Tasia, whom he has not seen in fifteen years. The scene shifts back and forth between the narrator's troublesome college days (D. himself had been married for two years, 1960–1962) and the hellish but very funny Slavic conference. The narrator continually assures his present wife by telephone that everything is fine. In truth, nothing "bad" happens, except that Tasia "borrows" virtually all of D.'s money. *Inostranka* is a more successful work, but the equally satirical *Filial* is of interest for its autobiographical depictions of mixed-up Soviet youth. The novel was reprinted in the Soviet journal *Zvezda* in 1989.

Of D.'s four collections of stories, three have been translated into English and are of special interest: *Kompromiss* (1981; *Compromise*, 1983), *Nashi* (1983; *Ours*, 1989), and *Chemodan* (1986; *Suitcase*, 1990). Each offers an artifice for assembling a collection. The first tells the "real" story behind eleven human-interest stories, most of them comic, published by D. for an Estonian newspaper in the 1970s; the second offers a dozen portraits of D.'s varied and eccentric family members: Jews, Armenians, and Russians, both communists and anticommunists, from Leningrad in the west, to farthest Siberia in the east: a true Soviet family; and the third reveals the autobiographical significance of each of eight items that had filled the single battered suitcase taken by D. to the new world. The stories in all three collections, despite their satirical content, demonstrate a profound love and respect for humanity.

D.'s most important journalistic work, *Marsh odinokikh* (1983; march of the lonely), is a collection of editorial columns that D. had written for a weekly émigré newspaper, *Novyi amerikanets* (new American), he had founded in 1980. As D. makes clear, the popular publication was forced to close in 1982 by the established émigré press. (In other words, Russians in the U.S. turned out to be only a little better than those in the U.S.S.R.) D.'s main purpose in his editorial columns was to teach his fellow émigrés the way of democracy and the way of true liberalism—things he had managed to learn himself in the Soviet Union. The most basic feature of D.'s editorial philosophy—and it appears in all his writings—is the rejection of all ideology. For D. the only thing worse than a communist was an anticommunist. He had become an important figure of reconciliation between East and West when he died.

FURTHER WORKS: *Solo na Undervude: Zapisnye knizhki* (1980); *Zapovednik: Povest'* (1983); *Remeslo: Povest' v dvukh chastiakh* (1985); *Predstavlenie* (1987); *Ne tol'ko Brodskii* (1989); *Zapisnye knizhki* (1990)

BIBLIOGRAPHY: Loseff, L., "D., S. D.," in Weber, H. B., ed., *The Modern Encyclopedia of Russian and Soviet Literatures* (1981), Vol. 5, 239–41; Brown, E., *Russian Literature since the Revolution,* rev. ed. (1982), 385–86; Goodman, W., on *Compromise, NYT,* 30 Aug. 1983, C14; Fiene, D. M., on *Compromise, SEEJ,* 28, 4 (Winter 1984), 552–53; Clark, K., on *The Zone, NYTBR,* 27 Oct. 1985, 45; Grimes, W., on *The Zone, Christian Science Monitor,* 21 Jan. 1986, 26; Fiene, D. M., on *Compromise* and *The Zone,* in Magill, F. N., ed., *Masterplots II: World Fiction Series* (1987), Vol. 1, 295–99, Vol. 4, 1808–13; Kasack, W., *Dictionary of Russian Literature since 1917* (1988), 87–88; Fiene, D. M., "S. D.," in Magill, F. N., ed., *Cyclopedia of World Authors II* (1989), Vol. 2, 452–54; Ruta, S., "Russia without Tears," *NYTBR,* 30 Apr. 1989, 1, 21–22; Fiene, D. M., on *Compromise* and *The Zone,* in Magill, F. N., ed., *Cyclopedia of Literary Characters* (1990), Vol. 1, 317–18, Vol. 4, 1770–71; Gladysz, T., "A 'Suitcase' of Soviet Satire," *San Francisco Chronicle,* 12 Aug. 1990, 6

DONALD M. FIENE

DRAGÚN, Osvaldo

Argentine dramatist, b. 7 May 1929, Paraná

In Argentina, where the theater has enjoyed popularity since the beginning of the 19th c. and where this genre has been cultivated in an unbroken line with varying degrees of success, D. is one of its most talented and innovative dramatists of the last four decades. His first years were spent in Paraná, but he soon moved to Buenos Aires, where at an early age he established contacts with various independent theater groups that purported to rebel against the tenets of commercial theater by offering an alternative to the predominant theater, which was aimed at middle-class values and tastes. These were groups that were established in the 1950s, fashioned after the North American Provincetown Players and off-Broadway groups. These groups were united in a common effort. Their aim was to entertain and to make the public politically and socially aware.

D.'s indebtedness to Roberto Arlt (1900–1942), the Argentinean novelist and short-story writer who created a world populated by grotesque, alienated individuals has been thoroughly documented. Both underscore a deep-felt concern for human values. Both insist that human bonds must exist on a basis of reciprocity, in existential terms, and not on a basis of seriality.

In D.'s first successful play, *La peste viene de Melos* (1956; the plague comes from Melos), based on historical fact and depicting the struggle of the Greek isle of Melos against Athens in 416 B.C., the underlying theme is a social one. It emphasizes the negative effects of materialism on humans as it depicts the classic struggle of the business middle class against the peasant workers. On another plane, this play has been seen as an allegory that details the North American invasion of Guatemala and the fall of the Arbenz government in 1954. It is an indictment of tyranny and oppression.

Tupac Amaru (1957; Tupac Amaru), is another historical play set between 1780 and 1781 treating the uprising of the Inca José Gabriel Condorcanqui against the repressive Spanish colonial regime in Peru. It is a play that points to the continuing battle of Third World countries in our own days as they seek to undo injustices that have reigned for hundreds of years.

D.'s unquestioned masterpiece is a series of one-act vignettes entitled *Historias para ser contadas* (1957; stories to be told). In these short pieces, which depict a "new realism," the scenery has been abolished and four actors assume interchangeable roles as they establish a direct bond with the public. The basic theme of human suffering in a society that has lost all values is presented in exaggerated situations that have been magnified to ridiculous proportions. D. employs Brechtian techniques to show the alienating effect of capitalism and the degradation of the individual trapped in his or her daily work. In *Historia de un flemón, una mujer y dos hombres* (1957; the story of an abscess, a woman, and two men), D. depicts the total disintegration of a family unit where each member is so concerned with financial gain that all levels of communication are severed. *Historia de como nuestro amigo Panchito Gonzales se sintió responsable de la epidemia de peste bubónica en Africa del Sur* (1957; the story of how our friend Panchito Gonzalez felt guilty for being responsible for the outbreak of bubonic plague in South Africa), in addition to showing the degrading effect of work, also treats the theme of racial discrimination and the failure of the intellectual to assume an active political role. On a more subtle plane the story indicts prevailing business practices of industrial nations in their relationship to Third World countries.

La historia del hombre que se convirtió en un perro (1957; the story of the man who turned into a dog) is so preposterous that the audience is forced to search for a deeper meaning on an allegorical level. A man loses all dignity when he is forced to turn into a dog in order to obtain a job. When the play was first produced, the audience empathized with the predicament of the character. In 1979 the same play in Buenos Aires produced entirely different results. The economic and political situation was so catastrophic that when the man turned into a dog he was actually happy and the audience cheered. As D. said, it was easier making a living as a dog than having to go out and work at the docks.

Historia de mi esquina (1957; story of my corner) and *Los de la mesa 10* (1957; the couple at table 10) are plays that treat the theme of alienated youths separated from the values of their parents. It is during this period that D. begins to incorporate in his plays popular songs and a chorus effect to heighten the anguish of his characters.

From 1961 to 1963 D. lived in Cuba, where he organized a series of workshops and where he dedicated himself to the writing of *Y nos dijeron que eramos inmortales* (1963; and they told us we were immortal) and *Milagro en el mercado viejo* (1964; miracle in the old marketplace). The first is a strong indictment of war as well as a condemnation of the family and its failure with the youth of today. The children are emotionally crippled and ill-equipped to face everyday life. The second play hinges on the theme of cruelty. The vagabonds that inhabit the marketplace are excluded from economic participation. The ending of the play with the killing of the powerful merchant points to the need for class change, by violent means if need be.

Heróica de Buenos Aires (1966; epic of Buenos Aires) is an extremely ambitious play that recreates Bertolt Brecht's (q.v.) *Mother Courage*. Written in a popular language, it portrays the epic of marginal beings who live with political ideologies that have not been totally assimilated. There is also the appearance of the intellectual, whose political position is well defined, and whose every word is correct, but who is cold and indifferent toward the sufferings of the masses.

Un maldito domingo (1968; a damned Sunday), produced in Spain and subsequently in Buenos Aires under the title of *El amasijo* (1968; mishmash), treats the theme of alienation in existential terms. It is the story of a middle-aged couple that leads a sterile existence. Each character takes turns hurting the other as they act out their fantasies in an effort to break their monotonous lives.

D. maintains the format of the *Historias* with his play *Historias con carcel* (1973; stories with a jail theme). At a time when Latin America was witnessing political persecutions in many of its countries, this play, which depicts the repression and loss of freedom that was so prevalent, was a finalist in the Casa de Las Américas Literary Prize for that year.

D.'s interest in the theater has never waned. In 1981, together with a group of dramatists, he founded the Teatro Abierto (Open Theater). Dramatist and artists worked together to create a new alternative theater that could be enjoyed and easily afforded by the masses. Many of the plays produced were political in nature, and their theater mysteriously burned down after the first week. They reopened at another location to great public acclaim.

One of D.'s latest plays is *Arriba corazón* (1987; take heart). It is the story of the main protagonist Corazón in different stages of his life. It closely parallels the history of contemporary Argentina with its social and political ills.

FURTHER WORKS: *Amoretta* (1957); *Hoy se comen al flaco* (1981); *Al violador* (1981); *Mi obelisco y yo* (1983); *Los hijos del terremoto* (1986)

BIBLIOGRAPHY: Reynolds, B. E., "The Theater of O. D.," in Lyday, L. F., and G. W. Woodyard, eds., *Dramatists in Revolt* (1976), 77–94; Leonard, C. C., "D.'s Distancing Techniques in *Historias para ser contadas* and *El amasijo*," *LATR,* 16, 2 (Spring 1983), 37–42; Pross, E. E., "Open Theatre Revisited: An Argentine Experiment," *LATR,* 18, 1 (Fall 1984), 83–94

JOHN F. GARGANIGO

DU BOIS, W(illiam) E(dward) B(urghardt)

American essayist, historian, novelist, sociologist, biographer, poet, and editor, b. 23 Feb. 1868, Great Barrington, Mass.; d. 27 Aug. 1963, Accra, Ghana

There is an almost too obvious symbolism in the fact that the death of D., in Africa, occurred on the eve of the March on Washington for Jobs and Freedom in 1963. Through a long life D., who held degrees from Fisk University and Harvard, had been one of those most influential in preparing the way for such a gathering, and, indeed, in establishing what would prove to be important guidelines for the Civil-Rights Movement and for the Black Power movement that was soon to emerge as a significant force in American racial politics. D. was one of those present at the creation in 1909 of the NAACP (National Association for the Advancement of Colored People) and would be the hugely influential editor of that organization's publication, the *Crisis,* from its inception in 1910 until 1934. He had in his life played many roles, including those of scholar, propagandist, artist, activist, political candidate, and radical. In addition to the harassment that might be expected by any man of color who dared to challenge the racist structures of American society in the early part of the 20th c., D. was more than once the target of the nation's periodic red scares, to the point of being indicted in 1951 for failing to register as a foreign agent; the judge directed a verdict of not guilty. D. was also involved in controversy within the black community, as an eloquent critic of what he regarded as the excessive accommodationism of Booker T. Washington, the demagoguery of Marcus Garvey, and the timidity of the NAACP. His joining the Communist Party in 1961 and his assumption of Ghanaian citizenship in 1962 may both be regarded as reflecting a late pessimism as to the possibility of significant reform within the structures of capitalist America. Whether his pessimism or the optimism of the demonstrators in Washington, who paused for a moment of mourning when his passing was announced, was the more appropriate response to the American reality is a question whose answer may still be debated.

The concerns of D. the man determine to a considerable extent the activities of D. the writer. It was as a historian that he was awarded the doctoral degree from Harvard University, and his dissertation, *The Suppression of the African Slave-Trade to the United States of America,* was published in 1896 as the inaugural volume of the Harvard Historical Studies series. The book demonstrates D.'s mastery of the principles of Germanic scholarship then in vogue, while at the same time reflecting D.'s commitment to the cause of arriving at a true understanding of the African-American past and its relation to American history at large. The same concern would later produce one of D.'s most important works, *Black Reconstruction.* By 1935, when this work was published, D. had become convinced that historical scholarship and advocacy, while not identical, could not be entirely separated. Thus *Black Reconstruction,* while a thoroughly responsible work of scholarship, is also a conscious attempt to undo the harm perpetrated by white racist historians, who had portrayed the era of Reconstruction as a mixture of scandal and farce, and to evoke a proper appreciation of the many substantial achievements of the black masses and of their political representatives in the years immediately following the end of the Civil War.

D. also turned his historian's attention to the subject of Africa and of those who trace their origins to that continent in a number of works, of which the foundation is *The Negro,* published in 1915. This text was expanded in 1939 to *Black Folk, Then and Now: An Essay in the History and Sociology of the Negro Race.* The later text reflects the growing influence of Karl Marx on D.'s thought. *The World and Africa: An Inquiry into the Part Which Africa Has Played in World History* (1947) is a further treatment of this subject.

As the subtitle of *Black Folk* suggests, D.'s scholarly interests included both history and sociology. His *The Philadelphia Negro: A Social Study* (1899), a pioneer work of ethnic and urban sociology, by examining with the objectivity of the social scientist the role of the environment in the shaping of character and conduct, also makes a subtle but compelling case against notions of innate racial inferiority. D.'s editorship from 1897 to 1910 of the annual publications of the Atlanta University conferences, substantial contributions to the sociology of black America, enhanced his reputation as a social scientist.

Scholarly writing, however, constitutes only a portion of D.'s total work. His five novels are perhaps not to today's critical taste, but none of them is without interest, especially when viewed as attempts to give imaginative form to the thought of one of the towering intellects of this century. Critics have tended to prefer *The Quest of the Silver Fleece* (1911), which combines social realism (q.v.) and romance in its symbolic depiction of the Southern cotton economy, its effect on black lives, and the transfiguration that follows when the black characters take control of their own lives. *Dark Princess: A Romance* (1928), which relates the struggles of black Americans to revolutionary unrest in what we have come to call the Third World, seems to have been D.'s favorite. The "Black Flame" trilogy, consisting of *The Ordeal of Mansart* (1957), *Mansart Builds a School* (1959), and *Worlds of Color* (1961), must be regarded as his most ambitious work of fiction, attempting to depict what it was like to be black in America in the last quarter of the 19th and the first half of the 20th cs. through the portrayal of four generations of a black family.

At least one critic has expressed regret that D. turned to the novel to deal with the materials of the trilogy, suggesting that a personal memoir might have been more powerful. And most critics would rate D.'s autobiographical *Dusk of Dawn: An Essay toward an Autobiography of a Race Concept* (1940) more highly than any of his novels. As the subtitle suggests, D. is not primarily concerned in this work to provide us with the intimate details of his personal life. Rather, we are to see that life in the light of the concept; it is the concept that gives significance to the life. One hardly knows whether to describe D.'s willingness to see himself as standing for the "race concept" as an instance of the arrogance of which he has sometimes been accused or as an indication of a humility that leads him to believe that his life is of moment only insofar as it may provide insight into such a concept. The posthumously published *The Autobiography of W. E. B. D.* (1968), while hardly confessional, is rather more personal.

If any one work by D. is to be singled out as his masterpiece, most critics agree it is *The Souls of Black Folk* (1903), a book of essays and sketches in which, by a combination of scholarship, personal reminiscence, reflection, and polemic, D. draws aside the veil of stereotype, condescension, and bigotry that had rendered black America invisible and affirms the full humanity, pathos, dignity, and promise of his people.

In his role as editor of the *Crisis*, D. was involved in publishing the work of a number of important black writers, including Langston Hughes (q.v.) and other luminaries of the Harlem Renaissance of the 1920s. He was also engaged in the effort in that period to define the terms of a black literature and to spell out the criteria by which such a literature might be judged. Although Claude McKay (q.v.) and others regarded D. as incorrigibly genteel in his literary preferences, his practices as an editor and his pronouncements as a critic suggest that the truth was more complicated.

In fact, the truth about a man of such protean talents as D. must be complicated. That he lived a long and productive life in such eventful times adds to the complication, as does the fact that he was for much of his life a man in intellectual motion, constantly reexamining and moving beyond earlier formulations. Only in the last years of his life, and not entirely even then, does one have a sense of thought hardening into dogma.

FURTHER WORKS: *John Brown* (1909); *Darkwater: Voices from Within the Veil* (1920); *The Gift of Black Folk: The Negroes in the Making of America* (1924); *Africa—Its Place in Modern History* (1930); *Africa—Its Geography, People, and Politics* (1930); *Color and Democracy: Colonies and Peace* (1945); *In Battle for Peace: The Story of My 83rd Birthday. With Comment by Shirley Graham* (1952); *An ABC of Color* (1963); *W. E. B. D. Speaks: Speeches and Addresses* (1970); *The Education of Black People* (1973); *The Correspondence of W. E. B. D.* (3 vols., 1973–1978); *Prayers for Dark People* (1980); *Writings by W. E. B. D. in Non-Periodical Literature Edited by Others* (1982); *Writings by W. E. B. D. in Periodicals Edited by Others* (1982); *Writings in Periodicals Edited by W. E. B. D.: Selections from the "Crisis"* (1983); *Writings in Periodicals Edited by W. E. B. D.: Selections from the "Horizon"* (1985); *Against Racism: Unpublished Essays, Papers, Addresses 1887–1961* (1985); *Creative Writings by W. E. B. D.: A Pageant, Poems, Short Stories, and Playlets* (1985)

BIBLIOGRAPHY: Broderick, F. L., *W. E. B. D.: Negro Leader in a Time of Crisis* (1959); Meier, A., "From 'Conservative' to 'Radical': The Ideological Development of W. E. B. D.," *Crisis*, 66 (1959), 527–36; Wesley, C., "W. E. B. D., Historian," *Freedomways*, 5 (Winter 1965), 59–72; Howe, I., "Remarkable Man, Ambiguous

Legacy," *Harper's*, March 1968, 143–49; Clarke, J. H., et al., eds., *Black Titan: W. E. B. D.* (1970); Brodwin, S., "The Veil Transcended: Form and Meaning in W. E. B. D.'s *The Souls of Black Folk*," *JBlS*, 2 (1972), 303–21; Moon, H. L., ed., *The Emerging Thought of W. E. B. D.* (1972); Tuttle, W. M., Jr., ed., *W. E. B. D.* (1973); Moses, W., "The Poetics of Ethiopianism: W. E. B. D. and Literary Black Nationalism," *AL*, 47 (1975), 411–27; Rampersad, A., *The Art and Imagination of W. E. B. D.* (1976); Byerman, K., "Hearts of Darkness: Narrative Voices in *The Souls of Black Folk*," *ALR*, 14 (1981), 43–51; Stewart, J., "Psychic Duality of Afro-Americans in the Novels of W. E. B. D.," *Phylon*, 44, 2 (1983), 93–107; Andrews, W. L., ed., *Critical Essays on W. E. B. D.* (1985); Marable, M., *W. E. B. D.: Black Radical Democrat* (1986); McKay, N. Y., "The Souls of Black Women Folk in the Writings of W. E. B. D.," in Gates, H. L., Jr., ed., *Reading Black, Reading Feminist* (1990), 227–43

W. P. KENNEY

DUNQUL, Amal

Egyptian poet, b. 23 June 1940, Al-Qal'a, governorate of Qina; d. 21 May 1983, Cairo

D. was the eldest son in a fairly comfortable, traditional, small family of Upper Egypt where he completed his secondary school. By age fifteen D. started writing his first poems in the traditional prosodic forms of Arabic verse primarily for school competitions and religious ceremonies. His introduction to the Arabic and Islamic literary heritage came very early during his childhood; his father had been a teacher, the first male in the village to obtain a degree from the foremost religious institution Al-Azhar, and owned a library that was constituted mainly of religious, philological, and literary texts. In 1958 D. moved to Cairo, thus becoming part of the young literary generation of the 1960s that included, among many other figures, D.'s close Upper Egyptian friends, the short-story writer Yahyā al-Tāhir 'Abdallāh (1938–1981) and the poet 'Abd al-Rahmān al-Abnūdī (b. 1937). D.'s initial encounter with the capital was soon to be interrupted by long periods of residence and work in Alexandria, where he was enrolled for two years in the department of history at Alexandria University, and in Suez. D. finally returned to Cairo, where he settled until his untimely death in 1983 after a four-year struggle against cancer.

In Cairo D. lived in poverty, refusing to accept jobs that would compromise him as a poet. The only position that D. occupied was an honorary one in the Organization of Afro-Asiatic Unity, which guaranteed him a meagre but regular salary. In 1979, a few months before his illness was discovered, D. married the journalist ʿAbla Al-Ruwaynī who, after his death, wrote the biographical text *Al-Janūbī* (1983; the southerner), titled after an autobiographical poem by D.

D.'s first published collection of poems, *Al-Bukāʾ bayna yaday Zarqāʾ al-Yamāmah* (lament before Zarqāʾ al-Yamāma), which appeared in Beirut in 1969, quickly established him as one of the Arab world's leading poets. The collection introduces the dialogical relationship between the poet, his present, and the historical past, whether that past be Roman, as in the poem "Kalimāt Spartakus al-akhīrah" (Spartacus's last words) or Christian as in "Al-ʿashāʾ al-akhīr" (the last supper) or Arab as in the poem that gives the collection its title. Written during the later Nasser period in Egypt, when the régime was becoming increasingly sensitive and intolerant to criticism, the poems of this collection rely on the historical and the intertextual to parody the poet's present reality. D.'s rereading and rewriting of history continue to be of crucial importance throughout his poetic career as can be easily demonstrated in all other volumes of his poetry where he revives and reworks historical incidents and figures. Furthermore, the poems of the first collection announce the first instance of the prophetic and nationalist voice of the poet where D. foresees the 1967 Arab defeat in the war against Israel. D.'s subsequent collections are renewed instances of reading, interpretation, and critique of the Arab present.

D. believed that poetry derives its raison d'être from its audience. As such, it has an important sociopolitical function and is instrumental in the elaboration of a national identity. Hence his work foregrounded the political poem and fused it with elements of the classical Arabic tradition about which he was so knowledgeable. It is therefore no surprise that D.'s poetic language is characterized by the modernity of its lexicon and its ability to mediate between classical and spoken Arabic. Even though D.'s Cairo experience and encounters had led him to experiment with conventional forms and genres of classical Arabic poetry, he still continued to integrate traditional rhyme patterns as part of the musicality and orality of his work. It is for these reasons that some of D.'s poems became manifestos, memorized and recited both within Egypt and the Arab world at large. It is also for the same reasons that his poetry was eventually banned in Egypt and reimported to it through its publication elsewhere in the Arab World. Such was the fate of his 1972 poem "Safar al-khurūj: Ughniyat al-kaʿkah al-hajariyyah" (exodus: chant of the stone cake), written for, and chanted by, the student movement in Egypt. In

fact, the literary journal *Sanābil* was closed down by the Egyptian authorities because it published the poem. Similarly, D.'s "Maqtal Kulayb" (Maqtal Kulayb), published in 1975, uses the historical war of Basūs, and the last words of the murdered Kulayb to his brother Al-Zīr Sālim, as a parody of Egypt's prospective peace with Israel: The poem opens with the line "Lā tusālih" (do not make peace).

If D.'s first five volumes of poems can be regarded as fulfilling predominantly his public role as an Arab nationalist poet, then certainly his last collection, *Awrāq al-ghurfa thamāniya* (papers of room eight), offers us his more private, contemplative, sometimes even hermetic self. Whereas the earlier work belonged to the period of struggle for freedom and for life, these poems belong to the four-year period of struggle against cancer and death. The title of the collection bears the room number that D. occupied in the cancer institute in Cairo. These poems provide not only reflections on life and death but, more importantly perhaps, an attempt at rereading the self, especially in D.'s much celebrated poem "Al-janūbī" (the southerner).

FURTHER WORKS: *Taʿliq ʿalā mā hadath* (1971); *Maqtal al-qamar* (1974); *Ahādīth fi ghurfa mughlaqah* (1974); *Al ʿahd al-āti* (1975); *Awrāq al-ghurfa thamāniyah* (1983); *Al-Aʿmāl al-shiʿriyyah al-kāmilah* (1983)

SAMIA MEHREZ

DURCAN, Paul

Irish poet, b. 16 Oct. 1944, Dublin

D. studied archaeology and medieval history at University College, Cork, and received the Patrick Kavanagh Award and Creative Writing Bursaries from the Irish Arts Council in 1976 and 1980. He has also represented Ireland at the Struga Poetry Festival in Yugoslavia and the Poetry International in Rotterdam. In 1983 he traveled in the Soviet Union by invitation of the Union of Soviet Writers.

He rose to prominence among a new wave of Irish poets to emerge in the 1970s and 1980s, but stands alone for his reputation as a biting satirist of political, social, and sexual conventions in Ireland. In book sales and reading attendances, he now rivals the "grand master" of Irish poetry, Seamus Heaney (q.v.), perhaps because, like no other Irish poet today, he is read widely by academicians and lay audiences alike.

While he may at first appear to be a mere iconoclast, out to shake the social foundations of an Ireland recalcitrant to change, D. stands out from his peers for his unprecedented penchant for the satirical and the surreal. The sacred institutions of family, marriage, and Catholicism are exposed to D.'s scrutiny, in the voice of a boy soprano.

D. is like a priest celebrating the mass of the ordinary and the unpretentious. But the ordinary, in this case, is juxtaposed with the extraordinary in the form of the sacred. In "10:30 a.m. Mass, June 16, 1985," from *The Berlin Wall Café* (1985), the ordinariness of the scene depicted urges us to skip over the poem until we get to lines like "[the Priest] was a small stocky man in his forties / With a big mop of curly grey hair / And black, horn-rimmed, tinted spectacles. / I am sure that more than half the women in the church / Fell in love with him on the spot— / Not to mention the men. / Myself, I felt like a cuddle." This is a characteristic line of D.'s, for it shows his inability to resist a poke at elevated authority, but we also get the feeling that the speaker himself is on a sacred quest for spiritual elevation, even in the most satirical poetry.

In probably his greatest poem, "Six Nuns Die in a Convent Inferno," from *The Selected P. M.* (1982) and based on G. M. Hopkins's (1844–1889) "The Wreck of the Deutschland" (1875), D. mourns the deaths, but also celebrates the lives, of the six elderly nuns who died in the fire in 1986. While the title has D.'s characteristic journalistic ring, the persona is the devout, meek voice of one of the dying nuns who, at the moment of death, evaluates her life with the confidence of one whose destiny is being fulfilled, "Now tonight in the convent Christ is the fire in whose waves / We are doomed but delighted to drown." But D. can never resist the surreal touch: "Remember us for the frisky girls that we were, / Now more than ever—kittens in the sun."

D. confronts in his work the social and political turmoil in Northern Ireland. His poetry often admonishes what he perceives to be the inaction and apathy of the government of the Republic in response to the crisis in the north. In poems such as "The Anglo-Irish Agreement, 1986," from *Jesus and Angela* (1988), the political and social distance created by the border between Northern Ireland and the Republic is obliterated by D.'s surreal pen.

D. often seems determined to shock the Irish out of the nightmare of history and overdependence on the authority of politician and priest alike. In "Margaret Thatcher Joins the I.R.A.," also from *Jesus and Angela,* the speaker juxtaposes two polar opposites with the ironic wit of Swift. The reader is forced to look at a kind of unifying dialectic between the extremes of British imperialism and Irish separatism that explodes their differences and joins them in an absurd dance of death: "Margaret Thatcher joined the IRA /

And the IRA joined Margaret Thatcher. / Black Dresses were worn by all for the occasion / In which a historical union was consummated."

D.'s established reputation in Ireland and Europe has now spread to the U.S., where in 1988 he was recognized by his appointment as poet in residence at The Frost Place, New Hampshire.

FURTHER WORKS: *Endsville* (1967); *O Westport in the Light of Asia Minor* (1975); *Teresa's Bar* (1976); *Sam's Cross* (1978); *Jesus, Break His Fall* (1980); *Ark of the North* (1982); *Jumping the Train Tracks with Angela* (1983); *Going Home to Russia* (1987); *Daddy, Daddy* (1990); *Crazy about Women* (1991)

BIBLIOGRAPHY: Dawe, G., "The Permanent City: The Younger Irish Poets," in Harmon, M., ed., *The Irish Writer and The City* (1984), 180–96; Mahon, D., "Orpheus Ascending: The Poetry of P. D.," *Irish Review,* 1 (1986), 15–19; Gahern, K., "Masks and Voices: Dramatic Personas in the Poetry of P. D.," *CJIS,* 13, 1 (June 1987), 107–20; Grennan, E., "A Different World: Reading P. D." in Brophy, J. D., and E. Grennan, eds., *New Irish Writing* (1989), 203–31; Longley, E., "Poetic Forms and Social Malformations" in Brown, T., and N. Grene, eds., *Tradition and Influence in Anglo-Irish Poetry* (1989), 159–80; Foden, G., "A Permanent Performance," *TLS,* 23 Nov. 1990, 1273

FERGAL O'DOHERTY

ECHEGARAY, José

Spanish dramatist, b. 19 Apr. 1832, Madrid; d. 27 Sept. 1916, Madrid

Trained as a mathematician and an engineer, E. taught at the School of Civil Engineering until the revolution of 1868. Subsequently, he was elected to the Spanish Parliament and became the minister of finance. He was the founder of the Modern Bank of Spain and held other prominent public posts. He began to write plays while in exile. In 1875 he became extremely popular with his *En el puño de la espada* (1875; at the hilt of the sword). In fact, he clearly dominated the Spanish stage until the end of the 19th c. In 1904 he shared the Nobel Prize for literature with Frédéric Mistral (1830–1914). The literary generation that followed E., the so-called Generation of 1898, reacted negatively to this award in that to this group he represented Spain's decadence in political, social, and literary terms.

In 1874, under the pseudonym/anagram of Jorge Hayaseca, he published *El libro talonario* (the checkbook), a drawing-room comedy in which a young wife ingeniously turns tables on her unfaithful husband and in so doing demonstrates that crime is always punished. Even though after the staging of this play he held other important government positions, E. devoted himself almost exclusively to the theater as evidenced by the scores of plays he wrote.

A master of melodrama, E. brought new life to the dull Spanish stage that preceded him. At times, his characters are mere cardboard representations of human beings. His major virtue lies in the power to create and maintain suspense despite the relatively simple plots of his works, a trait that explains to an extent his association by critics with romantic drama. E.'s theater is one of extreme exaggeration. According to him, he often began his plays at the end in order to find very theatrical and, at times, high-handed conclusions to plots that were to him of secondary importance to the overall effect provoked by what he wrote. Generally speaking, it is accepted that E.'s theater lacks authenticity (referentiality) as it portrays a humanity possessed and dominated by unsubstantial—unauthentic—passion and truth. Thus, critics confront special difficulties in discussing his favorite themes (among them, honor, love, duty, religion, hypocrisy, and envy) in that their portrayal by E. had little to do with their exploration; they were used as excuses to awaken the interest of a public concerned with experiencing extreme superficial emotions during a given theatrical representation. In this sense, E. not only provided a useful indication of artistic sensitivity in Spain during the late 19th and the early years of the 20th c. (that is, after the revolution of 1868), but of a phenomenon labeled by the Spanish philosopher José Ortega y Gasset (q.v.) "the revolt of the masses," a concept that is nowadays very much valued by those interested in, among others, the influence of mass communication in the postmodern era. E., to the extent that he successfully wrote dramatic texts appealing to the masses of his day, was a craftsman in that he was very much aware of the effect provoked by his plays; he was someone who calmly calculated the best way possible to appeal to his audience.

Among E.'s best plays is *O locura o santidad* (1887; *Madman or Saint,* 1912), a work that attempts to make a moral statement as its protagonist, Lorenzo Avendaño, does his best to surrender a fortune he has inherited after discovering he is not the real heir of this wealth. His actions are, however, frustrated by greedy relatives who declare him insane and, therefore, place him in an asylum. All of this is communicated by means of the extreme verbiage so typical of E., speech excesses that were much welcome by Spanish audiences of the time.

E.'s masterpiece was *El gran galeoto* (1881; *The World and His Wife,* 1908), a work with clear connections with high comedy. In this play, society is blamed for the tragic developments that befall the play's main character as a result of the apparent unlimited power of public opinion. As is the case with many of his other works, this play documents E.'s tendency to juxtapose oversimplified and exaggerated themes in order to achieve intense theatrical effects. Thus, it is not surprising that the great Spanish playwright Ramón del Valle-Inclán (q.v.) used *El gran galeoto* as a source of inspiration as to the lack of authenticity prevailing in the modern world, a world in which human

193

beings were mere types, generic entities with passions that were mere abstractions, individuals who spoke words that were empty rhetoric.

E.'s style and approach to drama changed little during his career. In his case, the significance of his theatrical works lies not so much in the contribution made by a specific play but on his overall impact on the Spanish stage for several decades. From the 1870s to 1904, when he was awarded the Nobel Prize, E. was the fundamental Spanish dramatist, one able and willing to speak to the feelings of the Spanish masses, one in full communion with their views on the cosmos. Thus, E.'s theater is extremely significant in sociological terms as one attempts to understand a period of transition in Spanish history and aesthetics.

FURTHER WORKS: *La esposa vengador* (1874); *En el seno de la muerte* (1879); *La muerte en los labios* (1880); *Lo sublime en lo vulgar* (1890); *Un crítico incipiente* (1891); *El hijo de Don Juan* (1892; *The Son of Don Juan*, 1895); *Malas herencias* (1892); *Mariana* (1892; *Mariana*, 1895); *El estigma* (1895); *Mancha que limpia* (1895); *La duda* (1898); *El loco dios* (1900; *The Madman Divine*, 1908); *Recuerdos* (1917)

BIBLIOGRAPHY: Antón del Olmet, L., and A. García Carraffa, *Los grandes españoles: E.* (1912); Curzon, H. de, *Un théâtre d'idées en Espagne: le théâtre de J. E.* (1912); Martínez de Olmedilla, A., *J. E.* (1947); Newberry, W., "E. and Pirandello," *PMLA*, 81 (1966), 123–29; Mathías, J., *E.* (1970); Sánchez, R. G., "Mancha que no se limpia, o el dilema de E.," *CHA*, 297 (1975), 601–12; Sobejano, G., "E. Galdós y el melodrama," *A Gald* (1978), 94–115; Martín Fernandez, M. I., *Lenguaje dramático y lenguaje retórico* (1981); Ruiz Ramón, F., *Historia del teatro español (desde sus orígenes hasta 1900),* rev. ed., (1986), 350–58

LUIS T. GONZÁLEZ-DEL-VALLE

ECO, Umberto

Italian semiotician and novelist (writing in Italian and English), b. 5 Jan. 1932, Allesandria, Piedmont

E. studied philosophy at the University of Turin, receiving his doctorate in 1954. In 1956 he published his thesis, *Il problema estetico in San Tommaso* (repub. as *Il problema estetico in Tommaso d'Aquino*, 1970; *The Aesthetics of Thomas Aquinas*, 1988). From 1954 to 1959 E. helped elaborate cultural programs in the Milan office of the RAI, the Italian state television network, an experience that contributed to his understanding of the mass

media, which was to become a major subject of his writing. He was assistant lecturer of aesthetics from 1956 to 1963, and lecturer in 1963–1964, at the University of Torino. In 1964–1965 he was a lecturer in the architecture department of the University of Milano. From 1959 to 1976 E. was also a nonfiction editor for Bompiani Publishing House. He founded and now edits the journal of semiotics, *VS*, is the secretary general of the International Association for Semiotic Studies, and occupies the first chair of semiotics at the University of Bologna. Although a variety of interests made demands on his attention, E. was always attracted to the medieval world. In 1969 he published *Sviluppo dell'estetica madioevale* (development of medieval aesthetics), and his analysis of the Beato of Leibana's medieval manuscript was published in 1973 as *Beatus Apocalypses* (the apocalypses according to Beato of Leibana).

E. is internationally known for his contribution to the theoretical study of signs encompassing all cultural phenomena. Much of his study, including *A Theory of Semiotics* (1976), has been on the development of a methodology of communication. In 1980 and 1988, with the publications of *Il nome della rosa* (1980; *The Name of the Rose*, 1983) and *Il pendolo di Foucault* (1988; *Foucault's Pendulum*, 1989), E. extended the use of semiotics to the fiction genre. He has also demonstrated the practical applications of his theories in literary essays as well as newspaper and magazine articles.

At one time E. wrote for the literary magazine *Il Menabò*, edited by the socialist novelist Elio Vittorini (q.v.). One of the articles E. wrote for this magazine is "Del modo al formare come impegno sulla realtà" ("Form and Social Commitment"), since collected in *Opera Aperta* (1962; rev. ed, 1972; *The Open Work,* 1989). In this article E. expresses the desire that contemporary art seek solutions to contemporary crises by offering new ways of seeing, feeling, and understanding the universe. Art, therefore, in its special way is seen as an instrument for social change. A concern for social betterment is also E.'s leitmotiv in *Apocalittici e Integrati* (1964, rev. ed., 1977; the apocalyptic and the integrated). For E. the apocalyptic view is that of the intellectuals who think culture has been debased by mass media; and the integrated view is that of those intellectuals who see the nature of mass media as necessary and even desirable. E. takes an in-between position. He discusses the concepts of "kitsch" (which he defines as nonart that aspires to artistic status) and of entertainment (which acknowledges the complexity of the world in which we live). He advocates a form of entertainment that does not have a false artistic pretension. For E. entertainment must allow the viewers to be critical and to generate in themselves a sense of freedom of choice.

E. contributes regularly to daily newspapers *(Corriere della Sera)*, weekly magazines *(L'Espresso)*, and artistic and intellectual periodicals *(Quindici, Il Verri,* et al.). Some of his articles have been collected in books such as *Diario minimo* (1963; rev. ed., 1976; minimal diary), *Il costume di casa* (1973; the habits of home), and *Dalla periferia dell'impero* (1977; from the periphery of the empire). In these books the reader can enjoy E.'s journalistic style—extremely humorous with a number of parodies.

E. knows several languages. He is married to Renate Ramge, a German-born graphic artist, who helped translate *Il pendolo di Foucault* into German. Among English-speaking writers E. feels a special affinity with James Joyce (q.v.). Like Joyce, E. was raised a Catholic and then left the church. In 1989, during an interview with Thomas Stauder, E. said, "The person who lived the religious experience can lose God, but not the religious dimension."

E.'s *Opera Aperta* collects his major presemiotic writings on modern art and literature. *Opera Aperta* served as a theoretical manifesto for the Grupo '63. This group created an avant-garde literary movement that flourished in Italy during the late 1950s and 1960s. *Opera Aperta* is a work on general questions of aesthetics in marked conflict with the Crocean concept of pure intuition-expression. It explains and justifies the difference between modern and traditional art. In the former the artists leave the arrangement of some of their works' consituencies to the public, or to chance. On the contrary, classical or traditional art is unambiguous (even if it can elicit various responses). In fact, there is only one way to understand the text of a classical work. But modern forms of art require a much greater degree of collaboration and personal involvement on the part of the public. Modern art is associated with deliberate and systematic ambiguity. The whole notion of plurality of meaning overturns the Cartesian axes of the vertical and the horizontal, paradigm and syntagm. For E. a work of modern art is aesthetically successful when it produces "controlled disorder, organic fusion of multiple elements." For E. the modern open work is not entirely free. A formative intention is manifest in every work, and this intention must be a determining factor in the interpretative process. For E. modern art conveys a much higher degree of information, though not necessarily a higher degree of meaning. His interest in information theory was one of the factors that led to the study of semiotics.

While taking over many of the fundamentals of the structuralistic theory of Claude Lévi-Strauss

(q.v.) and Roman Jacobson (1896–1982) and of the theories of structural linguistics of Ferdinand de Saussure (q.v.), E. drastically differs from them. For Saussure meaning is the production of structure. E., however, maintains that structures are only methodological in the sense that they are provisional, hypothetical products of the mind and that they may only partially reflect the nature of things. E.'s first work on semiotics was *La strutture assente* (1968, rev. ed., 1983; the absent structure), followed by *Le forme del contenuto* (1971; the form of the content) and *Il segno* (1973; sign). E.'s most advanced and systematic semiotic work is *A Theory of Semiotics,* written originally in English and then translated into Italian as *Trattato di semiotica generale* (1975). *A Theory of Semiotics* was supplemented by the collection of essays *Semiotics and the Philosophy of Language* (1984).

Semiotics is the science of signs. All forms of intellectual, social, and cultural life can be viewed as sign systems. E.'s theory is mainly concerned with the general theory of signs. E. wants to develop a single framework for a comprehensive conceptual theory of signs within which all sign systems may be studied to facilitate a growing interaction among all of them.

For E. the process of communication entails a theory of "sign production" that depends upon a system of signification entailing a theory of codes. The latter are sets of conventions that connect systems of expression to systems of content. Through codes we recognize a gesture, a picture, or a word as standing for a particular meaning.

Although not a science, semiotics can nevertheless be used in a rational way to criticize literature, art, and films. In *Lector in fabula* (1979; reader in fable) E. gives a detailed study of reader responses to a work of art. In this work he develops general groups of categories that describe the process of interpretative cooperation between the text and the reader. At the same time E. attacks the structuralism (q.v.) of the 1960s that attributes objective properties to works of literary art. According to E., the reader uses two main concepts in the process of interpretative cooperation: the "frames" and the "possible worlds." The former are several situations or sequences of action the reader inserts in the text in order to complete its meaning. The latter are possible worlds the reader projects into the text. *Lector in fabula* concludes with an analysis of an "open work," *Un drame bien parisien* (a very Parisian drama) by Alphonse Allais (1854–1905).

E.'s first novel, *Il nome della rosa,* is written in the genre of the detective novel, with appeal to the general reader. On the jacket of the first Italian edition E. writes that his novel may be read by three different groups of readers: The first group will be involved with the plot; the second group "will attempt to establish connections with the present"; and the third group "will realize that this text is a textile of other texts, a 'whodunit of quotations,' a book built of books." *Il nome della rosa* pays homage to Leibniz, as it is a book we read long before it was written. Undoubtedly it sheds light on how modern people might read the Middle Ages. Our reading of the past cannot be innocent, because it is "produced by the discourse upon it." In *Postille a Il nome della rosa* (1983; *Postscript to The Name of the Rose,* 1984) E. claims that the title came by chance: "I liked it because the rose is a symbolic figure so rich in meanings that by now it hardly has any meaning left."

Il nome della rosa is an eclectic literary work. In it are present history and semiotics, biblical exegesis and anthropology, medieval studies and literary theory. The story is told by the eighty-year-old Adso of Melk, who narrates what happened sixty-two years before during one week in 1327. He was the Dr. Watson of Brother William of Baskerville, a Franciscan from England who was visiting a wealthy Benedictine abbey in northern Italy. William went to the monastery to mediate a discussion between representatives of the Avignon Pope John XXII and the leaders of the Franciscan order regarding their differences in approaching the Franciscan vow of poverty. William finds the abbey in turmoil over the sudden and violent death of a monk. William is asked to revive his once famous gift for investigation. He solves the murder, though not before several other monks have been killed. The murders are all connected with the labyrinthine library of the abbey. In it is preserved the manuscript of the lost second book of Aristotle's *Poetics,* which deals with the subject of comedy. The monks who died had read the book and aspired the poison smeared on it by Jorge de Burgos, an elderly blind monk who believed Aristotle's text was corrupt, and wanted to prevent its release. In the struggle that follows the discovery of the murderer, the monastery catches fire and burns down.

In the book two themes are clear: the conflict between intellectual freedom and repression; and the urge toward intellectual freedom. In *Il nome della rosa* the reader gets to know E.'s culture, love, doubts, sense of humor, and aesthetic tastes. The book is very humorous in the sense that it makes people laugh at the truth, as the only truth lies in learning to free ourselves from insane passion caused by truth. In the novel the Italian language is influenced by the languages in which E. reads, teaches, lectures, writes, and thinks. Latin is the common denominator, but if the read-

ers do not understand the Latin, the detective plot still makes sense. *Il nome della rosa* has been translated into more than sixteen languages. In 1981 it won two of Italy's main literary awards, the Premio Viareggio and the Premio Strega, and France's Medici Prize. In the summer of 1983 the American edition topped the *New York Times* bestseller list, and a film version of the novel was made by French director Jean Jacques Arnaud.

In 1988 E. published his second novel, *Il pendolo di Foucault.* While the action of *Il nome della rosa* takes place in the Middle Ages, E.'s second novel displays the scenery of the modern world from 1968 to 1984. However, through numerous references to past centuries, *Il pendolo di Foucault* encompasses the whole history of the world. The narrator is Casaubon, a young philosophy professor. While he is writing his thesis on the process to the Templarians, he meets Jacobus Belbo, who works for Garamond Publishing House. Belbo invites Casaubon and his colleague Diotallevi to select the most scientific manuscripts on the secret of the Templarians for the publisher. Within a few years, the three friends realize there was no such secret. In a playful way they decide to invent the secret of the Templarians by themselves. They make believe the Templarians had elaborated a plan that was going to lead them to the control of all the energy in the universe. The friends invent a map that six different diabolical groups had supposedly put together and placed under Foucault's pendulum in the Conservatoire des Arts et Métiers in Paris. Here they are waiting unsuccessfully to find the center of the world's energy. The plan, which had started as an ironic and playful mimesis of diabolic argumentation, leads the three friends to their deaths. E. apparently wants to teach his readers that there is no other reality than the one offered by the immanent world. It seems that the novel deals with the hazards of intellectual overreaching and the impossibility of achieving definite answers to questions that beset us all. However, throughout the book E. tries to come closer to the unreachable and authentic reality of the mystery of our human existence, as when he writes about the "epiphanic moment" Bembo felt while playing the trumpet during a funeral in the presence of the town's authorities.

In E.'s two novels we find the Peircian theory of unlimited semiosis and the Bakhtinian views of the novel as an incorporation of various genres and a linguistic hybrid. In the two novels we can trace theories and comments from E.'s essays on different aspects of modern culture ranging from Woody Allen and Snoopy to Jorge Luis Borges and John Barth (qq.v.) and so on. E.'s novels are also books about books. In *Il nome della rosa*

Adso says, "Now I realize that not infrequently books speak of books: it is as if they spoke among themselves."

In 1991 E.'s *Sguardi venuti da lontano* (looks come from afar) was published, launching a new discipline, "reciprocal anthropology." It is the result of a convention held in Italy. There a group of scholars from the African and Asian countries observed carefully the Western people and came to the conclusion that Westerners are barbaric. So the Westerners, who used to pay little or no attention to the way others understood them, now must come to grips with this new historical reality.

E. is only 59, and he is an energetic man with a prolific literary activity. We can expect many more books in the near future from him. However, he may not write any more novels. In a 1989 interview E. says in his usual playful manner, "to write the second novel means to show that I am able to produce more than one novel. To write a third novel is like to write thirty of them, and it doesn't make much sense."

FURTHER WORKS: *Filosofi in libertà* (1958); *Le poetiche di Joyce* (1965; repub. as *Le poetiche di Joyce dalla "Summa" al "Finnegan's Wake,"* 1966; repub. in English as *The Aesthetics of Chaosmos: The Middle Ages of James Joyce,* 1982); *La definizione dell'arte* (1968); *Il superuomo di massa* (1976; rev. ed., 1978); *Come si fa una tesi di laurea* (1977); *Sette anni di desiderio* (1983); *Sugli specchi e altri saggi* (1985). FURTHER VOLUMES IN ENGLISH: *Carnival!* (with V. V. Ivanov and Monica Rector, 1984); *Art and Beauty in the Middle Ages* (1986); *The Limits of Interpretation* (1990)

BIBLIOGRAPHY: Benson, T. W., on *A Theory of Semiotics, P&R,* 10 (Summer 1977), 214–16; Bruss, E., and M. Waller, "Interview with U. E.," *MR,* 19 (Summer 1978), 409–20; De Lauretis, T., *U. E.* (1981); Robey, D., "U. E.," in Caesar, M., and P. Hainsworth, eds., *Writers and Society in Contemporary Italy* (1984); Lewis, T. E., "Semiotics and Interpretation: Before or After the Fact? U. E.'s *Semiotics and the Philosophy of Language,*" *PoT,* 6, 3 (1985), 503–20; special E. issue, *SubStance,* 47 (1985); Richter, D. H., "E.'s Echoes: Semiotic Theory and Detective Practice in *The Name of the Rose,*" *StTCL,* 10, 2 (Spring 1986), 213–36; Haft, A. J., J. G. White, and R. J. White, *The Key to The Name of the Rose* (1987); Frentz, T. S., "Resurrecting the Feminine in *The Name of the Rose,*" *Pre/Text: A Journal of Rhetorical Theory,* 9, 3–4 (Fall–Winter 1988), 123–45; Inge, M. T., ed., *Naming the Rose: Essays on E.'s The Name of the Rose* (1988); Capozzi, R., "Palimpsests and Laughter: The Dialogical Pleasure of Unlimited Intertextuality in *The Name of the Rose,*" *Italica,* 66, 4 (Winter 1989), 412–28; Luke, A., "Open and Closed Texts: The Ideological/Semantic Analysis of Textbook Narratives," *JPrag,* 13, 1 (Feb. 1989), 53–80; Viegnes, M., "Interview with U. E.," *L'Anello Che Non Tiene: Journal of Modern Literature,* 2, 2 (Fall 1990), 57–75; Weaver, W., "Pendulum Diary," *SWR,* 75, 2 (Spring 1990), 150–78

MICHELA MONTANTE

"Semiotics," says U. E., the world's first professor of semiotics, "is concerned with everything that can be *taken* as a sign. A sign is everything which can be taken as significantly substituting for something else. This something else does not necessarily have to exist or to actually be somewhere at the moment in which a sign stands in for it. Thus *semiotics is in principle the discipline studying everything which can be used in order to lie.*" But this is not a work of ethics or metaphysics. E. proceeds with order, lucidity, and tact to define the boundaries of semiotics (all of culture, from zoosemiotics to rhetoric) and to elaborate two semiotic processes—communication and signification—and their associated methodological approaches.

E. defines communication as "the passing of a signal . . . from a source . . . to a destination." Acts of human communication are made possible by signification, the process by which a code links "present entities with absent units." From this distinction, E. bases a theory of codes which is in turn the foundation for a theory of sign production (and interpretation).

E. proposes a theory of codes in which the semantics has to do with the content, understood as a unit of culture. Hence, meaning is a matter of cultural conventions and not of states of an objective world. This distinction requires, for instance, definitions of denotation and connotation that do not make them extensional versus intentional processes.

Thomas W. Benson, on *A Theory of Semiotics, P&R,* 10 (Summer 1977), pp. 214–15

U. E.'s *Semiotics and the Philosophy of Language* engages readers in a discussion that is at once more and less ambitious than its title suggests. For many readers, the phrase "philosophy of language" will serve to designate those writings associated with Anglo-American analytic philosophy. Yet E. devotes only eight and seven pages respectively to an examination of the work of Hilary Putnam and of Saul Kripke; only once or twice each does he mention an idea put forward by Carnap, Quine, Russell, Searle, or Wittgenstein. Parts of the book do facilitate a future encounter between semiotics and analytic philosophy, however, while the book as a whole contributes immediately to clarifying and developing some of the most fundamental areas of semiotic inquiry. Indeed, the most ambitious aspect of *Semiotics and the Philosophy of Language* surfaces as an attempt to wrest control of a series of key concepts from those who would wish to pursue semiotics exclusively as a formalist enterprise. I believe that the book generally succeeds in this endeavor because its arguments may be seen to accord methodological privilege to a semiotics of signification over a semiotics of communication. . . .

E. never asserts explicitly in this book that he now considers that a semiotics of signification should be made to govern a semiotics of communication. That he has finally come to enact this view in his most recent work, however, need provoke little surprise. Of course, in *A Theory of Semiotics* (1976), even as he stresses the interdependence of a theory of codes and a theory of sign production, E. exercises great care in attempting to establish the relationship between a semiotics of signification and a semiotics of communication on the basis of their relative autonomy and lack of hierarchy. Yet there occur several moments in *Theory* in which such happy relations verge upon collapse.

Thomas E. Lewis, "Semiotics and Interpretation: Before or After the Fact? U. E.'s *Semiotics and the Philosophy of Language*," *PoT*, 6, 3 (1985), pp. 503–04

In U. E.'s *The Name of the Rose*, a murder mystery set in a medieval monastery, the learned Franciscan, Brother William of Baskerville, discovers that his misguided interpretation of the significance of a series of clues has led him to erroneously link several deaths that have taken place in the abbey. He comes to realize that there is ultimately no "right way" through and out of any labyrinth of clues, or signs. Although the signs themselves can be useful and valid, the idea that it is possible to create an enduring thread of meaning by linking them together and following them to a permanent truth is an illusion. "I have never doubted the truth of signs," says William to Adso, his young novice assistant; "they are the only things man has with which to orient himself in the world. What I did not understand was the relation among signs. . . ."

The pursuit of signs in the quest for truth—the structure of every detective novel—is most metaphorically embodied in *The Name of the Rose* by the monastery's library. A huge labyrinthine construction with secret passageways, cryptic indices, and rooms within rooms of ancient books and scrolls holding diverse cultures and philosophies, it is guarded by zealous monks and is open only to a select few. Through the twists and turns of a plot that is yet another maze, William and Adso end up trying to utilize the library's winding structure and coded contents to lead them to the murderer.

In this novel, a parallel search to the hunt for the murderer goes on at the same time. Casually introduced in the first few pages as the purported subject of the frame story, in this optional search (the whodunit can be enjoyed without undertaking it), the reader is the detective, and the discovery he or she seeks is no less than the text itself. In an attempt to learn the nature and authority of its creator and its ultimate truth and reality, if any, the reader must penetrate the labyrinth of the novel's structure, find a way through and, by its twists and turns of signs, genres, translated codes, par-

odies, and intertextual culture clashes, to an awareness of the shape of the novel's universe.

Jocelyn Mann, "Traversing the Labyrinth: The Structures of Discovery in E.'s *The Name of the Rose*," in M. Thomas Inge, ed., *Naming the Rose: Essays on E.'s The Name of the Rose* (1988), pp. 130–31

The difficulties in trying, for nearly a decade, to classify *The Name of the Rose* under a specific label (metaphysical, mystery, detective or anti-detective story, postmodern, historiographic metafiction; historical, gothic or essay novel; *bildungsroman*, etc.) derive primarily from the plurality of meanings, and the plurality of texts, implanted in E.'s first bestselling novel. Even before the novel reached the public, privileged critics and friends of the author, such as Maria Corti, were already debating whether or not *The Rose* was an *open* or *closed* work. My conviction is that E.'s semiotic fabula, from its very structure, proves that texts are made of unlimited semiosis and unlimited intertextuality, and that a narrative is essentially a literary and linguistic pastiche of signs and systems of signs from the great encyclopedia of literature and language(s). *The Rose* illustrates the notion that with an aesthetic test the semiotic practice of writing and reading, coding and decoding, constructing and deconstructing (in short: the whole process of signification, communication, and interpretation) is an "interdisciplinary dissemination" of linguistic and cultural codes and of encyclopedic competence, of both writers and readers. His second novel, just published, *Il pendolo di Foucault*, certainly reconfirms this.

The Rose seems to have been written to demonstrate both the Peircean theorization of unlimited semiosis and the Bakhtinian views of the novel as a "developing genre" and as a linguistic and literary hybrid. . . . In fact, E.'s novel is a perfect example of conscious (and unconscious) "hybridization"; it is a text in which many other texts merge, fuse, collide, intersect, speak to, and illuminate, one another—each with its own language and "ideologue." *The Rose*, succinctly put, is a skillful (con)structure of an intentionally ambiguous, polyvalent, and self-reflexive novel intended to generate multiple meanings. Moreover, it is a novel which wishes to be: an intersection of textual "traces" and "textures"; a dialogue with many texts; and a literary text generated through the endless process of writing and reading, re-writing and re-reading, etc.

Rocco Capozzi, "Palimpsests and Laughter: The Dialogical Pleasure of Unlimited Intertextuality in *The Name of the Rose*," *Italica*, 66, 4 (1989), pp. 412–13

EDWARDS, Jorge

Chilean novelist, short-story writer, and essayist, b. 29 July 1931, Santiago

Born into a prominent bourgeois family of English ancestry, E. graduated with a degree in law from the University of Chile and subsequently studied international relations at Princeton University. From 1957 until 1973 he was a member of the Chilean diplomatic corps. After his resignation he moved to Spain and in 1978 returned to Chile where he still maintains his residence. Known throughout the Hispanic world as a journalist, E. also served as president of the Chilean Commission on Human Rights during the Pinochet dictatorship.

E. is perhaps best known for his *Persona non grata* (1973; *Persona non grata: An Envoy in Castro's Cuba,* 1977). This volume of memoirs chronicles his experiences as the Chilean government's chargé d'affaires in Havana, where he was sent in 1970 by socialist President Salvador Allende to reopen diplomatic relations between the two countries. After three frustrating months in Havana, E. became disillusioned with the Cuban revolution and was asked by the Cuban government to leave his post.

With the publication of *Persona non grata* E. came under attack from the Latin American intellectual community because his book appeared at approximately the same time as the military coup in Chile, when unity among leftists was considered essential. E.'s memoirs, however, do not constitute a political tract inspired by right-wing sympathies, but rather a soul-searching quest undertaken by an intellectual who confronts the realities of a police state and expresses his negative reactions. In his short stories E. broke with the traditional depictions of Chilean rural life and introduced universal themes such as middle-class decadence and alienation stemming from dehumanizing government bureaucracy. Evident also in his stories are his experiments with innovative techniques and his explorations of the elusive boundaries between reality and fantasy.

E.'s first novel, *El peso de la noche* (1964; the weight of the night), portrays a conservative bourgeois family whose decline symbolizes middle-class decadence within Chile's rigidly stratified society. *Los convidados de piedra* (1978; the stone guests), E.'s most complex novel, is a mosaic of modern Chilean society. Its foreground action represents a fiesta in the home of Sebastián Agüero during the month of October 1973. Although it is Sebastián's birthday, the real occasion for the celebration is the recent overthrow of the socialist régime of Salvador Allende whose policies the host and his guests, all archconservatives, detest. The fiesta lasts an entire night during which the revelers evoke in desultory fashion episodes from the past involving characters from various levels of society. This intricate work unveils the political and social tensions that festered for decades prior to the military coup.

El museo de cera (1981; the wax museum) is best described as a political allegory, with occasional flights of fantasy, whose plot parallels events in Chile during the years immediately before and after Allende's fall from power. In the opening pages the aging Marqués de Villa Rica discovers his young wife Gertrudis and her Italian piano teacher Sandro making love in the music room of his mansion. Outraged, he expels the couple and hires a sculptor to create life-size wax figures of Gertrudis and Sandro making love, and another of the Marqués himself surprising them in their illicit act. The Marqués then places the wax figures in the music room of his mansion, which has remained unoccupied since the day Gertrudis and her lover left. The subsequent surrealistic episodes—an example is a modern dictator's television appearance in a medieval city—suggest that Chile under Pinochet was an anachronism and the Marqués de Villa Rica's wax museum, the symbol of a nation frozen in time.

In his most recent novel, *El anfitrión* (1987; the host), E. continues to quarry the rich vein of recent Chilean history, this time presenting a modern version of the Faust legend. Faustino Piedrabuena, a Chilean socialist exile bored with his life in East Berlin, meets Apolinario Canales (Mephistopheles), who treats him to the debauchery of capitalism in West Berlin and then offers him a new past, making him a noncontroversial figure and thus qualifying him to become Chile's post-Pinochet leader. E. has invented this fantasy as a vehicle for satirizing the political maneuvers in his native land along with the obstacles to healing old wounds.

Although E.'s fiction concentrates on recent Chilean history, his sensitively drawn characters, dreamlike fantasies, and complex structural techniques all but eliminate the national boundaries of his settings. One of Chile's most talented and widely read writers today, E. is steadily broadening his reputation both throughout and beyond the Hispanic world.

FURTHER WORKS: *El patio* (1952); *Gente de la ciudad* (1961); *Las máscaras* (1967); *Temas y variaciones. Antología de relatos* (1969); *Desde la cola del dragón: Chile y España, 1973–1977* (1977); *La mujer imaginaria* (1985)

BIBLIOGRAPHY: Dorfman, A., "¿Volar?: Un estudio de la narrativa de Skármeta y E.," *RChL,* 1 (1970), 133–54; Turner, J. H., on *Persona non grata, Chasqui,* 4, 1 (1974), 84–85; Vargas Llosa, M., "Un francotirador tranquilo," *Contra viento y marea (1962–1982)* (1984), 201–12; Moody, M., "J. E., Chile, and *El museo de cera," Chasqui,* 14, 2–3 (Feb.–May 1985), 37–42; Alegría, F., "J. E.," *Nueva historia de la novela hispanoamericana* (1986), 385–90; McMurray, G. R., on *La mujer imaginaria* by J. E., *WLT,* 61, 1 (Winter 1987), 93; Otero, J., "Subjetividad y mito

como modos narrativos en *Persona non grata* de
J. E.,'' *Confluencia,* 5, 1 (1990), 47–53

GEORGE R. MCMURRAY

EGYPTIAN LITERATURE

See Volume 2, page 3.

During the past two decades Egypt has gone
through a process of rapid social, economic, and
political change and development, something that
has produced a variety of effects within the cultural
sector. The move to a more open, market-oriented
economy and the development of a parliamentary
system, with a number of political parties and
press organs to reflect their points of view, has
offered Egyptian citizens new opportunities and
challenges, not all of them regarded as favorable
and beneficial by the indigenous populace. The
ever-growing size of the population and the problems of housing and agriculture, while long anticipated, continue to impinge upon the life-style and
expectations of most Egyptian families. These issues form an often problematic backdrop to literary
creativity within the country.

In the specific area of literary genres, the two
spheres in which change is most noticeable are
those of fiction and criticism. That is not, of
course, to maintain that everything has remained
static in the realm of poetry and drama, but rather
to suggest that a number of factors, some involving
the more overtly political aspects of the cultural
sector, others more subtle and complex, has led
to a gradual but perceptible realignment in the
relative prominence accorded the different literary
genres in Egypt and the attention that each receives
from critics, whether Egyptian or non-Egyptian.
A younger generation of poets and dramatists continues to produce large quantities of work, but the
cultural press will often contain articles whose
authors allude to problems associated with the
publication and reception of poetry and drama in
Egypt today.

Among significant trends in contemporary
Western literary criticism and theory that are providing new insights into the Egyptian literary tradition, one of the most interesting is that of wom-
en's literature and feminist criticism (q.v.). On
the public level, the role of Qāsim Amīn (1865–
1908) as the pioneer in the process of raising the
consciousness of his countrymen regarding the
status of women in Egyptian society has long been
acknowledged. At the turn of the century he published two famous works on the subject: *Tahrīr
al-mar'a* (1899; women's liberation) and *Al-Mar'a
al-jadīda* (1901; modern woman). Within the more
literary realm, recent research has shown that women
writers were recording their creative output, sending it to each other, and publishing their views in

a number of women's journals in the 19th c.
However, it was not until the emergence of a
series of women's movements throughout the region in the 1920s and the concomitant growth in
educational opportunities that women were to be
able to emerge as full contributors to the literary
tradition of Egypt. The increasing number of women
writers in Egypt who are making notable contributions to the literary tradition are successors and
beneficiaries of the often courageous efforts of
such prominent earlier figures as 'Ā'isha al-Taymūriyya (1840–1902), Hudā Sha'rāwī (1879–1947),
and Nabawiyya Mūsā (1890–1951).

Poetry

A number of Egyptian poets continue to retain
a position of prominence throughout the Arab
world: Ahmad 'Abd al-Mu'tī Hijāzī (q.v.), Muhammad 'Afīfī Matar (b. 1939), Mahmūd Ibrāhīm
Abū Sinna (b. 1937), Fārūq Shūsha (dates n.a.),
and Ahmad Suwaylim (b. 1942). The tragically
early death of Amal Dunqul (q.v.) deprived the
Egyptian and broader Arabic poetic tradition of
one of its most effective and beloved voices, as
seen in such collections as *Ta'līq 'alā mā hadath*
(1971; commentary on what happened), *Al-Bukā'
bayna yaday Zarqā' al-Yamāma* (1973; lament
before Zarqā' al-Yamāma), and *Maqtal al-qamar*
(1974; slaughter of the moon). Ahmad Fu'ād Nigm
(b. 1929) has earned a wide following in the realm
of colloquial poetry with collections such as *Bilādī
wa-habībatī* (1973; my country and beloved) and
Ishī yā Misr (1979; wake up, Egypt), as has 'Abd
al-Rahmān al-Abnūdī (b. 1938), who is also a
prominent scholar in the field of Egyptian folklore.

A good deal of poetry by younger writers is
published in Egypt, normally in one of the many
literary periodicals. These outlets, however, offer
only ephemeral recognition, and, while a number
of collections in book form continue to be published, no figures from this new generation of
poets have thus far emerged to a sufficient degree
to merit placement alongside the more prominent
names mentioned above. To the normal difficulties
of obtaining public recognition must be added the
fact that in Egypt poetry no longer seems to command the degree of public attention that it has
traditionally done since the beginnings of Arabic
literature. A number of possible factors are habit-
ually cited to explain this situation; the popularity
of short fiction and the close links between it and
the popular media certainly appear to be among
the most cogent.

Fiction

In recent years the world of Egyptian fiction has
been dominated by the award of the Nobel Prize

in literature in 1988 to the country's most illustrious novelist, Najīb Mahfūz (q.v.), an event that has brought his works in translation to the attention of a wider audience than has been the case with any other Arab author. Both the award itself and Western and Arab reaction to it have been the occasion for much debate concerning the role of fiction in the Arab world in general and in Egypt in particular, and the relative merits of the Arabic and Western novelistic traditions. The Nobel citation itself makes it clear that the award was granted on the basis of works that Mahfūz published before the June War of 1967, a period concerning which it can be said without exaggeration that he laid the groundwork for the development of an Arabic novel tradition upon which many others have been able to build. With regard to Mahfūz's own writing in recent times, he has produced a large number of works in both novel and short-story form. However, their appeal has not been as broad as was the case with his earlier works; the primary focus has been on local Egyptian issues, and he has often resorted to fictional techniques first essayed in novels written in previous decades. Among his most notable novels from this period are *Malhamat al-Harāfīsh* (1976; epic of the riffraff) and *Rihlat Ibn Fattūma* (1982; Ibn Fattūma's travels).

Among a younger generation there are a number of writers who have made significant contributions to the novel genre. Pride of place for originality must go to Jamāl al-Ghītānī (q.v.), who in a series of works has used the styles and structures of earlier types of Arabic narrative as a framework for fictions that discuss the dilemmas of the present; worthy of particular mention are *Al-Zaynī Barakāt* (1974; *Al-Zayni Barakat*, 1988), *Waqā'i' hārat al-Za'farānī* (1976; *Incidents in Zafrany Alley*, 1986); and *Kitāb al-tajalliyyāt* (3 vols., 1983–1987; book of revelations). The prominent Egyptian feminist writer and physician Nawāl al-Sa'dāwī (b. 1931) has written several novels that portray the status of women in Egyptian society in a graphic and often strident fashion that seems to diminish the gap between author and narrator; among her most famous works are *Mudhakkirāt tabība* (wr. 1959; *Memoirs of a Female Physician*, 1988), *Imra'a 'inda nuqtat al-sifr* (1977; *Woman at Point Zero*, 1983), and *Suqūt al-Imām* (1987; *The Fall of the Imam*, 1988). Only slightly less prolific than these writers are Sun'allāh Ibrāhīm (b. 1937), whose troubled career, emblematic of the issues of writers' freedom in the region, is reflected in the incidents recorded in his works of fiction such as *Tilka al-Rā'iha* (ca. 1960s; *The Smell of It*, 1971) and *Al-Lajna* (ca. 1970s; the committee); 'Abd al-Hakīm Qāsim (1935–1991), whose first novel, *Ayyām al-insān al-sab'a* (1969; *The Seven Days of Man*, 1989) was instantly

recognized as a major contribution to the Arabic novel genre and who, after his return from a lengthy period in East Berlin, produced a steady stream of fictional works; and Muhammad Yūsuf al-Qu'ayyid (b. 1944), whose works have moved from an early realism in describing events in the Egyptian countryside of his own childhood to a more symbolic approach, thus from *Akhbār 'izbat al-Minīsī* (1971; *News from the Meneisi Farm*, 1987) to *Shakāwā al-Misrī al-fasīh* (1983; complaints of the eloquent Egyptian). Among other contributors to the Egyptian novel in recent decades mention should be made of Abū al-Ma'ātī Abū al-Najā (b. 1932), Ibrāhīm Aslān (b. 1939), Hudā Jād (b. 1923), Edwar al-Kharrāt (q.v.), Sabrī Mūsā (b. 1932), and Bahā' Tāhir (b. 1935).

Almost all the writers just mentioned have also made contributions to the short story. In more recent decades Yūsuf Idrīs (q.v.), the acknowledged master of the genre in previous decades, made occasional contributions, but few, if any, of them managed to match the artistry and innovative quality to be found in examples from his earlier collections. He himself tended to concentrate much of his attention on short articles for the Cairo daily newspaper *Al-Ahrām*, many of which were collected in volumes such as *Shāhid 'asrihi* (1982; witness of his age).

Even if Idrīs's mastery of the short story is generally acknowledged, there is no shortage of other distinguished contributors to the genre. Edwar al-Kharrāt has written many stories marked by a symbolic and allusive language that seems at times more akin to that of poetry, while an equally careful craftsman and critic, Yūsuf al-Shārūnī (b. 1924) has contributed a smaller but valuable selection of realistic and symbolic stories. In addition to these two author-critics, a whole generation of younger authors has struggled in generally unfavorable political and economic circumstances to eke out some kind of career as creative writers; in addition to names already mentioned in connection with the novel, we may cite Yahyā al-Tāhir 'Abdallāh (1942–1980), 'Abd al-'Āl al-Hamamsī (b. 1932), Diyā' al-Sharqāwī (1938–1977), and Majīd Tūbiyā (b. 1938). Another distinctive voice that has emerged during the 1980s has been that of Alīfa Rif'at (b. 1930) who, like Nawāl al-Sa'dāwī, has been concerned with reflecting women's issues in her stories; while the tone of the narrative in Rif'at's fictions may be more muted, it is no less effective.

The popularity of the short story as a literary genre has led to the publication of a large number of individual stories and collections, although it has to be acknowledged that a great deal of the production is of purely ephemeral merit. Among emerging writers whose works seem destined to endure, Salwā Bakr (dates n.a.), Jār al-Nabī al-

Hilw (b. 1945), Muhammad al-Makhzanjī (b. 1950), Munā Rajab (b. 1953), and Mahmūd al-Wardānī (b. 1950) show considerable promise.

Drama

During the 1970s and 1980s the problems inherent in the production of Arabic drama on stage—the question of the appropriate level of dramatic language, the debates over public and private financing of production, issues of censorship or "reading committees," the competence and training of actors and directors, the overall political and cultural situation—all of these factors have conspired to pull the Egyptian dramatic tradition in a variety of directions; some might say that the result has been to pull it apart. Since the drama is the most public of all literary genres, it is perhaps hardly surprising that similar difficulties are being encountered in almost all the countries of the Middle East region. In the particular case of Egypt, theater seasons in recent times tend to be divided between productions of a seemingly endless stream of domestic farces—which, it has to be acknowledged, have been a staple of the Egyptian drama tradition from the outset—and adaptations or translations of works culled from the world tradition of drama.

As a consequence of the varying combinations of the above factors at different periods, most critics and dramatists look back on the era of the 1950s and 1960s, for all its political difficulties, as a golden age in Egyptian drama.

Criticism

The political uncertainties that accompanied the period both before and after the June War of 1967 have been particularly reflected in the realm of criticism. Several critics left Egypt or remained in exile for many years, among them Mahmūd Amīn al-ʿĀlim, ʿAlī al-Rāʿi, Ghālī Shukrī, and Sabrī Hāfiz (dates n.a.). In recent years the cultural environment has stabilized to a considerable degree, and many critics have felt able to return to their homeland and publish their views in the plethora of cultural journals that are available. There they have joined colleagues from various generations in forging a newly enlivened critical environment. A representative list of significant critics would include, in addition to those mentioned above, ʿAbd al-Qādir al-Qitt, Rajāʾ al-Naqqāsh, Jābir ʿAsfūr, Mahmūd al-Rabīʿī, Tāhā Wādī, and Muhammad al-ʿInānī (dates n.a.). The status of literary criticism has also been bolstered by the publication of two excellent journals specializing in criticism, *Fusūl,* edited by one of Egypt's most accomplished literary critics, ʿIzz al-

dīn Ismāʿīl, and *Alif*, edited by Ceza Qāsim (Kassem) (dates n.a.). These publications and a continuing series of conferences at which critics from Egypt, the Arab world, Europe, and the Americas meet to discuss issues of literary history, criticism, and theory are providing a solid basis for the fostering and development of a diverse and probing critical tradition in Egypt and continuation of the lively literary community that is its focus.

BIBLIOGRAPHY: Awad, L., "Problems of the Egyptian Theatre," in Ostle, R. C., ed., *Studies in Modern Arabic Literature* (1975), 179–93; Jād, A. B., *Form and Technique in the Egyptian Novel 1912–1971* (1983); Brugman, J., *An Introduction to the History of Modern Arabic Literature in Egypt* (1984); Allen, R., ed., *Modern Arabic Literature* (1987); Badawi, M. M., *Modern Arabic Drama in Egypt* (1987); Badran, M., and M. Cooke, eds., *Opening the Gates: A Century of Arab Feminist Writing* (1990); Booth, M., comp., *My Grandmother's Cactus: Stories by Egyptian Women* (1991)

ROGER ALLEN

EKMAN, Kerstin

Swedish novelist, b. 27 Aug. 1933, Risinge

Before she became a full-time author, E. was a teacher and literary critic and also active in the film and television industry. She began her writing career as the author of popular detective novels. One of them, *Tre små mästare* (1961; three little masters), earned her the prize for that year's best Swedish detective story. In *Dödsklockan* (1963; the death knell) the traditional elements of a detective story are still in evidence, although E. now places greater emphasis on psychological complications and on the way characters interact as a group. The author also gives particular attention to the description of milieu: The autumnal landscape and the details surrounding a moose hunt are based on exact observation and evoked with remarkable concreteness. Such realism became her hallmark when she left detective fiction and in subsequent works established herself as a leading novelist.

With *Menedarna* (1970; the perjurers) E. made her contribution to the "documentary genre" of the period by turning to a historical event, the execution in Utah of the Swedish labor agitator and songwriter Joe Hill in the early years of the IWW (Industrial Workers of the World). The novel attempts to separate the man from the myth and the legend and presents the protagonist as a victim of both hostile authorities and of "friendly" socialist organizations that wish to make use of Hill's innocence and martyrdom for political purposes. In *Mörker och blåbärsris* (1972; darkness and blueberry scrub), E. presents a tale about life in a remote village in northern Sweden. The erotic triangle drama involving seemingly insignificant characters is described with humor and moving pathos and without a trace of condescension.

The novel *Häxringarna* (1974; the witches' circles) is the first volume in a tetralogy that includes the volumes *Springkällan* (1976; the spring), *Änglahuset* (1979; house of angels), and *En stad av ljus* (1983; a town of light). In this series, her to date most ambitious undertaking, E. follows the example of a number of Swedish writers of the period, Sven Delblanc and Sara Lidman (qq.v) among them, in tracing the recent history and development of a region. E.'s focus is the town of Katrineholm, south of Stockholm, and its growth from a modest trading place in the 1870s to a modern industrial town. The changing face of the town forms the backdrop for a line of fictional characters, mainly women, beginning with the indomitable Sara Sabina Lans. The novels raise a monument to the toil and hardships of the women of past generations and depict the material progress of the emerging welfare state. But people's easier lot through improved social conditions has been achieved at a price, and the title of the last novel in the series, *En stad av ljus,* is largely ironic; E. manages to convey a sense of loss and alienation in the depiction of this modern town, its neon lights, concrete, and supermarkets. What emerges is a society in which both the older and the younger generations have lost their roots in exchange for economic security.

In her later works, the novel *Rövarna i Skuleskogen* (1988; the robbers in Skule forest) and the verse epic *Knivkastarens kvinna* (1990; the knife thrower's woman), E. experiments with a mixture of myth, dream, and realism. Her criticism of our technocratic world is here balanced by an exploration of the mystical correspondences between humans and nature.

E.'s reputation rests mainly on her strength as a realistic writer with an uncompromising respect for authenticity and minute observation. Her novels are the result of painstaking research and gathering of details and significant facts, which are elegantly incorporated in her art and frequently jolt the reader with shocks of recognition. With her tetralogy about the small Swedish town she has contributed to the renewal of Swedish historical fiction. As a writer about women and their world she has few equals in contemporary Swedish literature.

In 1978 E. was elected to the Swedish Academy. In 1989 she left her seat in the Academy as a protest against the Academy's unwillingness to take a forceful stand in the Salman Rushdie (q.v.) case. Also in 1989 she received the prestigious Selma Lagerlöf Prize.

FURTHER WORKS: *30 meter mord* (1959); *Han rör på sig* (1960); *Kalla famnen* (1960); *Den brinnande ugnen* (1962); *Pukehornet* (1967); *Hunden* (1986); *Mine Herrar . . .* (1986)

BIBLIOGRAPHY: Forsås-Scott, H., "Women's Worlds," *Swedish Books,* 2 (1979), 8–16; Wright, R., "K. E.: Voice of the Vulnerable," *WLT,* 55, 2 (Spring 1981), 204–9; Wright, R., "K. E.'s Crime Fiction, and the 'Crime' of Fiction: The Devil's Horn," *SBR,* 2 (1984), 13–16; Wright, R., "Theme, Imagery, and Narrative Perspective in K. E.'s *En stad av ljus,*" *SS,* 59, 1 (Winter 1987), 1–27; Algulin, I., *A History of Swedish Literature* (1989), 272; Zuck, V., ed., *Dictionary of Scandinavian Literature* (1990), 139–40; Wright, R., "Narration as Transformative Power: K. E.'s *The Robbers of Skule Forest,*" *SBR,* 1 (1991), 11–12

LARS G. WARME

EMECHETA, Buchi

Nigerian novelist and juvenile fiction writer (writing in English) b. July 1944, Lagos

E. was born and grew up in Lagos, speaking both Ibo and Yoruba. Her Ibo parents died when she was quite young. To her village, Ibusa, and to her father's sister, "Big Mother," she attributes her own desire to write, to tell stories of her own family history and traditions. Although her mother wished E. to be engaged at age eleven, E. insisted on studying at Methodist Girls' High School in Lagos on scholarship until she was sixteen, when she married. After the birth of her first baby, she followed her student husband to London. To support her growing family, she took various odd jobs at places like a library and a home for underprivileged youth. She separated from her abusive and indolent husband. Working, writing at odd hours, she also studied sociology at the University of London. E. obtained her bachelor's degree in 1974. She has won several awards: Daughter of Mark Twain (1975), Afro-Caribbean Post's Golden Sunrise Award (1978), Jock Campbell–New Statesman Award (1977), Best Third World Writer for 1976–1979 Award (1979), and Best Black Writer in Britain Award (1980). Her success and international reputation enabled her to devote her time to lecturing and writing, in Africa, in Europe, and in the U.S. She founded her own publishing house named Ogwugwu Afo for an Ibo goddess. She currently makes her home in London.

"Keeping her head above water" as a single parent, a second-class citizen, poor, black, and foreign in an alien world, she calls a miracle. Most of her works reflect her own experiences as an immigrant Nigerian working woman in London, or those of her relatives in the Nigerian colonial setting of World War II or of the Biafran War (1967–1970). E. first published a column of "Observations of the London Poor" in the *New Statesman*. She later consolidated these and other anecdotes of her own life on the dole in her novel, *In the Ditch* (1972). In 1974 she published *Second-Class Citizen,* her story of her struggle for independence from her husband and from penury. The two were published together as *Adah's Story* (1983). She could afford to move with her five children from county council housing to her own home in North London. Her next two novels, *The Bride Price* (1976), based on traditional Ibo marriage customs, and *The Slave Girl* (1977), modeled somewhat on her own mother's experience in Nigeria a generation ago, required sociological research as well as family oral histories. In her ironic novel *The Joys of Motherhood* (1979) she draws her main character from her own mother-in-law, a woman obedient to traditional values of fecundity in a changing world of urbanization and Western belief systems. In *Destination Biagra* (1981) her protagonist, a female military attaché, witnesses the devastation and atrocities of Nigeria's civil war, in which many of E.'s relatives suffered and died. Although she herself was in England at that time, she used eyewitness testimonies and letters to substantiate her war account.

E.'s juvenile fiction follows the course of her adult novels. *Nowhere to Play* (1980) mirrors the lives of her own children at the London housing project. *Titch the Cat* (1979) refers to their first pet in their own home. *The Moonlight Bride* (1980) describes a Nigerian village marriage custom. *The Wrestling Match* (1980) urges postwar youth against conflict and violence. *Niara Power* (1982) exposes faults of current, materialistic African society.

E. turned later to fiction not so literally based on her own experience. The novel *Double Yoke* (1982) is set at the University of Calabar where E. was a guest lecturer, but presents a student view of harassment and chicanery in academia. E.'s science-fiction novel *The Rape of Shavi* (1983) takes place in Europe and Africa, and pleads for world peace. In *Gwendolyn* (1990; pub. in the U.S. as *The Family,* 1990) E. uses a West Indian girl, sexually abused, as her protagonist, who grows up in Jamaica but moves to England and London's immigrant district. Thwarted in her hopes for schooling and security, she survives her hostile family environments and hopes that her daughter, with maternal support, will prosper. In E.'s auto-

biography, *Head above Water* (1986), E. recounts her own first forty years of endurance, hardship, and persistence. She includes some description of her television and radio work. She is justly proud that she has achieved stability for her family, security for herself, and the satisfaction of what had seemed an impossible goal: success as an author, a woman, writing in a "fourth" language in an alien atmosphere.

E.'s strength as a writer relies on the force of her own personality and her clear narrative style. Emulating her "Big Mother's" storytelling power E. succeeds in holding the reader's attention and sympathy. She paints her own adventures with realistic detail, warmth, sympathy, and humor. Her best work is compellingly human, not analytic nor lyric. She feels passionate about woman's position, but is not doctrinaire enough to satisfy all feminists. Her friend, novelist Flora Nwapa (b. 1931), who has written fiction over twenty years and also established a printing company, is a kind of model for E. However, Nwapa remains in West Africa and follows the changing Nigerian scene. E., if she continues to draw her stories from the events of her own life, must turn to England and its multicultural environment for her subjects. Her autobiography reads as easily as her novels, but does not reveal her future plans. She promises to update it from time to time.

BIBLIOGRAPHY: Bray, R., "Nefertiti's New Clothes," *Voice Literary Supplement,* June 1982, 13–14; Bruner, C., and D. Bruner, "B. E. and Maryse Conde," *WLT,* 59, 1 (Winter 1985), 9–13; Bruner, C., "The Other Audience: Children and the Example of B. E.," *AfrSR,* 29, 3 (Sept. 1986), 129–40; Davies, C. B., and A. A. Graves, eds., *Studies of Women in African Literature* (1986), 173–80, 241–56; James, A., ed., *In Their Own Voices* (1990), 34–45; Davies, C. B., "Private Selves and Public Spaces: Autobiography and the African Woman Writer," *Neohelicon,* 17, 2 (1990), 183–210

CHARLOTTE H. BRUNER

ENDŌ Shūsaku

Japanese novelist, dramatist, and essayist, b. 27 Mar. 1923, Tokyo

E. lived with his parents in Dalian, China, between the ages of three and ten; when his mother filed for divorce, she returned to Japan with E. and his brother, and there all three became Catholics. E. was eleven at the time of his baptism, and has often described the experience as having a suit of foreign clothing placed on him by his mother. His chief literary task, he has written, has been to retailor those foreign clothes to fit his Japanese body. E. graduated in French literature from Keiō University, and was among the first group of Japanese chosen for overseas study after World War II. In 1950 he sailed to France, where he lived for almost three years, studying Catholic writers at the University of Lyons. A serious lung ailment forced him to return to Japan, where he began publishing essays and fiction. A trip to Europe to study the Marquis de Sade (1740–1814) was cut short by another pulmonary illness, which forced E. into two and a half years of hospitalization and three operations, which resulted in the removal of one entire lung.

After recuperating, E. began writing about the persecution of Japanese Christians in the 17th c. He also undertook management of Kiza, the largest amateur theatrical troupe in Japan, and became editor of the major literary journal *Mita Bungaku*. He was elected to the Japan Academy of Arts in 1981, was voted president of the Japan chapter of P.E.N. in 1985, and was designated a "person of cultural merit" by the Japanese government in 1988.

E.'s earliest works, including the novella *Shiroi hito* (1955; white men) and its companion work, *Kiiroi hito* (1955; yellow men), and such novels as *Umi to dokuyaku* (1957; *The Sea and Poison*, 1972) and *Kazan* (1959; *Volcano*, 1978) raise large philosophical and moral questions about the differences in spiritual climates between Japan and the West. For the most part they argue, through the presentation of apostate foreign priests and unfeeling Japanese converts, that the sense of guilt and sin that informs the Christian West is absent in Japan. These works are largely pessimistic about the possibility of planting the seeds of Christian moral accountability in Asian soil.

With the publication of the short-story collection *Aika* (1965; elegies), however, and most especially the novel *Chimmoku* (1966; *Silence*, 1969), E. began to suggest the prospect of salvation from the spiritual "mud swamp" of Japan through acts of caring and selfless love on the part of weak, often ineffectual characters. In *Chimmoku*, it is a European priest who cannot stand up to the tortures of Japanese officials in the period of persecution who apostatizes in order to save the lives of innocent Japanese believers. His inverted "conversion" to a more internalized, passive form of worship sets the model for later E. protagonists.

If a highly Japanized version of Christianity emerges victorious in *Chimmoku*, in E.'s next major historical novel, *Samurai* (1980; *The Samurai*, 1982), both the passionately fervent Western priest and the withdrawn, hesitant Japanese samurai convert are allowed to follow their separate visions of Christian devotion. The mode of narration in *Samurai*, shifting between the first-person accounts of the dynamic Spanish priest and the omniscient passages that gently intimate the emotions of the Japanese warrior, allowed E. to affirm both the diversity and the viability of these very disparate approaches to Christ.

In his most recent novel, *Sukyandaru* (1986; *Scandal*, 1988), E. has departed from the historical-fiction genre to examine questions of the nature of evil in the contemporary age, framed in a simple doppelgänger tale. E. parodies his own position as the leading Japanese Christian writer in this work, proposing that the power of wealth and position can bury public scandals, but that scandals of the soul are what canker the individual's relationship with deity.

E. has also written a large number of humorous novels and essays, and in Japan is highly regarded for these lighter works. The entertainment novels include *Obakasan* (1959; *Wonderful Fool*, 1974), which examines the spiritual and cultural gap between Japan and the West from a gentler angle in its portrayal of a bumbling Frenchman loose in modern-day Tokyo; *Watashi ga suteta onna* (1963; the girl I left behind), in which E. presents his view of a contemporary saint in the form of a young woman who sacrifices her own happiness to work at a leper colony; and *Kuchibue o fuku toki* (1974, *When I Whistle*, 1979), in which self-centered high achievers of the modern age are contrasted with the bonds of friendship that linked young people during the war years.

E. has cut a unique and original niche for himself in contemporary Japanese fiction, exploring questions of moral responsibility and religious adherence that are largely anathema to his fellow writers. The contrasts between Japan and the West that he explores, the adroit construction of his novels, and the compassionate concern he has for the weak and suffering characters in his stories have made him one of the most controversial and widely read authors of his generation in Japan.

FURTHER WORKS: *Hechimakun* (1961); *Kekkon* (1962); *Tomoshibi no urumu koro* (1964); *Ichi ni san* (1964); *Ryūgaku* (1965; *Foreign Studies*, 1989); *Ōgon no kuni* (1966; *The Golden Country*, 1970); *Kin to gin* (1966); *Kyōsōkyoku* (1966); *Saraba natsu no hikari yo* (1966); *Yami no yobu koe* (1966); *Dokkoisho* (1967); *Kaidanji, kaidanji* (1968); *Kagebōshi* (1968); *Taihen daa* (1969); *Bara no yakata* (1969); *Rakuten taishō* (1969); *Haha naru mono* (1971); *Kurombō* (1971); *Tadaima rōnin* (1972); *Shikai no hotori* (1973); *Menamugawa no Nipponjin* (1973); *Iesu no shōgai* (1973; *A Life of Jesus*, 1978); *Piero no uta* (1974); *Kare no ikikata* (1975); *Minoue sōdan* (1975); *Suna no shiro* (1976); *Tetsu no kubikase*

(1977); *Kanashimi no uta* (1977); *Kirisuto no tanjō* (1978); *Jū to jūjika* (1979); *Jūichi no iro garasu* (1979); *Ōhi Marii Antowanetto* (1980); *Mahiru no akuma* (1980); *Chichioya* (1980); *Ōkoku e no michi* (1981); *Tenshi* (1982); *Onna no isshō; Kiku no baai* (1982); *Onna no isshō; Sachiko no baai* (1982); *Shukuteki* (1985); *Waga kou hito wa* (1987); *Hangyaku* (1989). FURTHER VOLUME IN ENGLISH: *Stained Glass Elegies: Stories by Shusaku Endo* (1985)

BIBLIOGRAPHY: Uyttendaele, F., "S. E.," *Japan Christian Quarterly*, Fall 1972, 199–205; Mathy, F., "S. E.: The Second Period," *Japan Christian Quarterly*, Fall 1974, 214–20; Woodward, K., "Finding Jesus in Japan," *Newsweek*, 1 Dec. 1980, 106; Wills, G., "Embers of Guilt," *NYRB*, 19 Feb. 1981, 21–22; Gessel, V. C., "Voices in the Wilderness," *MN*, 37, 4 (Winter 1982), 437–57; Ribeiro, J., "Of Martyrdom and Apostasy," *Asiaweek*, 21 Oct. 1983, 63–65; Gessel, V. C., "E. S.," *Encyclopedia of Japan* (1983), Vol. 2, 214; Ribeiro, J., "S. E.; Japanese Catholic Novelist," *America*, 2 Feb. 1985, 87–89; Gessel, V. C., *The Sting of Life* (1989), 231–81

VAN C. GESSEL

ENGLISH LITERATURE

See Volume 2, page 33.

Britain in the 1980s will long be linked with the rise to power of Margaret Thatcher and the Conservative Party. As prime minister, Thatcher presided over a series of highly controversial policies that brought about substantial cuts in government spending for a wide range of social and industrial programs. Thatcher's backers insisted that a return to market economics would enliven an economy that was sluggish throughout the 1970s; and, indeed, throughout the 1980s much of England enjoyed levels of prosperity rarely seen during the postwar era. But as the critics of "Thatcherism" often noted, unemployment in the nation stayed high throughout the decade, particularly in the industrial north, where—more than once—protestors took to the streets.

As the 1960s had revealed, art tends to thrive during periods of new prosperity and wide social debate; and, in fact, the 1980s proved to be a rich decade for British fiction, drama, and poetry. Much of this vitality has owed to the fact that many older authors have continued to produce works showing little or no diminution in their creative powers. Among younger writers—those born in the 1940s and 1950s—one finds many highly talented voices at work in both traditional and postmodern modes. The increasing cultural diversity

of contemporary Britain has also added vigor to its literature. Several of Britain's best new writers have roots outside the European tradition; others have backgrounds in the lower middle class.

Fiction

With the death of Graham Greene (q.v.) in 1991, the English-speaking world lost one of its finest storytellers, the creator of a distinctive world of intrigue, exoticism, and sin that critics came to call "Greeneland." Beginning with *Doctor Fischer of Geneva: or the Bomb Party* (1980), Greene's novels tended to become leaner, but continued to reveal a penchant for exploring questions related to politics and religion. In the picaresque *Monsignor Quixote* (1982), the best of his final novels, Greene combines his fine comic skills with a continuing interest in Marxism and Christianity—traits that have always marked much of his fiction. *The Captain and the Enemy* (1988), the last novel Greene published in his lifetime, deftly blends politics and suspense as it deals with several ambitious themes, including the meaning of fatherhood and the nature of love.

In 1983 William Golding (q.v.) won the Nobel Prize for literature—a decision that surprised many British and American journalists and critics who had come to assume, understandably, that the award would go instead to Greene. In *Darkness Visible* (1979), the most surreal of his more recent novels, Golding weaves a richly textured account of cruelty and social derangement in contemporary Britain, mixing realism and allegory along the way; in *Rites of Passage* (1980), he echoes both Laurence Sterne (1713–1768) and Joseph Conrad (q.v.) as he constructs a blackly comic account of a 19th-c. sea voyage, which he continues in *Close Quarters* (1987) and *Fire Down Below* (1989). Golding's underrated *The Paper Men* (1984) raises a series of provocative questions about fiction writing—and fame—as it follows the farcical, finally fatal battle between a celebrated English novelist and a crass American academic on his own quest for success.

Although he calls himself "a busy hack," Anthony Burgess (q.v.) will surely come to be ranked, with Golding and Greene, as one of his generation's leading literary figures. In such novels as *The End of the World News* (1982) and *The Kingdom of the Wicked* (1985) Burgess exhibits his exuberant wit, erudition, and stylistic bravura; in *Earthly Powers* (1980) he creates, in Kenneth Toomey, one of the decade's most fully realized fictional characters, and again explores moral issues in a cosmos he shows to be continually wracked by the struggle between good and evil. The most entertaining of Burgess's later books, however, is his candid and lively autobiography, published in two widely praised volumes, *Little Wilson and Big God* (1987) and *You've Had Your Time* (1990).

Others known for their philosophical fiction continued to publish notable work in the 1980s, among them Iris Murdoch, Muriel Spark, and John Fowles (qq.v.). In novels such as *The Philosopher's Pupil* (1983), *The Good Apprentice* (1985), and *The Message to the Planet* (1989) Murdoch persists in pairing striking characters with complex plots, focusing again on such concerns as power, enchantment, obsession, and chance; although less shapely than her earlier novels, these works remain filled with sparkling wit and intellectual vigor. Spark's more recent novels have also remained satisfying in their darkly comic way; in *A Far Cry from Kensington* (1988), the best of these, she explores with aplomb several of her favorite subjects—including wickedness and deceit—while providing a vivid portrait of the world of British book publishing in the grim postwar years of the early 1950s. Like Murdoch and Spark, John Fowles developed an enormous following in both Europe and America during the 1970s. But with *Mantissa* (1982)—a lively exploration of eros, gender, and creativity that some critics found self-absorbed and contrived—Fowles's reputation and readership began to decline. Convincingly set in 18th-c. Britain, Fowles's *A Maggot* (1985) is even more demanding, balancing several plots while displaying a keen interest—at once playful and serious—in a wide range of linguistic, social, and metaphysical matters.

Doris Lessing and Margaret Drabble (qq.v.) also continued to publish what might be called "novels of ideas." Lessing has often puzzled critics by declining to be confined to a particular style, voice, or even genre; for example, with *The Sirian Experiments* (1981), *The Making of the Representative for Planet 8* (1982), and *The Sentimental Agents in the Volyen Empire* (1983) she completed a series of five science-fiction novels (collectively entitled *Canopus in Argos: Archives*) that provided her with an unusual—and unusually expansive—canvas for displaying her deep interest in subjects ranging from politics to economics to Sufi thought. In *The Diary of a Good Neighbour* (1983) and *If the Old Could* (1984) Lessing returned to contemporary Britain and a precisely "realistic" style, but published both novels under the pseudonym "Jane Somers" in order to demonstrate the difficulties faced by unknown novelists in need of publicity and support. Although Margaret Drabble—one of Britain's most visible literary figures—is by no means as unpredictable as Lessing, she has now published several novels quite unlike those that first brought her wide notice

in the 1960s. *The Middle Ground* (1980) and the trilogy consisting of *The Radiant Way* (1987), *A Natural Curiosity* (1989), and *The Gates of Ivory* (1992), are more ambitiously structured—and generally darker—than *A Summer Bird-Cage* (1962), or *Jerusalem the Golden* (1967). Increasingly, Drabble has produced large, allusive, multilayered, highly self-conscious fictions that tend to show Britons searching for meaning and normality in a world grown increasingly bizarre and bleak.

In various forms, novels belonging to what Malcolm Bradbury (b. 1932) has termed "the socio-moral tradition of fiction" have continued to thrive in Britain, where—as Drabble's own work shows—the presence of such figures as Dickens, Disraeli, and Gaskell remains strong. Although John Mortimer (b. 1923) is probably best known in Britain as the creator of "Rumpole of the Bailey" and as an insightful interviewer skilled at drawing out the diverse likes of John Gielgud and Mick Jagger, he deserves wider fame for such novels as *Paradise Postponed* (1985) and *Titmuss Regained* (1990). Indeed, these works show a certain Victorian fondness for dark secrets and mysterious inheritances, while offering a sharp commentary on Thatcherite conservativism. Like Mortimer, the prolific Fay Weldon (q.v.) has written many plays for both television and the stage; as a novelist, she is known for a distinctive style that blends breezy plotting, dark—often bitter—humor, and an intrusive authorial voice. Weldon's *Darcy's Utopia* (1990) reflects well her continuing interest in political issues; in *Life Force* (1992) she turns again to the blunt treatment of gender issues and sexual themes.

Martin Amis (b. 1949), another writer much concerned with the state of modern society, first came to wide attention with *The Rachel Papers* (1973), a brash, funny, and wholly convincing account of adolescent romance and self-absorption. But his subsequent works, including the short-story collection *Einstein's Monsters* (1987) and the novel *London Fields* (1989), reveal more fully the fear and despair that often seemed dominant in the decade of Chernobyl, global warming, and AIDS. Understandably, Amis's work has often been criticized for its persistently nasty tone. But his *Money: A Suicide Note* (1984)—often moving, often annoying—is a postmodern masterpiece, the tragicomic account of one man's self-destruction in an era of rampant materialism and greed.

Like Martin Amis, Indian-born Salman Rushdie (q.v.) is also an experimental and controversial novelist. Rushdie's earlier fictions, including *Midnight's Children* (1980) and *Shame* (1983), were widely praised for their exuberance, erudition, and imaginative flights; many critics compared them favorably to works by such internationally acclaimed practitioners of magic realism (q.v.) as Jorge Luis Borges and Gabriel García Márquez (qq.v.). But others have found verbosity, tedium, and a kind of adolescent smugness in Rushdie's novels, including *The Satanic Verses* (1988), easily one of the most controversial works in recent literary history; protests over its treatment of certain aspects of Muslim culture and belief grew intense enough to prompt charges of blasphemy and, eventually, death threats that—in 1989—sent Rushdie into prolonged hiding. Rushdie's *Haroun and the Sea of Stories* (1990), written during his confinement, does not deal overtly with political or religious issues, but—in a style designed to appeal to both children and adults—recounts one storyteller's plight and grants him a happy ending.

Rushdie's *Imaginary Homelands* (1991), a collection of essays on culture and literature, was among the first titles published by Granta Books, an offshoot of *Granta* magazine, which emerged during the 1980s as Britain's most influential literary magazine. Artfully packaged and widely distributed through Penguin Books, *Granta* offered stories and essays by a large range of internationally acclaimed authors and often brilliantly chronicled the massive social and political change facing Europe as economic borders fell and communism collapsed. Indeed, few literary publications in recent decades have managed to sustain both quality and influence as well as *Granta*.

Julian Barnes (b. 1946) and J. G. Ballard (b. 1930) are also associated with more experimental forms of fiction. Barnes has published several novels using intriguing structural strategies; in *Flaubert's Parrot* (1984), for example, he constructs a largely comic tale of scholarly obsession that sparks various questions about the conventions of both fiction and literary biography; in *Talking It Over* (1991) he employs three narrators to tell a cleverly compelling tale about the pain of love and the comfort of words. Ballard, like Barnes, often bridges the gap between popular and ''serious'' literature, and eludes easy categorization. Such works as *Crash* (1973), *Vermillion Sands* (1973), and *High Rise* (1975) blend humor and fantasy with apocalyptic tendencies and a touch of the surreal, and are sometimes labeled ''science fiction.'' But as *The Day of Creation* (1987) particularly proves, Ballard's fantasy fiction has many qualities—including stunningly precise descriptions of landscape and place—that are rarely found in genre literature of any kind. He has, moreover, excelled in such ''mainstream'' fictions as *Empire of the Sun* (1984), which draws upon Ballard's boyhood in China during World War II, and *The Kindness of Women* (1991), another display of fictionalized autobiography.

The prolific Michael Moorcock (b. 1939) is also hard to classify. But fantasy, wit, and a fascination

with history and myth continue to combine in his fictions, including *The City in the Autumn Stars* (1987) and *Mother London* (1989). Robert Nye (b. 1939) displays a similarly lively sensibility; his novels *Faust* (1981), *The Memoirs of Lord Byron* (1989), and *The Life and Death of My Lord Gilles de Rais* (1990) show him successfully drawing inspiration from history and older literary sources.

Like Ballard, Angela Carter (1940–1991) began publishing usually imaginative fiction in the 1960s but only recently came to wide notice; such novels as *Nights at the Circus* (1984) and *Wise Children* (1991)—as well as several of the essays in *Expletives Deleted* (1992)—confirm her place as one of the most distinctive voices of recent years. Another unusual talent, Christine Brooke-Rose (b. 1923), is perhaps as well known for her literary scholarship as her fiction. To be sure, Brooke-Rose's many novels, ranging from *The Dear Deceit* (1961) to *Textermination* (1991) will never be widely popular, but their mix of sophisticated wordplay and rare erudition will undoubtedly attract more critical interest in the years to come.

Among other established British writers, Kingsley Amis, David Storey, and Alan Sillitoe (qq.v.), have continued to publish significant fiction in a more traditional vein. Two of Amis's recent novels, *Stanley and the Women* (1984) and *Difficulties with Girls* (1988), were widely praised for their solid plots and strong characterizations, but also drew fire from some critics who found them marred by misogynist overtones. Amis's *The Old Devils* (1986) was, however, more warmly received for its sympathetic—if unsentimental—depiction of a group of friends on the verge of old age. Storey produced, in *Saville* (1976), a lengthy, intricately shaped account of working-class life that won Britain's prestigious Booker Prize; *A Prodigal Child* (1982), and *Present Times* (1984)—as well as *Storey's Lives: Poems 1951–1991* (1992)—have confirmed his status as one of modern Britain's most versatile and accomplished writers. Sillitoe also centered on working-class characters in several works, including *Out of the Whirlpool* (1987), a novella, and *The Open Door* (1989), a strong addition to his series of novels dealing with the Seaton family of Nottingham. Other notable novelists maintain strong reputations with British critics and readers. These include Stanley Middleton (b. 1919), Elizabeth Howard (b. 1923), Keith Waterhouse (b. 1929), Isabel Colegate (b. 1931), David Pownall (b. 1938), and Rose Tremain (b. 1943).

Both Malcolm Bradbury and David Lodge (q.v.) continued to attract growing audiences outside the United Kingdom. Because both have superb comic skills and have written frequently—and irreverently—of academic life, they are sometimes referred to simultaneously as "Brodge." Bradbury's more recent fictions include *Cuts: A Very Short Novel* (1987), which lampoons British television while capturing the atmosphere of uncertainty that prevailed in the summer of 1986, when layoffs and firings were common in both government and industry, and talk of "privatization" was much in the air. Bradbury's best novel remains *The History Man* (1975), a brilliantly crafted account of moral confusion and radical chic. Lodge's *Changing Places* (1975) and *Small World* (1984), offering exaggerated but insightful depictions of the rivalries and anxieties of academic life, have acquired a kind of cult status among professors on both sides of the Atlantic. Lodge has also examined the role religion plays in modern life; in *How Far Can You Go?* (1980; pub. in the U.S. as *Souls and Bodies,* 1982), for example, he ably portrays a group of characters caught awkwardly between the demands of the church and the temptations of a newly permissive society.

Penelope Fitzgerald (b. 1916), Anita Brookner (q.v.), and Penelope Lively (b. 1933) also earned much critical praise during the 1980s. After establishing herself as a respected writer of literary biographies, Fitzgerald began producing novels that differ impressively in their selection of characters and settings; *Human Voices* (1980), for example, portrays BBC broadcasters at work during the early days of World War II; *Innocence* (1986) is set in Florence in the 1950s; *The Beginning of Spring* (1988) takes place in Moscow just before the Russian Revolution. Brookner's settings and situations are less varied; as *A Start in Life* (1981; pub. in the U.S. as *The Debut,* 1981), *Hotel du Lac* (1984), *A Friend From England* (1987), and the particularly fine *A Closed Eye* (1991) suggest, she has tended to focus on women facing the difficulties and illusions of romantic love. But Brookner is a precise stylist whose keen sense of irony tends to keep her work from becoming predictable or cloying. Penelope Lively published several well-regarded works of fiction for both children and adults in the 1970s, but her reputation and readership rose significantly after *Moon Tiger* (1987), a memorable meditation on time, history, and personal destiny that won the Booker Prize.

A. S. Byatt (b. 1936) and Emma Tennant (b. 1937) also found many new readers during the 1980s. Byatt, an astute reviewer and critic, became known as a novelist in North America with *The Virgin in the Garden* (1978); *Possession* (1990), her most successful novel, also shows an ambitious interest in history, myth, mystery, and 19th-c. literature. Like Byatt, Tennant often makes artful use of older literary sources while maintaining her own highly distinctive voice. In *The Bad Sister* (1978), for example, she adapts James Hogg's

(1770–1835) *The Private Memoirs and Confessions of a Justified Sinner* (1824), a vivid account of mayhem and demonic possession. Gothic elements also inform Tennant's *Woman Beware Woman* (1983; pub. in the U.S. as *The Half-Mother,* 1983), perhaps her best novel, a well-told tale of deception and revenge. In *The Adventures of Robina, by Herself* (1985), Tennant updates Daniel DeFoe; in *Faustine* (1992), she effectively recasts the Faust myth in modern guise.

Other novelists of promise emerged during the decade, including William Boyd (b. 1952), Graham Swift (b. 1949), and Kuzuo Ishiguro (b. 1954). With his first novel, *A Good Man in Africa* (1981), Boyd produced the best English comic novel since Kingsley Amis's *Lucky Jim* (1954); his *Stars and Bars* (1984) is a shrewdly funny commentary on both English reserve and American vulgarity. Boyd's *An Ice-Cream War* (1982) and *The New Confessions* (1987) show strong narrative skills and a discerning use of historical sources; *Brazzaville Beach* (1990), his most impressive work to date, focuses on scientific ethics and the rather exotic subject of chimpanzee research. With *The Sweetshop Owner* (1980) and the short-story collection *Learning To Swim* (1982), Swift was widely hailed as a writer to watch; his novels *Shuttlecock* (1981) and *Waterland* (1983) show well the tensions and terrors that often swirl beneath the surface of family life. The Japanese-born Kazuo Ishiguro came somewhat more slowly to public attention, first publishing two well-crafted but quiet novels, *A Pale View of Hills* (1982) and *An Artist of the Floating World* (1986); his bestseller *The Remains of Day* (1989) is a butler's tale that reveals overlooked similarities between Asian and English cultures.

During the 1980s, Timothy Mo (b. 1950), A. N. Wilson (b. 1950), Peter Ackroyd (b. 1949), and Bruce Chatwin (1940–1989) also established their careers. Mo, born in Hong Kong, first won wide praise with *The Monkey King* (1978) and *Sour Sweet* (1982), which draw richly on his Chinese background and display a fine comic sensibility; his *An Insular Possession* (1986) tackles Chinese history and proceeds far more ponderously. In *The Sweets of Pimlico* (1977), *Who Was Oswald Fish?* (1981), and *Wise Virgin* (1982), Wilson mixes farce, satire, and black comedy in a manner that echoes, but does not surpass, the early Evelyn Waugh (q.v.). Wilson's more recent novels, including *Gentlemen in England* (1985) and *Incline Our Hearts* (1988), show a certain maturing in tone and technique; his biographies of *Tolstoy* (1988) and *C. S. Lewis* (1990) won wide acclaim. Like Wilson, Peter Ackroyd has published several ambitious biographies, including *T. S. Eliot* (1984) and *Dickens* (1990); like Robert Nye and Emma Tennant, he is also a novelist skilled at making imaginative use of biographical and historical sources, as such works as *The Great Fire of London* (1982), *The Last Testament of Oscar Wilde* (1983), and *Chatterton* (1987) prove. Bruce Chatwin sparked a wide renewal of interest in travel writing with *In Patagonia* (1977), a vivid account of his journey to the African Sahara. Chatwin's subsequent works—including the novels *On the Black Hill* (1982) and *Utz* (1988) and many of the sketches in *What Am I Doing Here* (1988)—show that he was among the most promising writers of his generation, a superb storyteller often willing to take Flaubertian pains with his prose.

Those publishing notable short fiction in more recent years include V. S. Pritchett (b. 1900, q.v.), Ian McEwan (b. 1948), and Patrick McGrath (b. 1950). Pritchett's career began when H. G. Wells and Ford Madox Ford (qq.v.) were still publishing; his vast *Complete Collected Stories* (1991) includes six decade's worth of expertly crafted, rather Chekhovian stories that tend to cast an unusually clear-eyed look at lower-middle-class life. McEwan's versatile career now includes several superb novels, including *The Comfort of Strangers* (1981)—an unusually haunting account of violence and sexual desire—and *The Innocent* (1990), a gripping tale of cold-war intrigue that compares favorably to the best novels of John le Carré (q.v.). McEwan also remains well known, however, for the arresting stories contained in *First Love, Last Rites* (1975) and *In Between the Sheets* (1978). Like McEwan, Patrick McGrath clearly knows his craft, and frequently gravitates to grotesque characters and plots, but he is also more overtly whimsical and droll. The stories in *Blood and Water and Other Tales* (1988), for example, show McGrath producing pieces reminiscent of Roald Dahl (1916–1991).

A revival of interest in Dahl's work became evident as the 1980s came to a close; several collections of his previously published stories appeared, among them *The Best of Roald Dahl* (1983) and *Ah, Sweet Mystery of Life* (1989). Even more significant was the publication of *The Collected Stories of Angus Wilson* (1987), which includes titles from earlier volumes like *Such Darling Dodos* (1940) and *A Bit Off the Map* (1957) and proves anew why Wilson stands as one of the finest fiction writers of the past fifty years.

Drama

Theater in Britain has enjoyed some very lively periods in recent years, at least in part because of the rise to prominence of several figures initially called "fringe playwrights" because their early works were often staged in small theaters and routinely expressed far-left views. David Hare (b. 1947), the most prominent member of this group, first acquired wide critical attention in Britain with *Knuckle* (1974), which parodies the Hollywood thriller as it indicts, among other things, the materialism and hypocrisy that pervade modern life; he is probably best known, however, for the particularly powerful *Plenty* (1978), which centers on one woman's search for meaning in a postwar Britain, which Hare portrays as unmoored and corrupt, unable to face the future or digest the past.

Hare began collaborating with Howard Brenton (b. 1942) in the early 1970s; their *Pravda: A Fleet Street Comedy* (1985) is a satiric, farcical, melodramatic portrayal of contemporary British journalism that features—in the shape of a monstrous press lord called Lambert Le Roux—one of the decade's most memorable stage characters. Brenton has regularly expressed Marxist-radical sympathies, and his own works—with their frequent use of profanity, violence, and explicit sexuality—have often proved highly controversial. In *The Churchill Play* (perf. 1974, pub. 1986), for example, Brenton depicts a fascist takeover of England while savaging the most widely esteemed figure in 20th-c. British history. With *A Short Sharp Shock!* (1981) Brenton began a scathing attack on the Thatcher government, which he would sustain in such plays as *The Romans in Britain* (1982) and *Bloody Poetry* (1987). Because of its scenes of sexual violence and its blunt criticism of Britain's military presence in Northern Ireland, *The Romans in Britain* sparked a particularly intense reaction in the British press; however, a widely publicized attempt to prosecute the play under the Sexual Offenses Act of 1956 proved unsuccessful.

Like Brenton, Howard Barker (b. 1946) often employs satire and shock as a means of emphasizing his attacks on capitalism, militarism, and various forces he finds inimical to the survival of free expression. In *Downchild* (1985) Barker seeks to depict the ineffectiveness of Labour politicians in the postwar era; in *The Castle* (1985) he centers on the eternal battle of the sexes, here played out in the years just after the Crusades. The work of writer-actor Stephen Berkoff (b. 1937) is similarly flamboyant and politically charged. In *East* (1977) Berkoff constructs a ribald and angry "elegy" for the working-class district of London where he was born and reared; in *Decadence* (1982) he savages the "infantilism" he finds rife in Britain's upper class. In *Sink the Belgrano!* (1987) Berkoff attacks Britain's role in the 1982 Falklands War.

Because Brenton, Barker, and Berkoff tend to produce such deliberately provocative material, critical responses to their plays tend to range predictably from utter admiration to complete disgust. Edward Bond (q.v.), who vigorously defended *The Romans in Britain,* is himself no stranger to controversy; his *Saved* (1966) was widely condemned for its portrayal of infanticide, even as other critics praised its frank rendering of the process of dehumanization that pervades modern society. With their use of parody, fantasy, and sharp irony, Bond's more recent works—including *Restoration* (1981), *Summer* (1982), and *The War Plays: A Trilogy* (1985)—continue to show something of the influence of Bertolt Brecht (q.v.) as well as an increasingly didactic strain; his *Two Post-Modern Plays* (1990)—*Jackets* and *In the Company of Men*—includes a series of "Notes on Post-Modernism" illuminating many of his aesthetic and philosophical views.

Harold Pinter (q.v.), Britain's most distinguished living dramatist, has written frequently about power, violence, and victimization, but never so powerfully as in *One for the Road* (1984), a starkly staged one-act play written in support of Amnesty International and conveying the full evil and horror of torture as well as any work of literature in the 20th c. Pinter's *Mountain Language* (1988) also shows his more explicit interest in political issues as it deals with the horrors faced by political protestors and their families in a growing number of tyrannical states.

Tom Stoppard (q.v.) also remains an impressive force in British theater, winning praise for *The Real Thing* (1982), a study of love and infidelity that won wide praise not only for its wit and verbal dexterity, but its powerful treatment of a wide range of philosophical and aesthetic issues. In *Hapgood* (1988) Stoppard again cleverly parodies a literary convention—in this case the spy thriller—as he constructs an intricate line of action again examining the limits of perception while raising questions regarding, among other things, quantum mechanics and Einsteinian theories of light. *Hapgood* stands as one of Stoppard's most demanding—and rewarding—plays.

Several other prominent British dramatists—including Alan Ayckbourn (b. 1939), Simon Gray (q.v.), and Alan Bennett (b. 1934)—have maintained their flair for comedy with a willingness to address serious artistic concerns. Perhaps because of his insistence on placing himself "slap-bang in the middle of the English theater-going public," Ayckbourn has often been dismissed as little more than a lively entertainer with dazzling technical skills. But his *A Chorus of Disapproval* (1986) and *Man of the Moment* (1985) offer not only laughs but sharp, subtle, sometimes painful commentaries on contemporary manners and mores. Like Ayckbourn, Gray repeatedly combines wit, intelligence, and West End success; *The Common*

Pursuit (1984), his most ambitious work, ably follows the linked lives of several friends over the course of two decades. In *Melon* (1987), Gray again enters Ayckbourn country, tragicomically dealing with, among other things, the strains and disenchantments of middle-class married life. Bennett began his career writing and performing with Peter Cook, Jonathan Miller, and Dudley Moore in the still fresh *Beyond the Fringe* (1963); his more recent plays, including *Kafka's Dick* (1987) and *Single Spies* (1988), display well his always sophisticated use of verbal comedy. Like many of Britain's leading dramatists, Bennett also writes occasionally for television; his *Talking Heads* (1987)—a series of six "monologues" originally aired by the BBC—are especially compelling, offering convincing testimonies from the often overlooked corners of middle-class life.

Caryl Churchill (b. 1938) and Pam Gems (b. 1925) are among the most widely recognized of Britain's growing number of prominent women dramatists. Churchill's early plays, including *Owners* (1973), *Vinegar Tom* (1978), and *Cloud Nine* (1979), were among the most spirited and influential Marxist-feminist plays of the 1970s; her inventive *Serious Money* (1987), which consists largely of couplets, is a witty, searing indictment of the rapacious world of high finance. Pam Gems's *Camille* (1984) deals powerfully with the social and sexual exploitation of women; her *Loving Women* (1984) continues her exploration of gender roles.

Hanif Kureishi (b. 1954) is the best known among an increasing number of dramatists focusing on life among Britain's minorities. In *Borderline* (1981), for example, he deals with the reality of racism as faced by members of the nation's Asian immigrant community. A similar concern informs *My Beautiful Laundrette* (1986), one of several acclaimed screenplays included in Kureishi's *London Kills Me* (1992).

Poetry

The most widely discussed poet of the 1980s was very probably Craig Raine (b. 1944), whose first published volume, *The Onion, Memory* (1978), and whose *A Martian Sends a Postcard Home* (1979) displays a striking, punning, flamboyantly metaphorical style. Along with Christopher Reid (b. 1950), whose *Arcadia* (1979) and *Pea Soup* (1982) revealed similar stylistic tendencies, Raine's name became synonymous with the much imitated "Martian" school of poetry, so named by James Fenton (b. 1949) because of its attempt to view life from angles fresh enough to appear, at times, alien.

Fenton and Blake Morrison (b. 1950) must also be placed among the more prominent younger poets of the 1980s. Although probably better known as a travel writer and as a drama critic for the *Times* of London, Fenton won wide praise for the poetry he came to collect in *The Memory of War* (1982) and in *Children in Exile* (1983). This volume includes several exceptional poems drawing upon Fenton's experiences in war-torn Cambodia, and another, "A German Requiem," which is an especially notable example of the trend toward narrative forms in contemporary British poetry. In *The Ballad of the Yorkshire Ripper and Other Poems* (1987), Morrison reveals an interest in topical matters, as well as the ability to write convincingly in dialect, as he does in the volume's title poem, a disturbing but memorable monologue dealing with Peter Sutcliffe's ghastly, widely publicized crimes. With poet-critic Andrew Motion (b. 1952), Morrison has also edited *The Penguin Book of Contemporary British Poetry* (1982), helped direct further attention to the work of such poets as Jeffrey Wainwright (b. 1944) and Hugo Williams (b. 1942), both of whom display, in varying ways, the kind of spare, understated approach that—despite the presence of the "Martians"— has tended to prevail in in recent British poetry. However, Williams, in such appealing volumes as *Love-Life* (1979) and *Writing Home* (1985), writes in the kind of more bluntly autobiographical style that remains somewhat rare in contemporary British verse.

Of the other English poets featured in the volume, Carol Rumens (b. 1946) and Tony Harrison (b. 1937) are probably best known to American readers. In such volumes as *Unplayed Music* (1981) and *Star Whisper* (1983) Rumens made her mark as a poet of particular clarity and insight; in *Direct Dialing* (1985) and *From Berlin to Heaven* (1989) she shows her continuing interest in eastern Europe and its history. Harrison combines a working-class upbringing in Leeds with degrees in the classics and linguistics. His sensitivity to diction and the subtle rhythms of everyday speech—as well as his willingness to deal bluntly with various class-related issues—are found in several excellent volumes, including *Selected Poems* (1984), which features many of the sonnets in his continuing "The School of Eloquence" sequence, perhaps the most consistently interesting project undertaken in recent British poetry.

Although not included in the Penguin anthology, John Fuller (b. 1937), Michael Hofmann (b. 1957), and Wendy Cope (b. 1945) must also be ranked highly among the more gifted of Britain's contemporary poets. The versatile Fuller produced several of the decade's most original works, including *The Illusionists* (1980), a tale in verse

structured in the four-footed iambic of Pushkin's *Eugene Onegin,* and *Partingtime Hall* (1987), an irreverent collaboration with James Fenton. Hofmann is particularly full of promise. In *Acrimony* (1986), for example, he is gloomy and aloof but often compelling, the maker of stark images and well-shaped lines that linger long in the mind. Cope combines intelligence, accessibility, and a delightful wit; her *Making Cocoa for Kingsley Amis* (1986) displays her strong gift of parody, and won wide praise and high sales.

The 1977 appointment of John Betjeman (q.v.) as poet laureat surprised no one. Long identified as a somewhat eccentric presence on Britain's cultural scene, Betjeman's latter poems—including those represented in his *Collected Poems* (4th ed., 1979) and his *Uncollected Poems* (1982)— continue to reveal his preoccupation with such subjects as architecture and death, as well as the satirical and accessible style that made him one of Britain's most popular poets. Next to Betjeman, Philip Larkin (q.v.) was for many years Britain's most popular "serious" poet, as well known for his bookish, rather cranky bachelor persona as for the lucid, witty, and quotable quality of such poems as "High Windows" and "I Remember, I Remember," which both appear in his posthumously published *Collected Poems* (1988).

Stylistically, Ted Hughes (q.v.) has little in common with either Betjeman or Larkin; in fact, his appointment as poet laureate in 1985 surprised those who were most familiar with Hughes's earlier work, including *Crow* (1970), and who continued to associate him vaguely with violence and misanthropy. Although Hughes is certainly uneven, he is, at his best, a poet of unusual power and lyrical sensitivity; his *Selected Poems (1957– 81)* (1982) as well as *River* (1983) and *Wolfwatching* (1989) show his continuing interest in nature and myth and add to a body of work that is, all things considered, unmatched in modern British poetry.

Geoffrey Hill (b. 1932) and Elizabeth Jennings (b. 1926) were also among the well-established poets to publish significant volumes in recent years. Hill is a poet with a scholar's interest in language, Christian mysticism, and English history; his verse is allusive, complex, highly self-conscious, and always scrupulously crafted, as such recent volumes as *Tenebrae* (1978) and *The Mystery of the Charity of Charles Péguy* (1983) indicate. Like Hill, Jennings is deeply interested in Christianity, as her prose works—including *Christianity and Poetry* (1965)—reveal. But her varied body of verse is not as immediately formidable as Hill's; indeed, much of the more recent work in Jennings's *Collected Poems* (1986) features the same clarity of expression that helps explain her frequent appearance on the literature syllabi of Britain's secondary schools.

Other poets to publish significant collections during the 1980s include Peter Reading (b. 1946), whose *Essential Reading* (1986) displays well the work of one of Britain's most idiosyncratic poets. Peter Redgrove (b. 1932) is another highly original poet, as his *The Moon Disposes: Poems 1954–1987* (1987) shows. The more orthodox Robert Conquest (b. 1917), well known for his writings on Russian history, also published his *New and Collected Poems* (1988).

During the 1980s, other important poets published significant collections, among them Gavin Ewart (b. 1916), D. J. Enright (b. 1920), and Geoffrey Grigson (1906–1985). Ewart—for five decades an industrious and lively presence in the world of British letters—has continued to publish poems vividly expressive of his social, political, and erotic concerns; his *The Collected Ewart 1933–1980* (1980), *The New Ewart: Poems, 1980–1982* (1982), and *Late Pickings* (1987) show once more his varying tones and his mastery of an unusually wide variety of verse forms. Enright, like Ewart, can be both witty and grim, sometimes simultaneously; his later works, contained in *Collected Poems* (1987) and *Selected Poems* (1990), also show a continued willingness to engage current social issues in a wry, often satiric voice. Like Enright, Geoffrey Grigson also qualifies as a modern "man of letters" who has worked in a variety of modes, often mixing art with literary journalism. While the best of Grigson's verse can be found in his *Collected Poems 1963–80* (1982), a posthumously published volume, *Persephone's Flowers and Other Poems* (1986), is notable for its inclusion of "Entering My Eightieth Year," the finest poem of his final years. Many other younger poets of varying voices and styles attracted wide attention, including Lawrence Sail (b. 1942), David Scott (b. 1947), Jeremy Reed (b. 1951), Sean O'Brien (b. 1952), Fiona Pitt-Kethley (b. 1954), and David Dabydeen (b. 1956).

BIBLIOGRAPHY: Brown, J. R., ed., *Modern British Dramatists: New Perspectives* (1984); Booth, M., *British Poetry, 1964–1984: Driving through the Barricades* (1985); Thwaite, A., *Poetry Today; A Critical Guide to British Poetry 1960–1984* (1985); Haffenden, J., *Novelists in Interview* (1985); Stevenson, R., *The British Novel since the Thirties* (1986); Wandor, M., *Carry on, Understudies* (1986); Bradbury, M., *No, Not Bloomsbury* (1987); Chambers, C., and M. Prior, *Playwrights' Progress: Patterns of Postwar British Drama* (1987); McHale, B., *Postmodernist Fiction* (1987); Morrison, B., "The Filial Art: A Reading of Contemporary British Poetry," *YES*, 17 (1987), 179–217; Ritchie, R., ed., *The Joint Stock Book: The Making of a Theatre Collective* (1987); Cave, R. A., *New British Drama in Performance on the London Stage: 1970–1985* (1988); Dipple, E., *The Unresolvable Plot: Reading Contemporary Fiction* (1988); Hassan, S. K., *Philip Larkin and His Contemporaries* (1988); Kenyon, O., *Women Novelists Today* (1988); Robinson, A., *Instabilities in Contemporary British Poetry* (1988); Taylor, D. J., *A Vain Conceit: British Fiction in the 1980's* (1989); Anderson, L., ed., *Plotting Change: Contemporary Women's Fiction* (1990); Massie, A., *The Novel Today: A Critical Guide to the British Novel 1970–1989* (1990); Logan, W., "A Letter from Britain," *Poetry*, 4 (1991), 222–238; Innes, C., *Modern British Drama, 1890–1990* (1992)

BRIAN MURRAY

ESPRIU, Salvador

Spanish poet, dramatist, and novelist (writing in Catalan), b. 1913, Santa Coloma de Farners (Gerona); d. 22 Feb. 1985, Barcelona

E. is the most famous of Catalan post-Civil War poets. As a student in the vigorous Catalan university during the time of the Spanish Republic, E. received a fine classical formation and developed a keen sense of a Spain whose political organization was based upon mutual knowledge and respect among its linguistically and culturally distinct regions. After the Francoist victory, the attempt was made by central authorities to suppress all public use of the Catalan language among the approximately four million Spanish nationals whose mother tongue it was. Yet in 1946 E. published in Catalan his first book of poetry, *Cementeri de Sinera* (*Sinera Cementery*, 1988). Before the war, he mainly wrote novels; the turn to the lyric signified in part his intent to express himself in his native language in a genre that authorities more or less tolerated only because of its appeal to very small minorities. This first book of poetry evidences an abiding dimension of E.'s production: personal meditations about a lost past and death. Sinera is a town on the Catalan Mediterranean coast, and E., who uses it as the setting for several of his works, succeeds admirably in evoking the sounds, temperatures, sun, and sights that stimulate and accompany his thoughts.

Shortly after the end of the Civil War and the beginning of anti-Catalan measures, E. wrote the play *Primera historia d'Esther* (first history of Esther), but it was published only in 1948 and was first staged in 1957. More than his brooding poetry, this play signaled the public E., the man who became, for practical purposes, the national poet of Catalonia during the last decades of his life. For this play compares symbolically the persecution of the Jews under King Ahasuerus in Persia with that of the Catalans by Franco during and after the Civil War. The use of puppet actors and the metamorphoses of some puppets into people says much about the censorship of the period and the way E. perceived the time.

With his much translated *La pell de brau* (1960; *The Bullhide*, 1977), E. became a national literary figure in Spain. The title refers to all of Spain since the shape of the country on a map is much like that of an extended bullhide. The message of the book written in Catalan is one of national reconciliation, yet with respect for the different cultural-linguistic groups of Spain. E.'s way of putting his art at the service of society in this book made it rapidly a model of the aesthetic of social literature then in vogue among younger Spanish writers.

When E. died, critics, whether their mother tongue was Spanish or Catalan, united in the feeling that the seventy-two-year-old poet had died before his time. In great measure this was because along with his generation, region, and country E. had gone from the despair portrayed in "De tan senzill, no t'agradarà" (1954; "It's So Simple That You Won't Like It," 1975) to the weary acceptance of the national fate described in "Assaig de càntic en el temple" (1954; "Rehearsal of a Canticle in the Temple," 1975) and, most gratifyingly, to the fulfillment and optimism of post-Franco democracy. The poet, who had once merely wanted to die without mourning, was enjoying the new Catalonia in the new Spain, an experience that recalled and culminated the promise of the Republic. Just as his adopted Barcelona opened itself to the world by bidding for and winning the right to hold the 1992 Summer Olympics, the once pessimistic and persecuted E. was busy with the opportunities and challenges of freedom.

FURTHER WORKS: *El Dr. Rip* (1931); *Laia* (1932); *Aspectes* (1934); *Miratge a Citerea* (1934); *Ariadne al laberint grotesc* (1935); *Letízia i altres proses* (1937); *Antigona* (1939); *Les cançons d'Ariadna* (1949): *Obra lírica* (1952); *El caminat i el mur* (1954); *Final del laberint* (1955); *Evocacions de Roselló-Pòrcel i altres notes* (1957); *Obra poètica* (1963); *Narracions* (1965); *Ronda de mort a Sinera* (1966); *Per al llibre de salms d'aquests vells cecs* (1967); *Setmana Santa* (1971); *Formes i paraules: aproximació a l'art d'Apelles Fenosa, en homenatge* (1975); *Una altra Fedra, si us plau* (1978); *Obras completas* (4 vols., 1980–1985); *Les roques i el mar* (1981); *Per a bona gent* (1984). FURTHER VOLUMES IN ENGLISH: *Lord of the Shadow: Poems* (1975); *Death around Sinera* (1980); *Selected Poems of S. E.* (1989)

BIBLIOGRAPHY: Castellet, J. M., *Iniciación a la poesía de S. E.* (1971); Terry, A., *Catalan Literature* (1972), 114–18; Rosenthal, D. H., "S. E. and Postwar Catalan Poetry," *Contemporary Poetry*, 5, 1 (1982), 12–23; Cocozzella, P., "*Ronda de mort a Sinera:* An Approach to S. E.'s Aesthetics," in Durán, M., et al., eds., *Actes del Segon Colloqui d'Estudis Catalans a Nord-Amèrica* (1979), 307–30; Cocozzella, P., "S. E.'s Idea of a Theater: The *Sotajador* versus the Demiurge," *MD,* 29, 3 (Sept. 1986), 472–89; Cocozzella, P., "S. E.'s Prophetic Mode: The Voice of a Historicist Persona," *RCEH,* 14, 2 (Winter 1990), 209–34

STEPHEN MILLER

ESTERHÁZY, Péter

Hungarian novelist, short-story writer, and essayist, b. 14 Apr. 1950, Budapest

Born into the most famous aristocratic family of his country, E. spent much of his childhood in a small village because his family was deported to the countryside by the communist authorities in 1951. After the revolution of October 1956, the Soviet-type dictatorship became somewhat more tolerant, allowing the family to move to Budapest, where E. went to school. At Eötvös University he studied mathematics. In 1974 he got a job in an institute for computer science. In the same year his first writing was published in a periodical. Four years later, he gave up his job and became a free-lance writer.

His first volume, *Fancsikó és Pinta* (1976; Fancsikó and Pinta), is an autobiographical sequence of stories. The events are related from the perspective of a young boy. The action has two basic components: On one level the main characters are the hero's parents, but their conflicts are subordinated to and distorted by a world dominated by Fancsikó and Pinta, who exist only in the boy's imagination. This book and its successor, *Pápai vizeken ne kalózkodj!* (1977; don't sail as a pirate through the pope's waters), a collection of short stories, made an immediate impact on the part of the Hungarian reading public that cared for innovative prose, but the general reader did not recognize E. as a major writer until the publication of *Termelési-regény* (1979; production novel).

This work was published with two bookmarks, one red and the other black, to encourage the public to read the first part, a parody of a genre of Socialist Realism (q.v.), simultaneously with the second part, a spiritual autobiography of the author, written in the form of endnotes attached to the first part. A superficial reading will disclose no connection whatsoever between the main text and the metafictional notes. On closer consideration, however, the latter create an alternative teleology which contradicts that of the generic parody. The names of the printers working on the book are inserted in the notes, indicating the author's belief in the role of indeterminacy and even chance in creation. Additionally, this second part is also an attempt to abolish the distinction between life and art.

On the basis of the combination of the structural devices of the avant-garde with the techniques of earlier periods, the mixing up of visual effects and texts, this book was associated with postmodern writing by some critics. Similar tendencies are even more apparent in his *Bevezetés a szépirodalomba* (1986; an introduction to literature), a huge work that was originally published in parts, which seems to juxtapose apparently disparate linguistic utterances and let unexpected relationships of incompatible texts emerge. The various sections are meant to explore different possibilities of prose writing. The incessant flow of words characterizing "Függő" (1981; dependent) does not seem to be related to the extremely economical, decidedly artificial syntax of "Fuharosok" (1983; *The Transporters,* 1985), a short text full of quotations from Pascal, the story of a rape that can be read as an allegory of the Soviet occupation of Hungary. "Kis magyar pornográfia" (1984; a handbook of Hungarian pornography) is a collection of fragments, some of them ribald or political jokes, whereas "A szív segédigéi" (1985; *Helping Verbs of the Heart,* 1991) is a sublime and even religious testimony to the memory of the author's mother. This final section of the work proceeds on two levels. Each page, bordered in heavy black, carries at the top a narrative, and at the bottom, in capital letters, another text that is often some quotation.

Having completed this long work, E. wrote a short book that can be regarded as a hoax. *Tizenkét hattyúk* (1987; seventeen swans) was published as a work by an author called Lili Csokonai. Mihály Csokonai Vitéz (1773–1805) was a major Hungarian poet. E.'s above-mentioned book was presented as the work of a Hungarian woman who lived in the early 19th c. The imitation of the style of that period was so successful that except for a very few critics, most readers were taken in, until E. admitted his authorship.

From the beginning of his career, E. was a harsh critic of communism, and his works were censored on several occasions. When the totalitarian system crumbled in Hungary in 1988, he turned to essay writing and journalism. Although he decided not to belong to any of the political parties emerging after the fall of communism, his articles published in the monthly *Hitel,* an unofficial organ of the Hungarian Democratic Forum, greatly helped

the transformation of his country. When the change of the political system was complete, he continued to write fiction. His most recent novel, *Hrabal könyve* (1990; the book of Hrabal), is a tribute to the Czech prose writer Bohumil Hrabal (b. 1914), whose works gave him inspiration for his attempt to understand the situation of Eastern Europe, a region ruled by the Soviet Union for more than four decades.

Although E. is still in the middle of his career, his two longest works are regarded by many critics as the most significant contributions to Hungarian fiction since 1945. He has succeeded in changing reading habits by rejecting a fair number of the conventions of narrative prose. His ambition to create a diction that contains the quaint, the rare, the technical, the obsolete, the borrowed, the nonce, the local slang, together with his heavy reliance on puns and intertextuality make his style hardly translatable, yet his books have been published in such languages as German, French, English, Italian, Dutch, Polish, and Slovenian.

FURTHER WORKS: *A kitömött hattyú* (1988); *Biztos kaland* (1989)

BIBLIOGRAPHY: Szegedy-Maszák, M., "Postmodernism in Hungarian Literature," *Zeitschrift für Kulturaustausch* (Stuttgart), 1 (1984), 150–56; Szegedy-Maszák, M., "The Life and Times of the Autobiographical Novel," *Neohelicon,* 13, 1 (1986), 83–104; Szegedy-Maszák, M., "Teleology in Postmodern Fiction," in Calinescu, M., and D. Fokkema, eds., *Exploring Postmodernism* (1987), 41–57; Jastrzebska, J., *Personnages tragiques et grotesques dans la littérature hongroise contemporaine* (1989), 118–76

MIHÁLY SZEGEDY-MASZÁK

EZEKIEL, Nissim

Indian poet, critic, editor, and dramatist (writing in English), b. 16 Dec. 1924, Bombay

E., one of India's foremost intellectuals, belongs to Bombay's small Marathi-speaking Bene-Israel Jewish community. Educated in English-medium schools, he received his undergraduate degree from Wilson College (Bombay) and his M.A. in English from the University of Bombay in 1947, where he would later return as reader of English and one of its most distinguished faculty members. In 1948 he went to Britain and studied philosophy with C. E. M. Joad (1891–1953) at the University of London, and avidly pursued his other interests: theater, film, art, but especially poetry. Returning to India in 1952, he worked as a journalist, then as an advertising-copy editor, and later as a factory manager. In 1959 he started teaching English at various colleges and universities in Bombay. In addition to writing poetry, he regularly contributes book, art, and film reviews, and essays on social commentary to major Indian journals and newspapers. An active member of the Indian chapter of P.E.N., he received the Government of India's Padma Shree Award in 1988.

E.'s first volume of poetry, *A Time to Change* (1952), was published in London and received excellent critical notice. The influence of T. S. Eliot and W. H. Auden (qq.v.) is apparent. The second volume, *Sixty Poems* (1953), published in Bombay, contains a number of notable poems whose impact is diluted by the inclusion of some of his earliest poems which, critics generally agree, should not have appeared there. *The Third* (1959) marks a transition from E.'s early period to that of a mature stylist. *The Unfinished Man* (1960) is a collection of poems written in 1959, which he describes as, literarily, the most fruitful year of his life. This volume contains many of his most lyrical, yet most ironic, works, many of them dealing with marriage.

The Exact Name (1965) includes many of E.'s best-known pieces, including "Night of the Scorpion," often cited as one of the finest modern Indian poems. With large, brilliant images suggesting childhood awe, fear, and confusion, the speaker recalls the rainy monsoon night his/her mother was bitten by a scorpion and the elaborate rites and incantations performed by various people to save her from death. The mother's only comment is a terse thanks to God that the scorpion bit her and not her child. Other notable poems are the much-anthologized "In India" and "Poet, Lover, Birdwatcher."

Some poems in *Hymns in Darkness* (1976) explore the aesthetic possibilities of "Indian" English, the English spoken in urban centers as a second language with Indian-language grammatical patterns, idioms, and intonation patterns bleeding through. Though these poems were misunderstood as merely satirical, for which E. was criticized, the experiment was continued by a number of other poets. Poems of *Latter-Day Psalms* (1982) are modeled on the Book of Psalms, sometimes pleading, sometimes cynical, and often bittersweetly humorous.

As a critic and editor, E. has exerted a powerful influence on India's intellectual life. Before him much of what passed for criticism in India tended to be either lionizing or fault-finding. E. has done much to change this kind of simplistic approach. His criticism is distinguished by its lucidity, judiciousness, and honesty. Contrary to the hierarchical and tradition-bound thinking that prevails in much of Indian society, E. is unafraid to ques-

tion hallowed assumptions and received wisdom. He does so with a sense of humility, a lack of pretension, and a strong predisposition to irony. His most famous piece is an essay on *An Area of Darkness* (1964), a harsh critique of India and Indians by V. S. Naipaul (q.v.). Entitled "Naipaul's India and Mine" (1965), it asserts with candor and accuracy that while much of what repulses Naipaul about India is valid, such things repulse most Indians as well. Moreover, E. insists, Naipaul is unable to see India beyond his own "temperamental alienation"; thus, he has failed to make the proper commitment to his subject. Many of E.'s best reviews are collected in *Another India* (1990).

Since 1955 E. has also edited a number of important journals. In these he has encouraged individual literary creativity and has urged Indian writers to learn about intellectual trends from other parts of the world. He has also championed the art of literary translation from India's vernacular languages into English as a means of cross-fertilizing the country's many separate literary traditions.

E. is an urban poet, the poet of the city of Bombay. His earlier poems show technical virtuosity and an almost laconic quality; by contrast, many later poems are freer, looser, and more experimental in structure and expression. Predominant themes in the poetry are alienation and marginality, which some suggest are the result of both his Jewishness and elitist Westernization. Another theme is the disharmony and hurt that modern urban culture inflicts on people, and which desensitizes and dehumanizes them. He is also concerned with the lack of certitude and stability in relationships, including romantic ones, but most particularly marriage. One is struck by the hortative quality of many of the poems, and by the preponderance of travel and bird imagery, both of which suggest transience and instability. Many of these themes so thoughtfully and provocatively explored by E. also preoccupy the poetry of the younger generation of poets writing in English and in India's other languages.

FURTHER WORK: *Three Plays* (1969)

BIBLIOGRAPHY: Belliapa, M., and R. Taranath, *The Poetry of N. E.* (1966); Garman, M., "N. E.: Pilgrimage and Myth," in Naik, M. K., et al., eds., *Critical Essays on Indian Writing in English* (1968), 106–21; Verghese, C., "The Poetry of N. E.," *IndL*, 15, 1 (1972), 63–75; Karnani, C., *N. E.: A Study* (1974); Kher, I., " 'That Message from Another Shore': The Esthetic Vision of N. E.," *Mahfil, A Quarterly of South Asian Literature,* 8, 4 (1972), 17–28; special E. issue, *JSoAL,*

11, 3–4 (1976); Harrex, S. C., "A Critical Approach to Indo-English Poetry," in Harrex, S. C., and G. Λmirthanayagam, eds., *Only Connect: Literary Perspectives East and West* (1981), 148–76; Narula, S. C., "Negative Affirmation in N. E.'s Hymns and Psalms," *ArielE,* 14, 4 (Oct. 1983), 57–71; Birbalsingh, F., Interview with N. E., *JSoAL,* 22, 2 (1987), 130–38; Börner, K. H., "Indian Poetry in English," *A&E,* 33 (1987), 87–100

CARLO COPPOLA

FARAJ, Alfred

Egyptian dramatist, b. 1929, Alexandria

F. is one of the most prominent of a group of Egyptian dramatists who established a reputation for themselves during the period between the Egyptian revolution of 1952 and the 1967 June War. Born and educated in Alexandria, F. was much influenced by the work of Tawfīq al-Hakīm (q.v.), the great pioneer of modern Arabic drama. F. served as a drama critic for the weekly journal *Rūz al-Yūsuf* and in 1966 accepted a position as adviser to the Egyptian Theatre Administration. By that time, he had established a reputation as a dramatist of great gifts who could compose plays of considerable dramatic impact that made use of the national heritage to illustrate the issues confronting the emerging postrevolutionary society in Egypt and, by extension, throughout the Arab world. Regrettably, the political circumstances in Egypt following the June War were to prove as difficult for him as for many other litterateurs. F. preferred exile to remaining in his homeland; more recently he has returned to Egypt after spending many years in England.

F.'s first published play was *Suqūt Fir'awn* (1955; fall of the pharaoh), a work that explores the dilemma of the Egyptian Pharaoh Akhenaton, a ruler who is by personal inclination devoted to peace but whose status as ruler requires that he declare war; he resolves the issue by stepping down from power. During the uncertainties of the initial years of the Egyptian revolution and the rise to power of Jamāl 'Abd al-Nāsir (Gamal Abdel Nasser), the possibilities of a more contemporary interpretation of the play's import were not lost on the Egyptian public, turning it into a political and critical cause célèbre. Leaving aside *Sawt Misr* (1956; the voice of Egypt), a rather ephemeral and strident piece celebrating Egypt's role in the Suez

invasion of 1956, F. composed another play that derived its context from Egyptian history, *Sulaymān al-Halabī* (1964; Sulayman from Aleppo). Here the historical event in question is more recent, Napoleon's invasion of Egypt in 1798 and in particular the assassination of General Kléber by a Syrian student attending the Al-Azhar mosque-university in Cairo. The play is couched in Brechtian terms, with a chorus and a series of rapidly moving scenes; contemporary accounts of the production of the play make it clear that a good deal of the credit for its popular acclaim belonged to the producer who succeeded in staging such a complicated piece of theater in a convincing and appealing fashion.

Another source of inspiration that F. has utilized in several plays is that of tales culled from the tradition of popular Arabic narrative. One of his most successful comedies, *Hallāq Baghdād* (1963; the barber of Baghdad), makes use of the primary figure of a nosey barber, Abū al-Fudūl, to combine two traditional tales—one culled from *A Thousand and One Nights,* the other from a collection of tales attributed to the famous litterateur al-Jāhiz (d. 869)—in a humorous concoction of stock characters and situations. Less overtly humorous perhaps but more accomplished as contributions to drama in Arabic are *Al-Zīr Sālim* (1967; Prince Sālim) and *'Alī Janāh al-Tabrīzī wa tābi'uhu Quffa* (1968; 'Alī Janāh from Tabrīz and his henchman, Quffa). Similar to *Sulaymān al-Halabī,* these two plays also make use of many of the distancing devices associated with Brechtian theatrical techniques. In *Al-Zīr Sālim* the tale is culled from the pre-Islamic period, as a ruler endeavors to break out of a cycle of blood vengeance between two tribes. *'Alī Janāh al-Tabrīzī* is, like *Hallāq Baghdād,* inspired by tales from *A Thousand and One Nights,* most particularly the elaborate trick of the delayed caravan with fabled riches: The anticipation of profits from its wealth of goods and the promissory notes exchanged before its arrival cause the economy of an entire kingdom to collapse. In this piece the interplay of illusion and reality is explored in a comedy that transfers most successfully to the stage.

Although F. wrote some of his plays in the colloquial dialect, such as *'Askar wa-haramiyya* (1966; cops and robbers)—a rather facile exploration of opportunism in a socialist society—a major contribution that he has made to the development of modern Arabic drama has been in using the standard written language as a dramatic medium. He has been particularly concerned that his plays and, by extension, those of other dramatists composing in the Arab world, should be exportable from one Arab nation to another. He has therefore remained an advocate of the use of the literary level of the Arabic language—the only common means of communication among different dialect areas—as the discourse of dramatic dialogue during a period when many critics and writers, such as the great Egyptian critic Lewis ʿAwad (1915–1991), have been vociferously advocating the use of the colloquial as a requirement for a lively and authentic tradition of drama. In F.'s own case, the dialogue in his plays has been composed with the greatest artistry, providing the model for a lucid dramatic style that few other writers of drama have been able to match.

FURTHER WORKS: *Buqbuq al-kaslān, Al-Fakhkh* (1965); *Bi-al-ijmāʿ + wāhid* (1965)

BIBLIOGRAPHY: Allen, R., "Egyptian Drama after the Revolution," *Edebiyat*, 4, 1 (1979), 97–134; Allen, R., ed., *Modern Arabic Literature* (1987), 92–96; Badawi, M. M., *Modern Arabic Drama in Egypt* (1987), 171–82

ROGER ALLEN

FARIA, Almeida

Portuguese novelist, b. 6 May 1943, Montemor-o-Novo, Alentejo

F.'s fiction delves into the origins of the cultural and philosophical stagnancy of the Portuguese mentality in modern times. Raised in the rural Alentejo province, he studied law and philosophy at the University of Lisbon. He became the first president of the Portuguese P.E.N. Club (1978–1988), which had been prohibited under the Salazar-Caetano dictatorship. F. is currently a professor of aesthetics and philosophy at the New University of Lisbon.

F.'s artistic concern is the substance and image of the written word. As he reformulates earlier novelistic structures, such as the epistolary novel and memoirs, or artistic devices, such as the parody, his fiction pursues a philosophical debate on the ethics of existence in the Portuguese context.

F.'s first novel, *Rumor branco* (1962; white noise), published when he was nineteen, was awarded the Portuguese Society of Writers Award (1962) for a first work of fiction. Its content, style, and use of language, directly influenced by the "new novel" then in vogue, was seen as a challenge to the neorealist fiction that had dominated Portuguese prose since the end of World War II.

Four of his novels form the "Lusitanian Tetralogy": *A paixão* (1965; the passion); *Cortes* (1978; cuttings); *Lusitânia* (1980; Lusitania); and *Cavaleiro andante* (1982; knight errant). The series traces the lives of a tradition-laden family of landholders from the years of the Salazar-Caetano dictatorship through the Portuguese revolution of 1974 and into the postrevolutionary period.

Cortes, written just before the 1974 revolution, which overthrew the Salazar-Caetano dictatorship, views the continuing decadence of the family through telescopic, almost slidelike projections that mix dream and reality within a twenty-four hour period just weeks before the revolution. These flashes are often sarcastic, subtle puns or broad parodies of the classics of Portuguese letters, Portuguese laws, and popular slogans.

Lusitânia launches us into the immediate prerevolutionary period and through the first turbulent year of democracy. The novel's epigraph is from the illustrious Portuguese 19th-c. novelist Eça de Queiroz's (1845–1900) *O crime do Padre Amaro* (1876; *The Sin of Father Amaro*, 1963); it evokes the heavy burden of the past glories (explorations, conquests, colonies), which Eça and his generation (and F.) view as having led to the total stagnation of the nation in modern times. The author rhetorically questions: Is it possible that a nation can eternally live in its supposed past glories in the present? Can the Portuguese "condition" be corrected or reformed? Is there, indeed, a national future? F. uses a parody of the epistolary novel as the structure for this fiction. His characters are located in Venice, Luanda, Angola, and Lisbon and offer multiple points of view about the events. The author textually subverts the national "classics," from Gil Vicente (c. 1465–1536) to Marcelo Caetano (1906–1980), as a form of protest against the weight of this past.

F.'s most recent novel (and his contribution to the ongoing debate) is *O conquistador* (1990; the conqueror). The "conqueror" is a modern-day King Sebastião—quite a radical and polemical one—who has both a natural and (as befits a true descendant of Portuguese mythology) a supernatural birth in 1954. In seven symbolic and ironic chapters, highlighted with drawings by the late Portuguese artist Mário Botas, Sebastião narrates his life—up to 1978—in the form of a memoir, a quasi-bildungsroman. He has inherited some physical characteristics of the earlier Sebastião, but primarily he, like his 16th-c. ancestor, is preoccupied with conquests—which in this case are sexual rather than territorial. His world is one of unending marvels, nightmares, and phantasmagoric games in which myths turn into eternal sensual realities. His "real" life is a comic battle against ingrained Portuguese superstitions and prejudices. By the time he is twenty-four, he withdraws from the natural Portuguese reality to become an emotional expatriate in a state of self-analysis.

Here, as well as in his earlier works, F. weaves a devilish, black comedy of subtle double entendres on philosophical, linguistic, and ideological levels. The fluid, dreamlike atmosphere of this novel and earlier ones is surely a direct reflection of F.'s view of Portuguese existence since the 16th c.: The national inability to resolve the historical dilemma has left Portugal and her people afloat. F.'s grand novels are a biting commentary on this continuing dilemma.

FURTHER WORK: *Os passeios do sonhador solitário* (1982)

BIBLIOGRAPHY: Listopad, J., *"A paixão,"* *BA,* 41, 4 (Autumn 1967), 198; Stern, I., "Redefining Identity: Uses of Language in Recent Portuguese Fiction," in Nunes, M. L., ed., *Identity in Portuguese and Brazilian Literature* (1982), 34–42

IRWIN STERN

FARMĀN, Ghā'ib Tu'ma

Iraqi novelist, short-story writer, translator, and journalist, b. 1927(?), Baghdad; d. 18 Aug. 1990, Moscow, U.S.S.R.

F.'s life was his writing, and his life was his exile. He left Iraq as a young man to study at the University of Cairo, from which he graduated in 1954. While in Egypt, he published a number of short stories in some of the most prestigious periodicals. On returning to Iraq, he could not find a job due to his political activities, so he left to work in Syria, Lebanon, and China. He returned to Iraq in 1958, but left after one year, only to resume the life of the wandering intellectual. He spent the last two decades of his life in Moscow, working as a translator and editor, and was responsible for supervising many of the translations into Arabic of some outstanding Russian and Soviet literary works, such as the selected works of Turgenev and collections of short stories by Pushkin, Tolstoy, and Dostoevsky.

Despite his continued exile, his writings were always about his native Iraq, especially Baghdad and its popular quarters. F. started by writing short stories in the 1950s. The two collections *Hasīd al-rahā* (1954; millstone harvest) and *Mawlūd ākhar* (1959; another child) show a young writer in search of a path to take. These early stories witness the movement from a "romantic" to a "realistic" attitude. Some of them were, in fact, first encounters with topics and characters that were to be developed later into novels. This was the destiny of the short story "Salīmah al-khabbāzah" (1959; Salimah, the baker), which developed into his first novel, *al-Nakhlah wa-al-Jīrān* (1965; the palm tree and the neighbors). This novel was rightly considered the first Iraqi novel. It traces the lives of a group of poor people in an old quarter in

Baghdad in the post-World War II period. F. is able to portray the ordinary, the daily, and the mundane in a way that makes it heroic without exaggeration. The characters are not heroes endowed with extraordinary powers, they are the poorest of the poor and the most ordinary of the ordinary. The collapse of the dreams of those characters and their tragedy are those of Iraq. In his next novel, *Khamsat aswāt* (1967; five voices), the stage is assumed by intellectuals of different convictions and mentalities, searching for ideals, but unable to find paths toward the realization of their dreams. Their estrangement from their society and their virtual collapse is highlighted.

In *al-Makhād* (1974; labor pains) F. traces the developments in Iraqi society after the collapse of the ancien régime in 1958 and the rise of the new revolutionary fervor. He does this through the eyes of an exiled Iraqi who comes back to his homeland searching for the old quarter, only to find it destroyed. Looking for authenticity, he finds the products of false modernization.

The dream of return from exile is again the subject of his novel *Zilāl 'alā al-nāfidhah* (1979; shadows on the window) in which a university graduate returns to Iraq during the 1960s, full of ambitions to serve his country, only to become disillusioned and have his faith in the revolution collapse.

Ālām al-sayyid Ma'rūf (1982; the sorrows of Mr. Ma'ruf) shows very clearly F.'s ability to portray the forgotten and the ordinary human being as a hero. He does it not as much through empathy as through extracting the inner and hidden strength of such characters by tracing their daily struggles to live and survive in a vicious world.

F. was not a technical innovator. He was a writer sensitive to his characters and his people. F. was a committed socialist and member of the Iraqi Communist Party, but despite his own political convictions and the dominant Socialist Realism (q.v.) during the 1950s and the 1960s among socialist writers, he gave a lot of freedom to his characters. Not only did he let them develop freely, but he always portrayed them in a sympathetic manner, even when they contradicted his own ideological convictions. This applies to his earlier novels more than it does to the later ones, which is possibly the result of the length of his exile and the separation from his beloved city. F.'s achievement in the context of the modern Arabic novel was through the development of what might be termed the aesthetics of simplicity.

FURTHER WORKS: *al-Hukm al-aswad fī al-'Irāq* (1957); *Lā Shīn: 'imlāq al-thaqāfah al-sīnīyah* (1957); *al-Qurbān* (1975); *al-Murtajā wa-al-mu'ajjal* (1986); *al-Markib* (1989)

BIBLIOGRAPHY: Allen, R., *The Arabic Novel* (1982), 75–77; Ali, M. J., "The Socio-Aesthetics of Contemporary Arabic Fiction: An Introduction," *JArabL*, 14 (1983), 70, 80; Allen, R., ed., *Modern Arabic Literature* (1987), 96–100

WALID HAMARNEH

FEMINIST CRITICISM

The term feminist literary criticism is usually understood as designating the body of commentary about the various relations of gender to the written word that has developed in response to the current, post-1968 phase of the women's movement. It embraces both academic and nonacademic approaches, based on a variety of theoretical models that are often given the rough national labels "French" or "Anglo-American." So much attention has been devoted to the distinctions between the different kinds of feminist criticism that there is a tendency to neglect the core of common assumptions and goals that brought into existence the term feminist criticism and the modes of reading it describes.

Although this article concentrates on work published between 1968 and 1991, it would be a mistake to conclude that feminist criticism began only with the feminism of the late 1960s. There has always been an eager and informed audience for those female voices that were raised during the centuries when literature was a male preserve. And there has been at least intermittent recognition that the dominant literature was gendered masculine, representing the perspective of one sex about the nature and relations of both. Ellen Moers (1928–1980) documents the ways in which English-speaking women writers of the 19th c. read, commented on, and were influenced by one another's work, often seeing themselves, across the limits of time and space, as constituting a separate, definable literary tradition.

In the 20th c., a number of the major Western social theorists who considered the status and condition of women either began or ended with discussions of literature. Virginia Woolf's (q.v.) *A Room of One's Own* (1929) starts as a meditation on the general topic of "Women and Fiction." But, in order to arrive at the famous conclusion that, to write fiction, a woman must have five hundred pounds a year and a room of her own, Woolf pursues her argument through the entire range of women's economic, psychological, sexual, and cultural situation. By contrast, Simone de Beauvoir's (q.v.) *Le deuxième sexe* (1949; *The Second Sex*, 1953), whose central thesis is that one is not born a woman, but becomes one, explores the question of "The Woman Writer" and her relation to the written word as one chapter in her overview of female experience. *A Room of One's Own* is sometimes described as the first piece of feminist literary criticism, but it is also a powerful contribution to social theory; *Le deuxième sexe* is commonly regarded as a landmark in the theory of feminism, but it is also a work of literary criticism.

As feminism took on a new momentum in the early 1970s, a great many of the popular books that raised questions about the treatment of women in our society employed the approach of cultural criticism. The key texts of Western culture—not only fictional texts, but religious and psychological literature as well—were scrutinized for their role in helping to shape society's dominant attitudes toward women and even the institutions those attitudes inform. Books like Kate Millett's (b. 1934) *Sexual Politics* (1970), Shulamith Firestone's (dates n.a.) *The Dialectic of Sex* (1970), Eva Figes's (b. 1932) *Patriarchal Attitudes* (1970), Germaine Greer's (b. 1939) *The Female Eunuch* (1970), and Carolyn Heilbrun's (b. 1926) *Toward a Recognition of Androgyny* (1973) all proceed by reading the society and its formative texts as if both had coequal status as literary texts.

Two other phenomena testify to the relationship of women, literature, and criticism in the early years of the revived feminist movement. One is the way that certain works of fiction—from Charlotte Perkins Gilman's (1860–1935) *The Yellow Wallpaper* (1899) to Doris Lessing's (q.v.) *The Golden Notebook* (1962) to Alix Kates Shulman's (b. 1932) *Memoirs of an Ex-Prom Queen* (1972) to Erica Jong's (b. 1942) *Fear of Flying* (1973)—became part of the experience of consciousness-raising, as they crystallized a sense of identification and provided the raw materials for social analysis. As campus women's studies programs began to proliferate, courses on the work of women writers were many women's introduction to the issues of feminism. The feminist movement also gave rise to the emergence, within women's studies, of a criticism that was more directly focused on literary studies than were the popular works of cultural criticism that provide the charter documents of the contemporary women's movement.

In outlining the twenty-year history of the more specifically literary focus within feminist criticism, many commentators tend to apply a kind of biological fallacy to its development. That is, they imply that early approaches and methods were young and crude, essentially stages that more recent work has "outgrown." In making "early" a pejorative term, such an attitude not only displays ignorance of the processes of intellectual history and the way that ideas build upon the work of the past, it also ignores the fact that, rather than being superseded, some of the now unfashionable earlier approaches continue to be used by critics.

One of the earliest feminist approaches was to consider the male-dominated canon of the literary tradition as a source not only of ideology in the larger cultural sense, but also of specific and often stereotypical "images" of women. Sometimes these conventional images were compared and contrasted with those that emerge from study of the smaller number of women writers who have been acknowledged as part of the common Western cultural heritage. Mary Anne Ferguson's (b. 1918) collection *Images of Women in Literature* (1973), which has undergone five revisions in the past two decades, was designed as a textbook anthology of literary sources reflecting some of these images. A similar critical approach is also represented in one of the earliest collections of feminist critical essays, Susan Koppelman Cornillon's (b. 1941) *Images of Women in Fiction* (1972).

Contrasts between male and female writers, combined with the growing emphasis within many fields of feminist studies on women's "agency," led many feminist critics, from the early 1970s on, to valorize the work of female authors, rediscovering "lost" writers of the past, rereading and reinterpreting the known but undervalued and misunderstood figures, and reconsidering such characteristically "feminine" genres as domestic and sensational fiction. Mid-1970s studies by Moers, Patricia Mayers Spacks (b. 1929), and Elaine Showalter (b. 1941) laid the groundwork for this approach. Moers and Louise Bernikow (b. 1940) also suggested that women writers constituted a continuous alternative literary tradition, whose thematic and stylistic parallels to and subversions of the dominant tradition are the subject, notably, of such studies as Showalter's *A Literature of Their Own* (1977), Sandra M. Gilbert (b. 1936) and Susan Gubar's (b. 1944) *The Madwoman in the Attic* (1979), Nina Auerbach's (b. 1943) *Communities of Women* (1978), and Judith Newton's (b. 1941) *Women, Power, and Subversion* (1981).

Certain critics throughout the 1970s and 1980s were particularly involved with connecting feminist concerns to a materialist reading of culture, emphasizing that women, as authors, characters, and readers of literature, were also significantly influenced by society's tensions around race, ethnicity, class, and sexual identity. Lillian S. Robinson's (b. 1941) critical writings from 1968 through 1977, collected in *Sex, Class, and Culture* (1978), mark some of the stages of this effort, as do Jane Marcus's (b. 1938) collected essays in *Art and Anger* (1988) and those by various British and American critics anthologized by Newton and

Deborah Rosenfelt (b. 1942) in *Feminist Criticism and Social Change* (1985).

Texts of women writers of color were made popularly available in anthologies by Mary Helen Washington (b. 1941) and by Gloria Anzaldua (b. 1942) and Cherrie Moraga (b. 1952), while black women's writing was also discussed by such critics as Washington, Barbara Smith (b. 1946), Barbara Christian (b. 1943), Marjorie Pryse (b. 1948), Hortense Spillers (b. 1942), Deborah McDowell (b. 1951), Joanne Braxton (b. 1950), Hazel Carby (b. 1953), and Cheryl Wall (b. 1954). The lesbian tradition within women's literature and criticism was examined by Smith in *Toward a Black Feminist Criticism* (1980) and also by critics like Jane Rule (b. 1931), Karla Jay (b. 1947), and Bonnie Zimmerman (b. 1947). As outlined in Robinson's "Treason Our Text" (1983), this range of criticism led to an equally wide range of feminist challenges to the literary canon.

Theoretical writing closely related to the socially based mode of reading characterizes the essays in *Sex, Class, and Culture,* as well as those by such feminist writers of poetry and fiction as Tillie Olsen in *Silences* (1978), Alice Walker in *In Search of Our Mothers' Gardens* (1983), and Adrienne Rich (qq.v.) in *On Lies, Secrets, and Silence* (1979). Another application of theory—the version understood by some as constituting the only authentic definition of feminist literary theory—draws from French linguistically and psychoanalytically oriented models, including the work of such male thinkers as Jacques Lacan, Jacques Derrida, and Michel Foucault (qq.v.).

The common denominator of French-derived theory is its emphasis on discourse as the basic cause and the measure of social differences. With the notion of discourse as the base, feminist theories like those of Hélène Cixous, Julia Kristeva (qq.v.), and Luce Irigaray (b. 1939) center on the connection between control of bodily, linguistic, and narrative experiences. The extremely varied critical writings of Gayatri Chakravorty Spivak (b. 1942), Alice Jardine (b. 1951), Elizabeth Meese (b. 1943), and Jane Gallop (b. 1952) suggest some of the breadth of this tendency and also make it abundantly clear that the "French" national label is no longer adequate.

Showalter's terms for the respective tendencies, "gynocriticism" and "gynesis," embody both their commonality in their centering on women, and their differences in their approach to the nature of discourse and its subjects. It may be that, in the long run, the principal difference will be one of interpreting the nature of women's marginalization from the power of discourse—whether that oppression originates in the symbolic system or in the social system that the symbolic system reflects.

BIBLIOGRAPHY: Woolf, V., *A Room of One's Own* (1929); de Beauvoir, S., *Le deuxième sexe* (1949; *The Second Sex,* 1953); Foster, J. H., *Sex Variant Women in Literature* (1956); Ellmann, M., *Thinking about Women* (1968); Millett, K., *Sexual Politics* (1970); Figes, E., *Patriarchal Attitudes* (1970); Firestone, S., *The Dialectic of Sex* (1970); Greer, G., *The Female Eunuch* (1970); Cornillon, S. K., ed., *Images of Women in Fiction* (1972); Heilbrun, C. G., *Toward a Recognition of Androgyny* (1973); Spacks, P. M., *The Female Imagination* (1975); Cixous, H., "Le rire de la Méduse," *L'Arc,* 61 (1975), 39–54; Kolodny, A., *The Lay of the Land* (1975); Rule, J., *Lesbian Images* (1975); Moers, E., *Literary Women* (1976); Showalter, E., *A Literature of Their Own* (1977); Baym, N., *Woman's Fiction* (1978); Olsen, T., *Silences* (1978); Robinson, L. S., *Sex, Class, and Culture* (1978); Auerbach, N., *Communities of Women: An Idea in Fiction* (1978); Gilbert, S. M., and S. Gubar, *The Madwoman in the Attic* (1979); Kristeva, J., "Le temps des femmes," *33/44: Cahiers de recherche de sciences des textes et documents,* 5 (Winter 1979), 5–19; Rich, A., *On Lies, Secrets, and Silence* (1979); Christian, B., *Black Women Novelists* (1980); Jehlen, M., "Archimedes and the Parodox of Feminist Criticism," *Signs,* 6, 4 (1981), 575–601; Newton, J. L., *Women, Power, and Subversion* (1981); Abel, E., ed., *Writing and Sexual Difference* (1982); Russ, J., *How To Suppress Women's Writing* (1983); Walker, A., *In Search of Our Mothers' Gardens* (1983); Radway, J. A., *Reading the Romance* (1984); Christian, B., *Black Feminist Criticism* (1985); DuPlessis, R. B., *Writing beyond the Ending* (1985); Greene, G., and C. Kahn, eds., *Making a Difference* (1985); Irigaray, L., *This Sex Which Is Not One* (1985); Newton, J., and D. Rosenfelt, eds., *Feminist Criticism and Social Change* (1985); Showalter, E., ed., *The New Feminist Criticism: Essays on Women, Literature, and Theory* (1985); Jacobus, M., *Reading Woman: Essays in Feminist Criticism* (1986); Kaplan, C., *Sea Changes* (1986); Pryse, M., and H. J. Spillers, eds., *Conjuring: Black Women, Fiction, and Literary Tradition* (1986); Benstock, S., ed., *Feminist Issues in Literary Scholarship* (1987); Carby, H. V., *Reconstructing Womanhood: The Emergence of the Afro-American Woman Novelist* (1987); Meese, E. A., *Crossing the Double-Cross* (1987); Spivak, G. C., *In Other Worlds* (1987); Willis, S., *Specifying: Black Women Writing the American Experience* (1987); Bauer, D. M., *Feminist Dialogics* (1988); Marcus, J., *Art and Anger* (1988); Todd, J. M., *Feminist Literary History* (1988); Wall, C. A., ed., *Changing Our Own Words: Essays on Criticism, Theory, and Writing by Black Women* (1989); Braxton, J. M., and A. N. McLaughlin, eds., *Wild Women in the Whirlwind: Afra-American Culture and the Contemporary Literary Renaissance* (1990); Gates, H. L., Jr., *Reading Black, Reading Feminist* (1990); Hooks, B., *Race and Gender in the Cultural Marketplace* (1990); Jay, K., and J. Glasgow, eds., *Lesbian Texts and Contexts* (1990); Meese, E. A., *(Ex-)tensions* (1990); Spivak, G. C., *The Post-Colonial Critic* (1990); Zimmerman, B., *The Safe Sea of Women: Lesbian Fiction, 1969–89* (1990); DuPlessis, R. B., *The Pink Guitar* (1990); Warhol, R. R., and D. P. Herndl, eds., *Feminisms: An Anthology of Literary Theory and Criticism* (1991)

LILLIAN S. ROBINSON

FERRÉ, Rosario

Puerto Rican short-story writer, poet, essayist, and novelist, b. 28 Sept. 1942, Ponce

F. received world recognition as a writer after the publication of her first book, *Papeles de Pandora* (1976: Pandora's papers). Her literary career began in the 1970s, years before she decided to study Spanish literature and received her M.A. from the University of Puerto Rico, and her Ph.D. from the University of Maryland (1987). Her first poems, short stories, and essays were published during 1972–1974 in *Zona de carga y descarga,* a magazine she founded and directed in Puerto Rico. The emergence of this short-lived magazine became a literary manifesto for new writers. It represented for contemporary Puerto Rican literature an opportunity to voice new aesthetic visions that departed from the style of writers of previous generations. It combined aesthetics with politics and with a new and innovative perspective on Puerto Rico's socioeconomic conditions. F.'s main contribution to Puerto Rican and Spanish literature has been an in-depth exploration of feminine themes. F., the daughter of a former governor of Puerto Rico, was raised in a traditional upper-class home with the same cultural myths and taboos typical to all women of her social status in Latin America. It is out of this experience that in her work F. makes a deliberate effort to explore, unveil, and condemn the restrictive cultural values imposed by the dominating classes on society, especially on women.

F.'s first published collection of poems and short stories in *Papeles de Pandora* portrays a sociopolitical and psychological reality dominated by economic exploitation and racial and sexist prejudice in enigmatic texts that combine different styles, subtle irony, harsh satire, and fantasy. In accordance with the title of the text, these poems and short stories share the underlying idea that language (the word) is like the evils that escaped from Pandora's box, spreading suffering throughout the world. F.'s innovative meditation on the Greek myth proposes a relationship between the social problems that afflict America in general and the language, rhetoric, and discourses of power that control the way individuals interpret themselves in the world. In the enigmatic twists of her stories, hope for change is voiced in F.'s stories by the subversion and rebellion of her female characters.

In her second book, *Maldito amor* (1986: dammed love), a collection of one novel and three short stories, F. explores the political and economic dichotomy of Puerto Rico in its dependent-independent relationship with U.S. economic interests, as well as in the dynamics of social and psychological relationships between individual persons and social classes. In her novel, F. evokes life in Puerto Rico during the beginning of the 20th c., a period of economic decline on the island, when the old landowners were displaced by new capitalistic classes dominated by North American companies. This is also the theme and setting of her short story "Isolda en el espejo" (Isolda in the mirror), where F. juxtaposes the sociohistorical theme with a complex relationship between art, woman, and male fantasy. In most of her work, F. explores the concept of the feminine double. With it, F. reconjugates in its holistic complexities the image of "woman" as an individual deprived of her human potential, fragmented and adulterated by cultural values that stereotype all feminine figures as either good or bad, virgin or whore, nurturing mother or femme fatale. F.'s work condemns such polarizations and seeks to reunite the feminine self. Restricted from exploring their own human potentials, F.'s women characters cannot recognize themselves in the categories imposed on them by society and must break away from such ties in order to find who they really are.

In F.'s collection of biographical and autobiographical essays, *Sitio a Eros* (1980; Eros besieged), revised in 1986 with the addition of two more essays, "La cocina de la escritura" (the kitchen of writing) and "De la ira a la ironía" (from anger to irony), F. addresses the issue of women as writers, herself included. The text is basically an account of the lives of those women writers like George Sand (1804–1876), Virginia Woolf, Anaïs Nin, Sylvia Plath (qq.v.), Julia de Burgos (1917–1953), and others, whom F. considers exemplary feminine models for their aesthetic rigor, their passion, and their imagination. Recently, a number of her writings have been translated and gathered in two different volumes, *Sweet Diamond Dust* (1988) and *The Youngest Doll* (1991).

In much of her work, but especially in *El acomodador. Una lectura fantástica de Felisberto Hernández* (1986; the usher, a fantastic reading of Felisberto Hernández), F. reiterates the very contemporary view that every critical interpretation of any work of fiction is another work of fiction parallel to the one it tries to recapture. Here, as in most of her writings, F. addresses the themes of human loneliness, isolation, and noncommunication. Though F.'s work is a feminine interpretation of society, she rejects the concept of a feminine nature in favor of the idea that women live and share common experiences due to social stereotypes that make women simple creations of fantasy, molded and distorted through history by way of myths, misprojections, and taboos. In most of her work, F. subverts these stereotypes by inverting traditional androcentric points of view. This partly explains F.'s interest in children's stories, and in the incorporation into the structure of her texts of popular anecdotes and themes like "La bella durmiente" (Sleeping Beauty) or the title of a *plena*, a popular regional song and dance from Ponce, in "Cuando las mujeres quieren a los hombres" (when women love men). F.'s texts are charged with multiple and complex metaphoric and symbolic meanings through which women are portrayed as very complex beings. Her women characters resist any binary classifications like those previously presented in Latin America, and, in general, in Western literature. F.'s work, like her poems in *Fábulas de la garza desangrada* (1982; fables of the bled heron), is also a profound meditation on love, its manifestations, and its distortions.

FURTHER WORKS: *El medio pollito. Siete cuentos infantiles* (1976); *La caja de cristal* (1978); *La muñeca menor* (1980); *Los cuentos de Juan Bobo* (1981); *La mona que le pisaron la cola* (1981); *Sonatina* (1989); *Árbol y sus sombras* (1989); *Coloquio de las Perras* (1990)

BIBLIOGRAPHY: López, I., " 'La muñeca menor': ceremonias y transformaciones en un cuento de R. F.," *ExTL*, 11, 1 (1982–1983), 49–58; Umpierre, L. M., "Un manifiesto literario: *Papeles de Pandora* de R. F.," *BR/RB*, 9, 2 (May–Aug. 1982), 120–26; Fernández-Olmos, M., "Desde una perspectiva femenina: la cuentística de R. F. y Ana Lydia Vega," *Homines*, 8, 2 (June–Jan. 1984–1985), 303–11; Guerra-Cunningham, L., "Tensiones paradójicas de la femineidad en la narrativa de R. F.," *Chasqui*, 13, 2–3 (Feb. 1984), 13–25; Chaves, M. J., "La alegoría como método en los cuentos y ensayos de R. F.," *Third Woman*, 2, 2 (1984), 64–76; Lagos-Pope, M. I., "Sumi-

KJARTAN FLØGSTAD

MAVIS GALLANT

STEFAN HEYM

MIROSLAV HOLUB

sión y rebeldía: el doble o la representación de la alienación femenina en narraciones de Marta Brunet y R. F.," *RI*, 51, 132–33 (July–Dec. 1985), 731–49; Acosta Cruz, M. I., "Historia, ser e identidad femenina en 'El collar de camandulas' y 'Maldito amor' de R. F.," *Chasqui,* 19, 2 (Nov. 1990), 23–31

JULIA CUERVO HEWITT

FERRON, Jacques

Canadian dramatist, novelist, short-story writer, and essayist (writing in French), b. 20 Jan. 1921, Louiseville, Quebec; d. 22 Apr. 1985, Longueil

F. received his first instruction in his native Louiseville and pursued his studies at the Collège Jean-de-Brébeuf, the Collège Saint-Laurent, and the Collège de l'Assomption, receiving his baccalaureate degree in 1941. In the early 1940s he studied medicine at the Université Laval (M.D. 1945), and then went into the armed forces until 1946, at which time he began to practice medicine, first in the Gaspé peninsula and then in Montreal.

F. had been writing since his early years, but he became particularly involved in it in his early twenties, all the while pursuing his interest in medicine, an activity that provided abundant subject matter and inspiration for his literary pursuits. His first play, *L'ogre* (1949; the ogre), was presented in 1949. It was followed by *Le licou* (1951; the halter), *Le dodu; ou le prix du bonheur* (1956; the plump one or the price of happiness), *Le cheval de Don Juan* (1957; Don Juan's horse), *Les grands soleils* (1958; the great suns), *Cazou; ou le prix de la virginité* (1963; Cazou or the price of virginity), *La tête du roi* (1963; the king's head), and *Le cœur d'une mère* (1969; a mother's heart). His theatrical works, which develop, among other subjects, the world of love as well as contemporary issues in Quebec, were well received. The earlier plays show an awareness of Molière's theater, while the later works become more contemporary, more directly Québécois.

It is upon his prose works, however, and his many short stories and novels, that his popularity and fame rest. F. began to move increasingly in this direction in the early 1960s, when his collection of short stories *Contes du pays incertain* (1962; *Tales from the Uncertain Country,* 1984) and the longer work *Cotnoir* (1962; *Dr. Cotnoir,* 1973) appeared, followed by *Contes anglais et autres* (1964; *English Stories and Other Tales,* 1971), *La nuit* (1965; the night), *Papa Boss* (1966; title in English), *Le ciel de Québec* (1969; *The Penniless Redeemer,* 1984), *L'amélanchier* (1970; *The Juneberry Tree,* 1975), and *Les confitures de coings et autres textes* (1972; *Quince Jam,* 1977). In these works, in which whimsy and the world of the fairy tale exist side by side with the "real" world, with all its seriousness, F. shows his preoccupation with problems in contemporary Quebec society, problems of self-identification and of the relationship of the powerful groups with the dispossessed ones—whether these be Anglophones viewing Francophones as living in a world of ignorance and sordidness, or Francophones looking askance at other, different groups.

Throughout his works, F. displays a striking power of invention, of mischievousness, of irony, mixing purely fictitious legend with historical fact as if they were part and parcel of the same world. The reader must be prepared to find, in the everyday world, figures from the Bible or historical figures from other eras as well as heroes of legend and myth. Yet throughout this new world that F. creates there appears a concern for and an involvement in the world of the present; indeed, these contemporary preoccupations led F. to create a political party, the Rhinoceros party, which poked fun at politicians and their solutions and which enjoyed a considerable amount of popularity. F.'s concern was not limited to the parochial; he was very much concerned with problems confronting all of humankind in the 20th-c. Quebec and its concerns were always on his mind, however, and he was always eager to explore all avenues that would allow it to grow politically and spiritually.

The recipient of many awards, among them that of the Governor General (1963), that of France-Amérique (1973), and the David Prize (1977), F. is one of the most important writers of contemporary Quebec.

FURTHER WORKS: *La charrette* (1968; *The Cart,* 1981); *Les roses sauvages, petit roman suivi d'une lettre d'amour soigneusement présentée* (1971; *Wild Roses: A Story Followed by a Love Letter,* 1976); *La Saint-Elias* (1972; *The Saint-Elias,* 1975); *Escarmouches* (1975); *Les lettres aux journaux* (1985); *La conférence inachevée* (1987). FURTHER VOLUME IN ENGLISH: *Selected Tales of J. F.* (1984)

BIBLIOGRAPHY: Robidoux, R., and A. Renaud, *Le roman canadien-français du vingtième siècle* (1966), 185–96; Marcel, J., *J. F. malgré lui* (1970); Lemire, M., et al., *Dictionnaire des œuvres littéraires du Québec* (1982), Vol. 3, passim; (1984), Vol. 4, passim; (1987), Vol. 5, passim; Cagnon, M., *The French Novel of Quebec* (1986), 84–90; Hamel, R., et al, *Dictionnaire des auteurs de langue française en Amérique du Nord* (1989),

510–14; New, W. H., *A History of Canadian Literature* (1989), 281–82

PAUL BARRETTE

FLØGSTAD, Kjartan

Norwegian novelist, poet, short-story writer, and essayist, b. 7 June 1944, Sauda

F. has his origins in the Norwegian working class, having grown up in a small industrial community in western Norway. He also has traveled the world as a seaman in the Norwegian merchant marine, and has lived in the extreme northeastern part of the country. These geographical aspects of F.'s biography have had a marked effect on his work, but so have his wide-ranging ventures in the world of intellect; F. probably has the best background in literature and philosophy of all contemporary Norwegian writers.

F.'s first books were two volumes of modernist poetry, *Valfart* (1968; pilgrimage) and *Seremoniar* (1969; ceremonies). Unlike most other writers of his generation, he displayed no overt political engagement but offered deeply felt experience of both nature and city environments. His next book, a mixture of narrative and essayistic prose entitled *Den hemmelege jubel* (1970; the secret jubilation) showed that he was a widely read, incisive, and engaging man of letters. The short-story collection *Fangliner* (1972; painters) and the novel *Rasmus* (1974; Rasmus) drew on F.'s own experience as a sailor in the merchant marine and as a worker in industry. Unlike some Marxist-Leninist writers, the foremost among them being Dag Solstad (q.v.)—who admitted that his novels about workers from the same period of time were written for members of the intelligentsia and not for the workers themselves—F. offered genuine portraits of daily life in the factory and onboard the merchant ship, and wrote in such a manner that the common person would be able to identify with the stories. Two mystery novels, written in the mid-1970s, can also be regarded as literature for the people.

The foundation of F.'s literary reputation is the novel *Dalen Portland* (1977; *Dollar Road,* 1989), which is also his first foray into postmodernism (q.v.) and for which he received the Nordic Literary Prize. An account of the changes that were brought about in a small community in western Norway when the area was industrialized, the book is a blending of the realistic and the fantastic. The lives of several members of one family are chronicled, and the author takes his characters to a large number of places at home and abroad. The text contains elements of the picaresque and other popular literary forms. Its self-reflexivity is shown in an otherwise realistic scene where one of the characters encounters a figure who states that his name is Kj. Fløgstad, and that he is knocking on a boiler in a factory because he is listening for hollow ringing sounds in the language. The author's next book, *Fyr og flamme* (1980; fire and flame), went further along the postmodernist road. Subtitled *Av handling* (which can be translated both as "dissertation" and "from action"), it is, in a sense, both a traditional story and a discussion of its subject and, at the same time, neither of the two. A hybrid text difficult to categorize, *Fyr og flamme* encompasses many different discourses. Its central character, Hertigen, is, like the text, also larger than life.

F.'s next book reads more like a traditional novel. *U3* (1983; U3) takes its title from the U2 episode in the middle of the Cold War, and is more overtly political in the traditional sense than either of its two predecessors. The protagonist, Alf Hellot, is an officer in the Norwegian air force, and he becomes the reader's guide to the history of Norwegian defense policy during the postwar era. The story culminates with the news of the downing of the U2 spy plane, after which Hellot, ever loyal to his people, terminates his life while on a mission to warn of what is happening to Norway as a result of her collaboration with the U.S. through NATO. The postmodern aspects of this novel are found primarily in the relationship between the figures and the narrator, who has at his disposal such aids as the fictional *retrospectoscope,* by means of which he is able to gather the information he needs to tell the story.

F.'s most hotly debated book is *Det 7. klima* (1986; the seventh climate), the fictional biography of one Salim Mahmood, a Pakistani immigrant to Norway who becomes a writer and datalinguist. The novel offered the author's view of what was happening to Norwegian cultural and intellectual life at the time, but his views were presented in such a difficult manner that most of the critics reacted with a great deal of frustration and only limited understanding. F.'s contributions to the debate about the book have been collected in the volume *Tyrannosaurus Text* (1988; tyrannosaurus text).

F. is still very much in the middle of his career. He is almost universally recognized as Norway's most important living writer, and his literary reputation seems secure.

FURTHER WORKS: *Døden ikke heller* (1975); *Ein for alle* (1976); *Loven vest for Pecos* (1981); *Ordlyden* (1983); *Portrett av eit magisk liv; Poeten Claes Gill* (1988)

BIBLIOGRAPHY: Garton, J., "New Directions in Norwegian Literature," *RNL*, 12 (1983), 163–84;

Stegane, I., "The New Norse Literary Tradition," *RNL,* 12 (1983), 101–22; Rønning, H., "History, Identity, Communication: Trends in Recent Norwegian Fiction," *ScanR,* 76, 2 (1988), 95–102

JAN I. SJÅVIK

FONSECA, Rubem

Brazilian novelist and short-story writer, b. 11 May 1925, Minas Gerais

Born in Minas Gerais to Portuguese parents, F. moved with his family to Rio de Janeiro when he was a child. Having earned degrees in law and public administration, F. has been a criminal lawyer, professor, and researcher at the Getúlio Vargas Foundation, as well as an executive with a multinational company. Retired from corporate life, he now dedicates his time to writing. F. is a city creature, however, and he maintains an apartment in Rio de Janeiro, where he keeps his library, participates in writers organizations, and receives visitors from all over the world. He has been an activist for writers' rights and is committed to giving his time to promote Brazil's cultural development. He served as secretary of culture for the city of Rio de Janeiro from 1980 to 1981. F. has won travel grants to Germany, where he spent several months researching a recent novel that features action in Europe, *Vastas emoções e pensamentos imperfeitos* (1988; vast emotions and imperfect thoughts). His work has been translated into the major languages.

Sex and violence are weapons in F.'s fiction, manipulated to disturb the complacency of Brazil's ruling technocracy to the point that he has been accused of being a pornographer, and his volume of short stories, *Feliz Ano Novo* (1975; happy New Year), was banned by General Ernesto Geisel's administration (1974–1979). Using the format of the American-style detective novel in the tradition of Dashiell Hammett (q.v.), F. insists on the writer's role as the "subversive" to focus on the malaise of the modern human in the urban setting. Firmly placed in the tradition of great city novelists, such as Balzac, Dickens, and Dostoevsky, and with strong links to contemporary North American fiction writers like Donald Barthelme, John Barth, and William Burroughs (qq.v.), F. is a moralist and muralist of contemporary Brazilian life.

F. has created four particularly noteworthy characters who reappear throughout his work: Mandrake, Vilela, Guedes, and, recently, in *Agosto* (1990; August), Alberto Matos. Mandrake, a lawyer, is present in the short stories and reappears in *A grande arte* (1983; *High Art,* 1986) and has a tough amoral attitude toward life. He is a model

for street survival, and yet full of tender brutality. Vilela is the young vice cop in *A coleira do cão* (1965; the dog collar) who reappears in *O caso Morel* (1973; the Morel case) as a free-lance writer and private detective. Guedes, who appears in the title story of *O cobrador* (1979; the avenger) and again in *Bufo & Spallanzani* (1990; Bufo & Spallanzani), and Alberto Matos are the good cops, flatfooted and laconic, who cling obstinately to an ethic of morality in the midst of the chaos they doggedly attempt to right. They are cynical, ulcerous, sweaty, and deliberately unexciting. In most of F.'s narratives the poet, the lawman, and the criminal become one.

F. spent twenty years perfecting his short-story style while aspiring to be a serious novelist. His interest in film, clearly evidenced in his narrative style, has led him to write original screenplays, most recently *Stelinha* (1991; Stelinha), based on the title story "Lúcia McCartney," from the collection *Lúcia McCartney* (1967; Lúcia McCartney). His novels develop the themes of his short stories, albeit in some of the recent works the intensity and poignancy of his story art is diverted into a kind of postmodernist slapstick. F. is at his best with his treatment of human sexuality and the social and philosophical issues that sex raises. He forces the reader to face human weakness, anxiety, and vulnerability by creating characters so believable that their drama transcends the boundaries of fiction. The unsettling effect of F.'s narratives is the fishbowl illusion that the reader, indeed, may be the one at risk.

FURTHER WORKS: *Os prisioneiros* (1963); *O homem de fevereiro e Março* (1973); *Romance negro* (1992)

BIBLIOGRAPHY: Coutinho, A., *O erotismo na literatura: o caso R. F.* (1979); Lowe, E., *The City in Brazilian Literature* (1982), 124–34, 136–44, 146–59, 186–91, 214–16; Tolman, J., "The Moral Dimension in R. F.'s Prose," *New World,* 1 (1986), 61–81; Vargas Llosa, M., on *High Art, NYTBR,* 7 Sept. 1986, 7; Stern, I., ed., *Dictionary of Brazilian Literature* (1988), 133–34; Simpson, A. S., *Detective Fiction from Latin America* (1990), 78–79

ELIZABETH LOWE

FOUCAULT, Michel

French philosopher, b. 15 Oct. 1926, Poitiers; d. 25 June 1984, Paris

Next to Jean-Paul Sartre (q.v.), F. is often considered the most influential and fecund French philosopher of the century. Born to a provincial family of doctors, he studied philosophy at the

École Normale Supérieure and later earned a degree in psychology (1952). F.'s family background explains to some degree his lifelong interest in the history of medicine and psychiatry, along with philosophy, history, and literature. Among his numerous works, *Les mots et les choses; Une archéologie des sciences humaines* (1966; *The Order of Things: An Archeology of the Human Sciences,* 1971) represents a turning point in his oeuvre. Another significant break marks the eight-year gap that separates the publication of volume one of his *Histoire de la sexualité: La volonté de savoir* (1976; *The History of Sexuality I: An Introduction,* 1978) from volumes two and three: *L'usage des plaisirs* (1984; *The Use of Pleasure,* 1985) and *Le souci de soi* (1984; *The Care of the Self,* 1986). During his later years, he came to be associated with such causes as prisoners' rights, the problems of the boat people, and gay rights. After having taught at the universities of Lille, Uppsala, Warsaw, Clermont-Ferrand, and Vincennes, F. held a chair at the prestigious Collège de France when he died in 1984.

The early F. produced a series of illuminating studies devoted to the emergence of the concept of mental illness, culminating with his monumental *Histoire de la folie à l'âge classique* (1961; *Madness and Civilization,* 1965). F.'s aim was to demonstrate that the generalized practice of institutionalizing people considered to be mad is relatively recent, as can be seen by the systematic roundups of beggars, petty criminals, and prostitutes that took place in the 17th c. under absolute monarchy. In the 18th c. madness was criminalized through a series of legal moves and was reinforced by the creation of a uniform network of prisons that F. would later describe in his *Surveiller et punir: Naissance de la prison* (1975; *Discipline and Punish: The Birth of the Prison,* 1977). The hallmark of F.'s early work is to have shown that reason as defined by Descartes could only exist in its relation to madness, the latter being a defining other that is both fascinating and repressed. F.'s *Histoire de la folie à l'âge classique* is also an account of the birth of the modern state and its repressive and disciplinarian apparatuses, which a F. critic has labeled "the rise of unfreedom." It should be pointed out that F. himself acknowledged that his early work contained phenomenological residues and displayed a somewhat romanticized vision of madness.

F.'s next major project, *Les mots et les choses,* was an ambitious reconstruction of the history of human sciences and proffered the much debated concept of *episteme* that did away with the concept of a linear history. It also closed on the no less famous, if often misunderstood, statement that "Man is dead." Focusing on the evolution of

sciences, F. isolated three moments in the modern ages when knowledge and representation seem to rely on different foundations. In each of these periods a trilogy of sciences—natural history/analysis of wealth/general grammar, biology/economics/philology, and psychology/sociology/linguistics—appears to be organized according to common patterns ignored by these sciences. For F. this hidden structuring of knowledge, which he called *episteme,* gives each of these periods its intellectual identity; some of F.'s critics have claimed that he was never able to account for change from one *episteme* to another. Finally, by stating that "Man is dead" F. meant that the concept of humankind was a very recent one, as a product of history, and that it might very well disappear.

His next major work, *Surveiller et punir,* addressed the traditional view of power based on force and coercion. According to F., power should be analyzed from the point of view of a "microphysics" (of power) that would take into account, among other things, the body as a fragmented area permeated by thousands of unconscious procedures of discipline. In F.'s eyes, the history of prisons in Europe and the U.S. along with legal literature provided the ideal research material for investigating the constitution and rise of "modern" power. His approach to these various issues caused him to be more or less ambiguously associated with the so-called structuralist generation, that is, with Louis Althusser (1918–1990), Roland Barthes, and Claude Lévi-Strauss (qq.v.).

What critics have labeled "the final Foucault" is associated with the published volumes of his *Histoire de la sexualité.* In the first volume, F., who had earlier welcomed and praised the advent of psychoanalysis as a liberating technique, turned against it, claiming that it reproduced in a new guise the urge to confess inherited from Christian thought. In subsequent volumes, F. departed from his original stated project and turned his attention to ancient Greece as the producer of the very subjectivity Christian thought was to erase. F. was trying to contribute to what subjectivity and ethics could be and mean in a post-Christian era. Thus, the very philosopher who in the 1960s and the 1970s had delivered a devastating blow to the concept of the subject was reinstating it through his studies of ancient texts dealing with happiness, diet, sexual habits, and personal ethics. At the time of his premature death, F. was devoting his Collège de France lectures to the concept of *gouvernementalité* or "governmentality."

As a philosopher F. remained close to Nietzsche and Heidegger. His relativism and deep distrust of morality, which in the first part of his career he considered a power play always won by the rulers, is reminiscent of Nietzsche's *Genealogy of Morals* (1887). But the manner in which F. also conceived of the limited possibilities that are offered the human mind by each historical horizon, as well as his early rejection of subjectivity, evokes Heidegger.

It is the fate of works of this amplitude that have revolutionized fields including philosophy, psychiatry, history, and legal studies, to be submitted to intense critical scrutiny. Up to *Surveiller et punir* F. was often charged with accounting for the totalitarian world of the modern state without offering the alternatives he clearly endorsed as a left-wing political activist. After volume two of *Histoire de la sexualité* he was perceived by some as a newborn elitist who had dropped all social concerns. And, like Sartre's work, F.'s does not register the existence of other cultures and non-Europocentric experiences of life. This will not prevent F. from being regarded in the future as one of the most influential thinkers of the 20th c., after whom entire sectors of human knowledge will never again be the same.

FURTHER WORKS; *Maladie mentale et personnalité* (1954); *Maladie mentale et psychologie* (1962); *Naissance de la clinique: Une archéologie du regard médical* (1963; *The Birth of the Clinic: An Archeology of the Medical Perception*, 1973); *Raymond Roussel* (1963; *Death and the Labyrinth: The World of Raymond Roussel*, 1986); *L'archéologie du savoir* (1969; *The Archeology of Knowledge*, 1976); *L'ordre du discours* (1971; *Orders of Discourse*, 1971); *Résumés des cours au Collège de France* (1989). FURTHER VOLUMES IN ENGLISH: *Language, Counter-Memory, Practice: Selected Essays and Interviews* (1977); *Power/ Knowledge: Selected Interviews and Other Writings* (1980); *The F. Reader* (1983); *M. F.: Politics, Philosophy, Culture: Interviews and Other Writings* (1988)

BIBLIOGRAPHY: Baudrillard, J., *Oublier F.* (1977); Dreyfus, H. L., and P. Rabinow, *M. F.: Beyond Structuralism and Hermeneutics* (1982); Racevskis, K., *M. F. and the Subversion of Intellect* (1983); Poster, M., *F., Marxism and History: Mode of Production versus Mode of Information* (1984); Rajchman, J., *M. F.: The Freedom of Philosophy* (1985); Deleuze, G., *F.* (1986); Arac, J., ed., *After F.: Humanistic Knowledge, Postmodern Challenges* (1988); Bernauer, J., and D. Rasmussen, eds., *The Final F.* (1988); Canguilhem, G., ed., *M. F. philosophe: Rencontre internationale, Paris 9, 10, 11 janvier 1988* (1989); Fraser, N., *Unruly Practices: Power, Discourse and Gender in Contemporary Social Theory* (1989), 17–66

JEAN-FRANÇOIS FOURNY

FRENCH LITERATURE

See Volume 2, page 133.

With a second millennium in the offing, the last quarter of the 20th c. witnesses the distinctive dynamism that has marked the century. The social and political upheavals of the late 1960s, catalyzed by the death throes of the colonial empire and the student revolt of 1968, have continued to work, as noted by Germaine Brée, toward "disintegrating traditional structures [and] fostering the emergence of uncertain new ones."

The structuralist theorists and critics of the 1960s and 1970s, maligned for their formalism, nonetheless have left their stamp on the remarkable varieties of literary exploration following in their wake: semiotics as well as poststructuralism, postmodernism (qq.v.)—whose bewildering profusion of ideas has heralded a shift in the way we view the world and ourselves. Concepts that had come to be held as invariable truths little by little became open to question: subject, presence, origin, representation. As the end of the 19th c. witnessed a narrowing of the gap between the popular and the learned, the spoken and the written, so literature in the last two decades has increasingly sought to break down the barriers between genres. Structuralism's (q.v.) devalorization of the canonical great work has furthered this tendency to blend the educated and literary with the popular and commercial.

With the deaths in the late 1970s and the 1980s of many of the writers and thinkers instrumental in fashioning modern literature and literary thought—in 1976 André Malraux and Raymond Queneau, the year following Jacques Prévert, in 1980 Jean-Paul Sartre and Roland Barthes, in 1981 Jacques Lacan, in 1982 Louis Aragon and Georges Perec, in 1984 Michel Foucault and Henri Michaux, in 1986 Simone de Beauvoir and Jean Genet, in 1987 Marguerite Yourcenar and Jean Anouilh, in 1988 René Char, in 1989 Samuel Beckett (qq.v.)—one has the impression that an age has passed. With the crisis in French theater in recent years and the increasing alienation of the poet from the public, with the concern about the continued weakening of the reading habits of the French, and with the renewed debate over the mongrelization of the French language through the depredations of English (in 1988 the French Academy opened a "museum of [linguistic] horrors"), doomsayers have sketched scenarios forecasting the decline of literature as a central force of stabilization and innovation upon which French society paces itself.

Many events speak otherwise: the rich pluralism and experimental bent of modern literature and literary theory; the opening of the Centre Pompidou at Beaubourg (1977); the creation of the "Maison de la Poésie" by the City of Paris in 1983 and the "High Committee for Poetry and the French Language" by the French government in 1987 to safeguard "the role of dream and escape" among young people; the creation of "Les Éditions des Femmes" devoted to reediting women's writings of the past (1979); the appearance in 1987 of volume 1 of the first reedition in 50 years of the *Dictionnaire de l'Académie Française;* the election of two women (Marguerite Yourcenar in 1980 and Jacqueline de Romilly in 1989) to the august inner circle of the French Academy; and the announcement in 1989 that a new National Library, more vast than the present one, will open in 1995 in the suburb of Tolbiac—they all point to literary renewal and new and inviting byways for cultural expression.

French literature since the 1970s continues the tradition of such illustrious forebears as Paul Valéry, Marcel Proust, and Paul Claudel (qq.v.) who have left rich commentary on the act of writing. The contemporary writer has often pushed this metalinguistic dimension to its ultimate, blurring the line between fiction and criticism, making narrative a critique of itself. Yet another characteristic of recent writing is its sociopolitical involvement. Perhaps more than at any time in the past, the writer and critic begin to conceive of the inseparability of the literary work and the culture that engenders it.

Since the mid-1970s three significant reorientations have distinguished contemporary literary endeavor: writing by women, postcolonial or migrant literature, and what has been called postmodernist literature. These modes, for all the diversity of their approaches, share certain characteristics: that of speaking from the margin, the recognition of the irreducible character of "reality," and oppositionality.

Fiction

Since the mid-1970s the French literary world has been the scene of a remarkable flourishing of fictional narratives in an astounding diversity of modes. The arrival of the autumn literary season (the "rentrée") has come regularly to herald the appearance of more than 200 novels, in time for the literary prizes of November and December. Several of the experimental novelists who attained reputations in the 1950s and 1960s—the so-called new or new-new novelists such as Alain Robbe-

Grillet, Michel Butor, Marguerite Duras, Jean Cayrol, Nathalie Sarraute, Robert Pinget, and Claude Simon (qq.v.)—continue to create important innovative works. Among them are Robbe-Grillet's *Djinn* (1981; *Djinn,* 1982), Simon's *Géorgiques* (1981; *Georgics,* 1989) and *L'acacia* (1989; *The Acacia,* 1991), and Duras's *L'amant* (1984; *The Lover,* 1985). Novels of Philippe Sollers (q.v.) follow one another at a prodigious rate, from *Paradis* (1981; paradise) to *La fête à Venise* (1991; celebration in Venice), as do those of Michel Tournier (q.v.), from *Gaspar, Melchior et Balthazar* (1980; *The Four Wise Men,* 1982) to *Le médianoche amoureux* (1989; *The Midnight Love Feast,* 1991), which explore myths of all ages and realms. Moreover, Elie Wiesel (q.v.) has persevered in his dedicated vigil over the unforgotten past of the Holocaust in works like *Le cinquième fils* (1983; *The Fifth Son,* 1985). The Nobel committee awarded him the peace prize in 1986. These writers, in their characteristic unprogrammatic way, manifest an ever-renewed push to reform writing, to challenge traditional narrative and conventional ordering structures of plot, character, and story. Fittingly, the Nobel Prize for literature went to one of them in 1985—Claude Simon.

Despite their diversity, many present-day fictional narratives share common features inherited from the New Novel (q.v.); exploded narrative that dissolves the order and linearity of the conventional story line, the calling into question of subject (narrator/character) identity, *mise en abyme* (textural part mirroring the textural whole), ambiguity, plural voices, even contradiction, that result in a multiplicity of viewpoints, of possible interpretations. Moreover, writers have persisted in eroding barriers between genres. *La vie, mode d'emploi* (1978; *Life: A User's Manual,* 1987), the masterpiece of Georges Perec, presents a mixture of the detective story, history, biography, scientific writing, journalism, and popular literature.

The autobiographical genre has loomed more in evidence. Since 1975, an entire generation seems to be drawing back and looking over its past. Memoirs of Sartre, Beauvoir, Genet, Yourcenar, and Philippe Soupault (q.v.) have appeared, as well as of the generation following, of Robbe-Grillet and Sarraute. Autobiographical writing, owing to its immediacy and call to personal experience and authority, has become the instrument of predilection for many authors, particularly women, and more particularly women born in French-speaking areas outside France: Marguerite Duras and Assia Djebar (q.v.) stand out as examples.

After the purism of the "new novelists" and the belief of the writer of the 1960s and 1970s in "uncommitted" writing, the narrative since the late 1970s has tended to manifest political and social commitment, even while conveying that commitment very often through a nonmimetic style and experimental language that create the type of specific (ir)reality we observe in the work of Georges Perec and Maurice Blanchot (q.v.). The narratives of Patrick Modiano (q.v.) return to the Occupation years to resuscitate the past through the collective memory of the French people—from his film script *Lacombe, Lucien* (1974; *Lacombe, Lucien,* 1975) to *Fleurs de ruine* (1991; flowers in the ruins). Duras, while repudiating the label of feminist, has explored the timbres of the feminine voice in a social context in a way few authors preceding her have. Her work attained worldwide recognition in the 1980s. Hélène Cixous and Monique Wittig (qq.v.), on the other hand, though differing in crucial respects, have both engaged with undisguised fervor the question of woman's sexuality, as have Luce Irigaray (b. 1939), Annie Leclerc (b. 1940), and Julia Kristeva (q.v.). The migrant narratives of *beur* writers (writers of North African extraction born in France) like Leïla Sebbar (b. 1941) and Mehdi Charef (b. 1952), and writers born in French-speaking countries outside the metropole, like Edouard Glissant, Abdelkebir Khatibi, Tahar Ben Jelloun, Maryse Condé (qq.v.) and Sony Labou Tansi (b. 1947), have added other dimensions of political and social contestation through experimentation and innovation in the form of narrative and subject matter.

Several venerable authors continue to compose important works: Julien Green (q.v.) caps his career at the age of eighty-five with the 900-page novel *Les pays lointains* (1987; *The Distant Lands,* 1990), judged by some critics to be his masterpiece; André Pieyre de Mandiargues (q.v.) in his late seventies continues to publish works such as *Tout disparaître* (1987; let everything disappear), as does Christiane Rochefort (b. 1917) whose *La porte du fond* (1988; door at the rear) received the Medecis Prize in 1988. Along with established writers such as Lucien Bodard (b. 1914), Jacques Laurent (b. 1919), Maurice Roche (b. 1924), Jean D'Ormesson (b. 1925), Raymond Jean (b. 1925), Françoise Mallet-Joris (b. 1930), Pierre-Jean Rémy (b. 1937), and J.-M. G. Le Clézio (q.v.), who are still active, a battery of new and talented writers, many of the post-World War II generation, has emerged: Serge Doubrovsky (b. 1928), Jean Vautrin (b. 1933), René-Victor Pilhes (b. 1934), Danièle Sallenave (b. 1940), François Weyergans (b. 1941), Jean-Marie Rouart (b. 1943), Alain Gerber (b. 1943), Patrick Grainville (b. 1947), Georges-Olivier Châteaureynaud (b. 1947), Erik Orsenna (b. 1947), Bernard-Marie Koltès (b. 1948), Jean Echenoz (b. 1948), Yann Queffélec (b. 1949),

Marc Cholodenko (b. 1950), Jacques Almira (b. 1950), Raphaële Billetdoux (b. 1951), Muriel Cerf (b. 1951), and Patrick Thévenon (dates n.a.). Their narratives vary radically, from rather traditional forms to bold experimentation in such a narrative as that of Weyergans where a fetus narrates the story in *Vie d'un bébé* (1986; the life of a baby); from metanovels (novels about novel writing)—Almira's *Le voyage à Naucratis* (1975; voyage to Naucratis) or Weyergans's *Je suis écrivain* (1989; I'm a novelist)—autofiction/autobiography such as Doubrovsky's *Le livre brisé* (1989; the sundered book) or Orsenna's *L'exposition coloniale* (1988; *Love and Empire,* 1991), and works of postmodern myth and allegory such as Grainville's *La caverne céleste* (1984; *The Cave of Heaven,* 1990) or Wittig's *Virgile, non* (1985; *Across the Acheron,* 1987) to novels of social-political orientation—Grainville's *Les flamboyants* (1976; the flamboyants), which treats Africa and revolution; Pilhes's *L'imprécateur* (1974; *The Provocateur,* 1977), which takes as subject the failure of a multinational corporation; Ormesson's *Le bonheur à San Miniato* (1987; happiness at San Miniato), set in the days of fascism and Stalinism of World War II; Châteaureynaud's *Le verger* (1978; the orchard), which depicts a child in a death camp; Bertrand Poirot-Delpeche's (b. 1929) *L'été 36* (1984; summer '36), about the violence of the 1930s; finally, the novels of Modiano.

Feminist writing has assumed special importance in the work of Benoîte Groult (b. 1920), Catherine Clément (b. 1939), and Annie Ernaux (b. 1940). Gay and lesbian themes inform *L'étoile rose* (1978; the pink star) and *Dans la main de l'ange* (1982; in the hand of the angel) by Dominique Fernandez (b. 1929), *Le jardin d'acclimatation* (1980; *Cronus' Children,* 1986) by Yves Navarre (b. 1940), and the postmodern *Virgile, non* by Monique Wittig. In *Les quartiers d'hiver* (1990; winter quarters), Jean-Noël Pancrazi (b. 1949) treats the scourge of AIDS threatening the gay community.

The genre of the detective novel was marked by the death in 1989 of the Belgian Georges Simenon (q.v.), whose prolific pen had authored over 300 novels, and by the appearance in the "Série Noire" in 1985 of the 2000th detective novel—a measure of the genre's increasing respectability. San Antonio (pseud. of Frédéric Dard, b. 1921) continues to produce his unique brand of mystery thriller. The "new" mystery flourishing since the early 1970s displaces the mystery intrigue through a metaliterary movement, as in René Belletto's (b. 1945) *L'enfer* (1986; hell), often subordinating it to a radical social and literary reevaluation and contestation: Jean Vautrin's (b. 1933) *Canicule* (1982; dog days) and Joseph

Bialot's (dates n.a.) *Babelville* (1979; Babel city), which depict the racism and violence of materialistic society; the writings of A. D. G. (pseud. of Alain Camille, b. 1947) and Jean-Patrick Manchette (b. 1942), which excoriate society from their respective positions of right- and left-wing militancy. The espionage novel maintains its rank as the best-selling genre in France (20 million copies yearly), including among its legion of practitioners (many of inferior talent), the ubiquitous Vladimir Volkoff (b. 1932), awarded the French Academy's Grand Prize for the novel in 1982, for *Le montage* (1982; the setting).

Drama

The last echoes of the Theater of the Absurd (q.v.) resounded in theater corridors in the mid 1970s and early 1980s, with new plays by Samuel Beckett and Eugène Ionesco (q.v.), restagings of these dramatists and of Arthur Adamov, Fernando Arrabal (qq.v.), and Georges Shehadé (b. 1910), and new productions by their followers—Robert Pinget, Jean Tardieu (qq.v.), and René de Olbadia (b. 1918). New plays by Jean Anouilh appeared, the latest of which was the farce *Le nombril* (belly button) in 1981. But since the 1970s, critics like Alfred Simon have emphasized the artistic and economic impoverishment of French theater, the disappearance of major dramatists and actors, the tendency of directors to "dust off" the classics, their failure to encourage young authors, and, consequently, the diminishment of theatergoers to serious theater.

Other tendencies contributing to the changes wrought in theater include the numerous productions of foreign dramatists and directors and the influence of television, film, and radio. Since the 1970s theatrical fare has consisted primarily of popular theater (the boulevard theater and the *cafés-théâtres*) and restagings and revivals of time-honored plays. Moreover, a collective theater (*création collective*), in which authors, actors, directors, and even the public merge, arose in the 1970s in the stagings of Ariane Mnouchkine (b. 1939) of the spectacles or historical frescoes of *1798, 1793,* and *L'âge d'or* (the golden age) at the Théâtre du Soleil. The spectacles of Robert Hossein (b. 1927)—*Danton et Robespierre* (perf. 1979), *Les misérables* (perf. 1980), and *Un homme nommé Jésus* (perf. 1983)—have attracted theatergoers by elaborate staging and hundreds of actors. Finally, numerous private theaters failed, and the absorption of the Odeon by the Comédie Française marked the close of a famed state theater.

The decentralization of theater encouraged by the ministry of culture, viewed by many critics negatively, has accounted for a dramatic increase in regional theaters (Lyons, Strasbourg, Marseille, and Grenoble) and summer companies playing in provincial festival centers like Avignon and Nice. These events signal, first, a move of theater out of the dominant Parisian theatrical milieu, secondly, a strengthening of the tendency of theater to free itself from the restraints of the written script and conventional staging. Hence, despite its seeming impoverishment, profound changes in process, which account for the shift from the individual dramatist to the production, invest theater with a new dynamism.

Another notable exception to the sense of general impoverishment lies in the striking productivity of women dramatists such as Duras, Sarraute, Cixous, Wittig, Djebar, and Sylvia Montfort (dates n.a.). Wittig's and Cixous's work, like Montfort's, fastens on contemporary sociopolitical issues. Cixous's *L'histoire terrible mais inachevée de Norodom Sihanouk, roi du Cambodge* (1985; the terrible and unfinished story of Norodom Sihanouk, king of Cambodia) and *L'Indiade* (1988; the Indiad) take as subjects the Cambodian tragedy, Gandhi, and Indian independence. Far from being mere historical accounts, her plays depict the enigmatic contrarieties of historical personages. Outstanding among dramatists of the last two decades is Duras, whose plays like *L'Eden-cinéma* (1977; Eden-cinema) and *Savannah Bay* (1982; title in English) convey a style founded on absence and silence, which eloquently depicts the anguish of her characters.

The work of the accomplished dramatists François Billetdoux (b. 1927)—*Réveille-toi Philadelphie!* (1989; wake up Philadelphia!)—the *boulevardier* Jean Poiret (1927–1992)—*Les clients* (1987; the clients)—the author–director Roger Planchon (b. 1931), and Jacques Sternberg (b. 1923) have also helped to keep theater alive. New writers of promise include Loleh Bellon (b. 1925), a latecomer to playwriting, whose intimate dramas between women have met with deserved success (*Absence,* 1988; absence); Jean-Claude Grumberg (b. 1939), whose work handles serious social and artistic questions through the medium of humor (*L'Indien sous Babylone,* 1985; the Indian under Babylon); Jean-Claude Brisville (b. 1922), who presents the painful, human confrontation of two famous viewpoints, one anguished, the other reasoned, in *L'entretien de M. Descartes avec M. Pascal le jeune* (1986; conversation of Descartes and young Pascal); the bold theater of Michel Vinaver (b. 1927), which in such plays as *Les travaux et les jours* (1979; works and days) or *L'ordinaire* (1983; the ordinary), depicts modern humankind as in perfect communion with the very system that crushes it; the brilliant and impassioned theater of Copi (1939–1987), whose early death cut short a promising career, and whose last play, *Une visite inopportune* (1988; an inopportune visit), stages a character dying of AIDS; finally, the gifted and prolific Bernard-Marie Koltès (b. 1948), whose *Dans la solitude des champs de coton* (1986; in the solitude of the cotton fields) puts into words a stark dialogue between an addict and a dealer. The work of certain dramatists, including Vinaver, the Belgian René Kalisky (b. 1936), author of *Aida vaincue* (1990; Aida vanquished), and Michel Deutsch (b. 1928), was dubbed *le théâtre du quotidien* (the theater of daily life) for its treatment of the fragmented reality of contemporary life. (For example, Deutsch's *Partage*, ''sharing,'' deals with the tortured portraits of two of Charles Manson's women followers trying to make sense of their complicity in the murder of Sharon Tate.) Other dramatists whose work manifests talent and force include Yasmina Réza (b. 1955), Jacques-Pierre Amette (b. 1943), Edouardo Manet (b. 1927), Françoise Dorin (b. 1928), the Quebecer Michel Tremblay (q.v.), and the Senegalese Souleymane Cissé (b. 1940).

Poetry

In the last few years the voices of several major poets have fallen silent: Saint-John Perse, Pierre Jean Jouve, Jacques Prévert, Henri Michaux, Pierre Emmanuel, Francis Ponge, and René Char (qq.v.). But these years have also witnessed astounding poetic activity—a flowering of festivals, gatherings, and readings devoted to poetry, and the resounding success of the Maison de la Poésie in bringing poetry to the literary public. They have also seen a proliferation of reviews consecrating the work of established and new poets alike: *Poètes Présents, Poésie Présente, Po&sie, Poémonde, Poésie,* launched by the Maison de la Poésie in 1984, and the influential *Argile,* which unhappily folded in 1981 after seven years of outstanding publication. The firm of Seghers continued as the major publisher of poetry, even after the death of the venerable Pierre Seghers in 1987. Finally, poetry collections sprout everywhere—in 1988 alone more than 300 received partial subventions from the Centre National des Lettres.

Poets of earlier generations have continued to affirm their poetic presence: esteemed talents like Eugène Guillevic (b. 1907), Edmond Jabès (q.v.), and Alain Bosquet (b. 1919), and the generation of the 1920s and early 1930s of Jean-Claude Renard (b. 1922), Yves Bonnefoy (q.v.), André du Bouchet (b. 1924), the Swiss Philippe Jaccottet (b. 1925), Jacques Dupin (b. 1927), Michel Deguy (b. 1930), and Pierre Oster Soussouev (b. 1933). The poetry of these latter is a poetry of silence and loss, dealing more with the allegorical figur-

ation of absence than the concreteness of material existence, poetry stripped to the essentials of being, often conveyed in hermetic language.

Another trend marking contemporary poetry stems from agonistic modes of the 1960s and 1970s seeking to demystify poetry, often framed by a movement or evolving around a journal: *lettrism* under Isadore Isou (b. 1925) that sought to rehabilitate poetic language; the *Tel Quel* group with its political program set forth by Marcelin Pleynet (b. 1933) and Denis Roche (b. 1937) that challenged the generic bases of poetry; the revolutionary poetics of *Change* under Jean-Pierre Faye (q.v.), Jacques Roubaud (b. 1932), and Jacques Réda (b. 1929); and the Oulipian wild bunch and its triad of Roubaud, François Le Lionnais (1901–1984), and Jean Lescure (b. 1912), whose ludic experimentation with the help of mathematics and the computer transformed traditional poetic forms.

Some of the most accomplished poetry of the last two decades has come from poets born abroad: Andrée Chedid (Egyptian of Lebanese origin), Mohammed Dib (Algeria) (qq.v.), Edouard Glissant (Martinique), Gaston Miron (b. 1928, Quebec), Salah Stétié (b. 1929, Lebanon), Edouard Maunick (b. 1931, Mauritius), Jacques Izoard (b. 1926, Belgium), and Tahar Ben Jelloun (Morocco), who read his latest work, a 600-verse poem honoring the unknown Arab soldier killed in the Persian Gulf War at the Capri Festival in June 1991. Younger poets of notable talent include Bernard Noël (b. 1930), Claude-Michel Cluny (b. 1930), Jude Stéfan (b. 1930), Jean Pérol (b. 1932), Marie-Claire Bancquart (b. 1932), Pierre Dalle Nogare (b. 1934), Yves Martin (b. 1936), Jean Joubert (b. 1938), Jean Orizet (b. 1937), James Sacré (b. 1939), Daniel Biga (b. 1940), Jean-Pierre Lemaire (b. 1948), and Marc Cholodenko (b. 1950).

The new poetry has been described by many critics as ''exploded''—shattering into a multitude of fragments replete with powerful imagery, provocative rhythms, jarring disharmonies. Multiple currents have arisen, ranging from the lyrical, the search for the secular sacred and fascination with nature (Orizet), the corporeal (Noël) and the metaphysical (Dalle Nogare)—on the one hand—to a realistic vein—on the other hand—inspired in part by the events of 1968, that fastens on the urban setting with its pop artifacts, blaring noise, glaring lights, graffiti, and violence (Biga, Martin, Réda).

Theory and Criticism

With theory and criticism as with theater, critics have spoken of crisis and impoverishment without a sense of the rich dynamics of change postwar thought has wrought in seeking to free itself from the procrustean restraints of reductive, doctrinaire thinking that played a part in the political and social debacles of the 1930s, the events of World War II, and the Cold War. Recent years have seen literature and literary theory inflected by theorists from varied disciplines: philosophy, psychoanalysis, anthropology, sociology, and linguistics. The type of critical thought that compartmentalizes knowledge, that ceases to be critical and reproduces rather than renews the status quo has been challenged by the French poststructuralists Jacques Derrida, Jean-François Lyotard, Roland Barthes, and Michel Foucault (qq.v.). Their works constitute the most innovative development in contemporary French thought—from Derrida's *Éperons* (1978; *Spurs*, 1979) to *La carte postale* (1980; *The Post Card*, 1987) and the autobiographical work *Jacques Derrida par Geoffrey Bennington et Jacques Derrida* (1991; Jacques Derrida by Geoffrey Bennington and Jacques Derrida), from Lyotard's *Économie libidinale* (1974; libidinal economy) to *Le différend* (1984; *The Different: Phrases in Dispute*, 1988) and *L'inhumain* (1988; *The Inhuman*, 1992), and from Barthes's, *Barthes par Barthes* (1975; *Roland Barthes by Roland Barthes*, 1977) to his posthumous works such as *Le grain de la voix* (1981; *The Grain of the Voice*, 1985). They mutually undertake an adversarial counteraction against absolutist systems, against narratives of the legitimation of knowledge, against the terror of technology in the informational age; they share a belief in the irreducible character of human and cultural phenomena in the face of representational systems; they open to question assumptions and constructs of traditional thought: the notion of a stable subject, of the act of writing (*écriture*) as predetermined by a logo-centered bias; finally, they examine at length the complex questions of "alterity" and "marginality."

These propositions sound strong refrains among other contemporary critics and theorists: Blanchot's writings of the 1980s (*L'écriture du désastre*, 1980; *The Writing of the Disaster*, 1986, and *Le dernier à parler*, 1985; the last to speak); Julia Kristeva's *Pouvoirs de l'horreur* (1980; *Powers of Horror*, 1982) and *Soleil noir: Dépression et mélancolie* (1987; *Black Sun: Depression and Melancholia*, 1989), which views language as originating in loss; Paul de Man's *Blindness and Insight* (1985), which posits language as in constant pursuit of naming what is missing; Michel Serres's (b. 1930) *Le parasite* (1980; *The Parasite*, 1982); Michel de Certeau's (b. 1925) *Heterologies: Discourse on the Other* (1986); and Pierre Bourdieu's (b. 1930) *Ce que parler veut dire* (1982; what speaking means).

In the arena of contestation, these years saw numerous debates on sexuality, beginning with Marc Oraison's *La question homosexuelle* (1976; *The Homosexual Question*, 1977) and including Foucault's three-volume *Histoire de la sexualité* (1976–1984; *The History of Sexuality*, 1978–1986). But by far the most significant event was the proliferation of feminist theory and criticism: Hélène Cixous and Catherine Clément, *La jeune née* (1975; *The Newly Born Woman*, 1986); Benoîte Groult (b. 1920), *Ainsi soit-elle* (1975; thus it/she be); Wittig, *Le corps lesbien* (1973; *The Lesbian Body*, 1975); Irigaray, *Ce sexe qui n'en est pas un* (1977; *This Sex Which Is Not One*, 1985); Sarah Kofman (b. 1934), *L'énigme de la femme* (1980; *The Enigma of Woman*, 1985); and Kristeva, *Au commencement était l'amour* (1985; *In the Beginning Was Love*, 1987).

The work of theorists in other disciplines has impacted significantly on literary study. The influential *Séminaire* of Jacques Lacan continues to appear posthumously (vols. 8 and 17 in 1991). 1985 saw the publication of an important work by Claude Lévi-Strauss (q.v.), *La potière jalouse* (*The Jealous Potter*, 1988). The rich collaborative series of Gilles Deleuze (b. 1925) and Félix Guattari (b. 1930) entitled *Capitalisme et schizophrénie*, of which the last of two volumes, *Mille Plateaux*, appeared in 1980 (*A Thousand Plateaus: Capitalism and Schizophrenia*, 1988), radically revises the notions of schizophrenia and desire. From *Rhizome* (1976; *On the Line*, 1983) to *Le pli* (1988; the fold) Deleuze pursues his conception of the book and film as sites of "multiplicity," of interchange of diverse theories, genres, concepts, and desires. A. J. Greimas (b. 1917) presses his distinction between the concepts of semantic and semiotic, from the series of writings carrying the title *Du sens* (1970–1983; *On Meaning: Selected Writings*, 1987) to his collaborative work with Jacques Fontanille, *Sémiotique des passions* (1991; semiotics of passion), which proposes a semiotic description of the universe of passion and emotion. Jean Baudrillard (b. 1929) pursues his study of contemporary society in such works as *Les stratégies fatales* (1983; *Fatal Strategies*, 1990). René Girard (b. 1923), whose writing represents a renaissance of religious thought, investigates violence, desire, and the sacred in works like *Le bouc émissaire* (1982; *The Scapegoat*, 1986). The influential Marxist theorist Henri Lefebvre (b. 1901) was still publishing in the 1980s, along with Louis Althusser (b. 1918), and Cornelius Castoriadis (b. 1922). The psychoanalytic writings of Jean Bellemin-Noël (dates n.a.) have strongly influenced literary study. In *Interlignes: Essais de Textanalyse* (1988; intersections, essays on textanalysis), he rejects, as Barthes before him, the notion of an absolute reality underlying the text, seeking rather to seize how a text "constitutes" itself, what it reveals of the operation of the unconscious. Many other theorists and critics continued to produce works that have strongly influenced the direction of contemporary literary thought: Abdelkebir Khatibi, Vincent Descombes (dates n.a.), Lucette Finas (b. 1921), Gérard Genette (b. 1930), Philippe Lacoue-Labarthe (b. 1940), Jean-Luc Nancy (b. 1940), Michael Riffaterre (b. 1924), and Tzvetan Todorov (b. 1939), to mention only a few.

Conclusion

The years from the mid-1970s to the early 1990s witness a literature in turmoil. Contemporary writers have boldly forged alternate passages, peopled the landscape of modern thought with strange and often bizarre forms, and expanded the perimeters of our thinking to express a changing world. These efforts have often left in their train cries of condemnation and predictions of a dire future for literature. But final judgment must be left to posterity as to whether the brilliant flourishes of these years toll the decadence of a society that has misplaced its values or the birth throes of an exciting era opening before our mind and senses.

BIBLIOGRAPHY: Descombes, V., *Modern French Philosophy* (1980); Culler, J., *The Pursuit of Signs: Semiotics, Literature, Deconstruction* (1981); Bersani, J., and J. Lecarme, comps., *Littérature en France depuis 1968* (1982); Culler, J., *On Deconstruction: Theory and Criticism after Structuralism* (1982); Brée, G., *Twentieth-Century French Literature* (1983); Eagleton, T., *Literary Theory: An Introduction* (1983); Hamon, P., *Texte et idéologie* (1984); Bradby, D., *Modern French Drama 1940– 1980* (1984); Bishop, M., *The Contemporary Poetry of France: Eight Studies* (1985); Boisdeffre, P. de, *Histoire de la littérature française des années 1930 aux années 1980* (2 vols., 1985); Caws, M. A., *Reading Frames in Modern Fiction* (1985); Todorov, T., *Literature and Its Theorists: A Personal View of Twentieth-Century Criticism* (1987); Duchen, C., ed., *French Connections: Voices from the Women's Movement in France* (1987); Lecherbonnier, B., D. Rincé, P. Brunel, and C. Moatti, eds., *Littérature: Textes et documents. XXe siècle* (1989); special new French-fiction issue of *RCF*, 9, 1 (1989); Atack, M., and P. Powrie, eds., *Contemporary French Fiction by Women* (1990); Suleiman, S., *Subversive Intent: Gender, Politics, and the Avant-Garde* (1990); Jameson, F., *Postmodernism or, The Cultural Logic of Late Capitalism* (1990); Stamelman, R. H., *Lost beyond Telling: Representations of Death and Absence in Modern French Poetry* (1990); Chambers, R., *Room for Maneuver; Reading (the) Oppositional (in) Narrative* (1991)

JOHN D. ERICKSON

FRIEL, Brian

Irish dramatist and short-story writer, b. 9 Jan. 1929, Derry

F. grew up in the Irish province of Ulster, living in County Tyrone in Northern Ireland but spending extensive vacations in his mother's native County Donegal in the Irish Republic. F. was educated primarily in Derry, Northern Ireland's second largest city, where his father was born and worked as a teacher. At St. Patrick's College, Maynooth, the national seminary of the Republic, F. studied for the priesthood, but took a B.A. instead and taught for a decade in Derry. He currently lives in rural Donegal, and has earned an international reputation as Ireland's finest living dramatist.

Critics tend to categorize F.'s career: In its first phase he writes short fiction and tentatively tries theatrical form; F. then bursts upon Broadway and the world stage as a mature dramatist of character-based drama; that drama then develops a political-critical perspective and ensemble-acting style to accommodate historical fact and its cultural context; and in its current phase his plays identify and focus on language as the structural agency of both the ideological and dramatic dialectic. While within and across these categories doublings and larger groupings by theme and device proliferate, the basic taxonomy discovers a development in the writing of the plays and rediscovers the process of reading-seeing them by progressive contextualizing.

F.'s fiction, published regularly in the late 1950s and early 1960s in American magazines, rests firmly in the tradition of the great Irish short-story writers. Following the dictum and practice of Frank O'Connor (q.v.), the stories collected in *A Saucer of Larks* (1962) and *The Gold in the Sea* (1966) reveal the lives of an intimately observed subculture, the residents, mostly poor and working class, of the border territory and towns of Ulster. The epiphanies, or telling lack of them, that characterize James Joyce's (q.v.) short fiction appear in F.'s, with pronounced ambivalence. The charge that F. ignores the border and its political significance can be countered by claims that his work represents and demonstrates the stultifying, fallow politics of Northern Ireland, that the recurrent appearance in the stories of an outsider thematically implies a border, and that epiphanies map experiential and spiritual borders by transcending them.

The characters and their struggles and the mature, complex tone of the stories are also the strengths of F.'s early drama. After having several plays produced on radio and one on the stage, F. retired as a teacher and turned his talent toward the theater. In 1962 the Abbey Theatre produced *The Enemy Within* (1975), considered F.'s first successful play, a historical drama of St. Columba in exile on Iona, an island off western Scotland. Columba, who would become the patron saint of Derry, is tested, his blood ties to his troubled family set against his monastic vows and responsibilities, presenting in a dramatic character the borderland of conscience and how conflicting demands make exile, no matter what the choice, inevitable.

The second stage of F.'s career as a writer begins with a trip to Minneapolis in 1963 to study dramaturgy with the famous director Tyrone Guthrie. This commitment to drama resulted in *Philadelphia, Here I Come* (1965), which premiered at the Dublin Theatre Festival in 1964 and went on to become an international hit in New York on Broadway and in the West End in London. The play details the themes from *The Enemy Within* of exile and paralyzing ambivalence effected by conflicting desires and claims on the conscience; it also shows a new confidence in F.'s handling of dramatic form, incorporating flashbacks and the innovation of dramatizing the interior life and divided nature of the main character, Gar O'Donnell, by portraying him with two personae, Public Gar, who interacts with the other characters, and Private Gar, the embodied inner monologue of the thoughtful, willful, desperate, lonely protagonist. A less novel though more enduring invention is the town of Ballybeg (from *baile beag*, Irish for "small town"), the setting for *Philadelphia, Here I Come* and a number of other F. plays. Northern, dreary, socially stratified, with a church, a school, an aristocratic big house, and fields and forest and an army base hard by, Ballybeg provides ample ground for every conflict of class and creed, age and youth, desire and responsibility.

F.'s character-based drama continued with *The Loves of Cass Maguire* (1966), about a feisty, vibrant exile returned to Ireland to live out her days in a retirement home and slowly succumb to stagnant though sweet illusion, and *Lovers* (perf. 1967, pub. 1969), a pairing of two one-acts, *Winners*, an ironically titled tale of young love and hopes annihilated, and *Losers*, based on one of F.'s short stories about a man who gets his hoped-for love and whose life is diminished as a result. The experiments in dramatic form continue, too, with direct address to the audience, rhapsodic passages, and dramatic irony proceeding from manipulation of narrative. None are outright innovations, but their use demonstrates F.'s displacement of the conventions of his realistic fiction within the expressionistic poetic tradition of the drama of W. B. Yeats, John Millington Synge, Sean O'Casey, and Samuel Beckett (qq.v.). *Crystal and Fox* (perf. 1968, pub. 1970) opens with a play within the play and proceeds to reckon the withering effects of an itinerant performer's efforts to shed the artifice from his life; in *The Gentle Island* (perf. 1971, pub. 1973) the focus shifts from the traveling troupe of outsiders in the previous play to a family in sole possession of an island, Inishkeen, off Donegal, their sterile, stony existence, and the impact of visitors on the layered narratives of illusion and repressed truth.

Chronologically aberrant in this categorization is *The Mundy Scheme* (perf. 1969, pub. 1970), a farcical satire on the venality of Irish politics. Slight in the virtues of the serious drama from the same period, the work is less concerned with depth of character than it is with the shallow soundings of public life. Seriousness came with Bloody Sunday, 30 January 1972, when a civil rights march in Derry ended with the deaths of thirteen protesters (a fourteenth died months later) shot by the British army. F.'s response, *The Freedom of the City* (perf. 1973, pub. 1974), fictionally posits similar events, delves into their meaning for the doomed participants, and comments upon them in diverse discourses, both partisan and ostensibly objective, resulting in various "official" versions. Some critical opinion maintains that *The Gentle Island* has historical themes in a symbolic mode, Inishkeen, hardscrabble and abandoned, its society/family repressed and violent, standing for Ireland, but *The Freedom of the City* (another bitterly ironic title) is overtly, if equivocally, concerned with historical fact and how it is determined. *Volunteers* (perf. 1975, pub. 1979) returns to the theme of *The Mundy Scheme*, the state-abetted mortgaging of Ireland's heritage in the name of economic development. F.'s genius for dramatic compression is evident in the setting, the pit of an archaeological dig in Dublin soon to be the site of a hotel; the action is contained in claustrophobic quarters, while the whole history of the island is laid bare in the exposed earth.

The plays based on conflicts in the life of a single central figure—Columba, Gar, Cass—have given way to a drama of ensemble playing in which the conflict is among a social set of well-wrought characters; any historical truth can only be the sum total of their understanding. The return to Ballybeg in F.'s next two productions, *Living Quarters* (perf. 1977, pub. 1978) and *Aristocrats* (perf. 1979, pub. 1980, based on one of F.'s stories, "Foundry House"), domesticates this theme. Both works bring families together in re-unions; in the former, a narrator represents the factual history to which the surviving characters return in memory; in the latter, an outsider helps salvage the remnants of a family falling from ascendancy. The settings suggest borders, real and symbolic: the detached living quarters of a military man, where heroism and suicide define the limits of public and private struggle; and Ballybeg Hall, on the outskirts of town, the scene of shifting perspectives caused by slippage in the socioeconomic strata.

The Faith Healer (perf. 1979, pub. 1980) carries the theme of the cumulative, relative nature of truth to its logical formal conclusion. The drama is fractured into four monologues by three characters covering the same events. The characters do not, cannot, communicate with one another, and the audience must make a whole of the narrative. The breakdown of the ensemble indicates the reduction of the sociopolitical element in F.'s work to its deconstructed ground, the *logos* of the monologue, the word, speech, language. Voices, internal and official, accents, jargon, rhetoric, quotation, and song have filled F.'s oeuvre from the first radio plays, but in this next phase of his career, language moves from prominence to primacy as means and theme. The metaphor of the faith healer as artist does not exhaust the primal, visionary substance of the drama, but it does initiate a new perspective in F.'s writing from which to reconsider his craft to that point. His next effort, *Translations* (perf. 1980, pub. 1981), was the maiden production of the Field Day Theatre Company, of which F. was a founder. With its openly political agenda, Field Day found in this historical drama—set in an outdoor school outside Ballybeg in 1833, on the theme and occasion of the remapping of Ireland by the British army, symbolic of the indigenous population's disenfranchisement—an apt inauguration. But as the title implies, *Translations* most significantly concerns communication, education, the facility and futility of language when vernacular is outlawed and the idiom of conquest dominates even the illegal education of the peasantry hidden behind hedges and hay sheds. *The Communication Cord* (perf. 1982, pub. 1983) updates the theme and academic context, though ironically the setting is a gentrified peasant cottage near Ballybeg. Employing farcical situations with satirical significance, F. mines the comic potential in dislocations similar to those that result in more dire consequences in *Translations*. Still, language fails, history is trivialized, and education is by accident. Some comedy.

F.'s preoccupation with character, language, and ambivalence led him in 1981 to translate Anton Chekhov's (q.v.) *Three Sisters* into an Anglo-Irish idiom (this is the play he saw rehearsed during his apprenticeship at the Guthrie Theater). The fit is natural; a Chekhovian sensibility is apparent in a number of F.'s works, most notably *Aristocrats,* which has been called "The Potato Orchard." In 1987 *Fathers and Sons,* F.'s dramatization of Turgenev's novel, premiered. Its conflict of academic theory and frustrating nature, of language and action, of naming and being, defines behavioral borders of lethal subtlety.

F.'s latest plays pair off to demonstrate his range, reiterate his themes, and further develop his formal dexterity. *Making History* (1988) dramatizes the events surrounding the Battle of Kinsale, which resulted in the Flight of the Earls, the first important emigration of native Irish, and the subsequent plantation of protestant loyalists on their property, laying the foundation for the partition of Ulster in the 20th c. Astride this historical border at the turn of the 16th into the 17th c. stands the figure of Hugh O'Neill, Earl of Tyrone, heroic in accounts by Catholic partisans of the Counter-Reformation, by his own account compromised. The dialectic of events and accounts makes history; in *Dancing at Lughnasa* (1990) the terms of the dialectic are reduced to inaction and silence. Still, when circumstance and language fail the five Mundy sisters of Ballybeg, they find refuge and expression in music and dancing. Their brother, a failed missionary, reprises with characteristically pregnant pathos a character from F.'s 1963 stage and radio play *The Blind Mice;* the unsentimental narration that cuts hope off short and spares no innocent is classic F. The rituals that sustain culture and incarnate desire give *Dancing at Lughnasa* resources of nonverbal knowledge and communication that tap the motive powers and inspiration of drama itself. It seems that F.'s work is broaching another category of radical dramatic techniques and effects. The Broadway production won the 1992 Tony Award for best play.

A list of the salient features of F.'s drama makes apparent his talents: the vocal variety, including numerous tonalities of soliloquizing; the strategies and degrees of dramatic irony; the concentration of philosophical and sociopolitical significance in theatrical, often novel, modes of narrative representation; and his generous, ambivalent characterizations eroded by the entropic effects of circumstance and sentiment. F.'s plays are intelligent and incisive, complex and uncompromising, unsettling yet satisfying. Their parochialism is so finely realized that it achieves a universal expressiveness; their pathos is authentic, immediate, communal;

their craft is polished and innovative; their author, nominated to the Irish senate in 1986, the only Irish writer since Yeats to serve in such a capacity, is the leading living Irish dramatist on both sides of the island's bloody border.

FURTHER WORKS: *A Sort of Freedom* (perf. 1958); *To This Hard House* (perf. 1958); *A Doubtful Paradise* (perf. 1960); *The Founder Members* (perf. 1964); *Farewell to Ardstraw* (perf. 1976, with David Hammond); *Selected Stories* (1979); *American Welcome* (1981); *The Diviner* (1983); *Selected Plays* (1984)

BIBLIOGRAPHY: Maxwell, D., *B. F.* (1973); Johnston, D., "B. F. and Modern Irish Drama," *Hibernia*, 7 Mar. 1975, 22; Murray, C., "Irish Drama in Transition 1966–1978," *EI*, 4 (1979), 187–308; Schleuter, J., "B. F.," in Weintraub, S., ed., *DLB: British Dramatists since World War II, Part 1* (1982), 179–85; Kearney, R., "Language Play: B. F. and Ireland's Verbal Theatre," *Studies*, 72 (1983), 20–56; Deane, S., Introduction to *Selected Plays* (1984), 11–22; Dantanus, U., *B. F.: The Growth of an Irish Dramatist* (1984); Kiberd, D., "B. F's *Faith Healer*," in Sekine, M., ed., *Irish Writers and Society at Large* (1985), 106–22; Bertha, C., "Tragedies of National Fate: A Comparison between B. F.'s *Translations* and its Hungarian Counterpart, András Sutö's *A Szuzai menyegaö*," *IUR*, 17, 2 (Autumn 1987), 207–22; Grene, N., "Distancing Drama: Sean O'Casey to B. F.," in Sekine, M., ed., *Irish Writers and the Theatre* (1987), 47–70; O'Brien, G., *B. F.* (1990)

DENNIS PAOLI

FURUI Yoshikichi

Japanese novelist, short-story writer, and essayist, b. 19 Nov. 1937, Tokyo

F. graduated from the German literature department of Tokyo University in 1960 and stayed on to complete his master's degree in 1962. He then took a post as a German literature instructor at Kanazawa University and later at Rikkyō University in Tokyo. During his years as an academic, he published translations of the works of Hermann Broch and Robert Musil (qq.v.). F.'s involvement with German literature in his early career is reflected in the style and themes of his later stories and novels, particularly in his concern with the fragmentation and disorientation of the self in modern society.

In 1966 F. joined the literary coterie *Hakubyō no kai* (plain sketch club), and his first original short story, "Mokuyōbi ni" (on Thursday), was published in its magazine in 1968. Soon his stories began to appear in a wide variety of literary magazines, and F. resigned his teaching position to devote himself to writing on a full-time basis. His career as a writer was assured when he received the prestigious Akutagawa Prize for his novella *Yōko* (1970; Yoko) in 1971.

The title character in *Yōko*, a beautiful schizophrenic young woman, is one of many characters in F.'s works who experience the world from a distorted, but ultimately more discerning, perspective. Through a painstakingly detailed portrayal of the thoughts and perceptions of a human being under the duress of mental or physical illness or exhaustion, F. delves beneath the façade of everyday life in contemporary Japan to reveal the irrational forces lurking within. Subtle shifts in self-awareness rather than broad drama characterize his plots. Another early work, "Tsumagomi" (1971; "Wedlock," 1977), a glimpse into a day in the life of a young married couple living in a newly developed Tokyo suburb, illustrates a setting typical of F.'s works: that of the spatial borderland between virgin wilderness and urban sprawl that serves as a metaphor for the spiritual one between folk traditions and the monotonous, impersonal existence of the city dweller. The protagonist's brief illness and a chance meeting with an old woman who mistakes him for one of her converts to a new religion disrupt his complacent routine. F.'s protagonists, passive but unusually perceptive observers of life, often find themselves in the wryly humorous situation of being mistaken for someone else by strangers or inexplicably unrecognizable to friends, underlining the instability of human identity.

F.'s scrutiny of the inner experience of ordinary life marks a departure from the politically conscious writers of the 1960s. He and several other writers—among them Kuroi Senji (b. 1932), Abe Akira (b. 1934), Gotō Meisei (b. 1932), Ogawa Kunio (b. 1927), and Kashiwabara Hyōzō (1933–1972)—making their debuts in the early 1970s, came to be grouped together as the *naikō no sedai* (introverted generation), a term that has gradually lost its original derogatory slant. F. is generally regarded as the most representative of the group and is noted for the dense texture of his prose and his inaccessibility to the average reader. However, his works are not without implicit social commentary concerning the role of the individual in modern urban society and the pathogenic nature of society itself. Cancer, the metaphorical disease of modern life, frequently appears in F.'s stories.

The novel *Hijiri* (1976; a sage) further explores the power of the ambiguous realm where the Japanese past and present collide. An injured mountain climber temporarily takes on the role of the holy man who disposes of the dead in a remote village and finds himself drawn into rituals of defilement and purification which hearken back to Japan's most ancient myths. The Japanese classics and elements of folk culture play a surprisingly central and evocative role in F.'s portrayals of contemporary life.

More recent works show a greater emphasis on the subject of coming to terms with aging and death, beginning as early as the short-story collection *Aihara* (1977; plain of sorrow). These later collections have a more flexible, flowing structure reminiscent of the traditional Japanese essay. In *Yoru wa ima* (1987; now is night) F. expresses his perennial subjects of the nature of consciousness and the flux of identity in a stylistically complex shift between narrative and personal meditation. *Kari ōjō denshibun* (1989; a tentative attempt at a tale of salvation) juxtaposes elaborated versions of stories from the Heian Period of the death and rebirth of Buddhist monks in paradise, with vignettes of modern life that reveal "the hysteria lurking quietly in everyday life."

F. has also increasingly turned his attention to the Japanese essay proper as is the case with most established writers in Japan. His essays echo the concerns and themes of his novels and stories: the illusive nature of reality and the fluid boundaries of human identity.

F. may well be remembered as one of the definitive writers of his generation, a time when Japan was beginning to become aware of the clash between modern and traditional values and the problem of defining the individual subject in a mass society. His stories and essays show a deep sensitivity to the mystery and the dark humor inherent in the everyday life of ordinary people.

FURTHER WORKS: *Enjin o kumu onnatachi* (1970); *Otokotachi no madoi* (1970); *Yukigakure* (1972); *Mizu* (1973); *Kushi no hi* (1974); *Onnatachi no ie* (1977); *Yoru no kaori* (1978); *Sumika* (1979); *F. Y. zen essei* (1980); *Mukudori* (1980); *Oya* (1980); *Sansōfu* (1982); *F. Y. sakuhin* (1982–1983); *Asagao* (1983); *Shōkon no sasayaki* (1984); *Ake no akauma* (1985); *Biu* (1986); *Rara chūki* (1986); *Hi ya getsu ya* (1988); *Musil no kannen no eros* (1988); *Nagai machi no nemuri* (1990)

BIBLIOGRAPHY: Iwamoto Y., "F.: Exemplar of the 'Introverted Generation,' " *WLT*, 62, 3 (Summer 1988), 385–90

DONNA GEORGE STOREY

GAINES, Ernest J.

American novelist and short-story writer, b. 15
Jan. 1933, Oscar, La.

Born and raised on a plantation in Louisiana, G.
may claim an intimate knowledge of the folkways
of black Americans in the rural South and of the
complexities of relationship between black and
white in that region. Not surprisingly, this knowledge has been the source of much of his best
fiction. But G., who graduated from San Francisco
State College (now University) and who studied
creative writing under Walter Van Tilburg Clark
(1909–1971) at Stanford, has created work that
reflects as well a highly sophisticated literary culture, which has made it possible for him to absorb
and transform the influence, not only of such
Americans as Ernest Hemingway and William
Faulkner (qq.v.), but, perhaps with even greater
consequences for G.'s work, the great Russian
authors Gogol, Turgenev, and Tolstoy. Characteristically, G.'s work involves a high-level literary
treatment of an intimately, and often lovingly,
observed folk culture.

G. is best known as the author of *The Autobiography of Miss Jane Pittman* (1971), which has
acquired the status of a classroom classic; the
novel has been adapted as a film that, although
not entirely faithful to the text, is effective on its
own terms and has had widespread exposure. Unfortunately, this kind of success does not always
best serve a writer's critical reputation. Not only
may the one text overshadow the writer's other
work, thus creating a distorted image of the whole
career, but the writer must often contend with the
elitist suspicion that anything so widely and quickly
popular cannot be very good. Any attempt to do
justice to the art of G. must therefore involve both
taking a new look at *The Autobiography of Miss
Jane Pittman* and looking beyond it to the riches
of G.'s work as a whole.

Like other Southern writers, G. is always aware
of the presence of the past, and the relation of the
individual and the community to the past is one
of the major themes of his work. The past is our
history, shaping our identity in the present and
providing us with strength and perspective. Yet
the past also has a destructive potential, as it may
take the form of patterns of repetition that entrap
the individual and condemn the community to
stagnation. How to draw on the past without being
trapped by it is a question implicit in much of
what G. has written.

Some of G.'s characters seek merely to reject
the past. Jackson Guerin, in G.'s first novel, *Catherine Carmier* (1964), tries to follow this course,
intending to find his destiny far from the rural
community of his origins; the effort is unsuccessful, as Jackson finds he must confront communal
and paternal forces, and on their terms, not his.
Others are locked into rigid patterns established
years before; Raoul Carmier in the same novel
exemplifies the destructive consequences of such
rigidity. A third way is to acquiesce in established
patterns, while maintaining an inner ironic distance; this is the way, ultimately an unsatisfying
one, of Kelly, the narrator of G.'s second novel,
Of Love and Dust (1967). In the course of this
novel, Kelly comes to feel a grudging respect for
Marcus, a younger black man who represents still
another way: outright rebellion against the rules,
customs, and tacit understandings established before he was born. Marcus's rebellion, however,
although not without heroic resonance, moves inevitably toward a tragic resolution.

And tragedy, as Miss Jane Pittman knows, is
not the goal. Miss Jane, over one hundred years
old when we meet her, must be coaxed, by the
young black historian whose inquiries motivate
the narrative, to turn back to the past for her
story—a story, we come to realize, as much communal as individual. And that story is a story of
moving on. We are made, as we follow Miss
Jane's narrative, to understand her (the) past, to
value it (not to reject, not to forget, it), and to
move beyond it. The last words of the novel are,
"I went by him." "He" is the white plantation
owner, and he symbolizes that version of the
past—the past as repetition, stasis, stagnation—
that must be transcended. Miss Jane herself may
be said to represent another version of the past—
the past as source and resource—on which the
generations of the present and future may confidently draw.

Miss Jane is clearly offered as a representative
character. Thoroughly individualized, she also embodies the forces that have brought her community
out of slavery and toward freedom. The relation
of individual to community is a further informing

theme of G.'s fiction. In *The Autobiography of Miss Jane Pittman* the theme is reflected, not only in the representative qualities of Miss Jane herself, but in the search for "the One" that is a recurrent motif in the novel. In G.'s *In My Father's House* (1983), the relation of the civil-rights leader Phillip Martin to the community he has represented is troubled both by the inevitability of change and by the reappearance of a figure out of Martin's past: the son he had abandoned years before. Thus the themes of self and community and of past and present are made to converge. And the troubled relation here of father and son points to yet another recurrent theme of G.'s work.

A Gathering of Old Men (1984) embodies in a richly textured and complex narrative many of the themes of G.'s earlier work. Once again, patterns of conduct and attitude formed in a racist past work destructively in the present. At the same time, the "Old Men" of the title find in a renewed understanding of their individual and communal past, of the dynamics of that past, the strength to unite in the present crisis. But G. is not concerned, here, with the black community alone; he also offers an unsentimental but not unsympathetic portrayal of the Cajun community, which has in the past exercised dominance over the black. He shows us in both communities the tension between the desire to hold on and the need to move on. Both communities are forced to realize that they are affected by changes they have hardly acknowledged. And in the Cajun community another of the intergenerational clashes with which G. has often concerned himself works itself out.

G.'s novels are of considerable thematic interest, and they will no doubt be read by many for the insights they offer into relationships between the races and relationships within the black community. But, as was suggested above, G. is a sophisticated literary artist as well as a concerned and provocative observer of and commentator on the issues of his time. The blending in *A Gathering of Old Men* of a number of individual stories to form one communal story is an impressive formal accomplishment. The interplay, common in his work, of a multitude of voices, old and young, male and female, white and black, each with its own identity and rhythm, lends to his fiction a notable complexity and delicacy of tone. He is consistently assured in his choice of narrative viewpoint. And his exploitation of the possibilities of narrative voice—Kelly in *Of Love and Dust*, Miss Jane, a series of voices in the remarkable short story "Just Like a Tree" in his collection *Bloodline* (1968)—link his literary narratives to an oral folk culture that is G.'s proper heritage. G.'s is a self-effacing art—he scarcely strikes one on first reading as a formal or stylistic innovator—

but it is art, and of a high order. G. deserves to be recognized as one of the important American novelists of his generation.

BIBLIOGRAPHY: Stoelting, W., "Human Dignity and Pride in the Novels of E. G.," *CLAJ*, 14 (1970), 340–58; Gayle, A., Jr., *The Way of the New World: The Black Novel in America* (1975), 288–302; Macdonald, W., "You Not a Bum, You a Man: E. J. G.'s *Bloodline*," *Negro American Literature Forum*, 9 (1975), 47–49; Shelton, F., "Ambiguous Manhood in E. J. G.'s *Bloodline*," *CLAJ*, 19 (1975), 200–9; Burke, W., "*Bloodline*: A Black Man's South," *CLAJ*, 19 (1976), 545–58; Andrews, W., " 'We Ain't Going Back There': The Idea of Progress in *The Autobiography of Miss Jane Pittman*," *BALF*, 11 (1977), 146–49; Hicks, J., "To Make These Bones Live: History and Community in E. G.'s Fiction," *BALF*, 11 (1977), 9–19; Puschmann-Nalenz, B., "E. J. G.: 'A Long Day in November,' " in Bruck, P., ed., *The Black American Short Story in the 20th Century: A Collection of Critical Essays* (1977), 157–67; special G. issue, *Callaloo*, 1, 3 (1978); Wertheimer, A., "Journey to Freedom: E. G.'s *The Autobiography of Miss Jane Pittman*," in Bruck, B., and W. Karrer, eds., *The Afro-American Novel since 1960* (1982), 219–36; Byerman, K. E., *Fingering the Jagged Grain: Tradition and Form in Recent Black Fiction* (1985), 67–103; Bell, B. W., *The Afro-American Novel and Its Tradition* (1987), 290–95; Callahan, J. F., *In the African-American Grain: The Pursuit of Voice in Twentieth-Century Black Fiction* (1988), 189–216; Foster, M., "G.'s Louisiana Blues," *MAWAR*, 3, 1 (June 1988), 10–14; Jones, K., "God and Religion in *Of Love and Dust*," *MAWAR*, 4, 1 (June 1989), 4–9; Gaudet, M., and C. Wooton, *Porch Talk with E. G.: Conversations on the Writer's Craft* (1990)

W. P. KENNEY

GAITÁN DURÁN, Jorge

Colombian poet, essayist, dramatist, short-story writer, and journalist, b. 12 Feb. 1924, Pamplona, Santander; d. 22 June 1962, Pointe-a-Pitre, Guadeloupe, Antillas

G. D. studied philosophy and at an early age traveled to Paris, where he stayed for several years. Along with the Colombian poet Hernando Valencia Goekel (dates n.a.), he founded in 1955 the cultural periodical *Mito*, which became a highly significant Colombian journal dedicated to translating foreign writers, to promoting diverse editorial enterprises, and to inspiring a spirit of agitation among young writers. Between 1955 and

1962, when G. D. died in an airplane crash and *Mito* was dissolved, the journal published modern writers such as Jean-Paul Sartre, Alain Robbe-Grillet, Henry Miller, Vicente Aleixandre, Jorge Luis Borges, Alfonso Reyes, and Octavio Paz (qq.v.). To many Colombian intellectuals, *Mito* represented an important link to significant movements and writers in Europe and North America; for young writers *Mito* offered the chance to publish for the first time; and for sociologists and politicians it meant the opportunity to analyze national dilemmas through polemic articles, essays, and scholarly studies.

G. D. belonged to the literary generation that came after the era of the poetic group *Piedra y Cielo* (Stone and Sky). G. D. and his fellow writers shared the intent to endow Colombian poetry with greater intellectual depth while emphasizing contemporary forms and themes. The poets of *Mito* constantly fought for density of the content in their works as opposed to mere formal intensity, while pursuing the discovery of new dimensions of imagination.

G. D.'s literary style is limpid, sometimes surrealistic, sometimes serving to convey social messages. He expressed his preoccupation with his people's political and social destiny through essays published in *Mito* as well as in occasional articles published in newspapers and political gazettes. Among his essays revealing an unusual perspicacity is "La revolución invisible" (1959; the invisible revolution). To G. D. society should be structured according to ethical standards, which, however, when pursued in isolation and without a sense of balance and proportion, diminish our true creative potential. G. D. also sees the need to participate in the aspirations of his people, a conviction that coincided with the political turmoil in Colombia since the "Bogotazo" (The Bogotá Event). This nationwide rebellion in 1949 against the régime in power extended from the capital to the most remote towns of the country, and the bloodshed lasted for the next twenty years. It was G. D.'s hope to commemorate this national tragedy by serving as an example of courage and solidarity for his country's ongoing struggles.

G. D. left a series of works that are intensive and rich without being remote. These include poetic prose, short stories, critical commentaries on art and film, political and literary essays, translations, and several volumes of poetry that place him among the greatest lyric poets of his country. As a poet G. D. explored the dimension of such states as death, passion, indifference, anguish, voluptuousness, and beauty. His poetry is flashing and thought-provoking. In *Asombro* (1951; amazement) the poet intensively ponders eroticism and

attributes part of human anguish to our obedience to the instincts. In *Amantes* (1959; lovers) G. D. showed beautifully how eroticism is the culmination of all human lives and hopes. In his most important work, *Si mañana despierto* (1961; if tomorrow I wake up), eroticism is transcended to a spiritual love that elevates the ethical being of humans to a higher level.

As an intellectual G. D. fought vigorously against rhetoric, dogmatism, sectarianism, prejudice, and anything that degrades the human condition. Like his fellow contributors to *Mito*, G. D. proposed to use high culture as a means for political and social change. His poetry displays a sense of commitment to himself and to others, with a clear awareness of the precariousness of human destiny.

FURTHER WORKS: *Insistencia en la tristeza* (1946); *Presencia del hombre* (1947); *El libertino* (1954); *La revolución invisible* (1959); *Los hampones* (1961); *China* (1962)

BIBLIOGRAPHY: Núñez Segura, A. S. J., *Literatura colombiana* (1967), 461; Liscano, J., "G. D.: entre el erotismo y la pulsión de muerte," *Eco*, 223 (1980), 17–38; Romero, A., "Los poetas de *Mito*," *RI*, 128–29 (July–Dec. 1984), 689–755; Charry Lara, F., *Poesía y poetas colombianos* (1985), 121–22, 130–41; Cote-Baraibar, R., "Los últimos veinte años en la poesía colombiana," *Ínsula*, 44, 512–13 (Aug.–Sept. 1989), 43–44; Williams, R. L., *The Colombian Novel, 1844–1987* (1991), 77

VIRGINIA SHEN

GALLANT, Mavis
Canadian short-story writer and novelist, b. 11 Aug. 1922, Montreal

G.'s short stories are acclaimed throughout the English-speaking world for their explorations of postwar alienation and dispossession in the West. Although she was born in Montreal, where she began her education, G. went to a large number of schools in Ontario and the U.S., only returning to Montreal at the age of eighteen. She worked there for six years as a columnist for the *Montreal Standard*. Determined to make writing her life, G. left for Europe in 1950, settling eventually in Paris, where she has lived for the last thirty-five years.

Before G. left Montreal, she had published a few short stories in Canadian literary periodicals like *Preview,* but her longstanding connection with the *New Yorker*—she has been one of its steadiest contributors of short fiction over the last four decades—began in 1951 with the publication of "Madeline's Birthday," a typical G. story in its depiction of a family's misapprehensions of an isolated adolescent's unhappiness. The trials of children at the hands of adults who are lost in their own disordered or deluded worlds often merge in G.'s stories with the cultural displacements suffered by characters lost in the postwar period, or with the shallow, romanticized sense of European history that G.'s North American characters bring with them to a postwar landscape suddenly transformed. The title piece of G.'s first book of stories, *The Other Paris* (1956), is typical in its evocation of a young and naive North American woman's engagement in Paris to her American boss, a narrative traced against the backdrop of her romantic notions of Paris and of love. This story also demonstrates how G. has developed the Jamesian presentation of the American abroad, although G.'s style, with its spare and incisive irony and wit, is altogether different from the rhythms of Henry James's (q.v.) writing.

Although G. has published two very well received novels, *Green Water, Green Sky* (1959) and *A Fairly Good Time* (1970), she is best known for her eight books of stories. G.'s stories often close, not with the epiphany associated with the stories of writers like James Joyce (q.v.), but with a moment of misperception, with an opportunity for insight nearly apprehended, but then lost. This is the ironic rhythm informing Carol Frazier's perception at the end of "The Other Paris" that, happily married in North America, she will be able to look back on her European engagement and remember it as it never was. Memory's distortions and recreations of the past play a crucial role throughout G.'s fiction, particularly when characters' memories are shown to be at odds with the larger historical forces that G. evokes. In *The Pegnitz Junction: A Novella and Five Short Stories* (1973) this theme finds its most powerful expression as G. explores the culture of postwar Germany, where the recent past, never fully understood, always threatens to intrude into the present. In the celebrated title novella, an arduous train ride from France into Germany acquires several layers of metaphorical and allegorical meaning as the passengers traverse geographical and psychic landscapes that resonate with dimly perceived portents of the past.

From the Fifteenth District: A Novella and Eight Short Stories (1979) is G.'s finest work. Several of the stories in this collection are set in Liguria, a region on the Mediterranean coast of northern Italy where national borders have often shifted in the 20th c., providing G. with an apt setting for her explorations of the effects that cultural and historical fragmentation have on the lives and relationships of her characters. In this collection as in much of her fiction, many of G.'s most powerful portraits are of female characters who are revealed as complex, oppressed figures, beset by contradictory demands and impulses that all too often render them indecisive, at once determined to win their independence and tied to their past by the bonds of memory, like Netta Asher, the central character in "The Moslem Wife."

As its title suggests, *Home Truths: Selected Canadian Stories* (1981), for which G. was awarded the Governor General's Award for fiction (1982), focuses more specifically on Canadian characters and settings than any other of G.'s works, although several of the stories present Canadian characters adrift in Europe. In *Overhead in a Balloon: Stories of Paris* (1985) G. returns to her adopted city, which she knows intimately, for her deftly comic treatment of Parisian foibles and sensibilities.

G. has continued to write fine nonfiction throughout her career. Many of her best pieces—among them, her two-part diary of the May 1968 student uprising in Paris and her famous essay on the Gabrielle Russier case (1971), in which a young French schoolteacher was driven to suicide over her affair with a student—reveal G.'s thoroughgoing familiarity with French institutions and social codes. But her short stories and novellas remain her most enduring contribution to contemporary writing. In depth and breadth, G.'s vision of postwar Europe is one of the fullest and most searching fictional representations of recent history; given G.'s preference for the short story, with its stringent demands for economy and precision, her achievement is all the more remarkable.

FURTHER WORKS: *My Heart Is Broken: Eight Stories and a Short Novel* (1964); *The End of the World and Other Stories* (1974); *What Is To Be Done?* (1983); *Paris Notebooks: Essays and Reviews* (1986); *In Transit* (1988)

BIBLIOGRAPHY: Stevens, P., "Perils of Compassion," *CanL,* 56 (1973), 61–70; Merler, G., *M. G.: Narrative Patterns and Devices* (1978); special G. issue, *CFM,* 28 (1978); Jewison, D. B., "Speaking of Mirrors: Imagery and Narration in Two Novellas by M. G.," *SCL,* 10, 1–2 (1985), 94–109; Besner, N. K., *The Light of Imagination: M. G.'s Fiction* (1988); Keefer, J. K., *Reading M. G.* (1989); Skelton Grant, J., "M. G.," in Lecker, R., J. David, and E. Quigley, eds., *Canadian Writers and Their Works: Fiction Series* (1989), Vol. 8, 23–80; special G. issue, *ECW,* 42 (1990)

NEIL K. BESNER

GALLEGOS LARA, Joaquín

Ecuadorean novelist and short-story writer, b. 9 Apr. 1911, Guayaquil; d. 16 Nov. 1947, Guayaquil

G. L. was a key figure in the literary circle known as the Group of Guayaquil, a company of writers that included Enrique Gil Gilbert (1912–1973), José de la Cuadra (1903–1941), Demetrio Aguilera Malta, and Alfredo Pareja Diezcanseco (qq.v.). A self-taught individual, G. L. suffered physical ailments most of his life. He worked as a journalist because, like most Ecuadorean literary figures, he was unable to earn a living as a creative writer. Well versed in European and North American literature, he was also a student of classical Greco-Roman civilization.

The three original members of the Group of Guayaquil—G. L., Aguilera Malta, and Gil Gilbert—combined to produce a revolutionary collection of twenty-four short stories that altered the course of fiction writing in Spanish America. This volume, *Los que se van* (1930; those who leave), created a stir in Ecuadorean letters, shocking readers with its scenes of brutality and raw language. Unlike anything written previously, the book came under much harsh criticism, but it was well received by one noted Ecuadorean intellectual, Benjamín Carrión (1897–1979). The stories focus on life among the lower-class citizens living in the tropical coastal region of Ecuador, specifically the *cholos* (the indigenous inhabitants) and the *montuvios* (those of mixed black, white, and Indian ancestry). *Los que se van* may be considered a forerunner of *indigenismo,* although it contains less explicit protest and denunciation than many of the later works in this vein.

Violence, exploitation, and crude language are essential ingredients in G. L.'s fiction. His is a literature of protest against the injustices of the Ecuadorean social and political system. In denouncing these abuses he refuses to shy away from the sordid and unpleasant aspects of the oppressive social environment. For example, in the short story "¡Era la mamá!" (she was his mother) he creates scenes of graphic violence and sexual innuendo in which the black characters undergo physical and emotional suffering. The story relies heavily on dialogue stocked with G. L.'s faithful transcription of rural, uneducated speech.

After *Los que se van,* G. L. published only one book of fiction, the proletarian novel *Cruces sobre el agua* (1946; crosses on the water). This work deals with the 15 November 1922 strike in Guayaquil during which government troops massacred hundreds of workers. The novel's protagonist, a black man, is a popular hero who was one of those killed in the slaughter. The crosses in the title refer to the observance of the anniversary of this tragic event, an occasion marked by the placing of candles on rafts that float across the waters where the bodies of the victims were thrown. G. L. wrote two other novels, neither of which was published during his lifetime: *La bruja* (the sorceress), also known as *Cacao,* concerned with life on the cacao haciendas, and *Los guandos* (1982, with Nela Martínez; the stretchers), which portrays the indigenous litter bearers of the sierra.

The Group of Guayaquil was composed of young, politically committed writers who mixed regionalism with themes of protest in an attempt to interpret contemporary Ecuadorean reality. Of the group, G. L. was the most politically oriented and the most revolutionary. Although not prolific, he was influential in raising the level of social consciousness by helping to introduce social realism (q.v.) into Ecuadorean literature. His writings were an early indication that a new literary aesthetic was evolving, one in which art would once again come to be viewed as an appropriate and effective vehicle for protest. This outlook would exercise a considerable influence on Spanish American literature in the second half of the 20th c.

BIBLIOGRAPHY: Rojas, A. F., *La novela ecuatoriana* (1948), 180–84; Menton, S., *El cuento hispanoamericano* (1964), Vol. 1, 273, 279–80; Schwartz, K., *A New History of Spanish American Fiction* (1972), Vol. 2, 21, 42–43; Jackson, R. L., *The Black Image in Latin American Literature* (1976), 84–86; McMurray, G. R., *Spanish American Writing since 1941: A Critical Survey* (1987), 114–17; Pareja Diescanseco, A., "Los narradores de la generación del Treinta: El Grupo de Guayaquil," *RI,* 54, 144–45 (July–Dec. 1988), 691–707

MELVIN S. ARRINGTON, JR.

GAMBARO, Griselda

Argentine dramatist and novelist, b. 28 July 1928, Buenos Aires

Born to working-class, first-generation Argentines whose family originated from Italy, G. first started working in a business office until she began to win the prizes and awards that have enabled her to devote all her time to writing. G. started writing at an early age and has continued to produce steadily despite economic and political obstacles.

G. was among the Argentine dramatists closely associated with the experimental Buenos Aires art group at the Instituto Di Tella, an avant-garde foundation formed in 1958 to combine sociological investigations with the patronage of the fine arts, where a number of G.'s plays were produced and published, before the institute was forced to close in 1971.

At first G. developed her dramas at the same time that she worked on prose pieces; *Las paredes* (1964; the walls) and *El desatino* (1965; the blunder) are prize-winning plays as well as narratives. She continued this practice until 1972, after publishing *Nada que ver con otra historia* (1972; nothing to do with another story) and the play version *Nada que ver* (1972; nothing to see), both of which are parodies of the Frankenstein story placed in modern Argentina. These early works share a common preoccupation with ordinary people involved in unequal relationships of power, where the victim is usually too passive to fight against his oppressor, who is usually a member of his family or a supposed friend. Plays like *El desatino, El campo* (1965; *The Camp,* 1971), and *Los siameses* (1967; the Siamese twins) make good use of violent physical images to explore the ambiguities and cruelty of existence.

The early plays are divided into two acts and present generic characters involved in a series of situations rather than the developmental plot associated with conventional dramas. Since G. also avoided dialogue using the distinctive accent or nationalist motifs that would situate the plays within a specific Argentine context, critics easily associated these plays with the Theater of the Absurd (q.v.). G.'s work, however, is no mere imitation of European absurdists; rather, the elements of the grotesque and Black Humor (q.v.) are related more to the early-20th-c. Argentine popular theater form called "grotesco-criollo." Moreover, an allegorical reading of the plays reveals that they do relate to the real sociopolitical events of Argentina. G. may use general metaphors, such as the absurd Kafkaesque world that marks *Las paredes,* or the concentration camp in *El campo,* or Frankenstein's monster in *Nada que ver,* yet the kidnapings, mental abuse, and physical torture undergone by her characters parallel real acts perpetrated by the Argentine military beginning in the 1960s and during the so-called Dirty War that ended in 1983.

Although her work was always subtly critical of the repressive Argentine military régimes, she fell into official disfavor in 1977. G. and her family moved to Barcelona, where they stayed for three years. Upon her return she participated in Teatro Abierto (open theater), a vanguardist movement of dramatists, directors, and actors who joined together in 1981 to present a cycle of three one-act plays a day for seven different programs. The majority of the plays, like G.'s *Decir sí* (1981; to say yes), were political in nature and constituted an attack both on the commercialization of Argentine theater and on the military government, which

at that time proved too ineffectual to prevent the festival's existence.

As *Información para extranjeros* (perf. 1972, pub. 1987; information for foreigners) shows, G.'s skillful use of gestures and movements along with her manipulation of the space of the stage illustrate her development of theatrical ideas that coincide with Antonin Artaud's (q.v.) concept of "total theater." The stage directions call for a house in which the spectators are led by a guide who interacts with them as they wander through rooms in which some actors commit violent acts (kidnapings, torture, murders) and others engage in children's games. When the actor-guide insists that the spectators comment on their surroundings, they are soon forced to become more than passive witnesses to the scenes, and the boundary between stage and life becomes blurred. G.'s understanding of theatrical spectacle is joined by a knowledge of social ills, so that the play forces the spectators to recognize their general inaction and pliability and requires them to question and respond more fully to the nature of events in their environment. G. was not able to publish *Información para extranjeros* until 1987 because of its obvious political commentary.

Instead of remaining silent in the face of censorship, G. employed displacement techniques to veil her criticism and still transform the passivity of the Argentine public. *La malasangre* (1982; *Bitter Blood,* 1988), set in the 1840s during the period of the Rosas dictatorship, ostensibly develops a naturalistic plot that involves a love story. On the allegorical level it describes the awakening of the Argentine public from its passive state to a new consciousness about its oppressive government. *Del sol naciente* (1984; the rising sun) is set in Japan, yet its samurai warrior and geisha maiden are involved in a power relationship that is kindred to the military's treatment of the Argentine people during the Falklands crisis.

Although her fame rests on her plays, her narrative pieces reflect the same interest in Black Humor, parodic techniques, and striking visual images. In *Dios no nos quiere contentos* (1979; God doesn't want us content) the main character works in a second-rate circus where she is always exploited by the bosses. As a trapeze artist who is also a contortionist, her experiences of trying to maintain her equilibrium in an oppressive world serve as a metaphor for our lives today, as we are often tied up in knots and unbalanced by the pressures and ills of modern life. In a lighter vein, the tour de force *Lo impenetrable* (1984; *The Impenetrable Madam X,* 1991) reveals G.'s sarcasm and irony with regard to relations between the sexes. While Madam X eagerly awaits an erotic encounter with the young man who has declared his undying love, she allows herself to be distracted by the sexual play of a varied lot, including her maid, the coachman, and another mysterious stranger. This woman is clearly different from the victimized aging actress in the play *El despojamiento* (1981; the striptease), whose servile demeanor recalls early characters like Emma of *El campo*.

G. represents one of a number of Latin American women who are successful dramatists. Although her early plays did not reflect the specific problems of women in authoritarian societies, her work in general is recognized for its representation of metaphysical issues relating to the human condition as well as to the specific Argentine sociopolitical problems of the abuses of power. G. showed her gift of foresight in the way the physical and psychological torture experienced by her characters anticipated the institutional sadism prevalent during the Argentine Dirty War. An acknowledged master in the manipulation of verbal and nonverbal signs, her work continues to be highly regarded for its exciting physical images on stage and for the richness of her dramatic metaphors.

FURTHER WORKS: *Madrigal en ciudad* (1963); *Una felicidad con menos pena* (1968); *Sólo un aspecto* (1973); *Ganarse la muerte* (1976); *La cola mágica* (1976); *Conversación con chicos* (1976); *Teatro. Nada que ver. Sucede lo que pasa* (1983); *Teatro I. Real envido. La malasangre. Del sol naciente* (1984); *Teatro II. Dar la vuelta. Información para extranjeros. Puesta en claro* (1987)

BIBLIOGRAPHY: Holzapfel, T., "G. G.'s Theatre of the Absurd," *LATR*, 4, 1 (1970), 5–12; Cypess, S. M., "Physical Imagery in the Plays of G. G.," *MD*, 18 (1975), 357–64; Cypess, S. M., "The Plays of G. G.," in Lyday, L. F., and G. W. Woodyard, eds., *Dramatists in Revolt* (1976), 95–109; Gerdes, D., "Recent Argentine Vanguard Theatre: G.'s *Información para extranjeros*," *LATR*, 11, 2 (Spring 1978), 11–16; Foster, D. W., "The Texture of Dramatic Action in the Plays of G. G.," *HisJ*, 1, 2 (1979), 57–66; Garfield, E. P., "Una dulce bondad que atempera las cruel-dades: *El campo* de G. G.," *LATR*, 13, 2 (Summer 1980), 95–102; Podol, P. L., "Reality Perception and Stage Setting in G. G.'s *Las paredes* and Antonio Buero Vallejo's *La fundación*," *MD*, 24, 1 (Mar. 1981), 44–53; Méndez-Faith, T., "Sobre el uso y abuso de poder en la producción dramática de G. G.," *RI*, 51, 132–33 (July–Dec. 1985), 831–41; Nigro, K., "G. G. vista desde lejos: Primeros textos y contextos culturales," in Pelletieri, O., comp., *Teatro argentino de los '60* (1990), 169–81; Cypess, S. M., "Frankenstein's Monster in Argentina: G.'s Two Versions," *RCEH*, 14, 2 (Winter 1990), 349–61

SANDRA MESSINGER CYPESS

GARRO, Elena

Mexican novelist, dramatist, journalist, and short-story writer, b. 15 Dec. 1920, Puebla

G.'s plays, novels, and short stories are a complex blend of allegorical symbols, fantasy, and autobiography. The theme of power in its many sociopolitical and psychological manifestations permeates all of G.'s work and is reiterated in various forms always in close relationship with G.'s perception of the situation of women in society and her own experiences as a woman. Her constant fascination with the issues of power, violence, and history can be related to the fact that G. was born only ten years after the beginning of the Mexican Revolution, one of the most violent and historically important revolutions in Latin America, and raised during the difficult period of power struggles and political reorganization that followed the postrevolutionary years.

G.'s career as a writer began while she was still a student at the National Autonomous University of Mexico. Soon after her marriage in 1937 to the Mexican poet and essayist Octavio Paz (q.v.), G. began to write for the Mexican journal *Así*. As a reporter, she was bold and daring. On one occasion, in order to complete an article, she had herself locked up as a common prisoner in the Federal District's women's jail for three weeks, and her story, once published, caused the discharge of the director of the prison. It was this boldness that made her an aggressive social activist years later, a boldness that she also transfers to the characters in her writings. Later, in 1948, while traveling back to Mexico from California, she was denied entrance to her country for being the daughter of a Spaniard. G., in spite of the fact that her mother was Mexican and that she had been born and raised in Mexico, had to go through the process of naturalization, was treated as a foreigner, was given a three-month visa, and was forced to leave the country after that time. This experience of feeling like a foreigner in her own country, isolated and marginalized, would also be recaptured in different ways in her work in the life of several of her feminine characters.

In 1954 G. began to write for films, and also wrote her first play, *Felipe Angeles* (1967; Felipe Angeles). By 1958 she had achieved fame as a dramatist. Her first three plays were aired in the same season in "Poesía en voz alta" (spoken poetry) and later published along with several one-act plays in a single volume she entitled *Un hogar sólido y otras piezas en un acto* (1957; a solid house and other one-act plays; repub. as *Un hogar sólido,* 1986). She was also successful with the films *Sólo de noche vienes* (you only come at night) and *Las señoritas Vivanco* (the Vivanco ladies). During this time, G. became involved in the problem of peasants evicted from their land in Ahuatepec, Morelos. The urgent sense of justice that has always accompanied G. made her join in the fight in their favor. She succeeded in helping the workers regain their land and founded a weekly magazine, *Presente,* to voice a defense on behalf of the peasants. The magazine disappeared after several issues, but she became so well known that the peasants of Madera, Chihuahua, called on her for her support on similar demands. G. was then a journalist for *Sucesos,* and she worked together with Gabriel García Márquez (q.v.) and other well-known writers on these peasants' behalf.

Years before the publication of her first plays, G. became ill while she and Paz were living in Berne. During her convalescence she wrote her first novel, *Los recuerdos del porvenir* (1966; *Recollections of Things To Come,* 1969), a manuscript she put away in a trunk until it was rescued by Paz years later and published. The novel, the winner of the Xavier Villaurrutia Prize in 1984, recaptures the actions occuring in the Mexico of the 1920s in the small town of Ixtepec during the cruel days of the Cristero rebellion, a violent movement in favor of the Church, which emerged as an aftermath of the revolution. In G.'s novel, the town tells its own story against a background of political change, religious persecution, and social unrest. Here, as in her play *Felipe Angeles,* G. portrays the image of a revolution that, like all revolutions, ended up devouring itself.

Mexico's dual heritage, Spanish and Indian, became an important theme in all of G.'s work, especially in the first period of her production when she was fascinated by the ancient Mexican concept of a reality that simultaneously accommodates different levels. Against a background of violence with its many manifestations, G. experimented in her work with the presence of the past in the present, with the concept of an eternal present, and with the idea that women, in spite of having extraordinary potential as human beings, are usually not recognized in a male-oriented culture. In the first period of G.'s production, which also includes the collection of short stories *La semana de colores* (1964; week of colors), where G. again proved her versatility and ingenuity as a writer of fiction, she created a magical world where time can stand still to allow lovers to escape, and where past and present can flow intermittently into each other. In the work of this period, G. also explores the feminine pattern of

the Malinche as a Mexican cultural and psychological model in the conceptualization of Mexican women, as seen in her most anthologized short story, "La culpa es de los Tlaxcaltecas" (it's the fault of the Tlaxcaltecas). G.'s perception of the role of women in Mexico, her preoccupation with the pervasive presence of the past in the present, and her view of an eternal reduplication of performance can be seen in her work in the characterization of generations that follow each other, each one repeating the same acts and gestures as those that preceded it. Following this impressive first period of G.'s work, there came fifteen years of silence, which coincided with her divorce, and a self-exile caused by illness and financial hardships. Other incidences were to mark the second period of her production. After the government's massacre of the students in Tlatelolco in 1968, G. was wrongly accused of being an instigator. To escape from the difficult situation of being watched by some and threatened by others, G. fled to the U.S. and then to Spain where she had to become a Spanish citizen since her Mexican passport was confiscated by the Mexican government.

In her earlier writings, G. created characters who existed in two different but parallel and simultaneous times, and through them she explored the traditional myth of female behavior and subverted traditional views in favor of new models in society. In the work of G.'s second period, these characters are superseded by an angry voice exposing injustices committed by society on its weak members, especially women. To this second period belong her second collection of short stories, *Andamos huyendo Lola* (1980; we are fleeing Lola), and her last three novels: *Testimonios sobre Mariana* (1981; testimonies about Mariana), *Reencuentro de personajes* (1982; reencounter of characters), and *La casa junto al río* (1983: the house by the river). This latter work involves a magical encounter of the living with the dead, through a death that is seen not as an end but as a beginning, and as a return to a comforting past where the main character, a girl harassed by the townspeople, is able to reunite with her dead relatives as she crosses from one reality into another. The themes of violence and cruelty, which permeate all of G.'s work, are intensified in this novel, and presented now as a psychic and psychopathological phenomenon. Other changes are also noticeable. G.'s strong and individual woman in her first plays and novel becomes a heroine that falls into passivity and oppression. The heroine in G.'s last novel is, like the traditional hero in a quest, a woman who must confront the absurd and struggle with solitude, isolation, marginality, and the constant fear of rejection and death in search of identity, knowledge, and meaning. The highly allegorical figure of Consuelo in this novel dies a victim of the townspeople who have kept her from knowing the facts of her family's disappearance. Yet her death is not defeat. It is the encounter with a new model outside of a present decadent order of things, and the reunion with her relatives is the encounter with the long-sought Paradise denied to her in the world of the living.

In G.'s work, death is the other side of one and the same reality, and the antithesis of cruelty is not kindness, but freedom. G.'s skillful control of narrative structure, style, and theme allows her to play successfully with a magical fictional world where history and time, as in the Aztec tradition, possess neither a past nor a future. Through myth and magic, G.'s work has addressed many important issues of 20th-c. Latin America, especially those pertaining to violence and power. Her mastery of action, timelessness, poetry in prose, narrative structure, dramatic intensity and suspense, vivid impressions, and characters drawn with bold strokes allow her to paint the passionate and secret lives of women characters in a constant search for themselves, marginalized, oppressed, rejected, and at times driven to suicide, which for G. is also a form of freedom.

FURTHER WORKS: *La señora en su balcón. Tercera antología de obras en un acto* (1960); *La dama boba: pieza en tres actos* (1963)

BIBLIOGRAPHY: Rosser, H. E., "Form and Content in E. G.'s *Los recuerdos del porvenir*," *RCEH*, 2, 3 (Spring 1978), 282–94; Candelaria, C., "La Malinche, Feminist Prototype," *Frontiers*, 5 (1980), 1–6; Johnson, H., "E. G.'s Attitudes towards Mexican Society," *South Central Bulletin*, 40, 4 (Winter 1980), 150–52; Mora, G., "Rebeldes fracasadas: una lectura feminista de *Andarse por las ramas y la señora en su balcón*," *Plaza*, 5–6 (Fall–Spring 1981–1982), 115–31; Mora, G., "*La dama boba* de E. G.: Verdad y ficción, teatro y metateatro," *LATR*, 16, 2 (Spring 1983), 15–22; Leal, L., "Female Archetypes in Mexican Literature," in Miller, B., ed., *Women in Hispanic Literature: Icons and Fallen Idols* (1983), 227–42; Duncan, C., " 'La culpa es de los Tlaxcaltecas': A Reevaluation of Mexico's Past through Myth," *CH*, 7, 2 (1985), 105–20; Mendez Rodena, A., "Tiempo femenino, tiempo ficticio: *Los recuerdos del porvenir* de E. G.," *RI*, 51, 132–33 (July–Dec. 1985), 843–51; Anderson, R. K., "Myth and Archetype in *Recollections of Things To Come*," *StTCL*, 9, 2 (Spring 1985), 213–27; Larson, C., "Recollections of Plays To Come: Time in the Theater of E. G.," *LATR*, 22, 2 (Spring 1989), 5–17; Stoll, A. K., ed., *A Different Reality: Studies on the Work of E. G.* (1990)

JULIA CUERVO HEWITT

GERMAN LITERATURE

See Volume 2, page 214.

In many respects the years between 1984 and 1991 mark a drastic change in German-language literature, for it was a period of monumental endings and beginnings. On the one hand, several of the authors who profoundly influenced postwar literature passed away. They include: Uwe Johnson, Heinrich Böll, the Austrian Thomas Bernhard, the Swiss Friedrich Dürrenmatt, the Swiss Max Frisch (qq.v.), Rudolf Hagelstange (1912–1984), Ingeborg Drewitz (1923–1986), Hubert Fichte (1935–1986), the Austrian Erich Fried (1921–1988), the Swiss Hermann Burger (1942–1989), Horst Bienek (1930–1990), and the Austrian Hilde Spiel (1911–1990). The death of these respected authors spelled a deep loss for German belles lettres. In the same vein, the opening of the Berlin Wall on 9 November 1989 and the subsequent rapid unification of Germany on 3 October 1990 meant an end to East German literature as we knew it. Writers from the East, who had previously enjoyed a wide readership since they offered alternative information and an oppositional voice to the dictates of the party, were suddenly subjected to the same market conditions as their western counterparts. Some were criticized in the West for their supposed compromising positions with the G.D.R. regime. A case in point is Christa Wolf (q.v.), whose *Was bleibt* (1989; what remains) describes how she continued to live and work in the East even though she realized she was subjected to surveillance by the state security system (the Stasi). Others, who opposed the total abandonment of socialism and were thus against becoming a part of West Germany, like Stefan Heym (q.v.), were left rather isolated. It remains to be seen if such authors will be able to integrate themselves into the new German state. On the other hand, a unified Germany, together with the changing structure of Europe, with all its problems and accomplishments, should provide a fertile ground for older and newer authors alike to express their creative talents.

The 1980s saw a continuation of the debate as to whether one or several German literatures exist. While the question of a distinct East German literature will only be of historical interest, controversies still remain about the relative independence of Austrian and Swiss-German letters. Some see the literatures of these two countries as distinct entities, for their authors examine primarily the nature of Austrian and Swiss experiences and identities respectively. Others point out that since many of these authors are published in Germany and since they all share a common language, they all partake in a common "German-language literature." A few want to blur all distinctions and speak only of a world literature. While the debate will probably not be settled soon, Austrian and Swiss authors have been included in this essay if they have made a significant impact in Germany or if they have been expropriated by German readers and critics.

It is difficult to distinguish many trends, movements or groupings for German literature in the past few years. One exception might be what is alternately called guest workers', foreigners', or migrants' literature. This is the writing of non-Germans living in Germany and publishing in German. Authors like Aras Ören (b. 1929), Rafik Schami (b. 1949), and TORKAN (b. 1941, pseud. of Torkan Daneshfar-Pätzoldt) write about the problems that foreigners face in Germany, such as prejudice and the lack of understanding between different cultures. Their professed purpose is to reduce friction, increase awareness, and contribute to a more harmonious integration of various parts of society. The only difficulty that these authors face is that their works, often published in anthologies, remain out of the mainstream and are overlooked by the reading public.

Apart from this one group it is impossible to find any convenient nomenclature for the other 13,000 to 15,000 literary works that appear annually on the German market. Some have applied the term postmodern to the 1980s, and this characterization certainly holds true in some cases. Authors such as Botho Strauss (b. 1944), in several of his prose works like *Der junge Mann* (1984; the young man) or *Niemand anders* (1987; no one else) and in his plays like *Besucher* (1988; visitors), or Peter Handke (q.v.), in his prose such as *Die Wiederholung* (1986; the repetition) or *Nachmittag eines Schriftstellers* (1987; afternoon of a writer), or Patrick Süskind (b. 1949), in his popular best-seller *Das Parfum* (1985; *Perfume*, 1986), tend to display many of the characteristics associated with this movement. They mix a variety of styles that can appeal to different groups of readers simultaneously, they use a complicated if not ornate language, they call their own profession or the literary forms they are using into question (often through parody), and they show an interest in history and biography. One author, Marianne Fritz (b. 1948), carries this trend to an absurd degree. In her monumental novel *Dessen Sprache du nicht verstehst* (1985; whose language you do not understand), which is over three thousand pages long, she purposely leaves out words, places

false punctuation within the sentences, and collects over one thousand characters, often under varying names, to tell the history of a German family during the early part of this century.

Other authors, however, have merely prolonged trends begun earlier, yet in many instances they still managed to produce significant works of art. The realm of poetry was perhaps the least productive in this regard, for it has been highly derivative and repetitive. Nevertheless, a few new poets, like Ulla Hahn (b. 1945), were able to find a fairly wide readership, and a few established poets, like Heinz Czechowski (b. 1939), continued to impress the critics. In both cases one admired the timeliness of their messages and the powerful scope of their language. The world of the drama was more exciting, although it was dominated by two authors, Botho Strauss and the Austrian Thomas Bernhard. The latter's *Heldenplatz* (1988; heroes square) caused a major scandal and was also an overnight success due to the hyperbole of its criticism of contemporary Austrian society and the parallels it draws with the events of 1938. The neorealist Bavarian Franz Xaver Kroetz (b. 1946) continued to write plays at a furious rate, and most of them, like *Furcht und Hoffnung der BRD* (1984; fear and hope of the FRG), centered on the theme of unemployment, often with surrealist overtones. The newcomer Friederike Roth (b. 1948) won considerable respect for her radio play *Nachtschatten* (1984; night shadows), which is a feminist reflection on the concept of happiness.

Prose continued to be the most popular genre, and committed works that examined societal issues garnered the most notoriety. Günter Walraff (b. 1942) disguised himself as a Turkish worker and documents the horrible prejudices and maltreatment to which he was subjected on and off the workplace in *Ganz unten* (1985; down at the bottom). The book became a scandalous success. The famous Günter Grass (q.v.) uses an atomic disaster in *Die Rättin* (1986; *The Rat*, 1987) as a pretext to tell a story set in the future, but which has connections to his earlier Danzig trilogy. Jurek Becker (q.v.) examines contemporary generation conflicts caused by the Nazi years in *Bronsteins Kinder* (1986; *Bronstein's Children*, 1988). Martin Walser (q.v.) employs the framework of a spy novel to investigate the division of Germany in *Dorle und Wolf* (1987; *No Man's Land*, 1988). Rainald Goetz (b. 1954) shocked the public with his account of the Red Army Faction in 1977 in his book *Kontrolliert* (1988; checked over).

Other prose authors treated more personal issues. Brigitte Kronauer (b. 1940), after a series of books about female emancipation, describes the self-realization of a male protagonist in *Berittener Bogenschütze* (1986; mounted archer). Hermann

Burger tries to overcome the spectre of death and depression in *Brenners Leben* (1989; Brenner's life). Christoph Ransmayr (b. 1954), in one of the most critically acclaimed works of the decade, *Die letzte Welt* (1988; the last world), sends his main character in search of the Roman poet Ovid. He never reaches his goal, but his journey results in a new relationship with nature and the world, which ends in madness. In all three works the reader is confronted with linguistic perfection and the deep inner worlds of the soul.

The tumultuous and partially unforeseen social and economic upheavals that unification brought about have left many writers at a literal loss for words—they seem to be searching for appropriate topics and means of expression in a world suddenly grown extremely complex and unfamiliar. Several, particularly those from the east, feel that they have lost their credibility and relevance, since they did not participate directly in the events leading to the demise of the G.D.R, and have thus ceased writing completely. A number of publishing houses in eastern Germany have collapsed, because the reading public there has neither the money nor the time for literature: they prefer instead travel information, how-to-do-it books, or practical advice guides. Of the many authors who left the East for the West during the 1970s and 1980s, only two have returned: Erich Loest (b. 1926) to Leipzig and Joachim Seyppel (b. 1919) to East Berlin.

As might be expected, the problematics of a divided Germany and its subsequent unification is tentatively emerging as an important theme in German literature of the 1990s. Some authors, like the former head of the East German Writers' Association, Hermann Kant (q.v.), in his book *Abspann: Erinnerungen* (1991; end of the film: recollections), have tried to justify their role in the G.D.R and have earned few complimentary comments for their efforts. Others, like Loest, in such books as *Der Zorn des Schafes* (1990; the anger of the sheep), in which he describes his encounters with the Stasi, or *Katerfrühstück* (1992; hangover breakfast), in which he tries to show how the two former Germanies had grown psychologically far apart, have gained praise and admiration. Still other authors approach this topic on a personal and intimate basis. The heroine of Monika Maron's (b. 1941) novel *Stille Zeile sechs* (1991; quiet line six), experiences firsthand the collapse of East Germany with a concomitant range of emotions. The individuals in Gabriele Goettle's (b. 1947) four-hundred-page reportage *Deutsche Sitten: Erkundungen in Ost und West* (1991; German customs: research in east and west) present an image of a united Germany in dark and somber tones. The protagonist of Martin Walser's much

acclaimed novel *Die Verteidung der Kindheit* (1991; the defense of childhood) experiences great internal suffering during the years of German division. Such works will no doubt serve as models for literary creations in the coming years.

BIBLIOGRAPHY: Hage, V., ed., *Deutsche Literatur: Jahresüberblick* (1984 ff.—annual survey); Schöne, A., ed., "Vier deutsche Literaturen?," *Kontroversen, alte und neue: Akten des VII. Internationalen Germanisten-Kongresses Göttingen 1985* (1986, Vol. 10); Demetz, P., *After the Fires: Recent Writing in the Germanies, Austria, and Switzerland* (1986); Acker, R., and M. Burkhard, eds., *Blick auf die Schweiz: Zur Frage der Eigenständigkeit der Schweizer Literatur seit 1970* (1987); Arnold, H. L., ed., *Bestandsaufnahme Gegenwartsliteratur: Bundesrepublick Deutschland, Deutsche Demokratische Republik, Österreich, Schweiz* (1988); Suhr, H., "Minority Literature in the Federal Republic of Germany," *NGC*, 46 (1989), 71–103; Winkels, H., "Im Schatten des Lebens: eine Antwort an die Verächter und die Verteidiger der Gegenwartsliteratur," *Die Zeit*, overseas edition, 9 Mar. 1990, 15; Baumgart, R., "Boulevard—was sonst?" *Die Zeit*, overseas edition, 13 Apr. 1990, 25; special issue on literature of the 1980s, *GQ*, 63, 3–4 (1990)

ROBERT ACKER

GHALLĀB, ʿAbd Al-Karim

Moroccan novelist, short-story writer, and journalist, b. 1919, Fes

G. attended the Qarawiyyin college in Morocco and obtained his B.A. in Arabic literature from Cairo University. While in Egypt, he militated through various Maghrebi organizations for the independence of Morocco, Algeria, and Tunisia. Upon his return to Morocco in 1948, he worked as a journalist and a teacher. He was appointed editor in chief of the weekly magazine *Risālat Al-Maghrib* and contributed to the daily newspaper *Al-Ālam*. He became its editor in chief after his country's independence and is presently its editor and director.

G. militated assiduously for his national cause and was arrested and imprisoned more than once. He related his experience in prison in his largely autobiographical novel *Sabʿat Abwāb* (1965; seven gates). He was appointed a plenipotentiary minister for the Middle East from 1956 to 1959. G. then returned to journalism and writing, interrupting his work a second time from 1983 to 1985 upon his appointment as minister in the Moroccan government. G. is a prominent member of the Istiqlal party. He is a devout and dedicated nationalist and a committed writer. His prolific production reflects his deep patriotism and his belief in Arab nationalism and the need for Arab unity. A versatile writer, whose books cover such fields as literary criticism and political and historical analysis, G. is also a novelist and short-story writer and an active member of various writers and journalists associations.

His idealistic concepts of Arab unity were first voiced in his book *Nabadāt fikr* (1961; the beat of a thinking mind). They were the leitmotiv of three other books that followed and dealt with similar topics: *Risālat fikr* (1968; the message of a thinking mind), *Al-thaqāfah wa-al-fikr fī muwājahat al-tahaddī* (1976; culture and thought in the face of challenge), and *Al-fikr al-'Arabī bayna al-istilāb wa ta'kīd al-dhāt* (1977; Arab thought between spoliation and confirmation of the self). In the novel *Al-Mu'allim 'Alī* (1971; master Ali) the national awakening and the political maturity of factory workers are achieved only through the guidance of an intellectual Imam. The choice of an Imam is not a total coincidence as G. is a firm believer in God and is highly critical of the atheists who see in their attitude an exercise of the freedom of expression.

While advocating modernism (q.v.), G. neither wants a blind imitation of the West nor the loss of his country's individuality and Arab-Islamic character. It is clear in his essays and his fiction that he is weary of the widespread use of French language by the Moroccan people and Moroccan intellectuals. He sadly deplores the limited impact of his writings and those of his colleagues because of the high percentage of illiteracy in his country and the lack of circulation of the Arabic-written books outside Morocco's borders. He concluded his book *Nabadāt fikr* wondering whether anyone will ever read it. G. considers the poor reading habits of the Arabs as a whole as one of the causes of their cultural disarray. The great loser in literature is the theater, which lowered its standards to cater to an audience interested only in amusement. Its dependence on the spoken word is another threat to its survival as the written text, maintains G., prevails over the spoken word because of the greater depth and value it carries.

G.'s assessment of the decade of the 1960s presented in his book *Risālat fikr* is dictated by his conservative and rather puritan judgment on life. The world according to him turned mad, and materialism overcame spiritualism. He did not react favorably to the liberalism of the 1960s and expressed the need for a cultural revolution to improve the situation. G.'s idealism and deep sense of right and wrong dictated his dislike for the various phenomena of the modern times, although he is a modernist in his own way. He

manifests an almost obsessive concern for freedom and considers it a necessity for the development of any culture, a concept that is strongly expressed in two of his main books, *Risālat fikr* and *Al-thaqāfah wa-al-fikr fī muwājahat al-tahaddī*. He believes that intellectual backwardness can be remedied through education, training of personnel, development of public opinion, and moral reformation, and that backwardness is not due only to a weak economy.

Although about fifteen years separate *Nabadāt fikr* from *Al-fikr al-'Arabī bayna al-istilāb wa ta'kīd al-dhāt*, G.'s concepts of Arab unity and the role of Arab intellectuals in cementing it did not change in any noticeable way. G. is critical of superficial writers and particularly of poets who depend solely on inspiration to write poetry. He stresses the need for study and research as well as the necessity for constructive criticism to improve the standard of Arabic poetry, particularly in the 1960s. His preference for rhymed poetry over free verse reveals a rather conservative view in art, a position clearly reflected in his fiction works and Arabic style. Moreover, G. believes that good fiction can only derive from personal experience. Some of his assessments of Arabic literature are outdated, but they form part of the trend that characterized the Arabic literary scene, in the Maghreb in particular, during the 1960s, opposing the old and the new schools of thought.

The concepts expressed in *Risālat fikr* served as the basis for G.'s novels and short stories. His collections *Al-ard habībatī* (1971; the land is my beloved) and *Wa akhrajahā min al-jannah* (1977; he led her out of paradise) can be classified as realistic works, highly descriptive and extremely detailed, with an obvious desire to inform the reader of Morocco's customs and traditions. Both collections reveal the writer's deep nationalism and his love for the land. The importance of holding to one's land at any price and resisting tempting offers to sell it is also one of the messages of *Al-Mu'allim 'Alī* where the villagers are described as lacking national consciousness. Some of these works are highly autobiographical, a good example being his novel *Sab'at Abwāb* in which G. relates the arrest and imprisonment of a Moroccan political activist. The insertion of such an experience in the frame of a novel has given the author more immediacy to praise the courage, patience, and patriotism of the characters, especially that of the hero and his wife. G. describes life in the prison at length, stressing the bonding that develops between political prisoners. The same patriotic feeling is at the basis of another novel, *Dafannā al-mādī* (1966; we buried the past), which raises the question of the conflict of civilizations as well as the colonial policy in Morocco, partic-

ularly the Arab-Berber relations and the efforts of
the French at dividing the Moroccans along these
lines. While this novel ends with the independence
of Morocco and the return of the king to the
country, another novel, *Sabā wa yazhaf al-layl*
(1984; morning followed by the night), takes the
action to the postindependence period. It tackles
the traumatic impact of the French colonial policy
and the francophone tendencies of some Moroccans. G. points out the negative effect of such a
policy on Islam and on society as a whole through
the life of a French-educated young man who
resists his wife's efforts to convert him to Moroccan traditional ways. The confrontation between
the young couple is an opportunity for the novelist
to voice his opinion on Western culture. G. adopts
his usual didactic and moralizing approach to condemn the Westernized young man and his peers.

G.'s fiction is burdened by a tendency to give
lengthy accounts of events and detailed descriptions of places. Moreover, his style borrows heavily
from traditional classical Arabic. His writings sound
like a lone voice on the Moroccan literary scene,
conservative and even old-fashioned, at a time
when Arabic is undergoing a revolutionary rejuvenation. Also, his moral message is too blunt
and obvious for the taste of the modern reader
who is used to hints and allusions.

It is safe to say that G.'s greatest contributions
to the cultural scene in Morocco and the Arab
world are in the field of journalism, in the political
essay, and to a lesser extent in literary criticism.
His writings are in step with Morocco's political
evolution as is obvious from works such as *Tārīkh
al-harakah al-wataniyyah bi-al-Maghrib* (1988; the
history of the national movement in Morocco),
Ma'a al-sha'b fī al-barlamān (1984; with the people in the parliament), and *Sultat al-mu'assassāt*
(1987; the power of the institutions). His interest
extends to all Arab causes, particularly the Palestinian problem and the Zionist policy to which he
dedicates a whole work entitled *Ma'rakatunā al-
'Arabiyyah fī muwājahat al isti'mār wa-al-Sahyū-
niyyah* (1967; our Arab battle with colonialism
and Zionism). The Lebanese civil war caught also
his attention and is the subject of his latest publication entitled *Bayrūt* (1991; Beirut). He has also
published two books on his experience as a journalist, *Sahafī fī Amrīkā* (1963; a journalist in
America) and *Min Makkah ilā Mūskū* (1971; from
Mekka to Moscow). G.'s long list of publications
in the 1980s and the early 1990s reveals a concentrated interest in political analysis, with little contribution to fiction.

One of G.'s merits is his ability to remain open
to change in spite of his deeply rooted conservatism. He remains a monument on the cultural scene

and a productive mind whose ability to write seems
endless.

FURTHER WORKS: *Al-istiqlāliyyah* (1960); *Fī al-
islāh al-qarawī* (1961); *Hadhā huwa al-dustūr*
(1962); *Fi al-thaqāfa wa-al-adab* (1964); *Māta qarīr
al-'ayn* (1964); *Difā'un 'an al-dīmūqratiyyah* (1966);
Difā' 'an fann al-qawl (1972); *Sirā' madhhab wa-
al-'aqīdah fī al-Qur'ān* (1973); *Ma'a al-adab wa-
al-udabā'* (1974); *Al-fikr al taqaddumī fī al-īdi-
yulujiyyah al-ta'āduliyyah* (1979); *Mujtama' al-
mu'minīn* (n.d.); *'Ālam shā'ir al-Hamrā'* (1982);
Wa-'āda al-zawraq ilā al-nab' (1985?); *Al-Ta-
tawwur al-dustūrī wa-al-niyābī bi-al-Maghrib min
sanat 1908 ilā sanat 1978* (2 vols., 1988); *Li-
mādhā inhārat al-shuyū 'iyyah?* (1990)

BIBLIOGRAPHY: Tovimi, B. M., A. Khatibi, and
M. Kably, *Écrivains marocains du protectorat à
1965, Anthologie* (1974), 81–93

AIDA A. BAMIA

al-GHĪTĀNĪ, Jamāl
Egyptian novelist, short-story writer, and journalist, b. 9 May 1945, Juhaynah, Sūhāj Province

G. grew up in old Cairo. He was trained as a
carpet designer and worked in this profession from
1962 to 1968. Since then he has been a full-time
journalist with the daily *Akhbār al-Yawm*. Both
carpet design, as an intricate and complex activity,
and journalism have had an impact on the way he
structures his novels and on their smooth style.

G. started publishing short stories in 1963. His
first collection, *Awrāq shābb 'āsha mundhu alf
'ām* (1969; the papers of a young man who lived
one thousand years ago), already showed a number
of aspects that will characterize his later, more
mature writings. This and the other short stories
that he wrote and published can be seen as preliminary exercises in the process of writing his first
novel, *Al-Zaynī Barakāt* (1974; Al-Zayni Barakat,
1988). This novel has been rightly considered one
of the most interesting and important literary
achievements of the post-Mahfūz generation of
Egyptian writers. G.'s narrative strategy of juxtaposing many different narrative modes was a
breakthrough within the context of the Arabic
novel. He made use of the Mahfūzian realistic
mode and that of reports of travelers, especially
Europeans who visited the Middle East during the
18th and 19th cs. Yet the important addition was
using the narrative mode of the late medieval
Egyptian historian Ibn Iyās. With this G. opened
new venues for the blending of the indigenous
narrative traditions with those of the Western novel.

252

The intricate structuring of the novel—the novel takes place during the first two decades of the 16th c., around the time of the Ottoman invasion of Egypt—with its different narrators and characters, coupled with the many analogies to the situation in Egypt during Nasser's reign and the War of 1967, and the successful use of native narrative modes, immediately turned this novel into an event in modern Arabic literature.

With the publication of his next novel, *Waqā'i' hārat al-Za'farānī* (1976; *Incidents in Zafrany Alley*, 1986), G. was still probing the different ways of using the native historical narrative modes, especially those of official reports and cumulative or incremental repetition. He developed a new and interesting literary language that blends the journalistic with the popular and the old classical Arabic. All these devices are used in portraying what happens in one of the quarters of Cairo during the first years of the reign of Sadat (1971–1972). In *Khitat al-Ghītānī* (1980; Ghitani's khitat)—the title refers to those writings in Egypt called *khitat*: encyclopedic descriptions rich with historical, social, and geographical information about the country—the influence of the popular linguistic modes was manifest. But G.'s other discovery was the language of the Muslim sufis—the medieval Muslim mystics. This is most manifest in his three-volume novel *Kitāb al-tajalliyyāt* (1983–1987; the book of revelations). The richness of the sufi linguistic and literary traditions is further explored in *Risālah fī al-sabābah wa-al-wajd* (1987; epistle on passion and ecstasy) and *Risālat al-basā'ir fī al-masā'ir* (1989; epistle of insights into destinies). Among G.'s other writings are collections of short stories and book-length interviews with literary and cultural figures like Najīb Mahfūz (q.v.). He has also written much about the historical geography of Cairo, rendering masterfully the flavor of the old city. G. also wrote journalistic reports as a war correspondent, *al-Misriyyūn wa-al-harb* (1974; Egyptians and war) and *Hurrās al-bawwābah al-sharqīyyah* (1975; guards of the eastern gate), of high literary value, going well beyond mere journalistic descriptions of war heroism—comparable to his early collection of short stories, entitled *Ard . . . ard* (1972; surface to surface).

Despite the large amount of writing that G. has produced over two decades, he has generally been able to preserve the high quality that characterized his works since the beginning of his career. G.'s success has been the result of his ability to introduce formal innovations into the modern Arabic novel, especially through creative use of medieval Arabic prose traditions, without neglecting the traditions of Western realistic writing. His sense of history and place infuses his writings with a unique flavor. The enthusiastic reception of his works, especially the earlier novels, in Europe, and more recently in North America, is further proof that some of his works may become classics of Third World literature.

FURTHER WORKS: *al-zuwayl* (1975); *al-hisār min thalāth jihāt* (1975); *Hikāyāt al-gharīb* (1976); *al-rifā'ī* (1978); *Dhikr mā jarā* (1978); *Najīb Mahfūz yatadhakkar* (1980); *Mustafā Amīn yatadhakkar* (1983); *Malāmih al-Qāhirah fī alf 'ām* (1983); *Asbilat al-Qāhira* (1984); *Ithāf al-zamān bi-hikāyat Jalabī al-sultān* (1984); *Ahrāsh al-madīnah* (1984)

BIBLIOGRAPHY: Hegazy, S., *Littérature et société en Égypte* (1979), 71–72, 108–11; Ballas, S., *La littérature arabe et le conflit au proche-orient (1948–1973)* (1980), 150–51, 185–86; Tomiche, N., *Histoire de la littérature romanesque de l'Égypte moderne* (1981), 163–64, 197–200; Draz, C. K., "In Quest of New Narrative Forms," *JArabL*, 12 (1981), 140–44; Mehrez, S., "Al-Zayni Barakat: Narrative As Strategy," *Arab Studies Quarterly*, 8, 2 (1986), 120–42; Allen, R., ed., *Modern Arabic Literature* (1987), 100–104; Hamarneh, W., "How To Tell a Story in Arabic: Some Narrative Modes in the Contemporary Arabic Novel," *Mundus Arabicus*, 5 (1992); Mehrez, S., "Alternative Fictional Histories: The Case of *Khitat al-Ghitani*," *Mundus Arabicus*, 5 (1992)

                                              WALID HAMARNEH

GHOSE, Zulfikar

Indo-Pakistani-American novelist, poet, short-story writer, and essayist, b. 13 Mar. 1935, Sialkot, India (now Pakistan)

G. and his oeuvre defy categorization by nationality. Born in a city that was in India until 1947, and thereafter in Pakistan, he moved with his Punjabi-speaking family to Bombay in 1942, where he, a Muslim, was educated in an English-medium school run by Italian priests. He immigrated to England in 1952, graduating from the University of Keele in 1959 with a degree in philosophy. A journalist for the *Observer*, G. revisited India and Pakistan for the first time in 1965. He married the Brazilian painter Helena de la Fontaine, and in 1966 traveled extensively for the first time throughout Brazil, later the setting for six of his nine novels. In 1969 he joined the faculty of the University of Texas at Austin, where he teaches English literature and creative writing. His works are variously categorized as British, American,

Indian, Pakistani, Commonwealth, and even Brazilian or Latin American.

G. made his literary debut as a poet with *The Loss of India* (1964), many poems of which nostalgically recall his Indian boyhood and treat the persistent themes of rootlessness and alienness, which are found throughout much of his writing. These same themes dominate both his autobiography, *Confessions of a Native-Alien* (1965), and his second volume of poems, *Jets from Orange* (1967). In *The Violent West* (1972) the landscape of his poems shifts dramatically from the Indian subcontinent and Britain, and becomes distinctively American.

His first novel, *The Contradictions* (1966), is set partly in India during the Raj, partly in the Hampshire countryside. Many critics remarked on the elegant, concise, chiseled quality of the prose. G. has said that he deliberately set his second novel, *The Murder of Aziz Khan* (1967), in Pakistan to prove that he could, in fact, write such a piece. A classic case study of the violent confrontation of rural and urban, tradition and modernity, the story of the novel could be told about any Third World country. Critically acclaimed, the book is written in a prose that is often elevated to poetry.

G.'s next novels form a massive trilogy, *The Incredible Brazilian: The Native* (1972), *The Beautiful Empire* (1975), and *A Different World* (1978). Set in Brazil, these works follow their picaresque hero, Gregório Peixoto de Silva Xavier, through three reincarnations each in a different critical period of Brazil's history: the 17th, the 19th, and the 20th cs. respectively. Blending magic realism (q.v.), ultra-Byronic exploits, and sex, these works are considered G.'s finest to date.

His next two novels, set in Britain and the U.S. respectively, show a number of affinities: scathing indictments of contemporary Western civilization, a postmodern manipulation of the novel form, and a virtuosic handling of the English language. *Crump's Terms* (1976) presents the stream-of-consciousness cerebrations of the Middlesex schoolmaster Crump, a masterful punster and manipulator of quotes, who feels that Western civilization, especially that of Britain (which he abhors) and of France (which he adores), is rapidly decaying. Futility, in Crump's view, is the "final" human condition. The metafictionally dense *Hulme's Investigations into the Bogart Script* (1981) is a fabulation of nine separate scripts that often blend with and sometimes contradict one another as they excoriate contemporary American life.

For his remaining novels, all prodigally imbued with magical realism, G. returns to a South American setting. *A New History of Torments* (1982) is the story of Martin Kessel, an idealist gone awry

in his unbridled pursuit of money and power. *Don Bueno* (1984) recalls many features of the trilogy, with Don Bueno as the sobriquet of one Calderón, who is then reincarnated as three different men, each living out a different, but yet the same, destiny. Dreams are a major feature of *Figures of Enchantment* (1986), in which Gamboa, a government statistician, dreams of winning the lottery and retiring to an island; after his arrest at a political demonstration, Gamboa's dream is fulfilled, for he is banished to one.

In his writings G. seems to be obsessed with Brazil. It has been suggested that Brazil is, in fact, G.'s substitution in locale for South Asia. He readily admits that Rio de Janeiro put him in mind of 1940s Bombay, and that one could easily substitute a large Bombay or Hyderabadi family for that of *The Incredible Brazilian*. Because he defies a facile national categorization as a writer, G. might be called multicultural, a label he would probably deny, preferring instead to be called British.

In spite of publication by the best presses, consistently excellent reviews, and translation into the major European languages, G.'s works have not received extensive critical treatment, very likely because scholars have been unable to pigeonhole him by nationality. Recently, however, this situation has begun to change, in part thanks to South-Asian literary specialists who, in addition to admiring the structural sophistication and linguistic brilliance of his novels, view G.'s Brazil as both a substitute India or Pakistan and as Anywhere. These scholars have been instrumental in bringing G. to the attention of the larger academic community and in giving his works well-deserved critical attention.

FURTHER WORKS: *Statement against Corpses* (1964, with B. S. Johnson); *Hamlet, Prufrock and Language* (1978); *The Fiction of Reality* (1983); *A Memory of Asia: New and Selected Poems* (1984)

BIBLIOGRAPHY: Mukherjee, M., "G., Z.," *Contemporary Poets* (1975), 541–43; New, W., "G., Z.," *Contemporary Novelists* (1976), 511–13; Kohli, D., "Landscape and Poetry," *JCL*, 13, 3 (Apr. 1979), 54–70; Hobsbaum, P., "G., Z.," *Contemporary Poets* (1980), 644–46; Hashmi, A., "Tickling and Being Tickled à la Z. G.," *CNIE*, 1, 2 (1982), 32–38; Kanaganayakam, C., "Z. G.: An Interview," *TCL*, 32, 2 (Summer 1986), 169–86; Vassanji, M., "A Conversation with Z. G.," *Toronto South Asian Review*, 4, 3 (1986), 14–21; Stoerck, B., "New Fiction by Z. G.," *Pakistan Literature: The Contemporary English Writers,*

2nd ed. (1987), 97–104; special G. section, *RCF,* 9, 2 (1989), 103–237

CARLO COPPOLA

GIBRAN, Kahlil

(also known as Jubrān Khalīl Jubrān) Lebanese-American mystic poet, short-story writer, and artist (writing in Arabic and English), b. 6 Jan. 1883, Bsharri, Lebanon; d. 10 Apr. 1931, New York, N.Y., U.S.A.

Born in Lebanon, G. emigrated at twelve to the U.S. to settle first in Boston, then in New York. He returned to Beirut (1897–1901) to study Arabic at al-Hikma College, after which he spent two years in Paris (1908–1910) studying art at the expense of Mary Haskell, his lifelong friend and benefactress. Upon his death, his body was shipped back to his hometown in Lebanon, where alongside his tomb the G. Museum was later established.

G. began his literary career writing Arabic and contributing to journals published by the Lebanese and Arab communities in the U.S. He became the founding president of the Society of the Pen, a literary association of Arab-Americans whose aim was to revolutionize the classically conservative Arabic literature at home.

G.'s first work, *al-Mūsīqā* (1905; music), a short panegyric on music, displays in rudimentary form the basic elements that were to characterize his future writings: a resonant flowery language with a prophetic biblical tone and a deep sense of solitude coupled with nostalgia for a platonic homeland. Next followed two collections of short stories, *'Arā'is al-murūj* (1906; *Nymphs of the Valley,* 1949) and *al-Arwāh al-mutamarridah* (1908; *Spirits Rebellious,* 1949), and a novelette, *al-Ajnihah al-mutakassirah* (1912; *The Broken Wings,* 1957). These works, though hailed in their time as pioneer works of Arabic fiction, were actually no more than literary devices for G. to elaborate his ideas. The principal characters are made to denounce with prophetic authority the evils that disfigure the image of the cherished Lebanese homeland: a church order portrayed as the antagonist of Christ, allied with a despotic oligarchy. Typical is the protagonist of "Khalīl al-Kāfir" ("Khalil the Heretic") in *al-Arwāh al-mutamarridah,* who, in a kind of a Socratic apology in the village square, rallies all the villagers behind him and puts the priest and the landlord, his accusers, to flight.

As G.'s homeland becomes increasingly platonic, his prophetic attack in subsequent collections, particularly in *al-'Awāsif* (1920; the tempests), broadens to include humankind at large.

Humans are depicted in their terrestrial existence to be living as apes, heedless of their transcendental origin. Yūsuf al-Fakhrī in the title story finds it below his dignity to associate with humankind. His prototype in "Haffār al-Qubūr" (the grave digger) finds society stinking for lack of sufficient graves.

As English started to replace Arabic in G.'s works beginning with *The Madman* (1918), and as his audience became international, his rebellion became artistically more convincing. In this collection, the crude story form, hitherto rhetorical and didactic, gives way to the mystically impregnated parable, prose poem, and allegory in which G.'s poetic genius found its best expression.

Reassured by the immediate recognition brought him by *The Madman,* G. the rebel becomes more conciliatory in his second collection of parables, *The Forerunner* (1920). It was not until his main work, *The Prophet* (1923), however, that his rather biblical theme of prophet/condemner finally develops into the prophet/guide and redeemer. Almustapha breaks his twelve years of mystic silence among the people of Orphalese, presumably his and everybody's country of "exile," to answer their queries before he is divinely rehabilitated. The resulting twenty-six sermons are meant as passageways between humans in bondage and humans emancipated. A masterly blend in a biblical style of the poetic, the mystical, and the allegorical, *The Prophet,* for several years a best-seller in the U.S., remains G.'s masterpiece. Patterned after Almustapha in an attempt to give him a more masculine image, Jesus in *Jesus the Son of Man* (1928), proves too biblically exacting to be as freely molded as his prototype, and too poeticized to be historically convincing.

Published two weeks before his death, *The Earth Gods* (1931) is G.'s attempt at approaching *The Prophet* in poetic excellence. A dialogue in free verse between three titans on the human destiny, the book betrays the three mental states now struggling in G. for final supremacy: the rebel/nihilist, the prophet/redeemer, and a third who is disenchanted with both and ends up supreme in the dialogue. Standing for sheer human love, in preference to the divine, this third titan is indicative of a budding but short-lived new state in G.'s writing. Of the two posthumous works, *The Wanderer* (1932), a collection of parables, belongs to an earlier date, while *The Garden of the Prophet* (1933) is partly apocryphal.

This tendency toward the human in G.'s work, which only came to be stressed in his later writings, was always detectable in his art. Though concerned with the transcendental, his drawings and paintings are steeped with a human intimacy of exceptional tenderness. Naked human bodies of

both sexes, painfully supple and tenderly intertwined, form the basic language of G.'s art as
well as its distinctive feature.

A bilingual writer, G. has managed to excel in
both languages. In his country of origin, he is
associated with the literary revival that ushered
Arabic literature out of its medievalism into the
20th c. Orientally prophetic in expression, style,
and spiritual content, his English works, on the
other hand, especially *The Prophet,* address Western readers, and have succeeded in exercising on
them an effect akin to the biblical. G., it would
seem, is one of those few writers in modern times
in whose works East and West do actually meet.

FURTHER WORKS: *Dam'ah wa ibtisāmah* (1914; *A
Tear and a Smile,* 1950); *al-Mawākib* (1919; *The
Procession,* 1958); *al-Badā'i' wa-al-tarā'if* (1923).
FURTHER VOLUMES IN ENGLISH: *Twenty Drawings*
(1919); *Sand and Foam* (1926); *Prose Poems*
(1934); *Secrets of the Heart* (1947); *A Treasury
of K. G.* (1951); *Thoughts and Meditations* (1961);
A Second Treasury of K. G. (1962); *The Voice of
the Master* (1963); *Mirrors of the Soul* (1965);
The Wisdom of G.: Aphorisms and Maxims (1966);
Spiritual Sayings (1970); *Prophesies of Love* (1971);
Lazarus and His Beloved (1973); *K. G.: Paintings
and Drawings 1905–1930* (1989)

BIBLIOGRAPHY: Bragdon, C. F., *Merely Players*
(1939), 139–47; Young, B., *This Man from Leb-
anon* (1945); Naimy, M., *K. G.: His Life and His
Work* (1950); Otto, A. S., *The Parables of K. G.:
An Interpretation of his Writings and His Art*
(1963); Hawi, K. S., *K. G.: His Background,
Character, and Works* (1963); Gibran, J., and K.
Gibran, *K. G., His Life and World* (1974); Bush-
rui, S. B., and P. Gotch, eds., *G. of Lebanon:
New Papers* (1975); Naimy, N., *The Lebanese
Prophets of New York* (1985), 35–56; Shehadi,
W., *K. G.: A Prophet in the Making* (1991)

NADEEM NAIMY

GIRRI, Alberto

Argentine poet and translator, b. 27 Nov. 1919,
Buenos Aires

Except for occasional trips abroad, G. has lived
his entire life in Buenos Aires. He attended the
University of Buenos Aires, graduating in 1946.
A prolific poet and translator, he has also contributed frequently to important magazines such as
Sur and the literary supplement of *La Nación.* He
has received numerous prizes within Argentina,
including the First National Prize for Poetry (1967),
as well as foreign honors such as a Guggenheim

Foundation fellowship (1964 and 1977) and a Gold
Medal from the Italian Government (1962).

Although his poetry owes little allegiance to any
movement or school, G. began to publish contemporaneously with the Argentine "Generation of
1940," a group of poets who distanced themselves
from the avant-garde poetics practiced in the 1920s
and 1930s. According to critic Saúl Yurkievich,
G. shares with many poets of the "Generation of
1940" a return to the cultural cosmopolitanism of
the earlier "modernista" tradition. That is, in
opposition to the regional poetry of the Argentine
avant-garde, G. opted for an overt universalism,
crossing geographic and historical boundaries. This
international orientation is nowhere more evident
than in G.'s work as a translator, which spans the
tradition of poetry in English from John Donne to
Robert Lowell (q.v.) and beyond, as well as including Italian and Japanese poetry.

From his first book of poems, *Playa sola* (1946;
deserted beach), G.'s poetry showed great range
in terms of its cultural allusions, and this characteristic has not changed over time. His style,
however, developed in the opposite direction, becoming progressively more spare over the next
decade. This economy of means, now a signature
feature of G.'s work, frequently carries the poems
to laconic or aphoristic extremes. G. summed up
this attitude in a book of metapoetic prose fragments titled *El motivo es el poema* (1976; the
motive is the poem) when he said: "Consciousness
of limitations: consciousness of lucidity. Make do
with very little."

According to critic Guillermo Sucre, this lucidity is the central characteristic of G.'s poetry. For
Sucre this poetry reveals an intelligence that is
supremely self-critical, and critical of literature as
well. G. sees language and poetry as inherently
separated from reality. The poem cannot create or
recreate the world; it can only provide a way of
seeing it, of organizing it, and of filling it with
meaning. In his poetics the world is silent, and
the poem is directed toward that silence with the
understanding that it can never reach it. This idea
reveals G.'s philosophical debt to Taoism, expressed most noticeably in his collection *El ojo*
(1964; the eye). For G. silence is a version of the
void, which in Taoism is the origin and end of all
life. Poetry, in his view, brings poet and reader
close to this void, although one may never reach
it. Inherent to his poetics is an insistence on the
negation of the self and the creation of an impersonal and anonymous poetry. A similar philosophy
was espoused by T. S. Eliot (q.v.), whom G. has
translated extensively. G. also approaches Eliot in
his embracing of the poetic tradition and enthusiasm for intertextual play. This play, and the un-

derlying idea of literature as a shared venture, is openly alluded to by the title of one of G.'s recent collections, *Lo propio, lo de todos* (1980; one's own, that which belongs to all).

The objects of much of G.'s poetry are philosophical issues such as time, the self, and the nature and purpose of art. This last theme is especially important, and it has overflowed into a number of prose efforts which are crucial to an understanding of his poetics. These include *El motivo es el poema, Diario de un libro* (1972; diary of a book), and *Notas sobre la experiencia poética* (1983; notes on the experience of poetry).

G. is an extremely prolific poet known for his bare style and his penetrating explorations of difficult philosophical issues. His works, both poetry and prose, constitute a sustained meditation on the nature of poetry. G. is highly conscious of the limitations of all art, its inability ever to bridge the gap between the world and one's idea of the world. Nevertheless, poetry is seen as a way of approaching that point at which self disappears, language falls silent, and reality is experienced directly and authentically.

FURTHER WORKS: *Crónica del héroe* (1946); *Coronacíon de la espera* (1947); *Trece poemas* (1949); *El tiempo que destruye* (1951); *Escándulo y soledades* (1952); *Línea de la vida* (1955); *Examen de nuestra causa* (1956); *La penitencia y el mérito* (1957); *Propiedades de la magia* (1959); *La condición necesaria* (1960); *Elegías italianas* (1962); *Poemas elegidos* (1965); *Un brazo de Dios* (1966); *Envíos* (1967); *Casa de la mente* (1968); *Antología temática* (1969); *Valores diarios* (1970); *En la letra, ambigua selva* (1972); *Poesía de observación* (1973); *Quien habla no está muerto* (1975); *Galería personal* (1975); *Bestiario* (1976); *Obra poética I* (1977); *Prosas* (1977); *Árbol de la estirpe humana* (1978); *Obra poética II* (1978); *Obra poética III* (1980); *Homenaje a W. C. Williams* (1981); *Poemas* (1982); *Borradores* (1982); *Lírica de percepciones* (1983); *Páginas de A. G. seleccionadas por el autor* (1983); *Monodias* (1985); *Existenciales* (1986); *Noventa y nueve poemas* (1988)

BIBLIOGRAPHY: Vitale, I., "A. G., poeta de lo real," *Sin Nombre*, 5 (1975), 65–69; Torres Fierro, D., "A. G.: Repaso a una obsesión," *Plural*, 58 (1976), 48–51; Yurkievich, S., "A. G.: Fases de su creciente," *Hispam*, 10, 29 (Aug. 1981), 99–105; Borinsky, A., "Interlocución y aporía: notas a propósito de A. G. y Juan Gelman," *RI*, 49, 125 (Oct.–Dec. 1983), 879–87; Sucre, G., *La máscara, la transparencia: Ensayos sobre poesía hispanoamericana,* 2nd ed. (1985), 345–49; Pascoe, M. S., *La poesía de A. G.* (1986)

BEN A. HELLER

GLISSANT, Edouard

Martinican poet, novelist, and essayist, b. 21 Sept. 1928, Sainte-Marie

Though almost exclusively informed by the Caribbean island of Martinique, G.'s oeuvre extends its relevance far beyond the region. Born in the highlands in the commune of Sainte-Marie, where Creole is the language of the people, G. attended Lycée Schoelcher in Fort-de-France, the capital of Martinique. His teacher was Aimé Césaire (q.v.), one of the founders of the Négritude (q.v.) movement. In 1946 G. went to the Sorbonne in Paris, where he first studied history, and later philosophy, in addition to ethnology. He befriended many African and Caribbean intellectuals, among them his compatriot Frantz Fanon (1927–1962), the famous psychiatrist and political activist for decolonization. Following his formal studies, G. worked as an editor and wrote critical reviews and essays on the arts and literature. His early poetry and essays reveal his preoccupations with the ambiguities of his personal situation as an Antillean immersed in French culture, a thematic strand that weaves through his work. In 1956 he also published a long epic poem, *Les Indes* (the Indies), which retraces Columbus's voyage to America and poses questions on the destinies of the New World. Two years later, G. published his first novel, *La Lézarde* (1956; *The Ripening,* 1959), an exploration of Martinican time and space, which was awarded, not without controversy, the prestigious Renaudot Prize. During the 1950s, G. turned to politics and, together with other writers and intellectuals, founded a political group, the Front Antillo-Guyanais, which, among other things, called for the decolonization of the French overseas departments. Because of his political activities, G. was kept under virtual house arrest, and the Front was banned in 1961. G. resumed his creative work, published a play, *Monsieur Toussaint* (1961; *Monsieur Toussaint,* 1981), dealing with the tragedy of Toussaint Louverture, the leader of Haitian independence, and finished his second novel, *Le Quatrième siècle* (1964; the fourth century), which retraces, through chronologically disrupted sequences, the destinies of two families, the Longoués, the fugitive slaves, and the Belouses, the assimilable plantation slaves, whose descendants reappear in virtually all of G.'s novels. Permitted to return to Martinique in 1967, G. founded his own Institut Martiniquais d'Études, which offered educational programs as well as sponsored re-search and other cultural activities relevant to Martinican culture. In 1971 G. founded a journal, *Acoma,* dedicated to the study of Martinican society and culture. In 1975 he published his third novel, *Malemort* (foul death), which evokes, in moods of wry humor and a poignant sense of helplessness, scenes of the early days of slavery and contemporary Martinique, corrupt and culturally inauthentic. In 1980 G. returned to Paris to assume editorship of UNESCO publications. While in Paris G. published two novels and a collection of essays and poetry each. In 1988 he accepted a distinguished lectureship position at Louisiana State University. In 1989 G. published another collection of essays, *La Poétique de la relation* (cross-cultural poetics), which pursues his favorite topics of Europocentric cultural imperialism and the dynamics and dilemmas of intercultural relations.

Informed by Martinique and its people, G.'s oeuvre is reaching out to articulate global concerns and intone themes that deal with universal issues. His first novels focus primarily on a search for Martinican identity that necessitates the recovery of the lost past of the Afro-Caribbean, who, traumatized by slavery, the plantation system, and colonization in the past, is today victim of cultural assimilation and socioeconomic exploitation. To recover the authentic past, ignored or distorted by European historiography, G. probes folkloric materials, stories, and legends, which are, for G., the depositories of the untapped collective unconscious. G. is particularly interested in the rehabilitation of the maroon, the fugitive slave, the first authentic hero. This search for the past becomes an urgency as the present-day Martinicans have lost their identity under the impact of urbanization and tourism promoted by metropolitan interests.

G.'s later works, particularly the novel *Mahagony* (1987; Mahogany) and two collections of essays, *Le discours antillais* (1981; *Caribbean Discourse,* 1989) and *La Poétique de la relation,* reject the notion of cultural hierarchies and stress the urgent need to recognize the coexistence of different cultures. G.'s arguments are complex, predicated on the experience of the Afro-Caribbean who has suffered a series of discontinuities. Thus, the texture of G.'s writing is challenging to the reader who expects causality and chronology as the mainstays of writing. G.'s narratives are polymorphic, sometimes with changing perspectives and contrasting stylistic devices, including peculiar Creole speech patterns. Although G. has commented on many aspects of contemporary culture, his starting point is almost invariably his native land, the little island of Martinique, which can be seen as a microcosm in the image of the macrocosm. G. calls for the acceptance of what is called *créolité,* a cultural state that recognizes the inevitable intercontamination of cultures and languages. With the passing of Négritude as a viable cultural notion, G.'s ideas have given rise to a new generation of writers and intellectuals who call themselves Créolistes. The recognition of G. as perhaps the most visible intellectual figure in the francophone Caribbean and beyond is incontestable.

FURTHER WORKS: *Un champs d'îles* (1953); *La terre inquiète* (1955); *Soleil de la conscience* (1956); *Le sel noir* (1960); *L'intention poétique* (1969); *La case du commandeur* (1981); *Pays rêvé, pays réel* (1985)

BIBLIOGRAPHY: Boisdeffre, P. de, "L'épopée d'E. G.," *Une anthologie vivante de la littérature d'aujourd'hui* (1966), 745–49; Silenieks, J., "Deux pièces antillaises: du témoignage local vers une tragédie moderne," *KRQ,* 15, 3 (1968), 245–54; Case, F. I., "The Novels of E. G.," *BlackI* (1973), 3–12; Baudot, A., "D'un pays (re)possédé," *EF* (1974), 359–73; Roget, W., "The Image of Africa in the Writings of E. G.," *CLAJ* (1978), 390–99; Ormerod, B., "Discourse and Dispossession: E. G.'s Image of Contemporary Martinique," *CarQ,* 27, 4 (Dec. 1981), 1–12; Radford, D., *E. G.* (1982); special G. issue, *CARE* (1983); Cailler, B., *Conquérants de la nuit nue: E. G. et l'H(h)istorie antillaise* (1988); special G. Issue, *WLT,* 63, 4 (Autumn 1989)

JURIS SILENIEKS

GODBOUT, Jacques
Canadian novelist, screenwriter, and poet (writing in French), b. 27 Nov. 1933, Montreal

After receiving a classical education with the Jesuits, G. pursued his studies at the University of Montreal, where he received his B.A. in 1953 and his M.A. in 1954. He then taught in Addis Ababa for three years. Upon his return to Canada, he worked in film for the government.

G.'s novels and films reflect the political events and important changes taking place in Quebec during the last three decades and explore the role of the individual, especially the writer, within this culture and, beyond the borders of Quebec, within the North American context, English Canadian and American as well. Various ways are explored to achieve happiness within a clearly defined cultural context. One's identity is often best defined, according to G., through the act of writing.

G.'s literary career began with the publication of several collections of poems: *Carton pâte* (1956; papier-mâché), *Les pavés secs* (1958; dry paving stones), and *C'est la chaude loi des hommes* (1960; it is the hot law of men). After this, his principal effort turned to the novel and to film. *L'aquarium* (1962; the aquarium) is set in Ethiopia during the monsoon season and explores the lives and relationships of a group of foreigners waiting for the moment of change when they will leave the country. During this time, revolution is brewing in the land. The parallels to Quebec society are obvious: the long period of isolation, the otherness of the principal characters, outsiders in this land, waiting for change to come, yet often sinking into personal trivialities, uninterested for the most part in becoming involved in the political changes, some preferring simply to take the money and run. In *Le couteau sur la table* (1965; *Knife on the Table,* 1968) the action is closer to home, in both English- and French-speaking Canada, between a francophone hero and his anglophone significant other, Patricia, each one eventually acquiring a homolingual consort. The new anglophone couple fails; the francophone couple fares better, but the ties are cruelly broken when Madeleine dies in a motorcycle accident. The hero will then direct his energies to dealing with Patricia with the knife on the table. Although the hero is from a modest background and is clearly interested in the wealth and power associated with the English-speaking world, it is with his own people, committed to transforming their world into a better one, that he will group; however, though the Anglo world and Patricia are rejected, the knife remains on the table, still not used against her.

G.'s third novel, *Salut Galarneau!* (1967; *Hail Galarneau!,* 1970), was a resounding success. The hero, François Galarneau, tricked into getting married and, after freeing himself from his marital prison, betrayed by his new woman friend Marise, who prefers his brother to him, withdraws from the world, walling himself up and writing in order to better understand himself and to recover from his pain. His freedom, his being, will be achieved and found through this creativity. The work is sprinkled throughout with the realities of everyday Quebec, where the popular language is riddled with Anglicisms, where the ordinary young man dreams of making it in the North American world of commercial enterprise—François dreams of becoming the King of the Hot Dog through a chain of stands he will create. François's mother leaves for the U.S., as did so many of her compatriots in the last century and a half, and François will also head in that direction. Not only does G.'s language reflect contemporary middle-class usage, but the story line in part reflects social realities, where from a period of licking his wounds the hero will make his way, through his creativity, in the new world, as a new man. G. continued to

explore some of these interests in his next novels and films: *Kid Sentiment* (1967; title in English), a film about francophone youths in an anglophone world; the film *IXE-13* (1971; IXE-13); the novels *D'amour, P.Q.* (1972; Thomas d'Amour, P.Q.), which redirects our attention to involvement in Quebec's political world, and *L'île au dragon* (1976; *Dragon Island,* 1978), with its capitalist American invader; the film *Distortions* (1981; distortions), which explores the world of Africans and their relationships to the international press; and *Comme en Californie* (1983; as in California), presenting the ''new age'' and its influence on Quebec.

Une histoire américaine (1986; *An American Story,* 1988) finds its hero, Gregory Francoeur, spending time to begin his life anew in the new center of the universe, the Bay Area, exploring, as a university researcher, studying happiness, but becoming an unwilling participant in a detective thriller, and seeking refuge, after his arrest, in the writing of his story. As a native outsider in the North American experience, associated with other ''outsiders,'' the protagonist learns to evaluate himself through the ties that bind him to North America in general, and to Quebec in particular. The film *Alias Will James* (1988; title in English) tells of the experience of Ernest Dufault, a Quebecer who transformed himself into a writer, Will James, of stories about cowboys and who succeeded in passing himself off as one of them, with an ''Indian'' accent. G. explores the attractions of the U.S. for the residents of Quebec.

In addition to his creative works, G. is important for having founded and being president (1977–1978) of the Union of Quebec Writers. He has been the recipient of numerous awards, both from Canadian and French groups, and a number of his works have been published in France.

FURTHER WORKS: *La grande muraille de Chine* (1969); *Le réformiste. Textes tranquilles* (1975); *Les têtes à Papineau* (1981); *Le murmure marchand 1976–1984* (1984); *Souvenir shop. Poèmes et proses* (1984)

BIBLIOGRAPHY: Bellemare, Y., *J. G. romancier* (1984); Lemire, M., et al., *Dictionnaire des œuvres littéraires du Québec* (1982), Vol. 3, passim; (1984), Vol. 4, passim; (1987), Vol. 5, passim; Cagnon, M., *The French Novel of Quebec* (1986), 74–84; Coulombe, M., and M. Jean, *Le dictionnaire du cinéma québécois* (1988), 203–4; Hamel, R., et al., *Dictionnaire des auteurs de langue française en Amérique du Nord* (1989), 612–14

PAUL BARRETTE

GOLDEMBERG, Isaac

Peruvian novelist and poet, b. 15 Nov. 1945,
Chepén

G., born in the small town of Chepén to a Jewish
father and a European-Quechua mother, moved in
1953 to Lima, where, as he has said, "my father
[was] waiting for me and 5,700 years of Judaism
rain[ed] on my head." His crisis of identity as
Jew, Peruvian-European, and Quechua began in
earnest at this point; he entered a school for Jewish
boys and was shocked to see Hebrew, which he
could not read and did not speak, written on the
board. He began to become involved in the activities of the Jewish colony in Lima and to identify
more and more with his Jewish roots. G. places
his initiation as a writer in 1957, when he moved
to a new house with his father and discovered in
the library there, left by the former tenant who
was a friend of his father's, European and North
American literature, and especially the works of
Sholem Aleichem (pseud. of Solomon Rabino-
witz, 1859–1916).

G. began to write in 1958 and was heavily
influenced by the work of two Peruvian authors:
César Vallejo and Ciro Alegría (qq.v.). The poetry
of Vallejo influenced G. because it struck in him
sympathetic chords by its emphasis on family and
identity; and the novel *El mundo es ancho y ajeno*
(1941; *Broad and Alien Is the World,* 1941) by
Alegría, which dealt with the Indian experience,
was important to him because of the analogies
between the Indian and Jewish predicaments in a
European world. G. traveled to Israel and to Spain
between 1962 and 1964, returning to Peru at the
death of his father. After moving to New York,
he pursued university studies and published his
first book of poems, *Tiempo de silencio* (1970;
time of silence). He continues to live in New
York, where he is the codirector of the Latin
American Writers' Institute at City College and of
the Latin American Book Fair. He is currently
working on an anthology of Latin American Jewish writers and on a novel, tentatively titled "En
la puerta del horno" (in the door of the oven [on
the brink]), which concerns Chepén but will eschew concentration on Jewish thematics.

G. first came to critical attention in a rather
unusual manner: with the publication of his first
novel in an English translation. The novel, *La vida
a plazos de don Jacobo Lerner* (1980; first pub.
in English as *The Fragmented Life of Don Jacobo
Lerner,* 1976), received critical acclaim for its
complex narrative, which both tragically and comically portrays the career of its protagonist, a man
alienated not only from his adopted country of
Peru but also from the Ashkenazi Jewish immigrant community of which he originally formed

an active part. The ironic collage of entries from
the cultural organ of that community, *Alma hebrea*
(Hebrew soul), as well as the *Citizen Kane*-like
reminiscences and evaluations of the late Jacobo
by his erstwhile friends, acquaintances, relatives,
and lovers, realize, as commentators such as Judith
M. Schneider have noted, a powerful textual representation of the absence of the immigrant Jew
from participation in Peruvian society.

G. has worked both in narrative and poetry,
publishing an early collection of poems, *De Chepén a La Habana* (1973; from Chepén to Havana),
which combines his work and pieces by Cuban
exile poet José Kozer (b. 1940). Many of G.'s
poems from the 1973 collection have appeared in
revised form in *Hombre de paso/Just Passing
Through* (1981), in which the poems are published
with parallel translations. The poems of *Hombre
de paso* deal with themes similar to those in the
fiction of G.: the alienation experienced by the
ethnic outsider, the specific concerns of growing
up Jewish, and the general existential position of
modern consciousness. But the poems, while keenly
aware of the difficult position of Jews in a Chris-
tianized society, avoid extreme militant stances
that would preclude the integration of ethnic experiences into larger cultural participation. The
search for meaning in one's past experiences is
strongly emphasized.

G. has more recently published a novel, *Tiempo
al tiempo* (1984; *Play by Play,* 1985), which
continues his probing of the Jewish experience in
Peru, in a manner even more uncompromising
than in his first work of fiction. One critic has
pointed out that the protagonist Marcos is the
"spiritual son" of Jacobo in the first novel and
thus represents what Efraín (the illegitimate, mad
son of Jacobo) might have become had he lived.
The novel departs from the moment of the circumcision of Marcos, which metaphorically encapsu-
lates his initiation into Jewish society as well as
his alienation from the larger Peruvian culture.
The story of Marcos is told by using parallel
narrative techniques, which include the treatment
of his life story as a soccer game narrated by a
rather frantic sportscaster. Within the soccer sections, an interesting technique of fragmented contrapuntal narrative offers commentary on the narration by the sportscaster: a "newsreel" or ticker
tape, generally consisting of pieces about the
founding of Israel or about biblical history, runs
along the bottom of the page and appears to have
allusive connections with the larger narration.

G. is consistently a writer unwilling to adhere
exclusively either to more traditional narrative
technique or to stylistic forms developed in his
first novel. His poetry is sometimes accessible and
sometimes strikingly private. His voice, both in

poetry and in fiction, is an important part of the Latin American literary experience, since it has helped to foreground the largely neglected consciousness of marginalized groups such as the Jews of Peru.

FURTHER WORK: *La vida a contado* (1992)

BIBLIOGRAPHY: Goldman, M., on *Hombre de paso/Just Passing Through, LALR,* 11, 22 (Spring–Summer 1983), 114–16; Lindstrom, N., on *Hombre de paso / Just Passing Through, RIB,* 49 (1983), 659–60; Roses, L., "El lector como jurado: el monólogo interior en *La vida a plazos de don Jacobo Lerner,*" *DLit,* 2, 1 (1984), 225–32; Tittler, J., *Narrative Irony in the Contemporary Spanish-American Novel* (1984), 172–85; Goldemberg, I., "Crónicas / genealogías / cronologías," *Hispam,* 14, 42 (Dec. 1985), 73–78; Stavans, I., "Judaísmo y letras latinoamericanas: entrevista a I. G.," *Folio,* 17 (1987), 141–50; Schneider, J. M., "Cultural Meanings in I. G.'s Fiction," *Folio,* 17 (1987), 128–40; Rosser, H. L., "Being and Time in *La vida a plazos de don Jacobo Lerner,*" *Chasqui,* 17, 1 (May 1988), 43–49; Gazarian-Gautier, M.-L., *Interviews with Latin American Writers* (1989), 129–54; Mosier, P., in Kancllós, N., ed., *Biographical Dictionary of Hispanic Literature in the United States: The Literature of Puerto Ricans, Cuban Americans, and Other Hispanic Writers* (1989), 115–21; Marowski, D. G., and R. Matuz, eds., *Contemporary Literary Criticism* (1989), 163–69; Ryan, B., ed., *Hispanic Writers: A Selection of Sketches from Contemporary Authors* (1991), 227–28

KENNETH E. HALL

GOMRINGER, Eugen

Swiss poet (writing in German), b. 20 Jan. 1925, Cachuela Esperanza, Bolivia

G. is considered to be the founder of concrete poetry. He grew up with his grandparents in Switzerland and studied art history and economics in Bern and in Rome between 1946 and 1950. He is a graphic designer by profession. In 1952 he was the cofounder of the magazine *Spirale,* which was devoted to concrete art. From 1954 to 1958 he served as secretary to the artist Max Bill, who was the director of the Hochschule für Gestaltung in Ulm, Germany. In 1959 he founded his own short-lived publishing house. Between 1962 and 1967 hc was the business manager for the Schweizer Werkbund in Zurich. Between 1967 and 1985 he was the artistic advisor to the Rosenthal concern. Since 1976 he has served as a professor for aes-

thetic theory at the Art Academy in Düsseldorf. He now lives in Rehau-Wurlitz in Germany.

G. published his first poems in 1953 in *Spirale* and thus became the initiator of the concrete movement, whose influence was felt throughout Europe and the U.S., but particularly in Germany and Austria, where G. found many admirers. He terms his poetry concrete because it ignores conventional syntax, description, and metaphor and instead places individual words in a visual arrangement on the page. The poem is thus not "about" something but forms its own concrete reality using words as the building blocks. The poem becomes a real object and not an abstraction. G. calls these concrete poems "constellations," since meaning arises through the spacial relationships the words form with each other, as groups of stars may tend to form pictures in the sky.

G.'s best-known books are *das stundenbuch* (1965; *The Book of Hours and Constellations,* 1968) and *worte sind schatten: die konstellationen 1951–1968* (1969; words are shadows: the constellations 1951–1968). From these works we can discern that his poems fall into four distinct categories: purely visual constellations, visual-audio constellations that can also be read aloud, constellations in languages other than German, and constellations in book form, which develop a sequence of images over several pages, much like the individual frames of a film. In each of these categories a minimum of language is used, and there are usually a great number of combinations and permutations. As an example we can take his perhaps most famous poem "schweigen" (1954; silence). The word "schweigen" is printed fourteen times to form a rectangle on the page—there is an empty hole in the middle, which is the "silence" of the poem.

G. also wrote theoretical tracts to explain his poetry and to argue for its efficacy. The most important are *manifeste und darstellungen der konkreten poesie 1954–1966* (1966; manifestos and representations of concrete poetry 1954–1966) and *poesie als mittel der umweltgestaltung* (1969; poetry as a means for structuring the environment). Here he argues that the modern technological world needs a new, simple, direct, and universal language devoid of any irrationality. Poetry should help develop models for this new language and test them on global readers. If the author is successful, the readers should be able to understand immediately the models presented. Through this process readers can thus gain a heightened relationship to the objects of the real world, which are reflected in the language of this new poetry.

G.'s influence was strong, but short-lived. He helped a postwar generation in German-speaking countries question and examine the linguistic medium, and thereby initiated a whole range of linguistic experimentation. After about 1972, interest in this movement waned, and G. ceased writing poetry; he turned instead to writing monographs on artists and collaborating on art books. Critics began to realize that G.'s approach was too simplistic. His poems only required his readers to project their own knowledge onto the poem, and thus his poetry was unable to provide the hoped-for "new" information. In addition, the lack of any social or political parameters tended to confirm the status quo rather than suggest change.

FURTHER WORKS: *konstellationen* (1953); *5 mal 1 konstellation* (1960); *33 konstellationen* (1960); *die konstellationen* (1963); *15 konstellationen* (1965); *einsam gemeinsam* (1971); *lieb* (1971); *der pfeil* (1972); *1970–1972* (1973); *Richard Paul Lohse* (1973); *konkretes von Anton Stankowski* (1974); *wie weiß ist wissen die weisen* (1975); *konstellationen, ideogramme, studenbuch* (1977); *kein fehler im system* (1978); *Distanzsignale* (1980); *Gucken* (1980); *Identitäten* (1981); *Himmel, erde, frankenland* (1981); *Gewebte bilder* (1984); *wir verschweben—wir verschwinden* (1985); *Helle räume* (1987); *Inversion & öffnung* (1988); *Zur sache der konkreten* (1988)

BIBLIOGRAPHY: Bornscheuer, L., "E. G.s 'Konstellationen': konkrete Poesie als universale Sprachgestaltung unserer Zeit," *DU*, 1 (1970), 59–78; Schnauber, C., ed., *Deine Träume—mein Gedicht: E. G. und die Konkrete Poesie* (1980); Demetz, P., "E. G. und die Entwicklung der konkreten Poesie," in Weissenberger, K., ed., *Die deutsche Lyrik 1945–1975* (1981), 277–86; Zeller, M., *Gedichte haben Zeit. Aufriß einer zeitgenössischen Poetik* (1982), 47–85; Solt, M. E., "Charles Sanders Pierce and E. G.: The Concrete Poem As Sign," *PoT*, 3, 3 (Summer 1982), 197–209

ROBERT ACKER

GONÇALVES, Olga

Portuguese novelist, short-story writer, and poet, b. 12 Apr. 1929, Luanda, Angola

G.'s fiction has vibrantly documented the social changes wrought on Portuguese life during the post-1974 revolutionary period. C. spent her childhood in Angola. She later studied at King's College, London, and has worked as an English teacher. Although G.'s literary career began with lyric poetry in the 1960s, which she continues to write, she has distinguished herself as a novelist.

G.'s fiction may have been inspired by the testimonial literature form. It shows direct influence of the "new novel's" concern with detail. Using what appears to be the interview format, her characters narrate their personal situations and beliefs about the events of the revolution and beyond.

In *A floresta em Bremerhaven* (1975; the forest in Bremerhaven), awarded the Ricardo Malheiros Prize of the Lisbon Academy of Sciences (1975), the postrevolutionary turmoil is viewed through the eyes, ideas, and reactions of a family of Portuguese immigrants to Germany recently returned home. Their experiences abroad had opened their mind to concepts of freedom of expression and justice, neither of which they had enjoyed in dictatorial Portugal. They returned with money to purchase the land where they once had been sharecroppers and to open a guest house on the property. The "author" is present at the guest house and becomes a "sounding board" for these newborn Portuguese citizens.

Este verão o emigrante là-bas (1980; the emigrants down home this summer) presents the Portuguese immigrants to France who had remained in Paris and return *là-bas* (down there, that is, Portugal) only during their August vacations. G.'s characters offer testimonies about their clandestine emigration and life in France. The "interviews" make clear that these people had traveled from one set of repressions in Portugal (social abuse, rural poverty) to another set in France (discrimination based on "race," urban poverty). Their attempts to maintain Portuguese heritage are stymied. The key words of daily existence only have significance for them in French. The volume has a poetic, impressionistic leitmotiv: the immigrants' difficulties are compared to the hardships of Claude Monet's life.

G.'s *Ora esguardae* (1982; hark ye, now!) is a mural of Portuguese life of the early 1980s. She invokes the medieval chronicler Fernão Lopes (ca. 1380–ca. 1460) through the voices and complaints of the Portuguese *povo*, the common people, who had defiantly supported the nation's existence since medieval times. Linguistic subversion (present in the earlier works) assumes greater importance here. For example, the *retornados*, returnees from the old Portuguese African colonies, have brought with them a new register of speech; the political opening has given new connotations to old words; and the now popular Brazilian soap operas reveal new social and linguistic possibilities. This novel possesses an optimistic tone about Portugal's future. G. suggests that the young postrevolutionary generation will "cleanse" the language of its past linguistic and cultural dilemmas.

G.'s fiction has also expressed a special interest in women's situations. Her *Mandei-lhe uma boca* (1978; smarty-pants) describes the change taking place in the cultural situation of Portuguese teen-agers. Sara, the protagonist, is revisited, eight years later, in *Sara* (1986; Sara), upon obtaining her M.A. in philosophy. She is still confronting the changes in Portuguese women's lives. G.'s *Armandina e Luciano, o traficante de canários* (1988; Armandina e Luciano, the "canary" traf-ficker) is a striking stream-of-consciousness mono-logue-testimonial novel in which the voice belongs to a young ex-prostitute (often relapsing), Carla Cristina. Carla narrates her own and her family's background in the slums around Lisbon. She is an astute observer of the Lisbon underground—pimps, thieves, smugglers, drug traffickers, and bizarre bohemian spirits—about whom she can casually but earnestly reveal positive qualities. She views the woman's situation, racism, sexual perversion, abuse, and even incest without resentment. Once again, the literary level of the novel invokes the traditional literary concern of the Iberian peninsula with the *povo,* the people, and the picaresque.

G.'s fiction has earned for her the title of por-traitist of the sociocultural reality of today's Por-tugal, in particular the urban existence of Lisbon.

FURTHER WORKS: *Movimento* (1972); *25 compo-sições e 11 provas de artista* (1973); *Só de amor* (1975); *Três poetas* (1981); *Caixa inglesa* (1983); *O livro de Olotolilisobi* (1983); *Rudolfo* (1985); *Contar de subversão* (1990)

BIBLIOGRAPHY: Stern, I., on *Este verão o emi-grante là-bas, WLT,* 53, 4 (Autumn 1979), 659; Stern, I., "Redefining Identity: Uses of Language in Recent Portuguese Fiction," in Nunes, M. L., ed., *Identity in Portuguese and Brazilian Litera-ture* (1982), 34–42

IRWIN STERN

GORAN, Abdulla

(born Abdulla Sulayman) Kurdish poet and essay-ist, b. Sept. 1904, Halabja, Ottoman Empire (now Iraq); d. 18 Nov. 1962, Sulaimaniya, Iraq

G. is the outstanding Kurdish poet of the 20th c. He combined the rich heritage of classical and folk poetry with the spirit and techniques of mod-ern lyricism to endow Kurdish poetry with new forms and expanded subject matter. His creative powers evolved continuously from his earliest poems of the 1920s to his mature work of the 1950s as his knowledge of Kurdish society, especially the hard existence and the aspirations of ordinary peo-ple, deepened. At first, his poems were suffused with the romantic atmosphere and motifs charac-teristic of traditional and of much contemporary Kurdish verse, but after World War II his poetic

vision was, in a sense, socialized, and he came to be recognized as one of the founders of Kurdish realism. Yet, for him, the boundaries between romanticism and realism were never rigid.

G. was born in the city of Halabja, in present-day northeastern Iraq, the son of a petty function-ary. After attending the pedagogical institute at Kirkuk, he taught elementary school in his native city between 1925 and 1937. During this period he studied foreign languages and read widely in modern Turkish and western European literatures, explorations that profoundly influenced his later literary work and philosophical outlook. In the latter 1930s, while employed in the Iraqi ministry of communications, he found time at last to work systematically at his poetic craft. But he also accepted his responsibility as an artist to combat social injustice, and during the next two decades he joined reformers in their efforts to bring about fundamental political and economic change. In the early 1950s he achieved prominence as the editor of *Jin,* a weekly, which he transformed from a purely cultural journal into a militant voice of the poor and dispossessed of Kurdish society. But he paid a heavy price for his commitment to such causes: He was dismissed from his editorship and was repeatedly arrested and jailed. The revolution that overthrew the Iraqi monarchy in 1958 freed him from prison, and until his death he continued to write poetry that reflected undiminished support for long-cherished social causes.

As a conscious poetic craftsman G. set for himself the task of revealing the inherent artistic and expressive capabilities of the Kurdish lan-guage. In the process he brought a new vigor and freshness to Kurdish poetry by introducing the prose poem, blank verse, and a syllabic rhythm close to the rhythm of Kurdish folk poetry. In "Awati duri" (1950; distant longing), for ex-ample, he abandoned the traditional *aruz* or quan-titative meter altogether, turning instead to a pros-ody that allowed him to vary the number of syllables in each line and to introduce new rhyme schemes. He also experimented with a variety of forms. He was fond of verse dramas, which seemed espe-cially suited to his lyrical temperament. All his poetry is written in a remarkably pure, flowing language, and, because of its simple, easy rhythms, many pieces were put to music.

G.'s early poetry, of the 1920s and 1930s, was unabashedly romantic and brought him recognition as the head of the romantic current in Kurdish poetry. His favorite themes were nature and love. Two longer poems—"Gesht le Hewraman" (jour-ney to Hewraman) and "Gesht le Keredag" (jour-ney to Keredag), both of which appeared in the collection *Behesht u yadgar* (1950; paradise and remembrance)—reveal his skill as a painter of native landscapes. In the former tableaux of nature predominate, whereas the latter abounds in descriptions of the rites and traditions of everyday life, thereby suggesting his growing predilection for realistic detail. At the center of his love poetry is woman, portrayed as the source of all that was beautiful and good. But even his most idyllic poetry showed traces of the later, predominant realism, for he curbed the hyperbole of classical Kurdish verse and sought to move the reader by genuineness and depth of feeling. In his "romantic period" G. was animated by strong ethnic feelings. In "Demi raperine" (1943; the voice awakens), for example, he expressed his ardent love of country (Kurdistan) and his yearning for its liberation, and in "Derwêsh Ebdulla" (1950; Dervish Abdulla) he urged the famous Kurdish balladeer to assuage his melancholy by singing pure Kurdish melodies.

The romantic element was rarely absent from G.'s later, realistic poetry. In the lament "Awabunek" (1960; sunset), which he composed on the death of the Kurdish literary scholar Rafik Hilmi (dates n.a.), he interweaves the sorrow of immediate loss with the hope that Hilmi's "star in the heavens" will never cease to inspire Kurdish patriots. More decidedly realistic, despite their preoccupation with romantic love, were G.'s dramas in verse, a new genre in Kurdish literature, which matured between the 1920s and 1940s. They gave him freedom to express his growing civic sense by allowing him to confront contemporary social issues more directly than the traditional genres. Perhaps the most popular of these dramas was "Guli hiwênawi" (1950; the bloody rose), the story of tragic love in an unjust world, which became a modern Kurdish classic. An equally powerful piece, "Bûkêki nakam" (1950; an unhappy bride), emphasizes social themes as two lovers from different classes try to overcome deeply rooted family prejudices.

G. was an accomplished prose writer and translator. He wrote numerous sketches on a variety of themes, and in 1953 he published *Helbijarde* (selections), a volume of his translations of short stories by English and French writers. He was also a prolific essayist. Among his passions was the creation of a single Kurdish literary language, which, he was certain, would enable writers to express the true essence of the Kurdish genius and way of life. He thought that the two main dialects—Kûrmanjî, used in Turkey, Syria, Iran, and northwest Iraq, and Sorânî, the literary language of the Kurds of Iraq, which G. himself used—were gradually coming together, and he railed against "extremists" who would interfere with the process by removing all Arabic and Persian elements and replacing them with "dead" words and "false" neologisms.

G.'s innovative use of language and meter, his introduction of new themes, and his harmonious blending of form and subject, especially in his social poetry, constitute a watershed in the development of modern Kurdish poetry. The generation that followed him no longer composed in accordance with the classical canon and continued to assimilate the experience of everyday life and to seek new means of expression. The evaluation of G.'s work has been aided by the appearance of the first critical edition of his poetry by Muhammadi Mela Karim (dates n.a.), *Dîwanî Goran* (1980; collected poems of G.), which includes G.'s translations from Persian, Turkish, English, and Arabic poetry. The same editor has promised similar volumes of G.'s prose, which is not as well known as his poetry, and of critical articles about him.

FURTHER WORKS: *Firmêsk u hûner* (1950); *Sirûsht u derûn* (1968); *Lawuk u peyman* (1969)

KEITH HITCHINS

GOROSTIZA, José

Mexican poet, b. 10 Nov. 1901, Villahermosa (Tabasco); d. 16 Mar. 1973, Mexico City

G., a member of the Mexican Academy of the Language and winner of the 1968 National Literary Prize, came from a family that had strong ties to literature. One of his ancestors was the dramatist Manuel Eduardo de Gorostiza (1789–1851), author of the well-known play *Contigo, pan y cebolla* (1833; bread and onions with you). G.'s brother Celestino (1904–1967) also earned recognition as a dramatist, with several plays to his credit, among them the highly acclaimed *El color de nuestra piel* (1952; the color of our skin). G. spent much of his life in the Mexican diplomatic service. These assignments took him to various locales around the world, including London, Copenhagen, Rome, Guatemala, Havana, Bogotá, Rio de Janeiro, Florence, Paris, Holland, and Greece. In addition to assignments abroad, he also held numerous government posts at home, and in 1964 he was named minister of foreign affairs.

G. belonged to an influential generation of vanguard writers who contributed regularly to the seminal Mexican literary magazine *Contemporáneos* (1928–1931). International in its scope, this review published numerous translations of contemporary poets such as T. S. Eliot (q.v.). Among the most prominent members of the *contemporáneos* group were Xavier Villaurrutia, Carlos Pellicer, Jaime Torres Bodet, Salvador Novo (qq.v.), Bernardo Ortiz de Montellano (1899–1949), and Gilberto Owen (1905–1952). Inspired by European and North American models, they maintained a cosmopolitan attitude toward literature and fostered universal themes rather than purely regional or national ones in their writings.

As a poet G. produced only two books. His initial volume, *Canciones para cantar en las barcas* (1925; boat songs), was characterized by an abundance of sea imagery and a fascination with traditional verse patterns of Spanish popular poetry as well as a nonnative form, the haiku. His renowned masterpiece, *Muerte sin fin* (1939; *Death without End*, 1969), has been called one of the most accomplished extended poems in 20th-c. Spanish American literature. Highly intellectual in content, it is a philosophical composition dealing with the search for meaning in life. The poem's origins can be traced to G.'s reading of metaphysical poetry while living in London in 1927. Both of these works were reissued, along with previously unpublished poems, in a single volume entitled *Poesía* (1964; poetry).

In *Muerte sin fin* the object of the poet's meditation, a glass of water, leads him to the realization that God molds the spirit just as a glass gives water an identifiable form. Despite this discovery the poet wrestles with doubt concerning the existence of the eternal and expresses his existential anguish over the eventual dissolution of form into nothingness. *Muerte sin fin* is a quest for permanence, illustrating the conflict between order and chaos, form and substance, the intellect and irrationality. In its focus on death it is at once universal yet firmly rooted in the Mexican tradition.

Mexican vanguard writers in the 1920s and 1930s were typically linked to either the *estridentistas* (those inspired by Italian futurism and Spanish ultraism) or the *contemporáneos* (who, much like the *modernistas* before them, avoided social issues in order to focus on aesthetic matters). Rejecting nationalistic themes and eschewing politically engaged poetry, the *contemporáneos* concerned themselves instead with archetypal themes and the subconscious. Theirs was an avant-garde poetry intended for a select audience rather than the common reader. G. and the other *contemporáneos* were somewhat aloof, favoring a more intellectual brand of poetry. In many respects they anticipated the achievement of Mexican Nobel laureate Octavio Paz (q.v.). G.'s verse deals with metaphysical concerns and treats such eternal subjects as love, life, solitude, death, and God. His lyricism is complex, profound, and transcendent. The significance of G. and the *contemporáneos* lies in their search for the universal, their efforts

to link Mexican writing to international literary currents, and their emphasis on the aesthetic function of art rather than simple didacticism.

FURTHER WORK: *Prosa* (1969)

BIBLIOGRAPHY: Paz, O., *Las peras del olmo* (1957), 105–14; Gómez-Gil, O., *Historia crítica de la literatura hispanoamericana* (1968), 532–35; Franco, J., *Spanish American Literature since Independence* (1973), 180–84; Franco, J., *An Introduction to Spanish-American Literature* (1975), 263–66; Rodríguez Monegal, E., ed., *The Borzoi Anthology of Latin American Literature* (1977), Vol. 2, 600–1; McMurray, G. R., *Spanish American Writing since 1941: A Critical Survey* (1987), 165–66; Pacheco, J. E., "J. G.," in Solé, C. A., ed., *Latin American Writers* (1989), Vol. 2, 923–31

MELVIN S. ARRINGTON, JR.

GRAU (DELGADO), Jacinto

Spanish dramatist and essayist, b. 1877, Barcelona; d. 14 Aug. 1958, Buenos Aires, Argentina

G. was a singular writer. Much of his life was spent out of Spain in other European countries and, after the Francoist victory in the Civil War, in Argentina. Although G. was a contemporary of the great figures of the Spanish Generations of 1898 and 1914, the so-called "problem of Spain"—its national identity and position in the world—is distant from the center of his production. He is a classicist in the sense that he sees life in terms of the basic paradigms of biblical, classical, and national myths. Hence his dramas center on figures such as the prodigal son, Judas, Pygmalion, and Don Juan. In another sense he is a modernist because he views true art, especially in the theater, as diametrically opposed to the "industrialized" art favored by the businessmen of culture (theater owners and impresarios), the vitiated public, and, most tellingly, the bourgeois capitalists who run the society.

As did José Ortega y Gasset (q.v.), G. disdained realist-naturalist art. Both considered the best art to be a creation rather than a recreation. In order to foster such art, G. favored constant artistic innovation and experiment. Repeating a not always justified commonplace among Spanish writers of the 19th and 20th cs., G. felt there was no literary-theatrical criticism worthy of the name in his country. So he followed the example of George Bernard Shaw (q.v.) and came to write prologues (albeit much shorter than Shaw's) for his dramatic works. Forty years before the widespread currency of the idea, G. proposed the function of the reader and critic was to use the work of art, be it famous or not, as the stimulus to a personal creation. The prefaces would presumably help to guide the process.

As might be expected, G. was by no means a popular dramatist in Spain. His prologues, dedications of his works, and record of successes show that G.'s own frame of reference was much more European than peninsular. His greatest work in this regard may have been *El señor Pigmalión* (1923; Mr. Pygmalion). Karel Čapek (q.v.), director of the Prague City Theater and artistic director of National Art Theater, heard about the play and eventually had it translated and staged in Prague. Čapek, as author of *R.U.R.* (1920), was most interested in G.'s robot play. For G.'s Pygmalion is a Spaniard who emigrated to the U.S. where he learned the necessary technology to create the humanoid machines. As opposed to Čapek's work-oriented robots, G.'s are actors for whom his Pygmalion has created a repertory of some two hundred farces. Although this Pygmalion's dream is to use his increasing knowledge of robotics to create a better world for humankind, one of his female creations is so attractive that Pygmalion wavers in his purpose and other men are driven nearly crazy with desire for her. In the end Pygmalion is killed by others of his robots in their bid for freedom from their creator.

While G. is not a very nationally oriented writer, his Spanish origins probably suggest a special place in his production for his two very different versions of the myth of Don Juan. While the titular protagonist of *Don Juan de Carillana* (1913; Don Juan of Carillana) is more of a man who has loved many women, the one of *El burlador que no se burla* (1930; the trickster who doesn't play) is defined by his incessant seductions and his murder of the men who object. This second Don Juan is credited with reinvigorating the myth by bringing it closer to its origins in Tirso de Molina's creation, and then adding new dimensions to it.

G. is a significant author whose work has become poorly known. In addition to the titles already mentioned, *El hijo pródigo* (1918; the prodigal son), for example, can be easily read today as a meditation on the responsibilities society has for the homeless. And in a number of plays he gives his own version of the Nietzschean Superman. As a European-class intellectual and artist G. was very familiar with the cultural life of his time. His works reveal this knowledge and add to the body of texts that must be known by anyone who wishes to understand the period during which G. was active.

FURTHER WORKS: *Trasuntos* (1899); *Las bodas de Camacho* (1903); *El tercer demonio* (1908); *Entre llamas* (1915); *Cervantes y Shakespeare* (1916); *El conde Alarcos* (1917); *En Ildaria* (1917); *Conseja galante, La redención de Judas, Sortilegio, Horas de vida* (1919); *El rey Candaules* (1920); *El mismo daño* (1921); *El caballero Varona* (1929); *La señora guapa* (1930); *Los tres locos del mundo* (1930); *Unamuno y la angustia de su tiempo* (1943); *Don Juan en el drama* (1944); *Teatro* (1954)

BIBLIOGRAPHY: Giulano, W., "A Spanish Version of the Authentic Don Juan," *Hispania*, 34 (1951), 256–60; Torrente Ballester, G., *Panorama de la literatura española contemporánea*, 3rd ed. (1965), 254–57, 597; Rodríguez Salcedo, G., "Introducción al teatro de J. G.," *Papeles de San Armadans*, 42 (1966), 13–42; Torrente Ballester, G., *Teatro español contemporáneo*, 2nd ed. (1968), 288–95; Navascues, M., *El teatro de J. G.: estudio de sus obras principales* (1975); Navascues, M., "Fantasy and the View of Destiny in the Theater of J. G.," *REH*, 11 (1977), 265–85; Dougherty, D., "The Semiosis of Stage Decor in J. G.'s *El señor de Pigmalión*," *Hispania*, 67, 3 (Sept. 1984), 351–57

STEPHEN MILLER

GRAY, Simon
English dramatist and novelist, b. 21 Oct. 1936, Hayling Island, Hampshire

G.'s best plays are about academia and, except for an early period of dramas featuring farcical situations with colloquial dialogue, his stagecraft reflects the life of British intellectuals through verbal wit, literary allusion, and complex character study. G. has spent most of his adult life in university settings. During World War II he was sent to Canada by his father, a first-generation Canadian. G. returned to England after the war, attended Westminster School in London, then returned to Canada in 1954 to study English at Dalhousie University. In 1958 he was lecturer at the University of Clermont-Ferrand, France, but began a second degree in English at Cambridge University in 1959. Among a close group of writers and satirists at Cambridge, G. published his first satirical novel, *Colmain* (1963), while there. In 1964 he moved to Canada a third time to lecture in English at the University of British Columbia. G. became a supervisor in English at Trinity College, Cambridge, until 1966, when he began as lecturer in English at Queen Mary College, London University, where he remained until 1985. Since the production of his first play in 1967, G.

has spent most of his time on the teaching faculty while writing for stage, film, and television.

Two plays, *Wise Child* (1968) and *Dutch Uncle* (1969), received some critical attention, often being compared to the comedies of Joe Orton (1933–1967), but *Butley* (1971) became G.'s first popular and critical success. Wit is central to the style of this play, its characters using idiosyncratic phrases, rhetorical questions, literary allusion, and pithy remarks about themselves and others. Butley, a university English teacher, shares an office and home with a man whose presence so perturbs Butley that he hazes and misleads him about his promotion. There is some enjoyment of the stage villain here, and of the way Butley treats people. The most distinctive aspect of character in this dark comedy involves the interest the protagonist has in keeping others at a distance and protecting himself from not fully realized terrors. Butley's personal problems occur within a professional and institutional context, a feature of the play that might account for its popularity. Butley is alone at the end, but his isolation is self-induced, since he has estranged everyone around him. Reality remains unpleasant, and Butley's attempts to achieve freedom from others through avoidance and verbal aggression results in a kind of self-imprisonment. Not simply a victim, Butley seems to become what he is through his own actions. Butley's failed attempts to extricate himself from his entanglements is a clear ironic reversal. This hints at Sophoclean tragedy; in fact, the classical unities of action, place, and time are almost fully obeyed, as the plot consists of a succession of characters who enter Butley's office, confront him, then leave. G.'s earlier emphasis on physical action and convolutions of plot are replaced in *Butley* by psychological character study and the power of language both to deny and deceive.

Part of G.'s box office appeal is doubtless drawn from the fortunate collaboration of Harold Pinter's (q.v.) stage direction and Alan Bates's acting in the leading roles for most of the major plays. *Otherwise Engaged* (1976) won both the New York Drama Critics Circle Award and the Evening Standard Award for best play. As in *Butley*, the protagonist, Simon Hench, shows brilliance in keeping his significant others at arms length through the use of critical humor, an agnostic type of questioning that undermines the intentions of his listeners, and a uniquely low-key emotionality. Only at the end, as in *Butley*, is there a realization of how destructive such denial can be. G. seems to leave his audiences with a disturbing sense of the helplessness of modern intentionality. No one is able to break through the barriers of Simon's material preoccupation and self-centered insouciance (while others plead with him for his attention,

Simon only wants to play *Parsifal* on his stereo). The adeptness of this isolating behavior is a characteristic quality of many of G.'s protagonists.

Quartermaine's Terms (1981), another play about academe, is rife with bright dialogue, topical allusion, and humor derived from confrontational language. However, unlike G.'s previous plays about university teachers, a deep sadness pervades this dark comedy, a feeling derived perhaps from the barely disguised loneliness of the characters. Quartermaine is a teacher of foreign students at a language school in Cambridge. He is taken for granted by the other teachers, who follow lives of not-so-quiet desperation. Failing marriages, vocational disappointments, and the realization of artistic mediocrity all appear to preoccupy the people around Quartermaine. Although he remains the only stable person in the play, he is taken advantage of perhaps because of his stability. In the end he is fired from the school, ostensibly for budgetary reasons, in fact because it is assumed he is incompetent. The play is unique for G. in that the feeling of pathos is overwhelming, the comedy of manners style being overcast by the sense of injustice and a sympathy for the protagonist.

The Common Pursuit (1984) and *Melon* (1987) both demonstrate G.'s ability to recreate the educated dialogue of the Oxbridge world, but also reveal a fatalistic note, as the characters gradually lose their ideals and self-confidence to become glib and mannered.

G. builds his dramas around a sense of isolation and noncommunication inherent in both professional and private life; his best plays evoke strong fears that seem to result from the demands and hidden agendas of close relationships. Although some of G.'s plots leave the protagonist with at least a partial perception of his life, notably *Butley* and *Quartermaine's Terms,* the overriding effect, even in these plays, is one of spiritual resignation and emotional surrender, if not despair. What saves these dramas as performance pieces is particularly clever dialogue used in familiar social and professional situations, and the thematic connection between the ambiguities of conversational language and the denial of true communication and connectedness.

FURTHER WORKS: *Simple People* (1965); *Little Portia* (1967); *Sleeping Dog* (1968); *A Comeback for Stark* (1969); *Spoiled* (1971); *The Idiot* (1972); *Two Sundays* (1976); *Plaintiffs and Defendants* (1976); *Dog Days* (1977); *The Rear Column* (1978); *Molly* (1978); *Man in a Side Car* (1978); *Pig in a Poke* (1979); *Close of Play* (1979); *Stage Struck* (1979); *Tartuffe* (1982); *Chapter 17* (1982); *An Unnatural Pursuit and Other Pieces* (1985); *After*

Pilkington (1987); *A Month in the Country* (1987); *How's That for Telling 'Em, Fat Lady* (1988); *Old Flames* (1990); *Hidden Laughter* (1991)

BIBLIOGRAPHY: Taylor, J. R., *The Second Wave* (1971), 169–71; Blaydes, S. B., "Literary Allusion As Satire in S. G.'s *Butley*," *MQ*, 18 (1977), 374–91; Hamilton, J., *The New Review*, 3 (1977), 39–46; Kerensky, O., *The New British Drama: Fourteen Playwrights since Osborne and Pinter* (1977), 132–44; Shaw, P., on *Otherwise Engaged, Commentary,* 65 (1978), 88–90; Jones, J. B., "The Wit and the Wardrobe: S. G.'s Tragic (?) Comedies," *WVUPP*, 25 (1979), 78–85; Shafer, Y., on *Quartermaine's Terms, TJ*, 34, 4 (Dec. 1982), 532; Gordon, G., "Person to Person," *The Spectator*, 14 July 1984, 33–34; Hodgson, M., on *The Common Pursuit, The Nation*, 243 (1986), 617

WILLIAM OVER

GROSSMAN, David
Israeli novelist, short-story writer, journalist, and dramatist, b. 25 Jan. 1954, Jerusalem

After studying philosophy and theater at Hebrew University, Jerusalem, G. quickly established himself as one of the leading innovators in the Israeli fiction of the 1980s. His first collection of stories, *Ratz* (1983; jogging), developed a plastic prose, adopting rhythms of thought waves and vernacular in stream-of-consciousness writing. Even here, as for example in the title story, the narrator enters extreme situations of stress, in this case, that of a runner attempting to transcend the limitations of the body and to carry on running. The rhythm, vocabulary, and syntax match up with the situation.

G.'s writing welds the political and personal. Both in his fictional and in his journalistic work, the personal situation meets the national, political point of crisis. *Hiyukh hagdiy* (1983; *The Smile of the Lamb*, 1990) is a fictional representation of life in the West Bank under Israeli occupation, a story told by the protagonists, Jews and Arabs, governors and governed, where the personal lives and conflicts of the characters intersect with the political nexus, creating a tapestry of mixed motives and surprising resolutions. *Hazman hatsahov* (1987; *Yellow Wind*, 1988) is the sort of reportage made familiar by Amos Oz (q.v.) in *Po vesham beerets yisrael* (1983; *In the Land of Israel*, 1983), a piece of "straight" reporting, based on interviews and impressions of the material and the situation. But whereas Oz deliberately contrived a multifaceted composite of different views, so as to offer the reader a notion of the complexity of

Israeli opinion across the political spectrum, G.'s material is worked to present a specific point of view, arguing the case against Israeli military presence and control and in favor of Arab self-determination. This is a prophecy of doom and a plea for disengagement. *Hiyukh hagdiy*, although an earlier work, can be seen as a fictional equivalent of the piece of reporting, deconstructing the coherent, assured writing set up in the journalistic account, mixing up the motives, casting doubt on readers' certainties and presumptions. The good guy turns out to be ineffective, the bad guy resilient, and all positive thrust questionable. It does, however, make for confusion.

The later work reinforces this direction, where stories are told in a multiplicity of modes and voices. *Ayen erekh ahavah* (1986; *See Under: Love,* 1990) is a "novel," not only told in four parts through four different voices, but in four different modes, only tangentially related to each other. The first section, "Momik," establishes the subject, the Holocaust as reconstructed by a nine-year-old child, through his survivor relative, and his child's imagination. The next three sections are not chronologically sequential but, rather, parallel and alternative attempts at understanding through fantasy—Bruno Schulz's only apparent death and the song of the sea—through the grotesque vision of the relative, Anshel Wasserman, in Auschwitz, who was unable to die, and, finally, through the encyclopedic series of definitions to concepts raised by the novel as a whole. Indubitably experimental, this work enthusiastically challenges traditional narrative standpoint and chronology, so as to offer a full-blooded, linguistically exuberant, and imaginatively penetrative account of how reality might be grasped afresh and then conveyed.

The way to see the world anew in G.'s terms can be to enter the world of the child. This is carried out with rigid purity in the play *Gan riki* (1988; Riki's kindergarten), entirely set in a kindergarten where the sole participants are young children, and where there exists no mediating adult presence. Thus, the world of the child becomes self-authenticating, not seen as subsidiary or as a stage on the way to adulthood. A further step in this direction is made by the novel *Sefer hadiqduq hapnimiy* (1991; book of internal grammar).

G.'s work, while it attaches itself to objective political and national reality, moves freely into the consciousnesses of the characters in narrative. It particularly enters the mind of the child, tracing the contours of child thought from within, and thus renders a fresh view of the world.

BIBLIOGRAPHY: Yudkin, L. I., "Victims and Oppressors in the Writing of D. G.," *Remembering the Future* (1988), Theme 2, 1649–54; Ramras-Rauch, G., on *See Under: Love, WLT,* 64, 1 (Winter 1990), 189; Mazor, Y., on *The Smile of the Lamb, WLT,* 65, 4 (Autumn 1991), 762

LEON I. YUDKIN

GUIDO, Beatriz

Argentine novelist, short-story writer, and screenwriter, b. 13 Dec. 1925, Rosario; d. 4 Mar. 1988, Madrid, Spain

G. was born and raised in the interior city of Rosario amidst a stimulating intellectual atmosphere provided by her parents. She traveled extensively in Argentina and Europe with her father, a successful architect, and developed an early interest in philosophy. She spent three years at the University of Buenos Aires and then continued her studies in Rome, Naples, and Paris in 1948. Following her return to Argentina, she gravitated to Buenos Aires, wrote her first novel, *La casa del ángel* (1954; *The House of the Angel,* 1957), and met Argentine film director Leopoldo Torre Nilsson, whom she later married, and with whom she would collaborate on a score of full-length films, half of which were based on her own narratives.

From the outset, her novels and stories stressed psychological introspection and focused on adolescence and its conflicts. This is particularly noted in *La caída* (1956; the fall), her most autobiographical novel. In subsequent works she revealed a critical view of her society and a growing political awareness, as exemplified in *Fin de fiesta* (1958; party's end). The latter work evoked in realistic terms the grim political circumstances—torture, assassination, electoral fraud—of an earlier period, that of the decline of Argentina's last conservative government. But following the publication of a collection of short stories, *La mano en la trampa* (1961; the hand in the trap), she wrote a novel that dealt directly with the Peronist years, *El incendio y las vísperas* (1964; *End of a Day,* 1966). The novel covers the period from October 1952 to April 1953, which serves as historical backdrop for the account of the personal crisis of a wealthy Argentine landowner, Alejandro Pradere, morally compromised by his passive collaboration with the Peronist régime. G. thus joined the ranks of the numerous River Plate writers who, in the 1960s, undertook an examination and an evaluation of the economic, social, and spiritual deterioration of the decade (1945–1955) under Perón.

G.'s style during this period had gradually begun to incorporate a number of narrative techniques that could be ascribed to her intimate familiarity with cinematic devices, such as flashbacks and flashforwards and experiments in reproducing film's continuous present with almost exclusively present-tense verbs. These stylistic features culminate in her most original and ambitious novel, *Escándalos y soledades* (1970; scandals and solitudes).

G.'s subsequent work consists mainly of testimonials, reminiscences, personal essays, short fiction, and extensive interviews concerning her writing. The new democratic government in Argentina named her, now widowed, to a diplomatic post in Madrid, and it was there she died in 1988, tireless to the end in her pursuit of the appropriate images with which to convey a sense of her understanding of her life and times.

FURTHER WORKS: *Regreso a los hilos* (1947); *Estar en el mundo* (1950); *El único ojo de la ballena* (1971); *Una madre* (1973); *Los insomnes* (1974); *Piedra libre* (1976); *¿Quién le teme a mis temas?* (1977); *La invitación* (1979); *Apasionados* (1983); *Rojo sobre rojo* (1987)

BIBLIOGRAPHY: Yates, D. A., on *End of a Day, SatR,* 4 June 1966, 53; Anderson Imbert, E., *Spanish-American Literature,* 2nd ed. (1969), Vol. 2, 739; Orgambide, P. G., and R. Yahni, eds., *Enciclopedia de la literatura argentina* (1970), 305–6; Brushwood, J. S., *The Spanish American Novel* (1975), 192, 229–30

DONALD A. YATES

GUZMÁN, Nicomedes

(born Oscar Nicomedes Vásquez Guzmán) Chilean novelist and editor, b. 25 June 1914, Santiago; d. 26 June 1964, Santiago

Because his family was very poor, G., to be able to attend school, worked outside of the home even as a young boy. Principally self-taught, he wrote novels and short stories that depicted the plight of the poor in the slums of Santiago. In the little that he wrote about his own life, he stated that he was his own worst enemy. He eventually destroyed his first marriage with an affair that produced an illegitimate child, but then he continued living with both families for the next twenty years. To support his families, he worked at many different jobs: He was a newspaper journalist; he held positions in different branches of the government where he promoted literature and culture; he sold his books as he traveled around Chile giving lectures; and at one time he resorted to selling women's lingerie from office to office.

Though G.'s first book was a collection of poems, *La ceniza y el sueño* (1938; ashes and dreams), it was his novel *Los hombres obscuros* (1939; the obscure men) that caught the attention of the public. It has the innovation of four narrators, telling the tale in a present-tense, first-person point of view. Each narrator is a different voice of Pablo the shoeshine-boy protagonist, and the reader can identify the different voices because each has different punctuation.

La sangre y la esperanza (1943; blood and hope) is considered G.'s masterpiece, and it is required reading in Chilean high schools. It was awarded the Santiago Municipal Prize for Fiction (1943) and has gone through numerous editions and printings. Even in its antithetical title, the novel is an excellent example of neobaroque style, which became the trademark of the group G. belonged to, the Generation of 1938.

Many of G's chapters are interspersed with a prose-poem frame called a "stamp" in Chile. A metaphor of the slum environment in terms of beauty, not degradation, the sandwichlike stamp often appears at the beginning and ending of chapters or subchapters. This use of stamps was also a characteristic of the Generation of 1938.

Even though G.'s works can be classified as proletarian novels, they are currently praised as important works of testimonial literature, because they depict, as if they were autobiographies, the difficulties that the poor, hard-working Chileans have living in the slums. G.'s family considered *La sangre y la esperanza* to be a true autobiography, but besides obvious influence from Chilean works it shows influences of Michael Gold (1894–1967) of the U.S., Georg Fink (b. 1903) of Germany, Maxim Gorky (q.v.) of Russia, as well as other international proletarian writers of Socialist Realism (q.v.).

G. was a leader of the Generation of 1938, which helped establish through the authors' writings Marxist governments in 1938 and 1970. As an editor, G. published an anthology of his generation, *Nuevos cuentistas chilenos* (1941; new Chilean short-story writers), one of the group's main documents. He also edited and published novels and other writings of his colleagues, as well as anthologies of several important Chilean novelists.

An author with an ability to show human tenderness, a common motif in G.'s stories, as well as a brutal side to humanity, G. has created a poetic prose that has made an impact both in Chile and abroad.

FURTHER WORKS: *Donde nace el alba* (1944); *La carne iluminada* (1945); *La luz viene del mar* (1951); *Una moneda al río y otros cuentos* (1954); *Autorretrato de Chile* (1957); *El pan bajo la bota* (1960)

BIBLIOGRAPHY: González Zenteno, L., "N. G., figura representativa de la generación del 38," *Atenea*, 392 (1961), 116–27; special G. issue, *Cultura: Revista de educación*, 96 (1964); Dyson, J., "Los cuentos de N. G.," *Atenea*, 404 (1964), 228–49; Promis Ojeda, J., "El sentido de la existencia en *La sangre y la esperanza* de N. G.," *AUC*, 145 (1968), 58–68; Pearson, L., *N. G., Proletarian Author in Chile's Literary Generation of 1938* (1976); Ferrero, M., *N. G. y la generación del 38: Antología mínima* (1982)

LON PEARSON

HABĪBĪ, Emile

Palestinian novelist, short-story writer, and essayist, b. 28 Aug. 1921, Haifa, Palestine (now Israel)

Until the publication of his collection of short
stories *Sudāsiyyat al-ayyām al-sittah* (1968; sextet
of the six days), H. was better known as a political
activist and commentator than as a writer of imaginative fiction. For decades before that event, he
was a prominent member of the Israeli Communist
Party, which he joined in the early 1940s, when
it was still the Palestinian Communist Party. He
represented the party in the Knesset between 1951
and 1971 and served for many years as editor of
its biweekly *al-Ittihād* and its other political and
literary periodicals. His regular weekly column,
published under different pen names, was a mainstay of this Arabic newspaper.

Sudāsiyyat al-ayyām al-sittah first appeared serialized in the Party's monthly *al-Ghadd,* under
H.'s pen name Abū Salām. It immediately attracted wide attention for its originality and was
successively reprinted in several Arab periodicals
before it appeared in book form (with other stories)
in 1969.

Still more momentous was the publication of
H.'s masterpiece *Al-waqā'i' al-gharībah fī ikhtifā'
sa'īd abī al-nahs al-mutashā'il* (1974; *The Secret
Life of Saeed, the Ill-Fated Pessoptimist,* 1982).
This book has since been published independently
by several publishing houses inside Israel and in
the Arab world, and has appeared in a number of
printings. It has also been translated into several
languages, including English, French, Russian,
and Hebrew and was staged in both Arabic and
Hebrew in Israel. H.'s subsequent three works,
though not without literary and artistic merit, appear anticlimactic when compared with this outstanding work.

H. views his fiction writing in strictly political
terms. He defines himself primarily as a political

activist, and only secondarily as a fiction writer.
Moreover, he insists that an intrinsic connection
binds the two fields to which he has devoted the
larger part of his life. His stories initially drew
attention in the Arab world for their unique blend
of savvy political acumen and consummate artistic
quality. They were immediately viewed in the
Arab world as part of what came to be known as
"the literature of the Palestinian resistance" or
"the literature of the occupied land."

H.'s fiction deals exclusively with the concerns
and experiences of the Palestinian Arab minority
living in Israel. References and allusions to the
peculiar rules and conditions that govern daily life
in this community permeate these works to such
an extent that annotation is virtually necessary if
the works are to be fully grasped by the outsider.
Thus, the thematic thread that binds the six tableaux of *Sudāsiyyat al-ayyām al-sittah* is the
renewed contact between Palestinians from within
Israel and fellow Palestinians from the newly occupied territories of the West Bank and Gaza.

Although hardly the circumstances under which
they had hoped to be reunited after nearly twenty
years of forced separation, both parts of the Palestinian people derive some solace from their awkward reunion. This is particularly true of the Palestinians of Israel who were left behind and felt
abandoned. The six episodes of the collection
dramatize the healing effect of this reunion on
individuals whose lives had suffered from a fundamental lack. In all cases, the wounds are psychological in nature. They range in severity from
the schizophrenic condition of a man who could
not remember that he was the hero of a love story
that haunts him, "Wa-akhīran nawwar al-lawz"
(and finally the almond trees blossomed), to that
of a boy whose stunted growth and inferiority
complex are cured by the discovery that he has an
extended family in the West Bank. The stories
occupy a dramatic space between the political
imperative that requires an Israeli withdrawal from
the occupied territories, to which both the author
and his fictional characters subscribe, and the need
to spare the Palestinian individual the psychological trauma of a renewed separation from the
collective body.

The generic status of *Sudāsiyyat al-ayyām al-
sitta,* that is, the question whether it is a novel or
a collection of short stories, is somewhat problematic. The six parts of which it is comprised are
discrete enough to stand independently of each
other. But they are also bound by lines of continuity that give the whole a distinct sense of unity,
though perhaps not quite that of a tightly structured
novel.

Daring experimentation with narrative form is
one of several features that make H.'s *Al-waqā'i'*

al-gharībah fī ikhtifāʾ saʿīd abī al-nahs al-mu-tashāʾil unique in the annals of the Arabic novel. Here H. utilizes the rich rhetorical and stylistic tradition of the classical Arabic genre of maqāma to depict the predicament of the Arabs in Israel. His treatment of this grave subject, however, is shot through with irony and humor. In large measure, the novelty resides in the choice of a singularly unheroic Palestinian, Saʿīd, as the protagonist of this work. For Saʿīd is at once a willing collaborator with the Israeli authorities against other fellow Palestinians and a victim of the general conditions that govern the daily life of all Arabs in Israel. In a series of loosely connected episodes reminiscent of the picaresque novel H. parades Saʿīd through the labyrinth of Israeli officialdom, only to discover that it leads absolutely nowhere. H. takes these spatial terms quite seriously. Most of the movement in this novel occurs on a vertical, not a horizontal, axis. The novel begins with a series of letters that Saʿīd addresses to the author, presumably from outer space whither he had been conducted by his extraterrestrial rescuers, and ends with him practically impaled on a high post from which he is unable to descend. The fact that the Saʿīd letters originate in Acre, which in contemporary Arabic and Hebrew vernacular stands metonymically for the mental asylum in it, imparts to the whole story a fantastic and comic quality that relieves much of the tension inherent in the serious subject matter.

Much of the satirical humor is directed against the vagaries of the Israeli political establishment. But the inept Arab regimes and the backward Arab condition in general also come under H.'s scathing satire. The satire is all the more biting because it is couched in a high form of classical Arabic that deliberately evokes past Arab glory only to contrast it with the dismal condition of contemporary Arab life. Nor is the humor exclusively political. The novel literally bristles with linguistic and rhetorical puns that proclaim its literary status. In this respect, it is among a handful of serious Arab novels that consciously flaunt their literary artifice and technical virtuosity.

H.'s subsequent works carry experimentation a significant step farther. In one of them H. mixes the generic features of novel and play so thoroughly that the hybrid is neither. H. calls it mis-riwāyah, which is an acronym made up of parts of the words of "play" and "novel." On the whole, the literary value of these latter works may reside primarily in their experimental nature as they constantly press against the contours of established genres and redefine the norms of modern Arabic narrative.

FURTHER WORKS: Lukaʿ ibn Lukaʿ (1980); Ikhtayye (1985); Sarāyā bint al-ghūl (1991)

BIBLIOGRAPHY: Le Gassick, T., "The Luckless Palestinian," MEJ, 34, 2 (1980), 215–23; Jayyusi, S. K., Introduction to The Secret Life of Saeed, the Ill-Fated Pessoptimist (1982), 7–20; Mehrez, S., "Irony in Joyce's Ulysses and H.'s Pessoptimist," Journal of Comparative Poetics, 4 (1984), 33–54; Tamari, S., "Saeed, the Ill-Fated Pessoptimist," Merip Reports (Oct.-Dec. 1985), 53–55; Allen, R., ed., Modern Arabic Literature (1987), 104–9; Boullata, I. J., "Symbol and Reality in the Writings of E. H.," Islamic Cultures, 62, 2–3 (1988), 9–21

MUHAMMAD SIDDIQ

al-ḤĀJJ, Unsī Lūwīs

Lebanese poet, critic, and translator, b. 1937, Kaitouli

Born in the south of Lebanon, H. studied at a French lycée, the Collège de la Sagesse in Beirut. As a journalist he contributed to the dailies al-Hayāt and al-Nahār and became director of the weekly literary supplement of this journal. As a young poet he was associated with the avant-garde review Shiʿr from 1957 to 1964 and again from 1967 to 1969, in which he published his prose poetry. He translated poetic works of Antonin Artaud, André Breton, and Jacques Prévert (qq.v.) and also translated plays from Shakespeare, as well as Eugène Ionesco, Friedrich Dürrenmatt, Albert Camus, and Bertolt Brecht (qq.v.)

In the spirit of Shiʿr he published in 1959 his first collection of prose poems, Qasāʾid al-nathr (poems in prose), also entitled Lan (never). Later followed al-Raʾs al maqtūʿ (1963; the severed head) and Mādī al-ayyām al-ātiya (1965; the past of the days to come). In his poetry one notes a surrealistic tendency and estrangement from the conventional poetic language. Qasāʾid al-nathr should be in his eyes the framework for what is deepest and most genuine in poetry. Density, compactness, and organic unity are essential in this most liberal form of poetry. Together with Adūnīs (q.v.) he made himself the enthusiastic defender of this new poetic genre. In their hands prose poetry, which existed since Amīn al-Rayhānī (1876–1940) and Kahlil Gibran (q.v.) wrote their shiʿr manthūr in the beginning of the century, became an instrument of revolutionary poetic experiments and a revolt against all the existing metrical tradition. H. made himself the most extreme exponent of the exclusive use of prose as the poetic medium. Others reproached him that he demonstrated a conscious quest for originality and a desire to shock. Certainly he is the most outspoken representative of those who have been called al-shuʿarāʾ al-ghādibūn al-rāfidūn or "the angry refusing poets."

In fact, H.'s work shows a resemblance to the history of the American English verse and the role of Walt Whitman (1819–1892) in it. In his evolution to prose poems H. was certainly influenced by the Lebanese poet of prose poetry Fu'ād Sulaymān (1912–1951), himself a great admirer of Gibran.

FURTHER WORKS: *Mādhā sana't bi-l-dhahab mādhā fa'alt bi-l-warda* (1970); *al-Rasūla bi-sha'rihā al-tawīl hattā l-yanābī'* (1975)

BIBLIOGRAPHY: Moreh, S., *Modern Arabic Poetry, 1800–1970* (1976), 306–7; Boullata, I. J., *Edebiyat,* 1, 2 (1967), 133–35; Jayyusi, S. K., *Trends and Movements in Modern Arabic Poetry* (1977), Vol. 2, 632–38; Khcir Beik, K., *Le mouvement moderniste de la poésie arabe contemporaine* (1978), passim; Jayyusi, S. K., ed., *Modern Arabic Poetry: An Anthology* (1987), 247–51

ED C. M. DE MOOR

HAMMETT, Dashiell

American novelist, short-story writer, and screenwriter, b. 27 May 1894, St. Marys County, Md.; d. 10 Jan. 1961, New York, N.Y.

Before embarking on a literary career, H. had worked at a number of jobs, had served in the U.S. Army during World War I, and had spent some time in hospitals, undergoing treatment for tuberculosis. One looks in vain for early signs of literary genius, but one is intrigued by the fact that the creator of at least two of American literature's most memorable private detectives was for several years an operative of the Pinkerton Detective Agency.

Although H. lived to 1961, his claim to our attention as an important American writer is based almost completely on work that he produced between 1922 and 1934—barely over a decade. In that time, H. was, by critical consensus, the most important and influential participant in the development of what came to be called hard-boiled detective fiction, contributing to the establishment of a distinctly American idiom within a major popular genre. Moreover, H. developed and defined possibilities for authenticity and art within hard-boiled detective fiction itself, thus raising the standard by which work in this subgenre might be judged, and toward which later writers would aspire. Finally, H.'s work at its best goes beyond narrow considerations of genre, blurring the distinction between the popular and the serious.

Among the activities that involved H. after 1934 were some screenwriting, writing continuity for a comic strip, a good deal of drinking, service with the U.S. Army in the Aleutians during World War II (H. was forty-eight years old when he enlisted), and political activism that led to his spending six months in jail for contempt of court in 1951. During this period he was also involved as an advisor in the work of his longtime companion, the American dramatist Lillian Hellman (q.v.); and he worked sporadically on a novel he would never finish.

H. first made his mark as a writer in the so-called "pulp" magazines that flourished in the 1920s. Aimed at a male mass audience, the pulps specialized in fiction that stressed action and adventure. Most of H.'s best short stories appeared initially between 1923 and 1929 in *Black Mask,* the most respected of the pulps, and most of them follow pretty closely the formula of hard-boiled detective fiction. But H.'s stories are distinguished from those of his contemporaries by qualities of craftsmanship and style. Carroll John Daly (1889–1958) is today often recognized as the first of the hard-boiled detective writers; his "Knights of the Open Palm" appeared in *Black Mask* in June 1923, some four months before the publication in the same magazine of H.'s "Arson Plus," the first of H.'s "Continental Op" stories. Daly's hero, Race Williams, is swaggering, callous, brutal. He is as overstated as the events in which he becomes involved and the style in which, as first-person narrator, he recounts those events to us. The events in the stories H. devotes to the exploits of the Continental Op are often as extravagant as those in Daly's yarns; certainly the action is as fast, the violence as wild. But the Continental Op (H. doesn't give him a proper name) doesn't swagger, isn't brutal or callous; he is tough. And the ability to establish and maintain the distinction between toughness and its counterfeits is one measure of H.'s art.

Red Harvest (1929), H.'s first published novel, in many ways marks the culmination of the Op saga. The character himself is fully realized, and the novel's portrayal of corruption and violence in a western American city is a compelling achievement. The action was apparently inspired in part by H.'s experiences as a Pinkerton man. That H. had actually been a private detective no doubt contributes to the special quality of his fiction, especially of the Continental Op stories, but the result of that experience is hardly "realism" in any of the more restricted senses of that word; rather, it's a matter of the air of authenticity H. can sustain, however extravagant the material he exploits.

The Dain Curse (1929), the second of the Continental Op novels and the last narrative in which that character appears, is a lesser work, although certainly not a dull one. Instead of the narrative drive one finds in his best work, H. here offers mechanical elaboration of plot. And there are hints of a dangerous softening in H.'s portrayal of his protagonist; H.'s decision to abandon the Op at this point seems well advised.

Certainly no one can regret a change of direction that produced a novel as fine as *The Maltese Falcon* (1930). H. replaces the first-person narration of the Op stories with a rigorously objective point of view. We are always "with" Sam Spade, H.'s detective protagonist—the book contains no scene at which he is not present—but H. never admits us directly to Spade's thoughts and feelings. He is viewed, as are all the other characters, from the outside. This technique, combined with an air of moral ambiguity ("Don't be too sure I'm as crooked as I'm supposed to be," Spade says at one point), generates a detective story in which the most mysterious character is the detective.

Not that Spade is the only memorable character in the novel. The conspirators, the police, the women in Spade's life, his mediocre partner, are all vividly, economically, and unforgettably drawn. And the falcon itself is one of H.'s most impressive creations: jewel-encrusted object of fabulous history and wild imaginings, worthy goal of an endless quest; worthless leaden fake, reducing romantic quest to parody; in any event "the stuff that dreams are made of."

The Glass Key (1931) was apparently H.'s favorite among his novels and certainly represents a serious effort at the detective novel as literature. More than any other novel by H., this one tends to divide his critics and admirers. The stylistic objectivity that is a major strength of *The Maltese Falcon* strikes some readers as an annoyance in the later novel: an obstinate and perverse refusal, some argue, to satisfy the reader's desire, motivated by other qualities in the text, to go below the surface. Yet there is no denying the work's formal integrity—perverse or not, H. doesn't compromise. And there are many critics for whom *The Glass Key* is H.'s most impressive achievement.

The Thin Man (1934) was H.'s last novel. It was also his most successful in commercial terms and, perhaps, his least successful in critical terms. It is by no means without merit, but it is a novel of parts, of witty or otherwise arresting passages that never cohere to form a satisfying whole. It is perhaps symptomatic of where H. was at this point in his career that much of what is best in *The Thin Man* is peripheral to the detective interest, an observation one could not have made of *The Glass Key*. It had begun to seem that, in order to grow as an artist, H. would have to move beyond detective fiction.

This is the move he was never able to make. One may look to biographers—H. has already had several—for theories that might explain his si-

lence. Personal problems, including alcoholism, may certainly have contributed. But it seems that H.'s problem as an artist was his recognition that he had reached that point in his development at which he had to find his material within himself, without the disguise and protection that generic conventions, even when employed as creatively as in H.'s work, could provide. And he found that he could not take off the mask.

H.'s reputation seems secure. Indeed, it may well ascend, as postmodernism (q.v.), whatever its sins, properly encourages us to question such limiting oppositions as serious versus popular. Certainly H. deserves our lasting respect as one who achieved excellence in the world of pulp/pop fiction, a world in which, according to long-standing academic prejudice, excellence isn't supposed to matter.

FURTHER WORKS: *$106,000 Blood Money* (1943); *The Adventures of Sam Spade and Other Stories* (1944); *The Continental Op* (1945); *The Return of the Continental Op* (1945); *Hammett Homicides* (1946); *Dead Yellow Women* (1947); *Nightmare Town* (1948); *The Creeping Siamese* (1950); *The Woman in the Dark* (1951); *A Man Named Thin and Other Stories* (1962); *The Big Knockover* (1966); *The Continental Op* (1974)

BIBLIOGRAPHY: Chandler, R., "The Simple Art of Murder," *Atlantic Monthly,* Dec. 1944, 53–9; Bazelon, D., "D. H.'s Private Eye: No Loyalty beyond the Job," *Commentary,* 7 (1949), 467–72; Blair, W., "D. H., Themes and Techniques," in Gohdes, C., ed., *Essays on American Literature in Honor of Jay B. Hubbell* (1967), 295–306; Edenbaum, R., "The Poetics of the Private Eye: The Novels of D. H.," in Madden, D., ed., *Tough Guy Writers of the Thirties* (1968), 80–103; Malin, I., "Focus on *The Maltese Falcon*," in Madden, D., ed., *Tough Guy Writers of the Thirties* (1968), 104–9; Nolan, W. F., *D. H.: A Casebook* (1969); Wolfe, P., *Beams Falling: The Art of D. H.* (1980); Layman, R., *Shadow Man: The Life of D. H.* (1981); Porter, D., *The Pursuit of Crime: Art and Ideology in Detective Fiction* (1981), 130–45; Margolies, E., *Which Way Did He Go?: The Private Eye in D. H., Raymond Chandler, Chester Himes, and Ross Macdonald* (1982), 17–31; Johnson, D., *D. H.: A Life* (1983); Nakjavani, E., "*The Red Harvest:* An Archipelago of Micro-Powers," *Clues: A Journal of Detection,* 4, 1 (Spring–Summer 1983), 105–13; Naremore, J., "D. H. and the Poetics of Hard-Boiled Fiction," in Benstock, B., ed., *Art in Crime Writing* (1983), 49–72; Symons, J., *D. H.* (1985); Lehman, D., *The Perfect Murder* (1989), 126–30, 147–67

W. P. KENNEY

HAQQĪ, Yahyā
Egyptian short-story and novella writer, literary critic, and essayist, b. 7 Jan. 1905, Cairo

Born into a highly educated family, H. was brought up in a popular area of Cairo. In 1925 he graduated from the Sultaniya Law School. After practicing law for two years, he gained employment with the government, which sent him as a legal inspector to Upper Egypt. The two years he spent there had a profound impact on his literary career. The five short stories that he wrote there dwell on a topos addressed by many 20th-c. writers: the barriers that confront outsiders, particularly officials, as they try to penetrate the worlds of closed, traditional communities. In 1929 he joined the Egyptian foreign service and was sent to Jeddah. Subsequent posts were in Istanbul, Rome, Paris, Ankara, and finally Tripoli in 1953. From the foreign service he moved to the department of fine arts, and his last employment was as editor in chief of the literary magazine *Al-Majallah*. Although he officially retired in 1970, he continued to be active on the literary scene. His autobiography, entitled *Khallīhā ʿalā Allāh* (1959; leave it to God), gives a lively account of the highs and lows of his career.

H. is best known for his first collection of short stories, *Qindīl Umm Hāshim* (1944; *The Saint's Lamp*, 1976). The story that gave the book its title tells of an individual's reconciliation between Eastern and Western cultural values that until then had been portrayed as mutually exclusive. The plot may seem hackneyed today, but at the time of its publication it caused a stir. Although the protagonist clearly navigates between two cultures that have both good and evil in them, critics, including the Muslim fundamentalist Sayyid Qutb (1903–1966), hailed what they claimed to be the story's advocacy of Islamic values. H.'s other novella, *Sahh al-nawm* (1955; *Good Morning!*, 1987), schematically compares the lives of some villagers before and after the return of one of their members from studying in the capital. The analogy with Nasser was inevitable since it came out only three years after the Free Officers' Revolution. H.'s sharply etched vignettes of the village-tavern habitués take the reader into the heart of a society in transition. In the same year that *Sahh al-nawm* came out he published two collections of short stories, *Umm al-ʿawajiz* (1955; mother of miracles) and *Dimāʿ wa-tīn* (1955; blood and mud). Rural and urban subjects mix to tell the multiple stories of 20th-c. Egyptians of the less-privileged classes.

H. is esteemed for his literary criticism. His first collection of literary articles, which he had published in journals and newspapers from the late 1920s until the 1950s, was *Fajr al-qissa al-misriyyah* (1960; dawn of the Egyptian story). These essays deal with Egyptian fiction from 1914 until 1934. He subsequently published literary articles in three more collections: *Khutuwāt fī al-naqd* (1961; stages of criticism), which includes also articles written about non-Egyptian writers; *Itr al-ahbāb* (1971; the scent of loved ones), whose articles are more in the form of literary reminiscences than of criticism; and *Unshūda li-al-basāta* (1972; an anthem to simplicity), whose message is simplification of language so as to assure communication. H. was also prolific as an essayist. His four collections of wry commentaries on life in the Cairo street, such as *Nās fī al-zill* (1971; people in the shadows), or on his numerous travels, such as *Haqībah fī yad musāfir* (1969; a suitcase in a traveler's hand), represent only a small fraction of the essays that lie scattered among dozens of newspapers, magazines, and journals.

H.'s lucid, elegant style has won him the esteem of the leading literary figures in the Arab world. He has won several prizes and has played an important role in promoting young writers.

FURTHER WORKS: *ʿAntar wa Jūliyāt* (1960); *Damʿah fa-ibtisāmah* (1965); *Taʿālamaʿī ilā al-kūnsīr* (1969); *Yā layl yā ʿayn* (1972)

BIBLIOGRAPHY: Jomier, J., "Deux extraits des souvenirs de M. Y. H.," *Mélanges: Institut Dominicain des Études Orientales* (1960), Vol. 6, 325–30; Vial, C., "Y. H. Humoriste," *Annales Islamologiques* (1972), Vol. 11, 351–65; Cooke, M., *The Anatomy of an Egyptian Intellectual, Y. H.* (1984); Allen, R., ed., *Modern Arabic Literature* (1987), 124–29; Layoun, M. N., *Travels of a Genre: The Modern Novel and Ideology* (1990), 56–105

MIRIAM COOKE

HAUGE, Olav H.
Norwegian poet, b. 18. Aug. 1908, Ulvik

H. has spent most of his life on his father's smallholding in Ulvik in the Hardanger district of western Norway, where he has made his living tending a small apple orchard. A trained orchardist, H. has reaped both tangible fruit and a harvest of poetic inspiration from this activity; his literary work is firmly rooted in his native soil. But H. is no country bumpkin: He has received inspiration from a variety of poetic traditions and styles, including Japanese Haiku poetry, and has translated verse from German, French, and English.

H. was close to forty at the time of his literary debut. *Glør i oska* (1946; embers in the ashes) was considerably indebted to the works of two earlier poets, namely Olav Aukrust (1883–1929) and Olav Nygard (1884–1924), who, like H., had strong ties to their native soil and wrote in *nynorsk* (New Norwegian). His second volume of poetry, *Under bergfallet* (1951; beneath the crag), however, showed that H. was in the process of finding his own voice as a poet. He abandoned the abstractions and the romanticism of his predecessors and turned to physical nature for inspiration. *Seint rodnar skog i djuvet* (1956; slowly the woods redden in the gorge) and *På Ørnetuva* (1961; on the eagle's tussock) testify to years of laborious striving for a clarity of vision. His style was now further simplified and his images became increasingly powerful. *Dropar i austavind* (1966; drops in the east wind) and *Spør vinden* (1971; ask the wind) represented a further turning toward concrete, everyday subjects.

H. is extremely well informed about both the literature of his native land and world letters, having taught himself several foreign languages. Like the earliest poets in the *nynorsk* tradition, Ivar Aasen (1813–1896), A. O. Vinje (1818–1870), and Arne Garborg (1851–1924), and like his contemporary Tarjei Vesaas (1897–1970), H. has remained within a fixed native sphere and yet transcended it through his wide-ranging intellect. H. stands as one of the foremost modernists in postwar Norwegian poetry, and as one of the greatest poets in Norwegian literature. He is also one of Norway's most outward-directed writers, and has continued writing poetry into advanced age: The most recent edition of his works, *Dikt i samling* (1980; collected poems), contains a number of new poems under the common title *Janglestrå* (a few blades of grass), in which the poet comments on his experience of growing old.

FURTHER WORK: *Utanlandske dikt* (1967). FURTHER VOLUMES IN ENGLISH: *Don't Give Me the Whole Truth* (1985); *Trusting Your Life to Water and Eternity* (1987)

BIBLIOGRAPHY: Fulton, R., Introduction to *Don't Give Me the Whole Truth* (1985), 9–15; Stegane, I., "The New Norse Literary Tradition," *RNL*, 12 (1983), 101–22

JAN I. SJÅVIK

HAYDEN, Robert

(born Asa Bundy Sheffey) American poet, b. 4 Aug. 1913, Detroit, Mich.; d. 2 Feb. 1980, Ann Arbor, Mich.

Given the name by which we know him by his foster parents, William and Sue Hayden, H. made the traumatic discovery late in life that his name had never been legally changed; before the law, he was still Asa Bundy Sheffey, and he now had to effect the legal change himself, no easy task for an intensely sensitive man whose relationships with foster parents, stepfather, and, above all, natural mother were already sufficiently complicated. He could at any rate now claim as his own the name under which he had received his B.A., from Detroit City College (now Wayne State University) in 1936, and his M.A. from the University of Michigan in 1944. It was also the name under which he had written some of the finest poems yet produced by an African-American poet of any generation.

Writing in 1972 the editors of a comprehensive anthology of African-American literature could note that, although H. had "sustain[ed] a high quality of writing over the years," his poetry had "received little published critical attention." The relative neglect up to that time of a body of work that, while not large, was highly impressive both in quality and in variety, may be attributed to two causes. The first was the indifference to African-American poets on the part of a white-dominated literary establishment; it was not until 1966 that a book of poems by H. was published by a "mainstream" publisher, although H.'s first book had appeared as early as 1940. Second, and probably more painful to this sensitive black American, was the hostility toward him, his work, and what that work was taken to represent, by the mostly younger African-American writers and critics who, during the 1960s and 1970s, espoused the causes of Black Nationalism, Black Art, and the Black Aesthetic. The implication was that H. was not "black" enough. Ironically, the widespread renewal and awakening of interest in African-American art during the 1960s and 1970s did not lead directly to the discovery of H. and his recognition as an important American poet.

Although long deferred, the recognition has come, and with it honors that gave H. a sense, if any was needed, of vindication. In 1966 H. was the recipient of the Grand Prix de la Poesie conferred by the First World Festival of Negro Arts, held in Dakar, Senegal; Langston Hughes (q. v.) chaired the committee that made the selection. In 1969 the National Institute of Arts and Letters granted H. its Russell Loines Award for distinguished poetic achievement. In the same year, H. was offered, but felt unable to accept, appointment as consultant to the Library of Congress; offered a similar position in 1975, he did accept it, becoming the first African-American to be so honored.

Also in 1975, he was appointed a fellow of the Academy of American Poets. In the last years of his life, H. was awarded a number of honorary doctorates, signifying the belated recognition of his achievement by the academic community. Finally, on 24 February 1980, the Center for African-American and African Studies at the University of Michigan, whose department of English H. had joined in 1969, spent a day in tribute to R. H. Unfortunately illness made it impossible for H. to attend; he died the following day.

H.'s earlier poems tend to be dominated by the influence of the poets of the Harlem Renaissance of the 1920s and are more frequently in the mode of social protest than would be true of his mature work. In fact, H. would later all but disown the poems of his first collection, *Heart-Shape in the Dust* (1940), which he came to regard as apprentice work. As H. found his own voice, the inheritance of African-American folk culture and the traditions of African-American poetry, including that of the Harlem Renaissance, entered into a creative tension with the modernism (q.v.) of poets like T. S. Eliot and W. H. Auden (qq.v.). Thus a poem like "Middle Passage," in *A Ballad of Remembrance* (1962), deals with the experience of slavery (the "middle passage" is the sea voyage of the slaves from Africa) and affirms the exploits of Joseph Cinquez, whose leadership of a slave uprising aboard the ship *Armistad* has made him one of the heroes of black history and legend. But the formal strategies (montage, irony, allusion, indirection) are those of literary modernism. "Runagate Runagate," in *Selected Poems* (1966), brings the same modernist sensibility to bear on the Underground Railway and the work of Harriet Tubman.

African-American history, then, provided H. with material for some of his most powerful poems, and the modernist idiom provided him with strategies for the artistic realization of that material. But H. also found inspiration in black popular culture, in black religion, and in the folkways of the black community, especially in the urban setting he knew from his childhood. And in dealing with these varied materials, H. demonstrated mastery of a range of formal strategies, consistently finding the formal correlative to the thematic drive of the poems. The controlled elevation of rhetoric in his sonnet "Frederick Douglass," the blues feeling of "Homage to the Empress of the Blues," the echoes of Gospel in "Mourning Poem for the Queen of Sunday," the baroque elaboration of "A Ballad of Remembrance" and of "Witch Doctor," or the approach to unadorned statement in "Those Winter Sundays" can only begin to suggest the range and variety of H.'s achievement, an achievement that fully justifies the observation by the younger African-American poet Michael S. Harper (b. 1938) that H. is a poet of perfect pitch.

When one takes into account as well that, in poems like "The Diver" and the sequence "An Inference of Mexico," H. establishes that he is not limited to racial themes (not that those themes were in any way limiting for H.); it is all the more remarkable that in reading H.'s work one is always aware of the overall coherence, the "presence" of the poet. No doubt a major contribution to that coherence was made by H.'s profound commitment to the faith of Baha'i, to which he was converted, having been raised a Baptist, in 1942. The tenets of Baha'i certainly bear on the note of hope one finds even in those poems that confront most directly the tragic history of race relations in America: "Middle Passage," for instance, is a poem that affirms "The deep immortal human wish."

Some have noted an irony in the questioning of H.'s "blackness." At least one critic has wondered why H. was so adamant in rejecting the category "black poet," since much of H.'s best work deals with the black experience. But, for H., any category narrower than "human" was unacceptable. At the same time, no one knew better than H. that to be human is to be rooted in time, place, and history. It is in this spirit that, in his own words, H. "reaffirm[s] the Negro struggle as part of the long human struggle toward freedom."

FURTHER WORKS: *The Lion and the Archer* (1948); *Figure of Time: Poems* (1955); *Words in the Mourning Time* (1970); *The Night-Blooming Cereus* (1972); *Angle of Ascent* (1975); *American Journal* (1978; rev. ed., 1982); *Collected Prose* (1984); *Collected Poems* (1985)

BIBLIOGRAPHY: Davis, C., "R. H.'s Use of History," in Gibson, D. B., ed., *Modern Black Poets: A Collection of Critical Essays* (1973), 96–111; Stepto, R., "After Modernism, after Hibernation: Michael Harper, R. H., and Jay Wright," in Harper, M. S., and R. B. Stepto, eds., *Chant of Saints: A Gathering of Afro-American Literature, Art, and Scholarship* (1979), 66–84; Wright, J., "Homage to a Mystery Boy," *GaR*, 36 (1981), 904–11; Cooke, M. G., *Afro-American Literature in the Twentieth Century: The Achievement of Intimacy* (1984), 133–57; Fetrow, F. M., *R. H.* (1984); Hatcher, J., *From the Auroral Darkness: The Life and Poetry of R. H.* (1984); Fetrow, F., "Portraits and Personae: Characterization in the Poetry of R. H.," in Baxter Miller, R., ed., *Black American Poets Between Worlds, 1940–1960* (1986), 43–76; Kutzinski, V. M., "Changing Permanences: Historical and Literary Revisionism in R. H.'s 'Middle Passage,' '' *Callaloo,* 9, 1 (Winter 1986), 171–83; Williams, P. T., *R. H.: A Critical Analysis of His Poetry* (1987)

W. P. KENNEY

HEAD, Bessie

South African novelist, short-story writer, and historian (writing in English), b. 6 July 1937, Pietermaritzburg; d. 17 April 1986, Serowe, Botswana

H. is South Africa's best-known black woman writer. She has written novels, short stories, and a history of the royal Khama family of Botswana. She has also been a teacher and journalist. Born in a Pietermaritzburg asylum to a white mother and a black stable worker, she left South Africa for Botswana after having to contend for years with racism and discrimination. Before she left South Africa, H. had completed her teacher's diploma and taught school for a short while. Not satisfied with teaching, she became a journalist and lived in cities such as Johannesburg, Port Elizabeth, and Cape Town. She began to write seriously in Botswana.

All of H.'s novels, *When Rain Clouds Gather* (1969), *Maru* (1971), *A Question of Power* (1974), and *A Bewitched Crossroad: An African Saga* (1984), and her collections of short stories, *The Collector of Treasures and Other Botswana Village Tales* (1977) and *Tales of Tenderness and Power* (1989), deal extensively with the questions of racial discrimination, exile, the ill-treatment of women, and insanity. In so many ways, the themes are related to H.'s own life. A mixed-race person discriminated against by both the white minority and black majority of South Africa, she finds little peace in Botswana because the black majority dislikes her. The female characters in her novels and stories must all suffer, and freedom is an illusion; H. writes feelingly and powerfully about the pain her characters and herself must experience in Botswana. In *A Question of Power,* truly a landmark novel, she explores in detail the question of insanity and male domination. Using her own birth in an asylum as the focus for her study, H. examines in deep and painful detail the viciousness of these phenomena. In the process, she creates characters and situations that seem to emanate from hell.

Yet H.'s work has a healing quality. In both of her early novels and her collection of stories, she introduces the simple and kind people of Botswana. In a largely rural country H. learns to appreciate human compassion. Also when looking at the history of the Khama family, we learn about the kind people of this country. Though H. died prematurely when she was at the height of her creativity, in her short span of life she left both for Africa and the world a valuable creative legacy.

FURTHER WORKS: *Serowe: Village of the Wind* (1981); *A Woman Alone: Autobiographical Writings* (1990)

BIBLIOGRAPHY: Taiwo, O., *Female Novelists of Modern Africa* (1985), 185–214; Katrak, K. H., ''From Pauline to Dikeledi: The Philosophical and Political Vision of B. H.'s Protagonists,'' *Ba Shiru: A Journal of African Languages and Literature,* 12, 2 (1985), 26–35; Eko, E., ''Beyond the Myth of Confrontation: A Comparative Study of African and African-American Female Protagonists,'' *ArielE,* 17, 4 (Oct. 1986), 139–52; Geurts, K., ''Personal Politics in the Novels of B. H.,'' *PA,* 140 (1986), 47–74; Ola, V. U., ''Women's Role in B. H.'s Ideal World,'' *ArielE,* 17, 4 (Oct. 1986), 39–47; Chetin, S., ''Myth, Exile, and the Female Condition: B. H.'s *The Collector of Treasures,*'' *JCL,* 24, 1 (1989), 114–37; MacKenzie, C., *B. H.: An Introduction* (1989); Abrahams, C. A., ed., *The Tragic Life: B. H. and Literature in Southern Africa* (1990)

CECIL A. ABRAHAMS

B. H.'s reputation as a writer rests on three novels, a collection of stories and a book on Serowe village. The three novels—*When Rain Clouds Gather, Maru* and *A Question of Power*—form something like a trilogy. In each of them the novelist exhibits strong disapproval for the misuse of power by any individual or group. This dislike is evident in the way she dramatises the process of the abdication of power which gets more complex from the first novel to the last. By the time the reader gets to the end of the third novel the novelist's message is clear: the naked display of power by the racists in South Africa or any other bigots elsewhere can only lead to disaster. There is no way of avoiding the rewards of oppression whether it is of blacks by whites, whites by blacks, whites by fellow whites or blacks by fellow blacks. The wise thing to do is to conceive of power in a progressive evolutionary manner. But, given man's insatiable lust for power, this is hardly possible. The novelist considers at length the psychological basis of power and finds that this has been largely eroded in a world dominated by conflict and the desire for political ascendancy. It is because of this stated position that B. H. is, for example, said to express ''an indiscriminate repugnance for *all* political aspirations in *all* races.''

The collection of stories *The Collector of Treasures* affords the author a chance to display her mastery of the art of storytelling. She understandably concentrates on the position of women and takes every opportunity to project a feminist point of view. She needs all the artistic talents displayed in her previous works to succeed with *Serowe: Village of the Rain Wind*. Here she combines imaginative writing with the fruits of a year's research study to produce work of great distinction. She succeeds magnificently in her reconstruction of the village life of Serowe. The daily occupations, hopes and fears of the ordinary people of the village come alive in the reader's mind mainly because of the opportunity given the inhabitants to tell their own stories. The conception of history here is edifying—history is made out of the preoccupations of the common man, not out of the lofty ideals, cruelty or benevolence of the wealthy and powerful. This reflects the concern for the underprivileged and oppressed masses of the people which is easily discernible in B. H.'s writings.

Oladele Taiwo, *Female Novelists of Modern Africa* (1984), 185–86.

B. H. is a crusader for sexual and social justice for all men and women. Her favourite theme is the drama of interpersonal relationships and their possibility for individual growth and regeneration. She explores not only social harmony but also what is unique in each individual who contributes to it. In the realization of this task she employs an imaginative power and an original grasp of style which match her forceful moral vision. In all this, the woman's identity is fundamental; for it is still easy to encapsulate the central issues of all H.'s novels into the vital issues of power and identity. . . . She truly approaches her characters as individuals and, with her usual sensitivity and thoroughness, journeys through the innermost recesses of their lives. The product of this exploration is the emergence of that uniqueness which makes each of them special. To B. H., South Africa typifies power in its ugliest form, and the revulsion with which she views such a moral wasteland has aroused in her a special reverence for human life and dignity.

Virginia U. Ola, "Women's Role in B. H.'s Ideal World," *ArielE,* 17, 4 (Oct. 1986), 39

B. H. has created some powerful and unusual characters in the work she has so far produced. We have seen that they strive to treat people equally in both interpersonal and community relations. Then, through their struggles as expatriates, or leading their lives in exile, they dissolve feelings of alienation and work toward a firmer and deeper commitment to their friends and lovers and humanity on a global scale.

For her characters, this commitment is not abstract. We see it tangibly enacted in their efforts to share responsibilities, decision making, power and profits. But we also see their mental and spiritual process of reconnecting to the horrors of political oppression, especially in South Africa. Each character has personal experience with sexual inequality, caste discrimination, political oppression by white and black rulers alike, etc., etc. For them, "politics" (in the form of power relations and issues of social injustice) has always impinged upon their own personal lives. Each character, however, reaches a point where the pain he or she experiences

through having such a lucid consciousness (about the connection between personal and political problems) makes it impossible for them to go on. Some of the characters run away and deny that they care about anyone or anything; others have mental breakdowns but all find or choose some path through which they begin to dissolve their feelings of alienation and begin to reconnect with humanity. In fact, their "connection" far exceeds what we might expect. Their concerns do not remain selfish or even simply geared toward their local community. Rather, we see each character express his/her vision of the soul of Africa rising and transferring this power into a global unity and peace through the *"brotherhood of man."* . . .

H., herself, is very idealistic. She creates characters who have an incredible drive to "right the wrongs" of their local communities and who dream about such change for all of Africa and even the entire world. We come to respect her characters as admirable and ethical people. Her own hope that "those who rule" or "the powers that be" will also develop the kind of idealism her characters embody is certainly a dream with a political base. She is hoping for a better balance of power in society, a more egalitarian world where women and Masarwa people are not subordinate. She brings this dream to reality in the world of her fiction. She provides us with models or prescriptions for how such idealistic goals can actually be achieved. B. H.'s faith and her belief in the strength of common people shines through the thoughts and action, the spirit and commitment of the characters she creates.

Kathryn Geurts, "Personal Politics in the Novels of B. H.," *PA,* 140 (1986), 72–73

B. H.'s background has obviously influenced the way she perceives the narrative tradition of oral storytelling and the myths that have informed it. Born of mixed parentage in South Africa, raised primarily by white missionaries and self-exiled to Botswana, H. had no particular sense of belonging to a particular tribe or ethnic group. As a result, she is not only aware of her "outsider" status but self-consciously exploits this position in her art by deliberately distancing herself from the community whose tales she narrates so that her stories reveal a distinctly ambiguous, unresolved tone. Her intention is to reinforce not only her own outsider status but also her literate audience's "unknowingness," an audience who is forced to search for a way to enlarge their vision of a world from which they are exiled. H. uses for her point of departure the framework of the traditional dilemma tale in which the audience is expected to debate the moral questions raised by the storyteller, but she not only involves the real audience but also a fictive or "knowing" audience who are part of the communal structure of her stories. Unlike other storytellers who do not openly acknowledge the fictive audience but allude to it by subtly pretending to remind their listeners of half-forgotten historical events, H. frequently fills in the gaps by giving some kind of historical comment so that the "unknowing" reader may situate the stories within a specific cultural context, thereby acknowledging their realistic viability. Yet this structural tension becomes even more complex when in some of H.'s stories her own voice completely disappears or when she disconcertingly shifts her tone and narrative persona within the same story so that the "outsider" voice can no longer be heard. At times H. appears to purposely dissolve her own structural function and become part of the excluded audience, all the more aware of its limited vision. In the process, H. subtly leads her audience into the realm of myth where her characters become so stylized that no reader is allowed to identify with them—or even accept them as plausible—but must use his/her own imagination, as H. has done, to translate historical experiences into a larger symbolic context that questions the universal nature of existence. We must not only read her stories to learn about the experiences of her Botswana villagers and how their history has shaped their consciousness, but must also learn to use the mythic imagination to shape our own moral vision of a future where we will no longer remain "outsiders," exiled from ourselves and each other.

Sara Chetin, "Myth, Exile, and the Female Condition: B. H.'s *The Collector of Treasures*," *JCL*, 24, 1 (1989), 114–15

The title *A Question of Power* clarifies further what this novel is about. To B. H. whose daily life was shaped by the racist practices of South Africa and the sexist attitudes of the men she lived with, the question of who has the power is indeed important. Like Virginia Woolf, Zora Neale Hurston, and Doris Lessing, B. H. views the need of the male to see himself twice as big as he really is as one of the chief causes of unjust, undemocratic, and unkind behavior. In *A Question of Power* the male need to dominate and feel superior to others is represented by two men, Sello and Dan. They come to life and into power through the mad imaginings of Elizabeth. They are so real to her that she talks with them and feels her life literally threatened by them. It is because Sello and Dan use every power they have to try to destroy Elizabeth psychologically that she is mad. To regain her sanity, she must defeat them. . . .

B. H. chooses to focus on sexism rather than racism in *A Question of Power*. This forces her African readers, more familiar with racism, to see the similarities between the two and their common root in the philosophy of domination. Men degrade, manipulate, and abuse women in Elizabeth's nightmare, basically because they fail to perceive sacredness in them. Elizabeth advocates a philosophy that insists upon the sacredness of all life because of her subjection to this patriarchal behavior. This is typical of the evolution of feminist thought. That is why feminists speak of ecological and peace issues as well as equal rights; and that is why they speak of equal rights not only for women but also for the poor, the handicapped, and the racially oppressed.

Nancy Topping Bazin, "Venturing into Feminist Consciousness," in Cecil Abrahams, ed., *The Tragic Life: B. H. and Literature in Southern Africa* (1990), 51–56

HERBERT, Xavier

(pseud. of Alfred Herbert; pseud.: Herbert Astor, E. Norden) Australian novelist and short-story writer, b. 15 May 1901, Geraldton; d. 10 Nov. 1984, Alice Springs

Born in Western Australia, H. graduated from Perth Technical College in 1922 with a diploma of pharmaceutical chemistry. In 1935–1936 H. was the superintendent of Aborigines in Darwin, which contributed to the experience he would draw on for his first novel, *Capricornia* (1938). Throughout an illustrious literary career that also included a three-year stint (1942–1944) with the Australian Imperial Force, H. received numerous awards and honors, including the Commonwealth Sesqui-Centenary Literary Prize (1938), the Australian Literary Society's Gold Medal (1940), and doctors of letters from the Universities of Newcastle (1975) and Queensland (1976), among others.

H. is most famous for his controversial classic novel of protest against racism, *Capricornia*, and for his monumental *cri de cœur*, *Poor Fellow My Country* (1975)—the first and last novels of his literary career. *Capricornia* grew directly from H.'s realization that there was widespread ignorance in Australia of the continuing sexual exploitation of Aboriginal women that he had seen as a boy on the northern frontier of Western Australia. But it depended upon its author gaining a good deal more nonliterary experience than he had before he felt equipped to write it: frontier experience in the Northern Territory, as a swagman, drover, railway fettler, and pearl diver. *Capricornia* is shocking in its angry depiction of the treatment of Aborigines in the (thinly veiled) Territory. Yet its real focus is on the tragedy of the (then rapidly expanding) Creole population, and despite its social concern it is at least equally and imaginatively interested in the plight of a white society that H. believed has so alienated itself from its conquered environment that its only hope of spiritual survival is to connect with Aboriginality, through blood identification with mixed-race offspring. This, he claims, is why he made his main characters "halfcaste," and it gives his fiction much in common with the Jindyworobak movement of the 1930s (one of the major principles of which was "to join" on to Aboriginal culture as a way of bringing Australian literature into contact with its proper environmental values). This explains also, at least in part, the deeply personal theme of psychological relationship between fathers and sons that runs throughout much of H.'s oeuvre.

After twenty years of self-imposed isolation, self-analysis, and literary struggle, during which he made substantial progress on several novels only to abandon one after another in a continuing crisis of confidence, H. burst into print again with *Seven Emus* (1959), publishing four books in four years. In fact, *Seven Emus* had been completed much earlier, while H. was serving in the bush commando North Australia observer unit during World War II, but had escaped serious notice because it had been serialized in the popular-fiction magazine *The Australian Journal,* where most of his early short stories had also first appeared. A slim novella with a quirky style of punctuation, developed, according to its author, in order to discover and liberate "style," *Seven Emus* offers a satirical and cynical critique of the anthropological exploration of Aboriginal sacred sites in Northern Australia. As a type of modern culture hero, the anthropologist is caricatured as an exploitative and self-serving bully and thief who thus has much in common with the original European settler-invader of Australia. *Soldiers' Women* (1961) purports to be a study of women unfettered by moral convention and liberated by the absence of husbands and boyfriends fighting in World War II. Often defended by the author as his personal favorite, for in it he developed his highly idiosyncratic theory of sexuality, it is nevertheless the least critically popular of his works. The detailed description of women's clothing seems not only fetishist but an indication of the author's unwillingness to observe more deeply than external appearances allow, while the focus on feminine desire is obviously masculine and, for most readers, distorted.

The bread and butter of H.'s writing had always been his short stories. *South of Capricornia: Short Stories by X. H., 1925–34* (1990) collects the earliest of his writings in order to trace his literary career up to the writing of *Capricornia.* Written for the popular-magazine and newspaper market, and initially to romantic-fiction formulae, H.'s stories were often "pipe-openers" for his longer fiction—set pieces in the manner of burlesque, satire, mystery writing, and autobiography—and were recycled in many different shapes and combinations. *Larger Than Life* (1963) is the author's own selection, mostly later works, but still with the emphasis on narrative, for H.'s are obviously "contrived" stories, much in the manner of O. Henry (1862–1910). The subject matter ranges widely, but racial themes and republican sentiments are never far below the surface.

The psychological substructure of much of H.'s writing reveals a more personal dimension, a deep concentration on self-exploration, which often was the author's own acknowledged motive for composition. This makes for more enigmatic subject matter than at first might seem the case, and indeed the fascination of even his first novel lies partly in subtleties of imaginative vision, masked initially by stridency of voice, contrivance of plot, and intrusive polemicism. *Disturbing Element* (1963), H.'s autobiography of his youth, to the age of twenty-five, confirms the enigma. Written in the

genre of a rake's progress, it nevertheless provides glimpses of many of the myth-making personae that feed not only into his fiction but also into the highly public exercises in self-promotion that, in later life, inevitably accompanied H.'s occasional forays from the isolation of his home in northern Queensland into what he called "civilization," the cities of the South—Sydney and Melbourne.

Poor Fellow My Country, H.'s magnum opus—winner of the Miles Franklin Award (1976), and one of the longest novels written in the English language—marks a final return to the thematic concerns of *Capricornia,* extending the chronology from 1936, when that novel had left off, to 1942. The subtitles of the three "books" (or volumes) tell the story: "Terra Australis—Blackman's Idyll Despoiled by White Bullies, Thieves, and Hypocrites"; "Australia Felix—Whiteman's Ideal Sold Out by Rogues and Fools"; "Day of Shame—A Rabble Fled the Test of Nationhood." The last title refers to the Japanese bombing of Darwin and the infamous evacuation that became known subsequently (after a horse race) as the Adelaide River Stakes. Between 1935 and 1938, and again in 1942, H. had again been in the Territory—as a pharmacist, government medical officer, superintendent of the Aboriginal Compound, gold fossicker, member of the Japan-Australia Society, agitator for the Euraustralian League (fighting for the rights of people of mixed race), union organizer, and finally a sergeant in the armed forces. For *Poor Fellow My Country* he drew upon all of these experiences. He satirized his enemies of old, he revealed the absurdities and injustices of his society, and he dramatized what he regarded as his own personal tragedy—the tragedy of Australia as a nation: failure to connect, to identify, with Aboriginality and the spiritualized Land, and failure to uphold the ideals of the "True Commonwealth" of Australia.

H. did not regard himself as an artist by destiny, but as a social revolutionary by national necessity. His importance to Australian literature lies undoubtedly in his contribution to the continuing debate on race and nation, on land rights, as well as in his mastery of the art of yarn spinning. However, the complexity of H.'s writing goes beyond narrative complication, beyond even the social issues involved, because the other major subject is himself: a social, psychic, sexual, cultural, and national creature of masks, and of monumental mythopoesis.

BIBLIOGRAPHY: Buckley, V., *"Capricornia," Meanjin,* 19 (1960), 13–30; Atkinson, A., "Mixed Grill," *Meanjin,* 20 (1961), 237–38; Heseltine, H., *X. H.* (1973); Heseltine, H. P., "X. H.'s Magnum Opus," *Meanjin,* 34 (1975), 133–36; McQueen, H., *"Poor Fellow My Country," Arena,*

41 (1976), 79–81; Hergenhan, L. P., "An Australian Tragedy: X. H.'s *Poor Fellow My Country*," *Quadrant*, 21, 2 (1977), 62–70; McDougall, R., "*Capricornia:* Recovering the Imaginative Vision of a Polemical Novel," *ALS*, 10, 1 (May 1981), 67–78; McLaren, J., *X. H.'s Capricornia and Poor Fellow My Country* (1981); Clancy, L., *X. H.* (1981)

RUSSELL MCDOUGALL

HERNÁNDEZ, Felisberto

Uruguayan short-story writer, b. 20 Oct. 1902, Montevideo; d. 13 Jan. 1964, Montevideo

In spite of the loyal support of some of his contemporaries, and the recognition of a handful of critics, H. did not achieve a well-deserved reputation as a major Latin American writer until after his death. His childhood in Montevideo left quite an impact on his writings, most of which can be considered autobiographical. He was not a gifted student, and had serious problems with conventional institutions of learning. In fact, he barely made it through elementary school, and never completed his secondary education. He was, however, obsessively interested in music, and started playing the piano at an early age. Very enterprising as a young man, at age sixteen he started his own music conservatory and became a piano instructor. Around that time he was working in local movie houses, providing the musical background to silent films. He continued perfecting his technique, enhancing his knowledge of theory, and developing his musicianship. A few years later, he was known as a concert pianist, and that prompted Arturo Sergio Visca (b. 1917) to assert that "actually one doesn't know if he was a pianist who became a writer or a writer who during many years swerved away from his vocation as a narrator channeling it into that of a concert pianist." It is safe to say, however, that nobody would remember H. today as a pianist of any note. He was to become a writer, and that is exactly what he wanted to be, against all odds, and in spite of the fact that at the end of his life he was planning a comeback piano recital that never materialized.

His literary career was irregular. H. started writing in his early twenties, but there were significant lapses throughout his production. José Pedro Díaz (b. 1921) suggests a division of H.'s works in three periods or stages of development. Between 1925 and 1931 he published very short texts, which—though they might be considered somewhat experimental, or perhaps even tentative—prefigure much of his later works. These editions, poor, limited, and self-published, were distributed among friends, who constantly encouraged the young author to continue writing. Over

a decade later, a group of those loyal friends published, at their expense, a novella titled *Por los tiempos de Clemente Colling* (1942; in the times of Clemente Colling) immediately followed by *El caballo perdido* (1943; the lost horse), also a novella. A third and relatively long text, *Tierras de la memoria* (1965; lands of memory), was written in that same period, but was not published with the exception of a fragment that appeared in *El Plata*, a local newspaper. It came out shortly after H.'s death.

His second period is marked by an intense preoccupation with the remembrance of things past. (It is common among critics to consider these texts a Proustian trilogy.) After another hiatus of more than a decade, H. came up with a collection of short stories that Editorial Sudamericana published in Buenos Aires under the title *Nadie encendía las lámparas* (1947; nobody turned on the lamps), a rather successful book, followed by the publication in newspapers and magazines of some very interesting short stories, notably "Las Hortensias" (1949; the hydrangeas) and "El cocodrilo" (1949; the crocodile). This last phase showed a preference for texts that did not rely so much on the memory of actual events as it incorporated an abundance of purely imaginative circumstances. It must be said, however, that some of the most successful stories of this third period were written in the first person, and were still based upon the author's biography, but the deformation of the material is much more deliberate, and they often enter the realm of the fantastic.

H.'s texts are often hard to follow and abound in irregularities of style that might startle some readers. He was well aware of what he himself termed "ugliness" in his prose, but defended it, and indeed cultivated it, as something that endowed his work with a special character, a personality of its own. That prompted noted author and critic Italo Calvino (q.v.) to affirm that H. was "a writer unlike any other, European or Latin American; . . . . an 'irregular' who [could] not be classified or categorized, but revealed to us his uniqueness in every page."

H.'s most significant contribution to the literature of our times was his persistent inquiry into the mechanisms of memory and the processes of writing. His stories are constantly intertwined with metatextual considerations that ultimately become the most important elements of his work. He was in many ways a forerunner of the narrative of the "post-boom" in Latin America, and that might account for the abundant and enthusiastic criticism that his work has generated in recent years.

FURTHER WORKS: *Fulano de tal* (1925); *Libro sin tapas* (1929); *La cara de Ana* (1930); *La envenenada* (1931); *La casa inundada* (1960); *Obras completas* (4 vols., 1967–1983); *F. H. y yo* (1974, with Paulina Medeiros)

BIBLIOGRAPHY: Giraldi de Dei Cas, N., *F. H.: del creador al hombre* (1975); Sicard, A., ed., *F. H. ante la crítica actual* (1977); Rela, W., *F. H.: bibliografía anotada* (1979); Lasarte, F., *F. H. y la escritura de "lo otro"* (1981); Echavarren Welker, R., *El espacio de la verdad: práctica del texto en F. H.* (1981); special H. issue, *Escritura*, 7, 13–14 (1982); Pallares, R., and R. Reyes, *¿Otro Felisberto?* (1983); Antúnez, R., *El discurso inundado* (1985)

HORACIO XAUBET

HERNÁNDEZ, Luisa Josefina

Mexican dramatist and novelist, b. 2 Nov. 1928, Mexico City

Prolific and successful author of more than thirty plays and thirteen novels during the past thirty-five years, H. grew up in Mexico City, an avid early reader of literature and history. She has translated many English, French, and German plays and prose works into Spanish, and her own novels and dramatic works reflect her wide readings. She wrote her first play when she was twenty-two and studied drama with Rodolfo Usigli (q.v.), one of the foremost dramatists of modern Mexico. H. succeeded Usigli as a professor of dramatic composition at the National Autonomous University of Mexico, and has been teaching there for more than thirty years. Beginning in 1951, when she won the first prize at the Spring Festival for her play *Aguardiente de caña* (1951; sugarcane alcohol), H. has been very active as a dramatist and has won many prizes and competitions, even though her topics are often controversial.

H. writes out of anger and indignation. Most of her plays and novels decry the abuse suffered by her characters, most of whom are women. She writes about problems of individuals and also about social conflicts. Many of her plays about individuals deal with self-realization, identity, and the ability or inability of individuals to act effectively. Other plays consider the topic of social justice: the marginalization of certain groups, the relationship of authority to justice, and the equity of marriage and divorce practices.

Among the plays that center upon the individual, *Los frutos caídos* (1957; the fallen fruit) explores the frustrations of a divorced woman who feels stifled by social conventions. In *La hija del rey* (1959; the king's daughter), the main character's identity derives from how others see her. Many other plays also focus on identity crises and inhibited sexuality: *Los huéspedes reales* (1958; the real guests), *El ambiente jurídico* (1950; ju-

dicial surroundings), *Botica modelo* (1953; corner pharmacy), and *Los sordomudos* (1953; the deaf-mutes) arc somc of these. H.'s novel *El lugar donde crece la hierba* (1959; the place where grass grows) also focuses on a woman's identity crisis. Many plays dramatize the perils and problems of male-female relationships, where one partner may destroy the other's sense of identity. This is a central theme of such plays as *Agonía* (1951; agony) and *Los duendes* (1960; the elves), a farce, as well as novels such as *Los palacios desiertos* (1963; the deserted palaces) and *La cólera secreta* (1964; the secret wrath).

Plays that dramatize the failure to act or the heroism of those who do struggle to effect change include *Afuera llueve* (1952; it is raining outside), *Los frutos caídos*, *La hija del rey*, and *La corona del ángel* (1951; the angel's crown). The novel *La memoria de Amadís* (1967; the memory of Amadís) is also based on the tensions between a weak-willed husband and a stronger wife.

Social justice is the theme of most of H.'s strongest works, such as *Botica modelo*, *La paz ficticia* (1960; fictitious peace), and *Historia de un anillo* (1961; the story of a ring), about the massacre of a town that believes in justice. *La fiesta del mulato* (1979; first pub. in English as *The Mulatto's Orgy*, 1971) is a complex and multilayered play that analyzes legal and ecclesiastical justice and questions of private and public identity: the extent to which women wear many masks and how these are viewed by society. It is one of many of H.'s works that effectively dramatize periods of Mexican history and the ideological issues of those times, as well as ours. H.'s novel *La primera batalla* (1965; the first battle) discusses the ideals of the Mexican Revolution compared with those of the Cuban revolution.

The mystical transcendence of anger and injustice is a theme of many of H.'s plays and novels from the 1960s on. Mysticism is a central concern of the two versions of *Apostasía* (1974; rev. ed., 1978; apostasy), *Las fuentes ocultas* (1980; the hidden fountains), and *Apocalipsis cum figuris* (1982; apocalypse with figures). The mystical experience enables people to endure and transcend their immediate circumstances and confirms their faith in a higher and more meaningful spirit of humanity.

H. is widely recognized as a major contemporary dramatist and as one of the important Mexican novelists of the 20th c.

FURTHER WORKS: *La Plaza de Puerto Santo* (1961); *La calle de la gran ocasión* (1962); *Arpas blancas, conejos dorados* (1963); *Clemencia* (1963); *La noche exquisita* (1965); *El valle que elegimos* (1965); *Popol-vuh* (1966); *Quetzalcóatl* (1968); *Nostalgia de Troya* (1970); *Los trovadores* (1973);

Danza del Urogallo múltiple (1974); *La Pavana de Aranzazú* (1975); *Hecube* (1976); *Apocrypha* (1978); *Caprichos y disparates de Francisco Goya* (1979); *Carta de navegaciones submarinas* (1987)

BIBLIOGRAPHY: Pacheco, C., "Con L. J. H.: La misoginia no existe," *Siempre,* 1321 (1978), 41–3; Miller, B., and A. González, "L. J. H.," *Veintiséis autoras del México actual* (1978), 239–51; Fox-Lockert, L., "L. J. H.," *Women Novelists in Spain and Spanish America* (1979), 241–59; Knowles, J. K., *L. J. H.: Teoría y práctica del drama* (1980); Toro, F. de, *"La paz ficticia de L. J. H.,"* *Brecht en el teatro hispanoamericano contemporáneo* (1984), 122–34; Valdés, M. E. de, "L. J. H.," in Marting, D. E., ed., *Spanish American Women Writers* (1990), 241–53

MARY G. BERG

HEYM, Stefan

(pseud. of Helmut Flieg) German novelist and short-story writer (writing in German and English), b. 10 Apr. 1913, Chemnitz

After being expelled from school for publishing an antimilitaristic poem, H. eventually studied Germanic philology in Berlin. He emigrated to the U.S. in 1935, where he received his M.A. from the University of Chicago and then became editor of the weekly newspaper *Deutsches Volksecho* in New York. During the 1940s he joined the U.S. Army, became a specialist in psychological warfare, participated in the Normandy invasion, and worked as a newspaper editor in Munich during the early occupation period. After his return to the U.S. he began writing again, but his political attitudes caused him to return his Army medals in protest against McCarthyism and the Korean War. In 1953 he moved to the German Democratic Republic, where he remained active as a writer and journalist. Repeated conflicts with the communist régime eventually led to his expulsion from the East German Writers' Union and to his active participation in the protest actions that preceded the collapse of the government in 1989. Among the awards that he has received for his writing are the Heinrich Mann Prize (1953) and the East German National Prize for Art and Literature (1959).

H.'s novels and short stories, which exhibit the influence of American realism, are flavored by personal experience and marked by negative political and social criticism. They reflect his journalistic orientation toward the experiences of both everyday life and history. Among the most important features of his best narratives are skillfully crafted, absorbing plots, the successful combination of documentary and fictional elements, dra-

matically pointed dialogues, and the effective use of irony and satire.

Compelling development of characters is one of the most consistent strengths of H.'s works. Although an obvious lack of accurate knowledge concerning the workings of the Gestapo diminishes the realistic effect of H.'s first novel, *Hostages* (1942), that weakness is offset by powerful psychological penetration of the characters in the portrayal of a hostage situation set within the context of the Czechoslovakian resistance to Nazi terror. Mastery of the psychological element is also a significant strength of *The Crusaders* (1948), the most successful of his early novels. In *The Crusaders,* H. employs the American march from France into Germany and scenes from the first year of the occupation as a backdrop for the depiction of human conflicts, behaviors, corruption, and vice that result from individual failure to grasp the meaning of World War II. The struggle of individual conscience against corruption is again a central theme in *Goldsborough* (1953), H.'s response to the experience of a miners' strike in Pennsylvania.

The more interesting works of H.'s middle period are engaging historical novels that use settings and situations from the past as frameworks for the critical examination of modern problems. *Die Papiere des Andreas Lenz* (1963; *The Lenz Papers,* 1964) is a colorful treatment of the contradiction between dictatorship and freedom, presented in the trappings of the Baden revolution of 1849, while the biographical novel *Uncertain Friend* (1969) explores the relationship between revolution and liberty through illumination of the unhappy life of Ferdinand Lassalle (1825–1864).

From the literary standpoint, the best of H.'s historical creations are the novellas *Die Schmähschrift; oder, Königin gegen Defoe* (1970; *The Queen against Defoe,* 1974) and *Der König-David-Bericht* (1972; *The King David Report,* 1973). In a style reminiscent of the early 18th c., *Die Schmähschrift* focuses on the career of Daniel Defoe and presents an interesting treatment of the relationship between literature and its audience, while *Der König-David-Bericht* employs a new version of the biblical King David's life as a vehicle for examining the abuses of Stalinism.

H. reached the peak of his literary development with *Ahasver* (1981; *The Wandering Jew,* 1984). The title figure is the author's projection of the archetypal revolutionary intellectual who, at critical junctures in world history, stands in conflict with reactionary forces personified in the figure of Satan. To some extent the Wandering Jew also represents H.'s perception of his own role as a writer with the responsibility to speak out on contemporary issues such as the threat of nuclear destruction and the dangers of bureaucratic stagnation, and to be active in furthering the cause of true democracy. His attempt to carry out those obligations in the more recent creation *Schwarzenberg* (1984; Schwarzenberg), a rather naive political fairy tale about an ideal democratic republic in postwar Germany, lacks the artistic quality and depth that he achieved in *Ahasver*.

Although less well-known than his novels, H.'s short stories are significant reflections of his personal literary style and clear demonstrations of his ability to present barbed social criticism effectively in compact narrative form. The most representative collection of his short fiction is *Schatten und Licht* (1960; *Shadows and Lights*, 1963), with its sometimes humorous but penetrating examination of specific problems of divided Germany and life in the German Democratic Republic during the reconstruction era.

Unlike most writers who reached the peak of their careers in East German semi-isolation, H. must be credited with producing literary works that combine substantial artistic mastery and intellectual depth with qualities that also give them an unusually broad international appeal in the English-speaking world.

FURTHER WORKS: *Die Hinrichtung* (1935); *Tom Sawyers großes Abenteuer* (1952, with Hanus Burger); *Die Kannibalen, und andere Erzählungen* (1953; *The Cannibals, and Other Stories*, 1957); *So liegen die Dinge* (1953); *Forschungsreise ins Herz der deutschen Arbeiterklasse* (1953); *Im Kopf sauber* (1954); *Reise ins Land der unbegrenzten Möglichkeiten* (1954); *Offen gesagt* (1957); *Casimir und Cymbelinchen* (1966); *5 Tage im Juni* (1974; *Five Days in June*, 1977); *Cymbelinchen; oder, Das Ernst des Lebens* (1975); *Das Wachsmuth-Syndrom* (1975); *Erzählungen* (1976); *Die richtige Einstellung, und andere Erzählungen* (1977); *Erich Huckniesel und das fortgesetzte Rotkäppchen* (1977); *Collin* (1979; *Collin*, 1980); *Wege und Umwege* (1980); *Atta Troll: Versuch einer Analyse* (1983); *Märchen für kluge Kinder* (1984); *Gesammelte Erzählungen* (1984); *Reden an den Feind* (1986); *Nachruf* (1988); *Meine Cousine, die Hexe, und weitere Märchen für kluge Kinder* (1989); *Auf Sand gebaut* (1990). FURTHER VOLUMES IN ENGLISH: *Nazis in U.S.A.* (1938); *Of Smiling Peace* (1944); *The Eyes of Reason* (1951); *The Cosmic Age* (1959); *The Queen against Defoe, and Other Stories* (1974)

BIBLIOGRAPHY: Moskin, R., "The Creator and the Commissars: An Encounter with S.H.," in *The Queen against Defoe, and Other Stories* (1974), 115–26; Petr, P., "S. H. and the Concept of Misunderstanding," *AUMLA*, 48 (1977), 212–21;

Dorman, M., "The State versus the Writer: Recent Developments in S. H.'s Struggle against the GDR's *Kulturpolitik*," *ML*, 62, 3 (Sept. 1981), 144–52; Zachau, R., *S. H.* (1982); Lauckner, N. A., "S. H.'s Revolutionary Wandering Jew: A Warning and a Hope for the Future," in Gerber, M., ed., *Studies in GDR Culture and Society* (1984), Vol. 4, 65–78; Ecker, H. P., *Poetisierung als Kritik* (1987); Hutchinson, P., "Problems of Socialist Historiography: The Example of S. H.'s *The King David Report*," *MLR*, 81, 1 (Jan. 1986), 131–38; Graves, P. J., "Authority, the State, and the Individual: S. H.'s Novel *Collin*," *FMLS*, 23, 4 (Oct. 1987), 341–50

LOWELL A. BANGERTER

HIJĀZĪ, Ahmad ʿAbd al-Muʿtī
Egyptian poet, b. 1935

Born in a village of Lower Egypt, H. moved to Cairo after his elementary schooling and spent seven years studying Arabic at the Teachers' Training College. He then went to France for graduate work, having spent some time in Cairo as a journalist. In 1987 he took a position in Arabic studies at the University of Paris.

H. was a leading poet of the late 1950s, 1960s, and 1970s. He has also edited collections of poetry by Ibrāhīm Nājī (1898–1953) and Khalīl Mutrān (1872–1949) and written critical works. H. had begun writing while still in his village, but the move to the metropolis had a profound effect on him. His first collection, *Madīnah bi-lā qalb* (1959; heartless city), was immediately praised, and is the one for which H. is best known. It is a contemplation of the city, and although H. does not pioneer the treatment of this theme—he is preceded by the Iraqi Badr al-Shākir al-Sayyāb (q.v.), for example—it is his own move from village to city that remains an enduring theme throughout his oeuvre.

Madīnah bi-lā qalb reflects H.'s feelings of bewilderment and anguish: The poetry is for the most part plaintive, a search for meaning in the urban morass. Alienation, loneliness, and anonymity all find expression in writing that is beginning to show signs of the socialism and Nasserism that was later to emerge in his work. He is exemplary of a generation whose social realism was a reaction against the romanticism of its predecessors.

In three subsequent collections, *Lam yabqā illā al-iʿtirāf* (1965; there remained only confession), *Marthiyyat al-ʿumr al-jamīl* (1973; elegy on the handsome life), and *Kaʾināt mamlakat al-layl* (1978; creatures of the night kingdom), the predicament faced by the estranged inhabitants of the city (now including Paris) is still a concern, but the initial bewilderment is replaced by feelings of unavoidable vulnerability: The citizen is like a "naked corpse devoured by buzzards." Nasser, about whom the poet has already written in earlier works, is also the object of considerable attention. "Ibtada'at al-rihlah" (1971; the journey's begun) from *Marthiyyat al-'umr al-jamīl*, is an elegy to Nasser or, in H.'s words, "not elegy, but a page in the history of revolution and poetry." It first appeared in a collection edited by H. entitled *Kitābāt 'alā qabr 'Abd al-Nāsir* (1971; writings upon the grave of Nasser), which includes poems by other prominent poets including the Syro-Lebanese Adūnīs (q.v.). The influence of the latter's concern with the mythic Near Eastern past, song, and Western (especially American, French, and Spanish) cultural icons is unmistakable.

In the introduction to *Ūrās* (1959; Aurès), a collection of five poems devoted to the Algerian revolution, H. writes that his search for Arab unity found an exemplary prototype in a group of three writers he encountered, which included the contemporary Saudi novelist 'Abd al-Rahmān Munīf (q.v.). The second poem, "Ilā al-ustādh al-'Aqqād" (1960; to Professor 'Aqqād), is a response to that critic's attack on socialism and accusation that poets of the new generation were unaware of the roots of their poetic tradition. It is written on the classical model (hemistich, mono-endrhyme) and mockingly includes several lines consisting entirely of a classical metrical paradigm.

Ashjār al-ismant (1989; trees of cement) is H.'s most recent work. The search for Arab unity and authenticity begun in Cairo and continued in the streets of Paris in *Ka'ināt mamlakat al-layl* remains important, but the poet's attention has turned to the intellectual and personal influences upon him. *Ashjār al-ismant*, which includes a poem dedicated to Munīf, is an introspective collection whose unifying theme is the use and treatment of Time.

Throughout his career, H. has written in a free-verse style all his own. It is exemplified by repetition and reiteration of opening phrases and by an erratic metrical and rhyme scheme. His early poetry, that of the newcomer to the city who is startled by its soullessness, is now the poetry of one who has become somewhat inured to its victimization and who has turned inward. His language has become more fractured, and the logic of his metaphors more obscure. Although his collections are not of equal merit, all include examples of the intense, unpredictable, and sustained writing for which he became justly popular. Regrettably, none of his collections exist in translation, but selected poems are anthologized in English and in French.

FURTHER WORKS: *Dīwān* (1973); *Ru'ya hadāriyyah tabaqiyyah li-'urūbat Misr: dirāsah wa-wathā'iq* (1979); *al-Shi'r rafīqī* (1988); *Hadīth al-thalāthah* (1988); *Qasīdat lā: qirā'ah fī shi'r al-tamarrud wa-al-khurūj* (1989)

BIBLIOGRAPHY: Badawi, M. M., *A Critical Introduction to Modern Arabic Poetry* (1975), 218–19; Moreh, S., *Modern Arabic Poetry 1800–1970* (1976), 216–88; Jayyusi, S. K., *Trends and Movements in Modern Arabic Poetry* (1977), Vol. 2, 605–25, 640–57, 709–19; Bencheikh, J., ed., *Terre émeraude: poèmes* (1980); Enani, M., ed., *An Anthology of the New Arabic Poetry in Egypt* (1986), 20–25; Allen, R., ed., *Modern Arabic Literature* (1987), 143–46; Jayyusi, S. K., ed., *Modern Arabic Poetry: An Anthology* (1987), 32–33, 261–68

SHAWKAT M. TOORAWA

HISTORICISM

Broadly defined, historicism can refer to any method whereby we seek to understand the artifacts and traces of the past and our relationship to that past. According to a prominent figure of the so-called new historicism, Stephen Greenblatt (b. 1943), it begins "with a desire to speak with the dead." As recently as the mid-1970s, historicism occupied, under the rubric "historical criticism," the place of a neutral-seeming adjective, one of many possible modifiers for the activity called literary criticism. In the early 1980s, the response of various literary historians to literary theory led not only to historical criticism's acquisition of its new, more polemical suffix—historic*ism*—but also to its splitting into two basic kinds: new and old.

Because the terms new and old historicism are now in common parlance, and because they do offer convenient labels for some differing critical assumptions, they seem to be worth using, but only with the understanding that their use encourages biases of the kind that the new historicists themselves struggle to make us see. Just as the concept "Renaissance" necessitated the envisioning of a preceding period, the Middle Ages, which it could claim to revise, the new historicism was obliged to create its own ugly sister, old historicism. New historicists campaign against their inheritance of such notions of progress, but at the same time tolerate and even enjoy the irony of being called new. In any case, practitioners of the new historicism would agree that the labeling process erroneously suggests a unified school of thought, a doctrine, where, instead, we have only a related set of themes, attitudes, and preoccupations—various historicisms.

A good way to think of the new historicism is as a common label for the renewed interest of literary critics in history. This is to suggest, of course, that literary critics have gone through an essentially antihistorical phase. Thus, to understand historicism, new or old, one needs to be aware of the New Critics' and other formalists' (structuralism) case against historical approaches to literary analysis, and of the poststructuralist argument against the concept of history itself.

What explains the renewed interest of literary critics during the last decade or so in historical analysis? What caused that interest to decline in the first place? And how and who did historicism change in its process of restoration after the New Critical and structuralist interregnum? The last question is the sort new historicists tend not to ask. A striking tendency in their practice is the avoidance of both causal analysis and the positing of linear sequences of development. New historicists don't so much deny the value of studying change as they defend their wish to see some things that the conception of history as progress seems to them to obscure.

A new historicist conviction that encourages this essentially synchronic as opposed to diachronic approach to history is that aesthetic representations (texts) should be read not only in relation to each other but to nonliterary and nondiscursive texts (events) as well. The method of the new historicist is thus what has been called cultural montage. Carefully avoiding words implying causal relationships, new historicists speak of reading texts "against" or "with" other "cultural practices," a term taken from anthropology, specifically from the work of Clifford Geertz (b. 1926), who, along with Michel Foucault (q.v.), has had a major impact on new historicist thinking.

The kind of overlapping that the new historicist tends to find between an event in the culture and a text can tend toward the bizarre—for example, the trial of hermaphrodites read against Shakespeare's *Twelfth Night;* anti-Semitic charges of kidnapings and forced circumcisions by Jews in Renaissance England read against the pound of flesh in *The Merchant of Venice;* accounts of Queen Elizabeth's private showings of her collection of miniatures read with the English sonnet. This kind of new historicist method aims at seeing things in cross section; like Geertz's "thick description," it captures a given moment in spatial rather than in linear terms. Some scholars have noted in this respect that new historicism models itself not on the forward momentum of narrative, like traditional history, but on the vertical organization of the lyric poem.

Thick description represents a reaction against the fairly simple reflectionist model of the histor-

ical criticism that the New Critical movement of the 1930s worked to supplant. In this historical model, the critic would point, for example, to instances of anti-Semitism in the culture and use these to "explain" *The Merchant of Venice* as a reflection of a cultural reality. Literature, in this model, mirrored and imitated life. And so it followed that to understand literature one needed to get out of the text into its context—that is, the relevant "facts" about the culture revealed to us through historical research.

By contrast the new historicism posits a more complex relationship between literary texts and history, one in which neither is simply a mirror or background for the other. The new historicists argue that literary representations don't simply spring from what is happening in the culture, but that texts also make things happen because they shape human consciousness. Consequently, history is not used only in the service of interpreting the text, nor is the text "used" to explain history. Instead, both a particular cultural phenomenon (for instance, the trial of hermaphrodites) and particular kinds of literature (gender benders like *Twelfth Night* or *A Midsummer Night's Dream*) together illuminate the complex relationship a text has to other processes in the culture. So, for example, Roy Strong's (b. 1935) influential study *The Cult of Elizabeth* (1977) attempts to show how court pageantry and literature functioned similarly to enhance the power of the queen.

Historical approaches to literature like Greenblatt's or Strong's suggest that a direction of the new historicism is not only to move away from a simple reflectionist model, but to overhaul the entire text/context model so as to break down the traditional distinguishing of literary text and history as foreground and background. Yet, as recently as 1975, handbooks of literary terms defined historical criticism as having two largely unquestioned aims, both rooted in a reflectionist way of reading the relationship between text and context: to locate the meaning of a work of literature in terms of the social and historical context in which it was produced and, further, to recreate for readers the meaning and value the work may have possessed for its own time. The slightly but tellingly revised version of these two objectives in new historicist terminology is: refiguring the sociocultural field in which texts were originally produced, and studying the uses to which the present has put its version of the past.

The new historicist critique of traditional historicist aims is not entirely new. However, the New Critics, who in the 1930s attacked traditional literary historical objectives, did so, they thought, in order to free the text by explaining it in isolation from historical, biographical or other contexts.

Alienated by what seemed to them a deforming pressure to place literature at the service of ethical and political contexts—from seeing Dickens, for example, as an exhibitor of manly virtues or Balzac as representative of a decadent bourgeoisie—the New Critics proposed seeing a work of literature in its own terms, as a more or less self-contained entity operating according to its own rules. Although new historicists tend to deride New Criticism (q.v.) for its supposedly "empty" formalism, New Criticism interestingly anticipates certain new historicist strategies, and is thus worth looking at. New historicism, much more than the New Criticism, stresses the importance of historicizing, but like New Criticism, it rejects the traditional serial, progression-oriented notion of history and the idea of a simple relationship between historical facts and the meaning of literary texts.

The differing orientations of historical criticism and New Criticism are evident if one compares a classic from each, for example, E. M. W. Tillyard's (1889–1962) *The Elizabethan World Picture* (1944), a classic work of older historical criticism, with William Empson's (b. 1906) basically New Critical study, *Seven Types of Ambiguity* (1930; rev. 2nd ed., 1947; rev. 3rd ed., 1953). Tillyard seeks to explain central features of English Renaissance literature by relating them to a specific cultural context—in this case, Elizabethan cosmology and the essentially hierarchical views that it seemed to Tillyard to have engendered. So, for example, when Hamlet complains to Ophelia about man's awkward placement between two realms or ways of being ("What should such fellows as I do crawling between heaven and earth?"), Tillyard would point to the elaborate ranking of angel, human, animal, vegetable, mineral, etc. to be found in Elizabethan philosophy, science, and natural history (the Great Chain of Being) and assert the explanatory power of this context. Readers are thus enjoined, though indirectly, from making any "ahistorical" associations with Hamlet's phrase, for example, a Freudian one. (Freudian readings of literature, like structuralist readings, tend to be ahistorical, as their concern is with common features of the human psyche throughout time. Although historical critics readily allowed that the psychic structures Freud described didn't need the advent of Freud to exert their pressure on literature, historicist critics stress that modern notions of the meaning and importance of Freudian psychology are not readily transferable to the 16th c., and can, in fact, prevent us from seeing another century's values and ways of thinking.)

The New Critic's primary objection to Tillyard's and others' recourse to history as explanatory key is that such an interpretation too quickly focuses attention on information outside the text, with the result that the text's actual language—Hamlet's speech—is inadequately mined for meaning. To the New Critic, historical criticism at its worst replaced a rich and complex reading experience with a facile and ultimately rather arbitrary "answer."

The title alone of Empson's *Seven Types of Ambiguity,* suggests its New Critical difference from Tillyard's traditional historicism. A typical new historicist title is Stephen Greenblatt's (b. 1943) *Shakespearean Negotiations: The Circulation of Social Energy in Renaissance England* (1988). Tillyard's title, *The Elizabethan World Picture,* names not a tendency of a literary text, but a broad cultural phenomenon. In fact, it posits with striking confidence its author's ability to name *the* worldview of an entire culture. As we shall see, this is the new historicist's primary objection to uses of history like Tillyard's—that they create too homogeneous and thus too exclusive a picture, a tendency new historicists call "totalizing." New historicists prefer the analysis of local conflicts over an attempt to construct any holistic account of the elements directing a whole society. Empson's typically New Critical title does not aim, as does Tillyard's, at establishing a broad definition of a culture. Rather, the book applies the same basic method of analysis to works from many different historical periods, thus demoting the importance of historical contextualizing.

In its focus on categorizing and on a feature of language rather than a philosophical system, Empson's title announces an apparently more limited aim than Tillyard's. Interestingly, however, Empson's title reveals only slightly less confidence in its author's authority than Tillyard's, despite the reduced area of analysis Empson claims as his own—a tendency of literary texts rather than an all-encompassing worldview. Lack of a definite article before the Seven in Empson's title, for example, acknowledges that the author may have missed a few types; and yet the title's assertion that its author can comfortably reduce literary complexity to seven manageable categories remains. In fact, Empson's book, which virtually defines literature in terms of its deliberate exploitation of ambiguity as a means of positing the irreducible complexity of human and aesthetic experience, goes well beyond an exposition of technique into a worldview of its own, though Empson doesn't name it as such, nor does he historicize it in terms of his own century's experience.

Predictably, the penchant of New Criticism and related critical orientations—formalism, structuralism, and deconstruction (qq.v.)—for formal analysis and for the elevation of literary texts over other kinds of discourse and cultural practices impelled succeeding generations to examine the very thing that the New Critics marginalized—the connection between literature and culture. To clarify this progression, it may be helpful to offer a new historicist critique of the preceding analysis. The explanation I have provided of Tillyard's and Empson's book titles is essentially New Critical in technique. I try to draw my conclusions from the language itself. I supply no biographical information about Tillyard or Empson, nor do I look for other events and practices in their culture that might help to explain the attitudes they assume. In other words, I choose not to historicize Tillyard and Empson's critical practice. My formalist orientation moves toward a deconstructive formalism when I note that Empson's insistence on categorizing and labeling contradicts (deconstructs) his claim for the value and inescapability of a complex (ambiguous) approach to experience. As New Critic in technique and old historicist in purpose (that being to explain the evolution of the term "historicism"), I walk around but carefully avoid most of the issues that the new historicists invoke in their critique of both New Criticism and the older kind of literary historicism.

Summed up concisely, albeit somewhat reductively, the new historicist claims against the New Criticism and ensuing formalisms are that these critical practices are apolitical, sexist, elitist, and hermetic. New historicists argue that neither literature nor the act of studying it can be separated from ideology. The challenge of the new historicism to the political detachment of the New Critics draws on Foucault in its insistence that a work of literature survives not because of its supposed universality, but because it continues to serve powerful interests. In this respect the guiding philosophical light of the new historicism moves from the humanist's choice—Locke—to Hobbes, for whom everything could be revealed as a sign of power.

Another blow to the claims of New Criticism is the current insistence of historicism on the historical positioning not only of the text, but of the critic herself. An implicit assumption of traditional historicism is that historians could arrive at similar and demonstrably true readings of texts and of the past regardless of their own experiences. In line with the new historicist argument that all claims to objectivity are inevitably illusory, women, for example, have questioned the categories of both literary and social history, and the notions of progress and periodizing that an older historicism put in place. Joan Kelly-Gadol (b. 1928) has thus invited a rethinking of traditional literary historical categories by suggesting that there was, in a sense, no Renaissance for women.

A good example of a basically new historicist, as well as feminist critique of old historicist premises can be seen in Toril Moi's (dates n.a.) attack on reflectionist readings of the literature of courtly love. Old historicists C. S. Lewis (q.v.) and D. W. Robertson (b. 1914), among others, approached medieval and Renaissance courtly-love poetry largely by attempting to discover whether or not courts of love existed, that is, as historical "facts." Each of these scholars then analyzed courtly-love literature in morally evaluative terms by trying to decide to what extent courtly love was bad (or good) for the culture and for the literature that presumably reflected it. Moi asserts that it doesn't matter whether or not courts of love existed. Instead, she directs readers to consider other questions. Why, she asks, would someone want to invent a literature of this sort? Who benefited from it and why? What system of power relationships did the literature of courtly love negotiate, for example, the struggle of the Norman aristocracy to assert its cultural superiority over the rising English middle class, and/or the struggle of one gender, men, to define themselves by inscribing feared traits onto a distanced other—the alternately loved and loathed courtly love lady? Moi's new historicist position thus insinuates that literary texts produce at least as much as they reflect culture.

An argument like Moi's challenges not only the aims and methods of traditional literary historians but the discipline of history itself. First, she discounts the value of a long-standing (basically reflective) means of arriving at an understanding of older texts. Then, further, by pointing to the difficulty of locating a boundary between fact and representation, she questions the value of traditional kinds of historical evidence, and even the historian's claim to the discovery of facts. In her argument, Moi pursues another key new historicist strategy—she historicizes the critical engagement itself, questioning the possibility that critics can climb out of their own historical positions to arrive at an objective depiction of reality.

In this vein, other obvious influences away from the New Criticism and toward the assumptions of new historicist practice emerge in the related trends of multiculturalism and the reader-response school of criticism, both of which aim to diversify literary interpretation in the academy. Obviously, the multicultural perspective creates formidable challenges to modes of criticism that assume there is some ideal reading to be gleaned from literary texts and that meaning finally inheres in the object (the text) and not also in its readers.

One charge provoked by new historicist challenges like Moi's, along with other destabilizing trends in contemporary theory, is that they are so obsessively antiauthoritarian that they celebrate anarchy in the name of freedom. To E. D. Hirsch (b. 1928), for example, the insistence of some theorists on the idea that meaning is always historical opens the door to complete relativism from which historical reconstruction of authors' intended meanings is one of the only antidotes. Thus, for Hirsch, the older historicism's pressure on readers to construe meaning in accordance with a text's probable authorial intentions is an admittedly arbitrary but defensible tactic. Hirsch argues that without such an interpretive "norm" we are doomed to critical anarchy. New historicists and other contemporary theorists counter that reconstruction of an author's probable intention goes on within the critic's own historically and linguistically conditioned frames of perception so that the traditional historian's humanist goal of arriving at an unchanging, universal, and sublimely disinterested reading of a text is impossible. Multicultural and reader-response schools of criticism are as interested as Hirsch in the limits and validity of interpretation, but they argue from the opposite point of view—that relativity breeds complexity, not chaos.

The new historicism has its critics on the left as well as the right. Scholars whose orientation directs them to the study of cultural change and its causes—feminists, for example—take issue with the new historicism's lack of attention to the possibility and means of changing the status quo. This criticism in particular promises continued negotiation between the perspectives of the older historicism and the new.

In sum, approaches to literature that are threatening or inhibiting to some readers are revelatory and liberating to others. Such is the case, for example, with contemporary theory's assertion that selves and texts are not autonomous, but are instead, at least in part, created by both overt and obscure cultural forces. The new historicism accepts the implications of this view when it argues against literary interpretation as a means of accessing unchanging truths and acknowledges that literary historical critiques of cultural and textual practices are neither objective nor free from the conditions they describe. If, as Greenblatt observed, historicism begins "with a desire to speak with the dead," its results may be less a revivification of those voices from the past than a clearer hearing of ourselves in the present.

BIBLIOGRAPHY: Hirsch, E. D., Jr., *The Aims of Interpretation* (1976); Barthes, R., *Image-Music-Text* (1977); Bridenthal, R., and C. Koonz, eds., *Becoming Visible: Women in European History* (1977); Strong, R. C., *The Cult of Elizabeth* (1977); Iser, W., *The Act of Reading: A Theory of Aesthetic Response* (1978); Fish, S. E., *Is There a Text in This Class?* (1980); Greenblatt, S. J., *Renaissance Self-Fashioning, From More to Shakespeare* (1980); Lentricchia, F., *After the New Criticism* (1980); Tompkins, J., ed., *Reader Response Criticism: From Formalism to Post-Structuralism* (1980); Eagleton, T., *Literary Theory: An Introduction* (1983); Geertz, C., *Local Knowledge* (1983); Selden, R., *A Reader's Guide to Contemporary Literary Theory* (1985); Aers, D., ed., *Medieval Literature: Criticism, Ideology, and History* (1986); Ferguson, M. W., et al., eds., *Rewriting the Renaissance: The Discourses of Sexual Difference in Early Modern Europe* (1986); Dubrow, H., and R. Strier, eds., *The Historical Renaissance: New Essays on Tudor and Stuart Literature and Culture* (1988); Lodge, D., ed., *Modern Criticism and Theory, a Reader* (1988); Summers, C. J., and T. L. Pebworth, eds., "Historicism, New and Old: Excerpts from a Panel Discussion," *"The Muse's Common-Weale": Poetry and Politics in the Seventeenth Century* (1988), 207–17; Liu, A., "The Power of Formalism," *ELH*, 56, 4 (Winter 1989), 721–71; Veeser, H. A., ed., *The New Historicism* (1989)

JILL STEPHEN

HOFMANN, Gert

German novelist, b. 29 Jan. 1932, Limbach

H. initially studied sociology, French, and German at the universities of Leipzig, Freiburg, and Paris, and then taught German and comparative literature for many years in Klagenfurt, Austria. He first became known as a prolific author of radio plays, and he has published all of his prose works in the relatively short time since 1979 until the present. Recurrent themes in his work are the indictment of hypocrisy and bigotry in hierarchically structured communities, people put under extreme pressures by a hostile state or bureaucracy, the marginalized and social outcasts. While H. criticizes such closed societies, he does not offer a solution or a redemptive vision. The tenor of his works is one of apocalyptic pessimism and a melancholy that is characteristic of many postwar German writers in so far as it reflects their attitudes to Germany's Nazi past and its reverberations in the present.

H.'s first novel, *Die Denunziation* (1979; the denunciation), traces the impact of a Nazi crime on the lives of twin brothers who victimized their parents and their neighbors, a Jewish couple. While one brother remains in Germany and leads an unexamined bourgeois existence, the other emigrates to America after the war and is driven nearly insane by his memories of the war crimes and his feelings of guilt. *Die Fistelstimme* (1980; the small hoarse voice) describes the conflicts between a German university lecturer and the Yugoslavian institution at which he is employed to teach German. The protagonist's increasing paranoia leads him to believe that others are copies of real people and that he himself is in danger of being replaced. He is then exposed as a fraud and forced to return home where he blames his domineering mother for his failures and kills her. H. criticizes the dehumanizing influence of bureaucracies and exposes the attempt to colonize other countries through the imposition of the German language. *Gespräch über Balzacs Pferd* (1981; *Balzac's Horse and Other Stories,* 1988) continues the investigation of authoritarian structures in society that prevent the individual from being fully realized, by examining family relationships in different historical epochs—ranging from an imaginary encounter between the old Casanova and his mother to the German poet Siegfried Lenz (q.v.) and his unsupportive father, Balzac's manipulation of his audience through a theater of cruelty to the contemporary poet Robert Walser (q.v.) and a literary club that sponsors him. *Der Turm* (1984; *The Spectacle at the Tower,* 1985) exposes the cruelty of small-village society in Sicily, which reflects the sadistic power games the narrator plays with his wife, both of whom are German tourists stranded in the village. *Der Blindensturz* (1985; *The Parable of the Blind,* 1986) is set in 16th-c. Holland and details that society's inhuman treatment of a band of old men who have been blinded for various misdemeanors and who are now objects of horror who will be painted by a famous artist. One of H.'s best novels is the recent *Veilchenfeld* (1986; Veilchenfeld), which once again takes up the theme of scapegoating the other by chronicling the persecution of a Jewish philosopher by "ordinary" small-town Nazis, and is told from a child's perspective.

H. has established himself as one of the most incisive critics of postwar German society, his prolific writings describing Kafkaesque social structures that maim or deform the individual trapped in them.

FURTHER WORKS: *Die Überflutung: Vier Hörspiele* (1981); *Unsere Eroberung* (1984; *Our Conquest,* 1985); *Die Weltmaschine* (1986); *Unsere Vergeßlichkeit* (1987); *Vor der Regenzeit* (1988); *Das allmähliche Verstummen des Kinoerzählers* (1990)

BIBLIOGRAPHY: Schwartz, L., "Korrekte Verzweiflung. Zu G. H.s Romanen und Novellen," *Merkur,* 1 (1983), 108–12; Painter, K., "Writer Lives in Imagination," *The Oberlin Review,* 20

Apr. 1984, 6; Lützeler, P. "Der verstoßene Sohn," *Die Zeit,* 4 July 1986, 14; Pulver, E., "Die Zerstörung der Überwelt," *Schweizer Monatshefte* (1986), 527–29; Kosler, H. C., *G. H.: Auskunft für Leser* (1987)

HELGA DRUXES

HOLAN, Vladimir

Czechoslovak poet and translator (writing in Czech), b. 16 Sept. 1905, Prague; d. 31 May 1980, Prague

H.'s highly complex poetic work is considered to be one of the most important achievements of modern Czech literature. He dedicated to it the greater part of his life almost exclusively. Having completed his education at a *gymnasium,* H. was employed from 1927 as a clerk, but poor health made him retire in 1935. The rest of his years were largely spent in contemplative solitude. He withdrew into almost complete seclusion in the early 1950s after he had fallen into official disfavor with communist ideologists. The significance of his writing could be fully acknowledged only in the more liberal 1960s.

In the 1930s H. began to publish intellectually demanding hermetic poetry in collections such as *Vanutí* (1932; wafting) and *Oblouk* (1934; the arc). Multiplicity of meaning was couched in a style rich in imagery and permeated by paradoxes, inversions, misshapen words, and neologisms. It was in this type of poetry, reminiscent of Rainer Maria Rilke (q.v.) or Stéphane Mallarmé (1842–1898), that H. established his own poetic realm in which different modes of vision conflicted with each other. His imagination, bizarre yet based in reality, was shaped by this clash. H.'s meditations, his favorite means of approaching a subject, were filled with a dramatic tension emanating from the poet's essential metaphysical dualism, viewing the world as ever oscillating between good and evil, being and nothingness, the moment of time and eternity.

The national tragedy caused by the Munich Agreement about the dismemberment of Czechoslovakia in September 1938 and by German occupation six months later brought about a period of committed poetry: H.'s verse acquired an emotional and forcefully critical tone directed against the perpetrators of the country's betrayal. He conceived the political realities of the time as being part of a wider schism, and saw Nazism as a physical manifestation of the timeless evil. The tendency toward a simpler, down-to-earth style, reflected in particular in the use of a proselike free verse, culminated in H.'s postwar collections *Panychida* (1945; the wake) and *Tobě* (1947; to you), in which he celebrated the nation's regained freedom.

During the period of increased social and patriotic concern (1938–1947), H. also wrote *Terezka Planetová* (1943; Theresa Planet), the first of his poetic stories. These long poems, inspired by real-life events, are endowed with a strong epic sense. Each of the stories is presented as a symbol of the universal human condition and thus attains the quality of myth. Outstanding among them are *Příběhy* (1963; histories) and *Noc s Hamletem* (1964; *A Night with Hamlet*, 1980). The latter, a philosophical meditation in verse, contains the sum of H.'s thought on humans and the world, on existence, and on creativity and art.

Along with this narrative poetry H. kept up his output of lyric verse, which was collected in several volumes. In it he mainly attempted to transcend the world of the senses into a sphere of philosophical reflection.

The last four books of H.'s poetry represent the closing chapter of his creative development and are joined in an ideational and structural unity. They give the impression of a poetic diary in which he abandons the metaphor and reduces his style to gnomic terseness.

A considerable amount of H.'s effort was dedicated to the translation of poetry. Rilke, Charles Baudelaire (1821–1867), Luis de Gongóra y Argote (1561–1627), Charles Vildrac (1882–1971), Jean de La Fontaine (1621–1695), Pierre Ronsard (1524–1585), Adam Mickiewicz (1798–1855), and others found a kindred spirit in H., whose sympathetic interpretation assured them a permanent place in the wider context of Czech literature.

Although all of H.'s work was marked by contemplation, the angle from which he perceived the world changed with time: While in the 1930s his metaphysical dualism often assumed the manner of cold rationalistic construction, in the 1960s and 1970s his lyric poetry was inspired by a compassionate Christian understanding for the mysterious imperfection of human life. Posing oneself ever new questions about the fundamental aspects of existence was regarded by H. as the very purpose of writing poetry.

FURTHER WORKS: *Blouznivý vějíř* (1926); *Triumf smrti* (1930); *Kolury* (1932); *Torzo* (1933); *Kameni, přicházíš* . . . (1937); *Září 1938* (1938); *Sen* (1939); *Lemuria* (1940); *První testament* (1940); *Záhřmotí* (1940); *Chór* (1941); *Cesta mraku* (1945); *Dík Sovětskému svazu* (1945); *Zpěv tříkrálový* (1947); *Rudoarmějci* (1947); *Prostě* (1954); *Bajaja* (1955); *Tři* (1957); *Mozartiana* (1963); *Bez názvu* (1963); *Dvě jezera* (1963); *Na postupu* (1964); *Trialog* (1964); *Bolest* (1965); *Dva světy* (1966); *Na sotnách* (1967); *Asklépiovi kohouta* (1970);

Noc s Ofélií (1973); *Sebrané spisy V. H.* (11 vols., 1965–1988). FURTHER VOLUMES IN ENGLISH: *Selected Poems* (1971); *Mirroring* (1983)

BIBLIOGRAPHY: Milner, I., Introduction to *Selected Poems* (1971), 9–15; Mihailovich, V. D., et al., eds., *Modern Slavic Literatures* (1976), Vol. 2, 98–103; special H. issue, *La Revue de Belles-Lettres,* 1–2 (1991)

JAROSLAV MED

HOLUB, Miroslav

Czechoslovak poet, essayist, and translator (writing in Czech), b. 3 Sept. 1923, Plzeň

Having completed his secondary education at a *Gymnasium* during the German occupation in 1942, H. worked on the railways and could resume his studies only after the war. He obtained an M.D. from Charles University in Prague in 1953 and a Ph.D. in immunology in 1958. He worked as a research scientist in various institutes in Czechoslovakia and abroad, including the Public Health Research Institute in New York (1965–1967) and the Max Planck Institute in Freiburg (1968–1969). He is the author of well over a hundred scientific papers and monographs in his field.

H.'s first poem came out in print in 1947, but he did not attract serious attention until he joined, in the mid-1950s, a group of younger writers associated with the literary magazine *Květen,* who were challenging the pompous, bloated, and shamheroic clichés of Socialist Realism (q.v.). With his sober lyricism supported by intellectual analysis rather than spontaneity and instinct, H. was soon recognized as the foremost representative of this school referred to as "Poetry of Everyday Life." Conditions were not yet ready for a program of this kind, and after a brush with the political authorities, the magazine was closed down. However, many of the names that first appeared in its pages were later to reemerge as those of the best-known Czech poets and novelists.

H.'s first collection, *Denní služba* (1958; day duty), was followed two years later by *Achilles a želva* (1960; Achilles and the tortoise), and by 1970 he had produced another eight volumes of poetry. They met with almost unanimous praise from the critics, but the reception by the Czech public was more reserved. H.'s apparent trust in the near omnipotence of science and the emphasis he placed on a conscious human effort to improve the world seemed to be suspiciously close to official Marxist ideology. Moreover, the altogether cerebral nature of his verse was outside the traditional perception of poetry as experienced by his compatriots. Many of them had been nurtured on the romantic, emotional lyricism, the mellifluous language, and the dazzlingly beautiful imagery of earlier Czech poets, and found these qualities missing in H.

On the other hand, he was accorded the respect and admiration due to a major poet as soon as his work began to be published in the West. It was particularly well received in the U.S. and Britain, where in the 1960s an intellectualized conception of poetry was already well established through the efforts of William Carlos Williams (q.v.) and Lawrence Ferlinghetti (b. 1919), among others. It seemed that both in spirit and in style H.'s poetry was ideally suited for translation into English; in fact, some of it may read better in English than in the original Czech.

While he was steadily growing in stature abroad, at home H.'s scientific and poetic careers both suffered setbacks caused by the political repression that followed the Soviet invasion in 1968. In 1973 H. issued a statement in which he revoked his previously held "incorrect" views and which in effect contradicted the ethos of all his work. Afterward, he could publish and attend poetry festivals in the West, yet had to wait nine years to see a new collection of his verse appear in Czechoslovakia. When at long last *Naopak* (1982; *On the Contrary*, 1984) was published, it could not escape notice that a new note of skepticism had entered H.'s world of irrefragable scientific certainties and unrelenting rational progress, perhaps as a consequence of the recognition that reason need not always prevail. More questions were being asked than answers offered, but the mood was far from gloomy. Some poems, most notably "Sny" ("Dreams"), interpreted usually as alluding to the dismal situation in Czechoslovakia, in fact expressed hope of future change. A similar shift in attitude was noted in that part of H.'s work that up to 1982 had been known only in the West, such as *Notes of a Clay Pigeon* (1977 [*holub* means pigeon in Czech]), *Sagitální řez* (1988; *Sagittal Section*, 1980), and *Interferon čili o divadle* (1986; first pub. in English as *Interferon or On the Theater*, 1982).

As well as poetry, H. published a number of witty travelogues and several collections of refined essays in which his point of view advocating the necessity of a constant struggle to expand the realm of knowledge was applied to the discussion of aspects of contemporary life.

With a force stemming from the combination of art and science, H.'s poetry offers a terse comment on the state of humankind in the second half of the 20th c. It reflects the self-confidence of the first part of this period as well as the increasing doubt about the rationality of individual and social behavior as the end of the century approaches.

Nonetheless, the essential message of H.'s work remains one of moderate encouragement and hope for the advance of scientific humanism. Many critics and fellow poets regard H. as one of the dozen greatest living poets. The clinical precision of his style and the compact imagery of his verse has such a direct appeal that the reader may forget that the original had been written in Czech. It could be argued, however, whether H.'s poetry would have been as universally effective had it not been supported by the poet's unique east European experience.

FURTHER WORKS: *Slabikář* (1961); *Jdi a otevři dveře* (1962); *Anděl na kolečkách* (1963); *Kam teče krev* (1963); *Zcela nesoustavná zoologie* (1963); *Tak zvané srdce* (1963); *Anamnéza* (1964); *Tři kroky po zemi* (1965); *Žít v New Yorku* (1969); *Ačkoli* (1969); *Beton* (1970); *Události* (1971); *K principu rolničky* (1987; *The Jingle Bell Principle*, 1991); *Maxwellův démon čili o tvořivosti* (1988); *nePATRNÉne* (1989); *Syndrom mizející plíce* (1990; *Vanishing Lung Syndrome*, 1990); *Skrytá zášť věku* (1991). FURTHER VOLUMES IN ENGLISH: *Selected Poems* (1967); *The Fly and Other Poems* (1987); *Poems Before and After* (1990); *The Dimension of the Present Moment* (1990)

BIBLIOGRAPHY: Alvarez, A., Introduction to *Selected Poems* (1967), 9–17; Mihailovich, V. D., et al., eds., *Modern Slavic Literatures* (1976), Vol. 2, 103–6; Schechter, B., "A Man for Two Cultures," *Discover*, May 1982, 60–64; Young, D., Introduction to *Interferon or On the Theater* (1982), 9–22; Heaney, S., *The Government of the Tongue* (1989), 45–53; Milner, I., Foreword to *Poems Before and After* (1990), 13–16; Reynolds, O., "A Voice for the Mute," *TLS*, 4-10 May 1990, 467–68; Crawford, R., "The Transnationality of the Czech Immunologist," *PoetryR*, 80, 2 (Summer 1990), 8–10

IGOR HÁJEK

HOVEYDA, Fereydoun

Iranian novelist, essayist, and film critic (writing in French), b. 21 Sept. 1924, Damascus, Syria

H. was born in Syria, the son of an Iranian diplomat. He was educated in Beirut, Lebanon, and obtained a doctorate in law from the Sorbonne in Paris in 1948. H. joined the Iranian foreign service and was press attaché at the embassy in Paris from 1947 to 1951. He joined UNESCO in 1952 as a mass-communications specialist, but returned to Iran in 1965 to serve as undersecretary for international organizations in the foreign ministry. He was the Iranian ambassador to the United Nations from 1971 to 1978. H. now lives in the U.S. and paints, lectures, and writes books and articles, all on a range of political and literary subjects.

As an artist H. in his many shows in the U.S. developed a new technique of "papiers collés," leaving a very narrow white space between papers. In the words of Andy Warhol, H. "combines his literary sensitivity, his cinematic instinct, and his international experience, to create images that are beautiful, perceptive, and funny."

His first book, *Histoire du roman policier* (1956; history of the detective novel), was given a preface by Jean Cocteau (q.v.). H. became a regular contributor to *Mystère-Magazine,* the French counterpart of Ellery Queen's magazine *Fiction,* a science-fiction monthly, and to the celebrated *Les cahiers du cinéma* that in the early 1960s launched what was to be known as the "new wave" of film directors. H. is represented in two volumes of *Les cahiers du cinéma,* on the 1950s and 1960s respectively, which were published by Harvard University in 1985–1986 in an English translation.

H. published his first novel, *Les quarantaines* (1962; a many-faceted word whose possible meanings include medical quarantines and the state of being forty years old). Its plot was of a French-educated Arab living in France during the Algerian war, caught between his traditional Arab culture and his Western education. Using cinematic and psychoanalytic techniques, H. describes accurately and vividly the emotions of the growing group of multicultured Middle-Eastern people and their problems. The novel succumbed to polemics in the heat of the Algerian war, but was eventually honored as a "healer" between Western and Eastern cultures. H.'s second novel, *L'aerogare* (1965; the airport), recounted the production of a script, in two weeks, by a Paris-born American film director. In the course of his writing, many questions concerning the coming of the "age of image" and the relationship between cinema, literature, and metaphysics are illuminated for the filmmaker.

H.'s third novel, *Dans une terre étrange* (1968; in a strange land), is the story of a child who feels cheated by his own parents. In this novel H. applied to literature the techniques of comic books to underline the distance between the worlds of adults and children. A year later, he wrote *Le losange* (1969; the lozenge), a collection of science-fiction stories.

His next novel concerned a French-born American writer drifting toward alcoholism, *Les neiges du Sinai* (1973; the snows of the Sinai). It opens with the protagonist reading the Sunday edition of the *New York Times.* In this work H. used in many ways the techniques of the stream-of-consciousness (q.v.) novel, introducing "sounds" and "im-

ages" in combination with words. The book won the Leopold Senghor Prize for foreigners writing in French.

When the Iranian revolution was victorious and Khomeini returned to Iran after fourteen years of living in exile, H. published in English *The Fall of the Shah* (1979; pub. in French as *La chute du Shah,* 1980), a personal account of the events that led to the tragic death of his brother, the long-time prime minister of Iran.

H. wrote an autobiographical piece, *Les nuits féodales* (1983; the feudal nights), and his first historical novel, *Le glaive de l'Islam* (1985; the sword of Islam), treating the rise of Islam in the 7th c. and its first sixty years. His latest book is an essay on the Middle East, *Que veulent les Arabes* (1991; what do the Arabs want?).

H.'s novels concentrate on characters pertaining to two or more cultures simultaneously. Even in *Dans une terre étrange,* although the story is about the French, his young character is caught between childhood and adulthood, which in the view of H. are two completely separate "cultures." In *Le glaive de l'Islam* the hero, an Arab general, is influenced by the cultures of the conquered nations: Persia, Syria, Egypt, and North Africa. In all his works, H. searches for the ultimate unity of all human cultures.

As a writer, H. argues that the cultures, civilizations, political and religious systems complement each other rather than merge together. The vision of the world in his writings is strongly reflected in his collages and "papiers collés," where there is a sharp edge between colors and sometimes even a space between them, while their totality creates a pattern in which color and shape are complementary.

PETER J. CHELKOWSKI

HULTBERG, Peer

Danish novelist and short-story writer, b. 11 Nov. 1935, Vangede

An academic specializing in psychoanalysis and Polish literature and an author in voluntary exile, H. is one of the most widely traveled and internationally experienced authors of modern Danish literature. His doctoral dissertation is on Wacław Berent's (1873–1940) symbolistic authorship, and he has taught Polish at the universities of London and Copenhagen. Formerly a student in eastern Europe, he has since the late 1950s lived in Switzerland, West Germany, and London.

Mythical themes and musical tones are discernible throughout H.'s work. In his recent texts the myth has submerged beneath a realistic, almost minimalistic, surface from where it continues to offset a musical style. In his debut, the novel *Mytologisk landskab med Daphnes forvandling* (1966; mythological landscape with the transformation of Daphne), this interest in minute details is more maniacal and appears to reflect a neurotic suppression of essential concerns. Transformation of major frustrations into small activities breaks the deadlock, and diabolic short-circuits between separate levels of meaning deny the grand narrative a free-wheeling showoff. Whether exposed directly as a grand illusion or subjected to less direct romantic irony, it signifies a depersonalized and fragmented world in which any existential situation dissolves into possible or probable, but ultimately undecidable, alternatives.

With no certainty at hand, dialogues and plots either run parallel or collide; an erotic triangle is typically devoid of meaningful encounters. Human identities elude clarification, and stylistic repetitions only testify to the permanence of confusion. With barely visible borders between narration and dialogue, the distinctions between first- and third-person narratives become precariously fickle and beholden to the narrative viewpoint. No wonder that different pronouns are, too, used synonymously or with ambiguous reference. Pros and cons are intertwined.

In H.'s principal work, *Requiem* (1985; requiem), the musical score has been elevated to a mass for the repose of the dead, and yet this formidable choir of 537 independent voices, or texts, is the epitome of situational representation, verisimilitude, and everydayness. H. has accepted that his discourse be called stream-of-unconsciousness (q.v.) and merely added that his book is 537 snapshots of anonymous individuals' minds in the moment before they each formulate their sentiments to other people. Merciless hatred and obscure sexuality blend with projected despair and self-contempt, and petty vindictiveness teams with studied generosity. These are the moments when people say ''yes'' but mean ''no,'' and when conscious self-censorship is most ineffectual. While intended to set matters straight and right, this state of mind is held hostage by duplicity and self-righteousness. Insight in self-deception only serves to refute it, modesty is pride in disguise, openness a calculated risk, and confidence the last resort of the powerless.

The sounding board for these pessimistic tones is the classical rift between spirit and matter. It is a neurotic or psychotic frustration, but at least it is dynamic and live. The alternative resolution is dead and soulless, and to discharge the split, one must dispense with life itself—or at least with male supremacy. The narrative voices are mostly male, and there is an indirect feminism and a humanistic sense of balance involved in H.'s modern orchestration of classical European dilemmas in this vital and viable requiem.

In part one of *Slagne veje* (1988; beaten tracks) the scene has changed to the U.S. and the key to forty short narratives or verbal stills of modern Americans and their mores and ways. Whether successful or not in their particular endeavors, theirs are stories about human vanity—a patchwork of alarming uniformity.

Part two consists of six longer and more intimate monologues or streams-of-unconsciousness. Although ''personalities'' are conspicuous by their absence throughout his universe, H.'s characters experience circumstances so turbulent as to occasion unforeseen angles of incidence on their traumatic patterns of life. The narrative subtly escapes the confines of the narrated—leaving the reader with a sense of catharsis.

The title of the novel *Præludier* (1989; preludes) suggests a preliminary mode of fiction marked by improvising and by free and poetic movements, and the novel does indeed exude some refined naive insight into the childhood and adolescent years of Frédéric Chopin. Again, H.'s ''prelinguistic'' licentia poetica provides a blend of character and characterizer, of narrative segments and lyrical poems, and of French and Polish idioms— on the background of the protagonist's fear of death and deadly parental discipline. A conflict-ridden process of human maturation springs from the process of mature writing.

Because of H.'s all-European orientation, combined with his attempts at stylistic innovation, it took about two decades for his art and audience to meet and for critics and others to appreciate his artistic powers. When it finally happened—in *Requiem*—the occasion was commonly celebrated as a rare event, and his subsequent books seem to confirm that H. is a migratory bird whose literary offspring has come to stay.

FURTHER WORKS: *Desmond* (1968); *Fjerut fra Viborg* (1990)

POUL HOUE

HUNGARIAN LITERATURE

See Volume 2, page 412.

Hungarian literature, whose development and very character had been shaped traditionally by poets, has become considerably more prose-oriented in the past two decades. Several writers of fiction who remained on the sideline of literary life for much of their careers, either for political reasons or because they never met the litmus test for social relevance in art, have seen their reputation grow in recent years. Géza Ottlik (1912–1990) was one such loner. His *Iskola a határon* (1959; *School at the Frontier*, 1966), now recognized as one of the most significant Hungarian novels of the post-1956 period, focuses on the recollections of a group of former cadets in an old-style central European military academy, though the novel is just as concerned with the process of fiction itself, with the difficulties of conventional narration, the inconclusiveness of memory, and, in a larger sense, with the impossibility of truly objectifying reality. Miklós Mészöly (q.v.) is another more or less experimental writer, who in sparse and precise narratives—*Az atléta halála* (1966; the death of an athlete), *Saulus* (1968; Saulus), and *Film* (1976; film) are his most important fictions—offers bleak and open-ended studies of solitary individuals in the throes of excruciating though never fully comprehended spiritual crises. Mészöly's best short stories—"Jelentés öt egérről" (1958; "Report on Five Mice," 1982) and "Ló-regény" (1982; "A Tale of Horses," 1986)—which also revolve around dimly perceived existential dilemmas and struggles, are somewhat more accessible, and his essays contain even more forthright discussions of specifically east European political and cultural issues.

Both Ottlik and Mészöly used to be classified by Marxist critics as alienated, "existentialist" writers, yet they had a strong impact on a generation of younger prose writers who appeared on the literary scene in the 1970s, and whose allusive, self-reflective and parodistic fiction exudes a postmodern sensibility. Writers like Péter Esterházy, Péter Nádas (qq.v.), Ferenc Temesi (b. 1949), Péter Lengyel (b. 1939), and others clearly admire their masters' moral and artistic integrity, but their rejection of literary forms sanctioned by ideology or tradition led them away from Ottlik's painstaking, irreproachable fictional reconstructions or Mészöly's stark moral fables to a skeptically playful, stylistically far more exuberant and inventive treatment of personal and communal history. In the process they often revisit, always with satiric intent, traditional anecdotal realism and embrace other classical, popular, once-obligatory genres. For example, Péter Esterházy's first long work of fiction, *Termelési-regény* (1979; production novel), is a takeoff on the Socialist Realist (q.v.) "production novels" of the 1950s, and his *Kis magyar pornográfia* (1984; a handbook of Hungarian pornography), rooted also in the totalitarian experience, is a compendium of lusty anecdotes and vignettes about the political perversions of recent and not-so-recent Hungarian history. Péter Nádas is another self-consciously literary writer. His magnum opus *Az emlékiratok könyve* (1986; book of memoirs), first strikes the reader as a confessional *je roman* in the grandly modernist manner,

replete with Proustian and Mannian echoes, but what it really is is an endlessly refined and modified postmodern reprise of the European psychological novel. Ferenc Temesi has chosen yet another unusual narrative device. His two-volume *Por A-Zs* (1986–1987; dust A-Z) is a novel in encyclopedic form, in which alphabetical entries do coalesce into a narrative of sorts, though the author's real aim is to present an in-depth portrait of a single Hungarian town: its past and present, its official and underground history, including tantalizing local legends, scandals, and villains. Similarly, Péter Lengyel's *Macskakő* (1988; cobblestone), subtitled a "detective story," uses the formulas and clichés of this particular genre to explore the urban folklore of his native Budapest, focusing on the period of the turn of the century when the city was young and vital and its underworld, too, was enviably resourceful and robust. Both Temesi and Lengyel are in some ways indebted to another "old master," Iván Mándy (b. 1918), who in his impressionistic stories and sketches also evokes the lore and romance of old Budapest.

There are even more radical experimenters among the younger Hungarian prose writers, and they, too, have attracted critical attention of late. László Márton (b. 1959), for example, a Germanist and translator by profession, favors linguistic parodies of old literary texts, whereas László Krasznahorkai (b. 1954) describes a timeless world of utter desolation and hopelessness with curiously suggestive and lively language. Krasznahorkai's remarkable first novel, *Sátántangó* (1985; satan-tango), dealing nominally with a group of isolated and sullen peasants deceived by a would-be savior, becomes an unnerving depiction of spatial-temporal immobility.

In general, one could say that the innovative prose writers who revolutionized Hungarian fiction are obsessed with form and language. In various ways they all engage in subtle culture criticism, which includes conspicuous linguistic criticism. Behind their parodies and pastiches there is the recognition that in a society where public discourse is warped, language itself is hopelessly compromised. Postmodernism (q.v.), then, in the Hungarian context, is not simply a new way of telling old stories but an attempt to make language relevant again, to purge it of cant without being solemn about it. Approaches vary, of course. Péter Esterházy and Péter Nádas, by far the most versatile and accomplished members of this group, have opted for markedly different stylistic solutions. Esterházy fights off linguistic corruptions by producing some of his own. His texts are riddled with untranslatable puns, wordplays, and distorted literary allusions. Nádas, on the other hand, protects his work from the debased political and intellectual jargon of the day by creating a highly intricate, rarefied, and classically screne literary language.

Naturally, not all contemporary Hungarian novelists are quite this form-conscious, or are followers of experimental, postmodernist trends. A number of important recent Hungarian novels have closer ties with the still flourishing realist school of fiction. For example, György Spiró's (b. 1946) widely acclaimed *Az ikszek* (1981; the X's) is a fiction set in 18th-c. partitioned Poland. Concerned exclusively with the inbred world of Polish theatrical people of the time, this intriguingly modern-toned historical novel reveals a great deal about conflicts and compromises characteristic of all occupied east European societies. A lesser-known figure, Imre Kertész (b. 1929), achieved belated fame only recently with his novel *Sorstalanság* (1975; *Without Destiny*, 1992), a detailed and dispassionate account of a fourteen-year-old Jewish boy's ordeal in wartime concentration camps.

Actually, Kertész is one of many Hungarian writers whose prominence has been more clearly acknowledged since the historic "quiet revolution" of 1989. While quite a few previously active, popular, even stylish writers—Ferenc Karinthy (1921–1992), György Moldova (b. 1934), László Gyurkó (b. 1934), Gyula Hernádi (b. 1924)—have been eclipsed by these changes, others came to the fore since the fall of Hungary's communist régime. These latter artists had either been under publication bans before, or they simply did not want to subject their works even to mild forms of censorship. It is true enough that the cultural policies of the pre-1989 Kádár régime were much more liberal than those of other east European communist governments, and the number of taboo subjects in literature remained relatively small, but in the past several years the country's unfettered media made it amply clear that the manipulation of the arts, though subtle, had been nevertheless pervasive even during the latter phase of one-party rule. Writers who once again became full-fledged members of the Hungarian literary community include the poet and publicist István Eörsi (b. 1931), the documentarist Zsolt Csalog (b. 1935), the satirist György Dalos (b. 1943), and the poet György Petri (b. 1943).

But the best-known author to have reentered literary life in the late 1980s, and one of the few Hungarian writers who established an international reputation in the past two decades, is George (György) Konrád (q.v.). His masterful first novel, *A látogató* (1969; *The Case Worker*, 1974), a devastating, sociologically revealing depiction of Budapest lowlife was brought out in a modest edition in 1969. A slightly censored version of his second, more abstract, experimental fiction, *A városalapító* (1977; *The City Builder*, 1977), could still be published in Hungary, but after that Konrád became an internal exile, and his writings could be read inside the country only in the underground *samizdat* press. His third novel, *A cinkos* (1978; *The Loser*, 1982), is a more traditional, loosely episodic narrative concerned with the checkered life history of a disenchanted modern revolutionary, and his latest, *Kerti mulatság* (1989; *Feast in the Garden*, 1992), is an even more diffuse, essayistic examination of the life and hard times of a present-day Hungarian intellectual.

The publication, or republication, of George Konrád's works were among the first sensations of the new democratic era. The reappearance in print of actual émigrés—the seminal modernist Győző Határ (b. 1914), the popular lyricist György Faludy (b. 1910), the excommunist novelist Tamás Aczél (b. 1921), and above all the doyen of Hungarian literary exiles, Sándor Márai (1900–1989)—was likewise greeted with lively interest. Yet, ironically, the political changes also created an air of crisis in literature. To be sure, the proliferation of new, uncensored publications and private publishing ventures stirred great initial excitement, but as a result of slashed government subsidies and other reforms, serious literature has fallen on hard times—and this in spite of the fact that a number of well-known writers, journalists, and historians are members of the democratically elected government, including the president of the Hungarian Republic, Árpád Göncz (b. 1922), a noted translator of American literature.

The freewheeling and combative new political atmosphere favors literary journalism and the political essay, and it seems to have diminished the importance of imaginative literature. Moreover, some of the long-standing divisions in Hungarian cultural life—the antagonism between "populist" and "urban" writers—have also resurfaced and led to several acrimonious public debates, with undercurrents of intolerant nationalism and anti-Semitism.

With the death of Gyula Illyés in 1983, the mantle of national poet passed to Sándor Csoóri (qq.v.), the most prominent and influential populist literary figure. In his recent volumes of poetry and prose—*Kezemben a zöld ág* (1985; green twig in my hand); *Készülődés a számadásra* (1987; preparing for the reckoning); and *A világ emlékművei* (1989; memorials of the world)—Csoóri continues to focus on such themes as the erosion of Hungarian national values, the decline of rural life, and the fate of the Hungarian minorities in neighboring east European countries. Another populist, the playwright István Csurka (b. 1934), has become better known in recent years as a controversial political figure. The finest "urban" poets of the day—Dezső Tandori (b. 1938), Ágnes Gergely (b. 1933), Szabolcs Várady (b. 1943), Péter Kántor (b. 1949), Zsuzsa Rakovszky (b. 1950)—tend to be less visible. Influenced by the understated intellectualism of István Vas (1910–1991) and the objective lyricism of Ágnes Nemes Nagy (1922–1991)—and reacting against the overwrought wordiness of much Hungarian poetry—these poets write sparingly, and with ironic detachment, about recent upheavals. The one possible exception is the former dissident György Petri, whose forceful and explicit political poetry effectively fuses public and private traumas. With his first collected edition of his verses, *Petri György versei* (1991; the poetry of György Petri), the once-banned poet gained a wider readership. The poems of Dezső Tandori cannot be said to have broad popular appeal: The minimalism of his early poetry yielded to a more obsessive privatization of experience in his later work; yet Tandori is a formidable talent, and not only as a poet but as a prose writer, critic, and translator as well—his quiet virtuosity is evident in all of these areas. (A selection of Tandori's poems, *Birds and Other Relations,* was published in English in 1986.) Though a more traditional poet drawn to somber moods and wistful insights, Ágnes Gergely is equally versatile, and Szabolcs Várady was hailed, already at the beginning of his career, as a "complete" poet. Indeed, what Tandori, Gergely, and Várady share with other "urbanists" is unobtrusive formal sophistication, polish, and reticence. Like the new fictionists, they distrust words, but they prefer to use fewer rather than more words to express this distrust.

Hungarian drama, always more conservative and convention-bound, produced fewer surprises in the 1970s and 1980s. Among the younger playwrights Mihály Kornis (b. 1949) stands out as the most original. Kornis's affinity for symbolist and absurdist modes lends his down-to-earth, zany, and very Hungarian plays, notably *Halleluja* (1980; hallelujah) and *Kozma* (1981; *Kozma,* 1991), an air of universality. György Spiró achieves a similar effect by turning to historical subjects. His *Az imposztor* (1982; the imposter) is a highly successful adaptation of a section of his novel *Az ikszek.* In a more recent play, *Csirkefej* (1985; *Chicken Head,* 1991), Spiró uses the stylized naturalism preferred by some contemporary American playwrights to portray the crude and cruel world of Budapest slum dwellers. The more traditional historical dramas of the Transylvanian Hungarian writer András Sütő (b. 1927) have also received memorable productions in Budapest in the past decade. The frequent performances of Sütő's dramas *Csillag a máglyán* (1975; star at the stake)

and *Egy lócsiszár virágvasárnapja* (1978; *The Palm Sunday of a Horse Dealer,* 1991) attest to the renewed literary and political interest in the works of Hungarian writers living beyond the country's borders. Some of these authors—Lajos Grendel (b. 1948) in Slovakia, Nándor Gion (b. 1941) in Yugoslavia, Ádám Bodor (b. 1936), formerly of Romania—are very much in the mainstream of Hungarian literature, though their writings often reflect the double isolation of minority nationals in repressive or aggressively nationalistic east European societies.

Since the 1989–1990 watershed, as might be expected, the tone-setting, ideologically committed analysts of Hungarian literature have lost much of their power and influence. Literary criticism, too, has become more variegated, more relevant. In this field two new personalities emerged: the erudite Sándor Radnóti (b. 1946), whose training in philosophy and formal aesthetics enables him to view literary developments from a broader perspective, and Péter Balassa (b. 1947), who is particularly in tune with the world of the innovative prose writers of the 1970s and 1980s. The dramatic political changes also affected, inevitably, the institutions and organizational structure of cultural life. Even under new leadership, the large state publishing houses and theaters are struggling to stay solvent. Similarly, the established literary journals such as *Kortárs, Új Írás, Élet és Irodalom,* and *Nagyvilág* have lost much ground—they now have to compete with a plethora of new publications of varying quality. Of the newly founded literary periodicals, the most significant appear to be *Holmi, 2000,* the populist-oriented *Hitel,* and *Budapesti Könyvszemle* (The Budapest Review of Books), modeled after its sister publication in New York.

Hungarian literary life in the early 1990s is clearly in a state of flux. The excitement over new freedoms and opportunities has given way to concern that the commercial spirit of the new age may lead to the further marginalization of literature. Yet, since this is a society where the printed word still matters, the desire to see thoroughgoing literary treatments of the most recent turn of events—and in general, to see the literary validation of the nation's historical experience—remains strong.

BIBLIOGRAPHY: Vajda, M., ed., *Modern Hungarian Poetry* (1977); Klaniczay, T., ed., *A History of Hungarian Literature* (1982); Czigány, L., *The Oxford History of Hungarian Literature* (1984); Balassa, P., "On Recent Hungarian Prose: A Survey and Introduction," *Formations,* 3 (1986), 153–56; Sanders, I., "Budapest Letter: New Themes, New Writers," *NYTBR,* 10 Apr. 1988, 1; Brogyányi, E., ed., *DramaContemporary: Hungary* (1992)

IVAN SANDERS

HURSTON, Zora Neale

American novelist, short-story writer, folklorist, and essayist, b. 7 Jan. 1901 (?), Eatonville, Fla.; d. 28 Jan. 1960, Fort Pierce, Fla.

Raised in an all-black Southern town, one of eight children, H. attended Howard University for two years, where she learned short-story writing, then graduated from Barnard College in 1928. While at Barnard H. journeyed to Alabama to interview the ex-slave Cudjo Lewis, then published the result in 1927. With a Rosenwald Fellowship she attended Columbia University Graduate School to study anthropology under Franz Boas. She returned to her home state to record Black folklore from 1928 to 1932, which produced the collection *Mules and Men* (1935). H.'s first published novel, *Jonah's Gourd Vine* (1934), was praised for its authentic use of folklore but criticized for ignoring the influence of racism. From 1935 to 1937 she studied voodoo practices in Haiti and Jamaica under a Guggenheim fellowship, which produced *Tell My Horse* (1938; repub. as *Voodoo Gods: An Inquiry into Native Myths and Magic in Jamaica and Haiti,* 1939), a folklore collection. *Their Eyes Were Watching God* (1937), regarded as her best novel, was a response to an experience of unrequited love. H. continued collecting folklore in Florida for the WPA (1938–1939).

Her autobiography, *Dust Tracks on a Road* (1942), became her most popular work, wherein she stated that the race question always left her unmoved. H. spent years raising funds to study black folklore in Honduras, traveling there in 1947. Her final decade was beset with financial problems, failing health, isolation from family and old friends, and destitution, punctuated by a few freelance writing assignments, 1950–1956, as well as sundry part-time jobs as a librarian, maid, and school teacher.

H. gained early experience writing short fiction in college, contributing stories to the Howard literary magazine *Stylus,* and to the black journal *Opportunity,* whose editor, Charles S. Johnson, encouraged her to go to New York to broaden her literary development. During this formative period she began folkloric study from a scientific perspective, encouraged by Boas to combine empathic interviewing techniques with anthropological disinterest. She was known to stop Harlemites on the street to measure the shape of their heads. This combination of distance and empathy would characterize H.'s literary style

throughout her life. To some extent the distancing devices in her work were a response to a felt need. "It was only when I was off in college, away from my native surroundings, that I could see myself like somebody else and stand off and look at my garment. Then I had to have the spyglass of anthropology to look through at that." Her first folklore collection, *Mules and Men,* reflected both the intimacy and the distance of her writer's point of view. H. always included herself as part of the culture she represented, even at times appearing as her own character Zora to record folktales and humor on the front porches of the homes she visited. Then her role was that of an eccentric woman taken to writing down the "lies" of the townsfolk while they "killed groceries" and drank freely. Later H. was accused by some critics of making her fiction and plays mere recordings of what other people told her.

H.'s sharp ear for the sounds of spoken English was reflected in *Jonah's Gourd Vine,* which was loosely based on her father's career as a minister, the personality of her mother, and her hometown milieu of an all-black township. Throughout this novel H. alternates between elevated prose and the figurative language of rural dialect as she examines the inner lives and hidden emotions of her characters. The critical success of *Jonah's Gourd Vine* brought H. literary recognition and commissions for magazine stories and articles.

Although *Their Eyes Were Watching God* (1937) has been criticized for lacking suitable political orientation and literary theme, Richard Wright (q.v.) calling it "counterrevolutionary," it is now generally considered her greatest work. Written over an eight-week period in Haiti, the plot concerns Janie Crawford, whose self-awareness develops as a result of her experience with three successive husbands. Disappointed in love with her first husband, unable to endure the strictures of social propriety in her second marriage, Janie finally finds love and a measure of equality in her third marriage. However, she must kill her demented husband in self-defense when he threatens her life as a result of his hydrophobia brought about by a rabid dog's bite. Read from a feminist perspective, Janie's marital histories show a progression from conventional submissiveness to middle-class restrictiveness and finally to a kind of freedom with equality, resulting from a marriage based on mutual sharing instead of status and material worth. The "counterrevolutionary" climax is Janie's acquittal of her husband's murder by an all-white jury. As she returns to her all-black town, Janie is condemned by her black neighbors, who reject her self-defense motive, interpreting the killing as a willful act against her husband: "No nigger woman ain't never been treated no better." Rather than a condemnation of black society, or "a lack of bitterness towards whites," as one early reviewer saw it, H.'s novel seems to describe the social, economic, and patriarchal dominance that crosses over both black and white worlds.

Dust Tracks on a Road reveals signs of H.'s defensiveness toward the growing criticism of her novels and folklore collections. While the accounts of her childhood and parents seem straightforward, disclosure about important aspects of her adult life is lacking. Though Alice Walker (q.v.) called the autobiography's tendency to circumvent self-analysis "oddly false-sounding," H.'s ruminations on life's difficulties are often subtle and revealing in their own right.

A member of the Harlem Renaissance, H. intended to write about the black experience in its full humanity, with stories "incisive and intimate . . . from the inside." Her fiction abandons what she has called "the reversion to type," by which she meant the persistent reluctance of writers and critics to transcend traditional stereotyping and simplistic psychology when depicting black life in America. H. juxtaposed the cadences of folk dialect with an eloquent prose style that explored the inner world of black Americans. She sought realistic situations and dialogue conveyed through a sensitive prose narrative that at times approached the Homeric. H.'s ear for folk dialect and stories was so keen and her understanding of black life so integrated with her own personality that her fiction was often attacked as mere novelized folklore. Her works integrated so fully social environment with the inner lives of her characters that such misinterpretations might have been inevitable.

FURTHER WORKS: *Mule Bone: A Comedy of Negro Life in Three Acts* (1931, with Langston Hughes); *Fast and Furious* (1932, with Clinton Fletcher and Tim Moore); *Moses, Man of the Mountain* (1939; repub. as *The Man of the Mountain,* 1941); *Seraph on the Suwanee* (1948); *I Love Myself When I Am Laughing . . . And Then Again When I Am Looking Mean and Impressive: A Z. N. H. Reader* (1979); *The Sanctified Church* (1981); *Spunk: The Selected Short Stories of Z. N. H.* (1985)

BIBLIOGRAPHY: Turner, D. T., *In a Minor Chord: Three Afro-American Writers and Their Search for Identity* (1971), 89–120; Davis, A. P., *From the Dark Tower: Afro-American Writers (1900–1960)* (1974), 113–20; Hemenway, R. E., *Z. N. H.* (1977); Newson, A. S., *Z. N. H.: A Reference Guide* (1980); Howard, L. P., *Z. N. H.* (1980); Bloom, H., ed., *Z. N. H.* (1986); Washington, M. H., ed., *Invented Lives: Narratives of Black Women, 1860–1960* (1987), 237–54; Krasner, J.,

"The Life of Women: Z. N. H. and Female Autobiography," *BALF,* 23, 1 (Spring 1989), 113–26; Wall, C. A., "Mules and Men and Women: Z. N. H.'s Strategies of Narration and Visions of Female Empowerment," *BALF,* 23, 4 (Winter 1989), 661–80; Nathiri, N. Y., ed., *Zora!: Z. N. H., A Woman and Her Community* (1991)

WILLIAM OVER

HYDER, Qurratulain

Indian novelist and short-story writer (writing in Urdu), b. 1927, Aligarh

H., the Urdu-speaking world's most famous novelist, has also made a mark as a short-story writer and a journalist. She was born in Aligarh, where her father, Sajjad Hyder Yildirim (1880–1942), also a short-story writer and prose stylist, was at that time registrar of the Muslim University. Her mother, Nazr Sajjad Hyder (1894–1967) was also a well-known Urdu writer of her times who played a leading role in Muslim social reform. H. received her M.A. in English from the University of Lucknow, studied Urdu and Persian at home, and learned classical Indian and Western music and painting. She migrated to Pakistan in 1947 and worked for the ministry of information and at the Pakistan High Commission in London. On her return to India, she edited a literary magazine, *Imprint,* became a member of the editorial board of *The Illustrated Weekly of India,* served as advisor to the chairman of the Board of Film Censors, and was invited as visiting professor by the Aligarh Muslim University and the Jamia Millia Islamia, Delhi. As the most celebrated author in Urdu, she received the Indian Academy of Letters Award (1967), the Soviet Land-Nehru Award (1969), the Government of India's Civilian Honour (1984), the Ghalib Award (1985), the Iqbal Award (1987), and the Altar of Knowledge Award (1989).

The predicament of the modern human being, confronted with cruel and formidable forces, finds powerful expression in her novels and short stories. Her writings also reflect her preoccupation with India's cultural heritage and its relevance to modern civilization. The trauma of the partition of India on the basis of religion, the miseries that came in its wake, the divided loyalties and bruised psyches it created, and a sense of longing for the positive values of the feudal and aristocratic way of life are the prime concerns in her early novels, like *Mere bhi sanamkhane* (1949; my temples too) and *Safina-e-gham-e-dil* (1952; the barge of heart's sorrows), and also in all her major works.

Aag ka darya (1959; the river of fire), her most significant novel, is spread over three thousand years of India's rich and turbulent history. The Hindu, Muslim, British, and the modern periods of the country's history are depicted in different episodes, held together by a single cord of proto- type protagonists. These characters, in spite of their creative powers and indomitable spirits, ul- timately fall victim to the vicissitudes of the forces of history. In this voluminous novel, H. tries to reinterpret history, and while doing so unravels interesting and thought-provoking facts. Political upheavals, more often than not, result in blood- shed, destruction, and misery for the common person who stoically suffers and undergoes ex- ploitation. The horrors of war especially are graph- ically depicted. H.'s concerns with the plight of humans are not confined to her compatriots; her heart goes out to all the oppressed and the wronged—be they the victims of the Korean War, the dwellers on either side of the Berlin Wall, the Muslim and Hindu refugees in Pakistan and India respectively, the American blacks, or the German Jews. Nearer home, her heart bleeds for the divi- sion of India, an event she views as a deathblow to the composite cultural heritage that took cen- turies to evolve. The question of Hindu and Mus- lim identities is also examined minutely. Apart from its intellectual and philosophical overtones, the novel stands out as a great tribute to Indian civilization. *Aag ka darya* has been translated into fourteen languages and remains the most talked- about novel in both India and Pakistan.

Aakhir-e-shab ke humsafar (1979; travelers at the end of night) deals with revolutionary move- ments in politically sensitive Bengal. This novel satirizes the pseudointellectuals, armchair politi- cians, and half-hearted revolutionaries who in In- dia have invariably ended up becoming part of the establishment. Though largely political in content, the novel shows rare finesse in painting pictur- esque scenes of idyllic Bengal, its flora and fauna, its land and people, its culture and tradition.

Kar-e-jahan daraz hai (2 vols., 1978, 1979; the task of the world is unending), a family saga, which H. has chosen to designate as an autobio- graphical novel, again travels far and wide in time and space. Its tentacles are spread over eight hundred years of political, social, and cultural history. Even while H. recounts the lives and times of her own ancestors, there is never a dull moment. The reader breaks away from the shackles of the pre- sent and is taken on a conducted tour of bygone eras. The journey is crowded with people and events, and at times the scenario is resonant and throbbing, at others tragic and melancholic.

Gardish-e-rang-chaman (1987; changing hues of the garden) shows H.'s prowess as a master storyteller. The semidocumentary novel, spread over a century and a half, has a very poignant tale

and in-depth characterization. H. speaks of the insignificance of the human individual and our destiny in the cosmic scheme of things. Her char- acters put up a valiant fight, but in vain—they are mauled by the forces of history. A male protago- nist, however, finds salvation in the mystical pow- ers of the East.

Like H.'s novels, her short stories and novel- ettes unfold themselves not only on the narrative level but also on the philosophical and metaphor- ical plane. Her female characters have almost heroic dimensions, particularly in the novelettes.

H.'s creative process is highly personal. Her imagination is boundless. She does not follow any set pattern of thought and ideology. Her writings, though steeped in a particular social and cultural milieu, are a picture of common human experi- ence. Plots, settings, and characters keep chang- ing, but her sensibility and vision remain steadfast.

FURTHER WORKS: *Sitaron se aage* (1947); *Shishe ke ghar* (1952); *Patjhar ki awaz* (1967); *Roshni ki raftar* (1982); *Char novelettes* (1982); *Chandni begam* (1990). FURTHER VOLUMES IN ENGLISH: *Ghalib's Prose and Poetry* (1968, with Sardar Jafri); *Selected Indian Stories* (1970, with Khush- want Singh); *A Woman's Life* (1979)

HUMAYUN ZAFAR ZAIDI

IBARGÜENGOITIA, Jorge

Mexican novelist, dramatist, and short-story writer,
b. 22 Jan. 1928, Guanajuato; d. 27 Nov. 1983,
Madrid, Spain

I. graduated from Mexico's National University
with a degree in engineering in 1949 and two
years later returned to the same institution to study
dramatic art under Rodolfo Usigli (q.v.), one of
Mexico's best-known playwrights. In 1955 he received a fellowship from the Rockefeller Foundation to study theater in New York. After writing
more than a dozen plays, many of which were
never performed or published, he abandoned the
theater for prose fiction, the field for which he is
best known. I. has published many articles in
Mexican journals, including *Excélsior, Siempre,
Vuelta,* and *Revista de la Universidad de México.*
He lectured at several universities in the U.S. and
was residing in Paris when he was killed in an
airplane crash.

I. is best known for his humorous satires of
Mexican life, both present and past. His most
highly regarded play, which in 1963 won the Casa
de las Américas Prize in Cuba, is *El atentado*
(1978; the attempted murder). A farce with elements of the absurd, this tragicomedy depicts the
assassination of president-elect Alvaro Obregón in
1928 by a Catholic fanatic, José de León Toral.
The play dramatizes the return of ex-President
Obregón to the political scene after his first term
of office (1920–1924), the assassination of two of
his rivals, the election campaign, and the trial and
execution of the culprit, whose accomplice was a
nun, la madre Conchita. The influences of German
dramatist Bertolt Brecht (q.v.) on this work are
particularly evident: the rapid changes in scenes,
the use of signs instead of stage sets, and, most
important, the distancing effects designed to alien-
ate characters from spectators and thus allow the

didactic message to have its maximum impact. I.'s
criticism is also conveyed by absurd episodes,
ludicrous characters, and ironic juxtapositions,
which elicit guffaws from the audience despite the
appearance of many acts of violence.

For decades after the Revolution of 1910, numerous novels and an occasional volume of memoirs depicted the upheaval in tragic and heroic
tones. Realizing that the ideals motivating the civil
conflict had been betrayed from the beginning, I.
wrote his first novel, *Los relámpagos de agosto*
(1964; *The Lightning of August,* 1986) to discredit
those who led the struggle and/or profited from it.
The narrator and antihero is retired General José
Guadalupe Arroyo, a stupid, amoral incompetent
who pens his memoirs to disprove the "slander-
ous" statements made about him in the memoirs
of other military hacks. The period referred to is
1928–1929, when President Plutarco Elías Calles
was ending his term of office and President-elect
Obregón was assassinated. Having been named
the private secretary of the president-elect just
before the latter's untimely death (from apoplexy
in the novel), Arroyo is left to fend for himself in
the political arena. He participates in battles between ambitious generals, all of whom lie and
change allegiance according to the dictates of raw
power or financial gain. Skirmishes are won by
luck and lost through bungling. In the final pages
Arroyo is captured and sentenced to death, but the
general in charge of the execution allows him to
escape to the U.S., meanwhile having another man
shot to prove that the order was carried out. Replete with grotesque humor and irony (the unreli-
able narrator unwittingly exposes his ignorance
and hypocrisy), *Los relámpagos de agosto* is a
hilarious parody of the volumes written about the
Mexican Revolution before 1964. Its reexamina-
tion of the past exposes the beginnings of a bankrupt political system that has lasted for seven
decades.

I.'s second novel, *Maten al león* (1969; kill the
lion), is almost as funny as his first. It too is set
in the 1920s, but instead of in Mexico, its action
takes place on a fictitious Caribbean island (Arepa),
governed by a ruthless dictator (the lion) who is
ultimately assassinated. The history of Arepa is
compressed into the life span of the director (Belaunzarán), who rids the island of the Spaniards
but then proceeds to torture, murder, and execute
his enemies. (I. stated that Belaunzarán was patterned after Obregón, but that the former was
disguised as a Caribbean strongman to avoid problems with zealous government censors.) Virtually
all the characters are caricatures whose words and
actions border on the absurd. Belaunzarán is celebrated as a national hero, even though his exploits
to defeat the Spaniards were anything but heroic—

he attacked and killed everyone in the enemy stronghold after the Spaniards had left. The nation's greedy landholders oppose him only because they seek power, not social reform. When the carefully planned attempt to eliminate him fails, he is accidently murdered by an impoverished musician. And when he finally dies, he is replaced by his handpicked successor, Cardona, meaning that nothing will change. The novel's proper names also have a humorous ring, a case in point being Arepa (pancake in Spanish), which ridicules the size and importance of the island nation.

In the late 1970s I. published two murder mysteries, both of which parody the popular genre. *Las muertas* (1977; *The Dead Girls,* 1983) is based on a criminal case that made sensational headlines in 1964 when two brothel owners in a small Mexican community allegedly kidnaped and murdered dozens of prostitutes. In the course of his investigation I. discovered that Serafina and Arcángela Baladro, the fictional names of the accused sisters, while not free of guilt, had been forced to pay bribes to corrupt politicians, police officers, and court officials. I. reveals, moreover, that the alleged crimes were greatly exaggerated, the number of dead totaling only six, four of whom died from natural causes. The novel desensationalizes the entire case by discrediting the news media and placing much of the blame on corrupt government authorities.

Dos crímenes (1979; *Two Crimes,* 1984), I.'s other murder mystery, is a humorous and erotic tale, also set in a provincial town. Marcos González, the protagonist and narrator of the first half of the novel, escapes from Mexico City to the home of his wealthy Uncle Ramón after having been unjustly accused of arson. While staying with his uncle, he tries with some success to obtain money from the crusty old man by claiming to have knowledge of a mine he would like to exploit for considerable gain. He also has sexual encounters with his cousin Amalia and his niece Lucero. After both Ramón and Lucero are murdered by mistake (both murderers intended to kill Marcos), the local pharmacist Don Pepe Lara narrates his investigation of the case, leading up to the suspenseful denoucment. *Dos crímenes* is a tightly structured detective story sprinkled with allusions to social and political impropriety. But I.'s main thrusts are his ingenious structuring of plot and his ironic treatment—through narrative distancing—of character and social customs.

I's last novel, *Los pasos de López* (1981; López's footsteps; also published as *Los conspiradores,* 1981; the conspirators), dramatizes the beginnings of the War of Independence (1810) between Mexico and Spain. Because of his position as an army officer, the first-person narrator, Matías

Chandón, has been chosen by a group of conspirators to direct military operations against the Spaniards. Mainly *criollos* (people of Spanish parents born in the New World), the conspirators are inspired by Don Periñón (historically Father Miguel Hidalgo), whose name derives from a kind of champagne (Dom Perignon), and thus refers obliquely to Father Hidalgo's wine-making enterprise. Although sincere, Periñón and his followers are portrayed by Chandón as bunglers, as are the inept Spanish authorities, who are told of the impending revolt but refuse to believe their informants. The climactic capture and execution of Don Periñón are foreshadowed by a drama the conspirators rehearse just before the uprising begins, a drama in which Don Periñón plays the role of the eponymous conspirator López. Although it describes events a century earlier, *Los pasos de López* has been compared to *Los relámpagos de agosto,* both serving to demythicize heroic moments of the Mexican past. I.'s more recent novel, however, portrays a more human side of its protagonist.

In their entirety I.'s works lampoon Mexico's most revered institutions, utilizing as weapons caricature, satire, irony, and parody. I. is an important man of letters not only because of his unique views of Mexican society, but also because of his accessibility to a large portion of the reading public. An enemy of hypocrisy and amorality, he revised both past and present in order to spark badly needed change.

FURTHER WORKS: *Susana y los jóvenes* (1958); *Ante varias esfinges* (1960); *El loco amor viene* (1960); *Clotilde, El viaje, y El pájaro* (1964); *La ley de Herodes* (1967); *Viajes en la América ignota* (1972); *Estas ruinas que ves* (1975); *Sálvese quien pueda* (1975); *Autopsias rápidas* (1988); *Obras completas* (1989); *Piezas y cuentos para niños* (1989)

BIBLIOGRAPHY: Acevedo Escobedo, A., *Los narradores ante el público* (1967), 125–34; Langford, W. M., *The Mexican Novel Comes of Age* (1971), 190–92; Bruce-Novoa, J., and D. Valentín, "Violating the Image of Violence: I.'s *El atentado,*" *LATR,* 12, 2 (Spring 1979), 13–21; Rama, A., *Novísimos narradores hispanoamericanos en marcha, 1964–1980* (1981), 195; Azuela, A., "J. I.: Múltiples espejos de utopías gastadas," *CA,* 4, 255 (July–Aug. 1984), 75–79; Ugalde, S. K., "Beyond Satire: I.'s *Maten al león,*" *DLit,* 1, 2 (Spring 1984), 217–29; McMurray, G. R., *Spanish American Writing since 1941: A Critical Survey* (1987), 88–89, 251–52; Corral, I. del, "Humor: When Do We Lose It?" *TRev,* 27 (1988), 25–27; Campbell, F., "I.: La sátira históricopo-

lítica,'' *RI*, 55 (July–Dec. 1989), 1047–55; Leñero, V., *Los pasos de Jorge* (1989); González,
A., ''J. I.: The Mexican Mock Heroic,'' *Euphoria
and the Crisis: Essays on the Contemporary Mexican Novel* (1990), 52–63; Sklodowska, E., ''I. y
Giardinelli: Reconocimiento y cuestionamiento de
la novela negra,'' *La parodia en la nueva novela
hispanoamericana (1960–1985)* (1991), 120–27

GEORGE R. MCMURRAY

IBN HADŪQA, 'Abd al-Hamīd
Algerian novelist, short-story writer, and dramatist, b. 9 Jan. 1925, Al-Mansurah

I. H. contributed the first significant Arabic novel
in Algeria. He also wrote short stories and radio
and television plays in colloquial Algerian. He
studied in Algeria, Tunisia, and France. He received a solid education in Arabic at the hands of
his father, a teacher of Arabic and Islamic thought.
He pursued his education at the al-Hamlāwī Institute in Algeria, an affiliate of ibn al-Hamlāwī's
zāwiyah. I. H. went to Tunisia for his secondary
and higher education and joined al-Zaitunah Mosque
College where he graduated from its Arabic literature section. While in Tunis, he completed four
years of study at the Arab Drama Institute. Back
in Algeria, he spent two years at the faculty of
law at the University of Algiers. He studied French
at school while pursuing his education at a Koranic
school. In France he shifted his education toward
technology, spending three and a half years in
Marseille and Paris studying plastic transformation.

I. H. worked both as a journalist and as a
producer of radio plays during the colonial period.
After the independence of his country in 1962, he
occupied various positions in the Algerian broadcasting service up to the time he was nominated
cultural adviser at the general administration for
radio and television. In 1987 he retired but was
soon recalled to be appointed first as director
general of the National Book Foundation, then
president of the National Council for Culture, a
position he holds to the present day.

I. H. began his writing activities with a collection of short stories entitled *Zilāl Jazā'iriyyah*
(1960; Algerian shades). It was soon followed by
a second collection, *al-Ashi'ah al-Sab'ah* (1962;
the seven rays). Though published during the years
of the war of independence, his two collections
were generally removed from patriotic topics.
Whenever the events of a story touched on the
subject of the war, the primary concern of the
author was the human dimension of the characters
depicted in unusual situations. I. H. seems intent
on proving the humane nature of a soldier through

his story ''al-jundī wa-al-layl'' (1960; the soldier
and the night), in which a *mujāhid* is seen reflecting on his emotions and the attraction that an
unsuspecting young woman exercised on him.
Writing at a time of profound nationalism, when
the freedom fighter was glorified and endowed
with superhuman power, I. H. was more interested
in pointing out his humanity.

Love is central to many of I. H.'s fiction works.
He examines it in its various kinds and forms,
conjugal, filial, paternal and maternal, as well as
the love between a man and a woman; he does
not indulge, however, in any detailed description
of sexual relations. His story ''Zaytūnat al-hubb''
(1960; the olive tree of love) typifies his tendency
to maintain love on a platonic level, as the two
teenagers in love are fully satisfied with their mere
meetings under an olive tree and take pleasure in
inscribing their names on its trunk.

I. H.'s attitude in his writings is generally that
of a compassionate man, concerned for the fate of
the meek and the wronged members of society,
eager to see justice established wherever fairness
has been trampled. A clear preoccupation with
fairness is obvious in his novel *Nihāyat al-ams*
(1975; the end of yesterday) for the wife of a *harkī*
(an unpatriotic Algerian serving in the hated French
military) and generally for women who did not
receive their fair share from society. Most of I.
H.'s novels and to a lesser degree his short stories
reveal a deep affection and respect for women,
though at times maladroitly expressed in the form
of either a failed effort at emancipation as in *Rīh
al-janūb* (1971; the southern wind), or a trial-and-
failure effort as in *Bāna al-subh* (1980; the morning appeared). The best and most successful portrayal of a feminine character is that of Jāziyah in
al-Jāziyah wa-al-darāwīsh (1983; Jāziyah and the
dervishes), projecting a clear message of change
in the status of women within the boundaries of
the cultural entity of the country. This latter attitude reinforces both I. H.'s nationalist position as
well as his deep appreciation for Algerian folklore.

I. H. clearly wishes to see his society advance
on the path of affection and mutual understanding,
away from the hindering action of some outdated
and useless traditions. He refutes the restrictions
imposed by parents on their daughters' emancipation, the imposition of exorbitant dowries that
either delay marriages or force young men to
emigrate to France in search of high-paying jobs.
Whether referring to the negative impact of traditions or expressing compassion for the unfortunate
and wronged members of society, I. H. reverts to
dramatic situations and tragic ends. His tone is
often moralizing and didactic, reinforcing the concept of the writer as his society's guide. The short
story ''Thaman al-mahr'' (1962; the price of the

dowry) ends with the death of the protagonist, who reached his goal that consisted in saving enough money to pay the requested dowry but died of tuberculosis. *Rīh al-janūb* presents also a tragic conclusion to a courageous story of elopement as the enraged father of the heroine charges against a man he accuses arbitrarily of dishonoring him: Blinded by his anger, he does not even try to understand the situation before attacking the innocent shepherd.

The interest that I. H. manifested in the human experience throughout his fiction works stems from his socialist ideology and a particular concern for the human spirit and its capacity to face life's difficulties and injustices. The historical periods and the geographical settings designated in his books serve as a frame for the study of human behavior. The dire circumstances of the war of independence described in both *Rīh al-janūb* and *Nihāyat al-ams,* through the device of flashbacks, reveal the exploitative nature of Ibn al-Sakhrī and Ibn al-Qādī, two men who pursued their material gains at the cost of their fellow men. The author's preoccupation with the greedy nature of people in power extends to the postindependence period as he reveals the wide-spread hypocrisy that dictates human actions. I. H. seems to abhor those whose actions are in total contradiction to their words. He preached honesty in a world and time when opportunism prevailed.

I. H. promotes a number of specific topics, foremost among them is the emancipation of women. A devout admirer of country life, he seems to find it more virtuous and amenable to positive changes. The action in most of his fiction works takes place in rural settings, with the exception of *Bāna al-subh,* located in Algiers. The corrupt and hypocritical life of the characters, mainly from the Algerian bourgeoisie, stands in sharp contrast to the simpler and healthier world of the country. Another issue dear to I. H. is folk culture, which he revives in his novels in various ways, mainly through descriptions of pottery work and design. He also uses folk characters, the most famous being al-Jāziyah, whose name is given to the heroine of the novel *al-Jāziyah wa-al-darā-wīsh.* The personality of al-Jāziyah is central to a very popular love story in Algeria. I. H. successfully uses the symbol as a reward for a returning migrant young man in search of his identity. This dependence on folklore among postindependence writers is a reflection of a recovered pride in their national entity.

I. H.'s main contribution has been in the field of fiction writing—in short stories and novels as well as plays—mainly in Algerian dialect for radio broadcasting. He translated stories from foreign literature and wrote poetry, which he published in a collection entitled *al-arwāh al-shāghira* (1967; the free souls.)

Although I. II. holds some noticeably modernist positions in relation to various aspects of life in his society, he is rather a conservative in other areas. An example is his deep respect for the Arabic language; he maintains that its sanctity does not allow him to use it to tackle certain topics that he deems unworthy of its holy nature. This outlook explains his reluctance to describe in Arabic what he terms "the immorality of the Arab society."

I. H. remains one of the pioneers of Arabic fiction in Algeria with a slow but steady production. There is an obvious progress and mastery of both the style and the artistic concept of the novel from the first book he published to the latest one. I. H. relies on a simple style and a direct approach in most of his early fiction, with an obvious tendency toward symbolism and a greater sophistication in his later works such as his novel *al-Jāziyah wa-al-darāwīsh.* He makes heavy use of stream-of-consciousness (q.v.) and flashback, particularly in relating the events of the war of independence, which he recalls often to assess a character's behavior or justify a judgment or a condemnation.

FURTHER WORKS: *Al-Jazā'ir bayna al-ams wa-al-yawm* (1959); *Al-kātib wa-qisas ukhrā* (1972); *Qisas min al-adab al-ʿālamī* (1983); *Al-nisr wa-al-ʿiqāb* (1985)

BIBLIOGRAPHY: Makarius, R., and L. Makarius, *Anthologie de la littérature arabe contemporaine* (1964), 356–62; Dejeux, J., *La littérature algérienne contemporaine* (1975), 113–15; Bamia, A. A., "La littérature algérienne de langue arabe," *Europe,* 567–68 (July-Aug. 1976), 38–48; Bamia, A. A., "Le roman algérien de langue arabe depuis L'Indépendance," *Annuaire de L'Afrique du Nord,* 19 (1980), 1127–33; Bonn, C., *Anthologie de la littérature algérienne* (1990), 150–51

AIDA A. BAMIA

IGNATOW, David

American poet and editor, b. 7 Feb. 1914, Brooklyn, N.Y.

I. has spent most of his life in New York City, and the influence of the city, especially its dark side, is evident in much of his poetry. He graduated from New Utrecht High School in Brooklyn in 1932 and attended Brooklyn College for a short time. At his family's insistence he left school to work for his father's bindery firm. I. was not happy in business, and although he left the firm two year later, he was never entirely free of its demands until almost thirty years later when he sold the company, in 1962. His harshly negative view of this experience and of American business tactics in general informs much of his early work. In the 1930s and 1940s I. worked at various jobs, from reporter to handyman in a shipyard to night admitting clerk in a hospital. In 1949 he became coeditor of the *Beloit Poetry Journal,* a position he held for ten years. He also worked as poetry editor of the *Nation* from 1962 until 1963.

I.'s teaching career began in 1964 when he became an instructor at the New School for Social Research in New York City. He was visiting lecturer at the University of Kentucky at Lexington (1965–1966), at the University of Kansas at Lawrence (1966–1967), and at Vassar College (1967–1968). In 1969 he became poet-in-residence at York College of the City University of New York and adjunct professor in the writing program of the School of the Arts at Columbia University. I.'s honors and awards include the National Institute of Arts and Letters Award (1964), two Guggenheim fellowships (1965 and 1973), the Shelley Memorial Prize from the Poetry Society of America (1966), a Rockefeller Foundation grant (1968–1969), a National Endowment for the Arts grant (1970), the Bollingen Prize (1977), and the Wallace Stevens Fellowship (1977).

I.'s first volume, *Poems,* was published in 1948. His often matter-of-fact comments on everyday life and his rhetorical style show the influence of William Carlos Williams (q.v.), whom he greatly admired and who praised and encouraged I. Other influences I. acknowledges as playing major roles in shaping his thinking and writing include Walt Whitman (1819–1892), the great Russian writers, and the Bible. I.'s typical poem is the short lyric, and while his material is strongly autobiographical, he more often than not adopts personae. His simple, straightforward use of the urban American vernacular underscores the horror he sees and feels as he looks at the minute details of both his private and his public life. Although I.'s themes defy easy categorization, it can be said that his unrelenting focus on his personal response—sometimes guilty, sometimes angry, often wryly humorous—gives an overall sense of unity to his work.

His political and social poems reflect his lived experience: the Depression of the 1930s, World War II, Vietnam, the evils of the American lust for money, the pervasive violence and outright insanity that has become a given in late 20th-c. America. His personal poems rely more on his felt experience. These works often contain a tension generated by juxtaposing the difficulties in marital and family relationships with the blighted, crumbling landscapes the speakers of the poems perceive both inside as well as outside their windows. In many of the poems in *The Gentle Weight Lifter* (1955) I. seems to be experimenting with distancing his work from the urban setting and focusing on the isolation and alienation that results from social decay. The settings are biblical, classical, or timeless. It is with these poems that I. begins to work in parable form, and while he does not maintain the impersonal distancing stance (his later work returns to the concrete and specific here and now of his surroundings), much of his work in the early 1960s is parablelike, especially the social poetry. This technique is evident in many of the poems in *Say Pardon* (1961) and *Figures of the Human* (1964). The urban nightmares of violence and corruption are rendered in a slightly surreal manner, and I. often moves away from free verse into the less structured narration of the prose poem.

While *Figures of the Human* has been judged to contain some of I.'s weakest work—short, flat pieces hinting at emotional exhaustion—his next book, *Rescue the Dead* (1968), articulates a personal and, in I.'s case almost necessarily, a poetic rebirth. He presents and recasts the issues he has been dealing with in his earlier work: parents, children, romantic and sexual love, marriage, the violence of American society, and the personal threat the narrator perceives such violence to be. There are also poems that hint at themes that I. will go on to explore more fully—the individual's connection with and relationship to nature. It might be speculated that, as I. starts to spend more time living and writing in his home in East Hampton, Long Island, his poetry begins to reflect both his physical and his emotional distance from New York City.

Facing the Tree (1975) and *Tread the Dark* (1978) delve into the complexities and contradictions the poet discovers in exploring his place within the natural world. But, paradoxically, the comfort that might be derived from imagining oneself part of a cycle that hints at an eternal return seems to shatter at some point and become instead a longing for the release from time and its evils that death offers. Many of the poems in *Tread the Dark* are concerned with suicide and escape from self. This volume also contains a number of wry poems about poems that often employ the voice of the poem itself as the speaker.

Although I. has sometimes been compared in a negative light to those who have influenced his work, and for many years critical appreciation was slow in coming, his gifts are now well recognized. In his most recent collection, *Shadowing the Ground* (1991), his voice is as authentic as it is individual. The early bitterness has been transmuted into a deeper and more complex moral and intellectual vision full of strongly felt and strongly realized emotions, and I. has achieved the status of an American poet worthy of serious acclaim.

FURTHER WORKS: *Political Poetry* (1960); *Walt Whitman: A Centennial Celebration* (1963); *William Carlos Williams: A Memorial Chapbook* (1963); *Earth Hard: Selected Poems* (1968); *Poems 1934–1969* (1970); *Notebooks* (1973); *Selected Poems* (1975); *The Animal in the Bush* (1977); *Open between Us* (1980); *Whisper to the Earth* (1981); *Leaving the Door Open* (1984); *New and Collected Poems 1970–1985* (1986); *The One in the Many: A Poet's Memoirs* (1988); *Despite the Plainness of the Day: Love Poems* (1991)

BIBLIOGRAPHY: Bly, R., "Some Thoughts on *Rescue the Dead*," *Tennessee Poetry Journal*, 3 (Winter 1970), 17–21; Kazin, A., "The Esthetic of Humility," *APR* (April–May 1974), 14–15; Melange, G., "The Art of Poetry XIII: D. I.," *Paris Review*, 76 (Fall 1979), 55–79; Sjoberg, L., "An Interview with D. I.," *CanL*, 28, 2 (Summer 1987), 143–62

MARGARET D. SULLIVAN

İLHAN, Attilâ

Turkish poet, novelist, and essayist, b. 1925, Menemen

İ. cut his education at the faculty of law at the University of Istanbul short to become a journalist, a career that culminated in his serving as editor in chief of the Izmir daily *Demokrat İzmir* and as a columnist for several leading newspapers and magazines. He first attracted attention in 1946 when he won second prize in a poetry contest, probably the most important contest of that time, organized by the ruling People's Republican Party. In the early 1950s he lived and studied in Paris. He had a short-lived involvement with Marxism-Leninism, which he renounced later in the decade. From 1973 to 1980 he was editorial consultant for Bilgi Yayınevi, a major publishing house. He has also been a prolific writer for film and television.

Starting with his first collection of poems, *Duvar* (1948; the wall), İ. has enjoyed popular and critical acclaim. Many of his early poems exhibit the angst of the turbulent times after World War II. His shorter early verses are marked by their raw emotions and forceful style, and the longer ones by an epic flair. *Sisler bulvarı* (1954; boulevard of fogs) and *Yağmur kaçağı* (1955; fugitive from rain) are comprised of poems of unabashed neoromanticism that are remarkable for their lyricism and extravagant vocabulary. In these, İ. made

a synthesis of the aesthetic values of Ottoman classical verse, traditional folk poetry, and modern poetics. The two collections, published in quick succession, swiftly endeared İ. to the larger poetry-reading public.

Ben sana mecburum (1960; I am obliged to you) augmented İ.'s reputation as a lyric poet. Here the metaphors are more audacious than ever, passions erupt into a whirlwind, and the style, although hyperbolic at times, is admirably controlled. *Belâ çiçeği* (1962; the flower of turbulence) represents İ.'s attempt to reconcile his Turkish sensibilities with his heightened preoccupation with European culture. The result is a mixed blessing: The innate lyric gifts remain vibrant although the cultural admixture seems to leave a lot to be desired. A cycle of poems glorifying the military coup of 27 May 1960 appended to the collection tends to reduce the level even further. His *Yasak sevişmek* (1968; loving is banned), however, is a powerful combination of love and political oppression. The tragic sense is acute here, with tenderness and anger coalescing into very poignant poetic statements.

1973 saw the publication of *Tutuklunun günlüğü* (diary of a detainee), poems mainly about the suffering of a sensitive man in prison and under interrogation. For this book, which effectively delineates the plight of a public-spirited individual in a harsh oppressive regime, İ. was given the Poetry Award of the Turkish Language Society in 1974.

Elde var hüzün (1984; there remains sorrow) and *Korkunun krallığı* (1987; sovereignty of fear) represent the highlights of İ.'s poetic art. They contain many of his most accomplished poems of private joy and sadness as well as acute social concerns. Both collections possess the wealth of fresh metaphors, lilting rhythms, and the sensuous vocabulary that Turkish poetry lovers have come to cherish.

İ. enjoys high esteem as an essayist and newspaper columnist as well. His probing short prose pieces are remarkable for their unusual perspectives and insightful analyses of politics, culture, and literature. He has collected these, along with autobiographical essays, in numerous volumes including *Hangi sol* (1970; which left), *Hangi batı* (1972; which west), *Faşizmin ayak sesleri* (1975; fascism's footsteps), *Hangi seks* (1976; which sex), *Hangi sağ* (1980; which right), *Gerçekçilik savaşı* (1980; realism's crusade), *Hangi Atatürk* (1981; which Atatürk), *Batının deli gömleği* (1982; straitjacket of the west), and other volumes. İ.'s travel pieces, collected in *Abbas yolcu* (1959; must go), earned praise as first-rate specimens of the genre.

İ. showed great promise in fiction when he published *Sokaktaki adam* (1953; the man in the street) and *Zenciler birbirine benzemez* (1957; blacks don't resemble each other), both of them conventional novels whose characters lacked psychological depth, though presented with considerable narrative skill. With his two-volume *Kurtlar sofrası* (1963–1964; a feast for wolves) he established his credentials as a major novelist. This impressive work portrays the vast vista of a society in turmoil—Turkey's middle class and intellectual elite—after World War II. It moves very swiftly, like a film script, through many dramatic episodes that are fragmentary but interrelated. *Kurtlar sofrası* led directly into İ.'s magnum opus, *Aynanın içindekiler* (those in the mirror), a sprawling work consisting of five long novels, each one of which can be read independently. Collectively, this tour de force is a saga of Turkey in the 20th c. caught in political turbulence, spiritual crisis, and private anguish. Many of the characters are from real life, identified by name, although basically the work is a roman à clef. The first novel in İ.'s modern epic, *Bıçağın ucu* (1973; tip of the knife), did not generate much critical enthusiasm. The second, however, *Sırtlan payı* (1974; hyena's share), won the prestigious Yunus Nadi Prize (1974–1975). After the mild success of *Yaraya tuz basmak* (1978; rubbing salt on the wound), his *Dersaadet'te sabah ezanları* (1981; morning calls to prayer in Istanbul) became a *succès d'estime* with its captivating personae, narrative power, and fascinating plot. *O karanlıkta biz* (1988; we in that darkness), fifth in the series, is a gripping account of political intrigue and foreign interference in the Turkey of World War II.

Fena halde Leman (1980; Leman in a bad way) and *Haco Hanım Vay* (1984; oh Mme. Haco) are two of İ.'s acclaimed novels in which, with an unmistakable poetic touch, the author excelled in depicting the lives and psychological personalities of two vivid woman protagonists.

A versatile and prolific literary figure, İ. has claimed the legacy of classical Ottoman verse, modern lyric poetry, and late Ottoman and contemporary Turkish history as his terra firma, infusing into them brave new forms and interpretations, always putting on them his own stamp of originality.

FURTHER WORKS: *Böyle bir sevmek* (1977); *İkinci yeni savaşı* (1983); *Sağım solum sobe* (1985)

BIBLIOGRAPHY: Halman, T. S., "A. İ. and the Promise of Turkish Poetry," *BA* (Autumn 1963), 403–5

TALAT SAIT HALMAN

INDIAN LITERATURE

See Volume 2, page 432.

Not unlike their counterparts in other excolonial, Third World countries, Indian writers have been preoccupied with two major concerns since the country gained freedom in 1947. First is the profound sense of disillusionment in independence, which, many Indians believed, would usher in a halcyon age in which all things would be better than when the British were there. In fact, they have not been. This disappointment, especially among the educated urban classes, has sometimes given way to anger, alienation, despair, and even violence. Second, many writers address the dilemma of modernity versus tradition: What, they ask, should they accept or reject from the modern industrialized West as part of their own value system, and what from their own traditional cultural heritage should they retain or discard? Both themes are found in varying degrees in the dozen major literatures of India and in a number of the minor ones as well.

Fiction

Writers in India's national language, Hindi, such as Mohan Rakesh (q.v.), Rajendra Yadav (b. 1929), and Kamaleshwar (b. 1932), ushered in the *nai kahani* (new story) movement during the 1950s and 1960s. Influenced by existentialism (q.v.), it focused in both novels and short stories on urban, middle-class, often educated, characters who experience the world as incomprehensible and meaningless, and whose limited choices invariably turn out to be the wrong ones.

At the other end of the socioeconomic spectrum, village-based regional literature flourishes throughout India. Referred to by various names in different languages, it is called *anchalik* literature (*anchal* is the end of a woman's sari used to cover her head) in North India and concentrates on villagers—peasants and farmers—coping with the encroachments of modern technology, urbanization, and government into their lives. One of its leading exponents is the Hindi novelist Phanishwarnath Renu (b. 1921), whose voluminous *Maila anchal* (1954; soiled *anchal*) is an outstanding example of this type of writing. A strong *anchalik* movement is also found in Bengali.

One of the most controversial yet highly acclaimed postindependence novels is U. R. Ananthamurthy's (b. 1932) *Samskara* (1965; *Samskara: A Rite for a Dead Man,* 1976). Written in Kannada and set in a tiny southern Indian village community of highly orthodox Brahmins, it details the morally vacuous religious values and traditions of believers who, in pursuit of the subtle, often arcane, practices of their religion, have lost the true meaning of their faith.

In Tamil fiction T. Janakiraman (b. 1921) is a major figure. He began writing from a Marxist point of view, but rejected this ideology in the early 1960s to embrace a broader humanism. His works deal with themes from everyday middleclass life in small towns in Tamilnadu. He is especially concerned with changing family relationships, particularly between spouses and between parents and children.

Punjabi writer Gulzar Singh Sandhu (b. 1934) has published four major collections of short stories, most recently *Amar katha* (1979; immortal story). Dealing with both urban and rural themes, he depicts the conflicts and divided loyalties that face India's small but economically powerful Sikh community.

Poetry

A number of modernist, antiestablishment movements, often called *akavita* (nonpoetry), have emerged since the 1960s, several of them finding their roots in radical left-wing politics. In 1962 Allen Ginsberg (q.v.) made his first visit to India, which turned out to be important not only to him but to large numbers of young Indian writers as well. In Bengali, fledgling poets embraced his thinking, imitated his poetry, and formed the so-called "Hungry Generation," college-educated but unemployed writers in their twenties whose works reflect a sense of futility, disillusionment, and anger at the political and literary establishments. Five of these poets, notably Shaileshwar Ghose (b. 1938), Subimal Basak (b. 1939), and Malay Roy Choudhury (b. 1939), were arrested and tried on charges of obscenity.

Marathi *dalit* (oppressed) literature is the revolutionary writing of the downtrodden Untouchables. Foremost among this group is the poet Namdeo Dasal (b. 1949), who grew up in a Bombay slum. The title of his major work, *Golpitha* (1973; Golpitha), refers to one of Bombay's red-light districts, famous for its "cages" in which the prostitutes ply their trade. It contains his best-known poems, angry, surrealistic descriptions of the plight of those who live in this area. Other important poets in this movement are Daya Pawar (b. 1935) and Trymbak Sapkale (b. 1930).

Naxalite writers, whose political sympathies support in some degree the terrorist activities of a small, violent group of Maoist communists formed in the Naxalbari district of northern Bengali in 1970, are also found in many of India's languages. Notable among these are the Digambara poets of Telugu. The name of this latter group literally means "sky-clad," a reference to a type of ancient Jain monk who went about naked, having the sky as his clothing. However, the group preferred to translate the term into English as "bare-assed." Politically and literarily iconoclastic, many of these writers were at odds with the law. One of their most radical members, Baddam Bhaskara Reddy (pseud.: Cherabanda Raju, 1939–1982), was hounded by the authorities even as he lay dying of brain cancer. His "Vandemataram" (1970; hail to thee, mother) is a scathing parody of the poem of the same name (1882), India's first nationalist anthem, by Bankimk Chandra Chatterji (1838–1894).

Always quick to react to political events in their country, poets did so vocally when in 1975 Prime Minister Indira Gandhi suspended civil liberties, ushering in the so-called "Emergency" period, which continued until 1977. Perhaps no single event in India's recent history, save the assassination in 1948 of Mohandas Karamchand Gandhi has produced an equivalent literary response. Many of the best poems from the major languages have been collected by American poet John Oliver Perry (b. 1938) in *Voices of Emergency* (1983).

Munibur Rahman (b. 1924) is an outstanding example of a contemporary Urdu poet. Initially influenced by Marxist ideology, his poetry has moved beyond its ideological beginnings and reveals a poet concerned about the large but especially the small anomalies of the human condition. His two collections are *Bazid* (1965, expanded 1988; visitation) and *Shahr-e ghamnam* (1983; the obscure city).

Among India's many English-language poets, Nissim Ezekiel (q.v.) and Jayanta Mahapatra (b. 1928) are notable. The latter, a college physics teacher by profession, received the English literary prize of India's Sahitya Akademi in 1981 for his long poem *Relationships*. The author of eight collections, he is widely published in both India and in the West. He also edited *Chandrabhaga,* India's most important English-language poetry journal.

Women writers are extensively represented in postindependence Indian literature. Urdu novelist and short-story writer Qurratulain Hyder (q.v.) has long been a major feminist voice in Indian literature. In Gujarati, Pann Naik (b. 1938) has emerged as a major feminist force in poetry. Writing in Philadelphia, she has produced two major volumes of poems, *Pravesh* (1979; entrance) and *Philadelphia* (1981), which have attracted a great deal of critical attention, some of it negative from a conservative, male-dominated literary establishment.

Expatriate Writers

Living in Great Britain and the U.S., and writing in English, expatriate authors have made major contributions to Indian literature, though some of them would prefer to be treated as British or American. In fiction, Salman Rushdie (q.v.), who lives in Great Britain, is the best known and, in many ways, one of the most innovative and noteworthy writers in this category. Bharati Mukherjee (q.v.), currently writer-in-residence at the University of California, Berkeley, has treated the theme of biculturalism and marginality in her novels *The Tiger's Daughter* (1972), *Wife* (1975), and *Jasmine* (1989) and in several short-story collections.

In poetry, University of Chicago professor A. K. Ramanujan (b. 1929), author of three collections, *The Striders* (1966), *Relations* (1971), and *Second Sight* (1986), is known for his highly visual images sculptured with precision and concrete details.

Other notable writers include poet Meena Alexander (b. 1951), writer-in-residence at Columbia University, whose five collections, the most recent being *House of a Thousand Doors* (1988), have been critically acclaimed. Vikram Seth's (b. 1952) *The Golden Gate* (1986), "a novel in verse" about California yuppies, cleverly utilizes many traditional English poetic forms. Hanif Kureishi (b. 1954), who lives in London, has written a number of theatrical and screen plays, including *My Beautiful Laundrette* (1985) and *Sammy and Rosie Get Laid* (1987). His novel *The Buddha of Suburbia* (1990), like his plays and film scripts, portrays the expatriate experience with irreverence and honesty. Shashi Tharoor (b. 1956), who works at the United Nations, received the 1990 Commonwealth Writer's Prize for *The Great Indian Novel* (1990), an imaginative and humorous retelling of modern Indian history using some of the style and form of the Indian epic *Mahabharata*.

Scholars frequently debate whether an entity known as "Indian literature" truly exists. Recent political events, which often prefigure much of the country's literary activity, suggest that, instead of developing a single, integrated literary tradition, India is becoming balkanized and, politically and literarily, may end up resembling Europe.

BIBLIOGRAPHY: Coppola, C., ed., *JSoAL* (1963–present); Mukherjee, M., *The Twice Born Fiction: Themes and Techniques of the Indian Novel in English* (1971); Jussawalla, A., ed., *New Writing in India* (1974); special issue on the Indian novel, *Contributions to Asian Studies,* 6 (1975); Bald, S., *Novels and Political Consciousness: Literary Expression of Indian Nationalism 1919–1947* (1982); special issue on Indian literature, *NewL,* 48, 3–4 (1982); Bharucha, R., *Rehearsals of Revolution: The Political Theater of Bengal* (1983); Schomer, K., *Mahadevi Varma and the Chhayavad Age of Modern Hindi Poetry* (1983); Mukherjee, M., *Realism and Reality: The Novel and Society in India* (1985); Jamal, M., ed., *The Penguin Book of Modern Urdu Poetry* (1986); Coppola, C., ed., *Marxist Influences and South Asian Literature* (1988); Tharu, S., and K. Lalita, eds., *Women Writing in India* (2 vols., 1991)

CARLO COPPOLA

INGE, William Motter

American dramatist, novelist, and screenwriter, b. 3 May 1913, Independence, Kan.; d. 10 June 1973, Los Angeles, Cal.

I. gained a wide reputation throughout the 1950s for his moving exploration of the fractured lives of ordinary people. The strong sense of spiritual abandonment and loss of values in his Midwestern settings continued through the drama the tradition of alienation developed in the novel by Sinclair Lewis and Sherwood Anderson (qq.v.). As a writer, I. had the ability to build upon simple story lines. All four of his most important plays were expansions of earlier short stories and one-act plays. When *Come Back, Little Sheba* (1949) was revived on Broadway in 1974, critics, while acknowledging a certain superficial resemblance to soap-opera plots, still found I.'s powerful psychological portraits and stifling social settings credible and haunting. Each of his four major plays was successfully translated into Hollywood films, and he learned quickly the exigencies of screenwriting. The original screenplay of *Splendor in the Grass* (1961) won for I. an Academy Award.

Although I. was interested in acting since childhood and active in high-school and college dramatics, financial reasons prevented him from leaving Kansas for New York to study acting. He took sundry stage roles in summer stock and a tent show after his graduation from the University of Kansas (A.B., 1935). While a graduate student at George Peabody College for Teachers (A.M., 1938) in Nashville, Tennessee, he taught high school. Between 1938 and 1943, I. was an instructor at Stephens College, Columbia, Missouri, where he met Maude Adams, his first important mentor. For three years he worked under her in the drama department. With her encouragement he renewed his interest in drama and became a theater and film critic for the *St. Louis Star-Times* (1943–1946). In St. Louis he resumed teaching from 1946 to 1949 at Washington University. A meeting with Tennessee Williams (q.v.) led to a lifetime friendship and a contract with the Theatre Guild, which presented *Come Back, Little Sheba* in 1949, and its Broadway production in 1950. Throughout the 1950s and most of the 1960s, I. was able to sustain himself completely through his writing.

Following his Broadway successes, screenplays and television plays were bought, but he never regained success as an author after *The Stripper* (1963). In 1969 he taught drama at the University of North Carolina and in 1970 at the University of California, Irvine. His last years saw the publication of a novel, *Good Luck, Miss Wyckoff* (1970), and the largely autobiographical *My Son Is a Splendid Driver* (1971).

I. received the George Jean Nathan Award and the Theatre Time Award in 1950 for *Come Back, Little Sheba*, and the Pulitzer Prize, Outer Circle Award, New York Drama Critics Circle Award, and Donaldson Award (shared with Tennessee Williams) for *Picnic* (1953). I. has been one of the most frequently anthologized American dramatists, and his plays have often been performed in college and community theaters and studied widely on campuses.

Come Back, Little Sheba combines unadorned language, psychoanalytic character study, and tight unity of plot to create a striking example of extreme realism. Considered by many critics his best play, its strengths derive from the ability to dramatize the psychological lives of a childless couple who face middle age without fulfillment. The husband, Doc, a recovering alcoholic, faces remorse for what he has missed in life—true romance and spontaneous pleasure. The wife, Lola, lacking communication and intimacy with her husband, struggles to overcome her compulsive retreats into fantasy and her remorse for the inability to produce children. The adroit use of depth psychology, the typical nature of the characters, and the oppressive influence of their social background combine to create a naturalistic style of stagecraft. However, what saves the play from a cold and clinical tone is the credibility of the husband and wife with Midwestern roots, the accuracy of the colloquial dialogue, and the sympathetic treatment of the characters that avoids sentimentality.

I.'s most acclaimed drama, *Picnic,* retains a Midwest setting, but the locale is a small Kansas town, not an urban environment as in *Come Back, Little Sheba*. The action occurs on Labor Day, the end of summer, which is symbolic of the end of youthful visions, a recurring theme for I., and also indicative of the play's preoccupation with choice of vocations, or life's calling, which challenges the characters in different ways. Hal, a youthful and handsome vagrant, incites the women of the play to reveal well-hidden longings. As a result, the older women are confronted with the vacuity of their emotional and intellectual lives, while the two teenaged daughters come to accept themselves and their own destinies. Wearing veneers of respectability, each major character unleashes an inner world of unfulfilled needs. This occurs dur-

ing a very short period of time and within a very confined, claustrophobic space. The fact that the theatrical unities of time, place, and action are strictly observed helps intensify the play's overall effect. In this way, I. achieves dramatic intensity in spite of the conformist and complacent attitudes of the small-town characters he portrays.

Critics who dismiss I.'s approach to playwriting as colloquial rather than probing, as avoiding ideas in favor of regional color and character verisimilitude, overlook the thoughtful exploration of human relationships evident in *Bus Stop* (1955). In this expansion of I.'s one-act play *People in the Wind* (1953), its characters confront the question of how love can be sustained. *Bus Stop* departs from I.'s earlier full-length plays in its form, in its romantic comedy, and in its dialogue, which is witty and exuberant. Compared with I.'s other 1950s dramas, *Bus Stop* offers the most hopeful tone, departs most from the psychodynamics of family life, and is only indirectly concerned with Midwestern complacency and repression. I.'s thesis, that love is dependent upon the selfless opening of the heart, works its way through the main characters, who present a spectrum of human desire and loving. *Bus Stop* is able to dramatize the anatomy of love, in spite of a rather bare story line, through dynamic character relationships and finely crafted dialogue.

I. returned to the inner life of the family and to a more detached, clinical approach to characterization in *The Dark at the Top of the Stairs* (1958). Shrewd dialogue and intriguing situations contributed to the play's Broadway success. Much of the material was autobiographical and supported by Freudian presuppositions. I.'s Hollywood screenplay *Splendor in the Grass* deals with the Wordsworthian theme of the passing glory of youth and offers a particularly compelling treatment of adolescent perspectives. In the early 1970s I. turned to novel writing with mixed critical, and little popular, success. *Good Luck, Miss Wyckoff* (1970) is a return to the plays of the 1950s in both its Midwestern setting and strong character portrayals. I. reveals few new insights in this novel, in spite of attempts at more explicit dialogue and sexuality. His last published work, a novel written as a memoir, *My Son Is a Splendid Driver* (1971), contains many revealing autobiographical elements, yet remains objective and unsentimental in tone. It was, unhappily, ignored by the reading public and did not attract sufficient critical commentary.

FURTHER WORKS: *Farther Off from Heaven* (wr. 1947); *To Bobolink, for Her Spirit* (1950); *Glory in the Flower* (1958); *The Mall* (1959); *A Loss of Roses* (1960); *Summer Brave* (1962); *A Social*

Event (1962); *The Tiny Closet* (1962); *Memory of Summer* (1962); *Bus Riley's Back in Town* (1962); *The Rainy Afternoon* (1962); *An Incident at the Standish Arms* (1962); *The Strains of Triumph* (1962); *Natural Affection* (1963); *Where's Daddy?* (1966); *The Call* (1968); *The Disposal* (1968); *A Murder* (1968); *Midwestern Manic* (1969)

BIBLIOGRAPHY: Barko, N., "W. I. Talks about Picnic," *Theatre Arts*, 37 (July 1953), 66–67; Weales, G., "The New Pineros," *American Drama since World War II* (1962), 40–56; Newquist, R., "W. I.," *Counterpoint* (1964), 356–63; Lewis, A., "The Emergent Deans: Kimpley, I., and Company," *American Plays and Playwrights of the Contemporary Theatre* (1965), 143–63; Shuman, R. B., *W. I.* (1966); Gould, J., "W. I.," *Modern American Playwrights* (1966), 264–72; Mitchell, M., "Teacher As Outsider in the Works of W. I.," *MQ*, 17 (July 1976), 385–93; Burgess, C. E., "American Experience: W. I. in St. Louis, 1943–49," *Pennsylvania Language and Literature*, 12 (Fall 1976), 438–68; Smotle, G. M., "W. I.: Homosexual Spite in Action," *Like a Brother, Like a Lover* (1978), 121–33; Centola, S. R., "Compromise As Bad Faith: Arthur Miller's *A View From the Bridge* and W. I.'s *Come Back, Little Sheba*," *MQ*, 28, 1 (Autumn 1986), 100–13; Voss, R. F., *A Life of W. I.: The Strains of Triumph* (1989)

WILLIAM OVER

INOUE Yasushi

Japanese novelist, short-story writer, essayist, and poet, b. 6 May 1907, Asahigawa; d. 29 Jan. 1991, Tokyo

The son of a military physician who was subject to frequent transfers, I. spent his childhood years apart from his parents in the family's native village of Yugashima, Shizuoka Prefecture, in the care of his grandmother, a fact that may help to account for the themes of loneliness and alienation that appear in most of his works. After having his literary interests aroused by classmates at the Numazu Middle School, he began to write and to publish poetry while attending the Fourth Higher School in Kanazawa. Although he continued this pursuit while a university student, his first works of fiction, mostly winning entries in contests sponsored by popular magazines, also appeared during those years, and he might have begun to write professionally at that time had he wished to. However, after graduating from Kyoto Imperial University in 1936, he chose to become a reporter for the weekly magazine *Sandē Mainichi*, in which some of his stories had been published. It was not

until after World War II that he again attempted to write fiction.

Through the good offices of the novelist Satō Haruo (1892–1964), who had recognized his talent, I. was able to publish two short novels, *Ryōjū* (1949; *The Hunting Gun*, 1961) and *Tōgyū* (1949; the bull fight), in the prestigious journal *Bungakkai;* his literary career began in earnest when *Tōgyū* was awarded the Akutagawa Literary Prize in 1950. In 1951 he gave up his position with *Sandē Mainichi* to write full time.

Despite the fact that he became a novelist only after reaching middle age, I. proved to be remarkably prolific. During the next few years he produced a great number of short stories, as well as newspaper and magazine serials, for popular consumption. "Hira no shakunage" (1950; "The Azaleas of Hira," 1955), "Aru gisakka no shōgai" (1951; "The Counterfeiter," 1965), *Ashita kuru hito* (1954; those who come tomorrow), *Michite kuru shio* (1955; rising tide), and *Hyōheki* (1956; wall of ice) may be especially worthy of note, but represent a fraction of his total output during those years.

Stories with a historical setting were included among his early works, but it was not until his career was firmly established that he began to produce the kind of fiction for which he is celebrated—meticulously researched historical tales that ponder the littleness of the human being in the vastness of space, and the brevity of our existence in the flow of eternity. Representative are *Tempyō no iraka* (1957; *The Roof Tile of Tempyō*, 1975), which relates the experiences of Japanese monks studying in 8th-c. China; "Rōran" (1958; "Loulan," 1959), about the rise and fall of a small state in Central Asia; *Tonkō* (1959; *Tun-huang*, 1978), which offers an explanation for the Buddhist writings sealed in the caves at Tun-huang; *Aoki ōkami* (1959; the blue wolf), based on the life of Genghis Khan; and *Fūtō* (1963; *Wind and Waves*, 1989), which examines from the Koreans' point of view the Mongol invasions of Japan in the 13th c.

Although he continued to the end of his career to produce novels and stories about ordinary people in ordinary situations, as he grew older the usual lighthearted tone of such works became muted as he began to treat more seriously questions about the nature of the human spirit, what it means to have lived, social values, and the relationships that drive people apart and bind them together. *Shirobamba* (1960; shirobamba), a "coming-of-age" novel based on his own childhood experiences, *Kaseki* (1965; fossils), about a middle-aged man coming to terms with his impending death from cancer, and *Waga haha no ki* (1975; *Chronicle of My Mother*, 1982), actually a series of essays written over a ten-year period portraying his mother in her declining years, were especially successful.

I.'s historical fiction has won such acclaim that many readers associate his name with no other genre, but such stories and novels represent only a small part of his total oeuvre. Indeed, his success and his popularity can only be accounted for by his ability to write prolifically in a variety of genres, and for readers of widely differing tastes and intellectual levels. The lyric style and the tacit affirmation of life that pervades his works contribute to their wide appeal. Although first and foremost a storyteller, I. also produced numerous accounts of his extensive travels, critical essays, personal reminiscences, and a substantial collection of poems.

FURTHER WORKS: *Kuroi ushio* (1950); *Fūrin kazan* (1953); *Asunaro monogatari* (1953); *Kuroi chō* (1955); *Yodo dono nikki* (1955); *Shatei* (1956); *Gake* (1961); *Yōkihi den* (1963); *Go-Shirakawa-In* (1964); *Natsugusa fuyunami* (1964); *Oroshiya-koku suimutan* (1966); *Yoru no koe* (1967); *Nukata no Ōkimi* (1968); *Seiiki monogatari* (1968; *Journey Beyond Samarkand,* 1971); *Kita no umi* (1968); *Keyaki no ki* (1970); *Shikaku na fune* (1970); *Hoshi to matsuri* (1971); *Osanaki hi no koto* (1972); *I. Y. shōsetsu zenshū* (32 vols., 1972–1975); *Utsukushiki mono to no deai* (1973); *Waga ichigo ichie* (1975); *Kadan* (1975); *I. Y. zenshi shū* (1979); *Honkakubō ibun* (1981); *I. Y. rekishi shōsetsu shū* (11 vols., 1981–1982); *Kōshi* (1987). FURTHER VOLUMES IN ENGLISH: *The Counterfeiter and Other Stories* (1965); *Lou-lan and Other Stories* (1979); *Selected Poems of I. Y.* (1979)

B. M. YOUNG

IRANIAN LITERATURE

See Volume 2, page 453.

The Islamic revolution of 1978–1979 in Iran, given its magnitude and impact on the life of Iranians, can only be compared to the Soviet Revolution of 1917. In the sphere of literature, however, the comparison does not hold. For the majority of writers who made names for themselves in Iran before the revolution, the goals and accomplishments of the Islamic Republic stand in contradiction to the ideas and ideals for which they had fought with their pens since the 1950s. Those literary men and woman were socially committed liberals, if not radical leftists, who applauded the victory of the revolution during the first year after the Shah had left Iran. That year did not produce any literary or artistic masterpieces but allowed the intellectuals, writers, and artists to express

themselves without constraint. This permissive atmosphere, however, did not last long after the introduction by the government of new Islamic codes of life-style and conduct for Iranian citizens. As a result of various strictures, many prose writers, poets, and dramatists emigrated. The execution by firing squad in mid-1981 of a dramatist, Sa'id Soltanpur (dates n.a.), was an ominous signal for those writers who stayed in the country. Only one year before his execution, Soltanpur had won critical acclaim for his play *Abbas Aga, Kargar-e Iran Nasional* (1980; Abbas Aga, a worker at the Iran National Company).

Despite this, the last decade must be seen as a measured success for Iranian literature as a new generation of Iranian writers has appeared on the scene. In these new circumstances, a dramatic shift has occured in literary form and content. It has been a decade of the novel as the predominant literary form, succeeding a thousand-year-old Persian preference and indeed love for poetry. The new crop of novelists in Iran have come into their own without being influenced by their Western counterparts, owing in great part to the relative isolation of Iran from the rest of the world after its revolution. The only foreign influence that can be noticed is that of the contemporary Latin American literature. These writers found the right medium of expression for Iranian readers who had gone through the convulsions of the revolution and eight years of a bloody and heartbreaking war with Iraq. It is interesting to note that not only has the contemporary Persian novel, espousing realism as its vocabulary, surpassed contemporary poetry in popularity, but that foreign novels translated into Persian have experienced the same reception. In the last decade alone more than one-hundred-fifty novels worthy of mention have been written in Iran. The best example of the novel's esteem in today's Iran is the fact that 30,000 copies of the longest, ten-part, five-volume novel of some 2,800 pages by Mahmoud Dowlatabadi (b. 1941) entitled *Klidar* (1978–1984; Klidar) were sold as they appeared on bookstore shelves. It is a modern folk epic structured almost entirely in the pattern of the *Shahnameh,* the famous national epic of Ferdowsi of the 11th c. The same epical approach is found in a novel by a woman writer, Moniru Ravanipur (b. 1953), called *Ahl-e qharq* (1990; the drowned). In this novel she creates a mythical atmosphere in a village by the sea where earthly and underwater inhabitants struggle. Their conflict is the millennia-long preoccupation of Iranians with the never-ending duel between the forces of light and darkness, between good and evil. This Zoroastrian concept is transposed onto both allegorical and real situations in historical and contemporary times by another woman writer, Shahrnush Parsipur (b.

1946), in her novel *Tuba va Ma'na-ye Shab* (1989; tuba and the meaning of the night). One of the most gifted living writers of fiction is Abbas Ma'rufi (b. 1958); his *Semfoni-ye-mordegan* (1989; symphony of the dead) is just short of a masterpiece. Among established writers Ismail Fasih (b. 1935) should be included for making his readers think as they laugh over situations, others, and themselves. Hushang Golshiri (b. 1937) has contributed penetrating observations about human conditions, while Reza Baraheni (b. 1935) is known for his outspoken insights, in his creative writing as well as in literary criticism, published in 1987 as *Razha-ye sarzamin-e man* (secrets of my land). This two-volume, 1,275-page account of American secret involvements in Iran, especially in Azerbaijan, is a well-informed and acerbically written book. One of the great masters of the short story, Sadeq Chubak (q.v.), seems to have closed his writing pad since he settled in the West fifteen years ago. The short story is still a very popular vehicle for Persian prose but is not being used as much as it was in the 1960s and 1970s. In poetry, under the shadow of two long-established giants of Persian verse, Ahmad Shamlu (b. 1925) and the recently deceased Mehdi Akhavan-Saless (1928–1990), newcomers are not abounding. Shamlu's output during the last decade has been erratic compared with his prerevolutionary production. Nevertheless, most of his poetry is pregnant with the ideas of an intellectual genius and a visionary. Akhavan-Saless's poetry is rooted deeply in Iranian culture and will influence many generations of Persian poets to come. Nader Naderpur (b. 1929), who chose to live in the West, must be seen as a poet that any national literature would like to claim—he is a ship on an even keel, proudly unfurling the sails of Iranian poetic tradition.

On the whole, important poetry and fiction appear to have managed to avoid the pitfalls of censorship, although self-censorship has doubtless deprived us of many creative works. What is even more significant is that the great bulk of poetry and fiction managed to avoid the taint of propaganda. Such has not been the lot of drama, and especially not of children's literature. This last along with young-adult literature in the Islamic Republic of Iran occupies, calculated on the percentage of books published on these lines, second place after religion and before poetry and fiction. The prominence given to children's literature is due to the fact that the Iranian population has been for many years one of the fastest growing in the world, with more than ten million children in primary schools. A youthful population played a very important role in the revolution and especially in the war against Iraq, and the government is intent on making an Islamic revolutionary imprint on its young minds. The content of this literature is further supported by graphic illustrations of great imagination.

Drama has probably been the fastest-growing literary genre since the 1960s. Before the revolution there were two schools of dramatic craftsmanship in Iran. One was structured after the classical and modern Western drama, while the other turned to traditional Iranian performing arts: professional storytelling and religious passion plays. After the revolution the latter school was encouraged by the existing regime to propagate its weltanschauung. However, since a great number of Iranian dramatists, theater, and film directors, and actors left the country as a result of the revolution, drama as a form became politicized and polarized, with many dramatists in Iran and in the diaspora exalting and degrading the same issues. This is most evident in the plays of the greatest Iranian dramatist, Gholam-Hossein Sa'edi (q.v.), and Hamid Reza A'zam (dates n.a.). Sa'edi died in exile in Paris in 1985. His *Pardedaran-e a'ineh afruz* (1986; the mirror-polishing storytellers) and *Otello dar sarzamin-e ajayeb* (1986; Othello in wonderland), both published posthumously, are a sardonic attack on the governmental enforcement of behavior patterns acceptable to the new, revolutionary standards as well as the conduct of war. A'zam in his *Shegerd-e akhar* (1986; the final art) is apotheosizing a sacred war against Iraq. An interesting aspect is that both playwrights use *naqqals* or storytellers to advance their plots. A'zam uses a famous tea-house storyteller in the national epic *Shahnameh* as a point of departure from praising the heroic deeds of ancient champions to glorify the heroism of Iranian youth in the battlefields of the Iran-Iraq war. Sa'edi's storyteller, on the other hand, uses a traditional backdrop painting *(pardeh)* to show the audience how young men are being used, and die only to bring anguish to their families. With its progression, the play becomes a black comedy. The master of the black comedy is another exiled Iranian man of theater, Parviz Sayyad (b. 1937). His *Samad be jang mirevad* (1984; Samad goes to war) and *Samad az jang barmigerdad* (1988; Samad returns from war) are the most frontal attacks on the Iranian regime and how Iranian youth was brainwashed by the regime in order to wage war. In *Mohakemeh-ye sinema reks* (1987; the Cinema Rex trial) Sayyad accuses the Islamic regime of starting the fire in Cinema Rex in Abadan in 1978 to gain revolutionary momentum against the Shah. Four hundred people died in that fire. In his *Khar* (1983; jackass), Sayyad mocks the Iranian society, which could so easily be manipulated. Never in the history of Iranian theater have as many spectators attended dramatic performances as they now do in the U.S., Canada, and Europe as Sayyad travels with his theater, making a circuit of Iranian communities on both continents and performing these four plays for them. A new literary form that became prominent in postrevolutionary Iran is *filmnameh*. These are published screenplays. The major proponent of this form is Bahram Beyzai (b. 1938), a famous dramatist.

Iran's greatest success in the literary field during the last decade may be measured by the rapidly growing number of readers. Again probably as the result of the revolutionary conditions in the country, the Iranians now spend more time at home, and have more leisure time to read than before the revolution. The pace of life in Iran before the revolution was very fast, and there was a great variety of available entertainment, drawing potential readers away from serious literature. Today they read more of Persian classics, contemporary Persian literature, and translations from world literature than ever before. One of the factors helping to enlarge general readership is an increase of literacy in Iran by some twenty percent during the last fifteen years, and a vastly increased number of women readers.

BIBLIOGRAPHY: Hamalian, L., and J. D. Yohannan, eds., *New Writing from the Middle East* (1978), 271–400; Southgate, M. S., *Modern Persian Short Stories* (1980); Farrukhzad, F., *Another Birth: Selected Poems of Forugh Farrokhzad* (1981); Sa'edi, G.-H., *Dandil: Stories from Iranian Life* (1981); Farrokhzad, F., *Bride of Acacias* (1982); Hillmann, M. C., ed., *Iranian Society: An Anthology of Writings by Jalal Al-e Ahmad* (1982); special Iranian literature issue, *IranS*, 15, 1–4 (1982); special Iranian literature issue, *IranS*, 18, 2–4 (1985); Alishan, L. P., "Ahmad Shamlu: The Rebel Poet in Search of an Audience," *IranS*, 18 (1985), 375–422; Fasih, E., "The Status: A Day in the Life of a Contemporary Iranian Writer," *Third World Review*, 9 (1987), 825–47; Hillmann, M. C., "Iranian Nationalism and Modernist Persian Literature," *LE&W*, 23 (1987), 69–89; Kapuscinski, G., *Modern Persian Drama* (1987); Yarshater, E., ed., *Persian Literature* (1988), 291–402, 513–18; Ghanoonparvar, M. R., and J. Green, *Iranian Drama* (1989); Hillmann, M. C., *Iranian Culture: A Persianist View* (1990)

PETER J. CHELKOWSKI

IRISH LITERATURE

See Volume 2, page 458.

Writing in Ireland in the 20th c. is the outgrowth of two cultures and languages: Gaelic and English. Since modern Ireland is a postcolonial culture, the naming of territory and literature is closely bound up with politics and history. Thus, over the past four centuries, literature written in English in Ireland has been referred to as "Anglo-Irish," while "Irish literature" could mean literature written in either Gaelic or English. For the purposes of this article, the term "Irish Literature" is used to refer to literature written in either language.

Beginning in the 17th c. the common use of Gaelic was eroded by wave after wave of cultural attrition by English colonists so that the production of Gaelic literature had dwindled to a trickle by the end of the 19th c. This trend was temporarily reversed with the advent of the Gaelic Revival. The revival was spurred on by a series of important historical events: the land-reform movement, political pressure for Home Rule, and the emergence of a series of heroic political figures who were to influence greatly the course of politics and literature in the 20th c. Probably the most important of these was Charles Stuart Parnell (1846–1891), who waged a vehement political campaign for Home Rule. His rejection by political opponents and the hierarchy of the Catholic church in Ireland and his premature and tragic death after a bitter public scandal over his apparent involvement in an adulterous affair inspired the young William Butler Yeats (q.v.) and others to invest great energy in generating an Irish cultural revival as part of a more militant movement to remove British political and cultural control in Ireland. Parnell, after his death, was inducted into Yeats's heroic pantheon along with Cuchulainn, and thus became another recurring figure in the work of Yeats, James Joyce (q.v.), and others.

Yeats felt that the rise of middle-class values in England and the powerful influence of the Catholic church in Ireland were threats to what he saw as the heroic Irish tradition that predated Christianity. In Yeats's opinion, Ireland was one of the strongholds against the "filthy modern tide." He thus led a movement whose purpose was to reinvent an Ireland that had been lost to numerous waves of colonization by Vikings and Normans, but most especially the imperialist English. Yeats's form of nationalism came as a direct response to Ireland's postcolonial history, so he focused his energies at this time on the founding of the National Literary Society (1892), and later The Abbey Theatre (1904). These, along with the founding of The Gaelic League by Douglas Hyde (1860–1949) in 1893, led to widespread renewal of interest not only in the Irish language, but also in ancient Irish myth and folklore. While Irish political and social changes exerted their own forces on the production of literature in Ireland, we cannot dispute the stylistic influence of the continental realists and symbolists. As Yeats himself put it, "Every man everywhere is more of his age than of his nation."

Drama

In 1899, Yeats, along with George Moore (1852–1933), Lady Augusta Gregory (1852–1932), and Edward Martyn (1859–1923), founded The Irish Literary Theatre, later renamed the Irish National Theatre, which in 1904 found its permanent home at the Abbey Theatre. In 1899 the company produced Yeats's second play, *The Countess Cathleen,* which tells of a young countess who sells her soul to the devil to save the lives of a group of famine-stricken Irish. The Irish public, many of whom did not see the play, protested vehemently the play's unorthodox religious implications, and thus began Yeats's often stormy relationship with the Irish public and the inauguration of the Abbey as not only the country's national theater, but, most extraordinarily, a platform for political and social debate. This was one of the first times in modern European history when the staging of plays in a metropolitan theater had the persistent power to provoke riots. Along with Yeats's plays, the drama of John Millington Synge and Sean O'Casey (qq.v.) at times verged on the incendiary. After a series of riots over the plays of these three dramatists, the Abbey Theatre was thrust into the international public eye.

Yeats exploited the controversy surrounding *The Countess Cathleen* to produce a play with a similar theme, called *Cathleen ni Houlihan.* In this play, set in the rural west of Ireland during the 1789 uprising, an old woman, who is the embodiment of dispossessed Ireland, asks the young hero to forsake married life to become a martyr for his country. The old woman is magically transformed into a beautiful young maiden as the rejuvenating blood of the young male is spilled. *Cathleen ni Houlihan* came to represent, for all subsequent Irish literature, the bloodthirsty but irresistible spirit of Ireland who would call young men to their deaths. The Irish National Theatre also saw the production of the first play in Irish: Douglas Hyde's *Casadh an Tsugain (The Twisting of the Rope,* 1901), which was a remarkable event in that its production came at the twilight of the use of the Gaelic language and the culture that cradled it.

Lady Gregory, Yeats's mentor and collaborator, wrote over forty plays, mostly one-act plays, many of which were performed at the Abbey, including *Spreading the Word* (1904), *The Workhouse Ward* (1909), and *The Rising of the Moon* (1910). Synge was "discovered" in Paris by Yeats who advised him to go to the west of Ireland and write about the people there, to "express a life that had never found expression." In 1903 The Irish National Theatre Society produced Synge's *In the Shadow of the Glen,* one of a series of plays that explore the folkways of a dying rural culture. When his best-known play, *The Playboy of the Western World* (1907), was performed, riots occurred in Dublin because nationalist feeling had reached such a pitch that any perceived insult to the sacred "national character" or the "noble Irish country people" was virtually sacrilegious. Synge's plays are outstanding because he successfully reproduced on stage the authentic dialect of the western Irish: He had ostensibly stripped the English language of its "Englishness." But it was George Bernard Shaw (q.v.) who was to play masterfully with the stereotype of Englishman and Irishman on stage, using as his model the stage-Irishman popularized in the drama of the 19th-c. Irish-American dramatist Dion Boucicault. In the preface to *John Bull's Other Island* (1904), which was expressly written for Yeats's Irish Literary Theatre, Shaw states, "Ireland is the only spot on earth which produces the ideal Englishman of history."

In 1923, after the partition of the island and the formation of the Irish Free State, the Abbey was now state subsidized and ready to resume production after civil conflicts that began with the uprising of 1916. It was the new dramatist O'Casey whose plays were to take the stage at the Abbey by storm, beginning with *The Shadow of a Gunman* (1923), *Juno and the Paycock* (1924), and the notorious *The Plough and the Stars* (1926), the last of which caused riots in the streets of Dublin of the kind that had not been seen since Synge's *Playboy* nineteen years earlier. All three of O'Casey's early plays are set against the background of the political turmoil of 1916, to the war of independence, and the subsequent civil war; however, they are more of a social study of life in the Dublin slums, in which the male characters are music-hall stage-Irish caricatures and the women are rational, tolerant, and heroic in the face of tragedy. O'Casey's later drama tends toward the expressionist (q.v.). *The Silver Tassie* (1928) was rejected by the Abbey, causing a split between Yeats and O'Casey. The Dublin Gate Theatre took on more experimental works than the Abbey, particularly the work of Denis Johnston and Paul Vincent Carroll (qq.v.) in the late 1920s and the 1930s. Brendan Behan's (q.v.) drama is outrageous tragicomedy that contains the autobiographical elements of his involvement with the I.R.A. and subsequent imprisonment in 1939, but unfortunately it verges on self-caricature. *The Quare Fellow* (1954) is set in a prison the night before an execution; and probably his best play, *The Hostage* (1958), looks at the capture of a British soldier in a brothel.

Brian Friel (q.v.) is recognized as today's greatest Irish dramatist, whose *Philadelphia, Here I Come* (1964), *The Freedom of the City* (1973), *Aristocrats* (1979), and *Translations* (1981) examine the history and psychopathology of a people suffering from a profound sense of dispossession and failure. His characters are starved of love and filled with worthless fantasies of historical grandeur, but in *Dancing at Lughnasa* (1991) Friel makes a claim for the Dionysiac rituals among the most repressed country people. Thomas Murphy's (b. 1931) *A Crucial Week in the Life of a Grocer's Assistant* (1969) and *The Gigli Concert* (1984) expose the squalor and repressions of provincial small-town life, while Thomas Kilroy's (b. 1934) *The Death and Resurrection of Mr. Roche* (1969) and *Talbot's Box* (1979) focus on the isolation of being an outcast, in this case a homosexual, in Dublin. Frank McGuinness (dates n.a.) moves into the more experimental and challenging territory with *Innocence: The Life and Death of Michelangelo Merici, Caravaggio* (1987) and *Observe the Sons of Ulster Marching to the Somme* (1986), in which we follow the ironic political and tribal allegiances of a group of Irish soldiers on the front during World War I.

Poetry

Yeats dominates the poetic landscape both in Ireland and abroad, for he belongs to both the canons of Irish literature and high modernism (q.v.). As in his drama, Yeats's early poetry uses Irish myth and folklore as a means of expressing his romantic ideals, and his early style has the elaborate poise of the Pre-Raphaelites. In "The Stolen Child" (1886) we find wistful escapism in enchanting lines like "In pools among the rushes / That scarce could bathe a star." But Yeats also had the remarkable ability to transform himself from an imaginary wanderer in fairyland into a realist who could confront the violence in the streets of Dublin after the uprising of 1916 and the subsequent war of independence, as well as World War I. In "The Second Coming" (1920) the speaker expresses an overwhelming sense of helplessness in the maelstrom of violence at home and abroad: "The blood-dimmed is loosed, and everywhere / The ceremony of innocence is drowned." This poem also contains Yeats's important theory of the repetitive cycles of history and violence. The legacy that Yeats wanted his poetic inheritors to adopt in "Under Ben Bulben" (1939) was "Irish poets learn your trade, / Sing whatever is well made."

Yeats's death in 1939 left a seemingly unfillable void on the Irish literary scene, particularly in the enveloping dark of the war in Europe in which the Republic chose to be neutral. Austin Clarke (q.v.) adopted the idea of the poet as social commentator, attacking the powerful influence of the Catholic church. Patrick Kavanagh (q.v.), the first father figure of the northern poets, railed against the limitations of rural life, most especially in his great antipastoral masterpiece "The Great Hunger" (1942). He marked a geographical shift in the center of poetic activity from south to north. Louis MacNeice (q.v.), while he belonged to a circle of radical English poets of the thirties along with W. H. Auden and Stephen Spender (qq.v.), was a lyrical poet who elevated the pastoral west of Ireland and criticizes the encroachment of the modern world in urban Belfast, though he is less romantic and more skeptical that Yeats. Thomas Kinsella (q.v.) is one of a series of poets to look both backward, to Irish mythology, and outside Ireland, especially to Carl Gustav Jung and Ezra Pound (qq.v.), for poetic models. Richard Murphy (q.v.) writes on the starkness of life in confrontation with the elements on his native west coast. Probably his greatest poem is the nostalgic "The Battle of Aughrim," which attempts to bridge the gap between history and the self. John Montague (q.v.) made the north the definitive territory for Irish poetry, territory that had to be recovered from its colonial history, and resituated in mythology. Montague looks to the landscape itself for evidence of ancient history, to the neolithic remains that litter the countryside, especially in *The Rough Field* (1972). Seamus Heaney (q.v.) began his career by taking Montague's analytical gaze on the landscape a step further, to the point that he approaches the land more like a lover than an archaeologist. Having grown up in rural County Derry and a member of the Catholic nationalist minority in British Northern Ireland, Heaney is keenly aware of the tremendous pressure exerted on him to be a spokesman for the dispossessed nationalist community. He has persistently resisted this role, and has worked, especially in the 1980s, to expand his horizons within an artistically limiting situation. Nevertheless many of his poems tackle the thorny issue of violence in today's Northern Ireland, particularly in *North* (1975), in which the poet struggles to make connections between archaeological evidence of ritual slayings in prehistoric Europe with today's violence. In *Station Island* (1985) Heaney takes a spiritual and artistic pilgrimage to meet the spirits of dead father figures, not to mention Joyce. *The Haw Lantern* (1987) contains a brilliant and moving elegy, "Clearances," to the poet's mother. Derek Mahon (q.v.) much of whose work takes place in the landscape of urban Belfast, is more skeptical about history and politics then Heaney; his loyalties vacillate for he is less physically attached to the landscape than his fellow northerners, and thus sees it in a different light. John Hewitt (1907–1987) is an important northern pastoral Protestant poet, writing, as it were, from the other side of the barbed wire from Heaney. Paul Muldoon (b. 1951) has been hailed as the leader of the next generation of northern poets, with fine collections such as *Why Brownlee Left* (1980) and *Quoof* (1984), in which he casts a cold eye on the pressure placed on the poet to comment on politics, by painting ever-shifting, often surreal images to reinforce the freedom that he demands in poetry. Tom Paulin (b. 1949), another important northerner, instead confronts head-on the bigotry in war-torn Ulster in *Strange Museum* (1980) and *The Liberty Tree* (1983) and insists on the poet's role in offering a useful vision to his community. While the north seems to have been the solitary wellspring of poetry for the past twenty years, the south has also produced some important new poets, notably Paul Durcan (q.v.), whose easy conversational style contrasts with his acidic but humorous attacks on the conventions of family, the church, and art. North and south, a number of new women poets have emerged whose work proves to be even more diverse, more tangible in its imagery and less abstract than the work of their male counterparts. Medbh MacGuckian's (b. 1950) contemplative pastoral and Irish mythic topics and Eavan Boland's (b. 1944) sharp eye for detail and feeling for place have produced some of the finest nature poetry in the tradition, which in Ireland is rich. Nuala Ni Dhomhnaill (b. 1952), who is one of many poets today writing in Irish, has a unique feeling for the landscape of the coast of her native Kerry. She also resists the traditional projection of feminine imagery onto the landscape by replacing the female figure with a male one. In this case, an ancient tradition—poetry in Irish—has been merged with the modern feminist ideology.

Fiction

The revival of the Irish language, spearheaded by Douglas Hyde, spurred many prose writers to turn away from English and write in Irish. This is true not only of writers from the predominantly Irish-speaking west, but also the urban east. The problem, of course, is that by rejecting the language of the oppressor, one is also greatly narrowing one's audience. Padraic O'Conaire (1883–1928) wrote short fiction about the rebellion against English rule, as did Seamus O'Grianna (1891–1969). Irish-language folk writers in rural and western Ireland wrote stories about a dying culture

in its own dying language. Among the notable classics are Muiris O'Suilleabhain's (1904–1950) *Fiche blian ag fas* (*Twenty Years A-Growing,* 1933), and Peig Sayers's (1873–1958) *Peig* (1936).

James Stephen's (q.v.) writing gives us a vivid fictionalized account of the Easter 1916 rising in *The Insurrection in Dublin* (1916); and in *The Charwoman's Daughter* (1912) he provides a disturbing picture of squalid poverty in the Dublin of the time. In George Moore's first collection of short stories, *The Untilled Field* (1903), which was originally published in Irish in 1902, we find one of the central theme's of 20th-c. Irish fiction: the necessity of exile from an Ireland that is spiritually stifling. Moore also introduced continental styles to Ireland, notably those of Zola, Flaubert, and Mallarmé. The writing of a collection of thematically related short stories was also taken up by Joyce with *Dubliners* (1914) and by Samuel Beckett (q.v.) in *More Pricks than Kicks* (1934). Joyce's *A Portrait of the Artist as a Young Man* (1916) is a moral history of the development of the author's semiautobiographical persona, Stephen Dedalus, whose peregrinations we later follow in the modernist masterpiece *Ulysses* (1922). In Joyce's final work, *Finnegans Wake* (1939), the distinction between order and chaos has been removed, so that the reader is locked in a linguistic labyrinth that few have found penetrable. Samuel Beckett, a member of Joyce's literary circle in Paris, helped translate *Finnegans Wake* into French and adopted, or rather distilled, to his own use, many of Joyce's stylistic sleights of hand. His first novel, *Murphy* (1938), tells of the life and death of an Irish immigrant in London. But his later writings, notably the trilogy *Molloy* (1955), *Malone Dies* (1956), and *The Unnamable* (1958) (all of which he translated from the French in which they were first written), reduce plot and character and landscape to an absurd minimalism. Nevertheless, the ''Irishness'' of character and topography pervades the overwhelming anonymity and bleakness of his work.

Flann O'Brien (q.v.) wrote his first classic, *An Beal Bocht* (1941; *The Poor Mouth,* 1961), as a direct satiric attack on attempts to revive and edify the Gaelic language and culture in the west, but in *At-Swim-Two-Birds* (1939) we are delighted by his parody of Celtic mythical figures and the act of writing itself.

The 1930s and 1940s saw the rise of a new group of writers who launched a seemingly concerted attack on the parochialism of the new Irish Free State. Sean O'Faolain (1900–1991) was the central personality in this group. *The Bell,* the group's literary magazine, succeeded in embracing a wide range of regional Irish writers who might otherwise have gone unpublished. O'Faolain's three great novels, *A Nest of Simple Folk* (1934), *Bird Alone* (1936), and *Come Back to Erin* (1940), depict an Ireland that is populated by characters whose nationalist aspirations are doomed, or who yearn for the modern world and its freedoms but who are spiritually anchored in the strictness of Irish Catholicism. Frank O'Connor (q.v.) became the master of the Irish short story; his sense of ease with his audience has produced a writer whose warmth with his subject matter surpassed his peers. Liam O'Flaherty (1897–1984) was born on the Aran Islands off the west coast. He is best known for his short stories, many of which tell of life and death from an animal's point of view, such as in "The Cow's Death" (1923) and "The Wounded Cormorant" (1925). His fiction is consciously stripped of sentimentality. Mary Lavin (b. 1912) writes about the young female, who in many cases is forced to cling to love lost in the cold world of modern Ireland in her *Collected Tales* (1971). Much of Elizabeth Bowen's (q.v.) fiction is centered on the decay of the English ascendancy in her family home in County Cork. *The Death of the Heart* (1938) and *The Heat of the Day* (1949) are her best-known works. Edna O'Brien's (q.v.) novels and short stories follow the fortunes of young women who seek to escape rural and restraining Ireland. Her females are abused and self-abusing, while her males are treacherous, as in *The Country Girls* (1960), *Night* (1972), and *Johnny I Hardly Knew You* (1977).

James Plunkett's (b. 1920) *Strumpet City* (1969) fictionalizes the struggle of the labor leader James Larkin, who struggled to raise the consciousness of Dublin workers against the opposition of the employers and clergy. Benedict Kiely (b. 1919) examines the violent present in a community that believes firmly in fixed values, as in *Dogs Enjoy the Morning* (1971) and *Nothing Happens in Carrickmacross* (1985). Brian Moore's (q.v.) unrelentingly bleak vision of life in the north is best crafted in *Judith Hearne* (1955) (repub. as *The Lonely Passion of Judith Hearne,* 1959). His latest novel, *Lies of Silence* (1990), lacks the sharp ironies of his earlier work and verges on moralizing about paramilitary violence in the north. John McGahern's (b. 1934) vision is no less bleak than Moore's, for his characters in their search for love are led into alienation. We find the physical and spiritual illness of a people in *The Dark* (1963) and *The Pornographer* (1979), but in his best novel to date, *Amongst Women* (1990), we find the inevitable demise of a tyrannical father and his effects on his children as they grow up. William Trevor (q.v.) is a gifted storyteller, which shows in his short fiction, but his novels lack the same finesse, his finest collections being *The News From Ireland* (1986) and *Family Sins* (1990). John Ban-

ville (b. 1945) emerged in the early 1970s as an important new novelist, and his *Birchwood* (1973) is hailed as a masterpiece. Set in a background of famine and civil war, the memoirlike narrative is a nightmarish vision of the decay of the ascendancy and the accompanying social breakdown. Jennifer Johnston's (b. 1930) writing examines the shifting distinctions between social and moral values in the violent north of today. In *Shadows on Our Skin* (1975) a young Catholic woman who dates a British soldier is "tarred-and-feathered" by an outwardly genteel people. Bernard Mac Laverty's (b. 1942) fiction is set in the same tense situation, and his characters are as isolated as Moore's, especially in *Cal* (1983).

BIBLIOGRAPHY: Boyd, E. A., *Ireland's Literary Renaissance* (1922); Corkery, D., *Synge and Anglo-Irish Literature* (1931); Foster, J. W., *Forces and Themes in Ulster Fiction* (1974); Marcus, D., and R. Deutsch, *Northern Ireland 1921–1974, A Select Bibliography* (1975); Brown, T., *Northern Voices: Poets from Ulster* (1975); Hogan, R. G., and J. Kilroy, eds., *The Modern Irish Drama* (4 vols., 1975–1979); Rafroidi, R. P., and M. Harmon, eds., *The Irish Novel in Our Time* (1976); Hunt, H., *The Abbey: Ireland's National Theatre, 1904–1978* (1979); Lyons, F. S. L., *Culture and Anarchy in Ireland 1890–1939* (1979); Brown, T., *Ireland: A Social and Cultural History 1922–79* (1981); Kenner, H., *A Colder Eye: The Modern Irish Writers* (1983); Trevor, W., *A Writer's Ireland* (1984); Deane, S., *Celtic Revivals: Essays in Modern Irish Literature 1880–1980* (1985); Hederman, M. P., and R. Kearney, eds., *The Crane Bag Book of Irish Studies* (2 vols., 1987); Bradley, A., ed., *Contemporary Irish Poetry* (1988); Hildebidle, J., *Five Irish Writers: The Errand of Keeping Alive* (1989); Deane, S., ed., *The Field Day Anthology of Irish Writing* (3 vols., 1991)

FERGAL O'DOHERTY

IRVING, John
American novelist, b. 2 Mar. 1942, Exeter, N.H.

I. is an American novelist who has achieved both critical acclaim and widespread popularity. He was educated at Exeter Academy, the University of Pittsburgh, the University of New Hampshire (B.A. 1965), and the University of Iowa Writers Workshop (M.F.A. 1967), where he completed his first novel and later returned as a writer in residence. Between 1963 and 1964 he studied at the University of Vienna, and the city is a recurring setting in his novels.

I.'s first three novels—*Setting Free the Bears* (1969), *The Water-Method Man* (1972), and *The*

158-Pound Marriage (1974)—earned some critical praise but little popular success. All three are experimental in form and blackly humorous; all feature young adult protagonists. In *Setting Free the Bears,* two young men, Siggy and Hannes, take off on a motorcycle from Vienna to the countryside, where Siggy dies bizarrely, trapped under a truck and stung by bees; Hannes returns to Vienna to carry out his friend's plan of freeing the animals in the Vienna Zoo. The novel contains a mixture of narratives: Hannes's narrative of his and Siggy's actions, Siggy's zoo-watch journal, and Siggy's autobiography, the tale of his family's sufferings and persecution at the hands of Yugoslavian factions during World War II. *The Water-Method Man,* the story of a graduate student's successful attempts to turn his life around by finding a cure for a rare urinary-tract disorder, reconciling himself with his father and his former wife, and fully committing himself to marriage and parenthood with his current mistress, also introduces one of I.'s recurrent themes—the relationship between life and art—by using a wild mixture of narratives: present time, flashbacks, excerpts from the Old Norse epic the hero is translating for his dissertation, his tape recordings and letters, and excerpts from a documentary film about him. All come together at the end as the hero achieves personal fulfillment; this is I.'s most sweetly optimistic novel. In contrast, *The 158-Pound Marriage* is a bleak tale of a four-way affair between two married couples that ends up causing all of them pain; this novel also mixes present-time narrative and the past-time stories of how each couple met (in Vienna).

I.'s breakthrough book, in earning not just critical attention but widespread popularity, was *The World According to Garp* (1978). The novel was a best-seller in hardcover and mass-market paperback; one of I.'s phrases, the Under Toad (a child character's mistaken notion of "undertow," which becomes a metaphor for life's uncontrollable sadness and violence), is now listed in some dictionaries. Perhaps because of the topicality of some of its concerns—including feminism, rape, the assassination of public figures—and its mixture of exaggeration, violence, and black humor, the novel was controversial; since then, all of I.'s novels have been best-sellers. In the judgment of most critics, *Garp* was also—and to some it still is— I.'s best book. It tells the life story of T. S. Garp, a wrestler and a writer, from his bizarre conception to his assassination, and conveys a coherent vision of a world where "we are all terminal cases"— readers learn how almost all of the characters die— where violence is random but family patterns recur oddly through generations, a world "rich with lunacy and sorrow" that I. himself described as

"an artfully designed soap opera," modeled in part on the great 19th-c. novels, intended to make readers laugh and cry. It also continues I.'s preoccupation with life and art; it contains two of Garp's stories and the opening chapter of one of his novels and descriptions of the other three, all of which bear intriguing resemblances to I.'s own fiction. In fact, the title of the novel Garp is planning to write, *My Father's Illusions,* might well serve as the title of I.'s next book.

The Hotel New Hampshire (1981), which actually outsold *Garp* in hardcover, disappointed many critics. A novel I. described as "fairy-tale-like," *The Hotel New Hampshire* returns to some of *Garp's* settings—New England prep schools and coastal estates, Vienna—and themes: rape, politically motivated violence, revenge, family patterns, oddly recurring events, and the influence of childhood on adult identity. Black Humor abounds, but feels more strained, and I. uses, with more frequency and exaggeration, some of the literary techniques of *The World According to Garp,* like different typefaces for emphasis (italics and all caps) and the aphorism ("Sorrow floats"; "Life is serious but art is fun"). Compared with *Garp, The Hotel New Hampshire* is a thinner and more mannered book.

The Cider House Rules (1985) divided critics. It has two heroes, Dr. Wilbur Larch, who heads an orphanage where he also performs abortions on request, and his adopted son Homer Wells, who eventually after some moral struggle follows in his father's footsteps, and thus two major plot threads, and two settings, the orphanage in the Maine interior and an apple orchard on the coast. A few critics saw it as I.'s best work, his most successful in avoiding cuteness and exploring an important public issue—abortion—seriously. Others found it sentimental, dully written, and repulsive in its gynecological detail.

A Prayer for Owen Meany (1989) is I.'s soundest artistic, critical, and popular success since *Garp.* Its plot and symbols seem more carefully designed and intertwined; its narrator, John Wheelwright, tells his and Owen's story in retrospect, and Owen's destiny as a Christlike sacrificial figure is both frequently foreshadowed and known to Owen well before it takes place. In fact, John and Owen believe—and the novel seems to endorse them—that Owen's fate is God's plan; John says that he had become a Christian because of Owen. This Christian perspective is a radical departure in the world according to I. From *Setting Free the Bears* on, I. has seen patterns, resemblances between present and past too striking to be entirely coincidental, but he never offered a religious explanation for them, and formal religion never was an issue in his characters' lives. Besides suggesting a change in I.'s world view, *A Prayer for Owen Meany* may also indicate new literary influences: Robertson Davies (q.v.) and perhaps Stephen King (b. 1947).

I. has achieved what he said he wanted all along: a wide general audience for his work, a readership like that enjoyed by the great 19th-c. British novelists. Like Dickens and Hardy, I. is first and always a storyteller, a creator of genuinely sympathetic characters to whom terrible things may happen. Critical reaction to his mature work has been mixed—in fact, British reviewers have been particularly unsympathetic—but at least for *The World According to Garp* and *A Prayer For Owen Meany,* far more favorable than unfavorable. I.'s reputation as a serious, if uneven, novelist seems secure. For all his protests that he is an imaginative writer and not a sociologist, I.'s best work reflects the America of the last three decades. Like F. Scott Fitzgerald's (q.v.), the best of I.'s novels should endure both as representations of their time and as timeless works of art.

FURTHER WORK: *Three by I.* (1980)

BIBLIOGRAPHY: Drabble, M., "Muck, Memory, and Imagination," *Harper's* (July 1978), 82–84; Tyler, A., "Three by I.," *NewR,* 182 (26 Apr. 1980), 32–33; Wymard, E. B., "New Version of the Midas Touch: *Daniel Martin* and *The World According to Garp,*" *MFS,* 27, 1 (Summer 1981), 284–86; Priestley, M., "Structure in the Worlds of J. I.," *Crit,* 23 (1981), 82–96; Epstein, J., "Why J. I. Is So Popular," *Commentary,* 73 (June 1982), 59–63; Hill, J. B., "J. I.'s Aesthetics of Accessibility: Setting Free the Novel," *SCR,* 16 (Fall 1983), 38–44; Adams, R. M., "The Story Isn't Over," *NYRB,* 32 (18 July 1985), 20–23

SARAH ENGLISH

ISHIKAWA Jun

(born Shiba Kiyoshi) Japanese novelist and essayist, b. 7 Mar. 1899, Tokyo; d. 29 Dec. 1987, Tokyo

The second son of a local banker and politician in the old downtown quarter of Tokyo known as Asakusa, I. was adopted and raised by his maternal grandparents. The grandfather, Ishikawa Shōsai, had been a samurai and scholar of Chinese and Japanese poetry employed by the last Tokugawa Shogun. As a boy I. received training in classical Chinese texts such as the *Analects,* the repertoire of the Nō theater, and the popular fiction of the Edo period. He was also a fan of Mori Ōgai's (q.v.) translations of modern European literature. Later he studied French at the Tokyo School of

Foreign Languages and, coming under the influence of the French symbolists and antinaturalists, numbered among the first to translate into Japanese the works of André Gide (q.v.), such as *L'immoraliste* (1902) and *Les caves du Vatican* (1914) in 1924 and 1928, respectively.

After a period of artistic vagabondage and flirtation with anarchist politics, I. began to publish his first novellas or *récits.* His debut work, "Kajin" (1935; the beauty), is a definitive statement of his antinaturalism as well as a parody of the *shishōsetsu* or "I-novel." Also conceived in a tongue-in-cheek tone, *Fugen* (1936; *The Bodhisattva; or, Samantabhadra,* 1990) is the tale of an impoverished novelist who, beset by the quotidian realities of life in Tokyo, is driven by the dream of the millennium. His dream is manifest in writing about Joan of Arc and her chronicler Christine de Pizan, and in his madcap affair to save Yukari, a young woman involved in the Japanese political underground, from falling into the hands of the police. By drawing successive layers of parallels between "dust and flowers"—Japan in the 1930s and France in the 15th c.—the novel comes to the conclusion that there will be no "bodhisattva" to save Japan. The last line of defense for those who oppose the times are "gratuitous" acts of resistance. Awarded the fourth Akutagawa Prize for literature in 1937, this seminal novel is a powerful combination of parody, allegory, and satire that employs both the palimpsest construction of European modernist prose and the mystification style *(tōkai-buri)* of fiction of the Edo period.

I.'s next major sally, "Marusu no uta" (1938; song of the war god), a denunciation of the chorus of jingoism that swept Japan after the invasion of China in 1937, was banned by the authorities. Along with *Fugen,* this work establishes I.'s reputation as one of Japan's few "resistance" writers.

During the war, I. produced largely criticism, especially his famous critique *Mori Ōgai* (1941; Mori Ōgai) that treats Mori Ōgai's late historical novels as precursors of metafiction, and a theory of prose, *Bungaku taigai* (1942; all about literature), which espouses I.'s theory of automatic writing and spiritual vitalism. He wrote only one novel, *Hakubyō* (1939; line drawing), a roman à clef that takes Bruno Taut (1880–1938), the modernist architect who resided briefly in Japan, as its protagonist. During the war I. sought his "inner emigration" in Edo-period literature, especially the *kyōka* or comic verse of the Temmei era (1781–1789), in which he saw the incipience of modernist attitudes in Japanese writing.

In 1945 Dazai Osamu (q.v.), Sakaguchi Ango (1906–1955), and I. emerged as the new leaders of the postwar literary scene. They are often treated as members of the so-called "libertine" *(burai)*

or "new burlesque" *(shin-gesaku)* school—labels that refer to their iconoclastic attitudes toward traditional values, and their interest in the parody fiction of the Edo period. Couched in Christian analogies instead of Buddhist, I.'s short stories— allegories for the destruction and resurrection of Japan such as "Ōgon densetsu" (1946; legend of gold) and "Yakeato no Iesu" (1946, Jesus amidst the ruins)—are his best-known works, and his most representative short fiction.

Although I. faded from public attention as of the 1950s, he continued to be touted in Japanese literary circles as a "novelist's novelist" and a *shibui* writer. He divided his energies between his work as an essayist—writing an ongoing series under the name Isai and in the style of the *propos* of the French essayist Alain (pseud. of Émile-Auguste Chartier, q.v.)—and creating what he called *jikken shōsetsu* or experimental novels. Adopting third-person narration and a less-garrulous style, I.'s mature novels are deeper explorations of the terrain of metafiction and social satire: *Taka* (1953; bird of prey) speaks of a mysterious language called futurese; *Aratama* (1963; wild spirit), the story of Sata—embodiment of the darkling forces at the bottom of society—is both a parody of comic-book or *manga* heroes, and a prophesy of the "black mist" or *kuroi kiri* that enveloped Japanese politics in the 1970s. *Shifuku sennen* (1965; the millennium), an imaginary scenario in which bands of hidden Christians attempt to seize control of the city of Edo, is inspired no doubt by Gide's tale of the Vatican cellars, as well as the factionalism endemic to Japan's politics and its new religions.

I. was recipient of the Ministry of Education Prize for literature in 1957 for *Shion monogatari* (1956; *Asters,* 1961), and the Asahi Cultural Prize in 1982 after publication of his longest novel, *Kyōfūki* (1980; record of a mad wind). He was elected to permanent membership in the *Geijutsuin,* Japan Academy of the Arts, in 1963. At the time of his death, he was at work on *Hebi no uta* (1986; song of the snake), a "banquet" of sex, power, and money in contemporary Japan.

Generationally speaking, I. ranks alongside critics and writers such as Kobayashi Hideo (q.v.) and Yokomitsu Riichi (1898–1947), who called for an end to naturalist, first-person narration and raised the clarion call for the "pure novel." Clearly he was the first among his generation to advance the cause of modernism (q.v.) and metafiction, and what in the West is called "writing degree zero." Often he has been anthologized with his younger protégés Abe Kōbō and Ōe Kenzaburō (qq.v.) as an "internationalist" because of their shared love of French existentialist literature and desire to wrest the novel in Japan from subjects

particular to the culture. Moreover, he is often compared to Jorge Luis Borges and Vladimir Nabokov (qq.v.) because of his brilliance as a stylist, his mastery of parody, and his advocacy of experimental fiction. At the same time, it must not be forgotten that I. is equally heir to the *bunjin* or literati tradition that, introduced to Japan from China, starts from the *nanga* painters and *kyōka* poets of the Edo period and is transmitted to modern Japanese letters by Mori Ōgai and Nagai Kafū. Thus he has also been hailed as Japan's *saigo no bunjin,* "the last of the literati," and embodies the critical, epicurean, and cosmopolitan spirit of that tradition.

FURTHER WORKS: *Watanabe kazan* (1941); *Giteiki* (1943); *Isai hitsudan* (1951); *Isai rigen* (1952); *Isai seigen* (1954); *Shokoku kijinden* (1957); *Hakutōin* (1957); *Isai jōzetsu* (1960); *Isai yūgi* (1963); *Zenken yōin* (1975); *Isai zadan* (1977); *Edo bungaku jōki* (1980); *Shinsaku kojiki* (1983); *Rokudō yugyō* (1983); *I. J. zenshū* (14 vols., 1974–1975; 19 vols., 1989–1991)

BIBLIOGRAPHY: Keene, D., *Dawn to the West* (1984), Vol. 1, 1087–102; Tyler, W., "Art and Act of Reflexivity in I. J.'s *The Bodhisattva: or, Samantabhadra*" (1990), 139–66

WILLIAM J. TYLER

ISKANDER, Fazil Abdulovich

Russian novelist, short-story writer, and poet, b. 6 Mar. 1929, Sukhum, U.S.S.R. (now Abkhazia)

Of mixed Persian and Abkhazian descent, I. was born in Sukhum, the capital of Abkhazia, an autonomous republic in Georgia. I. has written that as a child he witnessed the passing of the patriarchal way of life in Abkhazia, which provides the setting for much of his prose. I. grew up speaking both Abkhazian and Russian, but writes only in Russian. A graduate of the Moscow Gorky Literary Institute (1954), I. for over three decades has divided his time between Moscow and Abkhazia. In the tradition of such Russian novelists as Gogol, Turgenev, and Vladimir Nabokov (q.v.), I. began his literary career as a poet. I. published five volumes of verse between 1957 and 1964 and continues to write poetry to this day. A selection of I.'s poetry from the 1950s through the 1980s appeared under the title *Put'* (1987; the path).

While I. is a competent poet, he has made an indelible impression on the Russian novel and short story. In 1962 I.'s short fiction began to appear in the journal *Iunost',* the bastion of the "young prose" movement. The publication of the satirical *Sozvezdie kozlotura* (1966; *The Goatibex*

Constellation, 1975) created a sensation and catapulted the young author to prominence. Several collections of I.'s fiction appeared in the late 1960s and 1970s. In 1973 excerpts from I.'s epic novel *Sandro iz Chegema* were published in *Novyi Mir.* The tortured publication history of I.'s masterpiece and one of the landmarks of postwar Russian literature outlines his literary career from the mid-1970s through 1989. The novel was issued as a separate book in 1977, but in a severly abridged form. Unable to publish the uncensored and complete text of *Sandro* in the U.S.S.R., I. resolved on publication in the West, and a full edition in Russian appeared in 1978. The following year saw the publication of the literary almanac *Metropol'* (1979; *Metropol,* 1982), in which I. figures not only as contributor, but also as one of the editors. I. was severely censured for his role in the *Metropol'* affair, his name disappeared from the pages of literary journals, and the publication of his books in press was halted. In 1981 a volume of additional chapters to *Sandro* was brought out in the West as *Novye glavy: Sandro iz Chegema,* followed the next year by his last major publication abroad, the parable *Kroliki i udavy* (1982; *Rabbits and Boa Constrictors,* 1989). The book *Zashchita Chika* (1983; the defense of Chik) signaled the beginning of I.'s gradual rehabilitation in the U.S.S.R. In 1983 *Sandro iz Chegema* was translated in part into English as *Sandro of Chegem;* the rest of the novel was translated the following year as *The Gospel According to Chegem.* In the late 1980s, the period of Gorbachev's glasnost, works by I. appeared in all the major journals, but, most important, a complete edition of *Sandro iz Chegema* was published in Moscow (3 vols., 1989). I. currently serves as an adviser to the the editorial board of the journal *Znamia,* he has facilitated the publication of many repressed and forgotten authors, and he continues to add new chapters to his *Sandro.*

Although I. began his career as prose writer in the pages of *Iunost'* and his work had much in common with the young-prose school, there are a number of traits that set his fiction apart. In general, young prose strived for contemporaneity, the setting was usually the city in the 1960s, and the protagonist was a young person embarking on adult life, a new career, or a journey. On the other hand, I.'s short fiction for the most part was set in his native Abkhazia in the 1940s and 1950s, and his first-person narrator was often a child. The fictional world I. has created in Abkhazia with its ever-expanding cast of the narrator's relatives, friends, and eccentrics has its own mythology and history. The comic events are seen from two points of view: through the eyes of the child and those of the adult narrator who is remembering his childhood. I.'s preference for first-person narration gradually gave way to a third-person narrator who chronicles the events of the young Abkhazian boy Chik.

Sozvezdie kozlotura, I.'s lightly veiled satire of journalism and politics in the Khrushchev era, in particular the agricultural "reforms" and Lysenko's pseudogenetics, is narrated in the same unhurried and ambling manner as the Chik stories. As in all of I.'s work, digression is the storyteller's trademark.

I. has written that *Sandro iz Chegema* began as a parody of the picaresque novel. Comprised of a series of loosely related chapters, the novel tells the story of Uncle Sandro from the 1880s to the 1960s, and concurrently offers a microcosm of the history of the Abkhazian people. While part of the fictional world is clearly grounded in reality—the fictional city Mukhus is an anagram of I.'s birthplace Sukhum—other place names and tribes are pure invention, which has prompted critics to see parallels between I.'s method and the magic realism of William Faulkner and Gabriel García Márquez (qq.v.). Chronology and plot development are largely ignored, so that Uncle Sandro becomes the only unifying principle in the novel. However, I.'s fondness for digression and framing a story within a story often leaves Sandro on the periphery of the narration. The concepts of family, tradition, honor, courage, and honesty that are central to the Abkhazian way of life have not yet been corrupted by "civilization," although Uncle Sandro will resort to trickery to achieve just ends. I.'s novel is not merely a gentle recreation of village life, but it is also a moral commentary on the contemporary world. The most overtly political chapter, "Piry Baltasara" (Belshazzar's feasts), depicts a banquet given in Stalin's honor. In essence, the banquet scene is a parody of a banquet—the noble traditions of feasting etiquette are completely debased. The story paints a psychological portrait of a tyrant whose paranoia instills fear in the guests. Sandro, who dances for Stalin, escapes unscathed, but without any illusion about his host.

I.'s *Sandro* alternates between comedy and tragedy, but humor largely prevails. Although his portrayal of Abkhazia sometimes borders on the idyllic, there are also stories of injustice and vengeance. The loose organization of the novel has prompted some critics to insist that it is not a novel at all. But it is precisely the open-endedness that allows I. to supplement and modify one of the great novels of 20th-c. Russian literature.

FURTHER WORKS: *Gornye tropy* (1957); *Dobrota zemli* (1959); *Zelenyi dozhd'* (1960); *Deti Chernomor'ia* (1961); *Molodost' moria* (1964); *Za-*

pretnyi plod (1966); *Trinadtsatyi podvig Gerakla* (1966); *Zori zemli* (1966); *Derevo detstva* (1970); *Pervoe delo* (1972); *Vremia shchastlivykh nakhodok* (1973); *Pod seniu gretskogo orekha* (1979); *Prazdnik ozhidaniia prazdnika* (1986); *Izbrannoe* (1988); *Kroliki i udavy. Proza poslednikh let* (1988); *Stoianka cheloveka* (1990). FURTHER VOLUMES IN ENGLISH: *Forbidden Fruit and Other Stories* (1972); *The Thirteenth Labor of Hercules* (1978); *Chik and His Friends* (1985)

BIBLIOGRAPHY: Babenko, V., "F. I.: An Examination of His Satire," *RLJ,* 106 (1976), 131–42; Burlingame, H., "The Prose of F. I.," *RLT,* 14 (1976), 123–65; Chapple, R., "F. I.'s *Rabbits and Boa Constrictors:* A Soviet Version of George Orwell's *Animal Farm,*" *GSlav,* 5, 2 (1985), 33–47; Frank, M., "F. I.'s View of Muslim Caucasia," *WLT,* 60, 2 (Spring 1986), 261–66; Lowe, D. A., *Russian Writing since 1953: A Critical Survey* (1987), 50–51, 91, 99, 114–115; Ryan-Hayes, K., "I. and Tolstoj: The Parodical Implications of the Beast Narrator," *SEEJ,* 32, 2 (1988), 225–36

RONALD MEYER

ISMĀ'ĪL, Ismā'īl Fahd

Kuwaiti novelist, short-story writer, dramatist, and critic, b. 1940, Basrah, Iraq

I. is little known outside the Arab world, although he is a prolific writer and a major contemporary Kuwaiti novelist. He was born and educated in Iraq, and most of the material in his early works is derived from life and society there.

His first published work was a collection of short stories, *al-Buq'ah al-dākinah* (1965; the dark spot), characterized by their experimentation. This was followed by his most celebrated work, a quartet of three short and one longer novel, *Kānat al-samā' zarqā'* (1970; the sky was blue), *al-mustanqa'āt al-daw'īyah* (1971; the light swamps), *al-Habl* (1972; the rope), and *al-difāf al-ukhrā* (1973; the other shores). In this quartet, I. attempts to provide a cross section of the divergent political and social attitudes of different characters that represent the different social groups in Arab society, especially Iraq, during the 1950s and 1960s— a period of significant transformation. What is also important and innovative is the way he juxtaposes dialogue, which dominates the quartet, with interior monologues, thereby weaving dual levels of narrative time, one usually moving very slowly, while the other may cover years or decades. His next novel, *Milaff al-hādithah 67* (1974; the file of incident 67), develops the techniques used in

the quartet by adding to dialogues and interior monologues excerpts from radio broadcasts that provide a background for the interrogation that is taking place in the novel. If I.'s earlier novels were about Iraqis, this novel emphasizes the Palestinian who is subjected to the repression of Arab régimes. Shortly after the beginning of the civil war in Lebanon, I. published his novel *al-Shiyyāh* (1976; al-Shiyyāh)—a title that refers to the name of a quarter in Beirut, destroyed in the early stages of the war—which emphasizes the meaninglessness of the war.

It was not until the 1980s that I. shifted his interest toward Egypt and started to develop a new mode of writing. Following the lead of novelists like Jamāl al-Ghītānī (q.v.), I. wrote a novel in two parts, entitled *al-Nīl yajrī shamālan: al-bidāyāt* (1981; the Nile flows northward: the beginnings) and *al-Nīl yajrī shamālan: al-nawātīr* (1982; the Nile flows northward: the keepers). The novel is about Egypt around the time of Napoleon's invasion of the country. Narrative assumes central position, and is reinforced by the abundant references to historical incidents and persons. Historical writings from that period, especially those by the 18th-19th-c. historian and witness of the Napoleonic escapade al-Jabartī (1754–1822) are also quoted verbatim in the text. But the novel has many references to the more recent history of Egypt.

This chapter of Egyptian history constitutes the subject matter of I.'s latest novel, *al-Nīl: al-ta'm wa-al-rā'ihah* (1988; the Nile: the taste and the smell) which can be read as a continuation of the two earlier Nile novels. If the earlier novels bear the traces of the 1967 defeat of the Arabs, it is the 1973 war and its aftermath that provides the background for the later works.

I.'s fascination with dialogue is not only apparent in his novels, but also in the fact that he has written a play, *al-nass* (1980; the text) and two books of drama criticism, *al-Fi'l wa-al-naqīd fī Ūdīb Sūfūkl* (1980; action and contradiction in Sophocles's *Oedipus*) and *al-Fi'l fī masrah Sa'd Allāh Wannūs* (1981; action in the theater of Sa'd Allāh Wannūs), the latter referring to the most prominent contemporary Syrian dramatist, Sa'dallāh Wannūs (q.v.).

I.'s output has been relatively large, but its quality has not been uniform. He sometimes repeats himself and overuses some literary devices. He also tends to treat some of his characters as mere puppets, especially when attempting to provide an ending that suits his ideological or political purpose. Yet I. remains probably the only Kuwaiti novelist who has been able to achieve a prominent place in the contemporary Arabic novel. This is due to his bold literary experimentation coupled with his rootedness in, and sensitivity to, the cultural and social life of the Arab world.

FURTHER WORKS: *al-Aqfās wa-al-lughah al-mushtarakah* (1974); *al-Qissah al-ʿArabiyyah fī al-Kuwayt* (1980); *Khatwah fī al-hulm* (1980); *al-Tuyūr wa-al-asdiqāʾ* (1980)

BIBLIOGRAPHY: Allen, R., *The Arabic Novel* (1982), 144–56; Allen, R., ed., *Modern Arabic Literature* (1987), 160–64

WALID HAMARNEH

ISRAELI LITERATURE

See Volume 2, page 465.

In the decade of the 1980s, it is fiction that has proved most adventurous and innovative among the genres in Israel. The quantity and variety of types of expression indicate some dissatisfaction with linear narrative, time-bound, place-bound, limited to the traditional restraints of Hebrew grammar and vocabulary. So narrative has been tensed and stretched, mixing the modes and the forms. Chronological moments have been juxtaposed, voices have been transposed, points of view shuffled, time sequences broken, narrative segments highlighted or challenged by alternative versions and statements.

Leading experimenters have included well-established authors. Amos Oz (q.v.) has discovered several ways of handling plot development. In *Qufsah shehorah* (1987; *Black Box,* 1988) he presents a story from different points of view, through an epistolary novel. This form, of its nature, extracts different views of the same objective materials; that is the point of the story. In a later novel, *Ladaat ishah* (1989; *To Know a Woman,* 1991), we have a principal narrative consciousness in the novel's hero, but the different time scales allow another perspective, as well as some skepticism regarding the author's own account. A. B. Yehoshua (q.v.) has continued to experiment with narrative technique, particularly in *Mar maniy* (1990; *Mr. Mani,* 1992), where the "telephone" technique is adopted: When we hear someone speaking on the telephone, we not only hear one side of what is a dialogue, we also inevitably construct the other side in our mind. The other technical surprise lies in the reversal of normal expectations. We expect time to move forward, and fiction often explores the results and implications in the seeds of earlier action. Human experience of time is progressive, although memory moves back. But *Mar maniy,* in a series of five

episodes, opens with the most recent, in the 1980s, and then moves backward over two centuries in an apparent attempt to explore the nature of the place in history of the Mani line. So Yehoshua has played with various approaches to narrative, including fantasy, surprise, reversal, stream-of-consciousness (q.v.), as well as with the traditional type of narrative in *Molkho* (1987; *Five Seasons,* 1989). The reader is involved in the understanding and even in the creation of the narrative.

Fundamental to recent developments has been the contribution of Yaakov Shabtai (q.v.) to the novel. His two works, *Zikhron dvarim* (1977; *Past Continuous,* 1983) and *Sof davar* (1984; *Past Perfect,* 1987), because of their artistic success, have suggested new ways of representing reality in fiction. The earlier novel is a string of consciousnesses presented from the outside, where time and association link motifs and narrative parts together. Here, time moves on, and the reader has all sorts of markers to facilitate the understanding of the plot. So external reality bears closely on the internal awareness and does much to engender it. On the other hand, the specific shape of the text is created by the individual consciousness, so that there is constant interplay between the inner and outer layers of reality. Although the story is told by the protagonists and seen through their various lenses, the novel as a whole bears the stamp of a unity of vision. Perhaps this is because of the way that these three lives intertwine, particularly over the nine months covered, and within the limited environment of Tel Aviv. The detailed observation, the linguistic precision, the mental associations, the humor, and the imagination have created a unitary text. The posthumous novel, in the main, adopts a quite different approach. Here, there is a single focus of consciousness, holding several different approaches to the protagonist's mental state at an especially critical phase in his life. Reality and fantasy, waking and dream world, are molded together, as eventually are present and past. The reader is unsure whether objective reality is being offered or whether it is an alternative version of that reality, with a cocktail of memory and fantasy added.

It is these flexible versions of reality that have done something to shift the vistas of recent Israeli fiction. One of the leading voices of the 1980s, David Grossman (q.v.), is much concerned with alternative versions of reality, not only within any one particular work, but in his ongoing opus. We can see *Hiyukh hagdiy* (1983; *The Smile of the Lamb,* 1990) and *Hazman hatsahov* (1987; *Yellow Wind,* 1988) as obverse and reverse sides of one coin. Both works purport to describe the situation under Israeli occupation in the West Bank and the course of the Intifada. But whereas the earlier work is a novel, with a complex view of character, time, motivation, and development (this makes it all very hard for the reader), the latter account is journalistic and polemical, tendentious in its straightforward attempt to persuade the reader of a certain view of events. Of course, these works represent different genres. But even so, the genres themselves are deliberately jumbled; there is, for example, a story inserted in *Hazman hatsahov.* Grossman's novel *Ayen erekh ahavah* (1986; *See Under: Love,* 1990) constitutes a very ambitious effort to see the Holocaust (and reality generally) afresh, this time, through the eyes of a child (the primary account), but also by a variety of narrative devices, including surrealism (q.v.), fantasy, and dictionary definition.

Other novelists who are interested in expanding fictional range through magic realism (q.v.) include Itamar Levy (b. 1956). Magic realism is on the one hand anchored to reality and seeks to explore it, but, on the other, it handles it freely, and so can dispense with the laws of fictional gravity. In this case, the limiting determinants are time sequence and place limitation. If time sequences can be shifted, speeded up or slowed down (as has been done in all fiction through the ages), skipped and reversed, if distance can be contracted and places moved, and if the narrative voice can allow itself the freedom to shift in and out of various characters at will and at need, then a kaleidoscope of effects can be achieved. Magic realism is the product of a growing need to absorb larger and more astonishing portions of actuality, to confront the incredible with the surprising, and to provide innovative tools in the search for representation.

Fiction has moved in all sorts of diverse directions, and much Israeli fiction is likewise experimental. As seen, Yehoshua has allowed the reader space in which to create the missing parts of the dialogue in his "telephone" novel. Yoel Hoffman (b. 1932) has his novels printed on one side of the leaf only, so that the reader is confronted by a blank page for every printed page. Is the reader to create his own story, his own counterpoint? He has indeed no alternative but to do this. Yuval Shimoni (b. 1955), in *Meof hayonah* (1990; the flight of the dove), writes two parallel stories on facing pages in different print types, and these stories intersect in time and place. One is the story of an American couple visiting Paris as tourists, and the second is of a lonely woman living there. But sometimes, plot is abandoned altogether, as by Aner Shalev (b. 1958) in *Opus 1* (1988; opus 1), where, as the title implies, narrative, as in Pater's motto, may aspire to the condition of

music. Instead of the normal components of narrative, namely, linear time, logical sequence, coherent plot, we have a sort of musical notation— staccato, legato, and so forth. Or we have, as in the novel by Avram Heffner (b. 1935), *Sefer hamforash* (1991; an annotated book), a novel with its own commentary attached to the text. So, in this case, the reader is not left alone to draw his own conclusions, but is bombarded with suggestions, options, and interpretations.

But, of course, literature is not music. It is made of words, and words have meanings, connotations, and implications for external reality. One line of experimentation in fiction can lead to its own demise or silence. Fiction, that is, invention, can invent prodigiously, not only materials, but also ways of looking at materials. Frustration is inevitable in the search for the nugget of truth that is thought to lie at the source, or for the catchall means of grasping that truth. Reality is enormous, and it is the function of the writer to sharpen its outlines and encapsulate it. Just as reality expands in our consciousness and we learn more, so literature has to expand its capacity. This, at any rate, seems to be the impulse behind the ambition.

Nevertheless, literary concerns, in that they are human, remain static, and our consciousness, as well as the means for its representation, limited. We want to know how people understand each other, how people see themselves, others, and their mutual interaction. One of the most notable features of recent Israeli literature is the increased articulateness of the woman writer. Amalia Kahana-Carmon (q.v.) has long given expression to a specifically female view of interpersonal contact. But now, many others, in prose and poetry, are also presenting an uninhibitedly female view of subjects that often are assumed to be the exclusive male preserve.

Israeli drama has become more adventurous in choice of subjects and in manner of presentation. Yehoshua Sobol (b. 1939) continues to mix document and fantasy in his semihistorical plays, and Hanoch Levin (b. 1943) presents his masochistic figures in grotesque situations, for amusement and distress.

BIBLIOGRAPHY: Yudkin, L. I., *Escape into Siege: A Survey of Israeli Literature Today* (1974); Abramson, G., *Modern Hebrew Drama* (1979); Joseph, H. S., ed., *Modern Israeli Drama* (1983); Yudkin, L. I., *1948 and After: Aspects of Israeli Fiction* (1984); Fisch, H., *A Remembered Future* (1984); Fuchs, E., *Israeli Mythogynies* (1987)

LEON I. YUDKIN

IWANIUK, Wacław

Polish poet, essayist, and translator (also writing in English), b. 4 Dec. 1915, Chełm

I. is one of the most renowned contemporary Polish poets. He has published fifteen volumes of poetry and is translated into numerous languages. Born in Chełm, in eastern Poland, I. studied law and economics at the Free University of Warsaw, specializing in emigration and colonial problems. In 1939, with the help of a state grant, he undertook consular training in Buenos Aires and was offered a further course of studies at the École Coloniale in Paris. At the outbreak of World War II, he joined the Polish army in France. After the capitulation of France, I. attempted to reach England via Spain. Caught by the Spanish police, he was first imprisoned in Figueras and then in the camp in Miranda, from which he escaped and eventually made his way to England. Enlisted in the First Armoured Division, I. fought in Holland, Belgium, France, and Germany, where he remained until 1946. He returned to England to study language and two years later emigrated to Canada. Despite adverse conditions I. found employment as an official interpreter for the tribunal of the Province of Ontario and settled in Toronto.

I.'s first volume of poems, *Pełnia czerwca* (1936; fullness of June), was welcomed by the critics as a promising debut. There he demonstrates his ability to evoke landscape in combination with rich poetical imagery—qualities that characterize his later writing. Following his second volume, *Dzień apokaliptyczny* (1938; day of the apocalypse), World War II interrupted this auspicious start and provoked his exile from Poland. From that moment, I.'s autobiography becomes pivotal to his output. There is an apparent rift between his pre- and postwar life. The former belongs to the lost paradise of his native country; the latter belongs to Western civilization, which he views with the eye of an outsider who is angry with the present political order. He raises a voice of protest against communism and accuses the West of acquiescence. A tone of disappointment appears alongside the attempts to adapt to the new life and culture. All these elements constitute the core of I.'s postwar volumes of poetry, of which *Ciemny czas* (1968; *Dark Times: Selected Poems of W. I.,* 1979) is the most significant.

I. adds a historical dimension to the everyday life of an émigré. He speaks as a survivor emerging from a monstrous catastrophe. He acts as a guardian of memory to those who perished and as witness of a cruelty that unfortunately may recur. Full of genuine despair over the brutality of humankind, *Ciemny czas* is a pessimistic and revealing volume commemorating the victims of a tragic past.

The mood of catastrophe permeates *Lustro* (1971; mirror) and *Nemezis idzie pustymi drogami* (1978; nemesis walks empty roads). It is intensified by the poet's alienation from society and a sense of ill-adjustment to the world. However, I. expresses a sensitive perception of the world around him through gentle nostalgia, sympathy for human failure, feeling for nature, and an awareness of the expansion of urban civilization.

In 1981, I. published his first volume written in English, *Evenings on Lake Ontario,* where he presents his Canadian ordeal in diary form. Here the clash between the exile from eastern Europe and a nation with few antecedents is most apparent. The "client of war," as he calls himself, encounters people for whom the tragic experience of the other continent remains a "complete mystery." Yet from this encounter emerges a lasting partnership. Canada offers a chance to rebuild his shattered life. It also presents a challenge that enhances creativity. This in turn helps I. to be reconciled with his feelings of estrangement. I. writes about Canada with respect and a quiet touch of admiration.

I. is a veteran of many battles. The longest one was fought with the communist regime in Poland. Labeled like many other uncompromising émigré writers as an enemy of the state, he was consigned at home to oblivion. Yet his continuing involvement with people and occurrences in Poland surfaces in *Nocne rozmowy* (1987; nocturnal conversations). Only recently, after the collapse of the communist regime, has he been rewarded with publication of his works in Poland. The volume, significantly called *Powrót* (1989; return), marks his rightful reinstatement as a Polish poet.

I.'s poetic style derives from observation of everyday life. His use of language is direct, tending to the succinct. He often oscillates between sharp irony and restrained emotion, and perhaps the most striking facet of his writing is an attempt to reconcile extremes in subject matter as well as in form. His art is a blend of involvement in past and contemporary life, while at the same time being detached from it. He has mastered the contemplative attitude to the turmoil of the world and the dramatic condition of an exile. In this way he brings a sense of constancy into the uncertainty of the human predicament. I.'s poetry exemplifies a search for lasting values in the midst of raving confusion.

FURTHER WORKS: *Czas Don Kichota* (1946); *Dni białe i dni czerwone* (1947); *Dziennik z podróży tropikalnej* (1951); *Pieśń nad pieśniami* (1953);

Milczenia (1959); *Wybór wierszy* (1965); *Podróż do Europy* (1982); *Moje obłąkanie* (1991)

BIBLIOGRAPHY: Grabowsky, Y., on *Lustro, UTQ,* 4 (Summer 1977), 497–98; Islam, S. M., on *Dark Times: Selected Poems of W. I., The Wig Standard Magazine,* 12 July 1980, 21; Colombo, J. R., "I.," in Toye, W., ed., *The Oxford Companion to Canadian Literature* (1983), 391–92; Miązek, B., *Teksty i komentarze* (1983), 97–113; Cybulska, M. E., *W. I. poeta* (1984); Colombo, J. R., "Our Cosmopolitans: The Ethnic Canadian Writer in a Provincial Society," *CanL,* Supplement 1 (1987), 90–101

MAJA E. CYBULSKA

JABRĀ, Jabrā Ibrāhīm

Palestinian poet, novelist, translator, and literary critic, b. 28 Aug. 1920, Bethlehem

J. is one of the leading creative writers of the Arab world today. Born in Bethlehem, where he grew up as a boy and first went to school, he moved with his family to Jerusalem, where he continued his education and won a fellowship to study English literature in England. He earned his B.A. (1943) and M.A. (1948) at Fitzwilliam House, Cambridge University, and returned to Palestine to teach at the Rashīdiyya College in Jerusalem (1943–1948). At the end of the British Mandate in Palestine in 1948, the hostilities leading to the establishment of Israel forced him into exile. In Iraq he became a lecturer in English literature at the College of Arts of the University of Baghdad (1948–1952), then won a two-year research fellowship in the U.S. at Harvard University (1952–1954). Returning to Iraq, he became head of publications at the Iraq Petroleum Company (1954–1977), then cultural consultant at the Iraqi Ministry of Culture and Information until his retirement (1977–1985). He continues to live and write in Baghdad.

His autobiography, al-Bi'r al-ūlā (1987; the first well), tells the story of his boyhood in Bethlehem and chronicles his many literary and artistic interests since early age. It is a good introduction to understanding the man he became, with his many talents and achievements, in each of which his modernizing thought, his strong personality, and his liberal values are abundantly clear.

A witness to many political and social upheavals in the Middle East, J. has been particularly affected by the loss of Palestine, his homeland. The feeling of being an exile pervades his writings, but he does not permit it to make him bitter and destructive. Nostalgic memories of the homeland abound in his poetry, and fictional characters searching for their identity and roots recur in his novels and short stories. Transcending personal feelings, however, he seeks a universal vision of humans in the 20th c. and a deep insight into their condition.

Writing in an age when urban growth has become a pronounced feature of the Arab world, as it is elsewhere, J. focuses a great deal of attention on the city, its people, its problems, and its opportunities, as well as its power to crush individuals and values while developing its own urban rules of living. His first collection of poems, Tammūz fī al-madīnah (1959; Tammuz in the city), laments the spiritual death that prevails in the city as its people move away from life-giving principles in their search for material gain and power. His second collection, al-Madār al-mughlaq (1964; the vicious circle), decries the constraints imposed on people undergoing dramatic change in the city and being forced to lose their natural selves and their real voice. His third collection, Law'at al-shams (1979; the anguish of the sun), reveals the evils that enslave humans caught in the mesh of city life, from which nothing but love can redeem them. A symbol of modern civilization, the city in his view—like T. S. Eliot's (q.v.) "wasteland"—needs a revivifying force to bring back fertility and happiness to it.

J.'s poetry is among that of a very few Arab poets who have daringly discarded the traditional Arab meters and rhymes to create, in prose, a new poetry that has a rhythm of its own, which is not quantitative like traditional Arabic verse, but qualitative in its attempt to capture a new vision of Arab life and generate a new poetic harmony.

J. has produced seven works of fiction, including a collection of short stories, a novel written with 'Abd al-Rahmān Munīf (q.v.), and five other novels of varying lengths. His characters are mostly drawn from a rising bourgeoisie and a declining propertied urban class of tribal origins. Their conflict and their search for identity and stability constitute J.'s major plots, but intellectuals dominate the dialogues as they discuss problems of their society and express aspects of their sense of alienation.

In al-Safīna (1970; The Ship, 1985), the passengers cruising the Mediterranean are escaping their social straits at home only to realize they are carrying them along, ending with the suicide of one character. In al-Bahth 'an Walīd Mas'ūd (1978; search for Walīd Mas'ūd), the characters assemble to discuss the mysterious disappearance of their friend Walīd Mas'ūd, a rich Palestinian in Baghdad, but they embark instead on uncovering their own relations with him and baring their complexities, while it is rumored that he has gone to join the PLO commandos in his occupied homeland. In *al-Ghuraf al-ukhrā* (1986; the other rooms), the protagonist is led into a labyrinthian building, where he is brought for a purpose he does not know, accused by mercurial persons of acts he never thought he committed, and then his very identity is put to question to an extent that he begins to doubt who he is. The idea of being besieged is an insistent one in J.'s fiction, and human beings in it try incessantly to break out of their vicious circle.

J.'s works in various genres have contributed in a large measure to the introduction of modern ideas and styles in Arabic letters and the Arab arts, and his name will remain eminently associated with other modernizing influences in the Arab world in the second half of the 20th c.

FURTHER WORKS: *Surākh fī layl tawīl* (1955); *'Araq wa qisas ukhrā* (1956); *al-Hurriyyah wa-al-tūfān* (1960); *al-Rihla al-thāminah* (1967); *al-Fann al-'irāqī al-mu'āsir* (1972; *Contemporary Iraqi Art*, 1972); *Sayyādūn fī shāri' dayyiq* (1974; first pub. in English as *Hunters in a Narrow Street*, 1960); *Jawād Salīm wa-nusb al-hurriyyah* (1974); *al-Nār wa-al-jawhar* (1975); *Yanābī' al-ru'yā* (1979); *'Ālam bilā kharā'it* (1982, with 'Abd al-Rahmān Munīf); *al-Sūnītāt li William Shakespeare* (1983); *al-Fann wa-al-hulm wa-al-fi'l* (1985); *Judhūr al-fann al-'irāqī* (1986; first pub. in English as *The Grass Roots of Iraqi Art*, 1983); *al-Malik al-shams* (1986); *Baghdād bayn al-ams wa-al-yawm* (1987, with Ihsān Fathī); *Ayyām al-'uqāb: Khālid wa-ma'rakat al-Yarmūk* (1988); *Ta'ammulāt fī bunyān marmarī* (1989). FURTHER VOLUMES IN ENGLISH: *Art in Iraq Today* (1961); *A Celebration of Life* (1988)

BIBLIOGRAPHY: Barakat, H., *Visions of Social Reality in the Contemporary Arab Novel* (1977), 21–25; Boullata, I. J., "The Concept of Modernity in the Poetry of J. and Sāyigh," in Boullata, I. J., ed., *Critical Perspectives of Modern Arabic Literature* (1980), 263–79; Allen, R., *The Arabic Novel* (1982), 69–71, 138–44; Haydar, A., and R. Allen, Introduction to *The Ship* (1985), 3–10; Moosa, M., "J.'s *Ship*," *Gilgamesh*, 1 (1988), 77–81

ISSA J. BOULLATA

JACOBSEN, Rolf

Norwegian poet, b. 8 Mar. 1907, Oslo

J. is one of Norway's most distinguished poets, one of the few to have achieved an international reputation. J. grew up in Oslo, then moved to Hamar, a city about 60 miles north of Oslo, where he earned his living as a journalist.

From his first book of poems, *Jord og jern* (1933; earth and iron), J. wrote modernist free verse distinguished by compelling rhythms and startling images. His strong, strange rapport with both the natural and urban world is conveyed in striking images and in a free verse that convincingly mimed the movements of the poet's feeling; this distinguished J.'s poetry from the start, making it hard to categorize. Because he wrote poems about such things as trains, electrical turbines, office windows, racing cars, and airplanes, he was often taken as a kind of futurist, like Filippo Tommaso Marinetti (q.v.), as if modern civilization had found in him another troubadour. But even his first book contained clear signs that J. was not really on the side of the machine.

Two years later, in *Vrimmel* (1935; tumult), a stronger undertone of sadness and compassion entered J.'s poetry. Age, decay, and rust began to evoke a gentle, undismayed sympathy from him. War, business, and industry seemed driven by an indifferent and unstoppable energy. One senses J.'s underlying dismay at the destructiveness inherent in modern civilization, but as an artist he refuses to react conventionally and simplistically to it. His poetry fixes the permanent natural world and the speeded-up world of the modern city in a kind of metaphorical mirror relationship to each other, each commenting on the other, each striving to overcome the other. J.'s sympathies are on the side of nature, but his intuition and long-sighted wisdom seem to suggest to him that even the gasoline-driven cities may simply be nature moving at another tempo, one ultimately indifferent to the fate of humans.

J. is a master poet, so it is difficult to say which are his best books. *Fjerntog* (1951; express train) and *Hemmelig liv* (1954; secret life) are perhaps the collections that display his gifts most abundantly. Many of these poems seem to spring from some passionate sixth sense that allows J. to look to the edge of the thing he is considering and render its aura more powerfully than the thing itself. Within these collections J. has refined his art to the point where it is mystical and realistic all at once. Describing the auras of fountains, the faces of old people, the scent of pine reminiscent of bread, J. celebrates the beauty and mystery of the world at the same time as he conveys a deep, troubled compassion for it.

In J.'s later poetry—*Sommeren i gresset* (1956; summer in the grass), *Stillheten efterpå* (1965; the silence afterwards), *Headlines* (1969; title in English), *Pass for dørene—dørene lukkes* (1972; watch the doors—the doors are closing), *Pusteøvelse* (1975; breathing exercise), and *Tenk på noe annet* (1979; think about something else)—one notices, very generally speaking, that he becomes less "modernistic" as time goes on. He becomes more of an explicit and public poet—not in a pompous way, but from a need to speak clearly and directly about ecological matters, taking the word in its widest and deepest sense.

FURTHER WORK: *Nattåpent: dikt* (1985). FURTHER VOLUMES IN ENGLISH: *Twenty Poems/R. J.* (1977); *The Silence Afterwards: Selected Poems of R. J.* (1985)

BIBLIOGRAPHY: Naess, H. S., "The Poetry of R. J.," *American Scandinavian Review* (1962), 265–69; Bly, R., "What Norwegian Poetry Is Like," *The Sixties,* 10 (1968), 37–77; Loanhead, S., *Five Norwegian Poets: Tarjei Vesaas, R. J., Olav Hauge, Gunvor Hofmo, Stein Mehren* (1976); Grinde, O., "R. J.," *ScanR,* 70, 4 (Dec. 1982), 49–59; Grinde, O., "Interview with R. J.," *SDR* (Spring 1983), 7–13; Hass, R., *Twentieth Century Pleasures: Prose on Poetry* (1984); Gouchet, O., "R. J.: La pierre, la lumière et l'être," *Revue Littéraire Mensuelle* (Mar. 1987), 11–35

WILLIAM E. MISHLER

JACOBSON, Dan

South African–English novelist and short-story writer, b. 7 Mar. 1929, Johannesburg, South Africa

The child of Baltic Jewish parents, J. grew up in Kimberley in the Cape Province (the model for his fictional Lyndhurst). After taking a degree in English at the University of the Witwatersrand (1948), he spent nine months in a kibbutz in Israel and a year teaching in a Jewish boys' school in London before returning to South Africa in 1951 to work in his family's business and to write his first short stories and his first two novels, *The Trap* (1955) and *A Dance in the Sun* (1956). Before returning to England permanently, he spent a year as a creative-writing fellow at Stanford University, an experience that gave him the material for *No Further West: California Visited* (1959), a brilliant examination of American society and culture that places him among the most significant foreign observers of the U.S. Except for visiting professorships in the U.S. and Australia, he has been since 1975 a professor of English at University College, London.

J.'s career can be sharply divided into two periods. His first five novels and almost all of his short stories, published in *The Zulu and the Zeide* (1959), *Beggar My Neighbour* (1964), and *Through the Wilderness* (1968; pub. in England as *Inklings: Selected Stories,* 1973), have South African settings.

The Trap deals with an essentially decent Afrikaner farmer and his African foreman, who conspires to steal his employer's sheep with a racist white neighbor who is able to betray him because of a social system that finds it easier to believe a white thief than a black one. *A Dance in the Sun* concerns two hitchhiking university students who, taken in for a night by a mad South African English racist and his Afrikaner wife, discover a terrible family secret about the woman's brother, his African mistress, and the African girl's brother, who asks the boys to help him but is primarily concerned to blackmail his employer. These two novels reveal the qualities of method and intention that characterize all of J.'s later works: exact diction, economy of exposition, and a preoccupation with moral concerns that avoids didacticism.

J.'s upbringing was almost entirely secular, and his sense of being Jewish is cultural and historical rather than religious, but he dealt frequently in his early work with Jewish subjects. "The Zulu and the Zeide," probably his most famous story, is a moving portrayal of an old Jew who turns to a Zulu servant for the attention and affection that he cannot get from his materially successful son, who wishes to show him his love but cannot. *The Price of Diamonds* (1957) deals with two Jewish business partners and the crisis that threatens their friendship when a diamond smuggler mistakenly leaves a package of illegal diamonds with one of them. *The Beginners* (1966), a major work of South African fiction, is a long panoramic novel that reveals the influence of the great 19th-c. Russian masters as well as certain similarities to J.'s own family. A chronicle of the descendants of two brothers, Jewish immigrants from Lithuania, and set in South Africa, England, and Israel, it is a social history of South Africa in the first half of this century.

J.'s other South African novel, the less successful *Evidence of Love* (1960), may be regarded as his contribution to what might be called a genre of South African fiction—the story of miscegenation.

A key work for understanding J.'s career and his decision to abandon his South African subject is the story "Fresh Fields," published in *Through the Wilderness,* a story of a young South African's encounter with a famous émigré South African writer who has produced little in recent years and thus advises the young writer to return home to his true subject. When the young man shows him some of his work and the older man plagiarizes it, the young man expresses J.'s own declaration of independence from his South African origins: he will find his subject wherever he happens to be.

The novels J. produced when he abandoned South Africa as a subject are remarkably experimental in their various ways of distancing the reader from their material and drawing attention to their artistry. *The Rape of Tamar* (1970) is based on the biblical story of Tamar and her brother Amnon, Absalom's murder of Amnon and rebellion against King David, and his death in battle, all told in a modern idiom and with frequent anachronisms from the point of view of Yonadab, a manipulator of the emotions of others and a troublemaker who enjoys the confusion he creates. *The Wonder-Worker* (1973) is a remarkable story told by a lunatic in a Swiss sanatorium who, in telling his own story, also tells the story of a young Englishman who possesses the power to transform himself into inert objects. *The Confessions of Josef Baisz* (1977) is a story of conspiracy, set in a fictitious country that resembles South Africa in many ways; its narrator is a police informant in a totalitarian state who practices betrayal in his personal life and achieves power and prestige when he practices it on behalf of the state.

In spite of his physical and artistic abandonment of South Africa, J. remains one of the major figures of South African literature in the latter half of the 20th c. Looking at South Africa from the special position of a member of a Jewish minority in an English-speaking minority in a white minority, he was able to see the paradoxes inherent in South African society with an artistic vision that is ironic and skeptical and yet sympathetic with all elements in South Africa's racially complex population. His later novels also reveal this remarkable insight into social relationships, and two of them, *The Rape of Tamar* and *The Confessions of Josef Baisz*, show greater understanding of what motivates people in actual political conflicts—and thus may tell us more about South African reality—than any number of more obviously "socially conscious" works.

FURTHER WORKS: *Time of Arrival* (1962); *The Story of the Stories* (1982); *Time and Time Again* (1985); *Her Story* (1987)

BIBLIOGRAPHY: Hicks, G., "No End to Beginnings," *SatR*, 19 Feb. 1966, 37–38; Wolff, G., " 'Such a World, We Have To Live In,' " *NewR*, 9 Apr. 1966, 21–24; Alter, R., "A Long Story," *Commentary*, 42, 2 (Aug. 1966), 64–66; Schneidau, H. N., "Desire and Gratification," *Commentary*, 51, 1 (Jan. 1971), 95–96; Kaplan, J., on *The Wonder-Worker*, *Commentary*, 57, 6 (June 1974), 94–96; Wilkinson, D. R. M., "A Comment on Race Relationships: D. J.'s *The Trap* and *A Dance in the Sun*," *DQR*, 5 (1975), 270–81; Baxter, C., "Political Symbolism in *A Dance in*</br>

the Sun," *EinA* 5, 2 (1978), 44–50; Roberts, S., D. J. (1984); Roberts, S., "Tamar and After: A Glance at D. J.'s Recent Work," in Diamond, M. J., J. U. Jacobs, and M. Lenta, eds., *Momentum: On Recent South African Writing* (1984), 141–46; Solotaroff, T., *A Few Good Voices in My Head* (1987), 227–31

ROBERT L. BERNER

JAIMES FREYRE, Ricardo

Bolivian poet, essayist, and historian, b. 12 May 1868, Tacna, Peru; d. 24 Apr. 1933, Buenos Aires, Argentina

Born to a prominent and intellectual Bolivian family, J. F. was predestined to a promising artistic life, which he fully realized. He became the first Bolivian author to gain an international reputation, a historian of distinction, and a diplomat representing his country abroad. J. F. spent a decisive early life in Buenos Aires and settled there to pursue his literary ambitions. He published there his first and most important work, *Castalia bárbara* (1899; drawn from a barbaric fountain). He then lived in the city of Tucumán in northern Argentina, where he did extensive research on local history. Back in Bolivia in the later part of his life, he was elected a house representative, then appointed ambassador to several countries, including the U.S. (1923–1927). He again settled in Buenos Aires, where he died. His remains were repatriated, and his tomb placed next to his father's in the cathedral of Potosí.

Argentinian Emilio Carilla, J. F.'s main biographer, divided the author's life into three main periods: his early residence in Buenos Aires, his university service in Tucumán, and his diplomatic and public work in Bolivia (almost to the end of his life). J. F.'s literary production can be easily placed within the same divisions.

Critics agree that the first of these three periods is the one that matters most to Spanish American letters. And some have also stated that J. F. was a one-book author and that it is for *Castalia bárbara* that he will be always remembered. At least as a poet he was not a prolific author. In 1888, when the Nicaraguan poet Rubén Darío (q.v.) launched his literary school that he himself named *modernismo,* J. F. became his most faithful ally and even economic supporter. They jointly edited *Revista de América,* organ of the new movement, published briefly during 1894. And in 1899 J. F. gave further strength to Modernismo by publishing his *Castalia bárbara.* The major part of the work contains poems that introduced to Latin Americans the exotic world of Norse mythology. Critics are right in mentioning Leconte de Lisle's (1818–

1894) *Poèmes barbares* (1862) as the model J. F. followed, but Wagner's operas, then quite fashionable, must have also been an influence. Dexterously combining the subtlety of symbolism with the perfectionistic obsession of Parnassianism (qq.v.), J. F. created a unique magical, medieval world utterly removed from Latin American reality, thus also meeting one of the main goals of Modernismos—escapism. Faithful to that movement, this work was a purely aesthetic effort.

Leyes de la versificación castellana (laws on Spanish versification) appeared only in 1912, but it was again a solid contribution. J. F. became one of the few Hispanics to set theories for the proper use of meters, melody, and harmony in poetry.

Five years later his second and last poetry work appeared. *Los sueños son vida* (1917; to dream is to live) also follows the changes that Rubén Darío had impressed into his own movement of modernism (q.v.). Although still pursuing aesthetics, exotic settings tended now to disappear, to be replaced by themes exposing the spiritual problems of human beings and the suffering of the exploited. To this day one of the poems of this second book by J. F. astonishes us: In "Rusia" (Russia), which he wrote in 1905, he predicted the Russian Revolution fully eleven years before it happened. But always a good Parnassian, J. F. continued to uphold stylistic perfection in poetry writing.

In prose this Bolivian did shine, albeit briefly. Two dramas he composed received no attention, but one of his five short stories, like the poem "Rusia," must have again frozen readers. "En las montañas" (1906; in the mountains) is a typical piece of social protest. It seems to have been influenced by J. F.'s famous countryman, the novelist Alcides Arguedas (q.v.), whose indigenist novel *Wata Wara* (1904; Wata Wara) ended with a massacre of landowners in the hand of rebellious Indians. So does, too, this short story by J. F., whose suffering highlanders cruelly torture the haughty oligarchs and indifferently watch their slow death. Thus, J. F. is also a pioneer of the vigorous literature of social protest that characterizes Bolivian letters.

Thereafter, J. F. spent some twenty years researching the history of Tucumán, in whose university he worked. He produced five valuable books and also founded in 1905 the *Revista de Letras y Ciencias Sociales*. Returning to Bolivia to take up public and diplomatic posts, he was able to travel widely. In the last six years of his life he settled in Buenos Aires. He belongs to Argentina for having efficiently researched its history; to Bolivia, for putting as a modernist his country on the literary map; and to Latin American letters, for pioneering, with Rubén Darío, the free

verse and the cosmopolitanism that then began to take hold of the continent.

FURTHER WORKS: *La hija de Jephté* (1899); *Tucumán en 1810* (1909); *Historia de la República de Tucumán* (1911); *El Tucumán del siglo XVI* (1914); *El Tucumán colonial* (1915); *Historia del descubrimiento de Tucumán* (1916); *Los conquistadores* (1928); *Poesías completas* (1944)

BIBLIOGRAPHY: Torres-Rioseco, A., "R. J. F. (1870–1933)," *Hispania,* 16, 4 (Nov.–Dec. 1933), 389–98; Jaimes Freyre, Raúl, *Anecdotario de R. J. F.* (1953); Carilla, E., "J. F., cuentista y novelista," *Thesaurus,* 16 (1961), 664–98; Carilla, E., *R. J. F.* (1962); Ocampo, E., *Personalidad y obra poética de don R. J. F.* (1968); Cáceres, A., and J. Ortega, *Diccionario de la literatura boliviana* (1970), 140–44; Guzmán, A., et al., *R. J. F.: estudios* (1978); Cortés, D., "R. J. F." in Solé, C. A., ed., *Latin American Writers* (1989), Vol. 1, 419–23

EVELIO ECHEVARRÍA

JANDL, Ernst
Austrian poet and dramatist, b. 1 Aug. 1925, Vienna

J. served in the army during World War II. After his release from an American POW camp in 1946, he began studying German and English at the University of Vienna, where he earned his doctorate in 1950. He has served on and off as a teacher at various high schools in Vienna. He started writing in 1952. In 1954 he began his lifelong friendship with the Austrian writer Friederike Mayröcker (q.v.). He has held guest lectureships at several universities in Germany and was a visiting writer at the University of Texas at Austin in 1971. In 1973 he was a cofounder of the Graz Authors Society. He often reads his works in connection with orchestral performances. He has won over fifteen prizes for his work, including the prestigious Büchner Prize in 1984. He still resides in Vienna.

Although J.'s works are usually ascribed to the concrete school, this classification is misleading, for he never expresses a radical mistrust of language, and his works always have some message connected with the outside world. His playful experimentation with the linguistic medium usually has a humorous, didactic, contemplative, or introspective intent, and his poems and plays are never just comments on language alone. J. has developed a whole scala of innovations, which he constantly improves and amplifies. This accounts for his continued popularity with the reading public, who quickly forgot other less versatile experimenters.

J.'s first collection of poems, *andere augen* (1956; other eyes), was fairly traditional, but he soon was to develop his unique style. His most important early collections are *laut und luise* (1966; sound and Luise) and *der künstliche baum* (1970; the artificial tree), both of which reflect his output for the preceding several years. These volumes contain a wide variety: visual poems, texts meant to be read aloud, dialect poems, puns on foreign languages, montages, poems which repeat phonemes, and combinations of all of these. Inevitably the last line shocks, surprises, or bemuses, and drives home the message. Thematically the poems run the gamut of human experience, with a concentration on the earthy and the mundane. Together with the anthology *sprechblasen* (1968; speech bubbles), which contains only acoustic poems, these books made J. extremely popular in Austria and Germany and firmly established him in literary circles. Contributing to his success was the wickedly wry humor of many of the poems as well as J.'s extraordinary ability to perform his work in public.

In the late 1970s and early 1980s, J. entered into a more somber stage of his writing. In a series of poetry volumes, *die bearbeitung der mütze* (1978; the treatment of the cap), *der gelbe hund* (1980; the yellow dog), and *selbstporträt des schachspielers als trinkende uhr* (1983; self portrait of the chess player as a drinking clock), he discusses old age, death, problems with writing, depressions, his uneasy relationship with Mayröcker, and an identity crisis. We see little of his usual caustic wit and instead meet a tortured individual whose writing appears to be his only solace. The language has been likened to guest workers' or children's German in that the structures are simple and verbal infinitives prevail. It is as if J.'s collapsing self-image is reflected in a decaying language. In his most recent volume, *idyllen* (1989; idylls), there is also a somber mood, but there are some indications J. is regaining a more positive outlook on life.

J.'s play *aus der fremde* (1980; from abroad) was extremely popular with audiences and was performed on dozens of German-language stages. It details a little over a day in the life of two writers, a "he" and a "she," who speak to each other in 655 triplets whose verbs are all in the subjunctive. The play is clearly autobiographical, with J.'s creative crisis, his friendship with Mayröcker, and his daily life at the foreground. In spite of the potentially depressing thematics the play is both humorous and fascinating.

J. may be Austria's best-known contemporary poet and one of its best. His works are both entertaining and incisive without being ponderous,

and this should ensure him a permanent place in literary history.

FURTHER WORKS: *lange gedichte* (1964); *klare gerührt* (1964); *mai hart lieb zapfen eibe hold* (1965); *Hosi-Anna!* (1965); *no music please* (1967); *flöda und der schwan* (1971); *fünf mann menschen* (1971, with Friederike Mayröcker); *dingfest* (1973); *übung mit buben* (1973); *die männer: ein film* (1973); *serienfuss* (1974); *wischen möchten* (1974); *für alle* (1974); *der versteckte hirte* (1975); *alle freut was alle freut* (1975); *drei hörspiele* (1975, with Friederike Mayröcker); *die schöne kunst des schreibens* (1976); *klatschmohn* (1977); *augenspiel* (1981); *falamaleikum* (1983); *das öffnen und schliessen des mundes* (1985); *gesammelte werke* (1985); *ottos mops hopst* (1988); *das röcheln der mona lisa* (1990)

BIBLIOGRAPHY: Acker, R., "E. J. and Friederike Mayröcker: A Study of Modulation and Crisis," *WLT*, 55, 4 (Autumn 1981), 597–602; Schmidt-Dengler, W., ed., *E. J.: Materialienbuch* (1982); special J. issue, *manuskripte*, 88 (1985); König, F., "E. J. and Concrete Poetry," in Daviau, D. G., ed., *Major Figures of Contemporary Austrian Literature* (1987), 265–92; Siblewski, K., ed., *E. J.: Texte, Daten, Bilder* (1990)

ROBERT ACKER

JAPANESE LITERATURE

See Volume 2, page 493.

The 1970s began with several significant deaths, which in turn announced a new era of uneasy cultural transition as well as of unprecedented economic growth. Mishima Yukio (q.v.) committed a ritual suicide of *seppuku* in 1971. One year after, his mentor, the Nobel Prize laureate Kawabata Yasunari (q.v.), took his own life too. There were also many bloody deaths as a result of infighting among factions of leftist students whose dream of revolution was simply gobbled up by the huge machinery of Japan's late capitalism. Literary culture looked threatened to be erased by the plethora of visual media, rock music, and copywriting in a computer-generated information society.

Fiction

The first significant group of writers to emerge in the 1970s promptly received the label of the "introspective generation." This group included Furui Yoshikichi, Ōba Minako (qq.v.), Gotō Meisei (b. 1932), Kuroi Senji (b. 1932), and Abe Akira (b. 1934). Many sensed in their works a tendency to turn away from society and politics and to turn inward in the hope of locating one's own place, however powerless it may be. Critics read their works as symptomatic of the general decline in the power of literature to speak to contemporary society.

New writers were of course also emerging. Nakagami Kenji (b. 1946), Murakami Ryū (b. 1952), Mita Masahiro (b. 1948), Tsushima Yūko (q.v.), and Aono Sō (b. 1943) were among the most prominent, though their works were first greeted with such weary captions as "the generation of blue," or "the generation of emptiness."

Nakagami Kenji stunned the literary world with the inordinate power of his writing when he began publishing short stories in the mid-1970s. His award-winning novel *Misaki* (1976; promontory) evokes a powerful sense of raw physicality through the character of a young day laborer who uncontrollably revolts against the already crumbling family institution in rural Japan. His subsequent works continue to show that he is indeed one of the few writers who can raise literature to a mythological height without being uprooted from his most significant site—his birth place, Kishū, rich with ancient myths that speak of primordial sexuality, violence, and undeniable vitality.

After his sensational debut in 1976 with a novel filled with drugs, sex, and rock music, Murakami Ryū has continued to write provocative works that touch on the most grotesque reality of our contemporary world. His third novel, *Koinrokkkā beibīzu* (1980; coin-locker babies), was highly acclaimed for its bold and imaginative treatment of the postmodern world, with its interrelated themes of autistic self, imaginative construction of reality, and the final destruction of all. In his most recent novel, *Kokku sakkā burūsu* (1991; cocksucker blues), he explores the underground sadomasochistic world in Tokyo, linking an unspeakable sexual crime to contemporary Japan's political and economical practices.

The daughter of the famous novelist Dazai Osamu (q.v.), Tsushima Yūko, has firmly established her own place in the literary world. Her works often deal with themes that seem to derive from her own life: the absence of father, divorce, single mother, death of her son. However, her work cannot be confined within the convention of the *shishōsetsu* or "I-novel," for it often incorporates surreal situations and appropriates classical literature as its framework. Her ability to produce the unforgettable image of a female physicality that is solitary yet inseparably tied to the flow of all-inclusive life on earth, marks her as one of the major writers of contemporary Japan.

One of the significant changes in contemporary Japanese literature is how foreign countries and cultures function in Japanese texts. Thanks to the strong yen, foreign travels are no longer a remote dream for the Japanese, who have come to be known as the most-traveled people on earth. Correspondingly, there is a noticeable increase of novels staged in foreign countries as some Japanese writers begin to seek, whether voluntarily or not, new situations to write in and about. Writers with foreign locales include the following recipients of the most prestigious award for new writers, the Akutagawa Prize: Ōba Minako in 1968, Ikeda Masuo (b. 1934) in 1977, Takahashi Michitsuna (b. 1948) in 1978, Aono Sō in 1979, Mori Reiko (b. 1928) in 1979, and Kometani Fumiko (b. 1930) in 1986. Ōba writes about her experiences in Alaska. Ikeda, a noted visual artist, wrote his highly erotic novels while living in East Hampton. Takahashi's works reflect his experiences of having been a student in California. Both Mori and Kometani reside in the U.S. and write about being wives to Americans. Aono, the son of an eminent literary critic, began writing fiction during his eleven years of roaming around the globe.

Ōe Kenzaburō (q.v.), who began his literary career in the late 1950s as the most outrageous innovator of Japanese fiction, continues to be an uncompromising avant-gardist of the field. Going beyond the existential mode of his early works, his later works show his distinctive employment of methodology informed by the writings of Mikhail Bakhtin (q.v.) as well as a unique appropriation of the style of the "I-novel." He also continues to explore and deepen the two most fundamental themes of his writing: the isolated, forestal village of his birthplace in Shikoku, and his relationship with his brain-damaged son. His foreign sojourns in Mexico and at Berkeley, California, also contribute to his vigorous production of new materials.

There have been many talented women writers in modern Japan, though their works are categorized separately from the mainstream "male" literature as *joryū bungaku* (women's literature). Among the established older generation of women writers, two names deserve mention for their life-long accomplishments: Nogami Yaeko (b. 1885) and Uno Chiyo (b. 1897). Nogami has been known as a steadfast, yet nonactivist liberal throughout her long literary career. At the age seventy-eight, she received the Women's Literature Prize for her historical novel *Hideyoshi to Rikyū* (1963; Hideyoshi and Rikyū). Uno, as an epitome of "new woman," has led a colorful life, on which many of her works are based. Her best-selling novel, *Irozange* (1935; *Confessions of Love*, 1989) deftly recounts a story of a failed double suicide, which her then lover, the noted painter Tōgō Seiji, actually had lived through.

As the changes of daily reality brought out by Japan's rapid economic growth took root, it became evident that conventional realism was no longer able to produce the gestalt of the contemporary Japanese woman. With its radical antirealist stance, the appearance of *Parutai* (1960; *Partei,* 1982) by Kurahashi Yumiko (b. 1935) showed the possibility of a new type of women's literature that moved away from the usual convention of sensitively detailing one's own life. Kōno Taeko (b. 1926) also succeeded in presenting the distinctive image of women in her highly conceptual and often fantastic style that explored the depths of human sexuality. She received the Tanizaki Prize for her novel *Ichinen no bokka* (1980; one year's pastoral song). There are also outstanding women writers whose works directly address social issues. Ariyoshi Sawako (q.v.) dealt with ecological issues as well as the problems of elderly people. After publishing highly literary works, Takenishi Hiroko (b. 1929) began to write about Hiroshima's unhealed wound. Hayashi Kyōko, whose debut work *Matsuri no ba* (1975; "Ritual of Death," 1978) received the Akutagawa Prize, continues to write about her experience as a victim of the atomic bomb dropped in Nagasaki.

No other novel has captured the situation of the postmodern consumer society better than *Nantonaku kurisutaru* (1981; somehow crystal) by Tanaka Yasuo (b. 1956), then a college student. It depicts the life of a college girl living amidst hundreds of mostly foreign brand names, for which the book provides a parallel text of notes that resemble those in a city guidebook. The city has become a map of consumer signs; and its inhabitants are defined by them. Murakami Haruki's (q.v.) emergence as a major literary figure of the 1980s cannot be explained without an understanding of the cultural and semiotic transformation of city life. Utterly divorced from the longstanding tradition of *jun bungaku* (serious literature), Murakami's works nonetheless seek a new framework to address the emptiness of signs, communication, and self.

Drama

After separating itself from the traditional drama of Kabuki and Nō, *Shingeki* (new drama) firmly established itself after World War II with talented dramatists including Kinoshita Junji (q.v.) and Mishima Yukio. Toward the end of the 1960s, however, a countermovement to such a modern establishment began to appear. Commonly known as the *angura* (underground) theater, it was led by Kara Jūrō (b. 1940) and Terayama Shūji (1936–1983) who advocated the need to move beyond the modernity represented by *Shingeki* through incorporating more primitive, spontaneous, and immediate aspects of a show-tent atmosphere.

The second generation of the underground movement was led by Tsuka Kōhei (b. 1948) who debuted in the early 1970s with his satirical plays seeped in black humor. While the earlier underground theater carried a politically revolutionary agenda, Tsuka's plays, free from such confrontational approaches, comically depicted grotesque figures trapped in the sameness of daily life. Another new playwright to emerge around this time was Inoue Hisashi (b. 1934), who is now also known as an important novelist. His light comedies, which embraced many aspects of popular culture, heralded the recent ascension of popular culture to the status of high culture.

Poetry

Beginning in the late 19th c. with awkward translations of Western poetry, modern Japanese poets absorbed various modernist schools—romanticism, symbolism, dadaism, surrealism (qq.v.)—with bewildering speed and produced highly original works of their own.

Shimazaki Tōson (q.v.), who later became a naturalist novelist, is commonly credited as the creator of modern Japanese poetry. His first collection of poems, *Wakana shū* (1897; seedlings), effectively conveys his romantic lyricism. Kambara Ariake (1876–1947) succeeded in producing his own symbolist poetry, though much inspired by Dante Gabriel Rossetti (1828–1882) and Stéphane Mallarmé (1842–1898). Kitahara Hakushū (1885–1942) was the most talented poet before Hagiwara Sakutarō (q.v.) who redefined the language of modern Japanese poetry with his use of colloquialism soaked with a modern sense of alienation in *Tsuki ni hoeru* (1917; *Howling at the Moon,* 1978). Hagiwara's contemporary Miyazawa Kenji (q.v.) is still revered as a poet-saint who led a life of altruism. The son of a famous sculptor, Takamura Kōtarō is remembered for his direct expressions of love for his mentally ill wife, recorded in *Chieko-shō* (1941; *Chieko and Other Poems,* 1980).

In the 1930s, centering around the modernist poet and scholar Nishiwaki Junzaburō (q.v.), some fine modernist poets began to appear: Kitagawa Fuyuhiko (b. 1900); the editor of the important journal *VOU,* Kitasono Katsue (1902–1978); Anzai Fuyue (1898–1965); and surrealist Takiguchi Shūzō (1903–1979). Less-experimental poets gathered around the journal *Shiki,* notably Miyoshi Tatsuji (1900–1964) and Nakahara Chūya (1907–1937). Nakahara, whose work was much inspired by Arthur Rimbaud (1854–1891), still invokes romantic adoration for his intense lyricism as well as for his tragically brief life.

From the ashes of World War II rose many original poetic voices. The vagabond poet Kaneko Mitsuharu (1895–1975) emerged as one of the few who dared to write antiwar texts during the war. The leading figure of *Arechi,* the first poetry journal to appear after the war, was Tamura Ryūichi (b. 1923). Arguably the most important postwar poet, Yoshioka Minoru (1919–1990) wrote distinctively sensual, surreal works. The important poet and critic Ōoka Makoto (b. 1931) began writing under the influence of Paul Éluard (q.v.); his erudition in classical Japanese literature has allowed him to revive a modern version of *renga* (Japanese linked verse) with foreign poets. The first Japanese "beat" poet, Shiraishi Kazuko (b. 1931), weaves her unabashed expression of sexuality with the pulsating rhythm of jazz. She could be seen as the precursor of the talented young women poets who began to emerge in the 1970s. The most gifted one among them seems to be Itō Hiromi (b. 1955), whose bold experimentation in poetic language and explicit expressions of sexuality exhibit a voice that is at the same time unique and reflecting of our contemporary situation at large.

BIBLIOGRAPHY: Miyoshi, M., *Accomplices of Silence: The Modern Japanese Novel* (1974); Kato, S., *A History of Japanese Literature* (1983), Vol. 3; Ueda, M., *Modern Japanese Poets and the Nature of Literature* (1983); Keene, D., *Dawn to the West: Japanese Literature of the Modern Era* (2 vols., 1984); Marks, A. H., and B. D. Bort, *Guide to Japanese Prose,* 2nd ed. (1984); Pronko, L. C., *Guide to Japanese Drama,* 2nd ed. (1984); Rimer, J. T., and R. E. Morrell, *Guide to Japanese Poetry* (2nd ed., 1984); Rubin, J., *Injurious to Public Morals: Writers and the Meiji State* (1984); Rimer, J. T., *A Reader's Guide to Japanese Literature* (1988); Fowler, E., *The Rhetoric of Confession: Shishōsetsu in Early Twentieth-Century Japanese Fiction* (1988); Vernon, V. V., *Daughters of the Moon: Wish, Will, and Social Constraint in Fiction by Modern Japanese Women* (1988); Goodman, D. G., ed., *Japanese Drama and Culture in the 1960s: The Return of the Gods* (1988); Gessel, V. C., *The Sting of Life: Four Contemporary Japanese Novelists* (1989); Miyoshi, M., and H. D. Harootunian, eds., *Postmodernism and Japan* (1990); Wolfe, A. S., *Suicidal Narrative in Modern Japan: The Case of Dazai Osamu* (1990)

HOSEA HIRATA

JOHNSON, B(ryan) S(tanley)

English novelist, poet, screenwriter, and editor, b. 5 Feb. 1933, London; d. 13 Nov. 1973, London

Born into a working-class family in a class-conscious society, J. persistently used the details of his varied life in his art; spokesman for innovation in the novel in a time of rigorous conservatism, he became a well-regarded if controversial writer. His mother, wife, children, friends, and former lovers appear in his novels (he refused to call them "fictions"). And he himself, both as man and as novelist, becomes a character in his books. Permeated by the fear of loss and betrayal, his works are nonetheless a celebration of life: rich in humor, in inventiveness, in wordplay, and in the willingness to feel and to express emotion. We are often tempted, unwisely, to seek for details of his life in his novels. But the broad connection is clear. J.'s suicide seems in some respects as much an act of his art as of his life.

At a time when most English novelists and critics were deploring the modernists' example, J. was virtually alone in following in their path. He insisted that there was much that his contemporaries could learn still from James Joyce (q.v.); he refused to accept for his own work the rubric "experimental"—used as a pejorative by English critics—contending that when he applied some innovative technique in a novel, it was no longer an experiment but that he had already tried it out and knew that it could work. We can learn much about his principles of art and the hostile environment in which he worked from the revealing personal essay included in the volume *Aren't You Rather Young To Be Writing Your Memoirs?* (1973). His novels in this atmosphere are as daring as his public statements. Although in recent years the tide in English fiction has turned away from denial and increasingly in J.'s direction, his own works seem destined to be read by a limited audience only. This is not because they are difficult or unrewarding or even because they sometimes have an unusual physical appearance. J.'s premature death, soon after he had completed his best novel, *See the Old Lady Decently* (1975), in the midst of his most ambitious project, may have cut him off from a potentially larger audience. Yet he remains a figure worthy of consideration, in some respects the most serious novelist of his English generation.

In *Travelling People* (1963), J. employs a different narrative technique in each chapter (following Joyce's example in *Ulysses*), running the range from omniscience to stream-of-consciousness (q.v.). Endeavoring to link form integrally to function, the narrative is at once playful in tone and serious in intent; thus pages turn gray as a character grows ill and blacken as he dies. The central metaphor is traveling, as characters reach out to one another, touch briefly, and then move apart, their emotional rootlessness a factor of modern life. For a first novel, this is quite sophisticated work (it won the

Gregory Award for 1963), but J. subsequently refused to allow it to be reprinted, effectively removing it from his canon.

It is in *Albert Angelo* (1964) that J. discovers the pattern that will serve for almost all of his subsequent novels: his own experience transmuted into art, the act of writing about his life becoming a vital part of both the art and the life. The self-reflexive act of writing his life is from now on a constant theme, but there is little of the self-conscious cleverness here that we find in so much contemporary American metafiction. For J., this is but one more way of seeking the truth, one of the oft-stated goals of his novel writing. J. distinguishes between "novel" and "fiction," arguing that it is only in the former that he can achieve "truth." These terms appear repeatedly in his essays and letters and even in his novels.

While *Albert Angelo* builds on J.'s activities as a substitute schoolteacher (his last resort when free-lance writing and film work had totally dried up), these are surely not his own experiences that are detailed here. For Albert Angelo is an architect working as a teacher, and—in a scene undoubtedly imagined by every substitute with a difficult class—he is murdered by his pupils. The funeral of their teacher is seen in the final chapter from the joint point of view of the students, one more of the many narrative possibilities explored in the novel—including elements from outside the text that become part of the text (letters, ads, student essays, excerpts from architectural tomes) and variations in the physical text itself (a shift between roman and italic typefaces for differing perspectives within the classroom, slits in certain of the pages so that the reader can peer into the future). It is in *Albert Angelo* that J. first understands—or so he tells us—what it means for him to be a novelist.

J. would later offer *Trawl* (1966) as illustration of his writer's need for personal experience on which to base his writing. He had the idea for a book set on an oceangoing trawler, and so he went to sea on one. His account of seasickness and lovesickness is the result of that experience. (The latter clearly predates the sea journey; the former is its immediate result.) Everything we see here is presented through the character J.'s interior monologue (which varies, of course, with the degree of his seasickness), yet this remains the most conventional of J.'s novels. It won the Somerset Maugham Award for 1967.

The most unusual of J.'s novels is *The Unfortunates* (1969), issued in a box of separately bound, variously sized folios, of which only the first and the last are labeled. The others can be shuffled and read in any order, however random or carefully arranged, that the reader desires. Based apparently on a newspaper sports story that the free-lancer J. was commissioned to write in Nottingham and on the news learned there of the impending death, from cancer, of a dear friend, one of the few who had encouraged the writer early in his career. The line between J. the character and J. the writer seems very thin at this point, and the intimate point of view may induce us to feel his/their emotional dilemma with special urgency. Similarly, the random shuffling of time sequences can be either inconsequential (it hardly matters at what point we hear that the narrator takes the bus back from the stadium) or powerfully emotive (learning that his friend, Tony, is dying after being told that his cancer had been cured). The fear of loss remains J.'s most persistent theme.

The connection to *House Mother Normal: A Geriatric Comedy* (1971) is not, at first, easy to find; it is more likely in the novel's form than in its content, since its events seem to have little to do with J.'s life. The text consists of nine almost perfectly symmetrical narratives from within the minds of the residents of a nursing home and of their head nurse. Some of the patients are infirm; at least one is senile; only the nurse is aware of her audience. And she reveals herself—her rigidity, her masochism, her strong sexual urges—quite consciously and without hesitation. She also reveals on a final, additional page (a page denied the other consciousnesses)—the one lack of symmetry in the novel—that behind her is an author, controlling all: not quite a Dickensian final page. The work is clever, comic, a playing with form, but it is not meant, perhaps, to be taken with full seriousness. It is one of the few J. novels in which neither J. the character nor any of his surrogates makes an appearance.

Rich in both narrative innovation and emotional content, *See the Old Lady Decently* is the first part of a planned trilogy, to be called The Matrix Trilogy, its combined titles to be read consecutively: *See the Old Lady Decently Buried Although Amongst Those Left Are You*. Although J. makes only, as it were, a cameo appearance, this is the most autobiographical of all his novels, the one that most forcefully relates life to art to the process of converting life to art. Its elaborate system of notations and sources barely disguises its impact. Impelled by the death of his mother, Emily, from cancer, in 1971, J. set out to reconstruct her life and to parallel it with that of modern-day Britain, the Mother Country, her early life at the height of the Empire, her death in the time of its decay. Outside the reconstruction, we learn of J.'s suicide shortly after he completed this novel, the ultimate act, we might say, of life intersecting with art.

FURTHER WORK: *Christie Malry's Own Double-Entry* (1973)

BIBLIOGRAPHY: Levitt, M. P., ''The Novels of B. S. J.: Against the War against Joyce,'' *MFS,* 27, 4 (Winter 1981–1982), 438–44; Ghose, Z., ''Bryan,'' *RCF,* 5, 2 (1985), 23–34; Levitt, M. P., *Modernist Survivors: The Contemporary Novel in England, the United States, France, and Latin America* (1987), 60–72

MORTON P. LEVITT

JOLLEY, Elizabeth

Australian novelist and short-story writer, b. 4 June 1923, Birmingham, England

J. came to Perth, Western Australia, where she still lives, with her family in 1959. She grew up in the industrial Midlands in England and was educated at home by her English father, a teacher, then at a Quaker boarding school. J.'s mother was Viennese. J. trained and worked as a nurse during World War II. Writing from an early age, J.'s first public recognition came when a children's story was broadcast on regional radio in England. During many years when her work was regularly rejected for publication, J. had a variety of casual jobs, including work as a geriatric night nurse and a door-to-door salesperson. More recently, J. has taught writing at a Perth University and worked with community writing groups. Years of rejection ended when the Western Australian publishers Fremantle Arts Centre Press released a collection of short fiction, *Five Acre Virgin and Other Stories,* in 1976.

The stories in this first collection reveal the preoccupations that characterize J.'s work; an ability to combine a sense of the significance yet absurdity of ordinary lives, an interest in the effects of displacement and exile on those lives, and a deep feeling for place. Recognition of J. as a major Australian writer occurred with the publication in 1983 of *Mr. Scobie's Riddle* and *Miss Peabody's Inheritance.* Nine novels and three further volumes of short stories have now been published, and a number of radio plays have been performed on Australian and British radio. While this output may seem prolific, it derives from writing over the last four or more decades. J. worked on the novel *Milk and Honey* (1984), for instance, at different times from the early 1960s, simultaneously with other manuscripts and ideas for novels and short stories. J.'s work should not be read as a progression, linked in a linear sense, but as a network of influences. Characters, incidents, and motifs or references are often repeated with a difference in a novel, a story, and a radio play; things constantly recur as they do in life, while the characters are used to explore central human problems: the nature of human love and

the capacity of human beings for idealism and manipulation.

Growing up in England in a German-speaking household has marked J.'s imagination and her writing, which is highly allusive, drawing on a huge range of reference from major religious and secular texts, both poetry and prose, in the Western cultural tradition. Music occupies an important place in her oeuvre. The cultural differences between life in Australia and Europe are often marked by those characters who are music lovers and others who are indifferent to or scorn music. J.'s prose structures are also often likened to musical forms, where the recurrences inside and among her novels and stories recall the classical musical practice of variation on a theme and counterpoint, or the interplay of independent themes or melodic fragments. The short story is J.'s favorite form, and her novels are episodic, often poetic, and compressed. Formally, J. constructs a recognizably realistic fictional world but one that is constantly interrupted or shifted by bizarre events or the interpolation of fantastic elements. Generic experimentation with modes such as the gothic, the romance, and the thriller is used to interrupt readers' singular generic expectations. These modes are used, too, as ways of exploring women's lives. Relationships between women are a major concern in J.'s writing; they sometimes involve lesbian sexuality and are presented through a range of configurations. Women and their creativity provide a constant theme, and the narratives, in which comedy and irony, the grotesque and the lyric form an unsettling blend, are often deliberately fragmented, fractured by a range of narrative modes and voices.

J. is now regarded as one of Australia's major writers, and her work has been translated into a number of European languages. While the metafictional aspect of her work constantly interrogates the categories of truth and fiction, the values espoused are deeply humanist, with a central belief in the possibility of a moment where truth may be discovered. The question of human responsibility, to oneself and to others, is always present and never lightly dealt with. J.'s depiction of Australian life is sharply idiosyncratic, and her work as a whole provides an unusually close-knit, witty yet compassionate observation of contemporary existence, and a meditation on its momentary joys and major limitations.

FURTHER WORKS: *The Travelling Entertainer and Other Stories* (1979); *The Newspaper of Claremont Street* (1981); *Woman in a Lampshade* (1983); *Stories* (1984); *Foxybaby* (1984); *The Well* (1986); *The Sugar Mother* (1988); *My Father's Moon* (1989); *Cabin Fever* (1990)

BIBLIOGRAPHY: Garner, H., "E. J.: An Appreciation," *Meanjin,* 42 (1983), 153–57; Riemer, A. P., "Between Two Worlds—An Approach to E. J.'s Fiction," *Southerly,* 43, 3 (1983), 239–52; Jones, D., "The Goddess, the Artist and the Spinster," *Westerly,* 29, 4 (1984), 77–88; Howells, C. S., "In Search of Lost Mothers: Margaret Laurence's *The Diviners* and E. J.'s *Miss Peabody's Inheritance,*" *ArielE,* 19, 1 (1988), 57–70; Daniel, H., *Liars* (1988), 269–300; Trigg, S., "An Interview with E. J.," *Scripsi,* 4, 1 (1988), 244–64; Kavanagh, P., "This Self the Honey of All Beings: A Conversation with E. J.," *Southerly,* 49, 3 (1989), 438–51; Bird, D., and B. Walker, eds., *E. J.: New Critical Essays* (1990)

DELYS M. BIRD

JORGE, Lídia

Portuguese novelist, b. 18 June 1946, Boliqueime

J. was born and raised in a rural community in the Algarve and studied at the University of Lisbon where she first became politically conscious. Upon completing her studies, she spent several years as a teacher in the African colonies of Angola and Mozambique. She returned to Lisbon to teach, first at the secondary level and later at the university. She began writing as a child, but it was at the age of thirty-three that she published her first book.

Her first novel, *O dia dos prodígios* (1980; the day of the prodigious events), acclaimed by an eminent Portuguese scholar as one of the key works of the Portuguese revolution of 1974, was an immediate success. It revealed already most of the characteristics that were to define her as a novelist: formal experiment, an idiosyncratic style marked by a pronounced orality, an inclination toward magic realism (q.v.), a fascination with her historical moment. Many novels were written about the 1974 revolution in the years immediately following it, but none of them records its failure as brilliantly as does J.'s. The author figures her commentary in the juxtaposition of two prodigious events: the revolution itself and the sudden appearance and equally sudden disappearance in the rural village of Vilamaninhos of a mysterious winged snake. For the villagers, the former is a remote "prodígio," far less real and far less fascinating than their own prodigious snake. By depicting these villagers as an insular, culturally deprived community, implicitly like many others throughout the country, J. questions the viability of a political program as sophisticated as the one espoused by the makers of the revolution. On a secondary level, the novel is as much about the art of narration as it is about the inability of political reform to penetrate the remote corners of Portugal. Early in the novel, J. reveals an interest in the dynamics of group storytelling. The task she sets for herself is not merely to describe the process but to reproduce it, to transpose the oral experience of simultaneous narration (essentially temporal) to the medium of writing (primarily spatial). For this novel, she won the Ricardo Malheiros Prize (1980).

J.'s second novel, *O cais das merendas* (1982; the snack wharf), is again a response to social change. Here the issue is an insidious colonization: the tourist invasion of the Algarve. The author exposes its devastating consequences for the inhabitants of a small rural village, lured by the perceived sophistication and economic promise of rededicating their lives to service at a thriving resort hotel. The price is the sacrifice of cultural identity and of selfhood in new roles that require J.'s characters to be no longer members of a culturally valid community but simply functionaries in the world of the tourist, a world that appropriates their time and space but systematically excludes them from full participation. J.'s artistic medium is again a brilliant use of language and form: shifting narrators and temporal planes, symbolic and allegorical detail, a touch of magic realism. Most impressive is her depiction of language itself in the process of being colonized, her revelation of the cultural charge that words carry, and the cultural and psychological ramifications of replacing one word with another.

Colonization of a more traditional, though no less devastating, kind is the subject of J.'s fourth novel, *A costa dos murmúrios* (1988; the coast of murmurs). As in the second novel, the setting is a hotel, this time one that houses the wives of military personnel in war-ravaged Mozambique during the final throes of the colonial enterprise. The author's primary intention is to expose the brutality of the war, but, as in the other two novels, there is a secondary, one might say literary, concern as well. This book is in reality two novels in one. The first is an account of a tragic war-related episode that once occurred at the hotel. The second, a telling of the "true story" of that event by a participant who twenty years later has just finished reading the account. The author's intention here is to explore the relationship of truth, reality, and history (history as the way in which reality is interpreted, recorded, and remembered). She intends not simply to question the events and the rationale of the colonial war but to challenge the way contemporary Portuguese society is processing the "memory" of that war. Again the novel is enriched by the oral style, the numerous and varied discourses of that African experience.

While all of these novels have met with a highly favorable reception, there is one group of readers that has been less than enthusiastic about J.'s work: the radical feminists. J. gives a prominent place to women in each of the works, but she does not privilege them, undoubtedly because it was the broader national picture that absorbed her. Her third novel, *Notícia da cidade silvestre* (1984; word from the sylvan city), focuses on two female characters through the first-person confessional narrative of one of them. The narrative appears at first to be the story of women's friendship, but it soon becomes evident that it is something quite different: an examination of the power struggles and the subliminal forces that inform human relationships whether they be with women, with men, or even with children. All are at issue in the novel, which in that sense continues to have a broader social theme. This work breaks with the others not only in dealing with more intimate, subjective material but in doing so in a more straightforward manner, shorn of the allegorical and magic realist cast that characterizes them. Orality alone continues. For this work J. received the City of Lisbon Fiction Award (1984). Since the publication of these novels, J. has written a play dealing with the early 20th-c. feminist and medical doctor Adelaide Cabete; plans for a stage production are under way.

In the scant decade since she began publishing, J. has become one of the central figures on the Portuguese literary scene. She is much sought-after in academic as well as literary circles not only in her own country but in Brazil and even in the U.S. She is one of the most imaginative and linguistically gifted of her contemporaries, and she is clearly a writer with a social mission.

BIBLIOGRAPHY: Sadlier, D. J., *The Question of How: Women Writers and New Portuguese Literature* (1989), 49–73

ALICE R. CLEMENTE

KAHANA-CARMON, Amalia

Israeli novelist and short-story writer, b. 18 Nov. 1930(?), Tel Aviv

K.-C.'s first collection of stories, *Bkhfifah ahat* (1966; under one roof), already testified to a literary maturity and decisiveness. Both in theme and in style, these stories deviate from the prevalent norms of Israeli fiction. They relate primarily to feeling, to the individual, and to the contact between individuals, particularly in respect to romantic attraction. This attraction is seen as ungraspable, perhaps irrational and mystical, but more significant than any other human emotion in the writing. The language of the stories is condensed, intricate, and elliptical. The sentences are short, and the phraseology alludes little to classical sources. The narratives here explore the relationships and feelings of narrator or narratee with a growing intensity, often playing off such feelings against external reality. The person to whom such feeling attaches may be totally unaware of what is happening. Such an infatuation is always modified by the narrative irony of an alternative voice. There is a commentator behind or at the side or in the action. The implied questions are posed: What is true reality? Is it the subject's version of the inner event, or is it the observer's or the object's version?

What makes for some difficulty in the reading of K.-C. is the paucity of "stage directions" or manifest context. Although the settings vary from Swiss villages through English country houses to Tel Aviv and Jerusalem, the material is interior. In K.-C.'s subsequent work, the novel, *Veyareah beemeq ayalon* (1971; and moon in the valley of Ayalon), material from the earlier collection, there seen as a story, here becomes part of the extended, ongoing narrative. The third-person account of Mrs. Talmor incorporates now this first-person account from an earlier phase of her life. So we see her both from within and without, sometimes wavering between accounts appropriate to the limited focus of a single character or within the province of the omniscient narrator. The unusual title of the novel is taken from *Joshua* 10:12, and refers to the stopping of the sun and moon in their tracks to give time to the Israelites to overcome the Amorites within one day.

The overall title of the triptych, *Sadot magnetiyim* (1977; magnetic fields), states the author's concern with the attraction between man and woman. The metaphor is suggestive of the fact that this attraction is neither consistent nor predictable. These magnetic fields delimit the range of the two individual paths. As often as not, K.-C. describes the encounter from the male point of view, as in the main unit of the triptych, "sham hadar hahadashot" (the newsroom is over there). In this case, the American girl, Wendy, holds they exist in two separate fields, and so they part.

Themes of attraction, support, and dependence are explored by K.-C. in her later work, *Lemaalah bemontifer* (1984; up in Montifer) and in *Livitiy otah baderekh levetah* (1991; I accompanied her home). In *Lemaalah bemontifer* the main section has a medieval setting, so the archaic style favored by the author seems ever more appropriate. The narrator is a Jewess, subject to the Christian Peter, previously a torture victim, but now ruminating her fate and her relationship to the master who has free access to Montifer. Her own account of the past and present situation is both realistic and masochistic.

K.-C.'s work is unique in Israeli narrative for its close analysis of relationships and for its condensed, yet metaphorical and unusual, language.

BIBLIOGRAPHY: Telpaz, G., *Israeli Childhood Stories of the Sixties* (1983), 121–46; Yudkin, L. I., *1948 and After: Aspects of Israeli Fiction* (1984), 97–111, 164–67; Fuchs, E., *Israeli Mythogynies: Women in Contemporary Hebrew Fiction* (1987), 87–104

LEON I. YUDKIN

KANAFĀNĪ, Ghassān

Palestinian novelist, short-story writer, and dramatist, b. 9 Apr. 1936, Acre, Palestine (now Israel); d. 8 July 1972, Beirut, Lebanon

During the 1948 Israeli-Arab war, when K. was twelve years old, his family fled their native city of Acre to Lebanon and thence to Syria, where they settled in a refugee camp near Damascus. After acquiring his secondary-school diploma in 1952, K. enrolled in the department of Arabic literature at the University of Damascus but was expelled for political activity three years later before completing his studies. From Damascus he moved to Kuwait, where he worked in journalism until his permanent relocation to Beirut in 1960. In Beirut K. wrote regularly for several major dailies and rapidly rose to editorial positions in a number of them. In 1969 he became spokesman for the Popular Front for the Liberation of Palestine and chief editor of its publication *al-Hadaf*. He retained both positions until his assassination in a car bomb planted by Israeli agents in Beirut in 1972. In 1975 K. was posthumously awarded the Lotus Prize for literature by the Conference of Afro-Asian Writers.

Although he died at the young age of thirty-six, K.'s relatively short adult life produced an extraordinarily prolific and diverse literary career. In addition to political commentaries, he wrote short stories, novels, plays, literary criticism, and historical expositions. He was also a painter of some standing. His literary fame, however, rests primarily on his fiction.

With a few exceptions, Palestinian concerns furnish the subject matter of K.'s fiction. His intense involvement in Palestinian national affairs gave him a unique vantage point from which he could closely observe the evolution of Palestinian political consciousness during a crucial phase of modern Palestinian history. K.'s short stories and novels preserve an imaginatively rendered record of that consciousness. But K. was no mere observer of the Palestinian scene. As a committed writer, he invariably sought to influence the course of the events he was describing in his fiction. His constant experimentation with narrative possibilities was largely motivated by the desire to make the formal means of fiction yield optimal political results. In response to this clear order of priorities, K.'s fiction grew progressively simpler in form and more direct and discursive in style. Of K.'s four novels, the first two reflect the supremacy of the literary imperative, while the last two reflect its subordination to a strict political agenda.

In theme and outlook K.'s first two novels, *Rijāl fi-al-shams* (1963; *Men in the Sun,* 1978) and *Mā tabaqqā lakum* (1966; *All That's Left to You,* 1990), bear the unmistakable marks of the period in which they were written. Since the Palestinian question was in deep limbo at the time, the outlook of both novels is quite bleak, though the second is far less so than the first. This correspondence between actual events and fiction is built into the plot of both novels. Thus, the three Palestinian refugees of *Rijāl fi-al-shams* perish in an empty water tank in the desert as they are being smuggled by a Palestinian driver into Kuwait in search of an alternative to life in the refugee

camps. What makes this gloomy ending even more harrowing is the symbolism with which K. invests the characters. The three men, being of different ages, represent three generations of Palestinians; the driver represents a fourth. But since he is a castrate and no one is left in the novel to perpetuate the Palestinian species, the conclusion virtually spells the physical end of the Palestinian people.

This ending enacts a recurrent pattern in Palestinian fiction, only here it is more graphic and more brutally stark than anywhere else. The outline of this pattern is as follows. Movement in the opposite direction to Palestine invariably leads to death and loss of identity, while movement in the direction of Palestine, even when it ends in physical death or captivity, leads to a symbolic recovery of the self and a reassertion of individual and national will.

Movement in K.'s second novel, *Mā tabaqqā lakum* begins in one direction and ends in the other. The Palestinian protagonist inadvertently encounters an Israeli soldier on his flight route from Gaza to Jordan and is thus forced to eschew his original escape plan and turn to confront his enemy. And even though the novel ends with the two protagonists practically locking horns, for the Palestinian the very act of confronting the enemy constitutes a symbolic victory. This thematic development reflects the change in the general condition after the initiation of the Palestinian armed struggle against Israel a year before the publication of the novel.

In form and narrative technique both of these novels rank among the most complex and experimental in all of Arabic fiction. Under the acknowledged influence of William Faulkner (q.v.), K. skillfully uses the techniques of interior monologue, flashback, and fragmentation to depict the psychological effects of dislocation and uprootedness on his characters. The symbolic treatment imparts a universal dimension to the specific Palestinian content of both novels. Artistically, they mark the zenith of K.'s literary achievement.

In the wake of the War of 1967, K.'s fiction underwent a fundamental change. Questions of technical and stylistic virtuosity were no longer relevant; the political imperative of reaching and mobilizing the masses became paramount. Both *Umm Saʿd* (1969; the mother of Saʿd) and *ʿĀʾid ilā Haifā* (1969; returning to Haifa) reflect this change in K.'s approach to fiction writing. In both novels straightforward narrative and dialogue replace the fragmented narrative and interior monologue of the earlier novels. In place of the tightly structured symbolic plots, episodic structures that K. calls tableaux constitute the "plot" of *Umm Saʿd*. In this novel it is the illiterate working class woman Umm Saʿd who speaks, often in the Palestinian vernacular, while the learned narrator-writer records "verbatim" her artless accounts.

From the posthumously published fragments of the three novels he was working on at the time of his assassination, it appears that K. continued to be preoccupied with the relationship of fiction to history. In one of these fragments he adopts the means and format of scholarly research by appending footnotes to the events of the fictional plot. Anticipating the rise of women in the Palestinian struggle for national liberation, K. entrusts the lead role in this novel to a woman who acts as his own female counterfoil. In this and other fundamental respects, K.'s pioneering contributions to Palestinian literature have remained unsurpassed.

FURTHER WORKS: *Mawt Sarīr Raqm 12* (1961); *Ard al-burtuqāl al-hazīn* (1963); *al-Bāb* (1964); *'Ālam laysa lanā* (1965); *Adab al-muqāwamah fī filastīn al-muhtalla 1948–1966* (1966); *Fī al-Adab al-sahyūnī* (1967); *al-Adab al-filastīnī al-muqāwim tahta al-ihtilāl: 1948–1968* (1968); *'An al-rijāl wa-al-banādiq* (1968); *al-'Āshiq* (1972); *al-A'mā wa-al-atrash* (1972); *Barqūq Naysān* (1972); *al-Qubba'ah wa-al-nabī* (1973); *Thawrat 1936–39 fī filastīn* (1974); *Jisr ilā al-abad* (1978); *al-Qamīs al-masrūq wa-qisas ukhrā* (1982)

BIBLIOGRAPHY: Kanafani, A., *G. K.* (1973); Wild, S., *G. K.: The Life of a Palestinian* (1975); Kilpatrick, H., "Tradition and Innovation in the Fiction of G. K.," *JArabL*, 7 (1976), 53–64; Kilpatrick, H., Introduction to *Men in the Sun* (1978), 1–7; Magrath, D. R., "A Study of *Rijāl fil-shams* by G. K.," *JArabL*, 10 (1979), 95–108; Allen, R., *The Arabic Novel* (1982), 108–19; Siddiq, M., *Man Is a Cause: Political Consciousness and the Fiction of G. K.* (1984); Allen, R., ed., *Modern Arabic Literature* (1987), 176–80

MUHAMMAD SIDDIQ

KANT, Hermann

German novelist and short-story writer, b. 14 June 1926, Hamburg

Shortly before the end of World War II, K. completed an electrician's apprenticeship and entered the army. From 1945 to 1949 he was a prisoner of war in Poland, where he became politically active in an antifascist group in a Warsaw labor camp. When he returned to Germany, he entered an experimental preparatory institute for students from working-class and farm families at the Ernst Moritz Arndt University in Greifswald, East Germany. He studied Germanic philology at the Humboldt University in East Berlin from 1952 to 1956, after which he worked as a journalist and news-

paper editor until 1962. Since then he has committed himself entirely to his literary career. In 1969 he became a member of the Academy of Arts of the German Democratic Republic, and in 1978 he took the highly controversial office of president of the East German Writers' Union. Among the awards that he has received for his writing are the Heinrich Heine Prize (1963), the Erich Weinert Medal (1966), the Heinrich Mann Prize (1967), and the National Prize of the German Democratic Republic (1973 and 1983).

In K.'s narrative prose, a focus on personal involvement in reality is combined with pointed, sometimes humorous or satirical, sometimes evenly objective but constructive social, cultural, and political criticism. Among the themes and problems that are central to his works are the establishment and justification of individual identity through coming to grips with the past, analysis of specific experiences, such as those of a prisoner of war, as a basis for perceptions of the world, and the contradictions, dilemmas, conflicts, and challenges that are visible on a private level in the process of building a new and different society. The general tone of his writing is optimistic, although in some instances the optimism seems forced and fails to convince the reader. Particularly visible elements of his best work include freshness and vitality of character portrayal, effective development of situational humor, the successful combination of didactic intent and readability, compelling presentation of human interaction, and penetrating interpretation of life in the German Democratic Republic during the reconstruction period.

In his first collection of stories, *Ein bißchen Südsee* (1962; a little South Pacific), with its autobiographical focus on themes such as childhood, first love, war, and confinement, K. presented flashes of the humor and witty satire that became attractive features of his more mature works. Later anthologies, however, including *Eine Übertretung* (1975; a transgression), *Der dritte Nagel* (1982; the third nail), and *Bronzezeit* (1986; Bronze Age), are not uniform in quality or literary effectiveness. In addition to subtle, realistic tales that are both compelling and entertaining, they also contain pieces in which satire and pointed irony lose much of their force because of the author's very visible unwillingness to risk transcending the limits imposed upon him by East German cultural politics. Social and political criticism are promoted and then immediately negated; attention is shifted from significant problems to trivial bureaucratic matters; attempts to reveal truth are reduced to apologies for existing conditions.

K.'s first novel, *Die Aula* (1964; the auditorium), is based in part on his personal experiences at the institute in Greifswald. It has become a classic of East German literature and remains his most important creation. Within the programed cultural context of the time, *Die Aula* is especially remarkable for its fresh, captivating style. A variety of literary devices, including internal monologues, flashbacks, humorous understatement, and reflective analysis are successfully employed in a presentation that examines complex problems of the reconstruction era on multiple narrative levels. An ironic skepticism colors the novel's refusal to justify the failings of the new society, while honest criticism and vibrant, believable characters become effective vehicles for conveying the spirit of the times.

In his subsequent novels, K. failed to maintain the vitality and spontaneity of presentation that set *Die Aula* apart from much of East German reconstruction literature. *Das Impressum* (1972; the journal), with its treatment of the relationship between individual self-realization and political necessity, also gives interesting insights into East German society, but it is more programmatic than the earlier novel, lacks authentic human conflicts, and comes across as a slightly inferior structural and stylistic imitation of *Die Aula*. Although *Der Aufenthalt* (1977; the stay), an autobiographically motivated reflection on the prisoner-of-war experience, did not have the public impact of *Die Aula*, it is a significant document of the subjective current in late-20th-c. German literature that has emphasized grappling with and overcoming the past.

While K. has not consistently produced narratives of high literary quality, his best writings are certainly among the most significant creations that appeared in the German Democratic Republic during the forty years of its existence. For that reason, he was able to exert a powerful—often sinister—influence upon cultural policy as it pertained to literature and upon the concrete efforts of other writers. Within that context he is a very important—though politically highly controversial—representative of what was the East German literary establishment.

FURTHER WORKS: *In Stockholm* (1971); *Anrede der Ärztin O. an den Staatsanwalt F. gelegentlich einer Untersuchung* (1978); *Zu den Unterlagen* (1981); *Unterlagen zu Literatur und Politik* (1982); *Schöne Elise* (1983); *Krönungstag* (1986); *Die Summe* (1987); *Abspan: Erinnerungen* (1991)

BIBLIOGRAPHY: Herd, E. W., "Narrative Technique in Two Novels by H. K.," in Siefken, H., and A. Robinson, eds., *Erfahrung und Überlieferung* (1974), 185–96; Gerber, M., "Confrontations with Reality in H. K.'s *Die Aula*," *Monatshefte*, 67 (1975), 173–84; Langenbruch, T., *Dialectical Humor in H. K.'s Novel "Die Aula"* (1975); Holmes, J. E., "An Interview with H. K.," *StTCL*, 4, 1 (Fall 1979), 89–102; Langenbruch, T., "H. K.'s *Die Aula*: Literary References in a Contemporary East German Novel," in Nelson, C., ed., *Studies in Language and Literature* (1976), 325–30; Krenzlin, L., *H. K.* (1980); Ertl, W., "A Poetry Lesson in K.'s *Die Aula*: Notes on the Theme of Socialist Education in the GDR," *Schatzkammer*, 8 (1982), 23–30; Krenzlin, L., "Erzählstruktur und Leserreaktion. H. K.'s Roman *Die Aula* in der zeitgenössischen Rezeption," *WB* (1986), 912–36

LOWELL A. BANGERTER

KAO Hsiao-sheng

(also romanized as Gao Xiaosheng) Chinese short-story writer and essayist, b. 6 July 1928, Tung-shu Village, Wu-chin County, Kiangsu

K. was born in a peasant village where many of his fellow villagers were near or distant relatives. His father held the distinction of local intellectual since he had attended a modern-style university established in Shanghai near the end of the last dynasty of imperial China. Despite a young life of field labor, poverty, and only irregular schooling, K. too managed to get into a university in Shanghai, where he was studying economics just before the Communist Party assumed power. The change in government allowed him to abandon these studies and engage in the literary career he had always desired. In 1957, however, he was labeled a rightist for having written a proposal for an independent journal. This forced his return to the harsh peasant life of his village for the next twenty-one years. After the political changes following Mao Tse-tung's death, K. began to write again. He was politically "rehabilitated" along with many other intellectuals in 1979 and allowed to move to the city of Ch'ang-chou, where he resumed his life as a professional writer of fiction.

K. is best known for his "peasant fiction" from the post-Mao period. Since the early 1940s, in accordance with the official political line and requirements of Socialist Realism (q.v.), Chinese authors had dutifully portrayed a heroic peasant type who was naturally patriotic and progressive in socialist terms. In "Li Shun-ta tsao-wu" (1979; "Li Shunda Builds a House," 1983) and his series of stories about Ch'en Huan-sheng, K. expressly challenges this mythic figure by replacing it with a peasant who is uneducated, generally unreflective, preoccupied with the need for food and shelter, and conditioned to an attitude of awe toward authority. The stories are a complex mix of humor and satire as the author simultaneously sympathizes with the plight of the peasants and regards with profound concern the political implications of their ignorance and passivity. The object of

K.'s satire, however, is not the particularly simpleminded and humble peasant who serves as his protagonist. Li Shun-ta and Ch'en Huan-sheng are both surrounded by a far more reprehensible crowd of greedy, manipulative cadres, friends, and even family, as well as an occasional cynical and powerless intellectual. Higher levels of authority in the stories, like the county party secretary, still retain a glow of socialist purity (necessary undoubtedly because of possible symbolic connection to more powerful figures in the real Chinese political structure). Yet even these characters are depicted as, if nothing else, willing to require sacrifice of their peasant brothers for the sake of that aura of purity.

While the thematic concerns of K.'s peasant fiction secured his most immediate significance in the post-Mao literary scene of China, his other writings may ultimately insure his longer reputation. Among these are a group of stories that critics refer to as K.'s "philosophical tales" or "parables." These are short pieces developed around an extraordinary event and thus reminiscent of the traditional Chinese *chih-jen chih-kuai* (records of men and anomalies). Like the traditional writings, K.'s accounts of odd, even grotesque occurrences offer the reader an exaggerated portrait of more "ordinary" human characteristics or behavior. The complex nature and effects of paranoia, greed, dishonesty, and moral evasiveness serve as focus in such pieces as "Shan-chung" (1981; on the mountain), "Ch'ien-pao" (1980; "The Briefcase," 1980), "Yu tiao" (1980; "Fishing," 1987), or "Sheng-tzu" (1982; the rope). Thematic ties to current political issues in China remain evident if not always immediately obvious in these stories. For instance, one can easily read the excessive timidity and paranoia presented in "Shan-chung" as describing a historically specific habit of mind made prevalent in China by several decades of constant political and physical struggles in the name of socialism. The spareness of historical detail in the story, however, both obscures this level of political satire and enhances interpretive richness. Not only does the traditional form of K.'s philosophical tales encourage reading them as broader cultural explorations, they also stand as more universal reflections on human nature.

Since the mid-1980s, K. has ventured with different degrees of success into new materials. Along with many other middle-aged writers, he has written some "reform literature," basically optimistic stories concerning the effects of recent economic reforms. Several of these have a rather prescriptive tone, recommending less conservative and more scientific methods in such sideline agricultural production as honey or fish. At the same time, K. has written a few works that might loosely be categorized as his "love stories": "Tieh-chiao yin-yüan" (1984; falling into a marriage), "Ts'un-tzu li te feng-ch'ing" (1990; amorous feelings in a village), and his first novel, *Ch'ing t'ien tzai shang* (1991; blue skies above). The love element of these stories, like K.'s peasants, is not heroic or glorious and, while subjected to scrutiny, not entirely the subject of the pieces. Rather the concern of the texts is the excessive interference at this personal level caused by social attitudes and abuse of power. *Ch'ing t'ien tzai shang* is more complicated, as it is an autobiographical novel about K.'s own first wife, who accompanied him in his exile to the countryside and died there of tuberculosis exacerbated by malnutrition and inadequate medical care. The author's deeply painful experience of loss and grief colors the narrative, which dwells on the beauty and gentle goodness of the young woman. Nonetheless, the relationship described retains an understated and ordinary dimension, as the novel reveals the devastating effect that the often absurd implementation of the rural policies of the Great Leap Forward had on this insignificant couple.

The satiric tone of K.'s writings, particularly in his depiction of peasants, has caused many critics to compare him to Lu Hsün (q.v.), a writer generally acclaimed as the father and best author of modern Chinese short stories. Narrative styles differ greatly, though, as K. prefers the voice of an apparently uninhibited storyteller, while Lu Hsün's narrator tends to be tersely omniscient or a self-conscious intellectual, frequently tormented by a sense of moral failure. K.'s storyteller, by contrast, is more openly entertaining. He delights in word play and never hesitates to comment on the characters or events of the story, sometimes in straightforward fashion, sometimes tongue in cheek. A detail of this story may take the narrator off on a tangent, offering, for instance, a diatribe on the Chinese preoccupation with sex or comic reflections on time and space. While this storyteller cast of K.'s style is a strength and major source of the appeal of his works, it arguably neglects the larger elements of narrative structure. The language is delightful but may seem arbitrary, superficially witty, and employed at the expense of the organization and significance of the story. The very pleasure of the text disguises the fundamental intellectual honesty and seriousness of purpose that underlie K.'s works.

FURTHER WORKS: *Chieh yüeh* (1955); *Kao Hsiao-sheng 1979 nien hsiao-shuo chi* (1980); *Kao Hsiao-sheng 1980 nien hsiao-shuo chi* (1981); *Kao Hsiao-sheng hsiao-shuo hsüan* (1983); *Kao Hsiao-sheng 1982 nien hsiao-shuo chi* (1983); *Kao Hsiao-sheng 1983 nien hsiao-shuo chi* (1984); *Sheng-huo, ssu-*

THOMAS KENEALLY

GEORGE KONRÁD

PRIMO LEVI

EARL LOVELACE

k'ao, ch'uang-tzo (1986); *Sheng-huo te chiao-liu* (1987). FURTHER VOLUME IN ENGLISH: *The Broken Betrothal, and Other Stories* (1987)

BIBLIOGRAPHY: Lee, L. O., "The Politics of Technique: Perspectives of Literary Dissidence in Contemporary Chinese Fiction," in Kinkley, J. C., ed., *After Mao: Chinese Literature and Society, 1978–1981* (1985), 159–90; Feuerwerker, Y. M., "An Interview with G. [K.]," *MCL*, 3, 1–2 (1987), 113–35; Wagner, R. G., "Documents Concerning *Tanqiuzhe* [the explorer], an Independent Literary Journal Planned during the Hundred Flowers Period," *MCL*, 3, 1–2 (1987), 137–46; Ye, Z. C., "The String That Will Never Break—Introducing the Writer G. [K.]," *The Broken Betrothal, and Other Stories* (1987), 212–18

MARGARET H. DECKER

KENAZ, Yehoshua

Israeli novelist, short-story writer, and translator, b. 2 Mar. 1937, Petah Tikva

The semipastoral environment in which K. grew up is reflected in the background of his first novel, *Aharey hahagim* (1964; *After the Holidays*, 1987), an invocation of the life of the veteran Hebrew colony Petah Tikva under the British Mandate. But the calm and order associated with this environment are a veneer over seething turmoil, conflict, and misery.

K.'s narrative is apparently naturalistic, relating to the surfaces of Israeli life, but the underlying currents are tempestuous and cruel. Through the Weiss family, the tensions within the Jewish sector, as well as those between Jews and Arabs, are exposed. Also exposed is the unbearable frustration of the crabbed life, pretending to imperturbable normality amongst the orchards and against the backdrop of the nationalist politics of the emergent *yishuv* (prestate Zionist establishment). The passions seem to be ignited by the heat of the summer, and relief beckons only "after the holidays," in the autumn. Yet there is violence and evil in this apparently placid setting. Limpid, transparent prose presents the narrative simply, so the violence of the emotions stands in stark contrast to the manner of the telling. What seems to be the gratuitous violence of the characters Baruch and Langfuss as well as the more oblique spite of the two Weiss daughters and Masha stem from the ubiquitous sexual frustration that is so rampant in the colony.

The concerns evinced in the first novel reappear in K.'s second, *Haishah hagdoiah min hahalomot* (1973; the great woman of the dreams). This again is a story taken from everyday Israeli life, this time based in Tel Aviv. The characters once more are not notably successful in the management of their business and personal affairs. Once more, we have the eruption of extreme situations within an apparent context of social naturalism. But here there is an explicit movement in the direction of the grotesque and the surrealistic. This is hinted at in the title, so that the reader is unsure whether the subject is waking reality or dream. The characters are inarticulate, either because they lack the vocabulary to put their feelings into words or because the words themselves are trimmed to the social needs of the environment, whereas their feelings are much stronger. For K.'s characters, violence is the normal means of expression. The prose is direct, allowing the action, unfiltered, to indicate the underlying emotions. But even in the case of the pathetic Shmulik, there is a shadow archetype that stands behind and beyond his actual wife, Malka—the great, dark woman who haunts his fantasies. The "great woman" stands on the outside, but it is the "mad dog" within him that does not allow him to sleep. And it is this mad dog that he feels might take its revenge on him at any moment.

If there is one subject that lies at the center of K.'s writing, it is the way in which individual passion accommodates itself within Israeli society. This society is represented by the veteran colony and its new immigrants, by the disadvantaged poor of Tel Aviv, by the child moving into adolescence, and by the new recruits facing their test, their rites of passage, in the Israeli army. The collection of long stories *Moment muziqaliy* (1980; musical moment) revolves around childhood. The title story, referring to Schubert's "Moments Musicaux," recalls the deep impression it made on him.

The theme of life's significant transitions is also handled in K.'s subsequent novel, *Hitganvut yhidim* (1986; infiltration of individuals), which tells of a platoon of new recruits in the Israeli army of the 1950s. The first-person narrative draws a complex, composite picture of different types, facing a grueling and fundamental experience. K. recalls not just his own initiation, but that of a collective within Israeli society, its maturation (reaching its potential) and its loss of previous attachments and old worlds.

BIBLIOGRAPHY: Yudkin, L. I., on *Moment muziqaliy*, *MHL*, 6, 1–2 (Summer 1980), 84–85; Ramras-Rauch, G., on *Moment muziqaliy*, *WLT*, 55, 1 (Winter 1981), 171; Vardi, D., on *Haishah hagdoiah min hahalomot*, *WLT*, 61, 3 (Summer 1987), 487–88; Mazors, Y., on *After the Holidays*, *WLT*, 62, 1 (Winter 1988), 174

LEON I. YUDKIN

KENEALLY, Thomas

Australian novelist and dramatist, b. 7 Oct. 1935, Sydney

K. is one of the most prolific Australian novelists of the 20th c. His work covers a wide range of styles and subject matters, including suspense novels and mysteries, historical fiction, expressionism, and realism. His constant experimentation with literary forms and the consistent, craftsmanlike quality of his work have established K. as a major figure in world literature.

K. was brought up in a Catholic family, and Catholicism is a recurring issue in his novels. At St. Patrick's College in New South Wales K. originally studied for the priesthood, and these experiences formed the backdrop of *Three Cheers for the Paraclete* (1968), a novel about a priest who struggles with the "local taboos" of the Australian church. K. received praise for the objective and compassionate portrayals of his principal characters, and this talent for characterization has served him well in his later novels, many of which feature actual historical figures as characters. K.'s early work earned him the Miles Franklin Award in 1967 and 1968 and the Captain Cook Bi-Centenary Prize in 1970.

Following a brief period with the Australian Citizens Military Forces (1968–1970), K. published *A Dutiful Daughter* (1971). This novel, the story of an Australian family of which the parents are half-human and half-bovine, was a departure for K., as he abandoned the realistic plots and characters of his earlier works and experimented with expressionistic techniques. Although he has never duplicated such an extreme departure from realism in any later novel, K. has continued to experiment. *Passenger* (1979), for example, features a narrative written from an unborn child's point of view.

Although several of K.'s early novels deal with his native Australia, he is a truly international writer. *The Chant of Jimmie Blacksmith* (1972) is a compelling story of an aborigine forced into a life of crime. K.'s first historical novel, *Blood Red, Sister Rose* (1974), is a recounting of the story of Joan of Arc, and the highly praised *Gossip from the Forest* (1975) takes place at the signing of the armistice ending World War I. In *Confederates* (1979) K. creates a mosaic of a group of soldiers at the second battle of Antietam, and critics lauded the writer for the accuracy and "American-ness" of his presentation of the American Civil War. One of K.'s best-known books, *Schindler's List* (1982; pub. in U.K. as *Schindler's Ark*, 1982), is the novelization of the real-life story of Oskar Schindler, a German manufacturer who helped European Jews escape the Holocaust. In *A Family Madness* (1985) K. deals with cultural

conflicts in Australia. K.'s most recent novel is *Flying Hero Class* (1991).

While primarily regarded as a novelist, K. has established a successful reputation in other genres. His plays include *Halloran's Little Boat* (perf. 1966), *Childermass* (perf. 1968), and *An Awful Rose* (perf. 1972), all of which were produced in Sydney. His 1987 novel *The Playmaker* was adapted by Timberlake Wertenbaker (dates n.a.) as the play *Our Country's Good*, which enjoyed successful runs in both London and New York. He has written teleplays: *Essington* (1974) and *The World's Wrong End* (1981); travel literature: *Outback* (1983); and even a children's book: *Ned Kelley and the City of Bees* (1978).

The critical response to K.'s work has varied. Although generally responding favorably, many critics have been reluctant to accept K. as a true literary artist because of his prolific body of work and his general popularity. The critical debate over whether K. is a major literary figure or a strictly popular writer continues. But due to his consistent creativity and sensitive depiction of internationally accessible plots and characters, K. has established himself as an important figure in modern world literature.

FURTHER WORKS: *The Place at Whitton* (1964); *The Fear* (1965); *Bring Larks and Heroes* (1967); *The Survivor* (1969); *Moses the Lawgiver* (1975); *Season in Purgatory* (1976); *A Victim of the Aurora* (1977); *Bullie's House* (perf. 1980); *The Cut-Rate Kingdom* (1980); *Australia: Beyond the Dream Time* (1987, with Patsy Adam-Smith and Robyn Davidson); *To Asmara* (1989)

BIBLIOGRAPHY: Beston, J. B., "K.'s Violence," *JCL*, 9 (1974), 71–73; Breitinger, E., "T. K.'s Historical Novels," *Commwealth Newsletter*, 10 (1976), 16–20; Vargo, E. P., "Struggling with a Bugaboo: The Priest Character in Achebe and Greene and K.," in Narasimhaiah, C. D., ed., *Awakened Conscience: Studies in Commonwealth Literature* (1978), 284–93; Brady, V., "The Most Frightening Rebellion: The Recent Novels of T. K.," *Meanjin*, 38 (1979), 74–86; Erhardt, M., "T. K.: A Checklist," *ALS*, 9 (1979), 98–117; McInherny, F., "Woman and Myth in T. K.'s Fiction," *Meanjin*, 40 (1981), 248–58; Hulse, M., "Virtue and the Philosophic Innocent: The British Reception of *Schindler's Ark*," *CritQ*, 25, 4 (1983), 43–52; Goodwin, K., "Political Power and Social Flexibility in African and Australian Novels," *WLWE*, 23 (1984), 96–108; Magill, F. N., ed., *Cyclopedia of World Authors II* (1989), Vol. 3, 824–26; Buckbridge, P. "Gossip and

History in the Novels of Brian Penton and T. K.,''
ALS, 14, 4 (Oct. 1990), 436–49

JASON BERNER

KENNEDY, William
American novelist, b. 16 Jan. 1928, Albany, N.Y.

Few writers have remained so inspired by their place of birth as K. His novels have consistently drawn from the three-hundred-year history of his home city, Albany, New York. He observed, ''I write . . . as a person whose imagination has become fused with a single place, and in that place finds all the elements that a man ever needs for the life of the soul.'' Yet K.'s regard for his roots is complex. As the only child of a working-class couple from the Irish neighborhood of the North End, he admits that he didn't like the Albany of his youth. His restlessness motivated his leave-taking, but he eventually returned to Albany to channel his dissenting views into fiction. K.'s novels seek to reveal both the turpitude and the moral stature of his native characters. His creative focus clearly advanced beyond the depiction of social milieu with *Ironweed* (1983), which continued his exploration of contemporary Albany life, but revealed a more lyrical approach that expressed the interior lives of its characters.

After receiving a B.A. from Siena College, Loudonville, New York, in 1949, K. became an assistant sports editor and columnist for the *Post Star* in Glen Falls, New York, for one year, then served in the U.S. Army as a sports editor and columnist from 1950 to 1952. Returning to his home town he worked as a reporter for the Albany *Times-Union* between 1952 and 1956, then moved to San Juan, Puerto Rico, to become an assistant managing editor and columnist for the *Puerto Rican World Journal.* In 1957, however, he was in Miami, Florida, as a reporter for the Miami *Herald,* where he received an award from the Puerto Rican Civil Association of Miami for investigative reporting. K. returned to Puerto Rico as a correspondent for Time-Life Publications and Knight newspapers from 1957 to 1959. He helped found the San Juan *Star* and was its managing editor between 1959 and 1961, but spent much of his time writing fiction. Returning to Albany when his father became ill in 1961, he decided to resume work at the Albany *Times-Union.* As a special writer for this newspaper from 1963 to 1970, K. asked to work only part-time so that he could continue his creative writing in earnest. His investigative reporting during this period earned him the Page One Award from the Newspaper Guild and the NAACP Award for responsible reporting. For a series of articles on Albany slums, he re-

ceived the New York State Publishers Award for Community Service in 1965. That year K. also was nominated for the Pulitzer Prize in reporting.

While an Albany reporter, K. wrote his first novel, *The Ink Truck* (1969), which sold only a few thousand copies and remained underreviewed until its republication. His fellow Albany writer Doris Grumbach (b. 1918) secured him adjunct teaching assignments in creative writing at Empire State College, and he became a lecturer at the State University of New York at Albany from 1974 to 1982. The publication of *Legs* in 1975 began the ''Albany cycle'' of novels that would include *Billy Phelan's Greatest Game* (1978) and *Ironweed.* Saul Bellow (q.v.), who had K. as a writing student at the University of Puerto Rico, approached Viking Press to publish *Ironweed,* remarking on K.'s talent as a writer as evidenced in *Legs* and *Billy Phelan.* Viking agreed, also deciding to republish his previous novels during 1983 and 1984. K. became professor of English and was given tenure at State University of New York, Albany, in 1983 following the critical and popular success of *Ironweed,* which won both the Pulitzer Prize for fiction and the National Book Critics Circle Award in 1984. He was visiting professor at Cornell University during 1982–1983 and founder of the New York State Writers Institute in 1983.

Critics were impressed by the brilliant dialogue and expressive power of language in *The Ink Truck.* Using jargon from the city desk of an urban newspaper, phrases from the police blotter, language from local politicos, and slang from the Albany demimonde, K. sustained interest through sheer verbal energy and the believable eccentricities of his social character types.

Legs, the first novel of a trilogy that chronicled the vibrant past of Albany, featured the legendary 1930s criminal Jack ''Legs'' Diamond, whose gangster associations touched every class and culture in Albany. The clash of ethnic groups, the mix of gangsters, gamblers, and corrupt politicians, vivified by a narrator who is the gangster's legal advisor, led the reviewer Peter S. Prescott to comment that the novel ''translated the career of a gangster into a shimmering witty story that combined fact and myth to prod at our national ambivalence toward celebrity criminals.'' Other reviewers, while acknowledging K.'s ability to present compelling social types through an accurate historical context, remarked on the lack of moral vision in *Legs. Billy Phelan's Greatest Game* continued the history of the Albany underworld with its corrupt politicians and crossover characters. The novel's hyperactive plot structure included numerous flashbacks—some reviewers judged them unnecessary—tangential character disclosures, and abundant subplots. The dialogue is teeming with wit and creative neologisms; the characters are well-oiled and exuberant; and the complicated plot structure is matched by complex character delineations. For most critics, K.'s superb dialogue, idiosyncratic but with the feel of historical authenticity, and his revealing period characters compensated for the novel's unfocused and overdeveloped plot structure. *Ironweed*, K.'s third novel in the series, departs substantially from his earlier fiction in its lyrical style, poetically charged with language that often approaches the surreal. Amidst the bleakness of vagrant existence the main characters seek the significance of their lives. The inner dialogue, supplely crafted and imaginative, produces both heartfelt and satirical perceptions, and contributes to the novel's lyricism. Plot construction also shows an advance over K.'s previous novels. For example, the economical device of a returning ghost allows K. to eschew the rhetorical flourishes on the father-son theme evident in *Billy Phelan*. The characters of *Ironweed* speak a variety of rhetorical idioms and at times seem Joycean in their texture and social context.

K.'s interest in the formative years of American history produced *Quinn's Book* (1988), a wide-ranging novel centered on Daniel Quinn, a Civil War reporter whose curiosity leads him to describe the tumultuous social life of that era. Spanning the years 1849 to 1864, the plot has been criticized for lacking cohesiveness, much as *Legs* and *Billy Phelan* had been. However, its compelling scenes reflect many of the social and political tensions of the period, so that the episodic structure seems less chaotic. K.'s gift for presenting strong, colorful characters in fast-paced scenes is evident, even though his 19-c. dialogue often seems anachronistic.

K.'s gift for situating interesting historical characters has offered a deep appreciation of American popular culture. Part of his ability to create personable and forceful characters results from a journalist's ear for dialogue grounded in idioms evocative of the attitudes and experiences of certain American professions and historical periods. In one novel, *Ironweed*, the subjective dimensions of human life are given lyric stature even as its characters are framed within a realistic social milieu.

FURTHER WORKS: *O Albany!: An Urban Tapestry* (1983); *The Cotton Club* (1984, with Francis Ford Coppola); *Charlie Malarkey and the Belly Button Machine* (1986, with Brendan Christopher Kennedy); *Ironweed* (film script, 1987); *Very Old Bones* (1992)

BIBLIOGRAPHY: Croyden, M., "The Sudden Fame of W. K.," *NYTMag* (26 Aug. 1984), 33ff.; Murtaugh, D. M., "Fathers and Their Sons," *Commonweal*, 116 (26 Aug. 1984), 32–35; Bonetti, K., "An Interview with W. K.," *Mississippi Review*, 8, 2 (1985), 71–86; Thompson, D., "The Man Has Legs: W. K. Interviewed," *Film Comment*, 21 (Mar.–Apr. 1985), 54–59; Whittaker, S., "The Lawyer As Narrator in W. K.'s *Legs*," *Legal Studies Forum*, 9, 2 (1985), 157–64; Black, D., "The Fusion of Past and Present in W. K.'s *Ironweed*," *Crit*, 27 (Spring 1986), 177–84; Clark, P. P., "Classical Myths in W. K.'s *Ironweed*," *Crit*, 27, 3 (Spring 1986), 167–76; Robertson, M., "The Reporter As Novelist: The Case of W. K.," *Columbia Journalism Review*, 24 (Jan.–Feb. 1986), 49–50; McCaffery, L., and S. Gregory, eds., *Alive and Writing; Interviews with American Authors of the 1980s* (1987), 157–74; Parini, J., "Man of Ironweed," *Horizon*, 30 (Dec. 1987), 35–36

WILLIAM OVER

KENYAN LITERATURE

See Volume 2, page 577.

Kenyan literature in English has its roots in autobiographical narratives that recount the personal and group histories of the authors. Although most African literature in European languages could also in some way lay claim to this putative genealogy, Kenya's experience as a settler colony perhaps gives the country its unique position in East Africa. Life in colonial Kenya was characterized by the expropriation of land by the settlers. The alienation of the land was later to enhance the proliferation of books panegyric of communal life and of its ties to the land. In those books, the struggle for the land and the Mau Mau movement occupy a special place.

With independence, however, came a host of new problems. The new state was unable to deliver on its promises. People were left to believe that political independence would be a panacea for all of their misery and deprivation. Without the promised solutions in sight, dashed hopes and unrealized dreams marked the Kenyan landscape. Themes dealing with this new reality are a major component of African postindependent literature. As the new realities took hold of an unsuspecting populace, some writers looked for a way out. Others found consolation in a nostalgic search for a golden past that perhaps never existed. The strength of Kenyan literature of this time lies in its avoidance of romanticization of the past. Ngugi wa Thiong'o's (q.v.) *Petals of Blood* (1977), which sets the pace for the literature of this era, shows his understanding of the dynamics of postindependent Kenya, and reflects his basic understanding that a romanticization of the past does not only breed a prisoner to a remote past but also blurs one's vision of the present and future—that by ruminating on a wistful past one loses twice. Most other Kenyan writers have successfully managed to steer away from an undue fascination with the past and are now trying to come to grips with the socioeconomic problems of the here and now.

The reluctance to delve into the past in search of clues and answers for contemporary issues may reflect three things. First, it reveals the need for a new analysis of Kenyan society as old issues such as white versus black, familiarized by some of the early books, become obsolete. Secondly, a revival of such issues as the Mau Mau will ironically show how independent Kenya is not yet free; it is perhaps in this sense that writers are wary of stepping on the government's toes. Finally, the reluctance to deal with the past may emanate from practical considerations on the part of publishers as to what is popular with the reading public. As a result of these new realities, Kenyan literature of the past decade has turned inward and in the process has become more reflective of the country's ethnic diversity.

With the compartmentalization of Kenyan society, the individual as an embodiment of communal values, typical of the more immediate postindependent literature, gave way to a portrayal of a more pronounced individual character. David Maillu (b. 1939), by some accounts Kenya's most successful popular writer, typifies authors who create such a character. In *Ayah* (1986; housemaid) he deals with the fate of a housemaid who is both exploited by a mean wife and raped by an unscrupulous master. In *Untouchable* (1987) he depicts the contumacy of two lovers who are determined to have their way in an environment that is not yet ready for an interracial relationship.

Asenath Bole Odaga (dates n.a.), like her more famous compatriot Grace Ogot (b. 1930), deals with Luo social realities in her novels and in her studies on the oral literature. In *A Bridge of Time* (1987) the disintegration of the family is shown first through a devastating power struggle between a man, his son, and his brother, and later through a heinous love triangle between the son, his cousin, and the beauty of the village. In her latest novel, *Riana* (1991), the eponymous heroine's defiance of such social institutions as polygamy and levirate among her people attests to women coming of age in Luo land and, by extension, Kenya.

In an attempt to reverse the thematic trend in African literature in which most writers attempting to show the inequality between town and village all too often focus on the influx of people from rural to urban centers, Meja Mwangi (b. 1948), undeniably one of the most talented writers on the East African literary scene, adopts the countryside as the setting of his latest novel *Striving for the Wind* (1991). Rampant corruption, flagrant injustice, and squalid living conditions caused by class and gender difference are realistically depicted. Reminiscent of Maillu's *After 4:30* (1974) but without its alleged pornographic aspects, Mwangi's novel, as well as Odaga's *Riana,* emphasize the need for an urgent reappraisal of the lot of women in Kenyan society. This preoccupation with women's issues, as we shall see later on, is a tendency that Kenyan literature in English shares with that in Swahili.

H(enry) R. Ole Kulet (b. 1946) has left behind the themes of his first two books, *Is It Possible?* (1971) and *To Become A Man* (1972). In both novels he had skillfully depicted the corrosive effects of colonial education and of culture shock on the Maasai. Kulet now champions the environmental cause, which has of late become an international concern since the African elephant is threatened with extinction. In *The Hunter* (1985) Kulet shows the intricacies and dangers involved in divulging the guarded secrets of the mafialike poaching business in Kenya. In *Daughter of Maa* (1987) he depicts how the arrival of a woman teacher at a village is viewed both with suspicion by the wives and with admiration by the husbands who surreptitiously covet her.

The keen observer of Kenyan literature cannot miss noticing the paucity of English drama and poetry writing. With the exception of Ngugi, Micere Mugo (b. 1942), Francis Imbuga (b. 1947), Jared Angira (b. 1947), and Jonathan Kariara (b. 1935), Kenya has not produced well-known dramatists and poets.

A discussion of Kenyan literature would be incomplete without a look at other languages, especially at the literature written in Swahili. Of the forty-six Kenyan languages, Swahili has certainly produced the most works. Writing in Swahili cuts across ethnic lines. In a marked difference with Kenyan literature in English, Swahili literature does abound with poetry and drama. Prose fiction, perhaps indicative of an overall tradition in Swahili literature, has lagged behind poetry and drama. Two recent novels in Swahili worthy of mention are Angaluki Muaka's (b. 1958) *Ushuhuda wa mwanachuo* (1986; testimony of a student), a story about the role of students in society, how they formulate and express the aspirations of the people, and how the university as an institution is a microcosm of Kenyan society; and Ari Katini

Mwachofi's (dates n.a.) *Mama ee* (1987; O mother), which shows the valiant struggle of women against male chauvinism and the dominant culture that produces it.

Two plays that also espouse the cause of women are Chacha Nyaigoti Chacha's (b. 1952) *Mke mwenza* (1982; cowife), which raises social and emotional issues such as jealousy and infertility; and Alamin Mazrui's (b. 1948) *Kilio cha haki* (1981; a cry for justice) about the exploitation of workers and the rise of a woman leader who spearheads the struggle for their rights.

Ahmed Sheikh Nabhany (b. 1927), one of the leading contemporary Swahili poets, has two recent collections of poems: *Umbuji wa mnazi* (1985; compositions about the coconut) and *Umbuji wa Kiwandeyo* (1985; compositions about Lamu), which deals with various aspects of life, language, and culture. Alamin Mazrui has also a collection of poems, *Chembe cha moyo* (1988; arrow in my heart). These love and hate poems are heavily laden with symbolism.

Writing in Kikuyu vies for second place in Kenyan literature of indigenous languages. Ngugi's commitment to writing in his mother tongue no doubt enhances its development. His latest novel, *Matigari* (1987; *Matigari,* 1989), shows a close affinity with the Ng'ano (narrative) tradition of his Kikuyu culture. The eponymous hero is endowed with superhuman qualities that frustrate his opponent's endeavors to label him as one thing or another. The omnipresence of Matigari and his immunity to death are adeptly employed to reveal the vulnerability and frailty of those in power. The novel is also a pertinent reminder that the Mau Mau movement is far from being jettisoned from Kenyan history.

Other Kenyan languages, such as Dholou and Kamba, have also produced written literatures. It is hoped, however, that the drive for the production of indigenous literatures would not lead to further fragmentation of Kenyan society. Rather, the proliferation of written indigenous literatures will, one hopes, contribute to the forging of a new Kenyan national consciousness.

BIBLIOGRAPHY: Ngugi wa Thiong'o, *Homecoming: Essays on African and Caribbean Literature, Culture and Politics* (1972); Baker, H. A., Jr., *The Journey Back* (1980); Killam, G. D., ed., *The Writing of East and Central Africa* (1984); Ngara, E., *Art and Ideology in the African Novel* (1985); Jeyifo, B., ed., *Wole Soyinka: Art, Dialogue and Outrage* (1988); Priebe, R. K., *Myth, Realism and the West African Writer* (1988); Wanjiku, M. K., and K. W. Muthi, *Gikuyu Oral Literature* (1988); Ngara, E., and A. Morrison, *Literature, Language and the Nation* (1989); Smith, A., *East African Writing in English* (1989); Harrow, K. W., ed., *Faces of Islam in African Literature* (1991)

ALI JIMALE AHMED

KHÁI-HƯNG

(anagrammatized pseud. of [Trần] Khánh Giư) Vietnamese novelist, short-story writer, and dramatist, b. 1896, Hai-duong; d. 1947, Nam-dinh

K.-H. was the cofounder in 1933 of the "Self-Reliant" literary group and also one of its most prolific writers. Son of a provincial mandarin, he had a traditional education in Sino-Vietnamese letters followed by a French education, and chose first to be a teacher. Later the French authorities arrested him for his anticolonial politics and deported him to the highlands of northern Vietnam. Upon his release in 1943, he resumed his political activities, especially after the "August revolution" of 1945, but as a member of the Vietnamese Nationalist Party he was murdered by the communist Vietminh shortly after the French-Vietnamese hostilities broke out in December 1946. The exact date of K.-H.'s death is unknown.

His first three novels were idealistic, but later he dealt with local customs and mores, with emphasis on psychological characterizations. *Hồn bướ mơ tiên* (1933; butterfly soul dreaming of immortals) is about the pure love between Ngọc and a Buddhist novice, who actually is a disguised beautiful young woman. Lan, the latter, torn between love and religion, decides that she is more dedicated to her religious faith and plans to escape to the highlands and enter a remote temple. But the young man talks her out of it, swears that in his continuing friendship he would control his desire and that he would remain a bachelor and "only live in the dream world of idealistic platonic love." He further expresses his noble sentiment to Lan, "A family? I don't have a family any more: my extended family now is humankind, the universe, while my small family is our two souls hiding under the merciful shadow of Buddha." In *Nửa chừng xuân* (1934; unfinished spring), Mai, a pretty, intelligent, and noble girl in love with a mandarin's son, is determined to end the "illicit life" they have spent together. In the light of her sacrifice, Lộc, her husband, is just an ordinary young man, who has given a son to this young woman, but abandoned her after his manipulating mother made him suspect her of being unfaithful. When he argues that he is going to convert his love for his family into love for humanity and to devote his talent and energy to help society, the reader realizes that the author simply does not want a reunion to take place, so that their love could become idealized.

In his third novel, *Trống Mái* (1936; rooster and hen), K.-H. gave the idealization of his fiction a new twist, the praise of physical beauty: Hiền, a city girl, falls in love with a humble fisherman, or rather with his well-built physique. The author wants her to like Vọi the way an artist likes a beautiful statue, but critics have found this case of platonic love unrealistic. *Thử-tự* (1940: heir) belongs to a different category: It is a psychological novel, in which the author examines various corrupt practices in traditional Vietnamese society, particularly that of choosing at any price a descendant to be one's heir, reflecting the ancestral cult. In contrast, *Hạnh* (1940: Hanh) is a short novel with an educational focus since it features a shy and weak schoolteacher with an inferiority complex, afraid to face women in general. K.-H.'s short stories reveal him to be a keen, observant writer about the young Vietnamese generation of his time. His style went from floweriness to simplicity, and was definitely typical of the unfettered, flowing style, slightly influenced by French writings, that won K.-H.—and his associates—the admiration of readers, especially female readers. K.-H. showed that he perfectly understood Vietnamese women, their feelings, prejudices, and maneuvers.

FURTHER WORKS *Gánh hàng hoa* (1934, with Nhất-Linh); *Đời mưa gió* (1934, with Nhất-Linh); *Dọc đường gió bụi* (1936); *Anh phải sống* (1937, with Nhất-Linh); *Tục-luy* (1937); *Tiếng suối reo* (1937); *Gia-đình* (1938); *Thoát-ly* (1939); *Đợi chờ* (1939); *Tiêu-sơn tráng-sĩ* (1940); *Đẹp* (1940); *Đôi Mũ lệch* (1941); *Những ngày vui* (1941); *Đồng bệnh* (1942); *Bắn-khoăn* (1943)

BIBLIOGRAPHY: Durand, M. M., and Nguyễn-Trần Huân, *An Introduction to Vietnamese Literature* (1985), 182–91 and passim; Bùi Xuân-Bào, *Le roman vietnamien contemporain* (1972), 143–64 and passim; Huỳnh Sanh Thông, "Main Trends of Vietnamese Literature between the Two World Wars," *The Vietnam Forum,* 3 (Winter–Spring 1984), 99–125

DINH-HOA NGUYEN

al-KHĀL, Yūsuf

Lebanese poet and critic, b. 1917, Tripoli; d. 1987, Paris, France

Born in a Christian family from Tripoli, where he attended secondary school, K. graduated in 1944 from the American University of Beirut in philosophy and English, and went into teaching. He left

Beirut in 1948 for the U.S., where he worked at the United Nations office first, then started an export business, while editing at the same time the Arabic paper *al-Hudā*. There he made the acquaintance of American poets like Archibald MacLeish, Ezra Pound, and T. S. Eliot (qq.v.). Back in Beirut in 1955, after a stay in Libya and Geneva, he advocated a new poetic mentality in addition to the new forms introduced by the young Iraqi poets Badr Shākir al-Sayyāb and Nāzik al-Malā'ika (qq.v.). It was this combination of a new mentality and the new form that marked the work of K. and his colleagues at the literary review *Shiʿr* which from 1957 to 1964 was the most important forum for ideas on change and modernism (q.v.) in Arabic literature.

However, the new review, founded in January 1957, did not fit in well with the spirit of *iltizām* or commitment that was propagated by the group of poets and writers at the other Beirutian review, *al-Ādāb,* started in 1953 by Suhayl Idrīs and still existing today. K. had to stop the experiment after a serious conflict with his most talented Syrian colleague, Adūnīs (pseud. of ʿAlī Ahmad Saʿīd, q.v.), and after persistent rumors from outside that the *Shiʿr* group was infiltrated by Syrian nationalist elements. In 1967 K. started publishing the review again in a new form and with another editorial board, but it was no longer the avant-garde review it had been. K. also founded an art gallery, Gallery One, and a publishing house, Dār Majallat Shiʿr, which published work of the main representatives of the New Poetry propagated by *Shiʿr*. For a short time he edited also the literary revue *Adab* which existed from 1965 to 1966. In the 1970s K. devoted himself to a new translation of the Bible. During the Lebanese civil war he lived in Paris, where he died after having been decorated with the Lebanese Order of Merit. He expressed his bitterness about the Lebanese situation in *Rasā'il ilā Dūn Kīshūt* (1979; letters to Don Quixote).

As a poet, K. followed first Saʿīd ʿAql (q.v.) and his symbolist interpretation of reality in his first volumes, *Hurriyyah* (1945; liberty) and *Hīrūdiya* (1954; Herodias). Then he started to translate poetry of American poets, which he published together with Adūnīs in an anthology in 1958, notably Eliot's *The Waste Land* (1922). This reading fundamentally transformed his ideas about poetry. In 1958 he published in free verse *al-Bi'r al-mahjūrah* (the forsaken well), followed in 1960 by *Qasā'id fī l-arbaʿīn* (poems at the age of forty). In the first selection, dedicated to Pound, K. presents the poet as a new Christ in his struggle to revive Arabic poetry, whose task it is to redeem people from the past and to face the reality of the present. In its vision, life in the Arab world is marked by sterility, and the poet prays for another and better world in which people will find the well and drink from it. In the second selection of poems one notes a metaphysical dimension and a hopeful vision of the world, which will transcend suffering and death. By his reliance on fertility myths K. ranges himself in the group of so-called Tammuz-ists, which include also al-Sayyāb, Adūnīs, Jabrā Ibrāhīm Jabrā, and Khalīl Hāwī (qq.v.). In later criticism K. advocated the use of the vernacular for serious literary purposes, but he never published poetry in dialect like, for example, Saʿīd ʿAql or Mīshāl Trād (b. 1913).

FURTHER WORKS: *Al aʿmāl al-shiʿriyya al-kāmila* (1973); *Al-Wilāda al-thaniyya* (1981)

BIBLIOGRAPHY: Jargy, S., "Poètes arabes d'avant-garde," *Orient*, 18 (1961), 147–72; Badawi, M. M., *A Critical Introduction to Modern Arabic Poetry* (1975), 241–45; Moreh, S., *Modern Arabic Poetry 1800–1970* (1976), 278–88; Jayyusi, S. K., *Trends and Movements in Modern Arabic Poetry* (1977), Vol. 2, 569–73; Kheir Beik, K., *Le mouvement moderniste de la poésie arabe contemporaine* (1978), passim; Zeidan, J., "Myth and Symbol in the Poetry of Adūnīs and Y. al-K.", *JArabL*, 10 (1979), 70–94; Jayyusi, S. K., ed., *Modern Arabic Poetry: An Anthology* (1987), 295–99; Allen, R., ed., *Modern Arabic Literature* (1987), 180–3

ED C. M. DE MOOR

al-KHARRĀT, Edwar

(also spelled Edward in English) Egyptian novelist, short-story writer, translator, and critic, b. 16 Mar. 1926, Alexandria

K. was born into a Coptic family and brought up and educated in Alexandria at Coptic and state schools. After his father's death in 1943, K. worked as a storeman for the British navy to help support his family while he completed his studies. He graduated in law from Alexandria University in 1946 and went to work as a clerk in the Egyptian National Bank. Active in a Trotskyist movement opposed to King Farouk and the British presence in Egypt, K. was arrested and held in concentration camps from 1948 to 1950. After his release he worked for an insurance company until 1955, when he resigned to finish writing his first collection of short stories. Subsequently he worked as press and public-relations officer for the Romanian embassy in Cairo and in 1959 joined the staff of the Afro-Asian Peoples' Solidarity Organization and the Afro-Asian Writers' Union, eventually becoming assistant secretary-general of both or-

ganizations. In 1983 he resigned to devote himself to writing.

The stories in K.'s first collection, *Hitān ʿāliyah* (1959; high walls), like much of his later work, are poetically rooted in the daily life of Alexandria or the Egyptian countryside. However, their concern with isolation and guilt and the introspective, experimental nature of the writing were out of keeping with the prevailing tradition in Egyptian fiction, which was still outward-looking, positive, and inspired by national pride. During the 1960s, with the changing political and cultural climate, K.'s work began to receive more critical acclaim, and, as a critic and as a writer, he became an influential figure in the "new wave" of Egyptian writing, the so-called Sixties Generation. He was on the editorial board of the avant-garde periodical *Galīrī 68,* where many of the best short-story writers and critics published their work in the late 1960s.

K. is fluent in English and French and has translated works of fiction into Arabic, including those of American and African writers. He demonstrated his continuing concern with the state of new writing, the publishing industry, and related social issues in Egypt when he compiled *Mukhtārāt al-qissah al-qasīrah fī'l-sabʿīnīyāt* (1982; an anthology of the short story in the 1970s), which has an extensive critical introduction.

His second collection, *Saʿāt al-kibriyāʾ* (1972; hours of pride), which won the State Prize for the short story, anticipates the radical stylistic features that were to characterize K.'s work increasingly over the next two decades, with characters whose identities merge at some points, contradictory accounts of the same events, abrupt movements back and forth in time and space, and an iconoclastic use of Christian and Pharaonic allusions and symbols. Female characters are almost always at the center of the action, sometimes assuming superhuman proportions as saint-whore figures for the invariably male narrator, and arousing in him feelings of compassion, guilt, suspicion, ecstasy, and moral bewilderment.

K.'s first novel, *Rāma wa'l-tinnīn* (1979; Rama and the dragon), was a literary event in the Arab world, acknowledged by critics and other novelists as having effectively severed connections with the structure of the modern novel in Arabic established by Najīb Mahfūz (q.v.). Each chapter is autonomous and yet related to the others. Legends from Eastern and Western traditions are used to illuminate and expand both each other and the new text, which is a blend of poetry, fiction, history, and philosophical debates on love, sex, and communication or its impossibility. Narrative traditions are ignored, questioned, or inverted, and the language is poetic and metaphorical throughout, but accessible, even demotic, in a way that much of experimental literary language is not.

From *Rāma wa-al-tinnīn* onwards, K.'s works are increasingly hard to classify in terms of genre. Although usually described as novels, they are more like interlocking stories with recurring autobiographical elements, such as the memories of wartime Alexandria in *Turābuhā za'farān* (1986; *City of Saffron,* 1989), which are worked and reworked in different combinations and contexts in a vivid portrayal of the alternating blissful security and bottomless terror of childhood experiences.

Sometimes the scenes and images are violently juxtaposed or change abruptly in ways that are not always successful, however the essentially cerebral context of words and silent imaginative responses may be stretched and modified in experimental writing. In addition, the dreamlike or surreal episodes appear to have too tenuous a relationship with the perceived meanings of the text and the physical reality so carefully and often exquisitely constructed by K. But he sees the novel form as being open to almost unlimited adaptations and developments. Through it he returns again and again to such subjects as the ambiguities of moral responsibility and choice, the spiritual aspects of sexual passion and human suffering, and the relationship between love and knowledge, treating them in such a fashion that the meanings remain fluid and open to varying interpretations. The immediately accessible sense and imaginative power of his writing come from the masterly way he evokes the distinctive qualities of places, characters, and events through a wealth of description of textures, smells, tastes, and sounds.

FURTHER WORKS: *Ikhtināqāt al-'ishq wa-al-sabāh* (1983); *Mahattat al-sikka al-hadīd* (1985); *Al-zaman al-ākhar* (1985); *Adlā' al-sahrā'* (1987); *Yā banāt iskandariyyah* (1990); *Makhlūqāt al-ashwāq al-tā'irah* (1990); *Amwāj al-layālī* (1991)

BIBLIOGRAPHY: Cobham, C., "'An Open Wound' by K.," *JArabL,* 15 (1984), 121–34; Ayyād, S., and N. Witherspoon, "Elation and Solitude," *Reflections and Deflections* (1986), 255–58; Barbulesco, L., and P. Cardinal, "Portrait: Entretien et questionnaire," *L'Islam en question* (1986), 87–92; Fontaine, J., "Le nouveau roman égyptien (1975–1985)," *IBLA,* 158 (1986), 245–58; al-Shārūnī, Y., S. Hāfiz, and N. 'Atiyya, "K.," in Allen, R., ed., *Modern Arabic Literature* (1987), 183–87; Cardinal, P., "K., les clés d'Égypte," *Liberation,* 9 Mar. 1988, 38; K., "The Mashriq," in Ostle, R. C., ed., *Modern Literature in the Near and Middle East 1850–1970* (1991), 180–92

CATHERINE COBHAM

KHATIBI, Abdelkebir

Moroccan novelist and essayist (writing in French), b. 1938, El Jadida

After attending Koranic school and the École Franco-Musulmane, K. went at the age of twelve to boarding school in Marrakesh where he discovered French literature and culture, an experience which he has described in his autobiographical novel, *La mémoire tatouée* (1971; the tatooed memory). K. studied sociology at the Sorbonne (1958–1964). His 1965 doctorat de 3ᵉ Cycle entailed a thesis on *Le roman maghrébin* (1968; rev. ed., 1979; the Maghrebian novel). He directed the Institut de Sociologie in Rabat from 1966 until it was integrated into the university in 1970. He is currently a university research professor at the Institute of Scientific Research in Rabat. K.'s dual vision as writer and sociologist has played a significant role in defining his writing, which often links creative impulses and such social phenomena as the cinema, urban layout or planning, onomastics, art appreciation, tattoos, superstition, the acts of reading and writing, and psychoanalysis.

The publication of K.'s first and best-known work, *La mémoire tatouée,* signaled a new approach to writing in Morocco. The fragmented postmodern structure of the work, so different from the earlier well-wrought novels of writers like Driss Chraïbi of Morocco, Mouloud Feraoun, Mohammed Dib, and Mouloud Mammeri of Algeria, and Albert Memmi (qq.v.) of Tunisia, reflects K.'s interest in modern linguistics and the critical theory of Roland Barthes, Jacques Derrida (qq.v.), and others.

With the possible exception of *La mémoire tatouée* and *Un été à Stockholm* (1991; a summer in Stockholm), K.'s works defy easy classification by genre, and even those two works do not have the tight structural integrity we associate with the conventional novel. His works labeled "novels" often seem to be essays, and his essays include highly poetic, oneiric, or anecdotal passages, and in most of the works there is a sense of ritual and drama due to K.'s extensive use of dialogue—the "images" liminary to *La mémoire tatouée*—framing of characters in stagelike or still scenes: *Le livre du sang* (1979; the book of blood) and *Ombres japonaises* (1988; Japanese shadow play). Paradoxically, actual drama, *Le prophète voilé* (1979; the veiled prophet), and poetry, *Le lutteur de classe à la manière taoïste* (1976; the ranking Tao-style wrestler) and *Dédicace à l'année qui vient*

(1986; a dedication for the coming year), are not K.'s strongest suits.

Both K.'s creative works and theoretical writings, which reinforce one another, have had considerable influence on Maghrebian writers of his generation. Tahar Ben Jelloun's (q.v.) first novel, *Harrouda* (1973; Harrouda), was inspired in part by *La mémoire tatouée*, and Nabile Fares (b. 1941) of Algeria and Abdelwahab Meddeb (b. 1946) of Tunisia may well have been encouraged in the pursuit of their own particular idioms as a result of K.'s success in exploiting code mixing and the use of "intersemiotics" in his works.

In such works as *La blessure du nom propre* (1974; the wound of the proper noun/name), *Amour bilingue* (1983; *Love in Two Languages,* 1990), and various essays on bilingualism and diglossia, especially *Maghreb pluriel* (1983; plural Maghreb), and the papers of a conference organized by K. and published under the title *Du bilinguisme* (1985; on bilingualism), K. has championed a constructive interpretation of interference in Maghrebian writing, in which the writer's mother tongue acts upon the acquired French in which he or she writes, providing a discourse based on "interior calligraphy" and resulting in an aesthetics of the "palimpsest" prominent, if not unique, in francophone and other bilingual literatures. It is when K. indulges in his passion for bilingualism and what he terms the "captation" of hidden psycholinguistic impulses—as in his reflections on parapraxis and word associations in *Amour bilingue* and *Par-dessus l'épaule* (1988; over one's shoulder) —or in the development of his narrative on a nonlinear basis—as in *Le livre du sang* and the passages reminiscent of vintage K. in the second half of *Un été à Stockholm*—that he is at his best. Even as K. brings into question the standard recipes that long governed literature, he loads language with a dynamics beyond entertainment and didacticism, giving it an importance akin to that generally accorded religion.

FURTHER WORKS: *Vomito blanco* (1974); *L'art calligraphique arabe* (1976, with Mohamed Sijelmassi); *De la mille et troisième nuit* (1980); *Le même livre* (1985, with Jacques Hassoun); *Figures de l'étranger dans la littérature française* (1987)

BIBLIOGRAPHY: Gontard, M., *Violence du texte* (1981), 80–114; Déjeux, J., *Dictionnaire des auteurs maghrébins de langue française* (1984), 242–43; Memmi, A., *Écrivains francophones du Maghreb* (1985), 194–99; Tenkoul, A., *Littérature maghrébine d'écriture française* (1985), 131–44; Buci-Glucksmann, C., et al., *Imaginaires de l'autre: K. et la mémoire littéraire* (1987); special K. issue, *CelfanR,* 8, 1–2 (Nov. 1988–Feb. 1989);

Sellin, E., "Obsession with the White Page, the Inability to Communicate, and Surface Aesthetics in the Development of Contemporary Maghrebian Fiction: The 'Mal de la page blanche' in K., Farès, and Meddeb," *IJMES,* 20, 2 (May 1988), 165–73

ERIC SELLIN

KIHLMAN, Christer Alfred

Finnish novelist (writing in Swedish), b. 14 June 1930, Helsinki

K.'s family background is important for an understanding of his work: His great-grandfather, Alfred Kihlman (1825–1914), was a provincial schoolmaster who, called to the Swedish Normal Lyceum, a new "model school" in Helsinki, carried on a distinguished pedagogical and political career while simultaneously becoming an industrialist; the "Kihlman Mansion," from the 1890s, still stands in the capital. His son Lorenzo (1861–1941) was a jurist remembered in particular for his opposition to Czarist rule; Lorenzo's sons were the critic and editor Erik (1895–1933) and the translator and novelist Bertel (1898–1977), who assumed the editorship of the important journal *Nya Argus* after Erik's death in a car accident. Thus Bertel's son, Christer, seemed destined for a life of literary activity and public responsibility. As an angry young man, revolting against his background (variously called "aristocratic" and "bourgeois" by him), he published the little magazine *Arena* together with Jörn Donner, was a member of the circle around the poet Gunnar Björling (qq.v.), and brought out two verse books of his own. Employed as a reviewer by the Helsinki afternoon paper *Nya Pressen* and occasionally by Stockholm's *Dagens Nyheter,* he caught general Scandinavian attention with an article, "Svenskhetens slagskugga" (1959; "The Shadow Cast by Swedishness," 1986), on what he considered the privileged, artificial, and sterile life led by Finland's Swedish-speaking patricianate.

The attack was a forerunner of the novel *Se upp salige!* (1960; pay heed, o blest!), in which K. depicted the allegedly rotten establishment of a small town, Lexå, modeled on Porvoo (Swedish: Borgå), a place of historical and cultural importance, where the venerated national poet Johan Ludvig Runeberg (1804–1877) had dwelt. A well-meaning newspaper editor, the scion of an eminent family, undertakes numerous efforts, egged on by a leftist Finnish friend, to reveal the manifold hypocrisies of his milieu, but these projects all fall flat. Simultaneously, erotically fascinated by the friend's adolescent daughter, he neglects his son, who commits suicide. The book was received in some quarters as "the best Finland-Swedish novel in a very long time" (in it, K. had displayed his wonderfully pliant style to the full); but other voices called it a hateful and distorted parody on K.'s own cultural tradition.

Den blå modern (1962; *The Blue Mother,* 1990) is a kind of sequel; much of it likewise takes place in Lexå, and more is learned about the circumstances surrounding the death of the editor's son. Its main focus, though, is on two brothers and their male cousin, all members of the Lindermann family. One brother is an author and an alcoholic, sporadically unfaithful to his wife; the other is a homosexual whose fantasies of himself as commandant at Auschwitz represent the most shocking passages of the book. The depiction of the larger social and economic background is shadowy (in contrast to Donner's later portrayals of somewhat the same world in his novels); what matters to K. is the plumbing of tormented souls: The soft blue mother of the title may be a dream, for the brothers' actual mother has been selfish and uncaring, partially responsible for their emotional deformations. Again, the novel caused a sensation; some critics found it turgid, in thrall to the torrents of words K. had found in William Faulkner and the Swedish novelist Lars Ahlin (qq.v.). The story was continued with *Madeleine* (1965; Madeleine); after the black comedy of *Se upp salige!* and the horrors of *Den blå modern,* the narrative, in diary form, has a curious idyllic tone—the marital storm eventually passes by.

Madeleine opens and closes on the day of John F. Kennedy's assassination, an event which—as K. asserted, not altogether logically—gave the final blow to his "belief and trust in a liberal bourgeois order of society." This claim was made in *Människan som skalv* (1971; the human being who trembled), a confession of K.'s alcoholism and his bisexuality, culminating in an encounter à trois between K.'s wife, a male friend, and himself. K. declared that, by his candor, he meant to contribute to a cleansing of a society defiled by capitalism. The book became a best-seller in Swedish and Finnish, a success that persuaded K. to go back on his pledge in 1966 to write no more novels since a Finland-Swedish author could not live by his pen alone. Subsequently, his production continued apace, divided between confessional and creative literature. Cultivating the former genre, he twice told about his involvements, during trips to South America, with male prostitutes: first in *Alla mina söner* (1980; *All My Sons,* 1984), where he likened himself to Saul and his ward (who had ambitions as a vocalist) to David, and again in *Livsdrömmen rena: Bok om maktlöshet* (1982; the pure dream of life: book about powerlessness), in which the author experiences the bliss of an au-

tomobile trip with a young companion through Uruguay, the living-out of a boyhood dream. *På drift i förlustens landskap* (1986; adrift in the landscape of loss) was much less ecstatic in tone, complaining bitterly about the infidelity of a neglected wife and about K.'s writer's block.

A decade before, K. had returned to the novel with *Dyre prins* (1975; *Sweet Prince,* 1983), about Donald Blaadh, a financial genius who comes out of nowhere after the Russo-Finnish War of 1941–1944, makes an opportunistic first marriage to a communist, and then weds a member of the wealthy Lindermann clan. The book has been called both a "Finland-Swedish *Buddenbrooks*" and a soap opera. Slowly, Donald realizes that he has neglected his children in pursuit of his career as an international financier—two of his six offspring commit suicide. (It was in search of more models for the Blaadh-Bladh family that K. first went to South America.) In *Gerdt Bladhs undergång* (1987; *The Death of Gerdt Bladh,* 1989) another branch of the clan has center stage. Recovered from his spiritual crisis, Donald lives in Spain with a new mistress, while his nephew Gerdt is the head of a great Helsinki department store. The old concerns of K. reappear (Gerdt has a weakness for young boys and is cuckolded by his wife); but the Finland-Swedish establishment, rapidly losing power in actual fact, is treated more gently than before, and an element of the supernatural has been added to K.'s complex intrigue. In Gerdt's youth, an admired older cousin committed suicide, and his energetic soul entered Gerdt's flabby body, transforming the boy into a "masculine" achiever, but leaving him, in fact, with two spirits, which cause "an ambivalence in his emotional life."

K.'s oeuvre offers serious problems of evaluation. The homosexual-bisexual thematology grows tedious, as do the ponderous essays, or editorials, that K. often allots to his characters or his narrative voice. Furthermore, in his constant earnestness, he can veer off into unintentional comedy. Yet, to balance these weaknesses, there are the incomparable grace and genuine evocative strength of K.'s prose, and his unfailing ability to recreate atmospheres and capture subtle emotional reactions. In much, he will remind an American reader of John Cheever (q.v.), although he has never reached Cheever's mastery of narrative form.

FURTHER WORKS: *Rummen vid havet* (1951); *Munkmonolog* (1953); *Inblandningar utmaningar* (1969); *De nakna och de saliga* (1983, with Henrik Tikkanen)

BIBLIOGRAPHY: Schoolfield, G. C., "The Postwar Novel of Swedish Finland," *SS,* 34 (1962), 85–110; Svedberg, I., "Extending the Bounds of

Reality: An Approach to the Work of C. K.,'' *BF*, 10 (1976), 7–10; Lillquist, H., "Die Bedingungen des Überlebens: Zum literarischen Werke C. Ks," *Jahrbuch für finnisch-deutsche Literaturbeziehungen,* 13 (1979), 80–89; Tate, J., "C. K.: Chronicles of Crisis," *BF,* 16 (1982), 141–43; Schoolfield, G. C., Afterword to *The Blue Mother* (1990), 281–308

GEORGE C. SCHOOLFIELD

KILLENS, John Oliver

American novelist, short-story writer, essayist, dramatist, and screenwriter, b. 14 Jan. 1916, Macon, Ga.; d. 27 Oct. 1987, Brooklyn, N.Y.

K., who attended a number of colleges and universities, served on the staff of the National Labor Relations Board from 1936 to 1942 and again in 1946. He served in the Pacific Amphibian Forces of the U.S. Army during World War II.

K.'s importance to African-American literature rests not only on his accomplishments as a writer, but also on his influence as a cofounder of the Harlem Writer's Guild—with Rosa Guy (b. 1922) and John H. Clarke (b. 1915)—as writer-in-residence at Fisk University, as professor of creative writing at the New School, as director of the Brooklyn Writers' Workshop, and, more generally, as a force in the Black Arts movement that emerged as an aesthetic extension of the Black Power movement in the 1960s and 1970s. K. was also active in the Civil-Rights Movement and was by the late 1960s identified with that movement's more militant wing, which had moved away from the commitment to nonviolence articulated by Martin Luther King, Jr.; this development in K.'s social and political attitudes is reflected in *Black Man's Burden,* a book of essays published in 1965.

K.'s early fiction is closely linked to the social, political, and artistic commitments suggested by these affiliations and activities. His themes in his first three novels include the struggle for black dignity in a racist society; the developing awareness of a black identity in individual characters; the gradual coming into being of a black communal consciousness; the translation of communal consciousness into political perception and action; and the troubled search for the ground on which a healthy and vital relation of black and white might be based. It is a limitation of all three of these novels that they may in varying degrees be read as illustrations of these thematic concerns rather than as fully created examples of the novelist's art. The writing is frequently stiff, the dialogue explanatory or exclamatory, the situations dictated by the desire to make a point, the manner didactic, the tone painfully high-minded.

Yet the three taken together represent a not ignoble attempt to move the African-American novel beyond the legacy of Richard Wright and away from the influence of Ralph Ellison (qq.v.), whose *Invisible Man* (1952) K. denounced as a "vicious distortion of Negro life." K. is not concerned, as Wright to a degree was, with victimhood and its causes. For K., literary realism is an instrument for social change through an affirmation of personal and communal awareness, commitment, and action. The emphasis on community, and on the black family as a source of strength, distances K. as well from the emphasis on the physical and spiritual solitude of the protagonist that is often a feature of the work of Wright and Ellison, and of K.'s younger contemporary James Baldwin (q.v.).

And Then We Heard the Thunder (1962) is K.'s most impressive novel in the mode of socially committed realism that characterizes his early work. Drawing on his own experience, during the war, K. attempts a "Big War" novel, of the sort of this time associated with writers like Norman Mailer and James Jones (qq.v.). But K.'s version is told from a black perspective, and K. examines unblinkingly the many ironies, comic and savage, involved in asking African-Americans to sacrifice themselves for a democracy whose benefits they are discouraged from claiming as their own. The novel reaches a powerful (and factually based) climax as a battle breaks out between black and white American troops in the streets of Bainbridge, Australia. K.'s development as an artist in the years since the publication of *Youngblood* (1954) is reflected in formal terms in his decision to end the novel as the battle is still in progress and as the fate of his protagonist is still in doubt; the openness of the ending is powerfully appropriate to the unfolding of the novel's themes. And if, as some critics observed, K.'s characters still have a tendency to become mouthpieces for attitudes and positions K. wants to affirm or expose, they transcend this function often enough to give this novel an occasional vitality beyond anything one finds elsewhere in K.'s earlier work. Finally, the novel is informed throughout by a comic sense, especially in the portrayal of character, that prevents the ruthless high-mindedness, to which the K. of this period is constantly tempted, from taking over.

K.'s third novel, *'Sippi* (1967), does not sustain the level of accomplishment achieved in *And Then We Heard the Thunder* and suggests that K. had gone as far as he could with the sort of realism these works represent. His fourth novel, *The Cotillion; or, One Good Bull Is Half the Herd* (1971), turns away from the formal strategies and, to a lesser degree, from the thematic emphases of the earlier work. K. here takes a comic-satiric look at absurdities within the black community. His primary target is the sort of absurdity that arises when black people try to imitate the hollow frivolities (the cotillion, or formal display of debutantes) of a decadent white society. But he looks with an equally jaundiced eye on the fashions, fads, and role-playing that may substitute for an authentic racial consciousness. At the same time, K. celebrates all that is beautiful and life-giving in black culture and continues to explore the familiar themes of the growth and interaction of personal and racial awareness. The novel is written in what the narrator calls "Afro-Americanese." K.'s formal and stylistic experiments are not uniformly successful, but they do represent the author's willingness to try new ways and to explore new possibilities for African-American fiction.

The possibilities opened up in *The Cotillion* were, however, not to be developed by K. himself. The remaining novels published in his lifetime were intended for the "young adult" audience. A novel based on the life of Pushkin, the Russian poet who was of partly African ancestry, was published posthumously.

K. produced at least two novels that stand every chance of living on as significant works of African-American literature; they deserve to be read by audiences of varying racial and ethnic backgrounds, and in fact K. has been translated into more than a dozen languages. His effort to build on the legacy of Richard Wright, constitutes an honorable contribution to the development of an authentic African-American literature. And even K.'s hostility toward Ellison, though perhaps misguided in itself, may have served the useful function of suggesting to younger black writers and critics that they need not be intimidated by "official" accounts of the African-American literary tradition, especially insofar as those accounts are the handiwork of white academicians. His role in the encouragement of younger writers and his interaction with writers of his own generation must figure in any attempt to evaluate his importance to the literary culture of his time. His ultimate rank is yet to be determined, but we may confidently say this much: He was one of the liberators.

FURTHER WORKS: *Slaves* (1969); *Great Gittin' Up Morning: A Biography of Denmark Vesey* (1972); *A Man Ain't Nothin' But a Man: The Adventures of John Henry* (1975); *The Great Black Russian: A Novel on the Life and Times of Alexander Pushkin* (1988)

BIBLIOGRAPHY: Berry, A., "Crossroads, Georgia," *Masses and Mainstream*, Sept. 1954, 16–19; Ihde, H., "Black Writer's Burden: Remarks on J. O. K.," *ZAA*, 16 (1968), 117–37; Wiggins, W., "Black Folktales in the Novels of J. O. K.," *Black Scholar*, 3 (1971), 50–58; Wiggins, W., "Structure and Dynamics of Folklore: The Case of J. O. K.," *KFQ*, 17 (1972), 92–118; Klotman, P., "The White Bitch Archetype in Contemporary Black Fiction," *Bulletin of the Midwest MLA*, 6 (1973), 96–110; Gayle, A., Jr., *The Way of the New World: The Black Novel in America* (1975), 260–77; Bigsby, C. W. E., "Judgment Day Is Coming! The Apocalyptic Dream in Recent Afro-American Fiction," in Lee, A. R., ed., *Black Fiction: New Studies in the Afro-American Novel since 1945* (1980), 149–72; Gayle, A., Jr., Foreword to *Youngblood* (1982), 7–10; Watkins, M., Introduction to *And Then We Heard the Thunder* (1983), v–xvi; Bell, B. W., *The Afro-American Novel and Its Tradition* (1987), 245–53; Gayle, A., Jr., Foreword to *'Sippi* (1988), 5–10; Harris, N., *Connecting Times: The Sixties in Afro-American Fiction* (1988), 140–65

W. P. KENNEY

KILPI, Eeva

Finnish novelist, short-story writer, and poet, b. 18 Feb. 1928, Hiitola

When K. was twelve years old, the family had to leave their Carelian hometown of Hiitola as a result of the Finnish Winter War in 1940. This experience, the topic of K.'s two long novels *Elämä edestakaisin* (1964; life back and forth) and *Elämän evakkona* (1983; refugees of life) as well as of her two memoir books, *Talvisodan aika* (1989; time of Winter War) and *Välirauha* (1990; provisionary peace), shaped K.'s outlook on life. As the theme of loss and pain or separation it structures much of K.'s production.

K.'s first collection of short stories, *Noidanlukko* (1959; noidanlukko), the name of a flower that never blooms, dealt with idyllic childhood experiences, which, however, were cut short by the war. In the autobiographical series of books, starting with *Talvisodan aika*, she returned to her childhood Carelia, but now in the documentary mode, focusing not only on the loss of the land itself but on what it meant for a girl to grow up in the midst of the family's many moves and the whole nation's attempts to come to terms with its new truncated existence. Ibsen's words "Kun det tapte evig eies" ("Only what is lost, is forever owned") describe admirably K.'s attitude to the lost province of Carelia. For K.'s and her parents' generation, Carelia functioned as the seat of authentic values; its shared loss gave the former Carelians a sense of togetherness, and the shared memories bestowed their lives with meaning. Realizing that with the demise of her fathers and mothers disappeared also the values of the era they represented, K. has felt compelled to record her own Carelian experiences based on diaries, old letters, and other documentary sources.

Women as creators and centers of creativity but also as the deprived ones, whose lives consist of a series of losses, are the protagonists of many of K.'s novels and short stories. The lost childhood experience of unity with one's environment can be recaptured through love and the sexual experience. But for a woman even love leads to losses, of lovers, of a husband, and, for the mother, of her sons. Finally, she has to face the increasing signs of physical deterioration, the augurs of old age and death. It is particularly this perspective of a middle-aged woman, rather scantily treated in literature, that gains prominence in K.'s works. More openly than perhaps any other Finnish woman writer of her generation K. has dealt with female sexuality. At times her attitude approaches the traditional male one where a one-night stand serves to validate the aging woman's self-worth and prowess. But more often, like in the erotic novel *Tamara* (1972; *Tamara,* 1978) and the fictional diary *Naisen Päiväkirja* (1978; a woman's diary), the sex act is the one experience that at least momentarily reestablishes a feeling of lost unity by erasing all alienating boundaries between male and female, body and soul, life and death. Identification with nature and its cycles of life and death, from trees to insects, offers a similar experience of almost pantheistic oneness with the universe. Stylistically K.'s detailed descriptions of nature are superb in their sensitivity and beauty.

While a male critic's retort that K.'s meticulous reporting of the female's bodily functions leaves readers cold greatly misjudged the sociological makeup of the readership, it did accurately reveal how K.'s works address women in particular. Both in her psychological analysis of the different phases in a woman's life and her openly confessional treatment of female sexuality, she has been the forerunner of the many women writers of the 1980s who have been both bolder and stylistically more experimental in their depictions of today's Finnish women. Also in her attunement and deference to nature K. anticipated the ecological consciousness of the 1990s. A good indication of the exceptionally warm reception K. has enjoyed among readers in Sweden are the numerous and almost instantaneous Swedish translations of her works.

FURTHER WORKS: *Kukkivan maan rannat* (1960); *Nainen kuvastimessa* (1962); *Uudet jumalat* (1965); *Lapikkaita* (1966); *Rakkauden ja kuoleman pöytä* (1967); *Kesä ja keski-ikäinen nainen* (1970); *Hyvän yön tarinoita* (1971); *Laulu rakkaudesta ja muita runoja* (1972); *Häätanhu* (1973); *Ihmisen*

ääni (1976); *Terveisin* (1976); *Runoja 1972–1976* (1978); *Se mitä ei koskaan sanota* (1979); *Ennen kuolemaa* (1982); *Kuolema ja nuori rakastaja* (1986); *Animalia* (1987); *Kootut novellit* (1987)

BIBLIOGRAPHY: Deschner, M., "E. K.: Home and Solitude," *BF,* 3 (1984), 118–28

VIRPI ZUCK

KINOSHITA Junji
Japanese dramatist, b. 2 Aug. 1914, Tokyo

Born in the Hongō district of Tokyo to a middle-class family, K. moved at the age of five with his family to ancestral holdings in the prefecture of Kumamoto on the island of Kyushu. There he was raised and educated at the Kumamoto Fifth High School in the prewar educational system. He returned to Tokyo in 1936 to enter the graduate school of Tokyo Imperial University, where he studied English literature and drama. He has lived in Tokyo since. K. is best known for his drama, but he has also published novels, criticism of drama and politics, and translations of Shakespeare, John Millington Synge (q.v.), and other English-language dramatists.

K. is considered the foremost postwar dramatist of *Shingeki* or the "New Theater" tradition of modern realistic drama of Japan. Arising from productions of Shakespeare, Ibsen, and other European dramatists in translation in the first decade of the 20th c., the New Theater had become inextricably involved with leftist politics in the 1930s when K. first became active in it through the introduction of his mentors, the director Okakura Shirō and the actress Yamamoto Yasue. His first play, *Fūrō* (1939; wind and waves), recounted modern Kumamoto history in the epic style of the socialist dramatists of the 1930s, who, in turn, had learned their art from a variety of sources— Anton Chekhov, Socialist Realism (qq.v.), proletarian literature, and the old history plays of the Kabuki.

During World War II K. began experimenting with a new form of drama based on Japanese folktales. Soon after, he published *Yūzuru* (1949; *The Twilight Crane,* 1956), the most famous of these, which has become a standard play in the modern Japanese repertory. The genre, known by the neologism *minwageki* or "folktale drama" was considered by many to be the first indigenous form of modern drama and thus equivalent to other purely Japanese forms such as the Nō and Kabuki. Throughout the 1950s, K. continued to write folktale drama, which he produced in conjunction with *Budō no kai* or the Grapes Company, founded together with Okakura and Yamamoto. By the end of the decade, he had adapted the form for a variety of subjects, the most famous being *Onnyoro seisuiki* (1957; the rise and fall of Onnyoro), an ironic comedy, based on a play from the post-1949 Chinese revolutionary theater, recounting an instance of "self-criticism" by an "unself-conscious" peasant.

Even while he worked with folktales, K. continued to explore themes of modern Japanese history, especially the Pacific War and its effect on Japan, through plays in the realistic mode. Seen in the context of his entire work, these plays form the core of his career, with the folktale plays as his introduction to the art of writing for the theater. In 1960 the attempt by a broad coalition of political forces left of center to block passage of the Japan–U.S. Mutual Security Treaty in the Japanese Diet was frustrated. As one deeply involved in the movement, K. wrote a series of plays that helped provide a historical framework for the intellectual currents and social forces that had led to the 1960 defeat. These are best represented in the plays *Ottō to yobareru Nihonjin* (1962; a Japanese called Otto) and *Okinawa* (1963; Okinawa). K.'s work exploring the effects of the Pacific War on contemporary Japan culminated in *Kami to hito to no aida* (1970; *Between God and Man*, 1979), a two-part play recreating in Part I the International Military Tribunal for the Far East (the Tokyo War Crimes Trials), and in Part II, the war crimes trial of a common soldier who manages to break out of the debilitating psychology of guilt that had marked virtually all of K.'s earlier heroes and, in his judgment, the Japanese people.

Since 1970 K. has produced only one more play, the epic *Shigosen no matsuri* (1978; requiem on the meridian), a choral rendition of a medieval Japanese military epic. Among its many other aspects, this last play highlights K.'s mastery of the various styles of classical and modern Japanese and his ability to feature language itself as a major element of interest throughout his drama. In the 1970s and 1980s, theater in Japan shifted focus from the text to production, and from the dramatist to the actor, as has been true in many contemporary theaters around the world. K.'s theater, the New Theater of Japan, had been created to feature the dramatist and the written word as the primary focus of theatrical activity, and it is possible that K. may be the last of the historian dramatists of modern Japan.

FURTHER WORKS: *Rajio dorama senshū* (1953); *Watashi no Shēkusupia* (1953); *Engeki no dentō to minwa* (1956); *Geijutsu to shakai e no me* (1956); *Nihon no minwa* (1960); *Minwagekishū* (3 vols., 1961); *K. sakuhinshū* (8 vols., 1962–1971); *Fuyu no jidai* (1964); *Nihon ga Nihon de aru tame*

ni wa (1965); *Hanawaka/Yoki na jigoku yaburi* (1966); *Mugen kidō* (1966); *Yumemi kozō* (1966); *Dorama no sekai* (1967); *Shiroi yoru no utage* (1967); *Dorama to no taiwa* (1968); *Zuisō Shēkusupia* (1969); *K. hyōronshū* (12 vols., 1972); *Shēkusupia no sekai* (1973); *Bōkyaku ni tsuite* (1974); *Rekishi ni tsuite* (1976); *Unmei no kochiragawa* (1976); *Koten o yakusu* (1978); *Rakutenteki na Nihonjin* (1980); *Zuisōshū: Ryokaku* (1980); *Dorama ga naritatsu toki* (1981); *Gikyoku no Nihongo* (1982); *K. gikyokusen* (3 vols., 1982); *Giron shinokoshita koto* (1986); *K. shū* (16 vols., 1988). FURTHER VOLUME IN ENGLISH: *To Be or Not To Be* (1972)

BIBLIOGRAPHY: Scott, A. C., *Twilight Crane*, in *Playbook, 5 Plays for a New Theater* (1956), 129–59; Mori, A., "Le dramaturge japonais K.," in Jacquot, J., ed., *Les théâtres d'Asie* (1961), 185–202; Gangloff, E. J., *Between God and Man: A Judgment on War Crimes* (1979)

ERIC J. GANGLOFF

KINSELLA, Thomas

Irish poet, translator, and publisher, b. 4 May 1928, Dublin

One of the major poets working in the English language, K. was born in Dublin into a socialist family. After graduating from University College, Dublin, with a degree in public administration (1949), he became a civil servant and remained one for nearly twenty years, until his parallel career as a poet branched into the twin professions of American academic and Irish publisher. He is still, first and foremost, what he has been since the publication of his first major collection of poetry, *Another September* (1958), a modern Irish poet of the first rank.

Winner of the Guinness Poetry Prize (1958), *Another September* inaugurates what would become an archetypal career for a successful poet of the post-World War II generation. The volume brims with talent and influence, its prosodic expertise and lyrical precision of feeling and statement recalling W. H. Auden and William Butler Yeats (qq.v.) in similar modes. The poise and pitch of rhyme remind the reader that K. is an Irish poet, familiar with the assonant architecture of Celtic bardic verse. The flint in the poems is the existential theme of ordeal as order, the images resolving in irony, as at the close of the collection's signature poem, "Baggot Street Deserta," where a cigarette flicked out a window rounds out a contemplation of the stars.

The collected *Poems* (1956) and *Moralities* (1960) exhibit the same virtues in service of the same themes. With *Downstream* (1962), K. moves on, gaining perspective with maturity. The struggle, often bitter, to create a self—and a poem—is reimagined as a quest, the poet in motion, reflecting on his passage, often through darkness, always bearing a burden of history. K. steps surely from poetic detachment to political engagement, Ireland's mythic and nationalist past providing a poetic heritage. The shallows of a river ford give rise to warrior, not Wordsworthian, associations in "A Country Walk," and the heroes of the 1916 Irish Uprising are remembered in a litany of names, as in Yeats, though in a typical early Kinsellan twist, the names are read from shop windows, reducing history and heroism to commodity.

In 1965 K., now a recognized poet and member of the Irish Academy of Letters, left the civil service to accept an invitation to be poet in residence at Southern Illinois University, a post that led to a professorship and began an academic career, primarily in America. *Wormwood* (1966), a short sequence of short poems full of nightmares, cold dawns, and bare, scarred trees, that traces and ultimately praises the existential ordeal of marriage, won the Dennis Devlin Memorial Award (1966). In *Nightwalker and Other Poems* (1968), K. is questing again, expanding his imagery into the gothic, extending his poetic form with fragments of liturgical and narrative forms, folktale, and allegory. The poems explore the psychological and political resonance of the theme of decay as devouring, but it is another theme, the dislocation of poetry and the inherent homelessness of poets, that sets K. wandering, through his heritage, invoking forebears from itinerant Irish bards of the 18th c. to Keats (1795–1821) to Yeats to Austin Clarke (q.v.), and through the two longer entries, "Phoenix Park" and "Nightwalker." Rhyme, a homing device, is abandoned, as K. gives up his poetry to the journey and rediscovers old ironies in fresh imagery, as when at the end of the title poem he stands in a desert of lunar dust and sees the earth, full, in the sky.

K. laments in *Nightwalker* the near destruction of the Irish language in the 18th c. and satirizes its institutionalization in the 20th. An Irish poet's heritage is bilingual, and most major Irish poets are translators, too. A Guggenheim fellowship in 1968 helped K. finish his prose and verse translation of the ancient epic cycle of heroic tales, *The Táin* (1969), source of the Cuchulain myth so important to Yeats and Ireland's literary revival. K.'s method is the reasonable reconstruction from various sources of the stories of warriors involved in the great cattle raid of Cooley, and the faithful translation of the language, even in attempting obscure prophetic verse. Over a decade later in *An Duanaire* (1981; the poem book), edited by

Seán Ó Tuama, K. translated a selection of the extant works of latter-day cultural warriors, the dispossessed Irish poets of the 17th to 19th cs. Drawn by the drama of their struggle to retain possession of their language and bardic status, K. engages in his own struggle to suggest an untranslatable prosody (in both bardic syllabic verse and later accentual forms) while recreating the images and ideas, the politics and pathos of the originals. His resolute scholarship and dexterous poetic technique bridge the vernaculars of Irish verse and bring all-but-forgotten voices memorably to life.

His own poetry underwent a major development in the 1970s; he began publishing it himself. After relocating his American academic affiliation in 1971 to Temple University in Philadelphia, he established Peppercanister Press in Dublin in 1972. Since then, most of K.'s verse has first appeared as occasional poetry or works in progress in series of limited editions published by Peppercanister. His work has become at once more public and more private, responsive to events, sensitive to the graphic potential of the page and concrete presence of the poem, allusive to his personal life and previous work. The first of the Peppercanister poems was "Butcher's Dozen," a broadside criticizing the official report on the deaths of thirteen Civil Rights demonstrators in Derry on "Bloody Sunday"; the second was "A Selected Life," a short sequence occasioned by the death of K.'s friend, the composer and musical scholar Sean O'Riada.

Both these works were included in K.'s next collection, *Notes from the Land of the Dead and Other Poems* (1973). The poetic quest begun in *Downstream* continues here, turning inward, the poet adopting C. G. Jung (q.v.) as a psychoanalytic guide/mentor. A dreaming consciousness and mythic resonance throw imagery into even stronger relief than in *Nightwalker* and put a metonymic stress on language. The rhythm of creation and destruction replaces rhyme, cracks syntax, and echoes across recurrent ellipses, ungrammatical enjambments and anomalies of typeface, illustration, and layout. This dynamic of a publisher's care and a poet's exploration characterizes all K.'s subsequent work: *Peppercanister Poems, 1972–1978* (1979), including poems in memory of O'Riada, John F. Kennedy on the tenth anniversary of his assassination, and the poet's father; and *Blood and Family* (1988), a refined volume of works within works, sequences taking geographical pattern ("Settings"), musical form ("Her Vertical Smile"), and fractured chronological order ("St. Catherine's Clock"), among other structures. Both volumes include self-reflexive commentary and notes, and the poems have begun to quote themselves.

K.'s progress as a modern poet, from prosody to experiment to self-reference, is typical, though his professional stature in its international acclaim is eminent. His participation, as an Irish poet, in the mythic and political history of his country is typical, though few, if any, contemporaries have made so important or impressive an impact. As an essayist—*Davis, Mangan, Ferguson? Tradition and the Irish Writer* (1970, with W. B. Yeats)—editor—*The New Oxford Book of Irish Verse* (1986)—translator, publisher, and teacher, he has practiced and studied poetry in all its aspects and made a significant contribution from every quarter, and that is unique. Judging by the poetry alone, however, K. is a major figure, regardless of label, among writers in English in the second half of the 20th c.

FURTHER WORKS: *The Starlit Eye* (1952); *Three Legendary Sonnets* (1952); *Per Imaginem* (1953); *Death of a Queen* (1956); *Poems and Translations* (1961); *Nightwalker* (1967); *Poems* (1968, with Anne Sexton and Douglas Livingstone); *Tear* (1969); *Finistère* (1972); *New Poems* (1973); *Vertical Man* (1973); *The Good Fight* (1973); *Selected Poems 1956–1968* (1973); *One* (1974); *A Technical Supplement* (1976); *Song of the Night and Other Poems* (1978); *The Messenger* (1978); *One and Other Poems* (1979); *Poems 1956–1973* (1979); *Fifteen Dead* (1979); *Songs of the Psyche* (1985); *Out of Ireland* (1987); *St. Catherine's Clock* (1987)

BIBLIOGRAPHY: Rosenthal, M. L., *The New Poets: American and British Poetry since World War II* (1967), 283–97; Skelton, R., "The Poetry of T. K.," *Éire*, 2 (1967), 86–108; Bedient, C., *Eight Contemporary Poets* (1974), 119–38; Harmon, M., *The Poetry of T. K.: "With Darkness for a Nest"* (1974); Kersnowski, F. L., *The Outsiders: Poets of Contemporary Ireland* (1975), 73–84; Young, V., "Raptures of Distress," *Parnassus*, 3 (1975), 75–80; McGuiness, A. E., " 'Bright Quincunx Newly Risen': T. K.'s Inward 'I,' " *Éire*, 4 (1980), 106–25; John, B., "Imaginative Bedrock: K.'s *One* and the *Lebor Gabála Érenn*," *Éire*, 1 (1985), 109–32; Johnston, D., *Irish Poetry after Joyce* (1985), 97–120; Garratt, R. F., *Modern Irish Poetry: Tradition and Continuity from Yeats to Heaney* (1986), 167–97; Skelton, R., *Celtic Contraries* (1990), 183–209

DENNIS PAOLI

KIPPHARDT, Heinar

German dramatist, b. 8 Mar. 1922, Heidersdorf; d. 18 Nov. 1982, Munich

K. qualified in medicine at Düsseldorf University and was dramatic adviser at the Deutsches Theater in East Berlin from 1951 to 1959. In 1959 he left East Germany for West Germany, because two of his more critical theater plays were censored. His primary concerns are with social injustice, mass hysteria, and individual accountability.

His early plays are satirical comedies that criticize the preoccupations and major social trends in both Germanies after the war: *Shakespeare dringend gesucht* (1954; desperately seeking Shakespeare) parodies the positivist portrayal of heroic socialist workers by East German writers in the 1950s; *Die Stühle des Herrn Szmil* (1958; the chairs of Mr. Szmil) criticizes profiteering and persistent capitalist and bourgeois practices under socialism, while lip service is being paid to socialist rhetoric; *Die Nacht, in der der Chef geschlachtet wurde* (1967; the night the boss was butchered) attacks the grotesque manifestations of materialism and egoism in West Germany during the "economic miracle" wonder years. The play *Der Hund des Generals* (1964; the general's dog) first appeared as a story and is a satire on war and Prussian discipline. K. is best known for two of his documentary plays, *In der Sache J. Robert Oppenheimer* (1964; in the matter of J. Robert Oppenheimer) and *Bruder Eichmann* (1983; brother Eichmann). The earlier play details the effects of McCarthyist hysteria in the U.S. in the trial against the inventor of the atom bomb who was accused of being a communist sympathizer and delaying the development of the hydrogen bomb, while the later play follows the Israeli trial of Adolf Eichmann, one of the most notorious Nazi officials. K.'s montage technique allows him to link an analysis of past injustices with their contemporary equivalents, for instance, anti-Semitism under the Nazis and xenophobia toward minorities, especially Turkish foreign workers, in present-day Germany. The play *Joel Brand: Die Geschichte eines Geschäfts* (1965; Joel Brand: the history of a deal) concerns the Nazi proposal to barter Hungarian Jews for trucks. The novel *März* (1976; März) is interested in schizophrenia and artistic creativity and indicts modern psychiatry's treatment of the poet Alexander März; it was made into a play in 1980. The poems *Angelsbrucker Notizen* (1977; notes from Angelsbruck) and the collection of diary entries *Traumprotokolle* (1981; dream notes) contain much autobiographical information about K.'s family, his own struggle with depression and feelings of inadequacy, and the Nazis' deportation of his father to Buchenwald. K. is one of the foremost leftist playwrights of the 1960s along with Peter Weiss, Hans Magnus Enzensberger, and Rolf Hochhuth (qq.v.), who used documentary material in their art because they felt that people needed to be exposed to historicopolitical facts rather than fiction to be educated as citizens of a more democratic society. The 1960s in West Germany brought many Nazi war-crime trials, which resulted in a public reckoning with the Nazi inheritance. K. is exemplary in linking his condemnation of Nazi practices with more recent processes of exclusion and repression in German society.

FURTHER WORKS: *Der Mann des Tages und andere Erzählungen* (1977); *Theaterstücke, Band 1 und 2* (1978)

BIBLIOGRAPHY: Kowal, M., "K. and the Documentary Theater," *American-German Review,* 5 (1966–1967), 20–30; Hilzinger, K. H., *Die Dramaturgie des dokumentarischen Theaters* (1976), 16–25, 70–76; Bartelheimer, L., and M. Nutz, *Materialien H. K. In der Sache Robert J. Oppenheimer* (1981); Carl, R. P., "Dokumentarisches Theater," in Durzak, M., ed., *Deutsche Gegenwartsliteratur* (1981), 99–127; Muschg, A., *Literatur als Therapie?* (1981); Naumann, U., ed., *H. K. Bruder Eichmann: Schauspiel und Materialien* (1983); Meyer, S., *Kunst als Widerstand* (1989)

HELGA DRUXES

KIRSCH, Sarah

(formerly Ingrid Bernstein) German poet and short-story writer, b. 16 Apr. 1935, Limlingerode

At an early age K. changed her given name to Sarah in protest against the persecution of the Jews during the years of the Third Reich. After completing her secondary education, she began an apprenticeship in forestry, then worked briefly in a sugar factory, before studying biology in Halle, where she received her degree in 1959. During her brief marriage to the author Rainer Kirsch (b. 1934), she became closely associated with members of the younger generation of East German writers, and from 1963 to 1965 she attended the Johannes R. Becher Literary Institute in Leipzig. Since then, she has devoted herself exclusively to her writing. In 1977 she moved to West Berlin, and since 1983 she has made her home in Schleswig-Holstein. She has received many awards for her poetry, including the Heinrich Heine Prize (1973), the Petrarch Prize (1976), the Austrian State Prize for Literature (1981), and the Friedrich Hölderlin Prize (1984).

K.'s poems focus on the fundamental elements of natural human experience, from personal encounters with the external world of lakes and forests, animals and birds, sun and moon, days and seasons, to intense inner confrontations with love, loneliness, uncertainty, and longing for self-realization and fulfillment. In language that is often reserved, even hesitant, sometimes terse and dissonant, she evokes images that are remarkable for their richness and depth, their fairy-tale quality, their successful communication of changes in mood and tone. Especially characteristic of her poetry are lines that draw the reader beneath the surface of apparently idyllic landscapes into undercurrents of disappointment, disillusionment, disenchantment, and despair. Even her love songs discreetly juxtapose individual moments of happiness with sadness and pain. Tendencies in her best works are related to currents found in German romanticism and in the writings of the poet Johannes Bobrowski (q.v.) that focus on the increasing alienation of human beings from the natural world.

The poems of K.'s East German period, in *Gespräch mit dem Saurier* (1965; conversation with the saurian), coauthored with Rainer Kirsch, *Landaufenthalt* (1967; a stay in the country), *Zaubersprüche* (1973; magic spells), and *Rückenwind* (1976; tail wind), reflect her artistic progress from cautious and triflingly simple creations to more meaningful explorations of weighty problems. Even in her earliest writings, she occasionally succeeded in combining imagination, originality, and power of expression in the reproduction of subjective experience, but her lyrics took on the character of fresh, unique poetic utterance only as they became the product of increased reflection about more complex existential questions of personal identity and purpose.

Important tendencies of K.'s more mature verse include refinement of perception and awareness, heightened poetic sensitivity, broadening of theme and substance, integration of the private dimension into a deeper penetration of the general human condition, and greater density of imagery. In *La Pagerie* (1980; the pagery), a series of prose poems based upon her experiences in the Provence region of France, she demonstrated a special facility for combining delicate language with cynicism, while the creations of *Erdreich* (1982; earth realm), with their images of canyons, highways, and other landscapes encountered during a trip to the U.S., are critically ironic, almost apocalyptic interpretations of perceived threats to the contemporary world.

The tone of more recent collections suggests a return to an emphasis on private experience with nature and self. Some of K.'s best and most complex nature poems appear in *Katzenleben* (1984; *Catlives,* 1990), an almost idyllic documentation of her new life in rural Schleswig-Holstein. The intimacy of the poet's relationship to the surrounding world grows more intense in the prose poems of *Irrstern* (1987; wandering star), with their sometimes startling arrays of images, unusual observations, and predominantly elegiac mood. An inclination toward retreat into self becomes especially pronounced in the melancholy songs of resignation found in *Schneewärme* (1989; snow warmth).

Two of the most representative collections of K.'s prose writings are *Die ungeheuren berghohen Wellen auf See* (1973; the monstrous mountain-high waves at sea) and *Allerlei-Rauh* (1988; potpourri-raw). The stories in the earlier book offer an unexpected mixture of satire and straight narration of factual substance. With their impact weakened by contrived endings in which characters always make the best of their situations, these pieces reflect external limiting factors that K. could not ignore and still be permitted to publish in East Germany. From that perspective, *Allerlei-Rauh*, with its elements of chronicle, fairy tale, legend, autobiography, and reflection about personal experience of nature and contemporary life in Schleswig-Holstein, documents K.'s progress toward richer, deeper literary expression and toward a prose that forms a definite complement to her poetry.

The major strength of K.'s writing lies in her ability to relate deeply private concerns to the general human condition of her time, and to convey her feelings about those relationships in a manner that enables her readers to share in her experiences on an intimate level. That fact alone has made her one of the most important poets in contemporary Germany.

FURTHER WORKS: *Die betrunkene Sonne—Der Stärkste* (1963, with Rainer Kirsch); *Berlin-Sonnenseite* (1964, with Thomas Billhardt and Rainer Kirsch); *Gedichte* (1967); *Hansel und Gretel* (1972); *Die Pantherfrau* (1973; *The Panther Woman,* 1989); *Es war dieser merkwürdige Sommer* (1974); *Caroline im Wassertropfen* (1975, with Erdmut Oelschläger); *Zwischen Herbst und Winter* (1975, with Ingrid Schuppau); *Die betrunkene Sonne* (1975; *The Drunken Sun,* 1978); *Blitz aus heiterm Himmel* (1975); *Musik auf dem Wasser* (1977); *Wiepersdorf* (1977); *Sommergedichte* (1978); *Wintergedichte* (1978); *Katzenkopfpflaster* (1978); *Ein Sommerregen* (1978, with Kota Taniuchi); *Erklärung einiger Dinge* (1978, with Urs Widmer and Elke Erb); *Sieben Häute* (1979); *Drachensteigen* (1979); *Wind* (1979, with Kota Taniuchi); *Schatten* (1979, with Kota Taniuchi); *Hans mein Igel* (1980); *Papiersterne* (1981); *Landwege* (1985); *Hundert Gedichte* (1985); *Galoschen* (1987); *Lyrik* (1987, with A. R. Renck); *Luft und Wasser* (1988); *Die Flut* (1990). FURTHER VOLUME IN ENGLISH: *Conjurations* (1985)

BIBLIOGRAPHY: Wittkowski, W., "S. K.: 'Der Milchmann Schäuffele,' " *GQ,* 54 (1981), 311–17; Figge, S. G., " 'Der Wunsch nach Welt': The Travel Motif in the Poetry of S. K.," in Gerber, M., ed., *Studies in GDR Culture and Society* (1981), Vol. 1, 167–84; Armster, C., " 'Merkwürdiges Beispiel weiblicher Entschlossenheit': A Woman's Story—by S. K.," in Gerber, M., ed., *Studies in GDR Culture and Society* (1982), Vol. 2, 243–50; Fehn, A., "Authorial Voice in S. K.'s *Die Pantherfrau,*" in Woodmansee, M., and W. F. W. Lohnes, eds., *Erkennen und Deuten* (1983), 335–46; Post, L., "The Poetry of S. K.," *RaJAH,* (1986), 81–94; Melin, C., "Landscape As Writing and Revelation in S. K.'s 'Death Valley,' " *GR,* 4 (1987), 199–204; Mabee, B., *Die Poetik von S. K.* (1989); Wagener, H., *S. K.* (1989); Arnold, H. L., *S. K.* (1989)

LOWELL A. BANGERTER

KIŠ, Danilo

Serbian novelist, short-story writer, and essayist, b. 22 Feb. 1935, Subotica, Yugoslavia; d. 15 Oct. 1989, Paris, France

K. was one of the best-known of contemporary Serbian writers internationally. Born in Subotica of a Jewish father and a Montenegrin mother, he and his family were subjected to persecution by the Nazis during World War II, during which time most of his relatives perished, including his father. He studied literature at the University of Belgrade and later taught Serbo-Croatian for several years at French universities. He spent the last years of his life in Paris.

K. was most successful in novels, but he also wrote short stories and was a discerning essayist and a passionate polemicist. He belongs to a group of young Serbian writers who entered the literary scene in the mid-1960s and immediately asserted themselves as the new wave of Serbian letters. His first work, a short novel, *Mansarda* (1962; the attic), is typical of a beginner, yet it shows remarkable maturity in depicting the growing pains of young people searching for their identity amid the tragic combination of love and suicide. His next novel, *Psalam 44* (1962; psalm 44), employs a theme that would dominate K.'s writings for the rest of his career: the suffering of people, especially the Jews and other minorities, during wartime, most often during World War II. In this and other works, he does not dwell on suffering in itself but shows instead the degrading compromises the victims are forced to make, almost invariably leading to most tragic consequences. K. reaches the apex in this respect in his next two novels, *Bašta, pepeo* (1965; *Garden, Ashes,* 1975) and *Peščanik* (1972; *Hourglass,* 1990). In the first, he weaves a story of his childhood and his reminiscences of his remarkable father, who was, among other things, an eccentric, an incorrigible dreamer, a frustrated genius, a poet, a philosopher, a grotesque Don Quixote, and a drunkard who squandered his many gifts. The fact that his father ended tragically during the Nazi terror only enhanced the aura of pathos and unreality to the already unreal experiences of a growing boy. *Peščanik* continues to build a monument to the remarkable father, except that now the father is telling his own story in a dazzling variety of narrative devices.

From his personal vantage point, K. moves to a more general depiction of human's inhumanity to humans in his next novel, *Grobnica za Borisa Davidovića* (1976; *A Tomb for Boris Davidovich,* 1978). In seven seemingly unrelated stories K. follows the paths of several people, all of whom end up as victims of persecution. The victims are again mostly Jews, but this time they suffer not only at the hands of Nazis but also of the Soviet authorities asserting their party discipline. K.'s mixture of historical facts and fiction caused a furor in Yugoslav literary circles and led to accusations of plagiarism, which he was able to refute easily. With this work, K. cemented his reputation as a champion of human rights and a defender of basic human dignity against the forces of evil.

By choosing a significant subject matter and by employing a remarkable artistic prowess, K. built a reputation as one of the best among contemporary writers. He is especially adept at transcending regional boundaries and appealing to readers everywhere, as attested by numerous translations of his works into many languages.

FURTHER WORKS: *Noć i magla* (1968); *Papagaj* (1969); *Rani jadi* (1969); *Po-etika* (1972); *Poetika, druga knjiga* (1974); *Drveni sanduk Tomasa Wulfa* (1974); *Čas anatomije* (1978); *Enciklopedija mrtvih* (1983; *The Encyclopedia of the Dead,* 1989)

BIBLIOGRAPHY: Vitanović, S., "Thematic Unity in D. K.'s Literary Works," *Relations,* 9–10 (1979), 66–69; Bynum, D. E., "Philosophical Fun and Merriment in the First Fiction of D. K.," *Serbian Studies,* 2, 4 (1984), 3–20; Czarny, N., "Imaginary—Real Lives: On D. K.," *CCur,* 3 (1984), 279–84; White, E., "D. K.: The Obligations of Form," *SWR,* 71, 3 (1986), 363–77; Gorjup, B., "D. K.: From 'Enchantment' to 'Documentation,'" *CSP,* 29, 4 (1987), 387–94; Shishkoff, S., "Košava in a Coffee Pot: Or a Dissection of a Literary Cause Célèbre," *CCur,* 6 (1987), 340–71; Oja, M. F., "Fictional History and Historical Fiction: Solzhenitsyn and K. as Exemplars," *History and Theory,* 27 (1988), 111–24; Matvejević, P., "D. K.: Encyclopedia of the Dead," *CCur,* 7 (1988), 337–49; Birnbaum, M. D., "The Fiction of D. K.," *CCur,* 8 (1989), 345–60

VASA D. MIHAILOVICH

KLÍMA, Ivan

Czechoslovak short-story writer, novelist, dramatist, and essayist (writing in Czech), b. 14 Sept. 1931, Prague

As a Jew, K. spent three years of his boyhood, during the German occupation, in the Terezín (Theresienstadt) concentration camp. Having completed his secondary education after the war, he went to study Czech and theory of literature at Charles University in Prague. From 1956 to 1963 he worked as an editor, first on a weekly magazine, later in a publishing house. In 1964 he joined the editorial staff of the Writers' Union journal *Literární noviny.* His controversial articles often brought him into conflict with the political authorities, and in 1967 he was expelled from the Communist Party. After the suppression of the Prague Spring reform movement, K.'s work was banned in Czechoslovakia, but continued to be published abroad in translation. In 1988 he became the first previously banned writer whose name was allowed to appear in print again, and the overthrow of the communist régime in the following year put an end to all restrictions.

K.'s first work of fiction was a collection of short stories, *Bezvadný den* (1960; a perfect day), in which he, like other young writers of the day, treated contemporary life with a frankness that would hardly have been tolerated a few years earlier. The wronged, abandoned, and betrayed characters in the short stories, victims of circumstances that were not supposed to exist in a socialist society, signaled K.'s concern with social ethics. In the novel *Hodina ticha* (1963; hour of silence), he tried to expose the damage inflicted in human terms on a farming community in eastern Slovakia by a callous collectivization drive. Although K. presented the excesses of Stalinism as a good idea badly executed, he was addressing a subject that was still regarded as risky and sensitive. Soon, however, writers like Ludvík Vaculík and Milan Kundera (qq.v.) were able to take an even more critical view of the recent past.

In the mid-1960s eastern European audiences and dramatists, such as Sławomir Mrożek and Václav Havel (qq.v.), discovered that many aspects of everyday life under communism lent themselves to presentation on stage in terms of the Theater of the Absurd (q.v.). When K. turned to drama, he, too, adopted some of its devices in *Zámek* (1964; the castle) and *Mistr* (1967; the master) and combined them with a Kafkaesque sense of a sealed world infested with intangible evil. The influence of Franz Kafka (q.v.) grew even more perceptible in a number of short stories and plays that were inspired by real-life experience. In *Cukrárna Myriam* (1968; Café Myriam), for instance, the poisoning of old people becomes an established and tolerated means of solving the housing shortage. A similarly haunting model situation, apparently abstracted from the 1950s show trials, was the basis of a meticulously constructed novella (originally a radio play), *Porota* (1969; "The Jury," in *A Ship Named Hope*, 1970).

During the 1970s and 1980s, when his work could only be published abroad, K.'s subjects became less sinister, although a young woman desensitized to the point of anomie appears again as the central character in *Milostné léto* (1979; rev. ed., 1985; *A Summer Affair*, 1987), the story of an older man's infatuation that inescapably leads to disaster. Some of the figures in *Má veselá jitra* (1979; *My Merry Mornings*, 1985) show similar signs of alienation, but there is also a touch of humor in the seven short stories that contemplate the ironies and peculiarities of life in a decaying socialist society. Another collection of short stories, *Moje první lásky* (1985; *My First Loves*, 1986), stands out as being least affected by the author's tendency to intellectualize in fiction social and ethical issues, a trait that is strongly detectable in *Soudce z milosti* (1986; *Judge on Trial*, 1991). The theme of conscience and moral fortitude in the face of pressure and persecution is combined in this novel, unusually for K., with that of religious faith.

A moral conflict of a private character is at the center of *Láska a smetí* (1988; *Love and Garbage*, 1990). A writer, who has taken on the job of a street sweeper, reminisces about his love affair with a life-hungry sculptress that he broke off, faced with deep feelings of guilt toward his wife and unable to continue living a lie. Although there is no hint of politics, the debris, both human and physical, that surrounds the narrator, seems to be symbolic of the disintegrating communist system.

K. has been one of the most prolific and erudite Czech writers of the second half of the 20th c. With the exception of poetry, he has been active in all literary genres as well as in quality journalism. While aiming to provide an artistic comment on his times in carefully worked-out novels, plays, and short stories, he has not attempted entirely to hide their ideational framework. His authorial intentions have been allowed to show in places through the narrative conducted in a clear, unperturbed style, which reflected his preference for

subtle sensitivity and refined reasoning. In this respect as well as in others, K.'s work paralleled trends manifest in contemporary Western fiction and in translation became an integral part of it.

FURTHER WORKS: *Mezi třemi hranicemi* (1960); *Karel Čapek* (1962); *Milenci na jednu noc* (1964); *Návštěva u nesmrtelné tetky* (1965); *Kokrhací hodiny* (1965); *Klára a dva páni* (1969; *Klara and Two Men,* 1983); *Ženich pro Marcelu* (1969); *Milenci na jeden den* (1969); *Pokoj pro dva* (1971); *Malomocní* (1972); *Ministr a anděl* (1990; *The President and the Angel,* 1979); *Franz a Felice* (1990; *Franz and Felice,* 1986); *Moje zlatá řemesla* (1990); *Markétin zvěřinec* (1990); *Už se blíží meče* (1990). FURTHER VOLUME IN ENGLISH: *The Games* (1985)

BIBLIOGRAPHY: Mihailovich, V. D., et al., eds., *Modern Slavic Literatures* (1976), Vol. 2, 130–35; Goetz-Stankiewicz, M., *The Silenced Theatre* (1979), 117–45; Hájek, I., "Profile of I. K.," *IonC,* 12 (1983), 39–41; Goetz-Stankiewicz, M., "K. under Kafka's Gaze—Kafka under K.'s Pen," *CCur,* 5 (1986), 333–36; Roth, P., "A Conversation in Prague," *NYRB,* 12 Apr. 1990, 14–22

IGOR HÁJEK

KOBAYASHI Hideo
Japanese literary critic, b. 11 Apr. 1902, Tokyo; d. 1 Mar. 1983, Tokyo

K. is regarded as Japan's first modern literary and cultural critic, and by many its greatest and most influential. He was born in Tokyo at a time of that city's most rapid expansion, and lived there through the turbulence of both the 1923 earthquake and World War II. He studied French literature at the University of Tokyo, and already as a student began to translate and write essays on Charles Baudelaire (1821–1867), Arthur Rimbaud (1854–1891), and André Gide (q.v.). He was also attracted to the critical writings of Montaigne and Paul Valery (q.v.). His own mature work is noted for its style, and read not just as commentary or criticism, but as literature.

K. wrote on a wide range of subjects, but always from a personal angle—that of an urban intellectual working to describe, but not define, the fast-changing contours of modern Japanese culture. His work in the late 1920s and the 1930s, most of it focused on contemporary Japanese, French, and Russian literature, seems most directly to address issues of Japan's complex, cross-cultural "modernity." His later work, addressed more to premodern or "classical" Japanese literature and aesthetics, can yet be seen as a continuing effort to record the culture of modern urban life, which by turns denies, invents, or takes refuge in the past.

The Japanese literary world that K. first entered was fraught with competing schools and ideologies: Marxism, aestheticism, populism. An early, prize-winning essay, "Samazamanaru isho" (1929; multiple designs), marked the young critic as hostile to any and all ideological systems and fixed critical positions. He confronted, in particular, critics who lacked self-criticism, who presented their beliefs without irony or any skeptical distance. For K., the object of criticism did not exist in isolation from the values, tastes, and style of the critic. And in modern Japan, where under the impact of translated literatures and ideas these values and tastes were undergoing incessant change and transformation, K. could not help but be skeptical of the "stability" of any announced position, whether it be reactionary or avant-garde, cosmopolitan or nationalist.

Throughout the 1930s, even after the government moved to censor and ban radical, especially proletarian, writing, K. resisted the trend to define a "pure" Japanese culture, insulated and beyond any Western or outside influence. In "Kokyō o ushinatta bungaku" (1933; literature of the lost home), he describes the culturally homeless situation of modern, urban Japanese, who respond as readily to the image of a Moroccan desert in a western film, as they do to the city before their eyes. He observes, too, that Western culture is so much part of the education and cultural pursuits of modern Japanese that categorical distinctions between the "purely Japanese" and the foreign could no longer be made.

From this vantage, K. wrote about the tradition of novel writing in the West, and the modern phenomenon of the Japanese shishōsetsu or the "I-novel," as related but historically determined events, and with confidence that he could comprehend Rousseau or Gide as thoroughly as he could Tayama Katai (1871–1930) or Shiga Naoya (q.v.). Similarly, the great study Dostoevsky no seikatsu (1939; life of Dostoevsky) demonstrates K.'s capacity to read foreign culture as expressive of tensions deeply felt in modern Japanese life—in this case, how Dostoevsky's portraits of youth "possessed" by imported ideas rendered them as homeless in their own land as 20th-c. Japanese are in their own.

The coming of war and the intense government pressure on writers moved K. toward more reflective, meditative topics and themes. His wartime writing, some of it accommodationist in tone, was not the work of a propagandist but of a writer who had grown weary of his century. The essays collected in Mujō to iu koto (1946; on evanescence)

mark K.'s "return" to the classics of medieval Japan. No doubt he was drawn to this period of warfare and cultural upheaval because of its resemblance to his own, and to its poets and tellers of tales because of a spirituality that allowed them to stand apart and observe the passing tragedy of worldly ambition.

Following the war, after the American occupation and the ensuing "economic miracle" had transformed a shattered country into a prosperous one, K. assumed a nearly legendary status for the integrity of his writing style and his iconoclastic, if by now highly refined and classical, tastes. His studies of Mozart, van Gogh, and the great 18th-c. scholar Motoori Norinaga (1730–1801) might be regarded together as the work of a mature critic, trying to provide perduring models of cultural conduct to a fashion-conscious youth culture of unstable and eclectic tastes.

Given the challenges to the political and cultural establishment that emerged in Japan in the 1960s, it is not surprising that K. would be denounced for his postwar conservatism. Still, it is a measure of K.'s real force and influence on Japanese letters in this century that both his admirers and his critics acknowledge the singularity of his style and his achievement. He remains the critical standard against which successive generations of Japanese critics have to measure themselves.

FURTHER WORKS: Kobayashi Hideo Zenshū (15 vols., 1979)

BIBLIOGRAPHY: Seidensticker, E., "K. H.," in Shively, D. H., ed., Tradition and Modernization in Japanese Culture (1971), 419–61; Keene, D., Dawn to the West: Japanese Literature of the Modern Era (1984), 582–610

PAUL ANDERER

KONRÁD, George (György)

Hungarian novelist and essayist, b. 2 Apr. 1933, Debrecen

K. is a writer whose works reveal a great deal about his life and career. Although he received a degree in literature at the University of Budapest, he worked for years as a social worker and then as a town planner at Budapest's Institute of Urban Planning. His first two novels, A látogató (1969; The Case Worker, 1974) and A városalapító (1977; The City Builder, 1977), were products of these professional activities. His celebrated essays on dissidence and censorship, notably "A függetlenség lassú munkája" (1977; "The Long Work of Liberty," 1978), "Az állami ember és a cenzúra" (1981; "Censorship and State-Owned Citizens,"

1983), written in the 1970s and early 1980s, reflected his own situation at the time. His most recent fiction, *Kerti mulatság* (1989; *Feast in the Garden,* 1992), is directly autobiographical, chronicling his childhood in a prewar market town in eastern Hungary, his miraculous survival of the Nazi Holocaust, his youthful infatuation with socialism, as well as his years as a barely tolerated dissident intellectual.

A látogató, which secured K.'s place as a major contemporary novelist, is a sociologically precise and at the same time stunningly lyrical and provocatively nonpolitical examination of urban squalor and degradation. The city is Budapest, though it may well be any other metropolis. The case worker himself is a universal figure, a lonely, doubt-ridden man trying to comprehend the scope and texture of human misery. At once compassionate and detached, he listens to the horror stories of his clients and does what he can, which is not much. Still, he is no mere observer and recorder. His daily dealings with the dregs of society do not make him indifferent—they simply teach him the limits of his effectiveness and turn his anguish into quiet stoicism. What makes the novel an extraordinary achievement—what transforms the sociological content of the work into art—is K.'s success in revealing, with his physical descriptions even more effectively than with the actual case histories, the true state of his charges. Almost in the manner of the French *nouveau roman,* K. constructs a world of precisely observed objects, but his objects speak, and their tales of woe remain vivid.

A városalapító, K.'s second novel, is more abstract and elusive, outlining the political, social, and economic history of an unnamed eastern European city, where rulers and ruling classes kept changing but where the intoxication with power remained constant. The central consciousness is that of a builder who sees everything from the vantage point of his profession. As a young city planner he had been "eager to sketch out the most daring visions of our collective history"; as a middle-aged, middle-echelon executive, however, he is content with his modest share of power and is glad that years of repression and regimentation have not dehumanized him completely.

In *A cinkos* (1978; *The Loser,* 1982) K. uses yet another approach. This novel fairly teems with narrative; scores upon scores of self-contained stories as well as realist mininovels crowd its pages. Yet, in its own way, *A cinkos* is also a piece of experimental fiction, an attempted synthesis of eastern European history. Everything important that happened in Hungary in the last sixty-odd years is somehow worked into the novel. The hero—whom we see alternately as a pampered child, an underground communist, a prisoner, a cabinet minister, an academic, a mental patient—is a composite figure, and others in the novel likewise become characters in a grim political parable.

All of K.'s fictions—the traditional narratives as well as the allegories—are also reflective and meditative. This is especially true of his latest novel, *Kerti mulatság,* a many-faceted, self-consciously stylized and somewhat diffuse recreation of personal and family history. In his political essays and cultural-historical inquiries—*Antipolitika* (1983; *Antipolitics,* 1984) or *Az autonómia kísértése* (1980; the temptation of autonomy)—an always judicious and eloquent K. is able to make self-evident truths pressingly relevant. K. coauthored two studies with the noted sociologist Iván Szelényi (b. 1936): *Új lakótelepek szociológiai problémái* (1969; the sociological problems of new housing estates) and *Az értelmiség útja az osztályhatalomhoz* (1978; *The Intellectuals on the Road to Class Power,* 1979); and though his contribution to both were much more than stylistic, there are few examples of "hard" sociology or books of political philosophy that are as literate and readable as these two works.

In his novels K. delves into private misery and public oppression, and details these corruptions with the concern of a moralist. Not only does he demonstrate a somewhat old-fashioned belief in the moral value of literature, he places the highest premium on human freedom. His quest for individual freedom met with considerable opposition in his own country. While his works were acclaimed in the West—he received prestigious literary prizes in Austria, Switzerland, and Germany, and was elected president of P.E.N., the international writers organization—he was under a publication ban during most of the 1970s and early 1980s. His works began to appear in Hungary again only after the dramatic political changes of the late 1980s.

FURTHER WORKS: *Kitörés* (1975, with Péter Bacsó and Péter Zimre); *Európa köldökén* (1990); *Az újjászületés melankóliája* (1991)

BIBLIOGRAPHY: Howe, I., on *The Case Worker,* NYTBR, 27 Jan. 1974, 1; Kauffmann, S., "G. K.," *Salmagundi,* 57 (1982), 87–91; Sanders, I., "Freedom's Captives: Notes on G. K.'s Novels," *WLT,* 57, 2 (Spring 1983), 210–14; Birnbaum, M. D., "The Tropics of Love and Loyalty in G. K.'s *The Loser,*" *CCur,* 7 (1988), 271–94

IVAN SANDERS

KOSTENKO, Lina

Ukrainian poet, literary critic, and screenwriter, b. 19 Mar. 1930, Rzhyshchiv, Kiev region

Born into a family of teachers, K. completed her secondary education in Kiev and was admitted in 1952 to the prestigious Gorky Institute of Literature in Moscow, from which she graduated with distinction (1956). Attracted to literature very early in life, K. began to write poetry as a child and published her first poems at the age of fifteen in the Kiev-based literary journal *Dnipro*. Later she joined the journal's editorial board, holding a position until 1966, when she was dismissed for defending fellow writers persecuted by the Soviet régime. In the early 1960s she was also employed by the Dovzhenko Film Studios in Kiev as a scriptwriter. In 1958 K. became a member of the Union of Writers of Ukraine. Today, she is a leading Ukrainian poet whose works enjoy immense popularity, both in Ukraine and abroad.

K. belongs to the so-called "shestydesyatnyky," the generation of Ukrainian poets who began to publish during the period of the first Thaw in the 1960s. K.'s three collections of poetry, *Prominnya zemli* (1957; the rays of earth), *Vitryla* (1959; sails), and *Mandrivky sertsya* (1961; *Wanderings of the Heart*, 1990), established her reputation as the premier Ukrainian poet both in Ukraine and in the diaspora, and at the same time unleashed a flood of criticism from many influential Soviet critics. Already in 1958, K. was accused of "formalism," "linguistic trickery, and a pessimism unworthy of a Soviet poet," "mannerism," "modernism," "sickly sorrow and skepticism," and a number of other "sins." After these attacks, K. did not publish for three years. The appearance of her third collection muted the criticism; and her work received considerable praise from various critics including those who had attacked it previously. However, soon the critical mood changed once more. In a *Pravda* article published 14 April 1963, Andry Skaba (b. 1905) attacked the ideological content of the poetry produced by the generation of young Ukrainian poets, singling out K., Ivan Drach (b. 1936), and Mykola Vinhranovsky (b. 1936). The viciousness of these attacks silenced K. for the next ten years. But while she did not publish, she continued to write, and her previous work was widely reprinted, read, and discussed by the Ukrainian émigré community in the West.

K.'s poetry is characterized by a sense of authenticity of expression, an innovative powerful use of language, refreshingly striking, an at times almost exotic imagery coupled with traditional metaphors cast in classical verse, and an uncompromising, almost violent individualism. Recog-

nizing no other law than her own poetic and philosophical convictions, she has been known to refuse even the slightest editorial changes, insisting on the inviolability of her poetic word. Thoroughly nonpolitical, highly lyrical, at times profoundly speculative, the thematic range of her poetry includes autobiography, Ukrainian history, and, more recently, life in medieval Europe. Her early love poetry, such as the poem "Bila symfoniya" (1962; "The White Symphony," 1969), in which unauthentic puppy love is contrasted with a more mature relationship, is a good example of her ability to judge human experience and to understand human nature. Her historical novel in verse, *Marusya Churay* (1979; Marusya Churay), a poetic biography of the legendary 17th-c. Ukrainian folksinger, was instrumental in reviving knowledge about Ukraine's distant past and its rich customs and traditions that had been all but forgotten in the age of Socialist Realism (q.v.). In that sense, K.'s poetry has performed a most important function: that of keeping alive the spirit of Ukrainian national identity during the dark days of enforced Russification and Sovietization of the Ukrainian people. In 1987, as a result of the policies of glasnost and perestroika, K. was finally awarded the coveted Shevchenko Prize for this work. *Marusya Churay* and her dramatic poem *Snih u Florentsiyi* (1989; snow in Florence), a subtle analysis of the interaction between religion and art, are now being staged in various theaters in Ukraine and performed by amateur groups in Ukrainian communities living in the West.

K. has been the leading poetical voice of Ukrainian literature for more than three decades. While remaining firm and constant in her convictions, she has grown in wisdom and knowledge. The political changes in the late 1980s enabled her to travel in the West and to establish direct contact with Ukrainian émigré intellectuals and poets and with many Western writers, which will no doubt have an impact on her future writings. Her popularity has now reached new heights. The latest collection of her poetry, *Vybrane* (1989; selected works), published in an edition of 60,000 copies and containing many of her previously banned poems, was immediately sold out; she continues to enjoy esteem and popularity both in Ukraine and abroad. Despite her considerable success, K. maintains a strong sense of self-criticism: "Poetry and popularity—is an ever-present polarity," she notes, reminding her readers and herself of the poet's true calling—to be a *vox humana*, to speak the truth and to serve the muse and the people.

Free from any didactic or dogmatic overtones, blessed with revealing insight, informed by ethical and moral concerns, K.'s poetry assures its author a prominent place in the pantheon of Ukrainian poetry.

FURTHER WORKS: *Nad berehamy vichnoyi riky* (1977); *Nepovtornist* (1980); *Skifska baba* (1981); *Sad netanuchykh skulptur* (1987); *Buzynovy tsar* (1987)

BIBLIOGRAPHY: Luckyj, G. S. N., Introduction to *Four Ukrainian Poets* (1969), i–iv; Marshal, H., "Soviet National Poets," *Bulletin of the Center for Soviet and East European Studies,* 12 (1973), 1–2; Ovcharenko, M. M., "The Poets of Spirit and Truth: L. K. and Vasyl Symonenko," *UkrR,* 20 (1973), 71–82; Mihailovich, V. D., et al., eds., *Modern Slavic Literatures* (1976), Vol. 2, 481–83; Naydan, M. M., "Floating Flowers: The Poetry of L. K.," *Ulbandus Review,* 1 (1977), 138–39; Naydan, M. M., Afterword to *Selected Works* (1990), 141–50

LEONID RUDNYTZKY

KOTSYUBYNSKY, Mykhaylo

Ukrainian novelist and short-story writer, b. 17 Sept. 1864, Vinnytsya; d. 25 Apr. 1913, Chernihiv

Son of a petty government official and his sickly wife, K. completed his secondary education at the Sharhorod Religious Boarding School in 1880 and continued his studies at the Kamyanets-Podilsky Theological Seminary, from which he was expelled for his political activities in 1882. Unable to pursue university studies and under constant police surveillance, K. became a self-taught scholar, passed his teacher's examination in 1891, and supported himself and his family, after his father lost his position and his mother went blind, by teaching and private tutoring. From 1892 to 1897, he worked for an agricultural commission engaged in grape-phylloxera control in Moldavia and in the Crimea, and in 1898 he moved to Chernihiv, where he became a government clerk. While fighting off poverty, K. was extremely active in Ukrainian cultural and political life and developed contacts with leading intellectuals, such as the writer Ivan Franko (q.v.) and the ethnographer and literary scholar Volodymyr Hnatyuk (1871–1926) in western Ukraine, at that time part of the Austro-Hungarian Empire.

An avid reader, K. was drawn to literature early in life. Influenced by Ukraine's national bard, Taras Schevchenko (1814–1861), as well as West European writers and thinkers, K. became Ukraine's leading prose writer of all time. His extensive travels to West European countries, including a sojourn (1909–1911) on the isle of Capri, are

reflected in his works. K. gained considerable fame in his later years; many of his stories were translated into several European languages already during his lifetime, and a three-volume Russian edition of his collected works was published in 1911–1914.

K.'s early stories, such as "Andry Soloveyko" (1884; Andry Soloveyko), "21 hrudnya, na Vvedeniye" (1885; the 21st of December of the day of presentation), "Na viru" (1891; a common-law marriage), are steeped in 19th-c. ethnographic realism and reflect the populist ideas prevalent at that time, but his later work is characterized by a sophisticated impressionistic style and subtle psychological probings into the human soul. Among his best are the short stories "Lyalechka" (1901; the dolly), an ironic account of an intellectual's assessment of his life, "Tsvit yabluni" (1902; "Apple Blossom," 1973), a story about a writer who plans to use artistically observations made of his dying daughter, and "Podarunok na imenyny" (1912; "The Birthday Present," 1973), a psychological study of a boy whose father takes him to a hanging for his birthday.

K.'s most famous works are the novella "Intermezzo" (1909; intermezzo), a stylistic masterpiece in which elements of realism and impressionism (qq.v.) serve to heighten the psychological effect, and the pastoral novel *Tini zabutykh predkiv* (1911; *Shadows of Forgotten Ancestors,* 1981), which, set in the Carpathian mountains, presents a hauntingly beautiful slice of life of the Hutsul folk by exploring local legends and beliefs. This work, along with four other stories of K., was made into a successful film of the same title in 1967.

A consummate stylist, unsurpassed as a writer of Ukrainian prose, K. has become a classic writer of Ukrainian literature. His work is required reading in schools and the subject of countless scholarly investigations. In both Vinnytsya and Chernihiv, K. museums have been established to honor his memory and his lasting achievement.

FURTHER WORKS: *V putakh shaytana i inshi opovidannya* (1899); *Po-lyudskomu: opovidannya z bessarabskoho zhyttya* (1900); *Opovidannya* (1903); *Poyedynok i inshi opovidannya* (1903); *Debyut* (1911); *Lysty do Volodymyra Hnatyuka* (1914); *Tvory* (1924); *Tvory* (5 vols., 1925); *Vybrani tvory* (1927); *Tvory* (5 vols., 1930); *Vybrani tvory* (1934); *Vybrani tvory* (1936); *Vybrani opovidannya* (1937); *Vybrani tvory,* (4 vols., 1948); *Opovidannya. Novely. Povisti* (1953); *Povisti ta opovidannya* (1954); *Tvory* (3 vols., 1955); *Vybrani tvory* (1957); *Tvory* (6 vols., 1962); *Tvory* (7 vols., 1975). FURTHER VOLUMES IN ENGLISH: *Chrysalis and*

Other Stories (1958); *Fata Morgana* (1976; rev. ed., 1980)

BIBLIOGRAPHY: Kalenichenko, N., Introduction to *The Birthday Present and Other Stories* (1973), 3–10; Mihailovich, V. D., et al., eds., *Modern Slavic Literatures* (1976), Vol. 2, 483–86; Kolesnyk, P., Introduction to *Fata Morgana and Other Stories* (1976), 5–10; Yaremenko, V., Introduction to *Fata Morgana and Other Stories* (1980), 5–11; Rubchak, B., "The Music of Satan and the Bedeviled World: An Essay on M. K.," in *Shadows of Forgotten Ancestors* (1981), 77–121; Nowosad, M. E., "Mysterious and Irrational Elements in the Works of M. K. and Theodor Storm," in Bristol, E., ed., *East European Literature: Selected Papers from the Second World Congress for Soviet and East European Studies* (1982), 43–56

LEONID RUDNYTZKY

KRISTEVA, Julia

French-Bulgarian literary theoretician and critic (writing in French), b. 24 June 1941, Sliven, Bulgaria

A literary critic, semiotician, psychoanalyst, and professor at the University of Paris VII, K. is one of the most important and original thinkers in France today. Educated in Bulgaria, K. emigrated to France in 1965. As a doctoral fellow at L'École Pratique des Hautes Études in Paris, she studied under Lucien Goldmann (1913–1970) and Roland Barthes (q.v.). Shortly after, she met Philippe Sollers (q.v.), whom she married.

K. chose one of the most propitious moments to make her debut on the Parisian intellectual scene. The years 1965–1966 were marked by what can only be called an explosion of French intellectual thought. Undaunted by the impact of Barthes, Michel Foucault, Jacques Lacan (qq.v.) Émile Benveniste (1902–1976), and Louis Althusser (1918–1990), K. succeeded in conquering the Parisian intelligentsia with such publications as "Bakhtine, le mot, le dialogue et le roman" (1967; "Word, Dialogue, and Novel," 1980) and "Pour une sémiologie des paragrammes" (1967; for a semiology of paragrams).

In 1970 she published the doctoral dissertation that she had written under Goldmann in 1966–1967, *Le texte du roman, Approche sémiologique d'une structure discursive transformationnelle* (the text of the novel, a semiological approach to a transformational discursive structure). This work analyzes the origins of the novel in the late Middle Ages from the perspective of Bakhtinian "post-formalism," which K. was among the first to

introduce in France. Her background in Russian formalism and training in linguistics made her invaluable to the *Tel Quel* team, whose editorial board she joined in 1970.

K. wrote an introduction to linguistics entitled *Le langage, cet inconnu* (1969; *Language: The Unknown,* 1989) under the name of Joyaux (the family name of Sollers). With *Séméiotiké, recherches pour une sémanalyse* (1969; séméiotiké, research for a semanalysis) she firmly established her reputation in France and abroad. In this volume of essays she brings literary practice and psychoanalysis to bear on semiotic theory, and thereby formulates an original "textual semiotics" that makes subjectivity a fundamental concern of language.

La révolution du langage poétique, L'avant-garde à la fin du XIXe siècle. Lautréamont et Mallarmé (1974; *Revolution in Poetic Language,* 1984) is still considered her major theoretical work. The culmination of years of research, this state-doctoral thesis *(doctorat d'état)* draws on linguistics, philosophy, pschoanalysis, and avant-garde literature to elaborate a theoretical discourse centered on the question of subjectivity in language and history. K. demonstrates how the epistemological and sociopolitical transformations of the latter part of the 19th c. can be discerned in avant-garde "texts of rupture," where the subversion of language reciprocally implies the subversion of the writing subject, and both imply a critique of the existing sociopolitical order.

In the spring of 1974 K. traveled to China with other members of the *Tel Quel* team. Upon her return to Paris, she published *Des Chinoises* (1974; *About Chinese Women,* 1977), which is as much about K. and the West as it is about the evolution of Chinese women under Mao Tse-Tung. A highly subjective work, it allows us to understand the impact that the Chinese Cultural Revolution had on French intellectuals during the late 1960s and early 1970s. K.'s interest in non-Western cultures is also the basis for the collective work that she coedited in 1975, *La traversée des signes* (the traverse of signs).

Polylogue (polylogue), a collection of essays published in 1977, reflects K.'s growing interest in questions pertaining to the place of femininity and motherhood in Western thought and culture. *Folle vérité* (1979; mad truth) is a collective work resulting from a seminar on psychotic discourse and truth directed by K. at a hospital in Paris. K.'s work as a practicing psychoanalyst has greatly influenced all her subsequent publications. In *Pouvoirs de l'horreur, Essai sur l'abjection* (1980; *Powers of Horror: An Essay on Abjection,* 1982) K. scrutinizes both biblical writings and contemporary literary texts to reveal the abjection that underlies religious, moral, and political codes. *Histoires d'amour* (1983; *Tales of Love,* 1987) stems from K.'s experiences as a psychoanalyst and a mother. She examines the notion of love in relation to psychoanalysis, literature, religion, and philosophy. In analyzing discourses on love from the ancient Greeks to the moderns, K. traces the evolution of subjectivity in the West. K.'s work on the psychoanalytic dimensions of love in *Histoires d'amour* and *Au commencement était l'amour. Psychanalyse et foi* (1985; *In the Beginning Was Love: Psychoanalysis and Faith,* 1987) led to her study on loss, mourning, and absence in *Soleil noir; dépression et mélancolie* (1987; *Black Sun: Depression and Melancholia,* 1989). She examines the melancholic imaginary from both clinical and aesthetic perspectives.

In 1990 K. published *Les samouraïs* (*The Samurai,* 1992), a semiautobiographical novel on the passions underlying Parisian intellectual life in the 1960s and 1970s. *Etrangers à nous-mêmes* (1988; *Strangers to Ourselves,* 1991) and *Lettre ouverte à Harlem Désir* (1990; open letter to Harlem Désir) are works that reflect the political preoccupations of the 1980s and 1990s. Arguing that being a foreigner seems to have become the normal condition for the citizen at the end of the 20th c., K. turns to the question of exile, which has been one of her fundamental preoccupations as a foreigner living in France. She contends that we shall never be able to tolerate others so long as we have not yet come to terms with the otherness that lies within us.

As a psychoanalyst and writer, K. brings new insights to the study of Western thought and culture. Interdisciplinary in perspective, K.'s work provides an original response to the contemporary debate on the human subject and its relation to language, sexuality, and politics.

FURTHER VOLUMES IN ENGLISH: *Desire in Language, A Semiotic Approach to Literature and Art* (1980); *The K. Reader* (1986)

BIBLIOGRAPHY: Lewis, P., "Revolutionary Semiotics," *Diacritics,* 4, 3 (1974), 28–32; Roudiez, L. S., Introduction to *Desire in Language* (1980), 1–20; Pajaczkowska, C., "Introduction to K.," *m/f,* 5–6 (1981), 149–57; Roudiez, L. S., Introduction to *Revolution in Poetic Language* (1984), 1–10; Barthes, R., "K.'s *Séméiotiké*," *The Rustle of Language* (1986), 168–71; Jardine, A., "Opaque Texts and Transparent Contexts: The Political Difference of J. K.," in Miller, N. K., ed., *The Poetics of Gender* (1986), 96–115; Moi, T., Introduction to *The K. Reader* (1986), 1–22; Lechte, J., *J. K.* (1990); Fletcher, J., and A. Benjamin, eds., *Abjection, Melancholia, and Love: The Work of J. K.* (1990)

DANIELLE MARX-SCOURAS

KRYNICKI, Ryszard

Polish poet, b. 28 June 1943, Sankt Valentin, Austria

K., one of the most significant figures of the New Wave in Polish poetry, began his literary career in the late 1960s under a banner of revolt against cultural and political uniformity. He graduated from Adam Mickiewicz University in Poznań (1967). During his student years, K., along with Stanisław Barańczak (q.v.), established the poetic group "Attempts." Both writers were considered the most outstanding representatives of the so-called "linguistic current" in poetry. They focused on a critique of the official language saturated with communist newspeak. By exposing this contaminated language they intended to reveal the captive conscience of the common individual under communism.

K.'s first volume of poetry, *Akt urodzenia* (1969; a birth certificate), was a promising representation of "linguistic poetics." Following the chief theoretician of the prewar Polish avant-garde, Tadeusz Peiper (1891–1969), in this volume K. adopted a style known as an "arrangement of blossoming." Each "blossoming poem" consisted of a whole set of ever more developed sentence structures reflecting the psychological process of cognition.

In the early 1970s, K., like Barańczak and Adam Zagajewski (q.v.), rejected the concept of the poet isolated from social realities and attempted to introduce political topics, such as the workers' bloody protests in December 1970, into his verses. His second volume, *Organizm zbiorowy* (1975; a collective organism), bears traces of such attempts. As a result of K.'s involvement in protests against restrictions of civil liberties, his name was put on the censor's black list in December 1975. Consequently, his next volume, *Nasze życie rośnie* (1978; our life grows), could only be published in the West.

K.'s poetry of the mid-1970s is characterized by the intertwining of two different kinds of sensitivity: visionary and ethical. While reading these works, one is impressed by the quality of strangeness. The internal world of the poet is placed on the border between a waking and a dreamlike state. This visionary imagination is backed by a feeling of ethical chaos and by the image of reality in which intimate experiences can no longer be a protective shelter against the storm of history. Many of K.'s poems have drawn from the prophetic tradition through both the use of devices and the poet's ethical passion.

In the late 1970s, K.'s name frequently appeared in the uncensored quarterly *Zapis* among the names of its editors and contributors. After Wojciech Jaruzelski's declaration of martial law in December 1981, K. chose to remain in Poland. During the 1980s, he published several volumes of poetry in the underground: *Niewiele więcej* (1980; not much more), *Jeżeli w jakimś kraju* (1983; if in some country), and *Niewiele więcej i nowe wiersze* (1984; not much more and new poems). These independent publishing activities did not fail to have an impact on the formation of K.'s literary language. Freedom from censorship contributed to the literalness and simplicity of the poet's recent works.

Since his debut in 1969, K.'s poetics has come a long way. His early visionary works often assumed a verbose form, rich in both wordplay and paradoxes. All of those devices were gradually replaced by a means typical of poetic aphorisms and, when martial law had been imposed on Poland, by moral or even political slogans. K.'s recent collection of poetry, entitled *Niepodlegli nicości* (1989; independent of nothingness), contains some of his old and new works. It was published by an official publishing house in Poland under the changing political circumstances. The new poems included in this volume represent an ecumenical position toward cognitive and ethical values, a position that no longer depends on any political encouragement or restrictions, but on the revelation of difficult, timeless truths.

K. has won several significant literary awards, among them the Kościelskis Prize (1973) and the Jurzykowski Prize (1989).

FURTHER VOLUME IN ENGLISH: *Citizen R. K. Does Not Live* (1985)

BIBLIOGRAPHY: Barańczak, S., Foreword to *Citizen R. K. Does Not Live* (1985), 7–9; Witkowski, T., "R. K.: Between Metaphysics and Politics," *Studium Papers*, 14, 1–2 (1990), 70

TADEUSZ WITKOWSKI

KUMIN, Maxine

American poet, essayist, novelist, short-story writer, and children's-book author, b. 6 June 1925, Philadelphia, Pa.

Although she has published essays and fiction, as well as a notable body of books for children, several in collaboration with fellow poet Anne Sexton (q.v.), K. is best known as a poet. Her work combines urban sophistication, an intellec-

tual awareness of the universe, with deep knowledge of and feeling for both nature and rural life. Her biography reflects a similar duality: After living for many years in the Boston area, where she was a student at Radcliffe College (A.B., 1946; M.A., 1948) and then taught creative writing at institutions in the region, including Tufts and Brandeis universities, the University of Massachusetts, and Newton College, she moved to a farm in New Hampshire, where she gardens extensively and raises Arabian and quarter horses.

One of the words most commonly used in reviews and commentaries on K.'s work is "survival." She does write about personal and social grief, but the emphasis is on things that grow, continuity between generations, and other forces that insist on life—apprehended emotionally, though unsentimentally. The title of K.'s first published collection of poems, *Halfway* (1961), suggests the traditional midpoint in the biblically allotted human lifespan of threescore and ten, Dante's "middle of the journey." K. was at mid-life, rhetorically, if not actuarially, but at the beginning of a poetic career that, over the next thirty years, was to witness the publication of eleven collections of her poems.

Halfway introduces themes that recur in K.'s work, particularly in *Up Country: Poems of New England* (1972), awarded the Pulitzer Prize for poetry in 1973, *Our Ground Time Here Will Be Brief* (1982), and *Nurture: Poems New and Selected* (1989). The particular survival of which she speaks in poems about fruits and vegetables, children, and animals is, throughout, what Sandra M. Gilbert (b. 1936) and Susan Gubar (b. 1944), writing in *The Norton Anthology of Literature by Women* (1985), call "a redemptive choice for sanity." K.'s close association with Anne Sexton and her references to her friend since the latter's suicide underscore the sense in which both physical and psychic survival represent conscious choices for her.

K.'s two collections of essays make a deliberate effort to connect the poet's experience of language with the lived experience of the natural world of New England. Thus, *To Make a Prairie* (1979) is subtitled "Essays on Poets, Poetry and Country Living," whereas the same relationship, at once metaphysical and metaphorical, is implied by the title of *In Deep: Country Essays* (1987). By contrast, K.'s fiction tends to concentrate on interpersonal relations; once more, a title, this time of a collection of short stories, *Why Can't We Live Together Like Civilized Human Beings?* (1982), suggests both subject and tone. The children's books that K. has published, the earliest of them predating her first collection of poems, are fantasies or nature stories, all represented with a poet's ear and a poet's wit. Illustrated (by other hands), they both stress and stimulate the imagination.

FURTHER WORKS: *Sebastian and the Dragon* (1960); *Spring Things* (1961); *Summer Story* (1961); *Follow the Fall* (1961); *A Winter Friend* (1961); *Mittens in May* (1962); *No One Writes a Letter to the Snail* (1962); *Eggs of Things* (1963, with Anne Sexton); *Archibald the Traveling Poodle* (1963); *More Eggs of Things* (1964, with Anne Sexton); *Speedy Digs Downside Up* (1964); *The Beach before Breakfast* (1964); *The Privilege* (1965); *Through Dooms of Love* (1965); *Paul Bunyan* (1966); *Faraway Farm* (1967); *Wonderful Babies of 1809 and Other Years* (1968); *The Passions of Uxport* (1968); *When Grandmother Was Young* (1969); *When Mother Was Young* (1970); *The Nightmare Factory* (1970); *The Abduction* (1971); *When Great-Grandmother Was Young* (1971); *Joey and the Birthday Present* (1971, with Anne Sexton); *Tilting the Barn Swallow* (1972); *The Designated Heir* (1974); *House, Bridge, Fountain, Gate* (1975); *The Wizard's Tears* (1975, with Anne Sexton); *What Color Is Caesar?* (1978); *The Retrieval System* (1978); *Closing the Ring* (1984); *The Microscope* (1984); *The Long Approach* (1985); *Looking for Luck* (1992)

BIBLIOGRAPHY: Green, C., *A Writer Is Essentially a Spy* (1972); Booth, P., "M. K.'s Survival," *APR,* 7, 6 (Nov.–Dec. 1978), 18–19; Estess, S. P., "Past Halfway: *The Retrieval System* by M. K.," *IowaR,* 10, 4 (Autumn 1979), 99–109; Hammond, K., "An Interview with M. K.," *WHR,* 33, 1 (Winter 1979), 2–15; Armitage, S., "An Interview with M. K.," *Paintbrush,* 7–8 (1980–1981), 48–58; George, D. H., "K. on K. and Sexton: An Interview," *Poesis,* 6, 2 (1985), 1–18; Harris, P., "Poetry Chronicle: Hunger, Hope, and Nurture: Poetry from Michael Ryan, the Chinese Democracy Movement, and M. K.," *VQR,* 67, 3 (1991), 455–77

LILLIAN S. ROBINSON

LACAN, Jacques

French psychoanalyst and psychoanalytic theorist,
b. 13 Apr. 1901, Paris; d. 9 Sept. 1981, Paris

L. studied medicine and psychiatry at the Faculté
de Médecine de Paris, and in 1932 he published
his doctoral thesis *De la psychose paranoïaque
dans ses rapports avec la personnalité* (rev. ed.,
1975, *De la psychose paranoïaque dans ses rapports avec la personnalité suivi de Premiers écrits
sur la paranoïa;* the paranoiac psychosis in relation to the personality; paranoiac psychosis and its
relations to the personality and early writings on
paranoia). In this same year, L. became clinical
director of the Faculté de Médecine de Paris. In
1934 he became a member of the Société Psychanalytique de Paris, and two years later he
served as staff psychiatrist at various Paris mental
hospitals. During this time, he became interested
in surrealism (q.v.), founded by André Breton
(q.v.), in its approach to the unconscious, and he
contributed to the surrealist publication *Le Mino-
taure.*

From the early 1950s to his death at age eighty,
L. initiated and dominated the renewal of popular
interest in psychoanalysis in France. L. developed
Sigmund Freud's (q.v.) psychological theory to
incorporate the foundations of structural linguistics. Although his theories were considered controversial, L. was generally acknowledged as one
of the most influential figures in the intellectual
circles of Paris. He is often associated with the
structuralist movement, which included, among
others, Louis Althusser (1918–1990), an interpreter of Marx, Claude Lévi-Strauss, Jacques Derrida, and Michel Foucault (qq.v.). These theorists
and practitioners of structural analysis recognized
the Swiss linguist Ferdinand de Saussure (1857–
1913) as the pioneer who served as the inspiration
of their methods.

In 1936, at the XIVth Psychoanalysis International Congress in Marienbad, L. made an astonishing debut into the psychoanalytic world with a
speech entitled "Le stade du miroir" ("The Mir-
ror-Phase," 1937). In this address, L. demonstrated the primordial role of "identification" in
early childhood, acknowledging several phases that
infants go through to acquire their own identity.
What L. called the "mirror stage" is defined as
the various reactions of a child placed in front of
a mirror. At first a child considers the reflection a
reality, exterior to himself, which he tries to catch;
then, realizing there is no one behind the mirror,
he stops looking for an Other; and finally he
recognizes that other person as himself. In other
words, from a fragmented vision of his own body
he comes to perceive its global form through an
exterior image. A child's primary identification
with the mirror reflection, which L. qualified as
imaginaire, works as a source of all the child's
further identifications. This fundamental discovery
for psychoanalysis was further explored in another
speech: " 'Le stade du miroir' comme formateur
de la fonction du 'je' " (1949; "The Mirror As
Formative of the Function of the I," 1968), delivered in 1949 at the XVIth Congress in Zurich.

In 1953 internal conflict within the organization
drove him to split from the Société de Paris and
to organize the Société Française de Psychanalyse.
Then, in 1964, his exclusion from the International
Society led L. to create the École Freudienne de
Paris. L.'s new school was designed to train future
analysts. Its unorthodox methods challenged the
traditional aspects of psychoanalytic training and
practice. In 1980, L. dissolved his École Freudienne de Paris and formed l'École de la Cause
Freudienne.

From 1951 to 1963 L. was a lecturer in psychoanalysis at St. Ann's hospital in Paris, and in 1963
he began lecturing at the École Normale Supérieure and later at the École Pratique des Hautes
Études. For about twenty years, L. gave a biweekly seminar attended by a generation of French
intellectuals, accounting for his great influence and
reputation in France. His wide-ranging knowledge
enabled him to broaden psychoanalysis to include
linguistics, rhetoric, anthropology, and philosophy, as well as various scientific fields such as
mathematics, solid geometry, and optics.

Throughout his career, L. advocated a return to
Freud. His essential theoretical contribution to
psychoanalysis consists of two main principles:
L'inconscient est le discours de l'Autre (the unconscious is the discourse of the Other) and *l'inconscient est structuré comme un langage* (the
unconscious is structured as a language). When
developing his theory, L. made use of the linguistics theories of Saussure and Roman Jakobson

(1896–1982) as well as the anthropological studies of Lévi-Strauss. L. was further influenced by philosophers such as Heidegger and Hegel.

In his 1953 paper "Fonction et champ de la parole et du langage" (1956; "Function and Field of Speech and Language," 1968) psychoanalytic theory is approached in terms of structuralist methodology. In this paper, L. expressed one of his major themes, "the unconscious is structured as a language," and went on to say that the instrument of psychoanalysis is speech. For that purpose, L. used the Saussurean concept of the "sign" as defined by its two components, the signifier and the signified. In order to demonstrate the mechanism by which repression works (as described by Freud), L. gave supremacy to the signifier. Faithful to Freud's intuitions that the laws of dream are equivalent to those of poetry, L. attempted to interpret the poetics of the unconscious via fundamental figures of speech such as metaphor and metonymy. Metaphor occurs when interpretation results from a substitution of signifiers, whereas metonymy is ensued by the presence of the former signifier in the *chaîne signifiante* but is shadowed by the presence of a new signifier. Hence, the role of the psychoanalyst is to help the patient to repossess the lost sign and understand the process by which it has been repressed.

L.'s masterpiece *Écrits* (1966; rev. ed., *Écrits, I–II*, 2 vols., 1970; writings) is a collection of his most significant theoretical writings dealing with both psychoanalysis and language. Beginning in 1973, transcripts of L.'s lectures appeared in a multivolume series entitled *Le seminaire de J. L.*, four of which had been published in English: *Livre XI: Les quatre concepts fondamentaux de la psychanalyse, 1964* (1973; *The Four Fundamental Concepts of Psycho-Analysis*, 1978); *Livre I: Les écrits techniques de Freud, 1953–1954* (1975; *Freud's Papers on Technique, 1953–1954*, 1988); *Livre II: Le moi dans la théorie de Freud et dans la technique de la psychanalyse, 1954–1955* (1978; *The Ego in Freud's Theory and in the Technique of Psychoanalysis, 1954–1955*, 1988); and *Livre VII: L'éthique de la psychanalyse, 1959–1960* (1986; *The Ethics of Psychoanalysis, 1959–1960*, 1992).

With the publication of *Écrits*, L. gained international reputation as a psychoanalytical theorist. His influence was strongly felt in other disciplines such as literary criticism both in the U.S. and Latin America. In France Lacan's theories were in part incorporated into feminist criticism (q.v.) in the 1970s and 1980s, notably in regard to the works of Luce Irigaray (b. 1939), Julia Kristeva, and Hélène Cixous (qq.v.) to explain the root of sexual identity. Other authors whose work has been influenced by L. include the French novelist

Claude Ollier and the Italian novelist Paolo Volpini as well as the Polish novelist and dramatist Witold Gombrowicz (qq.v.).

Speech being the object as well as the instrument of his practice, L. himself developed a unique style in his work. He was considered a creative writer, for he was gifted with the capacity of autocriticism, which enabled him to observe the ways his analytical principles were manifested through his style. L. willingly blended various styles. He could be as abstract in his writing as Stéphane Mallarmé (1842–1898) had been, and his speech might also be rich and replete with witticisms.

An eminent and controversial figure in the psychoanalytic and intellectual worlds, L. dealt with and in orality, yet his legacy, as it must be, is in print. His *Écrits* are the conscious voice of the unconscious, the tip of the iceberg that refers us to hidden depths. In its effect on literature, poetry, and criticism, Lacanian interpretation has had a lasting effect on language itself.

FURTHER WORKS: *Télévision* (1974; *Television*, 1990); *Le séminaire: Livre XX: Encore, 1972–1973* (1975); *Le sinthome* (1976); *L., J. Travaux et interventions* (1977); *L. in italia, 1953–1978=L. en Italie, 1953–1978* (1978; bilingual ed.); *Le séminaire: Livre III: Les psychoses, 1955–1956* (1981); *L'acte psychanalytique: Séminaire 1967–68* (1982); *Les complexes familiaux dans la formation de l'individu: essai d'analyse d'une fonction en psychologie* (1984); *Almanach de la dissolution* (1986); *Joyce avec L.* (1987); *Le séminaire: Livre VIII: Le transfert, 1960–1961* (1991); *Le séminaire: Livre XVII: L'envers de la psychanalyse* (1991). FURTHER VOLUMES IN ENGLISH: *The Language of the Self: The Function of Language in Psychoanalysis* (1968; rev. ed., *Speech and Language in Psychoanalysis*, 1981); *Écrits: A Selection* (1977)

BIBLIOGRAPHY: Palmier, J.-M., *L.* (1970); Hesnard, A., *De Freud à L.* (2nd ed., 1971); Fages, J.-B., *Comprendre J. L.* (1971); Lacoue-Labarthe, P., and J.-L. Nancy, *Le titre de la lettre* (1973); Georgin, R., *L.* (1977); Clément, C., *Vies et légendes de J. L.* (1981); Mitchell, J., and J. Rose, eds., *Feminine Sexuality: J. L. and the école freudienne* (1982); Georgin, R., *De Lévi-Strauss à L.* (1983); Dor, J., *Bibliographie des travaux de J. L.* (1984); Silhol, R., *Le texte du désir* (1984); Dor, J., *Introduction à la lecture de L.* (1985); Raglan-Sullivan, E., *J. L. and the Philosophy of Psychoanalysis* (1986); MacCannell, J. F., *Figuring L.: Criticism and the Cultural Unconscious* (1986); Andrès, M., *L. et la question du métalangage* (1987); Felman, S., *J. L. and the*

Adventure of Insight: Psychoanalysis in Contemporary Culture (1987); Bowie, M., *Freud, Proust, and L.: Theory As Fiction* (1987); Muller, J. P., and W. J. Richardson, *The Purloined Poe: L., Derrida, and Psychoanalytic Reading* (1988); Grosz, E., *J. L.: A Feminist Introduction* (1990); Hogan, P. C., and L. Pandit, eds., *Criticism and L.: Essays and Dialogue on Language, Structure, and the Unconscious* (1990); Bowie, M., *L.* (1991); Smith, J. H., *Arguing with L.: Ego Psychology and Language* (1991)

GENEVIÈVE TROUSSEREAU

LAFOURCADE, Enrique

Chilean novelist and editor, b. 14 Oct. 1927, Santiago

L.'s early education was in Santiago, but in the 1950s he spent considerable time abroad: in France, where he studied art history at the Sorbonne (1954), in Italy, as the recipient of an Italian government honor fellowship (1955), and in Spain, where he served as cultural attaché in Madrid (1959–1962). During the 1960s and early 1970s, he taught at numerous American universities (Iowa, Utah, UCLA, Illinois, New Mexico, California, Columbia), returning to some schools two or three different times. Since 1972 he has remained principally in Santiago, editing the literary supplement of the Santiago newspaper *El Mercurio,* working periodically in television, and writing essays for newspapers, magazines, and books.

Due to his caustic attacks on public figures and his liberal life-style, L. has had a stormy public and private life. However, he retains the devotion of numerous Chilean novelists and short-story writers who make up the Chilean Generation of 1950. While some critics insist that L. "invented" the Generation of 1950, there are indications that it was a true "generation" of postwar authors who chose to reject the established *Criollista* writers and their regional-sociological approach to Chilean problems. In truth, L. organized a short-story contest and thereby gave his young colleagues the chance to express themselves. Then he published in 1954 the results of that contest in the *Antología del nuevo cuento chileno* (anthology of the new Chilean short story)—which gave many of those young writers their beginnings, including José Donoso and Jorge Edwards (qq.v.), who are, together with L., three of Chile's leading novelists.

While numerous Chileans fled their country to avoid the conflicts with governments of the extreme left and right during the 1970s and 1980s, L. remained in Santiago, taking up battle with leaders and their decisions. Irrespective of the people in power, L. has openly voiced his opposition to many of the actions with which he disagreed. His outspokenness on social decadence is an outgrowth of L.'s nihilistic philosophy, which emerges in his fiction as his view of life. He cherishes his individuality and states that he has been a literary activist, "studying, investigating, observing, writing, commenting on, defending, attacking, exposing, traveling, giving classes, living, and . . . creating."

One of the predominant elements in L.'s prose fiction has been an utter pessimistic tone, which unites character and theme in a tight band. L.'s disillusionment with modern society, together with his nihilistic (Nietzschean) weltanschauung produces characters who, as antiheroes, become increasingly alienated, materialistic, sadistic, dehumanized, and aware of their own absurd state of existence.

Because of his narrative structures and his use of existentialist key words and titles, such as *Asedio* (1956; blockade), early critics saw L. as an existentialist, but he personally expressed in 1985 that he was incensed by any suggestion that he had ever been an existentialist or was ever influenced by that school of thought. Yet he is proud to be considered a nihilist. He feels that the world should not be portrayed in literature as simply Manichaean, as a dichotomy of good and evil.

L.'s later fiction does not appear to have varied far from his earlier molds: revolutionaries who terrorize and then go running home to mother or father when things work out badly; individuals who create their own religion, saying it is of God, but condemn or manipulate followers rather than saving them; obscenely conniving bureaucrats who usurp human freedoms; or obsessive manipulators who abuse others in the pursuit of materialistic gains as they lower themselves into the quagmire of the dilemma of modern life. Some of his novels, such as *Variaciones sobre el tema de Nastasia Filippovna y el príncipe Mishkin* (1975; variations on the theme of Nastasia Filippovna and Prince Mishkin) and *Adiós al Führer* (1982; farewell to the führer), are full of symbolism and are sometimes difficult to follow. But in *Novela de Navidad* (1965; Christmas novel), *Terroristas* (1976; terrorists), and numerous others it is easy to get caught up in the plot and his parody of the characters' causes. Often L. takes a sensationalist theme and thrusts his characters into a marasmic world that destroys them.

L. was one of the early writers to attack Latin American dictators—a theme that became popular in the "boom" period of Spanish American literature of 1965–1980—and he did it with his highly acclaimed *Fiesta del Rey Acab* (1959; *King Ahab's Feast,* 1963).

His most successful novel has been *Palomita blanca* (1971; little white dove), Chile's greatest best-seller. Chilean newspaper critics passed it off as a popular work influenced by Erich Segal's (b. 1937) *Love Story* (1970), but it is a spontaneous synthesis of the themes that L. had been elaborating in previous novels, which often lacked the human warmth, anguish, and spontaneity that *Palomita blanca* conveys. Published in several languages, it has never appeared in English. *Palomita blanca* depicts the popular optimism and the language changes occurring in Chile during the important historical period of the Allende campaign for the presidency in 1970.

L. has worked with many innovations, but not always successfully. He has won numerous important Chilean literary prizes for his novels, such as the Municipal Prize of Santiago in 1959 for *Fiesta del Rey Acab,* the coveted Gabriela Mistral Prize in 1961 for *El príncipe y las ovejas* (1961; the prince and the sheep), and in 1982 the María Luisa Bombal Prize in Literature. His total output of twenty novels and ten other books, most with numerous editions, has been impressive and effective, but the public is often polarized into readers who admire him and those who hate him.

FURTHER WORKS: *El libro de Kareen* (1950); *Pena de muerte* (1952); *Para subir al cielo* (1959); *Invención a dos voces* (1963); *Fábulas de L.* (1963); *Pronombres personales* (1967); *Frecuencia modulada* (1968); *En el fondo* (1973); *Salvador Allende* (1973); *Inventario I* (1975); *Buddha y los chocolates envenenados* (1977); *Nadie es la patria* (1980); *Animales literarios de Chile* (1982); *El escriba sentado* (1982); *El gran taimado* (1984); *Los hijos del arco iris* (1985); *Carlitos Gardel, mejor que nunca* (1985); *Humo hacia el sur* (1987); *Pepita de oro* (1990); *Hoy está solo mi corazón* (1990)

BIBLIOGRAPHY: Fleak, K., "Promotion of the Chilean Short Story," *LangQ,* 24 (1986), 31–32, 37; Godoy Gallardo, E., *La generación del 50 en Chile: Historia de un movimiento literario* (1991)

LON PEARSON

LAGUERRE, Enrique

Puerto Rican novelist, short-story writer, dramatist, essayist, and poet; b. 3 May 1906, Moca

L., an educator by profession, began his career at age nineteen and became a certified teacher two years later. In 1935 he published the novel *La llamarada* (the blaze), which brought him national and international acclaim. In 1936 he worked as a school administrator and the next year received

his B.A. in education from the University of Puerto Rico. From 1937 to 1938 L. taught at Fajardo High School. The next three years he worked as an educational author for the Puerto Rican Department of Public Instruction ("School of the Air" radio series), and in 1941 he obtained his M.A. from the University of Puerto Rico. Between 1943 and 1978 L. wrote eight novels, a play, several short stories, and four books of essays. He taught at the University of Puerto Rico and at several distinguished American universities. He received two honorary doctor's degrees and was named a fellow by the American Association of Teachers of Spanish and Portuguese (1980). In 1967 L. was elected president of the Society of Puerto Rican authors and the next year he became a member of P.E.N.

In *La llamarada* L. presents a conflict between the workers of a sugar mill and the absentee owners. The protagonist, Juan Antonio Borrás, is a recent university graduate whose conscience is split between materialistic interests and the problems of the poor Puerto Rican people (*jíbaros*). In the next novel, *Solar Montoya* (1941; Montoya plantation), the *jíbaros* who attempt to grow coffee face such powerful obstacles as hurricanes, poor management, and high tariffs. Unlike the previous two novels, *El 30 de febrero* (1943; the 30th of February) takes place in an urban locale and a university environment. The plot revolves around a hunchback, Teófilo Sampedro, who must live and compete in a merciless society.

La resaca (1949; the undertow) is L.'s masterpiece and constitutes a departure in theme and technique from his previous works. It covers a period of Puerto Rican history (from 1870 to 1898) in fictional form. To read *La resaca* is to get immersed in the late colonial times of the island and to experience the despotism practiced by the Spanish rulers. An omniscient narrator tells the story.

La ceiba en el tiesto (1956; the ceiba tree in the flower pot) and *El Laberinto* (1959; *The Labyrinth,* 1960) depict the lot of Puerto Ricans living in other parts of the U.S. In *La ceiba en el tiesto* the main protagonist avoids responsibility for his involvement with a political group and seeks refuge in New York City where he leads an anonymous life. *El Laberinto* is even more a New York novel than *La ceiba en el tiesto.*

L.'s most recent novels are *Cauce sin río* (1962; river bed without a river), *El fuego y su aire* (1970; fire and its air), and *Los amos benévolos* (1976; *Benevolent Masters,* 1983). *Cauce sin río* is an introspective novel. All the events of the novel are sifted through the protagonist's mind. *El fuego y su aire* continues the introspective vein. It is another novel of the quest for Puerto Rican identity. L. advances his technical experimentation in this work by the frequent use of interior monologues, perspectivism, and daring metaphors. In *Los amos benévolos* L. approaches the practice of magic realism (q.v.), a predominant trend of modern Spanish American fiction. It is an indictment against Puerto Rican nouveaux riches.

As a dramatist L. is credited with only one work, *La resentida* (1960; the resentful woman), a historical play, which was first staged in 1944.

L. is the most significant Puerto Rican novelist of the 20th c. He has thoroughly explored the culture, history, and psychology of his people. While he does not pontificate, his denunciation of Puerto Rico's evils does call for a social commitment: The Puerto Rican reader must seek better alternatives for his condition. L. uses both traditional and modern techniques and does link with the Latin American narrative "boom" in his espousal of magical realism and the frequent use of interior monologues. He is both a regional and a universal writer; while unveiling Puerto Rican culture and psychology, he shows a wider vision that readers from other cultures can comprehend and even espouse.

FURTHER WORKS: *Los dedos de la mano* (1951); *Pulso de Puerto Rico, 1952–1954* (1956); *El jíbaro de Puerto Rico: Símbolo y figura* (1968); *La poesía modernista en Puerto Rico* (1969); *Obras completas* (1974); *Palos de la cultura iberoamericana* (1977)

BIBLIOGRAPHY: González, J., "El laberinto," *Asomante*, 16 (1960), 70–76; Vientos Gastón, N., "La novela de L., *La ceiba en el tiesto*," *Indice Cultural*, 50 (1962), 239–42; González, J., "Cauce sin río," *Asomante*, 19 (1963), 63–66; Morfi, A., *E. A. L. y su obra: "La resaca"; cumbre en su arte de novelar* (1964); Meléndez, C., *La generación del treinta: cuento y novela* (1972), 31–36; Zayas Micheli, L. O., *Lo universal en E. A. L.* (1974); Casanova Sánchez, O., *La crítica social en la obra novelística de E. A. L.* (1975); Beauchamp, J. J., *Imagen del puertorriqueño en la novela* (1976), 71–160; special L. section, *Horizontes*, 38 (1976), 5–16, 27–66; García Cabrera, M., *L. y sus polos de la cultura iberoamericana* (1978); Irizarri, E., *E. A. L.* (1982); Ortega-Vélez, R. E., *La mujer en la obra de E. A. L.* (1989)

JORGE RODRÍGUEZ-FLORIDO

LARSEN, Marianne

Danish poet, novelist, and prose writer, b. 27 Jan. 1951, Kalundborg

L. is one of the foremost representatives of Danish vanguard prose and poetry in the 1970s. Born in a provincial district of Zealand, she studied Chinese at the University of Copenhagen and later translated a selection of Lu Xun's poetry into Danish. Her own debut, with a collection of texts called *Koncentrationer* (1972; concentrations), dates back to her first year at the university.

This volume, along with the following collection *Overstregslyd* (1972; crossed-out sound), marks an authoritative body of experimental prose and poetry in which dreamlike abstraction and surrealism come across in a language defiant of normal grammar and logic. Repressive orderly circumstances and societal norms are subjected to linguistic disruption, and the crossing of visual and auditory boundaries, as in "crossed-out sound," indicates a confrontational poetic strategy aimed at creating new and freer connections and identities.

In *Ravage* (1973; havoc) this exclusive scheme applies more directly to societal conditions as it unmasks the conflict between victims and perpetrators of political oppression. It affords an insight into revolution, love, and poetry that is indispensable for the underdogs to counter the havoc inflicted by the powers that be. *Cinderella* (1974; title in English) is a specific, gender-political deployment of these experiences.

In *Billedtekster* (1974; pictorial texts), with the subtitle "Un-calligraphy," and *Sætninger* (1974; sentences), textual and scripture-thematic underpinnings still provide a balance for L.'s sociopolitical rejection of the entire society of commercial exploitation; her location of disorders remains a matter of combining political analysis with sensitive reflections of human loneliness. L. wishes to liberate the abandoned individual, but for the effort to take effect, she concurrently must redefine societal frames. Increasingly concrete, her texts incorporate her abstractions and leave the reader with a synthesis of political criticism and political utopianism.

In *Modsætninger* (1975; contrasts) the political analysis of societal conflicts gets the upper hand while in *Fællessprog* (1975; common language) a reborn and purified sociolinguistic synthesis is proclaimed. An attempt to further simplify these social teachings is apparent in *Det må siges enkelt* (1976: it must be said in simple terms) and in the bold political poems of *Handlinger* (1976; actions). *Hvem er fjenden?* (1977; who is the enemy?) makes no bones about the implications: This is "class poetry," as the subtitle reads, and it is unambiguous class poetry to boot.

Not abandoning the victims of technocracy and male domination, L. succeeds in reopening her political agenda for poetic inquiry. *Under jordskælvet i Argentina* (1978; during the earthquake in Argentina) is a collage of photos and texts with discernible references to clashes between military rulers and rebelling masses, yet it shows few geographical restraints. In *Jeg spørger bare* (1982; I am only asking) the questioning referenced in the title is the guiding principle in the opening part of the book—before predictable left-wing answers follow at the end. In the meantime a series of sober examples, written in different poetic and narrative modes, gives compelling testimony to the typical hardships of society's little people, especially its children.

De andre, den anden (1986; the others, the other) recalls the dichotomy between collective situations and individual attachments. Myriads of outer sensations collide with notions of intimate love. This is not individualism, though. The "other" is a figment of one's imagination—until the others offer fulfillment. *En skønne dag* (1989; one fine day) may promise precisely that; but it may also be a bittersweet indulgence in wishful thinking.

A similar ambiguity adheres to L.'s two novels. *Fremmed lykke* (1990; alien happiness) submits that human progress comes with development and the recognition of otherness, but also that otherness is always alien and out of reach. It makes a formally compelling case for both possibilities.

Spanning from almost trivial verisimilitude to impenetrable abstractions, L.'s pivotal point is nothingness. Her language blueprints a universe that is moving, touching, and indicative of *Lysende kaos* (1990; shining chaos), "open texts—registrations of transition," written with Pernille Tønnesen (b. 1957). Plain wonder is a challenge to the unnatural boundaries behind which we live because it is nothing, really. But its volatility is captivating, and so is the author when she allows poetry to be her political dimension and to complicate her more gullible political pronouncements, so typical of the 1970s.

FURTHER WORKS: *21 digte* (1972); *Noget tegnet syv gange* (1973); *Aforismer* (1977); *Opgørelse følger* (1978); *Det kunne være nu* (1979); *Hinandens kræfter* (1980); *Der er håb i mit hoved* (1981); *Bag om maskerne* (1982); *Dagbogsleg* (1983, with Ib Hørlyck); *I dag og i morgen* (1983); *Kære levende* (1983); *Udvalgte digte 1969–82* (1983); *Direkte* (1984); *Pludselig dette* (1985); *Hvor du er* (1987); *I timerne og udenfor* (1987); *Giv bare kærlighed skylden* (1989); *Gæt hvem der elsker dig* (1989); *Fri stil—Fantomtid* (1991). FURTHER VOLUME IN ENGLISH: *Selected Poems* (1982)

POUL HOUE

LASKER-SCHÜLER, Else

German poet, dramatist, essayist, and storyteller, b. 11 Feb. 1869, Elberfeld-Wuppertal; d. 22 Jan. 1945, Jerusalem

L.-S. was born in the Ruhr region as the daughter of a banker. Her ancestors include rabbis, scholars, and community leaders, and her plays *Die Wupper* (1909; the Wupper River) and *Arthur Aronymus und seine Väter* (1932; Arthur Aronymus and his fathers) lovingly reflect her family background and the lore of her native Rhineland. Soon enough, however, she turned her back on her bourgeois background and lived the life of a bohemian. With her first husband, the physician Berthold Lasker, she moved to Berlin, where she became the *magna mater* of early expressionism (q.v.), frequenting such fabled cafés as the Café des Westens and the Romanisches Café, and befriending many members of the avant-garde. Although ten volumes of her poetry and prose had appeared by the outbreak of World War I, her material circumstances steadily worsened after the breakup of her second marriage in 1912. In 1933, the year after she had received the prestigious Kleist Prize, L.-S. fled to Switzerland. The following year she visited Palestine for the first time, but the reality of her poetic and spiritual homeland was such a shock to her that she soon returned to Zurich. Her prose work *Das Hebräerland* (1937; the land of the Hebrews) is a jumble of magnificent insights and misconceptions; like a number of her other books it was illustrated with some of her dreamily grotesque drawings. The outbreak of the war in 1939 turned her third visit to Palestine into an immigration. Her remaining years were marked by disappointment, disorientation, and destitution, for the terrestrial Jerusalem was no match for the heavenly city that she had hymned for so long, and the harsh reality of the land of the Hebrews ill accorded with her self-willed conception of primordial purity and an exemplary community. In *Ichundich* (1960; "IandI"), a curiously Faustian play she wrote in 1942, she split herself into a poet and a scarecrow. Her haunting poem "Ich weiß, daß ich bald sterben muß" (1943; I know that I must die soon) was recited at her burial on the Mount of Olives.

L.-S.'s penchant for mythmaking and mystification informed both her life and her work. When she signed some of her letters "Prince Yussuf of Thebes" or "Princess Tino of Baghdad," she was putting on poetic masks in an attempt to escape to a fantasy world and introduce a mystical strain into her person and her poetry. She also invented fanciful names for accomplished and admired friends, claimed that her son Paul (born in 1899 and probably the issue of a failed marriage) had been fathered by a Greek or Spanish prince, renamed her second husband (Georg Levin) "Herwarth Walden," and called Gottfried Benn (q.v.) "King Giselheer the Heathen," which is also the title of a cycle of love poems she addressed to him.

Her collections of poetry range from *Styx* (1902; Styx) to *Mein blaues Klavier* (1943; my blue piano). German did not seem to suffice her for the optimal expression of her ecstatic visions, and so she wrote some poems in a language of her own devising that she called "Mystic Asiatic." The poet's idiosyncratic language with its deep-pile texture of assonance, metaphors, neologisms, ambiguities, ellipses, and luxuriant "inward" imagery poses a challenge to readers and translators alike. L.-S.'s metaphysical longing for universal fellowship even led her to accept certain Christian ideas, and the unorthodox Judaism of this conciliatory spirit encompassed Jesus and the Madonna. Her *Hebräische Balladen* (1913; Hebrew ballads) presents an eminently personal allegorical evocation of biblical figures and legends, containing the sensual (and even sexual) imagery characteristic of so much of her poetry, notably "Mein Volk" (my people), "Versöhnung" (reconciliation), and "Ein alter Tibetteppich" (an old Tibetan carpet). However, what has been described as the oriental or exotic strain in her poetry is as much indebted to German romanticism as it is to the Song of Songs and other Eastern legends and ideas. L.-S. had great affection for eastern European Jews and their "wonder rabbis," and she yearned for *wilde Juden*—untamed, heroic Maccabean types.

L.-S., always a poet's poet, is properly ranked with Gertrud Kolmar and Nelly Sachs (qq.v.) as one of the greatest poets produced by German Jewry.

FURTHER WORKS: *Der siebente Tag* (1905); *Das Peter-Hille-Buch* (1906); *Die Nächte Tino von Bagdads* (1907); *Meine Wunder* (1911); *Mein Herz* (1912); *Gesichte* (1913); *Der Prinz von Theben* (1914; rev. ed., 1920); *Die gesammelten Gedichte* (1917); *Der Malik* (1919); *Die Kuppel* (1920); *Der Wunderrabbiner von Barcelona* (1921); *Theben* (1923); *Ich räume auf* (1925); *Konzert* (1932); *Arthur Aronymus* (1932); *Briefe an Karl Kraus* (1959); *Gedichte 1902–1943* (1959); *Verse und Prosa aus dem Nachlaß* (1961); *Prosa und Schauspiele* (1962); *Sämtliche Gedichte* (1966); *Lieber gestreifter Tiger* (1969); *Wo ist unser buntes Theben?* (1969); *Die Wolkenbrücke* (1972); *"Was soll ich hier? Exilbriefe an Salman Schocken* (1986). FURTHER VOLUMES IN ENGLISH: *Hebrew Ballads and Other Poems* (1980); *Your Diamond Dreams Cut Open My Arteries: Poems by E. L.-S.* (1982)

BIBLIOGRAPHY: Politzer, H., "The Blue Piano of E. L.-S." *Commentary*, 9 (1950), 335–44; Kraft, W., *E. L.-S.* (1951); Guder, G., *E. L.-S.: Deutung ihrer Lyrik* (1966); Elow (pseud. of E. Lowins), "E. L.-S.," *Jewish Spectator*, 34 (Sept. 1969), 21–25; Gertner, M., "E.-L.-S.'s Biblical Poems," *Jewish Quarterly*, 17 (1969), 26–34; Blumenthal,

B., "The Play Element in the Poetry of E. L.-S.," *GQ*, 43 (1970), 571–76; Cohn, H. W., *E. L.-S.: The Broken World* (1974); Hessing, J., "E. L.-S. and Her People," *ArielK*, 41 (1976), 60–76; Grunfeld, F. V., *Prophets without Honor* (1979), 96–145; Bauschinger, S., *E. L.-S.: Ihr Werk und ihre Zeit* (1980); Hessing, J., *E. L.-S.* (1985); Yudkin, L. I., "E. L.-S. and the Development of Jewish Expressionism," *Jewish Quarterly*, 32 (1985), 51–56

HARRY ZOHN

LE CARRÉ, John

(pseud. of David John Moore Cornwell) British novelist, b. 19 Oct. 1931, Poole, Dorset

Le C. is the author of a series of espionage novels written in the manner of Graham Greene (q.v.). Le C. had a troubled early life. His father was in and out of legal trouble, and his mother deserted the family while le C. was still a child. The family moved frequently, and le C. attended a series of boarding schools. Eventually, his father sent him to Switzerland where he studied German language and literature at the University of Bern. In 1949 le C. joined the Royal army and served in the intelligence corps. After a short tour in the army, he resumed his education, earning a degree in modern languages at Oxford in 1956. After graduation, he was a tutor in modern languages at Eton for two years. Somewhat dissatisfied with his experience in teaching, he tried his hand at various other vocations, eventually having a successful career with the British Foreign Office, until 1964 when he resigned to work on his writing full time.

Le C.'s first two novels, *Call for the Dead* (1961) and *A Murder of Quality* (1964), are more detective stories than espionage novels, but they do introduce the character of George Smiley, around whom most of le C.'s later novels will revolve. They also introduce the central conflict that will be developed in his later work: human beings versus their institutions. Both of these novels enjoyed moderate critical and commercial success, but his literary breakthrough was his third novel, *The Spy Who Came In from the Cold* (1963).

Unlike the two preceding novels, *The Spy Who Came In from the Cold* is a solid espionage novel that introduces the world of "the Circus," le C.'s construct of the British Intelligence establishment. The novel tells a story of great complexity, but the text is tightly focused through the perceptions and psychological insights of the central character and concentrates upon internal conflict rather than external action. Through this technique, le C. achieves the psychological depth and intricate characterization that distinguish his later work. This novel was an international best-seller, and its success allowed le C. to become a full-time author. His next novel, *The Looking Glass War* (1965), was equally successful and earned him the Edgar Allen Poe Award for 1965.

The centerpieces of le C.'s work are the George Smiley books: *Tinker, Tailor, Soldier, Spy* (1974), *The Honorable Schoolboy* (1977), *Smiley's People* (1980), and *The Secret Pilgrim* (1991). The first three of these novels form a trilogy that traces the latter part of Smiley's career in "the Circus," and the fourth is a retrospect of Smiley's life of espionage. Other novels, such as *The Little Drummer Girl* (1983), and the semiautobiographical *A Perfect Spy* (1986), do not involve Smiley directly but maintain a consistent depiction of the intelligence community and a similar concentration upon character and internal conflict.

Le C.'s novels have achieved great popular success. The Smiley books are among the best-selling thrillers of all time, and seven of le C.'s novels have been made into motion pictures. His work has evolved from the relatively simple early mysteries to very complex, intricately crafted novels of great psychological depth. Rather than merely maintain a successful formula, le C. has continued to elaborate and expand upon his themes and characters. Three aspects that distinguish his work are the elaborate depth and development of his characters, the attention given to the often mundane, almost ritualistic day-to-day activities within a bureaucracy, and the consistent depiction of his principal landscape, "the Circus," which rivals Thomas Hardy's "Wessex" or William Faulkner's (qq.v.) "Yoknapatawpha" in its solidity. The later novels in particular have drawn significant critical attention and elevated le C. beyond consideration as merely a genre author to consideration as a successful author of "straight" fiction.

FURTHER WORKS: *A Small Town in Germany* (1968); *The Naive and Sentimental Lover* (1971); *Vanishing England* (1987, with Gareth Davies); *The Russia House* (1989)

BIBLIOGRAPHY: Sauerberg, L. O., *Secret Agents in Fiction: Ian Fleming, J. le C. and Len Deighton* (1984); Lewis, P. E., *J. le C.* (1985); Barley, T., *Taking Sides: The Fiction of J. le C.* (1986); Homberger, E., *J. le C.* (1986); Monaghan, D., *Smiley's Circus: A Guide to the Secret World of J. le C.* (1986); Wolfe, P., *Corridors of Deceit: The World of J. le C.* (1987)

ROBERT GREENUP

LEUTENEGGER, Gertrud

Swiss novelist and poet (writing in German), b. 6 Dec. 1948, Schwyz

L. is one of the most outspokenly feminist and politically leftist novelists of the postwar generation in Switzerland. Her most important contributions are in the areas of drama and the novel, which are characterized by a combination of a highly lyrical style, autobiographical elements, and political allegory. She initially published short stories and poetry. L. was the daughter of a civil servant and was educated in Swiss schools as well as a French boarding school. She also lived in Florence, England, and Berlin, then specialized in early-childhood education, but also worked in a women's psychiatric clinic as well as being for a time the custodian of the Nietzsche House in Sils Maria. These diverse working and living experiences made her critical of Swiss society's self-perception as a well-regulated microcosm, with its unrelenting insistence on tradition and order. L. protests against deeply entrenched structures of order, normalcy, and sameness, which marginalize women, foreigners, especially the Italian working-class population in Switzerland, the mentally ill, and those with communist or socialist political leanings.

Her first novel, *Vorabend* (1975; the evening before), invokes the apocalyptic atmosphere on the eve of a political demonstration. The isolated female narrator feels alienated from her surroundings but chronicles her feelings of dread and rebellion in realistic detail on a walk through Zurich, remembering on the eve of a big protest march, which she wants to join, sudden and violent disruptions of the daily routine—a worker killed by electric current in the town square, an awakening lesbian relationship to a girlfriend in high school with the ridicule that went along with it, being a nurse in a women's psychiatric ward, where the old and the ill are kept medicated but no effort is made to reintegrate them into society or even treat them as human beings. L. voices her hope for a less hierarchical, more caring society, but her appeal is tempered by skepticism. In her second novel, *Ninive* (1977; Ninive), L. frames her plea for social innovation in a more biblical and allegorical vein. The narrative begins with a visitation, an embalmed whale is exhibited to the people of L.'s hometown, and ends with the whale's destruction. This narrative contains the childhood friendship and later love-story of two communist inhabitants whose vision of a better society survives the repression of state institutions, which the whale symbolizes.

In 1977 L. began taking classes in directing for the stage at the Zurich Academy of Theater and the Arts, and interned with the noted director Jürgen Flimm in Hamburg in 1978. This experience led to the publication of a play, *Lebewohl, gute Reise* (1980; farewell, have a good trip), which deals with the struggle between Gilgamesh and Enkidu for control of the world. Their brutality is opposed but not overcome by two marginalized and abused female protagonists. The play incorporates many fantastical and surrealist elements, which tend to dominate in L.'s next novel, *Gouverneur* (1981; governor), an allegory of a Nietzschean construction project on a mountain plateau in Switzerland, far from the cities yet subject to periodic checks by teams of hostile state inspectors. The narrator wishes to find or remember the governor (God), who planned the project originally. The governor does return unexpectedly in the guise of a knife seller at the end when most of the other protagonists have been killed or victimized, and the dramatic ending leaves it open whether he has returned to help or to kill the narrator.

Two of L.'s more recent prose works, *Komm ins Schiff* (1983; come onboard) and *Meduse* (1985; Medusa), demonstrate her mastery of evocative, lyrical language. While the political dimension of L.'s earlier writing is less foregrounded in these texts, they blend philosophy, fantasy, and autobiographical detail with a critique of male-female relationships in so far as they reproduce social inequalities. L. is most compelling in her ability to blend social critique and writing about everyday life in Switzerland with a richly poetic language.

FURTHER WORKS: *Wie in Salomons Garten* (1981); *Das verlorene Monument* (1985)

BIBLIOGRAPHY: Matt, B. von, "G. Ls Gouverneur," *Lesarten* (1985), 171–74; Köchli, Y. D., *Themen in der neuren schweizerischen Literatur* (1982), 12–34, 121–55

HELGA DRUXES

LEVI, Primo

Italian memorialist, novelist, and short-story writer, b. 31 July 1919, Turin; d. 11 Apr. 1987, Turin

As a child L. had a vague awareness of Jewish cultural tradition; but as a chemistry student at the University of Turin he had to deal with the racial laws promulgated in 1938 by the Fascist regime. In 1943 he joined an antifascist partisan group. Captured shortly thereafter, he was deported to Auschwitz, where he survived one year thanks to a series of fortuitous circumstances. Liberated by the Russians in January 1945, his return home turned into an eight-month odyssey. He resumed his career as a chemist in Turin and also found time to write his two classic memorials. Several collections of science fiction and short stories followed at intervals until he retired in 1977 to become a full-time writer. Throughout his career he was the honored recipient of several literary

prizes, including the Campiello Prize in 1963 and again in 1982 as well as the Bagutta Prize in 1967.

L.'s first memorial, *Se questo è un uomo* (1947; *Survival in Auschwitz: The Nazi Assault on Humanity,* 1961), sprang from a pressing need to recount his experience in the camp and make others participate in that experience. At the same time he documented how such a dehumanizing institution systematically deprived each individual of his and her identity and dignity, and brought about the annihilation of the internees. The astonishing revocation of his personal calamities alternates with those of a vast gallery of fellow internees, caught with striking psychological insight. His alert moral consciousness blocks any hate for the oppressors, and equally guarantees an incommensurable admiration for those who, in spite of the terrifying brutality to which they were subjected, never completely forgot they were human beings. With great skill, balance, and comprehension, L. transforms documentary fact into a profound civil and moral experience.

La tregua (1963; *The Awakening,* 1965) is a sequel. In a more tranquil tone L. portrays the absurd wanderings that he and his companions followed at Russian directive through a devastated eastern Europe. The account of the eight-month peregrinations is at once tragic, comic, and picaresque. But eventually a pessimistic view takes over. The prisoners' aimless meandering, their subjugation to blind bureaucracy, and their impotence are not only a documentation of a tragic destiny, but also an allegory of life itself. The idea emerges that the hate inherent to the camp necessarily engenders revenge and violence, and further, that the human being is perhaps living in a permanent state of war in or out of the camp. L.'s style is essential, concise, and precise. A wise use of adjectives renders a feel for the complexities and contradictory aspects of reality and human nature.

In his fictional works L. abstracted and applied this historically based thematic to modern society. If the camp was synonymous with the perversion of human reason and a concomitant perverted use of science and technology for the sake of power, then scientific and technological progress could be construed as a threat to nature and to humankind. He wrote two series of science-fiction short stories, collected in *Storie naturali* (1966; natural stories) and *Vizio di forma* (1971; vicious form). Selections from both works were published in *The Sixth Day, and Other Tales* (1990). In both series L. writes of quotidian cases where excessive technological development changes the true essence of our lives and of nature.

Taking a more positive slant, *Il sistema periodico* (1975; *The Periodic Table,* 1984) mirrors a chemist's professional life of victories and defeats scrupulously performed with precision and deep moral dedication. The obvious implication is that in the "trade" of living the same scrupulous precision and dedication are needed. This theme, together with L.'s admiration for those who choose their destiny in the face of social restrictions, is fully developed in *La chiave a stella* (1978; *The Monkey's Wrench*, 1986). *Se non ora, quando?* (1982, *If Not Now, When?*,1989) combines the emergence of Jewish consciousness and pride with the historical documentation of action taken on the Russian front by partisan Jewish groups against retreating Nazi forces. His last book, *I sommersi e i salvati* (1986; *The Drowned and the Saved*, 1988), poses the question of how much of the camp is alive and well in our time, and how long it will remain in our memories.

L. is considered a great memorialist since the publication of *Se questo è un uomo*, and recent attentive readings of his works have revealed the full-fledged literary stature of a complex writer very attuned to the problems of the contemporary human being.

FURTHER WORKS: *L'osteria di Brema* (1975; repub. as *Ad ora incerta*, 1984; *Collected Poems*, 1988); *La ricerca delle radici. Antologia personale* (1981); *Lilit, e altri racconti* (1981; *Moments of Reprieve*, 1986); *L'altrui mestiere (1985; Other People's Trades*, 1989); *Racconti e saggi* (1986; *The Mirror Maker*, 1989)

BIBLIOGRAPHY: Gunzberg, L., "Down among the Dead Men: L. and Dante in Hell," *MLS*, 16 (1986), 10–28; Epstein, A., "P. L. and the Language of Atrocity," *BSIS*, 20 (1987), 31–38; McRae, M., "Opposition and Reversal in P. L.'s *The Periodic Table*," *POMPA* (1988), 115–24; Mondo, L., "P. L.'s Muse: Curiosity," preface to *The Mirror Maker* (1989), ix–xi; Regge, T., Introduction to *Dialogo* (1989), vii–xviii; Schehr, L. R., "P. L.'s Strenuous Clarity," *Italica*, 4 (1989), 429–43; Motola, G., "The Varnish-Maker's Dream," *SR*, 98 (1990), 506–14; Sodi, R. B., *A Dante of Our Time: P. L. and Auschwitz* (1990)

ROSARIO FERRERI

LIHN, Enrique

Chilean poet, novelist, and short-story writer, b. 3 Sept. 1929, Santiago; d. 10 July 1988, Santiago

Born in the home of his maternal grandmother, L. lived there sporadically during what he called his "archliterary childhood," where he fell under her spell, and more importantly, under his uncle's, Gustavo Carrasco, who according to L., "was the first artist in my life." This uncle, a professor of drawing, instilled in the boy a love of art, which he later as a youth studied seriously at the School of Fine Arts as well as attending the German *lycée* in Santiago. L.'s interest in the pictorial arts never flagged—indeed, some of his books are charmingly illustrated with his own drawings, and later in life he made an amusing documentary movie in which he played a major role.

However, L.'s true artistic talents lay elsewhere, in the realm of poetry, and this he discovered early on. His first slim volume of verse, *Nada se escurre* (1949; nothing slips away), came out when he was twenty, and was followed by *Poemas de este tiempo y de otro* (1955; poems of our times and another).

La pieza oscura y otros poemas (1963; *The Dark Room and Other Poems*, 1978) established L. as a major poetic voice in Chile. Close upon the publication of this book came his next one, *Poesía de paso* (1966; occasional poetry), which brought him the prestigious Cuban award for poetry granted by La Casa de las Américas. These last two volumes received much acclaim not only in his native Chile but also abroad, in other Latin American countries, in Europe, and the U.S. In 1965 L. took his first trip to Europe, having won a UNESCO fellowship, where he traveled through various countries, being especially "obsessed," as he put it, with Italy. Later, he spent some time in Paris on a Guggenheim fellowship, and the "City of Light" figures prominently in his later collections of poems. On another tour, in 1974, this time to the U.S., he was heralded enthusiastically on college campuses where he gave readings of his poetry. This prompted various translators like Dave Oliphant in *If Poetry Is To Be Written Right* (1977) and Jonathan Cohen, John Felstiner, and David Unger in *The Dark Room and Other Poems* (1978) to publish selections of his poems in English.

From 1973 on L. held a teaching position as professor of literature at one of the branches of the University of Chile in Santiago. He also taught as visiting professor at the University of California, Irvine, in 1976, and at the University of Texas, Austin, in 1986. During the mid-1980s L. underwent a serious operation for a heart problem, and his health began to fail. He returned to Chile, where he died two years later of cancer.

Though often moody and morose in his last years, when in high spirits L. was a witty, theatrical, and highly entertaining person, charged with life and dynamism. These latter qualities are certainly reflected in his poetry, where he frequently reaches and maintains a high level of emotional intensity. Many of his poems dwell on the tragedies in life, the loss of love, the betrayal of the beloved, or sadness at death. And like many contemporary poets, L. speaks directly to the reader, employing an everyday vocabulary and a disarming conversational tone to let us know what he thinks of social and political injustice, and at the same time to cry out against his existential loneliness. In many of his poems we encounter alienation. Communication tends to break down; consequently, relationships must suffer and crack apart.

The magic of L.'s poetry resides in the subterranean, subjective dream world he depicts, dark and destructive, filled with fears and anxieties. The reader may well be shaken up by his poems, by their sweat and tears, pulsing with life. But not all of them are somber or violent; there are moments of quiet pleasure. In addition, we witness his inquiring mind at work: Most everything is called into question, even the values of poetry and those who write it. But the general impression we are left with after reading his poems is one of a world where little separates convention from nightmare and abominations.

Although one of L.'s last books of verse, *Al bello aparecer de este lucero* (1983; to the fair apparition of this morning star), is punctuated with moments of hope and desire, as its title would indicate, it is also pervaded with a deep sadness, as is his *Diario de muerte* (diary of death), published posthumously in 1989. When he died, L. left some twenty volumes of verse to his credit, almost all of them scant in length but extremely rich in substance, long poems and short ones, but mainly long poems, often intensely gripping and immensely readable. Undoubtedly, L. has made his niche in the gallery of distinguished 20th-c. Chilean poets, which includes Pablo Neruda, Gabriela Mistral, and Nicanor Parra (qq.v.). Like them, he has attained international stature.

Besides his poetry, L. published several collections of short stories, notably *Agua de arroz* (1964; rice water), for which he received the Atenea Prize (1964) at the University of Concepción, Chile, and several novels, such as *Batman en Chile o El ocaso de un ídolo o Solo contra el desierto rojo* (1973; Batman in Chile or the sunset of an idol or alone against the red desert), *La orquesta de cristal* (1976; the crystal orchestra), and *El arte de la palabra* (1980; the art of the word). In these novels L.'s ironic sense of humor reigns supreme. Pedro Lastra (b. 1931), his close friend of long standing and collaborator on several books, published an engaging series of interviews, *Conversaciones con E. L.* (1980; 2nd ed., 1990; conversations with E. L.), packed with interesting information about the writer and his views on literature, which also includes a useful and extensive bibliography.

FURTHER WORKS: *Escrito en Cuba* (1969); *La musiquilla de las pobres esferas* (1969); *Algunos poemas* (1972); *Por fuerza mayor* (1975); *París,*

situación irregular (1977); *L. y Pompier* (1978); *A partir de Manhattan* (1979); *Antología al azar* (1981); *Estación de los desamparados* (1982); *El paseo ahumada* (1983); *Pena de extrañamiento* (1986); *Mester de juglaría* (1987); *La aparición de la Virgen* (1987); *Album de toda especie de poemas* (1989). FURTHER VOLUME IN ENGLISH: *This Endless Malice* (1969)

BIBLIOGRAPHY: Lastra, P., "Las actuales promociones poéticas," *AUC*, 120 (1960), 181–92; Goic, C., "E. L. *La pieza oscura* (1955–1962)," *AUC*, 128 (1963), 194–97; special L. section, *Review*, 23 (1978), 5–37; O'Hara, E., "La poesía de E. L.," *Desde Melibea* (1980), 121–31; Rojas, W., "A manera de prefacio: *La pieza oscura* en la perspectiva de una lectura generacional," in *La pieza oscura* (2nd ed., 1984), 7–27; Cánovas, R., *L., Zurita, Ictus, Radrigan: Literatura chilena y experiencia autoritaria* (1986), 21–56; Coddou, M., *Veinte estudios sobre la literatura chilena del siglo veinte* (1989), 147–68; Lastra, P., ed., *Conversaciones con E. L.* (2nd ed., 1990)

GEORGE D. SCHADE

LIND, Jakov

(pseud. of Heinz Landwirth) Austrian novelist, short-story writer, and dramatist (also writing in English), b. 10 Feb. 1927, Vienna

As a Jewish boy endangered by Nazi persecution L. left his native city in late 1938 and emigrated to Holland. Having become fluent in Dutch, he posed as a Dutchman named Jan Gerrit Overbeek and worked on a Rhine barge, later living in Germany as a laborer at a metallurgic research institute of the German aviation ministry. After the end of World War II, L. went to Palestine under the name Jakov Chaklan. In 1950 he returned to Vienna and studied acting and stagecraft at the Max Reinhardt Seminar. After working at a variety of jobs—fisherman in the Mediterranean, beach photographer in Tel Aviv, orange picker in Netanya, private detective, traveling salesman, film agent—L. went to London, where he has made his home since 1954, with periods of residence in New York and on Majorca.

L. achieved international prominence as a writer with a collection of stories entitled *Eine Seele aus Holz* (1962; *Soul of Wood*, 1964). In the title story, which is by turns horrifying and hilarious, a paraplegic Jewish youth who has been entrusted to an Austrian male nurse when his parents are deported from Vienna is abandoned on a mountainside. L.'s first novel, *Landschaft in Beton* (1963; *Landscape in Concrete*, 1966), has been described by Daniel Stern as "one of the most piercing pictures of the nihilism of this century." In it L. paints the lunatic landscape of the waning Third Reich and describes in allegorical fashion the macabre odyssey of the demented Wehrmacht Sergeant Gauthier Bachmann.

In *Eine bessere Welt* (1966; *Ergo,* 1967), an intricate scatological satire full of wicked wit and grisly humor, L. continues his relentless exploration of the cloaca of contemporary consciousness. Using his hated native country as a metaphor for the dismal state of Western society, the author describes the running fight between two German-Austrian humanoids that represent the dregs of postwar society. After several radio plays and autobiographical works L. published *Travels to the Enu: Story of a Shipwreck* (1982), his first work of fiction written in English, a novel that details a phantasmagoric journey to a utopian, paradisiac island inhabited by strange bird-men. The epistolary novel *The Inventor* (1987) presents the contrapuntal lives of two Jewish brothers born in Poland and raised in England, one of whom has invented a sort of supercomputer that will determine the distribution of the world's resources.

Alvin Rosenfeld has characterized L.'s prose style as being "somewhere between Kafka and Günter Grass." L., however, does not regard himself as a grotesque or absurdist writer but as an old-fashioned moralist in the tradition of Peter Altenberg (1859–1919) and Karl Kraus (q.v.) who describes ordinary people (though these are often more loathsome and dangerous than fanatics). His literary stance clearly is that of a survivor, and Virginia Kirkus perhaps characterizes his work best when she writes: "With a proliferation of dreamily forlorn details, a Mephistophelian grin, and a superbly insouciant style he fashions fables for our age, post-Auschwitz vaudeville."

FURTHER WORKS: *Die Heiden* (1965); *Anna Laub* (1965); *Angst* (1969); *Hunger* (1969); *Israel: Rückkehr für 28 Tage* (1972); *Der Ofen* (1973). FURTHER VOLUMES IN ENGLISH: *The Silver Foxes are Dead, and Other Plays* (1968); *Counting My Steps* (1969); *Numbers: A Further Autobiography* (1972); *The Trip to Jerusalem* (1973)

BIBLIOGRAPHY: Stern, D., "A Contemporary Nightmare," *SatR,* 15 June 1966, 25–26; Potoker, E. M., "A Distillation of Horror," *SatR,* 21 Oct. 1967, 35–36; Kahn, L., *Mirrors of the Jewish Mind* (1968), 231–32; Rosenfeld, A. H., "J. L. and the Trials of Jewishness," *Midstream,* Feb. 1974, 71–75; Langer, L. L., *The Holocaust and the Literary Imagination* (1975), 205–49; Swanson, R. A., "Versions of Doublethink in *Gravity's Rainbow, Darkness Visible, Riddley Walker,* and *Travels to the Enu,*" *WLT,* 58, 2 (Spring 1984), 203–8.

HARRY ZOHN

LINDGREN, Torgny

Swedish novelist, poet, and short-story writer, b. 16 June 1938, Raggsjö

L. was born in the northern province of Västerbotten, a desolate region that has produced more than its proportionate share of outstanding writers; Sara Lidman and Per Olov Enquist (qq.v.) both hail from the same area. L. is the recipient of a number of literary prizes, among them the French *Prix Fémina Étranger* in 1986 for the novel *Bat Seba* (1984; *Bathsheba,* 1989). In 1991 he was elected to the Swedish Academy.

L.'s early works are highly critical of certain aspects of contemporary Swedish society. From his platform as a social democrat, he aims his criticism at his own party's excessive bureaucracy, the disparity between professed vision and actual practice, and the tendency to forget the everyday problems of citizens. The collection of poetry *Hur skulle det vara om man vore Olof Palme?* (1971; what would it be like to be Olof Palme?) offers examples of such censure. The collection of short stories with the long title *Skolbagateller medan jag försökte skriva till mina överordnade* (1972; school trivia, while attempting to write to my superiors) is set in a school milieu, familiar to L., who had a long career as a teacher behind him when he became a full-time writer in 1985. Here the failings of the school system are poignantly illustrated in the fates of a few students.

The novel *Skrämmer dig minuten?* (1981; does this minute frighten you?), a highly entertaining story but with treacherously buried barbs, was a popular and critical success. L.'s real breakthrough, however, came in 1982 with the novel *Ormens väg på hälleberget* (*Way of a Serpent,* 1990), a dark and powerful tale from the author's native Västerbotten. Set in the 19th c., it tells of abject poverty, ruthless exploitation, and power abuse, as the widow Thea is forced to pay her debts to the local merchant with her body, a practice her daughter inherits when Thea is worn out and no longer able to please. What raises the story to the level of great literature is L.'s highly stylized prose, a mixture of dialect and biblical and archaic turns of phrase. The effect of this style is frequently humorous in a manner that only heightens the pathos of this Job-like lamentation questioning the righteousness of the Lord. Ian Hinchliffe (b. 1952) has pointed out that "In the well-weighed words of this single slender novel L. expresses the pietism, the stoicism and melancholy which *is* the northern soul.'' The collection of short stories *Merabs skönhet* (1983; *Merab's Beauty and Other Stories,* 1990) is also set in the Arctic North and exemplifies a happy phenomenon in the Swedish literature of the 1980s: the noticeable return of fabulation, the joy of telling a good or suspenseful tale. The eleven stories are set in L.'s native province and he continues to employ— and to elaborate on—its expressive dialect. L. would again tap the resources of this Arctic region in the novel *Ljuset* (1987; the light), in which the fantastic and the darkly chaotic, pathos, and bizarre humor form a disturbing union. L. was brought up in a pietistic religious environment; as an adult he converted to Catholicism. It may not be farfetched to read into this strange story a plea for a divine order beyond human anarchy.

The Bible was one of L.'s earliest encounters with literature. In *Bat Seba* he retells the Old Testament legend of King David and Bathsheba, the beautiful wife of the warrior Uriah. The King uses his power to make her his own. The novel is the story of unbridled sensuality, possession, violence, cruelty, and tenderness. David, the Lord's Anointed, commits a number of crimes because of his love; in turn he becomes more helpless as the power of her love grows and constitutes a threat to his holiness. In an ironic reversal of roles she uses the same unscrupulous means as the king to gain her ends to secure ultimately the throne for her son Solomon. The novel can be read on several different levels, as an allegory of male versus female, as a study in the uses and abuses of power, and—as is often the case with L.'s stories—as a tale about the human being's relationship with the divine or as an exploration of the nature of God.

L. is one of the most widely translated of contemporary Swedish writers. His command of the resources of language is impressive; he is a natural storyteller, whose fantasy at times is reminiscent of the magic realism (q.v.) of Latin American writers. His best stories, often set in the times of history, myth, and legend, are ultimately existential and metaphysical explorations of the human condition.

FURTHER WORKS: *Plåtsax, hjärtats instrument* (1965); *Dikter från Vimmerby* (1970); *Övriga frågor* (1973); *Hallen* (1975); *Brännvinsfursten* (1979); *Markus* (1982); *Legender* (1986); *Kärleksguden Frö* (1988); *Till sanningens lov* (1991)

BIBLIOGRAPHY: special T. L. issue, *SBR, Supplement* (1985); Algulin, I., *A History of Swedish Literature* (1989), 274–75

LARS G. WARME

LIPKIN, Semyon Izrailevich

Russian poet, prose writer, and translator, b. 6 Nov. 1911, Odessa

For decades highly regarded for his translations of central Asian and Caucasian poetry, it was not until the 1980s that L. became known as a major poet in his own right. Born in Odessa in 1911, L. graduated from the Moscow Institute of Engineering and Economics in 1937. While a student in Moscow, L. became acquainted with the poet Osip Mandelstam (q.v.), an association that profoundly affected the beginning poet. L., who began to publish his verse in the late 1920s, embarked on his distinguished career as verse translator in the mid-1930s, a decision in part motivated by his refusal to subject his poetry to the political demands on literature. L. continued to write poetry, but published very little. L.'s experiences as a soldier in World War II are reflected in the prose book of sketches *Stalingradskii korabl'* (1943; the ship of Stalingrad) and in numerous poems. Three collections of L.'s verse appeared between 1967 and 1977, but they offered a highly selective and skewed sampling of the poet's work. L.'s courageous decision to contribute six poems to the literary almanac *Metropol'* (1979; *Metropol,* 1982) changed the course of what had been a relatively prosperous career. The publication of the almanac abroad resulted in official censure for most contributors, which included a ban on their works. L., his wife Inna Lisnyanskaya, and Vassily Aksyonov (qq.v.) resigned from the Union of Writers to protest the expulsion of two younger colleagues. For L., who had been a member of the Union since 1934, this was not merely a symbolic gesture. Freed from the constraints of Soviet censorship, L. prepared a large volume of poetry that was published in the West. *Volia* (1981; freedom) collected verse written over a period of more than forty years and showed L. to be an important poet. L.'s next major publication abroad, *Kochevoi ogon'* (1984; a nomadic flame), also presents some early verse, but the emphasis is on poems written after *Volia*. In addition to these two volumes, L. published three books of prose, and his work appeared in all the major émigré periodicals. The advent of glasnost in the U.S.S.R. paved the way for L.'s reinstatement in the Union of Writers. Since 1987 L.'s work has been published by most of the leading soviet journals, including *Novyi Mir, Druzhba Narodov, Ogonek,* and *Iunost'*. The literary rehabilitation of the *Metropol* group brought L. numerous public tributes for his staunch defense of the almanac.

L.'s close association as translator for the non-Russian nationalities of the U.S.S.R. made him acutely aware of the injustices perpetrated on these peoples, including the forced migration of entire ethnic groups. Consequently, L.'s *Volia* is deeply rooted in history and religion, both taboo subjects for Soviet literature of the time. The role of the lyric persona as indicated by the poem "Ochevidets" (eyewitness) is to record and preserve the memory of the oppressed. The cycle of narrative poems *Vozhd' i plemia* (leader and tribe) refers to arrests, murders, and the secret police, all ruthlessly engineered by Stalin and his lackeys. The final poem in the cycle, "Literaturnoe vospominanie" (a literary reminiscence), recounts the degradation of Eduard Bagritsky (1895–1934), L.'s one-time mentor, whose poetic talents were corrupted by politics. Merely the titles of many poems would have prevented publication: "Bogoroditsa" (mother of God) and "Odesskaia sinagoga" (the Odessa synagogue). Given the thematics of L.'s verse, it is not surprising that before the publication of *Volia* only a small circle of friends knew L. as a poet. That circle, however, included Anna Akhmatova (q.v.), who considered L. to be a leading poet of his generation.

L.'s *Kochevoi ogon'*, as the title suggests, highlights his interest in non-Russian themes and imagery. The volume, unlike *Volia*, emphasizes the short lyric over the long narrative poem. The poignant love poem "Est' prelest' gor'kaia v moei sud'be" (there is a bitter delight in my fate) sets the tone for the entire book, since in a larger sense it underscores both the lyric persona's gratitude for the life he has been privileged to live, yet acknowledges the difficult role he has chosen. Although death is a constant in the majority of the poems, the persona seeks solace in his belief in God. The volume closes with the narrative "Viacheslav. Zhizn' peredelkinskaia" (to Vyacheslav: life in Peredelkino), which represents a short history in verse of the writers colony located outside of Moscow. The poet Boris Pasternak (q.v.) and his young neighbor Vyacheslav Ivanov are the principal characters, but many others figure. The lyric persona is autobiographical, but not idealized, since he reproaches himself for choosing silence when friendship required action.

The novel *Dekada* (1983; a ten-day festival), L.'s fictionalized portrayal of the deportation of a non-Slavic minority from the Caucasus to Kazakhstan, should be read in conjuction with his poetry. One of the principal characters, the translator Stanislav Borodsky, is obviously modeled on L. The novel recounts the enormous losses, not only of lives, but of an entire culture. For all its sincerity, *Dekada* is not successful as a novel, and the reader wishes that L. would abandon the mask of Borodsky and tell the story without resorting to fiction. L.'s most rewarding prose book is the warm memoir of the writer Vassily Grossman

(1905–1964), published as *Stalingrad Vasiliia Grossmana* (1986; Vassily Grossman's Stalingrad). Drawing on his long friendship with Grossman, as well as letters and other documents, L. reconstructs a portrait not only of a friend, but also of an entire era.

L.'s role as eyewitness and chronicler of the fate of culture had been privately acknowledged for over half a century before the publication of *Volia* initiated public recognition of a major talent.

FURTHER WORKS: *Ochevidets* (1967); *Vechnyi den'* (1975); *Tetrad' bytiia* (1977); *Kartiny i golosa* (1986); *Lira* (1989)

BIBLIOGRAPHY: "L.," in Terras, V., ed., *Handbook of Russian Literature* (1985), 255–56; Lowe, D. A., *Russian Writing since 1953: A Critical Survey* (1987), 17, 130–31

RONALD MEYER

LISNYANSKAYA, Inna

Russian poet and translator, b. 24 June 1928, Baku, U.S.S.R. (now Azerbaijan)

L., who was born in the capital city of Azerbaijan, began to write poetry at the age of ten, although she was not from a literary family. Unbeknownst to her Jewish parents, L. was taken by her grandmother to be christened, an event that profoundly affected the young girl. L. did not attend university, even though she was invited to apply for admission to a literary institute on the merits of her early poems. A published poet in Baku since 1948, L. attracted the attention of Alexander Tvardovsky (1910–1971), the influential editor of the Moscow journal *Novyi Mir,* and in 1957 her poetry began to appear in that and other mainstream publications. L. became a member of the Union of Writers in 1957 and moved to Moscow in 1961, where she resides to the present day. Five volumes of L.'s verse were published from 1957 to 1978. In addition, L. worked as a translator of poetry, principally from Azerbaijan. The official censure of the literary almanac *Metropol* (1979; *Metropol,* 1982), to which L. had contributed seven poems, altered the course of L.'s career in the U.S.S.R. The Metropolians intended to publish an uncensored volume of works, chosen on the basis of artistic principles, rather than ideological criteria. Refused permission to publish the collection in the U.S.S.R., the writers defiantly opted for publication abroad. The majority of the participants suffered public and private harassment, which included a ban on their works, and two young writers were expelled from the Union of Writers. L., together with her common-law husband, Semyon

Lipkin, and Vassily Aksyonov (qq.v.), one of the principal organizers of the almanac, resigned from the Union of Writers in protest. L. did not publish in the U.S.S.R. until 1988, when the reform policies of Gorbachev paved the way for her reinstatement into the Union. Since that time she has published widely in the leading literary journals and has been publicly acknowledged for her resolute defense of the *Metropol* group and her own artistic independence.

In her "Nechto vrode avtobiografiia" (1990; something in the way of an autobiography) L. dismisses her early books as immature, but blames the censorship for the distortion of her talents in the succeeding volumes *Iz pervykh ust* (1966; right from the source) and *Vinogradnyi svet* (1978; grape light). From the beginning, L.'s poetry was marked by a distinctively un-Soviet character, since the primary emphasis is on private and not social concerns. In contrast to the "stadium" poets such as Yevgeny Yevtushenko (q.v.), whom detractors criticized for actively courting the crowd with political pamphlets in verse, L. has consistently eschewed rhetoric and politics in favor of lyric simplicity and intimacy. Consequently, L. has become a master of the short form, whose predominant stanzaic measure is the quatrain. However, L. does not restrict herself to the familiar territory of Russian women's verse, but invokes such ethical problems as conscience and memory.

During the ten years of nonpublication in the U.S.S.R. that followed the *Metropol* affair, two volumes of L.'s verse appeared in the émigré press: *Dozhdi i zerkala* (1983; rains and mirrors) and *Stikhotvoreniia: na opushke sna* (1984; poems: on the edge of sleep). The first volume, which collects works written over a span of more than fifteen years, reveals the full scope of L.'s poetry, in particular the religiosity that the Soviet censorship had previously found unacceptable. *Stikhotvoreniia,* too, includes poems from as early as 1966, but the vast majority date from the 1980s and unmistakably herald a new poetic voice. Perhaps L.'s enforced silence, as well as the freedom from translation work, provided the impetus. Whatever the cause, *Stikhotvoreniia* is generally considered L.'s most successful book, largely due to the unity in theme and style that is achieved. The volume is a lyrical diary in which the persona records her hopes and tragedies as woman, poet, and citizen.

Firmly grounded in the traditions of Russian lyric poetry, most notably the verse of Anna Akhmatova and Marina Tsvetaeva (qq.v.), L.'s work retains its own distinct character. The hallmarks of L.'s style are a conversational diction, a sense of self-irony, and an attention to everyday events or objects, all of which belie the gravity of the lyric persona's anguish and loss.

FURTHER WORKS: *Eto bylo so mnoi* (1957); *Vernost'* (1958); *Ne prosto liubov'* (1963); *Vozdushnyi plast* (1990)

BIBLIOGRAPHY: Heldt, B., "I. L.'s *Stikhotvoreniia: No opushke sna,*" *WLT,* 60, 1 (Winter 1986), 131; Lowe, D. A., *Russian Writing since 1953: A Critical Survey* (1987), 7, 131

RONALD MEYER

LITERATURE AND EXILE

The historical phenomenon of exile, with writers among those afflicted by its cruelty, has been recorded since the first banishment from communal life by any of its ruling factions. Modern literature of exile is, however, a unique mode of writing not only in its reflections of the experience of exile, but in the patterns of expression of response to the experience.

The sheer weight of exilic history in the 20th c. undoubtedly has led to consciousness of exile as a spiritual and psychological condition not easily rooted out by favorable turns of circumstance. In addition, the constants of alienation—angst, fragmentation, and dislocation that pervade 20th c. life and art—have turned modern writing into an emphatic and invidious literature of exile.

Early literature treats exile, and its awesome threats to the sanity and equilibrium of the individual, in a manner distinct from modern literature. Ovid and Dante, in reflecting on their own and projected conditions of exile, clearly saw the phenomenon as a sentence of prosecution and persecution; their chief aim was to commute the sentence and return to their native land. Banishment was not viewed by them with ambivalence, although the necessity of acceptance of their reality produced both stoic and defiant passages of rhetoric in their work. Nineteenth-century literature of exile reflects a similar response—the exiled writer yearns for return to his banished land, but he is not destroyed by resignation to historical currency, nor is he afflicted with the disease of anomie. Émile Zola and Vicente Blasco Ibáñez (q.v.) are but two of these 19th-c. writers who suffered exile but who did not allow the experience to dominate their sense of history.

Twentieth-century literature, in distinction, abounds with such a sense of exilic dislocation that it subsumes geographic and historic content into a deeper psychological being. Although historic roots are at the base of modern exilic literature, the resultant tiers of expression go beyond particular history to reflect timeless and universal perception of loss. Literature of exile becomes, in the process, social history and a lyric rupture of unrecoverable moment. Whether the experience is recorded of a T'ien-ah-men (Tienanmen) Square freedom fighter who escaped into exile—Zhang Xianliang (b. 1936)—or a Spanish Civil War Loyalist who fled his country with the victory of Franco—Francisco Ayala (b. 1906) or Benjamin Jarnes (1888–1948)—the reflections encompass a collective sense of loss as well as an immediate disjuncture of historical culture.

The 20th c.'s most horrendous example of genocide is the Holocaust, with its record of the murder of six-million Jews, but other modern genocides have occurred as well. The slaughter of the Armenians, the attempt at extinction of gypsies by Hitler's Aryan stalwarts, the execution of the Russian middle-class, the brutal massacre of Spanish Loyalists by victorious Franco squads, and the systematic killings of Kurds, are among such cataclysmic events. Masterpieces that record each of these genocides are found in many languages, some native to the historic event and some observed under foreign eyes. The experience of exile is reflected in the works of these writers who lived through the upheaval of exile or observed it from a distance. At least six writers stand as exilic literary giants: Bertolt Brecht, Thomas Mann, Vladimir Nabokov, Isaac Bashevis Singer, Aleksandr Solzhenitsyn, and Elie Wiesel (qq.v).

Those who did not feel the need to flee and remained in their country after the disruption and usurpation of tradition and political-social power may reflect a different attitude to events. For every Nabokov, for example, whose family lost a vast fortune with the coming of the Russian Revolution, there were those who rose to a sharing of wealth and power heretofore denied them or who gloried in the new system, as did Maxim Gorky and Ilya Ehrenburg (qq.v). Yet it is significant that both Gorky and Ehrenburg suffered exile, one before the Russian Revolution of 1917 and one several times after the Communist Party ascension to power in the U.S.S.R. The transiency in Ehrenburg's life may be seen as a variant on exilic feeling: a rooted impermanency.

Literature of exile may conveniently be schematized into categorical imperatives: political, religious, personal, and expatriate. Without question, political exile is the most quantitatively horrifying example of modern exile, but exclusive categorization is likely to provide problematic issues. The half-million citizens of Germany, Austria, and Czechoslovakia who fled their countries during the rise of Adolf Hitler and the National Socialist Party and through World War II were political refugees, for they were fleeing a national program of extinction, but their exile often had a religious cause as well. Similarly, those citizens, some of them writers, who fled Germany because of their sexual orientation may be considered political refugees since Nazi doctrine branded them as undesirable deviants and moral lepers. Thus

they are political exiles at the same time that they are sexual exiles. The literature about such experiences, in whatever genres, reflects this invidious multitexture. Among such writers forced into exile, and the regions from which they fled, are: Africa—Okot p'Bitek, Camara Laye (qq.v); South Africa—Peter Abrahams, Breyten Breytenbach, Dennis Brutus (qq.v.), Jack Cope (b. 1931), Bessie Head (q.v.), Mazisi Kunene (b. 1930), Alex La Guma (q.v.), Mongane Wally Serote (b. 1944); Austria—Hermann Broch; Jakov Lind, Robert Musil, Joseph Roth, Franz Werfel, Stefan Zweig (qq.v.); China—Bei Dao (b. 1949), Duo Duo (b. 1951); Czechoslovakia—Pavel Kohout (b. 1928), Milan Kundera, Arnošt Lustig, Josef Škvorecký (qq.v.); Germany—Theodor Adorno (1903–1969), Hannah Arendt (1906–1975), Johannes R. Becher (1891–1958), Walter Benjamin (1892–1940), Alfred Döblin, Stefan Heym, Thomas Mann (qq.v.), Heinrich Mann, Herbert Marcuse (1889–1979), Nelly Sachs, Ernst Toller, Arnold Zweig (qq.v.); Hungary—Tamas Aczel (b. 1921), George Faludy (b. 1910), Julius Hay (1900–1975), Arthur Koestler, György Lukács, Ferenc Molnar, Elie Wiesel (qq.v.); Argentina—Miguel Bonasso, Manuel Puig, Luisa Valenzuela (qq.v.); Chile—José Donoso, Ariel Dorfman, Pablo Neruda (qq.v.); Colombia—Gabriel García Márquez (q.v.); Cuba—Guillermo Cabrera Infante, Nicolás Guillén (qq.v.), Heberto Padilla (b. 1932), Severo Sarduy (q.v.), Armando Valladares (b. 1937); Uruguay—Eduardo Galeano (b. 1904), Juan Carlos Onetti (q.v.); U.S.A.—Eldridge Cleaver (b. 1935); Poland—Stanisław Barańczak, Marek Hłasko, Jerzy Kosinski, Czesław Miłosz (qq.v.), Zdisław Najder (b. 1930), Isaac Bashevis Singer, Israel Joshua Singer (qq.v.), Aleksander Wat (1900–1967), Adam Zagajewski (q.v.), Spain—Rafael Alberti, Max Aub, Luis Cernuda, Jorge Guillén (qq.v.), Jorge Semprun (b. 1920), Ramón Sender (q.v.); Romania—Nina Cassian (b. 1924), E. M. Cioran (q.v.), Andrei Codrescu (b. 1946); Ukraine—Vasyl Barka (b. 1908), Yuri Klen (1891–1947), Wira Wowk (b. 1920); U.S.S.R.—Yuz Aleshkovsky (b. 1929), Nina Berberova (b. 1901), Joseph Brodsky, Ivan Bunin, Sergey Dovlatov (qq.v.), Aleksandr Galich (1919–1977), Lev Kopelev (b. 1907), Vladimir Nabokov, Irina Ratunshinskaya (b. 1954), Andrey Sinyavsky (q.v.), Aleksandr Solzhenitsyn.

Another form of exile literature is that which deals with the sense of cultural exile. Although such exile is not overtly forced on an individual (the artist may argue otherwise, in that he cannot deny his perceptions of society and a consequent ostracism for expression of such perceptions), the force of separatism is keenly felt by the individual artist who often deserts his native land when pressures become overwhelming for him. Several giants of modern literature exemplify this kind of exile—

James Joyce, who found he could write only about Catholicism, Ireland, and his family by "escaping the nets" of their physical location; Samuel Beckett, who chose Paris as his home base because a troubled and parochial Ireland allowed him no vision to write; Joseph Conrad, who self-consciously chose English as his medium of literary expression and left his native Poland at age seventeen; D. H. Lawrence, who wandered the world in search of an ideal place to write and breathe in his visionary airs; V. S. Naipaul, Doris Lessing, and Salman Rushdie (qq.v.), who left their birth lands redolent of colonial life for a metropolitan and more sophisticated empirical environment.

Joyce's *Ulysses* (1922) is the modern masterpiece of cultural exile-and-return in its complexly simple tale of a father and son in search of a son and father within the confines of a 24-hour walk through the mean streets of Dublin. *En attendant Godot* (1952; *Waiting for Godot*, 1954), as but one example of Beckett's genius in cohering the symbolic waste of his generation's putative flames, is another instance of cultural exile in its presentation of memory and consciousness of the void of loss. Joseph Conrad's *Under Western Eyes* (1911), an early-20th-c. example of exile, treats the story of a Polish student in his czarist-occupied country who has less interest in politics and in national independence than in his personal career, but who through circumstance is forced into a choice that sends him into exile and a tormented conscience. He is subsequently forced to come to terms with an awareness of politics and community that will end his invidious disease of psychic exile.

The end of exile in the literature that treats this subject comes for some writers in the moment when the protagonist adopts a new identity, whether it be that of national citizenship, communal membership, or a more personal joining in the form of an adoption of language and customs of his new land. When the "growing pains" of a refugee are treated as domestic comedy, exile may be said to have been pushed from the center of the writer's matter, and emigration to have entered as a dominant concern. Nabokov's *Pnin* (1957) is an example of this kind of literature, as is the fiction of Sergey Dovlatov, Bharati Mukherjee (q.v.), and I. B. Singer. Language as a gauge of the end of exile is a complex matter, for in a writer's adoption of one language over another, he or she is signaling the end of allegiance to one root and the beginning of a graft onto another. Yet loss of early roots is not always transcended in the artist's new growth. Examples may clarify the issue: Joseph Conrad chose English as his means of literary expression; in his case there was never a sense of separation from his native language, though English was his third means of expression (he knew

French before he studied English). Isaac Bashevis Singer continued to write in Yiddish (with an occasional piece in English; he did not use Polish for his literary endeavors), though he lived in the U.S. for more than fifty years. Nabokov wrote in Russian and knew German and French well, but he decided to break with his past in 1941 by writing completely in English; it was in that year that his first novel in English, *The Real Life of Sebastian Knight,* took shape, signaling a break with his past that was never completely made, as Nabokov's further works showed.

Literature of exile may then be said to consist of work written by those who suffered the terrible impact of exilic experience and by those whose works treat the individious subject of exile. There is as much literature of exile treating the condition in an oblique (but pervasive) manner as there is of direct content of exilic experience. Nabokov's *Speak, Memory* (1966; orig. pub. as *Conclusive Evidence,* 1951) and Milan Kundera's *Le livre du rire et de l'oubli* (1979; *The Book of Laughter and Forgetting,* 1980) and *Nesnesitelna lehkost byti* (1984; *The Unbearable Lightness of Being,* 1984) are direct records of preserving memory before it is filtered into oblivion, yet Brecht's *Leben des Galilei* (1938; *Galileo,* 1957) and *Mutter Courage und ihre Kinder* (1939; *Mother Courage and Her Children,* 1941), Isaac Bashevis Singer's *The Slave,* and Thomas Mann's *Joseph und seine Brüder* (1933–1942; *Joseph and His Brothers,* 1934–1945) are just as intimate—if indirect—records of exilic consciousness. The experience of exile, whether immediately palpable in the work or subtly adduced through distanced modes of narrative, has changed the course of modern literature.

BIBLIOGRAPHY: Tabori, P., *The Anatomy of Exile: A Semantic and Historical Study* (1972); Spalek, J., and J. Strelka, *Deutsche Exilliteratur* (1976); Rosenfeld, A. H., *A Double Dying: Reflections on Holocaust Literature* (1980); Gurr, A., *Writers in Exile: The Creative Identity of Home in Modern Literature* (1981); Pachmuss, T., ed., *A Russian Cultural Revival: A Critical Anthology of Émigré Literature before 1939* (1981); Pike, D., *German Writers in Soviet Exile, 1933–1945* (1982); Pfanner, H. F., *Exile in New York: German and Austrian Writers after 1933* (1983); Terras, V., ed., *Handbook of Russian Literature* (1985); Seidel, M., *Exile and the Narrative Imagination* (1986); Dance, D. C., ed., *Fifty Caribbean Writers: A Bio-Bibliographical Critical Source Book* (1986); Marotos, D. C., and Hill, M. D., *Escritores de la Diaspora Cubana: Manual Biobibliografica/ Cuban Exile Writers: A Biobibliographic Handbook* (1986); Faulhaber, U., et al., eds., *Exile and Enlightenment: Studies in German and Compara-*

tive Literature (1987); Ugarte, M., *Shifting Ground: Spanish Civil War Exile Literature* (1989); Tucker, M., ed., *Literary Exile in the Twentieth Century: An Analysis and Biographical Dictionary* (1991)

MARTIN TUCKER

LITHUANIAN LITERATURE

See Volume 3, page 128.

The postwar Soviet occupation of Lithuania divided the Lithuanian literary community into two parts: writers at home, subject to the ideological constraints of Socialist Realism (q.v.), and writers forced into exile.

Poetry

The exilic community included poets Juozas Kėkštas (pseud. of Juozas Adomavičius, 1915–1981), Kazys Bradūnas (b. 1917), Alfonsas Nyka-Niliūnas (pseud. of Alfonsas Čipkus, b. 1920), and Bernardas Brazdžionis (b. 1907); prose writers Algirdas Landsbergis (b. 1924) and Antanas Škėma (1911–1961); and the dramatist Kostas Ostrauskas (b. 1926). A poet of tragic intensity is Liūnė Sutema (b. 1927), wife of the novelist Marius Katiliškis (1915–1981) and sister of poet Henrikas Nagys (b. 1920). The greatest conflicts in Sutema's poetry arise from the confrontation of her own life, and that of her fellow Lithuanian refugees, with the trauma of exile and dispossession. Similarly, the condition of exile dominates the poetry of Algimantas Mackus (1932–1964) and Henrikas Radauskas (q.v.).

Within Soviet-occupied Lithuania, after de-Stalinization, talents came forward only gradually, notably Eduardas Mieželaitis (b. 1919), an outstanding pioneer of the new self-reliant poetry, and Justinas Marcinkevičius (b. 1930), who uses Lithuanian history in an attempt to depict the moral crucibles of the nation.

Judita Vaičiūnaitė (b. 1937), a poet of vibrant personal emotions, has explored erotic love in her verses with urban settings, and deep mythological dimensions in poetry with a prehistoric focus. Janina Degutytė (1928–1990) is known for her deep, lyrical devotion to the land and to nature in general. Sigitas Geda (b. 1934) is a subtle poet of nature and of the soul, whose word magic is permeated with references to ancient myth and to medieval symbolism. Notable among the recent poets are also Jonas Juškaitis (b. 1933), a master of finely tuned, complex emotions; Albinas Bernotas (b. 1934), a friend of the nature that envelops the human soul; and Marcelijus Martinaitis (b. 1936), famous for his folksy-surrealist cycle *Kukučio baladės* (1977; the ballads of Kukutis).

The younger generation born from the 1940s through the 1960s seeks a much more direct confrontation with the contemporary political situation in Lithuania, is more militant about ecology, and at the same time is immensely concerned with the mysteries of the poet's craft. Gintaras Patackas (b. 1951), a poet of many moods, can write with powerful anger against the menace of tyranny in human affairs, as he does in his latest books, *Amuletai* (1988; amulets) and *Kapitono Homero vaikai* (1989; the children of Captain Homer). Similarly, Donaldas Kajokas (b. 1953) in some poems exploits the traditionally strong presence of nature in Lithuanian poetry to reveal with a sudden and revolting clarity the ugly mutilation of the countryside by the presence of Soviet concentration camps, notably in *Tylinčiojo aidas* (1988; the echo of the silent one). In the same book Kajokas reinforces his point by depicting unendurable mystical horrors in a poem dedicated to the beauty of Bach's St. Matthew Passion.

Julius Keleras (b. 1961) is also very angry about the destruction of his nation, and the Christmas wafer in the title of his latest book, *Baltas kalėdaitis* (1990; the white Christmas wafer), often tastes of blood and tears and of the bitter herbs of exile. Vytautas Cinauskas (b. 1930), Keleras's senior by some thirty years, who has only recently begun to appear in print and has not yet published a book, shares the same bitter outrage.

A broader view of exile is taken by Vytautas Bložė (b. 1930), who says in the preface to his book *Polifonijos* (1981; polyphonies) that he seeks "to give meaning to the universality of human existence in various planes of space and time." This he achieves by relating, in close-knit image sequences, the experiences of east European exiles to Siberia and those of Africans brought in ships to slavery, and those anywhere who weep for a lost home. He extends these visions to the historical dimension, writing in the seemingly dispassionate manner of a chronicler in the elaborately entitled *Miko Kėdainiškio laiškai sau pačiam ir kiti nežinomi rankraščiai rasti senų griūvančių mūrinių namų pastogėje* (1986; the letters of Mikas Kėdainiškio to himself, and other unknown manuscripts found in the attic of an old, crumbling stone house). In his latest book, *Noktiurnai* (1990; nocturnes), Bložė focuses upon the poet's self-consciousness as the entire universe, petty and grand, turns around him.

Tautvyda Marcinkevičiūtė (b. 1955) in her *Tauridė* (1990; Tauris) speaks in a lyrical voice of shifting realities evocative of the world of antiquity. Antanas A. Jonynas (b. 1953), in his *Parabolė* (1984; parabola), also conveys a strong "classical" flavor in the style and mood of his verse. Markas Zingeris (b. 1947), in his *Vakaras vaikystėje* (1989; an evening in childhood), writes verses that are sad and full of ancient Jewish wisdom filtering like a mournful light through the veil of reality. Eduardas Juchnevičius (b. 1942), a graphic artist, with his book of poems entitled *Vilkolakiai* (1988; the werewolves), illustrates another recent trend in Lithuania—the crossing of boundaries between the arts.

In the last two or three years, some of the established poets have at least partially succumbed to a malaise, a restless wandering of the spirit and even a revulsion against writing poetry. Considered by many to be the speakers of the nation, or at least of its conscience, they were swept away into a whirlwind of political activities where they felt forced to speak with a prophet's voice, rather than that of the artist. Nevertheless, some continue to publish new and interesting things. Among them, Sigitas Geda came out with *Septynių vasarų giesmės* (1990; songs of seven summers), a graceful collection of personal musings, and Gintaras Gutauskas (dates n.a.), a talented poet of sardonic bent, with *Pasivaikščiojimas be šuns* (1990; a walk without a dog), a small book of crisp verse.

In the meantime, a considerable number of new and eager poets, mostly but not always young, have sprung up, filling the shelves with rather small booklets of fledgling verse as ambitious as it is uneven in quality. One of the best is Gražina Cieškaitė (b. 1951). Her latest book, *Auka žvaigždžių vainikui* (1991; an offering for the wreath of stars), wanders through the shadowy philosophical realms of being and nonbeing, in the company of love and death. Also mentioned should be Alis Balbierius (b. 1954), with his new book *Alsavimų girios* (1990; deep-breathing forests), Raimondas Jonutis (dates n.a.), with *Vėžių maras* (1990; the crayfish plague), Angelė Jankauskytė (dates n.a.), with *Žemės rūbais* (1991; in the garments of the earth), Vytautas Rubavičius (dates n.a.), with *Dangus ir kitos gamtos jėgos* (1988; the sky and other forces of nature), Romas Daugirdas (b. 1951), with a small book of verse, strangely entitled "(. . .)" (1990), and Eugenijus Kubilinskas (dates n.a.), with his first book, *Vyzdžio veidrody* (1990; in the mirror of the eye). Among the youngest to appear are Elena Karnauskaitė (b. 1964), with *Briedė jūroje* (1990; a she-moose wading in the sea), Auris Radzevičius-Radžius (dates n.a.), with *Ornamentas vietoj laivo* (1990; an ornament in place of a ship), and Sigitas Parulskis (dates n.a.), with *Iš ilgesio visa tai* (1990; it all comes from yearning).

Fiction

Prose writers are not as productive as their colleagues in poetry; in particular, there remains only a waning interest in the large novel, a genre that in the past had helped to build a high reputation for Lithuanian literature with the readers of all the former Soviet republics. Among the older writers, Mykolas Sluckis (b. 1929) and Jonas Avyžius (b. 1922) have undertaken to explore new modes of consciousness open to an individual once free from the constrictions of Socialist Realism. Avyžius has written some powerful accounts of the violence done to Lithuanian peasantry during its enforced collectivization, and he continues to show interest in rural Lithuanian life and its problems in his two recent novels, *Degimai* (1982; burned forest clearings) and *Sodybų tuštėjimo metas. Trečia knyga* (1988; the time of emptying homesteads).

Romualdas Granauskas (b. 1939) and Juozas Aputis (b. 1936) have created an intense, as it were, magical reality, seemingly plain, yet both surreal and mythical, in which to place the human soul in the crucibles of our age. Granauskas has not been very productive lately, but Aputis published two collections of short stories in his familiar style: *Gegužė and nulūžusio beržo* (1986; the cuckoo on a broken birch tree) and *Skruzdėlynas Prūsijoje* (1989; an anthill in Prussia). Richardas Gavelis (b. 1950) has recently published a sensational novel, *Vilniaus pokeris* (1990; the Vilnius poker game), in which life under communism is depicted as a filthy nightmare of mixed pornography and horror. His latest book, called *Jauno žmogaus memuarai* (1991; memoirs of a young man), portrays the hero as a dead man exploring his mind and his past life from beyond the grave. The novel *Priešaušrio vieškeliai* (1985; predawn highways) by Bronius Radzevičius (b. 1940), and his collection of short stories *Link Debesijos* (1984; toward cloudland), have left a powerful imprint upon Lithuanian prose. They do not have any elaborate or even very coherent plots, and consist instead of intensely emotional sets of episodic images subject to such tight control that, under its pressure, they begin to function like poetry, where every word acquires a symbolic meaning in the battle between the author's aesthetic discipline and his heart.

Writers in the West are subject to the inevitable attrition of time, and there is no real hope at all that the children and grandchildren of exiles will take their place, because most of them either no longer speak Lithuanian, or know it so poorly that they could not possibly write either poetry or creative fiction. Some of the older writers are still productive, however, notably Kazimieras Barėnas (b. 1908), who continues his fictional chronicles of Lithuanian life before and during World War II with the novel *Meškos maurojimo metai* (1990; the year of the roaring bear), and the dramatist

Kostas Ostrauskas, with a new play, *Ars Amoris* (1991; the art of love). In general, Lithuanian cultural life in the diaspora has begun to gravitate more and more toward the home country itself. There are frequent visits by individuals, some of whom participate in cultural reconstruction of the country by teaching at academic institutions, supplying advice and material assistance to the economy, participating in worldwide conferences, held in Lithuania, of Lithuanian writers and scholars, attending national folk festivals, athletic events, and the like. The older and middle generations are increasingly regaining the feeling that "home" is the old country, and not the comfortable nests they had built in western lands over the years. Even many of the young people are more and more interested in the land of their forebears. Lithuania itself welcomes this interest and tries to involve the émigrés in its life as much as is possible. In one such effort, the émigré writers are being republished at home with increasing frequency. Among the most recent examples we find the collected works of Bernardas Brazdžionis under the title *Poezijos pilnatis* (1989; the full moon of poetry), of Kazys Bradūnas, *Prie vieno stalo* (1990; together at the table), of Henrikas Nagys, *Grižulas* (1990; the Pleiades), and of Juozas Kėkštas, *Dega vėjai* (1986; the winds are burning).

Lithuanian literature continues to develop in spite of the contingencies of exile or the lingering consequences of past Soviet occupation.

BIBLIOGRAPHY: Ciplijauskaitė, B., "Old Themes Experienced Anew in Recent Lithuanian Poetry," *JBalS*, 6, 2–3 (1975), 190–98; Vaškelis, B., "The Motif of Anxiety in the Contemporary Short Story of Lithuania," *JBalS*, 6, 2–3 (1975), 162–70; Šilbajoris, R., "Forbidden Thoughts, Permitted Voices: Poets in Lithuania and in the Leningrad Underground," *Lituanus*, 23, 4 (1977), 45–54; Šilbajoris, R., "Images of America in Lithuanian Prose," *Lituanus*, 27, 1 (1981), 5–19; Bukaveckas-Vaičkonis, K., "The Development of Lithuanian Literature in the West: Two Divergent Trends," *Lituanus*, 28 (1982), 41–54; Šilbajoris, R., "Translucent Reality in Recent Lithuanian Prose," *WLT*, 57, 1 (Winter 1983), 21–24; Šilbajoris, R., ed., *Mind against the Wall: Essays on Lithuanian Culture under Soviet Occupation* (1983); Straumanis, A., ed., *Fire and Night: Five Baltic Plays* (1986); Šilbajoris, R., "Time, Myth, and Ethos in Recent Lithuanian Literature," *WLT*, 60, 3 (Summer 1986), 432–35; Willeke, A., "Iconoclastic Voices in Lithuanian Exile Prose," *JBalS*, 17, 2 (1986), 133–43; Šilbajoris, R., "Folkloric Subtexts in Modern Lithuanian Poetry," *IFRev*, 5 (1987), 11–19; Kavolis, V., "The Radical Project in Lithuanian Émigré Literature," *Lituanus*, 34, 1 (1988), 5–17; Mandelker, A., and R. Reeder, eds., *The Supernatural in Slavic and Baltic Literature: Essays in Honor of Victor Terras* (1988); Šilbajoris, R., "Some Recent Baltic Poets: The Civic Duty To Be Yourself," *JBalS*, 20, 3 (Fall 1989), 243–59; Šilbajoris, R., "A Look at Recent Poetry from Lithuania," *WLT*, 65, 2 (Spring 1991), 225–29

RIMVYDAS ŠILBAJORIS

LODGE, David

English novelist and literary critic, b. 28 Jan. 1935, London

L. has successfuly pursued two careers, combining the writing of novels with the teaching of English literature, primarily at Britain's University of Birmingham. L.'s fiction is often richly comic, and frequently draws upon his experiences as a Catholic and an academic.

L.'s first novel, *The Picturegoers* (1960), focuses somewhat gloomily on a group of Catholics living in a lower-middle-class district in London; L. admits that much of its style and tone can be traced to his youthful admiration for the more bluntly theological novels of Graham Greene (q.v.). With *The British Museum Is Falling Down* (1965), his third novel, L. employs a more overtly comical style, but again focuses primarily on young English Catholics struggling to cope with the requirements of their faith at a time when traditional beliefs and practices were widely believed to be in steep decline. It also features highly skilled parodies of several other well-known writers, including James Joyce (q.v.), another major influence on L.'s art.

During the early 1970s, L. was still best known for his critical writings, which included *Graham Greene* (1966), *Evelyn Waugh* (1971), and, most importantly, *The Language of Fiction* (1966), a lively and influential investigation of the function of style in the works of several accomplished writers of imaginative prose, including Austen, Dickens, and Thomas Hardy (q.v.).

With his fifth novel, *Changing Places: A Tale of Two Campuses* (1975), L. began to acquire a wider readership in both Britain and North America. Its central characters are two English professors—one British and one American—who decide one academic year to exchange teaching positions and find themselves exchanging a good deal more, including spouses, in the bargain. Although the novel is largely comic in tone, and features many funny episodes, it also addresses a wide range of social and intellectual issues that had suddenly moved to the fore in the 1970s, including the sexual revolution and the future of the novel—

subjects that would continue to surface in L.'s later fictions.

In *How Far Can You Go?* (1980; pub. in the U.S. as *Souls and Bodies,* 1982) L. portrays ten Catholic men and women who reassess their practices and beliefs in the wake of Vatican II. This novel, like *The British Museum Is Falling Down,* makes clear L.'s own opposition to the Church's official teachings on birth control; it suggests that many Catholics of L.'s generation were unable to form an enlightened and happy understanding of human sexuality. But as his works show, L. is not motivated by an abiding hostility to Catholicism; in fact, his stance tends to be that of a reform-minded believer who recognizes that religion plays a major role in the lives of most people, many of whom have been left anxious and puzzled by recent social and theological trends, feeling "spiritually orphaned" rather than spiritually renewed.

L. continues his largely satirical portrayal of academic life in *Small World* (1984), which again features Philip Swallow and Morris Zapp, the principal figures of *Changing Places.* Swallow plays a smaller role in *Nice Work* (1989), which centers on the unlikely love affair between a rather conservative, hard-nosed British businessman and a young college teacher with feminist leanings. *Nice Work* is L.'s most ambitious novel to date, combining humor and sharp social criticism while deliberately, brilliantly evoking the 19th-c. tradition of such "Condition of England" novels as Disraeli's *Sybil* (1845), and Dickens's *Hard Times* (1854).

L. is, however, very much a writer of his times; his fiction repeatedly displays a wide range of postmodern assumptions and strategies. And yet, in L.'s case, this artistic self-consciousness is not obtrusive or pretentious, perhaps because—in the tradition of literary realism—he never discounts the importance of convincing characters and well-made plots. At its best, L.'s fiction provokes both laughter and thought—an uncommon achievement in any age.

FURTHER WORKS: *Ginger, You're Barmy* (1962); *Out of Shelter* (1970); *The Novelist at the Cross-roads and Other Essays on Fiction and Criticism* (1971); *The Modes of Modern Writing: Metaphor, Metonymy, and the Typology of Modern Literature* (1977); *Working with Structuralism: Essays and Reviews on Nineteenth- and Twentieth-Century Literature* (1981); *Write On: Occasional Essays '65–'85* (1986); *Paradise News* (1991)

BIBLIOGRAPHY: Bergonzi, B., "D. L. Interviewed," *The Month* (Feb. 1970), 108–16; Widdowson, P., "The Anti-History Men: Malcolm Bradbury and D. L.," *CritQ,* 26, 4 (1984), 5–32; Morace, R. A., *The Dialogic Novels of Malcolm Bradbury and D. L.* (1989); Holmes, F. M., "The Reader as Discoverer in D. L.'s Small World," *Crit,* 32, 1 (Fall 1990), 47–57

BRIAN MURRAY

LOVELACE, Earl

Trinidadian novelist, short-story writer, and dramatist, b. 13 July 1935, Toco

L.'s family history is grounded in a love of the land and a sense of their specialness as Amerindian-African West Indians. Born in Trinidad, L. was moved shortly thereafter to Tobago where he lived with his maternal grandparents who raised him. The women in his family made an enormous investment in time and resources to encourage his development and ensure his survival in a society plagued by unemployment and racial prejudice. L. attended Scarborough Methodist Primary School in Tobago and Nelson Street Boys, R.C., in Trinidad. In Port-of-Spain, he attended the Ideal High School from 1948–1953 before moving to Centeno, Trinidad, to attend the Eastern Caribbean Institute of Agriculture and Forestry from 1962 to 1971. L. earned his M.A. in English from John Hopkins University in Baltimore, Maryland, before being awarded a Guggenheim fellowship in 1977. L.'s first job as a professional proofreader for the *Trinidadian Guardian* in 1953 merged his love for the land and his interest in writing. As a field assistant and agricultural assistant for the department of forestry from 1956 to 1966, L. learned the real and the poetic dimensions of the land and the people, which he recreates in an unmatched use of natural imagery in his fictional work. He was an employee in the Civil Service when he was given the B.P. Independence Literary Award in 1964 for his first novel, *While Gods Are Falling* (1965). In 1966 he received the Pegasus Literary Award for Outstanding Contribution to the Arts in Trinidad and Tobago. L. spent a year as writer in residence at Howard University in 1966–1967, and published *The Schoolmaster* in 1968. Accepting a position as writer on the *Trinidad and Tobago Express Newspaper,* he moved to Port-of-Spain to divide his time between journalistic writing and the creation of fiction and dramatic work.

L.'s sense that one person's voice can make a difference in the way a community evolves imbues all of his protagonists with parts of his own life experiences. For instance, it is believed that the character Bolo in *The Wine of Astonishment* (1982) was based on a newspaper story of a man who acted out Bolo's fictional trauma in real life. In this work, L. also immortalized the social prototypes that have the greatest impact on grassroots communication and change: The Badjohn, the Street Prince, and the Schoolmaster. While these figures are not new in Trinidadian culture, L. has taken them to new heights of literary artistry. *While Gods Are Falling* has become the harbinger of L.'s stylistic depiction of the question of the 20th c.: Can we successfully make the jump from a rural, agrarian culture to a technological society centered in urban populations? In *The Schoolmaster* the protagonist rapes the daughter of the man who arranges for the establishment of the school where he will reign as headmaster. The rape is also a metaphysical rape of the culture and society he does not know how to preserve. The daughter's suicide marks the death of the idyllic disposition of the inhabitants of rural Trinidad who must now try to enter the world of the latter 20th c. on their own terms. In *The Dragon Can't Dance* (1979), L. articulates the hierarchical power relationship of poor and democratic governments in postcolonial economies. The Street Prince, the Badjohn, and the Calypsonian, innovators of strategies in the tradition of the resistance of black people in Trinidad, appear here in a masterfully intricate plot dealing with the lives of people that are controlled by "carnival economies/carnival cultures" all over the globe.

L.'s collection *A Brief Conversion and Other Stories* (1988) contains previously published stories and new short fictional works. They focus primarily on the lives of people in the great migration from the countryside to the city. A significant technical difference in this collection is that the women have voices—they are better developed here as people with opinions and feelings.

While L. has written and produced many plays, *Jestina's Calypso and Other Plays* (1984) is the only published collection. These three plays are portrayals of problems L. dealt with in his newspaper editorials or in his public-service work years before: *Jestina's Calypso* parodies the argument that Trinidadian women with African physical attributes have a different but by no means lesser kind of beauty that needs to be acknowledged and appreciated. *The New Hardware Store* examines the function of capitalism in a culture-specific context through the example of a business that changes ownership after a riot. If black ownership does not positively impact on the lives of the employees or the community, can the change be considered progress? *My Name Is Village* is the archetype Village Play that challenges the concept of Western progress: Progress should have many culture-specific roles besides massive urbanization. The play is also about individuals coming of age—a father, a son, and a young woman who confront dichotomies in gender roles and the ne-

cessity of self-love before being able to love someone else. The language ascends to poetry inside the dialogue, dance, stick-fight choreography, and singing.

BIBLIOGRAPHY: Barratt, H., "Michael Anthony and E. L.: The Search for Selfhood," *ACLALSB*, 5, 3 (1980), 62–73; Green, J., "Moving Spirit–*The Wind of Astonishment* by E. L.," *Race Today* (May-June 1982), 110; Reyes, A., "Carnival: Ritual Dance of the Past and Present in E. L.'s *The Dragon Can't Dance*," *WLWE*, 24, 1 (Summer 1984), 107–20; Cager, C., "E. L.: A Bibliography," *Contributions in Black Studies: A Journal of African and Afro-American Studies*, 8 (1986–1987), 101–5; Cary, N. R., "Salvation, Self, and Solidarity in the Work of E. L.," *WLWE*, 28, 1 (Spring 1988), 103–14; Callaghan, E., "The Modernization of the Trinidadian Landscape in the Novels of E. L.," *ArielE*, 20, 1 (Jan. 1989), 41–54

CHEZIA THOMPSON-CAGER

LYNCH, Marta

Argentine novelist, short-story writer, and journalist, b. 8 Mar. 1925, Buenos Aires; d. 8 Oct. 1985, Buenos Aires

L. studied liberal arts at the National University of Buenos Aires where she obtained her B.A. in literature in 1952. Ten years later she was awarded the Band of Honor of the Argentine Society of Writers for her novel *La alfombra roja* (1962; the red carpet). Finished with her university studies, L. undertook a series of trips to North and Central America, Europe, Africa, the Near Orient, and the Pacific Islands. She taught literature courses, gave conferences at Argentine and foreign universities and cultural institutions, and attended numerous conventions of writers. In 1970 she formed part of the jury of a contest organized by Casa de las Américas, a Cuban publishing house formed to establish an association of Latin American intellectuals and to publish their works. L. was also very active in politics, because, to her, politics was something noble, a transcendental expression of education, and an activity involving the most central values of human existence. She was the director of the national committee of the Radical Intransigent Union Party; she was actively involved in Juan D. Perón's return to Argentina, and she was one of the few to criticize the military government for waging the Falkland Islands war against Great Britain in 1983.

L.'s record of literary production is impressive both for its quality and quantity; within one fifteen-year period she produced five novels and three collections of short stories, subsequently translated into English, French, Portuguese, German, Russian, Italian, Swedish, Norwegian, and Croatian. L. is also well known in Argentina for her newspaper articles and television appearances. She is one of the most representative of feminist writers in Argentina, along with Silvina Bullrich (b. 1915), Victoria Ocampo (1890–1979), Olga Orozco (b. 1920), and Beatriz Guido (q.v.), a generation that renewed the Argentine narrative and lyric. L.'s literary works express her view of the condition of Argentine women as oppressed in the expression of their disquieting insights by speech patterns imposed by a prevailing patriarchal society. One of L.'s merits lies in her innovative treatment of this theme and her creation of female characters of universal significance. L. has affirmed that she began to write out of her own feelings of interior chaos and desperation. Additional motives included feelings of anguish, the need to find an appropriate language, and the wish to engage in dialogue with other writers.

L.'s most widely known novel is *La Señora Ordóñez* (1968; Mrs. Ordóñez), which went through five editions in its first year alone, and was also made into a film for television. In this novel, as in most of her other works, love is the prime mover. Like Blanca Ordóñez, many of L.'s female protagonists feel oppressed and resigned; as a result, they suffer from flawed psyches and inhabit an obsessive, enclosed world. In order to fill their spiritual emptiness, they are always in need of a lover, which often results in obsession for sexual encounters that only end in disillusionment. Fear of aging is another recurring characteristic of L.'s female figures, who sometimes experience the anguish of losing their physical attraction and with it their power to command male attention. This preoccupation was mentioned in her last letter, written shortly before L.'s suicide in 1985.

Because she was straightforward in her writing, L.'s works are a direct reflection of her thoughts. Since her novel—*Informe bajo llave* (1983; report under lock and key)—L.'s longer fiction is deeply concerned with politics. In *Informe bajo llave,* for instance, L. reveals her concern about the concentration of power in one individual, who thereby becomes dehumanized.

Although several book reviews, dissertations, and critical studies of L.'s works do exist, she has received relatively little critical attention in comparison with other major Argentine writers of her generation such as Jorge Luis Borges, Ernesto Sábato, Julio Cortázar, and Manuel Puig (qq.v.). The corpus of L.'s works offers a profound inquiry into the nature of Argentine social reality as well as the mindset of Argentine women who are alien-

ated from emotional, historical, and political realities. Her narratives are more than mere testimony or chronicle, for they transcend such categories both formally and conceptually. The problems her works concern belong to a recent past that touches even those who are either indifferent to the nation's destiny or intent on denying their own responsibility as participants in the life of the nation. As an analyst of the national reality and a voice for Argentine women, L. has made significant contributions to history by way of her writings.

FURTHER WORKS: *Al vencedor* (1965); *Crónicas de la burguesía* (1965); *Los cuentos tristes* (1966); *Cuentos de colores* (1970); *El cruce del río* (1972); *Un árbol lleno de manzanas* (1974); *Los dedos de la mano* (1976); *Apuntes para un libro de viajes* (1978); *La penúltima versión de la Colorada Villanueva* (1978); *Los años de fuego* (1980); *Toda la función* (1982); *Páginas de M. L. seleccionadas por la autora* (1983)

BIBLIOGRAPHY: Kaminsky, A. S. K., "The Real Circle of Iron: Mothers and Children, Children and Mothers in Four Argentine Novels," *LALR,* 9 (1976), 77–86; Lindstrom, N., "The Literary Feminism of M. L.," *Crit,* 20, 2 (1978), 49–58; Foster, D. W., "M. L.: The Individual and the Argentine Political Process. *La penúltima versión de la Colorada Villanueva,*" *Latin American Digest,* 13, 3 (1979), 8–9; Lindstrom, N., "Woman's Voice in the Short Stories of M. L.," *The Contemporary Latin American Short Story* (1979), 148–53; Birkemoe, D. S., "The Virile Voice of M. L.," *REH,* 16, 2 (1982), 191–211; Lewald, E., "Alienation and Eros in Three Stories by Beatriz Guido, M. L. and Amalia Jamilis," in Mora, G., ed., *Theory and Practice of Feminist Literary Criticism* (1982), 175–85; Lindstrom, N., "Women's Discourse Difficulties in a Novel by M. L.," *I&L,* 4, 17 (1983), 339–48; Díaz, G. J., Introduction to *Páginas de M. L. seleccionadas por la autora* (1983), 11–40; Esquivel, M., "M. L., novelista por naturaleza," *Tragaluz,* 2, 13 (1986), 17–19

VIRGINIA SHEN

LYOTARD, Jean-François

French philosopher, b 10 Aug. 1924, Versailles

L. was trained in Husserlian phenomenology at the Sorbonne; his first book, an overview of phenomenology (q.v.), bears the traces of such a training (*La phénoménologie* [1954; phenomenology]). He started his career as a teacher in 1950 and taught at the high-school level for ten years, including two years in Constantine, Algeria, shortly before the beginning of the Algerian War (1950–1952). His shock in front of the aggressivity of French colonialism marked the beginning of his active political involvement—first in Algeria itself, then, after 1954, in the radical leftist group *Socialisme ou Barbarie* (Socialism or Barbarism). After the split of the group in 1964 he joined one of the two dissident organizations, *Pouvoir Ouvrier,* until 1966 when he left the "active service of the revolution" and began an intense activity of writing: In his first major book, *Discours, Figure* (1971; discourse, figure), art, especially painting, replaces active practical political militancy. Since 1959 he has taught at the Sorbonne (1959–1966) and at the universities of Nanterre (1966–1970) and Vincennes (1970–1987). He has been a researcher at the National Center for Scientific Research (CNRS) and was the cofounder of the International College of Philosophy. He has been a visiting professor in numerous universities in the U.S., Brazil, Canada, and Germany; he is currently a professor at the University of California, Irvine.

L.'s career as a philosopher, writer, critic, and teacher spans more than four decades, and the phases of his trajectory—existentialist phenomenology, Marxism, Freudian psychoanalysis, poststructuralism (q.v.), analytic philosophy and pragmatism, Kantian philosophy—comprise almost all the major movements of postwar continental philosophy. His work appeals to a number of different disciplines: philosophy, aesthetics, psychoanalysis, political history, and theories of language.

One of L.'s privileged objects of philosophical investigation since the beginning of his career has been and remains Kant. *L'enthousiasme* (1986; enthusiasm) is an analysis of the Kantian critique of history. In *Du sublime* (1988; on the sublime) L. raises the question of interest in the Kantian sublime. His most recent book, *Leçons sur l'analytique du sublime* (1991; lessons on the analytic of the sublime), is a close reading of the section on the sublime in Kant's *Critique of Judgment.* If Kant's sublime occupies such an important place in L.'s thinking, it does so insofar as the sublime feeling (the shock of a combined pleasure and pain) stems from a failure of Imagination (the faculty of presentation) to provide a representation of its object, a failure testifying, *a contrario,* to Imagination's attempt to represent that which cannot be represented. The sublime feeling marks the disruption of thought by that which resists representation and articulation: What is at stake in L.'s analyses of Kant, and could be seen as his larger project, is to preserve the unrepresentable, the inarticulable, the heterogeneous.

It is from a philosopher's point of view—not quite that of the art critic or the art historian—that L. has approached aesthetics and, since *Discours, Figure,* regularly comments on contemporary art. For him, the artistic avant-gardes have to do with this figural space insofar as they are concerned with the shock of a presentation presenting nothing but "presence" itself. In painting, it is a question of color and matter; in music, of sounds and timbres. L. has written on such artists as Marcel Duchamp, Gianfranco Baruchello, Albert Aymé, Jacques Monory, Valério Adami, Shusaku Arakawa, and Daniel Buren. He even organized a major art exhibit in Paris in 1985 called *Les Immatériaux,* the "immaterials," which testified to this concern for matter.

The defense of the heterogeneous undertaken in *Discours, Figure* marked L.'s move from phenomenology to psychoanalysis. Indeed, it is from a psychoanalytic perspective (a reading of Freud's *Interpretation of Dreams*) rather than from a phenomenological perspective that L. analyzed the presence of the figural within discourse. *Des dispositifs pulsionnels* (1973; apparatuses of drives), *Dérive à partir de Marx et Freud* (1973; partially translated as *Driftworks,* 1984), and *Économie libidinal* (1974; libidinal economy) then extended the psychoanalytic notions of an apparatus of drives and of libidinal forces in such a way that economical, political, linguistic, and pictorial apparatuses could be approached from a libidinal perspective. What was at stake in L.'s rereading of Marx was to show that the political economy hides a libidinal economy.

However, after *Économie libidinale,* L. abandoned the libidinal perspective, and gradually elaborated a "philosophy of phrases," which reached its most complete development in *Le différend* (1984; *The Different: Phrases in Dispute,* 1988), drawing from Kant as well as from Wittgenstein's work on language. *La condition postmoderne* (1979; *The Postmodern Condition,* 1984), the book that gave him international recognition, already analyzed sociopolitical, economical, and aesthetic aspects of our contemporary society in terms of a pragmatics of narratives, hence of phrases. The phrase interests L. as an *event,* the fact *that* something happens, before all determination of *what* happens. To say "there is no phrase" is still a phrase: for there to be no phrase is impossible. To think is to link phrases, which raises the question of the incommensurability of phrases, that is, the question of the conflict—the *différend*—among possible linkages: a *différend* is a fundamental difference, unresolvable because it resists synthesis and linkage. The "philosophy of phrases," which is not a linguistic or semiotic approach of the sociopolitical, allowed L. to analyze our contemporary world in terms of phrases and of conflicts among phrases.

399

L., with Jacques Derrida, Michel Foucault (qq.v.), and Gilles Deleuze (b. 1925), is one of the key figures in contemporary French philosophy. He consistently pushes philosophical speculation to border zones that are potentially productive for a variety of disciplines.

FURTHER WORKS: *Rudiments païens* (1977); *Instructions païennes* (1977); *Les TRANSformateurs DUchamp* (1977; *Duchamp's TRANS/formers,* 1990); *Récits tremblants* (1977); *Le mur du Pacifique* (1977; *Pacific Wall,* 1990); *Au juste* (1979; *Just Gaming,* 1985); *L'altra casa* (1979); *La partie de peinture* (1980); *Sur la constitution du temps par la couleur* (1980); *L'histoire de Ruth* (1983); *Tombeau de l'intellectuel et autres papiers* (1984); *L'assassinat de l'expérience par la peinture* (1984); *Le post-moderne expliqué aux enfants* (1986); *L'enthousiasme* (1986); *Que peindre? Adami, Arakawa, Buren* (1987); *Heidegger et "les juifs"* (1988; *Heidegger and "the Jews,"* 1990); *L'inhumain* (1988; *The Inhuman,* 1992); *Lectures d'enfance* (1991). FURTHER VOLUMES IN ENGLISH: *Perigrinations: Law, Form, Event* (1988; publ. in French as *Périgrinations,* 1990); *The L. Reader* (1989)

BIBLIOGRAPHY: Gasché, R., "Deconstruction As Criticism," *Glyph,* 6 (1979), 177–215; Bennington, G., "Theory: They or We?," *Paragraph: The Journal of the Critical Theory Group,* 1 (1983), 19–27; special L. issue, *Diacritics,* 14, 3, (Fall 1984); Rorty, R., "Le cosmopolitisme sans émancipation (en réponse à J.-F. L.)," *Crit,* 456 (1985), 569–80; Carroll, D., *Paraesthetics: Foucault, L., Derrida* (1987), 23–52, 155–84; Bennington, G., *L.—Writing the Event* (1988); Carroll, D., "L'invasion française dans la critique américaine de lettres," *Crit,* 491 (April 1988), 263–79; Ruby, C., *Les archipels de la différence: Foucault, Derrida, Deleuze, L.* (1990); special L. issue, *ECr,* 31, 1 (Spring 1991); Readings, B., *Introducing L.* (1991)

ANNE TOMICHE

MADSEN, Svend Åge

Danish novelist, b. 2 Nov. 1939, Århus

After having studied Danish and mathematics at the University of Århus from 1958 to 1961, M. made his debut in the mid-1960s with four experimental works. They were strongly influenced by the French *nouveau roman* of Alain Robbe-Grillet and Michel Butor (qq.v.) and aimed at subverting the traditional novel genre in an attempt to formulate M.'s own concept of reality in a new form.

In his later works M. increasingly employs existing popular novel genres but disclaims their ability to describe reality. Instead he emphasizes playfulness and the fictitious basis, using the novel as a linguistic, cognitive model. With the years, M. has moved from the hermetic and exclusive to an open style somewhat more accessible, but without abandoning his persistent probing into the insecurity of modern life. In recognition of his prominent position in modern Danish literature the Danish Academy awarded him its Literature Prize in 1972.

The point of departure for M.'s oeuvre is a theory that a literary work should not attempt to recreate reality but rather create its *own* reality. To write fiction means to establish an identity through language, both that of the author and the reader, and even the characters of the narrative only exist inasmuch as they are able to build up their identity through their own story. This theory is exemplified in the extreme in *Tilføjelser* (1967; additions), a novel published as a cassette with five separate volumes with different narrators, who nevertheless comment on one another and quote from M.'s earlier books. It is up to the reader to choose the order of reading and thus to establish an identity through the text.

Already in M.'s first novel, *Besøget* (1963; the visit), he experiments with various narrative perspectives offering the reader different possibilities of leading the totally abstract story to a conclusion. In the "non-novel" *Lystbilleder* (1964; pictures of lust) the basic situation is described again from various viewpoints. It is apparently done to define the concept of lust but actually to allow the author to experiment with narrative angles, with identity changes, and, above all, with various styles and language itself. The work is atomized into seemingly absurd episodes that might serve as elements of a puzzle to create coherence. A similar technique is used in the short-story collection *Otte gange orphan* (1965; eight times orphan). In the first seven stories seven mentally abnormal conditions are portrayed in deliberately monotonous language that follows certain given rules. However, in the eighth story complete linguistic anarchy prevails as a reflection of the impossibility of the narrator—and the reader—to make any sense of chaos.

The second phase of M.'s writings is signaled formally by a shift from first-person to third-person narration. The narrator and the protagonists no longer create their own fixed version of reality; rather it is the structure of a given novel type that determines the language, action, and thought of the characters. At the same time M. abandons verbal abstraction and stylistic puritanism in favor of humor and imagination.

Whereas the five volumes in *Tilføjelser* are mutually contradictory, five coherent novels executed in five different traditional genres make up *Sæt verden er til* (1971; if the world exists). The one-track search for the self has been replaced by a susceptibility, the ambiguity of which illustrates that the world is indeed changeable, that life can be experienced in many different ways. Still, the reader has to make an existential, Kierkegaardian choice, as in *Dage med Diam eller Livet om natten* (1972; days with Diam or life at night), which has two titles. The novel can only be read when the reader constantly chooses between two possibilities. According to a specific system 63 short-story fragments can be combined into 32 completed texts, each with its own outlook on life—M.'s background as a mathematician shines through here as well as in other works.

In M.'s later novels the experiments serve to stir social and political awareness. The plot of the colossal two-volume pseudodocumentary *Tugt og utugt i mellemtiden* (1976; decency and indecency in the meantime) is located in contemporary Århus. The novel is, in fact, a succinct political and social analysis of Denmark during the 1970s, supposedly written after the year 2000 by a writer who, to understand that period better, makes use of its favorite novel genres: the love story and the detective novel.

In the tradition of Balzac and Zola, M. allows characters from previous works to resurface in later books. Thus, in *Se dagens lys* (1980; see the light of day) many threads go back to the previous *Tugt og utugt i mellemtiden*. This new work too is a science-fiction story, set in a society completely guided by a computer, which at regular intervals moves the characters around from one family to the next, constantly providing new challenges and new encounters with people. Openness and freedom have been introduced, loneliness and monotony abolished. As the only restriction one is not allowed to see again one's fellow beings; one thing is prohibited: love as a repetition. M.'s artistic coup is his intertwinement of capitalist consumer society and dogmatic, restrictive socialism as two ways of expressing the same nightmare.

In *Lad tiden gå* (1986; let time pass) M. has widened the scope from his earlier focus on the question of identity to a more universal existentialist discussion. The concept of repetition resurfaces again but only increases the confusion and suffering that is humankind's lot. If one tampers with time, death is also being eliminated and thereby that which could make our lives meaningful. Besides death, M. tells us, only art is able to create meaning in absurdity.

The search for truth is the only thing that unites the 126 characters in M.'s next tragicomic novel *At fortælle menneskene* (1989; to tell human beings), in which he expands the microcosm of his native Århus into a timeless realm of total abstraction. The characters appear and disappear seemingly without any logical reason, intermarry, or change names and sex on the spur of the moment. However, in spite of the unpredictable behavior and fantastic metamorphoses of the characters, as well as the insane twists of plot, M. demonstrates that it is precisely language that creates coherence in chaos and helps us to overcome hopelessness and human wickedness.

M. is one of the most sophisticated, speculative writers of modern Danish literature but, at the same time, also one of the most imaginative. Besides novels and short stories M. has also written dramas and radio and television plays focusing on the same issues as in his prose, but it is as a novelist that he proves himself to be a writer of international rank.

Reading M. presents an intriguing challenge. His demands on the reader are enormous. Like no one else in contemporary Scandinavian literature, he is able to juggle with language, turn concepts upside down, bend words, and create puns. His oeuvre abounds with intellectual subtlety, and it is the main objective of his writing to implicate the reader and thus his fellow humans in an artistic

experience. But whereas the world was nothing but fiction, according to M.'s earlier works, now fiction not only establishes our identity but has become the basis for an existential process that might help us to answer some of the perpetual questions about art, faith, and eternity.

FURTHER WORKS: *Et livstykke og andre stykker* (1967); *Liget og lysten* (1968); *Tredje gang så ta'r vi ham . . .* (1969); *Maskeballet* (1970); *Jakkels vandring* (1974); *Hadets bånd* (1978); *Narrespillet om Magister Bonde og Eline Mortensdatter* (1978); *Slægten Laveran* (1988); *Mellem himmel og jord* (1990)

BIBLIOGRAPHY: Schmidt, K., *Mandlighedens positioner. Studie i S. Å. Ms forfatterskab* (1982)

SVEN HAKON ROSSEL

al-MĀGHŪT, Muhammad

Syrian poet, dramatist, and journalist, b. 1934, Syria

Well known in the fields of Arabic poetry, drama, and journalism, the Syrian-born M. lived in self-imposed exile for many years in Lebanon, where he was an early and active proponent of modernism (q.v.) in literary movements dating from the late 1950s. Self-educated, M. has familiarized himself with foreign literatures in translation, but looked for inspiration to such maverick figures in the Arabic poetic tradition as Al-Hutay'a (d. 678) and Abū Nuwās (d. 810). He now enjoys success as a screenwriter in collaboration with the popular Syrian comedian Durayd Lahhām (b. 1933), and resides for the most part in Damascus.

Huzn fī daw' al-qamar (1959; grief in the moonlight), M.'s first volume of poems, was an experiment in the form of prose-poetry. Most notably, the book launched a new satiric voice in Arabic poetry, which had been little disturbed by self-directed irony or much intimation that humor and absurdity are implicit in the business of making poems. Often jeopardized by their political beliefs, Arab poets had maintained a sober view of their artistic missions; M.'s roguish persona was the antithesis of the poet-prophet, guilty of a panoply of misdemeanors against virtually every social convention. Yet, however irreverent, M.'s poetry can by no means be considered ''decadent'' or trivial. Even in images of defeat and self-indulgence, deprecation of the self merges with criticism of society—not in the tone of facile indictment, but with a naked cry from the heart.

M.'s first volume of poems had contained curiously powerful elegies for his adopted country,

Lebanon; the second, *Ghurfah bi-malāyīn judrān* (1964; a room with millions of walls), presented an image of the Arab world as a prison from which no one escapes: a room with millions of walls. The subject matter was the defeated Arab, homeless and downtrodden; the underlying concern was the Arab's perception of history. A society numbed with nostalgia for its past victories and heroes had produced a literature in which cynicism and despair were anathema and in which it was mandatory to graft an optimistic postscript onto each poem. In contrast, M.'s poetic purpose was clearly ignited by concerns of the immediate, physical, and known and loved world, not an envisaged better one of the future or, for that matter, of the past.

In his next volume of poems, *Al-farah laysa mihnatī* (1970; joy is not my profession), M. reached artistic maturity in both language and form. The poems are shorter and more tightly structured, no longer suffering from stretches of hastily developed ideas, and the curious images achieve maximum impact. The tragic leitmotiv continues to be the theme of the beloved country, depicted by turns as betrayer and betrayed, yet finally indifferent to its lesser denizens. These poems demonstrate yet more clearly that M.'s "country" is the Arab nation, which offers a precarious sense of identity. The betrayal experienced is that of Arab by Arab, the people by its governments, and ultimately, "man's inhumanity to man."

Though he is a prolific and popular playwright, only two of M.'s plays have been published, the most noteworthy being *Al-'Usfūr al-ahdab* (1967; the hunchbacked bird). In this surrealistic work, an odd assortment of characters is imprisoned for obscure misdeeds in an unknown cage in a nameless desert: an allegory for the capricious practices of political imprisonment imposed by suppressive regimes. M.'s unpublished plays show greater mastery of characterization and form, with fewer intrusive monologues.

His volumes of poetry are few, but it is as a poet that M. has made his most significant literary contribution. With the publication of his work in the late 1950s, the poet as antihero invaded the newly emerging modern Arabic poem. M.'s use of poetic language is also remarkable: it juxtaposes the modern idiom with literary Arabic in a startling manner, giving maximum effect to unusual images and intentionally mixed metaphors. In both poetry and drama, this electric imagery spotlights serious social themes, leavened generously with satire. The result is an oeuvre that is by turns realistic and surrealistic, preposterous and tragic—an exceedingly rare blend in Arabic literature.

FURTHER WORKS: *M. al-M. al-āthār al-kāmilah* (1973); *Al-Muharrij* (1973); *Sa'akhūnu watanī* (1987)

BIBLIOGRAPHY: Allen, R., ed., *Modern Arabic Literature* (1987), 187–92; Asfour, J. M., "Adonis and M. al-M.: Two Voices in a Burning Land," *JArabL*, 20 (1989), 20–30; Asfour, J. M., and A. Burch, "M. al-M. and the Surplus Man," *Edebiyat,* 1, 2 (1989), 23–40

JOHN M. ASFOUR

MAHON, Derek

Irish poet, b. 23 Nov. 1941, Belfast

M. spent his early years in Belfast, but left there to go to Dublin to attend Trinity College, from which he received a B.A. in 1965. Since graduation, M. has divided his time between England and Ireland, but in common with many modern Irish writers he has spent more of his adult life abroad than at home.

Irish poets have always been obsessed by all those objects and persons that are visibly there in front of them: parts of landscapes, modern buildings, lovers, and parents. However, even though all these are present as themes in M.'s poetry, they do not dominate his work as they do the work of others. Instead, one of M.'s great concerns, following in the footsteps of Samuel Beckett (q.v.), a fellow Protestant and Trinity alumnus, is absence. In his best-known poem, "A Disused Shed in Co. Wexford," which appears in *The Snow Party* (1975), he feels that it is the poet's responsibility to provide the dead, in both human and nonhuman forms, with a voice, because people who are no longer alive and objects that are no longer used are essences crying out to be given a voice for "their deliverance" from silent agony.

The silent Ireland that is so attractive to M. stands in stark contrast to the living Ireland in which he grew up, and which he is unable to come fully to terms with. He is clearly uncomfortable in Belfast, his hometown, and has written little about his childhood there, or his family, or the Troubles. Unlike his contemporaries Seamus Heaney (q.v.), James Simmons (b. 1933), and Michael Longley (b. 1939), M. refuses to lend his poetic gifts to the inflamed political situation in the North, and steers well clear of it. In the poem "Afterlives" (in *The Snow Party*) he admits that after five years of destruction he can "scarcely recognize the places I grew up in," and wonders if he "had lived it bomb by bomb" might he "have grown up at last and learnt what is meant by home." M. rebukes himself for abandoning

Belfast, though he is uncertain he would have found a sense of community had he remained there.

M.'s language is as eclectic as his themes, and over and over he has proven himself to be wonderfully inventive and dexterous. Like W. H. Auden and Louis MacNeice (qq.v.), who have exercised a strong influence on his work, he possesses a remarkable ability to introduce original contrasts, and to vary his syntax and diction, without ever appearing to be merely seeking to be clever.

FURTHER WORKS: *Night-Crossing* (1968); *Ecclesiastes* (1970); *Beyond Howth Head* (1970); *Lives* (1972); *The Man Who Built His City in Snow* (1972); *Light Music* (1977); *The Sea in Winter* (1979); *Poems: 1962–1978* (1979); *The Hunt by Night* (1982); *The Chimeras* (1982); *A Kensington Notebook* (1984); *High Time* (1985); *The School for Wives* (1986); *Selected Poems* (1991)

BIBLIOGRAPHY: Carpenter, A., "Double Vision in Anglo-Irish Literature," in Carpenter, A., ed., *Place, Personality, and the Irish Writer* (1977), 173–89; Donnelly, B., "From Nineveh to the Harbour Bar," *Ploughshares*, 6, 1 (1980), 131–37; Deane, S., *Celtic Revivals* (1985), 156–65; Deane, S., *A Short History of Irish Literature* (1986), 227–47

EAMONN WALL

MAIS, Roger

Jamaican novelist, short-story writer, dramatist, poet, and journalist, b. 11 Aug. 1905, Kingston; d. 20 June 1955, Kingston

M., a passionate advocate of cultural and political nationalism, is a central figure in the development of modern Caribbean literature. One of eight children, M. spent part of his childhood on a coffee plantation in the Blue Mountains to which his family moved in 1912. Here he was taught mainly at home by his mother. When he later returned to Kingston, M. attended Calabar High School for three years. He earned the terminal certificate, the Senior Cambridge, in 1922.

M. turned increasingly to writing after brief careers as civil servant, photographer, education officer, insurance salesman, overseer, and horticulturist, among others. As a journalist, he was an editor for *Jamaica Tit-Bits*, a short-lived Jamaican publication, and continued in this career with the *Daily Gleaner*, the ranking local newspaper. The turmoil of the 1930s, characterized by labor riots and strikes, led M. to reject eventually the politics and social values of his middle-class

background; radicalized by the events of 1938, he became unabashedly nationalist.

Much of M.'s writing was in the short-story genre, a choice that widened his audience. M. brought nationalist criteria to these stories—of which there are some one hundred—insisting on nationalist authenticity to the "real" Jamaica. This meant subject shifts to underprivileged characters, with realistic portrayal of their social environment. The majority of these stories were published in the popular *Public Opinion,* the organ of the People's National Party (PNP), one of the two Jamaican political parties. Others appeared in *Focus* (Jamaica) and *Bim* (Barbados), and some were broadcast on the B.B.C.'s *Caribbean Voices* program. In 1942 M. personally financed the publication of two collections of stories, *Face and Other Stories* and *And Most of All Man.*

M.'s poems also hold a significant place in Caribbean literature. Crafted and eloquent, poems such as "All Men Come to the Hills" (1940) and "Men of Ideas" (1948) are anthologized with frequency.

As a dramatist, M. created over thirty stage and radio plays. The plays were written during a period of furious creativity alongside poetry, including *Masks and Paper Hats* (perf. 1943), *Hurricane* (perf. 1943), and *Atalanta in Calydon* (perf. 1950). Only two of M.'s plays were published, *The Potter's Field* (1950) and *The First Sacrifice* (1956). By 1951 M. had won ten first prizes in West Indian literary competitions.

M. gained notoriety in 1944 when he published the anticolonial essay "Now We Know" in *Public Opinion.* He particularly blamed Winston Churchill for "hypocrisy and deception" toward the colonies. M. was accused of sedition, and jailed by the colonial court for six months. His political act of resistance and defiance earned him the stature of hero among the people.

It is his achievement as a novelist, however, that marks his literary eminence. His first novel, *The Hills Were Joyful Together* (1953), startled readers with its daring content and form, serving to expose the injustices in his society, particularly as experienced by the poor. As a work of social realism (q.v.), the novel was seen as brutally honest in its representations. Stylistically, it was a tour de force, for it had successfully fused the mode of social realism with an experimental one— a new format suitable to represent the different cultural textuality of the Caribbean "yard" culture. M. showed himself ahead of his time in his second novel, *Brother Man* (1954), in which he intuited the cultural significance of Rastafarianism, the indigenous religion that was then strongly denigrated by the middle class. Allegorical, the novel reworked older biblical myth to symbolize the Rasta character, Brother Man, as a Christ figure. *Black Lightning* (1955), his last published novel, was M.'s least typical narrative. Philosophic, and poetically affective, it dramatized the dilemma of the artist in society, one beset by his own hubris and duality.

M., partly through frustration with his native Jamaica, which he found filled with "philistines"—"Why I Love and Leave Jamaica" (1952)—journeyed to England in August 1952 to continue writing and painting. Later, while residing in France, M. began a novel (In the Sight of This Sun) that was never completed. M. became ill with cancer and returned to Jamaica in 1954. Until his death in 1955, M. mainly painted. His unpublished works in typescript, at the Mais Special Collection of the University of the West Indies, include the plays *Atalanta at Calydon, Ordinary People* (perf. 1943), *George William Gordon* (perf. 1949), *Apollo in Delos* (perf. 1950), and *Samson* (perf. 1950), and the critical and theoretical manuscript *Form and Substance in Fiction* (wr. 1942–1943).

M. was a journalist, poet, fiction writer, dramatist, and painter who dedicated his life to art and to achieving nationalism in Jamaica, a colonized country. He saw the major task of writers as that of creating national culture and identity. His influence continues in the "new" literature that finds its sources in the indigenous peoples, culture, and language of the now postcolonial society. M. was awarded the Order of Jamaica posthumously in 1978.

FURTHER WORKS: *Another Ghost in Arcady* (1942); *The Seed in the Ground* (1943); *Blood on the Moon* (1950); *Storm Warning* (1950)

BIBLIOGRAPHY: Hearne, J., "R. M.—A Personal Memoir," R. M. Supplement, *Daily Gleaner* (Jamaica), 10 June 1966, 2; Carr, W. I., "R. M.—Design from a Legend," *CarQ*, 13 (1967), 3–28; Creary, J., "A Prophet Armed: The Novels of R. M.," in James, L., ed., *The Islands in Between* (1968), 50–63; Ramchand, K., "The Achievement of R. M.," *The West Indian Novel and Its Background* (1970), 179–88; Lacovia, R. M., "R. M.: An Approach to Suffering and Freedom," *BlackI*, 1 (1972), 7–11; Brathwaite, E., Introduction to *Brother Man* (1974), v–xxi; D'Costa, J., *R. M.* (1978); Morris, D., Introduction to *The Hills Were Joyful Together* (1981), iii–xxii; Hawthorne, E. J., "Power from Within: Christianity, Rastafarianism, and Obeah in the Novels of R. M.," *Journal of West Indian Literature*, 2, 2 (Oct. 1988), 23–32; Hawthorne, E. J., *The Writer in*

Transition: R. M. and the Decolonization of Caribbean Culture (1989)

EVELYN J. HAWTHORNE

al-MALĀ'IKA, Nāzik
Iraqi poet and critic, b. 23 Aug. 1922, Baghdad

M. comes from a cultured, literary family, and her mother, Um Nizār al-Malā'ika, was herself a poet. She studied first at the Higher Teachers' Training College in Baghdad, then at the University of Wisconsin, where she obtained an M.A. in literature in 1956. Both as poet and critic M. enjoys an eminent place in modern Arabic literature. Her courage, her genuine creative energy, and her pioneering spirit enabled her to launch, at the end of the 1940s, in conjunction with her compatriot Badr Shākir al-Sayyāb (q.v.), the free-verse movement, which is the most radical revolution ever in the form of the Arabic poem.

For over fifteen centuries formal Arabic poetry had sustained the monorhymed, two-hemistich form characterized by a fixed number of feet in each line and by symmetry and balance. Influenced by readings in foreign poetries, 20th-c. Arab poets launched a sustained effort to break the domination of this form and create their own. It was M. and al-Sayyāb who eventually succeeded in this, building on earlier contemporary experiments. The free-verse movement was launched with the publication of M.'s second collection, *Shazāyā wa ramād* (1949; shrapnel and ashes), which had eleven free-verse poems and a preface in which M. elucidated the advantages of this new form. The most heated debate in the history of Arab poetics ensued in the 1950s, in which M. took a leading role on the side of free-verse writing; at the same time, she produced some of the most original poems of the period, thus giving concrete proof of her argument. By the end of the 1950s, M.'s theories on poetry, which she published in consecutive articles, had developed greatly in sophistication and depth. The publication of her collected articles, *Qadāyā 'l-shi'r al-mu'āsir* (1962; issues in contemporary poetry), was a major event, producing yet again a heated argument against some of the principles she laid down to secure free verse against what she believed to be its inherent chaotic freedom. The appearance of this book showed how necessary it was to reexamine the bold free-verse venture.

M.'s studies abroad helped her formulate her critical method based on the concepts of the New Criticism (q.v.) which concentrates on the literary work itself rather than on its sources and effects, or on the poet's social and psychological background.

It was also in the early 1950s that M. advocated a revolutionary feminist stance. In two resounding lectures that shocked the audience of the time, "Al-mar'a baina 'l-tarafain, al-salbiyya wa 'l-akhlāq" (1953; woman between passivity and positive morality), and "Al-tajzi'iyya fi 'l-mujtama' al-'Arabī" (1954; fragmentation in Arab society), she expounded, with unrivaled skill and incisiveness, her argument concerning women's historical grievances in a patriarchal, oppressive society, and her faith in woman's capacity to excel in all avenues of artistic and intellectual life. Although her religious revivalism since the late 1960s has introduced a moralistic streak into her writings, her faith in women's capabilities has never weakened.

In its eloquence, terseness of language, and strength of structure, M.'s poetry stems from the heart of the Arab poetic tradition, but in all other respects she is highly innovative. Her poetry passed through three phases: Throughout the 1940s it was introverted and characterized by romantic sorrow and despair; in her second phase, lasting throughout the 1950s and most of the 1960s, she produced her best and greatly modernized poetry, which demonstrated a wide versatility of themes and a great originality in the manipulation of form, diction, and metaphor. At the end of the 1960s M. turned to a more conservative approach, writing on Islamic and nationalistic themes and resorting often to the two-hemistich form. Some of her poetry during this phase acquired an ardent tone of Islamic piety.

In her best poetry M. is versatile, inventive, and unique, producing poems of high quality that lay bare the general dilemma of life in the Arab world and, while preserving a personal approach to universal problems, often explore the predicament of the human condition in general. M.'s vocabulary is sensuous, fresh, and unadulterated by use, and in many of her poems, which include some of the religious poems she wrote in the 1970s, she employs a diction of ecstasy and ardor. There is a search for original metaphors and for rare epithets in her work, and she can string them together in ways that produce aesthetic rapture. In several poems she resorts to the use of verbal paradoxes, but in others, such as "Al-shakhs al-thānī" (1951; the second person) and "Al-zā'ir al-ladhī lam yaji'" (1952; the visitor who never came), both poems in *Qarārat al-mawja* (1958; the trough of the wave), she employs broad paradoxes of wit that inform the whole poem, modifying dramatically our preconceived concepts of things. She also uses complex symbols, some, as in her poem "Al-uf'uwān" (1948; the serpent), entertaining double interpretation, where the personal and the communal are merged.

M. has worked as a university lecturer and professor, spending many years at the University of Kuwait, from which she took an early retirement. A festschrift was published in her honor in Kuwait in 1985, edited by 'Abdallah al-Muhannā (dates n.a.), containing twenty articles on her work.

M. has kept a diary all her life. When and if it is published, it should illuminate many aspects of Iraqi and Arab cultural, social, and political experience during a great part of the 20th c., offered from the point of view of one of its most brilliant Arab women writers.

There is much to be learned from Ṁ.'s deep concern for and love of poetry, her delicate ear for the music of verse, her great confidence and courage, her steadfast adherence to her artistic and moral principles, and, above all, her technical precision, her adroit handling of language and metaphor, and her great thematic range.

FURTHER WORKS: *'Āshiqat al-layl* (1947); *Shi'r 'Alī Mahmūd Tāhā* (1965); *Shajarat al-qamar* (1968); *Ma'sāt al-hayāt wa ughniyat al-insān* (1970); *Al-majmū'a 'l-kāmila* (2 vols., 1971); *Al-tajzi'yya fī 'l-mujtama' al-'Arabī* (1974); *Yughayyiru alwānahu 'l-bahr* (1977); *Li 'l-salāt wa 'l-thawra* (1978)

BIBLIOGRAPHY: Rossi, P., "Impressions sur la poésie d'Iraq. Jawahiri, Mardan, N. al-M., Bayati," *Orient,* 12 (1959), 199–212; Stewart, D., "Contacts with Arab Writers," *Middle East Forum,* 37 (Jan. 1961), 19–21; Martinez, M. L., "N. al-M.," *Cuadernos de la Biblioteca Española de Tétuan,* (1964), Vol. 2, 75–82; Rejwan, N., "Rejecting Europe's Cultural Influence: Protest of an Iraqi Poetess," *Jewish Observer and Middle East Review,* 15, 22 (3 June 1966), 16–17; Wiet, G., *Introduction à la littérature arabe* (1966), 302–3; Moreh, S., "N. al-M. and al-shi'r al-hurr in Modern Arabic Literature," *AAS,* 4 (1968), 57–84; Vernet, J., *Literatura árabe* (1968), 212–45; Montavez, P. M., "Aspectos de la actual literatura femina árabe," *Almenara,* 1 (1971), 85–110; Altoma, S., "Postwar Iraqi Literature: Agonies of Rebirth," *BA,* 46 (1972), 211–13; Badawi, M. M., *A Critical Introduction to Modern Arabic Poetry* (1975), 143–44, 225–26, 228–30; Moreh, S., *Modern Arabic Poetry 1800–1970: The Development of Its Forms and Themes under the Influence of Western Literature* (1976), 213–15 and passim; Fernea, E. W., and B. Q. Bezirgan, eds., *Middle Eastern Muslim Women Speak* (1977), 331–49; Jayyusi, S. K., *Trends and Movements in Modern Arabic Poetry* (1977), Vol. 1, 557–60, 672–73; Montavez, P. M., *Literatura iraqui contemporanea,* 2nd ed. (1977), 65–68, 155–56, 373–85; Berque, J., *Cultural Expression in Arab So-*

ciety Today (1978), passim; Abdul-Hai, M., *Tradition and English and American Influence in Arabic Romantic Poetry* (1982), 27–29, 110–12, 119; Ayyad, S., and N. Witherspoon, *Reflections and Deflections: A Study of the Contemporary Arab Mind through Its Literary Creations* (1986), 135–37

SALMA KHADRA JAYYUSI

MARÍN CAÑAS, José

Costa Rican novelist and short-story writer, b. 1904; d. 14 Dec. 1980, San José

M. C., one of Costa Rica's most famous novelists, has also made contributions as a short-story writer, dramatist, and essayist. Due to the financial ruin of his family, he did not complete university studies and had to support himself as a baker, stevedore, merchant, violist, movie distributor, and radio broadcaster. Except for three years spent in Spain when he was a teenager, he resided in San José all of his life and made a living as a journalist after founding the newspaper *La Hora* (1933). One of his most important novels was serialized in this paper: *El infierno verde* (1935; green hell). Throughout his life, he wrote hundreds of articles and chronicles. One cause of bitterness was the loss of his job as a professor of journalism at the University of Costa Rica for lack of an advanced degree. However, he received several distinctions during his life, including the Magón National Award for Literature (1967) and the Pío Viquez Award for Journalism (1970). In addition, M. C. was a member of the Costa Rica Academy of Language and served as president of the Hispanic Culture Institute.

M. C. uses the elements of the chronicle to create short stories and novels and is the first Costa Rican author to reconstruct a historical event of his country: *Coto, la guerra del 21 con Panamá* (1934; Coto, the war of 21 with Panama), a collection of essays. With this work he also breaks from the folkloric and picturesque trend of his national literature.

In *Los bigardos del ron* (1929; the marginal society of rum) M. C. pictures the life of the lowest stratum of society, and does so with humanity, lyricism, and poetic feeling. The author shares the suffering of his characters and anticipates hope and beauty in spite of the darkness of their lives. He denounces the system with sympathy and humor, at times reaching the frontiers of the absurd. With this work, M. C. initiates the picaresque genre in Costa Rica.

In *Pedro Arnáez* (1942; Pedro Arnáez), his masterpiece, M. C. shows clear and graphic perspectives on the land and its suffering people

through multiple levels of narration. The expression is direct and subjective, following the story of a man in search of himself. Pedro Arnáez is an exceptional character: idealistic, mysterious, humane, always confronting with strength adverse circumstances. M. C., in this novel, perceives chaos everywhere and makes obvious the inequities between the rural setting and the urban one in El Salvador. Humanity does not exist. Society is ruthless and meaningless. Life is uneasy, and the only redeeming factor is love. Revolution to liberate the masses cannot succeed.

M. C., as the most important author of his generation in Costa Rica, depicts with vigor and skill the uncertainty of fate in Central America. The masses do not know where to go and cannot avoid failure. They live and die without understanding the system, as shown especially in *Pedro Arnáez* and *El infierno verde,* the author's favorite works. In denouncing social, political, and economic evils and dilemmas, however, M. C. does not chastise anyone in particular, in spite of the severity of his exposition, and his final message is that we must not live in an isolated exercise but in function of the well-being of others.

FURTHER WORKS: *Lágrimas de acero* (1929); *Como tú* (1929); *Tú, la imposible* (1931); *Pueblo macho; o, Ensayos sobre la guerra civil española* (1937); *Tierra de conejos* (1971); *Ensayos* (1972); *Realidad e imaginación* (1974); *Valses nobles y sentimentales* (1981)

BIBLIOGRAPHY: "M. C. y *Pedro Arnáez,*" *La República,* 19 Jan. 1969, 13; Erickson, M., "Los clásicos y la joven literatura costarricense," *La República,* 11 Apr. 1971, 9; Castegnaro, E., "M. C., periodista y escritor," *La Hora,* 10 Dec. 1971, 4; Tovar, E., "J. M. C.," *La Nación,* 26 Aug. 1973, 10; Duverrar, R., Introduction to *Los bigardos del ron* (1978), 7–24; Cerutti, F., *Recuerdo de J. M. C.* (1981); Marín, M., "M. C. y el relato histórico," *Revista Revenar,* 3, 6 (1983), 26–29

INÉS DÖLZ-BLACKBURN

MARSHALL, Paule
American novelist and short-story writer, b. 9 Apr. 1929, Brooklyn, N.Y.

Born to parents who had emigrated from Barbados, M. graduated from Brooklyn College in 1953. As a journalist for the publication *Our World,* she was sent to the West Indies and to Brazil, experiences she would exploit in her fiction. In the course of the 1960s, she received recognition in the form of prizes and fellowships from the Guggenheim Foundation, the Ford Foundation, the National Institute of Arts and Letters, the National Endowment for the Arts, and the Yaddo Corporation. In 1984 she received the Before Columbus Foundation American Book Award.

In spite of these institutional honors, M. endured a period of relative neglect from serious literary critics; more recently, however, M. has begun to receive the sort of recognition her impressive, if not notably large, body of work deserves. The neglect perhaps had something to do with the fact that M. did not fit easily into the most available categories. Although a black novelist, and fully capable of militant responses to what she perceived as racism, M. could not in her work easily be identified with any political line; moreover, her West Indian background, marking her as a member of a minority within a minority, presented difficulties to any critic who might be less interested in the individual talent or, for that matter, in the complexities of that mysterious phenomenon we call "race" than in sweeping generalizations about the significance of black literature. And, although a woman writing eloquently about women, M. did not in her work reflect a narrowly or mechanically ideological (and therefore predictable) feminism; this is not to deny, of course, that what might be called a humane feminism, at once critical and compassionate in its portrayal of relationships between the sexes, makes itself felt as an informing presence in her work.

At the center of each of M.'s first three novels is a remarkable female character. Selina, the protagonist of *Brown Girl, Brownstones* (1959), grows from childhood to young womanhood; Merle, in *The Chosen Place, the Timeless People* (1969), is a strongly defined woman in her forties; Avey Johnson, in *Praisesong for the Widow* (1983), is a widow in her sixties. In these three novels M. has thus given us portraits of three women at three major passages in their lives.

She has also placed these women in clearly defined fictional worlds, the interaction of individual and environment being one of her compelling concerns. In *Brown Girl, Brownstones* the environment extends from the protagonist's family outward to Brooklyn's Barbadian community as a whole. M.'s portrayal of that community, filtered through the consciousness of a protagonist who must define herself in part by rebelling against it, impresses the reader by its balance of the critical and the sympathetic; M. sees more than her character does. But the portrayal of life within the family is the novel's greatest strength; a casual reading might stress Selina's relation to her father, but it may well be that the mother-daughter relationship constitutes the novel's richest and most resonant achievement. M. has said that the con-

versations she overheard in her own mother's kitchen have been a major resource in the development of her narrative art.

The Chosen Place, the Timeless People, set on a fictional island that bears more than a fleeting resemblance to Barbados, puts a personal portrayal of the character Merle ("the most alive of my characters," says M.) against a panorama of island society that reflects not only the struggles of the present, but also the legacy of an imperialist past, a past that itself remains chillingly present; this novel also includes M.'s most ambitious attempt to deal with relationships involving characters of different races.

Praisesong for the Widow affirms openly what may be implicit in the earlier novels: that environment, for M., is as much spiritual as social and historical. Avey Johnson's discovery of her spiritual identity through rediscovering the link to her African heritage, the experience arising out of what was to have been a Caribbean pleasure cruise, provides the organizing theme of the novel. But the power of the book stems not from its abstract theme, but from its rhythms and textures; the novel is saturated with the rituals, traditions, folk and formal literatures, and art forms (especially dance, a major motif in M.'s work) of African, Caribbean, and African-American cultures.

In her first novel, M. explored the experience of the West Indian immigrant to the U.S., opening up a subject area that had received little previous exposure in American fiction. In her second novel, she brought a group of American characters to a fictional island in the Caribbean. Both novels placed M. clearly and firmly within the realistic tradition in fiction. In her third novel, although her capacity for social observation remained undimmed, M. ventured beyond realism into the realm of the mythic; she proved still capable of surprising us.

The placing of women's experience within varying and specific cultural contexts, especially contexts reflecting African origins, may be M.'s primary concern as an artist, but some of the most memorable characters in her fiction are men. Selina's father in *Brown Girl, Brownstones* and Avey's husband in *Praisesong for the Widow* are especially impressive achievements in the art of characterization. And it is worth noting that they differ dramatically from each other; M. doesn't work from a simplified model of the male. *Soul Clap Hands and Sing* (1961), a collection of four short novels, each featuring a male protagonist/viewpoint character, confirms this aspect of M.'s talent.

In the fall of 1991 M.'s long-awaited fourth novel appeared. Set in both New York and the West Indies, *Daughters* finds its moral focus in Ursa, daughter of a West Indian father and an American mother, while introducing a cast of characters comparable in range and complexity to that of *The Chosen Place, the Timeless People*. Through such characteristic concerns as the explorations of tensions—especially daughter-parent tensions—within the family, the articulation of the family within the larger social setting, the probing of relationships that refuse to fit neatly within preestablished categories, and the affirmation of the continuing power and presence of folk culture as a force and source in black life, American and West Indian, set against images of a past that is at once and inextricably historical and mythic, M. undertakes her most ambitious examination of the politics of male-female relationships and of the sexual dimensions of the political. Although the novel begins with an abortion, it is typical of M.'s art that, rather than degenerating into an occasion of ideological orthodoxy, the abortion here becomes a dynamic, complex, and by no means unambiguous organizing symbol of the novel as a whole.

M. has recently begun to receive the critical recognition denied her earlier in her career; most of the incisive commentary on her fiction dates from the 1980s. The recognition is deserved, because M. is unquestionably one of the gifted American writers of her generation. But its significance goes beyond that. Because M. has refused to be pigeonholed, the recognition she receives suggests that we may be ready to expand our notions of what constitutes African-American fiction or the feminist novel. M. is one of those writers to whom we turn in search of our humanity.

FURTHER WORK: *Reena, and Other Stories* (1983)

BIBLIOGRAPHY: Brown, L., "The Rhythm of Power in P. M.'s Fiction," *Novel*, 7 (1974), 159–67; Christian, B., *Black Women Novelists: The Development of a Tradition, 1892–1976* (1980), 80–137, 239–53; Schneider, D., "A Feminine Search for Selfhood: P. M.'s *Brown Girl, Brownstones*," in Bruck, P., and W. Karrer, eds., *The Afro-American Novel since 1960* (1982), 53–73; Collier, E., "The Closing of the Circle: Movement from Division to Wholeness in P. M.'s Fiction," in Evans, M., ed., *Black Women Writers (1950–1980): A Critical Evaluation* (1984), 295–315; McCluskey, J., "And Called Every Generation Blessed: Time, Setting, and Ritual in the Works of P. M.," in Evans, M., ed., *Black Women Writers (1950–1980): A Critical Evaluation* (1984), 316–34; Christian, B., *Black Feminist Criticism: Perspectives on Black Women Writers* (1985), 103–18, 149–58; Spillers, H. J., "*Chosen Place, Timeless People*: Some Figurations on the New World," in Pryse, M., and H. J. Spillers, eds., *Conjuring: Black Women, Fiction, and Literary Tradition* (1985), 151–75; Willis, S., *Specifying: Black Women Writing the American Experience* (1987), 53–82; Busia, A., "What Is Your Nation? Reconstructing Africa and Her Diaspora through P. M.'s *Praisesong for the Widow*," in Wall, C. A., ed., *Changing Our Own Words* (1989), 196–211; Russell, S., *Render Me My Song: Afro-American Woman Writers from Slavery to the Present* (1990), 144–50; Kubitschek, M. D., *Claiming the Heritage: African-American Women Novelists and History* (1991), 69–89

W. P. KENNEY

MAS'ADĪ, Mahmūd

Tunisian dramatist, novelist, essayist, and politician, b. 28 Jan. 1911, Tazerka

Born in the village of Tazerka, where he attended the Koranic school, the young M. then left for Tunis to attend high school, first at a national institution, Al-Sadiqiya, and later at a French *lycée*. In Paris, at the Sorbonne, M. studied Arabic language and literature. When he returned to Tunisia in 1947, upon successful completion of his studies, he became a regular and noted contributor to *Al-Mabāhith*, a literary journal that actively espoused the nationalist agenda against the colonial order. Shortly after Tunisia's independence, M. became a minister of education, a position he held for ten years (1958–1968). He is generally credited with democratizing and secularizing the educational system in Tunisia.

M. was among the first Tunisian writers to have enjoyed the benefits of a bilingual education. Along with his profound knowledge and refined appreciation of classical Arabic literature, his thorough assimilation of French language, literature, and philosophy, especially existentialism (q.v.), have further sharpened his speculative and philosophical bent. Since his early writings, in particular in the fields of language and aesthetics, M. has consistently gone against the grain. While his contemporaries sought to establish a national literary tradition by drawing on local and oral literatures, and to simplify Arabic grammar and syntax in the name of modernism (q.v.) and identity, M.'s idea of *asālā* or authenticity, contrastively began with an advocacy for a return to the linguistic rigor, purity, and elegance of classical Arabic, and for a revamping and updating of archaic knowledge as well as rhetorical and aesthetic forms, to express a modern consciousness.

M.'s popular fame as Tunisia's premier Arabic writer rests mainly on the critical success of his play *Al-Sudd* (wr. 1942, pub. 1955; the dam). His narrative *Haddatha Abū Hurayra . . . qāla* (wr.

409

1939, pub. 1973; thus spake Abu Hurayra . . . he said) and his essay collection *Mawlid al-nisyān, wa-ta'ammulāt ukhrā* (wr. 1941, pub. 1974; the birth of oblivion, and other essays)—all Nietzschean titles—have received less critical attention mainly because of the hermetic and esoteric nature of their subject matter and their archaic and arcane language. Although it expounds a tragic vision of the world, his oeuvre stands as a testimony to human greatness in the face of adversity and other vicissitudes.

Al-Sudd is an existential drama revolving around the eternal poles of essence and existence. Ghaylān, who symbolizes rationality and intellect, is determined to build a dam in defiance of Sahabbā', the goddess of aridity, and against the council of his own wife Maymūnah (a symbol of love and intuition). Upon completion of this project, and as predicted, disaster befalls earth, and the couple is forever separated. Ghaylān ascends heavenward with Mayārā, the Egeria who helped him erect the dam, while Maymūnah is seen descending into earth. They leave behind an intelligent mule tied to a rock, as a symbol of permanence and rebirth. However, for M. a plot is mainly a pretext to explore the meaning of life and the secret of being.

This philosophical speculation is further pursued in *Mawlid al-nisyān, wa-ta'ammulāt ukhrā*. In these essays, very much in the vein of Jean-Paul Sartre's (q.v.) brand of existentialism, M.'s man is posited as a free agent in a godless world responsible for his own actions and master of his own destiny. Whether they are called Ghaylān, Sindbad, or Abū Hurayra, all of M.'s characters are questers, idealists, and wanderers. They are relentlessly driven by a desire to seek the absolute. This is particularly true of Abū Hurayra, the protagonist of the narrative *Haddatha Abū Hurayra . . . qāla,* who bears the same name as Prophet Muhammad's close companion.

In many respects, Abū Hurayra is M.'s spokesman and alter ego, and certainly the best proponent of his existential metaphysics. In this stylistically uncompromising text, M. couches contemporary philosophical preoccupations in a blend of such archaic narrative forms as *hadīth*—or extemporaneous accounts and propositions, in the fashion of Prophet Muhammad's—and *khabar* or literary history which, unlike the sacred discourse of *hadīth,* refers to lay and profane knowledge. More than any other text, *Haddatha Abū Hurayra . . . qāla* exemplifies M.'s elaborate style and highly metaphorical language that often remains abstruse to the point of incomprehensibility.

Reading M. is a demanding and arduous undertaking: His oeuvre demands of his readers exorbitant concentration and comprehension; but if successfully carried through, this effort yields im-

mense insight and delight. M.'s oeuvre seems to revolve around a paradox—that a contemporary sensitivity can be couched in an archaic form. Within the universal and ahistorical framework of his oeuvre one does indeed find symbols that are open to social and political interpretations, some of which are indeed of acute relevance to current events in Tunisia and in the Arab world as a whole.

BIBLIOGRAPHY: Khatibi, A., *Le roman maghrébin* (1968), 37–41; Ghazi, F., *Le roman et la nouvelle en Tunisie* (1970), passim; Zmerli, S., *Figures tunisiennes: Les contemporains et les autres* (1972), passim; Fontaine, J., *Vingt ans de littérature tunisienne 1956–1975* (1977), passim; Ostle, R. C., ''M. al-M. and Tunisia's 'Lost Generation,' '' *JArabL,* 8 (1977), 153–66; Baccar, T., and S. Garmadi, eds., *Écrivains de Tunisie* (1980), 11–54; Belhaj Naser, A., *Quelques aspects du roman tunisien* (1981), passim; Fawsi, A., *Arabic Literature in North Africa: Critical Essays and Annotated Bibliography* (1982), passim; Allen, R., ed., *Modern Arabic Literature* (1987), 211–14

HÉDI ABDEL-JAOUAD

MAYRÖCKER, Friederike

Austrian poet, prose writer, and dramatist, b. 20 Dec. 1924, Vienna

M. grew up in Vienna and first attended a business school. From 1942 to 1945 she was drafted as a helper in the Luftwaffe. At the same time she trained to be an English teacher. She served in this capacity from 1946 until 1969, when she became a full-time author. She began writing at an early age, and her first poems appeared in print in 1946. In 1954 she met the poet Ernst Jandl (q.v.), and their friendship has provided many collaborations. She has been on several reading tours throughout Europe as well as the U.S. and Russia. She has won numerous prizes for her work, including the Theodor Körner Prize (1963), the Georg Trakl Prize for poetry (1977), and the Great Austrian State Prize (1982). She still resides in Vienna.

M. is perhaps the most consequential experimental writer living in Austria. At an early age, she was influenced by prewar avant-garde literary movements, especially surrealism (q.v.), and her early texts from about 1944 to 1965 were thus somewhat simple and derivative. They were collected in her first important work, *Tod durch musen* (1966; death through muses). After this initial period of exploration M. went on to develop her own personal style. In such works as *Minimonsters traumlexikon* (1968; minimonster's dream dictionary), *Fantom fan* (1971; title in English),

LARRY MCMURTRY

BHARATI MUKHERJEE

ʿABD AL-RAHMAN MUNĪF

MURAKAMI HURUKI

ADOLF MUSCHG

and *Je ein umwölkter gipfel* (1973; each a cloud-covered peak) she presented structural principles that she has applied quite consistently in all her remaining works. She begins with bits of personal remembrances, experiences, and feelings to which she adds other linguistic material collected from a variety of sources (and which she puts down through the years on pieces of paper). Her works consist of a grand collage of all of these elements, which she subjects to a series of permutations, repetitions, and other manipulations reminiscent of concrete poetry. The result is a text that does not easily fit into one of the standard genres, and which displays rich simultaneous interrelationships between dream and reality. As she further refined her style, recognizable characters began to appear, like in *Das licht in der landschaft* (1975; the light in the landscape) or *Fast ein frühling des markus m.* (1976; almost a spring of Markus M.), and one can discover some bits of narrative, but she has always steadfastly avoided the traditional devices of plot and character development.

In the late 1960s and 1970s, M. wrote a large number of radio plays. The most important works are the collection *Fünf mann menschen* (1971, with Ernst Jandl; five man humans), *Message comes* (1975; title in English), and *Schwarmgesang* (1978; swarm song). Like her other texts, these plays contain no recognizable plots or protagonists but instead explore the possibilities of acoustic and linguistic montage.

In the late 1970s and into the 1980s, a change became apparent in M.'s writing. Works like *Heiligenanstalt* (1978; asylum for saints), *Die abschiede* (1980; farewells), *Reise durch die nacht* (1984; journey through the night), and *Mein herz, mein zimmer, mein name* (1988; my heart, my room, my name) are less hermetic than the earlier works and have thus accounted for a new popularity and recognition among critics and readers. In addition, these works are permeated by a certain degree of sadness and lamentation. They discuss the themes of aging, deteriorating personal relationships, and identity crises centering on the profession of writing. Yet amidst the pessimism in these highly personal writings one can still discern a glimmer of hope.

M. is one of the most famous authors on the contemporary Austrian scene. While some of her works might be too opaque for many, she has been able in recent years to find a wide readership that shares with her the quest to maintain personal identity in an increasingly dehumanized mass society.

FURTHER WORKS: *Larifari* (1965); *Metaphorisch* (1965); *Texte* (1966); *Sägespäne für mein herzbluten* (1967); *Sinclair sofokles der babysaurier* (1971);

Arie auf tönernen füszen (1972); *Blaue erleuchtungen* (1972); *In langsamen blitzen* (1974); *Augen wie schaljapin bevor er starb* (1974); *Meine träume ein flügelkleid* (1974); *Schriftungen: oder gerüchte aus dem jenseits* (1975); *Rot ist unten* (1977); *Heisze hunde* (1977); *Lütt' koch* (1978); *Ausgewählte gedichte 1944–1978* (1979); *Tochter der bahn* (1979); *Friederike mayröcker: ein lesebuch* (1979); *Pegas das pferd* (1980); *Schwarze romanzen* (1981); *Treppen* (1981); *Bocca della verità* (1981); *Ich, der rabe und der mond* (1981); *Gute nacht, guten morgen: gedichte 1978–1981* (1982); *Im nervensaal* (1983); *Magische blätter* (1983); *Das anheben der arme bei feuersglut* (1984); *Rosengarten* (1985); *Das herzzerreißende der dinge* (1985); *Das jahr schnee* (1985); *Configurationen* (1985); *Winterglück: gedichte 1982–1986* (1986); *Der donner des stillhaltens* (1986); *Magische blätter II* (1987); *Blauer streusand* (1987); *Zittergaul* (1989); *Aus einem stein entsprungen; aus einem verwandtschaftshimmel* (1989); *Gesammelte prosa 1949–1975* (1989); *Magische blätter III* (1991)

BIBLIOGRAPHY: Acker, R., "Ernst Jandl and F. M.: A Study of Modulation and Crisis," *WLT*, 55, 4 (Autumn 1981), 597–602; Bjorklund, B., "Radical Transformation and Magical Synthesis: Interview with F. M.," *LitR*, 25, 2 (Winter 1982), 222–28; special M. issue, *TuK*, 84 (Oct. 1984); Schmidt, S., ed., *F. M.* (1984); Bjorklund, B., "The Modern Muse of F. M.'s Literary Production," in Daviau, D. G., ed., *Major Figures of Contemporary Austrian Literature* (1987), 313–36

ROBERT ACKER

MCMURTRY, Larry

American novelist, essayist, and screenwriter, b. 3 June 1936, Wichita Falls, Tex.

Long regarded as an interesting and promising regional writer, M. has won both a solid reputation as a serious novelist and a wide popular audience for his work. He grew up on a ranch outside Archer City, Texas, where he listened to his uncle's and grandfather's tales of the Old West. Except for a semester at Stanford, he was educated in Texas, and he wrote his first four books while working as a college English instructor there. In 1970 he bought a rare-book store in Washington, D.C., and relocated. Since buying a ranch in Texas, M. divides his time between the two, with occasional trips to California; besides being an extremely prolific novelist, he is a book scout and a screenwriter.

M.'s first three novels are set in Texas and are preoccupied with the passing away of the Old

West and its values; the protagonists, generally adolescents, struggle to find identities in an increasingly confusing and diminished world. Lonnie, the first-person narrator of *Horseman, Pass By* (1961), has to choose whether to model himself on his grandfather Homer, a cattle rancher and representative of pioneer virtue; his step-uncle Hud, a rake with few moral scruples, representative of the new Texas; or hired hand Jesse, a drifting cowboy. Torn between love of the land and the desire to escape, Lonnie also has to cope with emerging sexuality that has no outlet. In *Leaving Cheyenne* (1963), a story about a lifelong triangular love affair, told in first-person narratives by each of the protagonists, the two males escape for a while when they are young, but are drawn back to their home country by their attachment to the same woman—who marries someone else. Unlike the first two novels, *The Last Picture Show* (1966) is set in town, not the country, has an omniscient narrator, and is frequently satiric; again the adolescent protagonists must cope with loneliness, the desire to escape, often-frustrated sexuality, and mostly inadequate adults.

Critics interested in Southwestern fiction paid these books some attention, but even though all three were adapted as films—and two of the films were critical and popular successes—they did little to win M. wide recognition.

After writing directly about his ambivalence about Texas, present and past, in the collection of essays called *In a Narrow Grave* (1968), M. produced his "urban trilogy," three novels of contemporary Houston: *Moving On* (1970), *All My Friends Are Going To Be Strangers* (1972), and *Terms of Endearment* (1975). All three have young adult protagonists who seek fulfillment in marriage and love affairs without finding much. These novels are less tightly structured than M.'s early work, perhaps reflecting the characters' deracinated lives. Critics generally faulted the shapelessness while continuing to praise M.'s sense of place, his characterization, and his dialogue.

In 1975 M. announced his intention to abandon Texas as a setting for his fiction, and he did so in his next three novels: *Somebody's Darling* (1978), set in Hollywood, *Cadillac Jack* (1982), set in Washington, D.C., and *The Desert Rose* (1983), set in Las Vegas. These novels have more protagonists who are mature in years—if not in feelings—than the early work, and the characters have to grapple with partings and endings, of friendships, love affairs, and careers.

M.'s next novel, *Lonesome Dove* (1985), is a great American Western, the book that finally made M. famous, garnering universally favorable reviews, smashing popular success, and a Pulitzer Prize. Like M.'s early fiction, *Lonesome Dove*

contains tension between nostalgia and antinostalgia. The main characters are both touchingly vulnerable human beings and larger-than-life heroes—and heroines—in their ability to cope with adversities like snakes, hail storms, life in a sod hut, kidnaping by Indians, and the U.S. Cavalry. The main plot is classically Western, a cattle drive from Texas to Montana undertaken by two ex-Texas Rangers who have made their state too civilized to have any use for them. However, neither protagonist is sure of the ultimate point of the journey. There are no climactic confrontations between good and evil, no satisfactory resolutions for any of the lovers, and finally no sense that the heroes' exploits will even be remembered very long. A number of the most engaging characters die, to be buried in shallow graves with fragile wooden signs. The tension between romance and antiromance helps make *Lonesome Dove* M.'s most richly satisfying book to date. Its commercial success—enhanced by its adaptation as a television miniseries in 1989—has ensured all of M.'s subsequent work a place on the best-seller list.

Since *Lonesome Dove,* M. has followed a pattern of alternating novels of the new and old West. In the contemporary Texas novels, he chronicles the middle age of characters from his earlier fiction: the protagonists of *The Last Picture Show* in *Texasville* (1987), Danny Deck from *All My Friends* in *Some Can Whistle* (1989). While the first book is comic, the second finally tragic, both are loosely structured, both explore random, senseless violence, both are sympathetic to the characters' efforts to connect to one another, and both are rich in detail—often satiric—about contemporary Texas. The novels of the Old West, *Anything for Billy* (1988) and *Buffalo Girls* (1990), are much less romantic than *Lonesome Dove,* although each features a "legendary" Western character, Billy the Kid and Calamity Jane respectively. M.'s Billy is a sad kid with a character disorder, and he's not even a good shot. M.'s Calamity is an engaging survivor, but falling into alcoholism and making up stories about her past, including a nonexistent love affair with Wild Bill Hickock and an imaginary daughter. Perhaps the most interesting theme in both novels is M.'s speculation about how the West of legend was created. The narrator of *Anything for Billy* is a dime novelist from Philadelphia, intent on writing Billy's life, whose prior fiction is almost all fabrication. Calamity has also been approached by a dime novelist; more importantly, she goes to London with Buffalo Bill's show, which misrepresents the frontier even as that frontier is passing away. All four of these novels achieved respectful reviews and some popular success, though none generated as much enthusiasm as *Lonesome Dove.*

M. has achieved solid popularity among general readers and wide attention from reviewers. His reputation as a serious American—not just regional—novelist is growing. M.'s sense of place, of regional details, and of speech patterns and character types may still be most acutely accurate when he writes about Texas and the West. M.'s themes—how we can know the past and measure the present against it, how men and women and parents and children and friends can connect to one another, how people cope with change and loss in an indifferent and randomly violent world—are universal.

FURTHER WORKS: *Film Flam: Essays on Hollywood* (1987); *The Evening Star* (1992)

BIBLIOGRAPHY: Peavy, C. D., "A L. M. Bibliography," *WAL,* 3 (1968), 235–48; Landess, T., *L. M.* (1969); Crooks, A. F., "L. M.—A Writer in Transition," *WAL,* 7 (1972), 151–55; Schmidt, D., ed., *L. M.: Unredeemed Dreams* (1978; 2nd ed., 1981); Ahearn, K., "L. M.," in Erisman, F., and R. W. Etulain, eds., *Fifty Western Writers: A Bio-bibliographical Sourcebook* (1982), 280–90; Rafferty, T., "The Last Fiction Show," *The New Yorker* (15 June 1987), 91–94; Adams, R. M., "The Bard of Wichita Falls," *NYRB* (13 Aug. 1987), 39–41

SARAH ENGLISH

MECKEL, Christoph

German poet and novelist, b. 12 June 1935, Berlin

M. is one of the most prolific and versatile writers of the postwar generation, comparable to Günter Grass (q.v.). The son of the poet and theater critic Eberhard Meckel (1907–1969), M. went to school in Freiburg, Munich, and Paris with the aim of becoming a graphic artist. Afterward, he traveled widely, and lived in Berlin, Provence, Africa, southern Europe, and Mexico, and taught German literature at Oberlin College, Ohio University, and the University of Texas.

M. chronicled his education as a visual artist and as a traveler in an autobiographical essay, *Bericht zur Entstehung einer Weltkomödie* (1985; account of the evolution of a world comedy). In the late 1950s, M. published several surrealist poetry collections, and received eight literary prizes between 1958 and 1974. His poetry collection *Wildnisse* (1962; wildernesses) evokes apocalyptic visions influenced by Goya and Bosch. The trilogy of poems *Säure* (1979; acid), *Souterrain* (1984; basement), and *Anzahlung auf ein Glas Wasser* (forthcoming; down payment on a glass of water) describes cyclical troubles in a love relationship.

The main character of the short novel *Tullipan* (1965; tullipan) embodies the genesis of the writing process for M.: A fantastical personage enters the author's study and claims his attention. This motif is continued in the short novel *Die Gestalt am Ende des Grundstücks* (1975; *The Figure on the Boundary Line,* 1983), in which a vagrant appears at a Mexican villa, where the author is an invited guest, then gradually draws the author into a friendship until he adopts his way of life and disappears with him over the boundary line of the property, of what is knowable. The novel *Licht* (1978; light) analyzes a male-female love relationship that begins to dissolve and thematizes deception and self-deception and the importance of memory for overcoming disaster. One of M.'s strongest works is the novel *Suchbild* (1981; visual puzzle), which is an accounting of the writer-father's involvement with Nazi ideology. It represents one of the best examples of the spate of postwar German novels of generational conflict as they appeared in the mid- to late 1970s.

The fantasy novels *Der wahre Muftoni* (1982; the real Muftoni) and *Plunder* (1986; junk) are playful fairy tales about objects and actions that resist integration into a society ruled by materialism. The short biography *Sieben Blätter für Monsieur Bernstein* (1986; seven prints for Monsieur Bernstein) tells of the author's encounter and eventual friendship with a Holocaust survivor in southern France. M.'s drawings attempt to express with a childlike simplicity the horror of the Nazi concentration camps, while his writing tries to commemorate the victim's suffering.

M. celebrates the redemptive power of imagination and memory, and combines a high level of realistic description with fantastical writing that attempts to subvert the ordered universe of time and space.

FURTHER WORKS: *Tarnkappe* (1956); *Hotel für Schlafwandler* (1958); *Nebelhörner* (1959); *Moël* (1959); *Manifest der Toten* (1960); *Im Land der Umbramauten* (1961); *Die Noticen des Feuerwerkers Christopher Magalan* (1966); *Der glückliche Magier* (1967); *Der Wind, der dich weckt, der Wind im Garten* (1967); *Bei Lebzeiten singen* (1967); *Die Balladen des Thomas Balkan* (1969); *Eine Seite aus dem Paradiesbuch* (1969); *Werkauswahl* (1970); *Lieder aus dem Dreckloch* (1972); *Tunifers Erinnerungen* (1980)

BIBLIOGRAPHY: Middleton, C., "A New Visual and Poetic Fantasy," *TLS,* 28 Apr. 1961, 269; Brackert-Rausch, G., "C. M.," in Nonnenmann, K., ed., *Schriftsteller der Gegenwart* (1963), 221–27; Maier, W., "C. M.," *Leserzeitschrift,* 4 (1963), 12–15; Segebrecht, W., "C. M.s Erfindungen,"

Merkur, 20 (1966), 80–85; Segebrecht, W., "C. M. als Erzähler," *Der glückliche Magier* (1967), 7–25; Reinig, C., "C. M.," in Kunisch, H., ed., *Handbuch der deutschen Gegenwartsliteratur* (1970), 64–65

HELGA DRUXES

MEGGED, Aharon

Israeli novelist, short-story writer, and dramatist, b. 18 Aug. 1920, Wolozabek, Poland

M. emigrated to Palestine with his parents as a child in 1926, and, except for periods of service abroad, has always lived in Palestine (later Israel). He early established himself as a journalist and editor, started writing children's stories in the 1940s, and published his first collection of stories for adults, *Ruah yamim* (spirit of the times), in 1950. Since then, he has produced a regular succession of plays, stories, and novels, increasingly favoring this last genre.

From his first novel, *Hedva vaaniy* (1954; Hedva and me), M.'s work has been concerned with the social fabric of the emergent Israeli society, seeing how quickly pioneering idealism has turned sour. In this work, town is contrasted with country, in the guise of Tel Aviv vis-à-vis the kibbutz. The naive young people from the collective settlement are converted by their parents and parents-in-law into the grasping and vacuous materialists now populating the young State of Israel. The form adopted is the early picaresque novel, and the context is the social satire appropriate to the form. M. conscripts an allusive, literary language replete with echoes and phrases from the classical literature. Although the story is presented as a first-person narrative, as conveyed by the simple but harassed Shlomik, the tone adopted is that of the ironic observer.

M.'s social satire was to deepen into bitter parody, Kafkaesque surrealism (q.v.), and, as in his recent work, notably in *Foiglman* (1987; Foiglman), into desperate nostalgia. The novels are well made, typically reserving the principal elements in the denouement to the finale, as in a detective story. The narrator's stance continues to be that of marginal individual, of observer, specifically the observer of modern Israel and the current Jewish situation, reduced to functional paralysis. Sometimes the brilliance of the metaphor is sustained throughout the course of the novel, as in *Hahay al hamet* (1965; *The Living on the Dead,* 1970), where the narrator is sued for failure to comply with the terms of his contract and produce a biography. It is he who is living on the dead (as a biographer), but he is also unable to flourish in his vocation as a writer until his name has been cleared. He can not produce the work, as the biographee has disappointed him, in that his mythical life has proven a lie. But neither can he yet move on to something else, as this is all that he has to feed on, at the moment.

The preeminent theme in this prolific output is disappointed idealism. The fate of the narrator is linked to the national fate. In *Foiglman* the death of the eponymous central figure represents, for the narrator, the death of the people (or of Yiddish or of the diaspora); something more is happening than the specific event, in its implications and suggestion. Like the hero of *Hahay al hamet,* the narrator here, Professor Zvi Arbel, is not sure that he will be able to proceed with his historical research (here, on Petluria) and bring it to a conclusion. For all the humor and zest of the writing, M.'s book seems to comprise a dirge, an act of mourning for a nation.

M.'s writing continually recognizes the compulsiveness in the act of writing, long after the rational justification for the word seems to have departed. M.'s heroes are always acting against their better, or their rational judgment and rather in accordance with some inner force. The narrator in *Foiglman* continues to pursue the Yiddish poet, into and beyond the grave. The detached observer finds himself plunged into commitment.

FURTHER WORKS: *Yisrael haverim* (1956); *Miqreh haksil* (1959; *Fortunes of a Fool,* 1962); *Habrihah* (1962); *Hahayim haqzarim;* (1972; *The Short Life,* 1980): *Haatalef* (1975); *Heinz uvno veharuah haraah* (1976): *Asahel* (1978; *Asahel,* 1982); *Masa beav* (1980); *Hagamal hameofef vedabeshet hazahav* (1982)

BIBLIOGRAPHY: Yudkin, L. I., *Escape into Siege: A Survey of Israeli Literature Today* (1974), 173–74; Feinberg, A., "An Interview with A. M.," *MHL,* 8, 3–4 (Spring–Summer 1983), 46–52; Lotau, Y., "Sweet Revenge," *MHL,* 9, 3–4 (Spring–Summer 1984), 67–68

LEON I. YUDKIN

MEJÍA VALLEJO, Manuel

Colombian novelist, short-story writer, and poet, b. 23 Apr. 1923, Jericó, Antioquia

M. V. is currently the best-known Antioquian short-story writer and one of the major contemporary narrators in Colombia. He attended the Bolivariana University in Medellín, Colombia, studied sculpture and drawing at the Institute of Fine Arts of Medellín, and completed courses in journalism in Venezuela and Guatemala. He taught literature at the University of Antioquia and directed the university journal *Editorial Universitaria*. M. V. has also worked as a journalist in Venezuela and Central America, and contributed articles to the newspapers *El Tiempo* and *El Espectador* of Bogotá. To date he has published four volumes of short stories and five novels. M. V. was the first foreigner to be awarded the Eugenio Nadal Award in Barcelona, Spain, in 1963, for his novel *El día señalado* (1964; the appointed day), and the National Novel Award in 1973 for *Aire de tango* (1973; air of tango). He has been judge and guest in numerous national and international literary contests. At present he writes for national and foreign newspapers and journals, and lives in Medellín, Antioquia.

M. V. belongs to the group of novelists associated with the period known as La Violencia (1946–1964), who are characterized by their critical vision of national economic, social, and political life. Although many novels of La Violencia have been criticized for their documentary style, immediacy, and lack of creative essence, M. V.'s works have been praised for their ingenious use of literary devices such as his method of converging separate plot lines within a single work and his symbolic depictions of various psychological states. His earlier novels and short stories were noted for their tendency to idealize lyrically landscapes overloaded with sentimentalism, and he is considered a continuation of the Antioquian literary tradition embodied by Tomás Carrasquilla (q.v.). M. V.'s prose is always vigorous and pleasant. Like other writers of his era, M. V. is greatly interested in everyday life and social milieu. The novelist himself has said that he wrote his first novel, *La tierra éramos nosotros* (1945; the land used to be ours), on the basis of characters he had known on his parents' farm. In this work the first-person narrator-protagonist tells the story of his youth with innocence and honesty and writes in an immediate present of his life among impoverished peasants who inhabit the land of Antioquia and who must face life as victims of both the natural and the human order. With fresh and authentic realism the novel presents a complex psychological problem of Colombian people: being confused and puzzled during the steps of social transition, not knowing where to go or what to do, and ignorant of the history that has produced them.

M. V.'s masterpiece, *El día señalado*, is an example of the multiple facets of his artistry as a novelist. The literary symbolism, imagery, and complex structure of the novel invite readers to become involved in the development of the story in a Faulknerian fashion. This extensive novel depicts the trauma of the period of La Violencia as experienced in a remote small town in Colombia. During this era of tremendous political unrest in Colombia, approximately three hundred thousand Colombians died as victims of either progovernment or antigovernment terrorism. The novel is essentially patterned on the psychology of its characters, who are human types inescapably tied to a fatal destiny. M. V. captured vividly the authentic spirit and atmosphere of La Violencia as well as the exploitation and hypocrisy that the country endured during this period of social and political turmoil. Unlike other novels of this period, M. V. incorporated social, economic and political sources without describing in an overly graphic manner scenes of physical conflict.

One needs to have knowledge of the historical context of La Violencia in Colombia to understand much of *El día señalado*, in which the spirit of violence functions as the driving force behind the atmosphere and action of the novel. The fear, the memory of death, the authoritarianism, the despoilment of land and persons, the official complicity, and the traditional violence of a small cockfighting town are so rendered by M. V. as to become emblematic of the social, moral, psychological, political, and economic decomposition of the nation. *El día señalado* is the most outstanding of the more than forty novels of La Violencia written in Colombia in the 1950s and 1960s. The novel successfully unifies many elements in its treatment of the topic, while undermining an ideological interpretation of La Violencia by showing that the determining factor of this period is not, in fact, partisan politics, but banal acts of human irrationality.

In spite of having won significant literary awards at the national and international levels, M. V.'s works still remain little studied by foreign critics and scholars in comparison with Gabriel García Márquez (q.v.), the Colombian Nobel Prize winner. Through his tense and vivid style and effective treatment of rural life, M. V. has been able to call attention to the fact that some of the most important novels of the last few decades can be fully understood only if readers are sensitive to the social conditions amid which novelists have forged new intellectual realities.

FURTHER WORKS: *Tiempo de sequía* (1957); *Al pie de la ciudad* (1958); *Cielo cerrado* (1963); *Cuentos de zona tórrida* (1967); *Las noches de la vigilia* (1975); *Prácticas para el olvido* (1977); *Las muertes ajenas* (1979); *Tarde de verano* (1981); *El viento lo dijo* (1981)

BIBLIOGRAPHY: Carlos, A. J., "*El día señalado*," *Hispania,* 48 (1965), 947–48; Núñez Segura, J. A., *Literatura colombiana; sipnosis y comentarios de autores representativos* (1967), 572–73; Ávila

Rodríguez, B., *"El día señalado* de M. M. V.: cuentos-base y funcionamiento de dos ejes narrativos,"* Thesaurus,* 31, 2 (1976), 358–66; Sánchez López, L. M., *Diccionario de escritores colombianos* (1978), 295–96; Mena, L. I., "La función de los prólogos en *El día señalado* de M. M. V.," *Hispam,* 25–26 (1980), 137–46; Bedoya, L. I., *La novela de La Violencia en Colombia. El día señalado de M. M. V.* (1981); Williams, R. L., *M. M. V., Una década de la novela colombiana* (1981), 77–89; Williams, R. L., *The Colombian Novel, 1844–1987* (1991), 47–50, 140–46, 195–96, 209–11, 221–28, 246–47

VIRGINIA SHEN

MELO NETO, João Cabral de

Brazilian poet, b. 9 Jan. 1920, Recife, Pernambuco

Born into a traditional family, M. N. spent his childhood on a sugarcane plantation and studied in Catholic schools. In 1941 he published his first essay on poetry. He moved to Rio de Janeiro in 1942 and entered the foreign service. M. N. served in Europe and Latin America; his sojourns in Spain clearly influenced his work. In 1968 he was elected to the Brazilian Academy of Letters. M. N. has received numerous awards, including the prestigious Camões Prize (1990) for lifetime literary achievement in Portuguese.

Chronologically, M. N. coincides with Brazil's so-called "Generation of '45," who perceived excesses in modernist free verse and proposed neoparnassian solutions. M. N. shared with this group a formal rigor and discipline in the most general sense, but he opposed their cult of the sonnet, focus on psychic states, and bias for an elevated poetic lexicon. M. N.'s verse is based on things, objects, tangible reality, and a belief in the materiality of words rather than romantic inspiration. He advocates rationality in composition instead of a conventional lyricism of self-expression. M. N. is a leading exponent of new objectivity in postwar Latin American poetry but commonly connects his language of objects to real settings and social facts.

In *Pedra do sono* (1942; sleep stone) visual imagery and the plasticity of language are valued over any emotive content or message. This early poetry of dream states and spirits has evident elements of surrealism (q.v.). *O engenheiro* (1945; the engineer) abandons the initial taste for the surreal and offers the poem as a calculated function, as a fully constructed artifact. M. N. works systematically against the picturesque, sentimentalism, and irrationalism, seeking, above all, awareness of the objects that shape modern consciousness. Setting the standard for the collections to follow, the poetry is functionally architectonic and exhibits geometric rigor, with careful metrification and manipulations of semantics. The three sections of *A psicologia da composição* (1947; the psychology of composition) all constitute metapoetry, contemplations of verse making. The subtitle of the third poem, "Antiode"—"against so-called profound poetry"—reflects the poet's rejection of intuition and passion in favor of calculated composition in the lineage of Poe. The values of exactness and balance are maintained throughout.

M. N. next turns to regional settings for his severe verse. Avoiding superfluous sentimental cadences, he sharpens his perception of human situations and landscapes in a very nominal poetry. He is socially aware and depicts abject living conditions with sober precision while remaining faithful to literary principles. *O cão sem plumas* (1950; the plumeless hound) is a long poem, sinuous like the river it describes. Less figurative is *O rio* (1954; the river), where M. N. uses folk narrative; the full subtitle reads "story of the voyage that the Capibaribe River makes from its source to the city of Recife." Public discourse is also foregrounded in the dramatic verse of *Morte e vida Severina* (1955; death and life of Severina), M. N.'s best-known work. A refugee from drought walks toward the city and finds death at every turn, but he finally encounters hope in a birth in a riverside slum. *Morte e vida Severina* had great success as a musical with settings by poet-composer Chico Buarque (q.v.) and won international recognition at the university festival in Nancy, France (1966). The dramatic verse was published in *Duas águas* (1956; dual waters) alongside the long poem "Uma faca só lâmina" (a knife all blade), another meditation on writing, in which the knife is a symbol of poetic language.

References to Castille and Andalusia are frequent in M. N.'s titles of the 1960s. Harsh realities are often seen through a dry, laconic language. In *A educação pela pedra* (1966; education by stone), stone symbolism figures prominently in the questioning of self. There is a further distillation of subjectivity and affectivity in a search for a durable objective lucidity. *Museu de tudo* (1975; museum of all), *A escola das facas* (1980; the school of knives), and *Agrestes* (1985; ruralities) contain mostly shorter poems. Although this later work may appear to be more casual and personal (the first person, so rare earlier, is much more frequent), there is no concession to sentimental rhetoric or the vice of confessionalism.

Most critics agree that M. N. is a singular case in Brazilian literature. He is a Valéry-like figure who has had a broad impact. His antilyrical aesthetic of self-containment especially influenced concrete poetry, poets of song, regional poets, and all those who value rigor over emotivity. M. N. is the most important poet to emerge in Brazil after modernism (q.v.).

FURTHER WORKS: *Os três mal amados* (1943); *Paisagens com figuras* (1955); *Quaderna* (1960); *Serial* (1961); *Dois parlamentos* (1961); *Auto do frade* (1985); *Crime na Calle Relator* (1987)

BIBLIOGRAPHY: Nist, J. A., *The Modernist Movement in Brazil* (1967), 179–90; Dixon, P., "The Geography-Anatomy Metaphor in J. C. de M. N.'s *Morte e vida severina*," *Chasqui*, 11, 1 (Nov. 1981), 33–48; Reckert, S., "João Cabral: From Pedra to Pedra," *PStud*, 2 (1986), 166–84; Zenith, R., "J. C. de M. N.: An Engineer of Poetry," *LALR*, 15, 30 (July–Dec. 1987), 26–42; Peixoto, M., "J. C. de M. N.," in Stern, I., ed., *Dictionary of Brazilian Literature* (1988), 196–99

CHARLES A. PERRONE

MEMMI, Albert

Tunisian-French novelist, essayist, and poet (writing in French), b. 15 Dec. 1920, Tunis

M., a Tunisian Jew who resides in Paris, is Tunisia's foremost writer in French. Born in Tunis, M. attended first the Rabbinical School and then the Jewish Alliance School, and later the prestigious Lycée Carnot. His philosophy studies at the University of Algiers were interrupted by World War II. During the German occupation of Tunisia, M. was interned in a concentration camp, an experience accounted for in his first novel. After the war, he went to Paris to pursue his philosophy degree at the Sorbonne. Upon his return to Tunis in 1949, he taught philosophy and practiced psychology. He also wrote for local newspapers and journals until Tunisia's independence in 1956, when he left again for Paris, where he still teaches and resides. His work is a crisscross between fiction and philosophical speculations.

His early writings, tinged with a Sartrian brand of existential anguish, reflect, in the autobiographical mode, his childhood and adolescent experiences, a time marked by a cleavage between his traditional milieu and family-oriented upbringing, and an aggressive but seductive modernity embodied by the European and particularly the French presence in his country of birth. M. is a man of two worlds, East and West, and two cultures, Tunisian and French. This dual heritage is the stuff of his fiction and of his philosophical writings.

His first novel, *La statue de sel* (1953; *The Pillar of Salt*, 1955), describes both the precariousness of his early life in the Jewish quarter in Tunis, with its psychological and material insecurities—M.'s mother was illiterate, and his father was a saddler—and the transition, both traumatic and salutary, from his traditional milieu to the discovery of modern European civilization and the outside world. Narrated in the bildungsroman fashion, *La statue de sel* deals, above all, with the difficulty of being at once an oriental Jew, a Tunisian, and a colonized. This threefold alienation is emblematized in the protagonist's hybridized French-Western, Jewish, and Arabic name: Alexandre Mordechaï Benillouche. The hero's predicament is that of the North African intellectual who is caught in the bind between many contradictory worlds: orient/occident, colonizer/colonized, conformity/individuality. Dissatisfied with his plight, the narrator repudiates his past and leaves for Argentina—his El Dorado—to seek a new and better life.

In his second novel, *Agar* (1955; *Strangers*, 1960), M. continues his preoccupation with the conflict between cultures. However, he explores this thematic from the point of view of the couple. Upon completion of his medical degree, the narrator, a Tunisian like M., returns to Tunis with his French bride. His family's resentment of the intruding foreign woman and the latter's inability to adapt to her husband's native culture and traditions prove to be insurmountable and ultimately tear the couple apart. *Agar* may be read as a case study of mixed marriages because the encounter with the other is examined in all its social, psychological, and political implications as a marriage of two culturally and mentally antithetical worlds: East and West.

His third novel, *Le scorpion: ou, la confession imaginaire* (1969; *The Scorpion; or, The Imaginary Confession,* 1971), follows a long period devoted to theoretical and philosophical questions already adumbrated in his earlier fiction. In *Le scorpion* M. broadens the scope and thematic of his two first novels as he delves, with poetic detachment, into the collective unconscious of a Tunisian society caught in transition between its aspiration for modernity and its nostalgia for time-honored traditions and values. This stream-of-consciousness novel, narrated by at least three voices, explores such social and psychological themes as patriarchy and the inevitable Oedipus complex as well as artistic problematics such as the relationship of fiction to reality.

Although still an integral part of his itinerary of self-discovery, M.'s fourth novel, *Le Désert, ou la vie et les aventures de Jubair Ouali El-Mammi* (1977; the desert, or the life and adventures of

Jubair Ouali El-Mammi), is markedly different in theme and conception from his earlier novels, especially of *La statue de sel*. It is a novel of maturity, wisdom, and irony. The self-discovery theme that marks his earlier fiction is explored here in the collective mode. Set in the 15th c., *Le désert* is a minisaga of the El-Mammi's mythical dynasty—that which he refers to as the kingdom within—whose descendant is the narrator. M. focuses his search on his cultural heritage, a kind of autobiography in the plural, and taps techniques of Maghrebian traditional and oral storytelling techniques.

Like *Le désert*, M.'s latest novel, *Le pharaon* (1988; the pharaoh), is an archaeological investigation of the Tunisian psyche (the narrator is an archaeologist by profession). The story evolves along two parallel lines, personal and collective. The narrator is caught between his nationalist aspirations—Tunisia's independence—and his desire to maintain his ties with his newly acquired French culture, between his love for his wife and children—who stand for stability, tradition, the mother, and the mother country (Tunisia), on the one hand, and his infatuation with Carlotta, his seductive mistress (France) on the other hand. At the end, the narrator chooses to leave his native city for the cosmopolitan anonymity of Paris. In many respects, *Le pharaon* is a revisitation and an updating of the major themes and preoccupations of his earlier fiction.

M. puts to good use this autobiographical material in his sociological and philosophical essays to explore the problematics of colonialism and other forms of oppression such as racism, dominance, and dependency. With his first major philosophical essay, *Portrait du colonisé, précédé du Portrait du colonisateur* (1957; *The Colonizer and the Colonized*, 1965), M. emerged as one of the main theoreticians of colonialism and decolonization. Based on concrete situations and firsthand acquaintance with the colonial experience, M. expounds a sociology of oppression in which colonizer and colonized are not only perceived and treated as each other's foil but seem to share, in a dialectical fashion, a common predicament. M. proposed foresightedly that alienation, a byproduct of the colonial situation, would perdure well after independence.

Portrait du colonisé, précédé du Portrait du colonisateur was also the blueprint for a series of other psychological and sociological types where forms of oppression and dependency are scrutinized. In *Portrait d'un juif* (1962; *Portrait of a Jew*, 1962) and its sequel, *La libération du Juif* (1966; *The Liberation of the Jew*, 1966), as in his other philosophical writings, personal observations—that which M. calls *l'expérience vécue* or

life experience—and theoretical speculations are interrelated activities. His fourth major essay, *L'homme dominé* (1968; *Dominated Man*, 1968), is a synthesis of his earlier findings: We are presented here, under the same rubric of oppression and domination, with portraits as varied as that of the Jew, the servant, the black, and the woman. M. examines these types in a Hegelian fashion. In his essay *Juifs et Arabes* (1974; *Jews and Arabs*, 1975), M.—who considers himself a Jew Arab—delves into the complex psychology of Arab-Jewish relations both from the perspectives of a sociologist and a polemist. This paradigmatic approach to the question of dependence/independence and oppressed/oppressor is also the subject of his essay *La dépendance: Esquisse pour un portrait du dépendant* (1979; *Dependence*, 1984). His latest philosophical essay, *Le racisme: Description, définition, traitement* (1982; racism: description, definition, treatment), examines the roots of racism and the psychological motivations of the racist. Like Jean-Paul Sartre (q.v.) in *Anti-Semite and Jew*, M. expounds in this essay a theory of racism by focusing on the portrait of the perpetrator, the racist, rather than the victim.

In addition to being the author of essays and fiction, M. is the main contributor to two important anthologies: *Anthologie des écrivains maghrébins d'expression française* (1964; anthology of Maghrebian writers of French expression) and *Anthologie des écrivains français du Maghreb* (1969; anthology of French writers of the Maghreb). He is also the author of a book of poems, *Le mirliton du ciel* (1990; the reed pipe of the sky). M.'s poetry dwells mainly on the interior landscapes of his Tunisian youth.

M. is credited not only with putting Maghrebian literature in French on the world literary map but also for his role as a leading theoretician of Maghrebian letters and ethos. He was the leading Maghrebian novelist and thinker to use a critical discourse theory was then the sole apanage of Western thinkers—to regain intellectual initiative and assert North African identity.

BIBLIOGRAPHY: Sartre, J.-P., "Portrait du colonisé," *Les Temps Modernes*, 13, 137–38 (July–Aug. 1957), 289–92; Khatibi, A., *Le roman maghrébin* (1968), 71–77; Yetiv, I., *Le thème de l'aliénation dans le roman maghrébin d'expression française* (1972), 145–201; Déjeux, J., *Littérature maghrébine de langue française* (1973), 301–31; Yetiv, I., "Du scorpion au désert: A. M. Revisited," *StTCL*, 7, 1 (Fall 1982), 77–87; Monego, J. P., *Maghrebian Literature in French* (1984), 90–107; Roumani, J., *A. M.* (1987)

HÉDI ABDEL-JAOUAD

MÉSZÖLY, Miklós

(pseud. of Miklós Molnár) Hungarian short-story writer, novelist, essayist, dramatist, and poet, b. 19 Jan. 1921, Szekszárd

Educated in his native town and at Pázmány University in Budapest, M. finished his Ph.D. in law and started writing short stories. Sent to fight on the Russian front in World War II, he became a prisoner of war. After his return from the Soviet Union, he worked as an editor in Szekszárd and published a collection of short stories entitled *Vadvizek* (1948; marshy tracts). When communist dictatorship started in Hungary in 1948, M. became one of the most consistent critics of the political system. Because of his intransigence, he had serious difficulties earning a living. In 1951–1953 he worked for a puppet-show theater in Budapest. Since he was not allowed to publish anything but fairy tales intended for children, his stories written before the outbreak of the revolution of October 1956 were published only later, in the collection *Sötét jelek* (1957; ominous signs). They reflect memories of the war and draw a dark picture of totalitarianism. "A stiglic" (1954; the goldfinch) is about mass deportations, and *Magasiskola* (1967; the estate), a short novel which had to wait eleven years before it was published, presents power as a force inevitably alienated from human values.

After 1956 M. was allowed to publish, but was constantly attacked by the political authorities for his pessimism. His novel *Az atléta halála* (1966; the death of an athlete) was published first in French as *Mort d'un athlète* (1965) and then in Hungarian. The message of his works is certainly at odds with communist ideology: Life is viewed from the perspective of death. The title story of *Jelentés öt egérről* (1967; *Report on Five Mice*, 1983), written in 1958, is a grotesque parable about cruelty. In *Az atléta halála*, a book that was also translated into German in 1966 and into Danish in 1967, the wife of an athlete tries to write a biography of her husband, who died under mysterious circumstances; in *Saulus* (1968; Saulus) the death of Jesus makes the hero examine his values and lose his old identity; and in *Film* (1976; film) history appears as an endless process of deaths caused by political terror.

Many of M.'s short stories focus on the shifting interpretations of the history of central Europe and suggest that the very concept of history is illegitimate, since it depends on the knowledge of the future. In "Öregek, halottak" (1973; the old and the dead) the past becomes the object of constant distortion; in "Térkép Aliscáról" (1973; a map of Alisca) the legacy of the author's native town is interpreted as a long series of incidents that have

left no trace; in "Magyar novella" (1979; a Hungarian novella) Jamma, a boy who was shot at the age of five, becomes a legendary figure whose story is reinterpreted after each war; and in "Lóregény" (1982; "A Tale of Horses," 1986) a question is asked about the legitimacy of all teleological constructs, including the story about the Resurrection.

M.'s early works are marked by an interest in the fantastic and the parabolic, whereas his later phase—anticipated by the short story "Film, az Emkénél" (1964; a film, near the Emke café)—is characterized by an interrelationship between autobiography and fiction. The haunting memories of the war reappear in several stories, including "Lesiklás" (1976; downhill), and the first-person narration often goes together with an emphasis on the difficulties of storytelling and with a technique somewhat reminiscent of the French New Novel (q.v.), as, for instance, in the title story of the collection *Alakulások* (1975; transformations), or in "Levél a völgyből" (1985; a letter from the valley), a self-reflexive meditation centered around texts by Pierre Reverdy and Ludwig Wittgenstein.

In the 1970s and 1980s M.'s goal became to blur the distinction between object and subject, narrated and narrator. This is especially true of *Merre a csillag jár* (1985; where the star moves), a collection of stories and verse. *Megbocsátás* (1984; forgiveness), a short novel, is not the author's latest work, but it can be regarded as one of his finest achievements, a synthesis of the best qualities of his art. The style of this short novel is laconic, the narrator is detached, yet the modality of the storytelling is elegiac. In the absence of teleology, life appears as a mosaic of fragments that are seen or visualized with exceptional clarity.

In the 1950s M. was a solitary figure who ignored the aesthetics of Socialist Realism (q.v.). A character of great moral and artistic integrity, he kept the impulse of experiment and innovation alive in Hungarian fiction in the darkest period of Hungarian history. No other single writer has made a more consistent, sustained, and significant contribution to Hungarian prose over the last fifty years.

FURTHER WORKS: *Hétalvó puttonyocska* (1955); *Fekete gólya* (1960); *Ablakmosó* (1963); *Bunker* (1964); *A hiú Cserépkirálykisasszony* (1964); *Hajnalfa* (1964); *Az elvarázsolt tűzoltózenekar* (1965); *Pontos történetek útközben* (1970; rev. ed., 1989); *A tágasság iskolája* (1977); *Érintések* (1980); *Esti térkép* (1981); *Sutting ezredes tündöklése* (1987); *A pille magánya* (1989); *Volt egyszer egy Közép-Európa* (1989); *Wimbledoni jácint* (1990)

BIBLIOGRAPHY: Jastzebska, J., *Personnages tragiques et grotesques dans la littérature hongroise contemporaine* (1989), 75–96
MIHÁLY SZEGEDY-MASZÁK

MEXICAN LITERATURE

See Volume 3, page 271.

Fiction

During the 1960s, Mexico's principal representative of the "boom" in Latin American prose fiction was Carlos Fuentes (q.v.), whose universal themes and avant-garde techniques typified the outstanding writers of that period. Mexican fiction of the "postboom," that is, the fiction of the past two decades, is characterized not only by the continued publication of established writers, but also by the appearance of numerous younger writers who have profited from the examples set by their predecessors, but who have not necessarily followed in their footsteps. In general, perhaps as a result of the 2 October 1968 massacre of student protesters in Mexico City's Tlatelolco Square, there currently seems to be less emphasis on self-conscious narration and metafiction and more on the representation of social reality, on the recreation of history, and, as John Brushwood has indicated, on a return to telling a story. But according to Danny Anderson, the reality depicted by the "postboom" writers is far more complex than that of traditional realism, which perhaps explains in part another characteristic of the period, namely, the wide diversity of themes.

In recent years Fuentes has enhanced his reputation as Mexico's best novelist. In 1987 he was awarded the Cervantes Prize, the most prestigious literary award given in the Hispanic world. Since the publication of *Terra nostra* (1975; *Terra Nostra,* 1976), his monumental inquiry into Spanish history and culture, four more novels have appeared. *Una familia lejana* (1980; *Distant Relations,* 1982) explores the cultural ties linking the old and new worlds; the dramatic vehicle here is the mysterious relationship between two families, one French and one Mexican, with the same surname. *Gringo viejo* (1985; *The Old Gringo,* 1985) is a lyrical speculation about what happened to the American writer Ambrose Bierce (q.v.), who disappeared in Mexico during the Revolution. Fuentes's most ambitious text since *Terra Nostra* is *Christobal nonato* (1987; *Christopher Unborn,* 1988), an hallucinatory vision of Mexico in 1992, the quincentennial of Columbus's discovery of the New World. The protagonist and principal narrator is an unborn fetus whose omniscience affords the

reader a series of apocalyptic glimpses of a nation plagued by grinding poverty, exploding population, incredible pollution, and an invasion by gringos determined to prevent Mexico's oil fields from falling into communist hands. For his latest novel, *La campaña* (1990; the campaign), Fuentes has turned to early 19th-c. Argentina to chronicle the epic struggle of that nation for independence from Spain.

Among the other writers of the 1960s who have maintained a high profile into the 1990s are Sergio Galindo (b. 1926) and Fernando del Paso (b. 1935). An inspired creator of tense, dramatic situations, Galindo won an important literary prize for his psychological novel *Otilia Rauda* (1986; Otilia Rauda). Del Paso writes long, difficult texts praised by the critics but read only by sophisticated readers. Two examples of these are *Palinuro de México* (1977; Palinuro of Mexico), a digressive meditation on politics, philosophy, and language; and *Noticias del imperio* (1987; news of the empire), a historical novel set in the 1860s during the Hapsburg intervention in Mexico.

Gustavo Sainz and José Agustín (qq.v.), the two leading representatives of *la onda,* (the wave), a group of irreverent young writers of the 1960s, have emerged as major literary voices today. Language becomes a predominant factor in Sainz's *La princesa del Palacio de Hierro* (1974; *The Princess of the Iron Palace,* 1987), the monologue of a frivolous young woman detailing her escapades with a circle of hedonistic companions, whereas *Fantasmas aztecas: Un pre-texto* (1982; Aztec phantoms: a pre-text) is a brilliant piece of self-conscious fiction based on the excavation of the Aztec Templo Mayor (Main Temple), in the heart of Mexico City. Agustín's two most important novels during the past decade are *Ciudades desiertas* (1982; deserted cities) and *Cerca del fuego* (1986; near the fire). The former reflects the author's negative views of the U.S., where he has lectured at many universities. In *Cerca del fuego,* Augustín's most important work to date, the narrator, having recovered from a six-year bout with amnesia, confronts the chaotic ambience of Mexico City at the end of President José López Portillo's term of office (1976–1982).

Prominent practitioners of the nonfiction novel, Elena Poniatowska and Vicente Leñero (qq.v.) also began their careers in the 1960s. Leñero's ventures into this genre include *Los periodistas* (1978; the journalists), an engrossing chronicle of a dispute between *Excélsior* (Mexico's most prestigious newspaper) and then President Luis Echeverría, and *La gota de agua* (1983; the drop of water), the entertaining account of Leñero's predicament when the supply of water to his home is shut off.

Now embedded in the Mexican collective subconscious, the Tlatelolco massacre has, not surprisingly, produced what some critics have labeled "the novel of Tlatelolco," typified by works such as *El gran solitario de palacio* (1968; alone in the palace) by René Avilés Fabila (b. 1935), *Con él, conmigo, con nosotros tres* (1971; with him, with me, with us three) by María Luisa Mendoza (b. 1931), *La plaza* (1972; the square) by Luis Spota (q.v.), and *La invitación* (1972; the invitation) and *Crónica de la intervención* (1982; chronicle of the intervention) by Juan García Ponce (b. 1932).

As indicated previously, numerous young writers began their careers during the "postboom." Although they reveal a profound sensitivity to conditions in Mexico, their fields of reference encompass the entire globe. Their imaginary worlds are also fraught with subtle meanings designed to stimulate and challenge their readers. Names high on the list of these writers include Arturo Azuela, Ignacio Solares (qq.v.), Homero Aridjis (b. 1940), Hugo Hiriart (b. 1942), Francisco Prieto (b. 1942), Héctor Manjarrez (b. 1945), Luis Arturo Ramos (b. 1947), and Alberto Ruy Sánchez (b. 1951). Two works are especially worthy of note: Hiriart's *Cuadernos de Gofa* (1981; notebooks of Gofa), a densely structured philosophical novel that questions the validity of Western civilization by playfully creating a fictitious oriental nation (Gofa), and Aridjis's *1492: Vida y tiempos de Juan Cabezón de Castilla* (1985; *1492: The Life and Times of Juan Cabezón de Castile,* 1991), which portrays a fourth-generation *converso* (a Jew converted to Christianity) whose narration recreates the bizarre period of Spanish history that prefigured the discovery of America.

During the past decade, women have achieved increasing prominence among Mexican writers of fiction. Elena Garro (q.v.), who became known during the 1960s, has published several poetic novels about complex human relationships, as has María Luisa Puga (b. 1944). Others have written best-sellers, including *Arráncame la vida* (1985; put an end to my life) by Angeles Mastretta (b. 1949), *Como agua para chocolate* (1989; like water for chocolate) by Laura Esquivel (b. 1950), and *La insólita historia de la santa de Cabora* (1990; the unusual story of the Saint of Cabora) by Brianda Domecq (b. 1942).

Finally, to underscore the diversity of contemporary Mexican fiction, mention should be made of the new gay and proleterian subgenres, represented respectively by Luis Zapata (b. 1951) and Armando Ramírez (b. 1950). Influenced by the mass media and popular culture, these two writers use Mexico City as their setting and street vernacular as their medium to document the most shocking aspects of daily life.

Poetry

Winner of the 1990 Nobel Prize in literature, Octavio Paz (q.v.) continues to be Mexico's leading poet and most esteemed man of letters. Although in his recent works he repeats many of his previous themes, his imagery remains fresh and his style impeccable. As Steven Bell observes, Paz has assimilated the modern age of Western civilization only to reject its decadence and dehumanization. Idealist and mystic, he is concerned above all with language, which he uses to capture a kind of paradisiacal ecstasy outside the temporal realm. His principal themes include existential solitude, death, physical love, the passing of time, and the creative process. Paz is fascinated by Mexico's pre-Columbian past, but he has been influenced more by oriental philosophy and surrealism (q.v.). He is essentially a dialectic poet; his poems achieve dynamic movement through the use of binary oppositions, which he seeks to synthesize into a luminous moment of vision. His recent collections include *Pasado en claro* (1975; *A Draft of Shadows,* 1979), which represents a search for self-knowledge, *Vuelta* (1976; return), written upon his return to Mexico after years of absence, and *Arbol adentro* (1987; tree inside), a group of verses conceived since the publication of *Vuelta.*

Contrasting sharply with Paz are Efraín Huerta (1914–1982) and Jaime Sabines (q.v.). Known for his sardonic tone, colloquial language, and unflagging Marxism, Huerta has had considerable influence on the younger generation. Sabines also uses popular language, but he is especially preoccupied with human solitude and the dehumanizing aspects of urban life. His *Mal tiempo* (1972; bad weather) and *Nuevo recuento de poemas* (1983; new recount of poems) helped to win him the National Prize for Literature in 1983. Another major poet is Marco Antonio de Oca (b. 1932), explorer of the mysteries of human existence through brilliant surrealistic imagery.

Frank Dauster states that because of the Tlatelolco massacre, the 1985 earthquake, and the economic depression of the 1980s, Mexican poetry has become increasingly pessimistic. Dauster also sees two major strands of poets since Tlatelolco: those concerned with philosophical issues and those committed to a social agenda. A member of the first group, José Emilio Pacheco (q.v.) is a versatile, widely admired poet who unveils the poetic in everyday life. He also poeticizes his metaphysical concerns with time, death, and a decaying world in collections such as *Irás y no volverás* (1973; you will go and won't return) and *Los trabajos del mar* (1983; the works of the sea). His *Miro la tierra: Poemas (1983–1986)* (1986; I look at the earth: poems, 1983–1986) elicited praise for its anguished depiction of the earthquake.

Other poets of considerable merit include Rubén Bonifaz Nuño (b. 1923), known for his metaliterary and love verses, Rosario Castellanos (q.v.), who sought to define her role as a woman in a male-dominated society, Homero Aridjis, compared frequently to Paz because of his surrealistic and erotic imagery, and Elsa Cross (b. 1946), who has found inspiration in existential English and Italian poets.

The Essay

In the area of the essay Mexico has a rich tradition dating back to the 19th c., and since the Revolution the relative freedom of press has encouraged the dissemination of ideas. The older practitioners of the genre, of whom Paz is the most universally known, have often demonstrated an interest in broad subjects such as *lo mexicano* (Mexican essence) whereas, as seen below, the younger generation responds to more immediate circumstances. After the massacre of Tlatelolco, Paz published *Posdata* (1970; *The Other Mexico,* 1972), in which he sees the massacre in mythical terms, relating it to the Aztec ritual of human sacrifice. Paz has also written prolifically on literature and international politics; examples include *Tiempo nublado* (1983; cloudy times), a pessimistic view of the arms race, *Pequeña crónica de grandes días* (1990; short chronicle of great days), about the fall of communist governments in eastern Europe, and *Sor Juana Inés de la Cruz, o Las trampas de la fe* (1982; *Sor Juana Inés de la Cruz, or The Traps of Faith,* 1988), a study of Mexico's 17th-c. nun-poet.

Martin Stabb asserts that Tlatelolco has served as a unifying theme for recent Mexican essayists. Carlos Fuentes, whose essays are almost as widely read as those of Paz, reacted strongly to the massacre in his *Tiempo mexicano* (1972; Mexican time), proclaiming the bankruptcy of Mexico's political system. Thus he (along with others of the younger generation) is not interested in mythical explanations of Tlatelolco, but rather in the conditions that precipitated the tragic loss of life. In this same collection Fuentes attacks Mexico's infatuation with economic development, which he believes will make Mexico City into another Los Angeles, with the accompanying environmental problems. His most recent work, *Valiente mundo nuevo* (1990; valiant new world), speculates on the role of culture in the search for solutions to Latin America's numerous problems.

Soon after the massacre of Tlatelolco, Carlos Monsiváis (b. 1938), an accurate barometer of the times, published a book of essays entitled *Diás de*

guardar (1970; days to remember), in which he attacked the political establishment, defended the changing values of young intellectuals, and pronounced the Mexican Revolution dead. In a subsequent volume, *Amor perdido* (1978; lost love), however, he took Mexican youth to task for its emulation of American culture.

Another major essayist, Gabriel Zaid (b. 1934), is a kind of Mexican Ralph Nader, but humorous and intellectual. In his *Como leer en bicicleta* (1975; how to read while riding a bicycle) he pokes fun at both the political right and left, and in his next book, *El progreso improductivo* (1979; unproductive progress), he deplores, among other things, the uprooting of peasants who move to the overcrowded capital to get rich and purchase a weekend country home.

Additional voices that have contributed to the wealth of ideas in contemporary Mexico are Cosío Villegas (1898–1976), a historian fascinated with the interaction between the youth movement and the government, Jorge Ibargüengoitia (q.v.), whose wry humor, like Zaid's, masks a serious intent, and Juan García Ponce and Alberto Dallal (b. 1932), both of whom defend the ideals of the younger generation.

Drama

Although Mexican drama still has not achieved the level of prestige generally accorded prose fiction, since World War II the genre has made steady gains. During the 1960s, Emilio Carballido (q.v.) emerged as the leading dramatist, a rank he still holds today; he is the founder of the country's most important theater journal, *Tramoya*, and the author of more than one hundred plays. Unlike many of his colleagues, Carballido is not overtly political, but rather, as critic Diana Taylor states, considers culture as fundamental to the people's struggle for liberation. Thus in his opinion Mexican theater should become a cultural instrument for debate and evolutionary change. A master of symbolic expression, Carballido has experimented with a wide variety of avant-garde techniques. Although his plays often deal with Mexican issues, they exude both personal and universal resonances. Two of his recent successes are *Fotografías en la playa* (1980; photographs on the beach), in which an egocentric family reveals some embarrassing secrets, and *Tiempo de ladrones: La historia de Chucho El Roto* (1983; time of thieves: the story of Chucho El Roto), an epic about a 19th-c. Mexican Robin Hood.

After Carballido, Luisa Josefina Hernández (q.v.) and Vicente Leñero are generally considered to be Mexico's most important dramatists. The trajectory of Hernández's career follows that of Carballido, her early works representing realistic psychological portraits of stifling provincial life and her later creations evolving innovative, experimental forms appropriate for a broader range of subjects. Typical of her more recent work is *La calle de la gran ocasión* (1981; the street of the grand occasion), which presents seven fast-moving dialogues covering a broad range of social issues. Leñero has continued writing historical documentaries, as illustrated by his *Martirio de Morelos* (1983; Morelos's martyrdom), which questions official versions of history. His *Alicia, tal vez* (1985; Alice, perhaps), on the other hand, launches a scathing feminist attack on the exploitation of women both in the home and in the workplace.

In the late 1960s a group of young dramatists began to participate in theater workshops under the direction of Carballido, Hernández, and Leñero. Although they have not achieved success comparable to that of their mentors, several are still active today. These dramatists present a pessimistic view of Mexican life; their subjects range from political corruption—the single most important theme—to sadism, machismo, isolation, the generation gap, and escape from an unbearable reality to one that is even worse. Their language tends to be realistic, often crude, and their structures fragmented, designed more than likely to capture an unstable reality created by, or imposed on, their hapless protagonists. Important names of this group are Jesús González Dávila (b. 1941), Oscar Villegas (b. 1943), Willebaldo López (b. 1944), Oscar Liera (b. 1946), Tomás Espinosa (b. 1947), and Carlos Olmos (b. 1947).

Mexican literature during the last twenty years reveals an astonishing number and variety of practitioners of all genres. If this panorama appears chaotic, it is also promising because it demonstrates the artistic vitality of a nation devastated by recent disasters. Though uneven, the quality of the works discussed here is generally high. In the early 1990s, Mexico appears to be making substantial gains, both politically and economically, and the publishing industry is thriving. One might assume that the vibrant literature of the past two decades is a prelude to even better things to come.

BIBLIOGRAPHY: Puga, M. L., *Literatura y sociedad* (1980); Brushwood, J. S., *La novela mexicana (1967–1982)* (1984); Foster, D. W., *Estudios sobre teatro mexicano contemporáneo: Semiología de la competencia teatral* (1984); Robles, M., *La sombra fugitiva: Escritoras en la cultura nacional* (1985); Young, D. J., "Mexican Literary Reactions to Tlatelolco 1968," *Latin American Research Review*, 20, 2 (1985), 71–85; Duncan, J. A., *Voices, Visions, and a New Reality: Mexican Fiction since 1970* (1986); Ruffinelli, J., "Al margen de la ficción: Autobiografía y literatura mexicana," *Hispania*, 69, 3 (Sept. 1986), 512–20; Bell, S. M., "México," in Foster, D. W., ed., *Handbook of Latin American Studies* (1987), 381–401; Dauster, F. N., *The Double Strand: Five Contemporary Mexican Poets* (1987); Klahn, N., and J. Fernández, eds., *Lugar de encuentro: Ensayos críticos sobre poesía mexicana actual* (1987); McMurray, G. R., *Spanish American Writing since 1941: A Critical Survey* (1987), 68–75, 86–95, 159–62, 164–68, 216–20, 239–57; Stabb, M. S., "The New Essay of Mexico: Text and Context," *Hispania*, 70, 1 (Mar. 1987), 47–61; González, A., *Euphoria and Crisis: Essays on the Contemporary Mexican Novel* (1990); Anderson, D. J., "Cultural Conversation and Constructions of Reality: Mexican Narrative and Literary Theories after 1968," *Siglo* 8, 1–2 (1990–1991), 11–31; Burgess, R. D., *The New Dramatists of Mexico, 1967–1985* (1991); Taylor, D., *Theater of Crisis: Drama and Politics in Latin America* (1991), 1–63, 148–80

GEORGE R. MCMURRAY

MEYER, E. Y.

(pseud. of Peter Meyer) Swiss novelist, short-story writer, essayist, and dramatist (writing in German), b. 11 Oct. 1946, Liestal

M. grew up in Pratteln and Biel. He studied history and philosophy at the University of Bern, but then decided to become a secondary-school teacher in 1971. While teaching, he began to write. Since his first works were successful, he gave up teaching in 1974. He has won several literary prizes, including the Swiss Schiller Foundation Prize (1984). He now lives in Bern.

M.'s works are known for their exactitude of description, which he achieves through complicated syntactical structures, and for their philosophical musings on the meaning of life. His early works are marked by a predominance of the dark and morbid sides of existence, but he has gradually worked his way through to a more harmonious concept of the world.

All of the characters in his first work, *Ein reisender in sachen umsturz* (1972; a traveler in matters of subversion), a collection of short stories, feel apprehensive in unreal situations from which they can find no escape. In the novel *In trubschachen* (1973; in Trubschachen) the narrator's visit to a small idyllic Emmental village turns into a gruesome discovery of disease, decay, and trepidation, and ends with his rejection of Kant's famous dictum that fulfillment of duty is to be the governing factor in our lives. In the stories in *Eine entfernte ähnlichkeit* (1975; a distant resemblance) we are presented with the idea that we are never able to perceive reality as it is. In all three works there is a central problem—the fear of death and the fear of madness. M.'s protagonists wander through a world governed by anonymous threats and loss of direction. Everything seems to be disintegrating around them. M. also explores these and related philosophical issues in several essays, some of which have been published under the title *Die hälfte der erfahrung* (1980; one half of experience).

A partial solution to his dilemma of existence and a more positive outlook on life can be found in M.'s best work to date, his novel *Die rückfahrt* (1977; the return trip). The protagonist, Berger, no doubt an alter ego for M., is a teacher who decides to give up his profession for the sake of writing. He barely escapes death in a traffic accident, and during his recuperation he reflects on the reason for his existence and comes to the realization, through conversations with his doctor, an artist, and a monuments official, that it is only through the creative energy of art that we can hope to overcome the fear of death and the meaninglessness of life in the technological age. One must study the artistic creations of the past and the world of nature in order to live more fully in the present. A justification for life is not to be found in the mechanical fulfillment of duty in a well organized society but in a search for new interpretations of the world through art. M. thereby criticizes Swiss and all capitalist societies.

In his plays M. explores similar philosophical themes. *Sundaymorning* (1981; title in English) deals, in dialect, with the significance of art in the contemporary world and with our relationship to nature. *Das system* (1983; the system) questions our standard concepts about the perception of reality.

M.'s comparatively small oeuvre has earned him the respect of critics and a wide readership in the German-speaking countries. His precise language and his critique of accepted norms have made him one of the most important contemporary Swiss writers.

FURTHER WORK: *Plädoyer—für die erhaltung der vielfalt der natur beziehungsweise für deren verteidigung gegen die ihr drohende vernichtung durch die einfalt des menschen* (1982)

BIBLIOGRAPHY: Pender, M., "The Tenor of German-Swiss Writing in the Nineteen-Seventies: E. Y. M." *NGS,* 8, 1 (1980), 55–69; von Matt, B., ed., *E. Y. M.* (1983); Wietlisbach, C., *Kritische Betrachtungen zu E. Y. Ms "In Trubschachen" und "Die Rückfahrt"* (1987); Durrer, M., *Leben ohne Wirklichkeit—Schreiben gegen das Unter-*

gehen: 3 Studien zum erzählerischen Werk E. Y. Ms (1988)

ROBERT ACKER

MĪNA, Hannā

Syrian novelist and short-story writer, b. 1924, Lattakia

M. is Syria's most prominent novelist and one of the most acclaimed contemporary Arab authors of this genre. Born to a poor family in Lattakia, M. started working at the age of twelve after he got his elementary degree, the only degree he has. He worked in several jobs, one of which was as a workman with a sailor, an occupation that appeared repeatedly in his writings later, and which won him the title "the novelist of the sea." M. also worked as a journalist for twelve years, and was one of the founders of the Arab Writer's Union in 1951. M. was imprisoned nine times because of his political activities, and lived in exile for ten years in China and Hungary. Since 1969 he has been working as an adviser on publications and translations at the ministry of education in Damascus. In 1968 M. was awarded the State's Encouragement Prize in Syria, and in 1990 he received Sultan Oweiss' Literary Prize, a distinguished award in the Arab world. Several of his novels have been translated into Russian, Chinese, Hungarian, and French.

M.'s first three novels established him as a novelist of Socialist Realism (q.v.). This sense of commitment is to remain with him throughout his literary career. *Al-Masābīh al-zurq* (1954; blue lamps) examines the effects of World War I on Lattakia. The title refers to Lattakia's inhabitants who paint their window panes blue to divert the attacking planes. M. states that he was influenced by Najīb Mahfūz's (q.v.) *Zuqāq al-Midaqq* (1947; *Midaqq Alley,* 1966) while writing this novel. Like Mahfūz's novel, it takes a quarter in Lattakia to stand for the whole country. M.'s second novel, *Al-shirā' wa-al-'asifa* (1966; the sail and the storm), deals with confronting history in an indirect manner by facing it symbolically through nature. The sail represents the determination of human beings in confronting the storm, which is French colonialism. This novel brought M. immediate recognition in the Arab world, and it was often compared to Ernest Hemingway's (q.v.) *The Old Man and the Sea* (1952). In *Al-thalj ya'tī min al-nāfidha* (1969; the snow comes in through the window) M. tackles the life of a political activist and how he faces an unjust society. M. believes in a socialist revolution that would enable humanity to prosper in a homogeneous universe. His realistic style embodies the dialectical materialistic concept of history where individuals struggle against odd circumstances. Although his first novel suffered artistically for its inability to synthesize the individual with his community, the other novels show M.'s stylistic development in the treatment of the individual who becomes in fact Everybody in her or his struggle against social oppression and injustice.

Class conflict is a major theme in M.'s entire literary oeuvre. *Al-Shams fī yawm ghā'im* (1973; the sun on a cloudy day) depicts this conflict within a single family where the unnamed bourgeois intellectual ''youth'' sympathizes and suffers with the working class. He believes that his father, by dealing with the colonizer, contributes to the misery of the underprivileged class. However, the youth's calls for progressive change are doomed to failure because of his family's class position. This novel is an outcry for the liberation of the human soul from the shackles of outmoded concepts and traditions. Such liberation from within is a prerequisite step in the liberation of one's country.

Baqāyā suwar (1974; fragments of pictures) and *Al-Mustanqa'* (1977; the swamp) established M. as a master of the autobiographical novel. The novels present the suffering and displacement of M.'s family in the 1920s and 1930s respectively. Although told through a child's eyes, the novels blend successfully the personal with the general to show the effects of the world's economic crisis in Syria.

M.'s literary corpus gives a faithful picture of the historical period in Syria after World War I. While M. sets most of his novels in the past, he is in fact commenting on the present, showing that social struggle is necessary for a better and prosperous future at all times. Although M.'s style had suffered at the beginning of his career from its overemphasis on the political and ideological message, he was able in his later works to blend these messages artistically where the dialectics of fear and courage, of weakness and strength, of failure and achievement are worked out in a profound and natural manner to show the complexity of human nature. M.'s poetic language, his usage of symbol and myth, his mastery of the internal monologue and free association, his employment of time as a main factor for change are demonstrated with great skill and convey his vision of an optimistic future. Although M. understands quite correctly the unavoidable clash between freedom and necessity, his ultimate commitment is to humanity itself. Hence his message is universal, and his position as one of the pillars of modern Arabic literature seems to be beyond doubt.

FURTHER WORKS: *Nazim Hikmat wa-qadāyā adabiyyah wa-fikriyyah* (1971); *Man yadhkur tilka al-ayyām* (1974, with Najāh 'Attār); *Al-yātir* (1975); *Al-abnūsah al-baydā'* (1976); *Al-marsad* (1980); *Hikāyat Bahhār* (1981); *Al-duqul* (1982); *Al-marfa' al-ba'īd* (1983); *Al-rabī' wa-al-kharīf* (1984); *Ma'sāt Dimetrio* (1985); *Al-qitāf* (1986); *Hamāmah Zarqā fī al-suhub* (1988); *Nihāyat rajul shujā'* (1989); *Al-wallā'ah* (1990)

BIBLIOGRAPHY: Allen, R., *The Arabic Novel* (1982), 72–74; Allen, R., ed., *Modern Arabic Literature* (1987), 219–24

SABAH GHANDOUR

MO Yen

(or Mo Yan; pseud. of Kuan Mo-yeh) Chinese novelist, short-story writer, and essayist, b. Mar. 1956, Kao-mi County, Shantung Province

M. is one of China's most prolific and versatile contemporary writers, known primarily for his contributions to ''Hsün-ken wen-hsüeh'' (root-seeking literature), which flourished in the mid-1980s. M.'s early education was interrupted by the Cultural Revolution in 1965. He spent the next ten years working in the fields and later at a cotton plant. The experience was not a total waste, for M. acquired valuable first-hand knowledge about hardships in life and distinguished himself with some penetrating treatments of the cruel and degenerated conditions of humankind. At the age of twenty, M. enlisted in the People's Liberation Army. It was not until 1984 that he was admitted to the department of literature at the PLA Academy of Arts, and subsequently the graduate program at Peking Normal University. His teenage memories, his military experience, and his academic training all provided major ingredients for his art.

M.'s early writings followed a realist path commonly taken by almost all postrevolution fiction writers in China. ''Ch'un-yeh yü fei-fei'' (1981; spring drizzles), for example, deals with the monotonous life of a soldier in a realist light. M.'s artistic breakthrough did not come until after he was enrolled in the PLA Academy of Arts. With the appearance of his prize-winning ''T'ou-ming te hung-lo-po'' (1985; transparent carrots) M. entered a most prolific as well as versatile phase. His popularity was reconfirmed with the appearance of his first full-length novel, *Hung kao-liang chia-tsu* (1986; *Red Sorghum*, 1993). (Part of the novel was later made into an equally popular film, ''Hung kao-liang'' [1987; the red sorghum], by Chang I-mou, which won the Golden Bear Award at the West Berlin Film Festival in 1988.) The period between 1985 and 1989 saw M. in a burst of creativity, with the publication of ''Chin-fa ying-er'' (1985; the golden-haired infant), ''Pao-cha'' (1985; explosions), ''Mao-shih huei-t'sui'' (1987; collected anecdotes about cats), ''Hung-huang'' (1987; red locusts), *T'ien-t'ang suan-t'ai chih ko* (1988; a song of garlic in Paradise County), *Shih-san pu* (1989; the thirteenth step), ''Ni te hsing-wei shih wo-men kan-tao k'ung-chü'' (1989; your behavior horrifies us), and other works. Whereas he achieved almost instant fame in 1985 as one of the contemporary writers in search of national roots, his more experimental pieces (such as ''Huan-le'' [joy] and ''Hung-huang'') attracted rather negative criticisms. Although the change in readers' response was not unrelated to the gradual inward turn of his narrative, as M. probed socio-political pressures on his protagonists, but ideological campaigns in favor of positive treatment of reality since 1986 also had something to do with the adverse criticisms he received. He has nevertheless kept up with his writing, and his latest novel, *Shih-ts'ao chia-tsu* (the herbivorous family), is scheduled to be published soon.

Like other root-seeking writers, M. chooses for his milieu his native village, Kao-mi Tung-pei hsiang, Shantung, despite his disclaimer that the place is more fictional than real. The location is known for the unique behavior of its inhabitants. Among other things, the villagers are extremely robust and individualistic, presumably as a result of the adverse environment and the turbulent age they live in. The orphan child in ''T'ou-ming te hung-lo-po,'' Grandpa in *Hung kao-liang chia-tsu,* Kao Ma (tall horse) in *T'ian-t'ang suan-t'ai chih ko,* and the protagonist in ''Hung huang'' are but a few examples of his indomitable characters. (By contrast, the contemporary world is peopled by soft and greedy weaklings.) To M., writing should be an unreserved and unimpeded dissemination of human energy, and these rugged characters clearly serve as vehicles for such unrestrained expression. These characters derive their vitality from their intuitive, almost animalistic, mode of life and, in some cases, their unorthodox behavior, including their herbivorous diet (''Hung huang'').

Related to the concept of the individual is the family, be it extended or nuclear. M.'s works invariably consider how an individual fares in a familial context. Characteristically, his characters are found trapped in a clan that is on the road to decline, and some revitalization is in order (for example, in *Hung kao-liang chia-tsu,* ''Pao-cha,'' and ''Hung-huang''). To highlight the crisis of the family, especially in the modern context, M. often puts families in a rural setting, but increasingly under the threat of urban forces. The prize-winning ''Pai-kou ch'iu-ch'ien chia'' (1985; the white dog and the swing) deals with the return of an intellectual to his native village to find his childhood girlfriend married to a deaf-mute and leading the life of a common peasant. The reunion induces

much remorse in him over the gap that has developed between himself and his friend. To M., an individual acquires identity through his or her relations with the family just as much as through individual efforts. Thus, to know a person, it is necessary to play one character against another as well as one family against another. The idea of doubles is thus often fully exhausted. One character is, for instance, described as defiant while the other is depicted as docile *(T'ian-t'ang suan-t'ai chih ko).* Furthermore, one dead character's identity may be given to his neighbor after the latter is given plastic surgery (with the dead man's head being sewn on to his body) in a funeral parlor *(Shih-san pu).*

M.'s works are mainly about quests for identity in terms of relationships. These quests are conducted in the context of traditional kinship systems and against the backdrop of an increasingly bureaucratized and commercial society in contemporary China.

FURTHER VOLUME IN ENGLISH: *Explosions and Other Stories* (1991)

BIBLIOGRAPHY: Chou, Y. H., ''Romance of the Red Sorghum Family,'' *MCL,* 5 (1989), 1–20; Zhang, J., ''Red Sorghum,'' *Film Quarterly,* 42, 3 (Spring 1989), 41–43

YING-HSIUNG CHOU

MODIANO, Patrick

French novelist, dramatist, and screenwriter, b. 30 July 1945, Boulogne-Billancourt

Although M. was born after the end of World War II, many of his writings reflect his fascination with the humiliating German occupation of France. A winner of more literary prizes than almost any other French novelist of his generation, M. enjoys a wide audience in the French-speaking world. Many of his books have been translated into English and other languages. His father, an eastern European Jew, lived an underground life during World War II and survived miraculously during the Holocaust by dealing in the black market. M.'s mother, Luisa Colpeyn, was a Belgian actress who had moved to Paris during the occupation where she married his father. The couple had two children, Patrick and Rudy; the latter was M.'s closest childhood friend. His death at an early age haunted the author throughout his existence, and most of his major works are dedicated to his brother. After the liberation of France, M.'s father became a successful financier and businessman. The taciturnity of his father concerning his past and the separation of his parents when he was eighteen years old in 1963 were the basis for the obsessive themes of M.'s later works. During an itinerant, unstable youth, M. attended various schools, the most important of which was the Collège Saint-Joseph in Thônes (Haute-Savoie) during 1960–1962, after which he received the baccalaureate degree at the prestigious Lycée Henri IV in Paris. After a year of study at the University of Paris in 1965–1966, M. abandoned further education to become a creative writer. Two years later, when he was twenty-three, Gallimard published M.'s first novel, *La Place de l'Étoile* (1968; the Place de l'Étoile), a work that not only won him instant fame but also two literary prizes, the Prix Roger Nimier in 1968 and the Prix Félix Fénéon in 1969.

In *La Place de l'Étoile* M. reveals several recurrent traits of his unique art: a mélange of historical veracity (the setting is the German occupation of Paris of 1940–1945) and of fictional inventiveness; also transparent is stylistic lucidity that paradoxically expresses an atmosphere of vague mystery. The novel depicts both flagrant anti-Semitism and a fascination with the beauty of Judaic values and virtues. The protagonist, Raphael Schlemilovitch (the very name suggests in Yiddish a buffoon who never succeeds at anything), is tormented by his love/hate relationships with his Jewish heritage. M.'s second novel, *Ronde de nuit* (*Night Rounds*, 1971) appeared in 1969. Once again the setting is the sinister world of Paris under German control, an infernal place governed by the Gestapo and characterized by countless police raids, incorporating dramatic shifts from examples of French collaborators to fighters of the French Resistance movement. Perhaps M.'s best known novel is his third work, *Les boulevards de ceinture* (*Ring Roads*, 1974), published in 1972, a novel for which he was awarded the prestigious Grand Prix du Roman (1972) of the French Academy. The protagonist is obsessed with an old photograph of his missing father; he eventually locates him, a pitiful and despicable Jew who is being hunted by the Nazis because of his black-market activities.

M. shifts the time and setting of his fourth novel, *Villa Triste* (1975; *Villa Triste,* 1977), from the Paris of 1940–1945 to a fashionable spa on the French side of the Lake of Geneva during the early 1960s. The eighteen-year-old narrator seeks incessantly to resuscitate the emotions of a lost past and to make relive a disappeared villa in which he had spent many joyous days of childhood. In 1977, M. published his fifth novel, *Livret de famille* (family book or album). Here one of his most frequently used themes—that of memories—becomes for this author a useful device that allows him to blend pure autobiography with pure fiction. One year later, in 1978, M. published

another novel, *Rue des boutiques obscures (Missing Person,* 1980). For this work M. finally won France's most coveted literary prize, the Prix Goncourt (1978), a fact that guaranteed that this work would become a best-seller almost overnight. M. poses this question: What sort of things does a dead human being leave behind after death? An old photograph, a birth certificate, a few letters and documents, several memories. But all of these begin to fade away with the passage of time. Life is like an echo that eventually becomes total silence. The central character, an employee with a private detective agency, begins to recognize his own personal traits in those of the missing person he has been trying to find—we suspect that the protagonist is the same man for whom he has been searching. The tone of uncertainty and mystery constitutes one of the unique characteristics of M.'s prose fiction.

A marked resemblance unites his three novels *Une jeunesse* (1981; youth), *Memory Lane* (1981; title in English), and *De si braves garçons* (1982; such good fellows): these three works deal with the memories of events that all occurred some twenty years earlier. In the latter work, M. emphasizes the disparity between what each of twelve boys dreamed of becoming and the actual reality of their destinies twenty years later.

Noteworthy is M.'s collaboration with the internationally renowned director Louis Malle in one of the most successful French films of the last two decades: *Lacombe, Lucien* (1974; *Lacombe, Lucien,* 1975).

Among the contemporary writers of France, M. stands virtually apart from the dominant post-World War II literary trends. And unlike many of the novels published by the other trailblazing innovators, M.'s works are highly readable. He relates an interesting story and does so in a style easy to understand. In many respects, he continues the tradition of classical French literature. His works seem simple, orderly, and are devoid of unnecessary stylistic ornateness; they are generally brief, compact, and sensibly structured. The ambience painted in them is contemporary: bars, cafés, modern cities, travel and tourism, resorts that are very much in vogue. M.'s works reflect the rapid pace and fragmentation of modern human existence. His characters conduct their lives in a hallucinatory atmosphere of uncertainty, mystery, amnesia, alienation, rootlessness. The combination of these ingredients lends to M.'s texts an aura of magical poetry.

FURTHER WORKS: *Interrogatoire* (1976, with Emmanuel Berl); *Quartier perdu* (1984); *Une aventure de Choura* (1986); *Dimanches d'août* (1986);

Une fiancée pour Choura (1987); *Vestiaire de l'enfance* (1988); *Fleurs de ruine* (1991)

BIBLIOGRAPHY: Chassequet-Smirgel, J., "La Place de l'Étoile de M.," in *Pour une psychanalyse de l'art et de la créativité* (1971), 217–55; Rambures, J.-L. de, "Comment travaillent les écrivains. P. M.: Apprendre à mentir," *Le Monde,* 24 May 1974, 24; Magnan, J.-M., "Un apatride nommé M.," *Sud,* 19 (3rd trimester 1976), 120–31; Bersani, J., "M., agent double," *NRF,* 298 (Nov. 1977), 78–84; Morel, P.-J., "Une dissertation de M.," *Les Nouvelles Littéraires* (18 Nov. 1982), 37–38; Nettlebeck, C. W., and P. A. Hueston, "Anthology As Art, P. M.'s *Livret de famille,*" *AJFS,*" 21 (May–Aug. 1984), 213–23; Richter S., "Silhouetten von P. M.," *WB,* 31, 10 (1985), 1710–20; Nettlebeck, C. W., and P. A. Hueston, *P. M., Pièces d'identité: Écrire l'entretemps* (1986); Prince, G., "Re-Remembering M., or Something Happened," *SubStance,* 49 (1986), 35–43; Warehime, M., "Originality and Narrative Nostalgia: Shadows in M.'s *Rue des boutiques obscures,*" *FrF,* 12, 3 (Sept. 1987), 335–45; Bridges, V., and S. Barbour, "P. M.: *Quartier Perdu,*" *YFS,* 1 (1988), 259–83; O'Keefe, C., "P. M.'s *La Place de l'Étoile:* Why Name a Narrator 'Raphael Schlemilovich'?" *LOS,* 15 (1988), 67–74; Golsan, R., "Collaboration, Alienation, and the Crisis of Identity," in Ayock, W., and M. Schoenecke, *Film and Literature* (1988), 16–123; Prince, G., "P. M.," in Brosman, C. S., ed., *DLB: French Novelists since 1960* (1989), 147–53

JACK KOLBERT

MOMADAY, N(atachee) Scott

American poet, novelist, and short-story writer, b. 27 Feb. 1934, Lawton, Okla.

As a writer M. has explored the ways of being both a contemporary Native American and a member of a heritage that includes European as well as Indian ancestry. His lifelong concern with the influence of myth and ritual upon the fates of individuals figures largely in his highly autobiographical novels, short stories, and memoirs. Of Kiowa origin, M. was raised in the Navajo and Jemez Indian traditions of Arizona and New Mexico. Both parents had academic backgrounds and influenced M.'s interests in tribal identity and the inherent tension between the Anglo-American and Native American cultures. Between 1936 and 1943 M. lived with his family on Navajo reservations, learning the Navajo language but returning periodically to the Oklahoma Kiowa country in a conscious attempt to deepen his ancestral roots through communion with the land. During World War II

he was exposed for the first time to the wider American culture when both parents took jobs in war-related industries. The imaginative world of sports stars, war heroes, and movie stars would affect him as profoundly as would his immersion in Kiowa and Navajo cultures. After graduating in political science from the University of New Mexico in 1958, M. spent a year teaching speech at a reservation school, where he found time to develop his poetry. He was accepted into the creative-writing program at Stanford University the following year, where Yvor Winters (q.v.) became his mentor. M. received an A.M. from Stanford in 1960, and a Ph.D. in 1963. Thereafter he remained an English teacher and writer at the University of California at Santa Barbara, 1962–1969; Berkeley, 1969–1972 (English and comparative literature); and since 1972 at Stanford.

For his first major work, *House Made of Dawn* (1968), M. was awarded—as the first Native American—a Pulitzer Prize. Concerned with the heartbreak and disillusionment of Abel, a young World War II veteran, the novel explores the contradictions apparent when he attempts to live in the Anglo world of a Los Angeles relocation center, and, later, when he attempts an interracial relationship with a visiting white woman on the San Ysidro reservation. M. involves his protagonist in the spectrum of violent confrontation, misdirected anger, and prejudiced reaction existing between the bifurcated world of Indian and urban Anglo culture. Paralleling this tensive world, however, is a positive treatment of the imaginative world of contemporary Native American culture. Characters such as the grandfather, who comes to represent the continuity of Pueblo tradition through his evocation of nature imagery and stories of tribal origin, and the Mexican priest of the village, whose Catholic tradition mixes with Indian mythology, serve to articulate the search for personal and tribal identity that lies at the heart of this novel. Central to the thought of *House Made of Dawn* is the prescription that the survival of a people is dependent upon the continual revaluation of their identities.

A journey to his ancestral graves in the Kiowa homeland left M. with a determination to present Kiowa oral tradition in *The Way to Rainy Mountain* (1969). The sense of separation he felt at his grandfather's graveside, where his past seemed to lie in oblivion, led him on an intensive search for the stories and storytellers of tribal tradition. This quest he regarded as necessary to better understand his identity, but also as a necessary act of retrieval, because many Indian oral traditions were in danger of extinction. Characteristic of M. in this memoir is his focus on the lives of the storytellers by means of descriptive character detail, his concern for a subjective accounting of his own thoughts while in pursuit of folkloric detail, and, finally, his careful reading of the mythic stories and legends. Structurally, *The Way to Rainy Mountain* reflects the polymorphic approach of a writer who would see the landscape of his past through many eyes. Twenty-four triads of mythical, historical, and personal narratives are framed by a prologue and epilogue, the entire work preceded by an explanatory introduction. Two poems of mythical origins lend further perspective to the whole, the first dealing with tribal origins, the second predicting the end of traditional Kiowa culture. The entire work offers a multiplicity of tones as well, running from the restrained, matter-of-fact approach of the prologue, which deals with the development and decline of the oral tradition, to the highly rhythmic archaic power of the first poem, which tries to evoke the manifold forces of nature beyond the grasp of poetic language. *The Way to Rainy Mountain* attempts to meld an Indian tradition of "geopiety," a theology of the land, with a recognition of the significance of the past—dying and yet alive—that will sustain a revaluation of individual and tribal identity.

In *The Names: A Memoir* (1976), M. continues an exploration of the physical and spiritual presence of the land as a supportive force in Native American life. More unified in structure and tone than *The Way to Rainy Mountain*, it documents the history and lore of his own family ancestry, which includes Kiowa Indians and white Kentucky tobacco farmers; M. regards both cultural groups as rooted in the cultivation and appreciation of the land. He was significantly influenced by the Danish writer Isak Dinesen (q.v.), who focused on the connection between the land and the people of Africa in her autobiographical *Den afrikanske farm* (1937; *Out of Africa*, 1937) and *Skygger på græsset* (1960; *Shadows on the Grass*, 1960). Although M. has called *The Names* "an evocation of the American landscape," time as much as place is evoked through the conviction that the ancestral spirits surround the writer, that they are part of his present being.

M.'s poetic collections include prose poetry as well as more formal techniques and concern subjects familiar to his prose works. Social criticism of modern industrialism and nuclear-arms development also appear, as well as moments of humorous verse on dark subjects; more lyrical poetry confronting the problems of loneliness and separation reflects a Native American pursuit of song and formulaic charms as a necessary response to life's vicissitudes.

Most characteristic of M.'s writings as a whole is his integration of personal quest with a more general search for tribal redefinition. He has said

before a group of Native American scholars, "We are what we image. Our very existence consists in our imagination of ourselves." As a writer, M.'s words become products of self-knowledge, part of the imaginative life that must now serve the contemporary Native American, who has "at last stepped out of the museum that we have made of his traditional world."

FURTHER WORKS: *The Journey of Tai-me* (1967); *Colorado: Summer, Fall, Winter, Spring* (1973); *Angle of Geese and Other Poems* (1974); *The Colors of Night* (1976); *The Gourd Dancer* (1976); *A Coyote in the Garden* (1988); *Ancestral Voice* (1989); *The Ancient Child* (1989); *In the Presence of the Sun: A Gathering of Shields* (1991)

BIBLIOGRAPHY: Hylton, M. W., "On the Trail of Pollen: M.'s *House Made of Dawn*," *Crit*, 14, 2 (1972), 60–69; Trimble, M. S., *N. S. M.* (1973); McAllister, H. S., "Be a Man, Be a Woman: Androgyny in *House Made of Dawn*," *AIQ*, 12 (1975), 14–22; Strelke, B., "N. S. M.: Racial Memory and Individual Imagination," in Chapman, A., ed., *Literature of the American Indians* (1975), 348–57; Evers, L. J., "Words and Place: A Reading of *House Made of Dawn*," *WAL*, 11 (1977), 297–320; Dickinson-Brown, R., "The Art and Importance of N. S. M.," *SoR*, 14 (1978), 31–45; Kerr, B., "The Novel As Sacred Text: N. S. M.'s Mythmaking Epic," *SWR*, 63, 2 (1978), 172–79; Berner, R. L., "N. S. M.: Beyond Rainy Mountain," *American Indian Culture and Research Journal*, 3, 1 (1979), 57–67; Fields, K., "More Than Language Means: Review of N. S. M.'s *The Way to Rainy Mountain*," *SoR*, 6 (1979), 196–204; Velie, A. R., "Post-Symbolism and Prose Poems: M.'s Poetry," *Four American Indian Literary Masters* (1982), 11–31; Schubnell, M., *N. S. M.: The Cultural and Literary Background* (1985); Antell, J. A., "M., Welch, and Silko: Expressing the Feminine Principle through Male Alienation," *AIQ*, 12, 3 (Summer 1988), 213–20; Wild, P., "N. S. M.: Gentle Maverick," *American West*, 25 (1988), 12–13

WILLIAM OVER

MON, Franz

(pseud. of Franz Löffelholz) German poet and dramatist, b. 6 May 1926, Frankfurt am Main

M. studied history, philosophy, and German at the University of Frankfurt, where he received his doctorate in 1955. He is now the business manager of a textbook publishing house in Frankfurt.

M. can be classified as one of the leading concrete poets, since the content of his experimental works is language itself. As is the case with most avant-garde writers, M. has compiled extensive theoretical texts to explain and justify his approach. Most of these have appeared in the anthology *texte über texte* (1970; texts about texts). Here M. argues that we can know reality only through language. Yet this language has stored up historical ideas and conventions that are no longer valid. To rid ourselves of these incrustations and to achieve a clearer perception of present-day reality, it is therefore necessary to analyze this language by isolating its parts and performing experiments on them. For example, one can recombine bits of language in montage fashion, one can stretch the syntax of the sentence to unmanageable lengths, or one can create optical images using letters, words, parts of words, or sentences. Through such playful procedures one can hope to begin understanding how language works and how it influences our perception of the world.

M. began writing in the surrealist tradition, and his early poems were full of grotesque images. He quickly moved, however, to a more radical experimentation with language in his first major collection of concrete texts, *artikulationen* (1959; articulations). In subsequent collections he refined and expanded his technique. In *sehgänge* (1964; paths of vision), for example, he manipulates given texts according to set procedures: expansions through grammatical associations or similarities of sound, rearrangement of words, or the creation of pictures and new words from parts of the text. In his *lesebuch* (1967; reader) he creates sentences that are so long as to be uninterpretable, thus forcing readers to concentrate on the form, or he creates sentences that are syntactically straightforward but which have such bizzare images that the reader is baffled by the semantic connotations. In all these works the combination of linguistic elements not usually found together in language usage or the creation of new linguistic forms are supposed to give us a heightened insight into the relationship between language and reality.

M.'s most famous work is *herzzero* (1968; heart zero). The book contains two parallel texts that are collages of sentences, words, colloquial speech, and familiar sayings. Readers are instructed to mark in the book; with a pencil they are to connect passages that belong together, with a pen they are to improve or supplement the texts, and with a felt-tipped pen they are to cross out superfluous texts. Readers thus actively restructure their own language-reality and in so doing interpret the world in a new light.

In the late 1960s and early 1970s, M. wrote several radio plays where he applied the same principles and techniques of language experimentation. The pieces have no plot or theme, except to examine language. These acoustic montages and permutations came to be viewed as paradigms for the then popular genre of the "new radio play."

M.'s influence on German literature was intense but short. He argued cogently for a rethinking of our linguistic consciousness and for a responsible use by authors of their medium. His contributions to the concrete school are considerable, and he will be remembered for his ingenuity and innovation, even if his theories found no long-lasting support or confirmation.

FURTHER WORKS: *movens* (1960); *protokoll an der kette* (1961); *verläufe* (1962); *weiss wie weiss* (1964); *rückblick auf isaac newton* (1965); *5 beliebige fassungen eines textes aus einem satz* (1966); *animal nur das alphabet gebrauchen* (1967); *text mit 600* (1970); *aufenthaltsraum* (1972); *maus im mehl* (1976); *hören und sehen vergehen oder in einen geschlossenen mund kommt eine fliege* (1978); *fallen stellen* (1981); *hören ohne aufzuhören 03 arbeiten 1952–1981* (1982)

BIBLIOGRAPHY: Brüggemann, D., "Die Aporien der konkreten Poesie," *Merkur*, 2 (1974), 148–65; Waldrop, R., "Songs and Wonderings," *CL*, 4 (1975), 344–54; special M. issue, *T + K*, 60 (1978); Hedges, I., "Concrete Sound: The Radio Plays of F. M.," *Dada*, 12 (1983), 60–69

ROBERT ACKER

MONTAGUE, John

Irish poet and short-story writer, b. 28 Feb. 1929, Brooklyn, N.Y., U.S.A.

M. spent the first four years of his life in New York City before moving to County Tyrone, Northern Ireland, where he was raised by his paternal aunts. He received his B.A. in English from University College, Dublin (1949), his M.A. in English from Yale University (1952), and his M.F.A. from the University of Iowa (1955). In common with many Irish writers, M. has spent much of his adult life outside Ireland, though almost all of his work has remained Irish-centered. However, unlike the work of many of his contemporaries, M.'s work has been strongly influenced by the poets of other countries, and by modern American and French poets in particular.

Although M. is usually associated with the group of northern Irish poets who emerged in the late 1960s—Seamus Heaney, Derek Mahon (qq.v.), and Michael Longley (b. 1939)—his work is perhaps better understood if it is considered in relation to that of his own contemporaries—Thomas Kinsella (q.v.), Anthony Cronin (b. 1926), and James Liddy (b. 1934)—all of whom graduated from

University College, Dublin, in the late 1950s and early 1960s, and became part of a stable of poets whose work was published by Liam Miller's Dolmen Press. All of these poets, influenced by Patrick Kavanagh (q.v.), believed that Irish poetry had to be rescued from the post-Celtic twilight slumber it had fallen into, and be reborn by combining Irish material with more experimental forms.

The dominant themes present in M.'s first four collections of poems, *Forms of Exile* (1958), *Poisoned Lands* (1961), *A Chosen Light* (1967), and *Tides* (1970), are Irish history, mythology, and place, and M.'s exploration of his more private self as revealed in his relationships with his family and lovers. In contrast with William Butler Yeats's (q.v.), M.'s view of the Irish past is both anti-heroic and anti-Yeatsian. The Irish landscape may well be beautiful to look at, but it is also full of poisons—lovelessness, hatred, and loneliness. In one of his best early poems, "The Siege of Mullingar, 1963," published in *A Chosen Light*, M., to his delight, discovers that religious oppression, which is at the heart of many of Ireland's problems, is being obliterated by the forces of change that emerged in the 1960s and he declares, parodying Yeats's "September 1913" (1914), that "Puritan Ireland is dead and gone, a myth of O'Connor and O'Faolain."

The outbreak of the troubles in Northern Ireland in 1969 forced M. to reexamine his career as a poet and his relationship with the North. *The Rough Field* (1972) is a collage in which old and new poems are set side by side with quotations, epigraphs, and woodcuts, all of which are used to describe the collapse of the North as a civilization. Although M. empathizes with the Catholic nationalists, he does not believe that a vibrant province will emerge from the battle for equality and reform. His poems of this period are remarkably successful as art, but also because they represent the most sustained attempt by a modern Irish writer to describe a region, and a people, in its moment of collapse. *The Dead Kingdom* (1984) is M.'s most personal and perhaps his greatest work to date. The book is structured around a journey from Cork, where M. now lives, to Fermanagh/South Tyrone, where he spent much of his youth, and is a meditation on personal and national history.

M.'s style has changed little throughout his career. From its beginning, he has basically written in two forms—poems with vigorous, longer, Yeatsian lines, and poems with short lines, often just two words, of the type that one will encounter in the poetry of William Carlos Williams (q.v.). The former is a feature of southern Irish poetry, while the latter dominates Northern verse, and shows that M. can be easily accommodated within either tradition.

FURTHER WORKS: *The Old People* (1960); *Death of a Chieftain* (1964); *All Legendary Obstacles* (1966); *Patriotic Suite* (1966); *Home Again* (1967); *Hymn to the Omagh Road* (1968); *Small Secrets* (1972); *The Cave of Night* (1974); *O'Riada's Farewell* (1975); *A Slow Dance* (1975); *The Great Cloak* (1978); *Selected Poems* (1982); *Mount Eagle* (1988)

BIBLIOGRAPHY: Kersnowski, F., *M.* (1975); Carpenter, A., "Double Vision in Anglo-Irish Literature," in Carpenter, A., ed., *Place, Personality, and the Irish Writer* (1977), 173–89; Deane, S., *Celtic Revivals* (1985), 146–86; Deane, S., *A Short History of Irish Literature* (1986), 227–47

EAMONN WALL

MORENO-DURAN, Rafael Humberto

Colombian novelist and short-story writer, b. 7 Nov. 1946, Tunja

M.-D. studied law and political science at the National University of Colombia in Bogotá. He has been associated with a number of journals published in Spain and Latin America, and since 1989 has directed the Latin American edition of *Quimera*. Like other postmodernists (q.v.), he has spent much of his life in Europe. A man of broad culture, he is most fascinated by the classical era and its revival and reinterpretation in 18th-c. Europe, particularly the salon society. He speaks approvingly of "the ironic and demythologizing, irreverent and festive climate of the 18th c."

M.-D. is known for his postmodernist tendencies. In his case these involve a greater concentration on language as such than on the topic at hand and, correspondingly, a certain hermeticism (q.v.). M.-D. places great value on the principle of ambiguity, the effect of which is to deny validity to anything purporting to be an authoritative discourse. Nevertheless, his latest novel, *Los felinos del canciller* (1987; the chancellor's felines), is a good deal less hermetic than his earlier works, even while continuing to concentrate on the philological concerns of both characters and narrator. At the same time, wit of the linguistic variety has become more prominent in his fiction.

In his early novels the author placed great emphasis on the role of women in society, having concluded that all the significant novels of Colombia concentrated on concerns inherent to the life of women. While his short stories written from a woman's perspective appear to many readers to ring true, some feminist critics claim to find them somewhat inauthentic in this regard.

His first book was an ambitious essay, *De la barbarie a la imaginación* (1976; from barbarity to imagination), which set the tone for his subsequent fiction. Although he had completed first drafts of the novels in his trilogy known as *Femina Suite* (woman suite) by 1976, they were published between 1977 and 1983. The first, *Juego de damas* (1977; game of checkers, literally "ladies' game"), has as its framework a party that is reminiscent of the 18th-c. salons, albeit in parodic fashion. The characters recall their student days, including their abortive attempt to mount an armed rebellion against the government, but, in postmodern fashion, the most important activity in the text is clearly its various forms of discourse. Rather than narrate events, M.-D. tends to allow his characters to recreate them in lengthy dialogues. Alvaro Pineda-Botero has commented that M.-D.'s characters and situations serve not as the revelation of a supposed external reality but as a framework for the true motive of the discourse, which is language and culture.

The text of *El toque de Diana* (1981; reveille, or Diana's touch) also continually calls attention to itself. The central characters are highly sophisticated people who converse in several languages. The two most prominent are a general, whose career has just come to an end, and his wife, the owner of an elegant millinery shop. At one point she offers her opinion that style controls culture. Even so, in this work, as in the first of the trilogy, culture tends to be reduced to sexuality.

Within M.-D.'s hermetic style in the trilogy, the reader perceives an increasing emphasis on humor, most notably in the sexual realm, and often involving a multiform satire on cultural forms. At one point in *Finale capriccioso con madonna* (1983; capricious finale with Madonna), a Colombian male finds himself in bed with his Arabic ex-wife and his Jewish lover, their three bodies forming a triangle. The narration of the event plays on the cabala and other esoterica, and at the same time suggests that this may be a parody of the *convivencia* or codwelling of three religious groups under Alphonse X in 12th-c. Spain. In this novel, too, all of culture is reduced to style and sexuality.

The ostensible topic of *Los felinos del canciller* is Latin American diplomacy. In its opening pages the years of violence in Colombia (1948–1958 and beyond) have begun, ironically in Bogotá, which has always taken pride in calling itself "the Athens of South America." The protagonist is in New York, exercising a diplomatic career, when he receives the news of violence in the halls of the Colombian legislature in Bogotá. He then rehearses his family's history through several generations by means of flashbacks. Subsequently he returns home to uncover some of the family's more profound secrets. As Raymond L. Williams has noted, the key activity in the work is manipulation, both of people and of language. The narrator comments, "Politics and philology were the same thing in this country. In the beginning was the word, and the word was made with power." In this work, as in *Los felinos del canciller*, language is sexualized as surely as sex is equated with philological exercises.

M.-D.'s finely crafted short stories were published as *Metropolitanas* (1986; metropolitan women) and *Epístola final sobre los cuáqueros* (1987; final epistle on the Quakers). The latter won the National Short Story Prize (1987). His stories often deal with the attempts made by European women to come to terms with a male-dominated world. The best of those in *Metropolitanas* is "Perpetua" (Perpetua), the narrator of which is an Italian woman who has suffered greatly from the ravages of World War II as well as her late husband's infidelity. Ultimately she creates an identity for herself within the boundaries of the eternal feminine principle, because, as she perceives the situation, time is irredeemably cyclical. True to M.-D.'s tendencies, she does so largely through double entendres, both conscious and unconscious.

M.-D. is currently preparing what he calls a "literary biography" entitled "La augusta sílaba" (the august syllable) and a novel, "El caballero de La Invicta" (the knight of La Invicta).

M.-D. has developed a public image as the writer's writer. His readership, in contrast to that of Gabriel García Márquez (q.v.), consists largely of a relatively small group of people interested in innovative fiction.

BIBLIOGRAPHY: Jaramillo, J. E., "*Los felinos del canciller:* Una crítica de las fundaciones," in Pineda-Botero, A., and R. L. Williams, eds., *De ficciones y realidades* (1989), 255–68; Pineda-Botero, A., *Del mito a la posmodernidad* (1990), 184–93; Siemens, W. L., "M.-D.: 'Perpetua' y la cartografía de la feminidad," in Oyarzún, K., ed., *The Latin American Short Story* (1990), 98–105; Williams, R. L., *The Colombian Novel, 1844–1987* (1991), 196–204

WILLIAM L. SIEMENS

MUKHERJEE, Bharati

Indian novelist, short-story writer, and prose writer (writing in English), b. 27 July 1940, Calcutta

Born into a well-to-do family, M. earned her B.A. in English at the University of Calcutta (1959) and her M.A. at the University of Baroda (1961) before attending the University of Iowa Writing Workshop, where she met her husband, Canadian novelist Clark Blaise (b. 1940). After marrying, they lived in Toronto and Montreal. M. taught English at McGill University before moving to the U.S. Her first novel, *The Tiger's Daughter* (1972) satirized Indian society from the vantage point of a Vassar-educated expatriate married to an American. With irony and insight, M. records Tara's attempt to reconcile two worlds, Indian and Western, neither of which she can inhabit completely.

In her second novel, *Wife* (1975), M. details the daily life of Dimple Basu, whose training as a devoted Indian wife fails to prepare her for life in New York City. Unable to fit into the Indian community and lacking a sense of self, Dimple becomes increasingly alienated, even from her husband. Caught in a cage of an urban apartment, the protagonist bursts her bounds in a single act of violence. Although M. portrays urban America as disorienting and dehumanizing, she also condemns the Indian cultural ideal of the passive woman for whom marriage and husband worship are the only acceptable goals.

The Middleman and Other Stories (1988), which won the National Book Critics Circle Award, is a collection of hard-nosed, bitter stories of immigrants to the U.S. from the Middle East, the Caribbean, and various parts of Asia. In sometimes shocking turns of plot, M. successfully represents the difficulties of Third World peoples adjusting to a fast-paced, mercenary society, as well as Americans who respond with insults, indifference, or sometimes curiosity. Set in Canada, her earlier collection of stories, *Darkness* (1985), similarly explores hostility between various ethnic minorities and the dominant culture. M.'s intelligent vision and startling vignettes fully measure the poorly aligned "hoops" of the immigrant experience. Her acerbic analysis of postcolonial life in the West, rendered in stark language and a tough-guy tone, bars no punches.

In *Jasmine* (1989), however, M. reaches new heights of narrative incandescence, creating a chameleonlike character capable of the fluidity demanded by contemporary American society. Born Jyoti in the Punjab, she first becomes Jasmine, a devoted wife who loses her husband to Hindu-Sikh communalism. Though Jasmine is bent on coming to the U.S. to commit *sati,* a widow's voluntary suicide, her survival instinct prevails, and she instead tries on several different lives, metamorphosing next into Jazzy and then Jane. Life in the urban Indian community proves as stifling as life in rural Iowa; California and a yuppie marriage offer alternatives. M. penetrates American life with daggerlike observations that simultaneously reveal and dissect the paradoxical emptiness and energy of U.S. society. Contrasts between the coping mechanisms of Du, an adopted Vietnamese teenager, and those of the first-person narrator spell out divergent yet parallel tracks for a common journey.

M., who has also written several prose works, has a genius for social critique. Although her writing is anything but subtle, it challenges because her characters are always thinking, always commenting on the insanity of the lives they lead. Sometimes outrageous, yet endlessly interesting, M.'s creations cause the reader to brush away improbabilities and concentrate instead on the peculiarities of a society that demands cultural gymnastics for mere survival. One also comes away from her work with a new appreciation for the ingenuity necessary in those forced to leap several centuries by emigrating to the West at this moment in time.

As a bright, new voice in Indo-American fiction, M. covers some of the same territory as Salman Rushdie (q.v.) in *The Satanic Verses* (1988), but differently. Her rendition of the immigrant experience, in a spare, clean prose style, is less of a verbal tour de force—it is a tour de force of improbable plots and astonishing characters. M., too, requires of the reader a willing suspension of disbelief, though not to the extent of Rushdie's magic realism (q.v.). Yet, her novels and short stories, read cumulatively, cause the reader to ponder thoroughly the transformations required of so many Third World citizens suddenly transported to Disneyland.

FURTHER WORKS: *Days and Nights in Calcutta* (1977, with Clark Blaise); *The Sorrow and the Terror: The Haunting Legacy of the Air India Tragedy* (1987, with Clark Blaise)

BIBLIOGRAPHY: "Oh, Calcutta," *TLS,* 29 June 1973, 736; Vaid, K. B., "Wife," *Fiction International,* 4–5 (1975), 155–57; Desai, A., "Outcasts," *LM,* 25, 9–10 (1985–1986), 143–46; Nazareth, P., "Total Vision," *CanL,* 110 (1986), 184–91; Raban, J., "The Middleman," *NYTBR,* 19 June 1988, 1, 22–23; Ward, E., "Notes from a New America," *Book World,* 3 July 1988, 3, 9

JANET M. POWERS

MUNĪF, 'Abd al-Rahmān

(also spelled Abdelrahman Munif) Saudi novelist, b. 1933, Jordan

M. has come to a career in creative writing relatively late in life, but during the 1970s and 1980s he published a large number of novels that are significant additions to the contemporary tradition of Arabic fiction. Born in Jordan of mixed Saudi-Jordanian parentage, he studied law in both Damascus and Cairo before going to Yugoslavia to complete a doctorate in petroleum economics. He began a career in oil marketing and edited the Iraqi journal *Al-Naft wa-al-Tanmiya*. While in Baghdad, he became a close colleague of the great Palestinian littérateur Jabrā Ibrāhīm Jabrā (q.v.), who seems to have served as a catalyst for M.'s decision to embark upon a writing career. In this context it is interesting to note that Jabrā and M. have written a joint novel, *'Ālam bi-lā kharā'it* (1982; world without maps). After living for several years in France, M. currently resides in Damascus.

M.'s novels reflect the wide variety of his experiences. The theme of oil and politics impinges into the narrative of *Sibāq al-masāfāt al-tawīla: rihla ilā al-sharq* (1979; long-distance race: a trip to the East), set during the period of Mossaddeg's prime-ministership in Iran in the 1950s, while the impact of the discovery of oil on the Gulf region of Saudi Arabia and its effect on the indigenous population provides the context for what is the most ambitious novelistic project in Arabic to date, M.'s monumental quintet, published under the general title *Mudun al-milh* (cities of salt). It includes *Al-Tīh* (1984; *Cities of Salt,* 1987), *Al-Ukhdūd* (1985; *The Trench,* 1991), *Taqāsīm al-layl wa-al-nahār* (1988; sections of day and night), *Al-Munbatt* (1988; the hobbled), and *Bādiyat al-zulumāt* (1988; desert of gloom). The alienation of the individual within modern Arab societies is reflected in several works, including his first published novel, *Al-Ashjār wa-ghtiyāl Marzūq* (1973; the trees and Marzūq's assassination), *'Ālam bi-lā kharā'it,* and most notably *Sharq al-Mutawassit* (1977; pub. in French as *À l'est de la Méditerranée,* 1985), one of the most harrowing portraits to date of the fate of an Arab intellectual imprisoned in his homeland and pressured while studying abroad and of the measures taken by the governmental apparatus against his family members during his absences. The detailed description in *Mudun al-milh* of the impact of oil exploration on the fragile desert environment clearly reflects M.'s deep concern for the ecology of an area of the world that he personally holds very dear; the same theme is intensified in an earlier work, *Al-Nihāyāt* (1978; *Endings,* 1988), where the traditional life of a desert community and the delicate natural balance that forms the basis of its life-style and values is portrayed in a work that provides descriptive passages of climate, animals, and people of quite unique quality.

M. has contributed to the tradition of modern Arabic fiction through his choice of themes and the unique contexts in which many of his novels are placed. Beyond this lie his experiments in the area of narrative itself. Like many of his contemporaries among Arab novelists, M. has resorted to pastiches and even quotations from earlier narrative sources as a means of linking the speakers in his Arabic novels of today with the earlier tradition of Arabic narrative, but several of his novels (and most notably *Al-Nihāyāt* and the five-volume *Mudun al-milh*) also make it clear that in crafting his narratives he is intent on replicating the narrative techniques of traditional storytellers: the lengthy asides, the provision of more than one version of many events, and, above all, an apparent lack of concern with time or the relative importance of one event over another, all the more carefully crafted because of the narration's very insouciance. Readers of M. find themselves forced to follow the priorities of his narrators, which often appear at odds with those of their counterparts in much Western fiction. Therein lies not a little of the originality of this most individual voice in modern Arabic fiction.

FURTHER WORKS: *Qissat hubb mājūsiyya* (n.d.); *Hīna taraknā al-Jisr* (1976)

BIBLIOGRAPHY: Allen, R., *The Arabic Novel* (1982), 156–62; Allen, R., *Modern Arabic Literature* (1987), 224–28; Allen, R., "Incorporating the Other," *The World and I* (Feb. 1989), 378–87; Siddiq, M., "The Contemporary Arabic Novel in Perspective," *WLT,* 60, 2 (Spring 1986), 206–11; Siddiq, M., "Cities of Salt," *The World and I* (Feb. 1989), 387–92

ROGER ALLEN

MUNRO, Alice

(formerly Alice Laidlaw) Canadian short-story writer (writing in English), b. 10 July 1931, Wingham, Ontario

Among the best short-story writers in English, M. has made the form her only genre, but for occasional nonfictional pieces. M. was born into a family of modest means: M.'s father bred silver foxes during the Depression while her mother, a former school teacher, attempted various means to contribute to the family's support. Educated in local schools and at the University of Western Ontario, M. married and moved to Vancouver in 1951, raising three daughters. Her first stories were published in periodicals (*Montrealer, Chatelaine, Canadian Forum, Queen's Quarterly, Tamarack Review*) and broadcast on the Canadian Broadcasting Corporation during the 1950s and 1960s. Her first short-story collection, *Dance of the Happy Shades* (1968), includes many of these stories, covering a thirteen-year compositional span. Divorced and remarried after returning to Ontario in 1972, M. lives in Clinton, near Wingham.

Although her earliest stories display a strong attraction to the romantic and gothic (revealing an acknowledged influence of American Southern writing), M.'s most characteristic early material is derived from her childhood experience of rural southwestern Ontario. Focusing sharply on its textures—sights, sounds, smells—M. creates characters whose recollections, often the first-person narrators', probe both the nature of being and, most especially, of the mysteries of human relations and connections. These are people rooted in a particular place: Huron County, Ontario. The autobiographical dimension, seen in stories such as "Boys and Girls" and "The Peace of Utrecht," in *Dance of the Happy Shades,* and in the whole of *Lives of Girls and Women* (1971), privileges M.'s own childhood generally and her relations with her parents most particularly. Throughout, M. displays an ability to make the ordinary extraordinary, showing "People's lives," in a phrase from *Lives of Girls and Women* (putatively a novel but actually interconnected short stories), to be "deep caves paved with kitchen linoleum." Thus her art works—at its most essential—through her deftly precise probing of what she has called the surfaces of life; its mysteries are found in their most profound forms during its most commonplace occasions.

Variously seen as a feminist, magic realist, or metafictionalist—the latter especially after her next volume, *Something I've Been Meaning To Tell You: Thirteen Stories* (1974)—M. disavows all labels, preferring instead to let her stories speak for themselves, and so for her. A meticulous stylist, M. works and reworks stories to the very last moment. In one instance, *Who Do You Think You Are?* (1978; pub. in the U.S. as *The Beggar Maid,* 1979), she almost went beyond publication. She had the book, in page proofs, pulled from the presses for restructuring. These reworkings take a variety of forms but most frequently involve shifts in point of view and, particularly, in the shaping and sharpening of story endings to offer more a sense of closure rather than any conclusive insight. The variety and extent of her compositional efforts have been made evident by her papers, collected at the University of Calgary.

Although many critics saw M. revisiting the material treated in *Lives* in *Who Do You Think You Are?,* the later volume displays far greater technical skill and detachment, and, most significantly, its insights are far more qualified and, finally, ambivalent. This ambivalence has been central to M.'s subsequent collections. It is not an attitude of uncaring, or of ennui, though; rather, what M. offers in such stories as "Chaddeleys and Flemings" and "The Moons of Jupiter" in *The Moons of Jupiter* (1982) might be called an ambivalence over ever really being able to identify, know, understand, and relate the myriad details and insights that affect a person's life. These stories reveal a writer whose art is borne by the mysteries of being, and who has no expectation of gathering them together conclusively anymore, but who finds herself driven to try, and then try again, anyhow.

During the late 1970s and early 1980s, M.'s stories began to appear first in American periodicals, most regularly in *The New Yorker.* These stories have made up the bulk of M.'s last three collections, *The Moons of Jupiter, The Progress of Love* (1986), and *Friend of My Youth* (1990). In them, she has retained her concern with personal materials—as in the title stories of each collection, each of which displays M.'s longstanding concern with daughter-parent (especially -mother) relations, derived from her own experience—yet they also suggest different directions, like the psychology of a murder-suicide (and how one reacts to such an occurrence) in "Fits" (from *The Progress of Love*) or, more unusually, in the 19th-c.-recreated gothic atmosphere which is "Meneseteung" (from *Friend of My Youth*).

But the significance of M.'s most recent work lies less with its subjects than with its style, for she has taken the first-person retrospective technique seen in her first two books—largely a matter of a past event seen from the perspective of the present—and pushed it to its logical extremes. Thus the stories in the last two collections juggle various points in time—and events—seen as each impinges on a central focal point, whether an event or a particular insight. This involves breaks and shifts in the narrative, which fragment it and, as well, perpetually reminds one of the partiality of any human understanding, and of its fundamental relativity.

Three of M.'s volumes have been awarded Canada's highest literary prize, the Governor-General's Award for Fiction (1968, 1978, and 1986), she has been runner-up for the Booker Prize, and in 1990 she received the Canada Council Molson Prize for lifetime contributions to her country's cultural life. Not for every taste, M.'s stories may be said to have a certain sameness about them that strikes some as repetitious, whatever momentary understandings they offer. Even so, her ultimate significance is as a writer of dazzling ability and irreproachable integrity, a person whose stories, above all else, communicate the textures, uncertainties, and mysteries of being, of being human, and, finally (with Munrovian paradox), of just being a human being.

FURTHER WORKS: *The A. M. Papers: First Accession* (1986); *The A. M. Papers: Second Accession* (1987)

BIBLIOGRAPHY: MacKendrick, L. K., ed., *Probable Fictions: A. M.'s Narrative Acts* (1983); Miller,

J., ed., *The Art of A. M.: Saying the Unsayable* (1984); Thacker, R., "A. M.: An Annotated Bibliography;" in Lecker, R., and J. David, eds., *The Annotated Bibliography of Canada's Major Authors* (1984), Vol. 5, 354–414; Dahlie, H., "A. M. and Her Works," in Lecker, R., J. David, and E. Quigley, eds., *Canadian Writers and Their Works, Fiction Series* (1985), Vol. 5, 215–56; Martin, W. R., *A. M.: Paradox and Parallel* (1987); Blodgett, E. D., *A. M.* (1988); Carrington, I. de Papp, *Controlling the Uncontrollable: The Fiction of A. M.* (1989); Hoy, H., " 'Rose and Janet': A. M.'s Metafiction," *CanL,* 121 (Summer 1989), 59–83; Rasporich, B. J., *Dance of the Sexes: Art and Gender in the Fiction of A. M.* (1990)

ROBERT THACKER

MURAKAMI Haruki

Japanese novelist, short-story writer, essayist, and translator, b. 12 Jan. 1949, Kyoto

M. grew up in Ashiya, Hyogo, as an only child. Both his parents were Japanese literature teachers in high school. Out of youthful rebellion against his parents, M. decided not to read Japanese literature; instead, he began reading cheap American paperbacks easily obtainable in the port town Kobe's secondhand bookstores. In 1968 he moved to Tokyo to study theater at Waseda University. But he hardly went to school because the late 1960s in Japan saw the height of student uprisings, and many universities, including Waseda, were occupied by leftist students and were forced to close down. In 1974 M. and his wife opened a jazz bar, which they managed until 1981, when M. decided to make a living solely by his writing. In between, in 1975, he did graduate from Waseda.

Without a doubt M. is the most successful writer of *jun bungaku* (serious literature) in modern Japan. His books have sold by the millions, forcing him into the role of cultural icon of contemporary Japan. Though there are many factors that may account for his popularity, one thing seems clear—his books have spoken for a new generation. Just as a decade before, Ōe Kenzaburō and Abe Kōbō (qq.v.) offered a new language to the generation of existentialists unsatisfied with the peculiar Japanese aesthetics of Tanizaki Jun'ichirō and Kawabata Yasunari (qq.v.), M. has offered a new language to a new generation of Japanese. Just as many of the postwar Japanese writers had begun writing out of the existentialist vacuum left by World War II, M. began writing out of the vacuum of the 1970s that was left by the collapse of the counterculture of the 1960s. A persistent sense of loss pervades his works. At the same time, his writings struggle against the ever threatening, all-engulfing silence in which we pretend to communicate.

M. first attracted attention in 1979 when he won the Gunzō New Writer's Award with his first novel, *Kaze no uta o kike* (1979; *Hear the Wind Sing,* 1987). This work introduced to Japanese literature bold stylistic innovations inspired by the works of two contemporary American writers, Kurt Vonnegut (q.v.) and Richard Brautigan (1935–1984): brief chapters, insertions of seemingly unrelated stories, deadpan humor, a hint of science fiction, and the overall light touch eluding the introverted seriousness that had pervaded modern Japanese fiction. In it he also introduced the two main characters that inhabit the trilogy consisting of this first novel and the two that followed, *Sen kyūhyaku nanajū san nen no pinbōru* (1980; *Pinball. 1973,* 1988) and *Hitsuji o meguru bōken* (1982; *A Wild Sheep Chase,* 1989): "I" and a friend, or alter ego, called "Rat."

Many of M.'s works revolve around a dualism of the self as well as a dualism of the world: "I" in search of a truer self in a dual world of "reality" and the "other world." His fourth novel, *Sekai no owari to hādoboirudo wandārando* (1985; *Hard-Boiled Wonderland and The End of the World,* 1991), is no exception. This highly allegorical work has a parallel structure of two seemingly unrelated stories alternatively narrated chapter by chapter, yet eventually forming an intricately related story of two worlds: a postmodern computer society and a fairyland of death and tranquillity where "I" is separated from his "Shadow"—his "heart" and reality. This work won the Tanizaki Prize (1985).

In his next novel, *Noruwei no mori* (1987; *Norwegian Wood,* 1989), M. departed from his previous experimental styles and presented a youthful love story in a convincing realism of his own, filled with lyrical gentleness, explicit sexual scenes, and ever haunting threats of death, insanity, and suicide.

M. has also published six collections of short stories, more than a dozen nonfiction writings, often in collaboration with illustrators or photographers, as well as translations of works by F. Scott Fitzgerald, Truman Capote, Raymond Carver, John Irving (qq.v.), Paul Theroux (b. 1941) and Tim O'Brien (b. 1946).

Mainly because of his immense popularity, some critics regard M.'s works as the epitome of a postmodern consumer product, strategically packaged and marketed for mass consumption. Some bemoan the perceived lack of political engagement in his works. Others find his style too "Americanized." Yet despite the predictable criticism, his works show an imaginative power able to represent the new, vital transnational culture of contemporary Japan without ever forfeiting the author's serious moral and spiritual concerns. The postmodern outlook of his work may baffle readers accustomed to the more traditional literature of modern Japan, yet his fresh treatment of such traditional themes as love, death, and self does place him at the forefront of a tradition called "modern Japanese literature" that began over a century ago.

FURTHER WORKS: *Zō kōjō no happīendo* (1983); *Kangarū biyori* (1983); *Chūgoku iki no surou · Bōto* (1983); *Nami no e. nami no hanashi* (1984); *Murakami asahidō* (1984); *Hotaru · naya o yaku · sonota no tanpen* (1984); *Hitsuji otoko no kurisumasu* (1985); *Kaiten mokuba no deddo · hīto* (1985); *Rangeruhansutō no gogo* (1986); *Panya saishūgeki* (1986); *Murakami asahidō no gyakushū* (1986); *'The Scrap' natsukashi no 1980 nendai* (1987); *Hi izuru kuni no kōjō* (1987); *Za · sukotto · fittsugerarudo · bukku* (1988); *Dansu · dansu · dansu* (1988); *Murakami asahidō haihō!* (1989); *TV pīpuru* (1990); *Tōi taiko* (1990); *Uten enten* (1990); *M. H. zen sakuhin 1979–1989* (8 vols., 1990–)

BIBLIOGRAPHY: Arensberg, A., on *A Wild Sheep Chase, NYTBR,* 3 Dec. 1989, 82; Leithauser, B., "A Hook Somewhere," *New Yorker,* 4 Dec. 1989, 182–87; Seigle, S. S., on *A Wild Sheep Chase, JASt,* 49 (1990), 161–63; Melville, J., on *A Wild Sheep Chase, TLS,* 16 Nov. 1990, 1233

HOSEA HIRATA

MUSCHG, Adolf

Swiss novelist, dramatist, and essayist (writing in German), b. 13 May 1934, Zurich

M. is one of the best-known contemporary Swiss-German authors. After studying German and English at the University of Zurich, he received his doctorate in 1959. He taught secondary school in Zurich until 1962, and then served as a guest lecturer at several Swiss and foreign universities. In 1970 he became a professor of German literature at the Federal Technical University in Zurich. He has won several awards, including the Swiss Schiller Foundation Prize (1965), the Conrad Ferdinand Mayer Prize (1968), and the Hermann Hesse Prize (1974). He now lives in Kilchberg.

M. began his literary career in the mid-1960s, and his first novel, *Im sommer des hasen* (1965; in the summer of the hare), was an immediate success. Six men are given the task of spending half a year in Japan to record their impressions, but in the course of the novel we learn more about

the Swiss mentality than about Japanese culture. Years later M. reintroduced the theme of examining Switzerland from afar (a device very popular with contemporary Swiss authors) in *Baiyun oder die freundschaftsgesellschaft* (1960; Baiyun or the friendship society). The death of the head of a Swiss delegation to China causes the other members of the group to comment at length on their own culture and proclivities.

It soon became clear that M. was to have as his central theme the nature of Switzerland and the problems of the middle class, from which he came. He examines this nexus from a critical, committed standpoint in a finely tuned and exactly polished language. Sometimes his language becomes too complicated, however, and this detracts from the thematic concerns of his works. This was the case with his next two novels, *Gegenzauber* (1967; counter magic), which deals with the futile attempts to prevent an old building from being demolished, and *Mitgespielt* (1969; playing along), where a teacher and his pupils become involved in a murder.

M. is particularly interested in the role of the intellectual and the artist in contemporary life. In the novel *Albissers grund* (1974; Albisser's reason) he explores why a high-school teacher becomes involved in the student protests of the late 1960s and why the teacher shoots his psychiatrist, the only person who is trying to help him understand his new relationship to politics. In *Das licht und der schlüssel* (1984; The Light and the Key, 1988) a vampire and expert on fine paintings, Constantin Samstag, discusses the positive effects of art. Several of the stories in *Der turmhahn* (1987; the tower rooster), on the other hand, demonstrate how life can be destroyed by art. In all these works M. indirectly examines his own position in society as a writer who is concerned with social issues. He investigates the historical dimensions of this same problem in his play *Die aufgeregten von goethe* (1971; the excited ones by Goethe), which portrays the famous German writer's reaction to the French Revolution, and in his biography *Gottfried Keller* (1977; Gottfried Keller), which describes in great detail the life and times of the well-known 19th-c. Swiss author. Finally, in his essay *Literatur als therapie?* (1981; literature as therapy?) he states that art, in the form of literature, is necessary for him as an intellectual to come to terms with the problems in life.

M. has also inspected the parameters of Swiss society in several collections of short stories: *Fremdkörper* (1968; foreign bodies), *Liebesgeschichten* (1972; love stories), *Der blaue mann* (1974; *Blue Man & Other Stories,* 1983), *Entfernte bekannte* (1976; distant acquaintances), and *Leib und leben* (1982; body and life). Many schol-

437

ars claim that he is at his linguistic best in these shorter formats. In general the stories deal with the Swiss malaise of alienation from society, which is often metaphorically expressed as sickness and disease (another common feature of contemporary Swiss-German letters). The many characters feel powerless to act or express themselves in an environment that inhibits personal growth, and they are thus forced to resign themselves to the status quo.

M.'s honest explorations of his own metier and his open confrontation with the social ills of Switzerland (and paradigmatically of the whole industrialized world) have earned him fame far beyond the Swiss borders.

FURTHER WORKS: *Rumpelstilz* (1968); *Das kerbelgericht* (1969); *Papierwände: aufsätze über japan* (1970); *High fidelity oder ein silberblick* (1973); *Kellers abend* (1975); *Von herwegh bis kaiseraugst: wie halten wir es als demokraten mit unserer freiheit?* (1975); *Besuch in der schweiz* (1978); *Noch ein wunsch* (1979); *Besprechungen 1961– 1979* (1980); *Die tücke des verbesserten objekts* (1981); *Übersee* (1982); *Ausgewählte erzählungen 1962–1982* (1983); *Unterlassene anwesenheit* (1984); *Empörung durch landschaften: vernünftige drohreden* (1985); *Goethe als emigrant: auf der suche nach dem grünen bei einem alten dichter* (1986); *Dreizehn briefe mijnheers* (1986); *Deshima: filmbuch* (1987); *Die schweiz am ende, am ende die schweiz: erinnerungen an mein land vor 1991* (1990)

BIBLIOGRAPHY: Waidson, H., "The Near and the Far: The Writings of A. M.," *GL&L*, 28 (July 1975), 426–37; Ricker-Abderhalden, J., ed., *Über A. M.* (1979); Voris, R., *A. M.* (1984); Ricker-Abderhalden, J., "An Interview with A. M.," *StTCL*, 8, 2 (Spring 1984), 233–48; Ossar, M., "Das Unbehagen in der Kultur: Switzerland and China in A. M.'s *Baiyun*," in Acker, R., and M. Burkhard, eds., *Blick auf die Schweiz* (1987), 113–30

ROBERT ACKER

MUTIS, Alvaro

(pseud.: Alvar de Mattos) Colombian poet and novelist, b. 25 Aug. 1923, Bogotá

Although M. was born in Bogotá, his family is from the Tolima province of Colombia, and the landscape of this area is important to much of his work. M.'s father was a government official and diplomat, and M. attended elementary and secondary school in Brussels. Upon returning to Colombia, he attended secondary school in Bogotá

but never finished his studies. He took refuge in Mexico in 1956 because of a lawsuit brought against him in Colombia. In Mexico he was incarcerated for over a year in 1959–1960. He has resided in Mexico since 1956, and in 1989 he received the Aztec Eagle for his contributions to Latin American letters.

M.'s first book was a volume of poetry, *La balanza* (1948; the balance), written in collaboration with Carlos Patiño (dates n.a.). M. formed part of a group that has been called the *Mito* poets, after a magazine that published many of their works. The *Mito* poets did not break completely with the tradition of Colombian poetry (represented most immediately by the preceding *Piedra y Cielo* or Stone and Sky group), but they did break with much of the traditional rhetoric. In M.'s case, the widening of poetic horizons resulted from his early assimilation of French surrealism (q.v.).

The most salient feature of M.'s work, and the one that distinguishes it from that of other Colombian poets, is the presence of a character who acts as an authorial double. This character, Maqroll el Gaviero, appears in several poems of M.'s first two collections, and comes into his own in a series of poems, "Reseña de los hospitales de ultramar" (review of hospitals overseas), contained in his third volume, *Los trabajos perdidos* (1965; the lost works). The importance of Maqroll is firmly established by the title of M.'s collected poems, *Summa de Maqroll el Gaviero (1947–1970)* (1973; summa of Maqroll el Gaviero). Maqroll is an inveterate traveler marked by solitude and an outsider's view of common human experience. His obsessions (which are those of all of M.'s early poetry) include trains, coffee plantations, sea and river voyages, hospitals and illnesses, and lovers. This poetry is more narrative than most Latin American poetry, and it succeeds in recreating a world (a tropical landscape) much as would a novel. M. avoids strict meter in his poetry, but tends toward a Whitmanesque extension and to the prose poem. His fourth volume of poetry, *Caravansary* (1981; caravansary), also extends the biography of Maqroll, and is a mixture of poetry and prose.

Although avowedly apolitical, M. is enthralled with the spectacle of certain periods of monarchic rule. This is obvious in his more recent poetry, especially *Crónica regia y Alabanza del reino* (1985; royal chronicle and in praise of the kingdom). The first part of this volume explores different aspects of the life and legacy of King Philip II of Spain. The second section contains poems that reflect M.'s experiences in the Andalucía region of Spain. These poems, as well as those of *Un homenaje y siete nocturnos* (1986; an homage and seven nocturnes), make no mention of Maqroll and depart from the ahistorical melancholy of this character for a sense of spiritual completion.

M.'s early prose work, *Diario de Lecumberri* (1960; Lecumberri diary), is a series of testimonial pieces that reflect M.'s experiences while incarcerated in Mexico. The stories recount incidences of prison life and are written in straightforward prose laced with Mexicanisms. M.'s second extensive prose work is a novella, *La mansión de Araucaíma* (1973; Araucaíma mansion). Subtitled "Relato gótico de tierra caliente" (gothic story from the hot lands), the novella extends M.'s obsession with characters on the margins of society and returns to the tropical landscape of his poetry. The novella's short chapters read like prose poems, and the emphasis on the grotesque betrays M.'s attentive reading of the Spanish novelist and dramatist Ramón del Valle Inclán (q.v.).

M.'s more recent narrative centers on the protagonist of his early poetry, Maqroll el Gaviero. These novels are among his most mature works, and they add considerable depth to the character known only fragmentarily in the poetry. The machinations of plot are of little interest, as M. concentrates his lyrical energy on Maqroll's philosophical reveries. *La nieve del almirante* (1986; the admiral's snow) is particularly interesting as it contains a diary ostensibly written by Maqroll during a voyage up a large tropical river. This setting links the novel to a large body of Latin American travel literature extending from the chronicles of the Iberian conquistadors to many important modern novels.

M. has published a number of short stories of which "El último rostro" (1978; the last face) is of special import. Dealing with the last days in the life of Simón Bolívar, this story was used as a starting point by M.'s close friend Gabriel García Márquez (q.v.) for his novel *El general en su laberinto* (1989; *The General in His Labyrinth,* 1990).

M. is among the most gifted stylists in Latin America today. His poetry, linked to the best of the Colombian tradition, is of continental importance, distinguished by its exploration of the tropical landscape and its narrative depth. While M.'s reputation is based primarily on his poetry, his later novels, contemplative and complex, are written in exquisitely crafted prose.

FURTHER WORKS: *Los elementos del desastre* (1953); *Poemas* (1978); *Poesía y prosa* (1981); *La verdadera historia del flautista de Hammelin* (1982); *Los emisarios* (1984); *Abel Quezada, la comedia del arte* (1985, with Carlos Monsivais); *Historia natural de las cosas* (1985); *Obra literaria* (1985); *Sesenta cuerpos* (1985); *Ilona llega con la lluvia* (1987); *La muerte del estratega* (1988); *Tras las rutas de Maqroll el Gaviero: 1981–1988* (1988); *La última escala del tramp steamer* (1989); *Un bel morir* (1989); *Amirbar* (1990). FURTHER VOLUME IN ENGLISH: *Maqroll: Three Novellas* (1992)

BIBLIOGRAPHY: Barnechea, A., and J. M. Oviedo, "La historia como estética: entrevista con A. M.," in *Poesía y prosa* (1981), 576–97; Elzaguirre, L., "A. M. o la transitoriedad de la palabra poética," *Inti,* 18–19 (1983–1984), 83–105; Romero, A., "Los poetas de Mito," *RI,* 50 (1984), 689–755; Cobo Borda, J. G., "Dos poetas de Mito: A. M. y Fernando Charry Lara," *RI,* 51, 130–31 (Jan.–June 1985), 89–102; Garganigo, J. F., "Aproximaciones a la poesía de A. M.: un viaje inacabado a través del texto," *Revista de la Universidad Central,* 3, 23 (1985), 181–93; Sucre, G., *La máscara, la transparencia: Ensayos sobre poesía hispanoamericana,* rev. ed. (1985), 320–30; O'Hara, E., *"Los emisarios:* Respuestas que son preguntas," *RCLL,* 11, 24 (1986), 263–68; Jaramillo Zudvago, J. E., "El espacio en blanco, el envés de un dios, *Los elementos del desastre,"* in CELAM, eds., *Presencia de Dios en la poesía latinoamericana* (1988), 309–19

BEN A. HELLER

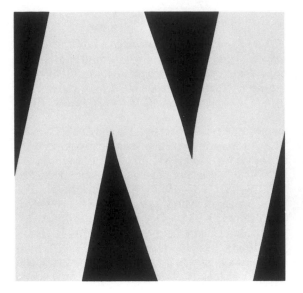

NÁDAS, Péter
Hungarian novelist, dramatist, and essayist, b. 14 Oct. 1942, Budapest

Considered an exquisitely refined intellectual writer, N. is actually one of the few novelists and dramatists of his generation without university training. He had intentions of becoming a chemist but dropped out of school and turned to photojournalism instead. During the late 1960s and early 1970s, N. worked as an editor, reader, and drama consultant, but soon thereafter became a self-supporting writer. In the early 1980s, he left Budapest and settled in Gombosszeg, a tiny village in southwestern Hungary.

N.'s first two volumes of short stories, *A biblia* (1967; the Bible) and *Kulcskereső játék* (1969; finding the key—a game), are almost wholly retrospective, dealing with children's perspectives of the grim early 1950s in Hungary. What makes these often autobiographically inspired stories particularly tense and ironic is that the young protagonists in question are the privileged children of powerful communist officials. N.'s own father had been a high-ranking party functionary. With great sensitivity and finesse N. depicts these children's easy identification with the values of the "new class," but he also suggests early stirrings of moral awareness.

In *Egy családregény vége* (1977; the end of a family novel), his first mature work of fiction, the author again assumes the point of view of a child growing up in Stalinist Hungary. Here the father is a dour and fanatical state-security officer who falls victim himself to one of the purges of the time. However, *Egy családregény vége* is much more than a political novel. By his own admission N. is attracted to the kind of literature that fuses "historical fact and fancy, myth, intuition, physicality and intellectuality." Thus, the shabby real-

ity of daily life in a police state is transfigured in the child-hero's mind into thrilling suspense stories, and the boy's grandfather, an even more seductive spinner of tales, regales his grandson with fascinating and often bizarre stories about their Jewish ancestors, tracing the family back to biblical times. Indeed this "family novel," until its sudden and strangely inconclusive end, becomes a capsule history of the Jewish people.

In his second monumental novel, *Emlékiratok könyve* (1986; book of memoirs), N. remains faithful to the confessional mode and once more weaves a very intricate yarn. But like some of the extravagant postmodern fabulists, he is more interested in subtle narrative and thematic correspondences, recurrences, and even subtler stylistic parodies than in the stories themselves. The novel alternates between the recollections of a young Hungarian writer finding himself passionately in love with another man, a German poet, in East Berlin, and the memoirs of a character of his own creation, an overrefined, turn-of-the-century aesthete. There is a third voice, toward the end of the novel: that of the narrator's childhood friend who, after the protagonist's return to his homeland and death several years later, concludes the memoir by describing his friend's last years, offering his own, seemingly far more objective and matter-of-fact version of their friendship.

A penetrating, analytical writer, N. is also a creator of elaborately literary prose. In highly cerebral essays and meditations, collected in *Játéktér* (1988; playing field) and *Égi és földi szerelem* (1991; heavenly and earthly love), or in more openly autobiographical reminiscences—*Évkönyv* (1989; yearbook)—he is just as likely to sketch out character, unravel motives, resort to myth and parable as he is in his fiction. His dramas, on the other hand, are stylistically more austere, narratively more static. He has written three plays—*Takarítás* (1977; housecleaning), *Találkozás* (1979; Encounter, 1988), *Temetés* (1980; funeral)—and all three are virtually plotless rituals of initiation and purification.

Yet even in his most stylized and abstract pieces N. remains a probing, sympathetic intellectual who longs for synthesis and harmony, a fusion of immanence and transcendence, of "heavenly and earthly love." Actually, human sexuality is a particularly important concern, including unconventional forms of sexuality, which are also seen as attempts to merge opposites.

In the past two decades N. has turned from promising innovator to a recognized master of Hungarian prose. Moreover, *Emlékiratok könyve,* which has been or is being translated into a number of languages, established him as a major central European literary figure.

FURTHER WORKS: *Leírás* (1979); *Nézőtér* (1983)

BIBLIOGRAPHY: Sanders, I., on *Egy családregény vége, WLT,* 52, 3 (Summer 1978), 496; Szegedy-Maszák, M., "P. N.," *The Hungarian P.E.N.,* 27 (1986), 44–45; Sanders, I., on *Emlékiratok könyve, WLT,* 61, 2 (Spring 1987), 322–23

IVAN SANDERS

NAGIBIN, Yury Markovich

Russian short-story writer, b. 3 Apr. 1920, Moscow

Perhaps the most distinguished contemporary Russian short-story writer, N. has also made his mark as an essayist and screenwriter. He grew up in a family of the Moscow intelligentsia and came by his love of literature early. After training at the Institute of Cinematography, he volunteered for service at the front during World War II and suffered a concussion in battle. He then worked as a war correspondent until 1945. For the next few years, he covered farm and village life for a newspaper. Several of these writings led to screenplays. By the mid-1950s, N. was looked on as one of the most promising young Russian writers. Since then, he has published in virtually every Soviet literary journal. He has traveled widely abroad, appeared frequently on Soviet television, and become one of the most prominent and widely published Soviet writers.

Despite N.'s many essays, reviews, and screenplays, it is as a short-story writer that he is best known. He has dealt with a wide range of subjects: war, children, sports, hunting and fishing, village life, art, life abroad, love, and historical personalities. N. began publishing at the outbreak of World War II, and the tone of his war stories is in keeping with the mood of the times. They are thoroughly patriotic, but suggest in their style and craftsmanship that their author is gifted. Much the same can be said about his stories of farm and village life in the late 1940s.

N. has said that the main theme of his stories is that of awakening, discovery: There turns out to be more to a person than one has thought; one sees into a person or thing as one has not seen before; appearances are deceptive, and one should not accept life at face value. This theme is present but less apparent in N.'s early stories about war and reconstruction. It was not until the 1950s that he hit his stride. Stories such as "Zimnii dub" (1953; "Winter Oak," 1955) and "Komarov" (1953; "Komarov," 1955) show his facility in portraying children. *Chistye prudy* (1962; Clear Ponds) and other collections are devoted largely to N.'s poignant memories of his youth. Stories

about sports recall his days as a promising athlete. And stories about hunting and fishing, such as those in *Pogonya, Meshcheriskie byli* (1964; the chase, Meshchera stories), are made up largely of the vivid descriptions N. is noted for. Much of N.'s fiction treats love affairs, as in "Olezhka zhenilsya" (1965; "Olezhka Got Married," 1979), and marriage, as in "Il'in den' " (1972; "Elijah's Day," 1979).

N. remarked that until 1960 he took all his stories from life, from what he had seen and heard, and that it was not until "Ekho" (1960; "Echo," 1961) that he relied on imagination. Since then, his imagination has come more and more into play, and his stories on historical figures are among his richest. Starting with "Kak byl kuplen les" (1972; "A Deal in Timber," 1982), N. has published fictional biographies of the Russian writers Avvakum Petrovich (1620 [or 1621]–1682), Vasily Kirillovich Trediakovsky (1703–1768), Aleksandr Sergeevich Pushkin (1799–1837), Anton Antonovich Delvig (1798–1831), Fedor Ivanovich Tyutchev (1803–1873), Apollon Aleksandrovich Grigorev (1822–1864), Afanasy Afanasevich Fet (Shenshin) (1820–1892), Nikolay Semenovich Leskov (1831–1895), Ivan Alekseevich Bunin, and Innokenty Fedorovich Annensky (qq.v.), as well as Christopher Marlowe, Stanislav Przybyszewski, August Strindberg, and Ernest Hemingway (qq.v.) and the composers Tchaikovsky, Rachmaninoff, and Bach. Many of these are included in the collection *Ostrov liubvi* (1977; *Island of Love,* 1982). The motif that runs through them all is that art calls for great sacrifices. Although the stories are based on the factual lives of personages, N. mixes fact with fiction. As a rule, the story takes place on a single day when the main character is moved to reflect on his life in an interior monologue and make a discovery. The language recalls the idiom of the period in question. The central theme or discovery is that the world of artists is quite different from that of others. It is hard for the two worlds to understand each other, but civilization needs both. In writing about artists who were not adequately recognized, N. does not overlook their shortcomings or the strengths of those who opposed them.

Although N. has written as independently as one could in the Soviet Union without being silenced, he has spoken up even more since 1985. His moving recollections of a boy in his largely autobiographical "Vstan' i idi" (1987; "Stand Up and Walk," 1988) throw a new light on his earlier memories of childhood. Other recent fiction has taken a caustic, satirical turn.

Despite N.'s stature and popularity at home, he has received less attention abroad than a number of other Soviet writers. There are several reasons.

He has not made news—he has not been arrested, officially reprimanded, or exiled. By and large, he has chosen to write about the eternal rather than about ephemeral topics of the day. And the forms that come naturally to him are the short story and the *povest'* (tale or novella), whereas the foreign audience may prefer novels.

N. has won many readers with his artistry and breadth. He is unusually skilled as a stylist and craftsman and is perhaps more aware of literary tradition than any other contemporary Russian writer. His eye for detail and the strength of his epiphanies are exceptional. And perhaps no other recent Russian writer has written about so many different subjects. N. has gradually become a spokesman for the Russian intelligentsia and for its permanence amid shifting ideologies.

FURTHER WORKS: *Chelovek s fronta* (1943); *Bol'shoe serdtse* (1944); *Dve sily* (1944); *Zerno zhizni* (1948); *Gosudarstvennoe delo* (1950); *Gospodstvuiushchaia vysota* (1951); *Partiinoe poruchenie* (1951); *Rasskazy* (1953); *Trubka* (1953); *Vsegda v stroiu* (1953); *Rasskazy o voine* (1954); *Mal'chiki* (1955); *Rasskazy* (1955); *Skalistyi porog* (1955); *Zimnii dub* (1955); *Na ozerax* (1957); *Rasskazy* (1957); *Boi za vysotu* (1958); *Chelovek i doroga* (1958); *Na ozere Velikom* (1958); *Skalistyi porog* (1958); *Poslednii shturm* (1959); *Pered prazdnikom* (1960); *Druz'ia moi liudi* (1961); *Rannei vesnoi* (1961); *Ekho* (1964); *Razmyshleniia o rasskaze* (1964); *Dalekoe i blizkoe* (1965); *Na tikhom ozere i drugie rasskazy* (1966); *Nochnoi gost'* (1966); *Zelenaia ptitsa s krasnoi golovoi* (1966); *Ne dai emu pogibnut'* (1968); *Chuzhoe serdtse* (1969); *Perekur* (1970); *Zabroshennaia doroga* (1970); *Pereulki moego detstva* (1971); *Nepobedimyi Arsenov* (1972); *Izbrannye proizvedeniia* (1973); *Moia Afrika* (1973); *Ty budesh' zhit'* (1974); *V aprel'skom lesu* (1974); *Pik udachi* (1975); *Literaturnye razdum'ia* (1977); *Berendeev les* (1978); *Rasskazy o Gagarine* (1978); *Zabroshennaia doroga* (1978); *Odin na odin* (1979); *Tsarskosel'skoe utro* (1979); *Zamolchavshaia vensa* (1979); *Sobranie sochinenii v 4-kh tt.* (1980); *Nauka dal'nikh stranstvii* (1982); *Ne chuzhoe remeslo* (1983); *Moskovskaia kniga* (1985); *Lunnyi svet* (1986); *Muzykanty* (1986); *Pushkin na iuge* (1986); *Moskva . . . kak mnogo v etom zvuke* (1987); *Poezdka na ostrova* (1987); *Sovetskie pisateli, stranitsy tvorchestva* (1987); *Chelovek s fronta* (1988); *Ispytanie* (1988); *Vdali muzyka i ogni* (1989); *Vstan' i idi* (1989). FURTHER VOLUMES IN ENGLISH: *Each for All* (1945); *Dreams* (1955); *Trubka* (1955); *Dreams* (1958); *The Pipe* (n.d., 1958?); *Selected Short Stories* (1963); *The Peak of Success, and Other Stories* (1986); *Unwritten Story by Somerset Maugham* (1988)

BIBLIOGRAPHY: Hager, R., "Die Evolution des literarischen Menschenbildes im Erzählschaffen Sergej Antonovs, Jurij Nagibins und Vladimir Tendrjakovs der 50-er Jahre," *ZS*, 20 (1975), 214–25; Porter, R. N., "The Uneven Talent of Jurij N.," *RLJ*, 32, 113 (1978), 103–13; Porter, R. N., "Jurij N.'s 'Istoricheskie rasskazy,' " *RLJ*, 34, 118 (1980), 127–35; Schefski, H. K., "Y. N.: Children and the Retreat from Collective Identity," *SSR*, 4 (Spring 1985), 99–106; Sampson, E. D., "The Poacher and the Polluter: The Environmental Theme in N.," in Connolly, J. W., and S. I. Ketchian, eds., *Studies in Russian Literature in Honor of Vsevolod Setchkarev* (1986), 222–32; Goscilo, H., "Introduction," and Cochrum, E., "Biography," in Goscilo, H., ed., *The Peak of Success, and Other Stories* (1986), 9–26, 27–33

RICHARD N. PORTER

NARANJO, Carmen

Costa Rican poet, novelist, short-story writer, and essayist, b. 1931, Cartago

N. is one of the most distinguished and best-known Costa Rican writers and public figures of the 20th c. The first of her books of poetry was published in 1961, but she soon became more acclaimed for her innovative prose. *Los perros no ladraron* (1966; the dogs did not bark) received the Costa Rican National Aquileo Echeverría Prize in 1966; *Camino al mediodia* (1968; on the way to noon) and *Responso por el niño Juan Manuel* (1971; requiem for the boy Juan Manuel) won the Central American Floral Games in 1967 and 1968, respectively; *Hoy es un largo día* (1974; today is a long day) was awarded the Editorial Costa Rica Prize; *Diario de una multitud* (1974; diary of a multitude) received the EDUCA Prize in 1974; and *Ondina* (1985; Ondina) won the EDUCA Prize in 1982. N. has also pursued a successful career in public administration, serving in both national and international organizations: in the Costa Rican Social Security System, as ambassador to India (1972–1974), as minister of culture, youth, and sport (1974–1976), and as Costa Rica's UNICEF representative in Guatemala and Mexico (1978–1982). In 1982 she became director of the Museum of Costa Rican Art, and since 1984 she has headed the Central American University Publishing House.

N.'s fiction and poetry reflect her double life as an administrator and as a writer. She writes of the inner workings of the bureaucratic system, and of the spiritual resources of the human beings who live in this materialistic society, numbed by daily routines. *Los perros no ladraron* depicts one day in the life of a middle-level bureaucrat who becomes aware of the extent to which he is trapped in the system. *Memorias de un hombre palabra* (1968; memories of a word man), like the essays of *Cinco temas en busca de un pensador* (1977; five themes in search of a thinker), explores the paralyzing fatalism, passivity, and other negative emotional states that are reactions to conventional society.

N.'s interest in women characters is apparent in all of her books. In *Sobrepunto* (1985; overpoint), the central character is a woman who struggles to define her identity. As in previous novels, N. explores the roles women play in Latin American society and analyzes the extent to which women are free to control their own destinies.

Another topic of recurrent concern to N. in her poems and in her fiction is the role of marginalized people. Both *Diario de una multitud* and *Homenaje a don Nadie* (1981; homage to Mr. Nobody) speak of all human beings as vulnerable to emotional and social deprivation: Anyone can become a Nobody, unloved, ignored, and unrecognized, even those who appear to have successful community identities. This is related to N.'s frequently expressed (especially in *Diario de una multitud* and *Sobrepunto*) anxiety that public images of Costa Rica as an exemplary democracy may lead to insufficient concern for the poor and underprivileged.

Ondina, Nunca hubo alguna vez (1984; once upon never), and *Mi guerrilla* (1984; my guerilla) emphasize the need to recognize the ambiguity and complexity of Latin American reality, which may best be described in bizarre and surreal imaginative metaphors. *Responso por el niño Juan Manuel,* too, stresses the role of imagination in interpreting reality. However, N. does not suggest that there are magical or mystical solutions to the problems she discusses in her fiction and poetry.

Both in her public career and in her writing, N. has emphasized concern for individual human beings. Her poetry and her fiction celebrate the human capacity for love, hate, compassion, imagination, and occasional heroism. Increasingly, N. is recognized as a major voice in 20th-c. Latin American literature.

FURTHER WORKS: *América* (1961); *Canción de la ternura* (1964); *Hacia tu isla* (1966); *Misa a oscuras* (1967); *Idioma de invierno* (1972); *Por las páginas de la Biblia y los caminos de Israel* (1976); *Cultura* (1978); *Estancias y días* (1985). FURTHER VOLUME IN ENGLISH: *Five Women Writers of Costa Rica: N., Odio, Oreamuno, Urbano, Vallbona* (1978)

BIBLIOGRAPHY: Cruz Burdiel de López, M., "Estudio de tres cuentos de C. N.," *Káñina,* 41 (1975), 101–10; Urbano, V., "C. N. y su voz plena en *Canción de la ternura,*" *Káñina,* 1, 2 (1977), 5–31; Arizpe, L., "Interview with C. N.: Women and Latin American Literature," *Signs,* 5, 1 (1979), 98–110; Minc, R., and T. Méndez-Faith, "Conversando con C. N.," *RI,* 51, 132–33 (July–Dec. 1985), 507–10; Martínez, L. I., *C. N. y la narrativa femenina en Costa Rica* (1987); Picón Garfield, E., "La luminosa ceguera de sus días: Los cuentos 'humanos' de C. N.," *RI,* 53, 138–39 (Jan.–June 1987), 287–301; Rubio, P., "C. N.," in Marting, D. E., ed., *Spanish American Women Writers* (1990), 350–59

MARY G. BERG

NASTASIJEVIĆ, Momčilo

Serbian poet, short-story writer, and dramatist, b. 6 Oct. 1894, Gornji Milanovac; d. 13 Feb. 1938, Belgrade, Yugoslavia (now Serbia)

N. was one of the most original and innovative writers in Serbian literature between the two world wars. Born in Gornji Milanovac, he became a high school teacher and spent most of his life in that capacity in Belgrade, where he died in 1938. He was also an accomplished violin player.

N. started out as a short-story writer and dramatist, but later turned more toward poetry. His collection of short stories, *Iz tamnog vilajeta* (1927; from the dark province), drew immediate attention to the critics for N.'s unusual approach to reality and his unique utilization of the language. His best play, *Medjuluško blago* (1927; the treasure of Medjulug), showed similar tendencies. But it was in poetry that he achieved his full potential. Between his first collection, *Pet lirskih krugova* (1932; five lyric cycles), and his last, *Pesme* (1938; poems), lies a brief but intensive creative period. There are two posthumous collections as well, *Rane pesme i varijante* (1939; early poems and variants) and *Sedam lirskih krugova* (1962; seven lyric cycles).

N. is perhaps the most enigmatic of Serbian poets. He developed independently of literary groups and movements, always endeavoring to create his own idiom. His unique style is characterized by extremely concise, ascetic, archaic, and often cryptic expressions, by which he enriched the modern language and tried to fathom the spiritual and religious character of his people. He drew heavily from folklore and the distant past, as well as from his deeply religious, even mystical outlook on life. He was often preoccupied with metaphysical and moral questions, which he tried to resolve through his own highly individualistic and hermetic art. As a poet, he remained a loner, understood and admired at first mainly by his closest friends. Lately, however, he has begun to exert considerable influence on younger Serbian poets and to be studied extensively by critics.

BIBLIOGRAPHY: Petrov, A., "Orphean Inspiration in Recent Serbian Poetry," *Literary Quarterly*, 2 (1966), 159–70; Kragujević, T., *Mitsko u N. delu* (1976); Milosavljević, P., *Poetika M. N.* (1978); Goy, E. D., "The Cycle 'Večernje' from the *Pet lirskih krugova* by M. N.," *Serbian Studies*, 1, 3 (1981), 31–49; Goy, E. D., "The Cycle 'Jutarnje' from the *Pet lirskih krugova* by M. N.," *Southeastern Europe*, 9, 1–2 (1982), 53–69; Goy, E. D., "The Cycle 'Bdenja' from the *Pet lirskih krugova* of M. N.," *Serbian Studies*, 4, 1–2 (1987), 29–51; Goy, E. D., "M. N.'s 'Gluhote' and 'Reči u kamenu,' " *SSR*, 8 (Spring 1987), 40–55; Vladiv, S. M., "The 'Lyrical Drama' of M. N.: Problems of Poetics and Translation," *NZSJ*, 1 (1988), 51–66

VASA D. MIHAILOVICH

NECATİGİL, Behçet

Turkish poet and translator, b. 16 Apr. 1916, Istanbul; d. 13 Dec. 1979, Istanbul

N. is one of Turkey's most highly esteemed poets. His life, which he spent almost entirely in Istanbul, was uneventful. After graduating from the Istanbul College for Teachers, he became a teacher of Turkish literature, briefly serving at the Kars Lycée, followed by many years at Istanbul's Kabataş Lycée and the Institute for Education, until his retirement in 1972. He enjoyed fame as a teacher of literature. Many of his students became major writers.

N.'s poetic career was devoted, as he observed, "to the private experiences of a citizen of median income from birth to death, to his real and imagined life in the triangle of home–family–close relations." Although he concentrated on daily living and ordinary subjects, his aesthetics emphasized formal innovation and an unusual style. Most critics characterize him as a consistent poet with a predictable world of his own. His unconventional use of the Turkish language, especially in his later work, occasionally made him difficult to understand and inaccessible. Nonetheless, his reputation as a major modern poet has remained high since the 1950s. His complete works, *Bütün eserleri*, published in seven volumes in the 1980s, continue to enjoy estimable sales. After his death, his family established the N. Poetry Prize, which has been awarded annually since 1980.

A leading writer of radio plays, N. collected them in four volumes, *Yıldızlara bakmak* (1965; stargazing), *Gece aşevi* (1967; night diner), *Üç turunçlar* (1970; three bitter oranges), and *Pencere*

(1975; window). Among his contributions are *Edebiyatımızda İsimler Sözlüğü* (1960; who's who in Turkish literature)—which he saw through many editions and which has been updated several times since his death—and *Edebiyatımızda Eserler Sözlüğü* (1979; guide to literary works), which contains the synopses of 750 novels, short-story collections, and plays by 220 Turkish writers. He also compiled a small dictionary of mythology. A selection of his essays and other prose pieces were collected in *Bile/Yazdı* (1979; even/wrote). He translated more than twenty books, including works by Heinrich Heine (1797–1856), Knut Hamsun, Miguel de Unamuno, and Heinrich Böll (qq.v.). The poems he translated were posthumously collected in a volume entitled *Yalnızlık bir yağmura benzer* (1984; loneliness resembles the rain).

In a poetic career that spanned four and a half decades beginning with the publication of his first poem in the influential journal *Varlık* in 1935, N. remained staunchly independent, shunning the literary schools and movements of his time. From the outset he turned a cold shoulder to the sentimental romanticism of his predecessors and most of his contemporaries. His first collection, *Kapalı Çarşı* (1945; grand bazaar), explores the life of the man in the street in a matter-of-fact and engaging style. His books that came out in quick succession in the 1950s—*Çevre* (1951; environment), *Evler* (1953; houses), *Eski toprak* (1956; old soil), and *Arada* (1958; in between)—refined this aesthetic approach in depicting the minutiae of ordinary life in objective terms, although the poet was able to augment his simple, direct statements with subjective symbols and asides.

Dar Çağ (1960; narrow age) marked a turning point: N. began to experiment with a new kind of poetry of intellectual search and abstract formulations. *Yaz dönemi* (1963; summer term) is a prismlike collection in which N. creates a brave new world of discovered and invented relationships. In some ways similar to Wallace Stevens (q.v.), N. appeared to marshal his creative energy to transforming visions and revisions of reality in the quest for higher meanings.

With *Divançe* (1963; little divan) N. returned briefly to the quintessence of classical Ottoman verse, whose hallmarks were abstract conceits, pure imagery, and a dominant euphony. Here N. not only captures the aesthetic values of his esoteric classical heritage but also succeeds in modernizing it and putting on it his own individualistic imprint. His later books, *İki başına yürümek* (1968; twosome solitary walk), *En/Cam* (1970; out/come), *Zebra* (1973; zebra), and *Kareler aklar* (1975; squares and whites), are indefatigable quests for paradoxical relationships between objects, actions, emotions, and concepts. In these collections, N.

forged new configurations of shapes and juxtaposed time and appearances into subjective formulations of what he saw or imagined. The syntax is sometimes dismembered, with phrases clipped and words employed out of context. Each poem, however, has a surface repose and a symmetry, proving that N. was one of Turkey's most meticulous practitioners of the poetic art.

In 1976 he published his selected poems, *Sevgilerde* (in loves), from the period 1935–1965. The culmination of his later work appeared in two collections, *Beyler* (1978; messieurs) and *Söyleriz* (1980; we shall tell), where his cubistic approach and formal purity were crowned by a much richer vocabulary. The eventual synthesis worked out by this superior craftsman is, in some ways, reminiscent of Paul Valéry (q.v.). Few Turkish poets have ever offered deeper insights into living experiences, into enigmas, into the life of the imagination with any comparable combination of intellectual complexity and smooth lyricism.

BIBLIOGRAPHY: Pazarkaya, Y., *B. N.: Gedichte* (1972)

TALAT SAIT HALMAN

NGUYỄN TUÂN

(pseud. Nhất Lang) Vietnamese essayist, short-story and novella writer, literary critic, and translator, b. 10 July 1910, Hanoi; d. 28 July 1990, Hanoi

N. T. started writing in 1938 for several Hanoi newspapers and magazines such as *Tiểu-thuyết thư bảy, Tao-đàn, Hà-nội Tân-văn,* and *Trung-Bắc Chủ-nhật.* His most successful work was *Vang bóng một thời* (1940; echoes of a past era), in which like the artist of an ancient painting N. T. recreated the picture of traditional life in Vietnam, a well designed picture presented in eleven vignettes, each with its own features and colors. Through ''Những chiếc ấm đất'' (terra-cotta kettles), ''Chén trà trong sương sớm'' (a cup of tea in early dew), ''Một cảnh thu muộn'' (late autumn), and other stories in this volume, the reader perceives the leisurely peaceful Vietnamese way of life, the simple and confident life-style of a Confucianist and Taoist society, represented by the laureates of literary examinations who indulged in orchid collecting, chrysanthemum planting, and alcohol drinking. The first essay, for example, is about two tea addicts, one of whom is an old beggar, like his companion drinker a real connoisseur of the art of tea brewing. *Tuỳ bút* (1941; essays) can be considered as ''echoes of the present era'': N. T. laid bare his cynicism, whether he wrote about the air-raid siren, about life in

Thanh-hoá, about his native town, about a wife expecting to give birth to twins, or about a Buddhist monk not quite detached from earthly life.

In the serialized novel *Thiếu quê-hương* (1943; lacking a native land) a restless young man feels the urge to travel constantly, just like N. T. himself. Indeed he confesses his own hereditary peripateticism in his travelogue *Một chuyến đi* (1941; a journey); in this essay N. T. shows that he simply wishes to move on and on without interruption, but the stop in Hongkong, where he took part in moviemaking, was described in humorous details—when a friend had to go to pass water in a famous hotel but showed more concern for the tip expected by the attendant, or when the Chinese music in the adjoining room made him down three cups of strong alcohol. *Nhà bác Nguyễn* (1940; Nguyen's house), as a short novel, presents charming sketches of typically Vietnamese life in a suburb, on a train, in the streets, and the like. But N. T. most excels in relating his trips to geisha houses and to opium dens: In *Chiếc lư đồng mắt cua* (1941; the copper incense burner) he depicts Thông Phu, a proud chess champion who runs a geisha house and whose heart attack, which he suffered when he lost a game, left him paralyzed and bedridden, and Bao, a Hanoi rake who took a geisha as his concubine. *Ngọn đèn dầu lạc* (1941; the peanut-oil lamp) is a two-part reportage on opium smokers, filthy and cynical characters pushed into inveterate lying, selfish behavior, and extortions just to satisfy their toxic habit.

N. T.'s remarkable talent was even more clearly shown after he had joined the ranks of resistance fighters in the anti-French war (1946–1954). After 1945 he abandoned his hedonistic and arrogant individualism as well as certain negative, doubtful literary tendencies. Both in *Đường vui* (1949; fun road) and in *Tình chiến-dịch* (1950; campaign sentiment) he related his experience in traveling with the troops, an opportunity for him to express his hatred for the enemy and his love for his people.

Between the late 1950s and the 1960s, his writings kept praising the beauty of his motherland—as he had already started doing in *Sông Đà* (1960; Da River)—and singing the unity of north and south in the anti-U.S. struggle: His essays assumed a clearly anti-American thrust. After being half jocular, half blasé—a mixture of cynicism and melancholic frustration—to help readers relive the past glory of a tranquil and complacent intellectual Vietnam of yore, N. T.'s style after 1945 had turned more positive in describing the exciting days of the anti-U.S. war ''for national salvation'' or the guerilla fighters in South Vietnam. N. T. was undeniably a master in the use of his native tongue, whose cadence and rhythm amidst lyric expansiveness he knew how to fully exploit. He qualifies as the greatest essayist in Vietnamese literature.

FURTHER WORKS: *Tóc chị Hoài* (1943); *Nguyễn* (1945); *Chùa Đàn* (1946); *Thắng càn* (1953); *Bút-ký đi thăm Trung-Hoa* (1955); *Tuỳ-bút kháng-chiến và hoà-bình* (2 vols., 1955, 1956); *Hà-nội ta đánh Mỹ giỏi* (1972); *Ký* (1976); *Tuyển-tập Nguyễn Tuân* (1981–1982)

BIBLIOGRAPHY: Xuân-Bào Bùi, *Le roman vietnamien contemporain* (1972), 269, 345–57; Nguyễn-Trần Huan, "The Literature of Vietnam, 1954–1973," in Tham Seong Chee, ed., *Essays on Literature and Society in Southeast Asia* (1981), 333–34; Huỳnh Sanh Thông, "Main Trends of Vietnamese Literature between the Two World Wars," *The Vietnam Forum,* 3 (Winter–Spring 1984), 99–125; Durand, M. M., and Nguyễn-Trần Huân, *An Introduction to Vietnamese Literature* (1985), passim

DINH-HOA NGUYEN

NIGERIAN LITERATURE

See Volume 3, page 389.

Because war is such a dramatic action that provides for easy historical periodizations, it is now habitual to see the Nigerian Civil War (1967–1970) as a turning point in the short history of modern Nigerian literature in English. That war duly brought about its own literature, but it produced no new social or political beginnings, and, if at all it started as a revolutionary war, it ended in victory for the forces of reaction that were to be found on both sides, and which came together more formidably than before.

The oil boom of the 1970s magnified all the social, moral, and economic wantonness of the prewar years, festering an unreal middle class whose ethics was consumerism, not productivity. The military sat tight in government and occupied its time building monuments to illusions of prosperity. More than the Civil War, it is this culture of collective self-abandon that forms the social action against which Nigerian literature since then has in several ways been a long reaction.

New and younger writers emerged to criticize the dissolute national life, and to reject what they perceived as the misplaced commitment of the earlier writers—Chinua Achebe, Wole Soyinka, Christopher Okigbo, J. P. Clark (qq.v.)—who had started the modern literary tradition.

Nigerian literature since the late 1970s has been characterized by reevaluations, rewritings and re-

definitions of the writer himself and his social role, of the matter to write about and its manner, and of the writer's relationship with his audience. The new writer is thus no longer one seeking aesthetic affects and spiritual values, but one striving to make his work have social effects. The older writers still dominate the scene, but such is the changed social environment that they too have somewhat modified their aesthetic stands.

Social expansion in Nigeria in the last two decades has been phenomenal, and so has literature; indeed, the 1980s might later come to be seen as the beginning of another literary renaissance. The prominent features of this expansion are a growth of the reading public brought about by the astronomical increase in the 1970s of schools and school populations, followed by a mushrooming of universities in which departments of English are usually quite large; the growth of a local publishing industry to provide both educational and leisure-reading materials for the ever-increasing literature populations; and the rapid expansion of the newspaper industry, especially in the early 1980s, manned in the main by academics and intellectuals who see a natural affinity between journalism and creative writing.

Before 1970, there were five universities in the country, four of them situated in the southern parts. Twenty years later the number has risen to more than twenty, with about eight in the northern parts. From its beginning to the present, modern Nigerian literature has remained tied to the universities. Thus, the expansion and spread of these institutions has meant the establishment of more potential centres of literary activity. The growth of an indigenous publishing industry has had two important effects on literature: easier access to publication by all and encouragement of new authors (the Association of Nigerian Authors has also played a prominent role in this); and the growth of popular literature side by side with the steady development of the elitist one. The newspapers have also played a major role by offering employment to needy young writers and by creating arts and culture pages where old and new works are regularly reviewed and talked about. What all this has meant is an outward and downward expansion in modern Nigerian literature—a making available of serious literature beyond academic journals, beyond its traditional home in the universities. To these trends may be added one other significant development: the rise of female writers in all three genres. Thus, the new aesthetic of social engagement, the situation of women, plus the call for a transethnic or "national" literature all combine to make current Nigerian literature a literature of issues.

Poetry

Poetry has taken the lead in the literary efflorescence. There are new and original ideas about the nature, function, and form of poetry, which also inform the practice; older poets have been challenged by younger ones, male and female; and such is poetry's popularity that there are now three living generations of poets in Nigeria.

Wole Soyinka, awarded the Nobel Prize for literature in 1986, followed up his 1976 one-poem volume *Ogun Abibiman* with *Mandela's Earth and Other Poems* (1988). In the latter, Soyinka continues his incipient concern with continental-racial emancipation by devoting the first section to the South African struggle centered around Nelson Mandela, then a Prometheus figure chained to the rocks of Robben Island. There is another section on the perennial evil of "cannibal leadership" in Africa. The two volumes are doubly political: They treat political subjects and the poet's revival of the idioms and styles of oral political poetry is an act of renewing and passing on, in usable form, an inherited tradition.

Also quite political is J. P. Clark-Bekederemo's (formerly J. P. Clark) *State of the Union* (1985), a collection in which the poet shrugs off his earlier aloofness and equanimity, to make direct and committed statements.

The descent by poets from the metaphysical, twilight zones of gods and myths to the lower, broader plain of history and mortals is most emphatic in the second generation of poets. These younger poets, who started being heard in the early 1980s, consider that broader plain where nothing is hidden and everything is material as the proper dwelling place of poetry. These poets are concentrated around the old universities at Ibadan and Nsukka; the Ibadan group is however the more successful. Its most important members are Niyi Osundare (b. 1947), Odia Ofeimun (b. 1950), and Tanure Ojaide (b. 1948).

An intellectual and university teacher of peasant background, Osundare had his higher education at Ibadan, Leeds, and Canada. He is a declared socialist, is uneasy in the elitist culture that the university institution in Nigeria has spawned, and is perpetually at war with the preceding poetic. Emotional and intellectual commitment to the peasantry and urban proletariat, clarity of expression, and the borrowing of folk idioms and saws constitute his poetic. His *The Eye of the Earth* (1986) was a joint winner of the Commonwealth Poetry Prize in 1986, and his *Waiting Laughters* (1990) won the Noma Award for 1991. *Moonsongs* (1988) is a collection of highly lyrical verse on a very intense mystical experience. In spite of his political aesthetic, Osundare is an artist who is very much concerned with the craft of poetry; in his poetry one can discern a great struggle to find English equivalents for the ample cadences of the music of his very tonal Yoruba language, with the verbal technology of orality meeting and diffusing with the "restructured consciousness" of literacy.

Ofeimun is also of peasant background and a socialist. Ofeimun is a restless man; he has been a teacher, a postgraduate student of political science, a private secretary to a major politician, and a journalist. In his two volumes to date—*The Poet Lied* (1980) and *A Handle for the Flutist* (1986)— Ofeimun does not consciously address the proletariat; instead, he has developed a muscular poetic idiom of hard-hitting tropes inspired by marxist historicism. Ofeimun's poetry succeeds in its efforts to be "national"; it is intellectual poetry of substantial individual talent, but it lacks reverberations and echoes in any particular tradition.

Ojaide is also a university teacher and critic. He is a quiet worker who has produced six volumes of verse so far; the first, *Children of Iroko,* was published in 1973. He is very sensitive to the cultural contradictions inherent in the office of the literary poet in a prevalently oral society, and how to overcome such conflicts has been a major burden of his poetry. His *Labyrinths of the Delta* (1986) gathers up all these themes and articulates them in a most economic manner. He has a strong but quiet voice; the conflicts he writes about are personalized, thus revealing the psychological dimensions attendant on the conflicts between politics and poetic imagination.

Molara Ogundipe-Leslie (b. 1940) is the most important female poet so far, though she has published only one slim volume, *Sew the Old Days and Other Poems* (1985). She graduated with honors in English at Ibadan in 1963, is vastly read, and has taught for several years at Ibadan. Ogundipe-Leslie has a mastery of tone, form, and language that shows evidence of long practice. In her poetry, militant feminism is expressed with deceptive simplicity and ease. She is thoroughly steeped in her Yoruba oral tradition and in western and oriental (haiku) traditions of poetry. In fact she tries to develop a new form, *Fìrí* ("eye-flash poem") based on haiku and imagism (q.v.). Ogundipe-Leslie possesses a freshness of vision that disturbs male-gender ways; she is introspective, playful, and ironic, and reminds one most of Emily Dickinson.

Drama

While Nigerian theater is still dominated by the now titanic figure of Soyinka, there have been significant developments in recent years: Attempts have been made to extend the modern theater in Nigeria beyond the universities; private theater companies now exist; two younger dramatists have firmly established their own names; the lone female dramatist of the 1970s, Zulu Sofola (b. 1935), has been joined by another, Tess Onwueme (b. 1954).

Soyinka's plays of the 1980s are *Opera Wonyosi* (1980), *A Play of Giants* (1984), and *Requiem for a Futurologist* (1985), but his *The Road* and *Death and the King's Horseman* have seen revivals on the stage, while the Jero plays continue to be popular. *Opera Wonyosi, A Play of Giants,* and *Requiem* are comic satires, again on the type and moral quality of leaderships in Africa. *A Play of Giants* is a particularly lively and humor-laden piece, although the reader-spectator must remember to separate the illusion on the stage from the horrific reality of Idi Amin's rule in Uganda. It is a play to which W. B. Yeats's (q.v.) line "Gaiety transfiguring all that dread" could serve as epigraph, and which teaches that the term "political relevance" has more than one meaning.

After a long period of absence, Clark-Bekederemo has returned to the stage in a double way: With his wife he now codirects his own theater (PEC Theater), and he has produced six new plays, three of which are a trilogy called *The Bikoroa Plays* (1987). The strong sense of locale and the tragic pessimism of his earlier plays are still present, although a beguiling simplicity has been added.

Between Soyinka and Clark-Bekederemo at one end and the two younger dramatists at the other stands Ola Rotimi (q.v.) whose dramaturgy has always tended toward the realistic and the popular. His last two plays, *If* (1981) and *Hopes of the Living Dead* (1989) view society through the bifocal lenses of humanism and socialism. In the latter, the inmates of a leper colony struggle to organize themselves into a union so as to assert their humanity rather than remain content as objects of charity. An accomplished theater director who seeks instant communication with his audience, Rotimi's forte lies in uncomplicated plots, suspense, sharp-edged dialogue, and "heavy" characters.

Femi Osofisan (q.v.) and Bode Sowande (b. 1947) are the two outstanding dramatists of the younger generation. Like the younger poets, they too believe in committed art. Osofisan is the more fecund and energetic, being also a newspaper columnist and popular short-story writer, a poet who has published a collection of poems (as Okinba Launko, *Minted Coins,* 1988), and a regular academic at Ibadan. All these creative activities constitute different aspects of one long endeavor to fuse elitist and popular literature in Nigeria. Propelled by the myth of dialectic materialism, and

opposing its archetypes of reason and social consciousness to those of the irrationality, blindness, and necessity of the tragic mythos, Osofisan has been rewriting some canonical Nigerian tragedies: Soyinka's *The Strong Breed* as *No More the Wasted Breed* (1982), and Clark-Bekederemo's *The Raft* as *Another Raft* (1988). This Nigerian Brecht has also recast local myths and history on the stage. His unpublished *Esu and His Vagabond Minstrels* (perf. 1986) is a political promotion of the Yoruba Esu as essentially an incarnation of the democratic spirit—in opposition to Soyinka's promotion of Ogun, the god who incarnates the tragic essence. In his most successful play to date, *Morountodun* (1982), Osofisan also rereads local myth and history along socialist revolutionary lines. But the intertextual character and interpellatory forms of his plays tell us to pay less attention to the ideologue in Osofisan and more to the artist in him, for it is in the latter that his real revolutionary endeavor lies.

Also a lecturer in drama at Ibadan, Bode Sowande has leaned more on the television in his own social crusade. He also founded a theater company that produces his own plays. His major plays to date are collected in *Farewell to Babylon* (1979) and *Flamingo and Other Plays* (1986). Clearly, the urge to reach a wider audience, plus the reformist zeal, have combined to influence the matter and manner of Sowande's plays: They are usually on subjects such as leadership problems, unemployment, and corruption, while his approach is that of the theater as a mirror of society. In the last play in the second collection, Sowande attempts a new kind of dramaturgy in which the Yoruba storytelling theater is enlarged, through the play-within-a-play technique, into a kind of opera.

Fiction

Narrative prose has diversified much, in response to the political whirlpool and other social undercurrents of the last two decades. The political uniformity enforced by prolonged military rule has engendered a stronger sense of national identity, thereby inviting the call for a "national literature" to underscore it; the old historical, cultural, and social differences that produced "ethnic literatures" persist, overlaid by the polarization of the entire society into the two economic classes of classical Marxism. This possible replacement of "ethnic literature" by "class literature" has found support in the rise of female novelists.

Achebe's *Anthills of the Savannah* (1987) is the most important novel yet produced in the labor for the great Nigerian novel. It takes off from where *A Man of the People* (1966) left off, and, if the former is on the blind necessity of military intervention, *Anthills of the Savannah* is on the double and triple irony of that intervention. Achebe in the novel gives a prominent place to a female character who survives the destruction of the male protagonists and takes on the role of priestess and healer to the grieving nation. The novel is a reflective one in which both author and characters are seeking to understand the banal misuse of power to produce absurd effects.

Kole Omotoso (b. 1943) was also educated at Ibadan and in the U.K. and is a scholar of Arabic literature. A prolific writer of short stories and short novels, he is an inveterate experimenter. He made his mark early with the novel *The Edifice* (1971), and his most significant work so far is also an experimental novel, *Just before Dawn* (1988). This work mixes elements of historical and fictional discourse to reveal how the present (of Nigeria) came to be. It is many stories in one, and the author has had to resort to a metonymic technique in which historical fragments imbricate. In this, he may have hit upon a correct strategy for handling politics and getting the attention of a significant segment of the Nigerian audience, which responds more vigorously to factual narratives. Indeed, both *Anthills of the Savannah* and *Just before Dawn* have to be read as the fictional obverse of the "national literature" coin, the other side being the personal accounts by military men, politicians, and other public officials of their roles in the political history of the nation.

The second—and main—trend is the old one in which the novel in Nigeria has been reflecting distinct group and/or ethnic, cultural, and historical identities. One novelist in this category who belongs to the first generation but still needs introduction is Elechi Amadi (q.v.). A physicist by education and an ex-military man, Amadi is an odd-man-out novelist in Nigeria. In his three characteristic novels—*The Concubine* (1966), *The Great Ponds* (1969), and *The Slave* (1978)—he deals with a rural past still untouched by colonialism; he is totally apolitical; and he holds not a tragic but a pessimistic view of life. Amadi is very conversant with the rural life he depicts so evocatively, and his subject is the gods and the fiery passions that rule the lives of the villagers. His latest novel, *Estrangement* (1986), is on a contemporary and "national" subject, but, both on its own and in comparison with earlier ones, it is weak.

Two of the younger novelists deserve mention: T. Obinkaram Echewa (b. 1940) and Ben Okri (b. 1959). Echewa's two novels so far, *The Land's Lord* (1976), awarded the English Speaking Union Literature Prize in 1976 and *The Crippled Dancer* (1986), are about the world of his Ibo people,

depicted in all its plenitude and chaotic vitality. Echewa concentrates on ordinary lives and their little, but no less significant, acts of failure and success. This focus has not come too soon, for a phenomenological depiction of the small politics of everyday life has received only secondary attention in the Nigerian novel.

By the age of nineteen, Okri had the manuscript of his first novel ready. He grew into adolescence in the now notorious 1970s and, judging by the vision projected in his first three works, simultaneously into despair. The heroes (antiheroes, really) of the first two novels, *Flowers and Shadows* (1980) and *The Landscapes Within* (1982), are still in their teens, early victims who are not even allowed to grow into adulthood before disillusionment sets in. He followed this with a collection of short stories, *Incidents at the Shrine* (1986), after which he changed the direction of his art completely. *Stars of the New Curfew* (1988), another short-story collection, is written in the magic-realism (q.v.) mode of Gabriel García Márquez and Salman Rushdie (qq.v.). If that book is a tentative but confident excursion into the supernatural world of African ontology, his next novel, *The Famished Road* (1991) and winner of the Booker Prize, is a narrative tour de force in the same mode. The hero is an *abiku,* or spirit child, who, in his combined roles as witness, participant, and narrator, embodies the novel's central theme: the transforming powers of imagination. Written in the sensuous language of poetry, *The Famished Road* reconnects with the inherited cultural imagination of the oral narratives that had been forced into retreat by the realistic mode in the African novel. But in Okri, that inherited imagination has found a powerful voice and is striking back by exposing the limitations of realism in dealing with the African universe. This novel also demonstrates that, contrary to prevalent belief, the free, autonomous imagination can be as responsive to social pains and ills as the one tied to commitment and relevance.

In the 1960s, Flora Nwapa (b. 1931) was the only female novelist in Nigeria; now there are five who have published at least two full-length novels each: Nwapa, Buchi Emecheta (q.v.), Adaora Ulasi (b. 1932), Ifeoma Okoye (b. 1945), and Zaynab Alkali (b. 1950). All of them except Ulasi are writing about the condition of women in a society of tyrannical patriarchal cultures and values. However, it is doubtful if they can be said to be writing from the "feminist" or "womanist" perspective. As of now, in Nigeria, women's movements tend either to be frustrated by the male-dominated government or assimilated into existing male institutions. There is no distinct female movement to provide the necessary political platform from which a theory and practice of feminist literature can emerge to challenge the patriarchal order. Moreover, a sizable sophisticated female audience is lacking; the majority of educated women wittingly or unwittingly subscribe to the prevalent social ideology, of which the feminine mystique forms a part. Thus, most of the novels by these female writers revolve around the conflict between that mystique (love, home, children), which glorifies woman, and its hidden ideology, which subjugates women socially and economically. In Nwapa's novels—*Efuru* (1966), *Idu* (1970), *One Is Enough* (1981), and *Women Are Different* (1986)—for instance, the heroines fail to live up to the feminine myth but, as if in compensation, succeed in storming the economic fortress occupied by men. And in *Women Are Different*, Nwapa preaches that marriage and childbearing are not the only ways for a woman to live "fully and fruitfully."

Buchi Emecheta is by far the most militant and progressive of the female novelists and, with seven adult novels already published, also the most prolific. The prolificness and militancy are partially explained by her permanent abode in Britain and her training in sociology. Where other female novelists plead for understanding or argue for equality on male terms, she is for outright emancipation. She sees women's oppression in materialist terms: Women are an oppressed socioeconomic class. In her early novels, paying a bride price is the same thing as buying a slave. In the later novels—the ironically entitled *The Joys of Motherhood* (1979), and *Double Yoke* (1982)—the heroines are transiting from the condition of wife-equals-slave to that of liberation. Here female subjectivity and sexuality are no longer traps for cooperating in the "myth of woman"; it instead finds expression in prostitution, a materialist weapon for gaining materialist emancipation.

There is neither a political platform nor a body of literary theory to give these novels an identity other than that of female authorship. However, in focusing on the injustices inherent in the fundamental experiences of love and sex, marrying and raising a family, working and feeding, it is the female novelists who, more than the male, are revealing that colonialism and neocolonialism are also internal conditions that have been contributing their own share to the dysfunctional politics so prevalent at the national level.

The major diversification in fictional prose has been in autobiography and biography, and the one and only important practitioner of both so far is Soyinka. His autobiographical work *Ake, The Years of Childhood* (1981) is a dramatist's recreation of life in a Yoruba town caught on the knife-edge of change in the 1930s and 1940s. *Ake* is definitely one of the best prose narratives in English from

Africa in this century. *Isara: A Voyage around Essay* (1989) is a son's recuperation (based on actual papers left behind) of a certain period in his father's life: that period when the few young men of education were beginning to assert themselves strongly and initiate changes in the affairs of their small communities. This fictional biography gives us an insight into how the emergent educated class began to displace the old political class. These two works reveal possibilities for other genres of imaginative writing in Africa; they also point to the kind of material to look for in linking literature and society in Africa. That link has so far been more speculated upon and theorized about by critics than researched into.

The last decade has witnessed an exhilarating growth and expansion in Nigerian literature. It has been a period of drive and confident expansiveness in which, paradoxically, the more some writers tried to subsume the literature under one social cause or the other, the more it established its own autonomy. The 1990s promise to be a period of consolidation of that tradition.

BIBLIOGRAPHY: Chinweizu, O. Jemie, and I. Madubuike, *Toward the Decolonization of African Literature* (1980); Achebe, C., *The Trouble with Nigeria* (1983); Ogunbiyi, Y., ed., *Perspectives on Nigerian Literature: 1700 to the Present* (2 vols., 1988); Jeyifo, B., ed., *Wole Soyinka: Art, Dialogue and Outrage* (1988); Otokunefor, H. C., and O. C. Nwodo, eds., *Nigerian Female Writers: A Critical Perspective* (1989); Wren, R. M., *Those Magical Years: The Making of Nigerian Literature at Ibadan, 1948–1966* (1991)

WOLE OGUNDELE

NISHIWAKI Junzaburō

Japanese poet, essayist, and translator, b. 20 Jan. 1894, Ojiya; d. 5 June 1982, Ojiya

Born to a well-established family in a rural town in Niigata, N. first aspired to become a painter. Though his true passion lay in art and literature, he was persuaded to study economics at Keiō University in Tokyo upon his father's death. Nonetheless, at college he read widely in foreign literatures and began to write poems in Latin, French, and English. In 1922 Keiō University sent N., then a lecturer at Keiō, to Oxford University to study English literature. In his three-year sojourn in England, N. encountered not only the poetry of T. S. Eliot and *Ulysses* (1922) by James Joyce (qq.v.), but various movements of modernism (q.v.) that were pouring in from the continent.

N.'s first book was a collection of his English poems entitled *Spectrum,* published in London in

CEES NOOTEBOOM

MILORAD PAVIC

NÉLIDA PIÑON

1925. Back in Japan with his newlywed British wife, N. became professor of literature at Keiō, teaching Old and Middle English, history of English literature, and linguistics. N. soon attracted poets and intellectuals interested in modernism and began to contribute poems and essays to modernist magazines. In 1929 N. published *Chōgenjitu shugi shiron* (1929; surrealist poetics), an influential collection of papers exploring and reexamining the notion of surrealist poetry. In this book N. did not merely introduce surrealism (q.v.) but tenaciously pursued the notion of poetry itself by tracing the surrealist rupture of images through the history of Western poetry since antiquity.

In 1933, at the age of thirty-nine, N. published his first collection of poems written in Japanese, albeit with a Latin title: *Ambarvalia* (1933; Ambarvalia). The poems collected in this volume proved to be truly ground-breaking in the history of modern Japanese poetry. The places evoked in the poems were not in Japan but somewhere in Europe—Greece, Rome, London, Paris—and time freely traveled between the ancient and modern worlds. Images and their surrealistic juxtapositions were clearly in the foreground, effectively eliminating any trace of the sentimentality that N. had despised in much of modern Japanese poetry. In sum, this work revolutionized the concept as well as the language of modern Japanese poetry by boldly incorporating a language of translation.

The luminous modernist language of *Ambarvalia* all but disappears in his second collection of Japanese poems, *Tabibito kaerazu* (1947; no traveler returns), published after a long silence precipitated by World War II. Many regard this work as N.'s return to Eastern poetics with the sentiment of *mujō* (transience) at its core. Not only the tone set by the sentiment of loneliness and transience but also the quasi classical language of the poem suggests a return to tradition. It is divided into one hundred and sixty-eight sections of varying length—from a single word to over forty lines—forming a loosely orchestrated whole that somehow resembles a *renga* (Japanese linked verse) sequence. However, the compelling beauty evoked by the entire poem does not simply come from N.'s nostalgic return to Japanese aesthetics but from his inimitable employment of repetitions, complex intertextuality, sudden imagistic and linguistic leaps, humor, and from his profound sense of lyricism that is simultaneously earthly and heavenly.

With his next collection, *Kindai no gūwa* (1953; modern fables), N.'s poetry comes to maturity. From the mode set by this work, all his subsequent poetic works do not diverge significantly except that his later works become increasingly lengthy. In this work one senses his unique, if not chaotic, fusion of opposing elements—frivolous and serious discourses, East and West, modern and ancient worlds, concrete images and abstract concepts—being encased in a most deftly crafted enclosure that is neither purely lyrical nor discursive.

With his keen interest in Joyce's linguistic experimentation, N.'s later works begin to resemble the polyglot text of *Finnegans Wake* (1939), though N.'s central tone of *mujō* never disappears in his freewheeling linguistic play. In the years between the age of sixty and his death at the age of eighty-eight, N.'s poetic production increased to an astonishing magnitude: ten volumes of poetry expanding over about one thousand pages. His text flowed on as a stream of consciousness, incorporating incessant insertions of allusions, of images of loneliness and eternity.

N. was also well known for his translations of works of such writers as Joyce, Eliot, D. H. Lawrence (q.v.), Stéphane Mallarmé (1842–1898), Shakespeare, and Chaucer. His erudition in world literature from antiquity to modern and in linguistics was lengendary. He was awarded a doctorate in philosophy for his dissertation *Kodai bungaku josetsu* (1948; an introduction to ancient literature) from Keiō University.

After Hagiwara Sakutarō (q.v.), to whom N. admitted indebtedness, N. commanded an uncontested position as the most respected leader of modern Japanese poetry. N.'s influence on the younger generation of poets is enormous. N. showed them the possibility of a poetry that is first and foremost a linguistic construct free from sentimentality. Yet the uniqueness of his poetic world remains unchallenged. Nurtured by his formidable learning, N.'s poetry brought an unprecedented intellectual and intertextual depth to modern Japanese poetry. At the same time, his clear imaging of often banal objects and voices only strengthened his distinctive lyricism.

FURTHER WORKS: *Dai san no shinwa* (1956); *Ushinawareta toki* (1960); *Hōjō no megami* (1962); *Eterunitasu* (1962); *Hōseki no nemuri* (1963); *Raiki* (1967); *Jōka* (1969); *Rokumon* (1970); *Jinrui* (1979); *N. J. zenshū* (12 vols., 1982–1983). FURTHER VOLUME IN ENGLISH: *Gen'ei: Selected Poems of N. J.* (1991)

BIBLIOGRAPHY: Keene, D., *Dawn to the West: Japanese Literature of the Modern Era* (1984), Vol. 2, 323–35; Hirata, H., "Return or No-Return: N.'s Postmodernist Appropriation of Literary History, East and West," in Dissanayake, W., and S. Bradbury, eds., *Literary History, Narrative, and Culture* (1989), 122–31; Claremont, Y., "A Turning Point in N. J.'s Poetic Career," *The*

Journal of Oriental Society of Australia (1990), 21–35

HOSEA HIRATA

NOOTEBOOM, Cees

Dutch novelist, poet, and short-story writer, b. 13 July 1933, The Hague

N. received his education at convent schools in the south of the Netherlands. Although he lives in Amsterdam, he has always spent large parts of the year traveling abroad. This is reflected in his travel stories, and many of his novels are set in foreign countries. Since 1967 he has been employed as the editor of the travel and poetry sections of *Avenue,* one of Holland's main magazines, for which he has also translated works by a number of foreign poets.

Poetry forms an important part of N.'s oeuvre. Although his poetry debut, *De doden zoeken een huis* (1956; the dead are looking for a house), is, stylistically, not as strong as his later poems, it already contains some of the main themes of his later work: time and, related to that, death. There has been a definite development in his poetical style; his poetry has become much more sober, notably in the volume *Gesloten gedichten* (1964; closed poems). In his work, time is seen as an extension of death, while death is the result of time. The rhythm of time, expressed in the natural order of day/night and change of seasons is connected with death and human mortality. In this, the poet is an observer; he does not express reality by his presence, but by his observations.

The same themes can be recognized in N.'s novels. He made his literary debut with the novel *Philip en de anderen* (1955; *Philip and the Others,* 1990), for which he was awarded the Anne Frank Prize (1957). It is the poetic account of a journey during which the main character explores the world and his inner self. The theme of time, so important in his later work, is already present. The novel *Rituelen* (1980; *Rituals,* 1983), for which he was given the Mobil Oil Pegasus Prize (1982), finally brought him deserved recognition. Its complex chronological structure, however, as well as its philosophical ideas, does not make it an easily accessible novel. The central themes of time and death are, again, all-important, while the title refers to the means by which the characters try to get a grasp on chaos and time. The rituals by which people live denote a higher order, a continuity that transcends ordinary lives. In *Een lied van schijn en wezen* (1981; *A Song of Truth and Semblance,* 1984) N. deals with another major theme in his work, the relationship between the author and his created characters, between reality

(time) and semblance (the world). If, N. wonders, the world is semblance only, why add to it something that is even more semblance, namely the world created by the author? The novel *In Nederland* (1984; *In the Dutch Mountains,* 1987), which was awarded the Multatuli Prize (1985), is set in a fictive Holland, which stretches from the north to the south of Europe. The story is told by a foreigner, an outsider, which produces a detachment in perspective also found in much of N.'s other work.

A large part of N.'s total oeuvre consists of travel literature. N. developed the genre in Dutch literature and is its undisputed master. N. has traveled extensively, and his stories are often very personal accounts of exotic and less faraway places, as in *Een avond in Isfahan* (1978; an evening in Isfahan). He mixes his travel stories with a large dose of history, notably in *Berlijnse notities* (1990; notes of Berlin).

Many of the central themes of his work are recurrent in all genres in which he has written. Because his work is often very philosophical, and his intricate play with time and space make his books not easily approachable, he is not read by the general public. However, his significance for Dutch literature is apparent. He cannot be classified under any particular literary movement, which contributes to making his work timeless.

FURTHER WORKS: *De verliefde gevangene* (1958); *De zwanen van de Theems* (1958); *Koude gedichten* (1959); *Het zwarte gedicht* (1960); *De koning is dood* (1961); *De ridder is gestorven* (1963); *Een middag in Bruay* (1963); *Een nacht in Tunesie* (1965); *Een ochtend in Bahia* (1968); *De Parijse beroerte* (1968); *Gemaakte gedichten* (1970); *Bitter Bolivia/Maanland Mali* (1971); *Open als een schelp, dicht als een steen* (1978); *Nooit gebouwd Nederland* (1980); *Voorbije passages* (1981); *Mokusei!* (1982); *Gyges en Kandaules* (1982); *Aas* (1982); *Waar je gevallen bent, blijf je* (1983); *Vuurtijd, ijstijd* (1984); *De zucht naar het Westen* (1985); *De brief* (1988); *Het gezicht van het oog* (1989); *De wereld een reiziger* (1989); *Het volgende verhaal* (1991)

WIJNIE E. DE GROOT

NORDBRANDT, Henrik

Danish poet, b. 21 Mar. 1945, Frederiksberg/ Copenhagen

At the University of Copenhagen N. has studied—independently—sinology since 1966, Turkish since 1969 (he has adapted Turkish poems and tales into Danish), and Arabic since 1975. Since his first journey to Greece in 1967, he has spent most of his life abroad, particularly in Asia Minor. A selection of articles and essays from N.'s stay here has been published as *Breve fra en ottoman* (1978; letters from an ottoman). N. earns a living as a free-lance journalist with various Danish newspapers and as a producer for Radio Denmark. He has received numerous awards, among them the Literature Prize of the Danish Academy in 1980.

The longing for greater openness than modern, rationalist civilization can provide and an attempt to dispel human isolation caused by a sense of inconstancy and absence even when close to natural objects or human beings has been a general theme in N.'s writing since his debut collection, *Digte* (1966; poems). The volume is dominated by fragmented modernist imagery conveying feelings of death and decay. Nevertheless, already in this volume, N. is successful in overcoming any stereotype of modernist poetry by merging acute observations with a romantic longing triggered by a sense of loss and instability, which is expressed in stanzas of exquisite beauty. The style is simplified, and the poetic technique further refined in *Miniaturer* (1967; miniatures). The metaphoric compactness—still retaining a penchant for the decadent—is replaced by sinuous · musical sequences frequently around one static nucleus.

With the volume *Syvsoverne* (1969; the sluggards) the worship of beauty is replaced by an increased awareness of total emptiness and a focusing on the poet's painful experience of loneliness even amidst a throng of other people, a sense of isolation that reaches a climax in the collection *Opbrud og ankomster* (1974; departures and arrivals). The previous nervousness has been replaced by a simple yet sonorous tone, the abrupt verses by lingering garlandlike structures.

Whereas nature and the seasonal changes are thoroughly integrated in N.'s earlier collections, the experience of love forces itself to the foreground as a—at least momentary—way out of the poet's present, desolate state, and a series of passionate, albeit melancholy love poems dominate the two next volumes, *Ode til blæksprutten* (1975; ode to the octopus) and *Glas* (1976; glass). Together the three volumes from 1974 to 1976 constitute a Mediterranean trilogy with nature still present—Greek islands and Turkish landscapes—but only as secondary points of orientation.

A philosophical and metaphysical tone becomes noticeable in the small but crucial collection entitled *Guds hus* (1977; *God's House*, 1979), describing the poet's attempt at holding on to the flighty but precious moments of happiness amidst restlessness, to establish meaning in life at least for a time. But already in *Istid* (1977; ice age) from the same year and the volume *Spøgelseslege* (1979; ghost games), much of the weariness and desper-

ation from the previous works are found again, but now they are expressed with classical calm, perhaps resignation, as well as humor.

An orientation toward current conditions is increasingly present in N.'s poetry, particularly in the volume *Istid,* with a series of topics from the alienating, technological reality of the Nordic welfare state. This orientation dominates the poems in *Forsvar for vinden under døren* (1980; defense for the wind under the door), focusing on a number of ecological themes. Thus N. confesses his reasons for leaving Denmark. In *Armenia* (1982; Armenia), which describes the genocide in Armenia in 1915, history is incorporated as a bogey of the destructive forces in humans. On the other hand, *84 digte* (1984; 84 poems) and, in particular, *Under mausolæet* (1987; under the mausoleum) mark, as the title of the latter volume indicates, a return to N.'s fascination with death and suffering on a more personal level. No direct cause is given, unless a subtle yet bitter reference to a finished love affair offers an indirect explanation.

Thus N. once again captures his favorite themes. Inspired by the 20th-c. Greek poetry of Constantine Cavafy (q.v.), and the medieval Turkish poetry of Ymus Emre, N. blends the concrete and the mystical, East and West, past and present. His oeuvre constitutes a series of infinitely varied poems sustained by glowing sensuality, sometimes in the form of subtle philosophical speculation, sometimes as precise registrations of the external world, observations that are almost a rebellion against the worship of beauty in N.'s poetry. External and internal are interwoven in a splendidly composed tapestry. It constitutes a romantic world, yet one of burning relevance that voices not only the poet's own destiny but also an all-encompassing, breathtaking attempt at reaching humankind as a whole.

N.'s evocative mastery of language and style is conspicuous already from his first book. With every new collection he has further consolidated his exceptional position or rather uniqueness as the most accomplished Danish poet of his generation. N. is a solitary figure in Danish lyrical poetry, alien to any relativity of values, to experiments in so-called "systemic" or "concrete" poetry, and to polemic and political attacks. As an indication of his status as an author, several selections of his poetry have already been issued, among them *Udvalgte digte* (1981; selected poems).

FURTHER WORKS: *Omgivelser* (1972); *Rosen fra Lesbos* (1979); *Finckelsteins blodige bazar* (1983); *Violinbyggernes by* (1985); *Håndens skælven i november* (1986); *Nissen flytter med* (1988); *Tifanfaya* (1990). FURTHER VOLUME IN ENGLISH: *Selected Poems* (1978)

SVEN HAKON ROSSEL

NORÉN, Lars

Swedish poet and dramatist, b. 9 Apr. 1911, Stockholm

Next to Göran Sonnevi, N. is the outstanding poet of his generation in Sweden. As a dramatist, he has been more successful internationally than any other Swede except August Strindberg (q.v.). Raised in the southernmost part of Sweden, N. has spent most of his mature life in Stockholm, where he still lives.

Starting out as a poet already in 1963, at the age of nineteen, N. employs a verbose, psychedelic kind of poetry in early collections like *Encyklopedi* (1966; encyclopedia) and *Stupor* (1968; stupor), where hallucinatory poems reflect a chaotic, schizophrenic experience of life. Adhering to a modernistic tradition represented by poets like Rainer Maria Rilke, Paul Celan (qq.v.), and Hölderlin, N.'s visionary talent and pregnant use of imagery characterize collections like *Revolver* (1969; revolver), *Order* (1978; order), and *Hjärta i hjärta* (1980; heart in heart). N.'s tendency to break through emotional barriers by means of "inflamed" imagery and shock effects is as apparent as his ability to create moods of an abstract, lucid beauty.

As a dramatist, N. is well known, especially in northern Europe. He has written some thirty plays, almost all of them after 1980. After a cool reception of the Renaissance drama *Fursteslickaren* (1973; the prince licker), N. achieved his first success as a dramatist with *Modet att döda* (1980; the courage to kill), depicting a traumatic oedipal parent-child relationship, a recurring theme in N.'s dramatic work.

The breakthrough came in 1982 with the publication of *Natten är dagens mor* (the night is mother of the day), where N.'s black humor helped to alleviate the play of its claustrophobic impact. (In 1984 an English version of the play, entitled *Night Is Mother to the Day*, was performed at the Yale Repertory Theatre in New Haven, Connecticut.) Being the first part of what may be seen as a family trilogy, the play was followed by *Kaos är granne med Gud* (1982; chaos is the neighbor of God), while the concluding part is called simply *Stillheten* (1986; the stillness). Like Eugene O'Neill's (q.v.) *Long Day's Journey into Night*—a drama that has had a tremendous impact on him—N.'s family trilogy is highly autobiographical.

In the six-hour drama *Nattvarden* (1985; the communion) two brothers demonstrate their contrasting attitudes to their recently dead mother, present on the stage in the form of an urn, while in *Höst och vinter* (1989; autumn and winter),

which opened in Copenhagen, the family interaction concerns two daughters and their parents. *Hebriana* (1989; Hebriana), first presented in the Hague, and *Endagsvarelser* (1990; one-day creatures), which had its premiere in Kassel, Germany, are thematically related. Both plays deal with representatives of a middle-aged "lost generation," caught between their own hopeful past (the spring of 1968) and the darkening future.

N.'s most recent play, entitled *Och ge oss skuggorna* (1991; and grant us the shadows), opened in Oslo as *En dag längre än livet* (a day longer than life). It is a play about Eugene O'Neill, his third wife, and his two sons. Set in the living room of the O'Neills on a grim October day in 1949 (O'Neill's sixty-first birthday) from morning to dusk, the play intentionally mirrors *Long Day's Journey into Night*, demonstrating how the family interaction described in that play (set in 1912) is ironically and fatefully repeated thirty-seven years later. As a semidocumentary "sequel play" to O'Neill's autobiographical masterpiece, *Och ge oss skuggorna* is probably unique in world drama.

Both as a poet and—especially—as a dramatist, N. has been astoundingly prolific. In his dramatic universe the unity of time and place has a thematic value, stressing the characters' ambivalent feeling that they are at once close to each other and imprisoned with one another. Confrontation is inevitable, separation—a key word with N.—necessary. As with O'Neill, the audience is asked to face the often strenuous interaction between the characters for a considerable time: four hours or more. Writing in a therapeutic era, N. depicts the "true" workings behind what is pretended. Role-playing, projections, and double-bind mechanisms abound in his psychoanalytically inspired oeuvre, which demonstrates a marked ear for subtextual innuendos.

FURTHER WORKS: *Syrener, snö* (1963); *De verbala resterna av den bildprakt som förgår* (1964); *Biskötarna* (1970); *Solitära dikter* (1972); *Viltspeglar* (1972); *I den underjordiska himlen* (1972); *Kung Mej och andra dikter* (1973); *Dagliga och nattliga dikter* (1974); *Dagbok augusti-oktober 1975* (1976); *Nattarbete* (1976); *Den ofullbordade stjärnan* (1979); *Akt utan nåd* (1980); *Orestes* (1980); *En fruktansvärd lycka* (1981); *Underjordens leende* (1982); *Demoner* (1984)

BIBLIOGRAPHY: Algulin, I., *A History of Swedish Literature* (1989), 276–79, 280–82; Törnqvist, E., "Strindberg, O'Neill, N.: A Swedish-American Triangle,'' *The Eugene O'Neill Review,* 15, 1 (1991), 65–76

EGIL TÖRNQVIST

NOVÁS CALVO, Lino

Cuban short-story writer, novelist, poet, and journalist, b. 22 Sept. 1905, Grañadas del Sol, Galicia, Spain; d. 24 Mar. 1983, New York, N.Y., U.S.A.

N. C. is one of the most important short-story writers in Cuba's literary history. He was an illegitimate child, born in northwestern Spain to a poor Galician family, and was only seven years old when his mother sent him to Cuba to live with an uncle. There, he experienced a life of economic difficulties as he lived with different families, working, out of necessity, in many different jobs throughout the island. In 1926 he went to New York but soon returned to Cuba ''with more scratches than dollars.'' From this experience he acquired sufficient knowledge of the language to later read and translate works by Balzac, Aldous Huxley, and William Faulkner, and Ernest Hemingway's (qq.v.) *The Old Man and the Sea* (1959), at the author's request. After returning to Cuba, N. C. found employment as a taxi driver, an experience he recaptures in several of his stories, especially in ''La noche de Ramón Yendía'' (''The Dark Night of Ramón Yendía''). This first-hand knowledge of life among the working classes, and the precarious existence of being poor in Cuba, became an important aspect of his world of fiction. Like N. C. himself, most of his characters are individuals who confront social and economic hardships, are haunted by a sense of not belonging, and must struggle for permanence in a world of change.

N. C.'s debut as a writer was the publication of nine poems in *Revista de Avance* under the pseudonym Lino María de Calvo. ''El camarada'' (1928; comrade) and ''Proletario'' (1928; proletariat) signal the emergence in Cuban literature of a proletarian poetic voice, a perspective also found in his first short story ''Un hombre arruinado'' (1929; a ruined man), where N. C. explores the psychological profile of a man whose materialism has isolated him from meaningful human contact. He was immediately singled out by other writers and editors, and rose from being a taxi driver without formal education to being a member of the Cuban intellectual circle.

Though N. C. was Spanish by birth, his short stories are uniquely Cuban. He experimented, especially, with the vibrant dialogue and the poetic stylization of colloquial Cuban speech. Aware of the new currents in literary expression, N. C. developed a literary style that was influenced by the great writers of his time, by poetic vanguard movements, and by the vibrant force of popular Cuban figures and colloquial language that were in vogue in the vernacular and burlesque theater during the 1920s. He was also particularly interested in Sherwood Anderson's techniques, as well as in Maxim Gorky, Joseph Conrad, John Steinbeck (qq.v.), and others.

In 1931 N. C. traveled to Spain as a correspondent for *Orbe,* a period that proved to be very important for him as a writer. During this time, he published three short stories in *Revista de Occidente,* contributed to other Spanish journals, became secretary for the literary section of the Ateneo of Madrid, began to write a novel, *El negrero: Vida novelada de Pedro Blanco Hernández de Trava* (1955; the slave trader, a novelized biography of Pedro Blanco de Trava), and published *Un experimento en el Barrio Chino* (1936; an experiment in the red-light district). During the Spanish Civil War, in 1937, N. C. was wrongly accused of writing articles against the miners of Asturias; he spent one night in prison, facing possible execution the next day, but he was released when the charges against him could not be proven. With the collapse of the Spanish Republic in 1939, N. C. fled to France and then, with the help of friends, returned to Cuba. There he worked as an editor and translator for *Ultra,* a journal directed by Fernando Ortiz, and, years later, for *Bohemia.*

Between 1942 and 1945, N. C. was awarded a degree in journalism by the National School of Journalism in Havana and received several literary awards: the Hernández Catá Prize for the short story (1942), the National Prize for the short story by the Cuban ministry of education (1944), and the Varona Prize for journalism for his book *No sé quién soy* (1945; I don't know who I am). A year later he published a second collection of short stories, *Cayo canas* (1946; palm key), in which, like in most of his fictional work, the narrative goes beyond traditional patterns and comes closer to the short novel. N. C.'s style became also strongly influenced by cinematographic techniques, in which emotions are not described, but are suggested through a series of images.

During the 1950s, the sociopolitical difficulties on the island and a general lack of interest in intellectual pursuits brought on a period of dissolusionment for N. C. during which his fictional production declined. In 1960, a year after the triumph of the Cuban revolution, N. C. sought political asylum at the Colombian embassy in Havana. Resettled in the U.S., N. C. worked for

Bohemia libre, and from 1967 to 1974 taught at Syracuse University. During these last years, he wrote several short stories for journals. Several of these were later published, with some of his previous work, in *Maneras de contar* (1970; narrative modes). In this second period of his productive career, N. C. followed the same narrative style and preoccupations of his earlier work, now including conflicts surrounding the Cuban revolution. N. C. continued to articulate basically the same sense of disorientation and irrationality that always accompanied his vision of the human being as a victim of social and psychological conditions.

But N. C.'s main contributions to Latin American literature belong to his earlier writings when he, and later Alejo Carpentier (q.v.), were the writers mostly responsible for the establishment of a modern tradition in Cuban prose fiction and the emergence of the Cuban short story as a mature and universal genre. Though N. C. was a prolific writer both in fiction and journalism, only part of his fiction has been published in collections. Several of his short stories have been translated into English and published in anthologies. Many of those that first appeared in journals in Cuba and in Spain are still unpublished in book form, while others have been lost.

FURTHER WORKS: *La luna nona y otros cuentos* (1942); *El otro cayo* (1959)

BIBLIOGRAPHY: Portuondo, J. A., "L. N. C. y el cuento hispanoamericano," *CA,* 35, 5 (Sept.–Oct. 1947), 245–63; Souza, R. D., "L. N. C. and the 'Revista de Avance,' " *Journal of Inter-American Studies,* 10, 2 (Apr. 1968), 232–43; Gutiérrez de la Solana, A., *Maneras de narrar: Contraste de L. N. C. y Alfonso Hernández Catá* (1972); special N. C. issue, *Symposium,* 29, 3 (Fall 1975); Ben-Ur, L., "La época española de N. C.: 1931–1939," *Chasqui,* 6, 3 (May 1977), 69–76; Clinton, S., "The Scapegoat Archetype As a Principle of Composition in N. C.'s 'Un dedo encima,' " *Hispania,* 62, 1 (Mar. 1979), 56–61; Souza, R. D., "The Early Stories of L. N. C. (1929–32): Genesis and Aftermath," *KRQ,* 26, 2 (1979), 221–29; Souza, R. D., *L. N. C.* (1981); special N. C. issue, *Symposium,* 29, 4 (Winter 1985); Roses, L. E., *Voices of the Storyteller: Cuba's L. N. C.* (1986)

JULIA CUERVO HEWITT

NOVO, Salvador

Mexican poet, dramatist, and essayist, b. 30 July 1904, Mexico City; d. 10 Jan. 1974, Mexico City

In 1917 N. attended Mexico City National Preparatory School with Xavier Villaurrutia, Jaime Torres Bodet, and Jose Gorostiza (qq.v.). In 1922 he met Pedro Henríquez Ureña (1884–1946) and became his protégé. In 1924 he was appointed the editorial chief of the Mexican ministry of education. Three years later he cofounded the Ulysses Theater and codirected with Villaurrutia *Ulysses* magazine. From 1930 to 1933 he held the History of Theater Chair at the National Conservatory. In 1933–1934 he worked as a recorder at the Seventh Panamerican Conference in Montevideo. N. received in 1946 the City of Mexico Prize for his essay "Nueva grandeza mexicana" (new Mexican grandeur). From 1937 to 1943 he wrote for the magazine *Hoy.* In 1946 he became director of the theater department of the National Institute of Fine Arts, a post he held until 1952. That same year he was elected a full member of the Mexican Academy of Language (a branch of the Spanish Royal Academy), and in 1965 was appointed the official historian of Mexico City.

N. wrote *XX poemas* (1925; XX poems), which he characterized as "visual poems." They satirize the monotonous, mechanized, impersonal characteristics of daily life. The twenty poems of *Espejo* (1933; mirror) recall his lost childhood. Like most of N.'s poetry, *Espejo* is extremely ironical and even cynical. In *Nuevo amor* (1933; new love) N. resumes the theme of dehumanization and develops it to the fullest, especially in the poem "Elegía" (elegy). *Nuevo amor* is considered N.'s ultimate poetry book by most critics. Love, a predominant theme in this collection, is "spiritual" not carnal. In 1934 N. published two volumes of poetry: *Seamen Rhymes* (title in English, bilingual ed.) and *Poemas proletarios* (proletarian poems). Other books of poetry are *XVIII sonetos* (1955; XVIII sonnets) and *Poesía* (1961; poetry), which includes previously published as well as unpublished poetry.

N. wrote over twenty dramatic pieces, some intended for children: *Don Quijote* (1947; Don Quixote) and *Astucia* (1948; astuteness). Others were composed as simple dialogues: *El tercer Fausto* (1934; Faust the third), *El joven II* (1951; young man II), and *Diálogos* (1956; dialogues). Among his short plays are *Divorcio* (1924; divorce) and *La señorita Remington* (1924; Miss Remington). N.'s four major plays are *La culta dama* (1950; the educated lady), *Yocasta o casi* (1961; Yocasta or almost), *La guerra de las gordas* (1963; the war of the fat women), and *A ocho columnas* (1965; at eight columns). *La culta dama* is a satire against Mexican high-class values. It indicts rich women who indulge themselves in volunteer works of mercy at the expense of their family duties. *Yocasta o casi* is a more cosmopolitan work. It draws from Greek mythology and modern psychology while presenting an alienated actress who must live out her role both in life and on stage. *La guerra de las gordas* is based upon pre-Columbian Mexican history. Moquihuix, king of Tlatelolco and his wife, Chalchiuhnenetzin, get entangled with Axayacatl, king of Tenochtitlan. The play depicts the end of the Tlatelolco kingdom. *A ocho columnas* is a dramatic denouncement of career opportunism and biased Mexican journalism.

N. was a prolific essayist. He published over twenty nonfiction prose works. Among these, the most famous is *Nueva grandeza mexicana* (1946; *New Mexican Grandeur,* 1967). This book has undergone several editions and has been frequently translated. It is a first person, comprehensive overview of Mexico City's neighborhoods, famous restaurants, movies, and play houses as well as architectural landmarks.

N.'s writing is exceptionally diverse. His poetry, plays, and essays bridge the gap between generations of writers. His poetry is decidedly ironical and iconoclastic and encompasses various literary modes: modernism, surrealism and postmodernism (qq.v.). N. the essayist captures in an original and passionate manner Mexican culture, literature, and history. N. the dramatist is a pivotal figure in Mexican theater. He excelled as a director and producer of many plays where, again, social criticism and a satirical view of life do not pass unnoticed.

FURTHER WORKS: *Return Ticket* (1928; title in English); *Jalisco-Michoacán: Doce días* (1933); *Décimas en el mar* (1934); *En defensa de lo usado y otros ensayos* (1938); *Diez lecciones de técnica de actuación teatral* (1951); *Este y otros viajes* (1951); *14 sonetos de navidad y año nuevo* (1955–1968); *El teatro inglés* (1960); *Breve historia de Coyoacán* (1962); *Cuauhtémoc* (1962); *Letras vencidas* (1962); *Breve historia y antología sobre la fiebre amarilla* (1964); *In ticitezcatl o El espejo encantado* (1965); *México: imagen de una ciudad* (1967); *La ciudad de México del 9 de junio al 15 de julio de 1867* (1967); *Cocina mexicana, o Historia gastronómica de la ciudad de México* (1967); *México* (1968); *Apuntes para una historia de la publicidad en la ciudad de México* (1968); *Un año, hace ciento: la ciudad de México en 1873* (1973); *Historia de la aviación en México* (1974)

BIBLIOGRAPHY: Dauster, F., "La poesía de S. N.," *CA,* 3, 116 (May–June 1961), 209–33; Arce, D. N., "Nómina bibliográfica de S. N," *Boletín de la Biblioteca Nacional,* 2a, época 13, 4 (1962), 61–89; Kuehne, A., "La realidad existencial y 'la realidad creada' en Pirandello y S. N," *LATR,* 2, 1 (Fall 1968), 5–14; Magaña-Esquivel, A., *S. N.* (1971); Muncy, M., *S. N. y su teatro: estudio crítico* (1971); special N. issue, *Reflexión,* 3–4 (1975); Roster, P., *La ironía como método de análisis: la poesía de S. N.* (1978); Forster, M., "S. N. como prosista," in Bleznick, D. W., and J. O. Valencia, eds., *Homenaje a Luis Leal* (1978), 129–43

JORGE RODRÍGUEZ-FLORIDO

NU'AYMA, Mīkhā'īl

(also spelled Mikhail Naimy) Lebanese poet, critic, essayist, dramatist, and biographer (writing in Arabic and English), b. 1889, Biskinta; d. 28 Feb. 1988, Beirut

N. attended the Russian elementary school that the Russian Imperial Orthodox Palestine Society had founded in 1899 in the village. In 1902 he qualified for admission to the Russian training college in Nazareth, and in 1906 he obtained a scholarship at the Diocesan Seminary in Poltava, Ukraine. After completion of a four-year course in 1911, N. left for the U.S. and became a student at the University of Washington, Seattle, where he received degrees in law and in English literature in 1916. After the completion of his studies, N. left for New York to join the Arab literary circle with whom he had become acquainted through correspondence. He made a living working at the Russian military mission to the U.S., until Russia withdrew from the war in November 1917 and N. was called up for active service. He was sent to France, where he spent the last week of the war on the frontline. While waiting for transport back to the U.S., he was allowed to follow courses in French language and literature at the University of Rennes. In 1919 N. returned to New York. Together with friends he founded the Society of the Pen. He gave it a charter and was its first secretary. To earn his livelihood, he became a traveling salesman, refusing to pursue a career in any of the fields open to him on the basis of his academic qualifications. In 1932 he left the U.S. for Lebanon, where he lived for the remainder of his life.

The spiritual development of N. can be divided into various phases. His destination seemed to be the clergy, but if he had ever cherished such thoughts he abandoned them during his stay in Poltava. The splendor displayed by the church may have affected his negative decision. Tolstoy's socialist ideas were more in accordance with his feelings. In Seattle he came into contact with the Theosophical Society and in 1925 he came to read Vivekananda's Raya Yogo and the Bagavatgita. Reincarnation and the purification of the soul were then to occupy a paramount place in his writings and literature.

The literary work of N. fills thirty-two volumes in Arabic. Two works were published originally in English and were later translated into Arabic. His work includes poetry, narrative prose, drama, biography, autobiography, literary criticism, and essay writing. He wrote his first poem in Russia, before 1911, his first critique in 1913, his first story in 1914. In 1917 he published, in New York, his play *al-Ābā' wa-al-banūn* (parents and children), which had been serialized in the literary magazine *al-Funūn*. It is the only work N. published in the U.S.

In 1923 *al-Ghirbāl* (the sieve), a volume of critical essays, was published in Cairo, where N. had contacts with the young and angry Dīwān group of 'Abbās Mahmūd al-'Aqqād (1889–1964) and Ibrāhīm al-Māzinī (1890–1949). *Al-Marāhil* (stages), another volume of essays, appeared in 1933 in Beirut. It contains only one essay on a literary subject, the other essays dealing with other subjects. N.'s biography *Gibrān Khalīl Gibrān. Hayātuhu, mawtuhu, adabuhu, Fannuhu* (1934; *Kahlil Gibran: His Life and His Work,* 1950) produced a shock among Gibran's admirers. Instead of a eulogy N. had produced a book revealing the weaknesses of Gibran. N. defended his choice by comparing the book to John Bunyan's (1628–1688) *The Pilgrim's Progress* (1684), seeing Gibran's life as a struggle against the forces of evil. In Arabic literary history it is the first *biographie romancée,* a genre that owes its renown to writers like André Maurois, Lytton Strachey, and Stefan Zweig (qq.v.).

N. has written more than eighty stories, which he collected in volumes like *Kān mā kān* (1937; once upon a time), *Akābir* (1956; notables), and *Abū Battah* (1959; the fat-calved man), also in volumes of miscellaneous content. He also wrote long pieces of narrative prose, among which *The Book of Mirdad* (1948), which he later translated into Arabic as *Kitāb Mirdād* (1952). N. considered this work as the summit of his thought. It is a book of metaphysical instruction that he wanted to leave behind as a spiritual guidebook for humankind. But N.'s most impressive piece of work may be his autobiography, *Sab'ūn* (3 vols., 1959–1960; seventy), covering three phases of his life: his early youth in Biskinta, Nazareth, and Poltava; his stay in the U.S.; and his return to Lebanon. Not limiting the biography to his own life, he gives vivid portrayal of the people around him and of the milieu in which he lived.

Lebanon respects N. as one of its great authors. In the wider field of Arabic literature he deserves to be celebrated as one of the critics, authors, and poets who have linked Arabic literature with the Western (Russian and English) narrative forms, and who have introduced ideas of romanticism—such as the poet as creator, priest, and prophet—into Arabic literature.

FURTHER WORKS: *Zād al-Ma'ād* (1936); *Hamsh al-Jufūn* (1943); *al-Awthān* (1946); *Karam 'alā darb* (1946); *Liqā'* (1946; *Till We Meet . . .* 1957); *Sawt al-'ālam* (1948); *Mudhakkirāt al-Arqash* (1949; *Memoirs of a Vagrant Soul,* 1952); *al-Nūr wa-al-Dayjūr* (1950); *Fī mahabb ar-rīh* (1953); *Durūb* (1954); *Ab'ad min Mūskū wa-min Washintun* (1957); *al-Yawm al-akhīr* (1963); *Hawāmish* (1965); *Ayyūb* (1967); *Yā ibn Ādam* (1969); *al-Majmū'ah al-kāmilah* (8 vols., 1970–1974); *Fī al-ghirbāl al-jadīd* (1972); *Mukhtārāt* (1972); *Nagwā al-ghurūb* (1973); *Min wahy al-Masīh* (1974); *Wamadāt. Shudhūr wa-amthāl* (1977)

BIBLIOGRAPHY: Naimy, N., *M. N.: An Introduction* (1967); Gabrieli, F., "L'autobiografia di M. N.," *Oriente Moderno,* 49 (1969), 381–87; Nijland, C., *M. N.: Promoter of the Arabic Literary Revival* (1975); Matar, N. I., "Adam and the Serpent: Notes on the Theology of M. N.," *JArabL,* 11 (1980), 56–61; Nijland, C., "M. N.: The Biography of Gibran and the Autobiography," *al-'Arabiyya,* 15 (1982), 7–15; Allen, R., ed., *Modern Arabic Literature* (1987), 237–44; Ghaith, A., *La pensée religieuse chez Gubrān Halīl Gubrān et M. N.* (1990)

CORNELIS NIJLAND

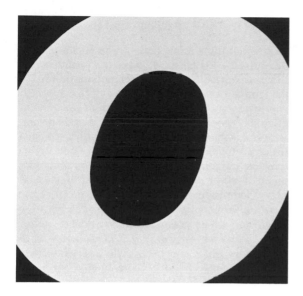

ŌBA Minako
Japanese novelist, short-story writer, essayist, and poet, b. 11 Nov. 1930, Tokyo

O. refers to herself as a "vagrant spirit," reflecting a life of wandering. As a child she changed schools fourteen times due to her father's transfers as a Navy doctor. An avid reader, she explored both the Japanese classics and masterpieces of world literature in translation. At age fourteen, in 1945, she assisted atomic-bomb victims in Hiroshima, a physical and mental landscape of despair, which at once shadows her writing with gloom and illuminates it with the inner strength gained from this experience. O. entered Tsuda Women's College in 1949, majoring in literature and drama. In 1955 she married "on the condition that I continue to write" and accompanied her husband, a representative for Alaska Pulp Company, to Sitka, Alaska, where she lived from 1959 to 1970. O. left periodically to study art and literature at the University of Washington and the University of Wisconsin, and to travel in the U.S. The pristine and fertile landscape of southeast Alaska and the harmony of traditional Native Alaskan life-styles contributed to her rich plant and animal imagery and to her concept of the human being as one small component of the biosphere. O.'s American experience, including her exposure to the doubts raised by U.S. involvement in Vietnam, increased her tendency to question the established order, strengthened her ability to perceive the relativism of so-called truths, and nurtured a flexible acceptance of other races and cultures. O. returned to Japan, not to put down roots, but with the determination to live her life as she wanted. She continues to travel widely and to write prolifically. In 1987 O. and Kōno Taeko (b. 1926) became the first women to sit on the selection committee of the coveted Akutagawa Prize for literature.

When O., a frustrated housewife, submitted "Sanbiki no kani" (1968; "The Three Crabs," 1978) to a literary magazine, she won immediate acclaim as recipient of the Gunzō New Writer Award and the 59th Akutagawa Prize for new talent in serious fiction. A repulsion for society's hypocrisy and the spiritual isolation of the individual are themes that form the basis of her later work. Rejecting the "coherence" of Western literature with its emphasis on structure and plot, O. has developed her own form, a kind of nonform, a spontaneous flow of thoughts and images permitting maximum freedom of time and space. O.'s work is recognized for its intellectual and witty dialogues, graphic and sensuous imagery, sensitivity, and lyricism. O. is a master of simile and metaphor in which plant and animal imagery are used to strip humans of their artificial clothing and housing, to lay bare our physical and mental state. More important than individual images is the manner in which they symphonize. This may be said of O.'s stories and novels, as well.

In *Garakuta hakubutsukan* (1975; the junk museum), recipient of the Prize for Women's Literature, O. focuses upon three women of diverse ethnicity, who, uprooted from their homeland, drift to a small Alaskan town. It is their individuality that is the key to their identity. They have attained their freedom, but at the cost of a certain loneliness.

O.'s protagonists are often found in triangular relationships, with a focus on the female role. As in "Yamauba no bishō" (1976; "The Smile of a Mountain Witch," 1982), traditionally expressionless women are depicted as the center of consciousness, as O. explores the price of suppressing fundamental thoughts and feelings to the point that one is anesthetized by social norms.

In *Katachi mo naku* (1982; formlessness and solitude), awarded the Tanizaki Prize for leading writers, O. seeks a state beyond the established "form" of marriage, dispelling the myths that have given shape to this institution. The fundamental nature of the relationship between heterosexual couples and the search for female identity is explored further in a series of autobiographical novels, *Kiri no tabi* (2 vols., 1980; journey through the mist) and *Nakutori no* (1985; of singing birds), which won the Noma Literary Prize (1986).

Umi ni yuragu ito (1989; lines that drift through the sea) is a collection of stories which finds the protagonists of *Nakutori no* revisiting a small town in Alaska. The narrator follows the thread of life, not attempting to untangle or determine its course, relating tales in such a way that the past lives in the present, Japanese legends merge with Tlingit Indian myths of southeast Alaska, characters from literature are juxtaposed to "real life" acquaintances, and dreams and reality are intertwined. The title story, "Umi ni yuragu ito" (1988), was awarded the Kawabata Yasunari Literary Prize in 1989.

O.'s feminist voice, sensitive cross-cultural comparisons, anecdotal style, and tendency to glide freely between different periods in time are seen in the biography *Tsuda Umeko* (1990; Tsuda Umeko), awarded the Yomiuri Literary Prize. After being raised and educated in the U.S., Umeko (1865–1929) returned to Japan and established Tsuda Women's College, creating the opportunity for students such as O. to acquire the education and self-confidence necessary to contribute to and find self-fulfillment in a society dominated by men.

O.'s work is distinguished by its fresh and immediate perception of life, its uninhibited expression of ideas, and its treatment of all aspects of life as part of a continuum, in which past and present, hope and despair, humans, plants and animals, self and other, lose their distinction in an exploration of the possibility of a new state of freedom and harmonious existence beyond established social systems.

FURTHER WORKS: *Funakuimushi* (1970); *Yūreitachi no fukkatsusai* (1970); *Uo no namida* (1971); *Sabita kotoba* (1971); *Tsuga no yume* (1971); *Kokyū o hiku tori* (1972); *O.-shū* (1972); *Shikai no ringo* (1973); *Yasō no yume* (1973); *Aoi kitsune* (1975); *Urashimasō* (1977); *Samete miru yume* (1978); *Aoi chiisana hanashi* (1978); *Hana to mushi no kioku* (1979); *Tankō* (1979); *Onna no danseiron* (1979); *Oregon yume jūya* (1980); *Shima no kuni no shima* (1982); *Watashi no erabu watashi no basho* (1982); *Yume o tsuru* (1983); *Bōshi no kiita monogatari* (1983); *Yumeno* (1984); *Yōbaidō monogatari* (1984); *Onna, otoko, inochi* (1985); *Dorama* (1985); *O. no taketori monogatari, Ise monogatari* (1986); *Miomotegawa* (1986); *Kagami no naka no kao* (1986); *O. no ugetsu monogatari* (1987); *Ōjo no namida* (1988); *Ikimono no hanashi* (1988); *Mahō no tama* (1989); *Niji no hashizume* (1989); *Shinshū otogisōshi* (1990); *O. zenshū* (10 vols., 1990–1991)

BIBLIOGRAPHY: Chambers, M., "Fireweed," *JapQ,* 28 (1981), 403–27; Tanaka, Y., Introduction to *This Kind of Woman* (1982), ix–xxv; Lippit, N. M., and K. I. Selden, eds., *Stories by Contemporary Japanese Women Writers* (1982), xxii, 182–96, 218

KAREN COLLIGAN-TAYLOR

ODIO, Eunice

Costa Rican poet, essayist, and short-story writer, b. Oct. 1922, San José; d. May 1974, Mexico City

One of the most remarkable Costa Rican poets of the 20th c., O. began to write very early in her life and started to publish her poems in 1945 in the journal *Repertorio Americano* of San José. She was awarded the prestigious "15th of September" prize for poetry for her volume *Los elementos terrestres* (the elements of earth), which was published in Guatemala in 1948. O. became a Guatemalan citizen, and continued to write poems, many of which were published only after her death in an anthology she edited herself, called *Territorio del alba y otros poemas* (1974; territory of dawn and other poems). She wrote her second book, *Zona en territorio del alba* (zone in the territory of dawn) between 1946 and 1948 and it was published in 1953 in Argentina, where it was much acclaimed. A year later, she completed a very long poem called *El tránsito de fuego* (1957; path of fire), which was published in San Salvador. After her move to Mexico in 1955, she worked as a reporter for *El Diario de Hoy* and wrote articles for many different journals. O. spent over two years in the U.S., and wrote extensively about the experience of exile. As well as poetry and essays, she wrote at least three stories in her later years, one of which, *El rastro de la mariposa* (1968; the trace of the butterfly), was published in booklet form.

O.'s poetry evolved over the course of her writing life from traditional verses in the early and mid-1940s to mystical-sensual-biblical allusion in *Los elementos terrestres* of 1948, to techniques of surrealism (q.v.) and other vanguard movements in *Zona en territorio del alba* of 1953, and finally to the lyric allegory of *El tránsito de fuego* of 1957 and subsequent poems and stories. Her early poems assimilate and use traditional lyric forms and often outspokenly advocate political activism, particularly in regard to the Spanish Civil War. *Los elementos terrestres,* a collection of eight long poems in free verse, derives its unity from the repeated lyrical insistence on natural cyclical process: night and day, the seasons, the rhythms of birth and death, love, and poetic creation. Allusions and interwoven paraphrases of the Song of Songs, Job, Genesis, and the Psalms intensify the fusion of mysticism and sensuality.

Zona en territorio del alba is far more experimental in form and in ideas. The book collects a varied series of poems in free verse about such themes as the importance of childhood, friendship, and the various artistic media: poetry, dance, and music. *El tránsito de fuego,* usually considered to be O.'s culminating masterwork, is an extensive poem, nearly five hundred pages long, in the form of an allegorical drama with many participant voices and choruses. The central plot revolves around the effort to understand Ion, the creator of the cosmos. O.'s passion for the creation and elaboration of myths culminated in her celebration of a cult to the Archangel Michael, dramatized in one of her best-known poems, "Arcangel Miguel" (archangel Michael).

O. has been widely recognized as a poet of extraordinary lyric intensity. Her poems celebrate creation, imagination, erotic love, and, above all, light. Her major poems have been interpreted in many different ways, but it is mainly the luminous harmony of her verse that impresses the reader.

FURTHER WORKS: *Los trabajos de la catedral* (1971); *En defensa del castellano* (1972); *Antología: Rescate de un gran poeta* (1975); *La obra en prosa de E. O.* (1980); *E. O. en Guatemala* (1983). FURTHER VOLUME IN ENGLISH: *Five Women Writers of Costa Rica: Naranjo, O., Oreamuno, Urbano, Vallbona* (1978)

BIBLIOGRAPHY: Liscano, J., "Eunice hacia la mañana," *Antología* (1975), 27–65; Huerta, E., "Deslindades costarricences," *Ancora,* 31 July 1977, 3–10; Vallbona, R. de, "E. O.: rescate de un poeta," *RIB,* 31, 2 (1981), 199–214; Vallbona, R. de, "Estudio valorativo de la obra de E. O.," *Atenea,* 1–2 (1985), 91–101; Albán, L., "E. O.: una mujer contra las máscaras," *RI,* 53, 138–39 (Jan.–June 1987), 325–30; Burdiel de las Heras, M. C., "La poesía bíblica y E. O.," *Foro literario,* 17 (1987), 42–50; Duverrán, C. R., "E. O.: su mundo transfigurado," *Andromeda,* 3 (1987), 2–5; Vallbona, R. de, "E. O.," in Marting, D. E., ed., *Spanish American Women Writers* (1990), 382–93

MARY G. BERG

OLSEN, Tillie

American novelist, short-story writer, and critic, b. 13 Jan. 1912 or 1913, Omaha, Neb.

The year of O.'s birth is uncertain. Her parents were Russian Jews who had fled to the U.S. after the 1905 revolution, and her father remained active in labor and leftist struggles, becoming secretary of the Nebraska socialist party. Although she dropped out of high school in the eleventh grade, O. continued her education through assiduous reading at public libraries and observation on her working-class jobs. A number of the "lost" writings by women that she helped to bring out of obscurity in the 1970s were works she initially discovered as a very young woman exploring libraries and second-hand bookshops. O. was also a labor activist, and was arrested organizing Midwestern packinghouse workers, as well as in the general strike in San Francisco, where she moved in the mid-1930s and has lived ever since. Since the 1950s, she has held a number of writing

fellowships and visiting teaching positions on the faculties of such institutions as Stanford, Amherst, MIT, and the University of Minnesota.

If the career of any single writer can be said to epitomize an entire movement and moment in literary history, O.'s represents the impact of feminism on American literature in the second half of the 20th c. Her fiction centers on the limitations that our culture places on women's lives and the ways that class and race, as well as gender, shape female experience. In her critical writing, too, O. focuses on both the restrictions on women as creative artists and their achievements despite those restrictions.

O.'s lifelong commitment to working-class, racial-justice, and peace movements informs her literary work, but, along with the effort of rearing four children and doing paid labor as well, it cut severely into the time and inner space she had available for writing. Her literary career is thus divided into two parts, separated by twenty years devoted almost exclusively to family, "everyday" jobs, and political life. In the earlier period, the 1930s, she published journalism, poetic prose drawn from her activist experience, and, in the 1934 *Partisan Review,* a short story that was the beginning of the novel *Yonnondio: From the Thirties* (1974) that she was to publish, still incomplete, some forty years later. It was not until the mid-1950s that O. began to write fiction again. Her three short stories from those years, "I Stand Here Ironing," "Hey Sailor, What Ship?," and "O Yes," offer realistic glimpses into the experience of working-class women, men, and children through use of experimental modernist techniques of narration. These three loosely connected stories are collected in a volume, *Tell Me a Riddle* (1961), along with O.'s novella of that title.

The novella "Tell Me a Riddle," which won the O. Henry Award for the best American short story of 1961, focuses on the last months in the life of an elderly Russian Jewish immigrant woman, a political activist who survived the revolution of 1905 only to witness the erosion of her own possibilities for a full life into the stifling experience of American working-class wife and motherhood. Embittered by the demands her experience has made on her, the dying woman's stream-of-consciousness (q.v.) is studded with the texts of suppressed idealism, the socialist humanism of her youth, in which she has never ceased to believe; these are words that make a vivid, ironic contrast with the ugly, self-satisfied world of America in the 1950s by which she is surrounded.

O.'s other fictional works include "Requa-I" (1971)—another long story—and *Yonnondio,* the novel begun in the 1930s and revised—though not completed—by the author in her maturity. *Yonnondio* is a narrative of the migrations of a working-class Midwestern family, with special attention to the way that the job and joblessness shape relationships between the sexes and the generations, as the violence of the workplace and the economy of which it is a part translates into domestic violence, marital rape, and child neglect.

As a critic, O. concentrates on the power of "circumstances," particularly race, class, and gender, to cut off creativity. *Silences* (1978) starts from her own experience as a "first generation" working-class writer and a woman and proceeds to elaborate a theory about the relation of material conditions to culture. O.'s efforts to make the work of such nearly forgotten authors as Rebecca Harding Davis (1831–1910) and Agnes Smedley (1890–1950) available to a new generation of feminist readers derives from this same sense of the social obstacles to creation and the great value of what is accomplished in spite of those obstacles.

FURTHER WORK: *Mother to Daughter, Daughter to Mother: A Daybook and Reader* (1984)

BIBLIOGRAPHY: Rosenfelt, D., "From the Thirties: T. O. and the Radical Tradition," *FSt*, 7, 3 (Fall 1981), 371–406; Orr, E. N., *T. O. and a Feminist Spiritual Vision* (1987); Coiner, C., "Literature and Resistance: The Intersection of Feminism and the Communist Left in Meridel LeSueur and T. O.," in Davis, L. J., and M. B. Mirabella, eds., *Left Politics and the Literary Profession* (1990), 162–85; Fishkin, S. F., "The Borderlands of Culture: Writing by W. E. B. DuBois, James Agee, T. O., and Gloria Anzaldua," in Sims, N., ed., *Literary Journalism in the Twentieth Century* (1990), 133–82; Pearlman, M., and A. H. P. Werlock, *T. O.* (1991); Fishkin, S. F., and E. Hedges, eds., *Listening to Silences* (1992)

LILLIAN S. ROBINSON

ONDAATJE, Michael

Canadian poet and novelist, b. 12 Sept. 1943, Colombo, Sri Lanka

O., one of the most influential writers of the contemporary period in Canada, has been recognized for his innovative work in two genres, poetry and prose fiction. He left Sri Lanka at the age of eleven, completing his secondary schooling in England before moving to Canada in 1962. He earned B. A. and M. A. degrees in English literature from the University of Toronto and Queen's University, Kingston, respectively. Since 1971, O. has taught at Glendon College, York University, in Toronto.

O.'s first poetry collection, *The Dainty Monsters* (1967), published when the author was only

twenty-four years old, reveals an impressive maturity. Its short, intensely visual domestic lyrics startle the reader with their sharp-edged imagery. This quality is honed in the later volume *Rat Jelly* (1973), which contains a number of O.'s best-known poems: "Spider Blues," "King Kong Meets Wallace Stevens," "Rat Jelly," and "White Dwarfs." Many of these poems meditate self-consciously on art, especially on the paradoxical notion of creativity as a violent act of "freezing" the flux of lived experience. O.'s most recent poems, however, collected in *Secular Love* (1984), show a more expansive, meditative tone, though the painfully sharp imagery is still there.

In 1970, O. was awarded Canada's highest literary prize, the Governor General's Award, for *The Collected Works of Billy the Kid: Left-Handed Poems* (1970). This work was probably the most influential poetic work of that decade in Canada, since it explored a fabricated version of a historical figure, the American outlaw William Bonney, through a daring, experimental mixture of poetry and prose.

In the late 1970s, O. continued this generic experimentation in *Coming through Slaughter* (1976), a poetic novel whose short, stabbing paragraphs and visual effects again showed Canadian readers a fresh innovator at work. O. recreates another historical figure, the legendary New Orleans jazz musician Buddy Bolden, in order to meditate on the meeting of order and chaos, violence and creativity. In his prose works of the 1980s, O. took these concerns in two different directions, the autobiographical and the sociopolitical. In *Running in the Family* (1982), O. turned to his own Sri Lankan family as the source of historical fictionalizing; in so doing he forged a hybrid genre: the fictionalized (auto)biography. In his most recent novel, *In the Skin of a Lion* (1987), the alternative history is that of those nearly forgotten, marginalized working-class immigrants in Canada who worked on large public projects.

More than any other Canadian writer working today, O. has brought to the literature of this country a cosmopolitan breadth of subject matter and a taste for stylistic and generic innovation. Like other contemporary writers dubbed postmodernist, he has moved the previously marginalized and excluded (process as opposed to product, popular culture, the outlaw, the immigrant) into the center of the reader's viewing frame. The fears of his earlier poetry, that art freezes and disempowers, are implicitly answered in this act of celebrating the undervalued.

FURTHER WORKS: *The Man with Seven Toes* (1969); *Elimination Dance* (1978); *There's a Trick with a*

Knife I'm Learning To Do: Selected Poems (1979); *Tin Roof* (1982); *The English Patient* (1992)

BIBLIOGRAPHY: Solecki, S., "Making and Destroying: M. O.'s *Coming through Slaughter* and Extremist Art," *ECW*, 2 (1978), 24–47; Solecki, S., "Nets and Chaos: The Poetry of M. O.," in David, J., ed., *Brave New Wave* (1978); Scobie, S., "His Legend a Jungle Sleep: M. O. and Henri Rousseau," *CanL*, 76 (1978), 6–21; Solecki, S., ed., *Spider Blues: Essays on M. O.* (1986); York, L. M., *The Other Side of Dailiness: Photography in the Works of Alice Munro, Timothy Findley, M. O., and Margaret Laurence* (1987), 93–120

LORRAINE M. YORK

OREAMUNO, Yolanda

Costa Rican novelist, short-story writer, and essayist, b. 8 Apr. 1916, San José; d. 8 July 1956, Mexico City, Mexico

Best known for her short stories and for her novel *La ruta de su evasión* (1948; the route of their escape), O. is one of the most prominent Costa Rican writers of the 20th c. Born in San José, O. was twenty when she published her first stories. Many of her stories and essays appeared in *Repertorio Americano,* of San José, a journal edited by O.'s mentor and friend Joaquín García Monge (1881–1958). In 1940, O.'s novel *Por tierra firme* (for native land) won the novel prize of the Congress of Spanish American writers sponsored by Farrar and Rinehart, but the manuscript was lost and never published. A second novel, *Casta sombría* (dark race), was also lost, but several fragments of it were printed in *Repertorio Americano.* After a bitter divorce and loss of custody of her son, O.'s health declined, and she was ill for much of the remainder of her life. "México es mío" (Mexico is mine), one of her most remarkable texts, appeared in 1945, "Valle alto" ("High Valley," 1978) was published in 1946, and in 1947 O. sent two novels to a literary contest in Guatemala. In 1948 she won the prestigious "15th of September" prize for the best novel of the year in Guatemala for *La ruta de su evasión;* the other novel manuscript, *De ahora en adelante* (from now on) was lost. O., who had left Costa Rica in 1943, became a Guatemalan citizen. She lived in Guatemala and later in Mexico, where she continued to write novels and stories, many of which were still unpublished at the time of her death in 1956.

Since her death, the publication of several volumes of her collected stories, essays, letters, and novel chapters has brought her wider recognition and admiration than she enjoyed during her life-

time. A new edition in 1984 of O.'s only extant complete novel, *La ruta de su evasión,* has met with extensive praise for the skill with which O. combines interior monologues, realistic description, and fantasy. The novel explores the interdynamics of the Vasco family through analysis of the motives of the women characters, their dreams and their aspirations. Many of O.'s better-known stories, such as "Las mareas vuelven de noche" (1971; "The Tide Returns at Night," 1978) and "Valle alto," are also written in surreal, powerful prose, the images stacked against each other, sensuous and poetic, bypassing rational logic of cause and effect.

Much of O.'s fiction is fragmentary and poetic, obsessed with time and with the definition of identity. Although her stories are set around the world, in Bogotá and Carthage and Hong Kong as well as in a mythic, mysterious Mexico or generic Central America, autobiographical elements are woven throughout O.'s fiction, and her tone of personal passion is convincing. She writes with hallucinatory intensity of the complexity of male-female relationships and of the simultaneous multiplicity of motives behind even the simplest of social acts. O.'s published work is not extensive, but it is highly accomplished and varied, ranging from humorous satire to poetic allegory. As her work has become more available to a reading public, she has become one of the most highly esteemed Costan Rican writers of the century.

FURTHER WORKS: *A lo largo del corto camino* (1961); *Relatos escogidos* (1977). FURTHER VOLUME IN ENGLISH: *Five Women Writers of Costa Rica: Naranjo, Odio, O., Urbano, Vallbona* (1978)

BIBLIOGRAPHY: Ramos, L., "Y. O. en mi recuerdo eviterno," in Chase, A., ed., *A lo largo del corto camino* (1961), 331–42; Urbano, V., *Una escritora costarricense: Y. O.* (1968); Vallbona, R., *Y. O. presentado por Rima de Vallbona* (1972); Fernández, R., "En busca de Y. O.," *Revista de Excélsior,* 7 Mar. 1976, 7; Bellver, C. G., "On 'The Tide Returns at Night,'" in Urbano, V., ed., *Five Women Writers of Costa Rica* (1978), 77–78; Vallbona, R., *"La ruta de su evasión* de Y. O.: Escritura proustiana suplementada," *RI*, 53, 138–39 (Jan.–June 1987), 193–217; Schrade, A., "Y. O.," in Marting, D. E., ed., *Spanish American Women Writers* (1990), 394–406

MARY G. BERG

OSOFISAN, Femi

Nigerian dramatist, literary critic, and novelist (writing in English), b. 15 June 1946, Ijebu Ode

O. is one of the most prolific and most successful of the Nigerian writers in what has been described as the post-(Wole) Soyinka, post-(Chinua) Achebe (qq.v) generation. After studying in Dakar and Paris, O. received his Ph.D, in French from the University of Ibadan in 1975. His first published work was a novel, *Kolera Kolej* (1975), but he is primarily a dramatist as well as a literary critic. His doctoral dissertation was entitled "The Origins of Drama in West Africa: A Study of the Development of Drama from the Traditional Forms to the Modern Theatre in English and French."

Kolera Kolej, named after a university that became an autonomous state because its home country saw that expedient as the most convenient way of dealing with an outbreak of cholera on the campus, is characteristic of O.'s strategy of using his art to expose the social problems in his society: disease, political corruption and opportunism, and totalitarianism. The same preoccupation marks his plays, for the performance of which he founded the Kakaun Sela Kompany at the University of Ibadan, where he is a professor of modern languages and dramatic arts. O. is currently the head of the department of dramatic arts.

Among his best-known works are *Once Upon Four Robbers* (1980) and *Morountodun* (1982). The former was inspired by the spate of public executions of armed robbers in the postcivil-war years in Nigeria. In it O. argues through a group of armed robbers about to be publicly executed that the structural inequities in the society, not individual perversities, were responsible for violent crimes. At the end the audience is posed the choice of siding with the authorities represented by the soldiers, or with the oppressed represented by the robbers. *Morountodun* is based on a Yoruba myth in which a patriotic princess (Moremi) sacrificed herself to win her society's deliverance from foreign marauders. In the play, however, O. revises the myth such that the heroine (Titubi) starts out with the intention of sacrificing herself on behalf of the elite pitted against the workers, but in the end switches her allegiance to the workers.

Although O. expresses admiration for the generation of writers before him, dedicating *The Chattering and the Song* (1977) to Soyinka and Christopher Okigbo (q.v.), he yet criticizes them for what he considers their elitism, escapism, and failure to grapple meaningfully with reality, signaled by their preoccupation with an elite audience, and their use of mythological materials. Such materials are legitimate, in his view, only for the sort of use he put them to in *Morountodun*—to effect their own unmasking and undermining. He identifies himself as one of the heirs to Cyprian Ekwensi (q.v.), the popular Nigerian

novelist, without whom he says literature would have remained the property of the privileged. These writers, according to him, are marked by "primal intention," if not by achievement, and for them literature is an active catalyst of social change, a vehicle for articulating and influencing this dynamic process of evolution.

Writing in 1985, the Nigerian leftist critic Biodun Jeyifo accepted the characterization of *The Chattering and the Song* as the most revolutionary play ever written in Nigeria, with the caveat, though, that Nigerian theater is not particularly revolutionary. But although warmly embraced by the left, O. disavows doctrinaire Marxism and refrains from the often combative rhetoric of his Marxist compatriots. Yet the agenda he promotes in his works, his undisguised antipathy for tradition and "animist gods," and his critical statements argue his close ideological affinity with them. He also shares the significant influence of Bertolt Brecht (q.v.), which critics have observed in African Marxist writers, especially in his use of sung commentaries, a discursive debate strategy, and other devices that undermine the stage as an arena for illusion. A combination of a keen sense of theater, incisive social analyses and criticism, and a lively sense of humor characterizes his plays, for which he has thrice been honored with the annual literature prize of the Association of Nigerian Authors.

FURTHER WORKS: *A Restless Run of Locusts* (1975); *Beyond Translation* (1985); *The Genre of Prose Fiction: Two Complementary Views* (1986, with Adebayo Williams); *Midnight Hotel* (1986); *A Farewell to Cannibal Rage* (1986); *Another Raft* (1988); *Birthdays Are Not for Dying and Other Plays* (1990)

BIBLIOGRAPHY: Enekwe, O. O., "Interview with F. O.," *The Greenfield Review,* 8, 1–2 (Spring 1980), 76–80; Emmanuel, I., "O. on His Ambitions," *Concord Weekly,* 14–21 Jan. 1985, 35; Akpederi, J., "A Chat with F. O.," *African Guardian,* 27 Mar. 1986, 42; Amuta, C., "Contemporary Contradictions and the Revolutionary Alternative: *Once Upon Four Robbers* and *Morountodun,*" *The Theory of African Literature* (1989), 167–75

OYEKAN OWOMOYELA

OSORGIN, M. A.

(pseud. of Mikhail Andreevich Il'in or Ilyin) Russian novelist, journalist, and short-story writer, b. 7 Oct. 1878, Perm; d. 27 Nov. 1942, Chabris, France

The son of a circuit-court judge, O. took a degree in law at Moscow University. As a lawyer he served the poor, published political brochures, and joined the terroristic, anti-Marxist Socialist-Revolutionary Party. During the December 1905 uprising O. was arrested, serving six months in solitary confinement. He was able to escape to Italy in 1906, where he was drawn to the anarchism espoused by the Maximalist wing of the Socialist-Revolutionary Party. From Italy he contributed to a variety of Russian periodicals, using the pseudonym Osorgin (his mother's maiden name). He also wrote a book on Italy, joined the Freemasons, and established a friendship with Maxim Gorky (q.v.). Returning to Russia in 1916, O. worked as a war correspondent, skillfully eluded the police, supported the February Revolution, published more political brochures "for the people," and contributed to and edited numerous democratic periodicals, all of which were finally closed down during the first months of 1918. During the next few years he published two collections of stories, translated Gozzi's *Princess Turandot* for theater director E. V. Vakhtangov (1883–1922), and became editor of a bulletin for the All-Russian Famine Relief Committee (a group that Lenin mistrusted)—leading to O.'s arrest and imprisonment, exile to Kazan, and finally in 1922 deportation to Berlin. O. worked for Kerensky's newspaper *Dni* in Germany, then moved to Paris where he wrote for P. N. Miliukov's *Poslednie novosti* until 1940. During his years in France, O. wrote for numerous émigré periodicals and published a dozen works of fiction. He avoided the anti-Bolshevik chorus of his fellow émigrés, frequently praised Soviet novels in his book reviews, and tended more and more to live as a recluse. In June of 1940, O. left Paris for the unoccupied zone, finally settling down in the village of Chabris. Now old, ill, and poverty-stricken, O. nevertheless continued to write, sending articles both to the U.S. and to Scandinavia. After all of France was occupied in 1942, O. was jailed for a short period as a suspected communist, and died the same year.

In addition to writing news articles, O. contributed stories, sketches, criticism, and reviews to the newspapers for which he worked. Most of the novels he published were first serialized in such newspapers. During his life, O. published some 2,300 items in over 100 Russian émigré periodicals—under at least 50 different pseudonyms ("Osorgin" being the most common). He published twenty books, of which six appeared posthumously. Two collections of stories that met with considerable success were *Tam, gde byl schastliv* (1928; there where I was happy) and *Chudo na ozere* (1932; miracle on the lake). Most

of these stories are narrated by the author and are obviously autobiographical, whether labeled as such or not. Though often humorous, they also tend to be nostalgic—first of all for Russia, for the birch forests and wide rivers of O.'s childhood, and, secondly, for Italy, where O. lived almost as a native for ten years. Not an experimenter except for one or two later works, O. was primarily a follower of traditional realistic narrative, employing a lyrical yet pure style pleasing to the Russian ear. Although his manner was that of conservative neorealism (q.v.), his views were often nonconformist. For instance, he lacked all interest in Christianity and seldom mentioned it in his writings.

Nature as the subject of O.'s many sketches was not limited to the nostalgic "birch-tree" school of writing. He also wrote about his small vacation cottage in a French village and its garden, which he so carefully tended. After eight or ten years, some thirty of O.'s feuilletons on this theme were collected under the title *Proisshestviia zelenogo mira* (1938; events of the green world). Here the major motif was the superiority of the country to the city, which O.'s Russian readers found congenial.

O. was best known for his novel *Sivtsev Vrazhek* (1928; *Quiet Street*, 1930), set in Moscow in the years 1917–1918. It became a best-seller in its American edition. The philosopher-protagonist, who represents the author, takes an existentialist view of the failure of the February Revolution to prevent the Bolshevik coup, concluding that all who had been responsible for the first revolution were in some sense also responsible for the second. O. expressed the view in this novel and in many of his later writings that he accepted both revolutions completely (even if he did not always agree with their tactics), and he regretted only that the October Revolution had rejected him by deporting him. He would rather live in Russia, even though he faced possible execution there, than live safely in bourgeois France.

O.'s only other novel to appear in English translation was *Povest' o sestre* (1931; *My Sister's Story*, 1931)—in which the author creates a believable intellectual woman of the fin de siècle period who refuses to accept the double standard in her failed marriage. She is based on O.'s own sister, Olga, who died in 1907.

The novel of his that O. liked best was *Vol'ny kamenshchik* (1937; Freemason). Relatively innovative in both style and subject, the novel treats an ordinary man, a Russian émigré, whose children speak French rather than Russian and whose marriage is falling apart. He finds the materialism of French society vastly tiresome and seeks to escape it by following the Masonic path to moral perfection. He only partly succeeds in this. The novel is not greatly didactic, while being virtually unique in its sympathetic presentation of Masonic philosophy.

Although O.'s dream of returning to Russia seemed hopeless, several of his short pieces were published in the Soviet Union in the 1960s and 1970s. Then in the late 1980s, seven major novels by him appeared in a variety of periodicals and books. *Sivtsev Vrazhek* appeared in three editions of up to 150,000 copies, and *Povest' o sestre* in two. This phenomenon attests to the fascination of Soviet intellectuals with the Russian émigrés of the first wave. More than that, it exhibits a particular fondness for O., who has implicitly been invited home by his fellow Russians—who have not forgiven O. for what he did, but rather have asked him to forgive them for what they did.

FURTHER WORKS: *Ocherki sovremennoi Italii* (1913); *Prizraki* (1917); *Skazki i neskazki* (1918); *Iz malen'kogo domika* (1921); *Veshchi cheloveka* (1929); *Svidetel' istorii* (1932); *Kniga o kontsakh* (1935); *Povest' o nekoei devitse* (1938); *V tikhom mestechke Frantsii* (1946); *Po povodu beloi korobochki* (1947); *Pis'ma o neznachitel'nom* (1952); *Vremena* (1955); *Zametki Starogo Knigoeda* (1989). FURTHER VOLUME IN ENGLISH: *Selected Stories, Reminiscences and Essays* (1982)

BIBLIOGRAPHY: Nazaroff, A., "Moscow Life during the Revolution," *NYT*, 19 Oct. 1930, 8; MacAfee, H., on *My Sister's Story*, *YR*, 21, 3 (Mar. 1932), vi–x; Gurvitch, G., "In Memory of Brother M. A. O.," *Masonic Club Rossia* (N.Y.), Bulletin 1 (April 1943), 13–15; "Ilyin, M. A.," in Harkins, W., ed., *Dictionary of Russian Literature* (1959), 150; "O., M. A.," in Florinsky, M., ed., *McGraw-Hill Encyclopedia of Russia and the Soviet Union* (1961), 403; Hagglund, R., "The Russian Émigré Debate of 1928 on Criticism," *SlavR*, 32, 3 (1973), 515–26; Barmache, N., D. Fiene, and T. Ossorguine, comps., *Bibliographie des œuvres de Michel Ossorguine* (1973); Fiene, D., "M. A. O.—The Last Mohican of the Russian Intelligentsia," *RLT*, 16 (1979), 93–105; Fiene, D., ed., *Selected Stories, Reminiscences and Essays* (1982); Sorokin-Vasiliev, O., on *Selected Stories, Reminiscences and Essays*, *SlavR*, 43, 1 (1984), 161; "O., M. A.," in Terras, V., ed., *Handbook of Russian Literature* (1985), 324

DONALD M. FIENE

OTERO, Blas de

Spanish poet, b. 15 Mar. 1916, Bilbao; d. 12 July 1979, Madrid

Together with Victoriano Cremer (b. 1908), José Hierro (b. 1922), Eugenio G. de Nora (b. 1923), and Gabriel Celaya (q.v.), O. formed the group of major poets who came to prominence during post-Civil War, Francoist Spain. Following earlier education with the Jesuits in Bilbao, O. took a degree in law from the University of Valladolid; but he never practiced law and instead went on to study literature in Madrid.

While most of the giants of pro-Republic, prewar poetry were either dead or in exile, O., along with Celaya especially, became identified as the most significant voice of Marxist-oriented liberalism and as the leading literary protester against injustice, oligarchy, and dictatorship. Although he visited the Soviet Union and China, stayed in Castro's Cuba for four years, and declared sympathy for North Vietnam, O. is not fundamentally a political poet. At the center of his best work are the Spaniards of his time and the conditions of their common life. In O. this so-called "social poetry" is generally not to be confused with the social realism (q.v.), which by decree treats only certain sectors of reality in specified manners.

Both in theory and practice O. at his best writes about what he personally feels strongly and sincerely. In often technically perfect and difficult poems, his treatment of suffering and outraged humanity becomes experience, not mere allusion or commentary. But such compositions of mid-century such as the sonnets "La tierra" (1950; the earth) and "Hombre" (1958; "Man," 1972) reveal what may be the more fundamental basis of his work: the post-World War II, existentialist questioning about the nature of God and the world he made, and the inquiry into the lot of humankind forced to live the horrors that history consistently revisits upon men, women, and children. In this context the Spanish Civil War, World War II, and the broken lives and countries of their aftermath are merely the portion of mortal misery that it has been O.'s lot to experience firsthand and to transform into his poetry. *Angel fieramente humano* (1950; fiercely human angel) and *Redoble de conciencia* (1951; drumroll of conscience), particularly in their reedition and augmentation in 1958 as *Ancia*, may contain the best of the O. being described here.

After O's death, there was a memorial service to him in Las Ventas bullring of Madrid, which some 40,000 attended. It is probable that those who went were attracted by the persona of O. as author of the "A la inmensa mayoría" (1955; "To the Immense Majority," 1972), the dedicatory opening poem of *Angel fieramente humano*. In a 1968 interview O. explained that even though his poetry was not the stuff around which mass audiences come to center themselves, it treated the vital concerns of the great majority of people. Now some sixteen years after Franco's death and the firm establishment of prosperous democracy in Spain, it seems that O.'s public reputation is somewhat on the wane. The anti-Francoism with which he was identified is largely irrelevant today. But the perdurance of O. will have nothing to do with Franco, but with his tremendously sensitive representation of human life as experienced during one of its epically trying periods.

FURTHER WORKS: *Cuatro poemas* (1941); *Cántico espiritual* (1942); *Poesías en Burgos* (1943); *Antología y notas* (1952); *Pido la paz y la palabra* (1955); *En castellano* (1959); *Esto no es un libro* (1963); *Que trata de España* (1964); *Mientras* (1970); *Historias fingidas y verdaderas* (1970); *Verso y prosa* (1974); *Todos mis sonetos* (1977); *Correspondencia sobre la edición de "Pido la paz y la palabra"* (1987). FURTHER VOLUMES IN ENGLISH: *Twenty Poems of B. de O.* (1964); *Selected Poems of Miguel Hernández and B. de O.* (1972)

BIBLIOGRAPHY: Alarcos Llorach, E., *La poesía de B. de O.* (1963); King, E. L., "B. de O.: The Past and Present of the Eternal," in Ferrán, J., and D. Testa, eds., *Spanish Writers of 1936* (1973), 125 33; Barrow, G. R., "Autobiography and Art in the Poetry of B. de O.," *HR*, 48 (1980), 213–30; Mellizo, C., and L. Salstad, eds., *B. de O.: Study of a Poet* (1980); Barrow, G. R., "Notions of Nowhere: A Poet in Francoist Spain," *MRRM*, 2 (1986), 111–25; Barrow, G. R., *The Satiric Vision of B. de O.* (1988); McDermott, P., "B. de O.: Cultural Memory in a Time of Silence: Alternative Voices *En castellano*," *Antípodas*, 2 (1989), 97–116

STEPHEN MILLER

OZICK, Cynthia

American novelist, short-story writer, and essayist, b. 17 Apr. 1928, New York, N.Y.

O. is one of the most significant, and most self-consciously "Jewish," literary voices to emerge in the past three decades. Born in New York City, O. received her B.A. in English from New York University and her M.A. from Ohio State. Equally at home with fiction and the literary essay, O. has published three novels, *Trust* (1966), *The Cannibal Galaxy* (1971), and *The Messiah of Stockholm* (1987); four collections of short fiction, *The Pagan Rabbi* (1971), *Bloodshed* (1982), *Levitation: Five Fictions* (1982), and *The Shawl* (1989); and two collections of essays, *Art and Ardor* (1983) and *Metaphor and Memory* (1988).

O. is the case of a writer who blossomed late (she blames her long, fruitless apprenticeship on an early fascination with the art novel of Henry James [q.v.]), but who has gradually emerged as the dominant voice for new directions in Jewish-American writing. If contemporary Jewish-American literature often seems dominated by those either estranged from or hostile to their Jewish roots, O. is a noteworthy exception. She is an observant Jew, a tireless student of Jewish ideas, and a fierce supporter of the State of Israel.

For O., it is essential that the Jewish-American writer think, and even dream, in centrally Jewish ways; and she goes on to define "centrally Jewish" as "whatever touches on the liturgical." The result has been a series of fictional works that pit Pan against Moses, unbridled passions against the fences of law. Moments in her first long and largely unsuccessful novel, *Trust,* intimate these themes; the stories in *The Pagan Rabbi* make them breathtakingly clear.

For many years O. so worried about the idol-making possibilities of fiction—in both her essays and her own fiction—that critics began to worry about her obsessive self-abnegation. Not since Hawthorne has a writer seemed so fatally attracted to the demonic, to the "pagan." However, *Metaphor and Myth* makes it clear that at least some imaginative work can be numbered on the side of the angels and that literature itself need make no apology for its potential as an abiding, even necessary, moral force.

O. continues to grow as an artist, but even at the midpoint of her career it seems safe to say that she will be regarded as a first-rate short-story writer and as one of America's most provocative literary essayists.

BIBLIOGRAPHY: Wisse, R., "American Jewish Writing, Act II," *Commentary,* 61 (1976), 40–45; Rosenfeld, A., "C. O.: Fiction and the Jewish Idea," *Midstream,* 23 (1977), 76–81; Walden, D., ed., *The World of C. O.* (1987); Epstein, J., "C. O., Jewish Writer," *Commentary,* 77 (1984), 64–69; Bloom, H., ed., *C. O.: Modern Critical Views* (1986); Pinsker, S., *The Uncompromising Fictions of C. O.* (1987); Lowin, J., *C. O.* (1988)
SANFORD PINSKER

PACHECO, José Emilio

Mexican poet, novelist, short-story writer, translator, essayist, and literary critic, b. 30 June 1939, Mexico City

P. is one of Mexico's most prolific and talented contemporary writers. He began publishing creative works in 1955 at the age of seventeen and has continued, unabated, producing literary works and literary criticism. P. has traveled widely, and he has taught and lectured throughout North America and Europe. In 1985 he was inducted into the Colegio de México as that institution's youngest member.

P. is viewed by critics as a premier poet. His poetry is found in nine collections, the first of which is *Los elementos de la noche* (1963; elements of the night). It contains poems written from 1958 to 1963 and is notable for its maturity, complex treatments of external reality, interplay of time planes, introspective musing, and solitude. *Los elementos de la noche* included various of P.'s "aproximaciones," translations into Spanish of English and French poets, thus establishing P. as a literary translator, a vocation in which he has excelled. His second collection, entitled *El reposo del fuego* (1966; the resting fire), is in large part a continuation of the themes and preoccupations found in *Los elementos de la noche*. Dedicated to P.'s friend Mario Vargas Llosa (q.v.), *El reposo del fuego* is divided into three cantos and focuses on nature and mortality, centering on the primary images of fire, wind, and water to inform a striking poetic reality.

In 1969 P. won the prestigious National Poetry Prize for his *No me preguntes cómo pasa el tiempo* (1969; don't ask me how the time flies). With this collection P.'s poetry enters a new cycle. Poetry itself becomes an object of examination—poetic language, poetic truth, poetic reality. Irony, cou-

pled with a critical and existential worldview, becomes an organizing principle. This new cycle is extended and intensified with *Irás y no volverás* (1973; you'll go and not return), a collection of verse written from 1967 to 1972. Amidst a kaleidoscopic array of utopic visions, notes of nobility and hope, desperation and disenchantment, P. finds poetic images in an international landscape, treating such diverse places as Illinois, Canada, Montevideo, and Rio de Janeiro.

Islas a la deriva (wr. 1973–1975; islands on course), P.'s fifth collection, appeared in 1976, followed by *Desde entonces* (1980; since then). In 1980 P. also published *Tarde o temprano* (sooner or later). This collection brought together the poems of all the previous collections into one volume.

Los trabajos de mar (1983; labors of the sea) represents a compilation of fifty-two poems that treat a large variety of topics. P.'s penchant for writing poems to and about other poets and artists is evident. There are numerous works treating Greek antiquity. More recently, P. has published the collections, *Miro la tierra* (1986; I look at the earth) and *Ciudad de la memoria* (1989; city of memories). These combined works contain most of P.'s poetry written during the 1980s, treating history and the human condition.

In addition to his poetry, P. is widely respected for his prose, particularly his short stories, which, according to P., are a "complement" to his poetry. He has published four major collections, several of which have grown in the number of stories they include with subsequent editions. His first collection, *La sangre de Medusa* (1958; blood of Medusa), was republished and greatly expanded in 1990. The later publication contains stories written from 1956 to 1984. It is a retrospective of works written mostly in youth and subsequently retouched and revived by a more mature author. *El viento distante* (1963; rev. ed., 1969; the distant wind) contains eight stories; these narratives, all of which have children or adolescents as protagonists, served to establish P. as a major short-story writer. His subsequent collection, *El principio del placer* (1972; the pleasure principle), not only furthered this reputation, but it earned P. the prestigious Xavier Villaurrutia Prize in 1973. Critics tend to divide P.'s short narratives into two thematic fields: youth (its problems, viewpoints, and evolution) and the fantastic. Within those themes is the preoccupation with time—its passage, past in the present, and temporal play.

P.'s two novels also merit comment. His first, *Morirás lejos* (1967; you will die far from here), won the Magda Donato Prize in 1968. It is a complicated work, which intertwines a variety of texts and has the central theme of the historical persecution and annihilation of Jews. *Las Batallas en el desierto* (1981; desert battles) is a short but incisive treatment of Mexico City in the late 1940s. Based on P.'s penchant for nostalgia, the author tries to come to terms with his personal past and the new Mexico City.

Aside from P.'s stature as a poet and prose writer, he has produced a large body of other works, including screenplays for movies and television. In collaboration with Arturo Ripstein (dates n.a.), he wrote *El castillo de la pureza* (1972; the castle of purity), which won the Ariel Prize. He won the Silver Goddess Award for *El santo oficio* (1974; the holy office), also written with Ripstein. In addition, P. is a literary translator of considerable stature, having translated into Spanish such authors as Beckett, Pinter, Pirandello, Tennessee Williams (qq.v.), Rimbaud, and many others. P. has also been responsible for a large number of literary anthologies, special editions, prologues, essays, and articles on literary topics. He has contributed (beginning in 1957) to numerous journals and newspaper literary supplements such as *Estaciones, México en la Cultura, Revista de la Universidad de México, La Cultura en México, Excélsior, Plural, Vuelta,* and *Proceso.* For this work he won the National Prize for Journalism in 1980.

P. is a major figure in Mexican letters. As a scholar, literary critic, and creative writer, P. is a principal personage in contemporary Latin American literature. His literary output has been astonishing both in terms of quantity and quality.

FURTHER WORKS: *Giménez Botey* (1964); *Al margen* (1976); *Ayer es nunca jamás* (1978); *Jardín de niños* (1978); *Breve antología* (1980); *Prosa de la calvera* (1981); *Fin de siglo y otros poemas* (1984); *Alta traición: antología poética* (1985)

BIBLIOGRAPHY: Campos, M. A., "J. E. P. o la palabra que se va," *El Rehilete,* 3a, 34 (1971), 57–61; Hoeksema, T., "J. E. P. Signals from the Flames," *LALR,* 3, 5 (1974), 143–56; Díez, L. A., "La narrativa fantasmática de J. E. P.," *TCrit,* 2, 5 (1976), 103–14; Gullón, A. M., "Dreams and Distance in Recent Poetry by J. E. P.," *LALR,* 6, 11 (1977), 36–42; Duncan, J. A., "The Themes of Isolation and Persecution in J. E. P.'s Short Stories," *Ibero-Amerikanisches Archiv,* 4, 3 (1978), 243–51; Jiménez de Báez, Y., et al., *Ficción e historia: La narrativa de J. E. P.* (1979); Duncan, J. A., "The Novel As Poem and Document: J. E. P.'s *Morirás lejos,*" *Ibero-Amerikanisches Archiv,* 6, 4 (1980), 277–92; Cluff, R. M., "Immutable Humanity within the Hands of Time: Two Short Stories by J. E. P.," *LALR,* 10, 20 (Spring–Summer 1982), 41–56; García Rey, J. M., "La poesía de J. E. P. o las palabras que dicta el tiempo," *CHA,* 380 (1982), 472–84; Villena, L. A. de, *J. E. P.* (1986); Verani, H. J., *J. E. P. ante la crítica* (1987)

SAM L. SLICK

PADILLA, Heberto

Cuban poet, novelist, and journalist, b. 20 Jan. 1932, Puerta de Golpe, Pinar del Río

P. is one of the most controversial literary figures of the Cuban revolution. Born in the province of Pinar del Río, P. has spent a great deal of time outside of Cuba. He lived in the U.S. off and on from 1949 to 1959. After the triumph of the revolution he returned to Cuba and worked for the news agency Prensa Latina. He also collaborated with Guillermo Cabrera Infante (q.v.) on *Lunes de Revolución,* the literary supplement of the newspaper *Revolución.* He later worked as a Prensa Latina correspondent in London (1960–1961) and in Moscow (1962–1963), and directed Cubartimex (a division of the ministry of foreign commerce in charge of culture), a position which took him to eastern Europe (1964–1966). The events known as the "Padilla Affair" began in 1968 when P. won the Julián del Casal Poetry Prize from the Cuban Writers and Artists Union for his collection *Fuera del juego* (1968; out of the game). Although the judges of the contest were respected authors, all of whom were in agreement on the awarding of the prize, the book drew severe criticism on account of its supposedly antirevolutionary content. The Cuban Writers and Artists Union published the book, but with a disclaimer expressing disagreement with its ideology. P. was allowed to work as a lecturer on literature at the University of Havana from 1969 to 1970, but in 1971 he was jailed for over a month after giving a poetry reading from his new collection, *Provocaciones* (1973; provocations). After his release he read a lengthy "autocriticism" at the Cuban Writers and Artists Union, chastising himself and many other contemporary Cuban writers—including his wife, the poet Belkis Cuza Malé (b. 1942)—for their critical attitudes. After a stint as a laborer on a governmental agricultural project, P. was allowed to return to Havana, but was only able to work as a translator from 1971 to 1980, when he was given permission to emigrate to the U.S.

P. belongs to a group of poets born between 1925 and 1940 who began to publish important works during the 1960s and who initially identified with the Cuban revolution. P.'s enthusiasm for the revolution is evident in his second book of poetry, *El justo tiempo humano* (1962; just, human time). In contrast to the poetry of the *Orígenes* group which dominated the Cuban literary scene from the mid-1940s through 1959 and which was known for its erudition and obscurity, the poems of this volume are simple in diction and relatively straightforward in their political endorsements.

When P. was arrested in 1971 he had completed a large portion of his first novel, *En mi jardín pastan los héroes* (1981; *Heroes Are Grazing in My Garden,* 1984). This novel received mixed reviews. His most recent repose work is a volume of memoirs, *Autoretrato del otro: La mala memoria* (1988; *Self-Portrait of the Other,* 1990), covering his life from the early 1950s to his departure from Cuba. The prose is direct and engaging, and avoids the self-indulgence of the author's first novel.

P. is a fine poet and a lesser novelist. His poetry is complex and allusive, yet largely rooted in colloquial diction. A singular contribution, however, has been his very public life, which drew attention to the excessive restrictions that revolutionary Cuba placed on artistic expression in the 1960s and 1970s.

FURTHER WORKS: *Las rosas audaces* (1948); *La hora* (1964); *El hombre junto al mar* (1981). FURTHER VOLUMES IN ENGLISH: *Sent Off the Field: A Selection from the Poetry of H. P.* (1972); *Poetry and Politics: Selected Poems of H. P.* (1974); *Legacies: Selected Poems* (1982); *A Fountain, a House of Stone* (1991)

BIBLIOGRAPHY: Casal, L., *El caso P.: Literatura y revolución en Cuba* (n.d.); Macklin, E., ''Paperweight,'' *Parnassus,* 10, 1 (Spring–Summer 1982), 125–39; Cohen, J. M., ''Prophet,'' *NYRB,* 30 June 1983, 32–35; Sucre, G., *La máscara, la transparencia: Ensayos sobre poesía hispanoamericana* (1985), 278–80; Zapata, M. A., ''Entre la épica y la lírica de H. P.,'' *Inti,* 26–27 (Fall–Spring 1987–1988), 273–84

BEN A. HELLER

PAI Hsien-yung

(also romanized as Bai Xianyong) Chinese short-story writer, novelist, essayist, and screenwriter, b. 11 July 1937, Kweilin

The son of a famous general of the Anti-Japanese Resistance War (1937–1945), P. migrated to Taiwan with his father after the 1949 communist takeover of mainland China. In 1960 P. founded with a group of young writers a small magazine, *Hsien-tai wen-hsüeh,* which played an instrumental role in introducing Western modernism (q.v.) to the Taiwan Chinese literary elites. Consequently, throughout the 1960s, the high-modernist

paradigm dominated and inspired the Taiwan Chinese literary production.

P.'s consistently brilliant short stories, collected in *Taipei jen* (1971; *Wandering in the Garden, Waking from a Dream: Tales of Taipei Characters,* 1982) and *Chi-mo ti shih-ch'i sui* (1976; lonely seventeen), are marked by a stylistic opulence that reminds critics of the canonized traditional 18th-c. narrative *Dream of the Red Chamber* by Ts'ao Hsüeh-ch'in (1715–1763); they skillfully employ Western fictional devices such as interior monologue, free association, and mediated narration to create psychologically rich portraitures. But unlike some of his contemporaries, P. always manages to avoid the derivative excesses often found in the overzealous imitations of the 1960s. Nearly all of P.'s stories focus on two character groups: the mainlanders who migrated with the Nationalists to Taiwan (the *Tai-pei jen,* or Taipei people) and those who exiled themselves to the U.S. (the *Niu-yüeh k'e,* or New York guests). The link between the two groups is their general disenchantment with life in domestic or foreign exile and their shared nostalgia for past glories real and imagined. This psychological obsession and dependence not only paralyzes them, but also disables them from adjusting to new realities. Dramatizing such pathos and melancholy are two themes that should be familiar to readers of *Dream of the Red Chamber,* a favorite of P. himself: the ravages of time and the transience of human affairs.

A totally different group of characters emerges in P.'s first novel *Nieh-tzu* (1983; *Crystal Boys,* 1990): young gay men living in the demimonde of illicit sex and rendezvous. Besides portraying for the first time in Chinese the young gays' incessant and arduous quests for emotional fulfillment, the novel also presents vividly the oppressive power of the Chinese patriarchy and its torturous effects on its sons. This compelling novel, as well as four memorable stories on the travails of Chinese womanhood, have been adapted into films, though predictably with uneven results. Long admired by readers in Taiwan, Hong Kong, and the overseas Chinese communities, P.'s works are now also known in mainland China.

FURTHER WORKS: *Mo-jan hui shou* (1978); *Yu-yüan ching-meng* (1982); *Ming-hsing k'a-fei kuan* (1984)

BIBLIOGRAPHY: Lau, J., ''Crowded Hours Revisited: The Evocation of the Past in *Taipei jen,*'' *JASt,* 34, 1 (1975), 31–47; Ouyang Tzu, ''The Fictional World of P.,'' *Renditions,* 5 (1975), 79–86; Lau, J., ''Celestials and Commoners: Exiles in P.'s Stories,'' *Monumenta Serica,* 36 (1984–1985), 409–23

WILLIAM TAY

PALACIO VALDÉS, Armando

Spanish novelist, short-story writer, and essayist, b. 4 Oct. 1853, Entralgo; d. 29 Jan. 1933, Madrid

Asturian by birth, P. V. studied in the city of Oviedo with Clarín (pseud. of Leopoldo Alas, 1852–1901), the famous author of *La regenta* (1884–1885; the regent). Subsequently he became a lawyer in Madrid. P. V. was very active at the Ateneo of Madrid, a cultural organization well known for its social gatherings. Besides editing the *Revista Europea,* he wrote for such newspapers as *El imparcial* and *La correspondecia de España.* In addition, he wrote on many contemporary writers in *Semblanzas literarias* (1871; literary biographical sketches), *Los oradors del Ateneo* (1878; the speakers of the Ateneo), *Los novelistas españoles* (1878; the Spanish novelists), and *Nuevo viaje al Parnaso* (1879; new journey to Parnassus). In collaboration with Clarín, he published a collection of critical essays entitled *Literatura en 1881* (1882; literature in 1881). In 1906 he was elected to the prestigious Spanish Royal Academy of the Language, an honor only afforded to well-connected figures of the cultural and political establishment in Spain (he was formally inducted as a member in 1920).

Even though P. V.'s first lengthy work of fiction, *El señorito Octavio* (1881; *Señorito Octavio,* 1896–1897), displayed aspects of his talent for character delineation and his Dickensian humor, it was with *Marta y María* (1883; *Martha and Mary,* 1896–1897) that some of his constant traits began to appear. In María de Elorza he portrays a repressive woman who reacts with a degree of physical pleasure when her maid flagellates her in the name of religion whereas she is unable to respond in a normal fashion to the affectionate advances of her fiancé and the warm feelings expressed by her family. On the surface, these traits of María seem to anticipate a disastrous ending for her, a conclusion which fails to materialize as the work finishes with a precipitous and preconceived happy ending reflecting P. V.'s unwillingness to face reality in a serious and rigorously intellectual manner.

With *La espuma* (1890; *Froth,* 1891), P. V. demonstrates his partial acceptance of naturalism (q.v.) as he attacks the high classes in Madrid as exploiters of Riosa's mercury miners, human beings who, by virtue of their hostile environment, remain ignorant as they provide the wealthy stockholders in the capital city with the resources they require to support their mistresses. A similar critical attitude is apparent in *La fe* (1892; *Faith,* 1892), a novel that attacks certain practices favored by the Roman Catholic church in Spain. Most of these novels, however, are not representative of P. V.'s works in that, as stated previously, his creations often avoid serious topics as evidenced by his most famous novels: *La hermana San Sulpicio* (1889; *Sister Saint Sulpice,* 1890), *José* (1885; *José,* 1901), *Riverita* (1886; Riverita), and *Maxima* (1887; *Maxima,* 1888). To a large extent, entertainment for the sake of entertainment became one of P. V.'s foremost objectives in many of his works.

Overall, P. V. published twenty-four novels, along with four collections of short stories, the fictionalized memoirs of his youth—*La novela de un novelista* (1921; the novel of a novelist)—and lengthy essays. Autobiographical elements clearly predominate in some of his novels (for instance, *Riverita* and *Maxima*). His characters delighted large numbers of readers in the Spanish-speaking world for many years in that his was a relaxing art form, one deliberately wishing to avoid crude referential reality. P. V.'s value today rests primarily in his humor and his ability to create atmospheres.

FURTHER WORKS: *El cuarto poder* (1888; *The Fourth Estate,* 1901); *La alegría del capitán Ribot* (1899; *The Joy of Captain Ribot,* 1900); *La aldea perdida* (1903); *Tristán o el pesimismo* (1906; *Tristán,* 1925)

BIBLIOGRAPHY: Cruz Rueda, A., *A. P. V. Estudio biográfico* (1949); Roca Franquesa, J. M., *P. V.: técnica novelística y credo estético* (1951); Baquero Goyanes, M., ''Estudio,'' *Tristán o el pesimismo* (1971); Pascuál Rodríguez, M., *A. P. V.* (1976)

LUIS T. GONZÁLEZ-DEL-VALLE

PALESTINIAN LITERATURE

See Volume 3, page 464.

Largely a product of the 20th c., Palestinian literature forms an integral part of modern Arabic literature and partakes of most of its major thematic and formal features. Perhaps the single most crucial characteristic of Palestinian literature is its total preoccupation with national concerns. And while involvement in social and political issues is a common feature of modern Arabic literature in general, it informs Palestinian literature to a far greater degree. Political consciousness and commitment to the national cause determines not only

471

the subject matter of Palestinian literature but also its division into periods and genres.

A general chronological division of Palestinian literature specifies three major, more or less distinct, periods demarcated by three historical events. The first period spans the years 1917–1948, from the Balfour Declaration, which promised the Jews a national homeland in Palestine, to the establishment of the state of Israel in 1948; the second from 1948 to 1967, from the first Arab-Israeli war to the June War of 1967; and the third from 1967 to the present. Like all periodization schemes, this one is useful only as a general outline.

The division into genres shows the exclusive preponderance of poetry during the first period, the emergence and rapid ascendancy of fiction during the second, and the intensification and proliferation of both during the third. The notable absence of a dramatic tradition from Palestinian literature is a direct result of the conditions of dispersion and instability that have characterized much of modern Palestinian history. All recent efforts to establish a regular Palestinian theater in East Jerusalem and the West Bank have faltered under the harsh and precarious conditions of life under Israeli military occupation. Although a number of Palestinian plays do exist, they are too few and too tentative to constitute a distinct literary tradition.

Poetry

Awareness of the unfolding Zionist schemes in Palestine impelled the first generation of Palestinian poets to devote much of their creative energy to sounding the bells of alarm. The task was made all the more urgent by the near universal ignorance of the impending danger to Palestine in the rest of the Arab world. All major Palestinian poets of the first half of this century, such as Iskandar al-Khūrī al-Baytjālī (1890–1978), Ibrāhīm Tūqān (1905–1941), 'Abd al-Rahīm Mahmūd (1913–1948), and 'Abd al-Karīm al-Karmī (pseud: Abū Salmā, 1910–1980), immersed themselves fully in the national struggle to save Palestine from Zionist colonization.

But even as they extolled the beauty of the Palestinian landscape and sought to imbue their listeners and readers with a spirit of sacrifice, these poets were profoundly pessimistic about the prospects of the homeland that was being dismembered and expropriated piecemeal before their very eyes. Palestinian national hymns, composed by these poets, were often sung collectively in public and became a common phenomenon during this period. Similarly, the image of both the martyr and the *fidā'ī* (freedom fighter) became major tropes of Palestinian poetry and through it imprinted themselves on the Palestinian collective consciousness.

In equally moving poems, both 'Abd al-Rahīm Mahmūd, who died in the battle of Sajara in 1948, and Abū Salmā simultaneously sang of Palestinian heroism and satirized official Arab impotence and treachery. Scathingly invective satire against the Zionists, the British Mandate, and the Arab kings, especially 'Abd-Allah of Jordan, provides a thematic counterpart to the panegyrics extolling heroism and patriotic virtues in this poetry.

Whatever the theme, the form of Palestinian poetry during this period is largely traditional and the language uniformly classical. To realize the intended political objective of rallying the people to the national cause, Palestinian poets readily availed themselves of the rich rhetorical tradition of classical poetry and fully used the intrinsic oratorical power of its established metrical and rhyme schemes. With the possible exception of Ibrāhīm Tūqān's occasional experimentation with new poetic forms, Palestinian poetry of this period shows little awareness of the revolutionary innovations that were transforming modern Arabic poetry in other parts of the Arab world, notably in Iraq.

In the wake of the Palestinian catastrophe of 1948, Palestinian poetry turned to nursing Palestinian wounds. Baffled and agonized soul-searching characterizes much of the poetry of the second phase, especially the poetry of the 1950s. The national tragedy finds its most painful expression in the fate of individual Palestinians who were transformed suddenly from citizens in their own country to refugees in foreign and often hostile lands. A mood of loss and abandonment is prevalent in much of the introspective poetry of Fadwā Tūqān (b. 1917), Salmā Khadrā Jayyūsī (b. 1926), Kamāl Nāsir (1925–1973), and Hārūn Hāshim Rashīd (b. 1930).

This inward turn was accompanied by a greater attention to the artistic-aesthetic aspects of poetry. While many Palestinian poets went on writing in the traditional style, some adopted the new forms and innovative techniques of modernist Arabic poetry. Foremost among the pioneers in this regard was Tawfīq Sāyigh (q.v.), who introduced the prose poem into Palestinian poetry. Sāyigh's poetry often uses mythic archetypes and symbolic patterns to grapple with personal experiences and existential questions. He alone among all Palestinian poets can be said to possess a metaphysical vision. Similar interests inform much of the poetic output of Jabrā Ibrāhīm Jabrā (q.v.) as well. On the whole, Palestinian poets who remained under Arab rule were far more daring and experimental than their counterparts who stayed behind in Israel.

A change in the bleak outlook and mood of Palestinian poetry begins to take form in the late

1950s and early 1960s at the hands of leftist poets like Muʿīn Bissīsū (1927–1988) and especially in the poetry of the Palestinian poets living in Israel. The distinctive quality of much of the poetry of Hannā Abū Hannā (b. 1931), Tawfīq Zayyād (b. 1932), Rāshid Husayn (1936–1977), Mahmūd Darwīsh (q.v.), and Samīh al-Qāsim (b. 1939) is its fiercely defiant tone. In highly rhetorical poems, these poets openly challenged official Israeli policies and attitudes and launched what came to be known as "the poetry of the occupied land" or, more generally, "the poetry of the Palestinian resistance."

Initially, most of this poetry was written in traditional form to be delivered in a declamatory style during political rallies. Its declared political objective was to strengthen the resolve of the Palestinians within Israel to stay put and resist Israeli attempts to dislodge them from the land. Much of this poetry was written under constant police harassment, which often included lengthy terms of imprisonment and house arrest. The relentless pressure eventually drove two leading poets, Rāshid Husayn and Mahmūd Darwīsh, into permanent exile.

Since 1967 Palestinian poetry has developed in several simultaneous directions. While it remains uniformly committed and keenly tuned to political developments, its form and techniques have evolved considerably. This change is perhaps most clearly evident in the poetry of the leading Palestinian poet, Mahmūd Darwīsh. The structure, imagery, diction, and style of Darwīsh's poetry have grown steadily more complex since he went into exile in 1971, and rival in this regard the most experimental trends in contemporary Arabic poetry.

A similar, though less drastic, tendency is evident in the recent poetry of Samīh al-Qāsim, Hannā Abū-Hannā, and other Palestinian poets. But while al-Qāsim, like Darwīsh and others, has steadily cultivated the prophetic voice through biblical and Koranic allusion in his poetry, Abū Hannā seems to gravitate more toward ancient Canaanite history, in light of which he seeks to read contemporary Palestinian reality.

Fiction

Of the two fiction genres, the achievements of the Palestinian novel far surpass those of the Palestinian short story, though these are by no means negligible. Both genres entered Palestinian literature in the first decades of the 20th c., but mature specimens of either began to appear only in the second half of the century. The short stories Jabrā Ibrāhīm Jabrā wrote in the 1940s but published in the 1950s, in the collection ʿAraq (1956; sweat), may have been the first credible specimens of the genre in Palestinian literature.

During the 1950s and early 1960s, Samīra ʿAzzām (1927–1967), Hannā Ibrāhīm (b. 1930), and Ghassān Kanafānī (q.v.) made significant contributions to this nascent genre. Their stories invariably dramatized the plight of Palestinian refugees, especially the psychological effects of dislocation on hapless Palestinian individuals. Though generally bleak, the outlook of some of these stories is occasionally brightened by a glimmer of political consciousness and the promise of change in the Palestinian condition.

With rare exceptions, these stories tend to depict Palestinian reality directly in an attempt to attract attention to the plight of the Palestinian people. As a result, the stories not infrequently subordinate literary and aesthetic considerations to political expediency. As thinly disguised commentaries on contemporary Palestinian reality, the documentary value of many of these stories may exceed their artistic merit.

A greater attention to artistic requirements is evident in much of the post-1967 output. Emile Habībī's (q.v.) Sudāsiyyat al-ayyām al-sitta (1968; sextet of the six days) exemplifies this tendency. The six "tableaux" of which the work is comprised broach political issues indirectly and elliptically, primarily through the experiences of marginalized individuals.

A similar authorial restraint informs the short stories of younger writers such as Tawfīq Fayyād (b. 1939), Zakī Darwīsh (b. 1944), ʿAlī Muhammad Tāhā (b. 1931), Zakī al-ʿEyla (b. 1950), and Gharīb ʿAsqalānī (b. 1948), among others. Much like Habībī, these writers frequently use framing devices and narrative techniques that are borrowed from the rich narrative heritage of classical Arab culture. A Thousand and One Nights is only one of many indelible sources to which these writers take frequent recourse.

The Novel

The roots of the Palestinian novel lie in journalistic writing. The two pioneers of the genre, Najīb Nassār (1862–1948) and Khalīl Baydas (1875–1949), were both newspaper publishers who introduced the genre by serializing their own novels in their newspapers before publishing them in book form. Intended primarily for light entertainment, these early attempts show little sophistication in form and narrative technique and possess hardly any artistic merit.

More artistically defensible specimens of the genre were written in the 1940s. Two works in particular have left a lasting impression: Mudhakkirāt dajāja (1943; diaries of a hen) by Ishāq Mūsā al-Husaynī (1904–1989) and Surākh fī layl tawīl (1955; screams in a long night) by Jabrā Ibrāhīm Jabrā. (According to the author's testimony, the latter novel was written before 1948.) The first is an allegorical work written in the style of animal fables but dealing with a philosophical issue that concerns humans, namely, how to contend with aggression. The second, far more realistic in plot, characterization, and narrative technique, deals with the perennial quest for rebirth and rejuvenation in the wasteland of modern life: the city. Neither work alludes directly to the Palestinian condition, though both evoke aspects of it indirectly.

By all accounts, the publication of Ghassān Kanafānī's first novel, *Rijāl fi-al-shams* (1963; *Men in the Sun,* 1978), was a high watermark in the development of Palestinian fiction. Though relatively short, this novel is a consummate work of art. Its plot relates the futile attempt of three Palestinian refugees to cross the Iraq-Kuwait border in search of an alternative to the abject humiliation of life in the refugee camps. All three die asphyxiated in the empty water tank of a truck that was supposed to smuggle them into Kuwait.

The rich symbolic significance of the novel's austere plot is further reinforced by adroitly sketched characters whose psychological motivation appears eminently compelling. Throughout, the pace of the narrative remains brisk, even as it shifts repeatedly from third-person omniscient narration to stream-of-consciousness (q.v.) and interior monologue. In this, as well as in his subsequent novel, *Mā tabaqqā lakum* (1966; *All That's Left to You,* 1990), Kanafānī successfully adapts the narrative techniques of the Western psychological novel, especially as practiced by William Faulkner (q.v.), to the specifically Palestinian subject matter of his fiction.

The pervasive ramifications of the 1967 war also touched the Palestinian novel. The humiliating defeat of the regular Arab armies left a vacuum that the Palestinian guerrilla organizations rushed to fill. Their ascendancy, for as long as it lasted, significantly boosted Arab morale and irreversibly transformed Palestinian political consciousness. All the Palestinian novels written since 1967 reflect these historical facts, on which, of course, each writer puts his or her interpretive slant.

Nowhere is the change in orientation more evident than in the works of Kanafānī, the leading Palestinian novelist at the time. After having written what may possibly be the two most complex novels in all of Arabic fiction, Kanafānī abandoned the techniques of the psychological novel and turned to the simple, almost artless style of social realism (q.v.). The two complete novels he wrote after 1967, *Umm Sa'd* (1969; the mother of Sa'd) and *'Ā'id ilā Haifā* (1969; returning to Haifa), are virtually plotless. In both, direct commentary and discursive dialogue replace artful narrative and interior monologue. Convinced of the permanence of the positive developments in the Palestinian condition, Kanafānī appears to have concluded that the time had come for Palestinian imaginative fiction to imitate Palestinian history, and not the reverse. The characters of both *Umm Sa'd* and *'Ā'id ilā Haifā* are presented in their unpolished and unadorned simplicity. In one of the posthumously published fragments of the three novels he left unfinished, Kanafānī attempted to narrow still further the gap between fiction and history by appending scholarly footnotes to the contrived fictional text.

Other major Palestinian writers responded to the new historical circumstances slightly differently. Thus Jabrā Ibrāhīm Jabrā continued to cultivate the revolutionary-cum-aesthetic sensibility of his elitist characters far from the misery of the refugee camps and the hubbub of the political street. In his masterpiece *al-Safīna* (1970; *The Ship,* 1985) the psychological effects of dislocation and homelessness on the main Palestinian character appear paradigmatic of angst-ridden and alienated modern life in general. A similar universalizing thrust informs Jabrā's subsequent novels, especially *al-Bahth 'an Walīd Mas'ūd* (1978; in search of Walid Mas'ūd), which, like Jabrā's earlier novels, uses a variety of sophisticated narrative techniques and poetic devices.

In a slightly different vein, Sahar Khalīfa's (b. 1941) novels thematize the feminist component within the political struggle for national liberation. The feminist agenda is prominently announced in the title of her first novel, *Lam na'ud jawārī lakum* (1974; no longer your maids), and is methodically pursued in both of her subsequent novels, *Al-Subbār* (1976; *Wild Thorns,* 1985) and *'Abbād al-shams* (1980; the sunflower).

Daring experimentation with form and narrative technique characterize Emile Habībī's fictional treatment of the experience of the Palestinians living in Israel. The five narrative works he wrote since 1967 systematically mix literary modes and confound generic distinctions. One of these, *Luka' ibn Luka'* (1980; Luka', son of Luka'), is written mostly in dialogue and is a hybrid between novel and play. Following Voltaire, Habībī takes a satirical view of human mindlessness and spares no one, least of all his fellow Arabs, the cutting edge of his biting satire. He is alone among Palestinian and Arab writers to dramatize antiheroes in lead roles. His masterpiece *Al-waqa'i' al-gharībah fī ikhifā' sa'īd abī al-nahs al-mutashā'il* (1974; *The Secret Life of Saeed, the Ill-Fated Pessoptimist,* 1982) employs the style of the classical Arabic genre of *maqāma* to depict contemporary Arab reality. The lofty style of the work accentuates the wide gap between the heroic past and the lowly present.

In sum, Palestinian literature continues to be profoundly nationalistic and political, even as it strives to field universal themes and to achieve wider international recognition of its literary merits. In its relatively short life, it has made significant inroads in that direction. But to do it adequate justice, a poetics of intrinsically political literature may have to be articulated more systematically and more forcefully.

BIBLIOGRAPHY: Aruri, N., and E. Ghareeb, Introduction to *Enemy of the Sun: Poetry of Palestinian Resistance* (1970), 25–68; Abu-Ghazaleh, A.M., "The Impact of 1948 on Palestinian Writers: The First Decade," *Middle East Forum,* 66, 2–3 (1970); Peled, M., "Annals of Doom: Palestinian Literature—1917–1948," *Arabica,* 29, 2 (1982), 143–83; Sulaiman, K. A., *Palestine and Modern Arab Poetry* (1984)

MUHAMMAD SIDDIQ

PALEY, Grace

American short-story writer and poet, b. 11 Dec. 1922, Bronx, N.Y.

Born and brought up in New York City, P. attended Hunter College for two years after graduating from Evander Childs High School. She also took various courses at New York University and the New School for Social Research where she studied poetry with W. H. Auden (q.v.). During the 1960s P. taught at both Columbia University and Syracuse University; currently she teaches at Sarah Lawrence College in Bronxville, N.Y. She is active in feminist and antimilitary groups and was one of the founders of the Greenwich Village Peace Center. P. was awarded a Guggenheim fellowship in fiction (1961) and a National Council on the Arts grant (1966). In 1970 she received the National Institute of Arts and Letters Award for short-story writing and was elected a member of the institute in 1980.

Although P.'s early interest was in poetry, she began writing short fiction in the 1950s, and her first collection of stories, *The Little Disturbances of Man: Stories of Women and Men at Love,* was published in 1959. Segments of a novel P. never completed appeared in several periodicals during the 1960s, but P.'s second book of stories, *Enormous Changes at the Last Minute,* was not published until 1974, some fifteen years after her first. Her third collection, *Later the Same Day,* was published in 1985. P. has been accused of sacrificing her art to life, and she admits that her family, her political concerns, and her teaching

are often distractions, but, as she told one interviewer, "There is a lot more to do in life than just writing." It is, however, the fact that P. has always lived her life fully and intensely that allows her to infuse her fictional world with the wry, witty glimpses of the ways in which her characters manage to live with and to love each other. P. is especially adept at exploring the turmoil that often bubbles just below the surface of what might appear to be lackluster everyday life. The influences of her childhood—the Russian and the Yiddish she heard spoken at home, the sights and sounds in the streets of The Bronx neighborhood she grew up in—her early love of poetry along with her devotion to her roles as wife and mother, all seem to have provided her with the ability to render the variety of voices, the precise inflections, the idioms, and the dialects that account for the enormous vitality of her wide range of characters.

As the title suggests, the major focus of *The Little Disturbances of Man* is on what might be viewed as commonplace issues confronting her vibrantly rendered characters. And as the subtitle hints, in these *Stories of Women and Men at Love,* the emphasis is on what happens as these ordinary people in working-class New York neighborhoods struggle with the "little disturbances" of their lives, sometimes succeeding, sometimes failing, "at love." In *Enormous Changes at the Last Minute,* some of the works move away from the traditionally structured short-story form that P. follows in her first collection. Many of the pieces are very short, almost sketches, while others seem to be plotless monologues. Yet they constitute a continuing investigation of love lost and love found, of family and of friendship, of death and of survival. *Later the Same Day* brings back many of the same characters found in the earlier collections, now somewhat older and wiser. P. still employs understatement, still avoids empty emotion and sentimentality. To be sure there is, as ever, a good deal of pathos in many of the stories, but it is always saved from any hint of melodrama by P.'s masterful use of humor and irony. Her characters' vulnerability is barely concealed by their wisecracks, but in the face of divorce, abandonment, old age, and death, they can still hope, can still see that there is possibility for change.

P. continues to hold before her readers the concept that the limitations of being human do not diminish the richness that is possible in life. If her prose has evolved into what might be considered postmodern form, her characters and their concerns transcend what seems trendy. They reinforce the importance of neighborhood, friendship, and community as antidotes to isolation and despair.

FURTHER WORKS: *Leaning Forward* (1985); *Long Walks and Intimate Talks: Poems and Stories* (1991); *New and Collected Poems* (1992)

BIBLIOGRAPHY: Mickelson, A. Z., *Reaching Out: Sensitivity and Order in Recent American Fiction by Women* (1979), 206–7, 221–34; Gelfant, B., "G. P.: Fragments for a Portrait in Collage," *NER*, 3 (Winter 1980), 276–93; DeKoven, M., "Mrs. Hegel-Shtein's Tears," *PR*, 48, 2 (1981), 217–23; Sorkin, A. J., " 'What Are We, Animals?': G. P.'s World of Talk and Laughter," *SAJL*, 2 (1982), 144–54; Isaacs, N. D., *G. P.: A Study of the Short Fiction* (1990); Taylor, J., *G. P.: Illuminating the Dark Lives* (1990)

MARGARET D. SULLIVAN

PARDO BAZÁN, Emilia

Spanish novelist, short-story writer, critic, essayist, folklorist, and journalist, b. 16 Sept. 1851, La Coruña; d. 12 May 1921, Madrid

P. B. is an extraordinary figure in Spanish letters. Although she began life conventionally enough—albeit within the aristocracy—as daughter and then wife and mother, P. B. became a major force in Spanish letters during nearly forty years. Most closely identified with the realist-naturalist novel of social observation and criticism, P. B. also published some 580 short stories and as many as 1,500 pieces of journalism, and founded and edited her own magazine, *Nuevo Teatro Crítico* (1891–1893). In 1916, and despite the gender-based opposition of the university council, she was named by the minister of national education to the chair of contemporary Romance literatures at the University of Madrid. During virtually all of her life she fought to make a place for women in every facet of Spanish national life; unfortunately, even such consecrated figures of national cultural life as Juan Valera (1824–1905) and Leopoldo Alas (pseud.: Clarín, 1852–1901) were early antagonists.

P. B.'s most famous works are her *La cuestión palpitante* (1882; the burning question)—a collection of diffuse articles about the naturalism that came into vogue in Spain in the late 1870s and early 1880s because of the translation of Zola's works—and her novel *Los pazos de Ulloa* (1886; *The Son of the Bondswoman,* 1908; rev. ed., 1976). But as happens with her generational companion Armando Palacio Valdés (q.v.), P. B. suffers from having her best-known works overshadow the rest of her production. If one accepts that the realist-naturalist group of Spanish novelists really belong to three different cultural generations in Ortega y Gasset's (q.v.) sense, it is

clear that P. B., along with Palacio Valdés and Alas, belongs to the third generation, whereas Valera, José María de Pereda (1833–1906), Pedro Antonio de Alarcón (1833–1891), and Benito Pérez Galdós (1843–1920) belong to the first two. Moreover, for being a woman, P. B. probably arrives on the literary scene with even more effective years of difference than Alas and Palacio with respect to the first two generations. And this means that the aesthetics of realism-naturalism bulk much less in her production than, for example, in that of Galdós and Pereda.

This difference reveals itself thematically more than technically. Whereas the masterpieces of realism-naturalism in Spain date from the mid-1880s, notably Alas's *Le Regenta* (4 vols., 1884–1885), Galdós's *Fortunata y Jacinta* (4 vols., 1886–1887), as well as other works including P. B.'s *Los pazos de Ulloa,* P. B.'s most important novel may well be *La quimera* (1905; the chimera). Although the novel uses the standard techniques of realism-naturalism, its protagonist is a young painter who lives the artistic and spiritual conflicts and crises of end-of-the-century Madrid and Paris. As in her subsequent and penultimate novel *La sirena negra* (1907; the black siren), *La quimera* is a novel no longer centered on society and its issues, but on the problematic individual for whom all received values are wanting and for whom new values are not forthcoming.

A gender-related difference adds to the thematic differences between P. B. and other novelists. More than in any other writer, P. B.'s narrators and main characters, in her longer and shorter fiction, may be masculine or feminine. In consequence the reader is usually aware of a constant subtext wherein the question of how men perceive women and women perceive men is present. This subtext is particularly compelling when the narrator is masculine and making observations about women. Hence, in one of her best novels, *Insolación* (1889; sunstroke), P. B. deftly has a male narrator tell the story of how a wealthy young woman, recently widowed, takes up her new life; in the telling the author makes important points about gender differences and roles.

P. B.'s short stories are effective narrations in which the people and problems of daily life, especially in the author's northwestern Spain, dominate. They were designated for a large, popular audience and in the main stay firmly within the realist-naturalist aesthetic of social observation and criticism. Her few works of theater are less important, but her play of social symbolism, *Cuesta abajo* (1906; downhill), compares favorably with Galdós's *El abuelo* (perf. 1904; the grandfather) and *La de San Quintín* (perf. 1895; the woman of San Quintin). As a historian and popularizer of then contemporary French and Russian literature, P. B. was a forerunner of the internationalization of Spanish culture that is actually associated with Miguel de Unamuno (q.v.) and Ortega y Gasset.

FURTHER WORKS: *Estudio crítico de Feijoo* (1876); *Pascual López* (1879); *Un viaje de novios* (1881); *San Francisco de Asís* (1882); *La tribuna* (1883); *La dama joven* (1885); *El cisne de Vilamorta* (1885); *La madre naturaleza* (1887); *Mi romería* (1888); *Obras completas* (47 vols., 1888–1922); *Morriña* (1889); *Al pie de la torre Eiffel* (1889); *Por Francia y por Alemania; Una cristiana* (1890); *Le prueba* (1890); *La piedra angular* (1891); *Cuentos de Marineda* (1892); *Polémicas y estudios literarios* (1892); *Cuentos nuevos* (1894); *Doña Milagros* (1894); *Los poetas épicos cristianos* (1895); *Por la España pintoresca* (1895); *Memorias de un solterón* (1896); *El tesoro de Gastón* (1897); *El nino de Guzmán* (1898); *Cuentos de amor* (1898); *El saludo de las brujas* (1898); *Cuentos sacroprofanos* (1899); *Cuarenta días en la Exposición Universal de Paris* (1900); *El destripador de antaño* (1900); *En tranvía* (1901); *Cuentos de Navidad y Reyes* (1902); *Cuentos de la patria* (1902); *Cuentos antiguos* (1902); *Por la Europa católica* (1902); *Misterio* (1903); *Novelas ejemplares* (1906); *Lecciones de literatura* (1906); *El fondo del alma* (1907); *Retratos y apuntes literarios* (1907); *Sud-exprés* (1909); *La literatura francesa moderna* (3 vols., 1910, 1911, 1914); *Dulce dueño* (1911); *Belcebú* (1912); *Cuentos trágicos* (1912); *La cocina española* (1913); *Hernán Cortés y sus hazañas* (1914); *Cuentos de la tierra* (1923); *Obras completas* (3 vols., 1947, 1956, 1973)

BIBLIOGRAPHY: Hilton, R., "E. P. B.'s Concept of Spain," *Hispania,* 34 (1951), 135–48; Hilton, R., "Doña E. P. B. and the Europeanization of Spain," *Symposium,* 6 (1952), 298–307; Hilton, R., "P. B. and the Literary Polemics about Feminism," *RR,* 44 (1953), 135–48; Brown, D. F., *The Catholic Naturalism of P. B.* (1957); Kirby, H. L., "P. B., Darwinism, and *La madre naturaleza,*" *Hispania,* 47 (1964), 733–37; Kronik, J. K., "E. P. B. and the Phenomenon of French Decadentism," *PMLA,* 81 (1966), 418–27; Dendle, B. J., "The Racial Theories of E. P. B.," *HR,* 38 (1970), 17–31; Pattison, W. T., *E. P. B.* (1971); Paredes Núñez, J., *Los cuentos de E. P. B.* (1979); Clemessy, N., *E. P. B. como novelista: de la teoría a la práctica* (1981); Scari, R. M., *Bibliografía descriptiva de estudios críticos sobre la obra de E. P. B.* (1982); Hemingway, M., *E. P. B.: The Making of a Novelist* (1983); Whitaker, D. S., *"La quimera" de B. P. y la literatura finisecular* (1988); Henn, D., *The Early P. B.:* *Theme and Narrative Technique in the Novels of 1879–89* (1988)

STEPHEN MILLER

PAREJA DIEZCANSECO, Alfredo

Ecuadorean novelist and historian, b. 12 Oct. 1908, Guayaquil

Over his long and productive career, P. D. has gained a solid reputation and today stands out as the most important novelist his country has produced. Born of an Ecuadorean father and a Peruvian mother, both of aristocratic families, P. D. spent his formative years in Guayaquil, the port city that later served as the setting for most of his novels. He had to abandon school at an early age and go to work because the family fortunes had dwindled away. As a youth, he performed many odd jobs, including work as a cabin boy on a ship and a dock laborer. Though he never finished his formal education, he was always a voracious reader of books on philosophy, history, literature, psychology, and social science, becoming virtually an autodidact.

Disciplined, hard working, and active, P. D. also became an inveterate traveler, venturing forth when only twenty-one on his first trip abroad to New York in 1929. There he continued to suffer economic hardship during the Depression and had to seek a variety of menial jobs, such as waiting on tables, to eke out an existence. This was the first in a series of sojourns in other countries. Later he served Ecuador in many diplomatic posts, in Argentina, Chile, and Mexico, crowning his diplomatic career as ambassador to France in 1983.

P. D. also devoted many years to teaching, starting with a high-school position in Guayaquil in 1931, next at the university there in 1934, and finally for many years at the University of Quito where he specialized in Ecuadorean history. He has also taught as a visiting professor in various Latin American countries and in the U.S., most recently at the University of Texas, Austin, in 1982, where he gave classes in Spanish American literature and political science. In 1988 the University of Guayaquil conferred on him the degree of doctor honoris causa, and in 1989 he became a member of the Ecuadorean Academy of History and Language. Today, an octogenarian, he lives tranquilly in Quito, revered as elder statesman and historian.

Writing novels has been "the fundamental passion of my spirit," as P. D. puts it. He has published fourteen novels in all, though he maintains that only thirteen should be counted, disclaiming the second, *La señorita Ecuador* (1930;

miss Ecuador), as negligible. Critics also tend to dismiss his first novel, *La casa de los locos* (1929; the madhouse), and the third, *Río arriba* (1931; upriver), as works of apprenticeship, though these earliest books contain virtues and the kernel of things to come. Like his major novels, they are set in the city and show P. D.'s preoccupation with political and social abuses quite graphically. The reader also realizes that P. D. does not have a political ax to grind, that he seems more interested in crafting his novels well.

The qualities just mentioned are strikingly evident in P. D.'s best works, among which one must cite *El muelle* (1933; the dock). In this naturalistic book, the first to bring him acclaim, he captures faithfully the squalid atmosphere of the coastal workers in Guayaquil, a motley group of mestizos—sailors, fishermen, stevedores, merchants, the jobless, the spoils of brothels and taverns. In this novel rife with scenes of violence, prostitution, and corruption, the descriptions are vivid and the dialogues ring with authenticity. As in most of P. D.'s novels, a feminine figure of great vitality stands out, here María del Socorro. The opening chapters, set in New York during the Depression, based on P. D.'s recent stay in that metropolis, protest against police brutality. P. D. implies that society is in bad shape, whether in New York or Guayaquil, and that the poor have no escape.

Among P. D.'s other novels, *Hombres sin tiempo* (1941; men without time), which describes the hideous conditions in a political prison, is based on the author's personal experiences during several months' incarceration, and *Las tres ratas* (1944; the three rats), which unfolds the tale of three sisters, again incorporates naturalistic Guayaquil scenes of drugs, sex, blackmail, political corruption, and tragedy. This novel met with such acclaim that a popular film version was made of it. In his more mature years, P. D. has continued to publish novels that have met with success, such as *Las pequeñas estaturas* (1970; small statures), which delves into the complexities of Ecuadorean politics, while at the same time displaying many of the technical complexities of the so-called Boom writers: long interior monologues, philosophical digressions, and baroque command over language.

P. D. has also published significant works in other fields, like his *Historia del Ecuador* (1954; history of Ecuador) in four volumes, several biographies, and literary essays, notably *Thomas Mann y el nuevo humanismo* (1956; Thomas Mann and the new humanism).

FURTHER WORKS: *La Beldaca* (1935); *Baldomera (La tragedia del cholo americano)* (1938); *Hechos y hazañas de don Balón de Baba y de su amigo Inocente* (1939); *La hoguera bárbara: Vida de*

Eloy Alfaro (1944); *Vida y leyenda de Miguel Santiago* (1952); *La lucha por la democracia en el Ecuador* (1956); *La advertencia* (1956); *El aire y los recuerdos* (1958); *Los poderes omnímodos* (1964); *La Manticora* (1974); *Ensayos de ensayos* (1981); *Notas de un viaje a China* (1986)

BIBLIOGRAPHY: Diez de Medina, F., "Tres libros de América. *El meulle*," *Atenea*, 28 (1934), 35–39; Latcham, R., "A. P. D., *El muelle*," *Atenea*, 29 (1935), 325–29; Rojas, A. F., *La novela ecuatoriana* (1948), 194–98; Schwarz, K., "A. P. D., Social Novelist," *Hispania*, 42, 2 (May 1959), 220–28; Carrera Andrade, J., *Galería de místicos y de insurgentes: La vida intelectual del Ecuador durante cuatro siglos (1555–1955)* (1959), 165–68; Pérez, G., *Pensamiento y literatura del Ecuador* (1972), 396–409; Pérez, G. R., *Historia y crítica de la novela hispanoamericana* (1983), Vol. 2, 158–64; Artieda, F., "Una democracia limitada. Entrevista con A. P. D.," *El secuestro del poder* (1987), 101–18; Ribadeneira, E., "La obra narrativa de A. P. D.," *RI*, 54, 144–45 (July–Dec. 1988), 763–69

GEORGE D. SCHADE

PAVIĆ, Milorad

Serbian novelist, short-story writer, poet, and literary historian, b. 15 Oct. 1929, Belgrade, Yugoslavia (now Serbia)

A native of Belgrade, P. graduated from the University of Belgrade and acquired his Ph.D. at the University of Zagreb. He now teaches history of Serbian literature at the University of Novi Sad. In that capacity, he was instrumental in bringing to attention and reevaluating some older Serbian writers and editing their neglected works. His chief occupation is writing.

P. began with a book of poetry, *Palimpsesti* (1967; palimpsests), followed by collections of short stories, *Gvozdena zavesa* (1973; iron curtain) and *Konji svetoga Marka* (1976; the horses of Saint Mark). In these early works, he showed traits that would become his trademarks: a meditative and erudite bent in poetry, and a successful merging of fantasy and a studied realistic approach, bolstered by an impeccable and controlled style.

It was not until his latest works, the novels *Hazarski rečnik* (1984; *Dictionary of the Khazars*, 1988) and *Predeo slikan čajem* (1988; *Landscape Painted with Tea,* 1990), that P. became known beyond the borders of his native land. He again mixes reality and fantasy, at times playfully but always purposefully, creating a complex world where the borders between the present, past, and future are erased and where humans seek, often unsuccessfully, to unravel the mysteries of existence. *Hazarski rečnik* is an attempt to solve the mystery of the Khazars, a tribe on the Black Sea, lost hundreds of years ago and now claimed equally by the Christians, Muslims, and Jews. In a dazzling display of fantasy, erudition, and wit, P. follows the story through the eyes of a Serbian leader, Muslim and Jewish missionaries and scholars, and an array of other characters, who all tell their version of the story in the form of a dictionary (hence, P. claims that the work can be read starting from any point in the book). The novel entails a mystery, numerous crime stories, historical forays, attempts at dream interpretation, and musing about life, death, and truth, all couched in a fashionable idiom of modern prose. Moreover, there are two versions, male and female, the difference being noticeable only on one page.

Predeo slikan čajem is equally fantastic and experimental and unbound by time and space. Even though the novel centered around a Serbian character, P. nevertheless roams through centuries and continents in his search for his roots and for the meaning of life and death, musing about the transience of time, the past and present, God, the devil, and the human being. The innovative twist in this work is that it is construed as a crossword puzzle, the solving of which is supposed to lead to the solution of the puzzle that is life. In the end, the solution depends on each individual, which, in most cases, yields no solution. P. is again dazzling in his mastery of the language and narrative techniques, which comes through in good translations.

P. has established himself as a leading Serbian writer and one of the most intriguing writers in world literature, as attested by his rising esteem all over the world and by numerous translations of his works.

FURTHER WORKS: *Istorija srpske književnosti baroknnog doba* (1967); *Mesečev kamen* (1971); *Vojislav Ilić i evropsko pesništvo* (1971); *Gavrilo Stefanović Venclović* (1972); *Istorija srpske književnosti klasicizma i predromantizma* (1979); *Ruski hrt* (1979); *Nove beogradske priče* (1981); *Duše se kupaju poslednji put* (1982); *Radjanje nove srpske književnosti* (1983); *Istorija, stalež i stil* (1985); *Izabrana dela* (1985); *Unutrašnja strana vetra ili roman o Heri i Leandru* (1991)

BIBLIOGRAPHY: Livada, R., "A Book of the Future," *Relations,* 1 (1985), 73–74; Coover, R., "He Thinks the Way We Dream," *NYTBR,* 20 Nov. 1988, 15–20; Golden, P. B., "The Khazars of Record," *The World and I,* 3, 11 (1988), 368–77; Mihailovich, V. D., "Parable of Nationhood," *The World and I,* 3, 11 (1988), 378–83; Palavestra, P., "Abracadabra, à la Khazar!" *The World and I,* 3, 11 (1988), 384–89; Simic, C., "Balkan Bizarre," *The World and I,* 3, 11 (1988), 390–97; Leonard, J., "Alphabeticon," *Nation* (5 Dec. 1988), 610–11, 613; Mihailovich, V. D., "The Novel As Crossword Puzzle," *The World and I,* 4, 1 (1989), 430–33

VASA D. MIHAILOVICH

PELLICER, Carlos

Mexican poet, b. 16 Jan. 1897, Villahermosa, Tabasco; d. 15 Feb. 1977, Mexico City

P. spent his early and very formative years in the tropical state of Tabasco. When P. was eleven, his father moved the family to Mexico City because of the Mexican Revolution. There P. studied at the National Preparatory School where he was influenced by important Mexican literary figures. Upon graduation, he went to Colombia and Venezuela to organize federations of students. These trips were the first of many voyages throughout P.'s life that took him all over the world (especially Europe and Latin America) and allowed him to meet and know many international literary figures. P. occupied a variety of public posts and duties. He was a member of the Mexican Academy of the Language and served as president of the Latin American Congress of Writers. In the early 1950s, P. had turned his attention to museums, helping found several important ones in Tabasco, Sonora, Palenque, Mexico City, and the state of Morelos. In 1976 he was elected to the Mexican Senate as a representative from the state of Tabasco.

In 1921 P. published his first collection of poetry, *Colores en el mar y otros poemas* (1921; colors in the sea and other poems), dedicated to his friend Ramón López Velarde (1888–1921). *Colores* was primarily focused on landscapes and seascapes, exalting nature and its connections with humans. Although somewhat traditional in theme and form, it announced great visual evocation supported by structural and lyrical virtuosity. The next two collections, *Piedra de sacrificio* (1924; sacrificial stone) and *6, 7 poemas* (1924; six, seven poems) were published in the same year, but they were almost diametrically opposed in orientation. The latter, *6, 7 poemas,* was in many ways an extension of the lyricism and optimism of *Colores,* and it helped establish P.'s poetry as one of major import. But *Piedra de sacrificio* was something very different. It embraced a strong voice of social protest directed primarily against the U.S. Moreover, *Piedra de sacrificio* revealed not only a newly discovered interest in indigenous culture, but also a clamorous affirmation of Pan-Americanism, a theme generated in large part by the ideas of P.'s close friend José Vasconcelos (1881–1959). P.'s next important work was *Hora de junio* (1937; hour of June), which firmly established him as an important writer. The collection had as an organizing principle a variety of love sonnets interspersed by landscape poems.

Although P. published two collections in 1941, *Recinto y otras imágenes* (corner and other images) and *Exágonos* (hexagons), they received mixed and essentially uninspired reviews. In 1949, however, P. produced another major work, *Subordinaciones: Poemas* (subordinations: poems). Dedicated to Gabriela Mistral (q.v.), the collection of twenty-six poems evidenced a continued fascination with pre-Hispanic myth and culture, the human connection to nature, and an exalted treatment of Hispanic heroes (Morales, Bolívar, Justo Sierra, and others). This collection of telluric verse mixes history, geography, flora, and fauna in a flashy, provocative series of varied poetic forms; it is poetry of movement and meditation, treating Greek myth, New World exoticism, and tropical musing. P.'s next important poetry collection was *Práctica de vuelo* (1956; flight practice), a far-reaching collection of verse written from 1929 to 1952. It contained mostly devotional sonnets in which P. affirmed his passion for the Creator and his universe.

In 1962 the National Autonomous University of Mexico honored P. by publishing *Material poético* (1982; poetic material). It contained all of P.'s poetry written from 1918 to 1961. Two years later, in 1964, P. was awarded the National Prize for Literature for his poetry. In 1978 *Reincidencias* (1978; reincidences) was published posthumously. It was important because it brought together the poet's diverse works that were written but not published from 1967 to 1976. It contained works of great color, movement, musicality, and intimacy. Included, as well, were poems of social protest and contemplative devotion.

Many critics have asserted that P. was Mexico's most important poet of the 20th c. Others have cited him as one of Latin America's greatest original voices. What is certain is that P. wrote some twenty collections of verse spanning a period of nearly sixty years. His poetry reflects New World lyricism and landscapes, a passionate tropical appeal, an uncanny correspondence to the plastic arts, a nativistic Pan-Americanism, and an unbridled optimism and faith in the message of Christianity.

FURTHER WORKS: *Oda de junio* (1924); *Bolívar* (1925); *Hora y veinte* (1927); *Camino* (1929); *Esquemas para una oda tropical* (1933); *Estrofas* *del mar marino* (1934); *Discurso por las flores: poema* (1946; rev. ed., 1977); *Sonetos* (1950); *Museo de Tabasco* (1959); *Con palabra y fuego* (1962); *Teotithuacán* (1965); *13 de agosto: ruina de Tenochtitlán* (1965); *Primera antología poética* (1969); *Noticias sobre Netzahualcóyotl y algunos sentimientos* (1974); *Cuerdas, percusión y aliento* (1976); *Miniantología poética* (1977); *Breve antología* (1977); *Cosillas para el nacimiento* (1978); *Poemas* (1979); *Obras* (1981); *Album fotográfico* (1982); *Cartas de italia* (1985); *Antología breve* (1986); *Cuaderno de Viaje* (1987), *El sol en un pesebre: nacimientos* (1987); *Esquemas para una oda tropical (a cuatro voces)* (1987)

BIBLIOGRAPHY: Forster, M. H., "El concepto de la creación poética en la obra de C. P.," *Comunidad*, 4 (1969), 684–88; Melnykovich, G., "C. P. and Creacionismo," *LALR*, 2, 4 (Spring–Summer 1974), 95–111; Debicki, A., "Perspectiva y significado en la poesía de C. P.," *Plural*, 5, 12 (1975), 33–38; Chávez, C., *Mis amigos poetas: López Velarde, P., Novo* (1977); Mullen, E. J., *C. P.* (1977); Mullen, E. J., *La poesía de. C. P.: Interpretaciones críticas* (1979); Prats Sariol, J., "La imagen en C. P.," *CasaA*, 20, 120 (May–June 1980), 3–17; Gamboa, R. A., "C. P.: Arte poética," *Káñina*, 5, 2 (July–Dec. 1981), 69–78; del Campo, D. M., *C. P.* (1987); Zaid, G., "Siete poemas de C. P.," *RI*, 55, 148–149 (July–Dec. 1989), 1099–118.

SAM L. SLICK

PEREC, Georges
French novelist, poet, essayist, and dramatist, b. 7 Mar. 1936, Paris; d. 3 Mar. 1982, Paris

Born into a family of Polish Jewish émigrés, P. was orphaned by World War II, an experience that would color every aspect of his literary work, if in strikingly different ways. His father, a soldier in the French army, was killed at the front in 1940; his mother was arrested in 1943 and deported to the German camps, where she was murdered. P. spent the rest of the war in a Catholic school in the unoccupied zone of France. After the war he returned to Paris, where he lived with a paternal aunt. After graduating from secondary school in 1954, he studied sociology at the Sorbonne, later working as a public-opinion pollster, a research librarian, and a crossword-puzzle maker. He died of lung cancer at the age of forty-five.

P.'s literary production includes a score of major works, and is characterized by its great diversity. Although he is principally known for his novels, he also wrote poetry, plays, essays, and film scenarios. His first novel, *Les Choses: Une histoire des années soixante* (1965; *Les Choses: A Story of the Sixties,* 1968), won the Renaudot Prize (1965), and launched P. on the literary scene. The story of a young couple living in an increasingly materialist milieu, *Les Choses* was hailed as a new "sociological" novel. It met with tremendous popular success and was eventually translated into sixteen languages.

La Disparition (1969; the disappearance) is a 300-page novel written without the letter E. It is conceived as a detective novel, the central conceit of which devolves upon the disappearance of the E from the alphabet. In a shorter novel, *Les Revenentes* (1972; the ghosts), the E is the only vowel used. P.'s work here testifies to the influence of the Oulipo (an acronym signifying Workshop of Potential Literature), a group of literary formalists he joined in 1967. P.'s contributions to the group's collective publications, such as *La Littérature potentielle: Créations, re-créations, récréations* (1973; potential literature: creations, re-creations, recreations), *Atlas de littérature potentielle* (1981; atlas of potential literature), and the three-volume *Bibliothéque oulipienne* (1987–1990; Oulipian library), are substantial.

The same sort of experimentation in form characterizes P.'s poetry. *Alphabets* (1976; alphabets), for example, is a series of heterogrammatic poems, each using only eleven letters of the alphabet. *La Clôture et autres poèmes* (1980; closure and other poems) includes bilingual poems (which can be read in French and English), palindromes, and acrostics. *Espèces d'espaces: Journal d'un usager de l'espace* (1974; species of space: journal of a user of space) is an extended essay. In it, P. reflects upon spaces of various kinds, and upon the manner in which they are represented in literature.

W ou le souvenir d'enfance (1975; *W or The Memory of Childhood,* 1988) is a hybrid text, in which chapters of autobiography alternate with chapters of fiction. It too is an exercise in literary representation; specifically, it tests the possibilities of representing the Holocaust and catastrophes, both personal and collective. The fictional narrative deals with a voyage to the island of W, where an Olympian society reveals itself as ever more oppressive; the autobiographical narrative centers upon the war years, and P.'s loss of his parents. As the two narratives alternate, it becomes clear that they are complementary, each saying things that the other cannot. They converge, moreover, upon a carceral, concentrationary locus of radical loss. In short, *W ou le souvenir d'enfance* is perhaps the most eloquent Holocaust narrative to appear in France.

P. worked on *La vie mode d'emploi* (1978; *Life: A User's Manual,* 1987), a 700-page novel, for ten years. It met with more immediate success than any of his books since *Les Choses,* and was awarded the Médicis Prize (1978). It is a work that elegantly melds the apparently irreconcilable traditions of the well-made novel and the experimental text. Recounting in minute detail the life of a Parisian apartment building, *La vie mode d'emploi* offers an astonishing multiplicity of stories, savantly interwoven. That interweaving, however, is based upon formal arcana that, although not apparent in a casual reading, constrain and order every aspect of the novel's structure. The principal image of the novel, that of the jigsaw puzzle, serves to encapsulate the novel itself, for the latter's construction, upon analysis, reveals itself to be that of a puzzle, a game studiously elaborated and offered as a participatory dynamic to the reader.

P. himself once suggested that his work responded to four concerns: a passion for the apparently trivial details of everyday life, an impulse toward confession and autobiography, a will toward formal innovation, and a desire to write "readerly" stories. It is undoubtedly in *W ou le souvenir d'enfance* and *La vie mode d'emploi* that those concerns find their most felicitous articulation, and it is those two books that have established P.'s reputation as one of the major writers in French of the 20th c. More generally, though, each of his works is a laboratory of writing, a place where the very possibilities of literature are tested. Yet the works themselves remain highly accessible, for one of the boundaries P. consistently interrogated was that between tradition and innovation. His great discovery as a writer was that those two orders were not mutually exclusive, but indeed shared many affinities and points of complementarity, and his literary production as a whole may be read as an elaborate, impassioned demonstration of that notion.

FURTHER WORKS: *Quel petit vélo à guidon chromé au fond de la cour?* (1966); *Un homme qui dort* (1967); *Petit traité invitant à la découverte de l'art subtil du GO* (1969, with Pierre Lusson and Jacques Roubaud); *Die Maschine* (1972); *La boutique obscure: 124 rêves* (1973); *Ulcérations* (1974); *Je me souviens* (1978); *Un cabinet d'amateur* (1979); *Les mots croisés* (1979); *La clôture et autres poèmes* (1980); *Récits d'Ellis Island: Histoires d'errance et d'espoir* (1980, with Robert Bober); *Théâtre* (1981); *Epithalames* (1982); *Tentative d'épuisement d'un lieu parisien* (1982); *Penser/Classer* (1985); *Les mots croisés II* (1986); *"53 Jours"* (1989); *L'infra-ordinaire* (1989); *Vœux* (1989)

BIBLIOGRAPHY: Motte, W., *The Poetics of Experiment: A Study of the Work of G. P.* (1984);

Pedersen, J., *P. ou les textes croisés* (1985); Raynaud, J.-M., *Pour un P. lettré, chiffré* (1987); Burgelin, C., *G. P.* (1988); Schwartz, P., *G. P.: Traces of His Passage* (1988); Magné, B., *Perecollages 1981–1988* (1989)

WARREN MOTTE

PERI ROSSI, Cristina

Uruguayan novelist, short-story writer, and poet, b. 12 Nov. 1941, Montevideo

P. R.'s father was a textile worker, her mother a school teacher. After graduation from the Artigas Institute for Teachers, P. R. started working as a journalist, and as a professor of literature in her native Montevideo. Her support of the Left, and her clear stance against a blatantly oppressive government, caused P. R. to seek political asylum in Spain, where she arrived in 1972. She still resides in Barcelona.

The noted Uruguayan essayist Angel Rama (1926–1983) includes P. R. among the writers he groups under the label "La generación crítica" (the critical generation), and suggests that some chapters of one of P. R.'s earlier texts, the novel *El libro de mis primos* (1969; the book of my cousins), represents "one of the freest examples of imagination that has been known in Uruguayan literature."

At age twenty-two, already quite a precocious member of the literary establishment, she published *Viviendo* (1963; living), a collection of three short stories that poignantly addresses the plight of women leading a life dominated by their daily boring rituals, and subtly explores lesbian relationships.

After what turned out to be the longest hiatus in P. R.'s prolific literary production—she has also been involved with journalism and criticism throughout her career—her second book of short stories, *Los museos abandonados* (1969; the abandoned museums), won the prize for young Uruguayan authors awarded by the publishing house Arca. Eroticism, the impact of social decay, and a constant feeling of sadness permeate the four stories. The first—and the longest of these—might be considered P. R.'s initial contact with the fantastic, a genre she continued to cultivate later on.

The same year, *El libro de mis primos* captured the first prize offered by *Marcha,* a weekly newspaper notorious for its incisive political analysis, but also acclaimed for its literary pages. Soon after, P. R. published *Indicios pánicos* (1970; signs of panic), a breakthrough in her production. Although she had already combined poetry and prose, and experimented with rhetorical figures and even typography in *El libro de mis primos,*

Indicios pánicos is the first text where P. R. challenges conventional notions of genre. If indeed a genuine preoccupation with social issues was already evident in her work, this book is boldly politicized. Its 46 sections—allegorical vignettes, conventional short stories, poems, short essays, aphorisms—are thoroughly independent and can be read in any order. The book, however, is remarkably integrated by the underlying feeling of sociopolitical decay. P. R. makes no serious effort to hide the fact that she is referring to the Uruguayan society where she lived and worked, and plainly reiterated it a few years later in the prologue to the Spanish edition of her text. *Indicios pánicos* turned out to be a grim prophecy of the heinous 1973 coup and subsequent period of unmerciful repression in Uruguay.

With the publication of her first book of poems *Evohé* (1971; Evohé), P. R. celebrates the female body, and unabashedly expresses passion and desire. Another collection of poems, *Diáspora* (1976; diaspora), her second publication in exile, won yet another prize. A few years later P. R. published her last book of poetry to date, *Lingüística general* (1979; general linguistics), which furthers her free-verse examination of art, the intricacies of language, and lesbian love.

Seix Barral, the Barcelona-based editorial house that had previously issued *El museo de los esfuerzos inútiles* (1983; the museum of the useless efforts)—another collection of brief texts of rather difficult generic categorization—published P. R.'s second novel. *La nave de los locos* (1984; *The Ship of Fools,* 1988) is a complex text. The chaotic narration of episodes where injustice and oppression affect a cast of characters—which includes a prostitute, a *desaparecido* (a person who "disappeared" for political reasons), and a desperate woman in need of an abortion—is interwoven with an impeccable, serene, detailed description of an 11th-c. tapestry depicting creation in all its splendor.

Her most recent novel, *Solitario de amor* (1988; solitaire of love), seems to be P. R.'s most conventional text to date. It is a tightly constructed love story, but not simply that. Lost love and an almost uncontrollable passion obsess the anonymous narrator, who at a certain point exclaims "I am Melibeo!" replicating Calixto's cry in *La Celestina* (1499; the go-between), when the young nobleman, "a prisoner of Melibea's love," surrenders his religion, his patrimony, and his very identity to the object of his desires. There are enough clues in P. R.'s text to suggest the androgynous nature of Aida's yearning lover ("I am a man without a key, that is to say, a man without sex"), and explicit references to their lovemaking quite clearly portray a lesbian encounter: "We make four-hands love, like a couple playing the piano . . . like two twins.'' Perhaps the carefully constructed ambiguity in *Solitario de amor* suggests a vision of love so pure—and so intense—as to transcend the constraints of gender.

P. R.'s literary merits have been further recognized with two other coveted prizes in Spain: the Palma de Mallorca Prize (1979), and the Benito Pérez Galdós Prize the following year. She writes without hesitations, with total control, and with an unyielding passion for the language. Her voice is eloquent, her style is elegant, and her literature, in the opinion of Julio Cortázar (q.v.), ''has been lived and said by a woman that knows the infernos of this earth—her own land, there in the south—and those of writing in our times—here and everywhere—.''

FURTHER WORKS: *Descripción de un naufragio* (1975); *La tarde del dinosaurio* (1976); *La rebelión de los niños* (1980); *Una pasión prohibida* (1986); *Cosmoagonías* (1988)

BIBLIOGRAPHY: Benedetti, M., ''C. P. R.: Vino nuevo en odres nuevos,'' *Literatura uruguaya siglo XX*, 2nd ed. (1969), 321–27; Brena, T. G., ''C. P. R.,'' *Exploración estética: Estudio de doce poetas de Uruguay y uno de Argentina* (1974), 463–84; Pereda, R. M., ''C. P. R.: la parábola de un naufragio,'' *Camp de l'Arp*, 13 (Oct. 1974), 27; Molina Campos, E., ''El naufragio de C. P. R.,'' *Camp de l'Arp*, 22 (July 1975), 26–27; Deredita, J. F., ''Desde la diáspora: entrevista con C. P. R.,'' *TCrit*, 9 (1978), 131–42; Mora, G., ''El mito degradado de la familia en *El libro de mis primos* de C. P. R.,'' in Pope, R. D., ed., *The Analysis of Literary Texts: Current Trends in Methodology* (1980), 66–77; Morello-Frosch, M., ''Entre primos y dinosaurios con C. P. R.,'' in Cunningham, L. G., ed., *Mujer y sociedad en América Latina* (1980), 193–201; Sosnowski, S., ''*Los museos abandonados* de C. P. R.: Reordenación de museos y refugios,'' *Actualidades*, 6 (1980–1982), 67–74; Verani, H. J., ''Una experiencia de límites: la narrativa de C. P. R.,'' *RI*, 48, 118–19 (Jan.–June 1982), 303–16; Verani, H. J., ''La rebelión del cuerpo y del lenguaje: A propósito de C. P. R.,'' *Revista de la Universidad de México*, 37 (Mar. 1982), 19–22

HORACIO XAUBET

PETRUSHEVSKAYA, Ludmila

Russian dramatist and short-story writer, b. 26 May 1938, Moscow

P.'s early childhood, coinciding as it did with World War II, personally familiarized her with the bleaker aspects of life: homelessness, starvation, abject poverty, orphanages, physical brutality, and loneliness without privacy. These experiences form the psychological backbone of her oeuvre. After studying journalism at Moscow State University, P., like many Soviet youths, journeyed to the virgin lands in Kazakhstan, before she found work as a hospital nurse, a radio reporter, and an editor at a television studio. Although she began writing short stories in 1963, she waited for almost a decade before the journal *Avrora* accepted two for publication in 1972: ''Rasskazchitsa'' (the storyteller) and ''Istoriia Klarissy'' (Clarissa's story). A similar fate met her plays, a genre she first tried that same year. Financial need forced P. to undertake translation from the Polish while she continued her solitary literary activity. Until the mid-1980s only a handful of P.'s more than forty stories and plays saw the light of day. Efforts to stage her works met with continued official resistance. The theaters that succeeded in presenting her plays tended to be experimental, amateur, or provincial. The two-act *Uroki muzyki* (1973; music lessons) was performed briefly at Moscow University in 1979; the diptych *Chinzano* (1973; *Cinzano*, 1989) and *Den' rozhdeniia Smirnovoi* (1977; Smirnova's birthday) premiered in 1978 in Estonian translation in Estonia. Only her one-act play *Liubov'* (1974; love) enjoyed a long, successful run in Moscow after its inclusion in the 1979–1980 season. Two decades of professional hardships finally ended in the mid-1980s, when Gorbachev instituted his policy of glasnost. Owing to the pendulum swing in her fortunes, P. has become the most popular dramatist in Moscow, with several plays simultaneously enjoying extended runs in major theaters. Her stories likewise have become staple fare in mainstream journals and newspapers. Under glasnost both P. and her plays travel abroad, to Europe and the U.S.

P. has provoked heated controversy as both prosaist and dramatist partly because her oeuvre portrays a nightmarish life on the edge of existence, devoid of palliative reassurances. Permeated with morbid humor and grotesquerie, her harshly unidealizing works deal with the underbelly of human relations—the nasty traffic in human desires and fears, where everything carries a literal and metaphorical price. Life for P. is the penalty we pay for having been born. Everyone in her grim universe tends to be cut adrift from a reliable mooring; is ruled by appetite and self-interest; falls into seemingly irreversible patterns of (self-)destructive behavior; abrogates moral responsibility; inflicts and experiences pain in an unbroken chain of universal abuse. Suicide, alcoholism, child abuse, fictitious marriages, one-night stands, prostitution, unwanted pregnancies, abortions, crushing poverty, theft, and physical and psychological violence constitute the stuff of P.'s fiction and drama.

P.'s stories, like her plays, concentrate on the middle class, largely the urban technical intelligentsia. The majority of her protagonists and narrators tend to be women whose lives are maimed through personal weakness, uncontrollable circumstances, male mistreatment, and relatives' interference or overbearing demands—numerous female protagonists must tend simultaneously to dependent children and needy, frequently hospitalized, mothers. Alienation, betrayal, and humiliation comprise the lot of these beasts of burden, because pragmatic calculation fuels relations between family members, spouses, and lovers: "Smotrovaia ploshchadka" (1982; "The Overlook," 1990), "Temnaia sud'ba" (1988; gloomy fate), "Strana" (1988; country), or "Takaia devochka" (1988; such a girl). Romantic love is a luxury to which P.'s characters rarely have access as they battle for a place to live and, minimally, find temporary shelter, as in "Skripka" (1973; "The Violin," 1989), or for clothes, food, sex, as in "Doch' Kseni" (1988; Ksenia's daughter), or for alcohol, as in "Ali-Baba" (1988; Ali Baba). In this Darwinian struggle, painted in largely physiological hues, ethical norms fall by the wayside.

Free of nature and psychological analysis, sparse in dialogue, and stripped of imagery, P.'s prose relies for its effects on the distinctive language of its ambiguous narrators. That language, like the lives it records, is a triumph of incongruities, synthesizing urban slang, cultural clichés, malapropisms, racy colloquialisms, and solecisms. These stream forth in a relentless monologic patter that strives to camouflage, or to defer confrontation with, what is most crucial and, usually, most painful. Revelation, not action, is the pivot on which P.'s stories turn. The seamy catastrophes in which her plots abound are conveyed in a monstrously calm narrative voice whose digressive, casual chatter is a stratagem of deflection, transference, and avoidance. The most chilling aspect of the narration is precisely the discrepancy between the extraordinary horrors that multiply implacably and the flat, casual tone of reportage that reduces everything to the same level of banality. Although P. divides her narratives into stories *(istorii)* and monologues *(monologi)*, they differ stylistically only in the use of free indirect discourse versus first-person narration, respectively.

"Svoi krug" (1979; "Our Crowd," 1990), P.'s longest and best narrative to date, offers the fullest, most nuanced glimpse of the ways in which the moral fabric of contemporary Russian society has unraveled. Her subsequent stories, "Novye

Robinzony" (1989; "A Modern Family Robinson," 1991) and "Gigiena" (1990; hygiene), belong to the substantial body of apocalyptic visions in Soviet fiction. With her recent publication *Skazki dlia vzroslykh* (1990; fairy tales for adults) P. has made a transition to a new genre: that of gnomic allegory and Kafkaesque parable.

P.'s plays mirror essentially the concerns of her prose and contain analogous types. Family as a synecdoche for society dominates P.'s drama, its microcosm reflecting the dissolution of human bonds—of kinship, support, and responsibilities—whereby relatives and husbands are estranged and instrumentalized. In *Syraia noga, ili vstrecha druzei* (1977; a raw leg, or a gathering of friends), Serezha the boxer steals money from his old mother's savings and beats his wife Natasha senseless; in *Liubov'* Evgeniia Ivanovna's selfish hostility to her son-in-law Tolia drives him and his new bride Sveta out onto the street on their wedding night; in *Moskovskii khor* (n.d.; Moscow chorus) savage family feuds, rife with vilification, erupt when members victimized by the purges return from the camps.

As setting P. favors kitchens and overcrowded rundown apartments whose spatial limitations symptomatize the psychological claustrophobia of its occupants, their entrapment in their situation. Lack of adequate space or a roof over one's head signals an absence of psychological refuge, of belonging, exemplified by Ira's dilemma in *Tri devushki v golubom* (1980; *Three Girls in Blue,* 1988). Spatial and temporal boundaries, however, are extended through P.'s technique of reminiscence and reference, whereby hearsay characters, their words and actions, become incorporated into a play when those present quote them or refer to incidents in which they participated. In *Syraia noga, ili vstrecha druzei* Volodia suggests to Sonia that they renew their former sexual intimacy, while blithely volunteering the information that one of his students in Kalinin supplies him with sex three times a week. While lying with his head in Ira's lap, he confesses that he cannot do without a woman for three days maximum, and recalls once propositioning ten women at a train station until one agreed to oblige him. By indirectly revealing the behavior of multiple hearsay characters, P. universalizes the moral dissoluteness of those we actually see. Fewer than twenty individuals inhabit the stage in *Tri devushki v golubom,* but over a hundred are mentioned, and the sheer volume depersonalizes people into a mass. When that technique resurrects relatives from the past, it also underscores the themes of heredity and continuity. Errors, vices, and weaknesses are one generation's legacy to the next. In *Uroki muzyki* eighteen-year-old Nina's mother, Grania, throws her parental duties, including the care of her baby, onto Nina's shoulders so as to concentrate on the violent, alcoholic ex-convict who fathered the child. When he returns uninvited to their apartment, revulsion and insufficient room force Nina to seek asylum at a neighbor's. Yet Grania's sole worry is her loss of a baby-sitter, especially when she has to check into a hospital for an abortion and fears leaving the baby with her unpredictable brute of a husband. Maternity, which serves as a key moral gauge in P.'s system of values, suffers endless violations, exemplified by Galia in *Lestnichnaia kletka* (1974; the stairwell), who plans to conceive a child with a stranger, only so as to mollify her hysterical mother.

The diversity of P.'s work for the theater is reflected in the five genres associated with her name: full-length plays, such as *Uroki muzyki, Tri devushki v golubom, Syraia noga,* and *Moskovskii khor,* which consist of two acts and casts averaging a dozen characters; her favorite genre of the one-act play, which observes the classical unities of time, place, and action and confines the cast to between three and six characters; dialogues, such as "Izolirovannyi boks"(1988; insulated box) and "Stakan vody" (1988; a glass of water); the monologues that double as prose narratives—"Pesni XX veka" (1988; songs of the 20th c.), "Seti i lovushki" (1974; "Nets and Traps," 1989), and "Takaia devochka"—and plays for children, which draw on puppet theater and include *Dva okoshka* (1975; two windows), *Chemodan chepukhi, ili bystro khorosho ne byvaet* (1975; a suitcase of nonsense, or things don't go well quickly), and *Zolotaia boginia* (1986; golden goddess).

Critics have commented on Chekhovian elements in P.'s drama, whereas the only common features are dialogues that are essentially sequentialized monologues and the habit of calling "comedies" works that audiences perceive as devastatingly somber. Others have remarked on P.'s debt to Aleksandr Vampilov (1937–1972), whose antiheroes, indeed, do prefigure the decidedly unadmirable types that predominate in P.'s plays. In response to queries about her unremittingly gloomy vision of life, P. claims to pose problems that invite audience's self-confrontation. Optimally, that process will catalyze one's humane impulses. P. scrupulously excludes all explicit judgment, sermonizing, and hope for moral progress from her fiction and drama. In fact, it would be difficult to imagine a world more desolate and bereft of hope than that portrayed by P., which may be summarized by the famous Sartrean formula "Hell is other people."

FURTHER WORKS: *P'esy* (1983); *Bessmertnaia liubov'* (1988)

BIBLIOGRAPHY: Smith, M. T., "*In Cinzano Veritas:* The Plays of L. P.," *SEEA,* 3, 1 (1985), 119–25; Condee, N., "L. P.: How the 'Lost People' Live," *Institute of Current World Affairs Newsletter,* 14 (Feb. 1986), 1–12

HELENA GOSCILO

PHELPS, Anthony

Haitian poet, novelist, short-story writer, and dramatist, b. 25 Aug. 1928, Port-au-Prince

Born into a bourgeois family in Port-au-Prince, P. is one of the most prestigious representatives of the new Haitian literature that emerged in reaction to the bloody dictatorship of François Duvalier in the early 1960s. P. studied various disciplines in the U.S. and Quebec, including chemistry, photography, filmmaking, ceramics, and sculpture, before returning home and devoting himself almost entirely to literature.

P. joins to his passion for literary invention a profound disgust inspired by the political situation of his country. His impact upon the politically conscious Haitian youth set the repressive machinery of the Duvalier dictatorship against him, and he was arrested in 1963. Freed after three weeks in prison, P. was finally forced to flee to Montreal in 1964 to live in an exile that would continue until the fall of the Duvalier régime in 1986.

In 1960 P. founded the group Literary Haiti with four other young poets: Davertige (pseud. of Villard Denis, b. 1940), René Philoctête (b. 1932), Roland Morisseau, and Serge Legagneur (dates n.a.). Denouncing the barriers imposed a priori on art by ideologies and traditions, the adherents to this school make only one demand on their poetry: that it have an incontestable richness of form. In that same year, P. also published his first volume of poetry; *Été* (summer) is a thin volume, but already, in its thematic and aesthetic concerns, it announces the direction his work will take. One finds in it traces of the old Haitian aesthetic, based on the three essential principles of Indigenism, Socialism, and Négritude (q.v.). This ideological aspect is one that P. will never abjure. His work expresses a constant struggle against enemies who seek to prevent his new humanism—extolling humankind's blossoming in liberty, peace, and universal brotherhood—from realizing itself. P.'s poetry, however, would be ill-defined if it were exclusively examined from the point of view of his militancy. It is first and foremost the expression of a literature comparable to the best contemporary productions.

P.s humanistic quest continues in *Présence* (1961; presence) and *Éclats de silence* (1962; bursts of silence), two small books of poetry, and in the

485

texts that appeared in 1962 in *Semence*, the organ of Literary Haiti, as well as the long "Poème de la montagne" (1964; poem of the mountain), the original version of which was published in *Conjonction*, the review of the French Institute of Haiti. This poem, in which the peasants are invited to fraternize with the poet, tells much about P.'s ideological romanticism.

During his exile in Montreal, P.'s work reaches its apogee. *Points cardinaux* (1967; cardinal points), published in Montreal, focuses on P.'s situation. In this introspective work the themes of militant inspiration, even if not entirely absent, are expressed only as if in a whisper. P. looks at himself through the prism of an exiled man's fantasies; on the threshold of exile, he surveys the chaos of his mind. For the first time, he completely cultivates the abstract language of surrealism (q.v.), before readjusting the cloak of his militancy, and altering his discourse once again to become accesible. *Mon pays que voici suivi de Les dits du fou-aux-cailloux* (1968; this country of mine, followed by the sayings of the fool of the rocks), a text nearly finished at the time P. went into exile, achieves perhaps the most spectacular success a collection of poetry signed by a Haitian author has ever obtained. The poem "Mon pays que voici," which exalts patriotism and stigmatizes the shameful régime of the "tontons-macoutes," touched the most sensitive fibers of the Haitian soul.

P. is, in fact, consecrated by Haitians as the poet of exile. For years, his creativity focused itself on the theme of exile; the problem for P., however, is not how the exile confronts his material obstacles, but rather the interior drama of such a person incapable of adapting himself to his new cultural environment. Far from his country, the poet is cut off from his natural source of inspiration; progressively he loses his sense of identity. Thus, returning to his native country appears to him such a vital necessity. That is the message of *Motifs pour le temps saisonnier* (1976; motifs for seasonal time). From an artistic point of view, the poems in this collection must be rated among the best P. has written.

La bélière caraïbe (1979; the Caribbean ram), awarded the Casa de las Américas Prize (1980), begins a new cycle. In principle the period of P.'s strict exile has ended with the demise of the Duvalier régime. He can finally see the country of his birth again, and he feels the rapture of the creator recapturing the sense of his roots. From this moment on, the need to proclaim his pride in his Caribbean identity supplants the theme of exile. One finds this same thematic preoccupation in *Orchidée nègre* (1985; black orchid), which earned P. a second prize from Casa de las Américas (1987).

Même le soleil est nu (1983; even the sun is naked) is an account of the emotions of the poet struck, upon his return to Port-au-Prince, by the terrible physical and moral decay that haunted the country. The paradise of his childhood had been ravaged. The brutal physical destruction of the people vied with the extreme brutality of the government. In 1984 P. asked for and received early retirement from Radio Canada in order to return to Haiti and devote himself entirely to literature. His anticipated repatriation was, however, delayed due to the brutality of the transitional period. P.'s disappointment at his continued exile, together with the desire to reassert the value of Haiti's cultural heritage, marks the most recent of P.'s works. The publication of "La mémoire dépiégée" (the untrapped memory) and "Femme-Amérique" (woman-America), two manuscripts completed several years ago, has been announced.

In addition to poetry, P. has always shown a great interest in theater. He has written some thirty radio plays, as yet unpublished, for Radio Cacique; he has only published one play, *Le conditionnel* (1968; the conditional), which has never been officially performed. Another manuscript, "Le mannequin enchanté" (n.d.; the enchanted mannequin), has recently resurfaced. These plays have two things in common: They are both comedies, and neither contains specific reference to Haiti. They can be performed without regard to the ethnicity of the actors, and this may account for their going nearly unnoticed on the Haitian literary scene.

P. has two major novels to his credit: *Moins l'infini* (1972; minus the infinite) and *Mémoire en colin-maillard* (1976; blind-man's-buff memory). Both texts feature an elegantly turned style and are marked by all the subtleties of P.'s poetic language. Written at the time when P. was still absorbed in anti-Duvalier activism, they belong to the prolific family of tales that, throughout the 1970s, strove to denounce the horrors of the dictatorship and, a corollary, to incite Haitians to continue unflinchingly to battle until the final victory. P.'s narrative structure well demonstrates processes one finds in the New Novel (q.v.), and, because of this, they may be inaccessible to many readers. But one can say about P.'s novels that, even though they may not spontaneously arouse popular enthusiasm, they possess, with respect to language and invention, everything necessary to resist the ravages of time.

P. is a complete writer. Because of the abundance, variety, and quality of his work, he represents the best that contemporary Haitian literature has to offer. He is in the advance guard of his generation of writers: engaged witnesses to one of the most dramatic periods in the history of their country, who understood they had to break through the barriers of insularity to participate equally in the fascinating literary experience of the modern world. Especially as a poet, P. must not be considered only as a Haitian writer, but also as one of the most illustrious representatives of contemporary literature written in French.

FURTHER WORKS: *Et moi je suis une île* (1973); *Haïti! Haïti!* (1985, with Gary Klang)

BIBLIOGRAPHY: Lacôte, R., "A. P.," *Lettres Françaises,* 19 Feb. 1969, 10; Bruner, C., "The Meaning of Caliban in Black Literature Today," *CLS,* 13 (1973), 240–53; Berrou, R., and P. Pompilus, *Histoire de la littérature haïtienne* (1977), Vol. 3, 344–59; Bruner, C., "Haitian Poets Cross Words," *The Gar,* 33 (1979), 22–24; Dash, M., *Literature and Ideology in Haiti, 1915–1961* (1981), 213; Hoffmann, L. F., *Le roman haïtien, ideologie et structure* (1982), 334; Ferdinand, J., "The New Political Statement in Haitian Fiction," in Luis, W., ed., *Voices from Under: Black Narrative in Latin America and the Caribbean* (1984), 127–46; Souffrant, C., "Une contre-négritude caraïbe, exode rural et urbanisation chez A. P.," in CIDIHCA, ed., *L'arme de la critique littéraire, littérature et idéologie en Haïti* (1988), 217–29

JOSEPH FERDINAND

PIÑERA, Virgilio

Cuban dramatist, short-story writer, novelist, poet, and literary critic, b. 4 Aug. 1912, Cárdenas; d. 19 Oct. 1979, Havana

P. is one of the leading and most prolific Cuban writers of the 20th c. He lived in Cuba all of his life, except for five years, from 1950 to 1955, which he spent in Argentina, where two of his major narrative works were published: the novel *La carne de René* (1953; René's flesh) and the volume of short stories *Cuentos fríos* (1956; *Cold Tales,* 1988). After the triumph of the Cuban revolution in 1959, he worked for the newspaper *Revolución* and directed the literary series "Ediciones Erre" for a number of years. He eventually fell into disgrace with the communist régime, but continued to write at a fast pace, although not a single creative piece by him was published in Cuba during the last years of his life. At his death, his apartment in Havana was sealed by Cuban authorities, and the manuscripts that he kept there were confiscated. The continued efforts of some Cuban literary critics and friends of P.'s succeeded in obtaining official permission in 1987 to publish some of these works.

As a poet, P. associated with José Lezama Lima (q.v.) and those who wrote for the literary journal *Orígenes.* His poetry evolved from the symbolism and surrealist traits of his early works, such as *La isla en peso* (1943; the island's full weight) to the shockingly prosaic style apparent in the late poems of his collected verse, *La vida entera* (1969; my entire life), or in *Una broma colosal* (1988; a colossal joke), published posthumously.

P. can be considered the initiator of the literature of the absurd in Cuba, both in the narrative and in the theater. Two of his novels, *Pequeñas maniobras* (1963; minor maneuvers) and *Presiones y diamantes* (1967; pressures and diamonds), as well as many of his short stories, seem to have a common theme, that of human degradation by a concatenation of disasters that the individual cannot control and which drag him into the darkest zones of human existence. His characters, when given an option, choose to retain the miserable condition to which they have been able to adapt and in which they have found an awkward kind of happiness. Some typical features of his narrative are circular plots, macabre humor, and grotesque characterizations.

His plays follow also, with a few exceptions, the absurdist trend. *Falsa alarma* (1948; false alarm) is reminiscent of Franz Kafka's (q.v.) *The Trial;* the protagonist ends up deranged after going through a comedic process of criminal justice that brings no punishment and no acquittal. In *El flaco y el gordo* (1959; the skinny guy and the fat one), the "skinny guy" eats the "fat one" out of both a desire of revenge and desperate hunger, to face a little later another "skinny guy" who will in turn, opening a new cycle, do the same to him. *Dos viejos pánicos* (1968; two ancient panics), in the line of Samuel Beckett's (q.v.) dramas about the predicament of aging, presents an old couple who play a "game of death" to prepare themselves for their impending final moments. The exceptions to the rule are *Electra Garrigó* (1943; Electra Garrigó) and *Aire frío* (1959; cold air). *Electra Garrigó* is a free adaptation of the classic tragedy, where the flaws of the Cuban bourgeoisie are depicted in a light satirical vein. Although exhibiting some distinctive grotesque elements, the very successful and much performed *Aire frío* is a departure from P.'s usual procedures; it is a realistic, semiautobiographical work, which portrays the life of a middle-class family throughout several decades. P.'s most poignant play to this date— several remain still unpublished in Cuba—is *Una caja de zapatos vacía* (1986; an empty shoe box), published posthumously in the U.S. This piece, smuggled out of Cuba in 1967, can be viewed as P.'s political testament. In it he presents, in the manner of Antonin Artaud's (q.v.) theater of cruelty, the sadistic methods that tyrants employ to rule over their subjects. He also suggests that those who are thus victimized can only earn the right to a fulfilling life through an act of liberating madness.

P. has been highly influential among the younger generations of Cuban writers. Outside Cuba his stature as a literary figure of universal appeal continues to grow.

FURTHER WORKS: *Las furias* (1941); *Poesía y prosa* (1944); *Teatro completo* (1960); *Cuentos* (1964); *El que vino a salvarme* (1970); *Un fogonazo* (1987); *Muecas para escribientes* (1987)

BIBLIOGRAPHY: McLees, A. A., "Elements of Sartrian Philosophy in *Electra Garrigó*," *LATR*, 7 (Fall 1973), 5–11; González-Cruz, L. F., "V. P. y el teatro del absurdo en Cuba," *Mester*, 5 (1974), 52–58; González-Cruz, L. F., "Arte y situación de V. P.," *Caribe*, 2 (1977), 77–86; Morello-Frosch, M., "La anatomía: mundo fantástico de V. P.," *Hispam*, 23–24 (1979), 19–34; Cabrera Infante, G., "Vidas para leerlas," *Vuelta*, 4, 41 (Apr. 1980), 4–16; Gilden, R. G., "V. P. and the Short Story of the Absurd," *Hispania*, 63, 2 (May 1980), 348–55; Arenas, R., "*La isla en peso* con todas sus cucarachas," *Mariel*, 2 (1983), 20–24; Matas, J., "Infiernos fríos de V. P.," *Linden Lane Magazine*, 4 (1985), 22–25; González-Cruz, L. F., *V. P.: "Una caja de zapatos vacía." Edición crítica* (1986); González-Cruz, L. F., "V. P.," in Martínez, J. A., ed., *Dictionary of Twentieth-Century Cuban Literature* (1990), 361–70

LUIS F. GONZÁLEZ-CRUZ

PIÑON, Nélida

Brazilian novelist and short-story writer, b. 1937, Rio de Janeiro

P. is a first-generation Brazilian, born of Spanish parents. She began serious writing in 1955, and has stated that it was not until this intense apprenticeship with the language that she truly came to identify herself as a Brazilian. Educated as a journalist at the Catholic University in Rio de Janeiro, she worked briefly for the newspaper *O Globo* before dedicating her efforts exclusively to creative writing. She has won Brazil's major literary prizes, and has taught at several universities, including Columbia and Johns Hopkins in the U.S. Her works have been translated into numerous languages, and she has traveled widely in Europe and the Americas.

P. challenges the imagination and interpretive skills of her readers. Her prose is rich with poetic devices. Narratives eschew linearity, and point of view often belongs to several different participants. Exposition of background information occurs gradually and sparingly. Shifts between interior monologue, dialogue, and narrated action are tenuously marked. Visual imagery is minimal. Lexical, syntactic, and logical combinations tend to be unconventional. P. has stated that part of her project is to act "against official syntax."

Like most of her compatriots, P. decries social ills. Perhaps her best example of this commitment is the short-story collection *O calor das coisas* (1980; the heat of things). However, her focal point is not the streets, the fields, the factories, or the homes, but primarily the individual's consciousness. She specializes in the profound analysis of isolated characters—forceful, eccentric, and self-conscious—and causes the social dimension gradually to unfold around such interior dramas. P.'s writings show also a fascination with religiosity, or more precisely, mysticism, since she stresses the individual experience over the institutional. For example, her first novel, *Guia-mapa de Gabriel Arcanjo* (1961; guide map of Archangel Gabriel) features an extended dialogue between the female protagonist and her alter ego/guardian angel, regarding guilt, expiation, and one's relationship with deity. Another salient mark of P.'s fiction is eroticism, which is exemplified by *A casa da paixão* (1972; the house of passion). The novel is a lyrical treatment of a young woman's sexual initiation, which presents interior monologues of the woman herself, as well as of her partner and other members of her household.

P. shows a profound interest in the myths that underlie human enterprises. In particular, she seems fascinated with the myth of origination. *Fundador* (1969; founder) explores the establishment of a new society, which in some sense repeats itself through several generations of individuals. A related concern in P.'s fiction is the experience of the immigrant. *A república dos sonhos* (1984; *The Republic of Dreams*, 1989), a semiautobiographical novel, explores this experience by means of succeeding generations of a Galician family that immigrates to Brazil. The story is primarily told by the patriarch-founder of this new Brazilian family, and by his granddaughter, a writer, who pays a return visit to her ancestral home. The structure of the work is rather like William Faulkner's (q.v.) *As I Lay Dying* (1930) in that the narrative content is developed as a series of flashbacks during the week in which the grandmother lies on her deathbed. This lengthy novel is generally considered to be P.'s most important work to date, as well as her most accessible to the general reader.

Because of her careful sculpting of language, her strong individualistic characters, and her orientation toward interior consciousness, critics often point out similarities between P. and Brazil's greatest female fiction writer, Clarice Lispector (q.v.). Feminist critics point to P.'s decentered narrations as examples of *écriture feminine* (feminine writing). Her texts are a fixture in courses on Latin American women writers; but in Brazil at least, her appeal and reputation place her squarely within the mainstream of current literary creativity.

FURTHER WORKS: *Madeira feita cruz* (1963); *Tempo das frutas* (1966); *Sala de armas* (1973); *Tebas do meu coração* (1974); *A força do destino* (1977); *A doce canção de Caetana* (1987)

BIBLIOGRAPHY: Crespo, A., and P. Gómez Bedate, ''N. P., de *Guia-mapa* a *Tempo das frutas*,'' *Revista de Cultura Brasileña,* 7 (1967), 5–27; Pontiero, G., ''Notes on the Fiction of N. P.,'' *Review,* 17 (1976), 67–71; Riera, C., ''Entrevista con N. P.: la vida es la literatura,'' *Quimera,* 54–55 (n.d.), 44–49; Maffre, C., ''Les chemins du rêve dans *A república dos sonhos* de N. P.,'' *Quadrant* (1988), 165–82

PAUL B. DIXON

PLASKOVITIS, Spyros

(born Spyros Plaskasovitis) Greek novelist, short-story writer, and essayist, b. 13 June 1917, Corfu

P. studied law at the University of Athens and philosophy of law in Paris. From 1935 to 1951 he worked as a civil servant, then joined the council of state (supreme administrative court) where he was promoted in 1959 and served until 1968 when the military dictatorship dismissed and exiled him. Charged for membership in the resistance group Democratic Defense, he was sentenced to prison. While incarcerated, he contributed a short story entitled ''To radar'' (''The Radar'') to the anti-junta miscellany *Dekaokhto Keimena* (1970; *Eighteen Texts,* 1972). Reinstated in his position after the collapse of the junta and promoted to counselor, he served until 1977, when he resigned, joined the Panhellenic Socialist Movement, and was elected member of parliament at large. He was reelected in all subsequent elections, first to the Greek and then to the European parliament, from which he retired in 1989.

P.'s first short story, ''Ta sperna'' (1947; memorial offerings), was published in the literary magazine *Nea Hestia*. Many stories and articles or essays have appeared to this day in prestigious periodicals, annuals, and newspapers. These were later collected in volumes. His second short-story collection, *He thyella kai to phanari* (1955; the tempest and the lantern), won a State Prize in 1956, as did his second novel, *He Poli* (1979; the city), in 1980; earlier he had received a prize from the Group of the Twelve for his first novel, *To phragma* (1960; the dam) in 1961.

P.'s diction and style are simple and straightforward with occasional touches of lyricism. His narrative technique, however, in either stories or novels, makes frequent use of time-plane changes in passages of memory, dreaming, or vagary, which tend to give it an aura of otherworldliness or fantasy verging on the surrealistic. He retains firm control of his material thanks to his skill in making the imaginary deflate at the end in an atmosphere of believable actuality which reestablishes the initially realistic setting of his fiction. A great asset of his art is the true-to-life depiction of his characters, who are indirectly and gradually analyzed in depth. Their idiosyncratic behavior and stubborn reaction to adversities earn the sympathy of the reader and help communicate P.'s thematic concerns. These are invariably issues involving crucial choices that lead to conflict with family, community groups, or the ruling establishment in the microcosm where his heroes and heroines live and function. In *He Poli,* for instance, his two protagonists are antagonized by the selfish, unprincipled, and corrupt in family and the social milieu of Corfu, before and after World War II. Their survival or vindication is painfully achieved thanks to their inherent human decency and integrity, however eccentric these may be.

Fundamentally P. is an existential moralizer not unlike Albert Camus (q.v.), whom he admires. His ideological stance as a moderate socialist emerges gradually but not in a doctrinaire fashion, as his spokespersons are governed by humanistic virtues that oppose the hypocrisy and moral dereliction of the conservatives or reactionaries who act as the pillars of society. This is also seen in his latest novel, *He kyria tes vitrinas* (1990; the lady of the showcase), which features the same heroine as *He Poli.* This time her vindication occurs on the personal rather than the sociopolitical level, as she finally earns the love and respect of a successful businessman who thus resists financial and sexual temptations that would only debase and destroy him. P. has the skill to elevate the personal onto a universal plane, and vice versa.

His novel *To phragma* has appeared in French, Russian, and Ukrainian. A number of his short stories were translated and included in anthologies of Greek literature in these three languages plus

English, German, Italian, Romanian, and Hungarian.

FURTHER WORKS: *To gymno dentro* (1952); *Hoi gonatismenoi* (1964); *To syrmatoplegma* (1974); *To trello epeisodio* (1984); *He pezographia tou ethous kai alla dokimia* (1986)

BIBLIOGRAPHY: Raizis, M. B., on *He Poli, WLT,* 54, 4 (Autumn 1980), 678; Raizis, M. B., on *He pezographia tou ethous kai alla dokimie, WLT,* 62, 1 (Winter 1988), 167

M. BYRON RAIZIS

POLISH LITERATURE

See Volume 3, page 551.

In Poland, owing to its challenging geopolitical situation, the literary process has always been strongly influenced by the country's turbulent history, and thus often motivated by political factors. Such factors have played a crucial role throughout the post-World War II period, but have acquired a new character in the 1970s, when the struggle of the Polish people against communist rule imposed by the Soviet Union led to the unusual alliance of workers, intellectuals, and the church, and culminated in the avalanchelike force called Solidarity. This spontaneous movement, spreading from cities to the countryside, embraced the entire country and, given the changes in the U.S.S.R., had to result, sooner or later, in the elimination of the oppressive régime, which became increasingly isolated from society. Indeed, as the "dissident" poet Stanisław Barańczak (q.v.) stated in his article "Kto jest dysydentem" (1982; who is a dissident?) published in *Kultura,* it was rather the government that found itself by 1980 in the role of a dissident group facing virtually the entire nation.

During the 1970s Polish literary life became increasingly emancipated from the political controls and ideological inspiration of the Communist Party. The events of 1968, when the government brutally suppressed a widespread student movement demanding freedom of speech and instigated a virulent anti-Semitic campaign, and the revolt of the Baltic coast workers in 1970, suppressed by the use of force, resulted in a sharp erosion of the ideological legitimacy of communist rule. The liberalization of cultural policies that followed the workers' revolt and lasted until mid-1973, detente, and the official fostering of consumerism, contributed further to the growth of a new cultural climate, in which writers sought to take advantage of the opportunities provided by the brief period of improved economic conditions and the expand-

ing role of the mass media, or to address the dissatisfied segments of society from a position of ideological and moral independence.

The former trend reflected as well as helped to shape a new kind of mass culture that took its inspiration and models from various Western currents, reflecting and adapting to Polish conditions and traditions such phenomena as the American and west European pop and countercultures. Manifestations of new sensibility and mores came to the fore among young writers in the 1960s and continued to spread in the 1970s, when poets found an outlet for reaching their public not only through print, but at numerous poetry readings and competitions, and through the medium of song.

One of the writers who expressed the earlier phase of the new sensibility was the poet Rafał Wojaczek (1945–1971), whose legend woven of aberrant behavior and psychological problems received tragic reinforcement as a result of his suicide. Among the most popular as well as controversial representations of the trend in the 1970s were Edward Stachura (1937–1979), also ending with suicide, and Janusz Głowacki (b. 1938). Stachura, who began his literary career as the author of highly stylized poetry and the lyrical quasinovels *Cała jaskrawość* (1969; all the flagrance) and *Siekierezada* (1971; axerezade) became in the 1970s a singer, a youth idol, and something of a religious guru. His prose *Oto* (behold), published in 1980, after his suicide, is interesting both as an experiment in modern gospel writing and for its blending of Buddhism, Christianity, and the teachings of Lao-Tse. His last work, "Pogodzić się ze światem" (1980; to become reconciled with the world), is a day-by-day record of his embracing death as the only way of testing the slenderest of religious hopes.

Głowacki's work includes several collections of short stories, such as *Nowy taniec la-ba-da* (1970; the new dance la-ba-da), *Paradis* (1973; paradise), and *My Sweet Raskolnikow* (1977; title in English), as well as plays and film scripts, of which "Kopciuch" (1979; *Cinders,* London premiere 1981), depicting the life of delinquent girls, was a reworking of the theme of the widely acclaimed film *Psychodrama,* directed in 1969 by Marek Piwowski. Głowacki represents precisely that world which Stachura's brand of counterculture tried to reject. His stories, which in their form reflect the penetration of narrative prose by film techniques, and display a strong predilection for the grotesque and parody, show the corruption both of values and of behavior that characterized in the 1970s the "playboyland" of the communist establishment.

The trend of political contestation and opposition also surfaced in the late 1960s, but expanded considerably as the 1970s moved toward an acute economic crisis and the Solidarity revolution. It initially comprised mostly young poets, such as Barańczak, who in 1976 gave up his party membership, Jacek Bierezin (b. 1947), Ewa Lipska (b. 1945), Krzysztof Karasek (b. 1937) Adam Zagajewski, Ryszard Krynicki (qq.v.), and others. Many of the so-called New Wave writers found ideological inspiration in such former communists-turned-oppositionists as Leszek Kołakowski (b. 1927), philosopher and author of excellent philosophical tales, and Wiktor Woroszylski (b. 1927), poet and prose writer; they gradually found common ground with the Catholic writers around the periodicals *Więź, Znak,* and *Tygodnik Powszechny,* as well as with the émigré *Kultura* circle abroad, which, although depleted by the deaths of Witold Gombrowicz and the essayist Jerzy Stempowski (1894–1969), still included Czesław Miłosz (q.v.), awarded the Nobel Prize for literature in 1980, and Gustaw Herling-Grudziński (b. 1919).

The reaction of the young poets against indirectness, stylization, and abstract symbolism, which characterized much of the poetry of the 1960s, had to take into account the negative lessons of Socialist Realism (q.v.), with its declaratory, rhetorical poetics and schematized imagination. The result was the adaptation of the so-called linguistic trend of the 1950s and 1960s, exemplified by Białoszewski and Karpowicz, to the task of exposing inauthentic and manipulative speech, which found its best expression in the poetry of Barańczak and Krynicki. Distrust of public forms of speech, subversion of official and common linguistic usage, objectivization of poetic idiom— these rather than the rhetoric of dissent became the features of the nonconformist and contestatory attitudes of the New Wave.

Although interesting as a phenomenon, the poets of the New Wave failed to challenge effectively the preeminence of the leading postwar poets; Herbert, Miłosz, Różewicz, and Szymborska. The latter two consolidated their position mainly through the publication of retrospective volumes, which in Różewicz's case comprised not only his collected poems (1971; 2nd ed., 1976) but also his experimental poetic drama and prose. Herbert and Miłosz developed further their respective modes of poetic discourse and reflection. In the case of Miłosz, perhaps the two most significant works were a volume of poems, *Gdzie wschodzi słońce i kędy zapada* (1974; *From the Rising of the Sun,* 1974), containing a remarkable long poem of the same title, and *Ziemia Ulro* (1977; *Land of Ulro,* 1981), an essay that examines various aspects of modern religious imagination in terms of Miłosz's own complex grappling with the problems of faith and unbelief. Herbert added another dimension to his ironic mode of expression by creating in *Pan Cogito* (1974; Mr. Cogito) a poetic persona whose multifaceted complexity enabled him not only to continue exploring in a profound way philosophical, moral, and contemporary themes, but to restate, in the famous poem "Przesłanie Pana Cognito" (1974; "Mr. Cogito's Envoy," 1977), the value of heroic idealism.

In prose the literary results of the new commitment and openness produced a number of interesting works that went beyond the allusive or naturalistic narratives of the 1950s and 1960s. Kazimierz Brandys's (q.v.) novel *Nierzeczywistość* (1977; *A Question of Reality,* 1980), published in the *Kultura* "without censorship" series, Tadeusz Konwicki's *Mała Apokalipsa* (1979; *A Minor Apocalypse,* 1983); and Jerzy Andrzejewski's (qq.v.) *Miazga* (1980; pulp)—all employed new means in depicting what Zagajewski and Julian Kornhauser (b. 1946) called "the unrepresented world" of Polish life and society. Perhaps the most interesting as an artistic experiment was Andrzejewski's *Miazga;* begun in the mid-1960s, and continued after 1969, it mixes various modes of discourse (narrative, essay, memoir, letters, diary, dialogues, and fictitious, yet representative, if parodic, biographical entries) in a discontinuous, patchwork fashion, in what is, in the end, an autothematic antinovel that fails to live up to the requirements of the genre in order to fulfil a complex mimetic and ideological function.

By the second half of the 1970s, a number of prominent older writers, including Andrzejewski, Konwicki, Brandys, and Marek Nowakowski (b. 1935), joined hands with the younger oppositionists around the Committee for the Defense of Workers (KOR, 1976), and several independent journals, such as *Zapis, Puls,* and *Spotkania.* By the late 1970s, independent journals and publishing ventures broke effectively the state's virtual monopoly on publishing.

The period of the Solidarity revolution, between August 1980 and December 1981, did not last long enough to generate new literary phenomena, but it did free the writers from some of the worst constraints of censorship and government control. Books hitherto banned began to appear, including the first book publication of Miłosz's poetry in Poland since 1945—although his collections of essays, such as *Ogród nauk* (1979; the garden of knowledge) were not allowed to appear. The imposition of martial law in December 1981, arrests, internments, and suspension of professional organizations, including the Union of Polish Writers, met with considerable resistance not only on the part of the writers associated with the opposition in the 1970s, and broadly sympathetic to the Solidarity movement, but also of a fairly large segment of those who were party members. Some, like Ernest Bryll (b. 1935), a poet and dramatist, renounced their party membership in protest; others, while retaining their membership, supported the efforts of the executive of the union to prevent the dissolution of the organization without compromising its autonomy. The attempt to save the organization proved, in the end, unsuccessful, and the union was dissolved by the authorities in August 1983. The subsequent creation of a party-controlled union was largely boycotted by the literary milieu, which on the whole showed a remarkable degree of solidarity.

The dissolution of the union was accompanied by the tightening of censorship, discrimination in state patronage, and the introduction of proscription lists. For instance, in March 1984 a government-controlled literary weekly published a list of twenty-eight names of writers whose works were not to be reissued by state publishing houses. Among those listed was the former president of the union, Jan Józef Szczepański (b. 1919), a fiction writer of distinction; Kornel Filipowicz (1913–1990), one of the best short-story writers in postwar Poland; Woroszylski; Konwicki; Stryjkowski; and Miłosz. However, harsh government policies failed to cow the literary community, which by the mid-1980s had at its disposal alternative means of publication: In addition to the Catholic journals and publishing houses, which the government did not dare to close, there emerged numerous underground presses, and periodicals, of which the most important were *Arka, Wezwanie, Obecność,* and *Brulion,* which became the organ of the now strongly politicized counterculture trend; moreover, many writers took advantage of the émigré publishing houses and journals, such as *Kultura* and *Zeszyty Literackie* in Paris and *Puls* in London. The underground presses reprinted works by Gombrowicz, Miłosz, Herling-Grudziński, Aleksander Wat (1900–1967)—whose autobiography, *Mój wiek* (1977; *My Century,* 1990), evoked special interest—Józef Mackiewicz, and many others, and published new work written in Poland, including Jarosław Marek Rymkiewicz's (b. 1935) topical novel *Rozmowy polskie* (1984; Polish conversations), Konwicki's autobiographical *Wschody i zachody księżyca* (1982; *Moonrise, Moonset,* 1987), Mrożek's satirical and absurdist tales, Adam Michnik's (b. 1946) historical and literary essays, and volumes of several young poets, such as Tomasz Jastrun (b. 1950), Jan Polkowski (b. 1953), and others.

The least harmed by the consequences of martial law was poetry. In the 1980s, Miłosz added to his substantial poetic achievement new work of outstanding quality, *Hymn o perle* (1981; hymn of the pearl), *Nieobjęta ziemia* (1985; *Unattainable Earth,* 1986), and *Kroniki* (1987; chronicles); the

appearance of these volumes as well as of his *Collected Poems* in English translation (1988) have further enhanced his standing as a major 20th-c. poet. Herbert came with one of the most important poetic documents of the troubled time, *Raport z oblężonego miasta i inne wiersze* (1983; *Report from the Besieged City and Other Poems,* 1987), in which he gives his poetic reaction to both the specifically Polish, but also universal, condition of the human being and society. The volume continues the earlier *Pan Cogito,* using the same versatile persona and developing further the philosophical and moral themes in the typically Herbertian mode of ironic complexity and intellectual integrity.

Of the poets who previously attained a level of excellence, Wisława Szymborska's new volume *Ludzie na moście* (1986; *People on a Bridge,* 1990) has gained wide acclaim as another example of the exquisite quality of her "Mozartian" verse. Several poets of the New Wave have now attained greater maturity and stature. Zagajewski's, Barańczak's, and Krynicki's growing to maturity received a special recognition by Miłosz, who in his diary *Rok myśliwego* (1990; a year of a hunter) expressed a high opinion of their work; Adam Czerniawski's (b. 1934) *Wiek złoty* (1982; age of gold) and *Jesień* (1989; autumn) testify further to the originality of his poetic development, achieved despite the fact that he had left Poland in early childhood; and among the youngest, Bronisław Maj (b. 1953) has already made his mark as the author of *Zagłada świętego miasta* (1986; annihilation of the holy city) and other volumes. Among retrospective volumes were Jan Twardowski's (b. 1916) *Nie przyszedłem pana nawracać* (1986; I did not come to convert you), Wacław Iwaniuk's (q.v.) *Powrót* (1989; return), Jan Darowski's (b. 1926) *Niespodziewane żywoty* (1990; unexpected lives), and Bogdan Czaykowski's (b. 1937) *Wiatr z innej strony* (1990; wind from another side).

The most affected by the regime's policies and the economic crisis was the theater. A boycott of state-run radio and television by the actors, which lasted for nearly a year, and the considerable state interference in theatrical life affected negatively the writing of plays and the desire to be staged. Attempts to create an alternative theater (such as performances in church halls) could not replace normally functioning theater. Nevertheless, an excellent journal devoted to drama and theater, *Dialog,* on the whole managed to maintain its high standards; some good plays did get published, including Różewicz's *Pułapka* (1982; *The Trap,* 1984), and Mrożek's *Portret* (1987; portrait), possibly the best of his plays since *Emigranci* (1974; émigrés). Also, such outstanding theater directors as Tadeusz Kantor; the brilliant representative of the "theater-of-happening" in Poland, Zygmunt Hübner; and Jerzy Jarocki were soon able to resume their theatrical experiments despite official restrictions, while Jerzy Grotowski (b. 1929) continued to exert influence both in Poland and abroad.

Both Mrożek's and Różewicz's development seems to have been going in the same direction as the Western absurdist dramatists, namely turning back, as it were, to the more traditional forms of drama and preoccupation with philosophical and psychological questions. Różewicz's *Pułapka* tackles in a highly successful manner the difficult problem of structuring a plotless "plot" around the dilemmas of an alienated individual by means of a series of monologues and conversations situated almost exclusively within the circle of a family. Nevertheless, it can still be classified as an absurdist play, as it deals with the situation of a man (Franz Kafka) whose entire life and work is one of the sources of inspiration of the whole concept of the Theatre of the Absurd (q.v.). Mrożek's case is in many respects similar.

In prose the pressure for topicality, commitment, witnessing, self-justification, affirmation of values, and painting the devil black (that is, mainly, red), thrust to the forefront paraliterary genres such as reportage, documentary fiction, diary, interview, apology, essay, polemic, and invective. One can mention here Brandys's mixture of diary, reminiscences, and commentary, *Miesiące* (3 vols., 1981–1984), *A Warsaw Diary: 1978–1981* (1983), and *Paris, New York: 1982–1984* (1988); Szczepański's report on his presidency of the Union of Writers during the Solidarity and martial-law period, *Kadencja* (1988; term of office); or fictionalized accounts of contemporary events, such as Marek Nowakowski's (b. 1935) *Raport o stanie wojennym* (1982; *The Canary and Other Tales of Martial Law,* 1984) and his other volumes in this genre, Głowacki's story of the August 1980 strike at the Lenin shipyard, *Moc truchleje* (1982; *Give Us This Day,* 1983), Konwicki's contemporary novel *Rzeka podziemna, podziemne ptaki* (1985; underground river, underground birds), or Hanna Krall's (b. 1937) *Okna* (1987; windows), none of which, however, equaled the highly successful transformation of journalism into literary form in the much earlier *Cesarz* (1978; *The Emperor,* 1983) by Ryszard Kapuściński (b. 1932).

Contrasting with the trend of topical fiction was the work of a number of young writers, such as Grzegorz Musiał (b. 1952) and Pawel Huelle (b. 1957), whose first novel, *Weiser Dawidek* (1987; *Who Was David Weiser,* 1990), which has been translated into more than a dozen languages, is remarkable if only as an example of the advantages that "makers of fictions" have over those who find it difficult to detach themselves in their narratives from actual happenings. Finally, one should not fail to mention new work of the master of satirical and philosophical science fiction, Stanisław Lem (b. 1921), such as *Golem XIV* (1981; included in *Imaginary Magnitude,* 1984) and *Wizja lokalna* (1982; official hearing on the spot).

Particularly popular was the genre of conversations, to mention only Ewa Czarnecka's (dates n.a.) *Podróżny świata; rozmowy z Czesławem Miłoszem* (1983; *Conversations with Czesław Miłosz,* 1987); Stanisław Nowicki's (dates n.a.) *Pół wieku czyśćca; rozmowy z Tadeuszem Konwickim* (1986; half a century of purgatory; conversations with Tadeusz Konwicki); Jacek Trznadel's (b. 1930) *Hańba domowa; rozmowy z pisarzami* (1986; native shame; conversations with writers), comprising interviews with twelve prominent writers concerning their communist past and rejection of communism; or Kazimierz Braun's (dates n.a.) and Tadeusz Różewicz's *Języki teatru* (1989; languages of theater), of considerable interest regarding the development of Różewicz's poetic drama and his literary views. There was also a great demand for diaries, a number of which by some of the most important 20th-c. writers appeared for the first time in print, offering often fascinating insights into various developments in Polish literature. Of particular value, despite some editorial deletions, are *Dzienniki* (5 vols., 1988; diaries) by Maria Dąbrowska (1889–1965), but mention should also be made of Jerzy Zawieyski's (1902–1969) *Kartki z dziennika, 1955–1969* (1983; pages from a diary, 1955–1969), and of the first printing in Poland of Gombrowicz's *Dziennik* (3 vols., first pub. in Paris, 1957, 1966, 1971; *Diary,* 1988–1989), with only minor deletions.

One of the major thematic concerns of the 1980s was the Jewish past, the Holocaust, and anti-semitism in Poland. Of the numerous writings dealing with this theme, Andrzej Szczypiorski's (b. 1924) *Początek* (1986; *Beautiful Mrs. Seidenman,* 1990), which deals in part with survival in Nazi-occupied Warsaw, has met with wide acclaim possibly because it is a deftly handled conventional novel; Jarosław Marek Rymkiewicz's (b. 1935) *Umschlagplatz* (1988; transit place), which eludes generic classification, exemplifies the need, felt by so many writers writing on the theme of *Shoah,* to go beyond the available literary forms, so as to do justice to a subject that defies imagination; and Jerzy S. Sito's (b. 1934) play *Słuchaj, Izraelu!* (1988; listen, Israel!), which deals with life (and death) in the Warsaw ghetto, has qualities of true dramatic power and tragic pity, especially in the presentation of its main character, Adam Czerniakow. A publication of an unusual documentary value is *Antologia poezji żydowskiej* (1983; anthology of Jewish poetry), selected and edited by Arnold Słucki, and comprising translators from Yiddish of over a hundred poems by poets, many of whom died in German and Soviet camps or in ghettos or were killed on the streets or while hiding in forests.

With the collapse of communist rule in 1989, Polish history, and with it Polish literature, have entered a new phase. While predictions would be unwise, it may be noted that the literary milieu has already become acutely aware of the fact that economic and political freedoms come together with the "laws of the free market" which, the pessimists say, means more demand for sex, crime, science fiction, and melodrama rather than for good literature. This may be so. But the cultural dynamics of postcommunist society, freed from ideological constraints, may yet give the lie to the pessimists, especially in a country with such literary traditions as Poland.

BIBLIOGRAPHY: Miłosz, C., *The Witness of Poetry* (1983); Ziegfeld, R. E., *Stanisław Lem* (1985); Davie, D., *Czesław Miłosz and the Insufficiency of Lyric* (1986); Barańczak, S., *A Fugitive from Utopia: The Poetry of Zbigniew Herbert* (1987); Czerwiński, E. J., *Contemporary Polish Theater and Drama* (1988); Możejko, E., ed., *Between Anxiety and Hope: The Poetry and Writing of Czesław Miłosz* (1988); Barańczak, S., *Breathing under Water and Other East European Essays* (1990); Fiut, A., *The Eternal Moment: The Poetry of Czesław Miłosz* (1990); Czerniawski, A., ed., *The Mature Laurel: Essays on Modern Polish Poetry* (1991); Donskov A., and R. Sokoloski, eds., *Slavic Drama, the Question of Innovation* (1991)

BOGDAN CZAYKOWSKI
ZBIGNIEW FOLEJEWSKI

PONIATOWSKA, Elena

Mexican novelist, short-story writer, and journalist, b. 19 May 1933, Paris, France

P.'s father, a Polish aristocrat, had emigrated to France, and her Mexican mother fled to Europe with her family during the Mexican Revolution. In 1942, during World War II, P., her mother, and her sister returned to Mexico, where her father joined them after the war. Having received her high-school education in British and American religious schools, P. learned Spanish from her family's servants, thus explaining her love of the colloquial idiom so evident in her works. In the mid-1950s P. was hired by the Mexican daily *Excélsior* to conduct interviews with a wide range of celebrities, a position that launched her career as a journalist and eventually inspired her to write documentary fiction. In 1978 she was awarded the

Mexican National Journalism Prize, and today she is perhaps Mexico's best-known writer after Octavio Paz and Carlos Fuentes (qq.v.).

P. achieved fame almost overnight with the publication of *La noche de Tlatelolco* (1971; *Massacre in Mexico,* 1975), a grouping of individual eyewitness accounts of the massacre of hundreds of unarmed civilians (P.'s younger brother was one of those killed) by government troops on Tlatelolco Plaza in the heart of the capital. The tragedy, which occurred on 2 October 1968 during a peaceful protest against government policies, has been the subject of many literary texts, but P.'s is by far the most widely read, having gone through more than fifty editions to date. It consists of a montage of oral testimonies, police records, photographs, newspaper articles, and political speeches, all of which have been edited and arranged in such a way that the reader feels caught up in the swirl of the events described. Almost two decades later P. utilized a similar technique to dramatize the earthquake that killed thousands of people in Mexico City on 19 September 1985. *Nada, nadie: Las voces del temblor* (1988; nothing, nobody: the voices of the earthquake) thrusts its readers into the center of the tragedy that, like the massacre of Tlatelolco, will remain embedded in the Mexican subconscious for generations. The searing descriptions of the terrible first-person experiences both during and after the quake are impossible to forget. Also memorable are the references to fraud on the part of contractors who had ignored building codes for personal gain, and the instances in which army and police personnel placed public order before rescue efforts. As in *La noche de Tlatelolco,* P. remains objective, allowing those she has interviewed to describe one of the major occurrences in recent Mexican history. *Nada, nadie: Las voces del temblor* reads almost like a novel, juxtaposing moments of suspense, heroism, and suffering. It is one of the most moving works ever published by a Mexican author.

P.'s best-known novel to date is *Hasta no verte, Jesús mío* (1969; *Until We Meet Again,* 1987), a testimonial of a poor, working-class woman who was born in southern Mexico about 1900, found herself caught up in the Revolution of 1910, and lived most of her life in Mexico City. P. came across her protagonist Jesusa Palancares by chance when she heard her conversing with coworkers in a laundry. With tape recorder and notebook in hand, P. spent two hours a week for many months with Jesusa, recording the old woman's recollections of her life. This novel is noteworthy for a number of reasons. Jesusa's language is a fascinating example of the colorful slang used by her class; her struggle to survive cannot fail to elicit our admiration; her everyday adventures while working for numerous employers in a wide variety of jobs liken her to a picaresque heroine; and her descriptions of the revolution and subsequent political events exude a combination of forthrightness and cynicism seldom observed in Mexican literature. While some critics see Jesusa as a feminist, a liberated woman in a *machista* society, others see her as a victim of male domination and social injustice. In a sense both opinions are correct, but one should recognize that in the course of the novel Jesusa evolves from an innocent adolescent, forced into a bad marriage at the age of fifteen, to a strong, resolute woman (she actually leads a combat unit during the revolution after her husband is killed), and she never again submits to male domination.

P.'s two other novels are *Querido Diego, te abraza Quiela* (1976; *Dear Diego*, 1986), in epistolary format, and *La "Flor de Lis"* (1988; the "Flor de Lis"), an autobiographical novel and a kind of bildungsroman about a girl who leaves France for Mexico with her mother and sister during World War II. P.'s best collection of short fiction is *De noches vienes* (1979; you come by night), which contains sixteen stories ranging in subject matter from social protest to the complex relations between social classes and the sexes.

P. is one of today's major practitioners of documentary fiction, a genre that has become increasingly important in Spanish America. Her popularity as a writer stems from her dramatic presentations of contemporary issues, her sympathy for the downtrodden, and her emphasis on colloquial language, which makes her writings accessible to most readers. For those seeking a better understanding of modern Mexico, P.'s oeuvre provides an excellent resource.

FURTHER WORKS: *Lilus Kikus* (1954); *Palabras cruzadas: Crónicas* (1961); *Todo empezó el domingo* (1961); *Los cuentos de Lilus Kikus* (1967); *El primer primero de mayo* (1976); *Gaby Brimmer* (1979); *Fuerte es el silencio* (1980); *La casa en la tierra* (1980): *Domingo siete* (1982); *El último guajolote* (1982); *¡Ay vida, no me mereces!* (1986); *Héctor García: México sin retoque* (1987)

BIBLIOGRAPHY: Miller, B., *Mujeres en la literatura* (1978), 65–75; Fox-Lockert, L., *Women Novelists in Spain and Spanish America* (1979), 260–77; Portal, M., *Proceso narrativo de la revolución mexicana* (1980), 285–92: Fernández Olmos, M., "El género testimonial: Aproximaciones feministas," *RevI*, 11, 1 (Spring 1981), 69–75; Young, D. J., and W. D. Young, "The New Journalism in Mexico: Two Women Writers," *Chasqui*, 12, 2–3 (Feb.-May 1983), 72–80; Hancock, J., " E. P.'s *Hasta no verte, Jesús mío:*

The Remaking of the Image of Woman," *Hispania,* 66, 3 (Sept. 1983), 355–59; Foster, D. W., "Latin American Documentary Narrative," *PMLA,* 99, 1 (Jan. 1984), 41–55; Chevigny, B. G., "The Transformation of Privilege in the Work of E. P.," *LALR,* 13, 26 (July–Dec. 1985), 49–62; Foster, D. W., *Alternate Voices in the Contemporary Latin American Narrative* (1985), 12–20 and passim; Friedman, E. H., "The Marginated Narrator: *Hasta no verte, Jesús mío* and the Eloquence of Repression," *The Antiheroine's Voice: Narrative Discourse and Transformations of the Picaresque* (1987), 170–87; Meyer, D., *Lives on the Line: The Testimony of Contemporary Latin American Authors* (1988), 137–38; Shea, M., "A Growing Awareness of Sexual Oppression in the Novels of Contemporary Latin American Women Writers," *Confluencia,* 4, 1 (Fall 1988), 53–59; Gazarian-Gautier, M.-L., *Interviews with Latin American Writers* (1989), 199–216; Martin, G., *Journeys through the Labyrinth: Latin American Fiction in the Twentieth Century* (1989), 344–50; Jörgensen, B. E., "E. P.," in Marting, D. E., ed., *Spanish American Women Writers: A Bio-Bibliographical Source Book* (1990), 472–82

GEORGE R. MCMURRAY

Feminist perspectives in literary analysis have seen frequent publication in the last few years. Works by such female authors as Sor Juana Inés de la Cruz, Gertrudis Gómez de Avellaneda, Gabriela Mistral, María Luisa Bombal, Marta Lynch, and Rosario Castellanos, to name only a few, have very recently been the subject of this specific kind of investigation. An important addition to this list is E. P.—novelist, short story and film script writer, journalist, editor, and feminist—whose production is both varied and fecund. One publication in particular, *Hasta no verte, Jesús mío* (1969), is a novel which may be considered a landmark in Mexican literature because it offers a fresh view and treatment of Latin American woman, and may represent a step toward the delineation of a new female image or role model. Intimately involved with the social realities of Mexico, the protagonist deviates radically from the commonly portrayed stereotypes of women. Her personality and conduct embody a blend of so-called feminine and masculine traits, thus approximating the androgynous figure which some feminist critics regard as essential. . . .

Hasta no verte, Jesús mío is based on the real life of Jesusa Palancares. Overhearing some vigorous statements made by a humble woman in a laundry room conversation, P. was so moved that she arranged to visit her at home in a poor neighborhood of Mexico City. This led to a series of interviews, many of them taped, which took place for more than a two-year period. . . . P. labels her work a *novela testimonial* rather than a sociological or anthropological document mainly because of what was involved in the writing. . . .

Women like Jesusa Palancares are not frequently represented in literature. In *Hasta no verte, Jesús mío,*

E. P. portrays a female character whose life, attitudes, and expression invalidate the erroneous and offensive stereotypes of women that have been perpetuated. Unlike many others depicted in fiction, Jesusa is a hardworking individual who survives situations with dignity. She has a keen sense of justice that compels her to censure whatever she judges to be a social injustice. Thus, a new alternative has been established: a liberated female hero; a positive role model who is independent, self-reliant, and physically, as well as emotionally, strong.

Joel Hancock, "E. P.'s *Hasta no verte, Jesús mío:* The Remaking of the Image of Woman," *Hispania,* 66, 3 (Sept. 1983), 353–57

The evanescent or invisible, the silent or the silenced, those who elude official history or vanish from it, make the subject of the two of P.'s works from which her fame and influence chiefly derive. Her testimonial novel, *Hasta no verte, Jesús mío* . . . presents in first-person narration the story of an adventuring peasant woman, fighter in the Mexican revolution and survivor of its inhospitable aftermath. Hitherto such characters had been presented only externally, and P.'s distillation of her subject's dense and highly-colored idiom became a new literary resource. *La noche de Tlatelolco* . . . is a dramatic collage of interviews with participants in the 1968 student movement and with witnesses to the massacre of hundreds during a peaceful meeting in Mexico City, an event obfuscated by government agencies and the press alike. . . .

P.'s choosing to cast her lot with Latin America and to write in Spanish with a highly Mexican inflection, point to a deliberateness of self-formation that is reinforced by other choices. For P.'s social roots are aristocratic and her political antecedents are conservative. Generations of exile from reform and revolution in Mexico and Poland produced in France P.'s parents and P. herself. Against such a background, P.'s two most celebrated works stand in high relief; they delineate the dual trajectory of her career. In *Hasta no verte, Jesús mío,* she journeys to the opposite end of woman's world of social possibility and in *La noche de Tlatelolco* she journeys to the alternate pole of political possibility. Each journey may be seen as metaphor and impetus of the other. Like her choice of Latin America, her choosing to write of a woman with no resources but her self and of political insurgents has everything to do with her authorial self-creation.

Bell Gale Chevigny, "The Transformation of Privilege in the Work of E. P.," *LALR,* 13, 26 (July–Dec. 1985), 49–50

Since the mid-1950s, when she began writing for newspapers in Mexico City as well as writing her own poetry and prose, P. has become an author identified with the voice of the Mexican people. This authentic, clear voice speaks through her work powerfully, whether in the testimonial novel based on interviews with the indomitable Jesusa Palancares—*Hasta no verte, Jesús mío*

. . . —or in the dramatic montage of first-person accounts of the 1968 student riots in *La noche de Tlatelolco*. . . . By bringing history to life in individual portraits, P. forces her reader to reconsider the personal dimensions of otherwise distant events or situations. She is particularly adept at conveying the experiences of women; prime examples would be the paralyzed *Gaby Brimmer* . . . a woman of great courage and determination, or the artist Angelina Beloff in *Querido Diego, te abraza Quiela* . . . , whom Diego Rivera spurned after having lived with her for ten years and fathering her son.

Doris Meyer, *Lives on the Line: The Testimony of Contemporary Latin American Authors* (1988), 137

E. P. . . . is one of Latin America's most remarkable narrators. Outside of [Octavio] Paz and [Carlos] Fuentes, she is probably the most important writer in Mexico today. Her father was a French-Polish émigré aristocrat, her mother the daughter of a Mexican landowning family which fled the country during the Revolution. The family returned to Mexico when Elena was nine years old, and she was sent to an English school, largely learning Spanish from the family servants. In later life she strived desperately to integrate herself into Mexican national life, and today is the country's best known journalist and arguably Latin America's most important producer of documentary narrative. *Until We Meet Again* . . . is the moving story of a Mexican working-class woman's experience of the 20th c., a work which makes most Social Realist novels seem artificial. *Massacre in Mexico* . . . is the single most influential record of any kind of the 1968 massacre, in which her brother Jan died, with a force reminiscent of the films of the Bolivian director Jorge Sanjinés. And her latest work, *"Nothing, No One"* . . . is a genuinely searing testimony to the experience of the [1985] earthquake. In short, P. has produced the most lasting memorials to the two most significant events of Mexican history in the last two decades, the Tlatelolco affair and the great earthquake, as well as a series of other works such as *Dear Diego* . . . , *Lilus Kilus* . . . , and *"The Fleur de Lys"* . . . . something like a fictionalized autobiography.

Gerald Martin, *Journeys through the Labyrinth: Latin American Fiction in the Twentieth Century* (1989), 346–47

Indeed, Tlatelolco has acquired such a profound meaning in contemporary Mexican culture that it has been the subject of a book-length essay by Octavio Paz and has inspired virtually a subgenre of recent Mexican literature. *La noche de Tlatelolco* . . . by E. P. . . . is the only documentary narrative besides [Julío] Cortázar's *El libro de Manuel* and [Miguel] Barnet's *Biografía de un cimarrón* that has been translated into English. It is the most documentary of the texts studied in this essay and, consequently, the least "novelistic" if viewed in terms of fictional elements or devices. Nevertheless, it is novelistic in the sense that it sustains a complex narrative structure. And, although *Noche* has a place in a bibliography of contemporary social history, it is frequently read as a contribution to the contemporary Latin American novel. To read *Noche* as more novel than document does not detract from its quality as documentary testimonial. Rather—as is true for all recent documentary and historical fiction in Latin America—such a reading testifies to the continuity in that culture of fiction and reality and the importance of productive "mythic" factuality.

David William Foster, *Alternate Voices in the Contemporary Latin American Narrative* (1985), 13

A quick review of E. P.'s published works reveals the variety of themes and literary forms which her writing embraces. A common thread, however, connects her political and social chronicles, her novels and short stories, her interviews and her testimonial works. That common thread is the profound commitment to interpreting contemporary Mexican society, with special attention to the silenced voices and the marginalized lives that constitute the majority experience in the vast human landscape of her country. Her books record such events as the 1968 Mexican student movement, a hunger strike by mothers of the "disappeared," and the 1985 earthquake in Mexico City; they offer as protagonists street vendors, a quadriplegic woman of the middle class, student dissidents, and political prisoners. For this reason most readers concur in considering P. to be a literary champion of the oppressed. In the process of allowing the other to speak for him or herself, P. often effaces her own participation in the dialogue . . . .

Beth E. Jörgensen, "E. P.," in Diane E. Marting, ed., *Spanish American Women Writers: A Bio-Bibliographical Source Book* (1990), 473

POSTMODERNISM

Postmodernism is a term generally used to describe a range of specific artistic and cultural phenomena that were created approximately after 1960; by extension, postmodernism often refers to a style or a mélange of stylistic features found generally throughout the fine arts during the last thirty years. Like many such critical terms, postmodernism thus has a narrow chronological meaning and a much broader and more contested use as a term that names either a "spirit," a particular set of formal and aesthetic qualities, or even a complex social and historical epoch and its dominant form of self-understanding. Further complicating any shared or usable sense of the term is a vast array of approaches to the relationship between social forces and artistic phenomena, and also the large number of possible critical and explanatory schemas that can be used to mediate such relationships. To complete the difficulty, postmodernism is itself often understood as positing its own radically

skeptical approach to the very idea of explanatory schema.

Postmodernism can nevertheless be used in a way that makes it no more imprecise, and hence no more unavoidable, a term than romanticism or neoclassicism. What usually generates disagreement about its more precise applications or analytic uses, however, is just what sort of weight or context should be given to the "post" part of the term. This conjures up in turn a field of possible disagreements about what will be understood by modernism (q.v.) itself. What many critics who use postmodernism as an explanatory term assume—and this may be the lowest common denominator of the meanings of postmodernism—is that modernism has by now become a thoroughly accepted cultural style that no longer possesses its radical or disruptive force, and postmodernism therefore serves as the completion, replacement, successor, or final eliminator of the modernist legacy.

Just how postmodernism relates to the legacy of modernism therefore determines its meaning. Fredric Jameson (b. 1934) has mapped out the various meanings of postmodernism by showing how the "post" attitude can be read as either a sign of approval or disapproval; in turn, modernism can have either a negative or positive valuation. This generates four possible variations on postmodernism: (1) a set of positive attitudes set against negatively viewed modernism; (2) a positive extension of an approved modernism; (3) a negative reaction to a modernism that is itself judged negatively; and (4) a negative reaction against an otherwise approved set of cultural values and achievements. The first position, for example, is occupied by Tom Wolfe (q.v.) while the fourth is occupied by Jürgen Habermas (b. 1929). Wolfe's stance, waggish and at times corrosively satirical, assumes that the classical phase of so-called "high" modernism now seems hollow, and it is all to the good that we develop new and different attitudes to replace what had become piously accepted as something like an establishment culture. On the other hand, it is one of Habermas's main points that the cultural work of modernism is essentially emancipatory, following as it does in the heritage of the Enlightenment, and postmodernism is largely dominated by those who have lost faith in modernity and modernism, its cultural expression. Jameson's map, which is very suggestive, works in part because the "post" in modernism differs from, say, the "neo" in neoclassicism. A term like neoclassicism involves more than historical revival; it usually implies a very positive, even worshipful, attitude toward the earlier values of a classical epoch. The "post" in postmodernism can be simply chronological, but it can also have a curiously judgmental stance, cautiously waiting to be filled with some sort of commitment or affectlessly avoiding it altogether.

Many critics of postmodernism, including Jameson, have remarked on its problematic relation to history itself. Postmodernism is frequently discussed as employing a pastiche of historically developed (and abandoned) styles as its own chief stylistic marker. Indeed, postmodernism can sometimes appear to be mocking the very idea of style, especially when style is considered as a guarantee of sincerity or self-expression. The pastiche of period styles was first highly evident in architecture, where the writings of Charles Jencks (b. 1939) and Robert Venturi (b. 1925) singled it out for particular praise. But such use of a formal device took place in painting as well, and throughout the visual arts, a use fomented in part by the domination of advertising and other mass media in the everyday life of postindustrial capitalist society. In the visual arts postmodernism covers a wide range of work, from the return of representational painting to the ever-increasing use of popular materials, so as to question radically the distinctions between "low" and "high" culture. Indeed, the flooding of the realm of public life with distributed and manipulated images is a phenomenon that critics often use to characterize the conflation of the postindustrial and the postmodern. These stylistic features would have analogues in literature. For example, the mixing of genres in the new journalism, and the experiments of Truman Capote and Norman Mailer with novels based on journalistic "facts," or John Ashbery's recycling of cliches with postromantic themes, as well as Ishmael Reed's (qq.v.) inventive play with popular genres and stereotypes, are all describable as part of postmodernism.

Since the development of genres and the ranking of subject matter have generally had historical sanction, postmodernism in effect attacks history as it attacks such traditional artistic values. But, to be more precise, postmodernism attacks a specific view of history, which can be generalized as the Enlightenment view that maintains that civilization and culture are steadily upward movements away from superstition and repression. In place of the Enlightenment view, postmodernism argues that history is merely linear, without any particular pattern except what might be subjectively imposed upon it, or that it is randomly recursive, throwing up repetitions that all too often seem like gross caricatures. In the first of these possibilities, and to a lesser extent in the other as well, the figure of Nietzsche especially dominates; he may in fact be the philosopher whose influence is most pervasive in postmodernism. What postmodernism's

historical sense also challenges is the belief, central to modernism, that cultural and social renewal are made possible by the discharge of revolutionary energies. Here the philosophy most immediately invoked—but only to be rejected as too subjective—is existentialism (q.v.). The work of Jean-François Lyotard (q.v.) especially makes the case against the viability of any grand narrative significance in history, whether derived from some transcendent force or the accumulated power of human will. Postmodernism is as resolute in its antiheroic feelings as in its antihierarchical attitude.

Because of its antihierarchical attitude to genres and subject matter, postmodernism may also be regarded as a certain sensibility, and in this context one of the more frequently discussed features is gross deadpan irony. Again, this can be seen as an extension of modernist irony, or its cancellation. The dark humor of Samuel Beckett's drama and the wry anomie of Milan Kundera's (qq.v.) fiction are two leading examples of this feature. Kundera, for example, while showing great respect for the historical development of the novel, employs a set of distancing devices that move the novelistic features of his work in the direction of the essay. This creates an irony like that found in many self-reflexive novels of the past, but in Kundera's case it also generates a sense that the novel, in generic terms, may be exhausted and yet remains the only available form for our cultural malaise. Set against this irony is a sense of paranoia, a feeling that the structures of ordinary experience are maintained by forces too complex to be revealed; sometimes this is extended to the point where even explanations themselves are felt to be inherently untrustworthy. Here the fiction of Thomas Pynchon (q.v.) is also notable. Complexity and irony can also be combined in postmodernism to generate a sensibility that borders on nostalgia and yet refuses that response as being too easy a solution; it is as if a simple, more straightforward ethos is invoked only to show how far from such simplicities we have come. This is one of the main elements in the short fiction of Donald Barthelme (q.v.). The French novelist Georges Perec employs an exceptionally rich mixture of high and low material, but also combines a fascination with mundane and even trivial details and activities with an uncanny complexity of form, in a way that suggests that one of postmodernism's main precursors is none other than James Joyce (qq.v.).

However, some currents in postmodernism mistrust the very idea of a sensibility. This mistrust is grounded in a larger questioning of the notion of a unified and distinctive self. Selfhood, though a highly debated notion, has been at the heart of

Western culture for centuries, underpinning as it does our sense of individuality and all our concomitant notions of personal identity and political and social rights. From such essays as Michel Foucault's "Qu'est-ce qu'un auteur?" (1969; "What is an Author?" 1977) and Roland Barthes's (qq.v.) notion of "the death of the author," postmodernism has drawn on a complex set of arguments that claims that the sources of meaning, and even the ability to create signs, are best located in systems of signification rather than in individual subjects. These arguments have been advanced in such a way that some have defined the postmodern era as marked by "the end of humanism." The development of such arguments was aided in significant measure by what is referred to as "the linguistic turn," or "the problematic of language," a set of philosophical and semantic problems that rejected the notion that language was a transparent means of establishing a truth that could otherwise exist without being put into words. While modernists as different as William Faulkner and T. S. Eliot (qq.v.) certainly raised these issues, it was postmodernism that pursued them, with a distinctive blend of thoroughness and skepticism. In some ways, postmodernism can be seen as the cultural expression of a body of thought known as "poststructuralism" (q.v.), which includes such figures as Lyotard, Foucault, Jacques Derrida, Julia Kristeva, Jacques Lacan (qq.v.), Paul de Man (1919–1983), and others. Certain writers, such as George Bataille and Michel Butor (qq.v.), have contributed fiction and essays that have added to the complexity of the movement; for example, Bataille introduced a fascination with transpersonal erotic desire and death, and their relation to the unexpressible, that has surfaced in many other places. Other writers, such as Jean Genet (q.v.), have used the emphasis on the insubstantial and even decreative features of language to stress the performative aspects of writing. Here the emphasis might begin with a juggling of perspectives, but would then move on to the undecidability of moral and social values, eventually calling into question most of the standard anchoring features of bourgeois epistemology. It is poststructuralism's pursuit of the linguistic turn, and its seeing the notion of a centered self as highly problematic, that allows it to contribute to postmodernism.

If postmodernism has a philosophical component it has a distinctive political understanding as well. When modernism is treated as the cultural expression of monopoly capitalism and bourgeois parliamentary democracy, then postmodernism can be understood as the cultural outgrowth of multinational capitalism and a postliberal hegemonic politics. In this light, we can approach postmodernism as the ground on which multiculturalism,

with its antihierarchical attitudes, might flourish. Conversely, if one sees contemporary society as dominated by consumerism, opinion polls, media spectacles, and sophisticated techniques of mass manipulation, then the paranoid views of postmodernism have more plausibility. Postmodernism can, however, be understood positively as contributing to (or being expressed in) movements of personal resistance to oppressive social formations, from gay liberation to feminism. The widespread acceptance of writers such as Audre Lorde (1934–1992) and Adrienne Rich (q.v.) depends to a large extent on the social movements that coexist with postmodernism. Equally significant here, at least in aesthetic terms, is an increasingly direct insistence on the political force of culture itself, so that such emerging fields as cultural studies are also part of postmodernism's development. Lorde's poetry and essays claim an authority that is based on her marginalized social status—as a black lesbian—and thus she demands a rethinking of the usual understanding of the relations between the centers of political power and its peripheral subjects. This can be seen as a rejection of the apolitical formalism that was thought by some to be central to modernism. The claims made for and against postmodernism's ability to energize new possibilities take place in a tangle of opposing truths.

Postmodernism has considerably more than its share of contradictions, on every level from the philosophical to the stylistic. But it remains a cultural movement that obviously delights in contradictions, and when it embraces paradox it does so without any self-deluding claims about the tragic view of life. As such, it has been accused, with some justification, of being a cynical and empty style. Its defense against such a charge might very well be that any defense is always and only a self-serving form of evasive justification.

BIBLIOGRAPHY: Jencks, C., *The Language of Postmodern Architecture*, rev. ed. (1977); Foster, H., ed., *The Anti-Aesthetic* (1983); Lyotard, J.-F., *The Postmodern Condition* (1984); Huyssen, A., "Mapping the Postmodern," *NGC*, 33 (Fall 1984), 5–52; Ross, A., ed., *Universal Abandon: The Politics of Postmodernism* (1988); Harvey, D., *The Condition of Postmodernity* (1989); Sayre H. M., *The Object of Performance: The American Avant-Garde since 1970* (1989); Norris, C., *What's Wrong with Postmodernism* (1990); Jameson, F., *Postmodernism, or, The Cultural Logic of Late Capitalism* (1991); McGowan, J., *Postmodernism and Its Critics* (1991); Hoesterey, I., *Zeitgeist in Babel: The Postmodernist Controversy* (1991); Rose, M. A., *The Post-Modern and the Post-*

Industrial: A Critical Analysis (1991); Birringer, J. H., *Theatre, Theory, Postmodernism* (1991)

CHARLES MOLESWORTH

POSTSTRUCTURALISM

The term poststructuralism refers to a critical epoch and interdisciplinary movement that succeeds structuralism (q.v.) but which incorporates the latter's most formal and radical features. One might begin by defining structuralism as a critical approach that explains the meaning of cultures and texts as a function of invariant structures (or constituent units) embodied in central myths and belief systems that transcend individuals but are recombined through their communications. The formalism of this approach, by which concrete social and personal phenomena would be interpreted in terms of a few stable patterns and organizing principles, would enable systematic classification. Roman Jakobson (1896–1982) and Claude Lévi-Strauss (q.v.) are often invoked as structuralists, although to rigorously define the movement that includes the best work in formal analysis of structures in life and culture one would have to name Georg Simmel (1858–1918) and Max Weber (1864–1920). More recently, Tzvetan Todorov (b. 1939) has advocated literary structuralism as a "science of literature." The avowed radicality of structuralism would, curiously enough, reside in its capacity for generalization or abstract universalism. This radicality, joined with a denial of certitude, lives on in such categories of poststructuralist theory as difference, power, and text, which are employed in readings of cultures and historical periods very different from the ones in which the categories were formulated.

Poststructuralism, less a school or method than a mode of thought to which a number of critical methods contribute, traces the discursive effects and sign relations that organize a text or cultural phenomenon not through a central myth or structure but in institutional strategies and economies of power and difference. There are no centers, origins, or permanent truths, only strategies, and these inhabit discourses that make certain events and forms of knowledge (such as war and logic) more legitimate than others. According to Roland Barthes (q.v.), there are also no authors, these being ruses of ideologies (for example, capitalism) that produce a "human person" for purposes of control and profit. In his *Les mots et les choses* (1966; *The Order of Things,* 1971) Michel Foucault (q.v.) proclaimed the "death of man." The distrust of central authority evinced in this approach comes from the 1968 strikes and student unrest in Paris; is epitomized in the critique of

institutions carried out by poststructuralists; and is phrased philosophically as the "critique of the subject." Wherever power pools in repressive ways, poststructuralism finds a subject lurking. One "deconstructs" this subject by unmasking the rhetoric and organizing principles by which it phrases the authority of its autonomy and perceptions, all a mirage of discourse mistaking itself for the immediacy of self-evidence. Organizing centers or essences are taken by poststructuralist critics as constructions, and these include classical myths and binary oppositions that have become hierarchies such as prose/poetry, nature/culture, male/female. Gender would be a function of discursive relations that institute a system of inclusion and exclusion by which men and women are empowered and marginalized.

Although its historical background is the 1960s, poststructuralism is indebted to a much earlier "linguistic turn" showing language and interpretation as prior conditions of reality and truth. One can trace this turn back to Friedrich Nietzsche (1844–1900), and the insights of Martin Heidegger (1889–1976) in such works as *Unterwegs zur Sprache* (1959; *On The Way to Language,* 1971) that language speaks itself, that the word "bethings the thing" and allows the world to "world"—as it were verbally and not as a noun or substance. One cannot underestimate the influence of such insights upon the academic study of literature, which became even more linked to linguistic speculation through readings of Ferdinand de Saussure (1857–1913). Saussure's work described language as a system of oppositions in sign relations whose signifying power is arbitrarily grounded in static reference of words to things. Radical readings of this work would affirm the dynamism of oppositional logic and the proximity of signs to other signs that are suppressed in everyday usage, and thus would lead to the concepts of textuality and intertextuality invoked by such theorists as Jacques Derrida and Julia Kristeva (qq.v.). A certain linguistic idealism and "anarchy of the signifier" would ensue, as would a litany of watchwords such as rupture, effacement, undecidability. The *Lebenswelt* or "life world," which for a phenomenologist such as Maurice Merleau-Ponty (1908–1961) had been both a concrete limit and possibility of discursive freedom, would now be an infinite text. For poststructuralists the self-performance of a text would in theory be uncontainable, the border between fiction and reality erasable. But the exigencies of life draw their own lines. The act of writing itself, which for certain theorists still encounters the enigmatic density of nature and history, has its own difficult conditions. It would be fair to say that the work of rigorous poststructuralists evinces these structural and phenomenal conditions while "playing" with their contradictions, which have been typically excluded from consideration.

The antihumanism of the viewpoint that has been sketched here, according to which language and texts dispense significance and sense as it were behind the backs of writers, speakers, readers, and audiences, has not gone unchecked. Certain theorists have claimed that the "metaphysical subject" is a pseudoproblem created solely by and for the decentralizing political arguments of many poststructuralists. In this regard the self-criticism of poststructuralism, of its own pretensions as a theory of discourse, would be immanent to its very projected aims. In his *Tropics of Discourse* (1979) Hayden White (b. 1928) says that "every discourse is always as much about discourse itself as it is about the objects that make up its subject matter." For this reason the so-called linguistic turn was perhaps more accurately a "rhetorical turn" or became consciously such as critics came to reflect on their own practices. The criticism leveled at Heidegger's theory of language by Paul de Man (1919–1983), that it gives priority to certain kinds of poetic discourse that are closest to Being and thus essentializes what is not essential but rhetorical, represents the first serious internal critique of linguistic ontology with *Jargon der Eigentlichkeit* (1964; *The Jargon of Authenticity,* 1973) by Theodor Wiesengrund Adorno (q.v.).

Another immanent critique has come from those critics and theorists who sustain some notion of a discourse community, or of dialogue consisting of separate but ethically obligated interlocutors. Rhetoric for them does not primarily operate in an abstract field of rules and differences called Being or *langue,* as it would for the interpreters of Heidegger and Saussure, but in what Hannah Arendt (1906–1975) calls the *vita activa,* public life defined as a discursive space of exposure. The philosopher Emmanuel Levinas (b. 1906) certainly recognizes the wisdom that a Heidegger sees contained in language and which can be disclosed as an unspoken possibility of Being. Yet Levinas himself is more interested in the responsibility of speakers for each other and for their risks of utterance, their face-to-face "saying," than in the truths mystically latent in what is "unsaid." The work of Levinas in *Autrement qu'être ou au-delà de l'essence* (1974; *Otherwise Than Being or Beyond Essence,* 1981) is poststructuralist because of its abiding concern with discourse and difference, but is equally "post-Auschwitz." Like such apparently diverse writers as Arendt, Mikhail Bakhtin (q.v.), and Paul Ricœur (b. 1913), Levinas endorses notions of personal responsibility and

the life of speech that link his theory to concrete experiences and encounters, including suffering.

Perhaps of the aforenamed theorists, Bakhtin, who defined discourse as "language in its concrete living totality" and whose work, like that of Roman Jakobson, sustains tacit links to the Russian oral tradition, will most leave his mark on the poststructuralist epoch. What will surely endure is Bakhtin's legacy of describing the manifold effects of voice that animate narrative as a "contact of personalities" in a context of choice amidst competing ideologies, revising our notions of social milieu and moral character. Bakhtin's critical writings on Dostoevsky have admirably brought these phenomena to our attention in a mode of interpretation Bakhtin calls "responsive understanding" in *Speech Genres and Other Late Essays* (1986).

The immanent critique (self-criticism) of poststructuralism has been shown here to have arisen from a concern with concreteness and linguistic community and personhood. Thus it has recently been argued that critics need to attend to the "embodiment" of literary discourse in expressions of bodily life and the tactile surface of signs. Other scholars have said that theory must analyze the mode of informational technology in which it and society operates. Still another concern for situational meaning has been articulated in the rise of a new critical pragmatism. All of these efforts, which represent a number of diverse viewpoints and political agendas, concur on the necessity of constraint in interpretation arising from concrete existence. A theory of constraint, which can be both an ethics and a literary materialism, comes to finally determine the possibilities of what are currently the most prominent issues in poststructuralist theory: gender, ethnic diversity, and the problem of the "canon," or body of texts that a curriculum would endorse for teaching and research. Having arisen from the problem of difference, which epitomizes the underlying political program of poststructuralism, these devisive issues remind us that the matter at stake for poststructuralist critics is above all institutional life, especially the life of radical theory. It is generally acknowledged that while conflict is positive for an institution so long as the basic values and assumptions on which its legitimacy depends are not contradicted, the life of an institution cannot be guaranteed if its members no longer share those beliefs. Thus the genuine test of poststructuralism will be its capacity to be tolerated and shared as a conflict, the capacity of its self-critique to sincerely respond to the institution of radicality.

BIBLIOGRAPHY: Sturrock, J., ed., *Structuralism and Since* (1979); Rorty, R., *Consequences of*

Pragmatism (1982); Frank, M., *Was ist Neostrukturalismas?* (1984; *What is Neostructuralism?* 1989); Barthes, R., *Le bruissement de la langue* (1984; *The Rustle of Language,* 1986); Ferry, L., and A. Renaut, *La Pensée 68* (1985; *French Philosophy of the Sixties,* 1990); Weber, S., *Institution and Interpretation* (1987); Scarry, E., ed., *Literature and the Body* (1988); Tavor Bannet, E., *Structuralism and the Logic of Dissent* (1989); Fraser, N., *Unruly Practices: Power, Discourse, and Gender in Contemporary Social Theory* (1989); Fuss, D., *Essentially Speaking: Feminism, Nature and Difference* (1989); Poster, M., *Critical Theory and Poststructuralism: In Search of a Context* (1989); Simons, H. W., ed., *The Rhetorical Turn* (1990); Cadava, E., P. Connor, and J.-L. Nancy, *Who Comes after the Subject?* (1991)

C. S. SCHREINER

PYM, Barbara

(born Barbara Mary Pym Crampton) English novelist, b. 6 June 1913, Oswestry, Shropshire; d. 11 Jan. 1980, Oxford

P. received a B.A. in English literature from St. Hilda's College, Oxford, and spent most of her life in the Oxford area. During World War II she worked in Postal and Telegraph Censorship and served a year in Italy with the Women's Royal Naval Service. Her most productive writing years, from 1946 until her retirement in 1958, were spent as a research assistant for the International African Institute and as assistant editor of the organization's journal, *Africa.*

P.'s novels of manners are filled with the social details of the ordinary, usually uneventful lives of rather well-off unmarried women involved in church life. Excitement and adventure are rare in the novels; characters are more often interested in observing the lives of others than in creating events in their own lives. The novels emphasize eating, drinking, and thinking about clothes; the pleasures of Earl Gray tea, and food that is well prepared. P. consistently provides exact observations of a limited scene, whether domestic, academic, or clerical. Her middle-aged protagonists cope with loneliness by filling their lives with observation and contemplation. Influenced by her years with the African Institute, P. displays the detachment of an anthropologist, yet sympathizes with her characters' peculiarities or failures.

P.'s characters often cherish a secret love; their affections are unannounced and unrequited, usually because the loved one is somehow "unsuitable," either too young, already married, or of an inappropriate class. P.'s first novel, *Some Tame Gazelle* (1950), begins the pattern that continues

in many of the novels. Two middle-aged sisters, modeled on P. and her sister Hilary, love men unsuitable for marriage: Belinda faithfully loves a former sweetheart now married to someone else, while Hilary loves a succession of young curates. In comparing their feelings with those of married people, the sisters conclude that remaining single is the way to preserve love. P. reverses the typical marriage plot so that the two women decide not to accept the proposals that come their way, but to remain unmarried and thus keep their love alive.

Characters satisfy their need for love in ways not necessarily associated with marriage or sexuality; characters love animals, young curates, church activities, persons who become surrogate children, or particular kinds of church services. *Excellent Women* (1952) and *Jane and Prudence* (1953) demonstrate that marriage is not necessarily any more fulfilling than the life of a "spinster" who does "good works" or has a succession of mild love affairs.

The ironic tone of P.'s work recalls Jane Austen (1775–1817). Protagonists maintain an ironic distance from the world; with independence of thought and a keen ability to observe and evaluate society, P.'s women rarely take themselves or their work very seriously; they see humor and irony associated with even their own favorite habits, and they find fulfillment in observation and a heightened consciousness of the society around them. In contrast, P.'s men, often anthropologists or clergymen, are usually selfish, vain, or arrogant, taking themselves seriously and expecting the devotion "excellent women" shower upon them. The novels often imply feminist subtexts, but P.'s characters rarely depart from proscribed behavior—the women see the ironies inherent in patriarchal culture, but they never rebel.

After publishing P.'s first six novels, Jonathan Cape in 1963 rejected *An Unsuitable Attachment* (1982) and inaugurated a period of sixteen years during which P. published nothing. The novels written after the mid-1960s, during the long period when her work was rejected, differ from the earlier ones; while the early work centers on English village life, with characters concerned about the habits and lives of their neighbors, the later novels are set in the city, where characters have more trouble admitting or expressing affection for one another. The later characters prefer to mind their own business rather than interfere; nor do they want their own freedom limited by neighbors, as when Leonora of *The Sweet Dove Died* (1978) is careful not to be seen by the woman who rents an upstairs apartment from her. In *Quartet in Autumn* (1977), four elderly office workers secretly care about one another, but their interaction is confined to the office; only after two of them retire and their routine avoidance of one another concludes do they attempt friendship. Although a village setting returns for *A Few Green Leaves* (1980), the intimacy of the early novels is absent, as is the emphasis on the church.

Despite the difference in the early and late novels, P.'s entire oeuvre is remarkable in its portrayal of daily life in 20th-c. England. P.'s attention to uneventful lives allows her to capture the essence of daily life. Her characters may lead what some consider dull existences, but through them P. displays the extraordinary capacity for observation and perception that accompanies an examined life.

FURTHER WORKS: *Less Than Angels* (1955); *A Glass of Blessings* (1958); *No Fond Return of Love* (1961); *A Very Private Eye: An Autobiography in Diaries and Letters* (1984); *Crampton Hodnet* (1985); *An Academic Question* (1986); *Civil to Strangers and Other Writings* (1987)

BIBLIOGRAPHY: Brothers, B., "Women Victimized by Fiction: Living and Loving in the Novels by B. P.," in Staley, T. F., ed., *Twentieth-Century Women Novelists* (1982), 61–80; Calisher, H., "Enclosures: B. P.," *NewC,* 1, 3 (Nov. 1982), 53–56; Nardin, J., *B. P.* (1985); Schofield, M. A., "Well-Fed or Well-Loved?: Patterns of Cooking and Eating in the Novels of B. P.," *UWR,* 18, 2 (Spring–Summer 1985), 1–8; Stetz, M. D., "*Quartet in Autumn:* New Light on B. P. As a Modernist," *ArQ,* 41, 1 (Spring 1985), 24–37; Salwak, D., ed., *The Life and Work of B. P.* (1987); Liddell, R., *A Mind at Ease: B. P. and Her Novels* (1989); Wyatt-Brown, A. M., *B. P.: A Critical Biography* (1992)

KAREN WILKES GAINEY

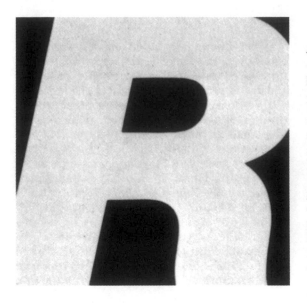

RADZINSKY, Edvard
Russian dramatist, b. 23 Sept. 1936, Moscow

R. was born into a Moscow family of the intelligentsia. His father was a prominent man of letters who translated from the French and adapted works of fiction for the stage. R. graduated from the Moscow State Historical-Archival Institute in 1960.

Probably no Soviet writer better deserves the title of "chronicler of his generation" than R. He made his stage debut in 1960 when his play, *Mechta moia, Indiia . . .* (1960; India, my dream . . .), written in collaboration with Liia Geraskina (dates n.a.), was performed at the Theater of the Young Spectator in Moscow. It was followed by *Vam 22, stariki!* (1962; you're 22, fellows!), a first in introducing the vernacular language of the younger generation into the Soviet theater. R.'s first critical success came in 1964 with his *104 stranitsy pro liub'vi* (1964; 104 pages about love). The play, which brought an ordinary love story onto the Soviet stage for the first time in the post-Stalin era, proved extremely popular in the Soviet Union where it was staged in 120 theaters as well as being made into a film and a ballet. Critical acclaim abroad followed as the play joined the repertory of major theaters in eastern Europe, West Germany, and Japan.

Snimaetsia kino . . . (1966; making a movie), an exposé of movie censorship, and *Obol'stitel' Kolobashkin* (1982; the seducer Kolobashkin), a savage satire of the Moscow intelligentsia (banned in 1968 after the dress rehearsal), led to the blacklisting of all R.'s plays for a period of seven years. During that time, R. returned to his first profession, history, and began working on a trilogy of historical dramas. In *Besedy s Sokratom* (1982; conversations with Socrates), *Lunin ili smert' Zhaka, zapisannaia v prisutstvii khoziana* (1982; I, Mikhail Sergeevich Lunin, 1982), and *Teatr vremen*

Nerona i Seneki (1982; theater in the time of Nero and Seneca) R. used historical fact to explore the plight of the intellectual in a totalitarian society. A masterpiece of Aesopean innuendo, the trilogy brought R. notoriety at home—where parallels were easily drawn between his historical characters and leading dissidents, including Aleksandr Solzhenitsyn (q.v.) and Andrei Sakharov—as well as international renown in the late 1970s.

With *Sportivnye stseny 1981 goda* (1981; *Jogging [Sporting Scenes, 1981],* 1988), R. directly confronted contemporary Soviet life, this time depicting the privileged and corrupt youth of the Kremlin leaders (the heroine and her husband are loosely based on Galina Brezhneva and her recently convicted husband, Yuri Churbanov). Its staging in 1986 at the Moscow Ermolova Theater was one of the first productions to usher in the new Gorbachev era of glasnost. It was followed by *Ub'em muzhchinu?; "Ya stoiu u restorana: zamuzh—pozdno, sdokhnut'—rano"* (1987; shall I kill the man?; I'm standing by a restaurant: too late to get married, too early to croak), about a neurotic actress and a philandering theater director; and *Nash Dekameron* (1988, Nash dekameron), a satire about a Moscow prostitute who becomes queen of an African nation.

During the 1980s, R. had as many as nine plays running simultaneously in Moscow. Equally successful abroad, he has become probably the most frequently staged Russian dramatist, second only to Anton Chekhov (q.v.). R.'s *Lunin,* about the Decembrist dissident, was widely performed in Europe to great critical acclaim. When his *Staraia aktrisa na rol' zheny Dostoevstogo* (n.d.; *An Old Actress in the Role of Dostoevsky's Wife,* 1986) was staged at the Odeon in Paris, the French press hailed R. as a "Russian Pirandello." New York audiences also had an opportunity to see R.'s work in performance at the Jean Cocteau Repertory Theatre's productions of his historical trilogy.

In the late 1980s, R. put aside dramaturgy and turned to writing "novellas in dialogue." Among the works in his first collection, published in 1989, are prose versions of a number of his dramas, including his trilogy of historical plays, as well as his first historical novella, *Posledniaia iz doma Romanovykh: Povesti v dialogakh (Toroplivaia proza)* (the last of the house of Romanovs: novellas in dialog [hasty prose]). Set in the 18th c. during the reign of Catherine the Great, it recounts one of the most enigmatic episodes in Russian history. This book was followed by the publication of a collection of short stories based on anecdotal versions of episodes from the life of Stalin. R. is currently completing a major historical novel about the circumstances surrounding the last days of Czar Nicholas II and his family. Based on fresh documentary evidence R. has collected, including detailed accounts of the murder of the royal family on the direct order of Lenin, excerpts from the novel created a sensation in the Soviet press.

R.'s great popularity as a dramatist is equally rooted in his mastery of language and in his ability to create tightly constructed plays susceptible to a variety of scenic interpretations. In his choice of themes and in their interpretation, R. has in the course of his career moved from writing about his own generation to exploring more universal historical, philosophical themes. While frequently banned by the authorities, R.'s plays have consistently won a following among leading directors and actors as well as audiences in the former Soviet Union.

FURTHER WORK: *Teatr vremen . . . teatr "pro liubov": . . . teatr v teatre . . .* (1986). FURTHER VOLUME IN ENGLISH: *A Pleasant Woman with a Geranium and Windows Facing North* (1985)

BIBLIOGRAPHY: Golub, S., "E. R.'s Masters of History, Servants to Illusion," *Newsnotes on Soviet and East European Drama and Theatre,* 3, 3 (1983), 9–14; Abensour, G., "Lorsque le roi est nu," *Slovo,* 6 (1984), 169–87; Kipp, M., "E. R.'s *Don Juan Continued:* The Last Return of Don Juan?," *SEEA,* 3, 1 (1985), 109–18; Leverett, J., "Worlds Apart: A Soviet Voice on the American Stage," *American Theatre,* 1 (1986), 26–27; Dementyeva, M., "E. R.'s Main Hero," *Culture And Life,* 12 (1987), 30–32

ALMA H. LAW

RAMÍREZ, Sergio

Nicaraguan novelist, short-story writer, and essayist, b. 5 Aug. 1942, Masatepe

R. studied law at the University of León, where he was a student activist opposed to the dictatorial régime of Anastasio Somoza. His interest in politics led to his fascination with the Nicaraguan patriot Augusto César Sandino (1895–1934), the subject of several of his best essays. But R. has also had a lifelong dedication to literature, which has at times conflicted with, and at times been enhanced by, his political career. After receiving his law degree in 1964, R. worked for several years in Costa Rica as a member of the Central American Inter-University Council. Soon thereafter he moved to West Berlin where he was supported by a grant from the German government. In 1977 he joined the Sandinista revolt against Somoza, who was overthrown in 1979. R. served as vice president of his homeland until the Sandinistas were defeated at the polls in 1990.

R.'s most important collection of stories is *Charles Atlas también muere* (1976; *Stories,* 1986), the unifying theme of which is the dependency of Nicaragua on the U.S. In the title story the puny narrator improves his physique after enrolling in Charles Atlas's course on physical culture, but upon traveling to the U.S. to meet the self-made Hercules, he discovers his hero to be a moribund old man. This portrait of demythification is enhanced by a subtle irony characteristic of the entire collection.

"Nicaragua es blanca" ("Nicaragua Is White") satirizes the influence, both cultural and economic, of the U.S. on the author's native land. In this absurd tale a meteorologist predicts snow for Managua on Christmas day, triggering elaborate preparations for the unprecedented event: fur coats, sweaters, and blankets are imported; heating systems are installed; and sleighs clog the streets. But the snow never materializes except in the backward areas of the country where subzero temperatures cause untold suffering.

Equally absurd, "A Jackie, con nuestro corazón" ("To Jackie with All Our Hearts") targets the social elite. The narrator is the president of the Virginia Country Club who, upon learning of Jackie (Kennedy) Onassis's trip to Nicaragua, pulls all strings to enable his organization to control every phase of her visit. Having been authorized by his club to purchase a boat to meet Jackie's yacht (and thus prevent other less prestigious groups from sharing the limelight), the narrator acquires the *Queen Elizabeth* and has it completely refurbished. The story ends with the image of the luxury liner filled with disgruntled passengers skirting the coast and anxiously scanning the horizon.

R.'s first novel, *Tiempo de fulgor* (1970; time of splendor), is set in the 19th c. in the city of León. Several plots are skillfully interwoven, the most important involving two families. Although this work emerges as something akin to the novel of customs, it differs from this traditional genre in that it is laced with fantasy and thereby shows unmistakable similarities to *Cien años de soledad* (1967; *One Hundred Years of Solitude,* 1970), by Colombia's Nobel laureate Gabriel García Márquez (q.v.).

¿Te dio miedo la sangre? (1977; *To Bury Our Fathers,* 1983), R.'s second novel, is considerably more complex than his first, its major theme being the armed struggle against the Somoza régime between 1930 and 1961, just before the foundation in 1962 of the National Sandinista Liberation Front. A tangle of six interrelated plot threads informs this densely populated work, whose characters in their entirety embody the collective voice of a nation in travail. Just as resonances of García

Márquez are discernible in *Tiempo de fulgor*, narrative strategies perfected by Peruvian novelist Mario Vargas Llosa (q.v.) have left their mark on *¿Te dio miedo la sangre?* These include the weaving of numerous plot threads into an artistically integrated whole; the frequent shifts in the narrative perspective; and the use of interior monologues, dreams, and abrupt temporal and spatial dislocations to keep the reader alert.

In the early 1930s the most sensational criminal case in Nicaraguan history focused the nation's attention on the city of León, where a law student from Guatemala was accused of poisoning his wife and two members of a prominent local family. *Castigo divino* (1988; *Divine Punishment*, 1991), R.'s most engrossing novel, dramatizes this case. The work is an excellent example of documentary fiction, that is, a combination of historical fact and authorial imagination, the former creating an air of authenticity and the latter generating dramatic tension.

R. is Nicaragua's leading writer of prose fiction and one of Latin America's most important men of letters of his generation. Despite his well-known commitment to socialism, his political convictions never mar his art, which in general terms can be described as poetic realism. Thus he makes use of figurative language, innovative techniques, and fantasy to condemn U.S. imperialism and depict the appalling conditions in his native land. He is not only a gifted storyteller but also a sensitive spokesman for the Third World.

FURTHER WORKS: *Cuentos* (1963); *Mis días con el rector* (1965); *Nuevos cuentos* (1969); *Mariano Fiallos* (1971); *De tropeles y tropelías* (1972); *El pensamiento vivo de Sandino* (1974); *Viva Sandino* (1976); *Biografía de Sandino* (1979); *El muchacho de Niquinohomo* (1981); *Los no alineados* (1981); *El alba de oro* (1983); *Balcones y volcanes y otros ensayos y trabajos* (1983); *Sandino, su ideología y los partidos políticos* (1984); *Estás en Nicaragua* (1985); *Seguimos de frente* (1985); *Julio, estás en Nicaragua* (1986); *Sandino* (1986); *Las armas del futuro* (1987); *Sandino siempre* (1988); *La marcha del Zorro* (1990)

BIBLIOGRAPHY: Arellano, J. E., "La primera novela de un joven cuentista," *PrensLit*, 20 Sept. 1970, 12; Arellano, J. E., *Panorama de la literatura nicaragüense* (1977), 138–39; Foster, D. W., on *Charles Atlas también muere*, *WLT*, 51, 2 (Spring 1977), 260; Rama, A., ed., *Novísimos narradores hispanoamericanos en marcha, 1964–1980* (1981), 34, 271; Dauster, F., on *¿Te dio miedo la sangre?*, *WLT*, 58, 4 (Autumn 1984), 573; Morales, A., "S. R.: 'Gobernar con el mismo esmero con que escribo,'" *CasaA*, 25, 151 (July–Aug. 1985), 70–74; Schaefer, C., "La recuperación del realismo: *¿Te dio miedo las sangre?* de S. R.," *TCrit*, 13, 36–37 (1987), 146–52; Fuentes, C., "Una novela centroamericana," *Suplemento Literario, La Nación* (Buenos Aires), 26 June 1988, 6; Santos, R., ed., *And We Sold the Rain: Contemporary Fiction from Central America* (1988), 9–24, 207; McMurray, G. R., on *Castigo divino, Chasqui*, 18, 1 (May 1989), 75–77; Beverley, J., and M. Zimmerman, *Literature and Politics in the Central American Revolutions* (1990), 40–48, 79–80, 182–88; McMurray, G. R., "S. R.'s *Castigo divino* as Documentary Novel," *Confluencia*, 5, 2 (Spring 1990), 155–59

GEORGE R. MCMURRAY

RASPUTIN, Valentin

Russian novelist, short-story writer, and essayist, b. 15 Mar. 1937, Atalanka

R. is one of the most artistically talented and politically controversial of Russia's postwar writers. Born in a village on the Angara River in Siberia, R. studied at Irkutsk University. From his college years until the mid-1960s, he worked as a journalist, reporting on such diverse topics as construction projects and the native peoples of Siberia. After 1966 he devoted his time primarily to fiction, with numerous forays into ethnographic and political essay writing. His primary home has remained Irkutsk in Siberia. In 1980 R. was severely beaten by thieves, an attack that interrupted his career for several years. Since the beginning of the Gorbachev era, R. has become increasingly involved in the "burning questions" of the day, from protection of the environment to the fate of Russia in the disintegrating U.S.S.R. Through his glasnost-era statements on nationalism, R. has been perceived both at home and abroad as belonging to the right-wing political camp, though not to its most extreme faction. R. served briefly in Gorbachev's government in 1990. Over the years he has played an active role in the Writers' Union of the Russian Republic and of the U.S.S.R., and has served on the editorial board of the influential conservative journal *Nash sovremennik*.

R. is primarily known for a series of four short novels: *Dengi dlya Marii* (1967; *Money for Maria*, 1981), *Posledniy srok* (1970; *Borrowed Time*, 1981), *Zhivi i pomni* (1974; *Live and Remember*, 1978), and *Proshchanie s Matyoroy* (1976; *Farewell to Matyora*, 1979). All of these works are set in the Siberian countryside and all focus on a moment of crisis in a peasant family or community. In *Dengi dlya Marii*, an innocent woman is faced with prison if her husband cannot collect enough money to cover losses at the government store where she works; what concerns the author most is the community's response to the crisis faced by one of its members. *Posledniy srok* focuses on a dying peasant woman who tries to reunite her family during her final days. *Zhivi i pomni* tells the story of a World War II deserter who secretly returns to his village, bringing tragedy in his wake. *Proshchanie s Matyoroy,* the best known of all R.'s works, shows an ancient village on an island in the Angara River just before it is to be flooded to make way for a new hydroelectric project. In all these works R. displays a talent for weaving together very specific details of life in the Siberian countryside with narratives of universal appeal. While avoiding the excessive folk stylization of some ruralists, R. has been remarkably successful in capturing the voices of contemporary peasants, especially the old women of the village. His longer narratives owe a great deal to the influence of 19th-c. writers, especially Dostoevsky, and virtually nothing to Soviet literature. Indeed, in R.'s work we see one of the best examples of the undermining of Socialist Realism (q.v.) in published literature during the period before glasnost.

Since the mid-1960s, R. has also written a number of shorter works that have gained a wide readership in Russia. Among his better-known stories are "Ekh, starukha" (1966; "The Old Woman," 1985), "Vasilii i Vasilisa" (1966; "Vasily i Vasilisa," 1989), "Vniz i vverkh po techeniyu" (1972; "Downstream," 1982), "Vek zhivi—vek lyubi" (1981; "Live and Love," 1986; rev., ed. 1989), and "Pozhar" (1985; "The Fire," 1989). "Vniz i vverkh po techeniyu," one of R.'s most autobiographical works, follows a writer traveling by boat down the Angara River to his native regions; it is a finely wrought story and an interesting companion piece to the novel *Proshchanie s Matyoroy.* "Pozhar" was one of the first major literary works to appear in the Gorbachev era, and while its somber tone seemed out of place in the euphoric early glasnost years, by the end of the 1980s it seems to have foreseen all too accurately the chaotic nature of post communist Russia. Like Dostoevsky, Aleksandr Solzhenitsyn (q.v.) and many other conservative Russian writers before him, R. sees his latter works as both a prophecy of the nation's decline and a plea to return to traditional ways.

In the second half of the 1980s, R. returned to the essay form that marked the beginning of his career, but with a far different focus. If, in the 1960s, he described with some enthusiasm the development of Siberia, twenty years later he was distraught over the same kind of development. And, while his earlier ethnographic work had concentrated on the non-Russian peoples of Siberia, by the 1980s he was concerned with the long history of Russian involvement in that region. These twin themes of the cost of progress and the need for recovering national roots came together in his campaign to save Lake Baikal, whose restoration he saw as being crucial not just to the environment, but to Russia's cultural and spiritual health as well.

R.'s work has marked important stages in Russia's political and literary life. He began in the Socialist Realist style, but abandoned it for a more traditional realism that was enriched by the rural idiom and universal themes. His novel *Proshchanie s Matyoroy* defines the end of the all-important Village Prose movement in 1976, and his story "Pozhar" marks the beginning of glasnost literature in 1985. His rhetorical shift to a more publicistic and less lyrical tone in the late 1980s reflects a process that was taking place throughout Russian literature. It is R.'s nonfictional statements from this latter period—specifically those that blame Russia's weakened state on Westerners and a host of non-Russians including Soviet Jews—that have gained him a prominence in the West that eluded him as a novelist and short-story writer. He has had the misfortune, mostly of his own making, to become well-known abroad as a Russian chauvinist, rather than as one of the finest writers of the post-Stalinist period.

FURTHER WORKS: *Kray vozle samogo neba* (1966); *Kostrovye novykh gorodov* (1966); *Chelovek s etogo sveta* (1967); *Dengi dlya Marii. Povest i rasskazy* (1968); *Posledniy srok. Povest i rasskazy* (1970); *Zhivi i pomni. Povest i rasskazy* (1975); *Vek zhivi—vek lyubi. Rasskazy* (1982); *Povesti i rasskazy* (1984); *Izbrannye proizvedeniya v dvukh tomakh* (1984). FURTHER VOLUMES IN ENGLISH: *You Live and Love and Other Stories* (1986); *Siberia on Fire: Stories and Essays* (1989)

BIBLIOGRAPHY: Shneidman, N. N., *Soviet Literature in the 1970s* (1979), 75–87; Corten, I., "Solzenitcyn's Matrena and R.'s Darja: Two Studies in Russian Peasant Spirituality," *RLJ*, 114 (1979), 85–98; Hosking, G., *Beyond Socialist Realism* (1980), 70–81; Brown, E. J., *Russian Literature since the Revolution,* rev. ed. (1982), 305–11; Gillespie, D., *V. R. and Soviet Russian Village Prose* (1986); Mikkelson, G., and M. Winchell, "V. R. and His Siberia," Introduction to *Siberia on Fire* (1989), ix-xxii; Polowy, T., *The Novellas of V. R.: Genre, Language and Style* (1989); Parthé, K., "Master of the Island," Introduction to *Farewell to Matyora* (1991), vii–xxiii; Parthé, K., "The Good Soldier's Wife," Introduction to *Live and Remember* (1992), v–xx

KATHLEEN PARTHÉ

REGLER, Gustav

German novelist, essayist, and poet (writing in German and English), b. 25 May 1898, Merzig; d. 14 Jan. 1963, New Delhi, India

R. had a strict Catholic upbringing, but his experiences in World War I, where he was wounded, and the subsequent chaotic years of inflation and mass unemployment in Germany, turned him into a socialist and a foe of organized religion. He joined the Communist Party in 1928. In 1923 he earned his doctorate in literature at the University of Heidelberg. He then worked at various jobs, such as managing a large department store and editing a liberal newspaper. He gradually turned to writing to express his social commitment. With the coming of Hitler in 1933 he was forced into exile, first to the Saarland and then to Paris. In 1934 he participated at the International Writers Congress in Moscow. Moved by a strong sense of justice, he fought against Franco in the Spanish Civil War between 1936 and 1937, where he was again wounded. Shortly thereafter, he was locked up in a French internment camp, but managed to emigrate to Mexico in 1940, where he renounced his communism and turned to a mystical, spiritual approach to life. In 1952 he returned to West Germany, but continued to write in this religious vein. He died of apoplexy in India, where he was doing research for a planned book on mysticism and the occult.

R.'s use of literature to effect social change is apparent from the start. One of his first works, the novel *Wasser, brot und blaue bohnen* (1932; water, bread, and blue beans), is a brutal critique of the German prison system. *Der verlorene sohn* (1933; the prodigal son) is an attack on the Catholic church, which he views as an oppressive institution. *Die saat* (1936; the sowing), which was written in exile and published in Amsterdam, is a historical novel about the medieval Peasants' Revolt and stresses the need for citizens to rise up against political suppression, an obvious parallel to Nazi Germany.

For several years, R. could write little because of his direct political activity and his injury. In 1940, however, he published in English *The Great Crusade*, which deals with the activity of the International Brigades during the Spanish Civil War. In it he describes the heroism of the troops, the atrocities of war, and the feeling of moral rectitude that enabled the poorly equipped soldiers to hold out against great odds.

R. gradually became disenchanted with communism (the failure of Stalin to support the Republican cause in Spain, the Hitler-Stalin pact) and was ostracized by his fellow exiles in Mexico because of his new apolitical stance. He turned

for solace to natural and supernatural phenomena, whereby he tried to synthesize the opposites of life. In several volumes of poetry (some written in English in an attempt to find a niche in the American market) he uses a plethora of nature symbols to stress the mystical, cosmic oneness of all matter. His poems are contained in *The Hour 13* (1943; the 13th hour), *Der brunnen des abgrunds* (1943; the bottomless pit), *Jungle Hut* (1946; title in English), and *Marielouise* (1946; Marielouise). In his prose works of the time he follows a similar bent. *Amimitl oder die geburt eines schrecklichen* (1947; Amimitl, or the birth of a monster) discusses Aztec prehistory and attributes war to the breakdown of cosmic harmony (women were deprived of their influence); *Vulkanisches land mexiko* (1947; volcanic Mexico), which was enlarged as *Verwunschenes land mexiko* (1954; *A Land Bewitched*, 1955), describes evil and suffering as part of the natural order and as a necessary component of progress.

Back in Germany R. expanded his new philosophy. The novel *Sterne der dämmerung* (1948; stars of twilight) seeks to find a confirmation of life beyond war and death through the unification of the male and female principles. His last novel, *Aretino* (1955; Aretino), a fictional biography of the Renaissance poet and libertine, is a diatribe against traditional religion as well as a harsh warning on the evils of excess.

R.'s life and works are fascinating for their diversity and for the way they document some of the most important and tumultuous upheavals of the 20th c. Since much of his work was first published outside of Germany, he is also an excellent example of German exile literature.

FURTHER WORKS: *Die ironie im werk goethes* (1923); *Zug der hirten* (1929); *Hahnenkampf—abenteuer eines französischen mädchens* (1931); *Im kreuzfeuer* (1934); *Der letzte appell* (1939); *Wolfgang Paalen* (1946); *Der turm und andere gedichte* (1951); *Das ohr des malchus* (1958; *The Owl of Minerva*, 1960)

BIBLIOGRAPHY: Acker, R., "G. R. and Ramón Sender: A Comparative View of Their Mexican Exile," in Moeller, H.-B., ed., *Latin America and the Literature of Exile* (1983), 311–22; Diwersy, A., *G. R.: Bilder und Dokumente* (1983); Schock, R., *G. R.—Literatur und Politik (1933–1940)* (1984); Grund, U., R. Schock, and G. Scholdt, eds., *G. R.—Dokumente und Analysen* (1985); Pohle, F., *Das mexikanische Exil* (1986), 140–67

ROBERT ACKER

REICH, Ebbe Kløvedal
Danish novelist, short-story writer, and essayist, b. 7 Mar. 1940, Odense

Since the late 1960s, R. has had a high profile in Denmark; not only is he a prolific writer, but he has also quite consciously assumed the role of a public figure with a message for his country. He seemed headed for a career as a politician in a moderate party, switched then to assume the editorship of a leftist magazine, but moved on to become one of the most eloquent and least predictable leaders of the so-called " '68-generation," That group of youthful rebels—one that had originated in the antinuclear movement—demonstrated not only against the American presence in Vietnam, but also against imperialism in general. The " '68-generation," mainly consisting of university students—a small, but influential, group that through dress, hair length, and language (often combined with experimentation with drugs) symbolically declared its distinct identity—tended to be quite dogmatically Marxist, but was reacting as well against the preceding generations' lack of any substantial idealism. Denmark became a stage for virulent disputes, violent demonstations, a very active feminist movement—and a blatant generation gap. R. was a frequent speaker at rallies and mass meetings, and some of his speeches and pieces of journalism were gathered in *Svampens tid* (1969; the age of the mushroom).

During those years R. lived with his friends in a commune called "Mao's Joy." R., however, was an "odd man out" among rigid Marxists, for he was profoundly fascinated with the occult, the cabala, astrology, and, to boot, Christianity. At that point R.'s worldview may seem obscure and fragmented, but it was headed for a synthesis of social radicalism, a sense of Christian solidarity, and a mysticism with a strong antiauthoritarian or anarchistic bent. The middle name "Kløvedal," a translation of J. R. R. Tolkien's (1892–1973) Rivendale from the *The Lord of the Rings* (3 vols., 1954–1955), was one he assumed, together with a group of likeminded contemporaries in 1970.

R. has contributed to all genres, but in the early 1970s, he began to settle into a role as a historical novelist who saw it as his mission to use fiction to send strong warnings to his compatriots about the impending loss of their national character. In *Holger danske* (1970; Holger the Dane) he composed a series of tales about a legendary Danish hero who is supposed to awaken from his slumber when the Danish nation is in distress. Thereby, R. established a method for his historical fiction; he operates with strong analogies between past and present and conjures up historical figures that serve as role models—they are intendedly without much depth—and have, as a rule, much in common with the free-spirited, antiauthoritarian " '68-generation."

This series of historical novels started in earnest with *Frederik* (1972; Frederik), which recorded how a prominent Danish preacher, poet, and pedagogue gained through love the personal strength that enabled him to become a mythmaker who would sustain his troubled nation. The book was a hit. It was followed by *Rejsen til Messias* (1974; the journey of Messiah), which records the disastrous rise of the repressive absolute monarchy. *Fæ of frænde* (1977; kith and kin) takes its readers back to the Iron Age and contrasts democratic, egalitarian Denmark with the rising Roman empire; and in *Festen for Cæcilie* (1979; the feast for Cæcilia), which is set in the Middle Ages, it is made obvious how greatly supranational organizations, such as the Catholic church, have intervened in Danish national affairs. Those novels have been followed up with a series of short-story collections tracing Danish history, *De første* (1981; the first ones), *Ploven og sværdet* (1982; the plough and the sword), and *Den bærende magt* (1983; the ruling power). The most recent installment in this defense of an independent Denmark is the novel *Bygningen af en bro* (1988; the building of a bridge).

These books, which all are filled with those fast-paced action scenes one expects in a historical romance, emerge as R.'s opposition to all attempts—such as making Denmark a member of the European Common Market—to interfere with his ideal nation. R. is a severe critic of his times, but one who always sees hope for the future. He is an energetic mythmaker, who sees myth as a tool for personal and national growth.

FURTHER WORKS: *Vietnam. Krigen i perspektiv* (1965, with Preben Dollerup); *Kina. Den ideologiske stormagt* (1967); *Billedalmanak fra en rejse i det fremmede* (1967); *Retning mod venstre* (1968); *Hvem var Malatesta* (1969); *Eventyret om Alexander 666* (1970); *Svampen og korset* (1973); *Du danske svamp* (1974); *Henry George* (1975); *Til forsvar for masselinien og den rette tro* (1976); *Svaneøglen* (1978); *Mediesvampen* (1980); *Viljen til Hanstholm* (1981); *David, de fredløses konge* (1982); *David, Guds udvalgte konge* (1983); *Kong Skildpadde* (1985); *Billeder og fortællinger fra Biblen* (1986); *Nornen fra Ygdrasil* (1988, with Gerhard Kaimer)

BIBLIOGRAPHY: Borum, P., *Danish Literature* (1979), 111–12; Kopp-Sievers, S., *Die Wiederentdeckung des Nationalen in Dänemark: Eine Analyse von E. K. Rs "Frederik"* (1985)

NIELS INGWERSEN

RENAULT, Mary

(pseud. of Mary Challans) British novelist, b. 9
Apr. 1904, London; d. 13 Dec. 1983, Cape Town,
South Africa

Of French Huguenot descent, R. studied English
literature at Oxford, then trained and made a career
as a nurse. Her first published novel, *The Purposes
of Love* (1939; pub. in the U.S. as *Promise of
Love*, 1939) is set in a provincial hospital in
England, the milieu she knew best. Its success
made it possible for her to consider writing as a
full-time occupation. But with the outbreak of
World War II she returned to nursing for the
duration. After the war, she settled in Durban,
South Africa, and became an opponent of her
adopted country's expanding system of apartheid
and censorship laws. Nonetheless, she remained
and over the next decade published several other
novels with contemporary settings, generally in
England, and contemporary themes, generally about
interpersonal relations. One of these novels, *Return to Night* (1947), won the $150,000 MGM
prize, although it was never made into a movie.

But it is with ancient Greece and its themes that
her name is irretrievably linked. Beginning in 1956
with *The Last of the Wine,* in a series of novels
spanning more than a quarter of a century, she
virtually created the modern reader's image of
Bronze Age and Classical and Hellenistic Greece.
Through impeccable research and imaginative reconstruction, she created an age and an ethos that
to modern readers remain totally convincing.
Whether she is writing of actors or of emperors,
of hero kings or common people, of Greeks at
home or abroad, whether her characters are drawn
from history or from myth or from her own imagination, she has total empathy for them and for
their culture. Her concern is with institutions and
people alike. R. has frequently been praised for
the historical accuracy of her novels. But she is
more than an historical novelist. We might more
accurately speak of her as a novelist of myth, even
as the creator of a new novel form that merges
history and myth.

The Last of the Wine only begins to set the
pattern; it is more a historical novel in the manner
perfected by Sir Walter Scott: characters and events
based on history in the background, invented characters to the fore. The setting is Athens and the
Aegean; the sources included Plato's *Phaedo* and
Xenophon's *Memorabilia;* the principal historial
figure is Alkibiades, and the principal events drawn
from history are those leading to the defeat of
Athens by Sparta in 404 B.C. We see everything
through the eyes of the fictional Alexias, son of a
noble Athenian family and witness to the events
leading to the downfall of the city and loss of her

freedom; it is a Greek tragedy of folly and excessive pride, taking place, ironically, in the midst
of a magnificent cultural era. The tragic hero is
the city itself.

The King Must Die (1958) and *The Bull from
the Sea* (1962) form together one of the most
evocative mythic narratives ever constructed, bearing comparison in this respect to such modern
masterworks as James Joyce's *Ulysses* (1922) and
Nikos Kazantzakis's (qq.v.) *The Odyssey: A Modern Sequel* (1958). In *The King Must Die,* Theseus, prince of Troizen, undergoes the adventures
attributed to him in myth, but R. adds to this
tradition knowledge derived from archaeology
(down to the jewelry worn by King Minos of
Crete), close familiarity with *The Golden Bough*
(her very title taken from one of its basic, archetypal concepts), and a penchant for logical explanations of events that must once have seemed
totally illogical.

The principal source of *The Bull from the Sea*
is Euripedes's *Hippolytus,* but R. has again made
characteristic changes. The fringe myth of Hip-
polyta, queen of the Amazons, is made the romantic core of the story. Hippolytus is an acolyte
of Artemis, following his dead mother. His own
death has been foreshadowed from early in *The
King Must Die,* and if forms part of a seamless,
fateful web: The power of the feminine principal,
which the young Theseus thought he had displaced
at Eleusis, is reasserted here, and Theseus's tragic
fate is worked out in the death of his son. With
The Mask of Apollo (1966) R. returns to history.
The time is the final years of Greek democracy;
the political plot revolves around the civil war in
Syracuse; the characters include Plato and members of his Academy, and the young Alexander of
Macedon appears in a scene ominous for the old
Hellenic ways but promising continuity for Hellenistic culture. Much of this is R.'s reconstruction, and the result is compelling—even if it seems
more scholarly at time than poetic. A similar
pattern is followed in *The Praise Singer* (1978),
whose subject is poetry and whose time is the
Lyric Age of Pisistratos (with Persian invasion
hovering in the future), and whose protagonist is
Simonides, a name known to us from history,
champion singer of odes at the great festival at
Delos. History, culture, politics, and personal
charateristics—as in every R. narrative—are part
here of a unified, inseparable whole.

Most of the last decade and a half of R.'s career
was devoted to her study of Alexander the Great,
resulting in a trilogy of novels—*Fire from Heaven*
(1969), *The Persian Boy* (1972), and *Funeral
Games* (1981)—and a history of sorts, *The Nature
of Alexander* (1975). This last provides us, in a
sense, with the remnants of her research and the

rationale for her fictional interpretations. It is thus a splendid companion to the novels, although it perhaps does not stand very well by itself for those who know little of R.—it may tell us more about R. than about her subject.

There is much in the trilogy to remind us of R.'s earlier Theseus series. Even the natures of the protagonists and their backgrounds (both raised by their mothers, devotees of the old religion, both inadvertent causes of the deaths of their fathers) are similar. Many of the old themes too are here; a responsiveness to foreign cultures, an acceptance of almost all forms of sexuality (here the hero's great love is not an Amazon but a eunuch); the recognition of the role played by fate in all human lives, but an insistence at the same time on individual responsiblity in the working out of those lives. Much of the first two volumes of the triology is predictable, albeit never dull. Her major imaginative leap occurs in the second novel: the Persian Boy of the title is Bagoas, Alexander's lover, and he serves as narrator. He provides the international viewpoint (he is writing in Egypt, many years later) that historians associate with the mature Alexander. He also provides a powerful mix of involvement and of distance, a vision at once intimate and universal.

The final volume of the trilogy, *Funeral Games,* begins with the death of Alexander and traces in human terms the disintegration of the empire he created. His heirs are given personalities that are consistent with their roles in recorded events. But there is a sense here also of larger events that goes well beyond the historical record (the rhythms of nature and of the individual psyche) and of the interaction of individuals with the patterns of history. Everything comes together in the end; human aspirations and fate, history and myth, imagination and scholarship. It is a fitting conclusion to R.'s distinguished career.

FURTHER WORKS: *Kind Are Her Answers* (1940); *The Friendly Young Ladies* (1944; pub. in the U.S. as *The Middle Mist,* 1945); *Return to Night* (1947); *North Face* (1948); *The Lion in the Gateway: The Heroic Battles of the Greeks and Persians at Marathon, Salamis and Thermopylae* (1948); *The Charioteer* (1953)

BIBLIOGRAPHY: Herbert, K., "The Theseus Theme: Some Recent Versions," *Crit,* 6, 3 (1960), 175–85; Burns, L. C., Jr., "Men Are Only Men: The Novels of M. R.," *Crit,* 6 (1963–1964), 102–21; Casey, B., "Nurse Novels," *SWR,* 49, 4 (1964), 332–41; Wolfe, P., *M. R.* (1969); Dick, B. F., *The Hellenism of M. R.* (1972); Hartt, J. N., "Two Historical Novels," *VQR,* 49, 3 (1973), 450–58;

Dick, B. F., "The Herodotean Novelist," *SR,* 81, 4 (Oct.–Dec. 1973), 864–69

MORTON P. LEVITT

RIBEIRO, Darcy

Brazilian novelist and prose writer, b. 26 Nov. 1922, Montes Claros, Minas Gerais

R. is his nation's premier investigator of the indigenous populations, publishing extensively, from a decidedly Marxian perspective, on underdevelopmental issues germane to the Brazilian subcontinent and to Latin America as a whole. Early on, his expertise and dedication brought him to the attention of reformist elements within several pre-1964 central governments, where he served as cofounder and head of the University of Brasilia, minister of education and culture, and presidential chief of staff. A lengthy exile followed—in Uruguay, Venezuela, Chile, and Peru—precipitated by the 1964 rightest coup that was to impose successive military regimes on the nation. In 1978, with an end to overt oppression, R. returned permanently to Brazil, first getting elected as vice governor of Rio de Janeiro State and, most recently, as its senator. At the same time, he began a late-blooming and highly successful novelistic career. Indeed, in a decade marked by intense extraliterary pursuits, he penned four narratives, three of which are quite lengthy and involved.

In *Maíra* (1976; *Maíra,* 1984) the author goes further than anyone, before or since, in redefining fictionally the Native American experience, pinpointing autochthonous ethnography within defined boundaries and exposing irreversible sociological tendencies. In so doing, he goes about allegorizing and synthesizing the dichotomy between European and indigenous populations, but from the viewpoint of a tribal nation. While the distressing findings are not surprising, nor the reasons new, R.'s empathy produces an explosive indictment of aboriginal mistreatment. The author's updated, factual, scientific New Indianism exposes a torrent of collateral ills, from continuing ecological abuse to governmental malfeasance and detrimental missionary work. The sometimes weighty approach, however, is tempered and embellished by the mock-heroic tone of omnipresent native deities. Much as in the classically inspired *Os lusíadas,* the supernatural dramas of the deities run parallel to, and intervene with, those of the earthly adversaries, further enriching Indian legends.

Externally, the novel is divided into four parts, titled to mirror those of the Catholic mass, itself so symbolic of death and sacrifice. Internally, structure draws mostly on the indigenous myths and traditions, whose spontaneous arrangement makes for a fragmented narrative, unfolding through an endless array of counterpoint. Thus, what immediatly comes into focus is the schism between the red and white nations, a pervasive thesis that polarizes every aspect of *Maíra*. The author presents *Maíra,* as well, through linguistic duality: colloquial Portuguese, enhanced by copious *Maírum* vocabulary for which no exact translation exists. Use of the indigenous tongue, along with its speech patterns, solidifies an autochthonous atmosphere already pregnant witih native flora and fauna. The rhythmic prose, multiple levels of symbolism, and lively descriptions all proved R. to be a competent, first-time novelist, while the committed tone and dialectic development of the novel make for convincing polemics.

O mulo (1982; the mule) is his first confessional novel. Its more than five hundred pages project the backward psyche of an old land baron whose *goiano* rusticity is encased in layers of somber eroticism, machismo, brutishness, violence, and intolerance. The novel has an oral spontaneousness heightened by the intimate and informal nature inherent in any dying person telling all, as well as by the rambling prolixity of its very opinionated and self-serving character.

In *Utopia selvagem* (1982; savage utopia) R. subverts genres, blending legends, (un)official history, essay, polemics, and pamphleteering into a loosely structured, satirical discussion of, and attack on current Brazilian society, its values and identity. R. juxtaposes luxuriant indigenous settings with echoes of concrete and steel metropolises. He sets his fable, as inferred in the title, around the sights, sounds, smells, and tastes of autochthonous nations still largely unscathed by *caraíba,* or white contact. Meanwhile, an obtrusive, humorous, and sardonic first-person narrator shortens the distance between himself, the reader, and the reluctant antihero. His constant intrusions, in an informal language studded with slang, foreign neologisms, indigenous terminology, and explicit sexual epithets, succeed in interpreting extraneous goings-on as much as they propel the protagonist forward. Such is the comedic intent of the piece, in fact, that even the hallowed tenants of traditional Indianism are relegated to providing little more than contrast in the form of a colorful if catalytic backdrop. The protagonist, on the other hand, is a passive and vulnerable main character-victim, definitely more comic than tragic. His major comedic thrust is the way in which his virility is progressively erased. His carnivalized reversal of the traditional, composite macho role is made that much more ironic, given his race, region of origin, and profession. He is apt to appear reluctantly and more often naked than

clothed; Amazons first depilate his body, then reduce him to being a humiliated, zoomorphic appendage of his genitalia—a sort of ritualistic male rape that may also be seen as a metaphoric reversal. Unlike in the real world, the Indians possess the upper hand as well as the secret to societal success.

Although uniquely autobiographical, R.'s *Migo* (1988) shares with *O mulo* the presence of an aging and overbearing male narrator-character, a prolixity in keeping with spontaneous, informal and repetitive mental meanderings, and a pervasive sense of ribald earthiness. Nonetheless, *Migo* is, in fact, a sophisticated cross section of the views, left and right, held by that generation of Brazil's intelligentsia most responsible for the nation's dismal state of affairs. A multiplicity of focus is elaborated throughout nearly two hundred short, titled chapter entries, many of which conclude with a brief, unidentified if often famous quote that serves as a kind of posterior motif. These fragmented entries are then arranged in six blocks, all but the first prefaced by the progressing dialectic discord surrounding a colossal womblike construction. The individual blocks may also be read out of conventional order, through an imaginative pattern, or *roteiro,* outlined at the beginning.

Rather than subverting style to fit the oftentimes radical notions that characterize his intellectual trajectory, R. has turned his works into a fictional and expository celebration of national consciousness. Telluric epic and allegory combine with scatology and eroticism; political treatise joins tragicomedy, farce, and parody; and ethnological essay is fleshed out through pulsating figures whose varying autobiographical bents aptly evoke, as well, facets of the Brazilian character. Indeed, for those willing to look, the author's fiction, to date, reinforces and synthesizes the numerous essays for which he is best known worldwide.

FURTHER WORKS: *Religião e mitologia Kadiwéu* (1950); *Línguas e culturas indígenas no Brasil* (1951); *A poética indígena brasileira* (1962); *A universidade necessária* (1969); *As Américas e a civilização* (1970); *Os índios e a civilização* (1970); *Configurações histórico-culturais dos povos americanos* (1975); *Uirá sai a procura de Deus* (1976); *O dilema da América Latina* (1978); *Ensaios insólitos* (1979); *Aos trancos e barrancos; como o Brasil deu no que deu* (1985); *Sobre o óbvio* (1986); *Testemunho* (1990)

BIBLIOGRAPHY: Johnson, R., "D. R.," in Stern, I., ed., *Dictionary of Brazilian Literature* (1988), 287–88; Silverman, M., on *Migo, WLT,* 63, 2 (Spring 1989), 287–88; Columbus, C. K., "Mother

Earth in Amazonia and in the Andes: D. R. and Jose Maria Arguedos,'' in Dennis, P. A., and W. Aycock, eds., *Literature and Anthropology* (1989), 165–80

MALCOLM SILVERMAN

RIBEIRO, João Ubaldo

Brazilian novelist and short-story writer, b. 23 Jan. 1940, Itaparica

R. was born and still resides in Itaparica, a large island across All Saints' Bay from the city of Salvador, the colonial capital of Brazil from 1549 to 1763. Proud of its multiracial heritage and its respect for tradition, Bahia, as Salvador and its surrounding areas are commonly known, is regarded as the place where the present and the past of Brazil meet, and where the roots of Brazilian culture are most authentically preserved. Although R. is by no means a regionalist writer, his work reflects the sense of both national history and national pride deeply ingrained in the Bahian mind. Trained as a lawyer at the University of Bahia, R. later attended the University of Southern California, where he earned his M.A. in political science and public administration and perfected his command of English to the point that he has been able to translate his own novels. Returning to Bahia upon completion of his degree, R. resumed his career as a journalist, taught for some time at the Federal University, and has dedicated increasingly larger amounts of time to writing fiction.

Although individually R.'s works are characterized by a great diversity of subject matter, settings, tone, and styles, they are linked by an awareness of the past history and present problems of Brazil, and by a concern for the controversial question of national identity.

R.'s first novel, *Setembro não tem sentido* (1968; September has no meaning), is a semiautobiographical account of the trials and tribulations of a group of young intellectuals in a still provincial city of Salvador. Although the novel is ostensibly set during the political turmoil that followed the abrupt resignation of President Jânio Quadros on 25 August 1961, it evokes the anxiety, insecurity, and hopelessness of R.'s generation as Brazil is about to enter the most authoritarian phase in the country's modern history, the dark years from 1969 to 1974 known as *sufoco* (choking). Written in a harsh poetic prose, R.'s next work, *Sargento Getúlio* (1971; *Sergeant Getulio,* 1978), is a rambling monologue by the title character, a gunman who has been hired by a political boss to capture and deliver one of the boss's enemies. Ordered by his boss to set the prisoner free when political conditions abruptly change, Getulio refuses to bend

and vows to carry out his assignment even as federal troops are sent after him and eventually kill him. Although Getulio is capable of the most savage actions against his fellow human beings, he is also somewhat of a tragic hero, who remains completely faithful to his principles, and whose unshakable sense of duty lies above opportunism and political expediency. *Sargento Getúlio,* is thematically and formally R.'s most subversive work. *Vencecavalo e o outro povo* (1974; Overcomes-Horses and the other people), a collection of five interconnected short stories, is an irreverent and iconoclastic satire, whose light tone masks a serious examination of a host of important national issues, ranging from government corruption and ineptitude to the consequences of colonialism and economic dependence. Published when censorship was just beginning to be relaxed, this work relies on parody, allegory, allusion, and a Rabelaisian delight in linguistic excess to create an antihistory of Brazil, which demystifies and deconstructs official history.

R.'s three most recent novels are products of both the growing liberalization that began in the late 1970s and of the increasing doubts of Brazilians about the prospects for their country. Rejecting the symbolism and stylization of the two preceding works, *Vila Real* (1979; Vila Real) is a straightforward incursion into the old problem of economic deprivation in the Brazilian Northeast. *Viva o povo brasileiro* (1984; *An Invincible Memory,* 1989) is a massive historical novel, intertwining imagined situations with well-known historical events, and spinning stories about the interconnections of dozens of characters from different segments of Brazilian society over a period ranging from 1647 to 1977. R.'s next novel, the more somber and bitter *O sorriso do lagarto* (1989; the lizard's smile), is a biting satire depicting a corrupted society that has lost its moral bearings. Parodying many of the devices used in soap operas, pornographic films, and popular fiction, this story of decadence can be viewed as a literary counterpart to the pessimism brought about by the aimlessness of José Sarney's government (1985–1990) and the worsening economic crisis of the late 1980s.

A masterful storyteller and an impeccable stylist, R. is one of the most talented contemporary writers from Brazil. As more translations of his works become available, R. is sure to gain the international recognition he unquestionably deserves.

FURTHER WORKS, *Livro de histórias* (1981); *Política* (1981); *Vida e paixão de Pandonar, o cruel* (1983); *Sempre aos domingos* (1988); *A vingança de Charles Tiburone* (1990); *Já podes da pàtria filhos* (1991)

BIBLIOGRAPHY, Solomon, B. P., "Dupes of Authority," *NYTBR,* 9 Apr. 1978, 11; Amado, J., Introduction to *Sergeant Getulio* (1978), ix–xii; Bumpus, J., on *Sergeant Getulio, PR,* 46, 4 (1979), 634–35; DiAntonio, R., "Chthonian Visions and Mythic Redemption in J. U. R.'s *Sergeant Getulio,*" *MFS,* 32, 3 (Autumn 1986), 449–58; Valente, L. F., on *An Invincible Memory, WLT,* 64, 2 (Spring 1990), 288–89; Stern, I., on *O sorriso do lagarto, WLT,* 64, 2 (Spring 1990), 286

LUIZ FERNANDO VALENTE

RICH, Adrienne

American poet and theorist, b. 16 May 1929, Baltimore, Md.

R.'s parents were cultivated upper-middle-class Southerners. Her father was Jewish and a professor of medicine, her gentile mother a former concert pianist and composer. This ethnic mixture and its cultural and emotional meanings for R.'s life have been a subject of her writings since the late 1970s. R.'s parents, particularly her mother, devoted a great deal of time and energy to her early education in literature and music. After graduation from Radcliffe College (1951), R. entered into her professional career as a writer, uneasily combining this work, in the early years, with her roles as Harvard faculty wife and mother of three young sons. The tensions inherent in this dual life are reflected in her collection of poems *Snapshots of a Daughter-in-Law: Poems, 1954–1962* (1963; rev. ed., 1967). From 1966 to 1979, after leaving Cambridge, R. lived in the New York area, where she taught at Columbia's School of the Arts, the City College of New York, and Rutgers University. She lived for several years in western Massachusetts, where she edited the lesbian feminist journal *Sinister Wisdom,* and since the mid-1980s has been established in California, where she holds a professorship in English and feminist studies at Stanford University.

R. is widely regarded as one of the major American poets and the single most important American woman poet of the second half of the 20th c. As her work has come increasingly to reflect the influence of feminism and to contribute to that movement, she has retained the recognition and respect that her mastery of poetic craft won her in literary circles; this situation is extremely rare for American writers who are identified as "ideological," especially those whose ideology tends to the left of center.

R.'s career as an author spans the forty years from her first published collection of poems, *A Change of World* (1951), to her most recent one, *An Atlas of the Difficult World* (1991). Hers is an exceptionally long and rich production for a writer just over sixty. Despite the conflicts and frustrations that many poems themselves record, R.'s is also a career in which recognition came early. *A Change of World* was selected for the Yale Series of Younger Poets Award in 1951 by W. H. Auden (q.v.), who wrote respectfully—if somewhat condescendingly—in the collection's preface of R.'s stylistic acumen. This elegance is mentioned by most of the critics who commented on her first several volumes. As early as her second collection, *The Diamond Cutters and Other Poems* (1955), however, Donald Hall (b. 1928) was able to contrast its immersion in lived experience with what he called the "smug" detachment of her first book; here, he claims, "the wolf is inside and is busy writing poems about its successful campaign."

Feminist themes began to emerge with *Snapshots of a Daughter-in-Law: Poems, 1954–1962,* published before there was an organized social or literary movement around such issues. Those themes became more explicit and more in touch with the collective insights of the women's movement in *The Will to Change* (1971) and *Diving into the Wreck: Poems, 1971–1972* (1973). By the time of the publication of *The Dream of a Common Language: Poems, 1974–1977* (1978), R.'s poetry had itself become a source for a feminist theory, and this volume has been described as a mythic feminist manifesto. R.'s feminism has also served her, from the 1970s on, as a way of apprehending and writing poems about the condition of other oppressed and colonized groups.

R.'s prose includes essays in feminist literary criticism—notably the essays "When We Dead Awaken" (1972) and "*Jane Eyre:* Secrets of a Motherless Daughter" (1978)—as well as contributions to social theory. The book-length study *Of Woman Born: Motherhood as Experience and Institution* (1976) examines motherhood, as its subtitle indicates, as both experience and institution and has become a landmark in feminist analysis of the maternal condition; the essay "Compulsory Heterosexuality and Lesbian Existence" (1980), with its key notion of the "lesbian continuum," is equally central to the development of radical feminist and lesbian theory.

One of the hallmarks of R.'s writing, throughout, has been her concern for language as both a tool and a conceptual universe. As her poetry and her life have become more explicitly political, she has managed neither to abandon that concern nor to identify discourse with action. Rather, as she maintains in her first volume of collected prose pieces, *On Lies, Secrets, and Silence: Selected Prose, 1966–1978* (1979): "Poetry is, among other things, a criticism of language. Poetry is, above all, a concentration of the power of language, which is the power of our ultimate relationship to everything in the universe."

FURTHER WORKS: *Necessities of Life: Poems, 1952–1955* (1960); *Selected Poems* (1967); *Leaflets: Poems, 1965–1968* (1969); *Poems: Selected and New, 1950–1974* (1974); *Twenty-One Love Poems* (1976); *A Wild Patience Has Taken Me This Far: Poems, 1978–1981* (1981); *Sources* (1983); *The Fact of a Doorframe: Poems Selected and New, 1950–1984* (1984); *Blood, Bread, and Poetry: Selected Prose, 1979–1986* (1986); *Time's Power, Poems 1985–1988* (1989)

BIBLIOGRAPHY: Gelpi, B. C., and A. Gelpi, *A. R.'s Poetry* (1975): Juhasz, S., *Naked and Fiery Forms* (1976), 177–204; DuPlessis, R. B., "The Critique of Consciousness and Myth in Levertov, R., and Rukeyser," in Gilbert, S. M., and S. Gubar, eds., *Shakespeare's Sisters* (1979), 280–300; Ostriker, A., "Her Cargo: A. R. and the Common Language," *APR*, 8, 4 (July-Aug. 1979), 6–10; Cooper, J. R., *Reading A. R.* (1984); Martin, W., *An American Triptych. Anne Bradstreet, Emily Dickinson, and A. R.* (1984); Keyes, C., *The Aesthesics of Power: The Poetry of A. R.* (1986)

LILLIAN S. ROBINSON

RICHARDSON, Dorothy Miller

English novelist, short-story writer, and essayist, b. 17 May 1873, Abingdon, Berkshire; d. 17 June 1957, Beckenham, Kent

R. was the third of four daughters in a nonconformist family. Her father, who inherited his tradesman father's fortune, devoted himself to the life of a gentleman patron of science until he was overtaken by financial disaster. Her mother, from the yeoman-landholding class, fostered what R. would call her own deep-rooted suspicion of "facts." Thus R.'s early experiences were dominated by sharp contrasts in outlook and mood as family life changed from order and comfort to actual penury.

Ultimately R.'s mother committed suicide, and R.'s three sisters escaped into marriage. But R., at seventeen, had secured a post as pupil-teacher in Hanover, Germany. After six months she returned to England and took various jobs as teacher, as governess, and eventually as clerk-assistant in a London dental office.

These and other autobiographical details are incorporated in the story of Miriam Henderson's "pilgrimage," a fictional transmutation of R.'s life from adolescence through the years when she was working in London, making friends with—and debating—avant-garde artists and intellectuals, anarchists, Russian Jews, suffragists, and Fabian socialists, including George Bernard Shaw and H. G. Wells (qq.v.).

In her early school years, R. had been a close friend of Amy Catherine Robbins, who was the wife of Wells. In 1907 R. had an affair with Wells, became pregnant, but miscarried. The relationship is mirrored in *Pilgrimage* when Miriam for a brief time becomes the mistress of Hypo G. Wilson, but somehow manages to maintain her friendship with her former classmate Alma. The parallel was not noticed at first because R. introduced Wells into the novel under his own name as well. With her multivolume *Pilgrimage*, an important example of modern psychological fiction, R. was one of the first writers to exploit the technique known as stream-of-consciousness (q.v.).

Leaving London for a time, R. lived on a Sussex farm with a Quaker family, an episode reflected in the twelfth part of *Pilgrimage*. One result of the appeal that mysticism had to her was the publication in 1914 of her first two books: *The Quakers Past and Present* and *Gleanings from the Works of George Fox*.

R. had been writing for publication since 1906, and she continued to supplement her limited income by writing reviews, essays on dentistry, cinema, and other topics, as well as translations of French and German works. In 1917, at age forty-four, she took on the domestic burdens of marriage to Alan Odle, an obscure artist-illustrator, fifteen years younger but in frail health. For more than thirty years they divided their time between London and Cornwall, often living in primitive conditions, but their life together was mutually supportive in spite of illness and other hardships, including the theft of many of Odle's prized artworks. Friends frequently rescued them from actual privation, and eventually secured for R. a Civil List pension.

R. began writing *Pilgrimage* in 1913. The first "chapter," *Pointed Roofs*, published in 1915, introduces Miriam Henderson as the young woman whose inner consciousness would dominate succeeding volumes produced over the next quarter century: *Backwater* (1916), *Honeycomb* (1917), *The Tunnel* (1919), *Interim* (1919), *Deadlock* (1921), *Revolving Lights* (1923), *The Trap* (1925), *Oberland* (1927), *Dawn's Left Hand* (1931), *Clear Horizon* (1936), and the twelfth "chapter," *Dimple Hill*, first published in the omnibus four-volume edition of *Pilgrimage* (1938). *March Moon-*

light, a posthumous fragment, was included in the 1967 edition.

In her use of a single-viewpoint character, R. was influenced by Henry James and Joseph Conrad (qq.v.). She was proud of the fact that both she and Conrad had been "discovered" by Edward Garnett (1868–1937), who denominated her innovative technique "feminine impressionism." But in a foreword to the 1938 edition of *Pilgrimage* R. declared her own intention had been to create "a feminine equivalent of the current masculine realism." And in that foreword she acknowledged what critics were doing in comparing her with Marcel Proust, Virginia Woolf, and James Joyce (qq.v.).

May Sinclair (q.v.), in a 1918 essay on R., was the first to apply in a literary discussion the metaphor "stream-of-consciousness," a term invented by William James (1842–1910) to suggest the complexities of human thought. R. herself seemed to prefer the terms "interior monologue" or "slow-motion photography."

Other critics found in her fiction qualities of imagist poetry. Joyce's epiphanies and Woolf's intense moments of illumination are paralleled in R.'s mystical perceptions of reality. Woolf herself, as evidenced in a 1919 review of *The Tunnel,* respected R.'s technical achievements although she saw dangers of solipsistic formlessness in a long work focused exclusively on the consciousness of a single individual. Woolf praised R. for crafting "the psychological sentence of the feminine gender."

Not all R.'s contemporaries were unqualified admirers of *Pilgrimage.* Graham Greene called her work "ponderous," and C. P. Snow (qq.v.) pronounced the "moment-by-moment" novel to be the most hopeless "cul-de-sac" in the history of fiction.

From her wide reading and associations R. gained perspective on literary art and on more abstruse problems like freedom and time. She found philosophers "more deeply exciting than the novelists." Bergsonian concepts of time find expression in her handling of the subtleties of Miriam Henderson's mingling of memory with perceptions of immediate reality.

But R.'s skill in conveying thoughts, sensations, and memories in a welter of moments past and present, occasionally punctuated by flashes of mystical illumination, is not the only basis for critical consideration.

Winifred Bryher (1894–1983), who befriended R. when she was in financial need, felt that *Pilgrimage* was the book to read for understanding transitions in English society between 1890 and World War I. R.'s fiction is undoubtedly useful for understanding the intellectual and political forces of her day.

Although R. followed the activities of Mrs. Pankhurst and other suffragettes with interest, even visiting a friend who was confined in Holloway Gaol, she was her own kind of feminist. Through Miriam Henderson's consciousness she accurately depicted the evolution of a feminine mind in a time when women were striving for a new identity. Miriam's and her creator's struggle against masculine domination and against the psychocultural structures that contribute to women's self-abasement has timeless relevance.

FURTHER WORKS: *John Austen and the Inseparables* (1930); *Journey to Paradise: Short Stories and Autobiographical Sketches* (1989)

BIBLIOGRAPHY: Sinclair, M., "The Novels of D. R.," *Egoist,* 5 (April 1918), 57–59; Powys, J., *D. M. R.* (1931); Blake, C., *D. R.* (1960); Gregory, H., *D. R., An Adventure in Self-Discovery* (1967); Rosenberg, J., *D. R., The Genius They Forgot: A Critical Biography* (1973); Staley, T. F., *D. R.* (1976); Fromm, G. G., *D. R.: A Biography* (1977)

CARL D. BENNETT

RIVE, Richard

South African novelist, short-story writer, and editor (writing in English), b. 1 Mar. 1931, Cape Town; d. 6 June 1989, Cape Town

R. received his teacher's diploma in 1951 from Hewat Training College and his B.A. and B.Ed. from the University of Cape Town (1962). He earned his M.A. from Columbia University (1966) and his doctorate from Oxford University (1973). R.'s brutal and unexplained murder ended the important career of this man of letters. In a sense this more general title is a better accolade of his achievement than novelist, for his editorial enterprise was significant in bringing South African writing to the attention of an international audience. *Quartet: New Voices from South Africa* (1963) was an anthology in which he introduced four major new talents, including his own. His often anthologized short story "The Bench" (1952) exemplified all the qualities that would direct African writing from that country. It became a metaphor for the sense of belligerent resentment that determined political resistance throughout the following decades. There were a number of other publications, of short stories, essays, and, since he was at heart an academic, the important project of editing the letters of Olive Schreiner (q.v.). Many titles are listed in his bibliography, but his reputation may ultimately rest on one major novel, *Emergency* (1964).

The term "emergency" in this context is specific and relates to the South African government's declaration of a state of emergency, which permitted it to withdraw all the constraints of the legal constitution. The actual events happened in Cape Town between 28 and 30 March 1960. This was the high point of the campaign against the odious Pass Laws that required all nonwhites to carry identity papers. The government response to the upsurge of protest was immediate and harsh: arbitrary arrests of individuals, bullets and tear gas against the demonstrating crowds. The confrontation culminated in the infamous shootings at Sharpeville. At one level, this is a realistic novel drawing upon actual events. If it were only that, however, it would be journalism. However, the incidents form the background against which a series of carefully developed fictional characters react to the intense political intolerance that conditions their existence. Their survival depends upon their courage and their ingenuity. The central people are "colored." The whites are at the periphery. They sometimes show real kindness, but their liberal convictions are questioned by others since they do not suffer the same persecution. Somewhat surprisingly, the blacks are portrayed as a threatening majority. They exhibit, albeit from the opposite pole, a racism as virulent as the white version and equally destructive to harmonious social change. The coloreds feel excluded from both sides. The characters are convincing in their variety. Altmann the dedicated teacher, Abe the idealist intellectual, Mrs. Hanslo the kindly landlady, Braam the self-consciously dirty hippie, and, inevitably, the tough, sadistic police. The main character, Andrew, is seeking an advanced education, which requires his dependence on the hospitality of his resentful, brutal brother-in-law. Andrew is drawn into a more radical stance by circumstance as much as by conviction. His ambitions are genuine. He is not by nature a radical. He is forced into that attitude in response to the persecutions of the Special Branch. They show no mercy when they discover that he is breaking the Immorality Act by having a love affair with Ruth, a white woman.

In spite of following the precise dates of the days of increasing social violence, R. creates his own fictional rhythm. Against the background of events the characters move with inescapable urgency toward their own tragic catastrophes. The conclusion suggests that a stoic determination to survive is the only weapon against the state. Abe decides upon the rational solution of exile. Andrew chooses to make the absurd gesture of remaining, knowing he will inevitably be arrested. In this way he exhibits the same defiance as the man in "The Bench." R.'s final moral is that commitment, rather than successful outcome, is the true measure of heroism.

It was twenty years before the next major work appeared: *Buckingham Palace* (1986), the rather improbable name for a series of shabby cottages, one of which is a thriving whorehouse. The book presents a series of intriguing characters who live within the boundaries of District Six, the area of Cape Town reserved for coloreds. In this book R. again draws upon the region of his own upbringing. He records, with a very touching fondness, a life no longer permitted, for the apartheid bulldozers have razed this amiable community where pigmentation did not match the patterns of city planners. These vignettes are conceived with mature skill. The language is sensitive and accurate—with lively patois and sometimes poetry: "the apricot warmth of a summer Sunday morning." What is most remarkable is the style, so wonderfully tongue-in-cheek innocent, as R. subtly makes his wry observations. The episodes are wildly comic, even satiric, yet depict no unkindness or overt criticism. A wife discovers her husband's adultery when he pretends he must go to band practice but leaves his huge visible bass drum at home. Milton September follows his namesake by writing satiric verse, including a complaint against the prison warder, who becomes so incensed he threatens that either he or Milton must leave and "as Milton had two more years to serve . . . he was granted a transfer." There are the adventures of Dubaas who, commanded to paint all the house, obeys precisely, and the walls inside and out and all the furniture and the refrigerator are coated in a hideous pink. There are riches here that beg recounting and a shared delight.

Ultimately R.'s greatest claim to recognition is *Emergency*, with its passionate commitment to a nonracial and liberated South Africa. *Buckingham Palace* indicates his advance as a writer and makes us more aware of how much was lost by his sadly premature decease.

FURTHER WORKS: *African Songs* (1963); *Modern African Prose* (1964); *Make Like Slaves* (1973); *Selected Writings* (1977); *Advance, Retreat: Selected Short Stories* (1983); *Olive Schreiner Letters* (1987); *Emergency Continued* (1990)

BIBLIOGRAPHY: Gorman, G. E., *The South African Novel in English since 1950* (1978), 15, 19, 21, 40; Gray, S., *Southern African Literature* (1979), 9, 133, 137–38, 196; Barnett, U. A., *A Vision of*

Order: A Study of South African Literature in English (1914–1980) (1983), 129–31, 246–49, 264–66, and passim; "An Interview with R. R.," *Current Writing: Text and Reception in Southern Africa,* 1, 1 (Oct. 1989), 45–55; Raju, J., and C. Dubbeld, "R. R.: A Select Bibliography," *Current Writing: Text and Reception in Southern Africa,* 1, 1 (Oct. 1989), 56–65

JOHN POVEY

RODOREDA, Mercè

Spanish-Catalan novelist and short-story writer (writing in Catalan), b. 1909, Barcelona; d. 22 Apr. 1983, Barcelona

R. is the most famous Catalan novelist of the post-Civil War period (and is often considered to be the most important female writer of the entire Mediterranean region in many centuries). She participated fully in the great cultural flowering of Spain in general and of Barcelona in particular before that war. Even before publishing her well-received first novel, *Sóc una dona honrada?* (1932; am I an honest woman?), the young R. was associated with the so-called Sabadell group, and her name was a familiar one in the pages of prestigious Catalan literary reviews such as *La Rambla, Mirador,* and *La Publicitat.* In 1937 she won one of the major Catalan literary prizes, the Creixelles. With the imminent entrance of victorious Francoist forces into Barcelona in 1939, she went into a thirty-year exile. She stayed in Paris until the advent of the Germans during World War II, and then established herself with the Spanish exile community in southern France along the border with Spain. In 1954 she began to place her life on a new footing by going to live in Geneva and by gaining economic security as a translator for the many international groups headquartered there. With much of the worst of her experience of war and exile now under control, she was able to return to literature and published *Vint-i-dos contes* (1958; twenty-two stories). In 1962 R. published *La plaça del Diamant* (*The Pidgeon Girl,* 1967; repub. as *The Time of Doves,* 1980), the novel that is considered her masterpiece, and which has been both widely translated and made into versions in film and television.

This novel exhibits what is probably R.'s most characteristic element of style: the continuous, at times lyrical, interior monologue of a female protagonist, in which the details of daily experience dominate over the sociohistorical context favored by 19th-c. realist-naturalists. This practice leads critics to place R. in world literature by studying her in relation to James Joyce, Virginia Woolf, and Gertrude Stein (qq.v.) among others. Never-theless, R. does have male narrators and protagonists, and does portray directly larger sociohistoric canvases, especially with reference to the Barcelona of her pre-exile life. In this she may be similar to her illustrious predecessor Emilia Pardo Bazán (q.v.); the reader of both novelists senses a need in them to see the world from a masculine point of view, almost as if they lacked confidence in or were not satisfied solely with their feminine one. R., in a 1982 television interview, went so far as to express conformity with the version of the basic male-female relationship given in Genesis: real and necessary subordination of the so-called second to the first sex. In this light the resilient strength in suffering and solitude of R.'s protagonists such as Natalia/Colometa of *La plaça del Diamant* and Cecilia of *El carrer de les Camèlies* (1966; Camellia Street) is ambiguous. It is probably for the reader to decide if those women have a worthwhile life and how their and their fellow women's prospects appear.

Some of R.'s shorter fiction is strikingly different from these long narratives. At times R. gives free rein to her fantasy and imagination to create tales that bear comparison to Franz Kafka (q.v.) and to works of mainstream horror and science fiction. In other stories, those more thematically related to her novels and often involving some kind of exile, R. explores the uncertain boundary between the feminine and the masculine in men and women.

R.'s place in literature is, so soon after her death, still being mapped out. As with certain other contemporary writers whose first language is Catalan, her fame is such that virtually all her important work has been translated into Spanish, especially in paperback collections of fine reputation and wide circulation. Moreover, contemporary female Hispanists especially read R. in Catalan, but then go on to include her in the broader contexts of Hispanic and Western literature. It seems, therefore, that R.'s wide and at the same time select present audience will guarantee continued reputation.

FURTHER WORKS: *Del que hom no pot fugir* (1934); *Un día en la vida d'un home* (1934); *Crim* (1936); *Aloma* (1938; rev. ed., 1969); *Jardí vora del mar* (1967); *La meva Cristina i altres contes* (1967); *Mirall trencat* (1974); *Obres completes* (2 vols., 1976, 1978); *Viatges i flors* (1980); *Quanta, quanta guerra . . .* (1980); *Una campana de vidre: antologia de contes* (1984); *Cartas a l'Anna Muria: 1939–1956* (1985); *Mort i la primavera* (1986). FURTHER WORKS IN ENGLISH: *Two Tales* (1983); *My Christina and Other Stories* (1984)

BIBLIOGRAPHY: Arnau, C., "La obra de M. R.," *CHA,* 383 (May 1982), 239–57; Ortega, J., "Mujer, guerra y neurosis en dos novelas de M. R. *(La plaza del Diamante y La calle de las Camelias),"* in Pérez, J. W., ed., *Novelistas femeninas de la post-guerra española* (1983), 71–83; Wyers, F., "A Woman's Voices: M. R.'s *La plaça del diamant,"* *KRQ,* 30 (1983), 301–9; Nichols, G. C., "Exile, Gender, and M. R.," *MLN,* 101, 2 (1986), 405–17; Galerstein, C. L., ed., *Women Writers of Spain: An Annotated Bio-Bibliographical Guide* (1986), 273–75; Martí-Olivella, J., ed., *Homage to M. R.* (1987); Nichols, G. C., "Sex, the Single Girl, and Other *Mésalliances* in R. and Laforet," *ALEC,* 12 (1987), 123–40; Pérez, J., "M. R.," *Contemporary Women Writers of Spain* (1988), 74–85

STEPHEN MILLER

ROMANIAN LITERATURE

See Volume 4, page 79.

In the late 1970s and throughout the 1980s, Romanian literature and intellectual life had to function under the most oppressive dictatorship in Europe, centered on Nicolae Ceaușescu and his relatives. The country's living standards fell to unprecedented lows, isolation from Europe and the world was consciously fostered, and normal social communication was impeded by pervasive government supervision and invasion of privacy. Official pressure was exerted to encourage the growth of a nationalist-communist synthesis in writing, which ended up producing an ideology not unlike right-wing populism. Its leading spokesmen were the novelist Eugen Barbu (b. 1924) and the poet Adrian Păunescu (b. 1943). The speculative theories of Edgar Papu (b. 1908) on the temporal priority of Romanian stylistic, cultural, and literary phenomena over Western ones (known as "protochronism") were used to bolster nationalist ideology. The novel *Căderea în lume* (1987; fall in the world) by Constantin Toiu (b. 1923) suggested that before World War II only communists and *legionari* (fascists) represented true social consciousness and that, at a deeper level, these were twin brothers. Anti-Semitic tones found their way into the magazines closest to officialdom. Luxurious volumes flattering the regime and its leader were constantly edited. Nevertheless it is striking to note that the best Romanian literary production of the 1970s and 1980s adopted a socially critical stance.

Prose writing, despite heavy censorship, often sent messages of disagreement, anger, and despair to the readers. Augustin Buzura (b. 1938) emerged as the most prominent novelist to depict contemporary Romania as a land of darkness and injustice, particularly in *Vocile nopții* (1980; voices of

the night) and *Refugii* (1984; kinds of refuge). Others, either inside Romania or in emigration, also developed the nightmare mode, using fantasy and allegory, among them Bujor Nedelcovici (b. 1936), Ioana Orlea (b. 1936), and Constantin Eretescu (b. 1938). Paul Goma (b. 1935), living in Paris since 1977, wrote a sequence of novels portraying the growth of a young man from the 1940s on, under constantly renewed strata of communist persecution and threat; although written in Romanian, many of his novels have been published so far only in their French translation. Long short stories or short novels by the younger writers Ioan Groșan (b. 1954), Mircea Nedelciu (b. 1950), and the postmodernist Ștefan Agopian (b. 1947) suggested the indirect but dire impact of dictatorship upon everyday lives, sometimes using the camouflage of historical distance. Even more impressive were the works by women novelists such as Gabriela Adameșteanu's (b. 1942) *Dimineața nimănui* (1983; nobody's morning) and Dana Dumitriu's (1943–1987) *Sărbătorile răbdării* (1980; the feasts of patience) in which the cruelty and tensions of male-female relationships in a warped society were pointed out with precision and subtlety, as well as with a clear feminist consciousness. Norman Manea (b. 1936) described movingly the sufferings of a concentration-camp Jewish childhood in his early short stories and devised later a complicated and insinuating modernist idiom to portray the anguishes and half-truths of the society surrounding him, most notably in *Plicul negru* (1986; black envelope). Ioan D. Sîrbu (1919–1989), in the collection of short stories *Șoarecele B* (1983; mouse B), but much more forthrightly and powerfully in his underground novel of ideas *Adio Europa* (1986; a farewell to Europe), pointed to the very roots of the system as one designed to destroy individual options and personal identity. Petre Creția (b. 1927) provided in his highly original *Norii* (1979; the clouds) a series of meditations on nature, intended as a record of social sensitivity and a defense of personal privacy.

The best poets of the 1970s and 1980s were in the forefront of dissidence. The poems of Ana Blandiana (q.v.), who had been known earlier for delicate eroticism and mild lyricism, had an explosive effect and circulated throughout the country. Mircea Dinescu (b. 1950), indirectly in *Proprietarul de poduri* (1976; the bridge owner) and *Exil pe o boabă de piper* (1983; exile on a peppercorn), and, in the end openly, in the banned *Moartea citește ziarul* (1989; death reading the newspaper), challenged dictatorship and Ceaușescu in a very personal style, blending elements of surrealism (q.v.) and street rap. Dorin Tudoran (b. 1945) picked up the the parodic and parabolic style that had been invented by Marin Sorescu (q.v.) and others, but gave it moral rectitude, a sarcastic edge, and combative immediacy, as seen perhaps best in his volumes *Semne particulare* (1979; distinguishing features) and *De bună voie* (1986; of my own free will). His activities as a relentless investigative journalist impelled the government to exile him in 1985.

A new poetic generation arose after 1980, abruptly altering the prevailing poetic idiom by opting for a tough colloquial language, cynical and disenchanted imagery, a tragic or hopeless view of life, and brooding over the asperities of the concrete. Among its prominent figures were Florin Iaru (b. 1955), Ion Stratan (b. 1954), Bogdan Ghiu (b. 1956), Mariana Marin (b. 1955), Liviu Ioan Stoiciu (b. 1950), and particularly Mircea Cărtărescu (b. 1955). The latter's novel in verse *Levantul* (1990; Levantine realm) is a postmodernist exercise in recuperating early romantic vision and meter in an ironic perspective.

Ştefan Augustin Doinaş (q.v.), now generally recognized as the greatest living Romanian poet, offered in *Vînătoare cu şoim* (1985; a-hawking) and in *Interiorul unui poem* (1991; a poem's insides) metaphoric statements of rage and resentment, often using the corruption and erosion of freedom in imperial Rome as a referential level. Ileana Mălăncioiu (b. 1940) emerged—along with Blandiana—as the leading woman poet within Romanian literature, particularly in volumes such as *Linia vieţii* (1982; life-line) and *Urcarea muntelui* (1985; climbing the mountain), which displayed enormous lexical variety and skillfully used the lyrical intensities of love and death as suggestions for political and social conflict.

Perhaps the most characteristic feature of Romanian literature in the 1970s and the 1980s was the fact that, because of dictatorial constraints on political and social debate, literary criticism and essay writing had to take over the functions of the former, in a coded manner. The most influential philosophical figure of the 1980s was Constantin Noica (1909–1987), who advocated a platonic detachment from social life and an option for the exclusive creativity of cultural elites, and at the same time urged the rejection of Western civilization and thinking patterns in favor of local and nationally identifiable styles. His disciples Andrei Pleşu (b. 1948) and, more markedly, Gabriel Liiceanu (b. 1943) have tended to modify Noica's teachings to allow for more openness toward modernist and humanist possibilities, as seen in Liiceanu's *Jurnalul de la Păltiniş* (1983; the Păltiniş diary) and in the collective volume *Epistolar* (1987; epistolary).

Others, unconnected with Noica, were presenting even more consistently the argument for Western and democratic values. Mihai Şora (b. 1917) used models drawn from aesthetics as an underpinning for epistemology and showed that any antimaterialist stance must be rooted in the respect for the individual person, rather than in tribal or ethnic patterns and frameworks. Nicolae Steinhardt (1912–1989), a Jewish-born Eastern Orthodox monk, maintained that true spiritual liberation and even national identity can be achieved only by firmly placing Romanian literature in its European contexts. The need for personal ethical responsibility and for a closer connection between the workings of imagination and desire and the practices of social behavior was pointed out by Alexandru Paleologu (b. 1919) and by Octavian Paler (b. 1926), one of the latter's more significant works being the autobiographical novel *Un om fericit* (1985; a happy man). Paler and Paleologu outlined a case for democratic development with social and liberal overtones. All these essayists were subjected over the years to imprisonment or house arrest, and their works were banned for longer or shorter periods of time.

Ileana Vrancea (b. 1929), who emigrated in the 1980s to Israel, and Mircea Martin (b. 1940) formulated their theories regarding the conflict between nativist and Westernizing trends in Romanian history by using as a vehicle a discussion about the literary criticism of George Călinescu (q.v.). Adrian Marino (b. 1921), a comparatist and literary theoretician, often promoted principles of democratic pluralism cloaked in the idiom of literary criticism; and Alexandru George (b. 1930) consistently defended the liberal tradition in Romanian literature. More than any of the above, Nicolae Manolescu (b. 1939), the country's leading critical voice, insisted on professionalism and aesthetic and ethical standards against an encroaching totalitarianism. His efforts were often supported by émigré critics such as Monica Lovinescu (b. 1923) and Virgil Ierunca (b. 1920), who castigated forcefully the political and ethical compromises of writers and highlighted genuine literary achievements. A deeper revision of the self-understanding of Romanian culture is now being advanced in the sociocultural studies of Z. Ornea (b. 1930), a moderate Marxist, and in the new histories of Romanian literature written by Manolescu and Ioan Negoiţescu (q.v.), the latter living in Germany since 1979.

One remarkable new phenomenon of the last two decades has been the emergence of regional intellectual, literary, and political movements in a number of Romanian larger cities. In a form less obvious before than after 1989, groups of young writers assumed the initiative of shaping public opinion and organizing efforts toward change. The dissident essayist Dan Petrescu (b. 1949), an acute diagnostician of Romanian social psychology, provided a focus for a larger number of socially conscious writers in the eastern city of Iasi. Novelists and scholars such as Vasile Popovici (b. 1956), Serban Foarţă (b. 1942), and Mircea Mihăieş (b. 1954) emerged as revolutionary leaders in the western city of Timisoara. Other young philosophers and writers constituted themselves as a group of articulate media leaders, among them Stelian Tănase (b. 1951), Dan C. Mihăilescu (b. 1953), and Radu Ţeposu (b. 1954). As political changes in Romania created the need for alternative political elites, the intellectual categories that had, to a certain point, preserved rational sociopolitical discourse showed themselves willing to switch over to a much more active political role.

BIBLIOGRAPHY: Cornis-Pope, M., "A Long-Rehearsed Revolution of Sensibility: Post-Modernism and the Historical Romanian Avantgarde," *South-Eastern Europe,* 11 (1984), 129–48; Spiridon, M., "Ideology and Fiction," *CREL,* 2 (1986), 85–96; Cornis-Pope, M., "Narration across the Totalistic Gap: On Recent Romania Fiction," *Symposium,* 43, 1 (Spring 1989), 3–19; Moraru, C., "Poetical Subject and Ontological Precariousness," *CREL* (1989), 102–9; Nemoianu, V., "Mihai Sora and the Traditions of Romanian Philosophy," *Review of Metaphysics,* 43 (Mar. 1990), 591–605

VIRGIL NEMOIANU

ROSEI, Peter

Austrian novelist, short-story writer, and poet, b. 17 June 1946, Vienna

R. studied law at the University of Vienna and earned his doctorate in 1968. He then held a variety of jobs, including working as the secretary for the artist Ernst Fuchs. In 1972 he moved to Bergheim (near Salzburg) to devote himself entirely to his writing. In 1981 he returned to Vienna, where he still lives.

R. began his career by writing dark and negative antihomeland literature, where scenes of death and inhuman conditions prevail. The stories of *Landstriche* (1972; tracts of land) and *Wege* (1974; paths) are populated by characters who succumb to the tyranny and domination of others. The persons in *Bei schwebendem verfahren* (1973; pending proceedings) are so driven by sex and avarice that the president of the country wishes to destroy all individuality through comprehensive legislation. In all these works any attempt to subjugate and control others ends in disaster.

R. entered a second stage of his writing with *Entwurf für eine welt ohne menschen, entwurf zu einer reise ohne ziel* (1975; plan for a world without people, plan for a trip without a goal). In this and in subsequent works the protagonists take long trips that are without purpose or direction. In the first story of this book the narrator makes a long journey where he does not encounter a single human being; in the second, a group of people travel endlessly through a country populated by quasi-barbarians. In *Wer war edgar allen?* (1977; who was Edgar Allen?) the protagonist travels to Italy where he tries to learn more about his psyche through drugs and alcohol. Karl, in *Von hier nach dort* (1978; from here to there), takes a long motorcycle trip, returns home, makes a lucrative drug deal, and then flies to a large city in the south, where he goes on long walks. Finally, Ellis, in *Die milchstrasse* (1981; the Milky Way), a compendium of R.'s ideas to date, is constantly on the move meeting friends and acquaintances. Everyone here seems to be lonely and isolated, and any type of happiness appears to be elusive.

R. explains his rather bizarre thematics in a series of essays collected under the title *Versuch, die natur zu kritisieren* (1982; attempt to criticize nature). Here he postulates that we are all on the journey of life, in search of happiness, which we can never achieve as long as we try to dominate nature and other individuals. Instead we should accept our isolation, try to be at one with nature, and look for happiness within ourselves and in our sense experiences.

The achievement of a modicum of happiness is the theme of a cycle of six prose pieces written between 1984 and 1988; *Mann & frau* (1984; man & woman), *Komödie* (1985; comedy), *15.000 seelen* (1985; 15,000 souls), *Die wolken* (1986; the clouds), *Der aufstand* (1987; the rebellion), and *Unser landschaftbericht* (1988; our landscape report). R. likens this project to a Gothic winged altar that portrays a central religious theme in a series of individual paintings. In all these works we learn that happiness cannot be achieved through human relationships or religion but by working hard, by living alone, and by assimilating nature.

R. is extremely prolific (averaging one or two works a year), and has developed into one of the most important and respected contemporary Austrian writers. He has conceived a unique vision of the postmodern world, which shocks, fascinates, and entertains his readers at the same time.

FURTHER WORKS: *Klotz spricht mit seinem rechtsanwalt* (1975); *Der fluss der gedanken durch den kopf* (1976); *Nennt mich tommy* (1978); *Alben* (1979); *Regentagstheorie: 59 gedichte* (1979); *Das lächeln des jungen: 59 gedichte* (1979); *Chronik der versuche, ein märchenerzähler zu werden* (1979); *Das schnelle glück* (1980); *Frühe prosa*

(1981); *Reise ohne ende: aufzeichnungsbücher* (1983); *Rebus* (1990)

BIBLIOGRAPHY: Von Schirnding, A., "Schreiben, weil Schweigen qualvoller ist: Über P. R.," *Merkur*, 33, 7 (1979), 714–20; Greiner, U., *Tod des Nachsommers* (1979), 139–54; Exner, R., "Stifter und die Folgen—Schreiben ohne Menschen, ohne Ziel? Reflexionen zu P. R.'s Prosa," *MAL*, 13, 1 (1980), 63–90; Von Bormann, A., " 'Es ist, als wenn etwas wäre': Überlegungen zu P. Rs Prosa," in Zeman, H., ed., *Studien zur österreichischen Erzählliteratur der Gegenwart* (1982), 156–88

ROBERT ACKER

ROTIMI, Ola

(born Emmanuel Gladstone Olawale Rotimi) Nigerian dramatist (writing mostly in English), b. 13 Apr. 1938, Sapele

R.'s family background brought him into contact with the English language, with the diversity of Nigeria, and with the performing arts from an early age. He spent part of his youth in the most cosmopolitan city in Nigeria, Lagos, and there, since his father was playing a leading role in the trade-union movement, he had firsthand contact with political activity. On completing his secondary education, he went to the U.S. and obtained his B.A. from Boston University and his M.F.A. from Yale University. He returned to Nigeria in 1966 and has held appointments at the universities of Ife and Port Harcourt.

Since the late 1950s Nigeria has been swept by a variety of political and intellectual movements, and these provide the background to R.'s approach to the theater. The intense nationalism of the independence movement was accompanied by an anxiety to affirm the vitality and validity of Nigerian cultural traditions and a concern that the historical experiences of the nation should be made familiar to generations emerging from a colonial educational system. Today there is in Nigeria, it appears, a spirit of vitality and excess that finds expression both creatively and destructively in politics, business, music, art, crime, fashions, the press, celebrations, and the very style in which people express themselves. It is appropriate that such a society should have produced a dramatist with R.'s commitment to plays on a grand scale in which monumental emotions are unleashed.

R.'s early foray into political drama, *Our Husband Has Gone Mad Again* (1974), first performed at Yale in 1966, reflected the intensity of nationalist feelings, and revealed the dramatist's desire to exploit various means of communication within

the "two-hour traffic of the stage." His next major work was characteristically ambitious: Seeking to exploit similarities between the cultures of Yorubaland and Ancient Greece, R. prepared an adaptation of *Oedipus Rex,* with the provocative title *The Gods Are Not To Blame* (1971). He created a compelling theatrical event in which issues of concern to all communities, such as incest and political stability, are explored through a drama rich in ritual, spectacle, and movement. The play is written in English, but an English heavily interlaced with elements from several Nigerian languages and rhetorical traditions, replete with incantations, proverbs, riddles, and direct translations of Yoruba verse forms. At the end of the 1960s, R. toured his production of the play to various theaters in Nigeria and Ghana; it attracted large audiences, and was appreciated even by those who had only a limited knowledge of English.

During the late 1970s and the 1980s, R. turned to history for his sources and wrote *Kurunmi* (1971) and *Ovonramwen Nogbaisi: An Historical Tragedy in English* (1974). He found his material in the Yoruba conflicts that preceded colonial rule and that affected the Kingdom of Benin—events in which he found conflicts that appealed to his taste for full-blooded theater and that had relevance for his contemporaries.

R.'s recent work focuses on suffering humanity in a contemporary setting. *If* (perf. 1979, pub. 1983), subtitled "A Tragedy of Our Times," is set in a crowded and poverty-stricken row of "quarters" whose residents' lives and experiences are representative of the pressures on "the wretched of the earth." Over the course of a weekend they go through what R. calls "the giddy gamut of survival imposed by the sociopolitical truths of present-day Nigeria."

In *Hopes of the Living Dead* (1989), set in a hospital for lepers during the 1930s, R. extends his pioneering experiments in communicating with audiences unfamiliar with English, even Pidgin English. The hospital patients are from different language groups, and important statements, particularly those made by the central character, Ikoli Harcourt White, are translated for their benefit. With this device, R. has found a way of keeping a substantial proportion of his audience informed about developments. The device inevitably slows the play down, but R. provides so much incident and action, so much broad comedy and high drama, that the necessary momentum is maintained.

R. has been accused of cultural and theatrical opportunism, as well as attacked on political grounds, by detractors who hold narrower views of what theater should be and who do not share his ideological perspectives. But R.'s true importance should be measured by the extent to which he has contributed to a popular and dynamic Nigerian theater tradition. His plays speak to large audiences in a variety of languages and, as they are intended to do, take the audience through the "giddy gamut" of emotions.

FURTHER WORKS: *Holding Talks* (1977); *Statements towards August 1983* (1983); *Everyone His Own Problem* (1987); *When Criminals Turn Judges* (1990)

BIBLIOGRAPHY: Adedeji, J., "Oral Tradition and the Contemporary Theatre in Nigeria," *RAL,* 2, 2 (1971), 135–49; Sekoni, O., on *Kurunmi, Ba Shiru,* 7, 1 (1976), 80–81; Adelugba, D., "Wale Ogunyemi, Zulu Sofola and O. R.: Three Dramatists in Search of a Language," in Irele, A., and O. Ogunba, eds., *Theatre in Africa* (1978), 201–20; Jeyifo, B., "The Search for a Popular Theatre," in Ogunbiyi, Y., ed., *Theatre and Drama in Nigeria* (1981), 411–21; Crow, B., "Melodrama and the 'Political Unconscious' in Two African Plays," *ArielE,* 14, 3 (1983), 15–31; Lalude, O. O., *Theatre Arts: O. R. and his Works—An Annotated Bibliography* (1984); Osofisan, F., *Beyond Translation: Tragic Paradigms and the Dramaturgy of O. R. and Wole Soyinka* (1986)

JAMES GIBBS

ROVINSKI, Samuel

Costa Rican dramatist, novelist, and short-story writer, b. 13 Nov. 1932, San José

R. was born in San José in 1932 and was educated there until going to the Universidad Autónoma in Mexico City, where he obtained his degree in civil engineering (1956). He pursued the engineering profession until 1971. R. lived in Paris for a time, where he studied filmmaking, and was an advising minister of the Costa Rican embassy in Paris from 1972 to 1975. He has held several important cultural positions in Costa Rica, including the presidency of the Association of Costa Rican Authors (1976) and, in addition to writing, is currently the president of the film enterprise ICARO Productions.

The Teatro Nacional of Costa Rica has premiered several of R.'s works, which have brought him to a position of prominence in Costa Rican theater. R. has also worked significantly in the novel, his only published work in that genre, *Ceremonia de casta* (1976; caste ceremony), receiving critical acclaim, and in the short story. His theater has wide range, from Theater of the Absurd (q.v.) to Brechtian experimentation to plays

concerning conflicts within typical Costa Rican families. He attained great popular success in Costa Rica with *Las fisgonas de Paso Ancho* (1971; the eavesdroppers of Paso Ancho), a farce about social mores in San José, the Costa Rican capital.

The primary concerns of the work of R. have included the impact of modernity on Costa Rican society and the concomitant loss of traditional values, as detailed in *Ceremonia de casta.* This novel recalls *All My Sons* (1947) by Arthur Miller as well as the Sartoris novels of William Faulkner (qq.v.) with its focus on a dying patriarch and his loss of influence over his resentment-ridden family, whose conflicts and historical faults are concentrated in the figure of his outcast bastard son, the narrator of the novel. The house which Juan Matías, the patriarch, tries to keep in the family becomes a metaphor for the changes in Costa Rican society, and which is surrounded by the modern San José. Other concerns important to R. have been political corruption and dictatorship, central to his plays *El laberinto* (1986; the labyrinth), *Gobierno de alcoba* (1986; bedroom government), and *El martirio del pastor* (1983; the martyrdom of the pastor), the latter dramatizing the murder of Archbishop Oscar Arnulfo Romero of El Salvador on 24 March 1980.

R.'s plays are usually experimental, although not forbiddingly so. In *El martirio del pastor,* for example, two film screens are placed on the stage, projecting newsreels showing scenes of rioting, public speaking, and inaugurations that form a counterpoint to the action in the text. *El laberinto* uses sound effects, while *Un modelo para Rosaura* (1974; a model for Rosaura) features an on-stage argument between some of the actors, the director, and the author, with direct address of the audience, about how to interpret and present the second part of the play.

The short stories of R., which have included those collected in *La hora de los vencidos* (1963; the hour of the vanquished), *La pagoda* (1968; the pagoda), and *Cuentos judíos de mi tierra* (1982; Jewish stories of my land), are varied in form and content. Some are relatively traditional in narrative style; others are more adventurous, recalling the intricate texture of his novel. The pieces in *La hora de los vencidos,* as the title indicates, present different protagonists who undergo forms of defeat, but who often—though not always—find some redemption or catharsis through their frustration. *Cuentos judíos de mi tierra* is a collection with apparent autobiographical content. R.'s approach to the Jewish experience is generally more concerned with issues of personal integrity, family survival, and economic problems than with the questions of historicity and political involvement dealt with by Mario Szichman or with the problems of identity emphasized by Isaac Goldemberg (qq.v.). R. has also worked with Jewish material in his play *La víspera del sábado* (1984; Saturday [Sabbath] eve).

R. has detailed his coming of age as a writer in the interesting *Cuarto creciente* (1964; growing quarter), an autobiographical narrative that presents the young R. as a rather introverted potential artist who began his first novel, never finished, as an homage to the doomed World War II struggle of the Jews in the Warsaw ghetto against Nazi occupiers. The book won the National Prize for Essay in Costa Rica in 1964 and was reissued with a new preface in 1987.

R. has been an important cultural force in Costa Rica, because of his triple positions as businessman, politician, and writer. He brings to his work a wide and judicious experience, allowing him to deal with numerous themes, especially in his surprisingly varied short stories. In more recent years, he has been heavily involved in the cinema but has continued to produce literary works. R. is a literary presence deserving of more attention from critics and readers abroad.

FURTHER WORKS: *La Atlántida* (perf. 1960); *Los agitadores* (perf. 1965); *Política cultural de Costa Rica* (1976; *Cultural Policy in Costa Rica*, 1978); *Los pregoneros* (1978); *La guerra de los filibusteros* (film script, 1981); *Los intereses compuestos* (1981); *Gulliver dormido* (1985); *Eulalia* (film script, 1987); *El embudo de Pandora* (1991)

BIBLIOGRAPHY: Herzfeld, A., and T. Cajiao Salas, *El teatro de hoy en Costa Rica: perspectiva crítica y antología* (1973), 47–54; Gallegos, D., Introduction to *Tres obras de teatro* (1985), 7–9; Souza, R. D., "Novel and Context in Costa Rica and Nicaragua," *KRQ*, 33, 4 (Nov. 1986), 453–62; Allen, R. F., ed., *Teatro hispanoamericano: una bibliografía anotada/Spanish American Theatre: An Annotated Bibliography* (1987), 71; Vallbona, R. de, "Costa Rica," in Foster, D. W., comp., *Handbook of Latin American Literature* (1987), 191–202; Rojas, M. A., "*Gulliver dormido* de S. R.: Una parodía del discurso del poder," *LATR*, 24, 1 (1990), 51–63

KENNETH E. HALL

RUDENKO, Mykola

Ukrainian poet, novelist, literary critic, journalist, and dramatist, b. 19 Dec. 1920, Yurivka, Luhansk region

Born into a miner's family, R. completed his secondary education in 1939, and began studies at the philosophical faculty of the Kiev University. He served in the Soviet army, survived the blockade of Leningrad, was severely wounded, recovered, and spent the last moments of World War II again at the front. For his war efforts, R. was awarded various medals including the Order of the Red Star and admitted to the Communist Party. Discharged from the army in 1946, he worked as poetry editor for the journal *Radyansky pysmennyk,* and from 1947 to 1950 he served as editor in chief of the literary journal *Dnipro.*

R.'s early poetic work such as the collection of poetry *Z pokhodu* (1947; from the campaign), his *Nezboryme plemya: Leninhradtsi* (1948; the invincible tribe, the people of Leningrad), as well as his early novels, *Viter v oblychchya* (1955; wind in the face) and *Ostannya shablya* (1959; the last sword) are informed by his war experiences and written, for the most part, according to the tenets of Socialist Realism (q.v.). A somewhat more liberal spirit pervades his science-fiction works, the novels *Charivny bumeranh* (1966; the magical boomerang) and *Slidamy kosmichnoyi katastrofy* (1962; on the tracks of a cosmic catastrophe), and his poetry of the early 1960s. Like many other Ukrainian writers of his generation, R. was influenced by the *shestydesyatnyky,* the young storm-and-stress generation of Ukrainian poets of the 1960s, whose entrance on the literary scene he heartily welcomed in an article published on 30 January 1962, in *Literaturna hazeta,* at that time the official organ of the Union of Ukrainian Writers.

The repression of Ukrainian writers in the 1970s caused R. to revolt. In his writings and his personal appearances he began to lodge various protests against the persecution of the Ukrainian intelligentsia. He was warned several times and finally arrested and tried. On 30 June 1977, R. was convicted of "anti-Soviet agitation and propaganda" and sentenced to seven years of imprisonment and five years of exile. Released in 1987, R. was allowed to emigrate to the West. On 27 January 1988, he arrived in the U.S., where he lived in New York and in Jersey City, N.J., working for the Ukrainian daily *Svoboda* and contributing to Radio Liberty. In 1991 R. returned to his native Ukraine.

R.'s poetry of the 1970s reflects the transition of his weltanschauung from Marxism to what may be termed a Christian humanism. R. realized that "a soulless world is the creation of a bureaucrat," and that the task of the poet, in these spiritless times, is to seek "the human being and the way," and to strive for "goodness and light." In his

SALMAN RUSHDIE

JOSÉ SARAMAGO

SIMONE SCHWARZ-BART

HANĀN AL-SHAYKH

HENRIK STANGERUP

prison poetry, for instance in "Tak prosto vse: napyshesh kayattya" ("Prison Poem," 1978) dated 18 August 1977, he rejects any kind of compromise, preferring the prison walls to "the prison hidden in the human being." His poetry, such as the collections *Prozrinnya* (1978; enlightenment) and *Za gratamy* (1980; behind bars), both published in the West, rejects all totalitarian coercion of the human spirit and restores human conscience to its position of primacy. R.'s metaphysical poetry reached its zenith in the long narrative poem *Khrest* (1979; *The Cross*, 1987), a philosophical attempt to explain the problem of evil, in which the author developed a poignant parallel between the Stalin-made famine in Ukraine (1932–1933) and the crucifixion of Christ.

Most important of R.'s prose works are the *Künstlerroman* entitled *Orlova balka* (1982; eagle's ravine), a search for the meaning of human existence, written under the influence of Dante and the Ukrainian philosopher Hryhory Skovoroda (1722–1794), and a study entitled *Ekonomichni monology* (1978; economic monologues), a trenchant critical analysis of Marxist economics based on his own thinking and on the work of François Quesnay (1694–1774).

R.'s philosophic poetry and imaginative prose, while influenced by such thinkers as Pascal, Kant, and Hegel, are steeped in the Ukrainian poetic tradition. A profound Christian mysticism coupled with a semiotic pantheism inform his work, which bears witness to a tragic period in his country's history.

FURTHER WORKS: *Poeziyi* (1949); *Muzhnist* (1952); *Svitli hlybyny* (1952); *Pereklyk druziv* (1954); *Poeziyi* (1956); *Bila akatsiya* (1962); *Vsesvit u tobi* (1968); *Ya vilny* (1977); *Na dni morskomu* (1981)

BIBLIOGRAPHY: Rudnytzky, L., Introduction to *The Cross* (1987), 7–10; Zyla, W. T., on *The Cross*, *WLT*, 62, 3 (Summer 1988), 478; Rudnytzky, L., "A Miracle in Continuity: Christian Themes and Motifs in Soviet Ukrainian Literature," *UQ*, 46 (1990), 34–44; Black, H., "By Way of Golgotha: Notes on M.R.'s *The Cross*," *America*, 19 Sept. 1991, 3, and 26 Sept. 1991, 4

LEONID RUDNYTZKY

RUKEYSER, Muriel

American poet, translator, and biographer, b. 15 Dec. 1913, New York, N.Y.; d. 12 Feb. 1980, New York, N.Y.

"What would happen if one woman told the truth about her life?" asks R. in her 1968 poem "Käthe Kollwitz," answering herself laconically in the next line, "The world would split open." Throughout an exceptionally prolific forty-five-year career as a poet, R. was notable for trying to tell the truth—not always as a feminist, but always as an honest and clear-eyed commentator on society and on the connection between historical forces and the inner life of individuals.

R.'s career as a writer and an outspoken one began early. While she was still at Vassar College, she joined with other students who were also to leave their mark on American literature—Elizabeth Bishop, Mary McCarthy (qq.v.), and Eleanor Clark (b. 1913)—to found an experimental alternative to the official campus literary magazine. At twenty-one, she received the Yale Series of Younger Poets Award, entailing publication of her first collection of poems, *The Theory of Flight* (1935). From that time until her death, R. remained involved as a writer and a social activist, supporting herself by teaching at Sarah Lawrence College and helping to run New York's House of Photography.

From the first, R.'s poems were recognized as a rare combination of the two meanings of "avant-garde": They showed a mastery of technique, an assimilation of modernism's (q.v.) formal explorations, but they addressed subjects of social concern. Philip Blair Rice in his review of *The Theory of Flight* pointed out that the poems in this collection "are among the few so far written in behalf of the revolutionary cause which combine craftsmanship, restraint, and intellectual honesty." In the 1930s and 1940s, R. wrote poems in support of the labor movement and the antifascist struggle in Spain and eventually throughout Europe. In the postwar period, as such topics became less modish, she continued to speak out—in person and in poetry—about human-rights abuses and against war and imperial aggression. Always sensitive to gender as it intersected with other social issues, her poems became more explicitly feminist in the 1970s.

Another aspect of R.'s modern sensibility is her interest in science and technology, particularly her adoption for poetic purposes of figurative language drawn from contemporary achievements in these areas. As her work developed, she continued to use such metaphors, but tended increasingly to place them at the service of what one reviewer called her "oracular, soothsaying quality." The two come together, for example, in the title of her collection *The Speed of Darkness* (1968), as well as in a number of the poems it contains.

R.'s social and scientific interests are also reflected in her biographies of Willard Gibbs (1942), Wendell Wilkie (1957), and Thomas Hariot (1971). She also published fiction and criticism, the latter in the essays collected in *The Life of Poetry* (1949) and her Clark Lectures, *Poetry and Undeniable Fact* (1968). R. was a sensitive translator and was responsible for making the work of Mexican poet Octavio Paz and Swedish poet Gunnar Ekelöf (qq.v.) available to readers of English.

R.'s involvement with social issues was never restricted to her writing. She was active in support of the causes to which she was committed and took part in protest demonstrations, as well as more decorous efforts. In her later years, she visited Hanoi to express her opposition to the U.S. role in the Vietnam War and, as president of P.E.N. American Center, led a vigil in Seoul in support of South Korean poets imprisoned for their writings. This continued commitment, along with the content of her poems exploring the condition of women, won her a new audience in those years among younger feminists—activists, writers, and critics.

FURTHER WORKS: *Mediterranean* (1938); *U.S. 1* (1938); *A Turning Wind* (1939); *The Soul and Body of John Brown* (1940); *Wake Island* (1942); *Beast in View* (1944); *The Children's Orchard* (1947); *The Green Wave* (1948); *Elegies* (1949); *Orpheus* (1949); *Selected Poems* (1951); *Come Back Paul* (1955); *Body of Waking* (1958); *I Go Out* (1961); *Waterlily Fire: Poems 1932–1962* (1962); *The Orgy* (1966); *Bubbles* (1967); *The Outer Banks* (1967); *Mages* (1970); *Twenty-Nine Poems* (1970); *Breaking Open* (1973); *Early Poems, 1935–1955* (1973); *Brecht's Uncle Eddie's Moustache* (1974); *The Gates* (1976); *The Collected Poems of M. R.* (1978); *More Night* (1981)

BIBLIOGRAPHY: Coles, R., "M. R.'s *The Gates*," *APR*, 7, 3 (1978), 15; DuPlessis, R. B., "The Critique of Consciousness and Myth in Levertov, Rich, and R.," in Gilbert, S. M., and S. Gubar, eds., *Shakespeare's Sisters* (1979), 280–300; Kertesz, L., *The Poetic Vision of M. R.* (1980)

LILLIAN S. ROBINSON

RUSHDIE, Salman
Indian novelist, short-story writer, and critic, (writing in English), b. 19 June 1947, Bombay

R. is perhaps the most controversial novelist of the late 20th c.; he lives under sentence of death at the hands of Islamic fundamentalists and the government of Iran, and thus remains in hiding, presumably somewhere in the British Isles. His books, moreover, have been banned in India, South Africa, and most of the Muslim world. Born in Bombay of Muslim parents, R. has spent most of his adult life in Great Britain but retains ties to three countries: India, Pakistan, and England. He graduated from the Cathedral School in Bombay and took an M.A. (honors) degree in history from King's College, Cambridge in 1968. He has one son from his first marriage in 1976. R. worked as an actor in London from 1968 to 1969 and as a freelance advertising copywriter there from 1970 to 1980. His second marriage, to an American, ended in divorce during his forced underground exile.

In his first novel, *Grimus* (1975), R. introduced his own distinctive narrative technique of magic realism (q.v.), which has been compared to the narratives of Gabriel García Márquez (q.v.). The hero of *Grimus* is Flapping Eagle, a Native American who discovers the meaning of life through a series of bizarre encounters with eccentric characters and supernatural experiences. Myth dominates the lives of all who live on Calf Island, where a Dantesque figure named Virgil serves as guide for Flapping Eagle's journey up Paradise Mountain. However, it was R.'s second novel, *Midnight's Children* (1981), that catapulted him to international literary attention and earned him the Booker McConnell Prize (1981), the English-Speaking Union Award (1981), and the James Tait Black Memorial Prize (1982).

Midnight's Children takes its title from Nehru's speech delivered at the stroke of midnight, 14 August 1947, as India gained its independence from England (coincidentally the year R. was born). R.'s central narrative device is a network of one thousand and one babies, born during the first hour of renascent India, all of whom share the ability to communicate with each other through extrasensory perception. This device permits the author to range widely across geography, caste, and class, as well as employ a multiplicity of perspectives as he handsprings his way through Indian history. Protagonist Saleem Sinai, a man in his early thirties, is both prematurely old and impotent, and must be taken as an allegory for India itself. R.'s fiction is funambulistic—an exhilerating admixture of languages, historical moments, and fantasy. His style, full of puns, allusions, autobiographical elements, satire, and slang, is perfectly suited to the task of plummeting through India's astonishing first three decades.

Having presented India's exuberant history as a historical farce, R. did much the same thing for Pakistan in *Shame* (1983), using an altogether darker lens. As the author admits, in one of many authorial intrusions, he experienced Pakistan in so many fragments that he tends to reflect it in bits of broken mirrors. Through an array of preposterous characters living outrageous lives, R. explores themes of shame and shamelessness, polar opposites that lead to violence. The story evolves into a thinly disguised allegory of two historical figures in the characters of Iskander Harappa, playboy turned politician, modeled on former Prime Minister Zulfikar Ali Bhutto, and General Raza Hyder, Iskander's valued associate and later his executioner, who stands for real-life military dictator Zia-al-Huq. With hyperbole, R. depicts the neglected wives and daughters of the two rivals and cruelly works through the triple whammy of being born a girl-child in an elite family of a patriarchal Islamic society. *Shame* won for R. election to the Royal Society of Literature (1983) and France's Foreign Book Prize (1985).

When *The Satanic Verses* (1988) appeared, it was clear that all of R.'s earlier novels had been merely rehearsals for this chef d'oeuvre that was to cause so much controversy worldwide and earn the Whitbread Award for Fiction (1988).

England, the obvious milieu for an exploration of the immigrant experience, is the setting for this brilliant and disturbing fantasy. The immigrant heroes are Gibreel Farishta, a Bombay film actor who plays Hindu gods, and Saladin Chamcha, a voice dubber who has been successful at "translating" himself into British culture. Victims of an airplane bomb explosion, both men fall to earth and soon after begin their respective physical and moral transformations into the Archangel Gibreel and Satan. These characters allow R. to explore not only the question of what it means to be fully human, but also what it feels like to change cultures abruptly. Although he briefly considers the encounter between different ethnic communities in London, it is R.'s own Islamic heritage that evokes extravagant satire and casts the two heroes in dualistic opposition.

R.'s Islamic critics insist that his creation of the character Mahound, a thinly veiled parody of the prophet Muhammad, is sheer blasphemy. But they would do well to look closely at what R. has chosen to ridicule: the prophet's nine wives, mullahs who refuse to countenance competing orthodoxies, and extreme sects that lead their followers into dangerous waters. These, R. insists, are elements of Islam that no educated Muslim can honestly acknowledge. To treat the prophet so cavalierly may be against the tenets of Islam, but R.'s exaggerated humanization of Mahound is a plea for Islam to make peace with the contemporary world by recognizing the prophet Muhammad as a historical figure and diminishing the rigidity of its belief system. R.'s satire has clearly found a target, for the Muslim world has reacted to his demand for self-scrutiny by rejecting all discussion and sentencing the heretic. To examine *The Satanic Verses* only in its religious dimensions, however, is to do injustice to what is a densely patterned Oriental carpet: boisterous language, film

archetypes, autobiographical experience, and high-spirited plots and subplots. Moreover, as with James Joyce's (q.v.) *Ulysses* (1922), a strong human truth emerges from R.'s multilingual welter: Chamcha/Satan regains his humanness only upon returning to Bombay to care for his dying father and to recognize the integrity of South Asian culture.

Haroun, and the Sea of Stories (1990) is a very different sort of novel, a fantasy of simple dimensions that begs to be read aloud and savored as a tale of good outwitting evil. Emerging from R.'s painful experience of having to live as a hunted criminal, this story depicts a kingdom of darkness that has stopped the motion of the earth so that it may forever keep its people unenlightened and miserable. (In this allegory born of R.'s private hell, read Iran). The heroes, Rashid, a storyteller who has temporarily lost his gift, and his son Haroun, together with Butt the Hoopoe and Iff the Water Genie, manage to defeat Khattam-Shud, Arch-Enemy of Stories and Foe of Speech, and rescue the princess. Weaving together strands from the *Ramayana* and classical Sanskrit story literature, as well as characters from Satyajit Ray films and houseboat life in Kashmir, R. produces an enchanting moral tale studded with puns and artifacts of classical Indian culture. R., like Thomas Pynchon, Gabriel García Márquez, and Günter Grass (qq.v.), is a fabulist whose apocalyptic visions of a disenchanted world both terrify and fascinate. R.'s diction, however, is the most densely exotic, for he stirs in bits of five or six languages, as well as a multitude of disparate contemporary voices. Yet this blend of eclecticism and energy is fully equal to the task of presenting a postcolonial world undergoing unpredictable transformations. In deconstructing the old stabilities and rewriting them, R. generates new cultural confluences awesome in their richness and promise of redemption. Because he does not apologize for the intrusion of an irrepressible South Asian culture, but instead revels in it, R.'s locutions and vision have gained a prominent place in contemporary literature, bringing to the forefront the global dimensions of postmodernism (q.v.).

FURTHER WORKS: *The Jaguar Smile: A Nicaraguan Journey* (1987); *In Good Faith* (1990); *Is Nothing Sacred* (1990); *Imaginary Homelands: Essays and Criticism (1981–1991)* (1991)

BIBLIOGRAPHY: Couto, M., *"Midnight's Children and Parents,"* *Encounter,* 58, 2 (1982), 61–66; Gorra, M., "Laughter and Bloodshed," *HudR,* 37, 1 (1984), 151–64; Grewal, I., "S. R.: Marginality, Women, and *Shame,*" *Genders,* 3 (1988), 24–42; Mukherjee, B., "Prophet and Loss: S.

R.'s Migrations of Souls," *Village Voice Literary Supplement*, 72 (1989), 9–12; Leithauser, B., "Demoniasis," *New Yorker*, 15 May 1989, 124–28; Pipes, D., "The Ayahtollah, the Novelist, and the West," *Commentary*, 87, 6 (1989), 9–17; Mazrui, A., "Is *The Satanic Verses* a Satanic Novel? Moral Dilemmas of the Rushdie Affair," *MQR*, 28, 3 (Summer 1989), 347–71; Tyssens, S., *"Midnight's Children* or the Ambiguity of Impotence," *CE&S*, 12, 1 (1989), 19–29; Srivastava, A., "The Empire Writes Back: Language and History in *Shame* and *Midnight's Children*," *ArielE*, 20, 4 (Oct. 1989), 62–78; Malak, A., "Reading the Crisis: The Polemics of S. R.'s *The Satanic Verses*," *ArielE*, 20, 4 (Oct. 1989), 176–86; Amanuddin, S., "The Novels of S. R.: Mediated Reality in Fantasy," *WLT*, 63, 1 (Winter 1989), 42–45; Edmundson, M., "Prophet of a New Postmodernism: The Greater Challenge of S. R.," *Harper's*, 297 (Dec. 1989), 62–71; King, B., "Satanic Verses and Sacred Cows," *SR*, 98, 1 (Winter 1990), 144–52

JANET M. POWERS

It is generally recognized that the modern novelist is "a special master of language in whom the energies of idiomatic usage, of etymological implication, declare themselves with obvious force," and that the main impulse of current literature is the search for ethnicity. *Midnight's Children* evokes this "lost centre" in language that conveys the ineffable and inescapable "Indianness" of the novelist. He dips into the rich store of religious and social customs, into the physical aspects of identity . . . for a splendid array of metaphor drawn from Indian reality. The rhythmic flow and the high figurative content of Indian languages, myth, fable, belief and superstition are integrated into English prose in joyful profusion to suggest India's many-tongued diversity. In its meandering interpolations, its paradoxical statements, its parabolic patterns, the novel strives to suggest the formlessness of India's all-encompassing form, its ability to "swallow the lot," "to encapsulate the whole of reality." Traditionally, the women of North India were in purdah, and from within its confines peered at a limited view of the world. The metaphor of the hole drawn from this custom suggests the development of a fractured self, and the manner in which the novel is written—gradually, in vignettes of finely observed detail—reveals a mosaic of experience spread over three generations.

Maria Couto, *"Midnight's Children* and Parents," *Encounter*, 58, 2 (1982), 61–66

Shame is in some small degree a *roman à clef* about the relationship between Pakistan's last two dictators, Zulfikar Ali Bhutto and General Zia ul-Haq, but any *clef* is strictly secondary to R.'s consideration of Pakistan itself as a failed act of the imagination. The country's very name is an acronym, he writes, meant to denote the peoples and regions of its western portion—while ignoring the Bengalis who comprised the bulk of its population until the founding of Bangladesh. That irony makes the country's history grotesque from the start, and yet R. hesitates before assaulting it. . . . "Is history," he asks, in one of the many passages in his own voice interpolated into, and commenting on, *Shame's* narrative line, "to be considered the property of the participants solely?" Well, perhaps—but if so, R. can take certain liberties with it, can avoid the "real-life material" that would otherwise "become compulsory," in favor of a symbolic version. R.'s compromise with history is to write about a country that is "not quite" Pakistan, one that occupies the "same space" but exists at "a slight angle to reality," an angle that gives him the freedom upon which this "modern fairy tale" is predicated. . . . His prose prances, a declaration of freedom, an assertion that *Shame* can be whatever he wants it to be, coy and teasing and ironic and brutal all at once. He's been compared to Sterne, but the 18th-c. novelist who comes to my mind is Fielding. To read R. is to re-experience the novel as novel, as new, to recapture Fielding's claim, in *Tom Jones*, to be "the founder of a new province of writing [in which] I am at liberty to make what laws I please." *Shame* is, like *Tom Jones*, full of narrative games, a fiction about fiction that is nevertheless crammed, and finally most concerned with, the vibrant stuff of life.

Michael Gorra, "Laughter and Bloodshed," *HudR*, 37, 1 (Spring 1984), 162

The Satanic Verses is in love with metamorphosis. The best-known of R.'s metamorphoses is, of course, his rather cruel rewriting of the political, personal, and religious life of the prophet Muhammad, who comes off, to the horror of the Islamic devout, looking like a shrewd opportunist. But what R. is trying to do with traditional narratives is what time itself inevitably does. As time separates us further from our stories, they're transformed, they come *to mean* differently. R., with no little presumption, wants to be ahead of time, doing some of history's work for it. (And history, of course, is what those who believe they possess the Word most want to resist: "History is the blood-wine that must no longer be drunk," thinks R.'s exiled imam.) In the case of his rewriting of Muhammad, that means speeding up the work of secularization by vaporizing—in good, negative postmodern fashion—the prophet's holy aura.

But I'm more affected by the kind of *positive* transforming work that *The Satanic Verses* undertakes. Shuttling from London to Bombay, the book dramatizes the blending of two cultures, conjuring a new version of England as a land of immigrants and of India as the potential site of a world culture, at once appalling and exhilarating. R.'s objective is to stand between these two worlds and encourage their fusion; he wants to persuade people on both sides to open themselves to each other, though he's not unsophisticated about the risks involved in such an opening. The book's visions of cultural conjoining tend to be executed with gusto and high good humor. . . .

The prose of *The Satanic Verses* is iridescent, fugue-like: It strives to outspeed as well as out-envision the camera. Perspectives supplant one another and idioms alternate ceaselessly. But the book is also dense, full of layered, striving meanings that sometimes work in clear collaboration, sometimes not.

Mark Edmundson, "Prophet of a New Postmodernism: The Greater Challenge of S. R.," *Harper's*, 297 (Dec. 1989), 66

R.'s imagination is cyclically Hindu and dualistically Muslim, with an extravagant inventiveness that seems pan-Indian. Certainly the Hindu and Islamaic cosmogonies are richer, fictionally speaking, than the Jewish Genesis, and R. uses them both for modern fictional purposes. According to Islam, humanity was brought into a world already seething with dangers, displacing the angels, who remain jealous, yet still subject to corruption by the subhuman, shape-changing djinns. *The Satanic Verses,* in spite of its much-reported brush with Islamic orthodoxy, is a *very* Muslim book. . . .

R. humanizes Mohammed—whose nondivinity is one of the pillars of the faith—but in decidedly contemporary terms. R.'s Mohammed patronizes whores, tolerates a few Arabian tribal gods, and splits the territory with the local competition, Jews and Christians, who've been expanding their franchises on Arabian turf. It's not Mohammed who comes out badly; it's his traditional interpreters, the mullahs, those who've institutionalized Mahound's own fear of self-scrutiny into an aggressive, fortressed denial of all criticism. . . .

One of R.'s more appealing notions (which I hope is not an unfounded flattery) is that immigration, despite losses and confusions, its sheer absurdities, is a net *gain,* a form of levitation, as opposed to Naipaul's loss and mimicry. Of course, the gain is equivocal. Many of us, R. included, trade top-dog status in the homeland for the loss-of-face meltdown of immigration. He dramatizes the pain, that confusion, with a thousand inventions and some very shrewd, dead-on observations. R.'s language is a mask, a way of projecting all the forms of Indian speech at once (bombastic, babu, bureaucratic, Vedantic, vehement, servile, and Sellersish, without mocking or condescending) while remaining true to the essentially damaged, ego-deficient, postcolonial psyche.

Bharati Mukherjee, "Prophet and Loss: S. R.'s Migrations of Souls,"*Village Voice Literary Supplement,* 72 (1989), 9–12

Writers . . . are naturally committed to free speech and to personal freedom; they expect justice and equality. Within nationalism there is increasingly a conflict between free thought and political and cultural unity, a conflict between two forms of modernization, the one experimental and open to change, the other looking to the past as a model. Fundamentalism is a radical traditionalism imposing orthodoxy and order on people who feel threatened by rapid change.

The Satanic Verses shows the conflict between modernization and traditionalism within the Islamic and Third World in the contrast between the exiled imam with his eyes continually on the past and the various immigrants, such as Saladin, who live in a multicultural changing world. But it also embodies the conflict by investigating and questioning traditionalism and the past. We live in an age of large movements of population through immigration, rapid international transportation and communication, global politics, and a world economy in which goods and people continually cross borders. Cultural movements or periods represent significant social, demographic, economic, or political changes . . . and the international controversy concerning *The Satanic Verses* tell[s] us much about what may be truly significant to our culture and time.

Bruce King, "Satanic Verses and Sacred Cows," *SR,* 98, 1 (Winter 1990), 151

RUSSIAN LITERATURE

See Volume 4, page 103.

With the election of Mikhail Gorbachev as secretary-general of the Communist Party of the U.S.S.R. in 1985 and his subsequent proclamation of perestroika, a policy of announced reform and renewal, Russian literature entered the age of glasnost. Usually defined as "openness," glasnost has affected Russian literature in a number of ways. First, it has gradually brought about the elimination of official censorship. There are no guarantees that governmental control over the printed word will not be reinstated, but for the time being the role of censor seems to have passed to editors and, in a sense, to Russian consumers.

The concept of the reader as a consumer leads to a second major consequence of perestroika and the disappearance of censorship, namely, the rapid commercialization of Russian culture as a whole and of literature in particular. Russian publishers now have to think about sales and profits. As a result, poetry, literary criticism, and scholarly editions have fallen on hard times, a situation that many writers and critics naturally view with alarm. As could have been predicted, popular culture is rapidly crowding out the pious highbrow literature that the Soviet state so long subsidized.

In a third significant development, glasnost has firmly resolved the question of whether Russian émigré literature and Russian literature originally written and published in the U.S.S.R. or Russia belong to the same body of writing. Clearly they do, although only now, for the first time since 1917, may one plausibly argue that the most significant Russian-language presses are all in Russia. There, with ever increasing zeal, publishers of newspapers, magazines, and books have been making available to readers works to which they lacked easy or indeed even legal access before the age of glasnost.

Now that glasnost has erased distinctions between writing published in Russia and writing published abroad, Russian literature has reemerged as a single but variegated literature. Naturally, its competing branches, schools, and tendencies reflect both Russian and Soviet tendencies and processes. Consequently, there exists an overtly didactic and ideological mainstream paralleled by a competing but less voluminous countertradition of Russian writing.

Finally, by way of a paradoxical disclaimer, it should be noted that future historians of Russian literature may conclude that glasnost, at least in its early stages, did not fundamentally alter the overall literary landscape that had been visible to commentators abroad well before 1985. After all, many of the works published in Russia within the last few years cannot count as new. Russian journals and publishing houses have been zealously filling in the "blank spots" in their literary history, but many of those spots were blank only in the Soviet Union. Not surprisingly, given the amount of writing only now being published in Russia but already known in *samizdat* or *tamizdat,* at least one critic has argued that Russian literature's present is actually its past.

Poetry

Several of the most interesting poets now publishing were in fact known earlier, if only to the select few who read their verses in limited copies. Now the broader public is making the acquaintance of these poets, several of whom have organized themselves in informal groups.

The two most acclaimed groups of poets, both of them quite heterogeneous in their makeup, are the Conceptualists and the Metaphorists. The Conceptualists number among their ranks Lev Rubinshteyn (b. 1947), Dmitry Prigov (b. 1940), Vsevolod Nekrasov, and Timur Kibirov (dates n.a.). Because of the sense of playfulness and high irony characteristic of Conceptualist verses, critics find in them echoes of such Russian schools of the 1920s as the Futurists and the Oberiu (the latter a Leningrad-based absurdist group).

The Metaphorists, also sometimes referred to as Metarealists or Presentalists, are represented by Aleksey Parshchikov (b. 1954), Aleksandr Yeryomenko (b. 1950), and Viktor Krivulin (dates n.a.), among others. Close to this movement, but younger than any of its members, is Tatyana Shcherbina (dates n.a.). An even less coherent school than the Conceptualists, the Metaphorists nonetheless reveal many of the same influences. On the whole, however, their verses are much less accessible than those of the Conceptualists, and in general the work of the Metaphorists invites the classification of postmodern.

Not associated with any group, but a poet who has recently attracted considerable attention both at home and abroad, is Olesya Nikolaeva (b. 1956). In her poetry, startlingly rich in its stylistic diversity, Nikolaeva shows a concern for spiritual and moral questions. All the poets mentioned here reveal a greater affinity with the techniques and concerns of Russian poets of the early part of the 20th c. than with those of their contemporaries and immediate predecessors.

Prose Fiction and Nonfiction

Broadly speaking, most genuinely new works of prose represent one of two traditions—the overtly ideological mainstream or the nonmainstream, nonideological countertradition. The mainstream itself consists of two competing but complementary orientations—conservative and liberal. Conservative writers, usually Russophiles opposed to liberal democracy, have grouped themselves around the journals *Nash Sovremennik, Molodaya Gvardia,* and *Moskva.* The liberals publish in such journals as *Druzhba Narodov, Znamia, Yunost,* and the venerable *Novy Mir.* The last two journals additionally provide a home for most of the nonmainstream, countertraditional writing.

Both conservatives and liberals admire, Aleksandr Solzhenitsyn (q.v.), in whose works one finds nearly all the themes that typify the literature of glasnost. At the nexus of those concerns lies the Stalinist past and its impact on Russian life today. Solzhenitsyn's aesthetics and ethics grow out of his fellow Russian writers, whether conservatives or liberals. The result is a decidedly monologic mainstream literature not always easily distinguishable from monochrome journalism.

No new names have arisen among the conservatives, many of whom represent village prose. The insularity and xenophobia that always marked much of the writing of that school have now evolved into undisguised Russian chauvinism, antidemocratism, anti-Westernism, and anti-Semitism. These aspects of conservative literary ideology are most apparent in the novella *Pechalny detektiv* (1986; a sad detective story) and the story "Lovlia peskarei v Gruzii" (1986; gudgeon fishing in Georgia) by Viktor Astafev (b. 1924); the novel *Vsyo vperedi* (1986; *The Best Is Yet To Come,* 1989) by Vasily Belov (b. 1932); the novel *Sudny den* (1988; judgment day) by Viktor Ivanov (b. 1932); and published remarks by the novelist Valentin Rasputin (q.v.).

Many of the liberals are no less overtly ideological than the conservatives, and their prose is often no less monologic, especially in such major works of glasnost as *Deti Arbata* (1987; *Children of the Arbat,* 1988) by Anatoly Rybakov (b. 1911), *Zubr*

(1987; *The Bison,* 1990) by Daniil Granin (b. 1919), and *Belye odezhdy* (1987; *White Garments,* 1989).

Several of the most interesting writers of the liberal traditionalist school, in fact, began publishing much earlier but did not really make their mark until the era of glasnost. Thus, most of the "new names" among the liberals are not particularly young or inexperienced writers. Several of these authors, each in his own way, write most of all about history. In *Nepridumannoe* (1989; true stories) Lev Razgon (b. 1908) reminisces about leading figures in the arts and politics both inside and outside the camps during the Stalin period. Boris Yampolsky (dates n.a.) shares Razgon's interest in depicting the Stalinist terror; his *Moskovskaya ulitsa* (1988; a Moscow street) paints a terrifying portrait of someone awaiting arrest in the late 1940s. In *Kapitan Dikshteyn* (1987; "Captain Dikshtein," 1990), *Nochnoy dozor* (1989; the night watch), and "Petya po doroge v Tsarstvie Nebesnoe" (1991; Pete on the way to the Heavenly Kingdom), Mikhail Kuraev (b. 1939) narrates Soviet history from the point of view of average people largely unable to make sense of the quite fantastic events transpiring around them. Vyacheslav Petsukh (b. 1946) offers witty, but ultimately superficial commentary on manifold aspects of Russian and Soviet history in his *Novaya moskovskaya filosofia* (1989; the new Moscow philosophy) and *Rommat* (1990; Rommat).

Other "new" authors identified with glasnost write about contemporary life. Of them, Anatoly Genatulin (b. 1925) is the most conventional. His favorite theme is the moral and physical rigors of life in the Bashkirian village. When not writing as a professional economist, Nikolay Shmelyov (b. 1936) pens straightforward tales about contemporary urban mores and morals. Gennady Golovin (b. 1941), whose most recent collection of stories bears the title *Terpenie i nadezhda* (1988; patience and hope), draws on the styles and themes of classical Russian writers for his tales of people hard-pressed by the vicissitudes of life today.

Critics have dubbed the current countertradition in Russian prose "the other prose." On the whole, this extremely heterogenous school of writing tries to ignore seventy years or so of Soviet Russian literature and to take up where the experimentalists and countertraditionalists of the 1920s left off. Some of the writers associated with "the other prose" evoke the greatest interest because of their stylistics, others because of their thematics. The brightest star among the former, Tatyana Tolstaya (q.v.), writes philosophical stories whose richly metaphorical style calls to mind Yury Olesha (q.v.). Several of Tolstaya's narratives are collected in the volume *Na zolotom kryltse sideli* (1987; *On*

the Golden Porch, 1989). Valeria Narbikova (b. 1960) shares Tolstaya's love of metaphor, while her intoxication with language itself suggests an affinity with the futurist poet Velemir Khlebnikov (q.v.). A very different sort of writer, Tatyana Nabatnikova (dates n.a), treats the age-old battle of the sexes with verve and insouciance.

The second group have caused the greatest stir not because of their styles, also nontraditional and worthy of comment, but because of their thematics. Their works consistently treat aspects of social and personal life generally excluded from the Russian literary tradition until now. As a consequence, such works are often referred to collectively as *chernukha,* a word that suggests unrelieved darkness and gloom. In his *Smirennoe kladbishche* (1987; *The Humble Cemetery,* 1990), Sergey Kaledin (b. 1949) portrays grave diggers at work and rest, for instance. Viktor Yerofeev (b. 1947) shocks readers with physiological detail and the depiction of mindless violence. The characters in the short stories of Lyudmila Petrushevskaya (q.v.) seem to have emerged from a social worker's case book. Svetlana Vasilenko (b. 1956) writes of women and death in tragic tones. All in all, because of its exploration of new possibilities for theme, language, and style, many critics, both at home and abroad, feel that the future of Russian literature now lies with "the other prose."

Drama

As with prose fiction, Russian dramas and dramatists working in the glasnost era fall into two general categories: traditionalist and alternative. The new plays published by the traditionalists in Russia since 1985 generally explore the past or expose the present. The dramatist who has shown the greatest interest in the early days of the Soviet regime is Mikhail Shatrov (pseud. of Mikhail Marshak, b. 1932). His *Brestsky mir* (1987; the peace of Brest-Litovsk) and *Vperyod, vperyod, vperyod* (1988; forward, forward, forward) explode many of the clichés of preglasnost official Soviet history while nonetheless leaving intact the Lenin cult.

The veteran dramatists Aleksandr Galin (b. 1947), Aleksandr Gelman (b. 1933), and Igor Gorin (b. 1940) have all had plays staged and published that reflect various aspects of perestroika. Representative is Galin's *Zvyozdy na utrennem nebe* (1988; *Stars in the Morning Sky,* 1988), which portrays the life of prostitutes, whose very existence as social group was officially denied before glasnost.

Petrushevskaya remains the most significant alternative dramatist. Such plays of hers as *Tri devushki v golubom* (1980; *Three Girls in Blue,* 1988) and *Chinzano* (1973; *Cinzano,* 1989) depict aimless lives in moral voids. Other noteworthy alternative dramatists include Nikolay Kolyada (b. 1957) and Viktor Korkia (dates n.a.). Like Petrushevskaya, Kolyada shocks Russian audiences with depictions of milieus previously unimaginable on the Soviet or Russian stage. Kolyada's *Rogatka* (1989; the slingshot), for instance, portrays a gay relationship between an older alcoholic cripple and a much younger man. Korkia's absurdist leanings are apparent in his *Cherny chelovek, ili ya bedny Soso* (1988; the black man, or, I am poor Soso), whose protagonists are Stalin and Beria. In both language and theme, plays by Petrushevskaya and other nontraditional dramatists invite comparison with "the other prose."

Criticism

Judged by Western standards, Russian literary criticism in the age of glasnost remains primarily a boundary genre in which history, philosophy, sociology, and polemical journalism sometimes commingle. Critics for whom literature is indisputably a matter of ideology fall, predictably, into two camps—conservatives and liberals. The most influential conservative critics, many of them opposed to liberal reform, include Vadim Kozhinov (b. 1930), Sergey Vikulov (b. 1922), and Mark Lyubomudrov (dates n.a.), the latter a theater critic.

The critic most identified with reform and glasnost is the talented Natalya Ivanova (b. 1945), whose articles are collected in *Tochka zrenia* (1988; point of view) and *Voskreshenie nuzhnykh veshchey* (1990; the resurrection of needed things). Other critics who treat literature in a way and tone congenial to Western liberals are Tatyana Ivanova (dates n.a.), author of *Krug chtenia* (1988; circle of reading); Igor Dedkov (b. 1934), a recent volume of whom bears the title *Obnovlyonnye zrenie* (1988; renewed vision); Igor Zolotussky (b. 1930), recent pieces by whom may be found in *Ispoved Zoila* (1989; Zoilus's confession); and the extraordinarily witty Natalya Ilina (b. 1914). Representing the countertradition of Russian criticism, what the 19th c. called "aesthetic criticism," is Viktor Yerofeev. His efforts to draw a line between literature and didacticism, imaginative writing and prophecy, often enrage Russian readers.

BIBLIOGRAPHY: Special Russian-literature issue entitled *Perestroika and Soviet Culture: The New Soviet Prose, MQR,* 28, 4 (1989); Zalygin, S., ed., *The New Soviet Fiction* (1989); Goscilo, H., and B. Lindsey, eds., *Glasnost: An Anthology of Russian Literature under Gorbachev* (1990)

DAVID A. LOWE

SABINES, Jaime

Mexican poet, b. 25 Mar. 1926, Tuxtla Gutiérrez, Chiapas

S. was born and has spent most of his life in Chiapas. He studied medicine and literature as a young man in Mexico City during the late 1940s and early 1950s. During that time, S. became involved with the so-called "América" group, which included such future literary figures as Emilio Carballido and Rosario Castellanos (qq.v.). But S. has steadfastly refused to live amidst or participate in the tumultuous and heady literary circles of the capital on a long-term basis, preferring instead the provincial Chiapas. Moreover, even though he enjoys considerable stature in Mexican letters, S. has chosen to make his living in the business world and not that of academia.

In spite of the fact that S. and his poetry have been critically acclaimed, the poet openly disavows poetic convention and technique. The result has been that S. has also produced some poetry of uneven quality. Most critics point to the obvious lack of trajectory or development throughout some thirty years of poetry, suggesting, therefore, a surprising lack of growth or maturation. Nevertheless, S. has received a wide variety of literary awards, including the Chiapas Prize (1960), the Xavier Villaurrutia Award (1972), and the National Prize for Literature (1983).

S. established himself in the 1950s as a major poet by producing four collections. The first, *Horal* (1950; horal), revealed a number of elements and preoccupations that S. would treat in his subsequent poetry: death, alienation, despair, and fear, all presented with shocking intensity. It was a highly lyrical poetry of transcendental inspiration. *La señal* (1951; the sign) continued in the vein of *Horal*, emphasizing death as the one constant of life. S. revealed deeper and darker shadows un-

derscoring a suffocating reality marked by the marginal time or mortality. Additionally, it was a poetry of bitterness and fear.

Perhaps S.'s most provocative work came in 1956 with *Tarumba* (tarumba), a kind of confessional-testimonial cry that is at once violent, sordid, and aggressive. It smacked of self-indulgence and self-preoccupation, but it caught the attention of writers and critics alike, many of whom were intrigued by its experimental nature. In the broadest sense, the work represents the author's intense reaction to his natural state. *Tarumba,* with its cynicism, clamoring, and disdain has helped support an image of S. as a counterhero of sorts, somewhat akin to the beat poets of the 1950s and 1960s in the U.S.

During the 1960s, S. published several collections of poetry and began experimenting with poetic prose, a literary form that he would continue to cultivate. Of particular interest is *Diario semanario y poemas en prosa* (1961; weekly diary and poetry in prose). Using a wide range of everyday topics, S. embarked on a lyrical investigation of the ordinary, in prose, that reflects his already established poetic view as poet. *Diario semanario* exhibits a socially conscious poet who, for the first time in his literature, espouses what might be considered an emerging ideological position.

Yuria (yuria), written in 1967, is a collection of twenty-six poems, thirteen of which were written in poetic prose. It has been judged by critics as extremely irregular in quality. Perhaps its most noteworthy feature is its political orientation relative to its defense of the Cuban revolution, coupled with a distinct anti-American point of view. *Maltiempo* (1972; bad times), S.'s last collection of published works, was also received with widely differing critical evaluations. It is laced with pessimism and despair, suggesting a futility of life. Some critics see in *Maltiempo* S.'s emerging view that poetry is no longer an efficacious manner in which to confront or examine the world.

Nuevo recuento de poemas (1977; new recompilation of poems) was a collection of all of S.'s poetry in one volume—a major testament to the poet's breadth and importance as an artist. Since *Nuevo recuento* S. has not continued to produce published poetry. Some critics suggest that S. has lost faith in poetry and no longer chooses to write.

Only time will tell whether S. will break his self-imposed poetic silence, but it is certain that S. occupies a major position in 20th-c. Mexican poetry. Both his poetry and poetic prose have earned the author recognition as an outstanding artist.

FURTHER WORKS: *Adán y Eva* (1952); *En mis labios te sé* (1961); *Recuento de poemas* (1962);

Dos poemas = Two poems (1967); *Poemas sueltos* (1981); *Crónicas del volcán* (1988)

BIBLIOGRAPHY: Durán, M., "J. S. and Mario Antonio Montes de Oca: A Study in Contrast," *Mundus Artium*, 3, 2 (1970), 44–55; Dietrick, C. P., "Breaking Myth, Making Myth: 'Así es' by J. S.," *Chasqui*, 4, 1 (1974), 34–49; Mansour, M., "J. S.: Malestares y desconciertos," *Plural*, 12, 4 (1983), 38–45; Mansour, M., "Estructuras rítmicas y ritmo semántico en la poesía: Un poema de J. S.," *TCrit*, 10, 29 (1984), 159–72; Hurtado, E., "J. S.: el inútil milagro del misterio," *México en el Arte*, 14 (1986), 125–26; *La poesía en el corazón del hombre: J. S. en sus sesenta años* (1987); Armenjol, A., "El experimento de J. S.: estudio de *Tarumba*," *Plural*, 17, 199 (1988), 25–35

SAM L. SLICK

SA'EDI, Gholam-Hossein

(pseud.: Gowhar Morad) Iranian dramatist, short-story writer, screenwriter, and novelist; b. 1935, Tabriz; d. 24 Nov. 1985, Paris, France

S. was born to the poverty-stricken family of a tailor apprentice turned civil servant. He spent his childhood in Tabriz, where he received his secondary education. From the time he learned to read, he was a lover of literature. Even when he was in medical school in Tabriz and Tehran, he said that for every medical book he read, he read ten novels. Writing became second nature, first for newspapers and then his own fiction and nonfiction. By the time he died one month short of his fiftieth birthday, he had more than forty works to his credit.

S. was an engaging writer committed to the improvement of the lot of the poor and downtrodden. His commitment to destitute people led him to open a doctor's office in the poor section of Tehran, where he offered psychiatric consultations free of charge. S. also became an amateur anthropologist who traveled around the country studying the living conditions of people in rural areas and writing about their experiences. He was arrested several times for these sociopolitical activities and in 1974–1975 spent eleven months in prison.

S.'s visit to the U. S. in 1978 under the auspices of a group of American writers and publishers turned into a crusade for freedom of expression in Iran, and was well-reflected in three articles in the *New York Times* and one in the *Washington Post*. S.'s desire for freedom of expression made him settle in France during the revolutionary upheaval in Iran. Heartbroken and far from home, he died in exile in Paris.

S. must be considered the leading dramatist of Iran. His plays, marked by political symbolism and allegory, combine elements of the traditional Iranian performing arts, Western classical drama, and the Theater of the Absurd (q.v.). Though S.'s plays are set predominantly in Iranian locales, they transcend national and artistic boundaries as they join the universal battle against tyranny, oppression, alienation, poverty, suffering, and ignorance. Even when S. objects to the blind copying of the Western life-style by Iranians, it has a universal dimension. He sees national customs, traditions, and ways of life as complementing other people and nations rather than creating separation.

S. began his career as a dramatist in 1957 with the publication in literary magazines of three short one-act plays. This was followed by a collection of one-act plays under the title *Panj namayesh-nameh az enqelab-e mashrutiyyat* (1966; five plays from the constitutional revolution). These one-act plays should be regarded as studies that S. wrote to test his skills in playwriting fundamentals such as unity of time and action. The action in these plays takes place in his native Azerbaijan during the constitutional movement from 1905 until the coup by Reza Khan, later Reza Shah. Social and national issues underline the action of the plays. In his next collection of one-act plays, *Khaneh rowshani* (1967; housewarming), S. brings in complex psychological problems that no doubt were drawn from his psychiatric practice. Some of the plays from the first and second collections were well received by television viewers. Symbolism and allegory play an important role in S.'s writing and go hand in hand with the stark realism. However, in his *Dah lal bazi* (1963; ten pantomimes) S. departs from a realistic portrayal and plunges into a surrealistic world bordering on the absurd.

S.'s first full-length play was *Karbafakha dar sangar* (1960; *Workaholics in the Trenches*, 1989). The play, which deals with the ecological dangers to the shores of the Persian Gulf posed by development of a sulfur mine and processing plant, probably would have fared well in the Western world today. Against this background, the play tells the story of a young, newly married engineer and his wife. It is a strong commentary on how rapid industrialization in a traditional society uproots individuals and groups of people. *Chub be Dastha-ye Varazil* (1965; the stick wielders of Varazil) is a highly symbolic play, in which the fields of poor villagers are being destroyed by wild boars. However, it is the hunters invited to take care of the boars who pose the greater threat to the villagers' meager wealth. It is easier for the villagers to cope with the hardship represented by boars than by their "liberators." Another community unable to fend off danger is portrayed in the play *A-ye bi Kolah, A-ye ba Kolah* (1967; *O Fool, O Fooled*, 1987). In *Mah-e Asal* (1978; *Honeymoon*, 1989), the last play he wrote in Iran before emigrating to Paris, he portrays the life of an individual in a police state. It is a strong condemnation of the Iran of the 1970s. S.'s last plays, written in exile and published posthumously, are *Pardedaran-e a'ineh afruz* (1986; the mirror-polishing storytellers) and *Otello dar sarzamin-e ajayeb* (1986; Othello in wonderland). Both are sardonic attacks on the Islamic Republic of Iran's enforcement of behavior patterns acceptable to the new, revolutionary standards as well as the war with Iraq, in which young men die only to bring anguish to their families.

S.'s screenplays are as powerful as his plays, and several movies based on his screenplays received international awards. *Gav* (the cow) won the 1971 Venice Film Festival Award, and *Day-ere-ye Mina* (the cycle) earned an award at the 1977 International Paris Film Festival. The screenplays are based on S.'s short stories. He has six stories to his credit: "Shabneshini ba Shokuh" (1960; the splendid evening party), "Azadaran-e bayal" (1964; the mourners of bayal), "Dandil" (1966; "Dandil," 1981), "Vahemenha-ye bi nam-o neshan" (1967; vague misgivings), "Tars-o larz" (1968; fear and trembling), and "Gur-o gahvareh" (1972; the grave and the cradle).

In both his dramas and short stories, S. is interested in the common human being's daily struggles, fears, hopes, and sorrows. The stories are like vignettes of Iranian life with real people and their national and religious customs, full of human irony and political metaphor. As a dramatist S. was influenced by Samuel Beckett, Eugène Ionesco (qq.v.), and the Theater of the Absurd.

S.'s novel is entitled *Tup* (1967; the cannon). The few issues of S.'s magazine *Alefba*, which he tried to continue in France, are further monuments to his genius and versatility.

FURTHER WORKS: *Kalate-ye gol* (1961); *Behtarin baba-ye donia* (1965); *Dikteh va zaviyeh* (1968); *Parvarbandan* (1969); *Janeshin* (1970); *Vay bar maghlub* (1970); *Aqebat-e qalam-e farsai* (1975); *In dar on dar* (1975). FURTHER VOLUME IN ENGLISH: *Dandil: Stories from Iranian Life* (1981)

BIBLIOGRAPHY: Hillmann, M. C., ed., *LE&W*, 20 (1976), 144–47; Southgate, M. S., *Modern Persian Short Stories* (1980), 180–201; Javadi, H., Introduction to *Dandil: Stories from Iranian Life* (1981), vii–xiii; Jabbari, A., and R. Olson, eds., *Iran: Essays on a Revolution in the Making* (1981), 130–33; Kapuscinski, G., *Modern Persian Drama* (1987), xiii–xvii, 101–73; Ghanoonparvar, M. R., and J. Green, *Iranian Drama* (1989), xxi–xxii, 1–132; Hillmann, M. C., *Iranian Culture: A Persianist View* (1990), 111–18

PETER J. CHELKOWSKI

SALAZAR BONDY, Sebastián

Peruvian dramatist, b. 1924, Lima; d. 4 July 1965, Lima

S. B. was one of the most successful and prolific 20th-c. Peruvian authors. His writings spanned the spectrum from drama and essay to poetry and prose fiction. A graduate of the University of San Marcos, he traveled widely abroad and worked for many years as a journalist and drama critic. From 1948 to 1950 he lived in Buenos Aires as a correspondent for *La Nación*. He received a scholarship from the French government enabling him to study at the National Conservatory of Dramatic Arts in Paris. In 1953, shortly after his return to Peru, he founded the Club de Teatro de Lima, an important theater group that staged foreign as well as local plays and became a major factor in the revitalization of Peruvian drama.

S. B. was the leading dramatist in his country during the first half of the 20th c. Productions of his plays had successful runs not only in Lima but also in Buenos Aires and other South American cities. Ranging from serious drama to comedy and including full-length as well as one-act pieces, his theatrical works made good use of dialogue while conveying irony and humor and allowing readers and spectators glimpses of the characters' psychological makeup. S. B.'s first play, the satirical farce *Amor, gran laberinto* (perf. 1946, pub. 1948; love, great labyrinth), won the national theater prize in 1947, an award he received again in 1952 for the historical drama *Rodil* (1952; Rodil). His two best plays were the three-act tragedy *No hay isla feliz* (1954; there is no happy island), a social drama on the theme of frustration that portrayed the spiritual downfall of a middle-class family, and *El fabricante de deudas* (perf. 1962, pub. 1964; the debt maker), a lighter work in two acts inspired by Balzac's *Le faiseur* and employing the Brechtian technique of allowing the characters to speak directly to the audience. In 1965 he won a third national theater prize (given posthumously) for the one-act drama *El rabdomante* (1965; the diviner), his final play. He also coauthored, with César Miró Quesada (b. 1907), a modern version of the Quechua drama *Ollantay* (1953; Ollantay) and collaborated on *La escuela de los chismes* (1965), an adaptation of a classic 18th-c. work, Sheridan's *The School for Scandal*.

SALAZAR BONDY

Although S. B. made his most important contributions in the field of drama, his initial publication was a volume of poetry, *Rótulo de la esfinge* (1943; sign of the sphinx), produced in collaboration with Antenor Samaniego (b. 1919). Numerous collections followed, and he maintained an active interest in the genre throughout the remainder of his life. At the time of his death in 1965, he was working on yet another book of verse, *El tacto de la araña* (1966; the spider's touch).

In addition to the drama and poetry S. B. also penned numerous journalistic pieces. In these nonfiction writings he was concerned with social problems relating to the indigenous population and was highly critical of Peru's social structure, especially the Lima aristocracy. His polemical book-length essay *Lima, la horrible* (1964; Lima the horrible) challenged the nostalgic, picturesque evocation of life during the Viceroyalty in Ricardo Palma's (1833–1919) famous *Tradiciones peruanas* (Peruvian traditions). According to S. B.'s revisionist X ray of the city, the portrait of society contained in the *Tradiciones peruanas* was incomplete and therefore false, because Palma, despite his incisive social and political satire, failed to denounce the exploitation of the country's indigenous citizens.

As a short-story writer S. B. examined philosophical questions as well as contemporary problems of urban life. The stories in *Náufragos y sobrevivientes* (1954; shipwrecked souls and survivors), written in an existentialist vein, dealt with distorted values, hypocrisy, and corruption. Another prose work, *Pobre gente de París* (1958; poor people of Paris), was composed of vignettes about young Latin Americans living in France and their common feeling of uprootedness. A posthumous novel, *Alférez Arce, Teniente Arce, Capitán Arce* (1969; Ensign Arce, Lieutenant Arce, Captain Arce), departed from the traditional linear format by employing multiple narrative perspectives and flashbacks.

S. B. was one of a group of Peruvians who in the 1950s began to write about the city, focusing on social and political problems and incorporating universal themes along with technical advances. Appearing on the literary scene at a time when support and interest were low, S. B. led a resurgence in the arts in his country. Perhaps the most revealing indication of S. B.'s significance can be seen in the influence he exerted on authors of his and the succeeding generation. The universally acclaimed Peruvian novelist Mario Vargas Llosa (q.v.) acknowledged his intellectual debt and paid homage to his fellow countryman by writing a prologue to S. B.'s *Obras* (3 vols., 1967; complete works) and by dedicating a book, the short novel *Los cachorros* (1967; *The Cubs*, 1979), to S. B.'s memory.

536

SÁNCHEZ

FURTHER WORKS: *Bahía del dolor, Sinfonía del alma y Tránsito a la muerte* (1944, with Antenor Samaniego); *Voz desde la vigilia* (1944); *Cuaderno de la persona oscura* (1946); *Poesía contemporánea del Perú* (1946); *Máscara del que duerme* (1949); *Tres confesiones* (1950); *Pantomimas* (1950); *Los ojos del pródigo* (1951); *Algo que quiere morir* (1956); *Antología general de la poesía peruana* (1957); *Seis juguetes* (1958); *Dos viejas van por la calle* (1959); *Conducta sentimental* (1960); *Teatro* (1961); *Confidencia en alta voz* (1964); *Poesía quechua* (1964)

BIBLIOGRAPHY: Monguió, L., *La poesía postmodernista peruana* (1954), 180–81, 232–33; Hesse Murga, J. H., Prologue to *Teatro peruano contemporáneo,* 2nd ed. (1963), 21–24; Powell, O. B., untitled article on S. B., *Américas,* Oct. 1965, 39; Aldrich, E. M., Jr., *The Modern Short Story in Peru* (1966), 147–49; Jones, W. K., *Behind Spanish American Footlights* (1966), 269–71; Gómez Gil, O., *Historia crítica de la literatura hispanoamericana* (1968), 730–31; Franco, J., *The Modern Culture of Latin America: Society and the Artist,* rev. ed. (1970), 225–38; Morris, R. J., *The Contemporary Peruvian Theatre* (1977), 28–40; McMurray, G. R., *Spanish American Writing since 1941: A Critical Survey* (1987), 118–19, 292–95

MELVIN S. ARRINGTON, JR.

SÁNCHEZ, Luis Rafael
Puerto Rican novelist, short-story writer, dramatist, and essayist, b. 17 Nov. 1936, Humacao

S. was born in a small Puerto Rican city, far from the capital, on the southern portion of the island, not far from the sea, and as a child he lived in the rather small quarters of a public-housing development. He completed a doctorate, and became a professor of literature, eventually joining the faculty at the University of Puerto Rico. His teaching career has been quite distinguished, and S. has often participated in international university conferences and literary symposia. He has recently accepted a teaching appointment at the City College in New York.

S. started his career as a dramatist with the publication of a few plays that have been performed in Puerto Rico since the late 1950s. These early works announced his talent but did not achieve the status of *La pasión según Antígona Pérez* (1968; the passion according to Antígona Pérez), a vigorous text that examines an archetypal Latin American dictatorship, and focuses on the unnecessary suffering of young people against a backdrop of false pretenses and indifference. Although indeed remarkable, the play does not approximate the impact of a previous work that reveals S.'s exceptional talent: his first collection of short stories, *En cuerpo de camisa* (1966; in shirt sleeves). The fifteen stories that comprise this volume—four have been added since the first edition—although seemingly unrelated, have in common a profound interest in people, especially the ones suffering from the incomprehension of others, the marginal, the weak, and the destitute.

S.'s style is rich in vernacular expressions and quite successfully explores the poetry of everyday language. In that sense it has been said that some, if not most, of his work has been written in "Puerto Rican," and although that is a fair assessment of one aspect of his writing, it is not all. The language of his characters accurately reflects their predicaments, and becomes an allusion to social stratification. The orality of S.'s style tends to open the text, rather than confine it to a specific region.

In addition to his teaching and multiple contributions in periodical publications, S. wrote a few more stage productions, and ten years after the publication of *En cuerpo de camisa* he published his first novel, *La guaracha del Macho Camacho* (1976; *Macho Camacho's Beat*, 1982). This text has enjoyed a great deal of critical attention, and it is by far the best known of S.'s works to date. S.'s poignant criticism of the manipulation of people's minds by the mass media, his vehement attack on political corruption, social discrimination, and sexual exploitation, make *La guaracha del Macho Camacho* a formidable document. Reality, however, is enhanced—and at the same time subtly subdued—by S.'s sense of humor and the incomparable richness of his imagery. S.'s exuberant narration betrays a certain bitterness about reality in Puerto Rico and the rest of "America the invaded." The characters are archetypal, and the situations are sufficiently distorted to become a parody of some elusive reality. It has been repeated that "nothing happens" in the novel. Nothing happens, except everything.

S.'s second novel, *La importancia de llamarse Daniel Santos* (1988; the importance of being called Daniel Santos), is a celebration of the language, the culture, and the peoples of Spanish-speaking America. An impressive inventory of popular culture, intertwined with nearly obsessive intertextual references to the most notable writings of the history of Western literature (Shakespeare, Kafka, Tennessee Williams, Borges, Sor Juana, Proust, Carpentier, Neruda, and Baudelaire, among a host of others), *La importancia de llamarse Daniel Santos* is a most enjoyable text. Daniel Santos, a popular singer, incarnates the multifaceted spirit of very dissimilar societies that in spite of their differences share language, misery, and an unquenchable desire for living. The text, again, is chaotic, repetitive—S. is particularly fond of the use of *anaphora*—and written with a particular flare for vernacular expressions that transcend the Puerto Rican dialect. There is a very reverent, and skillful, blending of very diverse linguistic manifestations, from the highly cultivated to the very foul, that enhances the carefully structured prose of a writer who knows exactly what he wants to say and exactly how he wants to say it.

FURTHER WORKS: *La espera* (1959); *Sol 13, Interior* (1961); *Farsa del amor compradito, o casi el alma* (1966); *Quíntuples* (1985)

BIBLIOGRAPHY: Rodríguez, M. C., "Poor-Black, Rich-White: Women in *La guaracha del Macho Camacho*," *Studies in Afro-Hispanic Literature*, 2–3 (1978–1979), 244–54; García Castro, R., "*La guaracha del Macho Camacho* de L. R. S. y 'que sepa abrir la puerta para ir a jugar' de Julio Cortázar," *Chasqui*, 9 (Feb.–May 1980), 71–74; Santos Silva, L., "*La pasión según Antígona Pérez*: La mujer como reafirmadora de la dignidad política," *RevI*, 11, 3 (Fall 1981), 438–43; Guinnes, G., "*La guaracha* in English: Traduttore traditore," *REH*, 8 (1981), 107–22; Agura, H. C., and J. A. Englebert, "L. R. S. Speaks about *Macho Camacho's Beat*," *Review*, 28 (1981), 39–41; Zalacain, D., "*La Antígona* de S.: Recreación puertorriqueña del mito," *ExTL*, 9, 2 (1981), 111–18; Colón Zayas, E. R., *El teatro de L. R. S.* (1985); Gelpi, J., "La cuentística antipatriarcal de L. R. S.," *Hispam*, 15, 43 (Apr. 1986), 113–20

HORACIO XAUBET

SANDEL, Cora

(pseud. of Sara Fabricius) Norwegian novelist and short-story writer, b. 20 Dec. 1880, Oslo; d. 3 Apr. 1974, Uppsala, Sweden

S. is one of 20th-c. Norway's most admired novelists and short-story writers. She was born in Oslo, and her family moved to the northern city of Trømso when she was twelve, a difficult move for the child who resented the provincialism of the smaller city as well as its cold climate and long periods of winter darkness. Aspiring to be a painter, S. moved to France in 1905 and for the next fifteen years struggled to scrape together a living while pursuing her artistic ambitions. In part she supported herself by writing articles for Norwegian newspapers and in this way began to develop her writing talent. Also during these years in France, she got married and divorced. In 1920 S. moved to Sweden, where she resided for the rest of her life.

S.'s major work is a trilogy of novels about her fictional alter ego, Alberte, the first volume of which was published when she was forty-six: *Alberte og Jakob* (1926; *Alberte and Jacob,* 1962). It tells the story of Alberte's childhood in her northern city above the polar circle. Through careful selection of sensuous detail S. vividly communicates Alberte's dread at the harsh climate, her family's near-poverty, and the awful respectability of the town's middle-class ladies with their "oil cloth sofas and porcelain dogs." As the first volume ends, Alberte half-heartedly attempts to commit suicide and then recovers her will to live. Volume two, *Alberte og friheten* (1931; *Alberte and Freedom,* 1963), relates the story of Alberte in Paris, where she ekes out a living by working as a model—lonely, almost morbidly sensitive, but with a toughness in her that ultimately saves her. The final volume, *Bare Alberte* (1939; *Alberte Alone,* 1966), chronicles Alberte's final, painful steps in becoming an artist. She returns to Norway and finally writes a novel very much like the Alberte trilogy.

S.'s other books include the novels *Kranes konditori* (1945; *Krane's Sweetshop,* 1968) and *Kjøp ikke Dondi* (1958; *The Leech,* 1960), also the following collections of short stories: *En blå sofa* (1927; a blue sofa), *Carmen og Maja* (1932; Carmen and Maja), *Mange takk, doktor* (1935; many thanks, Doctor), *Dyr jeg har kjent* (1945; animals I have known), *Figurer på mørk bunn* (1949; figures against a dark background), and *Vårt vanskelige liv* (1960; our difficult life). In these works S. turns her attention to struggles similar to those in the Alberte books, to portraits of children, dreamers, trapped housewives, passionate and inept people who struggle to maintain themselves against the forces of small-mindedness and bigotry.

Occasionally S. depicts her characters' struggles with the cold but angry objectivity of the outsider, as in the remarkable and chilling short story "Kunsten å myrde" (the art of murder).

FURTHER VOLUMES IN ENGLISH: *Selected Short Stories* (1985); *The Silken Thread, Stories and Sketches* (1987)

WILLIAM E. MISHLER

SANTOS, Bienvenido N.

Philippine novelist, short-story writer, and poet (writing in English), b. 22 Mar. 1911, Manila

An outstanding "practice teacher" with a B.S. in education from the University of the Philippines,

S. was sent abroad in 1941 for graduate courses at several American universities. When World War II broke out, his embassy asked him to lecture throughout the country on the merits of his people. The fact that he had left his own wife and children behind helped him sympathize with homesick Pinoys (overseas Filipinos) wherever he went. After the war he became president of Legaspi College and, later, of the University of Nueva Caceres, both in the rural Albay peninsula of Luzon. He returned to the U.S. on a Rockefeller grant (1958–1960), then extended his stay one year on a Guggenheim fellowship while he taught at the University of Iowa. From 1961 to 1972, he alternated teaching writing between Luzon and Iowa until martial law under President Ferdinand Marcos convinced him, in 1976, to become an American citizen. From 1973 to 1982 he served as writer-in-residence at Wichita State University in Kansas. In 1981, his collected stories, *Scent of Apples* (1980), won an American Book Award. Since then he has alternated between his homeland and his adopted country.

Compelled by circumstance to spend much of his life abroad, S. developed close ties with several generations of Filipinos in America. "Old-timers" particularly, those originally confined to bent-labor in California fields or to lonely lives in urban slums, he considered his fellow exiles. His first series of short stories, *You Lovely People* (1955), portrayed them with compassion but also with admiration for their courage in the face of economic and psychological adversity. With controlled sentiment, however, he ended that collection with the tale of Filipino returnees to an unrecognizable land so devastated by war that some immediately reemigrated. The best of those stories reappeared in *Scent of Apples,* along with selections from two interim volumes, *Brother, My Brother* (1960) and *The Day the Dancers Came* (1967). The title story in the latter group epitomizes the generation gap and cultural barriers between Filipinos abroad, when two "old-timers" become painfully invisible in the eyes of a visiting troupe of young, college-educated *bayanihan* dancers. The ideal of traditional *bayanihan* (togetherness) is recaptured in both *Brother, My Brother* and *Dwell in the Wilderness* (1985), largely unsophisticated stories of the Philippines before the war when the underclass occasionally pursued dreams away from their peasant origins but felt disgraced unless they revisited their parents in humble gratitude. Having often suffered rejection by others, they cannot in turn deny the embrace of their ordinary ancestors.

This same motif of memory as measurement of one's concern for others recurs in S.'s novels. In *Villa Magdalena* (1965) Fred Medallada, born poor but wed to the Conde leather fortunes, is nearly permanently corrupted by his passion for self-advancement. *The Volcano* (1965) dramatizes the rise and decline of relations between American missionaries and Filipino peasants between 1928 and 1958. During those years once gentle people, turned violent by their war experiences, reject those who had wished them well. The loss is irreparable. In *The Praying Man* (1982) the central character is a corrupt bureaucrat who, remembering sacred loyalties from his past in Manila's slums, finally makes peace with his conscience; Solomon King in *The Man Who (Thought He) Looked Like Robert Taylor* (1983) is a Pinoy who, after thirty years in the U.S., retires as an overseer in the stockyards and travels in search of friends, only to wonder if in his self-engrossment he ever did develop any real friendships; David Tolosa, narrator of *What the Hell For You Left Your Heart in San Francisco* (1987), is an intellectual and a writer, who discovers that nouveau riche Filipino professionals, potential sponsors of a magazine for their overseas countrymen, are too shallow culturally to keep their promises.

No Filipino has been more faithful in portraying the temptations faced by his compatriots abroad. Although all of these novels suffer from inconsistencies in character development and from dramatic lags, they share with the short stories of S. a genuine sense of Philippine ideals worth commemorating even as they erode.

FURTHER WORKS: *The Wounded Stag, 50 Poems* (1956); *Distances: In Time, Selected Poems* (1983)

BIBLIOGRAPHY: Bernad, M. A., *Bamboo and the Greenwood Tree* (1961), 33–41; Casper, L., *New Writing from the Philippines* (1966), 125–33; Manuud, A. G., ed., *Brown Heritage* (1967), 714–21; Galdon, J. A., ed., *Philippine Fiction* (1972), 101–12; Alegre, E. N., and D. G. Fernandez, *The Writer and His Milieu* (1984), 217–58; Casper, L., *Firewalkers* (1987), 21–34; Abad, G. H., and E. Z. Manlapaz, eds., *Man of Earth* (1989), 176–82

LEONARD CASPER

SARAMAGO, José

Portuguese novelist and short-story writer, b. 16 Nov. 1922, Azinhaga, Golegã

S.'s novels view the Portuguese existence within an artistic framework that seamlessly melds myth, history, and fiction. Raised in the Alentejo province, S. wrote fiction before the 1970s, but he was primarily a journalist. His membership in the illegal Communist Party led to repeated difficulties

with the Salazar-Caetano dictatorship. After the 1974 revolution, he abandoned journalism. In recent years, he has become Portugal's most widely read modern novelist both at home and abroad.

S. recreates significant moments of Iberian peninsular history from a Portuguese point of reference. National events are highlighted within the context of European existence, which was once quite foreign to Portuguese writers. His inspiration is purely peninsular, however. Social-class relationships—the relations between the nobility and the popular classes, between maids and guests in a hotel—and questions of ideology and the abuse of power are subtly debated with lyricism and humor.

Levantado do chão (1980; raised from the ground) is a three-generation saga of a poor sharecropper family from the post-World War I period through 25 April 1974, the date of the Portuguese revolution. The still prevailing medieval Portuguese mentality and organization of latifundia are evoked to explain the centuries-old disgrace of generations of a family. This portrait includes popular, fantastic elements of the rural existence—werewolves, talkative angels, and the dead actively participating in the lives of the living. The story is presented through mixed forms of monologue and dialogue. *Memorial do convento* (1982; *Baltazar and Blimunda*, 1987) is a complex memoir-chronicle of the sociopolitical, religious, and mystical fates of all strata of Portuguese life set during the 18th-c. construction of the Mafra Convent by King John V. The novel delightfully wavers at the point where reality collides head-on with fantasy, and the description of 18th-c. life may be seen as a symbolic discussion of the Portuguese present. In *O ano da morte de Ricardo Reis* (1984; *The Year of the Death of Ricardo Reis,* 1991) S. brings to fictional life Ricardo Reis, a heteronym of the illustrious Portuguese poet Fernando Pessoa (1888–1935), who supposedly returns to Portugal from Brazil upon learning of Pessoa's death. It is Portugal of the fascist 1930s, the years of the onset of the Spanish Civil War, and the rise of Hitler, Mussolini, Franco, and Salazar. S.'s melding of history, fiction, myth, and poetry once again produces a profoundly moving tale of the Portuguese and Iberian existence of the time.

In *A jangada de pedra* (1988; the stone raft) the Iberian Peninsula mysteriously separates from the rest of Europe owing to a crack in the Pyrenees—a symbolic story of Portugal's (and Spain's) centuries of exclusion from Europe and the recent integration into the European Economic Community and a new society. In *História do cêrco de Lisboa* (1989; history of the siege of Lisbon) S. skillfully interweaves the past with the present through two love stories: one medieval and one modern. The medieval story, of Moorish-Christian passion, and the modern tale are set against the backdrop of Lisbon of the past and the present.

S.'s panoramic and sweeping characterization of the Portuguese and peninsular existence has struck a chord not only among his compatriots in Portugal, but also in Spain and beyond. His fiction is not only a continual dialogue with the Portuguese character and the nation's history but also a revelation of basic human desires and fantasies.

FURTHER WORKS: *Os poemas possíveis* (1966); *Provàvelmente alegria* (1970); *Deste mundo e do outro* (1971); *A bagagem do viajante* (1973); *As opiniões que o DL teve* (1974); *O ano de 1993* (1975); *Os apontamentos* (1977); *Objecto quase* (1978); *Poética dos cinco sentidos. O ouvido* (1979); *A noite* (1979); *Que farei com este livro* (1980); *Viagem a Portugal* (1981); *O evangelho segundo Jesus Cristo* (1991)

BIBLIOGRAPHY: Howe, I., on *Baltasar and Blimunda*, *NYTBR*, 1 Nov. 1987, 1; Goodman, W., on *Baltasar and Blimunda*, *NYT*, 5 Dec. 1987, A12; Daniel, M. L., "Ebb and Flow: Place As Pretext in the Novels of J. S.," *LBR*, 27, 2 (Winter 1990), 25–40; Mitgang, H., on *The Year of the Death of Ricardo Reis*, *NYT*, 30 Apr. 1991, C17

IRWIN STERN

SĀYIGH, Tawfīq

Palestinian poet and critic (writing in Arabic and English), b. 14 Dec. 1923, Khirba, Syria; d. 3 Jan. 1971, Berkeley, Calif., U.S.A.

Although S. was born in Syria, he and his family were citizens of the British Mandate of Palestine, and S. grew up on the shore of the Sea of Galilee, in the town of Tiberias. After the establishment of Israel in 1948, the family fled to Beirut, where S. had obtained his B.A. degree from the American University in Beirut in 1946. Later in life, S. was haunted by this trauma, and his poetry constantly returns to the themes of exile and the search for identity.

S. was the son of a Protestant minister, and from his earliest days he was surrounded by an environment saturated in the Scriptures. Thus it is not surprising to find much biblical quotation and imagery in his poetry. Although he rejected conventional religiosity in later life, the Bible, and especially the figure of Christ in the New Testament, never lost its hold on his imagination.

In 1951 S. obtained a Rockefeller Foundation grant to study in the U.S., first at Harvard, and later at the University of Indiana (1952). In 1953–1954 he studied at Oxford and Cambridge, under

the auspices of the British Council. S. stayed in England for about a decade after finishing his studies, teaching at Cambridge and the University of London.

In 1961 S. agreed to serve as editor of an Arabic literary and cultural magazine, eventually entitled *Hiwār,* which was funded by an organization called the Committee for Cultural Freedom. This committee was exposed in 1966 as a CIA front organization. In the ensuing scandal, S.'s reputation was savagely attacked. Though S. steadfastly maintained that he had no knowledge of the committee's source of funding, and would not have accepted its support if he had known, in the politically charged atmosphere of the Middle East at the time such denials carried little weight. Thus, S. felt obliged to leave Beirut when he was offered the opportunity to spend a year lecturing at a number of U.S. universities, culminating in his appointment as a lecturer in Near Eastern languages and comparative literature at the University of California, Berkeley, in 1968. He died suddenly there, of a heart attack, in 1971.

From the first, English syntax and idiomatic structure had a strong stylistic influence on S.'s poetry. In fact, one of his early successes, "Sermon on the Mount" (1952), was initially composed in English and only later recast in Arabic. Ironically, this English influence has meant that S.'s poetry often reads more naturally in translation than in the original Arabic. It also explains some of the resistance shown by critics to S.'s poetry, which was reinforced by his thoroughgoing assimilation of a variety of trends in Anglo-American modernism (q.v.), during his studies in the U.S. and England. It is not without significance that all three of his collections of poetry, *Thalāthūn Qasīdah* (1954; thirty poems), *Al-Qasīdah K* (1960; the K poem), and *Mu'allaqat T. S.* (1963; the mu'allaqah [ode] of T. S.), were published during his sojourn abroad when he was actively engaged in assimilating modernist poetics.

S.'s later poetry resembles far more the postwar work of poets like William Carlos Williams (q.v.) and his objectivist followers than the more formalized metrics and rhymes found in the poetry of the Arab "Free-Verse Movement" with which S. is usually associated. For example, his well-known work "Bid'at as'ilah li-atrahhā 'alā al-karkadān" (1963; some questions I would ask the unicorn) reflects the influence of Williams's long poem *Paterson 5* both formally and thematically, especially in its exploration of the dynamics of male and female identity.

This concern with the male-female relationship, often expressed in highly charged erotic imagery, becomes more central to S.'s work in the late 1950s and early 1960s. It frequently fuses with the themes of exile and alienation. Like many Palestinian poets, S. often represented his lost homeland in the form of an unobtainable human beloved, an identification facilitated by the fact that the word "land" in Arabic is of feminine gender. For S. personally, the loss and despair he felt at becoming a stateless person was paralleled by the sufferings he endured during a long and painful love affair he had with an Englishwoman, Kay Shaw. This affair forms the main focus of his second collection of poetry, *Al-Qasīdah K,* and "K" continues to appear, in various forms, in his poetry throughout the remainder of his life.

In a very real sense, S.'s poetry was far in advance of its time. Whether it will fall in the center or more toward the margins in the eventual writing of the history of contemporary Arabic poetry, his work will continue to be of interest to literary historians as marking one limit of the Westernizing tendency in modern Arabic poetry.

FURTHER WORK: *Adwā' jadīdah 'alā Jubrān* (1966)

BIBLIOGRAPHY: Boullata, I. J., "The Beleaguered Unicorn: A Study of S.," *JArabL,* 4 (1973), 69–93; Khouri, M. A., "The Paradise Lost in S.'s Poetry," *Studies in Contemporary Arabic Poetry and Criticism* (1987), 139–47; Allen, R., ed., *Modern Arabic Literature* (1987), 275–79

TERRI DE YOUNG

SCHUTZ, David

Israeli novelist and short-story writer, b. 5 Aug. 1941, Berlin, Germany

S. arrived in Palestine on the eve of Israeli independence in 1948, and later studied history at the Hebrew University, Jerusalem. His first published work, a novel, *Haesev vehahol* (1979; the grass and the sand), went into four editions. Since then he has produced a collection of short stories, *Hahizdamnut haaharonah* (1980; the last chance), and three additional novels: *Ad olam ahakeh* (1987; I shall wait forever), *Shoshan lavan shoshan adom* (1988; white rose, red rose), and *Avishag* (1989; Avishag).

Although the narratives are set within the social reality of contemporary Israel, they also treat the past through the present. Many of the principal protagonists are immigrants and survivors; a main theme of S.'s work is the encounter between past and present, between outsider and insider. Another constant theme is the slippery face of reality, particularly female reality. A question posed throughout the S. opus is: Who is this woman— is she the person she seems to be—is there a

further reality behind the one that immediately presents itself?

Whether third- or first-person narrator, it is the male who observes, who loves, and who loses the love, either in reality or in imagination. *Ad olam ahakeh* opens with the observation that Peretz, out walking with his daughter "was already convinced that his wife was unfaithful." *Shoshan lavan shoshan adom* starts with "By chance I met Lily and by chance I lost her." And *Avishag* is really a novel in celebration of the eponymous heroine and in search of her. Here, the narrator tells us from his seemingly comfortable family situation how he is tortured by the floating identity of his wife. He is seen both in the first person, through his own narrative, and in the third, as the uncertain, dependent Amos, hanging onto the good will of his dominating father-in-law. That other man seems to serve as a model for all that Amos aspires to be, in his learning, in his confidence and competence, and in his material success. The two men, Avishag's father and her husband, represent past and present, together with their alternative claims.

Obsessive love is a linking theme of the novels. The title of *Ad olam ahakeh* indicates this posture. The social realism of the narrative is always partially undermined by the awareness that reality is a composite of disparate elements. The future, as contained by the daughter, is also full of ambiguity, as he notes how different she is from him, and how awkward are his efforts to approach her.

Shoshan lavan shoshan adom explicitly delves into the past, and takes as its point of departure those early days in April 1948 when the narrator (seemingly based on the author's own biography) found himself in Israel just before independence. His contact with Lily as a child is both physical and "unreal," as she can be transformed from a concrete creature of flesh and blood into "a princess of the night," "like a picture from a story book." An air of melancholy hovers over S.'s open narratives.

LEON I. YUDKIN

SCHWARZ-BART, Simone

Guadeloupean novelist and dramatist, b. 8 Jan. 1938, Saintes, France

S. is one of the francophone Caribbean's best-known writers. Born in France, she moved at a very early age to Guadeloupe where she lived and attended school until 1958, when she left for Paris to prepare for the baccalaureate exam and study law. There she met and married novelist André Schwarz-Bart (b. 1928) who won the Goncourt Prize for *Le dernier des justes* (1959; *The Last of the Just,* 1960). They would collaborate on *Un plat de porc aux bananes vertes* (1967; a plate of pork with green bananas) and *Hommage à la femme noire* (1988; homage to the black woman). She also studied at the universities of Dakar in Senegal and Lausanne in Switzerland. S. presently resides in Guadeloupe.

S.'s literary universe is the Caribbean. Her first two novels have women narrators who tell their life story. In *Un plat de porc aux bananes vertes* an old woman in a nursing home in Paris reflects on her past in Martinique. In *Pluie et vent sur Télumée Miracle* (1972; *The Bridge of Beyond*, 1981), S.'s first novel written by herself, the protagonist relates not only her life, but that of her mother and grandmother. This combination biography/autobiography of three generations of strong, courageous, rural women who triumph over adversity is recounted by the narrator while she stands in her garden. S. emphasizes the importance of women's oral culture and how mutual support, role models, and the transmission of knowledge to the young are essential to their survival. *Pluie et vent sur Télumée Miracle* is S.'s most widely read and studied work.

Ti-Jean l'Horizon (1979; *Between Two Worlds*, 1981) is based on a popular oral story. In this version Ti-Jean, attracted to a mythical Africa, leaves Guadeloupe in search of his identity. During his journey, which includes a visit to France, he undergoes several tests. Upon returning to Guadeloupe he realizes that his identity is to be found at home. In this novel S. transforms the Western literary identity quest into a traditional African and Caribbean initiation tale.

Ton beau capitaine (1987; *Your Handsome Captain*, 1988), her only published play, was inspired by her Haitian gardener who communicated with his wife in Haiti by way of audiocassettes. Set in a one-room shack in Guadeloupe, Wilnor, an agricultural worker, listens to the latest cassette sent by his wife in Haiti and records a response. The play explores the effects of separation on a couple, which is made even more poignant as Marie-Ange never appears on stage. The play, which has been performed on three continents, has broader meaning as it also exposes the plight of migrant workers who leave their native land only to suffer loneliness, economic hardship, and discrimination. On another level it condemns the original displacement and forced exile of Africans due to the slave trade.

While S.'s writing has evolved over the past twenty years, certain themes recur: the long-term effects of slavery, the island isolated from the rest of the world, exile and alienation in a foreign land, and the search for identity and stability—in short, the Caribbean landscape, cultural heritage, and experience. In addition, she is probably best known for her fully developed female characters.

S.'s works do not fit into traditionally defined genre categories. For example, *Ton beau capitaine* includes songs, dance, and music, while her novels incorporate proverbs, magic realism (q.v.), and the Creole language in an attempt to recreate the oral tradition. By privileging speech, S. places herself in the long line of oral storytellers.

BIBLIOGRAPHY: Scharfman, R., "Mirroring and Mothering in S.'s *Pluie et vent sur Télumée Miracle* and Jean Rhys's *Wide Sargasso Sea*," *YFS*, 62 (1982), 88–106; Bernabé, J., "Le travail de l'écriture chez S.," *PA*, 121–22 (1982), 166–79; Cailler, B., "*Ti-Jean l'Horizon* de S. ou la leçon du royaume des morts," *SFR*, 6 (1982), 283–97; Ormerod, B., "The Boat and the Tree: S.'s *The Bridge of Beyond*," *Introduction to the French Caribbean Novel* (1985), 108–31; Toureh, F., *L'imaginaire dans l'œuvre de S.* (1986); Smyley-Wallace, K., "The Female and the Self in S.'s *Pluie et vent sur Télumée Miracle*," *FR*, 59 (Feb. 1986), 428–36; Busia, A., "This Gift of Metaphor: Symbolic Strategies and the Triumph of Survival in S.'s *The Bridge of Beyond*," in Davies, C. B., and E. S. Fido, eds., *Out of the Kumbla: Caribbean Women and Literature* (1990), 289–301; Larrier, R., "The Poetics of Ex-île: S.'s *Ton beau capitaine*," *WLT*, 64, 1 (Winter 1990), 57–59

RENÉE LARRIER

SCLIAR, Moacyr

Brazilian novelist and short-story writer, b. 23 Mar. 1937, Porto Alegre

S. has attracted international recognition as one of the foremost Jewish writers of Latin America. The unusual fact that he has ten paperback books published in the U.S. in English translation has made him one of the most widely reviewed contemporary Brazilian writers in the American press. In Brazil he has been recognized with numerous literary prizes. S. grew up in Porto Alegre, the capital of the southern Brazilian state of Rio Grande do Sul. His father was a businessman who had emigrated to Brazil from eastern Europe. From early childhood, S. desired to become a fiction writer. This calling has been nourished by the experiences of a full professional life as a public-health physician in Porto Alegre. Perhaps because of what he has seen as a doctor, the characters and situations in his narratives are often macabre or grotesque. The ugly is, however, treated with irony, wit, and humor, a lightness of touch that lends charm and childlike innocence to his fiction. Indeed, S. is also a noted writer of children's literature, as well as the author of essays and commentaries on contemporary Brazil and public-health issues. S. offers a unique view of the realities of the Brazilian middle class through the various lenses of physician, member of the small Brazilian Jewish minority, and fabulist.

The universal themes of S.'s fiction are love, disease, death, and regeneration. Woven into this tapestry are the special concerns of a Jewish people exiled in a complex, multicultural society. The bestiary is a primary leitmotiv of the narratives; humans behave like animals, and animals have an angelic, transforming energy. The first book of S.'s long bibliography is the volume of short stories entitled *O carnaval dos animais* (1968; *The Carnival of the Animals,* 1985). Subsequent works that have been singled out as among his best are *O centauro no jardim* (1980; *The Centaur in the Garden,* 1985) and *A estranha nação de Rafael Mendes* (1983; *The Strange Nation of Rafael Mendes,* 1988).

O centauro no jardim is a picaresque fable that illustrates the human difficulty in accepting those not of one's own kind. This is the story of a young Jew who was born a centaur. It traces his early childhood exile because of his deformity, his flight from home, his encounter and marriage with a female centaur, their plastic surgery to remove their equine features, and their life as an almost-human couple. Their flaw is that of eternal longing for the life of the centaur, and the inability of both "species" to fully accept the other. *A estranha nação de Rafael Mendes* creates the endearing character of the Brazilian Jewish yuppie, whose existential angst is occasioned by numerous family and professional problems. Mendes strikes a Faustian deal with a cunning old genealogist, who sells him his family history. This novel makes a universal statement on the drama of being different, while offering a vivid portrait of the tensions and beauties of Brazil's unique cultural mix, its blends of Catholic and Candomblé, native Brazilian Indian and European, Eastern and Western elements.

The quality of S.'s writing has invoked comparisons to writers such as La Fontaine, Voltaire, Melville, Isaac Bashevis Singer, Jorge Luis Borges, and Gabriel García Márquez (qq.v.). Like other Latin American writers of his generation, S. crafts stories by linking and multiplying words, images, plots, subplots, and narrative points of view into a patterned whole. His trademark is a tender humor that keeps his narratives from becoming cerebral puzzles or stark statements of defeat. While his heroes may fail, they are treated with compassion. They are all travelers, and their destination, it is important to note, is always Jerusalem.

FURTHER WORKS: *A guerra no Bom Fim* (1972); *O exército de um homem só* (1973; *The One-Man Army,* 1986); *Os deuses de Raquel* (1975; *The Gods of Raquel,* 1986); *Os mistérios de Porto Alegre* (1976); *A balada do falso messias* (1976; *The Ballad of the False Messiah,* 1987); *O ciclo das águas* (1977); *Mães de cães danados* (1977); *Os voluntários* (1979; *The Volunteers,* 1988); *Doutor miragem* (1979); *Cavalos e obeliscos* (1981); *Max e os felinos* (1981; *Max and the Cats,* 1989); *Memórias de um aprendiz de escritor* (1984); *A massagista japonesa* (1984); *O olho enigmático* (1986; *The Enigmatic Eye,* 1989); *O tio que flutuava* (1988); *No caminho dos sonhos* (1988); *Os cavalos da república* (1989); *Um país chamado infância* (1989); *Pra você eu conto* (1991)

BIBLIOGRAPHY: Lowe, E., *The City in Brazilian Literature* (1982), 10, 19, 192, 204; Lindstrom, N., "Oracular Jewish Tradition in Two Works by M. S.," *LBR,* 12, 2 (Winter 1984), 23–33; Franco, J., on *The Strange Nation of Rafael Mendes, NYTBR,* 30 June 1985, 12; Vieira, N., "Judaic Fiction in Brazil: To Be or Not To Be," *LALR,* 14, 28 (July–Dec 1986), 31–45; Jackson, K. D., "The One-Man Army," *WLT,* 61, 2 (Spring 1987), 261–62; Donovan, L., "S.'s Mendes Differs from Usual Magic Realism," *Miami Herald,* 1 May 1988; Day, D., "The Beast in Us," *NYTBR,* 4 May 1986, 34; Stavans, I., on *The Strange Nation of Rafael Mendes, Review,* 39 (Jan.–June 1988), 63; Stern, I., ed., *Dictionary of Brazilian Literature* (1988), 313–14

ELIZABETH LOWE

SCOTT, Paul
English novelist, b. 25 Mar. 1920, London; d. 1 Mar. 1978, London

S., best known for the widely acclaimed work *The Raj Quartet,* was born in suburban North London, where he would continue to reside throughout most of his life. S.'s father was a commercial artist, his mother a former shop clerk with working-class roots. At sixteen, following his mother's wishes, S. left London's Winchmore Hill Collegiate School to train for a career in accountancy.

S. served as a supply officer during World War II; his duties took him to Malaysia, Burma, and India during the final phase of the British Empire. After the war, S. worked as a secretary at a small publishing firm; in 1950 he became a literary agent, and—by writing in his spare time—managed to publish a string of novels, including *Johnnie Sahib* (1952), *The Alien Sky* (1953), and *The Mark of the Warrior* (1958). All of these solid but rather undistinguished works deal in some way with British military figures on duty in foreign lands. In *A Male Child* (1956) S. effectively depicts the grim atmosphere of postwar Britain, but again centers on characters who spent the war years in Asian locales.

After *The Chinese Love Pavilion* (1960), the most deftly plotted and lushly written of his earlier novels, S. began writing fiction full-time. The fruits of his more focused attention soon began to show. Although *The Bender* (1963) is muddled and dull, both *The Birds of Paradise* (1962), a particularly fine novel, and *The Corrida at San Feliu* (1964), one of the more innovative English fictions of the 1960s, present characters of increasing intricacy while employing ever more sophisticated narrative techniques.

In 1964 S. revisited India and began to plan his next series of novels, including *The Jewel in the Crown* (1966), which revolves around the rape of a young Englishwoman during the closing years of English rule. In this novel—the first in what would become known as *The Raj Quartet*—S. reveals himself to be an absolute master of his craft, creating characters of considerable depth while using an abundance of historical material in a manner that is both imaginative and scrupulous.

In *The Day of the Scorpion* (1968), *The Towers of Silence* (1971), and *A Division of the Spoils* (1975), S. continues the story he began in *The Jewel in the Crown,* linking the series largely through the figure of Ronald Merrick, the tormented, sadistic British police official who emerges as one of the most complexly drawn and memorable figures in postwar fiction.

Some, including the novelist Salman Rushdie (q.v.), have criticized *The Raj Quartet* for perpetuating, perhaps unintentionally, a series of racial stereotypes and colonialist assumptions. It is true that S. does not demonize the British in these novels; and yet, as other critics have pointed out, S. successfully avoids prejudice, condescension, and sentimentality in his depiction of Indian life. And he repeatedly makes clear, through Merrick, that he has no sympathy for the practice of rule by force and intimidation that is inevitably a part of any colonialist enterprise.

S.'s best single novel is, arguably, his last, *Staying On* (1977). Connected loosely to *The Raj Quartet,* it focuses on two elderly Britishers— Tusker Smalley and his wife Lucy—who first appear, briefly, in *The Day of the Scorpion.* Here, the two are determined to live as long as possible in their Indian home, despite the fact that national independence has hastened the departure of most of their fellow countrymen. This brilliantly structured novel is informed by a rich comic sensibility that is, regrettably, rarely displayed in his earlier fiction.

Although *Staying On* won Britain's prestigious Booker Prize (1977), the great increase in critical and popular acclaim for S.'s work undoubtedly owes most to the enormous success of the superb adaptation, for television, of *The Raj Quartet* (called

The Jewel in the Crown), which features strong performances by a large cast of accomplished actors led by Dame Peggy Ashcroft.

As a growing number of critics and scholars have begun to suggest, *The Raj Quartet*—and many of S.'s other novels—will continue to survive on the strength of their own merit. S. was one of his generation's finest novelists, a gifted and disciplined artist who consistently offered humane portraits of men and women alive in turbulent times.

FURTHER WORKS: *I Gerontius: A Trilogy* (1941); *After the Funeral* (1979); *My Appointment with the Muse: Essays, 1961–75* (1986)

BIBLIOGRAPHY: Weinbaum, F. S., "P. S.'s India: *The Raj Quartet,*" *Crit,* 20, 1 (1979), 100–10; Swinden, P., *P. S.: Images of India* (1980); Rao, K. B., *P. S.* (1980); Tedesco, J., and J. Popham, *Introducing The Raj Quartet* (1985); Rubin, D., *After the Raj: British Novels of India since 1947* (1986), 103–56; Spurling, H., *P. S.: A Life of the Author of The Raj Quartet* (1990); Moore, R., *P. S.'s Raj* (1990); Rushdie, S., "Outside the Whale," *Imaginary Homelands* (1991), 87–101

BRIAN MURRAY

SCOTTISH LITERATURE

See Volume 4, page 177.

The 1980s marked a boom in modern Scottish fiction with an urge for new work and a growing opportunity to be published. Two distinct tendencies are obvious: sentimentalism and realism. One major shift is apparent: that from rural to urban subject matter. Some thirty-three Scottish novels were published from 1978 to 1981; first place goes to Alasdair Gray's (b. 1934) *Lanark* (1981) which Douglas Clifford praises as "a magnificent surrealist satire on the West of Scotland." Other novelists contending for recognition were Robert Jamieson with *Thin Wealth* (1986) continuing the promise of his first novel *Soor Hearts* (1983) and Ian Rankin (b. 1960) with his admirably deft and intense first novel *The Flood* (1986). Probably nobody strove more convincingly during this period than William McIlvanney (b. 1936). His *The Big Man* (1985), like his third and best-known novel *Docherty* (1975), concentrates on the working class; but, unlike *Docherty,* it turns to English, not Scots, for the dialogue.

The novelist Stuart Hood (dates n.a.) emerged in 1986 as a very skilled writer with publication of his second novel, *A Storm from Paradise,* which won the Scottish Book of the Year Prize. A competitor with Hood was Iain Banks (b. 1954) who published his psychosurreal mystery on the Forth Railway Bridge, *The Bridge,* in 1986. Neither Ronald Frame's (b. 1953) *A Woman of Judah,* an all-the-way English novel by a Scotsman, nor William Boyd's (b. 1952) *The New Confession* was so successful in 1987 as John Burrowes's (dates n.a.) Glaswegian *Incomers,* although the affectingly mythic fourth novel of Dominic Cooper (b. 1944), *The Horn Fellow,* came near. Closing out this decade were the republication of Fred Urquhart's (b. 1912) *Time Well Knit* (1988), and the powerfully elegiac *The Sound of the Sea* (1989) by the poet-dramatist Colin MacKay (b. 1944).

The short story as well as the novel flourished during the period 1975–1990; indeed, Scotsmen believe that Scotland all but invented the modern short story. That these stories are excellent can be read from *Modern Scottish Short Stories* (1978), which includes the work of twenty-nine authors representing contemporary Scottish fiction at its very best in their vigor and imagination and in their common love for and understanding of Scotland, various though their subjects and voices may be. Here again are the novelists Muriel Spark (q.v.), James Kennaway (1928–1968), Eric Linklater (1899–1974), and Robin Jenkins (b. 1912); here again the poets George Mackay Brown (b. 1921), Giles Gordon (b. 1940), and Iain Crichton Smith (b. 1928).

Each passing year marks new successes like the award-winning ones of Jackson Webb (b. 1940) and the 1980 *Prosepiece,* a volume of Carl Macdougall's (dates n.a.) short stories. Between 1980 and 1985, the reader had the stories of Ian Stephen's (dates n.a.) *Living at the Edge* (1982) and those of Alasdair Gray's *Unlikely Stories, Mostly* (1983). Thriving, the short story lost no force as manifested in the collection *I Can Sing, Dance, Rollerskate, and Other Stories by Scottish Writers* (1988), the work of eighteen authors, generally born in the 1950s. The poet Douglas Dunn (b. 1942) turned his powers of clinical observation to the short story, publishing his *Secret Villages* in 1986. Two years later, Irish-born Bernard MacLaverty (b. 1942) won a National Cash Register Award with his collection *The Great Profundo* (1988); and the following year, William McIlvanney published his first collection entitled *Walking Wounded* (1989), a volume loaded with this author's consistently intelligent observation and strong sense of character.

John Linklater's edition of short stories, *The Red Hog of Colima* (1989), presents mainly new writers like Ken Ross (b. 1941), as does Collin's *A Roomful of Birds* (1990). The outstanding short-story writer Fred Urquhart displays his technical mastery of both Scots and English in two volumes of his own short stories, both published in 1980:

A Diver in China Seas and *Proud Lady in a Cage.* Urquhart's collected stories *Full Scors* (1990) would support this judgment.

Some would argue that today the literature of Scotland may be described neither as "a cultural ruin" nor as "the rich harvest" forecast by Gunn in the 1930s; but never before has the Scots writer been offered at home more hope to be published, insufficient though the encouragement still appears to a few. Duncan Glen's (b. 1933) periodical *Akros* had life from 1965 to 1983. Since 1966, the University of Edinburgh Press has been publishing an impressive annual called *Scottish Poetry.* In 1969 Southside, a new Scottish imprint, announced its first publication as Sydney Goodsir Smith's (q.v.) *Fifteen Poems and a Play;* a year later the literary magazine *Chapman* first appeared; in 1970 Calder and Boyars published *Contemporary Scottish Verse,* edited by Norman MacCaig (q.v.) and Alexander Scott (b. 1920), as the first volume of the Scottish Library; and in 1972 Routledge & Keagan Paul published *The MacDiarmid Reader* as the first volume of the Scottish Series. Thomas Crawford at Aberdeen University became in 1974 the first editor of *The Scottish Literary Journal,* published by the Association for Scottish Literary Studies.

Tessa Ransford (b. 1938) founded "The School of Poets" in 1981, a time when the Hawthornden International Retreat for Writers was going strong. *Orbis* had its issue of Scottish poetry in 1985, the same year Peter Kravitz dropped "New" from *The New Edinburgh Review* and gave that literary magazine another motto: "To gather all the rays of culture into one whole." A year later, *New Writing Scotland* began to be published with Alexander Scott and James Hutchinson as editors; its intent has been to become "a showcase for new writers." *Lines Review* celebrated its one-hundredth number in 1987, and in January 1991 entered its thirty-ninth year. Today the phenomenon of the corporate sponsor behind such endeavors as the United Biscuit £5,000 check or, in 1987, the first McVitie Prize for Scottish Writer of the Year is accepted as is the Edinburgh Book Festival with its 1.6 miles of shelved books in its fourth year of 1989, a year that showed a 100 percent increase in ticket sales.

Among women writers, Spark has published more than seventeen novels since 1957, her latest being *Symposium* (1990), a "rich brew" about original sin, a fit subject for this Catholic expatriate novelist. Along the way of her career, she has turned from the novel to write a play, a children's book, poetry, criticism, and biography. Janet Caird (b. 1913) composes flowing free verse, but also traditional verse like her lovely "Black Night" (1987) in cinquains, opening "I could not sleep for sorrow''; in addition, as a prose writer, she has short stories, a children's book, and six novels to her credit. The homely muse of Helen B. Cruickshank (1886–1975) found its voice in Hugh MacDiarmid's (q.v.) editions of *Northern Lights* (1920–1922). Marion Angus (1866–1946), rooted like Cruickshank in the northeast, achieved technical mastery for the poetry of her *The Lilt and Other Poems* (1922). Anne Stevenson (b. 1933) had published seven volumes before Oxford published her *Selected Poems, 1956–1986* (1987), whereas Agnes C. Carnegie (d. 1984) was not heard until 1985 when the Aberdeen University Press posthumously published a selection from her poetry entitled *The Timeless Flow.*

The great efflorescence of women's writing in Scotland that leads to the 21st c. cannot be missed; faces of women seem everywhere. For Anne Born (b. 1924) it is translating *Spring Tide* (1990) from the Danish of Pia Tafdrup (q.v.) and, thus, extending the line from Willa Muir's (b. 1890) great translations of Kafka and Asch; for Tessa Ransford it is writing six volumes of poems, often metaphysical and religious, and then taking on (1989) the editing of *Lines*. Other Scots women like Judith Weir (b. 1954) have looked to music and the writing of a libretto for Scottish opera, such as her *The Vanishing Bridegroom* (1990), or like Mary Gladstone (dates n.a.) have written or adapted plays. Liz Lochhead (b. 1947) has published several volumes of poetry, none better than her first: *Memo for Spring* (1972). Her witty, natural, alert muse delights in sexual scenarios and aspects of womankind. Working usually in English, Lochhead has been turning more and more to composition of plays and revues. She has translated *Tartuffe* successfully into Scots and published in 1985 her *True Confessions and New Clichés,* hilariously satirical dramatic monologues, sketches, and reviews for live performance on the stage.

Numbers of other Scotswomen today favor writing novels or poems or both. First novels have come from Elizabeth Sutherland (b. 1926), *The Weeping Tree* (1980), and from Agnes Owens (b. 1926), *Gentlemen of the West* (1984). Canongate reprinted Nan Shepherd's (b. 1893) *The Quarry Wood* (1928) in 1987, and Faber and Faber reissued Emma Tennant's (b. 1937) *The Bad Sister* (1978) in 1989. Tennant's most recent novel *Two Women of London: The Strange Case of Ms Jekyll and Mrs. Hyde* (1989) alludes to Hogg's *Justified Sinner* and is Scottish through and through. Joan Lingard (b. 1932) worked the theme of Edinburgh's respectability into her *The Prevailing Wind* (1964); she has nine other novels and eighteen books for young people, which won her a coveted West German award for children's literature in 1987. Rosalind Brackenbury's (b. 1942) ninth novel,

Taxus (1988), is a fine example of how Scotland can evoke poetry in a Scotswoman; again, love of Scotland is written deeply into Margaret Elphinstone's (dates n.a.) *A Sparrow's Flight* (1990). Most recently, more than two-thirds of Scottish short stories have been written by women like Moira Burgess (b. 1936), editor with Hamish Whyte of *Scottish Short Stories* (1985).

Frequently, the latest women poets got their start in *Lines;* for example, almost one-third of the poets published in the September 1989 issue are women. Such are Anne Turner (b. 1925) and Valerie Thornton (b. 1954). Having found encouragement, such poets go on to a volume of their own; so it has been with Elizabeth Jennings (b. 1926) and Gail Fox (b. 1943).

Three of the best known women poets writing today are Val Warner (b. 1946), Valerie Gillies (b. 1948), and Sheena Blackhall (dates n.a.). Warner's *Before Lunch* (1986), published thirteen years after her first volume, displays a wide knowledge of languages. Gillies has published three volumes of clear, cool, sharp, poems as well as other books, radio scripts, and reviews. Blackhall has become an accomplished singer. An early volume *The Cyard's Kist* (1986) reveals the influence of ballad and folksong; the poetry of *The Spark O' the Land* (1987), *Hame-Drauchtit* (1988), and *The Nor'East Neuk* (1989) is composed refreshingly and naturally in Scots, the mastery of which is apparent elsewhere in Blackhall's collection of short stories entitled *A Nippick o' Nor'East Tales* (1989).

Scots writers, men and women, with their evergrowing output of new titles, make it seem as though a literary renaissance will mark the 1990s North o' the Tweed. Among the ranks, one sees no unified movement but rather a general agreement that Scots men and women choose to write about ''anything that comes up their backs and in whatever manner inspires them.''

Variety can be an index of vitality. Scotland's contemporary poets certainly include disparate accents: the Freudian tones of Robert Duncan (1919–1988), the surrealism of Tom Leonard (b. 1944), the symbolism of G. F. Dutton (b. 1924), the pastoralism of Margaret Gillies Brown (dates n.a.), the visual primer of Ian Hamilton Finlay (b. 1925), the free verse of Tom Scott (b. 1918), the "instamatic" poems of Edwin Morgan (b. 1920), the delightful rhymes of John Mole's (b. 1941) children's verses, the black humor of George Macbeth, the Orientalism of Ron Butler (b. 1949), the light verse of Gavin Ewart (b. 1916), the performance poetry of Brian McCabe (b. 1951), and the poetry of Andrew Greig (b. 1951) on radio.

This vitality has no geographical bounds in Scotland. Expatriates apart, in such far places as Australia and Nigeria, Canada and San Francisco,

Scots writers at home compose in every corner of the old kingdom. From the Burns Country come the scatological excursions of William S. Graham (b. 1948) and the consistently good poems of the Celtic scholar-poet William Neill (b. 1922) in eight collections—Gaelic, Scots, and English— the latest being *Making Tracks* (1988).

In the demotic speech of Glasgow invigorated by Irish and other foreign elements are Alan Hayton's (b. 1967) *Far Cry from 1945* (1988), Frank Kuppner's (b. 1951) poetry in four books (1984– 1989), William Montgomarie's (b. 1934) *From Time to Time* (1985) with its scholarly free verse, and Tom Leonard's "A Priest came on at Merkland Street." Maurice Lindsay (b. 1918) and Edwin Morgan are sons of Glasgow; so is Robert Crawford (b. 1959), a writer of ever-increasing stature. Glasgow University professor, coeditor of *Verse,* critic on Eliot or Kuppner, short-story writer in *Sterts and Stobies* (1985), and poet in *A Scottish Assembly* (1990), Crawford expresses his love for Glasgow and Scotland. His prize-winning verses are *pang'd fu' o'* interest in innovation, biting wit, and delightful humor.

Across from Glasgow, in Edinburgh, Stewart Conn (b. 1936), Alan Bold (b. 1943), and Alastair Fowler (b. 1930) take places in volumes of contemporary Scottish verse, as James Meek (b. 1962) puts Edinburgh at the heart of his first novel *McFarlane Boils the Sea* (1989), as Rayne Mackinnon (dates n.a.) makes an Edinburgh hospital the base of his first volume of poems, *Northern Elegies* (1986), and as Hugh McMillan (b. 1955) fills his first book of poetry, *Triumph of the Air* (1990), with the residents, pubs, and public places of Auld Reekie.

Above Edinburgh, in the east neuk o' Fife, are the four poets John Brewster (b. 1957), William Hershaw (b. 1957), Henry Holton (b. 1949), and Tom Hubbard (dates n.a.) composing verses on the Fife environment and community to be found in their *Four Fife Poets: Fower Brigs to a Kinrik* (1988). Nourished by Fife is also the poet and short-story writer Christopher Rush (b. 1944).

Sharing the northeast with Sheena Blackhall is the Aberdeen psychiatrist Ken Norrice (b. 1924) whose self-questioning punctuates the themes of sterility, escape, and maternity, most notably in *When Truth Is Known* (1989). Norrice's fellow poet David Morrison (b. 1941), vividly Scottish, offers poems that center on Caithness and isolation. The anthology *Ten Northeast Poets* (1985) represents older poetry of 1900–1950; the anthology *Moments in A Glass House* (1988) offers the verses of five young poets, serious and otherwise unpublished.

Far out to sea in the Shetlands, William J. Tait (b. 1918) recovers forty years of his poetry in *A Day between Weathers: Collected Poems 1938–*

1978 (1980), written in Scots, English, and Shetland speech. South in the Orkneys, George Mackay Brown has written Orcadian novels like *The Golden Bird* (1987) and short stories spoken of as "prose poems" like those in *The Masked Fisherman* (1990). Tait's *The Wreck of the Archangel* (1990) is excellent poetry with kennings, compounds, and archaisms, fine use of alliteration, and deep religious conviction.

The most illustrious island voice belongs to Iain Crichton Smith from the Hebridean Isle of Lewis. In a way, all of the more than fifty volumes by Smith may be said to be rooted in Lewis; for example, he tells the story of his life in the fifty-nine autobiographical poems of *A Life* (1986). A previous volume, *Selected Poems, 1955–1980* (1982), is Robert Fulton's choice of superlative poems from Smith's five earlier books of poetry; the most recent volume, *The Village and Other Poems* (1989), shows the continuing development of a major poet and the luminosity of his art. Subtle, gentle, original, complex: a poem by Smith is the statement of a true island poet. Much of Smith's recent work is a turning from the poem to the novel, such as *In the Middle of the Wood* (1987), to the short story (*Selected Stories,* 1990), to the essay replete with loyalty and allegiance to Lewis (*Towards the Human,* 1987), to translation from Gaelic into English (Duncan Ban MacIntyre's *Ben Dorain,* repub. 1988), and to editing (*Twelve More Modern Scots Poets,* 1987).

Today Gaelic, Scots, and English serve Scottish literature. Thus Iain Smith will compose in Gaelic and then make his own translation into English. The famous Scottish historian William Robertson (1721–1793) anticipated that, as a result of Scotland's union with England in 1707, English would eventually dominate almost to the exclusion of Scots. Now is the day of that "almost." Yet Scots hangs on with amazing tenacity as volumes like Tom Scott's (b. 1918) *The Ship, and Ither Poems* (1962), Goodsir Smith's (q.v.) *Collected Poems* (1975), Robert Garioch's *Selected Poems 1943– 1974* (1975), and the generous representation in the March 1989 issue of *Lines* attest. The diction of Duncan Glen is genuinely, everyday Scots diction (e.g., the poems in *Tales To Be Told,* 1988), and the poems in Raymond Vettese's (b. 1950) *The Richt Noise and Ither Poems* (1988) support that poet's belief that Scots is "the richt noise tae hurl at the storm's rattle."

Scots got one of its strongest boosts in 1984 when William Laughton Lorimer published his mind-boggling *The New Testament in Scots,* a volume Billy Kay called "the most important single book published in Scotland since World War II." Obviously it is likely to remain a major influence on the majority of Scottish writers far into the 21st c. Another big boost was given to

Scots in 1990 with the publication of Isabail Macleod's *The Scots Thesaurus*. Even without such upliftings, Scottish writers are not likely to renounce Scots just as long as any one of them gives ear to the utter beauty of lines like these, from William Soutar's (q.v.) "The Tryst" (1988): "A' thru the nicht we spak nae word, / Nor sinder'd bane frae bane, / A' thru the nicht I heard her hert, / Gane soundin' wi' my ain."

BIBLIOGRAPHY: Garioch, R., ed., *Made in Scotland* (1974); Lindsay, M., ed., *Modern Scottish Poetry* (1976); Aitken, W. R., *Scottish Literature in English and Scots* (1982); Royle, T., *The Macmillan Companion to Scottish Literature* (1983); Thomson, D. S., ed., *The Companion to Gaelic Scotland* (1983); Bold, A., *Modern Scottish Literature* (1983); Watson, R., *The Literature of Scotland* (1984); Scott, A., ed., *Voices of Our Kind,* 3rd ed. (1987); Craig, C., ed., *The History of Scottish Literature* (1988), Vol. 4; Gardner-Medwin, A., and J. H. Williams, eds., *A Day Estivall* (1990); Macleod, I., ed., *The Scots Thesaurus* (1990)

ROBERT DONALD THORNTON

SELVON, Samuel

Trinidadian novelist and short-story writer, b. 20 May 1923, Trinidad

S. began to write poetry and fiction after graduating from Naparima College in 1938. He continued writing while he worked as a wireless operator for the Royal Navy Reserve during World War II. When the war ended S. turned to journalism and became the fiction editor of the literary magazine of the *Trinidad Guardian*. But like so many promising West Indian writers, S. was forced to leave home if he wished to have his work reach an international audience. In 1950 he set out for England, but the journey was also an escape from the complacency and easy rhythms of Trinidad to which he found himself increasingly drawn. It was S.'s good fortune to live in London's Balmoral Hostel where he met several displaced West Indians, Africans, and Indians. These expatriate colonials inspired the creation of many of the ebullient characters of S.'s "London fiction." While he worked at a variety of jobs, S. contributed fiction to journals and newspapers, and his first novel, *A Brighter Sun,* was published in 1952. Nine additional novels, numerous short stories, articles, radio plays, television and film scripts followed. After living in England for some twenty-eight years, S. emigrated to Calgary, Canada, where he presently resides.

S.'s *A Brighter Sun* is a historically important novel in the development of West Indian fiction because the young hero's quest for self-awareness and wholeness in a colonial, pluralistic, and racially divisive society is a significant theme. The novel is a sensitive exploration of the growth of the callow Tiger from childish naïveté and ignorance to adult responsibility. Tiger's quest for maturity and self-knowledge is continued and consolidated in *Turn Again Tiger* (1958), which has some important links with *Those Who Eat the Cascadura* (1972). Both novels examine the individual's search for integrity in a society psychologically crippled by years of an effete colonialism. Sans Souci, the isolated and idyllic setting of *Those Who Eat the Cascadura,* is a microcosm of preindependent, colonial Trinidad complete with the three-tiered racial hierarchy and its antagonisms and divisiveness. The theme of individual integrity is crucial in this novel, and it emerges rather subtly in the female protagonist's relationship with an Englishman visiting Sans Souci. In *Turn Again Tiger* the hero's hunger for self-possession is dramatically conveyed in his violent sexual encounter with the white Doreen. The revenge motive, a feature of the black-male/white-female syndrome often explored in West Indian fiction, is rather prominent in the encounter.

Scholars have neglected S.'s *I Hear Thunder* (1963) and *An Island Is a World* (1955) in favor of his less ponderous, more satirical, and humorous fiction. However, these novels reveal S.'s meditative and philosophical side, and, furthermore, they call up a finely focused and particularly accurate picture of Trinidad society in the 1940s and 1950s. The characters are complex and fully embodied, and some of S.'s best female portraits appear in these two novels.

In his brilliant "London fiction" S. explores the harassed and sometimes bizarre lives of West Indians trying to survive in the hostile "Mother Country." The world of these novels, *The Lonely Londoners* (1956), *The Housing Lark* (1965), *Moses Ascending* (1975), and *Moses Migrating* (1983), is ferociously masculine. S.'s expatriates maintain a cohesive male community closed to women, most of whom are regarded as nuisances. More pertinently, S.'s West Indians have a psychological need to form a colony with a governor-leader if they are to survive in London. That governor is Moses, the charismatic Trinidadian in whose basement room "the boys" assemble each Sunday morning for sustenance.

S. is one of the brilliant writers who contributed to the remarkable development of a vibrant West Indian literature in the 1950s and 1960s. Increasingly scholars from several countries are discovering and elucidating the value of this contribution.

His pioneering work in the use of Trinidadian dialect, his incomparable gift for dialogue and pungent satire, and his sensitive treatment of alienated West Indians guarantee his place in the history of West Indian literature.

FURTHER WORKS: *Ways of Sunlight* (1957); *Carnival in Trinidad* (1964); *Lost Property* (1965); *A Cruise in the Caribbean* (1966); *Perchance To Dream* (1966); *Rain Stop Play* (1967); *Highway in the Sun* (1967); *A Drink of Water* (1968); *You Right in the Smoke* (1968); *El Dorado, West One* (1969); *Bringing in the Sheaves* (1969); *The Plains of Caroni* (1970); *Mary, Mary Shut Your Gate* (1971); *Voyage to Trinidad* (1971); *Cry Baby Brackley* (1972); *Water for Veronica* (1972); *The Harvest in the Wilderness* (1972); *Anansi the Spider Man* (1974); *Milk in the Coffee* (1975); *Zeppi's Machine* (1977); *Pressure* (1978); *Foreday Morning: Selected Prose 1946–1986* (1989)

BIBLIOGRAPHY: Brathwaite, E., "Sir Galahad and the Islands," *Bim,* 7 (1957), 8–16; Ramchand, K., *An Introduction to the Study of West Indian Literature* (1976), 58–72; Nazareth, P., "The Clown in the Slave Ship," *CarQ,* 23, 2–3 (1977), 24–29; Rohlehr, G., "S. S. and the Language of the People," in Baugh, E., ed., *Critics on Caribbean Literature* (1978), 153–61; Fabre, M., "S. S.," in King, B., ed., *West Indian Literature* (1979), 111–25; Baugh, E., "Friday in Crusoe's City: The Question of Language in Two West Indian Novels of Exile," *ACLALSB,* 3 (1980), 1–12; Barratt, H., "Dialect, Maturity, and the Land in S. S.'s *A Brighter Sun:* A Reply," *ESC,* 7, 3 (1981), 329–37; Ramchand, K., "Song of Innocence, Song of Experience: S. S.'s *The Lonely Londoners* As a Literary Work," *WLWE,* 21, 3 (1982), 644–54; Barratt, H., "Individual Integrity in S.'s *Turn Again Tiger* and *Those Who Eat the Cascadura,*" *Toronto South Asian Review,* 5, 1 (1986), 153–59; Nasta, S., ed., *Critical Perspectives on S. S.* (1988)

HAROLD BARRATT

SERENI, Vittorio

Italian poet and prose writer, b. 2 July 1913, Luino; d. 10 Feb. 1983, Milan

S. is the most complex poet, and perhaps the best, of his generation. From his native town, Luino, a continuous point of reference for the poet, S. followed his family to Brescia and to Milan in 1933, where he studied at the university. He was strongly influenced by Antonio Banfi's (1886–1957) teaching on the importance of a phenomenological approach to reality, and with a group of

Banfi disciples he cofounded and coedited the literary magazine *Corrente,* suppressed in 1940 by fascist authorities. In World War II, as an army lieutenant, S. served in Greece and Sicily. Captured by the Allies, he spent two years in a prison camp in Algeria. At the end of the war, after a few years of teaching, he joined the industrial sector, working first for the Pirelli company and later for the Mondadori publishing house. He has been awarded several prestigious prizes for poetry, including the Montefeltro Prize (1965), the Bagutta Prize (1981), and the Viareggio Prize (1982).

The prewar crisis, the experience of war and prison camp, and the exposure to the industrial world form the basis of S.'s poetic itinerary. Fully aware of the then dominant tradition of the hermeticist school and its pursuit of pure poetry, S. distanced himself from it, opting for a poetry that springs from the poet's relationship with objects and with life's events. This is evident even in his first collection of poems entitled *Frontiera* (1941; *Frontier,* 1990). The title is a reference to the actual boundary between fascist Italy and Switzerland and to the political boundary between fascist Italy and free European countries. The main feature of this early poetry is the delineation of an intimate and private world undermined by the presage of the war and disasters. Luino's stormy lake, the fog, and the changing of seasons are a part of the landscape and also signs of an alarming future.

The second collection of poems, *Diario d'Algeria* (1947; *Algerian Diary,* 1990), ripens along the lines of S.'s ordeal with war and prison camp. The tone is darker than in *Frontiera,* the language more intense and essential. S's identification with European civilization comes to grips with the reality of a divided Europe, and the poet finds himself unwillingly on the side of the oppressor. In a sense the wandering of Lieutenant Sereni through Europe is an initiation into life, but it paradoxically lands him in a prison camp where he remains impotent and totally idle. Beyond its autobiographical vicissitudes, *Diario d'Algeria* is the drama of a generation caught in a war it didn't fully understand, then defeated, confined, and limited to watching the unfolding of history. At the same time, the exemplary experience is an allegory of life as imprisonment.

Gli strumenti umani (1966; *The Human Implements,* 1990) appeared twenty years later. Once more by measuring his personal experience with the problems of his times, S. faces the upheaval of the Italian industrial boom, the rejection of the democratic values espoused by the antifascist resistance, and the political disarray of its present alienating industrial society. Such an implacable environment estranges the poet who feels as impotent as he had felt when he was a prisoner of war. A sense of perplexity, a lack of guidelines, and unanswerable questions are his perimeters. S.'s search for a language that would adequately represent the transformations of this historical reality produces a lyric language capable of handling colloquial forms of the dominant entrepreneurial class and, at times, anger and hate at the betrayal of democratic ideals.

In his last collection, *Stella variabile* (1981; *Variable Star,* 1990), S. still faces the issues of his day. However, the negativity of contemporary reality is more pervasive, and his feelings of alienation toward such an absurd society throw him into a state of nihilism. The poetic self is exploded into pieces, reduced to a sense of nothingness. Life is like a race from tunnel to tunnel with brightness appearing only momentarily in between tunnels of emptiness. However, his belief in poetry, though questioned, remains strongly committed. Moments of brightness are those moments in which poetry has the power to denounce and unmask hypocrisy, trickery, hate, and exploitation.

Special mention must be made of his prose works: *Gli immediati dintorni* (1962; the immediate surroundings), a literary diary, and *L'opzione e allegati* (1964; the option); they are closely related to his poetry and shed clarity on it. It was S.'s conviction that writing is an essential act of existing, and that his greatness as a poet would be measured by how well he had succeeded in mirroring the human condition. Without doubt he has remained faithful to his beliefs, and as time passes, it is evident that S. is one of the few great Italian poets of the century.

FURTHER WORKS: *Poesie* (1942); *Frammenti di una sconfitta. Diario bolognese* (1954); *La guerra girata altrove* (1969); *Ventisei* (1970); *Letture preliminari* (1973); *Il sabato tedesco* (1980); *Gli immediati dintorni primi e secondi* (1983); *Senza l'onore delle armi* (1986); *Tutte le poesie* (1986). FURTHER VOLUME IN ENGLISH. *Selected Poems of V. S.* (1990)

BIBLIOGRAPHY: Fortini, F., "S.," in Trevelyan, R., ed., *Italian Writing Today* (1967), 152–54; Dego, G., "A Poet of Frontiers," *LM* (Oct. 1969), 38; Merry, B., "The Poetry of V. S.," *IS,* 29 (1974), 88–102; Perryman, M., and P. Robinson, Introduction to *Selected Poems of V. S.* (1990), 11–27

ROSARIO FERRERI

SEXTON, Anne

(born Anne Gray Harvey) American poet, b. 9 Nov. 1928, Newton, Mass.; d. 4 Oct. 1974, Weston, Mass.

Raised in a well-to-do Massachusetts family, S. was educated in various Massachusetts public and boarding schools, and after graduation she worked as a bookstore clerk and fashion model while her husband served in the Korean War. Aside from a few poems published in her high-school yearbook, S. did not truly begin writing poetry until 1956, after the birth of her second child. At that time, S. was receiving regular psychiatric treatment, and one of her doctors encouraged S. to try writing as a form of therapy. Some four years later, the "results" of this therapy were published in the collection *To Bedlam and Part Way Back* (1960), which was nominated for the National Book Award. Although this collection received mixed reviews— some readers were disturbed by the confessional and extremely personal nature of the poems—it quickly established S. as an important American poet. Her second collection, *All My Pretty Ones* (1962), received the Levinson Prize from *Poetry* magazine.

Despite the fact that her literary career spanned less than twenty years and was cut short by suicide, S. is recognized as one of the premier poets of her generation. Her work is popularly classified as "confessional poetry." In this type of poetry there are no "rules" as to appropriateness of subject matter; highly personal, sometimes embarrassing, topics become grist for the poetic mill. S. wrote about such previously "taboo" topics as sex, abortion, and her own psychiatric problems and subsequent treatment. Her depiction of intimate and often depressing subjects in a clear and honest style, combined with a celebrity status earned by frequent readings of her own work, made S. a popular public figure as well as an accomplished literary artist.

Live or Die (1966) is S.'s best-known and most highly acclaimed collection. In this work S. continues to employ such familiar themes as death, madness, and depression; a number of the poems, including "Wanting To Die," "Suicide Note," and "Sylvia's Death," display S.'s fascination with suicide, and perhaps foreshadow her own tragic end. In *Live or Die* S. displays the fully developed poetic voice that would make her, along with Sylvia Plath and Adrienne Rich (qq.v.), one of the most influential female poets of her era. In 1967 she received both the Shelley Award from the American Society of Poetry and the Pulitzer Prize for this book, and in 1968 S. received an honorary Phi Beta Kappa from Harvard University.

Later poetry collections include *Love Poems* (1969), *Transformations* (1971)—an extremely popular collection in which S. retells a number of Grimm's fairy tales—*The Book of Folly* (1972), and *The Death Notebooks* (1974). Two more collections, *The Awful Rowing toward God* (1975) and *45 Mercy Street* (1976), were published post-humously. In addition to poetry, S. also wrote *Mercy Street* (1969), a play that enjoyed a successful off-Broadway run. S. collaborated with Maxine Kumin (q.v.) on a number of children's books: *Eggs of Things* (1963), *More Eggs of Things* (1964), *Joey and the Birthday Present* (1971), and *The Wizard's Tears* (1975).

Afraid that she was losing her creativity, S. committed suicide by carbon-monoxide poisoning in 1974, shortly before her forty-sixth birthday. In her brief literary career, S. produced a significant body of work that makes her one of the most significant poets of the late 20th c.

FURTHER WORKS: *Poems* (1968, with Thomas Kinsella and Douglas Livingstone); *A. S.: A Self-Portrait in Letters* (1977); *Words for Dr. Y.: Uncollected Poems with Three Stories* (1978); *The Complete Poems* (1981); *No Evil Star: Selected Interviews, Essays and Prose* (1985); *Selected Poems of A. S.* (1988)

BIBLIOGRAPHY: Northouse, C., and T. P. Walsh, eds., *Sylvia Plath and A. S.: A Reference Guide* (1974); McClatchy, J. D., ed., *A. S.: The Artist and Her Critics* (1978); Middlebrook, D. W., " 'I Tapped My Own Head': The Apprenticeship of A. S.," in Middlebrook, D. W., and M. Yalom, eds., *Coming to Light: American Women Poets in the Twentieth Century* (1985), 195–213; George, D. H., "How We Danced: A. S. on Fathers and Daughters," *WS*, 12, 2 (1986), 179–202; George, D. H., *Oedipus Anne: The Poetry of A. S.* (1987); George, D. H., "The Poetic Heroism of A. S.," *L&P*, 33, 3–4 (1987), 76–88; Bixler, F., ed., *Original Essays on the Poetry of A. S.* (1988); Colburn, S. E., ed., *A. S.: Telling the Tale* (1988); George, D. H., ed., *S.: Selected Criticism* (1988); Morton, R. E., *A. S.'s Poetry of Redemption: The Chronology of a Pilgrimage* (1988); Hall, C. K. B., *A. S.* (1989); Wagner-Martin, L., ed., *Critical Essays on A. S.* (1989); Middlebrook, D. W., *A. S.: A Biography* (1991)

JASON BERNER

al-SHĀBBĪ, Abū al-Qāsim

Tunisian poet, b. 24 Feb. or 3 Mar. 1909, Tozeur; d. 9 Oct. 1934, Tozeur

S. was born in Tozeur in southwestern Tunisia, a lush oasis where he spent an enchanting childhood. This joyous and carefree childhood, a recurrent theme in his poetry, contrasts with his unhappy adolescence, marred by depression, loneliness, and illness. After he attended the Koranic school in his native town, S. moved to Tunis, where he enrolled at Al-Zeituna University. Despite his frail

health, S. led a life effervescent with intellectual and political activities. While still a student at the university at Al-Zeituna, S. penned numerous literary and political articles and manifestos in the journals of the 1930s and delivered lectures where he expounded his ars poetica as well as his political views. He succumbed to consumption at the age of twenty-five.

S. is Tunisia's national poet. His patriotic verse found its way not only into his country's national anthem but also into the hearts of many generations of schoolchildren in the Arab world. But beyond the nationalistic appeal of his poetry, S. remains for many the poet of youth, of dreams, and of romantic love. His verbal inventiveness and audacious imagery rank him as one of the best poets in contemporary Arabic literature. His untimely death and unfinished work have, for generations, fostered among students and critics a Rimbaud-type myth—of the radical social rebel and of the prophetic poet. His only book of poems, *Aghānī al-hayāt* (hymns to life), was published posthumously in Cairo in 1954. His diary and correspondence—an invaluable source of bio-bibliographical information as well as an important social document on the period—were published in Tunis in 1965.

S. owes his patriotic and nationalistic credentials and reputation to a relatively small number of poems where he vehemently assails the colonial order and its oppressive policies, and where he castigates, with equal energy, his compatriots for their lethargy, childishness, and backwardness. More important, as one of the leaders of the literary and intellectual renaissance or *Nahdah* movement in Tunisia, S. strove to forge a new and modern Arab cultural identity and sensibility that would be locally inspired as well as expressive of contemporary reality and preoccupations. These new aesthetic and intellectual orientations are expounded particularly in his famous lecture *Al-Khayāl al-shi'rī 'inda al-'Arab* (1929; the poetic imagination of the Arabs). In this lecture he vigorously attacks contemporaries who dwell on the past glories of Arabic classical literature and who, for lack of imagination, continue a sterile poetic and rhetorical tradition that can no longer accommodate a modern sensibility and concerns. His active advocacy of *Tajdīd* or modernism, as a catalyst of social, political, and cultural change as well as a means of disenfranchisement from the vestiges of a suffocating past, is not, however, without contradictions.

Ironically, S.'s own poetry is hardly demonstrative of the aesthetic and original ideas and spirit he set forth in his lectures. His poetry adheres, except for a few promising but unconvincing attempts, to the metrical and rhetorical canons of the traditional *qasīda* as established by the classical and postclassical poets of long ago. However, his innovation is discernable in other aspects of his language; in the poems of *Aghānī al-hayāt*, S. eschews stock imagery and clichés and favors an individualistic, if not intimist, tone. A sense of tragic loss, especially of innocence, pervades the dominant themes of his poetic inspiration: love, death, and freedom. Some of S.'s poems hark back, via the poets of Al-Mahjar (Arab poets who emigrated to the Americas in the late 19th and early 20th cs.) to the European romantics whose angst and morbid imagination as well as suffusive language have struck a congenial cord with many Arab poets of the period.

Above all, S. remains the symbol of a whole generation of writers, poets, and intellectuals caught, as he was, in the bind between tradition and modernity, identity and difference. Although he remains Tunisia's best-known poet, whose poetry is still relished by the general public and especially the young, S. is, paradoxically, a lone and orphan voice as he neither inspired disciples nor initiated any recognizable literary or aesthetic following.

BIBLIOGRAPHY: Zmerli, S., *Figures tunisiennes: les contemporains et les autres* (1972), passim; Baccar, T., and S. Garmadi, eds., *Écrivains de Tunisie* (1981), 11–54; Allen, R., ed., *Modern Arabic Literature* (1987), 289–93

HÉDI ABDEL-JAOUAD

SHABTAI, Yaakov

Israeli novelist, short-story writer, and dramatist, b. 8 Mar. 1934, Tel Aviv; d. 4 Aug. 1981, Tel Aviv

S. began his literary work mainly as a playwright, although he also wrote stories in the early period. *Hadod peretz mamriy* (1972; Uncle Peretz takes off) is a collection of thirteen stories of the first stage of his work. His first novel (the only one that he himself completed for publication) was *Zikhron dvarim* (1977; *Past Continuous,* 1983); his posthumous novel, *Sof davar* (1984; *Past Perfect,* 1987), acquired its title at his own suggestion, and, although it was edited and brought to publication by his widow, Edna Shabtai, together with Dan Miron, no word was added to the original manuscript. Only existing alternatives were selected by the editors.

S.'s work is the product of a short life and a writing career of some fifteen years. The early works are lyrical, exuberant, and humorous, although, as throughout the S. opus, the theme of death predominates. The setting is very firmly the Israel of the 1960s, especially Tel Aviv, but it is an Israel that although located in the present is a very conspicuous witness to the shadow, the decay, and the death of the past: Over the existent secular society hovers another presence, that of the old world. The actuality of this world can become metaphor too, as in the story "Histalqut" (passing away). In *Hadod peretz mamriy,* which describes the death of the narrator's grandmother, and the manner in which the family increasingly rejects the traditional way of life that had been accepted under her influence. *Zikhron dvarim* was a new departure in narrative, not only for the author but for Israeli prose, marking a radical departure that is still very much a major influence in current Israeli fiction. The title is ambiguous, associating the senses of "protocol," a record of events, with memory. The typographical innovation that the author introduces is that the whole novel has no paragraph and chapter divisions, although it consists of 275 pages in the Hebrew edition (the English translation abandons this apparently difficult device).

S.'s final work yet again marked a new departure. This time, there are four sections in the novel, and they are all presented differently, although they all relate to one character, Meir. The first section adopts the flowing technique of the earlier novel, its tone, its preoccupation (with death), and its approach, although it abandons the use of the single paragraph. The second section moves at a slower pace and gives graver consideration to the actuality of death, in this case, the death of Meir's mother. The third section focuses on Meir's own attempt at self-renewal, here exemplified by a trip that he takes alone to Amsterdam and London. It is in Europe, away from his home, that he discovers how sick he is. The crisis occurs in Foyle's Book Shop in London, which follows a series of minor disappointments that, for him, are full of foreboding. Meir senses loss of control, and from here on he subjects his mind and faculties to close scrutiny to detect signs of abnormality. The last section, back in Tel Aviv, brings the narrative to a climax and conclusion, with a mixture of naturalism and surrealism (qq.v.).

S.'s fiction is marked by scrupulous, precise observation of consciousness, by attention to detail in full-blooded and appropriate narrative. The experimental nature of the prose derives from the pressure to push writing beyond the confines of the naturalistic and toward a grasp of the essential elements of life.

BIBLIOGRAPHY: Yudkin, L. I., *1948 and After: Aspects of Israeli Fiction* (1984), 112–16: Yudkin, L. I., "Transmission of Reality in the Fiction of Y. S.," *Jewish Book Annual* (1990–1991), 132–47

LEON I. YUDKIN

al-SHAYKH, Hanān
Lebanese novelist, b. 1945, Beirut

S. was brought up in Ras al-Naba, a very conservative, unfashionable sector of Beirut. She first attended the local Muslim girls' primary school and then the more sophisticated Ahliya School. While still at school, she contributed articles to newspapers like *al-Nahār*. In 1963 she went to Cairo to study at the American College for Girls. During the four years she lived in Egypt, she wrote her first novel, *Intihār rajul mayyit* (1967; suicide of a dead man). In 1967 she returned to Beirut to resume journalism. But she did not stay long. Subsequently she has lived in the Arabian Peninsula, where she wrote *Faras al-shaitān* (1971; praying mantis), and in London, where she published two more novels: *Hikāyat Zahrah* (1980; *The Story of Zahra,* 1987) and *Misk al-ghazāl* (1989; *Women of Sand and Myrrh,* 1990), as well as a collection of short stories, *Wardat al-sahrā'* (1982; the desert rose).

S. first came to international attention with the publication of *Hikāyat Zahrah.* Lebanese critics condemned its overt expression of sexuality, unprecedented for a woman. Many tried to dismiss the novel as artless. But this ploy for the suppression of women's writings failed; in 1986, the novel was translated into French under the title *L'histoire de Zahra,* and the following year it came out in English. European accolades found their echo at home, so that when *Misk al-ghazāl* was published, its sensationalist language and subject matter were not universally attacked. Indeed, some Arab critics in the West hailed it as a great novel.

Whereas her earlier works are more autobiographical in nature, *Hikāyat Zahrah* conveys little if anything of the author's life. It tells the story of a pathetic middle-aged woman who finds in the Lebanese Civil War an opportunity to escape the oppression and physical exploitation that had until then been her lot. After a brief sojourn in Africa, where she had stayed with her lecherous uncle and had to marry one of his undesirable associates, she returns to a Beirut at war with itself. Chaos transforms her and gives her a courage she had never before experienced. She initiates an affair with a sniper, which culminates in a pregnancy that she wants, but which he ends by killing her.

Misk al-ghazāl is more sexually explicit in its language than *Hikāyat Zahrah* and more critical of social mores. Set primarily in an expatriate community in an anonymous desert country, *Misk al-ghazāl* tells the story of four women, each from her own perspective. Two of the women are Arabs from the country in question, one is Lebanese, and the fourth is American. Each woman is seeking to fulfill herself in a context that militates

against women's self-assertion. Each woman chooses a different path that is ultimately self-destructive. The novel allows for few successful feminist options.

Although S. has become known as a novelist, her short stories are powerful and well crafted. They criticize patriarchal notions of how Arab women should behave, but they also praise Arab cultures that adhere to a premodern way of life and to traditions that give women a measure of power to negotiate their own realities.

BIBLIOGRAPHY: Cooke, M., *War's Other Voices: Women Writers on the Lebanese Civil War* (1988), 50–60; Larson, C. R., "The Fiction of H. al-S., Reluctant Feminist," *WLT,* 65, 1 (Winter 1991), 14–17

MIRIAM COOKE

SHEVCHUK, Valery
Ukrainian novelist, translator, literary historian, critic, and editor, b. 20 Aug. 1939, Zhytomyr

S. was born into a family of blue-collar workers. Upon completing secondary schooling in 1956, he received an additional year of technical training and found employment in the construction industry. In 1958 he enrolled at the Kiev University, from where he graduated in 1963 with a degree in history and archival sciences. S. worked briefly as a reporter for the newspaper *Moloda Hvardiya,* and served from 1963 to 1965 in the Soviet army in the Murmansk region. Upon discharge from the army, S. returned to Kiev, where he managed to obtain employment as a museum specialist. He lost his position in 1966, after the arrest of his brother, Anatoly, and took up writing as a full-time profession. S. is a member of the Union of Writers and a member of the International P.E.N. Club.

During the Thaw of the 1960s, S. made a name for himself with the publication of the collections of short stories *Sered tyzhnya* (1967; during the week) and *Vechir svyatoyi oseni* (1969; night of the sacred autumn), of which the miniature "Miy batko nadumav sadyty sad" ("My Father Decided to Plant Orchards," 1973), a beautifully gentle autobiographical tale of life and a father-son relationship, is a masterpiece of short prose. At that time he also published a collection of novels dealing with life in contemporary Ukraine, *Naberezhna, 12. Seredokhrestya* (1968; 12 Riverside. the crossroads), for which he was taken to task by Soviet critics and officially excluded from Ukraine's literary life until 1979. His superb translation of a collection of poems by Ukraine's premier philosopher, Hryhory Skovoroda (1722–1794), entitled

Sad pisen (1968; repub. 1972, 1980, 1983; orchard of songs), initiated a new phase in his activity. S. eventually established himself as a translator par excellence of Ukrainian baroque literature and of Polish poetry of the 17th and 18th cs.

S. broke his enforced silence in 1979 with the publication of his collection of novels entitled *Kryk pivnya na svitanku* (the cry of the cock at dawn), and in the 1980s his works began to appear regularly. A new collection of short stories, *Dolyna dzherel* (1981; valley of springs), featuring themes from lives of Ukrainian artists, was followed by a series of historical novels set in the 12th to 19th cs., in which fact and fiction, closely interwoven, provide an evolving portrait of the Ukrainian intellectual and his role in Ukraine's historical process. They include *Na poli smyrennomu* (1983; *The Meek Shall Inherit,* 1989), set in the days of Kievan Rus', and *Try lystky za viknom* (1986; three leaves outside the window), for which he was awarded the prestigious Shevchenko Prize for 1989. Of special significance among his recent publications are the novel *Dzygar odvichny* (1990; the eternal clock), a chronicle of contemporary family life presented from the perspective of a child, and the powerful short story *Ya duzhe kho-chu podyvytys* (1991; I very much like to see), written in 1962 in the form of the memoir of a dead man, about the horror of death, revolution, war, and life in a totalitarian system.

S.'s imaginative prose is informed by magic realism (q.v.), in which the elements of Ukraine's legends and mythology are interwoven with subtle psychological probings into the human soul. His is a *littérature désengagée,* nonpolitical and de-ideologized, focused on the human being's role in life and the history of the nation. In works that have a contemporary setting, S. seeks to eschew moral values and ethical norms for a society that has lost its spiritual absolutes. In this quest, the author journeys into Ukraine's historical past and into his own soul. His mission is to acquaint his reader with the complexities, enigmas, and mysteries of Ukrainian culture, a great part of which, according to him, has been forgotten or lost over the centuries. His ultimate goal is to rediscover and to redefine this culture in the light of objective truth, and to see himself and his contemporaries as its product.

S.'s work as compiler and editor of literary collections is of special significance for Ukraine's cultural renaissance of the 1980s and 1990s. Deftly combining literary scholarship with artistic taste and intuition, he has edited or coedited a number of anthologies of Ukrainian poetry, among them *Apollonova lyutnya: Kyyivski poety XVII–XVIII st.* (1982; Apollonian lute: Kievan poets of 17th–18th cs.), *Antolohiya ukrayinskoyi poeziyi. Ukrayinska*

dozhovtneva poeziya. Poeziya XI–XVIII st. (1984; an anthology of Ukrainian poetry: Ukrainian pre-October poetry. Poetry of the 11th–18th cs.), *Pisni Kupidona. Lyubovna poeziya na Ukrayini v XVI poch. XIX st.* (1984; the songs of Cupid: love poetry in Ukraine from the 16th c. to the beginning of the 19th c.), and an anthology of Ukrainian heroic poetry in two volumes entitled *Marsove pole* (1988–1989; the field of Mars). He has also edited the works of a number of Ukrainian classical authors, and written several full-length studies on Ukrainian literature and culture.

Selected works of S. have been translated into more than twenty languages. Most recently, some of his works have been dramatized and performed in Ukrainian theaters, and his popularity, both in Ukraine and outside its borders, is steadily increasing.

FURTHER WORKS: *Dim na hori* (1983); *Malenke vechirnye intermetstso* (1984); *Kamyana luna* (1987); *Myslenne derevo* (1989); *Ptakhy z nevy-dymoho ostrova* (1989); *Vybrani tvory* (1989); *Panna kvitiv* (1990)

BIBLIOGRAPHY: Luckyj, G. S. N., *Modern Ukrainian Short Stories* (1973), 226; Bilenko, A., "V. S.: *The Ferryman,"* *Ukraine,* 3 (Mar. 1987), 34–37; Pavlyshyn, M., "Mythological, Religious, and Philosophical Topoi in the Prose of V. S.," *SlavR,* 50 (1991), 905–13

LEONID RUDNYTZKY

SHUKSHIN, Vasily Makarovich

Russian short-story writer, screenwriter, and novelist, b. 25 July 1929, Srostki, Altai; d. 2 Oct. 1974, Stanitsa kletskaya, Volgograd Region

The year of S.'s birth coincided with the forced collectivization of peasant farmers in the U.S.S.R., a fact not lost on S.'s literary biography. The massive destruction of entire villages and the uprooting of families through inclusion into collective farms (kolkhozy) or migration into the cities haunt the histories of S.'s characters. Born in a small rural village, S. finished seven years of school, worked at his local kolkhoz, then at odd jobs in central Russian cities, before serving in the Soviet navy from 1949 to 1952. Finishing high school by correspondence, S. taught evening school in Srostki before entering the All-Union Institute of Cinematography in Moscow in 1954, where he studied directing with M. I. Romm. He began writing as part of his film training and published his first collection of short stories, *Selskie zhiteli* (1963; country folk), two years after graduating. His first full-length film, *Zhivyot takoy paren* (1964;

there lives this guy), won the Golden Lion of Saint Mark Award at the 16th Venice Film Festival. His second film, *Vash syn i brat* (1965; your son and brother), followed a year later and was awarded the Vasilev Brothers State Prize of the Russian Republic (RSFSR). Both films drew on S.'s short stories for their scripts. In 1965 S.'s first novel, *Lyubaviny* (the Lyubavins), was also published, whose sequel was posthumously discovered and brought out in 1987.

S.'s early stories introduce characters who normally hail from the country, particularly his own Altai region of Siberia. These characters are fiercely independent, simple people: drivers, mechanics, carpenters, librarians. Suspicious of the big city, they are prickly, uncompromising people whose moral discoveries often stem from the offenses and injustices they suffer at the hands of their spouses, neighbors, or friends. Description is spare. Plots are advanced primarily through character dialogues colored by local dialects and conversational turns of speech. The cinematic style of S.'s stories lends freshness and immediacy. Many stories are ironic or slightly humorous.

In tone and theme, *Lyubaviny* strikes a more somber note. Set in the 1920s on the eve of collectivization, it depicts an Altai village where Soviet reforms have yet to penetrate. Yegor Lyubavin is the first of the more elemental characters in S.'s prose who rebel against authority and seek some sort of higher transcendence. This spiritual deliverance—the search for *volya* (liberty or freedom) or a "holiday of the soul"—is a recurring theme in S.'s mature prose and figures in the title of S.'s second novel, *Ya prishel dat vam volyu* (1971; I have come to give you freedom). The latter is a treatment of Stenka Razin, the leader of a peasant rebellion against Czar Aleksey in 1670. S. admired Razin's intensely felt craving for immediate and complete justice, a trait shared by many of S.'s characters.

S.'s stories written in the mid-1960s and later are more complex thematically. Although neither collectivization nor World War II are treated directly by S., the uprooting of millions of Russians finds its reflection in the lives S. describes. These heroes of his mature works often cannot find a place for themselves. In seeking physical roots and spiritual transcendence, they become transient truth seekers who, through a combination of naïveté, misdirected passion, restlessness, rootlessness, or impulsiveness, clash with falsehood, complacency, and pettiness. In collections such as *Tam, vdali* (1968; there, in the distance), *Zemlyaki* (1970; men of one soil), *Kharaktery* (1973; types), and *Besedy pri yasnoy lune* (1974; conversations under a clear moon) S.'s protagonists suffer when their visions of spiritual release—often as vague

and boundless as their native Siberian landscapes—are clouded by petty bureaucrats, antagonistic colleagues, unsympathetic women, or the finality of death. S.'s characters often are depicted in transition, either moving from the country to the city or adapting to a changing countryside that is absorbing city culture and values. *Kalina krasnaya* (1974; *Snowball Berry Red,* 1979) treats all of these themes in its depiction of a recidivist thief's failed attempt to give up his former gang of urban criminals and reclaim the folk heritage of his rural childhood. The hero's rootlessness is seen as the cause for his life of crime. Controversial in its atypical themes and almost killed by censorship, the film—and through it, the novella—was nevertheless an incredible national success, for which S. was posthumously awarded the Lenin Prize in 1976.

S.'s later works are also pervaded by an urgent existential questioning, and it is his exploration of existential themes that makes him a more universally interesting and important author. S. resisted being labeled a writer of "village" or "country prose," insisting his interests lay primarily with humanity. How people are born, marry, and die is his self-professed interest as a writer. As if testifying to this fact, the titles of over half of his stories refer, through epithets, names, or quoted speech, directly to people. Moreover, the "eccentrics," "cranks," "strange people," and "scandal-mongers"—highlighted by critics as favorite subjects for S.—are really not country "types" or urban misfits so much as they are recognizable, even typical, representatives of the human race. Reflections on death and the purpose of life also inform S.'s later stories.

Today, S. is rightfully credited with revitalizing the short-story form in the Soviet Union. His anecdotal, powerfully economic authorial voice, and the wonderfully understated quality of his prose, have earned S. a distinct place in Soviet literary history.

FURTHER WORKS: *Brat moy* (1975); *Izbrannye proizvedeniya v dvukh tomakh* (1975); *Kinopovesti* (1975; rev. ed., 1988); *Rasskazy* (1975); *Osenyu* (1976); *Do tretikh petukhov* (1976); *Okhota zhit* (1977); *Nrastvennost est pravda* (1979); *Voprosy samomu sebe* (1981); *Rasskazy* (1984); *Sobranie sochineniy v tryokh tomakh* (1984); *Mgnoveniya zhizni* (1989). FURTHER VOLUMES IN ENGLISH: *I Want to Live* (1973); *Snowball Berry Red, and Other Stories* (1979); *Roubles in Words, Kopeks in Figures* (1985)

BIBLIOGRAPHY: Baklanov, G., et al., "Reality and the Writer's Vision: Round Table Discussion," *SovL*, 9, 330 (Sept. 1975), 123–38; le Fleming, S.,

"V. S.–A Contemporary Scythian," in Freeborn, R., R. R. Milner-Gullard, and C. A. Ward, eds., *Russian and Slavic Literature* (1976), 449–66; Dunlop, J. B., "The Search for Peace," *TLS*, 30 June 1978, 739–40; Heller, M., "V. S.: In Search of Freedom," *Snowball Berry Red, and Other Stories* (1979), 213–33; Hosking, G., *Beyond Socialist Realism* (1980), 162–79; Mann, R., "St. George in V. S.'s 'Kalina krasnaya,' " *SEEJ*, 28 (1984), 445–54; Ignashev, D. N., "V. S.'s *Srezal* and the Question of Transition," *SEER*, 66, 3 (July 1988), 337–56; Ignashev, D. N., "The Art of V. S.: *Volya* through Song," *SEEJ*, 32, 3 (Fall 1988), 415–27

JOHN R. GIVENS

SIBURAPHA

(pseud. of Kulap Saipradit) Thai novelist, essayist, and journalist, b. 31 March 1905, Bangkok; d. 16 June 1974, Beijing, China

Despite a modest family background S. attended the prestigious Thepsirin School in Bangkok, where his interest in writing was awakened. On leaving school he worked as a journalist while contributing fiction to various magazines. In 1928 he launched the short-lived but popular *Suphapburut* magazine, which established his reputation in journalistic and literary circles. For the next decade he held senior editorial posts on most of the major Bangkok dailies; disillusioned, however, by the failure of the 1932 revolution to institute genuine reform, S. became more outspoken in his views on social injustice and censorship, which led him increasingly into conflict with the government of Field Marshal Phibun Songkhram.

In 1947 S. went to Australia on a study trip; when he returned the following year, he became more active in his opposition to the ruling military régime. His criticisms were expressed both in newspaper articles and in short stories while he also became a prominent figure in the Thai branch of the worldwide Peace Movement set up to oppose the war in Korea. He was eventually arrested in 1952 as part of a broad military clamp-down on those suspected of communist sympathies. He was sentenced to thirteen years imprisonment but released in 1957 in an amnesty. He made trips to Moscow and Beijing, but, while in the latter, decided to seek asylum when he learned that Field Marshal Sarit Thanarat had seized power in a military coup in 1958. S. never returned to Thailand and died in exile in 1974.

S. achieved rapid popularity as a romantic novelist in the late 1920s when the Thai novel was beginning to develop its own identity. Many of his early novels were serialized in his own *Su-*

phapburut magazine. Works of this period such as *Luk phuchai* (1928; a real man), *Prap phayot* (1928; taming a shrew), *Hua chai pratthana* (1928; the heart's desire), *Lok sanniwat* (1928; life's destiny), *Man manut* (1928; the evil one), and *Phachon bap* (1929; encounter with sin) are characterized by complex plots that depend on improbable coincidences for their satisfactory resolution. There is evidence of S.'s concern with social injustice, especially in *Luk phuchai* and *Lok sanniwat,* but it does not constitute a major theme in his early works.

Throughout the 1930s S.'s fictional output was small, although it included two of his best-known novels, *Songkhram chiwit* (1932; the war of life) and *Khang lang phap* (1937; *Behind the Painting,* 1990). The former was a major departure from his early work and reflected a more mature appreciation of the role and responsibility of the writer. Influenced by Dostoevsky's *Poor Folk* (1846) and likewise written in an epistolary style, it is often described by Thai critics as a "humanitarian" novel; in fact, the novel is an outspoken attack on aspects of Thai society, the letters describing the miseries of poverty, the selfishness and vanity of the rich, religious hypocrisy, government corruption, inadequate medical facilities, and the lack of freedom of speech. By contrast, *Khang lang phap* set partly in Japan, is a confessional novel about a young man's infatuation with an older married woman and his subsequent awakening, after the death of her husband, to the frailty of his own romantic feelings. With its subtle undercurrent of frustrated sexuality and its attempt to deal with emotions in an honest way, it is considered by most Thais to be not only S.'s most stylistically accomplished work but also one of the best-written novels in Thai. *Khang lang phap* has been reprinted more than a dozen times, made into a film (directed by Piak Poster), studied in schools, and translated into Chinese, Japanese, and English.

In the decade that followed the appearance of *Khang lang phap* S.'s fictional output was minimal. On his return from Australia in 1948, however, he once again began to write prolifically. His nonfiction of the period included a series of articles on Marxism, and translations from Maxim Gorky and Anton Chekhov (qq.v.). Short stories such as "Khon phuak nan" (1950; "Those Kind of People," 1990), "Kho raeng noi thoe" (1950; "Lend us a Hand," 1990), and "Khao tu'n" (1952; "The Awakening," 1990), and the short novel, "Chon kwa rao cha phop kan ik" (1950; until we meet again), were blunt and uncompromising in their portrayal of social injustice and reflected S.'s politically committed view of literature. More ambitious in conception was *Lae pai khang na* (2 vols., 1955, 1957; look forward), conceived as a trilogy, but of which only the first two volumes appeared; in this work S. set out to provide a panoramic view of Thai history from the end of the absolute monarchy in 1932, through the experiences of a young boy studying and later working in Bangkok.

Throughout the 1960s S.'s links with communism made his name taboo in Thailand. In the liberal political climate of the 1970s, however, he was rediscovered and energetically promoted as a major figure in the struggle for social justice within Thailand. His later fiction was highly praised by progressive critics and became a model for many young writers in the 1970s. Conservative critics, though, regarded it as lacking literary merit but saw S.'s early novels as important in the development of the Thai novel. As a result of Thailand's stability in the 1980s S. is no longer regarded as a "dangerous" writer, and recent evaluations of his work acknowledge the significance of both his early "romantic" work and his later "political" writing in the development of Thai fiction.

FURTHER WORKS: *Amnat chai* (1930); *Saen rak saen khaen* (1930); *Tham ngan tham ngoen* (1934); *Phu thi ma chak lok borisut* (1934); *Phu'an tang phet* (1934); *Tai hon raek* (1934); *Thaeng thong* (1935); *Khang khu'n khang raem* (1935); *Kon taeng ngan* (1937); *Nop* (1938); *Sing thi chiwit tongkan* (1939); *Sunthari* (1942); *Kae thi phlat fung* (1949); *Nak bun chak chantan* (1949); *Mahaburut khong chantima* (1949); *Khao lu'ak lambarene nai sayam* (1949); *Kham khan rap* (1950); *Ai nu long thang* (1950); *Prakai mai nai duangta khong khao* (1951)

BIBLIOGRAPHY: Batson, B., "K. S. and the 'War of Life,' " *JSSB*, 69 (1981), 58–73; Smyth, D. A., "The Later Short Stories of S.," in Davidson, J. H. C. S., ed., *Lai Sü Thai: Essays in Honour of E. H. S. Simmonds* (1987), 98–115; Smyth, D. A., Introduction to *Behind the Painting and Other Stories* (1990), 1–44

DAVID A. SMYTH

SKÁRMETA, Antonio

Chilean novelist and short-story writer, b. 7 Nov. 1940, Antofagasta

After President Salvador Allende's socialist regime was overthrown by a military coup in September 1973, many Chilean writers took refuge abroad; among these, S. is perhaps the best known. The grandson of Yugoslavian immigrants who arrived in Chile in the late 19th c., S. graduated from the University of Chile with a degree in philosophy. With the aid of a Fulbright scholarship he completed his M.A. in Spanish literature at Columbia University and then returned to Chile to teach at his alma mater and work as a journalist. He lived in Buenos Aires from 1973 until 1975, after which he spent more than a decade in West Berlin, where he directed films and held a professorial post at the German Academy of Cinematography. In 1989 he returned to Chile.

S.'s first book, a collection of short fiction entitled *El entusiasmo* (1967; enthusiasm), depicts the vitality and spontaneity of youth on the threshold of adulthood. *Desnudo en el tejado* (1969; naked on the roof), S.'s second collection, initiates the author's preoccupation with social and political issues, for which he is well known today. Although not political in its subject matter, the best tale of this collection is "El ciclista del San Cristóbal" (the bicyclist of San Cristóbal), which is narrated by a young bicyclist before, during, and after a race. What determines the excellence of this story is its celebration of two victories, one sporting and the other spiritual. Thus the narrator not only wins the race, but also, through love and will power, effects the resurrection of his dying mother. Other virtues of this story are S.'s adept manipulation of the interior monologue and colloquial language, by which he brings the reader into direct contact with the emotions gushing from the mind of the bicyclist.

A fine example of S.'s politically inspired short fiction is "La llamada" (the telephone call), which appeared in his collection *Novios y solitarios* (1975; fiancés and lonely beings). This brief sketch portrays a professor of literature who has recently been intimidated by the police, perhaps because of something he said in the classroom; as he leaves the institution where he is employed, he is again accosted by two policemen, one formerly his student. An unnerving conversation ensues, after which the professor enters a café to make a telephone call. But upon seeing a man sitting nearby reading a newspaper, he changes his mind and leaves. S.'s technique is reminiscent of Ernest Hemingway's (q.v.), consisting of dialogue and unadorned narration, obliging the reader to discover possible cause-and-effect relationships from the limited material presented. "La llamada" depicts the terror and paranoia felt by Chileans, who prior to 1973 had taken democracy and freedom of speech for granted.

S.'s first novel, *Soñé que la nieve ardía* (1975; *I Dreamt the Snow Was Burning*, 1985), is a moving dramatization of events during and immediately following the Allende regime. The protagonist is a young, ambitious soccer player, Arturo, who comes from the backwaters of Chile to Santiago determined to make his fortune in a professional sports career. His materialistic, bourgeois agenda soon clashes with the values of idealistic Marxists sharing his boarding house. Revolutionary in its negation of classical syntax, the experimental style of this novel captures the intensity of a crucial period in recent Chilean history. S.'s next novel, *No pasó nada* (1980; nothing happened) stems directly from S.'s exile in West Germany. A bildungsroman, its subject matter is the rite of passage to manhood of a fourteen-year-old son of Chilean exiles in West Berlin. As in most of S.'s works, language plays an important role; in this case it reveals the protagonist's psychological adjustment to his new environment as he assimilates German slang and the vocabulary of sports, food, and pop art. As a story of exiles suddenly thrust into an unfamiliar environment, *No pasó nada* is both timely and universal. S.'s commitment to the socialist cause is nowhere more evident than in *La insurrección* (1982; *The Insurrection*, 1983), about the Sandinistas' revolt against Anastasio Somoza's dictatorial regime in Nicaragua. Described in epic form, the action takes place in the city of León, where the two leading characters become leaders in the movement, which triumphs on 19 July 1979. The use of many narrative voices in the text seems particularly appropriate because this technique, like the array of characters, expresses the collective will of Nicaragua in crisis.

S.'s most successful novel to date is *Ardiente paciencia* (1985; *Burning Patience*, 1987), the protagonists of which are the poet Pablo Neruda (q.v.) and Mario Jiménez, a seventeen-year-old fisherman's son who becomes Neruda's mailman and intimate friend. The novel's time frame covers the period between 1969 and 1973, that is, from the year before the election of Salvador Allende to less than a month after the military coup and Neruda's death. The most important theme is the power of poetry. *Ardiente paciencia* is a tragicomical tribute to Latin America's greatest poet, but it is also replete with passages reminiscent of Gabriel García Márquez's (q.v.) *Cien años de soledad* (1967; *One Hundred Years of Solitude*, 1970). Characterized by parody, irony, and the masterful use of metaphor, S.'s style in this novel is worthy of the highest praise.

Match Ball (1989; set point) marks a new direction in S.'s oeuvre because of its total lack of political commitment. Laced with irony and black humor, this novel is narrated by a middle-aged American antihero, who is married to a wealthy, aristocratic German woman. While successfully practicing medicine in West Berlin he falls madly in love with a fifteen-year-old tennis champion, for whom he sacrifices marriage and professional reputation. Perhaps the most entertaining of S.'s novels, *Match Ball* emerges as a satire of the

pleasure-seeking, cosmopolitan jet set, a satire enhanced by a sprinkling of erotic scenes, foreign words, and references to other literary works.

In both his novels and short stories S. has demonstrated a remarkable sensitivity to today's political climate. More important, however, are his mastery of poetic style, his insightful understanding of youth, and his subtle sense of humor. It is hardly surprising that he has become one of Spanish America's most admired and popular writers.

FURTHER WORKS: *El ciclista del San Cristóbal* (1971); *Tiro libre* (1973)

BIBLIOGRAPHY: Lyon, T., on *La insurrección*, *WLT*, 57, 3 (Summer 1983), 433; McMurray, G. R., "The Spanish American Short Story from Quiroga to Borges," in Peden, M. S., ed., *The Latin American Short Story: A Critical History* (1983), 131–32; Silva Cáceres, R., ed., *Del cuerpo a las palabras: La narrativa de A. S.* (1983); Rojo, G., "Explicación de A. S.," *Hispam*, 13, 37 (Apr. 1984), 65–72; Benavides, R. F., on *Soñé que la nieve ardía*, *WLT*, 58, 4 (Autumn 1984), 577; Filer, M. E., on *Ardiente paciencia*, *WLT*, 60, 3 (Summer 1986), 450; Rojo, G., and C. Steele, *Ritos de iniciación: Tres novelas cortas de Hispanoamérica* (1986), 65–75; McMurray, G. R., *Spanish American Writing since 1941* (1987), 138–40; Bannura-Spriga, M. G., "El juego y el deseo en la obra de A. S.," *Inti*, 24–25 (Fall–Spring 1986–1987), 155–61; Rodríguez, F. M., "A. S.: De *El entusiasmo* a *La insurrección*," *Atenea: Revista de Ciencia, Arte y Literatura de la Universidad de Concepción*, 455 (1987), 175–78; Rodríguez Hernández, R., "Nueva novela histórica hispanoamericana: *La insurrección* y *Un día en la vida*," *TCrit*, 13, 36–37 (1987), 153–63; Cortínez, V., "Polifonía: Isabel Allende y A. S.," *Plaza: Revista de Literatura*, 14–15 (Spring–Fall 1988), 73–80; Blanc, M., "A. S.: Cuentos y novelas," *Chasqui*, 13, 2 (Nov. 1989), 64–78; Tittler, J., "Toward a Revolutionary Writing: A. S.'s *La insurrección*," in Bevan, D., ed., *Literature and Revolution* (1989), 97–105

GEORGE R. MCMURRAY

SNYDER, Gary

American poet and essayist, b. 8 May 1930, San Francisco, Cal.

S. is a poet often identified with the San Francisco Renaissance of the 1950s and with the ecology movement that began in the 1960s and continues today. Born in San Francisco, he moved to Portland, Oregon, attended Reed College, studied anthropology, and briefly attended graduate school. But in 1956, after working as a logger and forest ranger in the Pacific Northwest, he went to Japan where he lived for over a decade, eventually becoming a practicing Buddhist. He returned to the U.S. in 1968 and now lives in the foothills of the Sierra Nevada range in California; he recently joined the faculty at the University of California, Davis.

S.'s poetry was deeply marked from the first by his interest in hiking and the closely observed— even intensely worshiped—processes and values of nature. As for poetic form, S. has claimed that the rhythms of his physical work determine the rhythms of his line. In *Myths and Texts* (1960; rev. ed., 1978) he demonstrated this claim in tightly constructed, meditative lyrics in a sequence that drew on imagism and Zen philosophy.

In *The Back Country* (1968) and *Regarding Wave* (1970) he began to move beyond imagism and its extension into objectivism by exploring more deeply the metaphoric basis of the common and mythic patterns of life and consciousness. He accomplished this largely by intensifying his commitment to a precise and even austere use of language and rhythm. His essays in *Earth House Hold* (1969) did a great deal to articulate the ecological consciousness that formed a valuable part of the social activism of the time. These essays are remarkably consonant with his poetry, and demonstrate a focus of intellect and feeling, combined with a social awareness and political commitment that set his work apart from the confessional and academic writing of many of his contemporaries. In 1977, he published another book of essays, *The Old Ways*, followed by a collection of interviews and talks, *The Real Work* (1980). *The Practice of the Wild* (1990) is the latest collection of S.'s prose, and continues his discussion of the crucial ethical and political issues associated with ecology and its critique of industrial capitalism.

In the poems of *Turtle Island* (1974), awarded the Pulitzer Prize, S. extended his explorations into myth and metaphor, invoking both the ancient fables of pre-Columbian America and the prophetic tradition and shamanistic practices more frequently found in the writings of anthropologists and students of comparative religion. After a decade in which S. published little, there appeared two more volumes of poetry, *Axe Handles* (1983) and *Left Out in the Rain* (1986). The latter volume contained poems from as far back as the earliest volumes and showed how consistent are S.'s concerns and how patient he is as a reviser and polisher of his work.

S.'s work has been widely appreciated and continues to influence poets, but also students of

ecology. Often seen by some as no more than a ''beatnik,'' S. has carved for himself a steady path from the imagism and bohemianism of his early work through to a more articulated and even cosmic view of modern experience. He is part of that culture of modernism which calls into question the very valuation of culture itself. His use of ''primitive'' values, and his suggestion that a life that is separated from natural rhythms and a respect for the biosphere is not worthy of human effort, makes him considerably bolder than many lyric poets.

FURTHER WORKS: *Riprap and Cold Mountain Poems* (1959; rev. ed., 1965); *Six Sections from Mountains and Rivers without End* (1970; rev. ed., 1977); *He Who Hunted Birds in His Father's Village* (1979)

BIBLIOGRAPHY: Parkinson, T., ''The Poetry of G. S.,'' *SoR*, 4 (Summer 1968), 616–32; Altieri, C., ''G. S.'s *Turtle Island:* Reconciling the Roles of Seer and Prophet,'' *Boundary 2*, 4 (1976); Steuding, B., *G. S.* (1976); Kern, R., ''Clearing the Ground: G. S. and the Modernist Imperative,'' *Criticism,* 19 (Spring 1977), 158–77; Molesworth, C., *G. S.'s Vision: Poetry and the Real Work* (1983); Murphy, P. D., *Critical Essays on G. S.* (1990)

CHARLES MOLESWORTH

SOKOLOV, Sasha

Russian novelist, essayist, and poet, b. 6 Nov. 1943, Ottawa, Canada

S. is the premier avant-garde stylist to appear in Russian literature during the 1970s and 1980s. Born in Canada, where his father (in reality a spy) was stationed as a military diplomat, S. returned to Moscow in 1946. After an unsuccessful period in a military foreign-language training institute, an undetected attempt at defection, and short stays in jail and a mental hospital, S. was a member of the short-lived modernist literary group SMOG, which was broken up by the KGB in the mid-1960s. During and after attending Moscow University, S. worked as a journalist in the provincial and Moscow press, before becoming a game warden so that he would have time to write. Completing his first novel in 1973, S. sent it abroad and began his long campaign to emigrate. S.'s arrival in the U.S. in 1976 was heralded by Vladimir Nabokov's (q.v.) rare praise for the young writer's work. For the next twelve years S. lived in the U.S. and Canada while gaining a reputation as a brilliant, if difficult, writer. In 1988 S. returned to Europe; first to Greece, and then, with the flowering of glasnost, to the U.S.S.R., where he was effusively welcomed as a major literary figure. S. returned to his native Canada in 1990.

Shkola dlia durakov (1976; *A School for Fools,* 1977) grows out of S.'s childhood encounters with Soviet educational institutions and the dreary duplicity of daily Soviet life. These experiences are depicted through the innocent eyes of the schizophrenic narrator, a student at a "special" school, who sees himself as two people. Much of the dialogue-free novel is in the form of exchanges between the boy's two competing personalities. There is no plot, and the narrative consists of a small number of scenes that recur in evolving variants. These center upon his attempts to understand the fundamental human experiences of love, sex, and death. The novel's central conflict is between the forces that oppress the boy: the misanthropic father, who is a public prosecutor, the psychiatrist and the hospital, and certain of the officials of the school for fools and those that promise freedom of person and imagination. Characters representing the latter are identified with nature and the liberating force of the wind. The narrative, which has no time line, progresses by a complex pattern of phonetic associations and recurrent images. The language is intensely poetic, full of wit and invention. Widely admired and much translated abroad, *Shkola dlia durakov* became an underground classic in the U.S.S.R. Finally published there thirteen years after its appearance in the West, it received an award as one of the best works published in 1989. It remains S.'s most popular work.

Mezhdu sobakoi i volkom (1980; between dog and wolf) differs radically in setting and complexity from S.'s first novel, which was set among the urban professional classes. S.'s duties as a game warden took him into the deep provinces of the upper Volga, a primitive timeless land of hunters and fishermen where his predecessor had died under mysterious circumstances. This provided the setting and central event of his second novel. Its title phrase "between dog and wolf" is an idiom meaning "twilight," that time of day when the shepherd cannot distinguish between his dog that guards his flock and the marauding wolf. All things blur indistinguishably: dog and wolf; day and night; life and death; reality and fantasy. In a broader sense the meaning of the title is "ambiguity," perhaps the key word in characterizing S.'s oeuvre. Groups of chapters are separated by sections of whimsical poetry that, in passing, provide glimpses of the real state of affairs. The book is a structural and stylistic tour de force, which has proved untranslatable. The novel has garnered much critical acclaim, but few readers. Nonetheless, the underground Leningrad literary journal *Chasy* awarded it its 1981 Andrey Bely Prize—an

award especially appropriate since Bely's (q.v.) masterpiece, *Peterburg* (1916, rev. ed., 1922; *Petersburg*, 1959, 1978) was one of the foundation works of literary modernism (q.v.).

Palisandriia (1985; *Astrophobia*, 1989) is an abrupt departure from the earlier, more involute novels. It is, in part, S.'s attempt to reach a wider audience. *Palisandriia* (the epic of Palisander) is a comic picaresque work with all the attributes of the mock epic: a hero of national importance, an extended journey, great obstacles surmounted, supernatural participation, and a baroquely ceremonious style. The book is also elegantly and perversely erotic. In a deliberate inversion of Nabokov's *Lolita* (1955), the very youthful Palisander is drawn to elderly women. Most of all, *Palisandriia* is a lampoon of several commercial genres: the juicy, name-dropping memoir, the political espionage thriller, the futurological fantasy, and the pornographic novel. *Palisandriia* is parody raised to the level of high art.

The heterogeneity of content and setting in S.'s novels is striking, but from a formal viewpoint, they are united by their obsession with language and by their tendency to dislocate the reader's consciousness and expectations. Time is not linear, but circumambient. Memories may be of the future as well as the past. The individual is not necessarily restricted to one gender; nor is incest to be avoided. Even the distinction between the living and the dead is blurred. S.'s novels contain no real plots; no temporal continuity, and little dialogue. Intended for sophisticated readers, they are elegant poetic structures, both disconcertingly elliptical and highly allusive. S. has discussed some of these matters in a series of essays initially delivered as lectures. No less than his novels, the essays are works of art, but in miniature.

S.'s highly stylized writing and his indifference to political and social concerns set him at odds with the realism that has dominated Russian prose in the 19th and 20th cs. He sees his goal as raising the level of Russian prose to that of poetry of the very highest order.

BIBLIOGRAPHY: Johnson, D. B., "A Structural Analysis of S. S.'s *School for Fools:* A Paradigmatic Novel," in Birnbaum, H., and T. Eekman, eds., *Fiction and Drama in Eastern and Southeastern Europe: Evolution and Experiment in the Postwar Period* (1980), 207–37; Matich, O., "S. S.'s *Palisandriia:* History and Myth," *RusR*, 45 (1986), 415–26; Johnson, D. B., "S. S.'s *Palisandriia*," *SEEJ*, 30, 3 (Fall 1986), 389–403; Johnson, D. B., "S. S.'s Twilight Cosmos: Themes and Motifs," *SlavR*, 45, 4 (1986), 639–49; special S. issue, *CASS*, 21, 3–4 (1987); Simmons, C., "Incarnations of the Hero Archetype in *School for*

Fools,'' in Mandelker, A., and R. Reeder, eds., *The Supernatural in Slavic and Baltic Literature: Essays in Honor of Victor Terras* (1988), 275–89; Johnson, D. B., ''S. S.: The New Russian Avant-Garde,'' *Crit,* 30, 3 (Spring 1989), 163–78; Johnson, D. B., ''The Galoshes Manifesto: A Motif in the Novels of S. S.,'' *OSP,* 22 (1989), 155–79; McMillin, A., ''Aberration or the Future: The Avant-Garde Novels of S. S.,'' in McMillin, A., ed., *From Pushkin to Palisandriia: Essays on the Russian Novel in Honor of Richard Freeborn* (1990), 229–43

D. BARTON JOHNSON

SOLARES, Ignacio

Mexican novelist and short-story writer, b. 15 Jan. 1945, Ciudad Juárez

S. has spent his professional life in Mexico City, where he works as a journalist and professor of literature at the National University of Mexico. From 1966 until 1976 he directed the cultural section of *Excélsior,* one of Mexico's leading newspapers. More recently he has edited several journals including *Revista de Revistas, Plural, Quimera,* and *Hoy.* Like many of Mexico's best-known men of letters, S. launched his career with the aid of a grant from the *Centro Mexicano de Escritores,* a workshop for aspiring young writers.

S.'s first novel, *Puerta del cielo* (1976; door to heaven), typifies his oeuvre. Its style is direct and readily accessible to most readers, its setting (Mexico City) and much of its action appear to be realistic, and its episodes bordering on the surreal or fantastic set it apart from the mainstream of Mexican fiction. The protagonist, a sixteen-year-old boy named Luis, is torn between religious fervor and sexual impulses that cause him intense feelings of anguish and guilt. The two narrative voices, that of the protagonist and that of the omniscient author, underscore the conflict between the natural desires of youth and an oppressive social environment. But it is the realistic presentation of Luis's religious hallucinations, and the fading thereof when he marries, that suggest the author's pessimistic view of the human experience.

In *Anómino* (1979; the anonymous note) the two protagonists emerge as psychological doubles, each complementing the other. Raúl Estrada, a middle-aged journalist and one of the two first-person narrators, awakens one night finding himself in the body of another man, Rubén Rentería. The story ends when the two protagonists fuse into a single identity bearing the name of Raúl Rentería. Though utterly fantastic, *Anónimo* is told in a straightforward manner both convincing and at times amusing to the reader. Its open ending creates the possibility of either a psychological or a metaphysical interpretation.

S.'s next novel, *El árbol del deseo* (1980; the wish tree) has been called the most intense and disturbing of his works. A psychological study of fear, it portrays a ten-year-old girl who, having been sexually abused by her father, flees from her home in terror, taking along her four-year-old brother. The novel is narrated by an objective, casual observer of surface reality, a strategy that stimulates the reader's imagination. The girl's adventures, one suspects, are more dream than reality, her nightmarish images of the city representing a fear-induced metaphor of pervasive evil and hopelessness.

S.'s fascination with Mexico City, both its past and its present, is nowhere as evident as in his most complex novel, *Casas de encantamiento* (1987; houses of enchantment). The plot derives from two principal narrative sources: the diary of a recently deceased journalist and the comments made by his friend as he reads the diary. An ingenious melange of science and self-conscious fiction, the novel not only depicts S.'s efforts to recreate the Mexican capital of four decades ago, but also includes within its text one of his stories, ''La ciudad'' (1975; the city). The fusion of dream and reality, together with temporal displacements and adroit use of different narrative perspectives, makes this work a significant achievement in literary technique.

S.'s best work to date is *Madero, el otro* (1989; Madero, the other), which combines elements of psychological and historical novels to paint a compelling portrait of Francisco Madero, the leader of the Mexican Revolution of 1910. In addition to the carefully researched historical events informing the plot, S. uses the second-person narrative voice to address ''the other Madero'' and thus delineate the dual nature of one of Mexico's most complex public figures. A spiritualist who sought to communicate with the dead, Madero was, on the one hand, a mystic and pacifist, and, on the other, a politician and revolutionary. This dichotomy in his psyche emerges not only from the narrative point of view, but also from the tragic turn of events when he fails to deal decisively with his enemies. S. admits that he invented scenes and dialogues and that in some instances he had to choose between conflicting versions of events. The end result of his endeavor is nevertheless a moving work of fiction with a ring of truth and a texture enhanced by the density of human experience.

S. emerges as one of contemporary Mexico's most talented novelists. His ability to capture the interest of his readers is one of his major assets, a feat he accomplishes by first representing a real, everyday situation and then effecting a smooth transition into the realm of the unreal. Although Mexico, its past, and its capital provide a familiar backdrop for his plots, his novels are also informed by the dreams, fears, and abnormal behavior of his protagonists. As critic Alfonso González states, S.'s works have the simplicity of a fairy tale and the complexity of a metaphysical treatise.

FURTHER WORKS: *El hombre habitado* (1975); *El problema es el otro* (1978); *Delirium tremens* (1979); *La fórmula de la inmortalidad* (1982); *Serafín* (1985)

BIBLIOGRAPHY: Beaupied, A. M., "La teoría de lo fantástico de Todorov en *Anónimo* de I. S.," *Chasqui*, 9, 2–3, (Feb.-March 1980), 59–64; Brushwood, J. S., "La realidad y la fantasía: Las novelas de I. S.," *La Semana de Bellas Artes*, 143 (27 Aug. 1980), 10–12; Ortega, M., "La 'Cristina' de S.," *El Machete*, 10 (Feb. 1981), 58; Brushwood, J. S., *La novela hispanoamericana del siglo XX* (1984), 344–46; Torres, V. F., on *Serafín*, "Sábado," supplement to *Uno Más Uno*, 14 Dec. 1985, 12; Brushwood, J. S., "Narrating Parapsychology: The Novels of I. S.," *Chasqui*, 18, 2 (Nov. 1989), 12–17; Prieto, F., on *Madero, el otro*, *Proceso*, 11 Dec. 1989, 56; Torres, V. F., "I. S.: Conocer al diablo para creer en Dios," *Narradores mexicanos de fin de siglo* (1989), 9–38; Brushwood, J. S., *"Casas de encantamiento,"* *Chasqui*, 19, 1 (May 1990), 121–22; González, A., "I. S.: Fear and Fantasy as Reality," *Euphoria and Crisis: Essays on the Contemporary Mexican Novel* (1990), 44–51

GEORGE R. MCMURRAY

SOLSTAD, Dag

Norwegian novelist, short-story writer, and dramatist, b. 16 July 1941, Sandefjord

S. is known as a leader in the so-called *Profil* generation, a group of writers associated with a student magazine who came to the fore in the late 1960s. Like most of the other members of the group, S. considered himself a Marxist-Leninist, and throughout the 1970s he consciously placed his art in the service of a hoped-for proletarian revolution in Norway. Many of his erstwhile compatriots have since given up on their radical politics, but S. has not been deterred by the absence of a Marxist revolution.

S. had his debut in 1965, when he published *Spiraler* (spirals), a Kafka-inspired volume of short stories dealing with loneliness and isolation. A collection of short prose, *Svingstol* (1967; a turn-

ing chair), followed; its terse style is reminiscent of that of Tarjei Vesaas (q.v.). S.'s first novel was *Irr! Grønt!* (1969; patina! green!). Its protagonist is a student from the country who is searching for liberation by consciously playing roles. The author got this idea from the Polish writer Witold Gombrowicz (q.v.), whom he also introduced in an article in the literary periodical *Vinduet* in 1969. S. found that liberation cannot be achieved, however, for everybody is subject to the roles that are imposed on them by late capitalism. S.'s next novel, *Arild Asnes, 1970* (1971; Arild Asnes, 1970), portrays an attempt at a far more radical break with society. Asnes, a writer, is a socialist intellectual who, paradoxically, is given freedom to write in order that he may confirm the basis for existence under capitalism. An important aspect of the story is how Asnes overcomes his distaste for the simple and direct language of the Marxists and, in the end, becomes able to make it his own.

Arild Asnes, 1970 created a big stir, but even more so did S.'s next novel, *25. september-plassen* (1974; the 25th of september square). It is a chronicle of the postwar era in Norway, in which the author wants to show that the working class was betrayed by its Labor Party leaders, who abandoned true socialism and collaborated with American capitalist interests. This novel was followed by a trilogy that consists of the volumes *Svik. Førkrigsår* (1977; betrayal: prewar years), *Krig. 1940* (1978; war: 1940), and *Brød og våpen* (1980; bread and weapons). Here S. gives his Marxist-inspired version of events before and during World War II, attempting, among other things, to show that the Norwegian Nazis, the German occupants, and the Norwegian bourgeoisie had common interests. But the story is also a highly readable one that contains skillfully drawn portraits of members of the working class and their lives during trying times.

At the end of the 1970s it became apparent both that the Norwegian working class had no desire for a Marxist-Leninist revolution and that it was extremely unlikely that such a desire could be generated despite the best efforts of the committed revolutionary writers. A number of committed writers found it necessary to pause and review their earlier activities and the ideology behind them. S.'s attempt at such an examination of his past came under the unwieldy title *Gymnaslærer Pedersens beretning om den store politiske vekkelsen som har hjemsøkt vårt land* (1982; high-school teacher Pedersen's account of the great political revival that has visited our country). S.'s next novel, *Forsøk på å beskrive det ugjennomtrengelige* (1984; an attempt to describe the impenetrable), on the other hand, represents a return to one of the author's earlier themes: The Labor

Party has created a society in which it is impossible for decent human beings to exist.

S.'s most recent book, simply titled *Roman 1987* (1987; novel 1987), earned him the Nordic Literary Prize the following year. It is another review of the history of the Marxist-Leninist movement and is, like *Gymnaslærer Pedersens beretning,* told in the first person. The protagonist abandons a promising career in teaching and research to become one with the working class by becoming a factory worker. His attempt fails, but he insists that the experience was nevertheless worth the effort. An apologia in the form of a novel, *Roman 1987* thus shows that S. has remained true to his convictions.

Most critics and literary historians would agree that S. is one of the most significant writers of contemporary Norway, second only to Kjartan Fløgstad (q.v.). He is clearly the outstanding representative of the politically committed writers who flourished in the 1970s, and his work in the 1980s has become even more interesting than his earlier books.

FURTHER WORKS: *Kamerat Stalin eller familien Nordby* (1975); *Artikler om litteratur* (1981); *Sleng på byen* (1983)

BIBLIOGRAPHY: Sehmsdorf, H. K., "From Individualism to Communism: The Political and Esthetic Transformation of D. S.'s Authorship," *PPNCFL,* 27, 1 (1976), 130–32; Sjåvik, J., "Language and Myth in D. S.'s *Arild Asnes, 1970,*" *PCP,* 18 (1983), 30–36; Rønning, H., "History, Identity, Communication: Trends in Recent Norwegian Fiction," *ScanR,* 76, 2 (1988), 95–102; Garton, J., "New Directions in Norwegian Literature," *RNL,* 12 (1989), 163–84; Kittang, A., *Allegory, Intertextuality and Irony in D. S.* (1989)

JAN I. SJÅVIK

SORESCU, Marin

Romanian poet, dramatist, novelist, translator, and essayist, b. 29 Feb. 1936, Bulzeşti, Dolj County

One of the most widely read and translated contemporary Romanian poets, S. was born in Bulzeşti, southern Romania, to a family of peasants with literary interests. After receiving his degree in philology from the University of Jassy (1960), S. worked as an editor for *Viaţa studenţească* and *Luceafărul,* where he also published his first poems. Between 1966 and 1972 he served as editor in chief of the Animafilm studio. Since 1978 he has been editing the literary magazine *Ramuri.* After his participations in the Edinburgh Festival (1971) and the International Writers' Program at the Uni-

versity of Iowa (1972), S.'s work has been published in several English translations. Among his many literary distinctions are the Poetry Prize of the Academia delle Muze, Florence (1978) and the International Fernando Riello Prize in Madrid (1983).

Singur printre poeţi (1964; alone amongst poets), a collection of spirited poetic parodies, and *Poeme* (1965; poems) announced S.'s exceptional gift for ironic observation. This gift was put to more earnest uses in *Moartea ceasului* (1966; the death of the clock) and *Tinereţea lui Don Quijote* (1968; *Don Quijote's Tender Years,* 1979), volumes that "defamiliarize" the familiar, constructing a new, self-ironic mythology from everyday realities. An instant favorite with readers, S.'s nonconformistic poetry contributed to the revival of poetic imagination in Romania after a decade of socialist pseudoart.

If the existential and metaphysical themes, such as life, death, creation, time—erotic love is conspicuously absent—predominate in the early poems, the following volumes balanced them with sociocultural concerns. *Tuşiţi* (1970; cough), *Suflete, bun la toate* (1972; soul, good for everything), *Astfel* (1973; thus), *Sărbători itinerante* (1978; movable feasts), probe psychological stereotypes, social fallacies, and skewed moral perspectives. The typical S. poem begins with a witty, pointed narrative that opens unexpected vistas of thought. This successful construction was imitated in the 1970s by lesser poets. Fortunately, at a time when S.'s poetry seemed inescapably caught in its own formula, the poet managed to surprise his readers with a collection of ironic love poems, *Descîntoteca* (1976; an archive of incantations), and with three volumes of prose-poetry entitled *La lilieci* (3 vols., 1973, 1977, 1981; among the lilacs), which recreated the mythic-autobiographical universe of S.'s native village from the perspective of a child, but with the refined self-consciousness of a postmodern poet who mixes archaic and contemporary idioms.

Though overshadowed by his success as a poet, S.'s playwriting has been remarkably innovative, bringing Romanian drama closer to the imaginative excellence of poetry. Under the influence of existentialism (q.v.), S.'s plays are concerned with the struggle of the self in a hostile environment, with survival and spiritual questing. *Iona* (1965; Jonah) rewrites a well-known myth, focusing on various forms of modern entrapment. In a dramatized monologue, the fisherman Jonah debates his position in time and space, seeking to recover the freedom of the outside world, but each effort projects him into the belly of a larger fish. *Paracliserul* (1970; the sexton) is another one-man play that explores the tensions between faith and historical change. Locked up inside an abandoned cathedral, the sexton burns candles and eventually his own body in a metaphoric-absurd attempt to restore a blackened glory to his church. *Matca* (1973; the matrix) portrays a more hopeful post-diluvian world in which contraries (youth and age, creation and destruction, male and female) strike a fragile balance that perpetuates life. The play's humble villagers are caught in a cosmic drama that ends with the reassertion of the life-giving "matrix" of motherhood.

Republished as *Setea muntelui de sare* (1974; *The Thirst of the Salt Mountain,* 1985), these "ontological tragedies" established S.'s reputation as Romania's foremost metaphysical playwright. As if to challenge this description, S. wrote simultaneously comedies that explored the absurd face of contemporary urban culture: *Există nervi* (1968; folks have nerves) and *Pluta meduzei* (1970; Medusa's raft). More recently, S. has taken an interest in recreative historical drama: *Răceala* (1976; *A Cold,* 1978) and *A treia ţeapă* (1978; *Vlad Dracula, the Impaler,* 1987) are well-documented plays with a large cast of characters and an anticonventional treatment of history that suggest ingenious parallels between the bloody medieval times of Vlad the Impaler and Ceauşescu's Romania.

S. has also published a novel, *Trei dinţi din faţă* (1977; three front teeth), an anthology of translations, *Tratat de inspiraţie* (1985; treatise on inspiration), and several volumes of critical essays: *Teoria sferelor de influenţă* (1969; the theory of impacting spheres), *Starea de destin* (1976; state of destiny), and *Uşor cu pianul pe scări* (1985; easy with that piano down the stairs). S.'s reputation, however, remains primarily linked to the "poetic revival" of the 1960s and 1970s. Often compared to Henri Michaux, Jacques Prévert, or Eugène Ionesco (qq.v.), S. is perhaps best seen as the skeptical-imaginative voice of an eastern Europe in pursuit of new cultural "transparencies" and connections.

FURTHER WORKS: *O aripă şi-un picior—Despre cum era să zbor* (1970); *Unghi* (1970); *Insomnii; Microeseuri* (1971); *Ocolul infinitului mic* (1973); *Norii* (1975); *Ceramică; Versuri* (1979); *Fîntîni în mare* (1982). FURTHER VOLUMES IN ENGLISH: *Frames* (1972); *This Hour* (1982); *Symmetries* (1982); *Selected Poems* (1983); *Let's Talk about the Weather* (1985); *The Biggest Egg in the World* (1987); *Hands behind My Back: Selected Poems* (1991)

BIBLIOGRAPHY: MacGregor-Hastie, R., Introduction to *Frames* (1982), 9–14; Hamburger, M., Introduction to *Selected Poems* (1983), 5–8; Silkin, J., Introduction to *Let's Talk about the Weather* (1985), viii–xi; Catanoy, N., on *Symmetries, Mioriţa,* 9, 1–2 (1985), 93; Dorian, M., on *M. S.: Selected Poems, WLT,* 59, 1 (Winter 1985), 86; Munteanu, R., "La poésie de M. S.," *La civilisation des livres* (1986), 263–79

MARCEL CORNIS-POPE

SOUTH AFRICAN LITERATURE

See Volume 4, page 285.

In Afrikaans

Afrikaans literature had undergone a transformation in the hands of the writers emerging in the 1960s, most notably André P. Brink, Breyten Breytenbach (qq.v.), and Etienne Leroux (1922–1989). This self-proclaimed group has been criticized for being all-male, all-white, and for looking toward Europe for their literary models; the subsequent developments in Afrikaans literature, however, are to be seen in the light of these initial challenges to the religious and moral values of the Calvinist fathers.

Of the writers of the 1960s, Brink and Breytenbach are still producing work; both, however, are increasingly writing through the medium of English. Of Breytenbach a number of works written in prison have appeared, among which are the five volumes of poetry collectively known as *Die ongedanste dans* (1983–1985; the undanced dance) and *The True Confessions of an Albino Terrorist* (1984). A novel, *Memory of Snow and Dust* (1989), has appeared, in which Breytenbach explores, as in much of his other work, the themes of exile and imprisonment. Brink's most recent novel, *States of Emergency* (1988), is, like Brink's novels from the 1970s, a portrayal of a love relationship against the backdrop of the violence and injustice of South African society. When the most distinguished novelist in Afrikaans, Etienne Leroux, died in 1989, he had completed eleven novels. The most important of these are contained in the Welgevonden trilogy: *Sewe dae by die Silbersteins, Een vir Azazel,* and *Die derde oog* (1962–1966; *To a Dubious Salvation,* 1972, comprising *Seven Days at the Silbersteins, One for the Devil,* and *The Third Eye*).

The most significant poet, following the death of N. P. van Wyk Louw (1906–1970), was D. J. Opperman (1914–1980). He recovered from a prolonged illness to write his most important work, *Komas uit 'n bamboesstok* (1979; comas from a bamboo stick). The work is presented as a voyage by the author (accompanied by Odysseus, Marco Polo, and other travelers) through the shadowy realm of the comas, from which he returns to be born as Adam and to recount the tales he has gathered. Opperman combines and mythologizes in this work the major themes of his own literary production, and that of Afrikaans literature in general, making of it one of the most important works in Afrikaans.

The 1970s marked the emergence of a strong voice in Afrikaans, Wilma Stockenström (b. 1933). Her first published work was a volume of poetry entitled *Vir die bysiende leser* (1970; for the near-sighted reader), followed by *Spieël van water* (1973; mirror of water), *Van vergetelheid en van glans* (1977; of oblivion and of splendor), *Monsterverse* (1984; monstrous verses), and *Die heengaanrefrein* (1988; refrain of departure). Her work is in turn fiercely satirical of the monster, namely, humankind, and a nostalgic longing for a time when nature (and the African landscape in particular) still revealed its own significance. Stockenström has also published a number of novels, chief among which is *Die kremetartekspedisie* (1981; *The Expedition to the Baobab Tree,* 1983). Through the subject of a slave woman in 15th-c. Africa, Stockenström explores the realm of dreams and death, in which polarities are fused and boundaries dissolved. The novel shares certain qualities with the novels of J. M. Coetzee (q.v.), who translated it. Stockenström's latest work is the novel *Abjater wat so lag* (1991; Abjater, the laughing one), in which the subject is an old nurse, helping her wards enter into death.

Antjie Krog (b. 1952), who published her first volume of poetry in 1970, has emerged as a significant poetic voice. In her most recent publication, *Lady Anne* (1989; Lady Anne), she examines her own historical situation (explicitly present in the text) by placing it alongside that of Lady Anne Barnard (1750–1825), diarist and traveler at the Cape, who is invoked as muse and metaphor.

Karel Schoeman (b. 1939), a novelist whose work has been compared to Chekhov (q.v.), has most recently published *Afskeid en vertrek* (1990; farewell and departure), a novel set in Cape Town after an unspecified war. The central character is a middle-aged poet, wandering through a wasteland devoid of meaning. Through the consciousness of the poet, however, Schoeman's text anticipates a "new language" through which significant utterances might again be made. Schoeman has also written a number of historical works, the most important of which is *Olive Schreiner: 'n lewe in Suid-Afrika 1855–1881* (1989; Olive Schreiner: a life in South Africa 1855–1881), a biography that contains a great deal of new information on these formative years of Schreiner's life.

Etienne van Heerden (b. 1954), after publishing some poetry and short stories, wrote *Toorberg*

(1986; *Ancestral Voices,* 1990), a novel in which a magistrate is called on to investigate the death of a child on an ancestral farm; the novel uses elements from Afrikaner folklore and myth in an attempt to emulate Gabriel García Márquez (q.v.). Van Heerden's most recent novel is *Casspirs en camparis* (1991; casspirs and camparis), a satirical novel about South African society.

Afrikaans literature is marked by the great number of women writers, of whom Lettie Viljoen (pseud. of Ingrid Gouws, b. 1948) is the most significant new writer in the 1980s. Her first novella, *Klaaglied vir Koos* (1984; lament for Koos), has as its subject a white woman who seeks an "entrance into history" for herself and her young daughter. Increasingly she chooses a life outside the kind of history her Marxist husband pursues, and opens her husband's garden to the *Lumpenproletariat,* marking the beginning of a new, and less oppressive, community. In her first full-length novel, *Belemmering* (1990; impediment), the central metaphor is that of mapping. The novel interweaves the geological and historical strata of Southern Africa.

The last two decades have seen an increasing popularization of Afrikaans fiction, a movement that parallels the early history of the literature. With the recent political changes in the country, the Afrikaner's dominance is at an end, and the status of the language is uncertain.

BIBLIOGRAPHY: Coetzee, J. M., "The Great South African Novel," *Leadership S A* (1982), 74–79; Brink, A. P., *Mapmakers: Writing in a State of Siege* (1983); Daymond, M. J., J. U. Jacobs, and M. Lenta, eds., *Momentum: On Recent South African Writing* (1984); special South African issue, *ArielE,* 16, 2 (1985); Breytenbach, B., *End Papers: Essays, Letters, Articles of Faith, Workbook Notes* (1986); Brink, A. P., and J. M. Coetzee, Introduction to *A Land Apart: A South African Reader* (1987), 7–15; Coetzee, J. M., *White Writing: On the Culture of Letters in South Africa* (1988)

CARLI COETZEE

In English

Despite the increasingly severe political repression and the poor economic climate, South African literary production has grown substantially over the last decade, partly because of developing interest in local writing, both in South Africa and abroad, partly because of an expansion of local resources in the face of the cultural boycott, and partly because of an articulated relation between revolutionary struggle and cultural activism. Writing and drama workshops started reaching out to aspirant writers; sometimes combining with literacy projects (South Africa has a fifty-percent illiteracy rate); performance poetry and popular theater have flourished; additional publishing companies have established themselves, as have a few more local journals and little magazines, some specifically devoted to black writing; and a large number of anthologies have been published, their focus often on current writing from marginalized groups or on hitherto neglected voices from the past.

During the last ten years, then, the contours of South African literature and literary history have begun to be radically revised. The recent unbanning of oppositional political organizations and the return of exiles promise to unite two strands of South African writing: writing produced, published, and marketed within the country, and writing produced and published beyond its boundaries or forced underground. Moreover, the category of "English writing" is continually becoming adjusted and expanded, both through the multilingual references of some contemporary black writing and through the turn made by certain Afrikaans writers, notably Breyten Breytenbach and André Brink (qq.v.), to writing in English.

Cultural activism is most in evidence in popular theater and in performance poetry. Popular theater is a continuation of African oral tradition, whose religious rituals, praise poems, and imaginative narratives included well-developed dramatic elements; using song and dance, and often remaining unscripted, popular theater attracts a wide, often not literate, audience, playing in local community halls as well as commercial theaters. After Zakes Mda (b. 1948) and Gibson Kente (b. ca. 1945), whose plays tend to idealize black South African community life, younger playwrights often deal with class and ethnic differences within this community. Performance poetry, which also reaches back to oral tradition, is delivered rather than read, often with bodily gesture and movement, the spoken words sometimes combining with chants, ululations, and songs. It is performed at mass meetings, trade union and community gatherings, funerals, and other public and political occasions. While much performance poetry is in African languages, with some multilingual work (as in popular theater), some is in English, notably by Mzwakhe Mbuli (b. 1959?) and Nise Malange (b. 1960). Malange is one of the very few women cultural workers associated with COSATU (Congress of South African Trade Unions).

South African cultural debate typically revolves around the political responsibility of writers and critics, and the relation between writing and history. A semblance of historical veracity combined with political optimism is the preferred mode in fiction and drama; and in poetry, the exhortative and declamatory takes precedence over the lyric voice. Nadine Gordimer and J. M. Coetzee (qq.v.), South Africa's two best-known novelists, are used to represent different literary and political directions in this debate. Coetzee's writing treats history as myth, both in his earlier work and his three most recent novels, *Life & Times of Michael K* (1983), *Foe* (1986), and *Age of Iron* (1990). Unlike Gordimer, he does not confine his vision to southern African themes. Gordimer—who was awarded the 1991 Nobel Prize in literature—is overtly concerned with "truth-telling" in relation to closely specified political moments in recent South African history; she follows what she sees as a more committed and more optimistic political line than Coetzee's. Her most recent novels are *July's People* (1981), *A Sport of Nature* (1987), and *My Son's Story* (1990); she has also published a novella, *Something Out There* (1984), and *Jump and Other Stories* (1991). Although many of the stories offer a positive political vision, some, unlike the novels, are dominated by despair.

Gordimer's and Coetzee's international successes, as well as the recognition of South Africa's leading playwright, Athol Fugard (q.v.)—whose most recent works include *A Lesson for Aloes* (1981), *"Master Harold" . . . and the Boys* (1982), and *The Road to Mecca* (1988)—have tended to eclipse other novelists and short-story writers of the same race and generational span, although some, like Dan Jacobson (q.v.), made careers after leaving South Africa. Among the best-established "minor" writers are Lionel Abrahams (b. 1928), Jillian Becker (b. 1932), Stephen Gray (b. 1941), Christopher Hope (b. 1944), Sheila Roberts (b. 1937), Peter Wilhelm (b. 1943), and Rose Zwi (b. 1928); many write satirically about white South African life. From a younger generation, two novels by Menán du Plessis (b. 1948)— *A State of Fear* (1983) and *Longlive!* (1989)— continue in the tradition of Gordimer, where the personal and political become deeply interfused in the life of a white South African woman. Yet *Longlive!* makes a particular turn Gordimer's work only points to: It portrays a community that represents itself by means of multiple, heterogeneous voices, and whose mode of existence breaks down the categories of apartheid. The text's use of political slogans, religious chants, graffiti, streetvendors' cries, along with dialogue, places it as part of a new South African writing that strives, to use the words of poet Jeremy Cronin, to "learn how to speak / With the voices of this land."

In poetry, too, generational difference makes itself felt in the course of the 1980s. After a strong set of poets, who are still writing, including Guy Butler (b. 1918), Patrick Cullinan (b. 1932), Jean Lipkin (b. 1926), Douglas Livingstone (b. 1932), and others, such as Ruth Miller (1919–1969), a younger generation looks back, self-critically and often satirically, at being brought up "white" in an apartheid culture. Particularly noteworthy among the younger generation are Jeni Couzyn (b. 1942), Ingrid de Kok (b. 1951), and Stephen Watson (b. 1953).

Whereas contemporary white writing tends to deal with white mythology, the social construction of whites in an apartheid culture, the possibilities of reconciliation between black and white, and (sometimes) the forging of a new, nonracial culture, black writing—counteracting the literary imbalances of the past—tends to focus on black communities and the possibilities of revolutionary change from within those communities. Black-consciousness writing, which began in the 1970s and continues into the present, takes its major philosophical position from an "African communalism" as opposed to "Western individualism." Mongane Serote's (b. 1944) novel *To Every Birth Its Blood* (1981) bases its fictional dynamic upon this distinction, turning, in the second half of the novel, to the revolutionary rebirth of a nation that has regained contact with its African heritage. Many black-consciousness novels, like Serote's, also give a close account of daily events in the life of those engaged in political struggle, including details of the intense physical and psychological torture inflicted on political detainees. Plot resolutions generally take the form of moments of deferral: Freedom is in the not-so-distant future. Sipho Sepamla's (b. 1932) *A Ride on the Whirlwind* (1981) figures the return from exile as a "second coming."

Black consciousness has proven hospitable to black women writers, despite its explicit patriarchalism. After Noni Jabavu (b. 1919), whose work formed a (marginalized) part of what has been called a black literary renaissance in the 1960s and 1970s, the first wave of writing in English by black women in South Africa concerns itself with the supportive role of women in the struggle, both practically and as emblems of Mother Africa. Lauretta Ngcobo's (b. 1932) *Cross of Gold* (1981) and Miriam Tlali's (b. 1933) *Amandla* (1981) address these themes from slightly different political perspectives. In later writing, including political autobiographies, and poems and short stories in anthologies, as well as a second novel from Ngcobo, *And They Didn't Die* (1990), and recent short stories by Tlali, *Footprints in the Quag,* also published under the title *Soweto Stories* (1989), the female subjects take on more active and powerful roles, sometimes in response to the disempowerment of black men. The title of *Call Me Woman* (1985) by Ellen Kuzwayo (b. 1914) is an ironic allusion to Mtutuzeli Matshoba's (b. 1950) *Call Me Not A Man* (1979). Like much other black-consciousness writing, Kuzwayo's text re-

fers, with mingled pride and anxiety, to the changed relations between parents and children after the schoolchildren's rebellion of 1976 and its aftermath.

Although the norm in black writing is to convey a close and unproblematic relation between writing and history, recent sets of short stories by Njabulo S. Ndebele (b. 1948) and Zoë Wicomb (b. 1948) complicate the picture. Wicomb's *You Can't Get Lost in Cape Town* (1987) focuses on acts of representation rather than on an "objective" reality. Ndebele's *Fools and Other Stories* (1983) shows an interest in releasing forms of cultural expression rather than in simply documenting oppression. Both writers represent an important moment in black South African writing: deeply committed to local political issues, yet at the same time part of an international intellectual debate.

Standard divisions between "black" and "white" writing are beginning to break down, most obviously in the broadly defined genre of political writing, which includes political autobiographies, collections of life-stories and interviews, and prison memoirs, and which incorporates, for instance, Mary Benson's (b. 1919) *A Far Cry: The Making of a South African* (1989), Hugh Lewin's (b. 1939) *Bandiet* (1981), and Emma Mashinini's (b. 1929) *Strikes Have Followed Me All My Life* (1989). Two major texts, both volumes of poems, to come out of prison experience are Jeremy Cronin's (b. 1949) *Inside* (1983) and Breyten Breytenbach's *Judas Eye* (1988).

During the course of the last decade, new reputations have been made. Most notable in this regard is Bessie Head (q.v.), who left South Africa in 1963, and who lived in and wrote about Botswana as a part of an African past and future not available to her in the land of her birth. Head wrote three novels, *When Rain Clouds Gather* (1967), *Maru* (1971), and *A Question of Power* (1973), a set of short stories, *The Collector of Treasures* (1977), and two works of nonfiction, *Serowe: Village of the Rain Wind* (1981) and *A Bewitched Crossroad* (1984). She is one of Africa's most ambitious, energetic, and challenging writers, not least for her interest in race and gender oppression and her simultaneous refusal of orthodox political positions. Two collections of her writing have been posthumously published: *Tales of Tenderness and Power* (1989) and *A Woman Alone* (1990), along with a set of letters, *A Gesture of Belonging* (1991).

Finally, South African literary criticism has also come into its own, not least because of a set of critical texts written by South African writers themselves.

BIBLIOGRAPHY: Barnett, U. A., *A Vision of Order: A Study of Black South African Literature in En-*

glish 1914–1980 (1983); Gray, S., ed., *The Penguin Book of Southern African Stories* (1985); Adey, D., et al., *Companion to South African English Literature* (1986); Coetzee, J. M., and A. Brink, eds., *A Land Apart: A South African Reader* (1986); Bunn, D., and J. Taylor, *From South Africa: New Writing, Photographs and Art* (1987); Coetzee, J. M., *White Writing: On the Culture of Letters in South Africa* (1988); Gray, S., ed., *The Penguin Book of Southern African Verse* (1989); Driver, D., "South Africa," *JCL*, Dec. issue each year; Smith, M. van W., *Grounds of Contest: A Survey of South African English Literature* (1990); Trump, M., ed., *Rendering Things Visible: Essays on South African Literary Culture* (1990); Lockett, C., ed., *Breaking the Silence: A Century of South African Women's Poetry* (1990); Van Niekerk, A., ed., *Raising the Blinds: A Century of South African Women's Stories* (1990)

DOROTHY DRIVER

SOYFER, Jura

Austrian dramatist, poet, storyteller, and essayist, b. 8 Dec. 1912, Kharkov, Russia; d. 6 Feb. 1939, Buchenwald, Germany

S. was born as the son of a wealthy businessman in the Russian steel industry. In late 1920 the family fled from the Bolshevik Revolution and reached Vienna in March of the following year. As a schoolboy S. experienced the political strife of Austria and became a leftist activist at an early age, writing poems, prose sketches, and reviews. After graduating from a *Gymnasium* in 1931 and taking courses at the University of Vienna, S. increasingly devoted himself to political journalism and contributed to *Arbeiter-Zeitung,* the organ of the Social Democratic Party. S.'s response to the events of February 1934 and clericofascist suppression was membership in a clandestine communist group. His best and most enduring work was done for the *Kleinkunst* stages of Vienna, the "little theaters" that presented political cabaret, such as ABC and Literatur am Naschmarkt, to which he contributed *Mittelstücke,* the centerpieces of their programs. These short dramas highlighted Austria's stature as a "proving ground for the destruction of the world," to use a phrase of Karl Kraus (q.v.), one of S.'s mentors. After three months of political imprisonment, S. was trapped by the Nazi invasion of Austria. He was taken to Dachau and from there to Buchenwald, where he died of typhoid fever at the age of twenty-six.

One reason why S. sometimes used such pseudonyms as Jura, Georg Anders, Fritz Feder, Norbert Noll, and Walter West may have been his sensitivity about the fact that his last name was a homonym of the German word *Säufer,* "drunkard." In his writings, moral indignation, cynical bitterness, and critical wit are coupled with lyrical lightness and poignant pathos. S.'s inspired use of language is reminiscent of his idols Kraus and Johann Nestroy (1801–1862) as he wedded elements of the old Viennese popular theater to the hard-hitting topical revue. His four plays, unpublished in his lifetime, are modern morality plays, powerful parables, and dramatic tracts for the times that move on both a realistic and a surrealistic plane. For example, in *Der Lechner-Edi schaut ins Paradies* (1936; *Eddie Lechner's Trip to Paradise,* 1971), a play that presents a down-and-outer chopping away at the capitalistic system, an attempt is made, during a backward ride on a sort of time machine, to undo centuries of so-called progress. *Astoria* (1937; *Astoria,* 1977), a farce with a factual basis about the promotion of a nonexistent state, a swindle turned into a utopia, is still relevant in an age of wholesale delusion via manipulation and exploitation by the mass media and political packaging. *Weltuntergang* (1936; *The End of the World,* 1972) is a mordant cosmic farce in the spirit of Kraus and Nestroy, and *Vineta* (1937; *Vineta,* 1977) is based on a north German legend about a dead city. Among the most noteworthy of S.'s poems are "Das Lied von der Ordnung" (1932; "The Song of Order," 1977), "Lied des einfachen Menschen" (ca. 1936; "Song of the 20th Century Man," 1977), and "Dachau-Lied" (1938; "Song of the Austrians in Dachau," 1977).

S. devoted his tragically brief life to a futile fight against Austrian fascism and the deleterious slackness, apathy, and fatalistic resignation of his compatriots. Only in recent years has this fearless spokesman for a dispossessed generation emerged in his full stature as a major political and social satirist who illuminates a dark chapter in European history.

FURTHER WORKS: *Vom Paradies zum Weltuntergang: Dramen und Kleinkunst* (1947); *Von Paradies und Weltuntergang* (1962); *Das Gesamtwerk* (1980). FURTHER VOLUMES IN ENGLISH: *The Legacy of J.S., 1912–1939: Poems, Prose and Plays of an Austrian Antifascist* (1977); *It's Up to Us!* (1992)

BIBLIOGRAPHY: Lehmann, J., *The Whispering Gallery* (1955), 294–302; Steinmetz, S., "J. S.," *Weg und Ziel* (Feb. 1959), 149–56; Wellwarth, G. E., "J. S.: An Attempt at Rehabilitation," *American-German Review,* 35 (1969), 22–26; Jarka, H., "Politik und Zauberei: Die Stücke J. S.'s," *MAL,* 5 (1972), 96–143; Jarka, H., *J. S.:*

Leben, Werk, Zeit (1987); Jarka, H., "J. S.: A Jewish Writer under Austro-Fascism," *Shofar*, 5 (1987), 18–27; Scheit, G., *Theater und revolutionärer Humanismus: Eine Studie zu J. S.* (1988)

HARRY ZOHN

SPANISH LITERATURE

See Volume 4, page 298.

Franco's death in November of 1975 ended the post-Civil War era of nearly four decades. Censorship in the totalitarian first quarter century was capricious and harsh—extremely so at first and moderately so later; by the mid-1960s, the regime began to become more pragmatic. In the 1960s and 1970s, expanding relations with the U.S., large-scale tourism, and economic development brought relaxed censorship and, in Franco's declining years, *aperturismo* (opening)—a move to accommodate internal diversity and resume relations with countries on the political left. Early 1970s educational reform legislation reestablished the legal status of Spain's vernaculars—Catalan, Galician, Basque—authorizing daily newspapers in these languages and their instruction in the schools. Together with women's recuperation of rights lost when the Republic fell, these events profoundly affect post-Franco culture and literature. One of the most significant developments of the past two decades in Spain has been the flowering of vernacular cultures and literatures, not only in Catalan and Galician, whose literary histories date from the late Middle Ages, but in Basque (heretofore primarily an oral culture), and dialectical areas threatened with total assimilation: Leonese, *Andalán* (Aragonese), *Bable* (Asturian), and even regional cultures not clearly differentiated on the linguistic level such as Extremaduran and Andalusian. The regional autonomy movements that go hand-in-hand with such geographically specific cultural phenomena are not merely a reaction to the four decades of Francoist repression of local autonomy but belong to a centrifugal tradition of centuries, going back to the 15th c. when linguistically and culturally distinct kingdoms were forcibly united under Ferdinand and Isabel.

Spanish literature under Franco exhibited several distinct aesthetic moments, all but the final one being representational. The Civil War years and those immediately following (1936–1942) are marked by *triunfalismo* (provictory propaganda) with its defiant Fascist rhetoric and glorification of violence and of Falangist values. An orgy of self-aggrandizement (with opposing voices silenced or in exile), *triunfalismo* produced no enduring masterworks, and quickly alienated most Spanish intellectuals. Although the dominant mode, it was not exclusive (several trends coexist throughout the Franco and post-Franco eras). *Tremendismo*, the most notorious mode of the 1940s and early 1950s, was named for the "tremendous" reader reaction elicited by accumulated violence, degradation, poverty, perversion, filth, and deformity. Derived from naturalism (q.v.), without the scientific grounding, and the *esperpento*, an expressionistic aesthetic of deformation invented by Ramon María del Valle-Inclán (q.v.), *tremendismo* was exploited by some writers to reflect their anguish at war's atrocities; akin to existentialism (q.v.), it was censored in Spain on religious grounds. "Social" literature or "critical realism," the first postwar movement affecting all genres, held sway from around 1950 until the late 1960s, featuring generic or collective protagonists, economic injustices, and social-class problems. "Social" meant political: Themes constituted a laundry list of things wrong with Spain, initiated or perpetuated by Franco. French objectivism and the techniques of Alain Robbe-Grillet (q.v.) were adapted as a methodology; skirting censorship was facilitated by an impassive stance, objective or pseudoscientific descriptions, and the absence of editorializing. Peninsular writers' ends differed, however, with techniques of studied indifference being employed only to spotlight cancers on Spain's body politic. Raised and educated under a repressive regime that had expunged liberal and progressive writers from the canon and excised their works from libraries and bookstores, some postwar writers "reinvented" naturalism, while others more closely followed György Lukács (q.v.), usually known indirectly via French writers or translations.

What these varied literary modes or moments shared, ideological differences notwithstanding, was the predominance of content over form. Variants of neorealism (q.v.) have a testimonial thrust and a propagandistic ax to grind, though techniques and methods diverge. Covert belligerence is a major motivating force of post-Civil War writing, possibly explaining why aesthetic considerations were slow in returning. In the 1960s, however, with the works of Luis Martín-Santos and Juan Benet (qq.v.), the obligatory pedestrian style, simplistic techniques, and repetitive themes of *engagé* literature (q.v.) yield to new interest in literary artistry. Increasingly during the final post-Civil War decade and most emphatically in the post-Franco period, aestheticism, questions of form and language per se, experimentalism, and interest in literary theory replace emphasis on content. Whether neobaroque, postmodern, or neovanguardist, aesthetic experiments constitute the primary literary link between the post-Civil War and post-Franco periods.

Some critics term the "mid-century generation" (cultivators of "social" literature) the "new romantics"; their obsession with national ills also links them to Spain's "Generation of 1898." By contrast the immediately following neobaroques, postmoderns, or experimental postneorealists (critics have yet to agree on a name) have closer ties to Spain's "Generation of 1927" (neo-Gongorists, late modernists, vanguardists, and surrealists). The analogic fit is imperfect but suggestive. Experimentalism, the most highly visible mode in the post-Franco era, shares the stage with surviving members of the Generation of 1927: Rosa Chacel, the late Nobel laureate Vicente Aleixandre, Rafael Alberti (qq.v.), María Teresa León (b. 1904), Ernestina de Champourcín (b. 1905), and Clementina Arderiu (1899–1976); and returned exiles, notably Francisco Ayala (q.v.); Mercè Rodoreda (q.v.), the greatest of contemporary Catalan novelists; Manuel Andújar (b. 1913); Teresa Pàmies (b. 1919); and Gonzalo Torrente Ballester (b. 1910) from the "Generation of 1936." Still active are many established writers of the post-Civil War era—Camilo José Cela, Miguel Delibes, Juan Goytisolo (qq.v.), and Juan Benet—joined by an exceptional number of women writers from both the postwar and post-Franco era: poets Carmen Conde (q.v.), Concha Zardoya (b. 1914), Gloria Fuertes (b. 1918), María Victoria Atencia (b. 1931), Ana María Fagundo (b. 1938), Clara Janés (b. 1940), and Elena Andrés (b. 1931), among others; novelists Ana María Matute, Carmen Laforet (qq.v.), Mercedes Ballesteros (b. 1913), Dolores Medio (b. 1914), Mercedes Salisachs (b. 1916), Elena Quiroga (b. 1921), Elena Soriano (1917), Concha Alós (b. 1922), Carmen Martín Gaite (b. 1925), and Maria Aurèlia Capmany (1918–1992) from the Franco era plus Esther Tusquets (b. 1936), Ana María Moix (b. 1947), Marina Mayoral (b. 1942), Lourdes Ortiz (b. 1943), Rosa Montero (b. 1951), Carme Riera (b. 1948), Maria Antònia Oliver (b. 1946), Soledad Puértolas (b. 1947), Paloma Díaz-Mas (b. 1954), and Carmen Gómez-Ojea (b. 1945); dramatists Ana Diosdado (b. 1938), Pilar Enciso (b. 1926), Lidia Falcón (b. 1935), Maribel Lázaro (1949), Paloma Pedrero (b. 1957), Carmen Resino (b. 1941), and María Manuela Reina (b. 1958).

Spain's "new novel" of the 1970s is only indirectly indebted to prior experiments of the French New Novel (q.v.). The term was used previously and more appropriately to refer to Objectivist texts of the 1950s and 1960s; subsequent aesthetic renovation owes more to recuperation of the works of modernist and vanguardist exiles, including

Mercè Rodoreda, Rosa Chacel, Francisco Ayala, and many others, almost unknown because their works appeared outside Spain. A slightly prior impetus derives from the influence of the Latin American "boom"—writers from Jorge Luis Borges through Gabriel García Márquez (qq.v.). Linguistic and structuralist theory also produced literary echoes, and a renewed emphasis on culture: Writers who accepted the depersonalized authorial unobtrusiveness imposed by ideologues during the *engagé* period revel in their distinct identities, cultural heritage, artistic expertise, and technical virtuosity. The phenomenon is best observed in fiction and poetry, although a somewhat distant parallel occurs in the "underground theater" of abstract political allegory. Survivors of modernism (q.v.) and vanguardism of the 1920s offer precedents and parallels for much postneorealist experimentation of the 1970s and 1980s. In the 1970s *novísimos* poets (as in the "new novel"), themes expand beyond the narrow realm of social literature to the subjective, intellectual, imaginative, speculative, and metaphysical. Problems become more typical of 20th-c. Western civilization, no longer restricted to Spain's politicoeconomic circumstances. Themes grow more abstract; vocabulary turns complex and international—neologisms abound, and foreign or scientific terms proliferate. Typographical and visual experimentation, arbitrary punctuation, suppression of conventional syntax, new structures and subdivisions, and baroque contorsions of language become almost commonplace. Non-Spanish characters and settings—foreign, international, fantastic, or allegorical personae and geography—appear, and temporal exoticism replaces the "here and now" ambience of prior neorealist modes. Everyday life ceases to dominate; the author, with his culture, his rhetoric, and his personal weltanschauung comes increasingly to the fore. No longer brandished as an instrument for changing society, literature escapes from utilitarian preoccupations, and theoretical concerns replace thesis (message) to the detriment of clarity.

Philosophy, Criticism, and the Essay

The legacy of José Ortega y Gasset (q.v.) colors most subsequent thought, beginning with disciples from the Generation of 1927—Xavier Zubiri (b. 1898), José Gaos (b. 1902), María Zambrano (b. 1905)—and from the Generation of 1936—Julián Marías (b. 1914), Manuel Granell (b. 1906), Paulino Garagorri (b. 1916), José Luis Aranguren (b. 1909), and others of the "School of Madrid." Dispersed by the Civil War, many have returned to newly democratic Spain and continue writing. Equally indebted to Ortega's "vital reason" are

Zubiri's profound metaphysics, the medical anthropology of Pedro Laín Entralgo (b. 1908), and much contemporary Spanish historiography, sociology, and aesthetics. Laín—one-time psychiatrist, professor of medical history, and author of numerous scientific treatises—also draws on Martin Heidegger (q.v.), Wilhelm Dilthey (1833–1911), and Max Scheler (1874–1928) for his own anthropological, Christian humanism in such works as *Teoría y realidad del otro* (1983; theory and reality of the other), *Antropología médica para clínicos* (1984; medical anthropology for clinicians), *La espera y la esperanza* (1984; waiting and hoping), *Teatro del mundo* (1986; theater of the world), and *Sobre la amistad* (1986; on friendship). Zubiri's Catholic liberalism, likewise derived from phenomenology (q.v.) and Heidegger, finds maximum expression in his massive trilogy, *Inteligencia sentiente* (1981; feeling intelligence), *Inteligencia y logos* (1982; intelligence and Logos), *Inteligencia y Razón* (1983; intelligence and reason), and his masterpiece, *Naturaleza, Historia, Dios* (9th ed., 1987; nature, history, God). Julián Marías, Ortega's major interpreter, adapts and develops the master's concept of historical reason, describing human life in its general and theoretical structures in *Antropología metafísica* (1970; metaphysical anthropology), echoed on the personal level with his three-volume memoirs, *Una vida presente* (1988–89; present life), and on the national plane with *España inteligible: razón histórica de las Españas* (1985; intelligible Spain: historical reason of the Spains). With generational peers, namely, Rof Carballo (b. 1906), leading spokesman for Catholic psychoanalysis of Eros and culture, José Antonio Maravall (b. 1911), José Ferrater Mora (b. 1912), and others, Marías represents the effort to impose order upon the received and to follow the imperative of reason. Under the aegis of Ortega and modernism, novelist Rosa Chacel contributes important essays on eroticism in *Saturnal* (1972) while María Zambrano (b. 1904) treats themes ranging from Seneca to liberalism, from the divine to democracy, from Spain as problem to love and knowledge of the soul. Indirectly influenced by German phenomenology, her primary study is of "poetic reason" or poetic intuition as a philosophical method, in works such as *Claros del bosque* (1978; clearings in the forest) and *Dos fragmentos sobre el amor* (1982; two fragments on love). Spain's most significant woman philosopher and essayist, Zambrano returned in 1984 from exile in Mexico, Cuba, Italy, and France to become the first female recipient of the Cervantes Prize (1988), Spanish literature's most prestigious literary award. *De la aurora* (1986; concerning dawn) metaphorically alludes to new life and perpetual rebirth and is symbolic of a new ontology, mystic expression of new ways of knowing. Countess María de Campo Alange (b. 1902), Teresa Pàmies (b. 1919), Lidia Falcón (b. 1935), and Maria Aurèlia Capmany, exponents of Spanish feminism, are also concerned with political ideologies and social problems. Pàmies, a revolutionary activist who spent more than thirty years in exile, has published some two dozen novels and collections of memoirs in Catalan since her return to Catalonia at the end of the Franco era.

Young thinkers of the democratic era, Fernando Savater (b. 1938), Eugenio Trías (b. 1942), Xavier Rubert de Ventós (b. 1943), and Eduardo Subirats (dates n.a.) attempt to transcend limitations of earlier generations and incorporate existentialism, Marxism, psychoanalysis, structuralism, poststructuralism (qq.v.), and other important European currents. Partially synthesizing antagonistic intellectual postures from the Franco era, they move between Christian humanism and antihumanist Marxism as represented by Enrique Tierno Galvan (b. 1918), an agnostic socialist who evolved from neopositivism to become a marxist opponent of vitalism and existentialism. The anarchist thought of Agustín García Calvo (b. 1926) also attracts some younger Spaniards, but many follow Tierno (enthusiastic proponent of a secular, rational, scientifically controlled society), who offers an extreme solution to the conflict between personal autonomy and the state in favor of identifying the individual with the species. Younger Spanish thinkers' neoromantic (q.v.) defense of the empirical subject's passional nature and liberty attempts to rescue the subject from all politically and socially restrictive theory. Brandishing the metaphor of the ideal city, they react against system, authority, and ideology. Savater, influenced by Friedrich Nietzsche and Michel Foucault (qq.v.) is especially concerned with society's peril for the individual in *Panfleto contra el Todo* (1982; pamphlet against the whole) and *La tarea del héroe* (1983; the hero's task). Rubert, with a cultural critique in the line of Savater, warns of danger in abstractions such as power, progress, unity, and history—powerful collective symbols that absorb the individual—and combats bureaucracy, the collectivity, and utopianism of whatever hue. Subirats plumbs the relationship between Eros and culture, attempting to strengthen principles of critical reason against dogmatic abstraction in *La ilustración insuficiente* (1981; the insufficient Enlightenment), *El alma y la muerte* (1983; the soul and death), *La crisis de las vanguardias y la cultura moderna* (1985; the crisis of vanguards and modern culture), and *La flor y el cristal: Ensayos sobre arte y arquitectura* (1986; flower and crystal: essays on art and architecture). Trías, in dialogue with Heidegger and Nietzsche, offers anthropological and ontological analyses of human passions and creativity, incorporating neo-Freudian metapsychology, philosophical dualism, and binary systems in *El artista y la ciudad* (1976; the artist and the city), *Tratado de la pasión* (1979; treatise on passion), *Lo bello y lo siniestro* (1982; the beautiful and the sinister), *La filosofía y su sombra* (1983; philosophy and its shadow), and *Filosofía del futuro* (1983; philosophy of the future). Common to all is a neoromantic concern for individual freedom and a rejection of absolutist thought in any form.

Fiction

Camilo José Cela, Spain's most controversial and visible post-Civil War novelist, was awarded the Nobel Prize for literature in 1989, largely thanks to his best-known early works, *La familia de Pascual Duarte* (1942; *The Family of Pascual Duarte*, 1964) and *La colmena* (1951; *The Hive*, 1953). The comparably little-known novels after *San Camilo, 1936* (1969; Saint Camilo's Day, 1936) are much more experimental and less representational, especially *Oficio de tinieblas, 5* (1973; service in darkness, 5) and *Mazurka para dos muertos* (1983; dance for two cadavers). The latter, inspired like *San Camilo* by the Civil War, is set in Galicia and moves hostilities to the realm of myth. *Cristo versus Arizona* (1988; Christ against Arizona), Cela's most recent novel to date, continues the fragmentary, lyric techniques of *Oficio* and *Mazurka*, adding little new save the setting. *Madera de boj* (boxwood) has been announced for release several times without being completed. Also extremely productive in the post-Franco era is Gonzalo Torrente Ballester, who received the Cervantes Prize in 1985; a master of erudite humor and metaliterary satire, he came to prominence with *La saga/fuga de J. B.* (1973; J. B.'s saga and fugue), first part of a "fantastic trilogy" comprising *Fragmentos de apocalipsis* (1977; pieces of apocalypse) and *La isla de los jacintos cortados* (1980; the isle of cut hyacinths). Two-time winner of the Critics' Prize, professional critic Torrente mocked Francoist power manipulation in *La princesa durmiente va a la escuela* (1983; Sleeping Beauty goes to school) and *La rosa de los vientos* (1985; the compass) and satirized international intrigue in *Quizá nos lleve el viento al infinito* (1984; perhaps the wind will take us to infinity). Academic criticism is parodied in *Yo no soy yo, evidentemente* (1987; I'm not me, evidently), a literary mystery based on the multiple heteronyms of Fernando Pessoa (q.v.). The numerous post-Franco works of Juan Benet include *En ciernes* (1976; in bloom), *El ángel del Señor abandona a*

Tobías (1976; the angel of God abandons Tobias), *En el estado* (1977; in the state), *Del pozo y del numa* (1978; of the well and the guardian), *Saúl ante Samuel* (1980; Saul before Samuel), and a series of three novels entitled *Herrumbrosas lanzas* (1983–1987; rusty spears), which revisit his mythical world of Región, to examine once again the microcosm of Spain and of the Civil War. Although seemingly simpler than novels of the Región series—maps, battle plans, and a more straightforward syntax deceptively suggest that the later books will clarify the ambiguities of Región—abundant contradictions, omissions, and ambiguities reflect Benet's conviction that knowledge and communication are impossible. Miguel Delibes continues probing impoverished rural Castile's forgotten and half-abandoned villages with their xenophobia, backwardness, and vanishing values in *Los santos inocentes* (1981; the holy innocents), *El tesoro* (1985; treasure), and *Castilla habla* (1986; Castile speaks). *Cartas de amor de un sexagenario voluptuoso* (1983; love-letters by a voluptuous sexagenarian) explores the anguish of aging, as Delibes did in *La hoja roja* (1959; the red leaf). Most significant is *377A, madera de héroe* (1987; 377A, of the stuff of heroes), Delibes's exploration of the meaning of heroism in the context of wartime Fascist rhetoric. Juan Goytisolo revels in Arabic culture and life-styles in *Makbara* (1979; *Makbara*, 1981), while his *Paisajes después de la guerra* (1982; landscapes after war) presents an apocalyptic vision of an Arabic "invasion" of the Sentier section of Paris where Goytisolo has lived for many years. *Coto vedado* (1985; no hunting), the first volume of his memoirs, demythifies his family and class, while *Las virtudes del pájaro solitario* (1987; virtues of the solitary bird) blends Spanish and Arabic mysticism with contemporary homosexuality and AIDS in a nightmarish experiment filled with bitter humor. Luis Goytisolo (Juan's brother, b. 1939), has lately emerged as a major novelist, thanks to completion of his tetralogy, collectively known as "Antagonía" (1973–1981): *Recuento* (recount), *Los verdes de mayo hasta el mar* (May greens to the sea), *La cólera de Aguiles* (Achilles' wrath), and *Teoría del conocimiento* (theory of knowledge), dense novels of complex psychological exploration in a Joycean vein that offer parody, satire, and radically innovative literary experimentation, functioning simultaneously on the levels of personal experience, political recapitulation, metaphysical inquiry, eroticism, and moral reflections. *Estela del fuego que se aleja* (1984; distant wake of fire) and *La paradoja del ave migratoria* (1987; paradox of the migratory bird) may be seen as implied responses to his brother's memoirs and latest novel. Francisco Ayala, Spain's most talented and significant exile, reestablished in Madrid in the post-Franco era and belatedly elected to the Royal Academy, has published dense volumes of essays and memoirs—*Las plumas del fénix* (1989; the feather of the phoenix) and *El escritor en su siglo* (1990; the writer in his century)—and more short fiction, but no new novels. Returned expatriate Rosa Chacel continues, as in the 1920s and 1930s, slowly perfecting her modernist novels in the style of James Joyce (q.v.). The autobiographical *Barrio de Maravillas* (1976; *The Maravillas District,* 1992) and *Desde el amanecer* (1972; since dawn) are supplemented by her diary, *Alcancía* (1982; potpourri), *Acrópolis* (1984; the acropolis), and a collection of articles, and *Rebañaduras* (1986; slices), with *Ciencias naturales* (1988; natural sciences) closing the autobiographical trilogy of her generation. Deserving more than passing mention is Carmen Martín Gaite (b. 1925), one of Spain's most respected, translated, and studied women novelists and essayists. Typical of feminist concerns in more than a dozen of her books are the novels *Entre visillos* (1958; *Behind the Curtains,* 1990) and *El cuarto de atrás* (1978; *The Black Room,* 1983). Other important writers who, like Martín Gaite, began writing "social" novels under the aegis of neorealism but have evolved, matured, and moved toward more aesthetically oriented narratives are Juan García Hortelano (b. 1928) and Juan Marsé (b. 1933), prolific and popular winners of numerous prizes for fiction. Marsé's *Ronda del Guinardó* (1984; Guinardo patrol) exploits the vogue of the thriller while constructing an artistic parable of wartime victory and defeat. Also from this period comes Catalan humorist, poet, and satirist Juan Perucho (b. 1920), whose novels and short stories have become known in Spain since the legalization of the vernaculars in the 1970s. Carlos Rojas (b. 1928) has carved a niche for himself by creating fantastic (de)mythologizations of well-known episodes of Spanish history. Lexicographer, art scholar, and poet José María Caballero Bonald (b. 1926) emerged as an original novelist of Andalucía with *Toda la noche oyeron pasar pájaros* (1981; they heard birds overhead all night) and *En la casa del padre* (1988; in the father's house). Francisco Umbral (b. 1935), a cultivator of the "new journalism" and an exceptional, highly personal stylist, has published more than sixty volumes: novels, essays, memoirs, literary portraits, and chronicles.

The current narrative scene is crowded not only with active survivors of the generation of Ortega (or of 1925) and generation of 1936 (ex-combatants and returned exiles), but also features ongoing activity by representatives of the several post-Civil War trends (*tremendismo,* social novel, neobaroque, or neovanguardist), together with newer writers who have appeared in the post-Franco era. Postneorealist emphasis on form over content demands more of the reader, offers more cosmopolitan and intellectual fare, and requires readers knowledgeable in narrative theory, intertextuality, and creative processes. In the post-Franco era, especially during the first five to seven years of transition to democracy, an explosion of interest in areas previously censored resulted in a pornopolitical fad and a renewed fascination with the Spanish Civil War viewed from the unaccustomed anti-Franco perspective, as well as works of exile. *Franquismo* per se likewise became a thematic nucleus, and memoirs (previously a genre little cultivated in Spain) gained in popularity, especially memoirs of war, exile, and clandestine opposition during the dictatorship.

The post-Franco era witnesses the emergence of the metanovel as a genre, an enormous use of intertextuality, and the cultivation of a new historical novel. For the first time, detective fiction, the thriller, and science fiction begin to be cultivated by major Spanish writers. Significant, mature authors from diplomatic or professional circles have moved into the narrative, offering original perspectives and intellectual verve, including philosopher José Ferrater Mora (1912–1991), banker-diplomat José Luis Sampedro (b. 1917), naval officer, essayist, and novelist Antonio Menchaca (b. 1921), educator Josefina Aldecoa (b. 1926), and essayist José Jiménez Lozano (b. 1930), whose themes in both historical investigation and the novel are drawn from a variety of religions and their recondite or esoteric backgrounds. Recently recognized as a distinct group, the "Generation of 1968" includes Juan J. Armas Marcelo (b. 1946), José María Guelbenzu (b. 1944), Ana María Moix (b. 1947), Esther Tusquets (b. 1936), Juan José Millás (b. 1946), Luis Mateo Díez (b. 1945), José María Merino (b. 1944), Juan Pedro Aparicio (b. 1942), Lourdes Ortiz (b. 1943), Marina Mayoral (b. 1942), Cristina Fernández Cubas (b. 1945), and Soledad Puértolas (b. 1947). Writing in Catalan are Miquel Angel Riera (b. 1930), Baltasar Porcel (b. 1936), Manuel Vázquez Montalbán (b. 1939), Robert Saladrigas (b. 1940), Terenci Moix (b. 1943), and Pau Faner (b. 1949), who appeared in Franco's twilight years. In the forefront of Galician fiction in the post-Franco era are Carlos Casares (b. 1941), Xosé Neira Vilas (b. 1939), X. L. Méndez Ferrín (b. 1938), Camilo Gonsar (b. 1931), and María Xosé Queizán (b. 1939). Writing in Castilian are Ramón Hernández (b. 1943), Germán Sánchez Espeso (1940–1991), Raul Guerra Garrido (b. 1935), José María Vaz de Soto (b. 1943), José Leyva (b. 1938), Enrique Vila-Matas (b. 1948), Vicente Molina Foix (b. 1946), Pedro Zarraluki (b. 1940), and Javier Tomeo (b.

1940), each having authored at least a half-dozen works, garnering significant prizes or critical recognition; there is no common denominator among them; some began as vanguardists or experimentalists and others as neorealists. Important new writers achieving acclaim in the 1980s include Alvaro Pombo (b. 1939), Félix de Azúa (b. 1944), Javier Marías (b. 1951), Mariano Antolín Rato (b. 1943), Ignacio Martínez de Pisón (b. 1960), Enrique Murillo (b. 1944), and Paloma Díaz-Mas (b. 1954). Whether subverting the narrative conventions of realism via paradox and enigma, diffusion of meaning, or absence of a sense of closure, through metaphorical density, ellipsis, structural manipulation, fundamental incongruity, or multivalent and contradictory meaning, most post-Franco narratives challenge the reader and elude easy classification.

Poetry

A major event for Spanish poetry was the long-awaited return from exile of Rafael Alberti; and of comparable import was the death of Nobel Prize–winning poet Vicente Aleixandre in 1984. Carmen Conde began publishing poetry of note in the 1920s, but her association with the Republic brought hard times under Franco. Today the dean of living Spanish women poets, she has published more than forty books, including some novels and essays, and in 1978 became the first woman elected to the Spanish Royal Academy. The half-dozen poetry collections in Catalan by Clementina Arderiu (1889–1976) span some six decades from 1916 until her death; returned exile Ernestina de Champourcín (b. 1905) likewise has a poetic career of over sixty years. *Primer exilio* (1978; first exile) brings together memories of some three decades in Mexico, while *La pared transparente* (1984; the transparent wall) seeks a "naked" poetry to communicate religious insights. The recent deaths of Angela Figuera (1902–1984), Blas de Otero, and Gabriel Celaya (qq.v.) removed the leaders of the "social poets," a much-studied movement that had essentially run its course by 1970 with the highly touted launching of the *novísimos* ("newest") poets who rejected neorealist *engagement* in favor of experimental modes ranging from surrealist to camp. Others made of poetry an existential inquiry, an epistemological methodology, or a linguistic avenue to confront life's basic verities; imbricated in this trend are Francisco Brines (b. 1932), Eladio Cabañero (b. 1930), Angel Crespo (b. 1926), Gloria Fuertes (b. 1918), Jaime Gil de Biedma (b. 1929), Angel González (b. 1925), Manuel Montero (b. 1930), Claudio Rodríguez (b. 1934), Carlos Sahagún (b. 1938), and José Angel Valente (b. 1929), all of whom

published their major works between 1956 and 1971. Numerous new poets were on the scene at the death of Franco, several coming from the *novísimos* group and all born between 1939 (the end of the Civil War) and 1951: Antonio Martínez Sarrión (b. 1939), Jesús Muñárriz (b. 1940), José María Alvarez (b. 1942), José Luis Giménez Frontín (b. 1943), Félix de Azúa (b. 1944), José Miguel Ullán (b. 1944), Pere Gimferrer (b. 1945), Marcos Ricardo Barnatán (b. 1946), Antonio Colinas (b. 1946), Vicente Molina Foix (b. 1946), Genaro Talens (b. 1946), José Luis Jover (b. 1946), Guillermo Carnero (b. 1947), Leopoldo María Panero (b. 1948), Jaime Siles (b. 1951), and Luis Antonio de Villena (b. 1951). In the decade just ended, María Victoria Atencia (b. 1931), Elena Andrés (b. 1931), Pureza Canelo (b. 1946), Juana Castro (b. 1945), Clara Janés (b. 1940), Paloma Palao (1944–1986), María del Carmen Pallarés (b. 1950), and Luzmaría Jiménez Faro (b. 1937) are among the better-published women poets writing in Castilian, with Ana Rosetti (b. 1950) being noteworthy for her erotic verse. Marta Pessarrodona (b. 1941) and Maria Mercè Marçal (b. 1952) are the major women poets writing in Catalan.

Theater

"Social" playwrights who have evolved beyond neorealist beginnings and continue to be important in the post-Franco era include Carlos Múñiz (b. 1927), José Martín Recuerda (b. 1925), and José María Rodríguez Méndez (b. 1925). Andalusian Antonio Gala (b. 1936) cultivates a more lyric, tragicomic vein in the tradition of Casona (q.v.), marked by wit and a plea for individual and sexual freedom. Jaime Salom (b. 1925), one of the few Catalans to achieve success on the Madrid stage under Franco, has evolved from conservative Catholicism to a libertarian stance. Cultivators of abstract political allegory and social satire, the "underground" dramatists such as José Ruibal (b. 1930), Antonio Martínez Ballesteros, and Eduardo Quiles continue to be ignored by the Spanish theatrical establishment, although other previously unknown dramatists have experienced varying degrees of acceptance: Miguel Romero Esteo (b. 1928), Francisco Nieva (b. 1927), Francisco Rojas Zorrilla, Angel García Pintado, Jesús Campos, Juan Antonio Castro, José Luis Alonso de Santos (b. 1942), Marcial Suárez, Jerónimo López Mozo (b. 1938), Domingo Miras, Alberto Miralles, Fermín Cabal (b. 1948), Luis Matilla, and Luis Riaza (dates n.a.). Post-Franco revivals of plays from the first third of the century, especially by pro-Republican writers—García Lorca, Valle-Inclán (qq.v.), Manuel Azaña (1880–1940), and returned exile Rafael Alberti—share the boards with contemporary versions of classics done by writers well-known outside the theater, like Gonzalo Torrente Ballester, Carmen Martín Gaite, and others. Established post-Civil War luminaries Antonio Buero Vallejo and Alfonso Sastre (qq.v.) have enjoyed productions both of new works and plays previously censored. Only limited success was accorded Fernando Arrabal (q.v.) when he returned from self-imposed exile. As a result of a more favorable cultural climate, a Centro Drámatico Nacional was created in the mid-1980s, and the theatrical review *Primer Acto* (suspended in 1975) was resuscitated at the same time that other specialized journals were founded, including *Pipirijaina, El Público,* and *Segismundo.* Significant trends during the 1980s included decentralization (moving theater beyond traditional established centers in Madrid and Barcelona), official stimulation of children's theater, and the emergence of a number of younger dramatists such as Fermín Cabal (b. 1948), Alvaro del Amo, Ernesto Caballero, Julián Egea (dates n.a.), and an unusual number of women, headed by Lourdes Ortiz (b. 1943), Paloma Pedrero (b. 1957), and María Manuela Reina (b. 1958). A thriving theater in Catalan presented not only established contemporaries such as Manuel de Pedrolo (q.v.), but also Ricard Bofill (b. 1940), Albert Boadella (b. 1943), Josep M. Benet i Jornet (dates n.a.), and many other newcomers.

Quite possibly the most significant trend in the post-Franco era is decentralization, the absence of any single literary or cultural dogma, the proliferation of cultures, norms and voices, together with the literary empowering of many previously suppressed and silenced constituencies: women, exiles, and representatives of the regional or vernacular languages.

BIBLIOGRAPHY: Amorós, A., *Introducción a la novela contemporánea* (1981); García Lorenzo, L., *Documentación sobre el teatro español* (1981); Ruiz de la Pena, A., *Introducción a la literatura asturiana* (1981); García de la Concha, V., ed., *El surrealismo* (1982); Sarasola, I., *Historia social de la literatura vasca* (1982); Triadu, J., *La novela catalana de posguerra* (1982); Alonso, S., *La novela en la transición* (1983); Daydí-Tolson, S., *The Post Civil War Spanish Social Poets* (1983); Pérez, J., ed., *Novelistas femeninas de la postguerra española* (1983); Pérez Stansfield, M. P., *Direcciones de teatro español de posguerra* (1983); Fortes, J. A., *La novela joven en España* (1984); Besas, P., *Behind the Spanish Lens: Spanish Cinema under Fascism and Democracy* (1985); Cabal, F., and J. L. Alonso de Santos, eds., *Teatro español de los 80* (1985); Edwards, G., *Dramatists in Perspective: Spanish Theater in the Twentieth Century* (1985); Galerstein, C. L., ed., *Women Writers of Spain: An Annotated Bio-Bibliographical Guide* (1986); Mantero, M., *Poetas españoles de posguerra* (1986); Villena, L. A. de., ed., *Postnovísimos* (1986); Fernández Heliodoro, A., *La novela española dentro de España* (1987); Fortes, J. A., *Novelas para la transición política* (1987); Landeira, R., and L. T. González-del-Valle, eds., *Nuevos y novísimos: Algunas perspectivas críticas sobre la narrativa española desde la década de los 60* (1987); Mangini González, S., *Rojos y rebeldes: La cultura de la disidencia durante el franquismo* (1987); Palomero, M. P., *Poetas de los 70* (1987); Rodríguez Puértolas, J., *Literatura fascista española* (1987); Amell, S., and S. García Castañeda, eds., *La cultura española en el posfranquismo* (1988); Halsey, M. T., and P. Zatlin, eds., *The Contemporary Spanish Theater: A Collection of Critical Essays* (1988); Mainer, J.-C., *Historia. Literatura. Sociedad* (1988); Mantciga, R. C., ct al., cds., *Feminine Concerns in Contemporary Spanish Fiction by Women* (1988); O'Connor, P. W., *Dramaturgas españolas de hoy* (1988); Pérez, J., *Contemporary Women Writers of Spain* (1988); Provencio, P., *Poeticas españoles contemporáneos. La generación del 50* (1988); Vázquez de Gey, E., *Queimar as Meigas (Galicia: 50 años de poesía de mujer)* (1988); Oliva, C., *El teatro desde 1936* (1989); Gil Casado, P., *La novela deshumanizada española (1958–1988)* (1990); Pérez, G. J., and J. Pérez, eds., *Monographic Review: Hispanic Women Poets* (1990); Valis, N., and C. Maier, *In the Feminine Mode: Essays on Hispanic Women Writers* (1990); Brown, J. L., ed., *Women Writers of Contemporary Spain* (1991); Fortes, J. A., *La nueva narrativa andaluza* (1991); Perna, M. L., ed., *DLB: Twentieth Century Spanish Poets* (1991)

JANET PEREZ

SPOTA, Luis

Mexican novelist, b. 13 July 1925, Mexico City; d. 20 Jan. 1985, Mexico City

The son of an Italian merchant who immigrated to Mexico in the late 19th c. and a Mexican woman of Spanish descent, S. dropped out of school after finishing the sixth grade. In his struggle to support himself he worked as a bullfighter, a waiter, a sailor, a wetback in the fields of Texas, an encyclopedia salesman, an office boy, and a journalist. This broad experience, along with his voracious reading and keen observation of human behavior, enabled him to become Mexico's best-selling novelist as well as a major newspaper and television commentator. Although some critics consider him shallow and unworthy of serious literary investigation, his vivid portraits of contemporary Mexican society, including a total of twenty-eight novels, have elicited comparisons with Balzac's oeuvre.

S.'s second novel, *Murieron a mitad del río* (1948; they died in the middle of the river), epitomizes its author's writings in several respects: It dramatizes a well-known sociopolitical issue, in this case the maltreatment of wetbacks; it emphasizes dialogue and action rather than description and character development; and it holds the reader's attention from beginning to end. This novel portrays three young wetbacks, one of whom (José Paván) is probably a fictionalized portrait of the author himself. Although only one of them dies in a physical sense, they all experience a spiritual demise as a result of their encounter with injustice. Another of S.'s best early works is *Más cornadas da el hambre* (1951; *The Wounds of Hunger*, 1957), an exciting tale about bullfighting. Here too the protagonist exhibits characteristics of the author, who describes the triumphs and reverses of a young torero following the bullfighting circuit in provincial towns throughout Mexico. Perhaps S.'s best novel, *Casi el paraíso* (1956; *Almost Paradise*, 1964), is a clever satire of Mexico's greedy, shallow nouveaux riches. Although the characters emerge as sketchily drawn types, their actions and dialogues rivet the reader's attention throughout. Another important aspect of this novel is its structure, which alternates between the protagonist's present and past, enhancing suspense and irony. S.'s diverting exposé of the rampant corruption among Mexico's social climbers, politicians, and police has made this his most widely read work. Whereas *Casi el paraíso* flays Mexico's upper class, *La sangre enemiga* (1959; *The Enemy Blood*, 1961) stands out as a sordid, condemnatory portrayal of the urban poor. Like its predecessor, *La sangre enemiga* experiments with innovative structural techniques, shifting between different time frames and thus requiring greater reader participation. One of the major themes is jealousy and its disastrous ramifications, including deceit, murder, and police brutality. As in many of S.'s works, sex drives much of the action. Condemned is the strong element of *machismo* in Mexican society, that is, the harsh treatment of women by the insensitive, domineering male.

El tiempo de la ira (1960; the time of wrath) is one of many fine portraits of dictators in Latin American literature. Here S. presents a chronological account of César Darío's political career, including his eight-year dictatorial reign. Despite the length of this work (more than 500 pages), the reader's interest never flags, perhaps because of the vivid descriptions of setting and greater attention to character development. *El tiempo de la ira* marks the beginning of S.'s maturity as a writer.

Between 1975 and 1980 S. published a series of six political novels entitled *La costumbre del poder* (the custom of power). Although the setting of these traditionally structured, gripping tales is an unnamed Latin American country, they obviously depict conditions that have existed in Mexico. Critics have generally hailed *Palabras mayores* (1975; important words), the second of the series, as the best.

S. has been accused by critics of neglecting literary art to please the tastes of the unsophisticated reader, and it is true that, with a few notable exceptions, his novels are written in a direct, unadorned, almost journalistic style. He is nevertheless an exceptionally gifted storyteller whose suspenseful plots and forceful attacks on corruption have made him a highly visible and significant figure in contemporary Mexican fiction.

FURTHER WORKS: *José Mojica, hombre, artista, y fraile* (1944); *De la noche al día* (1945); *El coronel fue echado al mar* (1947); *Miguel Alemán en una semblanza* (1947); *Dos obras de teatro* (1949); *La estrella vacía* (1950); *Vagabunda* (1950); *Las grandes aguas* (1953); *Las horas violentas* (1958); *El aria de los sometidos* (1962); *La carcajada del gato* (1964); *La pequeña edad* (1964); *Los sueños del insomnio* (1966); *Lo de antes* (1968); *La plaza* (1972); *¿Qué pasa con la novela en México?* (1972); *Las cajas* (1973); *El viaje* (1973); *Retrato hablado* (1975); *Sobre la marcha* (1976); *El primer día* (1977); *El rostro del sueño* (1979); *La víspera del trueno* (1980); *Mitad oscura* (1982); *Los días contados* (1983); *Paraíso 25* (1983); *Días de poder* (1985)

BIBLIOGRAPHY: González, M. P., "L. S., gran novelista en potencia," *RHM*, 26 (Jan.–Apr. 1960), 102–6; Selva, M. de la, "Tres novelistas de nuestra América," *CA*, 114, 1 (Jan.–Feb. 1961), 283–95; Ocampo de Gómez, A. M., and E. Prado Velázquez, eds., *Diccionario de escritores mexicanos* (1967), 374–75; Brown, D. F., "Germinal's Progeny," *Hispania*, 51, 3 (Sept. 1968), 424–32; Langford, W. M., *The Mexican Novel Comes of Age* (1971), 103–26; Foster, D. W., and V. R. Foster, eds., *Modern Latin American Literature* (1975), Vol. 2, 356–63; Selva, M. de la, "Actualidad de L. S.," *CA*, 204, 1 (Jan.–Feb. 1976), 225–35; Trejo Fuentes, I., "¿Conoce usted a L. S.?: Un acercamiento a su obra," *La Semana de Bellas Artes*, 79 (6 June 1979), 12–14; Sefchovich, S., *Ideología y ficción en la obra de L. S.* (1985); Slick, S., on *Días de poder*, *WLT*, 60, 2 (Spring 1986), 291–92; García Nuñez,

F., "Notas sobre la frontera norte en la novela mexicana," *CA*, 2, 4 (1988), 159–68; Cota-Cárdenas, M., "Visión de la frontera México-Texana, 1959: *Murieron a mitad del río* por L. S.," *ExTL*, 18, 1 (1989–1990), 72–87; Vélez, J. F., *Escritores mexicanos según ellos mismos* (1990), 11–18

GEORGE R. MCMURRAY

STANGERUP, Henrik

Danish novelist, screenwriter, and critic, b. 1 Sept. 1937, Frederiksberg/Copenhagen

After four years' study of theology at the University of Copenhagen, S. began in 1960 a career as a journalist and a literature and film critic with various Copenhagen newspapers. As a reporter he has traveled extensively throughout Europe, in particular in France, where he studied film in 1964, and he feels strongly affiliated with pan-European sentiments and movements as well as the new French, anti-Marxist philosophers, such as Bernard-Henri Lévy (b. 1948). Journeys to Brazil in the 1970s have provided S. with new inspiration for a juxtaposition of exotic zest for life and European tepidity and sober-mindedness.

S.'s first and only short-story collection, *Grønt og sort* (1961; green and black), is written in the neorealistic style that dominated Danish literature in the early 1960s. The focus is primarily on problems caused by the modern welfare state among young people from the upper class. Under their polished surface S. discovers glimpses of madness and ferocity that forcefully break through in the characters of his later writings.

The transition to the following self-centered novels took place with the humorous and self-ironic stories and reportage in the travelogue *Veritabel pariser* (1966; a veritable Parisian) based on S.'s previous experiences in France. Autobiographical elements also dominate the novels *Slangen i brystet* (1969; the snake in the breast), S.'s breakthrough work, and *Løgn over Løgn* (1971; lie upon lie). The first novel is a penetrating psychological study of paranoia and existential insecurity. The protagonist is a middle-aged Danish correspondent stationed in Paris and fighting against the envy and criticism of his colleagues and against destructive forces in his environment and, in particular, in himself. The vague attempts at rebellion, which are also those of S. himself, erupt in his second novel. The previous satirical tone becomes more extrovert in a violent attack on the "politically correct" Danish cultural elite and their exploitation of other human beings.

With *Manden der ville være skyldig* (1973; *The Man Who Wanted To Be Guilty,* 1981), a major European success, S. combines the genre of the political novel in the tradition of Aldous Huxley and George Orwell (qq.v.) with science fiction. He departs from his former subjectivity and widens the scope of his polemic, focusing it on the social and political development, the final goal of which is the authoritarian state. His antidogmatic attitude, advocating the freedom and rights of the individual, is more directly voiced—also against reactionary conservatism—in several collections of essays and articles throughout the 1970s.

The final step into pure confession, related to S.'s first two novels, is taken with *Fjenden i forkøbet* (1978; anticipating the enemy). However, in contrast to these works, the depression and collapse lead to a state of clarification—the work is an exercise both in self-accusation and in self-defense. S. finds himself both as an artist and as a human being inspired by his experiences in Brazil. *Fjenden i forkøbet* concludes with a hymn to this newly discovered sensuous and colorful reality, which is juxtaposed to the one-dimensional Danish everyday grayishness.

This daily routine is brought up for discussion from a theological point of view in S.'s first feature film, *Giv Gud en chance om søndagen* (1970; give God a chance on Sunday), and from an erotic perspective in his next film, *Farlige kys* (1972; dangerous kisses), in which S. analyzes the attitude of his own generation toward love and sexuality. Later in his career as a film director S., together with the Brazilian writer Fausto Wolff (dates n.a.), reworked an 18th-c. comedy by the Danish dramatist Ludvig Holberg (1684–1754), *Erasmus Montanus,* into an imaginative movie influenced by the commedia dell'arte about a Brazilian student who returns from Portugal in the mid-17th c. The script was published in 1976, entitled *Jorden er flad* (the earth is flat); the film itself was a fiasco in Denmark and a success in France.

Brazil is also the setting for *Vejen til Lagoa Santa* (1981; *The Road to Lagoa Santa,* 1984), which marks a new development in S.'s writing, taking it to an absolute zenith and opening it up to an international audience. The volume is the first in a series of three documentary novels, in fact a trilogy, based on painstaking research of source material and structured on the three stages in Søren Kierkegaard's philosophy. They have in common three Danes whose destiny is defined through their wrestling with foreign environments, three historical figures who in S.'s universe become three spiritual types given mythic dimensions. For *Det er svært at dø i Dieppe* (1985; *The*

Seducer: It Is Hard To Die in Dieppe, 1990) S. has chosen an opposite character, the prolific 19th-c. man of letters P. L. Møller, an aesthetic character in a Kierkegaardian sense, attempting to live in the moment but perpetually dissatisfied and, like the protagonists of S.'s earlier novels, in a permanent state of catastrophe. With *Broder Jacob* (1991; brother Jacob) S. has reached the highest Kierkegaardian category, the religious stage. Jacob, the brother of the Danish Renaissance king Christian II, becomes a representative of the Catholic Church, not only its faith but also its spiritualism and cosmopolitan outlook that he could not find in Denmark. With a superbly developed stylistic beauty and narrative skill S. has returned to his initial cultural criticism of Danish mentality, against its rationalism, pettiness, and puritan sense of guilt.

Here, as well as in his entire oeuvre, S. centers on the relationship between the individual and his confining, hypocritical, and, in the final account, destructive environment. Whereas S. originally was unable to point to a way to escape from chaos and catastrophe, his last novel suggests a metaphysical solution represented by Catholicism, which has succeeded in incorporating the physical world, art, and longing in a universal utopia.

FURTHER WORKS: *Lille Håbs rejse* (1958); *Kunsten at være ulykkelig* (1974); *Mens tid var* (1978); *Retten til ikke at høre til* (1979); *Fangelejrens frie halvdel* (1980); *Samba* (1982)

BIBLIOGRAPHY: Monty, I., "An Unsentimental Dane," *Danish Journal,* 72 (1972), 14–19; Lasky, M. J., "In the Shadow of Northern Lights. A Conversation with the Danish Novelist, H. S.," *Encounter,* 63, 2 (1984), 97–123

SVEN HAKON ROSSEL

STRAND, Mark
American poet, b. 11 Apr. 1934, Summerside, Prince Edward Island, Canada

Like many American poets who are also professors of literature, S. has led a peripatetic life. He received his B.A. from Antioch College (1957); a B.F.A. from Yale University (1959) and his M.A. from the University of Iowa (1962). In the course of a distinguished career he has taught at such colleges and universities as Mount Holyoke, Columbia, Brooklyn College, Yale, Brandeis, Princeton, Harvard, and the universities of Iowa, Washington, Virginia, California, and Utah. In 1960–1961 he was a Fulbright scholar in Italy; in 1965–1966, a Fulbright lecturer in Brazil. In 1990 he was named America's fourth poet laureate—

the first laureate to be appointed at the height of his career.

S.'s poetry is distinguished from that of his contemporaries primarily by its persona, who is so alert to ontological mysteries that he experiences himself as double. In the collection *Sleeping with One Eye Open* (1964), S. makes clear that one of the two selves of his persona lives in the objective, physical world; the other self (the vehicle of consciousness in the poems) seems real only in the narrator's subjective awareness. The poem "Keeping Things Whole" defines the persona famously as a not-field moving through a field of reality and keeping the field whole by moving on, careful not to displace any aspect of the field with his comparatively insufficient being. The extraordinary impact of such poems derives from the coolness with which the persona recounts his sense of double existence. While he is clearly harrowed by his relationship to nothingness, his tone is far from being confessional. He affects to stand outside his trauma even while he strives conversationally to give it definition and even while he experiences it as personal dissolution.

Such ontological awarenesses are rendered surrealistically in the poems of *Reasons for Moving* (1968). The persona is awakened at midnight by a weeping mailman who seems his alter ego; he is run over by a train whose engineer whispers intimately in his ear; he leaves Rio de Janeiro in a death bus, comforted by a woman with tombstones in her eyes. In "The Man in the Mirror" he confronts an alter ego in the glass, frightened both that the image will desert him and that it will endure. Such poems extend the imaginative reach of *Sleeping with One Eye Open* and advance considerably its level of technique. Indeed, the increasing "dis-ease" of the poet's vision and the gathering ease of his craft become in *Reasons for Moving* an important counterpoint.

Several of the poems in *Darker* (1970) more than justify their collective title, notably such poems as "My Life By Somebody Else" and "The Way It Is," in both of which the persona continues to probe a nothingness that seems to contain the secret of his being. But other poems, like "Breath," "From a Litany," and especially "The New Poetry Handbook," look to poetry as an alternative to nothingness. Poetry is not in these texts a vehicle of expressing the self but a process of being that authenticates being. The S. persona subsequently approaches reality not so much through his shadow of nothingness as through his creative imagination. Indeed, the seven relatively long poems of *The Story of Our Lives* (1973) drift from the propositional mode to the interrogative as the persona strives to create a substantial world out of his emptiness. A new and daunting balance of ontologies is the result in poems like "Elegy for My Father" and "The Untelling."

The Monument (1978) is in many ways the persona's ultimate statement of selfhood as a nonexperience. A sequence of fifty-two prose statements, it intermingles almost seamlessly the voice of the S. persona and quotations from Shakespeare, Sir Thomas Browne, William Wordsworth, Friedrich Nietzsche, Wallace Stevens (q.v.), and others. Ostensibly engaged in creating a monument to selfhood—addressing, even, his future translator (the texts affect to be already translated)—the persona moves from an initial show of egotism to a self-effacement so entire that it is impossible to discern where he exits the sequence and fades into the voices of literary tradition. Ultimately, the volume is both monument and antimonument: a developing tabula rasa that configures the presence-through-absence of the persona's essential being.

In the wake of *The Monument*, the poems of *The Late Hour* (1978), of a "New Poems (1980)" section in the *Selected Poems* (1980), and of *The Continuous Life* (1990) seem the gentle aftermath of a storm. The concerns of the poems are more varied than before and less ontologically harrowed; the author's trademark commitment to self-effacement is only a sporadic concern; the persona is notably older, hopeful, almost at peace; his eruptions of anxiety are governable. There is no apparent rejection of the persona's earlier stance, for a poem like "An Old Man Awake in His Own Death" worries questions of ego and anonymity as much as the earlier poems. In the majority of these poems, however, the persona has abandoned his lonely vigil at the abyss of nothingness for more comfortable, even domestic terrain. One of the effects of this domestication is a more affective level of statement. Poems like "For Jessica, My Daughter," "My Mother on an Evening in Late Summer," and the almost blithesome "Night Piece" have enormous authority as testaments of felt experience, their authority all the greater for the poet having deferred affective statements for so long.

S. is generally recognized as an austerely eloquent and spiritually intrepid poet in the tradition of his acknowledged mentors, Elizabeth Bishop and William Carlos Williams (qq.v.), but his voice is entirely his own: subdued and quietly intense in the best manner of recent poetry; but plainer, sterner, and more spiritually harrowed than that of his mentors and of his contemporaries alike. Few voices in American poetry seem more authentic today, and few command a more respectful audience.

FURTHER WORKS: *The Sargeantville Notebook* (1973); *Elegy for My Father* (1978); *The Planet of Lost Things* (1982); *Art of the Real: Nine American Figurative Painters* (1983); *Mr. and Mrs. Baby and Other Stories* (1985); *The Night Book* (1985); *Rembrandt Takes a Walk* (1986); *William Bailey* (1987)

BIBLIOGRAPHY: Howard, R., *Alone with America: Essays on the Art of Poetry in the United States since 1950* (1969), 507–16; Crenner, J., "M. S.: Darker," *Seneca Review*, 2 (Apr. 1971), 87–97; Bloom, H., "Dark and Radiant Peripheries: M. S. and A. R. Ammons," *SoR*, 8 (Winter 1972), 133–41; Gregerson, L., "Negative Capability," *Parnassus: Poetry in Review*, 9 (1978), 90–114; Kirby, D., "The Nature of No One," *TLS*, 15 Sept. 1978, 1009; McClanahan, T., "M. S.," in Greiner, D. J., ed., *DLB: American Poets since World War II*, Part 2 (1980), 303–9; Shaw, R., "Quartet," *Poetry*, 139 (1981), 171–77; Stitt, P., "Stages of Reality: The Mind/Body Problem in Contemporary Poetry," *GaR*, 37 (1983), 201–10; Olsen, L., "Entry to the Unaccounted for: M. S.'s Fantastic Autism," in Murphy, P. D., and V. Hyles, eds., *The Poetic Fantastic: Studies in an Evolving Genre* (1989), 89–96; Kirby, D. K., *M. S. and the Poet's Place in Contemporary Culture* (1990)

ROBERT F. KIERNAN

STUS, Vasyl

Ukrainian poet, literary critic, and translator, b. 8 Jan. 1938, Rakhmanivtsi, Vinnytsya region; d. 4 Sept. 1985, Concentration Camp Nr.36-I Perm, Ural Region, Russia

Born into a rural Ukrainian family, S. was destined to become his country's leading intellectual poet and the unrelenting champion of its national resistance movement. After studying at the Donetsk Pedagogical Institute, S. served in the Soviet army and, upon his discharge, taught school and worked as a journalist. In 1964 he joined the Institute of Literature of the Ukrainian S.S.R. in Kiev, but lost his position in 1965 because of his repeated intercessions on behalf of persecuted Ukrainian intellectuals. In 1966 he obtained a position with the State Archives of History, but was dismissed from it later that year. S. was first arrested in 1972, and after nine months of interrogation in Kiev was sentenced to five years of forced labor and three years of exile. Having served the imprisonment in Mordovia and two years of exile in Kolyma, S. returned to Kiev in August of 1979 unbroken in spirit but with severely impaired health. In October 1979 he joined the Ukrainian Helsinki Group, was rearrested in May for "anti-Soviet agitation and propaganda," and was sentenced on

8 August 1980 to fifteen years of forced labor. His plight attracted considerable attention, both in Ukraine and in the West, and his death in the concentration camp, where he was deprived of medical treatment and tortured, rendered him a martyr of the Ukrainian cause.

S. began publishing poetry and articles on literature as early as 1959 in the Kiev-based literary journal *Dnipro*. Because of his activities on behalf of human rights, he soon became a dissident poet whose works could not be published in the Soviet Union. As a result, his major collections have appeared in the West, having been smuggled out of the Soviet Union, while hundreds of his poetic works have been destroyed by his jailers, and are thus irretrievably lost.

A highly original and powerful poet, S. combines autobiographical and patriotic motifs with intellectual introspection. Already his first collection, *Zymovi dereva* (1970; trees of winter), published in Brussels, manifests his extraordinary, Rilkean talent to transform life into poetry. Motifs of love for his native land and its beautiful natural settings, of joy and suffering, of love and hatred, and eternal questions concerning the human condition are almost always presented *sub specie aeternitatis*. S.'s poetry, even while intensely autobiographical or national, never fails to transcend personal and geographical confines and soars into the universal realm of thought and human spirit. In this sense, S. is an intensely religious poet, whose work is often a hymn to the Creator.

While S.'s early poetry is characterized by an ever-present *amor fati,* his later work, especially that written in prison, is informed by an intensely tragic sense of life. In the collection *Svicha v svichadi* (1977; a candle in a mirror), published in New York, motifs of manliness and courage vie for supremacy with feelings of sorrow and despair. His poetic farewell to Ukraine, for example, entitled significantly "Ostannya pisnya" (the last song), and his nine-line poem "Synovi" (to my son) from the collection with the revealing title *Vesely tsvyntar* (1971; the joyful cemetery), reflect what he ascribed to Beethoven: the "harmonized suffering" of his own "many-troubled soul" and his quest to preserve within himself the pristine purity of the human spirit.

Like Rilke and Goethe, whose work S. admired and translated (the bulk of these translations, too, was lost in the concentration camps), S. perceived in poetry a redemptive quality endowed with the power to change the world and the self. To S. poetry was both "beauty and delight" without which life was hardly imaginable; he sought it within himself, in his own Ukrainian tradition, and in the Western world from which he was separated. Within prison walls, poetry became a

way of life, a world unto itself without vanity and terror. At times it was perhaps more real than the cruel reality surrounding him because it reflected more accurately his true state of being. S. the poet often dwelled on sorrow and even despair; S. the man was always uncompromisingly heroic. For a while, his heroic biography tended to overshadow his poetic achievement. However, the continued interest in his poetry and its translation into many foreign languages, including English and German, provide assurance that his poetic oeuvre will endure and prevail.

FURTHER WORKS: *Palimpsesty* (1986); *Doroha bolyu* (1990). FURTHER VOLUME IN ENGLISH: *Selected Poems* (1987)

BIBLIOGRAPHY: Wolffheim, E., "Unter der Eisscholle schlägt das Herz der Erde," Introduction to *Du hast dein Leben nur geträumt* (1982), 5–11; Horbatsch, A., "Sein Verbrechen ist der Widerstand," Introduction to *Ein Dichter im Widerstand. Aus dem Tagebuch des Wassyl Stus* (1984), 5–7; Levytsky, M., "V. S.: Doomed to Death and Immortality," *Religious Rights*, 1 (1985), 6–7; Shevelov, G. Y., "Potion and Poison," Introduction to *Selected Poems* (1987), xv–xxx; Rudnytzky, L., "V. S. und die deutsche Dichtung," *Jahrbuch der Ukrainekunde* (1988), 162–76

LEONID RUDNYTZKY

SWEDISH LITERATURE

See Volume 4, page 376.

Toward the end of the 1970s, Swedish literature is marked by tenuous orientations in new directions after the unprecedented rallying around the radical leftist banners that took place in the period from the mid-1960s to the mid-1970s. As many of the ideologues and "culture workers" of the so-called Generation of '68 doffed their Mao jackets for equally becoming garments boasting Pierre Cardin labels and replaced the Fidel Castro and Che Guevara posters on their walls with art works of greater financial investment value, the benefits or casualties of the recent cultural revolution still remained to be evaluated—computed may be a better term in the age of electronics, which Sweden embraced more readily and thoroughly than most nations. It is still debatable whether the politicizing of literature and art in general provided a new and salutary definition of the whole concept of "culture" as intended or whether it constituted an act of vandalism through a radical break in the continuity of the cultural heritage. This heritage, kept alive under siege through the undaunted efforts of already established writers, had come to be viewed as a luxury or even as one more instrument of oppression and exploitation; the "difficulty," inaccessibility, or political irrelevance of traditional art for an imagined "average consumer" was seen as a further sign of the inequality inherent in the class society, even in the Swedish welfare state. The term *finkultur* (exclusive culture) was used as opposed to the new gospel that "everything is culture." The attempts to lower the standards to the imagined needs of the culturally "underprivileged" were often unwittingly condescending albeit well-meaning. The Swedish Academy, more than ever viewed as the stronghold of conservatism, weathered the storm and was able to celebrate its two hundredth anniversary in 1986. The literary legacy of the rebellious decade—"new simplicity" in poetry and in general contempt for traditional poetic expression, denial of existential-metaphysical dimensions of the novel in favor of political demonstration, and agitprop and "happenings" as substitutes for drama (in 1991 Ingmar Bergman laments the loss of a whole generation of professionally trained and disciplined actors and directors)—presented a shaky foundation for growth and development of the literary genres in the postmodernist (q.v.) era.

A further threat to the future of Swedish literature was economic: The modest size of the population with a proportionately small readership in combination with very high production costs makes book publishing unprofitable. Few authors in Sweden are able to support themselves solely from the results of their creative writing. Contributing factors are also competition from literature in translation and readily available sources of entertainment in the electronic media age. In this situation, a national "cultural policy" was adopted in 1975 involving among other things government support of literature aimed at safeguarding the variety and the quality of Swedish literature; the fact that the government has only a minority voice in determining the ultimate worthiness of recipients is of course crucially important.

In the last decade, there have been three highly publicized collective undertakings in Sweden that could be viewed as signs of a different climate or a major effort to restore and to summarize a battered cultural heritage: the initiation of a new national encyclopedia; the completion in 1990 of the seven-volume richly illustrated history of Swedish literature, *Den svenska litteraturen;* and the mammoth so-called National Edition of August Strindberg's works, which will comprise seventy-four annotated volumes when completed.

In a speech given in England in 1983, Swedish critic Ruth Halldén (b. 1927) compared the novel in Sweden and in Britain: "Swedish novelists have a different temperament and rarely seek recogni-

tion as entertainers and wits. They have less respect for common sense, and tend to be of a more mystical or revolutionary turn of mind, aspiring to the immodest heights of a genius, a saint, or a savior. Whereas an English writer is content to produce novels with an exciting plot elegantly and competently narrated, and selects another literary form if he wishes to argue a case, defend a cause, or put forward a new theory, a Swedish writer is likely to use the novel for such purposes." The observation is astute, and it may explain the readiness with which the Swedish novel became an instrument of radical political propaganda in the 1960s and 1970s, when documentary novels and a large number of "report books" threatened to obliterate the distinctive features of the various genres. Voices continued to proclaim the imminent death of the novel, or the "sclerosis of the Swedish novel" in the words of Lars Gustafsson (q.v.), himself a major novelist whose position as an observer in Austin, Texas, provides him with a critical distance to his native land and its literature. Notwithstanding such dire predictions, the novel has continued to defend its position and to develop in new directions.

One such direction, uniquely Swedish at this time, is a significant trend to explore a fairly recent past. Some of the best novelists set their clocks back from a critical today and its utopian concerns for tomorrow to a historical yesterday. A number of impressive multivolume works were produced in which social and family history and myth were built into stories around fictive characters in meticulously authentic historical settings. Per Anders Fogelström (b. 1915) had already presented an immensely popular traditionally realistic five-volume series about Stockholm during the last hundred years from a proletarian perspective (1960–1968); in the 1980s he extends the chronicle in four additional novels to include well-researched accounts of life in 18th- and 19th-c. Stockholm. Sven Delblanc (q.v.), more experimental in his narrative style, who wrote a tetralogy centered on a rural Hedeby (1970–1976), now continues in another tetralogy (1981–1985) to trace a dark saga about the ancestor Samuel and his descendants, partly based on the author's own family. Kerstin Ekman (q.v.) follows three successive generations of women from the 1870s to the present in a tetralogy (1974–1983) against the background of the growth and development of the town of Katrineholm. Perhaps most remarkable of all these historical chronicles is Sara Lidman's (q.v.) five-volume series (1977–1985) about the building of the railroad and colonization of her native province Västerbotten close to the arctic circle. Other writers also found their material in the recent past of their native regions: Göran Tunström (b. 1937), whose Värmland figures prominently in his novels, and Torgny Lindgren (q.v.), another native of Västerbotten. More personal explorations of the past are undertaken in Jan Myrdal's (b. 1927) recreation of his childhood in three volumes (1982–1989) or in Heidi von Born's (b. 1936) basically autobiographical tetralogy (1981–1989) set in Stockholm, while Sigrid Combüchen (b. 1942) presents a remarkable "metafictional" biography of Lord Byron (1988). In most of these novels, as well as the novels of Per Olov Enqvist (q.v.), traditional realism is undermined by a high degree of narrative artistry or flights of imagination, at times reminiscent of Latin American magic realism (q.v.).

Critic Halldén's comment on the traditional neglect of entertainment aspects in the Swedish novel is countered by a number of works in the 1980s, which justify the term *berättandets återkomst* (the return of storytelling). P. C. Jersild (q.v.) remains one of the most popular writers; his social criticism is tempered with ironic humor in novels of high literary merit. Göran Hägg (b. 1947) writes eminently readable satires of intellectual life in Sweden. Lars Gustafsson experiments with such popular genres as the spy thriller and science fiction, Delblanc even writes a novel in the style of a Jackie Collins best-seller, and Klas Östergren (b. 1955) presents an adventure story about smugglers; in all of these novels, the popular form is a deceptive front for a continued discussion of more serious moral, social, and literary issues.

A number of novels in the 1980s have religious or metaphysical undertones. Lars Ahlin (q.v.), one of the great novelists of the century, made his literary comeback in the early part of the decade after a silence of over twenty years. Birgitta Trotzig (q.v.) continues offering a specifically Catholic perspective in her novels. A note of Job-like lamentation coupled with implied social protest in the face of inhuman sufferings is noticeable in her works, and also in those of Delblanc, Tunström, and Lindgren. Of interest is the specifically religious vision, the "Christian socialism," in the novels of Hans Granlid (b. 1926). From an agnostic-existentialist position Lars Gyllensten (q.v.) continues his Kierkegaardian explorations of the human condition with an increased employment in the 1980s of religious "models" in intertextual dialogues with, among many others, Pär Lagerkvist's (q.v.) works.

The large number of immigrants in Sweden will undoubtedly add significantly to the texture and variety of Swedish literature in years to come. A leading position among the immigrant writers is held by Theodor Kallifatides (b. 1938), whose work alternates between contemporary descriptions of life in his adopted country and reminiscences from his native Greece.

Several authors who made promising debuts in the previous decade consolidated their positions in the 1980s, among them Inger Alfvén (b. 1940), Jacques Werup (b. 1945), Ernst Brunner (b. 1950), and Lars Andersson (b. 1954). Stig Larsson (b. 1955), active in all the major literary genres, is the foremost interpreter of a postmodernist sensibility and the writer who has most radically broken with established narrative conventions.

The shift in attitude toward poetry from the 1960s to the 1980s is illustrated in the fate of one of the great poetic geniuses of the century, Harry Martinson (q.v.), who fell silent, or was silenced, in the harsh public-media climate of the 1960s; a rich harvest of his unpublished poetry has appeared posthumously in the more appreciative 1980s. In this decade, poetry shows greater individual variations than prose fiction. In general, the poets are more concerned with existential probings than social issues. The earlier political involvement has all but disappeared; if "issues" are discussed, they tend to concern ecology. One of the most visible poets of the 1960s, Göran Palm (b. 1931), writes a broad and satirical epic in blank verse, *Sverige—en vintersaga* (1984; Sweden—a winter's tale). When he returns in 1989 with a second part, he expresses concern for the threatened environment. Similar ecological concerns are found in the poetry of Elisabet Hermodsson (b. 1927), Bengt Emil Johnson (b. 1936), and Ulf Eriksson (b. 1958). The poetic scene is still dominated by such masters as Tomas Tranströmer (q.v.) and Lars Gustafsson, both widely translated. Tranströmer's poetry is the subject of a study by Kjell Espmark (b. 1930), himself an outstanding poet and, as a professor of literature, the author of brilliant works about poetry. Lars Forssell (q.v.) again proves his versatility with a noted epic-dramatic poem, which was set to music; it is based on the Book of Ruth in the Old Testament. Niklas Rådström (b. 1953) displays stylistic brilliance in poems full of paradoxes, while Kristina Lugn's (b. 1948) poetry offers a specifically feminine perspective of self-mocking irony. As in his prose fiction, Stig Larsson performs acts of linguistic sabotage in his poetry. A problematic relationship to language is also evident in the tentative explorations of reality in the poetry of Katarina Frostenson (b. 1953).

Sweden is a theatergoing nation. Stockholm has a higher density of theaters than any capital in the world. One reason may be that interest is early fostered through Sweden's tradition of excellent children's theater. Ingmar Bergman retired from filmmaking with *Fanny and Alexander* and returned to his first love, theater. He remains a towering presence. As director at Dramaten, Sweden's national stage, he produced in the 1980s a line of brilliant interpretations of classics—Shakespeare, Ibsen, Strindberg, and O'Neill. Per Olov

Enquist and Lars Norén (q.v.) consolidated their reputations as Sweden's leading and most exportable contemporary dramatists. Agneta Pleijel (b. 1940), Stig Larsson, and Staffan Göthe (b. 1944) have added to the native repertoire, while a number of works by novelists, such as Anders Fogelström and Inger Alfvén, have been dramatized for the stage or the screen.

BIBLIOGRAPHY: Egholm Andersen, F., and J. Weinstock, eds., *The Nordic Mind: Current Trends in Scandinavian Literary Criticism* (1987); Scobbie, I., ed., *Aspects of Modern Swedish Literature* (1988); Algulin, I., *A History of Swedish Literature* (1989); Zuck, V., ed., *Dictionary of Scandinavian Literature* (1990)

LARS G. WARME

SZICHMAN, Mario

Argentine novelist and essayist, b. 2 Jan. 1945, Buenos Aires

S., born into an Argentine Jewish family, now lives in New York, where he is an editor in the Latin American department of Associated Press. In addition to his work in fiction, he has been a correspondent and editor for several newspapers and journals in Latin America, the U.S., and Israel. S. lived in Venezuela from 1967 to 1971, where he worked as a news editor, then returned to Buenos Aires. He left Argentina in 1975, living again in Venezuela until 1980, where he was an editor and a professor of Hispanic American literature at the Universidad Andrés Bello in Caracas. While in Venezuela, he published two socially conscious studies on Venezuelan writers Arturo Uslar Pietri (q.v.) and Miguel Otero Silva (1908–1985): *Uslar: cultura y dependencia* (1975; Uslar: culture and dependence) and *Miguel Otero Silva: mitología de una generación frustrada* (1975; Miguel Otero Silva: mythology of a frustrated generation). In 1980 he directed the cultural supplement of the newspaper *Últimas Noticias* in Caracas; the supplement won the National Prize for journalism that year. He left Caracas in 1980 for the U.S., where he has worked as a journalist, including, from 1981 to 1987, as editor in the Latin American department of United Press International in New York and then in Washington. Besides his journalistic work, he has published numerous stories, especially in the journal *Hispamérica*.

S. continues the prolific 20th-c. tradition of Argentine Jewish writing but, as commentators such as Naomi Lindstrom have noted, with a more radical and cynical stance than many of his predecessors such as Alberto Gerchunoff (1884–1950). His first effort as a novelist, *Crónica falsa* (1969;

false chronicle), is now seen by him as an apprentice work; he revised it as *La verdadera crónica falsa* (the true false chronicle) in 1972. The revision represents the first in a series of novels that employ cinematic devices (such as traveling shots), techniques from vaudeville, Yiddish humor, and other radical narrative techniques to detail the efforts of the Pechof family, Polish-born Jewish immigrants to Argentina, to maintain their identity within a nationalistic Argentine culture. At the same time, the nature of their Jewish cultural identity is questioned, examined, falsified, or shown to be historically elusive though perhaps "true" in the memory of the protagonists (thus the "true false chronicle").

A striking aspect of the work of S. is his rather bizarre, Marx-Brothers-like humor in presenting the saga of the Pechofs through several generations of Argentine life in the 20th c. The Pechof "saga" is presented in three novels: *La verdadera crónica falsa*; *Los judíos del Mar Dulce* (1971; the Jews of the freshwater sea); and *A las 20:25, la señora entró en la inmortalidad* (1981; At 8:25 Evita Became Immortal, 1983). A fourth novel in the series, *La tercera fundación de Buenos Aires* (the third founding of Buenos Aires), will soon be published. The novels are set against the backdrop of Argentine cultural and political history and especially of the rise and decline of Peronism and its cultural mythology, which is severely questioned. The use of Yiddish phrases, epithets, and scatological humor realizes the ethnic ambience of the characters and lends them individuality; one protagonist, for instance, normally reveals his foreignness by substituting "g" for "r" in his speech. But S. eschews any cheap sentimentalization or endearment of his characters; while memorable and attractive as human creations, they are subject to sharp criticism and revelation of their faults.

S. is now at work on a new novel, *Botín de guerra* (war booty), concerning one of the characters from *A las 20:25*. His work is an important part of the ongoing critical reevaluation by Argentine Jews concerning their history and their place within Argentine culture. As the criticism on S. has pointed out, his novels also contribute in a substantial way to the evaluation of the Peronist period, critiquing the effects of the cult of Juan Perón and his wife Eva on the politics and social relationships of Argentines.

BIBLIOGRAPHY: Sarlo, B., "Judíos y argentinos: el linaje de la literatura," *Quimera*, 21–22 (July–Aug. 1982), 70–73; Lindstrom, N., "Problems and Possibilities in the Analysis of Jewish Argentine Literary Works," *Latin American Research Review*, 18, 1 (1983), 118–26; Senkman, L., *La identidad judía en la literatura argentina* (1983), 269–83; Sosnowski, S., "Latin American Jewish

Writers: A Bridge toward History,'' *Prooftexts,* 4, 1 (1984), 71–92; Lipp, S., "Jewish Themes and Authors in Contemporary Argentine Fiction,'' in Minc, R. S., ed., *El Cono Sur* (1985), 49–55; Morello-Frosch, M., "Textos inscriptos al margen de la literatura argentina: *A las 20:25, la señora entró en la inmortalidad,* de M. S.,'' in Minc, R. S., ed., *El Cono Sur* (1985), 137–45; Senkman, L., "De la legitimación del israelita argentino a la asunción de la identidad de algunos escritores judeoargentinos,'' in Minc, R. S., ed., *El Cono Sur* (1985), 56–71; special issue on Jewish writers, *Folio,* 17 (1987), 24–56; Gardiol, R. M., "Jewish Writers: An Emerging Force in Contemporary Argentine Literature,'' *Hispano,* 31, 1 (1987), 65–76; Lindstrom, N., *Jewish Issues in Argentine Literature: From Gerchunoff to S.* (1989), 146–57, 181

KENNETH E. HALL

SZYSZKOWITZ, Gerald

Austrian novelist and dramatist, b. 22 July 1938, Graz

Born in Graz, S. began his literary career while still a student in his hometown. After receiving a Ph.D. in theater history and German from the University of Vienna in 1960, he traveled extensively to such exotic places as Martinique, Tokyo, Rangoon, and Calcutta. Subsequently he held positions at a number of theaters in West Germany—Bonn, Dortmund, Wilhelmshaven—initially as a director's assistant, later as a director. In 1968 he returned to Graz to become senior producer and director at the local state theater. Four years later, he joined the drama department of the Austrian Television Company. Having been responsible for numerous highly regarded, internationally acclaimed productions, S. is still better known as a television producer than as an author in his own right.

S. has taken a rather independent literary course, ignoring trends, distancing himself from experiments and extremes, avoiding firm programs and rigid theories but following, instead, a tradition of 19th- and early 20th-c. novelists such as Theodor Fontane (1819–1898) and Joseph Roth (q.v.), two of his favorite writers. S. is, above all, a storyteller, a literary chronicler of Austria's recent past. In all of his novels he has skillfully combined historically accurate events with fictitious portrayals of convincingly pictured individuals.

S.'s first novel, *Der Thaya* (1981; Mr. Thaya), and the fifth one, *Puntigam oder Die Kunst des Vergessens* (1988; *Puntigam or The Art of Forgetting,* 1990), are his masterpieces. *Der Thaya* is the first part of a trilogy in which the author

describes the life and the gradual decline of a manorial family from northern Austria. The trilogy captivates its readers not only through a well-defined, action-filled plot—family idylls are skillfully interwoven with odysseys of refugees and melodramatic love affairs—but also through its atmosphere. The basic tone is melancholy, overlaid with humor and subtle irony. While *Der Thaya* portrays the family patriarch, its sequel, *Seitenwechsel* (1982; changing sides), describes the attempts of his daughter-in-law to break out of the confinements of her marriage. The final volume, *Osterschnee* (1983; Easter snow), focuses on the younger Thaya's increasing alienation. Following the breakup of his marriage and disillusioned by the lethargy and the corruption in his country, he commits suicide. In *Osterschnee* S. shows the dilemma of what he calls the "sandwich generation,'' those men standing between their powerful fathers, who rebuilt Austria after World War II, and the younger, more dynamic generation. In *Furlani oder Die Zährtlichkeit des Verrats* (1985; Furlani or the tenderness of betrayal) S., remaining faithful to his montage technique, combines political events of the 1980s, with a spy thriller and a romance.

A best-seller in Austria, *Puntigam oder Die Kunst des Vergessens* exposes what many consider the Austrians' collective amnesia about their Nazi past. Moving between the present and the war years and including many allusions to the controversy surrounding Austrian President Kurt Waldheim, the novel portrays events following Hitler's annexation of Austria in 1938 from three points of view: old Puntigam, who operates a mill in Graz and welcomes the economic upsurge; his daughter, Marianne, who struggles to keep her Austrian identity; and her opportunistic, mindless cousin, Friedemann, the ultimate "artist of forgetfulness.'' Rightly, *Puntigam* has been called a "courageous and much-needed book.'' A stage play version of the novel was released in 1991.

It is against the background of international politics that S. presents two compelling love stories in his most recent novels. *Auf der anderen Seite* (1990; *On the Other Side,* 1991) deals with the opening of the Austro-Czechoslovakian border; *Moritz und Nathalie oder Die Angst vor der Sehnsucht* (1991; Moritz and Nathalie or fear of longing) is set during the war in Yugoslavia that followed Slovenia's declaration of independence in the summer of 1991.

The majority of S.'s plays, with their very Austrian tone, are a sequence of variations on one theme: Interpersonal relationships are generally unhappy. *Grillparzer oder Die drei Schwestern* (1991; Grillparzer or the three sisters) is about unrequited love; *Am Irrsee* (1991; on Lake Irrsee) shows the disappointments and the despair of five women, while *Der Liebe lange Weile* (1989; love's leisure) centers on the erotic adventures of students amidst political turmoil.

S. is a genuinely gifted author, whose books provide enjoyable reading and reflect his basic philosophy: A good novel must present an essential theme as ''entertainingly as possible.''

FURTHER WORK: *Theater-Stücke* (1991)

BIBLIOGRAPHY: *G. S.: Beiträge und Materialien* (1988); Binder, C. H., ''Anmerkungen zum Roman *Puntigam oder Die Kunst des Vergessens* von G. S.,'' *MAL,* 23, 3–4 (1990), 155–66; Koppensteiner, J., ''Gespräch mit G. S.,'' *Deutsche Bücher,* 2 (1990), 85–97; Koppensteiner, J., Afterword to *Puntigam or The Art of Forgetting* (1990), 261–66; Koppensteiner, J., Afterword to *On the Other Side* (1991), 135–39

JÜRGEN KOPPENSTEINER

TAFDRUP, Pia
Danish poet, b. 29 May 1952, Copenhagen

During the 1980s, T. clearly emerged as one of Denmark's most outstanding poets, and in 1988, at a remarkably young age, she became a member of the prestigious Danish Academy. She graduated in 1977 from the University of Copenhagen; she has traveled widely, including the U.S., and her experiences as a traveler have echoed in her poetry.

T.'s debut, *Når det går hul på en engel* (1981; when an angel has been grazed), reflects a young person's double experience of knowing that the world is fragmenting—wars, relationships, sudden death—and of being able to probe that world with and through words: to write poetry. This dual attitude, simultaneous desperation and joy, marks T.'s body of poetry and gives it an undeniable tension. T. is, however, not an ideological or philosophical writer, for her emphasis is always on experience—often in its minutest nuances. In particular, she devotes much detail and attention to sexual desire and that awareness of the body, or bodies, to which such sensuality leads. Perceptively, she has characterized her own poetry in that vein as not merely trying to write about desire but to demonstrate it through language—what she calls "the syntax of desire."

T.'s collections of poetry—*Intetfang* (1982; nohold), *Den inderste zone* (1983; the innermost zone), *Springflod* (1985; *Springtide*, 1989), *Hvid feber* (1986; white fever), and *Sekundernes bro* (1988; the bridge of the seconds)—may not startle the reader with any abrupt changes in form or outlook, but the language gradually seems more vibrant and rhythmical. T. is a skilled performer of her own texts, and the oral quality of them suggests very strongly that they be read aloud and not merely read. As is the case in all oral poetry

of quality, the full impact of the nuance of detail, the suggested pauses, the implied intonation are realized only when the text is given voice.

T., whose background in literature is impressive, once in an article—which might be seen as the draft for a poetics—noted that aesthetics should not be perceived as a straitjacket from which the poem dreams of being liberated; aesthetics is, rather, the reason why the poem is not destroyed by chaos. T.'s texts may be seen as acts of resistance against chaos, and in her exploration of desire and the language of desire, the moments of lust, ecstasy, intimacy, and joy grant her a sense of a fullness and fulfillment that, at least momentarily, keeps the existential darkness at bay. In some ambitious poems she attempts, as did the poets of yore, to reach for the unfathomable. Such sensual moments offer, in addition, a sense of self and self-assurance, which permit an openness and sensitivity to a partner; thus, T.'s poetry, even if it records much loneliness, cherishes a sense of togetherness.

Such moments, however, never make T.'s experience of the world simplistic or idyllic, for she is astutely aware that her world, as well as the world in general, is fragile and that death may be imminent. In fact, her rhythmic, sensuous language—laden with rich, innovative images—refutes any clear-cut, mundane perception of existence but conjures up, rather, the complexity and richness of the experience of the one whose senses are open to the world.

Lately, T. has tried her hand at drama, *Døden i bjergene* (1988; death in the mountains), and in *Sekundernes bro* there are rhythmic prose sketches that suggest that she may attempt the form of the short story.

It is, however, as a poet that T. has earned her prominent position in Danish letters. Her quest for fulfillment is rendered with a burning, pleading, proud, painful, and joyful intensity; thus, she has found for desire a language that is her own.

BIBLIOGRAPHY: Wamberg, B., ed., *Out of Denmark* (1985), 149–50; Heitmann, A., ed., *No Man's Land: An Anthology of Modern Danish Women's Literature* (1987), 11–12

NIELS INGWERSEN

TAKTSIS, Costas
Greek novelist, poet, and translator, b. 8 Oct. 1927, Thessalonike; d. 28 Aug. 1988, Athens

Born in Thessalonike, T. moved with his family to Athens when he was a boy, and he spent there most of his life in Greece. In the late 1940s he studied law for three years without earning a degree. He traveled extensively during 1954–1964 and again in 1968–1969. He visited, or lived in, France, England, the U.S., Australia, and Africa. While overseas, he supported himself by doing all sorts of odd jobs, just as he had done in Athens, although at the same period he published several books. During 1964–1967 he worked for the literary magazine *Pali*. In 1969 he openly opposed the military régime in Athens as he had done while abroad. Apart from writing and temporary positions he also did excellent translations of Aristophanes and some modern authors until his sudden death: He was found murdered in his apartment. Although the exact circumstances of his loss have not been unraveled, the consensus attributes it to homosexual foul play.

T.'s first literary publication was the verse collection *Deka poiemata* (1951; ten poems), followed by two other collections in 1952 and 1953. Later he quietly disavowed them. Another two books of poetry appeared in 1954 and 1958, but he never made a reputation as a poet although some of his pieces reflected personal experiences from the literary Café Byzantion and the homosexual circle of Café Brazilian in postwar Athens. Giving up poetry, he worked on his only novel, *To trito stephani* (1962; *The Third Wedding*, 1967; repub. as *The Third Wedding Wreath*, 1985), a tour de force of psychological fiction, which became a best-seller and was soon translated into English, French, German, Polish, and Hungarian. The great success of *To trito stephani* was due to T.'s unsurpassed skill in recording the sensibility and behavior of his spirited women protagonists through a sequence of interior monologues offering varying or conflicting viewpoints on personal, family, and national happenings over a time span covering the first half of this century in Greece. His heroines bring to mind Euripides's Hecuba and other tragic characters from the Trojan War cycle, as do some of the motifs and analogues in the complex plot. However, T.'s purpose was not to modernize the classical myth or to recreate a tragic saga, but to achieve a relentless and compassionate exposure of the female psyche in reaction to an intensely felt sequence of national agonies. "Read this book and you will know more about Greece than you could learn from a dozen histories," commented Dilys Powell. "It makes you think of Charles du Bos's remark on *Anna Karenina:* 'This is how life would speak, if it could speak!' " observed Robert André, and Seymour Smith wrote that this novel "shows a creative wisdom that places T. in the forefront of contemporary European writers."

T.'s only book of short stories, *Ta resta* (1972; the rest), was inspired by experiences of his adventurous youth. His last two books were nonfic-

tion: sketches and anecdotes from Athenian life entitled *He yiayia mou he Athena* (1979; my grandmother Athens), plus his controversial memoirs, *To phovero vema* (the terrible tribune), posthumously published in 1989.

FURTHER WORKS: *Mikra poiemata* (1952); *Peri horan dodekaten* (1953); *Symphonia tou Brazilian* (1954); *Kafeneio to Vyzantio* (1958)

BIBLIOGRAPHY: Mackridge, P., on *He yiayia mou he Athena*, WLT, 55, 2 (Spring 1981), 359–60; Chioles, J., Introduction to *The Third Wedding Wreath* (1985), i–xiii

M. BYRON RAIZIS

TĀMIR, Zakariyyā

Syrian short-story writer and journalist, b. 1931, Damascus

One of the most accomplished writers of short stories in the Arab world in recent decades, T. has devoted his career as a litterateur to this single genre. Apparently self-taught to a large extent, he has worked in television and journalism; among other posts within the government's cultural apparatus, he has served as editor of the prominent Syrian literary journal *Al-Ma'rifa*. The offer of a position in journalism at an Arab newspaper in London took him away from his homeland, and he now resides in the British capital.

A prolific writer of instinctual genius, T. produced a number of short stories of the highest quality beginning in the late 1950s. They are characterized by an extremely economical and clear style, one that often makes use of the techniques of the visual media in which he had worked, as, for example, in "Sayf" (1960; "Summer," in *Modern Arabic Short Stories*, 1974), in which he brings together a cluster of minor incidents that take place as a young man is endeavoring to seduce a young woman during the heat of summer. While T.'s allegorical and allusive style has enabled him to produce some of the most notable additions to the corpus of modern Arabic short stories, this very same quality has also made him a successful writer of stories for children, as in the collection *Li-mādhā saqat al-nahr* (1973; why did the river fall), which contains many examples of allegorical fables.

It is clearly a reflection of T.s impoverished upbringing and the kind of society in which he and many of his fellow authors have had to write for many years that allegory and symbol are used in his fictions to create nightmarish worlds full of alienated, oppressed people and oppressors of singular callousness. In stories of disconcerting terseness T. manages to capture the tragedy of human failure, demolishing the world of reality as he fashions scenarios where spite and injustice are the governing principles and the logic of normal life is absent. Any number of stories could be cited as reflections of these facets of his style. The effects of political oppression on the individual are seen in a story such as "Mulakhkhas ma jarā li-Muhammad al-Mahmūdī" (1978; pub. in English as "A Summary of What Happened to Mohammed al-Mahmoudi," in *Tigers on the Tenth Day and Other Stories,* 1986, and as "What Happened to Muhammad al-Mahmūdī," in *JArabL,* 13, 1982). "Al-Aʿdāʾ" (1978; "The Enemies," 1981) shows some of the consequences of such societal priorities, constituting a wholesale condemnation of the Arab nation in the wake of the June 1967 defeat couched within a sequence of numbered sections that make use of the most withering sarcasm.

Another subject to which T. has often turned his attention is the sexual morality that is forced upon both men and women in Middle Eastern society and the resulting psychological tensions. This is seen at its most powerful in "Wajh al-qamar" (1973; pub. in English as "The Face of the Moon," in *JArabL,* 3, 1972, as "The Moon Unmasked," in *JArabL,* 16, 1985, and as "The Face of the Moon," in *Tigers on the Tenth Day and Other Stories,* 1986), a story that is remarkable both for its creative use of symbols and for examples of that imagery for which T.'s writing is justifiably famous, as, for example, when the eyes of a madman in the street seem to Samīha, a young woman whose emerging sexuality is the subject of the story, like "two sick tigers drowsing on the grass of some thick jungle."

Since leaving Syria T. has devoted himself to journalism, something that has deprived readers of Arabic short fiction of one of its most excellent practitioners. Fortunately, he has left a large collection of short stories of considerable variety and quality to serve as a basis on which future generations may build. For, while the short story may be the most popular literary genre in the Arab world today, the number of those who may be counted as its masters, as T. undoubtedly is, are relatively few.

FURTHER WORKS: *Sahīl al-Jawād al-Abyad* (1960); *Rabīʿ fī al-ramād* (1963); *Al-Raʿd* (1970); *Li-mādhā saqat al-nahr* (1973); *Dimashq al-harāʾiq* (1975?)

BIBLIOGRAPHY: Allen, R., ed., *Modern Arabic Literature* (1987), 313–17; al-Khateeb, H., "A Modern Syrian Short Story: 'Wajh al-qamar,' " *JArabL,* 3 (1972), 96–105, Baldissera, E., "La formation du récit moderne en Syrie," *Quaderni di studi arabi,* 5–6 (1987–1988), 83–90

ROGER ALLEN

TAMMUZ, Benjamin

Israeli novelist, short-story writer, and art critic, b. 10 July 1919, Karkov, Ukraine; d. 20 July 1989, Tel Aviv

T. reached Palestine in 1924, growing up in Tel Aviv. He was active in the "Canaanite" movement as a young man, and then studied art at the Sorbonne in Paris. He was always active in journalism, at an early stage editing the youth journal *Haaretz shelanu* and, from 1965, serving as literary editor of *Haaretz.*

His first literary genre was the short story, and his first collection, *Holot hazahav* (1950; golden sands), attracted considerable attention and critical acclaim. In these stories, the central figure is usually a boy, growing up with his immigrant parents in the emergent yishuv (Jewish entity in Palestine), seeing himself as doubly alienated, from his family on the one hand, and from the crass environment of his peers, on the other. Such themes preoccupied the author in other guises in later works. His trilogy, *Hayey elyakum* (1963; life of Elyakum), *Bsof maarav* (1966; *Castle in Spain,* 1973), and *Sefer hahazayot* (1969; the book of hallucinations), pursues an individual trying to establish his own identity, often by removing himself from his own natural environment. In the third volume of the trilogy, the narrator returns narcissistically to his primary subject, himself. T. is the archetypal creator of a characteristic figure of the Israeli fiction of the 1960s, the antihero.

In the 1970s, T. sought new subjects and new ways of treating them. First, he wrote a long autobiography in fictional form, *Yaakov* (1971; Jacob). The author adopts as his hero one Jacob, but this name and the circumstances of his life act as a thinly veiled disguise for the author's own, from his birth, through his childhood emigration, his youth, and his maturity. One of T.'s fictional preoccupations is the question of national identity, of his own people and the status of Israel. Just as Jacob serves as the hero of the novel by that name so *Hapardes* (1972; *The Orchard,* 1984) is written in the manner of a parable concerning the ownership of an orchard. T. was much occupied in his writing with relations between Jew and Arab, which can be seen as rivalry between siblings over the birthright. *Hapardes* is open-ended, concluding with a tentatively expressed Messianic hope for a "solution."

The final phase of T.'s writing, in the 1980s, is more abstract. *Minotaur* (1980; *Minotaur,* 1981), perhaps his most achieved novel, is about a secret agent, and has the shape of a detective story. Typically, the female figure in the novel, his beloved Thea, is the idealized woman, adored but distanced by the Minotaur, the secretive hero. He loves her, but they must never meet. T.'s final work, *Haziqit vehazamir* (1989; the chameleon and the nightingale), is not only a puzzling amalgam of tales, but also presents a view of Jewish history through two types or approaches. One is the chameleon, who slots into his environment inconspicuously, and the other is the nightingale, who adds color to life. For all the suggestive allegorization of this story, it is the strong narrative line that gives the text its thrust and forces the reader to read on. As with so many of T.'s works, the practice can override a rather unsatisfactory theory.

FURTHER WORKS: *Mishley baqbuqim* (1975; *A Rare Cure,* 1981); *Reqviem lnaaman* (1978; *Requiem For Naaman,* 1982); *Pundaqo shel yirmiyahu* (1984)

BIBLIOGRAPHY: Yudkin, L. I., *Escape into Siege: A Survey of Israeli Literature Today* (1974), 91–92, 174–6; Yudkin, L. I., *1948 and After: Aspects of Israeli Fiction* (1984), 153–54, 159–60; Chertok, H., "The Number Two Canaanite in the World; a Conversation with B. T.," *Jewish Frontier,* 53, 3 (Apr.–May 1986), 9–12

LEON I. YUDKIN

TAYMŪR, Mahmūd

Egyptian novelist, short-story writer, dramatist, literary historian, and critic, b. 16 June 1894, Cairo; d. 25 Aug. 1973, Lausanne, Switzerland

T. is one of the most prolific Egyptian writers, with more than 300 short stories, seven novels, and numerous plays to his credit, as well as studies on literary history, literary criticism, language, aesthetics, and travels. On 5 April 1947 he was elected to the Egyptian Academy.

He is a scion of an aristocratic family, whose members held senior positions at the court of Egypt's rulers throughout the 19th c. and were noted for their interest in literature. Three other members of the family preceded T. as creative writers: the poet 'Ā'isha al-Taymūriyya (1840–1902), T.'s aunt, Ahmad Taymūr (1871–1930), his father, and Muhammad Taymūr (1892–1921), his older brother.

The last, who had considerable influence on the writers of his generation, strove to create authentic Egyptian literature, which he tried to do both in his short stories and plays. To make his writing truly Egyptian he made liberal use of 'ammiyyah (the spoken dialect), thus challenging the convention that literature should be written in the *fushā,* literary language, only. His influence on his younger brother, T., was immense. As described by T., his brother aroused in him the passion for creating an "Egyptian literature to the core" that would reflect "national features, national events, national spirit, where the national character would be emphasized in expression and description." It was not a call to shun European literature, which they both read and admired, but a reaction against the then current tendency to imitate it. His brother's early death left T. helpless and fearful that his brother's dream might remain unrealized. Eventually he recovered and determined to continue his brother's work by putting his ideas into practice. Thus he started his long literary career, never relenting in his efforts to bring Egyptian literature up to a level equal to the best in the world's literature. His works were translated extensively into a large number of languages.

The notion that a realistic Egyptian literature should depict Egyptian characters speaking 'ammiyyah was initially self-evident to T. He felt that making his characters speak *fushā* would give the story a false ring. Yet, writing in 'ammiyyah violated an age-old canon; so gradually he gave up the use of 'ammiyyah and systematically rewrote his stories and plays in *fushā.* Explaining his belated preference for the *fushā,* T. pointed out that in the earlier period of his creative writing *fushā* was too lofty for the ordinary reader and sounded too artificial in modern stories. But in time *fushā* had become simplified, while the rising level of education in Egypt made it easier for the readers. But even then he maintained that plays should be written in 'ammiyyah when depicting the present (thus excepting historical plays)—meant to be performed on the stage—because the 'ammiyyah is the language that people are used to hearing, whereas *fushā* is the language they are used to reading. A result of this vacillation is that many of T.'s plays and stories are available in two versions. In many cases the titles, too, were altered to *fushā* or 'ammiyyah. No systematic analysis of all of T.'s double versions has been made yet.

Critical comments on this dual procedure were voiced when the story "Abū 'Alī 'āmil artiste," first published in 1934, was turned in 1954 into "Abū 'Alī al-fannān" (Abu Ali the artist), questioning the author's right to alter a work that has become part of a people's literary stock. T. replied that he felt he had every right to reshape his works in a manner conforming to his more mature understanding of the requirements of good literature.

In his many years of creative writing, T. felt free to adopt any literary trend that seemed to him appropriate for the piece at hand. So we can find pieces written in the romantic, the realist, and even the surrealist vein. For his mode of narrative he has adopted, as the case may be, straight third-person narrative, first-person narrative, interior monologue, or any combination of them. With the advent of the psychological novel he had shown great interest in Freudian psychoanalysis and delved into his protagonists' subconscious. His way of writing has been, therefore, labeled *al-lā madh-habiyya,* or nondoctrinal.

FURTHER WORKS: *Al-shaykh jum'a* (1925); *'Amm Mitwallī* (1927); *Al-shaykh sayyid al-'abīt* (1928); *Tāriq al-andalusī* (1930); *Al-mawkib* (1932); *Al-atlāl* (1934); *Nidā' al-majhūl* (1939); *Fir'awn al-saghīr* (1939); *'Arūs al-nīl* (1941); *Al-makhbā' raqam 13* (1942); *Qanābil* (1943); *Salwā fī mahabb al-rīh* (1944); *Kull 'ām wa-antum bi-khayr* (1950); *Abū al-shawārib* (1953); *Abū 'ali al-fannān* (1955); *Shamrūkh* (1958); *Anā al-qātil* (1961); *Ma'būd min tīn* (1969); *Zawjatī al-mazād* (1970)

BIBLIOGRAPHY: Widmer, G., *M. T.* (1932); Johnson-Davies, D., comp., *Modern Arabic Short Stories* (1967), 169–75; Haywood, J., *Modern Arabic Literature, 1800–1970* (1971), 204–5, 235–40; Stetkevych, J., "Classical Arabic on Stage," in Ostle, R. C., ed., *Studies in Modern Arabic Literature* (1975), 152–78; Peled, M., "Reading Two Versions of a Story by M. T.: A Study in the Rhetoric of Fiction," *Israel Oriental Studies,* 7 (1977), 309–30; Badawi, M. M., *Modern Arabic Drama in Egypt* (1987), 88–111; Allen, R., ed., *Modern Arabic Literature* (1987), 317–23

MATTITYAHU PELED

TCHICAYA U TAM'SI

(born Gérald Félix Tchicaya) Congolese poet and novelist (writing in French), b. 25 Aug. 1931, M'Pili; d. 22 Apr. 1988, Paris, France

T. came from a prominent Congolese family. His father, Félix Tchicaya, became a deputy to the French national assembly in 1946, with the result that T. spent his formative years in Paris. He attended the Lycée Janson-de-Sailly and, after holding various jobs, joined UNESCO, where he worked until 1985. T., who had been in ill health, died of cardiac arrest during the night of 21–22 April 1988.

T.'s poetry is characterized by oneiric imagery, elliptical discourse, and semantic discontinuities, due in part, no doubt, to the blend of, on the one hand, African objective referents, linguistic cadences, and narrative predilections, and, on the other hand, European literary influences, such as the work of Arthur Rimbaud (1854–1891).

T. gained recognition in his mid-twenties with the publication of his first collections of poems, *Le mauvais sang* (1955; bad blood) and *Feu de brousse* (1957; *Brush Fire,* 1964). With the English translation of *Brush Fire,* published by the small but prestigious Mbari Publications press in Ibadan, Nigeria, as well as a *Selected Poems* (1970) in Heineman's widely-distributed African Writers Series, T. became known throughout the world as one of Africa's leading poets. Other collections, in the same mode as that of the first two, include *Á triche-coeur* (1958; a game of cheat-heart), *Épitomé* (1961; epitome), *Le ventre* (1964; the belly), and *La veste intérieure suivi de notes de veille* (1977; the indoor coat followed by waking notes).

T.'s career took a significant turn in 1980 with the publication of his first novel, *Les cancrelats* (the roaches). This brilliant work had, according to T., been composed in the 1950s but had been repeatedly rejected by publishers. *Les cancrelats* is the first volume of a loosely knit tetralogy spanning Congolese history in the 20th c. This novel interweaves the stories of two families over two generations during the first half of the century: a French colonial family and the family of one of its servants. It was followed by *Les méduses ou les orties de la mer* (1982; *The Madman and the Medusa,* 1989), which takes place against the somewhat remote backdrop of World War II. *Les phalènes* (1984; the moths), among whose main characters we find the children of the servant in *Les cancrelats,* covers the years from the rescission in 1946 of the double-standard legal system known as the *Indigénat* to Congolese independence in 1960; and *Ces fruits si doux de l'arbre à pain* (1987; those sweet, sweet fruits of the breadwood tree) deals with the tumultuous post-independence years during and immediately following the presidency of Abbé Fulbert Youlou (who appears in the novel as Abbé Lokou) and is an indictment of the period's loss of traditional values and of the corruption that overwhelms and destroys the book's honorable characters.

Though more accessible to the general reader than his poetry, T.'s novels do contain labyrinthine subplots and mysterious happenings reminiscent of supernatural events found in African folktales. Couched in a highly charged poetic prose and recounting hauntingly enigmatic tales, the novels warrant placement of T. among the major novelists of the world.

T. also wrote short stories, collected in *La main sèche* (1980; the dry hand), and plays: *Le Zulu, suivi de Vwène le fondateur* (1978; the Zulu, followed by Vwène the founding father) and *Le destin glorieux du maréchal Nniku Nniku* (1979; *The Glorious Destiny of Marshal Nniku Nniku*, 1986).

T.'s work as a whole is bold in style and often surreal in content. He compellingly intertwines narration of the experiences of individuals with the cultural givens of their society and the larger political events that impact on their lives. Despite T.'s extensive European experience and consummate manipulation of the French language, the main thrust of his work remains Afrocentric.

FURTHER WORKS: *Arc musical précédé de Épitomé* (1970); *Le pain et la cendre, Le ventre* (1978); *Légendes africaines* (1979)

BIBLIOGRAPHY: Herdeck, D. E., *African Authors* (1973), 450–52; Blair, D. S., *African Literature in French* (1976), 171–78; Kom, A., ed., *Dictionnaire des œuvres littéraires négro-africaines de langue française* (1983), passim; Zell, H. M., et al., eds., *A New Reader's Guide to African Literature*, rev. 2nd ed. (1983), 284–85, 503–6; Sellin, E., Introduction to *The Madman and the Medusa* (1989), xi–xvi; O'Grady, B., "Tchicayu U Tam'si: Some Thoughts on the Poet's Symbolic Mode of Expression," *WLT*, 65, 1 (Winter 1991), 29–34

ERIC SELLIN

TEILLIER, Jorge

Chilean poet and editor, b. 24 June 1935, Lautaro

The grandson of French immigrants to southern Chile, T. has chosen his homeland in the agricultural south as a setting for most of his poetry, even though Santiago has become a second home. He had been preparing to be a history professor when an older writer, Teófilo Cid (1914–1964), poet of the Generation of 1938, introduced T. to surrealism (q.v.) and inspired him to abandon history for poetry. One writer hinted that Cid may also have infected T.'s soul at the same time with his own devastating disease: alcoholism. His father's being a militant communist has caused T. anguish because he prefers to omit propaganda from his writings, feeling that ideology and poetry do not mix. (One critic jokingly said that the only Marx influence in his writings is high-brow slapstick from the Marx brothers.) Although he has not been a militant leftist in verse, T. sympathized with the Popular Front and suffered the loss of a daughter to exile.

T. says that much of the poetry of his first book, *Para ángeles y gorriones* (1956; for angels and sparrows), was composed at his student desk during high school. The book was widely reviewed

in Chile. In the press it received much praise, as a masterpiece for such a young poet. There are images in T.'s early writing that several critics attribute to Pablo Neruda (q.v.). Such motifs appear in his poetry as a combination of negative images—a world that falls apart—which can be seen, for example, in the title of his second book, *El cielo cae con las hojas* (1958; the heavens fall with the leaves). Yet for the most part T. has devised his own special poetic vision of the world. In 1962 he won the Municipal Prize of Santiago for Poetry and the Gabriela Mistral Prize for his third book, *El árbol de la memoria* (1961; the memory tree). In *Poemas del país de nunca jamás* (1963; poems from never-never land), T. continues the creation of fanciful metaphors of the Chilean southland which he had learned to evoke in his early writings. The predominant setting in these works is a landscape that is magical. It comes from the poet's own "metarealism" or secret realism in that it invokes memories, images, mystery, and daydreams that are innovative and very subjective. These elements can also be interpreted as tricks or secrets in his composition whereby he uses signifiers that have hidden meanings for other realities. For example, death is often disguised. *Los trenes de la noche* (1964; trains of the night) was written during an all-night train ride from Santiago south to Lautaro. The poet views his magic land at night, but also recalls other train rides. Trains have become motifs in many poems in his books.

Muertes y maravillas (1971; death and marvels) is an important anthology of his first twelve years of writing. It also includes a short autobiography, a complete bibliography to 1970, and a short criticism by Alfonso Calderón (b. 1929).

In some of his later writing T. continues his frustration with lost dreams. For example, in *Cartas para reinas de otras primaveras* (1985; letters for queens of other springs) his disillusionment continues to surface. But now he is less apt to stay in his southern microcosm, first writing of a burlesque hall in Panama and later about problems of censorship with the Pinochet military dictatorship. Some poems have beautiful, striking images, but, on the whole, this book is not as strong as his earlier efforts.

Fernando Alegría (q.v.) and others have included T. in the Generation of 1950, but even though he is a close friend of many of the writers, he does not identify with that group, which he considers too bourgeois. T. did belong to the Trilce Group (at the Austral University in Valdivia) and the Poets of the Lar. If one were to classify T.'s poetry, it would basically be romantic in theme with an occasional vanguardist metaphor. T. is a brilliant, erudite poet, who has read and traveled extensively. For some readers his setting may be limited, because he prefers to write about the land of his inheritance, but he is an artful poet who can capture the reader's imagination with his innovative images.

FURTHER WORKS: *Romeo Murga, poeta adolescente* (1962); *Otoño secreto* (1964); *Actualidad de Vicente Huidobro* (1964); *Poemas secretos* (1965); *Crónica del forastero* (1968); *Cuando todos se vayan: homenaje a Ray Bradbury* (1968); *El pasajero del Hotel Usher* (1975); *Los trenes que no has de beber* (1977); *Para un pueblo fantasma* (1978). FURTHER VOLUME IN ENGLISH: *From the Country of Nevermore: Selected Poems of J. T.* (1990)

BIBLIOGRAPHY: Sánchez Latorre, L., *Los expedientes de Filebo* (1965), 161–65; Alegría, F., *Literatura chilena del siglo XX* (1967), 53–54; Mengod, V., *Historia de la literatura chilena* (1967), 121–22; Villegas, J., "La mitificación de la pobreza en un poema [Aparición de Teófilo Cid] de J. T.," *Inti,* 9 (Spring 1979), 13–25; Guerra-Cunningham, L., "The Concept of Marginality in 'To a Ghost Town' by J. T.," *PCP,* 16 (1981), 45–55; Valdés, E., "Cincuenta años en la poesía de J. T.," *RCLL,* 13, 25 (1987), 185–88

LON PEARSON

TELLES, Lygia Fagundes
Brazilian novelist and short-story writer, b. 19 Apr. 1924, São Paulo

T. holds a position of prominence in contemporary Brazilian letters. She has been compared in stature to the late Clarice Lispector (q.v.) and is one of three women in the Brazilian Academy of Letters. She has over twenty published books, many of which are translated into several languages. Although her concern is with modern Brazilian women in an urban setting, T. grew up in the interior of the state of São Paulo in small cities, where her father served as judge. She completed her studies in the capital, where she graduated in law from the University of São Paulo. She began to write at an early age, but she dismisses these first efforts as products of a too-innocent girlhood. Her writing has been a process of empowerment, overcoming what she terms the ignorance and fear of her girlhood.

T.'s first published novel, *Ciranda da pedra* (1954; *The Marble Dance,* 1986), introduced the dialectic of imprisonment and liberation that moves through her entire oeuvre. Like in Clarice Lispector's fiction, family ties are prison chains that impede the protagonists from achieving growth.

This theme is encapsulated in the metaphor of the aquarium in *Verão no aquário* (1963; summer in the aquarium), which in the novel signifies the childhood that dooms the protagonist to dependency. The claustrophobic social ambience of most of T.'s narratives is that of an upper middle class bankrupt of both money and morals. T. documents the inner turmoil of women who need to escape but are ill equipped to function in a rapidly changing world.

T. is best known for her novel *As meninas* (1973; *The Girl in the Photograph,* 1982), which opens new directions in her prose style and introduces the element of specific political protest against the military dictatorship, then in one of its most repressive phases. The three women in this story are inmates not of the family home but of a pension in São Paulo. The fluid, alternating narrative perspectives of the novel offer intimate portraits of lives complicated by the contradictory dynamics of megacity life in a regressive moment of Brazilian history.

T.'s most recent work is *As horas nuas* (1989; the naked hour), which continues the revolutionary path of *As meninas* and has been compared to Clarice Lispector's *A hora da estrela* (1977; *The Hour of the Star,* 1986). This book, which won the Pedro Nava Prize for best novel of 1989, is the story of an aging alcoholic actress, a character as "polluted" and devastated as the country Brazil, for which she is clearly a symbol. The vision of São Paulo is one of prevailing misery; the city is "occupied" by street people, economic refugees of ecological and economic decline. One of the several narrators is Rahul, the cat, who gazes on the chaos with a calm, experienced eye.

T. distinguishes herself from peers such as Lispector and Nélida Piñon (q.v.) with a direct testimonial prose that contrasts with the famous abstract approaches of Lispector and Piñon to the themes shared by these three writers. T. offers keen observations on contemporary Brazilian society and politics, addressing the precarious situation of women in this aggressive environment. While they are very different stylists, T. and her colleagues find common ground in their commitment to social change.

FURTHER WORKS: *Histórias do desencontro* (1958); *Antes do baile verde* (1971); *Seminário dos ratos* (1977; *Tigrela and Other Stories,* 1986); *A disciplina do amor* (1980); *Mistérios* (1981)

BIBLIOGRAPHY: Oliveira, K., *A técnica narrativa em L. F. T.* (1972); Silverman, M., *Moderna ficção brasileira 2: ensaios* (1981), 162–84; Tolman, J., "New Fiction: L. F. T.," *Review,* 30 (1981), 65–70; Burgin, R., on *Seminário dos ratos*, "Tigrela and Other Stories," *NYTBR*, 4 May 1986, 40; Stern, I., ed, *Dictionary of Brazilian Literature* (1988), 337–38; Abreu, C. F., on *As horas nuas*, "As horas de Lygia," *Isto É/ Senhor*, 6 June 1989, 88

ELIZABETH LOWE

THERIAULT, Yves

Canadian novelist, short-story writer, radio and television scriptwriter, dramatist, and essayist (writing in French), b. 28 Nov. 1915, Quebec; d. 20 Oct. 1983, Rawdon, Province of Quebec

T. received his education in Montreal at the Notre-Dame-de-Grâce Parochial School and the Mont-Saint-Louis School before embarking on a number of professions, as trapper, truck driver, boxer, salesman, radio announcer, and scriptwriter, carrying out these activities in various cities, among them Montreal, Trois-Rivières, and Hull. A grant from the French government enabled him to go to France in 1950; from there he left on a trip around the world. Following this period of exploration and self-discovery, he devoted himself to literature, except for interruptions brought about by his work for the government—from 1965 to 1967 he was director of cultural affairs in the ministry of cultural affairs—and by illness—in 1970, a heart problem forced him to cease all activities temporarily.

T. is Quebec's most prolific and one of its most successful writers, among the few to live exclusively from writing. His first book, *Contes pour un homme seul* (1944; tales for a man alone), a collection of short stories, was a popular success and set him on the road to his literary career. In it, we find rebellious individuals with larger-than-life temperaments, the very type of psychological and physical traits that can be seen in characters in his later novels, works such as *Le dompteur d'ours* (1951; the bear tamer), *Aaron* (1954; Aaron), *Agakuk* (1958; *Agakuk*, 1963), *Ashini* (1961; *Ashini*, 1972), *Cul-de-sac* (1961; *Cul-de-sac*, 1973), and *Kesten* (1968; *Kesten*, 1973).

Many of his works can be read in the context of the recent history of Quebec, with the isolation of the Francophones in a sea of Anglophones, the opposition of two cultures in one nation, the group's oppression of the individual, and the gradual fulfillment of individuals confronted by forces tugging at them. In addition to societal polarizations, sexual opposition and harmony are repeatedly explored in T.'s works.

T. presents the reader with "outsiders" who must constantly struggle to assert their identity. In *Aaron*, Jews are the protagonists. Moishe, with orthodox values, confronts not only the "other"

world around him, but, within his own, Aaron, his grandson, who rejects his heritage. Aaron in turn seeks to liberate himself from his surroundings in a poor section of Montreal and to become part of the English world. Transposed into the traditional Catholic world of Quebec, we have the confrontation of the upholders of tradition against the newer generation eager for change and for the world of the future.

In T.'s most successful work, *Agakuk*, which has been translated into approximately twenty languages, the hero, an Inuit, leaves the traditional life of the village to go live alone with his wife Iriook, herself an outsider, a bearer of different customs and outlooks, in a remote arctic area several days' journey away. There he carries on the struggle for survival against nature, the wilderness, aided by Iriook, who is more instructed than ordinary Inuit women, more resourceful, and more independent-minded. The oppositions are between the individual and the group, the native culture and the white world with its different values, laws, and degrees of civilization, and, not least, between a husband and his wife. Rich in detail about the daily life of the residents of inhospitable climates, with vivid descriptions of the hunt, the building of living quarters, the sexual life of the couple, and the birth of their children, the work portrays the successful self-fulfillment of Agakuk, who is nevertheless forced to accept the nontraditional values of his wife, who is every bit as successful and even more evolved than he.

In recognition of the quality and quantity of his work—forty novels and stories, twenty books for children, numerous plays, over one thousand scripts for radio and television—T. has been the recipient of many awards, for example, from the Province of Quebec in 1954 and 1958, and from the governor general in 1960. In 1959 he was elected to the Royal Society of Canada. Although not known for modern approaches to creative writing, T. has nonetheless succeeded in developing a lively, energetic style appropriate to his narratives, and he has treated topics that have had a wide appeal. He has been called the father of Quebec letters.

FURTHER WORKS: *Roi de la côte nord* (1960); *Le vendeur d'étoiles* (1961); *Séjour à Moscou* (1961); *Si la bombe m'était contée* (1962); *La rose de Pierre* (1964); *N'Tsuk* (1968; *N'Tsuk*, 1972); *Tayaout, fils d'Agakuk* (1969); *Le haut pays* (1973); *Agoak, l'héritage d'Agakuk* (1975; *Agoak, The Legacy of Agakuk*, 1979); *Œuvre de chair* (1975; *Ways of the Flesh*, 1977); *Le partage de minuit* (1980); *L'étreinte de Vénus. Contes policiers* (1981); *La femme Anna et autres contes* (1981); *Valérie et le grand canot. Récits* (1981); *L'herbe de tendresse. Récits* (1983)

BIBLIOGRAPHY: Bessette, G., "French Canadian Society As Seen by Contemporary Novelists," *QQ*, 69 (1962), 177–97; Robidoux, R., and A. Renaud, *Le roman canadien-français du vingtième siècle* (1966), 92–103; Edmond, M., *Y. T. et le combat de l'homme* (1973); Carrier, D., *Bibliographie analytique d'Y. T. 1940–1984* (1985); Cagnon, M., *The French Novel of Quebec* (1986), 55–59; Talbot, E. J., "T.'s *Agakuk:* The Matter of Closure," *Québec Studies,* 4 (1986), 127–34; Lemire, M., et al., *Dictionnaire des œuvres littéraires du Québec* (1982), Vol. 3, passim; (1984), Vol. 4, passim; (1987), Vol. 5, passim; Hamel, R., et al., *Dictionnaire des auteurs de langue française en Amérique du Nord* (1989), 1283–86

PAUL BARRETTE

THURBER, James

American short-story writer and essayist, b. 8 Dec. 1894, Columbus, Ohio; d. 4 Nov. 1961, New York, N.Y.

T. was born in Columbus, Ohio, where he spent most of an unhappy childhood. Accidentally blinded in his left eye by his brother William, T. was unable to participate in games and sports with other children. This isolation caused him to develop a rich fantasy life through books and daydreams, which would serve to inspire his later fiction. As a young man T. worked in France for some time as a reporter for the Paris edition of the *Chicago Tribune* before returning to the U.S. in 1926. In 1927 T. was hired as an editor-writer for the then fledgling *New Yorker* magazine. Although he disdained the editorial tasks, T. would find this experience valuable for his later literary career. It was during his time at the *New Yorker* that T. developed the clear, concise prose style for which he (and the magazine as well) would become famous.

In 1929 T. published his first book in collaboration with his friend and fellow *New Yorker* staffer E. B. White (q.v.). *Is Sex Necessary? or Why You Feel the Way You Do* is a spoof of contemporary theorists who had been attempting to reduce sex to a scientifically and psychologically understandable level. White and T., assuming the personae of Drs. Walter Tithridge and Karl Zaner, wrote alternating chapters of the book, explaining such topics as White's "How To Tell Love from Passion" and T.'s "The Nature of the American Male" (a title that anticipates a theme prevalent throughout a great deal of T.'s later fiction). The book met with great popular success and instantly established T. as a true comedic talent.

The publication of *My Life and Hard Times* (1933) brought critical acclaim and public recognition of T. as a major American literary figure, and prompted Ernest Hemingway (q.v.) to call T.'s writing "the best . . . coming out of America." *My Life and Hard Times* is a collection of semiautobiographical essays that ostensibly tell of T.'s life growing up in Ohio. The pieces establish T.'s "family" as perhaps the oddest in American history, including "Grandfather," a sporadically senile old man who lives half his life in early-20th-c. Columbus and half in the Civil War era. The humor of these essays springs from T.'s craftsmanlike use of irony in narrative and tone. The characters are comical due to their ironic preoccupations with events that are feared but never happen. The subdued narrative ironically undercuts the frantic action of the narrative to create a humorous effect.

T.'s fiction generally deals with the themes of man versus woman and imagination versus reality. These two themes often merge in his short stories, and the best-known example is "The Secret Life of Walter Mitty" (1939)—far and away T.'s most famous short story. "The Secret Life of Walter Mitty" tells the story of the title character, a meek, mild-mannered, henpecked husband who escapes from the tedium and hopelessness of his everyday existence through a series of swashbuckling, escapist fantasies. Although the story is just over 2,000 words long, T. spent more than eight weeks writing it. The care he put into its construction is evident in the flawless way Mitty's dream sequences are blended with real-world events: A newsboy shouting about a spectacular murder trial causes Mitty to imagine himself as the defendant; a subsequently imagined courtroom outburst—"You miserable cur!"—causes the "real" Walter Mitty to remember a shopping errand for "puppy biscuit." The terms "Walter Mitty" and "Walter Mittyish" have gained generic status and today can be found as entries in English dictionaries—denoting an unassuming person who escapes from reality by dreaming of being heroic or successful. "Mittyish," or "Mittyesque," characters appear throughout T.'s fiction, for example, in "The Curb in the Sky" (1931), "The Unicorn in the Garden" (1939), "The Catbird Seat" (1942), and "The Lady on 142" (1943).

In addition to his fame as a writer, T. was a highly respected artist and cartoonist as well. Compared to such legendary figures as Pablo Picasso and Henri Matisse, T.'s surreal sketches first appeared in *Is Sex Necessary?* and were thereafter a regular feature of the *New Yorker,* where they became the prototypes for the offbeat sophisticated cartoons that appear in that magazine today. T.'s cartoons are best described as minimalist non-

MÄRTA TIKKANEN

TATYANA TOLSTAYA

WILLIAM TREVOR

LUISA VALENZUELA

sequitur snapshots, which defy attempts at conventional explanation. The "title piece" in the collection *The Seal in the Bedroom and Other Predicaments* (1932) is a good example. A man and woman are in bed, the woman lecturing the man who stares despondently in the opposite direction. Above the headboard is a bemused looking seal who gazes off in the opposite direction from the man and woman. The caption has the woman saying "All right, have it your way—you heard a seal bark." The humor lies in the utter inexplicability of the situation, and T. himself was often hard-pressed to explain the origin of his cartoon ideas.

In 1941 T. became totally blind and this obviously affected his later work. From that point on, he mainly confined his writing to more "simplistic" or childlike forms: fables and children's books, including *Fables for Our Time and Famous Poems Illustrated* (1940–1941), *Many Moons* (1942), *The Great Quillow* (1944), *The White Deer* (1945), *The 13 Clocks* (1950), *Further Fables for Our Time* (1956), and *The Wonderful O* (1957). It seems that he was unable or unwilling to deal with his personal crises, and thus he withdrew, Walter Mitty-like, into a childlike realm of fantasy. However, despite the innocent nature of these later genres, T.'s work at this time does show a great deal of bitterness. His fables frequently end with bleak morals of death and/or apocalyptic destruction. His children's tales, although more overtly optimistic, also display a cynical undercurrent, particularly *The White Deer*, whose heroes' "valiant deeds" are undermined by the ironic ease with which they are accomplished and the ultimate absence of any real danger in accomplishing them.

T. died in 1961, but his works have stood the test of time. His stories, with their elements of surrealism and fantasy, influenced later writers such as Kurt Vonnegut, Jr., and Joseph Heller (qq.v.). T. is generally acknowledged as the greatest American humorist since Mark Twain (1835–1910) and one of the most important figures in 20th-c. American literature.

FURTHER WORKS: *The Owl in the Attic and Other Perplexities* (1931); *The Middle-Aged Man on the Flying Trapeze* (1935); *Let Your Mind Alone!* (1937); *The Last Flower* (1939); *The Male Animal* (1939, with Elliott Nugent); *My World—And Welcome to It* (1942); *T.'s Men, Women and Dogs* (1942); *The T. Carnival* (1945); *The Beast in Me and Other Animals* (1948); *The T. Album* (1952); *T. Country* (1953); *T.'s Dogs* (1955); *Alarms and Diversions* (1957); *The Years with Ross* (1959); *Lanterns and Lances* (1961); *Credos and Curios*

(1962); *Vintage T.* (1963); *T. and Company* (1966); *Selected Letters of J. T.* (1981)

BIBLIOGRAPHY: Morsberger, R. E., *J. T.* (1964); Tobias, R. C., *The Art of J. T.* (1969); Black, S. A., *J. T., His Masquerades: A Critical Study* (1970); Holmes, C. S., *The Clocks of Columbus: The Literary Career of J. T.* (1972); Holmes, C. S., ed., *T.: A Collection of Critical Essays* (1974); Bernstein, B., *T.: A Biography* (1975); Kenney, C. M., *T.'s Anatomy of Confusion* (1984); Maharg, R. A., "The Modern Fable: J. T.'s Social Criticisms," *CLAQ,* 9 (1984), 72–73; Long, R. E., *J. T.* (1988); Sheed, W., *Essays in Disguise* (1990), 90–95

JASON BERNER

TIKKANEN, Märta

Finnish novelist (writing in Swedish), b. 3 Apr. 1935, Helsinki

The daughter of a distinguished educator, T. was employed as a young woman at Finland's leading Swedish-language newspaper, *Hufvudstadsbladet,* and then followed the pedagogical career of both her parents, teaching at an upper school and becoming director of an institute for adult education. A first marriage ended in divorce; a second union, in 1963, with the writer and artist Henrik Tikkanen (1924–1984), wrought a profound change in her life. Deeply devoted to her gifted and difficult husband, she was nonetheless drawn to the feminist movement and emerged, in time, as a leading northern European advocate of women's liberation; however, her militancy has been tempered all along by a sense of her individualism and a distinct pride in her role as the mother of five children.

Her first two novels, *Nu imorron* (1970; now tomorrow) and *Ingenmansland* (1972; no-man's-land), deal with a couple, easily recognized—with the aid of her own later works and her husband's autobiographical books—as a somewhat fictionalized portrayal of their marriage. The wife's situation is made ever more difficult by the husband's alcoholism, erotic adventures, and jealousy, and by her constant exhaustion (as a working woman, a mostly loving wife, and a conscientious mother), her growing awareness of male domination, and her sense that she is wasting her own gifts. T.'s next two books, sometimes characterized as "pamphlet novels," turn away from immediate personal concerns to other problems of oppressed or neglected women. In *Vem bryr sej om Doris Mihailov?* (1974; who cares about Doris Mihailov?) the central if invisible figure is a lonely and emotionally damaged single parent; the story of her life is pieced together by a female television reporter and a self-centered male psychiatrist. T.'s *Män kan inte väldtas* (1975; *Manrape,* 1977) marked her entrance into international fame, not least because of its sensational nature: Raped by a man whom she has accompanied to his apartment, a divorcee plots and triumphantly (if somewhat unbelievably) inflicts a counterrape on her assailant. Widely translated, the book was made into a film (1978) by Jörn Donner (q.v.). From this *succès de scandale* T. went on to *Århundradets Kärlekssaga* (1978; *Love Story of the Century,* 1984), in which, using what might be called a narrative series of prose poems, she took revenge on her husband for his complaints about her emotional coldness and aggressiveness. Concentrating not only on the husband's drunkenness but his egocentricity, the book (and a subsequent dramatization) reached a huge audience of women who found it a reflection, in some measure, of their own marital lot; T.'s remarkable reputation in Germany in particular was built upon her bitter story of an unbearable but evidently inescapable relationship.

As the health of her husband declined, T.'s attention went to other domestic miseries. In *Mörkret som ger glädjen djup* (1981; the darkness that gives happiness depth) she interlarded—in still more narrative-lyrical poems—the account of a contemporary adolescent's emotional illness with the tale of the devotion, and self-accusation, of the mother of Josef Julius Wecksell (1838–1907), a Finland-Swedish poet who had gone incurably insane while still in his early twenties. A companion work, in topic if not in tone, *Sofias egen bok* (1982; Sofia's own book), was the factual chronicle of the illness and treatment of her youngest child, afflicted with minimal brain dysfunction. With *Rödluvan* (1986; Little Red Ridinghood) T. took up her own case for analysis: the little girl with a gently domineering father and a compliant mother who moved into the lair of a demanding husband, a shaggy wolf more vulnerable in life than in the fairy tale. Nonetheless, aware though she was of the childhood situation that, she believed, created her acquiescence to male tyranny, and proud of her revolt, she told, in *Storfångaren* (1989; the great huntsmen), of her longing for her new love, a distinguished Danish author, during a visit to women's centers in Greenland.

T. is one of Finland's best-known authors, because of her ability to combine feminist messages with personal revelations in a variously passionate, wry, or sentimental way. Her ejaculatory style is a particularly apt instrument for attracting and holding her readership: Extremely conversational at the start of her career, her verbal mode has grown more and more exalted with the years, so

that it is almost impossible (save in the case history of her daughter) to draw a line between prose and poetry. Similarly, the genre description "novel" on the dust jacket of what is probably her best book, *Rödluvan,* seems to be a misnomer for what is part of her own ongoing autobiography.

FURTHER WORK: *Henrik* (1985)

BIBLIOGRAPHY: Koch-Klenske, E., "Über M. Ts Roman, 'Wie vergewaltige ich einen Mann?' " *Das häßliche Gesicht der schönen Frau: Literarische Porträts* (1982), 191–251

GEORGE C. SCHOOLFIELD

TOLSTAYA, Tatyana

Russian short-story writer, b. 3 May 1951, Leningrad

If heredity influences choice of vocation, T.'s literary genealogy preordained her role of writer. On her father's side, she is the great-grandniece of Lev Tolstoy (1828–1910) and the granddaughter of the novelist Aleksey N. Tolstoy (q.v.) and the poet Natalia Krandievskaya (1888–1963). Her maternal grandfather, Mikhail Lozinsky (1886–1955), translated the plays of Shakespeare and Molière, among others, and produced the acclaimed standard Russian version of Dante's *Divine Comedy.* Half a dozen lesser-known literati are also among the ancestors of T.'s highly cultured family. At Leningrad State University, T. specialized in classics in the School of Languages and Literatures. Upon graduation in 1974, she moved to Moscow and worked for eight years at the publishing house Nauka before making her debut with " 'Na zolotom kryltse sideli . . .' " (1983; "On the Golden Porch," 1989). Readers' enthusiastic reception of her story "Peters" (1986; "Peters," 1989) three years later established T.'s reputation as a unique voice in contemporary Russian fiction and launched her career. Her collection of stories, *"Na zolotom kryltse sideli . . ."* (1987; *On the Golden Porch,* 1989), translated into ten languages, brought her international fame. Since 1988 she has divided her time between Moscow and the U.S., where she teaches, lectures on Russian culture, and writes review essays for mainstream publications.

Time, language, and imagination are the reigning divinities of T.'s fictional universe. With the aid of myth, folklore, and numerous intertexts, her inordinately condensed narratives offer meditations on eternal universal concerns: the elusive significance of a given life in "Sonia" (1984; "Sonia," 1989), "Peters," "Samaia liubimaia" (1986; "Most Beloved," 1991), "Somnambula v tumane'' (1988; ''Sleepwalker in a Fog,'' 1991); the isolation of the individual personality in ''Peters,'' ''Spi spokoino, synok'' (1986; ''Sweet Dreams, Son,'' 1989), ''Krug'' (1987; ''The Circle,'' 1989); the conflicting claims of spirit and matter in ''Okhota na mamonta'' (1985; ''Hunting the Wooly Mammoth,'' 1989), ''Ogon' i pyl' '' (1986; ''Fire and Dust,'' 1989), ''Poet i muza'' (1986; ''The Poet and the Muse,'' 1990); the complex nature of, and interplay between, perception and language in '' 'Na zolotom kryltse sideli . . .' '' ''Fakir'' (1986; ''The Fakir,'' 1989), ''Noch'' (1987; ''Night,'' 1990), and ''Liubish'—ne liubish'' (1987; ''Loves Me, Loves Me Not,'' 1989); and the transforming power of imagination and memory in '' 'Na zolotom kryltse sideli . . .,'' ''Svidanie s ptitsei'' (1983; ''Date with a Bird,'' 1989), ''Reka Okkervil'' (1985; ''Okkervil River,'' 1989), and ''Milaia Shura'' (1985; ''Sweet Shura,'' 1989). Yet throughout her oeuvre, as T. herself has acknowledged, style has primacy over thematic novelty and psychological insight.

T.'s narratives move at an irregular pace, combining minimal plots and sparse dialogue with extravagant poetic description as they slip unobtrusively in and out of temporal frames and characters' thoughts through quasi-direct discourse. Those characters, often situated at the two extremes of the age spectrum, are rendered memorable through T.'s vividly grotesque depiction of their simultaneously risible and pitiable features. A comparably synthetic technique for portraying ''losers'' in amorous endeavors allows T. to demythologize romance, as in ''Peters'' and ''Vyshel mesiats iz tumana'' (1987; ''The Moon Came Out,'' 1992), just as multiple perspectives on a given individual destabilize a single, unilinear interpretation of character. T.'s fiction teems with dreamers, self-abnegators, failures, pragmatists, egotists, and misanthropes shuttled between largely unrealizable desires and brute reality. That gap may be bridged by the transfiguring capacities of the imagination, which flourishes virtually unchecked in childhood, but diminishes with time's passage. Hence the melancholy sense of loss and helplessness that permeates T.'s texts.

T. compensates for her protagonists' deprivations by conjuring up for the reader an Aladdin's cave of stylistic riches. To enter Tolstayaland is to step simultaneously into the magical realm of the fairy tale and the oppressive dinginess of a grimy kitchen. The endless array of startling contrasts yields not only sensual pleasure, but also fresh perspectives on phenomena that acquire multiple dazzling hues. Scrambling temporal and spatial categories, alternating poetic lyricism with satirical irony, shifting from one narrative perspective to another, leaping from colloquialisms and popular slogans to elevated diction and citations from ''sacrosanct'' sources, T. packs her kaleidoscopic narratives to the brim. Critics have responded above all to the bold originality of her metaphors, which sometimes swell to Homeric proportions; to her breathtakingly unconventional, subversive juxtapositions; to her idiosyncratic, garrulous Sternian narrator; and to her skill at creating a densely palpable atmosphere through eloquent detail and accumulation of rhetorical devices. Her iridescent, luxurious prose—laden with vivid tropes, apostrophes, exclamations, rhetorical questions, and allusions—isolates her stylistically from the majority of contemporary Soviet authors. It allies her with such creative innovators of the 1920s as Yury Olesha and Isaak Babel (qq.v.), as well as Nikolay Gogol (1809–1852), Ivan Bunin, Andrey Bely, and Vladimir Nabokov (qq.v.). Moreover, it corroborates T.'s claim that the desire to display the spectacular range of the Russian language, to explore its boundless expressive powers, was the chief stimulus for her metamorphosis into a writer.

Early in her career T. focused on the lost paradise of childhood, relying on the Edenic myth as algorithm. Whatever the diversity of her subsequent narratives, including experiments in moral allegory, notably ''Serafim'' (1986; ''Serafim,'' 1992) and ''Chistyi list'' (1984; ''A Clean Sheet,'' 1989), they never addressed nakedly political issues or engaged in topical debates. In that regard, her latest publication, ''Limpopo'' (1991; ''Limpopo,'' 1992), signals a dramatic reorientation. Longer, more digressive, and less tightly constructed than any of her previous stories, it verges on a novella and offers transparently ironic commentary on Russia's current situation of impotent chaos and spiritual indigence: Crushed by a compromised past, Russians foresee no tenable future and dwell in anomie. Its verbal pyrotechnics and hilariously comic passages notwithstanding, ''Limpopo'' has affinities with the apocalyptic strain of literature that has proliferated during Gorbachev's policy of glasnost.

Since her debut in 1983, T.'s texts have grown progressively longer. One could reasonably classify her last two publications, ''Somnambula v tumane'' and ''Limpopo,'' as *povesti* (novellas) rather than short stories. If her recently professed intention of authoring a novel in the near future signals a search for new directions, then the first phase of her creative development unequivocally guarantees her status as the stylistically most venturesome and complex modernist practitioner of the short story in Russia during the 1980s. Although modest in quantity, her oeuvre amply justifies Joseph Brodsky's (q.v.) assertion that T. is "[t]he most original, tactile, luminous voice in Russian prose today."

FURTHER WORK: *Somnambula v tumane* (1992). FURTHER VOLUME IN ENGLISH: *Sleepwalker in a Fog* (1992)

BIBLIOGRAPHY: Goscilo, H., "T. T.'s 'Dome of Many-Coloured Glass': The World Refracted through Multiple Perspectives," *SlavR,* 47, 2 (1988), 280–90; Barker, A., "Are Women Writing Women's Writing in the Soviet Union Today? T. and Grekova," *Studies in Comparative Communism,* 21, 3–4 (1988), 357–64; Goscilo, H., "Tolstajan Love as Surface Text," *SEEJ,* 34, 1 (1990), 40–52; Goscilo, H., "Paradise, Purgatory, and Post-Mortems in the World of T. T.," *Indiana Slavic Studies,* 5 (1990), 97–113; Goscilo, H., "Tolstaian Times: Traversals and Transfers," in Sharma, S., ed., *New Directions in Soviet Literature* (1992), 36–62

HELENA GOSCILO

TORRENTE BALLESTER, Gonzalo

Spanish novelist and essayist, b. 13 June 1910, Ferrol

T. B. has spent most of his professional life as a teacher in high schools in Spain, with a short stay at the State University of New York at Albany (1966–1970) as a professor of literature. Although he has won recognition as a critic and literary historian, and is a member of the prestigious Royal Academy of the Spanish Language, his prominence stems primarily from his novels.

T. B. cannot be placed easily into a generation of writers or be viewed as a member of a specific literary movement in post–Civil War Spain. Rather, he stands radically apart from most authors of his time during nearly fifty years of writing literature. Even when he has drawn upon dominant trends of literary fashion in Spain—the social realism of the 1950s or the experimental techniques of the 1970s— he has reshaped them in unique ways and enriched their potential for complexity. Although his early works have at times a clear political and social component, as did the novels of many Spanish novelists during the Franco regime, T. B.'s fiction is most consistently shaped by the recurrent concern for myth, parody, the writing of history, and the nature of literary characterization.

Many of T. B.'s early novels have been praised in recent critical writing but received scant attention when first published. His first significant body of work is the trilogy *Los gozos y las sombras* (joys and shadows): *El señor llega* (1957; the master arrives), *Donde da la vuelta el aire* (1960;

where the air turns around), and *La Pascua triste* (1962; the sad Easter). These novels are set in T. B.'s native Galicia in northwest Spain and focus on the material-spiritual conflict between a physician who has returned to his hometown after studying abroad, and an engineer who has lived in the town all of his life. Two other novels of the 1960s, although relatively unknown during the time of their publication, are important in the author's development. *Don Juan* (1963; Don Juan) hints at the imaginative play that will eventually dominate T. B.'s novels after 1970, while *Off-Side* (1969; title in English) reveals the realistic undercurrent of pessimism that several critics attribute to the early years of his writing.

With the publication of *La saga/fuga de J. B.* (the saga/fugue of J. B.) in 1972, winner of the National Novel Prize (1972), T. B. moved to the forefront of Spanish novelists. The work represents less a break with his previous novels than a complex elaboration of the principal narrative determinants that shape his earlier fiction: concern for the theory of narration; multiple perspectives on the real and the invented in the telling of a story; the fragmentation of time; parody of literary modes; and the play of history amid reality and imagination. The thin story line of the novel resists synthesis but turns upon the life of José Bastida and his growing awareness of his mythical status in the city of Castroforte. The novel ultimately destroys many of the myths upon which Spain has constructed its own image (T. B. attacks social institutions, sexual mores, religion) and parodies recent critical theories that seek to reduce fiction to mere structure or psychological case studies. Above all, however, *La saga/fuga* stands at the forefront of post-Civil War narrative that promotes the postmodern expression of ambiguity and chaos as essential values of the novelistic process.

The late 1970s to the present represent the most productive and inventive period of T. B.'s career. In a series of novels that intensify the metafictional pattern and technical complexity established in *La saga/fuga* T. B. explores the nature of the literary process and the contingencies of narration. *Fragmentos de apocalipsis* (1977; fragments of apocalypse), awarded the Critics' Prize (1977) and *La isla de los jacintos cortados* (1981; the isle of cut hyacinths) both examine how characters are at once fictional and real, and both explore T. B.'s interest in historiography and the way that events in past time are framed by narration and given meaning in the present as components of a story. *La rosa de los vientos* (1985; the rose of the winds) focuses more specifically on the nature of history and reveals how the real and the imaginary are enmeshed in similar narrative structures. T. B.'s most recent novel, *Yo no soy yo, evidentemente*

598

(1987; it's not me, obviously), represents a summing up of his intensely theoretical concerns. The novel undercuts the creation of characters in fiction by placing their very existence in doubt, and also parodies textual exegesis and the industry of literary criticism that produces meaning in fiction.

T. B. has played a significant role in bringing contemporary fiction in Spain into the mainstream of postmodern writing. His forceful imagination stands behind a theory of the novel that seeks to commingle literature and life, meaning and being. He frequently parodies the fictional process, not to destroy it, but to reveal the richness of its workings and the contingency of its meanings. Indeed, his parodies do not disparage the novel, but rather celebrate its pleasures and bring to the fore its existential importance.

FURTHER WORKS: *El viaje del joven Tobías* (1938); *El casamiento engañoso* (1939); *Lope de Aguirre* (1941); *Siete ensayos y una farsa* (1942); *Javier Mariño* (1943); *República Barataria* (1944); *El retorno de Ulises* (1946); *El golpe de estado de Guadalupe Limón* (1946); *Compostela* (1948); *Ifigenia* (1949); *Literatura española contemporánea (1898–1936)* (1949); *Farruquino* (1954); *Panorama de la literatura española contemporánea* (1956); *Teatro español contemporáneo* (1957); *El "Quijote" como juego* (1975); *Cuadernos de La Romana* (1976); *Nuevos cuadernos de La Romana* (1976); *Obra completa, I* (1977); *Acerca del novelista y de su arte: Discurso* (1977); *Las sombras recobradas* (1979); *Teatro, I, II* (1982); *Ensayos críticos* (1982); *Cuadernos de un vate vago* (1983); *Daphne y ensueños* (1983); *La princesa durmiente va a la escuela* (1983); *Quizá nos lleve el viento al infinito* (1984); *El "Quijote" como juego y otros trabajos críticos* (1984); *Cotufas en el golfo* (1986); *Hombre al agua* (1987); *Ifigenia y otros cuentos* (1987)

BIBLIOGRAPHY: *Homenaje a G. T. B.* (1981); Becerra, C., *G. T. B.* (1982); Giménez González, A., *T. B. en su mundo literario* (1984); Perez, J., *G. T. B.* (1984); Blackwell, F. H., *The Game of Literature: Demythification and Parody in Novels of G. T. B.* (1985); special T. B. issue, *Anthropos,* 66–67 (1986); Pérez, J., and S. Miller, eds., *Critical Studies on G. T. B.* (1989); Loureiro, A. G., *Mentira y seducción: La trilogía fantástica de T. B.* (1990)

DAVID K. HERZBERGER

TREMBLAY, Michel

Canadian dramatist, novelist, short-story writer, screenwriter, and translator (writing in French), b. 25 June 1942, Montreal

T. studied until the eleventh grade at the Saint-Stanislas School, at which point he became a linotypist and then a worker in the costume department of Radio Canada, 1966–1967. After writing a play and a collection of short stories, *Contes pour buveurs attardés* (1966; *Stories for Late Night Drinkers,* 1977), T. exploded onto the literary scene with his play *Les belles sœurs* (1968; *The Sisters-in-law,* 1974), written in 1965 and first performed in 1968. Subsequent plays in the same vein, referred to as the cycle of the *Belles-Sœurs,* made him the most important theatrical figure in Canada; the many performances of his works outside of the country have added an international dimension to his fame.

Les belles-sœurs originally met with resistance on the part of theater directors who all refused to perform it when it was first proposed to them; even after its overwhelmingly positive popular reception, it was denied support by the provincial and federal governments for performance in France. In both instances, the decisions were made because of the "vulgarity" of the language spoken by the women from the working-class neighborhood of Montreal. Nevertheless, when it finally appeared before the public in March 1968, it was immediately recognized as a turning point in Quebec theater. Ostensibly the representation of a party given by Germaine Lauzon to have fifteen of her friends help her glue the one million green stamps she won in a contest into stamp books, the dialogues—duets, trios, choruses—soon reveal the lives of the many *belles-sœurs,* solidly anchored in their trivialities, pushed around by men and the religious establishment, stealing small pleasures by watching television, becoming involved with a brush salesman, having a drink at a club once a week, being addicted to bingo, or being torn by personal conflicts. Many of them, in the course of the evening, steal filled stamp books for themselves. In addition to the novelty of representing this slice of society, the play's striking feature is the use of the language of the common people, *joual,* with its colorful imagery, its Anglicisms, its unusual grammatical turns, and its provincial-dialectal pronunciation. The public immediately recognized itself in these women, found the work unique, and observed, between laughs, some unsettling elements of their lives and society.

Among T.'s other plays are *À toi, pour toujours, ta Marie-Lou* (1971; *Forever Yours, Marie-Lou,* 1975), a much more somber work, pitting Carmen against her sister Manon and in confrontation with their dead parents—Carmen, intending to free herself from her oppressive surroundings, Manon clinging to her millieu. Despite the overwhelming tragic atmosphere, the play was a great success, the most successful of the cycle after *Les belles-*

sœurs. Carmen reappears in *Sainte Carmen de la Main* (1976; *Sainte Carmen of the Main*, 1981), in which she tries to launch a career as a country-western singer. *Damnée Manon, sacrée Sandra* (1977; *Damnée Manon, Sacrée Sandra* 1981) brings the series to an end, although the same cycle spirit is taken up again in *Albertine, en cinq temps* (1984; *Albertine in Five Times*, 1986).

Following his many theatrical successes, T. turned to the novel, creating a series, *Chroniques du Plateau Mont-Royal,* in which many of his best known characters reappear. *C't à ton tour, Laura Cadieux* (1973; it's your turn, Laura Cadieux), *La grosse femme d'à côté est enceinte* (1978; *The Fat Woman Next Door Is Pregnant,* 1981), *Des nouvelles d'Édouard* (1984; news from Edward), *Le Cœur découvert: Roman d'amours* (1986; open heart: novel of love). As is the case with his plays, we find the characters speaking the language of the people, with the structure sometimes betraying a certain theatricality, and these novels sometimes contain sections that seem to have been written for the stage; indeed, some have been presented as dramatic readings.

The society represented by T. reveals not only the problems found in everyday life, but represents the greater problems of Quebec society, where individuals living lives as Canadians are alienated, never quite fitting in because of their otherness.

Recognized as one of Quebec's most important writers, T. has been the recipient of numerous awards, among them that of being named the most important theatrical figure in Montreal in the preceding twenty years in 1978, receiving the France-Québec Prize in 1981, and being named Chevalier de l'Ordre des arts et des lettres de France in 1984.

FURTHER WORKS: *Demain matin, Montréal m'attend* (1972); *Hosanna (suivi de) La Duchesse de Langeais* (1973; *Hosanna,* 1974); *La Duchesse de Langeais and Other Plays* (1976); *Bonjour, là, bonjour* (1974; *Bonjour, là, bonjour,* 1975); *Mademoiselle Marguerite* (1975); *L'impromptu d'Outremont* (1980; *The Impromptu of Outremont,* 1981); *Thérèse et Pierrette à l'école des Saints-Anges* (1980; *Thérèse and Pierrette and the Little Hanging Angel,* 1984); *Les anciennes odeurs* (1981; *Remember Me,* 1984); *La duchesse et le roturier* (1982)

BIBLIOGRAPHY: Dorsinville, M., in New W. H., ed., *Dramatists in Canada: Selected Essays* (1972), 179–95; Usmiani, R., "The T. Opus: Unity in Diversity," *CTR,* 24 (Fall 1979), 12–25; Ripley, J., "From Alienation to Transcendence, the Quest for Selfhood in M. T.'s Plays," *CanL,* 85 (1980) 44–59; Usmiani, R., *M. T.* (1982); Lemire, M., et al., *Dictionnaire des œuvres littéraires du Qué-*

bec (1984), Vol. 4, passim; (1987), Vol. 5, passim; Weiss, J. M., *French-Canadian Theater* (1986), 27–48; Hamel, R., et al., *Dictionnaire des auteurs de langue française en Amérique du Nord* (1989), 1301–4; New, W. H., *A History of Canadian Literature* (1989), 248–50

PAUL BARRETTE

TREVOR, William

(pseud. of William Trevor Cox) Irish novelist and short-story writer, b. 24 May 1928, Mitchelstown

An Irishman who has lived most of his adult life in England, T. first established himself as an acute, ironic observer of contemporary English society, but in recent years has increasingly written about his native country and about the sectarian violence in Northern Ireland. He was born into a middle-class Protestant family in County Cork, and earned a degree in history from Trinity College, Dublin, in 1950. After teaching school for several years in Dublin and in the North, he moved to London and devoted himself to sculpting and, later, writing while working as an advertising copywriter. After his reputation as a writer was secured, he settled in the Devon countryside, where he still lives.

T.'s novels published in the 1960s are characterized by a precise, wry, understated brand of irony that caused him to be associated with Evelyn Waugh and Kingsley Amis (qq.v.). Typical of these is the novel that first put T. on the literary map, *The Old Boys* (1964), a satirical, often extremely comic portrayal of various intrigues among a group of elderly Englishmen who attended the same public school. A number of T.'s English novels are, however, considerably broader and more ambitious than this. *The Boarding-House* (1965), *Miss Gomez and the Brethren* (1971), and *Elizabeth Alone* (1973) rely on large, somewhat Dickensian, casts of characters and cut across many segments of English society: from upper-middle-class suburban life to the seedy underside of contemporary London, a world of petty criminals, con artists, and lonely men and women living in bed-sitters that T. has made his own. Through them all runs T.'s view of contemporary life as fundamentally alienated, a view that is countered to some extent by an essentially humanistic faith in the principles of compassion and connection. In his last two English novels, *The Children of Dynmouth* (1976) and *Other People's Worlds* (1980), this view is worked out in part through a critique of the divisiveness of the class system.

Although these novels never shrink from exposing bleak corners of contemporary life, their pessimism is tempered by a fine sense of comedy, as well as by T.'s humanism. T.'s short stories, however, tend to be darker; in them, characters rarely discover the means of breaking out of their moral and social alienation, or of overcoming the crippling illusions with which they mask their various inadequacies. One of T.'s most impressive achievements in this genre is a sequence of three stories entitled "Matilda's England," from *Lovers of Their Time, and Other Stories* (1978), in which the madness that steadily descends on the protagonist is seen to be the madness of a civilization irreparably maimed by two world wars.

T.'s Irish fiction, which accounts for most of his work in the 1980s, tends to fall into two categories. There are a number of short stories and one novella, *Nights at the Alexandra* (1987), that examine the middle-class provincial Ireland that T. knew growing up—the territory of much of the fiction of Frank O'Connor (q.v.)—depicting it somewhat relentlessly as morally, socially, and emotionally paralyzed. The best of these stories are nearly flawless in design, but they are not as ambitious, nor as fully satisfying, as the more politically conscious Irish fiction that T. has written in recent years: two novels, *Fools of Fortune* (1983) and *The Silence in the Garden* (1988), and several of T.'s best short stories—"Attracta," from *Lovers of Their Time, and Other Stories,* and the title stories of *Beyond the Pale, and Other Stories* (1981) and *The News from Ireland, and Other Stories* (1986). In their impressive moral understanding of Irish history, these works indirectly but powerfully confront the troubles in Ulster, exposing many of the forces—political, historical, and emotional—that lie behind them.

Although T. has often been described as an ironist preoccupied with society's losers and eccentrics, there is an impressive range to his writing. He has written, for example, as much about life in middle-class suburbs as he has about people wasting away in London's down-and-out quarters or Ireland's remote provinces. He has also written convincingly about love and marriage, a central concern of his fiction, at all levels of society. Finally, and perhaps most important, he has written with genuine depth about some of the most pressing social issues of his day, including those in Northern Ireland. There is a remarkable consistency of quality in all of T.'s work, but it seems likely that in the long run his writing about Ireland will be that for which he is most justly acclaimed.

FURTHER WORKS: *A Standard of Behaviour* (1958); *The Love Department* (1966); *The Day We Got Drunk on Cake, and Other Stories* (1967); *Mrs. Eckdorf in O'Neill's Hotel* (1969); *The Ballroom of Romance, and Other Stories* (1972); *Angels at the Ritz, and Other Stories* (1975); *The Stories of*

W. T. (1983); *Family Sins, and Other Stories* (1990); *W. T.: The Collected Stories* (1992)

BIBLIOGRAPHY: Mortimer, M., "W. T. in Dublin," *EI,* 4 (1975), 77–85; Gitzen, J., "The Truth-Tellers of W. T.," *Crit,* 21, 1 (1979), 59–72; Rhodes, R., "W. T.'s Stories of the Troubles," in Brophy, J. D., and R. J. Porter, eds., *Contemporary Irish Writing* (1983), 95–114; Mortimer, M., "The Short Stories of W. T.," *EI,* 9 (1984), 161–73; Stinson, J., "Replicas, Foils, and Revaluation in Some 'Irish' Short Stories of W. T.," *CJIS,* 11, 2 (1985), 17–26; Morrison, K., "W. T.'s 'System of Correspondence,'" *MR,* 28 (1987), 489–96; Schirmer, G. A., *W. T.: A Study of His Fiction* (1990)

GREGORY A. SCHIRMER

TRIANA, José

Cuban dramatist, b. 4 Jan. 1931, Hatuey, Camaguey

T. spent the early part of his life in a number of small towns around the Cuban countryside before moving to Madrid in the mid-1950s. Like many other young Cuban writers, T. sought to leave behind the repression of the Batista regime, which held power until the Marxist revolution of 1959. Afterward T. returned to his native country, where his career flourished during the 1960s due to the Castro government's support of a national Cuban artistic program. In 1966 T.'s most significant work, *La noche de los asesinos* (1965; *The Criminals,* 1971), was produced in Havana, firmly establishing T. as an influential voice in 20th-c. Latin American literature.

As a young man in Cuba, T. worked as a teacher and studied liberal arts at the University of Oriente. It was not until moving to Europe in 1955 that he committed himself to a literary career. In 1957 he wrote *El mayor general hablará de teogonia* (1962; the major general will speak of theogony), which was first produced in 1960. This play features several characteristics of the Theater of the Absurd (q.v.), which places characters in surreal and occasionally horrifying situations in an attempt to represent the futile nature of human existence. The play tells the story of a lower-class Cuban family that has been supported by the charity of its landlord (the major general). The family anxiously anticipates a visit from the general, who is perceived variously by the wife as a figure of divine generosity, and by the husband and his sister-in-law as a figure of divine retribution. Upon the general's arrival, it becomes apparent that the deified figure has nothing more than a sort of disinterested contempt for his idolators, and thus the play succeeds mainly as a satirical attack upon weak-willed worshipers of a supreme being.

After the success of this first play, T. went on to produce three more dramas set among the lower classes of Cuban society. *Medea en el espejo* (perf. 1960, pub. 1962; Medea in the mirror) is a modern retelling of Euripides's *Medea* set in the slums of Cuba. *El Parque de la Fraternidad* (1962; brotherhood park) deals with the failure of three stock characters of Cuban drama to establish meaningful communication. *La muerte del ñeque* (perf. 1963, pub. 1964; the death of the bogeyman) is another play reminiscent of Greek tragedy, wherein a gangster is killed by three other criminals who symbolize the three fates of Greek drama. All three plays lend a mythic status to the everyday occurrences of postrevolutionary Cuba.

In 1966 T. produced his most critically acclaimed work, *La noche de los asesinos*. The drama takes place in a run-down basement, where three Cuban youths engage in a bizarre role-playing game: They pretend to murder their parents, and then go on to enact their own arrest and trial. The youngsters play all the parts in the surreal drama, including parents, police, and courtroom figures. When their "story" is over, the teenagers switch parts and begin the role-playing again. Like *El mayor general hablará de teogonia, La noche de los asesinos* is an absurdist work that deals with the issues of guilt and innocence. The play won the prestigious Casa de las Américas Prize for drama (1965) and the Gallo de La Habana Award for best play (1966).

T.'s career as a dramatist flourished in the late 1960s. He served as literary adviser to the Consejo Nacional de Cultura, the Instituto Cubana del Libro, and the publishing house of Letras Cubanas, and in 1967 he traveled to Europe for the international premiere of *La noche de los asesinos*. This prestige, however, was short-lived, as hardliners in the Cuban government questioned the value of absurdist works to revolutionary ideals. Since absurdism, by definition, does not deal overtly with recognizable elements of everyday life, it was deemed worthless by those in power, who encouraged artistic works that featured Marxist propaganda. Furthermore, *La noche de los asesinos* was perceived as a thinly veiled attack on authoritarianism, and thus it and T.'s other plays were officially banned. T. himself was sentenced to a life of manual labor until 1980, when Castro allowed Cuban dissidents to leave the country, and T. voluntarily exiled himself to France, where he has lived ever since. T. came to the U. S. in 1981 as a visiting professor at Dartmouth College, and received a Cintas Fellowship for 1985–1986. In 1986 T.'s *Worlds Apart*, translated from the Spanish, premiered in London.

Despite his eventual discontent with the outcomes of the 1959 revolution and the subsequent exile from his homeland, T. remained committed to socialist ideals both personally and artistically. He is recognized as one of the most powerful literary voices of postrevolutionary Cuba.

FURTHER WORKS: *De la madera de los sueños* (1958); *La casa ardiendo* (perf. 1962); *La visita del angel* (perf. 1963); *Ceremonial de guerra* (1989)

BIBLIOGRAPHY: Dauster, F. N., "The Game of Chance: The Theatre of J. T.," *LATR*, 3, 1 (1969), 3–8; Miranda, J., "J. T. o el conflicto," *CHA*, 230 (1969), 439–44; Murch, A. C., "Genet-T.-Kopit: Ritual as 'Danse Macabre,' " *MD*, 15, 4 (1973), 369–81; Dauster, F. N., "J. T.: El juego violento," *Ensayos sobre teatro hispanoamericano* (1975), 9–36; Palls, T. L., "The Theatre of the Absurd in Cuba After 1959," *LATR*, 4, 7 (1975), 67–72; Nigro, K., *"La noche de los asesinos:* Playscript and Stage Enactment," *LATR*, 11, 1 (1977), 45–57; Campa, R. V. de la, *J. T.: Ritualización de la sociedad cubana* (1979); Neglia, E., "El asedio a la casa: Un estudio del decorado en *La noche de los asesinos,*" *RI*, 46, 110 (1980), 139–49; Dauster, F. N., "J. T.," in Sole, C. A., ed., *Latin American Writers* (1989), Vol. 3, 1415–18; Escarpenter, J. A., and L. S. Glaze, "J. T.," in Martinez, J. A., ed., *Dictionary of Twentieth Century Cuban Literature* (1990), 466–70

JASON BERNER

TROTZIG, Birgitta

Swedish novelist, short-story writer, and essayist, b. 29 Sept. 1929, Gothenburg

T. was raised in Sweden's southernmost province, Skåne, which provides the setting for a number of her works, a landscape of bleak plains, an undramatic Baltic coast line, and often oppressive skies. With her artist husband, T. lived in France from 1954 to 1969; in the words of Adma d'Heurle (b. 1924), "Her intimate knowledge of the art world, her continuing interest in world affairs, and her identification with the poor and oppressed of the world were intensified throughout this period of expatriation. It was also at this time that T. came in contact with the vigorous progressive Catholic movements of the 1950s and joined the Catholic church." From her debut in 1951, T.—unaffected by the vagaries of literary fashion—has remained faithful to an original vision of existence and presented a profile uniquely her own. She is the recipient of a number of prestigious literary prizes, among them the Selma Lagerlöf Prize (1984) and the Pilot Prize (1985), and has enjoyed critical acclaim, not least in France.

T.'s vision of existence is basically religious, but her novels and short stories (she often refers to the latter as fairy tales or legends) are not vehicles for abstract theological discourse; they are palpably and painfully concrete; the concept of God-made-flesh is fundamental in her works. Her early novel *De utsatta* (1957; the exposed) is set in Skåne against a background of war in the 17th c. The novel *En berättelse från kusten* (1961; a tale from the coast) is set in Skåne in the Middle Ages. Her later novels, *Sveket* (1966; the betrayal), *Sjukdomen* (1972; the illness), and *Dykungens dotter* (1984; the marsh king's daughter), are set in more recent times. In most of T.'s stories the protagonists are from the lowest strata of society, people who are poor, downtrodden, and betrayed by life and fellow beings. They are suffering pain, hardships, and indignities, sometimes to the limits of the endurable; the pessimistic vision of existence that emerges through T.'s descriptions is relentless and seemingly unrelieved by grace and only redeemed by the dark intensity of her language. Critics have suggested that T. has made her uncompromising vision an end in itself, effective and compelling, but ultimately aesthetic. It may also be tempting to suggest a deliberate "pious manipulation" behind the creation of such a bleak, implacable, and hopeless universe in order to offer redemption through Christ as the only possible salvation. T. had an early traumatic experience of unmitigated evil when confronted with the exposed horrors of Nazi concentration camps; she also repeatedly points to the predominance of hunger, poverty, oppression, and torture in the world at large as ample justification for her vision. The suffering of children in particular makes T. approach the timeless theodicy problem: how to reconcile the concept of a loving God with the existence of so much evil. Although T.'s political orientation toward a socialist-Marxist worldview may at times conflict with her religious convictions, the search for justice, divine or social, remains a constant. The descriptions in T.'s stories are often unstated indictments of intolerable social conditions; *Dykungens dotter*, for example, is on the mythical and allegorical level patterned on the Hans Christian Andersen fairy tale of the same title; on the realistic level it offers a highly critical account of the social development in Sweden, seen from the perspective of three generations of disenfranchised people. *De utsatta* is more than a historical novel; the descriptions of war in 17th-c. Skåne reverberate with the author's strong emotional involvement with contemporary events in Algeria. The malady implied in the title of the novel *Sjukdomen* is not only that of the mentally

retarded protagonist: his birth in 1914 and his first internment in 1939 are significant dates in his life, but also in world history. T. admits that she intended the novel to be both an individual story and a myth of our century.

T.'s primary concern, however, is to depict the individual at the intersection of life and death, order and disorder, hope and despair. The ritual movement is downward, to the lowest and the most degraded state, in an imitation of or rather identification with the passion of Christ toward metamorphosis and resurrection.

In her essays T. offers comments on her own activity as an author. Repeatedly she asserts her belief in the potentials of art and in the power of the artist as outsider and rebel: Unfettered art is one of the most effective weapons against what she terms "the insufferable order."

FURTHER WORKS: *Ur de älskandes liv* (1951); *Bilder* (1954); *Ett landskap, dagbok—fragment 54–58* (1959); *Utkast och förslag* (1962); *Levande och döda* (1964); *Ordgränser* (1968); *I kejsarens tid* (1975); *Berättelser* (1977); *Jaget och världen* (1977); *Anima* (1982)

BIBLIOGRAPHY: d'Heurle, A., "Introducing B. T.," *SBR*, 1 (Oct. 1983), 24–26; d'Heurle, A., "The Image of Woman in the Fiction of B. T.," *SS*, 55, 4 (1983), 371–82; Algulin, I., *A History of Swedish Literature* (1989), 266–67; Zuck, V., ed., *Dictionary of Scandinavian Literature* (1990), 626–28

LARS G. WARME

TSIRKAS, Stratis

(pseud. of Yannis Hadjiandreas) Greek prose writer, critic, and poet, b. 10 July 1911, Cairo, Egypt; d. 27 Jan. 1980, Athens

T. was a prolific writer of fiction and a pioneer commentator on the Alexandrian poet C. P. Cavafy (q.v.). After his graduation from the Ambeteios School of Commerce in Cairo (1928), he worked for a year in the National Bank of Egypt, then was an accountant in small cotton concerns of the Nile area until the late 1930s when he settled in Alexandria as manager of a tannery. His contact with communist circles started in 1930 and continued through the end of his life, although his books caused friction with party leaders of doctrinaire persuasions. He was very active in prewar antifascist and peace movements, helped Greek resistance fighters during World War II, and continued his political activism in the 1950s when he also traveled to France, Switzerland, Germany, and Greece. In 1963 he settled permanently in

Athens, where he contributed the short story "Alaxokairia" ("Weather-Change") to the resistance volume *Dekaokhto Keimena* (1970; *Eighteen Texts,* 1972). His studies of the Cavafy era and his Middle East trilogy made him famous in Greece and abroad in the 1970s.

T.'s literary career began with the publication of a fairy tale, "To phengari" (1927; the moon), in the Alexandrian magazine *Panegyptia* when he was only sixteen. The first collection of short stories, *Hoi Fellahoi* (1937; the Fellahs), presented his leftist ideology both in subject matter and themes. His sympathy for the poor, downtrodden, exploited, and those vanquished in personal or communal life continued to be the hallmark in his two books of verse, three volumes of short stories, and the novella *Noudendin Bompa* (1957; Nurendin Boba) that he published before settling in Athens.

T.'s narrative technique and style in realistic fiction were conventional although quite effective for his humanitarian concerns. In contrast, the pronounced Marxist coloration of his verse left it outside the aesthetic climate that was being developed by modernist poets like Angelos Sikelianos, George Seferis, and Odysseus Elytis (qq.v.), or the more sophisticated Marxists Kostas Varnalis, Yannis Ritsos (qq.v.), and Nikiforos Vrettakos (b. 1911). T. won his reputation as a novelist of great breadth and cosmopolitan vision with the publication of the epic trilogy *Akyvernetes politeies* (*Drifting Cities,* 1974), which consists of the novels *He leskhe* (1961), *Ariagne* (1962), and *He nykhterida* (1965) (respectively *The Club, Ariagne,* and *The Bat* in the English translation of 1974). Comparable in spirit, narrative structure, and characterization technique to Lawrence Durrell's (q.v.) contemporaneous tetralogy *The Alexandria Quartet* (1957–1962) this *roman-fleuve,* in its 1971 French translation, won the prize for best foreign book of the French critics and publishers in 1972. Its English version offered the scenario for the international television serial released in the 1980s. By then, it had appeared in Spanish, Italian, and Romanian as well. Its arresting but not complex plot features a fascinating gallery of Greek and international characters from many walks of life as they go through dramatic crises set in wartime Jerusalem, Alexandria, and Cairo. T.'s well-rounded and colorful heroes and heroines are drawn into a vortex of intrigue, spying, fighting, and love affairs that are typical of the exotic locale and its nebulous atmosphere.

Encouraged by the popularity of his trilogy, he started working on a new one, set in Greece. He completed only the first novel, *He khamene anoixe* (1976; the lost spring), whose main hero, now a middle-aged, tired, and disappointed leftist activist, not unlike the author, becomes involved in the dramatic political developments of 1965 in Greece that led to the 1967 military takeover. In most artistic and thematic respects this last novel is a continuation of the commendable achievement of the Middle East trilogy. A French translation appeared in 1982.

T.'s reputation as a literary critic was secured with the publication of the treatise *Ho Kavaphes kai he epokhe tou* (1958; Cavafy and his times), which won a State Prize for essay. It explores, from a Marxist angle, the cultural milieu and sociopolitical events in the international society of early 20th-c. Egypt where Cavafy lived and wrote. This study was complemented by the volume of essays *Ho politikos Kavaphes* (1971; the political Cavafy), which offered additional information and, like the monograph that preceded it, provoked a spirited but enlightening dialogue with disagreeing scholars, Greek and foreign.

Apart from the translation of *Akyvernetes politeies* into five languages and of his Nile novella into French and Arabic, several of T.'s short stories appeared in these two languages plus English, German, Hungarian, Polish, and Russian. His poems were collected in a volume posthumously.

FURTHER WORKS: *To lyriko taxidi* (1938); *Allokotoi anthropoi kai alla diegemata* (1944); *Proteleftaios apokhairetismos kai to ispaniko oratorio* (1946); *Ho Apriles einai pio skleros* (1947); *Ho hypnos tou theriste kai alla diegemata* (1954); *Ston kavo kai alla diegemata* (1966); *Ta hemerologia* (1973); *Ta poiemata* (1981)

BIBLIOGRAPHY: Raizis, M. B., on *He khamene anoixe, WLT,* 51, 4 (Autumn 1977), 658–59

M. BYRON RAIZIS

TSUSHIMA Yūko

(pseud. of Tsushima Satoko) Japanese novelist, short-story writer, and essayist, b. 30 Mar. 1947, Tokyo

T. is the daughter of Tsushima Shūji, who wrote under the pen name Dazai Osamu (q.v.), and his wife, Tsushima Michiko. After her father's death in 1948, when she was one year old, T. and her brother and sister were brought up by their mother. T. was close to her older brother, who had Down's syndrome, and who died when he was fifteen and she was twelve. The loss of the language-free world they had shared, and a desire to find value in human existence by some measure other than the intellect, led T. to begin writing fiction in her late teens while she was an English literature major at Shirayuri Women's College. An important inspiration, for its innovations in style and form, was the work of William Faulkner (q.v.), particularly *The Sound and the Fury* (1929).

T.'s first published short story, "Rekuiemu—inu to otona no tame ni" (1969; requiem for a dog and an adult), was written in her senior year of college. Her early stories present a closed world of family relationships, often from a child's viewpoint; many contain macabre and surreal elements. Inevitably first identified as Dazai's daughter, T. soon began to establish an independent reputation. "Kitsune o haramu" (1972; conceiving a fox) was nominated for the Akutagawa Prize; the collections *Mugura no haha* (1975; the mother in the house of grass) and *Kusa no fushido* (1977; a bed of grass) were awarded the Tamura Toshiko Prize (1976) and the Izumi Kyōka Prize (1977), respectively; and the novel *Chōji* (1978; *Child of Fortune*, 1983) received the Women's Literary Award (1978).

The protagonist of *Chōji* is a thirty-six-year-old divorced mother who believes herself to be pregnant again. Through her experience of the pregnancy and the conventional attitudes of the people around her, the novel explores two of T.'s major themes: the tensions between motherhood and other dimensions of identity and sexuality, and the social marginality of a woman raising a family alone. (T. married in 1970 and divorced in 1976, when her daughter was four; her son was born the same year.) T.'s characteristic use of light and water images as symbols of vitality and sexuality is at its most effective in this work. T. has carried on the efforts of earlier women writers such as Okamoto Kanoko (1889–1939) and Enchi Fumiko (q.v.) to portray sexual love as experienced by a woman. Often employing narrative techniques close to those of the confessional *shishōsetsu*, or "I-novel," she has reexamined the language available to express a woman's sexuality—a concern she shares with many contemporaries writing in other languages.

The newspaper serialization of her novel *Yama o hashiru onna* (1980; *Woman Running in the Mountains*, 1991) brought T. a wider audience, while the story "Danmari ichi" (1982; "The Silent Traders," 1984) earned her the Kawabata Yasunari Prize (1983). Both works employ vivid images of nature in the interstices of the city, and draw on folkloric sources. The novel's heroine, a young single mother, dreams of living like the indigenous hunter-gatherers of the far north. The deadening urban routine and the control of bureaucracy over her life (through records of her child's illegitimacy) can barely contain her intuitive, wild energy. Associations with the *yamanba*, or mountain witch, and Japan's preagricultural

peoples give mythic force to a novel of minutely detailed realism.

After the sudden loss of her son in 1985, T. turned to an intensely personal contemplation of grief in which she strips away modern technological society's insulation from the inevitability of death. The novel *Yoru no hikari ni owarete* (1986; driven by the light of night) retells the 11th-c romance *Yowa no nezame* (*The Tale of Nezame*, 1979). In three chapters in letter form, the contemporary narrator addresses the woman author of the tale, Sugawara no Takasue no Musume (1008–?). In her lifetime, death must have been an ever-present reality, yet her words have survived for nearly a thousand years—facts that sustain the narrator, herself a writer, as she resolves to continue her own work.

T.'s prolific output and the autobiographical basis of her writing have resulted in some repetitive reworking of materials in her short stories. Over her twenty-year career, however, her fiction has evolved a distinctive fusion of realistic social content, critically observed from the margins, and transcending elements of myth, dream, and natural imagery employed with considerable imaginative power.

FURTHER WORKS: *Shanikusai* (1971); *Dōji no kage* (1973); *Ikimono no atsumaru ie* (1973); *Waga chichitachi* (1975); *Tōmei kūkan ga mieru toki* (1977); *Yorokobi no shima* (1978); *Yoru no tī pātī* (1979); *Hyōgen* (1979); *Hikari no ryōbun* (1979); *Saigo no shuryō* (1979); *Moeru kaze* (1980); *Yoru to asa no tegami* (1980); *Shōsetsu no naka no fūkei* (1982); *Suifu* (1982); *Watakushi no jikan* (1982); *Hi no kawa no hotori de* (1983); *Danmari ichi* (1984); *Ōma monogatari* (1984); *Osanaki hibi e* (1986); *Mahiru e* (1988); *Yume no kiroku* (1988); *Hon no naka no shōjotachi* (1989); *Kusamura* (1989); *Afureru haru* (1990); *Ōinaru yume yo, hikari yo* (1991). FURTHER VOLUME IN ENGLISH: *The Shooting Gallery, and Other Stories* (1988)

BIBLIOGRAPHY: Monnet, L., "Mord, Inzest und Schwachsinn: Die weibliche Mythologie Tsushima Yukos," in Antoni, K., P. Portner, and R. Schneider, eds., *Referate des VII. Deutschen Japanologentages in Hamburg* (1988), Vol. 3, 218–27; Dunlop, L., on *The Shooting Gallery, LitR*, 32 (1989), 288–93; Schierbeck, S. S., "T. Y.," *East Asian Institute Occasional Papers 5: Postwar Japanese Women Writers* (1989), 149–52; Drabble, M., and Yūko Tsushima, "Career and Family—for the Woman Writer and in Women's Writing," in Takano, F., ed., *Margaret Drabble in Tokyo* (1991), 59–112; Cheever, S., on *Woman Running in the Mountains, Los Angeles Times Book Review*, 26 May 1991, 2; Miyoshi, M., "T. Y.,"

Off Center: Power and Culture Relations between Japan and the United States (1991), 212–16

GERALDINE HARCOURT

TURKISH LITERATURE

See Volume 4, page 474.

The 1980s were an eventful decade in Turkey: ideological and economic turmoil, repressive military regime, multiparty parliamentary system dominated by a single party, transition to free-market economy, restoration of democratic freedoms, and the establishment (in 1991) of a coalition government. Literature experienced, within ten years, the worst repression and the widest freedom. While academic freedom remained curtailed to some extent in the early 1990s, literature enjoyed a virtually unprecedented ability to deal with any themes and ideas, including those that had sometimes brought retribution to literary figures in the past. Consequently, as the 20th c. draws to a close, Turkish literature is enjoying a period of ideological and erotic openness and of brave innovations in substance, structure, and style. Its diversity seems wider and bolder than ever.

Poetry

Many of the prominent modern poets, including Fazıl Hüsnü Dağlarca, Melih Cevdet Anday, Necati Cumalı (qq.v.), İlhan Berk (b. 1915) and others, continue to be prolific and to explore new creative dimensions. Dağlarca, often referred to as "Turkey's leading living poet," published in the 1980s hundreds of lyric and philosophical poems remarkable for their luminosity. Anday pursued his interest in Near Eastern mythology as well as modern mythopoesis, while Cumalı achieved an ever stronger synthesis of social concerns and private sensibilities. Berk, a foremost experimenter since the 1950s, produced several volumes, each one of which represents a striking innovation of poetic technique.

Several poets, highly promising in the previous two decades, fulfilled their potential. Of these, perhaps the most productive was Özdemir İnce (b. 1936), who published several volumes of his new powerful poems and translations of Ritsos, Lautréamont, Char, and others and first-rate criticism, became a member of the Mallarmé Academy, and organized the First Istanbul International Poetry Forum (1991). İnce's poems, full of fresh evocations, metaphors, and compelling human drama, exhibit an admirable virtuosity. One of his major accomplishments is a four-volume anthology of modern world poetry, which he edited together with Ataol Behramoğlu (b. 1942) who also achieved

premier status in the 1980s with exquisitely crafted poems of love, exile, and protest.

Ahmet Oktay (b. 1933) stands as one of contemporary Turkey's eminent intellectual poets and masters of literary theory. His poetry shares some of the features of the best work of Wallace Stevens and Rilke. Hilmi Yavuz (b. 1936) enjoys considerable esteem for his stimulating blend of traditional Turkish aesthetic values and many of the values of European poetry. Perhaps the most original of the living Turkish poets is Ece Ayhan (b. 1931), who is renowned for his imaginative distortions of syntax, for calculated obscurantism, and strange syncopations. Sabahattin Kudret Aksal (b. 1920), by contrast, is a poet of lucidity even when he deals with elusive themes.

Between 1985 and 1990, several prominent poets died: Edip Cansever (q.v.), Oktay Rifat (1914–1988), Turgut Uyar (1927–1985), Metin Eloğlu (1927–1985), Tahsin Saraç (1930–1989), and Cemal Süreyya (1931–1990), all of whom had introduced to Turkey new dimensions of poetic experience.

In the early 1990s, ideologies and social protest became less of a force among Turkish poets compared with their dominance from 1960 to 1980. Nonetheless, political commitment continues to motivate many socialists including Gülten Akın (b. 1933), Turkey's leading woman poet.

Neosurrealism, which was in vogue as an antipode to the social realists in the pre-1980 period, seems to have lost much of its appeal. Essentially, Turkish poetry has entered an era when no specific school or movement prevails. Also, there is a growing group of poets, including many young ones, who are creating ultramodern poems inspired by some of the basic values and aesthetic norms of classical Ottoman verse. Neoclassicism, which attempts to keep alive the stanzaic forms and the prosody of that tradition, is still going strong.

Fiction

A restless quest for fresh techniques and textures has characterized Turkish novels and short stories since the early 1980s. As the so-called "village fiction" of the earlier decades steadily lost ground, writers became more responsive to the modern fiction of Europe, the U. S., and Latin America. Translation activity, mainly from English and French, has gained momentum—as well as greater impact thanks to strides in the art of translation.

Yashar Kemal (q.v.), still Turkey's strongest Nobel candidate, has continued to write the saga of his southwestern Anatolian region in further volumes of *İnce Memed* (slim Memed), the first volume of which was translated into English as *Memed, my hawk* (1961), and *Demirciler çarşısı cinayeti* (1974; *The Lords of Akchasaz: Murder in the Ironsmiths Market,* 1979). Much of Kemal's fiction since the late 1970s has dealt with fishing communities and urban life. His books are being translated into numerous languages at an impressive rate. Most recent English translations, all by Thilda Kemal, include *Al Gözüm Seyreyle Salih* as *Seagull* (1981), *Deniz küstü* (1978) as *The Sea-Crossed Fisherman* (1985), *Kuşlar da gitti* (1978) as *The Birds Have Also Gone* (1987), and *Yılanı Öldürseler* (1976) as *To Crush the Serpent* (1991).

The legendary satirist Aziz Nesin (q.v.) has published in the 1980s several collections of short stories and essays and his first book of lyric poems. Satire continues to fire the imagination of the Turkish public: Sales of humorous books (many of them with illustrations and cartoons) enjoy more substantial sales than virtually all other genres—and a whole new generation of humorists and satirists has emerged in recent years.

A remarkable development in fiction is the ascendancy of a large group of woman writers. This group which includes Adalet Ağaoğlu (q.v.), Tomris Uyar (b. 1941), Pınar Kür (b. 1943), Nazlı Eray (b. 1945), Leylâ Erbil (b. 1931), Sevim Burak (1931–1983), Füruzan (b. 1935), Gülten Dayıoğlu (b. 1935), Ayla Kutlu (b. 1938) and others, have brought vitality to novelistic techniques. Aysel Özakın (b. 1942) has produced stories drawn on the experiences of the Turkish guest workers in Germany; one of her books is available in English translation: *The Prizegiving* (1988, trans. by Celia Kerslake). A first novel, *Sevgili arsız ölüm* (1983; dear shameless death) by Latife Tekin (b. 1957), burst on the literary scene with a gripping narrative and a brave new language steeped in quaint provincial expressions and an unaccustomed urban lumpen lingo. Hailed by many critics as nothing short of a small masterpiece, the Tekin novel documents the trials and tribulations of a rural family struggling to survive in the big city.

The 1980s also witnessed the meteoric rise of Orhan Pamuk (b. 1952). His first novel, *Cevdet Bey ve oğulları* (1982; Cevdet Bey and his sons), a family saga reminiscent of Thomas Mann's (q.v.) *Buddenbrooks,* is a sprawling conventional narrative. *Sessiz ev* (1983; the silent house) is a powerful Faulknerian novella, which won the 1984 Madaralı Award. Pamuk's *Beyaz kale* of 1985 has been a major success not only in Turkey but also in the English-speaking world when it came out in 1991 as *The White Castle,* translated by Victoria Holbrook, winning extensive praise from American critics (the *New York Times,* John Updike in the *New Yorker,* and many others). It is perhaps the most successful postmodernist Turkish novel. Set in Istanbul in the 17th c., it depicts the confrontation and merger of East and West in the

persons of a young Italian and a Turkish intellectual who cooperate and sometimes conspire to find solutions for the Ottoman state. Pamuk's huge novel of 1990, entitled *Kara kitap* (black book), which went through a dozen printings in one year, has established him as one of Turkey's great novelists. It is a masterful intellectual exercise in postmodernist fiction with vivid and elusive characters and an obscurantist plot.

Mobil Corporation's prestigious Pegasus Prize, however, for the best novel published in Turkey between 1980 and 1990, went to Bilge Karasu (b. 1930), for his intriguing novel *Gece* (1985; night). Karasu, a master of the stream-of-consciousness (q.v.) technique and a conjurer of modern myths, shares with Ferit Edgü (b. 1916), Selim İleri (b. 1949), Murathan Mungan (b. 1955) and others a subtle aesthetics of narration and character portrayal.

The Turkish novel is currently enjoying a period of quest for regeneration based on an awareness of the best of world literature and the private and social crises of Turks at home and abroad.

Drama

Theater is vibrant in Turkish cities—with hundreds of plays, native and foreign, produced by the state, city, and independent theaters. Regional theatrical activity has also gained momentum.

Turkish playwrights have feverishly written about historical, mythological, and contemporary subjects in a wide variety of dramatic forms. A. Turan Oflazoğlu (b. 1932) and Orhan Asena (b. 1922) are among the leading figures of historical drama. Oflazoğlu has concentrated on Ottoman sultans in plays that have a Shakespearean structure and tone. Güngör Dilmen (q.v.) is a foremost playwright who has dealt with ancient myths and many phases of Turkish and non-Turkish history.

A major figure to emerge in the 1980s is Mehmet Baydur (b. 1952) whose ingenious plots, whimsical characters, and rich and sometimes lyrical dialogue have made his plays popular in Turkey and, some, in translation, in France. *Güneyli bayan* (1984; southern lady) by the woman playwright Bilgesu Erenus (b. 1943) attracted considerable attention. It is a poignant play based on the life of Lillian Hellman (q.v.). Murathan Mungan (b. 1955) is the author of some striking modern plays as well as the one-actor dramatization of the life and poetry of Orhan Veli Kanık (1914–1950), which has been presented with great success by the prominent actor Müşfik Kenter.

As the 20th c. draws to a close, Turkish literature shows both maturity and a restless energy to introduce new creative dimensions. It seems secure and confident about its authentic cultural identity, and eager to embrace influences from abroad and to generate new aesthetic values from within its own resources.

BIBLIOGRAPHY: Halman, T. S., "Life of Literature and Death of Ideologies in Turkey," *Translation: The Journal of Literary Translation,* 19 (Fall 1987), 3–7; Güneli Gün, "Comets on the Turkish Literary Horizon: Woman Writers," *Translation: The Journal of Literary Translation,* 19 (Fall 1987), 76–82; Reddy, N. M., *Twenty Stories by Turkish Women Writers* (1989); Halman, T. S., *Living Poets of Turkey* (1989)

TALAT SAIT HALMAN

TUURI, Antti

Finnish novelist and short-story writer, b. 1 Oct. 1944, Kauhava

T. is one of Finland's most highly regarded postwar writers. Born in the western Finland province of Ostrobothnia and trained as an engineer, he brings these two elements into his literary output. He has worked in a number of jobs requiring a high level of technical skill, and even his rather flat and matter-of-fact style serves to juxtapose the impersonal industrial milieu he often chooses as the background for his stories and his all too human characters who try to survive in this world.

After T.'s early novels and short-story collections in the 1970s, his *Joki virtaa läpi kaupungin* (1977; a river flows through the town) presents a richer narrative technique. The lives of three people accidentally touch—a foreman who breaks loose from the shackles of technocracy, a fragile artist, and an old university professor who wishes to die naturally rather than have his life prolonged by the life-support systems of the modern hospital. In his short-story collection *Maailman kivisin paikka* (1980; the stoniest place in the world) T. uses the classical short-story technique of the narrator and the frame.

T. is convinced that people are shaped by their heredity, economic factors, and even the landscape they live in. Most of his characters come from Ostrobothnia, the flat "breadbasket" province of Finland. His novel *Pohjanmaa* (1982; Ostrobothnia) was awarded the Nordic Prize for literature in 1985. It describes the events of one summer day; a farm family has gathered for the reading of the will of a grandfather who emigrated to the U.S. in the 1920s. The tone is matter-of-fact and often ironic, the narrator viewing the activities of his relatives as a black comedy. The book has been translated into several languages (not includ-

ing English) and was made into a film by the same title in Finland in 1988.

The Ostrobothnian province of Finland has probably contributed most to the Finnish emigration to the U.S. and Canada. T. has continued to explore the lives of his neighbors in several books that take them to the "new world" of which they had an idealized picture. *Ameriikan raitti* (1986; the American road), set in the present, describes the life of more recent Finnish emigrants in Florida, many of whom have fled there to avoid taxation in Finland. When the hero decides to visit the town where his grandfather had emigrated in the 1920s, he finds an entire parallel family they knew nothing about in Finland. The style is laconic and made more interesting still by the use of unusual verb forms, such as present and past perfect indicative. A Finnish movie was made of the book in 1990. The harsh reality of life in the Canadian mines where Finns were brought as strikebreakers in the 1930s is described in *Uusi Jerusalem* (1988; the new Jerusalem) and *Maan avaruus* (1989; the wide earth), where the utopian community praised to the hero as harboring "no dogs, no witches, no whores, no murderers, and no idol worshipers" turns out to be the very opposite. Another topic that has occupied T. is World War II as it was fought in Finland. Again, Ostrobothnians play the main parts. When T. was doing his research, he discovered that almost all of the many books about the war were written by people above the rank of colonel, to whom the war seemed like a game of chess. The regimental diaries kept by sergeant majors or clerks provided a much more personal view of the war. In *Talvisota* (1984; the winter war), the soldier is an unassuming hero who carries out his killing as a job that must be done. Because of the narrative style chosen, the book has few named characters. When the Finnish movie of this book was made in 1989, T. collaborated in the writing of the script. In 1990 T. published *Rukajärven tiellä* (on the road to Rukajärvi) and its sequel, *Rukajärven linja* (1991; the Rukajärvi line), which describe the Continuation War (1941–1944).

T. is undoubtedly one of the major contemporary Finnish writers. Besides novels and short stories, he has published plays and written articles and documentary texts. Between 1971 and 1987 he was awarded thirteen literary prizes, and his novels and short stories have been translated into many languages, although the English-reading public still has to depend on a few short stories published in *Books in Finland* and some anthologies. The reason may be found in the specifically Finnish associative contexts of T.'s characters that may not be immediately clear to non-Finnish readers, who nevertheless would enjoy the laconic wry humor that these heroes exhibit in the absurd situations where life—and T.—places them.

FURTHER WORKS: *Asioiden suhteet* (1971); *Lauantaina illalla* (1971); *Seitsemän kertomusta* (1972); *Marraskuun loppu* (1973); *Vuosi elämästä* (1975); *Perhokalastuksen alkeet* (1978); *Asiantuntija* (1979); *Kertomus järvestä* (1981); *"Juhani Aho kalastuskirjailijana,"* *Suomalaisia kirjailijoita* (1982); *Samuttajat* (1983); *Novellit* (1983); *Viisitoista metriä vasempaan* (1985); *Maakunnan mies* (1986); *Voiman miehet* (1986); *Vääpeli Matala lentää* (1987); *Maan avaruus* (1989)

BIBLIOGRAPHY: Salokannel, J., "Unusual Men," *WLT*, 54, 1 (Winter 1980), 24–27; Tarkka, P., "A. T.: The Engineer's Story," *BF*, 2 (1981), 46–48

MARGARETA MARTIN

TY-CASPER, Linda

Philippine novelist and short-story writer (writing in English), b. 17 Sept. 1931, Manila

As the daughter of a textbook writer for public schools and the operations manager of the Philippine National Railways, T.-C. was expected to prepare for a career of service in the postwar Philippines. She became valedictorian of the 1955 class at the University of the Philippines College of Law, and began to write short fiction while waiting for results of the bar examination. In 1956 she proceeded, on scholarship, to Harvard Law School where she received her LL.M. in 1957. At Widener Library meanwhile she discovered prejudicial statements about her country in supposedly authoritative sources. Consequently she decided neither to practice law nor to teach it, but to become an advocate for her people through researching and writing historical fiction. T.-C. became the first Filipina to receive a grant from the Radcliffe Institute (1974–1975); in 1984 she held a Djerassi Foundation in-residence grant in California; and in 1988 she received a Massachusetts Artists Foundation Award. With each opportunity she persisted in dramatizing the difficulty of Filipinos, during centuries of Spanish and American colonialism, to find satisfactory terms for self-definition and -determination.

The Peninsulars (1964) set a precedent for reconstructing confrontations in Manila, during the 19th c., between Spanish liberals and conservatives, which so weakened the colonial administration that incursions by the Dutch and later by the British were possible. In 1979, T.-C. published *The Three-Cornered Sun,* a novel of the ill-fated revolution of 1896–1898. Not only were the Span-

iards far better equipped militarily than the Filipino insurgents, but the latter were divided into factions. The novel shows how aristocratic dilettantes, at first in combat as if at play, learned in their defeat the rightness of the national cause and the need for solidarity. The same pattern of naïveté gradually and painfully enlightened appears in *Ten Thousand Seeds* (1987). This time, however, it is the Americans who, coming as liberators, found themselves substitute rulers instead, and understood such realities better only at the outbreak of the Philippine-American War in 1899.

T.-C.'s later novels have concentrated on oppression of Filipinos by their own countrymen who have put greed, nepotism, and factionalism before the national interest, especially during the martial-law years of President Ferdinand Marcos (1972–1981). *Dread Empire* (1980) reveals how a provincial strongman managed to imitate Marcos's tactics locally; *Hazards of Distance* (1981) pictures how ordinary citizens became caught between government violence and the Communist New People's Army; and *Fortress in the Plaza* (1985) dramatizes the impact on decent families of the political opposition's actual massacre, in a Manila public square, in 1972. As censorship tightened, T.-C., found her audience in London, with *Awaiting Trespass* (1985), a novel of the martyrdom of a presumed wastrel secretly helping imprisoned detainees; and *Wings of Stone* (1986), a tale of an expatriate's return from America during the election of 1984 which, along with the 1983 assassination of a more illustrious returnee, Ninoy Aquino, ignited the final stages of revolt against Marcos. *A Small Party in a Garden* (1988) personalizes the régime's brutality through the gang rape of a politically neutral woman, one of Imelda Marcos's lesser staff, by men in uniform.

Despite marriage to an American, T. C. has retained her Philippine citizenship. Yet she has tried not to be chauvinistic in her judgments, but to distinguish persons of good will among the Spaniards and Americans, as well as—when necessary—to indict Filipinos who have betrayed the ideals of self-sacrifice and service.

FURTHER WORKS: *The Transparent Sun, and Other Stories* (1963); *The Secret Runner, and Other Stories* (1974); *Common Continent, 19 Stories* (1991)

BIBLIOGRAPHY: Casper, L., *New Writing from the Philippines* (1966), 134–37; Galdon, J., ed., *Philippine Fiction* (1972), 193–202; Casper, L., *Firewalkers* (1987), 158–61; Valeros, F. B., and E. Valeros-Gruenberg, eds., *Filipino Writers in English* (1987), 52

LEONARD CASPER

TYLER, Anne

American novelist, b. 25 Oct. 1941, Minneapolis, Minn.

T. was raised and educated in North Carolina and has lived in Baltimore for much of her adult life. She considers herself a Southern writer and has stated that the influence of Eudora Welty (q.v.) was crucial in her decision to write fiction. The South is often the setting for her fiction and, in her hands, small-town Maryland is definitively part of that region. T. studied writing with Reynolds Price (b. 1933) at Duke University, but her major in Russian preserved her from what she calls the hardest time for many writers, "that dead spot after college . . . and before their first published work." After graduation from Duke, T. did graduate work in Russian studies at Columbia and worked, among other miscellaneous jobs, as a bibliographer, ordering books from the Soviet Union, before publishing her first novel, *If Morning Ever Comes* (1964). The professional "dead spot" was not only filled with various lively activities, but was also notably brief. From that first book through *Saint Maybe* (1991), T. has published a total of twelve novels to increasing critical praise and public attention.

Despite her acknowledged debt to Welty, T. is not a Southern writer in the gothic sense of the term, nor does she write regional chronicles of loss. Rather, the South is the essential, realistically conceived background for snapshots of persons and places, images designed and executed with meticulous craft. All the commentators on her earlier work remarked on their sense of T.'s careful attention to the means of expression. Some of them saw it as excessive caution, the failure or deliberate refusal to take risks, whereas others admired the concern for technique. Only in the second part of her oeuvre did critics regularly begin to note T.'s subtle wit and the way it informs not only the writing itself but the rendering of character.

Since *Searching for Caleb* (1976), T.'s novels have been recognized for their power in combining comic and serious elements, and their frequent creation of a particular comic figure. Thus, Morgan Gower of *Morgan's Passing* (1980) is described by Stella Nesanovich in the *Southern Review* (1981) as "a genuine eccentric in an urban setting, a comic anti-hero." And Benjamin DeMott, writing in the *New York Times* (1982), calls *Dinner at the Homesick Restaurant* (1982) "an extremely beautiful book," and also characterizes it as "funny, heart-hammering, [and] wise." *The Accidental Tourist* (1985), which shares these qualities, had an even better reception, especially since it was adapted into a popular film without their being

lost. In this and her work since, the hallmark of sensitivity to the eccentric in the ordinary continues to develop, such that the pains T. takes are no longer perceived as a false or unfortunate emphasis, but rather an organic support for content that manages to embrace the tragic and the comic at once.

T. is one of the very few contemporary American writers whose work effortlessly crosses the boundary between "high" and "popular" fiction. As the themes of her novels frequently involve the quirks and eccentricities of characters or events in ordinary life, the experience of reading one of her novels also involves the sense of crossing over, this time from the mundane to the nearly surreal and back again.

FURTHER WORKS: *The Tin Can Tree* (1965); *A Slipping-Down Life* (1970); *The Clock Winder* (1972); *Celestial Navigation* (1974); *Earthly Possessions* (1977); *Breathing Lessons* (1988)

BIBLIOGRAPHY: Linton, K., *The Temporal Horizon: A Study of the Theme of Time in A. T.'s Major Novels* (1989); Voelker, J. C., *Art and the Accidental in A. T.* (1989); Stephens, C. R., ed., *The Fiction of A. T.* (1990); Petry, A. H., *Understanding A. T.* (1990)

LILLIAN S. ROBINSON

al-'UJAYLĪ, 'Abd al-Salām

Syrian novelist, short-story writer, travel writer, and essayist, b. July 1918 or 1919, Raqqah

U. was born at Raqqah on the Euphrates, and comes of a family that claims descent from the Prophet Muhammad. The absence of birth registration in Syria at the time of his birth has made it uncertain whether U. was born in 1918 or 1919. After schooling at Raqqah and Aleppo, he entered the University of Dasmascus to study medicine, and was admitted to the degree of Doctor of Medicine in 1945. Soon afterward, he entered politics, and was elected a representative for Raqqah in the Syrian National Assembly in 1947. For a brief period (April–September 1962) he was a minister in the Syrian government, but he does not seem to have relished political power and instead devoted himself to the practice of his profession of medicine.

U. has traveled widely, and he has written a number of travel books. Nevertheless he has continued to make his home in Raqqah, and has thereby retained close ties with the Syrian countryside and traditional Arab life only indirectly touched by Western influences.

U. made his first attempts at literary composition when he was only twelve, and his first published work, the bedouin story "Nūmān" (1936; Numan), appeared before he was twenty. Since then he has contributed to many literary genres, but most significantly to the essay, the novella, and the short story. His first collection of short stories, *Bint al-Sāhirah* (daughter of the sorceress), appeared in 1948. Examples of his work have been translated into a number of languages, including English, French, German, and Spanish. U.'s work has been the subject of a great deal of attention from Arab critics: the two published bibliographies devoted to him list nearly 400 critical articles and books by Arab authors dealing with his literary production.

U. sees human existence as a continual struggle between inadequate human strength and ineluctable fate. He is thus much influenced by the ancient Arab concept of *qadar* (predestination), but he believes at the same time in the stubborn resilience of humans in the face of a threatening universe.

U. sets a distance between himself and the play of human interests and human actions, while finding in them rich and fertile material for portrayal and comment. He is a keen-eyed observer of the social scene but has not tried to analyze the structure of social struggles or the clash of class interests in his fiction. One cause, however, about which U. feels deeply is that of the dispossessed Palestinians. He has dealt with this subject in political articles and in some of his short stories, notably "Nubū'āt al-shaykh Salmān" (1965; the prophecies of shaykh Salman), which portrays the almost mystical yearning of the Palestinians for their lost land.

U.'s attitude of detachment is closely connected with his engrained scepticism. This is well illustrated in his short story "al-Ru'yā" (1953; "The Dream," 1967), in which an ignorant village religious dignitary interprets the dream of one of the superstitious villagers as meaning that the man will shortly die. The local schoolmaster, appalled by this, fights fire with fire by persuading the man that with supernatural aid his imminent demise can be avoided. The ironic twist at the end of the story in no way detracts from the sceptical note struck throughout the narrative.

"Al-Ru'yā" deals with scepticism towards superstitious and religious obscurantism; the novella *Hikāyat majānīn* (1971; *Madness,* 1988) is informed with a more comprehensive scepticism. It takes the form of an account of a car ride in which the lives and careers of the passengers are contrasted with the life of a madwoman, and presents a comparison between two sorts of madness: madness in the sense of insanity and madness in the sense of the pursuit of futility and illusion. In this novella U. seems to have moved some way from his accustomed realism toward symbolism (q.v.).

U.'s scepticism is, however, not totally unshakable. In one of the most interesting and suggestive of his essays, entitled "Ishhad yā tabīb" (1978; bear witness, o physician!), U. describes an extraordinary Sufi ceremony performed at his family residence in Raqqah. This ceremony involves the self-infliction of wounds on themselves by religious devotees, which leave no mark and leave the victims apparently none the worse physically. U. uses the inexplicable events of this so-called *darb* (blow) ceremony to point up the perplexity experienced by those like himself educated in

Western science, who are brought face to face with phenomena and aspects of traditional Eastern life that cannot be reconciled with their scientific knowledge—and yet which cannot be refuted by it.

Much of U.'s work displays an attractive sardonic humor. This is seen to best advantage in his *Maqāmāt* (1962; assemblies), a collection of comic dramatic anecdotes in rhymed prose, in the Arabic tradition of Badī' al-Zamān al-Hamadhānī (968–1008) and al-Qāsim b. 'Alī-al-Harīrī (1054–1122).

U.'s style has changed little during his long career as an author, although his work as a whole shows great diversity of theme and treatment. He disposes of a very wide vocabulary, and writes exclusively in literary Arabic, eschewing the use of colloquial dialects favored by some modern writers of Arabic fiction. His literary output is large, and some of it will probably prove to be ephemeral, but there can be no doubt that among his contributions to the art of the short story and the essay there are works that will have a permanent place in Arabic literature.

FURTHER WORKS: *Sā'at al-mulāzim* (1954); *Ashyā' shakhsiyyah* (1968); *Ahādīth al-'ashiyyāt* (1971); *Fāris madīnat al-qantarah* (1971); *Qulūb 'alā al-aslāk* (1974); *al-Sayf wa-al-tābūt* (1974); *Azāhīr tishrīn al-mudammah* (1976); *al-Hubb al-hazīn* (1977); *'Iyādah fī al-rīf* (1978); *al-Maghmūrūn* (1979)

BIBLIOGRAPHY: Young, M. J. L., "A. S. U. and his Maqāmāt," *Middle East Studies,* 14, 2 (1978), 205–10; Allen, R., ed., *Modern Arabic Literature* (1987), 329–32; Ramos Calvo, A. M., "Visión de España en la literatura árabe contemporanea: dos ejemplos sirios," in Agreda, F. de, ed., *La traducción y la crítica literaria: actas de las jornadas de Hispanismo árabe* (1990), 255–62

M. J. L. YOUNG

UKRAINIAN LITERATURE

See Volume 4, page 492.

The historical events of the late 1980s and early 1990s have had a profound impact on the development of Ukrainian literature. Gorbachev's policy of glasnost and perestroika eventually led to the birth of the "Rukh" (movement), an umbrella organization for reformers that initially defined itself as "the Popular Movement in Support of Perestroika." Rukh was the child of poets. Its nine-man coordinating committee, which came into being in Kiev early in 1989, included personalities of Ukrainian literature such as the renowned poets

Ivan Drach (q.v.) and Dmytro Pavlychko (b. 1929), the literary scholar Vyacheslav Bryukhovetsky (b. 1947), the literary critic and editor Vitaly Donchyk (b. 1932), the writer Anatoly Shevchenko (b. 1932), and the theater specialist Les Tanyuk (b. 1938). Rukh held its founding congress in Kiev in September 1989, with 1,109 delegates attending, representing some 280,000 members. Ivan Drach was elected as its first chairman, and the noted novelist Volodymyr Yavorivsky (b. 1942) chairman of its "Grand Council." The emergence of Rukh was a most important factor in Ukrainian literary and cultural life. The movement provided vigor and vitality to Ukrainian literature and set new directions for its future development. Additional important events that influenced literary life in Ukraine are the proclamation of Ukraine's independence on 24 August 1991 by the Ukrainian Rada (Parliament), and the subsequent overwhelming affirmation of that proclamation by a popular referendum. Perhaps the most important factor in the recent development of Ukrainian literature, however, was the tragedy of Chernobyl on 26 April 1986, which not only found wide reverberation in Ukrainian literature, both in Ukraine and in the diaspora, but also gave rise to a rage that engendered determined resistance.

As a result of these events, several important and very positive developments have occurred: Freedom of expression prevails, and the phenomenon of "dissidentism" has been relegated to history; the restoration of hundreds of writers whose names were taboo during the so-called era of stagnation is taking place—the Kiev-based literary scholar Mykola Zhulynsky (b. 1940) speaks of a total of 300 of such individuals; and the task of the inclusion of Ukrainian émigré writers, both dead and alive, into the mainstream of literary life in Ukraine has been initiated. In light of these developments one can speak of a unification process of Ukrainian literature. If allowed to continue, this process will lead to an unprecedented unity of Ukrainian literature. For the first time in history, Ukrainian literature will be without any artificial barriers or divisions and without "forgotten" names or forbidden books.

Among the former dissidents who are now active are the poet Ihor Kalynets (b. 1939), the poet and essayist Yevhen Sverstyuk (b. 1928), the poet and critic Ivan Svitlychny (1929–1992), and the poet and novelist Mykola Rudenko (q.v.) who recently returned to Ukraine from the U.S. Among the deceased victims of Stalinism who have been rehabilitated are the writer and political activist Mykola Khvylovy (1893–1933), the dramatist Mykola Kulish (1892–1937?), and the neoclassical poets Mykola Zerov (1890–1941) and Mykhaylo

Dray-Khmara (1889–1939), as well as the most recent victim, Vasyl Stus (q.v.), whose posthumously published collection *Doroha bolyu* (1990; the way of pain) has been received with great acclaim. Heading the list of rehabilitated dead émigré literati is the novelist and dramatist Volodymyr Vynnychenko (1880–1951). He is followed by Yevhen Malanyuk (1897–1968), Olena Teliha (1907–1942), and Oleh Olzhych (pseud. of Oleh Kandyba, 1908–1944)—all known previously as "bourgeois nationalist" poets—the neoclassicist poet Yury Klen (pseud. of Oswald Burkhardt, 1891–1947), and the novelist Ivan Bahryany (1907–1963). The living émigré writers now appearing in print in Ukraine include Bohdan Boychuk (b. 1927) and Bohdan Rubchak (b. 1935), both of the New York Group of Ukrainian poets, the Rio de Janeiro-based poet and dramatist Vira Vovk (pseud. of Vira Selyanska, b. 1926), whose plays have helped invigorate contemporary theater in Ukraine, and the poet and essayist Ostap Tarnavsky (1917–1992), the president of SLOVO, The Association of Ukrainian Writers in Exile.

Poetry

Traditionally the strongest genre in Ukrainian literature, poetry has experienced a tremendous revival in the late 1980s. A whole new coterie of poets known as *visimdesyatnyky* (the generation of the eighties) has come into being, united in love for the Ukrainian language and in their zest for innovation and experimentation, but at the same time highly individualistic and distinct, each with his or her own poetic profile. The leading voices of this generation are Yury Andrukhovych (b. 1960), Natalka Bilotserkivets (b. 1954), Pavlo Hirnyk (b. 1956), Oleksandr Hrytsenko (b. 1957), Viktor Kordun (b. 1946), Oleh Lysheba (b. 1949), Sofiya Maydanska (b. 1948), Viktor Neborak (b. 1961), Oksana Pakhlovska (b. 1956), Mykola Ryabchuk (b. 1953), Volodymyr Tsybulko (b. 1964), Oksana Zabuzhko (b. 1960), and Ihor Rymaruk (b. 1958), whose collection *Nichni holosy* (1991; voices of the night) reflects most succinctly the new directions of contemporary Ukrainian poetry.

Especially noteworthy are five women poets whose most important works were published between 1988 and 1990. Sofiya Maydanska's *Povnolittya nadiyi* (1988; hope coming of age), a collection of subjective lyrical poetry written in an optimistic mood celebrating life and beauty of nature, and her *Osvidchennya* (1990; declaration), which consists of seventy letters written to the reader, are fine examples of her art. The pithy and often compressed form of these poems enables the

author to communicate to the reader in a highly poetic manner her intellectual and social concerns and her love for her country and her people. A vivid imagination coupled with a pleasant sense of humor characterizes the collection *Chayna tseremoniya* (1990; tea ceremony) by Iryna Zhylenko, while Oksana Zabuzhko's *Dyryhent ostannoyi svichky* (1990; the bearer of the last candle) is informed by feelings of strong anger, a sense of profound sorrow, and an all-pervasive touch of bitter-sweet irony. Noteworthy is also Mariya Vlad's (b. 1940) poetry, such as her collection *Virshi ta poemy* (1990; poems and narrative poems), which is steeped in the natural beauty of the Hutsul region and its rich folklore tradition, but transcends aesthetically its regional confines. Lina Kostenko's (q.v.) *Vybrane* (1989; selected works) occupies a special place in this poetry written by women. Characterized by a universal, human concern, these works display no marked feminist tendencies; they are, for the most part, nonideological, apolitical, and intensely personal.

An important event in the annals of contemporary Ukrainian poetry is the publication of *Ikar na metelykovykh krylakh* (*Icarus on the Wings of a Butterfly,* 1991) by Vasyl Holoborodko (b. 1942), who made his literary debut in the 1960s, but whose work had been suppressed. The tragic history of Ukraine and the sufferings of its people form the subject matter of this collection, in which the author's personal reminiscences and observations are interspersed with historical motifs. Equally moving is Hryhory Chubay's (1949–1982) poetry with the revealing title *Hovoryty, movchaty i hovoryty znovu* (1989; to speak, to be silent, and to speak again), which expresses the tragic ethos of the 1970s, while the collections *Pohulyanka odyntsem* (1990; walking alone) by Mykola Vorobyov (b. 1941) and *Khymera* (1989; chimera) by Vasyl Ruban (b. 1942) display an interesting bent for experimentation with language. Two books by Hennady Moroz (b. 1948), *Veresnevi dni* (1985; days of September) and especially his latest, *Zemlya* (1989; the earth), show great promise.

The thematic diversity of contemporary Ukrainian poetry is astounding. Religious themes and motifs abound. While some poets champion Christianity, others bemoan the passing of the pagan age and accuse Christianity of eliminating it. There are frequent allusions to ecological problems that beset contemporary Ukraine, and the vicissitudes of life in the 20th c. are confronted there. The Ukrainian language and its sorrowful state are the subject of many poems and Ukraine's tragic plight throughout its history is acknowledged. Poetry in the 1980s and 1990s appears to serve as a form of catharsis, which enables both the poet and the reader to come to terms with personal and national dilemmas.

Fiction

Just like poetry, Ukrainian prose experienced a revival in the latter part of the 1980s. Roman Ivanychuk (b. 1929), author of significant historical prose, wrote a number of short stories, and was awarded the Shevchenko Prize (1985) for his latest novels, *Voda z kamenyu* (1982; water from the stone) and *Chetverty vymir* (1984; the fourth dimension). The prolific prize-winning novelist Yury Mushketyk (b. 1929) attracted considerable attention with his work *Yasa* (1987; Yasa), which celebrates in a heightened poetic manner the Ukrainian Cossack past. The novel portrays the Cossacks as fierce and brave warriors and their leaders as cultured, intelligent people whose heroic struggle against czarist Russian imperialism flows from the natural desire for freedom and sovereignty. The Chernobyl catastrophe, which received its due in poetry, notably by Drach, Kostenko, and Maydanska, among others, was best captured in prose by Volodymyr Yavorivsky's (b. 1942) novel *Mariya z polynom u kintsi stolittya* (1988; Maria with wormwood at the end of the century). Divided into 109 brief chapters (some of them less than half of a page), the work succeeds in conveying the suffering and sorrow of the simple people affected by the disaster. A kind of neo-Rousseauism informs the work of Oleksandr Hyzha (b. 1936) as evident from his two novels *Hlyboka mezha* (1987; the deep furrow) and its sequel, *Zhytni plachi* (1990; the laments of rye), which portray the Ukrainian peasants as simple yet noble human beings whose contact with the soil keeps them pure and unspoiled. In sharp contrast to the people are the dehumanizing forces of the collective system that cripple the human soul and destroy humanity.

Mykola Olynyk's (b. 1923) novel *Dochka Prometeya* (1990; daughter of Prometheus) and Valentyn Tarnavsky's (b. 1951) *Porozhny pedestal* (1990; the empty pedestal) are also works that will stand the test of time.

The thematic range of Ukrainian prose is just as wide as that of poetry. Traditional style alternates with "neo-avant-garde" mannerisms. Young authors attempt to establish themselves, and the older ones strive to reinvigorate or to restructure the creative process.

The Essay

The other avenues of literary expression—the essay and literary criticism—also flourish. Of special importance is Oles Honchar's (q.v.) *Chym*

zhyvemo: Na shlyakhakh do ukrayinskoho vidrodzhennya (1991; how we live: on the path to a Ukrainian rebirth), a collection of essays, speeches, interviews, and notes written on various occasions from 1966 to 1991, which reflect the zeitgeist of the three decades and chronicle the struggle of Ukrainian intellectuals for cultural and national independence: and Valery Shevchuk's (q.v.) *Doroha v tysyachu rokiv* (1990; the way into the millennium), which seeks to portray a deeper understanding of Ukrainian history and culture. A new rigorous scholarly approach is seen in Ivan Dzyuba's (b. 1931) examination of Taras Shevchenko's relations with the Slavophiles, *U vsyakoho svoya dolya* (1989; each has his own fate), and in Anatoly Pohribny's (b. 1942) trenchant studies of the writer and lexicographer Borys Hrinchenko (1863–1910), published in 1988 and 1990.

The new freedom has given rise to lively literary discussions on the pages of the *Literaturna Ukrayina* and in other journals. To reflect more accurately the new reality, some journals have changed their names. *Radyanske Literaturoznavstvo* (Soviet literary studies) has become *Slovo i Chas* (word and time), and many new literary journals and magazines have been founded. Among them is *Svito-Vyd* (the organ of the Kiev branch of the Writers Union and the New York Group, the first issue of which appeared in 1990), *Ternopil* (founded in January 1991), and a number of children's magazines.

Drama

The drama is traditionally the weakest genre of Ukrainian literature. Centuries of statelessness and the colonial status of Ukraine within the Soviet Union have precluded the development of a bona fide national theater. Such talented dramatists as Volodymyr Vynnychenko (1880–1951), Mykola Kulish (1892–1942), and to a lesser degree Ivan Kocherha (1881–1952) were frequently not afforded the opportunity to see their plays on Ukrainian stages. On the other hand, the works of Oleksandr Kornychuk (1905–1972), written and produced in accordance with the doctrine of Socialist Realism (q.v.), enjoyed considerable success, as did the plays of Mykola Zarudny (b. 1921), who is still active in the contemporary Ukrainian theater.

Among the leading dramatists in the 1980s is Larysa Khorolets (b. 1948), whose plays, such as *Trety* (1982; the third) and *V okeani bezvisti* (1985; in the ocean of obscurity), enjoy great popularity and have been translated into several languages; Oleksy Kolomiyets (b. 1919), whose plays *Uby leva* (1984; kill the lion) and *Zlyva* (1985; deluge) have received wide acclaim; and Vasyl Melnyk

(b. 1937), author of numerous one-act plays, among them the vaudeville comedy *Molodyata* (the young couple) and the historical drama *Dolya i pisnya* (fate and song), about the life of the bard of Bukovyna, Yury Fedkovych (1834–1888).

Some contemporary dramatists write both for the theater and the film industry. Among these are Bohdan Chaly (b. 1924), Ihor Malyshevsky (b. 1936), Vsevolod Nestayko (b. 1930), and Yury Shcherbak (b. 1934). Nelya Sheyko-Medvedyeva (b. 1947) is successful as a children's dramatist as attested by her collection of plays, *Kvitka shchyastya* (1986; flower of happiness), and as a scholar of the theater and drama.

In an article aptly entitled, "Istorychna patoheneza ukrayinskoyi dramy" (the historical pathogenesis of Ukrainian drama), published in the November 1991 issue of the journal *Sučasnist'* (Newark, New Jersey), Lina Kostenko analyses the "catastrophic" state of Ukrainian theater and drama. Although focusing on the negatives of past and present, she nonetheless predicts an imminent revival of both theater and drama in Ukraine.

Ukraine's newly won independence and statehood assure Ukrainian literature a prominent place in the family of national literatures in the 21st c.

BIBLIOGRAPHY: Rubchak, B., "Homes As Shells: Ukrainian Émigré Poetry," in Rozumnyj, J., ed., *New Soil, Old Roots* (1983), 87–123; Bahry, R. M., ed., *Echoes of Glasnost in Soviet Ukraine* (1989), 123–29, 151–70; Sajewych, G., and A. Sorokowski, eds., *The Popular Movement of Ukraine for Restructuring* (1989); Rudnytzky, L., "A Miracle in Continuity: Christian Themes and Motifs in Soviet Ukrainian Literature," *UQ*, 46 (1990), 34–44; Rubchak, B., "Because We Have No Time: Recent Ukrainian Poetry," *Agni*, 33 (1991), 278–304; Onyshkevych, L. M. L., "On the Stages of Ukraine 1990: From Sholom Aleichem to Mykola Kulish," *Soviet and East European Performance: Drama. Theater. Film*, 11 (1991), 49–57; Luckyj, G. S. N., *Ukrainian Literature in the Twentieth Century: A Reader's Guide* (1992)

LEONID RUDNYTZKY

UPPDAL, Kristofer

Norwegian novelist, poet, and essayist, b. 19 Feb. 1878, Beitstad, Nord-Trøndelag; d. 26 Dec. 1961, Oppdal, Sør-Trøndelag

U. is notable for his proletarian novels and lyric poetry, particularly his free verse, all of which he wrote in a version of New Norwegian strongly influenced by the dialect of his native Trøndheim. Born in the northern Trøndelag region, U. spent his youth as a farm laborer, shepherd, and hired hand in his father's livery stable. After some brief studies in folk high schools in Norway and Denmark, he worked for the next twelve years as a miner and itinerant laborer, occasionally as a newspaper reporter, traveling the length and breadth of Norway. In 1899 U. joined Norway's burgeoning labor union, at the time perhaps the most radical in Europe, in which he later served in several elected positions. In his fiction U. set himself the task of recounting the unfolding saga of Norway's new industrial worker—the miner, the railroad worker, the union organizer. The period after World War I was one of rapid industrialization in Norway when men by the thousands were leaving their villages and joining railroad crews or flocking to the cities in search of factory jobs. For U. these men represented, at the least, a new phase in the history of class relations, if not a new type of humanity altogether. In U.'s view, these workers, thanks to their newly acquired skills and political power, could look forward to a degree of freedom and self-confidence that was greater than at any previous point in history.

U. embodied this vision in a series of ten novels with the collective title of *Dansen gjennom skuggeheimen* (1911–1924; dance through the world of shadows). U.'s first novel, *Ved Akerselva* (1910; by Aker river), a realistic account of the life of an itinerant railroad worker, was originally conceived as an independent work, but after completing it U. conceived the idea for his larger work, and in 1923 he integrated the novel into the series in a revised version under the title of *Vandringa* (travels). While not autobiographical in a narrow sense, these ten novels retrace the course of U.'s life and career. In the first half of the series he tells the stories of young men as they grow up, leave home, and launch into life as itinerant laborers. In the latter half, particularly volumes seven and ten, U. focuses his attention on the complex relationships that arise between the worker and the labor union, the organization that both empowers and restricts him. The novels in their order of composition (not narrative sequence) are *Dansen gjennom skuggeheimen* (1911; dance through the world of shadows), *Trolldom i lufta* (1912; magic in the air), *Bas-Ola storbas og laget hans* (1913; big boss Ola and his crew), *Røysingfolke* (1914; people on the move), *Stigeren* (1919; the climber), *Kongen* (1920; the king), *Domkyrkjebyggaren* (1921; the cathedral builder), *I skiftet* (1922; the change), *Vandringa* (1923; travels), and *Herdsla* (1924; Herdsla). From an aesthetic standpoint, it is perhaps the first novel, from which the series derives its name, that is the most accomplished. The later novels, however, are interesting from the way in

which they reveal the almost religious significance
U. attributed to the labor movement in Norway,
and his growing pessimism when it failed to meet
his expectations.

U.'s first volumes of poetry, *Kvæde* (1905;
lament) and *Ung sorg* (1905; young sorrow), are
chiefly of historical value today, marked as they
are by conventional language and naive, nationalistic sentiment. However, his subsequent volumes, *Sol-laug* (1905; sun league), *Villfuglar* (1909;
wild birds), *Snø-rim* (1915; snow rhyme), *Solblø-
dling* (1918; sun bleeding), *Elskhug* (1919; love),
and *Altarelden* (1920; altar fire), show a steady
progression in artistry and creative freedom. As
in his fiction, U. directs his attention to the working man, portraying his passions and disappointments with immediacy and power, employing the
technique of free verse long before it became
popular in Scandinavia. In the earlier volumes,
U.'s vision is informed by a kind of pantheistic
eroticism; in the later volumes, certainly as a result
of World War I, his vision becomes darker, verging on the apocalyptic. U. devoted the final years
of his life to an immense poetic work in three
books, *Galgberget* (1930; gallows mountain), *Ha-
gamannen* (1939; Haga man), and *Løysinga* (1947;
the solution), published under the collective title
Kulten (1947; Kulten). Kulten is the name of the
protagonist of this epic work of dark Nietzschean
prophecy. He is a farmer-prophet who preaches a
dark religion of suffering and eternal return, and
as such embodies the pessimistic conclusion of
U.'s philosophical and religious speculation in his
final years.

FURTHER WORKS: *Ved Akerselva, og andre fortel-
jingar* (1910); *Jotunbrunnen* (1925); *Dikt i utval,
1878–1961* (1960); *Hestane mine; etterlatne dikt*
(1963); *Om dikting og diktarar; litterære artiklar
i utval* (1965)

BIBLIOGRAPHY: Solumsmoen, O., *K. U., Cathe-
dral-Builder* (1967)

WILLIAM E. MISHLER

VALENZUELA, Luisa
Argentine novelist, short-story writer, and journalist, b. 26 Nov. 1938, Buenos Aires

V. is one of the best-known, most critically acclaimed, and most translated contemporary Latin American authors. As the daughter of a successful Argentine novelist, Luisa Mercedes Levinson (b. 1912), V. grew up in an atmosphere of literary excitement and expectation. She worked as a journalist and editor, and published her first short story when she was eighteen. Her first novel, *Hay que sonreír* (1966; *Clara*, 1976), was written when she was homesick for Buenos Aires while living in Paris from 1959 to 1961. She participated in the University of Iowa's International Writers Program in 1969 while she wrote her second novel, *El gato eficaz* (1972; the effective cat). In 1978 V. settled in New York, where she has conducted creative writing workshops at New York University and Columbia University and has been the recipient of many grants and honors. In recent years, she has divided her time between New York City, Buenos Aires, and Tepoztlán, Mexico, all of which enter into her fiction. As well as being a prolific writer who has published six novels and five collections of short stories and novellas, V. is also vigorously involved in combating repression and censorship, both in her writing and as an active member of various international human-rights organizations.

In all of her fiction, V. has focused on the interrelated themes of politics, language, and women. She often demonstrates how language can deform the reality it purports to describe and how it can be used to oppress and manipulate, on both personal and political levels. Concern for human rights and individual freedoms permeates V.'s writing, as does her interest in the social role of gender, the factors that determine the identity of women, and sexuality. She is fascinated by myths and by dreams, frequently weaving them into her multilayered fictions, which are often complex metaphors or parables of political and social realities.

Much of V.'s fiction is recognizably descriptive of Argentina. *Aquí pasan cosas raras* (1975; *Strange Things Happen Here,* 1979), written in Argentina during a period of political terrorism, focuses on the oppression of human beings by other human beings. In the title story, two poor men are torn between their desire to improve their lives and their terror of being noticed by the police. "Los mejor calzados" ("The Best Shod") is an ironic description of how the beggars of Buenos Aires wear elegant shoes because they can appropriate the footware of the bodies dumped in heaps by the torture squads.

Como en la guerra (1977; *He Who Searches,* 1977) is a novel of multiple simultaneous levels: a mythic journey, a search for truth, and an exploratory investigation of the essence of terrorism and the relationship of torturers and victims. Although the majority of stories in *Donde viven las águilas* (1983; *Up among the Eagles,* 1988) are abstract, magical, and metaphorical, many of them also have a powerful political component. In "Los censores" ("The Censors"), a dissident becomes a supporter of repression, even though it means his own execution, and "La historia de Papito" ("Papito's Story") is a moving tale of fear and empathy in the face of military violence. *Novela negra con argentinos* (1990; *Black Novel [with Argentines],* 1992) is a surrealistic murder mystery, a metaphor of violence in contemporary Argentina, and *Realidad nacional desde la cama* (1990; national reality seen from bed) recounts the startling experiences of a woman who returns to Argentina after an absence of ten years. In a series of hilarious, bizarre encounters, the horrors of inflation, poverty, and militarism are described, mocked, and made vivid.

V. has shown herself to be immensely skillful at both realistic and imaginative description, and nearly all of her fiction combines the two levels. She celebrates the capacity of human culture for myth and invention, while denouncing the repressive political misuses of these same powers. Each of her novels and short-story collections has enhanced her reputation as one of the most important voices in contemporary Latin American literature.

FURTHER WORKS: *Los heréticos* (1967); *Libro que no muerde* (1980); *Cambio de armas* (1982; *Other Weapons,* 1985); *Cola de lagartija* (1983; *The Lizard's Tail,* 1983). FURTHER VOLUMES IN ENGLISH: *Clara: Thirteen Short Stories and a Novel* (1976); *Strange Things Happen Here: Twenty-Six*

Short Stories and a Novel (1979); *Open Door: Stories by L. V.* (1988)

BIBLIOGRAPHY: Martínez, Z. N., *El gato eficaz* de L. V.: La productividad del texto," *RCEH*, 4 (1979), 73–80; Picón Garfield, E., "Muerte—metamorfosis—modernidad: *El gato eficaz* de L. V.," *Insula*, 400–1 (1980), 17; Ordoñez, M., "Máscaras de espejos, un juego especular: Entrevista-associaciones con la escritora argentina L. V.," *RI*, 51, 132–33 (1985), 511–19; Paley Francescato, M., "*Cola de lagartija:* Látigo de la palabra y la triple P.," *RI*, 51, 132–33 (1985), 875–82; special L. V. issue, *RCF*, 6, 3 (1986); Magnarelli, S., *Reflections/Refractions: Reading L. V.* (1988); Gazarian-Gautier, M.-L., "L. V.," *Interviews with Latin American Writers* (1989), 293–322; Magnarelli, S., "L. V." in Marting, D. E., ed., *Spanish American Women Writers* (1990), 532–45

MARY G. BERG

VELOZ MAGGIOLO, Marcio

Dominican Republic novelist and short-story writer, b. 13 Aug. 1936, Santo Domingo

V. M. is one of the most important contemporary Dominican novelists. He has also written theater, poetry, essay, and history. He studied philosophy at the University of Santo Domingo, where he received his Licenciatura in 1961, and he obtained a Ph.D. in history at the University of Madrid (1970). He has been a university professor since 1962, having also been a prominent diplomat for his country in Mexico, Italy, Peru, Bolivia, Egypt, and Romania.

V. M.'s first novel was *El buen ladrón* (1960; the good thief), which obtained a mention from the William Faulkner Foundation as the best Dominican novel written after World War II. With *La vida no tiene nombre* (1965; life has no name) and *Los ángeles de hueso* (1966; angels made of bone) V. M. broke away from the traditional Dominican novel, thus initiating a renewal in that country's narrative, which culminated in *De abril en adelante* (1975; from April onward), one of the novels selected for the Seix Barral Prize in Barcelona, Spain. The novel obtained a resounding success, and initiated V. M. in the barrio and dictatorship themes, both of which became central to his later work. In 1981, with *Biografía difusa de Sombra Castañeda* (1981; diffuse biography of Sombra Castañeda), V. M. obtained the National Prize for the Novel in the Dominican Republic, followed by the National Prize for Short Stories with *La fértil agonía del amor* (1982; love's fertile

agony). With *Materia Prima* (1988; raw material) he again won the National Prize for the Novel.

His work had begun to attract attention as of the early 1970s when critics had noticed the recurrence of the theme of dictatorship, and of the figure of the dictator, as basic to V. M.'s narrative. V. M. focuses his work on experiences that, while appearing to be local on a first reading, develop universal dimensions. In his most recent novel, *Ritos de cabaret* (1991; nightclub rites), V. M. tries, as in his previous work, to transform the local Caribbean experience into material of a larger interest. He is considered a poet of prose writing, and frequently uses experimental techniques to intersperse the more traditional realist prose with the magical and hallucinatory elements characteristic of his production.

FURTHER WORKS: *El prófugo* (1962); *De donde vino la gente* (1978); *Novelas cortas* (1980); *Cuentos, recuentos y casi cuentos* (1986)

BIBLIOGRAPHY: González Cruz, L., "Desde el absurdo. La narrativa de V. M.," *ALHis*, 8 (1979), 119–25; García, J. E., "M. V. M. en el centro del cuento dominicano," *Isla abierta*, 16 (1982), 4–16; Sommer, D., *One Master for Another* (1983), 197–228; Mármol, J., "El cerco infranqueable del pasado," *Coloquio*, 4 (1989), 6–7; Amarante, H., "*Materia Prima:* el discurso del barrio," *Coloquio*, 4 (1989), 13–14; Tejada Holguín, R., "*Materia Prima:* una novela caótica o una representación del caos?," *Coloquio*, 4 (1989), 14–15

NICASIO SILVERIO

VIETNAMESE LITERATURE

See Volume 4, page 560.

After the communists took over the south in 1975, scores of writers were jailed, and their works seized and burned as "specimens of a depraved culture." In 1979 a collection of "prison songs" written between 1954 and 1978 was smuggled out to Europe. Unlike other writers who remained in the north at the time the Geneva armistice agreements partitioned Vietnam and whose works stayed close to the party line, the frail author of those poems, Nguyễn Chí Thiên (b. 1933), had spent time in various prisons, punished for daring to use poignant stanzas entitled *Hoa Ụịa-ngục* (1980; *Flowers from Hell*, 1984) to denounce communist atrocities. A worldwide movement was launched in the 1980s to demand the release of this 1985 Poetry International Prize winner as well as that of Doãn Quốc Sỹ (b. 1923), a renowned writer who moved south in 1954 and who was accused after the collapse of the Saigon government in 1975 of "ties with the U.S. and the puppet régime." After the Hanoi régime authorized some "untying" policies regarding artists and writers—one can speak of perestroika in socialist Vietnam—a "high tide" protest movement emerged between 1986 and 1990. But Dương Thu-Hương (b. 1947), a woman novelist, was condemned for her bold exposés of communist cadres' corrupt practices and her stern denunciations of the total failures of socialist functionaries. Dương's works, for example, *Thiên-đường mù* (1988; pub. in French as *Les paradis aveugles,* 1991), caused her expulsion from the Communist Party and from the Writers' Association. These three writers were released in November 1991 thanks to international pressure.

Writers in exile since the fall of Saigon have kept up the tempo of literary output overseas, facilitated by the appearance of several publishing houses, which started with pirate editions of the most popular pre-1975 writings by South Vietnam's authors. Monthly and weekly literary magazines, published in California (for example, *Văn* and *Tạp-chí Văn-học*), Texas, Washington, and Louisiana, as well as in Canada (for example, *Làng Văn*), France (for example, *Quê Mẹ*), and Germany (for example, *Độc-lập*), provide recreational readings to a large refugee audience.

The best-known authors are Võ Phiến (b. 1925), Mai Thảo (b. 1927), Duyên Anh (b. 1935), Nguyễn Mộng Giác (b. 1940), Lê Tất Điều (b. 1942), and Nguyễn Ngọc Ngạn (b. 1945). Võ Phiến's works published in the U.S. are either reprints of novels and short stories published in South Vietnam prior to 1975 or completely new creations, including delightful short stories and several volumes of excellent essays. Mai Thảo has kept up his productivity in prose and poetry besides being the publisher-editor of a monthly magazine, *Văn.* Nguyễn Mộng Giác has had short stories as well as two trilogies published in the U.S.: *Mùa biển động* (1986–1987; season of rough seas) and *Sông Côn Mùa lũ* (1990; Côn River at flood season). Lê Tất Điều has contributed novels, short stories, and essays as well as satirical writings with political overtones. Duyên Anh, who before his self-exile in France used to write stories about street urchins, has had two of his novels published in Paris: *Một người Nga ở Saigon* (1983; pub. in French as *Un Russe à Saigon,* 1986) and *Đồi Fanta* (1983; pub. in French as *La colline de Fanta,* 1989). The most prolific is certainly Nguyễn Ngọc Ngạn, who, besides *The Will of Heaven* (1982, with E. E. Richey), has turned out dozens of novels and short stories in Vietnamese, notably *Sân khấu cuộc đời* (1986; life as a stage), *Biển vẫn đợi chờ* (1984; the sea is still waiting), *Cõi đêm* (1982; night world), *Nước* (1986; muddy

waters), and *Truyện ngắn* (2 vols., 1982, 1986; short stories). Memoirs by former political and military figures of South Vietnam are of uneven quality.

The overseas writers' ranks have also been consolidated by young faces, including some remarkable female refugees, notably Phan Thị Trọng-Tuyến (b. 1951), Lê Thị Huê (b. 1953), Vũ Quỳnh-Hương (b. 1957), and Trần Diêu Hằng (b. 1952).

BIBLIOGRAPHY: Huỳnh Sanh Thông, "Main Trends of Vietnamese Literature between the Two World Wars," *The Vietnam Forum,* 3 (1984), 99–125; Durand, M. M., and Nguyễn-Trần Huân, *An Introduction to Vietnamese Literature* (1985); Võ-Phiến, "Writers in South Vietnam, 1954–1975," *The Vietnam Forum,* 7 (1986), 176–99; Xuân-Diêu, "Apport de la poésie française dans la poésie vietnamienne moderne," *The Vietnam Forum,* 5 (1985), 146–63

DINH-HOA NGUYEN

VIÑAS, David

Argentine novelist, critic, and essayist, b. 1929, Buenos Aires

V. studied philosophy and letters at the University of Buenos Aires and later at the University of Rosario, where he received a Ph.D. in 1963. He forms part of Argentina's so-called Generation of 1950, ideologically centered around opposition to the régime of Perón. In a continental context he is linked to the well-known "boom" of the 1960s. His writings all reveal his concerns for the masses; he is an excellent example of a Latin American social realist with strong Marxist tendencies.

Two vital and related ideas unite nearly all his essays, novels, and short stories: an analysis of the political history of Argentina and, to a lesser extent, that of all Latin America; and a search of Argentina's sociopolitical identity and heritage as expressed in his creative art and literature. The first idea pervades the essays *Argentina: Ejército y oligarquía* (1967; Argentina: the military and the oligarchy), *México y Cortés* (1978; Mexico and Cortes), and *Yrigoyen entre Borges y Arlt* (1989; Yrigoyen between Borges and Arlt). The works *Literatura argentina y realidad política* (1964; Argentine literature and political reality) and *Indios, ejército y frontera* (1982; Indians, the military, and the border) represent the second theme, exploring the complexities of Argentine society and literature.

Interest in Argentine identity pervades all of V.'s novels and stories. He published his first short story, "Los desorientados" (1952; the disoriented), during the height of Peronism yet did not shrink from criticizing the social ills that then beset Argentina. His earliest novels, *Cayó sobre su rostro* (1955; he fell on his face), *Los dueños de la tierra* (1959; the lords of the land), and *Dar la cara* (1962; turn the other cheek), examine and occasionally propose Marxist-oriented political solutions for his ailing country. In *Un Dios cotidiano* (1957; an everyday god) V. explores the difficulty of adopting radically independent religious or political positions; those who do are either completely rejected or are forcibly brought in line by the "establishment." V.'s essays are courageous and straightforward, never seeming to fear the censorship and possible repression that have plagued much of Argentina in the last half of the 20th c.

In 1955 V. received the esteemed Gerchunoff Prize as well as the Buenos Aires Municipal Prize for his first novel; other novels have also been honored by awards from Argentina's Kraft and Losada publishing houses in 1957 and 1958 respectively. The author's best-known work, *Los hombres de a caballo* (1967; men on horseback), received the 1967 Casa de las Américas Prize for best novel of the year, an indication that his national concerns were now appreciated and understood on a continental level. The novel's story line is rather simplistic, but the frequent flashbacks, difficult monologues, bits of conversations, and fragmented narration link the novel's complex structure to similar experiments by Julio Cortázar and Carlos Fuentes (qq.v.) during the same decade. False notions of patriotism, irrational family loyalties, and supposed continental unity all come under some fire, but the military is always the main target.

In recent years V.'s committed literature has delved into the "Dirty War" and the persecution of Argentine leftists and intellectuals. *Cuerpo a cuerpo* (1979; body to body) is an autobiographical testimonial of deep human suffering during the 1976–1977 period of repression, told through the eyes of a journalist who is writing a biography of one of Argentina's famous generals. In keeping with his vital concerns for his native country, V. published *Carlos Gardel* (1979; Carlos Gardel), a type of literary homage to that national hero/ singer; the book is an analysis of immigration as a basic component of the national character.

V. has also written and produced several plays and television shows, often based on his novels or short stories, but few have enjoyed the success of his novels. Argentina also knows him as a thoughtful newspaper columnist and editor. In this medium he has continued the same intellectual concerns with the relationship between the individual Argentine and society, and the conflicts between the elites in power and those with none. To date

his works have not been published in English translation. His eleven novels, thirteen books of essays, one collection of short stories, *Las malas costumbres* (1963; bad habits), poetry, theatrical works, movie scripts, and numerous articles and stories make him one of the most prolific Argentine writers of the 20th c.

FURTHER WORKS: *Los años despiadados* (1956); *Laferrère: del apogeo de la oligarquía a la ciudad liberal* (1965); *En la semana trágica* (1966); *Cosas concretas* (1969); *Rebeliones populares argentinas* (1971); *Grotesco, inmigración y fracaso: Armando Discépolo* (1973); *Juaría* (1974); *Literatura argentina y realidad política. Apogeo de la oligarquía* (1975); *Qué es el fascismo en Latinoamérica* (1977); *Ultramar* (1980); *Anarquistas en América Latina* (1983)

BIBLIOGRAPHY: Grossi, H. M., "Angry Young Argentine: D. V. Speaks His Mind," *Américas* (Jan. 1960), 14–17; Dellepiane, A. B., "La novela argentina desde 1950 a 1965," *RI,* 34, 66 (Dec. 1968), 253–59; Rasi, H., "D. V., novelista y crítico comprometido," *RI,* 42, 95 (June 1976), 259–65; Glickman, N., "V.'s *En la semana trágica:* A Novelist's Focus on Argentine Pogrom," *Yiddish* (Fall 1984), 64–71; Valverde, E., *D. V.: en busca de una síntesis de la historia argentina* (1989)

THOMAS E. LYON

VOYNOVICH, Vladimir Nikolaevich
Russian novelist, short-story writer, and dramatist, b. 26 Sept. 1932, Dushanbe

One of Russia's finest contemporary satirists, V. began writing during the Thaw of the 1960s. His formal education was limited to one and a half years at a pedagogical institute in Moscow. While in the Soviet army (1951–1955), V. began writing poetry. In 1960 one of his songs became the unofficial "Anthem of Soviet Cosmonauts." His literary career soared after January 1961 with the publication of his novella "My zdes' zhyvem" (1961; "We Live Here," 1979) in the prestigious *Novyi Mir*. By the early 1970s, V. was recognized as a leading Soviet writer.

During the late 1960s and early 1970s V. became a fighter for human rights, gradually becoming a dissident. This process began after he signed letters defending Andrey Sinyavsky (q.v.) and Yuly Daniel (b. 1925), and later Aleksandr Solzhenitsyn (q.v.); it continued when, in 1969, he published abroad the opening sections of *Zhizn' i neobychainye prikliucheniia soldata Ivana Chonkina* (1975; rev. ed., 1990; *The Life and Extraor-*

dinary Adventures of Private Ivan Chonkin, 1977), part of which had been circulating in *samizdat* since 1963. Finally, his 1973 letter satirizing the formation of the All-Union Authors' Rights Agency (VAPP) was perceived as an open challenge to the Soviet establishment. As a result, in 1974, he was expelled from the Union of Soviet Writers, officially "for actions defaming the title of Soviet Citizen." His name became anathema, his books were banned, and he was subject to constant KGB harassment. In 1980 V. was forced to leave the Soviet Union, emigrating to West Germany. The following year he was stripped of Soviet citizenship and proclaimed an "enemy of the people."

In exile V. has taught at Princeton University, been a fellow of the Kennan Institute in Washington, D.C., and lectured widely in the West. Since glasnost, all of his works have been published in Russia and his plays performed in Moscow and other cities of the former Soviet Union. In 1990 he was fully rehabilitated and his citizenship restored. He now resides in Moscow and Stockdorf, near Munich, Germany.

V.'s early works published in *Putem vzaimnoi perepiski* (1979; *In Plain Russian,* 1979) are brutally realistic portrayals of life in rural Russia, set in villages, collective farms, and provincial towns, during the 1950s and 1960s. His characters are poorly educated, rootless, isolated, and lonely peasants, town dwellers, workers, and soldiers. He exposes the moral and spiritual poverty, the atrophy of imagination and vision, and their boredom, hardships, and gray existence.

A brilliant satirist, V. uses grotesque imagery, caricature, and exaggeration to ridicule and describe an incongruous and incredible world in which all moral and ethical values are turned upside down. This talent is best revealed in his picaresque novel *Zhizn' i neobychainye prikliucheniia soldata Ivana Chonkina*. It is a hilarious attack on the sacred cows of the Soviet system: the NKVD (later KGB), the Soviet Red Army, collectivization, Lysenkovism, and even the morality of a society in which a little girl, when asked by Chonkin whom she loves better, "her mother or her father," replies: "Comrade Stalin!" V. views the world through the naive eyes of Ivan Chonkin who, like the proverbial Russian fairy-tale hero Ivan the fool, sees objects in their primary, unsophisticated, and defamiliarized sense. *Pretendent na prestol* (1979; rev. ed., 1990; *Pretender to the Throne,* 1981) continues Chonkin's adventures and misadventures. Set in a Soviet prison and under Nazi occupation, it is even more bitter, somber, and grotesque.

Many of V.'s works are permeated by strong autobiographical elements. This is particularly true of *Ivan'kiada* (1976; *The Ivankiad,* 1977), *Anti-*

sovetskii Sovetskii Soiuz (1985; *The Anti-Soviet Soviet Union,* 1986), and *Moskva 2042* (1986; rev. ed., 1990; *Moscow 2042,* 1987). His works give clear insight into *homus sovieticus*. *Ivan'kiada* is an autobiographical account of V.'s trials and tribulations during his purchase of a larger apartment. In this Kafkaesque world, V. lashes out at the official Soviet writers' establishment with its system of privileges. He paints a vivid portrait of the talentless party apparatchik Ivanko, who upon becoming a diplomat uses his position to amass material goods, especially the legendary blue diamond-studded American toilet, on which, in a surreal, fantasmagoric nightmare, Ivanko charges through a brick wall into V.'s apartment. In this work, Ivanko, a concrete, living figure, is transformed into a monster threatening the individual writer. Ivanko becomes a symbol of Soviet society and a metaphor for the whole system.

Antisovetskii Sovetskii Soiuz consists of essays, stories, parables, "fairy tales," vignettes, and anecdotes presenting a composite picture of various aspects of life, especially private lives, in the Soviet Union of the 1960s, 1970s, and 1980s. In *Shapka* V. again attacks and satirizes hack writers, the Soviet literary establishment, and the Union of Soviet Writers. Like Gogol in "The Overcoat," he uses clothing as a status symbol and form of identity.

Moskva 2024 has been called a parody of George Orwell's (q.v.) *1984* (1949) and has been compared to the works of Gogol and Andrey Bely (q.v.). Antiutopian, it is a dystopia in which V. describes a future Soviet Union as a bankrupt, demoralized, and disintegrated country. Moscowrep (The Moscow Republic) is all that remains. The novel's protagonist, the exiled writer Kartsev (modeled on V. himself), travels through time and returns to his native Moscow in 2042, sixty years into the future, after the Great August Revolution (an eerie, clairvoyant depiction of August 1991 reality). V.'s humor and satire spares nothing and no one, including the inefficient Soviet system with its inability to make anything work. He criticizes the writers' establishment, and individual writers, both in the Soviet Union and abroad. He singles out Solzhenitsyn, whom he attacks as Karnavalov (later, Czar Serafim), for his anti-Western attitudes, reactionary views, and monarchist longings. This time, V.'s comments are not limited to the Soviet Union but include his own impressions of the West, and observations of other contemporary Soviet dissident émigé writers.

V. has earned his place in the canon of Russian satirical literature, alongside Gogol, Mikhail Zoshchenko, and Vladimir Mayakovsky (qq.v.). A great satirist, he portrays an accurate picture of the world through a distorted, exaggerated, and skewed vision. He strips pretensions and verbal falsehood from words, presents things for what they really are, and makes us laugh. V.'s work is distinguished by moral integrity, honesty, and unwillingness to compromise his beliefs.

FURTHER WORKS: *My zdes' zhivem* (1963); *Povesti* (1972); *Stepen' doveriia* (1972); *Tribunal* (1986); *Shapka* (1988; *The Fur Hat*, 1989); *Khochu byt' chestnym* (1989)

BIBLIOGRAPHY: Szporluk, M., "V. V.: The Development of a New Satirical Voice," *RLT*, 14 (1976), 99–121; Hosking, G., *Beyond Socialist Realism: Soviet Fiction since Ivan Denisovich* (1980), 136–54, 243–46; Kasak, W., "V. and His Undesirable Satires," *AN*, 2 (1980), 305; Porter, R. C., "V. V. and the Comedy of Innocence," *FMLS*, 16 (1980), 97–108; Brown, E. J., *Russian Literature since the Revolution*, rev. ed. (1982), 365–70; Dunlop, J., ed., "V. V.'s *Pretender to the Throne*," in Brostrom, K. M., ed., *Russian Literature and American Critics* (1984); Starr, S. F., on *The Anti-Soviet Soviet Union*, *NYTBR*, 31 Aug. 1986, 5; Fanger, D., "Back to the Future," *PR*, 56, 3 (1989), 499–504; Baley, J., on *The Fur Hat*, *NYRB*, 3 (1990), 26; Ryan-Hayes, K., "Decoding the Dream in the Satirical Works of V. V.," *SEEJ*, 34, 3 (Fall 1990), 289–307

HELEN SEGALL

VŨ HOÀNG CHƯƠNG

Vietnamese poet and dramatist, b. 5 May 1916, Nam-định; d. 7 Sept. 1976, Saigon

One of the most active and prolific poets of modern Vietnam, French-educated in Nam-định, then Hanoi, V. H. C. studied law and worked as a railroad inspector before starting to write poetry in 1939, with his first collection published as *Thơ say* (1940; drunk poetry). People have dubbed him Vietnam's Li Po since his verse revealed someone drunk with alcohol, with music and songs, with unrequited love, with opium, and with Western dancing. In his youth V. H. C. switched to science studies, but quit early to publish his second collection, *Thơ mây* (1943; cloud poetry). He also authored the play *Trương Chi* (1944; Trương Chi, the boatman). In the early days of the resistance war against the French, he continued his productivity with *Thơ lửa* (1947; poetry of fire), appearing in the Maquis. While being a schoolteacher between 1950 and 1953, he produced two new plays in verse, before moving to the south when the Geneva armistice agreements brought about the partition of Vietnam in 1954. The first collection of poems that appeared in South Vietnam was

Rừng phong (1954; autumnal forest), followed by *Hoa đăng* (1959; flowered lantern). The public thinks a great deal of *Cảm-thông* (1960; communion). A man of delicate health, V. H. C. represented South Vietnam at the 4e Biennale Internationale de Poésie in Knokke-le-Zoute, Belgium, in 1959, and at meetings of P.E.N. International in Thailand (1964), Yugoslavia (1965), and Ivory Coast (1967).

His favorite themes were romantic love, alcohol, and opium, and his writings between 1940 and 1945 showed a mixture of classicism and modernism (q.v.). A carefully polished style continued to characterize the later creations of this bard of the prewar period, during which his poems already expressed some degree of weariness typical of his contemporaries. In later decades, when he was also a part-time teacher of Vietnamese literature, his poetry breathed more optimism in the stabilized atmosphere of anticommunist South Vietnam, which enabled all literary talents to execute long and exacting projects. Many of the poems of this period dealt with historical events, notably *Bài ca bình Bắc* (epic of the northern pacification), a narrative poem that praised the military talent of Nguyễn Huê and his victory over the Chinese Ch'ing in 1789. V. H. C. philosophically wondered about "all the question marks that completely encircle a human life."

In the early 1970s he turned away from politics and concentrated on his childhood love, Zen, the flame of Buddhist mercy, and indulged in playfully rearranging Nguyễn Du's (1765–1820) words in *Đoạn-trường Tân-thanh* (n.d.; *The Tale of Kieu*, 1983), as well as his own melodious words into twenty-eight-word sentences. In an interview in 1970 he said he was waiting for his death, and even contemplated suicide. "I no longer write poetry, and even if I write something, there will be no reader." Nobody believed him then, as South Vietnam had been offering the refugee writers and artists freedom, security, prosperity, and hope.

Arrested on 13 May 1976, more than a year after the fall of Saigon, V. H. C. died shortly after his release from Chí-Hoà prison. Overseas Vietnamese audiences still consider him their greatest poet, one whose subjectivity and sensuality are illustrated by means of metrical coherence and musical cadence.

FURTHER WORKS: *Mây* (1943); *Tâm-sự kẻ sang Tần* (1961); *Tâm-tình người đẹp* (1961, pub. in French as *Les 28 étoiles*); *Trời một phương* (1962); *Thi-tuyển* (1963, pub. in French as *Poèmes choisis*); *Ánh trăng đạo* (1966); *Bút nở hoa đàm* (1967); *Cành mai trắng mộng* (1968); *Ta đã làm chi đời ta* (n.d.)

BIBLIOGRAPHY: Bùi Xuân-Bào, *Le roman vietnamien contemporain* (1972), 270, 312–13; Nguyễn-Trần Huân, "The Literature of Vietnam, 1954–1973," in Tham Seong Chee, ed., *Essays on Literature and Society in Southeast Asia* (1981), 337; Durand, M. M., and Nguyễn-Trần Huân, *An Introduction to Vietnamese Literature* (1985), 171–72 and passim

DINH-HOA NGUYEN

VYSOTSKY, Vladimir

Russian poet, b. 25 Jan. 1938, Moscow; d. 25 July 1980, Moscow

Adored by millions of his compatriots, V. was the closest the Soviet Union has ever come to producing a genuine superstar. His extraordinary popularity as a poet-bard cut across all class lines to encompass laborers, truck drivers, soldiers, and students as well as prominent public figures. V. was born in Moscow, the child of a career military officer and translator of German. After spending the war years in evacuation in Orenburg with his mother, in 1947 V. joined his father and stepmother in occupied Germany. Two years later, V. returned to Moscow, where he finished school and entered an engineering-construction institute. But his interests lay elsewhere, and a year later, in 1957, he left the institute and entered the Moscow Art Theater School-Studio to study acting. Upon graduation V. worked in several Moscow theaters before joining the newly reorganized Taganka Theater under the leadership of Yuri Lyubimov. V. made his formal debut at the Taganka in 1964, in Lermontov's *A Hero of Our Time*. Two years later, at twenty-eight, V. played the title role in Bertolt Brecht's (q.v.) *The Life of Galileo*. Despite his coarse features and unimposing stature, V.'s bold interpretation of the great Italian astronomer established him almost overnight as one of the most promising young actors in the Soviet theater.

V. continued to perform at the Taganka until his death, always bringing to each role his unique combination of raw vigor and audacity. As the runaway convict Khlopush in the Taganka's production in 1967 of *Pugachev*, Sergey Yesenin's (q.v.) verse drama about the Pugachev uprising, the hard-drinking actor seemed to become one with the character. His other major roles in the 1970s included a guitar-playing hippie Hamlet, Lopakhin in *The Cherry Orchard*, and Svidrigailov in *Crime and Punishment*.

V. also worked as a film and television actor, appearing in more than thirty films and videos during his twenty-year career. He played a wide variety of roles, from mountain climber to Don Juan, frequently appearing with his guitar, singing ballads he himself had composed. V.'s first major role was as a wireless operator in *Vertical'* (1967; vertical). Among his other roles were the geologist Maxim in Kira Muratova's *Korotkie vstrechy* (1967; brief encounters), a White Guard lieutenant in *Sluzhili dva tovarishcha* (1968; two comrades served), and the lead in the spy thriller *Chetvortyi* (1972; the fourth man).

But for all his popularity as an actor, it was as a poet and author of some 800 songs that V. won the hearts of his countrymen. Begrudgingly tolerated but never officially recognized, during his lifetime V. saw the publication in his homeland of only fifteen of his songs and one of his poems. Yet in spite of the fact that his performances were never televised or heard on the radio, his fame rapidly spread to the farthest reaches of the Soviet Union. By the time of his death in 1980, he had become a national hero, a singer loved by people from all walks of life. V. traveled extensively throughout the country performing in factories and clubs, as well as at more formal concerts, none of which were ever publicly advertised. Tapes of his songs made by loyal fans were endlessly copied and circulated, so that his gravelly voice could be heard everywhere coming through open windows and sounding from the cabs of trucks and passing taxis.

V.'s success as a poet-bard rested largely on his ability to convey in his verses the reality of everyday life in the vernacular, often ironic language of the street. Saturated in metaphors, lyrics such as his "Okhota na volki" (the wolf hunt), reflected the fears and the yearnings of his fellow citizens. He sang of average people worn down by endlessly waiting in lines and mocked the privileged elite with access to special stores. He satirized phony veterans, their chests full of medals, and the mouthings of pompous bureaucrats. His songs of wartime heroes and ordinary soldiers were so vivid that his listeners were convinced he had served in the military; equally graphic were his "criminal songs," leading many to believe that he had served time in a labor camp.

V. was an individualist to the core. His extravagant life-style, particularly after his marriage to the French film actress Marina Vlady in 1969, only added to his stature as a folk hero. A hard drinker given to periodic binges and a wild driver, V. seemed to invite an early death, even prefiguring it in his many songs in which the hero rushes headlong toward his death. Worn down by alcohol, narcotics, and exhaustion, the forty-two-year-old V. died in a Moscow hospital of a heart attack on 25 July 1980.

Not since the death of Stalin did Moscow see such an outpouring of mourners as it did when word spread of V.'s death. On the day of his funeral, tens of thousands of people filled the streets around the Taganka Theater and along the highway leading to the cemetery. Since his death, thousands of ordinary citizens daily visit his grave in Bagankovskoe Cemetery to pay homage to the poet who "gave voice to his generation." Denied official recognition during his lifetime, V. has been posthumously canonized by the state, an irony he himself would have appreciated. In 1987, on the seventieth anniversary of the Revolution, V. was awarded the U.S.S.R. State Prize, the country's highest cultural honor. Currently, in addition to a steady stream of articles, books, recordings, and documentaries, plans are also under way to establish a museum in his honor.

FURTHER WORKS: *Nerv* (1981); *Pesni i stikhi* (2 vols., 1983); *Chetyre chetverti puti* (1988); *Ya, konechno, vernus'* . . . (1988); *Chetyre vechera s V. V.: po motivam televizionnoi peredachi* (1989)

BIBLIOGRAPHY: Smith, G. S., "V. V.," *Songs to Seven Strings* (1984), 145–79; Valdy, M., *Vladimir ou le vol arrêté* (1987); Sosin, G., and G. D. Sosin, "Moscow Coopts V.," *The New Leader*, 71 (22 Feb. 1988), 13–24; Lazarski, C., "V. V. and His Cult," *RR*, 51 (Jan. 1992), 58–71

ALMA H. LAW

ALICE WALKER

FAY WELDON

WANG MENG

A. B. YEHOSHUA

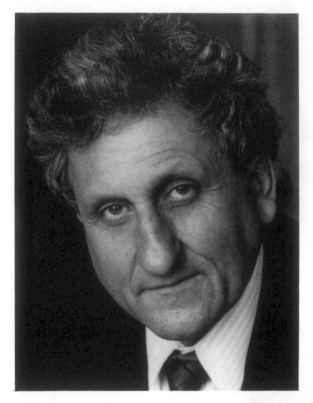

ADAM ZAGAJEWSKI

WALKER, Alice

American novelist, short-story writer, poet, critic, and essayist, b. 9 Feb. 1944, Eatonton, Ga.

W. grew up in the rural South, the youngest of eight children whose parents were sharecroppers. Blinded in one eye by an accident at the age of eight, W. was a shy and solitary child who found comfort and solace in reading books. She finished first in her class in high school and attended Spelman College in Atlanta (1961–1963), where she became involved in the Civil-Rights Movement. She completed her B.A. at Sarah Lawrence College in Bronxville, N.Y. (1965). In 1967 W. was named consultant on black history to the Friends of the Children of Mississippi. She was writer-in-residence and teacher of black studies at Jackson State College (1968–1969) and at Tougaloo College (1970–1971), and then became lecturer in literature at both Wellesley College and the University of Massachusetts in Boston (1972–1973). She was appointed Distinguished Writer in Afro-American Studies at the University of California, Berkeley, in the spring 1982 term, and Fannie Hurst Professor of Literature at Brandeis University in the fall of 1982. W. is a member of the board of trustees of Sarah Lawrence College and continues to lend her voice as a spokesperson for black women.

By the time W. published her first volume of poetry, *Once* (1968), she had already been a Bread Loaf Writer's Conference Scholar (1966), won first prize in an essay contest sponsored by *The American Scholar* (1967), and received both a Merrill Writing Fellowship and a McDowell Colony Fellowship (1967). The latter fellowship was awarded to W. again in 1977–1978. Among the many awards she has earned are two National Endowment for the Arts grants (1969 and 1977) and a Radcliffe Institute fellowship (1971–1973).

Her poetry collection *Revolutionary Petunias and Other Poems* (1973) won the Southern Regional Council's Lillian Smith Award and was nominated for a National Book Award. In 1977–1978 W. was the recipient of a Guggenheim award.

Most of the poems in her first collection, *Once,* which the then writer-in-residence at Sarah Lawrence, Muriel Rukeyser (q.v.), read and brought to the attention of an editor, were inspired by a period in W.'s senior year of college when she had to confront an unwanted pregnancy. Desperate and suicidal, W. began writing of her fears and her concerns about how her family would respond. She surmised they would react with sorrow should she kill herself, but that they would only feel shame and outrage in regard to her pregnancy. It was her recognition of the role that family/societal forces played in her life and in the lives of so many other women that allowed W. to reject the idea of suicide, to terminate the pregnancy, and then to acknowledge publicly that she had had an abortion. The poems in *Once* reflect her delight in being alive, but also contain the seeds of her attempt to promote unity among women in an effort to change not just the ways in which society defines women, but also the ways in which women define themselves.

W.'s lifelong commitment to battling sexism and racism comes directly out of her own background and experience. Much of her work focuses on the horrors of the lives of poor, uneducated black women who are emotionally and physically abused—often murdered—by black men who are themselves victims of a racist society. But she also explores the victimization of the black woman who manages to become "accepted" by white society because she has become "raceless" through education and a desire to escape her background. By cutting herself off from her African-American heritage, by rejecting her past and her family, such a woman may escape the physical pain and abuse, but must pay a devastating price in psychological and spiritual suffering. Yet such a victim in W.'s fiction usually allows W. to introduce the subject of the possibility of change, the sense, almost unthinkable before the events of the 1960s, that there are options and choices available to such women, that their futures need not resemble their pasts. Many of W.'s characters offer the hope that black women can struggle successfully against poverty and oppression, that they can and should be politically active, and that their ultimate goals must be to reclaim, reexamine, and reestablish their roles in and their relationships to their background and their heritage. And in so doing, many of W.'s female characters institute a restructured relationship between themselves and their men. It is this freedom—the ability to carve a space for themselves within white society without rejecting their roots or selling out—that for W. makes the pain and effort of the struggle worthwhile.

W.'s novel *The Third Life of Grange Copeland* (1970) and her short-story collection *In Love and Trouble: Stories of Black Women* (1973) focus directly on the fight of black women against oppression and abuse by black men. In *Meridian* (1976) W. moves into a deeper and more complex investigation of her heroine's struggle toward self-realization and autonomy. The protagonist's life serves as an extended metaphor for the black woman's fight to change what is blindly held to be valid just because it is traditional. Published some five years after *Meridian,* the stories in *You Can't Keep a Good Woman Down* (1981) indicate that W.'s themes are evolving, and that her characters are attempting to shape their futures from a more politically conscious and self-aware perspective. Many of the pieces move away from the traditional form of the short story as a finished product in favor of womanist prose, pieces in process—a technique meant to reflect the belief that women view life as unfolding, growing, and emerging out of personal histories and political contexts. *The Color Purple* (1982) is written in epistolary style (letters as the only acceptable form of women's writing in white-male-dominated society) and is strongly feminist in its emphasis on the importance of sisterhood in liberating women from oppression. The novel enjoyed enormous popularity, conferring best-seller status on W.'s work, and the film version was nominated for an Academy Award. But *The Color Purple* was a critical success as well. It was awarded the 1983 Pulitzer Prize and the American Book Award.

The primary focus of W.'s writing, whether fiction, poetry, or commentary, continues to be the African-American woman, but the scope and the power of W.'s work transcend easy sterotyping. She continues to evolve as a major American literary figure.

FURTHER WORKS: *Langston Hughes: American Poet* (1974); *Good Night, Willie Lee, I'll See You in the Morning* (1979); *In Search of Our Mother's Gardens: Womanist Prose* (1983); *Horses Make a Landscape Look More Beautiful: Poems* (1984); *To Hell With Dying* (1988); *The Temple of My Familiar* (1989); *Living by the Word: Selected Writings, 1973–1987* (1989); *Finding the Green Stone* (1991); *Her Blue Body, Everything We Know: Earthling Poems, 1965–1990* (1991); *Possessing the Secret of Joy* (1992)

BIBLIOGRAPHY: Harris, T., "Violence in *The Third Life of Grange Copeland*," *CLAJ,* 19 (Dec. 1975), 238–47; Washington, M. H., "An Essay on

A. W.," in Bell, R. P., B. J. Parker, and B. G. Sheftall, eds., *Sturdy Black Bridges: Visions of Black Women in Literature* (1979), 133–49; McDowell, D. E., "The Self in Bloom: A. W.'s *Meridian,*" *CLAJ,* 24 (Mar. 1981), 262–75; Parker-Smith, B. J., "A. W.'s Women: In Search of Some Peace of Mind," in Evans, M., ed., *Black Women Writers (1950–1980): A Critical Evaluation* (1984), 478–93; Early, G., "*The Color Purple* as Everybody's Protest Art," *AR* (Summer 1986), 270–75; Bloom, H., ed., *A. W.* (1989); Banks, E. D., and K. Byerman, *A. W.: An Annotated Bibliography 1968–1986* (1989); Winchell, D. H., *A. W.* (1992)

MARGARET D. SULLIVAN

WALTER, Otto F.

Swiss novelist (writing in German), b. 5 June 1928, Rickenbach

W. is one of the leading experimental authors of Switzerland. After studying the book trade, he held a series of minor jobs in the publishing business. In 1956 he became the head of the literary program for his father's publishing house, the Walter Verlag. He served in this capacity until 1966, when he accepted a similar position at Luchterhand publishers in Germany. Here he succeeded in obtaining a foothold for several Swiss authors in the West German market. He quit his job in 1972 to return to Switzerland to become a full-time writer. He now lives in Solothurn.

W.'s first five novels are set in the imaginary town of Jammers, near the Jura mountains in the canton of Solothurn. The first two in this series, *Der stumme* (1959; the mute) and *Herr tourel* (1962; Mr. Tourel) are very much like the French *nouveau roman* in that they avoid the use of plot and characterization in favor of highly subjective introspection. The narrator of the first novel tries to reconstruct the past of the silent protagonist, who lost his voice because of his father, through a series of speculations and conjectures. The second book is a mixture of recollections, associations, overheard conversations, and imaginary dialogues. W. was reacting here to a widespread literary skepticism in the German-speaking world, whereby standard language and conventional literary forms were no longer considered adequate to cope with the perversion of language under the Nazis and the demands of a new technological age.

W. outgrew his fascination with the purely subjective, and his next works show an increased concern with contemporary political and social issues. In *Die ersten unruhen* (1972; the first unrests) Jammers has become a large town dominated by capitalism, and this has split the populace into several groups alienated from each other. Lawlessness and loneliness abound and everyone seems to have lost his or her purpose in life. The alienation and inequalities that capitalism engenders are also the theme of *Die verwilderung* (1977; growing wild). A group of dropouts try to form a democratic commune in an abandoned factory outside of Jammers, but their presence cannot be tolerated by the local citizens, who violently disband them. Through his mouthpiece, the journalist Blumer, W. expresses the fear that the encroachment of the political and economic system into every aspect of our lives will result in a severe curtailment of our freedom and will ultimately lead to a return to fascism. Both of these novels have a strong documentary flavor, for they include numerous passages quoted from other sources. Stylistically they are linked to the first two novels, in that they consist of collages, but this time the collages are on a much grander scale and incorporate a wide variety of material, including fictive texts, authorial comments, and newspaper articles.

The novella *Wie wird beton zu gras: fast eine liebesgeschichte* (1979; how does concrete turn to grass: almost a love story) reverts to a more conventional style, but the thematics remain constant. Three siblings demonstrate against the construction of a nuclear power plant and thereafter become gradually alienated from Swiss society and its imposed restrictions. This familial aspect is expanded to epic proportions in *Zeit des fasans* (1988; time of the pheasant), a long novel, which chronicles the history of the industrialist family Winter, who lives in Jammers. The main question of the plot—who is responsible for the mother's murder—takes a backseat to the theme W. has been developing in his previous novels, namely capitalism and its concomitant evils. W. is particularly interested in the family's history in the 1930s and 1940s, thus trying to show the links between capitalism and fascism. Once again the novel is a montage of fictive texts, flashbacks, comments from the author, quotations, and other materials.

Through his literature W. has developed into one of the foremost critics of Swiss society and of Western consumer culture. His works call on us to critically reflect on the dangers that our political and social systems hold for our personal development and for the environment.

FURTHER WORKS: *Elio oder eine fröhliche gesellschaft* (1965); *Das staunen der schlafwandler am ende der nacht* (1983); *Eine insel finden* (1983); *Gegenwort* (1988)

BIBLIOGRAPHY: Weber, W., *Tagebuch eines Lesers* (1965), 232–50; Bucher, W., *Schweizer Schriftsteller im Gespräch* (1971), 219–40; Mattes, M., *Das Bild des Menschen im Werk O. F. Ws* (1973); Zeltner-Neukomm, G., *Das Ich ohne Gewähr* (1980), 81–100; Acker, R., ''O. F. W.'s *Die Verwilderung:* Swiss *Engagement* in the 70's,'' *UDR*, 16, 3 (Winter 1983–1984), 33–38

ROBERT ACKER

WANG Meng

Chinese novelist and short-story writer, b. 15 Oct. 1934, Beijing

W. became a member of the Chinese Communist Party before his fourteenth birthday in 1948, and in 1949 began work as a party secretary in the New Democratic Youth League while studying political theory at the Central League Academy in Beijing. W. was attacked during the 1957 Anti-Rightist Campaign and exiled to the countryside, where he performed manual labor for five years before returning to Beijing in 1962. After teaching in the Chinese department of Beijing Normal College for one year, W. was sent to the Xinjiang Province branch of the Chinese Writers Association, and in 1965 he went to a commune to work in manual labor. In 1973 W. was transferred to the Xinjiang ministry of culture where he worked as a translator, and in 1979 he returned to Beijing as a writer. In 1986 W. was appointed minister of culture but stepped down in 1989 and was replaced by Ho Ching-chih (He Jingzhi).

W.'s writing career began in 1953 with *Ch'ing-ch'un wan-sui* (long live youth), which was not published until 1979. He gained fame with a short story, ''Tsu-chih-pu lai-le ke nian-ch'ing-jen'' (1956; ''The Young Newcomer in the Organization Department,'' 1983). Foreshadowing the themes of a later novel—*Pu-li* (1979; *Bolshevik Salute,* 1989)—this story depicts a young and naive office worker who rejects the corruption and sterility of party bureaucracy and attempts to make reforms. As the Anti-Rightist Movement gained momentum and many well-established literary intellectuals were criticized for individualism and antiparty ideas, W. became one of the younger victims. Like many writers forced to work in the countryside or jailed during the Cultural Revolution (1966–1976), W. published little during that period.

After the death of Mao Zedong (Mao Tse-tung) and the fall of the Gang of Four in 1976, W. and other writers from the 1950s and earlier reemerged. In 1980 W. published a series of short stories, including ''Yeh te yen'' (''The Eyes of Night,'' 1983), ''Hu-tie'' (''The Butterfly,'' 1983), and ''Ch'un chih sheng'' (''Voices of Spring,'' 1983), which utilized techniques similar to stream-of-consciousness (q.v.), fragmented plot, and interior monologue to reevaluate the psychological and social damage done by the Cultural Revolution. These stories and W.'s novel *Pu-li*, the story of a young party member who retains loyalty throughout years of senseless criticism, formed part of a modernist movement that challenged the forty-year supremacy of Socialist Realism (q.v.) and called for new, more critical roles for the literary intellectual.

In 1980 critics attacked W.'s contemporary works as antirealist, non-Marxist, and un-Chinese. This critique of certain cultural productions as violating the emphasis on the masses that Socialist Realism had espoused culminated in the Anti-Spiritual Pollution Campaign of 1983, during which W.'s experiments with modernist techniques were branded as foreign, elitist, and politically unprogressive. Although many were afraid the campaign would develop into a second Cultural Revolution, it stopped abruptly at the end of 1983, and W. continued to write. The fact that in July of 1983, as the campaign was warming up, W. became editor in chief of *People's Literature* shows that criticism of his works as pollution had only a mild effect on his career.

Recently W. has been a prolific writer, publishing the novels *Hsiang-chien shih nan* (1982; *The Strain of Meeting*, 1989) and *Huo-tung pian-jen-hsing* (1987; *The Movable Parts*, 1989), as well as numerous stories and a few essays on literary creativity. W.'s work investigates themes such as party corruption, the effect of political movements on daily life, and human relations in adverse circumstances. He remains a writer whose career has spanned the existence of the People's Republic of China and whose work stands as a testimony to the political upheavals that defined contemporary culture and from which no Chinese writer could escape.

FURTHER WORKS: *Yeh te yen chi ch'i-t'a* (1981); *W. M. Chin-tso hsüan* (1981); *W. M. hsiao-shuo pao-kao wen-hsüeh hsüan* (1981); *W. M. t'an ch'uang-tso* (1983); *W. M. chung-p'ian hsiao-shuo-chi* (1985); *Ch'uang-tso shih i-chung jan-shao* (1985); *Wen-hsüeh ti yu huo* (1987). FURTHER VOLUMES IN ENGLISH: *The Butterfly and Other Stories* (1983); *Selected Works of W. M. I: The Strain of Meeting* (1989); *Selected Works of W. M. II: Snowball* (1989)

BIBLIOGRAPHY: Tay, W., "W. M., Stream of Consciousness, and the Controversy over Modernism," *MCL*, 1, 1 (Sept. 1984), 7–24; Larson, W., Introduction and "*Bolshevik Salute:* The Chinese Intellectual and Negative Self-Definition," *Bolshevik Salute: A Modernist Chinese Novel*

(1989), xiii–xx, 133–54; Tay, W., "Modernism and Socialist Realism," *WLT*, 65, 3 (Summer 1991), 411–13

WENDY LARSON

WANNŪS, Saʿdallāh

Syrian dramatist, producer, and drama critic, b. 1941, Syria

Trained in Syria, Egypt, and France, W. has made major contributions to the theater tradition of his homeland as well as to the development of a corpus of theoretical writing about drama, most notably that connected with performance and the relationship between actors and audience.

The turning point in his career came with the performance of his play *Haflat samr min ajl al-khāmis min Huzayrān* (1968; evening entertainment for the 5th of June). Before that, W. had written a number of plays with clear political messages but belonging more to the category of *théâtre des idées*. In *Haflat samr* he addressed himself to the issues surrounding the June defeat of 1967 in a carefully organized theatrical event through which the audience found itself drawn into a corporate condemnation of the power structures that had failed the Arab people. Although productions of the play were soon banned, some 20,000 people are said to have attended a later series of performances in Damascus in 1972.

Haflat samr has been characterized by some critics as an ephemeral piece. It is certainly the case that the parameters that W. established in that play have been explored with greater dramatic effect in the plays that he has written since that time. W.'s basic aim, expressed in a series of articles, reviews, and retorts, has been to break down the barriers separating the actors involved in the performance on stage and the audience watching in the auditorium; it is not surprising that, in his discussions of drama theory, the names of Erwin Piscator (1893–1966) and Bertolt Brecht (q.v.) are among those cited. He regards this development as a necessity for Arabic drama, not least because a lively interchange between actors and audience was a prominent feature of drama performances in the 19th c. He has written at length on what he terms *masrah al-tasyīs* (theater of politicization) and has provided copious directions and suggestions regarding the means of performing his works.

W. explored these ideas in two plays of the early 1970s: *Mughāmarat ra's al-mamlūk Jābir* (1972; the adventures of Mamlūk Jābir's head), based on a tale of treachery from the Abbasid era of Islamic history; and *Sahra ma'a Abī Khalīl al-Qabbānī* (1972; an evening entertainment with

Abū Khalīl al-Qabbānī). The first of these plays makes use of an "audience" of actors of the stage and the manipulative figure of the *hakawātī* (the traditional storyteller) to orchestrate the reactions and, W. even hopes in an introduction, the participation, of the audience. In *Sahra* we encounter the "play within a play" format, through which W. attempts to explore some of the issues associated with modern Arabic drama through an illustration of the trials of al-Qabbānī (1833–1902) in producing and performing a play culled from the tales of *A Thousand and One Nights* in Ottoman-controlled Syria in the 19th c.

Later in the decade W. published *Al-Malik huwa al-malik* (1977; the king's the king), a play inspired by tales from the Hārūn al-Rashīd cycle in *A Thousand and One Nights,* in which a henpecked husband is spirited away to the Caliph's palace and made ruler for the night. The modern twist to the plot is that no one seems to notice the difference; at the end of the play the ruler who decided to have some fun at someone else's expense has come to regret the game he has initiated. In this play, too, W. makes use of a number of theatrical devices, puppets, and the manipulating orchestrators of the action, Zāhid and 'Ubayd.

Besides his obvious desire to experiment with the dynamics of drama in the Arab world context, W. has made a radical and interesting decision regarding the problem of dramatic language in Arabic (the language of speech, the various colloquial dialects, not being considered a "literary" language by many critics). In the introduction to *Mughāmarat ra's al-mamlūk Jābir* he suggests that the published text of the play should be regarded as merely a blueprint, and that producers in the various regions of the Arab world should feel free to adapt the dialogue to conform with the local dialect and indeed choose props and music appropriate to the local audience's taste.

Accounts of performances of W.'s plays make it clear that theater directors and audiences have had considerable difficulty carrying out his agenda for Arabic drama; critics report audience discomfort over the confusion as to who were the real actors and who were the audience. It is also clear that the import of almost all W.'s plays has not been to the taste of governmental authorities who use various means of censorship to keep a very close watch on dramatic productions. This will probably account for W.'s extended silence throughout the 1980s. Even so, the corpus of plays that he has published thus far remains a significant contribution to the development of an indigenous tradition of modern Arabic drama.

FURTHER WORKS: *Al-Fīl, yā Malik al-Zamān* (1970); *Ma'sāt bā'i' al-dibs al-faqīr* (1977)

BIBLIOGRAPHY: Allen, R., "Arabic Drama in Theory and Practice: The Writings of S. W.," *JArabL,* 15 (1984), 94–113; Cccccato, R. D., "Il teatro contemporaneo in Siria: L'impegno di S. W.," *Quaderni di studi arabi,* 1 (1983), 53–65; Gouryh, A., "Recent Trends in Syrian Drama," *WLT,* 60, 2 (Spring 1986), 216–21

ROGER ALLEN

WATTĀR, al-Tāhir

Algerian novelist and short-story writer, b. 15 Aug. 1936, near Sedrata

W. received most of his education in Tunisia while his country was fighting for its independence. He worked for many years as a journalist in Algeria and was later appointed as political adviser in the National Liberation Front. He became the director of Algerian radio and television in 1990. W. is Algeria's most prominent fiction writer and the most outspoken defender of the country's socialist policy adopted after its independence in 1962. He published one play, *Al-Hārib* (1969; the fugitive), as well as novels and short stories. W.'s approach is both explicit and daring even while discussing topics traditionally considered taboo in his society. His short stories in particular raised the question of suppressed feelings among the Algerian youth and compared life to a barren desert. Such a complaint was strongly voiced by the hero of "Sahrā' Abadan" (desert forever) and other stories in his collection *Dukhkhān min qalbī* (n.d.; smoke from my heart). In spite of W.'s early concern for the absence of love in his society he gave it very little attention in his novels. Love themes are practically nonexistent in his books, where the relation between men and women is reduced to a sexual adventure, serving more as an escape from life's enduring problems of poverty and repression.

Women do not play a significant role in W.'s early novels, particularly those dealing with the war of independence. Whenever he portrays feminine characters, they are generally singled out in unusual situations and do not represent the Algerian woman in real life. Thus, while the heroine of his short story "Nawwāh" (n.d.; Nawwāh) reveals a panicking mother trying to save her children during an air raid on her village, *Rummānah* (1981; Rummanah), on the other hand, is the image of the woman as sex symbol, the way men in her society conceive her. She serves to point out men's vices rather than women's virtues. This tendency to use women as symbols characterizes W.'s novels; used as such, they are stiff and even artificial, with the possible exception of the prostitutes in his novel *'Urs baghl* (1978;

marriage of a mule). In fact, W. does not do justice to the women of his country. So far, the most successful portrayal of a feminine character has been Fajriyyah in *Tajribah fī al-'Ishq* (1989; an experience in passion). She is undoubtedly the most human of his feminine characters, though manifestly symbolic, and even endowed with magical powers.

W.'s novels present an assessment of Algeria's long march through history, old and new, and the various pitfalls on the way from the days of French colonialism to the postindependence period. This concern with history takes precedence over the fiction side of W.'s works. Both the novels and most of the short stories relate the political realities in Algeria, depending in most cases on symbols to convey the author's message. In *Al-zilzāl* (1974; the earthquake), for example, the choice of the geographical setting of the city of Constantine and the reference to a natural disaster to denote the huge changes that took place in Algeria as a result of the war of independence, mark a successful approach. A more direct use of history and political reality is apparent in *Al-lāz* (1974; al-Laz), *Al-'ishq wa-al mawt fī-al-zaman al-harrāshī* (1978; passion and death in the Harrashi time), and *Tajribah fī al-'Ishq*. Recent and contemporary political figures and events dominate the scene in the three novels. Facts are mentioned bluntly without any effort to camouflage names or incidents or even the author's feelings and emotions toward them. Some of the situations described here were prefigured in the short stories of *Al-Shuhadā' ya'ūdūn hādhā al-usbū'* (1974; the martyrs are coming back this week). Phony communists and the opportunists of the war of independence are particularly highlighted. The optimistic tone of *Al-'ishq wa-al mawt fī-al-zaman al-harrāshī* gives way to a melancholic despair and a moral nonchalance.

It is difficult to foresee the future trend of W.'s literary path, especially with the recent political changes in Algeria. So far he has proved to be a prolific writer, whose in-depth study of the social and the political Algerian scene as well as juggle of history and fiction brought him universal renown. W. is the best-known Algerian writer in the Arab world.

FURTHER WORKS: *Al-hawwāt wa-al-qasr* (1980); *Al-Ta'anāt* (1981)

BIBLIOGRAPHY: Makarius, R., and L. Makarius, *Anthologie de la littérature arabe contemporaine* (1964), 404–8; Déjeux, J., *La littérature algérienne contemporaine* (1975), 116; Bamia, A. A.,"La littérature algérienne de langue arabe," *Europe*, 567–68 (July–Aug. 1976), 38–48; Bamia, A. A., "Le roman algérien de langue arabe depuis l'indépendence," *Annuaire de l'Afrique du Nord*, 19 (1980), 1127–33; Allen, R., *The Arabic Novel* (1982), 74–75; Bamia, A. A., "L'homme dans l'œuvre de T. W.," *Littératures du Maghreb*, 4–5 (1984), 339–49; Allen, R., ed., *Modern Arabic Literature* (1987), 340–42; Bonn, C., *Anthologie de la littérature algérienne* (1990), 107–8, 151–54, 223–34

AIDA A. BAMIA

WELDON, Fay

British novelist, dramatist, and critic, b. 22 Sept. 1933, Alvechurch, Worcestershire

W. grew up in an all-female household in London after her parents' divorce when she was ten. She was educated at Hampstead Girls' High School and St. Andrews University, Fife, where she gained an M.A. in economics and psychology in 1954.

W. has written many novels, most of which tend to have a married or unmarried mother at their center. Her work takes up some of the issues that are of concern to the women's movement, such as friendship and rivalry between women, motherhood, women and work, the oppressive nature of heterosexual relationships, patriarchal attitudes toward women, etc., but suggests that, while women can do something to alter their situation, such activity will ultimately tend toward greater accommodation within existent expectations of how women are to fulfill their patriarchally determined roles. There seems little hope for attitudinal changes toward women in society at large in W.'s work. In her novels, many of her female characters experience lack of control, the "blindness" of having children, the no-win situation that society places them in. W.'s second novel, *Down among the Women* (1971), follows the lives and explores the survival instincts of a group of women of whom W. says, "Men are irrelevant. Women are happy or unhappy, fulfilled or unfulfilled, and it has nothing to do with men." Alternating between blaming women and blaming men for women's lot, W. is clear-sighted enough to see the shortcomings of both sexes and exploit these for her comic representations of life in 20th-c. Britain.

Female Friends (1975) gives an account of the enduring friendship of Marjorie, Chloe, and Grace through the various stages of their lives. Stylistically this novel is interesting because much of the dialogue is set apart from the rest of the text by being written in play form with the name of the speaking character appearing before each bit of speech. The result is a curious sense of stagedness of the conversations, which points to the artificiality of individuals' preoccupations. In *Remember Me* (1976) the same stylistic device is employed; not only is dialogue set out as if in a play, the reader is also offered a second version of the conversations in which what people "really mean" is revealed.

Little Sisters (1978) changes the scenario from "ordinary" people to the ultrarich. Elsa and her lover spend a weekend with his wealthy friends Hamish and Gemma, who is wheelchair-bound. Embedded in the story of that weekend, which turns into a disaster, is Gemma's story. This story-within-story device, used also in *Praxis* (1978), allows W. to present different time sequences within one work, thus giving the impression of the repetition of women's experience through time.

Puffball (1980) describes the interactions of Liffey, a pregnant woman, with the rural community in Somerset where she stays while her husband continues to work in London, and where he joins her for weekends. Liffey finds herself at the mercy of various members of the community. W. in this novel invokes the supernatural and witchcraft to express Liffey's uneasiness at her situation. She suggests similar forces in the title of *The Life and Loves of a She-Devil* (1983). Here a large woman uses her abilities, supernatural or otherwise, to revenge herself upon her unfaithful accountant husband by gradually breaking down the popular woman novelist with whom he has been having an affair. In the end the "she-devil," through a number of means such as ensuring that her husband is in prison for a prolonged period of time during which she undergoes extensive plastic surgery, manages to change her exterior to match that of her husband's ex-lover, and, in effect, takes over completely that lover's role and life, including her home and her professional career. She becomes that other woman. Other novels include *The President's Child* (1982) and *The Shrapnel Academy* (1986), which uses an intrusive narrator to distance the reader from the awful and violent events; and most recently W. has consolidated her reputation with the novels *Darcy's Utopia* (1990) and *Life Force* (1992).

W. has become known to a wider audience, both through the publication of short stories in magazines such as *Cosmopolitan*, *Company*, and *Woman's Own*, and through numerous adaptations and plays she has written both for radio and television. Her first original television serial, *The Heart of the Country* (1987), is a black comedy that probes marital relationships and the myth of rural living through the experiences of a middle-class wife who lives through the destruction of her cozy, affluent world. W.'s stories were collected in two volumes, *Watching Me, Watching You* (1981) and *Polaris and Other Stories* (1985). She won the SFTA Award for the Best Series for Episode 1 of *Upstairs, Downstairs* (1971), and

the Giles Cooper Award for Best Radio Play for *Polaris* (1978). W. was chairwoman of the Booker Prize in 1983, and of the Sinclair Prize in 1986. She is on the Video Censorship Appeals Committee, and was a member of the Arts Council literary panel.

(Adapted from *British Women Writers*, 1989, edited by Janet Todd)

FURTHER WORKS: *The Fat Woman's Joke* (1967); *Permanence* (1969); *Time Hurries On* (1972); *Words of Advice* (1974); *Moving House* (1976); *Friends* (1978); *Mr. Director* (1978); *Action Replay* (1978); *I Love My Love* (1981); *Woodworm* (1981); *After the Prize* (1983); *Letters to Alice* (1984); *Rebecca West* (1985); *The Hearts and Lives of Men* (1987); *The Rules of Life* (1987); *Leader of the Band* (1988); *The Cloning of Joanna May* (1989); *Moon over Minneapolis, or, Why She Couldn't Stay* (1991)

BIBLIOGRAPHY: Zeman, A., *Presumptuous Girls: Women and Their World in the Serious Woman's Novel* (1977), 64–65; Krouse, A. N., "Feminism and Art in F. W.'s Novels," *Crit*, 20, 2 (1978), 5–20; Wilde, A., " 'Bold, But Not Too Bold': F. W. and the Limits of Poststructuralist Criticism," *ConL*, 29, 3 (Fall 1988), 403–19

GABRIELE GRIFFIN

WHITE, E(lwyn) B(rooks)

American essayist, journalist, editor, poet, short-story writer, and children's-book author; b. 11 July 1899, Mount Vernon, N.Y.; d. 1 Oct. 1985, North Brooklin, Maine

W. served as a private in the U.S. Army during World War I and received his A. B. from Cornell University in 1921. After his graduation he became a reporter for United Press and American Legion News Service and then joined the *Seattle Times*. In 1924 he returned to New York to work as a production assistant and copywriter at an advertising agency. W. began submitting pieces to the *New Yorker* soon after the magazine started publishing in 1925. Editor Harold Ross was impressed with W.'s work and invited him to join the staff of the magazine. For the next eleven years, W. wrote and edited the "Talk of the Town" section of the *New Yorker* which is comprised of topical expository pieces ranging in subject matter from the often serious political commentary in "Notes and Comment" to the two or three light, amusing, and sometimes frivolous reports that present slices of New York life. In 1929 W. married the literary editor of the *New Yorker*,

Katherine Sargeant Angell (1892–1977), with whom he edited *A Subtreasury of American Humor* (1941). In 1936 W. and his family moved to Maine, and W. commuted to New York only when necessary. From 1938 to 1943 he wrote and edited a column called "One Man's Meat" for *Harper's*. He continued to be a regular contributor to the *New Yorker* for the rest of his working life. W. was awarded the Presidential Medal of Freedom (1963) and the National Medal for Literature (1971). He died in Maine of Alzheimer's disease at the age of eighty-five.

W.'s first books were published in 1929, *The Lady Is Cold*, a collection of light poems, and the humorous *Is Sex Necessary? or Why You Feel the Way You Do*, which he wrote in collaboration with his friend and colleague at the *New Yorker*, James Thurber (q.v.). W. later published a second volume of poetry, *The Fox of Peapack* (1938). His short stories and entertaining commentaries are collected in *Alice through the Cellophane* (1933), *Quo Vadimus?* (1939), and *The Second Tree from the Corner* (1954).

It is W.'s clear and graceful prose style, sometimes amusing but more often satirical, that makes him one of America's finest essayists. A master of the informal personal essay, W.'s writing has the ability to convey a sense of whimsy while maintaining a tone that remains modest though ironical. He is often credited with establishing the crisp, light, and slightly playful style that has long been associated with the *New Yorker*.

In 1957 the *New Yorker* published W.'s sketch of his late professor at Cornell, "Will Strunk," which describes parts of the short rhetoric Strunk had published privately called *The Elements of Style*. The piece caught the attention of editors at the publishing house of Macmillan, and W. was asked to revise and expand Strunk's book. Since its republication in 1959, *The Elements of Style* has become a mainstay of high-school and college English courses in the U.S. It is the rare American student who has not used what Strunk had called "the *little* book," now often referred to simply as "the Strunk and White."

Although W. was a shy, introverted man, the strength of his ethical, moral and intellectual convictions is always evident, even if just below the surface of his writing. His children's books, *Stuart Little* (1945), *Charlotte's Web* (1952), and *The Trumpet of the Swan* (1970), show his empathy for, and understanding of, the pain, the loss, and the fears connected with the child's emotional struggles in moving toward maturity.

W. was always a humane and sensitive spokesman for the freedom of the individual and a keen advocate of the right to privacy. While he often wrote from the perspective of slightly ironic on-

looker, there was never anything of the merely superficial about his crisp, direct, and engaging prose.

FURTHER WORKS: *Ho-Hum: Newsbreaks from The New Yorker* (1931); *Another Ho-Hum* (1932); *Every Day Is Saturday* (1934); *Farewell to the Model T* (1936); *One Man's Meat* (1942); *The Wild Flag: Editorials from The New Yorker on Federal World Government and Other Matters* (1946); *Here is New York* (1949); *The Points of My Compass* (1962); *An E. B. W. Reader* (1966); *Letters of E. B. W.* (1976); *Essays of E. B. W.* (1977); *Poems and Sketches of E. B. W.* (1981); *Writings from The New Yorker, 1927–1976* (1991)

BIBLIOGRAPHY: Thurber, J., "E. B. W.," *Saturday Review of Literature*, 18 (15 Oct. 1938), 8-9; Hasley, L., and W. R. Steinhoff, " 'The Door,' 'The Professor,' 'My Friend the Poet (Deceased),' 'The Washable House,' and 'The Man Out in Jersey,' " *CE*, 23 (Dec. 1961), 229–32; "The Talk of the Town and the Country: E. B. W.," *Connecticut Review*, 5 (Oct. 1971), 37–45; Sampson, E. C., *E. B. W.* (1974); Updike, J., *Hugging the Shore* (1983), 187–95; Elledge, S., *E. B. W.: A Biography* (1984)

MARGARET D. SULLIVAN

WIESEL, Elie

(born Eliezer Wiesel) French-language novelist, essayist, and short-story writer, b. 30 Sept. 1928, Sighet, Hungary (now Romania)

A survivor of the horrors of the German concentration camps and of the Holocaust (characterized by W. as "The Event"), W. represents the conscience if not the voice of the Jewish people throughout the world. He does nearly all of his most serious writing in French and must be considered as a member of the tradition of contemporary French literature. Among the authors who played a meaningful part in his intellectual and literary formation are Albert Camus, André Malraux, François Mauriac, and Jean-Paul Sartre (qq.v.). His hometown of Sighet was a center for Hasidic Jewish learning, a fact that has colored much of his writing. From his father and mother he learned Yiddish; in Hebrew School he studied biblical Hebrew; and after being liberated from Auschwitz and Buchenwald, he went to Paris, received a French university education, and mastered French. Later on, as a journalist, he went to the U.S. and learned English. Dodye Feig, his maternal grandfather, played a critical role in imbuing in W.'s boyhood soul the love for Hasidic culture, customs, and storytelling. After a happy childhood in a tightly united, traditional Jewish family, the sixteen-year-old adolescent was arrested by the Germans with his parents and sisters as well as with the 15,000 other Jews of Sighet and deported to Auschwitz. His earliest writings relate the inhumane and nightmarish existence of the concentration camps, where his parents and a sister as well as most of his relatives and closest friends perished from starvation or in the gas chambers. In April 1945, having miraculously survived, he was liberated by the U.S. Third Army. Thanks to the intervention of General Charles de Gaulle, he and many of the survivors of his group were sent to France, where he remained until 1951. After studying philosophy, psychology, and literature at the Sorbonne in Paris, he found a job as journalist for the Franco-Jewish newspaper *L'Arche,* and eventually was assigned to cover the fledgling state of Israel. In 1952 he became a reporter for the Tel Aviv newspaper *Yediot Ahronot,* and eventually was sent to New York to cover the United Nations in 1956. Naturalized in 1963, he has since resided in New York and, in 1969, married Marion Erster Rose, herself a survivor of the German concentration camps. She became his principal translator into English. In 1972 the couple had their only child, a son, Shlomo Elisha. W. travels frequently to France and to Israel, and in many respects these countries are second homes to him. An inspiring speaker, he has given thousands of lectures at college campuses, synagogues, and at other public forums around the world. Since 1976 W. has been Andrew Mellon Professor of the Humanities at Boston University, and he commutes to Boston weekly during the academic year to give courses in several humanistic disciplines. Enjoying an immense international reading public, W. received in 1986 the Nobel Peace Prize.

The experiences of the concentration camp were such a cataclysmic event in W.'s life that although he yearned to be a writer, he could not gather the courage to recount what he had witnessed there. Nor could he find words adequate to recapture the agony of the nightmare. For ten years he anguished over this dilemma: Should he try to share with a reading public what he had seen or should he forever remain silent? Finally, he could no longer contain himself, and he published an 800-page tome in Buenos Aires, writing in Yiddish, the only language he felt comfortable with at the time, the detailed account of his concentration-camp experience: *Und di Velt hot Geschvign* (1956; and the world was silent). The principal theme dealt with the silence of the entire world while Hitler and his forces exterminated six million Jewish adults and children. Relatively few readers could appreciate this initial publication, and in 1958, encouraged by François Mauriac, the Nobel Prize laureate and

celebrated French Catholic writer, he reduced the dimensions of his first book from 800 to only 127 pages; but this more concise version he wrote in French, and it appeared in 1958 under the title of *La nuit* (*Night,* 1960).

La nuit became an instantaneous best-seller around the world and was immediately translated into every major language. A genuine modern classic, it recaptures with terrifying precision the excruciating barbarism of life in the camps: the torture, suffering, brutalities, as well as the personal poignancy of W.'s loss of his parents and sister.

Not only did W. gain international notoriety from the publication of *La nuit,* but he realized that he could verbalize in French, one of the great languages of Western civilization, the memories stirring within his soul. Once he gained confidence in himself, almost one book per year has since flowed from his prolific pen. Instead of retelling repeatedly the agonies of the Holocaust, he turned immediately to the aftermath of "The Event" and began to concentrate on the adventures lived by the generations surviving the gas chambers, notably in *L'aube* (1960; *Dawn,* 1961) and *Le jour* (1961; *The Accident,* 1962). In the first work a survivor of the camps seeks to kill the enemies of the nascent Jewish state of Israel; in the second book, another survivor unconsciously lets himself have a serious automobile accident in New York because he really does not desire to live any longer—he feels a sense of guilt at having survived while his dearest friends and family had perished at Auschwitz.

In *La ville de la chance* (1962; *The Town beyond the Wall,* 1964), the author depicts the silence of a non-Jewish spectator who remains passive as his Jewish neighbors and lifelong friends pass through the streets of Sighet, moving toward the cattle cars where they will be sent to the camps of death. W. cannot comprehend the silence of the non-Jews, most of whom did nothing to save their fellow Jews from destruction. This theme of a silent, immobile, and passionless gentile world reasserts itself obsessively throughout W.'s literature.

In 1968 W. wrote one of his most exuberant novels, *Le mendiant de Jerusalem* (*Beggar of Jerusalem,* 1970), the subject of which is the triumphant victory of the state of Israel during the Six-Day War over the overwhelming odds of the entire Arab world. Recipient of the coveted Prix Médicis in Paris (1968), it was an enormously successful work on both sides of the Atlantic.

One of his finest works of fiction is *Le crépuscule au loin* (1987; *Twilight,* 1988). This complicated work deals with a question that ceaselessly fascinates W.: the nature of sanity and insanity. Often, according to W., the insane have a clearer understanding of reality than those who are regarded as sane. Were the highly educated, refined, and cultured henchmen of the Nazi era truly sane people? Where are the frontiers that divide madness from sanity?

But W. has published much more during his prodigious career than novels, most of which are based on his Holocaust memories. He has written collections of Hasidic tales like *Célébration hassidique* (1972; *Souls on Fire,* 1972) and biblical stories like *Célébration biblique: Portraits et Légendes* (1975; *Messengers of God,* 1976). He has written collections of essays on the scandalous situation of the Soviet Jews, essays and thoughts on contemporary human problems, interreligious relations, war and peace. Noteworthy is a three-volume collection edited by Irving Abrahamson in 1985 entitled *Against Silence; The Voice and Vision of E. W.;* it is a vast compendium of his public lectures, scattered essays and thoughts, maxims and aphorisms, and informal speeches delivered for decades around the world.

W.'s style is that of a minimalist; he compares writing to the work of the sculptor who must chisel away all the excess marble, leaving only the absolute essentials. His principal themes deal with "man's inhumanity toward man," not only during the Holocaust but throughout the world wherever human suffering, discrimination, and racial genocide have taken place. Despite seemingly hopeless circumstances, W. never despairs and pleads for the human race to come to its senses by realizing that the most precious commodity on earth is human life itself. Another recurrent theme is that of silence versus verboseness. Sometimes words are simply too feeble to convey with authenticity the depth of human suffering and joy. Indifference for him is the most terrible sin; his life's motto is "Indifference to evil is evil." This motto is engraved on the gold surface of the Congressional Medal of Achievement he received from President Ronald Reagan in 1984.

One of the world's most honored men of letters, in addition to the Nobel Peace Prize, he holds honorary doctorates from dozens of prestigious universities around the globe and is Commander of the French Legion of Honor. The chairman of the Nobel Prize committee called him a "Messenger to Mankind."

FURTHER WORKS: *Les portes de la forêt* (1964; *The Gates of the Forest,* 1966); *Les Juifs du silence* (1966; *The Jews of Silence: A Personal Report on Soviet Jewry,* 1966); *Les chants des morts* (1966; *Legends of Our Time,* 1968); *Zalmen ou la folie de Dieu* (1968); *Entre deux soleils* (1970; *One Generation After,* 1970); *Le serment de Kolvillag* (1973; *The Oath,* 1973); *Ani Maamin:*

Un chant perdu et retrouvé (1973); *Un Juif aujourd'hui* (1977; *A Jew Today,* 1978); *Le procès de Shamgorod (tel gu'il se déroula le 25 février 1649)* (1979; *The Trial of God,* 1979); *Le testament d'un poète juif assassiné* (1980; *The testament: Five Biblical Portraits,* 1981); *Contre la mélancolie: Célébration hassidique II* (1981; *Somewhere a Master: Further Hasidic Portraits and Legends,* 1982); *Paroles d'étranger* (1982); *Le cinquième fils* (1983, *The Fifth Son,* 1985); *Signes d'exode* (1985); *Job ou Dieu dans la tempête* (1986); *Silences et mémoire d'hommes* (1989); *L'oublie* (1989). FURTHER VOLUMES IN ENGLISH: "The Holocaust As Literary Dimension," in *Dimensions of the Holocaust: Lectures at Northwestern University* (1977); *Four Hasidic Masters and Their Struggle against Melancholy* (1978); *The Golem: The Story of a Legend As Told by E. W.* (1983); *The Six Days of Destruction* (1988, with Albert H. Friedlander); *From the Kingdom of Memory* (1990)

BIBLIOGRAPHY: Halperin, I., *Messengers from the Dead* (1970), 65–106; Abramowitz, M., comp., *E. W.: A Bibliography* (1974); Joseloff, S. H., "Link and Promise: The Works of E. W.," *SHR,* 8 (Spring 1974), 163–70; Langer, L., *The Holocaust and the Literary Imagination* (1975), 75–89; Green, M. J., "Witness to the Absurd: E. W. and the French Existentialist," *Renascence,* 29 (Summer 1977), 170–84; Rosenfeld, A. H., and I. Greenberg, eds., *Confronting the Holocaust: The Impact of E. W.* (1978); Berenbaum, M., *The Vision of the Void: Theological Reflections on the Works of E. W.* (1979); Estess, T. L., *E. W.* (1980); Rabi, W., "E. W.: Un homme, une œuvre, un public," *Esprit,* 9 (1980), 79–92; Fine, E. S., *Legacy of Night: The Literary Universe of E. W.* (1982); Friedman, J., *Le rire dans l'univers tragique* (1982); Stern, E. N., *E. W.: Witness for Life* (1982); Brown, R. M., *E. W.: Messenger to All Humanity: Critical Essays by Major Jewish and Christian Scholars* (1983); Diamond, D., "E. W.: Reconciling the Irreconcilable," *WLT,* 57, 2 (Spring 1983), 228–33; Freedman, S. G., "Bearing Witness: The Life and Work of E. W.," *NYTMag* (23 Oct. 1983), 32–36; McCain, N., "E. W.: The Struggle To Reconcile the Reality of Evil with Faith in God," *The Chronicle of Higher Education* (13 Apr. 1983), 21–22; Friedman, J. S., "The Art of Fiction LXXIX: E. W.," *Paris Review,* 26 (Spring 1984), 130–78; Cohen, B.-F., *E. W.—Qui êtes-vous?* (1987); Rittner, C., ed., *E. W.: Between Memory and Hope* (1990)

JACK KOLBERT

Night is an account of a young boy's divorce from life, a drama of recognition whose scenes record the impotence of the familiar in the face of modern atrocity; at its heart lies the profoundest symbolic confrontation of our century, the meeting of man and Auschwitz (a meeting reenacted by Rolf Hochhuth in the culminating episode of *The Deputy*)—and this confrontation in turn confirms (as in Anthony Hecht's "More Light! More Light!") the defeat of man's tragic potentiality in our time, and the triumph of death in its most nihilistic guise . . .

Throughout *Night,* W. displays a remarkable talent for investing the "items" of reality, and of the fantastic "irreality" that replaces it, with an animistic quality, and then setting both on a pathway leading to an identical destination: death.

Lawrence L. Langer, "The Dominion of Death," in Henry James Cargas, ed., *Responses to E. W.* (1978), 34–35

All of W.'s writings are concerned with the ramifications of the Holocaust for man, God, and Israel. Peter Berger has argued that death is the marginal experience *par excellence* which threatens to reveal the innate precariousness of all socially constructed universes. If death is the marginal experience *par excellence,* then the death of six million Jews in the Holocaust is the marginal experience *extraordinaire* which has undermined the socially constructed universe of normative Judaism. W.'s writings are an attempt to come to terms with that marginal experience and to construct a new universe to replace the one that was shattered.

The progression in W.'s first three novels, *Night, Dawn,* and *Le Jour (The Accident),* from night to dawn to day, is not merely a positive progression from a world of darkness to a world of light, but also a progression from a world in which God is present (at the beginning of *Night*), to a world in which God is killed so that man can live (in *Dawn*), and finally to a world in which God is absent (in *Le Jour*). In *Le Jour* God's presence is no longer felt, and the individual lives without meaning and without God. It is ironic that W.'s titles become brighter as the presence of God becomes dimmer, but this irony reflects W.'s reliance upon man in a world devoid of God. Nonetheless, the transition from a God-filled world to a Godless world is not easy for W. He continually emphasizes not only the initial suffering that brought him to his view of a Godless world, but also the internal pain that accompanies this new consciousness. He yearns to return to the God-filled world and to the shtetl in the Carpathian Mountains from which he was prematurely snatched and taken into the kingdom of night.

Michael Berenbaum, *The Vision of the Void* (1979), 9–10

"In truth," states Elie Wiesel, "I think I have never spoken about the Holocaust except in one book, *Night,*—the very first—where I tried to tell a tale directly, as though face to face with the experience." Correct . . . but only to a degree. Wiesel has stated, *"Night* was the foundation; all the rest is commentary." All events are linked, and thus Wiesel's writings are rarely more than

once-removed from the flames and smoke of Auschwitz. Indeed his continuing accomplishment is that of having the courage to remember and interrogate the Holocaust—forecast, real, and aftermath—in ways that honor the victims and teach the living.

This man does not see himself primarily as a philosopher, theologian, or political theorist. Instead he is a storyteller. Storytellers can explore questions without answering them straight out, and that possibility attracts Wiesel as a way of confronting what can now be called a Holocaust Universe. Its reality and significance elude words, at least those that are direct. Thus, the prospects afforded by theory-building disciplines seem less fruitful to Wiesel than those offered by the indirect approach of telling tales. And yet, in the midst of recounting stories linked to—if not of—the Holocaust, philosophy, theology, politics come to life in ways that theory alone never yields.

Writing mainly in French, Wiesel employs varied forms of prose and poetry, fact and fiction, as he draws heavily on Jewish legend and tradition. Echoes of modern thinkers such as Kierkegaard, Kafka, Buber, and Camus can be heard in his writings, too. He is transforming all of these resources into a literature of lasting power and moral authority. In spite of and at the same time because of this success, the gift of Elie Wiesel—born in suffering and silence—remains mysterious. Perhaps more than anyone, he is troubled by the meanings of his own survival and achievement, and by the duties that both lay upon him: "Man is responsible not only for what he says, but also for what he does not say."

John K. Roth, *Consuming Fire: Encounters with E. W. and the Holocaust* (1979), 25–26

In W.'s novels there is a general progression from witnessing to bearing witness. The survivor-protagonist, whose voice has been silenced by nocturnal flames, struggles to express himself and to recover the faculty of speech. He slowly learns to reach out to others and to reaffirm his identity as a member of the human community. The assertion of the voice is linked to the vocation of witness and is at the core of the thematic development. In their quest for a voice, the Wieselean characters pass through various stages, reflecting the author's own spiritual-intellectual itinerary. Their story is basically his, for his is very much a part of many of his protagonists. Yet, transposed into a fictional mode, W.'s story exposes the reader to the intensely problematic nature of the witness. The contradictions inherent in the act of testifying are revealed in both conscious and unconscious forms. A close study of the texts discloses an underlying tension between the compulsion to tell the tale and the fear of betraying the sanctity of the subject. The author has created characters who allow him to confront himself, and a new kind of protagonist—emblem of our times—issues forth from the literary mind after Auschwitz: *the protagonist as witness.*

W.'s novels lend themselves to a chronological investigation. They follow a logical sequence, each exploring a particular option open to the survivor after the journey to the end of night: killing, suicide, madness, faith and friendship, return from exile, silence, and involvement in revolutionary movements, in history itself. "The books came one after the other to answer the questions I was asking myself," W. tells us. "Each time a gate closed, the possibilities diminished, and one hope after another was stripped away." But if each text shuts a door, it also points the way to the volume that follows. The continuity and cumulative force of his oeuvre are sustained by the repetition of themes and the reappearance of characters who resemble one another.

Ellen S. Fine, *Legacy of Night: The Literary Universe of E. W.* (1982), 3

How is contact made between E. W.'s world, *l'univers concentrationnaire,* and our world?

The connecting link is story.

E. W. is not a historian (though he deals with the stuff of history), nor is he a collector of data (though every line he writes provides data for a new geography of the soul and of hell), nor a systematician (though systematic reflection can follow from his words). No, he is a teller of tales. You want to know about the kingdom of night? There is no way to describe the kingdom of night. But let me tell you a story . . . You want to know about the condition of the human heart? But let me tell you a story. . . You want a description of the indescribable? There is no way to describe the indescribable. But let me tell you a story. . . .

If we are to learn from E. W., we must listen to stories. His stories. They challenge our stories. They open horizons we had never seen before. They smash barriers we had thought were impregnable. They leave us desolate. They also bind us in new and deeper relationships.

Robert McAfee Brown, *E. W.: Messenger to All Humanity* (1983), 6–7

As a storyteller, E. [W.] speaks with a quiet intensity that holds the audience totally attentive. No one can adequately or fully appreciate W. the writer who has not heard him tell a story; for his writing, in the end, is nothing other than a mosaic of tales, a written embodiment of the living voice. But what I have appreciated equally as much as W.'s gifts as a storyteller is his wonderful, genuine, and subtle sense of humor. Although his present life is a happy and full one—an all too full one—he bears the unimaginable burden of his memoirs of the Holocaust as a touchstone of reality for our time. That precisely he should live and speak with such a rich interweaving of humor is a grace for which those of us who know him can only be grateful in the fullest and most religious sense of that term. If it were not for his humor, he would not be thoroughly genuine, and his witness would not be as compelling as it is. Humor is the milk brother of faith, Martin Buber said when speaking of his friend Franz Rosenzweig. This is equally true for E. W.

Maurice Friedman, *Abraham Joshua Heschel and E. W., You Are My Witnesses* (1987), 110

W. is the voice of the Jew in the Western world. When he speaks to the President in the White House, he is also the conscience of our society. When he teaches and publishes, when he lectures and dreams, he breaks the conspiracy of silence which has become the malady of our time. . . .

Indifference leads to silence. There must be words for those who care. Ignorance leads to silence. There must be records of past and present cruelties done in the world, so that each generation can remember—not only the evil of the past, but also the glowing goodness, the courage and the decency, which existed in the darkest days. In this test, W. brings us words to destroy indifference and to awaken remembrance. The words are small, glowing embers of despair. And hope. They are history. And they are prayers.

Albert H. Friedlander (and E. W.), *The Six Days of Destruction* (1988), 8–9

WILLIAMS, John A.

American novelist, biographer, and essayist, b. 5 Dec. 1925, Jackson, Miss.

W. is a remarkably prolific writer who has published ten novels, along with biography, other nonfiction books and articles, and two anthologies. His fiction occupies an uneasy place between art, popular genres, and polemic, and he himself falls between two African-American literary generations. The result of these multiple ambiguities—none of which has anything to do with the uniformly high quality of his writing—has assured that W. has so far attracted a less wide audience than his work deserves.

There is a sense in which W.'s early work shows the influence of the Beat writers and belongs in any consideration of that movement. To situate it there, however, would entail a redefinition of the Beat Generation that could encompass the directly racial anger of a young black, as well as W.'s insider's view of jazz music and its culture. The alienation that characterizes the white authors usually identified with the beat scene, their relation to masculinity, even their devotion to black music, all take on different meanings when seen through the lens of the black author's alienation, struggle for manhood, and involvement with jazz.

As the black movement in society and in the arts took on new energy through the 1960s and 1970s, W.'s work became clearly identified with that struggle. He compiled two anthologies of African-American writing, *The Angry Black* (1962) and *Beyond the Angry Black* (1967), wrote articles and reviews calling attention to the new black writers, and produced biographies of Richard Wright (q.v.)—*The Most Native of Sons* (1970)—and of Martin Luther King, Jr.—*The King God Didn't Save* (1970). At the same time, his fiction reflects the major themes of race and the search for a viable identity that are salient in much black literature.

In a number of his novels, W. brings both the rhetoric of political struggle and the diction of sensational popular fiction to bear on the questions of individual identity and race relations. He places his characters within the history of American (and, to some extent, international) racism, and he illuminates that history. At the same time, he attributes an intentionality to that history that gives a number of his novels the tonality of thrillers or spy fiction. Given what has happened to black people in the past several hundred years, he seems to be saying, we should consider whether there is an intentional conspiracy. This is the polemicist's hypothesis. The novelist's contribution is to imagine what such a conspiracy would look and sound like, to people it, and give it a voice.

Thus, *Sons of Darkness, Sons of Light* (1969), takes place in a proximate Mafia-run future. *The Man Who Cried I Am* (1967), W.'s best-known novel, introduces the discovery of a "final solution"-type plot for the extermination of the black population of the U.S. And *Captain Blackman* (1972), a fictionalized survey of black military history from the American Revolution through Vietnam, posits actual meetings of the ruling white elite throughout that history, in which decisions are made about how best to exploit the blacks without granting them the material or civic benefits of their service.

W.'s work is sometimes reminiscent of Ralph Ellison's (q.v.), in the combination of hyperrealism and surrealism (q.v.) with which social themes are treated. The rapid pace of his novels, however, and their dependency on plotting brings them much closer to the world of fiction for the mass audience, an audience that W. has only rarely been able to reach.

FURTHER WORKS: *The Angry Ones* (1960); *Night Song* (1961); *Sissie* (1963); *The Protectors* (1964); *This Is My Country, Too* (1965); *Africa: Her Lands and People* (1969); *Flashbacks: A Twenty-Year Diary of Article Writing* (1973); *Mothersill and the Foxes* (1975); *One for New York* (1975); *Minorities in New York* (1975); *The Junior Bachelor Society* (1976); *!Click Song* (1982); *The Berhama Account* (1985); *Jacob's Ladder* (1987)

BIBLIOGRAPHY: Karrer, W., "Multiperspectives and the Hazards of Integration: J. W.'s *Night Song* (1961)," in Bruck, P., and W. Karrer, eds., *The Afro-American Novel since 1960* (1982), 75-101; Muller, G. H., *J. A. W.* (1984); Nadel, A., "My Country Too: Time, Place and Afro-American Identity in the Work of J. A. W.," *Obsidian II,* 2 (1987), 25-41; Reilly, J. M., "Thinking History in *The Man Who Cried I Am,*" *BALF,* 21 (1987), 25–42; Salaman, F., "To Be or Not To Be a Part of the United States: Itinéraire de l'écrivain noir dans *The Man Who Cried I Am* de J. A. W.," in Martin, J.-P., ed., *Les États-Unis: Conformismes et dissidences* (1987), 33–57

LILLIAN S. ROBINSON

WILSON, August

American dramatist and poet, b. 27 Apr. 1945, Pittsburgh, Pa.

The most honored American dramatist to emerge in the 1980s, W. grew up in poverty in a slum community in Pittsburgh, Pennsylvania. Raised by his mother, he never knew his biological father and had an often troubled relationship with his stepfather; the relationship of father and son is one of the recurrent concerns of W.'s plays. A high-school dropout at the age of fifteen, W. educated himself at the public library, where he discovered the writings of black American authors; this first acquaintance with writers like Langston Hughes, Richard Wright, and Ralph Ellison (qq.v.) gave to the disaffected adolescent a sense of possibilities that his formal education had somehow excluded. He began to think of himself as a writer.

W. has published poetry that is by no means without interest, but he has in recent years established himself as primarily a dramatist, and it is certainly his work in the theater that has brought him the attention and acclaim of a growing audience. His association with the theater began in Pittsburgh, where he was the cofounder of the Black Horizon Theatre, a black activist company that produced several of his earliest plays. By the late 1960s, W. had become involved with the Black Power movement, and these early plays reflected a belief that a function of theater is to raise the political consciousness of the audience. W. still regards himself as a Black Nationalist, but his mature work has not been overtly political.

In 1978 W.'s *Black Bart and the Sacred Hills* was staged at the Penumbra Theatre in St. Paul, Minnesota, where W. had moved earlier in the year. But it was when he received a Jerome fellowship in 1980 for his play *Jitney,* which would have its first full-scale production in Pittsburgh in 1982, that W. began to think of himself as a playwright rather than as a poet who happened to be writing plays. As a reflection of this new seriousness of purpose, in 1980 W. submitted three plays to the Eugene O'Neill Conference: *Black Bart, Fullerton Street,* and *Why I Learned to Read.* The plays were rejected, but W.'s commitment remained firm; he began work on the play that would become *Ma Rainey's Black Bottom,* which he submitted to the O'Neill Conference in 1982. This time his play was selected for workshops and readings, bringing W. into contact with Lloyd Richards, who would eventually direct this and all of W.'s later works as they made their way to Broadway.

Ma Rainey's Black Bottom (1985) is the first of four outstanding plays that have established W. as a major force in the contemporary American theater, winner of two Pulitzer Prizes, three New York Drama Critics Circle awards, and a number of other honors. The play, set in Chicago in the 1920s, is meant to be one of what is ultimately to be a series of ten plays, the series as a whole to constitute a depiction of the struggles of African-Americans during each decade of the 20th c. *Fullerton Street,* set in the 1940s, fits the general pattern, but it is not clear whether that play, not one of W.'s successes, will, at least in its present form, remain W.'s last word on that decade. The other three plays that W. has completed in the series are all set in Pittsburgh: *Fences* (1986) in the 1950s, *Joe Turner's Come and Gone* (1988) in 1911, and *The Piano Lesson* (1990) in the 1930s. W.'s most recent play, *Two Trains Running,* set in the 1960s, opened on Broadway in 1992. Whatever the specific geographical setting of the individual play, the South is a felt presence, as is the history of black America before the 20th c., including the experience of slavery and its aftermath. Further, W. is concerned, especially in the two more recent plays, with exploring the continuing African dimension in the African-American experience. That black Americans are an African people is for W. a given, and to bring his audience, especially his black audience, to a shared awareness of this perception is one of his goals.

Ma Rainey's Black Bottom and *Fences* are both written in the mode of social realism verging on naturalism (qq.v.). Both explore tensions among black characters: musicians in the first play, the family group in the second. In both, these tensions arise ultimately out of situations created by racism: the exploitation of black musicians, the exclusion in the first half of this century of black athletes from major-league professional sports. Yet the tensions also arise from the specific traits and frustrations of the individual characters. W.'s ability to sustain this sort of dual vision is an important source of the plays' emotional power and complexity, as well as a tribute to his honesty.

The most recent plays reflect both thematic and structural developments in W.'s art. Thematically, *Joe Turner's Come and Gone* and *The Piano Lesson* give greater emphasis than the earlier work to the affirmation of the healing power of African-

American folk culture; essentially, the characters' chance of survival is closely related to their willingness to accept that cultural tradition. Structurally, W. moves toward more imaginatively open forms, less bound by the conventions of social realism, that are able to accommodate without condescension or apology elements of magic and the supernatural; the plays thus formally enact the very acceptance of folk cultural traditions that they thematically affirm.

Although W. regards himself as a Black Nationalist, the recognition he has enjoyed, as reflected in awards, critical acclaim, and at least some measure of commerical success, attests to the general appeal of his work. There is not the slightest reason to doubt the genuineness of W.'s nationalism, but, at least as reflected in his plays, it is a nationalism that is neither narrow nor negative. W. is committed to exploring the life of black Americans. His work provides us with compelling images of that life as black, as American, as human.

BIBLIOGRAPHY: Smith, P., "*Ma Rainey's Black Bottom:* Playing the Blues as Equipment for Living," in Hartigan, K. V., ed., *Within the Dramatic Spectrum* (1986), 177–86; Freedman, S., "A Voice from the Streets," *NYTMag,* 10 June 1987, 36, 40, 49, 70; Staples, B., "A. W.," *Essence,* Aug. 1987, 51, 111, 113; Poinsett, A., "A. W.: Hottest New Playwright," *Ebony,* Nov. 1987, 68, 70, 72, 74; Ching, M. C., "Wrestling against History," *Theater,* 19, 3 (1988), 70–71; Glover, M., "Two Notes on A. W.: The Songs of a Marked Man," *Theater,* 19, 3 (1988), 69–70; Reed, I., *Writin' Is Fightin': Thirty-Seven Years of Boxing on Paper* (1988), 161–81; Brown, C., "The Light in August," *Esquire,* Apr. 1989, 116, 118, 120, 122–27

W. P. KENNEY

WILSON, Lanford

American dramatist, b. 13 Apr. 1937, Lebanon, Mo.

W. is considered one of the most influential contemporary American playwrights. Raised in a small town and on a farm, he presents a Midwestern perspective in many of his important works. After working in factories and studying art briefly at Southwest Missouri State College and San Diego State College (1955–1957), he moved to Chicago to work as a commercial artist. In 1959 he discovered a talent for playwriting and gave up art and short-story writing. W. moved to Greenwich Village, New York City, in 1962 and became acquainted with the Theater of the Absurd (q.v.) at

Caffe Cino. Joe Cino produced his *So Long at the Fair* in 1963, a work inspired by the madcap but serious plays of Eugène Ionesco (q.v.). During the next few years, W.'s plays became the mainstay of Caffe Cino. In 1965 his full-length plays were produced successfully on the larger stage of Ellen Stewart's La Mama Experimental Theatre. W. and friends organized the nonprofit Circle Repertory Theatre in 1969, which proved the most successful locus for his playwriting. The ensemble policies and varied repertoire of this institution allowed W. to create certain roles for known actors and to envision locales in familiar acting spaces. His three most significant plays won box-office approval and critical acclaim at the Circle Repertory Theatre. Among these were *The Hot-l Baltimore* (1973), which received the New York Drama Critics Circle Award, the Outer Circle Award, and the Obie Award; *The Mound Builders* (1975), the Obie Award; and *Talley's Folly* (1980), the Pulitzer Prize.

The Hot-l Baltimore shows life among the remnants of a vanishing era, a theme that W. would return to, particularly in *The Mound Builders*. A portrait of a marginalized and down-and-out community, the play follows the dramatic traditions of Maxim Gorky's *The Lower Depths* (1912), Eugene O'Neill's *The Iceman Cometh* (wr. 1939, pub. 1946), and most especially William Saroyan's (q.v.) *The Time of Your Life* (1939), whose wayward but somewhat sentimentalized characters W. at times redraws. The play is set in the early 1970s in a soon-to-be demolished railway hotel built during the Gilded Age; everything is allowed to deteriorate without repair. The characters are prostitutes, homosexual partners, the dispossessed, the put-upon, and the despairing. A golden age of travel (and of personal dreams) has given way to a hard reality, which has left the characters little sense of hope or fulfillment. W. reveals a spectrum of individual responses to this condition: Some of the characters, especially The Girl, a street prostitute, show an awareness of what has been lost. As a child, W. was fascinated by the American railroads, and this vanishing transportation system functions as a symbol in the play of life's elusive goals.

In *The Mound Builders,* W. returns to the American Midwest, and to a strong Middle-American presence, for his inspiration. Two archaeologists and their wives live in a farmhouse, itself fast becoming an artifact and locus for nostalgic reflection on a more ideal time in American life. Structurally the play follows a pattern of parallel-and-contrast between the vanished society for which the archaeologists are digging and the vacuities of their own lives. During periodic flashback scenes, photographic slides are projected by August, the senior archaeologist, which depict alternately the significant people in his life—the other characters in the play—with shots of the decaying glory in the dig site. W.'s humor is based on the wit of the characters, their self-deprecating commentary and their ironic perception of the futility of all attempts at meaning in civilization, including above all their own. *The Mound Builders* seems to expose our general complicity in the destruction of meaning in American life, even as we pursue such ideals as a greater understanding of past history.

With *Talley's Folly* W. began what was planned as a five-play cycle dealing with the history of the Talley family of Lebanon, Missouri, from the Civil War era to the present. Only two other plays of the cycle have been completed: *War in Lebanon* (1980) and *Talley and Son* (1986). *Talley's Folly* garnered critical and popular acclaim for its unusual performance structure—the main character both opens and closes the stage action in a framing device spoken directly to the audience—as well as for the effective simplicities of plot and character. Using only two characters, one setting, and a very restricted time frame—the ninety-six-minute running time of the performance—the play focuses on the developing relationship of the two characters and their tensive dialogue. Set in 1944, the plot is an episode in the history of the Talleys, a respected Missouri family. Matt, a Jewish-American, successfully courts Sally Talley, who rejects his love overtures until she is convinced of his sincerity.

Burn This (1987) presents the ills of urban living with dialogue and characterization somewhat more acerbic than W.'s earlier plays, although, as in *Talley's Folly,* it reveals a continued interest in the dynamic chemistry between a romantic odd couple. Anna is invaded late at night in her downtown Manhattan loft by Pale, her deceased roommate's brother. They are immediately drawn to each other, but soon digress into frenetic musings brought about by the pressures of their modern life-styles and their complex psychologies.

As a dramatist, W. follows the traditions of Tennessee Williams, Lillian Hellman, and William Inge (qq.v.) in presenting character and conflict from America's heartland. His straightforward realism is enhanced by elements of lyricism and nostalgia for a bygone era when ideals were still believed in. His people strive for meaning in life, often failing, but at times achieving some sort of perception. In the tradition of Anton Chekhov (q.v.), the characters often express through humor and reflection an earnest desire for fulfillment and an end to aimlessness and spiritual vacuity. Although W.'s plays have been criticized for insufficient character motivation and occasional sentimentality, his sense of human speech patterns, his sympathy for a wide range of characters, and his experiments with play structure, particularly with layered dialogue and choric commentary, have been exemplary.

FURTHER WORKS: *Balm in Gilead* (1965); *Days Ahead* (1965); *Home Free!* (1965); *This Is the Rill Speaking* (1967); *Days Ahead* (1967); *The Madness of Lady Bright* (1967); *The Rimers of Eldritch* (1967); *Wandering* (1967); *The Gingham Dog* (1969); *Lemon Sky* (1970); *The Sand Castle* (1970); *Sextet (Yes)* (1970); *Stop: A Turn* (1970); *Summer and Smoke* (1972, libretto adaptation, with Lee Hoiby); *The Family Continues* (1973); *The Great Nebula in Orion* (1973); *Ikke, Ikke, Nye, Nye, Nye* (1973); *Victory on Mrs. Dandywine's Island* (1973); *Serenading Louie* (1976); *Brontosaurus* (1978); *5th of July* (1979); *A Tale Told* (1981); *Angels Fall* (1982); *Thymus Vulgaris* (1982); *Halls of North American Forests* (1988); *The Moonshot Tape* (1988)

BIBLIOGRAPHY: Barnett, G. A., *L. W.* (1987); Barnett, G. A., "Recreating the Magic: An Interview with L. W.," *BSUF*, 25 (Spring 1984), 57–74; Dasgupta, G., "L. W.," in Marranca, B., and G. Dasgupta, eds., *American Playwrights: A Critical Survey* (1981), 27–39; Dreher, A., "L. W.," in MacNicholas, J., ed., *DLB: Twentieth-Century American Dramatists*, Part 2 (1981), 350–68; Harriet, E., "L. W.: To Vanish without a Trace," *American Voices* (1989), 19–35; Jacobi, M. J., "The Comic Vision of L. W.," *SLitI*, 21 (1988), 119–34; Kellman, B., "The American Playwright in the Seventies: Some Problems and Perspectives," *Theatre Quarterly*, 8, 29 (1978), 45–58; Schvez, H. I., "Images of the Past in the Plays of L. W.," in Bock, H., ed., *Essays in Contemporary American Drama* (1981), 225–40; Witham. B. B., "Images of America: W., Weller and Horovitz," *TJ*, 21 (Fall 1988), 119–34

WILLIAM OVER

WITTIG, Monique
French feminist writer, b. 1935, Belgium

W. has been secretive about her life. Allegedly the daughter of the Belgian poet Henri Dubois, she earned a degree in modern literature at the Sorbonne; studied oriental languages; and then worked first in the Bibliothèque Nationale and later as a proofreader. Her first novel, *L'opoponax* (1964; *The Opoponax*, 1966), was hailed by Marguerite Duras, Mary McCarthy, and Claude Simon (qq.v.). It won the prestigious Médicis Prize. In 1970 W. contributed to writing the official anthem of the Mouvement de Libération des Femmes; she also

became the leader of the Féministes Révolutionnaires; and she created a well-publicized scandal by trying to place a wreath under the Arc de Triomphe to honor the wife of the Unknown Soldier. In 1976 she emigrated to the U.S. She moves frequently, by choice, among the colleges and universities where she teaches. She has contributed important articles on the lesbian identity to *Questions féministes* and to *Feminist Issues*.

L'opoponax forcefully depicts the oppressive atmosphere of a convent school and its indoctrination of girls into partriarchal culture. The impressionistic style and focus on group interactions recalls Nathalie Sarraute (q.v.). Over the years, the class gradually achieves a limited autonomy and critical detachment, while the heroine discovers herself through her love for a classmate. The gender-neutral pronoun *on* is used throughout. *Les guérillères* (1969; *The Guérillères*, 1971), a utopian epic, shows an independent society of warrior women who learn to create their own traditions without being bound by them; to appreciate their bodies without worshiping them; to fight, win, and to dismiss with laughter derogatory clichés about women. They then conquer men, and rehabilitate a few men of good will as they pursue a worldwide revolution. *Le corps lesbien* (1973; *The Lesbian Body*, 1975) evokes the Song of Songs with a cycle of prose poems that praise the lover's body, including the internal organs and the secretions. Lesbian love, at times violent, is glorified as complete and democratic. The *Brouillon pour un dictionnaire des amantes* (1976, with Sande Zeig; *Lesbian Peoples: Material for a Dictionary*, 1979) depicts a utopian future society and offers sample articles for a feminist revision of all knowledge. All references to males are erased; "lesbian" is redefined as "companion lover." "History," the long central entry, rejects *l'écriture féminine* (femininitude). *Virgile, non* (1985; *Across the Acheron*, 1987) parodies Dante's *Divine Comedy* and is set in San Francisco. Hell is filled with horrific processions of women enslaved, battered, and mutilated by men; Limbo is occupied by cruising lesbians, isolated in their hedonism; and Paradise is emotional and sensual fulfillment. "Wittig" and her angelic guide try mostly in vain to persuade the women in Hell to take up their arms and escape. *Le voyage sans fin* (1985; pointless [or endless] voyage), an experimental playscript and video, recreates *Don Quixote* by Miguel de Cervantes (1547-1616) with female characters. Quichotte (the French spelling of Quixote) is opposed by her own conventional mother and sister. Independent series of words and of pantomime are interwoven.

W. is the leader of the militant French feminists who seek to attack and subvert the concept of the difference between the sexes, a concept they denounce as the foundation of the patriarchal hierarchy, male domination, and the enslavement of women. She has called for a worldwide revolution in which writing would constitute only an initial call to arms. Thus she opposes the countervailing French feminist movement led by Hélène Cixous (q.v.) advocating the glorification of woman's difference in *l'écriture féminine*. The accessible *L'opoponax* remains highly regarded as a narrative of childhood. In academic circles, *Les guérillères* is considered a model of feminist fiction. The *Brouillon* has greatly influenced the "Women's Language" debate and Cheris Kramarae (b. 1938) and Paula Treichler's (b. 1943) monumental *Feminist Dictionary* (1985). W.'s experiments with rejecting plot, and her consistent, idealistic attempts to replace the cult of personality with a collectivist ethic have made her works less appealing to conventional readers than to those familiar with the New Novel (q.v.) and with poststructuralist theories of language. Her major thrust has been to reappropriate language and culture for women.

BIBLIOGRAPHY: McCarthy, M., "Everybody's Childhood," *The Writing on the Wall and Other Literary Essays* (1970), 102–11; Higgins, L., "Nouvelle, nouvelle autobiographie: M. W.'s *Le corps lesbien*," *SubStance*, 14 (1976), 160–66; Wenzel, H. V., "The Text as Body/Politics: An Appreciation of M. W.'s Writing in Context," *FSt*, 7 (1981), 264–87; Shaktini, N., "Displacing the Phallic Subject: W.'s Lesbian Writings," *Signs*, 8 (1982), 29–44; Crowder, D., "Amazons and Mothers? M. W., Hélène Cixous, and Theories of Women's Writing," *ConL*, 24 (1983), 117–44; special W. issue, *Vlasta*, 4 (1985); Duffy, J., "M. W.," in Brosman, C. S., ed., *DLB: French Novelists since 1960* (1989), 330–44; Porter, L. M., "Writing Feminism: Myth, Epic and Utopia in M. W.'s *Les guérillères*," *ECr*, 29 (1989), 92–100

LAURENCE M. PORTER

WOLFE, Tom

(born Thomas Kennerly Wolfe, Jr.) American essayist, journalist, and novelist, b. 2 Mar. 1930, Richmond, Va.

W. is one the most original and influential American prose writers of the 20th c. He played a major role in helping create a more experimental style of nonfiction writing that came to be widely called "the New Journalism." In 1957, W. earned a doctorate in American studies from Yale. After working as a reporter and feature writer for the *Washington Post* and the *New York Herald Tri-*

bune, he gained national attention in 1963 with a lengthy feature story on customized cars published in *Esquire* magazine.

In this piece, "There Goes (Varoom! Varoom!) The Kandy-Kolored Tangerine-Flake Streamline Baby," W. employs the slangy, hyperbolic, and highly descriptive style that he would continue to refine in the years to come. In two early collections of essays, *The Kandy-Kolored Tangerine-Flake Streamline Baby* (1965) and *The Pump House Gang* (1968), W. also first showed his interest in examining closely a variety of subcultural groups—among them surfers, gamblers, and stock-car drivers—who were then still largely ignored by mainstream journalism.

W.'s *The Electric Kool-Aid Acid Test* (1968) focuses on novelist Ken Kesey (q.v.) and his band of "Merry Pranksters" as they travel the country shooting a movie, ingesting hallucinogens, and, eventually, finding themselves in conflict with the law. This book, a major best-seller, demonstrates not only W.'s capacity for exhaustive research, but his ability to use artfully the novelist's techniques in the writing of nonfictional prose. Here, for example, W. seeks to narrow the mental and verbal distance between himself and the Pranksters, in part by carefully recording—and often imitating—the distinctive flair and rhythm of their highly colloquial speech. Morever, he shifts points of view, and builds drama through the careful pacing of precisely detailed scenes. W.'s especially creative use of such strategies encouraged their wide adoption; in fact, by the mid-1970s, a more subdued form of this "New Journalism" could be found in a wide variety of books, newspapers, and magazines.

Although some critics complained that W. looked too sympathetically at the drug-promoting Pranksters, a more careful reading of the book shows that his interest in the group and their various mystical and social pursuits was less personal than intellectual, and that his own cultural biases were fairly conservative—a fact that became clearer during the 1970s, a period W. indelibly dubbed "the Me Decade."

Indeed, in *Radical Chic & Mau-Mauing the Flak Catchers* (1970), his most acid book, W. savages what he believed to be a growing trend among affluent white liberals (such as the composer Leonard Bernstein) to court and support far-left groups, many of whom were calling for the revolutionary transformation of American society, and thus, ironically, of the very system that made both affluence and liberalism possible.

In another controversial work, *The Painted Word* (1975), W. remained on the attack, this time seeking to debunk many of the more celebrated practitioners and promoters of modern art. Essentially, W. argues that modern art, particularly in America, has been characterized chiefly not by an explosion of unique and innovative talent, but by a widespread and rather slavish adherence to fashionable aesthetic theories. Although many critics found *The Painted Word* to be a witty and valuable exposé of hype and pretentiousness in the arts, others found it inaccurate and simplistic, revealing primarily the large gaps in W.'s knowledge of the painters and theoreticians he was attempting to analyze.

In *The Right Stuff* (1979), W. strikes a more celebratory tone as he describes the lives of the elite group of astronauts involved in the American space program during its earliest—and most dangerous—phase. There would seem to be little in common between a clean-cut corps of fighter pilots and the many eccentrics, outsiders, and outlaws who had previously appeared in W.'s writing. But the themes and concerns of *The Right Stuff* can also be found in such works as *The Electric Kool-Aid Acid Test*. Once again, W. is interested in examining the rhetoric—and thus the belief system—of a group who not only live well outside the mainstream of American society, but who continually seek escape from the predictability of daily life.

W.'s first novel, *The Bonfire of the Vanities* (1987), was widely hailed as one of the decade's most significant fictions. In this large, lively bestseller, W.'s principal target is the American legal system, but he also looks satirically at the world of journalism, and at the spirit of greed and social climbing that often seemed to prevail in the 1980s. Although the book contains no sympathetic characters, many critics praised its bold sweep and linguistic vitality. In various essays and interviews, W. indicated that he wrote the novel to illustrate the qualities of fiction writing he most admires and associates with a tradition of "realism," which includes Dickens, Balzac, and Zola. Moreover, W. has condemned the trend toward fantasy, self-obsession, and "minimalism" that he finds dominant in much recent American fiction.

These observations provoked an often heated discussion on the aims of fiction that raged for months in various journals and magazines. W.'s own writings—as well as his famously dapper, white-suited persona—came under severe attack. Once again, W. was accused of being old-fashioned and elitist, and of simplifying complex aesthetic and cultural issues.

But even many of the harshest of these critics have been forced to admit that, over the years, W. has expressed his beliefs with a force and verve that few of his literary contemporaries have been able to match. Indeed, in many respects, W. can be likened to H. L. Mencken (q.v.), who played a similarly provocative role in the 1920s and 1930s. Like Mencken, W. is an erudite, articulate, and wide-ranging author whose distinctive and seriously playful style will ensure that many of his works are likely to endure for years to come.

FURTHER WORKS: *Mauve Gloves & Madmen, Clutter & Vine, and Other Short Stories* (1976); *In Our Time* (1980); *From Bauhaus to Our House* (1981); *The Purple Decades: A Reader* (1982)

BIBLIOGRAPHY: Hersey, J., "The Legend on the License," *YR*, 75, 2 (Winter 1986), 289–314; Anderson, C., *Style As Argument: Contemporary American Nonfiction* (1987), 8–47; Epstein, J., "T. W.'s Vanities," *NewC*, 6, 6 (Feb. 1988), 5–16; Crawford, S., "T. W.: Outlaw Gentleman," *Journal of American Culture*, 13, 2 (1990), 39–50; Grunwald, L., "T. W. Aloft in the Statussphere," *Esquire*, Oct. 1990, 146–60

BRIAN MURRAY

WOLFF, Egon
Chilean dramatist, b. 13 Apr. 1926, Santiago

W. was born of German immigrant parents and grew up in an atmosphere of solid social values and a strong work ethic. He graduated from the Catholic University in Santiago with a degree in chemical engineering. Although he studied science and worked in the development of chemicals, he was always interested in literature, the classics, and the humanities in general.

W. began writing his plays at a time when there was a great deal of theatrical creativity in his country, especially at the University of Chile and the Catholic University in Santiago. Almost every play he wrote earned him a first prize in one competition or another. While he is perhaps not the most radically innovative of recent Latin American playwrights, he is one of the most powerful and most widely performed. He himself has been invited to premieres of his plays throughout the world. A recurring theme in his work concerns the threat of some kind of Other, a chaotic, anarchic force from the "outside" on a comfortable but fragile order built on illusion.

W.'s first plays are in the tradition of the social realism (q.v.) begun in Latin America in the first decade of the 20th c. by Florencio Sánchez (q.v.). *Mansión de lechuzas* (1956; mansion of owls), depicts the struggle of two sons to resist their fearful mother's efforts to protect them from the dangers of the outside world. *Discípulos del miedo* (1957; disciples of fear) reverses this image of the mother figure; the character Matilde is almost pathologically concerned with her quest for psychological security through the acquisition of material things and her dreamed-of entry into the entrepreneurial class. A third play, *Niñamadre* (1962; childmother), portrays a variety of characters from the lower class. It deals primarily, however, with a good-hearted, sentimental prostitute who wants to have her baby in spite of the psychological insecurity her desire precipitates in her macho lover. These early plays are strongly mimetic, involve the audience emotionally with the characters and the conflicts, and are well constructed with rising tension in each of the three acts and an unambiguously resolved conflict with a clear social message. Objects and lighting are used in effectively, albeit rather conventionally, symbolic ways.

Los invasores (1963; the invaders) marks a change in W.'s dramatic method if not in his worldview. While it may not be his best work, it remains his most popular and most critically discussed. The social message remains clear—the "secure" world of the middle class is falsely constructed on the sands of their indifference to the plight of the poor. It is the latter, under the leadership of the enigmatic character China who invade, insidiously take over, and eventually destroy the home of the industrialist Lucas Meyer. The play is charged with ambiguities that allude to terrifying psychological and metaphysical insecurities beyond the mere social order. China is a fascinatingly ambivalent character—reassuring, threatening, constructive, sinister, priestly, revolutionary—Christ, Lucifer, Lenin, Che Guevara, and Robespierre all rolled into one. The play's resolution, too, is open-ended. Although it has all been Lucas's dream, it is a dream that threatens to repeat itself in reality. Numerous defamiliarization devices are used in the play to create an unreal atmosphere. The result is an artistic blending of social realism, surrealism, and the Theater of the Absurd (qq.v.).

Most experts would agree that *Flores de papel* (1970; *Paper Flowers,* 1971), is probably W.'s masterpiece. It is similar in theme to *Los invasores* but more intense in that it is restricted to two characters and has a more claustrophobic atmosphere with its strict limitation of scene. Here the elegant, middle-class apartment of Eva, a refined middle-aged woman who lives alone, is gradually destroyed by the derelict known as The Hake, who intrudes into her world, unobtrusively at first, by offering to carry home her groceries. The play goes beyond *Los invasores* also in the devastating nature of the destruction that takes place, for here the very structure of Eva's psyche is undermined as she is utterly stripped by The Hake of her individuality, her femininity, and her identity. This play has had a wide variety of interpretations—

social, psychological, metaphysical, even aesthetic—but continues to resist closure. In the almost allegorical reductionism of the portrayal of character and scene, in the emotional detachment of the dialogue, in its dependence on language for dramatic effect, and in the strange unreality of the atmosphere, one is reminded of the plays of Harold Pinter (q.v.).

W. is not only a craftsman of the first order. He is a dramatist of profound vision as well. Although he deals locally with Chilean social reality, he has at the same time great universal appeal. He fascinates because he gives dramatic form to our most fundamental human fears and forces us to face the fragility of the structures on which we build our society, our psyches, and our views of reality. For these reasons he is one of the outstanding dramatists of Latin America today.

FURTHER WORKS: *Parejas de trapo* (1959); *El signo de Caín* (1969); *Kindergarten* (1977); *Espejismos* (1978); *José* (1980); *Alamos en la azotea* (1981); *La balsa de la Medusa* (1984)

BIBLIOGRAPHY: Peden, M. S., "Three Plays of E. G., *LATR,* 3 (1969), 29–35; Lyday, L. F., "E. W.'s *Los invasores*: A Play within a Dream," *LATR,* 6, 1 (1972), 19–26; Peden, M. S., "The Theater of E. W.," in Lyday, L. F., and G. Woodyard, eds., *Dramatists in Revolt* (1976), 190–201; Peden, M. S., "*Kindergarten:* A New Play by E. W.," *LATR,* 10 (Spring 1977), 5–10; Chrzanowski, J., "Theme, Characterization, and Structure in *Los invasores*," *LATR,* 11, 2 (Spring 1978), 5–10; López, D., "Ambiguity in *Flores de papel*," *LATR,* 12 (1978), 43–50; Lyday, L. F., "Whence W.'s Canary: A Conjecture on Commonality," *LATR,* 16, 2 (Spring 1983), 23–29; Taylor, D., "Art and Antiart in E. W.'s *Flores de papel*," *LATR,* 18, 1 (Fall 1984), 65–68

ROBERT SCOTT

WRIGHT, James

American poet, b. 13 Dec. 1927, Martins Ferry, Ohio; d. 25 Mar. 1980, New York City, N.Y.

W. grew up the son of a factory worker in Martins Ferry, Ohio, which is both a literal and a ghostly presence in his poetry, life there the apparent source of his trademark identification with the lonely, the derelict, and the damned. The rich literary tradition of Kenyon College, where he was a student from 1948 to 1952, is another ghostly presence in his work. It stands clearly behind the closed-form poetry of his first collections, and it survived in a continued reverence for Horatian craft, restraint, distance, and elegance even as he shifted from closed to open forms under the influence of the poet Robert Bly (q.v.) and under the stimulus of translating such surrealistic Spanish American poets as Pablo Neruda, César Vallejo, and Juan Ramón Jiménez (qq.v.). After earning a Ph.D. at the University of Seattle (1959), where he studied with Theodore Roethke (q.v.), W. taught at the University of Minnesota, at Macalester College in St. Paul, and from 1966 until his death in 1980 at Hunter College in New York City.

W.'s first collection, *The Green Wall* (1957), was selected for publication in the Yale Series of Younger Poets by W. H. Auden (q.v.). Most of its poems are neo-Georgian in style, written in rhyme and meter, as are a substantial number of the poems in *Saint Judas* (1959). Especially striking in these volumes at the time because of their unexpected sympathies, striking now because they symptomize a darkening tone and an increasing pressure of personality, are a trio of poems about men condemned to death; "A Poem about George Doty in the Death House," "American Twilights, 1957," and "At the Executed Murderer's Grave." Other poems have as their subjects mad girls, black prostitutes, deaf children, and the poet Sappho. Traditional form seems to be proffered in these early poems as aesthetic compensation for the way things are.

W. remarked upon the publication of *Saint Judas* that whatever he wrote thereafter would be completely different, and so it is generally thought to have been. The early poems only hint at the spare, colloquial, raggedly personal style of *The Branch Will Not Break* (1963), and they have few glimmers of the natural beauty that is allowed in the latter volume to transform the act of perception into something deeply affecting. Indeed, the new poems of *The Branch Will Not Break, Shall We Gather at the River* (1968), and the *Collected Poems* (1971) possess an alertness to the particulars and to the particular moments of experience that is extraordinarily resonant, for the logically discursive progression and elaborate closure of the earlier poetry give way in those collections to anecdotal non sequiturs and a flatness of statement that reach downward to the emotional gestalt of what has come to be termed "the deep image." Poems like "Lying in a Hammock at William Duffy's Farm in Pine Island, Minnesota" and "A Blessing" became instantly famous for sudden shifts of feeling that are responses to such deeply buried figures of understanding. Like other Deep Imagists—Robert Bly, Robert Kelly (b. 1935), James Dickey (q.v.), Jerome Rothenberg (b. 1931), Diane Wakoski (b. 1937)—W. was reacting in part against the tendency of the so-called New York Poets to fragment perception into an apparently discontinuous stream of images. Famously,

he rebuked the New York Poets in the poem "Many of Our Waters: Variations on a Poem by a Black Child" for their disdain of the "pure clear word."

In the wake of his *Collected Poems* and the Pulitzer Prize that it earned him, W. experimented unsuccessfully with prose poems in *Two Citizens* (1973), a collection he later regretted, and in *Moments of the Italian Summer* (1976), a collection of fourteen prose poems published in limited edition. A number of such poems, some of them recycled from the latter volume, also appear in W.'s last collections, *To a Blossoming Pear Tree* (1977) and the posthumously published *This Journey* (1982). The late poems are colloquial in their diction, loose in their rhythms, and elliptical in their structures, but a firm technique of lineation, a talismanic sense of the word, and an unmannered fluidity lend them classical grace. Even when their anecdotes are riven suddenly by auctorial intrusions, the poems tend to be shapely psychological wholes—the poems in particular that are inspired by the landscape of Italy and that speak of irredeemable loneliness opened inexplicably to joy even under the shadow of W.'s approaching death.

Above the River: The Complete Poems (1990) makes clear that loneliness was W.'s abiding subject, with death looming large as the final loneliness. His is a particularly American strain of loneliness because it is permeated with both a Jamesian sense that the inner life has no home in the Martin Ferries of America and a Whitmanesque recognition that loneliness admits one to the fraternity of outsiders. It is also a loneliness particularly W.'s own in his turning to the place within, only to discover Martin Ferry there, too, even in Italy. One of the most appealing strategies of his poetry, because it sets off chiaroscuricly this preoccupation with loneliness, is the irradiating shaft of joy that tends to emanate in the early poems from communication with the natural world; in the later poems, from love of his wife. At its best, the interplay of the two lends extraordinary psychological drama to lyrics of high technical achievement and establishes W. in the first rank of American poets in his generation.

FURTHER WORKS: *The Lion's Tale and Eyes: Poems Written Out of Laziness and Silence* (1962); *Salt Mines and Such* (1971); *I See the Wind* (1974); *Old Booksellers and Other Poems* (1976); *The Summer of James and Annie Wright: Sketches and Mosaics* (1981, with Ann Wright); *In Defense against This Exile: Letters to Wayne Burns/J. W.* (1985); *The Delicacy and Strength of Lace: Letters between Leslie Marmon Silko and J. W.* (1986)

BIBLIOGRAPHY: Saunders, W. S., *J. W.: An Introduction* (1979); Smith, D., ed., *The Pure Clear*

Word: Essays on the Poetry of J. W. (1982);
Mazzaro, J., "Dark Water: J. W.'s Early Poetry,"
CentR, 27 (1983), 135–55; Graves, M., "Crisis
in the Career of J. W.," *HC,* 22, 5 (1985), 1–9;
Blakely, R., "Form and Meaning in the Poetry of
J. W.," *SDR,* 25, 2 (1987), 20–30; Dougherty,
D. C., *J. W.* (1987); Lammon, M. D., "Making
Acquaintance: Second Hand Notes on J. W.,"
IowaR, 17, 1 (1987), 55–71; Bly, R., "J. W. and
the Slender Woman," *APR,* 17, 3 (1988), 29–33;
Stein, K., *J. W.: The Poetry of a Grown Man:
Constancy and Transition in the Work of J. W.*
(1989); Stitt, P., and F. Graziano, eds., *J. W.:
The Heart of the Light* (1990)

ROBERT F. KIERNAN

YEHOSHUA, A(braham) B.

Israeli novelist, dramatist, and essayist, b. 19 Dec. 1936, Jerusalem

Y. started publishing stories in 1957, and his first collection, *Mot hazaqen* (death of the old man) appeared in 1962. Characteristic stylistic features are already discernible in his early work, although they underwent conscious modification, change, and transformation in his subsequent fiction. These early stories are distinguished by the starkness of the sentences, the shocking transitions, the surprising shifts in plot, the blankness of the narrator, the symbolism of the action and names, and overall allegorization. These features were continued and refined in his second work, a volume of novellas, *Mul hayearot* (1968; facing the forests), still considered by many the author's major achievement. On the whole, allegorization gives way to metaphor, and the metaphor works both on the abstract level in the particular narrative circumstances and in the transforming suggestion.

Y. is adept at setting up extreme and ambivalent situations indicating mixed and contrasting motives within the characters. In the novella *Bithilat qayits 1970* (1972; *Early in the Summer of 1970*, 1973) a father tells of the death of his own son, victim of the ongoing war. Only it transpires that there has been a case of mistaken identity; it is not his son. We then see that he, the narrator, the "bereaved" father, is in love with his role and cannot exist without it. The features noticeable then are role reversal, shock, surprise, psychological attack, and national implications. In all his work, Y. has displayed a preoccupation with form. *Bithilat qayits 1970* is constructed in a circular pattern, where the final chapter repeats the first, with variations, as though time could be played with. When Y. started to write novels, this preoccupation was dominant. His first novel, *Hameahev*

(1977; *The Lover*, 1978), consists of a series of monologues uttered by separate voices, where each successive section takes up the story from the previous. Again we have a mystery, a mystery of motivation and impulse. Even clearer in its national and radical connotations is *Gerushim meuharim* (1982; *A Late Divorce*, 1984), where the divorce that is projected by the old man, living in America, coming to finalize matters in Israel, is paralleled by the national situation. The two are inextricably linked, and the reader will have difficulty in disentangling the surface narrative elements from the metaphorical and allegorical leads.

In a later novel, *Molkho* (1987; *Five Seasons*, 1989), Y. attempted to return to a more traditional form, writing a third-person narrative of the eponymous hero, recently widowed, who attempts to make a new life for himself in late middle age. Absent here are the typical elements of Y.'s prose— the odd images, the shock reverses, the surprising developments, the allegorical leads. Here we have a tale of a very average, not to say boring, man, in his routine ambition and attempted reengagement. Molcho is a man removed from history. This is not the same sort of story as is told in *Mar maniy* (1990; *Mr. Mani*, 1992), where both the obsessional pursuit after the meaning of Israeli, Jewish history and the interest in technique return. Here, the manner of telling adopted is of the telephone conversation. We only hear one side of a dialogue, and have to infer the other. An even greater surprise is the direction of the narrative. Spaced over 200 years or so, in five episodes, the story begins almost in the present, in the early 1980s, and goes back through key episodes in Jewish history to the accompaniment of a "Mani" representative. Mani, unlike Molcho (so unrelated to history) is always by the side of great events, although he himself does not forge them. The first of the Manis to appear (in the final chapter) wonders whether he is to be the last of the line. Here, technique, in pursuit of meaning, has shunted meaning aside, and displayed itself on the stage as exclusive exhibit.

FURTHER VOLUMES IN ENGLISH: *Three Days and a Child* (1971); *The Continuous Silence of a Poet* (1988)

BIBLIOGRAPHY: Yudkin, L. I., *Escape into Siege: A Survey of Israeli Literature Today* (1974), 108–11; Yudkin, L. I., *1948 and After: Aspects of Israeli Fiction* (1984), 35–36, 116–19, 154–55, 167–73; Fisch, H., *A Remembered Future: A Study in Literary Mythology* (1984), 56–57, 96–97, 126; Fuchs, E., "The Sleepy Wife; a Feminist

Consideration of A. B. Y.'s Fiction,'' *HAR*, 8 (1984), 71–81

LEON I. YUDKIN

YEROFEEV, Venedikt

Russian novelist, dramatist, and essayist, b. 28 Oct. 1938, Poyakonda, Murmansk oblast; d. 11 May 1990, Moscow

Y. was Russia's preeminent prose-poet of the 1970s and 1980s whose art and perception of the world were dominated by alcohol. Unpublished in his homeland until late 1988, his *samizdat* writings were nonetheless widely known. After his father was arrested and he was abandoned by his impoverished mother, Y. was raised in a state orphanage in the Murmansk region north of the arctic circle. Dropping out of Moscow University at the end of his first year (1956), Y., a chronic alcoholic, wandered the country as menial laborer. A brief stay at the Vladimir Pedagogical Institute led to his expulsion as ringleader of a Christian student group (1962). In spite of his sketchy formal education, Y. had a wide knowledge of history, literature, and music. His writing, mostly done in spurts at long intervals, was circulated by friends who also sent it abroad where it garnered critical acclaim. Only with the advent of glasnost did Y., by now stricken with fatal throat cancer, become a public figure in the U.S.S.R. Y.'s long existence on the fringe of Soviet society and, more recently, his own irascibility, heavy irony, and whimsy make much of his life, his views, and his work difficult to assess.

Y.'s fame with both public and critics derives from *Moskva-Petushki* (1973; *Moscow to the End of the Line,* 1980), which has now appeared in more than a dozen languages. It was written in 1969 or 1970 while E. (like his eponymous hero, Venichka) was working as a cable layer, the title referring to an interurban train line to a village some seventy miles from Moscow. In the mind of the drunken narrator, Petushki is heaven on earth. Awaiting him there are his beloved mistress and, a bit further on, his three-year-old son. Having spent the night drunk in a stairwell, Venichka makes his way to the train station stopping to fill his suitcase with bottles on the way. During the drunken journey, he reflects on events from his sad life and talks with angels, the devil, and the Sphinx, as well as with fellow passengers who join him in drinking. The train arrives at the village, which mysteriously contains wide streets and high buildings. The hero is pursued by four hooligans who kill him in the Moscow stairwell, which he has apparently never left. It has been

suggested that the murderous villains are Marx and Engels, Lenin and Stalin.

Moskva-Petushki, subtitled an epic poem but more accurately a mock epic, has little plot. Punctuated by the numerous station stops on the journey, the hero's rambling monologue is a series of wry anecdotes, witty aphorisms, and paradoxes, ranging from the personal to the cosmic. The novel, whose exuberant language and action is thoroughly uninhibited, abounds in playful humor such as cocktail recipes containing cologne, foot antiperspirant, and furniture polish, and bearing names like ''Tears of a Komsomol Girl.'' Much of the humor is, however, of the blackest hue. All of European cultural history and a grandiose, meretricious, Soviet pseudoculture are hilariously reassessed in terms of alcohol, that universal solvent of Soviet society. Alcohol plays a dual role in *Moskva-Petushki,* as it does in Russian culture. It serves as both a release from a harsh external reality and as a mechanism for the expression of mystical transcendence. The former role provides a playing field for Y.'s ribald humor; the latter, for his religious pathos. The novel draws upon an extraordinary range of historical and cultural figures for its allusions, but the single most important source is the Bible. Venichka sees himself as a Christ figure, and, significantly, his last journey falls on Friday, the day of the crucifixion. The tale's most frequent motif is a series of variants on *talipha cumi,* ''. . . I say unto thee, arise,'' Christ's words to a resurrected girl.

Y. has proclaimed the arch conservative Russian journalist and philosopher Vasilii Rozanov (1856–1919) as his forebear. Y., whose iconoclastic outlook and aphoristic style evoke Rozanov's, expressed his admiration in a curious story-essay *Vasilii Rozanov glazami ekstsentrika* (wr. 1973, pub. 1982; Vasilii Rozanov through the eyes of an eccentric). The alcoholic narrator, deserted, attempts to kill himself with three pistols. Missing, and in hope of obtaining poison, he goes to see a pharmacist friend who gives him a dose of hemlock and three volumes of Rozanov, an author forbidden in enlightened Soviet society. Rozanov's iconoclastic condemnation of conventional pieties and his rejection of rationalism in favor of ''a tender idea,'' revives the despondent hero.

During the 1980s Y. devoted himself to drama. *Valpurgieva noch; ili, 'shagi komandora'* (1985; Walpurgis Night, or the commandant's steps) is set in a Soviet psychiatric hospital on May Day eve. The hero, an alcoholic, involves the other patients in a drinking bout that ends fatally for all of the participants. The grim setting and even grimmer denouement provide a framework for the same sort of riotous language play and debunking of official reality found in *Moskva-Petushki.* Again the theme is the clash between the joys of an irrational humanity and a repressive "rational" social order. *Valpurgieva noch* was to be the second part of a trilogy collectively called *Drei Nächte* (three nights)—the first night, being Saint John's eve and the third night, Christmas eve. Y. whimsically, but accurately, noted that the outrageous—only partly published—trilogy observes Boileau's classical unities of time, place, and action. Not long before his death, Y. also spoke of a play called *Fanny Kaplan,* the antibolshevik radical who attempted to assassinate Lenin in 1919, as being almost ready for publication.

Although Y. was apolitical in any strict sense, he produced one curious piece that might be described as political, *Moia malenkaia Leniniana* (1990; my little Leniniana). The common view is that Lenin was a great and decent man whose ideas were perverted into the nightmare created by Stalin. In 1988 Y. gathered a selection of quotes from Lenin's correspondence showing him to have been scarcely less bloodthirsty than his notorious successor. The quotes are framed by Y.'s wry introductory remarks and tongue-in-cheek commentary. On the occasion of E.'s death, *Literaturnaia gazeta,* the organ of the Writer's Union, published a short selection of aphorisms gathered from his writer's notebook "Ot pravoslavnogo novogo goda 1981" (from the orthodox new year 1981). The selection was entitled "Mne khorosho, ia zhivu v stabilnoi sverkhderzhave" (1990; I am glad that I live in a stable superpower). Since Y.'s death, publication of some of the early writings and late notebooks has been promised. Among the works unpublished at the time of his death are *Zapiski psikhopata* (wr. 1955–1956; notes of a psychopath), *Blagaia vest* (wr. 1963; glad tidings), and essays on the Norwegian writers Henrik Ibsen (1828–1906), Bjørnstjerne Bjørnson (1832–1910), and Knut Hamsun (q.v.). The only manuscript copy of his novel *Dmitrii Shostakovich* (wr. 1972; Dimitry Shostakovich) was stolen during a drunken train journey.

Y. was an enormously gifted writer—part holy fool, part social and aesthetic provocateur. His wit, linguistic exuberance, and almost perverse delight in shattering idols made him unique in the "stagnation" of the 1970s and 1980s. In his dark view of the human condition (Soviet and otherwise) and in the religious yearnings he expressed in his art, he is akin to both Gogol and Dostoevsky and, more immediately, to the masters of the Silver Age, that last flare-up of artistic and intellectual creativity before the Soviet period. Y.'s oeuvre is small, and his style laconic, but as the author of *Moskva-Petushki* he is assured a place in the pantheon of 20th-c. Russian literature.

BIBLIOGRAPHY: Paperno, I. A., and B. Gasparov, "Vstan' i idi," *Slavica Hierosolymitana,* 5–6 (1981), 387–400; Hosking, G., "Drinking Mystically, Traveling Sentimentally," *TLS,* 15 Jan. 1982, 63; Brown, E. J., *Russian Literature since the Revolution,* rev. ed. (1982), 376–79; Lowe, D. A., *Russian Writing since 1953: A Critical Survey* (1987), 104–5, 190–92; Yerofeyev, V., "I'll Die before I Understand It . . . ," interview, *Moscow News,* 50 (1989), 13

D. BARTON JOHNSON

YOSANO Akiko

(formerly Hō Shō) Japanese poet, essayist, translator, and short-story writer, b. 7 Dec. 1878, Sakai; d. 29 May 1942, Tokyo

The third daughter of a confectionery shop owner in Sakai in western Japan, Y. was drawn as a girl to the Japanese classics and the new romantic literature of the Meiji period (1868–1912). After publishing her first poems in the local Kansai literary journals in the late 1890s, she joined the progressive New Poetry Society founded by Yosano Hiroshi (pseud. of Yosano Tekkan, 1873–1935) in Tokyo and began to publish her poems in its literary journal, *Myōjō.* Soon her passionate love for Hiroshi compelled her to leave her family in 1901 for Tokyo to be with him. The five years after their marriage in that same year witnessed a remarkable surge of creative energy in Y., resulting in the publications of some of the poetry collections for which Y. was best known, namely *Midaregami* (1901; *Tangled Hair,* 1935), *Koōgi* (1904; little fan), *Koigoromo* (1905; intimate love, with Yamakawa Tomiko [1879–1909] and Masuda Masako [1880–1946]), and *Maihime* (1906; the dancing girl). Having established herself as a noteworthy and innovative romantic poet before she turned thirty, she continued to publish an extraordinary number of poems throughout the late Meiji and into the Taishō era (1912–1926). Her love for her eleven children provided the impetus for a series of poetic works and children's tales such as *Yatsu no yoru* (1914; eight nights) and *Uneunekawa* (1915; meandering river).

In 1912 Y. went to France, her first experience abroad, to join Hiroshi, and stayed in Europe for about half a year. While the trip partly inspired another one of Y.'s poetry collections, entitled *Natsu yori aki e* (1914; from summer to fall), more importantly it further stimulated Y.'s already burgeoning interest in feminist issues. After returning to Japan, she began to publish social commentaries on a wide range of topics related to women and education, including such collections as *Hito oyobi onna to shite* (1916; as a human being and a woman), *Warera nani o motomuru ka* (1917; what are we seeking?), *Ai, risei oyobi yūki* (1917; love, reason, and courage), and *Gekidō no naka o yuku* (1919; walking into the midst of upheaval). To practice what she preached about women's education, she became in 1921 the school superintendent of the Academy of Culture, a school that advocated a liberal educational philosophy.

Among Y.'s extensive publications were fifteen collections of essays and three volumes of critical writings on the art of poetry. She was also an indefatigable translator of some of the major works of classical Japanese literature into modern Japanese, the most noteworthy of which was her unprecedented four-volume translation of the 11th-c. romance *Genji monogatari* (*The Tale of Genji*) entitled *Shin'yaku Genji monogatari* (1912–1913; a modern translation of *The Tale of Genji*). Toward the end of her life, she even renewed her efforts in producing yet another eight-volume translation of the same work called *Shin shin'yaku Genji monogatari* (1938–1939; the newest translation of *The Tale of Genji*).

Y. continued to publish collections of her poetry and essays in the early part of the Shōwa period (1926–1989) such as *Kokoro no enkei* (1928; the distant scene in the heart), *Hikaru kumo* (1928; the glistening clouds), and *Man-mō yūki* (1930; travels in Manchuria and Mongolia). But among her later works, the most notable was probably her collection *Hakuōshū* (1942; a collection of white cherry blossoms). Published posthumously, many of the poems imparted Y.'s feelings of melancholy and loneliness after the death of Hiroshi as well as her reflections on her own illness. She died at the age of sixty-three (sixty-five by Japanese count).

The most prolific and well-known of modern Japanese women poets, Y. has been best remembered for the sensual quality of her poems and their innovative imagery enlivened by a vibrant, imaginative diction. This was especially true of her romantic love poems collected in her most widely read and most thoroughly studied collection, *Midaregami*. Her long poem "Kimi shi ni tamōkoto nakare" (1904; "Heaven Forbid That You Shall Die!" 1951), published in the midst of the Russo-Japanese War and harshly criticized by the contemporary poet Ōmachi Keigetsu (1869–1925) as unpatriotic, has been cherished by some critics after 1945 as one of the most celebrated antiwar poems in prewar Japan, while others have noted its limitations. All her other poetry collections and her writings in other genres are much lesser known and are awaiting scholarly attention both in Japan and abroad.

FURTHER WORKS: *Dokugusa* (1904); *Yume no hana* (1906); *Kurokami* (1907); *Eihon otogibanashi* (1908); *Byakkō* (1908); *Jōka* (1908); *Suohime* (1909); *Hana* (1910, with Enami Bunzō); *Joshi no fumi* (1910); *Shōnen shōjo* (1910); *Shundeishū* (1911); *Ichigū yori* (1911); *Seikaiba* (1912); *Kumo no iroiro* (1912); *Pari yori* (1914, with Yosano Hiroshi); *Sakurasō* (1915); *Yosano Akiko shū* (1915); *Zakkichō* (1915); *Uta no tsukuriyō* (1915); *Shuyōshū* (1916); *Akarumi e* (1916); *Tanka sanbyakukō* (1916); *Maigoromo* (1916); *Akiko shinshū* (1917); *Myōjōshō* (1918); *Wakaki tomo e* (1918); *Shintō zassō* (1919); *Itte mairimasu* (1919); *Hi no tori* (1919); *Akiko kawa* (1919); *Akiko tanka zenzhū* (1919–1920); *Nyonin sōzō* (1920); *Taiyō to bara* (1921); *Ningen reihai* (1921); *Tabi no uta* (1921); *Kusa no yume* (1922); *Akiko renkashō* (1923); *Ai no sōsaku* (1923); *Ryūsei no michi* (1924); *Rurikō* (1925); *Deido jizō* (1925); *Suna ni kaku* (1925); *Ningen ōrai* (1925); *Fujitarō no tabi* (1925); *Akiko shihen zenshū* (1929); *Kirishima no uta* (1929); *Gaitō ni okuru* (1931); *Yosano Akiko zenshū* (13 vols., 1933–1934); *Yūshōsha to nare* (1934); *Tanka bungaku zenshū. Yosano Akiko hen* (1936); *Gendai tanka sōsho. Yosano Akiko hen* (1940); *Rakkashō* (1942); *Yosano Akiko shokanshū* (1948); *Teihon Yosano Akiko zenshū* (20 vols., 1979–1981)

BIBLIOGRAPHY: Honda, H., *The Poetry of Y. A.* (1957); Shinoda, S., and S. Goldstein, Introduction to *Tangled Hair* (1971), 1–23; Ueda, M., *Modern Japanese Poets and the Nature of Literature* (1983), 53–94; special Y. issue, *JATJ*, 25, 1 (Apr. 1991)

CHIA-NING CHANG

YÜ Kwang-chung

(also romanized as Yu Guangzhong) Chinese poet and essayist, b. 9 Sept. 1928, Nanking

Y. is a leading poet, essayist, critic, and translator, well known to readers in Taiwan, Hong Kong, and, recently, mainland China. A graduate of the Foreign Languages and Literature Department, National Taiwan University, Y. received his M.F.A. from the University of Iowa. He has been a professor of English literature at universities in Taiwan, Hong Kong, and the U.S. Since 1985 he has been dean of the Liberal Arts College, National Sun Yat-sen University in Kaohsiung.

He has written some forty books, fifteen of which are in verse, and has received half a dozen major literary awards in Taiwan. Though he is regarded by some as a Taiwan writer, both his life experience and the scope of his writings prove that he is a veritable Chinese writer. A native of Fukien, before he came to Taiwan at twenty-two, he had resided and traveled in many cities in China, including Hang-chou, Kun-ming, Chung-king, Nanking, and Amoy. Not only is China his obsession, his beloved motherland, but Chinese classical literature and history furnish rich vision and imagery to his imaginary world.

Y. is a great master of the Chinese language. His early poetry and lyrical prose abound in newly coined phrases and ingeniously rearranged syntactical structures. He forges a new style that fuses classical language, modern Chinese vernacular, and English syntactical structure into one. The following subject matters are his main concerns: fervent patriotism, passion for natural beauty, especially that of Hong Kong and southern Taiwan, conservationism, friendship, and romantic love, which is the major theme in his poetry collection *Lien ti lien-hsiang* (1964; associations of the lotus). W. B. Yeats (q.v.) and the Chinese poet Tu Fu (712–770) are the two writers who have had greatest impact on him. His tone is sometimes serious and passionate, sometimes witty and intellectual, but always conveys an imposing tension. His poetry is well-structured and often enriched with well-wrought conceits.

His early poetic style shows a heavy imprint of Chinese poetry written in the 1930s and 1940s. Then, influenced by existentialism and modernism (qq.v.), his poetry collection *Wan-sheng-chieh* (1960; Halloween) deals with his experiences in the U.S. and shows ingenuity in both form and technique. Using an outspoken, audacious voice, his poetry collections *Wu-ling shao-nien* (1967; a youth of T'ang) and *Tien-lang-hsing* (1976; Sirius) are permeated with modern images, strong moods such as anger, despair, and anxiety, and an acute sense of contention. On the other hand, *Lien ti lien-hsiang* marks a return to Chinese classicism, to the graceful poetic world of ancient China. The poetry collections *Chiao-ta hsüeh* (1969; music percussive) and *Pai-yü k'u-kua* (1974; white jade bitter gourd) unravel his profound love for his ailing mother and motherhood. Poems like "Tang wo szu shih" (when I die) and "Pai-yü k'u-kua" (white jade bitter gourd) are so touching that they have become classics extolled by Chinese readers all over the world. Contemplating the Vietnam War, *Tsai leng-chan ti nien-tai* (1959; in years of cold war) uncovers the poet's conscientiousness. The style of his later poetry such as *Tzu-ching-fu* (1986; bauhinia) and *Meng yü ti-li* (1990; dream and geography) has become more temperate, smooth, and mature.

Some consider that his achievements in prose writing exceed those in poetry. His lyrical essays in *Tso-shou ti miu-szu* (1963; the left-handed muse),

Hsiao-yau-yu (1963; the untrammeled traveler), and *T'ing-t'ing na leng-yü* (1974; listen to the cold rain) are highly experimental and innovative. Forging an elaborate style unrivaled by any modern Chinese writer, he presents new combinations or new correlations in his diction, phrase, syntax, tone, and metaphor. Meanwhile, his consciousness expands to the classical literary world of thousands of years. His recent essays, such as those dealing with natural beauty in *Ko-shui hu-tu* (1990; calling for the ferry), are fraught with keen observation, wit, and warmth. Some of his Chinese translations are very popular. *Fan-ku chuan* (1957), his translation of *Lust for Life: The Story of Vincent van Gogh* by Irving Stone (1903–1989) is itself a classic, and his rendering of Oscar Wilde's *The Importance of Being Earnest* has been a stage success in Taiwan, Hong Kong, and mainland China. Y. also participated actively in compaigning for the modern poetry movement in the 1960s and in protesting against pollution in the 1980s. In the past three decades he has sponsored and intermittently edited the poetry journal *Lan Hsing*.

The quality and quantity of Y.'s poetry and prose, as well as his mastery of the Chinese language, secure him a position of a major Chinese writer of this century.

FURTHER WORKS: *Chou-tzu ti bei-ke* (1952); *Lan-se ti yü-mau* (1954); *Chung-ju shih* (1960); *Chang-shang yü* (1964); *Wang-hsiang ti mu-shen* (1968); *Tien-kuo ti yeh-shih* (1969); *Fen-ho-jen* (1972); *Yü Kuang-chung san-wen hsüan* (1975); *Ch'ing-ch'ing pien-chou* (1977); *Yü Yung-heng pa-ho* (1979); *Wen-hsüeh ti sha-tien* (1981); *Fen-shui-ling shang* (1981); *Yü Kuang-chung shih-hsüan* (1981); *Ko-shui kuan-yin* (1983); *Chi-i hsiang Pieh-kuei i-yang chang* (1987); *Yü Kuang-chung shih-hsüan* (1988); *Yü Kuang-chung i-pai-shou* (1988; rev. ed., 1989). FURTHER VOLUME IN ENGLISH: *Acres of Barbed Wire* (1971)

BIBLIOGRAPHY: Hsia, C. T., "The Continuing Obsession with China: Three Contemporary Writers," *RNL*, 6, 1 (1975), 76–99; Donath, A., "Ein Langgedicht von Y.," *China: Kultur, Politik und Wirtschaft* (1976), 51–56; Hou, S. S., "The Phoenix Bathing in Fire: Y. tso-p'in p'ing-lun chi, by Wong Wai-leung," *CLEAR*, 7, 1–2 (1987), 201–9; Chien, C. C., "Y.: Writing As the Phenomenal World of Exile," *Chung-hsing ta-hsüeh wen-shih hsüeh-pao*, 21 (1991), 1–28

CHUNG LING

ZAGAJEWSKI, Adam

Polish poet, novelist, and essayist, b. 21 June 1945, Lwów (Lvov), U.S.S.R.

Z. appeared on the Polish literary stage at the threshold of the 1970s as one of a group of Cracow poets calling themselves "Now," and from the beginning was considered one of the leaders of the literary New Wave. A graduate in philosophy from the Jagiellonian University in Cracow, he introduced many philosophical motifs into his writing and was an advocate of "plain speaking" in poetry. This term did not mean a rejection of devices considered poetic. In fact, Z., like other poets of the so-called "Generation of 68," extensively used metaphors, syntactic and lexical repetitions, and adopted irony. In his view, "plain speaking" was a matter of representing reality as openly as possible and directly communicating human experiences in their richness and complexity.

Most of Z.'s programmatic ideas were directed against the dominating tendencies of the 1960s, especially against a concept of poetry devoid of the specific "here and now," and exclusively using allusion and abstract symbols. His motifs were explained in a series of articles published in the student literary press and subsequently included—along with Julian Kornhauser's manifestos—in the collection of essays *Świat nie przedstawiony* (1974; unrepresented world). Z.'s first two volumes of poetry, *Komunikat* (1972; the communiqué) and *Sklepy mięsne* (1975; meat shops), were both an attempt at representing reality and, at the same time, a document of the poet's struggle with communist censorship. This attempt to represent the human condition under existing socialism was also characteristic of Z.'s first novel, *Ciepło, zimno* (1975; warm and cold). However, the idea of "truth" connected with "plain speak-

ing" could hardly be implemented under the circumstances prevailing in the mid-1970s. In 1975 Z. became involved in political protests and, like several other poets of the New Wave, started publishing beyond the pale of censorship. Along with Stanisław Barańczak and Ryszard Krynicki (qq.v.), he published the underground quarterly *Zapis*. He also issued a new collection of poems, *List* (1981; a letter) outside official channels.

Since the late 1970s, Z. has been residing in the West, chiefly in Paris. When visiting Poland in 1981, he became an eyewitness of the imposition of martial law. In his collection *List—Oda do wielości* (1982; a letter—ode to plurality) the thematic layer of the new poems has been penetrated by the spirit of solidarity with those remaining in Poland. The more recent books by Z. reflect a different sensitivity. According to his articles contained in the volume *Solidarność i Samotność* (1986; *Solidarity, Solitude,* 1990), the artistic production of the 1970s and the 1980s was, in the case of many Polish writers publishing underground, a negative reflection of "official" literature. Its vision of the world was often reduced to two colors, black and white, symbolizing good and evil. Its predominant tone was negation. For Z. the important question became whether it was possible to accept a world that, from the moral point of view, was quite unacceptable. In the place of an ethical attitude he proposed one that he termed "ecstatic." This category was to designate a spontaneous perception of the world in all its richness and variety.

In his volumes of poetry *Jechać do Lwowa* (1985; to go to Lwów) and *Płótno* (1990; canvas) Z. gradually turns away from political-ethical problems, and moral issues are pushed into the background by ontological and epistemological questions. Also, a tone of affirmation is predominant. Instances from general history take the place of events connected with contemporary Polish affairs. More and more often Z. focuses on ecumenical questions, while the history depicted in his poems contends with objects that release wonder and a sense of mystery of existence.

Z. is the winner of several Polish and international literary prizes, among others the Kościelskis Prize (1975), the Tucholsky Prize (1985), and the Kijowski Prize (1986).

FURTHER WORKS: *Drugi oddech* (1978); *Cienka kreska* (1983). FURTHER VOLUME IN ENGLISH: *Tremor: Selected Poems* (1985)

BIBLIOGRAPHY: Levine, M. G., "A. Z., *Jechać do Lwowa i inne wiersze. Tremor: Selected Poems,*" *PolR,* 32, 1 (1987), 113–15; Witkowski, T., "The Poets of the New Wave in Exile," *SEEJ,* 33, 2

(Summer 1989), 204–16; Barańczak, S., "Alone But Not Lonely," *Breathing under Water and Other East European Essays* (1990), 214–18; Witkowski, T., "A. Z.: In Praise of Multiplicity," *Studium Papers*, 14, 3–4 (1990), 168–69

TADEUSZ WITKOWSKI

ZAPATA OLIVELLA, Manuel

Colombian novelist, short-story writer, dramatist, and anthropological essayist, b. 17 Mar. 1920, Lorica

Z. O. is by profession a physician, who has spent his life working and writing on behalf of the lower economic classes and Afro-Colombian people. His work, always directed toward social problems and racial prejudice, includes fiction and anthropological essays on the condition, history, and cultures of Afro-Colombians. He has been very active fomenting organization of folkloric groups, conferences, and other educational activities in his country, and is currently director of the Colombian journal *Letras nacionales*. Born in a poor community of Lorica, Z. O. has had firsthand knowledge of the plight of poor Afro-Colombians and the violence to which the lower economic classes are subjected to in his country. His literary work has been a monumental effort to give voice to this silent majority and to unveil the psychological complexities of social, economic, and racial discrimination. His sense of curiosity and his urgent desire to learn about the world, influenced by his readings of Maxim Gorky (q.v.) and other writers and thinkers, inspired him at age twenty-two to travel north in spite of his difficult economic circumstances. In 1942 he started out by boat through the Amazon on his way to Panama, where he was arrested for "looking suspicious." After a series of similar experiences, and bold experimentations, he reached first Mexico City, where he earned his living writing for the Mexican journals *Sucesos, Así*, and *Tiempo*. Later, in New York City, he met Langston Hughes (q.v.), who became a decisive influence in Z. O.'s life and career. Z. O.'s experiences in Harlem were later recaptured in *He visto la noche* (1954; I have seen the night), a testimonial autobiography of his trip to the U.S. during the 1940s, and his testimony of the prejudice he experienced and witnessed in the U.S. toward African-Americans and Latinos.

When Z. O. reached New York he was carrying with him a rough draft of what was going to be his first novel, *Tierra mojada* (1947; wet land). The famous Spanish American novelist Ciro Alegría (q.v.), who was also at this time in New York and read the manuscript on Z. O.'s request, writes in his prologue to Z. O.'s first novel that, in spite

of its awkwardness and exuberant rhetoric, while reading it he felt that with *Tierra mojada* the black Spanish American novel was about to be born. This text, as well as all of Z. O.'s work since then, communicates, with the same direct and simple style that characterizes Z. O.'s writing, a deep sense of injustice and a deep feeling of compassion toward the oppressed.

In 1948 Z. O. published his second book, *Passion vagabunda* (roaming passion), an account of personal experiences. It was a few years later, however, with the publication of *Cuentos de muerte y libertad* (1956; stories of death and freedom), *El galeón sumergido* (1963; the sunken galleon), and *¿Quién le dio el fusil a Oswald?* (1967; who gave Oswald the rifle?) that Z. O. finally showed his true talent as a writer with a mature style, in narratives where the fantastic, the marvelous, and the crude reality he lived and witnessed are intertwined. In all of these stories, the poor, the black, the oppressed are always victims of a system that robs humans of dignity and hope. Z. O.'s fictional world is a world of deep-rooted political, economic, and psychological violence, in which the victim's attempt to revolt and to cry for justice is always destroyed, as can be seen in his short stories "La ciénaga cercada" (sieged swamp), "Siembra nocturna" (night crop), and "La tinaja en la sombra" (the clay pot in the shadow). Violence, in Z. O.'s work, not only targets the powerless, it is also a psychological phenomenon that accompanies the many manifestations of vengeance, because for Z. O. violence, in Colombia, like anywhere where there is discrimination and class struggle, becomes a state of mind, and, ultimately, a self-devouring way of life.

In some of Z. O.'s short stories there are surrealistic and fantastic elements characteristic of postwar vanguard movements and of what later came to be called in Latin America magic realism (q.v.). The interpolation of these elements in Z. O.'s work shows the writer's interest in blending social realism (q.v.) with innovative techniques, for example, in his short stories "La telaraña (the spiderweb), "El ausente" (the absent man), and "Un extraño bajo mi piel" (another under my skin), a fantastic account of a black man who turns white at a moment of racial danger only to turn black again when threatened with violent discrimination. In this excellent short story the main character lives at the edge of two different racial worlds, experiencing prejudice on both barriers of colors, like, allegorically, the experience of mulattos and of educated African-Americans.

The theme of violence, reiterated in various forms throughout Z. O.'s work, is also the theme of *La calle 10* (1960; 10th street), for which he received the Colombian National Award for the

Novel. Different modalities of the same theme of violence can also be found in *En Chimá nace un santo* (1974; *A Saint Is Born in Chimá,* 1991), a gripping story of superstition, where a fetish religion of hope is born out of poverty and despair, and in *Chambacú: Corral de negros* (1963; *Chambacú, Black Slum,* 1989), the story of a destituted community that attempts to voice its demands for justice and is crushed for it. With the publication of *Detrás del rostro* (1969; behind the face), for which Z. O. received the Colombian National Novel Award given by the Colombian Language Academy, Z. O. shifts toward a more innovative and experimental style. This complex text is narrated by several voices from different perspectives, all of which serve as windows to many different individual interests that are all equally oppressive in Colombian society.

In a more recent book, *Changó, el gran putas* (1983; Changó, the great whore/devil), Z. O.'s research on the history and mythologies of Afro-Colombian lore, his mature style, and his simple and direct narrative techniques come together to produce a complex text that blends poetry and prose, investigation and fiction, concrete reality and myths. This text is a monumental invocation in the style of an African *oriki,* as a chant of praise in which indigenous beliefs and the mythologies brought by African slaves to America come together in a majestic cry for freedom and justice. The text is a dance and an embrace between humans and *orishas,* in the memory of Changó, the Yoruba deity of thunder, lightning, and justice.

Although Z. O.'s themes and motifs have changed little since his first writings, his shift away from social realism to a mythological text that interpolates in its pages the memory of ancient African traditions in America, is also a shift in Afro-Colombian literature toward a new demarginalized zone of racial, ethnic, and historical awareness— and a shift that brings Z. O.'s work closer to the poetic sensitivity of other Afro-Caribbean writers like the Cuban poet Nicolás Guillén (q.v.) and the Puerto Rican poet Luis Palés Matos (1899–1959).

FURTHER WORKS: *China 6 a.m.* (1955); *El cirujano de la selva* (1962); *Teatro por Manuel y Juan Zapata Olivella* (1972); *El hombre colombiano* (1974); *El fusilamiento del diablo* (1986); *Nuestra voz; aportes del habla popular latinoamericano al idioma español* (1987); *Las claves mágicas de América* (1989); *Levántate mulato (por mi raza hablará el espíritu)* (1990)

BIBLIOGRAPHY: Jackson, R., "Myth, History and Narrative Structure in M. Z. O.'s *Chango, el gran putas,*" *RevI,* 13, 1–4 (1983), 108–19; Clemons, B. F., "M. Z. O.'s 'Un extraño bajo mi piel': A Study of Repression," *AHR,* 2, 3 (Sept. 1983), 5–7; Carullo, S., "La dialéctica hambre-agresión en *Chambacú: Corral de negros,*" *AHR,* 2, 3 (Sept. 1983), 19–22; Captain Hidalgo, Y., "El espacio del tiempo en *Chango, el gran putas,*" in Williams, R. L., ed., *Ensayos de literatura colombiana* (1985), 157–66; Kooreman, T., "Integración artística de la protesta social en las novelas de M. Z. O.," *AHR,* 6, 1 (Jan. 1987), 27–30; Heredia, A., "Figuras arquetípicas y la armonía racial en *Chambacú: Corral de negros* de M. Z. O.," *AHR,* 6, 2 (May 1987), 3–8; Mose, K., *"Changó, el gran putas* y el negro en la novelística del colombiano Z. O.," *AHR,* 7, 1–3 (Jan.–Sept. 1988), 45–48; Kooreman, T., *"Pasión vagabunda,* comienzo de una creación ficcionesca," *AHR,* 8, 3 (Sept. 1989), 3–6

JULIA CUERVO HEWITT

Index

This index covers the entire *Encyclopedia of World Literature in the 20th Century,* volumes one to five.

Because of different methods of transliteration and national variations in the sequence of name elements, certain names may not appear at the expected place. The reader is therefore advised to look under other elements or spellings of such names.

Aafjes, Bertus, III 377
Aakjær, Jeppe, I 536
Aasen, Ivar, III 399; V 276
Aavik, Johannes, II 62
Aba, Noureddine, V 17
Abad, Antonio M., III 523
Abadilla, A. G., III 526
Abai Qunanbaiev, I 144
Abashidze, Grigol, II 213
Abashidze, Irakli, II 213
Abasıyanik, Sait Faik, IV 478
Abati, Joaquín, V 47
Abaza literature. *See under* North Caucasian literatures
Abbasi, Tanvir, III 460
al-Abbāssī, Muhammad Sa'īd, IV 365
Abbau. See deconstruction
Abbe Gubegna, II 64, 65
Abbòndio, Valerio, IV 388
'Abbūd, Mārūn, III 34
'Abd, 'Abdallāh, IV 398
'Abd al-'Āl al-Hamamsī, V 201
'Abd al-'Alī Razzā, V 14
'Abd al-Hakīm Qāsim, V 201
'Abd al-Karīm al-Karmī (Abū Salmā),
   V 472
Abdallah, Hemed, IV 417
'Abdallāh, Yahyā al-Tāhir, II 6
'Abdallah al-Muhannā, V 406
'Abd al-M'utī Hijāzī, Ahmad, V 200
'Abd al-Qādir al-Qitt, V 202
'Abd al-Rahīm Mahmūd, V 472
'Abd al-Rahmān, 'Abdallāh, IV 365
'Abd al-Rahmān, Jaylī, IV 366
'Abd al-Rahmān al-Abnūdī, V 190, 200
'Abd al-Sabūr, Salāh, II 5; V 1–2
Abdïramanov, Shabdanday, II 589
Abdoel Moeis, II 441
Abdul Ghani Hamid, IV 233
Abdulla, M. S., IV 418
Abdullaev, Sagid, III 398
Abdullah bin Abdul Kadir Munshi,
   III 189
Abdullah-oghli, Abdurahim. *See*
   Ghayratiy
Abdullah Sidik, III 189
Abdullin, B., IV 481
Abdullin, Khizmet, IV 520
Abdul Rahim Kajai, III 189
Abdul Samad bin Ismail. *See* Asmal
Abdul Samad Said, III 189, 190
Äbdüräshid, Rāzzaq, IV 522
Äbdürāzzaq, Äziz, IV 522
Abe Akira, V 238, 334
Abedi, Amri, IV 417
Abe Kōbō, I 3–4; II 497, 498;
   V 322, 436
Abelaira, Augusto, III 568
Abell, Kjeld, I 4–5, 538
Abkhaz literature. *See under* North Caucasian literatures
Abma, Gerben Willem. *See* Daen, Daniël
Abovian, Katchadour, I 122
Abraham-Razafimaharo, Michel Paul, III
   185
Abrahams, Lionel, V 566

Abrahams, Peter, I 5–6; III 49; IV 289–
   90; V 391
Abrahamson, Irving, V 634
Abramov, Fyodor, IV 112; V 2–3
Abramov, Kuźma, II 105
Abramovitsch, Sholem Jacob. *See* Mendele Mokher Sforim
Abrams, M. H., I 75
Abro, Jamal, III 460
Abruquah, Joseph, II 226
Absatz, Cecilia, V 41
Abse, Danny, IV 609
absurd, the. *See* Theater of the Absurd.
   See also: Black Humor;
   existentialism
Abū al-Ma'ātī Abū al-Najā, V 201
Abū Dibs, Munīr, III 34
Abū Hannā, Hannā, V 473
Abulhasan, Alekperzade, I 166
Abū Mādī, Īliyyā, V 3–4
Abū Nuwās, V 402
Abū Salām. *See* Habībī, Emile
Abū Salmā. *See* 'Abd al-Karīm al-Karmī
Abū Shabaka, Ilyās, III 33
Abū Shādī, Ahmad Zakī, II 4
Acar In, I 386
Accioly, Marcus, V 88
Acevedo Díaz, Eduardo, IV 515
Achard, Marcel, II 142
   on Feydeau, Georges, II 91–92
Achchygyya, Amma, IV 671
Achdiat Karta Mihardja, I 6–7;
   II 441, 442
Achebe, Chinua, I 7–9, 491; III 391–92;
   V 23, 446, 448, 464
A Cheng. *See* Ah Ch'eng
A-chin Panchaphan, IV 431
Achleitner, Friedrich, I 158
Achterberg, Gerrit, I 9–10; III 376
Ackroyd, Peter, V 209
Acorn, Milton, V 108
Acosta de Samper, Soledad, V 145
Ács, Károly, IV 700
Aczél, Tamás, II 416; V 297, 391
Adab, II 628
Adam, Paul, II 137
Adameşteanu, Gabriela, V 519
Adami, Valerio, V 399
   as subject, V 169
Adamic, Louis
   criticism on, IV 721
Adamiyat, Roknzadeh, II 453
Adamov, Arthur, I 10–11; II 147, 148;
   IV 433, 434; V 232
Adamovich, Georgy, II 584; IV 104, 106
Adams, Henry, I 11–12, 274; II 489;
   III 573
   influence of, III 611
Adams, Léonie
   on Bogan, I 287
   influence of, IV 70
Adams, Richard P.
   on Jones, James, II 522
Adams, Valmar, II 61
Adamson, Hendrik, II 60–61
Ādamsons, Ēriks, III 17

Aderca, Felix, IV 81
Adereth, Maxwell
   on Aragon, I 108
A. D. G. *See* Camille, Alain
Adib, Anam, III 460–61
Adib, Hoda, III 35
Adibah Amin, III 190
Adiloğlu, Mustafa, I 519
Adıvar, Halide Edib, I 12–13; IV 477
Adler, Alfred, IV 320
   influence of, II 75; III 326
Adler, Yankev, IV 683
Adomavičius, Juozas. *See* Kekštas, Juozas
Adonias Filho, I 322; III 77
Adorno, Theodor W., I 13–15, 239; III
   81–82; IV 122; V 391, 501
   on Benjamin, I 241–42
   criticism on, IV 333
   influence of, II 220
Adotevi, Stanislas Spéro, I 237
Adson, Artur, IV 505
Adūnīs ('Alī Ahmad Sa'īd), I 15–17; II 5;
   III 33; IV 400; V 37, 272, 286,
   353, 354
'Adwān, Mamdūh, IV 400, 401
Ady, Endre, I 17–18, 172; II 412, 413
   influence of, I 527; II 531, 533; IV 401
Adyghe literature. *See under* North Caucasian literatures
AE. *See* Russell, George William
Aeschylus, V 180
Afawarq Gabre Yesus, II 64
Afghani, 'Ali Mohammad, II 454
al-Afghani, Jamal al-din, III 458
Afghan literature, I 18–20
   in Dari, I 18–20
   in Pashto, I 18–20
'Afīfī Matar, Muhammad, V 200
Afinogenov, Alexandr, IV 114
Africa, 20th-c. *See also under the literatures of individual African countries*
   colonialism in (general), I 237, 531,
   532 (*see also under:* colonialism;
   independence struggles)
   post-, IV 491
Afrikaans literature. *See under* South African literature
Afro-Cubanism, I 20, 414, 415; II 299;
   IV 315–16
Afzal, Ghamil, IV 421
Ağaoğlu, Adalet, IV 479; V 4–5, 607
Agarwal, Bharatabhushan, II 437
Agarwal, Jyoti Prasad, II 436
Agatstein, Mieczysław. *See* Jastrun,
   Mieczysław
Agbossahessou, I 237
Agee, James, I 21
Agel, Jerome, V 108
Agha, Vazir, III 458
Aghbalian, Nigol, I 121
Agîrbiceanu, Ion, IV 79
Agliati, Mario, IV 388
Agnon, S. Y., I 21–23; II 465, 466;
   IV 123
Agopian, Stefan, V 519

655

Aguilera Garramuño, Marco Tulio,
V 146, 147
Aguilera Malta, Demetrio, II 1, 2;
V 5–6, 244
Aguirre, Domingo de, IV 310
Aguirre, Isadora, V 133
Aguirre, José María de. *See* Lizardi,
Xabier de
Aguirre, Raúl Gustavo, V 41
Agustín, José, I 23–24; III 272; V 420
Agustini, Delmira, IV 515
Ah Ch'eng (A Cheng), 137
Ahlfors, Bengt, V 62
Ahlin, Lars, I 24–25; IV 379; V 357, 582
Ahlsen, Leopold, II 223
Ahmad, Aziz, III 459
Ahmad, Muhammad Sulaymān. *See* al-Ja-
bal, Badawī
Ahmad Bachtiar, III 189
Ahmad Lutfi, III 189
Ahmed, Faiz. *See* Faiz, Faiz Ahmed
Aho, Juhani, II 100
Aichelburg, Wolf von, IV 84
Ai Ch'ing, I 25–26, 458, 459–60
Aichinger, Ilse I 26–27, 157; II 10; V 55
Aidoo, Ama Ata (Christina Ama Ata Ai-
doo), II 227; V 6–7
Aiken, Conrad, I 27–28, 65, 71; II 161;
III 83
on García Lorca, Federico, II 198
influence of, II 47; IV 650
Ai Pei (Ai Bei), V 137
Aistis, Jonas, I 28–29; III 130
Aitmatov, Chinghiz. *See* Aytmatov,
Chïngïz
Aiyar, Ullur Parameswara, II 434; III
265–66
Ajemian, Kevork, I 121
Akar, John, IV 215
Akatdamkoeng Raphphat, IV 430
Akbal, Oktay, IV 478
Aken, Piet van, I 220
Åkesson, Sonja, I 29–30; IV 380
Akhavan-Saless, Mehdi, II 455; V 314
Akhmadulina, Bella, I 30–31; IV 107
Akhmatova, Anna, I 30, 31–32, 98, 340,
341; II 304; III 206; IV 104–5,
106, 112; V 389, 390
criticism on, IV 11; V 142, 143
on Mayakovsky, III 257
Akilandam, P. Vaithialingam, II 438
Akilimali, IV 417
Akimov-Arui, Mikhail F., I 466
Akın, Gülten, V 606
Akpan, Ntieyong U., III 392
Akritas, Loukis, I 518, 519
Aksal, Sabahattin Kudret, V 606
Akselrod, Zelik, IV 684
Aksyonov, Vasily Pavlovich, I 32–33; II
572; IV 112, 113; V 388, 390
Akula, Kastuś, I 376
Akurāters, Jānis, III 16
Akutagawa Ryūnosuke, I 33–34; II 496,
624; IV 210
'Alā' al-dīn, Hasan, III 34
Aladji, Victor, IV 448
Alain (Émile-Auguste Chartier), I 34–35;
II 138, 143, 144; IV 597; V 322
influence of, III 253
on Valéry, IV 529
Alain-Fournier, I 35–36; II 138
Alamayyawh Mogas, II 64–65
Alarcón, Pedro Antonio de, V 476
Alas, Leopoldo. *See* Clarín
Alavi, Buzurg, I 36–37; II 454
Al-Azad, Alauddin, I 187
Alazraki, Jaime
on Borges, I 306
Albanian literature, I 37–39
in Yugoslavia, IV 699
Albany, Jean, IV 25
Albee, Edward, I 39–41, 74; IV 355,
433; V 28
influence of, II 223

Albérès, R.-M., II 148
on Butor, I 373
Albert, Caterina. *See* Català, Victor
Alberti, Rafael, I 41–42; IV 304–5, 372;
V 145, 391, 570, 574, 575
on Guillén, Jorge, II 297
Albert i Paradis, Caterina. *See* Català,
Victor
Alcântara, Oswaldo. *See* Silva, Baltasar
Lopes da
Aldecoa, Ignacio, IV 308
Aldecoa, Josefina, V 573
Aldington, Richard, I 578; II 33, 116,
432; III 140
Aldridge, John W.
on Dos Passos, I 582
on Jones, James, II 523
Al-e Ahmad, Jalal, II 454; V 7–9
Alecsandri, Vasile, III 530
Alegre, Caetano da Costa, IV 147
Alegría, Ciro, I 42–43; III 509–10; V
260, 652
Alegría, Claribel, V 9–10
Alegría, Fernando, I 454; V 10–12, 131,
132, 591
on Neruda, III 371
Aleichem, Sholem. *See* Sholem Aleichem
Aleixandre, Vicente, I 43–45; IV 304,
305, 372; V 242, 570, 574
Aleksandravičius, Jonas. *See* Aistis, Jonas
Alemán, Vicente. *See* Barrera, Claudio
Alepoudhelis, Odysseus. *See* Elytis,
Odysseus
Aleramo, Sibilla, II 469
Aleshkovsky, Yuz, IV 113; V 391
Aleut literature. *See* Eskimo literature
Alexander, Meena, V 310
Alexander, Pamela, V 28
Alexandru, Ioan, IV 82
Alexis, Jacques-Stéphen, II 154
Alfon, Estrella, III 525
Alfons, Sven, IV 379
Alfvén, Inger, V 582, 583
Algerian literature, I 45–48; V 12–17
in Arabic, I 45–46; V 13–15
Beur literature, V 13, 14, 16, 17, 231
in French, I 46–48; V 15–17
the "generation of 52" of, III 205
the "generation of 54" of, I 562
independence as subject of, I 45, 47,
392; IV 221
Maghrebian literature, *see* Maghrebian
literature
major writers of, in French, *see:* Boud-
jedra; Dib; Djebar; Feraoun; Kateb;
Mammeri
in Arabic, *see:* Boudjedra; Ibn Ha-
dūqa; Kateb; Wattār
Algren, Nelson, I 48–49, 70
on Dreiser, I 590
Ali, Ahmed, II 439; III 458; V 17–19
Ali, Aziz, III 191
Ali, Bachir Hadj, I 47
Ali, Sabahattin, III 373; IV 478
alienation
effect, I 327; II 97
and society, IV 258
al-'Ālim, Mahmūd Amīn, II 7; V 202
Ali Majod, III 190
Alishan, Ghevont, IV 540
Alithersis, Glafkos, I 518
Alkali, Zaynab, V 449
Alkio, Santeri, II 100
Allais, Alphonse, IV 195
Allan, Robert, II 153
Alle, August, II 60
Allégret, Marc, III 456
Allen, Hervey, I 64
Allen, Walter
on Amis, I 77
on Greene, II 46
Allen, Woody, V 196
Allende, Isabel, V 19–20, 131
critical excerpts on, V 20–21

Allgood, Molly, IV 394
Alliksaar, Artur, II 61, 63
Allott, Kenneth, II 37
on Greene, II 291
Alloula, Malek, V 17
Almada-Negreiros, José de, III 512, 567;
IV 118
Almăjan, Slavco, IV 700
Almeida, José Américo de, I 322; III 616
Almira, Jaques, V 231
Almqvist, C. J. L., IV 265
Alnæs, Finn, III 401
Alomar, Gabriel, IV 314
Aloni, Nissim, I 49–50; II 467
Alonso, Amado, III 96
Alonso, Dámaso, I 50; III 96;
IV 304, 305
Alonso de Santos, José Luis, V 574
Alós, Concha, V 570
Alphonsus, João, I 323
Altenberg, Peter, I 152; II 166, 607, 608;
IV 342; V 387
influence of, III 550
Altendorf, Wolfgang, II 223
Alter, Robert
on Nabokov, III 349
Alterman, Natan, I 51; II 465
Altgeld, Peter, III 74
Althusser, Louis, III 93;
V 228, 234, 372, 376
Aluko, Timothy M., III 390, 392
Alunāns, Juris, III 15
Alvarez, A., II 53
Álvarez, José María, IV 306; V 574
Álvarez Enparantza, José Luis. *See*
Txillardegi
Alvarez Gardeazabal, Gustavo, V 21–23,
126, 145, 146
Álvarez Lleras, Antonio, I 485; V 145
Álvarez Quintero, Joaquín, I 51–52; IV
301
Álvarez Quintero, Serafín, I 51–52; IV
301
Alvaro, Corrado, I 52–54; II 470, 472
Alver, Betti, I 54; II 61; IV 412, 506
Alves Antunes Filho, José, V 90
Alves de Souza, Naum, V 90
Alves Redol, António. *See* Redol, Antó-
nio Alves
Alvim, Chico, V 89
Alyn, Marc, II 148
Alzaga, Toribio, IV 310
Amadi, Elechi, III 392; V 24, 449
Amado, Jorge, I 55–56, 322; II 97; III
295; IV 9, 550; V 88
influence of, IV 18
Amado Carballo, Lois, IV 315
Amalrik, Andrey, IV 112
Amar, Yasmin, I 47
Amaral, Maria Adelaide, V 90
Amarasekara, Gunadasa, IV 322, 323
Amaya Amador, Ramón, V 123
Ambrogi, Arturo, V 122
Ambrus, Zoltán, I 56–57; II 413
America, 20th-c., as literary subject, I
586–89; III 62–64, 264, 265; IV
140–41, 230–31
agrarian movement in, Southern,
IV 12–13
the American Dream of, I 588; III 321;
IV 230, 617
civil-rights movements in, I 182, 451–
52; IV 587
the cold war of, with Russia, I 135; II
92; IV 227
the Jazz Age of, I 60–61; II 107–8; III
320; IV 642
the McCarthy persecutions in (HUAC),
II 353; III 279, 280; IV 43
migrant farmers of, IV 331, 332
the New Deal in, I 581; III 265; IV 642
and Puerto Ricans in New York,
IV 282–83
the Rosenberg trial in, I 572; II 92

657

André, Robert
on Taktsis, V 587
Andreas-Salomé, Lou, IV 46
influence of, IV 47
Andrée, S. A.
as subject, IV 368
Andreev, Leonid, I 89–91; II 262, 618;
IV 108, 114
Andrés, Elena, V 570, 574
Andres, Stefan, I 91–92; II 219
Andresen, Sophia de Melo Breyner,
III 569
Andrewes, Lancelot
influence of, II 17
Andriamalala, E. D., III 185
Andrianjafy, Romain, III 184
Andrian-Werburg, Leopold von, I 150
Andrić, Ivo, I 92–94; IV 692
Andricki, Mikławš, III 155
Andriušis, Pulgis, III 132
Andrukhovych, Yury, V 613
Andrzejewski, Jerzy, I 94–95; III 557,
558; IV 255; V 491
Andújar, Manuel, V 570
Angel, Albalucía, V 145–47
Angelet, Jaume, IV 311
Angell, Katherine Sargeant, V 632
Ângelo, Ivan, V 89
Angelou, Maya, V 31–32
critical excerpts on, V 32–34
Angel Riera, Miquel, V 572
Anger, Kenneth, II 95
Angira, Jared, II 578; V 351
Ang-khan Kalayanaphong, IV 431
Anglo-American literature. See under
American literature, major writers
of
Anglo-Indian literature. See under Indian
literature, major writers of
Anglo-Irish literature. See under Irish lit-
erature
Anglo-Welsh literature. See Welsh litera-
ture, in English
Angolan literature, I 95–97
creolized, I 97; IV 559
independence as subject of, IV 559
in Kimbundu, I 95; IV 559
major writers of, in Portuguese, see
Vieira, José Luandino; see also
Soromenho
neorealism in, IV 282
in Portuguese, I 96–97; IV 559
Angus, Marion, IV 178; V 546
Anhava, Tuomas, II 102
al-'Ānī, Yūsuf, II 458
Aniebo, I. N. C., III 393
Anil. See Deshpande, A. R.
Anīs, 'Abd al-'Azīm, II 7
Anker, Nini Roll, III 399
Annensky, Innokenti, I 97–99; IV 105
as subject, V 441
Annist, August, II 61, 62
Annunzio, Gabriele D'. See D'Annunzio,
Gabriele
Anouilh, Jean, I 99–101; II 142, 144,
146, 447, 502; IV 262;
V 229, 232
critical excerpts on, I 101–2
Anski, S., IV 687
An Su-gil, II 601
Anthias, Tefkros, I 518
Anthony, Michael, II 54; V 34–35
antitheater. See Theater of the Absurd
Antokolsky, Pavel, IV 106
Antolín Rato, Mariano, V 574
Antonenko-Davydovych, Borys, IV 495
Antoni, Robert
on Allende, V 21
Antoninus, Brother, I 72
Antônio, João, V 89
António, Mário, I 96
Antonioni, Michelangelo, II 96
Antonov-Ovseenko, Vladimir, III 406

Antonych, Bohdan Ihor, IV 496
Antschel, Paul. See Celan, Paul
Anwar, Chairil. See Chairil Anwar
Any Asmara, II 444
Anzai Fuyue, V 336
Anzaldua, Gloria, V 222
Aono Sō, V 335
Aparicio, Juan Pedro, V 573
Apitz, Bruno, II 225
Apollinaire, Guillaume, I 102–4, 433,
476, 477, 513; II 138, 140, 409,
471, 482, 502; III 92; IV 26, 283,
370, 372, 692; V 117, 154
influence of, III 420; IV 692
on Czechoslovak literature, I 521;
IV 185
Appel, Alfred
on Nabokov, III 347
Appelfeld, Aharon, II 467; V 35–36
Aprieto, Pacifico, III 525
Áprily, Lajos, IV 85
Apter, T. E.
on Mann, Thomas, III 217–18
Aputis, Juozas, III 133; V 394
'Aql, Sa'īd, III 33; V 36–37, 353, 354
al-'Aqqād, 'Abbās Mahmūd, II 4, 5, 7
Aquilina, Ġużè (Joseph), III 203
Aquin, Hubert, I 399; V 37–38, 109
Aquinas, Thomas. See Thomas Aquinas
Arab-American literature. See Lebanese,
literature
Arabic literature
See Algerian, Egyptian, Iraqi, Le-
banese, Moroccan, Palestinian, Su-
danese, Syrian, Tajik, and Tu-
nisian literatures
See under Nigerian, Senegalese, and
Somali literatures
Al-Mahjar poets of, IV 472
''The Awakening'' of, III 318
Aragon, Louis, I 103, 104–6, 591; II 24,
140, 141, 143, 144; III 80; IV
254–55, 371, 486; V 229
critical excerpts on, I 106–8
influence of, II 362; III 257
on Sollers, III 267
al-A'raj, Wasini, V 12–14
Arango, Gonzalo, V 146
Aranguren, José Luis, IV 300–301; V 570
Aranha, José da Graça, I 108–9, 320,
321; III 295
Arany, János, I 172
Arato, Andrew
on Lukács, III 153–54
Arayal, Bhairav, III 367
Arbasino, Alberto, II 474
Arbaud, Joseph d', II 152
Arbó, Sebastià Juan, IV 312, 313
Arcellana, Francisco, III 525
Archer, David, I 191
Archer, William, II 38
Arciniegas, Germán, I 485
Arcos, Joaquim Paço d', III 568
Arden, John, I 109–10; II 40
on O'Casey, III 414–15
Arderiu de Riba, Clementina, IV 311; V
570, 574
Ardila Casamitjana, Jaime, V 145
Arenas, Reinaldo, IV 317; V 38–40
Arendt, Hannah, V 391, 501
on Benjamin, I 242
on Broch, I 228
Aresti, Gabriel de, IV 310
Aretino, Pietro
as subject, V 508
Arévalo Martínez, Rafael, I 434–35;
V 121
Argentine literature, I 110–14; V 40–43
Black Humor in, I 272, 273; V 245
the Boedo group of, I 111, 117
the Florida group of, I 111
the *invencionismo* movement in, I 111
major writers of, see: Arlt; Bioy Cas-

ares; Borges; Cortázar; Costantini;
Denevi; Dragún; Gálvez; Gambaro;
Girri; Guido; Güiraldes; Lugones;
Lynch; Mallea; Marechal; Martínez
Estrada; Mujica Láinez; Payró;
Puig; Sábato; Szichman; Valen-
zuela; Viñas
modernism in, I 110–11; III 148, 225,
293
Perón regime as subject of, IV 121
post-, III 235; IV 121
phenomenological, III 518
Socialist Realism in, I 112
surrealism in, I 111; IV 372; V 41, 43
symbolism in, IV 392
Theater of the Absurd in, I 113;
V 42, 245
ultraism in, I 111, 302; III 225
Arghezi, Tudor, I 114–15, 409; IV 80,
514
Arguedas, Alcides, I 115–16, 289; V 333
Arguedas, José María, I 116–17;
III 509–10
Argueta, Manlio, V 43–44, 122
Arguilla, Manuel, III 525
Argyle, Barry
on White, IV 623
Arias, Arturo, V 121
Arias Trujillo, Bernardo, V 145
Aridjis, Homero, III 273; V 421, 422
Arifin C. Noer, II 443
Arion, Martinus, I 605
Ariosto
criticism on, III 85, 86
Arishima Takeo, II 496; V 44
Aristophanes, V 587
influence of, II 314
Aristotle, V 196
influence of, III 124, 151
criticism on, V 81
Ariyoshi Sawako, V 44–46, 336
Arland, Marcel, II 141, 142
Arlt, Roberto, I 112, 117–18, 496; V
187, 619
Armah, Ayi Kwei, I 118–19; II 226
Armas Marcelo, Juan J., V 573
Armattoe, Raphael, II 226
Armen, Mgrditch, I 122
Armenian literature, I 119–22
major writers of, see: Charents; Mate-
vossian; Oshagan, Hagop; Sevag;
Varoujan; Zohrab
the Mehian Group of, I 120
revolution as subject of, I 120
the Turkish massacre as subject of, I
120, 121, 442; IV 197, 716
and of other literatures, IV 614
Armijn Pane, II 441
Armijo, Roberto, V 122
Arnaud, Jean Jacques, V 196
Arnér, Sivar, I 123; IV 379
Arnheim, Rudolf
on film, II 94
Arniches, Carlos, IV 301; V 46–47
Arnim, Achim von
influence of, IV 370–71
Arnold, Matthew, II 52; IV 466
influence of, III 112; IV 466
Aron, Raymond, V 146
Aron, Robert, I 127
Arp, Hans (Jean), I 530; II 216
influence of, II 617
Arpiarian, Arpiar, I 120
Arrabal, Fernando, I 123–25; II 148, 228;
IV 303, 433; V 232, 575
Arraiz, Antonio, IV 542–43, 544
Arreola, Juan José, I 125–26; III 272
Arrigucci, Jr., Davi, V 90
Arriví, Francisco, IV 316
Arrué, Salvador Salazar. See Salarrué
'Arsān, 'Alī 'Ukla, IV 400
Arsiennieva, Natalla, I 126–27, 375, 376
Arsovski, Tome, IV 698

Backman, Sigrid, II 100
Bacovia, George, I 176–77, 410; IV 80
Baczyński, Krzysztof K., III 557
Baden-Powell, Robert, IV 712
Badi, Hasan, II 453
Badī 'al-Zamān al-Hamadhānī, V 612
Badian, Seydou Kouyaté, III 194
Badr, Tāhā, II 7
Baduev, Saidbek, III 398
Báez, Cecilio, III 473
Baghdādī, Shawqī, IV 398
Baghio'o, Jean-Louis, II 154
Bagounts, Axel, I 122
Bagritsky, Edvard, I 177–78; III 488; IV 106; V 389
Bagryana, Elisaveta, I 178–79, 359; V 181
Bahar, Mohammad Taqi, II 454
Baharuddin Zainal, III 191
Bahdanovich, Maksim, I 126, 179, 376
Bahele, Jacques N., IV 703
Bahnīnī, Ahmad, III 319
Bahr, Hermann, I 150, 179–81; III 106
criticism on, III 107
Bahryany, Ivan, IV 497; V 613
Bahushevich, Frantsishak, I 374
Baierl, Helmut, II 223
Bai Hua. See Pai Hua
Baillon, André, I 223
Bainbridge, Beryl, I 181–82; II 48
Baissac, Charles, III 252
Bai Xianyong. See Pai Hsien-yung
Baker, Carlos
on Hemingway, II 358
Baker, Elliot, I 273
Baker, George Pierce, IV 655
Bakhtin, Mikhail Mikhailovich, III 100; IV 115; V 58–59
influence of, V 335
Bakhtiya, Ilya, IV 520
Baklanov, Grigory, IV 111
Bakr, Salwā, V 201
Bakst, Léon, II 138
Bakunin, Mikhail, I 174, 342
Balaguer, Joaquín, IV 316
Bălăiţă, George, IV 83
Balakrishnan, V. See Elangkanan, M. A.
Bălan, Ion, IV 700
Balassa, Péter, V 298
Balbierius, Alis, V 394
Baldini, Antonio, II 471
Baldini, Gabriele, II 239
Baldwin, James, I 69, 182–83; IV 363; V 358
Balestrini, Nanni, II 474
Balewa, Abubakar Tafawa, III 389
Balinese literature. See under Indonesian literature
Balisidya, N., IV 418
Balkt, Herman Hendrik ter, III 377
Ball, Hugo, I 530
on Hesse, II 369
Balla, Giacomo, II 185
Ballagas, Emilio, I 20; V 59
Ballard, J. G., V 208
Ballesteros, Mercedes, V 570
Balmaceda, Pedro, I 544
Balmont, Konstantin Dmitrievich, I 183–84; III 98, 294; IV 104, 106, 391
influence of, II 305; IV 265
Balmori, Jesús, III 523
Balochi literature. See under Pakistani literature
Baloyi, Samuel Jonas, IV 292
Baltazar, Camil, IV 81
Balti literature. See under Pakistani literature
Baltrušaitis, Jurgis, III 129
Balzac, Honoré de, III 519; V 184, 229, 288, 402, 576
criticism on, I 517; III 89, 105, 151; V 94
influence of, II 487; III 444, 602; IV 259; V 535, 642

on English literature, I 246; IV 251
as subject, V 291
Bambara literature. See under Mali literature
Bamoun literature. See under Cameroonian literature
Banchs, Enrique, I 111
Bancquart, Marie-Claire, V 233
Bancroft, David
on Cocteau, I 479
Banda, Innocent, III 188
Bandeira, Manuel, I 184–85, 321, 322; III 295
Bandopadhyaya, Manik, II 438
Banerji, Bibhuti-Bhusan, I 185–86; II 438
Banfi, Antonio, V 549
Bang, Karin, III 401
Bangladeshi literature, I 186–88
Banks, Iain, V 544
Banville, John, V 319
al-Banna, Muhammad 'Umar, IV 365
Bannānī, Ahmad, II 319
Banu, Zaitun, III 461
Bănulescu, Ştefan, IV 83
Bänziger, Hans
on Frisch, II 170
Baquero Diego, Gastón, IV 316
Barac, Antun, IV 696
Baradulin, Ryhor, I 375
Baraheni, Reza, V 314
Baraka, Amiri, I 72, 73, 74, 188–89
Barakāt, Halīm, III 34
Baranauskas, Antanas, III 129
Barańczak, Stanisław, III 559; V 59–61, 373, 391, 490–92, 651
Baratashvili, Nikoloz, II 211, 213
Baratynsky, Yevgeny
influence of, IV 702
Barba Jacob, Porfirio, I 483
Barbadian literature. See under English-Caribbean literature
Barbarani, Berto, II 476
Barbeitos, Arlindo, I 97
Barbier, Jean, II 150
Barbilian, Dan. See Barbu, Ion
Barbosa, João Alexandre, V 90
Barbosa, Jorge, I 402
Barbu, Eugen, IV 83; V 519
Barbu, Ion, I 189–90; III 139; IV 80
Barbusse, Henri, I 190–91, 311; II 496; IV 121, 260
Bárcena, Catalina, III 235
Bārda, Fricis, III 15
Barea, Arturo
on Unamuno, IV 504
Barenas, Kazimieras, V 394
Barfield, Owen, II 52; III 59
Bargonne, Charles. See Farrère, Claude
Bargum, Johan, V 61–62
Baritz, Loren, I 76
Barka, Vasyl, IV 497; V 391
Barker, George, I 191–92; II 37
Barker, Howard, V 210
Barlach, Ernst, I 192–93; II 70, 217
Barnard, Chris, IV 287
Barnard, Lady Anne, V 565
Barnatán, Marcos Ricardo, V 574
Barnes, Djuna, I 194–95
Barnes, Julian, V 208
Barnes, William, II 328
Baroja, Pío, I 195–96; IV 299, 306–7; V 69
criticism on, III 436
Baronas, Aloyzas, III 132
Barons, Krišjānis, III 15
Barra, Eduardo de la, I 544
Barrault, Jean-Louis, I 127; II 91, 141, 145, 228
Barrenechea, Ana María
on Borges, I 305
on Cortázar, I 498
Barreno, Maria Isabel, III 569
Barrera, Claudio (Vicente Alemán), V 123

Barrès, Maurice, II 137; III 35
criticism on, III 91
influence of, I 180
Barreto, Bruno, II 97
Barreto, Henriques Afonso de Lima, I 320–21, 323
Barrie, James M., I 196–97; III 571; IV 178
Barrios, Eduardo, I 198, 454
Barroso, Maria Alice, V 89
Barsacq, André, II 141, 145
Bartalis, János, IV 85
Bartels, Adolf, III 107
Bartevian, Souren, I 120
Barth, John, I 70, 199–200, 272, 273; III 518; IV 362; V 24, 25, 150, 227
criticism on, II 205; V 196
Barthelme, Donald, I 70, 201, 273; II 205; V 150, 227, 498
Barthelme, Frederick, V 26
Barthes, Roland, I 201–3; II 98, 148, 149; III 80, 93, 94; IV 359, 361, 362; V 228, 229, 234, 355, 498, 500
on Butor, I 201
influence of, I 343; IV 147; V 355, 372
on Robbe-Grillet, I 201; IV 61
Baruchello, Gianfranco, V 399
al-Bārūdī, Mahmūd Sāmī, II 3
Barzini, Luigi
on Sciascia, IV 176
Basak, Subimal, V 309
Basdekis, Demetrios
on Unamuno, IV 504–5
Bashev, Vladimir, I 360
Bäshir, Ghömär, IV 421
Bashīr, Tijānī Yūsuf, IV 366
Bashkir literature, I 203–4
in Bashkir, I 203–4
in Russian, I 203
in Tatar, I 203
Bashō, IV 414
Basic English, supporters of use of, IV 41–42
Başkut, Cevat Fehmi, IV 479
Basman, Rivke, IV 687
Basner, Miriam, III 50
Basque literature. See under French and Spanish literatures
Bassani, Giorgio, I 204–5; II 472
Bastida, José, V 597
Bataille, Félix, II 137
Bataille, Georges, I 205–6; II 148; III 41; V 499
criticism on, I 279; IV 268
Bataille, Nicholas, II 447
Batalvi, Ahsan, III 461
Batchelor, R. E.
on Unamuno, IV 505
Bate, Walter Jackson, III 125
Bates, H. E., II 46, 50–51; V 62–63
on Garnett, Edward, II 50
Bateson, F. W., III 118
Batikuling. See Balmori, Jesús
Battal, Salikh, IV 421
Batu, IV 521
Batukezanga, Zamenga, IV 703
Baturin, Nikolai, II 61
Baty, Gaston, II 141, 145
Baudelaire, Charles, IV 370, 389, 390; V 292, 537
criticism on, I 240, 241; III 81
French, II 146; III 59, 92, 93, 94, 520; IV 155
influence of, III 293, 307
on American literature, IV 422
on Danish literature, V 161
on Finnish literature, III 39
on French literature, III 89
on Hungarian literature, IV 401
on Italian literature, I 410
on Portuguese literature, III 566
on Romanian literature, I 114, 409
on South African literature, I 389

on Spanish literature, II 295
as subject, V 367
Baudoin, Charles, III 83
Baudouin, Charles Pierre. *See* Péguy, Charles
Baudrillard, Jean, V 234
Baucr, Walter, I 206–7; II 219
Bauer, Wolfgang, II 322, 395; V 54, 63–65
Baumanis, Arturs, III 18
Baumann, Gerhart
on Musil, III 338
Baxter, James K., I 207–8; III 383
Bayalinov, Kasïmalï, II 588
Bayanov, Äkhsän, IV 421
Baybars, Taner, I 519
Baydas, Khalīl, III 465; V 473
Baydur, Mehmet, V 607
Bayer, Konrad, I 128, 158
Baykurt, Fakir, IV 478
Bayley, John, III 333
on Auden, I 138–39
on Solzhenitsyn, IV 277
Baynton, Barbara, I 145
Bayr, Rudolf, I 158
al-Baytajāli, Iskandar al-Khūrī, III 464
Baytursin-ülï, Aqmet, II 570
al-Bayyātī, ʿAbd al-Wahhāb, I 208–9; II 457
Bazarrabusa, Timothy B., IV 489
Bazhan, Mykola, IV 496
Bazin, André, II 93, 98
Bazin, Nancy Topping
on Woolf, Virginia, IV 662
on Head, 280
Bazin, René, II 137
Beato of Leibana, V 194
Beatson, Peter
on White, IV 624
Beattie, Ann, V 65 66
Beauchamp, Kathleen. *See* Mansfield, Katherine
Beauchemin, Yves, V 110
Beaujardière, Pitot de la, III 252
Beaulieu, Victor-Lévy, V 110
Beauvoir, Simone de, I 209–10, 596; II 144, 145, 146, 147, 149; III 38, 57; IV 154, 665; V 221, 229, 230
influence of, IV 125
on Montherlant, III 305
Bebey, Francis, I 388
Bec, Pierre, II 153
Bec, Serge, II 153
Becher, Johannes R., II 70, 216, 221, 222, 623; V 391
Becke, Louis, I 145
Becker, Jillian, V 391
Becker, Jurek, I 210–11; II 225; V 249
Becker, Jürgen, II 225
Becker, Knuth, I 538
Becker, Lucille
on Montherlant, III 306
Beckett, Samuel, I 211–14, 343, 600; II 40, 45, 68, 147, 148, 217, 375, 462; III 381, 517, 518, 532, 534; IV 257, 303, 343, 355, 433, 434; V 5, 73, 129, 133, 232, 236, 318, 392, 403, 469, 487, 498
criticism on, II 205, 372; IV 333; V 180
excerpts of, I 214–15
influence of, I 455, 539; II 456; III 401; IV 83; V 535
Bećković, Matija, I 215–16; IV 694
Bédier, Joseph, IV 25
Bednall, John
on Hofmannsthal, II 387
Beeharry, Deepchand, III 253
Beer, John
on Forster, II 124
Beer-Hofmann, Richard, I 150, 216–17
Beg, Mirza Qalich, III 460
Begović, Milan, I 217–18; IV 694

Béguin, Albert, II 146; III 93, 502, 520; IV 386
Behan, Brendan, I 218; II 460; V 316
Beh'azin, II 454
Behbudiy, Mahmud Khoja, I 219; IV 521
Behramoğlu, Ataol, V 606
Behrangi, Samad, II 454
Behrman, S. N., I 73
Bei Dao. *See* Pei Tao
Beier, Ulli, III 391, 455
Beitab, Sufi Abdul Haq, I 19
Belamri, Rabah, V 15, 17
Belcheva, Elisaveta. *See* Bagryana, Elisaveta
Belcheva, Mara, IV 246
Beleño, Joaquín, I 435; V 125
Belghoul, Farida, V 17
Belgian literature, I 219–26
Cobra movement in, I 475
expressionism in, I 222, 511; II 70, 228; III 446; IV 425
in Flemish, I 219–23
in French, I 223–26
the Hainault group of, I 225
literary criticism in, IV 551
magic realism in, I 220, 535
major writers of
also writing in English, *see* Gijsen
in Flemish, *see:* Boon; Brulez; Claes Claus; Daisne; Elsschot; Gijsen; Ostaijen; Pillecijn; Roelants; Streuvels; Teirlinck; Timmermans; Vermeylen; Walschap; Woestijne
in French, *see:* Crommelynck; Ghelderode; Gijsen; Maeterlinck; Mallet-Joris; Michaux; Simenon; Verhaeren
the Monday group of, I 223–24
neorealism in, I 222
surrealism in, I 221, 225
symbolism in, I 221, 224; III 174; IV 391, 649
the ''vijfenvijftigers'' of, I 222
the ''vijftigers'' of, I 222
World War II, Nazi occupation during, as subject of, IV 582
Belhassan, Ammar, V 14
Belizean literature. *See under* Central American literature
Bell, Clive, IV 346, 658
Bell, Julian, II 37
Bell, Lindolf, V 88
Bell, Madison Smartt, V 25, 26
Bell, Marvin, V 26
Bell, Steven
on Paz, V 421
Bell, Vanessa, IV 658
Bellemin-Noël, V 234
Belletto, René, V 231
Bell-Gam, Leopold, III 390
Belli, Carlos Germán, III 511; V 66–67
Belli, Gioconda, V 124
Belli, Giuseppe Gioacchino, II 475, 476
Bellman, Carl Michael, II 89, 411
Bello, Andrés, III 148
Belloc, Hilaire, I 226–27; II 53
on Pitter, II 546
Bellon, Loleh, V 232
Bellow, Saul, I 69, 227–30; II 161; V 24, 170, 349
criticism on, I 504; II 205
excerpts of, I 230–31
Belov, Vasily, II 572; IV 112; V 530
Bels, Alberts, III 18–19
Belser, Raymond de. *See* Ruyslinck, Ward
Belševica, Vizma, III 19
Bely, Andrey, I 183, 231–32, 282; II 247, 584; III 98, 294, 531; IV 104, 105, 107, 108, 240, 391, 469; V 560, 597, 621
criticism on, IV 114
influence of, II 305; IV 107, 109
Belyaev, Alexandr, IV 113

Bemba, Sylvain, V 67–68
Bemba literature. *See under* Zambian literature
Ben-Amots, Dan, II 467
Benavente, Jacinto, I 232–34; IV 299, 301
Benawa, Abdur Rauf, I 19
Bencheikh, Jamal-Eddine, V 17
Bencúr, Matej. *See* Kukučín, Martin
Benda, Julien, II 138, 141; III 88, 284
influence of, IV 700
Bender, Hans, II 224
Bendezú, Francisco, III 511
Bendre, Dattatreya Ramachandra, II 435, 437
Bendrupe, Mirdza, III 17
Benedetti, Mario, I 234; IV 516
Benediktsson, Einar, II 425–26
Ben Eliezer, Israel, I 351
Beneš, Eduard, III 405
Beneš, Jan, I 524
Benešová, Božena, I 520
Benet, Juan, V 309; V 68–70, 570, 572
Benét, Stephen Vincent, I 65, 234–36
Benét, William Rose
on Beer-Hofmann, I 217
Benet i Jornet, Josep Maria, IV 314; V 575
Bengali literature. *See* Bangladeshi literature *and under* Indian literature
Bengtsson, Frans G., I 236; IV 378
Beniak, Valentín, I 526
Beniak, Valentín, I 526
Beninian literature, I 236–38
in Fon, I 237–38
in French, I 236–37
Benítez, Justo Pasto, III 473
Beniuc, Mihai, IV 82
Benjámin, László, I 238; II 414–15
Benjamin, Walter, I 238–41; III 81, 151, 551; V 391
on Brecht, I 329
criticism on, IV 333
excerpts of, I 241–43
on Fleisser, II 113
influence of, II 220
Benjayamoyo, Storm, IV 705
Ben Jelloun (Benjelloun), Tahar, III 320; V 70–71, 231, 233, 356
Ben-Jellūn, ʿAbd al-Majīd, III 319, 320
Benn, Gottfried, I 177, 243–46; II 70, 71, 216, 218, 221; III 106, 547
as subject, V 381
Bennett, Alan, V 211
Bennett, Arnold, I 246–47; II 42, 49; IV 248, 349
criticism on, I 584; II 42; IV 579
Benoît, Pierre, II 142
Benoît, Réal, I 398
Bense, Max, II 222
Benson, Jackson J.
on Hemingway, II 358
Benson, Mary, V 567
Benson, Thomas W.
on Eco, V 197
Bentley, Eric, I 327
on Brecht, I 329
on Chekhov, I 449–50
on O'Neill, Eugene, III 433–34
on Pirandello, III 543
on Shaw, George Bernard, IV 206
on Williams, Tennessee, IV 633
Benviste, Émile, V 372
Béranger, Pierre-Jean de, III 252
Berberova, Nina, II 583; V 391
Berdnyk, Oles, IV 497
Berdyaev, Nikolay, III 98
Berenbaum, Michael
on Wiesel, IV 635
Berent, Wacław, III 554
as subject, V 294
Berg, Alban, IV 595
Bergamín, José, IV 300
Berge, H. C. Ten, V 71–72
Bergelson, Dovid, I 247–48; IV 683

661

Bergengruen, Werner, II 219, 221
Berger, Raimund, I 158
Berger, Thomas, I 70, 272; V 72–73
Berggren, Tobias, IV 381
Bergler, Edmund, II 162
Bergman, Bo Hjalmar, IV 376
Bergman, Hjalmar, I 248–49;
    IV 377, 381
Bergman, Ingmar, II 97, 121; IV 381; V
    581, 582
  criticism on, V 183
Bergmann, Hugo
  influence of, I 339
Bergonzi, Bernard
  on Eliot, T. S., II 20–21
  on Powell, III 583
Bergroth, Hugo, IV 265
Bergson, Henri, I 249–51, 360; III 167;
    IV 36
  criticism on, III 113; V 141
Bergsson, Guðbergur, I 251; II 427
Berk, Ilhan, IV 477; V 606
Berkeley, George
  influence of, I 303
Berkoff, Stephen, V 210
Berková, Alexandra, V 155
Berl, Emmanuel, II 141, 143
Berlin, Isaiah
  on Pasternak, Boris, III 484
Bermúdez, Ricardo J., V 125
Bernanos, Georges, I 251–53, 290; II
    142, 143, 144; III 502
Bernard, Carlo. See Bernari, Carlo
Bernard, Harry, I 398
Bernard, Jean-Jacques, II 142
Bernard, Tristan, II 136
Bernari, Carlo, I 253–54; II 472
Bernášek, Antonín. See Toman, Karel
Bernhard, Thomas, I 158–59, 159, 254–
    55; V 53, 54, 248, 249
Bernhardt, Sarah, II 137
Bernier, Hector, I 398
Bernikow, Louise, V 222
Bernlef, J., III 377
Bernotas, Albinas, V 393
Bernstein, Aline, IV 655, 656
Bernstein, Henry, II 137
Bernstein, Ingrid. See Kirsch, Sarah
Bernstein, Michael
  on Pound, III 579
Berrigan, Ted, I 73
Berryman, John, I 71, 255–56
Bersani, Leo
  on Proust, III 604
Bersianik, Louky, V 110
Berthelot, Philippe, II 242
Berthoud, Jacques A.
  on Conrad, Joseph, I 493
Bertin, Charles, I 226
Berto, Giuseppe, I 256–57; II 472, 473,
    474; III 366
Bertoni, Brenno, IV 387
Bertram, Ernst, III 103
Bertrana, Prudenci, IV 312
Bertrand, Louis, II 137
Bērziņš, Uldis, III 19
Bērzs, Alfrēds. See Tauns, Linards
Bessette, Gérard, I 399; V 110
Beti, Mongo, I 257–58, 387–88
Betjeman, Sir John, III 172; V 73–74,
    212
Betocchi, Carlo, I 259; II 361, 471
Betti, Ugo, I 259–60; II 475; IV 391
Beur literature. See under Algerian litera-
    ture
Beutler, Maja, IV 383
Bevk, France, IV 697
Bewley, Marius, III 117
  on James, Henry, II 490
Beyatlı, Yahya Kemal, IV 476
Beynon, Richard, I 149
Beyshenaliev, Shükürbek, II 589
Beyzai, Bahram, II 456; V 315
Bezbarua, Lakshminath, II 436

Bezoro, Édouard, III 185
Bezruč, Petr, I 260–61, 520
Bezzola, Eduard, IV 388
Bhali, Ahmad Nassir bin Juma, II 578
Bharati, Subramania, I 261–62; II 434
Bhattacharya, Bhabani, II 439
Bhattacharya, Birendra Kumar, II 439
Bhattacharya, Jitendra Nath, II 436
Bhatti, Abdul Majid, III 460
Bhatti, Muhammad Azim, III 460–61
Bhêly-Quénum, Olympe, I 237
Bhengu, Kenneth, IV 296
Bhikshu, Bhavani, III 368
Biadula, Zmitrok, I 375
Bialik, Chayim Nachman, I 262–63;
    II 465
Białoszewski, Miron, I 263–64; III 558–
    59; V 491
Bialot, Joseph, V 231–32
Bianco, José, V 40
Bianconi, Piero, IV 388
Bichel-Zahnetava, Danuta, I 376
Bichsel, Peter, III 382; V 74–75
Bičole, Baiba, III 17
Bidyalankarana, Prince, IV 431
Biebl, Konstantin, III 386
Biedma, Jaime Gilde, IV 305
Bieler, Manfred, II 225
Bien, Peter
  on Kazantzakis, II 575
Bienek, Horst, II 222; V 248
Bierce, Ambrose, I 60; V 75–77
  as subject, V 420
Bierce, Lucius Verus, V 76
Bierce, Marcus Aurelius, V 76
Bierezin, Jacek, V 491
Biermann, Wolf, I 264–65; II 221, 222,
    362; V 86
Biert, Cla, IV 389
Biga, Daniel, V 233
Bigongiari, Piero, I 265–66; II 361,
    471
Bikal, Ramesh, III 367
Bilac, Olavo, I 320
Bildungsroman, the, as vehicle for litera-
    ture of society, IV 257
Bille, S. Corinna, IV 386
Billetdoux, François, V 233
Billetdoux, Raphaële, V 231, 232
Billinger, Richard, I 155, 156
Bilotserkivets, Natalka, V 613
Binde, Ilze, III 19
Bingel, Horst, II 222
Binkis, Kazys, III 130
Binswanger, Ludwig, III 515, 520
Bioy Casares, Adolfo, I 112, 266–67,
    303; III 149; V 40
Biqtash, Mirzaq, V 13
Birnbaum, Milton
  on Huxley, II 421
Birney, Earle, I 396
Bisayan literature. See under Philippine
    literature
Bishop, Elizabeth, I 71, 267–68; V 525,
    579
Bissīsū, Mū 'īn, V 473
Bista, Daulat Bikram, III 368
Bitov, Andrey, IV 113, 115
Bixler, Jacqueline Eyring
  on Carballido, V 115
Biyidi, Alexandre. See Beti, Mongo
al-Bizim, Muhammad, IV 400
Bjerke, André, I 268–69; II 11; III 403
Bjero, Wylem, III 155
Björksten, Ingmar
  on White, IV 624
Björling, Gunnar, I 269–70, 413; II 100;
    III 294; V 356
Bjørneboe, Jens, I 270; III 400, 402
Bjørnkjær, Kristen, I 541
Bjørnseth, Finn, III 400
Bjørnson, Bjørnstjerne, I 360–61; III 398
  criticism on, V 648
  influence of, IV 43

Bjørnvig, Thorkild, I 270–71, 538–39;
    V 161
Black, Stephen, IV 289
black experience, the, as literary subject,
    I 20
  American, II 23; III 321–22; IV 665
  South African, III 325
Black Humor, I 271–73, 430; II 102; IV
    1, 106, 434, 523, 645
  American, I 199, 271–73; II 351, 581;
    III 610; IV 572; V 320
  Argentine, V 245
  Canadian, I 399; IV 44
  Chilean, V 133
  Ecuadorean, V 6
  precursors of, IV 616, 617
  Scottish, V 546
black identity, awareness of, as literary
  subject. See also: black experi-
    ence; Négritude
  African, I 95–96, 159–60, 487; III 3,
    323; IV 290
  American, I 68, 69, 73, 182, 188–89,
    345–46, 361–62, 451–52, 514; II
    405, 517; IV 19, 454, 665
  Caribbean, I 20, 535, 604–5; II 54,
    155; IV 283
  South American, I 322
black liberation as literary subject. See
    also: black identity; civil rights
    struggles
  African, I 6, 8, 258; IV 292, 296 (see
    also apartheid, under South Afri-
    can literature)
  American, I 73, 188, 361; III 260
black literature
  See: Afro-Cubanism; American litera-
    ture, Harlem Renaissance of; black
    identity; black liberation; Négritude
  See also individual literatures of Afri-
    can and Caribbean countries
Blackburn, Paul, I 72, 506
Blackhall, Sheena, V 546, 547
Blackmur, R. P., I 67, 75, 256, 274–75;
    III 111, 122–23, 270
  on James, Henry, II 490
  on Yeats, William Butler, IV 678
Blackwood, Caroline, III 141
Blaga, Lucian, I 275–76; IV 80, 81
  influence of, IV 82
Blair, John G.
  on Auden, I 139
Blais, Marie-Claire, I 276–77, 398, 399;
    V 109
Blaise, Clark, V 109, 433
Blake, George, IV 180
Blake, Nicholas. See Day Lewis, C.
Blake, William, II 66; IV 70; V 27
  criticism on, II 177; III 117, 118, 124,
    125; IV 5
  influence of, I 146, 418, 419, 505; II
    140, 237, 600; III 104; IV 334,
    335, 564, 591, 674, 676
Blaman, Anna, I 277–78; III 377
Blanchot, Maurice, I 278–80; II 146; III
    93, 94; V 231, 234
Blanco, Yolanda, V 124
Blanco-Amor, Eduardo, IV 315
Blanco Fombona, Rufino, IV 542, 543
Blanco Hernández de Trava
  as subject, V 455
Blandiana, Ana (Otilia-Valeria Coman),
    V 77–78, 519, 520
Blasco Ibáñez, Vicente, I 280–81; II 496;
    IV 306; V 118, 390
Blatter, Silvio, V 78
Blaumanis, Rūdolfs, III 15
Blažková, Jaroslava, I 526–27
Blecher, M., I 281–82; IV 81
Blei, Franz, I 156; II 69; IV 335
Blend, Charles D.
  on Malraux, III 201–2
Blest Gana, Alberto, I 454
Blin, Roger, I 127

Braque, Georges, I 102, 441
  criticism on, IV 26
  influence of, I 512
Brasillach, Robert, II 141, 143, 144
  on Giraudoux, II 245
Brassai, Viktor, IV 85
Brathwaite, Edward Kamau (Lawson Edward Brathwaite), II 54; V 85–86
Bratny, Roman, III 559
Brault, Jacques, V 111
Braun, Edward
  on Gorky, II 264–65
Braun, Felix, I 155
Braun, Kazimierz, V 493
Braun, Volker, II 222, 223; V 86–87
Brautigan, Richard, I 70, 72
  influence of, V 436
Braxton, Joanne, V 222
Bray, Arturo, III 473
Brazdžionis, Bernardas, III 130; V 393, 395
Brazilian literature, I 320–24; V 87–91
  and Afro-Brazilianism, I 55
  the Anta (Tapir) group of, IV 38
  the Antropofagia group of, I 321
  "deep regionalism" in, III 77
  existentialism in, IV 550
  expressionism in, IV 324
  the Generation of '45 of, I 323; V 416
  literary criticism in, I 87, 88, 184
  major writers of, see: Amado; Andrade, Carlos Drummond de; Andrade, Mário de; Andrade, Oswaldo de; Aranha; Bandeira; Boal; Buarque; Callado; Fonseca; Freyre; Lispector; Lobato; Meireles; Melo Neto; Piñon; Queiroz, Rachel de; Ramos, Graciliano; Rego; Ribeiro, Darcy; Ribeiro, João Ubaldo; Ricardo; Rodrigues, Nelson; Rosa, João Guimarães; Scliar; Telles; Veríssimo, Érico
  also writing in English, see Freyre
  modernism in, see under modernism
  the New Novel in, I 322, 323
  the Pau Brazil group of, I 321
  plantation system, decline of as subject of, IV 22
  the "region-tradition" movement in, IV 21
  the social chronicle in, IV 259
  surrealism in, I 87, 323; IV 68; V 416
  symbolism in, I 185, 320; III 263; IV 37–38, 392
  verde-amarelismo in, I 321
Breban, Nicolae, IV 83
Brechbühl, Beat, IV 384
Brecht, Bertolt, I 4, 155, 245, 270, 324–28, 599; II 70, 90, 97, 112, 168, 217, 218–19, 220, 221, 274; III 150, 262; IV 254, 255, 262, 359, 718; V 68, 81, 272, 391, 392, 448, 623
  criticism on, I 241; III 81; IV 333
  excerpts of, I 328–30
  influence of
    on Argentine literature, I 113; V 42, 188
    on Austrian literature, I 156
    on Brazilian literature, V 99
    on Chilean literature, V 133
    on Costa Rican literature, V 523
    on Egyptian literature, V 218
    on English literature, I 110, 295; II 38, 40; III 443; IV 197; V 211
    on French literature, II 148
    on German literature, I 239; II 314, 623; III 330
    on Mexican literature, V 302
    on Nigerian literature, V 464
    on Norwegian literature, III 401, 402
    on Peruvian literature, V 535
    on Romanian literature, IV 84
    on Spanish literature, I 355; IV 314
    on Swiss literature, IV 383
    on Syrian literature, IV 399, 400; V 628
  on Kaiser, Georg, II 551
  precursors of, IV 596, 666
  on Wedekind, IV 596
Brée, Germaine, V 229
  on Aragon, I 107
  on Camus, I 393–94
  on Gide, II 235
  on Malraux, III 201
Breines, Paul
  on Lukács, III 153–54
Bremond, Abbé Henri, II 143; III 91; V 36
Brennan, Christopher John, I 146, 330–31
Brenner, Paul A., IV 384
Brenner, Yosef H., II 466
Brentano, Clemens
  criticism on, III 108
Brenton, Howard, V 210
Breslin, James E.
  on Williams, William Carlos, IV 639
Breton, André, I 102, 103, 104, 127, 281, 331–33, 530, 545; II 24, 26, 140, 161; III 92, 386; IV 283–84, 370, 371, 372, 373, 525; V 272, 376
  on Aragon, I 107
  on Césaire, I 437
  on Desnos, I 560
  influence of, I 124; II 269
  on Roussel, IV 96
Breton literature. See under French literature
Brewster, Elizabeth, V 108
Breytenbach, Breyten (B. B. Lasarus), IV 287; V 91–92, 391, 564, 566, 567
Breza, Tadeusz, III 558
Březan, Jurij, III 156
Březina, Otokar, I 333–34, 520; IV 133
Briand, Aristide, II 242
Bridges, Robert
  criticism on, III 123; IV 644
Bridie, James, I 334–35; IV 179
Briedis, Leons, III 19
Brieux, Eugène, II 136
Briffa, Ružar, III 203
Briffault, Robert, II 278
Brigadere, Anna, I 335–36; III 16
Brik, Lily, III 256
Brines, Francisco, IV 305; V 574
Brink, André P., IV 287, 288; V 92–93, 564, 566
Brinkmann, Richard
  on Broch, I 338
Brinkmann, Rolf Dieter, II 222; V 93–94
Brissenden, Robert F.
  on White, IV 623
Brisville, Jean-Claude, V 232
Britiaty Elbyzdyqo, III 445
Brito, Antônio Carlos de. See Cacaso
Britten, Benjamin, III 173, 450, 549
  on Forster, II 125
Broch, Hermann, I 154–55, 336–38; II 538; V 238, 391
  critical excerpts on, I 338–39
  influence of, I 539
Brock-Sulzer, Elisabeth
  on Dürrenmatt, I 602
Brod, Max, I 153, 339–40; II 544; IV 455, 613
  on Kafka, II 547
Brode, Hanspeter
  on Grass, II 277
Broderzon, Moyshe, IV 683
Brodkey, Harold, V 26
Brodsky, Joseph, I 340–41; III 132; IV 107; V 391, 597
Bródy, Sándor, I 341–42; II 413
Brøgger, Suzanne, V 160
Brolsma, Reinder, III 379
Brombert, Victor
  on Malraux, III 201
Broniewski, Władysław, I 342–43; III 555, 556–57
Bronowski, Jacob, III 516
Brontë, Anne, IV 229; V 3, 49
  influence of, IV 228
Brontë, Charlotte, IV 229; V 3, 49
  influence of, IV 43, 228
Brontë, Emily, IV 229; V 3, 49
  influence of, IV 228
Brooke-Rose, Christine, I 343–44; III 118, 382; V 208
Brookner, Anita, V 94–95, 209
Brooks, Cleanth, I 67, 75, 344–45; III 113, 119, 121, 122, 124; IV 587
  on Faulkner, II 84
Brooks, Gwendolyn, I 345–46
Brooks, Jean R.
  on Hardy, Thomas, II 332–33
Brooks, Peter
  on Genet, II 209
Brooks, Van Wyck, I 67; III 78, 112
  on Dreiser, I 590
  on Hughes, Langston, II 404
  on James, Henry, II 489
Brophy, Brigid, I 346–47; II 462
Brossa, Joan, IV 313
Brossard, Nicole, V 110
Brossky, Iosif, V 185
Brotherston, Gordon, III 497
Brouwer, Jelle Hindriks, III 379
Brouwers, Jeroen, V 95–96
Brower, Reuben A.
  on Frost, II 175
Brown, Clarence
  on Nabokov, III 347
Brown, Deming
  on Solzhenitsyn, IV 277
Brown, Douglas
  on Hardy, Thomas, II 332
Brown, Ford Madox, II 115
Brown, George Douglas, IV 178
Brown, George Mackay, IV 181; V 545, 547
Brown, Margaret Gillies, V 546
Brown, Norman O., II 157
Brown, Robert McAfee
  on Wiesel, V 636
Browne, Sir Thomas, V 579
Brownell, William Crary, I 67
Browning, Robert, III 113, 115; IV 120, 146
  criticism on, III 91
  influence of, III 141, 575, IV 335
Broyard, Anatole
  on Genet, II 209
  on Updike, IV 512
Brú, Heðin, I 542
Bruccoli, Matthew J.
  on Fitzgerald, F. Scott, II 112
Bruckner, Ferdinand, I 155–56, 157, 347–48; II 223
Bruggen, Jochem van, IV 286
Bruggen, Nic van, I 222
Brulez, Raymond, I 220, 348–49
Bruller, Jean. See Vercors
Brumaru, Emil, IV 83
Brunclair, Victor J., I 222
Brunetière, Ferdinand, II 138; III 88, 112
Brunner, Ernst, V 582
Brushuski literature. See Pakistani literature
Brushwood, John
  on González Martínez, II 256
Brustein, Robert
  on Chekhov, I 450
  on Pirandello, III 544
Brutus, Dennis, I 349; IV 290; V 391
Bruyn, Günter de, II 225
Bryce Echenique, Alfredo, III 509, 510; V 96–97
Bryher, Winifred, 516

665

Campos Cervera, Hérib, III 473
Camprubi, Zenobía, II 510
Campton, David, IV 433
Camus, Albert, I 95, 390–93; II 68, 88,
    144, 145, 146, 180; III 8, 38, 303,
    381, 441, 517, 573; IV 66, 156,
    262; V 272, 489
  criticism on, III 94, 125
    excerpts of, I 393–95
  influence of, I 454; II 220; III 419,
    503; IV 270, 538
  on Kazantzakis, II 575
  precursor of philosophy of, IV 131
  on Sábato, IV 121
  on Wiesel, V 632
Canadian literature, I 395–99; V 108–10
  Black Humor in, I 399; IV 44
  cultural conflict as subject of, III 171
  in English, I 395–97; V 108–9
  film technique in, IV 44
  in French, I 397–99; V 109–111
  Group of the Sixties of, I 395–96
  literary criticism in, II 277–78
  major writers of
    in English, see: Atwood; Callaghan;
      Cohen, Leonard; Davies; Frye;
      Gallant; Klein; Laurence; Layton;
      Leacock; MacLennan; Munro; On-
      daatje; Pratt; Richler
    in French, see: Aquin; Blais; Ferron;
      Godbout; Hébert, Anne; Langevin;
      Nelligan; Ringuet; Roy, Gabrielle;
      Theriault; Tremblay
  Maple Leaf school of, I 396
  Montreal Group of, I 396
  symbolism in, I 398; III 362
Cañas, Alberto, I 435
Cândido, Antônio, V 89
Candinas, Theo, IV 389
Canelo, Pureza, V 574
Canetti, Elias, I 157, 399–400
Cankar, Ivan, I 400–401; IV 697, 721
Cansever, Edip, IV 477; V 111–12, 606
Capécia, Mayotte, II 155
Čapek, Josef, I 403
Čapek, Karel, I 403–5, 522, 523; IV 536;
    V 155, 266
  critical excerpts on, I 405–7
Čapek-Chod, Karel Matěj, I 520
Cape Verdean literature, I 401–3
  in Creole, I 402–3
  in Portuguese, I 401–3
Capmany, Maria Aurèlia, IV 313; V 570,
    571
Capote, Truman, I 68, 407–8, 569; IV
    261; V 436, 498
Capozzi, Rocco
  on Eco, V 198
Capuana, Luigi, IV 547
Caragiale, Ion Luca, I 408; IV 79, 514
Caragiale, Mateiu, I 408–9; IV 81
Caraion, Ion, I 409–10; IV 82
Caratsch, Reto, IV 389
Carballido, Emilio, III 274; V 112–13,
    422, 423, 533
  critical excerpts on, 114–15
Carballo, Rof, V 571
Carby, Hazel, V 222
Cárcamo, Jacobo, V 123
Cárceres, Adolfo, I 289
Carco, Francis, II 139, 142
Carcopino-Tusoli, François. See Carco,
    Francis
Carda, R. I. See Huch, Ricarda
Cardarelli, Vincenzo, I 410–11; II 470,
    471
Cardenal, Ernesto, I 434; V 115–17, 123,
    124
Cardoso, António, I 96
Cardoso, Lúcio, I 322; III 77
Cardoso Pires, José. See Pires, José
    Cardoso
Cardoza y Aragón, Luis, I 435; V 121

Cardozo, Efraím, III 473
Carducci, Giosuè, III 478, 479; IV 120
  influence of, I 298
Carême, Maurice, I 225
Carey, Peter, V 51
Carías Reyes, Marcos, V 123
Carías Zapata, Marcos, V 123
Caribbean literatures. See Dutch-Carib-
    bean, English-Caribbean, French-
    Caribbean, and Spanish-Caribbean
    literatures
Carilla, Emilio, V 332
Carling, Finn, I 411–12; III 400, 402
Carlyle, Thomas, I 272
  influence of, IV 500
Carman, Bliss, I 395–96
Carmen Pallarés, María del, V 574
Carné, Marcel, III 595
Carnegie, Agnes C., V 546
Carner, Josep, II 114; IV 311
Carnero, Guillermo, V 574
Carnot, Maurus, IV 389
Caron, Louis, V 110
Carossa, Hans, I 412–13; II 221
Carpelan, Bo, I 413–14; II 102
Carpenter, Edward, IV 173
Carpentier, Alejo, I 20, 414–16; III 177;
    IV 57, 316; V 132, 456, 537
Carrà, Carlo, II 185
Carranza, Eduardo, I 483; V 117–18, 145
Carranza, María Mercedes, V 147
Carrasco, Gustavo, V 385
Carrasquilla, Tomás, I 484; V 100, 118–
    19, 145, 415
Carré Alvarellos, Leandro, IV 315
Carrera, Margarita, V 121
Carrera Andrade, Jorge, I 416–17
Carrier, Roch, I 399; V 110
Carrión, Alejandro, II 2
Carrión, Benjamin, II 2; V 244
Carroll, Paul Vincent, I 417–18; II 460;
    V 316
Carruth, Hayden, V 26
Cărtărescu, Mircea, V 520
Carter, Angela, V 208
Carus, C. G., II 403
Carvajal, María Isabel. See Lyra, Carmen
Carvalho, André Agostinho Mendes de.
    See Xitu, Uanhenga
Carvalho, Maria Judite de, III 568
Carvalho, Ronald de, I 321
Carvalho, Ruy Duarte de, I 97
Carver, Raymond, V 26, 119–20, 436
Cary, Joyce, I 418–19; II 45
Casabar, Constante, III 526
Casaccia, Gabriel, III 473
Casal, Julián del, III 293; IV 392
Casalduero, Joaquín
  on Guillén, Jorge, II 295
Casalis, Alfred, III 295
Casares, Carlos, IV 315; V 573
Casellas, Ramon, IV 312
Casely-Hayford, Adelaide, II 226
Casey, Gavin, I 147
Casey, John, 25
Casey, Kevin
  on O'Casey, III 413–14
Caso, Antonio, III 273
Casona, Alejandro, I 419–20; IV 302;
    V 574
Cassady, Neal, II 237, 579, 580
Cassian, Nina, IV 82; V 391
Cassiano, Ricardo, III 295
Cassirer, Ernst, III 99
Cassola, Carlo, I 420–22; II 472
Castellanos, Rosario, I 422; III 273; V
    422, 533
Castelli, Carlo, IV 388
Castillo, Otto René, V 121, 122
Castillo, Roberto, V 123
Castoriadis, Cornelius, V 234
Castrén, Gunnar, IV 265
Castro, Alfonso, V 145

Castro, Américo, III 95; IV 300
Castro, Consuelo de, V 89
Castro, E. M. de Melo e, III 569
Castro, Eugénio de, III 294, 566; IV 392
Castro, José Maria Ferreira de, I 422–23;
    III 568
Castro, Juana, V 574
Castro, Juan Antonio, V 574
Castro, Luis, IV 542
Castro, Rosalía de, IV 314
Castro Soromenho, Fernando. See Soro-
    menho, Fernando Castro
Čašule, Kole, IV 698
Català, Victor (Caterina Albert i Paradís),
    IV 312
Catalan literature. See under Spanish
    literature
Cather, Willa, I 59, 60, 423–25
Caudwell, Christopher, II 37, 52; III 80
Cavafy, C. P., I 425–26; II 281; V 603,
    604
  criticism on, IV 668
  influence of, I 425–26, 518; IV 182;
    V 453
Cavell, Stanley, II 97
Caws, Peter
  on Sartre, IV 159
Cayrol, Jean, I 426–27; II 145, 147;
    V 230
Cazamian, Louis, IV 25
Cecchi, Emilio, II 471; III 87
Čech, Svatopluk, III 169
Cecil, David
  on de la Mare, I 552
Cela, Camilo José, I 427–29; IV 308,
    314; V 570, 572
Celan, Paul, I 157, 429–30; II 71, 221;
    IV 84
  influence of, V 454
Celaya, Gabriel, I 430–31; IV 305; V
    466, 574
Çelebi, Asaf Halet, IV 477
Céline, Louis-Ferdinand, I 431–32, 491
  criticism on, V 83
  influence of, I 432
Céline, Paul, II 143–44
Celliers, Jan F. E., IV 286
Cendrars, Blaise, I 432–34, 513, 530; II
    139; IV 386
  influence of, I 225, 433
censorship, 20th-c., IV 162, 263, 707
  African, IV 188, 216
    South, IV 287, 288, 290, 295, 296
  American, I 589; III 21
  Brazilan, IV 9
  British, I 436; III 21, 360, 590;
    IV 713
  Catholic, III 501
  Communist, I 377; II 214, 390; III 4,
    294, 330, 344; IV 59, 413, 485,
    497, 521, 577
    of Chinese writers, I 460, 463; III
      11, 454; IV 446
    of Czechoslovak writers, I 522, 523,
      524, 526, 603; II 343, 399, 621,
      622; IV 243, 523
    of East German writers, II 221, 222,
      223
    of Hungarian writers, II 431, 561; III
      351, IV 711
    of Latvian writers, I 335, 379; III 19;
      IV 7
    of Polish writers, II 378, 598; III
      558, 560
    of Romanian writers, I 190; III 209,
      360; IV 82, 568
    of Russian writers, I 33, 90; II 629;
      III 481; IV 103, 115, 272, 575,
      679, 705–6
  underground circumvention of, IV
    272, 496
  see also Communist Party, criticism
    by

Chinese literature (*continued*)
criticism on, III 576
during the Cultural Revolution, I 459;
III 146; V 135–37, 372, 425, 627,
628
Epoch Society of, I 460
literary criticism in, IV 611
major writers of, *see:* Ai; Chang Ai-
ling; Chao Shu-li; Chou Li-po; Ho
Ch'i-fang; Hsü; Hu; Kao Hsiao-
sheng; Kuo; Lao She; Liu Ya-tzu;
Lu Hsün; Mao Tun; Mo Yen; Pa
Chin; Pai Hsien-yung; Su Man-
shu; Ting Ling; Ts'ao Yü; Wang
Meng; Wen; Yü Kwang-chung
the Mandarin Duck and Butterfly
School of, I 457
the Modernist School of, I 460;
V 470, 650
the Nan-shê group of, IV 364
New Cultural movement in, III 146
New Literature movement in, III 11
Socialist Realism in, I 456, 463, 466;
V 345, 628
Southern Society of, III 133, 134
in Taiwan, I 460; V 137
For non-Chinese writing in China, see
Mongolian, Tibetan, *and* Uyghur
literatures
Chinese-Indonesian literature. *See under*
Indonesian literature
Chinese-language literatures
See Chinese literature
See under Japanese, Malaysian, *and*
Singapore literatures
See also Vietnamese literature
Chin Kee Onn, III 192
Chinnov, Igor, IV 104, 106
Chipasula, Frank, III 188
Chirico, Giorgio de, I 102
Chistalev, Venyamin, II 105
Chitepo, Herbert, IV 714
Chitty, Sir Thomas Willes. *See* Hinde,
Thomas
Ch'iu Chin, I 456
Chobanzade, Bekir Sidqi, IV 421
Chocano, José Santos, I 461; III 293
Chodziesner, Gertrud. *See* Kolmar,
Gertrud
Cholodenko, Marc, V 232, 233
Cholpan, IV 521
Chomsky, Noam, II 85; III 126; IV 359;
V 139
Chŏng Chi-yong, II 600
Chŏng Hyŏn-jong, II 601
Chong Ruiz, Eustorgio, V 125
Chŏn Kwang-yong, II 601
Cho'oe Nam-sŏn, I 599
Chopin, Frédéric
as subject, V 296
Chopin, Kate, V 76
Choquette, Gilbert, I 398
Chor, Olga. *See* Deschartes, O.
Chorell, Walentin, I 461–62; II 102
Chornovil, Vyacheslav, IV 496
Chorny, Kuzma, I 375
Chothia, Jean
on O'Neill, Eugene, III 435
Chotjewitz, Peter, II 225
Choudhury, Malay Roy, V 309
Chou Li-po, I 463
Chou Shu-jen. *See* Lu Hsün
Chou Yang, I 463
Chraïbi, Driss, III 319; V 138–39, 355
Chrestien, François, III 252
Christensen, Inger, I 540; V 139–40, 160
Christian, Barbara, V 222
Christiansen, Sigurd, III 401
Christie, Agatha, V 128
Christine de Pizan, V 321
Christov, Solveig, I 463–64; III 400
Chrysanthis, Kypros, I 518
Chubak, Sadeq, I 464–65; II 454; V 314

Chubay, Hryhory, V 613
Chu Hsi-ning, I 460
Chukchi literature, I 465
Chukovskaya, Lidia, IV 111, 112
Chukovsky, Korney, I 340; II 8
Chuprynka, Hryhory, IV 494
Churchill, Caryl, V 211
Churchill, Winston, III 380; V 404
as subject, V 210
Chute, Carolyn, V 25
Chuvash literature, I 465–66
Ch'ü Yüan, II 626
Chwa Daudi, IV 489
Chydenius, Kaj, II 103
Cid, Teófilo, V 591
Cielava-Zigmonte, Dagnija, III 18
Cieškaitė, Gražina, V 394
Čietek, Ján. *See* Smrek, Ján
Cigáň, Janko. *See* Krasko, Ivan
Cíger-Hronský, Jozef, I 525
Cihlar-Nehajev, Milutin, IV 695
Cilmi Bowndheri, IV 278
Cinatti, Rui, III 569
Cinauskas, Vytautas, V 393
cinema and literature. *See* film and
literature
Čingo, Živko, IV 698
Cingria, Charles-Albert, IV 386
Ciobanu, Mircea, IV 83
Cioculescu, Șerban, IV 80
Cioran, E. M., II 148–49; V 140–42,
391
Čipkus, Alfonsas (Niliūnas), V 393
Cisek, Oskar Walter, IV 84
Cissé, Souleymane, V 233
civil-rights struggles, as literary subject.
See also black liberation
American, I 182, 451–52; IV 587
South African, III 4 (*see also* apartheid,
under South African literature)
Cixous, Hélène, II 149; V 142–43, 222,
231, 232, 234, 377, 641
Claes, Ernest, I 220, 466–67; IV 350
Claesson, Stig, IV 380–81
Clampitt, Amy, V 27, 28
Clare, John, IV 70
Clarín (Leopoldo Alas), V 471, 476
Clark, Eleanor, IV 587; V 525
on Genet, II 208
Clark, John Pepper (J. P. Clark) *See*
Clark-Bekederemo, J. P.
Clark, Sir Kenneth
on Sitwell, Edith, IV 242, 586
Clark-Bekederemo, J. P. (John Pepper
Clark, J. P. Clark), I 467–68; III
391, 392; V 446–48
Clarke, Austin, I 468–69; II 460; V 317,
362
criticism of, II 566
Clarke, Basil, V 74
Clarke, Gillian, IV 609
Clarke, John H., V 358
Claudel, Paul, I 469–72; II 135, 138,
139, 143, 145, 146, 233; III 89;
IV 391; V 230
critical excerpts on, I 472–74
influence of, I 492; IV 11, 193, 412
Claus, Hugo, I 221, 222, 223, 475–76;
III 329
Clavuot-Geer, Ursina. *See* Girun, Gian
Cleaver, Eldridge, I 69; III 573; V 391
Clemens, Samuel. *See* Twain, Mark
Clément, Catherine, V 142, 231, 234
Clementis, Vladimír, III 405
Clifford, Douglas, V 544
Cloetta, Gianet, IV 388
Closson, Herman, I 226
Cloutier, Eugène, I 398
Clouts, Sydney, IV 289
Cluny, Claude-Michel, V 233
Clurman, Harold
on Anouilh, I 102
on O'Neill, Eugene, III 434

Cobb, Carl W.
on Jiménez, II 513
Coblenz, Ida, II 210
Cobo Borda, Juan Gustavo, V 147
Cochofel, João José, III 569
Cocteau, Jean, I 476–78; II 95, 115,
140–41, 142, 146, 242, 502; III
38; IV 3; V 294
critical excerpts on, I 478–79
influence of, IV 3, 692
on Roussel, IV 96
Codrescu, Andrei, V 391
Coe, Richard N.
on Ionesco, II 451
Coenen, Frans, III 376
Coetzee, J. M., IV 289; V 143–44, 565,
566
Coghill, Nevill, III 59
Coghlan, Brian
on Hofmannsthal, II 387–88
Cohen, Jonathan, V 385
Cohen, Leonard, I 273, 397, 479–80;
II 592
Cohen, Robert
on Giraudoux, II 246
Cohn, Dorrit C.
on Broch, I 338–39
on stream-of-consciousness technique,
IV 349
Cohn, Ruby
on Beckett, I 214
Cold War, the, as literary subject, I 135;
II 92; IV 227
Cole, Robert, II 517; IV 215
Colegate, Isabel, V 208
Coleman, Alexander
on García Márquez, II 202
Coleridge, Samuel Taylor, III 57
criticism on, III 113, 118, 120, 122; IV
587, 601
influence of, IV 655
Coles, Robert
on Williams, William Carlos, IV 639
Colette, Sidonie-Gabrielle, I 480–82; II
135, 137
Colinas, Antonio, V 574
Colinet, Paul, I 225
Colliander, Tito, II 101
Collin, V 545
Collingwood, R. G., III 84
Collins, Jackie, V 582
Collins, Tom. *See* Furphy, Joseph
Collodi, Carlo (Carlo Lorenzini), V 151
Colombian literature, I 483–85; V 144–47
civil war as subject of, I 484; II 200
magic realism in, I 485; III 177
major writers of, *see:* Alvarez Gardeazábal; Buenaventura; Caballero
Calderón; Carranza; Carrasquilla;
Cepeda Samudio; Gaitán Durán;
García Márquez; Mejía Vallejo;
Moreno-Duran; Mutis; Rivera; Zapata Olivella
symbolism in, IV 392
colonialism, 20th-c., as literary subject,
III 498
and American territories, IV 282–83,
317
Belgian, I 221; IV 582
British, I 145, 367, 399; III 189, 190,
354, 383, 454, 455; IV 252
in Africa, I 8, 237, 531, 532; II 194,
227; III 188, 387; IV 49, 63, 64,
712, 714
in the colonialists' literature, II 44,
48; III 560
in India, III 357; IV 13–14, 481
in South Africa, IV 289, 290–96
passim
criticism of, I 97, 237, 399; II 445,
478; III 223, 354; IV 63, 64, 194,
472, 473, 481, 490, 712
by colonialists, III 303; IV 282

cultural conflict under, II 441; III 357, 455; IV 282–83, 559
   in Africa, I 8, 46, 96, 237, 387–88; II 194, 227, 479; III 185, 387, 498; IV 193, 196, 490, 714
   in South Africa, IV 290–96 passim
   Dutch, I 604, 605; II 441, 445; III 549
   French, I 531, 532; III 185, 252, 361
     in Africa, I 268, 387–88; II 478, 479; III 451; IV 193, 194, 196, 472, 473, 703
     in Algeria, I 45, 46; III 206
     in the colonialists' literature, III 303
     in Martinique, I 437; III 223
     in Vietnam, III 388
   Portuguese, I 96, 97; IV 147, 282, 559
   reaction against, I 45, 46, 258, 367, 387, 437, 531, 532; III 252, 361, 388, 451 (see also: independence struggles; liberation movements)
Colum, Padraic, II 459
Coman, Otilia-Valeria. See Blandiana, Ana
Combüchen, Sigrid, V 582
communism, as literary subject, IV 320, 344, 615. See also: Communist Party; Maoism; Marxism; Socialist Realism; Stalinism
   adaptation to, I 94, 95; III 284
   anti-, I 456, 460; II 78, 595; III 267; IV 58, 238, 402, 455 (see also criticism of below)
   criticism of, I 465, 466; II 371; III 27, 28; IV 14
   ideology of, III 4–5
     in China, I 25, 456, 458, 459
     in Communist countries, I 39, 208, 307, 342, 358, 359; II 362, 404, 509, 532; III 291
     in the Soviet Union, I 375; II 72, 86, 194, 212, 213, 390, 570–71; III 19, 256; IV 116 (see also: Marxism; Socialist Realism; and in Communist countries under this entry)
     in Western countries, I 37, 298, 326, 435; II 616; III 369, 375, 384, 480; IV 95, 130 (see also: in France and in Spain under this entry)
     in Yugoslavia, I 494, 500, 546; II 615
   satire of, IV 106, 109, 717
   and socialism, IV 577 (see also socialism)
Communist Party, II 595, 625; IV 222, 435, 523. See also communism
   criticism by, of writers in the following literatures (see also under censorship)
     Czechoslovak, III 405, 474; IV 186
     East German, II 315
     Hungarian, I 238; III 149, 150, 351; IV 401
     Italian, II 114
     Kazakh, II 570
     Romanian, I 276
     Russian, II 564, 593; III 47, 469, 470, 531, 548; IV 702
     Tatar, IV 421
     Uzbek, I 219; IV 521
     Yiddish, III 228, 396
     Yugoslav, I 217
   official writers for, III 405, 406, 425, 490; IV 124, 211, 253, 486, 522, 594, 653
     Chinese, III 11, 133, 222; IV 446
Compton-Burnett, Ivy, I 485–86; II 45
   criticism on, IV 152
Comte, Auguste
   influence of, IV 544
Conde (Abellán), Carmen (Florentina del Mar), V 148–49, 570, 574

Condé, Maryse, II 155; V 149–50, 231
confessional literature, I 223; IV 119, 121, 609
   American I 71, 72; III 547; IV 94
   Japanese, I 550; II 423, 424, 494, 495
Confucius, IV 611
Congolese literature, I 486–87
   major writers of, see: Bemba; Tchicaya U Tam'si
Congrains Martín, Enrique, III 510
Coninck, Herman de, I 222
Conn, Stewart, V 547
Connaroe, Joel
   on Williams, William Carlos, IV 639
Connelly, Marc, I 73; II 520
Connolly, Cyril, II 52, 53; III 111; IV 319
   on Orwell, III 441
Conquest, Robert, II 37; V 213
Conrad, Joseph, I 95, 487–92; II 41–42, 44, 49, 115, 116, 489; IV 348; V 206, 392, 516
   criticism on, II 162; III 31, 116; IV 467, 587
   excerpts of, I 492–93
   influence of, I 419, 491; II 251; III 199; V 455
Conrad, Patrick, I 222
Conscience, Hendrik, I 219, 223
Constantin, Ilie, IV 82
consumerism, as literary subject, IV 306
Contini, Gianfranco, III 87
   on Montale, II 471
   on Pizzuto, II 473
   on Tozzi, II 470
Conton, William, II 194; IV 215
Cony, Carlos Heitor, V 88, 89
Cook, David, IV 489
Coolidge, Calvin, III 265
Cooper, Dominic, V 545
Cooper, James Fenimore, I 57, 58
Coover, Robert, I 70, 272; V 26, 150–51
   criticism on, II 205
Cope, Jack, V 391
Cope, Wendy, V 212
Copeau, Jacques, II 138, 590
Copi, V 232
Ćopić, Branko, I 494–95; IV 693
Copland, Aaron, I 310
Coppard, A. E., I 495, II 49
Coppola, Francis Ford, I 491; II 96
Corazzini, Sergio, II 470–71
Corbière, Tristan, I 177; IV 390
   influence of, IV 245, 486
Corbin, Henri, I 155
Cordero-Fernando, Gilda, III 525
Cordes, Léon, II 152
Cordle, Thomas
   on Gide, II 235
Corkery, Daniel, II 462–63
Corm, Charles, III 35
Corn, Alfred, V 28
Corneille, Pierre
   criticism on, III 85
Cornford, John, II 37
Cornillon, Susan Koppelman, V 222
Cornwell, David John Moore. See le Carré, John
Coronel Urtecho, José, I 434; V 115, 123
Corrington, John William, I 68–69
Corso, Gregory, I 72
Cortázar, Julio, I 112, 118, 495–98; II 96; III 328, 382; IV 372; V 40, 42, 76, 97, 131, 132, 398, 620
   critical excerpts on, I 498–99
   influence of, I 323
   on Marechal, III 225
   on Peri Rossi, V 483
Cortesão, Jaime, III 567
Cortez, Alfredo, III 567
Cortezón, Daniel, III 315
Ćosić, Branimir, IV 693
Ćosić, Dobrica, I 499–501; IV 693

Cossa, Roberto, V 42
Cossío, Jose María de, IV 300
Costa, Maria Velho da, III 569
Costa, Nino, II 476
Costa, René de
   on Neruda, III 372
Costa Lima, Luís, V 90
Costantini, Humberto, V 40, 152
Costa Rican literature. See under Central American literature
costumbrismo. See also regional literature
   Portuguese, IV 20
   Spanish, IV 301
   Spanish-Caribbean, II 69; IV 315
   Venezuelan, IV 544
Cote Lamus, Eduardo, I 483–84
Cotruş, Aron, IV 80
Couchoro, Félix, I 237; IV 448
Coulibaly, Augustin Sondé, IV 513
Coulter, John, I 397
Coupe, C. See Wilderode, Anton van
Couperus, Louis, I 501–2; II 445; III 375, 379
Cour, Paul la, I 537
Courtenay, Baudoin de, III 98
Courthope, William J., II 52; III 110–11
Coutinho, Afrânio, V 89
Coutinho, Carlos, III 570
Coutinho, Sônia, V 90
Couto, Maria
   on Rushdie, V 528
Couzyn, Jeni, V 567
Covici, Pat, IV 331
Cowan, Peter, I 147
Coward, Noel, I 502–3
Cowley, Malcolm, I 503–4; II 579
   on Aragon, I 106–7
   on Faulkner, II 83
   on Woolf, Virginia, IV 662
Cox, James M.
   on Frost, II 175
Cox, William Trevor. See Trevor, William
Cozzens, James Gould, I 68, 504–5
Craib, Ian
   on Sartre, IV 159
Craig, David, IV 178
   on Lukács, III 152–53
   on MacDiarmid, III 166
Crainic, Nichifor, IV 80
Crampton, Barbara Mary Pym. See Pym, Barbara
Crane, Hart, I 65, 505–6; II 97; IV 141, 373, 391, 636
   criticism on, III 122; IV 644
   influence of, II 238
Crane, R. S., I 75; III 124
Crane, Stephen, I 57, 255, 488; II 489; V 76
   influence of, I 255
Crashaw, Richard
   criticism on, III 87
Cravierinha, José, III 323
Crawford, Isabella Valancy, I 395
Crawford, Robert, V 547
Crawford, Thomas, V 545
Crayencour, Marguerite de. See Yourcenar, Marguerite
Creangă, Ion, IV 79
Creeley, Robert, I 72, 396, 506–7; III 428; V 26, 27
Creixells, Joan, IV 314
Cremer, Jan, III 378
Cremer, Victoriano, V 466
Crémieux, Benjamin, II 143
   on Giraudoux, II 245
Cremona, John, II 203
creolized languages, literatures using. See under Angolan, Cape Verdean, Dutch-Caribbean, French-Caribbean, Guinea-Bissau, Mauritian, Réunion, and Sierra Leonean literatures

669

dialect literatures (*continued*)
   sian, II 445; Croatian, IV 695;
   Cypriot, I 518; Finnish, II 411;
   German, II 616, III 330, 331 (*see
   also under* Swiss literature); Indian
   (South American), II 424; Indo-Fi-
   jian, III 454; Italian, II 475–76, III
   479, 542; Luxembourg, III 157–
   58; Norwegian, III 399; Occitan, II
   152–53; Polish, III 49, 561; Ro-
   mansh, IV 388–89; Scots, IV 179;
   Ukrainian, IV 327; Welsh, IV 607;
   Yugoslav (Montenegrin), I 215
Diallo, Assane, IV 192
Dias, João, III 322
Diawaky, Noé, IV 703
Díaz, Jorge, I 455; V 133
Díaz, José Pedro
   on Hernández, Felisberto, V 282
Díaz Icaza, Rafael, II 2
Díaz Jácome, Xosé, IV 315
Díaz Lozano, Argentina, V 123
Díaz-Mas, Paloma, V 570, 574
Díaz Mirón, Salvador, III 271
Díaz Plaja, Guillermo, III 97
Díaz Rodríguez, Manuel, III 294; IV 543,
   544
Díaz Sánchez, Ramón, IV 544
Díaz Valcárcel, Emilio, IV 316
Dib, Mohammed, I 46, 47, 562–63; II
   88; V 13, 16, 17, 233, 355
Dicenta, Joaquín, V 46
Dickens, Charles, II 94; IV 348; V 95,
   207, 227, 288, 321, 471
   criticism on, III 31, 117, 120, 125; IV
     146, 640, 644; V 395
   influence of, II 487; III 10–11, 63,
     591; V 642
   as subject, V 209
Dickey, James, I 68, 73, 563–64; V 26
   on Kazantzakis, II 575–76
Dickinson, Emily, I 58; III 547; IV 249,
   470; V 26, 447
   criticism on, III 122
   influence of, I 438; IV 70
Dickinson, Goldsworthy Lowes, II 121
Diderot, Denis
   criticism on, III 105
Didion, Joan, I 70, 564–65; V 25
Diebold, Bernhard, III 106
Diego, Gerardo, IV 500; V 145
Dierx, Léon, IV 25
Dieste, Rafael, IV 315
Dietrich, Marlene, III 210
Dietz, Gertrud. *See* Fussenegger, Gertrud
Díez, Luis Mateo, V 573
Díez de Medina, Fernando, I 289
Diggelmann, Walter Matthias,
   IV 382, 383
Di Giacomo, Salvatore, I 565–66; II 469,
   470, 476
Diharce, Jean, II 151
Diktonius, Elmer, I 566–68; II 100, 101,
   102; III 294; IV 266
   influence of, I 537
Diller, Edward
   on Grass, II 276
Dillier, Julian, IV 385
Dilmen, Güngör (Güngör Dilmen Kal-
   yoncu), IV 479; V 179–80, 607
Dilong, Rudolf, I 526
Dilthey, Wilhelm, III 126
   criticism on, III 82
   influence of, I 351; III 95, 102; V 571
Dimitrova, Blaga, I 360; V 180–82
Dimov, Dimitur, I 359
Dimov, Leonid, IV 82
Dine, Spiro, I 38
Dinescu, Mircea, IV 83; V 519
Dinesen, Isak (Karen Blixen), I 144, 271,
   538, 568–69; IV 280; V 140
   influence of, I 539, 569; V 428
Dionísio, Mário, III 568, 569

Diop, Alioune, IV 194
Diop, Birago, I 569–70; III 361; IV 192,
   194
Diop, Cheikh Anta, IV 194
Diop, David, IV 95, 193–94
Diop, Massyla, IV 193
Diop, Ousmane Socé, IV 193, 194
Diosdado, Ana, V 570
Disengomoka, Émile, IV 703
Disraeli, Benjamin, V 207, 396
Ditlevsen, Tove, I 539; V 159
Ditzen, Rudolf. *See* Fallada, Hans
Diviš, Ivan, V 156
Diyāb, Mahmūd, II 7
Djabarly, Djafar, I 166
Djafer, Ait, I 47
Djaout, Taher, V 12
Djavid, Husein, I 166
Djebar, Assia (Fatima-Zohra Imalayen), V
   15, 182–83, 230, 232
Djibril Tamsir Niane, II 302
Djoleto, Amu, II 226
Djurhuus, Hans Andrias, I 541
Djurhuus, Jens Hendrik Oliver, I 541
Dlamini, John C., IV 296
Dniprovsky, Ivan, IV 495
Doãn Quốc Sỹ, V 618
Dobles, Fabián, I 435; V 124
Döblin, Alfred, I 245, 570–72; II 71,
   219, 402, 485; IV 347, 348;
   V 391
   criticism on, III 151
   influence of, II 275
Dobrogeanu-Gherea, Constantin, IV 79
Dobrolyubov, Nikolay, IV 253
Dobru, I 605
Dobrushin, Yekhezkil, IV 683
Dobson, Rosemary, V 52
Doctorow, E. L., I 70, 572–73; V 25,
   150
Doderer, Heimito von, I 157, 573–74;
   IV 260
Dodo, Jean D., II 479
Doelwijt, Thea, I 605
Doesburg, Theo van. *See* Bonset, I. K.
Dogbe, Yves-Emmanuel, IV 448
Dogbeh, Richard, I 237
Dohmann, Barbara
   on García Márquez, II 202
Doig, Ivan, V 25
Doinaş, Ştefan Augustin, I 574–75; III
   360; IV 82; V 520
Doke, Clement, IV 714
Dokmai Sot, I 575; IV 431
Domaška, Romuald, III 155
Dombrovsky, Yury, IV 111
Domecq, Brianda, V 421
Domin, Hilde, I 575–76; II 222
Domínguez, José Antonio, V 123
Domínguez, Manuel, III 473
Dominican literature. *See under* English-
   Caribbean literature
Dominican Republic literature. *See under*
   Spanish-Caribbean literature
Domjanić, Dragutin, IV 695
Domontovych, Viktor, IV 497
Donaldson, Scott
   on Hemingway, II 359
Don-brgyud-ñi-ma, IV 444
Dončević, Ivan, IV 696
Donchev, Anton, I 359
Donchyk, Vitaly, IV 612
Donckers, M. H. L. T. *See* Insingel,
   Mark
Dondavitra, III 184
Donelaitis, Kristijonas, III 128
Đông-hồ Lâm Tan Phát, IV 560, 561
Donker, Anthonie, III 376
Donkersloot, Nicolaas Anthonie. *See* Don-
   ker, Anthonie
Donleavy, J. P., I 271; II 462
Donnadieu, Marguerite. *See* Duras,
   Marguerite

Donne, John, II 356; V 256
   criticism on, III 87, 105, 115, 116, 122
Donner, Jörn, V 61, 183–84, 356, 357,
   596
Donoghue, Denis, II 463
   on Bellow, I 231
   on Lukács, III 154
   on Yeats, William Butler, IV 679
Donoso, José, I 455, 577–78; V 131,
   378, 391
Dons, Aage, I 538
Dontsov, Dmytro, IV 494
Dooley, D. J.
   on Lewis, Sinclair, III 65
Doolittle, Hilda, I 54, 64, 578–79; II 33–
   34, 116, 161, 432; III 140
   criticism on, I 594
Doppo. *See* Kunikida Doppo
Dorbe, Herberts, III 19
Dorfman, Ariel, I 455; V 131–33, 184–
   85, 391
Dorin, Françoise, V 233
D'Ormesson, Jean, V 231
Dorn, Edward, I 72, 506; III 428
Dorosh, Yefim, IV 112
Dorris, Michael, V 25
Dorssen, Hendrika Akke van, III 379
Dorst, Tankred, II 223
Dosach, Olha Drahomanov. *See* Pchilka,
   Olena
Dos Passos, John, I 57, 60, 61, 68, 579–
   81; II 97–98, 219; V 125
   on Cendrars, I 433
   criticism on, III 92, 151
   excerpts of, I 581–83
   influence of, IV 544
     on American literature, III 180;
      IV 40
     on French literature, II 143
     on German literature, II 224
     on Hungarian literature, III 350
Dostoevsky, Fyodor, I 24; II 66; III 99;
   IV 98, 103, 256, 348; V 186, 220,
   227, 507, 556, 648
   criticism on, III 88, 96, 117; IV 152,
     159; V 58
     American, III 125; IV 333
     Russian, II 477; III 98, 100, 266;
      IV 115
   Freud on, II 159, 160
   influence of
     on American literature, I 227, 228,
      III 503; on Argentine literature, IV
      121; on Armenian literature, III
      444; on Australian literature, IV
      42; on English literature, I 246,
      488; on Estonian literature, IV
      414; on expressionism, II 69; on
      French literature, II 144, 207, 232,
      III 198; on German literature, IV
      184; on Greek literature, III 472;
      on Japanese literature, II 315; on
      Polish literature, III 607; on Rus-
      sian literature, I 340, II 86, III 46,
      IV 109, 706; on Scottish literature,
      III 165; on Thai literature, V 556
   opposition to, IV 253
   as subject, V 368, 501
Dosvitny, Oles, IV 495
Doszhanov, Dukenbay, II 571
Douangchampa, III 10
Doubrovsky, Serge, III 521; V 231
Doughty, Charles
   influence of, III 165
Douglas, Gavin
   criticism on, IV 250
Douglas, Keith, I 583–84; II 37
Douglas, Norman, II 115
Douglass, Frederick
   as subject, V 277
Dourado, Autran, V 88
Dovlatov, Sergey, IV 113; V 185–87,
   391

Dovydėnas, Liudas, III 131
Dovzhenko, Olexandr, IV 496
Dowlatabadi, Mahmoud, V 313
Dowson, Ernest, IV 674
Dox. *See* Razakandrainy, J. V. S.
Doxas, Takis, II 283
Drabble, Margaret, I 584–85; II 42, 48;
    V 207
Drach, Ivan, I 585–86; IV 497; V 612,
    614
Dragún, Osvaldo, I 113; V 42, 187–88
Drahomanov, Mykhaylo, IV 492
    influence of, II 132
Drakul, Simon, IV 698
Dravidian literatures. *See* Indian literature
Dray-Khmara, Mykhaylo, IV 495;
    V 612–13
Drda, Jan, I 523
Dreimane, Valda, III 17
Dreiser, Theodore, I 59, 60, 579, 586–89;
    criticism on, III 111, 120, 264; IV 466,
    587
    excerpts of, I 589–91
    influence of, I 227; II 78
Drewitz, Ingeborg, V 248
Dreyer, Carl, II 94
Drieu la Rochelle, Pierre, I 591–92; II
    143, 144
Droguett, Carlos, I 454
Droste-Hülshoff, Annette von, II 616
Drummond de Andrade, Carlos. *See* Andrade, Carlos Drummond de
Drutse, Ion, III 297, 298
Dryden, John, III 141
    criticism on, III 115
Dsida, Jenő, IV 85
D'Sola, Otto, IV 543
Du'ājī, 'Ali, IV 472–73
Duarte, Fausto, II 301
Dube, John L., IV 295–96
Dubois, Henri, V 640
Du Bois, W. E. B., III 260; IV 666;
    V 188–90
Du Bos, Charles, II 143; III 89, 91;
    V 587
Dubowka, Uladzimier, I 375
Duchamp, Marcel, I 530; II 95; IV 371;
    V 399
Ducharme, Réjean, I 399; V 111
Duchene, François
    on Auden, I 140
Duchscher, Andreï, III 158
Dučić, Jovan, I 592, IV 691
Dudás, Kálmán, IV 700
Dudek, Louis, V 108
Dudintsev, Vladimir, IV 681
Dufrenne, Michel, III 115
Duhamel, Georges, I 593–94; II 142,
    143, 144; IV 76
    on Claudel, I 473
Duinkerken, Anton van, III 376
Dujardin, Édouard, IV 348
Dukore, Bernard F.
    on Ionesco, II 450
Dullin, Charles, II 141, 145; IV 130, 131
Dumarchey, Pierre. *See* Mac Orlan, Pierre
Dumas, Alexandre, père, IV 547
    influence of, II 453
Dumbadze, Nodar, II 213
Dumitrescu, Geo, IV 82
Dumitriu, Dana, V 519
Dumitriu, Petru, IV 82
Dunbar, William, II 391; III 165
    influence of, I 110
Duncan, Isadora, IV 679
Duncan, Quince, V 124
Duncan, Robert, I 71, 594–95; III 394,
    428; V 546
Dune, Edmond, III 159
Dunham, Vera, IV 227
Duniets, Khatskl, IV 684
Dunn, Douglas, IV 179, 181; V 545
Dunne, John Gregory, I 564

Dunqul, Amal, II 5; V 190–91, 200
Duo, Duo, V 391
Duodu, Cameron, II 226
Dương Thu-Hương, V 619
Dupee, F. W.
    on James, Henry, II 489
Dupin, Jacques, V 233
Duque López, Alberto, V 147
Duran, Manuel
    on Cortázar, I 498
Durand, Jules, IV 131
Durand, Luis, I 454
Durand, Mercedes, V 122
Durand, Oswald, II 153
Duras, Marguerite, I 595–96; II 147, 148,
    149; III 381; V 230–32, 640
Durcan, Paul, V 191–92, 318
Durdï, Agakhan, IV 480
Durkheim, Émile, II 138; IV 76
Durrell, Lawrence, I 194, 207, 425, 426,
    491, 596–98; II 46; III 281, 394;
    V 92, 604
    on Rilke, IV 50
Dürrenmatt, Friedrich, I 599–602; II 71,
    217, 551; IV 262, 355, 383, 596;
    V 248, 272
    critical excerpts on, I 602–3
Durych, Jaroslav, I 522, 603–4
Durzak, Manfred
    on Böll, I 294
Dušek, Václav, I 524; V 155
Dušić, Stanko. *See* Begović, Milan
Dutch-Caribbean literature, I 604–6
    in Creole, I 604, 605
    in Dutch, I 604–6
    in the Netherlands Antilles, I 605–6
    Our Own Things group of, I 604–5
    in Surinam, I 604–5
Dutch-language literatures
    See Netherlands literature
    See under Dutch-Caribbean *and* Indonesian literatures
    See also Belgian literature, in Flemish
Dutt, Sudhindranath, II 435
Dutt, Toru, II 434; III 352
Dutton, G. F., V 546
Duun, Olav, I 606–7; III 399–400
Duwlat-ŭlï, Mir Jaqib, I 607; II 570
Duyên Anh, V 619
Dwelshauvers, Jacques, IV 551
Dwinger, Edwin Erich, II 219
Dy, Robert Mélot du, I 225
Dyce, J. R.
    on White, IV 624
Dygasiński, Adolf, III 552
Dygat, Stanisław, I 607–8; III 556
Dyk, Viktor, I 520
Dykstra, Jan. *See* Spanninga, Sjoerd
Dylan, Bob, V 161
Dyson, Edward, I 145
Dyson, H. V. D., III 59
Dzanaity Ivan, III 445
Dzhusoity Nafi, III 445
Dziļums, Alfrēds, III 16
Dzyubin, E. Georgievich. *See* Bagritsky,
    Edvard

Earle, Peter G., V 41
    on Allende, V 20
Easmon, Raymond Sarif, IV 215
Ebdulla, Derwêsh, V 264
Ebejer, Francis, III 203
Ebekenov. *See* Ibrahim, Erkish
Ebeoğlu, Nazif Süleyman, I 519
Eberhart, Richard, III 140
Eble, Kenneth
    on Fitzgerald, F. Scott, II 110
Ebner-Eschenbach, Marie von, I 150
Eça de Queiroz, José Maria, V 219
Echad Haam, I 262, 352
Echegaray, José (Jorge Hayaseca), I 233;
    IV 301; V 193–94

Echenoz, Jean, V 231
Echeruo, Michael, III 391
Echeverría, Aquileo J., V 124
Echeverría, Luis, III 43
Echeverría, Marilín. *See* Ríos, Lara
Echewa, T. Obinkaram, V 449
Eco, Umberto, II 474; III 88; V 194–97
    critical excerpts on, V 197–98
Ecuadorian literature, II 1–2
    Group of Guayaquil of, II 1
    Madrugada group of, II 2
    magic realism in, II 1, 424
    major writers of, *see:* Aguilero Malta;
        Carrera Andrade; Gallegos Lara;
        Icaza; Pareja Diezcanseco
Edel, Leon, I 76; III 83; IV 642
    on James, Henry, II 487, 489, 491
Edelshtat, Dovid, IV 683
Edfelt, Johannes, IV 379
Edgell, Zee, V 121
Edgü, Ferit, V 607
Edib, Halide. *See* Adıvar, Halide Edib
Edison, Thomas, II 94
Edmundson, Mark
    on Rushdie, V 529
Edschmid, Kasimir, II 69, 71; III 106
    on expressionism, II 69
Edwards, James Morgan, IV 605
Edwards, Jorge, I 455; V 131–33, 198–
    200, 378
Edwards, O. M., IV 606
Edwards Bello, Joaquín, I 454
Eeden, Frederik Willem van, II 2–3;
    III 375
Eekhoud, Georges, I 223
Ee Tiang Hong, III 192–93
Efendi, Hilmi, I 519
Efendiev, Ilyas, I 166
Effersøe, Rasmus, I 541
Eftimiu, Victor, IV 81
Egbuna, Obi, III 392, 393
Egea, Julián, V 575
Egge, Peter, III 399, 401
Eggiman, Ernst, IV 385
Eghivart, I 121
Eglītis, Andrejs, III 17
Eglītis, Anšlavs, III 17
ego-futurism. *See* futurism, Russian
Egri, Viktor, I 527
Eguren, José María, III 511
Egyptian literature, II 3–8; V 200–202
    the Divan school of, II 4, 7
    in Lebanon, II 4, 5
    and literary criticism, II 7–8, 417
    major writers of, *see:* 'Abd al-Sabūr;
        Chedid; Dunqul; Faraj; al-Ghītānī;
        al-Hakīm; Haqqī; Hijāzī; Husayn;
        Idrīs; al-Kharrāt; Mahfūz; Taymūr
    the 1960s as subject of, III 179
    revolution as subject of, II 5
    the Six Day War as subject of, II 6
    Theater of the Absurd in, II 317, 428–
    29
Ehrenburg, Ilya, I 298; II 8–9; III 80,
    470; IV 109, 110, 111; V 391
Ehrenstein, Albert, II 71
Eich, Günter, I 26; II 10, 71, 221, 223
Eichelbaum, Samuel, I 113
Eichenbaum, Boris, III 98, 99; IV 114–
    15
Einstein, Albert, I 360; II 549; IV 231;
    V 211
Einstein, Carl, II 71
Eisenman, Peter, V 169
Eisenreich, Herbert, I 158
Eisenstadt, Jill, V 26
Eisenstein, Sergey, II 94, 98; III 365;
    IV 231
Eisler, Hanns, I 265
Eisner, Kurt, IV 449
Eissler, Kurt R., II 162

Fernandez, Dominique, V 231
Fernández, Macedonio, I 111
Fernandez, Ramon, II 143; III 88–89
Fernández, Sergio, III 272
Fernández Almagro, Melchor, IV 300
Fernández Alvarez, Luis, IV 542, 543
Fernández Cubas, Cristina, V 573
Fernández de Castro, José Antonio, I 20
Fernández Moreno, César, I 111; V 41
Fernández Retamar, Roberto, IV 316
Fernando, Basil, IV 324
Fernando, Caio, V 90
Fernando, Lloyd, III 193
Fernando, Patrick, IV 324
Ferraté, Joan, IV 314
Ferrater, Gabriel, IV 313
Ferrater i Mora, Josep, IV 314; V 571,
    573
    on Unamuno, IV 504
Ferrater Mora, José. See Ferrater i Mora,
    Josep
Ferré, Rosario, V 223–25
Ferreira, Ascenso, I 322
Ferreira, José Gomes, III 569
Ferreira, Vergílio, III 568
Ferreira de Castro, José Maria. See Cas-
    tro, José Maria Ferreira de
Ferreiro, Celso Emilio, IV 315
Ferron, Jacques, I 399; V 109, 225–26
Fet, Afanasy Afanasievich (Shenshin),
    IV 103
    influence of, I 350
    as subject, V 441
Feuchtwanger, Lion, II 89–91, 112, 219
    on Brecht, I 328–29
    criticism on, III 151
Feuerbach, Ludwig, IV 253
Feydeau, Ernest, II 91
Feydeau, Georges, II 91–92, 136
Fiallos Gil, Mariano, V 124
Fiawoo, Kwasi, IV 448
Fichte, Hubert, II 225; V 248
Ficker, Ludwig von, I 152; IV 461
Fiedler, Leslie A., I 75; II 92–93, 398
    on Roth, Henry, IV 91
Field, Edward, I 73
Field, Frank
    on Kraus, II 610
Fielding, Henry, III 308
Fierro, Humberto, II 1
Fierstein, Harvey, V 29
Figes, Eva, V 221
Figueiredo, Fidelino de Sousa, III 97
Figuera, Angela, V 574
Fiji literature. See under Pacific Islands
    literature
Filipowicz, Kornel, V 492
Filippini, Enrico, IV 388
Filippini, Felice, IV 388
film
    influence of, on literary technique, II
        97–98; III 198, 256, 609; IV 11,
        27, 39–40, 44, 68, 110, 137, 308,
        671
    and literature, I 476–77, 491; II 70,
        93–99, 141, 555; III 366, 427,
        480
    surrealism and, II 95, 141; IV 373
Filosofov, Dmitry, III 266
Filyansky, Mykola, IV 494
Finas, Lucette, V 235
Finch, Peter, IV 609
Finch, Robert, I 396
Finlay, Ian Hamilton, IV 179; V 546
Findley, Timothy, V 109
Fine, Ellen S.
    on Wiesel, V 636
Fink, Georg, V 270
Finnish literature, II 99–104
    civil war (1918) as subject of, I 567; II
        100–101, 102; III 39, 76; IV 219,
        562
    Continuation War as subject of, II 101–
        2, 103; III 76

existentialism in, IV 132
expressionism in, III 40
"Finlandization" of, II 103
in Finnish, II 99–104
Flame Bearers group of, II 101
major writers of
    in Finnish, see: Diktonius; Haanpää;
        Haavikko; Kallas, Aino; Kilpi,
        Eeva; Kilpi, Volter; Lehtonen;
        Leino; Linna; Manner; Meri; Saari-
        koski; Salama; Sillanpää; Tikka-
        nen; Tuuri; Viita
    in Swedish, see: Bargum; Björling;
        Carpelan; Chorell; Diktonius;
        Donner; Enckell, Rabbe;
        Huldén; Jansson; Kihlman; Söder-
        gran
modernism in, I 567; II 100, 313; III
    294; IV 266
the New Novel in, II 313
in Swedish, II 99–104
the Tampere circle of, IV 131
Theater of the Absurd in, II 313
the Winter War as subject of, II 101;
    III 76
World War II, conditions during, as
    subject of, II 313–14
Finno-Ugric literatures of the Soviet
    Union, II 104–5
    Estonian literature, II 259–63
    Karelian (Finnish) literature, II 104
    Khanty literature, II 104
    Komi literature, II 104, 105
    Mansi literature, II 104
    Mari literature, II 104, 105
    Mordvin literature, II 104, 105
    Nenets literature, II 105
    Udmurt literature, II 104, 105
Fîntîneru, Constantin, IV 81
Firbank, Ronald, II 44–45, 105–6
    influence of, II 45; IV 592
Firchow, Peter
    on Huxley, II 421
Firdaus Abdullah, III 191
Firestone, Shulamith, V 221
Firpo, Edoardo, IV 476
Fischer, Ernst, III 151
    on Musil, III 338
Fischer, Otokar, III 83
Fishburn, Katherine
    on Lessing, Doris, III 54
Fishman, Rokhl, IV 687
Fishta, Gjergj, I 38
Fitilov, Mykola. See Khvylovy, Mykola
Fitrat, Abdalrauf, II 106–7; IV 521
Fitzgerald, F. Scott, I 60–61, 62, 63, 68,
    491, 588; II 107–10, 354, 356; III
    535; IV 328; V 321, 436
    criticism on, II 110–12
    influence of, I 460; III 180
Fitzgerald, Penelope, V 209
Fitzgerald, Robert, III 415
    on Cavafy, I 425–26
FitzGerald, Robert D., I 147
Fitzgerald, Zelda Sayre, II 107
Flakoll, Darwin J., V 9
Flaubert, Gustave, III 92, 571; IV 60,
    348; V 95, 210,
    criticism on, III 151; IV 538
    American, III 487
    French, II 68; III 90, 91, 93; IV 156
    influence of
        on American literature, I 227; II 487;
            III 141
        on Australian literature, IV 42
        on English literature, I 246; II 105,
            116
        on French literature, II 137
        on German literature, II 131; III 210
        on Hungarian literature, I 57
        on Irish literature, II 528; V 318
Fleishman, Avrom
    on Conrad, I 493
    on Woolf, Virginia, IV 662–63

Fleishman, Lazar
    on Pasternak, Boris, III 482, 485–86
Fleisser, Marieluise, II 112–13, 223
    influence of, II 616
Flemish literature. See under Belgian
    literature
Flers, Robert de, II 136
Fletcher, Angus, II 162
Fletcher, John Gould, I 64; II 432; III 140
    on Beckett, I 215
Fletcher, Valerie, II 18
Flimm, Jürgen, V 383
Flint, F. S., II 33, 116, 432
Fløgstad, Kjartan, V 226–27, 563
Floqi, Kristo, I 39
Flora, Francesco, II 471; III 86
Flora, Ioan, IV 700
Flora, Radu, IV 700
Florentino, Alberto, III 525
Flores, Ángel, III 177
    on Andrade, Eugénio de, V 30
Florit, Eugenio
    on Jiménez, II 512–13
Flower, J. E.
    on Mauriac, François, III 251–52
Flying Officer X. See Bates, H. E.
Fo, Dario, II 113–14, 475
Foarţă, Serban, V 521
Foerster, Norman, III 112
Fogelström, Per Anders, V 581, 583
Foix, J. V., II 114–15; IV 312, 372
Földi, Mihály, II 414
Fondane, Benjamin. See Fundoianu,
    Barbu
Fon literature. See under Beninian
    literature
Fonseca, António Branquinho da, III 567;
    IV 20
Fonseca, Rubem, I 323; V 89, 90, 227
Fontana, Gian, IV 389
Fontane, Theodor, II 215; V 584
    on Hauptmann, III 341
    influence of, II 217
Fontanille, Jacques, V 234
Fontinhas, José. See Andrade, Eugénio de
Foote, Shelby, I 69
Forbáth, Imre, I 527
Ford, Charles Henri, IV 373
Ford, Ford Madox, I 363, 488; II 42,
    115–18, 290, 489; III 21; IV 33;
    V 210
    on Bogan, I 287
    critical excerpts on, II 118–20
    influence of, II 42, 115, 116, 288, 431
    on Joyce, II 530
Ford, George
    on Lawrence, D. H., III 25
Ford, John, II 95, 96
Ford, Richard, V 26
Foreman, Richard, V 28
Forêts, Louis-René des, I 296
formalism, 20th-c., II 391; IV 645; V 288
    American, I 71; III 141, 363; V 101
    anti-, I 72
    and literary criticism, III 79, 98–99
    Russian, I 232, 325; III 94, 98–99; IV
        114–15
Forsh, Olga, IV 109–10
Forssell, Lars, II 120–21; IV 380, 381;
    V 582
Forster, E. M., I 491; II 44, 50, 53, 121–
    24; III 21, 83, 111, 120; IV 346,
    453, 658; V 18
    on Conrad, Joseph, I 492
    critical excerpts on, II 124–25
    on Desani, I 559
    on James, Henry, II 489, 490
Fort, Paul, II 136
Fortes, Corsino, I 402
Fortune, George, IV 714
Fortuyn-Leenmans, Margaretha Droog-
    lever. See Vasalis
Foscolo, Ugo, IV 547
Foster, David, V 52

677

Friedell, Egon, I 155; II 165–66; III 551
Friedlander, Albert H.
  on Wiesel, V 636
Friedman, Bruce Jay, I 69, 271, 273
Friedman, Maurice
  on Wiesel, V 636
Friedrich, Hugo
  on Guillén, Jorge, II 295
Friel, Brian, II 460; V 235–38, 317
Frisch, Max, I 71, 166–70, 217, 551; IV
    382, 383; V 248
  on Brecht, I 329
  critical excerpts on, II 170–71
Frischmuth, Barbara, I 159; V 53, 54
Frisian literature. See under Netherlands
    literature
Fritsch, Gerhard, V 54
Fritz, Marianne, V 249
Fritz, Walter Helmut, II 222
Friulian literature. See under Italian
    literature
Frobenius, Leo, V 104
Fröding, Gustaf, II 89; IV 376
Frohock, Wilbur M.
  on Malraux, III 200–201
Frost, Robert, I 64, 71; II 171–74; IV 12,
    261, 440, 628
  criticism on, I 274
    exerpts of, II 174–76
  influence of, III 141, 162–63
  on Thomas, Edward, IV 440–41
Frostenson, Katarina, V 582
Frutos, Eugenio
  on Guillén, Jorge, II 296
Fry, Christopher, II 39, 176–77; V 45
Frye, Northrop, II 177–78, 538; III 28,
    124; V 108
Fu'ād Nigm, Ahmad, V 200
Fuad Salim, IV 233
Fubini, Mario, III 86
Fučík, Julius, I 621
Fuenmayor, Alfonso, V 125
Fuentes, Carlos, II 178–79; III 272, 274,
    382; V 76, 97, 420, 422, 494, 620
  on Cortázar, I 498
  on Goytisolo, Juan, II 267–68
Fuertes, Gloria, V 570, 574
Fugard, Athol, II 179–80; IV 289; V 566
Fuhrmann, Dieter, IV 84
Fuks, Khaim L., IV 1
Fuks, Ladislav, I 523, 524; II 180–81;
    V 155
Fulani literature. See Cameroonian and
    under Mali literatures
Fuller, John, V 212
Fuller, Roy, II 37, 182
Fulton, John, V 547
Fulton, Robin, IV 178
Funck, Joseph, III 158
Fundoianu, Barbu, III 522; IV 81
Furmanov, Dmitry, IV 109, 253
Furphy, Joseph, I 146; II 182–83
Furui Yoshikishi, V 238–39, 334
Füruzan, IV 479; V 607
Fussenegger, Gertrud, I 157
Füst, Milán, II 412
Fuster, Joan, IV 314
Futabatei Shimei, II 183–84, 495
futurism
  in Hungarian literature, II 414
  influence of
    on East European literatures, I 165,
      375, 442, II 212, III 16, 130, 228,
      IV 495–96; on expressionism, II
      69; on modernism, III 294; on
      Spanish American literatures, III
      273; on ultraism, IV 499; on West-
      ern European literatures, II 216, III
      567, IV 299
    Italian, I 298, 531; II 184–85, 362,
      471; III 226–27, 385, 463; IV 17,
      336, 347, 370, 509
    criticism of, I 410
    and expressionism, II 69

and literary criticism, III 86
  in Japanese literature, II 496
  in Polish literature, III 554, 555, 605
  in Portuguese literature, IV 118
  Russian, I 177, 513, 531; II 181, 185–
    86, 582–83; III 255–57, 385,
    481–82; IV 105, 470
    and constructivism, IV 105–6
    and literary criticism, III 98
    see also cubism
Fylypovych, Pavlo, IV 495
Fyodorov, Mikhail R., I 466

Gaadamba, Shanjmyatavyn, III 300
Gáal, Gábor, IV 85
Gabeira, Fernando, V 90
Gadamer, Hans-Georg, III 522
Gadda, Carlo Emilio, I 53; II 187–88,
    471, 472–73; III 243
Gaddis, William, I 70; II 188–89; V 24
Gadeau, Germain Coffi, II 478
Gädiaty Seka, III 445
Gadjiev, Zagid, III 398
Gaelic literature. See under Irish and
    Scottish literatures
Gafudzi, Tito Yisuku, IV 703
Gagnon, Madeleine, V 111
Gailit, August, II 62
Gaillard, Roger
  on Roumain, IV 95
Gaines, Ernest, I 69; V 240–41
Gaiser, Gerd, II 224
Gaitán Durán, Jorge, I 483–84; V 241–42
Gaitskill, Mary, V 26
Gajcy, Tadeusz, III 557
Gál, Laszlo, IV 700
Gala, Antonia, V 574
Galaction, Gala, I 114; IV 79
Galapatti, Buddhi, IV 323
Gałczyński, Konstanty Ildefons, II 189;
    III 555, 557
Gäle, Rita, III 17
Galeano, Eduardo, V 391
Galich, Alexandr, III 424; IV 107; V 391
Galician literature. See under Spanish
    literature
Galin, Alexandr, V 531
Galindo, Sergio, V 420
Gallagher, D. P.
  on Borges, I 306
  on García Márquez, II 203
  on Paz, III 496
Gallagher, Tess, V 27, 119
Gallant, Christine, II 538
Gallant, Mavis, V 95, 109, 242–43
Gallegos, Daniel, V 124
Gallegos, Rómulo, II 190–91; IV 543,
    544, 545
Gallegos Lara, Joaquín, IV 1; V 5, 244
Gallop, Jane, V 222
Galsworthy, John, I 489; II 39, 42, 49,
    115, 191–92, 556; IV 349; V 184
  criticism on, II 42
  influence of, IV 517
Galvão, Walnice, V 91
Gálvez, Manuel, I 111; II 192–93
Gama, Sebastião de, III 569
Gamaléya, Boris, IV 25
Gambaro, Griselda, I 113; V 42, 244–46
Gambian literature, II 193–94
  major writers of, in English, see Peters,
    Lenrie
Gamero de Medina, Lucila, V 123
Gamsakhurdia, Konstantine, II 194–95,
    212, 213
Gamzatov, Rasul, III 398
Ganda literature. See under Ugandan
    literature
Gandhi, Mahatma, II 434; III 351, 352;
    IV 404
  influence of, IV 75
Gandiaga, Bitoriano, IV 310
Ganem, Chekri, III 35

Ganeshalingam, Selliah, IV 323
Gaos, José, V 570
Gaos, Vicente, IV 305
Gao Xiaosheng. See Kao Hsiao-sheng
Gaprindashvili, Valerian, II 211, 212
Garagorri, Paulino, V 570
Garaudy, Roger, III 80
  on Aragon, I 107
Garay, Blas, III 473
Gäräy, Räshit, IV 421
Garborg, Arne, V 276
Garcés, Tomàs, IV 311
García, Santiago, V 147
García Alvarez, Enrique, V 47
García Calderón, Ventura, III 509
García Calvo, Agustín, V 571
García Hortelano, Juan, V 573
García Lorca, Federico, I 41–42, 420; II
    195–98, 296; III 167, 196, 368,
    477; IV 256, 301, 302, 304, 372,
    392; V 30, 81, 574
  critical excerpts on, II 198–99
  influence of, I 586; III 420; V 152
García Lorca, Francisco
  on García Lorca, Federico, II 198
García Márquez, Gabriel, I 323, 484–85;
    II 199–203; III 177; IV 57; V 6,
    19, 21, 22, 40, 97, 103, 125, 131,
    145–47, 208, 247, 323, 391, 415,
    432, 449, 505, 506, 526, 527,
    543, 558
  criticism on, IV 538; V 133
  excerpts of, II 202–3
  film adaptations of, II 97
  influence of, V 51, 126, 565, 570
García Marruz, Fina, IV 316
García Monge, Joaquín, I 435; V 124,
    463
García Morente, Manuel, IV 300
García Pintado, Angel, V 574
García Ponce, Juan, V 421, 422
García Sarmiento, Félix Rubén. See
    Darío, Rubén
García Terrés, Jaime, III 273
Garcilaso de la Vega, I 50, 436
  criticism on, III 96
Gardies, André
  on Robbe-Grillet, IV 62
Gardner, Erle Stanley, V 128
Gardner, John, III 571
Gárdonyi, Géza, II 413
Garents, Vahakn, I 122
Garfield, Evelyn Picon
  on Cortázar, I 499
Gargiulo, Alfredo, III 86
Garioch, Robert, IV 178, 180, 250;
    V 547
Garland, Hamlin, I 58
Garmadi, Salah, IV 474
Garmendia, Julio, IV 544
Garmendia, Salvador, IV 544
Garneau, Michel, I 398
Garner, Helen, V 52
Garnett, David, II 44, 50
Garnett, Edward, I 488; II 50; III 21; V
    62, 516
Garro, Elena, III 274; V 246–48, 421
Garrod, H. W., II 52; III 111
Garroni, Emilio, II 98
Garten, Hugh F.
  on Hauptmann, II 342
  on Kaiser, Georg, II 553
Gascar, Pierre, I 147, 203–4
Gasché, Rodolphe
  on Derrida, V 178
Gascoyne, David, II 37, 38; IV 373
Gaskell, Elizabeth Cleghorn, V 207
Gass, William, I 70, 273; II 204–5
  on James, Henry, II 491
  on Singer, Isaac Bashevis, IV 237
Gasset, Eduardo, III 436
Gassner, John, V 80
  on Cocteau, I 479
  on O'Casey, III 413   679

255–56, 272, 273, 458
influence of, II 248; IV 366
Gibson, Wilfred, II 35
Gibson, William, I 74
Gicaru, Muga, II 577
Gide, André, I 469, 491, 513; II 135,
138, 139, 142, 143, 144, 230–34,
240, 242, 286, 502; III 90, 232;
IV 77, 224, 360, 391, 526; V 321
on Claudel, I 473
criticism on, II 500; III 120; V 367,
368
excerpts of, II 234–35
influence of, I 476; II 233, 251; IV 81;
V 322
Gifford, Emma Lavinia, II 328, 330
Gijsen, Marnix, I 220; II 236–37; IV 69
Gilbert, Mary E.
on Hofmannsthal, II 387
Gilbert, Sandra M., V 222, 374
on Lawrence, D. H., III 25
Gilbert-Lecomte, Roger, I 545; IV 525
Gilboa, Amir, II 466
Gilchrist, Ellen, V 25, 26
Gil de Biedma, Jaime, V 574
Gil Gilbert, Enrique, II 1; V 5, 244
Gill, Claes, III 402
Gill, Eric, II 521
Gill, Georgine Bélanger. See Montreuil,
Gaétane de
Gill, Walter, III 454
Gillès, Daniel, I 224
Gilliams, Maurice, I 222
Gilliard, Edmond, IV 386
Gillies, Valerie, V 546
Gilman, Charlotte Perkins, V 221
Gilman, Richard
on Brecht, I 330
on Chekhov, I 450–51
on Ionesco, II 450–51
Gilmore, Mary, I 146
Gils, Gust, I 221, 222
Giménez Caballero, Ernesto, IV 300
Gimferrer, Pere, IV 313; V 574
Ginastera, Alberto, III 328
Ginsberg, Allen, I 72, 188; II 237–39,
579; IV 637; V 26, 309
on Pound, III 579
Ginsberg, Asher Hirsch. See Echad Haam
Ginzburg, Leone, II 239
Ginzburg, Natalia, II 239–40
Ginzburg, Yevgenia, I 32; IV 111
Gioia, Dana, V 28
Gion, Nándor, V 298
Giono, Jean, II 142, 143, 144, 240–41;
III 456; IV 95, 425
Giovanni, Nikki, I 73
Gippius, Zinaida. See Hippius, Zinaida
Girard, René, V 234
Giraudoux, Jean, I 4; II 138, 142, 144,
146, 241–44; III 310
on Alain-Fournier, I 36
criticism on, II 500
excerpts of, II 244–46
Gironella, José María, II 246–47; IV 260,
307
Girourard, Laurent, I 399
Giroux, André, I 398
Girri, Alberto, I 111; V 41, 256–57
Girun, Gian, IV 388
Gissing, George
influence of, I 246
Githae-Mugo, Micere, III 387
Giuliani, Alfredo, II 474
Giurjian, Melkon. See Hrend
Giurlani, Aldo. See Palazzeschi, Aldo
Gjedsted, Rolf, I 541
Gjerku, Enver, IV 699
Gladilin, Anatoly, II 572; IV 112–13
Gladkov, Fyodor Vasilievich, II 247–48;
IV 108, 110, 253
Gladstone, Mary, V 546
Glants-Leyeles, Aron, II 248; IV 374, 683

Glasgow, Ellen, I 58–59
glasnost, V 3, 323, 389, 483, 504, 506,
507, 529–32, 559, 597, 612, 621,
647
Glatshteyn, Yankev. See Glatstein, Jacob
Glatstein, Jacob (Glatshteyn, Yankev), II
248–49; IV 683, 685
Glauser, Friedrich, IV 382
Glazarová, Jarmila, I 522
Glazman, Borekh, IV 685
Glen, Duncan, V 545, 547
Gligorić, Velibor, IV 694
Glissant, Edouard, II 154–55; V 231,
233, 257–58
Głowacki, Aleksander. See Prus, Boles-
ław
Głowacki, Janusz, V 490, 493
Glucksman, André, II 149
Godard, Barbara
on Davies, Robertson, V 167
Godard, Jean-Luc, II 96, 97
Goday, Juan, I 454
Godbout, Jacques, I 399; V 110, 258–59
Godin, Gerald, V 110
Godin, Marcel, I 399
Godoy Alcayaga, Lucila. See Mistral, Ga-
briela
Godwin, Gail, V 25
Goemans, Camille, I 225
Goes, Albrecht, II 218, 224, 249–50
Goetel, Ferdynand, II 250–51; III 556
Goethe, Johann Wolfgang, I 412; II 66,
132, 403, 609; III 151, 214; V 580
criticism on, II 162; III 82, 85, 96;
IV 146
Freud on, II 159, 160
influence of, II 12, 585; III 40
on Austrian literature, II 385, 609;
IV 48
on French literature, II 231; IV 76
on German literature, II 367
and psychology, II 535, 538
as subject, V 437
Goettle, Gabriele, V 250
Goetz, Rainald, V 249
Goffin, Robert, I 225
Goga, Octavian, IV 80
Gogarty, Oliver St. John, II 462, 566
Gogh, Vincent van, I 592
influence of, I 567
Gogol, Nikolay, III 326; IV 108; V 186,
322, 597, 621, 648
criticism on, III 99, 104, 346; IV 115;
V 58
influence of, I 232; II 86; III 531; IV
414, 493; V 240
Goh Poh Seng, IV 233
Gökalp, Ziya, IV 475
Gökçeli, Yaşar Kemal. See Kemal, Yaşar
Gokhale, G. K., III 352
Gold, Herbert, I 69
Gold, Michael, V 270
Goldemberg, Isaac, V 260–61, 524
Golden, Louis, IV 472
Goldfaden, Avrom, IV 686
Golding, William, II 42, 43, 47, 251–52;
IV 262; V 206
Goldman, Emma, II 453
Goldmann, Lucien, II 148; III 80, 151
on Genet, II 209
on Kristeva, V 372
on Robbe-Grillet, IV 61–62
Goldscheider, Ludwig, I 156
Goll, Yvan, II 70, 218
Golovin, Gennady, V 531
Golshiri, Hushang, V 314
Gołubiew, Antoni, III 558
Goma, L. K. H., IV 704
Goma, Paul, IV 83; V 519
Gombrowicz, Witold, II 252–54; III 325,
556, 558; IV 174, 214; V 377,
491–93
influence of, I 607; V 562

Gomes, Joaquim Soeiro Pereira, III 568
Gomes, Manuel Teixeira, III 568
Gómez, Vicente, II 190
Gómez Carillo, Enrique, III 294; V 121
Gómez de la Serna, Ramón, I 128; II
254–56; IV 307, 372; V 126
Gómez-Ojea, Carmen, V 570
Gómez Picón, Rafael, V 145
Gomringer, Eugen, II 221, 222; IV 384;
V 261–62
Gonçalves, Egito, III 569
Gonçalves, Olga, III 569; V 262–63
Göncz, Árpád, V 297
Gondra, Manuel, III 473
Góngora (y Argote), Luis de, I 41, 50; III
70, 95; IV 304; V 66, 292
criticism on, III 96, 97
Gonne, Maud, IV 674
Gonsar, Camilo, V 573
Gönül, Engin, I 519
González, Alfonso, V 562
González, Angel, V 574
González, Natalicio, III 473
Gonzalez, N. V. M., II 256; III 525
González Dávila, Jesús, V 423
González Martínez, Enrique, II 256–57;
III 273, 293
González Prada, Manuel, I 42; II 257–58;
III 510
González Tuñón, Raúl, II 303
González Zeledón, Manuel, V 124
Goodman, Paul, II 398
Gooneratne, Yasmine, IV 324–25
Goonewardena, James, IV 324
Gopaleen, Myles na. See O'Brien, Flann
Goran, Abdulla (Abdulla Sulayman), II
628; V 263–64
Gorbanevskaya, Natalya, IV 107
Gordimer, Nadine, II 258–59; IV 289;
V 566
Gordin, Jacob, IV 686
Gordin, A. D., I 352
Gordon, Caroline, I 63; II 115, 259–60;
III 415; IV 422
Gordon, E. V., IV 448
Gordon, Giles, IV 179, 181; V 545
Gordon, Lyndall
on Eliot, T. S., II 21
Gordon, Mary, V 25
Gorenko, Anna Andreevna. See Akhma-
tova, Anna
Gorin, Igor, V 531
Goris, Jan-Albert. See Gijsen, Marnix
Gorky, Maxim, I 89, 90, 164, 446; II 86,
260–63, 584; IV 108, 114, 706; V
391, 465, 556, 639
on Bryusov, I 350
criticism on, III 151
excerpts of, II 263–65
influence of, II 247, 263; III 425; IV
75; V 270, 455, 652
on Leonov, III 46
on Mayakovsky, III 257
and Socialist Realism, IV 253
Gorodetsky, Sergey, II 305; IV 104
Gorostiza, Carlos, V 42
Gorostiza, Celestino, III 274; V 264
Gorostiza, José, III 273; V 264–65,
456
Gorostiza, Manuel Eduardo de, V 264
Gorra, Michael
on Rushdie, V 528
Gorter, Herman, I 308
influence of, III 375
Gosse, Edmund, I 488; II 52; III 110,
351, 352
Gostandian, Harout, I 121
Gothale, Govinda Bahadur, III 367
Göthe, Staffan, V 583
Gotō Meisei, V 238, 334
Gotthelf, Jeremias, IV 382
Gottwald, Klement, III 405
Gotuta, L., II 213

Goudeket, Maurice
  on Cocteau, I 479
Gourmont, Remy de, II 138; III 89
  influence of, II 599
Govoni, Corrado, II 184, 471, 472
Govshut, Ata, IV 480
Gouws, Ingrid. See Viljoen, Lettie
Goya, Francisco de, I 355, 429; II 254
Goyen, William, I 69
Goytisolo, Juan, II 265–67; IV 309;
    V 570, 572
  critical excerpts on, II 267–68
Goytisolo, Luis, V 572
Gozzano, Guido, II 268–69, 470; IV 120
Gozzi, Carlo, V 465
Grab, Hermann, I 156
Grabbe, Christian Dietrich, II 70
Graça, José Vieira Mateus da. See Vieira,
    José Luandino
Gracq, Julien, II 269–70
Grade, Chaim, II 270–71; IV 684, 685
Graf, Oskar Maria, I 156; II 219, 271–72
Graff, Gerald, III 126
Graft, Joe de, II 227
Graham, R. B. Cunninghame, I 488;
    IV 178
Graham, Shirley, V 190
Graham, William S., V 547
Graham, W. S., IV 179
Grainville, Patrick, V 231
Grameno, Mihal, I 38
Gramsci, Antonio, II 469; III 81, 480
Granauskas, Romualdas, III 133; V 394
Grandbois, Alain, I 398
Granell, Manuel, V 570
Granin, Daniil, IV 113; V 531
Granlid, Hans, V 582
Granovsky, Alexandr, IV 686
Grant, Duncan, IV 658
Grant, Judith Skelton
  on Davies, Robertson, V 167
Grants, Valdis. See Krāslavietis, Valdis
Gräs, Ulrik, V 159
Grass, Günter, I 273; II 220, 222, 223,
    224, 272–76; III 44, 45; IV 260,
    333, 433; V 54, 249, 387, 413,
    527
  criticism on, II 273
    excerpts of, II 276–77
Grau (Delgado), Jacinto, IV 302; V 265–
    66
Grau, Shirley Ann, I 69
Graves, Robert, II 29, 33, 34, 35, 36,
    277–79
  influence of, II 38
Gray, Alasdair, V 544, 545
Gray, Sir Alexander, IV 178
Gray, Ronald
  on Kafka, II 548
Gray, Simon, II 41; V 211, 266–68
Gray, Stephen, V 566
Gray, Thomas
  criticism on, III 116, 122
Great Depression, as literary subject
  in America, I 48, 58, 380, 580; III
    170, 418; IV 150, 331, 617, 642
  in Canada, I 383
  in Europe, I 537; II 426; III 26
  and postrealism, III 572
  social chronicles of, IV 261
Greek literature, II 279–84. See also Cyp-
    riot literature
  Asia Minor disaster (1922) as subject
    of, III 593
  civil war as subject of, II 282, 573;
    IV 54
  and Crete, II 52
  dhimotiki (demotiki; demotic)/kathare-
    vousa conflict in, II 279–81 pas-
    sim, 573; III 342, 343, 462; IV
    183, 539
  the Generation of the Thirties of, IV
    436

Greek Parnassians of, see New School
    of Athens below
  Ionian School of, II 280
  kathomiloumeni in, IV 668
  literary criticism in, IV 183, 428, 539,
    668
  major writers of, see: Cavafy; Elytis;
    Haris; Kambanellis; Karyotakis;
    Kazantzakis; Myrivilis; Palamas;
    Panayotopoulos; Papadiamantis;
    Plaskovitis; Prevelakis; Ritsos; Sa-
    marakis; Seferis; Sikelianos, Ange-
    los; Taktsis; Terzakis; Theotokas;
    Tsirkas; Varnalis; Vassilikos; Ve-
    nezis; Xenopoulos
  the military junta (1967–74) as subject
    of, IV 137–38, 540–41
  New School of Athens of, II 280;
    III 462
  Old School of Athens of, II 280
  stream of consciousness in, IV 428
  surrealism in, II 27, 282
  symbolism in, II 280, 281; III 462;
    IV 182
  World War II as subject of
    the Albanian front during, IV 218
    Nazi occupation during, II 282, 334;
      III 467; IV 542
    pre-, III 467
Green, Dorothy, V 51
Green, Henry, II 45, 284–85
Green, Julien, II 142, 144, 285–87; III
    502; V 231
Green, Martin
  on Golding, II 252
Green, Paul, IV 665
Greenacre, Phyllis, II 162
Greenberg, Herbert
  on Auden, I 139–40
Greenberg, Richard, V 29
Greenberg, Uri Zvi, II 287–88, 465, 466;
    III 228; IV 684, 687
Greenblatt, Stephen, V 286–88, 290
Greene, Graham, I 290, 491; II 41, 46,
    50, 51, 285, 288–90; III 356; IV
    159; V 107, 206, 382
  on Andres, I 92
  on Bates, H. E., V 62
  criticism on, V 395
    excerpts of, II 290–92
  on Ford, Ford Madox, II 118
  influence of, II 395; III 503
  on Richardson, Dorothy Miller, V 516
  on Sábato, IV 121
Greenland literature. See Eskimo literature
Greer, Germaine, V 221
Gregh, Fernand, II 136
Gregor-Tajovský, Jozef, I 525
Gregory, Horace, I 71
Gregory, Lady Augusta, II 459; IV 393,
    674
  criticism of, II 566; V 316, 317
Gregory of Narek, I 120
Greiff, León de, I 483
Greig, Andrew, V 546
Greimas, A. J., III 93; V 234
Greiner, Donald J.
  on Updike, IV 513
Greiner, Ulrich, V 53, 54
Greitz, Torgny, II 310
Gréki, Anna, I 47
Grekova, I., IV 113
Grendel, Lajos, V 298
Grene, Nicholas
  on Synge, IV 397
Grenier, Jean
  on Camus, I 394
Grenier, Paul-Louis, II 152
Grenville, Kate, V 52
Greshoff, Jan, II 24; III 376
Greyerz, Otto von, IV 384
Griboedov, Alexandr Sergeevich, IV 110
Grieg, Nordahl, II 292–93; III 401, 402

Grieg, Solveig Fredriksen. See Christov,
    Solveig
Grierson, John, III 365
Grieve, Christopher Murray. See Mac-
    Diarmid, Hugh
Griffith, D. W., II 94
Griffiths, John Gwyn, IV 605
Grigorev, Apollon Aleksandrovich,
    V 441
Grigorev, Sergey, II 105
Grigson, Geoffrey, V 213
Grillparzer, Franz, I 172; IV 342; V 53
  as subject, V 584
Grimm, Hans, II 218
Grimm, Reinhold
  on Dürrenmatt, I 602
Grímsson, Stefán Hörður, II 293, 427
Grīns, Aleksandrs, III 17
Grīns, Ervins. See Rīdzinieks, Richards
Gripenberg, Bertel, V 99
Gröber, Gustav, I 516
Grobéty, Anne-Lise, IV 386
Grochowiak, Stanisław, III 559
Groethuysen, Bernard, II 143
Grogger, Paula, I 156
Gronicka, André von
  on Mann, Thomas, III 217
Groșan, Ioan, V 519
Grosman, Ladislav, I 527
Gross, Walter, IV 384
Grosskopf, J. F. W., IV 286
Grossman, David, V 268–69, 325, 326
Grossman, Vassily, V 389
Grotius, Hugo, III 378
Grotowski, Jerzy, II 180; V 493
Groult, Benoîte, V 231, 234
Grove, Frederick Philip, I 396
Grudziński, Gustaw Herling, III 560
Gruffydd, W. J., IV 605
Grumbach, Doris, V 349
Grumberg, Jean-Claude, V 232
Gründgens, Gustaf, II 372
Grundtvig, N. F. S., III 332
Grünthal, Ivar, II 61
Gruša, Jiří, V 156
Grušas, Juozas, II 293–94; III 131
Guadeloupe literature. See under French-
    Caribbean literature
Guanes, Alejandro, III 473
Guardia de Alfaro, Gloria, V 125
Guare, John, V 29
Guarnieri, Gianfrancesco, V 81, 89
Guatemalan literature. See under Central
    American literature
Guattari, Félix, V 234
Gubar, Susan, V 222, 374
Gu Cheng. See Ku Ch'eng
Guðmundsson, Tómas, II 294–95, 426
  influence of, IV 330
Guéhenno, Jean, II 141, 143
Guelbenzu, José María, V 573
Guennoun, 'Abd Allāh, III 319
Guérard, Albert
  on Conrad, Joseph, I 489
  on Gide, II 235
Guerra, Ruy, V 98
Guerra Garrido, Raúl, V 573
Guerrero, Wilfrido, III 525
Guest, Barbara, I 73
Guevara, Che, III 329
Guèvremont, Germaine, I 398
Gufstafson, Ralph, V 109
Guggenheim, Kurt, IV 382
Guglielmi, Angelo, II 474
Guglielminetti, Amalia, II 268
Gu Hua. See Ku Hua
Guicharnaud, Jacques
  on Anouilh, I 101
Guido, Beatriz, I 112; V 40, 269, 398
Guiette, Robert, I 225
Guiler, Hugh. See Hugo, Ian
Guillen, Claudio
  on Jiménez, II 513

Guillén, Jorge, II 195, 295–97; IV 304;
　V 145, 391
　critical excerpts on, II 297–99
Guillén, Nicolás, I 20; II 299–300; IV
　316; V 391, 653
Guillevic, Eugène, II 145; V 233
Guilloux, Louis, II 144, 300–301
Guimaraens, Alphonsus de, I 320
Guimarães Rosa, João. *See* Rosa, João
　Guimarães
Guimerà, Angel, IV 312
Guinea-Bissau literature, II 301
　in Creole, II 301
　in Portuguese, II 301
Guinean literature, II 301–2
　major writers of, in French, *see* Camara
　Négritude in, I 385
Güiraldes, Ricardo, I 111; II 302–3
Guirao, Ramón, I 20
Guiton, Margaret
　on Aragon, I 107
　on Malraux, III 201
Guitry, Sacha, II 141–42
Gujarati literature. *See under* Indian
　literature
Gulácsi, Irén, IV 85
Güleranja, III 300
Guilia, Dimitri, III 398
Gulia, Wallace, III 203
Gullar, Ferreira, I 323; V 89
Gullberg, Hjalmar, II 303–4; IV 379
Gullón, Ricardo
　on Jiménez, II 513
　on Paz, III 496
Guma, Enoch S., IV 295
Guma, Samson Mbizo, IV 291
Gumilyov, Nikolay Stepanovich, I 31, 98;
　II 304–6; III 206; IV 104, 105,
　469
　influence of, I 177
Gunasinghe, Siri, IV 322, 323
Gundolf, Friedrich, II 215; III 101–2
Gunn, Neil M., IV 179, 180, 181
Gunn, Thom, II 38
Gunnarsson, Gunnar, II 306–7, 416
Güntekin, Reşat Nuri, IV 478
Guramishvili, Davit, II 213
Gurchan Singh, III 192
Gurdjieff, Georges, IV 454
　influence of, I 545, 546
Guri, Chayim, II 466
Gurney, A. R., V 28
Gürpınar, Hüseyin Rahmi, IV 477
Gurra, A., I 38
Gusein, Mehti, I 166
Gustafson, Alrik
　on Strindberg, IV 357
Gustafsson, Lars, II 307–8; IV 380; V
　581, 582
Gutauskas, Gintaras, V 394
Gütersloh, Albert Paris von, I 157, 573; II
　308–9
Gutiérrez, Joaquín, V 124
Gutiérrez Nájera, Manuel, III 271, 293
　influence of, III 373
Guy, Rosa, V 358
Guyanese literature. *See under* English-
　Caribbean literature
Guyot, Charly, IV 386
Guyot, Gabriele. *See* Wohmann, Gabriele
Guyotat, Pierre, I 201; II 149
Guzel, Bogomil, IV 698
Guzmán, Augusto, I 289
Guzmán, Martín Luis, II 309–10; III 272
Guzmán, Nicomedes (Oscar Nicomedes
　Vásquez Guzmán), I 454; V 269–
　70
Gwala, Mafika Pascal, IV 290
Gwayi, Joice J., IV 296
Gwenallt. *See* Jones, D. Gwenallt
Gwynn, F. L.
　on Jones, James, II 522
Gyaw, James Hla, I 366

Gyllensten, Lars, II 310–11; IV 379–80;
　V 582
Győry, Dezső, I 527
Gyr, Radu, IV 80
Gyurkó, László, V 297
Gzhytsky, Volodymyr, IV 495

Haanpää, Pentti, II 102–3, 312–13
Haarla, Lauri, II 101
Haasbroek, P. J., IV 287
Haasse, Hella, III 378
Haava, Anna, II 60
Haavardsholm, Espen, III 400
Haavikko, Paavo, II 102, 103, 313–14
Habermas, Jürgen, V 497
　on Benjamin, I 243
Habibi, Abdul Hai, I 19
Habībī, Emile (Abū Salām), III 465; V
　271–72, 473, 474
Hacene, Leila. *See* Amar, Yasmin
Hacker, Marilyn, V 27
Hackl, Erick, V 54
Hacks, Peter, II 223, 314–15
Haddad, Malek, I 47
Haddād, Tāhir, IV 472
Hadejia, Mu'azu, III 389
Hadi, Mähmud. *See* Batu
Hadj-Ali, Bashir, V 17
Hadjiandreas, Yannis. *See* Tsirkas, Stratis
Hadūga, 'Abd al-Hamīd ibn. *See* Ibn Ha-
　dūqa, 'Abd al-Hamīd
Hadzidimitriou, Michael. *See* Alithersis,
　Glafkos
Hadzopoulos, Konstandinos
　influence of, IV 428
Haeckel, Ernst, II 338; IV 219
Haff, Bergljot Hobæk, III 401
Hāfiz
　influence of, III 359
Hāfiz, Sabrī, II 7; V 202
Hagelstange, Rudolf, II 221; V 248
Hagerup, Helge, III 401
Hagerup, Inger, III 403
Hägg, Göran, V 582
Haggard, H. Rider, II 538
Hagiwara Sakutarō, II 315–16, 497;
　V 336, 451
Hagopian, Jacques, I 121
Hahn, Beverly
　on Chekhov, I 451
Hahn, Oscar, V 132
Hahn, Ulla, V 249
Haigh-Wood, Vivienne, II 17
Haïk, Farjalla, III 45
Haisma, Nyckle J., III 380
Haitian literature. *See under* French-Carib-
　bean literature
Haji Hasan Mustapa, II 444
al-Hājj, Unsī Lūwīs, III 33; V 272–73
Håkanson, Björn, IV 381
al-Hakīm, Tawfīq, II 5, 6, 316–18; V 218
Halas, František, I 521; II 318–19, IV
　186
　influence of, I 521
Haldas, Georges, III 387
Haley, Alex, I 68, 69
Hali, Khwaja Altaf Husain, III 458
Halkin, Shmuel, IV 684
Hall, Adam, III 535
Hall, Donald, V 27, 514
Hall, Rodney, I 148; V 52
al-Hallāj, V 1
Hallāj, Mustafā, IV 400
Halldén, Ruth, V 581, 582
Hallström, Per, III 377
Halman, T. S., V 154
Halpé, Ashley, IV 324, 325
Halper, Leyvik. *See* Leivick, H.
Halpern, Joseph
　on Genet, II 209
　on Sartre, IV 159

Halpern, Moyshe Leyb, II 248, 319;
　IV 683
Halter, Toni, IV 389
Hamasdegh, I 121
Hamdan, III 189
Hamdī, Ahmad, I 46
Hamesh, Ahmad, III 460
Hamilton, Alice
　on Beckett, I 215
Hamilton, Kenneth
　on Beckett, I 215
al-Hammāmī, Tāhir, IV 473
Hammett, Dashiell, II 352, 353; III 571;
　V 128, 129, 227, 273–74
Hamnett, Ian, IV 180
Hamsun, Knut, II 319–21, 327; III 40,
　399, 401; IV 220, 425; V 444
　criticism on, V 648
　influence of, III 130; IV 414, 706
Hamutyinei, Mordikai, IV 714
Hamzah Hussein, III 190
al-Hamzāwī, Rashād, IV 473
Hancerlioglu, Orhan, IV 478
Hancock, Joel
　on Poniatowska, V 496
Handel-Mazzetti, Enrica von, I 155
Handke, Peter, I 159; II 98, 321–23, 395;
　V 53, 54, 249
Hang Thun Hak, I 387
Hanley, Clifford, IV 180
Hanley, James, II 50, 323–24
Hanley, William, I 74
Hàn Mặc Tử, IV 561
Hanrahan, Barbara, V 52
Hansberry, Lorraine, I 74; II 324–25
Hansen, Anton. *See* Tammsaare, A. H.
Hansen, Jørgen Christian, V 159
Hansen, Martin A., I 538; II 325–27
Hansen, Ron, V 26
Hansen, Thorkild, I 541, II 327, V 159
Han Shao-kung (Han Shaogong), V 137
Han Sŏr-ya, II 600
Hansson, Ola, IV 377
Han Yong-un, II 599–600
Hao Jan, I 459
Haqqī, Yahyā, II 5; V 275
Harapi, Zef, I 38
Harding, Gunnar, IV 381
Harding, Warren G., III 265
Hardwick, Elizabeth, III 141, 142
Hardy, Barbara
　on Auden, I 140–41
Hardy, Thomas, II 33, 36, 46, 327–31;
　V 62, 321, 383
　criticism on, I 584; III 104; V 395
　excerpts of, II 331–33
　influence of, I 419; II 33, 37, 330–31;
　III 13; IV 228, 588
Hare, David, V 210
Hare, Richard
　on Gorky, II 264
Haretski, Maksim, I 126, 375
Hariot, Thomas, V 525
Haris, Petros, II 283, 333–34
Harkins, William E.
　on Čapek, Karel, I 406
Harlem Renaissance. *See under* American
　literature
Harlem Writers Guild. *See under* Ameri-
　can literature
Harling, Robert, V 29
Harmos, Ilona, II 604
Haroche, Charles
　on Aragon, I 107
Haroutiunian, Ardem, I 122
Haroutiunian, Hovaness. *See* Telkadintsi
Harper, Michael S.
　on Hayden, V 277
Harris, Arthur Hammond. *See* Fry,
　Christopher
Harris, Mark, I 69
Harris, Wilson, II 54, 334–35
Harrison, Jane, II 278; III 84

683

Harrison, Tony, V 212
Harss, Luis
  on García Márquez, II 202
Hart, Clive
  on Joyce, II 531
Hart, Francis
  on Spark, IV 317
Hart, Moss, I 73
Hart, Patricia
  on Allende, V 21
Hart, Robert Edward, III 252
Hartley, L. P., II 50, 335–36; III 535
Härtling, Peter, II 221
Hartman, Geoffrey, I 75–76; III 125, 126, 521
  on Derrida, V 177
Hartmann, Eduard von
  influence of, IV 595
Hartmann, Nicolai, III 515
Hartmann von Aue
  criticism on, III 103
Hartnett, Michael, II 461
Hartog, Jan de, III 377
Harun, Aleś, I 375
Harun Aminurrashid, IV 232
Harvey, Anne Gray. See Sexton, Anne
Harvey, John
  on Anouilh, I 101
Harvey, Lawrence E.
  on Beckett, I 215
Harwood, Gwen, V 52
Hasan, 'Abd al-Qādir, III 319
Hasan, Ismā'īl, IV 366
al-Hasan, Tāj, IV 366
Hasani, Sinan, IV 699
Hasegawa Tatsunosuke. See Futabatei Shimei
Hašek, Jaroslav, I 155, 520–21; II 336–37
Hasenclever, Walter, II 70, 217; IV 471, 613
Hashim Rashīd, Hārun, V 472
Hasim, Ahmet, IV 476
Haskell, Mary, V 255
Haslinger, Josef, V 54
Hassan, Ihab, III 521
Határ, Győző, V 297
Hatfield, Henry
  on Mann, Thomas, III 216–17
Hatvany, Lajos, II 532
Hatzopoulos, Konstandinos, II 280, 281
Hauge, Alfred, III 401
Hauge, Olav H., V 275–76
Haugen, Helge, III 403
Hauptmann, Gerhart, II 215, 218, 338–41, 527, 609; III 101; IV 391
  critical excerpts on, II 341–42
  influence of, IV 84
  reaction against, I 327
Hausa literature. See under Nigerian literature
Hausmann, Raoul, I 531
Havel, Václav, I 524; II 342–44; IV 433; V 156, 157, 366
Havrevold, Finn, III 401
Hāwī, Khalīl, I 16; II 344; III 33; V 354
Hawkes, John, I 70, 194, 271; II 344–45; III 415; V 26, 150
  criticism on, II 205
Hawks, Howard, II 95
Hawthorne, Nathaniel, I 58, 59; III 142; V 467
  criticism on, III 83, 117, 120, 123; IV 644
  influence of, II 335, 487
Hay, Eloise Knapp
  on Conrad, Joseph, I 493
Hay, George Campbell, IV 178
Háy, Gyula, II 416
Hay, J. MacDougal, IV 180
Hay, Julius, V 391
Haya de la Torre, Victor Raúl, II 257
Hayama Yoshiki, II 496
Hayaseca, Jorge. See Echegaray, José

Hayashi Fumiko, II 345–46, 496
Hayashi Kyōko, V 336
Haydar, Haydar, IV 398
al-Haydarī, Buland, II 457
Hayden, Robert (Asa Bundy Sheffey), I 73; V 276–78
Hay-Holovko, Olexa, IV 497
Haykal, Muhammad Husayn, II 5, 7
Hayman, David, IV 268
Hayman, Ronald
  on Pinter, III 537
Hayton, Alan, V 547
Hayward, Max
  on Pasternak, Boris, III 484–85
Hazari, Abdul Ghani, I 187
Hazaz, Chayim, II 466
Hazlitt, William
  influence of, II 4
Hazoumé, Paul, I 237
Hazzard, Shirley, V 52
H. D. See Doolittle, Hilda
Head, Bessie, I 308; V 278–80, 391, 567
Heaney, Seamus, II 346–47, 461, 567; III 165; V 191, 317, 318, 403, 430
Heard, Gerald
  influence of, II 419
Heartfield, John, IV 471
Heath, Stephen, IV 362
  on Robbe-Grillet, IV 62
Hebare, A. R., II 437
Hébert, Anne, I 398, 399; II 347–48; V 109
Hébert, Maurice, II 347
Hebrew literature. See Israeli literature
  See also Asch, Bialik, Tchernichowsky
Hečko, František, I 526
Hedayat, Sadeq, II 348–49, 453–54
Hedberg, Olle, IV 378
Heer, Jakob Christoph, IV 382
Heerden, Ernst van, IV 286
Heerden, Etienne van, V 565
Heeresma, Heere, III 378
Heever, C. M. van den, IV 286
Heever, Toon van den, IV 286
Heffner, Avram, V 327
Hegel, Friedrich, II 66; V 168, 418
  criticism on, V 175
  influence of, I 205; III 81, 82, 86, 121, 150, 377, 525
    on surrealism, IV 371
    on literary criticism, I 279, 510
Heiberg, Gunnar, III 401
Heiberg, Hans, III 401
Heidegger, Martin, I 137; II 66–67; III 107–8, 515, 516–17, 520, 521, 522; V 167, 169, 228, 229, 500, 501
  criticism on, III 109; IV 334
  influence of, I 279; III 95; IV 154; V 142, 377, 571, 572
Heidenstam, Verner von, IV 376
Heijermans, Herman, II 349–50; III 375
Heilbrun, Carolyn, V 221
Heilman, Robert B.
  on Williams, Tennessee, IV 634
Hein, Nicolas, III 158
Hein, Piet, I 539
Heine, Heinrich, V 44
  criticism on, III 82
  influence of, III 40, 262; IV 246, 335, 498
Heinesen, Jens Pauli, I 542
Heinesen, William, I 542
Heiremans, Luis Alberto, I 455; V 133, 134
Heise, Hans-Jürgen, II 222
Heisenberg, Werner, III 516
Heislers, Harijs, III 18
Heissenbüttel, Helmut, II 222, 225, 350–51
Helbo, André
  on Butor, I 374
Helder, Herberto, III 569
Helds, Juris, III 19

Hellaakoski, Aaro, II 102
Hellens, Franz, I 224
Heller, Erich
  on Kraus, II 610
  on Rilke, IV 51
Heller, Joseph, I 68, 69, 231, 432; II 351–52; V 24, 595
Hellingrath, Norbert von, III 103
Hellman, Lillian, I 66, 73; II 352–53; V 273, 639
  as subject, V 606
Hellström, Gustaf, IV 377
Helman, Albert, I 605
Helmsdal, Guðrið, I 542
Hel Sumphar, I 386
Heltai, Jenő, II 413
Hemingway, Ernest, I 57, 60, 61, 62, 68, 85, 228, 382, 491, 563, 579; II 42, 81–82, 97, 115, 353–59; III 137, 170, 366; IV 224, 257, 328; V 35, 424, 455, 457
  criticism on, I 503; II 81; III 122; IV 587; V 96
  excerpts of, II 357–59
  influence of
    on American literature, II 78; IV 558; V 119, 240
    on Canadian literature, I 396
    on Colombian literature, V 125, 126
    on Danish literature, I 537
    on English literature, II 50
    on French literature, II 143
    on German literature, II 220, 224; III 45; IV 650
    on Spanish literature, II 201
    on Swedish literature, I 533; IV 379
  as subject, V 441
Hemmer, Jarl, II 100
Hémon, Louis, I 398
Hemon, Roparz, II 151
Hempel, Amy, V 26
Henderson, Archibald
  on Shaw, George Bernard, IV 205–6
Hendriks, A. L., II 54
Henisch, Peter, V 54
Henkes, Paul, III 158
Henley, Beth, V 28, 29
Hennecke, Hans, III 108
  on Hauptmann, II 341
Henries, Doris, III 71
Henriot, Émile, II 143
Henríquez Ureña, Pedro, III 97; IV 29, 316; V 456
Henry, O., I 60; V 281
Henryson, Robert, III 165
Henshaw, James Ene, III 391
Henz, Rudolf, I 157
Heppenstall, Rayner, II 359–60; III 382
Heras León, Eduardo, IV 317
Herbert, John, I 397
Herbert, Zbigniew, II 360–61; III 558; V 491, 492
Herbert, Xavier (Alfred Herbert, Herbert Astor, E. Norden), I 147; V 51, 280–82
Herburger, Günter, II 220, 222, 225
Herczeg, János, IV 700
Herczeg, Ferenc, II 413; IV 699
Herdal, Harald, I 538
Hérédia, José-Maria de, I 190; III 293
Hergesheimer, Joseph
  criticism on, III 112
Hériat, Philippe, II 143
Herlihy, James, I 273; III 394
Herling-Grudziński, Gustaw, V 491, 492
Hermans, Frederik, III 377–78
Hermant, Abel, II 137
Hermes Trismegistus, II 361
hermeticism, I 259, 265, 388; II 205, 361–62, 471; III 159, 301, 302, 625; IV 509; V 431
  and literary criticism, III 86
Hermlin, Stephan, I 156; II 222, 362–63
Hermodsson, Elisabet, V 582

Hernádi, Gyula, V 297
Hernandez, Amado V., III 526
Hernández, Felisberto, IV 516; V 282–83
  as subject, V 224
Hernández, José, I 110; II 303
Hernández, Luisa Josefina, III 274;
  V 283–84, 422
Hernández, Miguel, II 363–64; IV 305;
  V 148
Hernández, Ramón, V 573
Hernández Rueda, Lupo, IV 316
Herreman, Raymond, I 222; IV 69
Herrera, Darío, V 125
Herrera, Fernando de, V 66
Herrera y Reissig, Julio, II 364–65; III
  293; IV 392, 515
Herreweghen, Hubert van, I 222
Hersey, John, IV 261
Hershaw, William, V 547
Hervé, J. A., II 69
Herzen, Alexandr, IV 103
Herzl, Theodor, I 351
Herzmanovsky-Orlando, Fritz von,
  I 157
Herzog, Émile. See Maurois, André
Hesse, Hermann, II 217, 219, 365–69,
  538
  critical excerpts on, II 369–70
Heurle, Adma d'
  on Trotzig, V 602
Hewett, Dorothy, V 51, 52
Hewitt, John, V 318
Heyke, Leon, III 561
Heym, Georg, II 69, 216, 218
  influence of, II 362; IV 505–6
Heym, Stefan, V 248, 286–87, 391
Hibberd, John
  on Kafka, II 548–49
Hicks, Granville, I 67; III 80
Hicks, John, II 328
Hieniyush, Larysa, I 376
Hierro, José, IV 305; V 466
Higginbotham, Virginia
  on García Lorca, Federico, II 199
Highsmith, Patricia
  influence of, II 322
Hijāzī, Ahmad 'Abd al-Mu'tī, II 5;
  V 287–88
Hikmet, Nazım, II 370–72; IV 476
  influence of, IV 701
Hildesheimer, Wolfgang, II 223, 372–73;
  IV 433
Hilevich, Nil, I 375
Hill, Geoffrey, II 373–74; V 212
Hill, George Roy, II 96
Hill, Joe, V 202
Hiller, Kurt, II 69
Hilmi, Refik (Rafik), II 628; V 264
Hilst, Hilda, V 90
Hiltbrunner, Hermann, IV 384
Himes, Chester, I 69; II 374–75
Hinchliffe, Arnold P.
  on Pinter, III 536
Hinchliffe, Ian
  on Lindgren, V 387
Hinde, Thomas, III 375–76
Hindemith, Paul, IV 347
Hindi literature. See under Indian and Pa-
  cific Islands literatures
Hindko literature. See under Pakistani lit-
  erature
Hindrey, Karl August, II 62
Hindus, Milton
  on Fitzgerald, F. Scott, II 111
  on Proust, III 604
Hippius, Zinaida, I 376–77; III 266; IV
  104, 106, 470
hippy movements, as literary subject,
  IV 575
Hirabayashi Taiko, II 496
Hiraoka Kimitake. See Mishima Yukio
Hiriart, Hugo, V 421
Hiriart-Urruty, Jean, II 150
Hirnyk, Pavlo, V 613

Hiroshima, destruction of, as literary sub-
  ject, II 423; IV 261, 664
Hirsch, E. D., III 126; V 290
Hirshbein, Peretz, IV 686
Hisar, Abdülhak Şinasi, IV 478
historicism, V 102, 286–90
Hitchcock, Alfred, I 491; II 95; V 129
Hitler, Adolf, II 381; IV 58
  attempted assassination of, III 61
  as subject, IV 259, 459, 598
Hivnor, Robert, I 74
Hjartarson, Snorri, II 377–78, 427
Hjortø, Knud, I 536
Hkin Hnin Yu, I 367
Hłasko, Marek, II 378–79; III 559; V 391
Hlaváček, Karel, I 520
Hlibov, Leonid, IV 493
Hlybinny, Uladzimier, I 376
Hnatyuk, Volodymyr, V 371
Hoàng Đạo, IV 561
Hoang Lien, V 91
Hoàng Ngọc Phách, IV 560
Hobbes, Thomas, V 289
Hochhuth, Rolf, II 71, 223, 379–81;
  V 363
Ho Ch'i-fang, I 458, 459–60; II 379
Hø Ching-chih, I 460
Hochwälder, Fritz, I 157–58; II 71,
  381–83
Hoddis, Jakob van, II 69, 216
Hodza, Aaron, IV 714
Høeck, Klaus, V 160
Hoel, Sigurd, II 70, 383–84; III 400
  on Sandemose, IV 142
Hoerschelmann, Fred von, II 223
Hoffer, Klaus, V 54
Hoffman, Daniel, I 71
Hoffman, Frederick J., II 162
  on Beckett, I 214
  on Dos Passos, I 582–83
Hoffmann, Charles W.
  on Frisch, II 170
Hoffmann, E. T. A., II 158; IV 241
  influence of, II 132, 567; III 46;
  IV 109, 113, 370–71, 493
Hoffmann, Fernand, III 158
Hofmann, Gert, V 290–91
Hofmann, Michael, V 212
Hofmannsthal, Hugo von, I 150, 151,
  154, 216; II 210, 216, 384–87;
  III 103, 104; IV 170, 171, 391
  criticism on, III 103, 107
  exerpts of, II 387–88
Hofmiller, Josef, III 104
Hofshteyn, Dovid, IV 683
Hogaş, Calistrat, IV 79
Hogg, James, V 209, 546
Hohl, Ludwig, IV 382
Hohoff, Curt
  on Fleisser, II 113
Højholt, Per, I 540; V 160
Hokusai, II 498
Holan, Vladimír, I 523, 524; V 291–92
Holappa, Pentti, II 103
Holban, Anton, IV 81
Holberg, Ludvig, V 577
Holbrook, Victoria, V 607
Holden, Raymond, I 286
Hölderlin, Johann Christian Friedrich, II
  28, 66; IV 600
  criticism on, I 279; III 82, 93, 103, 108
  influence of, I 300, 436; II 366; IV
  370–71; V 454
  and psychology, II 535
Holland, Laurence
  on James, Henry, II 489, 491
Holland, Norman N., II 162–63; III 83
Hollander, John, I 71; V 27, 28
Höllerer, Walter, II 221, 222, 388–89
Hollis, James R.
  on Pinter, III 537
Hollmerus, Viveca, V 61
Holloway, John, III 119
  on Lewis, Wyndham, III 68

Holm, Peter R., III 402
Holm, Sven, I 540
Holmes, Charles M.
  on Huxley, II 241
Holmqvist, Bengt, I 269
Holoborodki, Vasyl, V 613
Holocaust literature, IV 14; V 35, 36,
  369, 391, 413, 481, 493, 632–34.
  See also: Jewish experience; Nazis;
  World War II
  American, IV 94, 235, 364
  Austrian, I 430; IV 320
  Canadian, III 28
  French, V 230, 426
  German, II 221, 380; IV 122–23
  Hungarian, III 529
  Indian, V 178
  Israeli, I 51; V 268, 326
  Yiddish, II 249, 270, 287; IV 235,
  374, 685
Holovko, Andry, IV 495
Hølsen, Ragnhild, III 399
Holt, Kåre, II 389–90; III 400
Holtby, Winifred, IV 259–60
Holthusen, Hans Egon, II 221; III 109
  on Rilke, IV 50
Holton, Henry, V 547
Holub, Miroslav, I 523; V 156, 292–93
Holz, Arno, II 215
Holz, Detlev. See Benjamin, Walter
Holzapfel, Tamar
  on Carballido, V 114
Hölzer, Max, II 221
Homer, I 142
Honchar, Oles, II 390–91; IV 496; V 614
Honduran literature. See under Central
  American literature
Honegger, Arthur, IV 527
Honig, Edwin
  on García Lorca, Federico, II 198
Honwana, Luís Bernardo, III 323
Hood, Hugh, V 108
Hood, Stuart, V 544
Hooft, Pieter Corneliszoon, III 378
Hoornik, Eduard, III 377
Hooson, I. D., IV 605
Hope, A. D., I 148; II 391–92; V 52
Hope, Christopher, V 566
Hopkins, Gerard Manley, I 274; II 34;
  V 192
  criticism on, III 31, 116; IV 644
  influence of, I 255; III 547; IV 439
Hora, Josef, I 521; II 392–93
  influence of, IV 656
Hordynsky, Svyatoslav, IV 494
Hořejší, Jindřich, I 521
Horia, Vintilă, IV 82
Hori Tatsuo, II 496
Horniman, Annie, IV 674
Horonchik, Shimen, IV 684
Horovitz, Israel, V 29
Hörspiel. See under German literature
Horta, Glória, V 90
Horta, Maria Teresa, III 569
Horton, James Africanus, IV 215
Horváth, Ödön von, I 155, 156; II 223,
  393–95
  influence of, II 616
Horvath, Violet
  on Malraux, III 202
Hō Shō. See Yosano Akiko
Hospital, Jane Turner, V 52
Hossein, Robert, V 232
Hostovský, Egon, I 522; II 395–96
Hough, Graham
  on Lawrence, D. H., III 25
Houm, Philip
  on Sandemose, IV 142
Houseman, John, IV 329
Housman, A. E., II 396–97
Houston, Veline Hasu, V 45
Houten, Ulbe van, III 380
Hovaness, Tavit, I 122
Hoveyda, Fereydoun, V 293–94

685

Ikhlāsī, Walīd, IV 400
Ikromi, Jalol, IV 409, 410
Ilchenko, Olexandr, IV 496
İleri, Selim, V 607
Ilf, Ilya, II 429–30; IV 109
  on Bulgakov, I 357
İlhan, Attilâ, IV 479; V 307–8
Il'in, Mikhail Andreevich. *See* Osorgin,
  Mikhail
Ilina, Natalya, V 532
Illyés, Gyula, II 414, 415, 430–31;
  V 153, 297
Iloko literature. *See under* Philippine liter-
  ature
Ilyin, Mikhail Andreevich. *See* Osorgin,
  Mikhail
imagism, II 33–34, 36, 116, 431–32;
  III 574
  in American poetry, I 64; II 432; III
    139–40; IV 635
  in Chinese literature, V 136
  in Finnish poetry, III 218
  and hermeticism, II 361
  influence of, I 396; II 248, 566; IV 15,
    643
  and literary criticism, III 113; IV 229
  in Nigerian literature, V 447
  in Romanian poetry, III 210
  Russian, I 375; III 16; IV 679, 680
Imalayen, Fatima-Zohra. *See* Djebar,
  Assia
Imam, Abubakar, III 389
Imber, Samuel Jacob, II 319
Imbuga, Francis, II 578; V 351
Im Chudet, I 386
impressionism, 20th-c., literary
  in American literature, I 58, 67
  criticism on, III 88, 89
  in East European literature, I 520; II
    194, 604; III 16, 130; IV 413,
    495; V 371
  in Western European literature, I 152,
    168, 309, 310; II 215–18 passim,
    320, 554; III 307, 308, 375; IV
    299, 307
al-'Inānī, Muhammad, V 202
Inber, Vera, IV 105
İnce, Özdemir, V 606
Ince, W. N.
  on Valéry, IV 530
independence struggles, 20th-c., as liter-
  ary subject. *See also:* nationalism;
  revolution
  African colonial
    Algerian, I 392; IV 221
    Angolan, IV 559
    Cape Verdean, I 402
    Guinean, II 302
    Ivory Coast, II 479
    Moroccan, III 319
    Nigerian, IV 297
    Senegalese, IV 188
    Tanzanian, IV 418
  Asian colonial
    Burmese, I 367, 368
    Indian, III 193; IV 239, 405
    Indonesian, III 508
    Singapore, IV 232, 233
  Bashkir, I 203
  Icelandic, IV 443
  Irish, I 309 (*see also under* Ireland)
  Israeli, II 466
  Korean, II 599, 600
  Kurdish, II 628
  Latvian, IV 7, 242
  Turkish, IV 476, 477
  Ukrainian, IV 498
Indian literature, I 187–88; II 432–40;
  V 308–10
  in Assamese, II 433, 436
  in Bengali, II 433, 434, 435, 436, 438;
    V 309
  Chhaya-vada movement in, II 435

  in English, II 433, 434, 435, 436, 437–
    40; V 309, 310
  in Gujarati, II 433, 436; V 309
  in Hindi, II 433, 435, 437, 438, 439;
    V 308
  independence, as subject of, III 193; IV
    239, 405 (*see also under* colonial-
    ism, British)
  in Kannada, II 432, 435, 437, 438,
    439; V 308
  in Kashmiri, II 433
  in Maithali, II 433
  major writers of
    Anglo-, *see* Jhabvala
    in Bengali, *see:* Banerji; Chatterji;
      Das; Saratchandra; Ghose, Auro-
      bindo; Nazrul Islam; Tagore
    in English, *see:* Anand; Desai; De-
      sani; Ezekiel; Ghose, Aurobindo;
      Ghose, Zulfikar; Iqbal, Muham-
      mad; Malgonkar; Markandaya;
      Mukherjee; Naidu; Narayan; Rao,
      Raja; Rushdie; Singh, Khushwant;
      Tagore
    in Hindi, *see:* Premchand; Rakesh
    in Kannada, *see* Karanth
    in Malayalam, *see* Menon
    in Marathi, *see* Khandekar
    in Oriya, *see* Mohanty, Gopinath
    in Persian, *see* Iqbal, Muhammad
    in Tamil, *see* Bharati
    in Urdu, *see:* Hyder; Iqbal, Muham-
      mad; Premchand
  in Malayalam, II 432, 434, 435–36,
    438
  in Marathi, II 433, 435, 436–37, 439;
    V 309
  in Nepali, II 433
  the "New Short Story" movement in,
    IV 8
  in Oriya, II 433, 435, 436, 438
  in Pali, II 433
  partition of India as subject of, III 193;
    IV 239
  Pragati-vada (Progressive) movement
    in, II 434, 435
  in Punjabi, II 433, 435, 439; V 309
  in Rajasthani, II 433
  in Sanskrit, II 432–33, 436, 437
  in Sindhi, II 433
  in Tamil, II 432, 433, 434, 438; V 309
  in Telugu, II 432, 435; V 309
  in Urdu, II 433, 434–35, 437, 438,
    439, 440; V 300, 309
Indo-Aryan literature. *See* Indian literature
Indo-English literature. *See* Indian literature
Indonesian literature, II 440–46
  in Balinese, II 444–45
  in Chinese-Indonesian dialect, II 445
  in Dutch, II 445–46
  independence as subject of, III 508
  in Indonesian, II 441–43
  Japanese occupation as subject of, II
    441–42; III 587; IV 411
  in Javanese, II 443–44
  major writers of
    in Indonesian, *see:* Achdiat; Chairil;
      Pramoedya; Takdir
    also writing in Dutch, *see* Takdir
    also writing in English, *see* Takdir
  in Minangkabau, II 444–45
  revolution as subject in, II 441–42; III
    587
  post-, III 587
  in Sundanese, II 444
Indra, I 120
industrialization, 20th-c., as literary
  subject
  criticism of, II 320; IV 442
  effects of, IV 405, 478, 516, 713, 714
  and Italian "literature and industry,"
    III 447–48, 570–71

  and urbanization, II 74; IV 37, 286,
    291–96 passim, 413, 428, 516,
    683
Ingarden, Roman, III 99, 515; IV 602
Inge, William Motter, I 74; V 310–12,
  639
Inglin, Meinrad, IV 382
Ingolič, Anton, IV 697
Ingush literature. *See under* North Cauca-
  sian literatures
Injannashi, III 300
Innaurato, Albert, V 29
Innerhof, Franz, V 54
Inner Mongolian literature. *See* Mongolian
  literature
Innes, Michael. *See* Stewart, J. I. M.
Inoue Hisashi, V 336
Inoue Yasushi, I 497; V 312–13
Insingel, Mark, I 222
interior monologue. *See* stream-of-con-
  sciousness technique, the
Iñurritza, IV 310
Ionesco, Eugène, II 45, 68, 147, 149,
  217, 446–50; III 517; IV 81, 303,
  355, 433, 434; V 133, 141, 232,
  272, 563
  on Claudel, I 474
  criticism on, V 81
    excerpts of, II 450–51
  on Feydeau, Georges, II 91
  influence of, I 455, 539; II 372, 456;
    III 401; V 535, 639
  on Roussel, IV 96
  on Urmuz, IV 514
Iorga, Nicolae, IV 80
Iosif, Ştefan O., IV 80
Ipatava, Volha, I 376
Ipchi, Omer, IV 421
Iqbal, Muhammad, II 434–35, 451–52;
  III 458
Iqbal, Zafar, III 458
al-Īrānī, Mahmūd Sayf al-dīn, III 465
Iranian literature, II 453–56; V 313–15
  in Azerbaijani, I 167
  existentialism in, II 348
  in Kurdish, II 627–28
  literary criticism in, I 37
  major writers of, *see:* Alavi; Al-e Ah-
    mad; Chubak; Farrokhzad; He-
    dayat; Hoveyda; Lahuti; Sa'edi
    also writing in German, *see* Alavi
    also writing in English, *see* Alavi
    also writing in French, *see* Hoveyda
    also writing in Tajik, *see* Lahuti
  the "new wave" in, II 79
Iraqi literature, II 456–58. *See also under*
  Kurdish literature
  the Ba'th party as subject of, II 458
  major writers of, *see:* al-Bayyātī; Far-
    mān; al-Malā'ika; al-Sayyāb
  political conditions (1960s) as subject
    of, II 457
  Socialist Realism in, I 208; II 458;
    V 220
  World War II as subject of, post-,
    II 457–58
Iratzeder, Xabier. *See* Diharce, Jean
Irbe, Andrejs, III 18
Iredyński, Ireneusz, III 559
Ireland, David, I 149; V 52
Ireland, 20th-c., as literary subject
  civil war in, II 460, 461, 462; III 412,
    514
  the Easter Rising in, II 459–60, 520;
    III 412; IV 102, 676
  and the Irish "situation," II 460
  the "Troubles" of, III 412
Irigaray, Luce, V 222, 231, 234, 377
Irish literature, II 458–63; V 315–19. *See
  also* Ireland, 20th-c.
  Anglo-, II 33, 38, 39, 40, 41, 46, 49,
    50, 51
  in English, II 458–63

Irish literature (*continued*)
expressionism in, II 70, 460; III 412; V 316
in Gaelic, II 458–59, 461
the Irish Renaissance and, II 459, 462, 463, 566; IV 674
literary criticism in, II 462–63; III 417; IV 200
major writers of, *see:* Durcan; Friel; Kinsella; Mahon; Montague; Trevor, William
Anglo-, *see also:* Bowen, Elizabeth; Cary; Hanley, James; MacNeice; Moore, George; Shaw, George Bernard
in English, *see also:* Beckett; Behan; Brophy; Carroll; Clarke, Austin; Heaney; Johnston; Joyce; Kavanagh, Patrick; Moore, Brian; Murphy; O'Brien, Edna; O'Brien, Flann; O'Casey; O'Connor, Frank; Russell, George William; Stephens, James; Synge; Yeats, William Butler
also writing in French, *see* Beckett
also writing in Gaelic, *see* Behan; O'Brien, Flann
the Rhymers' Club of, IV 674
symbolism in, IV 673–74, 675
Theater of the Absurd in, I 218
Irkaev, Nikolay, II 105
Irving, John, I 70; V 24, 319–21, 436
Irving, Washington, I 57
Isaac, Jorge, I 483
Isaksson, Folke, IV 380
Isaksson, Ulla, IV 379
Iser, Wolfgang, III 110, 522
Ishak Haji Muhammad, III 189
Is'haqi, Muhammad Ghayaz, IV 421
Isherwood, Christopher, I 310; II 39, 45, 463–64; IV 319
on Green, Henry, II 285
Ishidanzanwangjil, III 300
Ishiguro, Kuzuo, V 209
Ishikawa Jun (Shiba Kiyoshi), V 321–22
Ishikawa Shōsai, V 321
Ishikawa Takuboku, II 464–65, 494, 498
influence of, II 465
Ishkhan, Moushegh, I 121
Iskander, Fazil Abdulovich, IV 112, 115; V 322–24
Ismaaciil Mire, IV 278
Ismā'īl, Ismā'īl Fahd, V 324–25
Ismā'īl, 'Izz al-dīn, II 7; V 202
Ismā'īl, Sidqī, IV 399
Ismail bin Haji Omar. See Noor S. I.
'Ismat, Riyāḍ, IV 400
Isou, Isadore, V 233
Israel, as literary subject, IV 374. See also Zionism
Israeli literature, II 465–68; V 325–26.
See also: Israel; Palestinian literature
major writers of
in Hebrew, *see:* Agnon; Aloni; Alterman; Amichai; Appelfeld; Greenberg, Uri Zvi; Grossman; Kahana-Carmon; Kenaz; Megged; Oz; Schutz; Shabtai; Tammuz; Yehoshua
Hebrew, pre-Israel, *see* Bialik; Tchernichowsky
in Yiddish, *see:* Agnon; Bialik; Greenberg, Uri Zvi; Sutskever
"Palmach," II 466
symbolism in, I 263
in Yiddish, IV 687–88
Israil, Zulfiya, IV 521
Issahakian, Avedik, I 122
Istarú, Ana, V 124
Istrati, Panait, IV 81
Isyangul, Farit, I 203
Italian literary criticism, I 410; II 470; III 84–88; IV 143, 453, 708

Crocean, II 84–86, 87, 88
major writers of, *see:* Bigongiari; Croce; Marinetti
structuralist, III 88
Italian literature, II 468–76. *See also* Italian literary criticism
Crepuscolarismo in, II 268, 362, 470–71; IV 164
existentialism in, I 410–11; II 470–71; III 88, 313; IV 17
expressionism in, I 298; IV 17
fascism as subject of, *see under* fascism
in Friulian, IV 476
futurism in, *see under* futurism
the Group 63 of, II 474; IV 143
hermetic, *see* hermeticism
life under Mussolini as subject of, II 526; III 588, 615; IV 260, 447
and linguistic theory, IV 708
"literature and industry" trend in, III 447–48; IV 570–71
major writers of, *see:* Alvaro; Bacchelli; Bassani; Bernari; Berto; Betocchi; Betti; Bontempelli; Brancati; Calvino; Campana; Cardarelli; Cassola; D'Annunzio; De Filippo; Deledda; Di Giacomo; Eco; Fenoglio; Fo; Gadda; Gatto; Ginzburg, Natalia; Gozzano; Jovine; Landolfi; Levi, Carlo; Levi, Primo; Luzi; Marinetti; Mastronardi; Montale; Morante; Moravia; Ortese; Ottieri; Palazzeschi; Pascoli; Pasolini; Pavese; Piccolo; Piovene; Pirandello; Pratolini; Prisco; Quasimodo; Rea; Rèbora; Saba, Umberto; Sanguineti; Sbarbaro; Sciascia; Sereni; Silone; Soldati; Svevo; Tobino; Tomasi di Lampedusa; Tozzi; Ungaretti; Verga; Vittorini, Elio; Volponi; Zanzotto
also writing in English, *see* Eco
also writing in French, *see* Marinetti
also writing in Friulian, *see* Pasolini
see also under Italian literary criticism
neorealism in, *see under* neorealism
Officina in, group around, IV 570
postrealism in, III 570
in regional dialects, II 475–76
the Solaria group of, IV 576
structuralism in, III 243
surrealism in, I 298; II 205
symbolism in, I 298, 542; III 85, 86; IV 391
verismo in, I 566; II 468, 469–70 (*see also* Verga *article*)
World War II as subject of
American occupation during, IV 14
conditions during, III 615; IV 14, 509
effects of, I 53, 384
post-, IV 567
resistance movement during, II 87, 471, 472; III 588; IV 447
For further writing in Italian, see under Maltese *and* Somali literatures
Itō Hiromi, V 337
Itote, Waruhiu, II 577
Ivănescu, Mircea, IV 82
Ivanov, Alexey Andreevich. *See* Künde
Ivanov, Georgy, IV 104, 106
influence of, IV 412
Ivanov, Konstantin, I 466
Ivanov, Viktor, V 530
Ivanov, Vsevolod, IV 108
Ivanov, Vyacheslav Ivanovich, I 350; II 477–78, 582, 592; III 98, 294; IV 104, 106, 391
Ivanova, Natalya, V 532
Ivanova, Tatyana, V 532
Ivanychuk, Roman, IV 497; V 614
Ivasiuc, Alexandru, IV 83
Ivask, Ivar, II 62

Ivaska, Astrīde, III 17
Ivchenko, Mykhaylo, IV 495
Ivnik, Ivan, I 466
Ivory Coast literature, II 478–79
major writers of, *see* Dadié
Iwaniuk, Wacław, III 556; V 327–28, 492
Iwano Hōmei, II 495
Iwan Simatupang, II 442
Iwaszkiewicz, Jarosław, II 479–80; III 554, 556, 557
Iyayi, Festus, III 393
Iyer, C. Subramania. *See* Bharati, Subramania
Izoard, Jaques, I 225; V 233
Izumi Kyōka, II 480–81, 495
Izumi Kyōtarō. *See* Izumi Kyōka

Jaamac Cumar Ciise, IV 278
al-Jabal, Badawī, IV 400
al-Jabartī, V 324
Jabavu, Noni, V 567
Jabès, Edmond, II 148, 482; V 233
Jābirī, Shakīb, IV 398
Jabrā, Jabrā Ibrāhīm, III 464, 465; V 329–30, 354, 434, 472–74
Jabrī, Shafīq, IV 400
Jac, F. P., V 161
Jacinto, António, I 96
Jackson, Esther Merle
on Williams, Tennessee, IV 634
Jackson, Moses J., II 396
Jackson, Robert Louis
on Chekhov, IV 450
Jacob, Fred, I 397
Jacob, Max, I 102, 513; II 140, 482–84; IV 26
influence of, I 225; III 532
Jacob, Violet, IV 178
Jacobsen, Jens Peter
influence of, IV 42, 47
Jacobsen, Rolf, III 402; V 330–31
Jacobsen, Steinbjørn, I 542
Jacobsohn, Siegfried, IV 471
Jacobson, Dan, IV 289; V 331–32, 566
Jacottet, Philippe, II 148; IV 387; V 233
Jād, Hudā, V 201
Jæger, Frank, I 539; II 484–85
Jaensson, Knut, I 144
Ja'far, Hasab al-Shaykh, II 457
Jahier, Piero, I 53
al-Jāhiz, V 218
Jahn, Janheinz, III 391
Jahnn, Hans Henry, II 219, 223, 485–86
Jaimes Freyre, Ricardo, I 289, 544; III 293; V 332–33
Jakobsdóttir, Svava, II 427
Jakobson, Roman, III 57, 94, 98, 99, 118; V 500, 501
influence of, V 195, 376
Jakobsson, Jökull, II 428
Jakubāns, Andris, III 18
Jalāl, 'Uthmān, II 4
Jalandoni, Magdalena, III 526
Jaleb, Iftikhar, III 459
Jalebi, Jameel, III 458
Jalil, Rahim, IV 409
Jaloux, Edmond, II 137
Jamaican literature. *See under* English-Caribbean literature
Jamaldini, Azah, III 461
Jamalzadeh, Mohammad 'Ali, II 453
James, Brian. *See* Tierney, John
James, E. O., II 278
James, Henry, I 57, 58, 60, 67, 488, 491; II 42, 49, 486–90; III 111; IV 348, 453, 619; V 94, 95, 243, 644
the "central intelligence" technique of, II 260
criticism on, II 489; III 83, 91; V 50
American, III 112, 113, 117, 120, 123, 124; IV 641, 644
English, III 31, 116; IV 318

Jonson, Ben
  criticism on, IV 641
  influence of, I 110
Jonsson, Thorsten, IV 379
Jonsson, Tor, III 403
Jonutis, Raimondas, V 394
Jonynas, Antanas A., V 393
Jooris, Roland, I 222
Jordan, Archibald C., IV 295
Jorge, Lídia, V 340–41
Jörgensen, Beth E.
  on Poniatowska, V 497
Jose, F. Sionil, III 525
Josephson, Hannah
  on Aragon, I 106–7
Joshi, Umashankar Jethalal, II 436
Jotuni, Maria, II 99
Joubert, Elsa, IV 288
Joubert, Jean, V 233
Jouhandeau, Marcel, II 142, 143, 523–24
journalism as social chronicle, IV 261
Jouve, Pierre Jean, II 141, 145, 524–25;
    V 233
  influence of, II 28
Jouvenel, Henry de, I 481
Jover, José Luis, V 574
Jouvet, Louis, II 141, 142, 145, 242,
    243, 244
Jovine, Francesco, II 470, 525–26; III
    366
Joyce, James, I 84, 200, 211, 298, 336,
    589; II 35, 42, 43, 50, 81, 98,
    115, 161, 219, 310, 432, 459,
    461, 462, 463, 526–30, 574; III
    12, 170, 220, 225, 410, 427, 571,
    574; IV 171, 258–59, 329, 360,
    375, 439, 453, 641; V 151, 195,
    243, 315, 317, 318, 350, 392,
    450, 451, 510, 516, 518, 527,
    572, 573
  criticism of, II 567; IV 578
  criticism on, I 152; II 163, 500; III
    151, 410; IV 268, 318
    American, II 398; III 113, 119
    excerpts of, II 530–31
    German, I 517; II 372; III 105; IV
    169
  influence of, I 160, 454, 460; II 592;
    III 165, 567; IV 544, 579
    on American literature, I 195; II 78;
    IV 175, 363, 629, 655; V 170,
    171
    on Brazilian literature, V 107
    on English literature, I 365; II 43,
    47; V 337
    on expressionism, II 71
    on French literature, II 143; IV 226;
    V 142
    on German literature, II 224; IV 650
    on Irish literature, V 235
    on Japanese literature, V 451
    on Spanish literature, V 126
    on Swedish literature, II 311; IV 380
  and postmodernism, V 498
  and psychology, II 537
  and stream-of-consciousness technique,
    IV 348–50
  as subject, V 396
József, Attila, II 414, 531–32
Juana Inés de la Cruz, Sor, III 373
Juan de la Cruz, San, I 50
  criticism on, III 96
Juarroz, Roberto, V 41
Jubrān, Jubrān Khalīl. See Gibran, Kahlil
Jubrān, Sālim, III 464
Juchnevičius, Eduardas, V 394
Júdice, Nuno, III 570
Juhász, Ferenc, II 414, 415
Juhász, Gyula, I 172; II 412, 531, 532–
    33
Juin, Hubert, I 224
Juliana, Elis, I 605
690 Julqunbay. See Gadiriy, Abdullah

Juminer, Bertene, II 155
al-Jundi, 'Alī, IV 401
Jung, Carl Gustav, II 533–39; V 81, 165
  influence of, I 275, 337, 562; II 538–
    39; III 124
    on American literature, I 284; II 92;
    IV 199
    on English literature, II 53
    on French literature, I 10; III 92
    on German literature, II 219, 366,
    367
    on Irish literature, V 317
  and stream-of-consciousness technique,
    IV 348
  as subject, V 362
  See also under psychology
Jünger, Ernst, II 218, 219, 223, 269,
    539–41
Jünger, Friedrich Georg, II 218
Jura. See Soyfer, Jura
Juškaitis, Jonas, V 393
Justice, Donald, I 71
Juvonen, Helvi, II 102
Jylha, Yrjo, II 101

Ka, Abdou Anta, IV 194
Kaalep, Ain, II 61, 63
Kabardian literature. See under North
    Caucasian literatures
Kachingwe, Aubrey, III 188
Kachurovsky, Ihor, IV 497
Kačič, Vladimir, IV 698
Kaden-Bandrowski, Juliusz, II 542–43;
    III 555
Kadima-Nzuji, Mukala, IV 703
Kadiri, Rozi, IV 520
Kael, Pauline, II 96, 98
Kaffka, Margit, II 412, 543–44
Kafka, Franz, I 26, 152–53, 281, 339; II
    68, 161, 544–47; III 326, 327,
    427, 551, 573–74; IV 60, 122,
    174, 257, 360, 598, 613; V 73,
    84, 119, 171, 245, 291, 387, 414,
    487, 518, 536, 537, 546, 621
  criticism on, I 241, 279; III 81, 93,
    125, 208
    excerpts of, II 547–49
  influence of, II 547
    on Chinese literature, I 460
    on Czech literature, V 367
    on Danish literature, I 539
    on English literature, II 40
    on French literature, II 144
    on German literature, II 623; IV 583
    on Hungarian literature, I 558
    on Iranian literature, II 348
    on Norwegian literature, III 400;
    V 562
    on Romanian literature, IV 83
    on Russian literature, V 484
    on Swedish literature, I 533
    on Swiss literature, I 599
  as subject, V 493
Kaganovski, Efrayim, IV 685
Kagwa, Apolo, IV 489
Kahana-Carmon, Amalia, II 467; V 326,
    342
Kahanovitsh, Pinkhes. See Der Nister
Kahiga, Samuel, II 578
Kahler, Erich
  on Mann, Thomas, III 217
Kahn, Coppélia, II 163
Kahn, Gustave, II 136; IV 390
Kailas, Uuno, II 101; IV 266
Kailasam, T. P., II 437
Kailasapathy, K., IV 323
Kaiser, Georg, II 70, 217, 218, 549–52;
    IV 336
  criticism on, III 106
    excerpts of, II 552–53
  influence of, II 381, 551
Kaiser, Ingeborg, IV 383

Kajava, Viljo, II 101
Kajokas, Donaidas, V 393
Kakabadze, Polikarp, II 213
Kakar, Hasan, I 19
Kalandadze, Ana, II 213
Kale, Pokware, III 455
Kaleb, Vjekoslav, IV 696
Kaledin, Sergey, V 531
Kalimugogo, Godfrey, IV 490
Kalisky, René, V 233
Kallas, Aino, II 101, 553–54; III 41
Kallas, Oskar, II 553
Kallifatides, Theodor, V 582
Kallio, Kyösti, I 567
Kalma, Douwe, III 379
Kalniņš, Jānis, III 19
Kalniņš, Viktors, III 19
Kalve, Aivars, III 18
Kalynets, Ihor, IV 497; V 612
Kalyoncu, Güngör Dilmen. See Dilmen,
    Güngör
Kamaleshwar, V 308
al-Kamālī, Shafīq, II 457
Kamba literature. See Kenyan literature
Kamban, Guðmundur, II 426
Kambanellis, Iakovos, II 284, 554–55
Kambas, Nikolaos, II 280
Kambara Ariake, V 336
Kamensky, Vasily, II 185; IV 105
Kaminska, Esther Rokhl, IV 686
Kaminska, Ida, IV 686
Kamlongera, Chris, III 188
Kampanellis, Yorghos, II 284
Kampmann, Christian, I 286, 541; II 555;
    V 159
Kampov, Boris. See Polevoy, Boris
Kamran, Jilani, III 459
Kamu, Kemalettin, IV 476
Kamugungunu, L., IV 489
Kanafānī, Ghassān, III 465; V 342–44,
    473, 474
Kan'ān, 'Alī, IV 400
Kandinsky, Wassily, II 70; IV 347
Kandoro, Saadan, IV 417
Kandyba, Oleh. See Olzhych, Oleh
Kandyba, Olexandr. See Oles, Olexandr
Kane, Cheikh Hamidou, IV 193
Kaneko Mitsuharu, V 337
Kang Bun Chhouen, I 386
Kangro, Bernard, II 61, 62, 63
Kani, John, II 180
Kanié, Léon Maurice Anoma, II 478
Kanık, Orhan Veli, I 81; IV 476–77; V
    154, 607
Kannada literature. See under Indian liter-
    ature
Kant, Hermann, II 225; V 250, 344–45
Kant, Immanuel, III 79, 516; V 168, 169,
    423
  influence of, I 537; III 95; IV 601; V
    399, 525
Kántor, Péter, V 298
Kantor, Tadeusz, V 492
Kao Hsiao-sheng (Gao Xiaosheng), V
    135, 345–47
Kapinski, Jaan, II 61
Kapuściński, Ryszard, V 493
Karahasan, Mustafa, IV 701
Kara Jūrō, V 336
Karakalpak literature. See under Uzbek
    literature
Karanth, Kota Shivaram, II 437, 438, 556
Karaosmanoğlu, Yakup Kadri, II 556–57;
    IV 477–78
Karasek, Krzysztof, V 491
Karásek ze Lvovic, Jiří, I 520
Karashev, Sīdīk, II 588
Karaslavov, Georgi, I 359; IV 255
Karasu, Bilge, V 607
Karatkevich, Uladzimier, I 375
Karay, Refik Halit, IV 473
Karelian literature. See under Finno-Ugric
    literatures of the Soviet Union

Kariara, Jonathan, V 351
Karim, Abdul, IV 417
Kärim, Mostay, I 204
Karim, Muhammadi Mela, V 264
Karinthy, Ferenc, II 558; V 297
Karinthy, Frigyes, II 412, 413, 557–58
Karinthy, Gábor, II 557–58
Kariuki, Josiah, II 577
Karkala, John A., II 438
Kārkliņš, Valdemārs, III 17
Karl, Frederick R.
    on Lessing, Doris, III 53
Karlee, Varfelli, III 70–71
Karlfeldt, Erik Axel, IV 220, 376
Karm, Dun. See Psaila, Carmelo
Karmansky, Petro, IV 494
Karnad, Girish Ragunath, II 437
Karnauskaite, Elena, V 394
Karnowski, Jan, III 561
Károlyi, Amy, IV 612
Karpenko-Kary, IV 493
Karpowicz, Tymoteusz, III 559; V 491
Kartini, II 445
Karvaš, Peter, I 526; II 558–59
Karyotakis, Kostas, II 280, 281, 559–60
Kasack, Hermann, I 92
Kasaipwalova, John, III 455
Kaschnitz, Marie Luise, II 223, 560–61
Kaseem, Hassan, I 19
Kashiwabara Hyōzō, V 238
Kashubian literature. See under Polish
    literature
Kasïmbekov, Tolegen, II 589
Kasoma, Godfrey, IV 705
Kasprowicz, Jan, III 552, 607
Kasrai, Siavash, II 455
Kassák, Lajos, II 414, 561–62
Kassem, Ceza. See Qāsim, Ceza
Kassim Ahmad, III 191
Kassner, Rudolf, III 104
Kaštelan, Jure, IV 696
Kästner, Erich, II 219, 562–63; IV 596
Kataev, Valentin Petrovich, II 8, 429,
    563–64; III 488; IV 109, 110, 112
Kataev, Yevgeny. See Petrov, Yevgeny
Katate, A. G., IV 489
Katay Don Sasorith, III 9
Kateb Yacine, I 46–47; II 565–66; V 12
Katigula, Barnabas, IV 419
Katiliškis, Marius, III 132; V 393
Katiyo, Wilson, IV 712
Katsenelson, Yitskhok, IV 684
Katsizne, Alter-Sholem, IV 684, 687
al-Kattānī, Muhammad, III 318
Kaudzīte, Matīss, III 15, 16
Kaudzīte, Reinis, III 15, 16
Kaufman, Fritz
    on Mann, Thomas, III 216
Kaufman, George S., I 73; II 520
Kaufmann, Walter F., III 103
Kaun, Alexander
    on Gorky, II 263
Kaunda, Kenneth, IV 705
Kaus, Gina, I 156
Kavafis, Konstantinos Petrou. See Cavafy,
    C. P.
Kavanagh, Patrick, II 460, 566–67; V
    317, 431
Kavanagh, Peter, II 566
Kaverin, Veniamin, II 567–68; IV 109
Kawabata Yasunari, II 481, 496, 568–69;
    III 286; IV 688; V 334, 436
Kawahigashi Hekigodō, II 497
Kawere, Edward E. N., IV 489
Kay, Billy, V 547
Kaya, Fahri, IV 701
Kayamba, Martin, IV 418
Kayira, Legson, III 188
Kayper-Mensah, Albert, II 227
Kazakh literature, II 569–71
    major writers of, see: Auezov;
        Duwlat-ŭlï
    in Russian, II 570

Kazakov, Nikolay, II 105
Kazakov, Yury, II 571–72; IV 112
Kazan, Elia, IV 630, 631
Kazantzakis, Nikos, II 93, 281, 282–83,
    572–74; III 593; IV 137, 218,
    539; V 510
    critical excerpts on, II 574–76
Kāzim, 'Ādil, II 458
Kazimi, Mushfik, I 167
Kazin, Alfred, II 398
    on Dos Passos, I 582
    on Dreiser, I 589–90
    on Lukács, III 152
    on Roth, Henry, IV 90–91
    on Singer, Isaac Bashevis, IV 237
    on Snow, IV 251
Keats, John, V 362
    criticism on, III 91, 105, 116, 117–18,
        120
    influence of, I 235, 514; III 140, 375;
        IV 366, 611
Kebebe Mikael, II 64
Keilhau, Carl, IV 45
Keita, Fodéba, II 302
Kekilov, Aman, IV 480
Kckilov, Annasoltan, IV 480
Kekilov, Shalï, IV 480
Kekštas, Juozas (Juosas Adomavičius), III
    131; V 393, 395
Keleras, Julius, V 393
Keller, Gottfried, I 152; II 166, 366; III
    214; IV 382
    criticism on, III 83, 108
    influence of, III 342
    as subject, V 437
Keller, Stefan, IV 385
Kelly, Robert, V 644
Kelly-Gadol, Joan, V 289
Kemal, Namık, IV 474, 475
Kemal, Orhan, IV 478
Kemal, Thilda, V 607
Kemal, Yaşar (Yashar), II 576–77; IV
    478; V 606, 607
Kemény, Simon, II 412
Kemp, Robert, II 143; IV 180
Kempowski, Walter, II 220
Kenaz, Yehoshua, V 347
Keneally, Thomas, I 148; V 51, 348–
    49
Keng Vannsak, I 387
Kennaway, James, IV 181; V 545
Kennedy, Leo, I 396
Kennedy, William, V 25, 349–50
Kenner, Hugh
    on Beckett, I 214
    on Lewis, Wyndham, III 66
    on Pound, III 578
Kente, Gibson, V 566
Kenworthy, B. J.
    on Kaiser, Georg, II 552
Kenyan literature, II 577–79; V 350–52
    civil war as subject of, II 577, 578
    in English, II 577–78
    in Kikuyu, II 579
    major writers of, see Ngugi wa
        Thiong'o
    in Swahili, II 578
Kenyatta, Jomo, II 577
Ker, W. P., II 52; III 111
Kerbabaev, Berdï. See Kerbaba-oghli,
    Berdï
Kerbaba-oghli, Berdï, III 614; IV 480
Keris Mas, III 190
Kerler, Yoysef, IV 687
Kermode, Frank, III 118–19
    on Eliot, T. S., II 20
    on Lawrence, D. H., III 26
    on Musil, III 338–39
Kerouac, Jack, I 69, 188, 432; II 237,
    579–80; III 137
    criticism on, V 110
Kerr, Alfred, III 106
    on Fleisser, II 113

Kerrigan, Anthony
    on Borges, I 305
Kerslake, Celia, V 607
Kertész, Imre, V 297
Kerverzioù, Gwilherm Berthou, II 151
Kesey, Ken, I 70, 432; II 580–81
    as subject, V 641
Kette, Dragotin, IV 721
Keulkut, Viktor, I 465
Key, Ellen
    influence of, IV 377
Keynes, John Maynard, IV 346, 658
    influence of, II 52
Keyserling, Eduard Graf, II 217
Kezilahabi, Euphrase, IV 417, 418
Khaddūr, Fayez, IV 401
Khadi, Mukhamedi, I 165
Khadijah Hashim, III 190
Khadilkar, K. P., II 436
Khái-Hùng (Trần Khánh Giù), III 389; IV
    561; V 352–53
Khair-Eddine, Mohammed, III 319–20
Khaketla, Bennett, IV 50
al-Khāl, Yūsuf, I 15; III 33; V 37,
    353–54
Khālid, Abū Bakr, IV 366–67
Khalid, Riza, IV 421
Khalid, Tasaduq Hussain, III 459
Khalīfa, Sahar, V 474
Khalili, Khalilullah, I 19
al-Khalīlī Ja'far, II 457
Khamchan Pradith, III 10
Khammār, Abū al-Qāsim, I 46
Khamphun Bunthawi, IV 430
Khamrayev, M. K., IV 520
Khamsing Sinok. See Lao Khamhom
Khandekar, Vishnu Sakharam, II 439,
    581–82
Khanty literature. See under Finno-Ugric
    literatures of the Soviet Union
Khanzadian, Sero, I 122
Kharats, Meyer, IV 687
Kharfī, Sālih, I 46
Kharik, Izzi, IV 684
Kharms, Daniil, IV 106
al-Kharrāt, Edwar (Edward), II 6; V 201,
    354–55
Khatibi, Abdelkebir, III 320; V 69, 70,
    231, 235, 355–56
Khatkov, Akhmet, III 398
Khatri, Kishin Chant Tirathdas, III 460
Khaytov, Nikolay, I 360
Khechoumian, Viken, I 122
Khesigbatu, III 300
Khetagkäty Kosta, III 445
Khlebnikov, Velemir Vladimirovich (Vik-
    tor), I 513; II 185, 186, 582–83;
    III 98; IV 105; V 531
    influence of, IV 575, 702
Khodasevich, Vladislav Felitsianovich, I
    340; II 583–84; IV 106
    on Nabokov, III 347
Khorloo, Püreviin, III 300
Khorolets, Larysa, V 614
Khösni, Fatikh, IV 421
Khotkevuch, Hnat, IV 493
Khowar literature. See under Pakistani
    literature
Khristov, Kiril, IV 246
Khudayberdi, Hälimä, IV 521–22
Khuluqī, 'Alï, III 398
Khurayif, Bashīr, IV 473
al-Khūrī, Bishāra, III 32; V 36
Khūrī, Colette, IV 398
Khūrī, Ilyās, III 35
Khūrī, Jalāl, III 34
al-Khūrī al-Baytjālī, Iskandar, V 472
Khusangay, Petr, I 466
Khvylovy, Mykola, IV 495; V 612
Kiacheli, Leo, II 212
Kianto, Ilmari, II 100–101
Kibera, Leonard, II 578
Kibirov, Timur, V 530

Kidde, Harold, I 536
Kiehtreiber, Albert Konrad. See Güters-
    loh, Albert Paris von
Kielland, Alex, III 401
Kielland, Alexander, III 398
Kiely, Benedict, II 461; V 320
Kierkegaard, Søren, II 67, 621; V 140,
    141, 401, 577, 578, 582
    criticism on, V 127
    influence of, I 599; II 38, 66, 311;
        V 159
Kiernan, Brian
    on White, Patrick, IV 624–25
Kieser, Rolf
    on Frisch, II 171
Kiestra, Douwe Hermans, III 379
Kihlman, Alfred, V 356
Kihlman, Bertel, V 356
Kihlman, Christer, II 103; V 61, 183,
    356–58
Kihlman, Erik, V 356
Kihlman, Lorenzo, V 356
Kiimbila, J. K., IV 418
Ķikauka, Tālivaldis, III 18
Kiki, Albert Maori, III 455
Kikongo literature. See under Zairian
    literature
Kikuchi Kan, II 496
Kikuyu literature. See under Kenyan
    literature
Killens, John Oliver, V 358–59
Kilpi, Eeva, V 359–60
Kilpi, Volter, II 101, 584–85
Kilroy, Thomas, V 317
Kim, Richard E., II 601
Kim, Tomaz, III 569
Kim, Yong Ik, II 601
Kimbangu, Simon, IV 703
Kimbugwe, Henry. See Seruma, Eneriko
Kimbundu literature. See under Angolan
    literature
Kim Ch'un-su, II 601
Kimenye, Barbara, IV 490
Kim-Hak, I 386
Kim Ŏk, II 599
Kim So-wŏl, II 600
Kim Sŭng-ok, II 601
Kim Su-yŏng, II 601
Kim Tong-in, II 599
Kim Tong-ni, II 600
Kinck, Hans, III 399, 401
King, Bruce
    on Rushdie, V 529
King, Stephen, V 321
Kinnell, Galway, I 73; II 585–86
Kinoshita Junji, V 336, 360–61
Kinsella, Thomas, II 460; V 317, 361–
    63, 430
Kipling, Rudyard, I 303; II 42, 49, 586–
    88
    criticism on, III 120
    influence of, III 514; IV 265
Kipnis, Itsik, IV 685
Kipphardt, Heinar, II 71, 223, 380; V
    363–64
Kirgiz literature, II 588–90
    major writers of, see Aytmatov
    also writing in Russian, see
        Aytmatov
    Muslim revolt as subject of, II 588–89
    in Russian, II 589; IV 112
Kirikiño, IV 310
Kirillov, Pyotr, II 105
Kirillov, Vladimir, IV 105
Kirk, Hans Rudolf, I 538; II 590
Kirkus, Virginia
    on Lind, Jakov, V 387
Kirša, Faustas, III 129
Kirsanov, Semyon, IV 106
Kirsch, Rainer, II 222; V 364
Kirsch, Sarah (Ingrid Bernstein), II 221;
    V 364–65
Kirsten, Wulf, II 222

Kiš, Danilo, IV 694; V 365–66
Kısakürek, Necip Fazil, IV 476
Kishida Kunio, II 498, 590–91
Kiss, Jenő, IV 85
Kiss, József, II 413
Kitagawa Fuyuhiko, V 336
Kitahara Hakushū, II 497; V 336
Kitasono Katsue, V 336
Kittner, Alfred, IV 84
Kitzberg, August, II 63
Ki Umbara, II 444
Kivi, Aleksis, II 99, 100, 101, 103; III
    268
Kizer, Carolyn, V 26
Kjær, Nils, III 401
Klein, A. M., I 396, 397; II 591–92
Klein, Marcus
    on Bellow, I 230
Klein, Melanie, II 157
Kleist, Heinrich von
    criticism on, III 85, 102; V 142, 143
    influence of, IV 48, 184
Klen, Yury. See Burghardt, Oswald
Klīdzējs, Jānis, III 16
Klíma, Ivan, I 524; V 156, 366–67
Kline, Franz, III 419
Klinger, Kurt, I 158; V 55
Kloos, Willem, I 308; III 375; IV 552
    reaction against, IV 552
Kloosterman, Simke, III 379
Klopstock, Friedrich Gottlieb, III 103
    influence of, IV 48
Klyuev, Nikolay Alexeevich, II 592–93;
    IV 105
Knap, Josef, I 522
Knight, Etheridge, I 73
Knight, G. Wilson, III 84, 118
    on Pinter, III 536
Knights, L. C., III 117
Knopf, Alfred, V 165
Knopfli, Rui, III 323
Knudsen, Erik, I 539
Knudsen, Jakob, I 536–37
Kobayashi Hideo, V 322, 367–68
Kobayashi Takiji, II 496; IV 210
Kober, Arthur, II 352
Köbey-ŭlï, Ispandiyar, II 570
Kobylanska, Olha, IV 493
Kobylyansky, Volodymyr, IV 495
Kocbek, Edvard, IV 697
Koch, Jurij, III 156
Koch, Kenneth, I 72–73; III 419; V 47
Koch, Martin, IV 377
Kochar, Hrachia, I 122
Kocherha, Ivan, IV 495, 497; V 614
Kočić, Petar, IV 692
Kodály, Zoltán, IV 612
Kodituwakku, Parakrama, IV 323
Kodolányi, János, II 414
Koenders, Julius Gustaaf Arnout, I 604
Koenegracht, Frank, III 377
Koenig, Alma Johanna, I 156
Koeppen, Wolfgang, II 224, 593–94
Koestler, Arthur, I 491; II 594–96; IV
    321; V 391
    influence of, I 533; III 440
Kofman, Sarah, V 234
Kogawa, Joy, V 109
Kohout, Pavel, I 524; V 156, 391
Kohzad, Ahmad Ali, I 19
Koidula, Lydia, II 60
Koirala, B. P., III 367–68
Koirala, Mohan, III 367
Koirala, Prasad, III 367
Kok, Ingrid de, V 567
Koka, Şecaettin, IV 701
Kokoschka, Oskar, I 152; II 70; IV 347
Kołakowski, Leszek, V 491
Kolas, Yakub, I 179, 375
Kolb, Annette, II 219, 596–97
Kolbenheyer, Erwin Guido, II 219
Kolhatkar, Shreepad Krishna, II 436–37
Koliqi, Ernest, I 38–39

Kollár, Ján, I 525
Kolleritsch, Alfred, V 55
Kolmar, Gertrud, II 218, 597–98; V 382
Kolnik, Arthur, IV 213
Kolomiyets, Oleksy, V 614
Koltès, Bernard-Marie, V 231, 233
Kolumb, Valentin, II 105
Kolyada, Nikolay, V 532
Komb, Anton de, I 604
Komi literature. See under Finno-Ugric
    literatures of the Soviet Union
Komitas, IV 197
Kommerell, Max, II 215; III 103, 108
Kometani Fumiko, V 335
Konadu, Asare, II 226, 227
Kondé, Kwame, I 402
Konert, Nicolas, III 159
Koneski, Blaže, IV 698
Konitsa, Faik, I 39
Konopnicka, Maria, III 552
Kōno Taeko, V 45, 336, 459
Konrád, György (George), II 416; V 297,
    368–69
Konstantinov, Aleko, IV 246
Kontoglou, Fotis, II 283
Konwicki, Tadeusz, II 598–99; III 559; V
    491, 492
Kooning, Willem de, III 419
Kopelev, Lev, IV 111; V 391
Kopit, Arthur, I 74; IV 433
Kops, Bernard, II 40
Kör, Kazinczy, I 527
Korda, Alexander, III 456
Kordun, Viktor, V 613
Korean literature, II 599–601
    conditions in Korea as subject of, II
        600
    divided Korea as subject of, II 601
    Korean War as subject of, II 601 (see
        also Korean War)
    Kŭk yesel yŏn'guhoe group of, II 601
    left-right controversy as subject of,
        II 600
    major writers of, see: Pak Tu-jin; Sŏ
        Chŏng-ju
    "new tendency" movement in, II 600
    T'owŏrhoe group of, II 601
Korean War, as subject
    of American literature, II 504
    of Chinese literature, I 439; III 454
    of Czechoslovak literature, III 386
    of Korean literature, 601
Korepanov, Dmitry, II 105
Kõressaar, Viktor, II 62
Korkia, Viktor, V 532
Kornaros, Vitzentzos, III 594
Kornhauser, Julian, V 491, 651
Kornis, Mihály, V 298
Kornychuk, Olexandr, IV 495, 497;
    V 614
Korolenko, Vladimir, II 262
Koroleva, Natalena, IV 494
Korotych, Vitaly, IV 497
Korsakas, Kostas, III 130
Korsi, Demetrio, V 125
Koryürek, Enis Behiç, IV 475–76
Korzeniowski, Apollo, I 488
Korzeniowski, Józef Teodor. See Conrad,
    Joseph
Korzhavin, Naum, IV 106–7
Koš, Erih, IV 693
Kósa, Ferenc, V 153
Kosach, Olha Drahomanov. See Pchilka,
    Olena
Kosach, Yury, IV 494
Kosinski, Jerzy, II 601–3; V 64, 391
    influence of, II 254
Koskenniemi, V. A., II 99
Kosmač, Ciril, IV 697
Kosola, Vihtori, II 101
Kossak, Zofia, II 603–4; III 556
Kostenko, Lina, IV 497; V 370–71,
    613–15

Kostić, Laza
  criticism on, IV 692
Kostiuk, Hryhory, IV 577
Kostra, Ján, I 526
Kostrowitzky, Wilhelm Albert. See Apol-
    linaire, Guillaume
Kosynka, Hryhory, IV 495
Kosztolányi, Dezső, I 172; II 412, 532,
    604–5; IV 458, 699
Kötlum, Jóhannes úr. See Jóhannes úr
    Kötlum
Kōtoku Shūsui, II 464
Kotsoity Arsen, III 445
Kotsyubynsky, Mykhaylo, IV 493;
    V 371–72
Kourouma, Ahmadou, II 479
Kouwenaar, Gerrit, III 377
Kovačić, Ivan Goran, IV 696
Kovaļevska, Margarita, III 16
Kozer, José, V 260
Kozhinov, Vadim, V 532
Kracholov, Peyo Totev. See Yavorov,
    Peyo
Krag, Vilhelm, III 402
Krains, Hubert, I 223
Králik, Štefan, I 526
Kralis, Manos, I 518
Krall, Hanna, V 493
Kramarae, Cheris, V 641
Kramer, Theodor, I 156; II 606
Krämer-Badoni, Rudolf, II 224
Krandievskaya, Natalia, V 596
Kranjec, Miško, IV 697
Krapiva, Kandrat, I 375–76
Krapoth, Hermann
  on Broch, I 339
Krasilnikoff, Arthur, V 159
Krasilnikov, Gennady, II 105
Kraśko, Ivan, I 525; II 606–7
Krāslavietis, Valdis, III 17
Krasniqi, Mark, IV 699
Krasznahorkai, László, V 296
Kraujiete, Aina, III 17
Kraus, Karl, I 151–52, 153–54; II 607–9;
    III 107, 551; IV 342; V 387, 568
  criticism on, I 241; III 81
  excerpts of, II 609–11
  influence of, I 400; IV 456
Krause, David
  on O'Casey, III 414
Kravitz, Peter, V 545
Kravtsiv, Bohdan, IV 496
Kreft, Bratko, IV 697
Kreisel, Henry, I 397
Křelina, František, I 522
Kresh, Paul
  on Singer, Isaac Bashevis, IV 237
Kreuder, Ernst, II 224
Kreutzwald, Friedrich Reinhold, II 60
Krėvė, Vincas, II 611–12; III 129
Krėvė-Mickevičius, Vincas. See Krėvė,
    Vincas
Kridl, Manfred, III 99, 100
Kriegel, Leonard
  on Jones, James, II 522
Krieger, Murray, III 125, 126
Krige, Uys, IV 286
Krikorian, Hovaness, I 122
Krile, Velga, III 19
Krinaios, Pavlos, I 518
Kripalani, Krishna
  on Tagore, IV 407–8
Kris, Ernst, II 157, 162; III 83
Krishnan, P., IV 232, 233
Kristensen, Tom, I 537; II 612–13
Kristeva, Julia, II 149; III 522; IV 267; V
    222, 231, 234, 372–73, 377, 499,
    500
Kristmundsson, Aðalsteinn. See Steinarr,
    Steinn
Kristoforidhi, Konstantin, I 38
Kristol, Irving, IV 319

Krivulin, Viktor, V 530
Krklec, Gustav, IV 695
Krleža, Miroslav, II 613–15; III 82; IV
    255, 695
Krmpotić, Vesna, IV 696
Kroetsch, Robert, V 108, 109
Kroetz, Franz Xaver, II 223, 395, 615–
    16; V 249
Krog, Antjie, V 565
Krog, Helge, III 401
Krokann, Inge, III 400
Krolow, Karl, II 221, 616–17
Kronauer, Brigitte, III 249
Kronbergs, Juris, III 17–18
Kroon, Willem E., I 605
Kropotkin, Pyotr, III 453
Kropyvnytsky, Marko, IV 492
Kross, Jean, II 63
Kross, Rudi, I 605
Kruchonykh, Alexey, II 185, 186; IV 105
Kruczkowski, Leon, II 617–18; III 556,
    557
Krúdy, Gyula, II 414, 618–19
Krusenstjerna, Agnes von, IV 378
Krushyna, Ryhor, I 376
Krustev, Krustyo, I 358; IV 245, 246,
    672
Krutch, Joseph Wood, III 83
Krymsky, Ahatanhel, IV 494
Krynicki, Ryszard, V 59, 60, 373–74,
    491, 492, 651
Kshatri, Lil Bahadur, III 368
Kuan Mo-yeh. See Mo Yen
Kubašec, Marja, III 155
Kubheka, I. S., IV 296
Kubilinskas, Eugenijus, V 394
Kubin, Alfred, I 152
Kublanovsky, Yury, IV 107
Kübler, Arnold, IV 382
Ku Ch'eng (Gu Cheng), V 136
Kuhar, Lovro. See Prežihov, Voranc
Kühn, C. H. See Mikro
Kühn, Dieter, II 225
Kuhn, Thomas S., III 127
Ku Hua (Gu Hua), V 137
Kukrit Pramoj, II 619–20; IV 430
Kukučín, Martin, I 525; II 620–21
Kulaaskar, Serafim Aramaanabys. See
    Ellyay
Kulachikov, Serafin Romanovich. See
    Ellyay
Kulakovsky, Alexey Yeliseevich, IV 670
Kulap Saipradit. See Siburapha
Kulbak, Moyshe, IV 684, 687
Kulet, H(enry) R. Ole, V 351
Kulish, Mykola, IV 495; V 612, 614
Kulish, Pantaleymon, IV 492
Külvet, Ilmar, II 63
Kumaranatunga, Munidasa, IV 322
Kumbirai, Joseph, IV 714
Kume Masao, II 496
Kumin, Maxine, V 374–75, 551
Kun, Béla, III 350
Kuna, Franz
  on Kafka, II 548
Kuncewiczowa, Maria, III 556
Kuncz, Aladár, IV 85
Künde, IV 670
Kundera, Milan, I 524; II 621–22; IV
    255; V 156, 366, 391, 392, 498
Kunene, Mazisi, IV 296; V 391
Kunert, Günter, II 222, 225, 622–24
Kunikida Doppo, II 495, 624–25
Kunikida Tetsuo. See Kunikida Doppo
Kunitz, Stanley, I 71; V 26
Kunze, Reiner, II 221, 222, 625
Künzegesh, Yury, IV 484
Kuo Mo-jo, I 458, 459; II 625–26
Kupala, Yanka, I 179, 375
Kuppner, Frank, V 547
Kuprin, Alexandr Ivanovich, II 626–27;
    IV 108
Kür, Pınar, V 607

Kuraev, Mikhail, V 531
Kurahashi Yumiko, V 45, 336
Kuratov, Ivan, II 104
Kurban, Sukur, III 397–98
Kurbas, Les, IV 495
Kurdish literature, II 627–29; V 263–64
  in Iran, II 627–28
  in Iraq, II 627–28
  in the Soviet Union, II 628–29
  in Syria, II 627–28
  in Turkey, II 627–28
Kureishi, Hanif, V 211, 310
Kureishy, Maki, III 458
Kurek, Jalu, III 555, 557
Kuroi Senji, V 238, 334
Kurosawa Akira, II 97
Kurup, G. Shankar, II 436
Kušan, Ivan, IV 696–97
Kushner, Alexandr, IV 107
Kutateli, Alexandre, II 212
Kutlu, Ayla, V 607
Kuwaiti literature, V 324–25
Kuyper, Sjoerd, III 377
Kuzebai, Gerd. See Chaynikov, Kuzma
Kuzmin, Mikhail Alexeevich, II 582,
    629–30; IV 105
Kuzuo Ishiguro. See Ishiguro, Kuzuo
Kuzwayo, Ellen, V 567
Kvalstad, Louis, III 402
Kvaran, Einar H., I 425
Kvitka, Laryssa Kosach. See Ukrayinka,
    Lesya
Kvitko, Leyb, IV 684
Kyi, U, IV 429
Kyin Hswei, U. See Thaw-da Hswei
Kymytval, Antonina, I 465
Kyrklund, Willy, IV 380
Kyukhelbeker, Karlovich, IV 110
Kzwayo, Z., IV 296

Laaban, Ilmar, II 61, 62
Laberge, Marie, V 111
Labhām, Durayd, V 402
Labiş, Nicolae, IV 82
Lacan, Jacques, II 149, 163, 253; III 93,
    427; IV 571; V 168, 229, 234,
    376–78, 499
  influence of, V 222, 372
Lacerda, Alberto de, III 569
La Cierva, Juan de, I 168
Lacis, Asja, I 239
Lacoue-Labarthe, Philippe, V 235
Lacretelle, Jacques de, II 142
Ladin literature. See Swiss literature, in
    Romansh
Ladipo, Duro, III 390, 391
Ladurie, Emmanuel LeRoy, II 149
Lafitte, Pierre, II 150
Lafont, Robert, II 152
La Fontaine, V 292, 543
  criticism on, III 105
Laforet, Carmen, III 1; IV 308; V 570
Laforgue, Hugo, III 293
Laforgue, Jules, I 177; II 34; III 293;
    IV 391
  criticism on, III 115
  influence of, II 17
Lafourcade, Enrique, I 455; V 131, 378–
    79
Lafuente Ferrari, Enrique, IV 300
Laganovskis, Jezups, III 18
Lagarde, Paul de
  influence of, III 315
Lagerkvist, Pär, II 70; III 1–3; IV 377,
    381; V 582
  influence of, III 401
  on Strindberg, IV 356
Lagerlöf, Selma, IV 122, 376
Lago, Mary M.
  on Tagore, IV 407
Laguerre, Enrique, V 379–80
La Guma, Alex, III 3–4; IV 290; V 391   **693**

Macbeth, George, V 546
MacBride, John, IV 674
MacCaig, Norman, III 162–63; IV 178, 179, 180, 250; V 545
MacCarthy, Desmond, III 111
on Lawrence, D. H., III 24
MacColla, Fionn, IV 178, 180
MacDiarmid, Hugh, III 163–65; IV 178, 179, 250; V 546
critical excerpts on, III 165–67
criticism of, IV 179
influence of, III 165; IV 285
on Smith, Sydney Goodsir, IV 180
MacDonagh, Thomas, I 468
Macdonald, Ross
on Cain, V 106
Macdougall, Carl, V 545
Macedo, Donaldo Pereira, I 403
Macedonian literature. See under Yugoslav literature
Macedonski, Alexandru, I 114; III 209, 529; IV 79
Mačernis, Vytautas, III 131
MacGuckian, Medbh, V 318
Mácha, Karel Hynek, I 520; II 393
criticism on, IV 133
Machado, Antonio, III 167–68; IV 301, 304, 392
Machado, Antônio de Alcântara, I 323
Machado, Manuel, III 167, 168, 294; IV 301
Machado de Assis, Joaquim Maria. See Assis, Joaquim Maria Machado de
Machaka, Samson Rasebilu, IV 291
Machar, Josef Svatopluk, I 520; III 169–70; IV 133
Machel, Samora, III 322
Machen, Arthur, IV 607
Macherey, Pierre, III 81
MacIntyre, Duncan Ban, V 547
MacIntyre, John. See Brandane, John
Mačiulevičus-Mačiulis, Jonas. See Maironis
Mackail, J. W., III 241
Mackay, Agnes
on Valéry, IV 530
MacKay, Colin, V 545
Mackenzie, Compton, IV 180
Mackie, Alastair, IV 178
Mackiewicz, Józef, III 560; V 492
Mackinnon, Rayne, V 547
Mackus, Algimantas, III 132; V 393
MacLaverty, Bernard, V 319, 545
Maclean, John
influence of, III 165
Maclean, Somhairle, IV 178
MacLeish, Archibald, I 65, 71; II 70; III 170–71; V 353
MacLellan, Robert, IV 179
MacLennan, Hugh, I 397; III 171–72; V 108
Macleod, Isabail, V 548
Macleod, Joseph, IV 178
MacNeice, Louis, I 548; II 36; III 172–73; IV 318; V 317, 404
Mac Orlan, Pierre, II 142
Madagascar literature. See Malagasy literature
Madanī, al-Amīn 'Alī, IV 366
Madanī, 'Izz al-dīn, IV 473
Madariaga, Salvador de, III 95; IV 300
Madden, C. F.
on Boyle, I 312
Madden, David, I 69
Maddy, Yulisa Amadu, IV 216
Made, E. H. A., IV 296
Made Sanggra, II 445
Madge, Charles, IV 5
Madima, E. S., IV 294
Maditsi, Thipagkolo, IV 290–91
Madsen, Svend Åge, I 540; V 160, 401–2
Maeterlinck, Maurice, I 224, 225; III 173–75, 571; IV 391, 667
criticism on, III 553

influence of, I 90; II 105; III 607; IV 47, 265, 347, 666
Maeztu, Ramiro de, I 195; III 95; IV 300
Magarshack, David
on Chekhov, I 449
Magdaleno, Mauricio, III 175–76, 272
Mageza, Bill T., IV 292
Maghrebian literature, V 70, 71, 83, 84, 138, 139, 250–52, 356, 418
al-Māghūt, Muhammad, IV 400; V 402–3
magic realism, III 176–78; IV 83, 84, 518
Australian, V 51
Belgian, I 220, 535
Central American, I 132, 434; III 177; V 122
Chinese, V 138
Colombian, I 485; III 177
Ecuadorian, II 1, 424; V 6
English, V 208
and film, II 97
French-Caribbean, II 154
German, I 298; II 468
Guadeloupean, V 542
Indian, V 433, 526
Israeli, V 326
Italian, I 298; II 468
Nigerian, V 449
Pakistani, V 254
Paraguayan, III 473
Puerto Rican, V 380
Portuguese, V 340
Russian, V 323
Spanish-Caribbean, I 415; III 177
Swedish, V 388, 582
Ukrainian, V 554
Venezuelan, III 177; IV 518
Magnus, Judah L., I 353
Magny, Claude-Edmonde, III 93
on Radiguet, IV 3
Magris, Claudio, V 53, 54
Magritte, René, IV 371
Maha Hswei, I 367
Mahakavi, IV 324
Mahapa, Lesiba, IV 291
Mahapatra, Jayanta, V 309
Mahari, Kourken, I 122
Maha Sila Viravong, III 9
Maheux-Forcier, Louise, V 110
Mahfūz, Najīb, V 5–6; III 178–79; V 201, 252, 253, 354, 424
Mahieu, Vincent, II 445–46
Mahjūb, Muhammad Ahmad, IV 366
Mahlangu, Peter S., IV 713
Mahler, Alma, V 613
Mahler, Margaret, II 163
Mahmud, III 398
Mahmūd, 'Abd al-Rahīm, III 464
Mahmud, Mamadali, IV 521
Mahmūd al-'Aqqād, 'Abbās, V 458
Mahon, Derek, V 317, 403–4, 430
Mahsuri Salikon, III 190
Maignot, Émile. See Henriot, Émile
Mailer, Norman, I 68, 69; II 179; III 179–81; V 24, 170, 171, 358, 498
influence of, III 419
Maillet, Antonine, V 110
Maillu, David, II 578; V 351
Mainali, Prasad, III 367
Mainza, M. C., IV 704
Maiorescu, Titu, IV 79
Maironis, III 129
Mais, Roger, V 404–5
Maissen, Michel, IV 389
Mai Tháo, V 619
Maj, Bronisław, V 492
al-Majdhūb, Muhammad al-Mahdī, IV 366
Majerová, Marie, I 522; III 181–82; IV 255
Majevskis, Hermanis Margers, III 19
Majkowski, Alexander, III 561
Major, André, I 398, 399; V 110

Major, Clarence, I 69
Major, Nándor, IV 700
Majrooh, Bahauddin, I 19
al-Mak, 'Alī, IV 367
Makarfi, Shu'aibu, II 389
Makayonak, Andrei, I 376
Makgoana, P. M., IV 292
Makhali Phal, I 387
Makhalisa, Barbara, IV 713
al-Makhzanjī, Muhammad, V 202
Makkai, Sándor, IV 85
Makonnen Endalkachew, II 64
Maksimović, Desanka, III 182–83; IV 692
Malagasy literature, III 183–86
in French, III 185–86
in Malagasy, III 183–85
al-Malā'ika, Nāzik, II 4, 457; V 353, 405–7
al-Malā'ika, Um Nizār, V 405
Malakasis, Miltiadis, II 280, 281
Malamud, Bernard, I 68, 69; III 186–87
Mălăncioiu, Ileana, V 520
Malang, Khalifah Rahmat, III 461
Malange, Nise, V 566
Malanyuk, Yevhen, IV 496; V 613
Malaparte, Curzio, I 297, 356
Malawian literature, III 187–88
in English, III 187–88
in Nyanja, III 187
in Tumbuka, III 187
Malayalam literature. See under Indian literature
Malay literature. See under Malaysian and Singapore literatures. See also Indonesian literature in Indonesian
Malaysian literature, III 189–93. See also Singapore literature
Asas '50 in, III 190
in Chinese, III 191–92
in English, III 192–93
major writers of, in Malay, see: Shahnon; Usman
in Malay, III 189–91
in Tamil, III 192
Maldoror, Sarah, IV 559
Malenkov, Georgy, III 80
Malerba, Luigi, II 474
Maleski, Vlado, IV 698
Malevich, Kazimir, II 185
Malgonkar, Manohar, II 439; III 193–94
Malherbe, D. F., IV 286
Malherbe, François de
influence of, III 562
Malhi, Govind, II 439
Mali literature, III 194–95
Malinké literature. See Guinean and under Mali literatures
Malinovski, Ivan, I 540; III 195
Malinowski, Bronisław, II 644
Malla, Vijaya, III 367, 368
Mallarmé, Stéphane, I 470; II 139, 210; III 90, 93, 488, 566; IV 96, 360, 362, 389, 390; V 291, 336, 377, 451
criticism on, I 279; III 91, 95, 96, 97, 115
influence of, I 330; II 231; III 89; IV 118, 370, 526; V 36, 161, 318
as subject, V 372
Malle, Louis, V 427
Mallea, Eduardo, I 112, 113; III 196–97; V 41
Mallei, III 398
Mallet-Joris, Françoise, II 147; III 197–98; V 231
Malmanche, Tangi, II 151
Malmberg, Bertil, IV 377
Malmberg, Richard, II 99
Malonga, Jean, I 487
Malope, R. M., IV 293
Malouf, David, V 51
Malraux, André, I 134, 491; II 68, 141, 144, 146, 147; III 80, 92, 198–

Ma'rufi, Abbas, V 314
Marugg, Tip, I 605
Marut, Ret. *See* Traven, B.
Marx, Karl, I 311; III 82; IV 253. *See also:* Marxism; Marxist criticism
  influence of, I 442; III 88, 150; IV 200, 326, 376; V 189, 590
  as subject, V 376, 399
Marx, Leo, I 76
Marxism. *See also:* communism; Marxist criticism; socialism
  anti-, II 430–31
  versus Christianity, IV 546
  conflicts within, III 531
  criticism of, III 28
  versus existentialism, II 146; IV 156
  in American literature, I 136, 188, 189; III 137, 260; IV 664
  in Arabic literature, II 457
  in Asian literatures, I 3–4, II 591, IV 480; Chinese, II 379 (*see also* Maoism); Indian, II 435, 452, 581, III 360
  in Canadian literature, III 28
  in East European literatures, I 358, 520, 526; II 261, 314, 416, 430–31, 618; III 531; IV 83 (*see also* Socialist Realism)
  in Latin American literatures, I 87, 112, 323, 324, 434, 454; II 154; III 170; IV 27, 535
  neo-, III 260
  in South African literature, I 6
  in Third World literatures, I 96; IV 561
  and Socialist Realism, IV 252, 254
  in Western European literatures, II 101, 314, 515, 557, III 568, IV 303, 310, 378; Austrian, II 393, 394, IV 320; Danish, I 537, 538, II 590, III 195; English, I 548–49, II 38, 182; French, II 143, 144, 146, III 397; German, I 325–27, II 219, 221, 222, IV 584; Italian, II 113, III 312, 480, IV 143
Marxist criticism, I 78, 314; III 79–82, 84, 365; IV 338, 612, 641. *See also:* Marxism; Socialist Realism
  American, I 67; III 80, 119, 120, 126; IV 334
  English, II 52; III 116
  French, I 202, 278; II 68, 143, 148; III 80–81
  German, I 239–41; III 79, 81–82, 110
  Hungarian, III 150–51
  Italian, III 81, 86, 88
  and Jewish culture, I 239
  Polish, III 82
  Soviet, III 79, 97, 100; IV 115 (*see also* Socialist Realism)
  structuralist, III 57–58, 80
März, Alexander, I 363
Mas'adī, Mahmūd, IV 473; V 409–10
Masaoka Shiki, II 494, 497; III 238–39
Masaoka Tsunenori. *See* Masaoka Shiki
Masaryk, Thomas G., I 403; III 169; IV 133
Masebenza, B. J., IV 293
Masefield, John, II 35; III 239–40
Masegabio, Philippe, IV 703
Masekela, Paul Selaelo Mosehle, IV 294
Masferrer, Alberto, V 122
Mashinini, Emma, V 567
Mashuwa, Pal Tshindane, IV 294
Masing, Uku, II 61; III 240–41
Mason, Ann L.
  on Grass, II 276
Mason, Bobbie Ann, V 25
Mason, H. T.
  on Montherlant, III 306
Massa, Ann, III 75
Massaki, André, IV 703
Massis, Henri, II 143; III 88
Masson, André, I 127; III 42, 252

Masson, Loys, III 252
Masters, Edgar Lee, I 60, 65; III 75, 241–42; IV 141
  influence of, I 567; II 623
Masters, Olga, V 52
Mastretta, Angeles, V 421
Mastronardi, Lucio, II 473; III 243
Masuda Masako, V 648
Masuri S. N., IV 232
Materer, Timothy
  on Lewis, Wyndham, III 69
Matevossian, Hrant, I 119, 122; III 243–44
Matevski, Mateja, IV 698
Mathers, Peter, I 149
Mathewson, Rufus W., Jr.
  on Pasternak, Boris, III 485
  on Solzhenitsyn, IV 276
Mathieu, Noel. *See* Emmanuel, Pierre
Mathivha, M. E. R., IV 294
Matić, Dušan, IV 693
Matilla, Luis, V 574
Matip, Benjamin, I 388
Matković, Marijan, IV 696
Matlala, Elias, IV 291
Mätmurad, Tölepbergen, IV 522
Matoš, Antun, IV 695
Matos Paoli, Francisco, IV 316
Matras, Christian, I 542
Matsepe, Kgadime, IV 291
Matshili, R. R., IV 294
Matson, Alex, IV 562
Matsuo Bashō, II 495
Matta, Joaquin Dias Cordeiro da, I 95
Matthew, Brian, V 51
Matthews, W. K.
  on Brigadere, III 16
Matthey, Pierre-Louis, IV 387
Matthiessen, F. O., III 113, 120; V 47
Matthiessen, Peter, V 26
Mattos, Alvar de. *See* Mutis, Alvaro
Mattsson, Guss, II 99
Matuška, Alexander
  on Čapek, Karel, I 407
Matute, Ana María, II 265; III 244–45; IV 307–8; V 570
Maunick, Edouard, V 233
Matveeva, Novella, IV 107
al-Matwī, al-'Arūsī, IV 473
Maugham, Robin, III 535
Maugham, W. Somerset, II 39, 49; III 245–46; IV 586
  on Frank, Bruno, II 131
Mauliņš, Jānis, III 18
Maulnier, Thierry, II 143
Maumela, Titus N., IV 294
Maung Gyi, U, I 367
Maung Hmaing, Mit-sata. *See* Thahkin Ko-daw Hmaing
Maung Htin, I 367, 368
Maung Lun. *See* Thahkin Ko-daw Hmaing
Maung Tha-ya, I 368
Maunick, Édouard J., III 252
Maupassant, Guy de, II 487
  film adaptations of, II 96
  influence of, I 49, 116, 191, 624; III 245, 246, 591
Maura, Antonio, I 168
Maurhut, Richard. *See* Traven, B.
Mauriac, Claude, III 246–47, 381
Mauriac, François, II 138, 142, 143, 144, 286; III 246, 247–50; V 632
  on Claudel, I 473
  on Wiesel, V 632, 633
  critical excerpts on, III 250–52
  on Genet, II 208
  on Greene, II 291
  influence of, III 286; V 458
  on Montherlant, III 305
  on Sollers, IV 266
Mauriņa, Zenta, III 17
Mauritian literature, III 252–53
  in Creole, III 252, 253

in English, III 252–53
in French, III 252, 253
Maurois, André, II 143; III 253–55
  on Alain, I 35
Mauron, Charles, II 148; III 83–84
Maurras, Charles, I 252; II 134, 138, 144; III 88
Mauss, Marcel
  influence of, I 205
Mauthner, Fritz
  influence of, III 315
Mavor, Osborne Henry. *See* Bridie, James
Maxamed Cabdulle Xasan, Sayid, IV 278
Maximov, Vladimir, IV 113
May, Keith M.
  on Huxley, II 421–22
May, Rollo, III 515
Mayakovsky, Vladimir Vladimirovich, I 104, 379, 513; II 71, 185, 186, 564; III 98, 255–57, 482; IV 105, 114, 253; V 180, 181, 621
  on Balmont, I 183
  influence of, I 177; II 38, 371; III 420; IV 476, 575, 611, 681, 683
Maydanska, Sofiya, V 613, 614
Maylin, Beyimbet, II 570
Mayoral, Marina, V 570, 573
Mayorov, Yakov, II 105
Mayröcker, Friederike, I 158; V 53, 55, 333, 410–11
Mayzel, Nakhman, IV 683
Mazālī, Muhammad, IV 473
Mazeline, Guy, II 143
Mazhari, Kubra, I 19
al-Māzinī, Ibrāhīm, II 4, 5; V 458
Mazrui, Alamin, V 352
Mazumdar, Anita. *See* Desai, Anita
Mazzaro, Jerome
  on Lowell, Robert, III 143
Mbhombhi, E. G. W., IV 292
Mbise, Ismail, IV 419
Mbotela, James Juma, II 578; IV 418
Mbuli, Mzwakhe, V 566
McAlmon, Robert, IV 635
McArthur, Alexander, IV 180
McAuley, James, I 147–48
McCabe, Brian, V 546
McCarthy, Cormac, I 69
McCarthy, Desmond
  on Cocteau, I 478
McCarthy, Mary, I 541; III 257–58; IV 641; V 525, 640
McClatchy, J. D., V 28
McClure, Michael, I 72
McCorkle, Jill, V 26
McCourt, James, I 70
McCrae, Hugh, I 146
McCullers, Carson, I 74, 569; III 258–59; IV 630
McDermott, Alice, V 25
McDowell, Deborah, V 222
McElroy, Joseph, V 26
McEwan, Ian, V 210
McEwen, Gwendolyn, I 396
McGahern, John, V 319
McGrath, Patrick, V 210
McGrath, Thomas
  on Neruda, III 371–72
McGuane, Thomas, I 273
McGuffie, Jessie, IV 179
McGuinness, Frank, V 317
McHale, Tom, I 70
McIlvanney, William, IV 181; V 544, 545
McInerney, Jay, V 26
McKay, Claude, II 54; III 259–60; V 190
McKeon, Richard, III 124
McLuhan, Herbert Marshall; V 108, 109
  on Dos Passos, I 583
McMillan, Hugh, V 547
McMurtry, Larry, V 24, 411–13
McNally, Terrence, V 28
McPherson, Jay, I 396

Mda, Zakes, IV 290; V 566
Mead, George H.
  influence of, II 78
Meavenn, Fant Rozenn, II 151
Mechakra, Yamina, V 13
Meckel, Christoph, II 222; V 413–14
Meckel, Eberhard, V 413
Meckier, Jerome
  on Huxley, II 420–21
Mécs, László, I 527; II 414
Meddeb, Abdelwahab, IV 474; V 356
Medeiros, Tomás, IV 147
Medenis, Jānis, III 16–17
Meder, Cornel, III 158
Medina, Enrique, V 40
Medina, Fernando, I 290
Medio, Dolores, V 570
Medoff, Mark, V 29
Medrano, Francisco, V 66
Medu, Jemba, I 387
Medvedev, Pavel, III 100
Medvedev, Roy, IV 212
Medzarentz, Missak, I 119
Meek, James, V 547
Meese, Elizabeth, V 222
Meffre, Joël, II 153
Megged, Aharon, II 466; V 414
Mehren, Stein, III 260–61, 402
Mehring, Franz, III 79
Mehring, Walter, I 156; III 261–63
Meigs, Mary, V 109
Meier, Gerhard, IV 384
Meier, Herbert, IV 383
Meir, Veijo, II 102–3
Meireles, Cecília, I 321; III 263–64, 295
Meister, Ernst, II 221
Mejía Sánchez, Ernesto, V 123
Mejía Vallejo, Manuel, I 484; V 145, 146, 414–16
Mekas, Jonas, II 95
Mekul, Esad, IV 699
Melas, Spyros, II 284
Melhau, Jan dau, II 153
Méliès, Georges, II 94
Melkonian, Zareh, I 121
Mell, Max, I 156
Melle, Johannes van, IV 286
Melnyk, Vasyl, V 614
Mellos, Elias. See Venezis, Elias
Melo Neto, João Cabral de, I 87, 323; III 295; V 88, 89, 416–17
Meltzer, David, I 72
Melville, Herman, I 57, 58, 59, 488, 505; III 142; V 543
  criticism on, III 87, 120, 125, 428; IV 587, 644
Memmi, Albert, IV 473; V 355, 417–18
Menai, Huw, IV 608
Menart, Janez, IV 698
Menasse, Robert, V 53, 54
Menchaca, Antonio, V 573
Menchú, Rigoberta, V 121
Mencken, H. L., I 67, 589; III 62, 111–12, 264–65; V 105, 642
  influence of, III 74; IV 29
  on Wells, IV 603–4
Mendele Mokher Sforim, II 465; IV 682–83
Mendeleeva, Lyubov, I 282, 283
Mendelson, Edward, III 612
Mendès, Catulle, III 293
  influence of, I 190
Mendes, Murilo, I 321
Mendes, Orlando, III 323
Méndez Ferrín, X. L., IV 315; V 573
Mendoza, Jaime, I 289
Mendoza, María Luisa, V 421
Menéndez Pidal, Ramón, III 96; IV 29, 300
Menéndez y Pelayo, Marcelino, III 95; IV 300
Meneses, Vidaluz, V 124
Menga, Guy, I 487

Menghini, Felice, IV 388
Menghistu Lemma, II 64, 65
Menil, René, II 154
Menon, Vallathol Narayana, II 434; III 265–66
Menshutin, A., IV 240
Menton, Seymour
  on Heras León, IV 317
M. E. R., IV 286
Mera, Juan León, II 1
Mercan, Hasan, IV 701
Mercanton, Jacques, IV 386
Merchant, Vivien, III 534
Meredith, George, II 328, 330; IV 348, 552
Merezhkovsky, Dmitry Sergeevich, II 376; III 98, 266–67, 294; IV 103
Mergeai, Jean, I 224
Meri, Veijo, III 267–69
Meriluoto, Aila, II 102; IV 562
Merino, José María, V 573
Merleau-Ponty, Maurice, II 146; III 57, 151, 515, 517; V 500
Merquior, José Guilherme, V 91
Merrill, Charles E., III 269
Merrill, James, I 71; III 269–70; V 27
Merrill, Stuart, IV 390–91
Mertens, Pierre, I 224
Merton, Thomas, I 434; IV 102
Merwin, W. S., I 73; III 270–71; V 27, 28
Meschendörfer, Adolf, IV 84
Mesens, E. L. T., I 225
Mestel, Jacob, III 319
Mesterton, Erik, I 311
Mészöly, Miklós (Miklós Molnár), V 296, 419–20
Metcalf, John, V 109
Metz, Christian, III 98
Mew, Charlotte, II 36
Mexican literature, III 271–75; V 420–23
  the Atheneum of Youth group of, II 256; III 271, 273–74; IV 29
  the *Contemporáneos* group of, II 257; III 273; IV 565
  Cristero rebellion (1926–28) as subject of, IV 27
  the *Estridentistas* of, III 273
  existentialism in, I 125; III 273
  film techniques in, IV 27, 671
  literary criticism in, II 179; III 97, 274, 373; IV 517
  major writers of, see: Agustín; Arreola; Azuela, Arturo; Azuela, Mariano; Carballido; Castellanos; Elizondo; Fuentes; Garro; González Martínez; Gorostiza; Guzmán, Martín Luis; Hernández, Luisa Josefina; Ibargüengoitia; Leñero; López y Fuentes; Magdaleno; Nervo; Novo; Pacheco; Paz; Pellicer; Poniatowska; Revueltas; Reyes; Romero, José Rubén; Rulfo; Sabines; Sainz; Solares; Spota; Usigli; Villaurrutia; Yáñez
  also writing in English, see Fuentes
  in literary criticism, see Reyes
  the Mexican Revolution as subject of, I 169; II 309–10; III 138, 176, 271–72, 273, 274; IV 27, 671; V 56, 57, 422
  post-, III 272
  modernism in, II 257; III 293, 373; V 457
  the New Novel in, II 21, 179; III 272, 382
  "novel of revolution" in, IV 28
  the Obregón assassination as subject of, III 274
  the *Onda* (Wave) movement in, I 23; III 272; IV 130
  stream-of-consciousness technique in, IV 27, 100–101, 565

student demonstration (1968) as subject of, III 272, 273, 495
  surrealism in, III 273, 494; IV 27, 671; V 421, 457
  symbolism in, III 271, 494; IV 392
  ultraism in, III 273
Meyer, Bernard C., II 162
Meyer, Conrad Ferdinand, I 152; IV 382
  influence of, IV 342
Meyer, Doris
  on Allende, V 21
  on Poniatowska, V 496
Meyer, E. Y., IV 383; V 423–24
Meyer, Gustav. See Meyrink, Gustav
Meyerhold, Vsevolod, I 90; IV 114, 269
Meyers, Jeffrey
  on Lewis, Wyndham, III 69
Meylan, Elisabeth, IV 383
Meyrink, Gustav, I 153; III 275–76
Meysenbug, Malwida von, IV 74
Mezu, Sebastian O., III 392
Mgombe, James, III 188
Mhac an tSaoi, Maire, II 461
Miao Hsiu, IV 232
Micaelsen, Stubb, III 403
Michael, Ib, V 161
Michaelides, Vassilis, I 518
Michaux, Henri, I 224–25; II 141, 144; III 276–78; IV 371; V 229, 233, 564
Michelangelo
  Freud on, II 159, 160
Michelet, Jules, I 202; III 501
Micheli, Silvia, III 366
Michiels, Ivo, I 221
Michnik, Adam, V 492
Mickel, Karl, II 222
Mickiewicz, Adam, II 318; V 292
  criticism of, IV 666–67
Middleton, Christopher, V 72
Middleton, Stanley, V 208
Miedzyrzecki, Artur, III 556
Mielzinger, Jo, IV 630
Mieses Burgos, Franklin, IV 316
Mieželaitis, Eduardas, III 133; V 393
Mifsud-Bonnici, Carmelo, III 203
Miguéis, José Rodrigues, III 568
Miguel, André, I 225
Mihăescu, Gib, IV 81
Mihăieş, Mircea, V 521
Mihăilescu, Dan C., V 521
Mihalić, Slavko, IV 696
Mihardja, Achdiat Karta. See Achdiat Karta Mihardja
Mihura, Miguel, IV 303
Mikanza, Mobyem M. K., IV 703
Mikhaylov, Nikolay. See Liliev, Nikolay
Mikhoels, Solomon (Shloyme), III 229; IV 684
Mikolla, Millosh Gjergj, I 39
Mikro, IV 286
Mikszáth, Kálmán, II 619
Mileck, Joseph
  on Hesse, II 370
Miles, David H.
  on Hofmannsthal, II 388
  on Lukács, III 153
Miles, John, IV 287
Miles, Keith
  on Grass, II 276
Milev, Geo, I 358
Milgate, Rodney, I 149
Miliukov, P. N., V 465
Miliusz, József, IV 85
Millás, Juan José, V 573
Millàs-Raurell, Josep M., IV 312
Millay, Edna St. Vincent, I 65; III 278–79
  criticism on, III 103
Miller, Arthur, I 73–74; II 97, 179; III 279–80; V 28, 523
  influence of, III 511
Miller, Henry, I 70, 432; II 161; III 280–

82, 394, 488, 617; IV 257; V 242
criticism on, IV 199
Miller, J. Hillis, I 75–76; III 125, 521;
  V 168
  on Eliot, T. S., II 20
  on Williams, William Carlos, IV 638–
    39
Miller, Liam, V 431
Miller, Ruth, V 566
Millett, Kate, V 221
Millgate, Michael
  on Faulkner, II 84
Millin, Philip, III 282
Millin, Sarah Gertrude, III 282–83; IV
  288
Milner, Marion, II 157
Miłosz, Czesław, III 283–84, 555, 557,
  558, 560; V 391, 491, 492
  on Herbert, Zbigniew, II 361
  on Różewicz, IV 99
  as subject, V 493
Milton, John
  criticism on, II 30, 178; III 113, 114,
    116, 118
Mimouni, Rachid, V 12, 16
Mīna, Hannā, IV 399; V 424–25
Minangkabau literature. *See under* Indone-
  sian literature
Minatti, Ivan, IV 697
Minco, Margo, III 378
Mine, Urkiye, I 519
Minkoff, Nokhum Borekh, II 248; IV 683
Min Kyaw, I 367
Minne, Richard, I 222; IV 69
Min Shin, I 367
Minter, David
  on Faulkner, II 85
Minulescu, Ion, IV 79
Miraji, III 459
Miralles, Alberto, V 574
Miranda, Jaime, V 134
Mirande, Jean, II 151
Miras, Domingo, V 574
Mirbeau, Octave, II 137; III 174
Miriam, III 553
Miró, Gabriel, I 441; III 284–85; IV 307
Miró, Joan, III 42; IV 371
Miró, Ricardo, V 125
Miron, Dan, V 552
Miron, Gaston, I 398; V 233
Miró Quesada, César, V 535
Mirshakar, Mirsaid, IV 408–9, 410
Mirsky, D. S.
  on Khodasevich, II 583
Mirzo, Ghaffor, IV 409
Mishima Yukio, II 481, 494, 497; III
  285–87; V 334, 336
Mishra, Godavaris, II 436
Mishra, Lakshminarayan, II 437
Mishra, Vijay C., III 455
Misiṇa, Māra, III 19
Miškinis, Antanas, III 130
Mistral, Frédéric, II 152; V 193
Mistral, Gabriela, I 455; III 287–89, 294;
  V 104, 386, 480
Mita Masahiro, V 335
Mitchell, James Leslie. *See* Gibbon,
  Lewis Grassic
Mitchell, Ken, V 109
Mitchison, Naomi, IV 180
Mithat, Ahmet, IV 475
Mitko, Thimi, I 38
Mitrei, Kedra. *See* Korepanov, Dmitry
Mittelholzer, Edgar, II 54; III 289–90
Mitterer, Felix, V 54
Mitxelena, Salbatore. *See* Iñurritza
Miyamoto Kenji, II 496
Miyamoto Yuriko, II 496
Miyazawa Kenji, II 496; III 290–91;
  V 336
Miyoshi Tatsuji, V 336
Mizener, Arthur, III 582
  on Fitzgerald, F. Scott, II 110

Mjedja, Ndre, I 38
Mkhas-btsun-bzaṅ-po, IV 444
Mkhize, E. E. N. T., IV 296
Mkufya, W. E., IV 419
Mlilo, Sithembile O., IV 713
Młyńk, Jurij, III 156
Młyńkowa, Marja, III 156
Mmileng, Masego T., IV 293
Mňačko, Ladislav, I 526; III 291
Mnthali, Felix, III 188
Mnyampala, Mathias E., IV 417
Mo, Timothy, V 209
Moatsou, Dora, IV 539
Moberg, Vilhelm, III 292–93; IV 378,
  381
Mochtar Lubis, II 442
Mocoancoeng, J. G., IV 292
modernism, II 455; III 293–95; V 497
  American, I 310; V 277, 525
  Asian, III 460; IV 688; V 322, 402,
    450, 470, 540, 622, 650
  Brazilian, I 86–87, 88, 108–9, 185,
    321–22; III 135, 263, 294–95; IV
    21, 38; V 417
  Central American, I 544, 545; III 294;
    V 123
  East European, I 217, 275–76, 358,
    359, 520, 525; II 606; III 294,
    552–54, 563; IV 108–9, 493–94,
    575, 683, 694–95, 697; V 560
  and expressionism, II 69
  Mexican, II 257; III 293, 373; V 457
  North African, V 130, 251, 409
  opponents of, I 268; III 618
  precursors of, I 483; III 294, 577
  Spanish American, I 20, 289, 454; II 1,
    364–65; III 293–94; IV 31, 515–
    16, 542, 543; V 146, 332, 333
    Argentine, I 110–11; III 148, 225,
      293
    Peruvian, I 461; II 258; III 293, 509,
      510
  and symbolism, I 110; III 293, 294;
    IV 392
  Western European, I 321; II 293, 377,
    427, 510; III 167, 294, 567; IV
    20, 118, 189, 301, 304, 307, 311,
    312, 382, 531, 532; V 317, 353,
    570
  Scandinavian, I 539, 540, 567; II 11,
    100, 313; III 2, 73, 74, 195, 294;
    IV 45, 217, 266, 330, 377, 563
Modiano, Patrick, V 231, 426–28
Modisane, Bloke, IV 289–90
Modupe Paris, II 302
Moen, Petter, III 400
Moens, Wies, I 222
Moers, Ellen, V 221, 222
Mofokeng, Sophonia Machabe, IV 291
Mofolo, Thomas, III 49, 194, 295–96;
Mohamed, M. S., IV 418
Mohamed, S. A., IV 418
Mohamad Ambri, II 444
Mohammed, Z. H., IV 417
Mohanty, Gopinath, II 438; III 296–97
Mohanty, Khanu Charan, III 296
Mohapi, Michael, III 50
Mohd, Affandi Hassan, III 190
Moholy-Nagy, Laszlo
  on Joyce, II 530
Moi, Toril, V 289
Moiloa, James Jantjies, IV 291
Moix, Ana María, V 570, 573
Moix, Terenci, IV 313; V 573
Moldavian (S.S.R.) literature, III 297–98
Molden, Ernst, III 592
Moldova, György, IV 416; V 297
Mole, John, V 546
Molema, Moliri Silas, I 307
Molière, V 596
  influence of, I 99, 532; IV 335, 399,
    517; V 225
Molina, Enrique, V 41

Molina, Juan Ramón, V 123
Molina Foix, Vicente, V 574
Molinari, Ricardo E., I 111
Møller, P. L., V 577
Molnár, Ferenc, II 413; III 298–99;
  V 391
Molnár, Miklós. *See* Mészöly, Miklós
Moloney, Michael F.
  on Mauriac, François, III 251
Moloto, D. P., IV 293
Momaday, N(atachee) Scott, V 428–29
Mombert, Alfred, II 216
  influence of, IV 265
Momigliano, Attilio, I 265; III 86
Mon, Franz (Franz Löffelholz), II 222;
  V 429–30
Monaghan, David M.
  on Davies, Robertson, V 167
Mondlane, Eduardo, III 322
Monet, Claude, I 250; V 263
Mongolian literature, III 299–301
  See also under Buryat literature
Monnerot, Jules, II 147, 154
Monnier, Jean-Pierre, IV 386
Monokutuba literature. *See* Congolese
  literature
monologue intérieure. See stream-of-con-
  sciousness technique, the
Monory, Jacques, V 399
Monroe, Harriet, III 278; IV 140, 337
Monroe, Marilyn, III 279, 280
Monsiváis, Carlos, V 422
Mont, Paul de, I 223
Montague, John, II 460; III 165; V 317,
  430–31
  on MacDiarmid, III 166
  as subject, V 367
Montaigne, Michel Eyquem de, V 367
Montale, Eugenio, II 185, 361, 468, 470,
  471, 472; III 159, 301–2, 527; IV
  120, 164, 452, 707
  on D'Annunzio, II 469
  influence of, II 471
Montalvo, Juan, II 1
Monteforte Toledo, Mario, I 435
Monteiro, Adolfo Casais, III 567
Monteiro, Luís de Sttau, III 569
Monteiro-Grillo, Joaquim Tomás. *See*
  Kim, Tomaz
Monteiro Lobato. *See* Lobato, Monteiro
Montejo, Victor, V 121
Montello, Josué, V 88
Montenegro, Carlos, I 289
Montero, Manuel, V 574
Montero, Rosa, V 570
Montes de Oca, Marco Antonio, III 273
Montfort, Sylvia, V 232
Montgomerie, William, V 547
Montgomery, Marion, I 69
Montherlant, Henry de, II 142, 143, 145,
  147; III 302–5
  critical excerpts on, III 305–6
  influence of, II 359
Monti, Ricardo, V 42, 43
Montiel Ballesteros, Adolfo, IV 516
Montis, Kostas, I 518
Montreuil, Gaétane de, I 398
Monyaise, D. P. Semakaleng, IV 293
Monzón, Telesforo, II 151
Moodie, Susannah, I 396
Moody, William Vaughn, I 64
Moorcock, Michael, V 208
Moodie, Susannah, I 396
Moody, William Vaughn, I 64
Moorcock, Michael, V 208
Moodie, Bai, III 71
Moore, Bai, III 71
Moore, Brian, II 462; III 307; V 319
Moore, Douglas, I 235
Moore, G. E., II 121, 122
Moore, Geoffrey
  on Lewis, Sinclair, III 64
Moore, George, II 41, 49, 459, 461, 462;
  III 307–9; IV 674; V 316, 318
  influence of, I 246
Moore, Gerald
  on Osofisan, III 393   **701**

Moore, Marianne, I 65, 71, 515; III 309–10; IV 635
  criticism on, I 274, 286; IV 644
  influence of, I 267; III 377; IV 627
Moore, Mary Warner, III 309
Moore, T. Sturge
  criticism on, III 123; IV 644
Moorhouse, Frank, V 52
Mopeli-Paulus, Attwell Sidwell, III 49, 50; IV 291
Móra, Ferenc, II 414
Morad, Gowhar. See Sa'edi, Gholam-Hossein
Moraes, Wenceslau de, III 566
Moraga, Cherrie, V 222
Morais, Vinícius de, I 321–22
Morand, Paul, II 142; III 310–11
  on Giraudoux, II 244
Morante, Elsa, II 473; III 311–12
Moravia, Alberto, II 472, 474; III 311, 312–14
Morax, René, IV 387
Mørch, Dea Trier, V 160
Morcinek, Gustaw, III 556
Mordell, Albert, II 162
Mordinov, Nikolay Yegorovich. See Achchygyya, Amma
Mordvin literature. See under Finno-Ugric literatures of the Soviet Union
More, Paul Elmer, I 67; III 112
Moréas, Jean, I 190; II 136; IV 389, 391
  influence of, IV 649
Moreau, Marcel, I 224
Moreno, Fulgencio R., III 473
Moreno-Duran, Rafael Humberto, V 145–47, 431–32
Morgan, Charles, II 53; III 93
Morgan, Edwin, V 546, 547
  on MacDiarmid, III 166
Morgan, Elena Puw, IV 606
Morgan, Eluned, IV 606
Morgenstern, Christian, II 216; III 314–15, 595
Móricz, Zsigmond, I 172; II 412–13, 543; III 316–18
Mörike, Eduard
  influence of, II 366
Mori Ōgai, II 485, 496; III 315–16, 349; V 321, 322
Mori Reiko, V 335
Mori Rintarō. See Mori Ōgai
Morisseau, Roland, V 485
Morley, Patricia A.
  on White, IV 623–24
Mörne, Arvid, II 99; IV 265
Moro, Artur, II 105
Moro, César, III 511
Moroccan literature, III 318–20
  in Arabic, III 318–19; V 250–52
  in French, III 319–20; V 70–71, 138–39, 355–56
  See also Maghrebian literature
Moroke, S. A., IV 293
Moroz, Hennady, V 613
Morrell, Lady Ottoline, III 21
Morris, Andrés, I 435
Morris, C. B.
  on Guillén, Jorge, II 298
Morris, Charles W.
  influence of, III 121
Morris, Lewis, IV 607
Morris, Mary, V 26
Morris, Robert K.
  on Powell, III 582–83
Morris, William
  influence of, I 235; IV 674
Morris, Willie, II 522
Morris, Wright, I 68; III 320–21
Morris-Jones, Sir John, IV 605
Morrison, Blake, V 212
Morrison, David, V 547
Morrison, John, I 147
Morrison, Toni, I 69; III 321–22; V 24

Morrissette, Bruce
  on Robbe-Grillet, IV 61
Morstin, Ludwik Hieronim, III 556
Morsy, Zaghloul, III 320
Mortensen, Henning, V 160
Mortimer, John, V 207
Mortimer, Penelope, III 535
Mosendz, Leonid, IV 496
Mosley, Nicholas, III 535
Moss, Howard, I 71
Mostaghānmī, Ahlām, I 46; V 14
Mota, Mauro, I 323
Motherwell, Robert, III 419
Motinggo Boesye, II 442
Motion, Andrew, V 212
Motoori Noringa, V 368
Motta, Giuseppe, IV 387
Motzan, Peter, IV 84
Moule, Horace, II 328
Moulier, Jules, II 150
Mounier, Emmanuel, II 143, 146; III 502
Mourão-Ferreira, David, III 569
Mourselas, Kostas, II 284
Moussali, Antoine, V 84
Mouzat, Joan, II 152
Movsessian, Alexander. See Shirvanzadeh
Mo Yen (Mo Yan, Kuan Mo-yeh), V 137, 425–26
Moyo, Aaron, IV 714
Mozambican literature, III 322–24
  in Portuguese, III 322–24
  in Ronga, III 322
  war with Rhodesia as subject of and of other literatures, IV 297
Mozart, Wolfgang Amadeus, II 372; V 368
  influence of, II 250; IV 200
Mpashi, Stephen, IV 704
Mphahlele, Ezekiel, III 324–25; IV 289–90, 705
Mphande, Lupenga, III 188
Mpofu, Isaac N., IV 713
Mqhayi, Samuel Edward Krne, IV 294–95
Mrevlishvili, M., II 213
Mrevlishvili, Vakeli, II 213–14
Mrożek, Sławomir, III 325–26, 559; IV 433; V 366, 492, 493
Msimang, C. T., IV 296
Mtombeni, B. K. M., IV 292
Mtshali, Oswald Mbuyiseni, IV 290
Mt. Suphardi, II 443–44
Mtutuzeli, Matshoba, V 567
Muaka, Angaluki, V 351
Muchnic, Helen
  on Gorky, II 264
  on Solzhenitsyn, IV 276
Mudimbe, V. Y., IV 704
Mugo, Micere, V 351
Mugur, Florin, IV 82
Muhammad V, King (of Morocco), III 318
Muhammadi, Umar, IV 520
Muhammad Latiff Muhammad, IV 233
Muhammed Haji Salleh, III 191
Muhando, Penina, IV 418
Muhtar, Ahmad, II 628
Muir, Edwin, II 35, 36; III 326–28; IV 179, 180
  on Woolf, Virginia, IV 662
Muir, Willa, V 546
Mujica Láinez, Manuel, I 112; III 328–29
Mukařovský, Jan, III 99, 100
  on Čapek, Karel, I 405
Mukasa, Ham, IV 489
Mükhamedzhanov, Qaltay, I 164; II 570
Mukherjee, Bharati, V 109, 310, 392, 432–33
  on Rushdie, V 529
Mukhtar, Asqad, IV 521
Mukhtarov, Guseyn, IV 481
Mukka, Timo K., II 103
Mulaisho, Dominic, IV 704

Mulder, Tiny, III 380
Muldoon, Paul, V 318
Mulikita, Fwanyanga, IV 704
Mu Ling-Nu, IV 233
Mulisch, Harry, III 329–30, 378
Müller, Dominik, IV 385
Müller, Heiner, II 223; III 330–31
Müller, Inge, III 330
Müller-Guttenbrunn, Adam, IV 84
Multatuli, II 445; III 375, 379
Muñárriz, Jesús, V 574
Münchhausen, Börries von, II 216
Munch-Petersen, Gustaf, I 537
Mungan, Murathan, V 607
Mungoshi, Charles, IV 712
Munīf, 'Abd al-Rahmān (Abdelrahman), II 458; V 286, 329, 433–34
Muñiz, Carlos, I 355; IV 303; V 574
Munk, Georg. See Winckler, Paula
Munk, Kaj, I 537–38; III 331–33
Munonye, John, III 392–93
Muñoz Seca, Pedro, IV 301
Munro, Alice (Alice Laidlaw), I 397; V 109, 434–36
Munro, Harold, II 35
Munro, Neil, IV 180
Munson, Gorham B.
  on Giraudoux, II 244–45
Muordinap, Nyukulay Jögyörebis. See Achchygyya, Amma
Muoth, Giachen Caspar, IV 389
Muqimiy, Muhammad Khoja-oghli, IV 521
Murad, Gowhar. See Sa'edi, Gholam-Hossein
Murakami Haruki, V 336, 436–37
Murakami Ryū, II 497; V 335
Murasaki Shikibu, II 31
Muratova, Kira, V 623
Murdoch, Iris, I 310; III 45, 47, 48; III 333–34, 518–19; V 207
Murillo, Enrique, V 574
Murillo, Rosario, V 124
Murn-Alexandrov, Josip, IV 721
Murname, Gerald, V 52
Murnau, F. W., II 94
Murphy, Richard, II 460; III 334–35; V 317
Murphy, Thomas, V 317
Murray, Charles, IV 177
Murray, Gilbert, III 84
Murray, Les, V 52
Murray, Margaret, II 278
Murry, John Middleton, III 21, 84, 117–18
Murugaiyan, R., IV 324
Muryalelana, II 444
Mūsā, Nabawiyya, V 200
Mūsā, Sabrī, V 201
Mūsā al-Husaynī, Ishāq, V 473
Muscat-Azzopardi, Gużè, III 203
Muschg, Adolf, IV 382–83; V 437–38
Muschg, Walter, III 109
Muse, Clarence, II 405
Mushakoji Saneatsu, II 496
Mushketyk, Yury, V 614
Musiał, Grzegorz, V 493
Musiba, E. A., IV 418
Musil, Robert, I 154, 156; III 335–37; IV 360; V 238, 391
  critical excerpts on, III 337–39
Müsrepov, Ghabit Makhmud-ūlï, II 570
Musset, Alfred de, II 66
Mussolini, Benito, II 87, 185; IV 58
  criticism of, II 187
Müstafin, Ghabiden, II 570
Mustaghni, Abdul Ali, I 19
Mustapha Kamal Yassin, III 191
Mutis, Alvaro (Alvar de Mattos), I 483; V 438–39
Mutrān, Khalīl, II 4; III 32; V 36, 285
Mutswairo, Solomon M., IV 714
Muuse Cumar Islaam, IV 278

Nenzhelele, P. H., IV 294
neorealism, I 222; II 142–43; III 365–66;
    IV 298, 301, 302, 308, 414, 451,
    548; V 135, 465, 569, 570. *See*
    also: postrealism; realism
  Danish, I 286, 536, 541; II 555
  Italian, I 257; II 471, 472–73; III 56,
    365–66, 491
  Portuguese, III 545, 568; IV 18, 19,
    256
    in Angola, IV 282
  precursors of, I 253, 423; II 471–72;
    IV 548
neoromanticism, I 351; II 425–26; III 15,
    40; IV 217, 413, 496, 505; V 571
  and literary criticism, III 117–18
Nepalese literature, III 366–68
Nepali literature. *See* Nepalese literature
  and under Indian literature
Neris, Salomėja, III 130
Neruda, Pablo, I 87, 455; III 368–71,
    477; IV 372; V 9, 81, 131–33,
    386, 391, 537, 591
  criticism on, III 96
    excerpts of, III 371–72
  influence of, I 586; III 257; IV 543; V
    610, 644
  as subject, V 558
Nerval, Gérard de
  criticism on, III 93
  influence of, II 140
Nervo, Amado, III 271, 293, 372–73;
    IV 392
Nesanovich, Stella
  on Tyler, V 610
Nesin, Aziz, III 373–74; IV 478–79;
    V 607
Nesin, Mehmet Nusret. *See* Nesin, Aziz
Nessi, Angelo, IV 388
Nestayko, Vsevolod, V 614
Nestroy, Johann, II 608
  influence of, I 601; V 568
Netherlands Antilles literature. *See under*
  Dutch-Caribbean literature
Netherlands literature, III 374–80
  in Dutch, III 374–79
  expressionism in, II 70
  the *Forum* group in, III 376; IV 555
  in Frisian, III 379–80
  literary criticism in, III 375; IV 73, 553
  major writers of, *see:* Achterberg;
    Berge, Ten; Blaman; Bordewijk;
    Boutens; Braak; Brouwers; Coupe-
    rus; Deyssel; Eeden; Heijermans;
    Leopold; Lucebert; Marsman, Hen-
    drik; Mulisch; Nijhoff; Noote-
    boom; Perron; Roland Holst; Ro-
    land Holst-van der Schalk;
    Schendel; Slauerhoff; Verwey;
    Vestdijk
  the Movement of the Eighties in, I 308;
    II 2; III 374–75, 378
  Nazi occupation as subject of, III 376,
    378, 380; IV 555
  new factualism in, I 301
  De Stijl movement in, III 376
  symbolism in, I 308; III 47, 375
  De Vijftigers of, III 147, 377
  the Young Frisian movement of, III 379
Neto, António Agostinho, I 96, 97
Neto, Henrique Coelho, I 320
Neto, João Cabral de Melo. *See* Melo
  Neto, João Cabral de
Netshilema, Elias S., IV 294
neue Sachlichkeit. See new factualism
Neubauer, Carol E.
  on Angelou, V 33
Neuhaus, Volker
  on Grass, II 277
Neuhuys, Paul, I 225
Neumann, Erich, II 278
Neumann, Robert, I 155
Neumann, Stanislav Kostka, I 520
  influence of, III 181; IV 185, 656

Neumukovhani, Michael N., IV 294
Neustroev, Nikolay Denisovich, IV 670
Neutsch, Erik, III 331
Neveux, Georges, II 142
new factualism *(neue Sachlichkeit),* I 156,
    301; IV 92
  German, I 206; II 218, 562, 563; III
    350, 365; IV 184
New Criticism. *See under* American literary criticism
Newes, Tilly, IV 595
new historicism. *See* historicism
Newman, C. J., V 109
New Novel, the, I 371, 595; II 147, 148–
    49; III 247, 381–82, 427, 533; IV
    39, 59, 225, 267, 268; V 37, 68,
    230, 486, 641
  and existentialism, II 68
  and film, II 97
  New, IV 59–60
  and phenomenology, III 519
  and postrealism, III 570
  precursors of, I 426; II 240, 359;
    III 382; IV 96, 152
  rejection of, III 197
  and structuralism, IV 362
  techniques of
    in European literatures (non-French),
      I 343, 524, 540; II 55, 181, 220,
      313; III 382, 499, 568; IV 308,
      310, 382; V 127, 419, 570, 626
    in Latin American literatures, I 322,
      323; II 21, 179; III 272, 382; IV
      148
new realism
  German (Cologne School), II 220–21
  Hungarian, II 415
Newton, Judith, V 222
New Uyghur literature. *See* Uyghur litera-
  ture
New Zealand literature, III 382–84, 455
  major writers of, *see:* Baxter; Frame;
    Sargeson
Nexø, Martin Andersen, I 536; III 384–
    85; IV 254; V 159
Nezval, Vítězslav, I 521; III 385–87
Ngal, Mbwila Mpaang, IV 704
Ngcobo, Lauretta, V 567
Ngcobo, Moses, IV 296
Ngô, Tất Tố, IV 561
Ngubane, Jordan K., IV 296
Ngugi, James. *See* Ngugi wa Thiong'o
Ngugi wa Mirii, II 579; III 387
Ngugi wa Thiong'o, I 491; II 577–78,
    579; III 387–88; V 350, 357
Nguyễn Bá Học, IV 560
Nguyễn Chí Thiện, IV 562; V 618
Nguyễn Công Hoan, III 388; IV 561
Nguyễn Đình Thi, IV 561
Nguyễn Du, V 622
Nguyễn Hồng, IV 561
Nguyễn Mộng Giác, V 619
Nguyễn Ngọc Ngạn, V 619
Nguyễn Tuân (Nhất Lang), V 445–46
Nguyễn Trọng Thuật, IV 560
Nguyễn Tường-Tam. *See* Nhất-Linh
Nguyễn Văn Vĩnh, IV 560
Ngwana, D. M., IV 294
Nhất Lang. *See* Nguyễn Tuân
Nhất-Linh, III 388–89; IV 561
Nh. Dini, II 442
Nhok-Them, I 387
Nhouy Abhay, III 9
Niane, Djibril Tamsir, II 302; III 194
Niang, Lamine, IV 194
Nicaraguan literature. *See under* Central
  American literature
Nicholas, T. E., IV 606
Nicodin, Dinu, IV 81
Nicol, Davidson, IV 215
Nicolson, Harold, I 389
Niebuhr, Reinhold
  on Graves, II 278
Niedra, Aīda, III 16

Nielsen, Hans-Jørgen, I 540; V 160
Nielsen, Jørgen, I 538
Nielsen, Morten, I 538
Niemöller, Martin, IV 625
Nietzsche, Friedrich, II 66, 215; V 141,
    168, 228, 229, 500, 579, 616
  criticism on, III 82, 103, 126; IV 467
  influence of
    on American literature, II 504; III
      137, 430
    on Armenian literature, III 444
    on Australian literature, I 146; IV 42,
      43
    on Austrian literature, I 351; IV 47
    on Belgian literature, IV 551
    on Bulgarian literature, IV 246
    on Canadian literature, III 28
    on Chilean literature, V 378
    on Czech literature, III 169
    on Dutch literature, I 313
    on expressionism, II 69
    on Finnish literature, II 585; III 40;
      IV 265
    on French literature, I 205, 279; II
      138, 231; III 198
    on Georgian literature, II 194
    on German literature, I 244; II 215,
      219, 549; III 210, 315; IV 335,
      336, 595
    on Greek literature, II 573
    on Icelandic literature, IV 217
    on Irish literature, IV 674, 676
    on Italian literature, I 410, 543
    on Japanese literature, II 315, 316
    on Norwegian literature, II 75
    on Pakistani literature, III 458
    on Polish literature, II 254; III 607
    on Romanian literature, I 189, 275
    on Russian literature, I 90
    on Spanish literature, V 266, 571,
      572
    on Swedish literature, II 12; IV 352
  and postmodernism, V 498
  and psychology, II 536, 538
  as subject, V 410
Nieva, Francisco, V 574
Niger. *See* Dzanaity Ivan
Nigerian literature, III 389–93; V 446–50
  in Arabic, III 389
  the Biafran war as subject of, III 392,
    422, 423; IV 297
  in English, III 390–93
  in Hausa, III 389
  independence of as subject of, IV 297
  major writers of, in English, *see:* Ach-
    ebe; Amadi; Clark-Bekederemo;
    Ekwensi; Emecheta; Osofisan;
    Okara; Okigbo; Rotimi; Soyinka;
    Tutuola
  Mozambique/Rhodesian war as subject
    of, IV 297
  in Yoruba, III 389–90
Nijhoff, Martinus, III 376, 393–94
Nijlen, Jan van, I 221–22
Nikolaev, Sergey, II 105
Nikolaeva, Olesya, V 530
Nikolaides, Melis, I 518
Nikolaides, Nikos, I 518–19
Nilin, Pavel, IV 111
Niliūnas. *See* Čipkus, Alfonsas
Nima Yushij, II 454–55
Nimit Phumithawon, IV 430
Nimmanhemin, M. L. Buppha K. *See*
  Dokmai Sot
Nin, Anaïs, I 194; III 394–96; V 224
Nirala. *See* Tripathi, Suryakant
Nirk, Endel, II 62
Nishimura Yōkichi, II 465
Nishiwaki Junzaburō, V 336, 450–52
Nissaboury, El Mostefa, III 320
Der Nister, III 396–97; IV 683, 685
Niyazi, Munir, III 460–61
Niyaziy, Hamza Hakimzada, IV 521
Nizan, Paul, II 143; III 397

O'Connor, Flannery, I 68; III 415–16
  influence of, III 503
O'Connor, Frank, II 50, 461, 462, 463;
  III 416–17; V 235, 319, 601
  influence of, II 566
October Revolution, the. *See* Russian
  Revolution
Oculi, Okello, IV 490
Odaga, Asenath Bole, V 351
Odets, Clifford, I 66; III 417–18
Odian, Ervand, I 120
Odio, Eunice, V 124, 460–61
Ó Direáin, Máirtin, II 461
O'Donovan, Michael. *See* O'Connor,
  Frank
O'Dowd, Bernard, I 146
Ōe Kenzaburō, II 497; III 419; V 322,
  335, 436
O'Faoláin, Sean, II 50, 461; V 318
  on Greene, II 291
Ofeimum, Odia, V 447
O'Flaherty, Liam, II 50, 461; V 319
Oflazoğlu, Turan, IV 479; V 607
Ogali, Ogali A., III 393
Ogawa Kunio, V 238
Ogden, C. K., III 115; IV 41
Ogiwara Seisensui, II 497
Ognyanov, Khristo, I 360
Ogot, Grace, II 578; V 351
Ó Grianna, Séamus, II 461; V 318
Ogunde, Hubert, III 390
Ogundele, Ogunsina, III 390
Ogundipe-Leslie, Molara, V 447
Ogunmola, E. Kola, III 390
Ogunyemi, Wale, III 391
O'Hara, Frank, I 73; III 419–21; IV 373;
  V 47, 93
O'Hara, John, I 63; III 421–22; V 50
Ojaide, Tanure, V 447
Ojo, Gabriel E., III 390
Okai, Atukwe, II 227
Okakura Shirō, V 360
Okamoto Kanoko, V 605
Okara, Gabriel, III 392, 422
O'Kelly, Seamus, II 461
Oki, Ashaítsi. *See* Vekshina, Lina
Okigbo, Christopher, III 391, 422–23;
  V 446, 464
Økland, Einar, III 403
Okopenko, Andreas, I 158
Okot p'Bitek, III 497–98; IV 489, 490; V
  391
Okoye, Ifeoma, V 449
Okpewho, Isidore, III 393
Okri, Ben, V 449
Oks, Jaan, II 60
Oktay, Ahmet, V 606
Okudzhava, Bulat Shalvovich, III 424; IV
  107, 111
Ola, Virginia U.
  on Head, V 279
Olabimtan, Afolabi, III 390
Olbadia, René de, V 232
Olbracht, Ivan, I 522; III 425
O'Leary, John, IV 674
O'Leary, Juan E., III 473
Oles, Olexandr, IV 493, 494
Olesha, Yury Karlovich, III 425–26; IV
  109; V 531, 597
Oliphant, Dave, V 385
Olivares Figueroa, Rafael, IV 543
Oliveira, Carlos de, III 568, 569
Oliver, Joan, IV 312, 313
Oliver, Maria Antònia, V 570
Oliver, Mary, V 27
Oliver, Roger W.
  on Pirandello, III 545
Oliver, William I.
  on Carballido, V 114
Oliver Belmás, Antonio, V 148
Olivier, Juste, IV 385
Olivier, Laurence, III 173
Oller, Narcís, IV 312

Ollier, Claude, II 147; III 381, 426–28;
  V 377
Olmo, Lauro, IV 303
Olmos, Carlos, V 423
Olnyk, Mykola, V 614
Ologoudou, Émile, I 237
Olsen, Ernst Bruun, I 540
Olsen, Tillie, I 69; V 222, 461–62
Olson, Charles, I 72, 396; III 55, 428–29;
  IV 637
  influence of, I 506
Olson, Elder, III 124
Olsson, Hagar, I 566; II 100, 101; III
  294; IV 266
Ölvedi, László, I 527
Olzhych, Oleh (Oleh Kandyba), IV 496;
  V 613
Ōmachi Keigetsu
  on Yosano Akiko, V 649
Omar, Kaleem, III 458
Omari, C. K., IV 418
Omötbaev, Mökhämmätsälim Ishemghol-
  ulï, I 203
Omotoso, Kole, III 392, 393; V 499
Omurbaev, Sagïndïk, II 589
Ondaatje, Michael, I 396; V 109, 462–63
O'Neale, Sondra
  on Angelou, V 33
O'Neill, Alexandre, III 569
O'Neill, Eugene, I 66, 73, 74, 194, 491;
  II 70, 161, 551; III 429–33; IV
  355; V 582, 639
  critical excerpts on, III 433–35
  influence of, I 188; IV 468; V 454
  on Strindberg, IV 356
O'Neill, James, III 429
Onerva, L., II 99; III 41
Onerva Lehtinen-Madetoja, Hilja. *See*
  Onerva, L.
Onetti, Juan Carlos, I 118; III 435–36; IV
  516; V 391
Onís, Federico de
  on García Lorca, Federico, II 198–99
  on Salinas, IV 135
O'Nolan, Brian. *See* O'Brien, Flann
Onwueme, Tess, V 448
Ooi Cheng Teck, III 192
Ōoka Makoto, V 337
Opatoshu, Yoysef, IV 685
Opdahl, Keith Michael
  on Bellow, I 230–31
Oppenheimer, Joel, I 72
Oppenheimer, Robert, IV 231
Opperman, D. J., IV 286; V 564, 565
Oraison, Marc, V 234
Oras, Ants, II 61–62
Ordubady, Mamed Said, I 166
Oreamuno, Yolanda, V 124, 463
Oreana, Francisco de, V 6
Orelli, Giorgio, IV 388
Ören, Aras, V 249
Orhon, Orhan Seyfi, IV 475–76
O'Riada, Sean, V 362
Ó Ríordáin, Seán, II 461
Orixe, IV 310
Oriya literature. *See under* Indian
  literature
Orizet, Jean, V 233
Ørjasæter, Tore, III 402
Orkan, Władysław, III 554
Örkény, István, II 416
Orlea, Ioana, V 519
Ormaechea, Nicolás. *See* Orixe
Ormond, John, IV 609
Ornea, Z., V 520
Ørnsbo, Jess, I 540

Orozco, Olga, V 41, 398
Orr, Gregory, V 26
Ors, Eugeni d', III 96–97; IV 34, 311,
  312, 314
Orsenna, Eric, V 231
Országh, Pavol. *See* Hviezdoslav

Ortaç, Yusuf Ziya, IV 476
Ortega, Daniel, V 124
Ortega Munilla, José, III 436
Ortega y Gasset, José, III 95–96, 234,
  436–38; IV 299, 300, 301, 360; V
  126, 193, 265, 476, 477, 571
  criticism on, I 517
  influence of, I 134; III 436; IV 307;
  V 127
Orten, Jiří, I 523
Ortese, Anna Maria, II 473; III 438–39
Ortiz, Adalberto, II 1
Ortiz, Fernando, I 20; V 105, 455
  influence of, IV 316
Ortiz, Juan L., V 41
Ortiz, Lourdes, V 570, 573, 575
Ortiz de Montellano, Bernardo, V 265
Ortiz Guerrero, Manuel, III 473
Orton, Joe, V 267
Ørum, Poul, I 539
Orwell, George, I 77, 80; II 44, 49, 53,
  359, 395; III 439–41; IV 109,
  262, 578, 706; V 126, 185, 577
  criticism on, IV 579
  excerpts of, III 441–42
  on Greene, II 290–91
  influence of, I 365; V 98
  as subject, V 621
Orzeszkowa, Eliza, III 552
Osadebay, Denis, III 390
Osborne, John, II 40; III 442–44; IV 197
Oshagan, Hagop, I 120; III 444
Oshagan, Vahé, I 121
Osherovitsh, Hirsh, IV 687
Osipov, Petr N., I 466
Óskar, Jón, II 427
Osmachka, Todos, IV 493, 496, 497
Osmonov, Alïkul, II 588
Osofisan, Femi (Okinba Launko), III 393;
  V 448, 463–64
Osorgin, M. A. (Mikhail Osorgin, Mik-
  hail Andreevich Il'in *or* Ilyin), IV
  109; V 464–66
Osorio, Luis Enrique, V 145
Osorio, Miguel Ángel. *See* Barba Jacob,
  Porfirio
Osório, Oswaldo, I 402
Osses, Esther María, V 125
Ossetic literature, III 444–45
Ossietzky, Carl von, IV 471
Ostaijen, Paul van, I 222; II 70;
  III 445–47
Oster, Pierre, II 148
Östergren, Klas, V 582
Osterle, Heinz D.
  on Broch, I 339
Österling, Anders, IV 377
Ostornol, Antonio, V 131
Ostrauskas, Kostas, III 132; V 393, 395
Ostrovsky, Nikolay Alexeevich, III 447;
  IV 110
Ostwald, Wilhelm
  influence of, IV 219
Ó Súilleabháin (O'Suilleabhain), Muiris,
  II 461; V 318
Osundare, Niyi, V 447
Osvát, Ernő, II 412
Otčenášek, Jan, I 523
Ötep, Äbdiraman, IV 522
Otero, Blas de, IV 305; V 466–67, 574
  influence of, IV 310
Otero Pedrayo, Ramón, IV 315
Otero Silva, Miguel, IV 542, 543, 544,
  545; V 583
Otte, Jean Pierre, I 224
Otten, Karl, II 70
Ottieri, Ottiero, II 474; III 447–48
Ottlik, Géza, V 295, 296
Ó Tuama, Seán, II 461; V 362
Ouary, Malek, II 88
Ouologuem, Yambo, III 194
Outer Mongolian literature. *See under*
  Mongolian literature

Pavlović, Miodrag, III 491–92, 563; IV 694
Pavlovski, Radovan, IV 698
Pavlovsky, Eduardo, V 42
Pavlychko, Dmytro, V 612
Pavšič, Vladimir. *See* Bor, Matej
Pawar, Daya, V 309
Payelle, Raymond Gérard. *See* Hériat, Philippe
Payeras, Mario, V 121
Payró, Roberto Jorge, I 111; III 492–94
Paz, Octavio, III 273, 274, 494–96; IV 372; V 242, 246, 265, 421, 494, 525
  critical excerpts on, III 496–97
  on Guillén, Jorge, II 298
Pazwak, Abdur Rahman, I 19
p'Bitek, Okot. *See* Okot p'Bitek
Pchilka, Olena, IV 492, 498
Peabody, Endicott, V 49
Peacock, Ronald
  on Synge, IV 395–96
Pearce, Roy Harvey
  on Stevens, IV 341
  on Williams, William Carlos, IV 638
Pearse, Padraic, II 461
Peate, Iorwerth C., IV 605, 606
Pécout, Roland, II 153
Peden, Margaret Sayers
  on Carballido, V 114
Pedersen, Knud. *See* Hamsun, Knut
Pedi literature. *See under* South African literature
Pedreira, Antonio S.
  influence of, IV 315
Pedrero, Paloma, V 570, 575
Pedretti, Erica, IV 383
Pedro, António, III 569
Pedrolo, Manuel de, III 498–500; IV 313; V 575
Pedroso, Reginio, I 20
Pedullà, Walter, II 474
Peer, Andri, IV 389
Péguy, Charles, I 250; II 138, 289; III 89, 500–503
  influence of, I 251; II 144; IV 11
Peiper, Tadeusz, III 555, 605; V 373
Peirce, Charles Sanders, V 196
Pei Tao (Bei Dao), V 136, 137, 391
Pekkanen, Toiva, II 101
Pellegrini, Domingos, V 90
Pellegrini, Vincenzo Maria, III 203
Pellicer, Carlos, III 273; V 264–65, 479–80
Peltonen, Vihtori. *See* Linnankoski, Johannes
Pena, Cornelio, III 77
Pendse, Shripad Narayan, II 439
Pennanen, Eila, II 102
Pepetela, I 97
Peppard, Murray B.
  on Dürrenmatt, I 602
Peralta, Alejandro, III 511
Peralta, Bertalicia, V 125
Perbosc, Antonin, II 152
Percy, Walker, I 68; III 503–4
Perec, Georges, V 229–31, 480–82, 498
Pereda Valdés, Ildefonso, I 20
Pereira, José Maria dos Reis. *See* Régio, José
Pereleshin, Valery, IV 106
Perelman, S. J., IV 616
Péret, Benjamin, IV 371, 372
Peretz, Yitskhok Leybush, IV 683
  influence of, IV 685, 686
Pereverzev, Vladimir, IV 115
Pérez, Genaro J.
  on Goytisolo, Juan, II 268
Pérez de Ayala, Ramón, III 504–5; IV 307
Pérez Galdós, Benito, III 284, 506–8; IV 301, 306; V 476
  influence of, III 506; IV 259

Pérez Petit, Victor, IV 67, 515
Pérez Sánchez, Manuel António, IV 314–15
Périer, Odilon-Jean, I 225
Peri Rossi, Cristina, V 482–83
Perk, Jacques, III 375
Perkens, Duco. *See* Perron, Edgar du
Perkins, Maxwell, I 380; IV 655, 656
Perkonig, Josef Friedrich, I 156
Pernath, Hugues C., I 222
Pérol, Jean, V 233
Perón, Juan, III 225
Perosa, Sergio
  on Fitzgerald, F. Scott, II 111
Perpessicius, IV 80
Perron, Edgar du, III 376, 508–9; IV 69, 555
  influence of, I 438
  on Slauerhoff, IV 245
Perry, John Oliver, V 309
Perse, Saint-John. *See* Saint-John Perse
Persian literature
  See Iranian literature
  See also Afghan, Indian, *and* Pakistani literatures
Perucho, Joan (Juan), IV 313; V 573
Perumal, K., IV 233
Peruvian literature, III 509–11
  feudal system, decline of, as subject of, IV 37
  indianismo as subject of, I 42; III 511
  literary criticism in, IV 538
  major writers of, *see:* Alegría; Arguedas, José María; Belli, Carlos Germán; Bryce Echenique; Chocano; Goldemberg; González Prada; Ribeyro; Salazar Bondy; Vallejo, César; Vargas Llosa
  modernism in, I 461; II 258; III 293, 509, 510
  Odría régime as subject of, IV 537
  surrealism in, III 511; V 66
Pervomaysky, Leonid, IV 496
Peshkov, Alexey Maximovich. *See* Gorky, Maxim
Pessanha, Camilo, III 566; IV 392
Pessarrodona, Marta, V 574
Pessemesse, Pierre, II 153
Pessoa, Fernando, III 511–13, 567; IV 118; V 30, 539, 572
  influence of, IV 118
Pestalozzi, Karl
  on Dürrenmatt, I 602
Pestana, Artur. *See* Pepetela
Peterman, Michael
  on Davies, Robertson, V 167
Peters, Frederick G.
  on Musil, III 339
Peters, Jánis, III 19
Peters, Lenrie, II 194; III 513
Petersen, Jonatan, II 59
Petersen, Kaj. *See* Munk, Kaj
Petersen, Nis, I 537; III 513–14
Peterson, Kristjan Jaak, II 60
Peterson, Karen
  on Carballido, V 114
Petlyura, Symon, IV 494
Petőfi, Sándor
  influence of, I 238
Petrėnas-Tarulis, Juozas, III 130
Petrescu, Camil, III 139, 514–15; IV 81
Petrescu, Cezar, III 522; IV 81
Petrescu, Dan, V 520
Petrescu, Radu, IV 83
Petri, György, V 297, 298
Petrie, Flinders
  influence of, II 504
Petrov, Dimitur Talev. *See* Talev, Dimitur
Petrov, Mikhail, II 105
Petrov, Valeri, I 360
Petrov, Viktor. *See* Domontovych, Viktor
Petrov, Yevgeny, II 429–30; IV 109
Petrović, Rastko, IV 692

Petrovich, Avvakum, V 441
Petrushevskaya, Ludmila (Lyudmila), V 483–85, 531, 532
Petsukh, Vyacheslav, V 531
Pétursson, Hannes, II 377
Peul literature. *See under* Senegalese literature
Peyre, Henri
  on Malraux, III 201
  on Mauriac, François, III 250–51
  on Saint-Exupéry, IV 127
Pfeiffer, Johannes, III 108, 521
Pfemfert, Franz, II 69, 216
Phala, Mampšhe, IV 290
Phạm Duy Tôn, IV 560
Phạm Quỳnh, IV 560
Phan Bội Châu, IV 560
Phan Châu Trinh, IV 560
Phan Thị Trọng-Tuyến, V 619
Pharis, Gwen, I 397
Phatudi, Cedric, IV 291
Phelps, Anthony, V 485–87
phenomenology and literature, III 515–22, 562; IV 60; V 398, 571
Phetsarath Ratanavongsa, Prince, III 9
Philcox, Richard, V 149
Philippe, Charles-Louis, II 137
Philippide, Alexandru, III 522–23; IV 81
Philippine literature, III 523–26
  in Bisayan, III 526
  in English, III 524–26
  in Iloko, III 526
  major writers of, in English, *see:* Gonzalez; Joaquin; Santos, Bienvendo N.; Ty-Casper; Villa
  Philippine-American War as subject of, III 526
  in Pilipino, III 526
  Sakdal uprisings as subject of, III 525
  in Spanish, III 523
Phillips, Jayne Anne, V 25
Phillips, William, II 162
Philoctète, René, V 485
Philombe, René, I 388
philosophy and literature. *See:* phenomenology; positivism
Phiri, Masauto, IV 705
Phoumi Vongvichit, III 10
Phouvong Phimmasone, III 9
Piaget, Jean, II 157; III 57
Piatier, Jacqueline
  on Montherlant, III 306
Picabia, Francis, IV 371
Picard, Raymond, I 202; III 94
Picasso, Pablo, I 102, 103, 441, 476; II 25, 140, 482; III 42, 200; IV 328, 371, 487
  criticism on, IV 26
  influence of, I 512
Piccolo, Lucio, II 473; III 526–27; IV 452
Pichette, Henri, II 145
Picon, Gaëtan, I 296; II 148; III 93
Picón-Salas, Mariano, IV 545
Pidmohylny, Valerian, IV 495
Pielmeier, John, V 29
Pien Chih-lin, I 458
Piepka, Jan, III 561
Pierro, Albino, II 476
Pieyre de Mandiargues, André, III 527–28; V 321
Piglia, Ricardo, V 41
Pignatari, Décio, I 323; V 88
Pignotti, Lamberto, II 474
Pilar, Marcelo H. del, III 523
Pilhes, René-Victor, V 231
Pilinszky, János, II 415; III 528–29
Pilipino literature. *See under* Philippine literature
Pillai, Raymond C., III 454
Pillai, Thakazhi Sivasankara, II 438
Pillat, Ion, III 209, 529–30; IV 80
Pillecijn, Filip de, I 220; III 530–31

Pilnyak, Boris, III 531–32; IV 24, 108, 110
  influence of, IV 109
Pim, Job. *See* Pimentel, Francisco
Pimentel, Francisco, IV 545
Piña, Nicolás, I 605
Pindale, Keshav Raj, III 367, 368
Pindar
  criticism on, III 103
Pineda Botero, Alvaro
  on Moreno-Duran, V 432
Piñera, Virgilio, IV 316; V 487–88
Pinero, Arthur Wing, II 39
Pinget, Robert, II 147, 148; III 532–33; IV 59, 387; V 230, 232
Piñón, Nélida, I 323; V 89, 488–89, 592
Pinski, Dovid, IV 686
Pinter, Harold, II 40, 41; III 518, 533–36; IV 343, 433, 434; V 133, 211, 267, 469, 643
  critical excerpts on, III 536–38
Pinthus, Kurt, II 70, 216; IV 613
  on Sachs, Nelly, IV 123
Pinto, Julieta, V 124
Pinzón, Germán, V 146
Piontek, Heinz, II 221, 222; III 538–39
Piovene, Guido, II 471, 473; III 539
Piper, Henry Dan
  on Fitzgerald, F. Scott, II 111
Piramerd, Tawfik, II 628
Pirandello, Luigi, II 185, 469; III 540–43; IV 164, 177, 301, 355, 461, 547; V 469, 504
  criticism on, II 470
  excerpts of, III 543–45
  influence of, I 99; II 40, 142, 168, 207, 317; III 298; IV 568
Piraten, Fritiof Nilsson, IV 378
Pires, José Cardoso, III 545–46, 568
Pirozhkova, Antonina
  on Babel, I 172
Pisani, Ġorġ, III 203
Piscator, Erwin, I 155, 325; II 216; V 628
Pitoëff, Georges, II 141, 145
Pitter, Ruth, II 36; III 546–47
Pitt-Kethley, Fiona, V 213
Pius XII, Pope, II 223
Piwowski, Marek, V 490
Pizarnik, Alejandra, V 41
Pizer, Donald
  on Dreiser, I 591
Pizzuto, Antonio, II 473
Plá, Josefina, III 473
Pla, Josep, IV 313
Plaatje, Sol T., IV 289, 293
Planchon, Roger, II 145; V 232
Plaskovitis, Spyros (Plaskasovitis), V 489–90
Platen, August von
  influence of, II 12
Plath, Sylvia, I 71; III 547–48; V 41, 224, 550
  criticism on, I 564
Plato, V 127, 168, 175, 510
  influence of, III 174; IV 73, 175
Platonov, Andrey Platonovich, III 548–49; IV 108
Pleijel, Agneta, V 583
Plekhanov, Georgy, III 79
Plenzdorf, Ulrich, II 225
Plessis, Menán du, V 566
Pleşu, Andrei, V 520
Pleynet, Marcelin, II 148; V 233
  on Ponge, III 562
Pliekšāns, Jānis. *See* Rainis, Jānis
Plievier, Theodor, II 223; IV 260
Plisnier, Charles, I 223
Pliya, Jean, I 237
Ploeg, Durk van der, III 380
Plomer, William, III 549–50; IV 289
Plūdonis, Vilis, III 16
Plunkett, James, II 461; V 319
Pluzhnyk, Yevhen, IV 495

P. Mo-hin, I 367
Pocaterra, José Rafael, IV 543, 544
Podbevšek, Anton, IV 697
Podrimja, Ali, IV 699
Podro, Joshua, II 278
Poe, Edgar Allan, I 57, 58, 59; IV 169; V 76
  criticism on, III 83, 90, 105, 122, 123; IV 644
  influence of, I 261, 311, 409; II 315, 348; III 293; V 416
    on French literature, IV 526, 528
    on Russian literature, II 567; IV 109
Poethen, Johannes, II 221–22
Pogodin, Nikolay, IV 114
Pohribny, Anatoly, V 614
Poincaré, Henri, II 138
Poincaré, Raymond, II 242
Poiret, Jean, V 232
Poirier, Louis. *See* Gracq, Julien
Poirier, Richard
  on Bellow, I 230
  on Eliot, T. S., II 20
  on Frost, II 176
Poirot-Delpeche, Bertrand, V 231
Pokharel, Bal Krishna, III 367
Polak, Alfred. *See* Polgar, Alfred
Polanski, Roman, V 64
Polari, Alex, V 90
Põldmäe, Asta, II 63
Põldmäe, Jaak, II 62
Polemis, Ioannis, II 280
Polevoy, Boris, IV 254
Polgar, Alfred, I 155, 156; II 165; III 550–51
Poli, Umberto. *See* Saba, Umberto
Polish literature, III 551–61; IV 174–75; V 490–94
  Black Humor in, IV 645
  "condemned generation" of, III 557
  cubism in, IV 594
  expressionism in, II 542; III 554; IV 646
  Kashubian literature, III 561
  literary criticism in, I 528; II 503; III 49, 99, 100, 606–7; IV 594
  major writers of, *see:* Andrzejewski; Barańczak; Białoszewski; Borowski; Brandys; Broniewski; Czechowicz; Dąbrowska; Dygat; Gałczyński; Goetel; Gombrowicz; Herbert, Zbigniew; Hłasko; Iwaniuk; Iwaszkiewicz; Jastrun; Kaden-Bandrowski; Konwicki; Kossak; Kruczkowski; Krynicki; Lechoń; Leśmian; Miłosz; Mrożek; Nałkowska; Parandowski; Parnicki; Przyboś; Przybyszewski; Reymont; Rostworowski; Różewicz; Schulz, Bruno; Sienkiewicz; Słonimski; Szymborska; Tuwim; Ważyk; Wierzyński; Witkiewicz; Wittlin; Wyspiański; Zagajewski; Żeromski
  also writing in English, *see* Miłosz
  also writing in German, *see* Przybyszewski
  in Yiddish, *see:* Asch; Rabon; Singer, I. J.
  modernism in, III 552–54
  Pikador writers of, *see* Skamander poets of *below*
  the "Quadriga" group of, II 189
  the Skamander poets of, I 342; III 36, 554–55; IV 246–47, 484, 626
  Socialist Realism in, I 318; II 598, 618; III 555, 558, 559, 606; IV 255, 402; V 491
  the "Suburbs" of, II 618
  surrealism in, IV 594
  symbolism in, I 528; II 542; III 553, 555, 607
    (*see also* Young Poland movement *below*)

Theater of the Absurd in, III 325, 559; V 493
  in Yiddish, IV 682, 683, 684, 685, 686
    (*see also under* major writers of *above*)
  the Young Kashubian movement in, III 561
  the Young Poland movement in, III 48, 355, 552–53, 606; IV 32, 666, 667
Politis, Linos
  on Papadiamantis, III 472
Politis, Nikolaos, II 280
Politzer, Georges, II 146
Politzer, Heinz
  on Kafka, II 547–48
Polkowski, Jan, V 492
Pollmann, Leo
  on Camus, I 394–95
Pollock, Jackson, III 419
Pollock, Sharon, V 109
Polorussov-Shelebi, Nikolay I., I 466
Polotan-Tuvera, Kerima, III 525
Polynesian literature. *See* Pacific Islands literature
Pombo, Alvaro, V 574
Poncela, Enrique Jardiel, IV 303
Ponge, Francis, II 145; III 561–63; V 233
Poniatowska, Elena, III 273; V 420, 494–95
  critical excerpts on, V 495–97
Pons, Josep Sebastià, IV 311
Pontes, Paulo, V 98
Poor, Harold, IV 472
Poortinga, Ype, III 380
Pop, Ion, IV 83
Popa, Ştefan. *See* Doinaş, Ştefan Augustin
Popa, Vasko, III 491, 563–64; IV 694, 700
pop art, influence of, on literature, IV 384, 698
Pope, Alexander, I 272
  criticism on, III 116, 122
Popescu, Dumitru Radu, III 564; IV 83
Popescu, Petru, IV 83
Poplavsky, Boris, IV 106
Popov, Leonid Andreevich, IV 671
Popović, Bogdan, IV 692
Popovici, Vasile, V 521
Poradeci, Lasgush, I 39
Porcèl, Baltasar, IV 314; V 573
Porfyras, Lambros, II 280, 281
Porta, Antonio, II 474
Porta, Carlo, II 475, 476
Porter, Countee. *See* Cullen, Countee
Porter, Hal, I 148
Porter, Katherine Anne, I 63; III 415, 564–66
  on Hardy, Thomas, II 332
  on Pound, III 578
Porter, Peter, V 52
Porter, William Sydney. *See* Henry, O.
Porto-Riche, Georges de, II 137
Portugal, José Blanc de, III 569
Portuguese Creole literatures. *See under* Angolan, Cape Verdean, Guinea-Bissau, *and* São Tomé and Príncipe literatures
Portuguese-language literatures
  See Brazilian, Portuguese, and São Tomé and Príncipe literatures
  See under Angolan, Cape Verdean, Guinea-Bissau, and Mozambican literatures
Portuguese literature, III 566–70. *See also* Spanish literature: Galician literature
  in Africa, III 569
  costumbrismo in, IV 20
  dictatorship as subject in, III 568, 569
  First Portuguese Republic as subject of, IV 36

709

Portuguese literature (*continued*)
interseccionismo in, IV 118
literary criticism in, III 97, 512, 570;
 IV 189
major writers of, *see:* Andrade, Eugénio de; Brandão, Raúl; Castro,
 José María Ferreira de; Faria; Gonçalves; Jorge; Namora; Pessoa;
 Pires; Redol; Régio; Ribeiro,
 Aquilino; Sá-Carneiro; Saramago;
 Sena; Teixeira de Pascoaes; Torga
Angolan, *see* Soromenho
also writing in English, *see* Pessoa
modernism in, I 321; III 294, 567; IV
 20, 118, 189
neorealism in, III 545, 568; IV 18, 19,
 256
the New Novel techniques in, III 568
paùlismo in, IV 118
the Poetry 61 movement in, III 569
the Portuguese Renascence movement
 in, III 566
postrealism in, III 570
the *presencistas* group of, III 567, 568
saudosismo in, III 512, 566–67; IV 426
the *Seara nova* group of, III 567; IV 36
surrealism in, III 569; IV 189
symbolism in, III 566, 567; IV 392
World War II conditions as subject of,
 III 356
Poruks, Jānis, III 15
positivism and literature, II 137–38, 328;
 III 84; IV 515, 544, 602
Posse, Abel, V 40
Post, Laurens van der, III 549
Post, Lipkje Beuckens. *See* Fear, Ypk
 fan der
Poster, Piak, V 556
Postma, Obe, III 379
postmodernism, V 497–500
 American, V 23, 274
 Colombian, V 431
 English, V 211
 French, V 229
 Hungarian, V 216, 296
 Indian, V 527
 Mexican, V 457
 Norwegian, V 226
 Russian, V 530
 Swedish, V 581
Postoli, Foqion, I 38
postrealism, III 570–74
poststructuralism, V 229, 399, 499, 500–
 502, 571, 641
 and historicism, V 287
 and postmodernism, V 499
Potebnya, Alexandr, III 99
Potokinov, Bohdan J. *See* Krasko, Ivan
Poular literature. *See* Guinean literature
Poulenc, Francis, I 252
Poulet, Georges, II 148; III 93, 125, 520
 on Guillén, Jorge, II 297–98
Poulet, Robert, I 224
Poulin, Jacques, V 110
Pound, Ezra, I 60, 64, 65, 71, 364, 491,
 506, 594; II 17, 18, 33–36, 42,
 70, 117, 172, 354, 356, 431–32,
 486, 528, 534n; III 21, 66, 89,
 113, 114, 139, 574–78; IV 256,
 328, 340, 635, 636, 675; V 91,
 353
 criticism on, III 31, 115; IV 199, 644
 excerpts of, III 578–79
 on Ford, Ford Madox, II 116
 on Hardy, Thomas, II 331
 on Housman, III 397
 influence of, III 110, 577
 on American literature, I 515; III 428;
  IV 720
  on Canadian literature, I 396
  on Central American literature, I 434;
   V 115
  on Danish literature, V 161
  on Dutch literature, V 72

on English literature, II 38, 116
on Greek literature, IV 183
on Icelandic literature, II 427
on Indian literature, II 435
on Irish literature, V 317
on Lithuanian literature, III 133
on Pakistani literature, III 459
on Scottish literature, III 165
on Yiddish literature, II 248
influence on, II 17
on Moore, Marianne, III 309
reaction against, IV 441
on Tagore, IV 404, 406–7
Pourtalès, Guy de, IV 386
Pous i Pagès, Josep, IV 312
Powell, Anthony, II 42, 45, 46–47, 106;
 III 579–82
 critical excerpts on, III 582–84
Powell, Dilys
 on Taktsis, V 587
Powell, Padgett, V 25
Pownall, David, V 208
Powys, John Cowper, II 46; III 584–85
 on Masters, III 241
Powys, Llewelyn, III 584
Powys, T. F., II 44, 50; III 584, 585–86
Prada, Renato, I 289, 290
Prado, Pedro, I 454
Pramoedya Ananta Toer, II 441–42; III
 586–88
Prasad, Kamla, III 454
Prasad, Shyam, III 367
Pratolini, Vasco, II 205, 471, 472, 473;
 III 366, 588–89
Pratt, E. J., I 396; III 589
Praz, Mario, III 87
Preda, Marin, III 590; IV 83
Premchand, II 435, 438; III 590–91
Preradovíc, Paula von, I 156; III 592–93
Prescott, Frederick, III 83
Prescott, Peter S.
 on Kennedy, William, V 349
Prevelakis, Pandelis, II 283; III 593–94
 on Kazantzakis, II 575
Prévert, Jacques, II 145; III 594–96; IV
 371; V 229, 233, 272, 564
 influence of, IV 420
Previn, André, IV 344
Prežihov, Voranc, IV 697
Prezzolini, Giuseppe, II 470
Price, Alan
 on Synge, IV 396–97
Price, Reynolds, I 69; V 24
Price-Mars, Jean, II 153
Pricha Intharapalit, IV 430
Prichard, Katharine Susannah, I 146
Prieto, Francisco, V 421
Priestley, J. B., II 53; III 596–98
Prigov, Dmitry, V 530
Prijatelj, Ivan, IV 697
Primo de Rivera, José Antonio, IV 300
Prince, Frank, II 37
Prince, Gérald Joseph
 on Sartre, IV 158
Príncipe literature, IV 147
Pringle, Thomas, IV 289
Pringsheim, Katia, III 212
Prisco, Michele, II 473; III 598
Prishvin, Mikhail Mikhailovich, III 598–
 99; IV 24, 108
Pritam, I 435
Pritchard, William H.
 on Lewis, Wyndham, III 68
 on Yeats, William Butler, IV 679
Pritchett, V. S., II 50, 51, 53; III 599–
 600; V 210
 on Lavin, II 462
 on Powell, III 582
Procházka, Jan, I 523
Proctor, Raja, IV 324
Prokofiev, Alexandr, IV 1–6
Pronko, Leonard
 on Anouilh, I 101
Proust, Marcel, I 211, 250, 476, 491; II

138, 139, 142; III 90, 310, 535,
 572–73, 574, 600–603; IV 60,
 125, 256, 348, 453, 641; V 96,
 230, 282, 296, 516, 537
criticism on, I 241, 517; III 81, 89, 90,
 93, 94, 96, 105, 119, 126, 436;
 IV 152
excerpts of, III 603–5
influence of, III 603
 on Armenian literature, III 444
 on Austrian literature, I 156
 on Brazilian literature, V 107
 on English literature, III 581; IV 251
 on French literature, II 207; III 248;
  IV 226
 on Hungarian literature, I 558
 on Netherlands literature, IV 555
 on Portuguese literature, III 567
 on Romanian literature, I 382; IV 81
 on Spanish literature, V 69, 127
 on Venezuelan literature, IV 544
 on Roussel, IV 96
Provençal literature. *See* French literature,
 in Occitan
Prøysen, Alf, III 403
Prudencio, Eustache, I 237
Prus, Bolesław, III 552
Pruszyński, Ksawery, III 556
Pryse, Marjorie, V 222
Przesmycki, Zenon. *See* Miriam
Przyboś, Julian, III 555, 557, 605–6
Przybyszewski, Stanisław, III 553–54,
 606–8; V 441
Psaila, Carmelo, III 203, 608
Pshavela, Vazha, II 211, 212
psychoanalytic criticism. *See under* litera-
 ture and psychology
psychology, 20th-c. *See* literature and
 psychology
Psykharis, Ioannis, II 280
Ptáčník, Karel, I 523
Puddicombe, Ann A. *See* Raine, Allen
Pudovkin, Vsevolod, III 365
Puértolas, Soledad, V 570, 573
Puerto Rican literature. *See under* Span-
 ish-Caribbean literature
Puga, María Luisa, V 421
Puhvel, Heino, II 62
Puhvel, Jaan, II 62
Puig, Manuel, I 112; III 608–9; V 40,
 147, 391, 398
Puig i Ferreter, Joan, IV 312
Pujmanová, Marie, I 522; IV 255
Pulver, Max, IV 382, 383
Punch, Petro, IV 494, 496
Punjabi literature. *See* Indian *and* Paki-
 stani literatures
Pürbü, Sergey Bakizovich, IV 484
Purdy, Al, V 108
Purdy, James, I 70, 273; III 609–10
Purtscher, Nora W.
 on Rilke, IV 51
Pushcha, Yazep, I 375
Pushkin, Alexandr, IV 103; V 220
 criticism on, II 584; III 98, 346; IV 115
 influence of, I 350; II 393; IV 702;
  V 212
 as subject, V 359, 441
Putík, Jaroslav, I 524
Putinas, Vincas. *See* Mykolaitis, Vincas
Putrament, Jerzy, III 559
Puzo, Mario, II 96
Pym, Barbara (Barbara Mary Pym Cramp-
 ton), V 95, 502–3
Pynchon, Thomas, I 70, 272, 273, 491;
 III 610–12; V 150, 498, 527

al-Qabbāj, Muhammad, III 319
al-Qabbānī, Abū Kalīl, IV 399; V 629
Qabbānī, Nizār, III 613; IV 400; V 14
Qābul, Nuräli, V 521
Qadiriy, Abdullah, III 613–14; IV 521
Qähhar, Äbdullah, IV 521

Qangule, Zitobile Sunshine, IV 295
Qarizada, Zia, I 19
Qāsim, 'Abd al-Hakīm, II 6; V 201
al-Qāsim, 'Alī-al-Harīrī, V 612
al-Qāsim (Kassem), Ceza, V 202
al-Qāsim, Samīh, III 464; V 473
Qasmi, Ahmad Nadim, III 459
Qayïpbergen, Tölek, IV 522
al-Qaysī, Jalīl, I 458
Qazbegi, Alexander, II 211
Qlïch, Muhammed, IV 480
Quadros, António. See João, Mutimati Bernabe
Qualtinger, Helmut, I 158
Quart, Pere. See Oliver, Joan
Quasimodo, Salvatore, II 361, 471, 472, 474; III 302, 614–15
Quaye, Cofie, II 227
al-Qu'ayyid, Muhammad Yūsuf, V 201
Queffélec, Yann, V 231
Queiroz, José Maria Eça de, III 566, 567
Queiroz, Rachel de, I 322; III 615–16; V 88
Queizán, María Xosé, V 573
Queneau, Raymond, II 144, 447; III 594, 616–18; V 229
    criticism on, III 94
    influence of, IV 420
Quennell, Peter
    on Greene, II 291
    on Montherlant, III 306
Quental, Antero de, III 512, 566
Quesada, José Luis, V 123
Quesnay, François, V 525
Quessep, Giovanni, V 147
Quevedo (y Villegas), Francisco Gómez de, I 50; IV 308; V 66
    criticism on, III 96
Quezon, Manuel, III 523
Quigley, Austin E., III 537–38
Quiles, Eduardo, IV 303; V 574
Quiller-Couch, Arthur, II 52; III 111
Quintana, Mário, V 88
Quintero, José, V 29
Quiroga, Elena, V 570
Quiroga, Horacio, I 111–12; III 618–19; IV 515–16
Quiroga, Marcelo, I 289
Qulmohammed-oghli, Abdulhäkim, IV 480
Qŭnanbay-ŭli, Ibrahim, II 569–70
Quoirez, Françoise. See Sagan, Françoise

Raab, Esther, II 466
Raabe, Wilhelm, II 215
Rabary, Andriamatoa, III 184
Rabassa, Gregory, I 497
    on Lispector, III 77
Rabe, David, I 75; V 28
Rabearivelo, Jean-Joseph, III 185, 186
Rabelais, V 76, 513
    criticism on, III 100; V 58
Rabemananjara, Jacques, III 185, 186
Rabemanantsoa, Naka, III 184
Rabestimanandranto, Fidelis-Justin, III 184
Rabie, Jan, IV 287
al-Rabī'ī, 'Abd al-Rahmān. See al-Rubaya'ī, 'Abd al-Rahmān
al-Rabī'ī, Mahmūd, V 202
Rabinovitsh, Sholem. See Sholem Aleichem
Rabon, Israel, IV 1, 684–85
Raboy, Isaac, IV 685
Rachedi, Ahmed, V 84
Rachmatullah Ading Affandie, II 444
Racine, Jean
    criticism on, I 202; III 94, 105
    influence of, III 286
Rada, Jeronim de, I 37
Radauskas, Henrikas, III 132; IV 1–2; V 393
    criticism on, IV 11

Raddall, Thomas, I 396
Radek, Karl, IV 253
Radichkov, Yordan, IV 255
Radiguet, Raymond, II 142; IV 3–4
Raditladi, Lettle Disang, I 307
Radnóti, Miklós, II 414; IV 4–5
Radnóti, Sándor, V 298
Radrigán, Juan, V 134
Rådström, Niklas, V 582
Radvanyi, Netty Reiling. See Seghers, Anna
Radzevičius, Bronius, V 394
Radzevičius-Radžius, Auris, V 394
Radzinsky, Edvard, V 504–5
Raes, Hugo, I 221
Raet, Lodewijk de, IV 551
Rafat, Taufiq, III 458
Raffi, I 122
Ragana, Marija Pečkauskaitė-Šatrijos, III 129
Ragimov, Suleiman, I 166
Rahamin, S. Fyzee, II 437
Raharolahy, Elie, III 184
al-Rāhib, Hānī, IV 399
Rahidy, Basilide, III 184
Rähim, Yaqut, IV 521
Rahman, Munibur, V 309
Rahman, Rustäm, IV 521
Rahman, Salimur, III 459
Rahman, Shamsur, I 187
al-Rā'ī, 'Alī, II 7; V 202
Raičković, Stevan, IV 694
Raine, Craig, V 211
Raine, Kathleen, IV 5–6
Rainio, Ritva, III 313
Rainis, Jānis, III 15; IV 6–7
Rainitovo, Ingahibe, III 184
Rainizanabololona, Justin, III 184
Rajab, Munā, V 202
Rajan, Balachandra, II 438
Rajaofera, Fredy, III 184
Rajaonah, Tselatra, III 184
Rajemisa-Raolison, Régis, III 184, 185
Rajoelisolo, Charles, III 184
Rajoro, Justin, III 184
Raju, Cherabanda. See Reddy, Baddam Bhaskara
Rakesh, Mohan, II 437; IV 7–8; V 308
Rakíc, Milan, IV 691–92
Rakitin, Nikola, I 359
Rákosi, Jenő, II 413
Rakotobe, Alexis, III 184
Rakovszky, Zsuzsa, V 298
Ralea, Mihai, IV 80
Raleigh, Sir Walter, II 52; III 111
Ralin, Radoy, I 360
Rama, Angel, IV 516; V 482
Ramaila, Mogagabise, IV 291
Ramanantoanina, III 184
Ramanujan, A. K., V 310
Ramat, Silvio, II 471, 474
Ramathe, A. C. J., IV 291
Ramge, Renate, V 195
Ramírcz, Armando, V 421
Ramírez, Sergio, V 124, 505–6
Rammala, Maggie, IV 291
Ramo, Şükrü, IV 701
Ramonas, Vincas, III 132
Ramón y Cajal, Santiago, IV 300
Ramos, Graciliano, I 322; III 295; IV 8–10
Ramos, Lilia, V 124
Ramos, Luis Arturo, V 421
Ramos, María Eugenia, V 123
Ramos, Samuel, III 274
Ramsey, Priscilla R.
    on Angelou, V 33
Ramuz, Charles-Ferdinand, IV 10–11, 385
    criticism on, IV 386
    influence of, IV 386
Rana, Diamond Shumshere, III 368
Rana, Pushkar Shumshere, III 367
Ranaivo, Flavien, III 185, 186

Ranasinghe, Anne, IV 324
Randall, Dudley, I 73
Rangnekar, Motiram Gajanan, II 437
Rank, Otto, II 162; III 83, 394
Rankin, Ian, V 544
Rannit, Aleksis, IV 11–12
Ransford, Tessa, V 545, 546
Ransmayr, Christoph, V 53, 54, 250
Ransom, John Crowe, I 65, 67, 71; III 119, 121, 140; IV 12–13, 422, 587
    criticism on, III 123
    on Hardy, Thomas, II 331
    influence of, II 500; IV 587, 588
    on Jarrell, II 501
Ranudo, Vicente, III 526
Rao, Kshama, II 436
Rao, Raja, II 439; IV 13–14
Rao, Srirangam Srinivas, II 435
Raos, Ivan, IV 696
Rapin, Christian, II 153
Rapoport, Shloyme Zanvl. See Anski, S.
Raptanov, Timofey, II 105
Rasamizafy, Jean-Louis, III 185
Rasamuel, Maurice, III 184
Rashed, N. M., III 459
Rashidov, Sharaf R., IV 521
Rashiid Maxamed Shabeele, IV 278
Rasi, Mauro, V 90
Rasim, Ahmet, IV 477
Rasmussen, Bent William, V 159
Rasmussen, Halfdan, I 538
Rasputin, Valentin, II 572; IV 112; V 506–7, 530
Rato, Manuel Antolín, IV 309
Ratsimiseta, Jasmina, III 184
Ratunshinskaya, Irina, V 391
Rauch, Men, IV 388
Raudsepp, Hugo, II 63
Ravales, Robin. See Dobru
Ravanipur, Moniru, V 313
Ravelomoria, Wast, III 184
Raven, Simon, II 48
Ravitsh, Melekh, II 287; III 228; IV 684
Ravoajanahary, Alphonse, III 185
Rawet, Samuel, I 323
Rawlings, Marjorie Kinnan, I 64
Ray, Jean, I 224
Ray, Man, II 25, 95
Raychev, Georgi, I 359
Rayfield, Donald
    on Chekhov, I 451
al-Rayhānī, Amīn, V 272
Raymond, Marcel, II 146; III 93, 520; IV 387
Razafimahefa, Charles-Aubert. See Dondavitra
Razafiniaina, Charlotte, III 184
Razakandrainy, J. V. S., III 184
Razakarivony, Arthur. See Rodlish
Razgon, Lev, V 531
Rázus, Martin, I 525
Rea, Domenico, II 473; III 366; IV 14–15
Read, Herbert, II 35, 53; III 84, 118; IV 15–16, 373
Reading, Peter, V 213
Réage, Pauline, V 487
realism in 20th-c. literature. See also: Italian literature, verismo in; neorealism; postrealism
    African, IV 286, 288, 366, 367, 703–4, 712
    American, I 58–59, 63, 68, 228, 505; II 79; III 186
    Asian, I 120, 443, 444; II 435, 628; IV 410, 561
    Canadian, I 277
    comic, see Black Humor
    cynical, I 359
    East European, I 342, 494; I 62, 87, 605, 621; III 16, 169; IV 32, 107–8, 413, 492–93, 494, 697, 710; V 371
    and the influence of 19th-c. realism on, 711

realism (*continued*)
I 99, 145, 235; III 552, 570, 571–
72; IV 251, 256, 259
and literary criticism, III 82, 105, 150–
51; IV 133
Near Eastern, IV 477, 479
regional, III 540
and Socialist Realism, IV 252, 253,
254 (*see also* Socialist Realism)
and society, IV 255, 256, 257 (*see also*
social realism)
Spanish American, I 115, 169, 289,
454; III 492; IV 515
super-, IV 139
Western European, I 224, 246; II 137,
219, 224, 273, 462–63, 554; III
399, 402–3, 540; IV 45, 301, 306,
389, 428
Reaney, James I 397; V 108
Rebello, Luiz Francisco, III 569
Rèbora, Clemente, II 470, 471, 472;
IV 17
Rebreanu, Liviu, IV 17–18, 81
Recabarren, Luis Emilio, V 11
Rechy, John, I 68
Recto, Claro, III 523
Recuerda, José Martín, V 574
Réda, Jacques, V 234
Reddy, Baddam Bhaskara (Cherabanda
Raju), V 309
Redgrove, Peter, V 213
Redol, António Alves, III 568; IV 18–19
Reed, Carol, I 491
Reed, F. A.
on Kazantzakis, II 575
Reed, Henry, II 37
Reed, Ishmael, I 69, 273; IV 19–20; V
24, 498
Reed, James, V 213
Reed, T. J.
on Mann, Thomas, III 217
Reedy, William Marion, III 241, 242
Rees, Richard
on Orwell, III 441–42
Reeson, Margaret, III 455
Régio, José, III 567; IV 20–21
regionalism in literature, I 223–24, 536,
538; II 433, 435; III 71, 292, 402;
IV 248, 430, 431, 441–42, 445,
478, 479, 718. *See also: costum-
brismo;* dialect literatures
American, IV 141 (*see also* American
literature, Southern)
Brazilian, I 322; III 77, 295; IV 87–88,
550–51
East European, I 494; III 561; IV 327,
412, 493, 680, 691, 692
Italian, II 87–88; III 540, 542, 615
Portuguese, III 567; IV 18–19, 36, 457
Spanish, IV 308, 314–15
Spanish American, I 111, 169, 454; III
509; IV 56, 86
Regler, Gustav, V 508
Regman, Cornel, IV 82
Régnier, Henri de, II 136
Rego, José Lins do, I 322; III 295; IV
21–22
Rehberg, Hans, II 218
Reich, Ebbe Kløvedal, I 541; V 159, 509
Reich, Wilhelm, III 329
influence of, IV 199
Reichart, Elisabeth, V 54
Reich-Ranicki, Marcel
on Böll, I 294
Reid, Alastair
on Borges, I 306
on Neruda, III 372
Reid, Alexander, IV 179
Reid, Christopher, V 211
Reid, James H.
on Böll, I 293
Reid, Victor S., II 54
Reina, María Manuela, V 570, 575

Reindof, Carl, II 226
Reinfrank, Arno, II 222
Reinhardt, Max, I 4, 151, 180, 216, 324,
347; II 166, 216, 308, 384
Reinhart, Josef, IV 385
Reis, Marco Konder, I 323
Reisel, Vladimír, I 526
Reisen, Abraham. *See* Reyzen, Avrom
Reiss, Frank
on Neruda, III 372
Reiss-Andersen, Gunnar, III 402
Reizenstein, Elmer Leopold. *See* Rice,
Elmer
Rela, Josip, IV 699
Remal, Walter. *See* de la Mare, Walter
Remark, Erich Paul. *See* Remarque, Erich
Maria
Remarque, Erich Maria, II 219; IV 22–
23, 260
Reményik, Sándor, IV 85
Remizov, Alexey Mikhaylovich, III 531;
IV 23–25, 108
influence of, IV 24
Rémy, Pierre-Jean, V 231
Renan, Ernest, III 501
Renard, Jean-Claude, II 148; V 234
Renaud, Jacques, I 399
Renault, Louis, IV 284
Renault, Mary (Mary Challans), V 510–
11
Rendra, II 443
Renn, Ludwig, II 219
Renoir, Jean, II 95; III 595
Renu, Phanishwarnath, V 308
Resink, Getrudes Johannes, II 446
Resino, Carmen, V 570
Resnais, Alain, I 426; IV 59
Réunion literature, IV 25–26
in Creole, IV 25–26
in French, IV 25–26
Reve, Gerard Cornelis van het, III 377,
378
Reverdy, Pierre, I 513; II 140, 141, 409;
IV 26–27, 371–73; V 419
influence of, I 225; III 420
revolution, 20th-c., as literary subject,
IV 260
See also independence struggles: Alge-
rian, I 45, 47; Armenian, I 120;
Bolivian, I 289; Central American,
I 434–45 (*see also* Cuban *below*);
Chinese, I 459–60, III 133, 134,
198–99, IV 446; Cuban, II 299;
Egyptian, II 5; Indonesian, II 441–
42, III 587; Mexican, *see under*
Mexican literature; Russian, *see*
Russian Revolution; Somali, IV
278; Turkish, II 557; Zanzibar
(Tanzanian), IV 417
Revueltas, José, III 272; IV 27–28
Rexroth, Kenneth, I 72; IV 28–29
Reyes, Alfonso, III 97, 274; IV 29–31;
V 242
Reyes Basualto, Neftalí. *See* Neruda,
Pablo
Reyles, Carlos, IV 31, 515
Reymont, Władysław Stanisław, III 554;
IV 31–33
Reynold, Gonzague de, IV 386, 387
Reyzen, Avrom, IV 685
Réza, Yasmina, V 233
Řezáč, Václav, I 522
Rhodesian literature. *See* Zimbabwean
literature
Rhodesian-Mozambique war. *See under*
Mozambican literature
Rhys, E. Prosser, IV 606
Rhys, Jean, II 50, 54: IV 33–34
Rhys, Keidrych, IV 608
Riaza, Luis, V 574
Riba, Carles, II 114; IV 34–35, 311, 313,
314
Ribas, Tomás, III 568

Ribeiro, Aquilino, III 567; IV 18–19, 35–
37
Ribeiro, Darcy, V 89, 511–13
Ribeiro, João, I 184
Ribeiro, João Ubaldo, V 90, 513–14
Ribeyro, Julio Ramón, III 509, 510; IV
37
Ricardo, Cassiano, I 321, 323; IV 37–38
Ricardou, Jean, III 382; IV 38–39, 362
on Robbe-Grillet, IV 63
Rice, Elmer, I 66, 73; II 70, 551; IV 39–
41
Rice, Philip Blair
on Rukeyser, V 525
Rich, Adrienne, I 71; V 26, 222, 499,
514–15, 550
on Bogan, I 287
Richard, Jean-Pierre, II 148; III 93, 125,
520
Richards, I. A., I 67; II 29, 52; III 113,
114, 115–16, 121, 122; IV 41–42
criticism of, III 124
influence of, I 344; II 52; III 110, 116
Richardson, Dorothy Miller, II 43; IV
348; V 515–16
criticism on, IV 229
influence of, IV 229
Richardson, Henry Handel, I 146; IV 42–
43; V 51
Richardson, Jack, I 74
Richardson, James
on Hardy, Thomas, II 333
Richardson, Samuel
criticism on, IV 640
Richardson, Tony, III 443
Richey, E. E., V 619
Richler, Mordecai, I 397; IV 43–44; V
109, 110
Richter, Bernt, III 551
Richter, Hans Werner, I 82; II 220
Richter, Harvena
on Woolf, Virginia, IV 662
Richter, William
on Malraux, III 202
Richthofen, Frieda von, III 21, 23
Ricketts, Ed, IV 330–31
Ricœur, Paul, III 521; V 501
Ridala, Villem, II 60
Riddel, Joseph N.
on Stevens, IV 341
Riding, Laura, II 29, 36, 277
Ridruejo, Dionisio, IV 305
Rīdzinieks, Richards, III 18
Riemersma, Trinus, III 380
Riera, Carme, V 570
Riera, Miguel Angel, V 573
Ries, Nicolas, III 159
Rif'at, Alīfa, V 201
Rifat, Oktay, I 81; IV 476–77; V 606
Rifbjerg, Klaus, I 540; IV 44–46
Riffaterre, Michael, V 235
al-Rīhānī, Amīn, III 32
al-Rīhānī, Najīb, II 4, 6
Riis, Annie, III 403
Rijal, Prasad, III 366, 367
Rilke, Rainer Maria, I 152, 245; III 90;
IV 46–50, 256, 386, 391, 470; V
291, 292, 580, 606
on Beer-Hofmann, I 217
criticism on, I 271, 279; III 88, 108–9,
126; IV 11
excerpts of, IV 50–51
on Hauptmann, II 340
influence of, I 222, 438, 539; II 348;
III 482; IV 696; V 454
on American literature, II 501; III
611
on German literature, I 300; II 131
Rimal, Gopal Prasad, III 366, 367
Rimbaud, Arthur, I 190, 342; II 66; III
49; IV 389, 390; V 91, 469
criticism on, III 93, 281, 553; IV 133
influence of, I 325, 389, 518; II 140;

III 89, 420; IV 118, 175, 370,
462; V 161, 336, 590
as subject, V 132, 367
Rim-Kin, I 387
Rinchen, Byamba, III 300
Ring, Barbra, III 399
Ringuet, I 398; IV 51–52
Rintala, Paavo, II 102
Río, Ángel del
on García Lorca, Federico, II 199
on Unamuno, IV 504
Rios, Cassandra, V 90
Ríos, Lara (Marilín Echeverría), V 124
Riou, Jakez, II 151
Ripstein, Arturo, V 469
Risco, Vicente, IV 315
Rīsha, 'Umar Abū, IV 400
Rishtya, Said Qassim, I 19
Risi, Nelo, II 474
Risse, Heinz, II 224
Ristić, Marko, IV 694
Ristikivi, Karl, II 62; IV 53–54
Ritsos, Yannis, II 282; IV 54–55; V 30,
604, 606
Rivaz, Alice, IV 386
Rive, Richard, IV 289–90; V 516–18
Rivera, José Eustasio, I 484; IV 55–56; V
144, 145
Rivera, Pedro, V 125
Rivers, Conrad, I 73
Rivers, J. E.
on Proust, III 605
Rivers, Larry, III 419
Rivers, W. H. R., II 277
Rivière, Jacques, I 36, 128, 469, 470; II
139; III 90–91, 562
on Claudel, I 472
Rixt. See Dorssen, Hendrika Akke van
Rizal, José, III 523
R. Kovid, I 386
Roa Bastos, Augusto, III 473–74; IV 56–
58
Robakidse, Grigol, II 211, 214; IV 58–59
Robbe-Grillet, Alain, I 343; II 68, 97,
147, 148–49; III 381, 382, 518,
519–20; IV 59–61, 362; V 230,
242, 401
criticism on, I 201
excerpts of, IV 61–63
influence of, IV 148; V 107, 151, 569
on Roussel, IV 96
Robberechts, Daniël, I 221
Robert, Shaaban, IV 63–64, 417
Robertis, Giuseppe de, II 470; III 87
Roberts, Charles G. D., I 395
Roberts, Elizabeth Madox, I 64
Roberts, Kate, IV 606
Roberts, Michael, I 191
Roberts, R. Silyn, IV 605
Roberts, Sheila, V 566
Robertson, D. W., IV 289
Robertson, Ethel Florence. See Richard-
son, Henry Handel
Robertson, J. Logie, IV 178
Robertson, William, IV 180; V 547
Robinary, Michel-François, III 185
Robinson, Edwin Arlington, I 64;
IV 64–65
Robinson, Lillian S., V 222
Robinson, Mary, V 26
Roblès, Emmanuel, II 88; IV 66–67
Robleto, Hernán, V 124
Robson, William W., III 119
Rocha, Adolfo Correia da. See Torga,
Miguel
Roche, Denis, II 148; V 233
Roche, Mazo de la, I 396
Roche, Maurice, V 231
Roche, Roselyne, II 153
Rochefort, Christiane, II 149; V 231
Rod, Édouard, IV 385
Rodange, Michel, III 158
Rodas, Ana María, V 121

Rodin, Auguste
influence of, IV 46, 47–48
Rodlish, III 184
Rodó, José Enrique, III 294; IV 67–68,
515
Rodoreda, Mercè, IV 313; V 518–19, 570
Rodrigues, Eustáquio, V 90
Rodrigues, Nelson, I 324; IV 68
Rodrigues, Urbano Tavares, III 568
Rodriguez, Buenaventura, III 526
Rodríguez, Claudio, V 574
Rodríguez Álvarez, Alejandro. See Ca-
sona, Alejandro
Rodríguez Buded, Ricardo, IV 303
Rodríguez Cárdenas, Manuel, IV 542,
543
Rodríguez Castelao, Alfonso, IV 315
Rodríguez de Francia, José Gaspar, III
473; IV 57–58
Rodríguez Feo, José, IV 316
Rodríguez Méndez, José María, V 574
Rodríguez-Monegal, Emir
on Cortázar, I 498–99
on Neruda, III 372
Rocdel, Reto, IV 388
Roelants, Maurice, I 220; III 508; IV 68–
69
Roethke, Theodore, I 73, 286; IV 69–71;
V 644
on Bogan, I 287
influence of, II 586
Roffé, Reina, V 41
Rogers, Pattiann, V 28
Rogers, Sam Shepard, Jr. See Shepard,
Sam
Roggeman, Willy, I 222
Rogoff, Gordon
on Williams, Tennessee, IV 634
Roh, Franz, III 177
Roiç de Corella, Joan, IV 311
Rojas, Carlos, V 573
Rojas, Jorge, I 483; V 117, 145
Rojas, Manuel, IV 71–72
Rojas, Pablo, II 303
Rojas, Ricardo, I 112–13; III 97; IV 30
Rojas Herazo, Héctor, V 145–47
Rojas Zorrilla, Francisco, V 574
Rokpelnis, Jānis, III 19
Roland Holst, Adriaan, III 375, 376; IV
72–73
Roland Holst-van der Schalk, Henriëtte,
III 375; IV 72, 73–74
Roll, Ştefan, IV 81
Rolland, Romain, II 137, 138, 496, 524;
III 181, 285; IV 74–76, 723
criticism on, III 151
influence of, II 379
on Robakidse, IV 58
Rolland de Renéville, André, I 545; II
146
Rolleston, James
on Kafka, II 548
on Rilke, IV 51
Romains, Jules, I 593; II 138, 143, 144,
524; III 573; IV 76–79, 259, 260
Romanian-language literatures
See Moldavian and Romanian literatures
See under Yugoslav literature
See also Tzara, Tristan, who also has
written in Romanian
Romanian literature, IV 79–84; V 519–21
the Bucharest group of, IV 82
collectivization as subject of, III 590;
IV 124
existentialism in, IV 80; V 563
expressionism in, I 275, 276; IV 80, 85
in French, IV 81
in German, IV 84
Gîndirea (Gândirea) group of, III 523,
529; IV 568
in Hungarian, IV 85–86
Iaşi group of, III 523

literary criticism in, I 190, 381–82,
575; III 139, 523; IV 83
magic realism in, IV 84
major writers of, see: Arghezi; Bacovia;
Barbu, Ion; Blaga; Blandiana;
Blecher; Călinescu, George; Caragiale, Mateiu; Caraion; Cioran;
Doinaş; Eliade; Lovinescu; Maniu;
Papadat-Bengescu; Petrescu,
Camil; Philippide; Pillat; Popescu,
Dimitru Radu; Preda; Rebreanu;
Sadoveanu, Mihail; Sorescu; Stă-
nescu; Urmuz; Voiculescu
also writing in English, see Eliade
also writing in French, see: Cioran;
Eliade
in literary criticism, see Negoiţescu
in Yiddish, see Shteynbarg
modernism in, I 275–76
peasant revolt (1907) as subject of, IV
18
populist movement in, IV 79–80
Sibiu group of, IV 82
Socialist Realism in, I 115
surrealism in, I 409; IV 81, 82, 514;
V 519
symbolism in, I 176, 177, 189, 276;
IV 79
the Transylvania Helicon group of,
IV 85
World War I, effects of, as subject of,
IV 81
World War II conditions as subject of,
III 590
post-, III 564
in Yiddish, IV 683, 684, 686
Youth (Junimea) group of, III 139
Romanowiczowa, Zofia, III 560
Romansh literature. See under Swiss
literature
romanticism in 20th-c. literature, I 58,
289; IV 288, 470, 494, 495; V 48,
123, 336
Arabic, II 4; III 33; IV 366
criticism on, III 113
European, III 338–39, 366, 515; IV
303–4, 387
and existentialism, II 66
and Socialist Realism, IV 254
Romero, Elvio, III 473
Romero, José Rubén, III 272; IV 86–87
Romero, Luis, IV 308
Romero, Sílvio, I 320
Romero Esteo, Miguel, V 574
Romero García, Manuel Vicente, IV 543
Romilly, Jacqueline de, V 230
Rondeaux, Madeleine, II 230
Ronga literature. See under Mozambican
literature
Rong Wong-savun, IV 431
Ronsard, Pierre, V 292
Rooij, René de, I 605
Roosevelt, Theodore, IV 64
Roppel, Leon, III 561
Rorem, Ned, III 419
Rorty, Richard, 169
on Derrida, V 177
Rosa, António Ramos, III 569
Rosa, João Guimarães, I 322, 323; III 77,
295; IV 87–88; V 88
Rosario, Guillermo, I 605
Rosas, Juan Manuel de, II 193
Røsbak, Ove, III 403
Rose, Marion Erster, V 633
Rosei, Peter, V 54, 521–22
Rosenberg, Isaac, II 34; IV 88–89
Rosenfarb, Chava, V 685
Rosenfeld, Alvin
on Lind, Jakov, V 387
Rosenfeld, Morris, IV 683
Rosenfelt, Deborah, V 222
Rosengarten, Theodore, I 69
Rosenstock, Samuel. See Tzara, Tristan   713

in Yiddish, IV 684, 686
Young Prose in, II 572
the Zavety (Behests) school of, IV 108
the Znanie group of, IV 108
For literatures of the U.S.S.R., see Soviet Union literatures
Russier, Gabrielle
on Gallant, Mavis, V 243
Russo, Ferdinando, II 476
Russo, Luigi, II 184; III 81
Russolo, Luigi, II 185
Ruswa, Mirza, III 458
Rutherford, Peggy, IV 292
Ruuth, Alpo, II 103
Ruvanpathirana, Monica, IV 323
al-Ruwaynī, 'Abla, V 191
Ruyra, Joaquim, IV 312
Ruy Sánchez, Alberto, V 421
Ruysbroeck, Jan van
influence of, III 174
Ruyslinck, Ward, I 221
Ryabchuk, Mykola, V 613
Rybakov, Anatoly, V 530
Rycroft, Charles, II 157
Ryga, George, I 397; V 108
Rygulla, Ralf-Rainer, V 93
Rylsky, Maxym, IV 116–17, 494, 495, 497
Rymaruk, Ihor, V 613
Rymkiewicz, Jarosław Marek, V 492, 493
Rynōsuke Akutagawa, V 76
Ryōkan, IV 414
Rytkheu, Yury, I 465
Rza, Rasul, I 166

Saagpakk, Paul, II 62
Saar, Ferdinand von, I 150
Saarikoski, Pentti, II 103; IV 119
Saba, Umberto, II 470, 471, 472; IV 120–21
Saba, Ziya Osman, IV 476
Sabatier, Robert, II 148
Sábato, Ernesto, I 112, 118; III 382; IV 121–22; V 40, 41, 398
Sabbān, Rafīq, IV 399
Sabines, Jaime, III 273; V 421, 533–34
Sabir, Mirza Alekper, I 165
Sá-Carneiro, Mário de, III 512, 567; IV 118–19, 392
Sachs, Hanns, III 83
Sachs, Maurice, III 38
Sachs, Nelly, II 71, 221; IV 122–23; V 382, 391
Sackville-West, Victoria (Vita), I 389; IV 660
Sacré, James, V 233
al-Sa'dāwī, Nawāl, V 201
Saddlemyer, Ann
on Synge, IV 397
Sade, Marquis de, III 87, 488; IV 60; V 205
criticism on, IV 268
influence of, I 205; II 254; V 151
Sadeh, Pinchas, II 466, 467
Sadīkov, Jalil, II 589
Sadoveanu, Ion Marin, IV 81
Sadoveanu, Mihail, IV 81, 123–25
Sa'edi, Gholam-Hossein (Gowhar Morad, Gowhar Murad), II 456; V 314, 534–35
Saenz, Carlos Luis, V 124
Safa, Peyami, IV 478
Safadī, Mutā', IV 399
Sagan, Françoise, IV 125–26
Sagan-ool, Oleg, IV 484
Sagarra, Josep M. de, IV 312
Sahagún, Carlos, V 574
Sahian, Hamo, I 122
Sahle Sellassie, II 65
Saichungga, III 301
Sa'īd, 'Alī Ahmad. *See* Adūnīs
Saïd, Amina, IV 474

Said, Edward W.
on Derrida, V 176
Saigyō, IV 414
Saiko, George, I 157; V 54
Sail, Lawrence, V 213
Sainchogtu, Na. *See* Saichungga
Saint Augustine, V 127, 176
Saint-Denis, Michel, II 145
Saint-Denys Garneau, Hector de, I 398; II 347
Sainte-Beuve, III 88
criticism on, III 90, 602
Saint-Exupéry, Antoine de, II 144, 146; IV 126–27
Saint Georges de Bouhélier, II 136
Saint-Hélier, Monique, IV 386
Saint-John Perse, I 16; II 138, 141, 145; III 170; IV 127–29, 391; V 233
influence of, IV 193, 562
Saint-Léger Léger, Alexis. *See* Saint-John Perse
Saint-Pierre, Jean, II 150
Saint-Pol-Roux, II 136
Saintsbury, George, II 52; III 110
Sainz, Gustavo, III 272; IV 129–30; V 420
Saipradit, Kulap. *See* Siburapha
Saitō Mokichi, II 465, 498
influence of, II 465
Saizarbitoria, Ramón, IV 310
Saja, Kazys, III 133
Sajjad, Anvar, III 459–60
Sakaguchi Ango, V 321
Sakchai Bamrungphong. *See* Seni Saowaphong
Sakharov, Andrei, V 504
Sakubita, M. M., IV 704
Salacrou, Armand, II 142, 144, 146; IV 130–31
Saladrigas, Robert, V 573
Salama, Hannu, II 103; IV 131–32
Salamon, Ernő, IV 85
Šalamun, Tomaz, IV 697
Salarrué (Salvador Salazar Arrué), I 435; V 122
Salaverri, Vicente A., IV 516
Salaviei, Aleś, I 376
al-Salawī, 'Abd al-Ghanī, IV 365
Salazar Arrué, Salvador. *See* Salarrué
Salazar Bondy, Sebastián, III 511; V 535–36
Šalda, František Xaver, I 520; IV 132–33, 656
on Čapek, Karel, I 406
on Seifert, IV 185
on Wolker, IV 657
Sale, Roger
on Bellow, I 230
Saleh, Christiane, III 35
Salgado, Plínio, I 321; IV 38
Sālih, al-Tayyib, IV 367
Salinas, Pedro, I 435–36; II 195, 296; IV 133–35, 304
Salinger, J. D., I 70; IV 135–37
influence of, III 468
Salinš, Gunars, III 17
Salisachs, Mercedes, V 570
Salivarová, Zdena, V 155
Salkey, Andrew, II 54
Salleh Ghani, III 189
Sallenave, Danièle, V 231
Sallinen, Aulis, II 313
Salmā, Abū, III 464
Salmi Manja, III 190
Salmon, André, I 102, 513; II 140
Salo, Arvo, II 103
Salom, Jaime, V 574
Salomon, Ernst von, II 224
Salten, Felix, I 155
Salter, Mary Jo, V 27
Saltykov-Shchedrin, Mikhail
influence of, IV 240
Salustri, Carlo Alberto. *See* Trilussa
Salvador, Carles, IV 312

Salvat-Papasseit, Joan, IV 312
Sama, Bal Krishna, III 366, 367, 368
Samain, Albert, I 177
Samaniego, Antenor, V 536
Samantar, Mohamed Said, IV 279
Samarakis, Andonis, II 283; IV 137–38
Samchuk, Ulas, IV 497
Sami, I 37–38
Samkange, Stanlake, IV 712
Sam-Long, Jean-François, IV 25
al-Sammān, Ghāda, IV 398
Sammut, Frans, III 203
Samné, Georges, III 35
Samokovlija, Isak, IV 692
Samoyed literature. *See* Finno-Ugric literatures of the Soviet Union, Nenets
Samoylov, David, IV 107
Sampedro, José Luis, V 573
Samper Ortega, Daniel, V 145
Samuels, Charles Thomas
on Fitzgerald, F. Scott, II 110–11
Samylenko, Volodymyr, IV 493
Sanadhya, Totaram, III 454
San Antonio. *See* Dard, Frédéric
Sánchez, Florencio, I 113; IV 138–39, 515; V 642
Sánchez, Luis Rafael, IV 316; V 536–37
Sanchez, Sonia, I 73
Sánchez Espeso, Germán, V 573
Sánchez Ferlosio, Rafael, IV 139–40, 308, 309
Sánchez Gómez, Gregorio, V 145
Sand, Arne, IV 380
Sand, George, V 224
Sandburg, Carl, I 65, 345; IV 140–41
influence of, II 623
Sande, Jakob, III 402
Sandel, Cora (Sara Fabricius), III 400; V 537–38
Sandemose, Aksel, III 400; IV 142–43
Sandhu, Gulzar Singh, V 309
Sanguineti, Edoardo, II 474; IV 143–44
Sankawulo, Wilton, III 71
Sanskrit, literatures using. *See* Indian *and* Nepalese literatures
Sansom, William, II 51; IV 144–45
Sánta, Ferenc, II 416
Sant'Anna, Affonso Romano de, V 90
Santareno, Bernardo, III 569
Santayana, George, I 67, 274; III 115; IV 145–47
criticism on, IV 467
influence of, IV 146, 337
Santiago, Silviano, V 90
Santo, Alda Espírito, IV 147
Santos, Aires de Almeida, I 96
Santos, Arnaldo, I 96
Santos, Bienvenido N., III 524–25; V 538–39
Santos, Lope K., III 526
Santos, Marcelino dos, III 323
Santos Chocano, José, III 510
Sanu, Yaqub, II 4, 6
Saoli, Jacob Russell, IV 291
São Tomé and Príncipe literature, IV 147
Sapegno, Natalino, III 81
Sapkale, Trymbak, V 309
Sappho, V 644
al-Saqr, Mahdī, II 458
Sára, Sándor, V 154
Sarabhai, Bharati, II 437
Saraç, Tahsin, V 606
Sarachchandra, Ediriwira, IV 322–23
Sarafian, Nighohos, I 121
Saraiva, António José, III 570
Saramago, José, V 539–40
Sarcey, Francisque, II 91
Sarduy, Severo, IV 147–48, 317; V 391
Sargeson, Frank, III 383; IV 148–49
Sarkia, Kaarlo, II 101, 102
Sarma, Sundersena, II 437
Sarmiento, Domingo Faustino, I 110, 112; II 303; V 42
Sarnogoev, Bayïlda, II 589

Saroyan, William, I 63, 66; IV 149–51; V 125, 639
Sarraute, Nathalie, I 596; II 68, 147, 148, 149; III 381, 382; IV 59, 151–52; V 230, 232, 640
Sarris, Andrew, II 98
Sarton, George, IV 152
Sarton, May, I 286; IV 152–54
Sartre, Jean-Paul, I 202, 209, 391, 392, 491; II 67–68, 144, 145, 146, 147, 149; III 38, 41, 57, 80, 92, 151, 365, 381, 391, 515, 517, 520–21; IV 61, 154–57, 195, 257, 665; V 141, 227, 229, 230, 242, 410, 418, 484
  on Butor, I 372
  on Camus, I 393
  on Césaire, I 437
  criticism on, I 278; III 93; IV 467
    excerpts of, IV 157–59
  on Dos Passos, I 582
  on Genet, II 206, 207, 208
  on Giraudoux, II 245
  influence of, I 454; III 419; IV 121, 125, 538, 562; V 632
  on Négritude, III 361, 362
  on Nizan, III 397
  on Ponge, III 562
  precursor of philosophy of, IV 131
  on Sarraute, IV 151
Sarvig, Ole, I 538; IV 159–60
Saryg-ool, Stepan, IV 484
Sassoon, Siegfried, II 34, 277; III 450; IV 160–61
Sastre, Alfonso, I 355; IV 161–63, 303; V 575
Sastri, Mathuranatha Kavi, II 436
Satie, Erik, I 476; II 140
Satō Haruo, II 496; V 312
Satomi Ton, II 496
Sauser, Frédéric Louis. See Cendrars, Blaise
Saussure, Ferdinand de, III 57; IV 359; V 500, 501
  criticism on, V 175
  influence of, III 93–94; V 195, 376
Savard, Félix-Antoine, I 398
Savater, Fernando, V 571
  on Cioran, V 141
Savchenko, Yakiv, IV 494, 495
Savickis, Jurgis, III 131
Savin, Viktor, II 105
Savvin, S. See Jiribine, Kün
Sayers, Dorothy L., V 128
Sayers, Peig, II 461; V 318
Sāyigh, Tawfīq, III 464; V 472, 540–41
al-Sayyāb, Badr Shākir, II 4, 457; IV 163–64; V 285, 353, 354, 405
Sayyad, Parviz, V 314, 315
al-Sayyid, Mahmūd, II 457
Sbarbaro, Camillo, II 470, 471; IV 164–65
  influence of, IV 164
Scanziani, Piero, IV 388
Scève, Maurice, I 297
Schade, Jens August, I 537; IV 165
Schaffner, Jakob, IV 382
Schaik-Willing, Jeanne van, III 376
Schallück, Paul, II 225; IV 165–67
Schami, Rafik, V 249
Scharang, Michael, I 159; V 54
Scharen, Peter, IV 324
Scheerbart, Paul, II 70
Scheer-Schäzler, Brigitte
  on Bellow, I 231
Schehadé, Georges, II 148; III 35
Scheler, Max, III 515; V 571
  influence of, I 517; III 95
Schendel, Arthur van, III 375–76; IV 167–68
Scherfig, Hans, I 538
Scherg, Georg, IV 84
Schevchenko, Taras, V 371
Schickele, René, II 69

Schierbeek, Bert, III 377
Schietekat, Edmond. See Snoek, Paul
Schildt, Runar, II 99, 100; V 62
Schiller, Friedrich, III 79
  criticism on, III 82, 85, 103, 215
  influence of, I 331
Schirach, Baldur von, II 218
Schirmbeck, Heinrich, II 224
Schirò, Zef, I 37
Schisgal, Murray, I 74
Schleiermacher, Friedrich, III 126
Schlesak, Dieter, IV 84
Schmid, Max
  on Hesse, II 369
Schmidt, Arno, II 225; IV 168–69
Schmidt, Augusto Frederico, IV 9
Schmitz, Ettore. See Svevo, Italo
Schmitz, Paul. See Muller, Dominik
Schnabel, Ernst, II 223
Schnackenberg, Gjertrud, V 27, 28
Schneider, Benno, IV 686
Schneider, Elisabeth
  on Eliot, T. S., II 21
Schneider, Hansjörg, IV 383
Schneider, Judith M.
  on Goldemberg, V 260
Schneider, Reinhold, II 218
Schneider, Rolf, II 225
Schnitzler, Arthur, I 150–51, 154, 216; II 216; IV 169–72; V 53
  criticism on, III 107
  influence of, III 298
Schnurre, Wolfdietrich, II 222, 224
Schodjaie, Ghulam Ghaus, I 19
Schoeman, Karel, IV 288; V 565
Scholem, Gershom, I 239
  on Benjamin, I 242
Scholes, Robert, III 126
  on Durrell, II 46
Schönberg, Arnold, IV 360
Schopenhauer, Arthur
  influence of, II 549; III 315, 430, 607
    on American literature, III 430
    on Argentine literature, I 303
    on Armenian literature, III 444
    on English literature, I 488; II 329
    on Finnish literature, II 585
    on French literature, II 231
    on German literature, II 549; III 315
    on Japanese literature, II 315, 316
    on Polish literature, III 607
    on Russian literature, I 90
    on Spanish literature, I 195
Schöpflin, Aladár, II 413
Schorer, Mark
  on Lewis, Sinclair, III 65
Schoultz, Solveig, II 102
Schreiner, Olive, IV 172–74, 288; V 516, 565
Schreyer, Lothar, III 106
Schriber, Margrit, IV 383
Schröder, Rudolf Alexander, II 216, 218; III 103, 104
Schulz, Bruno, I 281; III 556, 558; IV 174–75
Schulz, Max F.
  on Singer, Isaac Bashevis, IV 237
Schürer, Ernst
  on Kaiser, Georg, II 553
Schurer, Fedde, III 379
Schuster, Paul, IV 84
Schutting, Julian, V 54
Schutz, Alfred, III 515
Schutz (Schütz), David, II 467–68; V 541
Schuyler, James, I 73; V 27, 47
Schwaiger, Brigitte, V 54
Schwalbach, Eduardo, III 567
Schwartz, Delmore, I 229, 256; IV 175–76
  on Eliot, T. S., II 20
Schwartz, I. J., IV 683
Schwartz, Kessel
  on Goytisolo, Juan, II 267
Schwartz, Maurice, IV 686

Schwartz, Murray M., II 163
Schwartzmann, Leo. See Shestov, Lev
Schwarz, Manfred, IV 383
Schwarz, Roberto, V 90
Schwarz-Bart, André, V 541
Schwarz-Bart, Simone, V 541–42
Schweitzer, Charles, IV 154
Schwellnus, Paul Erdmann, IV 294
Schwellnus, Theodor, IV 294
Schwitters, Kurt, I 530, 531
Sciascia, Leonardo, II 473; IV 176–77
Scliar, Moacyr, V 90, 542–43
Scott, Alexander, IV 180; V 544, 545
Scott, David, V 213
Scott, Duncan Campbell, I 395–96
Scott, F. R., I 396; V 108
Scott, Francis George
  influence of, III 165
Scott, Gabriel, III 399
Scott, J. D., II 406
Scott, Paul, II 48; V 543–44
Scott, R. D.
  on Jung, II 535
Scott, Tom, IV 180; V 546, 547
Scott, Sir Walter, IV 547; V 510
  criticism on, III 85, 151; IV 179, 640
  influence of, I 396
Scottish literature, IV 177–81; V 544–48
  in English, IV 177–81
  in Gaelic, IV 178
  the Kailyard school of, I 196–97; IV 177–78
  literary criticism in, III 327; IV 250
  major writers of
    in English, see: Barrie; Bridie; MacCaig; MacDiarmid; Muir; Soutar; Spark
    in Scots, see: MacDiarmid; Smith, Sydney Goodsir; Soutar
  the Saltire Society of, IV 178
  in Scots, IV 178–79, 180, 250
  the Scottish Renaissance and, III 163, 165; IV 178, 179, 285
Scriabin, Alexander, III 481
Scribe, Eugène, II 91
Scutenaire, Louis, I 225
Sears, Sallie
  on James, Henry, II 491
Seaver, Edwin, IV 665
Sebastian, Mihai, IV 81
Sebbar, Leïla, V 16, 231
Seboni, Michael Ontepetse, I 307
Sebukima, Davis, IV 490
Seduro, Vladimir. See Hlybinny, Uladzimier
Sędzicki, Franciszek, III 561
Seeberg, Peter, I 539, 540; IV 181–82
Seers, Eugene. See Dantin, Louis
Seferiadhis, Yorghos. See Seferis, George
Seferis, George, I 426; II 27, 281, 283; IV 182–83; V 604
  influence of, I 518
Sefrioui, Ahmed, III 319, 320
Segal, Erich, V 379
Segal, Hannah, II 157
Segal, J. I., IV 685
Šegedin, Peter, IV 696
Seghers, Anna, II 219, 221, 225; IV 184–85, 320
  influence of, IV 653
Seghers, Pierre, II 145; V 233
Segoete, Everitt, III 49
Segrè, Cesare, III 88
Seidlin, Oskar
  on Hauptmann, II 341
Seifert, Jaroslav, I 521; III 385; IV 185–86; V 156
Seillière, Ernest, III 88
Šeinius, Ignas, III 130–31
Sein Tin, U, I 367
Seisensui Ogiwara
  influence of, IV 414
Sekera, Mahagama, IV 323
Sekese, Azariele, III 49

717

Shvarts, Yevgeny, IV 114
Shvartsman, Osher, IV 683
Shwei U-daung, I 367
Siadniou, Masiei, I 376
Siamanto, I 119–20; III 243; IV 540
Sibale, Grieve, IV 705
Sibelius, Jean, I 567
Siburapha (Si Burapha, Kulap Saipradit), IV 430; V 556–57
al-Siddīq, Muhammad 'Ashrī, IV 366
Sïdïkbekov, Tügelbay, II 588
Sidqī, Najātī, III 465
Sienkiewicz, Henryk, III 302, 552; IV 213–15
  on Przybyszewski, III 607
Sierra, Justo, III 271
Sierra Leonean literature, IV 215–16
  in Creole (Krio), IV 216
  in English, IV 215–16
Sieveking, Alejandro, V 133, 134
Siew Yang, III 191
Sigogo, Ndabezinhle, IV 713
Sigurðardóttir, Jakobína, II 427
Sigurðsson, Ólafur Jóhann, II 426; IV 216–17
Sigurjónsson, Jóhann, II 426; IV 217–18
Sigússon, Hannes, II 427
Sigwavhulimu, W. M. R., IV 294
Sík, Sándor, II 414
Sikelianos, Angelos, II 281; IV 218–19, 539; V 604
Sikelianos, Penelope, IV 218
Sikhat, Abbas, I 165
Šiktanc, Karel, V 156
Siles, Jaime, V 574
Siliqi, Llazar, IV 699
Siljo, Juhani, II 101
Sillanpää, Frans Eemil, II 101, 102; IV 219–20
Sillitoe, Alan, II 47, 48, 51; IV 220–21; V 208
Silone, Ignazio, II 470, 472; III 366; IV 221–23, 260
Silva, Alírio. See Talcalhe
Silva, Baltasar Lopes da, I 402
Silva, Domingos Carvalho da, I 323
Silva, José Marmelo e, III 568
Silva, Medardo Ángel, II 1
Silveira, Onésimo, I 402
Silveira, Tasso da, I 321
Sima, Joseph, I 545
Simbamwene, J. M., IV 418
Simenon, Georges, I 224; IV 223–25; V 231
  influence of, II 14
Šimić, Antun Branko, IV 695
Simic, Charles, V 26
Simionescu, Mircea Horia, IV 83
Simmel, Georg, III 149; V 500
  influence of, I 351; III 95
Simmons, James, V 403
Simões, João Gaspar, III 567; IV 20
Si-Mohand, Mohand, V 15
Simon, Alfred, V 232
Simon, Claude, II 147; III 381; IV 59, 225–26, 362; V 230, 640
Simon, John
  on Musil, III 338
Simon, Neil, V 28
Simon, Pierre-Henri
  on Camus, I 393
Simonaitytė, Ieva, III 130
Simonian, Simon, I 121
Simonov, Konstantin Mikhaylovich, IV 110, 226–28
Simons, Hi
  on Stevens, IV 340
Simpson, N. F., IV 433
Simukwasa, William, IV 705
Šimunović, Dinko, IV 695
Sinán, Rogelio, I 435; V 125
Şinasi, İbrahim, IV 474–75
Sinclair, Lister, I 397

Sinclair, May, IV 228–29; V 516
Sinclair, Upton, I 59; II 2; III 26, 572; IV 229–31
  influence of, III 350
Sinda, Martial, I 487
Sinden, Margaret
  on Hauptmann, II 342
Sindhi literature. See Indian and Pakistani literatures
Singapore literature, IV 232–34
  Asas '50 of, IV 232
  in Chinese, IV 232–34
  in English, IV 232–34
  in Malay, IV 232–34
  symbolism in, IV 233
  in Tamil, IV 232–34
Singer, Burns
  on MacDiarmid, III 165–66
Singer, I. J., IV 234, 238–39, 684; V 391
  influence of, IV 235
Singer, Isaac Bashevis, I 69; IV 234–36, 685; V 391, 392, 543
  critical excerpts on, IV 236–37
Singh, Jagjit, IV 490
Singh, Khadga Man, III 368
Singh, Khushwant, II 439; IV 239–40
Singh, Nanak, II 439
Singleton, Mary Ann
  on Lessing, Doris, III 53
Sinhala literature. See under Sri Lankan literature
Sinisgalli, Leonardo, II 361
Sinjohn, John. See Galsworthy, John
Sinkó, Ervin, IV 700
Sinna, Muhammad Abū, II 5; V 200
Sinopoulos, Takis, II 282
Sinxo, Guybon B., IV 295
Sinyavsky, Andrey Donatovich, IV 113, 240–41; V 391, 620
  on Pasternak, Boris, III 485
Sion, Georges, I 226
Sipikim, Mudi, III 389
Sîrba, Ioan D., V 519
Sirisena, Piyadasa, IV 322
Sisouk Na Champassak, III 9
Sit, Madame, I 386
Sithole, Ndabaningi, IV 712, 713
Sito, Jerzy S., V 493
Sitor Situmorang, II 442–43
Sitwell, Edith, II 35; III 450, 609; IV 241–42
  criticism on, IV 586
  on Villa, IV 564
Sitwell, Osbert, IV 241
Sitwell, Sacheverell, IV 241
Siwertz, Sigfrid, IV 377, 381
Sjarif Amin, II 444
Sjöberg, Birger, II 89; IV 377
Sjöstrand, Östen, IV 380
Skaba, Andry, V 370
Skæraasen, Einar, III 402
Skagestad, Tormod, III 402
Skala, Jan, III 155
Skalbe, Kārlis, III 16; IV 242–43
Skard, Sigmund, III 403
Skármeta, Antonio, I 455; V 131, 132, 557–58
Skelton, Robin
  on Synge, IV 397
Škėma, Antanas, III 131, 132; V 393
Skerlić, Jovan, IV 692
  influence of, IV 693
Skif, Hamid, V 17
Skinner, B. F., IV 262
Šķipsna, Ilze, III 18
Skjoldborg, Johan, I 536
Sklyarenko, Semen, IV 496
Skouen, Arne, III 401
Skou-Hansen, Tage, I 539
Skourtis, Yorghos, II 284
Skovoroda, Hryhory; V 553
  influence of, I 586; V 525

Skujenieks, Knuts, III 19
Skujiņš, Zigmunds, III 18
Škvorecký, Josef, I 523, 524; II 622; IV 243–44, 255; V 156, 391
Slančíková, Božena. See Timrava
Slater, Francis Carey, IV 289
Slauerhoff, Jan Jacob, III 376; IV 245
Slaveykov, Pencho, I 358; IV 245–46, 672, 673
Slaveykov, Petko Rachov, IV 245
Slavica, Tomislav, IV 696, 697
Slavici, Ioan, IV 79
Slavutych, Yar, IV 497
Sleptsov, P. A. See Oyunsky, Bylatan Ölöksüöyebis
Slessor, Kenneth, I 147
Slisarenko, Olexa, IV 495
Šlitr, Jiří, I 524
Slonim, Marc, II 584
  on Gorky, II 264
  on Simonov, IV 227
Słonimski, Antoni, III 554, 556, 557; IV 246–47
Slovak literature. See under Czechoslovak literature
Slovene literature. See under Yugoslav literature
Słowacki, Juliusz, II 318, 618
Słucki, Arnold, V 494
Sluckis, Mykolas, III 133; V 394
Slutsky, Boris, IV 106
Small, Adam, IV 287
Smart, Christopher, IV 70
Smedley, Agnes, V 462
Smilansky, Yizhar, II 466
Smirnenski, Khristo, I 358
Smit, Bartho, IV 287
Smith, A. J. M., I 396
Smith, Barbara, V 222
Smith, Bernard, III 80
Smith, Florence Margaret. See Smith, Stevie
Smith, Henry Nash, I 76
Smith, Iain Crichton, IV 178, 181; V 545, 547
Smith, Lee, V 25
Smith, Maxwell A.
  on Mauriac, François, III 252
Smith, Pauline, IV 248, 288
Smith, Seymour
  on Taktsis, V 587
Smith, Sidonie Ann
  on Angelou, V 32
Smith, Stevie, II 36; IV 248–49
Smith, Sydney Goodsir, IV 178, 180, 249–51; V 545, 547
Smithyman, Kendrick, III 383
Smolych, Yury, IV 495
Smrek, Ján, I 525
Snellman, Johan Vilhelm, II 103
Sniķere, Velta, III 17
Snodgrass, W. D., I 71; V 26, 516
Snoek, Paul, I 222
Snow, C. P., II 42, 47, 52; IV 251–52, 257
  criticism on, III 31
  on Tvardovsky, IV 485
Snyder, Gary, I 72; II 579; V 26, 558–59
Soaba, Russell, III 455
Soare, Iulia, IV 82
Sobol, Yehoshua, V 326
Sŏ Chŏng-in, II 601
Sŏ Chŏng-ju, II 600–601; IV 252
social chronicle, the, IV 259–61
socialism in literature, IV 722. See also: communism; Marxism
  African, IV 194, 366, 417, 418, 419
  American, III 418; IV 230–31
  Asian, II 443, 464, 600; III 10; IV 323, 561
  and communism, IV 577
  East European, I 238, 264–65, 521–22,

Soyinka, Wole, III 390, 391, 392; IV 297–98; V 23, 174, 446–48, 450, 464
Soysal, Sevgi, IV 479
Spacks, Patricia Mayers, V 222
Spagnoli, John J.
on Proust, III 603
Spalter, Max
on Brecht, I 330
Spanish America. *See also the literatures of individual Spanish American countries*
costumbrismo in the literatures of, III 69; IV 315, 544
the *criollista* novel of, I 454; III 196
magic realism in the literatures of, I 132, 415, 434, 485; II 1, 424; III 176–78, 473; IV 518
modernism in the literatures of, *see under* modernism
political conditions in, as subject of, I 497; IV 324
ultraism in the literatures of, I 111, 302, 455; II 409; III 225, 273
Spanish-Caribbean literature, IV 315–17; V 105
Afro-Cubanism in, I 20; IV 315–16
costumbrismo in, III 69; IV 315
Cuba, 20th-c., as subject of
Batista dictatorship in, I 378; IV 148
Castro revolution in, II 299
in Cuba, IV 315–17
in the Dominican Republic, IV 315–17
existentialism in, IV 283
Generation of 1940 in, IV 316
literary criticism in, IV 316
and literary theory, IV 147
major writers of
in Cuba, *see:* Arenas; Ballagas; Cabrera, Lydia; Cabrera Infante; Carpentier; Guillén, Nicolás; Lezama Lima; Novás Calvo; Padilla; Piñera; Sarduy; Triana
in Dominican Republic, *see:* Veloz Maggiolo
in Puerto Rico, *see:* Ferré; Laguerre; Marqués; Sánchez, Luis Rafael; Soto
Négritude in, II 299; V 59
Orígenes in, group around, IV 316
Puerto Rico, 20th-c., as subject of, IV 315
American domination in, III 230–31
natives of, in New York, IV 282–83
structuralism in, IV 283
symbolism in, IV 392
Theater of the Absurd in, III 231; V 601
Transcendentalist group of, III 69; IV 316
Spanish Civil War, the, as literary subject, IV 262
causes of, IV 582
interpretations of, IV 307–8
in the literatures of: Belgium, IV 582; Canada, IV 43; England, II 37, 595, III 66, 440; France, I 252, 592, II 25, III 199, IV 155; Ireland, III 412; Portugal, I 423, IV 189; Spain, I 135, 355, 436, II 246, 265, 266, 364, III 244, IV 35, 190, 299, 302, 305, 307–8, 313, 315; Spanish America, III 370; IV 534; the United States, II 356
post-, III 244–45; IV 43, 189
social chronicles of, IV 260
Spanish-language literatures
See Argentine, Bolivian, Central American, Chilean, Colombian, Ecuadorian, Mexican, Paraguayan, Peruvian, Spanish, Spanish-

Caribbean, Uruguayan, *and* Venezuelan literatures
See under Philippine literature
Spanish literature, IV 298–310; V 569–75
Andalán (Aragonese) literature, V 569
Andalusian literature, V 569, 574
Bable (Asturian) literature, V 569
Basque literature, IV 310–11; V 569
Castilian literature, V 573, 574
Catalan literature, IV 34–35, 311–14; V 213–14, 569, 570, 573–75
the Noucentisme movement in, IV 34–35, 311–12
civil war as subject of, *see* Spanish Civil War
costumbrismo in, IV 301
the *esperpento* in, IV 301–2, 306, 531, 532, 533
existentialism in, I 427; III 437, 438, 499; IV 300, 304, 306, 310; V 569, 571
expressionism in, I 168; IV 306
and *nova-expresionismo,* IV 309
Extramaduan literature, V 569
the Franco régime as subject of, I 124, 354–55, 390, 428
the Falangists of, IV 300
and of American literature, IV 666
see also: censorship; Franco; Spanish Civil War; *and* of sociopolitical commitment *under this entry*
Galician literature, IV 314–15; V 569, 573
the Irmandades da Fala group of, IV 315
Rexurdimento in, IV 314
the Generation of '98 (1898) of, I 167, 195; II 254; III 167, 436–37, 507; IV 298, 299, 300, 304, 306, 531; V 193, 570
the Generation of 1925 (or 1927) of, I 50, 436; II 363; IV 298, 299, 304, 306, 307, 500; V 128, 148, 570
the Generation of 1936 of, I 427; IV 298, 299, 305, 306; V 148, 570
Gongorism in, IV 304; V 570
Leonese literature, V 569
literary criticism in, II 266, 499–500; III 95–97, 436; IV 35, 162, 300, 314
exile, versus at-home, IV 299
major writers of, *see:* Alberti; Aleixandre; Alonso, Dámaso; Arniches; Aub; Ayala; Azorin; Baroja; Benavente; Benet; Blasco Ibáñez; Buero Vallejo; Casona; Cela; Celaya; Cernuda; Chacel; Conde; Cunqueiro; Delibes; Echegaray; Espriu; García Lorca, Federico; Gironella; Gómez de la Serna; Goytisolo, Juan; Grau (Delgado); Guillén, Jorge; Hernández, Miguel; Jarnés; Jiménez; Laforet; Machado, Antonio; Martín-Santos; Martínez Sierra; Matute; Miró, Gabriel; Ortega y Gasset; Otero, Blas de; Palacio Valdés; Pardo Bazán; Pérez de Ayala; Pérez Galdós; Rodoreda; Salinas; Sánchez Ferlosio; Sastre; Sender; Torrente Ballester; Unamuno; Valle-Inclán
in Catalan, *see:* Espriu; Foix; Pedrolo; Riba; Rodoreda
also writing in French, *see* Arrabal
in Galician, *see* Cunqueiro
in literary criticism, *see* Alonso
in philosophy, *see:* Ortega y Gasset; Unamuno
modernism in, II 510; III 167, 294; IV 301, 304, 307, 310, 312, 531; V 570
neobaroque in, IV 306, 309
neorealism in, IV 299, 301, 302, 308

New Novel techniques in, III 499; V 127, 570
the Novísimos group of, IV 305–6, 309
objectivism in, IV 308
of sociopolitical commitment, IV 299, 302, 303, 305, 308; V 569
surrealism in, *see under* surrealism
symbolism in, I 233; III 95, 167; IV 303–4, 311, 313, 315, 392
Theater of the Absurd in, III 499; IV 314, 433
tremendismo in, I 427; IV 298–99, 306, 308
the Turia group of, II 265
ultraism in, IV 499–500
Spanninga, Sjoerd, III 380
Spark, Muriel, II 47; IV 181, 317–18; V 207, 545
Sparks, Tryphena, II 328
Späth, Gerold, IV 382
Spears, Monroe K.
on Auden, I 139
Spence, Lewis, IV 179
Spencer, Bernard, II 37; III 172
Spencer, Elizabeth, I 69
Spencer, Herbert
influence of, III 137; IV 544
Spencer, Michael
on Butor, I 373–74
Spender, Stephen, I 548; II 34, 36, 37, 53; III 172, 450; IV 318–19, 438; V 317
influence of, II 70, 182
Spengler, Oswald
influence of, II 504
Sperber, Manès, I 157; IV 319–21
Sperr, Martin, II 223, 395
Spescha, Hendri, IV 389
Spiel, Hilde, V 248
Spilka, Mark
on Lawrence, D. H., III 24–25
on Lessing, Doris, III 53
on Woolf, Virginia, IV 663
Spillane, Mickey, III 571
Spiller, Robert, I 67
Spillers, Hortense, V 222
Spingarn, Joel Elias, I 67; III 84
Spinoza
influence of, III 47; IV 73, 552
Spiró, György, V 297, 298
Spitteler, Carl, IV 321–22, 383
and psychology, II 536, 538
Spitzer, Leo, III 105
Spivak, Gayatri Chakravorty, V 222
Spota, Luis, III 273; V 421, 575–77
Sprigg, Christopher St. John. *See* Caudwell, Christopher
Sprinchorn, Evert
on Strindberg, IV 358
Spurling, Hilary
on Powell, III 583–84
Spurling, John
on Beckett, I 215
Squarzina, Luigi, II 475
Squires, Radcliffe
on Frost, II 175
Šrámek, Fráňa, I 520
influence of, II 656
Sranan Tongo literature. *See* Dutch-Caribbean literature, in Surinam
Sri Lankan literature, IV 322–25
the ''Aesthetes'' of, IV 323
in English, IV 324–25
Free Verse group of, IV 323
the Progressives of, IV 323
in Sinhala, IV 322–23
in Tamil, IV 323–24
use of stream-of-consciousness technique in, IV 322
Youth Insurgency (1971) as subject of, IV 323, 324
Sri Sri. *See* Rao, Srirangam Srinivas
Srivastav, Dhanpat Rai. *See* Premchand

E. Y.; Muschg; Spitteler; Walser, Robert; Walter, Otto
in Romansh, IV 388–89
student uprisings (1960s) as subject of, IV 383
surrealism in, IV 384
in Swiss-German, IV 384–85
Syad, William J. F., IV 279
Sybesma, Rintsje Piter, III 379
Sybille, I 120
Sychta, Bernard, III 561
Syed Alwi, III 191
Syed Sheikh al-Hady, III 189
Sygietyński, Antoni, III 552
Sylejmani, Hivzi, IV 699
Sylvain, Georges, II 153
Sylvain, Normil, II 154
symbolism, IV 389–92
  American, I 58, 64, 67; III 141, 170, 269; IV 391
  Australian, I 330
  Belgian, I 221, 224; III 174; IV 391, 649
  Brazilian, I 185, 320; III 263; IV 37–38, 392
  Canadian, I 398; III 362
  Czechoslovak, I 403, 525; II 606
  Dutch, I 308; III 47, 375
  Eastern, II 423, 497, 599; III 461; IV 233; V 336
  East European, I 358, 401, 592; II 211; III 16, 129, 341; IV 116, 242, 495, 566, 673, 698 (see also Czechoslovak, Estonian, Hungarian, Polish, Romanian, and Russian under this entry)
  Estonian, I 54; II 60; III 241; IV 412
  French, I 102–3, 190, 469, 470; II 135, 136, 139, 231; III 552; IV 26, 528
  French-African, III 252
  French-Caribbean, II 153
  and hermeticism, II 361
  Hungarian, I 527; II 412, 604
  influence of, IV 391, 392, 641
  influences on, IV 390
  and literary criticism, I 67; II 542; III 85, 86, 89, 95, 98, 101, 104, 119, 553; IV 132–33, 602, 641
  and modernism, I 110; III 293, 294; IV 392
  Near Eastern, I 263; III 33; IV 475; V 611
  Polish, I 528; III 553, 555, 607; IV 666, 667
  post-, IV 118
  and psychology, II 534–35
  Romanian, I 176, 177, 189, 276; IV 79, 85, 568
  Russian, I 98, 231–32, 282–84, 350; II 247, 477, 593, 627; III 46, 266, 552; IV 103–4, 107, 114, 268, 269, 391, 403, 470
    opposition to, II 305; IV 104–5
  Yiddish, III 396
  South African, IV 287, 288, 289
  Spanish, I 233; III 167; IV 35, 303–4, 311, 313, 315, 392
  Spanish American, II 364; III 271, 494; IV 392, 515; V 82
  Western European, I 248, 298, 536, 542; II 210, 215, 280, 281; III 402, 462, 566, 567; IV 182, 217, 241, 377, 391, 392, 539, 607, 673–74, 675; V 546 (see also Belgian, Dutch, French, and Spanish under this entry)
symbolism, Freudian, II 157
Symonenko, Vasyl, IV 497
Symons, Arthur, II 52; III 110, 351; IV 391, 674
  influence of, II 17
  on Yeats, William Butler, IV 677–78

Synge, John Millington, II 459, 463, 520; III 411; IV 392–95, 674; V 316, 236, 360
  critical excerpts on, IV 395–97
  criticism of, II 566
Syrian literature, IV 397–401. See also under Kurdish literature
  Egypt, dissolution of union with, as subject of, IV 399
  major writers of, see: al-Māghūt; Mīna; Qabbānī; Tāmir; al-'Ujaylī; Wannūs
  Lebanese, see Adūnīs
  the Palestine Liberation Movement as subject of, III 613
  the Six Day War as subject of, III 613; IV 399
  World War II conditions as subject of, IV 399
Szabó, Béla, I 527
Szabó, Dezső, II 413
Szabó, Lőrinc, II 412, 414; IV 401–2
Szabó, Magda, II 416
Szabó, Pál, II 414
Szaniawski, Jerzy, III 556, 557
Szczepański, Jan Józef, V 492, 493
Szczypioski, Andrzej, V 493
Székely-Lulofs, Madelon Hermina, II 445
Szelényi, Iván, V 369
Szenteleky, Kornél, IV 699–700
Szép, Ernő, II 412
Szichman, Mario, V 41, 126, 524, 583–84
Szilágyi, András, IV 85
Szomory, Dezső, II 413
Szymborska, Wisława, III 559; IV 402; V 491, 492
Szyszkowitz, Gerald, V 54, 584–85

Taban lo Liyong, IV 490–91
Tabasaran literature. See under North Caucasian literatures
Tabéry, Géza, IV 85
Tabet, Jacques, III 35
Tabidze, Galaktion, II 211, 212; IV 403
Tabidze, Titsian, II 211, 212
Tablada, José Juan, III 271
Tadijanović, Dragutin, IV 695–96
Tafdrup, Pia, V 161, 546, 586
Tagalog literature. See Philippine literature, in Pilipino
Tagger, Theodor. See Bruckner, Ferdinand
Tagore, Rabindranath, I 187, 444; II 400, 434, 436; III 352, 360; IV 403–6; V 163, 164
  criticism on, IV 404
    excerpts of, IV 406–8
  influence of, II 248; IV 75
Tāhā, 'Alī Mahmūd, II 4
Tāhā, 'Alī Muhammad, IV 473
Tāhir, Bahā', II 7; V 201
Tahir, Kemal, IV 479
al-Tahīr 'Abdallāh, Yahyā, V 190, 201
Tai Hou-ying (Dai Houying), V 136
Tailleferre, Germaine, III 527
Taine, Hippolyte, III 88, 501, 570
  influence of, IV 699–700
Tait, William J., V 547
Taiwanese literature. See under Chinese literature
Taiwo, Oladele
  on Head, V 279
Tajik literature, IV 408–10
  collectivization as subject of, IV 408, 409
  major writers of, see: Ayni; Lahuti; Tursunzoda
    also writing in Persian, see Lahuti
    also writing in Uzbek, see Ayni
  Socialist Realism in, IV 408–9
Tajik-Farsi literature. See Uzbek literature
Takahama Kyoshi, II 497, 498

Takahashi Michitsuna, V 335
Takamura Kōtarō, V 336
al-Takarlī, Fu'ād, II 458
Takdir Alisjahbana, Sutan, II 441, 442; IV 410–11
Takeda Taijun, II 497
Takenishi Hiroko, V 336
Takiguchi Shūzō, V 336
Takizawa Bakin, II 494
Taktsis, Costas, V 586–87
Talabani, Reza, II 628
Talcalhe, I 402
Talens, Genaro, V 574
Talesnik, Ricardo, V 42
Talev, Dimitur, I 359; IV 411–12
Tall, al-Hajj Umar ibn Saïd, IV 192
Tallet, José Zacarías, I 20
Talvik, Heiti, I 54; II 61; IV 412–13
  criticism on, IV 11
Talviken, Heiti. See Talvik, Heiti
Talvio, Maila, II 100
Tamási, Aron, IV 85
Tamayo, Franz, I 289
Tambal, Hamza, IV 366
Tamer, Ülkü, IV 477
Tamil literature. See under Indian, Malaysian, Singapore, and Sri Lankan literatures
Tāmir, Zakariyyā, IV 398; V 587–88
Tam Lang, IV 561
Tamminga, Douwe Annes, III 380
Tammsaare, A. H., II 62, 63; IV 413–14
Tammuz, Benjamin, V 588–89
Tamsanqa, Witness K., IV 295
Tamura Ryūichi, V 337
Tanaka Yasuo, V 336
Tănase, Virgil, IV 82
Tản-Đà Nguyễn Khac Hiếu, IV 560
Tandori, Dezső, V 298
Taneda Santōka, II 497–98; IV 414–15
Taneda Shōichi. See Taneda Santōka
Taner, Haldun, IV 478, 479
Tănese, Stelian, V 521
Tangour, Habib, V 15
Tanguy, Yves, IV 371
Tanizaki Jun'ichirō, II 31, 496; IV 415–16; V 436
Tank, Maksim, I 375
Tan Kok Seng, IV 233
Tanner, Ilona, I 172
Tanner, Tony
  on Bellow, I 231
Tanpınar, Ahmet Hamdi, IV 476
Tansi, Sony Labou, V 231
Tanyuk, Les, V 612
Tanzanian literature, IV 416–19
  in English, IV 418–19
  literary criticism in, IV 419
  the Maji Maji war as subject of, IV 417, 418
  major writers of, in Swahili, see Robert
  oral traditions in, IV 419
  in Swahili, IV 417–18
  the Wameru expulsion as subject of, IV 419
  the Zanzibar revolution as subject of, IV 417
Tāqa, Shādhil, II 457
Taraki, Noor Mohammad, I 19, 20
Tarancı, Cahit Sıtkı, IV 476
Tarar, Mustansar Husain, III 461
Tardieu, Jean, II 148; IV 419–20; V 232
Tardivaux, René. See Boylesve, René
Tardon, Raphael, II 155
Tarhan, Abdülhak Hamit, IV 475
al-Tarīs, 'Abd al-Khaliq, III 319
Tarkovsky, Arseny, IV 106
Tarn, Adam, III 559
Tarnavsky, Ostap, IV 497; V 613
Tarnavsky, Valentyn, V 614
Tarnawsky, Yuriy, IV 497
Tarzi, Mahmud Beg, I 18
Tashmuhämmäd-oghli, Musa. See Aybek

Tin Mo, I 368
Tiofe, Timóteo Tio. *See* Varela, João
Tirso de Molina (Gabriel Téllez), V 266
Titel, Sorin, IV 83
Titta, Cesare de, II 476
Titus-Carmel, Gérard, V 169
Tiusanen, Timo
  on Dürrenmatt, I 602–3
  on O'Neill, Eugene, III 434
Tlali, Miriam, V 567
Tlili, Mustapha, IV 473
Tobar García, Francisco, II 2
Tobilevych, Ivan. *See* Karpenko-Kary
Tobino, Mario, II 473; IV 447
Todd, Ruthven, IV 373
Todorov, Petko, IV 246
Todorov, Tzvetan, II 394; V 142, 235, 500
Toghïs-ŭlï, Kölbey, II 570
Togolese literature, IV 447–48
  in Ewe, IV 447–48
  in French, IV 447–48
Tōgō Seiji, V 335
Tố Hữu, IV 561
Toit, Jacob Daniel du. *See* Totius
Țoiu, Constantin, IV 83; V 519
Toka, Salchak, IV 483–84
Toki Zemmaro, II 464
Toklas, Alice B., IV 328, 329
Tokobaev, Moldogazi, II 588
Tokombaev, Aalï, II 588, 589
Tokuda Shūsei, II 495
Toland, Gregg, II 96
Tolkien, J. R. R., II 44; III 59; IV 448–49; V 509
Toller, Ernst, II 70, 217, 218, 520; IV 449–50; V 391
Tolstaya, Tatyana, V 531, 596–98
Tolstoy, Alexey Nikolaevich, IV 110, 254, 260, 430–32; V 596
Tolstoy, Lev, I 418; II 262; III 29, 481; IV 46, 74, 107–8, 259, 348; V 220, 596
  criticism on, III 98, 151, 266; IV 114–15, 333
  influence of, IV 259
    on American literature, V 240
    on Australian literature, IV 42
    on Bulgarian literature, IV 412
    on English literature, II 191; IV 251
    on French literature, II 138; III 232
    on German literature, IV 184
    on Indian literature, III 591
    on Lebanese literature, V 457
    on Polish literature, III 607
    on Russian literature, I 362, 447; II 72; IV 109
  opposition to, I 446; IV 253
  as subject, V 209
Toma, Velta, III 17
Toman, Karel, II 392
Tomashevsky, Boris, III 98
Tomasi di Lampedusa, Giuseppe, I 204; II 473; IV 177, 261, 452–54
Tomeo, Javier, V 573
Tonegaru, Constant, IV 82
Tonga literature. *See under* Zambian literature
Tongkat Waran. *See* Usman Awang
Tønnesen, Pernille, V 381
Toomer, Jean, IV 454–55
Topalian, Puzant, I 121
Topelius, Zachris, II 493
Topîrceanu, Gheorghe, IV 79–80
Torberg, Friedrich, I 155; IV 455–56
Torga, Miguel, III 567; IV 456–57
TORKAN. *See* Daneshfar-Pätzoldt, Torkan
Torre, Guillermo de, III 96
Torre Nilsson, Leopoldo, V 269
Torrente Ballester, Gonzalo, IV 308; V 570, 572, 575, 598–99
Torres, Alberto, I 321

Torres, Màrius, IV 313
Torres, Xohana, IV 315
Torres Bodet, Jaime, III 273; V 265
Torsvan, F. or T. *See* Traven, B.
Tóth, Árpád, II 412; IV 458
Totius, IV 286
Totovents, Vahan, I 122; III 243, 244
Toumanian, Hovaness, I 122
Touré, Sadan-Moussa, II 302
Touré, Samori, II 478
Touré, Sekou, II 302
Tourian, Bedros, I 119
Tournier, Michel, IV 458–60; V 230
Toussaint L'Ouverture (Louverture), Pierre Dominique, V 258
Tousseul, Jean, I 223
Toyen, III 386
Toynbee, Philip
  on Dennis, I 557
Tozzi, Federigo, II 470; IV 164, 460–61
Traba, Marta, V 40–42
Trād, Mīshāl (Michel), III 33; V 354
Traill, Catherine Parr, I 396
Trakl, Georg, I 152, 177; II 38, 69, 216, 607, 608; IV 461–62
  influence of, I 156; IV 506
Trần Diêu Hằng, V 619
Trần Khánh-Giư'. *See* Khái-Hưng
Tranquilli, Secondo. *See* Silone, Ignazio
Tranströmer, Tomas, IV 380, 462–63; V 582
Traoré, Mamadou, II 302
Trausti, Jón, II 425
Traven, B., IV 463–65
Traversi, Derek, III 117
Trayanov, Teodor, I 358
Traz, Robert de, IV 386
Trediakovsky, Vasily Kirillovich, V 441
Trefossa, I 604
Treichler, Paula, V 641
Tremain, Rose, V 208
Tremblay, Michel, V 109, 111, 599–600
Trend, John B.
  on Jiménez, II 512
Trenyov, Konstantin, IV 253
Třešňák, Vlastimil, V 156
Trevisan, Dalton, I 323
Trevisan, João Silvério, V 90
Trevor, Elleston. *See* Hall, Adam
Trevor, William (William Trevor Cox), II 51; V 319, 600–601
Triadú, Joan, IV 314
Triana, José, IV 316; V 601–2
Trías, Eugenio, V 571
Tribhuvandas, Manilal, II 436
Trifonov, Yury Valentinovich, IV 111, 113, 115, 465–66
Trilling, Lionel, I 69, 75; II 162, 398; III 83, 120, 127; IV 466–68
  on Agee, I 21
  on Dos Passos, I 582
  on Frost, II 174
  on Orwell, III 441
  on Snow, IV 251
Trilussa, II 476
Trinidadian literature. *See under* English-Caribbean literature
Triolet, Elsa, I 104–5; II 143
Tripathi, Suryakant, II 435
Tripp, John, IV 609
Trist, Margaret, I 147
Trollope, Anthony, V 95
  influence of, IV 251
Trọng Lang, IV 561
Trotsky, Leon, III 79
Trotzig, Birgitta, V 582, 602–3
Trubetskoy, Nikolay, III 98
Truffaut, François, II 96, 97
Trunk, Yekhiel Yeshaya, IV 684
Trương Vĩnh Ký, Petrus, IV 560
Trzebiński, Andrzej, III 557
Trznadel, Jacek, V 493
Ts'ai Yen, II 626

Tsang, K'o-chia, I 458, 460
Ts'ao Hsüeh-ch'in, II 401; V 470
Ts'ao Ts'ao, II 626
Ts'ao Yü, I 458, 459, 460; IV 468–69
Tscharner, Gion, IV 389
Tschumi, Bernard, V 169
Tsegaye Gabre-Medhin, II 64, 65
Tseng P'u, I 456
Tsereteli, Akaki, II 211
Tshaka, R. M., IV 295
Tshans-dybyans-rgya-mtsho, IV 444
Tshe-dban-don-ldan, IV 444
Tshiakatumba, Matala Mukadi, IV 703
Tsinberg, Yisroel, IV 684
Tsirkas, Stratis (Yannis Hadjiandreas), II 283; V 603–4
Tsonga literature. *See under* South African literature
Tsou Yung, I 456
Tsuda Umeko, V 460
Tsuka Kōhei, V 336
Tsuruya Namboku, V 45
Tsushima Shūji. *See* Dazai Osamu
Tsushima Yūko (Tsushima Satoko), V 335, 604–6
Tsvetaeva, Marina Ivanova, I 30, 340; IV 105, 106, 469–71; V 390
  criticism on, IV 470; V 143
  influence of, IV 469, 575
Tsvetkov, Alexey, IV 107
Tswana literature. *See under* Botswana *and* South African literatures
Tsybulko, Volodymyr, V 613
Tudoran, Dorin, V 519
Tūbiyā, Majīd, II 6; V 201
Tucholsky, Kurt, II 218; III 551; IV 471–72, 596
Tucker, James
  on Powell, III 583
Tuéni, Nadia, III 35
Tu Fu, V 650
Tuglas, Friedebert, II 62; III 72
Tu Hung, IV 232
Tuktash, Ilya, I 466
Tumas-Vaižgantas, Juozas, III 129
Tumbuka literature. *See under* Malawian *and* Zambian literatures
Tú Mỡ, IV 561
Tumunov, Zhamso, I 370
Tumusiime-Rushedge, IV 490
Tunisian literature, IV 472–74
  in Arabic, IV 472–73; V 409–10, 551–52
  in French, IV 473–74; V 417–18
  Maghrebian literature, *see* Maghrebian literature
  the Taht al-Sūr group of, IV 472
Tunström, Göran, V 581, 582
Tu P'eng-ch'eng, I 459
Tūqān, Fadwā, III 464; V 472
Tūqān, Ibrāhīm, III 464; V 472
Tuqay, Ghabdullah, IV 421
Turcios, Froylán, V 123
Turdi, Kayyum, IV 520
Turel, Adrien, IV 382, 383
Turèll, Dan, V 160
Turgenev, Ivan, II 489; IV 103, 112; V 220, 237, 322
  criticism on, III 600
  influence of, II 50, 116, 131, 191, 624; IV 42, 108; V 240
Türkay, Osman, I 519
Turki literature. *See* Uzbek literature
Turkish literature, IV 474–80; V 606–8
  the *Garip* movement in, IV 477
  independence as subject of, IV 476, 477
  major writers of, *see:* Adıvar; Ağaoğlu; Anday; Cansever; Cumalı; Dağlarsa; Dilmen; Hikmet; İlhan; Kalyoncu; Karaosmanoğlu; Kemal, Yaşar; Necatigil; Nesin
  also writing in English, *see:* Adıvar; Dilmen

Valgirin, Mikhail, I 465
Valladares, Armando, V 391
Vallak, Peet, II 62
Valle, Martino della, IV 388
Valle-Inclán, Ramón del, II 254, 409; IV
    301–2, 306, 392, 531–33; V 193,
    569, 574
  influence of, IV 315; V 439
Vallejo, César, III 510, 511; IV 372,
    533–35; V 260, 644
Vallejo, Georgette de, IV 534
Vallenilla Lanz, Laureano
  influence of, IV 544
Valle Peña, Ramón María. See Valle-Inclán, Ramón del
Vampilov, Alexandr, IV 114; V 485
Vančura, Vladislav, I 522; IV 535–37
Vandercammen, Edmond, I 225
Van der Meersch, Maxence, II 143
Van Doren, Mark
  influence of, I 255
Van Dyke, Henry, I 69
Van Ghent, Dorothy
  on Lawrence, D. H., III 24
Van Gogh, Vincent, V 368
  as subject, V 169
Vanhakartano, Helga, II 585
Van Itallie, Jean-Claude, I 75; IV 433
Várady, Szabolcs, V 298
Varela, João, I 402
Varerkar, Bhargavaram Vithal, II 437
Vargas, Germán, V 125
Vargas, Suzana, V 90
Vargas Llosa, Mario, III 509, 510; IV
    537–38; V 43, 97, 468, 506
  on Alegría, Ciro, I 43
  on Belli, Carlos Germán, V 67
  on Salazar Bondy, V 536
Vargas Osorio, Tomás, V 117, 145
Vargas Vila, José María, V 145
Varma, Ramkumar, II 437
Varnalis, Kostas, II 281; IV 538–39;
    V 604
Varoujan, Daniel, I 119, 120; III 244,
    444; IV 539–40
Vartio, Marja-Liisa, II 102, 313
Vaś, Iĺĺa. See Lytkin, Vasily
Vas, István, I 415; V 298
Vasalis, III 377
Vasconcelos, Joaquim Pereira Teixeira de.
    See Teixeira de Pascoaes
Vasconcelos, José, III 274; V 480
Vasconcelos, Mário Cesariny de, III 569
Vašek, Vladimír. See Bezruč, Petr
Vasilenko, Svetlana, V 531
Vasilev, Flor, II 105
Vasilev, Vladimir, I 358
Vasilev, Yordan, V 182
Vasiliev-Borogonsky, Sergey Stepanovich,
    IV 671
Vasiliu, George. See Bacovia, George
Vasin, Kim, II 105
Vásquez Guzmán, Oscar Nicomedes. See
    Guzmán, Nicomedes
Vassallo, Karmenu, III 203
Vassilikos, Vassilis, II 283–84; IV 540–
    41
Vasylchenko, Stepan, IV 493
Vatshavski, Oyzer, IV 684
Vaughan, Hilda, IV 608
Vaughan, Madge, IV 660
Vautrin, Jean, V 231
Vaykhert, Mikhl, IV 686
Vaysenberg, Itskhok Meyer, IV 684
Vaz de Soto, José María, V 573
Vazov, Ivan, I 358, 359
  criticism of, IV 246
  influence of, IV 412
Vázquez Montalbán, Manuel, IV 306;
    V 573
Veblen, Thorstein, III 62
Veen, Adriaan van der, III 378
Vegri, Saša, IV 697
Veiga, J. J., V 88

Veiga, Marcelo, IV 147
Veigelsberg, Hugo. See Ignotus
Vejvoda, Jaroslav, V 156
Vekshina, Lina, II 105
Velan, Yves, IV 386
Velázquez, Diego Rodriguez de Silva y,
    I 355
Velde, Rink van der, III 380
Velea, Nicolae, IV 83
Veliev, Ali, I 166
Veloz Maggiolo, Marcio, IV 316; V 618
Ven, Tima. See Chistalev, Venyamin
Venclova, Antanas, III 130
Venclova, Tomas, III 132–33
Venda literature. See under South African
    literature
Vendler, Helen
  on Stevens, IV 314
Venegas Filardo, Pascual, IV 543
Venezis, Elias, II 283; IV 541–42
Venezuelan literature, IV 542–45
  costumbrismo in, IV 544
  the Generation of 1918 of, IV 542
  the Gómez dictatorship as subject of,
    IV 544
  magic realism in, III 177; IV 518
  major writers of, see: Gallegos; Uslar
    Pietri
  mestizaje as subject of, IV 518
  modernism in, III 294; IV 542–43
  the Sardio group of, IV 544
  surrealism in, IV 543
  Viernes in, group around, IV 543
Venkatacharya, Tiru, II 437
Venkataramanayya, C., II 437
Venkitarattinam, III 192
Vennberg, Karl, I 131; IV 379
  influence of, III 195
Venttsel, Yelena. See Grekova, I.
Ventura, Adão, V 90
Venturi, Robert, V 498
Verbitsky, Bernardo, I 112
Vercors, II 147, 249; IV 545–46
Verga, Giovanni, II 468–69; IV 177,
    546–48
  criticism on, II 470; III 86
  influence of, II 470; IV 548
Vergil
  criticism on, III 103
Verhaeren, Émile, I 224, 225; IV 391,
    548–50
  influence of, I 350; II 138; IV 566, 723
Verhesen, Fernand, I 225
Verheyen, Renat, II 228
verismo. See Verga, Giovanni. See also
    realism
Veríssimo, Érico, I 322; IV 550–51; V 88
Veríssimo, José, I 184
Veríssimo, Luís Fernando, V 90
Verlaine, Paul, I 544; II 210, 599; IV
    389, 390; V 117
  influence of, III 47, 566
Vermeylen, August, I 219; IV 425,
    551–52
Verne, Jules
  influence of, II 44, 453
Vernet, Florian, II 153
Vernois, Paul
  on Ionesco, II 451
Vernon, Barbara, I 149
Vertov, Dziga, II 95
Verwey, Albert, I 308; III 375; IV 552–
    53
  influence of, IV 73
Very, Jones
  criticism on, III 123
Vesaas, Halldis Moren, III 402
Vesaas, Tarjei, III 400, 402; IV 553–55;
    V 276, 562
Veselis, Jānis, III 17
Veselovsky, Alexandr, III 99
Vesper, Will, II 218
Vestdijk, Simon, III 232, 330, 375, 376,
    377, 379; IV 555–56

Vetemaa, Enn, II 62–63
Vettese, Raymond, V 547
Vezhinov, Pavel, I 360
Vian, Boris, III 617; IV 556–57
Viana, Javier de, IV 515, 516
Viana Filho, Oduvaldo, V 88, 89
Vianen, Bea, I 605
Vianu, Tudor, I 189; IV 80
Viaud, Louis Marie Julien. See Loti,
    Pierre
Vicens Vives, Jaume, IV 314
Vicente, Gil, V 219
  influence of, I 324
Vicente, José, V 90
Vickery, Olga
  on Faulkner, II 84
Vico, Giambattista, I 510; III 57
  influence of, II 504
Vidal, Gore, I 70; III 394; IV 558–59;
    V 24
Vidmar, Josip, IV 697
Vidrić, Vladimir, IV 694–95
Vieira, Afonso Lopes, III 566
Vieira, Arménio, I 402
Vieira, José Luandino, I 96–97; III 569;
    IV 559–60
Viélé-Griffin, Francis, IV 390–91
Viertel, Berthold, I 152; II 607
Viese, Saulceríte, III 19
Vietnamese literature, IV 560–62; V 618–
    19. See also Vietnam War
  collectivization as subject of, IV 561
  the Dông-kinh School of the Just Cause
    of, IV 560
  literary criticism in, IV 561
  major writers of, see: Khái-Hưng;
    Nguyên Công Hoan; Nguyên Tuân;
    Nhát-Linh; Vũ Hoàng Chương
  the Self-Reliant group of, III 388; IV
    560–61
  Socialist Realism in, IV 561
Vietnam War, the, as literary subject, II
    565; III 71, 181, 258, 400; IV 185
Vieux, Damoclès, II 153
Viganò, Renata, III 366
Vigée, Claude, II 148
Vigneault, Gilles, I 398
Vihalemm, Arno, II 61
Vi Huyèn Đắc, IV 560, 561
Viirlaid, Arved, II 63
Viita, Lauri, II 102; IV 562–63
Vik, Bjørg, III 401
Vikulov, Sergey, V 532
Vilakazi, Benedict W., IV 296
Vilalta, Maruxa, III 274
Vila-Matas, Enrique, V 573
Vilar, Jean, I 327; II 141, 145
Vilde, Eduard, II 62, 63
Vilde, Iryna, IV 497
Vildrac, Charles, I 593; II 142; V 292
Vilhjálmsson, Thor, II 427; IV 563–64
  on García Márquez, II 203
Vilinska-Markovych, Maria. See Vovchok, Marko
Viljoen, Lettie (Ingrid Gouws), V 565
Vilks, Ēvalds, III 18
Villa, Jose Garcia, III 526; IV 564–65
Villaespesa, Francisco, II 510; III 294; IV
    301
Villalonga, Llorenç, IV 312, 313
Villaurrutia, Xavier, I 125; III 273, 274;
    IV 565–66; V 264, 456
Villaverde, Cirilo, V 39
Villegas, Cosío, V 422
Villegas, Oscar, V 423
Villemarqué, Théodore Hersart de la,
    II 151
Villena, Luis Antonio de, V 574
Villiers de l'Isle-Adam, Philippe Auguste
    Mathias de, IV 390, 391
  influence of, I 409
Villon, François, IV 486
  influence of, I 325; III 262
Viñas, David, I 112; V 40, 42, 619–20   727

Vinaver, Michel, V 232, 233
Vinaver, Stanislav, IV 692
Vinchevsky, Morris, IV 683
Vinea, Ion, IV 81, 486
Vinhranovsky, Mykola, IV 497; V 370
Vinje, Aasmund (A. O.), III 399; V 276
Vinkenoog, Simon, III 377
Vinokurov, Yevgeny, IV 106
Virrès, Georges, I 223
Virshsawmy, Dev, III 252
Virza, Edvarts, III 16; IV 566
Visca, Arturo Sergio
  on Hernández, Felisberto, V 282
Visconti, Luchino, II 96; III 366; IV 548
Visnapuu, Henrik, II 60, 61
Visser, A. G., IV 286
Visser, Germant Nico, III 380
Vitaly, Georges, II 145
Vitéz, Mihály Csokonai, V 215
Vitier, Citio, IV 316
Vitrac, Roger, I 127
  on Roussel, IV 96
Vittor, Ńobdinsa. See Savin, Viktor
Vittorini, Domenico
  on Pirandello, III 543–44
Vittorini, Elio, II 471, 472; III 243, 366;
    IV 177, 567–68; V 194
  influence of, IV 568
  on Ortese, III 439
Vivas, Eliseo
  on Lawrence, D. H., III 25
Vivier, Robert, I 225
Vlad, Mariya, V 613
Vladimov, Georgy, IV 111
Vlysko, Olexa, IV 496
Vočadlo, Otakar
  on Čapek, Karel, I 407
Vodanovich, Sergio, I 455; V 133, 134
Vodnik, Anton, IV 697
Voeten, Bert, III 378
Vogau, Boris Andreevich. See Pilnyak, Boris
Vogler, Elkhanon, IV 684
Vogt, Nils Collett, III 401, 402
Vogt, Walter, IV 383
Voiculescu, Vasile, IV 80, 568–69
Voigt, Ellen Bryant, V 27
Voisard, Alexandre, IV 387
Vojnović, Ivo, IV 569–70, 695
Vold, Jan Erik, III 402
Volkoff, Vladimir, V 232
Voloshin, Maximilian, IV 104, 469
Voloshinov, N., III 100
Volpe, Edmund L.
  on Faulkner, II 83
Volpe, Galvano della, III 81
Volponi, Paolo, II 474; IV 570–71; V 377
Voltaire, V 76, 543
  criticism on, III 105
  influence of, IV 335; V 474
Vondel, Joost van den, III 379
Vonmoos, Schimun, IV 388
Vonnegut, Kurt, Jr., I 70, 271, 272, 432;
    II 96; IV 137, 362, 571–73; V 24,
    25, 436, 595
Voorde, Urbain van de, I 222
Võ Phiến, V 619
Vormweg, Heinrich, II 350
Vorobkevych, Sydir, IV 493
Vorobyov, Mykola, V 613
Voronca, Ilarie, IV 81, 514
Voronny, Mykola, IV 493, 494
Voronsky, Alexandr Konstantinovich, III
    79; IV 252
Vörösmarty, Mihály
  influence of, I 238
Voskovec, Jiří (George), I 523; IV 573–74
Voss, Richard, V 76
Vossler, Karl, III 84, 104–5
Vovchok, Marko, IV 492
Vovk, Vira (Vira Selyanaska), V 613

Voynovich, Vladimir Nikolaevich, IV
    111; V 620–22
Vozáry, Dezső, I 527
Voznesensky, Andrey, IV 107, 574–76,
    682
Vrahimis, Nikos, I 518
Vrancea, Ileana, V 520
Vrchlický, Jaroslav, III 169
Vree, Paul de, I 222
Vreto, Jan, I 38
Vrettakos, Nikiforos, II 282; V 604
Vries, Abraham H., de, IV 287
Vriesland, Victor van, III 376
Vrioni, Mehmet, I 37–38
Vroman, Leo, III 377
Vroon, Ronald
  on Solzhenitsyn, IV 277
Vrugt, Johanna Petronelle. See Blaman, Anna
Vũ Băng, IV 561
Vučo, Aleksandar, IV 693
Vũ Đình Chí. See Tam Lang
Vũ Dình Long, IV 560
Vũ Hoàng Chương, V 622–23
Vũ Khắc Khoan, IV 561
Vũ Quỳnh-Hương, V 622–23
Vurgun, Samed, I 165–66; IV 576
Vvedensky, Alexandr, I 340; IV 106
Vyartsinski, Anatol, I 376
Vylka, Tyko, II 105
Vynnychenko, Volodymyr, IV 493, 576–
    77; V 613, 614
Vyshnya, Ostap, IV 495
Vysotsky, Vladimir, III 424; V 623–24

Waarsenburg, Hans van, III 377
Wādī, Tāhā, V 202
Wadman, Anne Sybe, III 380
Waggerl, Karl Heinrich, I 156; V 54
Wägner, Elin, IV 377
Wagner, Geoffrey
  on Lewis, Wyndham, III 68
Wagner, Jane, V 29
Wagner, Richard
  influence of, IV 200
Wahba, Sa'd al-dīn, II 7
Wain, John, II 30, 47, 48, 375; IV 578–
    79
  influence of, II 182
Wainwright, Jeffrey, V 212
Wakayama Bokusui, IV 498
Wakoski, Diane, V 644
Walcott, Derek, II 54–55; IV 579–80;
    V 86
Walden, Herwarth, II 69, 216; IV 347
Waldinger, Ernst, I 156; IV 580–81
Waley, Arthur, II 35
Waliullah, Syed, I 187
Walker, Alice, V 25, 222, 625–26
  on Hurston, V 299
Walker, Kath, V 51
Walker, Melissa G.
  on Lessing, Doris, III 54
Wall, Cheryl, V 222
Wallace, Edgar
  influence of, II 14
Wallach, Yona, IV 467
Wallant, Edward Lewis, I 69; IV 581–82
Walraff, Günter, V 249
Walschap, Gerard, I 220; IV 69, 582–83
Walser, Martin, II 223, 224; IV 583–84;
    V 249, 250
Walser, Robert, IV 382, 584–85; V 291
Walsh, William
  on Enright, II 56
Waltari, Mika, II 101, 102
Walter, Otto F., IV 382; V 626–27
Walter, Silja, IV 384
Walton, Eda Lou, IV 90
Walton, William, III 173; IV 241
Walzel, Oskar, III 105
Wan Chia-pao. See Ts'ao Yü

Wang An-i (Wang Anyi), V 136
Wang Chen-ho, I 460; V 137
Wang Gungwu, III 192
Wang Meng, V 136, 627–28
Wang Shuo, V 137
Wang Wei
  influence of, IV 611
Wang Wen-hsing, I 460; V 137
Wannūs, Sa'dallāh, IV 399–400;
    V 628–29
  as subject, V 324
Wantwadi, Homère-Antoine, IV 703
al-Wardānī, Mahmūd, V 202
Warhol, Andy, II 95; V 294
Warmond, Ellen, III 377
Warner, Rex, I 548
Warner, Sylvia Townsend, II 36, 50; IV
    586–87
Warner, Val, V 546
Warren, Austin, I 75; III 113; IV 601
Warren, Robert Penn, I 63–64, 65, 67,
    68, 491; II 115; III 119, 121, 122,
    573; IV 12, 13, 257, 422, 587–89
  criticism on, III 122
  on Dreiser, I 590–91
Waryński, Ludwik, I 342
Wasin Inthasara, IV 430
Wassermann, Jakob, II 217; IV 589–90
Wasserstein, Wendy, V 28, 29
Washington, Mary Helen, V 222
Wästberg, Per, IV 380, 590–91
Wat, Aleksander, III 555, 557; V 391,
    492
Watanabe Junzō, II 465
Waten, Judah, V 51
Waterhouse, Keith, V 208
Watkins, Vernon, IV 591–92, 608
Watson, George, III 119
Watson, Harold
  on Claudel, I 474
Watson, Sheila, I 397
Watson, Stephen, V 567
Wattār, al-Tāhir, I 45, 46; V 12, 629–30
Watts, Harold H.
  on Huxley, II 421
Waugh, Alec, IV 592
Waugh, Auberon, IV 592
  on Waugh, Evelyn, IV 593
Waugh, Evelyn, II 44, 45, 106, 285; III
    579, 581; IV 592–94, 640; V 73,
    209, 600
  criticism on, V 395
  on Greene, II 290
  influence of, III 503; V 165
  on Sitwell, Edith, IV 241
Wayan Gobiah, II 445
Wayhu Wibisana, II 444
Ważyk, Adam, III 557, 559; IV 594–95
Weales, Gerald
  on Williams, Tennessee, IV 633–34
Weaver, William, II 187
Webb, Jackson, V 545
Weber, Batty, III 158
Weber, Max, III 149; V 500
  influence of, III 611
Webster, Grant, III 127
Wecksell, Josef Julius, V 596
Wedd, Nathaniel, II 121
Wedekind, Frank, II 70, 216, 217, 607,
    608; III 335, 595–97
  criticism on, III 106
  influence of, IV 335, 596
  on Schnitzler, IV 171
Wegener, Paul, II 70
Weideli, Walter, IV 387
Weidlé, Wladimir
  on Pasternak, III 482
Weigand, Hermann J.
  on Rilke, IV 50
Weigel, Hans
  on Artmann, I 129
Weigel, Helene, I 325
Weil, Simone, II 146; IV 597–98
  on Alain, I 35

Weill, Kurt, I 325, 326; II 219; IV 40;
    V 99
Weinheber, Josef, I 156
Weinstein, Arnold, I 74
Weinstein, Nathan. *See* West, Nathanael
Weintraub, Rodelle
    on Shaw, George Bernard, IV 207
Weinzierl, Ulrich, III 551
Weir, Judith, V 546
Weisenborn, Günther, II 402
Weiss, Ernst, I 153; IV 598
Weiss, Konrad, II 218
Weiss, Peter, II 71, 220, 223, 381; IV
    599–600; V 363
Weisstein, Ulrich
    on Frisch, II 171
Weizmann, Chaim, I 351
Weldon, Fay, V 207, 630–31
Welhaven, Johann S., III 398
Wellek, René, I 75; IV 600–602
    on Čapek, I 406
Wellershoff, Dieter, II 220, 225
Welles, Orson, II 97
Wells, H. G., I 403, 488; II 42, 49, 115,
    252, 331; III 21, 596; IV 262,
    349, 451, 603–5, 618; V 210, 515
    criticism on, II 42, 43
    influence of, II 44; III 440
Wellwarth, George E.
    on Dürrenmatt, I 602
    on Frisch, II 170
Welsh literature, IV 605–9
    in English, IV 607–9
    literary criticism in, III 61
    major writers of
        Anglo-, *see:* Hughes, Richard; Jones,
            David
        in English, *see:* Davies, W. H.;
            Hughes, Richard; Jones, David;
            Lewis, Saunders, Thomas, Dylan;
            Thomas, R. S.; Watkins
        in Welsh, *see* Lewis, Saunders
    symbolism in, IV 606
    in Welsh, IV 605–7
Welti, Albert J., IV 382
Welty, Eudora, I 63, 68; II 115; IV 609–
    11
    influence of, III 503; V 610
    on Pritchett, III 599
Wenders, Wim, II 96, 98
Wendian literature. *See* Lusatian literature
Wendt, Albert, III 455
Wen I-to, I 458; II 400; IV 611–12
Weöres, Sándor, II 414, 415; IV 612–13
Werfel, Franz, I 153, 156; II 70; IV 613–
    15; V 391
    criticism on, III 107
    on Torberg, IV 455
Wergeland, Henrik, I 360; III 398
Werich, Jan, I 523; IV 573–74
Wertenbaker, Timberlake, V 348
Werup, Jacques, V 582
Wesker, Arnold, II 40; IV 615–16
West, Anthony, IV 618
West, Nathanael, IV 616–18
West, Paul, I 70
West, Rebecca, II 45–46; IV 618–19
West, Walter. *See* Soyfer, Jura
Western Samoan literature. *See under* Pa-
    cific Islands literature
Westhoff, Clara, IV 46
West Indian literature. *See* English-Carib-
    bean literature
Westphalen, Emilio Adolfo, III 511
Weyergans, François, V 231
Weygandt, C.
    on Synge, IV 395
Weyrauch, Wolfgang, II 222
Whalen, Philip, I 72
Wharton, Edith, I 58, 59, 60; II 489; IV
    619–20; V 50, 94
    on Cocteau, I 478–79
    criticism on, IV 644
Wheeler, Richard, II 163

Wheelock, Carter
    on Borges, I 305
Wheelock, John Hall, I 71
Wheelwright, Philip, III 124–25
Whipple, T. K.
    on Lewis, Sinclair, III 64
White, E(lwyn) B(rooks), V 594, 631–32
White, Hayden, V 501
White, Kenneth, V 72
White, Patrick, I 148, 149; II 43, 128; IV
    621–23; V 51
    critical excerpts on, IV 623–25
Whitehead, Alfred North, I 250
    influence of, II 52
Whiting, John, II 40
Whitman, Walt, I 57, 58; II 97; IV 141,
    636; V 26, 273, 438, 644
    criticism on, III 120, 123; IV 146, 199
    influence of, I 146; II 138, 561, 600;
        III 165, 477; IV 165, 193, 265,
        606
    on American literature, I 514; II 238,
        586; IV 71, 655; V 306
    on expressionism, II 69
Whyte, Hamish, V 546
Wićaz, Ota, III 155
Wickert, Erwin, II 223
Wickham, Anna, II 36
Wickramasinghe, Martin, IV 322
Wicomb, Zoë, V 567
Widi Widajat, II 444
Wiebe, Rudy, V 109
Wiechert, Ernst, II 219, 223; IV 625–26
Wied, Gustav, I 536
Wied, Martina, I 155
Wiene, Robert, II 70
Wiener, Oswald, I 158
Wierzyński, Kazimierz, III 544, 556, 558;
    IV 626–27
Wiesel, Elie(zer), V 230, 391, 632–34
    critical excerpts on, V 634–36
Wijaya Mala, III 190
Wijenaike, Punyakante, IV 324
Wikkramasinha, Lakdasa, IV 324, 325
Wilbur, Richard, I 71; IV 627–28; V 26
Wilcox, James, V 25
Wilde, Alan
    on Forster, II 124–25
Wilde, Oscar, I 469; II 49, 231, 254; IV
    391; V 650
    criticism on, IV 467
    influence of, III 298; IV 30, 335, 413,
        414, 674
    as subject, V 210
Wildenvey, Herman, I 268; III 402
Wilder, Billy, V 129
Wilder, Thornton, I 60, 66, 73; II 70,
    185, 217; IV 628–30
    influence of, I 601; II 168
Wilderode, Anton van, I 222
Wildgans, Anton, I 152
Wilhelm, Peter, V 566
Wilhelm II, Emperor, II 608
Wilker, Gertrud, IV 383
Wilkinson, Ann, I 396
Will, George
    on DeLillo, V 171
Willebrand-Hollmerus, Margaret von,
    V 61
Willems, Paul, I 226
Willet, John
    on Brecht, I 329
Williams, C. E.
    on Kraus, II 611
Williams, Charles, III 59; IV 449
    influence of, II 38
Williams, C. K., IV 27
Williams, D. J., IV 606
Williams, Eliseus, IV 605
Williams, Ella Gwendolen Rees. *See*
    Rhys, Jean
Williams, Emlyn, IV 608
Williams, Hugo, V 212
Williams, John A., I 69; V 636–37

Williams, Jonathan, I 72
Williams, Maslyn, III 455
Williams, Oscar, I 191
Williams, Raymond L.
    on Alvarez Gardeazabal, V 22
    on Cepeda Samudio, V 125
    on Moreno-Duran, V 432
    on Orwell, III 442
Williams, Rhydwen, IV 606
Williams, Tennessee, I 73–74; III 259; IV
    355, 630–33; V 28, 310, 311,
    469, 537, 639
    critical excerpts on, IV 633–35
    influence of, I 223
Williams, Thomas Lanier. *See* Williams,
    Tennessee
Williams, William Carlos, I 65, 73, 506,
    513, 515; II 70, 237, 238, 432; III
    574; IV 256, 337, 340, 373, 617,
    635–37; V 119, 293, 431, 540
    criticism on, IV 199, 644
    excerpts of, IV 637–39
    influence of, I 188; III 141, 377, 420,
        428; IV 637, 643, 650, 720; V
        306, 579
    on Layton, III 28
    on Moore, Marianne, III 309
    on Zukofsky, IV 720
Williams, William Crwys, IV 605
Williamson, Alan
    on Lowell, Robert, III 144
Williamson, David, I 149; V 52
Williamson, Henry, II 46
Willmann, Asta, II 62, 63
Willumsen, Dorrit, V 159
Wilson, A. N., V 209
Wilson, Angus, II 42, 45, 47–48, 51, 53;
    IV 639–41; V 210
    on Green, Henry, II 284
Wilson, August, V 29, 637–38
Wilson, Edmund, I 61, 67, 75, 286; III
    80, 83, 119–20, 127, 257; IV 146,
    334, 466, 641–43
    on Ady, I 17
    on Fitzgerald, F. Scott, II 110
    on Hemingway, I 357
    influence of, IV 29
    on James, Henry, II 489
    on Marcelin, IV 437
    on O'Neill, Eugene, III 433
    on Shaw, George Bernard, IV 206
    on Thoby-Marcelin, IV 437
    on Yeats, William Butler, IV 678
Wilson, Ethel, I 397
Wilson, Jason
    on Paz, III 497
Wilson, John Anthony Burgess. *See* Bur-
    gess, Anthony
Wilson, Lanford, I 75; V 28, 638–40
Wilson, Woodrow, III 265; IV 230
Wimsatt, William K., I 75, 344; III 124
Winger, Jurij, III 155
Winkler, Josef, V 54
Winkler, Paula, I 351
Winnicott, D. W., II 163
Winternitz, Friderike Maria Burger von,
    IV 724
Winters, Yvor, I 67; III 113, 121, 123;
    IV 643–44; V 428
    on Pound, III 113
    on Williams, William Carlos, IV 638
Winton, Tim, V 52
Wirz, Otto, IV 382
Wiseman, Adele, I 397
Wispelaere, Paul de, I 222
Witkacy. *See* Witkiewicz, Stanisław
    Ignacy
Witkiewicz, Stanisław Ignacy, III 325,
    556, 558; IV 174, 644–46
Witkojc, Mina, III 155
Witte, Bernd
    on Benjamin, I 242
Wittgenstein, Ludwig, I 128, 152; IV
    461; V 419

729